Housing Allocation and Homelessness

Fifth Edition

D1339510

Housing Allocation and Homelessness

Fifth Edition

HHJ Luba QC
Circuit Judge

Liz Davies
Barrister, Garden Court Chambers

Connor Johnston
Barrister, Garden Court Chambers

Tessa Buchanan
Barrister, Garden Court Chambers

Members of the LexisNexis Group worldwide

United Kingdom	RELX (UK) Limited, trading as LexisNexis, 1-3 Strand, London WC2N 5JR
Australia	Reed International Books Australia Pty Ltd trading as LexisNexis, Chatswood, New South Wales
Austria	LexisNexis Verlag ARD Orac GmbH & Co KG, Vienna
Benelux	LexisNexis Benelux, Amsterdam
Canada	LexisNexis Canada, Markham, Ontario
China	LexisNexis China, Beijing and Shanghai
France	LexisNexis SA, Paris
Germany	LexisNexis GmbH, Dusseldorf
Hong Kong	LexisNexis Hong Kong, Hong Kong
India	LexisNexis India, New Delhi
Italy	Giuffrè Editore, Milan
Japan	LexisNexis Japan, Tokyo
Malaysia	Malayan Law Journal Sdn Bhd, Kuala Lumpur
New Zealand	LexisNexis New Zealand Ltd, Wellington
Singapore	LexisNexis Singapore, Singapore
South Africa	LexisNexis, Durban
USA	LexisNexis, Dayton, Ohio

© 2018 RELX (UK) Limited
Published by LexisNexis

ISBN 978-1-7847-3407-7

9 781784 734077

ISBN for the set: 9781784734077

Printed and bound by CPI Group (UK) Ltd, Croydon, CR0 4YY

Visit LexisNexis at http://www.lexisnexis.co.uk

Stop Press

The Immigration Act 2016, s 67 (sometimes referred to as the 'Dubs amendment', after Lord Dubs, who introduced it in response to the plight of children affected by the refugee crisis) provides that: 'The Secretary of State must, as soon as possible after the passing of this Act, make arrangements to relocate to the United Kingdom and support a specified number of unaccompanied refugee children from other countries in Europe.'

On 6 July 2018, changes to the Immigration Rules, including a new rule 352ZA, came into effect, establishing a system for granting leave to remain to children brought to the UK pursuant to Immigration Act 2016, s 67. The new rules provide for the granting of five-year residence permits with the potential for the young person (and their dependents) to be granted indefinite leave to remain thereafter.

To complement this, on 9 July 2018, the Allocation of Housing and Homelessness (Eligibility) (England) (Amendment) Regulations 2018, SI 2018/730 came into force, allowing this group to access mainstream housing and homelessness assistance from their local housing authority. This will be achieved by means of two new classes of eligible person: class G (in respect of the allocation of social housing) and class H (in respect of homelessness assistance). These classes are added to regulations 3 and 5(1) respectively of the Allocation of Housing and Homelessness (Eligibility) (England) Regulations 2006, SI 2006/1294. The text of the Regulations, as amended, appears at Appendix 2 of this book.

On 18 June 2018, the Ministry of Housing, Communities and Local Government wrote to all Chief Executives, Chief Housing Officers and Chief Officers for Children's Services of Local Authorities in England, explaining the changes and the role that local housing authorities and children's services are expected to play in implementing them.

CHAPTER 3 and CHAPTER 11 of this text should be read with these changes in mind.

Preface to the Fifth Edition

Each successive edition of this book has been framed by the context of a continuing housing crisis in England and Wales. Like its predecessors, this edition is intended to help those readers who are dealing with the two starkest aspects of that housing crisis – the need to make provision for the homeless and the difficulties in securing an allocation of housing from the dwindling social rented sector.

It is no accident that the first chapters of this book focus on access to social housing. The demand for such housing still far outstrips supply. Many thousands of people are desperate to gain even a chance to be allocated a home from a council or housing association landlord. Among them are many applicants exhausted by a sequence of short-term and insecure stays in privately rented homes. But the social landlords to which they look have, not least as a result of the 'right to buy' and heavily limited new-build pro- grammes, only a diminishing stock in which vacancies become available. In England, in the last full year (2016/2017), lettings by councils fell by 9% – a continuation of their long-term trend. Lettings by housing associations decreased by 11% – continuing the fall from the previous year[1]. There is less, not more, but demand is accelerating.

It is precisely because the crisis in social housing is becoming ever more acute, that this edition opens with nearly 300 pages of legal text devoted to helping social landlords, applicants and their advisers to work through the law and procedure related to allocation of social housing. The material has been reviewed and revised to include all the latest case law and other developments.

The 'right' approach to social housing allocation remains a matter of both political and legal controversy. It had been anticipated that our highest court, the UK Supreme Court, might agree to hear another wide-ranging appeal on the topic but, just before this work went to the publishers, that opportunity was lost. The Court refused permission to appeal and, in effect, 'parked' several of the key issues for determination in later cases[2]. Meanwhile, this text should offer some help as to steer the reader through the legal maze of the world of social housing allocation.

---

[1] *Social Housing Lettings: April 2016 to March 2017, England* (Ministry of Housing, Communities and Local Government, January 2018).

[2] *R (on the application of H and others) (Appellants) v Ealing London Borough Council (Respondent)* UKSC 2017/0209. Permission to appeal from the judgment of the Court of Appeal (see [2017] EWCA Civ 1127) was refused on 15 March 2018.

It is no less tragic that the remaining 1000 pages of text in this edition, excluding the appendices, have had to be devoted to the topic of help for the homeless in England and Wales.

Since the last edition of this text, central government has accepted the need to improve the legal framework of arrangements for homelessness in England so as to address, at an earlier stage, the prevention of homelessness. The result is the *Homelessness Reduction Act 2017*. To make the most of the commencement of its provisions in April 2018, local housing authorities in England needed early guidance, training and resources for implementation. As usual, it has been a case of too little, too late. CHAPTER 15 outlines the new provisions and offers such illumination as the authors can.

Much might have been learned from the earlier implementation of similar legislative arrangements for homelessness prevention in Wales (described in CHAPTER 17). But that opportunity for cross-learning from experience, in framing new law, has not been taken by government either. It has been left to the authors of this work, and other independent commentators, to offer what help they can – both to users of the new services and to those expected to provide them. This edition of this work contains what I hope will be the essential and accessible material to guide the reader around the new arrangements.

The new legislation was itself the trigger for the long overdue replacement of previous statutory guidance on homelessness in England which had fallen out-of-date by a decade. The issue of the new Code of Guidance[3] has required a comprehensive revision of every element of this book that deals with homelessness. Just as that revision was being completed, there were two further, long overdue, revised guidance documents – one dealing with homeless teenagers[4], the other with referrals of the homeless between local housing authorities[5]. Thankfully, it has been able to capture their provisions in the revised text.

Of course, this new fifth edition also updates the chapters on homelessness with significant commentary on much new and developing case law. None of us, however, can stem the tide of ever more obscure statutory changes to the eligibility arrangements for homelessness assistance and, until the next edition, readers will have to work as best they can with such complexities as the recently enacted *Persons Subject to Immigration Control (Housing Authority Accommodation and Homelessness) (Amendment) Order 2018*, SI 2018/729 and the *Allocation of Housing and Homelessness (Eligibility) (England)*

---

[3] *Homelessness Code of Guidance for Local Authorities* (Ministry of Housing, Communities and Local Government, February 2018) in force from April 2018.

[4] *Prevention of homelessness and provision of accommodation for 16 and 17 year old young people who may be homeless and/or require accommodation* (Ministry of Housing, Communities and Local Government and the Department for Education, April 2018).

[5] *Procedures for referrals of homeless applicants to another local authority* (Local Government Association, May 2018).

(Amendment) Regulations 2018, SI 2018/730[6]. We join our readers in despair at the prospect.

On a happier note, the preparation of this edition has seen further significant and positive changes to the writing team. The initial co-authors, myself and Liz Davies, were joined for the last edition by Connor and, for this edition, have had the considerable additional benefit of writing by Tessa. This work is dedicated to the readers whom all of us serve – advisers and housing staff trying their very best to uphold the legal rights of those seeking access to housing in a very demanding context. We hope our writing is of some little help.

Jan Luba
June 2018

---

[6]   See the 'Stop Press' notice at p v.

Introduction

This fifth edition of Housing Allocation and Homelessness: Law and Practice is published shortly after the amendments to the Housing Act 1996, Part 7, inserted by the Homelessness Reduction Act 2017 (HRA 2017) have come into force. We welcome the new approach in the HRA 2017. More assistance from local housing authorities should now be available to those homeless persons who, for example, are not deemed to be vulnerable or do not have dependent children. The HRA 2017 also emphasises early assistance, with the laudable aim of helping people to avoid homelessness altogether. If, in a few years' time, there will be fewer people hitting the crisis point of homelessness in the first place, as its sponsor, Bob Blackman MP, hopes, then the HRA 2017 will have been a success. We applaud the homelessness charity, Crisis, and other groups who drew up the HRA 2017 and worked hard to steer it through Parliament.

The HRA 2017 draws on the Welsh legislation, namely the Housing (Wales) Act 2014, Part 2, which came into force in April 2015. Overall, the experience in Wales has been positive. Two-thirds of households have been helped to prevent their homelessness, and two-fifths of applicants have been helped to find alternative accommodation. Significantly, it is reported that the culture of local housing authorities has changed, with the ethos being towards a more preventative, person-centred and outcome-focussed approach. This change in culture has assisted groups of applicants who were previously ignored, particularly adults without children (Homelessness Monitor: Wales, Crisis, 2017).

The HRA 2017 forms part of a wider policy agenda to tackle homelessness generally and rough sleeping in particular. The end of 2017 saw the government announce a target of halving rough sleeping by 2022 and eliminating it completely by 2027. The adoption of this target has been accompanied by the appointment of various rough sleeping teams, task forces and advisory panels.

We very much hope that these announcements and appointments prove to be more than just fine words, because urgent action is needed. Both official statistics and everyday experience paint a bleak picture of homelessness in 2018. In both England and Wales, the levels of rough sleeping are rising, a phenomenon that is visible in most towns and cities. The winter of 2017–18 saw a number of well-reported instances of rough sleepers freezing to death. The number of homeless households placed in temporary accommodation in England has risen constantly since 2010. Nearly 6,000 of those households are accommodated in bed and breakfast style accommodation and, of those, around 2,000 are households with dependent children, a significant proportion of whom have been living in such accommodation for longer than the six-week statutory limit. Homelessness campaigners draw attention to the 'hidden homeless', who do not feature in these statistics, who have not sought help from local housing authorities or whose applications were not accepted, and who sleep on friends' floors or sofas, moving from place to place.

Against this backdrop, we agree with Shelter, Crisis, and other housing campaigners that much more is needed in order to resolve homelessness. An increased supply of genuinely affordable accommodation is necessary, including social housing let at low rents, and more emergency and easily accessible accommodation. Local housing authorities also need adequate resources in order to carry out their new duties effectively. Many consider that the government's additional funding of £72 million to finance the HRA 2017 is simply not enough effectively to implement the new duties.

We also agree that homelessness cannot be eliminated without a serious political commitment to tackle poverty. For some years now, the most frequent cause of homelessness has been the loss of an assured shorthold tenancy, the most common, and one of the most precarious, forms of tenancy available in the private sector. Frequently such tenancies end because the landlord wishes to increase the rent to a level which is unaffordable to the tenant. The combination of the freeze in the local housing allowance, the benefit cap, and rising market rents has made the private rented sector unaffordable for too many. Preventing homelessness by helping to keep people in their existing homes requires significant resources to ensure that those homes are affordable for those on low incomes. The time may also have come to reconsider rent regulation and security of tenure in the private sector more generally. In saying this, we are mindful that the HRA 2017 encourages the use of private sector accommodation as a means to tackle homelessness to a greater extent than ever before. It is imperative that the new measures do not simply create a revolving door to homelessness.

This book cannot begin to tackle these political issues around homelessness. However, we hope that it provides a guide to the intricacies of the duties on local housing authorities in both England and Wales. Since April 2015, the two jurisdictions have diverged in respect of homelessness law, but not the law on allocation on social housing. Part 1 – allocation of social housing – therefore considers the two jurisdictions together, with acknowledgement where there are legal differences. In Part 2 – homelessness – most of the chapters deal with the law as applicable in both England and in Wales. However, there are two new chapters setting out the new duties on local housing authorities in England. CHAPTER 15 contains the duties to *help* applicants in England: the new prevention and relief duties. CHAPTER 16 contains the new, and amended, duties to *accommodate* applicants in England. CHAPTER 17 describes the similar duties for local housing authorities in Wales.

The fifth edition of this book has been written by ourselves, without the direct assistance of HHJ Luba QC. He remains a contributing author, however, since much of the text still derives from earlier editions of this book. He and Liz Davies began this project and we are grateful for the work put into earlier editions, allowing us to build on those foundations, and for his constant encouragement. He has provided a preface to this edition. Tessa Buchanan has stepped in to fill his shoes.

As always, we are grateful to our publishers and our editor at LexisNexis.

Our professional colleagues and clerks have been long-suffering, as we endeavoured to manage our legal practices and our writing commitments. We have benefitted from collective discussions of the new duties with our housing law colleagues at Garden Court Chambers and thank them for their insight. Any mistakes, of course, are our sole responsibility.

Inevitably, our families have had to shoulder the burden of sharing their lives with distracted legal writers. We apologise and thank them for their love and support, without which this project would not be possible.

Liz Davies, Connor Johnston and Tessa Buchanan
Garden Court Chambers
April 2018

Biographical Notes

Liz Davies

Liz Davies is a barrister practising at Garden Court Chambers, London. She specialises in all types of legal work for tenants, other occupiers and homeless applicants. Before coming to the Bar, she was a solicitor specialising in housing law. She assisted Crisis in drafting the Homelessness Reduction Act 2017 and is known for her writings and talks on homelessness law and policy.

In 2001, she published *Through the Looking Glass* (Verso, 2001), an account of her two years' membership of the Labour Party's National Executive Committee. She is Honorary Vice-President of the Haldane Society of Socialist Lawyers.

Connor Johnston

Connor Johnston is a barrister practising at Garden Court Chambers, London. He specialises in housing, homelessness, asylum support, public law and community care and was junior counsel for Shelter in the recent challenges to the legality of the benefit cap. In July 2015, he was named Legal Aid Lawyer of the Year (newcomer category). He was co-chair of Young Legal Aid Lawyers between 2011 and 2015 and remains an active member. He is a committee member of the Junior Housing Law Practitioners Association. He writes regularly on housing law and legal aid.

Tessa Buchanan

Tessa Buchanan is a social welfare law barrister, with particular expertise in housing and homelessness. She practises at Garden Court Chambers, London. She appeared in a recent test case before the Court of Appeal on the meaning of 'vulnerable' and is the Vice-Chair of the Housing Law Practitioners Association.

Jan Luba QC

Jan Luba QC was appointed as a Circuit Judge (Civil) in December 2015. He is a resident judge at the County Court for Central London and also sits at the Mayor's and City Court. At the time of writing, he was also the (acting) Designated Civil Judge for all the other London County Courts. A significant proportion of the work at the county courts is housing-related.

Jan had previously been in practice at Garden Court Chambers in London where he specialised in housing law with particular emphasis on homelessness, housing management law, the allocation of social housing and housing conditions. He is a co-author of two other major Housing Law textbooks: *Defending Possession Proceedings* (Legal Action Group, 8th edn, 2016) and *Repairs Tenants Rights* (Legal Action Group, 5th edn, 2016). For over 25 years he has written 'Recent Developments in Housing Law' for the journal *Legal Action*.

He is a Patron (and past chair) of the London welfare benefits and housing advice charity 'Z2K' and also a Bencher at Middle Temple. He is a former chair of the Free Representation Unit and of the Legal Action Group.

Contents

Contents

Contents

Contents

Contents

Chapter 10   Homeless or Threatened with Homelessness

Chapter 11   Eligibility for Assistance

Contents

Contents

Chapter 18   Suitability of Accommodation

Contents

Contents

Other Materials

Table of Statutes

Table of Statutory Instruments

Table European Material

Table of Cases

Table of Cases

Table of Cases

D

E

F

Table of Cases

Table of Cases

K

L

M

N

O

P

Table of Cases

Q

R

Table of Cases

Table of Cases

Table of Cases

Table of Cases

S

Table of Cases

T

U

V

Part I

ALLOCATION

Chapter 1

ALLOCATION OF SOCIAL HOUSING: AN OVERVIEW

Contents

PREFACE TO THIS PART OF THE BOOK

1.1 The first part of this book is concerned with the process of distribution, or 'allocation', of tenancies of social housing in England and Wales. The topic is not free of political controversy or legal complexity. As a former President of the UK Supreme Court has said:

'The allocation of social housing is a difficult and potentially controversial matter, which gives rise to very hard choices, at all levels of decision making, whether strategic, policy or specific.[1]'

[1] Lord Neuberger in *R (Ahmad) v Newham London Borough Council* [2009] UKHL 14, [2009] 3 All ER 755 at [25].

1.2 The important role of housing allocation in shaping communities has been repeatedly recognised. The most recent statutory guidance for England states that:

'Social housing – stable and affordable – is of enormous importance for the millions who live in it now and for those who look to it to provide the support they need in future. The way it is allocated is key to creating communities where people choose to live and are able to prosper.[1]'

[1] *Providing social housing for local people: statutory guidance on social housing allocations for local authorities in England* (DCLG, December 2013) (the Supplementary English Code) reproduced in APPENDIX 1 of this book.

1.3 Similarly, the statutory guidance for Wales makes clear that:

'The Welsh Government believes that the allocation of housing can play an important role in broader regeneration, sustainability and inclusion. For example, allocations can make a contribution towards meeting the objectives set out in a local authority's Homelessness Strategy, Housing Strategy and Community Strategy. It recognises that allocation schemes will need to form part of an integrated range of measures and initiatives to address social issues at the local level.[1]'

[1] *Code of Guidance for Local Authorities on the Allocation of Accommodation and Homelessness* (Welsh Government, March 2016) (the Welsh Code), paras 1.1–1.2, reproduced in the CD Rom with this book.

1.4 The rest of this opening chapter introduces the topic of allocation, relates some of its history, and ventures some comments about possible future developments relating to housing allocation. Until relatively recently, the law relating to social housing allocation applied in precisely the same way in both England and Wales. However, that is no longer the case and the text of this part of this book seeks to explain the differences in the way the law now operates in each of the two countries.

1.5 The five chapters which follow provide a detailed analysis of every stage of the allocation process. Readers seeking the primary source materials on social housing allocation, rather than descriptive text, will find that we have gathered in the **Appendices** and on the **CD Rom** the essential statutory materials, the statutory Codes of Guidance and other relevant documents.

INTRODUCTION

1.6 For the purposes of this part of this book, 'social housing'[1] is taken to embrace the portfolio of residential accommodation for rent held by local authority landlords and by other providers of social housing. In this part of this book the term 'private registered provider' or 'registered social landlord' is used to refer to social landlords other than local authorities[2]. These landlords are mainly, but not exclusively, housing associations.

[1] A term now technically defined, for other purposes, by the Housing and Regeneration Act 2008, s 68(1).
[2] The term 'private registered provider' is used in England and the term 'registered social landlord' is used in Wales. Therefore, to embrace all non-local authority social landlords whether operating in England or Wales, the modern statutory language uses the rubric 'a private registered provider of social housing or a registered social landlord': eg Housing Act 1996, s 159(4A)(b) (HA 1996).

1.7 In both England and Wales the allocation of most social housing is organised through the 'local housing authority'[1] for the area in which the housing is situated. These local housing authorities not only allocate their own stock (if they have any)[2] but also make nominations to other social landlords such as local housing associations and housing co-operatives.

[1]   HA 1996, s 230.
[2]   Local housing authority owned properties now represent less than half of the social housing stock in England (*Local authority housing statistics: year ending March 2017* (MHCLG, January 2018), p 1).

1.8 This Part of this book deals with:

(1)   how local housing authorities which hold their own stock of properties allocate the homes that they have available to rent;
(2)   lettings arising from nominations made by local housing authorities to other providers of social housing (which are the most numerically significant form of letting for those landlords); and
(3)   direct allocations, by private registered providers or registered social landlords, of their remaining vacancies[1].

[1]   For a historical perspective, see also Chapter 10 of Alder & Handy *Housing Association Law and Practice* (Sweet & Maxwell, 4th edn, 2003) and Robert Latham 'Allocating social housing: the registered social landlord context' (2008) October *Legal Action*, p 42.

1.9 Local housing authorities in many areas face a difficult task in the distribution of their available rented homes. Demand for such social housing often far exceeds supply, and the supply of affordable housing has been generally diminishing[1]. Pressure on what remains of the stock is increasing[2].

[1]   There were 1.16m households on local authority waiting lists in England on 1 April 2017: *Local authority housing statistics: year ending March 2017* (MHCLG, January 2018). Yet, in England, the number of homes delivered in the affordable housing sector (which comprises social rent, affordable rent, intermediate rent, shared ownership, and affordable home ownership) was only 41,530 in 2016–17: *Affordable Housing Supply: April 2016 to March 2017 England* (DCLG, November 2017). That number bears no resemblance to the numbers achieved in the heyday of social house-building during which in excess of 100,000 new homes in social housing became available each year. The lack of social housing has been recognised as the primary cause of increased homelessness: *Report from the House of Commons Committee of Public Accounts: Homeless Households*, HC 462 (December 2017).
[2]   That pressure has increased in England as a result of measures to re-stimulate the exercise by social housing tenants of the right to buy which took effect in England on 1 April 2012 and have been subsequently stepped up: *Reinvigorating Right to Buy and one for one replacement: Information for Local Authorities* (DCLG, March 2012). As a result of such measures, the number of properties sold under the right to buy increased from 16,659 in 2012–13 to 23,186 in 2016–17: *Social Housing Sales: 2016–17, England* (DCLG, November 2017). The pressure is likely to increase yet further if and when the measures to extend the right to buy to housing association tenants and to force the sale of high-value local housing authority homes contained in the Housing and Planning Act 2016, Pt 4, come into force. At the time of writing, no dates had been given for the implementation of either measure, although money was made available in the Autumn 2017 budget for a pilot of the right to buy extension in the Midlands (see 'Delayed Right to Buy pilot for housing association tenants to go ahead', *Inside Housing* 22 November 2017) which at the time of writing was due to proceed in 2018. The House of Commons Library produced a briefing paper explaining the background to the policy and progress to date: *Introducing a voluntary right to buy for housing association tenants in England* (House of Commons Library, CBP-7224, 24 May 2018). In Wales, the Abolition of the Right to Buy and Associated Rights (Wales) Act 2018 will end the right to buy for all local housing authority and housing association tenants as of 26 January 2019.

1.10 In each local housing authority area, those seeking the allocation of social housing will include, among many others:

(1) applicants for Housing Act 1996 (HA 1996), Pt 7[1] (Homelessness) or Housing (Wales) Act 2014 (H(W)A 2014), Pt 2 (Homelessness) assistance who are in temporary accommodation provided by the local housing authority[2];

(2) people staying with family or friends but needing a home of their own;

(3) tenants in the private sector who occupy unsuitable accommodation or who want the relative permanence of a secure or assured tenancy in social housing;

(4) tenants of social housing who may occupy unsuitable or overcrowded accommodation, or who may need to move for work or family reasons;

(5) people from outside a local housing authority's own area needing to move into it; and

(6) rough sleepers.

[1] As amended by the Homelessness Reduction Act 2017 (HRA 2017), for applications for homelessness assistance made to a local housing authority in England on or after 3 April 2018.

[2] See CHAPTERS 7, 16 AND 17.

1.11 All of those people may apply to the local housing authority and ask that they be allocated somewhere suitable and secure to live.

1.12 Local housing authorities can meet some of that demand by selecting applicants for secure or introductory tenancies of properties from their own stock (if they hold any), or by nominating applicants to other local housing authorities or to other social landlords. Each time a local housing authority selects an applicant, or nominates in this way, it has, in legal terms, 'allocated' accommodation[1].

[1] Subject to exceptions set out at HA 1996, s 159(4A) and (4B) (England), s 159(5) (Wales), s 160(2) and (3) and in regulations; see **1.23–1.27**.

1.13 How does the local housing authority decide which deserving case gets priority over other deserving cases and therefore who should get the next available property? The answer, in broad terms, is that each local housing authority is free to draw up its own policy on how it will prioritise its applicants, provided that the policy adopted complies with certain statutory requirements and with basic legal principles of fairness and rationality.

HISTORY

Allocation law prior to April 1997

1.14 Before 1 April 1997[1], local housing authorities could organise the allocation of social housing as they saw fit, subject only to legal principles of rationality and fairness, their statutory duties towards applicants for homelessness assistance under what is now HA 1996, Pt 7[2] (England) and H(W)A 2014, Pt 2, (Wales) and a long-standing statutory obligation to give reasonable preference to certain groups[3]. Provided that they complied with those obligations, the priority accorded to different groups of applicants was left to the discretion of each local housing authority[4]. Local housing authorities also enjoyed a general discretion as to when, and in what circumstances, they would exclude certain applicants from consideration for the allocation of social housing⁵. Commonly, local housing authorities would use this discretion to exclude applicants who were in rent arrears, or who had a history of nuisance behaviour. Many also operated policies suspending applicants from consideration if they refused a certain number of offers of suitable accommodation or for other reasons.

¹ When HA 1996, Pt 6 came into force.
² As amended by the Homelessness Reduction Act 2017 (HRA 2017), for applications for homelessness assistance made to a local housing authority in England on or after 3 April 2018. It was then Housing Act 1985, Pt III.
³ Re-enacted in Housing Act 1985, s 22 and giving reasonable preference to: those occupying insanitary or overcrowded houses; those with large families; those living in unsatisfactory housing conditions; and applicants for homelessness assistance to whom duties were owed.
⁴ Housing Act 1985, s 21 vests the general management of its houses in a local housing authority.
⁵ *R v Canterbury City Council ex p Gillespie* (1986) 19 HLR 7, QBD.

1.15 The decisions of the courts and the Ombudsmen about the operation of social housing allocation before April 1997 now offer little relevant guidance on the correct application of the current statutory regimes.

Allocation law between April 1997 and January 2003

1.16 From 1 April 1997, HA 1996, Pt 6 ('Allocation of Housing Accommodation') as enacted provided a new statutory basis for the allocation of social housing by local housing authorities in England and Wales. The big change was the requirement¹ for local housing authorities to maintain a 'Housing Register' – one list that would contain all the different applicants entitled to be considered for an allocation of social housing, except internal applicants for transfer. Within the list of applicants held on that register, local housing authorities were required to give reasonable preference to particular groups. Importantly, no specific preference was required to be given to applicants entitled to assistance under HA 1996, Pt 7 ('Homelessness'), thereby abandoning the explicit statutory duty to that effect which had been contained in the earlier Housing Act 1985. At the same time, HA 1996, Pt 7, had introduced the concept that local housing authorities' duties to applicants for assistance under that Part (who had a priority need and had not become homeless intentionally) were simply to provide accommodation for a period of two years. The idea was that applicants for assistance under HA 1996, Pt 7, would be provided with safety-net accommodation and, during those two years, they would either rise to the top of the list of those on the local housing register and be allocated social housing accommodation or would find their own accommodation in the private sector. Homelessness was no longer to be an automatic passport into long-term social housing. Some of that changed with the election of a new government (in May 1997), and, from 1 November 1997, the effect of a ministerial order was that homeless people, who were in priority need and had not become homeless intentionally, were included among the groups of people to whom 'reasonable preference' had to be given in the allocation of social housing.

¹ HA 1996, s 162(1), as originally enacted.

1.17 Subject to those 'reasonable preferences', however, a local housing authority could draw up its own policies as to how to recognise the different types of need for an allocation of accommodation among those on the housing register. Local housing authorities could also continue to operate policies excluding certain categories of applicants, provided that they scrutinised each applicant's case individually and fairly[1]. Many local housing authorities therefore continued to operate policies, adopted before 1997, of excluding people with rent arrears and those who had committed acts of nuisance, and of suspending applicants who had refused offers of accommodation[2]. They were also entitled to operate policies excluding applicants from outside their own areas[3]. Local housing authorities were additionally required by statute to exclude asylum-seekers and other persons subject to immigration control from their registers[4].

1   *R v Wolverhampton Metropolitan Borough Council ex p Watters* (1997) 29 HLR 931, CA.
2   See eg *R (Giles) v Fareham Borough Council* [2002] EWHC 2951 (Admin), (2003) 35 HLR 36, Admin Ct (acquiescence in nuisance behaviour); and *R v Southwark London Borough Council ex p Mason* (1999) 32 HLR 88, QBD (refusal of offers). One survey of 74 housing organisations found that 47 had an exclusions policy in place, with a further eight operating a deferral/refusal policy: *Exclusions from the housing register* (Northern Housing Consortium, May 2000).
3   *R (Conway) v Charnwood Borough Council* [2002] EWHC 43 Admin, (2002) March *Legal Action*, p 16, Admin Ct.
4   HA 1996, s 161(2).

1.18 The housing register scheme did not apply to existing tenants seeking transfers within the same landlord's stock. As far as those transfers were concerned, local housing authorities retained the broad general discretion to operate any policy they wished, subject to public law considerations of fairness and rationality, and limited statutory requirements to consider housing need[1]. Many local housing authorities operated policies of excluding tenants who had a certain level of rent arrears or who were accused of nuisance behaviour from being eligible for a transfer[2], and suspending from transfer schemes those tenants who had refused an offer of a property[3].

1   *R v Newham London Borough Council ex p Watkins* (1993) 26 HLR 434, QBD.
2   *R v Lambeth London Borough Council ex p Njomo* (1996) 28 HLR 737, QBD (rent arrears); *R v Southwark London Borough Council ex p Melak* (1996) 29 HLR 223, QBD (rent arrears); and *R v York City Council ex p Wilson* (1997) June *Legal Action*, p 18, QBD (nuisance).
3   *R v Wandsworth London Borough Council ex p Lawrie and Heshmati* (1997) 30 HLR 153, QBD.

Allocation law between January 2003 and June 2012

1.19 In January 2003, HA 1996, Pt 6 was substantially amended by the Homelessness Act 2002, ss 13–16, which applied in the same way in both England and Wales[1]. The concept of a compulsory local housing register was abolished and replaced by a requirement to have a comprehensive local housing allocation scheme. The categories of reasonable preference were altered. New codes of statutory guidance were issued[2] to which local housing authorities were required to have regard when making allocation schemes and decisions on allocations[3]. The application of HA 1996, Pt 6 was extended to include existing secure or introductory tenants who had themselves applied for a transfer. Although barely referred to in the statutory amendments made by

the Homelessness Act 2002, running through the revised approach to allocation of social housing from 2003 to 2012 was the concept that applicants
should have a choice of accommodation, rather than be the subject of a
take-it-or-leave-it allocation[4].

1   In force from 27 January 2003 (Wales) and 31 January 2003 (England).
2   In England, *Allocation of Accommodation: Code of Guidance for local housing authorities*
     (Office of the Deputy Prime Minister, November 2002), parts of which were subsequently
     replaced by the further statutory guidance given in *Fair and flexible: statutory guidance on
     social housing allocations for local authorities in England* (DCLG, December 2009) which has
     itself been replaced by *Allocation of accommodation: guidance for local housing authorities in
     England* (DCLG, June 2012) and *Providing social housing for local people: statutory guidance
     on social housing allocations for local authorities in England* (DCLG, December 2013). In
     Wales, *Code of Guidance for local housing authorities on allocation of accommodation and
     homelessness* (National Assembly for Wales, April 2003) which has itself been replaced by
     *Code of Guidance for Local Authorities on the Allocation of Accommodation and Homeless-
     ness* (Welsh Government, March 2016).
3   HA 1996, s 169(1).
4   See Chapter 5.

Allocation law since June 2012

1.20 Since June 2012 the legal position has become significantly more
complex. The provisions of HA 1996, Pt 6, as amended by the Homelessness
Act 2002, remain in force in Wales and continue to operate in essentially the
same way as they have done since last significantly amended in 2003. However,
in England, the provisions of HA 1996, Pt 6, were substantially modified by
the Localism Act 2011, ss 145–147, with effect from 18 June 2012[1]. The two
key differences are that local housing authorities in England:

(1)   can now designate classes of applicants who can and cannot qualify for
       housing allocation under their local allocation schemes[2]; and
(2)   no longer need to include non-priority transfer applicants in their
       statutory allocation arrangements[3].

1   Localism Act 2011 (Commencement No 6 and Transitional, Savings and Transitory
     Provisions) Order 2012, SI 2012/1463, art 3.
2   HA 1996, s 160ZA. See **3.91–3.150**.
3   HA 1996, s 159(4A). See **2.55–2.65**.

1.21 This legislative dichotomy in the law of social housing allocation as it
applies between each of the two countries has been achieved by the insertion
of the words 'in Wales' into many of the substantive sections of HA 1996, Pt 6,
and the insertion into that Part of whole new sections and new subsections
containing the words 'in England'. The law as it presently stands is represented
by the amended terms of HA 1996, Pt 6, as set out in Appendix 1 to this edition
of this book. The effect of the present arrangements is fully described in
Chapters 2–5 of this book[1].

1   And is also briefly outlined in Dr T Baldwin and J Luba QC, 'The Localism Act 2011:
     allocation of social housing accommodation' (2012) January *Legal Action*, p 23.

1.22 As before, separate statutory guidance applies in England and in Wales[1].
In England, the current guidance is contained in *Allocation of accommodation: guidance for local housing authorities in England* which is referred to

throughout this part of this book as 'the English Code'[2]. This expressly replaces all other previous statutory guidance on housing allocation in England[3]. It is to be read with the further guidance issued in December 2013, *Providing social housing for local people: Statutory guidance on social housing allocations for local authorities in England*, which is referred to throughout this part of this book as 'the Supplementary English Code'[4] and with the additional statutory guidance issued in March 2015, *Right to move*, which is referred to in this part of the book as the 'RTM Code'[5]. In Wales, the current guidance is that issued by the Welsh Government which is referred to throughout this book as 'the Welsh Code'[6]. In both cases, the guidance has been issued in exercise of the powers granted by HA 1996, s 169. The English Code is reproduced in full in APPENDIX 1 to this book and on the accompanying CD Rom. The Welsh Code is included on the CD Rom.

[1] HA 1996, s 169.
[2] *Allocation of accommodation: guidance for local housing authorities in England* (DCLG, June 2012), reproduced in APPENDIX 1.
[3] English Code, para 1.2.
[4] *Providing social housing for local people: Statutory guidance on social housing allocations for local authorities in England* (DCLG, December 2013), reproduced in APPENDIX 1.
[5] *Right to move: Statutory guidance on social housing allocations for local housing authorities in England* (DCLG, March 2015), reproduced in APPENDIX 1. At the time of writing, the Government is considering responses to a consultation on issuing further guidance on *Improving access to social housing for victims of domestic abuse* (DCLG, October 2017).
[6] *Code of guidance for local authorities on the Allocation of Accommodation and Homelessness* (Welsh Government, March 2016), reproduced on the CD Rom with this book.

WHAT DOES AND DOES NOT COUNT AS AN 'ALLOCATION'?

'Allocation' defined

1.23 An 'allocation' is defined as occurring when a local housing authority selects a person to be its own secure or introductory tenant, nominates a person to be a secure or introductory tenant elsewhere, or nominates a person to be an assured tenant of another social landlord[1]. The selection or nomination of a person for the initial grant of a 'flexible' or 'affordable' tenancy of social housing will also be an 'allocation' because those tenancies are simply variants of secure or assured tenancies[2].

[1] HA 1996, s 159(2).
[2] English Code, para 1.4.

1.24 The process of allocation is essentially one of identifying a person apt to be made an offer of a social housing tenancy and then the making of that offer. The allocation process does *not* include the actual entry by the applicant into the tenancy agreement for a particular property. That is a housing management function beyond the scope of HA 1996, Pt 6[1].

[1] 'Part [6] of the 1996 Act is concerned with, indeed limited to, establishing and then managing priorities between applicants for residential accommodation (which may or may not be owned by the local authority in question) as it becomes available for letting, which effectively is preliminary to, and not part of, the actual letting of such accommodation, which is governed by Pt [2] of the 1985 Act': *Birmingham City Council v Qasim* [2009] EWCA Civ 1080, [2010] HLR 19, CA per Lord Neuberger MR at [18].

Exceptions

1.25 The allocation provisions set out in HA 1996, Pt 6, do not apply to each and every situation in which a person may come to be a tenant of social housing.

1.26 The Codes each identify the common situations in which social housing can come to be occupied by a new tenant *without* the statutory provisions on housing allocation engaging at all[1]. Some of these exceptions, outlined in the next few paragraphs, are the result of express provisions in the HA 1996, Pt 6 (and regulations made under them), and others are the result of the term 'allocation' in HA 1996 being defined as applying only when a local housing authority nominates or selects a person for a specified type of tenancy[2]. If the tenancy to be granted will not be secure, introductory or assured – for example, because it will be a form of tenancy without security of tenure (such as a 'family intervention tenancy'[3]) – selection or nomination for that tenancy will not count as an allocation.

1   English Code, para 1.9; Welsh Code, Annex 1.
2   HA 1996, s 159(2).
3   A form of social housing tenancy created by the Housing and Regeneration Act 2008.

1.27 The provisions of HA 1996, Pt 6, do not apply where someone obtains a tenancy of social housing as a result of:

(1)   the vesting by succession of a periodic secure or introductory tenancy on the death of the tenant[1]; or

(2)   the devolution of a fixed term secure tenancy on the death of the tenant[2]; or

(3)   the assignment of a secure tenancy as part of a mutual exchange[3]; or

(4)   the assignment of a secure or introductory tenancy to a person who would have been qualified to succeed to the tenancy on the tenant's death[4]; or

(5)   the vesting or disposal of a secure or introductory tenancy pursuant to a court order made under the specified provisions of three family law statutes identified in HA 1996, Pt 6[5]; or

(6)   an order made under specified provisions of the Civil Partnership Act 2004 in relation to a secure or introductory tenancy[6]; or

(7)   an order made under the Family Law Act 1996, Sch 7, Pt II in relation to a social housing tenancy[7]; or

(8)   a transfer initiated by the landlord of a secure or introductory tenant (ie not initiated by the making of an application for a transfer by the tenant)[8]; or

(9)   the local housing authority providing a tenant or owner-occupier who has been displaced from his or her previous accommodation with suitable alternative accommodation under the Land Compensation Act 1973, s 39[9]; or

(10)   the grant of a secure tenancy to a former owner-occupier or statutory tenant of a defective dwelling-house acquired by the local housing authority under Housing Act 1985 ss 554–555; or

(11)   the grant of a tenancy to a person who is currently and lawfully occupying a property held on a family intervention tenancy[10]; or

(12)   in England only, a transfer of a social housing tenant who applied for such a transfer, who was previously a secure, introductory or assured tenant of social housing, and who the local housing authority was satisfied was not in a category qualifying for a 'reasonable preference'[11]; or

(13)   in England only, the tenancy being granted as part of the surrender and re-grant procedure available where two social housing tenants in England wish to exchange their homes and one of the tenants holds a flexible tenancy or an assured shorthold tenancy[12].

In none of these cases will there have been an 'allocation' for HA 1996, Pt 6, purposes.

[1]   HA 1996, s 160(2)(a) and (3)(b).
[2]   HA 1996, s 160(2)(b).
[3]   HA 1996, s 160(2)(c).
[4]   HA 1996, s 160(2)(d) and (3)(c).
[5]   HA 1996, s 160(2)(e)(i)–(iii) and (3)(d)(i)–(iii).
[6]   HA 1996, s 160(2)(e)(iv) and (3)(d)(iv).
[7]   An order under those provisions moves the tenancy from the existing tenant to a new tenant by 'virtue of the order and without further assurance' (FLA 1996, Sch 7, para 7(1)) and therefore there is no intervention by the local housing authority and no allocation for HA 1996, Pt 6 purposes.
[8]   HA 1996, s 159(4B)(b) (England) and s 159(5) (Wales).
[9]   HA 1996, s 160(4); Allocation of Housing (England) Regulations 2002, SI 2002/3264, reg 3; and Allocation of Housing (Wales) Regulations 2003, SI 2003/239 (W 36), reg 3.
[10]   Allocation of Housing (England) (Amendment) (Family Intervention Tenancies) Regulations 2008, SI 2008/3015.
[11]   HA 1996, s 159(4A) and (4B)(c) (England).
[12]   HA 1996, s 160(2)(da).

Allocation to current non-tenant occupiers

1.28 Local housing authorities receive many requests for tenancy allocation from non-tenants who are occupying existing local housing authority accommodation and are seeking the grant of a tenancy for that particular property[1]. Such an occupier may have no statutory right to the tenancy, but may have been occupying that accommodation as his or her home for some time and wish to remain there. Examples would include:

*   where one joint tenant has terminated the tenancy, by serving a notice to quit on the landlord, and the other former joint tenant remains in the home[2]; or

*   where a tenant has died and the remaining household member has no statutory succession rights but had lived with the tenant for some time, or was the tenant's carer or former partner, or needs to live in the property to care for the tenant's dependants[3]; or

*   where a tenant has moved to a care home, and the remaining household member has no right to an assignment of the tenancy but had lived with the tenant for some time[4].

[1]   See CHAPTER 4 at **4.187–4.191**.
[2]   The factual scenario of *R (Dixon) v Wandsworth London Borough Council* [2007] EWHC 3075 (Admin), (2008) February *Legal Action*, p 40, Admin Ct.
[3]   The factual scenario of *R (Neville) v Wandsworth London Borough Council* [2009] EWHC 2405 (Admin), (2009) December *Legal Action*, p 17, Admin Ct, *R(Moore) v Wandsworth*

London Borough Council [2012] All ER (D) 66 (Jan), (2012) April *Legal Action*, p 46, Admin Ct and of *Leicester City Council v Shearer* [2013] EWCA Civ 1467, [2014] HLR 8, CA.

⁴ The factual scenario of *R (George) v Hammersmith & Fulham London Borough Council* [2012] EWHC 2369 (Admin), (2012) July *Legal Action*, p 36, Admin Ct.

1.29 An allocation of a new tenancy in those situations *will* be subject to HA 1996, Pt 6, and will ultimately be governed by the terms of the local housing authority's allocation scheme. The Welsh Code recommends that local housing authorities set out in their allocation schemes whether they will grant tenancies in these circumstances and, if so, on what basis. If the local housing authority *does* include provisions for these classes of case within its allocation scheme then, when deciding whether to evict the non-tenant who is in occupation, it should consider whether to:

(1) give the non-tenant advice and/or information about the relevant provisions of its scheme; and

(2) encourage an application from a person who might be within such a class[1].

Where the property is owned by a private registered provider or registered social landlord, in a case such as one of these, the arrangements described in CHAPTER 6 will apply.

¹ *Leicester City Council v Shearer* [2013] EWCA Civ 1467, [2014] HLR 8, CA.

REGULATION OF SOCIAL HOUSING PROVIDERS

1.30 Matters relating to housing allocation schemes are subject to regulation by the national regulatory authorities.

England

1.31 In England, the body responsible for regulation of social housing is the Regulation Committee. This is a statutory committee of the Homes and Communities Agency[1] which was established by the Housing and Regeneration Act 2008 (HRA 2008)[2]. It has the power to set standards to be followed by registered providers of social housing[3]. The Secretary of State may direct the regulator to issue such standards[4].

¹ On 11 January 2018 the Homes and Communities Agency's investment arm adopted the trading name of Homes England whilst the regulation directorate re-named itself the Regulator of Social Housing. At the time of writing, a draft Statutory Instrument was before Parliament (the Legislative Reform (Regulator of Social Housing) Order 2018) which if made will abolish the Regulation Committee of the Homes and Communities Agency, create a Regulator of Social Housing, and transfer the functions of the Regulation Committee to the Regulator of Social Housing. The way in which registered providers of social housing are regulated is not expected to change.

² HRA 2008, s 1(1).

³ HRA 2008, s 193(1).

⁴ HRA 2008, s 197(1). The current directions are set out at Annex A of *Implementing Social Housing reform: Directions to the Social Housing Regulator – Consultation: a summary of responses* (DCLG, November 2011).

1.32 A provider of social housing is defined, in respect of low cost rented accommodation, as the landlord of such accommodation[1]. This includes both local housing authorities[2] – where they have not disposed of all their stock – and other social landlords such as housing associations. The regulator must maintain a register of providers of social housing which must be available for inspection by the public[3].

¹ HRA 2008, s 80(1).
² Housing and Regeneration Act 2008 (Registration of Local Authorities) Order 2010, SI 2010/844, art 3.
³ HRA 2008, s 111.

1.33 The standards set by the Regulation Committee require registered providers of social housing to comply with specified rules about criteria for allocating housing accommodation[1]. The current regulatory standards are contained in *The Regulatory framework for social housing in England from April 2015*[2].

¹ HRA 2008, s 193(2)(a).
² Homes and Communities Agency, March 2015.

1.34 In England, the current regulatory standard for housing allocation in England (part of a broader Tenancy Standard) provides[1]:

'1 Allocations and mutual exchange

1.1 Registered providers shall let their homes in a fair, transparent and efficient way. They shall take into account the housing needs and aspirations of tenants and potential tenants. They shall demonstrate how their lettings:
• make the best use of available housing
• are compatible with the purpose of the housing
• contribute to local authorities' strategic housing function and sustainable communities

There should be clear application, decision-making and appeals processes.'

¹ *Tenancy Standard* (Homes and Communities Agency, April 2012), part of *The regulatory framework for social housing in England from April 2015* (Homes and Communities Agency, March 2015). The current regulatory framework was published in March 2015 but the Tenancy Standard remained unchanged from 2012. The passages of the current regulatory standard dealing with *mutual exchange* have not been reproduced in these extracts.

1.35 The regulatory standard then sets out the following Specific Expectations[1]:

'1 Allocations and mutual exchange

1.1 Registered providers shall co-operate with local authorities' strategic housing function, and their duties to meet identified local housing needs. This includes assistance with local authorities' homelessness duties, and through meeting obligations in nominations agreements.

1.2 Registered providers shall develop and deliver services to address under-occupation and overcrowding in their homes, within the resources available to them. These services should be focused on the needs of their tenants, and will offer choices to them.

1.3 Registered providers' published policies shall include how they have made use of common housing registers, common allocations policies and local letting policies. Registered providers shall clearly set out, and be able to give reasons for, the criteria they use for excluding actual and potential tenants from consideration for allocations, mobility or mutual exchange schemes.

1.4 Registered providers shall develop and deliver allocations processes in a way which supports their effective use by the full range of actual and potential tenants, including those with support needs, those who do not speak English as a first language and others who have difficulties with written English.

1.5 Registered providers shall minimise the time that properties are empty between each letting. When doing this, they shall take into account the circumstances of the tenants who have been offered the properties.

1.6 Registered providers shall record all lettings and sales as required by the Continuous Recording of Lettings (CORE) system.

1.7 Registered providers shall provide tenants wishing to move with access to clear and relevant advice about their housing options.'

The Housing and Regeneration Act 2008 (HRA 2008) gives the regulator considerable powers of inspection and enforcement to ensure that these standards are complied with[2].

[1]   *Tenancy Standard* (Homes and Communities Agency, April 2012), part of *The regulatory framework for social housing in England from April 2015* (Homes and Communities Agency, March 2015).
[2]   HRA 2008, ss 192–269.

Wales

1.36 In Wales, the regulatory function falls to the Welsh Ministers. A Housing Regulation Team undertakes the regulation activity on their behalf and its work is overseen by the Regulatory Board for Wales. Under HA 1996, s 33A the Welsh Ministers may set performance standards to be met by registered social landlords in connection with their functions relating to the provision of housing. The Welsh Ministers may issue guidance relating to and amplifying a performance standard under HA 1996, s 33B.

1.37 In contrast to England, these regulatory standards apply only to housing associations and other non-profit-making housing bodies[1]. It does not apply to local housing authorities.

[1]   HA 1996, ss 1A and 2.

1.38 The current performance standards and guidance are contained within *The Regulatory Framework for Housing Associations Registered in Wales*[1]. This has the stated purpose of improving and strengthening the Welsh Government's approach to regulation but the guidance it provides in respect of allocations is minimal. Performance Standard 5 requires housing associations to demonstrate 'A track record of achieving positive outcomes, responding appropriately to new challenges and performance issues'. The guidance accompanying this standard recommends that the association demonstrate 'how lettings make the best use of available housing, compatible with the core purpose of the Registered Social Landlord'.

[1]   Welsh Government, May 2017.

1.39 More general guidance is available in the introduction to the Framework, which confirms that:

> 'Key elements of the risk based approach of the 2011 Framework remain unchanged
> * Tenants remain at the heart of regulation with improved accountability and transparency to tenants and other stakeholders
> * The underpinning principles of proportionality, transparency and openness, consistency and promotion of learning and development, are unchanged
> * The approach to regulation continues to be founded on co-regulation.

HOW ARE THE MODERN ALLOCATION SCHEMES OPERATING?

England

1.40 Despite the major legislative changes relating to social housing allocation brought into force in England in 1997, 2003 and 2012 respectively, there has been no recent major national research programme to investigate or monitor the lawfulness or effectiveness of the housing allocation schemes subsequently adopted and operated by the hundreds of local housing authorities across England.

1.41 In 2004–05 an independent survey was conducted of the allocation schemes operated by 12 local housing authorities in the London area[1]. Its conclusions were that:

* local housing authorities were not disclosing all aspects of their allocation procedures in their published allocation schemes as required by HA 1996, Pt 6[2];
* requests for copies of allocation schemes were not being met promptly by many local housing authorities and in some cases copies of allocation schemes were only available under threat of litigation;
* there was an urgent need for DCLG to provide further guidance to ensure that local housing authorities comply with their statutory duties; and
* to ensure that social housing is allocated in a fair and transparent manner, targets must be set and outcomes monitored and published[3].

[1] Robert Latham 'Allocating accommodation: reconciling choice and need', published in two parts at (2005) March *Legal Action*, p 16 and (2005) May *Legal Action*, p 15.
[2] HA 1996, s 167(1).
[3] R Latham 'Allocating accommodation: reconciling choice and need' (2005) May *Legal Action*, pp 18–19.

1.42 In 2007–08, the Department for Communities and Local Government commissioned a small scale review by other independent researchers. Its findings presented only a snapshot of practice across a relatively modest selection of local housing authorities[1].

[1] *Exploring local authority policy and practice on housing allocations* (DCLG, July 2009).

1.43 In 2016 the Local Government Ombudsman[1] published a special focus report about complaints it had received regarding housing allocation[2]. It noted that in the year 2014–15 it had received 978 complaints and enquiries about housing allocation, a 13% increase on the previous year[3]. Where a detailed investigation had been carried out, fault had been found in 42% of cases. Some of the main areas of fault were:

- delay in dealing with cases;
- decisions which were not in accordance with the local housing authority's allocation scheme;
- failure to take into account relevant information;
- failure to notify an applicant of their right of review; and
- removing an application from the register or reducing an applicant's priority without properly considering his or her circumstances[4].

[1] As of 19 June 2017, the Local Government and Social Care Ombudsman.
[2] *Full House: Councils' role in allocating social housing* (LGO, January 2016), p 4.
[3] *Full House: Councils' role in allocating social housing* (LGO, January 2016), p 4.
[4] *Full House: Councils' role in allocating social housing* (LGO, January 2016), p 4.

1.44 These limited reports do demonstrate that, despite the wholesale restructuring of housing allocation law made by the successive amendments to HA 1996, Pt 6, too many local housing authorities have taken too long to catch up with changes in the modern law of social housing allocation and to devise and implement wholly lawful housing allocation schemes. In England it has been left to inspectors, the courts and the Ombudsmen to turn up instances of poor or unlawful practices which may, in fact, be widespread. For example, an Audit Commission inspection of one major English city council's allocation arrangements found:

> 'the allocation policy and practice . . . is poor and lacks clarity, clear policies and procedures and there is no effective mechanism of control or audit to ensure the allocation of homes is done fairly and transparently.[1]'

[1] *Nottingham City Homes – Nottingham City Council* (Audit Commission, March 2006).

1.45 In March 2009 the Local Government Ombudsman[1] in England identified one local housing authority which had not operated a lawful allocation scheme since September 2002[2].

[1] As of 19 June 2017, the Local Government and Social Care Ombudsman.
[2] Complaint against Medway Council 08/008/647, 23 March 2009, (2009) May *Legal Action*, p 30.

Wales

1.46 In Wales, the much smaller number of local housing authorities, which were operating from 1997 to 2012 under essentially the same legal framework as those in England, have been subject to significant scrutiny and that scrutiny has thrown up issues equally relevant to social housing allocation by local housing authorities in England. For example, in February 2006, the Public Services Ombudsman for Wales published a special report containing an examination of how the modern legal structure for social housing allocation was operating in Wales[1]. The report found that:

- a significant number of Welsh local housing authorities had yet to adopt allocation policies that fully complied with the law and took account of the statutory guidance;
- in particular, the changes introduced by the Homelessness Act 2002 had still not been sufficiently implemented, some three years after those changes had come into force;
- as a result, the lawfulness of each allocation decision since January 2003 was potentially questionable;
- some local housing authorities continued to operate unlawful policies of blanket exclusions[2]; and
- some local housing authorities were failing to accord preference to the categories of applicants entitled to a reasonable preference[3].

[1]   *Housing Allocation and Homelessness: A Special Report by the Public Services Ombudsman for Wales* (Public Services Ombudsman for Wales, 2006).
[2]   See **1.17** and CHAPTER **3**.
[3]   See **4.27–4.112**.

1.47 Local housing authorities in Wales were asked to take expert legal advice and to review their allocation schemes as a matter of urgency. Some Welsh local housing authorities had already started that process as a result of the Public Services Ombudsman's investigations of individual complaints.

1.48 In response to the Ombudsman's Special Report, and to further letters of complaint being received by the Welsh Assembly Government and by Shelter, officials of the Welsh Assembly Government carried out a joint review with Shelter Cymru of the 22 local housing authority allocation schemes in Wales. That review was published in March 2007[1]. It found that all the allocation schemes scrutinised required some level of further review. Issues identified ranged from failure to adopt schemes meeting statutory requirements to the need to clarify or elaborate those schemes which did satisfy the legal basics. The report contained a series of recommendations for both the Welsh Assembly Government and for local housing authorities. The latter included a recommendation that every Welsh local housing authority 'undertake a fundamental review of their allocation schemes to ensure they are compliant with the law, Code of Guidance and good practice and review them annually thereafter'.

[1]   *Review of Local Authority Allocation Schemes (2006): report by Welsh Assembly Government and Shelter Cymru* (March 2007).

1.49 The response of the Welsh Assembly Government was to commit itself to 'undertaking a full review of allocation schemes every three years, to issue strengthened guidance to local housing authorities and housing associations on allocations', and to ensuring that the 'revised guidance addresses the issues raised by the Ombudsman'[1]. While the content of that revised guidance was being formulated, the Chartered Institute for Housing in Wales reported that, at least in respect of the operation of provisions excluding applicants from social housing, 'not all the exclusion policies and procedures examined during the project were legal'[2].

[1]   Leighton Andrews AM (National Assembly for Wales, Deputy Minister for Housing) answering WAQ50133 on 4 July 2007 in the Welsh Assembly.

1.50 In April 2010, in its new National Housing Strategy for Wales, the Welsh Assembly Government identified as a priority the need to 'extend the legal powers available to the National Assembly for Wales so that it is able to do more to help meet housing need'[1]. That bore fruit in an order made in July 2010 by which the Assembly acquired jurisdiction to make legislation relating to 'the arrangements under which social housing is provided'[2]. However, the power given has yet to be significantly exercised by the Assembly in respect of social housing allocation notwithstanding the adoption of a significant legislative programme in relation to housing matters[3]. The subsequent H(W)A 2014 has re-cast the law on homelessness in Wales, but its impact on social housing allocation is confined to minor consequential amendments.

[1] *Improving Lives and Communities Homes in Wales*, para 3.8 (WAG, April 2010).
[2] The National Assembly for Wales (Legislative Competence) (Housing and Local Government) Order 2010, SI 2010/1838, art 2(2), matter 11.4.
[3] *Homes for Wales A White Paper for Better Lives and Communities* (Welsh Government, May 2012).

1.51 However, the need to address the new regime on homelessness in Wales has required a revised set of statutory guidance on housing allocation and homelessness. The current statutory guidance in Wales was subject to a consultation exercise in early 2015 and the final version of new guidance was issued in April 2015. It was revised and reissued on 24 March 2016[1].

[1] The Welsh Code, reproduced in the CD Rom with this book.

THE FUTURE FOR SOCIAL HOUSING ALLOCATION

1.52 Whilst there is no statutory obligation to keep allocation schemes under review, many local housing authorities do so as a matter of good practice. A survey of local housing authorities and social landlords conducted by the Chartered Institute of Housing in October 2013 found that most respondents 'have either carried out a review of their allocations scheme in the last 12 months (60%) or plan a review in the next 12 months (29%)'[1].

[1] *Under pressure? Emerging issues for allocations* (Chartered Institute of Housing, November 2013). See also 'Why should you be considering reviewing your approach to allocations?' in *New Approaches to Allocations* (Chartered Institute of Housing, June 2014).

1.53 Particular events may lead to the amendment of local housing authorities' allocation schemes. In England, the expectation was that – starting from no later than December 2013[1] – every local housing authority would reconsider the terms of its housing allocation scheme in the light of the amendments made to HA 1996, Pt 6, by the Localism Act 2011 which came into force in June 2012. In the foreword to the current English Code, the then Housing Minister explained that the intention was 'to assist councils to make full use of these new freedoms – and the existing flexibilities within the allocation legislation – to encourage work and mobility, and to tailor their allocation priorities to meet local needs and local circumstances'[2].

1 *Providing social housing for local people* (DCLG, December 2013) at [4].
2 English Code, p 4.

1.54 In Wales, the publication of the revised Welsh Code in March 2016 may well trigger a review of local housing authority allocation schemes across that country[1].

1 See Welsh Code, para 1.46 explains changes made since the last code was issued in April 2015.

1.55 In the special focus report published in 2016, the Local Government Ombudsman[1] stated that it would 'criticise a local housing authority for failing to review its housing allocation scheme in response to a court judgement [sic] against a different authority that raises an issue which is clearly relevant to the authority's own scheme'[2]. As discussed in CHAPTER 4, there have been several important decisions recently which are likely to have implications for most or all local housing authorities. Three particular issues that have come before the courts repeatedly are:

- The requirement to avoid discrimination in allocation schemes[3];
- The obligation to give a reasonable preference in the allocation scheme to certain groups of people[4]; and
- Ensuring that the best interests of children are treated as a primary consideration in the formulation and amendment of allocation schemes[5].

Local housing authorities are likely to want to review their allocation schemes carefully in light of the recent decisions on these questions.

1 As of 19 June 2017, the Local Government and Social Care Ombudsman.
2 *Full House: Councils' role in allocating social housing* (LGO, January 2016), p 3.
3 *R (H) v Ealing London Borough Council* [2017] EWCA Civ 1127, [2018] HLR 2; *R (C) v Islington London Borough Council* [2017] EWHC 1288 (Admin), [2017] HLR 32; *R (XC) v Southwark London Borough Council* [2017] EWHC 736 (Admin), [2017] HLR 24; *R (YA) v Hammersmith and Fulham London Borough Council* [2016] EWHC 1850 (Admin), [2016] HLR 39; *R (Fartun Osman) v London Borough of Harrow* [2017] EWHC 274 (Admin); and *R (HA) v Ealing London Borough Council* [2015] EWHC 2375 (Admin), [2016] PTSR 16.
4 *R (Fartun Osman) v London Borough of Harrow* [2017] EWHC 274 (Admin); *R (Woolfe) v Islington London Borough Council* [2016] EWHC 1907 (Admin), [2016] HLR 42; and *R (HA) v Ealing London Borough Council* [2015] EWHC 2375 (Admin), [2016] PTSR 16.
5 *R (C) v Islington London Borough Council* [2017] EWHC 1288 (Admin), [2017] HLR 32; and *R (Woolfe) v Islington London Borough Council* [2016] EWHC 1907 (Admin), [2016] HLR 42.

Chapter 2

INFORMATION, APPLICATIONS AND DECISION-MAKING IN RESPECT OF SOCIAL HOUSING ALLOCATION

Contents

INTRODUCTION

2.1 Access to straightforward information about how the local housing allocations scheme operates is crucial to applicants having confidence in the process. Consequently, in the Housing Act 1996 (HA 1996), Pt 6 ('Allocation of Housing Accommodation'), there are specific obligations on local housing authorities to inform members of the public about the content of their allocation schemes, and to provide applicants with advice and information about their individual applications. In addition, local housing authorities are subject to the provisions of the General Data Protection Regulation 2016, the Data Protection Act 2018[1], and the Freedom of Information Act 2000, which may respectively enable applicants to access records relating to their own applications and obtain information about specific aspects of housing allocation locally.

¹   Which replaced the Data Protection Act 1998 as of 25 May 2018.

2.2 HA 1996, Pt 6, also makes reasonably detailed provision about what local housing allocation schemes must contain in relation to the receipt and processing of applications, and the notification of decisions. Those provisions are supplemented by statutory guidance[1].

¹   *Allocation of accommodation: Guidance for local housing authorities in England* (DCLG, June 2012) (the English Code), *Providing social housing for local people* (DCLG, December 2013) (the Supplementary English Code), *Right to Move: Statutory Guidance on Social Housing Allocations for Local Housing Authorities in England* (DCLG, March 2015) reproduced in APPENDIX 1 of this book and *Code of Guidance for Local Authorities on the Allocation of Accommodation and Homelessness* (Welsh Government, March 2016) (the Welsh Code), reproduced on the CD Rom with this book.

2.3 Some applicants will, inevitably, be dissatisfied with decisions affecting their applications. In some, but not all, of those cases, HA 1996, Pt 6, gives applicants the right to request a review of those decisions or requires that such a right be provided under the terms of a local allocation scheme. An applicant dissatisfied with the result of a review could bring judicial review proceedings to challenge the decision on review or the process by which it was reached[1]. There is no provision within HA 1996, Pt 6, for an appeal to the county court. For those cases in which reviews are not specifically provided for in HA 1996, Pt 6, the local housing authority may provide an extra-statutory review. In any event, legal challenge to an initial decision, a statutory review decision, or an extra-statutory review decision can only be by way of judicial review.

¹   For 'judicial review proceedings', see CHAPTER 19 of this book.

2.4 Additionally, a complaint about the handling of an individual application can be made via the local housing authority's internal complaints procedure, or be raised with its monitoring officer or, ultimately, be pursued with the Local Government and Social Care Ombudsman (LGSCO) in respect of local housing authorities in England or the Public Services Ombudsman (PSO) for Wales. An applicant who is or has become a tenant of social housing could also complain to the statutory regulator of social housing. In England, that is presently the Regulation Committee of the Homes and Communities Agency. In Wales, the 'regulators' are the Welsh Government and the Welsh Ministers[1]. The complainant can seek redress if it appears that the local housing authority has not complied with the relevant regulator's published national standards (described in CHAPTERS 1 AND 6)[2].

¹   See **1.36–1.39**.
²   Housing and Regeneration Act 2008, Pt 2 as amended by Localism Act 2011, Sch 17 (England). See **1.30–1.39** and **6.14–6.21**.

2.5 This chapter reviews, in sequence, the statutory duties upon local housing authorities to provide information for applicants, to receive and process applications, and to notify decisions on those applications. Readers concerned with applications being made directly to housing associations and other private registered providers or registered social landlords will find assistance in CHAPTER 6.

INFORMATION

General information and advice about local social housing allocation

2.6 HA 1996, Pt 6, requires local housing authorities to ensure that advice and information about the right to apply for social housing accommodation is available free of charge to everyone in their districts[1]. Although HA 1996, Pt 6, elsewhere specifically requires the publication of a free summary of the allocation scheme[2], this general duty to make information and advice available goes much wider than that.

[1]   HA 1996, s 166(1)(a).
[2]   HA 1996, s 168(1).

2.7 The information provided by local housing authorities should include information about housing allocation procedures and also potential stock availability. Statutory guidance advises that information should also be available about qualification and prioritisation criteria[1].

[1]   English Code, para 5.4, Welsh Code, para 3.15.

2.8 Local housing authorities may also wish to provide general information about the profile of their stock, including the type, size and location of the housing, whether it is accessible or could be adapted, whether there is access to a shared or private garden, and how old it is. Where stock is in short supply, an indication of how frequently it is likely to become available would also be helpful.

2.9 The Chartered Institute of Housing (CIH) has identified that:

'the publication of accessible and free information is vital in enabling people to take responsibility for their own housing solutions. This should additionally include information about housing options that exist within a local area. Where local authorities have stock or have nomination rights to partners' stock, it is important how that stock will be used and who is eligible for help is clear to everyone. This will be particularly important in the light of the local variations and additions that government is proposing to allow local authorities to introduce. The variety of local differences mean that clarity of local conditions and eligibility will be even more important to help people navigate local circumstances and make effective and empowered choices for themselves[1].'

[1]   *How to . . . consider new approaches to allocations and lettings* (CIH, April 2012).

2.10 Care must be taken to ensure that this advice and information is accessible to all. The Welsh Code advises that information should be easy to understand and that it should be available on request in translation, in alternative formats (Braille, large print, and audiotapes, etc), and through a variety of media, including printed hard copy, online, and via the telephone[1]. The former Commission for Racial Equality's Code of Practice on Racial Equality in Housing[2] includes this pertinent example of the care that needs to be taken in preparing information:

'A local council (or housing association) fails to make sure that information about its lettings services reaches people from all racial groups; for example, by not advertising the service in outlets which it knows are preferred by ethnic minority residents. This could amount to indirect discrimination' (Example 35).

¹ Welsh Code, paras 1.25–1.29 and 3.49.
² See **4.227**.

2.11 Prospective applicants may also have the right to obtain a broader range of information about social housing allocation under the General Data Protection Regulation 2016, the Data Protection Act 2018 and the Freedom of Information Act 2000¹.

¹ English Code, para 5.7 and see **2.28–2.29**.

2.12 For some enquirers, the provision of information will suffice. But the statutory duty under HA 1996, s 166(1)(a), also requires that *advice* must be available free of charge. This can be particularly important where the local housing authority has adopted a choice-based letting scheme that requires applicants to be proactive in securing an allocation. Suitable advice could be provided by the local housing authority itself, a social landlord, or the voluntary sector, and is likely to be most effective if the adviser has appropriate housing-related experience and is properly trained to sensitively meet the needs of a diverse client group.

Information about a particular local allocation scheme

2.13 Each local housing authority is required by HA 1996, Pt 6, to publish a summary of its allocation scheme and to make a copy of that summary available free of charge to 'any member of the public who asks for one'¹. The request for a copy can come from 'any member of the public'. There is no requirement that the person making the request should also be an applicant under the local housing authority's allocation scheme, or even a prospective applicant. Indeed, there is no requirement that the person should have any connection with that particular local housing authority's district. Any member of the public, anywhere in the country, is entitled to receive a free summary of any local housing authority's allocation scheme on request. Obviously, it is this provision that allows advisers to collect summaries of any allocation schemes that might be useful to them in advising members of the public.

¹ HA 1996, s 168(1).

2.14 There is no requirement to publish the whole of the allocation scheme, although many local housing authorities do put their full scheme on their website¹ and in Wales the expectation is that all local housing authorities will do so². However, each local housing authority must 'make the scheme available for inspection at their principal office'³. The principal office is usually the town hall, or the central address for the housing department. Members of the public do not, however, need to attend the principal office, in person, in order to see the full scheme. If they ask for a copy (in person, by post, by phone, or by email), and pay any required fee (which can only be a reasonable amount), the local housing authority 'shall provide' a copy of the full scheme⁴.

Again, advisers may consider purchasing copies of the allocation schemes operated by the local housing authorities which deal with the majority of their clients, or may simply download copies from websites.

1   Local housing authority websites are usually at the government's domain name: thus, a typical address would be www.anytown.gov.uk. In preparing the report *Exploring local authority policy and practice on housing allocations* (CLG, July 2009) researchers found that only 71% of local housing authorities surveyed had published the full scheme on their websites. Even among those operating choice-based letting schemes, 15% had not done so.
2   Welsh Code, paras 3.15 and 3.49.
3   HA 1996, s 168(2).
4   HA 1996, s 168(2).

2.15 Sadly, not all local housing authorities readily embraced the statutory requirement to make the full scheme available for purchase on demand. The full scheme, which must cover 'all aspects of the allocation process'[1], will often be a substantial document and there is not infrequently a degree of reticence in supplying copies. In 2004/2005 one limited exercise in requesting copy schemes from 12 local housing authorities in London produced only four responses within 14 days, five further responses within 28 days, and the remaining three only after complaints to the monitoring officer for each local housing authority and service of a pre-action protocol letter threatening judicial review proceedings[2]. A good deal of time and legal expense can be wasted when a failure to respond promptly to a request for a copy of the scheme leads to a claim for a mandatory order in judicial review proceedings[3]. Such claims will almost never come to trial, for obvious reasons, but will leave local housing authorities with substantial legal costs easily exceeding the expense of supplying a copy of the scheme promptly in response to the initial request.

1   HA 1996, s 166A(1) (England), s 167(1) (Wales).
2   Robert Latham 'Allocating accommodation: reconciling choice and need' (2005) March *Legal Action*, p 16 and (2005) May *Legal Action*, p 15.
3   As in *R (Onuegbu) v Hackney London Borough Council* [2005] EWHC 1277 (Admin), (2005) August *Legal Action*, p 17, Admin Ct.

Information about applications

2.16 When a person applies for an allocation of social housing, he or she must be informed by the local housing authority of his or her relevant statutory rights, or the local housing authority must secure that someone else informs the applicant of those rights[1]. The relevant rights are:

- the right to request such general information as will enable the applicant to assess how his or her application is likely to be treated under the scheme, including whether he or she is likely to fall within any of the groups entitled to a reasonable preference[2];
- the right to request such general information as will enable him or her to assess whether accommodation appropriate to his or her needs is likely to be made available and, if so, how long it is likely to be before an offer is made[3];

- the right (if the application is made to a local housing authority in Wales) to be notified in writing of any decision that he or she is *not* to be given any reasonable preference that he or she would ordinarily have been entitled to receive, and of the reasons for that decision[4];
- the right to ask the local housing authority to inform him or her of any decision about the facts of his or her case which has been, or is likely to be, taken into account when considering whether to allocate accommodation[5];
- the right to request a review of any decision that he or she is *not* to be given reasonable preference, any decision as to the facts of his or her case, any decision that he or she is *not* eligible for an allocation, or (if the application is made to a local housing authority in England) any decision that he or she is not a qualifying person for an allocation[6]; and
- the right to be informed of a review decision and the grounds for that review decision[7].

1   HA 1996, s 166A (England) and s 166(2) (Wales). The Welsh Code suggests that this duty should be implemented within the context of 'a constructive housing options approach, so that applicants will understand their prospects of being rehoused into the accommodation they are seeking': Welsh Code, para 3.205.
2   HA 1996, s 166A(9)(a)(i) (England), s 167(4A)(a)(i) (Wales).
3   HA 1996, s 166A(9)(a)(ii) (England), s 167(4A)(a)(ii) (Wales).
4   HA 1996, s 167(4A)(b) (Wales only).
5   HA 1996, s 166A(9)(b) (England), s 167(4A)(c) (Wales).
6   HA 1996, s 166A(9)(c) (England), s 167(4A)(d) (Wales).
7   HA 1996, s 166A(9)(c) (England), s 167(4A)(d) (Wales).

2.17 Such information must be given to *every* applicant and, plainly, the terms of the statutory provision indicate a policy intention that the information should be provided when the application is first received, in a written acknowledgement of, or response to, the application or as accompanying information to the acknowledgement or response.

2.18 As is clear from the first two items in the list above, the applicant may request 'general information' which will enable him or her to assess how the application is likely to be treated, whether he or she will be entitled to any preference, whether he or she is likely to receive accommodation and, if so, after what period. There is no time limit specified within which this information must be requested. It follows, therefore, that the applicant may request this information *at any time*, once he or she has made the application. Of all the available information, it is this – a realistic appraisal of the prospects of obtaining a suitable local allocation – that the applicant is most likely to want. Many advisers will have drawn up pro-forma requests for this information, to enclose when writing to a local housing authority about individual applications.

2.19 The statutory Codes of Guidance on social housing allocation do not contain much guidance on what sort of information the applicant could expect to receive, having made his or her request. Local housing authorities might usefully maintain lists of properties earmarked for special groups (eg properties adapted for disabled use, etc), and make those lists available to relevant applicants. However, only a small number of applicants will benefit from that sort of information[1].

[1] See **4.165–4.171**.

2.20 For most applicants, the information that they receive in response to such a request should include:

- whether or not they have been accepted as eligible for an allocation;
- whether or not (in England) they qualify for an allocation;
- the type of property they are likely to be allocated;
- the method that will be used in assessing their needs, whether by awarding points or by inclusion in a specific group or band, or otherwise;
- the number of other applicants with equal or greater priority; and
- an assessment of the likely time that they will have to wait to receive an offer (or to make a successful bid in a choice-based letting scheme), by reference to average waiting time or to the number of lettings of similar properties in the previous year or quarter.

2.21 This sort of information allows the applicant an opportunity to assess his or her realistic (if sometimes depressing) chances of receiving an offer. It may usefully be accompanied by a copy of the free published summary of the particular local housing authority's allocation scheme. In short, the thrust of the statutory provisions is that the local allocations process, and information about it, should be transparent and open:

> 'we want a really open and transparent allocation scheme so that anybody can see what a particular council's scheme is, and can understand why they have been included or excluded and whether it is appropriate for them to appeal[1].'

[1] Andrew Stunnell MP, Under-Secretary of State, House of Commons Public Bill Committee on the Localism Bill, 3 March 2011, col 765.

2.22 These aspects of HA 1996, Pt 6, dealing with the provision of information, make it unnecessary for applicants to rely on the general rights to provision of information by a local housing authority set out in Housing Act 1985, s 106. That section was specifically amended by the Homelessness Act 2002 to disapply its provisions so far as they impose requirements corresponding to those to which a local housing authority is now subject under HA 1996, s 168[1].

[1] Housing Act 1985, s 106(6).

2.23 Of course, in order to be able to measure the information that he or she has received against what actually happens in practice - in terms of the distribution of housing under a local housing authority's allocation scheme – an applicant will need access to information about the outcomes applicants generally achieve under the local scheme. Indeed, one function of the current statutory guidance in England is 'to encourage authorities to be open and transparent about who is applying for and being allocated social housing in their area'[1]. That guidance specifically advises that:

> 'It is important that applicants and the wider community understand how social housing is allocated in their area, and that they know who is getting that social

housing, so that they can see that the allocation system is fair and the authority is complying with its allocation scheme. We would encourage housing authorities to consider how accurate and anonymised information on waiting list applicants and lettings outcomes could be routinely published, to strengthen public confidence in the fairness of their allocation scheme[2].'

---

[1] *Providing social housing for local people* (DCLG, December 2013) (the Supplementary English Code), para 10.
[2] The Supplementary English Code, para 28.

2.24 However, it does not follow from the duty to publish the scheme, or to provide either person-specific or more general information about likely or actual outcomes, that:

'an applicant is entitled to be able to predict when and if he will actually be accorded accommodation. There are many uncertainties, thus, for instance, the Authority cannot know for certain which of its properties will become vacant or what size they will be. Some people who were on the list may leave the area or, for other reasons, no longer be eligible to bid. Other people may move into the area or join one of the categories to whom reasonable preference must be given. The two Codes of Guidance specifically contemplate that an Authority may use quotas and confine bidding for specific properties to particular groups on its list. I recognize . . . that this will mean that the operation of the Scheme is not as transparent as it might otherwise be . . . [1].'

---

[1] *R (Babakandi) v Westminster City Council* [2011] EWHC 1756 (Admin), (2011) August *Legal Action*, p 40, at [20].

2.25 On an application for permission to appeal in that particular case, Lord Justice Sullivan said:

'The mere proposition that [an allocation scheme] might be more transparent is not sufficient to establish unlawfulness. To a degree there is bound to be a trade off between simplicity and the complexity inherent in any scheme that tries to monitor and adjust to ensure that particular targets are being met. What precisely results from that trade off is very much a matter for the judgment of the local authority: the more sensitive the scheme, it may well be the more complex it will be, and therefore it can be said that the less transparent it will be, but it seems to me that it could not be said that this scheme is so opaque as to be unlawful[1].'

---

[1] *R (Babakandi) v Westminster City Council* [2011] EWCA Civ 1397, (2012) January *Legal Action*, p 21, CA at [5].

Information about specific facts

2.26 The applicant has the right to ask the local housing authority to inform him or her of any decision about the facts of his or her case which is likely to be, or have been, taken into account in considering whether to allocate housing accommodation to him or her[1]. This right is supplemented by the right of every applicant to have made available, on request, at all reasonable times and without charge, details of the particulars which he or she has given to the authority about himself or herself and about his or her family and which the authority has recorded as being relevant to the application for accommodation[2]. These rights to information are only triggered if the applicant requests the information; there is no automatic requirement on the local housing authority to give this information to the applicant as a matter of course. The right first mentioned above is a right to be informed of any decision taken 'about the facts of his [or her] case'[3]. The 'facts' relied upon by the local housing authority in reaching its decision may have come from various sources: from the applicant, but also from housing officers, doctors, schools, other professionals or agencies, or even neighbours.

[1]   HA 1996, s 166A(9)(b) (England), s 167(4A)(c) (Wales).
[2]   Housing Act 1985, s 106(5) (earlier disapplied by the Access to Personal Files Act 1987 which has itself now been repealed). Note that s 106 only operates in this context to the extent that HA 1996, Pt 6 itself gives no statutory right to the information sought: s 106(6).
[3]   HA 1996, s 166A(9)(b) (England), s 167(4A)(c) (Wales).

2.27 The right to be informed about decisions made on factual issues is not limited to the facts which the local housing authority takes into account in determining general issues about whether to allocate accommodation to the applicant, for example, as to his or her eligibility or priority. The wording is sufficiently broad to enable an applicant to ask to be informed about any decisions, for example, about decisions as to whether he or she will be considered for, or why he or she was not considered for, a particular property.

2.28 Local housing authorities are also subject to the information disclosure requirements of the General Data Protection Regulation 2017 and the Data Protection Act 2018, giving any individual the right to obtain confirmation as to whether or not 'personal data' concerning him or her is being processed and, if so, access to that personal data.[1] The individual also has the right to be told the purposes of the processing, what categories of personal data are involved, to whom the personal data has been or will be disclosed, for how long the personal data will be stored, his or her right to request rectification or erasure of the personal data or to lodge a complaint, from where the personal data has been collected if not the individual, and information in respect of any automated decision-making that is occurring.[2] 'Personal data' means any data relating to a natural person who is identified or can be identified directly or indirectly, including by reference to an identification number.[3] A request may be made verbally or in writing. The local housing authority must comply with the request without undue delay and at the latest within one month.[4] The information must be provided free of charge, except where the request is manifestly unfounded or excessive, in which case the local housing authority may charge a reasonable fee or refuse the request.[5] The advice given in the English Code in respect of the Data Protection Act 1998, namely that if local housing authorities remain unclear about their obligations and responsibilities in the context of social housing allocation they may wish to contact the office of the Information Commissioner[6], remains valid.

[1]   General Data Protection Regulation 2016, Art 15, and Data Protection Act 2018, s 45.
[2]   General Data Protection Regulation 2016, Art 15, and Data Protection Act 2018, ss 15 and 45.
[3]   General Data Protection Regulation 2016, Art 4, and Data Protection Act 2018, s 3.
[4]   General Data Protection Regulation 2016, Recital 59, and Data Protection Act 2018, ss 4 and 45.
[5]   General Data Protection Regulation 2016, Art 12, and Data Protection Act 2018, ss 2 and 53.

⁶   English Code, para 5.7. The website of the Information Commissioner is at https://ico.org.uk. See generally *Findings from ICO advisory visits to social housing organisations* (Information Commissioner's Office, February 2014).

2.29 Local housing authorities are also subject to the information disclosure provisions of the Freedom of Information Act 2000. An individual is entitled to make a written request to a public authority, which includes a local housing authority, and to be informed by the public authority whether it holds information of the description specified in the request and, if so, to have that information communicated to the individual, unless the information is exempt[1]. 'Personal data' is exempt from disclosure, as it is provided to the public authority in confidence[2]. The Freedom of Information Act 2000 can therefore be used to obtain the local housing authority's policies[3], procedures and other general information about social housing allocation, but not confidential information about a particular application. The duties imposed by the Freedom of Information Act 2000 are *additional* to the duties imposed by HA 1996, Pt 6, to provide information. For example, an applicant may use a request under the Freedom of Information Act 2000 to obtain a list of local housing authority properties in a particular area or throughout a local housing authority's district in order to know what properties *might* become available[4]. However, where a local housing authority was asked to give the addresses of properties owned by a private registered provider operating in its area it was entitled to provide that information in a way that did not allow individual occupiers to be identified[5].

¹   Freedom of Information Act 2000, s 1; exemptions are at ss 21–44 inclusive.
²   Freedom of Information Act 2000, s 40.
³   See, for example, *W v West Lothian Council*, Decision 074/2015, 3 June 2015, Scottish Information Commissioner.
⁴   See *Decision Notice concerning Mid Devon DC* [2006] 4 May, Information Commissioner Ref FS50082890, (2006) July *Legal Action*, p 26; and *Decision Notice concerning Braintree DC* (2006) 4 May, Information Commissioner Ref FS50066606, (2007) March *Legal Action*, p 13.
⁵   *Turcotte v Information Commissioner* [2008] 12 June, Information Tribunal Case no EA/2007/0129.

Confidentiality

2.30 The applicant has the personal right to confidentiality, in that the fact that an application has been made cannot be divulged to any other member of the public without the applicant's consent[1]. Routinely, of course, local housing authorities request consent from applicants so that they can seek information from others, such as doctors or social workers, to help them determine an application for social housing. This consent should not, however, be treated as a general consent permitting the local housing authority to inform others, who do not need to know, that an application has been made. In practice, a considerable issue has arisen about the sharing of information between local housing authorities and private registered providers or registered social landlords about applicants nominated to such landlords for housing allocation. Local housing authorities could usefully draw up information sharing protocols to cover such situations, but any sharing of personal information about an applicant can only be achieved by consent of the applicant and only in compliance with the General Data Protection Regulation 2016. To facilitate the drawing up of information-sharing protocols, the former Housing Corporation published a national standard protocol on sharing information about applicants for re-housing[2].

1 HA 1996, s 166(4).
2 *Access to Housing: Information sharing protocol* (Housing Corporation, November 2007).

APPLICATIONS

Making an application

2.31 Local housing authorities are under no duty to seek out those most in need of any available social housing. Their statutory responsibilities are confined to responding to, and considering, applications made to them by those seeking allocation of any available stock. So, for all those seeking social housing, everything turns on successfully making an application and then pursuing its proper consideration under the terms of the allocation scheme adopted by the local housing authority to which the application is made.

2.32 However, to ensure that the most vulnerable are not disadvantaged in gaining access to what might be available, each local housing authority must ensure that free advice and information is available in its district about the right to make an application for social housing[1]. Each local housing authority must also ensure that free assistance is provided to anyone who is likely to have difficulty in making an application[2].

1 HA 1996, s 166(1)(a); see **2.6–2.12**.
2 HA 1996, s 166(1)(b); see **2.44–2.47**.

2.33 Many of those most in need of social housing will have sought the help of the local housing authority because they were homeless or facing the prospect of homelessness. An application for homelessness assistance (made under HA 1996, Pt 7 'Homelessness: England' or Housing (Wales) Act 2014, Pt 2 'Homelessness') does *not* automatically count as an application for an allocation of social housing (under HA 1996, Pt 6), and therefore local housing authorities receiving applications for homelessness assistance should ensure that applicants also complete any separate application forms required for their allocation schemes[1].

1 The *Homelessness Code of Guidance for Local Authorities* (MHCLG, February 2018) (the English Homelessness Code) para 3.7, suggests that 'many people concerned about a risk of homelessness will be seeking practical advice and assistance' and that advice on a number of issues, including 'how to apply for social housing' may help to prevent people from becoming threatened with homelessness. In one case, a delay of six months between a young applicant approaching a local housing authority for homelessness assistance and him being helped to complete a social housing allocation application compounded a catalogue of maladministration: *Complaint against Dover City Council*, 09 017 510, 31 July 2012, Local Government Ombudsman, (2012) October *Legal Action*, p 36.

2.34 Although HA 1996, Pt 6, does not explicitly say so in terms, everyone has a right to make an application to any, or indeed every, local housing authority, although they may not necessarily qualify or be eligible for an allocation by that authority[1]. Applications cannot be restricted or rejected simply because the local housing authority to which the application has been made has little or no vacant housing currently available. The chosen local housing authority may not even own any property to rent, perhaps having disposed of its housing stock, but it must still receive and process applications under its allocation scheme and then 'allocate' by making nominations to local private registered providers or registered social landlords, or to other local housing authorities, under that scheme[2].

[1]   HA 1996, s 166(1), which deals with the provision of information, refers to 'the right to make an application' and the English Code, para 5.4, uses the term 'right to apply for an allocation'.
[2]   HA 1996, s 159(2)(c).

2.35 There is no minimum age restriction on applications and nothing in the statutory scheme suggests that a person who is 'dependent' on another cannot apply[1].

[1]   In contrast to an application for homelessness assistance: see **8.40–8.46**. See also *R v Oldham Metropolitan Borough Council ex p Garlick* [1993] AC 509, HL.

2.36 There is no statutorily prescribed form for the making of an application. The only requirement, in order to have an application considered, is that the application must be made in accordance with the procedural requirements (if any) set out in the allocation scheme of the local housing authority to which the application is directed[1]. If the scheme requires that a particular application form should be completed, the form should ideally be straightforward to complete but might well also be sufficiently detailed to enable a wide range of information to be obtained from the applicant (eg as to age, religion, sexual orientation, ethnicity, disability, gender, any support needs, immigration status, and composition of the household). The Welsh Code suggests that the forms should be accompanied by guidance notes which are themselves easy to understand and 'in plain language'[2].

[1]   HA 1996, s 166(3).
[2]   Welsh Code, para 3.202.

2.37 Separate applications must be made to each local housing authority from which the applicant seeks consideration for an allocation. To make the process easier for applicants, local housing authorities and private registered providers or registered social landlords which are collaborating in regional or sub-regional allocation arrangements might usefully have a single application form that can be treated as constituting an application to them all[1].

[1]   See **6.53–6.59**.

2.38 There are no statutory pre-conditions to the making of an application. The local housing authority cannot impose a charge for receiving an application or for its consideration. Even if the local housing authority believes that the applicant is highly likely to be found to be ineligible for an allocation or (in England) not to qualify, or is likely to be given a very low priority under the local scheme, it must still accept an application from anyone, whether that person is physically in its district or elsewhere, if the application is made in accordance with the relevant procedural requirements (if any) of the local housing authority's scheme (although see **2.73–2.74** in respect of repeat applications)[1]. It is important to emphasise that every application culminates in a written decision. No applicant should be prevented or dissuaded from making an application even if it may be determined, in due course, that he or she is not eligible or (in England) is not within a qualifying class.

¹ HA 1996, s 166(3). For an example of allocations arrangements which unlawfully prevented applicants from submitting an application, see *Complaint against Bristol City Council*, 16 003 575, 3 April 2018, Local Government and Social Care Ombudsman, (2018) June *Legal Action*, p 34.

2.39 Again, so as to ensure that the most vulnerable are not excluded, local housing authorities are advised to ensure that applicants who have no fixed address can make applications[1].

[1] Welsh Code, para 2.71.

2.40 Some local housing authorities require applicants to 'renew' their applications (essentially by re-applying) at regular intervals. This can work to the disadvantage of those applicants with unsettled accommodation, who are in consequence highly mobile, or those applicants who have difficulties with paperwork or bureaucratic processes. Nevertheless, in one challenge to a scheme for the allocation of local housing authority mobile home pitches for Gypsies and Travellers, a judge said[1]:

> 'Nor, in my view, is it irrational to require that registration on the list must be renewed. Given the small number of pitches and the intense competition for the few pitches that do become available, it is essential that those on the list have a continuing interest and continue to meet the criteria. Without an effective sift of that nature, the list could well become unmanageable and would retain on it those who either had no serious interest in securing a pitch in Hackney, or who had far inferior claims in terms of connection with Hackney. A policy that neglected that requirement might indeed be vulnerable to a challenge on the grounds of irrationality.
>
> I fully recognise . . .   that some travellers might well find it burdensome to re-register each year and to keep abreast of any changes in relevant policy, especially those relating to allocation criteria. If a traveller is not able to read and write, as is the case with the claimant, there may be special difficulties in effectively communicating from both sides. However, I am not persuaded that such difficulties, which can potentially lead to unfortunate consequences, vitiate the policy as a whole. The traveller may take appropriate steps to ensure, so far as is practicable, that the person at the c/o address is responsible and is aware of the relevant policy, and is alert to the need for re-registration. The traveller may put in place arrangements by which such person either herself provides the necessary documentation, or takes steps to remind the traveller of what is needed so that the latter can herself take the necessary steps. From the evidence in the case, it is clear that the traveller can attend the Council offices to re-register in person, or to get someone to do that for her, provided the documentation is provided – an extra facility that gives some degree of flexibility to the administrative arrangements.'

[1] *R (McDonagh) v Hackney London Borough Council* [2012] EWHC 373 (Admin), (2012) April *Legal Action*, p 46, Admin Ct per Kenneth Parker J at [29]–[30].

Offences in relation to applications

2.41 It is a criminal offence for a person knowingly or recklessly to make a statement which is false in a material particular or knowingly to withhold information which the local housing authority reasonably requires the applicant to give, in connection with the exercise of any of a local housing authority's functions under HA 1996, Pt 6[1]. A suitable warning to this effect should be included with the information that the applicant receives on, or prior to, making an application. The offence can be committed when making an application or when giving the local housing authority any further information. Guidance suggests that the offence may also be committed during any review procedure[2]. If the false information actually results in the grant of a *secure* tenancy, it may be possible for the local housing authority to recover possession through the civil courts[3]. Likewise, a private registered provider or registered social landlord that has granted an *assured* tenancy in such circumstances may recover possession by court proceedings[4].

[1]   HA 1996, s 171.
[2]   English Code, para 5.11. Welsh Code, para 4.40(ii) and 4.40(iii).
[3]   Housing Act 1985, Sch 2, Ground 5; English Code, para 5.12; and Welsh Code, para 4.41.
[4]   Housing Act 1988, Sch 2, Ground 17.

2.42 Of course, providing false information can also constitute an offence under the general criminal law. Recent prosecutions under the Fraud Act 2006 and under the Forgery and Counterfeiting Act 1981 have been brought against applicants for housing who have given false information or failed to disclose plainly relevant information. Successful prosecutions in housing allocation fraud cases have led to custodial sentences[1] or significant non-custodial penalties[2].

[1]   See, for example, the 18-month term imposed in *R v Opaleye*, Wood Green Crown Court, 11 May 2015, (2015) September *Legal Action*, p 53, the 30-month sentences in *R v Odulate*, Kingston Crown Court, 14 August 2015, (2015) October *Legal Action*, p 41, and the 15-month sentence in *Ealing London Borough Council v Qayum*, Isleworth Crown Court, 15 June 2015, (2015) October *Legal Action*, p 41.
[2]   See *Ealing London Borough Council v Asifiri*, Uxbridge Magistrates' Court, 26 June 2015, (2015) October *Legal Action*, p 41, and *Wolverhampton City Council v Mpofu and Mpofu*, Wolverhampton Magistrates' Court, 12 November 2013, (2014) February *Legal Action*, p 30: 3 and 12-month community orders for fraudulent homelessness applications.

2.43 Although the title of the Prevention of Social Housing Fraud Act 2013 suggests that it might contain offences and penalties relating to applications for social housing, that Act is primarily concerned with sub-letting of social housing by current tenants. However, the 2013 Act does contain regulation-making powers designed to assist social landlords in conducting investigations into social housing fraud more widely, including in relation to an offence 'under the Fraud Act 2006 relating to an application for an allocation of housing accommodation under Pt 6 of the Housing Act 1996'[1].

[1]   Prevention of Social Housing Fraud Act 2013, s 7(7)(c). The regulations made pursuant to the power are the Prevention of Social Housing Fraud (Power to Require Information) (England) Regulations 2014, SI 2014/899 and the Prevention of Social Housing Fraud (Detection of Fraud) (Wales) Regulations 2014, SI 2014/826 (W 84). See Welsh Code, paras 4.42–4.44.

Assistance in making an application

2.44 As already explained[1], local housing authorities are required to ensure that free *advice* and *information* about the right to make an application for an allocation of social housing is available to people in their districts[2]. But they are also required to ensure that free *assistance* is provided to anyone in their districts who is likely to have difficulty in making an application[3]. Local housing authorities may provide this assistance directly through their own staff (eg in Housing Advice Centres), or may contract the services out to independent advice agencies or other providers[4].

[1] See **2.6–2.12**.
[2] HA 1996, s 166(1)(a).
[3] HA 1996, s 166(1)(b), English Code, para 5.5, Welsh Code, paras 3.51 and 3.202.
[4] See CHAPTER **21**.

2.45 The Welsh Code recommends that the written advice and information available to those needing assistance should be available in a range of formats and languages, as appropriate to the needs of the area[1], including audio tapes, large print versions or Braille copies, as well as copies in the different languages commonly used in the district[2]. Those likely to need information in a different format will obviously also be more likely to need specialist support in making their application for an allocation. The local housing authority will need to have addressed these issues in any equality impact assessments (under the Equality Act 2010) made in relation to the adoption of (or changes to) the allocation scheme[3]. The Welsh Code advises that local housing authorities should ensure that language and interpretation support is available for those applicants who have difficulty speaking or reading in English[4].

[1] Welsh Code, paras 3.202–3.203.
[2] Welsh Code, paras 3.51, 3.202–3.203.
[3] See **4.193–4.209**.
[4] Welsh Code, paras 2.28 and 3.202.

2.46 Particular issues arise where a local housing authority operates a choice-based letting scheme requiring applicants to bid for advertised properties. Assistance must be made available to those who may need help to bid regularly[1]. The housebound, prisoners, and Gypsies and Travellers may obviously need special help to make applications, as they will not necessarily have access to the internet or be able to attend at pick-up points to collect free sheets describing available properties. Guidance given by the Equality and Human Rights Commission (EHRC) emphasises that[2]:

> 'providers will need to ensure that the online materials are available in accessible formats and that arrangements are in place for those applicants without computer access to get information, in accessible formats, about properties and how to bid for them.'

Local housing authorities might usefully consider how to meet the needs of applicants who are deaf, blind or partially sighted, who have learning disabilities or who cannot read English. Obviously, any reasonable adjustment sought by an applicant on account of his or her disability should be made. For example, an applicant who could not read printed material could require that the local housing authority advise him or her by telephone of suitable properties available. In one case, in which the re-housing of a housebound disabled tenant depended on her husband and full-time carer checking every week what properties had been advertised under a local housing authority's scheme, the Local Government Ombudsman[3] (LGO) said that 'it was insensitive to expect someone in [his] position to devote time and energy to bidding for properties'[4].

[1]   Welsh Code, para 3.51.
[2]   *Guidance for social housing providers* (EHRC, September 2017).
[3]   As of 19 June 2017, the Local Government and Social Care Ombudsman (LGSCO).
[4]   *Complaint against Leeds City Council* 05/C/13157, 20 November 2007, (2008) January *Legal Action*, p 37.

2.47 In *Housing and the Disability Equality Duty: A guide to the Disability Equality Duty and Disability Discrimination Act 2005 for the social housing sector*, the former Disability Rights Commission suggested that when local housing authorities make impact assessments of choice-based lettings arrangements, they should consider these questions:

- Is advertising accessible?
- Are a property's accessible features advertised?
- Does a mechanism exist to identify the requirements of disabled applicants?
- Is there a mechanism to allow extra time for disabled applicants if they need it?
- Is there a mechanism for providing support in making applications[1]?

[1]   *Housing and the Disability Equality Duty: A guide to the Disability Equality Duty and Disability Discrimination Act 2005 for the social housing sector* (DRC, 2006) p 56. See now Welsh Codes, paras 3.97–3.104.

Processing applications

2.48 When an application has been received, the local housing authority will normally consider, first, whether an applicant is 'eligible' and, if in England, 'qualified' for an allocation of social housing under the terms of the statute and its own allocation scheme[1]. It is important that the local housing authority decides eligibility and qualification at the initial application stage, because an applicant permitted to engage with the allocation scheme (eg by being allowed to bid for properties in a choice-based letting scheme) may have a legitimate expectation[2] that he or she will receive full consideration for an allocation. However, the issues of eligibility and qualification may be revisited immediately prior to any prospective allocation to take account of any changed circumstances since the initial application 'particularly where a substantial amount of time has elapsed since the original application'[3].

[1]   See CHAPTER 3.
[2]   For a further discussion of 'legitimate expectation' see **4.50–4.53**.
[3]   English Code, para 3.2.

2.49 If the local housing authority decides that the applicant *is* eligible (and, in England, *is* within a class of qualifying persons), it should then consider, by applying the provisions of its housing allocation scheme:

- whether he or she falls into any of the categories to which it must give reasonable preference[1];
- whether he or she is entitled to any additional preference[2];

- (if the application is made to a local housing authority in Wales) whether the applicant's behaviour permits the local housing authority to give him or her no preference at all[3]; and
- what increased or reduced priority the applicant is entitled to under the scheme as compared to other applicants[4].

[1] HA 1996, s 166A(3) (England), s 167(2) (Wales). See also **4.54–4.112**.
[2] HA 1996, s 166A(3) (England), s 167(2) (Wales). See also **4.113–4.144**.
[3] HA 1996, s 167(2B) and (2C) (Wales only). See also **4.150–4.158**.
[4] HA 1996, s 166A(5) (England), s 167(2A) (Wales). See also **4.113–4.144**.

2.50 There is no statutory deadline or time limit within which the local housing authority must decide these questions once it has received an application, although a commitment to process applications within a particular period might well be made by a local housing authority in its own allocation scheme. If it becomes plain that the application is not being considered at all, the applicant may need to seek a mandatory order in a claim for judicial review. If the application is being considered, but progress is unduly slow, the applicant may wish to make a complaint under the local housing authority's own complaints procedure[1] or, if that proves unsatisfactory, seek the help of the LGSCO (in England) or the PSO (in Wales)[2].

[1] Information about the local housing authority's own complaints procedure should be supplied to applicants by the local housing authority itself.
[2] See **2.109–2.120** and more generally http://www.lgo.org.uk and www.ombudsman-wales.org.uk.

2.51 Where a local housing authority is operating a choice-based letting scheme, it may wish to make only a preliminary assessment of an initial application (in order to avoid spending resources on examining in detail applications from applicants who have no realistic prospect of successfully bidding), and to reserve detailed scrutiny to a later stage (eg when an applicant has bid for, and appears to qualify for, the allocation of a particular property).

2.52 Some local housing authorities, operating choice-based letting schemes, may arrange to review applications in detail *twice*, ie at both the initial application stage and again at the bidding stage. On that model, at the second stage, the application will again be assessed to determine whether the applicant:

- is still eligible; and
- (in England) is still a qualifying person; and
- meets any specific letting criteria for the particular property; and
- still has the appropriate priority for an allocation to be made; and
- matches any size criteria for the property (in light of the composition of the applicant's household).

2.53 Local housing authorities adopting this approach may find that they are required to notify decisions[1] on more than one occasion for each applicant and will need to include the detail of the procedures that will be operated at each stage in their allocation schemes.

[1] See **2.100–2.102**.

2.54 The advice in the English Code relating to double-testing for eligibility and qualification (at the stage of determining the initial application and at the pre-offer stage) does not sit happily with the drafting of the eligibility regulations[1]. At least in terms of transitional provisions, those regulations focus on the position when an applicant's *application* was first made[2].

[1] See CHAPTER 3.
[2] Allocation of Housing and Homelessness (Eligibility) (England) Regulations 2006, SI 2006/1294, reg 8, reproduced in APPENDIX 2.

Transfer applications (from current tenants of social housing)

2.55 Not all transfer cases will be handled through the housing allocation scheme arrangements made under HA 1996, Pt 6. That Part does not apply in England or in Wales *unless* the transfer is tenant-initiated, ie the tenant has made the application for a transfer himself or herself[1]. A transfer offered to a tenant at the landlord's initiative (usually called a 'management transfer'), eg as part of a decanting programme, does not count as triggering the provisions of HA 1996, Pt 6, at all[2].

[1] HA 1996, s 159(4B)(b) (England), s 159(5) (Wales).
[2] English Code, para 1.9, Welsh Code, paras 2.10 and 3.18.

2.56 Where the transfer *is* tenant-initiated, the secure, assured, introductory, or other tenants of social housing wishing to apply for transfers to alternative social housing accommodation have the same rights as applicants who are not existing social housing tenants:

• to make applications;
• to have their applications considered;
• to be notified as to their rights to information and review; and
• to have the fact of their application kept confidential[1].

Applications to a local housing authority by current tenants of social housing can be made not only by tenants of that local housing authority but also by tenants of any other social landlord (whether a different local housing authority or a private registered provider or registered social landlord)[2]. However, as explained below, the provisions of HA 1996, Pt 6, relating to transfers operate differently in respect of applications made to local housing authorities in Wales from the way they operate in England.

[1] Welsh Code, paras 3.17–3.18.
[2] English Code, para 1.5.

2.57 In both England and Wales, transfer applications will initially be treated in the same way as all other applications[1], *except* that the local housing authority should not make inquiries into the eligibility of transfer applicants. That is because secure or introductory tenants, and assured tenants of social landlords, are eligible for a further allocation regardless of their immigration or habitual residence status[2].

[1] Welsh Code, paras 3.17–3.18.
[2] HA 1996, s 160ZA(5) (England), s 160A(6) (Wales). Note that, in respect of assured tenants, the exemption from the eligibility requirement in Wales is only available to those who were

granted that tenancy as a result of an allocation by a local housing authority in Wales. English Code, para 3.4 and Welsh Code, para 2.13(i). For 'eligibility' see CHAPTER 3.

2.58 In Wales, subject to that exception, all transfer applications made to local housing authorities will be handled through the local allocation scheme. Local housing authorities in Wales have been asked by the Welsh Government to ensure that social housing tenants who are under-occupying get particular assistance when they apply for transfers[1].

[1]   Welsh Code, para 3.17.

2.59 In England, however, even if a tenant of social housing makes an unsolicited application for a transfer, the provisions of HA 1996, Pt 6, will still not apply unless the local housing authority is satisfied that the transfer applicant qualifies for a 'reasonable preference' under HA 1996, s 166A(3)[1]. Deciding whether a transfer applicant is within a 'reasonable preference' category is therefore a preliminary issue for local housing authorities in England.

[1]   HA 1996, s 159(4B)(c), English Code, para 2.3.

2.60 If the transfer applicant *does* fall into such a category, he or she will be dealt with under the allocation scheme[1]. For *non-priority* transfer applicants, ie applicants who do not qualify for a reasonable preference, the local housing authority can operate separate arrangements either outside, or alongside, the local allocation scheme. Alternatively, all applicants could be dealt with through one overarching housing allocation system applying both to HA 1996, Pt 6 applicants and non-priority transfer applicants[2]. The local housing authority will have to decide what prioritisation arrangements it will apply as between that transfer applicant and all others and, perhaps most crucially, whether to expose a newly available letting to demand from the applicants on the local allocation scheme or, instead, to offer it to one or more of those on the non-priority transfer list[3].

[1]   English Code, paras 1.5 and 2.3.
[2]   English Code, para 1.8.
[3]   The latter alternative may be particularly compelling if there a significant numbers of current social housing tenants under-occupying their homes and willing to move.

2.61 Taking non-priority transfer applicants out of the HA 1996, Pt 6, regime was perceived to be a means of facilitating greater mobility within social housing. The statutory guidance accordingly encourages local housing authorities to use this flexibility, particularly to assist tenants who are presently under-occupying social housing[1]. However, this policy intention of stimulating greater mobility among social housing tenants was not immediately realised. The 2010–15 UK Coalition Government was particularly concerned about tenants wishing to move to take up employment or training opportunities and in September 2014, it undertook a consultation[2] on proposals designed to achieve what would have amounted to a 'right to move' for such transfer applicants within the framework of HA 1996, Pt 6[3]. The latest statutory Code of Guidance issued in England in 2015 is solely concerned with this issue and encourages local housing authorities to take a 'flexible approach' to applicants for transfers wanting to move for work-related reasons[4]. The Welsh Government considers that the flexibility sought to be achieved by the new regulations made in England 'already exists within the reasonable preference hardship grounds'[5].

[1]   English Code, paras 1.6–1.7.
[2]   *Right to Move Consultation* (DCLG, September 2014) and *Right to Move: Response to Consultation* (DCLG, 2015).
[3]   *Housing Mobility Schemes* (House of Commons Library, Standard Note SN04696, 14 November 2014) contains a useful review of the relevant issues.
[4]   *Right to Move: Statutory Guidance on social housing allocations for local housing authorities in England* (DCLG, March 2015).
[5]   Welsh Code, para 3.36.

2.62 Even with this guidance, it appears that few local housing authorities are making use of the greater latitude. A poll published in 2015 found that only 30% of the respondent social landlords had used the increased flexibility to assess transfer applications separately[1].

[1]   The poll was conducted by the Chartered Institute of Housing and reported in *Inside Housing* (February 2015).

2.63 Local housing authorities in England which have exercised their powers to specify classes of applicants as qualifying (or not qualifying) for allocation under HA 1996, Pt 6[1], may decide to apply the same or different qualifying criteria to those *transfer* applicants to whom HA 1996, Pt 6, applies (ie those in the reasonable preference categories). The statutory guidance suggests that there might be sound policy reasons for applying different (more relaxed) criteria to transfer applicants[2]. In response to an amendment to the Localism Bill[3], which would have prevented any qualification requirements being applied to transferring tenants, the government minister said:

> 'We are producing secondary legislation that will outline when local authorities can and cannot prevent people transferring. If there were any evidence that local authorities were disqualifying transferring tenants inappropriately, that would be covered by that secondary legislation, which will not be on hand immediately but is coming[4].'

[1]   HA 1996, s 160ZA(7).
[2]   English Code, para 3.24.
[3]   Which subsequently became the Localism Act 2011.
[4]   *Hansard*, Lords Debates, 5 September 2011, col 32.

2.64 Such regulations have since been made to prevent the qualification criteria of 'local connection' being applied to applicants for transfers from one housing authority area to another for work-related reasons[1].

[1]   Allocation of Housing (Qualification Criteria for Right to Move) (England) Regulations 2015, SI 2015/967.

2.65 Transfer applicants to whom the provisions of HA 1996, Pt 6, apply will enjoy the same rights to be notified of decisions on their applications (and to be informed of their rights to request information) as those described above in relation to new applicants[1]. Those non-priority transfer applicants in England being dealt with outside the provisions of HA 1996, Pt 6, have no formal statutory rights in relation to decision-making or notification and will need to rely on any references made to their circumstances in documents published by the local housing authority, such as a non-statutory Transfers Policy or Transfers Scheme. The local housing authority is only legally obliged to maintain rules relating to transfers by *secure* tenants and to publish a summary of those rules[2].

1 See **2.16**.
2 HA 1985, s 106(1)(a) and (2).

Procedure for handling applications

2.66 There is no prescribed national code in either England or Wales as to the way in which applications must be processed. The respective national authorities have the reserve power to prescribe by regulations the 'principles' that should govern allocation procedures, but the power has not been used except to limit the role of elected members in allocation of properties (see **2.75–2.76**)[1]. The procedure being followed will therefore be that set out in the particular local housing authority's own allocation scheme. This must cover all aspects of the allocation process, including the identity (or description) of the staff by whom decisions will be taken[2]. The relevant statutory regulators of social housing in each country will set and enforce national standards for housing allocation in exercise of their respective statutory powers[3].

1 HA 1996, s 166A(10) (England), s 167(5) (Wales).
2 HA 1996, s 166A(1) (England), s 167(1) (Wales).
3 See **1.31** and **1.36**.

2.67 In dealing with an application for an allocation of social housing, there is no statutory duty upon the local housing authority to 'make . . . inquiries' into the application (in contrast to the position in relation to applications for homelessness assistance in England)[1] nor a duty to make an 'assessment' (of the type required on an application for homelessness assistance in England and Wales)[2]. The extent of any investigation of an application will be outlined in the local allocation scheme. It will, however, be subject to the public law duty which requires a decision-maker to ask the right questions and take reasonable steps to acquaint him or herself with the relevant information to enable him or herself to answer them correctly[3]. Further, where the information before the local housing authority raises a real possibility that the applicant or member of their household may be disabled, the public sector equality duty is likely to impose a duty to make further inquiries[4]. Where, for example, a letter from a GP stated that the local housing authority should send a medical questionnaire and fee form if more information was required, the local housing authority was at fault in deciding that the medical evidence did not address the applicant's mobility needs and suitability of his accommodation without contacting the GP to seek more information[5].

1 HA 1996, s 184(1). See Chapter 9. Indeed, the local housing authority will not owe an applicant a 'duty of care' in the handling of the application at all: *Darby v Richmond Upon Thames London Borough Council* [2015] EWHC 909 (QB), (2015) June *Legal Action*, p 45 QBD. An application for permission to appeal to the Court of Appeal was refused: [2017] EWCA Civ 252. See also *CN and GN (through their Litigation Friend) v Poole Borough Council* [2017] EWCA Civ 2185, CA, in which the Court of Appeal struck out a claim

that was 'in fact a criticism of the housing functions of the local authority' which had been 'shoe-horned into a claim arising from duties and powers under the Children Act 1989', per Irwin LJ at [104].

2 H(W)A 2014, s 62. See CHAPTERS 15 AND 17.
3 *Secretary of State for Education and Science v Tameside Metropolitan Borough Council* [1977] AC 1014, HL per Lord Diplock at 1065B.
4 *Pieretti v London Borough of Enfield* [2011] HLR 3 at [36].
5 *Complaint against Royal London Borough of Kensington and Chelsea*, 16 007 264, 11 January 2017.

2.68 The absence of rigorous statutory control of the process of allocating social housing, and the corresponding flexibility given to local housing authorities, can lead to situations in which both applicants and officials are free to abuse local arrangements for social housing allocation. It is therefore important that local housing authorities not only have detailed procedures, and structures for delegation of decision-making, set out in their allocation schemes but also that these are properly monitored and enforced by the local housing authorities themselves. The English Code advises local housing authorities to consider taking action to minimise the risks of staff fraud and error in allocations, including the vetting of junior staff and the use of senior staff to randomly check and validate decisions on applications[1]. The guidance was drawn up in the light of a striking instance of a member of staff having access to, and abusing, the allocation processes in the largest local housing authority in England (Birmingham)[2].

1 English Code, para 5.13.
2 *Birmingham City Council v Qasim* [2009] EWCA Civ 1080, [2010] HLR 19, CA.

2.69 A lack of clarity as to how applications are determined is also likely to result in unfairness to the applicant. The LGO[1] was asked to investigate a case where the applicant had not been informed that he was required to submit evidence by a certain date and had not been warned that failure to respond in time would lead to his application being removed from the register. The local housing authority was found to be at fault for these omissions[2].

1 As of 19 June 2017, the LGSCO.
2 *Complaint against Epping Forest District Council*, 16 004 599, 7 November 2016.

Applications which trigger other responsibilities

2.70 It may be plain, from the terms in which the applicant has completed the local housing authority's application form, that there is a need for other assistance, even before consideration of the application for social housing allocation is completed.

2.71 If the form provides material which gives a local housing authority in England reason to believe that the applicant may be homeless or threatened with homelessness, it *must* make the inquiries necessary to establish whether it owes the applicant a duty under the homelessness legislation[1]. This is because an application for social housing is an application 'for accommodation', which may trigger the threshold for inquiries into any potential homelessness[2]. If the application for social housing allocation is made to a local housing authority in Wales and it appears to the local housing authority that, on the material in the application form, the person may be homeless or threatened with homelessness, the local housing authority must then conduct the 'assessment' required by homelessness legislation in Wales, in addition to processing the social housing application[3].

1   HA 1996, Pt 7 ('Homelessness: England') as amended by the Homelessness Reduction Act 2017 (HRA 2017) for applications for homelessness assistance made to local housing authorities in England on or after 3 April 2018, see CHAPTER 9.
2   HA 1996, ss 183–184, as amended by HRA 2017, ss 4(3) and 5(3), for applications for homelessness assistance made to local housing authorities in England on or after 3 April 2018. Discussed further in CHAPTER 9; and see *R (Bilverstone) v Oxford City Council* [2003] EWHC 2434 (Admin), [2003] All ER (D) 170 (Oct), Admin Ct and *English Homelessness Code* (MHCLG, February 2018), para 18.6.
3   H(W)A 2014, s 62. See CHAPTER 17.

2.72 Likewise, if the local housing authority is also an adult care and children's services authority, the application may trigger responsibilities under community care or child care legislation[1]. For example, if the application reveals that:

(1)   the applicant is a 'child in need' under the age of 18; and
(2)   he or she is seeking accommodation because the person with parental responsibility is unable to accommodate any longer,

the children's services authority may itself owe a statutory duty to accommodate under the Children Act 1989 (in England) or the Social Services and Well-being (Wales) Act 2014 (in Wales)[2].

1   Welsh Code, para 1.35 and *R v Tower Hamlets London Borough Council ex p Bradford* (1997) 29 HLR 756, QBD.
2   Children Act 1989, s 20. See also *R (M) v Hammersmith and Fulham London Borough Council* [2008] UKHL 14, [2008] 1 WLR 535, HL, and *R (G) v Southwark London Borough Council* [2009] UKHL 26, [2009] 1 WLR 1299, HL; and see **12.145–12.147, 20.39–20.68** and **20.85–20.98**. Note that, on 6 April 2016, Children Act 1989, s 20, in so far as it related to Wales, was replaced by Social Services and Well-being (Wales) Act 2014, s 76. See **20.85–20.98**.

Repeat applications

2.73 In principle, there is nothing to stop an unsuccessful applicant from making a further application at any stage. However, in practice, unless the applicant's circumstances have changed, the decision will be likely to be the same. Indeed, if an application has been fully considered, fairly and on its merits, a local housing authority is entitled to deal with a later re-application on the same facts by asserting that the matter has already been determined, in the absence of any material change of circumstances[1].

1   *R (George) v Hammersmith & Fulham London Borough Council* [2012] EWHC 2369 (Admin), (2012) June *Legal Action*, p 36. Note that permission to appeal to the Court of Appeal was later granted in this case – see [2012] EWCA Civ 1768, (2013) March *Legal Action*, p 20 – but the appeal was never heard.

2.74 HA 1996, Pt 6, specifically provides for re-applications in two circumstances:

(1)   an applicant who has been treated as ineligible by a local housing authority in Wales on account of his or her conduct can make a fresh application at any time, and the Code suggests that, in such a case, it will be for the applicant to show that his or her behaviour or circumstances have changed[1]; and

(2)   if a local housing authority in England decides that a person is not qualified for an allocation because he or she does not fall within a category of qualifying persons, that person can re-apply if he or she considers that he or she should be treated as a qualifying person[2]. The Code suggests that on such a re-application it would be for the applicant to show that his or her circumstances have changed[3]. This is incorrect: and in any event it may be that there has been no change of personal circumstances but the local housing authority may have simply changed its qualifying criteria.

[1]   HA 1996, s 160A(11); Welsh Code, para 2.40.
[2]   HA 1996, s 160ZA(11).
[3]   English Code, para 3.30.

DECISION-MAKING

The role of councillors

2.75 Elected members are prohibited from taking part in any decisions on an individual allocation if the accommodation is in their electoral ward or if the person subject to the allocation decision has a sole or main residence in their electoral ward[1]. Elected members can, of course, seek and obtain information on behalf of their constituents, and participate in more general policy decisions that affect their wards[2].

[1]   Allocation of Housing (Procedure) Regulations 1997, SI 1997/483, reg 3(2) (England) and Local Housing Authorities (Prescribed Principles for Allocation Schemes) (Wales) Regulations 1997, SI 1997/45, reg 3, Sch 1, para 1. See also English Code, paras 4.35–4.37; Welsh Code, paras 4.35–4.37. In *Heesom v Public Services Ombudsman for Wales* [2014] EWHC 1504 (Admin), [2014] 4 All ER 269, Admin Ct, a fact-finding tribunal determined that a particular councillor's conduct 'drove a coach and horses through the Council's housing policy. Certainly, it undermined the Council's policy in respect of housing allocation (based upon the 1997 Regulations), in a particularly persistent manner, and in a way designed deliberately to cross the dividing line between the functions of council members and their officers', per Hickinbottom J at [116].
[2]   A local housing authority's practice of inviting elected councillors to comment at the point of a potential allocation was criticised by the Public Service Ombudsman for Wales as giving the impression that there might be undue influence: *Housing Allocation and Homelessness in Wales: A Special Report by the Local Ombudsman for Wales* (February 2006).

2.76 In *R (Hussain) v Sandwell Metropolitan Borough Council*[1], the claimant councillor's application for judicial review to prevent the defendant council continuing its investigations into his conduct was dismissed. An internal report had raised a number of concerns about the claimant's conduct, including issues relating to housing allocations over twenty years. An investigation into the allocation of ten local housing authority owned properties found:

'patterns of behaviour exhibiting features of a conspiracy to defraud and / or misconduct in public office. The outcome of a number of housing allocation decisions appeared to benefit members of the Claimant's family. The evidence suggested a *"repeat pattern of use of a number of factors that allowed members of Councillor Hussain's family to be allocated Council properties"*[2].'

Green J found that on the evidence before the court, there was a 'serious prima facie case' against the claimant councillor and that the allegations against him should be investigated.

[1]   [2017] EWHC 1641 (Admin), [2017] ACD 97.
[2]   *R (Hussain) v Sandwell Metropolitan Borough Council* [2017] EWHC 1641 (Admin), [2017] ACD 97 per Green J at [98].

Decisions on applications

2.77 As already noted (see **2.50**), there is no statutory time limit within which a decision must be reached or within which the applicant must be notified of the outcome of his or her application for social housing, although any local housing authority may include such a time limit in its local scheme and the LGSCO has repeatedly found fault with local housing authorities which have delayed making decisions on applications.

2.78 For some applicants, the outcome of the application will be notification of successful entry onto the waiting list for a housing allocation. This may be a simple letter indicating that the applicant will in future be considered for an allocation based on the material provided in the application form or, where there is a local choice-based letting system, that the applicant is free to make bids for available properties. What the applicant most probably wants to know, and may not have been automatically told, is when, realistically, the application will result in an allocation of social housing (ie selection for the offer of a tenancy of a house or flat). The applicant is entitled to ask for information, in writing, about precisely that: whether housing accommodation is likely to be made available and, if so, how long it is likely to be before it is made available[1].

[1]   HA 1996, s 166A(9)(a)(ii) (England), s 167(4A)(a)(ii) (Wales); see **2.18–2.20**.

2.79 For other applicants, however, the notification will be that their application has been wholly or partly unsuccessful. The most serious adverse decision that an applicant could receive is that he or she is 'ineligible for an allocation' or (in England) not qualified for allocation[1]. The legal framework for decisions on eligibility or qualification and the obligations when notifying such decisions are discussed in CHAPTER 3[2]. Other adverse decisions, and the notification obligations attaching to them, are dealt with in this and later chapters[3].

[1]   HA 1996, s 160ZA (England), s 160A(9) (Wales).
[2]   See CHAPTER 3.
[3]   See **2.89–2.93** and CHAPTERS 3 AND 4.

Notifying decisions

2.80 Curiously, while every local housing authority must accept applications for social housing made in accordance with its allocation scheme and determine them, there is no express statutory obligation on local housing authorities to give written notification of all decisions or to give reasons for them. No doubt these matters were thought so central to good administrative practice as not to require explicit mention in HA 1996, Pt 6, because they will be included in the allocation scheme adopted by any reasonable local housing authority.

2.81 However, if a local housing authority decides that an applicant is 'ineligible' for its allocation scheme[1], or (in England) that he is not a 'qualifying' person[2], or (in Wales) that he or she is not to be given any preference on the grounds of unacceptable behaviour[3], those decisions must be notified to the applicant in writing[4].

[1]   See CHAPTER 3.
[2]   See CHAPTER 3.
[3]   See **4.150–4.164**.
[4]   HA 1996, s 160ZA(9) and (10), (England), and s 167(4A)(b) (Wales).

2.82 In each of the above cases, the decision must be 'notified' to the applicant, meaning that it should actually be received by him or her[1]. However, in the case of a decision that the applicant is not eligible or not qualified, the decision is additionally treated as having been given to the applicant:

'if it is made available at the authority's office for a reasonable period for collection by him [or her] or on his [or her] behalf[2].'

[1]   '"Notify" requires the giving of a notice which imports a degree of formality sufficient to constitute the document, as it will usually be, a notice', per May LJ in *Ali v Birmingham City Council* [2009] EWCA Civ 1279, [2011] HLR 17, CA at [39]; see **9.90–9.94** and **19.180–19.184**.
[2]   HA 1996, s 160ZA(10) (England), s 160A(10) (Wales); Welsh Code, para 2.53.

2.83 This treating provision only applies if the applicant does not actually receive the decision notice. If the applicant does receive the decision, any time limits run from the date of receipt, not from a notional date when the applicant could have collected the decision. An attempt to supplement the statutory rubric by the addition of the words 'and the applicant has previously been informed that the notice will be available and how it can be collected' was rejected by the government because the effect of the additional words 'is really a matter of good administrative practice, and might well be expected of local authorities as a matter of course'[1].

[1]   Andrew Stunnell MP, Under-Secretary of State, House of Commons Public Bill Committee on the Localism Bill, 3 March 2011, col 758.

2.84 The applicant is also entitled to be given *reasons* for those three types of decisions. The statutory guidance suggests that the notification should give clear grounds for the decision 'based on the relevant facts of the case'[1] and that where a particular applicant may have difficulty understanding the implications of the decision 'it would be good practice to make arrangements for the information to be explained verbally in addition to providing a written notice'[2]. Obviously, the reasons should be carefully considered. If the local housing authority gives several distinct reasons for its decision on an application for an allocation, it may find the whole decision is rendered unlawful even if only one of the reasons was given in error[3] although, conversely, if it is highly likely that the decision would not have been substantially different had the illegality not occurred, then a challenge to the court will fail[4].

[1] English Code, para 5.16, Welsh Code, para 2.51.
[2] English Code, para 5.16, Welsh Code, para 2.52.
[3] *Pirie v City of Aberdeen District Council* [1993] SLT 1155, Court of Session (Outer House).
[4] Senior Courts Act 1981, s 31(2A).

2.85 Even if the statutory rights of notification do not apply, good administrative practice and procedural fairness will require that an applicant be notified of a decision on his or her application[1]. He or she should in addition be given reasons for a decision that is against their interests. In a case concerning Birmingham City Council, the LGO[2] found fault where the local housing authority's letter telling the applicant that she had not been awarded medical priority failed to explain the reasoning for the decision[3].

[1] In the case of *Complaint against Epping Forest District Council*, 16 004 599, 7 November 2016, the LGO found fault where the council did not inform the applicant that it had decided to suspend his application.
[2] As of 19 June 2017, the LGSCO.
[3] *Complaint against Birmingham City Council*, 16 009 622, 8 March 2017.

REVIEWS

Right to a review

2.86 A local housing authority is free to provide in its allocation scheme that all of the decisions it takes on an application for social housing will carry a right to a review by the authority at the applicant's request. However, HA 1996, Pt 6, imposes a minimum requirement that all allocation schemes must be framed so as to provide a right to a review of certain important decisions. Strictly speaking, the review being undertaken is never a statutory review. It is always a review provided for by the allocation scheme and not pursuant to an absolute statutory right. This is not a mere matter of semantics. If, for some reason, a badly drafted scheme had not been framed so as to include the minimum review rights envisaged by HA 1996, Pt 6, it would be necessary for an applicant first to apply for a mandatory order (by way of judicial review proceedings) requiring the local housing authority to amend its scheme so as to include the review rights and then, once they were included, that applicant could exercise them.

2.87 HA 1996, Pt 6, requires that rights to review of the following categories of decisions made by a local housing authority relating to an applicant are included in any allocation scheme:

(1)   a decision that the applicant is not eligible for an allocation[1];
(2)   a decision concerning the facts of his or her case which are likely to be, or have been, taken into account in considering whether to allocate accommodation[2];
(3)   a decision by a local housing authority in England that he or she is not within a class of persons qualifying for an allocation[3]; and
(4)   a decision by a local housing authority in Wales that he or she is not to be awarded any reasonable preference, to which he or she would

otherwise be entitled, on the grounds of unacceptable behaviour[4].

[1]   HA 1996, s 160ZA(9)(a) and s 166A(9)(c) (England), s 160A(9) and s 167(4A)(d) (Wales).
[2]   HA 1996, s 166A(9)(b) and (c) (England), s 167(4A)(c) and (d) (Wales).
[3]   HA 1996, s 160ZA(9)(b) and s 166A(9)(c).
[4]   HA 1996, s 167(4A)(b) and (d).

2.88 The first, third and fourth categories of decisions listed refer to decisions taken under specific statutory provisions, and the applicant will have been notified in writing of those decisions with reasons.

2.89 The second category of decision carrying a right to a review is much more wide-ranging. From the wording, it is reasonable to assume that it includes decisions about:

(1)   the type of property for which an applicant will be considered;
(2)   the extent of the applicant's household to be considered for housing with him or her[1];
(3)   the applicant's medical condition or other welfare needs;
(4)   other facts used to determine whether the applicant is entitled to a reasonable preference;
(5)   whether the applicant should receive additional preference on the grounds of urgent housing needs or otherwise; and
(6)   determining the applicant's priority, including his or her financial resources, behaviour (or that of his or her family), and local connection where the scheme renders any of these relevant.

[1]   *R (Ariemuguvbe) v Islington London Borough Council* [2009] EWCA Civ 1218, [2010] HLR 14, CA.

2.90 This second category carrying a right to request a review, therefore, opens the door for an applicant to request an internal review, and consequent reconsideration, of nearly all the adverse decisions (if any) that are made on his or her application.

2.91 However, unlike the decisions on eligibility, qualification (in England) or unacceptable behaviour (in Wales), there is no automatic *notification* of the initial decision to the applicant in this second category of decisions. If the applicant has not been notified of the decision in question then, for him or her even to access the right to request a review, he or she must first request the local housing authority to inform him or her of its decision about a particular fact, or set of facts, about his or her case[1]. Only having made that request, and having received the response, can the applicant then sensibly request a review although there is no statutory obligation on the local housing authority to provide reasons when notifying this class of decision.

[1]   See **2.26–2.29**.

2.92 As already indicated (see **2.86**), the statutory requirements relating to reviews of decisions, on applications for social housing allocation, represent the legal minimum. There is nothing to prevent a local housing authority from adopting an allocation scheme which allows for a review of additional categories of adverse decisions or of all adverse decisions.

2.93 On the *nature* of the review that needs to be undertaken, it is reasonable to assume that Parliament at least intended reviews of decisions made within HA 1996, Pt 6, to have the same function as reviews within HA 1996, Pt 5 ('Conduct of Tenants')[1] and Pt 7[2] ('Homelessness'), ie a reconsideration of all the relevant facts and law at the time that the review is decided, not a narrow review confining itself to the legality or fairness of the original decision[3].

---

[1] HA 1996, s 129 gives an introductory tenant the right to request a review of his or her landlord's decision to seek an order for possession and the Introductory Tenancy (Review Procedures) Regulations 1997, SI 1997/72 regulate the procedure on review.

[2] As amended by HRA 2017 for applications for homelessness assistance made to local housing authorities in England on or after 3 April 2018, see CHAPTER 19.

[3] For a discussion of the scope of reviews in the homelessness context see **19.166–19.174**.

Procedure on review

2.94 There are no statutory provisions governing review procedure in relation to social housing allocation. There are, for example, no statutorily specified time limits within which a review must be requested and no statutorily prescribed form or procedure for making the request for a review. All and any procedural requirements must be set out in the particular allocation scheme under which a review is being pursued.

2.95 The Secretary of State and Welsh Ministers are empowered to make regulations governing 'the procedure to be followed' on housing allocation, which appears, from the wording, to encompass any procedural matters under the allocation scheme, including any procedure relating to requests for review[1]. However, no regulations have been made in exercise of that power.

---

[1] HA 1996, s 166A(10) (England) and s 167(5) (Wales).

2.96 In this procedural vacuum, it will be for every local housing authority to spell out the review procedures in its own allocation scheme. This will inevitably mean different review procedures in almost every part of the country, subject to the usual public and administrative law protections of natural justice and procedural fairness and the high standards of administration which applicants should be entitled to expect from a local housing authority.

2.97 The English Code suggests that review procedures should be clearly set out in allocation schemes, should include 'timescales for each stage of the review process, and must accord with the principles of transparency and fairness'[1]. It sets out six general principles of good administrative practice that local housing authorities are expected to apply when making provision for review procedures in their allocation schemes and when undertaking reviews. They are as follows[2]:

'1. Applicants should be notified of the timescale within which they must request a review. 21 days from the date the applicant is notified of the decision is well-established as a reasonable timescale. A housing authority should retain the discretion to extend this time limit in exceptional circumstances.

2. Applicants should be notified that the request for review should be made in writing, and that it would also be acceptable for the request to be submitted

by a representative on their behalf. Applicants should also be advised of the information which should accompany the request.

3. Authorities should consider whether to advise that provision can be made for verbal representations, as well as written submissions, to be made.

4. The review should be carried out by an officer who is senior to the person who made the original decision. Alternatively, authorities may wish to appoint a panel to consider the review. If so, it should not include any person involved in the original decision.

5. The review should be considered on the basis of the authority's allocation scheme, any legal requirements and all relevant information. This should include information provided by the applicant on any relevant developments since the original decision was made – for instance, the settlement of arrears or establishment of a repayment plan, or departure of a member of the household responsible for anti-social behaviour.

6. Reviews should be completed wherever practicable within a set deadline. Eight weeks is suggested as a reasonable timescale. The applicant should be notified of any extension to this deadline and the reasons for this.'

[1] English Code, para 5.19.
[2] English Code, para 5.19.

2.98 In relation to adverse decisions on 'eligibility', or 'no preference' made by local housing authorities in Wales, the Welsh Code recommends that allocation schemes adopt the following as 'fair procedure' in relation to reviews:

- ensuring that notifications of decisions include advice on the right to request a review, the time within which the request must be made, and sources of advice and assistance;

- ensuring that applicants have an opportunity to request further information about any decision about the facts of their case;

- advising applicants that they may request a review by way of an oral hearing or a written submission;

- ensuring that the review is carried out by a person who was not involved in the original decision and, if the reviewer is to be another officer, one senior to the original decision-maker;

- ensuring that the circumstances of the applicant at the time of the review, not just at the time of the original decision, are taken into account;

- if there is not to be a hearing, allowing the applicant to make written representations, and informing the applicant of the date by which those representations must be received, giving the applicant at least 5 clear days' notice;

- if there is to be a hearing, giving notice to the applicant of the date, time and place no sooner than five days after the request for a hearing (unless the applicant consents to lesser notice);

- ensuring that the reviewer determines the procedure to be adopted for hearings, and that the procedure gives the applicant the right to be heard, to be accompanied, to be represented by a lawyer or other person, to call witnesses to give evidence, to put questions to any witness and to make written representations;

- ensuring that, if a person having been given notice should fail to appear at the hearing, the reviewer has regard to all the circumstances, including any explanation offered for the absence and should be able to proceed with the hearing or give any directions he or she thinks proper for the conduct of a further review;
- ensuring that the reviewer will allow applicants to be able to request a postponement of a hearing, and will grant or refuse the request as the reviewer sees fit;
- ensuring that the reviewer should be able to adjourn the hearing at any time during the hearing on the applicant's application, or if the reviewer otherwise sees fit. If, at a re-scheduled hearing, the identity of the reviewer has changed, the hearing should be a complete re-hearing of the case;
- ensuring that, where more than one person is conducting the review, the review should only proceed in the absence of one of the reviewers if the applicant consents;
- ensuring that the applicant is notified of the decision on the review and, if the decision confirms the original decision, of the reasons for it;
- ensuring that the applicant is notified of any right to re-apply; and
- ensuring that the review is conducted in the applicant's language of choice[1].

[1]   Welsh Code, para 2.55.

2.99 In the absence of explicit statutory provisions and given a wide variety of locally adopted procedures, it has been left to the courts to scrutinise individual review decisions and review procedures on a case-by-case basis applying traditional administrative law principles (outlined in Chapter **19**)[1]. The courts have developed some expertise in scrutinising the role of reviewing officers in reviews conducted of decisions made within the introductory tenancy and homelessness regimes of HA 1996[2], so that the move to judicial scrutiny of review procedures in the housing allocation field has been relatively straightforward (see **2.103**).

[1]   For examples of challenges to internal review arrangements on decisions about social housing allocation see: *R v Tower Hamlets London Borough Council ex p Spencer* (1995) 29 HLR 64, QBD (a challenge brought under Housing Act 1985) and *R v Southwark London Borough Council ex p Mason* (2000) 32 HLR 88, QBD (a challenge to a review panel's decision on the suitability of accommodation offered under the allocation scheme).
[2]   HA 1996, Pt 5 ('Conduct of Tenants') and Pt 7 ('Homelessness') as amended by HRA 2017 for applications for homelessness assistance made to local housing authorities in England on or after 3 April 2018 respectively.

Notifying review decisions

2.100 Each allocation scheme must be framed in terms that provide for an applicant who has sought a review to be notified of the decision on review and the grounds for it[1]. This requirement is interpreted in the statutory guidance as meaning that there should usually be provision in the allocation scheme for delivery of a written statement of the review decision and of the reasons for it[2].

[1]   HA 1996, s 166A(9)(c) (England), s 167(4A)(d) (Wales).
[2]   English Code, para 5.19(viii), Welsh Code, para 2.55(m).

2.101 In one case, in which the adequacy of the reasons given in a review decision was challenged, despite the decision being set out in a lengthy letter to the applicant, a judge said[1]:

> 'In my view proper, adequate and intelligible reasons are set out in the decision letter. The reasons are stated "in sufficient detail" to enable [the Claimant] to know what conclusion [the decision maker] has reached on the "principal important controversial issues" (*Bolton Metropolitan Borough Council v Secretary of State for the Environment* [1995] 3 PLR 37, 43C, Lord Lloyd; and see *William v Wandsworth LBC* [2006] HLR 42 at para 18). Moreover [the reviewing officer] balanced competing factors and explained why he concluded that some outweighed others.'

[1]   *R (Dixon) v Wandsworth London Borough Council* [2007] EWHC (Admin) 3075, (2008) February *Legal Action*, p 40, Admin Ct per Deputy Judge Supperstone QC at [26].

2.102 In another case, the local housing authority's correspondence relating to a decision on eligibility was described as 'opaque', but a challenge based on inadequate reasons was rejected as the claimant himself was well apprised of the issues being addressed[1].

[1]   *R (M) v London Borough of Hackney* [2009] EWHC 2255 (Admin), (2009) May *Legal Action*, p 26, Admin Ct.

Challenges to review decisions (and non-reviewable decisions) about particular applications

2.103 Any legal challenges to review decisions, or to any decisions about individual applications that do not carry the right to request a review, can only be brought by judicial review, on the grounds that the local housing authority has infringed some requirement of public or administrative law, or has failed to comply with the duty to supply the grounds for the decision[1].

[1]   The duty to supply reasons in an allocation case is set out at **2.84**. The classic grounds upon which judicial review claims can be mounted are discussed at **19.225–19.231**.

2.104 Judicial review challenges to allocation decisions tend to fall into two distinct categories:

(1)   challenges to the allocation scheme itself (or to some part of it); and
(2)   challenges to particular decisions made relating to particular applicants.

2.105 This part of this chapter is concerned only with the latter. Challenges to the contents of allocation schemes are dealt with in CHAPTER 4[1]. Of course, occasionally, both forms of challenge may be available in a particular case. For an example of a judicial review which involved both forms of challenge see *R (Woolfe) v Islington London Borough Council*[2].

[1]   See **4.258–4.267**.
[2]   [2016] EWHC 1987 (Admin), [2016] HLR 42.

2.106 As far as individual decisions are concerned, an applicant seeking to challenge such a decision would have to show that it was made contrary to the provisions of HA 1996, Pt 6, or of the local housing authority's allocation scheme, or that it had been reached by applying an unfair or unlawful procedure, or that it was based on some other mistake of law (or, in some circumstances, a mistake of fact[1]). In one unsuccessful case, the challenge to the decision of a reviewing officer on an issue about eligibility for social housing allocation was described as containing 'the familiar complaints that he had misdirected himself, failed to take into account relevant circumstances, and/or failed to give adequate reasons'[2]. Familiar as they may be, those complaints can sometimes be made out by an applicant in an appropriate case. For example, when considering whether to apply a discretionary provision in an allocation scheme, a local housing authority must act fairly by giving an applicant an opportunity to deal with matters likely to be weighed against him or her[3]. In another case, the local housing authority had misapplied its own policy and in consequence had failed lawfully to consider whether the claimant was entitled to 'New Generation' points[4]. Local housing authorities have also been found to have erred by failing to take into account or to give proper weight to relevant evidence, namely the conclusions of their own Children's Services assessment[5].

1   *E v Secretary of State for the Home Department* [2004] EWCA Civ 49, [2004] QB 1044. As to 'mistake of fact' as a ground of challenge see **19.230**.
2   *R (Dixon) v Wandsworth London Borough Council* [2008] EWCA Civ 595, (2008) July *Legal Action*, p 22, CA.
3   *R (Moore) v Wandsworth London Borough Council* [2012] All ER (D) 66 (Jan), (2012) April *Legal Action*, p 46, Admin Ct.
4   *R (Woolfe) v Islington London Borough Council* [2016] EWHC 1907 (Admin), [2016] HLR 42 at [55]–[70].
5   *R (J and L) v Hillingdon London Borough Council* [2017] EWHC 3411 (Admin) per Nicklin J at [66] and *R (KS) v London Borough of Haringey* [2018] EWHC 587 (Admin) per HHJ Walden-Smith (sitting as a Judge of the High Court) at [49]–[50].

2.107 Claims for judicial review have been particularly successful in relation to decisions on medical needs assessment for the purposes of allocation schemes. In one case, a local housing authority's assessment failed to address issues raised by the applicant's medical advisers and gave insufficient reasons for a refusal to accord the highest medical priority in the local scheme[1]. In another, the medical assessment was based on medical advice commissioned by the local housing authority, but that advice had failed to address particular points and specific materials put forward by the applicant's advisers[2]. In a third case, the decision to refuse a claimant entry to the housing register was flawed because it had relied 'word for word' on a medical assessment in which the doctor had improperly commented on issues that had no medical dimension[3]. In a fourth case, a local housing authority's decisions were:

'insufficiently reasoned as to the criteria applied as to how medical need can or fails to come within the doctrine of reasonable preference and how the evidence has been related to the criteria that are applied[4].'

1   *R (Sawalha) v Westminster City Council* [2008] EWHC 1216 (Admin), (2008) July *Legal Action*, p 22, Admin Ct.
2   *R (Ghandali) v Ealing London Borough Council* [2006] EWHC 1859 (Admin), [2006] All ER (D) 134 (Jul), Admin Ct.
3   *R (J and L) v Hillingdon London Borough Council* [2017] EWHC 3411 (Admin), Admin Ct per Nicklin J at [64]–[66].
4   *R (Ahmad) v Newham London Borough Council* [2007] EWHC 2332 (Admin) at [24], (2007) November *Legal Action*, p 34, Admin Ct – not appealed on this point.

2.108 In a fifth case, the medical advisers engaged by the local housing authority had gone beyond their remit and advised as to the relative priority of the applicant to others in housing need. The local housing authority had wrongly taken into account those non-medical opinions and relied upon them[1].

1   *R (Bauer-Czarnomski) v Ealing London Borough Council* [2010] EWHC 130 (Admin), [2010] All ER (D) 101 (Jan), Admin Ct.

2.109 Where judicial review is unavailable, the applicant should invoke the local housing authority's own internal complaints procedure and, if still dissatisfied, can then complain of maladministration to the LGSCO (in England)[1] or the PSO (in Wales). Dissatisfied applicants for social housing can also seek redress through the intervention of the relevant national regulators of social housing providers[2].

1   See Sanderson, *Unfair Allocation* [2007] 124 *Adviser* 35.
2   See **1.30–1.39**.

2.110 Complaints to the Ombudsmen may be pursued by complainants personally or by their legal advisers. The latter will need to consider carefully how such assistance might be remunerated[1].

1   See *R (Adams) v Commission for Local Administration in England* [2011] EWHC 2972 (Admin), (2012) January *Legal Action*, p 21, Admin Ct.

2.111 Both the English and Welsh Ombudsmen Services have produced fact-sheets for applicants who may want to complain about housing application matters. For applicants, the LGSCO has identified the sorts of complaints against a local housing authority that he or she may investigate[1]:

> '•   It is using an allocation scheme that is not clear or fair;
> •   It has failed to apply the allocation scheme properly or fairly failed to follow the Government's code of guidance on housing allocation;
> •   It did not take relevant information into account in reaching its decision, or took irrelevant information into account;
> •   It failed to give you information you should have (for example, about the priority awarded to your application or how to challenge the priority given to it); or
> •   It delayed in dealing with your application, changes in your situation, or with an appeal from you about the priority given to your application.'

1   *Fact Sheet – H2 Complaints about your housing application* (LGO, March 2014).

2.112 The LGSCO has provided a similar indicative list relating to complaints arising from *transfer* applications. The complaints likely to be investigated include[1]:

> '•   delay in processing your application;
> •   losing your application or other documents;
> •   turning down or suspending your application for no good reason;
> •   not assessing your application in line with the council's allocations policy;
> •   making a mistake, such as getting your application date wrong, not giving you the points you should have, or putting you in the wrong band;

- failing to take special factors into account, such as overcrowding or medical problems;
- not offering accommodation to you, including losing a bid made through a choice-based lettings scheme; or
- unreasonable delay in responding to correspondence.'

However, since April 2013, the LGSCO has only had responsibility for complaints relating to transfer applications that fall within HA 1996, Pt 6. Complaints relating to management transfers or to transfer applications from those outside the 'reasonable preference' categories are instead within the jurisdiction of the Housing Ombudsman.

1   *Fact Sheet – H1 Complaints about your housing transfers* (LGO, March 2013).

2.113 Since April 2013, the LGSCO website has carried details of all housing allocation complaints examined, in the interests of greater transparency. The details are posted after three months have expired from the last stage of the consideration of the particular complaint[1]. Some of the most important decisions noted on the LGSCO website appear later, in summary form, in the monthly column Recent Developments in Housing Law in *Legal Action* magazine.

1   The housing allocation decisions are gathered (in reverse chronological order, latest first) at www.lgo.org.uk/decisions/housing/allocations.

2.114 In January 2016, the LGO[1] issued a special focus report on its handling of complaints about housing allocation[2]. The report 'highlights the severe impact on people when councils have got it wrong and the common issues we find in our investigations into housing allocations'.

1   As of 19 June 2017, the LGSCO.
2   *Full House: Council's role in allocating social housing* (LGO, January 2016).

2.115 Where such faults caused injustice, the report indicated that the LGO[1] asked local housing authorities to:

- backdate an application or priority award;
- correctly allocate priority or waiting time;
- enhance priority or waiting time (particularly appropriate if there has been a delay);
- carry out a medical assessment and make appropriate provision;
- carry out a review of a decision; or
- allow a person to go on the housing list.

1   As of 19 June 2017, the LGSCO.

2.116 The LGSCO may also ask a local housing authority to review not just individual decisions but also its allocation scheme in general. In one recent case the local housing authority was asked to review the definition of 'child' in its scheme, which was unclear[1]. In another, the LGO[2] recommended that the local housing authority 'review its scheme to clarify the definition of "settled accommodation" and clarify how it deals with circumstances where someone moves out of the area into less settled accommodation'[3].

1   *Complaint against Kettering Borough Council*, 16 012 028, 3 August 2017, (2017) November *Legal Action*, p 41.

²   As of 19 June 2017, the LGSCO.
³   *Complaint against Epping Forest District Council*, 15 020 774, 9 September 2016.

2.117 The Public Services Ombudsman for Wales (PSOW) has indicated that, in relation to both new applications and transfer requests, he can look at[1]:

'•   whether your housing application has been dealt with properly.
   •   whether the Council or housing association has properly applied its policy to your housing application e.g. are you in the correct band?
   •   whether the organisation has told you how it has dealt with your housing application e.g. has it sent you a letter detailing any points awarded?
   •   whether the organisation has delayed dealing with changes in your situation which you have told it about e.g. you have been asked to leave your home.
   •   why your application may have been suspended e.g. has the Council followed the correct procedure if the reason(s) for suspension is your behaviour?'

¹   *Housing Application Factsheet* (PSOW, undated).

2.118 The Welsh Code suggests that applicants for local housing authority or housing association accommodation may complain to the PSOW if they consider they have been treated unfairly, or have received a bad service through some failure on the part of the organisation and that local housing authorities and housing associations are 'obliged by law' to inform applicants of their rights to complain to the PSOW[1].

¹   Welsh Code, para 4.47.

2.119 Recent investigation reports from the LGSCO and PSOW indicate that significant awards of compensation may be recommended if maladministration has caused injustice to individuals who have applied for the allocation of social housing:

•   A family of six, with four children aged between 14 and 18, two of whom had disabilities, lived in a three-bedroom house. They had been on the local housing authority's housing register for thirteen years when they were asked to complete a new application. The Ombudsman found that the information provided should have prompted the local housing authority to visit the property to ascertain whether the family were statutorily overcrowded, which it did not do; further, it had wrongly said it could only consider the needs of one household member; it should have recognized that this was a complex case requiring a cross-agency referral, but did not; it failed to consider exercising its discretion to take account of the family's exceptional circumstances; it failed to explain to the family how it could help them secure private rented accommodation; and it provided inaccurate information about what properties they would be able to bid on. The Ombudsman found that, as a result of the local housing authority's fault, the amended family had lived in unsuitable accommodation for nearly two and a half years longer than was necessary. The Ombudsman recommended that the local housing authority pay the family £8,650 and apologise to them[1].

- A middle-aged single disabled man living with his mother (who was a tenant of the local housing authority) made repeated applications for rehousing on the grounds that his accommodation was unsuitable for his disabilities and was in disrepair. The Ombudsman found extensive maladministration including: (1) systemic failures in approach to the rehousing applications; (2) failure to follow relevant legislation, statutory guidance and policies and procedures; and (3) poor record-keeping. He recommended a wide-ranging re-training of staff, a review of the local housing authority's policies, systems and procedures, an apology and £1,500 compensation[2].

- In 2008 a local housing authority had allocated a property to a disabled man which it subsequently said could not be adapted to meet his needs (although it had been fully aware of his needs prior to allocating the property). It advised him to apply for a transfer but he did not wish to move again as his family had become settled. The local housing authority carried out no adaptations for over three years until it reassessed the complainant's needs following the complaint to the Ombudsman's office in 2011. It then agreed to carry out all the adaptations requested. The Ombudsman found maladministration in the allocation process and throughout the request for adaptations at the property. There had been no occupational therapist's (OT) assessment prior to allocation, nor was there a full assessment of the need for adaptations by either an OT or social services for over three years after the complainant had moved in. The local housing authority did not appear to recognise its statutory social care duties to him, or that his human rights may have been engaged. The Ombudsman made a number of recommendations including an apology and payment of £3,000[3].

- A tenant applied for a transfer in 2004 on the grounds that her accommodation was overcrowded. She complained that the local housing authority had failed to deal with her application properly. On investigation, the Ombudsman found that: (1) for the period from January 2003 to May 2006 the local housing authority had failed to have a lawful allocation scheme; (2) it had failed to visit the accommodation to assess overcrowding; (3) in making its paper assessment of the overcrowding, it had considered only one of the two overcrowding standards in HA 1985, s 326[4] and had failed to conduct an overcrowding assessment under the Health and Safety Hazards Rating System introduced by Housing Act 2004[5]; (4) it had failed to record receipt of and reply promptly to correspondence; and (5) it had failed to consider whether the accommodation might no longer be 'reasonable to continue to occupy': HA 1996, s 175[6]. The Ombudsman recommended an apology, compensation, staff training and a proper assessment of the complainant's application[7].

[1] *Complaint against Thanet District Council*, Case 15000234, 3 August 2016, (2016) October *Legal Action*, p 41.
[2] *Complaint against Wrexham County Borough Council*, Case 201002076, 25 January 2012, (2012) April *Legal Action*, p 46.
[3] *Complaint against Carmarthenshire County Council*, Case 201001198, 22 December 2011, (2012) April *Legal Action*, p 46.
[4] See **4.82–4.86**.
[5] See **4.82–4.86**.

⁶   See **10.73**.
⁷   *Complaint against Blaenau Gwent County Borough Council*, Case No 09016302, 24 January 2011, (2011) April *Legal Action*, p 30.

2.120 Sadly, the most common source of dissatisfaction with social housing allocation concerns the length of time that applicants have to wait before being made an offer of accommodation or succeeding in a bidding process in a choice-based letting scheme. Invoking legal remedies, or complaints procedures, rarely cures that grievance where the root cause of it is an excess of demand over supply.

Chapter 3

ELIGIBILITY AND QUALIFICATION FOR ALLOCATION

Contents

AN OVERVIEW

3.1 The statutory scheme for social housing allocation contained in Housing Act 1996 (HA 1996), Pt 6[1] has some features which are common to England and Wales and other features which apply differently in the two countries. This chapter first explores one of the common features – a restriction on eligibility for an allocation which is primarily based on immigration status – and then addresses, in turn, two aspects in which the statutory allocation arrangements apply differently:

(1)   the ability to exclude applicants from allocation based on criteria of 'qualification', available only to local housing authorities in England; and

(2)   the ability to exclude applicants on the basis that past misconduct has rendered them 'ineligible', now available only to local housing authorities in Wales[2].

---

[1]   Statutory guidance on allocation schemes made under HA 1996, Pt 6 is given in *Allocation of Accommodation: Guidance for local housing authorities for England* (Department for Communities and Local Government, June 2012) (the English Code), *Providing social housing for local people* (DCLG, December 2013) (the Supplementary English Code), *Right to Move: Statutory Guidance on Social Housing Allocations for Local Housing Authorities in England* (DCLG, March 2015) and in *Code of Guidance for Local Authorities on the Allocation of Accommodation and Homelessness* (Welsh Government, March 2016) (the

Welsh Code). See **Appendix** **1** of this book for the English Codes and see the accompanying CD ROM for the Welsh Code.

2 This was available to local housing authorities in both countries until 18 June 2012. Readers considering the position for local housing authorities in England prior to 18 June 2012 may wish to refer to the text setting out the current position in Wales at **3.151–3.200**.

3.2 If an applicant is found to be 'ineligible', the local housing authority is statutorily barred from allocating housing accommodation to him or her[1]. Further, only an applicant who is also found to be a 'qualifying' person by a local housing authority in England will be allocated housing accommodation by that authority.

1 HA 1996, s 160ZA(1) and (6) (England), s 160A(1) (Wales).

3.3 In relation to eligibility, a local housing authority in England or Wales *must* decide that people who are subject to immigration control (with limited exceptions), and other people who are to be treated as persons from abroad, are ineligible *unless* either:

(1) they are currently secure, introductory or, in certain cases, assured tenants of social housing[1]; or

(2) they fall within one of the exceptional classes prescribed by regulations as being eligible for allocation notwithstanding their immigration or residence status[2].

1 HA 1996, ss 159(4B) and 160ZA(5) (England) and 160A(6) (Wales). English Code, para 3.4, Welsh Code, para 2.13(i).

2 HA 1996, s 160ZA(2), (3) and (4) (England), s 160A(3), (4), (5) and (6) (Wales); Allocation of Housing and Homelessness (Eligibility) (England) Regulations 2006, SI 2006/1294, regs 3–4 as amended; Allocation of Housing and Homelessness (Eligibility) (Wales) Regulations 2014, SI 2014/263 (W 257), regs 3–4.

3.4 In relation to 'qualification', the position is much more flexible. Local housing authorities in England are free to decide for themselves what classes of eligible persons are or are not also qualifying persons[1]. That flexibility is subject to a back-stop in that the Secretary of State can prescribe by regulations that certain classes must be treated as qualifying persons or are not to be so treated[2]. At the date of writing, such regulations had only been made in respect of the treatment of applicants with connections to the armed forces (see **3.128–3.133**) and those applicants seeking to move for work-related reasons (see **3.134–3.135**).

1 HA 1996, s 160ZA(7).

2 HA 1996, s 160ZA(8).

3.5 In relation to 'eligibility' turning on past misconduct, a local housing authority in Wales *may* choose to adopt and apply a rule that applicants who have been guilty of unacceptable behaviour, serious enough to make them unsuitable to be tenants of the local housing authority, are ineligible for an allocation[1]. This is a discretionary power available to all local housing authorities in Wales but they are not obliged to use it[2]. If a local housing authority does choose to use it, considers an applicant's behaviour, and concludes that the behaviour is *not* so serious as to make the applicant unsuitable to be a tenant, but that he or she should be penalised in some way, it could decide that the applicant *is* eligible for an allocation, but that he or she should receive a lower priority than other applicants[3].

1   HA 1996, s 160A(7) and (8); Welsh Code, para 2.30.
2   HA 1996, s 160A(2) and (7); Welsh Code, para 2.29.
3   HA 1996, s 167(2A) and Welsh Code, para 3.41(b). See **4.128–4.135**.

3.6 The various categories of ineligibility and qualification are examined in detail in the remainder of this chapter.

3.7 If an applicant is found by a local housing authority to be ineligible or not qualified for an allocation, that decision and the reasons for it must be notified to him or her in writing[1]. The applicant is then entitled to request a review of the decision and to be notified of the review decision and the reasons for it[2]. There is no provision for any appeal against the review decision to the county court, so any challenge by legal proceedings could only be by judicial review[3].

1   HA 1996, s 160ZA(9) and (10) (England), s 160A(9) and (10) (Wales).
2   HA 1996, s 166A(9)(c) (England), s 167(4A)(d) (Wales).
3   For three examples of challenges to eligibility decisions by way of judicial review see *R (McQ) v Bolton Metropolitan Borough Council* [2005] EWHC 1285 (Admin), (2005) August *Legal Action*, p 17, Admin Ct; *R (Dixon) v Wandsworth London Borough Council* [2008] EWCA Civ 595, (2008) July *Legal Action*, p 22, Admin Ct; and *R (M) v Hackney London Borough Council* [2009] EWHC 2255 (Admin), (2009) May *Legal Action*, p 26, Admin Ct.

3.8 If an applicant is ineligible for an allocation of accommodation for any reason, he or she must not be allocated a sole tenancy, nor be allocated a joint tenancy with others, under the allocation scheme[1]. So, if a couple apply for an allocation of a property to be let on a joint tenancy and only one of them is eligible, a joint tenancy cannot be granted. The tenancy can only be granted to the eligible applicant in his or her sole name. In respect of 'qualification'[2] the rule is different. While an allocation may not be made to a non-qualifying person as a sole tenant, a joint tenancy may be granted as long as at least one of the joint tenants is a qualifying person (and both are eligible)[3].

1   HA 1996, s 160ZA(1) (England), s 160A(1) (Wales). However, once a person has been granted a secure or assured tenancy, that tenancy does not come to an end, nor is the landlord entitled to apply for possession, simply because he or she is ineligible for a grant of a secure or assured tenancy. The landlord can only obtain possession under the grounds for possession at Housing Act 1985, Sch 2 (secure tenants) or Housing Act 1988, Sch 2 (assured tenants), or if the tenant loses his or her security of tenure (*Akinbolu v Hackney London Borough Council* (1997) 29 HLR 259, CA).
2   For local housing authorities in England.
3   HA 1996, s 160ZA(6)(b); English Code, para 3.29.

3.9 The eligibility and qualification restrictions apply to *applicants*, not to their dependants or others in the household with whom they seek to be accommodated. However, the previous unacceptable behaviour of a household member may allow a local housing authority in Wales to treat the applicant himself or herself as ineligible[1].

1   See **3.171–3.173**.

3.10 If an eligible applicant has ineligible or non-qualifying family members, their needs must still be taken into account when the local housing authority considers the type and size of accommodation to be allocated, provided they form part of the applicant's household[1]. However, a local housing authority is free to take into account the immigration status of family members in deciding whether they do indeed form part of an applicant's 'household'[2]. If an ineligible household member is a 'restricted person'[3], that fact will not render the otherwise eligible applicant ineligible, but it may affect his or her entitlement to a reasonable preference[4].

[1] *R (Kimvono) v Tower Hamlets London Borough Council* (2001) 33 HLR 78, Admin Ct.

[2] *R (Ariemuguvbe) v Islington London Borough Council* [2009] EWHC 470 (Admin), (2009) April *Legal Action*, p 21, Admin Ct, upheld on appeal in *R (Ariemuguvbe) v Islington London Borough Council* [2009] EWCA Civ 1308, [2010] HLR 14, CA.

[3] A 'restricted person' is a person: who is not eligible for assistance under HA 1996, Pt 7 (as amended by the Homelessness Reduction Act 2017 (HRA 2017) for applications for homelessness assistance made to local housing authorities in England on or after 3 April 2018) or Housing (Wales) Act 2014 (H(W)A) 2014) Pt 2; who is subject to immigration control within the meaning of the Asylum and Immigration Act 1996; and either who does not have leave to enter or remain in the United Kingdom or whose leave to enter or remain is subject to a 'no recourse to public funds' condition. HA 1996, s 184(7) (England); Housing (Wales) Act 2014, s 63(5) (Wales). See **4.148–4.149.**

[4] HA 1996, s 166A(4) (England), s 167(2ZA) (Wales) and **4.148–4.149.**

3.11 Ineligible or non-qualifying applicants are not prevented by HA 1996, Pt 6, from acquiring a tenancy in cases where those provisions do not apply, eg where the grant of a tenancy to them does not count as an allocation at all[1].

[1] HA 1996, s 159(4A)–(5), s 160(2), (3) and (4). See also **1.23–1.27.**

INELIGIBILITY ON THE GROUNDS OF IMMIGRATION STATUS (ENGLAND AND WALES)

Overview

3.12 The provisions governing ineligibility on the basis of immigration status are tortuous and complicated. The Codes of Guidance each have several annexes to help with the assessment of eligibility[1].

[1] English Code, Annexes 2–4 inclusive; Welsh Code, Annexes 4–6 inclusive.

3.13 The immigration status of an existing secure or introductory tenant, or an assured tenant who was nominated to his or her landlord by a local housing authority, who has applied for an allocation (eg by way of a transfer) is irrelevant[1]. Those applicants are eligible for an allocation irrespective of their immigration status[2].

[1] HA 1996, s 160ZA(5) (England), s 160A(6) (Wales).

[2] Immigration Act 2014, Pt 2 prohibits certain persons from occupying premises under a residential tenancy agreement on the grounds of their immigration status. However, this does not apply to allocations under HA 1996, Pt 6: Immigration Act 2014, Sch 3, para 1.

3.14 The general rule in HA 1996, Pt 6, is that applicants who are 'people from abroad' are not eligible[1]. They fall into two distinct categories:

- those subject to immigration control:
    - they are *not eligible* for assistance;

- – *unless* they fall within a class prescribed as 'eligible' in regulations made by the Secretary of State or the Welsh Ministers[2];
- • those not subject to immigration control but who are nevertheless prescribed by regulations as being 'persons from abroad':
  - – they are *not eligible* if they are not habitually resident in the Common Travel Area *unless* they are prescribed as exempt from the habitual residence test; or
  - – they are *not eligible* if they are prescribed as ineligible because of their particular rights of residence under EU law[3].

[1] HA 1996, s 160ZA(1) (England), s 160A(1)(a) (Wales).
[2] HA 1996, s 160ZA(2) (England), s 160A(3) (Wales).
[3] HA 1996, s 160ZA(4) (England), s 160A(5) (Wales).

3.15 It can be seen that the Secretary of State and the Welsh Ministers each have the power to make regulations exempting some people from abroad from the exclusory rule[1]. They each also have the power to make regulations excluding people who would otherwise be eligible. Each of these powers has been exercised in both England and Wales[2].

[1] They cannot designate as eligible any person who is excluded from entitlement to housing benefit or universal credit by the Immigration and Asylum Act 1999, s 115 (HA 1996, s 160ZA(3) (England), s 160A(4) (Wales)). Immigration and Asylum Act 1999, s 115 prescribes that 'a person subject to immigration control' is not eligible for housing benefit or universal credit unless he or she falls within one of the classes of people prescribed by the Secretary of State. Classes of person subject to immigration control who are entitled to housing benefit are prescribed in the Social Security (Immigration and Asylum) Consequential Amendment Regulations 2000, SI 2000/636, reg 2 and Sch 1, Pt 1 and the Housing Benefit Regulations 2006, SI 2006/213, reg 10(3B).
[2] This chapter does not deal with the regulations in effect prior to 1 June 2006 (for applications to local housing authorities in England) or 31 October 2014 (for applications to local housing authorities in Wales). Reference can be made to the three previous editions of this book if necessary (Luba and Davies *Housing Allocation and Homelessness* (1st edn, 2006; 2nd edn, 2010; 3rd edn, 2012).

3.16 For England, the Secretary of State has made the Allocation of Housing and Homelessness (Eligibility) (England) Regulations 2006[1], which apply to all applications for an allocation of social housing made to local housing authorities in England on or after 1 June 2006[2]. Those regulations have since been amended by:

- • the Allocation of Housing and Homelessness (Eligibility) (England) (Amendment) Regulations 2006[3];
- • the Allocation of Housing and Homelessness (Eligibility) (England) (Miscellaneous Provisions) Regulations 2006[4];
- • the Allocation of Housing and Homelessness (Eligibility) (England) (Amendment No 2) Regulations 2006[5];
- • the Allocation of Housing and Homelessness (Eligibility) (England) (Amendment) Regulations 2009[6];
- • the Allocation of Housing and Homelessness (Eligibility) (England) (Amendment) Regulations 2012[7];
- • the Allocation of Housing and Homelessness (Eligibility) (England) (Amendment) Regulations 2013[8];
- • the Allocation of Housing and Homelessness (Eligibility) (England) (Amendment) Regulations 2014[9]; and

- the Allocation of Housing and Homelessness (Eligibility) (England) (Amendment) Regulations 2016[10].

[1] SI 2006/1294. References in these regulations to Immigration (European Economic Area) Regulations 2006, SI 2006/1003 should be read as referring to Immigration (European Economic Area) Regulations 2016, SI 2016/1052 at Appendix 2 of this book. See SI 2016/1052, Sch 7, para 1.

[2] Any applications for an allocation of social housing made before 1 June 2006 to local housing authorities in England are determined according to the Homelessness (England) Regulations 2000, SI 2000/701, amended by Allocation of Housing and Homelessness (Amendment) (England) Regulations 2004, SI 2004/1235 and further amended by the Allocation of Housing and Homelessness (Amendment) (England) Regulations 2006, SI 2006/1093.

[3] SI 2006/2007, in force for applications made to local housing authorities in England on or after 25 July 2006.

[4] SI 2006/2527, in force for applications made to local housing authorities in England on or after 9 October 2006.

[5] SI 2006/3340, in force for applications made to local housing authorities in England on or after 1 January 2007.

[6] SI 2009/358, in force for applications made to local housing authorities in England on or after 18 March 2009.

[7] SI 2012/2588 in force for applications made to local housing authorities in England on or after 8 November 2012.

[8] SI 2013/1467, in force for applications made to local housing authorities in England on or after 1 July 2013.

[9] SI 2014/435. Came into force on 31 March 2014. The Regulations contain no transitional provisions and will hence apply to any application outstanding at that date irrespective of when the application was made.

[10] SI 2016/965. In force from 30 October 2016. The regulations contain no transitional provisions and presumably apply to any application outstanding at that date irrespective of when the application was made.

3.17 Appendix 2 of this book contains the text of the Allocation of Housing and Homelessness (Eligibility) (England) Regulations 2006[1] as amended by all of the above regulations. Guidance is provided at paras 3.2–3.17 and Annexes 2–4 of the English Code[2].

[1] SI 2006/1294.
[2] These Annexes are not kept up to date and should be read with caution.

3.18 For Wales, the Welsh Ministers made the Allocation of Housing and Homelessness (Eligibility) (Wales) Regulations 2014[1], which apply to all applications to local housing authorities in Wales made on or after 31 October 2014[2].

[1] SI 2014/2603 (W 257).
[2] For the relevant regulations in Wales before 31 October 2014, see Luba and Davies *Housing Allocation and Homelessness* (1st edn, 2006; 2nd edn, 2010; 3rd edn, 2012).

3.19 The text of the Allocation of Housing and Homelessness (Eligibility) (Wales) Regulations 2014 is contained in the CD ROM which accompanies this book[1]. Guidance is provided at paras 2.13(ii)–2.28 and Annexes 4–6 of the Welsh Code.

[1] SI 2014/2603 (W 257).

3.20 There will be applicants whose applications were made before June 2006 (to a local housing authority in England) or before 31 October 2014 (to a local housing authority in Wales). The question of whether or not they were eligible for an allocation fell to be considered under the regulations in effect at the date that they made their applications. However, the English Code advises that authorities consider applicants' eligibility at the time of the initial application and again when considering making an allocation to them, particularly where a substantial amount of time has elapsed since the original application. This two-stage checking of eligibility will affect applicants:

- who either made their applications before 1 June 2006 and were eligible under one of the classes in the previous regulations[1] but do not fall within any of the classes prescribed as eligible in the current regulations; or

- whose immigration status may have changed since they made their applications.

[1]   For applications to a local housing authority in England before 1 June 2006, the relevant regulations were the Allocation of Housing (England) Regulations 2002, SI 2002/3264. Those regulations were amended by the Allocation of Housing and Homelessness (Amendment) (England) Regulations 2006, SI 2006/1093, with effect to applicants whose applications were made between 20 April 2006 and 31 May 2006.

3.21 The regulations in both England and Wales set out classes of persons who are subject to immigration control, but are prescribed as nevertheless eligible. They also set out classes of persons who are not subject to immigration control, but are nevertheless ineligible. Since the coming into force of the Allocation of Housing and Homelessness (Eligibility) (Wales) Regulations 2014[1] on 31 October 2014, the respective classes in England and Wales have been virtually identical[2]. However, the classes prior to 31 October 2014 contained a number of important differences. Readers interested in these historic differences may wish to refer to the previous editions of this book[3].

[1]   SI 2014/2603 (W 257).
[2]   There are minor semantic differences between SI 2006/1294 (England) and SI 2014/2603 (W 257) (Wales), for example SI 2014/2603 (W 257) is gender neutral, but in substance the law is now identical.
[3]   Luba and Davies *Housing Allocation and Homelessness* (1st edn, 2006; 2nd edn, 2010; 3rd edn, 2012).

3.22 The rules that tell us whether a person falling within either of the two categories (those subject to immigration control and those not subject to such control) is eligible for assistance need careful examination. The rules that apply to the first category are discussed at **3.31–3.47**. The rules that apply to the second category are discussed at **3.48–3.75**. But first it is necessary to work out which category an applicant is within. That depends on whether or not the applicant is 'subject to immigration control'. References will be made, where appropriate, to the fuller commentary on this topic contained in **CHAPTER 11**.[1]

[1]   See **11.26–11.93**.

Who is, and is not, subject to immigration control?

3.23 There is a special meaning of 'subject to immigration control'[1]. The HA 1996, s 160ZA(3) (England), s 160A(3) (Wales) refer to:

' . . . a person subject to immigration control within the meaning of the Asylum and Immigration Act 1996.'

[1] See **11.26–11.93** for a fuller discussion of who is, and is not, subject to immigration control including a detailed exposition of the various rights of residence available to EEA nationals. What follows is simply an outline.

3.24 The Asylum and Immigration Act 1996 defines 'a person who is subject to immigration control' as being a person[1]:

' . . . who under the 1971 Act requires leave to enter or remain in the United Kingdom (whether or not such leave has been given).'

[1] Asylum and Immigration Act 1996, s 13(2).

3.25 Tracing that route back to the Immigration Act 1971[1] reveals that:

- British citizens;
- Commonwealth citizens with the right of abode in the UK;
- European Economic Area (EEA) and Swiss nationals[2] exercising certain Treaty rights[3];
- family members and others exercising rights derived from those EEA or Swiss nationals exercising, or who had previously exercised, certain Treaty rights[4];
- certain people who are exempt from immigration control under the Immigration Acts (diplomats and their family members based in the UK, and some military personnel); and
- Irish citizens with a Common Travel Area entitlement[5];

do *not* require leave to enter or remain in the UK and therefore cannot be persons 'subject to immigration control'[6]. Those applicants will be eligible *unless* they fall within the second sub-category of persons prescribed as being 'persons from abroad' and not eligible[7].

[1] Immigration Act 1971, ss 1–3.
[2] From 1 June 2002, Swiss nationals have had the same rights to freedom of movement and social security within the EEA as EEA nationals and Swiss nationals now fall within the definition of 'EEA nationals' at Immigration (European Economic Area) Regulations 2016, SI 2016/1052, reg 2. All references to EEA nationals in this book therefore include Swiss nationals.
[3] Immigration Act 1988, s 7; Immigration (European Economic Area) Regulations 2016, SI 2016/1052, regs 13–15. For a full discussion of the various rights of residence available to EEA nationals and whether, consequently, an EEA national is, or is not, subject to immigration control, see **11.26–11.93**. It is to be expected that the law relating to the rights of EEA nationals to reside in the UK will change significantly following Brexit. What these changes may be and when they may come into effect are, at the time of writing, a matter of speculation. This chapter states the law as in force at the time of writing.
[4] Immigration (European Economic Area) Regulations 2016, SI 2016/1052, reg 16. For those derivative rights, see **11.66–11.87**.
[5] In the case of *McCarthy v Brent London Borough Council* (2016) November *Legal Action*, p 41, County Court at Central London, the local housing authority unsuccessfully sought to persuade the court that Irish Citizens with a Common Travel Area entitlement were subject to immigration control.
[6] Immigration Act 1971, ss 1–3; Immigration Act 1988, s 7; Immigration (European Economic Area) Regulations 2016, SI 2016/1052. See English Code, paras 3.7–3.9; Welsh Code, para 2.3.

[7] HA 1996, s 160ZA(4) (England), s 160A(5) (Wales); Allocation of Housing and Homelessness (Eligibility) (England) Regulations 2006, SI 2006/1294, reg 4 and Allocation of Housing and Homelessness (Eligibility) (Wales) Regulations 2014, SI 2014/ 2603 (W 257), reg 4.

3.26 The legal definition of 'The United Kingdom' and its related parts is given in Box 1.

Box 1

Key Geographic Terms:

England: counties established by Local Government Act 1972, s 1, Greater London area and the Isles of Scilly[1].

Great Britain: England, Wales, and Scotland[2].

United Kingdom: England, Wales, Scotland and Northern Ireland[3].

Common Travel Area (CTA): England, Wales, Scotland, Northern Ireland, Republic of Ireland, Isle of Man, and the Channel Islands[4].

---

[1] Interpretation Act 1978, s 5 and Sch 1.
[2] Union of Scotland Act 1706.
[3] Interpretation Act 1978, s 5 and Sch 1.
[4] Immigration Act 1971, s 1(3).

3.27 Box 2 shows which countries are members of the European Union (EU) and/or members of the wider European Economic Area (EEA). Obviously, the list will fluctuate from time to time[1]. For these purposes, nationals of Iceland, Liechtenstein, Norway, and Switzerland have the same rights to enter or reside as nationals of most of the EU Member States[2]. Rights for nationals of Croatia[3] are slightly different from those enjoyed by nationals of other EEA states[4]. We refer throughout this chapter to nationals of EEA Member States, by which we mean all the EU Member States plus the three additional EEA Member States and Switzerland.

Box 2

The European Union (EU):

Member States: Austria, Belgium, Bulgaria, Cyprus, Czech Republic, Denmark, Estonia, Finland, France, Germany, Greece, Hungary, Ireland, Italy, Latvia, Lithuania, Luxembourg, Malta, Netherlands, Poland, Portugal, Romania, Slovakia, Slovenia, Spain, Sweden and the UK; and

Accession States acceding in 2013: Croatia

The European Economic Area (EEA):

All EU States[5] plus Iceland, Liechtenstein and Norway.

Switzerland is not part of the EEA, but its nationals are treated as EEA nationals for these purposes[6].

---

[1]   Croatia acceded to the European Union on 1 July 2013. Albania, Montenegro, Serbia, Turkey and the former Yugoslav Republic of Macedonia are 'candidate countries' for accession to the EU. Bosnia and Herzegovina, and Kosovo are potential 'candidate countries'. See www.europa.eu/about-eu/countries/index_en.htm for an up-to-date list.
[2]   Immigration (European Economic Area) Regulations 2016, SI 2016/1052, as amended.
[3]   See **11.88–11.92**.
[4]   The nationals of new member states are typically treated differently upon accession to the EU. Rights for nationals of the eight 2004 Accession States (A8 states) were initially subject to derogation between 1 May 2004 and 30 April 2009 (Accession (Immigration and Worker Registration) Regulations 2004, SI 2004/1219). This period was subsequently extended to 30 April 2011 (Accession (Immigration and Worker Registration) (Amendment) Regulations 2009, SI 2009/892). This extension was recently held to be unlawful by the Court of Appeal in *Secretary of State for Work and Pensions v Gubeladze* [2017] EWCA Civ 1751, CA. The nature and extent of the practical ramifications of this decision remain to be seen. But, in any event, from 1 May 2011 nationals of the A8 member states have been treated in the same way as nationals of any other EEA member state, save that retained worker status is slightly different. The A8 states were the Czech Republic, Estonia, Hungary, Latvia, Lithuania, Poland, Slovakia and Slovenia. Rights for nationals of the two 2007 Accession States (A2 states) were subject to derogation between 1 January 2007 and 31 December 2013 (Accession (Immigration and Worker Registration) Regulations 2006, SI 2006/3317). From 1 January 2014 nationals of the A2 member states have been treated in the same way as nationals of any other EEA member state, save that retained worker status is slightly different. The A2 states were Romania and Bulgaria. Rights for Croatian nationals have been subject to derogation since 1 July 2013. After 30 June 2018, Croatian nationals are to be treated in the same way as other EEA nationals. See **11.88–11.92**.
[5]   The Channel Islands, Isle of Man and Gibraltar are not part of the EEA.
[6]   Immigration (European Economic Area) Regulations 2016, SI 2016/1052, reg 2.

3.28 If the applicant, even if newly arrived in the UK, does not require leave to enter or remain in the UK, he or she will usually be 'eligible' *unless* rendered ineligible by falling within the second sub-category[1]. For these purposes, it is important to emphasise that a person, usually an EEA national, or a person claiming to exercise rights derived from an EEA national, who does not require leave to enter but who does require leave to remain and does not have it, is a person subject to immigration control[2]. It is only a person who requires neither leave to enter nor leave to remain who is not subject to immigration control. Strangely, a person can be ineligible for an allocation of social housing even if he or she was born in the UK and has never left it, simply because he or she does require leave to enter or remain in the UK and does not have it[3].

1 See **3.48–3.75**.
2 *Abdi v Barnet London Borough Council, Ismail v Barnet London Borough Council* [2006] EWCA Civ 383, [2006] HLR 23, CA.
3 *Ehiabor v Kensington & Chelsea Royal London Borough Council* [2008] EWCA Civ 1074, [2008] All ER (D) 104 (May), CA.

3.29 Everyone else is a 'person subject to immigration control' and is *not* eligible for assistance *unless* he or she falls into one of the classes prescribed by the Regulations[1]. In some instances it will be easy to establish whether an individual falls within the list of persons not subject to immigration control at **3.25**. For example, it will often be fairly easy to establish whether an individual has British Citizenship, from which it can then be concluded that he or she is not subject to immigration control. Difficulties tend to arise in cases involving EEA nationals. In these cases it is not sufficient to inquire whether the individual has citizenship of a country within the EEA in order to determine whether he or she is subject to immigration control. In addition to that inquiry it will be necessary to establish whether he or she is exercising treaty rights, or has derived a right to reside from another person who is exercising his or her treaty rights. Answering these questions is rarely straightforward. For that reason, a detailed discussion of the various rights to reside available to EEA nationals and their family members can be found at **11.32–11.93**.

1 Allocation of Housing and Homelessness (Eligibility) (England) Regulations 2006, SI 2006/1294, reg 3 as amended; Allocation of Housing and Homelessness (Eligibility) (Wales) Regulations 2014, SI 2014/2603 (W 257), reg 3.

3.30 The resolution of any uncertainty about an applicant's immigration or asylum status, or the relevant dates (eg of entry into the UK or application for asylum) may require the help of the Home Office[1]. Local housing authorities are advised to contact the Home Office if there is any uncertainty arising from an application, and to inform the applicant that an inquiry will be made before doing so[2]. This allows the applicant an opportunity to withdraw his or her application for if he or she does not want such an inquiry to be made. The Home Office advises on an applicant's immigration status, but the decision on eligibility is for the local housing authority itself[3].

1 The English Code refers to the UKBA, which ceased to exist in 2013. The functions of the UKBA have, for the most part, been subsumed by United Kingdom Visas and Immigration (UKVI): a subsidiary of the Home Office. Contact details can be found at Welsh Code, Annex 5.
2 English Code, para 3.10; Welsh Code, para 7.15.
3 English Code, para 3.10.

Working out whether the applicant is eligible

Sub-category one: those who are subject to immigration control

3.31 Anyone who requires leave to enter or remain in the UK is a person subject to immigration control[1] and will not be eligible for an allocation unless he or she falls within one of the classes prescribed as eligible in regulations made by the Secretary of State or the Welsh Ministers[2].

[1]   See **3.23–3.30** and **11.26–11.93** for a detailed discussion of who is, and who is not, subject to immigration control.
[2]   HA 1996, s 160ZA(2) (England), s 160A(3) (Wales).

3.32 The Secretary of State and the Welsh Ministers cannot designate as 'eligible' anyone who is excluded from entitlement to housing benefit or universal credit by the Immigration and Asylum Act 1999, s 115[1].

[1]   HA 1996, s 160ZA(3) (England), s 160A(4) (Wales). Immigration and Asylum Act 1999, s 115 prescribes that 'a person subject to immigration control' is not eligible for housing benefit or universal credit unless he or she falls within one of the classes of people prescribed by the Secretary of State. Classes of persons subject to immigration control who are entitled to housing benefit or universal credit are prescribed in the Social Security (Immigration and Asylum) Consequential Amendment Regulations 2000, SI 2000/636, Sch 1, Pt 1 and the Housing Benefit Regulations 2006, SI 2006/213, reg 10(3B).

3.33 The Secretary of State and the Welsh Ministers have exercised their powers given by HA 1996, s 160ZA(2) (England) and s 160A(3) (Wales) to set out classes of persons subject to immigration control who are nevertheless eligible for an allocation of accommodation.

3.34 The basic rule is that a person subject to immigration control is *not eligible*. The exceptions to that basic rule are contained in classes set out in regulations. Regulation 3 of the Allocation of Housing and Homelessness (Eligibility) (England) Regulations 2006[1] and Reg 3 of the Allocation of Housing and Homelessness (Eligibility) (Wales) Regulations 2014[2] prescribe that the following classes of people from abroad are eligible even though they are subject to immigration control:

(1)   Class A:[3] a person recorded by the Secretary of State as a refugee and who has leave to enter or remain in the UK.

(2)   Class B[4]: a person who has:
 (a)   exceptional leave to enter or remain in the UK; and
 (b)   whose leave is not subject to conditions requiring him or her to maintain and accommodate himself or herself and any dependants without recourse to public funds.

(3)   Class C[5]: a person:
 (a)   who is habitually resident in the 'common travel area' (CTA); and
 (b)   who has current leave to enter or remain in the UK which is not subject to any limitation or condition; but
 (c)   is not someone who has—
  (i)   been given leave to enter or remain in the UK upon a written undertaking from a sponsor that he or she will be responsible for maintenance and accommodation; and
  (ii)   has been resident in the CTA for less than five years beginning on the date of entry or the date of the undertaking (whichever is the later date); and
  (iii) whose sponsor is still alive.

(4)   Class D[6]: a person who has humanitarian protection granted under the Immigration Rules.

CLASS C: A PERSON WITH CURRENT LEAVE TO ENTER OR REMAIN IN THE UK WITH NO CONDITION OR LIMITATION AND WHO IS HABITUALLY RESIDENT IN THE CTA

3.42 The type of leave contemplated by this class is commonly referred to as 'indefinite leave to enter or remain'[1] and cannot be granted subject to conditions[2]. Anyone granted indefinite leave will be eligible if he or she is also habitually resident in the CTA[3].

[1] Allocation of Housing and Homelessness (Eligibility) (England) Regulations 2006, SI 2006/1294, reg 3(c); Allocation of Housing and Homelessness (Eligibility) (Wales) Regulations 2014, SI 2014/ 2603 (W 257), reg 3(c). See English Code, para 3.11(iii).
[2] Immigration Act 1971, s 3(1)(b) and (c).
[3] For the meaning of 'habitually resident' see **3.55–3.61** and **11.130–11.136**. For the meaning of 'CTA' see **3.26**, Box 1.

3.43 If leave to enter or remain was granted on a written undertaking that a sponsor would be responsible for the applicant's maintenance and accommodation, the applicant will *not* be eligible under this class for an allocation for the five years running from:

- the date of his or her arrival in the UK, or
- the date the sponsorship undertaking was given,

starting from whichever is the later event.

3.44 After those five years, or during the five years if the sponsor (or at least one of several sponsors) has died, an applicant will be eligible under this class (subject to satisfying the test of habitual residence)[1].

[1] See **3.55–3.61** and **11.130–11.136**.

CLASS D: A PERSON GRANTED HUMANITARIAN PROTECTION UNDER THE IMMIGRATION RULES

3.45 'Humanitarian protection'[1] is granted to those people whose claims for asylum do not succeed, but who have international protection needs (ie they face a serious risk of the death penalty, unlawful killing, torture, inhuman or degrading treatment or punishment if removed from the UK). The status must be granted pursuant to the Immigration Rules.[2] People with humanitarian protection are entitled to family reunion in the same way as refugees.[3]

[1] Allocation of Housing and Homelessness (Eligibility) (England) Regulations 2006, SI 2006/1294, reg 3(d); Allocation of Housing and Homelessness (Eligibility) (Wales) Regulations 2014, SI 2014/2603 (W 257), reg 3(d). See English Code, para 3.11(iv).
[2] See Immigration Rules, HC 395 (23 May 1994 as amended), paras 339C–339H.
[3] Immigration Rules, HC 395 (23 May 1994 as amended), paras 352FA–352FI.

CLASS E: A RELEVANT AFGHAN CITIZEN GRANTED LEAVE TO ENTER UNDER *IMMIGRATION RULES*, PARA 276BA1, WHO IS HABITUALLY RESIDENT IN THE CTA

3.46 This class[1] consists of persons habitually resident[2] in the CTA[3] and who have limited leave to enter the United Kingdom as a relevant Afghan citizen under para 276BA1 of the Immigration Rules[4]. This is a niche category of leave offered to locally engaged staff in Afghanistan who worked in particularly challenging or dangerous roles in Helmand province[5].

[1] Allocation of Housing and Homelessness (Eligibility) (England) Regulations 2006, SI 2006/1294, reg 3(1)(e); Allocation of Housing and Homelessness (Eligibility) (Wales) Regulations 2014, SI 2014/2603 (W 257), reg 3(1)(e).
[2] See 3.55–3.61.
[3] See Box 1 at 3.26.
[4] HC 395 (23 May 1994 as amended).
[5] See Letter DCLG to Chief Housing Officers of Local Authorities in England, 5 March 2014, found at APPENDIX 2.

CLASS F: PERSON WHO HAS LIMITED LEAVE TO ENTER OR REMAIN IN THE UK ON FAMILY OR PRIVATE LIFE GROUNDS UNDER ARTICLE 8, WHO IS NOT SUBJECT TO A NO RECOURSE TO PUBLIC FUNDS CONDITION

3.47 To fall within this class a person must[1]:

(a)   have limited leave to enter or remain in the United Kingdom on family or private life grounds under Art 8 of the European Convention on Human Rights, such leave granted under para 276BE(1), para 276DG or Appendix FM of the Immigration Rules[2], and
(b)   not be subject to a condition requiring that person to maintain and accommodate himself, and any person dependent upon him, without recourse to public funds[3].

This class was introduced in 2016 in England and 2017 in Wales[4]. In broad terms, the class encompasses those granted leave to remain in the UK pursuant to Art 8. The policy background to this class is described in detail at 11.117–11.121.

[1] Allocation of Housing and Homelessness (Eligibility) (England) Regulations 2006, SI 2006/1294, reg 3(1)(f); Allocation of Housing and Homelessness (Eligibility) (Wales) Regulations 2014, SI 2014/2603 (W 257), reg 3(1)(f).
[2] Immigration Rules, HC 395 (23 May 1994, as amended).
[3] The requirements of SI 2006/1294, reg 3(1)(f), strictly, do not make grammatical sense: a point highlighted in the Joint Committee on Statutory Instruments Thirteenth Report of Session 2016–17, 16 November 2016 at para 2.4. However, if one refrains from an overly technical reading, the scope of the class is clear and the requirements have been set out here so as to avoid reproducing the error. This grammatical error has been avoided in SI 2014/2603 (W 257), reg 3(1)(f).
[4] SI 2006/1294, reg 3(1)(f) was added by the the Allocation of Housing and Homelessness (Eligibility) (England) (Amendment) Regulations 2016, SI 2016/965, in force from 30 October 2016. SI 2014/2603 (W 257), reg 5(1)(g) was added by the Allocation of Housing and Homelessness (Eligibility) (Wales) (Amendment) Regulations 2017, SI 2017/698 (W 164).

Sub-category two: other 'persons from abroad'

OVERVIEW

3.48 Ordinarily, persons not subject to immigration control[1] would be eligible for an allocation of social housing. However, the Secretary of State and the Welsh Ministers are permitted to make regulations treating some people who are not subject to immigration control as 'persons from abroad' and therefore not eligible for allocation[2]. Both the Secretary of State and the Welsh Ministers have exercised these powers.

1　See **3.23–3.30** and **11.26–11.93** for the rules on how to determine who is, and who is not, subject to immigration control.
2　HA 1996, s 160ZA(4) (England), s 160A(5) (Wales).

3.49 In the Allocation of Housing and Homelessness (Eligibility) (England) Regulations 2006[1], and the Allocation of Housing and Homelessness (Eligibility) (Wales) Regulations 2014[2], the Secretary of State and the Welsh Ministers have exercised their powers to treat some people who are not subject to immigration control as 'persons from abroad'[3]. This means that some British citizens, nationals of EEA Member States, and others who are exempt from immigration control may nevertheless be denied an allocation on the grounds that they are 'not eligible'. The primary function of these provisions is to confine new allocations of social housing to the ordinary residents of the UK, ie those habitually resident here, and to EEA nationals exercising Treaty rights.

1　SI 2006/1294, as amended.
2　SI 2014/2603 (W 257).
3　For applications made before 1 June 2006 in England and before 31 October 2014 in Wales, see the first and third editions of this book respectively.

3.50 Allocation of Housing and Homelessness (Eligibility) (England) Regulations 2006, reg 4, and Allocation of Housing and Homelessness (Eligibility) (Wales) Regulations 2014, reg 4, establish three classes of people who are to be treated as 'persons from abroad' and therefore *ineligible* for an allocation despite not being subject to immigration control.

3.51 The *first class*[1] comprises persons who are 'not habitually resident'[2] in the CTA[3]. But that test of habitual residence is subject to a number of exemptions[4].

1　Allocation of Housing and Homelessness (Eligibility) (England) Regulations 2006, SI 2006/1294, reg 4(1)(a); Allocation of Housing and Homelessness (Eligibility) (Wales) Regulations 2014, SI 2014/2603 (W 257), reg 4(1)(a).
2　See **3.55–3.61**.
3　See Box 1 at **3.26**.
4　See **3.62–3.65**.

3.52 The *second class* comprises EEA nationals and their family members whose only right to reside in the UK is derived from their status as job-seekers, as family members of job-seekers, from their initial right to reside in the UK for a period not exceeding three months, by having a derivative right to reside in the UK as the primary carer of a British citizen, or by having a right to reside derived from Art 20 of the Treaty on the Functioning of the EU[1].

1　SI 2006/1294, reg 4(1)(b); SI 2014/2603 (W 257), reg 4(1)(b). See **3.66–3.71**.

3.53 The *third class* comprises EEA nationals and their family members whose only right to reside in the rest of the CTA (Channel Islands, Isle of Man or the Republic of Ireland) is derived from their status as job-seekers, as family members of job-seekers, from their initial right to reside in the UK for a period not exceeding three months, by having a derivative right to reside in the CTA as the primary carer of an Irish or British citizen, or by having a right to reside derived from Art 20 of the Treaty on the Functioning of the EU[1].

---

[1]   SI 2006/1294, reg 4(1)(c); SI 2014/2603 (W 257), reg 4(1)(c). See **3.72–3.75**.

3.54 Each of the three classes will be examined in turn.

THE FIRST CLASS: NOT HABITUALLY RESIDENT

3.55 'Habitual residence'[1] is not a term of reference to someone's immigration status. A person may be a British citizen, but if he or she is not habitually resident in the CTA[2], he or she will not be eligible[3]. Nor is the term 'habitual residence' defined in either HA 1996, Pt 6 or in the regulations.[4] It is a question of fact for the local housing authority to decide. Happily, there is some guidance in the Codes of Guidance[5].

---

[1]   SI 2006/1294, reg 4(1)(a); SI 2014/2603 (W 257), reg 4(1)(a).
[2]   See Box 1 at **3.26**.
[3]   Unless he or she is exempt from the habitual residence test. See **3.62–3.65**.
[4]   SI 2006/1294 and SI 2014/2603 (W 257).
[5]   English Code, paras 3.16–3.17 and Annex 4; Welsh Code, paras 7.13 and 2.18–2.24 and Annex 6.

3.56 A person who is not habitually resident will also not be entitled to non-contributory social security benefits. If the person is receiving one of those social security benefits, it must follow that the Department for Work and Pensions (DWP) has determined that he or she is habitually resident[1]. A determination by the DWP is not necessarily binding on a local housing authority[2] but in the interests of good administration and consistent decision-making, such a determination should certainly be taken into account by the local housing authority during the decision-making process[3] and reasons should be given if the local housing authority elects to depart from the determination[4].

---

[1]   A person who has a derivative right of residence contained at SI 2016/1052, reg 16(5) (the 'Zambrano' right of residence) is treated as not habitually resident for the purposes of entitlement to income support, jobseeker's allowance, state pension credit, and housing benefit (SI 2012/ 2587, in force 8 November 2012) and for Universal Credit (SI 2013/376 reg 9).
[2]   See *Mangion v Lewisham London Borough Council* [2008] EWCA Civ 1642, (2009) January *Legal Action*, p 26, CA and *Simpson-Lowe v Croydon London Borough Council* [2012] EWCA Civ 131, (2012) April *Legal Action*, p 47, CA dealing with the different question of whether findings made in relation to disability related benefits were binding on a local housing authority when assessing vulnerability; see **9.76**.
[3]   See *R (Clue) v Birmingham City Council* [2010] EWCA Civ 460, [2011] 1 WLR 99, CA on the importance of consistent decision making across government departments and local authorities.
[4]   See **9.111–9.125** on the duty to give reasons.

3.57 There are two aspects required to be present in order to constitute habitual residence:

(1)   a settled purpose of establishing residence in one of the territories of the CTA[1]; and
(2)   an appreciable period of such residence.

---

[1]   For 'CTA', see Box 1 at **3.26**.

3.58 Whether each aspect is satisfied is a question of fact for the local housing authority to decide. The Codes advise that normally, if someone has lived in one of the territories of the CTA for two years continuously prior to his or her application, he or she should be considered to be habitually resident without further inquiry[1]. However, that should not be taken as meaning that a person cannot be habitually resident if he or she has not lived in one of the territories of the CTA for two years. The point is simply that there is little point in a local housing authority wasting resources by making inquiries into whether or not an applicant who came to the UK more than two years ago is habitually resident. In *R (Paul-Coker) v Southwark London Borough Council*[2], a number of instances where people had been resident for periods of time that were shorter than two years, but had been sufficient to constitute 'an appreciable period', were cited to the judge. He said: '[i]t is therefore clear that what constitutes an appreciable period of time for these purposes will vary from case to case and will depend on the facts of the individual case'[3]. In that particular case the local housing authority was wrong in law to have directed itself that an applicant had to have been resident for six months before she could be considered to be habitually resident.

1   English Code, para 3.17 and Annex 4, para 1; Welsh Code, paras 2.22 and 7.13 and Annex 6, para 4.
2   [2006] EWHC 497 (Admin), [2006] HLR 32, Admin Ct.
3   *R (Paul-Coker) v Southwark London Borough Council* [2006] EWHC 497 (Admin), [2006] HLR 32, Admin Ct, Forbes J at [22].

3.59 Establishing a 'settled purpose' will obviously involve consideration of an applicant's subjective intentions and motivations. Someone in stable employment may be more likely to be able to establish his or her 'settled purpose' to be habitually resident than someone in transitory employment, or dependent on benefits. However, local housing authorities must be careful not to give too much weight to an applicant's lack of finances and not enough weight to other factors such as the applicant's nationality, ties with the UK, and future intentions[1].

1   *Barnet London Borough Council v Shah* [1983] 2 AC 309, HL; and *Olokunboro v Croydon London Borough Council* (2003) February *Legal Action*, p 37, Croydon County Court.

3.60 What constitutes an 'appreciable period of residence' likewise varies according to the circumstances of each individual's case. If a former British resident returns to the UK after living and working abroad, he or she may be habitually resident from the first day of his or her return[1]. When someone is coming to live in the UK for the first time, there must be an appreciable period of residence before habitual residence is obtained. To determine how long that period of residence should be in any particular case, local housing authorities should consider all the circumstances, including:

- whether the person is seeking to bring any family members to the CTA;
- whether he or she has brought his or her personal property and possessions to the CTA;
- whether he or she has done everything necessary to establish a residence before coming;
- whether he or she has a right of abode; and

- what 'durable ties' there are with the CTA[2].

[1]   *Swaddling v Adjudication Officer* [1999] All ER (EC) 217, CJEU, and see CIS/1304/1997 and CJSA/5394/1998; and English Code, Annex 4, paras 7.
[2]   *Nessa v Chief Adjudication Officer* [1999] 1 WLR 1937, HL. English Code, Annex 4, paras 5–20.

3.61 In *R (Paul-Coker) v Southwark London Borough Council*[1] the local housing authority erred in failing to take into account that the applicant had, in fact, been resident for seven months, had given birth to a child who was a British national, had spent her formative years in the UK and had returned for extended holidays in the three years preceding her arrival, that she had travelled to the UK on a one-way ticket and had family and friends in the UK. All of those factors should have been considered.

[1]   [2006] EWHC 497 (Admin), [2006] HLR 32, Admin Ct.

EXEMPTIONS FROM THE HABITUAL RESIDENCE TEST

3.62 The following people are eligible for assistance even if they are not habitually resident:

- an EEA national who is a 'worker'[1]; or
- an EEA national who is self-employed[2]; or
- until 30 June 2018, a person who is an Accession State national subject to worker authorisation who is authorised in accordance with the Accession Regulations 2013[3] (a 'Croatian national')[4]; or
- a family member of an EEA national who is a worker, a self-employed person, or an Accession State national subject to worker authorisation who is authorised in accordance with the Accession Regulations 2013[5]; or
- a person who has one of certain permanent rights to reside in the UK[6]; or
- a person who is in the UK as a result of having been deported, expelled or otherwise removed by compulsion of law from another country to the UK[7].

[1]   Allocation of Housing and Homelessness (Eligibility) (England) Regulations 2006, SI 2006/1294, reg 4(2)(a); Allocation of Housing and Homelessness (Eligibility) (Wales) Regulations 2014, SI 2014/2603 (W 257), reg 4(2)(a). For 'worker' see **11.40–11.46**.
[2]   SI 2006/1294, reg 4(2)(b); SI 2014/2603 (W 257), reg 4(2)(b). For 'self-employed' see **11.47–11.49**.
[3]   Accession of Croatia (Immigration and Worker Authorisation) Regulations 2013, SI 2013/1460.
[4]   SI 2006/1294, reg 4(2)(c)(ii); SI 2014/2603 (W 257), reg 4(2)(c)(ii). For 'Accession State national subject to worker authorisation' see **11.88–11.92**.
[5]   SI 2006/1294, reg 4(2)(d); SI 2014/2603 (W 257), reg 4(2)(d). For 'family member' see **11.54–11.60**.
[6]   SI 2006/1294, reg 4(2)(e); SI 2014/2603 (W 257), reg 4(2)(e). For 'permanent right to reside' see **11.61–11.65**.
[7]   SI 2006/1294, reg 4(2)(g); SI 2014/2603 (W 257), reg 4(2)(f). This group of people who are eligible, even if not habitually resident, is likely to be small.

3.63 Most of these categories refer to those persons exercising rights of freedom of movement enjoyed under EU law, and to the Immigration (European Economic Area) Regulations 2016[1], which are the current regulations transposing EU freedom of movement legislation into domestic law.

¹ SI 2016/1052.

3.64 The penultimate exemption requires some elaboration. This exemption from the habitual residence test only applies to three sub-classes of persons who are entitled to a permanent right of residence¹. Those three sub-classes give permanent rights of residence to:

(1)   an EEA national who was a worker or self-employed person who has ceased activity²;

(2)   the family member of such an EEA national³; and

(3)   a person who was:

- the family member of an EEA national who was a worker or self-employed person; and
- the EEA national has died; and
- the family member had resided with the EEA national immediately before his or her death; and
- either the EEA national had resided in the UK for at least two years immediately before his or her death; or
- the death was the result of an accident at work or an occupational disease⁴.

¹ For 'permanent right of residence' see **11.61–11.65**.
² Immigration (European Economic Area) Regulations 2016, SI 2016/1052, reg 15(1)(c).
³ SI 2016/1052, reg 15(1)(d).
⁴ SI 2016/1052, reg 15(1)(e).

3.65 'Worker or self-employed person who has ceased activity' is defined at Immigration (European Economic Area) Regulations 2016, reg 5¹. For 'family member', see **11.54–11.60**. For 'worker', see **11.40–11.46**. For 'self-employed person' see **11.47–11.49**.

¹ SI 2016/1052.

THE SECOND CLASS: EEA NATIONALS WITH CERTAIN RIGHTS TO RESIDE IN THE UK

3.66 Anyone who falls exclusively within this class cannot be eligible for a housing allocation¹. The habitual residence test is not relevant. If an EEA national is:

(a)   a jobseeker²; or

(b)   a family member³ of a jobseeker; or

(c)   only entitled to remain in the UK by virtue of the initial right to reside for three months⁴; or

(d)   has a derivative right to reside because he or she is the primary carer of a British citizen⁵; or

(e)   has a right to reside derived from Art 20 of the Treaty on the Functioning of the EU, where the right to reside arises because a British citizen would otherwise be deprived of the genuine enjoyment of the substance of those rights as an EU citizen⁶, he or she cannot be eligible.

1.   Allocation of Housing and Homelessness (Eligibility) (England) Regulations 2006, SI 2006/1294, reg 4(1)(b); Allocation of Housing and Homelessness (Eligibility) (Wales) Regulations 2014, SI 2014/2603 (W 257), reg 4(1)(b). See English Code, para 3.12(ii) and (iii).
2.   See **11.39**.
3.   See **11.54–11.602**.
4.   See **11.35–11.36**.
5.   SI 2006/1294, reg 4(1)(b)(iii); SI 2014/2603 (W 257), reg 4(1)(b)(iii). For 'derivative right to reside because he or she is the primary carer of a British citizen', see **11.80–11.85**.
6.   SI 2006/1294, reg 4(1)(b)(iv); SI 2014/2603 (W 257), reg 4(1)(b)(iv). For 'a right to reside derived from Art 20 of the Treaty on the Functioning of the EU, where the right to reside arises because a British citizen would otherwise be deprived of the genuine enjoyment of the substance of those rights as a EU citizen', see **11.93**.

3.67 This second class operates to ensure that any EEA national, or family member of an EEA national, whose *only* right of residence in the UK is the initial 3-month right of residence is not eligible for an allocation of social housing.

3.68 The second class excludes 'jobseekers'[1] from an allocation of social housing. EEA nationals who are 'jobseekers' are 'qualified persons'[2] and therefore are entitled to the extended right of residence[3]. A 'jobseeker' is defined as 'a person who enters the UK in order to seek employment and can provide evidence that he is seeking employment and has a genuine chance of being engaged'[4]. If the jobseeker had previously been employed, he or she may still have retained worker status and so be a 'worker' in certain circumstances and therefore potentially eligible[5].

1.   See **11.39**.
2.   Immigration (European Economic Area) Regulations 2016, SI 2016/1052, reg 6(1)(a). See **11.38**.
3.   See **11.37–11.60**.
4.   SI 2016/1052, reg 6(1)(a) and (4).
5.   See **11.42–11.46**.

3.69 Also excluded is any person who is entitled to an EU right of residence that is derived from being the primary carer of a British national[1]. He or she is also to be treated as not habitually resident and thus excluded from receiving non-contributory benefits[2] including housing benefit. The 'derivative right of residence' which forms the basis of this exclusion was recognised by the CJEU in the case of *Zambrano v Office national de l'emploi*[3] and is now identified in the Immigration (European Economic Area) Regulations 2016[4]. People entitled to any of the four other derivative rights of residence in reg 16 of the Immigration (European Economic Area) Regulations 2016[5] do not fall within this second class of people excluded from eligibility.

1.   SI 2006/1294, reg 4(1)(b)(iii); SI 2014/2603 (W 257), reg 4(1)(b)(iii). This exclusion reverses the effect of *Pryce v Southwark London Borough Council* [2012] EWCA 1572, [2013] 1 WLR 996, [2013] HLR 10, CA. See further T Vaneghan 'The Pryce of Eligibility' *Legal Action*, February 2013, pp 31–32 for commentary on the background to, and legality of, these regulations. See **11.80–11.85** for a discussion of this derivative right to reside.
2.   Social Security (Habitual Residence) (Amendment) Regulations 2012, SI 2012/2587, and Universal Credit Regulations 2013, SI 2013/376, reg 9. A challenge to these regulations as discriminatory was unsuccessful in *R (Sanneh) v Secretary of State for Work and Pensions* [2015] EWCA Civ 49, [2015] HLR 27, CA. There is no exclusion prohibiting the person who has this derivative right of residence from working or from receiving contributory benefits. However, if the person is not in or cannot work (not least because of his or her caring

responsibilities), has no entitlement to contributory benefits, and the household is destitute, the recourse is likely to be to adult care or children's services for financial and accommodation assistance. See CHAPTER **20**.
3   Case C34/09, [2012] QB 265, CJEU.
4   SI 2016/1052, reg 16(5). See **11.80–11.85**.
5   SI 2016/1052. See **11.66–11.87**.

3.70 In addition, a person who has a right derived from Art 20 of the Treaty on the Functioning of the EU, in a case where the right to reside arises because a British citizen would otherwise be deprived of the genuine enjoyment of the substance of his or her rights as an EU citizen, is also excluded from eligibility[1]. This new provision appears to exclude anyone who has a right of residence which is not, as yet, identified in the Immigration (European Economic Area) Regulations[2], but which is subsequently declared by the CJEU. Article 20 of the Treaty contains the right of nationals of EU member states to be citizens of the EU and to move and reside freely within the territories of the EU member states. This provision does not exclude all the rights of EU residence that might, in the future, be recognised in CJEU case-law but simply those that are:

* derived from Art 20 of the Treaty; and
* arise because otherwise a British citizen would be deprived of the genuine enjoyment of the substance of his or her rights under EU law.

For rights declared by the CJEU, see **11.93**[3].

1   SI 2006/1294, reg 4(1)(b)(iv); SI 2014/2603 (W 257), reg 4(1)(b)(iv).
2   SI 2016/1052.
3   The DCLG has written to Chief Housing Officers of Local Authorities in England in relation to these rights, see letter dated 17 October 2012 found at APPENDIX **2**.

3.71 If a person has more than one right of residence, such as being both a job-seeker and being the family member of a worker or self-employed person, then his or her right to reside is not 'only' derived from his or her status as a job-seeker, or from any of the other four provisions in this second class, and he or she will not fall within this second class of persons (not subject to immigration control) who are not eligible.

THE THIRD CLASS: EEA NATIONALS WITH CERTAIN RIGHTS TO RESIDE IN THE REST OF THE COMMON TRAVEL AREA

3.72 This third class[1] refers to people who have been residing in the Channel Islands, the Isle of Man or the Republic of Ireland. The rest of the CTA is dealt with by the second class.

1   Allocation of Housing and Homelessness (Eligibility) (England) Regulations 2006, SI 2006/1294, reg 4(1)(c); Allocation of Housing and Homelessness (Eligibility) (Wales) Regulations 2014, SI 2014/2603 (W 257), reg 4(1)(c). See English Code, para 3.12(iv).

3.73 For 'jobseeker' see **11.39**. For 'family member' see **11.54–11.60**. For 'initial right to reside' see **11.35–11.36**. For 'Common Travel Area' see **3.26**, Box 1. For 'persons with a right to reside derived from Art 20 of the Treaty on the Functioning of the EU', see **11.93**.

3.74 The derivative right to reside referred to in this class is the same as that identified in the Immigration (European Economic Area) Regulations 2016[1], but is separately identified because those Regulations do not apply to the remainder of the CTA. The derivative right arises as a result of the CJEU's decision in *Zambrano v Office national de l'emploi*[2]. That decision recognised rights of residence which are directly effective in the remainder of the CTA: ie the Channel Islands, Isle of Man and the Republic of Ireland. A person will have this derivative right of residence if he or she is the primary carer of a British citizen residing in the Channels Islands or the Isle of Man, or of an Irish citizen, residing in the Republic of Ireland, and the British or Irish citizen would have to leave that country of residence if his or her primary carer did not have an EU right of residence. The derivative right of residence will be enjoyed by people who are not nationals of any EEA member state.

[1]   SI 2016/1052.
[2]   C34/09, [2012] QB 265, CJEU.

3.75 As with the second class, if a person has more than one right of residence, then his or her right to reside is not 'only' derived from his or her status as a jobseeker, or the other four provisions in this class, and he or she will not fall within this third class of persons (not subject to immigration control) who are not eligible for an allocation of social housing.

QUALIFICATION FOR ALLOCATION (ENGLAND)

Background to the current arrangements

3.76 From 1996 to 2003, each local housing authority in England and Wales had the power to exclude from its statutory housing register whole classes of applicant which it chose to designate as 'non-qualifying persons'[1].

[1]   HA 1996, s 161(4) repealed by Homelessness Act 2002, Sch 2. See **1.16–1.18**.

3.77 However, in 2002 the then UK Labour Government expressed concern at the 'extensive use' being made of 'this broad power to effectively exclude categories of applicants from access to social housing, regardless of housing need'[1]. HA 1996, Pt 6, was amended to remove the power to impose blanket exclusions of classes of person[2]. Local housing authorities were left with only a limited power to lawfully exclude *individual* applicants in narrow circumstances. As a result, from early 2003 to June 2012, a local housing authority in England or Wales only had the ability to treat an applicant as ineligible for allocation as a result of his or her immigration status or because of unacceptable behaviour by the applicant or a member of his or his household[3].

[1]   *Parliamentary Joint Committee on Human Rights First Report, Appendix: The Homelessness Bill, Memorandum by the Department for Transport, Local Government and the Regions*, para 3.3, November 2001.
[2]   HA 1996, s 161(4); repealed by Homelessness Act 2002, Sch 2.
[3]   See **3.151** et seq for a description of these arrangements, which still apply in Wales.

3.78 Several of the relatively small number of cases in which the conditions for exclusion were treated by local housing authorities as having been fulfilled led to applications for judicial review[1]. Against that background, local housing authorities often preferred to permit access by all applicants to their allocation schemes but then to use other powers to remove or reduce the preferences which certain applicants would otherwise have enjoyed in the local allocation schemes. In consequence, the number of applicants on waiting lists grew steadily from 2003 onwards[2]. This led to a further policy change, described in the next few paragraphs, after the election of the UK Coalition Government in 2010.

[1]   See for example *R (McQ) v Bolton Metropolitan Borough Council* [2005] EWHC 1285 (Admin), (2005) August *Legal Action*, p 17, Admin Ct and *R (Dixon) v Wandsworth London Borough Council* [2008] EWCA Civ 595, (2008) July *Legal Action*, p 22, Admin Ct.

[2]   'In 1998 waiting list numbers [of households] were 1.02 million, and remained below 1.1 million until 2002. The introduction of open waiting lists in 2003 coincided with a steep rise in waiting list numbers, which reached 1.77 million in 2008. In 2009, overall waiting list numbers remained stable at 1.76 million. This represents a 61% rise over 2002 levels.' *Localism Bill: A fairer future for social housing – Impact Assessment* (DCLG, January 2011), p 15.

The policy change

3.79 In its May 2010 programme, the incoming UK Coalition Government proclaimed its intention to 'promote decentralization' and 'end the era of top-down government' by 'giving new powers to local councils, communities, neighbourhoods and individuals'[1].

[1]   *Freedom Fairness Responsibility, The coalition – our programme for Government* (Cabinet Office, May 2010), p 11.

3.80 In the context of social housing allocation, this approach paralleled calls made during 2010 by some local housing authorities in England, and by some housing policy makers, for greater local flexibility in relation to decision-making about access to social housing[1] and for a move away from the open access needs-based approach to allocation to one more attuned to prioritising local circumstances and local residents[2].

[1]   See, for example, *Allocations and Local Flexibility* (Chartered Institute of Housing, February 2010), *Allocating social housing: opportunities and challenges* (Chartered Institute of Housing, July 2010), and *Fairer access to social housing: a consultation proposal* (National Housing Federation, August 2010).

[2]   *Making Housing Affordable: A new vision for housing policy* (Policy Exchange, August 2010).

3.81 The new Government's detailed proposals for change to social housing allocation arrangements in England were issued for consultation in November 2010. The published summary stated that under the proposals[1]:

'Councils will be able to set the rules which decide who qualifies to go on the housing waiting list. At the moment they have to keep 'open' waiting lists, which means that people can get onto any council's waiting list whether they need social housing or not.'

[1]   *Local decisions: a fairer future for social housing: A summary* (DCLG, November 2010).

3.82 The main consultation paper suggested that in areas where there was not enough housing, 'continuing to operate an open waiting list raises false expectations and is likely to fuel the belief that the allocation system is unfair'. In addition, it was anticipated that shorter waiting lists would be 'simpler – and as a result cheaper – to administer'[1]. The paper envisaged a return to the pre-2003 position in which local housing authorities in England would once again be able to set their own local criteria for admission to, or exclusion, from their allocation schemes.

1   *Local decisions: a fairer future for social housing* (DCLG, November 2010).

3.83 Around two-thirds of the local housing authority respondents to the consultation welcomed the proposed flexibility, or indicated that they would consider setting restrictive qualification criteria[1]. In light of that, the proposals were pursued in the form of the Localism Bill.

1   *Local decisions: next steps towards a fairer future for social housing – Summary of responses to consultation* (DCLG, February 2011), para 4.3.

3.84 During its parliamentary passage, the provisions of the Bill addressing this aspect of social housing allocation received relatively little scrutiny. The Localism Act 2011 achieved Royal Assent in November 2011 and the relevant changes to the allocation provisions of the HA 1996, Pt 6 were brought into force on 18 June 2012[1].

1   Localism Act 2011 (Commencement No 6 and Transitional, Savings and Transitory Provisions) Order 2012, SI 2012/1463, art 3.

3.85 Between January and March 2012 the UK Government carried out a consultation exercise on the draft of a new statutory Code of Guidance about social housing allocation for local housing authorities in England. Although more than half of the responses to the consultation considered that the draft guidance on the implementation of the new qualification criteria for allocations was sufficiently clear, 'a significant minority sought further guidance on framing qualification criteria as they were concerned about the risk of legal challenge'[1]. Despite these requests, the guidance that was eventually published in June 2012 dealt with the new arrangements for 'qualification' in only 13 short paragraphs, underscoring the thrust of the UK Government's policy of leaving it to local housing authorities to decide how best to apply the statutory provisions in their districts[2].

1   *Allocation of accommodation: guidance for local housing authorities in England Summary of responses to consultation* (DCLG, June 2012), paras 3.21–3.22.
2   English Code, paras 3.18–3.31.

3.86 In summary, the policy intention behind HA 1996, Pt 6 as amended[1] was to provide local housing authorities in England with the power to decide locally, based on local circumstances, which classes of applicants can or cannot access social housing in their districts. The result is that there may be considerable variation between different local housing authorities as to which 'classes' of persons are qualified to apply for social housing or are disqualified. The differences in qualifying classes for allocation schemes, between even neighbouring local housing authorities in England, have created a national patchwork of qualifying criteria.

1   By the Localism Act 2011.

3.87 By 2013, the UK Coalition Government had become concerned that fewer local housing authorities in England than expected had embraced the possibilities offered by the Localism Act 2011 changes. It decided that additional statutory guidance specifically aimed at helping local authorities 'make full use of their new allocation freedoms'[1] might encourage their take up.

[1] *Providing social housing for local people Strengthening statutory guidance on social housing allocations: A consultation paper* (DCLG, October 2013) para 2.

3.88 Following a consultation exercise – which ran for only five weeks and received only 140 responses – on 31 December 2013 the new guidance was issued, in virtually identical terms to the draft[1]. The UK Government's haste was such that the document could not be published, as would be normal, at the same time as the Summary of Responses[2] and the Equality Impact Assessment[3]. Those documents were published, much later, in April 2014.

[1] *Providing social housing for local people: statutory guidance on social housing allocations for local authorities in England.* (DCLG, December 2013).
[2] *Providing social housing for local people Statutory guidance on social housing allocations for local authorities in England: Summary of responses to Consultation* (DCLG, April 2014).
[3] *Providing social housing for local people: statutory guidance on social housing allocations for local authorities in England: Equality statement* (DCLG, April 2014).

3.89 A particular function of the December 2013 statutory guidance (referred to in this part of this book as the 'Supplementary English Code') was to encourage local housing authorities in England to use the new powers in ways that would ensure that local residents secured the available social housing. Another was that increased emphasis should be given to meeting the needs of current and former members of the armed forces. In a statement accompanying the issue of his new guidance[1], the Secretary of State said[2]:

'For years hard-working families have watched helplessly as local council homes go to people without jobs or any connection to the local area. We're calling time on this blatant unfairness. That's why we've published guidance that will ensure local people and members of the Armed Forces are made the top priority for council homes in their community. It's part of a package of reforms to tackle unsustainable immigration, which will also ensure councils are completely transparent about who they have given social homes to, so those people who make a valuable contribution to their community can be confident they are not losing out.'

[1] Issued under HA 1996, s 169.
[2] DCLG Press Release, 31 December 2012.

3.90 It appears that the policy emphasis in the December 2013 statutory guidance is being reflected in changes to local housing allocation schemes. A survey published in 2016 found that over half of the local housing authority respondents had introduced a local connection requirement. The results from the respondents revealed that since the Localism Act 2011 came into effect, nearly 300,000 people had been removed from waiting lists and a further 43,000 new applicants had been refused entry[1].

[1] *Inside Housing*, 'Applicants barred by local connection rules', 11 March 2016, https://www. insidehousing.co.uk/home/home/applicants-barred-by-local-connection-rules-46435, accessed 26 September 2017.

The new arrangements

The scope of the new power

3.91 With effect from 18 June 2012, the Localism Act 2011 amended HA 1996, Pt 6, so as to:

(1)   restore to local housing authorities in England the power that they enjoyed between 1996 and 2003, as described at **1.16–1.18** and **3.76**, to exclude applicants 'by class'; and

(2)   add a new power for local housing authorities in England to positively prescribe, by class, the only applicants entitled to be allocated social housing under their allocation schemes[1].

[1]   Localism Act 2011, s 146, inserting HA 1996, s 160ZA.

3.92 A local housing authority in England can now regulate access to social housing in its district by exercising the power to identify 'classes' of persons who are – and/or who are not – qualifying persons for allocation of such housing[1].

[1]   HA 1996, s 160ZA(7).

3.93 The only statutory limit on the exercise of these powers by a local housing authority is that they cannot be used to treat as qualifying persons those who are rendered ineligible by their immigration status[1]. The scope for the adoption of very restrictive qualifying classes, or designation of very broad non-qualifying classes, is obvious. As a potential restraint on any abuse of these new powers, the Secretary of State has retained a regulation-making power to:

(1)   prescribe classes of persons who are or are not to be treated as qualifying; and

(2)   prescribe criteria which cannot be used by local housing authorities to decide which classes of persons are not qualifying persons[2].

[1]   HA 1996, ss 160ZA(2) and (4).
[2]   HA 1996, s 160ZA(8).

3.94 The former power has yet to be used but the latter power has been exercised in respect of applicants who are, or are related to, current or former armed services personnel (see **3.128–3.133**) and for the benefit of applicants for social housing accommodation who were seeking to move for work-related reasons (see **3.134–3.135**).

3.95 During the parliamentary passage of the Localism Bill, concern was expressed about the scope of the regulation-making powers and an amendment was moved designed to impose on the Secretary of State a requirement to consult with local housing authorities, over a minimum 12-week period, before exercising the power.[1] The Minister opposed the amendment on the basis that it simply reflected 'good administrative practice' which was already observed by the UK Government. He also declined to give examples of the 'type of scenario' in which the powers might be used on the (incorrect) basis that the precise powers already existed and were simply being re-enacted[2]. The

Government had previously indicated that the powers would be used if 'there is evidence that people in housing need are being excluded from social housing without good cause'[3].

1   House of Commons Public Bill Committee of the Localism Bill, Amendment No 223.
2   *Hansard*, Commons Public Bill Committee of the Localism Bill, col 756, 3 March 2011.
3   *Local decisions: a fairer future for social housing* (DCLG, November 2010), para 4.11.

Amending the schemes

3.96 Many local housing authorities in England needed to amend or re-cast their allocation schemes to reflect their policy choices about the exercise of these new powers[1]. If the local housing authority was also a registered social landlord it needed to comply with the statutory regulator's requirement to 'clearly set out, and be able to give reasons for, the criteria it uses for excluding actual and potential tenants from consideration for allocations'[2].

1   For the process of amending an allocation scheme see CHAPTER **4**.
2   *Tenancy Standard* (Homes and Communities Agency, April 2012), part of *The regulatory framework for social housing in England from April 2015* (Homes and Communities Agency, March 2015). See **1.31–1.35**.

3.97 The UK Government made some projections of the likely cost of the exercise of reviewing and revising local allocation schemes in the light of these changes:

'All 326 local authorities are expected to incur a one-off cost from familiarising themselves with the new arrangements, at a cost of between £290,000 in the advantageous scenario and £1.2m in the disadvantageous scenario (central case £770,000).

Those authorities that decide to adapt their policies and procedures will also face costs; these could amount to as little as £400,000 or as much as £3.7m, depending on how many local authorities adapt their waiting list policies and how much staff time is involved.'[1]

1   *Localism Bill: A fairer future for social housing – Impact Assessment* (DCLG, January 2011), p 25.

3.98 The projection was that these costs would normally be offset, for those local housing authorities choosing to exercise their discretion to limit waiting lists, by the saved costs of receiving and processing applications which have no prospect of securing an allocation.

3.99 The Secretary of State's view was that the adoption of qualifying criteria would form 'part of an allocation scheme' as distinct from forming part of some pre-scheme policy or procedure[1]. If that is correct, identifying in the allocation scheme the classes who qualify and/or those who do not qualify will be highly likely to amount to a 'major change of policy' to any current allocation scheme. Such a change triggers an obligation to consult housing associations and other private registered providers in the local housing authority's district with which it has nomination arrangements[2].

1   English Code, para 4.1.
2   HA 1996, s 166A(13). See **4.13** et seq.

3.100 No transitional provisions were made, when the new arrangements were brought into force, to deal with the situation of those persons who had already successfully made applications to join local allocation schemes before 18 June 2012. In the absence of any such provision, each local housing authority in England that decides to revise its allocation scheme to incorporate qualifying and/or non-qualifying classes will need to spell out whether those classes will be applied only to new applicants or to all applications[1].

[1] See **4.20–4.21**.

3.101 Sadly, the adoption and exercise of these new powers has not gone as smoothly as might have been hoped. They have triggered a surge in complaints to the Local Government and Social Care Ombudsman who has recorded that: 'A significant proportion of these are from applicants who have been denied access to their council's housing register as a result of the new qualification requirements introduced to allocation schemes. In many cases we have found councils at fault in the way they have implemented these changes.[1]'

[1] *Full house: Councils' role in allocating social housing – Focus report: learning lessons from complaints* (LGO, January 2016).

Setting the classes

3.102 Defining with precision the classes who qualify or do not qualify for social housing allocation will require very careful consideration. The objective will be to produce terminology which is clear, fair and transparent (so that applicants can easily see precisely what classes the local housing authority has adopted) and also be readily applicable with certainty and assurance by local housing authority officers and staff. So, for example, if a non-qualifying class is drawn to exclude former tenants who lost their tenancies as a result of misconduct, that wording alone will not disqualify the partner of such a former tenant[1].

[1] *Pirie v City of Aberdeen District Council* [1993] SLT 1155, Court of Session (Outer House).

3.103 Two specific points will, for practical reasons, need to be addressed:

(1) whether the description of the class should have a built-in override enabling a designated officer to waive the requirements in particular or exceptional cases; and/or

(2) whether the description of the class should apply to all allocations or should be limited by reference to either (a) some types of applicants and/or (b) particular parts of the housing stock.

As to the first of these points, the possible requirement for an overriding discretion is discussed in CHAPTER 4[1].

[1] See **4.248–4.257**.

3.104 As to the second of these points, the statutory guidance advises that local housing authorities may wish to set different qualifying and non-qualifying classes as between:

(a) new applicants and transferring tenants; and/or

(b) different types of housing stock (for example, in relation to hard to let housing)[1].

[1] English Code, para 3.24. The local housing authority must ensure that any such measures do not contravene the requirement to give reasonable preference to certain classes: see CHAPTER 4.

3.105 For example, in relation to qualifying classes drawn by reference to *residence* (see **3.118–3.121**), the Supplementary English Code issued in December 2013 suggests that:

(1) they may be defined differently as between current social housing tenants and new applicants for social housing;
(2) they might be waived for current tenants who are down-sizing; and
(3) they might not be applied to hard-to-let stock[1].

[1] *Supplementary English Code* (DCLG, December 2013), para 20.

OTHER LEGAL CONSIDERATIONS

3.106 In taking the policy decisions about the parameters of qualifying and non-qualifying classes, local housing authorities will need to take account of their general equality duties under the Equality Act 2010[1], the impact that any fixed residence requirements may have on the free movement of EU workers[2], and the importance of avoiding provisions which may be directly or indirectly discriminatory[3]. However, beyond stating those obvious propositions, the main 2012 statutory guidance provides no further assistance[4].

[1] See **4.192–4.209**.
[2] In *R (Winder) v Sandwell MBC* [2014] EWHC 2617 (Admin), [2015] PTSR 34, Admin Ct, the council had introduced residence requirements in its local scheme for means-tested reductions in council tax. It could not justify either the indirect discriminatory effect or the adverse impact on the free movement rights of EU workers.
[3] See **4.210–4.230**.
[4] English Code, para 3.20.

3.107 Each local housing authority in England, when modifying an allocation scheme to introduce new qualifying and non-qualifying classes, must also take account of any relevant content of[1]:

(a) its current homelessness strategy adopted under Homelessness Act 2002, s 1[2];
(b) its current tenancy strategy adopted under Localism Act 2011, s 150; and
(c) in the case of a local housing authority that is a London borough council, the London Housing Strategy.

[1] HA 1996, s 166A(12).
[2] See CHAPTER 7.

3.108 Once the policy decisions on the new classes have been taken, the consultation has been completed, the final wording has been adopted and the new allocation scheme has been published, it will fall to officers of local housing authorities in England to apply the new qualifying and non-qualifying classes to applicants for social housing allocation.

Equality Act 2010 and qualifying classes

Guidance on the Equality Act 2010 and qualifying classes

3.109 The Supplementary English Code issued in December 2013, which deals directly with the introduction of qualifying classes, simply states that[1]:

> '16. Whatever qualification criteria for social housing authorities adopt, they will need to have regard to their duties under the Equality Act 2010, as well as their duties under other relevant legislation such as s 225 of the Housing Act 2004.[2]'

---

[1] *Supplementary English Code* (DCLG, December 2013), para 16.

[2] Housing Act 2004, s 225 was repealed as of 12 July 2016 by Housing and Planning Act 2016, s 124. In its place, Housing Act 1985, s 8 was amended to make clear that the existing duty on local housing authorities to review housing needs in their districts included an obligation to consider the needs of people living in caravans or houseboats.

3.110 That guidance followed a consultation exercise in which 'a few respondents queried the potential for a residency test to indirectly discriminate against certain groups of applicants, such as gypsies and travellers'[1]. The UK Government's response was that the Supplementary English Code 'makes clear that local authorities should consider providing for appropriate exceptions to the residency requirement, to take account of special circumstances. It also reminds local authorities of the need to have regard to equalities and other relevant legislation when framing their local residency criteria'[2].

---

[1] *Providing social housing for local people Statutory guidance on social housing allocations for local authorities in England Summary of responses to Consultation* (DCLG, April 2014) at para 12.

[2] *Providing social housing for local people Statutory guidance on social housing allocations for local authorities in England Summary of responses to Consultation* (DCLG, April 2014) at para 12.

3.111 The Local Government Association has identified that 'changes to housing allocation plans that have the net effect of negatively impacting on those with protected characteristics, such as disability race or age, may well be against equality laws, and would be subject to legal challenge' and has encouraged local housing authorities to cross-check their arrangements against its Social Housing Equality Framework[1].

---

[1] *Councils must consider equality laws when changing services* (LGA Media Release, 16 February 2012); *Social Housing Equality Framework* (LGA, 2012).

3.112 The Chartered Institute of Housing (CIH) has advised that 'establishing criteria for people to be able to go onto the housing waiting list is not without risk of legal challenge and so housing authorities will need to be mindful of unlawfully discriminating, either directly or indirectly' and that 'full consideration of provisions in the Equality Act 2010 and a comprehensive equality analysis will be required to ensure a fair and accessible approach to allocations'[1]. In more recent guidance the CIH has added that local housing authorities should 'consider, for example the impact [of] policies which treat applicants who are in work and those on benefits differently; such as allowing or not allowing applicants to be allocated a property they are under occupying based on their employment status. Policies like this adversely impact upon people on benefits and could therefore be open to challenge. You should also assess the impact the introduction of a residency test as a qualification criterion may have on different protected groups. Through our research we have come across authorities who have introduced residency tests of up to ten years; consider the negative impact this policy will have on migrants from the European Union, for example'[2].

[1]   *Allocation of accommodation: guidance for local authorities in England: Briefing paper* (CIH, July 2012), p 7.
[2]   *New approaches to allocations* (CIH, June 2014), p 12.

3.113 That last point is echoed in the Equality Statement on the Supplementary English Code. It states that[1]:

'How the guidance affects lettings to different ethnic groups and nationalities will depend on how authorities respond to the guidance, as well as the supply, demand and need for social housing in each area: for instance, impacts are likely to vary between larger, urban areas where there is likely to be a more ethnically diverse population, and small, rural communities.

There are likely to be some impacts in relation to recently arrived migrants unless they fall within the exceptions which local authorities adopt to take account of special circumstances. Otherwise, impacts in relation to race and ethnicity are likely to be highly area specific and for local authorities to consider and mitigate, in relation to their equality duties.'

[1]   *Providing social housing for local people: statutory guidance on social housing allocations for local authorities in England: Equality statement* (DCLG, April 2014).

Equality Act 2010 and qualifying classes in the courts

3.114 An example of unlawful qualifying criteria is found in *R (HA) v Ealing London Borough Council*[1]. The local housing authority's allocation scheme disqualified applicants that had not been resident in the borough for the last five years[2]. This was challenged by an applicant who had recently fled to the borough with her children to escape domestic violence. The residency requirement was held to be unlawful for a number of reasons, including that it indirectly discriminated against female victims of domestic violence and no rational justification for the discrimination had been advanced.

[1]   [2015] EWHC 2375 (Admin), [2016] PTSR 16, Admin Ct.
[2]   See **3.118–3.121**.

3.115 In contrast, a scheme which disqualified applicants who had been 'guilty of unacceptable behaviour which makes them unsuitable to be a tenant' was lawful, despite the fact that it discriminated against care leavers. The discrimination was found to be justified as excluding those with behaviours that would have an adverse impact on others being allocated housing would 'improve the environment for relevant residents in general' as well as reduce 'the risk of the defendant expending limited resources on legal proceedings' to evict such persons[1].

[1]   *R (YA) v Hammersmith and Fulham London Borough Council* [2016] EWHC 1850 (Admin), [2016] HLR 39, Admin Ct at [84]. See **4.210–4.230** for further discussion of discrimination in the context of housing allocation schemes.

Common classes

3.116 In line with its generally non-prescriptive approach to the new powers, the statutory guidance issued by the Secretary of State does not offer any suggested list of qualifying or non-qualifying classes from which local housing authorities may wish to select[1].

[1]   'We have decided to maintain a light-touch approach, in the spirit of localism, and in order to maximise the opportunities for local authorities to innovate and to think creatively about how social housing can best be used to improve people's lives.' *Allocation of accommodation: guidance for local housing authorities in England: Summary of responses to consultation* (DCLG, June 2012), para 4.2.

3.117 The only class directly addressed in the 2012 guidance is that of current *homeowners*. The guidance encourages local housing authorities to avoid allocation of social housing to applicants in that class and suggests that the rule should only be departed from in exceptional circumstances eg where an elderly homeowner needs to move into sheltered social housing accommodation[1].

[1]   English Code, para 3.23. In contrast the Welsh Code advises that local housing authorities are 'expected to consider the housing needs of owner-occupiers in the same way as other applicants', para 2.69.

3.118 The *Supplementary English Code* issued in December 2013 expressly invites all local housing authorities in England to consider framing qualifying or non-qualifying classes by reference to *residence* criteria. It states that the Secretary of State 'believes that including a residency requirement is appropriate and strongly encourages all housing authorities to adopt such an approach'[1].

[1]   Supplementary English Code (DCLG, December 2013), para 12.

3.119 Admission to such a qualifying class might require a minimum period of residence in an area (or alternatively a non-qualifying class could exclude those with less than a minimum period of residence). The Supplementary English Code suggests that a reasonable minimum period of residency would be two years[1] but local housing authorities have often gone beyond this, with at least one authority's scheme requiring continuous residency of seven years[2].

[1]   Supplementary English Code (DCLG, December 2013), para 12.
[2]   House of Commons Library, *Allocating social housing (England)*, Briefing Paper 06397, 9 June 2017.

3.120 The statutory guidance suggests that where local housing authorities do set residency criteria they may wish to consider at least four exceptional categories to be exempted from the normal residency requirements. They are:

(1)   people who are moving into the district to take up work or escape violence[1];

(2)   people who have been placed temporarily outside the local housing authority's district but are children in the care of that authority or are applicants for homelessness assistance and therefore need to return to the local housing authority's own district[2];

(3)   people who are existing tenants of social housing seeking to move to a smaller home or to take up a work opportunity[3]; or

(4)   people connected with the armed forces (see **3.128–3.133**)[4].

[1]   English Code, para 3.22 and Supplementary English Code (DCLG, December 2013), paras 19 and 22.
[2]   English Code, para 3.22 and Supplementary English Code (DCLG, December 2013), para 22.
[3]   English Code, para 3.24 and Supplementary English Code (DCLG, December 2013), paras 20 and 21.
[4]   Supplementary English Code (DCLG, December 2013), para 25. In October 2017, the Government consulted on proposals to issue new guidance which would 'strongly [encourage] local authorities to exempt from their residency requirements victims of domestic abuse who have escaped violence from another area and are currently living in refuges in their area' (*Improving Access to Social Housing for Victims of Domestic Abuse: Consultation* (DCLG, October 2017).

3.121 Additionally, the Supplementary English Code issued in December 2013 states that 'When adopting a residency test, we expect housing authorities to also consider the wider needs of the Armed Forces community, and to be sympathetic to changing family circumstances, recognising, for example, that the spouses and partners of Service personnel can also be disadvantaged by the need to move from base to base.'[1] This guidance became necessary when it was realised that regulations designed to protect the armed forces community from the effects of the introduction of qualifying classes defined by local connection (see **3.128–3.133**) would not impact upon qualifying classes drawn by simple reference to residency requirements[2].

[1]   Supplementary English Code (DCLG, December 2013), para 25.
[2]   This is because local connection and residency are not coterminous. Local connection may be acquired on the basis of normal residence, but the residence must be voluntary and of a quality sufficient to give rise to a local connection. Local connection may also be acquired by other means such as employment: HA 1996, s 199, as amended by HRA 2017, s 8, for applications made to local housing authorities in England on or after 3 April 2018. See **14.43–14.122**.

3.122 Some local housing authorities in England might be attracted to the possibility of framing their qualifying or non-qualifying classes by reference to criteria which already have statutory definitions and well developed case-law such as:

•   'local connection'[1];
•   'reasonable preference'[2]; and
•   'priority need'[3].

[1]   HA 1996, s 199(1) and see **4.27–4.112**.
[2]   HA 1996, s 166A(3) (England) and s 167(2) (Wales), see **4.28–4.114**.
[3]   HA 1996, s 189 and see CHAPTER **12**.

3.123 Local housing authorities could specify that those terms, when used in their allocation schemes, have the same meanings as those used in HA 1996, Pts 6 and 7.

3.124 Others may wish to define, supplement or limit qualifying and non-qualifying classes by reference to other criteria such as:

- age;
- (participation in) anti-social behaviour;
- community involvement/participation;
- employment in the local area[1];
- family associations with an area[2];
- housing need (eg homeless households and overcrowded families)[3];
- means (eg excluding those with sufficient financial resources to rent or buy privately)[4];
- local residence (see **3.1318–3.121**); or
- previous tenant history (eg rent arrears).

[1] Referred to in the Supplementary English Code (DCLG, December 2013), para 15.
[2] Referred to in the Supplementary English Code (DCLG, December 2013), para 15.
[3] This example is given in *Local decisions: a fairer future for social housing: Consultation* (DCLG, November 2010), para 4.9.
[4] This example is also given in *Local decisions: a fairer future for social housing: Consultation* (DCLG, November 2010), para 4.9.

3.125 Local housing authorities would need to define in their allocation schemes what these criteria mean and how decisions about them will fall to be taken. One commentator has suggested that making 'housing need' a require-ment for qualification could have the adverse effects of (1) generating a large number of reviews of decisions that applicants do not fall within a 'need' category and (2) making it difficult to give those owed a homelessness duty a 'reasonable preference' if their immediate housing need has been met by the provision of suitable temporary accommodation[1].

[1] M Mackreth, 'Localism and allocations: is it yesterday once more?' [2012] 150 *Adviser* 20.

3.126 The last of the criteria listed above, previous tenant history, has been taken up with enthusiasm by several local housing authorities which have adopted classes of non-qualifying applicants by reference to their housing-related debts.[1] A survey of 50 allocation schemes found that after 'local connection' the three next most common qualification criterion adopted were: (1) making false or misleading statements to obtain a tenancy; (2) owning a home; and (3) exceeding capital or income threshold limits[2].

[1] See M Mackreth, 'Housing allocation and debt: left out in the cold' [2013] 158 *Adviser* 17.
[2] Bevan and Cowan, 'Use of Macro Social Theory: A Social Housing Case Study' [2016] 79 *Modern Law Review* 76.

Special cases

3.127 As already noted (at **3.4**), HA 1996, Pt 6 contains reserve powers enabling the Secretary of State to protect certain classes from the full rigour of the freedom of local housing authorities to set their own qualifying criteria. To date, two classes of applicant have been singled out for special treatment. These are (1) applicants who have a particular connection with the armed forces and (2) those who are seeking to move within the social housing stock for work related reasons.

3.128 From the outset of its policy programme to enable local housing authorities in England to set local qualifying and non-qualifying classes of applicants, the 2010–15 UK Coalition Government was keen to ensure that no disadvantage would be suffered by members of the *armed forces* and their families who were seeking to access social housing[1]. However, in responses to the consultation about the scope of the changes, it became clear that some local housing authorities would be introducing quite restrictive qualifying and non-qualifying categories which might exclude ex-services personnel. The Secretary of State has therefore used his regulation-making power[2] to make regulations[3] which prescribe that when deciding which classes of persons are not qualifying persons a local housing authority cannot use the criterion that a person must have a local connection to the district of a local housing authority, if that category applies to a person who is a 'relevant person'[4].

[1]   Members of the Armed Forces who have to leave their married quarters were singled out for mention in *Local decisions: a fairer future for social housing: Consultation* (DCLG, November 2010), para 4.11.
[2]   HA 1996, s 160ZA(8)(b).
[3]   Allocation of Housing (Qualification Criteria for Armed Forces) (England) Regulations 2012, SI 2012/1869, reproduced in APPENDIX 1.
[4]   Allocation of Housing (Qualification Criteria for Armed Forces) (England) Regulations 2012, SI 2012/1869, reg 3.

3.129 The Regulations came into force on 24 August 2012[1]. They give effect to the UK Government's commitment that those who serve in the regular and reserve armed forces are not disadvantaged in their access to social housing by the requirements of their service[2].

[1]   Allocation of Housing (Qualification Criteria for Armed Forces) (England) Regulations 2012, SI 2012/1869, reg 1(2).
[2]   Supplementary English Code (DCLG, December 2013), para 24.

3.130 For the purposes of the regulations the following are 'relevant' persons:

(a)   members of the armed forces and former service personnel, where the application for social housing is made within five years of discharge; and

(b)   bereaved spouses and civil partners of members of the armed forces leaving services family accommodation following the death of their spouse or partner where that death was wholly or partly attributable to military service; and

(c)   serving or former members of the reserve forces who need to move because of a serious injury, medical condition or disability wholly or partly attributable to their service[1].

[1]   Regulation 3(3) and English Code, para 3.27. The reserve forces consist of the Royal Fleet Reserve, the Royal Naval Reserve, the Royal Marines Reserve, the Army Reserve, the Territorial Army, the Royal Air Force Reserve, and the Royal Auxiliary Air Force (Armed Forces Act 2006, s 374).

3.131 The intention is to recognise the special position of:

(1)   members of the armed forces (and their families) whose employment requires them to be mobile and who are likely therefore to be particularly disadvantaged by local connection requirements; and

(2)   those injured reservists who may need to move to another local housing authority district to access treatment, care or support[1].

[1]   English Code, para 3.28.

3.132 The UK Government had initially been inclined simply to provide for an armed forces exception to any 'residence' requirements that might be used to frame non-qualifying classes. However, when it became clear from consultation responses that some local housing authorities might additionally or alternatively require an employment or family membership connection to a district as an aspect of qualification for an allocation, the UK Government decided to broaden the reach of its draft regulations so as to give exemption from any qualifying rules based on 'local connection' as a criterion[1]. The regulations use the same definition of local connection as that used elsewhere in housing legislation[2].

[1]   *Explanatory memorandum to the Allocation of Housing (Qualification Criteria for Armed Forces) (England) Regulations 2012*, paras 7.4 and 8.8.
[2]   Regulation 3 and HA 1996, s 199, as amended by HRA 2017, s 8, for applications made to local housing authorities in England on or after 3 April 2018, see **14.43–14.103**.

3.133 The net effect is that, in practical terms, if a local housing authority elects to use 'local connection' as a criterion for qualifying persons under its local allocation arrangements, it cannot adopt the same approach in relation to armed forces personnel and the other related categories of 'relevant' persons. Those persons cannot be excluded from being 'qualifying persons' due to the absence of a local connection (although they may, of course, fail to qualify under qualifying classes framed by some other criteria, even a simple residency criteria (see **3.118–3.121**))[1].

[1]   This is because local connection and residency are not coterminous. See **3.122** fn 1 and **14.43–14.122**.

NEED TO MOVE ON WORK-RELATED GROUNDS

3.134 The Government also decided to make provision for special treatment of current social housing tenants who wished to move for *work-related reasons*. From 20 April 2015 new regulations provided that local housing authorities must not disqualify specified applicants on the grounds that they do not have a local connection with the authority's district[1]. As the accompanying statutory guidance explains, local connection may not be applied to existing social tenants seeking to transfer from another local authority district in England who:

•   have reasonable preference under s 166(3)(e) because of a need to move to the local housing authority's district to avoid hardship; and

•   need to move because the tenant works in the district; or

•   need to move to take up an offer of work[2].

The policy objective is to ensure that existing social housing tenants who are seeking to move between local authority areas in England in order to be closer to their work, or to take up an offer of work will not be disadvantaged by local qualifying criteria based on residence conditions or other requirements for a 'local connection'. The policy was adopted following a consultation exercise about a 'right to move' which ran from September 2014 to early 2015[3].

¹ Allocation of Housing (Qualification Criteria for Right to Move) (England) Regulations 2015, SI 2015/967, reproduced in **Appendix 1**.
² *Right to Move: Statutory guidance on social housing allocations for local housing authorities in England* (March 2015, Department for Communities and Local Government) reproduced in **Appendix 1**.
³ *Right to Move: Response to Consultation* (March 2015, Department for Communities and Local Government).

3.135 In October 2017, the Government stated its view that people who had fled to another area to escape domestic abuse should also be exempt from residency requirements[1]. It announced proposals to achieve this, not by regulations, but by issuing new guidance which would 'strongly [encourage] local authorities to exempt from their residency requirements victims of domestic abuse who have escaped violence from another area and are currently living in refuges in their area'[2]. The consultation on these proposals closed on 5 January 2018. At the time of writing, the Government response had not been published.

¹ *Improving Access to Social Housing for Victims of Domestic Abuse: Consultation* (DCLG, October 2017).
² *Improving Access to Social Housing for Victims of Domestic Abuse: Consultation* (DCLG, October 2017).

Qualification and reasonable preference

3.136 The text of the amended statutory scheme in HA 1996, Pt 6, does not make clear whether a local housing authority in England may specify a class of non-qualifying persons which includes (and therefore disqualifies from allocation) a person – or class of persons - who would otherwise fall within one of the categories[1] required to be given a reasonable preference in the local allocation scheme. What follows in this subsection is a discussion about the legality of qualifying classes judged against the obligation under HA 1996, Pt 6 to give reasonable preference to certain classes of person[2].

¹ HA 1996, s 166A(3).
² The wider issue of discrimination in respect of housing allocation schemes is considered in **Chapter 4**.

3.137 The 2010–15 UK Coalition Government had seemingly intended that the June 2012 changes in the statutory regime should not lead to those in the reasonable preference categories losing out:

'It is important that those who are vulnerable and in housing need do not lose out under these changes and that they continue to be in the frame for social housing, together with appropriate support as necessary . . . This applies not just to victims of domestic violence forced to flee their home, or members of the Armed Forces who have to leave their married quarters, but also to those leaving prison with no family to return to. We believe that the statutory duty on local authorities to frame their allocation scheme to give 'reasonable preference' to certain groups, together with local authorities' wider equalities duties, should serve to ensure that local authorities put in place allocation systems which are fair and that those who are vulnerable and in housing need are properly protected.[1]

> ¹ *Local decisions: a fairer future for social housing: Consultation* (DCLG, November 2010), para 4.11.

3.138 The Government's approach was that somehow a balance must be struck between, on the one hand, the exercise of the power to use non-qualification to exclude whole classes of applicants and, on the other, the need to give certain groups of applicants a reasonable preference:

> 'We want to provide local authorities with the power to decide who should qualify to be considered for social housing, while retaining a role for government in determining which groups should have priority for social housing through the statutory reasonable preference requirements . . . [1]'

If a person does not 'qualify' for an allocation it is difficult to understand how they can be expected to be given a 'reasonable preference' in an allocation scheme. Despite this, on the literal wording of HA 1996, Pt 6, there is the clear potential for local housing authorities to adopt classes which exclude even those applicants who, if they were permitted to join the allocation scheme, would be entitled to a statutory 'reasonable preference'[2].

> ¹ *Local decisions: a fairer future for social housing: Consultation* (DCLG, November 2010), para 4.10.
> ² HA 1996, s 166A(3).

3.139 In light of this confusion it was virtually inevitable that there would be an early legal challenge brought by an applicant who had been told that he or she fell within a non-qualifying class but would otherwise have been given a reasonable preference under a local allocation scheme.

3.140 In *R (Jakimaviciute) v Hammersmith & Fulham London Borough Council*[1] the council's social housing allocation scheme contained a non-qualifying class comprising homeless applicants whom the council had provided with suitable temporary accommodation under its homelessness functions (HA 1996, Pt 7)[2]. The claimant fell into that class. As a result she would normally have been entitled to a statutory 'reasonable preference' in any allocation scheme (see **4.67–4.79**) but the council notified her that she did not qualify for its scheme at all. She sought a judicial review, contending that it was unlawful to exclude from an allocation scheme a person who would otherwise be entitled to a reasonable preference. In the Administrative Court, she was refused permission to seek a judicial review on the grounds that the case was 'unarguable'[3]. The Court of Appeal granted permission to appeal and permission to seek a judicial review. It heard and decided the judicial review claim for itself. It held that the council's qualifying class had been specifically drawn to disqualify a sub-set of a category of applicants whom HA 1996, Pt 6, had required be given a reasonable preference. That was unlawful. The court appeared to accept that, on the other hand, it was not unlawful to devise a 'rule excluding individual applicants by reference to factors of general application, such as lack of local connection or being in rent arrears'[4].

> ¹ [2014] EWCA Civ 1438, [2015] 3 All ER, 490, CA.

² As amended by HRA 2017 for applications made to local housing authorities in England on or after 3 April 2018. See CHAPTER **16**.
³ [2013] EWHC 4372 (Admin), 20 December 2013, [2014] March *Legal Action*, p 23. See the commentary on the High Court decision in this case by M Makreth, 'Allocations update: going even more local' [2014] 163 *Adviser* 27 and M Coates, 'To have and to have not: "reasonable preference" and allocation policy' [2014] 164 *Adviser* 24.
⁴ [2014] EWCA Civ 1438, CA at [45].

3.141 In *R (Alemi) v Westminster City Council*[1] the council decided not to set a qualifying class disqualifying applicants who were entitled to a reasonable preference by virtue of being owed a homelessness duty but to achieve the same effect by a provision preventing them from bidding under its choice-based letting scheme for one year. It introduced an amended scheme to achieve that effect. The Administrative Court quashed those parts of the amended scheme. The judge said at para [32]:

'This amended Scheme carves out a whole sub-group which is altogether excluded from the potential of being allocated social housing for 12 months. They have no preference. Part VI of the Act does not permit the removal of a whole sub-group from a group which section 166A(3) requires be given reasonable preference in the allocation of social housing, when that sub-group is not defined by reference to differentiating features related to the allocation of housing, but applies a simple time bar to all who otherwise qualify. It is unlawful.'

¹ [2015] EWHC 1765 (Admin), [2015] PTSR 1339, Admin Ct.

3.142 Much the same approach was followed in *R(HA) v Ealing London Borough Council*[1]. In that case, the applicant was owed the main housing duty as an unintentionally homeless person in priority need: HA 1996, s 193(2)[2]. Her online application for social housing allocation was met with an automated rejection because she could not meet the qualifying criteria that the local housing authority had adopted: 'Households will not be able to register for housing in future unless they are able to demonstrate that they have been resident in the borough for five years'. The Administrative Court declared the allocation scheme unlawful. The judge said at [23]:

'Although a residency requirement is an entirely appropriate and encouraged provision in relation to admission onto a social housing list, it must not preclude the class of people who fulfil the "reasonable preference" criteria. The Defendant's policy does not provide for the giving of reasonable preference to prescribed categories of persons as required by section 166A(3) of the Act. In this respect the policy is unlawful.'

¹ [2015] EWHC 2375 (Admin), [2016] PTSR 16, Admin Ct.
² See **16.94–16.199**.

3.143 A different conclusion was reached in *R (Woolfe) v Islington London Borough Council*[1]. As in *R (HA) v Ealing*, the applicant was owed the main housing duty as an unintentionally homeless person in priority need: HA 1996, s 193(2)[2]. She was admitted onto the local housing authority's waiting list but was unable to bid because she had only been awarded 110 points and the local housing authority operated a points threshold pursuant to which applicants with fewer than 120 points were not allowed to bid.

¹ [2016] EWHC 1907 (Admin), [2016] HLR 42, Admin Ct.

3.144 The argument that this threshold was unlawful because it meant that she was not given a reasonable preference was rejected. The Administrative Court distinguished *R (Jakimaviciute) v Hammersmith & Fulham London Borough Council*¹, *R (Alemi) v Westminster City Council*², and *R(HA) v Ealing London Borough Council*³ on the basis that, in *R (Jakimaviciute) v Hammersmith & Fulham London Borough Council*⁴ and *R (HA) v Ealing London Borough Council*⁵, the applicants had been excluded altogether from the register, and in *R (Alemi) v Westminster City Council*⁶ the applicant had been barred from bidding for 12 months regardless of the strength of her case. In contrast, Ms Woolfe had been allowed onto the scheme and had been allocated points, including points for her homelessness, so 'the scheme does make some preference for her homelessness' and the court would not 'subvert the policy and decision of the housing authority as to the number of points to be awarded'⁷. This reasoning suggests that there is a key distinction to be drawn between being given reduced preference and no preference at all. Reduced priority and no priority are conceptually different, even though for the applicant, the practical result may be the same, in that either way he or she has little prospect of being allocated social housing⁸.

¹   [2014] EWCA Civ 1438, [2015] 3 All ER, 490, CA.
²   [2015] EWHC 1765 (Admin), [2015] PTSR 1339, Admin Ct.
³   [2015] EWHC 2375 (Admin), [2016] PTSR 16, Admin Ct.
⁴   [2014] EWCA Civ 1438, [2015] 3 All ER, 490, CA.
⁵   [2015] EWHC 2375 (Admin), [2016] PTSR 16, Admin Ct.
⁶   [2015] EWHC 1765 (Admin), [2015] PTSR 1339, Admin Ct.
⁷   [2016] EWHC 1907 (Admin), [2016] HLR 42, Admin Ct at [34]–[37].
⁸   For further discussion of this topic see Johnston, 'Allocations: testing the boundaries' [2017] JHL 7.

3.145 In *R (Jakimaviciute) v Hammersmith & Fulham London Borough Council*¹, *R (Alemi) v Westminster City Council*², *R (HA) v Ealing London Borough Council*³, and *R (Woolfe) v Islington London Borough Council*⁴, the disadvantage facing the claimants arose not from any default on their part but because of their membership (or non-membership) of a particular group. A case in which the applicant's own conduct made him liable to exclusion from the scheme is the pre-HA 1996, Pt 6, case of *R v Wolverhampton Metropolitan Borough Council ex p Watters*⁵ which was considered by the court in the case of *R (Woolfe) v Islington London Borough Council*⁶. In *R v Wolverhampton Metropolitan Borough Council ex p Watters*⁷, the claimant was in a category of persons entitled to reasonable preference, but she had accrued rent arrears which meant that, under the council's policy, she would not be admitted onto their waiting list. The Administrative Court in *R (Woolfe) v Islington London Borough Council*⁸ noted that:

> '*Watters* clearly establishes that "other factors" may diminish or "even nullify the preference" after applying a balancing exercise, provided the applicant is first given a "reasonable head start". In my view, however, there is a material distinction from the facts of the present case. In *Watters*, there were factors adverse to the applicant, viz. the rent arrears, which outweighed and "nullified" the head start. In the present case, the claimant is not in rent arrears and her application has no adverse or

outweighing factors. All that can be said is that she has an absence of factors which would otherwise entitle her to more points.'"

1 [2014] EWCA Civ 1438, [2015] 3 All ER, 490, CA.
2 [2015] EWHC 1765 (Admin), [2015] PTSR 1339, Admin Ct.
3 [2015] EWHC 2375 (Admin), [2016] PTSR 16, Admin Ct.
4 [2016] EWHC 1907 (Admin), [2016] HLR 42, Admin Ct.
5 (1997) 29 HLR 931, CA.
6 [2016] EWHC 1907 (Admin), [2016] HLR 42, Admin Ct.
7 (1997) 29 HLR 931, CA.
8 [2016] EWHC 1907 (Admin), [2016] HLR 42, Admin Ct.
9 [2016] EWHC 1907 (Admin), [2016] HLR 42, Admin Ct at [20].

3.146 In line with *R v Wolverhampton Metropolitan Borough Council ex p Watters*[1], qualification (or disqualification) criteria which refer to an individual's conduct have been accepted as lawful by the courts, even if the individual thereby disqualified would otherwise be entitled to a reasonable preference[2]. Indeed use of a qualifying class based on former housing misbehaviour or some other default appears to be increasing[3].

1 (1997) 29 HLR 931, CA.
2 As in the case of *R (Edward) v Royal Borough of Greenwich* [2016] EWHC 3410 (Admin) and *R (YA) v Hammersmith and Fulham London Borough Council* [2016] EWHC 1850 (Admin) although it appears that in neither case was the challenge brought on the basis that the reasonable preference requirement was breached.
3 A recent article, 'Uses of macro social theory: a social housing case sutdy' (2016) 79 MLR 76, reflects on what is said to be the growing category of households excluded from allocation schemes due to former housing misconduct or some other default.

3.147 This is consistent with the provisions for the individual ineligibility of applicants on grounds of unacceptable behaviour which previously applied in England and now only apply in Wales (see **3.151–3.200**). It would also explain the otherwise somewhat confusing guidance given in the English Code[1]:

'Housing authorities should avoid setting criteria which disqualify groups of people whose members are likely to be accorded reasonable preference for social housing, for example on medical or welfare grounds. However, authorities may wish to adopt criteria which would disqualify individuals who satisfy the reasonable preference requirements. This could be the case, for example, if applicants are disqualified on a ground of anti-social behaviour.'[2]

1 Which has been described as 'obscurely worded': M Robinson, 'Home page: keep on knocking' [2013] 159 *Adviser* 23.
2 English Code, para 3.21.

3.148 The above decisions do not all sit easily together. What follows is an attempt to draw out some common themes, and a suggestion as to how the case-law might best be reconciled, pending further guidance from the higher courts[1]:

(1)   A scheme which disqualifies a class of people by reference to the very criterion which entitles them to a 'reasonable preference', such as being homeless as defined by HA 1996, Pt 7[2], will be unlawful: *R (Jakimaviciute) v Hammersmith & Fulham London Borough Council*[3] and *R (Alemi) v Westminster City Council*[4].

(2)   Entirely excluding from the scheme a person entitled to a reasonable preference is likely to be unlawful (*R (HA) v Ealing London Borough Council*)[5] unless the exclusion relates to his or her individual conduct (*R v Wolverhampton Metropolitan Borough Council ex p Watters*)[6] or is related to the statutory purpose of allocation (*R (Alemi) v Westminster City Council*)[7].

(3)   A scheme which permits a person with reasonable preference to be on the waiting list for an allocation of social housing but which prevents him or her from bidding, regardless of the strength of his or her case, will be unlawful. The applicant's exclusion from bidding means that he or she has been given no preference at all, contrary to HA 1996, Pt 6: *R (Alemi) v Westminster City Council*[8].

(4)   A scheme which permits a person with reasonable preference to be on the waiting list for an allocation of social housing but which prevents him or her from bidding because of the strength (or weakness) of his or her case will be lawful: *R (Woolfe) v Islington London Borough Council*[9]. In contrast to the proposition outlined in (3), the applicant is being given preference, albeit at a reduced level such that he or she cannot bid. The applicant has not been completely excluded from the scheme because if his or her circumstances change, or further evidence is forthcoming, he or she may then be entitled to bid.

[1]   For more detailed discussion see Johnston, 'Allocations: testing the boundaries' [2017] JHL 7.

[2]   As amended by HRA 2017 for applications for homelessness assistance made to local housing authorities in England on or after 3 April 2018.

[3]   [2014] EWCA Civ 1438, [2015] 3 All ER, 490, CA.

[4]   [2015] EWHC 1765 (Admin), [2015] PTSR 1339, Admin Ct. See also para 2.46 of the *English Homelessness Code of Guidance* (MHCLG, February 2018), which states that local housing authorities 'should not apply qualification criteria which would exclude from their allocation schemes homeless households who would be entitled to reasonable preference in the allocation of housing'.

[5]   Cf. [45] of *R (Jakimaviciute) v Hammersmith and Fulham London Borough Council* [2014] EWCA Civ 1438, CA.

[6]   (1997) 29 HLR 931, CA.

[7]   [2015] EWHC 1765 (Admin), [2015] PTSR 1339, Admin Ct.

[8]   [2015] EWHC 1765 (Admin), [2015] PTSR 1339, Admin Ct.

[9]   [2016] EWHC 1907 (Admin), [2016] HLR 42, Admin Ct.

When to consider qualification

3.149 As with the approach to the eligibility of applicants (see **3.201–3.203**), the statutory guidance recommends that local housing authorities in England which have adopted qualifying or non-qualifying classes should consider whether an applicant qualifies for an allocation both at the time of the initial application and then again when considering making an allocation, particularly where a long time has elapsed since the original application[1].

[1]   English Code, para 3.26.

Decisions on qualification

3.150 A decision that an applicant does not fall within a qualifying class or falls within a non-qualifying class must be notified to the applicant in writing with the grounds for that decision[1]. The local housing allocation scheme must provide the applicant with a right to have a review of such a decision and to be notified in writing of the grounds for any review decision[2]. For information on challenging review decisions see CHAPTER 2[3].

[1] HA 1996, s 160ZA(9)(b) and see **2.81**.
[2] HA 1996, s 166A(9)(c) and see **2.87(3)**.
[3] See **2.103–2.120**.

INELIGIBILITY DUE TO UNACCEPTABLE BEHAVIOUR (WALES)

Introduction

3.151 If a person is eligible for an allocation of social housing, because he or she is not caught by the provisions relating to immigration status explored in the first part of this chapter, he or she would ordinarily be able to be considered alongside all other applicants seeking a social housing allocation. However, from early 1997 to 18 June 2012, the provisions of HA 1996, Pt 6, enabled local housing authorities in both England and Wales to decide, on a case-by-case basis, that certain applicants were ineligible for allocation on account of their previous misconduct.

3.152 When HA 1996, Pt 6, was amended in June 2012 to allow local housing authorities in England to introduce qualifying classes of applicants, in the manner described in the second part of this chapter[1], the specific power to decide that certain individual applicants were ineligible on grounds of past misconduct became redundant and was repealed in relation to England[2].

[1] See **3.76–3.150**.
[2] English Code, para **2.4**.

3.153 However, the misconduct-related eligibility provisions remain fully in force in Wales and the text which follows deals primarily with their effect on applications made to local housing authorities in Wales. The text may also be of interest in respect of any outstanding issues arising from their use by local housing authorities in England in relation to decisions made before 18 June 2012[1].

[1] See too the 2002 English Code reproduced in APPENDIX 1 of the third edition of this book.

An overview

3.154 A local housing authority in Wales may decide, but is not required to decide, that an applicant is to be treated as ineligible for the allocation of social housing as a result of his or her past unacceptable behaviour, or the behaviour of a member of his or her household[1]. The wording of the statutory provision (HA 1996, s 160A) prevents local housing authorities in Wales from operating blanket exclusions, and requires them to consider, if they are minded to use the ineligibility provision, the behaviour of each applicant, or of a member of his or her household, individually.

[1] HA 1996, s 160A(7)–(8) and Welsh Code, para **2.29**.

3.155 A local housing authority's decision that an applicant is 'ineligible' on behaviour grounds, and thus excluded from consideration for an allocation, requires consideration of two stages:

(1)   Does the applicant meet certain statutory conditions? If so,
(2)   Should the local housing authority, in the exercise of its discretion, elect to treat the applicant as 'ineligible' as a result of the applicant fulfilling those conditions[1]?

[1]   HA 1996, s 160A(7).

3.156 As far as the *first stage* of the test for ineligibility on behaviour grounds is concerned, there are two statutory conditions:

(1)   that the applicant, or a member of his or her household, has been guilty of past unacceptable behaviour of a specified standard (described in the rest of this chapter as Condition One)[1]; and
(2)   that in the circumstances at the time when the application for allocation is considered, the applicant is unsuitable to be a tenant of the local housing authority by reason of that past behaviour (described in the rest of this chapter as Condition Two)[2].

[1]   HA 1996, s 160A(7)(a).
[2]   HA 1996, s 160A(7)(b).

3.157 At the *second stage* the local housing authority is deciding, in the exercise of an unfettered discretion, whether to treat an applicant who satisfies both of the two statutory conditions as ineligible for its scheme.

3.158 It was confirmed by the then UK Government during the passage of what became the Homelessness Act 2002 that the two statutory conditions of the *first stage* constitute a 'high test', intended to exclude 'only those applicants whose behaviour would genuinely render them unsuitable to be a tenant'[1].

[1]   *DTLR memo to the Joint Select Committee on Human Rights*, para 6.3, reproduced in the Appendix to the report of the Joint Committee dated 7 November 2001.

3.159 The UK Government emphasised that the power to decide that an individual was ineligible for allocation was a discretionary power, that local housing authorities were not required to use it, and that it could only be used in a manner that was compatible with an applicant's Convention rights[1]. Even an applicant who met the *first stage* conditions may not necessarily be found ineligible in the exercise of the *second stage* discretion. The Government also referred to the safety net of accommodation available to those excluded from an allocation under the National Assistance Act 1948 and the Children Act 1989[2], and noted that persons declared ineligible by virtue of their behaviour would still be eligible for housing benefit, and thus able to access private rented accommodation[3].

[1]   Rights under the European Convention of Human Rights set out in Human Rights Act 1998, Sch 1.
[2]   These statutes have been replaced in respect of Wales by the Social Services and Well-being Act 2014. See **20.69–20.98**. The relevant powers and duties to provide accommodation under the National Assistance Act 1948 have been replaced in respect of England by the Care Act 2014. See **20.19–20.38**.

3   *DTLR memo to the Joint Select Committee on Human Rights*, reproduced in the Appendix to the report of the Joint Committee dated 7 November 2001.

3.160 The Joint Select Committee remained concerned that those excluded from eligibility by their behaviour might suffer degrading treatment by reason of homelessness affecting their health and welfare, or suffer a failure of respect for their home and family life but nevertheless concluded that the provision was compatible with Convention rights[1].

1   The ineligibility provision relating to misconduct has yet to generate any litigation claiming that it is incompatible with the provisions of Human Rights Act 1998, although it has been unsuccessfully contended that a decision that an applicant is not eligible for an allocation engages (and may infringe) the right to respect for a home protected by Human Rights Act 1998, Sch 1, Art 8: *R (Dixon) v Wandsworth London Borough Council* [2007] EWHC 3075 (Admin), (2008) February *Legal Action*, p 40, Admin Ct at [28]–[30] and *R (Dixon) v Wandsworth London Borough Council* [2008] EWCA Civ 595, (2008) July *Legal Action*, p 22, CA at [11].

The statutory conditions

Condition One: guilty of unacceptable behaviour

3.161 The first condition is that the local housing authority must be satisfied that the applicant or a member of his or her household has been guilty of unacceptable behaviour serious enough to make him or her unsuitable to be a tenant of that authority[1].

1   HA 1996, s 160A(7)(a). The local housing authority should not take into account behaviour which relates to a spent conviction: *R (YA) v Hammersmith and Fulham London Borough Council* [2016] EWHC 1850 (Admin), [2016] HLR 39, Admin Ct.

THE STATUTORY DEFINITION OF 'UNACCEPTABLE BEHAVIOUR'

3.162 Parliament has defined 'unacceptable behaviour' as only such behaviour, by the applicant or by a member of his or her household, which would, if the applicant were a secure tenant of the local housing authority, entitle it to a possession order on any ground in Housing Act 1985, s 84A or in Sch 2, Pt 1, (other than Ground 8)[1].

1   HA 1996, s 160A(8) as amended.

3.163 This rather curious phrasing generates four important preliminary points.

(1) Literal or hypothetical approach

3.164 The test may arise for application either literally or hypothetically, in that the applicant may or may not have been a secure tenant of the local housing authority against whom a possession order was made on one of the relevant grounds. If the applicant, or a relevant member of his or her household, was at that time a secure tenant of the same local housing authority and a possession order was obtained, then the definition can be readily and literally applied[1]. But in many more circumstances – where the applicant was not a secure tenant of the local housing authority, or no possession order has been made – the question will be hypothetical. The local housing authority will be asking itself: 'What if the applicant had at that time been one of our secure tenants?'

¹   Welsh Code, para 2.33.

3.165 Indeed, Condition Two of the statutory conditions (discussed at **3.192–3.200**) also contains an element that requires either a literal or a hypothetical approach, relating to the identity of the likely future landlord. If the likely future landlord is the local housing authority itself, a literal approach can be taken: 'Is the applicant 'unsuitable' for one of our own tenancies?' But the ineligibility test is also available where a successful applicant could only expect to be nominated to a different landlord (a registered social landlord in Wales or a different local housing authority)¹. In such a case, the test is one of suitability to be the local housing authority's tenant even though there is no prospect or possibility of such a tenancy.

¹   Because the local housing authority may have disposed of all of its stock to one or several other social landlords.

(2) The meaning of 'entitle'

3.166 The second general point to emerge from the definition is the curious use of the word 'entitle' in the phrase 'would . . . entitle the authority to a possession order . . . "¹. Most of the relevant grounds for possession are not mandatory grounds². Instead, most of them require the court to find that 'it is reasonable to make the order' for possession³. Strictly speaking, it is impossible to say that any landlord is 'entitled' to possession where possession is sought on a ground that depends (for the grant of an order) on the exercise of discretion by the court. A judge has accepted that 'the effect of the provisions is to require the local housing authority to be satisfied that a notional county court judge would probably make an outright order for possession in the circumstances of the case'⁴.

¹   HA 1996, s 160A(8)(a).
²   See Housing Act 1985, Sch 2.
³   Under Housing Act 1985, s 84(2)(a). These grounds are therefore commonly referred to as 'discretionary grounds' for possession.
⁴   *R (Dixon) v Wandsworth London Borough Council* [2007] EWHC 3075 (Admin), (2008) February *Legal Action*, p 40, admin Ct at [17].

3.167 Since 19 May 2015, the special 'mandatory ground for possession' in Housing Act 1985, s 84A has been added as a relevant ground of possession for these purposes¹. It might be thought that this would make it easier to establish with certainty that the local housing authority would be 'entitled' to a possession order but, as the Welsh Code recognises² the new ground is subject to the caveat that the court may decline to make a possession order where to grant one would infringe a tenant's Convention rights³. Moreover, the court may refuse to make a possession order where the possession claim amounts to discrimination under the Equality Act 2010 or the local housing authority has failed to comply with its public sector equality duty[4]. However, if an order is made then it will be an outright order for possession, because the usual provisions for postponing or suspending an order (Housing Act 1985, s 85) do not apply to that ground.

[1] HA 1996, s 160A(8)(aa) added by Anti-social Behaviour, Crime and Policing Act 2014 (Consequential Amendments) (Wales) Order 2015, SI 2015/1321, art 2(2)(a) with effect from May 2015; Welsh Code, para 2.49.

[2] Welsh Code, para 2.34.

[3] Housing Act 1985, s 84A(1). It was confirmed in *Manchester City Council v Pinnock* [2010] UKSC 45, [2011] 2 AC 104 that where possession proceedings are instituted by a public body, and the tenant does not have any right to remain in their home under domestic law, they may in an appropriate case seek to defend the claim by relying on s 6 of the Human Rights Act 1988 and Art 8 of the European Convention on Human Rights.

[4] Equality Act 2010, s 149. Defences brought under the Equality Act 2010 to possession claims were considered by the Supreme Court in *Akerman-Livingstone v Aster Communities Ltd* [2015] UKSC 15, [2015] AC 1399.

(3) The meaning of 'behaviour'

3.168 The statutory wording is concerned with the 'behaviour' of the applicant, or, where relevant, that of a member of his or her household. Indeed, the terminology used is 'guilty of unacceptable behaviour'[1]. This would naturally be understood to require some past action or activity on that person's part. But in this context it must, at least arguably, also include an applicant's omission, failure to act, passivity or inactivity in circumstances where there has been an expectation of action. Otherwise it would not embrace common cases of 'unacceptable behaviour' such as:

(1) failing to pay rent or other charges; or
(2) simple inactive non-compliance with obligations under a tenancy, eg failing to maintain the garden; or
(3) failing to control the actions of lodgers or visitors.

[1] HA 1996, s 160A(7)(a).

3.169 Such a wide construction would be consistent with the judicial approach to the term 'guilty of conduct causing or likely to cause a nuisance or annoyance' in a statutory ground for possession[1]. It is rather surprising that, in this context, parliamentary counsel did not adopt the now familiar rubric of 'deliberately does or fails to do anything' to be found in other provisions of HA 1996[2].

[1] Housing Act 1985, Sch 2, Ground 2. See also *Kensington and Chelsea Royal London Borough Council v Simmonds* (1997) 29 HLR 507, CA.

[2] Such as the test of becoming homelessness intentionally in HA 1996, s 191(1) or H(W)A 2014, s 77. See **13.42–13.48**.

3.170 The statutory emphasis on the behaviour of the applicant (or a member of the applicant's household) was relied upon by the claimant in *R (McQ) v Bolton Metropolitan Borough Council*[1]. He had given up his former home for reasons associated with the anti-social behaviour of third parties with whom he had been involved. He argued that that conduct (being neither his conduct nor that of any member of his household) was irrelevant. The Administrative Court held that the claimant's former association with the third parties – members of a paramilitary organisation in Northern Ireland which had undertaken the anti-social conduct – itself constituted ample factual material to support the decision that *his own* behaviour would have notionally made out the statutory grounds for possession.

1   [2005] EWHC 1285 (Admin), (2005) August *Legal Action*, p 17, Admin Ct.

(4) Household membership

3.171 Plainly, the policy of HA 1996, Pt 6, reflected in the wording used, is to avoid the ineligibility control from being circumvented by an application being made in the name of an innocent member of the household rather than by the actual perpetrator of the misconduct. Accordingly, local housing authorities may consider not only the applicant's own behaviour but also that of 'a member of his [or her] household'.[1] HA 1996, Pt 6 contains no statutory definition of the term 'household'. It will therefore be for the local housing authority to decide which persons constitute the applicant's household for these purposes. The local housing authority's allocation scheme might set out how membership of a household will be ascertained[2] or may be silent on the issue, leaving the decision to be made by officers on the facts of individual cases interpreting 'household' by reference 'to its ordinary, everyday usage'[3].

1   HA 1996, s 160A(7)(a).
2   The Local Government and Social Care Ombudsman has criticised a local housing authority whose scheme failed to clarify how adult children would be dealt with: *Complaint against Kettering Borough Council*, 16012028, 3 August 2017, (2017) November *Legal Action*, p 41.
3   *R (Ariemuguvbe) v Islington London Borough Council* [2009] EWCA 1218, [2010] HLR 14, (2010) January *Legal Action*, p 35, CA.

3.172 HA 1996, Pt 6, appears to be looking to the *present* household composition. So, an applicant with an unblemished past may find that he or she is rendered ineligible by having formed a common household with a person who brings to that household past misconduct, either the new partner's own misconduct, or that of any other person. As will be seen, the innocent applicant is only saved from any adverse consequence of the new partner's past misconduct if that history is immaterial to the applicant's own present suitability to be a tenant[1].

1   See **3.193**.

3.173 But the statutory provision could be interpreted as also engaging with the *past* composition of the applicant's household. HA 1996, Pt 6, when defining unacceptable behaviour, does so in terms that include past 'behaviour of a member of his [or her] household'. Given that the statutory language is taking attention back to past misbehaviour, arguably it could be capable of being satisfied by the misconduct of a person who was at that time a member of the applicant's household but is no longer. If correct, this would protect against the situation in which an applicant may have temporarily separated from a past member of his or her household to avoid the prospect of ineligibility through misconduct, with every intention of resuming residence together once a tenancy has been allocated. It does mean, however, that an innocent applicant, whose former miscreant household member has permanently departed, may nevertheless still be disqualified. Whilst a safeguard is provided by the requirement that the past misconduct must presently render the applicant unsuitable as a tenant (Condition Two – discussed at **3.192–3.200**), that requirement may well be met, even where the perpetrator is long gone, if it is considered material that the applicant failed to bring to an earlier end the other person's misconduct.

APPLYING THE STATUTORY DEFINITION OF 'UNACCEPTABLE BEHAVIOUR'

3.174 On detailed examination, the definition in HA 1996, s 160A(8), itself breaks down into three constituent questions, each of which the local housing authority needs to address in succession:

(1)   Is one, or are more than one, of the relevant grounds for possession made out by the circumstances of the past behaviour?
(2)   If so, would a court make an absolute order under Housing Act 1985, s 84A or consider it reasonable to make an order for possession under Housing Act 1985, Sch 2, Pt 1, Grounds 1–7 on the basis of that behaviour?
(3)   If so, would a court make an *outright* order for possession?

3.175 The applicant is only guilty of 'unacceptable behaviour' for the purposes of this statutory provision if the local housing authority is able to answer 'Yes' to all three questions. It can be readily envisaged that different local housing authorities may well give different answers to some or all of these questions, even when considering the same set of facts. Indeed, it might be thought common knowledge that a county court judge sitting at one court would certainly evict for a particular level of misconduct which, had the matter been tried before the county court judge at another court, would have resulted in dismissal or adjournment of the possession claim or the making of a suspended or postponed order for possession. Precisely because the making of a possession order will often require a discretionary decision, the statutory definition is sensitive to such variables[1].

1   See **3.178**.

Grounds for possession

3.176 The first step in applying the statutory definition is to be clear as to the wording of the relevant statutory grounds for possession. The current wording of Housing Act 1985, Sch 2, Pt 1, Grounds 1–7 and of Housing Act 1985, s 84A, is given in Tables A and B respectively[1].

1   See also Welsh Code, form 2.33, paras 2.56–2.58, paras 2.66–2.67 and Annex 10.

Table A
Grounds For Possession Under Housing Act 1985, s 84, Sch 2, Pt 1, Grounds 1–7

Ground 1   Rent lawfully due from the tenant has not been paid or an obligation of the tenancy has been broken or not performed.
Ground 2   The tenant or a person residing in or visiting the dwelling-house:

(1) has been guilty of conduct causing or likely to cause a nuisance or annoyance to a person residing, visiting or otherwise engaging in a lawful activity in the locality; or

(2) has been guilty of conduct causing or likely to cause a nuisance or annoyance to the landlord of the dwelling-house, or a person employed (whether or not by the landlord) in connection with the exercise of the landlord's housing management functions, and that is directly or indirectly related to or affects those functions[1]; or

(3) has been convicted of:

   (i) using the dwelling-house or allowing it to be used for immoral or illegal purposes; or

   (ii) an indictable offence committed in, or in the locality of, the dwelling-house[2].

Ground 2A[3]   The dwelling-house was occupied (whether alone or with others) by a married couple, a couple who are civil partners of each other[4], a couple living together as husband and wife or a couple living together as if they were civil partners[5] and:

(a) one or both of the partners is a tenant of the dwelling-house;

(b) one partner has left because of violence or threats of violence by the other towards:

   (i) that partner, or

   (ii) a member of the family of that partner who was residing with that partner immediately before the partner left; and

(c) the court is satisfied that the partner who has left is unlikely to return.

Ground 3   The condition of the dwelling-house or of any of the common parts has deteriorated owing to acts of waste by, or the neglect or default of, the tenant or a person residing in the dwelling-house and, in the case of an act of waste by, or the neglect or default of, a person lodging with the tenant or a sub-tenant of his, the tenant has not taken such steps as he ought reasonably to have taken for the removal of the lodger or sub-tenant.

Ground 4   The condition of furniture provided by the landlord for use under the tenancy, or for use in the common parts, has deteriorated owing to ill-treatment by the tenant or a person residing in the dwelling-house and, in the case of ill-treatment by a person lodging with the tenant or a sub-tenant of his, the tenant has not taken such steps as he ought reasonably to have taken for the removal of the lodger or sub-tenant.

Ground 5   The tenant is the person, or one of the persons, to whom the tenancy was granted and the landlord was induced to grant the tenancy by a false statement made knowingly or recklessly by:

(a) the tenant; or

(b) a person acting at the tenant's instigation.

Ground 6   The tenancy was assigned to the tenant, or to a predecessor in title of his who is a member of his family and is residing in the dwelling-house, by an assignment made by virtue of s 92 (assignments by way of exchange) and a premium was paid either in connection with that assignment or the assignment which the tenant or predecessor himself made by virtue of that section.

In this paragraph 'premium' means any fine or other like sum and any other pecuniary consideration in addition to rent.

Ground 7   The dwelling-house forms part of, or is within the curtilage of, a building which, or so much of it as is held by the landlord, is held mainly for purposes other than housing purposes and consists mainly of accommodation other than housing accommodation, and:

(a)   the dwelling-house was let to the tenant or a predecessor in title of his in consequence of the tenant or predecessor being in the employment of the landlord; or of

– a local authority;

– a new town corporation;

– a housing action trust;

– an urban development corporation; or

– the governors of an aided school; and

(b)   the tenant or a person residing in the dwelling-house has been guilty of conduct such that, having regard to the purpose for which the building is used, it would not be right for him to continue in occupation of the dwelling-house.

---

[1]   This sub-paragraph was inserted by Anti-social Behaviour, Crime and Policing Act 2014, s 98(1) with effect from 13 May 2014: Anti-social Behaviour, Crime and Policing Act 2014 (Commencement No 1 and Transitory Provisions) (Wales) Order 2014, SI 2014/1241, art 2(a).

[2]   'Indictable' was inserted by Serious Organised Crime and Police Act 2005, s 111 and Sch 7, in force from 1 January 2006 (Serious Organised Crime and Police Act 2005 (Commencement No 4 and Transitory Provision) Order 2005, SI 2005/3495, art 2(1)(m)).

[3]   Ground 2ZA is not included in this table as it applies only to secure tenancies of dwellings in England: Anti-social Behaviour, Crime and Policing Act 2014, s 99(1).

[4]   Inserted by Civil Partnership Act 2004, s 81, s 263(2) and Sch 8, in force from 5 December 2005 (Civil Partnership Act 2004 (Commencement No 2) Order 2005, SI 2005/3175).

[5]   Inserted by Civil Partnership Act 2004, s 81, s 263(2) and Sch 8, in force from 5 December 2005 (Civil Partnership Act 2004 (Commencement No 2) Order 2005, SI 2005/3175).

Grounds For Possession Under Housing Act 1985, s 84A

Sections 84A(1)-(8) provide:

(1)   If the court is satisfied that any of the following conditions is met, it must make an order for the possession of a dwelling-house let under a secure tenancy.

This is subject to subsection (2) (and to any available defence based on the tenant's Convention rights, within the meaning of the Human Rights Act 1998).

(2)   Subsection (1) applies only where the landlord has complied with any obligations it has under section 85ZA (review of decision to seek possession).

(3) Condition 1 is that—

   (a) the tenant, or a person residing in or visiting the dwelling-house, has been convicted of a serious offence, and

   (b) the serious offence—

      (i) was committed (wholly or partly) in, or in the locality of, the dwelling-house,

      (ii) was committed elsewhere against a person with a right (of whatever description) to reside in, or occupy housing accommodation in the locality of, the dwelling-house, or

      (iii) was committed elsewhere against the landlord of the dwelling-house, or a person employed (whether or not by the landlord) in connection with the exercise of the landlord's housing management functions, and directly or indirectly related to or affected those functions.

(4) Condition 2 is that a court has found in relevant proceedings that the tenant, or a person residing in or visiting the dwelling-house, has breached a provision of an injunction under section 1 of the Anti-social Behaviour, Crime and Policing Act 2014, other than a provision requiring a person to participate in a particular activity, and—

   (a) the breach occurred in, or in the locality of, the dwelling-house, or

   (b) the breach occurred elsewhere and the provision breached was a provision intended to prevent—

      (i) conduct that is capable of causing nuisance or annoyance to a person with a right (of whatever description) to reside in, or occupy housing accommodation in the locality of, the dwelling-house, or

      (ii) conduct that is capable of causing nuisance or annoyance to the landlord of the dwelling-house, or a person employed (whether or not by the landlord) in connection with the exercise of the landlord's housing management functions, and that is directly or indirectly related to or affects those functions.

(5) Condition 3 is that the tenant, or a person residing in or visiting the dwelling-house, has been convicted of an offence under section 30 of the Anti-social Behaviour, Crime and Policing Act 2014 consisting of a breach of a provision of a criminal behaviour order prohibiting a person from doing anything described in the order, and the offence involved—

   (a) a breach that occurred in, or in the locality of, the dwelling-house, or

   (b) a breach that occurred elsewhere of a provision intended to prevent—

      (i) behaviour that causes or is likely to cause harassment, alarm or distress to a person with a right (of whatever description) to reside in, or occupy housing accommodation in the locality of, the dwelling-house, or

      (ii) behaviour that causes or is likely to cause harassment, alarm or distress to the landlord of the dwelling-house, or a person employed (whether or not by the landlord) in connection with the exercise of the landlord's housing management functions, and that is directly or indirectly related to or affects those functions.

(6) Condition 4 is that—

   (a) the dwelling-house is or has been subject to a closure order under section 80 of the Anti-social Behaviour, Crime and Policing Act 2014, and

(b)   access to the dwelling-house has been prohibited (under the closure order or under a closure notice issued under section 76 of that Act) for a continuous period of more than 48 hours.

(7)   Condition 5 is that—

    (a)   the tenant, or a person residing in or visiting the dwelling-house, has been convicted of an offence under—

        (i)   section 80(4) of the Environmental Protection Act 1990 (breach of abatement notice in relation to statutory nuisance), or

        (ii)   section 82(8) of that Act (breach of court order to abate statutory nuisance etc.), and

    (b)   the nuisance concerned was noise emitted from the dwelling-house which was a statutory nuisance for the purposes of Pt 3 of that Act by virtue of section 79(1)(g) of that Act (noise emitted from premises so as to be prejudicial to health or a nuisance).

(8)   Condition 1, 2, 3, 4 or 5 is not met if—

    (a)   there is an appeal against the conviction, finding or order concerned which has not been finally determined, abandoned or withdrawn, or

    (b)   the final determination of the appeal results in the conviction, finding or order being overturned.

3.177 In practice, behaviour that falls within either or both of Grounds 1 or 2[1] in Table A (arrears, breach of tenancy, and/or nuisance) is likely to be the most common form of 'unacceptable behaviour' considered by local housing authorities. But when considering the applicant's behaviour, or that of a member of his or her household, local housing authorities should take care to ensure that the behaviour would in fact have given rise to a ground for possession by satisfying the precise wording of the statute. For example, the only 'rent' that counts for Ground 1 purposes is 'rent lawfully due', and not unpaid instalments of overpaid housing benefit, or arrears owed by a previous tenant[2]. Likewise, nuisance behaviour or indictable offences committed *away* from the locality of the dwelling-house do not fall within Ground 2[3].

[1]   Housing Act 1985, Sch 2.
[2]   *Tickner v Clifton* [1929] 1 KB 207, Div Ct.
[3]   Save as now provided-for by the enlargement of Ground 2 in May 2014, as shown in the table, in relation to conduct directed at the landlord.

Reasonableness

3.178 However, if the applicant's behaviour, or that of a member of his or her household, demonstrably does fall within the precise words of one or more of the grounds for possession in Table A, the next question is whether it would have been reasonable for a court to make an order for possession on those facts. The question arises because all of those prescribed grounds are discretionary grounds upon which the landlord must be able to satisfy the court that 'it is reasonable to make' a possession order (of whatever type)[1]. The test of reasonableness is a very broad one, and will depend on the individual circumstances of each case. The courts themselves are warned by judicial precedent against applying hard and fast rules[2]. The Welsh Code suggests that in deciding whether it is reasonable to make an order a court may consider 'the conduct of both parties and the public interest'[3] and that the court must have regard to the interests and circumstances of the tenant (and of his or her household), the local housing authority and the wider public[4].

1   Housing Act 1985, s 84(2). But the grounds in Table B are not 'discretionary'.
2   *Cresswell v Hodgson* [1951] 2 KB 92, CA and, more recently, *Whitehouse v Lee* [2009] EWCA Civ 375, [2010] HLR 11, CA.
3   Welsh Code, Annex 10.
4   Welsh Code, para 2.34.

3.179 Where the behaviour consists of allowing 'rent arrears' to accrue, a court hearing possession proceedings would normally consider, on the question of reasonableness:

- the level of the arrears;
- the reason for the arrears accruing, including the degree of personal culpability for those arrears;
- any outstanding housing benefit issues;
- any offers to repay; and
- the tenant's, and his or her household's, personal circumstances[1].

1   *Woodspring District Council v Taylor* (1982) 4 HLR 95, CA; *Second WRVS v Blair* (1987) 19 HLR 104, CA; *Haringey London Borough Council v Stewart* (1991) 23 HLR 557, CA; *Lambeth London Borough Council v Thomas* (1998) 30 HLR 89, CA; and *Brent London Borough Council v Marks* (1999) 31 HLR 343, CA. See also Luba et al *Defending Possession Proceedings* (Legal Action Group, 8th edn, 2016).

3.180 If relevant past behaviour was 'nuisance or annoyance', the court hearing a possession claim under Sch 2, Ground 2 is required to consider:

- the effect that the nuisance or annoyance has had on persons other than the person against whom the order is sought;
- any continuing effect the nuisance or annoyance is likely to have on such persons; and
- the effect that the nuisance or annoyance would be likely to have on such persons if the conduct is repeated[1].

1   Housing Act 1985, s 85A, inserted by Anti-social Behaviour Act 2003, s 16 (with effect from 30 June 2004).

3.181 The court hearing a possession claim based on nuisance behaviour under Sch 2, Ground 2 should also consider:

- the tenant's personal circumstances and those of his or her household;
- the landlord's obligation to its other tenants and to the neighbours;
- the degree of personal culpability of the tenant;
- any factors explaining or mitigating the behaviour (such as a medical condition or a disability);
- the degree of compliance since notices were served and/or proceedings issued;
- any assurances as to future conduct; and
- any other relevant circumstances[1].

1   *Cresswell v Hodgson* [1951] 2 KB 92, CA; *Woking Borough Council v Bistram* (1993) 27 HLR 1, CA; *Wandsworth London Borough Council v Hargreaves* (1994) 27 HLR 142, CA; *Kensington and Chelsea Royal London Borough Council v Simmonds* (1996) 29 HLR 507, CA; *West Kent Housing Association v Davies* (1998) 31 HLR 415, CA; *Camden London Borough Council v Gilsenan* (1999) 31 HLR 81, CA; *Croydon London Borough Council v Moody* (1999) 31 HLR 738, CA; *Portsmouth City Council v Bryant* (2000) 32 HLR 906, CA;

Newcastle upon Tyne City Council v Morrison (2000) 32 HLR 891, CA; *Lambeth London Borough Council v Howard* [2001] EWCA Civ 468, (2001) 33 HLR 636, CA; *North Devon Housing Association v Brazier* [2003] EWHC 574, [2003] 35 HLR 59, QBD; *Manchester City Council v Higgins* [2005] EWCA Civ 1423, [2006] 1 All ER 841, CA; and *North Devon Homes v Batchelor* [2008] EWCA Civ 840, (2008) September *Legal Action*, p 23 are some of the reported cases on whether it would be reasonable to make a possession order in respect of nuisance or other anti-social behaviour. See also Luba et al *Defending Possession Proceedings* (Legal Action Group, 8th edn, 2016).

3.182 Where the behaviour in question consists of the commission of a serious criminal offence in the dwelling-house or in the locality of the dwelling-house, it would only be in exceptional circumstances that the court dealing with a Ground in Table A would consider that it is not reasonable to make an order for possession[1] (although, in such a case, a court should also consider the possibility that an order for possession, suspended or postponed on conditions, could succeed in controlling the tenant's behaviour)[2].

1   *Bristol City Council v Mousah* (1997) 30 HLR 32, CA, but see also *North Devon Homes v Batchelor* [2008] EWCA Civ 840, (2008) September *Legal Action*, p 23.
2   *Norwich City Council v Famuyiwa* [2004] EWCA Civ 1770, (2005) February *Legal Action*, p 34, CA; *Sheffield City Council v Shaw* [2007] EWCA Civ 42, [2007] HLR 25, CA; and *Sandwell Metropolitan Borough Council v Hensley* [2007] EWCA Civ 1425, [2008] HLR 22, CA.

3.183 In *R (McQ) v Bolton Metropolitan Borough Council*[1], the applicant argued that the local housing authority's decision on his application for social housing had failed to address the question of whether a judge would have found it 'reasonable' to make an order for possession (assuming that a ground for possession based on anti-social behaviour would have been made out). In refusing permission to bring judicial review proceedings, the Administrative Court held that there was only one answer to the question of whether it would have been reasonable to make an order for possession on the facts of the applicant's case, which was that it would have been reasonable.

1   [2005] EWHC 1285 (Admin), (2005) August *Legal Action*, p 17, Admin Ct.

3.184 For guidance on the application of the reasonableness requirement as operated in relation to the other relevant prescribed grounds of possession in Table A, see the discussion in Luba, Gallagher, McConnell and Madge *Defending Possession Proceedings*[1].

1   *Defending Possession Proceedings* (Legal Action Group, 8th edn, 2016).

Nature of the order

3.185 The final question for the local housing authority, in applying the 'unacceptable behaviour' limb of the ineligibility test, is whether the court did make (or, in the hypothetical cases, would have made) an outright or a suspended/postponed (conditional) order. HA 1996, Pt 6, is silent as to whether suspended or postponed (conditional) possession orders fall within the statutory definition, which refers only to 'a possession order'[1]. However, the Code of Guidance is very clear that only behaviour that would result in an outright order for possession falls within the statute[2]. During the Parliamentary debate on the then Homelessness Bill[3], the opposition quoted figures for the number of possession actions brought by social landlords in 2000, showing that in 82% of possession cases the social landlord had believed that it was entitled to an outright order for possession, but the court decided that it was not[4]. In response, the Minister gave assurances that only behaviour justifying an outright, rather than a suspended or postponed (conditional), possession order would fall within this section:

' . . . the authority would need to be satisfied that, if a possession order were granted, it would not be suspended by the court.[5]'

[1] HA 1996, s 160A(8).
[2] Welsh Code, para 2.35.
[3] Subsequently the Homelessness Act 2002.
[4] *Hansard*, HL Deb, vol 629, ser 6, col CWH 48 (10 December 2001) (Baroness Maddock): 150,000 actions were started (the vast majority being for rent arrears); 65% resulted in an order being made; but only 18% resulted in an outright order for possession.
[5] *Hansard*, HL Deb, vol 629, ser 6, col CWH 51 (10 December 2001) (Lord Falconer).

3.186 If an outright order was in fact granted in relation to the past misconduct, there is, perhaps, little difficulty with this element of the definition. But applying it to hypothetical cases[1] is probably the most difficult part of the local housing authority's decision-making on ineligibility for misbehaviour. Whether an order is made outright, or is suspended or postponed on terms, is a very broad discretionary decision for the court dealing with a Table A ground, taking into account all the circumstances as at the date of the decision[2]. It is not sufficient for the local housing authority to conclude that, on the facts as they have emerged, it would have requested that the court make an outright possession order. For the applicant not to be eligible, the local housing authority must be able to conclude that a court *would* in all probability have actually made an outright possession order and *not* a suspended or postponed (conditional) possession order.

[1] See **3.164–3.165**.
[2] Housing Act 1985, s 85(2) and see *Birmingham City Council v Ashton* [2012] EWCA Civ 1557, [2013] HLR 8, CA.

3.187 Examples of behaviour that may lead to only a suspended or postponed possession (conditional) order are given in the Code:

- modest rent arrears, absence of persistent default, delays in housing benefit, liability for a partner's debts, the applicant was not in control of the household finances or was unaware of the accrual of arrears, the local housing authority failed to provide help and advice[1]; or
- where allegations of nuisance are relatively minor, or the nuisance was caused by a member of the household who has since left, or the court would have been satisfied that a suspended or postponed (conditional) order would be sufficient to control the household's future behaviour[2].

[1] Welsh Code, para 2.36.
[2] Welsh Code, para 2.37.

3.188 Local housing authorities frequently request that courts make outright possession orders, but they do not always obtain them[1].

[1] Of landlord possession orders being made in county courts in England and Wales in the last quarter of 2017, 35% were suspended. (*Mortgage and landlord possession statistics in*

England and Wales: October to December 2017 (Provisional), Ministry of Justice, February 2018). This figure covers all landlord possession claims, including those in which the court had no power to suspend the order, eg those brought by private landlords against assured shorthold tenants.

3.189 As far as *rent arrears* are concerned, day-to-day practice in the courts suggests that suspended or postponed (conditional) possession orders are made regularly. Postponed or suspended (conditional) possession orders are not confined to cases of arrears that are the responsibility, but not the fault, of the tenant. In practice, suspended or postponed (conditional) possession orders are made where there are realistic offers by the tenant to repay the arrears, however the arrears accrued[1].

1   *Lambeth London Borough Council v Henry* (1999) 32 HLR 874, CA; and *Taj v Ali (No 2)* (2001) 33 HLR 259, CA.

3.190 In *nuisance cases*, the question is whether there is (or would have been) a sound basis, supported by cogent evidence, for hope that the tenant will observe the terms of their tenancy agreement in future[1]. Suspended or postponed (conditional) possession orders have been approved by the Court of Appeal where the behaviour appears to have ceased, or where the court considers that a postponed (conditional) possession order should be a sufficient deterrent from future misconduct[2]. Often the principal considerations for the court are whether the tenant has some insight into the nuisance caused to his or her neighbours, and whether the court can accept the tenant's assurances as to future behaviour: the tenant does not have to give a cast-iron guarantee, but a social landlord does not have to accept a tenant who sets out to breach the terms of his tenancy[3]. The prescribed statutory criteria which apply in a nuisance case and may have driven the court to be satisfied that it was 'reasonable' to order possession do not expressly apply to the stage at which the court is deciding whether the order should be outright, suspended or postponed, but they are intended to remind the court that the focus is on the effect that nuisance and annoyance has on others, and it would be appropriate to consider them again at this stage[4]. Of course, if the particular conduct under consideration meets one of the conditions for the making of an order under Housing Act 1985, s 84A (see Table B above), a possession order may have been actually (or hypothetically) granted under that provision. However, the new absolute ground is intended only 'for the most serious cases of antisocial behaviour and landlords should ensure that the ground is used selectively'[5].

1   *City West Housing Trust v Massey* [2016] EWCA Civ 704, [2017] 1 WLR 129, CA.
2   *Kensington and Chelsea Royal London Borough Council v Simmonds* (1996) 29 HLR 507, CA; *West Kent Housing Association v Davies* (1998) 31 HLR 415, CA; *Portsmouth City Council v Bryant* (2000) 32 HLR 906, CA; *Greenwich London Borough Council v Grogan* (2001) 33 HLR 12, CA; *Gallagher v Castle Vale Housing Action Trust* [2001] EWCA Civ 944, (2001) 33 HLR 72, CA; and *Sheffield City Council v Shaw* [2007] EWCA Civ 42, [2007] HLR 25, CA.
3   *City West Housing Trust v Massey* [2016] EWCA Civ 704, [2017] 1 WLR 129, CA at [48].
4   Housing Act 1985, s 85A, added by Anti-social Behaviour Act 2003, s 16(1) (with effect from 30 June 2004), *Lambeth London Borough Council v Debrah* [2007] EWCA Civ 1503, (2008) May *Legal Action*, p 44, CA. As to the more general question of whether a conditional or outright order would be made in a nuisance case see *Moat Housing Group-South Ltd v Harris & Hartless* [2005] EWCA 287, [2005] HLR 33, CA; *Manchester City Council v Higgins* [2005] EWCA Civ 1423, [2006] 1 All ER 841, CA per Ward LJ at [29]; and *Birmingham City Council v Ashton* [2012] EWCA Civ 1557, [2013] HLR 8, CA.

3.191 Two cases well illustrate the operation of this element of the statutory conditions for ineligibility on behaviour grounds:

(1)   In *R (Dixon) v Wandsworth London Borough Council*,[1] the applicant had a history of drug-related incidents at his former home. He accepted that a ground for possession would have been made out and that a judge would have found it reasonable to have made a possession order. However, he challenged the decision of the local housing authority – that he was not eligible for an allocation – on the grounds that his conduct would not have led to the making of an outright order, but only to a suspended or postponed (conditional) order. His claim failed. The judge was satisfied that, in reaching the decision that a county court would probably have granted an outright order, the reviewing officer had applied the correct test, had regard to the relevant considerations, made proper findings of fact (in a lengthy decision letter) and had not reached an irrational conclusion. The applicant's renewed application for permission to appeal was rejected by the Court of Appeal, which said:

> 'it was open to the authority to conclude that an outright order was likely to be made on the facts of this case. The applicant had a history of drug abuse for a period of ten years, during which time the flat was raided three times. The raid that resulted in this conviction had caused £1000 worth of damage to the flat itself, and each raid must have been very disturbing for the applicant's neighbours.[2]'

(2)   In *R (M) v Hackney London Borough Council*[3], the applicant was an elderly council tenant living alone and seeking a transfer. He had a long history of convictions for sexual offences and in 2004 he had been made subject, by consent, to a sexual offences prevention order which recited activities relating to a teenage boy. The local housing authority decided that the events of 2004 were so serious that, had possession been sought on the basis of them, the court would have granted an outright order. Dismissing a claim for judicial review of that decision, the judge emphasised that the judgment as to whether an outright order would have been made was one for the housing authority not the reviewing court. He said:

> 'The Council took the view that the incident of 2004 constituted anti-social behaviour sufficient to justify an outright possession order. In considering that matter I have regard to two background factors. In *Hensley*[4] Gage LJ referred to the need for a council, as a provider of social housing, to make sure that its properties are properly managed and kept free from undesirable activity. It is in my view also necessary to underline the remarks in the judgment of Otton LJ, which I have quoted, that the judicial and administrative functions should not be elided[5]. Admittedly the remarks were in a somewhat different context. But the message to me is clear: it is not for me to allocate Hackney's housing.[6]'

4   *Sandwell Metropolitan Borough Council v Hensley* [2007] EWCA Civ 1425, [2008] HLR 22, CA.
5   Referring to the judgment of Otton LJ in *City of Bristol v Mousah* (1998) 30 HLR 32 at [40].
6   Per Cranston J at [36].

Condition Two: unsuitable to be a tenant

3.192 The second condition necessary to sustain a decision of ineligibility on behaviour grounds is that, at the time that the application for allocation falls to be considered, the applicant is still unsuitable to be a tenant of the local housing authority by reason of past behaviour[1]. It must be noted that the relevant date for applying this test is the date on which the local housing authority reaches a decision on eligibility or concludes a review of that decision, *not* the date that the application for allocation was made.

1   HA 1996, s 160A(7)(b). Welsh Code, para 2.38.

3.193 In determining whether past behaviour renders the applicant currently 'unsuitable', local housing authorities should consider whether the tenant's behaviour has improved[1], whether the circumstances that caused the behaviour have changed (eg in the case of nuisance behaviour that was caused by drug or alcohol problems whether the tenant has successfully resolved those problems), whether the member of the household who was responsible for the behaviour remains a member of the applicant's household, and whether it can accept any assurances from the applicant as to future behaviour[2].

1   Welsh Code, para 2.38.
2   *Hansard*, HL Deb, vol 629, ser 6, col CWH 52, (10 December 2001), the Minister, Lord Falconer, referred to the circumstances as 'all the relevant matters before it. Those will include all the circumstances relevant to the particular applicant, whether health, dependents or other factors'.

3.194 If the local housing authority has reason to believe that the past unacceptable behaviour was due to physical, mental or learning difficulties, it should consider whether the applicant could now maintain a tenancy with appropriate care and support. Local housing authorities cannot adopt a blanket approach of treating all applicants who were in the past guilty of nuisance behaviour, or were in substantial rent arrears, as ineligible[1].

1   Welsh Code, para 2.38.

The exercise of the local housing authority's discretion

3.195 Even if the statutory conditions for ineligibility on the basis of past behaviour are made out, the local housing authority must go on to consider whether to exercise its discretion to treat the applicant as ineligible due to that unacceptable behaviour. The word used in HA 1996, Pt 6, s 160A(7) is 'may' and not 'shall', making it clear that the local housing authority has such a discretion[1].

1   HA 1996, s 160A(7).

3.196 The local housing authority must take into account, in exercising this discretion, the applicant's particular circumstances, any health needs, any dependents and any other relevant factors[1]. The importance of the discretion is most acutely demonstrated in cases where the applicant meets the statutory conditions for ineligibility by reason of previous default in payment of rent and still has arrears outstanding. The local housing authority must be careful not to automatically bar such applicants but instead must exercise discretion on a case-by-case basis. It is essential to avoid loose language which suggests that a fixed rule rather than a discretion is being exercised, eg 'It is the policy of this Council not to make offers to applicants who owe property related debts'[2].

[1]   Welsh Code, para 2.39.
[2]   That text is taken from a decision letter cited in *R (Joseph) v Newham London Borough Council* [2008] EWHC 1637 (Admin), (2009) September *Legal Action*, p 34 Admin Ct. The claimant went on to succeed in the claim for judicial review because the property related debt on which the council was relying was an irrecoverable overpayment of housing benefit: *R (Joseph) v Newham London Borough Council* [2009] EWHC 2983 (Admin), (2010) May *Legal Action*, p 23, Admin Ct.

3.197 The local housing authority, faced with a case meeting the statutory conditions, could nevertheless decide to accept the applicant as eligible for its allocation scheme, but give him or her no preference (even if he or she would otherwise have been entitled to a statutory reasonable preference)[1]. The Code reminds local housing authorities that they are not obliged to find that an applicant is ineligible on the grounds of unacceptable behaviour, but could instead give the applicant no preference[2]. However, the local housing authority cannot refuse to give any preference at all to an applicant in a category entitled to a reasonable preference except on the same specified grounds as the 'unacceptable behaviour' test of eligibility[3].

[1]   HA 1996, s 167(2B); Welsh Code, para 2.41.
[2]   Welsh Code, para 2.41.
[3]   HA 1996, s 167(2A), (2B) and (2C); Welsh Code, para 2.42.

3.198 The Welsh Code sets out detailed policy considerations for local housing authorities to take into account when they are deciding whether or not to treat applicants as ineligible on the grounds of unacceptable behaviour. Starting from the view that 'barriers to social housing should be minimised', the Code recommends that local housing authorities should:

- consider their role as providers of social housing in order to meet housing need in their area;
- develop their own 'unacceptable behaviour' policies specifying the grounds when a person is likely to be thought ineligible;
- keep restricted access measures to a minimum;
- work collaboratively with the police, probation services and other statutory and voluntary agencies to share information;
- avoid unreasonable application requirements;
- monitor and evaluate their policies and practice;
- develop common restricted access policies with housing association partners; and
- be prepared to consider applicants with former tenant rent arrears[1].

[1]   Welsh Code, para 2.44.

3.199 The Welsh Code suggests that policies regarding the application of sanctions on the grounds of unacceptable behaviour should:

> 'accommodate the broader Welsh Government policy aims of equality of opportunity, social inclusion and sustainability. Therefore, sanctions to exclude people from social housing should be kept to a minimum and support mechanisms developed to maximise opportunities for people to secure social housing.[1]'

[1] Welsh Code, para 2.29.

3.200 There has been no systematic national monitoring of the operation of the ineligibility provisions relating to behaviour, even during the period when the provisions applied in both England and Wales. It is simply not known how many applicants have been held to fall within the statutory conditions and how many of those have gone on to be excluded from an allocation scheme in the exercise of a local housing authority's discretion. A limited study of local housing authorities in England[1] found that 'considerable staff member discretion is often used in determining appropriate treatment of applicants with rent arrears or believed previously responsible for anti-social behaviour. Whether actions taken are fully recorded and monitored is a question beyond the scope of this research'[2]. In Wales, 11 local housing authorities participated in a study specifically looking at exclusions from allocation schemes[3]. Of those, eight local housing authorities provided copies of their relevant policies. The researchers found that 'not all the exclusion policies and procedures examined were lawful' and that, during the single year 2006–07, just four of those authorities had excluded a total of 129 applicants.

[1] *Exploring local authority policy and practice on housing allocations* (CLG, July 2009).
[2] *Exploring local authority policy and practice on housing allocations* (CLG, July 2009), para 4.6.
[3] *Am I on the list? Exclusion from and re-inclusion on social housing waiting lists* (CIH Cymru, May 2008).

WHEN TO DETERMINE ELIGIBILITY AND QUALIFICATION

3.201 Under HA 1996, Pt 6, as originally enacted, the *eligibility* test operated as a control on the admission of an applicant to the local housing register. With the abolition in 2003 of the requirement to keep housing registers, the scheme now works by prohibiting the allocation of housing to ineligible applicants. This has led to the practice of testing eligibility twice in respect of any given applicant. First, the eligibility tests are operated when an applicant initially applies for consideration under the particular local allocation scheme. Second, assuming satisfaction of the tests at that stage, they are applied again later when the allocation of a specific property is being contemplated. For an applicant who passed the eligibility test when he or she initially applied, this can mean that changed circumstances might render him or her ineligible just prior to the point at which he or she would have been allocated a property. The English Code advises that a similar approach should be taken in relation to checking at both stages for 'qualification'[1].

[1] English Code, para 3.26 and see **3.149**.

3.202 There are two obvious justifications for this double testing[1]. First, if an applicant is admitted for consideration under the local scheme, he or she will reasonably believe the local housing authority has satisfied itself that he or she is entitled to be allocated property under that scheme and he or she is likely to put time and effort into bidding on properties. It is important, therefore, that eligibility and/or qualification is tested on initial application. Second, there must be a further check just prior to the later prospective allocation of a specific property, because otherwise the local housing authority may mistakenly infringe the statutory injunction that it 'shall not allocate' to an ineligible person[2]. That second check may identify a person who was initially eligible, on his or her earlier application, but is not eligible when a specific allocation is about to be made. It is therefore particularly important that when a person from abroad receives an initially favourable decision on eligibility, he or she is informed that any changes to his or her immigration status – or, indeed, changes to the complex statutory rules about eligibility and immigration status – could affect eligibility later for a particular allocation of property.

[1] Which is specifically recommended by the Secretary of State in the English Code, para 3.2.
[2] HA 1996, s 160ZA(1) (England), s 160A(1) (Wales).

3.203 If there is no change of circumstances between the first and second checks, but the local housing authority simply reaches a different conclusion which is adverse to the applicant – perhaps because the decision-maker takes a different view of the facts, or material factors were previously overlooked – then the applicant may be able to challenge this second, unfavourable, decision. In the homelessness context, it has been held that a local housing authority cannot revisit a decision that the applicant was eligible where there had been no fraud or deception on the part of the applicant and no fundamental mistake of fact[1]. Further, the applicant may be able to show that he or she has a legitimate expectation arising from the first decision[2].

[1] *R (Sambotin) v Brent London Borough Council* [2017] EHWC 1190 (Admin), [2017] HLR 31, Admin Ct.
[2] The issue of 'legitimate expectation' arises where a person is, contrary to his or her expectations, deprived ' . . . of some benefit or advantage which either (i) he had in the past been permitted by the decision-maker to enjoy and which he can legitimately expect to be permitted to continue to do until there has been communicated to him some rational grounds for withdrawing it on which he has been given an opportunity to comment; or (ii) he has received assurance from the decision-maker that they will not be withdrawn without giving him first an opportunity of advancing reasons for contending that they should not be withdrawn': *Council of Civil Service Unions v Minister for the Civil Service* [1985] AC 374, HL per Lord Diplock at 408. See also *R v North and East Devon Health Authority ex p Coughlan* [2001] QB 213, CA, and *R (Bhatt Murphy (a firm)) v The Independent Assessor* [2008] EWCA Civ 755, CA. For a recent discussion of these cases in the context of housing allocation see *R (Alansi) v Newham London Borough Council* [2013] EWHC 3722 (Admin), [2014] HLR 25, Admin Ct, in which Stuart-Smith J held that 'the test to be applied is whether frustrating the claimant's expectation is so unfair that to take a new and different course will amount to an abuse of power' (at [35]).

NOTIFICATION OF DECISIONS AND RIGHTS TO REVIEW

3.204 All applicants who have been found ineligible (whether on grounds of immigration status or of past misconduct) should have the right under the local allocation scheme to written notification of that decision and of the grounds for it[1]. The grounds must be firmly 'based on the relevant facts of the case.[2]' The applicant should also have the right under that scheme to request a review of that decision, and to be informed of the review decision and the grounds on which it was made[3]. The reviewer should reconsider afresh the whole of the information put before him or her, and consider the facts as at the date of the review decision[4]. As to the procedure to be followed on the review, see **2.94–2.99**. The Welsh Code contains extensive guidance as to how a review of a decision on eligibility should be organised and conducted to ensure procedural fairness[5].

[1]   HA 1996, s 160ZA(9)(a) (England), s 160A(9) (Wales).
[2]   English Code, para 5.16 and Welsh Code, para 2.51.
[3]   HA 1996, s 166A(9)(c) (England), s 167(4A)(d) (Wales).
[4]   English Code, para 5.19v.
[5]   Welsh Code, para 2.55.

3.205 In relation to a decision that an applicant to a local housing authority in England is not a 'qualifying person' there should be a similar right in the local allocation scheme for that person to be given written notice of the decision and of the grounds for it[1]. It is to be hoped that there will be no return to the practices, adopted in some areas from 1996–2003, of deflecting genuine applicants to local housing authorities at their first point of contact by telling them (in person or over the telephone) that they do not meet the local qualifying conditions or that they fall within a class that does not qualify and therefore should not apply. An applicant dissatisfied with such a decision should have the right to request a review of that decision, and to be informed of the review decision and the grounds on which it was made[2].

[1]   HA 1996, s 160ZA(9)(b).
[2]   HA 1996, s 166A(9)(c).

3.206 If the review upholds the original decision in any case relating to eligibility or qualification, there is no mechanism to appeal to the county court and the only available legal challenge to the review decision is by judicial review, alleging an error of law in the review process, in the tests applied by the local housing authority in reaching its decision on review, or in the review decision itself[1].

[1]   Further information on challenging review decisions is given at **2.103–2.120**.

3.207 In *R (Dixon) v Wandsworth London Borough Council*[1] the applicant complained that the reviewing officer had failed to give the 'grounds' for the review decision because the notice of the review decision (a lengthy document) gave insufficient reasons. The judge rejected the claim and that decision was upheld by the Court of Appeal which said that 'the reasons were stated in sufficient detail to enable the applicant to know what conclusion the decision maker had reached on the principal important controversial issues.[2]' In another case, the local housing authority's correspondence relating to a decision on eligibility was described as 'opaque', but a challenge based on inadequate reasons was rejected as the claimant himself was well apprised of the issues being addressed[3].

[1]   [2007] EWHC 3075 (Admin), (2008) February *Legal Action*, p 40, Admin Ct.
[2]   [2008] EWCA Civ 595, (2008) July *Legal Action*, p 22, CA at [9].

[3]   *R (M) v London Borough of Hackney* [2009] EWHC 2255 (Admin), (2009) May *Legal Action*, p 26, Admin Ct.

RENEWED APPLICATIONS

3.208 The decision reached by a local housing authority on an applicant's eligibility (whether on immigration-related grounds or behaviour-related grounds) or whether he or she is a qualifying person does not bind any other local housing authority to reach the same decision. Disappointed applicants unable to overturn the adverse decision may be advised to apply elsewhere. In England that is particularly true of decisions relating to qualification because every local housing authority in England will have adopted different qualifying classes and criteria.

3.209 Alternatively, the applicant could make a further application to the same local housing authority[1]. Plainly, a person who has been declared ineligible on immigration-related grounds will wish to apply again, as soon as his or her immigration status alters.

[1]   See 2.73–2.74 on 'Repeat Applications'.

Wales

3.210 HA 1996, Pt 6 expressly envisages that an applicant found to be ineligible by a local housing authority in Wales on behaviour-related eligibility grounds may want to re-apply on the basis that he or she should no longer be treated as ineligible. It provides for the making of 'a fresh application' in such cases[1]. This is no doubt because the two statutory conditions for ineligibility in the behaviour category link past misconduct and present suitability to be a tenant.

[1]   HA 1996, s 160A(11).

3.211 Inevitably, that link will become weaker with the passage of time and with other changes in an applicant's circumstances. The Welsh Code suggests that the burden will be on the applicant to show that his or her circumstances or behaviour have changed[1].

[1]   Welsh Code, para 2.40.

England

3.212 An applicant who has received a decision from a local housing authority in England that he or she does not qualify can re-apply if he or she considers that he or she should be treated as a qualifying person[1]. The most obvious example will be where the initial application was made at the time when the applicant was unemployed and the local qualifying class was 'persons in employment'. The applicant may re-apply as soon as he or she obtains employment. Similarly, a person caught by a residency requirement may re-apply on accruing the requisite period of residence. The statutory guidance suggests that on any re-application it would be for the applicant to show that his or her circumstances have changed[2]. However, there is no need for there to have been any change of personal circumstances – the local housing authority may simply have changed its qualifying criteria.

1   HA 1996, s 160ZA(11).
2   English Code, para 3.30.

Chapter 4

ALLOCATION SCHEMES

Contents

INTRODUCTION

4.1 Each local housing authority in England and Wales is required by the Housing Act 1996 (HA 1996), Pt 6 ('Allocation of Housing Accommodation'), to have a scheme for the allocation of social housing[1]. Even those local housing authorities which have transferred the whole of their housing stock, and no longer have any properties to let, are required to have an allocation scheme, not least because they retain nomination rights (to other local housing authorities and to non-local authority social landlords) and the exercise of those nomination rights constitutes an 'allocation'. The obligation to have an allocation scheme remains in place even if the local housing authority has contracted out delivery of its allocation functions[2]. However, research has found that several local housing authorities in England, which had transferred their housing stock to private registered providers, perceived themselves as 'retaining no such role'[3].

[1] HA 1996, s 166A(1) (England), s 167(1) (Wales). Statutory guidance on allocation schemes is given in *Allocation of Accommodation: Guidance for local housing authorities in England* (Department for Communities and Local Government [DCLG], June 2012) (the English Code), *Providing social housing for local people* (DCLG, December 2013) (the Supplementary English Code), *Right to Move: Statutory Guidance on Social Housing Allocations for Local Housing Authorities in England* (DCLG, March 2015) and in *Code of Guidance for local authorities on the Allocation of accommodation and homelessness* (Welsh Government, March 2016) (the Welsh Code). See Appendix 1 of this book for the English Code and the Supplementary English Code and see the accompanying CD Rom for the Welsh Code.

[2] English Code, para 4.2; Welsh Code, Annex 9.

[3] *Exploring local authority policy and practice on housing allocations* (DCLG, July 2009) para 2.15.

4.2 This chapter discusses how these local housing allocation schemes must be framed (whether from the outset or by amendment) in order to comply with HA 1996, Pt 6 and how they must work to enable a lawful assessment of each applicant's application. The process of actual allocation to those who have had their applications assessed is reviewed in the next chapter. HA 1996, Pt 6, states that everything that counts as an 'allocation'[1] must be undertaken in accordance with the local allocation scheme or it will be unlawful[2]. As long as a local housing authority complies with the basic requirements set out in this chapter, it is allowed to exercise its own discretion in settling on a scheme for determining how it actually makes allocations and to whom[3].

[1] For the definition see HA 1996, s 159(2); and see also the discussion at **1.23–1.27** of circumstances in which a person can become a tenant of social housing without an allocation.

[2] HA 1996, s 166A(14) (England), s 167(8) (Wales).

[3] HA 1996, s 159(7) (England and Wales), s 166A(11) (England) and s 167(6) (Wales).

ADOPTING OR AMENDING AN ALLOCATION SCHEME

Adopting a scheme

4.3 Most local housing authorities will have long since adopted an allocation scheme, as required by HA 1996, Pt 6, as amended. But some new local housing authorities are from time to time created (eg by establishing new unitary authorities in areas with multiple layers of local government). Where a new local authority has been established as a local housing authority for a district it will need to formulate and adopt an allocation scheme. There are two essential statutory pre-requisites before any new local allocation scheme can be adopted.

4.4 The first is that the local housing authority must undertake any impact assessments required under equalities legislation and by the local housing authority's own statements of equality policy[1].

[1] See **4.193–4.209**.

4.5 The second requirement is one of limited consultation. Before an allocation scheme is adopted, the local housing authority is required to consult every private registered provider (or, in Wales, every registered social landlord) with which it has nomination arrangements. As part of that consultation, it must send those landlords a copy of the draft scheme and give them a reasonable opportunity to comment on the proposals[1]. A reasonable opportunity is identified in the Welsh Code as being a minimum period of 12 weeks[2].

1   HA 1996, s 166A(13) (England) and s 167(7) (Wales).
2   Welsh Code, para 4.34. A similar provision originally appeared in the English Code (2002 edn), para 6.6.

4.6 These are, of course, the *minimum* statutory prerequisites. A local housing authority drawing up a scheme for the first time might well be expected to undertake a much wider range of measures before finally adopting its scheme. There is no *statutory* requirement to consult any other people or organisations before adopting a scheme, but much might usefully be gained by eliciting the views of local tenants' organisations, housing advice agencies and the like. The Welsh Code advises that any such consultation should be broad based and should use a variety of methods to ensure that it is representative and that it addresses the needs of people with protected characteristics[1]. It also recommends that local health boards, Supporting People teams, relevant voluntary sector organisations and other recognised referral bodies should be consulted[2].

1   Welsh Code, para 4.27. For the 'protected characteristics' see Equality Act 2012, ss 5–12.
2   Welsh Code, para 4.28.

4.7 Indeed, local housing authorities may wish to engage with and involve all interested groups and the wider community[1] before they produce their first allocation scheme so that local people are given the opportunity to contribute to the development of the allocation priorities. The Chartered Institute of Housing has suggested that 'allocation schemes should be developed in consultation with local registered providers, partners working in health and the local economy and tenants, residents and communities themselves'[2].

1   Welsh Code, para 4.29.
2   *Allocation of accommodation: guidance for local housing authorities in England, Briefing paper* (CIH, July 2012), p 7.

4.8 A local housing authority should take into account the findings and conclusions of its own homelessness review and strategy when settling upon an allocation scheme and, conversely, the homelessness strategy should take into account the local allocation scheme[1]. Indeed, if a local housing authority in England is preparing an allocation scheme it must have regard to:

(1)   its homelessness strategy;
(2)   its tenancy strategy[2]; and
(3)   (if it is a local housing authority in London) the London housing strategy[3].

1   Homelessness Act 2002, s 1(5). Welsh Code, para 3.8. See Chapter 7 of this book and *English Homelessness Code of Guidance* (MHCLG, February 2018) at para 2.48.
2   Adopted in order to comply with Localism Act 2011, s 150.
3   HA 1996, s 166A(12).

4.9 A local housing authority in Wales should have regard, in drawing up an allocation scheme, to the local housing strategy or the strategic housing element of the local Single Integrated Plan[1].

[1] Welsh Code, paras 3.8–3.9.

4.10 The content and degree of detail required in the finished scheme is considered later in this chapter[1].

[1] See **4.22–4.26**.

Amending the current local allocation scheme

4.11 There is no statutory obligation on a local housing authority to keep the terms of its allocation scheme under review or to revise it regularly[1]. However, the Welsh Code suggests that it would be 'good practice' to review allocation policies at least every two years[2]. The *English Homelessness Code of Guidance* encourages local housing authorities to 'keep under review the impact of their allocations policies upon people at risk of homelessness'.[3] Further, review or revision of an allocation scheme may be prompted by a number of different factors.

(1)   If a court declares the whole or a part of a housing allocation scheme to be unlawful the local housing authority will need to replace or vary its scheme[4].

(2)   A court's decision in respect of a different local housing authority may also be relevant. The Local Government Ombudsman (LGO)[5] has said 'we would criticise a local housing authority for failing to review its housing allocation scheme in response to a court judgement [sic] against a different authority that raises an issue which is clearly relevant to the authority's own scheme'[6].

(3)   An event affecting the housing situation in a local housing authority's area may prompt an amendment to its scheme. In 2017, after the devastating fire at Grenfell Tower in London, which destroyed 129 flats and took 72 lives, the local housing authority concerned adopted an exceptional rehousing policy for those affected.

(4)   A significant change in legislation is also likely to require review and, if necessary, revision of an allocation scheme. Since June 2012, all local housing authorities in England were expected to undertake reviews of, and make possible amendments to, their allocation schemes in the light of the changes to HA 1996, Pt 6, made by the Localism Act 2011[7]. The revision of allocation schemes in England has been positively promoted by the Supplementary English Code[8] which particularly encourages revisions to adopt or change classes of qualifying and non-qualifying applicants. This guidance appears to have been followed as, since the Localism Act 2011 came into effect, 95% of local authorities have reported changing their waiting list criteria due to the new legislation[9]. In addition, the *English Homelessness Code of Guidance* states that local housing authorities may need to review their allocation schemes in response to the Homelessness Reduction Act 2017,[10] in order to 'ensure that they deliver the requirements of the legislation and are sufficiently geared towards preventing homelessness'.[11]

(5) In Wales, there will have been a need to review local allocation schemes to take account of the new national guidance on local housing allocation published in the Welsh Code in March 2016[12].

If a local housing authority proposes to make any significant change to the local allocation scheme, two sets of statutory requirements are triggered.

1   In contrast to the requirements in relation to homelessness strategies set out in Homelessness Act 2002, ss 1–4. See **7.169–7.177.**
2   And to review published information about them annually, see Welsh Code, paras 3.83 and 4.52.
3   *English Homelessness Code of Guidance* (MHCLG, February 2018), at para 2.48
4   An application by the local housing authority for permission to appeal from such a declaration does not operate as an automatic 'stay' of that requirement. Either an application for a stay must be made to the appellate court or the local housing authority must adopt a new or modified scheme – even if an interim one: *R(HA) v Ealing London Borough Council (No 2)* [2015] EWHC 4108 (Admin), [2016] February *Legal Action* p 44, Admin Ct.
5   As of 19 June 2017, the Local Government and Social Care Ombudsman (LGSCO).
6   *Full house: Councils' role in allocating social housing. Focus report: learning lessons from complaints* (LGO, January 2017) at p 3.
7   The major change made by the Localism Act 2011 is discussed at **3.91.**
8   *Providing social housing for local people* (DCLG, December 2013) at Appendix 1.
9   *Local authority housing statistics: year ending March 2017, England* (MHCLG, January 2018).
10 This substantially amends Part 7 of the Housing Act 1996 with respect to applications for homelessness assistance made to local housing authorities in England on or after from 3 April 2018.
11 *English Homelessness Code of Guidance* (MHCLG, February 2018), at para 2.45.
12 See the Welsh Code.

4.12 First, the local housing authority will need to make any impact assessment necessary to achieve compliance with the requirements of equalities legislation and with its own equality policies[1].

1   See **4.192–4.230.**

4.13 Second, if an alteration is to be made which amounts to 'a major change of policy', the local housing authority is required to notify and consult with local private registered providers (or, in Wales, registered social landlords) with which it has nomination arrangements and give them a reasonable opportunity to comment on the proposed changes[1]. A minimum consultation period of 12 weeks is recommended[2].

1   HA 1996, s 166A(13) (England), s 167(7) (Wales).
2   Welsh Code, para 4.34. A similar provision originally appeared in the English Code (2002), para 6.6.

4.14 But what is 'a major change of policy'? The Welsh Code advises that 'a major change of policy' for these purposes would include any amendment affecting the relative priority of a large number of people being considered for an allocation of social housing, and any significant alteration to allocation procedures[1]. In a case concerning Brent London Borough Council, the LGO[2] decided that a change in policy under which working applicants were awarded an additional five years' priority constituted a major change of policy[3].

1   Welsh Code, para 4.26. A similar provision originally appeared in the English Code (2002), para 6.3.
2   As of 19 June 2017, the Local Government and Social Care Ombudsman (LGSCO).

³   *Complaint against London Borough of Brent*, 16 010 013, 24 March 2017.

4.15 The question was considered by the Court of Appeal in *R (A) v Lambeth London Borough Council*¹. The court was concerned with Lambeth's decision to change the proportions of allocations ('quotas') made available to different groups within its scheme, so that three of the seven groups would receive no allocations whatsoever. Arguably, this constituted 'a major change of policy', certainly as far as the applicants in those three groups were concerned. The prospects of any of them receiving an allocation had suddenly become 'zero'. The allocation scheme itself did not refer to the quotas of allocations that each group could expect, merely stating 'the effect of preference on each applicant group is also reviewed, and targets changed if necessary'. The Court of Appeal, whilst holding that other aspects of the scheme were unlawful², held that since the actual proportion of allocations between the different groups was not part of the published scheme, and there was no requirement for it to be published, a change in the proportion did not constitute 'a major change of policy' and there was no need to consult or inform applicants. It follows that 'a major change of policy' must at least be a change relating to the information which is contained, or should be contained, in the published allocation scheme.

¹   *R (A) v Lambeth London Borough Council* [2002] EWCA Civ 1084, [2002] HLR 57, CA.
²   See **5.34**.

4.16 Until recently, the most commonly proposed 'major change of policy' was either a shift from officer-led allocation to the adoption of at least some choice-based element in an allocation scheme or the complete replacement of the previous arrangements with a wholly choice-based letting scheme.

4.17 The broadest possible approach should be taken to involving the local community in consultation on the variation of any allocation scheme¹. The Welsh Code suggests that anyone who is affected by or interested in the way social housing is allocated should be included when consulting on changes to an allocation scheme and local housing authorities in Wales are encouraged to engage with a wide range of stakeholders in the statutory, voluntary and community sectors, as well as applicants and the general public². In any event, a local housing authority which is also a social landlord will also need to comply with the requirements of its own statutory scheme³ for consulting current tenants and with the statutory regulator's expectations⁴ as to consultation with, and participation by, tenants in respect of major changes of policy.

¹   Welsh Code, paras 3.60 and 4.28–4.33.
²   Welsh Code, paras 3.60 and 4.28–4.33.
³   Housing Act 1985, s 105.
⁴   For example, the *Tenant Involvement and Empowerment Standard* (updated in July 2017), part of *The regulatory framework for social housing in England from April 2015* (Homes and Communities Agency, March 2015), requires that 'Registered providers shall ensure that tenants are given a wide range of opportunities to influence and be involved . . . in the formulation of their landlord's housing related policies and strategic priorities'.

4.18 If an alteration is made which reflects a 'major change of policy', the local housing authority must take such steps as it considers reasonable to bring the effects of the change to the attention of those likely to be affected by it¹. Most obviously, that will be the pool of actual or prospective applicants and those likely to be advising them. Very little guidance is given in the Codes as to what steps might be considered 'reasonable'. The Welsh Code suggests that a major policy change will require 'each potential applicant to be informed personally by letter', leaving unanswered the question as to how a local housing authority can identify potential, as opposed to actual, applicants[2].

1   HA 1996, s 168(3) as amended.
2   Welsh Code, para 4.26.

4.19 Plainly, those applicants already being dealt with under the current allocation scheme can be directly written to[1]. However, potential applicants and other members of the public will have to be informed through the usual information mechanisms available to the local housing authority, such as publication on the website, notice in the local newspapers, informing housing advice agencies, etc. Given that some existing tenants of social housing who are seeking transfers will fall within the allocation scheme arrangements, and would therefore be likely to be affected, arguably the local housing authority should inform all social housing tenants and tenants' organisations in its district of any 'major change of policy' to be reflected in the revised allocation scheme.

1   In *R (Alansi) v Newham London Borough Council* [2013] EWHC 3722 (Admin), [2014] HLR 25, Admin Ct the local housing authority proposed a revision of its allocation scheme which, among other matters, would remove one particular group of applicants from a 'reasonable preference' category. The council wrote to every current applicant, consulting them on the proposed changes. When the particular change had been made, it wrote to each applicant in the group affected, inviting the provision of any new or additional information and providing the opportunity of a review.

4.20 One of the most difficult aspects of adopting extensive amendments to a local housing allocation scheme is the need to deal with those applicants who have already been considered and assessed under the old scheme. This should be made clear in the scheme, but in the absence of any such provision, the assumption would be that the requirements of the amended scheme would apply immediately to all applicants.

4.21 In September 2005 a local housing authority in London changed its housing allocation scheme from being points-based to one using wholly new assessment bands in which priority operated by reference to registration dates. The new scheme did not address how applicants registered on the old scheme would be dealt with under the new one. The Court of Appeal declined to fill that gap, holding that it was 'questionable' on what basis the local housing authority could give any applicant a registration date under the new scheme earlier than the date of the adoption of the new scheme – while also indicating that if any such provision was to be made, it should be published as part of the revised allocation scheme[1].

1   *R (Faarah) v Southwark London Borough Council* [2008] EWCA Civ 807, [2009] HLR 12, CA.

ENSURING THAT THE SCHEME IS SUFFICIENTLY DETAILED

4.22 HA 1996, Pt 6, prescribes that the new local housing allocation scheme must set out:

(1)   how the local housing authority will determine priorities between applicants; and

(2)   what procedures it will follow in allocating housing accommodation[1].

[1]   HA 1996, s 166A(1) (England), s 167(1) (Wales).

4.23 Where the local housing authority has adopted a choice-based letting arrangement, the formal allocation scheme ought to set out the procedures and priorities as they apply not only to the initial consideration of an applicant's application but also to the treatment of any bid made by the applicant for specific accommodation.

4.24 Experience would suggest that local housing authorities sometimes overlook the fact that, for these purposes, 'procedure' includes 'all aspects of the allocation process, including the persons or descriptions of persons by whom decisions are to be taken'[1]. In short, the statutory requirement is that the published scheme deals with both 'why' and 'how' allocations are made. Obviously, the statements as to who does what in the allocation process should reflect actual practice. In one case, an allocation scheme provided that particular decisions would be taken by the area housing manager and the rehousing manager jointly. A decision later taken by one of those officers, acting alone, was outside the terms of the scheme and was, accordingly, unlawful[2].

[1]   HA 1996, s 166A(1) (England), s 167(1) (Wales) Welsh Code, para 3.6.
[2]   *R (Moore) v Wandsworth London Borough Council* [2012] All ER (D) 66 Jan, (2012) April *Legal Action*, p 46, Admin Ct.

4.25 The courts have not taken an altogether consistent line as to how much *detail*, on the prioritisation of applications or the procedures to be followed in processing them, is required in a local allocation scheme. The range of approaches taken by the courts is illustrated by the following examples:

• A scheme which did 'not explain what criteria apply or indicate that they will be applied' was held to be unlawful in that respect[1].

• An allocation scheme provided for nominations by social services but did not explain what sort of communication from what part of social services would qualify as such a nomination. That was insufficient[2].

• A scheme enabled an applicant to obtain substantially increased points if he was imminently required to give up accommodation leased from the private sector. It wrongly failed to indicate precisely at what stage the extra points would accrue[3].

• A local housing authority had adopted targets for achieving allocations to particular classes of applicant. The targets were not part of the procedure of the scheme, so the scheme did not need to be amended each time they were changed[4].

• On a challenge to the sufficiency of detail in a local housing authority's scheme, in respect of allocation to particular priority groups, a judge said:

> 'The scheme must set out all aspects of the allocation process but it is not necessary to do more than . . . explain what criteria apply to each group and to indicate that an officer will allocate in accordance with those criteria which may be general[5].'

- An allocation scheme which was already 'very long and detailed' did not set out the precise criteria under which applicants in medical need were to be admitted to a particular priority category. That level of detail did not need to be added to the scheme[6].

- A local housing authority operated a policy whereby, at shortlisting stage, bidders from the same bands would have the presence (or otherwise) of a local connection taken into account. The policy was not initially mentioned in the published allocation scheme but was added on a later revision. The court held that the matter was one of minor detail, the omission of which was not unlawful[7].

- It was implicit in a local housing authority's scheme that direct offers would only be made to applicants with at least 120 points. However, it emerged during the hearing that in practice offers would be made to applicants with only 100 points. This was not ascertainable from the scheme and there was nothing in the scheme to indicate what criteria were used to make direct offers. The scheme was unlawful in this regard[8].

[1] *R (Cali, Abdi and Hassan) v Waltham Forest London Borough Council* [2006] EWHC 302 Admin, [2007] HLR 1, Admin Ct.
[2] *R (Yazar) v Southwark London Borough Council* [2008] EWHC 515 (Admin), (2008) May *Legal Action*, p 46, Admin Ct.
[3] *R (Lin) v Barnet London Borough Council* [2007] EWCA Civ 132, [2007] HLR 30, CA.
[4] *R (A) v Lambeth London Borough Council* [2002] EWCA Civ 2084, [2002] HLR 57, CA.
[5] *R (Lynch) v Lambeth London Borough Council* [2006] EWHC 2737 (Admin), [2007] HLR 15, Admin Ct per HHJ Hamilton QC, sitting as a deputy High Court judge, at [51].
[6] *R (Ahmad) v Newham London Borough Council* [2008] EWCA Civ 140, (2008) April *Legal Action*, p 34, CA.
[7] *R (Van Boolen) v Barking & Dagenham London Borough Council* [2009] EWHC 2196 (Admin), (2009) September *Legal Action*, p 34, Admin Ct.
[8] *R (C) v Islington London Borough Council* [2017] EWHC 1288 (Admin), [2017] HLR 32, Admin Ct at [56]–[63].

4.26 A particular issue has been the extent to which the local allocation scheme must be a comprehensive document, containing all aspects and details of the scheme, or whether it can include material by reference to other documents. Some allocation schemes simply set out broad policy statements, unlawfully leaving the mechanics to be detailed in unpublished procedure manuals or staff training materials. However, it seems that if the allocation scheme refers to relevant details to be found in another published document, the failure to include that material in the allocation scheme itself may not be unlawful. In one case, the Introduction to the published scheme said that it had to be read in connection with the annual and mid-year reports made to the council by the cabinet member with responsibility for housing, which were published on the internet. Responding to an assertion that that did not meet the statutory requirements the judge said '[i]t may be cumbersome to have to look at two (and possibly more) documents, but it is not unlawful'[1]. In refusing permission to appeal against that decision, another judge said: 'The mere proposition that it [publication in one place] might be more transparent is not sufficient to establish unlawfulness'[2].

[1] *R (Babakandi) v Westminster City Council* [2011] EWHC 1756 (Admin), (2011) August *Legal Action*, p 40, Admin Ct per Nicol J at [21].

2   R *(Babakandi) v Westminster City Council* [2011] EWCA Civ 1397, (2012) January *Legal Action*, p 21, CA per Sullivan LJ at [5].

DETERMINING PRIORITY FOR ALLOCATION – REASONABLE PREFERENCE CLASSES

4.27 The primary function (and requirement) of a local allocation scheme is that it sets out the local housing authority's priorities in allocating housing accommodation. It represents the local housing authority's policy choices about discrimination between applicants. It sets out which applicants are to have more priority than others and, where priorities are broadly evenly matched, which applicant is to be preferred. The scheme needs to explain to those operating it, or advising about it, the circumstances in which Applicant A will have greater or lesser preference than Applicant B.

4.28 HA 1996, Pt 6, leaves a local housing authority free to adopt its own locally agreed policies and principles, subject to the terms of HA 1996, Pt 6 itself (and to any regulations made under HA 1996, Pt 6)[1]. Of course, although the whole process is one of discrimination about access to services, any unlawful discrimination is to be avoided[2]. The most significant constraint on the local housing authority's freedom to select particular applicants is the requirement that the scheme must be framed to give a preference to those groups of applicants set out in HA 1996, Pt 6.

1   HA 1996, s 166A(11) (England) and s 167(6) (Wales).
2   See **4.210–4.230**.

Giving a 'reasonable preference'

4.29 In relation to prioritisation between applicants, HA 1996, Pt 6, states that every local allocation scheme must be drawn up so as secure a 'reasonable preference' for the groups of people specified in HA 1996, Pt 6[1]. Local housing authorities must design and operate schemes that broadly comply with the statutory list. This does not mean that the local allocation scheme must adopt precisely the same text as that given in HA 1996, Pt 6. All that is required is that the local scheme does actually give a reasonable preference to applicants falling into one or more of the statutory groups. The statutory list contains five broad groups. Each of the five groups is described and discussed in detail later in the chapter[2] after a consideration of what the concept of a 'reasonable' preference entails.

1   HA 1996, s 166A(7) (England) and s 167(3) (Wales) respectively permit the Secretary of State for Communities and Local Government and the Welsh Ministers to specify further groups of people, or to amend or repeal the groups specified in HA 1996, Pt 6. Neither the Secretary of State nor the Welsh Ministers have exercised these powers.
2   See **4.54** et seq.

How much preference is 'reasonable'?

4.30 HA 1996, Pt 6, does not require a local allocation scheme to be framed so as to accord *absolute* preference to those in the listed groups[1]. Local housing authorities need give them only a *'reasonable* preference' in the allocation scheme[2]. The term 'reasonable preference' is not new. In an early case, it was established that it requires:

> ' . . . that positive favour should be shown to applications which satisfy any of the relevant criteria. To use colloquial language they should be given a reasonable head start[3].'

As the Welsh Code puts it, what is important is that an allocation scheme makes a clear distinction between those applicants who fall within the reasonable preference categories and those who do not[4].

[1] *R (Ahmad) v Newham London Borough Council* [2009] UKHL 14, [2009] HLR 41, HL at [18].
[2] HA 1996, s 166A(3) (England) and s 167(2) (Wales); emphasis added by the authors.
[3] *R v Wolverhampton Metropolitan Borough Council ex p Watters* (1997) 29 HLR 931 per Judge LJ at [938].
[4] Welsh Code, para 3.12.

4.31 However, the degree of preference that is reasonable is a matter for the discretion of the local housing authority[1]. Provided that their allocation schemes comply with the broad statutory 'reasonable preference' categories, local housing authorities may otherwise decide for themselves on the principles for determining priorities in the local allocation scheme[2]. In 2009, the House of Lords decided that the amendments made to HA 1996, Pt 6, by the Homelessness Act 2002 had given local housing authorities even greater flexibility than had previously been thought and that the statutory flexibility is such that it would be 'impossible to argue that an authority's allocation scheme is unlawful unless the basis on which it accords priority as between those applicants [in the reasonable preference categories] is irrational'[3].

[1] *R (Lin) v Barnet London Borough Council* [2007] EWCA Civ 132 per Dyson LJ at [28].
[2] HA 1996, s 166A(11) (England), s 167(6) (Wales).
[3] *R (Ahmad) v Newham London Borough Council* [2009] UKHL 14, [2009] HLR 41, HL at [49]. It follows that, whether the cases decided on the pre-amendment terms of HA 1996, Pt 6, had been rightly decided or not, they can no longer be relied upon.

4.32 Nevertheless, despite this wide discretion, it is possible to identify a number of principles governing how reasonable preference is to be given and assessed.

4.33 First, the language of HA 1996, Pt 6, relating to 'reasonable preference' deals with groups of people. It does not address the relative standing of any individual applicants within an allocation scheme precisely because it only requires a 'reasonable preference' to be given to particular groups rather than to specific applicants[1].

[1] *R (Ahmad) v Newham London Borough Council* [2009] UKHL 14, [2009] HLR 41, HL at [15] and [18].

4.34 Second, the obligation is only to give some preference, and preference 'should not be confused with prospects of success'[1]. It would be 'quite possible for a lawful scheme to give reasonable preference to a person within s 167(2)[2] and for that person never to be allocated Pt 6 housing'[3]. A scheme which imposes a points threshold below which an applicant cannot even place a bid, even though he or she is in a reasonable preference category, may not be unlawful[4]. However, a residence requirement which precludes a person entitled to a reasonable preference from accessing the waiting list at all may be unlawful[5].

[1]   *R (Lin) v Barnet London Borough Council* [2007] EWCA Civ 132, [2007] HLR 30, CA per Dyson LJ at [25].
[2]   HA 1996, s 167 now applies only to local housing authorities in Wales. The relevant provision for local housing authorities in England is now HA 1996, s 166A.
[3]   *R (Lin) v Barnet London Borough Council* [2007] EWCA Civ 132, [2007] HLR 30, CA per Dyson LJ at [25].
[4]   *R (Woolfe) v Islington London Borough Council* [2016] EWHC 1907 (Admin), [2016] HLR 42, Admin Ct.
[5]   *R (HA) v Ealing London Borough Council* [2015] EWHC 2375 (Admin), [2016] PTSR 16, Admin Ct.

4.35 Third, HA 1996, Pt 6 prohibits local housing authorities from adopting a scheme which awards *no preference at all* to a person within one of the preference groups unless:

(1)   the applicant is ineligible by reason of his or her immigration status or insufficient residence in the UK[1];

(2)   the applicant is not within a qualifying class (or is within a non-qualifying class) as defined by the local housing authority in England to which the application has been made. The qualifying case must itself, of course, be consistent with the requirement to give the specified groups reasonable preference[2];

(3)   a local housing authority in Wales has decided that the applicant is not eligible on account of his or her past behaviour[3];

(4)   a local housing authority in Wales has decided that the applicant is eligible but has been guilty of 'unacceptable behaviour' within the statutory definition of that term[4]; or

(5)   the applicant is entitled to a preference solely because he or she is in one of the first two reasonable preference categories and that category is only satisfied because of the presence in the applicant's household of a 'restricted person'[5].

[1]   See **3.12–3.75**.
[2]   But see the discussion of this point at **3.136–3.148**.
[3]   See **3.151–3.200**.
[4]   HA 1996, ss 167(2B) to (2D) applying s 160A(8); see **4.150–4.158**.
[5]   HA 1996, s 166A(4) (England) and s 167(2ZA) (Wales). English Code, para 4.6. See HA 1996, s 184(7), H(W)A 2014, s 63(5), **4.149** and **10.47** for the definition of 'restricted person'.

4.36 Fourth, there is no requirement to give equal weight to each of the reasonable preference categories, provided that, overall, reasonable preference has been given to all of them[1].

[1]   English Code, para 4.5.

4.37 Fifth, HA 1996, Pt 6, does not require that people in the reasonable preference groups must be given preference in relation to every property which is let under the scheme. It is the scheme taken as a whole that must give a reasonable preference to the statutory groups. Accordingly, a scheme which enabled a mere 5% of its available properties to be open to bids from transfer applicants who were not in the reasonable preference categories did not fail to give those statutory priority groups a 'reasonable' preference overall[1]. The difficulty is to identify the point at which allocation, to applicants without a reasonable preference, of a higher percentage of properties than 5% would prevent the scheme from giving overall priority to the reasonable preference classes[2]. The Welsh Code suggests that the percentage used by particular local housing authorities is a matter for individual consideration of how to best meet the strategic needs of the area[3].

[1] *R (Ahmad) v Newham London Borough Council* [2009] UKHL 14, [2009] HLR 41, HL at [17]–[21].
[2] In *R (H) v Ealing London Borough Council* [2017] EWCA Civ 1127, [2018] HLR 2, CA an allocation scheme which reserved 20% of the available lettings for 'working households' and 'model tenants' was found to be unlawful. However, it was not challenged on the basis that it breached the obligation to give reasonable preference to the specified groups and therefore there was no discussion of its lawfulness in that respect.
[3] Welsh Code, para 3.10.

4.38 Sixth, the obligation to give reasonable preference is 'a continuing one' and 'in that sense is absolute and required to be complied with at all times'. Nevertheless, 'it would be wrong to assess whether or not it is being complied with by simply taking a snapshot of the operation of the scheme on a particular day or a particular week'[1]. The obligation does not require that reasonable preference is given 'at all times and in relation to all properties': it will be sufficient if reasonable preference is given 'over the course of a reasonable period'[2]. However, this does not mean that a scheme which suspends a reasonable preference group from bidding for a certain period of time will be lawful. In *R (Alemi) v Westminster City Council*[3], the local housing authority's scheme provided that applicants to whom the main housing duty under HA 1996, s 193(2)[4] had been accepted were suspended from bidding for social housing for 12 months. An argument that the scheme was lawful if assessed over a reasonable period of time was unsuccessful: the reasonable period proposed was 'totally arbitrary' and 'unrelated to the statutory purpose of *allocating* social housing'[5]. Further, the effect of the provision was that the applicant was wholly excluded from the potential of being allocated social housing for 12 months and therefore she had no preference at all in that period[6].

[1] *R (Babakandi) v Westminster City Council* [2011] EWCA Civ 1397, (2012) January *Legal Action*, p 21 at [3]–[4].
[2] *R (Babakandi) v Westminster City Council* [2011] EWCA Civ 1397, (2012) January *Legal Action*, p 21 at [22].
[3] [2015] EWHC 1765 (Admin), [2015] PTSR 1339, Admin Ct.
[4] See **16.94–16.199**.
[5] [2015] EWHC 1765 (Admin), [2015] PTSR 1339, Admin Ct at [31].
[6] [2015] EWHC 1765 (Admin) at [32].

4.39 Seventh, it is not necessary for an allocation scheme to provide a mechanism for cumulative or composite assessments[1] or, put another way, for a scheme to 'afford greater priority to applicants who fall within more than one reasonable preference category (cumulative preference) over those who have reasonable preference on a single, non-urgent basis'[2]. While the statutory provisions[3] enable such an approach to be adopted, they do not require it[4]. However, the local housing authority must still consider the needs of all household members[5].

1   *R (Ahmad) v Newham London Borough Council* [2009] UKHL 14, [2009] HLR 41, HL; see 5.38–5.42.
2   English Code, para 4.5; Welsh Code, para 3.10.
3   Particularly the sentence in HA 1996, s 166A(3) (England) and s 167(2) (Wales) starting 'The scheme may also be framed . . . ' when read with the opening words of s 166A(5) (England) and s 167(2A) (Wales).
4   *R (Ahmad) v Newham London Borough Council* [2009] UKHL 14, [2009] HLR 41, HL at [41].
5   *Complaint against Thanet District Council*, 15000234, 3 August 2016, (2016) October *Legal Action*, p 41.

Reasonable preference: formulating the scheme

4.40 Notwithstanding the degree of flexibility thus permitted, local housing authorities must actually identify the criteria for determining priorities within their allocation schemes[1]. They will have to decide, for example, how to choose between applicants who fall into the different 'reasonable preference' categories and also how to organise people within each of those different groups (whether according to their comparative need or according to some other locally adopted criteria). The scheme will also need to address the priority to be given to applicants who are not in the reasonable preference categories at all. A scheme which did not clearly identify and define the criteria for awarding a reasonable preference was held not to comply with the requirements of HA 1996, Pt 6[2]. Moreover, as one judge has also said:

' . . . it goes without saying that whatever criteria are adopted must be rational and must be related to the particular policy and housing needs . . . [3].'

1   HA 1996, s 166A(1) (England), s 167(1) (Wales); Welsh Code, para 3.14.
2   *R (Cali) v Waltham Forest London Borough Council* [2006] EWHC 302 (Admin), [2007] HLR 1, Admin Ct at [31].
3   *R (George) v Hammersmith & Fulham London Borough Council* [2012] EWHC 2369 (Admin), (2012) June *Legal Action*, p 36 per Deputy Judge Catchpole QC at [19]. Note that permission to appeal to the Court of Appeal was later granted in this case – see [2012] EWCA Civ 1768, (2013) March *Legal Action*, p 20 – but the appeal did not proceed to a hearing.

4.41 Beyond the requirement to frame an allocation scheme to reflect the statutory list of reasonable preference groups, local housing authorities are permitted a good deal of autonomy to decide the procedures and principles they wish to apply locally. HA 1996, Pt 6 does, however, offer a steer towards other specific factors. Local housing authorities are, for example, expressly permitted to give 'additional preference' to people with 'urgent housing needs' who fall within any of the reasonable preference categories[1], and to take account of such an applicant's financial resources, his or her behaviour (good or bad), any local connection with a particular local housing authority's area, or any other matter[2]. Other distinguishing factors may include:

- Nature of tenure: a scheme which prioritised overcrowded applicants living in social housing over overcrowded applicants living in private rented sector housing was not unlawful[3].
- Length of time the applicant has been waiting for an allocation[4]: in *R (Ahmad) v Newham London Borough Council*[5] the House of Lords was persuaded that a scheme based on banding together those appli-

cants in *any* of the reasonable preference categories and then prioritising between them by reference to waiting-time had the merit of being 'quantifiable, transparent and hard to manipulate'[6], in contrast to schemes for the affording of relative priority by case-by-case assessment of housing need reflected in the awarding of points.

1 HA 1996, s 166A(3) (England), s 167(2) (Wales); see **4.113–4.118**.
2 HA 1996, s 166A(5) (England), s 167(2A) (Wales); see **4.124–4.144**.
3 *R (Fartun Osman) v Harrow London Borough Council* [2017] EWHC 274 (Admin). At the time of writing there was an outstanding application for permission to appeal against this decision.
4 Welsh Code, para 3.14.
5 *R (Ahmad) v Newham London Borough Council* [2009] UKHL 14, [2009] HLR 41, HL.
6 *R (Ahmad) v Newham London Borough Council* [2009] UKHL 14, [2009] HLR 41, HL at [52].

4.42 'Need' for housing which brings an applicant within any of the reasonable preference categories must, of course, be assessed objectively by the local housing authority. Schemes which rely upon applicants assessing their own needs have been held to be unlawful in that they run the risk of encouraging applicants to assess themselves as requiring accommodation which would in fact be unsuitable for them, in the hope of benefiting from a shorter waiting period for less desirable accommodation[1].

1 *R (A) v Lambeth London Borough Council, R (Lindsay) v Lambeth London Borough Council* [2002] EWCA Civ 1084, [2002] HLR 57, CA and *R (Cali) v Waltham Forest London Borough Council* [2006] EWHC 302 (Admin), [2007] HLR 1, Admin Ct.

4.43 An allocation scheme could therefore be based on awarding points to applicants, or grouping applicants into bands, or both. Either method should accord some preference to those in the 'reasonable preference' categories. In some allocation schemes, a combination of the two methods is used. The most straightforward scheme of allocation, strict date order for all applicants, simply cannot work in the modern statutory framework, which requires some classes of applicants to be given a reasonable preference over others.

4.44 In a *points-based scheme*, points could be awarded to reflect different categories of need, for example for medical and welfare needs, overcrowding, etc, and further points may reflect the length of time that an applicant has been waiting for accommodation after having been accepted onto the scheme. Some have suggested that points-based systems can be complex, lacking in transparency and difficult to understand. Local housing authorities retaining such schemes have previously been encouraged to consider simplifying them[1].

1 English (2009) Code, para 74. Reproduced in APPENDIX 1 to the second edition of this book.

4.45 If a *banding system* is adopted, applicants within each band may be prioritised by points and/or by date order, reflecting the degree of their need and/or their waiting time. The now withdrawn English (2009) Code strongly suggested this as a preferred model but the present guidance for England does not express any preference for any particular method of identifying relative priorities[1].

1 English (2009) Code, paras 70–73. Reproduced in APPENDIX 1 to the second edition of this book.

4.46 Self-evidently, an allocation scheme that placed in the same band or group those applicants who were entitled to 'reasonable preference' and those who were not so entitled, and then treated the non-reasonable preference applicants equally – or even more favourably - would be unlawful[1]. A local housing authority must be able to distinguish between applicants who are entitled to the benefit of the 'reasonable preference' categories and those who are not[2]. A scheme which gave existing secure tenants seeking a transfer an additional 100 points each, when not all of them were entitled to a reasonable preference, was held to be unlawful because it artificially raised the points threshold to the detriment of applicants who were not existing tenants and were entitled to a statutory preference[3].

1   *R (A) v Lambeth London Borough Council, R (Lindsay) v Lambeth London Borough Council* [2002] EWCA Civ 1084, [2002] HLR 57, CA.
2   English Code, para 4.5, Welsh Code, para 3.12.
3   *R (Lin) v Barnet London Borough Council* [2006] EWHC 1041 (Admin), [2006] HLR 440, Admin Ct; Barnet London Borough Council successfully appealed to the Court of Appeal *(R (Lin) v Barnet London Borough Council* [2007] EWCA Civ 132, [2007] HLR 30, CA) but not on that point.

4.47 An emphasis on prioritisation by combinations of 'reasonable prefer-ence' and the assessment of a particular household's 'need'[1] can produce bizarre results. An applicant could be ceaselessly moving, yo-yo fashion, up and down the list of those eligible (and/or qualified) for an allocation as his or her own housing circumstances and needs change and as others apply for an allocation.

1   HA 1996, s 166A(3) (England) and s 167(2) (Wales).

4.48 For example, a household with no children may find itself almost at the top of the list of those awaiting a bed-sit or other small unit of accommoda-tion, only to be taken towards the bottom of the list of those waiting for larger accommodation when a child arrives. One local housing authority's scheme survived a challenge to its provision that, where the applicants' needs had changed, so that they required a two-bedroom rather than a one-bedroom unit, they should be put at the bottom of the two-bedroom property list, and lose their points awarded for the time that they had waited on the one-bedroom property list[1]. Another local housing authority's scheme had the same effect, by re-adjusting a registration date to reflect the date of a move to a new priority band, even when the extent of accommodation needed had decreased. It was nevertheless lawful[2]. The judge said:

> 'The final resting place of the submissions advanced on behalf of Ms Kabashi was by reference to *Yemlahi*. In the light of *Ahmad*, however, it is no longer tenable to contend that a scheme that provides for the alteration of effective dates when an applicant up-sizes would be rational but which does not provide for such an alteration is irrational[3].'

1   *R (Yemlahi) v Lambeth London Borough Council* [2002] EWHC 1187 (Admin), (2002) August *Legal Action*, p 31, Admin Ct. The court held that either scenario created injustice: if the applicants had been placed towards the top of the list for two-bedroom properties (reflecting their waiting time on the list for one-bedroom properties), those below the applicants who had a longer standing need for two-bedroom properties would rightly feel aggrieved.

2 *R (Kabashi) v Redbridge London Borough Council* [2009] EWHC 2984 (Admin), (2010) October *Legal Action*, p 32, Admin Ct.
3 At para [19].

4.49 Similarly, in any scheme based on housing need, a household provided with temporary accommodation under HA 1996, Pt 7[1] (Homelessness: England)[2] or H(W)A 2014, Pt 2 (Homelessness: Wales)[3] may find that the prospects of securing an early allocation under HA 1996, Pt 6 actually diminish if the household is moved to a higher standard of self-contained temporary accommodation. In one case considered by the LGO[4], a homeless couple rejected temporary accommodation from the local housing authority precisely because its superior quality was such that they would fall into a lower priority category under the allocation scheme if they accepted it[5].

1 As amended by the Homelessness Reduction Act 2017 (HRA 2017) for applications for homelessness assistance made to local housing authorities in England on or after 3 April 2018.
2 See CHAPTER 16.
3 See CHAPTER 17.
4 As of 19 June 2017, the Local Government and Social Care Ombudsman.
5 *Complaint against Hounslow London Borough Council*, 14 April 2009, No 07/A/14215, (2009) June *Legal Action*, p 34.

Reasonable preference and legitimate expectation

4.50 There is one form of prioritisation not accorded by HA 1996, Pt 6, and which does not turn on 'need'. It arises where applicants have been given a 'legitimate expectation' that they will be allocated local housing authority tenancies, or nominated to a private registered provider or registered social landlord[1].

1 The issue of 'legitimate expectation' arises where a person is, contrary to his or her expectations, deprived: ' . . . of some benefit or advantage which either (i) he had in the past been permitted by the decision-maker to enjoy and which he can legitimately expect to be permitted to continue to do until there has been communicated to him some rational grounds for withdrawing it on which he has been given an opportunity to comment; or (ii) he has received assurance from the decision-maker that they will not be withdrawn without giving him first an opportunity of advancing reasons for contending that they should not be withdrawn': *Council of Civil Service Unions v Minister for the Civil Service* [1985] AC 374, HL per Lord Diplock at 408. See also *R v North and East Devon Health Authority ex p Coughlan* [2001] QB 213, CA, and *R (Bhatt Murphy (a firm)) v The Independent Assessor* [2008] EWCA Civ 755, CA. For a discussion of 'legitimate expectation' in an allocation context see *R v Brent London Borough Council ex p Jerke* CO/2069/97 (unreported) 8 May 1998, QBD; *R v Lambeth London Borough Council ex p Trabi* (1998) 30 HLR 975, QBD; *R (Tout a Tout) v Haringey London Borough Council* [2012] EWHC 873 (Admin), (2012) May *Legal Action*, p 39, Admin Ct; and *R (Alansi) v Newham London Borough Council* [2013] EWHC 3722 (Admin), [2014] HLR 25, Admin Ct.

4.51 Such an expectation may be difficult to establish. No 'legitimate expectation' argument is likely to succeed simply where there has been a failure in communication[1] or where the applicant has not relied on the representation[2]. Even where there has been a clear and unambiguous representation on which the applicant has relied, that will not be sufficient: the question is whether frustrating that expectation would be so unfair that to take a different course would be an abuse of power[3]. Findings that the local housing authority's conduct amounts or would amount to an abuse of power are likely to be rare. Decisions about housing allocations have been held to fall within the realm of 'macro' policy making where:

> ' . . . the court should be cautious before substituting its own judgment for that of the democratically elected local authority about what is the appropriate balance to strike and when and to what extent it is proportionate to affect individual interests adversely in striking that balance[4].'

[1] *R (Tout a Tout) v Haringey London Borough Council* [2012] EWHC 873 (Admin), (2012) May *Legal Action*, p 34, Admin Ct at [24].
[2] *Kingsley Edward v Royal Borough of Greenwich* [2017] EWHC 1112 (Admin).
[3] *R (Alansi) v Newham London Borough Council* [2013] EWHC 3722 (Admin), [2014] HLR 25, Admin Ct at [35].
[4] *R (Alansi) v Newham London Borough Council* [2013] EWHC 3722 (Admin), [2014] HLR 25, Admin Ct at [50].

4.52 However, the possibility of such an expectation being generated cannot be entirely ruled out. A 'legitimate expectation' of this type arose where homeless applicants, who had been accepted as such under the Housing Act 1985, Pt 3, were told that they would be given a local housing authority or housing association tenancy in performance of the homelessness duty[1]. It may also arise where a local housing authority has announced a policy of giving carers the right to take over tenancies on the death of tenants for whom they were caring.

[1] The facts of *R (Bibi and Al-Nashed) v Newham London Borough Council* [2001] EWCA Civ 495, (2001) 33 HLR 84, CA.

4.53 The local housing authority must therefore make provision for such an eventuality in its allocation scheme so that such applicants receive points or are placed in a specific band in order to take account of those expectations[1]. Of course, an allocation scheme may subsequently be altered (provided the procedures described above, for amending a scheme, are properly followed) so as to remove a preference or priority that a particular applicant or class of applicants had a 'legitimate expectation' of receiving[2].

[1] *R (Bibi and Al-Nashed) v Newham London Borough Council* [2001] EWCA Civ 495, (2001) 33 HLR 84, CA; *R (Ibrahim) v Redbridge London Borough Council* [2002] EWHC 2756 (Admin), (2003) February *Legal Action*, p 35, Admin Ct; and *R (Bibi) v Newham London Borough Council* [2003] EWHC 1860 (Admin), (2003) September *Legal Action*, at p 28, Admin Ct.
[2] *R (Alansi) v Newham London Borough Council* [2013] EWHC 3722 (Admin), [2014] HLR 25, Admin Ct.

The 'reasonable preference' groups

4.54 Five groups of people must be accorded a 'reasonable preference' in housing allocation schemes framed under HA 1996, Pt 6. They are:

(1)   people who are 'homeless', within the meaning of either HA 1996, Pt 7[1], (England) or H(W)A 2014, Pt 2 (Wales)[2];
(2)   people who are owed a particular statutory duty by any local housing authority under certain provisions of homelessness legislation[3];
(3)   people occupying insanitary or overcrowded housing or otherwise living in unsatisfactory housing conditions;

(4)   people who need to move on medical or welfare grounds, including (in England) grounds relating to a disability[4]; and

(5)   people who need to move to a particular locality in the district of the local housing authority, where failure to meet that need would cause hardship, to themselves or to others[5].

[1]   As amended by HRA 2017 for applications for homelessness assistance made to local housing authorities in England on or after 3 April 2018.

[2]   See CHAPTER 10.

[3]   In England, the relevant duties are those set out in HA 1996, s 190(2) (as amended by HRA 2017, s 5(5) for applications for homelessness assistance made to local housing authorities in England on or after 3 April 2018), s 193(2) and s 195(2) (as amended by HRA 2017, s 4(2) for applications for homelessness assistance made to local housing authorities in England on or after 3 April 2018). The equivalent duties under the Housing Act 1985 (HA 1985) were set out in HA 1985 s 65(2) and s 68(2)). HA 1996, s 190(2) and s 193(2) contain the accommodation duties owed to applicants with a priority need which arise once the HA 1996, s 189B(2) relief duty (as inserted by HRA 2017, s 5(2) for applications for homelessness assistance made to local housing authorities in England on or after 3 April 2018) has come to an end. HA 1996, s 195(2) contains the prevention duty owed to all applicants who are eligible and threatened with homelessness. See CHAPTERS 15 AND 16. In Wales, this reasonable preference category covers 'people who are owed any duty by a local housing authority under H(W)Act 2014, ss 66, 73 or 75': HA 1996, s 167(2)(b) as amended by H(W)A 2014, s 100 and Sch 3, para 3. See CHAPTER 17.

[4]   HA 1996, s 166A(3)(d) (England) and s 167(2)(d) (Wales) prospectively amended by Housing Act 2004, s 223, adding '(including grounds relating to a disability)' but yet to be brought into force in Wales.

[5]   HA 1996, s 166A(3) (England), s 167(2) (Wales).

4.55 The list may be extended or reduced by ministerial regulations without the need for primary legislation[1]. No such regulations have been made since that power was enacted.

[1]   HA 1996, s 166A(7) (England), s 167(3) (Wales).

4.56 Each of the present five categories entitled to 'reasonable preference' requires detailed and careful consideration (offered in the next sections of this chapter) but it will be readily appreciated that some of the categories are very broadly expressed. The result is that a huge number of applicants will be covered by at least one 'reasonable preference' category. In 2016–17 there were 479,000 households on local housing authority waiting lists in England who were within those categories[1]. The largest reasonable preference group was 'People occupying insanitary or overcrowded housing or otherwise living in unsatisfactory housing conditions', which covered 250,600 households. The second largest group was 'People who need to move on medical or welfare grounds, including grounds relating to a disability', which covered 108,900 households. These groups have been the largest and second largest groups since 2013[2]. The reasonable preference category applicants therefore formed a little under half of the total of 1.16 million households on local housing authority waiting lists in England but that proportion varies wildly between regions and particular local authorities. In some metropolitan areas, and in particular in inner London, almost all applicants qualifying for consideration for an allocation are likely to be in one – or several – of the reasonable preference categories.

[1]   *Local authority housing statistics: year ending March 2017* (MHCLG, January 2018), p 7.

²   *Local authority housing statistics: year ending March 2017* (MHCLG January 2018), p 8 and chart 5.

4.57 A person who comes within a 'reasonable preference' category may, if the local scheme so provides, obtain 'additional preference' if they have 'urgent housing needs'¹.

¹   HA 1996, s 166A(3). See **4.113–4.118**.

People who are 'homeless'

4.58 'Homelessness'¹ is a concept defined in England by HA 1996, Pt 7² and in Wales by H(W)A 2014, Pt 2³. Under those definitions, a person is homeless if he or she has no accommodation available for his or her occupation, in the UK or elsewhere, which he or she is entitled to occupy:

(1)   by virtue of an interest in it;
(2)   because of an order of a court;
(3)   by an express or implied licence to occupy;
(4)   by virtue of an enactment or rule of law giving him or her the right to remain in occupation; or
(5)   by reason of a restriction on the right of another person to obtain possession⁴.

¹   HA 1996, s 166A(3)(a) (England), s 167(2)(a) (Wales).
²   As amended by HRA 2017 for applications for homelessness assistance made to local housing authorities in England on or after 3 April 2018.
³   HA 1996, ss 175–177 and H(W)A 2014, ss 55–58; see Chapter 10 of this book.
⁴   HA 1996, s 175(1) (England), H(W)A 2014, s 55(1) (Wales).

4.59 A person who has somewhere to live is therefore 'homeless' *unless* he or she has at least one of these forms of entitlement to occupy – so a person living in a squat is 'homeless'.

4.60 A person is also homeless if he or she has a right to occupy accommodation but cannot secure entry to it, or it is not available, or it is not reasonable for him or her to continue to occupy it¹. Accommodation is only regarded as 'available' if it is available to be occupied by all the members of the applicant's family who normally reside with him or her, and also by any other person who might reasonably be expected to reside with him or her². Occupiers of caravans, mobile homes, and houseboats are homeless if they have no place where they are permitted both to place and to reside in their vehicle or vessel³. In October 2017, the UK Government stated its belief that people who were living in a refuge to escape domestic abuse were homeless, as it would not be reasonable for them to continue to occupy that accommodation on a long-term basis⁴. It proposed to issue guidance making clear the circumstances in which local housing authorities would be expect to apply this category to victims of domestic abuse who were living in refuges⁵. This guidance if issued will apply to local housing authorities in England only.

¹   HA 1996, s 175(2)(a) and (3) (England), H(W)A 2014, s 55(2)(a) and (3) (Wales).
²   HA 1996, s 176 (England), H(W)A 2014, s 56 (Wales).
³   HA 1996, s 175(2)(b) (England), H(W)A 2014, s 55(2)(b) (Wales).

4 *Improving Access to Social Housing for Victims of Domestic Abuse: Consultation* (DCLG, October 2017). This drew on a proposition well-established from case-law: *Birmingham City Council v Ali* [2009] UKHL 36, [2009] 1 WLR 1506, HL.
5 *Improving Access to Social Housing for Victims of Domestic Abuse: Consultation* (DCLG, October 2017).

4.61 To fall within the definition of 'homeless', an applicant need not have made an application for homelessness assistance to any local housing authority, let alone have received a decision on such an application. Indeed, the Welsh Code explicitly states that in no circumstances should allocation practices encourage the view that people have to apply as homeless to the local housing authority in order to obtain a tenancy of social housing[1]. The assessment of whether the applicant is 'homeless' will need to be made by the local housing authority to which the application for an allocation has been directed[2]. A person who has already applied to a local housing authority as 'homeless', has been accepted as such and has then been provided with accommodation in compliance with that local housing authority's duty may in consequence have ceased to be 'homeless' (and thus would normally fall within the second reasonable preference category – category (2) – which specifically deals with those formerly homeless persons owed housing duties)[3]. In one case, however, it was rightly conceded that a person provided with interim accommodation by a local housing authority pending the determination of an application for homelessness assistance remained 'homeless', for the purposes of this reasonable preference category, while in that accommodation[4].

1 Welsh Code, para 12.20.
2 An applicant for social housing accommodation who gives the local housing authority sufficient reason to believe that she or he may be homeless must also be dealt with under the homelessness provisions in HA 1996, Pt 7 (England) (as amended by HRA 2017 for applications for homelessness assistance made to local housing authorities in England on or after 3 April 2018) or H(W)A 2014, Pt 2 (Wales). See **8.69**.
3 See **4.67–4.79**.
4 *R (Alam) v Tower Hamlets London Borough Council* [2009] EWHC 44 (Admin), (2009) March *Legal Action*, p 24, Admin Ct.

4.62 To obtain a 'reasonable preference' under the 'homeless' category, applicants need not have a 'priority need'[1]. Nor should the local housing authority consider whether or not applicants have become homeless intentionally[2]. These issues are relevant only to the question of what further duty, if any, is owed following the end of the HA 1996, s 189B(2)[3] relief duty[4]. Regardless of priority need or intentional homelessness, all homeless people fall within this reasonable preference category[5] – even those who are not entitled to, for example, the final main housing duty under the statutory provisions for homelessness assistance because they have no priority need[6].

1 English Code, para 4.4(a). See Chapter 12 of this book for the definition of 'priority need'.
2 English Code, para 4.4(a). See Chapter 13 of this book for the definition of 'becoming homeless intentionally'.
3 As inserted by HRA 2017, s 5(2) for applications for homelessness assistance made to local housing authorities in England on or after 3 April 2018.
4 Although where there is reason to believe an applicant may have a priority need (and may be homeless and eligible for assistance), the local housing authority will be under a duty to provide interim accommodation: HA 1996, s 188 (as amended by HRA 2017, s 5(4) for applications for homelessness assistance made to local housing authorities in England on or after 3 April 2018) and H(W)A 2014, s 68.

⁵ Applicants who are 'threatened with homelessness' (defined in HA 1996, s 175(4) and (5) (England) (as amended by HRA 2017, s 1(2) and (3) for applications for homelessness assistance made to local housing authorities in England on or after 3 April 2018) and H(W)A 2014, s 55(4)) will not fall within the category until they are actually homeless.

⁶ *R (Alam) v Tower Hamlets London Borough Council* [2009] EWHC (Admin) 44, (2009) March *Legal Action*, p 24, Admin Ct.

4.63 Precisely because statutory homelessness duties provide a safety net to pick up and accommodate those who are in priority need and are unintentionally homeless, this first category of 'reasonable preference' works to ensure that all *other* homeless people also secure a reasonable preference in allocation: those other homeless people being fit and healthy individuals, couples without children, those who have become homeless intentionally, etc.

4.64 The policy behind HA 1996, Pt 6, is therefore unashamedly to ensure that every allocation scheme is open to, and gives preference to, those who are homeless for any reason and in any circumstances. It is intended to 'include rough sleepers and all others who do not have a home, for whatever reason'¹.

¹ *Hansard*, HL Deb, vol 630, ser 6, col 1013 (15 January 2002), Lord Falconer.

4.65 Indeed, in Wales, the statutory guidance goes further than a strict reading of HA 1996, Pt 6, requires and suggests that local housing authorities define homelessness for these purposes as arising 'where a person lacks accommodation or where their tenure is not secure'¹. This approach, unlike the statutory definition, includes persons who are threatened with homelessness and those who have no suitable alternative accommodation, whether they are leaving institutions, required to leave by family or friends or due to relationship breakdown, or facing a possession order². When deciding whether or not a person is 'homeless' for these purposes, Welsh local housing authorities must have regard to the Welsh Code's more generous approach, although it is expressly recognised to be guidance which is 'broader' than the legal definition³.

¹ Welsh Code, para 5.22.
² Welsh Code, para 5.22, giving examples of people who are living in insecure/temporary housing, are subject to possession proceedings, or are under the threat of eviction, as people whose tenure is not secure.
³ Welsh Code, para 5.22. HA 1996, s 167(2)(a) (Wales) provides that to get within the first category of 'reasonable preference' the person must be homeless 'within the meaning of' H(W)A 2014, Pt 2.

4.66 A person in this first 'reasonable preference' category may, if the local scheme so provides, also obtain 'additional preference' if his or her housing needs are 'urgent'¹ or if he or she also falls into another of the preference categories². A person who would otherwise be in this first 'reasonable preference' category will not in fact be entitled to benefit from it if the only reason he or she comes within it is because regard has been had to a 'restricted person' in determining his or her application³. The remaining four categories deal with applicants who already have accommodation.

¹ See **4.113–4.118**.
² Although this is not mandatory: see **4.39**.
³ HA 1996, s 166A(4) (England), s 167(2ZA) (Wales). For more on 'restricted person' see **4.148–4.149**.

People who are owed certain homelessness duties

4.67 This category[1] encompasses applicants for an allocation of social housing who have already applied to a local housing authority for homelessness assistance and have received a decision that a local housing authority owes them a relevant duty. The relevant duties are specified differently in England and in Wales.

---

[1] HA 1996, s 166A(3)(b) (England), s 167(2)(b) (Wales).

4.68 In England, the relevant duties are the following duties as set out in HA 1996, Pt 7[1]:

(1) The **main housing duty** (in HA 1996, s 193(2))[2]. Prior to its amendment by the Homelessness Reduction Act 2017 (HRA 2017)[3], this applied where a person was homeless, eligible, had a priority need, and did not become homeless intentionally. As amended[4], it applies where a person is homeless, eligible, has a priority need, did not become homeless intentionally, and in respect of whom the local housing authority's relief duty under HA, s 189B(2)[5], has come to an end[6].

(2) The **prevention duty** (in HA 1996, s 195(2))[7]. Prior to its amendment by the HRA 2017, this was a duty to take reasonable steps to secure that accommodation did not cease to be available for the applicant's occupation. It applied to applicants who were eligible, threatened with homelessness, had a priority need and did not become threatened with homelessness intentionally. As amended[8], it is a duty to take reasonable steps to help *the applicant* to secure that accommodation does not cease to be available for his or her occupation. It applies to all those who are threatened with homeless and eligible. The requirements for priority need and to have been threatened with homelessness unintentionally have been dispensed with.

(3) The **duty to persons who became homeless intentionally** (in HA 1996, s 190(2))[9]. Prior to its amendment by the HRA 2017, this was owed to a person who was homeless, eligible, had a priority need, and became homeless intentionally. As amended[10], it applies to an applicant who is homeless, eligible, has a priority need, became homeless intentionally, and in respect of whom the local housing authority's relief duty under HA, s 189B(2)[11], has come to an end[12].

---

[1] As amended by HRA 2017 for applications for homelessness assistance made to local housing authorities in England on or after 3 April 2018. Pursuant to HA 1996, s 166A(3), reasonable preference also applies to applicants owed duties under the Housing Act 1985, s 65(2) and s 68(2): these sections were repealed by HA 1996, Sch 19, para 1 and are unlikely to be of any practical relevance.

[2] See **16.94–16.199**.

[3] Which came into force for applications for homelessness assistance made to local housing authorities in England on or after 3 April 2018.

[4] By HRA 2017, s 5(7) for applications for homelessness assistance made to local housing authorities in England on or after 3 April 2018.

[5] As inserted by HRA, s 5(2) for applications for homelessness assistance made to local housing authorities in England on or after 3 April 2018. See **15.138–15.195**.

[6] HA 1996, s 193(1) as amended by HRA 2017, s 5(7) for applications for homelessness assistance made to local housing authorities in England on or after 3 April 2018. However, the main housing duty under HA 1996, s 193(2) will not apply where the applicant, having been informed of the consequences of refusal and of his or her right to request a review of the suitability of the accommodation, refuses a 'final accommodation offer' or a 'final Pt 6 offer':

HA 1996, s 193(1A) (as amended by HRA 2017, s 7(2) for applications for homelessness assistance made to local housing authorities in England on or after 3 April 2018) and s 193A(1) and (3) (as inserted by HRA 2017, s 7(1) for applications for homelessness assistance made to local housing authorities in England on or after 3 April 2018). A 'final accommodation offer' is defined by HA 1996, s 193A(4) and a 'final Pt 6 offer' is defined by HA 1996, s 193A(5). See **15.195**. It will also not apply where a local housing authority has given notice to the applicant under HA 1996, s 193B(2) that they consider that the applicant has deliberately and unreasonably refused to take any step under HA 1996, s 189A (as inserted by HRA 2017, s 3(1) for applications for homelessness assistance made to local housing authorities in England on or after 3 April 2018) that he or she had agreed to take to secure suitable accommodation or that the local housing authority had considered it would be reasonable to require the applicant to take to secure suitable accommodation: HA 1996, s 193(1A) (as amended by HRA 2017, s 7(2) for applications for homelessness assistance made to local housing authorities in England on or after 3 April 2018) and s 193C(1) and (4) (as inserted by HRA 2017, s 7(1) for applications for homelessness assistance made to local housing authorities in England on or after 3 April 2018). See **15.195**.

7 See **15.87–15.137**.
8 By HRA 2017, s 4(2), for applications for homelessness assistance made to local housing authorities in England on or after 3 April 2018.
9 See **16.81–16.93**.
10 By HRA 2017, s 5(5) for applications for homelessness assistance made to local housing authorities in England on or after 3 April 2018.
11 As inserted by HRA 2017, s 5(2) for applications for homelessness assistance made to local housing authorities in England on or after 3 April 2018. See **15.138–15.95**.
12 This reasonable preference category used to include applicants who were homeless, did not have a priority need, and had not become homeless intentionally, and in respect of whom the local housing authority had decided to exercise its power under HA 1996, s 192(3) to provide accommodation. However, the section containing this power was repealed by HRA 2017, s 5(6) for applications for homelessness assistance made to local housing authorities in England on or after 3 April 2018.

4.69 In Wales, the relevant duties are the following duties as set out in H(W)A 2014, Pt 2:

(1) the relief duty (in H(W)A 2014, s 73) to help to secure that suitable accommodation is available for a person who is homeless and eligible[1]; or

(2) the housing duty (in H(W)A 2014, s 75) to help some of those persons previously owed the s 73 duty for whom that duty ended in circumstances described in ss 74(2) or (3)[2]; or

(3) the prevention duty (in H(W)A 2014, s 66) to help to secure that suitable accommodation does not cease to be available for occupation by a person who is threatened with homelessness and eligible[3].

1 See **17.73–17.117**.
2 See **17.146–17.188**.
3 See **17.45–17.72**.

4.70 By definition, these applicants for social housing allocation must have made applications for homelessness assistance, and have received decisions that a duty of the prescribed type is owed to them. The duty need not be owed by the same local housing authority as the local housing authority to which the applicant is applying for an allocation. So an applicant who has applied as homeless to District A, and has been placed by that local housing authority, pursuant to one of the prescribed duties, in District B might wish to apply for an allocation to the local housing authorities for both Districts A and B. He or she will have an entitlement to 'reasonable preference' in both the local housing authorities' schemes.

4.71 It must be noted that the terms of this second category of 'reasonable preference' are very tightly drawn. They certainly do *not* cover all applicants who have applied to a local housing authority as homeless, nor all of those who have benefited from a duty under HA 1996, Pt 7[1] or H(W)A 2014, Pt 2. For example, the following persons who have made applications for homelessness assistance to local housing authorities in England, and are now applicants for an allocation of social housing, would fall outside the second of the 'reasonable preference' categories because they are not owed one of the prescribed statutory homelessness duties:

- people provided with interim accommodation because there is reason to believe they may be homeless, eligible, and have a priority need[2];
- people provided with accommodation pending a review of an unfavourable decision or pending an appeal[3];
- people accommodated pending a local connection referral[4];
- people who are not eligible for homelessness assistance[5];
- people who are owed the HA 1996, s 189B(2)[6] relief duty[7]; and
- people who are owed the HA 1996, s 193C(4)[8] final accommodation duty[9].

[1] As amended by HRA 2017 for applications for homelessness assistance made to local housing authorities in England on or after 3 April 2018.

[2] HA 1996, s 188(1). See **16.37–16.46**. They would still be 'homeless' and entitled to a reasonable preference under the first 'reasonable preference' category: *R (Alam) v Tower Hamlets London Borough Council* [2009] EWHC 44 (Admin), (2009) March *Legal Action*, p 24, Admin Ct.

[3] HA 1996, ss 188(3) and 204(4). See **16.233–16.257** and **16.258–16.277**.

[4] HA 1996, ss 199A(2) and 200(1). See **16.217–16.232**.

[5] HA 1996, s 185. See CHAPTER **11**.

[6] As inserted by HRA 2017, s 5(2) for applications for homelessness assistance made to local housing authorities in England on or after 3 April 2018.

[7] This is a duty owed to an applicant for homelessness assistance to a local housing authority in England who is homeless and eligible. The duty requires the local housing authority to take reasonable steps to help the applicant to secure that suitable accommodation becomes available for his or her occupation for at least six months. See **15.138–15.195**.

[8] As inserted by HRA 2017, s 7(1) for applications for homelessness assistance made to local housing authorities in England on or after 3 April 2018.

[9] This is a duty owed to an applicant for homelessness assistance to a local housing authority in England who is homeless and eligible, who has a priority need, and who did not become homeless intentionally, but in respect of whom the HA 1996, s 189B(2) relief duty (as inserted by HRA 2017, s 5(2) for applications for homelessness assistance made to local housing authorities in England on or after 3 April 2018) ended pursuant to the local housing authority giving the applicant a notice under HA 1996, s 193B (as inserted by HRA 2017, s 7(1) for applications for homelessness assistance made to local housing authorities in England on or after 3 April 2018). A notice under HA 1996, s 193B may be given where the local housing considers that the applicant has deliberately and unreasonably refused to take any step under HA 1996, s 189A (as inserted by HRA 2017, s 3(1) for applications for homelessness assistance made to local housing authorities in England on or after 3 April 2018) that he or she had agreed to take or that was recorded by the authority as being reasonable for him or her to take to secure accommodation. The duty requires the local housing authority to secure that accommodation is available for occupation by the applicant. See **16.200–16.216**.

4.72 Similarly, in Wales, despite the array of duties that might be owed by a local housing authority to a homeless person under H(W)A 2014, Pt 2[1], it is only the current beneficiaries of the three specific duties identified at **4.69**

above who obtain a 'reasonable preference' under this category.

¹   See Chapter 17.

4.73 Those persons who do not fit into this second 'reasonable preference' category may, depending on their circumstances, fit into the first category, or into one or more of the third to fifth categories¹.

¹   See **4.58–4.66** for the first category and **4.80–4.112** for the third to fifth categories.

4.74 Amendments made by the Localism Act 2011¹ to HA 1996, Pt 7 allow a local housing authority in England to bring to an end the duty owed to an unintentionally homeless person in priority need (the 'main housing duty') by the making of an offer of suitable private rented sector accommodation². A similar provision also allows a local housing authority in Wales to bring to an end the duty owed to an unintentionally homeless person in priority need by the making of an offer of suitable private rented sector accommodation³.

¹   Localism Act 2011, ss 148–149.
²   HA 1996, s 193(7AA). For 'private rented sector offer' see **16.153–16.179**.
³   H(W)A 2014, ss 76(3) and 4). See Chapter 17.

4.75 Several respondents to the November 2010 consultation paper on social housing, issued by the 2010–15 UK Coalition Government, noted that this change could have a considerable impact on social housing allocation to those in this preference category¹. To counter the possibility that some local housing authorities might, in consequence, consider it unnecessary to continue to afford the relevant applicants for homelessness assistance a reasonable preference under this category, the English Code says in terms that the category remains in place 'notwithstanding the amendments to Pt 7 made by the Localism Act'².

¹   *Local decisions: next steps towards a fairer future for social housing: Summary of responses to consultation* (DCLG, February 2011), para 4.34.
²   English Code, para 4.7.

4.76 Of course, the local housing authority is entitled to discriminate (provided it does so lawfully) among those within this reasonable preference category to reflect the particular nature of the homelessness duty owed to the applicant, or the way it is being performed, or the applicant's particular circumstances. For example, an allocation scheme may give a greater degree of preference to an applicant owed the main housing duty than to an applicant owed one of the lesser relevant housing duties.

4.77 An allocation scheme may even draw distinctions, in terms of priority, between applicants owed the same relevant homelessness duty. For example, people owed the main housing duty in England (HA 1996, s 193(2))¹ and who are accommodated in good quality and stable temporary accommodation may be afforded less preference than applicants owed the same duty whose temporary accommodation will shortly become unavailable (eg because the lease from a private landlord is shortly to expire). In one local housing authority's scheme, 10 points were awarded to applicants owed the main housing duty during the period that private sector leased accommodation was provided for them but 300 points were awarded shortly before the termination of their leases to enable the households to compete realistically for allocations at that particular time. That aspect of the scheme was perfectly lawful[2].

1   See **16.94–16.199**.
2   *R (Lin) v Barnet London Borough Council* [2007] EWCA Civ 132, [2007] HLR 30, CA.

4.78 In the same vein, the Welsh Code advises that local housing authorities in Wales which have placed homeless households in private sector leased accommodation should review the circumstances of those households at least annually. Those applicants who wish to move out of the private leased accommodation could be awarded 'full homelessness points' while those content to remain could have such points deferred until the lease expires[1].

1   Welsh Code, paras 3.43–3.44.

4.79 A person who would otherwise be in this second 'reasonable preference' category will not in fact be entitled to benefit from it if the only reason he or she comes within it is because regard has been had to a 'restricted person' in determining the application[1]. Further, an applicant who receives 'reasonable preference' by being in this category remains subject to any other provisions in the local allocation scheme eg may be subject to the deferral of his or her application where suitable offers of accommodation under the allocation scheme have been made but refused[2].

1   HA 1996, s 166A(4) (England), s 167(2ZA) (Wales). For 'restricted person' see **4.148–4.149**.
2   *R (Cranfield-Adams) v Richmond upon Thames London Borough Council* [2012] EWHC 3334 (Admin), (2012) August *Legal Action*, p 27, Admin Ct.

People occupying insanitary or overcrowded housing or otherwise living in unsatisfactory housing conditions

4.80 Nothing in HA 1996, Pt 6, defines the three key adjectives in this 'reasonable preference' category: 'insanitary', 'overcrowded', and 'unsatisfactory'[1]. Nor does HA 1996, Pt 6, provide a direct link to the meanings that those words have in other legislation, even other housing legislation.

1   HA 1996, s 166A(3)(c) (England), s 167(2)(c) (Wales).

4.81 As a result, local housing authorities are largely free to develop, and incorporate into local allocation schemes, their own approach to determining the circumstances in which an applicant would fall into this 'reasonable preference' category.

4.82 The general law governing insanitary conditions, overcrowding, and unsatisfactory housing standards is scattered over a number of statutes. The Environmental Protection Act 1990, Pt 3 is designed to address unhealthy premises. The rules on overcrowding are set out in the Housing Act 1985, Pt 10. The law relating to hazardous housing is contained in the Housing Act 2004, Pt 1. These statutory provisions should be taken into account by local housing authorities when drawing up their criteria for admission to this third 'reasonable preference' category[1]. However, local housing authorities could, and many do, adopt a more generous approach than the statutory minimum standards when operating this category.

¹ See Welsh Code, para 3.30 which also refers to statutory controls on houses in multiple occupation.

4.83 For example, local housing authorities have adopted a variety of definitions of 'overcrowding', many of which are broader than the statutory minimum¹. Indeed, one judge has said that this reasonable preference category:

'must include those who live in unsatisfactory housing conditions but need not necessarily statutorily be overcrowded².'

¹ *Exploring local authority policy and practice on housing allocations* (CLG, July 2009), para 14 and *Allocation of accommodation: guidance for local housing authorities in England: Summary of Responses to consultation* (DCLG, June 2012), paras 3.38–3.39. The statutory definition is in HA 1985, ss 325–326.
² *R (Ahmad) v Newham London Borough Council* [2007] EWHC 2332 (Admin), (2007) November *Legal Action*, p 38, Admin Ct per Blake J at [64]. This part of his decision was not subject to appeal.

4.84 There are a number of possible approaches which local housing authority could adopt.

(1) Applying the statutory definition given in HA 1985, ss 324–326. Pursuant to this, a dwelling will be overcrowded if the number of people sleeping in it contravenes either the 'room standard' or the 'space standard'. The room standard is breached where the number of people sleeping in a dwelling¹ and the number of rooms available as sleeping accommodation² is such that two people of the opposite sex, who are not partners, must sleep in the same room³. The space standard is breached where the number of people sleeping in a dwelling⁴ exceeds the permitted number, which is calculated by reference to either the number or floor area of rooms available as sleeping accommodation⁵.

(2) Using the Secretary of State's *bedroom standard*. This is held out in the English Code as 'an appropriate measure of overcrowding for allocation purposes' and recommended 'as a minimum'⁶. The bedroom standard⁷ allocates a separate bedroom to each:
  • married or cohabiting couple;
  • adult aged 21 years or more;
  • pair of adolescents aged 10–20 years of the same sex; and
  • pair of children aged under 10 years regardless of sex.

(3) Using a variant of the *bedroom standard*. This usually involves applying different age limits for particular occupants from those in the mainstream bedroom standard.

(4) Applying the Local Housing Allowance size criteria⁸.

(5) Awarding priority according to whether the overcrowding is sufficiently severe to present a category 1 hazard under the Housing Health and Safety Rating System contained in the Housing Act 2004, Pt 1.

(6) Devising a local definition.

¹ Children under the age of ten are not taken into account: HA 1985, s 325(2)(a).
² This is defined as a room of a type normally used in the locality as a bedroom or living room: HA 1985, s 325(2)(b).
³ HA 1985, s 325(1).

4 Children under the age of one are not taken into account and children aged between one and ten are counted as a half-unit: HA 1985, s 326 (2)(a).

5 HA 1985, s 326(1) and (3). A room is available for sleeping accommodation if it is a room of a type normally used in the locality as a bedroom or living room: HA 1985, s 326(2)(b).

6 English Code, para 4.8.

7 English Code, para 4.8.

8 Local housing allowance rates are used to determine how much housing benefit is payable where a tenant rents from a private landlord. The rate of local housing allowance will depend on where the tenant lives and how many bedrooms he or she is entitled to: Housing Benefit Regulations 2006, SI 2006/213.

4.85 It is clear that there is something of a lottery in England as to whether any particular degree of overcrowding would fall within or outside this reasonable preference category for the purposes of any particular local allocation scheme. One survey asked respondents to specify the numbers of households on their list who were 'in the reasonable preference category of overcrowding'. They found that:

> 'On average, these accounted for 18 per cent of all new applicants on authorities' housing registers. However, the proportions cited were wide-ranging – from over half in two authorities to less than one per cent in four others. While the incidence of overcrowding is certain to vary from area to area these findings suggest that local definitions of the phenomenon as incorporated within allocations policies may well vary more[1].'

1 *Exploring local authority policy and practice on housing allocations* (DCLG, July 2009), para 4.28.

4.86 The approach taken in the housing benefit scheme towards the number of bedrooms in a property[1] is unlikely to be of assistance.

1 See Housing Benefit (General) Regulations 2006, SI 2006/213, as amended, reg B13.

4.87 As to the scope of 'unsatisfactory' housing conditions, the Codes of Guidance each provide a list of suggested criteria, said to be for illustrative purposes only, although many local housing authorities will adopt most, or all, of the criteria in their own schemes as examples of what conditions are accepted by that particular local housing authority as amounting to unsatisfactory housing conditions[1]. The Codes emphasise that the lists are not comprehensive or exhaustive (the English Code also describes its list as simply providing 'possible indicators'[2]) and that there may, in particular, be *local* factors that an individual local housing authority would wish to acknowledge in its allocation scheme[3].

1 English Code, para 4.12 and Annex 1; Welsh Code, para 3.37 and Annex 3.

2 English Code, para 4.12.

3 English Code, para 4.12 and Annex 1; Welsh Code, para 3.37 and Annex 3.

4.88 'Under-occupation' is included in the illustrative list contained in the Welsh Code[1] but has been omitted from the list in the latest English Code[2]. That omission is probably the result of a desire to encourage local housing authorities in England to treat transfer applicants who are under-occupying as *not* falling within this reasonable preference category as defined in their local allocation schemes[3]. In that way, the provisions of HA 1996, Pt 6, will not apply to their transfer applications which can be dealt with outside the normal

HA 1996, Pt 6, arrangements[4].

1   Welsh Code, Annex 3.
2   English Code, Annex 1.
3   See **2.55–2.65**.
4   HA 1996, s 159(4B)(c) and see **2.55–2.65**.

4.89 Whether to include under-occupation as a criterion in assessing 'unsatisfactory housing' remains a matter for each local housing authority, provided it has had regard to the relevant national guidance. All those local housing authorities in England which responded to a consultation exercise conducted in early 2012 reported that they 'give priority in their allocation scheme to social tenants who are under-occupying their property, or are reviewing their allocation scheme in order to do so'[1]. In one case in which a local allocation scheme gave considerable preference to under-occupying applicants, none of the parties 'suggested that the very favourable treatment given to under-occupation transfers is unlawful'[2].

1   *Allocation of accommodation: guidance for local housing authorities in England: Summary of Responses to consultation* (DCLG, June 2012), para 3.2.
2   *R (Ahmad) v Newham London Borough Council* [2009] UKHL 14, [2009] HLR 41, HL at [19]

4.90 Local housing authorities are often keen to transfer their own tenants who want a smaller property, so as to free up the larger property for an allocation. Since April 2013 the reduction in housing benefit, for working age tenants of social housing who are under-occupying, has provided a further incentive for registered providers to agree to transfers to smaller homes. Of course, where such a transfer is at the *landlord's* initiative, there is no 'allocation' at all and the allocation scheme does not apply[1]. In England, where a social housing tenant's own application to a local housing authority for a transfer to a smaller property is prompted by the impact of the 'bedroom tax' (or 'removal of the spare room subsidy')[2], the local housing authority will need to treat that as an application under HA 1996, Pt 6, *only* if its own allocation scheme has placed 'under-occupation' in its 'unsatisfactory housing conditions' category. Otherwise, the application can be dealt with outside of HA 1996, Pt 6 as a non-priority transfer[3], unless the applicant falls into one of the other 'reasonable preference' categories.

1   HA 1996, s 159(4B) (England) and s 159(5) (Wales). See **1.27(8)**. This may explain why under-occupation has hitherto *not* attracted such high priority within allocation schemes as might otherwise have been expected: see *Exploring local authority policy and practice on housing allocations* (DCLG, July 2009), para 16.
2   Housing Benefit (General) Regulations 2006, SI 2006/213, reg B13.
3   See **2.60**.

4.91 Neither the statutory minimum definitions, nor the illustrative lists contained in the Codes, should inhibit advisers from assisting applicants to press for a local housing authority to treat them as within this third 'reasonable preference' category where circumstances suggest that the present home is 'overcrowded', 'insanitary' or otherwise 'unsatisfactory'. Advisers will need to consider the wording used to reflect this broad statutory category in the particular local allocation scheme and then do their best to bring their clients within that wording.

People who need to move on medical or welfare grounds (including, in England, grounds relating to a disability)

4.92 This fourth 'reasonable preference'[1] category should be reflected in every local housing allocation scheme so as to include any applicant for accommodation whose health or welfare, or that of a member of his or her household, is impaired by remaining in the accommodation currently occupied, and thus there is a 'need to move' elsewhere. For obvious reasons, no 'reasonable preference' must be accorded simply because an applicant *wishes* to move on welfare or medical grounds, for example to a warmer part of the country or to be nearer friends or relatives. The category is designed for those who 'need' to move.

[1] HA 1996, s 166A(3)(d) (England), s 167(2)(d) (Wales).

4.93 Again, none of the terms 'medical grounds', 'welfare grounds' or 'grounds relating to a disability' are defined by HA 1996, Pt 6. Nor are there any direct links made to the definitions of these terms in any other statutes. In the first instance it is for local housing authorities to decide what the categories mean and to apply them when framing an allocation scheme.

4.94 The terms do not relate exclusively to the impact, on health or welfare, of the present accommodation alone, although any detrimental effect caused by the present accommodation would obviously fall within this test. As one judge put it:

'the relevant question is whether the current housing conditions are having an adverse effect on the medical condition of the claimant, which itself creates a particular need for her to move[1].'

[1] *R (Ghandali) v Ealing London Borough Council* [2006] EWHC 1859 (Admin), at [34], (2006) September *Legal Action*, p 14, Admin Ct per Leveson J.

4.95 The detrimental effect on health or welfare could be caused by the location of the present accommodation as much as by the physical conditions of that accommodation.

4.96 Thus, 'medical grounds' could relate to an adverse impact of the current accommodation on health (such as dampness having an effect on health, or the presence of inaccessible washing and toilet facilities) or there may be sound medical grounds for changing location, eg to relocate closer to a particular medical facility or to a carer[1], or to escape adverse environmental factors in the present location.

[1] Welsh Code, para 3.128.

4.97 'Welfare grounds' would seem to refer to care and support needs or other social needs that do *not* require medical care or support. Examples given in the Codes are the needs of those leaving care or other vulnerable persons who need a stable base from which to build a secure life, and the needs of vulnerable people who are not able to find their own accommodation[1]. The English Code advises that this category would also include any need to move of those providing (or intending to provide) care and support to certain children:

'[t]his would include foster carers, those approved to adopt, or those being assessed for approval to foster or adopt, who need to move to a larger home in order to accommodate a looked after child or a child who was previously looked after by a local authority. It would also include special guardians, holders of a residence order and family and friends carers who are not foster carers but who have taken on the care of a child because the parents are unable to provide care[2].'

1   English Code, para 4.10; Welsh Code, para 3.32.
2   English Code, para 4.10.

4.98 Specialist advice is obviously helpful when assessing whether the applicant's health or welfare necessitates a move. The Welsh Code recommends that the health or social care professional with direct knowledge of the applicant's condition is contacted by the local housing authority for an opinion on the applicant's health and its impact on the applicant's housing needs[1]. Such a person will usually be the applicant's GP, consultant or social worker.

1   Welsh Code, para 3.31.

4.99 The local housing authority must, however, be careful in its treatment of the medical advice it receives. It must not delegate to a medical adviser its decision about whether an applicant meets those terms of its local allocation scheme which give effect to this reasonable preference category. The adviser advises, the local housing authority makes the decisions. A local housing authority should not confine itself to reliance on an assessment by its own medical adviser. It should seek information from the applicant's own doctors or other relevant professionals. When the report from an external or in-house medical adviser is obtained, the local housing authority should not rely on any expressions of opinion or value judgments that it contains and which are beyond the remit of truly medical advice[1].

1   *R (Bauer-Czarnomski) v Ealing London Borough Council* [2010] EWHC 130 (Admin), (2010) March *Legal Action*, p 30, Admin Ct and see **2.107–2.108**.

4.100 After a local housing authority's medical adviser has advised on the evidence available at the time, and the local housing authority has made a decision as to the applicant's entitlement to reasonable preference and priority under its scheme, if there is then further medical evidence or social work opinion, and/or subsequent events, the medical adviser is under a duty to consider that new information once brought to his or her attention. In a case where the medical adviser's advice was not based on a proper consideration of new evidence and events, the local housing authority's decision not to award the applicant any reasonable preference under this category was quashed and was required to be reconsidered[1].

1   *R (Ghandali) v Ealing London Borough Council* [2006] EWHC 1859 (Admin), (2006) September *Legal Action*, p 14, Admin Ct and see **2.107–2.108**.

4.101 The additional words '(including any grounds relating to a disability)' were first introduced into HA 1996, Pt 6, in England on 27 April 2005[1] so as to make it clear that those applicants whose need to move relates to a disability (but who are not ill or otherwise in 'medical' need) would fall within this 'reasonable preference' category. However, they have never formed part of the applicable provisions in Wales and were not introduced there by the amendments made by the Localism Act 2011 or the H(W)A 2014[2].

1   The then HA 1996, s 167(2)(d). As amended by Housing Act 2004, s 223.
2   HA 1996, s 167(2)(d) (Wales).

4.102 The wording '(including any grounds relating to a disability)' embraces those with a learning disability as well as those with a physical disability[1]. Prior to the statutory amendment in England, the view that medical needs should be taken to include those needs relating to a disability was recommended by the then statutory guidance in any event. The Welsh Code provides extensive guidance on issues relating to disability in the context of social housing allocation even though the statutory amendment has not been brought into force in Wales[2].

1   English Code, para 4.9.
2   Welsh Code, paras 3.33–3.34.

4.103 It is plain from the additional wording that the 'disability' referred to is not restricted to a disability of the applicant; it could be the disability of any member of the applicant's household. Alternatively, the wording would be satisfied where a non-disabled applicant needs to move so as to be nearer to a disabled relative or some other disabled person. An argument that a local housing authority's allocation scheme was unlawful because it did not allocate points to reflect 'disability' failed when the points awarded for health needs were shown to have included needs arising from disabilities[1].

1   *R v Lewisham London Borough Council ex p Pinzon* (1999) 2 CCLR 152, QBD.

4.104 Local housing authorities may wish to consider whether an applicant's needs could be met by providing aids and adaptations to the current accommodation, enabling him or her to remain in his or her present home.

4.105 The Codes provide illustrative lists of different types of 'medical grounds' and 'welfare grounds'[1]. Those illustrations encompass the types of accommodation that may be needed (adapted, improved, sheltered or ground floor), the type of medical condition that might fall within this criterion (mental illness or disorder, physical or learning disability, chronic or progressive medical conditions), and other types of vulnerability (such as young people at risk, people with behavioural difficulties or those recovering from the effects of violence). The needs of those who provide care, as well as those who receive it, are included in the illustrative lists. The need to be near friends, relatives or medical facilities for medical reasons is also mentioned. The Welsh Code, but not the English Code, includes recovery from alcohol or drug problems as a type of 'medical ground' that could fall within this category[2]. The English Code uses the less specific terminology of 'ability to fend for self restricted for other reasons'[3].

1   English Code, Annex 1; Welsh Code, Annex 3.
2   Welsh Code, Annex 3.
3   English Code, Annex 1.

4.106 The Welsh Code recommends that once accommodation is allocated to a person falling within this category, his or her support and care needs should be assessed and there should be liaison with social services, Supporting People, Local Health Boards and other relevant agencies[1].

[1]   Welsh Code, para 3.33.

4.107 In October 2017, the UK Government stated its belief that there was 'good cause' for including within this category 'those who are recovering from the effects of domestic abuse, and who need to move on from a refuge in order to build a stable life'[1]. It consulted on proposals to issue guidance to 'make clear the circumstances in which' local housing authorities would be expected to apply this category to victims of domestic violence living in refuges. Any such guidance would apply to local housing authorities in England only.

[1]   *Improving Access to Social Housing for Victims of Domestic Abuse: Consultation* (DCLG, October 2017).

People who need to move to a particular locality in the local housing authority's district where hardship would be caused if they did not move

4.108 This is the most recently created 'reasonable preference' category[1] and was first introduced in January 2003[2]. The Codes suggest that people may fall within it if they need to move in order to give or receive care, to be able to access specialised medical treatment, or to take up particular education, employment or training opportunities in some particular locality[3]. Some, but not all, of those examples would fall within 'medical or welfare grounds' in the fourth category, but those applicants who overlap are now entitled to be placed in both categories. Again, the emphasis is on 'need' to move, not a desire to move. This fifth category will also be suitable for victims of harassment or violence needing to move to safer areas.

[1]   HA 1996, s 166A(3)(e) (England), s 167(2)(e) (Wales).
[2]   Homelessness Act 2002, s 16(3).
[3]   English Code, para 4.11; Welsh Code, para 3.35.

4.109 A particular locality to which the applicant needs to move should be identified and, in order to get the benefit of this reasonable preference category, that locality must be within the district of the local housing authority to which application is made. Any need to move outside the district of the local housing authority in which the applicant presently resides requires either application to the other local housing authority in whose district the specific locality falls, or the use of any reciprocal agreements or nomination rights agreed between the two local housing authorities involved[1].

[1]   In its report into a *Complaint against London Borough of Ealing and London Borough of Brent*, 14 019 234 and 15 016 582, 8 August 2016, (2016) November *Legal Action* p 41 the LGO criticised a reciprocal rehousing agreement intended for rehousing victims fleeing domestic violence which 'did not work effectively' (p 1) and failed to make clear that the receiving borough could reject a referral if it did not consider the applicant to be in priority need (p 12).

4.110 The need to move must be sufficiently great that 'hardship' would otherwise be caused, either to the applicant or to others. Neither HA 1996, Pt 6, nor the Codes define 'hardship', or the degree of severity required for an applicant to fall within this category. The hardship that might be caused to *the applicant* if he or she is not moved may well be fairly self-evident: deterioration in health, inability to take up education, employment or training opportunities, etc. The hardship that might be caused to *others* includes situations where an applicant needs to move to a particular locality to provide care to a friend or relative already living in that locality. The category is not limited to personal hardship. It may include financial hardship, for example, so as to accord preference to an applicant of limited means who needs to move from a high rent to a low rent district. This will become increasingly relevant as changes to welfare benefits limit the maximum benefits certain claimants can receive – whether as a cap on housing costs or as an overall cap on benefit receipts. The category could therefore include people subject to housing benefit restrictions (such as the 'bedroom tax') or other constraints on their incomes from benefits (such as benefit sanctions).

4.111 In 2015, new statutory guidance was issued to encourage more local housing authorities in England to treat applicants seeking to move for work purposes as falling within this 'reasonable preference' category[1]. The new guidance states that:

> 'This guidance goes further [than previous guidance] and strongly encourages all local authorities to apply the hardship reasonable preference category to tenants who are seeking to transfer and who need to move within the local authority district or from another local authority district to be closer to work, or to take up an offer of work[2].'

[1] *Right to Move: Statutory guidance on social housing allocations for local housing authorities in England* (DCLG, March 2015). In addition to this guidance, the UK Government also made regulations stipulating that a person who needed to move to the district of a local housing authority for work-related reasons could not be disqualified from that local housing authority's allocation scheme on local connection grounds: Allocation of Housing (Qualification Criteria for Right to Move) (England) Regulations 2015, SI 2015/967.

[2] *Right to Move: Statutory guidance on social housing allocations for local housing authorities in England* (DCLG, March 2015) at [38]. For the Welsh response to this development, see Welsh Code para 3.36.

4.112 Having reviewed the importance of the allocation scheme making provision for classes of applicants falling within the statutory categories to be afforded 'reasonable preference', this chapter will next consider how a local housing allocation scheme can:

(1)   award *additional* preference; and/or
(2)   *reduce* preference.

Additional preference

4.113 HA 1996, Pt 6 gives a local housing authority the discretion to frame its allocation scheme so as to give 'additional preference' to particular descriptions of people who are already within the reasonable preference categories[1]. The scheme does not need to contain a provision for this form of enhanced priority but *may* do so. HA 1996 does not define the scope of 'additional preference' or offer illustrations of its application.

¹   HA 1996, s 166A(3) (England) and s 167(2) (Wales), last sentence in each case.

4.114 Local housing authorities are advised by the Codes that they should consider whether they have a local need to exercise this discretion and include such provisions in their schemes, taking into account their local circumstances, and presumably the particular circumstances of likely applicants¹. It should be noted that the provision does not enable the allocation scheme to be framed so as to simply afford additional preference to particular individuals. Under this statutory provision the scheme can be framed so as to give additional preference to 'particular descriptions of people' with urgent housing needs who are already within the reasonable preference classes.

¹   English Code, para 4.13; Welsh Code, para 3.38.

4.115 Examples of descriptions of people who may be identified by a local housing authority in its allocation scheme as entitled to additional preference, by having more urgent housing needs than other reasonable preference applicants, are included in both Codes of Guidance.

4.116 The English Code suggests local housing authorities 'should consider' giving additional preference to three specific groups¹:

- those who need to move urgently because of a life-threatening illness or sudden disability;
- families in severe overcrowding which poses a serious health hazard; and
- those who are homeless and require urgent re-housing as a result of violence or threats of violence, including intimidated witnesses, and those escaping serious anti-social behaviour or domestic violence.

¹   English Code, para 4.13.

4.117 The Welsh Code gives the following examples of applicants to whom the local housing authority 'should' consider awarding additional preference¹:

- those owed a homelessness duty as a result of being forced to leave their homes by actual or threatened violence (including intimidated witnesses);
- those who need to move for urgent medical reasons;
- those who have reasonable prospects of an offer of accommodation within a relatively short period but who suddenly lose their existing homes as a result of a disaster;
- those who are under-occupying and wish to move to smaller premises; and
- certain applicants with connections to the armed forces (see **4.119–4.123**).

¹   Welsh Code, para 3.38.

4.118 Both Codes are clear, however, that these are only examples¹. The intention is that the local scheme should spell out the sorts of circumstances in which additional preference, and thus priority, will be given in respect of the most urgent housing needs. Thus, the House of Lords has upheld as lawful a scheme which gave additional priority (beyond ordinary reasonable preference) to only a small proportion of applicants and only on satisfaction of 'stringent' and 'very strict' criteria[2].

1   English Code, para 4.13; Welsh Code, para 3.39.
2   *R (Ahmad) v Newham London Borough Council* [2009] UKHL 14, [2009] HLR 41, HL at [54].

Armed forces

4.119 The UK Government has been particularly keen that local housing authorities should frame their schemes to give additional preference to applicants within the reasonable preference categories who have some connection with the armed forces. A circular issued in April 2009 recommended that any scheme which made provision for additional preference should give additional preference to[1]:

> 'any applicant who needs to move to suitable adapted accommodation because of a serious injury, medical condition or disability which he or she, or a member of their household, has sustained as a result of service in the Armed Forces.'

1   *Communities and Local Government Circular 04/2009*, 9 April 2009 reproduced in Appendix 1 of the second edition of this book.

4.120 The 2010–15 UK Coalition Government took this a stage further and in 2012 exercised its regulation-making powers[1] to amend HA 1996, s 166A(3). The amendments made by the HA 1996 (Additional Preference for Armed Forces) England Regulations 2012[2] 'require' local housing authorities to frame their allocation schemes to give additional preference to the following categories of people connected with the military, who fall within at least one of the reasonable preference categories and who have urgent housing needs[3]:

(1)   former members of the armed forces;
(2)   serving members of the armed forces who need to move because of a serious injury, medical condition or disability sustained as a result of their service;
(3)   bereaved spouses and civil partners of members of the armed forces leaving services family accommodation following the death of their spouse or partner; and
(4)   serving or former members of the reserve forces who need to move because of a serious injury, medical condition or disability sustained as a result of their service.

1   HA 1996, s 166A(7) (England).
2   SI 2012/2989 at Appendix 1 of this book. The purpose and extent of the regulations was explained to the House of Lords Grand Committee by Baroness Hanham on 20 November 2012 (Lords Debates, col GC 153) and is set out in the Explanatory Memorandum published with the regulations.
3   *The Housing Act 1996 (Additional Preference for Former Armed Forces Personnel) (England) Regulations* 2012, SI 2012/2989 at Appendix 1 of this book, amending HA 1996, s 166A(3) (England). English Code, para 4.14.

4.121 For these purposes 'armed forces' means the regular forces ie the Royal

Navy, the Royal Marines, the regular army or the Royal Air Force[1].

[1]   Armed Forces Act 2006, s 374.

4.122 If they wish, local housing authorities in England may structure their allocation schemes to give more general priority to those with military connections than the regulations require - but they will do so under different powers[1].

[1]   See **4.141**.

4.123 Although there has been no equivalent amending legislation in Wales, the Welsh Code invites local housing authorities to give additional preference to two categories of armed forces applicant[1]:

- any applicant who needs to move to suitable adapted accommodation because of a serious injury, medical condition or disability which he or she, or a member of their household, has sustained as a result of service in the armed forces;
- people needing accommodation as a result of leaving the armed forces and the loss of military accommodation;

and encourages local housing authorities to give 'high priority' to injured or disabled servicemen[2].

[1]   Welsh Code, para 3.38.
[2]   Welsh Code, paras 3.168–3.173.

Adding, or reducing, preference for other reasons

4.124 Whilst it may seem unnecessary, given the existing power to grant additional preference which is discussed in the previous section, HA 1996, Pt 6, expressly provides a further power to enable local housing authorities to frame an allocation scheme so as to prioritise between applicants who *are already* within one or more of the 'reasonable preference' categories[1]. Local housing authorities are therefore able to design schemes so as to give additional or reduced priority to people in the reasonable preference categories for any reasons that they choose to set out in those allocation schemes.

[1]   HA 1996, s 166A(5) (England) and s 167(2A) (Wales).

4.125 Enhancing priority for those in the reasonable preference categories by reference to the length of time an applicant has been waiting is an increasingly popular method adopted in allocation schemes[1]. The use of waiting time is probably the simplest way of determining priorities between those with a similar level of need and its use as a criterion may have benefits of simplicity and transparency.

[1]   See the encouragement to take this approach given, for example, in the Welsh Code, para 3.45.

4.126 HA 1996, Pt 6, directs local housing authorities towards three particular factors that they might wish to take into account in framing their schemes so as to enable prioritisation between those in the reasonable preference categories. The three are:

(1)   the *financial resources* available to the person; and/or
(2)   any *behaviour* of the person or a member of his or her household which affects his or her suitability to be a tenant; and/or
(3)   any *local connection*[1] which exists between the person and the local housing authority's district[2].

[1]   Within the meaning of HA 1996, s 199 as amended by HRA 2017, s 8, for applications made to local housing authorities in England on or after 3 April 2018, or H(W)A 2014, s 81. For more on 'local connection' see CHAPTER 14.
[2]   HA 1996, s 166A(5) (England) and s 167(2A) (Wales).

Financial resources

4.127 The 'financial resources' category permits a local housing authority to give a higher priority in the allocation scheme to applicants who cannot afford to pay a market rent or to take out a mortgage, and, as the other side of that coin, a lower priority to applicants who are in a better financial position. An online survey of local housing authority practice in two English regions found that household resources (including, in some cases, capital in the form of equity and/or savings) were taken into account under the allocation policies of most local housing authorities responding to the survey. Troublingly, it also found that in rare cases local housing authorities were using resources as a complete bar to allocation at a time when exclusion for such a reason was unlawful[1]. The English Code suggests[2] that the reference to 'financial resources' includes property ownership and that, in consequence, a scheme may be framed so as to give reduced priority to an applicant who falls within a 'reasonable preference' category if he or she is a home-owner (assuming that the local housing authority has declined to follow that Code's earlier guidance[3] and make home owners a non-qualifying category). That Code also suggests that, if it adopts 'financial resources' as a criterion for reducing preference, a local housing authority could make provision for disregarding any lump sum received by a member of the armed forces as compensation for an injury or disability sustained on active service[4]. The Welsh Code simply suggests that the power could be used to give less preference to an applicant who is financially able to buy or rent privately[5].

[1]   *Exploring local authority policy and practice on housing allocations* (CLG, July 2009), para 12. See **3.77**.
[2]   English Code, para 4.16.
[3]   English Code, para 3.23 and see **3.117**.
[4]   English Code, para 4.25.
[5]   Welsh Code, para 3.41(a).

Behaviour

4.128 The 'behaviour' category permits local housing authorities to include provision in an allocation scheme to reward good behaviour and penalise bad behaviour among those who fall into the reasonable preference categories. During the debate in the House of Lords on this provision, the then Housing Minister, Lord Falconer, contrasted the examples of two applicants: one who had:

' . . . . a history of persistent but minor rent arrears not caused by any problems with housing benefit and another . . . who has demonstrated that he is a model tenant[1].'

[1]   *Hansard*, HL Deb, vol 630, ser 6, col 1017 (15 January 2002), (Lord Falconer).

4.129 The latter could be accorded priority over the former. The 'model tenant' example of relevant 'behaviour' has been carried into the statutory guidance for England with the additional example of an applicant who has 'benefited the community'[1].

[1]   English Code, para 4.17.

4.130 In *R (Osei) v Newham London Borough Council*[1] the local allocation scheme enabled the housing authority to take into account former tenant arrears as an aspect of 'behaviour' when prioritising between applicants who would otherwise qualify for urgent rehousing on domestic violence or other emergency grounds. The court held that such a provision would not be unlawful provided it was applied with a flexibility which allowed for the personal circumstances of an applicant which might justify not taking into account that past behaviour in a particular case. In *R (Joseph) v Newham London Borough Council*[2] the allocation scheme enabled account to be taken of 'property-related debts' and gave the example of housing benefit overpayments. The court held that this did not permit the local housing authority to reduce preference where an overpayment had been outstanding so long that it could not be recovered by any legal process. The operation of this 'property-related debt' provision in Newham's allocation scheme has spawned not only these two judicial reviews but also a successful complaint to the LGO[3].

[1]   *R (Osei) v Newham London Borough Council* [2010] EWHC 368 (Admin), (2010) March *Legal Action*, p 30, Admin Ct.
[2]   [2009] EWHC 2983 (Admin), (2010) May *Legal Action, p 23, Admin Ct.*
[3]   *Complaint against Newham London Borough Council*, 11 006128, 29 October 2012, (2012) December *Legal Action*, p 30.

4.131 A local housing authority will not be able to take into account behaviour relating to a spent conviction[1]. Under the Rehabilitation of Offenders Act 1974, s 4(1) where a rehabilitated person's conviction is spent, he or she is to be treated 'for all purposes in law as a person who has not committed or been charged with or prosecuted for or convicted of or sentenced for' the offence or offences which were the subject of the conviction. In considering whether to change a person's priority under a housing allocation scheme because of his or her behaviour, the Rehabilitation of Offenders Act 1974, s 4(1) prohibits the local housing authority from taking into account behaviour relating to a conviction which is spent. If, however, it is possible to identify reprehensible behaviour which does not form part of conduct constituting spent offences, this may be taken into consideration[2].

[1]   By analogy with the decision in *R (YA) v Hammersmith and Fulham London Borough Council* [2016] EWHC 1850 (Admin), [2016] HLR 39, Admin Ct, which held that behaviour relating to a spent conviction could not be taken into account when deciding whether an applicant fell within a non-disqualifying class.
[2]   *R (YA) v Hammersmith and Fulham London Borough Council* [2016] EWHC 1850 (Admin), [2016] HLR 39, Admin Ct per Mr Peter Marquand at [4].

4.132 Two examples of 'good' behaviour given in the English Code, as potentially justifying provision for additional preference in an allocation scheme, are where:

(1)   the applicant is in a household where at least one member is in work or seeking work[1]; or

(2)   the applicant's actions have otherwise directly benefited the community[2].

It seems that several local housing authorities have adopted either or both of these classes of additional preference in their allocation schemes. Research conducted by the Chartered Institute of Housing in late 2013 found 'a number of landlords incentivising applicants that are in work or contributing to their community through volunteering. Some are awarding priority in their allocation scheme while others are advertising properties with a preference for those that are working or are making a community contribution'[3].

[1]   English Code, para 4.27.
[2]   English Code, para 4.17.
[3]   'New approaches to allocations' (CIH, June 2014), p 10.

4.133 An allocation scheme which gives additional priority to working tenants may be indirectly discriminatory against disabled people and women with childcare responsibilities, as they are less likely to be able to work. However, a recent challenge brought on this basis was unsuccessful[1]. It was not disputed that the measure had a legitimate aim, 'namely . . . the creation of sustainable and balanced communities and encouraging residents to make a contribution to the local community', nor that the policy had a 'rational connection to that objective'[2]. The 'real question' was whether the scheme 'was the least intrusive measure which could be used without unacceptably compromising the objective'[3]. The judge decided that it was: the local housing authority had made provision for 'those with priority need, for the homeless and vulnerable, for those who need to move on medical or welfare or hardship grounds'. It was entitled to favour workers and volunteers. Extending the class would reduce the benefit of being within it. The scheme contained an overriding discretion for exceptional cases[4].

[1]   *R (XC) v Southwark London Borough Council* [2017] EWHC 736 (Admin), [2017] HLR 24, Admin Ct. At the time of writing there was an outstanding application for permission to appeal against this decision.
[2]   *R (XC) v Southwark London Borough Council* [2017] EWHC 736 (Admin), [2017] HLR 24, Admin Ct at [85]. At the time of writing there was an outstanding application for permission to appeal against this decision.
[3]   *R (XC) v Southwark London Borough Council* [2017] EWHC 736 (Admin), [2017] HLR 24, Admin Ct at [86]. At the time of writing there was an outstanding application for permission to appeal against this decision.
[4]   *R (XC) v Southwark London Borough Council* [2017] EWHC 736 (Admin), [2017] HLR 24, Admin Ct at [97]–[100]. At the time of writing there was an outstanding application for permission to appeal against this decision. For an example of an allocation scheme which sought to reward 'working households' and 'model tenants' by setting aside a proportion of lettings for such applicants, rather than awarding them additional priority, see *R (H) v Ealing London Borough Council* [2017] EWCA Civ 1127, [2018] HLR 2, CA.

4.134 The Welsh Code deals with the 'behaviour' category only in relation to the possibility of reducing priority for previous poor behaviour[1] but reminds local housing authorities in Wales that policies regarding the application of sanctions on the grounds of unacceptable behaviour should accommodate the Welsh Government's broader policy aims of promoting equality of opportunity, social inclusion and sustainability[2].

1   Welsh Code, para 3.41(b).
2   Welsh Code, para 2.44.

4.135 Some local housing authorities also choose to penalise applicants who fail to bid, or who refuse offers of accommodation, by reducing their priority within the scheme. Any such sanction should be clearly set out within the scheme. In addition, it should be made clear to the individual applicant what is expected to them. One recent complaint to the Local Government and Social Care Ombudsman (LGSCO) concerned a couple whose priority had been reduced from Band 1 to Band 4 because, the local housing authority said, they had 'not actively expressed interest in suitable advertised homes'. The LGSCO found that the local housing authority was at fault because it had not explained to the couple what was expected of them: 'While it gave general advice on the need to bid, it did not provide advice on what the Council thought reasonable'[1].

1   *Complaint against South Tyneside Metropolitan Borough Council*, 16 002 288, 31 August 2016.

Local connection

4.136 The 'local connection' category enables discrimination in a housing allocation scheme, among those within the reasonable preference categories, in favour of local applicants[1]. 'Local connection' is defined in both HA 1996, s 199[2] and H(W)A 2014, s 81 as existing where a person has a connection with an area: because he or she is or was normally resident there of his or her own choice; because he or she is employed in the area; due to family associations; or in special circumstances. A person is also deemed to have a local connection with an area if he or she was at any time provided with accommodation there under the Immigration and Asylum Act 1999, s 95 and, in England, if he or she is or was owed certain duties under the Children Act 1989[3]. A local housing authority is entitled, should it so choose, to make provision in its scheme so as to give a higher priority to an applicant who has a local connection with its district (either personally or because a member of his or her household has a local connection). On the face of it, this seems perfectly rational in the distribution of limited resources. In dealing with a challenge to the allocation scheme that Hackney London Borough Council operated for the distribution of pitches on its official Gypsy and Traveller sites, which included a local connection requirement, a judge said:

> 'For my part, I discern no irrationality in the starting point of Hackney's policy that requires a residential connection with the borough, nor in the requirement that residence must be contemporary, in the sense that the traveller can show either continuing physical presence, or that the traveller has retained a c/o address in the borough. It must make sense to afford priority to those who are in fact living in Hackney, or who have lived there and have retained a firm point of contact with Hackney[4].'

1   HA 1996, s 166A(5)(c) (England), s 167(2A)(c) (Wales).

2 As amended by HRA, s 8 for applications for homelessness assistance made to local housing authorities in England on or after 3 April 2018.

3 For more on 'local connection' see CHAPTER **14**.

4 *R (McDonagh) v Hackney London Borough Council* [2012] EWHC 373 (Admin), (2012) April *Legal Action*, p 46, Admin Ct per Kenneth Parker J at [27]. However, in *R (VC) v North Somerset Council (EHRC intervening)* (2016) October *Legal Action*, p 33, a challenge to a 'local connection' requirement within the local housing authority's housing allocations scheme which had been extended to cover Gypsy/Traveller site allocations was compromised by way of a consent order under which the local housing authority agreed to place the claimant on its housing register and review its scheme.

4.137 Local housing authorities in Wales are advised in the Welsh Code that they should be careful, when using this provision, to comply with the Equality Act 2010 and not to detract from the overall requirement that the allocation scheme must give an overall preference to those in the reasonable preference categories[1]. Some local housing authorities have operated 'sons and daughters' policies whereby children of local residents are given priority over applicants who have moved into the area more recently. This provision for enhanced priority by reference to local connection permits local housing authorities to operate such policies, provided that they ensure that the local allocation scheme adopted is not contrary to the Equality Act 2010 and, more generally, does not run counter to other equal opportunities considerations[2].

1 Welsh Code, paras 2.68 and 3.41(c).

2 See **4.192–4.230**.

4.138 Where the allocation scheme gives additional weighting based on local connection, it is likely to result in greater complexity, particularly if the scheme generally uses a banding system to confer priority. It is well recognised that a scheme which attaches particular priority to local connection could disadvantage some applicants. Nevertheless, allocation schemes frequently reflect local political priorities by providing for enhanced priority for local connection cases which are also within the reasonable preference categories. In *R (van Boolen) v Barking & Dagenham London Borough Council*[1] the local housing authority's policy was to take account of local connection when there was more than one bidder, in the same high priority band, shortlisted for a property under its choice-based letting scheme. The bidder in that band with a local connection would normally be preferred to a bidder without such a connection. Although the practice had resulted in the claimant being repeatedly shortlisted, but never successful, her claim that the policy was unlawful was rejected.

1 *R (van Boolen) v Barking & Dagenham London Borough Council* [2009] EWHC 2196 (Admin), September *Legal Action*, p 34, Admin Ct.

4.139 The Codes of Guidance particularly highlight recent changes to the statutory definition of 'local connection' which have improved the standing of serving military personnel[1].

1 English Code, para 4.18; Welsh Code, para 3.41(c).

4.140 More recently, supplementary statutory guidance issued to local housing authorities in England has suggested that the statutory power to give additional preference in an allocation scheme to those with a local connection might usefully be exercised in two particular ways:

(1)   to give priority to those with a local connection to a particular parish, within a local housing authority's district, where lettings in rural villages need to be dealt with sensitively as part of a local lettings scheme; or

(2)   to give priority to those with a local connection to a particular local housing authority's district where a group of local housing authorities collectively apply a broader residency test for qualification for admission to a common allocation scheme[1].

[1]   Supplementary English Code, para 27.

Other examples of reasons to enhance, or reduce, preference

4.141 HA 1996, Pt 6 contains no limit on the features that a local housing authority could include in an allocation scheme so to determine priorities between those entitled to a reasonable preference[1]. Local housing authorities are reminded by the Codes of Guidance that the three particular factors that the legislation suggests might be included in an allocation scheme (discussed at **4.127–4.140** above), so as to enhance or reduce relative priorities among those entitled to a reasonable preference, are not mandatory or exhaustive[2]. Within local housing allocation schemes, local housing authorities may give priority to, or downgrade, yet further classes of applicant who are otherwise within the 'reasonable preference' categories. However, they are also reminded by the Codes that each application has to be considered on its own merits[3].

[1]   HA 1996, s 166A(5) (England) and s 167(2A) (Wales) each provide that a housing allocation scheme 'may' contain provisions for determining such priorities and that the factors taken into account in any such provisions 'may' include the three specified ones.
[2]   English Code, para 4.15; Welsh Code, para 3.41.
[3]   For example, Welsh Code, para 3.39. See too the guidance relating to those with a history of rent arrears given at Welsh Code, paras 2.44(iii) and 3.50.

4.142 A local housing authority must not add or reduce priority in a way which is unlawfully discriminatory. In *R (Fartun Osman) v Harrow London Borough Council*[1] the local housing authority's scheme originally awarded Band A priority to all severely overcrowded households. This was amended with the effect that severely overcrowded households in the private rented sector had their priority reduced to Band C. Severely overcrowded households in the social housing sector remained in Band A. The rationale put forward by the local housing authority to justify the change was that severely overcrowded households in the private rented sector had been remaining in unsuitable accommodation in the hope of receiving an offer of an allocation of social housing, when they could in fact move to more suitable accommodation within the private rented sector. This was held not to be an option for households in the social housing sector, who could not be expected to give up their security of tenure. A challenge to the amended scheme on the grounds that it unlawfully discriminated against private rented sector tenants failed. Whilst it did discriminate against tenants in the private rented sector when compared to tenants in social housing, the measure was a proportionate means of achieving a legitimate aim.

[1]   [2017] EWHC 274 (Admin), Admin Ct. At the time of writing there was an outstanding
      application for permission to appeal against this decision.

4.143 The scope of the statutory discretion to set priorities among those within the 'reasonable preference' categories is plainly wide but the bottom line is that (save in respect of the circumstances described at **4.147–4.158**) the effect of any reduction in priority must not be to eliminate all preference, with the result that a person in a 'reasonable preference' category is in practice getting *no* preference at all. A scheme which 'defers' applications made by those within 'reasonable preference' categories may also be unlawful. In *R (Alemi) v Westminster City Council*[1], the scheme prohibited applicants who were entitled to a reasonable preference by virtue of being owed a homelessness duty from bidding under its choice-based letting scheme for one year. The judge quashed those parts of the amended scheme on the basis that:

> 'Part VI of the Act does not permit the removal of a whole sub-group from a group which section 166A(3) requires be given reasonable preference in the allocation of social housing, when that sub-group is not defined by reference to differentiating features related to the allocation of housing, but applies a simple time bar to all who otherwise qualify[2].'

However, the judge did indicate that a provision which suspended the bidding rights of a particular 'reasonable preference group' which had been 'securing a greater proportion' of properties than planned in order to allow another reasonable preference group to 'catch up'[3] might be lawful, if its purpose was 'to distribute the limited stock of available housing on rational grounds of relative priority'[4]. In addition, another court has been prepared to hold that provisions in an allocation scheme enabling the 'deferral' of applications made by those within 'reasonable preference' categories (eg for the refusal of a suitable offer) would not be unlawful[5].

[1]   [2015] EWHC 1765 (Admin), [2015] PTSR 1339, Admin Ct.
[2]   [2015] EWHC 1765 (Admin), [2015] PTSR 1339, Admin Ct at [32].
[3]   [2015] EWHC 1765 (Admin), [2015] PTSR 1339, Admin Ct at [23].
[4]   [2015] EWHC 1765 (Admin, [2015] PTSR 1339, Admin Ct at [31].
[5]   *R (Cranfield-Adams) v Richmond upon Thames London Borough Council* (2012) August
      Legal Action, p 27 and as to 'refusals' generally see **5.83–5.86**.

4.144 Precisely 'how' reasonable preference is enhanced or reduced by the exercise of these powers is a matter for the particular local housing allocation scheme. For example, if an applicant in a reasonable preference category has rent arrears his or her priority might be reflected in a reduction in points (in a points-based scheme), a move to a lower band (in a banded scheme) or a date adjustment (in a date-order scheme).

SUSPENSION

4.145 For many years it has been unclear whether the statutory powers enable an applicant or application to be *suspended* from a scheme or from bidding under a scheme (for example until arrears were cleared or reduced). For the time being, that issue appears to have been resolved in favour of suspension being a lawful exercise of these powers by a case involving Westminster

City Council's allocation scheme. Section 10 of that scheme suspended applicants from bidding if they owed more than a week's rent, subject to the possibility of the Director of Housing permitting bidding by an applicant with arrears in exceptional cases. In a challenge to that provision, it was conceded by the claimant that suspension might be lawful but it was argued that it was not lawful where it was triggered by an absolute threshold applied in every case (subject to the exceptional override). That argument was rejected at trial[1]. However, in dismissing an application for permission to appeal from that decision, the appeal court judge put the matter much more broadly. He said[2]:

' . . . we are concerned with someone who has been given preference but who has been temporarily suspended from bidding under the choice-based scheme while they have rent arrears. That is lawful within [HA 1996, s 167] subsection (2A)(b) . . .

As I understand it, there is no quarrel with the proposition that the council may in principle have a scheme which suspends from bidding those who have arrears of rent. The only criticism of this scheme is that the suspension is automatic provided a certain rental arrears threshold is reached; and it is then open to the person who is suspended to seek to persuade the Director of Housing that they ought to be allowed to bid "in exceptional circumstances". Again, it seems to me that it cannot possibly be said that the scheme is so irrational as to be unlawful. It is clearly sensible to have a fixed threshold so that not every arrears of rent, however minor, will trigger suspension, but so that everybody knows that if they go over a certain level then they will be suspended. The scheme contains the necessary safety valve to enable those who are in arrears to explain to the Director of Housing that there is some good reason for them being in arrears, for example because they are ill in hospital or whatever. In those circumstances the Director of Housing can then allow bidding to take place "in exceptional circumstances", and that indeed is precisely what happened in the appellant's case.

. . . It is plainly sensible to have a clear-cut arrears threshold over which one will not be allowed to bid unless one can persuade the director of housing that there are exceptional circumstances. It seems to me that there is nothing arguably unlawful about that policy.'

1   *R (Babakandi) v Westminster City Council* [2011] EWHC 1756 (Admin), (2011) August *Legal Action*, p 40, Admin Ct at [23]–[25].
2   *R (Babakandi) v Westminster City Council* [2011] EWCA Civ 1397, (2012) January *Legal Action*, p 21, CA per Sullivan LJ at [6]–[8].

4.146 If the local housing authority does wish to be able to suspend applicants, a rule to that effect must be included in the scheme and be properly applied in each individual's case[1]. In *Complaint against Cymdeithas Tai Eryri*[2], the registered social landlord had a policy enabling it to suspend a housing application for 'unacceptable behaviour' of a type making the applicant unsuitable to be a tenant but it wrongly used that policy to suspend an applicant for providing misleading information in an application form. The Ombudsman said that if it wished to suspend for that reason, its published policies should be amended to make that clear.

1   *R v Wandsworth London Borough Council ex p Lawrie and Heshmati* (1997) 30 HLR 153, QBD.
2   Public Services Ombudsman for Wales, Ref 201102854, 2012.

REMOVING 'REASONABLE PREFERENCE' ALTOGETHER

4.147 An applicant who falls within one or more of the 'reasonable preference' categories may be deprived of that status, and given no preference at all, but only if either:

(1)   the applicant is entitled to a reasonable preference under the first or second of the statutory reasonable preference categories and his or her entitlement to reasonable preference would not have arisen but for the presence in his or her household of a 'restricted person'[1]; or

(2)   a local housing authority in Wales decides that he or she or a member of his or her household has been guilty of 'unacceptable behaviour'[2].

[1]   HA 1996, s 166A(4) (England), s 167(2ZA) (Wales).
[2]   HA 1996, s 167(2B) and (2C).

The presence of a 'restricted person'

4.148 The first ground for removal of a reasonable preference arises where[1]:

(1)   the reasonable preference is made out by satisfaction of the first or second categories for such a preference (homelessness or a specific duty owed to the homeless)[2]; and

(2)   the application would not have fallen within those categories without the local housing authority having had regard to a 'restricted person' (within the meaning of HA 1996, Pt 7[3] (England) or H(W)A 2014, Pt 2 (Wales))[4].

[1]   HA 1996, s 166A(4) (England), s 167(2ZA) (Wales).
[2]   HA 1996, s 166A(3)(a) and (b) (England), s 167(2)(a) and (b) (Wales). See **4.58–4.66** for the first category and **4.67–4.79** for the second category.
[3]   As amended by HRA 2017 for applications for homelessness assistance made to local housing authorities in England on or after 3 April 2018.
[4]   A 'restricted person' is a person who is not eligible for assistance under HA 1996, Pt 7 (as amended by HRA 2017 for applications for homelessness assistance made to local housing authorities in England on or after 3 April 2018) or H(W)A 2014, Pt 2, Ch 2; who is subject to immigration control within the meaning of the Asylum and Immigration Act 1996; and either who does not have leave to enter or remain in the United Kingdom or whose leave to enter or remain is subject to a condition of no recourse to public funds: HA 1996, s 184(7) (England); Housing (Wales) Act 2014, s 63(5) (Wales).

4.149 A 'restricted person' is defined at HA 1996, s 184(7) (England) and H(W)A 2014, s 63(5) (Wales)[1]. Only if *both* the conditions in **4.148** are fulfilled is the applicant deprived of the reasonable preference to which he or she would otherwise have been entitled. This provision illustrates the policy intention that homeless households with 'restricted persons' should be looking to the private rented sector, rather than to social housing, for their long-term accommodation needs. An applicant entitled to a reasonable preference under any of the third to fifth statutory categories retains that preference even if it has been triggered by the needs of a restricted person[2].

[1]   See **10.47**.
[2]   HA 1996, s 166A(3)(c), (d) and (e) (England), s 167(2)(c), (d) and (e) (Wales). See **4.80–4.91** for the third category, **4.92–4.107** for the fourth category and **4.108–4.112** for the fifth category.

The 'unacceptable behaviour' test: local housing authorities in Wales

4.150 Until 18 June 2012, local housing authorities in both England and Wales could remove entirely, on 'unacceptable behaviour' grounds, the reasonable preference of a person otherwise entitled to it. However, since that date local housing authorities in England have had the power to adopt classes of persons who do not qualify at all for social housing allocation in their districts[1]. This left the 'removal of preference' power unnecessary – those who would have lost preference on 'unacceptable behaviour' grounds can now be kept out of allocation arrangements altogether.

[1] See Chapter 3.

4.151 That has left the power to remove preference altogether on 'unacceptable behaviour' grounds only available to local housing authorities in Wales.

4.152 A local housing authority in Wales may *only* treat an applicant otherwise entitled to a 'reasonable preference' as having no preference when it is satisfied that:

- the applicant, or a member of his or her household, has been guilty of unacceptable behaviour serious enough to make him or her unsuitable to be a tenant of the local housing authority; and
- at the time that the application is being considered and by reason of that behaviour, the applicant deserves not to be treated as a member of a group of people who are given 'reasonable preference'[1].

[1] HA 1996, s 167(2B) and (2C). See Welsh Code, paras 2.41–2.42 and 3.46.

4.153 The definition of 'unacceptable behaviour' is the same as that applied in determining eligibility for an allocation in Wales. That is to say, behavior, by the applicant or by a member of his or her household, which would, if the applicant were a secure tenant of the local housing authority, entitle it to a possession order on any ground in Housing Act 1985 (HA 1985), s 84A or in Sch 2, Pt 1 (other than Ground 8)[1].

[1] HA 1996, s 167(2D) applying HA 1996, s 160A(8). For a full discussion see **3.151–3.191**.

4.154 Before removing any 'reasonable preference' to which an applicant would otherwise be entitled, a local housing authority in Wales must therefore ask itself:

(1) Would the applicant's behaviour, or that of a member of his or her household, have come within one of the grounds for possession[1]?

(2) Would the court make an absolute order under HA 1985, s 84A or consider it reasonable to make an order for possession under HA 1985, Sch 2, Pt 1, Grounds 1–7?

(3) Where the order would be made under HA 1985, s 84 (not HA 1985, s 84A, where there is no power to suspend or postpone), would the order be an outright, not a suspended or postponed, possession order?

[1] The local housing authority should not take into account behaviour which relates to a spent conviction: *R (YA) v Hammersmith and Fulham London Borough Council* [2016] EWHC 1850 (Admin), [2016] HLR 39, Admin Ct.

4.155 Only after it has considered those three questions (where applicable) and answered them all in the affirmative, may the local housing authority then decide whether, at the time that the application is being considered, the applicant deserves not to be given the reasonable preference to which he or she would otherwise be entitled. The key issue that the local housing authority should consider is whether there has been a change of circumstances since those events that led to the affirmative answers to the three questions identified above[1].

[1] For a fuller discussion of the correct approach to this part of the statutory test, see **3.192–3.194**.

4.156 If a local housing authority in Wales decides that an applicant should have his or her 'reasonable preference' removed on the grounds of 'unacceptable behaviour', it must notify the applicant in writing of the decision and of the grounds for it. The applicant has the right to request a review of that decision and to be informed of the review decision and of the grounds for it.[1] Any further challenge to the review decision would be by judicial review[2] or by complaint, ultimately to the Public Services Ombudsman for Wales[3].

[1] HA 1996, s 167(4A)(b) and (d). See also **2.86–2.102**.
[2] See **2.104–2.108** and CHAPTER **19**.
[3] See **2.109–2.120**.

4.157 This provision, permitting the removal of preference, operates as an alternative to the power available to a local housing authority in Wales to treat an applicant as wholly ineligible for an allocation by reason of his or her unacceptable behaviour[1]. It may therefore be used in respect of an applicant where the local housing authority in Wales has considered his or her behaviour for the purposes of eligibility and concluded that he or she is eligible but nevertheless considers that the behaviour should deprive him or her of the 'reasonable preference' that would otherwise be accorded.

[1] Discussed at **3.151–3.200**. One local housing authority's policy that an applicant in rent arrears would be allowed onto its allocation scheme and entitled to points, but would not receive an offer whilst the arrears continued was found to be an attempt to apply this provision, rather than to hold the applicant ineligible: *R (Onuegbu) v Hackney London Borough Council* [2005] EWHC 1277 (Admin), (2005) August *Legal Action*, p 17, Admin Ct. That interpretation, however, does not sit easily with the statutory provision which does not allow for suspension but simply a removal of a reasonable preference to which the applicant would otherwise be entitled.

4.158 Even if an applicant in Wales, with a background of unreasonable behaviour, survives both the eligibility test and the removal of 'reasonable preference' test, he or she may still be accorded a lower preference than others in similar circumstances by being given a lower priority than he or she would otherwise receive[1].

[1] In exercise of the power at HA 1996, s 167(2A). See **4.128–4.135**.

PRIORITY FOR OTHER CLASSES OF APPLICANT (WHO DO NOT FALL WITHIN ANY REASONABLE PREFERENCE CATEGORY)

4.159 Although HA 1996, Pt 6 requires an allocation scheme to be framed so as to give a reasonable preference to the five statutory classes of applicant described above, it does not prohibit a local housing authority from also framing its allocation scheme to give preferences or priorities to other groups or classes of applicant reflecting local circumstances. Local housing authorities in England and Wales are free to adopt other priority classes of their own choosing, provided that the overall requirement that the statutory classes receive a reasonable preference in the scheme is not displaced[1]. Indeed, the Secretary of State has positively encouraged local housing authorities in England to 'take advantage of this flexibility'[2] and many are actively doing so[3]. As the Codes put it, local housing authorities are free to prioritise groups of applicants who do not fall into the reasonable preference categories provided that:

(1)   they do not dominate the scheme, and
(2)   overall, the scheme operates to give reasonable preference to those who are in the statutory reasonable preference categories over those who are not[4].

[1]   Welsh Code, para 3.40.
[2]   English Code, para 4.19.
[3]   See the examples given in *New approaches to allocations* (Chartered Institute of Housing [CIH], June 2014), *Under pressure? Emerging issues for allocations* (CIH, November 2013), *How to . . . consider new approaches to allocations and lettings* (CIH, April 2012) and *Allocations and Local Flexibility* (CIH, March 2010).
[4]   English Code, para 4.19; Welsh Code, para 3.40.

4.160 If this advice is followed and unlawful discrimination is avoided, there is no limit as to the number of categories that may be given preference in a local allocation scheme nor any limit as to the size of the class of prospective or actual applicants each category may embrace.

4.161 By virtue of the fact that local housing authorities are required to have regard to statutory guidance, the Secretary of State (in England) or the Welsh Minister (in Wales) are able to identify and promote particular classes of applicant they would wish local housing authorities at least to consider prioritizing through the Codes. The guidance ranges in emphasis from mere suggestion that local housing authorities may like to consider giving one particular group priority to local housing authorities being 'strongly encouraged' or 'urged' to give preference to other suggested groups[1].

[1]   Contrast, for example, the language used within English Code, paras 4.22–4.32.

4.162 The English Code particularly singles out for possible priority treatment within local allocation schemes the following groups (to the extent that they do not already fall within the reasonable preference categories adopted in those schemes):

•   current and former members of the armed forces and their family members[1];
•   applicants who are in work or seeking work or living with others who are in work or seeking work[2];

- prospective adopters and foster carers[3]; and
- former social housing tenants forced to move into the private sector by housing benefit penalties for under-occupation who later wish to move back to social housing[4].

[1] English Code, paras 4.24–4.25.
[2] English Code, para 4.27. Some of the difficulties in framing a priority class for this group are set out in *Allocation of accommodation: guidance for local housing authorities in England Summary of responses to consultation* (DCLG, June 2012), paras 3.66–3.77. For an example of a challenge to an allocation scheme which set aside 20% of lettings for 'working households' and 'model tenants' see *R (H) v Ealing London Borough Council* [2017] EWCA Civ 1127, [2018] HLR 2, CA.
[3] English Code, para 4.30–4.32. Some of the issues around affording special priority for this group are set out in *Allocation of accommodation: guidance for local housing authorities in England Summary of responses to consultation* (DCLG, June 2012), paras 3.78–3.87. In *R (Aslamie) v London & Quadrant Housing Trust* [2016] EWHC (Admin) 2396, the court upheld a decision to refuse to consent to a mutual exchange on the grounds that the claimant would be under-occupying, despite his desire to adopt. The court agreed that the defendant was 'not obliged to grant consent by reference to the future intentions of the claimant' (at [5]).
[4] English Code, para 4.23.

4.163 The Welsh Code suggests that priority might be given under allocation schemes to:

- promote job-related and training-related mobility;
- help those who are under-occupying (given the changes in welfare benefits);
- meet the needs of extended families; and
- sustain rural or Welsh-speaking communities[1].

[1] Welsh Code, para 3.67.

4.164 Local housing authorities in England and Wales are free to adopt, modify or reject the suggested classes for prioritisation put forward in the statutory guidance provided they can demonstrate that they have at least 'had regard' to the relevant code in making their choices when framing their schemes[1]. Some local housing authorities may share the views of the Chartered Institute of Housing that 'there is very little detail in the new guidance [for England] in ensuring the needs of all communities are taken into account'[2] or the views of those who responded to the consultation on the draft English Code and who, according to the DCLG's Summary of Responses, 'were concerned that the guidance lacked clarity or would have preferred more detailed guidance, and were concerned about the risk of legal challenge, or that this would lead to a wide variety of approaches and inconsistency between local authority areas. In particular, there was a call for more guidance on how to strike an appropriate balance between the reasonable preference requirements, local policy priorities and the Government's policy priorities'[3].

[1] HA 1996, s 169(1).
[2] *Allocation of accommodation: guidance for local housing authorities in England: A Briefing paper* (CIH, July 2012), p 7.
[3] *Allocation of accommodation: guidance for local housing authorities in England Summary of responses to consultation* (DCLG, June 2012), para 3.90.

PRIORITY FOR PARTICULAR TYPES OF ACCOMMODATION

4.165 An allocation scheme does not need to apply uniformly to the whole of a local housing authority's available housing stock, or to all the available nominations to private registered providers or registered social landlords. HA 1996, Pt 6, provides that a scheme may, in effect, identify that specified accommodation is available to be allocated:

(1)   only to those who make specific applications for it; or

(2)   only to a particular group or groups of applicants (whether or not in one of the statutory reasonable preference categories)[1].

[1]   HA 1996, s 166A(6) (England), s 167(2E) (Wales).

4.166 By these means, HA 1996, Pt 6, allows the local allocation scheme to be drawn so that, in respect of certain types of accommodation specified in the scheme, the normal 'reasonable preference' categories do not, in effect, apply. Care must be taken in framing these provisions in any local allocation scheme. These two special provisions are still subject to the over-arching requirement that the scheme must be framed so as to secure a reasonable preference for all five of the statutory reasonable preference categories. The position remains that the scheme must be drawn in terms ensuring that, *overall*, a reasonable preference is given to applicants who fall within the reasonable preference categories over those who do not[1].

[1]   English Code, paras 4.5 and 4.19; Welsh Code, paras 3.68 and 3.71.

4.167 The function of the first special provision – that the scheme may provide for the allocation of particular accommodation to those who specifically apply for it – is to facilitate 'choice'. It enables the adoption of advertising schemes whereby applicants can apply for particular properties which have been advertised as vacant by the housing authority. It is thus the lynch-pin for the concept of choice-based lettings[1], although it is a rather roundabout way of achieving that objective.

[1]   See 5.6–5.47.

4.168 In local allocation schemes not structured on choice-based letting, the type of accommodation most likely to be specifically earmarked for those who make 'a specific application' for it[1] is what is commonly known as 'hard to let' housing – in respect of which there is little point in operating the normal allocation scheme, because offers are likely to be refused[2]. Indeed, where there is housing stock of that sort, local housing authorities in England are invited to consider adopting different, less stringent, qualification criteria than they operate for the rest of their stock[3].

[1]   HA 1996, s 166A(6)(a) (England), s 167(2E)(a) (Wales).
[2]   Welsh Code, para 3.75.
[3]   English Code, para 3.24.

4.169 The form of accommodation most likely to be earmarked, under the second special provision, for a particular group or groups of applicants (in the statutory language, 'persons of a particular description'[1]) is the stock of purpose-built or adapted accommodation designed for use by the disabled[2] or elderly[3]. Inclusion of such a provision in an allocation scheme can ensure that such specialist housing is available to those who most need it. The current Codes of guidance give particular emphasis to the needs of injured or disabled armed services personnel[4] whilst the Welsh Code specifically promotes the use of Accessible Housing Registers[5].

1   HA 1996, s 166A(6)(b) (England), s 167(2E)(b) (Wales).
2   Welsh Code, paras 3.97–3.104 and see *No place like home: five million reasons to make housing disability friendly* (Leonard Cheshire Disability, December 2014).
3   Welsh Code, paras 3.120–3.122.
4   English Code, paras 4.24–4.25; Welsh Code, paras 3.168–3.170.
5   Welsh Code, paras 3.99–3.104.

4.170 The use of the power to make special provision for particular classes of persons, who need not be within a reasonable preference category, can sometimes produce unusual results. For example, a local housing authority may have a surfeit of applicants for general accommodation who fall within one or more 'reasonable preference' categories, but its scheme may have excluded particular accommodation from the general pool and earmarked it for the elderly or disabled. If there is little demand for that earmarked accommodation, an elderly or disabled applicant could receive an offer almost immediately, even if his or her circumstances would otherwise command no reasonable, or other, preference at all under the local allocation scheme.

4.171 There is at least one other circumstance in which a local allocation scheme could usefully make provision in respect of allocation of particular properties only for particular applicants. That is to ensure that property is not allocated to an applicant in a particular locality in the local housing authority's district in which he or she has previously been the victim (or, perhaps, perpetrator) of anti-social behaviour. In *R (Carney) v Bolton-at-Home Ltd*[1] an allocation scheme, which utilised choice-based letting, contained a provision enabling a bypass to be applied to the applicant at the top of the shortlist for any property if the allocation would result in a person previously evicted for anti-social behaviour being rehoused in the same area as that where the behaviour took place, even if the applicant was otherwise eligible and qualified to be allocated any other accommodation. The provision was not unlawful and had been lawfully applied in the particular case.

1   *R (Carney) v Bolton-at-Home Ltd* [2012] EWHC 2553 (Admin), (2012) November *Legal Action*, p 22, Admin Ct.

LOCAL LETTINGS SCHEMES

Local lettings schemes: guidance

4.172 Statutory guidance[1] suggests that the power to make special provision for particular classes of persons, who need not be within a reasonable preference category, in relation to particular housing accommodation provides 'the statutory basis for so-called 'local lettings policies' which may be used to achieve a wide variety of housing management and policy objectives'[2]. Specific attention is given in both Codes of Guidance to suggestions that local housing authorities identify particular types or clusters or locations of housing for particular types of applicants and deal with allocation of them by way of local lettings policies[3].

1   See generally, *Exploring local authority policy and practice on housing allocations* (DCLG July 2009), chapter 5 – *Local lettings policies*.
2   English Code, para 4.21. Welsh Code, para 3.68.
3   See the Welsh Code, paras 3.68–3.74. The suggestions made in the English Code are not gathered in one discrete section.

4.173 For example, the English Codes suggest that local housing authorities in England might:

- set aside a proportion of properties for 'former members of the armed forces' under a local lettings policy[1];
- use a local lettings policy to 'ensure that specific properties, or a specified proportion of properties, are allocated to households in particular types of employment where, for example, skills are in short supply'[2];
- set aside a 'quota of properties each year for people who need to move to larger accommodation in order to foster or adopt a child on the recommendation of children's services'[3];
- use a local lettings policy for allocation of accommodation in rural villages and give priority within that policy to applicants with a connection to a particular parish[4]; or
- set a quota for the proportion of properties that it expects to allocate each year to transferring tenants who need to move into their district for work related reasons (the Right to Move quota). The Secretary of State strongly encourages all local authorities to adopt such an approach and considers that an appropriate quota would be at least 1%[5].

1   English Code, para 4.25.
2   English Code, para 4.27.
3   English Code, para 4.31.
4   Supplementary English Code, para 27.
5   *Right to Move: Statutory guidance on social housing allocations for local housing authorities in England* (DCLG, March 2015) at [42].

4.174 The Welsh Code suggests that local housing authorities in Wales can use local letting policies to address a range of issues including[1]:

- creating more mixed communities;
- dealing with a concentration of deprivation;
- ensuring properties that are particularly suited to being made accessible (eg ground floor flats) are prioritised for those with access needs;
- relocating essential workers such as teachers, nurses and police officers within a reasonable travelling distance from their work;
- supporting people in work/volunteering or who are seeking work or seeking to take up volunteering opportunities;
- dealing sensitively with lettings in rural areas to sustain communities by giving priority to those with a local connection to the local area;
- taking account of the needs of mobile workers such as those in the armed forces; and
- where the child to adult ratio could be lowered on an estate where there is high child density or, conversely, young single people could be

integrated into an estate via this route.

[1] Welsh Code, paras 3.69.

4.175 Providing somewhat more practical guidance, the Chartered Institute of Housing (CIH) has suggested that proposals for local lettings policies should set out the following[1]:

- a clear definition of the objective(s) to be achieved, backed up by clear evidence;
- a method which is likely to achieve the objective(s);
- a potential (equality) impact assessment;
- how the scheme will be monitored and who will be involved;
- mechanisms of reporting and reviewing the scheme;
- how the views of local communities have shaped the scheme; and
- a clear exit strategy.

[1] *Allocations and local flexibility: A Practice brief* (CIH, March 2010).

4.176 A survey conducted by CIH in late 2013 found that[1]:

'Local lettings policies have been used by organisations to achieve a wide variety of housing management and policy objectives. They allow properties to be allocated to certain categories of applicants, whether or not they fall within the reasonable preference categories, provided that overall the landlord is able to demonstrate compliance with statutory requirements. Local lettings policies can be used on new developments or in existing communities having regard to housing management considerations such as the social mix of tenants, density, age range, and vulnerability of tenants. They may also be used to encourage working people or people who contribute to their local community through volunteering to move to a particular area[2].'

[1] *New approaches to allocations* (CIH, June 2014), p 10.
[2] Local housing authorities in England seeking an understanding of how local lettings policies and schemes are being operated by others may also find helpful material in the results of a research survey published by DCLG in July 2009: *Exploring local authority policy and practice on housing allocations* (DCLG, July 2009), chapter 5.

4.177 The Welsh Code suggests that any local lettings policies should have clear aims linked to community sustainability and be supported by clear evidence of the need for the approach being taken[1].

[1] Welsh Code, para 3.72.

4.178 All local housing authorities are reminded by the statutory guidance that local lettings arrangements must not be used in such a way that there will be a failure to meet the requirement to give a reasonable preference to statutorily specified groups. In other words, an allocation scheme may include local lettings policies provided that:

- they do not dominate the scheme; and
- overall, the scheme operates to give reasonable preference to those in the statutory reasonable preference categories over those who are not[1].

[1] English Code, para 4.19, Welsh Code, para 3.71.

Local lettings schemes in court

4.179 Two different types of local lettings schemes have recently come before the courts. In *R (H) v Ealing London Borough Council*[1], the claimant challenged a policy whereby 20% of all available lettings were set aside for 'working households' and 'model tenants'[2]. The scheme was challenged on the grounds that the provisions were unlawfully discriminatory against women with childcare responsibilities, the disabled, and the elderly, under the Equality Act 2010, s 19[3]; the provisions were unlawfully discriminatory under Art 14 of the European Convention on Human Rights (ECHR), in conjunction with Art 8 ECHR[4]; the public sector equality duty had not been complied with[5]; and Children Act 2004, s 11[6] had been breached. The claim was allowed in the Administrative Court on all four grounds. However, the local housing authority's appeal to the Court of Appeal was allowed in part. The Court of Appeal found that any discrimination arising from the scheme was justified and that the local housing authority had had the Children Act 2004, s 11 duty in mind. Although the court had concerns regarding the degree of consideration given to the public sector equality duty when the priority scheme had been implemented, it held that there was no need to grant substantive relief given that the scheme was under review[7].

1   [2017] EWCA Civ 1127, [2018] HLR 2l, CA.
2   For an example of a challenge to a housing allocation scheme which rewarded working tenants by giving them additional priority, see *R (XC) v Southwark London Borough Council* [2017] EWHC 726 (Admin), [2017] HLR 24. At the time of writing there was an outstanding application for permission to appeal against this decision.
3   See **4.211–4.216** and **4.220–4.230**.
4   See **4.217–4.230**.
5   See **4.193–4.209**.
6   See **4.241–4.247**.
7   *R (H) v Ealing London Borough Council* [2017] EWCA Civ 1127, [2018] HLR 2, CA.

4.180 In *R (C) v Islington London Borough Council*[1], the local housing authority operated a local lettings policy which prioritised the letting of new homes to people currently living on the estate on which they were built. The claimant argued that this unlawfully discriminated against the homeless and victims of domestic violence, who were more likely to be women. The Administrative Court dismissed this ground of challenge (although the claim was upheld on other grounds):

' . . . in the context of the 2015 scheme as a whole, the effect of the local lettings policy, as was intended, has a beneficial effect upon the provision of social housing within the borough, in that it facilitates the securing of reasonable preferences to those, including the claimant, who are entitled to it under s 166A(3) of the 1996 Act. It may be that it is always possible to think of possible ways in which to create less intrusive policies in general. However, I do not consider that the defendant's local lettings policy could be any less intrusive, in the sense of being less detrimental to the claimant, and still maintain its legitimate aim. Certainly, the defendant's decision on this point, is not manifestly without reasonable foundation. Furthermore, in relation to the issue of proportionality, I consider that, bearing in mind the extent to which the local lettings policy contributes to that aim, the local lettings policy does strike a fair and proportionate balance between the severity of the consequences for the claimant, and the importance of the aim[2].'

1   [2017] EWHC 1288 (Admin), [2017] HLR 32, Admin Ct.

2   *R (C) v Islington London Borough Council* [2017] EWHC 1288 (Admin), [2017] HLR 32, Admin Ct at [93].

Particular types of accommodation

4.181 Beyond local lettings schemes, three specific forms of accommodation may be suitable for special treatment under these statutory powers in an allocation scheme:

- accommodation with linked support;
- accommodation particularly suited for agricultural workers; and
- accommodation subject to an application from a former tenant or other occupier of it.

4.182 Each of these three suggested categories requires careful consideration.

Accommodation with linked support

4.183 Certain applicants may not only seek accommodation but also have needs for support[1]. Where an applicant's household includes a child who needs accommodation on medical and welfare grounds, local housing authorities are advised to consult with children's services about the appropriate level of priority, what support needs are present, and how those support needs will be met[2]. Where applicants for an allocation are cared for by people who do not live with them, local housing authorities are advised that the applicant will need a spare bedroom (for overnight stays)[3].

1   Welsh Code, para 3.51.
2   The guidance *Working together to safeguard children: A guide to inter-agency working to safeguard and promote the welfare of children* requires co-operation between departments in the same authority, but the duty of co-operation imposed by Children Act 1989, s 27 does not apply to two departments within the same authority: *R (M); R (A) v Islington London Borough Council* [2016] EWHC 332 (Admin), [2016] HLR 19.
3   Welsh Code, para 3.127.

4.184 Single parents aged under 18, who are not living with their parents, should be offered semi-independent accommodation with support. A joint assessment of the applicant's housing, care and support needs should be undertaken by the housing and children's services departments, provided that the applicant consents to the involvement of children's services. It would be unusual for a young single parent to be given an independent tenancy, but arrangements should be made for the young parent to move on from supported accommodation as he or she reaches adulthood[1]. Local housing authorities should not be deterred by the legal problems associated with the granting of a tenancy to a minor: children's services authorities may underwrite the tenancy agreement, and the tenancy itself can be treated as a trust for land (giving the minor the beneficial interest) or as a contract for a lease[2].

1   Welsh Code, paras 3.132–3.142.
2   Welsh Code, para 3.142, Annex 11; *Kingston upon Thames Royal London Borough Council v Prince* (1999) 31 HLR 794, CA; *Newham London Borough Council v Ria* [2004] EWCA Civ 41, (2005) March *Legal Action*, p 23, CA and *Alexander-David v Hammersmith & Fulham London Borough Council* [2009] EWCA Civ 259, [2009] HLR 39, CA.

4.185 Access to the allocation of accommodation with support should also be available for rough sleepers and people at risk of sleeping rough. Many rough sleepers will need support with other problems: mental health, alcohol or drug problems, and basic life skills. Local housing authorities should work with adult care services and (in Wales) Supporting People Teams to provide such support[1]. Where sex offenders are allocated accommodation, there should be joint working with the police, probation services, adult care services, health professionals and other bodies to manage any risk to the community[2].

1   Welsh Code, paras 3.174–3.175.
2   Welsh Code, paras 3.176–3.179. See too the discussion of *R (M) v Hackney London Borough Council* [2009] EWHC 2255 (Admin), (2009) May *Legal Action*, p 26, Admin Ct, noted at **3.191**.

Accommodation particularly suited for agricultural workers

4.186 Local housing authorities are required by the Rent (Agriculture) Act 1976 to use their best endeavours to provide accommodation for displaced agricultural workers where they are satisfied that the dwelling house from which the worker is displaced is needed to accommodate another agricultural worker, that the farmer cannot provide suitable alternative accommodation for the displaced worker and that the displaced worker needs to be rehoused in the interests of efficient agriculture[1]. Local housing authorities should include within their allocation schemes a policy statement in respect of the priority that will be accorded to displaced agricultural workers[2].

1   Rent (Agriculture) Act 1976, ss 27–28 and see the leaflet *Agricultural Lettings* (ODPM and Welsh Assembly Government, June 2006).
2   Welsh Code, paras 3.180–3.183.

Accommodation subject to an application from a former tenant or other current occupier

4.187 The exercise of these statutory powers to separate from the general allocation provisions certain accommodation which would otherwise be available for letting might be particularly apt where an applicant seeks the specific allocation of just one property – the home in which he or she is already living[1]. For example, this might arise where the applicant:

- has married an existing tenant and they both seek the grant of a fresh tenancy into their joint names;
- is a former joint tenant and the joint tenancy has ended;
- is a relation of the previous tenant who has died without there being a right of succession;
- has otherwise occupied the particular property for a considerable time; or
- was placed in the accommodation under a non-secure tenancy but now wishes to be granted a secure or introductory tenancy of the same property[2].

1   See **1.28** et seq for an introduction to this topic.
2   The *English Homelessness Code of Guidance* (MHCLG, February 2018) recommends that local housing authorities give consideration to allocating temporary accommodation under a

secure or assured tenancy, especially where 'a household has been living in a particular property for anything other than a short-term emergency stay': para 2.50.

4.188 Unless the local housing authority has used the power in HA 1996, Pt 6[1], to identify in its scheme the special treatment of applicants in such cases, distinct from the general allocation provisions, it would be in difficulty in lawfully allocating the specific property to the applicant, given the entitlement of many others to a 'reasonable preference' in allocation. The position will be all the more acute where a scheme provides that 'all' allocations will be by way of choice-based letting. A local housing authority will need to ensure that its scheme is framed sufficiently flexibly to take account of these particular cases.

[1]   HA 1996, s 166A(6)(b) (England), s 167(2E)(b) (Wales).

4.189 For example, when a former joint tenancy has ended, a local housing authority may be asked to decide whether to grant a sole tenancy to the former joint tenant who remains in the property. One of the joint tenants may have terminated the former joint tenancy by service of a notice to quit on the landlord[1]. Local housing authorities need to set out in their allocation schemes the circumstances in which they will exercise their discretion to grant a new sole tenancy in this situation[2]. Of course, if the couple are married, have a civil partnership, or have children, a family court has jurisdiction to decide that a joint tenancy should be transferred to a sole tenancy in one of the partners' names and such a transfer made following the court's decision is not subject to the allocation scheme[3].

[1]   *Hammersmith and Fulham London Borough Council v Monk* [1992] 1 AC 478, HL.
[2]   *R (Hussey) v Southwark London Borough Council* [2002] EWHC 1142 (Admin), [2002] All ER (D) 332 (May), Admin Ct and *R (Dixon) v Wandsworth London Borough Council* [2007] EWHC 3075 (Admin), (2008) February *Legal Action*, p 40, Admin Ct.
[3]   Transfers made by virtue of Matrimonial Causes Act 1973, s 24; Matrimonial and Family Proceedings Act 1984, s 17(1); Children Act 1989, Sch 1 para 1; and Civil Partnership Act 2004, Pt 2, Sch 5 are excluded from counting as allocations by HA 1996, s 160(2)(e) and (3)(d). See also **1.27**. For transfers ordered under the Family Law Act 1996 see **1.27**.

4.190 Similarly, when a secure tenant dies, and there is no entitlement to a statutory succession, local housing authorities may consider granting a tenancy to somebody who has been living with the tenant. To do so they must specifically provide for that scenario in their allocation schemes and set out the circumstances that they will take into account in determining applications[1]. For example, local housing authorities might consider granting a tenancy where the applicant is a former household member who was living with the tenant for the year prior to the tenant's death, had been providing care for the tenant, or has accepted responsibility for the tenant's dependants, and needs to live with them[2]. If the local housing authority has included a provision of this type in its allocation scheme, it should consider whether it might be utilised *before* it takes proceedings to recover possession of the particular property from the person in occupation[3]. An occupier who has been refused an allocation in these circumstances may be able to challenge the decision by way of judicial review[4] or as a defence to possession proceedings[5]. For example, in one case, a mother and her children had not been living with the father (who was a social housing tenant) at the date of his death although they returned to his home shortly afterwards. On those facts there could be no statutory succession. The local allocation scheme provided for the possible allocation of a new tenancy of the same property to the non-successor in such exceptional circumstances. The local housing authority was found to have behaved unlawfully in not soliciting an application from the mother for consideration under that provision and its possession claim against her was dismissed[6].

1   *R v Islington London Borough Council ex parte Blissett* (unreported) 9 September 1997, QBD (noted at (1998) 75 P&CR D4) concerned an allocation scheme which provided for a deceased tenant's same-sex partner to be offered a tenancy if they could establish 12 months' residence. A judicial review challenge, based on a claim that the claimant's evidence made out his fulfilment of that qualifying period, failed on the facts.

2   Welsh Code, para 3.26. See *R (Sleith) v Camden London Borough Council* [2003] EWHC 347 (Admin), (2003) May *Legal Action*, p 33, Admin Ct, in respect of which an application for permission to appeal was refused: *R (Sleith) v Camden London Borough Council* [2003] EWCA Civ 347, CA. For a more recent example of this scenario, see *R (Neville) v Wandsworth London Borough Council* [2009] EWHC 2405 (Admin), (2009) December *Legal Action*, p 17, Admin Ct.

3   *Leicester City Council v Shearer* [2013] EWCA Civ 1467, CA.

4   *Jack Jones v Luton Borough Council* [2016] EWHC 2036 (Admin).

5   *Leicester City Council v Shearer* [2013] EWCA Civ 1467, [2014] HLR 8, CA.

6   *Leicester City Council v Shearer* [2013] EWCA Civ 1467, [2014] HLR 8, CA.

4.191 Although not mentioned in the Codes, an allocation scheme should make provision for applications for allocation of specific properties where applicants were placed in their accommodation under a non-secure tenancy but now wish to be granted a secure or introductory tenancy of the same property. For example, an applicant for homelessness assistance who has been granted a non-secure tenancy of local housing authority accommodation under the main housing duty owed to homeless applicants under HA 1996, Pt 7[1] could apply to his or her local housing authority for a secure or introductory tenancy of that property. Likewise, a person who had a non-secure tenancy because the accommodation was provided as a term of his or her employment might seek a secure or introductory tenancy when the employment ended[2]. A local housing authority could only allocate a secure tenancy to an applicant covered by these examples if its allocation scheme made provision for those circumstances or in the exercise of an overriding discretion[3].

1   See **16.94–16.199**.

2   See, for example, *Barnsley Metropolitan Borough Council v Norton* [2011] EWCA Civ 834, [2011] HLR 46, CA.

3   HA 1996, s 159(3).

AVOIDING DISCRIMINATION AND ENHANCING EQUALITY OF OPPORTUNITY IN ALLOCATION SCHEMES

4.192 The statutory guidance on housing allocation reminds local housing authorities that their allocation schemes, and the detailed policies and procedures they contain, should take account of their statutory duties under equalities legislation and should not unlawfully discriminate between applicants[1]. But neither of the Codes gives any detailed practical guidance on what compliance with these requirements means in the context of framing an allocation scheme.

¹ English Code, para 3.20; Welsh Code, paras 3.78–3.85.

The public sector equality duty

The equality duty at Equality Act 2010, s 149

4.193 The most important of the relevant statutory duties imposed by the Equality Act 2010 (EA 2010) is the public sector equality duty, which states that a public authority, such as a local housing authority, in the exercise of its functions must:

> 'have due regard to the need to—
> (a) eliminate discrimination, harassment, victimisation and any other conduct that is prohibited by or under this Act;
> (b) advance equality of opportunity between persons who share a relevant protected characteristic and persons who do not share it;
> (c) foster good relations between persons who share a relevant protected characteristic and persons who do not share it[1].'

¹ Equality Act 2010, s 149.

4.194 Each of these elements is expanded upon in the various subsections of EA 2010, s 149. Having due regard to the need to advance equality of opportunity between people who share a relevant protected characteristic and people who do not involves having due regard to the need to:

* remove or minimise disadvantages suffered by persons who share a relevant protected characteristic that are connected to that characteristic;
* take steps to meet the needs of persons who share a relevant protected characteristic that are different from the needs of persons who do not share it; and
* encourage persons who share a relevant protected characteristic to participate in public life or in any other activity in which participation by such persons is disproportionately low[1].

¹ Equality Act 2010, s 149(3).

4.195 Having due regard to the need to foster good relations between people who share a protected characteristic and people who do not involves having due regard to the need to:

* tackle prejudice; and
* promote understanding'[1].

¹ Equality Act 2010, s 149(5).

4.196 Complying with the public sector equality duty may involve treating some people more favourably than others[1]. The 'protected characteristics' mentioned in the duty are age, disability, gender reassignment, marriage and civil partnership, pregnancy and maternity, race, religion or belief, sex, and sexual orientation[2].

1   Equality Act 2010, s 149(6).
2   Equality Act 2010, ss 5–12.

4.197 EA 2010, s 149 does not impose a statutory duty on public authorities requiring them to conduct a formal equality impact assessment when carrying out their functions. At the most, it imposes a duty on a public authority to consider undertaking an impact assessment, along with other means of gathering information, and to consider whether it is appropriate to have one in relation to the function or policy at issue, when it will or might have an impact on the protected characteristics[1]. However, in order to avoid discrimination, and to be best able to demonstrate compliance with the public sector equality duty, when considering any substantial variation of its housing allocation scheme a local housing authority will probably first wish to undertake such an assessment.

1   For an illustration of the difficulties that can arise where an equality impact assessment inadequately addresses the impact of a proposed amendment to a housing allocation scheme, see *R (H) v Ealing London Borough Council* [2016] EWHC 841 (Admin) [2016] HLR 20, Admin Ct and [2017] EWCA Civ 1127, [2018] HLR 2, CA. For a helpful summary of other relevant cases, and academic commentary upon them, see *The Public Sector Equality Duty and Equality Impact Assessments* (House of Commons Library, 22 May 2014) at pp 19–21.

4.198 In Wales, the position is made more explicit. The Equality Act 2010 (Statutory Duties) (Wales) Regulations 2011[1] require that local housing authority policies should be subject to an equality impact assessment and the impact monitored to help ensure and demonstrate compliance with the objectives of the Equality Act 2010. The Welsh Code suggests that this is done by identifying any potential negative impact on people with protected characteristics and adopting an action plan to mitigate this impact[2].

1   SI 2011/1064.
2   Welsh Code, para 3.80.

Guidance on the public sector equality duty

4.199 The importance of the public sector equality duty in the context of housing allocation cannot be overstated. Comprehensive guidance is offered in *The essential guide to the public sector equality duty*[1]. The public sector equality duty is given particular emphasis in Wales by supplementary regulations[2] which are referred to in the Welsh Code[3]. Both the Local Government Association and the Chartered Institute of Housing have advised of the importance of complying with the duty[4].

1   *The essential guide to the public sector equality duty: England (and non-devolved public authorities in Scotland and Wales)* Revised (third) edition (Equality and Human Rights Commission (EHRC)) November 2012 (England) and *The essential guide to the public sector equality duty: An overview for listed public authorities in Wales* (EHRC, April 2011) (Wales). See also *Equality Act 2010: Public sector equality duty – What do I need to know? A quick start guide for public sector organisations* (Home Office, June 2011) and *The Public Sector Equality Duty and Equality Impact Assessments* (House of Commons Library, 22 May 2014).
2   Equality Act 2010 (Statutory Duties) (Wales) Regulations 2011, SI 2011/1064 (W 155).
3   Welsh Code, para 3.80.

⁴   *Councils must consider equality laws when changing services* LGA Media Release 16 February 2012 and *Allocation of accommodation: guidance for local authorities in England: Briefing paper* (CIH, July 2012), p 7.

4.200 The Equality and Human Rights Commission (EHRC) advises that decision-makers in public authorities need to:

'•   be aware of their responsibilities under the duty
- make sure they have adequate evidence (including from consultation, if appropriate) to enable them to understand the potential effects of their decisions on different people covered by the duty
- consciously and actively consider the relevant matters, in such a way that it influences decision-making
- do this before and at the time a decision is taken, not after the event
- be aware that the duty can't be delegated to third parties who are carrying out functions on their behalf[1].'

¹   *FAQs on the equality duty: What public authorities need to do on assessing impact on equality under the general equality duty* (EHCR website, August 2012). For more general guidance see *Meeting the equality duty in policy and decision-making England (and non-devolved public authorities in Scotland and Wales)* EHRC, Revised (second) edition, January 2012 (formerly published as *Equality Analysis and the Equality Duty: a guide for public authorities*).

4.201 In relation to the protected characteristic of 'disability', the publication *Housing and the Disability Equality Duty: A guide to the Disability Equality Duty and Disability Discrimination Act 2005 for the social housing sector* from the former Disability Rights Commission (DRC) is still available online and offers considerable advice (and examples of good practice) on drawing-up allocation schemes[1]. The Department of Health (DH) commissioned and published research on the experiences of the disabled in accessing choice-based letting schemes[2] and associated guides for social landlords establishing such schemes[3] and for people with learning difficulties who try to use them[4].

¹   *Housing and the Disability Equality Duty: A guide to the Disability Equality Duty and Disability Discrimination Act 2005 for the social housing sector* (DRC, 2006), pp 54–57.
²   *Choice Based Lettings and People with Learning Disabilities* (DH, February 2008).
³   *Making Choice Based Lettings work for People with Learning Disabilities: A Guide for Choice-based lettings schemes and landlords* (DH, February 2008).
⁴   *Choice Based Lettings: A guide to choosing a home through the council* (DH, February 2008).

4.202 Regard must obviously be had to the various elements of the duty when taking strategic decisions about, for example, consultation arrangements on changes to allocation schemes and the formulation of their major elements. Local housing authorities should ensure that they consult with a wide range of groups when drawing up or revising their allocation schemes, and particularly engage with those who are currently under-represented in social housing[1]. Translation of the scheme into different languages spoken in the local community is recommended[2]. The Welsh Code advises that local housing authorities should be particularly sensitive to the housing needs of refugees, Gypsies and Travellers, people with disabilities, older people, people with mental health problems, and lesbian, gay and bisexual people[3].

¹   Welsh Code, para 4.27
²   For example, Welsh Code, para 1.27.

³ Welsh Code, chapter 3.

4.203 Local housing authorities would also be well advised to monitor the operation of their current allocation schemes in order to identify and prevent discrimination and to review their schemes if particular groups are shown to be disadvantaged[1].

¹ Welsh Code, para 4.49–4.52.

4.204 The Chartered Institute of Housing (CIH) has published useful guides for local housing authorities and other housing organisations seeking to give effect to the duties imposed by the equality legislation by carrying out equality impact assessments or an equality analysis of services[1].

¹ *How to . . . undertake an equality analysis* (CIH, February 2013) and *How to . . . mainstream equality and reflect diversity* (CIH, September 2013).

4.205 Perhaps reflecting a new emphasis on the importance of measuring the likely equality impact of housing allocation schemes and policies, the UK Government published a free-standing equality statement on its latest statutory guidance about social housing allocation in England[1].

¹ *Providing social housing for local people: statutory guidance on social housing allocations for local authorities in England: Equality statement* (DCLG, April 2014).

The public sector equality duty in the courts

4.206 Case law has established a number of general principles applicable to the exercise of the public sector equality duty. These include the following:

- The aim of the public sector equality duty is to 'bring equality issues into the main-stream, so that they become an essential element in public decision making'[1].
- The duty is a matter of substance, not form. The decision-maker must be aware of the duty to have due regard to the relevant matters. The duty must be exercised 'in substance, with rigour and with an open mind'. It is not about 'ticking boxes'. Simply mentioning the statutory provision will not show that the duty has been performed, but equally 'a failure to refer expressly to the statute does not of itself show that the duty has not been performed'[2].
- The duty must be fulfilled before and at the time that a particular policy is being considered. Ex post facto attempts to justify a decision as being consistent with the duty will not be enough to discharge the duty[3].
- The duty may involve a duty of inquiry: the public authority must be properly informed before taking the decision which may involve a duty to acquire the relevant material[4].
- The duty is a continuing one[5].
- The duty is non-delegable, although in practice another organisation may undertake practical steps to fulfil the duty[6].
- The requirement to have due regard is different from an obligation to give the equality considerations 'specific weight. It is not a duty to achieve a particular result'[7].

- Whilst there must be 'a rigorous consideration of the duty'[8], if there has been a 'proper and conscientious focus on the statutory criteria', the court cannot interfere with the decision simply because it would have given greater weight to the equality implications of the decision than the decision maker did[9].
- It is good practice for an adequate record to be kept showing the steps taken to fulfil the duty[10].

[1] *Hackney London Borough Council v Haque* [2017] EWCA Civ 4, [2017] HLR 14, CA per Briggs LJ at [21]. See also *R (Elias) v Secretary of State for Defence* [2006] EWCA Civ 1293, [2006] 1 WLR 3213, CA per Arden LJ at [274].

[2] *Hackney London Borough Council v Haque* [2017] EWCA Civ 4, [2017] HLR 14, CA per Briggs LJ at [22]. See also *R (Brown) v Secretary of State for Work and Pensions* [2008] EWHC 3158 (Admin), [2009] PTSR 1506, Admin Ct and *R (Baker) v Secretary of State for Communities and Local Government* [2009] EWCA Civ 141, [2009] PTSR 809, CA.

[3] *R (Brown) v Secretary of State for Work and Pensions* [2008] EWHC 3158 (Admin), [2009] PTSR 1506, Admin Ct per Aikens LJ at [91] and *Bracking v Secretary of State for Work and Pensions* [2013] EWCA Civ 1345, (2013) CCLR 479, CA at [25].

[4] *R (Hurley and Moore) v Secretary of State for Business, Innovation and Skills* [2012] EWHC 201 (Admin), Admin Ct per Elias LJ at [89]–[90], *Bracking v Secretary of State for Work and Pensions* [2013] EWCA Civ 1345, (2013) CCLR 479, CA at [25].

[5] *R (Brown) v Secretary of State for Work and Pensions* [2008] EWHC 3158 (Admin), [2009] PTSR 1506, Admin Ct per Aikens LJ at [95].

[6] *(Brown) v Secretary of State for Work and Pensions* [2008] EWHC 3158 (Admin), [2009] PTSR 1506, Admin Ct per Aikens LJ at [94]. See also *Panayiotou v Waltham Forest London Borough Council* [2017] EWCA Civ 1624, [2017] HLR 48.

[7] *Hackney London Borough Council v Haque* [2017] EWCA Civ 4, [2017] HLR 14, CA per Briggs LJ at [23]. See also *R (Brown) v Secretary of State for Work and Pensions* [2008] EWHC 3158 (Admin), [2009] PTSR 1506, Admin Ct per Aikens LJ at [81].

[8] *Hotak v Southwark London Borough Council* [2015] UKSC 30, [2015] WLR 1341 per Lord Neuberger at [74].

[9] *R (Hurley and Moore) v Secretary of State for Business, Innovation and Skills* [2012] EWHC 201 (Admin), Admin Ct per Elias LJ at [78], *Hackney London Borough Council v Haque* [2017] EWCA Civ 4, [2017] HLR 14, CA per Briggs LJ at [23], *Bracking v Secretary of State for Work and Pensions* [2013] EWCA Civ 1345, (2013) CCLR 479, CA at [25].

[10] *R (Brown) v Secretary of State for Work and Pensions* [2008] EWHC 3158 (Admin), [2009] PTSR 1506, Admin Ct per Aikens LJ at [96] and *Bracking v Secretary of State for Work and Pensions* [2013] EWCA Civ 1345, (2013) CCLR 479, CA at [25].

4.207 The application of the public sector equality duty in the context of a local lettings scheme was considered in *R (C) v Islington London Borough Council*[1]. The local housing authority operated a local lettings policy which prioritised the letting of new homes to people currently living on the estate on which they were built. The claimant argued that this breached EA 2010, s 149. This ground of challenge was rejected. The judge noted that 'when the original local lettings policy was introduced, the whole of the defendant's housing allocation scheme, which necessarily included the local lettings policy, was subjected to an extensive analysis, for the express purpose of enabling the defendant to fulfil its statutory duty of having due regard to the public-sector equality duty'[2]. The judge found that 'sufficiently rigorous and conscientious consideration' had been given to the duty[3].

[1] [2017] EWHC 1288 (Admin), [2017] HLR 32, Admin Ct.
[2] [2017] EWHC 1288 (Admin), [2017] HLR 32, Admin Ct per Baker J at [101].
[3] [2017] EWHC 1288 (Admin), [2017] HLR 32, Admin Ct per Baker J at [104].

4.208 The role of the public sector equality duty in housing allocation decision-making was recently considered by the Court of Appeal in *R (H) v*

Ealing London Borough Council[1]. This was a challenge to two priority schemes under which 20% of available lettings were set aside for 'working households' and 'model tenants'. It was claimed that in enacting and maintaining the new policies the local housing authority had been in breach of the public sector equality duty. The court considered the degree of detail required for an equality impact assessment, noting that it was not a 'precise mathematical exercise' and that 'a relatively broad brush approach' may be sufficient[2]. The local housing authority in fact accepted that the initial equality impact assessment had been deficient and stated that it was undertaking a review. Although the court had concerns as to whether or not these deficiencies had been remedied, it decided not to grant any substantive relief given that a full review was underway.

[1]   [2017] EWCA Civ 1127, [2018] HLR 2, CA.
[2]   [2017] EWCA Civ 1127, [2018] HLR 2, CA per Sir Terence Etherton MR at [113], quoting *R (West Berkshire District Council) v Secretary of State for Communities and Local Government* [2016] EWCA Civ 441, [2016] 1 WLR 3923 per Laws and Treacy LJJ at [83] and [85].

4.209 The courts have also confirmed that having due regard to the elements of the public sector equality duty is not only a requirement in relation to 'strategic' decision-making. It will, in relevant circumstances, also need to infuse and inform decision-making by local housing authorities in individual cases[1]. Those parts of a local housing allocation scheme which deal with the procedure on applications, and particularly with the making of decisions on applications, will need to indicate that those taking decisions have been alerted to the need to comply with the duty. In *Barnsley Metropolitan Borough Council v Norton*[2] the local housing authority had failed to consider the public sector equality duty in respect of the eviction (and possible rehousing) of a family which included a disabled person. The Court of Appeal said:

'The decision of this appeal may serve to reinforce that which the courts have been saying for some time, calling on public authorities to face up to their obligations under [what is now] section 149 of the 2010 Act. It seems to me that the practical problem needs to be resolved by proper consideration being given by the Council, with the cooperation of the Norton family, to the question where they are to be accommodated in the future, whether under [HA 1996] Pt 7 or under Pt 6[3].'

[1]   *Pieretti v Enfield London Borough Council* [2010] EWCA Civ 1104, [2011] HLR 3, CA at [26].
[2]   [2011] EWCA Civ 834, [2011] HLR 46, CA.
[3]   [2011] EWCA Civ 834, [2011] HLR 46, CA at [35].

Non-discrimination

4.210 In addition to complying with the public sector equality duty, local housing authorities must ensure that their allocation schemes do not unlawfully discriminate under either the Equality Act 2010 or Art 14 of the European Convention on Human Rights.

Discrimination under the Equality Act 2010

4.211 Discrimination may be direct or indirect. Direct discrimination occurs when a person is treated less favourably than others because of a protected characteristic[1]. It cannot be justified save where the protected characteristic is age[2]. Indirect discrimination occurs when:

- A applies, or would apply, a provision, criterion, or practice;
- the provision, criterion, or practice puts, or would put, persons with a protected characteristic at a particular disadvantage when compared with persons without that characteristic;
- B has that protected characteristic;
- the provision, criterion, or practice puts, or would put B at that disadvantage; and
- A cannot show it to be a proportionate means of achieving a legitimate aim[3].

[1]   EA 2010, s 13.
[2]   EA 2010, s 13.
[3]   EA 2010, s 19.

4.212 There is also a particular type of discrimination which relates only to disability. This applies where:

- A treats B, who is disabled, unfavourably;
- the unfavourable treatment is because of something arising in consequence of B's disability;
- A knows, or could reasonably have been expected to know, that B had that disability; and
- A cannot show that the treatment is a proportionate means of achieving a legitimate aim[1].

[1]   EA 2010, s 15.

4.213 Section 29 EA 2010 prohibits discrimination by a person providing services to the public or exercising a public function. Section 33 of the Equality Act prohibits discrimination in the disposal of premises. In deciding whether a discriminatory provision is justified, the court must consider:

- Whether the measure pursues a sufficiently important objective.
- Whether the measure is rationally connected to that objective.
- Whether it is the least intrusive action that could be taken without unacceptably compromising that objective.
- Whether a fair balance has been struck between the importance of achieving the objective and the effect of the discrimination[1].

[1]   *Akerman-Livingston v Aster Communities Ltd* [2015] UKSC 15, [2015] AC 1399, SC per Baroness Hale at [28] and *Bank Mellat v Her Majesty's Treasury (No 2)* [2013] UKSC 39, [2014] AC 700, SC per Lord Sumption at [20]. This approach was applied in *R (YA) v Hammersmith and Fulham London Borough Council* [2016] EWHC 1850 (Admin), [2016] HLR 39, Admin Ct; *R (H) v Ealing London Borough Council* [2017] EWCA Civ 1127, [2018] HLR 2, CA; *R (XC) v Southwark London Borough Council* [2017] EWHC 736 (Admin), [2017] HLR 24, Admin Ct; and *R (C) v Islington London Borough Council* [2017] EWHC 1288 (Admin), [2017] HLR 32, Admin Ct.

4.214 Service-providers are subject to a duty to make reasonable adjustments in certain circumstances[1]. Where a provision, criterion or practice of a service-provider puts a disabled person at a substantial disadvantage compared with a non-disabled person, the service-provider must take such steps as it is reasonable to take to avoid the disadvantage[2]. They must also take reasonable steps to avoid disadvantage where a physical feature puts a disabled person at a substantial disadvantage, or to provide an auxiliary aid where the lack of such an aid puts a disabled person at a substantial disadvantage[3].

[1] EA 2010, ss 20–22, 29, and Sch 2.
[2] EA 2010, s 20(3) and Sch 2, para 2.
[3] EA 2010, s 20(4) and (5) and Sch 2, para 2.

4.215 Controllers of premises to let are also subject to a duty to make reasonable adjustments[1] in respect of a disabled person who is considering taking a letting of the premises[2]. The duty will, however, only arise if they have received a request by or on behalf of the disabled person to do so[3]. It may require them to take reasonable steps to avoid a disadvantage arising from a provision, criterion, or practice of the controller of premises to let, or to provide an auxiliary aid. It does not extend to removing disadvantages arising from physical features[4].

[1] EA 2010, ss 20–22, 36, and Sch 4.
[2] EA 2010, Sch 4, para 3(3).
[3] EA 2010, Sch 4, para 3(5).
[4] EA 2010, s 20 and Sch 4, para 3.

4.216 A failure to comply with the duty to make reasonable adjustments will constitute discrimination[1]. The protected characteristics under the Equality Act are age, disability, gender reassignment, marriage and civil partnership, pregnancy and maternity, race, religion or belief, sex, and sexual orientation[2].

[1] EA 2010, s 21(2).
[2] EA 2010, s 4. EA 2010, Pt 3 does not apply to the protected characteristics of age, so far as relating to a person under 18, or civil partnership: EA 2010, s 28(1). EA 2010, Pt 4 does not apply to the protected characteristics of age or civil partnership: EA 2010, s 32(1).

Discrimination under Article 14 ECHR

4.217 Discrimination is also prohibited by Art 14 ECHR but only where it impacts upon 'the enjoyment' of other Convention rights. Article 14 provides:

'The enjoyment of the rights and freedoms set forth in this Convention shall be secured without discrimination on any ground such as sex, race, colour, language, religion, political or other opinion, national or social origin, association with a national minority, property, birth or other status.'

It is not necessary to show a breach of this other right but the matter must have a connection, which is more than tenuous, to the 'core values' which the right protects[1]. The right most likely to be applicable in housing allocation decision-making is Art 8, the right to respect for a person's private and family life, home, and correspondence. In a number of decisions the courts have accepted that Art 8 is engaged in housing allocation cases[2]. However, a recent Court of Appeal decision has cast doubt on the subject, with two of the three judges stating (obiter) that it was not engaged and the third judge finding that it was engaged in respect of one provision of the allocation scheme (which affected single parent families who were not in secure accommodation), but not in relation to another (which concerned families who were already housed under secure tenancies)[3]. However, the court indicated that it had only heard limited argument on the point[4] and it appears that relevant cases may not have been cited[5] so the matter cannot be regarded as closed.

[1] *Smith v Lancashire Teaching Hospitals NHS Foundation Trust* [2017] EWCA Civ 1916, [2018] PIQR P 5, CA per Sir Terence Etherton MR at [48] and [55]. See also *R (H) v Ealing London Borough Council* [2017] EWCA Civ 1127, [2018] HLR 2, CA per Sir Terence Etherton MR at [92]–[94].

[2] *R (HA) v Ealing London Borough Council* [2015] EWHC 2375 (Admin); *R (YA) v Hammersmith and Fulham London Borough Council* [2016] EWHC 1850 (Admin); *R (C) v Islington London Borough Council* [2017] EWHC 1288 (Admin).

[3] *R (H) v Ealing London Borough Council* [2017] EWCA Civ 1127, [2018] HLR 2, CA per Sir Terence Etheron MR at [101]–[102], Davis LJ at [128]–[130] and Underhill LJ at [131]–[133].

[4] *R (H) v Ealing London Borough Council* [2017] EWCA Civ 1127, [2018] HLR 2, CA per Underhill LJ at [131].

[5] Such as *Petrovic v Austria* (2001) EHRR 14.

4.218 The characteristics protected by Art 14 include not only sex, race, colour, language, religion, political or other opinion, national or social origin, association with a national minority, property, and birth, but also 'other status'. A 'wide and generous' approach will be taken to whether or not the claimant has some 'other status'[1]. The courts have tended to focus more on whether alleged differential treatment is justified than on the question of status[2]. The Court of Appeal has recently observed that 'if the alleged discrimination falls within the scope of a Convention right, the question of status will normally be answered in the claimant's favour'[3]. Examples of 'other status' include the status of being homeless[4], or a care leaver[5] or a private rented sector tenant as opposed to a secure tenant[6].

[1] *Stevenson v Secretary of State for Work and Pensions* [2017] EWCA Civ 2123, CA per Henderson LJ at [36].

[2] *AL (Serbia) v Secretary of State for the Home Department* [2008] UKHL 42, [2008] 1 WLR 1434 at [24]–[25].

[3] *Stevenson v Secretary of State for Work and Pensions* [2017] EWCA Civ 2123, CA per Henderson LJ at [41].

[4] *R (RJM) v Secretary of State for Work and Pensions* [2008] UKHL 63, [2009] 1 AC 311, HL.

[5] *R (YA) v Hammersmith and Fulham London Borough Council* [2016] EWHC 1850 (Admin) at [68].

[6] *R (Fartun Osman) v Harrow London Borough Council* [2017] EWHC 274 (Admin). At the time of writing there was an outstanding application for permission to appeal against this decision.

4.219 When deciding whether a discriminatory provision or practice is justified, the court will consider the same four-stage test which applies to discrimination under the Equality Act 2010 (see **4.213** above)[1]. However, as discussed below (at **4.220–4.226**), the standard of scrutiny to be applied is not necessarily the same.

[1] *Bank Mellat v Her Majesty's Treasury (No. 2)* [2013] UKSC 39, [2014] AC 700, SC per Lord Sumption at [20]. It was confirmed that this approach applies to claims of discrimination under Art 14 ECHR by the Supreme Court in *Brewster v Northern Ireland Local Government Officer's Superannuation Committee* [2017] UKSC 8, [2016] 1 WLR 519, SC per Lord Kerr at [66].

Standard of scrutiny

4.220 When the court is considering whether a measure which is discriminatory under either the Equality Act 2010 or Art 14 ECHR is justified, how strict a level of scrutiny should it apply? Should it treat the decision-maker's actions with a significant degree of respect, upholding the policy unless it is manifestly without reasonable foundation? Or should it apply a more exacting test?

STANDARD OF SCRUTINY UNDER ARTICLE 14 ECHR

4.221 It is well-established that, 'when it comes to general measures of economic or social strategy', policy choices by the legislature will generally be respected unless they are manifestly without reasonable foundation[1]. Thus in the context of state benefits, a difference of treatment amounting to discrimination will be upheld unless it is 'manifestly without reasonable foundation'[2].

1   *Stec v United Kingdom* (2006) 43 EHRR 1017 at [51].
2   *R (DA) v Secretary of State for Work and Pensions* [2018] EWCA Civ 504.

4.222 Local housing authorities are distinct from national governments, and housing allocation schemes do not amount to macroeconomic and/or social policy. However, it is well-established that 'housing allocation policy is a difficult exercise which requires not only social and political sensitivity and judgment, but also local expertise and knowledge'[1] which local housing authorities are best placed to undertake.

1   *R (Ahmad) v Newham London Borough Council* [2009] UKHL 14, [2009] HL 31, HL per Lord Neuberger at [46].

4.223 The approaches taken by the court have varied:

* In *R (HA) v Ealing London Borough Council*[1], the standard of scrutiny applied was not specified, although it appeared to be somewhat higher than 'manifestly without reasonable foundation'. The judge noted that 'the defendant, as a public body, is entitled to the appropriate measure of respect in relation to its decision' but found that 'no rational justification' had been advanced for the discriminatory treatment[2].
* In *R (YA) v Hammersmith and Fulham London Borough Council*[3], the parties agreed that 'there was a wider margin of appreciation in this case for any justification and that the burden of establishing the justification is on the defendant'[4]. The judge applied a significantly higher level of scrutiny than 'manifestly without reasonable foundation', making positive findings that the measure was rational, proportionate, and the least intrusive option available[5].
* In *R (Fartun Osman) v Harrow London Borough Council*[6] the scrutiny applied appeared to go beyond 'manifestly without reasonable foundation'. The judge found that the policy was not 'so ill-founded' or 'manifestly unfair or otherwise disproportionate' as to be unlawful under Art 14[7].
* In *R (C) v Islington London Borough Council*[8], the local housing authority argued that each of the four parts of the test should be answered in its favour unless the policy under challenge was 'manifestly without reasonable justification'. The claimant argued that, whilst that

may be the correct test to apply to the first three questions, the last question was essentially a matter to be determined by the court. The judge accepted the claimant's position, whilst recognizing that 'significant weight should be accorded to the defendant's decision' given that 'the policy also concerns the allocation of finite resources, namely social housing, by a body that not only has considerable expertise and experience in these matters, but has been entrusted with this task by Parliament'[9].

• In *R (H) v Ealing London Borough Council*[10], the judge at first instance held that the 'manifestly without reasonable foundation' test was insufficiently exacting, 'although of course due regard must be paid to the choices facing the council when distributing scarce resources like housing'[11].

The judge's decision in *R (H) v Ealing London Borough Council*[12] was challenged in the Court of Appeal[13]. Unfortunately, however, the court did not decide the matter either way, finding simply that the judge had not been entitled to reject the justification defence for the reasons given. The matter therefore remains uncertain.

1   [2015] EWHC 2375 (Admin), [2016] PTSR 16, HC.
2   [2015] EWHC 2375 (Admin), [2016] PTSR 16, HC per Goss J at [30].
3   [2016] EWHC 1850 (Admin), [2016] HLR 39, HC.
4   [2016] EWHC 1850 (Admin), [2016] HLR 39, HC per Mr Peter Marquand at [75].
5   [2016] EWHC 1850 (Admin), [2016] HLR 39, HC per Mr Peter Marquand at [84]–[85].
6   [2017] EWHC 274 (Admin), Admin Ct. At the time of writing there was an outstanding application for permission to appeal against this decision.
7   [2017] EWHC 274 (Admin), Admin Ct per Robin Purchas QC at [73].
8   [2017] EWHC 1288 (Admin), [2017] HLR 32, Admin Ct per Baker J at [79]–[81].
9   [2017] EWHC 1288 (Admin), [2017] HLR 32, Admin Ct per Baker J at [81].
10 [2016] EWHC 841 (Admin), [2016] HLR 20, Admin Ct.
11 [2016] EWHC 841 (Admin), [2016] HLR 20, Admin Ct per HHJ Waksman QC at [99]. The judge proceeded to find that the measure was not justified even if the manifestly without reasonable foundation test was applied.
12 [2016] EWHC 841 (Admin), [2016] HLR 20, Admin Ct.
13 *R (H) v Ealing London Borough Council* [2017] EWCA Civ 1127, [2018] HLR 2, CA.

Standard of scrutiny under the Equality Act 2010

4.224 The 'manifestly without reasonable foundation' threshold would appear to have no purchase in respect of justification defences under the Equality Act 2010. It is well-established that when the court is considering the four-stage test (see **4.213**), it does not limit itself to a rationality assessment but must reach its own judgment as to whether the conditions for justification are met[1]. The reasons given for a discriminatory measure will not be uncritically accepted[2].

1   *Akerman-Livingston v Aster Communities Ltd* [2015] UKSC 15, [2015] AC 1399, SC per Baroness Hale at [23]–[34], *Essop v Home Office* [2017] UKSC 27, [2017] 1 WLR 1343, SC per Baroness Hale at [29].
2   *Akerman-Livingston v Aster Communities Ltd* [2015] UKSC 15, [2015] AC 1399, SC, *Essop v Home Office* [2017] UKSC 27, [2017] 1 WLR 134, SC per Baroness Hale at [29], *Secretary of State for Defence v Elias* [2006] EWCA Civ 1293, [2006] 1 WLR 3213, CA per Mummery LJ at [164]–[181].

4.225 There are several reasons for this distinction. Article 14 ECHR is potentially open-ended, in that the protected characteristics include 'other status', in contrast to the protected characteristics under EA 2010, which are narrowly defined. Article 14 ECHR applies only to public authorities, unlike EA 2010. The 'manifestly without reasonable foundation' threshold derives from decisions as to what latitude should be given to national governments in questions of macroeconomic and/or social policy whereas EA 2010 protects individuals' rights not to be discriminated against.

4.226 Notwithstanding these differences, it has recently been argued on behalf of local housing authorities that the 'manifestly without reasonable foundation' level of scrutiny applies to justification defences under EA 2010. This submission was rejected by the court in *R (XC) v Southwark London Borough Council*[1]. The same argument was made by the local housing authority in *R (H) v Ealing London Borough Council* and it was hoped that some clarification might be forthcoming from this decision. However, the Court of Appeal did not decide the point. Without clear authority to show that the 'manifestly without reasonable foundation' test is applicable, the preferred view must be that it is not[2].

---

[1]   [2017] EWHC 736 (Admin), [2017] HLR 24, Admin Ct. At the time of writing there was an outstanding application for permission to appeal against this decision.
[2]   In *R (C) v Islington London Borough Council* [2017] EWHC 1288 (Admin), [2017] HLR 32, Admin Ct, the judge appeared to treat the questions of whether discrimination was justified under Art 14 ECHR and EA 2010 as coterminous: see [98]. However, it does not appear that argument on the applicability of the 'manifestly without reasonable foundation' test to EA 2010 claim was heard.

Guidance on avoiding discrimination

4.227 The former Commission for Racial Equality's *Code of Practice for Racial Equality in Housing* (of which there were separate versions for England, Scotland and Wales respectively)[1] contained the following examples of potential unlawful discrimination on grounds of 'race' relating to social housing allocation schemes (in the version for England):

'A council generally allocates the worst properties to homeless applicants, whereas tenants transferring to housing association accommodation receive better properties. Ethnic minority households are disproportionately represented among those whom the council has a duty to house because they are homeless. This policy would be unlawful direct discrimination[2], unless the council could show it to be a proportionate means of achieving a legitimate aim. It may also be unlawful under the Housing Act 1996' (Example 30).

'A housing association's allocation policy gives priority for lettings to tenants' sons and daughters. If the racial profile of tenants does not reflect the racial profile of people in need of housing in the association's catchment area, the policy could disadvantage prospective tenants from under-represented racial groups and could amount to unlawful indirect discrimination. It would therefore need to be carefully considered, and the justification for the policy tested against any possible discriminatory effects' (Example 31).

'A local council (or housing association) fails to make sure that information about its lettings services reaches people from all racial groups; for example, by not advertising the service in outlets which it knows are preferred by ethnic minority residents. This could amount to indirect discrimination' (Example 35).

'A CRE inquiry into a major public sector landlord's "choice-based" lettings scheme found that:

- the city council had not done a race equality impact assessment of the scheme;
- it had not consulted affected groups and agencies in the community adequately;
- ethnic monitoring of applications and allocations was poor; and
- information about the new scheme was not available in relevant languages.

The CRE concluded that there had been contraventions of the duty to promote race equality, and that these failings should be rectified' (Example 38).

'Analysis of a council's housing allocations shows that people from certain racial groups are consistently offered inferior accommodation. This constitutes direct discrimination' (Example 39).

[1]   All the versions of the CRE's Code are available on the EHRC website.
[2]   This appears to be an error: the discrimination described would constitute indirect discrimination.

4.228 The former statutory guidance in the Disability Rights Commission's publication *Duty to Promote Disability Equality: Statutory Code of Practice England and Wales* also contained a number of examples of unlawful discrimination on the grounds of disability in the housing and social housing area[1].

[1]   Disability Rights Commission, October 2006. The statutory guidance on gender discrimination was *Gender Equality Duty: Code of Practice for England and Wales* (Equal Opportunities Commission, November 2006). All of these Codes are available on the EHRC website.

Examples of court decisions on discrimination

4.229 An example of unlawful discrimination on the grounds of sexual orientation is the case of *Rodriguez v Minister of Housing of Gibraltar*[1] in which a tenant asked her social landlord to agree to make her long-term same sex partner a joint tenant of her home (so that her partner would be secure in the event of her death). The allocation policy was only to agree to such requests if the couple were married or had children. The landlord claimed that the policy was not discriminatory because a heterosexual childless couple would also have been refused. Alternatively, if there was discrimination, it was justified by the aim to support families and children. The Privy Council held that the policy did discriminate against same-sex partners and that there was no rational justification for that discrimination.

[1]   [2009] UKPC 52, (2009) 28 BHRC 189, PC.

4.230 Issues about discrimination in the housing allocation context have become more prominent as local housing authorities take advantage of the opportunities to increase or reduce preference or create qualifying classes. The court have considered claims of discrimination in a number of different schemes:

- In *R (HA) v Ealing London Borough Council*[1] the local housing authority had adopted a qualifying criterion based on local residence which operated to exclude women who had fled into the local housing authority's area from elsewhere to seek refuge from domestic violence. The criterion was successfully challenged on the basis that it constituted unlawful indirect discrimination against women contrary to Equality Act 2010, s 29.

- In *R (YA) v Hammersmith and Fulham London Borough Council*[2] a qualifying class which excluded applicants who had been guilty of unacceptable behaviour was, although discriminatory against care leavers, justified as it improved the environment for other residents and reduced the risk of the council spending limited resources on legal proceedings to evict misbehaving tenants.

- In *R (Fartun Osman) v Harrow London Borough Council*[3] the local housing authority revised its scheme with the effect that overcrowded households in the private rented sector had their priority reduced to Band C whilst overcrowded households with secure tenancies remained in Band A. The judge found that the discrimination was a proportionate means of achieving a legitimate aim and therefore justified.

- In *R (XC) v Southwark London Borough Council*[4] the judge found that the award of a priority star to applicants who were in voluntary or paid work indirectly discriminated against disabled persons and women. However, the discrimination had the legitimate aim of creating sustainable communities and encouraging residents to contribute to the local community; the system was rationally connected to those objectives; and the measure adopted was the least intrusive to achieve those aims. Of relevance was the fact that the authority had retained a discretion to waive the practice in exceptional circumstances.

- In *R (C) v Islington London Borough Council*[5] a local lettings policy which gave local residents priority for new homes on existing estates was found to be discriminatory, but justified when looked at in the context of the scheme as a whole. The court held that it should accord significant weight to the authority's decision as the matter concerned the allocation of finite resources by a body with considerable expertise which had been entrusted by Parliament with the task.

- In *R (H) v Ealing London Borough Council*[6] the Court of Appeal allowed in part an appeal against a judge's finding that two schemes which set aside a number of lettings for 'working households' and 'model tenants' was unlawfully discriminatory. It was conceded that each scheme was indirectly discriminatory but the court found that the judge had not been entitled to reject the council's justification defence. In finding that the schemes were not the least intrusive way of achieving the legitimate aim in question, the judge had relied on other allocation schemes which were radically different from Ealing's and had stepped 'over the line of unacceptable incursion by the court into the practical running of a housing allocation scheme'[7].

1   [2015] EWHC 2375 (Admin),[2016] PTSR 16, [2015] BLGR 954, Admin Ct.
2   [2016] EWHC 1850 (Admin), [2016] HLR 39, Admin Ct.
3   [2017] EWHC 274 (Admin). At the time of writing there was an outstanding application for permission to appeal against this decision.
4   [2017] EWHC 736 (Admin), [2017] HLR 24, Admin Ct. At the time of writing there was an outstanding application for permission to appeal against this decision.
5   [2017] EWHC 1288 (Admin), [2017] HLR 32, Admin Ct.
6   [2017] EWCA Civ 1127, [2018] HLR 2, CA.

[7] In *Complaint against London Borough of Brent*, 16 010 013, 24 March 2017, the Local Government Ombudsman considered an allocations policy which reserved 80% of lettings for homeless households in temporary accommodation was found to be lawful. However, it appears that no discrimination arguments were raised.

Allocation and migration

4.231 Despite the measures that local housing authorities are – or should be – taking to involve local communities in setting, or at least understanding, priorities in housing allocation and the need to avoid discrimination and inequality, recent surveys have found that many people perceive that the way that social housing is allocated is unfair. A UK Government-commissioned study published in 2009 found that less than a quarter (23%) of the public agreed that the way social housing is allocated is fair[1].

[1] *Attitudes to Housing: Findings from the Ipsos MORI Public Affairs Monitor Omnibus Survey (England)* (DCLG, 2009), chapter 7.

4.232 A particularly popular misconception has been that the majority of available social housing is allocated to new arrivals from overseas[1]. Research commissioned by the EHRC, for example, identified anxieties about housing allocation schemes putting British families at a disadvantage[2].

[1] Readers seeking to probe further the relationship between allocation and migration may find helpful material in *Immigration and the Access to Social Housing in the UK*, CEP Discussion Paper No 1264 and *Migrants and Housing in the UK: Experiences and Impacts*, The Migration Observatory, Oxford University, September 2015.

[2] *Social housing allocation and immigrant communities* Jill Rutter and Maria Latorre Migration, Equalities and Citizenship Team, IPPR, 2009.

4.233 In fact, studies have consistently shown this to be incorrect. The aforementioned research commissioned by the EHRC found that less than 2% of all social housing residents are people who have moved to Britain in the last five years and that nine out of ten people who live in social housing were born in the UK[1]. An earlier study had found that, on the available data, relatively small numbers of new immigrants and migrants were accessing the social rented sector[2]. Research from 2012 showed that UK-born and foreign-born individuals have similar levels of participation in social housing (about 17–18% of each group live in social housing)[3]. A recent note produced by the Parliamentary Office of Science and Technology confirmed that less than a fifth of migrants live in social rented accommodation and, when differences in household structure, area of residence, and economic circumstances are taken into account, migrant households are significantly less likely than comparable UK-born households to live in social housing. The note concluded that 'There is no evidence that social housing allocation favours migrants'[4]. The proportion of social lettings to UK nationals remained virtually unchanged from 2012–13 (91%) to 2016–17 (90%) for general needs accommodation[5].

[1] *Social housing allocation and immigrant communities* Jill Rutter and Maria Latorre Migration, Equalities and Citizenship Team, IPPR, 2009.

[2] *New immigrants and migrants in social housing in England* (Local Government Association, 2008).

3   *Housing and migration May 2012 A UK guide to issues and solutions* (Housing and Migration
    Network, May 2012) and see *Migrants and Housing in the UK: Experiences and Impacts* (The
    Migration Observatory, Oxford University, September 2015).
4   Parliamentary Office of Science and Technology, *POSTnote: Migrants and Housing*, No 560,
    August 2017, p 1.
5   *Social Housing Lettings: April 2013 to March 2014*, England (DCLG, October 2013) and
    Social *Housing Lettings: April 2016 to March 2017* , England (MHCLG, January 2018).

4.234 In an attempt to correct these misconceptions, emphasis has been placed on improving the transparency of social housing allocations. The Welsh Code recommends that local housing authorities provide regular, accurate and generalised information on how social housing is allocated and how waiting lists are managed, working actively to dispel any myths and misconceptions which may arise[1]. The Supplementary English Code advises that[2]:

'It is important that applicants and the wider community understand how social housing is allocated in their area, and that they know who is getting that social housing, so that they can see that the allocation system is fair and the authority is complying with its allocation scheme. We would encourage housing authorities to consider how accurate and anonymised information on waiting list applicants and lettings outcomes could be routinely published, to strengthen public confidence in the fairness of their allocation scheme.'

1   Welsh Code, paras 4.3 and 4.49–4.52.
2   Supplementary English Code, para [28]. See also Welsh Code, para 3.57.

4.235 In October 2013 local housing authorities were encouraged to do more to improve the data collected and made available on social housing lettings. The UK Government told local housing authorities in England that[1]:

'Good quality data on social lettings is critical to enabling local authorities to effectively discharge their functions and understand how their assets are used and allocated. Local authorities should have up-to-date information about prospective tenants' characteristics, *including nationality and immigration status*, in order to ascertain their priority and eligibility for social housing. In the spirit of transparency and public accountability, this information should be readily available.' [Emphasis added]

1   *Provision of Social Lettings Data: Advice to Local Authorities* (DCLG, October 2013) at
    para 9.

4.236 In light of the referendum vote to leave the European Union, the future relationship between social housing allocation and EU migrants is very uncertain. However, despite the fact that access to social housing was one of the topics raised by the UK Government during the EU Membership Negotiations of February 2016, only 4% of new social lettings each year go to EU migrants. This means that, even if new rules meant EU migrants were denied social tenancies, the effect on supply generally would be 'very small'[1].

1   Chartered Institute of Housing, *What you need to know about Brexit and how it might affect
    migration, housing need and eligibility*, undated.

SOCIAL HOUSING ALLOCATION AND HUMAN RIGHTS

4.237 The only 'human rights' directly enforceable in the courts in England and Wales are those set out in Sch 1 of the Human Rights Act 1998 (HRA 1998). As explained later in this book, those rights can be deployed in some circumstances to force public bodies to arrange accommodation for particularly vulnerable individuals[1]. However, none of those specified human rights confers on any person a right to obtain a home in *social* housing[2].

1   See **20.110** et seq.
2   The submission that a decision that an applicant is not eligible for an allocation engages (and may infringe) the right to respect for a home protected by Human Rights Act 1998, Sch 1, Art 8 has been rejected: *R (Dixon) v Wandsworth London Borough Council* [2007] EWHC 3075 (Admin), (2008) February *Legal Action*, p 40, Admin Ct at [28]–[30] and *R (Dixon) v Wandsworth London Borough Council* [2008] EWCA Civ 595, (2008) July *Legal Action*, p 22, CA at [11].

4.238 This does not mean that the HRA 1998 can be ignored by those concerned in the allocation of social housing. The Equality and Human Rights Commission has included valuable coverage of the interface between the HRA 1998 and social housing allocation in its current guidance for social landlords[1].

1   *Human Rights at home: guidance for social housing providers* (EHRC, March 2011) at pp 161–9. The guidance was referred to and applied in *R (H) v Ealing London Borough Council* [2016] EWHC 841 (Admin), [2016] HLR 20, Admin Ct at [86]. An appeal against this decision was allowed by the Court of Appeal: [2017] EWCA Civ 1127, [2018] HLR 2, CA.

4.239 Perhaps the most obvious point of interface between the HRA 1998 and the legislative scheme governing housing allocation in HA 1996, Pt 6, arises if a local housing authority or other social landlord performs its public, mainly statutory, functions relating to social housing allocation in a discriminatory way. That may trigger the application of HRA 1998, Sch 1, Art 14 which provides that the other rights protected in Sch 1 'shall be secured without discrimination on any ground such as sex, race, colour, language, religion, political or other opinion, national or social origin, association with a national minority, property, birth or other status'[1].

1   See **4.217** et seq.

4.240 The human rights protected by HRA 1998, Sch 1 also include the right, in Art 6, to a fair and just determination of a dispute about civil rights within a reasonable time. That has been interpreted as including the right to obtain a reasonably prompt enforcement of a judgment. Indeed, the benefit of such a court judgment may become a person's possession protected by Art 1 of Protocol 1. So where, as in the UK, the state has provided a statutory system of distribution of social housing, a failure to comply with a court judgment requiring the provision of such social housing to an individual may be a breach of Art 6 and/or of Art 1 of Protocol 1[1].

1   *Gerasimov and Others v Russia* [2014] ECHR 680, ECtHR and *Stetsenko v Russia* [2014] ECHR 433, (2014) June *Legal Action*, p 433, ECtHR.

ALLOCATION SCHEMES AND THE BEST INTERESTS OF CHILDREN

4.241 Local authorities, including local housing authorities, must make arrangements for ensuring that their functions are discharged having regard to the need to safeguard and promote the welfare of children[1]. This applies not only to the formulation of general policies but also to decisions in individual cases[2].

---

[1]   Children Act 2004, s 11.
[2]   *Nzolameso v Westminster City Council* [2015] UKSC 22, [2015] All ER 942 at [24].

4.242 The Supreme Court has explained that the Children Act 2004, s 11 duty requires decision-makers to treat the best interests of children as a primary consideration, although not as 'the' primary consideration[1]. The Children Act 2004, s 11 duty means that local housing authorities who are formulating or amending their allocation schemes must do so with regard to the need to safeguard and promote the welfare of children. 'Welfare' is to be given a broad meaning, 'encompassing physical, psychological, social, educational and economic welfare'[2]. The local housing authority must not simply 'safeguard' the welfare of children but actively promote it[3]. It is also likely that decision-makers will be obliged to interpret housing allocation schemes consistently with the Children Act 2004, s 11 duty[4].

---

[1]   *ZH (Tanzania) v Secretary of State for the Home Department* [2011] UKSC 4, [2011] 2 AC 166, SC at [22]–[26].
[2]   *Nzolameso v Westminster City Council* [2015] UKSC 22, [2015] 2 All ER 942, SC per Lady Hale at [23], quoted by Goss J in *R (HA) v Ealing London Borough Council* [2015] EWHC 2375 (Admin), [2016] PTSR 16, Admin Ct at [35].
[3]   *R (J and L) v Hillingdon London Borough Council* [2017] EWHC 3411 (Admin), Admin Ct per Nicklin J at [46] and *R (HC) v Secretary of State for Work and Pensions* [2017] UKSC 73, [2017] 3 WLR 1486, SC per Baroness Hale at [46].
[4]   *R (J and L) v Hillingdon London Borough Council* [2017] EWHC 3411 (Admin), Admin Ct per Nicklin J at [72] (obiter).

4.243 The Children Act 2004, s 11 duty also requires local housing authorities to treat the best interests of any children involved as a primary consideration when making decisions in individual cases. On the facts of one case, that was met by the housing department contacting social services when considering what points to award the application[1]. The obligation was further satisfied by welfare categories which awarded points for households that included someone with 'a need for settled accommodation on welfare or medical grounds who cannot reasonably be expected to find accommodation for themselves in future'. It was held that this was 'clearly wide enough to include consideration of children'[2]. However, in another case, the obligation had not been met: the local housing authority had been required to identify the principal needs of the children and then have regard to the real risks to their safety and well-being, but had not done so.[3]

---

[1]   *R (Woolfe) v Islington London Borough Council* [2016] EWHC 1907 (Admin), [2016] HLR 42, Admin Ct at [51].
[2]   *R (Woolfe) v Islington London Borough Council* [2016] EWHC 1907 (Admin), [2016] HLR 42, Admin Ct at [42]–[54]. This interpretation may be seen as support for the proposition that housing allocation schemes must be construed consistently with Children Act 2004, s 11 as far as possible.

3   *R (KS) v London Borough of Haringey* [2018] EWHC 587 (Admin) per HHJ Walden-Smith (sitting as a Judge of the High Court) at [62].

4.244 The Children Act 2004, s 11 duty may well involve the housing department seeking the active involvement of its Children's Services department in its housing allocation decision-making. Whilst the duty under s 27 of the Children Act 1989 which requires co-operation between authorities does not apply to two departments within the same authority, a similar degree of co-operation between such departments is required by the statutory guidance *Working together to safeguard children: A guide to inter-agency working to safeguard and promote the welfare of children*[1].

1   *R (M); R (A) v Islington London Borough Council* [2016] EWHC 332 (Admin), [2016] HLR 19, Admin Ct.

4.245 This duty of co-operation was considered, and found to have been breached, in *R (KS) v London Borough of Haringey*[1]. In that case, a social worker had made clear to the local housing authority that the children's accommodation was unsuitable. The judge found that local housing authority had been obliged, in response to this, to make a decision based upon the issues highlighted by the social worker. The local housing authority's decision that the family should simply remain where they were was deficient. The duty of co-operation was also breached in *R (J and L) v Hillingdon London Borough Council*[2]. This case concerned a severely disabled 8-year-old boy (L) living with his mother in unsuitable accommodation in which his health and safety were at risk. The Children's Services department had completed a Child and Family assessment which, as the judge found, concluded that the risks to L were tolerable pending alternative accommodation which could be provided through 'the usual housing application and bidding process'[3]. The local housing authority obtained a medical assessment which stated that the current accommodation was suitable and in reliance on that assessed the claimant as having no identified medical or housing need. As a consequence, she was not allowed onto the housing register. The judge found that there had been a failure of co-operation between the local housing authority and Children's Services:

- the Child and Family assessment failed to clearly communicate to the local housing authority that Children's Services were not going to accommodate the family because his needs would be met through the allocation process;
- the local housing authority's decision letter contained no reference to, 'or apparent consideration of', the recommendations in the Child and Family assessment (or the previous Occupational Therapy assessments);
- the local housing authority's decision letter failed 'so comprehensively' to grasp the nature of the risks to L and how they were to be addressed, as set out in the Child and Family assessment, that it was 'impossible' to conclude that there had been any co-operation with the Children's Services department; and
- Children's Services had then failed to pick up on the negative housing allocation decision, which should have prompted a referral back to

Children's Services for further consideration[4].

1   [2018] EWHC 587 (Admin).
2   [2017] EWHC 3411 (Admin), Admin Ct.
3   [2017] EWHC 3411 (Admin), Admin Ct per Nicklin J at [57]–[57].
4   [2017] EWHC 3411 (Admin), Admin Ct per Nicklin J at [60]–[69].

4.246 In contrast, the Children Act 2004, s 11 duty was found to be satisfied in another case[1] where:

* the local housing authority had discussed the scheme, including in particular the welfare points element, with the children's services department prior to its introduction;
* the housing department had a joint working protocol with the children's services department; and
* when considering whether points should be allocated on welfare grounds, the housing department would contact the children's services department.

1   *R (Woolfe) v Islington London Borough Council* [2016] EWHC 1907 (Admin), [2016] HLR 42, Admin Ct at [42]–[54].

4.247 As when it comes to considering compliance with the public sector equality duty[1], judges should not be 'too exacting' when deciding whether or not the Children Act 2004, s 11 duty has been breached[2]. However, it should be clear that 'proper consideration' has been given to the relevant matters: the local housing authority must be able to show that the obligation has been properly discharged[3]. This was not shown in *R (J and L) v Hillingdon London Borough Council*[4] where the decision letter did 'not even recognise' the Children Act 2004, s 11 duty 'as a factor in the decision-making'[5]. The court will not 'assume' that a local housing authority has performed its functions conscientiously[6]. Whilst the court will not take over the role of decision-maker, it will 'scrutinise with care' what the local housing authority has done[7].

1   See **4.193–4.209**.
2   *R (H) v Ealing London Borough Council* [2017] EWCA Civ 1127, [2018] HLR 2, CA at [122].
3   *Nzolameso v Westminster City Council* [2015] UKSC 22, [2015] All ER 942, SC at [32] and [37].
4   [2017] EWHC 3411 (Admin), Admin Ct.
5   [2017] EWHC 3411 (Admin), Admin Ct per Nicklin J at [69].
6   *R (KS) v London Borough of Haringey* [2018] EWHC 587 (Admin) per HHJ Walden-Smith (sitting as a Judge of the High Court) at [35].
7   *R (KS) v London Borough of Haringey* [2018] EWHC 587 (Admin) per HHJ Walden-Smith (sitting as a Judge of the High Court) at [35].

THE ROLE OF 'DISCRETION' IN ALLOCATION SCHEMES

4.248 One of the most difficult tasks in framing an allocation scheme is to determine the extent to which flexibility should be retained, on the part of identified officers of the local housing authority, to depart from the normal rules or to deal with exceptional or unusual cases. Sadly, the judicial guidance is not altogether clear on the extent to which the inclusion of a broad discretion is lawful, or the absence of such unlawful.

4.249 At one extreme it is plain that a scheme cannot lawfully allow so much discretion to depart from the rules that, in reality, there is no scheme other than the exercise of discretion on a case-by-case basis. The examples of allocation schemes which were unlawful in that respect include:

- *R v Islington London Borough Council ex p Reilly & Mannix*[1]. That case was concerned with a points-based system. There was discretion to award as many additional points as were needed to bring a particular household to the head of the queue and to gain the needed priority. The judge said[2]:

  ' . . . the residual discretion is not a satisfactory way of bridging the gap between the outcome of the category-based points calculation and the true assessment of need. It is too vague and uncertain and results in a disproportionately large element of need being subject to assessment on an undefined and unguided discretionary basis.'

- *R (Cali) v London Borough of Waltham Forest*[3]. The local housing authority had adopted a banding scheme and choice-based letting. The published scheme gave unfettered power to a panel of officers to move an applicant from one category to another, depending upon their perceived housing need. Applying *Reilly & Mannix* the judge said[4]:

  'First, the practice identified appears to be the exercise of a broad discretion to promote a household from one category to another. . . . In the absence of published criteria, the mechanism described in the letter depends excessively on discretion . . . As in *Reilly & Mannix*, the discretion identified . . . is too vague and would result in decisions as to comparative need being taken on "an undefined and unguided discretionary basis" which could lead to inconsistency and arbitrary results.'

In the second case, the effect of introducing an unlimited discretion was that the published allocation scheme failed to meet the statutory obligation that it must set out the local regime for determining priorities.

[1]   [1998] EWHC Admin 912, (1998) 31 HLR 651, QBD.
[2]   [1998] EWHC Admin 912, (1998) 31 HLR 651, QBD at p 666.
[3]   [2006] EWHC 302 (Admin), [2007] HLR 1, Admin Ct.
[4]   [2006] EWHC 302 (Admin), [2007] HLR 1, Admin Ct at [39].

4.250 A more difficult question is whether the terms of an allocation scheme may remove or exclude all possibility of the exercise of residual discretion, even in an exceptional case. This issue arises particularly in the context of setting qualifying classes for local allocation of social housing. The statutory guidance suggests that there may be exceptional circumstances where it is necessary to disapply the generally adopted qualifying criteria in the case of individual applicants. It encourages local housing authorities to 'make explicit provision for dealing with exceptional cases within their qualification rules', offering the example of the need to move an intimidated witness quickly[1]. This guidance is no doubt intended to meet one of the criticisms made in respect of the equivalent pre-2003 statutory scheme which had the effect that:

' . . . where an applicant falls within a class of non-qualifying persons (eg persons with rent arrears), the housing authority rejects the application and does not make a balanced decision based on consideration of the particular circumstances of the case (eg weigh the degree of housing need against the severity of the rent arrears)[2] .'

1   English Code, para 3.25.
2   *Parliamentary Joint Committee On Human Rights First Report, Appendix: The homelessness bill, Memorandum by the Department for Transport, Local Government and the Regions,* para 6.1.

4.251 This issue has been further developed in the Supplementary English Code issued in December 2013. Under the heading 'Providing for exceptions' that guidance states[1]:

'19. It is important that housing authorities retain the flexibility to take proper account of special circumstances. This can include providing protection to people who need to move away from another area, to escape violence or harm; as well as enabling those who need to return, such as homeless families and care leavers whom the authority have housed outside their district, and those who need support to rehabilitate and integrate back into the community . . .

21. These examples are not intended to be exhaustive and housing authorities may wish to consider providing for other appropriate exceptions in the light of local circumstances. In addition, authorities retain a discretion to deal with individual cases where there are exceptional circumstances.'

1   Supplementary English Code (DCLG, December 2013), reproduced at Appendix 1 to this book, p 6.

4.252 Departure from this guidance was, however, sanctioned by the court in the case of *R (Hillsden) v Epping Forest District Council*[1]. The local housing authority in this case had adopted a residency test to identify those qualifying for housing allocation in its district. The allocation scheme set out the residency rules and specific exceptions to them but did not include any discretion for specific exceptional cases. An applicant unable to meet the terms of the allocation scheme's residency test contended that her circumstances were exceptional and sought a judicial review[2]. The Administrative Court held that nothing in HA 1996, Pt 6, as amended by the Localism Act 2011, required a local housing authority to retain an override facility for individual, exceptional cases to be treated as falling within carefully drawn qualifying classes the specific conditions of which they could not satisfy. The encouragement in the Codes to include such a facility was simply that, ie 'encouragement'.

1   *R (Hillsden) v Epping Forest District Council* [2015] EWHC 98 (Admin), Admin Ct.
2   *R (Hillsden) v Epping Forest District Council* [2015] EWHC 98 (Admin), Admin Ct.

4.253 However, this is contrary to other decisions where a residual discretion has been viewed as essential. For example, in a case decided in 2002, when the law allowed for the exclusion of classes from a housing register, a local housing authority had adopted a new fixed rule that an applicant who was a tenant of other social housing accommodation and was aged under 60 could not join the local housing register[1]. A housing association tenant aged only 36 applied to join the register and was refused. The judge said: 'I am clear that it would be unlawful for the defendants to apply their new policy in such a way as to preclude their acceptance of an application which fell foul of it but of which the circumstances were exceptional' and held that: 'the policy is lawful, provided that the defendants never forget that indeed it is but policy which, of its nature, must never be so applied as to preclude acceptance in exceptional circumstances of an application which falls foul of it'[2]. Similarly, in *R (Osei) v Newham London Borough Council*[3] the local allocation scheme enabled the housing authority to take into account former tenant arrears as an aspect of 'behaviour' when prioritising between applicants who would otherwise qualify for urgent rehousing on domestic violence or other emergency grounds. The court held that such a provision would not be unlawful provided it was applied with a flexibility which allowed for the personal circumstances of an applicant which might justify not taking into account that past behaviour in a particular case.

[1] *R (Conway) v Charnwood Borough Council* [2002] EWHC 43 (Admin), [2002] NPC 11, Admin Ct.
[2] *R (Conway) v Charnwood Borough Council* [2002] EWHC 43 (Admin), [2002] NPC 11, Admin Ct per Wilson J at [22].
[3] *R (Osei) v Newham London Borough Council* [2010] EWHC 368 (Admin), (2010) March *Legal Action*, p 30, Admin Ct.

4.254 In another case, a rule in an allocation scheme suspended all applicants from bidding where they owed in excess of one weeks' rent arrears, save where the Director of Housing considered there were exceptional circumstances. No-one suggested that the presence of such discretion rendered the scheme unlawful and an appeal court judge said[1]:

'The scheme contains the necessary safety valve to enable those who are in arrears to explain to the Director of Housing that there is some good reason for them being in arrears, for example because they are ill in hospital or whatever. In those circumstances the Director of Housing can then allow bidding to take place "in exceptional circumstances" . . . '

[1] *R (Babakandi) v Westminster City Council* [2011] EWCA Civ 1397, (2012) January *Legal Action*, p 21, CA at [7].

4.255 In *R (XC) v Southwark London Borough Council*[1] an allocation scheme which discriminated against women and people with disabilities was found to be lawful because the measure was the least intrusive possible to achieve a legitimate aim and struck the right balance. The judge was reinforced in this view 'by the existence within the scheme of provision for exceptional cases' through which 'the Council has, very properly, reserved to itself the right to remedy particular incidents of unfairness thrown up by the operation of the scheme'[2].

[1] [2017] EWHC 736 (Admin), [2017] HLR 24, Admin Ct. At the time of writing there was an outstanding application for permission to appeal against this decision.
[2] [2017] EWHC 736 (Admin), [2017] HLR 24, Admin Ct at [100].

4.256 In *Hillingdon London Borough Council v Holley*[1], the local housing authority argued that the effect of the Supreme Court's decision in *R (Ahmad) v Newham London Borough Council*[2] was to eliminate any requirement for an allocation scheme to include a residual discretion. This submission was rejected, the Court of Appeal noting that the scheme in Ahmad plainly contained a residual discretion[3]. However, the occupier's appeal was still dismissed. The court considered that, 'viewed as a whole', Hillingdon's scheme 'arguably' contained 'a form of residual discretion to address exceptional cases'[4]. In any event, even if that discretion was too narrow, or even if the respondent had failed to consider applying it, the appellant's case must fail:

> His case for allocation of this house, however much it may generate human sympathy, simply came nowhere near that degree of exceptionality that gave him a real rather than fanciful prospect of success under a residual discretion, however widely framed, as to allocation of public housing[5].

[1]   [2016] EWCA Civ 1052, [2017] HLR 3, CA.
[2]   [2009] UKHL 14, [2009] HLR 41, HL.
[3]   [2016] EWCA Civ 1052, [2017] HLR 3, CA at [27].
[4]   [2016] EWCA Civ 1052, [2017] HLR 3, CA at [26].
[5]   [2016] EWCA Civ 1052, [2017] HLR 3, CA at [31].

4.257 Moreover, the LGSCO – in guidance issued post-*Hillsden* – has indicated that it expects exceptional cases to be individually considered as a matter of good administration. Its guidance states that 'We take the view that, whether or not a council has included an exceptional circumstances provision in its policy, if an applicant's exceptional circumstances have not been considered, we are likely to find it to be at fault'[1]. Where a discretion does exist, it must be exercised (or not exercised) lawfully: in one case, a local housing authority's failure to exercise its discretionary power was irrational in light of social services' assessment that the property was a risk to the children's health and safety.[2]

[1]   *Full house: Councils' role in allocating social housing - Focus report: learning lessons from complaints* (LGO, January 2016).
[2]   *R (KS) v London Borough of Haringey* [2018] EWHC 587 (Admin) per HHJ Walden-Smith (sitting as a Judge of the High Court) at [49].

CHALLENGES TO ALLOCATION SCHEMES

4.258 Ordinarily, an applicant will only be concerned with whether his or her particular application has been correctly considered under the terms of the relevant local housing allocation scheme - in other words, whether decisions have been correctly made on questions of eligibility and qualification and whether the application has been attributed to the right band (in a banding scheme) or accorded the appropriate points (in a points-based scheme). Disputes about these and other case-specific matters can be dealt with by reviews, complaints and litigation[1].

[1]   See **2.86–2.120** for general information about reviews, complaints and judicial review litigation and **3.204–3.207** for challenges to decisions about eligibility and qualification.

4.259 But, not infrequently, a particular applicant's case may demonstrate that there is – at least arguably – something wrong with the local allocation scheme more generally. In those circumstances the applicant may need to challenge the legality of the scheme or some part of it. That is normally done by proceedings for judicial review[1].

[1]   For a fuller description of judicial review principles and procedures, see **19.306** et seq.

4.260 For example, it might be suggested that:

- the scheme has failed to comply with some express statutory requirement of HA 1996, Pt 6;
- it has been adopted or varied without the requisite prior consultation[1];
- it fails to set out the local housing authority's policies on priority or procedures for allocation[2];
- it has been drafted without regard to the statutory Codes of Guidance – or is contrary to them (without explanation)[3];
- the scheme is discriminatory in an unlawful respect[4]; or
- the scheme does not comply with Children Act 2004, s 11[5].

[1] See **4.5** and **4.13**.
[2] See **4.22–4.26**.
[3] HA 1996, s 169(1).
[4] See **4.210–4.230**.
[5] See **4.241–4.247**.

4.261 In short, a housing allocation scheme adopted by a local housing authority must 'be lawfully and fairly operated, for example without unlawful discrimination'[1].

[1] *R (Ahmad) v Newham London Borough Council* [2009] UKHL 14, [2009] HLR 41, HL at [14].

4.262 Very exceptionally, it may be said that the whole or part of a scheme is irrational in the sense that no reasonable local housing authority could have framed its scheme in that way. Between 1996 and 2008, several schemes adopted under HA 1996, Pt 6, were described in those terms by the courts. But, in 2009, the House of Lords emphasised just how difficult it would be to sustain such a criticism, given the very broad terms in which the statute is now framed since the amendments made to HA 1996, Pt 6, by the Homelessness Act 2002. As Lord Neuberger put it:

'once a housing allocation scheme complies with the requirements of section 167[1] and any other statutory requirements, the courts should be very slow to interfere on the ground of alleged irrationality[2].'

[1] Now s 166A (England) and s 167 (Wales).
[2] [2009] UKHL 14, [2009] HLR 41, HL, at [55].

4.263 Indeed, the judicially approved examples of schemes that might be irrational are extreme:

'one possibility might be a policy which ensured that small families had priority over large ones, or that people coming from outside the borough had priority over those living within it, or that people who had been waiting the shortest time had preference over those waiting the longest[1].'

[1] [2009] UKHL 14, [2009] HLR 41, HL, at [16].

4.264 Where, in such a very exceptional case, a scheme or part of a scheme is described as 'irrational', the relevant court will probably do no more than declare that to be the position and leave it to the local housing authority to work out how to revise or amend the scheme to address the particular problem:

'Castigating a scheme as irrational is of little help to anyone unless a rational alternative can be suggested. Sometimes it may be possible to do this. But where the question is one of overall policy, as opposed to individual entitlement, it is very unlikely that judges will have the tools available to make the choices which Parliament has required a housing authority to make[1].'

[1]   [2009] UKHL 14, [2009] HLR 41, HL, at [22].

4.265 However, shortly after setting out the high hurdle that would need to be surmounted to establish that an allocation scheme was in whole or in part irrational, the House of Lords itself declared unlawful an irrational provision in the allocation scheme adopted by the largest housing authority in England[1]. In that case, the allocation scheme gave greater priority to a person owed a homelessness duty if they had been provided with suitable temporary accommodation than if they had remained in the unsuitable accommodation in which conditions were so bad that they were accepted as being 'homeless'. The Court of Appeal decided that the scheme was, in that respect, unlawful. On a further appeal, the House of Lords held that[2]:

'The council's explanation for this priority is to "assert the premise on which the Allocation Policy is based [namely] that those in greatest need are dealt with first". This bald statement is not enough to justify the priority accorded to those in new temporary accommodation over those left temporarily in their existing accommodation. Both groups are in accommodation which is temporary. Indeed, at least on the face of it, if anything, it would appear that the latter group would have the more pressing claim. They are, *ex hypothesi*, in accommodation which has been found to be such that it would not be reasonable for them to continue in occupation. No such finding will necessarily have been made as to the accommodation now occupied by the former group. It may be that the council could have shown that, as a matter of fact, applicants in the former group are normally in worse accommodation than those in the latter group: if so, the priority would be justifiable. It may be, for example, that when the council refer to "temporary accommodation" they are referring to bed and breakfast hotels or hostels. But no such evidence, not even an opinion to that effect, has been put forward in the evidence. Accordingly, on this, relatively narrow aspect, we would agree with the decision of the Court of Appeal.'

[1]   *Birmingham City Council v Ali* [2009] UKHL 36, [2009] 1 WLR 1506, HL.
[2]   *Birmingham City Council v Ali* [2009] UKHL 36, [2009] 1 WLR 1506, HL at [63].

4.266 Following this warning from the House of Lords that allocation schemes should not readily be held unlawful, subsequent rationality challenges have manifested a judicial approach of reluctance to intervene. For example:

•   It was argued that an allocation scheme was unlawful because it contained an auto-bid facility for homeless applicants who had not successfully bid during a fixed period of two months. Dismissing the claim, the judge held that:

'It is trite law that the court should be very slow to second-guess the judgments made by [local housing authorities] in the formulation of policies for the allocation of social housing: see, most authoritatively, *R (Ahmad) v London Borough of Newham* . . . per Lady Hale at para. 22. I am not prepared to say that the Council's judgment that a two-month bidding period gave persons in the Claimants' position an opportunity to exercise a reasonable degree of choice failed to conform to the requirements of the Code or was otherwise irrational[1].'

- A scheme for allocating pitches on official local authority Gypsy and Traveller sites was not irrational, applying the *Ahmad* approach, even though it gave priority to applicants with a local connection and required them to renew applications annually[2].
- An allocation scheme which automatically suspended applicants with rent arrears of more than a threshold amount was not irrational. It enabled applicants in exceptional circumstances to obtain a lifting of the suspension[3].
- In a scheme adopted by Redbridge London Borough Council which prioritised by combined band and application date, it was not irrational to bring forward an applicant's date when he or she moved to a different priority band. The judge said:

  'It is first to be noted that Redbridge has put forward several reasons [for] the particular policy that operates to bring forward an effective date when property requirements alter. It is not for the court to assess these reasons since, to do so, it would have to examine all relevant aspects of the Scheme before reaching a conclusion as to whether the overall Scheme was rational or not. This policy also excludes any exercise of a residual discretion to modify the details of the selection scheme. It is clear from *Ahmad* that it is both rational and fair to exclude any residual discretion from being exercised when allocations are known. The court should not second guess the policy decisions taken by a local authority in settling the details of how it will allocate properties within a particular banding[4].'

---

[1] *R (Tout a Tout) v Haringey London Borough Council* [2012] EWHC 873 (Admin), (2012) May *Legal Action*, p 34, Admin Ct at [19].

[2] *R (McDonagh) v Hackney London Borough Council* [2012] EWHC 373 (Admin), (2012) April *Legal Action*, p 46, Admin Ct.

[3] *R (Babakandi) v Westminster City Council* [2011] EWHC 1756 (Admin), (2011) August *Legal Action*, p 40, Admin Ct.

[4] *R (Kabashi) v Redbridge London Borough Council* [2009] EWHC 2984 (Admin) at [16]–[17], (2010) October *Legal Action*, p 32, Admin Ct.

4.267 These cases demonstrate how difficult it would now be to successfully contend that an allocation scheme was unlawful because it was irrational. A challenge is only likely to succeed if the irrationality is 'obvious'. For example, in one case concerning the allocation of pitches on a local authority Gypsy Traveller site, permission to bring a challenge by way of judicial review would have been granted if the local housing authority had applied a rule that pitches would only be granted to those considered compatible with others already on site[1].

---

[1] *R (Ward) v South Cambridgeshire District Council* [2014] EWCA Civ 1736, (2015) April *Legal Action*, p 45, CA.

Chapter 5

BEING ALLOCATED A PROPERTY

Contents

INTRODUCTION

5.1 Successfully establishing eligibility and/or qualification for allocation of social housing and securing consideration under a local housing authority's housing allocation scheme are only the first stages in obtaining a rented home from a social landlord. What the applicant will usually want from his or her application is an early opportunity to consider an actual offer of a tenancy of a house or flat.

5.2 Most social landlords experience a regular turnover in their housing stock and need to make rapid and effective arrangements to re-let properties falling vacant (or to fill newly constructed or acquired property available for first letting), not least because rapid re-letting maximises rental receipts. For local housing authorities, the question will be whether to re-let pursuant to an 'allocation' within the terms of the allocation scheme established under the Housing Act 1996, Pt 6 (HA 1996)[1], or whether to grant a tenancy which does not constitute an allocation[2], in which case the letting can be made free of the legal constraints of its ordinary allocation scheme. For private registered providers or registered social landlords (such as housing associations), the question will be whether to make the property available for nomination of a tenant by the local housing authority (which would then count as an 'allocation' by that local housing authority), or whether to keep it as part of their own pool of properties for re-letting to their existing tenants or to those making applications directly to them[3].

---

[1]   Statutory guidance on allocation schemes made under HA 1996, Pt 6 is given in *Allocation of Accommodation: Guidance for local housing authorities in England* (Department for Communities and Local Government (DCLG), June 2012) (the English Code), *Providing social housing for local people* (DCLG, December 2013) (the Supplementary English Code), *Right to Move: Statutory Guidance on Social Housing Allocations for Local Housing Authorities in England* (DCLG, March 2015) and in *Code of Guidance for local authorities on the*

Allocation of Accommodation and Homelessness 2012 (Welsh Government, March 2016) (the Welsh Cod'). See APPENDIX 1 of this book for the English Codes and see the accompanying CD ROM for the Welsh Code.

2   See **1.23–1.27** for a review of the circumstances in which a person may become a tenant of social housing without that process constituting an allocation.

3   For a discussion of lettings by private registered providers or registered social landlords see CHAPTER **6**.

5.3 If a property, whether owned by a local housing authority or another social landlord, is to be re-let in circumstances which *do* count as an 'allocation', that will trigger the operation of the local allocation scheme arrangements described in this book. To whom, and when, an actual offer of that accommodation will be made depends entirely on the detailed operation of the particular local allocation scheme. Beyond the requirements of the scheme, a local housing authority's only duty – when selecting a tenant – is to lawfully exercise its general discretion as to the management of its own housing stock[1]. The allocation scheme is, however, only a process of selection or sifting among potential candidates for a tenancy, or nomination for a tenancy. Following the selection or nomination, the actual offer and acceptance of the tenancy agreement (or 'grant' of a tenancy) is separate from the process of allocation and will take place after that process has completed[2]. The offer and acceptance of any tenancy will be dictated by rules of contract and by any relevant statutory or regulatory controls on the ability of the local housing authority, private registered provider or registered social landlord to let property[3].

1   Housing Act 1985, s 21 (see *R v Canterbury City Council ex p Gillespie* (1987) 19 HLR 7, QBD). There is no general 'duty of care' owed by a local housing authority arising from the management of its housing allocation scheme: *Darby v Richmond Upon Thames London Borough Council* [2015] EWHC 909 (QB), (2015) June *Legal Action* p 45, QBD. An appeal against this decision was dismissed: [2017] EWCA Civ 252.

2   *Birmingham City Council v Qasim* [2009] EWCA Civ 1080, [2010] HLR 19, CA.

3   For example, the powers of local housing authorities to let or otherwise dispose of the housing they own are controlled by Housing Act 1985, Pt 2.

5.4 Essentially, in a true 'allocation' situation, prospective candidates for any available property will be identified through one of two routes:

(1)   by self-selection, in the sense that candidates for the tenancy will put themselves forward or 'bid' for the property in a choice-based letting scheme; or

(2)   by the local housing authority itself selecting a prospective tenant from among the applicants who fall to be considered under its allocation scheme (commonly known as 'direct offers').

5.5 Which route is available will depend upon whether and to what extent the particular local housing authority has adopted a choice-based letting element in its allocation scheme. Because a previous UK Government's target – that every local housing authority in England should be operating some form of choice-based letting scheme – was largely achieved, this chapter first considers those choice-based arrangements. The second part of the chapter covers the alternative, ie selection made by the local housing authority. Finally, this chapter reviews more general points affecting offers and refusals of tenancies under both routes.

CHOICE-BASED LETTINGS

The policy background

5.6 In 2000, the then Labour Government issued Green and White Papers on Housing Policy, both entitled *Quality and Choice: A Decent Home for All*[1]. Those Papers emphasised that applicant 'choice' would be a feature of the new allocation regime to be brought in by what became the Homelessness Act 2002. The rationale behind introducing customer choice into housing allocation was to reduce the number of offers of accommodation that were rejected by applicants. If applicants selected their own property, rather than being offered a property selected by the local housing authority, there were likely to be far fewer refusals. With the same aim in view, applicants were encouraged to provide as much information as possible on the type and location of accommodation that they would accept, in advance of being offered a property.

[1] *Quality and Choice: A Decent Home for All* (Green Paper, DETR, April 2000); *Quality and Choice: A Decent Home for All – the Way Forward for Housing* (White Paper, DETR, December 2000).

Pilot choice-based lettings schemes

5.7 In 2001, the UK Government funded 27 local housing authorities to conduct pilot schemes to test the scope for choice-based lettings[1]. The pilots ended in March 2003, and the evaluation reports were published[2]. The 27 English local housing authorities that participated in the pilot scheme between April 2001 and March 2003 were, on the whole, positive about the experience. Choice-based letting was considered, both by local housing authorities and by the applicants, to be more transparent and the system itself more open and simpler to understand. The system required greater participation from applicants than previously, in that they were expected to monitor advertised properties and bid themselves but generally, applicants seemed to consider that the benefits were worth the extra effort. There was an overall reduction in the rate of refusal of offers. Local housing authorities found that there were fewer households with difficulties than they had expected.

[1] See *How to Choose Choice: Lessons from the First Year of the ODPM's CBLs Pilot Schemes* (Office of the Deputy Prime Minister, October 2002).
[2] *Piloting Choice-Based Lettings: An Evaluation* (ODPM, August 2004); and *Applicants' Perspectives on Choice-Based Lettings* (ODPM, March 2004).

5.8 It was, however, noticeable, and concerning, that homeless households seemed to bid less frequently than other households. Whether this was because those households were more vulnerable and had more difficulty in accessing or understanding the system, or because they were less anxious to move from their temporary accommodation than existing tenants waiting for transfers, was unclear.

5.9 The pilot schemes included areas of high and low demand for social housing. However, in none of those areas, even those of low demand, was a truly 'choice-based' lettings scheme implemented, nor could it be. All of the schemes had a mechanism for prioritising candidate households who were entitled to reasonable preference under HA 1996, Pt 6 (and, in particular, for prioritising homeless households), as a failure to do so would have been unlawful.

5.10 In 2005, Shelter published a separate evaluation of the pilot schemes, based on direct contact with eight local housing authorities, information publicly available from others, and the experiences of their own housing advisers and clients[1]. Shelter confirmed that choice-based letting was perceived by both applicants and local housing authority staff as fairer and more transparent, the process was quicker and there were fewer refusals than under previous schemes. However, Shelter also discovered 'a disturbing pattern' that homeless applicants were given less choice, and were compelled to bid more often or more quickly for properties than other applicants, resulting in an increasing concentration of previously homeless households in low-demand areas[2]. It was also concerned that most local housing authorities had not allocated extra resources to help vulnerable applicants with the bidding process. Shelter concluded by identifying the difficulties of providing choice, given the lack of social housing available, and warning:

> 'choice is a hollow concept when there is a chronic housing shortage . . . given the current lack of available social housing, choice-based letting cannot realise its full potential.'

[1] *A Question of Choice: Good Practice and Issues in Choice-Based Letting* (Shelter, June 2005).
[2] Principally through the use of time-limited priority cards; see **5.31**.

5.11 Based upon the perceived successes of the pilot scheme, and the general policy shift towards 'choice' in the provision of public services[1], in 2005 the then UK Government set a target in its 5-year plan[2] that 25% of local housing authorities should adopt some form of choice-based letting scheme by the end of 2005 and that all local housing authorities should be offering choice to applicants by 2010[3]. Considerable progress was made towards that target. By April 2011, 87% of local housing authorities in England (283 of 326 local housing authorities) participated in choice-based lettings, an increase from 80% in 1 April 2010[4], although there were wide regional variations[5].

[1] See House of Commons Public Administration Select Committee report, *Choice, Voice and Public Services*, Fourth Report of Session 2004–05, March 2005.
[2] *Sustainable Communities: Homes for All – A Five Year Plan* (ODPM, January 2005); and *Sustainable Communities: Homes for All – A Strategy for Choice Based Lettings* (ODPM, June 2005).
[3] A useful overview of how choice-based lettings schemes worked, and of government policies and targets for their implementation, is given in '*Choice-Based Lettings: A Factsheet*' (ODPM, March 2005).
[4] *Local Authority Housing Statistics, England: 2010/2011: Housing Strategy Statistical Appendix and Business Plan Statistical Appendix* (DCLG, November 2011).
[5] *Local Authority Housing Statistics, England: 2010/2011: Housing Strategy Statistical Appendix and Business Plan Statistical Appendix* (DCLG, November 2011).

Evaluation of choice-based lettings schemes

5.12 A major study of 13 schemes, which had each been operating for over 18 months, was published in October 2006[1]. It found that:

- the significance of 'waiting time' as a factor in allocation had increased compared to pre-choice arrangements;
- the vast majority of lettings continued to go to high need applicants;
- many applicants saw bidding as a positive proactive way of looking for a home, but some who had been bidding unsuccessfully over long periods expressed frustration with the systems and lack of confidence in their fairness;
- while most applicants understood the bidding system, many reported having less understanding of the rules by which bidders were ranked[2];
- the schemes appeared to have improved rather than damaged the prospects of statutory homeless households;
- in most cases, there had been improvement in tenancy sustainment (measured by the proportion of tenancies lasting more than 12 months); and
- the additional costs of the schemes were more than offset by tenancy management savings (in faster re-lets and lower turnover).

[1] *Monitoring the Longer Term Impact of Choice-Based Lettings* (CLG, October 2006) summarised in Housing Research Summary No 231 (CLG, 2006).
[2] A point later emphasised by the report's author, Professor Hal Pawson: see 'Choice Ranking Rules Not Always Fully Understood' (2007) *Inside Housing* 15, 7 September 2007.

5.13 In 2008, the Department of Health (DH) commissioned and published research on the experiences of disabled individuals in accessing choice-based letting schemes[1] and associated guides for social landlords establishing such schemes[2] and for people with learning difficulties who try to use them[3].

[1] *Choice Based Lettings and People with Learning Disabilities* (DH, February 2008).
[2] *Making Choice Based Lettings Work for People with Learning Disabilities: A Guide for Choice-Based Lettings Schemes and Landlords* (DH, February 2008).
[3] *Choice Based Lettings: A Guide to Choosing a Home Through the Council* (DH, February 2008).

5.14 A concern with choice-based letting has been the impact on members of black and minority ethnic (BME) communities in areas where choice-based letting has been introduced. Unpublished research for the Federation of Black Housing Organisations in 2004 showed that the proportion of BME tenants responding to suitable advertised properties was small[1]. One study showed that black and ethnic minorities, and especially those using choice-based letting schemes, were the most likely to end up in deprived neighbourhoods[2].

[1] 'Choice-Based Lettings Threat to BMEs' (2004) *Inside Housing*, 12 November 2004. Others have expressed similar concerns: see, for example, T Soares 'Needs Must' (2009) *Inside Housing*, 24 July 2009.
[2] *Choice-based Letting, Ethnicity and Segregation in England*, Manley and van Ham, *Urban Studies* (November 2011), p 48.

5.15 The move to choice-based letting was given a significant push in the summer of 2008 by the publication of *Allocation of Accommodation: Choice-based Lettings*[1] – a code of statutory guidance issued by the Secretary of State to local housing authorities in England under the powers given by HA 1996, s 169. That now-repealed Code, and the earlier statutory guidance issued to English local housing authorities, had advised that the UK Government believed that choice should be provided in housing allocation wherever possible.

1   DCLG, 2008.

5.16 In 2007, the Welsh Government published its report on Welsh social landlords' approaches to choice in letting accommodation. The report identified some 11 choice-based schemes which covered the whole of a social landlord's available stock[1]. The report describes the key features of those schemes, recording a shift away from 'time waiting' to 'housing need' as the main means of prioritising among applicants. It found that the weakest general feature of the schemes was the late provision of feedback on bid outcomes and patchy content of that feedback. The report's recommendations were non-prescriptive as to the type of scheme a local housing authority in Wales should adopt.

1   *A Review of Welsh Social Landlords' Approaches to Increasing Choice in Letting Accommodation* (Welsh Assembly Government, 2008).

5.17 The 2010–15 UK Coalition Government took a less enthusiastic approach to choice-based letting than its predecessors. As a result, the current Codes of Guidance contain no steer towards choice-based letting, or any other particular mechanism for allocation, preferring to leave the matter entirely to the decision of the local housing authority[1].

1   See, for example, Welsh Code, para 3.48.

5.18 The only material that the 2010–15 UK Coalition Government published on choice-based letting was two research reports[1] commissioned by the previous government. Those local housing authorities that have already adopted, or are minded to adopt, a choice-based letting element in their local allocation schemes may find the two reports useful as they focus on an aspect of choice-based lettings previously under-explored, ie their effects on 'accessible housing registers'[2].

1   Delia Lomax and Hal Pawson *Choice-based lettings, potentially disadvantaged groups and accessible housing registers: a summary guide to positive practice* and *Choice-based lettings, potentially disadvantaged groups and accessible housing registers: a guide to positive practice* (DCLG, 2011) and Colin Jones and Mark Lordon *Costs and effectiveness of accessible housing registers in a choice-based lettings context* (Incisive Minds Ltd, DCLG, 2011).
2   An accessible housing register is 'a list of suitable homes for disabled people with access needs': *Disability Equality Report by the Secretary of State for Communities and Local Government* (DCLG, 2008), p 28. See further on 'accessible housing registers': the Welsh Code at paras 3.99–3.104 and 4.5–4.11.

5.19 The Welsh government has taken a similarly non-prescriptive approach. The Welsh Code does not recommend any one system of allocation and encourages local housing authorities to determine housing need in, and strategic priorities for, their own areas, after consultation[1]. It briefly mentions three different approaches – choice-based lettings, mid-way schemes, and hybrid schemes – but offers no further elaboration of them[2]. It simply emphasises that any scheme will, in reality, include both an element of choice and also an attempt to meet need. The difference between the three approaches lies in the balance that each attempts to strike between choice and need. In general, the Welsh Code suggests that maintaining common housing lists, rather than separate lists for different groups of applicants, encouraging mobility between different areas and different types of tenure, providing good quality information, making the widest practicable range of options available to applicants and, above all, operating a simple and transparent system, should be hallmarks of an allocation scheme[3].

1   Welsh Code, paras 1.4 and 3.5.
2   Welsh Code, para 4.50.
3   Welsh Code, paras 3.47–3.48 and 3.57–3.58.

The statutory basis for choice-based lettings

5.20 Despite all the emphasis on 'choice', at least in *policy* terms, during the decade 2000–10, there is not now – and never has been – any *statutory* obligation on local housing authorities to implement choice-based letting schemes. HA 1996, Pt 6, merely provides that applicants should be informed of any local policy on offering either:

(1)   'a choice of housing accommodation'; or
(2)   'the opportunity to express preferences' about what is to be allocated to them[1].

1   HA 1996, s 166A(2) (England), s 167(1A) (Wales).

5.21 In either case that need only be by way of a statement in the local housing allocation scheme. There is no requirement to notify every individual applicant of the opportunities for choice or for expressing preferences in local housing allocation arrangements.

5.22 Strictly speaking, this obligation to deal with choice and preferences in the local housing allocation scheme could be met by a simple statement in the allocation scheme to the effect that there is *no* local policy on 'choice' or customer 'preferences'. At a minimum, however, local housing authorities could be expected to allow applicants an opportunity to express a preference for accommodation of a particular type or in a particular location.

5.23 There is no statutory duty positively to give effect to applicant choice or preference in HA 1996, Pt 6. The position in relation to allocations is no different to that in respect of the statutory duty to provide temporary accommodation for the homeless, ie unless the local scheme expressly provides to the contrary, an applicant is not entitled to any choice[1].

1   *R (Khatun) v Newham London Borough Council* [2004] EWCA Civ 55, (2004) 36 HLR 29, CA.

5.24 In summary, therefore, HA 1996, Pt 6, simply permits, but does not require, local housing authorities to contain within their allocation schemes any provisions allowing applicants opportunities to state preferences or make choices. For those local housing authorities wishing to adopt choice-based letting, HA 1996, Pt 6, expressly enables local allocation schemes to include provision for the allocation of particular units of accommodation in response to specific applications for that accommodation[1]. This is the sole statutory basis for local housing authorities to implement 'choice' by means of enabling applicants to 'bid' for specific properties.

¹ HA 1996, s 166A(6) (England) and s 167(2E) (Wales), discussed further at **4.165–4.171**.

5.25 In this absence of any legislative compulsion, the direction of travel towards choice-based letting is a matter for local policy choices on methods of housing allocation. All the statutory guidance previously issued in England – which positively promoted choice – has been withdrawn¹ and the Welsh Code does not recommend any one system of allocation.

¹ The main current guidance – *Allocation of Accommodation: Guidance for local housing authorities in England* (DCLG, June 2012) (the English Code) – replaced: (1) *Allocation of Accommodation: Code of Guidance for local housing authorities for England* (ODPM, November 2002); (2) *Allocation of Accommodation: Choice-based Lettings Code of Guidance for Local Housing Authorities* (CLG, August 2008); and (3) *Fair and flexible: statutory guidance on social housing allocations for local authorities in England* (CLG, December 2009). The Codes which have been replaced appeared in APPENDIX 1 of the first two editions of this book. The current English Code and the Supplementary English Code are reproduced in APPENDIX 1.

5.26 Indeed, one recent report suggested that some local housing authorities have abandoned choice-based lettings in favour of direct allocations. This is frequently done with the intention of saving costs but there is doubt as to whether it does indeed save money, given the consequential increased expense of dealing with challenges to direct lettings¹.

¹ *Building Bridges: A guide to better partnership working between local authorities and housing association*, published by the Chartered Institute of Housing in association with the Association of Retained Council Housing and VIVID Housing, September 2017, p 97.

The practicalities of a choice-based scheme

5.27 Those local housing authorities that have adopted the choice-based letting route have generally arranged for their available properties to be advertised on their websites or in magazines or by emails or texts sent to those eligible to 'bid' for them.

5.28 Such local housing authorities have needed to identify mechanisms for ranking those who bid for advertised properties and most have adopted allocation schemes which attribute to applicants a relative rank or priority as against other prospective bidders. Broadly, either of two alternative systems will be in operation:

(1) a 'banding' system, so that applicants are placed in different bands reflecting their different needs, and, within those bands, applicants are prioritised according to the length of time they have waited; or

(2) a 'points-based' system simply giving those applicants with the most urgent housing needs priority over others with less urgent needs by affording them more points¹.

¹ Whether by a simplified points system or by 'time limited priority cards' which would enable an applicant with the most urgent need to have priority over other applicants for a specified period.

5.29 Both types of scheme can take account of the length of time an applicant has been waiting for an allocation under the local housing allocation scheme. In the banding schemes, waiting time can be used as a factor to fix relative priority for those applicants within the same band. In points-based schemes, waiting time can be recognised by the award of additional points for specific periods spent waiting. One survey found that the adoption of choice-based letting tended to put a greater focus on the relative waiting times among applicants:

> 'Waiting time made some contribution to applicant priority in most authorities. As perceived by survey respondents, however, its significance tended to be much greater under CBL than under traditional allocations schemes. Whereas 19 of the 20 CBL authorities considered waiting time to be "quite significant" or "very significant" here, this was true for only seven of the other 32 authorities.[1]'

[1]   *Exploring local authority policy and practice on housing allocations* (CLG, July 2009), p 7.

5.30 Where available properties are openly advertised, so that applicants can apply for particular properties, the advertising will usually state the level of priority and/or the waiting time required by the likely successful applicant. The thinking is that providing this information will allow applicants to assess their chances of success, and so to refrain from bidding if they would have no prospect of being allocated the accommodation.

5.31 Some local housing authorities in England have allocation schemes under which 'choice' (ie freedom to bid) is only available to certain classes of applicants, most often homeless households, for limited periods. When the period expires, the local housing authority reverts to the officer-led form of allocation described later in this chapter (sometimes called 'direct lettings')[1]. Shelter's evaluation of the pilot choice-based lettings schemes in England, published in June 2005[2], was highly critical of time-limited choice for those in greatest need, arguing that the effect was to put pressure on those applicants to bid for unpopular properties. Shelter also identified at least two local housing authorities that refused to accept bids from homeless applicants for high-demand properties. Shelter recommended that, if time-limited priority cards were to be used, they should be valid for a long enough period of time (at least six months) to allow for a suitable range of properties to become available, and that the applicant's needs should be reviewed at the end of the period.

[1]   See **5.48–5.52**.
[2]   *A Question of Choice: Good Practice and Issues in Choice-Based Letting* (Shelter, June 2005). See also **5.10**.

5.32 In one case, a local housing authority's allocation scheme enabled homeless applicants to bid freely alongside other applicants for social housing for two months before the system would auto-bid for the next available property sufficient for their needs. A challenge to the lawfulness of that arrangement failed. The judge said that he was 'not prepared to say that the Council's judgment that a two-month bidding period gave persons in the claimants' position an opportunity to exercise a reasonable degree of choice failed to conform to the requirements of the Code or was otherwise irrational'[1].

[1] R *(Tout a Tout) v Haringey London Borough Council* [2012] EWHC 873 (Admin), (2012) May *Legal Action*, p 34, Admin Ct at [19].

The courts' approach

1996–2009

5.33 In the first decade of operation of HA 1996, Pt 6, the courts discerned the meeting of housing 'need' as the primary policy driver in the legislation[1]. The central problem identified by the litigation in this period was how to establish a system that was easy to operate and understand, that gave priority to customer choice, but that also took account of the vast range of needs exhibited by applicants and ranked them in a way which gave effect to the perceived statutory purpose that those in the greatest need should be housed first. The courts had a number of opportunities to consider these issues.

[1] Notwithstanding later developments in the case law, the UK Government's policy is still one of 'ensuring that priority for social housing goes to those in the greatest need': English Code, para 2.1.

5.34 An early attempt to implement a choice-based lettings scheme, reconciling freedom of choice with providing reasonable preference to those groups falling within the statutory categories by the adoption of broad priority bands, was made by the London Borough of Lambeth[1]. The Court of Appeal considered that attempt in the linked cases of *R (A) v Lambeth London Borough Council and R (Lindsay) v Lambeth London Borough Council*[2] and concluded that Lambeth had been unsuccessful and had failed to give effect to the statutory scheme properly. Lambeth's bands, recognising different categories of needs, were organised in such a way that applicants who did not fall within any of the reasonable preference categories could have the same priority as those who did. The Court of Appeal also criticised Lambeth's policy of allowing applicants to define their own needs, by specifying the size and location of accommodation they sought (and being encouraged to do so as widely and flexibly as possible), as haphazard and not capable of ensuring that the categories of applicants falling within the statutory 'reasonable preference' groups were given preference. The court expressed concern that applicants might under-estimate their own needs, in order to stand a greater chance of being allocated accommodation, but that some applicants, such as families with young children, would have fewer chances of being allocated accommodation as they would not find it possible to under-estimate their needs. In reality, the main 'choice' offered by the Lambeth scheme was a freedom to opt for poorer quality or less satisfactory accommodation in the hope of an earlier offer. Having been declared unlawful in July 2002, it was replaced by a new allocation scheme in February 2004.

[1] The Lambeth experiment with choice-based letting is well-charted by Cowan and Marsh 'From Need to Choice' (2004) 67 MLR 3, p 478.
[2] [2002] EWCA Civ 1084, (2002) 34 HLR 57, CA.

5.35 In the London Borough of Newham, where a choice-based scheme had been operating (with amendments) since September 2002, at least two early judicial review applications were launched. The first resulted in an undertaking to amend the scheme in June 2003[1]. The second was again settled on terms that the local housing authority would further amend its allocation scheme[2]. Some of those amendments were later revoked by the local housing authority's Director of Housing, and others were incorporated into a scheme that reached its seventh revision before being upheld as lawful[3].

[1]   *R (Nazma Begum) v Newham London Borough Council* CO/566/2003 (unreported) 26 June 2003.
[2]   *R (Heather Phillip) v Newham London Borough Council* CO/1731/2004 (unreported) 22 June 2004. See also 'Choice Scheme Revised After Challenge' (2004) *Inside Housing*, 30 July, p 7l. In *R (Najha Al-Juboori) v Ealing London Borough Council* [2002] EWHC 2726 (Admin) permission had been granted for a challenge to the local choice-based allocation scheme in a judicial review claim. The trial was adjourned to enable other local housing authorities in London to join the proceedings. By the time it was restored, the claimant had been re-housed and the scheme amended so that no judgment on the merits of the claim was delivered
[3]   See **5.38–5.41.**

5.36   In *R (Cali) v Waltham Forest London Borough Council*[1], a choice-based scheme containing a banding system was declared to be unlawful because it did not provide for the identification of a household's cumulative needs and so could not effectively offer additional preference[2]. Nor did it identify, within the published scheme, the criteria by which an applicant qualified for reasonable preference.

[1]   [2006] EWHC 302 (Admin), [2007] 39 HLR 1, Admin Ct.
[2]   See **4.39.**

5.37   In *R (Lin & Hassan) v Barnet London Borough Council*[1], a points-based scheme of choice-based letting was held to be unlawful as its provision giving 100 points to its existing tenants, seeking transfers, artificially raised the points threshold (above which a bid might succeed) to the detriment of applicants who were not existing tenants and who were entitled to a statutory preference. That decision was not disturbed on an appeal pursued (for the most part unsuccessfully) by the claimants, who sought to establish that the choice-based scheme gave insufficient opportunity to the homeless to secure long-term housing[2].

[1]   [2006] EWHC 1041 (Admin), [2006] HLR 440, Admin Ct. See **4.46.**
[2]   *R (Lin) v Barnet London Borough Council* [2007] EWCA Civ 132, [2007] HLR 30, CA.

2009 onwards

5.38   The legal landscape changed dramatically in March 2009 with the first House of Lords decision on a choice-based letting scheme[1]. Newham had adopted a banding scheme with three bands:

(1)   applicants in reasonable preference categories;
(2)   transfer cases with no reasonable preference; and
(3)   non-transfer applicants with no reasonable preferences[2].

[1]   *R (Ahmad) v Newham London Borough Council* [2009] UKHL 14, [2009] HLR 41, HL.
[2]   In common with the schemes of many other authorities, Newham's allocation scheme included a 'top slice' facility enabling a very small number of those in the most acute housing need to obtain a priority higher than the main bandings. Subsequently published research has shown

that across local housing authorities which assess housing 'need' among applicants, the proportion of the 'top banded' applicants was in most cases under 3% of all applicants: *Exploring Local Authority Policy and Practice on Housing Allocations* (CLG, July 2009), para 10.

5.39 Unsurprisingly, the vast majority of advertised properties went to bidders from the first band. But within that band applicants were afforded relative priority as between one another, not by reference to housing need (in the sense of particular assessments of cumulative or composite need), but by date order. The applicant waiting longest among the highest banded bidders for a particular property would be allocated it. In both the High Court and Court of Appeal the scheme was held to be unlawful[1].

[1] *R (Ahmad) v Newham London Borough Council* [2007] EWHC 2332 (Admin), (2007) November *Legal Action*, p 38, Admin Ct; and *R (Ahmad) v Newham London Borough Council* [2008] EWCA Civ 140, (2008) April *Legal Action*, p 38, CA.

5.40 The House of Lords allowed the local housing authority's appeal. It decided that nothing in HA 1996, Pt 6, as amended by the Homelessness Act 2002, *required* allocation to those in the greatest need, nor *required* a facility for cumulative or composite assessment of needs. A local housing authority such as Newham, where demand vastly outstripped supply, was entitled to adopt a simple banding scheme which met the statutory obligation to give a reasonable preference to the statutory categories but then prioritised amongst them by waiting time.

5.41 This dramatic change in the judicial perception of HA 1996, Pt 6 (as amended), gave new impetus to simplified choice-based banding schemes. For the reasons explained in CHAPTER 4[1], many fewer legal challenges to allocation schemes can now be expected.

[1] See **4.262–4.267**.

5.42 While the current English Code certainly promotes the use of these flexibilities it offers no guidance on 'banding', 'points' or 'choice'. The Chartered Institute of Housing (CIH) has suggested that the whole emphasis in the Code, on a more managed approach to waiting lists, 'may present challenges to local housing authorities also intending to keep a choice-based letting scheme'[1]. Those local housing authorities deciding to retain an element of choice, whilst also seeking to address housing need, might find the extended guidance available from the CIH[2] of more assistance than the current English Code.

[1] *Allocation of Accommodation: Guidance for Housing Authorities in England – Briefing paper* (CIH, July 2012), p 7.
[2] *Allocations & Local Flexibility* (CIH, March 2010).

The effectiveness of choice

5.43 Despite the use of the name 'choice-based letting' to describe the process, the ultimate allocation of any particular property by a local housing authority will lie with the local housing authority itself. Many individuals may have expressed their wish (usually through a 'bid') to be allocated a particular property advertised as vacant – it will then be for the local housing authority to select one household from among them (or none of them)[1]. Of course, the terms of the local allocation scheme may, and should, spell out precisely how the choice is to be made between them, and by whom. For example, the scheme might specify that the property is to be offered to the candidate with the highest banding, longest waiting time, greatest number of points, or whatever[2]. The scheme may also specify who is to be considered next, if the highest bidder pulls out.

1   Or, where the property is owned by a private registered provider, registered social landlord or a different local housing authority, to decide which applicant(s) to *nominate* to that landlord.
2   For example, in *R (van Boolen) v Barking and Dagenham London Borough Council* [2009] EWHC 2196 (Admin), (2009) September *Legal Action*, p 34, Admin Ct, the policy of the local housing authority was to identify the bidders in the highest band and then to give further preference as between them to those applicants with a local connection.

5.44 In this sense, 'choice-based letting' is a misnomer. Almost all the schemes adopted by local housing authorities are, in reality, choice-based *applications* schemes. They simply facilitate the expression of interest by bidders in particular properties available for letting. It does not necessarily follow that the highest ranked bidder at the closing date *will* be allocated the property. For example, most schemes incorporate an element of re-assessment of shortlisted bidders to ensure that they are still eligible or qualified and have maintained their initially awarded degree of priority. That element of re-checking (or evaluating the bids) is not at all uncommon and many schemes retain some form of override enabling the rejection of bids from applicants who are considered, by officers, to be unsuitable for the particular property. These practices are all perfectly lawful, provided they are spelt out in the published allocation scheme.

5.45 In many avowedly 'choice-based' schemes, not all the available properties are advertised. Some empty homes are often reserved for applicants entitled to or required to accept what schemes may describe as 'direct lets' or 'direct offers'. In some schemes, advertised properties may be withdrawn to be offered outside the allocation scheme or to direct-let cases. In others, properties are offered subject to multiple qualifications as to the type of bid that will be considered. In yet others, bidding preferences expire if not used within a fixed period or on the refusal of offers. In some schemes, provision is made for 'choice' to be available only for a fixed period and thereafter for bids for appropriate properties to be automatically made on an applicant's behalf[1].

1   The circumstances in *R (Tout a Tout) v Haringey London Borough Council* [2012] EWHC 873 (Admin), (2012) May *Legal Action*, p 34, Admin Ct.

5.46 It has yet to be seen whether the courts will recognise any enforceable 'legitimate expectation' on the part of the candidate who would be due to receive the offer of a particular property under the strict terms of the choice-based allocation scheme[1], although the Ombudsman has frequently criticised and sanctioned local housing authorities for failures which have led to applicants being wrongly prevented from bidding for a property[2]. Could, for example, the local housing authority withdraw a property, advertised under the choice-based scheme, and offer it to another applicant, or let it in circumstances that do not constitute an 'allocation' after the bid process had closed? What would be the legal effect of mistakenly overlooking the bidder with the highest priority under the scheme, and offering the property, inadvertently, to the next person in the queue of bidding candidates[3]? It is unlikely that a simple failure of communication[4] would give rise to a claim of breach of 'legitimate expectation' but a clear departure from the published scheme may well do so[5].

[1] For a discussion of 'legitimate expectation' in an allocation context see *R v Brent London Borough Council ex p Jerke* CO/2069/97 (unreported) 8 May 1998, QBD; *R v Lambeth London Borough Council ex p Trabi* (1998) 30 HLR 975, QBD; *R (Tout a Tout) v Haringey London Borough Council* [2012] EWHC 873 (Admin), (2012) May *Legal Action*, p 39, Admin Ct; and *R (Alansi) v Newham London Borough Council* [2013] EWHC 3722 (Admin), [2014] HLR 25, Admin Ct. See also **4.50–4.53**.

[2] See for example *Complaint against London Borough of Camden*, 16 008 603, 13 February 2017, *Complaint against Bristol City Council*, 16 003 575, 3 April 2018, (2018) June *Legal Action*, p 34, and *Complaint against Royal Borough of Windsor and Maidenhead Council* 16 003 062, 1 February 2018, (2018) May *Legal Action*, p 37.

[3] In *Globa v Ukraine* [2012] ECHR 1375, Mr Globa had been at the top of the waiting list for a Town Council apartment. A vacant apartment was wrongly allocated to someone below him on the list. He took court proceedings and obtained a judgment that: the occupiers be evicted; he be allocated the flat; and the occupiers be rehoused. The Town Council failed to comply with the order and enforcement measures failed. The European Court of Human Rights awarded him €5,000 compensation.

[4] *R (Tout a Tout) v Haringey London Borough Council* [2012] EWHC 873 (Admin), (2012) May *Legal Action*, p 34, Admin Ct at [24].

[5] See also **4.50–4.53**.

5.47 Applicants who believe that they have not been treated appropriately under a choice-based scheme will need to obtain access to the courts very quickly if they are to prevent letting of a property for which they and others have bid. Unless an application for judicial review is launched very quickly and, if necessary, an injunction obtained to prevent the property being let, the disappointed applicant may well find that the claim has become academic[1] or at best reduced to an attempt to prevent any future departure from the published arrangements[2].

[1] As happened in *R (Fidelis-Auma) v Octavia Housing and Care* [2009] EWHC 2263 (Admin), (2009) November *Legal Action*, p 25, Admin Ct.

[2] *Birmingham City Council v Qasim* [2009] EWCA Civ 1080, [2010] HLR 19, CA at [39].

LOCAL HOUSING AUTHORITY LED ALLOCATION (DIRECT LETS)

5.48 If a local housing authority is not operating a choice-based allocation scheme, all allocation decisions will be made by officers of the local housing authority applying the principles set out in the local allocation scheme. The scheme must identify the procedure for making actual allocation decisions, including the name or designation of the responsible officer(s)[1].

[1] HA 1996, s 166A(1) (England), s 167(1) (Wales).

5.49 Planning for such allocations usually starts well before a specific property becomes available to offer. Once an applicant has been accepted onto the allocation scheme, and the preference to which he or she is entitled has been assessed and accorded, the local housing authority must decide what type of property the applicant should be offered, and whether there is any particular geographic area in which an allocation would or would not be appropriate.

5.50 HA 1996, Pt 6, permits local housing authorities to target certain properties at certain groups of applicants[1]. Building on that provision, many have established 'local lettings' policies and schemes within their published allocation schemes[2]. Others have decided to make provision in their allocation schemes for a specific quota of properties to be allocated to particular groups of applicants. The English Code, for example, suggests that local housing authorities might set aside an annual quota of properties for prospective adopters and foster parents[3] or a specified proportion of the stock for workers with skills that are in short supply locally[4]. However, none of these arrangements must be allowed to produce an allocation scheme that fails to give an overall preference to those in the reasonable preference groups or that unlawfully discriminates against people with protected characteristics under the Equality Act 2010[5].

[1]   HA 1996, s 166A(6)(b) (England) and s 167(2E)(b) (Wales).
[2]   See **4.172–4.191**.
[3]   English Code, para 4.31.
[4]   English Code, para 4.27.
[5]   English Code, para 4.5. In *R (H) v Ealing London Borough Council* [2017] EWCA Civ 1127, [2018] HLR 2, CA, the local housing authority's allocation scheme set aside twenty percent of lettings for 'working households' and 'model tenants'. The Court of Appeal held that these provisions were indirectly discriminatory but that the judge in the Administrative Court had erred in his approach to finding that the discrimination was not justified. The question as to whether the provisions were in fact justified was not remitted as the local housing authority was reviewing its scheme. See CHAPTER 4 in respect of avoiding discrimination in allocation schemes.

5.51 Once a property of the requisite description in the appropriate area becomes available for letting, the local housing authority must decide from among the pool of available applicants which of them should first be offered it. This is the most sensitive aspect of allocation and the stage at which greatest transparency will be needed. Many authorities will use 'banding' or 'points' to rank the relative priority of those in the pool of available applicants[1]. How the actual selection is made will fall to be determined by the particular local allocation scheme.

[1]   See **4.44–4.45**.

5.52 Some local housing authorities reserve a 'direct letting' function for use by officers in tandem with, or as a variant of, what is otherwise a choice-based letting scheme. It is particularly common for such hybrid schemes to be adopted where applicants, who are being accommodated in temporary accommodation under the homelessness provisions of HA 1996, Pt 7[1], would be reluctant to bid under a choice-based scheme for less desirable properties than the temporary homes they occupy. In one case, a local allocation scheme dealt with that scenario by allowing such applicants a 'free' bidding opportunity for a fixed period but thereafter the scheme 'auto-bid' for any appropriate properties which applicants were offered if they were the highest ranked bidders. A legal challenge to that arrangement, based on the argument that it was inconsistent with the statutory guidance then in place, failed[2].

[1]   As amended by HRA 2017 for applications for homelessness assistance made to local housing authorities in England on or after 3 April 2018, see CHAPTER 16.

GENERAL POINTS

The offer of accommodation

5.53 Under either of the two routes described earlier in this chapter, a particular applicant will be identified to be allocated an available property. At that stage the strict 'allocation' process, which involves simple selection or nomination of a candidate, comes to an end[1]. The actual letting will normally be handled by housing management staff of the relevant social landlord (which may be the local housing authority itself) who will sign up the new tenant following the offer and acceptance of a tenancy.

1   *Birmingham City Council v Qasim* [2009] EWCA Civ 1080, [2010] HLR 19, CA.

5.54 Once an allocation of particular accommodation has been made, the Welsh Code advises that an applicant should be given 'a reasonable period' to consider whether to accept it[1]. 'Reasonable period' is not defined in HA 1996, Pt 6, or the Codes. The applicant should be given sufficient time for careful consideration and the length of time provided should depend on the individual circumstances of each applicant. Vulnerable applicants, or applicants who are unfamiliar with the property, are likely to need longer. An applicant who is in hospital or who needs to arrange a support worker to be present at the viewing may also need longer, as may those who are working or have childcare commitments[2].

1   Welsh Code, paras 3.65. The *Homelessness Code of Guidance for Local Authorities* (MHCLG, February 2018) gives the same advice in respect of offers of accommodation that would bring the main housing duty to an end at para 15.48.
2   See these, and further examples, at Welsh Code, para 3.66.

How many offers?

5.55 The local housing allocation scheme may allow unlimited bids for available properties or the making of an unlimited number of offers by officers to applicants. Alternatively, the scheme may cap the number of bids or offers that may be made. There is no nationally prescribed maximum or minimum number.

5.56 Some local housing authorities have allocation schemes that discriminate among classes of applicant, enabling certain applicants to enjoy a greater number of bids or offers than others. In the past this had been particularly true in relation to households owed housing duties under the homelessness assistance provisions of HA 1996, Pt 7, who have often been restricted to limited bids or offers. However, the 2012 Welsh Code made it plain that if it was previously expected that homeless households would be discriminated against in that way, the position has changed. It stated in terms that:

'It is no longer an expectation that homeless people should be given a single offer of accommodation. Wherever possible, they should receive the same number of offers, or range of choices, as existing tenants or Part 6 applicants (general waiting list applicants).[1']

[1] 2012 Welsh Code, para 4.47. There is no equivalent guidance in the English Code.

5.57 Of course, the current Codes now recognise that a single suitable offer may have the effect of releasing a local housing authority from its homelessness duties[1].

[1] Welsh Code, paras 3.61–3.62 and, in England, *Homelessness Code of Guidance for Local Authorities* (MHCLG, 2018), para 15.37 and 15.41. See CHAPTERS 15 AND 16 (England) and CHAPTER 17 (Wales) for discussion of the effect of an offer on homelessness duties.

5.58 The effect of refusal of an offer on an application for social housing allocation is discussed later in this chapter[1].

[1] See 5.83–5.86.

Types of tenancies to be offered

Size and location

5.59 The extent and circumstances of the applicant's household as assessed under the allocation scheme obviously determines the number of bedrooms that the applicant may expect to find in an allocated property[1]. It will be for each local housing authority to frame its own rules in its allocation scheme dealing with the size of property to be offered. The scheme should be clear as to how members of the applicant's household will be calculated[2]. Provided that the result is not the allocation of a property which would be statutorily overcrowded[3], local housing authorities are free to set their own criteria[4]. Some may wish to adopt the 'bedroom standard' promoted by the Secretary of State in England[5]. If a property is being allocated to a working-age applicant who would be under-occupying it, the local housing authority will need to be aware of the housing benefit implications[6].

[1] *R v Lewisham London Borough Council ex p Pinzon* (1999) 2 CCLR 152, QBD. This may not be a straightforward task. In *R (Bibi) v Camden London Borough Council* [2004] EWHC 2527 (Admin), [2005] HLR 18, Admin Ct, the local housing authority offered a woman a one-bedroom property, overlooking the fact that she had a joint residence order in respect of her children with her former husband. It was required to reconsider the offer, taking into account that order, as well as the other demands on its housing stock and any potential under-occupancy of the property. For a discussion of 'household' in this context see 3.171–3.173.
[2] In *Complaint against Kettering Borough Council*, 16 012 028, 3 August 2017, (2017) November *Legal Action*, p 41, the scheme was unclear as to in what circumstances adult children would be assessed as forming part of the household.
[3] *Complaint against York City Council*, 11 018 683, 16 October 2012, (2012) December *Legal Action*, p 30 well illustrates the care that a local housing authority must take in determining what rooms, in the property to be allocated, actually constitute 'bedrooms' (or, more technically, 'sleeping accommodation') for the purposes of the statutory overcrowding standards.
[4] English Code, para 4.22.
[5] See 4.84(2).
[6] English Code, para 4.22.

5.60 An applicant, or a member of his or her household, may have a medical need for a ground floor property or an accessible bathroom, or an additional bathroom or toilet. The Codes advise that applicants who receive support from a carer, who does not live with them, should have their need for a spare bedroom taken into account wherever possible[1]. In Wales, local housing authorities are reminded that elderly applicants who are awaiting an allocation of accommodation have particular needs[2]. In England, local housing authorities considering applications from those proposing to foster[3] or adopt are encouraged to balance the case for allocation of a larger property against the risk that any placement may fail to materialise or break down[4].

1   English Code, para 4.29; Welsh Code, paras 3.127–3.129.
2   Welsh Code, paras 3.120–3.122. Note also the guidance in the Welsh Code, paras 4.19–4.24, relating to pets in social housing.
3   In *R (Aslamie) v London & Quadrant Housing Trust* [2016] EWHC (Admin) 2396, the court upheld a decision to refuse to consent to a mutual exchange on the grounds that the claimant would be under-occupying, despite his desire to adopt. The court agreed that the defendant was 'not obliged to grant consent by reference to the future intentions of the claimant' (at [5]).
4   English Code, para 4.30.

5.61 When determining the extent and circumstances of the applicant's household, the local housing authority must take all of the members of the household into account, whether they were eligible or qualified for an allocation in their own right or not, unless the local allocation scheme otherwise provides. There is no statutory provision permitting local housing authorities to ignore the needs of members who would not have satisfied the eligibility or qualification test had they been the applicant, although the authority may take into account a family member's immigration status when deciding whether they form part of the applicant's household at all[1]. The matter is one to be determined by the terms of the local scheme[2].

1   See *R (Ariemuguvbe) v Islington London Borough Council* [2009] EWCA Civ 1218, [2010] HLR 14, CA.
2   See *R (Ariemuguvbe) v Islington London Borough Council* [2009] EWCA Civ 1218, [2010] HLR 14, CA.

5.62 An applicant may need or prefer a property to be in a particular location, or there may be locations that the applicant cannot be placed in, for example, if the applicant has left an area due to violence. Alternatively, a local allocation scheme might provide that an applicant will not be made an allocation of property in a locality within the local housing authority's district in which he or she has previously been the perpetrator (or, perhaps, victim) of anti-social behaviour[1].

1   *R (Carney) v Bolton-at-Home Ltd* [2012] EWHC 2553 (Admin), (2012) November *Legal Action*, p 22, Admin Ct. In *Complaint against Royal Borough of Windsor and Maidenhead Council* 16 003 062, 15 February 2018, (2018) May *Legal Action*, p 37, the housing association to which the complainant had been nominated refused the nomination because the property was too close to his ex-wife.

Sole or joint tenancy?

5.63 The allocation cannot be made of a property to be held on a joint tenancy where one of the joint tenants is not eligible for an allocation[1]. However, the tenancy could be granted as a sole tenancy to the eligible applicant in those circumstances. There is no similar difficulty if one of the applicants to a local housing authority in England is not in a qualifying class[2]. Such a joint applicant can be included in a joint tenancy[3].

[1]   HA 1996, s 160ZA(1)(b) (England) and s 160A(1)(c) (Wales). Welsh Code, para 2.17. For eligibility, see Chapter 3.
[2]   English Code, para 3.29. As to 'qualifying class' see **3.76–3.150**.
[3]   HA 1996, s 160ZA(6)(b).

5.64 Where there are joint applicants, or a partner, friend or live-in carer is included as part of an individual applicant's household, local housing authorities will normally offer joint tenancies so that either person would continue as tenant if the other died[1]. To avoid any unlawful discrimination, same-sex partners should be treated in the same way as heterosexual partners[2]. If prospective tenants ask to be granted a joint tenancy, and are refused, the local housing authority should give clear, written reasons for the refusal[3]. Applicants with children may prefer to take a tenancy which offers contractual rights of succession to the children because new secure and assured tenancies of social housing in England no longer carry *statutory* rights of succession by family members, other than partners[4].

[1]   *Solihull MBC v Hickin* [2012] UKSC 39, [2012] 4 All ER 867, [2012] 1 WLR 2295, SC: Welsh Code, para 3.21.
[2]   See *Rodriguez v Minister of Housing of the Government of Gibraltar* [2009] UKPC 52, (2009) 28 BHRC 189, PC noted at **4.229**. See also Welsh Code, para 3.23 suggesting that if a sole tenancy is initially granted to a person who later enters into a civil partnership that tenant may be 'entitled' to vary it into a joint tenancy with his or her new partner.
[3]   Welsh Code, paras 3.22.
[4]   See the amendments made by Localism Act 2011, ss 160–161 to the succession provisions of the Housing Act 1985 and Housing Act 1988, applying to tenancies granted on or after 1 April 2012 in England. Housing and Planning Act 2016, Pt 4 and Sch 8, further amend the Housing Act 1985 to make the rules governing succession to secure tenancies granted before 1 April 2012 the same as those for tenancies granted from that date and, in addition, to stipulate that family members other than spouses, civil partners, or those living together as husband and wife, will only be given a five year fixed term tenancy where they are allowed to succeed. Housing and Planning Act 2016, Pt 4 and Sch 8 amend the Housing Act 1996 to make corresponding changes to the rules governing succession in respect of introductory and demoted tenancies. It is not known if and when these provisions will be brought into force.

What tenure to offer?

5.65 An allocation of accommodation made under the local allocation scheme may produce the offer of a secure, introductory or assured tenancy[1]. But even within those categories there may be variants as to the form of tenancy and security of tenure.

[1]   HA 1996, s 159(2). Note that, when the provisions of the Renting Homes (Wales) Act 2016 takes effect, people who rent from housing associations will have the same rights as tenants of local housing authorities: Welsh Code, para 1.17.

5.66 It has always been possible for local housing authorities to grant *secure* tenancies either on a periodic or fixed term basis. However, since 1 April 2012, it has also been possible for local housing authorities in England to offer a variant of the latter, known as a 'flexible tenancy', which carries a mandatory right to re-possession at the end of the term[1]. As a flexible tenancy is a form of secure tenancy, it can be offered as the result of an allocation. Part 4, Ch 6 and

Sch 7 of the Housing and Planning Act 2016 will, when enacted, phase out 'tenancies for life' meaning that virtually all new secure tenancies will be for fixed terms. There is at the time of writing no date yet set for when they will come into force.

¹ Housing Act 1985, s 107A, inserted by Localism Act 2011, ss 154–155.

5.67 *Assured* tenancies of social housing are only allocated through allocation schemes by way of nomination to private registered providers or registered social landlords. Assured tenancies can also be periodic or for a fixed term. An assured *shorthold* tenancy is a form of assured tenancy carrying a mandatory right to recovery of possession. Such assured shorthold tenancies can be offered by private registered providers or registered social landlords¹. In practice, if a periodic assured shorthold tenancy is offered as an allocation, it may be intended to fulfil the same function as an introductory tenancy, ie that it should be probationary and cease to be an assured shorthold tenancy (and thus become a fully assured tenancy) after a specified period. Alternatively, the property may be offered by the private registered provider or registered social landlord on a fixed term assured shorthold tenancy, perhaps at an 'affordable' rent, rather than an ordinary 'social housing' rent². In the statutory guidance for local housing authorities in England, the Secretary of State has indicated that he expects both local housing authorities and private registered providers to make 'affordable rent' homes available through the local allocation scheme, in the same way that other rented properties are made available³.

¹ HA 1996, s 230; Housing Act 1988, ss 1 and 19A–20.
² See, for England, the regulatory guidance given by the *Tenancy Standard*, para 2 (Homes and Communities Agency, April 2012), part of *The Regulatory Framework for Social Housing in England from April 2015* (Homes and Communities Agency, March 2015).
³ English Code, para 6.4.

5.68 For the first time, in 2012/13, social landlords were asked to record what numbers of their tenancies were granted on a fixed-term rather than periodic basis. The data collected indicated that of over 370,000 social housing lets, 12,597 were fixed-term lets of general needs social housing and there were 7,475 fixed-term lets at affordable rents¹. These figures indicate than less than 10% of lettings made by social landlords were on a fixed-term basis². By 2016/17 the proportion of general needs private registered provider lettings let at social rent levels on a fixed term basis had increased to 23%. The majority of general needs fixed-term tenancies (75%) were issued for between three and five years but for supported housing 83% of fixed-term tenancies were for two years or less in length³.

¹ *Social Housing Lettings: April 2012 to March 2013: England* (DCLG, October 2013), Accompanying Table 2b Length of Fixed Term Letting.
² See also F Priest-Stephens 'Fixed Term Tenancies Under the Spotlight' (2014) *Inside Housing* 16 June.
³ *Social Housing Lettings: April 2016 to March 2017*, England (MHCLG, January 2018).

5.69 In England, the tenancy strategy, published by the local housing authority, will explain which forms of tenancy of social housing are likely to be available in any particular district, whether from the local housing authority or from other social landlords within that district[1]. The local allocation scheme will have been drawn up having regard to the content of that tenancy strategy[2].

[1]   Localism Act 2011, s 150.
[2]   HA 1996, s 166A(12)(b).

Furnished or unfurnished?

5.70 The allocation scheme will govern selection or nomination for both furnished and unfurnished properties. Most local housing authority stock is let unfurnished, but a significant proportion of properties designed for the elderly or others with support needs will be partly or wholly furnished. The same general pattern is true of the stock made available by other social landlords for nominations from local housing authorities.

5.71 An applicant cannot insist on the provision of (or removal of) furnishings. However, local housing authorities have very broad powers to furnish and fit out their properties and/or sell or hire furniture to tenants[1]. The economies of scale that can be achieved by a local housing authority in bulk-buying furniture and selling it on to incoming tenants should not be underestimated. The golden rule must be that it is always open to an applicant to ask. A local housing authority which responded to a request with a pronouncement that it never provided furniture would be guilty of unlawfully fettering its discretion, and the relevant decision should be quashed in proceedings for judicial review. The question of whether furniture will be provided in lettings by other social landlords will be subject to the terms of any relevant guidance from national regulatory authorities and the terms of that landlord's own governing instrument (for example, any Articles of Association). However, social landlords have been invited by other commentators to let a greater proportion of their properties on a furnished basis[2].

[1]   Housing Act 1985, s 10.
[2]   See, for example, *Why social landlords should provide fully furnished properties*, Guardian Housing Network Blog, 20 November 2012.

Quality of accommodation offered

5.72 There is no minimum standard of accommodation that a property must achieve before a local housing authority or other social landlord offers a particular unit to an applicant selected or nominated under a local allocation scheme. Indeed, it may be precisely the least desirable properties that are most frequently on offer.

5.73 In contrast to the law relating to homelessness, there is no requirement that the offered property be 'suitable' or 'available for occupation'[1]. Advisers must be careful to ensure that this distinction between offers under HA 1996, Pts 6 and 7, is made clear to applicants[2]. Of course there may be an overlap: for example, an allocation under HA 1996, Pt 6, may be made to an applicant who is owed a homelessness duty, perhaps in order to release the local housing authority from that duty. Such an allocation would have to be of a 'suitable' property in order to achieve that effect[3].

1   See CHAPTER 18 of this book for 'suitable' and CHAPTER 10 for the concept of 'available for occupation'.
2   *Brent London Borough Council v Sharp* [2003] EWCA Civ 779, [2004] HLR 65, CA.
3   For example, in England a homeless applicant owed the main housing duty is free to *accept* any Pt 6 offer (HA 1996, s 193(6)(c)) but an offer which has been *refused* must have been 'suitable' in order to effect a discharge of that duty (HA 1996, s 193(7)). See CHAPTER 16. However, in Wales, a homelessness duty owed to an applicant will only come to an end where an applicant *accepts* or refuses an offer of 'suitable' accommodation: H(W)A 2014, s 76(2) and (3). See CHAPTER 17.

5.74 The principle in operation is 'caveat lessee' or 'let the prospective tenant beware'. It is for the prospective tenant to decide whether he or she wants to accept or reject what is offered, having carefully considered it. Accordingly, a tenant who accepts the property can later have no complaint in law if he or she subsequently finds that it is in a more noisy location or situation than expected[1], or if there is a pungent smell which the tenant erroneously thought could be removed by cleaning[2].

1   *Southwark London Borough Council v Tanner and Mills* [2002] 32 HLR 148, HL.
2   *Smith v Wrekin Housing Trust* [2004] EWCA Civ 1792, CA. In one case, the Local Government Ombudsman did find the local housing authority guilty of maladministration where it had allocated a property to an applicant which the Ombudsman described as 'so filthy it could not be lived in': *Complaint against Nottingham City Council 05/C/2965*, 19 April 2007, (2007) June *Legal Action*, p 37.

5.75 There is, at present, no general legal rule in England that the properties of a local housing authority landlord or other social landlord must meet minimum standards at the date of letting[1]. The previous statutorily implied term that a property must be 'fit for human habitation' at the date of letting currently has no practical application as a result of a failure to up-rate the rent thresholds that govern its operation[2]. What is left is only the old common law rule that a property let furnished (which is itself unusual in social housing[3]) must be fit for occupation at the date of letting[4]. However, at the time of writing the Homes (Fitness for Human Habitation) Bill had passed its second reading in the House of Commons, having secured government backing. If enacted, this would require landlords of residential property, including local housing authority landlords and other social landlords, to ensure that the dwelling is fit for human habitation and remains so throughout the tenancy. In Wales, the Renting Homes (Wales) Act 2016 will also, when brought into force, require that all rented property must be fit for human habitation[5].

1   *Siney v Dublin Corporation* [1980] IR 400.
2   Landlord and Tenant Act 1985, s 8(1) and (4), only applicable to properties let on low rents (the threshold is now unrealistically low).
3   See 5.70–5.71.
4   See Luba, Prevatt and Forster *Repairs: Tenants Rights* (LAG, 5th edn, 2016), pp 14–15.
5   Welsh Code, para 1.18.

5.76 Of course, a new tenant who finds that the property is unsatisfactory for some reason may give it up, by notice to quit or surrender, if he or she has somewhere else to go, or could pursue a complaint about the allocation (to the social landlord and thereafter to an Ombudsman) and/or apply for a transfer to more satisfactory accommodation under the allocation scheme. The new tenant can, of course, additionally expect that any repairing obligations, imposed on the social landlord by the tenancy agreement, will be met within a reasonable time of commencement of the tenancy.

Offers to transfer applicants

5.77 Where the offer is made to an applicant who is already a tenant of the local housing authority or another social landlord[1], two particular issues arise:

(1)   getting the type of tenancy right; and
(2)   determining the old tenancy.

[1]   For the current policy emphasis on facilitating tenancy transfers see **2.55–2.65**.

5.78 If the transferring tenant is currently a secure or assured tenant (but not an assured shorthold tenant), whether under a sole or a joint tenancy, the new tenancy to be offered of any local housing authority property can only be a secure tenancy and not an introductory tenancy, even if the local housing authority normally only offers introductory tenancies to new tenants[1].

[1]   HA 1996, s 124(2).

5.79 If the allocation process has resulted in a tenant being nominated to a different social landlord (not currently that tenant's landlord) and has produced an offer of a tenancy from that landlord, the tenancy may be offered as an assured tenancy or assured shorthold tenancy irrespective of the applicant's current form of tenancy. In practice, most private registered providers or registered social landlords will offer a full assured tenancy to an incoming tenant who has been the secure or assured tenant of another social landlord.

5.80 Offering an equivalent form of tenancy to that which a transferring social housing tenant has previously enjoyed has become of more acute importance since the changes to security of tenure and succession made in respect of social housing tenancies in England from 1 April 2012 by the Localism Act 2011[1] and will become even more so when the changes contained in the Housing and Planning Act 2016 come into effect[2]. In order to ensure that transferring tenants – especially those ceasing to be periodic tenants in order to take fixed-term tenancies – do not inadvertently lose accrued rights, the social housing regulator for England requires that:

> 'Registered providers shall grant those who were social housing tenants on the day on which section 154 of the Localism Act 2011 comes into force [1 April 2012], and have remained social housing tenants since that date, a tenancy with no less security where they choose to move to another social rented home, whether with the same or another landlord. (This requirement does not apply where tenants choose to move to accommodation let on Affordable Rent terms).[3]'

[1]   See M Robinson 'Keep on Moving' (2012) 152 *Adviser* 18 on the issues relating to social housing tenants who move within the social housing sector after 1 April 2012.
[2]   At the time of writing, it is not known if or when this will happen.
[3]   *Tenancy Standard*, para 2.2.8 (Homes and Communities Agency, April 2012), part of *The regulatory framework for social housing in England from April 2015* (Homes and Communities Agency, March 2015).

5.81 It will be important for the local housing authority or other social landlord to ensure that the successful applicant's current tenancy is brought to an end at, or immediately following, the commencement of the new tenancy. Unless (unusually) the tenancy is of the same property, the grant of the new tenancy does *not* automatically determine the old one. The old tenancy will need to be determined by a tenant's notice to quit or by surrender, the latter being most safely achieved by deed. If the landlord and tenant have overlooked the need to determine the old tenancy before the new one commences, it will usually be possible for the old one to be immediately surrendered or subject to a notice to quit, with, perhaps, both parties agreeing to short notice[1].

[1] See *Hackney London Borough Council v Snowden* (2001) 33 HLR 49, CA and *Ealing Family Housing Association v McKenzie* [2003] EWCA Civ 1602, [2004] HLR 21, CA.

5.82 A common issue will be whether any arrears of rent outstanding on the old tenancy can be transferred to the new one. Although the parties can make an agreement as to how those arrears will be cleared, that agreement cannot be enforced in proceedings for possession of the new home in respect of those arrears, unless either:

(1)   the parties have agreed that any payments made after the date of transfer will be first applied to meet the old debt, in which case arrears will accrue in the new tenancy unless the tenant makes double payment; or

(2)   the parties have agreed that compliance with the arrears agreement will be a term of the new tenancy[1].

[1] *Notting Hill Housing Trust v Jones* [1999] L&TR 397, CA.

Refusal of offers

5.83 No applicant can be compelled to accept an offer of accommodation made under a HA 1996, Pt 6 allocation scheme. Where the offer has been made to a homeless applicant, however, the effect of a refusal may, in narrowly prescribed circumstances, operate to bring a homelessness duty to an end[1].

[1] See the discussion in CHAPTER 15 and CHAPTER 16 (England) and CHAPTER 17 (Wales).

5.84 In other cases, the effect (if any) of a refusal will be dealt with in the allocation scheme itself. An applicant who has rejected a property cannot properly be subject to some form of penalty or suspension under an allocation scheme unless a rule to that effect appears in the published scheme and has been properly applied[1]. Indeed, even if such a provision did appear in a published scheme, if the scheme itself was based on a needs-led priority system, it would be difficult to impose any sanction unless the refusal itself evidenced a change in assessed need. However, a period of deferral resulting from the refusal of an offer would, it seems, be lawful where such a refusal was a reasonable matter for an allocation scheme to take into account in affording relative priority between applicants[2].

[1] *R v Wandsworth London Borough Council ex p Lawrie and Heshmati* (1997) 30 HLR 153, QBD.

² *R (Cranfield-Adams) v Richmond upon Thames London Borough Council* [2012] EWHC 3334 (Admin), (2012) August *Legal Action*, p 27, Admin Ct.

5.85 If the penalty provision for a refusal is legitimately included in a local allocation scheme, the local housing authority must still ensure that its operation is considered on a case-by-case basis, having regard to the circumstances of each refusal[1]. Indeed, many allocation schemes make provision for 'appeals' against, or for the 'review' of offers, made under the scheme and a significant proportion of such challenges made are successful[2]. The Welsh Code recommends that the allocation scheme should include rights to a review for those penalised by refusal of an offer[3]. The inclusion or application of a penalty can, of course, be challenged by way of judicial review if the local housing authority is not willing to waive it in any particular case[4].

1   *R v Gateshead Metropolitan Borough Council ex p Lauder* (1996) 29 HLR 360, QBD and *R v Westminster City Council ex p Hussain* (1999) 31 HLR 645, QBD.
2   A survey conducted in 2006/07 found that a significant proportion of appeals had been upheld. The average 'appeal success rate' ('success' from an applicant perspective) was 40%: *Exploring local authority policy and practice on housing allocations* (CLG, July 2009), para 2.14.
3   Welsh Code, para 3.62.
4   *R (Cranfield-Adams) v Richmond upon Thames London Borough Council* [2012] EWHC 3334 (Admin), (2012) August *Legal Action*, p 27, Admin Ct.

5.86 The local housing authority must also be clear that an applicant has in fact refused a property before imposing any sanction. The local housing authority should not act solely on information received from a third party but should confirm this with the applicant him or herself[1].

1   *Complaint against Horsham District Council*, 15 018 987, 7 September 2016.

Chapter 6

LETTINGS BY SOCIAL LANDLORDS (OTHER THAN LOCAL HOUSING AUTHORITIES)

Contents

DEFINITIONS

6.1 As a result of changes to the relevant statutory provisions in England and Wales, there are now several different technical descriptions of the major social landlords that may be involved in the allocation of social housing. They are:

(1)   registered providers of social housing in England[1], of which there are two sub-categories:
    (a)   public registered providers ie local housing authority landlords; and
    (b)   private registered providers (mainly housing associations);
(2)   social landlords in Wales, of which there are two sub-categories:
    (a)   local housing authority landlords; and
    (b)   registered social landlords[2].

---

[1]   Registered providers in England, of both categories, are regulated by the Regulation Committee of the Homes and Communities Agency, following amendments made by the Localism Act 2011, Pt 7 to the Housing and Regeneration Act 2008 with effect from 1 April 2012. See **1.31–1.35**.
[2]   Registered social landlords in Wales are regulated by the Welsh Ministers pursuant to the provisions of Housing Act 1996, Pt 1. See **1.36–1.39**.

6.2 This chapter is concerned with lettings by social landlords other than local housing authority landlords ie by private registered providers in England and by registered social landlords in Wales.[1]

[1]   We acknowledge our indebtedness to our former professional colleague Robert Latham. His stimulating article *Allocating social housing: the registered landlord context* (2008) October *Legal Action*, p 43, provided the inspiration for much of the material in this chapter.

OVERVIEW

6.3 In England, the stock of social housing for rent owned by private registered providers now exceeds two million units. In Wales, the number of homes owned by registered social landlords is over 141,000[1]. With the development of new housing schemes, the acquisition of properties through funding from the Homes & Communities Agency (in England) and the Welsh Government, and the transfer of local housing authority homes to other social landlords, that stock had been gradually increasing and in Wales that is still the case[2]. In England, however, the number of private registered provider dwellings has not increased since 2014[3] and with the planned introduction of the right-to-buy for private registered provider tenants in England the number may remain static or even start to fall[4]. Nevertheless, these social landlords now hold more housing stock for rent than do local housing authorities. In consequence, significantly more lettings of social housing homes in England are now made by private registered providers than by local housing authorities[5].

[1]   In 2016 there were 4 million dwellings in the social housing sector in England of which 2.4 million were held by housing associations and 1.6 million by local authority landlords: *English Housing Survey: Headline Report 2016–2017* (MHCLG, January 2018). In Wales, as at 31 March 2017, there were 228,684 units of social housing of which 141,378 were held by registered social landlords and only 87,306 by local authority landlords: *Social Housing Stock and Rents as at 31 March 2017* (Welsh Government, August 2017) at Table 2.

[2]   The number of social housing units held by registered social landlords has increased from 137,406 in 2012–13 to 141,378 in 2016–17. *Social Housing Stock and Rents as at 31 March 2017* (Welsh Government, August 2017) at Table 1.

[3]   The number of private registered provider dwellings has remained constant at 2.4 million since 2014 (*English Housing Survey: Headline Report 2014–2015* (DCLG, February 2016) and *English Housing Survey: Headline Report 2016–2017* (MHCLG, January 2018).

[4]   In October 2015, an agreement was reached between the National Housing Federation and the Government under which housing associations agreed to extend the right-to-buy to their tenants on a voluntary basis. At the time of writing, one pilot scheme had been completed and a further, large-scale regional pilot had been announced. The House of Commons Library produced a briefing paper explaining the background to the policy and progress to date: *Introducing a voluntary right to buy for housing association tenants in England* (House of Commons Library, CBP-7224, 24 May 2018). In contrast, an Act to abolish the right to buy for tenants of local authorities and registered social landlords in Wales received royal assent on 24 January 2018.

[5]   In England in 2015/16 there were 110,312 general needs lettings by private registered providers and 89,206 such lettings by local housing authorities. There were a further 79,159 lettings of supported housing by private registered providers and only 11,383 such lettings by local housing authorities. In 2016/17 private registered providers made 65% of all social lettings in England compared to 60% in 2007/08. *Social housing lettings: April 2016–March 2017, England* (MHCLG, January 2018).

6.4 However, there is no equivalent in this part of the social housing sector to the over-arching statutory control on allocations imposed on local housing authorities by HA 1996, Pt 6. Each private registered provider or registered social landlord will, within the terms of its own governing legal instrument, be free to let its available homes to such applicants as it pleases (subject to the applicable constraints of the general law – eg as to the prohibition of certain forms of discrimination[1]). There is nothing preventing a private registered provider or registered social landlord from letting, for example, to a person who would not meet the statutory eligibility or qualification requirements[2] for local housing authority accommodation in the same district.

[1]   For a discussion of discrimination in the context of social housing allocation see **4.210–4.230**.
[2]   Described in CHAPTER 3 of this book.

6.5 A private registered provider or registered social landlord may deal with the letting of its homes in a number of ways. For example:

* It may, if it chooses – operate a *transfer* scheme enabling its existing tenants to seek alternative homes within its stock. Most such landlords take that course[1].

* For *non-transfer* applicants, a private registered provider or registered social landlord may operate an 'open list' or 'direct applications' system so that anyone who applies may be considered for a tenancy in its stock, and it may then order or organise that list in such manner as it chooses.

* It may, additionally or alternatively, make available some part or the majority of its stock to the local housing authority or other social landlords to make nominations of prospective tenants – whom it may then accept or reject as it pleases[2].

* It may, if it chooses, advertise its available properties through a choice-based letting scheme. That may be the social landlord's own scheme, a scheme operated jointly with a local housing authority, or even a common scheme[3] shared with other social landlords and local housing authorities.

[1]   See **6.60–6.65**.
[2]   For 'nominations' see **6.25–6.59**.
[3]   For 'common schemes' see **6.53–6.59**.

6.6 The relative freedom enjoyed by private registered providers and registered social landlords is held in check only by the requirements of the national regulatory authorities. In England, the regulator is the Homes & Communities Agency's Regulation Committee[1]. It has the power to set standards to be followed by the providers of social housing[2]. Those standards require registered providers of social housing to comply with specified rules about criteria for allocating housing accommodation[3]. The current regulatory standards are contained in *The Regulatory framework for social housing in England from April 2015*[4]. The Housing and Regeneration Act 2008 gives the regulator considerable powers of inspection and enforcement to ensure that these standards are complied with[5]. The regulator issues regulatory standards to social housing providers as directed by the Secretary of State[6].

[1]   On 11 January 2018 the Homes and Communities Agency's investment arm adopted the trading name of Homes England whilst the regulation directorate re-named itself the Regulator of Social Housing. At the time of writing, a draft Statutory Instrument was before Parliament (the Legislative Reform (Regulator of Social Housing) Order 2018) which if made will abolish the Regulation Committee of the Homes and Communities Agency, create a

Regulator of Social Housing, and transfer the functions of the Regulation Committee to the Regulator of Social Housing. The way in which registered providers of social housing are regulated is not expected to change.

2   HRA 2008, s 193(1).
3   HRA 2008, s 193(2)(a).
4   Homes and Communities Agency, March 2015.
5   HRA 2008, ss 192–269.
6   The current directions are set out at Annex A of *Implementing Social Housing reform: Directions to the Social Housing Regulator – Consultation: a summary of responses* (DCLG, November 2011).

6.7 In Wales, the regulatory function falls to the Welsh Ministers. A Housing Regulation Team undertakes the regulation activity on their behalf and its work is overseen by the Regulatory Board for Wales. Under HA 1996, s 33A the Welsh Ministers may set performance standards to be met by registered social landlords in connection with their functions relating to the provision of housing. The Welsh Ministers may issue guidance relating to and amplifying a performance standard under HA 1996, s 33B. The current performance standards and guidance are contained within *The Regulatory Framework for Housing Associations Registered in Wales*[1].

1   Welsh Government, May 2017.

6.8 Some of the largest private registered providers and registered social landlords are those that were created specifically to acquire the housing stock of particular local housing authorities in large scale voluntary transfers. Most local housing authorities engaging in such transfers took the opportunity, before transfer of their stock, to entrench the new social landlord's future arrangements for allocation of the transferred stock (and, in some cases, allocation of stock subsequently acquired) through contractual commitments. Those contractual obligations operate as a fetter on the freedom in letting that most other social landlords enjoy[1].

1   For contractual 'nomination agreements' see **6.25–6.43**.

6.9 A private registered provider's or registered social landlord's responsibility in housing allocation may not necessarily be confined to the letting of *its own* stock. Several have contracted to operate housing allocation services for local housing authorities[1]. Those services are contracted out to them pursuant to the arrangements described in Chapter 21 of this book. Such a social landlord may thus find itself directly allocating some of its own stock, managing allocation of local housing authority stock and also operating the local housing authority's system for nomination of prospective tenants to itself[2]. However, even in a situation where functions are contracted out to a social landlord, which acquired the stock through a large-scale transfer, local housing authorities must remain active participants in allocation arrangements[3].

1   For contracting out of allocation functions see **6.66–6.68**.
2   See **6.66–6.68**.
3   One survey found that at least a significant minority of local housing authorities had unlawfully treated a large scale transfer, combined with the contracting out of allocation arrangements, as releasing them from any further concern with the allocation of that housing: *Exploring local authority policy and practice on housing allocations* (DCLG 2009, paras 2.15–2.16).

DIRECT APPLICATIONS

Duty to maintain a lettings policy

6.10 Most, if not all, private registered providers or registered social landlords retain at least some of their available housing stock for lettings to new applicants – those who have directly applied to that social landlord for housing (direct applications) – or to their own current tenants who wish to move within their stock. Lettings to current tenants are dealt with separately later in this chapter[1].

[1] See 6.60–6.65.

6.11 The private registered provider's or registered social landlord's governing body will have adopted a lettings policy relating to direct applications (and other lettings) and there will usually be a procedure guide or manual setting out the way in which housing staff are to implement the policy. In 2015/16, 42% of general needs lettings by private registered providers in England were to direct applicants[1].

[1] *Social Housing Lettings in England, 2016–17: Continuous Recording (CORE) Summary Tables* (MHCLG, January 2018), Table 3j.

6.12 As CHAPTERS 1–5 of this book have explained, HA 1996, Pt 6, requires local housing authorities, but not other social landlords, to incorporate a statement of their policies for selection priorities and lettings procedures into a single local allocation scheme, copies of which must be available on request. A similar, but not precisely the same, statutory obligation is cast on private registered providers and registered social landlords by Housing Act 1985, s 106. This requires any 'landlord authority' (a term defined to embrace private registered providers and registered social landlords)[1] to maintain two sets of rules:

(1) the rules for determining *priority* as between applicants in the allocation of its housing accommodation[2]; and

(2) the rules which it has laid down governing the *procedure* to be followed in allocating its housing accommodation[3].

[1] Housing Act 1985, s 114.
[2] Housing Act 1985, s 106(2)(a).
[3] Housing Act 1985, s 106(2)(a).

6.13 A private registered provider or registered social landlord is under a statutory duty to publish a summary of the first set of rules but not of the second[1]. Although any applicant can *ask* for a full copy of both sets of rules, there is no statutory duty to make them available at the landlord's offices. Copies need only be sent to the relevant statutory regulator and to any local housing authority in the district of which the social landlord still has stock let on secure tenancies[2]. An applicant could inspect the rules, or take copies of them, at the office of any such local housing authority[3]. All the regulatory guidance, reproduced earlier in this chapter, emphasises the need for transparency and fairness in fixing the terms of, and operating allocation schemes – although it falls short of requiring the production and publication of a formal lettings policy or allocation scheme.

[1] Housing Act 1985, s 106(1)(a).
[2] Housing Act 1985, s 106(3).
[3] Housing Act 1985, s 106(4).

Guidance on contents of lettings policies

6.14 Statutory guidance on the content of allocation policies is limited. In England, the current regulatory standard for housing allocation in England (part of a broader Tenancy Standard) provides[1]:

'1 Allocations and mutual exchange

1.1 Registered providers shall let their homes in a fair, transparent and efficient way. They shall take into account the housing needs and aspirations of tenants and potential tenants. They shall demonstrate how their lettings:

- make the best use of available housing
- are compatible with the purpose of the housing
- contribute to local authorities' strategic housing function and sustainable communities

There should be clear application, decision-making and appeals processes.'

[1] *Tenancy Standard* (Homes and Communities Agency, April 2012), part of *The regulatory framework for social housing in England from April 2015* (Homes and Communities Agency, March 2015). The passages of the current regulatory standard dealing with *mutual exchange* have not been reproduced in these extracts.

6.15 The regulatory standard then sets out the following Specific Expectations[1]:

'1 Allocations and mutual exchange

1.1 Registered providers shall co-operate with local authorities' strategic housing function, and their duties to meet identified local housing needs. This includes assistance with local authorities' homelessness duties, and through meeting obligations in nominations agreements.

1.2 Registered providers shall develop and deliver services to address under-occupation and overcrowding in their homes, within the resources available to them. These services should be focused on the needs of their tenants, and will offer choices to them.

1.3 Registered providers' published policies shall include how they have made use of common housing registers, common allocations policies and local letting policies. Registered providers shall clearly set out, and be able to give reasons for, the criteria they use for excluding actual and potential tenants from consideration for allocations, mobility or mutual exchange schemes.

1.4 Registered providers shall develop and deliver allocations processes in a way which supports their effective use by the full range of actual and potential tenants, including those with support needs, those who do not speak English as a first language and others who have difficulties with written English.

1.5 Registered providers shall minimise the time that properties are empty between each letting. When doing this, they shall take into account the circumstances of the tenants who have been offered the properties.

1.6 Registered providers shall record all lettings and sales as required by the Continuous Recording of Lettings (CORE) system.

1.7 Registered providers shall provide tenants wishing to move with access to clear and relevant advice about their housing options.'

---

[1]   *Tenancy Standard* (Homes and Communities Agency, April 2012), part of *The regulatory framework for social housing in England from April 2015* (Homes and Communities Agency, March 2015).

6.16 In Wales, the current guidance is even less detailed. The revised *Regulatory Framework for Housing Associations Registered in Wales* has the stated purpose of improving and strengthening the Welsh Government's approach to regulation but the guidance it provides in respect of allocations is minimal. Performance Standard 5 requires registered social landlords to demonstrate 'A track record of achieving positive outcomes, responding appropriately to new challenges and performance issues'. The guidance accompanying this standard recommends that the association demonstrate 'how lettings make the best use of available housing, compatible with the core purpose of the Registered Social Landlord'.

6.17 More general guidance is available in the introduction to the Framework, which confirms that the Framework is underpinned by the 'principles of proportionality, transparency and openness, consistency and promotion of learning and development'.

6.18 This guidance is, in part, supplemented by provisions in the Welsh Code[1], which suggests that registered social landlords are required by their regulators to retain responsibility for their own allocations policies[2]. The Welsh Government's Housing Association Circular *RSL 004/15* directs registered social landlords in Wales to 'take account' of the Welsh Code when addressing their key delivery outcomes reproduced above[3]. The Welsh Code suggests that registered social landlords in Wales:

•   consider carefully the information they provide about their allocation policies[4];
•   should not involve board members in decision-making on individual allocations[5]; and
•   should monitor their allocation outcomes[6].

---

[1]   *Code of Guidance for Local Authorities on the Allocation of Accommodation and Homelessness 2012* (Welsh Government, March 2016) (the Welsh Code).
[2]   Welsh Code, para 4.16.
[3]   *RSL 004/15: Code of Guidance for Local Authorities on the Allocation of Accommodation and Homelessness* (Welsh Government, July 2015). Reproduced on the CD Rom provided with this book.
[4]   Welsh Code, paras 1.25–1.27 and 1.33.
[5]   Welsh Code, para 4.37.
[6]   Welsh Code, paras 4.49–4.50.

6.19 Private registered providers and registered social landlords must also ensure that their lettings policies comply with the requirements of the general law. In particular, private registered providers and registered social landlords must comply with their obligations under the Equality Act 2010. Allocating social housing is a public function and private registered providers or registered social landlords exercising those functions will constitute public bodies when doing so[1]. This means that they must comply with the public sector equality duty, which requires public authorities to:

'have due regard to the need to—
(a)   eliminate discrimination, harassment, victimisation and any other conduct that is prohibited by or under this Act;
(b)   advance equality of opportunity between persons who share a relevant protected characteristic and persons who do not share it;
(c)   foster good relations between persons who share a relevant protected characteristic and persons who do not share it[2].'

In addition, lettings policies must not unlawfully discriminate under either the Equality Act 2010 or Art 14 of the European Convention on Human Rights[3].

[1]   *R (Weaver) v London and Quadrant Housing Trust* [2009] EWCA Civ 587, [2010] 1 WLR 363, CA.
[2]   Equality Act 2010, s 149. See **4.193–4.209**.
[3]   See **4.210–4.230**.

6.20 Private registered providers and registered social landlords must also ensure that their functions are discharged having regard to the need to safeguard and promote the welfare of children[1]. This applies not only to the formulation of their lettings policies but also to their decisions in individual cases[2].

[1]   Children Act 2004, s 11.
[2]   See **4.241–4.247**.

6.21 The limited nature of the guidance suggests, as already indicated, that, subject to the constraints of the general law as referred to above, private registered providers and registered social landlords have a relatively free hand in the arrangements they make for direct applications and in the organisation of what will usually be a waiting list where demand exceeds supply. They may, for example, include policies explaining:

•   how applications will be prioritised;
•   in what circumstances, if any, applicants will be excluded or suspended from their schemes[1];
•   whether access is to be restricted to those with a particular connection to an area; and
•   what choice applicants will be given before being allocated a property.

In short, it is for each private registered provider or registered social landlord to set its own categories for prioritising applicants and its own arrangements for allocating particular properties.

[1]   In *Complaint against Cymdeithas Tai Eryri* (Public Services Ombudsman for Wales, ref 201102854, 2012) the registered social landlord had a policy enabling it to suspend a housing application for 'unacceptable behaviour' of a type making the applicant unsuitable to be a tenant but it wrongly used that policy to suspend an applicant for providing misleading information in an application form. The Ombudsman said that if it wished to suspend for that reason, its published policies should be amended to make that clear. The Welsh Government has indicated (Welsh Code, paras 2.44(vii) and 2.45) that it is in the process of developing regulatory guidance which will require that registered social landlords restrict access to housing only in circumstances which mirror the unacceptable behaviour provisions under HA 1996, Pt 6, but none has been forthcoming at the time of writing.

Information about lettings policies and procedure

6.22 The starting point for any applicant considering a direct application to any particular private registered provider or registered social landlord will be to obtain details of its letting scheme. The obligation of a private registered provider or registered social landlord to have a scheme and make it available is described at **6.12**.

6.23 Although no applicant for a direct letting has a statutory right to make an application, or even to be informed of the outcome, the regulatory guidance suggests at least some basic procedural requirements should be observed. The guidance for England requires that 'clear application, decision-making and appeals processes' are in place and that allocations processes are developed and delivered 'in a way which supports their effective use by the full range of actual and potential tenants, including those with support needs, those who do not speak English as a first language and others who have difficulties with written English'[1].

[1]   See **6.15**.

Disputes about direct lettings

6.24 A dissatisfied applicant under a direct letting scheme has access to a range of options to press matters beyond any internal review or appeal opportunity that the scheme itself may contain. Disputes may be progressed through complaints procedures, with the relevant social housing regulator, to the Housing Ombudsman or Public Services Ombudsman for Wales and/or through the courts[1].

[1]   See further **6.69–6.81**.

NOMINATIONS BY LOCAL HOUSING AUTHORITIES

The legal basis

6.25 HA 1996, Pt 6, requires that every private registered provider or registered social landlord will, on request from a local housing authority, 'co-operate to such extent as is reasonable in the circumstances in offering accommodation to people with priority under the authority's allocation scheme'[1].

[1]   HA 1996, s 170. This duty to co-operate with a local housing authority to a reasonable extent mirrors the duty imposed on private registered providers or registered social landlords to co-operate in assisting a local housing authority in discharging its homelessness functions under HA 1996, s 213(1)(a) (England) or H(W)A 2014, s 95(2) (Wales).

6.26 This statutory obligation to co-operate over housing allocation arises only 'on request'[1]. A generic request from a local housing authority might cause a private registered provider or registered social landlord to offer nomination arrangements or to negotiate a common housing register or some other joint scheme with the requesting local housing authority. But the request may also be applicant specific. The local housing authority may, for example, owe a duty to accommodate a particular applicant needing accommodation of a particular type held by the private registered provider or registered social landlord and may make a request accordingly.

¹   HA 1996, s 170.

6.27 The duty to co-operate is limited to 'such extent as is reasonable in the circumstances'. A reasonable response to such a request might include an invitation to the local housing authority to transfer a unit of its stock to the private registered provider or registered social landlord or to accept a reciprocal nomination in return for the provision of the requested assistance.

6.28 The duty is not, however, restricted to requiring co-operation in respect of those in the statutory 'reasonable preference' categories. A local housing authority may also have identified other applicants in its scheme as having 'priority'¹.

¹   See CHAPTER 4 of this book at **4.159–4.164**.

6.29 This provision is the only statutory underpinning for strategic co-operation between local housing authorities and private registered providers or registered social landlords. Presumably Parliament expected that formal arrangements for day-to-day co-operation between local housing authorities and other social landlords would be set out in individually negotiated agreements. These locally agreed arrangements may be highly informal or, at the other extreme, may be set out in legally binding contractual documents.

6.30 The latter are more common in the cases of those private registered providers or registered social landlords which have taken a large-scale transfer of local housing authority stock. Indeed, the arrangements governing stock transfers from local housing authority landlords to private registered providers in England now expressly state that a local housing authority submitting a request for ministerial consent to transfer its stock must supply 'the transfer contract' governing the sale of the housing and the relationship between the local authority and the private registered provider and that that contract 'should include all agreements entered into by the local authority and private registered provider in respect of the transfer'¹. Further, in considering the application for consent, the Secretary of State will apply the criteria that the local authority will be able to fulfil its statutory obligations under the HA 1996, Pt 6, and has 'adequate nomination rights'².

¹   *Housing Transfer Manual: Period to 31 March 2016*, para 6.11. The matter was also covered in non-statutory guidance *Housing Allocation, Homelessness and Stock Transfer – A Guide to Key Issues* (ODPM, 2004) and, in Wales, the *Welsh Government Housing Transfer Guidelines 2009* (see Welsh Code, para 4.18).

²   *Housing Transfer Manual: Period to 31 March 2016*, para 7.2.

6.31 Save in those cases where the private registered provider or registered social landlord has entered into a contractual commitment to take local housing authority nominations, however, there is no legal obligation on that landlord to agree to take local housing authority nominations, either generally or for specific properties.

Guidance on co-operation

6.32 In the absence of any strict legal obligation, the matter of private registered provider or registered social landlord participation in nomination arrangements is simply another issue covered by the current statutory guidance.

6.33 The statutory Codes of Guidance issued to local housing authorities in England and Wales concerning housing allocation contain very little guidance about nominations to private registered providers or registered social landlords, in contrast to the ample non-statutory guidance[1]. The current statutory guidance in England simply suggests that nomination agreements should identify:

- the proportion of lettings that will be made available;
- any criteria which the private registered provider has adopted for accepting or rejecting nominees; and
- how any disputes will be resolved[2].

[1] See, for example, *Effective Co-operation in Tackling Homelessness: Nomination Agreements and Exclusion* produced jointly by Communities and Local Government (formerly the ODPM), the Housing Corporation, the National Housing Federation and the Local Government Association in November 2004 and *Building Bridges: A guide to better partnership working between local authorities and housing associations*, published by the Chartered Institute of Housing in association with the Association of Retained Council Housing and VIVID Housing, September 2017.
[2] English Code, para 6.3.

6.34 Local housing authorities are encouraged by the same guidance to monitor effective delivery of the nomination agreement 'so they can demonstrate they are meeting their obligations under Pt 6'[1]. Those 'obligations' are presumably the obligations to ensure that those in the prescribed categories are actually being afforded the 'reasonable preference' to which HA 1996, Pt 6, entitles them[2].

[1] English Code, para 6.3.
[2] CHAPTER 4 of this book.

6.35 The present Welsh Code provides that registered social landlords in Wales should actively work with local housing authorities to help them fulfil their functions and deliver good housing outcomes[1]. It expressly encourages partnership working between local housing authorities and registered social landlords in order to meet the needs of the local community and maximise the best use of the housing stock available[2]. It also advises that local housing authorities should develop common policies on restricting access to allocations with partner registered social landlords to maximise consistency in approach and improve efficiency in nominations procedures[3] and suggests that, where a local housing authority has transferred its stock to a registered social landlord, it is important that the local housing authority and registered social landlord have a clear nomination agreement and effective arrangements for allocations[4].

[1] Welsh Code, para 1.6.
[2] Welsh Code, paras 1.4–1.7
[3] Welsh Code, para 2.44(vii).
[4] Welsh Code, para 4.18.

6.36 Some guidance on the subject has also been given by the relevant national regulators. In England, the guidance requires co-operation with 'local authorities' strategic housing functions, and their duties to meet identified local housing needs. This includes assistance with local housing authorities' homelessness duties, and through meeting obligations in nominations agreements'[1]. The Welsh Regulatory Framework simply stipulates that housing associations are accountable to organisations, 'such as local authorities' that 'play a vital role in meeting local housing needs'[2].

[1] See the extract set out at **6.15**.
[2] *The Regulatory Framework for Housing Associations Registered in Wales* (Welsh Government, May 2017), p 4.

6.37 In parallel to all the emphasis in the old statutory guidance in England on the negotiating position of local housing authorities, in formulating nomination agreements, the now defunct Housing Corporation, for its part, reminded housing associations of the need to protect their own interests. Its guidance stated that, in order to preserve such a landlord's independence, any nomination agreement must:

- reflect the housing association's own objectives both as set out in its governing instrument and as agreed by the governing body;
- be approved by the governing body;
- be subject to regular and timely review; and
- run for such a term as would enable the parties to exit from it should circumstances or requirements change[1].

[1] Housing Corporation Circular 02/03, para 4.2. See also *Building Bridges: A guide to better partnership working between local authorities and housing associations*, published by the Chartered Institute of Housing in association with the Association of Retained Council Housing and VIVID Housing, September 2017.

6.38 This advice was mirrored in the previous version of the *English Homelessness Code of Guidance*, now withdrawn, which reminded local housing authorities to:

'bear in mind that RSLs are required to retain their independence. They must honour their constitutional obligations under their diverse governing instruments, and will make the final decision on the allocation of their housing, within their regulatory framework[1].'

This advice has not been replicated in the current *English Homelessness Code of Guidance.*[2]

[1] *English Homelessness Code of Guidance* (DCLG, July 2006) Annex 5, para 9 (see Appendix 2 of the fourth edition of this book).
[2] *English Homeless Code of Guidance* (MHCLG, February 2018).

6.39 Most nomination agreements also include 'carve out' provisions designed to allow registered social landlords to refuse applicants in appropriate circumstances. One report has recommended that these 'take account of the association's objectives and policies, striking a balance between the duty to cooperate and an association's right to refuse a nomination that is not 'reasonable' from its point of view"[1].

[1] *Building Bridges: A guide to better partnership working between local authorities and housing associations*, published by the Chartered Institute of Housing in association with the Association of Retained Council Housing and VIVID Housing, September 2017, pp 95–96.

Co-operation in practice

6.40 Arrangements made between a private registered provider or registered social landlord and any particular local housing authority may provide for that local housing authority to nominate applicants for general consideration by that landlord, or for consideration for a particular property, or may involve the private registered provider or registered social landlord supplying details of its premises to be advertised as available to nominees under a local housing authority's choice-based letting scheme.

6.41 From the perspective of the local housing authority, nominating an applicant to be an assured tenant of housing accommodation held by a private registered provider or registered social landlord constitutes an 'allocation' of accommodation – unless it falls within one of the exceptions discussed in CHAPTER 1[1] – and is therefore governed by the local allocation scheme adopted by that particular local housing authority[2].

[1] See **1.23–1.29**.
[2] HA 1996, s 159(2)(c).

6.42 In practice, most private registered providers and registered social landlords co-operate to the extent of making at least some proportion of their lettings available to applicants who are nominees of local housing authorities. Indeed, in England in 2015/16, more than 44% of general needs lettings by private registered providers were made to local housing authority nominees[1].

[1] *Social Housing Lettings in England, 2016–17: Continuous Recording (CORE) Summary Tables* (MHCLG, January 2018), Table 3j.

6.43 However, a report published in September 2017[1] found that the relationship between local housing authorities and private registered providers had come under strain in recent years. The root of the problem was said to be Government decisions to 'refocus' social registered landlords' programmes towards shared ownership, intermediate rent, and Affordable Rent. This had led to a 'sharp decline' in the availability of properties at social rents, with some private registered providers even questioning whether they could provide such accommodation at all. At the same time, local housing authorities were using their powers under the Localism Act 2011 to 'severely trim' their lists with the results that the registers 'tend to focus on applicants for social rent lettings' and did not 'generate the steady stream of appropriate applicants for housing association Affordable Rent, intermediate and market rent, and homeownership products'[2]. In addition to this, welfare reform was adversely affecting applicants' ability to afford properties for which they were nominated, with the result that 'Housing associations feel that some local authorities are nominating households who cannot afford their homes and are therefore set up to fail'[3].

1   *Building Bridges: A guide to better partnership working between local authorities and housing associations*, published by the Chartered Institute of Housing in association with the Association of Retained Council Housing and VIVID Housing, September 2017.
2   *Building Bridges: A guide to better partnership working between local authorities and housing associations*, published by the Chartered Institute of Housing in association with the Association of Retained Council Housing and VIVID Housing, September 2017, pp 91–94.
3   *Building Bridges: A guide to better partnership working between local authorities and housing associations*, published by the Chartered Institute of Housing in association with the Association of Retained Council Housing and VIVID Housing, September 2017, p 95.

Information sharing

6.44 Where private registered providers or registered social landlords and local housing authorities are working closely together over social housing allocation, there will inevitably be a need to share information. But information sharing relating to the particulars of individual applicants requires very careful handling.

6.45 Those who have applied to a local housing authority for accommodation under HA 1996, Pt 6, have the statutory assurance that even the simple fact that they have applied will not be shared with others (including private registered providers or registered social landlords) without their consent,[1] as well as the protection of the General Data Protection Regulation and the Data Protection Act 2018.[2]. It will therefore be essential for the local housing authority to have the written consent of each and every applicant before sharing access to such information with a private registered provider or registered social landlord.

1   HA 1996, s 166(4). See CHAPTER 2 of this book at **2.30**.
2   See **2.30**.

6.46 Against this background, both the former Housing Corporation and previous UK governments produced publications designed to help local housing authorities and private registered providers or registered social landlords to resolve information sharing issues[1].

1   See, in particular, *Access to Housing: Information Sharing Protocol* (Housing Corporation, November 2007).

'Failed' or 'problematic' nominations

6.47 A particular difficulty with the operation of nomination agreements, in practice, has been the rejection of nominated applicants by private registered providers or registered social landlords. These have been described as 'failed nominations' or 'problematic nominations'[1]. In a survey conducted in October 2013, local housing authorities were 'concerned that housing associations are refusing their nominations' and the researchers reported that 'this is a particular problem for non-stock holding authorities who have homelessness duties to discharge'[2].

1   D Cowan et al *Problematic Nominations* (School of Law, Bristol University, December 2007).

2   *Under Pressure? Emerging issues for allocations* (Chartered Institute of Housing, November 2013), p 5. For an example of a failed nomination see *Complaint against Royal Borough of Windsor and Maidenhead Council* 16 003 062, 15 February 2018, (2018) May *Legal Action*, p 37.

6.48 Three common reasons for rejection of nominations have been identified. The first cause is information mismatching, ie the local housing authority and the private registered provider or registered social landlord both hold information about the applicant, but the content differs. For their part, local housing authorities should provide details about nominated households that are clear, comprehensive and up to date, including any available information about vulnerability, support needs and arrangements for support. Failure to get this sort of information sharing right could undermine a nomination process, whilst getting it right will ensure the best chances of new tenancies being sustained[1].

1   See Welsh Code at para 3.51 and *Access to Housing: Information Sharing Protocol* (Housing Corporation, November 2007).

6.49 A second common reason for failed nominations occurs where applicants, whilst meeting the local housing authority's criteria for nomination (under the local allocation scheme), do not meet the particular private registered provider's or registered social landlord's letting criteria for the specific property (or, in some cases, for any letting by that social landlord)[1]. All such criteria should, of course, be the subject of consultation and subsequent incorporation into the written nominations agreement between the particular private registered provider or registered social landlord and the local housing authority[2]. If rejection of nominations on these grounds occurs frequently, it may seriously impair a local housing authority's statutory obligations, eg to give a 'reasonable preference' to particular categories of its applicants[3].

1   For a recent discussion of the issue see *Housing associations should have some say in who lives in their homes*, Guardian Housing Network Blog, 12 August 2014 and *Why housing associations should not be able to pick and choose their tenants*, Guardian Housing Network Blog, 15 August 2014.
2   See **6.25–6.43**.
3   For the meaning of 'reasonable preference', see CHAPTER 4 of this book.

6.50 The particular problems arising from inconsistent criteria relating to nominated applicants are thrown into sharp focus when accommodation made available for local housing authority nominees by a private registered provider or registered social landlord is advertised through the local housing authority's choice-based lettings scheme. The highest ranked bidder for that property will expect to be offered the tenancy if he or she meets the local housing authority's own criteria and will not expect to be denied it for failing to meet the private registered provider's or registered social landlord's criteria, eg because the housing association landlord has wider exclusion criteria than the local housing authority or because it gives particular emphasis to local connection or local lettings policies[1]. In an attempt to avoid such difficulties, the now-withdrawn English CBL Code advised that:

'the exclusion policy of each participating RSL should be clearly set out in the published CBL scheme details. In addition, where this is feasible, the exclusion criteria applied by an RSL should be stated in the advertisement of any relevant vacancy, so that applicants are clear about the basis on which the property is offered[2].'

1   As to 'legitimate expectation' in the housing allocation context see **4.50–4.53**.
2   English CBL Code, para 6.7. The code was reproduced in the second edition of this book at APPENDIX 1.

6.51 Because most nominations will be made under the auspices of the local housing authority's own allocation scheme, it will be the local housing authority which has ultimate responsibility to the applicant for any difficulties. It may well be that an aggrieved applicant seeks redress against that local housing authority. However, a 'nominated' applicant will also have access to avenues of redress against the private registered provider or registered social landlord, where appropriate[1].

1   See **6.69–6.81**.

6.52 If a private registered provider or registered social landlord does not co-operate in the face of a request from the local housing authority, the local housing authority could pursue the matter with the relevant regulator or through the courts (because the statutory duty is mandatory)[1]. Alternatively, the individual (if there is one) who is the subject of the request could use the private registered provider's or registered social landlord's complaints procedure or could pursue one of the other means of redress[2]. However, the better course is obviously for the degree and level of co-operation to be improved. Research conducted in October 2013 found that 40% of the local housing authority and private registered provider respondents were reportedly 'working to strengthen relationships with their partners with a view to resolving differences and challenges'[3].

1   HA 1996, s 170 says '*shall* co-operate' (emphasis added).
2   See **6.69–6.81**.
3   *Under pressure? Emerging issues for allocations* (Chartered Institute of Housing, November 2013), p 5.

Common housing registers and allocation schemes

6.53 Some local housing authorities and private registered providers or registered social landlords choose to operate common housing registers and/or common allocation schemes. The former was defined in the English CBL Code[1] as an arrangement under which a local housing authority and another social landlord developed a single list or database of all applicants for housing allocation who had applied to either of them[2]. The latter consists of a framework for enabling common criteria to be applied in assessing applications (eg to ascertain eligibility and priority). As a report on such matters in Wales indicated:

'The presence of a common housing register in an authority area is not necessarily a requisite for a common allocations policy. 29% of respondents have common registers but no common allocations policy. However, in the 3 authorities where a common allocations policy is in operation, 2 of the authorities also have a common register operating[3].'

¹   Reproduced in the second edition of this book at Appendix 1.
²   English CBL Code, para 6.16.
³   Homelessness Strategy Working Group Report: *Housing Association Lettings* (Community Housing Cymru).

6.54 The modern impetus for the adoption of 'common' allocation schemes between local housing authorities and other social landlords in England was given in August 2008 by publication of the English CBL Code in which the Secretary of State recommended that all local housing authorities work with other social housing partners to provide 'joint choice-based lettings schemes which extend to all or the majority' of local social housing vacancies[1]. The Secretary of State considered that the adoption of common housing registers had advantages:

- for applicants (because a single application form and a single access point obviates the need to register separately);
- for local housing authorities (because the register provides a more reliable assessment of housing need in their districts, providing important information for the development of their housing strategy, and enabling the best use to be made of existing stock)[2]; and
- more generally, because the process of negotiating and drawing up such registers can build trust between local housing authority partners and other social landlords[3].

¹   English CBL Code, para 6.1 and English (2009) Code, para 99. Both codes were reproduced in the second edition of this book at Appendix 1.
²   English CBL Code, para 6.17 and English (2009) Code, para 99.
³   English (2009) Code, para 100.

6.55 The current regulatory guidance in England contains no particular recommendations on such arrangements and the regulatory guidance in Wales is silent on the issue. However, the Welsh *Code* is emphasises the advantages of common housing registers[1] and provides its own list of their perceived benefits:

- they provide a single point of access to all social housing in the area;
- they help improve joint working between an authority and housing associations and help in meeting strategic housing objectives;
- they support the development of more strategically planned and integrated lettings schemes in an area;
- they give a better understanding of the pattern of local housing needs; and
- they can reduce void levels[2].

¹   Welsh Code, para 3.52 and 4.12–4.18.
²   Welsh Code, para 4.12. See too Welsh Code, para 3.52, reporting that 90% of housing associations in Wales are part of at least one common housing register.

6.56 Nevertheless, considerable care is needed in drawing up such schemes. As already explained[1], if an applicant on the common register is applying for a property to be let directly by a private registered provider or registered social landlord, the only eligibility criteria will be those adopted by that social landlord. But if the applicant is going to be a local housing authority nominee for a private registered provider or registered social landlord vacancy, the statutory *eligibility* or *qualification* criteria of HA 1996, Pt 6, and the local housing allocation scheme must be met[2].

[1] See **6.4–6.8** and **6.14–6.21**.
[2] Those terms are explained in CHAPTER 3.

6.57 These complications are thrown into even sharper relief when a private registered provider or registered social landlord participates in a common registration scheme with more than one local housing authority or with a number of local housing authorities and other social landlords. Ambitious plans to amalgamate registers and allocations policies, to produce common schemes, involving private registered providers or registered social landlords but run by a single central organisation exercising the delegated powers of all participants, have run into difficulties. Previous statutory guidance in England has advised that local housing authorities cannot use their general statutory powers of delegation to operate such common lettings schemes together with other social landlords although 'it would be possible to include within such a scheme [those] vacancies to which a local authority had nomination rights'[1].

[1] English CBL Code, para 7.8.

6.58 All social landlords have also been encouraged to monitor their participation in choice-based lettings schemes with other local housing authority and social landlord partners[1]. Where private registered provider or registered social landlord property is advertised through a joint choice-based lettings scheme in which the private registered provider or registered social landlord participates with local housing authorities which each have their own allocation scheme:

(1) the partners in the scheme should be clear as to which local housing authority is the nominating local housing authority; and
(2) there should be clear information available for applicants as to which local housing authority's allocation scheme applies to that property (and therefore how priority will be determined).

[1] See, for example, Welsh Code, para 4.50.

6.59 In the latest supplementary statutory guidance on housing allocation issued to local housing authorities in England (the 'Supplementary English Code')[1], the Secretary of State acknowledged that common allocation policies are operating in some areas and advised as follows in relation to the consequences of the adoption, by one or more of the participants, of a qualifying class limited by residence requirements[2]:

'We are aware that in some parts of the country, housing authorities share a common allocation policy with their neighbours and may wish to adopt a broader residency test which would be met if an applicant lives in any of the partners' districts. Such an approach might be particularly appropriate where an established housing market area spans a number of local authority districts, and could help promote labour mobility within a wider geographical area.'

1 The Supplementary English Code – *Providing social housing for local people* (DCLG, December 2013) – is reproduced in Appendix 1.
2 The Supplementary English Code, para 14.

TRANSFERS (CURRENT TENANTS WHO WANT TO MOVE)

6.60 All private registered providers and registered social landlords will have arrangements in place to handle the receipt, and subsequent determination, of requests from existing tenants to move to other homes within that land-lord's stock, ie applications from tenants seeking a transfer. Indeed, in 2015/16 in England 15.4% of general needs lettings by private registered providers were internal transfers[1].

1 *Social Housing Lettings in England, 2016–17: Continuous Recording (CORE) Summary Tables* (MHCLG, January 2018), Table 2f.

6.61 The applicable statutory requirements are minimal. They only oblige the minority of private registered providers or registered social landlords which have *secure* tenants to publish a summary of their transfer rules governing cases where their secure tenants wish to move to other dwelling-houses let under secure tenancies by that landlord[1]. Where that obligation does apply, the private registered provider or registered social landlord must also make a copy of the transfer rules available at its principal office for inspection at all reasonable hours, without charge, by members of the public[2].

1 Housing Act 1985, s 106(1). Private registered providers and registered social landlords will usually only have 'secure tenants' if they were letting properties before early 1989 (when Housing Act 1988 introduced the assured tenancy for most housing association lettings).
2 Housing Act 1985, s 106(1).

6.62 Although the adoption of such transfer arrangements (ie published transfer rules and policies) might be thought in any event to represent sensible housing management for all private registered providers or registered social landlords, the matter has in the past been the subject of statutory guidance. Housing associations were previously directed to ensure that their written lettings policies 'take account of the need to give reasonable priority to transfer applicants'[1]. The current regulatory guidance in England simply specifies that tenants of private registered providers wishing to move should be provided 'with access to clear and relevant advice about their housing options'[2].

1 *Regulatory Code of Guidance* (Housing Corporation, August 2005) para 3.6f.
2 See **6.15**.

6.63 If all the stock of a particular private registered provider and registered social landlord is ring-fenced for allocation only through a nomination arrangement or a common allocation scheme, some requests for transfers will fail because they would not meet the criteria for allocation under those arrangements or schemes[1].

[1] See, for an example, the facts of *R (Fidelis-Auma) v Octavia Housing & Care* [2009] EWHC 2263 (Admin), (2009) November *Legal Action*, p 25, Admin Ct.

6.64 The precise detail of a particular private registered provider's or registered social landlord's internal transfer scheme is not regulated by any statutory parameters or guidance and such landlords have, essentially, a free rein. This is, of course, subject to the constraints of the general law (eg the need to avoid unlawful discrimination) and the requirement[1] to act fairly and in accordance with the particular landlord's own published scheme. The private registered provider or registered social landlord may even differentiate between the criteria it applies to transfer applicants and those applying to direct applicants. For example, the now-withdrawn Housing Corporation Circular 02/07 suggested that a housing association may take a stricter view of the effect of rent arrears on eligibility for allocation if the arrears are owed by its own tenant[2].

[1] This requirement is discussed further (in the context of judicial review) in CHAPTER **19**.
[2] Circular 02/07: *Tenancy Management: Eligibility and Evictions* (Housing Corporation, April 2007).

6.65 The published information generally provided by the private registered provider or registered social landlord about its lettings arrangements[1] should be made available to transfer applicants. Complaints by, and redress for, dissatisfied transfer applicants are considered later in this chapter[2].

[1] See **6.22–6.23**.
[2] See **6.69–6.81**.

PRIVATE REGISTERED PROVIDERS OR REGISTERED SOCIAL LANDLORDS AS LOCAL HOUSING AUTHORITY CONTRACTORS

6.66 Local housing authorities may not contract out of ultimate responsibility for the local housing allocation scheme[1]. Responsibility for adopting or altering the scheme, for the principles of the scheme, for consulting social landlords and for ensuring that the allocation scheme is available for inspection by the public cannot be contracted out[2]. However, local housing authorities may contract out the functions of:

- inviting and/or receiving applications;
- making inquiries into an application;
- making decisions as to eligibility or qualification;
- carrying out reviews of decisions;
- making arrangements to secure that advice, information and necessary assistance is available; and
- making the actual allocation decision, arranging the tenancy sign-up, etc.

[1] See generally CHAPTER **21**.
[2] Local Authorities (Contracting out of Allocation of Housing and Homelessness Functions) Order 1996, SI 1996/3205, applying to both England and Wales. See also English Code, paras 6.5–6.11, Welsh Code Annex 9, and **21.43–21.49**.

6.67 The local housing authority remains legally responsible for any acts or omissions of the contractor and for decisions made in its name[1].

¹   See **21.2**.

6.68 CHAPTER 21 of this book deals more fully with both contracting out and stock transfer. The report *Housing allocation, homelessness and stock transfer: A guide to key issues* contains advice for private registered providers, registered social landlords and local housing authorities on all three subjects – stock transfer, contracting-out and housing allocation nominations – in a single publication, but this must now be read with some caution as it has not been revised since 2005[1].

¹   *Housing allocation, homelessness and stock transfer: A guide to key issues* (CLG, 2005).

COMPLAINTS, APPEALS AND LEGAL CHALLENGES

6.69 Before deciding whether or how to dispute a decision made on an application for (or nomination for) a housing allocation by a private registered provider or registered social landlord, an applicant should first obtain such details as he or she can about the particular private registered provider's or registered social landlord's housing allocation scheme[1]. At the same time, he or she should ask the private registered provider or registered social landlord to provide the details of the particulars which he or she has given to the local housing authority about 'himself and his family'[2] and which the private registered provider or registered social landlord has recorded as being relevant to the application for accommodation. The applicant has the statutory right to have that information made available on request at all reasonable times and without charge[3]. Complying with the request will require disclosure of not only the application form but also of any details the private registered provider or registered social landlord has subsequently obtained in its consideration of the application. Most simply, the applicant can ask for and will usually be provided with a copy of the application file. Armed with the file and the copy scheme, the applicant (or an adviser) will usually be able to identify, and draw to the private registered provider's or registered social landlord's attention, any simple error, missing material or other mishap that has occurred in considering the application.

¹   See **6.22–6.23**.
²   Housing Act 1985, s 106(5).
³   Housing Act 1985, s 106(5).

6.70 In case any difficulty is not so easily resolved, every private registered provider or registered social landlord is required to have a complaints procedure. The Housing Ombudsman Service publishes a useful leaflet for complainants pursuing a complaint to a private registered provider in England under its complaints procedure: *Making a complaint*[1]. The regulatory guidance in England requires that:

> 'Providers shall offer a range of ways for tenants to express a complaint and set out clear service standards for responding to complaints, including complaints about performance against the standards, and details of what to do if they are unhappy with the outcome of a complaint. Providers shall inform tenants how they use

261

complaints to improve their services. Registered providers shall publish information about complaints each year, including their number and nature, and the outcome of the complaints. Providers shall accept complaints made by advocates authorised to act on a tenant's/tenants' behalf[2].'

[1]   Available at www.housing-ombudsman.org.uk.
[2]   *Tenant Involvement and Empowerment Standard*, para 2.1.2 (updated July 2017), part of *The regulatory framework for social housing in England from April 2015* (Homes and Communities Agency, March 2015).

6.71 If the complaints procedure does not resolve the matter, an applicant with a continuing grievance concerning a private registered provider operating in England can press the complaint to the Housing Ombudsman service. The Ombudsman is established by statute[1] and provides a free and independent service. Private registered providers are expected to comply with his recommendations. Information about how a complaint can be made is available on the Housing Ombudsman's website. The Localism Act 2011 modified other arrangements for complaints to the Housing Ombudsman in England with effect from April 2013 but complaints relating to allocation decisions of private registered providers are still within his jurisdiction.

[1]   HA 1996, s 51 and Sch 2.

6.72 Complaints about registered social landlords operating in Wales can be directed to the Public Services Ombudsman for Wales[1]. A *Housing Allocation Factsheet* is available on his website[2].

[1]   See further, **2.117–2.120.**
[2]   In 2006 he published *Housing Allocations and Homelessness: A Special Report* summarising findings in relation to housing allocation complaints. This is available to download at the PSOW website.

6.73 Particular difficulties face applicants who have been nominated by a local housing authority but whose applications have been rejected by the private registered provider or registered social landlord to whom the nominations were made. In theory, they may need to pursue the matter with both the local housing authority and the housing provider. The reality is that most simply give up. Research conducted in England did not find a single case of an applicant exercising their right to a review of a HA 1996, Pt 6 allocation decision where a nomination had been rejected and the researcher commented that[1]:

'Put simply, applicants disappeared from the process. The issue was regarded as being between the RSL and the local authority. Most usually, the applicant themselves did not appreciate that they had even been the subject of a nomination. Their applications might have been considered by the RSL, they might even have been interviewed by the RSL, but they were unlikely to know that they were the subject of a nomination let alone a problematic one.'

[1]   D Cowan, 'Nominations: A Practical Issue' [2008] 11 *Journal of Housing Law* 26.

6.74 However, one determined applicant did obtain relief from the Local Government Ombudsman[1] in a failed nomination case[2]. The applicant was a homeowner. He wished to move nearer to a school which was able to meet the needs of his disabled child. He applied for accommodation under the local housing authority's choice-based allocation scheme, was allocated priority Band B, and was able to bid under the scheme. In response to a successful bid, the local housing authority nominated him for a housing association property which suited his needs and he agreed to take it. However, the association operated an additional letting criterion - it would not let to an applicant who was a property owner. No such criteria appeared in the local housing authority's allocation scheme. The association refused to rent the property to the complainant. The local housing authority accepted the association's position. When the complainant sought a review, the local housing authority said that it could not hold a review because the decision had been made under the association's policy. When the matter was raised with the Local Government Ombudsman[3], both the local housing authority and the association agreed that they had acted wrongly. The Ombudsman found maladministration because the local housing authority had lacked a clear understanding of its arrangements for nominations and consequent housing association letting and had simply accepted the association's withdrawal of the tenancy. The refusal of a review had compounded those errors. Recommendations made included £3,800 compensation, a direct let and a review of both staff training and the content of nomination agreements made with local housing associations.

[1] As of 19 June 2017, the Local Government and Social Care Ombudsman (LGSCO).
[2] *Complaint against Kettering Borough Council*, 11 011 766, 16 January 2013, (2013) March *Legal Action*, p 20.
[3] As of 19 June 2017, the Local Government and Social Care Ombudsman (LGSCO).

6.75 That example was followed by another successful complaint, to the Public Services Ombudsman for Wales, arising from a failed nomination[1]. A stock-transfer housing association (TCC) entered into a partnership agreement with the local housing authority under which all its housing stock was to be let in accordance with the local housing authority's housing allocation scheme. An applicant under the scheme was a previous tenant of TCC, which considered that she owed it a former tenant debt. The local housing authority nominated her to TCC. Three TCC properties became available for which the applicant was the highest qualified under the scheme but she was bypassed for an offer by TCC because of her alleged debt. The Ombudsman found that TCC had taken matters into its own hands in 'complete disregard for the partnership agreement . . . the law and government guidance and all good practice' (para 36). However, TCC considered that other partners in the common housing register had similarly departed from the partnership agreement and circulated the draft embargoed PSOW report to other registered social landlords, which then wrote to the Ombudsman. The PSOW considered that this conduct demonstrated that there may be wider problems with stock transfer landlords in Wales and referred his report to the Welsh Government. The PSOW recommended an apology and £1,000 compensation for the complainant.

[1] *Complaint against Tai Ceredigion Cyf*, 2012 04677, 26 November 2013, (2014) February *Legal Action*, p 30.

6.76 In Northern Ireland, a failed nomination applicant has succeeded in an application for judicial review of the relevant housing association[1]. He had applied for social housing accommodation under the allocation scheme adopted by the Northern Ireland Housing Executive (NIHE). He was awarded 330 points. This was the highest points score of any applicant for two-bedroom accommodation in the area where he wished to live. A local housing association had a development of two-bedroom units in that area and it had agreed to allocate its housing accommodation in keeping with the rules of the published NIHE allocation scheme. However, the association decided that it should let the new units only to transfer cases, rather than to new applicants such as Mr Turley. The properties were then allocated to tenants with fewer points than he had. One was a board member of the association who had 112 points, another was a management transfer applicant with 90 points and the third was the niece of a board member, who was not a transfer applicant, and had only 34 points. Horner J held that the allocation decisions were unlawful. They had not been made fairly because the two board members ought to have declared their interests in the lettings and taken no part in the relevant decision-making. The decision to let only to transfer applicants had not accorded with the rules of the scheme. The association had failed to consider the application made by Mr Turley alongside the others and had fettered its discretion in deciding only to consider transfer applicants. The failure to deal with the claimant fairly had also been in breach of his legitimate expectation[2] and of the Human Rights Act 1998, Sch 1, Art 8[3].

[1]   *Turley's application for judicial review* [2013] NIQB 89, (2013) November *Legal Action*, p 32.
[2]   See **4.50–4.53** and **5.46**.
[3]   See **4.237–4.240**.

6.77 Although a private registered provider or registered social landlord may operate a system of complaints handling, reviews of decisions or even appeals, there is strictly no right of appeal to the courts or tribunals from any decision of a private registered provider or registered social landlord or of the Ombudsmen.

6.78 The Divisional Court and the Court of Appeal have held that the decision of a private registered provider or registered social landlord in relation to the allocation of social housing can be amenable to judicial review – at least to the extent that, in allocating its housing, the private registered provider or registered social landlord might be described as undertaking a 'public function'[1]. The housing association involved in that case was refused permission to appeal to the Supreme Court. Therefore, unless and until – in some other case – the Supreme Court overrules the decision of the Court of Appeal, a dissatisfied applicant is now able to invoke the jurisdiction of the Administrative Court to review a private registered provider's or registered social landlord's decision-making on a housing allocation application (whether the applicant was seeking a transfer[2], was a direct applicant, was a nominee from a local housing authority[3], or was simply a tenant of that social landlord seeking a mutual exchange[4]). The grounds on which the court will interfere with such a decision are narrowly drawn and are described later in this book[5].

[1]   *R (Weaver) v London & Quadrant Housing Trust* [2008] EWHC 1377 (Admin); [2009] 1 All ER 17, Divisional Court, and [2009] EWCA Civ 587, [2009] 4 All ER 865, [2009] HLR 40, CA. For an example of a case in which the refusal of a mutual exchange request by a housing association was not an exercise of its 'public functions' see *R (Macleod) v Governors of the Peabody Trust* [2016] EWHC 737 (Admin).

2   As in *R (Fidelis-Auma) v Octavia Housing & Care* [2009] EWHC 2263 (Admin), (2009) November *Legal Action*, p 25, Admin Ct and *R (Podkowka) v Women's Pioneer Housing Association* [2014] EWCA Civ 208, (2014) April *Legal Action*, p 26, CA.
3   *R (Carney) v Bolton at Home Ltd* [2012] EWHC 2553 (Admin), (2012) November *Legal Action*, p 22, Admin Crt and in *Turley's application for judicial review* [2013] NIQB 89, (2013) November *Legal Action*, p 32.
4   As in *R (McIntyre) v Gentoo Group Ltd* [2010] EWHC 5 (Admin), (2010) March *Legal Action*, p 28, Admin Ct. For an example of a case in which the refusal of a mutual exchange request by a housing association was not an exercise of its 'public functions' see *R (Macleod) v Governors of the Peabody Trust* [2016] EWHC 737 (Admin), [2016] HLR 27, Admin Ct.
5   See CHAPTER 19.

6.79 The Divisional Court and the Court of Appeal have also decided that the act of a private registered provider or registered social landlord in granting or terminating a tenancy of social housing is, where it is done pursuant to a function of a public nature, an act to which the requirements of the Human Rights Act 1998 (HRA 1998) apply[1]. HRA 1998 prohibits a public authority from acting in a manner contrary to an individual's Convention rights as set out in those articles reproduced in HRA 1998, Sch 1[2]. Although no Convention right gives an applicant a right to a home from a private registered provider or registered social landlord, the Convention rights might assist an applicant who has been denied a proper hearing of an application or an appeal by such a landlord (Art 6), who has been denied a transfer and thus is left in an unsatisfactory home let by a private registered provider or registered social landlord (Art 8) or who has been a victim of discrimination in consideration of his or her application (Art 14)[3]. Obviously, an applicant seeking to conduct a judicial review or to assert his or her Convention rights against a private registered provider or registered social landlord should be referred for specialist legal advice.

1   *R (Weaver) v London & Quadrant Housing Trust* [2008] EWHC (Admin) 1377, Divisional Court; [2009] 1 All ER 17, [2009] EWCA Civ 587, [2009] 4 All ER 865, [2009] HLR 40, CA.
2   HRA 1998, s 6(1). For an example of a successful claim for breach of Art 14 in a housing allocation context see *R (HA) v Ealing London Borough Council (No 1)* [2015] EWHC 2375 (Admin), [2016] PTSR 16, Admin Ct.
3   See further Chapter 4 at 4.237–4.240. For an example of a successful discrimination claim in a housing allocation context see *R (HA) v Ealing London Borough Council (No 1)* [2015] EWHC 2375 (Admin), [2017] PTSR 16, Admin Ct.

6.80 Additionally, where the applicant considers that there has been unlawful discrimination[1] or an infringement of human rights, the assistance of the Equality and Human Rights Commission can be sought[2].

1   See further CHAPTER 4 at **4.210** et seq.
2   At www.equalityhumanrights.com..

6.81 It is theoretically possible for individual complaints to be made to the national regulatory authorities[1] about allocation decisions made by private registered providers or registered social landlords but in practice they will be diverted to the private registered provider's or registered social landlord's complaints procedure or to the relevant Ombudsman. However, where the individual complaint reflects a systemic malfunction by the private registered provider or registered social landlord it may be worthwhile seeking to involve the regulator.

¹ In England, the Homes and Communities Agency's Regulation Committee and in Wales, the Housing Regulation Team.

Part II

HOMELESSNESS

Chapter 7

LOCAL HOUSING AUTHORITIES' HOMELESSNESS REVIEWS AND STRATEGIES

Contents

INTRODUCTION

7.1 This chapter and the following chapters of this book deal with 'Homelessness'. Like the statutory schemes for the homeless in the Housing Act 1996 (HA 1996), Pt 7[1], for local housing authorities in England, and the Housing

(Wales) Act 2014 (H(W)A 2014), Pt 2, for local housing authorities in Wales, this book's primary focus is on the individual applicant for assistance and the powers and duties of a local housing authority in dealing with the application. However, over recent years, increasing attention has been focused on the need to take a more strategic approach to the problem of homelessness beyond simply operating the safety net mechanism for individual applicants now contained in the HA 1996, Pt 7[2], or H(W)A 2014, Pt 2.

[1]   As amended by Homelessness Reduction Act 2017, (HRA 2017), for applications for homelessness assistance made to local housing authorities in England on or after 3 April 2018.
[2]   As amended by HRA 2017 for applications for homelessness assistance made to local housing authorities in England on or after 3 April 2018.

7.2 The steady rise, between 2001 and 2004, in the number of applications for homelessness assistance in all parts of the UK, and the consequent growth in the numbers of households in temporary accommodation, caused the focus of attention to shift towards methods of preventing homelessness and to dealing more effectively with it when it does arise. Central government began encouraging a more proactive rather than reactive approach to the issue of homelessness.

7.3 After 2004, the number of applications for homelessness assistance to local housing authorities in England and Wales fell steadily until 2010[1]. The fall has been attributed to various factors including the former Labour government's policy of encouraging local housing authorities in England to halve their use of temporary accommodation by the year 2010. Critics observed that another reason might be that the laudable policy of taking action to prevent homelessness in practice became 'gate-keeping', in that potential applicants for homelessness assistance were dissuaded from making applications.

[1]   Statistics from local housing authorities in England are available at: https://www.gov.uk/gov ernment/collections/homelessness-statistics. Statistics from local housing authorities in Wales are available at: https://statswales.gov.wales/Catalogue/Housing/Homelessness

7.4 From mid-2010, as the recession began to impact, the number of applications for homelessness assistance increased in both England and Wales. In England, the number of acceptances (applicants who were owed the HA 1996, s 193(2), main housing duty[1]) in the *second* quarter of 2017 was 53% higher than the numbers in the last quarter of 2009[2]. In Wales, there was a smaller, but still significant, increase[3]. Commentators noted that the figures of acceptances of applications for homelessness assistance could not provide a true picture of the extent of homelessness for two reasons. The first was that only applicants who are eligible for assistance[4], have a priority need[5] and have not become homeless intentionally[6] are accepted, so most single homeless adults are not included in the figures[7]. The second was that local housing authorities were increasingly using a prevention and housing options approach, rather than assisting applicants to make an application for homelessness assistance under HA 1996, Pt 7[8], or H(W)A 2014, Pt 2[9].

[1]   HA 1996, s 193(2), see **16.94–16.199**.
[2]   The last quarter of 2009 saw the lowest number of acceptances of applications for homelessness assistance: 9,430. The number of acceptances in the second quarter of 2017 was 14,400: Statutory Homelessness and prevention and relief, April to June (Q1) 2017: England

(DCLG, 28 September 2017). Strangely, the number of acceptances in the second quarter of 2017 was considerably lower than the number in the first quarter of 2017, which was 28,430.

3   It is not possible to compare directly the figures of acceptances by local housing authorities in Wales in 2010 and 2017, because of the impact of the Housing (Wales) Act 2014, (H(W)A 2014), Pt 2, see CHAPTER 16.

4   See CHAPTER 11.

5   See CHAPTER 12.

6   See CHAPTER 13.

7   See Support for single homeless people in England Annual Review 2016 (2016 Homeless Link); the annual publication *Homelessness Monitor, England* (Fitzpatrick, Pawson, Bramley, Wilcox & Watts, Crisis) and *The Green Book Report: 50 years on* (Shelter 2016).

8   As amended by HRA 2017 for applications for homelessness assistance made to local housing authorities in England on or after 3 April 2018.

9   See, for example, *The Homelessness Monitor, England 2015* (Fitzpatrick, Pawson, Bramley, Wilcox & Watts, Crisis, 2015), chapter 4.

7.5 The housing charity and campaigning organization Shelter, in a review of housing conditions since its inception in 1966, highlights those people who are "hidden homeless": sofa surfing between friends or relatives, or living in unsuitable accommodation. It is not possible to ascertain how many people are living in these conditions. In addition to the hidden homeless, 250,000 people are known to be homeless in the UK at any one time, and at least 3,500 people are known to sleep rough on any given night[1]. Shelter concludes that radical action is necessary.

1   *The Green Book Report: 50 years on* (Shelter 2016).

7.6 In August 2017, the homelessness charity Crisis published *Homelessness Projections*, which considered what the level of homelessness might be in the future[1]. Crisis reported that all forms of core homelessness had increased over the previous five years and that if government policies remained unchanged, the most acute forms of homelessness were likely to keep rising. Crisis predicted an increase in rough sleeping of 76% over the next ten years. Shelter has calculated that at any one time, there are 307,000 recorded as homeless, which equates to one in 200 people across the UK as a whole[2].

1   *Homelessness Projections: Core homelessness in Great Britain* (Bramley, Crisis, 2017)

2   *Far from alone: Homelessness in Britain in 2017* (Shelter, November 2017). Shelter's analysis is based on figures for people sleeping rough, single people in hostels, households owed a duty under HA 1996, Pt 7, or H(W)A 2014, Pt 2, and homeless household accommodated by social services obtained through freedom of information requests.

7.7 The governments in both England and Wales responded to these increases by encouraging greater use of the private rented sector. In England, the 2010–15 UK Coalition Government introduced the Localism Act 2011, ss 148–149, which permits local housing authorities in England to bring the HA 1996, s 193(2) main housing duty to an end by making an applicant a private rented sector offer[1]. In Wales, the National Assembly for Wales passed H(W)A 2014, Pt 2[2], which gives local housing authorities in Wales the power to make private rented sector offers[3]. In addition, H(W)A 2014, Pt 2, aims to help a much larger number of homeless people. It concentrates on prevention and helping applicants to stay in their existing homes, or to find new ones, without needing local housing authority accommodation, where possible[4].

1   For 'main housing duty' at HA 1996, s 193(2), see **16.94–16.199**. For 'private rented sector offer' at HA 1996, s 193(7AA)–(7AC), see **16.161–16.180**.

² In force for applications for help made to a local housing authority in Wales on or after 27 April 2015: Housing (Wales) Act 2014 (Commencement No 3 and Transitory, Transitional and Saving Provisions) Order 2015, SI 2015/1272 (W 88), see the CD Rom with this book.

³ H(W)A 2014, s 76(3)–(4), see **17.173–17.177**.

⁴ See **17.6–17.18**.

7.8 In 2016, Crisis worked with Bob Blackman MP to put forward a Homelessness Reduction Bill as a Private Members' Bill. The Bill received Government and indeed all-party support and was enacted as the Homelessness Reduction Act 2017 (HRA 2017). It applies to local housing authorities in England and has come into effect substantially in April 2018[1]. It is modeled on the Welsh approach, in H(W)A 2014, Pt 2, of early intervention, prevention and helping applicants to secure their own accommodation. All applicants who are eligible, and either homeless or threatened with homelessness, are to be helped. The issues of whether an applicant has a priority need and/or has become homeless intentionally only become relevant in relation to the provision of accommodation[2]. We discuss the potential impact of the amendments to HA 1996, Pt 7, by HRA 2017, in CHAPTERS **15** AND **16** of this book.

¹ Royal Assent 27 April 2017. In force for the power of the Secretary of State to make regulations 27 April 2017 (HRA s 13). Remainder to be brought into force by statutory instrument (HRA s 13(3)).

² A number of organisations had reported concerns at the lack of help and support available to homeless people who do not have any priority need: see *Support for single homeless people in England: Annual Review 2016* (Homeless Link, 2016); *Stop the scandal: an investigation into mental health and rough sleeping* (St Mungos, February 2016); *It's no life at all: and Rough Sleepers' experiences of violence and abuse on the streets of England and Wales* (Sanders & Albanese, Crisis, December 2016). After HRA 2017 had received Royal Assent, but before its coming into force, the All-Party Parliamentary Group for Ending Homelessness published its findings into support available for particular vulnerable groups: Homelessness Prevention for care leavers, prison leavers, and survivors of domestic violence (July 2017). In October 2017, Crisis published *Moving on: Improving access to housing for single homeless people in England* (Crisis, October 2017) which recommended that the government should take urgent steps to ensure that there is a supply of affordable housing available to single people who are homeless.

7.9 Both HA 1996, Pt 7[1], for local housing authorities in England, and H(W)A 2014, Pt 2, for local housing authorities in Wales, require local housing authorities to take a strategic and corporate approach to tackling homelessness.

¹ As amended by HRA 2017 for applications for homelessness assistance made to local housing authorities in England on or after 3 April 2018.

7.10 This chapter reviews the consequences of this strategic approach. It considers, in turn, the development of 'homelessness strategies' at national, regional and local level. Most of the focus is upon the latter, particularly as a result of statutory duties imposed on local housing authorities to draw up their own local homelessness strategies[1]. Those duties are considered in particular detail.

¹ Homelessness Act 2002 (HA 2002), ss 1–4; H(W)A 2014, ss 50–52.

NATIONAL STRATEGIES

7.11 At national level, policy-making relating to homelessness is undertaken by central government for England, and by the devolved governments of Wales, Scotland and Northern Ireland[1]. The UK Government has no single national strategy directed towards the prevention of homelessness or to tackling homelessness when it arises.

[1] For government policy in England, see https://www.gov.uk/government/collections/homelessne ss-guidanceFor Welsh Government policy see http://gov.wales/topics/housing-and-regeneratio n/services-and-support/homelessness/?lang=en. For Scottish Executive policy, see https://beta. gov.scot/policies/homelessness/. For Northern Ireland Housing Executive policy, see www.ni he.gov.uk/index/corporate/strategies/homelessness_strategy.htm.

7.12 In the absence of a UK-wide strategy, we consider each of the four national policies on homelessness in turn.

England

A review of recent history

1997–2010 LABOUR GOVERNMENTS

7.13 In 2001, the former Department for Transport, Local Government and the Regions (DTLR) consulted on the development of a National Homelessness Strategy for England, but no national strategy emerged from that exercise[1]. Then, between July 2004 and January 2005, the Parliamentary Select Committee on the work of the Office of the Deputy Prime Minister (ODPM)[2] carried out an Inquiry into the effectiveness of implementation of the Homelessness Act 2002[3].

[1] A national homelessness strategy: an invitation to comment (DTLR, 21 September 2001).
[2] Now the Communities and Local Government Parliamentary Select Committee. The ODPM was the relevant government department with responsibility for housing policy at the time.
[3] Select Committee on Office of the Deputy Prime Minister 'Housing, Planning, Local Government and the Regions, Third report of session 2004–2005'.

7.14 In January 2005, the ODPM published a five-year national housing strategy, *Sustainable Communities: Homes for All*[1], and then followed it, in March 2005, with a strategy for tackling homelessness, *Sustainable Communities: settled homes; changing lives*[2]. A Housing Green Paper *Homes for the Future: more affordable, more sustainable* was published in July 2007[3]. The most ambitious aim was to halve the number of households living in temporary accommodation between 2005 and 2010. Increased emphasis on prevention was seen as the key to achieving this. This was reflected in the guidance contained in chapters 1–5 of the 2006–2018 *Homelessness Code of Guidance for Local Authorities*, published in July 2006[4]. Another priority was reducing youth homelessness, and a commitment to end the use of bed and breakfast accommodation for 16- and 17-year-olds by 2010. The numbers of households in temporary accommodation did indeed fall between 2005 and 2010, so that by December 2010 the policy aim had been achieved. However, the figures started to rise again from mid-2011, as applications for homeless-

273

ness assistance increased[5].

1   ODPM, January 2005.
2   ODPM, March 2005.
3   Department for Communities and Local Government, July 2007.
4   Homelessness Code of Guidance for Local Authorities (Department for Communities and
      Local Government, Department for Education and Skills, Department of Health, July 2006)
5   MHCLG statutory homelessness statistics, Table 775.

2010–15 COALITION GOVERNMENT

7.15 Shortly after the UK Coalition Government assumed office in May 2010, the Minister for Housing announced the formation of a cross-government Ministerial Working Group on homelessness. The Minister also changed the methodology used by local housing authorities to count the numbers of people sleeping rough[1]. In July 2011, the Working Group published *Vision to End Rough Sleeping? No Second Night Out Nationwide*[2].

1   *Evaluating the extent of Rough Sleeping: A New Approach* (DCLG, 2010).
2   DCLG, 2011.

7.16 In November 2011, the UK Coalition Government published *Laying the Foundations: a Housing Strategy for England*[1]. In relation to homelessness duties owed under HA 1996, Pt 7, the Government's policy was enacted in the Localism Act 2011, permitting local housing authorities to bring the main housing duty to an end with offers of suitable private rented sector accommodation[2]. The strategy continued the previous government's commitment to implement measures to prevent homelessness[3]. It also committed the Government to 'tackle rough sleeping' through the Ministerial Working Group on Homelessness. The 'No Second Night Out' scheme was originally piloted in London and subsequently applied across the country[4].

1   HM Government, November 2011.
2   Chapter 3, para 21 of *Laying the Foundations*. See **16.94–16.199** of this book for the main
      housing duty and **16.161–16.180** for private rented sector offers.
3   Chapter 6, para 4 of *Laying the Foundations*.
4   See **7.56–7.61**.

7.17 In August 2012, the then Department for Communities and Local Government (DCLG) published *Making every contact count, a joint approach to preventing homelessness*[1], the second publication of the Ministerial Working Group on Homelessness. In March 2015, the Ministerial Working Group published Addressing complex needs: improving services for vulnerable homeless people[2]. It advises local housing authorities to commission, rather than provide, services for homeless people who have complex needs, and to work with other statutory and voluntary agencies to try to meet those needs.

1   DCLG, 2012.
2   DCLG, March 2015.

THE 2015–17 CONSERVATIVE GOVERNMENT AND
CURRENT CONSERVATIVE GOVERNMENT

7.18 As already noted[1], the Homelessness Reduction Bill 2016, introduced as a Private Members' Bill, received government and cross-Party support and was enacted as HRA 2017, receiving Royal Assent on 27 April 2017. HRA 2017 responds to concerns that the duties and powers to assist the homeless at HA 1996, Pt 7, are not available to all homeless people. Mirroring H(W)A 2014, Pt 2[2], it introduces new duties to help all eligible applicants[3] prevent their imminent homelessness[4] (for those who are threatened with homelessness)[5] and to help all eligible applicants secure their own accommodation[6] (for those are homeless)[7]. The issues of whether an applicant has a priority need[8] and/or whether he or she has become homeless intentionally[9] only arise in relation to whether the local housing authority has any duty to secure accommodation for the applicant. This model envisages increased use of the private rented sector so that local housing authorities work with private landlords, and refer applicants, rather than secure accommodation from their own stock. The scheme envisages early intervention, during a two month period when an applicant is threatened with homelessness. The days when local housing authorities would refuse to assist until an applicant was at crisis point should become a thing of the past[10].

[1]   See **7.8**.
[2]   See **15.3–15.52**; **16.1–16.3** and CHAPTER **17**.
[3]   For 'eligible', see CHAPTER **11**.
[4]   HA 1996, s 195, as amended by HRA 2017, s 4, for applications for homelessness assistance made to local housing authorities in England on or after 3 April 2018. See **15.87–15.137**.
[5]   For 'threatened with homelessness', see HA 1996, s 175(4) as amended by HRA 2017, s 1, for applications for homelessness assistance made to local housing authorities in England on or after 3 April 2018, and see **10.144–10.147**.
[6]   HA 1996, s 189B as inserted by HRA 2017, s 5, for applications for homelessness assistance made to local housing authorities in England on or after 3 April 2018. See **15.138–15.195**.
[7]   HA 1996, s 175(1)–(3), see **10.1–10.10**.
[8]   See CHAPTER **12**.
[9]   See CHAPTER **13**.
[10]   See Local Government Ombudsman Report: *Homelessness: how councils can ensure justice for homeless people Focus Report: learning the lessons from complaints* (Local Government Ombudsman, 2011).

7.19 In anticipation of the changes required by the amendments to HA 1996, Pt 7, inserted by HRA 2017, the government announced a Homelessness Support Grant to local housing authorities in England, paid for two years from April 2017. Campaigners and local government organisations have voiced fears that the money will not be sufficient and that additional money is required beyond the two year period. The government consulted on a draft *Homelessness Code of Guidance for Local Authorities*[1] between October and December 2017. The final *Homelessness Code of Guidance for Local Authorities* (the English Code) was published in February 2018[2] and amended in June 2018.

[1]   DCLG, October 2017.
[2]   *Homelessness Code of Guidance for Local Authorities* (MHCLG, February 2018) (the English Code), see APPENDIX **2**.

7.20 As already noted[1], the English government's progress in tackling homelessness has been subject to criticism by Crisis which, from 2011, has been publishing an annual report. The most recent publication at the date of writing is *The Homelessness Monitor: England 2018*[2]. It notes an ongoing upward trend in officially estimated rough sleeper numbers by 169% , and an increase in acceptances of applications for homelessness assistance by 34% since the low point in 2009/2010[3]. The authors estimate that the third category of homeless people, the 'hidden homeless' living in insecure and concealed households, could compromise 3.38 million adults. The vast bulk of the recorded increases are from people who have been made homeless from the private rented sector and thus the driving force behind the increase in homelessness is poverty. The authors also note that welfare cuts (including the shared accommodation rate, the benefit cap and universal credit) are likely to increase the numbers of people who are homeless. They comment that the increase in rough sleeping numbers, and the attention paid to households living in temporary accommodation particularly bed and breakfast accommodation, has driven the issue of homeless up the political agenda. They note cross-Party and cross-sector support for HRA 2017 and also high-profile political commitments to address homelessness from government, and from elected Mayors in London, Greater Manchester, Liverpool and the West Midlands. They doubt that the government's current targets for house-building will be met, or that those houses will be sufficient to resolve the crisis of homelessness. They describe as unprecedented 'the profile and energy now being given to homelessness as an acknowledged 'national crisis", which they welcome.

[1] See **7.5–7.6**.
[2] *The Homelessness Monitor*, Crisis, 2018. Parallel *Homelessness Monitors* are published for Wales, Northern Ireland and Scotland, see **7.37**, **7.44** and **7.53**.
[3] For discussion of the statistics, see **7.4–7.6**.

7.21 It remains to be seen whether local housing authorities in England will have access to sufficient supplies of affordable, suitable accommodation, including private rented sector, accommodation, to be able to fulfil their new duties to help applicants prevent their own homelessness[1] and to help applicants secure their own accommodation[2].

[1] HA 1996, s 195, as amended by HRA 2017, s 4, for applications for homelessness assistance made to local housing authorities in England on or after 3 April 2018. See **15.87–15.137**.
[2] HA 1996, s 189B inserted by HRA 2017, s 5, for applications for homelessness assistance made to local housing authorities in England on or after 3 April 2018. See **15.138–15.195**.

7.22 There is no statutory obligation on any local housing authority in England to have regard to the government's national housing or homelessness strategies, either in formulating its own homelessness strategy or when it comes to the performance of its homelessness functions. However, local housing authorities should ordinarily take national government policy into account.

Wales

7.23 When the National Assembly for Wales was formed in 1999, it was given competence to make secondary legislation in the areas of housing and homelessness, but not primary legislation[1]. Those functions were passed to the Welsh Assembly Government in 2006, which became the Welsh Government in 2011[2]. Following a referendum in March 2011, the National Assembly of Wales acquired the right to pass primary legislation in the areas of housing and homelessness[3]. The Assembly exercised this power when it passed the H(W)A 2014, Pt 2, which created a new statutory structure for homelessness in Wales.

[1]   Government of Wales Act 1998, s 22.
[2]   Government of Wales Act 2006.
[3]   Government of Wales Act 2006, s 108 and Sch 7, para 11 amended by National Assembly for Wales (Legislative Competence) (Amendment of Schedule 7 to the Government of Wales Act 2006) Order 2007, SI 2007/2143.

7.24 Upon formation, the National Assembly for Wales made a commitment to set up a Homelessness Commission to advise it on how it should be tackling homelessness in Wales. Following the Commission's report[1], the Welsh Assembly Government published the 2003 *National Homelessness Strategy*[2], based on an overall strategic national housing policy document, *Better Homes for People in Wales – National Housing Strategy for Wales*[3].

[1]   The Homelessness Commission report to the Minister for Finance, Local Government and Communities, August 2001.
[2]   Welsh Assembly Government, March 2003.
[3]   Welsh Assembly Government, July 2001.

7.25 Following a general review of the housing and homelessness situation in Wales in 2005[1], the Welsh Assembly Government published its second *National Homelessness Strategy for Wales (2006–2008)*[2].

[1]   Report to the Welsh Assembly Government, *Tackling Homelessness – Key issues for consideration by Welsh Local Authorities* (Tarki Technology Ltd, June 2005).
[2]   *National Homelessness Strategy for Wales (2006–2008)* (Welsh Assembly Government, November 2005).

7.26 In February 2006, the Public Services Ombudsman for Wales published an account of practices by local housing authorities in Wales: *Housing Allocations and Homelessness: A Special Report by the Local Government Ombudsman for Wales*[1]. The Ombudsman summarised his findings:

> 'A significant number of the 22 Welsh local authorities have failed to introduce housing allocation and homelessness policies and procedures that implement in practice the relevant legislative requirements.'

[1]   Public Services Ombudsman for Wales, 2006.

7.27 The current national strategy – *Ten Year Homelessness Plan for Wales 2009–2019* – was published by the Welsh Assembly Government in July 2009. This was more ambitious and far-reaching than the previous plans and demonstrated considerable autonomy from the UK Government.

7.28 The *Ten Year Homelessness Plan for Wales 2009–2019*[1] aims to reduce homelessness 'to a minimum' by 2019 and to eliminate rough sleeping altogether. It will achieve those goals by preventing homelessness wherever possible, and working across organisational and policy boundaries. The Plan requires prevention services to recognise 'the need for a holistic approach to break cycles of homelessness', so that housing advice services should be providing not only advice on homelessness, and on sustaining existing homes, but also referrals for employment, training, education, help with financial problems and debt, and health advice. The needs of veterans, young homeless people, care-leavers, former prisoners, those fleeing domestic abuse, asylum-seekers and refugees are specifically addressed, as is rural homelessness.

¹ Welsh Assembly Government, July 2009.

7.29 The Plan concluded that the statutory framework in place at the time (HA 1996, Pt 7) 'does not allow everyone to receive the level of service that they need to ensure that their housing needs can be met'. '[K]ey areas of homelessness legislation and the duties placed on Local Authorities, especially around the area of priority need, intentionality, local connection and the discharge of duty into the private rented sector' were to be revised. The aim of the review was to achieve a situation where 'everyone can have access to the help that they need, to secure a home that meets their needs and provides a platform from which to address their aspirations'.

7.30 In May 2012, the Welsh Government published *Homes for Wales: A White Paper for Better Lives and Communities*¹, a consultation on proposals for new legislation and for other action. Attached to the White Paper was a research report: *Impact analysis of existing homelessness legislation in Wales*². The report found strong concerns about how HA 1996, Pt 7 was interpreted and applied differently across Wales, particularly in relation to homelessness prevention, and application of the tests for determining priority need and whether applicants might have become homeless intentionally.

¹ Welsh Government, May 2012.
² January 2012, Cardiff University and others.

7.31 The White Paper proposed a 'long-term vision' of 'ending family homelessness by 2019'¹. It sought to achieve a more flexible housing system, where people can move between social housing, private rented accommodation and home ownership, to suit their needs at different times of their lives. Beyond 2019, the Welsh Government wanted to see a future where 'homelessness does not exist'. It will achieve that by building more homes, bringing empty homes and other empty properties back into use, and improving the quality of existing homes. One chapter deals with prevention of homelessness².

¹ Introduction to the White Paper.
² Chapter 8 of the White Paper.

7.32 The plans for legislation contained in the White Paper were then brought forward in the Housing (Wales) Bill. The Bill was debated by the National Assembly in 2013–14 and received Royal Assent on 17 September 2014. H(W)A 2014, Pt 2, came into effect on 27 April 2015 and applies to all applications for help made to local housing authorities in Wales on or after that date¹.

¹ Housing (Wales) Act 2014 (Commencement No 3 and Transitory, Transitional and Saving Provisions) Order 2015, SI 2015/1272 (W 88), see the CD Rom with this book.

7.33 The Welsh Government consulted on a draft *Code of Guidance for Local Authorities on the Allocation of Accommodation and Homelessness* for consultation on 26 January 2015 and a *Code of Guidance for Local*

Authorities on the Allocation of Accommodation and Homelessness was published on 28 April 2015[1]. A revised *Code of Guidance* for *Local Authorities on the Allocation of Accommodation and Homelessness* (the Welsh Code) was published on 24 March 2016[2]. The Welsh Code noted and endorsed[3] the recommendations from Shelter Cymru on good practice for service users in homelessness services: Equal Ground Standard a guide to the service user standard for Welsh homelessness services[4].

[1] *Code of Guidance for Local Authorities on the Allocation of Accommodation and Homelessness* (Welsh Government, April 2015).
[2] *Code of Guidance for Local Authorities on the Allocation of Accommodation and Homelessness* (Welsh Government, March 2016), see the CD Rom with this book.
[3] Welsh Code, para 5.41.
[4] Shelter Cymru, January 2015.

7.34 The provisions of H(W)A 2014, Pt 2, emphasise the prevention of homelessness and the role of local housing authorities in helping applicants to secure accommodation for themselves. As well as providing accommodation as a safety-net for applicants who are homeless, eligible for help, have a priority need and, in some cases, have not become homeless intentionally[1]. Local housing authorities can make greater use of the private rented sector in order to perform their duties under H(W)A 2014, Pt 2. The Welsh Government's intention is that the test of 'becoming homeless intentionally' should be gradually phased out. H(W)A 2014, Pt 2, seeks to achieve this by:

- requiring local housing authorities in Wales, from 1 July 2015, to opt into using the 'becoming homeless intentionally' test[2]; and
- containing a provision, which will not come into force until 2019, whereby the duty to accommodate applicants with priority need will include applicants who have become homeless intentionally if they have children or young people in their household[3].

[1] H(W)A 2014, s 75(1), see **17.146–17.199**.
[2] H(W)A 2014, s 78, see **17.17–17.23**.
[3] H(W)A 2014, s 75(3), see **17.24–17.167**.

7.35 There have been three evaluations of the implementation of H(W)A 2014, Pt 2, since it was brought into force in April 2015. In 2016, Shelter Cymru published *Reasonable Steps: Experiences of Homelessness Services under Housing (Wales) Act 2014*[1]. The report had interviewed 50 service-users on how they felt they were treated when they approached local housing authorities as homeless. Generally, there was clear evidence of good practice, although the report commented that sometimes the response left people feeling that they had not been offered adequate levels of support. Some people had told to remain in their homes despite having received valid notices to quit. The report noted that use of the private rented sector was very much 'front and centre', there was some pro-active help providing including assisting people making their own searches for accommodation and financial help was often offered. Other interventions, such as advice on finances or benefits, or mediation, were under-used. Overall, some people had been effectively helped and some felt brushed aside. There was not, as yet, a culture of assessing housing needs in the round.

[1] Shelter Cymru & Oak Foundation, 2016.

7.36 In 2017, the Welsh Government published an interim post-implementation evaluation of the homelessness legislation (Pt 2 of the Housing (Wales) Act 2014)[1]. The evaluation drew on the experiences of local housing authorities and various 'stakeholder' organisations, along with interviews with service-users. Local housing authorities and stakeholders were overwhelmingly positive about the introduction of H(W)A 2014, Pt 2, and the new services provided. Their figures suggested that the preventative approach was working. Service-users were broadly positive about the help that they had received but some were concerned about lack of support. The main prevention activity was financial assistance in the form of rent guarantees, payments of deposits or bonds or help to reduce rent arrears. It was found that a larger number of people had been helped to prevent their own homelessness than before the implementation of H(W)A 2014, Pt 2.

[1]   Welsh Government, August 2017.

7.37 The most recent Homelessness Monitor was published by Crisis in 2017: *The Homelessness Monitor: Wales 2017*[1]. In general, its findings were positive. It reported that there was an overwhelming consensus that the new framework in H(W)A 2014, Pt 2, had had an array of positive impacts, including re-orientating the culture of local housing authorities towards a more preventative, person-centred and outcome-focussed approach, and providing a much better service for single homeless people in particular. The numbers of household accommodated under the H(W)A 2014, s 75(1), main housing duty[2], was much lower than under the previous HA 1996, Pt 7, framework. However, there was still a substantial cohort of applicants for homelessness assistance for whom local housing authority offers of assistance had not succeeded in finding a solution to their housing crisis. The largest group in this cohort of applicants were those who had been assessed as not having a priority need and so were not eligible for the (W)A 2014, s 75(1), main housing duty[3], after the H(W)A 2014, s 73(1), relief duty[4] had come to an end. There was also concern at the numbers of applicants who had been found not to have co-operated and so had fallen out of the system[5]. In April 2018, the Welsh Assembly's Equality, Local Government and Communities Committee published a report noting that the numbers of people sleeping rough had increased and calling for the Welsh Government to consider abolishing priority need altogether, failing which it should extend the categories of priority need to include prison leavers and widen the definition of 'vulnerable'.[6]

[1]   Fitzpatrick, Pawson, Bramley, Wilcox, Watts and Woods (Crisis, September 2017).
[2]   See **17.146–17.199**.
[3]   See **17.146–17.199**.
[4]   See **17.73–17.143**.
[5]   5% of applicants owed the H(W)A 2014, s 66(1), prevention duty, and 6% of applicants owed the H(W)A 2014, s 73(1), relief duty had been given a decision that the relevant duty had ended because they had not co-operated: H(W)A 2014, s 79(5), see **17.195–17.197**.
[6]   *Life on the Streets: Tackling and Preventing Rough Sleeping in Wales* (Equality, Local Government and Communities Committee, Welsh Assembly, April 2018).

7.38 The Welsh Government published statistics on applications for homelessness assistance between April 2016 to March 2017 on 27 July 2017[1]. 9,210 applicants had been assessed as threatened with homelessness and 62% of those had been helped to prevent their homelessness. 10,884 applicants had been assessed as homeless and eligible for help, and owed the H(W)A 2014, s 73(1), relief duty[2]. 41% of those had been helped to secure accommodation and had their homelessness successfully relieved. 2,076 applicants had been assessed as homeless, eligible for help, having a priority need and having not become homeless intentionally and owed the H(W)A 2014, s 75(1), main housing duty[3]. Of those, 81% accepted an offer of suitable accommodation. Between 5–6% of applicants had been notified of a decision that they had not co-operated and that the relevant duty had come to an end[4], as Crisis had noted[5].

[1] *Homelessness in Wales, 2016–2017* (Welsh Government, July 2017).
[2] See **17.73–17.143**.
[3] See **17.146–17.199**.
[4] H(W)A 2014, s 79(5), see **17.195–17.197**.
[5] *Homelessness in Wales 2016–2017* (Welsh Government, July 2017). See **7.37** for Crisis.

7.39 Local housing authorities in Wales should take into account both the Ten Year Homelessness Plan[1], and the Welsh Code[2], when formulating their own homelessness strategies. The homelessness strategies should be part of each local housing authority's local planning framework, particularly the Well-being Plan[3]. Each local housing authority's homelessness strategy should reflect a corporate approach, involving other departments of the local housing authority and external organisations[4].

[1] Welsh Code, para 5.7.
[2] H(W)A 2014, s 98(1).
[3] Welsh Code, para 5.4; *Shared Purpose – Shared Delivery* (Welsh Government, December 2012). Local authorities in Wales were required to prepare and publish a local Well-being Plan by the Well-being of Future Generations (Wales) Act 2015, s 39.
[4] Welsh Code, chapter 5.

Northern Ireland

7.40 Since the restoration of the Northern Ireland Executive in May 2007, policy on housing, including homelessness, has been the responsibility of the Department for Social Development. Statutory responsibility for dealing with homeless people lies with the Northern Ireland Housing Executive. Supervision is conducted by the Northern Ireland Audit Office.

7.41 In July 2007 and after a three-year consultation period, the Department for Social Development published *Including the Homeless, a Strategy to promote the social inclusion of homeless people, and those at risk of becoming homeless, in Northern Ireland*[1].

[1] Department for Social Development, July 2007.

7.42 Housing (Amendment) Act (Northern Ireland) 2010, s 1, placed a statutory duty on the Northern Ireland Housing Executive to develop and publish a 5-year homelessness strategy. In 2011, the Housing Executive consulted on a draft *Homelessness Strategy 2011–2016*[1]. It then published its *Homelessness Strategy for Northern Ireland 2012–2017* in April 2012[2]. This contained similarly ambitious targets to those of the Welsh Government[3] or Scottish Executive[4]: to eliminate long term homelessness and rough sleeping across Northern Ireland by 2020.

¹ Northern Ireland Housing Executive, 2012.
² Northern Ireland Housing Executive, 2012.
³ See 7.30–7.31
⁴ See 7.47.

7.43 Between December 2016 and February 2017, the Northern Ireland Housing Executive consulted on a new draft *Homelessness Strategy*. It then adopted published a new strategy: *Ending Homelessness Together: Homelessness Strategy for Northern Ireland 2017–2022* in April 2017[1]. As the title suggests, its vision is of 'ending homelessness together' which it aims to do by helping people prevent their own homelessness, supporting households who are homeless to find suitable accommodation as quickly as possible, and working across departments. Like all the other jurisdictions in the United Kingdom, the emphasis is on early intervention and prevention. The new Strategy contains an evaluation of the 2012–2017 Strategy and finds that, whilst there had been some positive developments, progress in delivering the strategy had not always been rapid. That was particularly true in the case of developing prevention services. More housing advice was recommended and the lack of affordable housing across Northern Ireland highlighted. The new Strategy recommends more work on understanding the causes of rough sleeping and chronic homelessness and use of the Housing First model[2].

¹ Housing Executive.
² 'Housing First' is a new approach towards supporting homeless people with high and complex needs, which aim to help those people find an independent tenancy as quickly as possible and then provide the support needed in order to sustain the tenancy. It has been piloted in Northern Ireland, Liverpool and elsewhere. See *Housing First Feasibility Study for the Liverpool City Region* (Blood, Copeman, Goldup, Place, Bretheron & Dulson, Crisis, 2017).

7.44 In 2016, Crisis published *The Homelessness Monitor: Northern Ireland 2016*[1]. It finds that the levels of homelessness in Northern Ireland has been at historically high levels since 2005 and continue to rise. Acceptances were higher than in the other jurisdictions, which the authors attribute to Northern Ireland having yet, at that time, to move to a prevention model. A large proportion of applicants are discharged into social housing, and this is likely to change when the 2017–2022 Strategy is implemented. There has been controversy over rough sleeping, following six deaths, although the levels are low in comparison with other jurisdictions. The implementation of the 2012–2017 Strategy is described as 'disappointing'. They note a decline in social lettings available, but an increase in the supply of private sector properties available for rent. There was concern at the impact of anticipated welfare reform measures, which had been implemented earlier in the rest of the United Kingdom but delayed in the case of Northern Ireland. The new Strategy, with a Housing First and prevention approach, was anticipated.

¹ *The Homelessness Monitor* (Fitzpatrick, Pawson, Bramley, Wilcox & Watts, Crisis, 2016).

Scotland

7.45 At national policy level, homelessness in Scotland is the responsibility of the Scottish Executive. Soon after devolution in 1999, the Executive established a Homelessness Task Force charged with mapping out a programme to address the issue of homelessness in Scotland.

7.46 The initial report of the Task Force (in April 2000) led in due course to the amendment of the statutory homelessness scheme in Scotland, until then contained in the Housing (Scotland) Act 1987, by the Housing (Scotland) Act 2001.

7.47 The final report of the Task Force in 2002, Homelessness: an action plan for prevention and effective response[1], set out a 12-year action programme to eliminate and thereafter prevent homelessness in Scotland. The subsequent Homelessness etc (Scotland) Act 2003 contained radical statutory measures designed to implement the Task Force recommendations. It included an ambitious target to abolish the priority need test by 2012, so that everyone who had not become homeless intentionally would be entitled to a permanent home. This ambition was realised in the Homelessness (Abolition of Priority Need) Test) (Scotland) Order 2012[2], which came into effect on 31 December 2012. From that date, the priority need test has been abolished in Scotland.

[1]   Homelessness Task Force, February 2002.
[2]   SI 2012/330 (Scottish SI).

7.48 The current Code of Guidance was published in May 2005: *Code of Guidance on homelessness*[1]. It has since been updated by three additions: *Prevention of Homelessness Guidance* (2009)[2], *Guidance on the Best Interests of Children* (2011)[3], and *Guidance on the Housing Support Duty to Homeless Households* (2013)[4].

[1]   Scottish Executive, 2005.
[2]   Scottish Executive, June 2009.
[3]   Scottish Executive, 2011.
[4]   Scottish Executive, June 2013.

7.49 As the titles of the first and third additions to the Code of Guidance suggest, the Scottish Executive has adopted the prevention and housing options agenda. Five regional Housing Options Hubs, designed to co-ordinate and develop policy and practice were established in 2010. The Scottish Housing Regulator published a fairly critical report on housing options practice in 2014, recommending greater clarity and guidance and also noting that the diversion of people from a homelessness assessment to housing options approach was not always appropriate[1].

[1]   Housing Options in Scotland: A Thematic Inquiry (Scottish Housing Regulator, 2014).

7.50 It would have been expected that the abolition of the priority need test in 2012 would lead to a corresponding increase in the numbers of applications for homelessness assistance, and in the numbers of applications accepted. However, the statistics show a significant drop in applications for homelessness assistance since 2010[1]. The drop is attributed, by both the Scottish Executive and by commentators, to the use of prevention and housing options. However, the authors of the *Homelessness Monitor: Scotland 2015*[2] argue that combining the numbers of applications for homelessness assistance with the numbers of people approaching housing options gives a truer picture of the level of homelessness and that the level has remained fairly steady since 2010[3].

1   From nearly 60,000 in 2010, to 34,100 applications between 1 April 2016 and 31 March 2017 (Homelessness in Scotland 2016–2017, Scottish Executive, 2017).
2   Fitzpatrick, Dawson, Bramley, Wilcox & Watts, Crisis, 2015.
3   See **7.53**.

7.51 The statutory responsibility for providing homelessness services in Scotland falls upon the Scottish local authorities. The Scottish Executive monitors Scottish local authorities by the publication of homelessness statistics based on returns from local authorities.

7.52 Scottish local authorities are required by Housing (Scotland) Act 2001 to publish local housing strategies[1] and homelessness strategies[2]. The homelessness strategy must be based upon an assessment of homelessness in a local authority's area. The Scottish Executive has published guidance to local authorities on formulating their housing strategy[3]. That guidance includes advice on the preparation of homelessness strategies[4]. The Executive's Minister[5] has power to reject local homelessness strategies submitted by those local authorities[6].

1   Housing (Scotland) Act 2001, s 89.
2   Housing (Scotland) Act 2001, s 1.
3   *Local Housing Strategy Guidance* (Scottish Executive, August 2014).
4   *Local Housing Strategy Guidance* (Scottish Executive, August 2014), paras 8.1–8.8.
5   The Cabinet Secretary for Social Justice, Communities and Pensioners' Rights.
6   Housing (Scotland) Act 2001, s 1(6).

7.53 The authors of *The Homelessness Monitor: Scotland 2015*[1], noted the decrease in the number of applications for homelessness assistance. They commented that this is the result of the introduction of housing options model of homelessness prevention. However, when taking the number of approaches to housing options into account, they conclude that the overall annual level of homelessness presentations in recent years has remained fairly steady, at around 54,000. Scottish local authorities make less use of the private rented sector than local housing authorities elsewhere in the UK and the authors note that "right to buy" was due to be abolished and that should prevent further losses to the social rented sector[2]. They also noted, as they had done in other jurisdictions, the impact on expected levels of homelessness of cuts to welfare benefits.

1   Fitzpatrick, Pawson, Bramley and Wilcox, Crisis, December 2015.
2   'Right to buy' was abolished by the Scottish Executive from 31 July 2016: Housing (Scotland) Act 2014, s 1.

REGIONAL STRATEGIES

7.54 In England, steps were taken towards the development of regional homelessness strategies. In 2003, Regional Housing Boards were established to develop strategic housing policy for the regions. That role passed to the eight Regional Assemblies in England, plus the Mayor of London, in September 2006. Except for the Greater London Assembly, Regional Assemblies in England were abolished between 2008 and March 2010, and replaced by

Local Authorities' Leaders Boards: voluntary associations of council leaders. Those Boards were abolished by the UK Coalition Government in 2010.

7.55 All of the Regional Assemblies had Regional Housing Strategies. The West Midlands Regional Assembly, the East of England Regional Assembly, the North West Regional Assembly and the East Midlands Regional Assembly also published Regional Homelessness Strategies.

London

7.56 In London, responsibility for housing and homelessness strategy was given to the Mayor in 2006. The London Boroughs retain the statutory responsibility for the delivery of homelessness services under HA 1996, Pt 7, and must also publish their own homelessness strategies and reviews.

7.57 The then Mayor of London, Ken Livingstone, published a draft housing strategy for London in 2007. His successor as Mayor of London, Boris Johnson, published the first statutory housing strategy for London in February 2010[1]. In the foreword, the Mayor wrote:

'Tackling homelessness and reducing overcrowding are two of my key priorities, with targets to end rough sleeping by 2012 and to halve severe overcrowding among social tenants by 2016.'

[1]   Mayor of London, February 2010.

7.58 From April 2012, the Mayor of London, with the Greater London Assembly, has been responsible for strategic housing policy in London[1]. A new housing strategy was published in June 2014: *Homes for London: the London housing strategy*[2]. The strategy emphasised the need for an increase in the supply of housing to meet London's 'affordability crisis' and 'rising housing costs'.

[1]   Greater London Authority Act 1999, s 333A as amended by Localism Act 2011, s 188.
[2]   Mayor of London, June 2014.

7.59 The priority to end rough sleeping led to the launch of the London Delivery Board in 2009, tasked with tackling rough sleeping. The Board in turn piloted the No Second Night Out initiative in 2011 across ten London boroughs, expanding it to cover all of the London boroughs in June 2012. No Second Night Out aimed to identify people sleeping rough, and provide them with advice through hub facilities which are open 24 hours a day. The hubs make an assessment of each individual and then provide support, such as helping the individual find accommodation or helping him or her to return to a home area (other parts of the UK or abroad). The initiative has also been adopted by local housing authorities outside of London[1].

[1]   See 7.16.

7.60 The 2016–2020 Mayor of London, Sadiq Khan, established a Rough Sleeping Taskforce in 2016. The Taskforce adopted a No Nights Sleeping Rough plan. Various London local housing authorities and voluntary groups are represented and the aim is to identify interventions that will tackle rough sleeping in London and either implement those interventions, or lobby for their implementation. The focus is to prevent people from sleeping rough, and prevent those who are sleeping rough from becoming entrenched rough sleepers[1].

[1] See No Nights Sleeping Rough Taskforce at https://www.london.gov.uk/what-we-do/housing-and-land/homelessness/no-nights-sleeping-rough-taskforce

7.61 The Mayor of London 2016–2020, Sadiq Khan, published a draft Housing Strategy for consultation in September 2017[1]. 'Helping tackle homelessness' is one of the five priorities. He aims to achieve this by working with London Borough Councils, government and charities to support a greater focus on the prevention of homelessness, pressing government for adequate funding for local housing authorities to deliver the new duties required by HRA 2017, investing in more affordable homes, lobbying government to overturn cuts to welfare benefits (particularly those affecting youth people) and working to eliminate rough sleeping through the No Nights Sleeping Rough taskforce.

[1] *London Housing Strategy* (Mayor of London, 2017).

LOCAL HOMELESSNESS STRATEGIES AND REVIEWS

Overview

7.62 The Homelessness Act 2002[1] (HA 2002) introduced a statutory duty on local housing authorities in England and in Wales to formulate and publish local homelessness strategies. The relevant provisions came into force on 31 July 2002 for local housing authorities in England and 30 September 2002 for local housing authorities in Wales[2].

[1] HA 2002, ss 1–4, see Appendix 2.
[2] For local housing authorities in Wales, the statutory duty is now at H(W)A 2014, ss 50–52.

7.63 Local housing authorities were required to publish their first local homelessness strategy within a year, ie by 2003 . They are required to keep the local strategies under review, and modify them if necessary. At the very least, they must publish new strategies every five years[1]. So most local housing authorities in England, and all local housing authorities in Wales, were required to publish new homelessness strategies in 2008 and 2013. Local housing authorities in England are required to publish new homelessness strategies by July 2018.

[1] HA 2002, s 1(3) and (4).

7.64 On 27 April 2015, the statutory obligation on local housing authorities in Wales to formulate, adopt and publish a homelessness strategy moved to H(W)A 2014, ss 50–52. New homelessness strategies are to be adopted in 2018 and every four years after that[1].

[1] H(W)A 2014, s 50(2).

7.65 The provisions of H(W)A 2014, ss 50–52, for local housing authorities in Wales, are very similar to those of HA 2002, ss 1–4 for local housing authorities in England. We note in this chapter where there are differences between the law in England and the law in Wales. At the end of each section – on homelessness reviews and on homelessness strategies – we provide a paragraph summarising any different legal obligations for local housing authorities in Wales[1].

[1] See **7.126** for homelessness reviews for local housing authorities in Wales. See **7.78** for homelessness strategies for local housing authorities in Wales.

7.66 The purpose of preparing a local strategy is to enable local housing authorities to have an accurate picture of the levels of homelessness in their district, and to set out the steps to be taken in order to tackle and prevent homelessness.

7.67 Of course, to devise an effective local strategy, the local housing authority must have access to the raw data on the extent of homelessness in its area and on the current prevention programmes and local initiatives to tackle it. HA 2002, and H(W)A 2014, Pt 2, therefore, require every local housing authority to conduct a 'review' of such matters, in relation to its area, so that the design and content of the local strategy may be undertaken on the best possible information[1].

[1] HA 2002, s 1(1)(a); H(W)A 2014, s 50(1)(a).

7.68 In short, the review is meant to paint the picture on homelessness locally and the strategy is intended to set out how the problem is to be addressed.

7.69 The fundamental objectives underlying the requirement both for a review and for a strategy are:

(1)   identifying action that can be taken to prevent homelessness;
(2)   providing suitable services and accommodation for people who are, or may become homeless; and
(3)   supporting people who are homeless or potentially homeless and those who were formerly homeless and need support, to prevent them becoming homeless again[1].

[1] HA 2002, ss 2(2) and 3(1); H(W)A 2014, ss 51(1)(b) and 52(1).

7.70 HA 2002, H(W)A 2014, Pt 2 and the Codes of Guidance emphasise a multi-agency approach[1]. They require cooperation between local housing authorities and adult care and children's services, and encourage consultation and joint working with other public authorities, voluntary organisations and individuals in the undertaking of the review and in the formulation of the strategy[2].

[1] *Homelessness Code of Guidance for Local Authorities* (MHCLG, 2018) (the English Code), see Appendix 2; *Code of Guidance for Local Authorities on the Allocation of Accommodation and Homelessness* (Welsh Government, March 2016) (the Welsh Code) on the CD-Rom with this book, and Prevention of homelessness and provision of accommodation for 16 and 17 year old young people who may be homeless and/or require accommodation (MHCLG and Department for Education, April 2018), Chapter 6, on the CD-rom with this book.
[2] HA 2002, s 1(2) and s 3(2)–(4); H(W)A 2014, ss 50(4), and 52(3); English Code, chapter 2; Welsh Code, chapter 5. For example of guidance on joint working, see *Prevention of*

Homelessness and Provision of Accommodation for 16 and 17 year old young people who may be homeless and/or require accommodation (MHCLG and Department for Education, April 2018) and *Provision of Accommodation for 16 and 17 year old young people who may be homeless* (Welsh Assembly Government, September 2010).

7.71 The strategies, once produced, should not be filed away to gather dust. Both local housing authorities and the relevant adult care and children's services authorities are required to take the contents of the local homelessness strategy into account when exercising other statutory functions, such as decisions on homelessness and allocation and the performance of duties owed to young people, families with children and other vulnerable people[1]. As this chapter indicates, the requirement to have regard to them in day-to-day work will enable strategies to be used as legal tools, where appropriate[2].

[1]   HA 2002, s 1(5) and (6); H(W)A 2014, s 50(4).
[2]   See **7.183–7.185**.

7.72 There is no statutory timetable for the undertaking, production or publication of the initial homelessness review (or any subsequent reviews). In practice, many local housing authorities published both their initial review and initial strategy documents together or, indeed, incorporated the homelessness review into the first local homelessness strategy. Since the strategy must be based on the findings in the review, it follows that a review should always be carried out first.

7.73 Because the statutory requirement to prepare a homelessness strategy was entirely novel when brought into force in 2003, considerable resources were deployed to assist local housing authorities with the task of formulating their first strategies. The UK Government provided additional financial resources to assist local housing authorities in England in drawing up their local reviews and strategies. Substantial written guidance was provided to local housing authorities. This included: *Homelessness Strategies: A Good Practice Handbook*[1] and *Preventing tomorrow's rough sleepers: A Good Practice Handbook*[2], and they were in turn followed by publication of the Homelessness Codes of Guidance providing more assistance.

[1]   Department for Transport, Local Government and the Regions, 13 March 2002.
[2]   ODPM, June 2001. See also English Code, para 1.4 and Annex 1.

7.74 At local level, the individual reviews and strategies are expected to take into account other local authority and national government plans and strategies relevant to addressing the causes of homelessness[1]. The strategies adopted by local housing authorities in England must also take into account the local housing authority's own allocation scheme and tenancy strategy[2]. London borough councils must take into account the current London housing strategy[3]. Joint working with adult care and children's services departments or authorities (in the case of non-unitary authorities) is a statutory requirement[4], and local housing authorities are encouraged to involve other public authorities, such as health authorities, the police, private registered providers or registered social landlords and private landlords, voluntary organisations and other organisations and individuals[5].

[1]   English Code, paras 2.67–2.69; Welsh Code, para 5.7 which specifically mentions the Welsh Government's Ten Year Homelessness Plan.

2   HA 2002 s 3(7A)(a) and (b).

3   HA 2002 s 3(7A)(c). For the current London housing strategy see **7.60–7.61**.

4   HA 2002, s 1(2) and (6); H(W)A 2014, ss 50(4) and 52(6).

5   English Code, paras 2.4–2.9; for local housing authorities in Wales, joint working is provided for at H(W)A 2014, s 52(3) and (6) and Welsh Code, chapter 6.

7.75 By the end of 2003, every local housing authority in England and Wales had complied with the duty to conduct a review and had adopted and published a strategy, and most local housing authorities had repeated that exercise in 2008. Copies of those strategies are relatively easy to obtain. Local housing authorities generally post their reviews and strategies on their websites[1]. Hard copies of local reviews and strategies are available from individual local housing authorities on request[2].

1   Local housing authorities in Wales are required to publish the homelessness review and strategy on their website, if they have one: H(W)A 2014, ss 51(2)(a) and 52(9)(a).

2   HA 2002, ss 2(3) and 3(9); H(W)A 2014, ss 51(2)(c) and 52(9)(c); and see **7.123–7.125** and **7.167–7.168**.

7.76 A review of the content or methodology in the many hundreds of local housing authorities' published reviews and strategies is beyond the scope of this book. However, between 2003 and 2008, there were several useful reviews of initial local homelessness strategies.

7.77 In January 2004, Shelter published *The Act in Action, an assessment of homelessness reviews and strategies*[1]. Shelter's conclusion was that:

' . . . compiling reviews and strategies appears to have produced positive outcomes beyond simply delivering an assessment of homelessness levels and patterns. In a broader sense, it has enabled authorities to identify gaps in their knowledge (even where these gaps are yet to be tackled), build stronger relationships with other departments and agencies and develop a multi-agency approach not just to homelessness, but also to wider issues.'

1   *The Act in Action, an assessment of homelessness reviews and strategies* (Shelter, January 2004).

7.78 A more detailed national picture was given in *Homelessness strategies – a survey of local authorities* published by the LGA[1]. It contained the troubling finding that only 52% of local housing authorities thought that the exercise of preparing a strategy would help to any extent in determining likely future levels of homelessness in their areas.

1   Homelessness Strategies: A Survey of Local Authorities, Research Briefing 6.04 (Local Government Association, October 2004).

7.79 During the first half of 2004, Housing Quality Network Services carried out an evaluation of homelessness strategies on behalf of the UK Government (and consulted a number of local housing authorities in England). A summary of that evaluation was published (*Local Authorities' Homelessness Strategies: Evaluation and Good Practice*)[1] and local housing authorities were encouraged to refer to it in carrying out future local homelessness reviews and drawing up further local strategies. The research considered both homelessness reviews and homelessness strategies.

[1] *Local Authorities' Homelessness Strategies: Evaluation and Good Practice* (ODPM, 2004).

7.80 The ODPM issued a policy briefing *Homelessness Strategies: Moving Forward* based on this evaluation[1]. The document recommended that local housing authorities in England bring forward plans for comprehensively reviewing their homelessness strategies. It suggested that they should be:

- ensuring greater involvement from the voluntary sector;
- engaging in more cooperation with other authorities, regions and agencies;
- working with Supporting People authorities; and
- taking a more multi-agency approach.

[1] ODPM, November 2004.

7.81 Much of the material in the Policy Briefing was taken forward into the content of the 2006 edition of the *Homelessness Code of Guidance for Local Authorities*[1].

[1] CLG July 2006.

7.82 Following publication of the 2006 Code, the CLG published *Preventing Homelessness: A Strategy Health Check*[1], which will have been used by local housing authorities in preparing their new strategies in 2008. There was no attempt to repeat the earlier exercise of calling in, for review and evaluation, the individual strategies of local housing authorities in England. Indeed, there have been no further publications from government on the subject of homelessness strategies since 2006.

[1] CLG, September 2006.

7.83 The remainder of this chapter will outline the detailed legal duties imposed on local housing authorities in relation to local homelessness reviews and strategies, the powers given to them, and the guidance that has been provided. All statutory references in this chapter, unlike the rest of this book, are to the Homelessness Act 2002 (HA 2002), and not to the Housing Act 1996 unless specifically stated. For local housing authorities in Wales, from 27 April 2015, the relevant legislation is H(W)A 2014, ss 50–52.

7.84 To avoid confusion, it is necessary to emphasise that a local 'Homelessness Strategy' is not the same thing as a local 'Housing Strategy' nor the local 'tenancy strategy'. The housing strategy was, until 26 May 2015, required by the terms of any direction made to local housing authorities in England and in Wales under the Local Government Act 2003[1]. Since 26 May 2015, the obligation to have a housing strategy only applies to local housing authorities in Wales[2]. Local housing authorities in England are required to prepare and publish a tenancy strategy by the Localism Act 2011[3]. Both strategies are beyond the scope of this book[4].

[1] Local Government Act 2003, s 87.
[2] Local Government Act 2003, s 87, amended by Deregulation Act 2015, s 29.
[3] Localism Act 2011, s 150.

⁴   English Code, para 2.8.

A power or a duty to have local reviews and strategies?

7.85 Strictly speaking, HA 2002, only gives a power to local housing authorities in England to carry out homelessness reviews for their districts and to formulate and publish homelessness strategies based on the results of those reviews¹.

¹   HA 2002, s 1(1).

7.86 However, HA 2002 also set out mandatory time-scales for the publication of the first local homelessness strategies and of further strategies thereafter. It thereby converted the power to formulate and publish the local homelessness strategy into a duty¹.

¹   HA 2002, s 1(3) and (4).

7.87 The intention is that strategies will follow the local homelessness review. Homelessness strategies are defined as being 'based on the results of that review'¹. It follows that local housing authorities in England are under a duty both to conduct reviews and to formulate and publish strategies.

¹   HA 2002, s 1(1)(b).

7.88 For local housing authorities in Wales, the position is much clearer. H(W)A 2014, s 50(1) imposes a duty on local housing authorities to carry out reviews and formulate and adopt homelessness strategies. They are also under a duty to publish the results¹.

¹   H(W)A 2014, s 51(2).

A power or a duty to have regard to the local strategy?

7.89 Once the strategy has been published, the local housing authority is under a duty to take its content into account when exercising its homelessness functions or, indeed, any of its other statutory functions¹. The strategy should therefore inform, for example, a local housing authority's adoption of a housing allocation scheme as well as the decisions on any individual homelessness application.

¹   HA 2002, s 1(5); H(W)A 2014, s 50(4); further discussed at **7.183–7.185**.

7.90 In *R (Ho-Sang) v Lewisham London Borough Council*¹, an applicant for homelessness assistance, who had not been provided with interim accommodation to which she was entitled, brought a test case challenging the local housing authority's routine and systematic practice of turning away applicants without providing interim accommodation. The judicial review claim cited the local housing authority's homelessness review, which had identified the provision of interim accommodation as being a major problem for the local housing authority, and challenged the homelessness strategy, which only made provision for 50 additional units of temporary accommodation. The local housing authority settled the judicial review claim by conceding that the strategy was inadequate and agreeing to take measures to acquire additional units of interim accommodation (in addition to accepting that it owed the claimant a duty to provide interim accommodation which it would perform).

1   *R (Ho-Sang) v Lewisham London Borough Council* (2004) CO/5652/03, (2004) July *Legal Action*, p 19, Admin Ct.

Duty on adult care and children's services to cooperate

7.91 In the case of non-unitary authorities in England, the adult care and children's services authorities are under a duty to give their local housing authority (or authorities) such assistance as the local housing authority (or authorities) may reasonably require with both the carrying out of the local review and the formulation of the homelessness strategy[1]. Examples of the types of assistance that might be required are given in the Homelessness Codes of Guidance for both England and Wales. They range through:

- providing information to the local housing authority, as part of the review process; to
- providing financial assistance so as to prevent homelessness; and
- providing support with homeless persons' associated needs[2].

1   HA 2002, s 1(2). There is no equivalent obligation in H(W)A 2014, Pt 2 because Welsh local housing authorities are all part of unitary authorities: counties or county boroughs. However, the Welsh Code emphasises a corporate approach to preventing and tackling homelessness, including from children's services: Welsh Code, para 5.10. There is also a general obligation on county or county borough councils to promote cooperation between officers exercising social services functions and officers exercising local housing authority functions with a view to achieving the prevention of homelessness, and the provision of suitable accommodation and support: H(W)A 2014, s 98.
2   English Code, paras 2.21–2.22; Welsh Code, paras 5.10–5.14.

7.92 Once the exercise has been completed and a local homelessness strategy has been drawn up, the adult care and children's services authorities are under a duty to take the homelessness strategy into account when carrying out their functions[1]. This duty may particularly assist young people, or disabled people, who are homeless and also have needs for support or assistance from adult care or children's services authorities or departments. The English Code advises 'since a large proportion of people who are homeless or at risk of homelessness will be vulnerable adults or have children in their care, it will always be necessary to seek assistance from the social services authority to formulate an effective homelessness strategy'[2].

1   HA 2002, s 1(6); H(W)A 2014, s 50(4).
2   English Code, paras 2.212–2.22.

7.93 In the case of unitary authorities, the same obligations apply to the adult care and children's services departments to provide assistance at the strategy design stage and to take account of the strategy in the performance of their own functions[1].

1   HA 2002, s 1(6); H(W)A 2014, s 50(4); English Code, para 2.21; Welsh Code, paras 5.10–5.14.

Duty on private registered providers and registered social landlords to cooperate

7.94 Private registered providers (England) and registered social landlords (Wales) are under a duty to cooperate with local housing authorities to assist them in performing their functions under Housing Act 1996, Pts 6 and 7[1], and H(W)A 2014, Pt 2, if requested, and so far as is reasonable[2]. They would normally expect to be consulted by local housing authorities before homelessness strategies are adopted or modified[3].

[1] As amended by HRA 2017 for applications for homelessness assistance made to local housing authorities in England on or after 3 April 2018.
[2] HA 1996, ss 170 and 213(1); H(W)A 2014, s 98(2)–(5).
[3] HA 2002, s 3(8); H(W)A 2014, s 52(8).

7.95 Prior to 31 March 2015, the Homes and Communities Agency's Regulatory Framework, which contains the requirements that private registered providers of social housing must meet, included advice that private registered providers should cooperate with local housing authorities. The current Regulatory framework encourages private registered providers to contribute to the environmental, social and economic well-being of the area[1].

[1] *Regulating the Standards* (Homes and Communities Agency, 2017).

7.96 In Wales, the previous *Regulatory Framework for Housing Associations Registered in Wales*[1] required registered social landlords to support local housing authorities in the delivery of their strategic housing roles. That advice has not been replicated in the current Framework[2]. The Welsh Code advises that local housing authorities, housing associations and voluntary sector organisations should be working together to address housing need[3].

[1] Welsh Government, December 2011.
[2] *The Regulatory Framework for Housing Associations registered in Wales* (Welsh Government, May 2017).
[3] Welsh Code, paras 6.8–6.12.

LOCAL HOMELESSNESS REVIEWS

7.97 Since the local homelessness strategy must be based on the results of the homelessness review, the review must logically be carried out and concluded first, although generally many local housing authorities publish both documents simultaneously, or publish their review and strategy within the same document[1].

[1] HA 2002, s 2; H(W)A 2014, s 51.

7.98 The review is an audit of the local scene in relation to homelessness. It is defined to mean a review of:

(1)   the levels and likely future levels of homelessness in the local housing authority's district[1];

(2)   the activities which are carried out in the district for the purpose of preventing homelessness, securing accommodation for people who are or may be homeless, or providing support for those people or for formerly homeless people who need support to prevent them becoming homeless again[2]; and

(3)   the resources available to the local housing authority, the adult care and children's services authorities, other public authorities, voluntary organisations and other persons in the district for carrying out these activities[3].

[1]   HA 2002, s 2(1)(a); H(W)A 2014, s 51(1)(a).
[2]   HA 2002, s 2(1)(b) and (2); H(W)A 2014, s 51(1)(b).
[3]   HA 2002, s 2(1)(c); H(W)A 2014, s 51(1)(c).

7.99 Each of those aspects will be considered in turn.

What is meant by 'homelessness' for the purposes of conducting the review?

7.100 To be able to assess current and future levels of homelessness with any accuracy, the review must apply the relevant meaning of 'homelessness'. But there can be different interpretations of that concept. Does it mean the likely numbers of applicants to the local housing authority for HA 1996, Pt 7[1], or H(W)A 2014, Pt 2, assistance? Or does it have a more practical interpretation, referring to the likely number of people who will be homeless, whether they seek the help of the local housing authority or not? Does it refer simply to literal street homelessness or does it also include those living in temporary or insecure accommodation?

[1]   As amended by HRA 2017 for applications for homelessness assistance made to local housing authorities in England on or after 3 April 2018.

7.101 The English Code advises local housing authorities that 'the review must take account of all forms of homelessness within the meaning of the [HA] 1996, and should therefore consider a wide population of households who are homeless or at risk of becoming homeless. This will include people sleeping rough and those whose accommodation and circumstances make them more likely than others to become homeless including sleeping rough'[1]. Local housing authorities in England should not, therefore, consider only those applicants towards whom the HA 1996, s 193(2), main housing duty[2] has been accepted in the past, or would be accepted in the future. They should ensure that homeless people who do not have a priority need, or who are or have become or may become homeless intentionally, also fall within the scope of the review. The Codes specifically refer to 'people sleeping rough', as well as 'those who might be more difficult to identify'[3]. The review should therefore consider those who are likely, in future, to have no accommodation that they are entitled to occupy and also those who do have (or will have) accommodation that is not reasonable for them to continue to occupy.

[1]   English Code, para 2.17.
[2]   HA 1996, s 193(2). See **16.94–16.199**.

3   For a discussion on the definition of homelessness contained in HA 1996, ss 175–177, or H(W)A 2014, ss 55–58, see Chapter 10. See further English Code, para 2.17; Welsh Code, paras 5.22–5.24.

7.102 The Welsh Code contains a different definition of homelessness drawn up by the Welsh Government: 'where a person lacks accommodation or where their tenure is not secure' – and gives examples of the types of people, and the types of accommodation, that would fall within that definition[1].

1   Welsh Code, para 5.22.

7.103 Both Codes therefore draw attention to the needs of those in insecure accommodation as well as those who are literally roofless. The statutory emphasis (on preventing homelessness, identifying those who might become homeless in the future, and providing support to those who are potentially homeless) should mean that local housing authorities in England and Wales are considering various different groups of people when undertaking their reviews.

Current and future levels of homelessness in the local housing authority's district

7.104 In order to ascertain what levels of homelessness there are currently are, and to predict what levels there may be in the future, the review will need to analyse data on local homelessness in the recent past, on current homelessness, and on likely future homelessness[1].

1   Homelessness Act 2002, s 2(1)(a); English Code, para 2.18; H(W)A 2014, s 51(1)(a); Welsh Code, paras 5.25–5.32.

7.105 The local housing authority will have its own records and statistics of the number of homelessness applications it has received in the past, and the outcome of those applications. It will also regularly compile returns for the UK and Welsh governments' statistics[1]. However, the review should not be confined to those records of past homelessness alone.

1   In England: *Statutory Homelessness and Homelessness Prevention and Relief* (Department for Communities and Local Government). In Wales, *Homelessness Statistics* (Welsh Government).

7.106 The local housing authority should take into account any information it possesses (or can find with reasonable diligence) on the local homelessness problem. That will include counts or estimates of the numbers of people sleeping rough and estimates of the numbers of people who are staying with family or friends on a temporary or insecure basis. The local housing authority can also consider its own records of the numbers (and outcomes) of possession proceedings it has brought, and the records held by the local court and by local private registered providers or registered social landlords. Local advice agencies may hold records and statistics on the numbers of clients who seek homelessness or housing advice. Hospitals, prisons, the armed forces, and the National Offender Management Service[1] should all have records of people discharged from their various services who had nowhere to live. Children's services departments or authorities should be asked for their statistics on homeless families with children, young people leaving care and children in need requiring accommodation. Local hostels and refuges should also be asked for figures[2]. This should provide, in its totality, a fairly accurate picture of both past and current homelessness.

[1] Formerly the Probation Service.
[2] English Code, paras 2.19–2.20; Welsh Code, paras 5.25–5.29.

7.107 In order to predict future levels of homelessness in the district, the local housing authority will need to identify those groups of people most likely to be at risk of homelessness, the reasons why they might become homeless and the extent to which the supply of affordable accommodation locally is likely to increase or decrease.

7.108 The Welsh Code suggest that young people estranged from their families or leaving care, vulnerable people leaving the armed forces or prison, people exposed to domestic or other violence or abuse, vulnerable people with mental health problems, learning disabilities, age-related problems or ill health, people with drug and alcohol problems, people with debt problems, those suffering harassment or abuse from outside the home, and former asylum-seekers given permission to stay in the UK, are likely to be amongst those with a higher risk of homelessness[1]. It also recommends drawing up a profile of those who have experienced homelessness[2].

[1] Welsh Code, paras 5.33–5.37. There is particular emphasis in the Welsh Code on identifying the extent of rough sleeping, so as to try to eliminate it: Welsh Code, para 5.35.
[2] Welsh Code, paras 5.30–5.32.

7.109 The English Code does not contain similar recommendations, except to the effect that a large proportion of people who are homeless will be vulnerable adults or have children in their care[1]. Instead it refers to 'a wide population of households' who are homeless or at risk of becoming homeless, including those sleeping rough[2]. It recommends considering the profile of households who have experienced homelessness in the district but does not contain any guidance as to the contents of that profile[3].

[1] English Code, para 2.21.
[2] English Code, para 2.17.
[3] English Code, para 2.18(d).

7.110 The identification of the current and future levels of homelessness in the district is a substantial task, involving social and economic mapping and projections. Bare statistics of current or recent applications for homelessness assistance, whilst of importance in contributing to the review, will not suffice on their own[1].

[1] Welsh Code, paras 5.25–5.29.

7.111 The UK Government-commissioned evaluation of homelessness strategies in 2003 found that many local housing authorities in England had difficulties in assessing future levels of homelessness. Local housing authorities that tackled the issue well had used: population trends; indicators of needs, demands and aspirations from Housing Needs Surveys; trends in homelessness data; and plans for prevention through, for example, advice to those leaving prison, hospital or care[1]. In recent years, the homelessness statistics published by both the UK Government and the Welsh Government have recorded a significant increase in the numbers of people being made homeless from private rented accommodation[2]. It follows that homelessness reviews should consider preventative efforts to keep private tenants in their own homes, such as funding court-based duty advice schemes or making assistance available to tenants in financial difficulties.

[1]   *Local Authorities' Homelessness Strategies: Evaluation and Good Practice* (ODPM Homelessness Research Summary, Number 1, 2004). See also **7.79**.

[2]   See **7.20** (England) and **7.38** (Wales).

Current activities being carried out

7.112 This is the second matter that HA 2002 and H(W)A 2014, Pt 2, require to be considered within the local homelessness review[1]. The required review of activities currently being carried out should not be confined to the activity of the local housing authority's own homeless persons' department or housing options officer(s).

[1]   HA 2002, s 2(1)(b); H(W)A 2014, s 51(1)(b); English Code paras 2.14–2.22, 2.25–2.62; Welsh Code, paras 5.17–5.40.

7.113 The current 'activities' to be reviewed are defined as activities for the purposes of:

(1)   preventing homelessness in the local housing authority's district;

(2)   securing that accommodation is or will be available for people who are currently homeless or may become homeless; and

(3)   providing support for those people and for people who were formerly homeless and need support to prevent them becoming homeless again[1].

[1]   HA 2002, s 2(2); H(W)A 2014, s 51(1)(b). For local housing authorities in Wales, the support provided for people who may become homeless in the future is also relevant: H(W)A 2014, s 51(1)(b)(iii).

7.114 The Codes recommend that the activities, and resources, of public, private and voluntary sectors should be considered[1].

[1]   English Code, paras 2.19, 2.27–2.29; Welsh Code, para 5.32.

7.115 Activities for the prevention of homelessness, for securing accommodation and for providing support to homeless people (or those likely to become homeless) go much further than simply providing a roof over someone's head. They can include the 'activities' of giving advice on the availability of benefits and employment, on debt management and on other financial issues. Local housing authorities and adult care and children's services authorities have statutory powers to provide assistance in the form of rent deposits, rent guarantees and disabled facilities grants for adaptations. The exercise of those powers is a relevant activity. Local charities, or even local businesses, may provide limited financial assistance to the homeless and they too would be relevant 'activities'. The local housing authority should also consider what other 'activities' are being carried out to provide support for the homeless and for those potentially homeless, including support with their other needs, such as health care, education, food (through the provision or funding of food banks) etc.

Resources currently available for such activities

7.116 This is the third matter that HA 2002 and H(W)A 2014, Pt 2, require to be considered within the local homelessness review[1]. The local housing authority should obviously consider its own resources, and also those available to the adult care and children's services authorities, other public authorities, voluntary organisations and any other persons. 'Resources' in this context means far more than just the financial resources available to tackle local homelessness. Both current Codes of Guidance place even more emphasis than earlier editions did on the importance that each government attaches to a move away from the historic local housing authority role as the potential provider of the resources (and, most particularly, homes) for relieving homelessness and into a more modern role of encouraging and facilitating provision by others. The focus has very much shifted from inviting attention to the resources that might be supplied by the local housing authority itself to those which may be marshalled from others in relation to homelessness. As elsewhere in the current Codes, the primary emphasis is on those resources which may be directed to homelessness prevention in the first instance[2]. For local housing authorities in England, the provisions first of the Localism Act 2011, and now of the HRA 2017, make it even clearer that the government views the local housing authority as housing enabler rather than as housing provider. The provisions of H(W)A 2014, Pt 2, for local housing authorities in Wales, take a similar approach, emphasising prevention and use of the private rented sector.

[1]   HA 2002, s 2(1)(c); H(W)A 2014, s 51(1); English Code, paras 2.19–2.20, 2.34–2.62; Welsh Code, paras 5.38–5.40.
[2]   See English Code, paras 2.25–2.62; Welsh Code, paras 5.38–5.40.

7.117 When it comes to their own resources in relation to prevention, local housing authorities are advised to consider their own infrastructure and those of other service providers[1].

[1]   English Code, paras 2.27–2.29; Welsh Code, paras 5.37–5.38.

7.118 Physical resources available for securing accommodation to those actually homeless obviously include the local housing authority's own housing stock and that of private registered providers, registered social landlords and private landlords in the district. The availability of hostel and refuge spaces should also be considered.

7.119 The mechanisms available to increase the supply of accommodation should be taken into account. These include:

- securing affordable accommodation through planning conditions[1];
- future developments by private registered providers or registered social landlords[2];
- the resources made available by the government to the local housing authority; and

- the extent of new development, self-build homes, shared ownership schemes, etc[3].

1 English Code, paras 2.37–2.42.
2 English Code, paras 2.42–2.50.
3 Welsh Code, paras 5.19 and 5.3–5.40.

7.120 The local housing authority should consider what initiatives could increase the supply of affordable accommodation. Can the local housing authority increase the proportion of lettings made available by private registered providers or registered social landlords or that of affordable homes obtained through planning conditions, etc?

7.121 Local housing authorities are advised to take all available steps to identify the housing resources that might be available in their districts[1]. This includes taking the opportunity of filling any empty accommodation in the district[2]. Such a 'strategy for minimising empty homes' should be an integral part of the homelessness review and strategy and should include tackling any hard-to-let properties, bringing empty private sector properties back into use and encouraging landlords to let flats over shops. The local housing authority should consider what financial resources are available that could be used to encourage private homeowners to repair empty properties and make them available for letting. The powers to take over and manage empty properties[3] should also be considered. 'Resources' for these purposes also includes the resources available to provide 'support' to homeless people, to those likely to become homeless and to those formerly homeless people who need support to prevent them losing their accommodation[4]. This will embrace the availability of housing benefit and other welfare benefits locally, the provision of easily accessible advice, and accommodation with specific levels of support (for single people, rough sleepers, families, victims of domestic abuse, and those in temporary accommodation etc)[5]. In keeping with the modern policy emphasis on sustainability of new homes for the homeless[6], the current English Code deals with the importance of reviewing resources available locally for 'support'[7].

1 English Code, para 2.34; Welsh Code, para 5.19.
2 English Code, para 2.54.
3 Given by the Housing Act 2004, ss 132–138.
4 HA 2002, s 2(2)(c); H(W)A 2014, s 51(1)(b).
5 English Code, paras 2.57–2.74; Welsh Code, paras 5.38–5.40
6 See, for example, the Housing First model, described in *Housing First in England: the principles* (Homeless Link, 2017) and *Housing First Feasibility Study for the Liverpool City Region* (Blood, Copeman, Goldup, Place, Bretheron & Dulson, Crisis, 2017).
7 English Code, paras 2.19–2.29.

Consultation

7.122 There are no formal obligations on a local housing authority to consult over the contents of its homelessness review[1]. However, local housing authorities in Wales are advised in the Welsh Code to consult homeless people, seeking their views about their own situations, their needs, their experiences of services and 'what works', any barriers to services and any suggestions for improvement[2].

[1] In contrast, there are obligations on local housing authorities in both England and Wales to consult over the contents of their homelessness strategies, see **7.138–7.147**.

[2] Welsh Code, para 5.20, see **7.145**.

Publication and inspection

7.123 Once the review is completed, the local housing authority is required to ensure that the results of the review can be inspected by any member of the public, free, at its principal office[1].

[1] HA 2002, s 2(3)(a); H(W)A 2014, s 51(2)(b). Lewisham London Borough Council was found to have acted in breach of the Freedom of Information Act 2000 when it failed to provide, in response to a request, updated information on material originally published in its homelessness review (Information Commissioner's Office Decision Notice FS50092310, 7 August 2006, (2006) October Legal Action, p 25).

7.124 It is also required to provide a copy of those results to any member of the public who requests one. The local housing authority may charge a reasonable fee for copying[1].

[1] HA 2002, s 2(3)(b); H(W)A 2014, s 51(2)(c).

7.125 Local housing authorities in Wales are required to make the results of their review available on their websites (if they have them), and local housing authorities in England are advised to do the same[1]. In practice, many local housing authorities make the whole of their review (and strategy) available on their website whether required to do so or not. Local libraries may provide free internet access enabling these documents to be read online free of charge.

[1] H(W)A 2014, s 51(2)(a); English Code, para 2.12.

Wales

7.126 The following points apply to local housing authorities in Wales, but not to local housing authorities in England. Local housing authorities in Wales:

- are under an express duty to carry out a homelessness review for the local housing authority's area[1];
- must apply a broad definition of homelessness: 'where a person lacks accommodation or where their tenure is not secure'[2];
- should ensure that the scope of the review, when considering what accommodation and support is available, should include people who may become homeless as well as those who are homeless[3];
- are under a duty to make the results of the review available on the local housing authority's website, if it has one[4]; and
- are subject to a recommendation in the Welsh Code that the views of homeless people should be sought when the local housing authority is carrying out the review and drawing up the strategy[5].

Guidance on these points is given at paras 5.17–5.40 of the Welsh Code.

[1] H(W)A 2014, s 50(1)(a); see **7.88**.

² H(W)A 2014, ss 55–59; Welsh Code, paras 5.22–5.24; see **7.102–7.103**.
³ H(W)A 2014, s 51(1)(b)(ii) and (iii); see **7.108**.
⁴ H(W)A 2014, s 51(2)(a); see **7.125**.
⁵ Welsh Code, para 5.20; see **7.122** and **7.145–7.149**.

LOCAL HOMELESSNESS STRATEGIES

Overview

7.127 Once the local housing authority has assembled the raw material and completed its review, it can begin to formulate its strategy (or to reconsider an earlier strategy)[1].

[1] HA 2002, s 3; H(W)A 2014, s 52.

7.128 The required content of the local homelessness strategy is defined in HA 2002, s 3 and H(W)A 2014, s 52[1]. The strategy to be formulated by the local housing authority must be a strategy for:

(1)   the prevention of homelessness in the local housing authority's district[2];
(2)   the securing of suitable accommodation for those people in the local housing authority's district who are, or may become, homeless[3]; and
(3)   the provision of satisfactory services to those people in the local housing authority's district who are actually or potentially homeless, including those who used to be homeless and now need support in order to prevent them becoming homeless again[4].

[1] HA 2002, s 3; H(W)A 2014, s 52.
[2] HA 2002, s 3(1)(a); H(W)A 2014, s 52(1)(a).
[3] HA 2002, s 3(1)(b); H(W)A 2014, s 52(1)(b).
[4] HA 2002, s 3(1)(c); H(W)A 2014, s 52(1)(c). H(W)A 2014, s 52(1)(c) does not include the reference to those who were previously homeless and might become homeless again.

7.129 The strategy is based on the results of the homelessness review[1] and must identify specific objectives for the local housing authority and specific action as to how the local housing authority aims to achieve those objectives[2]. It must also take into account the local housing authority's current allocation scheme, the local tenancy strategy once published and, for London borough councils, the current London Housing Strategy[3].

[1] HA 2002, s 1(1)(b); H(W)A 2014, s 50(1)(b).
[2] HA 2002, s 3(2); H(W)A 2014, s 52(2) where the wording is 'may' rather than 'must'.
[3] HA 2002, s 3(7A) inserted by LA 2011, s 153; this does not apply to local housing authorities in Wales.

7.130 A multi-agency approach[1] enables the local housing authority to identify specific objectives and action, not only for itself, but also for the local adult care and children's services authorities or departments[2]. The local housing authority can also identify specific action to be taken by any of the other organisations involved, but only if each organisation agrees to that action being included in the strategy[3].

[1] See **7.138–7.144**.
[2] HA 2002, s 3(2)(a) and (b); H(W)A 2014, s 52(2).

[3]   HA 2002, s 3(3) and (4); H(W)A 2014, s 52(3) and (4).

7.131 As with the homelessness review[1], the strategy, once completed, must be made available free for inspection and the public permitted to purchase copies[2]. Local housing authorities in Wales are required to publish the strategy on their websites, if they have them[3].

[1]   See **7.123–7.125.**
[2]   HA 2002, s 3(9); H(W)A 2014, s 52(9)(b) and (c).
[3]   H(W)A 2014, s 52(9)(a).

7.132 Local housing authorities in Wales are required to include in the strategy provision for specific action to be taken by the local housing authority, and by other public authorities, voluntary organisations and anyone else involved in the multi-agency approach, to assist any person who may be in particular need of support if they are or may become homeless. Five groups of such people are identified but the list is not exclusive. Those five groups are:

- people leaving prison or youth detention accommodation;
- young people leaving care;
- people leaving the regular armed forces of the Crown;
- people leaving hospital after medical treatment for mental disorder as an in-patient; and
- people receiving mental health services in the community[1].

[1]   H(W)A 2014, s 52(6); Welsh Code, para 5.65.

7.133 Importantly, both the local housing authority and the local adult care and children's services authorities are required to take the homelessness strategy into account when exercising their statutory functions[1]. Obviously, the local housing authority should take the strategy into account when making decisions on applications for homelessness assistance, or under its housing allocation scheme. It might also be argued that the local housing authority should take the strategy into account when exercising its housing management functions, for example, in considering whether or not to bring possession proceedings in respect of a property occupied by one of its own tenants[2].

[1]   HA 2002, s 1(5) and (6); H(W)A 2014, s 50(4) which requires county and county borough councils in Wales to take the homelessness strategy into account in the exercise of any its functions, not just those relating to housing, adult services or children's services, so planning, education and any other statutory functions are included.
[2]   In *Barnsley Metropolitan Borough Council v Norton* [2011] EWCA Civ 834, [2011] HLR 46, CA, the Court of Appeal held that a local housing authority was required to take into account its public sector equality duty (now contained at Equality Act 2010, s 149) when considering whether or not to bring possession proceedings against one of its tenants whose household contained a disabled person. For local housing authorities in Wales, H(W)A 2014, s 50(4) is quite clear that the homelessness strategy should be taken into account when exercising any of its functions, including its housing management functions.

7.134 The children's services authority or department should take the local housing authority's homelessness strategy into account when exercising its functions under the Children Act 1989, so that assistance can be given to homeless young people or to homeless families with children[1]. The strategy should also be taken into account when the adult care authority or department considers its obligations under community care legislation towards those with mental health needs, drug and alcohol abuse problems, the disabled, and ill or elderly people[2].

1 HA 2002 s 1(6); H(W)A 2014, s 50(4).
2 See Chapter 20 for an outline of some of those powers and duties under which a local authority can provide accommodation.

Identification of objectives for the strategy

7.135 The English Code gives examples of the types of specific objectives and actions that might be included in a homelessness strategy for the local housing authority and for the adult care and children's services authorities or departments[1]. Obviously, the strategy must be drawn with relevant consideration of the local housing authority's wider responsibilities in relation to equality and diversity issues.

1 English Code, paras 2.21–2.74.

7.136 The Welsh Code advises that four themes, underpinning the Welsh Government's *Ten Year Homelessness Plan*[1], should be taken into account in planning homelessness services:

- preventing homelessness wherever possible; and
- working across organisational and policy boundaries; and
- placing the service user at the centre of service delivery; and
- ensuring social inclusion and equality of access to services[2].

1 See 7.27.
2 Welsh Code, para 5.41.

7.137 It also advises that local housing authorities should be working with 'partners' to prepare a strategic approach to tackling homelessness, so that partners can assist with prevention work, securing accommodation, securing access to support services, provision of Supporting People and other support services and collaboration with the NHS, Criminal Justice and Community Safety agencies. Services should be designed around the needs of users, so that they are accessible, flexible, responsive to each homeless household's needs. The Code advises that '[t]he empowerment of service users should lie at the heart of all homelessness planning'[1], and that good practice includes adopting the Equal Ground Standard[2] developed by Shelter Cymru.

1 Welsh Code, paras 5.42–5.43.
2 See 7.33.

Consultation and the multi-agency approach

7.138 The local housing authority is required to consult before adopting a homelessness strategy or modifying it[1]. HA 2002 and H(W)A 2014, Pt 2, give local housing authorities a very broad discretion as to which organisations should be consulted, being such public or local authorities, voluntary organisations or other persons as it considers appropriate. The English Code offers a list of those with whom a local housing authority in England may wish to consult[2]. The Welsh Code contains a whole chapter on partnership working with other organisations[3].

[1] HA 2002, s 3(8); H(W)A 2014, s 52(8).
[2] English Code, para 2.10.
[3] Welsh Code, chapter 6, para 6.13 contains guidance on organisations to be consulted over the contents of the homelessness strategy.

7.139 Adult care and children's services authorities are required to cooperate with the local housing authority to the extent that the local housing authority may reasonably require[1]. Examples of joint working between the local housing authority and children's services include joint assessments of homeless families with children[2]. The Welsh Code makes it clear that joint working is expected to assist people who may be in particular need of support if they are or may become homeless, particularly the five groups of people identified at H(W)A 2014, s 52(6)[3].

[1] HA 2002, s 1(2). There is no equivalent provision in relation to homelessness strategies in H(W)A 2014, Pt 2, but H(W)A 2014, s 95, requires social services departments to cooperate in the exercise of any of the local housing authority's functions under H(W)A 2014, Pt 2. Chapters 5 and 6 of the Welsh Code make it very clear that social services departments are expected to cooperate with housing and homelessness functions, see Welsh Code, para 6.3.
[2] English Code, paras 2.21 and 2.70; Welsh Code, para 5.57.
[3] For the five groups, see **7.178**; Welsh Code, para 5.65.

7.140 Both HA 2002 and H(W)A 2014, Pt 2, require a multi-agency approach, reaching far beyond the local housing authority or even other public authorities. This multi-agency approach has been strengthened in recent years by the statutory duties to co-operate at H(W)A 2014, s 95 for certain bodies in Wales[1] and HA 1996, s 213B[2] for public authorities in England. The local housing authority is required to consider whether any of the objectives can be achieved through joint action with the adult care or children's services authorities or departments, with other public authorities, with voluntary organisations or with other people whose activities might contribute to their achievement[3]. The strategy should then identify which of those organisations will take what specific action, either individually or in association with other organisations[4]. The strategy should only identify specific action to be taken by other public authorities if those other authorities or organisations consent to their inclusion[5].

[1] See **17.206–17.215**.
[2] Inserted by HRA 2017, s 10, for applications for homelessness assistance made to local housing authorities in England on or after 3 April 2018. See **15.222–15.228**.
[3] HA 2002, s 3(3) and (5); H(W)A 2014, s 52(3) and (5).
[4] HA 2002, s 3(3); H(W)A 2014, s 52(3).
[5] HA 2002, s 3(4); H(W)A 2014, s 52(4).

7.141 The other organisations that should be consulted over the contents of the homelessness strategy, and the extent to which the actions within the strategy can be performed by them, fall into two categories:

(1)   public authorities (other than the local housing authority and adult care or children's services authority) which have functions that are capable of contributing to the achievement of the objectives of preventing homelessness, securing sufficient accommodation, and securing the satisfactory provision of support[1]; and

(2)   any voluntary organisation or other person whose activities are capable of contributing to the achievement of the objectives[2].

[1]   HA 2002, s 3(3)(a); H(W)A 2014, s 52(3)(a).
[2]   HA 2002, s 3(3)(b); H(W)A 2014, s 52(3)(b).

7.142 Public authorities whose functions may contribute to the objectives of the homelessness strategy include the health authority and other health organisations, the police, the National Offender Management Service, the Department for Work and Pensions, UK Visas and Immigration, the armed forces, education and employment programmes, etc.

7.143 The voluntary organisations and 'other persons' mentioned in the legislation would obviously include housing advice agencies and citizens' advice bureaux, local private registered providers or registered social landlords, private landlords and their representative forums. Casting the net wider, youth action groups, refuges, faith groups, victim support groups, refugee organisations, local businesses and the Samaritans are also suggested as possible organisations to contribute to the strategies[1]. Local housing authorities are advised, in the English Code, to consider 'public, private and voluntary sectors'[2]. In particular, local housing authorities should be entering into partnerships with local private registered providers or registered social landlords[3].

[1]   Welsh Code, para 5.58.
[2]   English Code, para 2.19; Welsh Code, paras 6.13–6.14.
[3]   Welsh Code, paras 6.8–6.12.

7.144 The UK Government-commissioned evaluation in 2004 of the initial local housing authority homelessness strategies in England[1] noted that the involvement of adult care and children's services at a strategic level tended to be disappointing, and that other statutory agencies, such as health and probation services, were also hard to engage. When those other agencies did play a part, they provided helpful input.

[1]   *Local Authorities' Homelessness Strategies: Evaluation and Good Practice* (ODPM, 2004). See also **7.79**.

Consulting the homeless

7.145 There is no specific requirement in either HA 2002 or H(W)A 2014, Pt 2, to consult the former or current users of the local housing authority's services, homeless people, or people who have been or might become homeless. However, the broad discretion given to local housing authorities to consult 'such . . . voluntary organisations or other persons as they consider appropriate'[1] certainly permits them to consult both representative forums for the homeless and individual homeless people themselves. The English Code suggests that local housing authorities should consult service users and specialist agencies that provide support to homeless people[2]. The Welsh Code describes the views of homeless people as 'important to developing a successful strategic approach to homelessness'. It recommends that they should be consulted about their own views on their situation; their needs; their experience of services and 'what works'; any barriers to services; and any suggestions for improvement[3]. Any consultation carried out by a local housing authority must be framed in accordance with the public law requirements of fairness, ensuring that all the different alternative options are fully set out to the public[4].

[1] HA 2002, s 3(8); H(W)A 2014, s 52(8).
[2] English Code, para 2.10.
[3] Welsh Code, para 5.20.
[4] *R (Stirling) v Haringey London Borough Council* [2014] UKSC 56, [2014] 1 WLR 3947, SC.

7.146 Many local housing authorities have taken the opportunity to consult homeless people in their district. Shelter's review of homelessness strategies in 2004 noted[1]:

' . . . consultation with users has enabled authorities to identify and distinguish between the needs of different groups and plan for services which meet their particular needs, rather than providing a "blanket" approach to the problem of homelessness. Importantly, they have identified the need to adopt a proactive approach to tackling homelessness.'

[1] *The Act in action: an assessment of homelessness reviews and strategies* (Shelter, January 2004). See also 7.77.

7.147 The UK Government-commissioned evaluation of initial strategies noted that, in general, local housing authorities found it difficult to engage with homeless people and users of homelessness services. Local housing authorities said to have addressed this problem creatively had gone to speak to homeless people on the street, or gone into hostels or day centres to talk with them[1].

[1] *Local Authorities' Homelessness Strategies: Evaluation and Good Practice* (ODPM Homelessness Research Summary, Number 1, 2004). See also 7.79.

The three matters the strategy must address

7.148 As already indicated[1], HA 2002 and H(W)A 2014, Pt 2, require a local homelessness strategy to address three essential matters: prevention; provision of accommodation; and support.

[1] See 7.128.

7.149 Following consideration and evaluation of the first homelessness strategies in England published in 2003, the opportunity was taken in the 2006 edition of the English Code to expand substantially the advice previously given by government on the content of the strategies. The current edition of the English Code has far less detail in it[1].

[1] English Code, chapter 2; see also Welsh Code, chapter 12.

7.150 Each of the three essential components of a local homelessness strategy is considered in the following paragraphs.

(1)   Prevention of homelessness

7.151 This is the first of the three matters that HA 2002 and H(W)A 2014, Pt 2, require the strategy to address[1]. 'Prevention of homelessness' is now a key policy aim for both the UK and Welsh Governments[2]. In addition, there are now new duties on local housing authorities in both England and Wales to help applicants prevent their own homelessness[3]. Any strategy to prevent homelessness will obviously include ensuring that general advice and information on homelessness, housing benefit and other welfare benefits, occupiers' rights, etc is available, and is both comprehensive and effective[4]. The local housing authority has a statutory obligation to ensure that free advice and information on homelessness assistance is available to any person in its district[5].

[1]   HA 2002, s 3(1)(a); H(W)A 2014, s 52(1)(a); English Code, paras 2.25–2.56; Welsh Code, paras 5.44–5.48.
[2]   See **7.17–7.31** and **7.27–7.34**.
[3]   For local housing authorities in England, HA 1996, s 195 (as amended by HRA 2017 s 4, for applications for homelessness assistance made to local housing authorities in England on or after 3 April 2018; see **15.87–15.137**. For local housing authorities in Wales, H(W)A 2014, s 66; see **17.45–17.72**.
[4]   English Code, para 2.30; Welsh Code, paras 5.44–5.48 and CHAPTER **12**.
[5]   HA 1996, s 179(1), as inserted by HRA 2017, s 2, for applications for homelessness assistance made to local housing authorities in England on or after 3 April 2018; see **8.4–8.4**; H(W)A 2014, s 60(1). See **8.9–8.11**.

7.152 It might be expected that local housing authorities will want to take into account the good practice on homelessness prevention published by the government in *Homelessness Strategies – A Good Practice Handbook*[1] and *Preventing tomorrow's rough sleepers – A Good Practice Handbook*[2], as well as the comprehensive government publication on the subject: *Homelessness Prevention: A guide to good practice*[3]. It would also be expected that local housing authorities should take into account the MHCLG or Welsh Government quarterly homelessness statistical[4].

[1]   DTLR, March 2002.
[2]   Rough Sleepers Unit, 2001.
[3]   CLG, June 2006.
[4]   *Statutory Homelessness and Homelessness Prevention and Relief* (MHCLG; Homelessness Statistics, Welsh Government).

7.153 The previous edition of the English Code, and the current Welsh Code, contain some detailed guidance. In order to contribute to homelessness prevention by minimising the number of evictions for rent arrears, the local housing authority itself should aim to have an effective arrears collection policy and should ask local private registered providers or registered social landlords to ensure that their arrears policies take into account the homelessness strategy's aims. The objective is that all local social landlords should facilitate access to financial and housing advice. The local housing authority is advised to ensure that its housing benefit service is efficient. The Department for Work and Pensions should be asked by local housing authorities to ensure speedy access to budgeting loans or any other financial assistance available.

The children's services authority should be asked by the local housing authority to exercise its functions under the Children Act 1989 to give children, or families with children, financial assistance with deposits, rent payments in advance, and/or rent guarantees. Tenants in financial difficulties should be enabled to obtain local advice to help them manage their finances or negotiate with any creditors[1].

[1] Welsh Code, para 5.47.

7.154 The previous edition of the English Code, and chapter 12 of the Welsh Code, offer local housing authorities a range of advice on homelessness prevention initiatives. For example:

- actions to help applicants who have been asked to leave accommodation by their parents, relatives or friends[1], such as ensuring that any accommodation provided at the outset is suitable, operating mediation and reconciliation services[2], and providing children services support for young people;
- mediation schemes can also help with neighbour disputes that might otherwise lead to one of them leaving his or her home and making an application for homelessness assistance; and
- adaptations can ensure that people with disabilities remain in their own homes, rather than having to apply for accommodation from adult care services.

[1] Homelessness statistics in both England and Wales show that this is the second highest cause of homelessness, after loss of an assured shorthold tenancy.
[2] But see *Robinson v Hammersmith & Fulham London Borough Council* [2006] EWCA Civ 1122, [2007] HLR 7, CA, holding that mediation should not be used to delay inquiries and thus deprive a homeless applicant of a benefit he or she would otherwise have been entitled to. See **8.69** and **12.136–12.139**. Under the modern approach in HA 1996, Pt 7 (as amended by HRA 2017, for applications for homelessness assistance made to local housing authorities in England on or after 3 April 2018) and H(W)A 2014, Pt 2, an applicant in Ms Robinson's position should be assessed as homeless and owed the relief duty (HA 1996, s 189B(2), as inserted by HRA 2017, s 5 (2), for applications for homelessness assistance made to local housing authorities in England on or after 3 April 2018 or H(W)A 2014, s 73(1)) and the contacts with her mother and the suggestion of mediation (with a view to the mother agreeing to permit Ms Robinson to return to her former home) would be reasonable steps taken to help Ms Robinson secure suitable accommodation. See **15.138–15.195** and **17.73–17.143**.

7.155 The UK Government-commissioned evaluation of homelessness strategies in England published in 2004 recommended a number of 'good practice ideas' on prevention[1]. They included[2]:

- refocusing the housing allocation arrangements to reflect the main causes of homelessness, so that an assessment of potential homelessness could be undertaken when someone applies for an ordinary housing allocation;
- improving housing advice services so that there are systems to identify a housing problem and provide advice to prevent homelessness, before an application for homelessness assistance is made;
- mediation schemes to prevent the loss of homes resulting from exclusion by parents, relatives or friends;
- family reconciliation work;
- working with private landlords to develop accreditation schemes;

- improving housing benefit systems so that the payment of housing benefit is speeded up;
- tackling domestic violence and trying to prevent repeat applications for homelessness assistance from victims of domestic violence;
- identifying the triggers for repeat homelessness;
- addressing homelessness for ex-prisoners (by work with prison advice services);
- addressing the needs of vulnerable tenants at risk from crack dealers;
- reviewing the rent arrears policies of local private registered providers or registered social landlords; and
- providing floating support.

[1] Later contained in *Homelessness Prevention: A Guide to Good Practice* (CLG, June 2006).
[2] *Local Authorities' Homelessness Strategies: Evaluation and Good Practice* (ODPM, 2004). See also 7.75.

7.156 These, and all other relevant local opportunities to prevent homelessness, should be considered and addressed in each local housing authority's homelessness strategy.

(2) Securing that sufficient accommodation is (and will be) available for people who are (or may become) homeless

7.157 This is the second statutory objective of the local homelessness strategy[1]. Its fulfillment is, of course, primarily the responsibility of the local housing authority itself, but private registered providers, registered social landlords, local planning authorities and private landlords should be working with the local housing authority to ensure that the supply of affordable and suitable accommodation is maximised[2].

[1] HA 2002, s 3(1)(b); H(W)A 2014, s 52(1)(b); English Code, paras 2.31–2.56; Welsh Code, paras 5.49–5.53.
[2] English Code, paras 2.37–2.42.

7.158 While both Codes of Guidance outline the ways in which accommodation can be secured by local housing authorities in order to meet statutory obligations towards particular homeless applicants for homelessness assistance, the English Code places special emphasis on the role of the local homelessness strategy in enabling a local housing authority to meet likely demand for alternative homes. Paragraphs 2.37–2.56 of the English Code provide guidance, not only as to how the strategy should address the need to secure an increased supply of new housing (through the distribution of financial aid and by planning measures), but also guidance as to the steps that can be taken to maximise the use of existing housing stock, including:

- increasing the supply of new housing by local planning authorities to plan for a mix of housing, identify the size, type, tenure and range of housing and set policies to meet any identified need for affordable housing within development sites[1];
- maximising use of the private rented sector[2];
- making best use of existing social housing[3];
- exercising powers over empty privately-owned property[4]; and
- using housing renewal policies and the disabled facilities grant to

maximise use of existing dwellings[5].

1   English Code, paras 2.37–2.42.
2   English Code, para 2.43.
3   English Code, paras 2.44–2.50.
4   English Code, para 2.54.
5   English Code, para 2.55–2.56.

7.159 The advice in the Welsh Code is that homelessness strategies should reflect the critical role played by the private rented sector, both in relation to prevention (so that private tenants are assisted to remain in their homes) and in moving on. Local housing authorities should be working proactively with the private rented sector to increase access to affordable, well-managed accommodation[1].

1   Welsh Code, para 5.53.

7.160 The UK Government-commissioned evaluation of the initial homelessness strategies in England published in 2004 noted that, in practice, the proportion of lettings by private registered providers to homeless households (via the local housing authority) is not always at a significant level[1].

1   *Local Authorities' Homelessness Strategies: Evaluation and Good Practice* (ODPM, November 2004), para 3.175. See 7.75.

7.161 Commenting on this second statutory objective, one judge has said[1]:

'Local authorities such as the defendant may reasonably say that, given the reduction in its housing stock and the pressure of numbers of those seeking accommodation, it is well-nigh impossible at present to achieve what is set out in [Homelessness Act 2002] s 3(1)(b). However, it is important to note that Parliament has clearly placed an understandable emphasis upon the need for authorities to take measures to try to avoid homelessness.'

1   *R (Aweys) v Birmingham City Council* [2007] EWHC 52 (Admin), [2007] HLR 27, Admin Ct, at [12] per Collins J. The case subsequently reached the House of Lords, but not on this point.

(3)   Providing support for people who are (or were, or may be) homeless

7.162 For local housing authorities in England the 'support' envisaged, under this third category of matters that must be embraced by the homelessness strategy, falls into two sub-categories[1]:

(1)   ongoing support for those who already are, or may soon become, homeless; and
(2)   help for formerly homeless people who need support to stay in their new homes[2].

1   HA 2002, s 3(1)(c); H(W)A 2014, s 52(1)(English Code, paras 2.57–2.75; Welsh Code, paras 5.54–5.59.
2   HA 2002, s 3(1)(c)(i) and (ii); H(W)A 2014, s 52(1)(c) which omits the second category.

7.163 Local housing authorities in Wales are required by H(W)A 2014, s 52(1)(c) to achieve the objective of satisfactory support being available for people who are or may become homeless. That does not, however, exclude the possibility of support for formerly homeless people who need support to stay in their new homes, not least because without that support those formerly homeless people may become homeless in the future.

7.164 People in the first sub-category have a greater need for support than the provision of bare advice or minimal services to prevent homelessness. For these purposes, 'support' can include help with a homeless person's drug or alcohol addiction, or mental health problems. Rough sleepers and those in temporary accommodation should be able to have access to primary health care, to employment opportunities and to education[1].

[1]   For examples of recent research into the support – or lack of support – available to people who are, or may become, homeless, see *Support for single homeless people in England Annual Review 2016* (Homeless Link, 2016); *Stop the Scandal: an investigation into mental health and rough sleeping* (St Mungos, 2016); *Rough Sleepers: access to services and support (England)* (House of Commons Library, 2016); and *It's no life at all: Rough Sleepers' experiences of violence and abuse on the streets of England and Wales* (Sanders & Albanese, Crisis, 2016).

7.165 The objectives, and the activities to be carried out, in relation to the second sub-category are very similar to those within the prevention of homelessness objective[1]. Obviously, advice should be available, both from the statutory sector and the voluntary sector, to enable occupiers to stay in their homes. Sources of financial and other assistance should be identified and made available.

[1]   See **7.182–7.185**.

7.166 Both Codes emphasise joint working with key partners and support agencies[1].

[1]   English Code, paras 2.57–2.75; Welsh Code, paras 5.54–5.59.

Publication and inspection

7.167 Once the strategy has been completed, the local housing authority is required to make a copy available at its principal office for inspection at all reasonable hours, free, by any member of the public[1]. It must also provide a copy of the strategy to any member of the public who requests one, and can charge a reasonable fee for doing so[2]. These statutory provisions mirror the general requirement on local authorities under the Freedom of Information Act 2000 to provide such information. A local housing authority in Wales must also publish the strategy on its website[3], and local housing authorities in England are advised to publish the strategy on their website[4].

[1]   HA 2002, s 3(9)(a); H(W)A 2014, s 52(9)(b); English Code, para 2.12.
[2]   HA 2002, s 3(9)(b); H(W)A 2014, s 52(9)(c); English Code, para 2.12.
[3]   H(W)A 2014, s 52(9)(a).
[4]   English Code, para 2.12.

7.168 Since the local housing authority and the local adult care and children's services authorities are all required to take the homelessness strategy into account in the exercise of their functions[1], it should be expected that the strategy will be readily available to housing and adult care and children's services staff making decisions related to homelessness or to homeless people.

[1] HA 2002, s 1(5) and (6); H(W)A 2014, s 50(4).

New strategies

7.169 Local housing authorities in England were required to have published their first statutory homelessness strategies by 31 July 2003 and local housing authorities in Wales were required to have published by 30 September 2003[1]. By the end of 2003 all local housing authorities had a first strategy in place.

[1] 12 months after the HA 2002 was brought into effect.

7.170 But homelessness presents a changing landscape. Local housing authorities can keep up to date with the changing local picture by regularly undertaking the homelessness review function[1]. The power to conduct a statutory homelessness review can be exercised at any time.

[1] See **7.66**.

7.171 Changing circumstances locally, whether identified by a statutory review or otherwise, may require the local homelessness strategy to be re-visited. There is, accordingly, a general statutory duty to keep the strategy under review and a statutory power to modify it from time to time[1]. Local housing authorities may therefore publish modified strategies at any time. Some anticipated that their initial strategies would stand for three or more years before requiring reconsideration; others revisited their strategies earlier than that.

[1] HA 2002, s 3(6); H(W)A 2014, s 52(7).

7.172 Before producing a revised or replacement strategy, the local housing authority may conduct another homelessness review and, in any event, must consult those public and local authorities, voluntary organisations and members of the public whom it considers appropriate to be consulted[1].

[1] HA 2002, s 3(8); H(W)A 2014, s 52(8).

7.173 Any modified or replacement strategy must be made available to the public in the same way as the initial strategy[1].

[1] See **7.167–7.168**.

7.174 The English Code advises that local housing authorities might consider modifying their strategies at various key stages including anything that may affect the composition of homelessness and/or the risk of homelessness in the district; anything that may change the delivery of the strategy; changes to the relationships between the partners involved in the strategy; or changes to the organizational structure of the housing authority[1]. The Welsh Code advises that any change which is likely significantly to affect homelessness, or how it is tackled, including stock transfer, will require modifications to homelessness strategies[2].

[1] English Code, para 2.13.

² Welsh Code, para 5.68.

7.175 For local housing authorities in England, a new strategy must be published within five years of the publication of the last strategy[1].In effect, therefore, most local housing authorities had updated and published their homelessness strategy by July 2008 and again by July 2013. Again, before a new strategy is adopted, the appropriate organisations should be consulted. Once the new strategy is adopted, it must be published and made available to members of the public. The next date for publication of a new strategy is July 2018 and those new stratagies should take into account the amendments to HA 1996, Pt 7, made by HRA 2017.

1 There was previously an exemption for excellent, 4-star and 3-star local housing authorities. This exemption was revoked with effect from 1 April 2015: Local Audit and Accountability Act 2014 and the English Code advise that all local housing authorities are required to publish homelessness strategies by 1 April 2017: English Code, para 2.3.

7.176 Local housing authorities in Wales were required by HA 2002 to publish their homelessness strategies in September 2003 and to update and publish new homelessness strategies by September 2008 and again by September 2013. H(W)A 2014, Pt 2, came into force on 27 April 2015. H(W)A 2014, Pt 2, requires local housing authorities in Wales to adopt a new homelessness strategy by 2018 and to adopt a new homelessness strategy every fourth year after 2018[1].

1 H(W)A 2014, s 50(2).

7.177 The obligation to keep a homelessness strategy under review and to consult upon necessary modifications to it was considered in *R (Calgin) v Enfield London Borough Council*[1]. The local housing authority had adopted a homelessness strategy in October 2003, but in spring 2004 it implemented a policy for out-of-borough placements of some homeless households without modifying the strategy or consulting upon its modification. In a challenge brought by judicial review, it was contended that this rendered both the strategy and the policy unlawful. The court found that, at the time of adoption of the strategy, an earlier version of the out-of-borough policy had been in place and the strategy had made reference to households placed out of the borough. The new policy was being applied only to a small proportion (1%) of homeless households. In those circumstances, it was held that there had been no unlawfulness in the failure to modify the strategy or consult upon proposed modification. The judge said[2]:

'Furthermore it cannot be the case that every variation of each specific policy relating to the homeless and directed to implementing the strategy has to be made the subject of a formal amendment to the strategy document. The time and cost would take valuable resources away from front line services. I accept that in theory the adoption of a major new homelessness policy could involve such a shift from the strategy that a reasonable authority would need to reflect it in a modified strategy and go through the consultation mechanism laid down in the Act.'

1 [2005] EWHC 1716 (Admin), [2006] HLR 4, Admin Ct.
2 R (Calgin) v Enfield London Borough Council [2005] EWHC 1716 (Admin), [2006] HLR 4, Admin Ct per Elias J at [50].

Wales

7.178 The following points apply when local housing authorities in Wales are drawing up their homelessness strategies, but not to local housing authorities in England:

- the strategy must include provision for specific action expected to be taken by the local housing authority and other public authorities, voluntary organisations and other person for people who may be in particular need of support if they are or may become homeless[1];
- five groups of people who may be in particular need of support are identified[2]; and
- the homelessness strategy must be published on the local housing authority's website, if it has one[3].

[1]   H(W)A 2014, s 52(6); Welsh Code, para 5.65.
[2]   H(W)A 2014, s 52(6); Welsh Code, para 5.65; see **7.138**.
[3]   H(W)A 2014, s 52(9)(a), see **7.167**.

WHO SHOULD DRAW UP THE STRATEGIES AND REVIEWS?

7.179 As already emphasised, the drawing up of the local homelessness strategy and homelessness review is a key task for the local housing authority. These documents will inform all decisions taken by local housing authority officers under HA 1996, Pt 7[1], or H(W)A 2014, Pt 2, and will also set out the local housing authority's policy commitments, the extent to which it works in partnership with private registered providers, registered social landlords, other statutory agencies and voluntary organisations, and what present and future users of the homelessness service can expect from that service.

[1]   As amended by HRA 2017, for applications for homelessness assistance to local housing authorities in England made on or after 3 April 2018.

7.180 Elsewhere in this book, we discuss the extent to which local housing authorities are permitted to contract out any of the activities that they carry out under HA 1996, Pts 6 and 7[1] or H(W)A 2014, Pt 2[2]. The Local Authorities (Contracting Out of Allocation of Housing and Homelessness Functions) Order 1996[3] only applies to activities carried out under HA 1996, Pts 6 and 7[4], and H(W)A 2014, ss 53–100, and not to activities carried out under HA 2002, ss 1–4 or H(W)A 2014, ss 50–52.

[1]   As amended by HRA 2017, for applications for homelessness assistance to local housing authorities in England made on or after 3 April 2018.
[2]   See CHAPTER 21.
[3]   SI 1996/3205 as amended by the Housing (Wales) Act 2014 (Consequential Amendments) Regulations 2015, SI 2015/752 (W 59). See APPENDIX 1.
[4]   As amended by HRA 2017, for applications for homelessness assistance to local housing authorities in England made on or after 3 April 2018.

7.181 By HA 2002, s 1, or H(W)A 2014, s 50(1), a local housing authority is under a 'duty' to formulate a homelessness strategy, and that homelessness strategy must be informed by the raw data contained in the homelessness review[1]. There are similar duties imposed by HA 2002, and H(W)A 2014, Pt 2, on a local housing authority to arrange for its homelessness strategy and its homelessness review to be available for inspection at all reasonable hours, and to provide a copy of those documents on request on payment of a reasonable charge[2]. Any failure to draw up a homelessness strategy would be a breach of the local housing authority's duty.

[1]   See **7.85–7.88**.
[2]   HA 2002, ss 2(3) and 3(9); H(W)A 2014, ss 51(2) and 52(9) where the duty to publish the review and strategy extends to publishing it on the local housing authority's website, if it has one.

7.182 The task of formulating the homelessness review and strategy may be contracted out, in that it might be appropriate for a local housing authority to seek assistance in the formulation of those documents from other organisations, such as staff working for private registered providers, registered social landlords, etc. However, the final content of the homelessness review and strategy should be the local housing authority's decision.

USING THE STRATEGIES AND REVIEWS

7.183 The local homelessness review document will contain essential data on the local homelessness (and prevention of homelessness) scene. It will therefore be an invaluable source of data for those providing, or planning to provide, housing-related services in a local housing authority's district. It will also help the local housing authority itself in dealing with the exercise of judgment in individual homelessness cases. For example, in assessing whether a person is 'homeless' or 'has become homeless intentionally' a local housing authority may (for limited purposes) have regard to 'general circumstances prevailing in relation to housing in the district'[1]. The local homelessness review should provide an up-to-date snapshot of those 'general circumstances' for easy reference by officers and advisers alike.

[1]   HA 1996, s 177(2); H(W)A 2014, s 57(3). See **10.104–10.106**.

7.184 The local homelessness strategy document is an essential additional ingredient in the local housing authority's own work in dealing with individual applications for homelessness assistance and/or housing allocation. The requirement on local housing authorities to 'take their homelessness strategy into account' makes the strategy document, in effect, a local mini-Code of Guidance[1]. Failure to take the strategy into account where it contains material relevant to a particular decision would potentially render that decision unlawful (for failure to have regard to a relevant consideration). The strategy should certainly help officers to make decisions which are consistent with local strategic objectives[2].

[1]   HA 2002, s 1(5); H(W)A 2014, s 50(4).
[2]   See *R (Seabrook) v Brighton & Hove City Council* (2005) CO/5670/2004, (2005) March Legal Action, p 23, Admin Ct; HA 1996, ss 195(2) and 189B(2) (as amended and inserted by HRA 2017, ss 5(2) and 4(2) for applications for homelessness assistance to local housing authorities in England made on or after 3 April 2018), see **15.87–15.137** and **15.138–15.195** H(W)A 2014, ss 66(1) and 73(1), see **17.45–17.72** and **17.73–17.143**.

7.185 Both documents will, of course, be relied upon by advisers assisting the homeless. They may well contain material which can be referred to when making representations on behalf of a particular applicant or in making a complaint under the local housing authority's complaints procedure. It might be expected that the Local Government and Social Care Ombudsman[1] will ask to see copies of the current strategy when investigating homelessness complaints. Indeed, as has already been demonstrated, the review and strategy may well provide material which can be deployed (on both sides) in litigation concerning an individual applicant for homelessness assistance or a local housing authority's policies and procedures on services for the homeless[2].

[1]   Public Services Ombudsman in Wales.
[2]   See *R (Ho-Sang) v Lewisham London Borough Council* (2004) CO/5652/03, (2004) July Legal Action, p 19, Admin Ct and *R (Calgin) v Enfield London Borough Council* [2005] EWHC 1716 (Admin), [2006] HLR 4, Admin Ct as examples of such an approach in practice. See also **7.90**.

Chapter 8

ADVISORY SERVICES AND APPLICATIONS FOR HOMELESSNESS ASSISTANCE

Contents

INTRODUCTION

8.1 Anyone seeking assistance with homelessness from a local housing authority must take the initiative and approach that local housing authority or its contracted provider of homelessness services. There is no legal duty on local housing authorities in England or Wales to seek out homeless people within their districts in order to offer their services to them. That is as true for those who are 'vulnerable' in housing terms[1] as it is for all the homeless[2].

---

[1] See CHAPTER 12.
[2] Note that, in England, there is a duty on certain public authorities to ask a person whom it considers, may be homeless or threatened with homelessness for permission to make a referral to a local housing authority: HA 1996, s 213B, in force from 3 April 2018 although the implementation date for the specified public authorities is 1 October 2018, see **15.222–15.228**. The English Code advises local housing authorities that receipt of the referral is not, in itself, a receipt of an application for homelessness assistance, but that local housing authorities should respond to the referral by trying to contact the person: English Code, para 4.19. See **15.228**.

8.2 As this chapter explains, at the point of first contact, a local housing authority has twin responsibilities:

- to ensure that an information and advice service is available in its district for those who want help in preventing or dealing with their homelessness; and
- to receive applications made to it for accommodation (or for assistance in obtaining accommodation).

8.3 This chapter outlines the statutory requirements relating to information and advice before reviewing the considerable body of law on the treatment of applications.

INFORMATION AND ADVICE

Local housing authorities in England

8.4 Each local housing authority must make arrangements so that free information and advice is available to everyone in its district[1].The information and advice must cover the following topics:

- preventing homelessness;
- securing accommodation when homeless;
- the rights of people who are homeless or threatened with homelessness;
- the duties of the local housing authority under Housing Act 1996, Pt 7 (HA 1996);
- any help that is available from the local authority, whether under HA 1996, Pt 7, or otherwise for persons in the local housing authority's district who are homeless or may become homeless (whether or not they are threatened with homelessness);
- any help that is available from anyone else for persons in the local housing authority's district who are homeless or may become homeless (whether or not they are threatened with homelessness); and
- how to access that help[2].

---

[1]   Housing Act 1996, s 179(1) (HA 1996) as amended by Homelessness Reduction Act 2017 (HRA 2017), s 2, in force from 3 April 2018.
[2]   HA 1996, s 179(1) as amended by HRA 2017, s 2, in force from 3 April 2018.

8.5 The information and advice must be 'available . . . to any person in the authority's district' and be designed to meet the needs of all 'persons in the authority's district'[1]. In addition, the service must be designed to meet the needs of particular groups of people, who are more at risk of homelessness, or more likely to experience detrimental effects if homeless. Those groups of people are:

- persons released from prison or youth detention accommodation[2];
- care leavers[3];
- former members of the regular armed forces[4];
- victims of domestic abuse[5];
- persons leaving hospital[6];
- persons suffering from a mental illness or impairment[7]; and
- any other group that the local housing authority identifies as being at

particular risk of homelessness in its district[8].

1 HA 1996, s 179(1) and (2) as amended by HRA 2017, s 2, in force 3 April 2018.
2 'Youth detention accommodation' means '(a) a secure children home, (b) a secure training centre, (c) a secure college, (d) a young offender institution, (e) accommodation provided by or on behalf of a local authority for the purpose of restricting the liberty of children, (f) accommodation provided for that purpose under Children Act 1989 s 82(5), or (g) accommodation or accommodation of a description for the time being specified by order under Powers of Criminal Courts (Sentencing) Act 2000, s 107(1)(e) (youth detention accommodation for the purposes of detention and training orders' (HA 1996, s 179(5), inserted by HRA 2017, s 2, in force from 3 April 2018). For the circumstances in which members of this group might have a priority need, see **12.180–12.186** (England) and **12.228–12.228** (Wales).
3 'Care leavers' are defined as 'persons who are former relevant children' within the meaning given by Children Act 1989, s 23C(1) (HA 1996, s 179(5) inserted by HRA 2017 s 2 and in force from 3 April 2018). For 'former relevant children' and the circumstances in which members of this group might have a priority need, see **12.160–12.179** (England) and **12.214–12.219** (Wales). For the circumstances in which care leavers (under a slightly different statutory definition) might require a local connection, see **14.95–14.103**.
4 'Regular armed forces' means 'the Royal Navy, the Royal Marines, the regular army or the Royal Air Force' (HA 1996, s 179(5) as inserted by HRA 2017, s 2, applying the definition at Armed Forces Act 2006, s 374, and in force from 3 April 2018). For the circumstances in which members of this group might have a priority need, see **12.174–12.186** (England) and **12.220–12.222** (Wales).
5 'Domestic abuse' means 'a) physical violence, b) threatening, intimidating, coercive or controlling behaviour; or c) emotional, financial, sexual or any other form of abuse, where the victim is associated with the abuser' (HA 1996, s 179(5) inserted by HRA 2017, s 2, and in force from 3 April 2018). 'Financial abuse' includes '(a) having money or other property stolen, (b) being defrauded, (c) being put under pressure in relation to money or other property, and (d) having money or other property misused' (HA 1996, s 179(5) inserted by HRA 2017, s 2, and in force from 3 April 2018). For the circumstances in which members of this group might be homeless, see **10.79–10.91** (England) and **10.92–10.98** (Wales). For the circumstances in which members of this group might have a priority need, see **12.187–12.194** (England) and **12.208–12.211**.
6 'Hospital' means '(a) any institution for the reception and treatment of persons suffering from illness, (b) any maternity home, and (c) any institution for the reception and treatment of persons during convalescence or persons requiring medical rehabilitation, and includes clinics, dispensaries and out-patient departments maintained in connection with any such home or institution' (HA 1996, s 179(5) as inserted by HRA 2017, s 2, applying the definition at National Health Service Act 2006, s 275(1) and in force from 3 April 2018). For the circumstances in which members of this group might have a priority need, see **12.106–12.115** (England) and **12.199–12.206** (Wales).
7 For the circumstances in which members of this group might have a priority need, see **12.106–12.110** (England) and **12.199–12.206** (Wales)
8 The local housing authority would be expected to identify groups in its homelessness review, see **7.97–7.126**, and its homelessness strategy, see **7.127–7.178**.

8.6 This duty to provide information and advice has been greatly expanded by the amendments to HA 1996, s 179, inserted by the Homelessness Reduction Act 2017 (HRA 2017), s 2[1]. These amendments reflect an increasing concern that particular groups are not receiving appropriate services and are at greater risk of homelessness, or of suffering detrimental effects if homeless[2].

1 In force from 3 April 2018: The Homelessness Reduction Act 2017 (Commencement and Transitional and Savings Provisions) Regulations 2018, SI 2018/167 at Appendix 2.
2 See, for example, *Stop the scandal: an investigation into mental health and rough sleeping* (St Mungos, 2016); and the Report of the All-Party Parliamentary Group for Ending Homelessness: *Homelessness prevention for care leavers, prison leavers and survivors of domestic violence* (2017).

8.7 The scope of the information and advice provided should obviously include an outline of what different housing options might be available in the particular district[1]. The information and advice should also try to address some of the common reasons why people may become homeless. Since the most common cause of homelessness is the loss of a private rented sector tenancy, information and advice to assist with financial difficulties or delays with housing benefit or universal credit payments, will be relevant. The English Code sets out eleven different issues in respect of which advice might help to prevent people from becoming threatened with homelessness[2]. HA 1996, Pt 7, as amended by HRA 2017, contains a power for local housing authorities to give any person, or organisation, who is providing an information and advice service financial assistance, by way of grants or loans[3]. Local housing authorities can also permit those people, or organisations, to use their premises, can provide furniture or other goods and can even make the services of local housing authority staff available[4].

[1] *Homelessness Code of Guidance for Local Authorities* (Ministry of Housing, Communities and Local Government, 2018) (the English Code), para 3.7.
[2] English Code, para 3.7.
[3] HA 1996, s 179(3), as inserted by HRA 2017, s 2, in force from 3 April 2018.
[4] HA 1996, s 179(4), as inserted by HRA 2017, s 2, in force from 3 April 2018.

8.8 Local housing authorities may also assist voluntary organisations concerned with homelessness or matters relating to homelessness, by making grants or loans to them, together with allowing them to use their premises, providing furniture or other goods and even providing local housing authority staff[1].

[1] HA 1996, s 180(1). The Secretary of State has a similar power: HA 1996, s 180(1). Assistance can only be provided if the recipient undertakes to use the money, furniture, other goods or premises for a purpose specified by the Secretary of State and also undertakes to provide any information reasonably required by the donor as to how the assistance is being used within 21 days of asked in writing to give the information. The donor must also require the voluntary organisations to keep proper books of account, have them audited in any manner specified, keep records indicating how the money, furniture etc has been used and submits the books and record for inspection. If the recipient used those facilities for a different purpose, the local housing authority or Secretary of State must take steps to recover the amount provided: HA 1996, s 181.

Local housing authorities in Wales

8.9 Local housing authorities in Wales must also make arrangements for the provision of free advice and information. The Housing (Wales) Act 2014 (H(W)A 2014), Pt 2, contains specific requirements that local housing authorities in Wales must comply with[1]. The service must include the publication of information and advice on:

- the system for making an application for homelessness assistance, and how that system operates;
- whether any other help for people who are homeless or may become homeless is available in the local housing authority's area; and
- how to access the help that is available[2].

The local housing authority should also ensure that the service is designed to meet the needs of groups at particular risk of homelessness, including but not limited to:

- people leaving prison or youth detention accommodation;
- young people leaving care;
- people leaving the regular armed forces of the Crown;
- people leaving hospital after receiving in-patient medical treatment for mental disorder; and
- people receiving mental health services in the community.

Targeting those groups, and any other groups of people at particular risk of homelessness, should be achieved through joint working with other public authorities, voluntary organisations and any other persons[3].

[1]   Housing (Wales) Act 2014 (H(W)A 2014) s 60(2)–(6); Code of Guidance for Local Authorities on the Allocation of Accommodation and Homelessness (Welsh Government, March 2016) (the Welsh Code), chapter 9, on the CD Rom with this book.
[2]   H(W)A 2014, s 60(2); Welsh Code, paras 9.18–9.30.
[3]   H(W)A 2014, s 60(4); Welsh Code, paras 9.45–9.46.

8.10 The service must also include assistance in accessing help under the homelessness provisions of H(W)A 2014, Pt 2, or any other help available for people who are homeless or may become homeless[1]. That assistance should be available whether or not a person is threatened with homelessness within the meaning of H(W)A 2014, Pt 2 and must include assistance in accessing help to prevent that person from becoming homeless[2].

[1]   H(W)A 2014, s 60(1)(b).
[2]   H(W)A 2014, s 60(3). See **10.144–10.147** for 'threatened with homelessness'.

8.11 The services of information, advice and assistance provided by local housing authorities in Wales may be jointly secured by two or more local housing authorities[1]. The services may also be integrated into a local authority's other functions of providing people with information, advice and assistance in accessing care and support[2].

[1]   H(W)A 2014, s 60(5); Welsh Code, paras 9.9–9.12, recommends collaboration with other providers.
[2]   H(W)A 2014, s 60(6); Social Services and Well-being (Wales) Act 2014, s 17; Welsh Code, para 9.23.

How to provide an information and advice service

8.12 The advice and information service may either be provided by the local housing authority itself, or the local housing authority may fund or otherwise support other organisations to enable them to provide the advice and information[1]. The Welsh Code recommends that the service should be 'impartial'[2]. The English Code refers to 'comprehensive, tailored advice and information', delivered 'in a targeted and planning way when it is most likely to be needed'[3].

[1]   HA 1996, s 179(3)–(4) as amended by HRA 2017, s 2, and in force from 3 April 2018; English Code, para 3.8; H(W)A 2014, s 60(1)
[2]   Welsh Code, para 9.20.
[3]   English Code, paras 3.1 and 3.6.

8.13 Information and advice could be provided before someone has made an application for homelessness assistance[1]. It could also be provided once an application for homelessness assistance has been made, in performance of either of the duty to prevent or relieve homelessness[2].

[1] HA 1996, s 183(1); H(W)A 2014, s 62(1) see **8.4–8.19**.
[2] For the prevention duty, see HA 1996, s 195(2), as amended by HRA 2017, s 4(2), for applications for homelessness assistance made to local housing authorities in England on or after 3 April 2018; H(W)A 2014, s 66 for applications for homelessness assistance made to local housing authorities in Wales, see **15.87–15.137** (England) and **17.45–17.72** (Wales). For the relief duty, see HA 1996, s 189B(2), as inserted by HRA 2017, s 5(2), for applications for homelessness assistance made to local housing authorities in England on or after 3 April 2018; H(W)A 2014, s 73 for applications for homelessness assistance made to local housing authorities in Wales, see **15.138–15.195** (England) and **17.73–17.143** (Wales).

APPLICATIONS

Applying to a local housing authority

8.14 Local housing authorities are obliged to have arrangements in place so that anyone who wants to make an application for homelessness assistance can do so[1]. In practice, that means that there must be, at the very least, a locally accessible contact point where an applicant can make an application. Usually this will be an office of the local housing authority where applications can be made face to face and, if necessary, in private. There must also be an emergency 24-hour service enabling applications to be made and received day or night[2]. Local housing authorities should publicise the opening hours, address and telephone number of the homelessness service and the 24-hour emergency contact details, translate the information into any 'main languages' in their district, and ensure that interpreters are accessible for less frequently spoken languages[3]. They should ensure that emergency services, such as the police and adult care and children's services, have details of the opening hours and contact numbers[4]. An application need not be directed to any particular department of the local authority[5]. A letter giving details of an applicant's homelessness and containing a request for accommodation which is sent, for example, to the local housing authority's own housing or adult care or children's services departments should be sufficient to trigger the duty to make inquiries[6].

[1] HA 1996, s 183(1); H(W)A 2014, s 62(1). See also English Code, chapter 18; Welsh Code, chapter 10.
[2] *R v Camden London Borough Council ex p Gillan* (1988) 21 HLR 114, QBD; English Code, para 18.2.
[3] English Code, para 18.4; Welsh Code, para 10.7.
[4] English Code, para 18.
[5] English Code, para 18.5.
[6] *R (Edwards) v Birmingham City Council* [2016] EWHC 173 (Admin), [2016] HLR 11, Admin Ct per Hickinbottom J at [38].

8.15 A local housing authority's practice of requiring an applicant for homelessness assistance to go through a 'home options interview' before the local housing authority accepted that the applicant had made an application and triggered duties under HA 1996, Pt 7, was conceded, by that local housing authority, to be unlawful after an applicant had brought a challenge in judicial review proceedings[1]. The judge said:

'the Home Options Scheme . . . cannot lawfully be used to defer consideration of a homeless application. All steps taken to avoid homelessness are of course laudable. But any such steps must be taken in parallel to the carrying out of the duty under Pt [7][2].'

1   *R (Aweys) v Birmingham City Council* [2007] EWHC 52 (Admin), [2007] HLR 27, Admin Ct. The case was later considered by the House of Lords under the name of *Ali v Birmingham City Council* [2009] UKHL 36, HL, but not in relation to that specific point.
2   *R (Aweys) v Birmingham City Council* [2007] EWHC 52 (Admin), [2007] HLR 27, Admin Ct per Collins J at [17]. See also *Complaint against Cardiff City Council*, 20060749, 16 April 2008, (2008) June *Legal Action*, p 32, and *Complaint against Conwy County Borough Council*, 200702044, 11 December 2008, (2009) April *Legal Action*, p 22.

Applications made to other organisations

Contracted out homelessness services

8.16 If the local housing authority has contracted out its homelessness services, applications may need to be directed to, or referred to, that contractor[1]. No doubt the contractor will be anxious to demonstrate that its arrangements for receiving applications are at least as wide-ranging and flexible as the arrangements the local housing authority itself would have made.

1   See **21.23–21.30** and **21.39–21.41**.

8.17 Local housing authorities may choose to contract out the delivery of housing advice and information, or, indeed, the administration of part or all of their mainstream homelessness services. If they do, they remain responsible for the acts or omissions of the contractor in the exercise of the local housing authorities' advice and homelessness functions[1]. Local housing authorities in England cannot contract out:

• their strategic functions of drawing up homelessness strategies and reviews;
• their duty to ensure that housing information and advice is provided free to any person in their district;
• their power to fund voluntary organisations concerned with homelessness; or
• their duty to cooperate with other local housing authorities[2].

1   Local Authorities (Contracting Out of Allocation of Housing and Homelessness Functions) Order 1996, SI 1996/3205, as amended, at Appendix 1. See also English Code, chapter 5; Welsh Code, Annex 9; and chapter 21.
2   Local Authorities (Contracting Out of Allocation of Housing and Homelessness Functions) Order 1996, SI 1996/3205, as amended, at Appendix 1.

8.18 Local housing authorities in Wales can contract all of their functions under H(W)A 2014, Pt 2, except their duty to cooperate with other local housing authorities: H(W)A 2014, s 95[1].

[1]   Local Authorities (Contracting Out of Allocation of Housing and Homelessness Functions) Order 1996, SI 1996/3205, amended by the Housing (Wales) Act 2014 (Consequential Amendments) Regulations 2015, SI 2015/752 (W 59). See also Welsh Code, Annex 9. See **21.30–21.34**.

8.19 Local housing authorities in both England and Wales remain responsible for decisions made on applications for homelessness assistance, the performance of any duties owed and the exercise of any powers. Whilst the decisions and other functions may be contracted out, the responsibility for those decisions and their consequences remains with the local housing authority[1].

[1]   See **21.1–21.2** and **21.23–21.34**.

DUTY ON SPECIFIED PUBLIC AUTHORITIES TO REFER

8.20 HA 1996, s 213B[1] requires specified public authorities to notify a local housing authority in England of the details of any person in respect of whom the public authority exercises functions and whom it considers is, or may be, homeless or threatened with homelessness. The relevant public authorities are specified at reg 10 and Schedule of the Homelessness (Review Procedure etc.) Regulations 2018[2]. They are broadly prisons, secure training centres, social services authorities and NHS Trusts[3]. The duty on them to refer does not come into force until 1 October 2018[4].

[1]   As inserted by HRA 2017, s 10, and in force from 3 April 2018 although the regulation specifying the public authorities does not come into force until 1 October 2018: Homelessness (Review Procedure etc.) Regulations 2018, SI 2018/223, reg 1(4) and 10 and Schedule. See **15.222–15.228**
[2]   SI 2018/223, at APPENDIX 2.
[3]   The full list at Sch 1 is: a governor of a prison within the meaning of Prison Act 1952, s 53(1); a director of a contracted out prison within the meaning of Criminal Justice Act 1991, s 84(4); a governor of a young offender institution provided under Prison Act 1952, s 43(1)(a); a governor of a secure training centre provided under Prison Act 1952, s 43(1)(b); a director of a contracted out secure training centre within the meaning of Criminal Justice and Public Order Act 1994, s 15; a principal of a secure college provided under of Prison Act 1952, s 43(1)(c); a youth offending team established under Crime and Disorder Act 1998, s 39(1); a provider of probation services, an officer designated for these purposes by the Secretary of State for Work and Pensions employed at a Jobcentre Plus office; a social services authority; a person who performs a function of a local authority pursuant to a direction under Education Act 1996, s 497A(4) or (4A) applying to social services functions relating to children under Children Act 2004, s 50, and relating to childcare by Childcare Act 2006 s 15; a NHS Trust and an NHS Foundation Trust in relation to emergency departments, urgent treatment centres and in-patient treatment; and the Secretary of State for Defence in relation to members of the regular armed forces.
[4]   Homelessness (Review Procedure etc.) Regulations 2018, SI 2018/223, regs 1(4) and 10 and Schedule.

8.21 The notification can only occur if the person has consented to the referral and has identified which local housing authority he or she would like the notification to be made to. Once or she has consented, the public authority must notify the relevant local housing authority of its opinion that the person may be homeless or may be threatened with homelessness and give details as to how that person may be contacted by the local housing authority[1]. Guidance as to the procedure for making and receiving the referral is at

Chapter 4 of the English Code.

1   HA 1996, 213B(1)–(3), as inserted by HRA 2017, s 10, and in force from 3 April 2018, see **15.222–15.228**.

8.22 The English Code contains advice that the receipt of the referral 'will not in itself constitute an application' for homelessness assistance[1]. Local housing authorities in England receiving the referral are advised to contact the individual being referred by phone, email or letter. If direct contact is not made, information should be provided as to how the person can access advice and assistance from the local housing authority. It advises that an application for homelessness assistance under HA 1996, s 183(1), will only be triggered if the local housing authority's subsequent contact with the individual, after receipt of the referral, reveals details that provides it with reason to believe that he or she may be homeless or threatened with homelessness[2]. Whilst this may be practical advice, because if the individual fails to respond to an approach, he or she may no longer wish to make an application for homelessness assistance, it is not strictly consistent with the wording of HA 1996, s 183(1). The better analysis might be that receipt of the referral constitutes an application for homelessness assistance, and that the information contained in the referral is likely to be sufficient to give the local housing authority reason to believe that the person named may be homeless or threatened with homelessness. The local housing authority's subsequent attempt to contact him or her would be the first step in it making inquiries into whether the person is homeless or threatened with homelessness[3].

1   English Code, paras 4.19 and 18.7.
2   English Code, para 4.19.
3   HA 1996, s 184(1), see **9.21–9.24**.

To which local housing authority can an application be made?

8.23 There are 326 local housing authorities in England and 22 local housing authorities in Wales. People seeking accommodation or assistance in obtaining accommodation can apply to any local housing authority they choose, in England or in Wales. They need not fulfil any residence requirement or other preliminary condition[1]. Indeed, applications can be made consecutively or concurrently to several local housing authorities[2]. As it is not necessary to make an application in person, applications can be directed to widely dispersed local housing authorities.

1   HA 1996, s 183(1); H(W)A 2014, s 62(1); and *R v Slough Borough Council ex p Ealing London Borough Council* [1981] QB 801, CA.
2   See **8.55–863**.

8.24 The statutory scheme is obviously based on the premise that the applicant will apply to the local housing authority for the area in which he or she wishes to be accommodated. Not surprisingly, therefore, if the local housing authority to which the application is made decides to accept and perform the HA 1996, s 189B(2)[1], or H(W)A 2014, s 73(1)[2], relief duty to help the applicant to secure accommodation or the HA 1996, s 193(2)[3], or H(W)A 2014, s 75(1), main housing duty[4] by providing accommodation in its area, the applicant has no redress against that decision, even if he or she would have preferred to have been referred to a different local housing authority for it to perform that duty[5].

1   As inserted by HRA 2017, s 5(2) for applications for homelessness assistance made to local housing authorities in England on or after 3 April 2018; see **15.138–15.195**.
2   See **17.73–17.143**.
3   See **16.94–16.199**.
4   See **17.146–17.199**.
5   *Hackney London Borough Council v Sareen* [2003] EWCA Civ 351, (2003) 35 HLR 54, CA.

8.25 It is notorious that local housing authorities have different approaches to the strictness with which they apply homelessness legislation. In areas of acute housing shortage, applicants must expect the law to be tightly applied. In areas where there is a surplus of housing accommodation available, applicants may find that their applications receive very little scrutiny and promptly result in the acceptance of the main housing duty.

8.26 Those considering making applications could therefore often benefit from early advice as to the appropriate local housing authority to approach with an application. If their home local housing authority takes a very strict approach to applications, they may be better advised to apply to a more generous local housing authority in the hope that the duties will be promptly accepted and then referred back to their home area[1].

1   Under the 'local connection' provisions described in CHAPTER **14**.

8.27 Indeed, the different tests in HA 1996, Pt 7[1], and H(W)A 2014, Pt 2, in relation to the definition of priority need[2], might render it advantageous for an applicant to direct an application for homelessness assistance to a local housing authority in one jurisdiction in the hope that he or she might benefit from the different test.

1   As amended by HRA 2017, s 5(2), for applications for homelessness assistance made to local housing authorities in England on or after 3 April 2018.
2   HA 1996, s 189(1) and Homelessness (Priority Need for Accommodation) (England) Order 2002, SI 2002/2054; H(W)A 2014, s 70. See CHAPTER **12**.

8.28 Of course, if an applicant is worried that he or she might be found to have 'become homeless intentionally'[1], then there is every advantage in the applicant considering which local housing authority should receive his or her application. From 1 July 2015, local housing authorities in Wales can only have regard to the 'becoming homeless intentionally' test if they have made a specific decision to have regard to that test and have specified the categories of applicant to whom the test might be directed[2]. It follows that an applicant might wish to consider the advantages of applying to a local housing authority in Wales, rather than to a local housing authority in England. He or she could also consider to which local housing authority in Wales to apply[3].

1   HA 1996, s 191; H(W)A 2014, s 77, see CHAPTER **13**.
2   H(W)A 2014, s 78; Welsh Code, paras 17.6–17.11, see **14.265–14.268** and **17.17–17.23**.
3   A local housing authority in Wales will have published a notice if it has decided to stop having regard to whether or not applicants failing within certain specified categories have become homeless intentionally: H(W)A 2014, s 78(3), see **17.17–17.23**.

8.29 There is no eligibility condition or geographic connection required to make an application. The local housing authority cannot therefore turn away applicants who appear to have just arrived in the UK from overseas, or those who seem to have no local connection with its district (even if they have an obvious and current connection with the district of another local housing authority) or anyone else. The proper course, if an applicant does not appear to have a local connection with the local housing authority's district, is for the local housing authority to make the usual inquiries into:

(1) whether the applicant is 'eligible' for assistance under HA 1996, Pt 7[1], or for 'help' under H(W)A 2014, Pt 2; and

(2) if so, whether any duty is owed under HA 1996, Pt 7[2], or H(W)A 2014, Pt 2, to the applicant[3].

[1] As amended by HRA 2017, s 5(2), for applications for homelessness assistance made to local housing authorities in England on or after 3 April 2018.

[2] As amended by HRA 2017, s 5(2), for applications for homelessness assistance made to local housing authorities in England on or after 3 April 2018.

[3] HA 1996, s 184(1); H(W)A 2014, s 62(1), (4) and (5). The language used by H(W)A 2014, Pt 2, is that the local housing authority 'must carry out an assessment of a person's case'. See **9.12–9.14**.

8.30 The scope of those inquiries may (but does not need to) include considering whether the applicant has a local connection with the local housing authority and, if not, whether he or she has a local connection elsewhere[1].

[1] HA 1996, s 184(2). There is no equivalent provision in H(W)A 2014, Pt 2, but the local housing authority has a discretion whether or not to make a referral: H(W)A 2014, s 80(1) and (2). This implies that it also has a discretion whether or not to make inquiries into local connection, as confirmed by Welsh Code, para 18.1. For further discussion of local connection see **14.26–14.34**.

8.31 A local housing authority in England must also accept an application for homelessness assistance made by an applicant who had previously accepted a private rented sector offer[1], made by a different local housing authority, in the first local housing authority's area. If the application is made within two years of acceptance of the private rented sector offer, the special provisions at HA 1996, s 195A will apply[2].

[1] For 'private rented sector offer' see HA 1996, s 193(7AA) and **16.161–16.180**.

[2] As amended by HRA 2017, s 4(4) for applications for homelessness assistance made to local housing authorities in England on or after 3 April 2018. See English Code, paras 18.16–18.26; and **8.100–8.106**.

8.32 The local housing authority in England to which the applicant has applied must accept the application, secure interim accommodation if required[1], make inquiries and notify the applicant of its decision as to whether any duty is owed. If the applicant is owed the HA 1996, 189B(2)[2], relief duty or the HA 1996, s 193(2), main housing duty[3], the local housing authority can then refer the applicant to the local housing authority which made him or her the private rented sector offer[4].

[1] The duty at HA 1996, s 188(1A) (as amended by HRA 2017, s 5(4), for applications for homelessness assistance made to local housing authorities in England on or after 3 April 2018)

does not require the local housing authority to consider whether or not it has reason to believe that the applicant may have a priority need, see **16.20–16.26**.

2   As inserted by HRA 2017, s 5(2) for applications for homelessness assistance made to local housing authorities in England on or after 3 April 2018, see **15.138–15.195**.

3   See **16.94–16.199**.

4   HA 1996, s 198(A1) (as inserted by HRA 2017, s 5(8) for applications for homelessness assistance made to local housing authorities in England on or after 3 April 2018), (1) and (2ZA); see **15.139–15.142**.

Form in which an application can be made

8.33 Whenever a person approaches a local housing authority for accommodation, or for assistance in obtaining accommodation, and the local housing authority has reason to believe that he or she may be homeless or threatened with homelessness, then he or she has made an application for homelessness assistance[1]. Indeed, it is the authors' view that receipt by a local housing authority in England of a referral made by a public authority under the HA 1996, s 213B, duty[2] is sufficient for a person to have made an application for homelessness assistance.

1   HA 1996, s 183; H(W)A 2014, s 62(1).

2   As inserted by HRA 2017, s 10, in force from 3 April 2018, see **8.20–8.22**and **15.222–15.228**.

8.34 Although it may be convenient for a local housing authority to have its own application form for applicants to complete, there is no legal requirement that an application should be in writing or in any specified form[1]. An application could perfectly properly be made in person, by letter, fax, telephone, text or email. So long as the communication seeks accommodation or assistance in obtaining accommodation and sets out an account that gives the local housing authority reason to believe that the person might be homeless or threatened with homelessness, it constitutes an application. As the Codes make clear, there is absolutely no requirement on applicants to specify that they are seeking services under HA 1996, Pt 7[2], or H(W)A 2014, Pt 2[3]. Obviously, there is room for possible disagreement as to whether what is said in the course of a conversation constitutes an application. In *R v Cherwell District Council ex p Howkins*[4], the applicant's solicitor telephoned the local housing authority shortly after it had evicted the applicant (who had been a council tenant) for rent arrears. The judge was quite satisfied that an application for homelessness assistance did not need to be in writing. He said that:

' . . . in order to be treated as an application it seems to me that an oral conversation has to be conducted in such a way that it is clear that it amounts to an application.'

Consequently, on the facts, the conversation had simply been an inquiry by the solicitor as to whether the local housing authority was going to offer temporary accommodation and was not itself an application for any accommodation.

1   English Code, para 18.5; Welsh Code, paras 10.7–10.8; *R v Chiltern District Council ex p Roberts* (1990) 23 HLR 387, QBD; and *R (Aweys) v Birmingham City Council* [2007] EWHC 52 (Admin), [2007] HLR 27, Admin Ct per Collins J at [8]. The case was later considered by the House of Lords under the name of *Ali v Birmingham City Council* [2009]

UKHL 36, [2009] 1 WLR 1506, HL, but not in relation to that specific point. See also *R*
(Edwards) v Birmingham City Council [2016] EWHC 173 (Admin), [2016] HLR 11, Admin
Ct per Hickinbottom J at [37].
2 As amended by HRA 2017 for applications for homelessness assistance made to local housing
authorities in England on or after 3 April 2018.
3 English Code, para 18.5; Welsh Code, paras 10.7–10.9.
4 *R v Cherwell District Council ex p Howkins* (unreported) 14 May 1984, QBD.

8.35 Local housing authorities should take particular care to identify when
someone may appear only to be applying for an allocation of social housing,
but is actually indicating that he or she might be homeless according to the
definitions at HA 1996, Pt 7¹, or H(W)A 2014, Pt 2², Where the information
on an inquiry about the allocation scheme, or on an application for an
allocation, gives the local housing authority 'reason to believe' that the
applicant might be homeless, that approach is also an application for
homelessness assistance. The courts and the Ombudsmen have criticised local
housing authorities who have failed to recognise such applications³.

1 As amended by HRA 2017 for applications for homelessness assistance made to local housing
authorities in England on or after 3 April 2018.
2 English Code, para 18.6. See Chapter 10 for the definition of 'homelessness'.
3 See **8.110**.

8.36 Once an application meeting the above (fairly minimal) requirements is
received, the local housing authority cannot ignore it until the applicant has
completed the local housing authority's standard application form. It must act
upon the application and start to make inquiries.

'Actual' and 'deemed' applications

8.37 The regime for homelessness assistance does not recognise the concept of
an implied, constructive or deemed homelessness application. The only
application which counts, and triggers the duty to make inquiries, is one
actually made.

8.38 This can be a source of frustration for a local housing authority that is
seeking to free itself from responsibility for particularly problematic tenants. It
is not uncommon for tenants, in both the social housing and the private rented
sectors, who are facing eviction for rent arrears or persistent anti-social
behaviour, to be forewarned that the local housing authority will not accept a
responsibility for rehousing them once evicted. If the tenant potentially has a
priority need, and chooses to refrain from making a homelessness application
until the moment of eviction (or very shortly beforehand), it is likely that the
local housing authority will have to provide further accommodation, at least
until the local housing authority can notify the applicant that it is satisfied that
he or she does not have a priority need¹.

1 HA 1996, s 188(1) and (1ZA)(b) as amended by HRA 2017, s 5(4), and HA 1996, s 189B(2)
as inserted by HRA 2017, s 5(2), for applications for homelessness assistance made to local
housing authorities in England on or after 3 April 2018; H(W)A 2014, s 68(1). See **16.37–16.**
80 (England) and **17.118–17.134** (Wales).

8.39 For this reason, some local housing authorities have in the past tried to
explore a concept of an implied or deemed application made well before the

eviction, allowing them to undertake inquiries while the tenants are still in their homes (and awaiting the bailiffs) and thus reducing any temporary accommodation responsibility to an absolute minimum. However, it seems that (very properly) this device has been abandoned.

Who can make an application?

8.40 Anyone can make a request for accommodation or for assistance in obtaining accommodation. If that person does not appear to be homeless or threatened with homelessness, he or she will be entitled to housing information and advice, free of charge, but the local housing authority will owe no further duty[1]. If the person appears to be homeless or to be threatened with homelessness, the local housing authority must treat the request as an application for homelessness assistance and start to make inquiries[2].

[1]   HA 1996, s 179(1) as amended by HRA 2017, s 2, in force from 3 April 2018; H(W)A 2014, s 60(1)(a), see **8.4–8.13**.
[2]   HA 1996, s 183(1) and English Code, paras 18.6 and 18.32; H(W)A 2014, s 62(1) and Welsh Code, paras 10.6–10.9.

8.41 There is no eligibility condition or geographic connection required in order to make an application. The local housing authority cannot therefore turn away applicants who appear to have just arrived in the UK from overseas, nor those who seem to have no local connection with its district (even if they have an obvious and current connection with the district of another local housing authority)[1].

[1]   See CHAPTER 14 for 'local connection'.

8.42 A person must have legal capacity in order to make an application for homeless assistance. Accordingly, those who lack the mental capacity to make an application cannot apply[1]. It is for the local housing authority, in the first instance, to decide whether the applicant has the mental capacity to make an application[2]. There is no right of statutory review or appeal if the application is refused on the basis of lack of capacity. The obvious practical route to achieving a reversal of the local housing authority's decision would be the submission of clear medical evidence that the applicant did have capacity. If the local housing authority persisted in its refusal to accept the application, proceedings for judicial review would need to be brought[3].

[1]   *R v Oldham Metropolitan Borough Council ex p Garlick, R v London Borough of Tower Hamlets ex p Begum* [1993] AC 509, HL; *R (MT) v Oxford City Council* [2015] EWHC 795 (Admin), (2015) May Legal Action, p 45, Admin Ct and, most recently, *WB v W District Council* [2018] EWCA Civ 928, CA. A local authority which has adult care responsibilities would almost certainly have duties under the Care Act 2014 (England) or Social Services and Well Being Act 2014 (Wales) towards someone who attempted to make an application for homelessness assistance but did not have the capacity to do so. Those duties can include the provision of accommodation. See **20.19–20.38** (England) and **20.72–20.84** (Wales).
[2]   It is presumed that capacity to make an application for homelessness assistance should be assessed applying the principles at Mental Capacity Act 2005, ss 1–3 and thus presumption was applied in *WB v W District Council* [2018] EWCAQ Civ 928, CA.
[3]   See *R (Halewood) v West Lancashire District Council* (2009) May 2010 *Legal Action*, p 24, where the local housing authority had decided that the claimant lacked capacity. Judicial

review proceedings were subsequently compromised when the claimant produced new evidence. See **19.306–19.333** for judicial review.

8.43 There is no minimum age for applicants[1]. In the absence of a statutory minimum age, the House of Lords has, in dealing with an application made by a 4-year old, held that applications from 'dependent' children should not be considered[2]. There is no statutory definition of that term[3]. It follows that an application may be made by any child who is no longer 'dependent'. As the House of Lords recognised:

> 'There will obviously be the case from time to time when a child leaves home under the age of 16 and ceases to be dependent on the parents or those with whom he or she was living[4].'

1   English Code, para 18.8. The Welsh Code states 'applications can be made by anyone 16 or over' (Welsh Code, para 10.7) although arguably a person younger than 16 is not excluded from making an application if he or she has capacity to do so.
2   *R v Oldham Metropolitan Borough Council ex p Garlick* [1993] AC 509, HL.
3   The English Code contains advice from the Secretary of State: 'local housing authorities may wish to treat as dependent all children under 16, and all children aged 16–18 who are in, or are about to begin, full-time education or training or who for other reasons are unable to support themselves and who live at home . . . The Secretary of State considers that it will be very rare that a 16 or 17-year-old child who is living at home will not be considered to be dependent.' (English Code, para 8.7); Welsh Code para 16.6 is less explicit; see **12.53** and **12.198**. The Secretary of State's advice should be taken into account but should not be read as meaning that children 16 or 17 are always dependent on their parents.
4   [1993] AC 509, HL at 517 per Lord Griffiths.

8.44 Such an individual can make his or her own application. Applicants need not show a history of independence from their parents or others. Plainly, the very first step that an applicant may have taken to demonstrate that he or she is no longer 'dependent' might be making the application[1].

1   See **12.41–12.75** (England) and **12.198** (Wales) for 'dependent children'. See also *R (SD) v Oxford City Council* [2015] EWHC 1871 (Admin), (2015) October *Legal Action*, Admin Ct where exactly that scenario occurred: a 16-year-old boy made an application for homelessness assistance after each of his parents had been found to have become homeless intentionally; Ouseley J refused permission to apply for judicial review, holding that, whilst it had not been appropriate for the local housing authority to refuse to accept an application, the claimant could not conceivably be in priority need since that category of priority need was directed to non-dependent children.

8.45 There are occasionally applications made by non-dependent young people under the age of 16[1], but applications by those aged 16 or 17 are more common. Since 1 March 2001 in Wales and 31 July 2002 in England, most 16- and 17-year-olds have been designated as being in priority need[2]. Guidance suggests that local housing authorities should have arrangements in place so that, when applications for homelessness assistance are received from 16- or 17-year-olds, assessments of their housing, care and support needs are carried out jointly with children's services and that the principal responsibility falls upon children's services[3]. Obviously, unless the local housing authority is a unitary authority, the consent of the young person will be required before his or her details are disclosed to the children's services department of a different authority.

1   For an example, see *Kelly v Monklands District Council* [1985] Lexis Citation 24, 1986 SLT 165, CtSess.

2   Homelessness (Priority Need for Accommodation) (England) Order 2002, SI 2002/2051, art 3; H(W)A 2014, s 70(1)(f). Until 2002, around 3–4,000 applicants in England each year were accepted as homeless and having priority need due to their vulnerability as young people. The number rose to 11,050 in 2003–04 and then fell to 4,070 in 2008/09. It has since fallen even further, to 1030 in 2016–17 presumably as a result of more young people being accepted as children in need and accommodated by children's services under the Children Act 1989 duties, see **12.133–12.159** and **20.58–20.64** (MHCLG, Homelessness Statistics, Table 773). Similarly, in Wales in 2004–05, 970 children were accepted as homeless and having a priority need due to their being aged 16 or 17. The numbers declined from 2005 onwards. The Welsh Government no longer collates figures on acceptances by different categories of priority need. See **12.133–12.159** (England) and **12.212–12.213** (Wales).

3   English Code, para 8.23; Welsh Code, paras 16.40–16.44. See *R (M) v Hammersmith & Fulham London Borough Council* [2008] UKHL 14, [2008] 1 WLR 535, HL; and *R (G) v Southwark London Borough Council* [2009] UKHL 26, [2009] 1 WLR 2399, HL. See *Prevention of Homelessness and Provision of Accommodation for 16 and 17 year old young people who may be homeless and/or require accommodation* (MHCLG and Department for Education, April 2018) paras 3.2–3.63. See **12.133–12.159** (England) and **12.212–12.213** (Wales).

8.46 Both the courts and the Ombudsmen have been extremely critical of local authorities passing 16- and 17-year-olds between housing departments and children's services departments, with neither agency accepting a statutory duty to the young person[1]. In one case, the Local Government Ombudsman found two councils guilty of maladministration where a 16-year-old homeless boy spent nine months sleeping in a tent or occasionally on friends' sofas because neither council had complied with its statutory duty to secure accommodation for him[2].

1   See **12.150–12.159** (England) and **12.212–12.213** (Wales).
2   *LGO Investigation into complaints about Kent County Council*, 09 017 510 *and about Dover District Council*, 09 017 512, 31 July 2012, (2012) October *Legal Action*, p 36; and *LGO Investigation into complaint about Doncaster Municipal Borough Council*, 13 001 144, 3 March 2014, (2014) May *Legal Action*, p 23.

Joint applications

8.47 The law does not recognise an application for accommodation, or for assistance in obtaining accommodation, made by a couple, a family or a household. Applications are made by individuals. Both HA 1996, Pt 7, and H(W)A 2014, Pt 2, refer to 'a person' making the application[1]. One judge has said:

'I am quite unable to conclude that an application for housing as a homeless person falls to be treated as being made by a family unit. It is, and must be, an application at the instance of an individual. Of course, if that individual is residing with others in a family, that will affect the accommodation he requires, and whether he has priority need, but it does not alter the fact that the application is the application of an individual[2].'

1   HA 1996, s 183(1); H(W)A 2014, s 62(1).
2   *MacLeod (aka Hynds) v Midlothian District Council* (1986) SLT 54, (1985) November SCOLAG 163 per Lord Ross.

8.48 Of course, there is nothing to prevent more than one individual in the same household from making an application. Indeed, several applicants from a single household may apply at the same time to the same local housing authority and even on the same application form. This is particularly common where there are two adult heads of household and both choose to apply.

8.49 There is some helpful judicial guidance on how to deal with such jointly made applications:

'It seems to me that where the application which is made to the authority is, as here, a joint application, it is a joint application which the authority must determine. If there is no request by one of two joint applicants for his or her case to be treated separately, there is no obligation upon the authority to deal with the application as being other than a joint application. However, in considering the joint application there may be an obligation on the housing authority to consider the separate circumstances of the individuals who are making the joint application[1].'

[1] *R v Wandsworth London Borough Council ex p Lord* (unreported) 8 July 1985, QBD per Woolf J.

8.50 In *Hemans v Windsor and Maidenhead Royal Borough Council*[1], the application for homelessness assistance had been made by solicitors acting for both husband and wife and had been expressed as a 'joint application'. There was some discussion before the Court of Appeal as to what that meant. One member of the Court of Appeal said:

'We were referred to the provision in the Interpretation Act 1978 that, unless the contrary intention appears, the singular includes the plural. In practice, joint homelessness applications are common. It is also common ground that in such cases, the council must look at the circumstances of both or all the applicants. In the vast majority of cases, it will make no practical difference whether technically it is to be regarded as a single application capable only of a single determination or two applications in a single document. I would leave further discussion of that arcane point until such time as a case may arise where it matters[2].'

[1] [2011] EWCA Civ 374, [2011] HLR 25, CA.
[2] *Hemans v Windsor and Maidenhead Royal Borough Council* [2011] EWCA Civ 374, [2011] HLR 25, CA per Toulson LJ at [23].

8.51 In practice, this judicial guidance enables local housing authorities to proceed on the basis that there is an identity of interest between the joint applicants unless and until material before the local housing authority indicates that separate consideration of each application is required. Such material could be a disagreement between the joint applicants in the course of interviews with the local housing authority or might be implied from the giving of mutually inconsistent accounts. The safer course must ordinarily be to treat even joint applicants with a degree of separate consideration.

8.52 This sense, in which even supposed joint applications are simply two applications contained in one single form, was emphasised in *Lewis v Brent London Borough Council*[1]. Mr and Mrs Lewis had applied together for homelessness assistance to the local housing authority. However, Mrs Lewis was unable to rely on her husband's circumstances in an appeal against a decision that she had become homeless intentionally. Although they had made a joint application, he was not a party to the appeal and so his – more favourable – circumstances could not be relied upon by her.

[1] [2005] EWCA Civ 605, (2005) July *Legal Action*, p 29, CA.

8.53 Where more than one individual in a household could apply, it may be sensible for one rather than the other to make the application. For example, one may be eligible for assistance under HA 1996, Pt 7[1], or H(W)A 2014, Pt 2, and the other may not be eligible; one may have a priority need and the other may not[2]; or one may be more likely to be found to have become homeless intentionally. There may even be an advantage in applicants in similar circumstances making consecutive applications in order to obtain not only the possibility of a second, and more favourable decision, but also to obtain at least a further period in interim accommodation whilst the second application is considered[3]. Where the application is a re-application for homelessness assistance, made within two years of the acceptance of a private rented sector offer made to the applicant by a local housing authority in England in order to bring the HA 1996, s 193(2), main housing duty to an end[4], the special provisions in HA 1996, s 195A[5] will only apply if the application is made by the same person who had accepted the private rented sector offer and is made to a local housing authority in England[6].

[1] As amended by HRA 2017, for applications for homelessness assistance made to local housing authorities in England on or after 3 April 2018.

[2] This is relevant where the application for homelessness assistance is to a local housing authority in England and one person has a form of priority need that is at HA 1996, s 189(1)(d) or one of those listed in the Homelessness (Priority Need for Accommodation) (England) Order 2002, SI 2002/2051 because each of those categories require that the applicant must have the requisite priority need. In the case of priority need acquired under one of the categories at HA 1996, s 189(1)(a)–(c), and all applications to local housing authorities in Wales under H(W)A 2014, Pt 2, the applicant has a priority need if either he or she, or a member of his or her household, has the requisite characteristics.

[3] See *R (SD) v Oxford City Council* [2015] EWHC 1871 (Admin), (2015) October *Legal Action*, Admin Ct where Ouseley J refused permission to bring a judicial review claim and an interim injunction requiring the provision of accommodation for a 16-year-old boy who had made an application for homelessness assistance after each of his parents had made applications and had been found to have become homeless intentionally, see **8.42–8.44**.

[4] HA 1996, s 193(7AA)–(7AC), see **16.161–16.180** for 'private rented sector offer'.

[5] As amended by HRA 2017, s 4(4) for applications for homelessness assistance made to local housing authorities in England on or after 3 April 2018.

[6] See **8.100–8.107**.

8.54 Where an application by one adult member of a household results in the acceptance of the HA 1996, s 193(2) main housing duty[1], or accommodation duties owed under H(W)A 2014, Pt 2[2], accommodation will be provided for the whole household[3]. What happens, however, if the applying adult rejects that offer and the other household members then make further applications? This occurred in *R v Camden London Borough Council ex p Hersi*[4]. In that case, the new applicant was a 19-year-old daughter of the first applicant, her own mother. After the mother had rejected an offer of accommodation, the local housing authority refused to accept the daughter's application. The Court of Appeal described the daughter as having 'no standing' to apply for homelessness assistance for the whole family (although the reasoning seems to suggest that this was because the younger children of the household were dependent on their mother and not on her). However, in that case Camden accepted (correctly) that had the new application been from another adult member of the household on whom the children were dependent, inquiries into that application would need to have been made.

[1] See **16.94–16.199**.

[2] H(W)A 2014, s 68(3), see **17.118–17.134**; H(W)A 2014, s 75(1), see **17.146–17.199**.

Multiple applications

8.55 There is nothing to prevent someone applying simultaneously to more than one local housing authority. Local housing authorities normally require an applicant for homelessness assistance to declare all recent or current applications for homelessness assistance made to other local housing authorities. Where there are concurrent applications to different local housing authorities, each local housing authority will be obliged to carry out its own inquiries, potentially resulting in a wasteful duplication of effort. As a result, both Codes suggest that the receiving local housing authorities should agree amongst themselves which one will be responsible for carrying out inquiries[1]. Presumably this is on the basis that the local housing authority which does undertake the inquiries does so both on its own behalf and as agent for (or delegate of) the others[2]. Each local housing authority should then make its own assessment of the results of the inquiries and reach its own decision[3]. It seems implicit in this suggested arrangement, however, that in practice the applicant will withdraw all other applications as soon as one of the local housing authorities accepts that it owes the applicant any duty under HA 1996, Pt 7[4] or H(W)A 2014, Pt 2.

1 English Code, para 18.9; Welsh Code, para 10.39.
2 As permitted by Local Government Act 1972, s 101(1)(b).
3 As both Codes recognise: English Code, para 18.9; Welsh Code, para 10.39.
4 As amended by HRA 2017, for applications for homelessness assistance to local housing authorities in England made on or after 3 April 2018.

Consecutive applications

8.56 As already stated, there is nothing to prevent an applicant applying first to one local housing authority and then to another. When an applicant has previously applied to one local housing authority (the first local housing authority), the second or subsequent local housing authority would normally seek the applicant's consent so that it is free (in the course of making inquiries into the second or subsequent application) to contact the first local housing authority and request information on the application made and on that local housing authority's decision (if any) on that application. The first local housing authority is under a duty to cooperate with any such request[1].

1 HA 1996, s 213; H(W)A 2014, s 92(2) and (5).

8.57 The second local housing authority, however, must not rely solely on the first local housing authority's decision in reaching its own decision on the application made to it, although it may take that decision into account. Nor may it merely adopt the first local housing authority's decision. It must make its own independent inquiries and reach an independent decision on the application it has received[1].

1 English Code, para 18.9; Welsh Code, para 10.39.

8.58 It may well be that the second local housing authority reaches a different decision from the first local housing authority. For example, it may decide that the applicant is owed a duty because he or she is eligible, even if the first local housing authority had decided that matter against the applicant[1].

---

[1] As occurred in *R (Sambotin) v Brent London Borough Council* [2017] EWHC 1190 (Admin), [2017] HLR 31, Admin Ct, where Waltham Forest London Borough Council had notified the applicant of its decision that he was not eligible for assistance. On a further application for homelessness assistance to Brent London Borough Council, Brent notified him of its s 184(1) decision that he was eligible, and that the conditions for referral were met, so that he would be referred to Waltham Forest. Brent subsequently attempted to re-open its s 184 decision. The Administrative Court judge held that a s 184(1) decision could only be re-opened in the event of fraud on the part of the applicant, or where the local housing authority which had made the decision had proceeded from a fundamental mistake of fact. See **14.182**.

8.59 Since local housing authorities in Wales now have a choice whether or not to apply the 'becoming homeless intentionally' test, an applicant who has been found to have become homeless intentionally is likely to be advised to consider directing a second application to a local housing authority in Wales which has not decided to have regard to the test[1].

---

[1] H(W)A 2014, s 78, see **17.17–17.26**. A local housing authority in Wales will have published a notice if it has decided to stop having regard to whether or not applicants failing within certain specified categories have become homeless intentionally: H(W)A 2014, s 78(3).

8.60 The second local housing authority may also decide that the HA 1996, s 189B(2)[1], relief duty or HA 1996, s 193(2), main housing duty[2] is to be referred to the first local housing authority on the grounds that the conditions for referral in HA 1996, s 198[3] are satisfied[4]. This can result in the first local housing authority being obliged to receive back and accommodate an applicant to whom it had previously notified an adverse decision[5].

---

[1] As inserted by HRA 2017, s 5(2) for applications to local housing authorities in England made on or after 3 April 2018, see **15.138–15.195**.
[2] Or, for local housing authorities in Wales, the H(W)A 2014, s 75(1), main housing duty, see **17.146–17.199**.
[3] Or, for local housing authorities in Wales, under H(W)A 2014, s 80, see **14.32**.
[4] For an introduction to the conditions for referral, including local connection, see **14.33–14.42**. Note that the H(W)A 2014, s 73(1), relief duty cannot be referred under local connection.
[5] For an example where two local housing authorities took different views on an applicant's eligibility for assistance (HA 1996, s 185, see Chapter 11), see *R (Sambotin) v Brent London Borough Council* [2017] EWHC 1190 (Admin), [2017] HLR 31, Admin Ct.

8.61 A dispute resolution mechanism is available where there is disagreement between two local housing authorities as to whether the conditions for referral are met. However, that mechanism does not apply in cases where there is no dispute over the local connection conditions, but where the local housing authority to whom the applicant has been referred does not agree with the referring local housing authority's decision that a duty to accommodate is owed to the applicant. In those circumstances, the first local housing authority cannot refuse to accept the referral unless it can successfully demonstrate, in the usual way, that the conditions for referral are not satisfied[1].

---

[1] *R v Slough Borough Council ex p Ealing London Borough Council* [1981] QB 801, CA; *R (Bantamagbari) v Westminster City Council and Southwark London Borough Council* [2003] EWHC 1350 (Admin), [2003] All ER (D) 163 (May), Admin Ct. See **14.184–14.190**.

8.62 If the first local housing authority believes that the second local housing authority has incorrectly reached a decision that the main duty is owed to the applicant, it cannot simply refuse the referral of the duty and wait for the applicant or the second local housing authority to bring legal proceedings[1]. Instead, it must take the initiative and bring judicial review proceedings to demonstrate that the decision-making by the second local housing authority was unlawful[2]. Obviously, the second local housing authority must apply the law correctly when making its inquiries and reaching its decision. If it has not done so, the first local housing authority will succeed in having the decision overturned. In *R v Newham London Borough Council ex p Tower Hamlets London Borough Council*[3], the Court of Appeal held that Newham would have been entitled to find that it owed the main housing duty to someone whom Tower Hamlets had previously found to have become homeless intentionally. Newham would have been, had it applied the law correctly, entitled to refer the applicant back to Tower Hamlets under the local connection provisions. However, Newham made an error of law when considering whether the applicant had become homeless intentionally, in that it took into account its own local housing conditions rather than those of Tower Hamlets. Tower Hamlets succeeded in having the Newham decision, and consequently the referral, set aside.

[1]   *R (Bantamagbari) v City of Westminster and Southwark London Borough Council* [2003] EWHC 1350 (Admin), [2003] All ER (D) 163 (May), Admin Ct.
[2]   English Code, para 10.45.
[3]   *R v Newham London Borough Council ex p London Borough of Tower Hamlets* [1991] 1 WLR 1032, CA.

8.63 In *R (Kensington & Chelsea Royal London Borough Council) v Ealing London Borough Council*[1], the applicant had first made an earlier application for homelessness assistance to Ealing London Borough Council, which had accepted that it owed her the main housing duty and made her an offer of accommodation. She had refused the offer and so the main housing duty owed to her by Ealing had come to an end[2]. She made then made a new application for homelessness assistance to Kensington & Chelsea Royal London Borough Council, which made inquiries into the reason why she had refused Ealing's offer of accommodation and concluded that she had not become homeless intentionally and that a main housing duty was owed[3]. Since she had no local connection with Kensington & Chelsea, it referred the main housing duty to Ealing under the conditions of referral[4]. Ealing refused to accept the referral, arguing that its main housing duty towards the applicant had come to an end. The judge held that Ealing's earlier discharge did not permit it to refuse the referral. Ealing had not sought argue to that Kensington & Chelsea had made an error of law in its decision-making. It could not therefore refuse the referral.

[1]   [2017] EWHC 24 (Admin), [2017] HLR 13, Admin Ct.
[2]   HA 1996, s 193(7), see **16.142–16.152**.
[3]   HA 1996, s 193(2), see **16.94–16.199**.
[4]   HA 1996, s 198(1) and (2), see CHAPTER **14**.

Applications from owners and tenants

8.64 It is not necessary for someone to be physically without a roof over his or her head in order to make an application for accommodation (or for assistance in obtaining accommodation) which requires consideration under HA 1996, Pt 7[1], or H(W)A 2014, Pt 2. An applicant cannot be treated as having accommodation unless it is accommodation which it would be reasonable for him or her to continue to occupy[2]. Such an applicant may be a freehold owner, long leaseholder or tenant who gives the local housing authority some reason to believe that it is no longer reasonable for him or her to continue occupying the present accommodation. The concept of reasonable continued occupation is discussed in detail elsewhere[3], but obvious examples of those who may be homeless include owners or tenants who might be victims of domestic violence[4], who cannot afford their accommodation, or who experience gross overcrowding or other adverse physical conditions[5].

[1]   As amended by HRA 2017 for applications for homelessness assistance made to local housing authorities in England on or after 3 April 2018.
[2]   HA 1996, s 175(3); H(W)A 2014, s 55(3).
[3]   See **10.73–10.134**.
[4]   HA 1996, s 177(1), see **10.79–10.91**; H(W)A 2014, s 57(1), see **10.79–10.80** and **10.97–10.98**. Such a scenario occurred in the *LGO investigation into complaint against Wiltshire Council*, 12 011 081, 16 July 2013, (2013) November *Legal Action*, p 32, although on the facts and the law at that time, Wiltshire Council had not made an error when it concluded that the applicant was not likely to be subject to violence or domestic violence if she continued to occupy her accommodation.
[5]   The Local Government Ombudsman found maladministration where a council tenant, having decided that it was no longer reasonable for her to continue to occupy her accommodation, tried to make an application for homelessness assistance and the local housing authority informed her that, as a secure council tenant, she was unable to make an application: *Complaint against Croydon London Borough Council*, 14 016 826, 8 January 2016 (2016) June *Legal Action*, p 42.

8.65 Local housing authorities need particular sensitivity to this type of application where an applicant is an existing tenant of that local housing authority. Local housing authorities should be aware that an application for alternative accommodation from one of their existing tenants might, in reality, be an application for homelessness assistance if the tenant is saying that it is not reasonable for him or her to continue to occupy the existing home. Generally, a local housing authority is entitled to presume that an application for a transfer from one of its existing tenants is exactly that – an application for a transfer – rather than an application under HA 1996, Pt 7[1], or H(W)A 2014, Pt 2[2]. However, where, from the circumstances of the application, it is clear that the tenant is saying that it is not reasonable for him or her to continue in occupation, the local housing authority would be in breach of its statutory duty if it treated the application as a simple application for a transfer rather than also as an application for HA 1996, Pt 7[3], or H(W)A 2014, Pt 2, assistance[4]. An obvious example, where a tenant apparently seeking a transfer is in fact asserting that his or her existing accommodation is not reasonable to continue to occupy, is where the tenant is complaining that he or she has to be transferred because of violence or harassment[5]. It is not necessary for the applicant to spell out that the application should be considered under HA 1996, Pt 7[6], or H(W)A 2014, Pt 2[7]. Where the applicant is complaining about the condition of his or her property, the local housing authority should consider carefully whether it has reason to believe that the accommodation might not be reasonable to continue to occupy, or whether the property could be repaired and it would not be unreasonable to expect the tenant to continue to live in the property until the remedial works have been carried out. If the latter is the case, the low threshold at HA 1996, 183(1), will not be met[8].

1   As amended by HRA 2017 for applications for homelessness assistance made to local housing authorities in England on or after 3 April 2018.
2   *R v Lambeth London Borough Council ex p Pattinson* (1996) 28 HLR 214, QBD.
3   As amended by HRA 2017 for applications for homelessness assistance made to local housing authorities in England on or after 3 April 2018.
4   *R v Islington London Borough Council ex p B* (1998) 30 HLR 706, QBD. See also *R v Sefton Metropolitan Borough Council ex p Healiss* (1995) 27 HLR 34, QBD; *Complaint against Tower Hamlets London Borough Council*, 91/A/2474 and *Complaint against Hounslow London Borough Council*, 99/A/03731. See also the findings of the Commissioner for Complaints relating to the Northern Ireland Housing Executive, where a tenant whose accommodation was unsuitable because of his disability wrote asking to be assessed as homeless, and no inquiries were made promptly: 200700491, 6 November 2008, (2009) April *Legal Action*, p 22 and Public Services Ombudsman for Wales investigation of a *Complaint against Blaenau Gwent County Borough Council*, 09016302, 24 January 2011, (2011) April *Legal Action*, p 30.
5   *Complaint against Hounslow London Borough Council*, 99/A/03731 and *Complaint against Southwark London Borough Council*, 12 011 599, 5 June 2013, (2013) September *Legal Action*, p 30; and *Complaint against Croydon London Borough Council*, 14 016 826, 8 January 2016 (2016) June *Legal Action*, p 42.
6   As amended by HRA 2017 for applications for homelessness assistance made to local housing authorities in England on or after 3 April 2018.
7   *R (Aweys) v Birmingham City Council* [2007] EWHC 52 (Admin), [2007] HLR 27, Admin Ct, later considered by the House of Lords under the name of *Ali v Birmingham City Council* [2009] UKHL 36, [2009] 1 WLR 1506, HL, but not in relation to that specific point. In these seven linked cases, tenants were accepted to be homeless because their tenancies were so overcrowded that it was not reasonable for them, and all the members of their households, to continue to occupy. See **10.122–10.123**.
8   *R (Edwards) v Birmingham City Council* [2016] EWHC 173 (Admin), [2016] HLR 11, Admin Ct per Hickinbottom J at [42].

8.66 Local housing authorities must take exactly the same approach with applications from those who are not existing local housing authority tenants but who apply for accommodation under the local housing authority's ordinary housing allocation scheme. A private sector tenant applying for long-term council accommodation (or for nomination to a private registered provider in England or a registered social landlord in Wales) who writes, on his or her application form, that the application must be considered urgently because the present home is grossly overcrowded, unfit for occupation, or is for some other reason no longer suitable to occupy, must likewise be the subject of inquiries under HA 1996, Pt 7[1], or H(W)A 2014, Pt 2[2]. In *Bury Metropolitan Borough Council v Gibbons*[3], the applicant had completed an application form for HA 1996, Pt 6 accommodation in which he stated that he could not afford his rent and had to move out of his home 15 days later when the notice expired. The Court of Appeal held that the HA 1996, Pt 6 housing application disclosed information triggering an obligation on the local housing authority to make inquiries and, had it done so, it would have concluded that Mr Gibbons was threatened with homelessness and that it owed him a duty to provide advice and assistance[4]. Self-evidently that information was sufficient to give the local housing authority reason to believe that the applicant may be homeless. The applicant did not need to spell out that he or she was applying for consideration under both HA 1996, Pt 6[5] and under HA 1996, Pt 7[6], or

H(W)A 2014, Pt 2[7].

1   As amended by HRA 2017 for applications for homelessness assistance made to local housing
     authorities in England on or after 3 April 2018.
2   Public Services Ombudsman for Wales *Complaint against Conwy County Borough Council*,
     200702044, 11 December 2008, (2009) April *Legal Action*, p 22 and Public Services
     Ombudsman for Wales *Complaint against Cardiff County Council*, 2011/02310, 24 October
     2012, (2012) December *Legal Action*, p 30.
3   [2010] EWCA Civ 327, [2010] HLR 33, CA.
4   HA 1996 s 195(2), as amended by HRA s 4, for applications for homelessness assistance made
     to local housing authorities in England on or after 3 April 2018, and see **15.87–15.137**.
5   See **2.31–2.76**.
6   As amended by HRA 2017 for applications for homelessness assistance made to local housing
     authorities in England on or after 3 April 2018.
7   See also *Complaint against Eastbourne Borough Council*, 14 016 569, 29 February 2016,
     (2016) September *Legal Action*, p 37.

Warnings

8.67 It is a criminal offence for an applicant knowingly or recklessly to make
a false statement in order to induce the local housing authority to believe that
he or she is entitled to accommodation or homelessness assistance. It is also a
criminal offence for the applicant knowingly to withhold information reasonably required by the local housing authority, or to fail to notify the local
housing authority of any change of facts material to his or her case[1]. Local
housing authorities are obliged to explain the duty to notify any change of
facts, and what that means, to each applicant, in ordinary language, and are
encouraged to explain it in a sensitive way, in order to avoid intimidating
applicants[2]. Where a person can show that the explanation was not given, or
that there is some other reasonable excuse for non-compliance, no offence will
have been committed[3].

1   HA 1996, s 214; H(W)A 2014, s 97(1) and (2). See also English Code, para 18.10;
     Welsh Code, paras 15.81–15.83.
2   HA 1996, s 214(2), English Code, para 18.10; H(W)A 2014, s 97(3).
3   HA 1996, s 214(3); H(W)A 2014, s 97(5).

8.68 For local housing authorities in Wales, if a mistake of fact is discovered
after a duty has been accepted, then, in addition to any possible criminal
offences committed, the duty will come to an end[1]. Obviously the 'mistake of
fact' might be an innocent mistake by the applicant or by someone else, in
which case the duty will come to an end, but there will not have been any
criminal offences committed.

1   H(W)A 2014, s 79(3); Welsh Code, paras 15.80–15.83, see **17.193**.

A local housing authority's immediate duties

8.69 As soon as a local housing authority has reason to believe that a person
who has made an application may be homeless or threatened with homelessness, it is obliged to make inquiries into whether the person is eligible for
assistance and, if so, whether any duty is owed to him or her under the
homelessness provisions[1]. The duty to make inquiries cannot be postponed[2].
However, the inquiries could be taken in stages. Since the immediate issue for

a local housing authority will be whether a HA 1996, s 195(2)[3] or H(W)A 2014, s 66(1)[4] prevention duty, or a HA 1996, s 189B(2)[5] or H(W)A 2014, s 73(1)[6] relief duty will be owed, those issues could be determined first. The issues of priority need and whether or not the applicant may have become homeless intentionally could be inquired into at a later stage.

[1] HA 1996, ss 183 and 184(1); H(W)A 2014, ss 62–63 where the terminology used is that the local housing authority in Wales must carry out 'an assessment of a person's case'.

[2] *Robinson v Hammersmith & Fulham London Borough Council* [2006] EWCA Civ 1122, [2007] HLR 7, CA; and *R (Edwards) v Birmingham City Council* [2016] EWHC 173 (Admin), [2016] HLR 11, Admin Ct per Hickinbottom J at [44].

[3] As amended by HRA 2017, s 4(2), for applications to local housing authorities in England made on or after 3 April 2018, see **15.87–15.137**.

[4] See **17.45–17.72**.

[5] As inserted by HRA 2017, s 5(2), for applications to local housing authorities in England made on or after 3 April 2018, see **15.138–15.195**.

[6] See **17.73–17.143**.

8.70 There have been a number of findings of maladministration by the Local Government and Social Care Ombudsman against local housing authorities in England which, instead of considering whether applicants were homeless or might be threatened with homelessness, refused to make inquiries, told applicants that they would not be helped (thereby pre-judging the result of inquiries), or told them that they should make their own accommodation arrangements[1]. The Local Government and Social Care Ombudsmen have indicated that it is essential to good administration that all applicants receive equal treatment, and that their applications are given fair consideration and are properly investigated before decisions are reached[2]. The Public Services Ombudsman for Wales has taken the same approach[3].

[1] *Complaint against Hammersmith & Fulham London Borough Council*, 09001262, 21 January 2010, (2010), March *Legal Action*, p 31; *Complaint against Richmond upon Thames Royal London Borough Council*, 10 009 069, 10 February 2011, (2011) April *Legal Action*, p 30; *Complaint against Islington London Borough Council*, 10 013 025, 24 February 2011, (2011) April *Legal Action*, p 31; *Complaint against Hounslow London Borough Council*, 10 019 388, 5 October 2011, (2011) December *Legal Action*, p 29; *Complaint against Newham London Borough Council*, 11 000 383, 8 March 2012, (2012) May *Legal Action*, p 34; *Complaint against Southwark London Borough Council*, 10 000 27, 10 004 245 and 11 000 195, 22 May 2012, (2012) August *Legal Action*, p 27; *Complaints against Kent County Council*, 09 017 510 and *Dover District Council*, 09 017 512, 31 July 2012, (2012) October *Legal Action*, p 36; *Complaint against Hounslow London Borough Council*, 11 008 191, 28 August 2012, (2012) November *Legal Action*, p 14; *Complaint against Newham London Borough Council*, 11 022 307, 27 November 2012, (2013) January *Legal Action*, p 41; *Complaint against Plymouth City Council*, 13 014 046, (2014) October *Legal Action*, p 50; *Complaint against Wandsworth London Borough Council*, 13 009 118, (2014) November *Legal Action*, p 40; *Complaint against Haringey London Borough Council*, 13 019 000, 10 July 2014, (2015) March *Legal Action*, p 45; *Complaint against Southwark London Borough Council*, 14 002 981, 9 October 2014, (2015) April *Legal Action*, p 46; *Complaint against Eastbourne Borough Council*, 14 016 569, 29 February 2016 (2016) September *Legal Action*, p 37 and *Complaint against Barnet London Borough Council*, 16 002 971, 8 March 2017, (2017) May *Legal Action*, p 42. See also the findings of the Commissioner for *Complaints relating to the Northern Ireland Housing Executive*, 200700491, 6 November 2008, (2009) April *Legal Action*, p 22.

[2] *Complaint against Cheltenham Borough Council*, 88/B/1795.

[3] *Complaint against Cardiff City Council*, 20060749, 16 April 2008, (2008) June *Legal Action*, p 32; *Complaint against Conwy County Borough Council*, 200702044, 11 December 2008, (2009) April *Legal Action*, p 22; *Complaint against Blaenau Gwent County Borough Council*,

09016302, 24 January 2011, (2011) April *Legal Action*, p 30; and *Complaint against Cardiff City Council* 2011/02310, 24 October 2012, (2012) December *Legal Action*, p 30.

8.71 Indeed, both Ombudsmen were so concerned at local housing authorities' failure to comply with their statutory duties, that each one issued a report into those failings. In 2006, the Public Services Ombudsman for Wales published *Housing Allocations and Homelessness: A Special Report by the Local Government Ombudsman for Wales*[1] in which he said 'I have found . . . shortcomings in the manner in which some authorities deal with applicants who approach them claiming to be homeless. Recording practices were found to be wanting as well as in some instances the quality of inquiries and decision making.'

[1]   (2006) Public Services Ombudsman for Wales.

8.72 In 2011, the Local Government Ombudsman published *Homelessness: how councils can ensure justice for homeless people Focus Report: learning the lessons from complaints*[1]. In the Focus Report, the Ombudsman said:

'complaints to the Local Government Ombudsman suggest that people who face homelessness do not always receive the help that they are entitled to from councils. Other organisations have coined the phrase "gatekeeping" to describe where councils refuse to accept a homelessness application or to provide interim accommodation where there is no legitimate reason . . . We know that councils are currently under pressure with limited resources and increasing numbers of people presenting as homeless. To avoid more people suffering personal injustice councils should always properly apply the law in practice.'

[1]   (2011) Local Government Ombudsman.

8.73 Given the absolute duty to make inquiries and, in some cases, to secure interim accommodation when an application for homelessness assistance is made[1], it is essential that local housing authority staff in direct contact with the public are well trained and can recognise and receive applications and ensure that inquiries are put in hand. Far too often, applicants are wrongly turned away by busy or inexperienced reception staff. It is not unknown for applicants to be told:

- 'you need to apply to a different local housing authority';
- 'we do not take homelessness applications from our own tenants';
- 'we only help the priority homeless here';
- 'we cannot help because you have made yourself homeless intentionally'; or
- 'please return with a passport and proof of employment'[2].

All of these responses to an application, and any other similar statements, are wrong in law.

[1]   HA 1996, s 188(1) and (1A) as amended by HRA 2017, s 5(4), for applications for homelessness assistance made to local housing authorities in England on or after 3 April 2018; H(W)A 2014, s 68(1). For interim accommodation duties, see **16.37–16.80** (England) and **17.118–17.134** (Wales).
[2]   For recent examples, see LGO investigations into *Complaint against Haringey London Borough Council*, 13 019 000, 10 July 2014, (2015) March *Legal Action*, p 45; *Complaint against Southwark London Borough Council*, 14 002 981, 9 October 2014, (2015) April *Legal Action*, p 46; *Complaint against Eastbourne Borough Council*, 14 016 569, 29 February

2016 (2016) September *Legal Action*, p 37 and *Complaint against Barnet London Borough Council*, 16 002 971, 8 March 2017, (2017) May *Legal Action*, p 42.

8.74 In January 2015, Shelter Cymru published its *Equal Ground Standard* following consultation with service users and those delivering homelessness services[1]. The Welsh Code advises that local housing authorities in Wales should adopt its recommendations which contain useful standards on treating applicants with respect and with as much openness as possible, so that applicants are equally open and honest[2].

[1]   *Equal Ground Standard, a guide to the service user standard for Welsh homelessness services* (2015, Shelter Cymru).
[2]   Welsh Code, paras 9.32 and 10.16. The *Equal Ground Standard* is at Annex 14 of the Welsh Code.

A local housing authority's first decision: interim accommodation

8.75 The very first issue that a local housing authority must consider when it has received an application for homelessness assistance is whether it has reason to believe that an applicant may be homeless, eligible for assistance and have a priority need[1]. If the local housing authority does have reason to believe that the applicant may fall into all of these categories and the application for homelessness assistance cannot be inquired into and concluded that day[2], it must provide accommodation for the applicant and his or her household pending notification of a decision on the application[3]. That duty cannot be postponed[4]. The threshold trigger is very low: the local housing authority need only have 'reason to believe' that the applicant 'may be' homeless, 'may be' eligible for assistance and 'may' have a priority need[5]. Both Codes remind local housing authorities that 'having reason to believe' is a lower test than 'being satisfied'[6]. If in doubt, interim accommodation should be provided.

[1]   A local housing authority in England will not need to consider whether it has reason to believe that an applicant may have a priority need if the applicant is making a new application for homelessness assistance within two years of having accepted a private rented sector offer from a local housing authority: HA 1996, ss 188(1A) and 195A, see **8.100–8.107** and **16.47–16.50**.
[2]   In one case, a judge said that an applicant had 'a highly arguable case that no s 184 inquiry was ever conducted' where the local housing authority had issued what purported to be a decision made under HA 1996, s 184(3) on the same day as the applicant had made his application for homelessness assistance: *R (IA) v Westminster City Council* [2013] EWHC 1273 (Admin), (2013) July/August *Legal Action*, p 23, Admin Ct.
[3]   HA 1996, s 188(1) as amended by HRA 2017, s 5(4) for applications for homelessness assistance made to local housing authorities in England on or after 3 April 2018; H(W)A 2014, s 68(1) and (2). See also English Code, paras 18.27–18.28; Welsh Code, paras 11.3–11.4; and see **16.37–16.80** (England) and **17.118–17.134** (Wales).
[4]   In *R (Ho-Sang) v Lewisham London Borough Council* (2004) CO 5562/03, (2004) July *Legal Action*, p 19, Admin Ct, the local housing authority conceded that it was in breach of its statutory duty by not immediately providing accommodation in those circumstances. See the Local Government Ombudsman's investigations into *Complaint against Southwark London Borough Council*, 12 011 599, 5 June 2013, (2013) September *Legal Action*, p 30; *Complaint against Plymouth City Council*, 13 014 046, (2014) October *Legal Action*, p 50; *Complaint against Wandsworth London Borough Council*, 13 009 118, (2014) November *Legal Action*, p 40; *Complaint against Haringey London Borough Council*, 13 019 000, 10 July 2014, (2015) March *Legal Action*, p 45; *Complaint against Southwark London Borough Council*, 14 002 981, 9 October 2014, (2015) April *Legal Action*, p 46; *Complaint against Eastbourne Borough Council*, 14 016 569, 29 February 2016 (2016) September *Legal Action*, p 37 and *Complaint against Barnet London Borough Council*, 16 002 971, 8 March 2017, (2017) May *Legal Action*, p 42. The Ombudsman ordered a total of £10,100 to be paid by two councils

where a homeless 16-year-old had had to sleep in a tent, and occasionally on friends' sofa, for nine months: *Complaints against Kent County Council,* 09 017 510 and *Dover District Council,* 09 017 512, 31 July 2012, (2012) October *Legal Action,* p 36. A *Serious Case Review in respect of 'Robert'* by North Yorkshire Safeguarding Adult Board, November 2012, was an investigation into the circumstances of the death of a long-term rough sleeper ('Robert') who had died after two local housing authorities had failed to secure interim accommodation for him.

5   *R (Aweys) v Birmingham City Council* [2007] EWHC 52 (Admin), [2007] HLR 27, Admin Ct, at [8]–[9] per Collins J. The case was later considered by the House of Lords under the name of *Ali v Birmingham City Council* [2009] UKHL 36, HL, but not in relation to that specific point. See also *R (Kelly & Mehari) v Birmingham City Council* [2009] EWHC 3240 (Admin), (2010) January *Legal Action,* p 35, Admin Ct. See **16.37** (England) and **17.118** (Wales).

6   English Code, para 15.5; Welsh Code, paras 11.3–11.4.

8.76 It was suggested in one case that a local housing authority was encouraging its officers to make decisions on applications for homelessness assistance on the same day as the application was received, so that the duty to secure interim accommodation in HA 1996, s 188(1) would not arise. The judge said:

'there is no doubt that a blanket "same day" policy, which requires a decision on the homeless application and, in consequence, the interim accommodation all in one day would be unlawful . . . it would only be "in the most straightforward of cases that a decision can be reached on the same day as the application itself"[1].'

1   *R (Khazai & others) v Birmingham City Council* [2010] EWHC 2576 (Admin) (2011) December *Legal Action,* p 37, Admin Ct per Foskett J at [47]; and *R (IA) v Westminster City Council* [2013] EWHC 1273 (Admin), (2013) July/August *Legal Action,* p 23, Admin Ct. In *R (Edwards) v Birmingham City Council* [2016] EWHC 173 (Admin), [2016] HLR 11, Admin Ct, Hickinbottom J found that there was no evidence that Birmingham City Council's current practices reflected a systematic failure of its duties under HA 1996, Pt 7. See also Welsh Code, para 11.4.

Repeat applications

8.77 There is no bar on someone who has made an earlier application for homelessness assistance, and had that application determined by the local housing authority, from re-applying to the same local housing authority for accommodation (or assistance in obtaining accommodation) at any later time[1]. The local housing authority must accept the application if there is reason to believe the applicant may be homeless or threatened with homelessness.

1   English Code, para 18.11.

Local housing authorities in England

8.78 For local housing authorities in England, there is nothing in HA 1996, Pt 7[1], that cuts down the right to make such repeat applications[2]. Indeed, HA 1996, Pt 7[3], specifically states that even a person whose previous application resulted in a local housing authority owing him or her the main housing duty can make a fresh application when that duty ends[4].

1   As amended by HRA 2017 for applications for homelessness assistance made to local housing authorities in England on or after 3 April 2018.

2   See English Code paras 18.11–18.13

3   As amended by HRA 2017 for applications for homelessness assistance made to local housing authorities in England on or after 3 April 2018.
4   HA 1996, s 193(9). See *R (Dumbaya) v Lewisham London Borough Council* [2008] EWHC 1852 (Admin) (2008) September *Legal Action*, p 25, Admin Ct; and *R (Dragic) v Wandsworth London Borough Council* [2012] EWHC 1241 (Admin), (2012) July *Legal Action*, p 42, Admin Ct.

8.79 In these circumstances it has been left to the courts to work out sensible limits to protect local housing authorities from having to investigate fully what are essentially repetitive applications. The broad rule established by the courts is that a local housing authority is entitled to preface any inquiries into a repeat application by simply considering whether the relevant factual circumstances have changed since the previous application was disposed of.

8.80 If there has been no factual change, the local housing authority is entitled to refuse to entertain the application and to rely on its previous decision (including any previous decision that the local housing authority's duty to the applicant had been discharged)[1]. If, however, there has been such a factual change of circumstances, the local housing authority can no longer rely on its previous decision and must make inquiries into the application in the usual way[2]. In *R v Harrow London Borough Council ex p Fahia*[3], the House of Lords held that there were no administrative short cuts available which would enable a local housing authority to avoid the duty to make at least that level of inquiries into a repeat application[4].

1   See *Johnston v Westminster City Council* [2015] EWCA Civ 554, [2015] HLR 35, CA, where the local housing authority agreed that the applicant could make a fresh application for homelessness assistance.
2   *R v Harrow London Borough Council ex p Fahia* [1998] 1 WLR 1396, (1998) 30 HLR 1124, HL.
3   [1998] 1 WLR 1396, (1998) 30 HLR 1124, HL.
4   See also *R (SD) v Oxford City Council* [2015] EWHC 1871 (Admin), (2015) October *Legal Action*, Admin Ct, where Ouseley J held that 'in order to decide whether it is an application, the sort of investigations envisaged by the later stages of the Act have to be gone through' at [20], see **8.42–8.44**.

8.81 The Court of Appeal applied this approach in *Begum v Tower Hamlets London Borough Council*[1]. Unless a repeat application discloses no new facts on the application form, or any new facts that are disclosed are merely fanciful or trivial, the local housing authority must accept the application, make its inquiries, comply with any other statutory duties that might arise (such as securing accommodation) and notify its decision in accordance with HA 1996, Pt 7. The English Code reflects this approach[2].

1   [2005] EWCA Civ 340, [2005] 1 WLR 2103, [2005] HLR 34, CA.
2   English Code, para 18.11.

8.82 Prior to the decision in *Begum v Tower Hamlets London Borough Council*[1], most local housing authorities were only prepared to accept repeat applications if there had been a 'material change of circumstances'. There was also a practice of asking repeat applicants if they had obtained and occupied settled accommodation since their earlier applications. The former approach was overruled by *Begum v Tower Hamlets London Borough Council*[2], and the latter practice is no longer appropriate. Unless a repeat application is based on precisely the same facts as an earlier application when that application was finally disposed of, then it should be accepted. Situations in which two applications for homelessness assistance are 'exactly the same' as likely to be rare[3]. Intervening settled accommodation might be a factor distinguishing the second application from the first, requiring a local housing authority to accept and determine a fresh application[4]. Equally, it is not the only factor.

1   [2005] EWCA Civ 340, [2005] 1 WLR 2103, [2005] HLR 34, CA.
2   [2005] EWCA Civ 340, [2005] 1 WLR 2103, [2005] HLR 34, CA.
3   *Begum v Tower Hamlets London Borough Council* [2005] EWCA Civ 340, [2005] 1 WLR 2103, [2005] HLR 34, CA per Neuberger LJ at [53].
4   The English Code gives as an example of a factual change of circumstances a further application following a relationship breakdown (English Code, para 18.13). Obviously, this does not exclude other factual changes in circumstances.

8.83 The various duties under HA 1996, Pt 7[1] can come to an end when the applicant refuses an offer of suitable accommodation that meets certain statutory requirements[2]. Can the applicant make a further application for homelessness assistance in those circumstances? The starting point will be for the local housing authority to consider whether the application is based on precisely the same facts as the previous application at the time when that previous application was disposed of. The English Code advises:

> '[i]n the majority of re-application cases where the applicant has previously refused an offer of suitable accommodation, the housing authority will be entitled to rely on the ending of its duties following the refusal of accommodation. However, if after the refusal of accommodation, the applicant's factual circumstances change, the housing authority can no longer rely on the completion of the earlier duty and must consider the fresh application[3].'

1   As amended by HRA 2017 for applications for homelessness assistance made to local housing authorities in England on or after 3 April 2018.
2   The HA 1996, s 195(2) (as amended by HRA 2017, s 4(2), for applications for homelessness assistance made to local housing authorities in England on or after 3 April 2018) prevention duty comes to an end when the local housing authority is satisfied that the applicant has refused an offer of suitable accommodation that would be available for at least six months: HA 1996, s 195(8)(d) (as amended by HRA 2017, s 4(2), for applications for homelessness assistance made to local housing authorities in England on or after 3 April 2018), see **15.118–15.122**. The HA 1996, s 189B(2) (as inserted by HRA 2017, s 5(2), for applications for homelessness assistance made to local housing authorities in England on or after 3 April 2018) relief duty comes to an end when the local housing authority is satisfied that the applicant has refused an offer of suitable accommodation that would be available for at least six months: HA 1996, s 189B(7)(c) (as inserted by HRA 2017, s 4(2), for applications for homelessness assistance made to local housing authorities in England on or after 3 April 2018) see **15.169–15.173**, or he or she has refused a final accommodation offer or a final Pt 6 offer: HA 1996, s 189B(9)(a) (as inserted by HRA 2017, s 4(2), for applications for homelessness assistance made to local housing authorities in England on or after 3 April 2018) see **15.181–15.188**. The HA 1996, s 193(2), main housing duty comes to an end when the local housing authority is satisfied that the applicant has refused a suitable offer of accommodation made under HA 1996, s 193(2), or a suitable offer of HA 1996, Part 6 accommodation or a private rented sector offer: HA 1996, s 193(5), (7) and (7AA), see **16.114–16.123, 16.142–16.152** and **16.163–16.179**.
3   English Code, para 18.12.

Local housing authorities in Wales

8.84 For local housing authorities in Wales, H(W)A 2014, Pt 2, has put the test on a statutory footing. Under H(W)A 2014, s 62(1) and (2), the duty to carry out an assessment of a person's case does not arise if the person has been assessed by a local housing authority on a previous occasion and the local housing authority is satisfied (i) that the person's circumstances have not changed materially since that assessment was carried out; and (ii) there is no new information that materially affects that assessment. If the answer is that the applicant's circumstances have not changed materially and there is no new information, the local housing authority can refuse to accept the new application for homelessness assistance[1]. There is no provision at H(W)A 2014, s 62(2), for the local housing authority to notify the prospective applicant that it has decided that these conditions are satisfied, and that it will not carry out an assessment of his or her case. It follows that there is no right for the prospective applicant to request a review of the decision not to carry out an assessment[2], and so any challenge to that decision would have to be brought by judicial review[3].

1 See Welsh Code, paras 10.11–10.12.
2 See H(W)A 2014, s 85, for the right to request a review and **19.70–19.85**.
3 See **19.306–19.333** for judicial review.

Factual changes

8.85 As explained[1], the effect of the decisions in *R v London Borough of Harrow ex p Fahia*[2] and *Begum v Tower Hamlets London Borough Council*[3] is that a local housing authority in England must ask, on a repeat application for homelessness assistance, whether there has been any change in relevant facts since the previous application was disposed of. A local housing authority in Wales must ask whether the applicant for homelessness assistance was assessed by a local housing authority on a previous occasion, whether the local housing authority is satisfied that the applicant's circumstances have not changed materially since that assessment was carried out and whether there is any new information that materially affects that assessment[4].

1 See **8.80–8.82**.
2 [1998] 1 WLR 1396, (1998) 30 HLR 1124, HL.
3 [2005] EWCA Civ 340, [2005] 1 WLR 2103, [2005] HLR 34, CA.
4 H(W)A 2014, s 62(1) and (2); Welsh Code, paras 10.11–10.12.

8.86 In *R v London Borough of Harrow ex p Fahia*[1], the applicant had occupied guest house accommodation originally provided by the local housing authority while it was making inquiries into her first application. After the local housing authority had decided that she had become homeless intentionally, she had been permitted by the guest house manager to stay on. She claimed housing benefit in order to pay the rent. Over a year later, she was asked to leave the guest house and applied again to the local housing authority. The local housing authority's refusal to accept her application was quashed as there had been a relevant change in her factual circumstances. The local housing authority had failed to address itself to whether the loss of the non-settled accommodation was a new or supervening event causing a new incidence of homelessness.

1 *R v London Borough of Harrow ex p Fahia* [1998] 1 WLR 1396, (1998) 30 HLR 1124, HL.

8.87 In *Begum v Tower Hamlets London Borough Council*[1], the presence of two additional adults in the applicant's accommodation, rendering it over-crowded, was a relevant change of factual circumstances sufficient for the local housing authority to have to accept a further application[2].

[1]   [2005] EWCA Civ 340, [2005] HLR 34, CA.
[2]   See **10.122–10.123**.

8.88 The Court of Appeal's decision in *Begum v Tower Hamlets London Borough Council*[1] on repeat applications was applied in *R (May) v Birmingham City Council*[2]. In that case, the local housing authority had accepted that it owed a HA 1996, s 193(2), main housing duty to the applicant. It made the applicant an offer of accommodation which she refused. She was at the time living with her grandmother. The local housing authority notified the applicant that it had decided that its main housing duty had come to an end as a result of her refusal of the offer. The applicant continued to live with her grandmother. Ten months later, the grandmother required the applicant and her children to leave and the applicant tried to make a fresh application for homelessness assistance. The local housing authority refused to accept the application stating that it was not satisfied that there had been a relevant change of circumstances. The judge held that the local housing authority's decision was irrational and that the circumstances of the applicant were not exactly the same as when she had made her first application for homelessness assistance. Accordingly, the local housing authority was obliged to accept a further application for homelessness assistance[3].

[1]   [2005] EWCA Civ 340, [2005] 1 WLR 2103, [2005] HLR 34, CA.
[2]   [2012] EWHC 1399 (Admin) (2012) July *Legal Action*, p 41, Admin Ct. See also *R (Daie) v Camden London Borough Council* [2006] EWHC 452 (Admin), (2006) May *Legal Action*, p 34, Admin Ct, where permission was given for an applicant to bring judicial review proceedings where the local housing authority had refused to accept a second application saying that there had been no 'material change of circumstances'. By the time that the judicial review claim came to a full hearing, the local housing authority had not only accepted the second application but had also concluded that the applicant was owed the HA 1996, s 193(2), main housing duty.
[3]   It should be noted that the local housing authority had notified the applicant that she was entitled to a review of its decision that there had been no relevant change of circumstances and the applicant had requested a review. This was plainly the wrong procedure since a decision that an application will not be accepted is not one of the decisions of which the applicant has a right to request a review at HA 1996, s 202(1) (see **19.12–19.69** (England) and **19.70–19.85** (Wales)). This was recognised by the applicant's legal representatives, who brought proceedings in judicial review in order to challenge the decision.

8.89 Case-law decided under the old test of material change of circumstances had held that events that might have been sufficient to require a local housing authority to entertain a second application included:

• the breakdown of the applicant's marriage[1];
• the award of Disability Living Allowance for night-time supervision (so that an applicant who originally needed one bedroom now needed two-bedroom accommodation)[2];
• a threat of possession proceedings combined with overcrowded accommodation[3]; and

- where a medical report showed that an applicant's health was poor and deteriorating and contained additional material relevant to the original decision that the applicant had become homeless intentionally (a case said to be unusual on its facts)[4]. Any of these circumstances would now be instances of changes in relevant facts.

---

[1] *R v Basingstoke and Deane Borough Council ex p Bassett* (1983) 10 HLR 125, QBD.
[2] *Ali v Camden London Borough Council* (1998) October *Legal Action*, p 22, Central London County Court.
[3] *R (Jeylani) v Waltham Forest London Borough Council* [2002] EWHC 487 (Admin), (2002) May *Legal Action*, p 30, Admin Ct.
[4] *R (Van der Stolk) v Camden London Borough Council* [2002] EWHC 1621 (Admin), (2002) July *Legal Action*, p 26, Admin Ct.

8.90 Changes of circumstances which, on their facts, the courts found, under the old test, were not sufficient to give rise to a duty to entertain a second application included:

- the illness and death of a friend who had been providing unsettled accommodation[1];
- pregnancy of the applicant[2];
- the failure of an arrangement made by a prisoner for his sister to pay the rent during his sentence[3]; and
- disrepair to the applicant's home[4].

Many of these would now constitute changed factual circumstances requiring the local housing authority to entertain a new application under the modern approach.

---

[1] *R v Brighton Borough Council ex p Harvey* (1997) 30 HLR 670, QBD.
[2] *R v Hackney London Borough Council ex p Ajayi* (1997) 30 HLR 473, QBD.
[3] *Stewart v Lambeth London Borough Council* [2002] EWCA Civ 753, [2002] HLR 40, CA.
[4] *R (Campbell) v Enfield London Borough Council* [2001] EWHC 357 (Admin).

8.91 Cases where the courts have held that, on their facts, there are new factual circumstances are:

- where the applicant had refused an offer of accommodation, then spent a period in overcrowded accommodation before making a fresh application when the overcrowding worsened[1];
- where the applicant had refused an offer of accommodation, and then spent ten months living with her grandmother before the relationship broke down and her grandmother asked her to leave[2];
- where an applicant who had been found not to be vulnerable or at risk of suicide presented fresh evidence of suicidal ideation[3];
- where the applicant's husband and three of the couple's nine children had moved out[4]; and
- where the applicant had been evicted from the property from which she had previously refused an offer of accommodation[5].

---

[1] *Begum v Tower Hamlets London Borough Council* [2005] EWCA Civ 340, [2005] HLR 34, CA.
[2] *R (May) v Birmingham City Council* [2012] EWHC 1399 (Admin), (2012) July *Legal Action*, p 41, Admin Ct.
[3] *R (Hoyte) v Southwark London Borough Council* [2016] EWHC 1665 (Admin), [2016] HLR 35, Admin Ct.

4 *R (Abdulrahman) v Hillingdon London Borough Council* [2016] EWHC 2647 (Admin), [2017] HLR 1, Admin Ct.
5 *R (Kensington & Chelsea Royal London Borough Council) v Ealing London Borough Council* [2017] EWHC 24 (Admin), [2017] HLR 13, Admin Ct, see **14.181**.

Abandoned and withdrawn applications

8.92 Having made an application, an individual may decide not to proceed with it or otherwise be unable to proceed with it. Although this must be commonplace, there is no statutory process for local housing authorities in England to deal with the deemed abandonment or withdrawal of applications. In the absence of such provision, local housing authorities will want to make sensible practical arrangements. For local housing authorities in Wales, H(W)A 2014, Pt 2, provides that any duties owed to the applicant will come to an end if the local housing authority is satisfied that the applicant has withdrawn his or her application and the applicant has been notified by the local housing authority to that effect[1].

1 H(W)A 2014, ss 79(1), (4) and 84; Welsh Code, paras 15.84–15.85; see **17.194**. The applicant has the right to request a review of any decision that he or she has withdrawn his or her application: H(W)A 2014, s 85(1)(b), see **19.77–19.80**

8.93 If the applicant dies before a decision is reached on the application, the local housing authority can simply substitute (with that person's consent) another member of the late applicant's household as applicant[1].

1 As was done in *R v Camden London Borough Council ex p Hersi* (2001) 33 HLR 577, CA; English Code, para 18.15.

8.94 Each local housing authority will have its own procedures and policies for allowing applicants to withdraw their own applications[1].

1 English Code, para 18.14; Welsh Code, para 10.84.

8.95 More controversial is the question of whether there are circumstances in which the local housing authority may itself treat an application as withdrawn. The English Code recommends that local housing authorities may wish to consider an application as 'closed' where there has been no contact from the applicant for three months or longer and that any further approach after that time may be treated as a fresh application; the Welsh Code gives a period of six weeks. If the applicant renews contact during the suggested period, the suggestion is that the local housing authority should resume its original inquiries, and consider all relevant matters, including whether there are any relevant new facts that affect those inquiries[1].

1 English Code, para 18.14; Welsh Code, para 10.84.

8.96 That guidance is somewhat at variance with HA 1996, Pt 7[1], which recognises that contact will be lost with at least some applicants, because it makes special provision for notice of decisions on applications to be retained for later collection at the local housing authority's offices[2]. This would suggest that the proper course is for every application to result in a decision even if the decision is that, on the material available to the local housing authority, it is not satisfied that the applicant is homeless or threatened with homelessness. This has the additional advantage of enabling a local housing authority to maintain comprehensive statistics for decisions on all applications (and the time it takes to reach them).

1   As amended by HRA 2017 for applications for homelessness assistance made to local housing authorities in England or after 3 April 2018.
2   HA 1996, ss 184(6) and 203(8).

Simultaneous applications to the same local housing authority

8.97 What happens when an applicant has made an application for homelessness assistance and the decision-making process (or any legal challenges to decisions made on the application) have not been concluded before another application is made to the same local housing authority? That was the case in *R (Konodyba) v Kensington & Chelsea Royal London Borough Council*[1] where the applicant had been notified of a decision that she was not eligible for assistance, had requested a review which upheld the original decision, had appealed unsuccessfully against the review decision to the county court and had applied for permission to appeal to the Court of Appeal. In the meantime, she had indicated to the local housing authority that she wished to make a fresh application for homelessness assistance because the legal position regarding eligibility had changed. The local housing authority responded that, while the applicant had an outstanding application for homelessness assistance, which was currently the subject of an application to the Court of Appeal for permission to appeal, she could not make a fresh application and that a local housing authority cannot entertain two applications for homelessness assistance at the same time.

1   [2011] EWHC 2653 (Admin), (2011) December *Legal Action*, p 30, Admin Ct.

8.98 The applicant then brought a judicial review claim challenging the local housing authority's refusal to secure interim accommodation[1] for her pending notification of a decision on her asserted new application. At an early stage in the case, a deputy High Court judge considered whether the claimant had a strong prima facie claim and found, for a number of reasons, that she did not. There was a discussion as to whether or not an application for homelessness assistance could be made when the previous application was still subject to legal proceedings. The judge said:

> '[i]f there is arguably a significant change in the circumstances there would be merit in the authority taking a fresh decision on that basis, particularly if the previous application is out of their hands because it is under appeal. If the fresh application is successful, it might render the appeal otiose and thus avoid the time and expense of the appeal being determined. If it is unsuccessful, why should the applicant be prejudiced by having had to withdraw his appeal which might otherwise have succeeded. On the other hand, how is an authority to decide if a new application is or is not on exactly the same facts as the previous one . . . If the further application is accepted on the grounds that it is not on exactly the same facts as the previous one, would the authority have to carry out the same statutory inquiries as in the former application, even on matters where it is not said that there had been any change . . . On this approach, and where the first application is under appeal,

it could lead to the appeal being pursued on a factual basis which is inconsistent with the facts of any subsequent application[2].'

---

1   HA 1996, s 188(1). See **16.37–16.80**.
2   HHJ Robinson at [53].

8.99 The judge found that it was arguable that the refusal to accept a second application for homelessness assistance in these circumstances was based on a misconstruction of HA 1996, Pt 7[1].

---

1   It should be noted that the facts of this case are unusual. The applicant's principal argument – that she was eligible for assistance (see Chapter **11**) – had been rejected by Kensington & Chelsea Royal London Borough Council, an appeal against that review decision was dismissed by a county court judge, she was granted permission to appeal the decision of the county court judge and in the Court of Appeal abandoned the main point on which she relied. The Court of Appeal dismissed the appeal, treating it as abandoned. On her second application to Kensington & Chelsea Royal London Borough Council, she sought to raise the same point on eligibility that she had abandoned before the Court of Appeal. The local housing authority found that she was not eligible; a county court judge dismissed her appeal against that decision and the Court of Appeal decided that she could not rely on a legal point that she had previously had the opportunity to raise and had abandoned (*Konodyba v Royal Borough of Kensington & Chelsea* [2012] EWCA Civ 982, [2012] HLR 45, CA).

Re-applying to a local housing authority in England within two years of acceptance of a private rented sector offer

8.100 Applicants:

*   who made an application for homelessness assistance to a local housing authority in England on or after 9 November 2012;
*   who accepted a private rented sector offer which brought the HA 1996, s 193(2), main housing duty triggered by that application to an end[1];
*   the private rented sector tenancy has subsequently come to an end;
*   have a right to make a further application for homelessness assistance[2].

---

1   HA 1996, s 193(7AA)–(7AC). See **16.161–16.180**.
2   HA 1996, s 193(9); English Code, paras 18.16–18.26.

8.101 If the application is made within two years of the date of the applicant's acceptance of the private rented sector offer, the applicant will be entitled to the HA 1996, s 193(2), main housing duty if the applicant is eligible for assistance, homeless, and did not become homeless intentionally[1]. In other words, the applicant need not still have a priority need in order to be entitled to the HA 1996, s 193(2), main housing duty again.

---

1   HA 1996, s 195A(1) as amended by HRA 2017, s 4(4) for applications for homelessness assistance made to local housing authorities in England on or after 3 April 2018.

8.102 This special provision will not apply where an applicant would only be entitled to the HA 1996, s 193(2), main housing duty again because of the presence in the applicant's household of a restricted person[1]. Where the applicant is homeless because of the presence in his or her household of a restricted person, he or she has to have a priority need in order to be entitled to the HA 1996, s 193(2), main housing duty.

¹   HA 1996, s 195A(5). For 'restricted person', see HA 1996, s 184(7) and **9.54–9.56** and **11.163–11.167**.

8.103 The special provision only applies once. Where an applicant has been the beneficiary of this special provision and has subsequently accepted another private rented sector offer, which then comes to an end within two years of the date of acceptance, the applicant must make a fresh application for homelessness assistance and would have to have a priority need in order to be entitled to the main housing duty again¹.

¹   HA 1996, s 195A(6).

8.104 The special provision will not apply to applicants whose applications for homelessness assistance are made more than two years after the date of acceptance of a private rented sector offer. Applicants in that position who may be homeless would have to have a priority need to be entitled to the HA 1996, s 193(2), main housing duty. It should be noted that the date from which the 2-year period begins is the date of acceptance of the private rented sector offer, not the date when the tenancy was granted or when the applicant actually moved in¹.

¹   HA 1996, s 195A(1) and (3).

8.105 An applicant who had accepted a private rented sector offer and is subsequently served with a Housing Act 1988, s 21 notice by his or her landlord should make his or her application for homelessness assistance as soon as he or she is served with the notice. Provided that the notice is valid, he or she will be found to be homeless on the date on which the notice expires and the HA 1996, s 189B(2)¹ relief duty will apply².

¹   As inserted by HRA 2017, s 5(2), for applications for homelessness assistance made to local housing authorities in England on or after 3 April 2018, see **15.138–15.195**.
²   For applications for homelessness assistance made on or after 3 April 2018, see **8.100–8.107** and **16.47–16.50**.

8.106 If the local housing authority has reason to believe that the applicant may be homeless, and may be eligible for assistance, it is under a duty to secure interim accommodation¹. There is no need to consider whether or not the applicant may have a priority need. That interim accommodation duty will come to an end when one of the following events occurs, whichever is the later event:

- the local housing authority notifies the applicant of a decision that the HA 1996, s 189B(2)², relief duty is not owed (because either the applicant is not eligible for assistance or is not homeless)³;
- the HA 1996, s 189B(2)⁴, relief duty has come to an end⁵; or
- the local housing authority notifies the applicant of what other duty, if any, will be owed to him or her following the coming to an end of the HA 1996, s 189B(2)⁶, relief⁷.

¹   HA 1996, s 188(1A), as amended by HRA 2017, s 5(4), for applications for homelessness assistance made to local housing authorities in England on or after 3 April 2018, see **16.47–16.50**.

2   As inserted by HRA 2017, s 5(2), for applications for homelessness assistance made to local housing authorities in England on or after 3 April 2018, see **15.138–15.195**.

3   HA 1996, s 188(1ZA)(a) and (1ZB)(a), as inserted by HRA 2017, s 5(4), for applications for homelessness assistance made to local housing authorities in England on or after 3 April 2018, see **16.51–16.80**.

4   As inserted by HRA 2017, s 5(2), for applications for homelessness assistance made to local housing authorities in England on or after 3 April 2018, see **15.138–15.195**.

5   HA 1996, s 188 (1ZB)(b), as inserted by HRA 2017, s 5(4), for applications for homelessness assistance made to local housing authorities in England on or after 3 April 2018, see **16.62–16.65**.

6   As inserted by HRA 2017, s 5(2), for applications for homelessness assistance made to local housing authorities in England on or after 3 April 2018, see **15.138–15.195**.

7   HA 1996, s 188(1ZB)(b), as inserted by HRA 2017, s 5(4), for applications for homelessness assistance made to local housing authorities in England on or after 3 April 2018, see **16.62–16.65**.

8.107 Prior to 3 April 2018[1], HA 1996 s 195A also provided that an applicant who had re-applied within two years of having accepted a private rented sector offer[2], and had been served with a valid Housing Act 1988, s 21, notice, would be threatened with homelessness[3], and that the duty at HA 1996, s 195(2), to take reasonable steps to help the applicant secure that accommodation did not cease to become available would apply whether or not the applicant had a priority need. Since HA 1996, Pt 7, as amended by HRA 2017, now provides that the HA 1996, s 195(2)[4], prevention duty applies to all applicants who are eligible[5] and are threatened with homelessness[6], there is no special provision for applicants who are threatened with homelessness and would have fallen under HA 1996, s 195A[7].

1   When the amendments to HA 1996, Pt 7, inserted by HRA 2017, came into force: the Homelessness Reduction Act 2017 (Commencement and Transitional and Savings Provisions) Regulations 2018, SI 2018/167 at Appendix 2.

2   HA 1996, s 193(7AA), see **16.161–16.180**.

3   HA 1996, s 175(4), see **10.144–10.147**.

4   As amended by HRA 2017, s 4(2), for applications for homelessness assistance made to local housing authorities in England on or after 3 April 2018, see **15.87–15.137**.

5   HA 1996, s 185(2), see Chapter 11.

6   As defined at HA 1996, s 175(4) and (5), as amended and inserted by HRA 2017, ss 1(2) and (3), for applications for homelessness assistance made to local housing authorities in England on or after 3 April 2018, see **10.144–10.147**.

7   See **8.100–8.107**.

Challenges to refusals to accept applications

8.108 If a local housing authority refuses to accept an application for homelessness assistance (and therefore declines to undertake inquiries into it) there is no right to any statutory review of that decision, or appeal against it[1]. The applicant could lodge a complaint through the local housing authority's complaints procedure[2], but if a swifter remedy is needed, the applicant should apply for a judicial review[3] and ask for a mandatory order requiring the local housing authority to accept the application and comply with its consequent statutory duties. Judicial review is also the proper course if the applicant is dissatisfied with a local housing authority's decision that it need not accept an application because it is a repeat application and there is no relevant change of facts[4].

1 Because a refusal to accept an application is not in the list of decisions which carry a right to request a review at HA 1996, s 202(1) as amended by HRA 2017, s 9 for applications for homelessness assistance made to local housing authorities in England on or after 3 April 2 018 (see **19.12–19.69**) or at H(W)A 2014, s 85(1) (see **19.70–19.85**).
2 See **19.333–19.335**.
3 See **19.306–19.353**.
4 See **8.50–8.82** and **8.85–8.91**.

8.109 If the judicial review claim results in the local housing authority being required to entertain and inquire into the application, then a decision must be reached on it by the local housing authority and notified with reasons. The applicant will then be entitled to seek a review of that decision (and, if necessary, appeal) in the usual way[1].

1 See **19.12–19.69** (England) and **19.70–19.85** (Wales).

8.110 Complaint can also be made to the appropriate Ombudsman that the local housing authority is guilty of maladministration by refusing to accept an application for homelessness assistance. In both England and Wales, Ombudsmen have been so concerned at the number of complaints against local housing authorities in this respect that special reports have been published[1].

1 *Homelessness: how councils can ensure justice for homeless people Focus Report: learning the lessons from complaints* (2011) Local Government Ombudsmen; *Housing Allocations and Homelessness: A Special Report by the Local Government Ombudsman for Wales* (2006) Public Services Ombudsman for Wales. See **8.70–8.73**.

Chapter 9

INQUIRIES AND DECISIONS

Contents

INQUIRIES INTO APPLICATIONS

Overview

Local housing authorities in England

9.1 Once a local housing authority in England has reason to believe that a person who has made an application for accommodation (or for assistance in obtaining accommodation) may be homeless or threatened with homelessness, it *must* make inquiries sufficient to enable it to answer three questions:

(1)   whether the applicant is 'eligible' for assistance;

(2)   if so, whether any duty under the Housing Act 1996 (HA 1996) Pt 7[1] is owed to the applicant; and

(3)   if so, what duty is owed[2].

---

[1]   As amended by Homelessness Reduction Act 2017 (HRA 2017) for applications for homelessness assistance made to local housing authorities in England on or after 3 April 2018.

[2]   HA 1996, s 184(1).

9.2 Following the coming into force of the Homelessness Reduction Act 2017 (HRA 2017) on 3 April 2018[1], local housing authorities will owe duties to all eligible[2] applicants who are either threatened with homelessness[3] or homeless[4]. Those duties are:

- to make an assessment of the applicant's case and try to agree a personalised housing plan[5]; and
- if the applicant is threatened with homelessness, to take reasonable steps to help the applicant to secure that accommodation does not cease to become available for his or her accommodation (the HA 1996, s 195(2) prevention duty)[6]; or
- if the applicant is homeless, to take reasonable steps to help the applicant secure that suitable accommodation becomes available for his or her occupation (the HA 1996, s 189B(2) relief duty)[7].

[1]   In force for applications for homelessness assistance made to local housing authorities in England on or after 3 April 2018: Homelessness Reduction Act 2017 (Commencement and Transitional and Savings Provisions) Regulations 2018, SI 2018/167, reg 3; see APPENDIX 2.
[2]   HA 1996, s 185, see CHAPTER 11.
[3]   HA 1996, s 175(4) and (5), as amended and inserted by HRA 2017, s 1(2) and (3), for applications for homelessness assistance made to local housing authorities in England on or after 3 April 2018. See **10.144–10.147** for 'threatened with homelessness'.
[4]   HA 1996, s 175(1)–(3), see CHAPTER 10 for 'homeless'.
[5]   HA 1996, s 189A, as inserted by HRA 2017, s 3(1), for applications for homelessness assistance made to local housing authorities in England on or after 3 April 2018. See **15.62–15.86**.
[6]   HA 1996, s 195(2), as amended by HRA 2017, s 4(2), for applications for homelessness assistance made to local housing authorities in England on or after 3 April 2018. See **15.87–15.137**.
[7]   HA 1996, s 189B(2), as inserted by HRA 2017, s 5(2), for applications for homelessness assistance made to local housing authorities in England on or after 3 April 2018. See **15.138–15.195**.

9.3 The assessment of the applicant's case must include an assessment of:

- the circumstances that have caused the applicant to become homeless or threatened with homelessness;
- the applicant's housing needs, including in particular what accommodation would be suitable for the applicant and for any other relevant persons defined as any persons with whom he or she resides or might reasonably be expected to reside[1]; and
- what support it would be necessary for the applicant and any other relevant persons to have in order to have and retain suitable accommodation[2].

[1]   For 'suitable accommodation' see CHAPTER 18.
[2]   HA 1996, s 189A(2), as inserted by HRA 2017, s 3(1), for applications for homelessness assistance made to local housing authorities in England on or after 3 April 2018. See **15.67–15.69**.

9.4 In practice, the assessment of the applicant's case will inform the local housing authority as to what reasonable steps it should be taking in the performance of either the HA 1996, s 195(2)[1], prevention or HA 1996, s 189B(2)[2], relief duty. It may also contain enough information for the local housing authority to be able to decide what further duty, if any, will be owed if accommodation has not been secured for the applicant at the conclusion of the HA 1996, s 195(2)[3], prevention or HA 1996, s 189B(2)[4], relief duties.[5]

1   As amended by HRA 2017, s 4(2), for applications for homelessness assistance made to local housing authorities in England on or after 3 April 2018. See **15.87–15.137**.

2   As inserted by HRA 2017, s 5(2), for applications for homelessness assistance made to local housing authorities in England on or after 3 April 2018. See **15.138–15.195**.

3   As amended by HRA 2017, s 4(2), for applications for homelessness assistance made to local housing authorities in England on or after 3 April 2018. See **15.87–15.137**.

4   As inserted by HRA 2017, s 5(2), for applications for homelessness assistance made to local housing authorities in England on or after 3 April 2018. See **15.138–15.195**

5   Government guidance advises that, in the case of applications for homelessness assistance by young people aged 16 or 17, the principal responsibility for assessment falls upon children's services (Children Act 1989, ss 17 and 20). However, guidance as to the contents of an assessment where the young person is assessed as part of an application for homelessness assistance is at Chapter 4 of Prevention of Homelessness and Provision of Accommodation for 16 and 17 year old young people who may be homeless and/or require accommodation (MHCLG and Department for Education, April 2018) at CD-rom of this book.

9.5 In addition, if the local housing authority has 'reason to believe' that an applicant 'may be' homeless, eligible for assistance and have a priority need, it has a duty to secure interim accommodation for the applicant and members of the applicant's household[1]. That interim accommodation duty will come to an end when one of the following events occurs, whichever is the later event:

- the local housing authority notifies the applicant of a decision that the HA 1996, s 189B(2)[2], relief duty is not owed (because either the applicant is not eligible for assistance or is not homeless)[3];
- the local housing authority notifying the applicant of a decision that, when the HA 1996, s 189B(2)[4], relief duty comes to an end, it will not owe the applicant any duty under HA 1996, ss 190[5] or 193[6], because it is not satisfied that the applicant has a priority need[7];
- the HA 1996, s 189B(2)[8], relief duty has come to an end[9]; or
- the local housing authority notifies the applicant of what other duty, if any, will be owed to him or her following the coming to an end of the HA 1996, s 189B(2)[10], relief[11].

1   HA 1996, s 188(1), as amended by HRA 2017, s 5(4), for applications for homelessness assistance made to local housing authorities in England on or after 3 April 2018. See **16.37–16.80**.

2   As inserted by HRA 2017, s 5(2), for applications for homelessness assistance made to local housing authorities in England on or after 3 April 2018, see **15.138–15.195**.

3   HA 1996, s 188(1ZA)(a) and (1ZB)(a), as inserted by HRA 2017, s 5(4), for applications for homelessness assistance made to local housing authorities in England on or after 3 April 2018, see **16.51–16.675**.

4   As inserted by HRA 2017, s 5(2), for applications for homelessness assistance made to local housing authorities in England on or after 3 April 2018, see **15.138–15.195**.

5   As amended by HRA 2017, s 5(5), for applications for homelessness assistance made to local housing authorities in England on or after 3 April 2018: duty to accommodate applicants who are homeless, eligible for assistance, have a priority need and have become homeless intentionally, see **16.81–16.93**.

6   Main housing duty to accommodate applicants who are homeless, eligible for assistance, have a priority need and have not become homeless intentionally, see 16.94–16.199.

7   HA 1996, s 188(1ZA)(b), as inserted by HRA 2017, s 5(4), for applications for homelessness assistance made to local housing authorities in England on or after 3 April 2018, see **16.56–16.59**.

8   As inserted by HRA 2017, s 5(2), for applications for homelessness assistance made to local housing authorities in England on or after 3 April 2018, see **15.138–15.195**.

[9] HA 1996, s 188 (1ZB)(b), as inserted by HRA 2017, s 5(4), for applications for homelessness assistance made to local housing authorities in England on or after 3 April 2018, see **16.60–16.65**.

[10] As inserted by HRA 2017, s 5(2), for applications for homelessness assistance made to local housing authorities in England on or after 3 April 2018, see **15.138–15.195**.

[11] HA 1996, s 188(1ZB)(b), as inserted by HRA 2017, s 5(4), for applications for homelessness assistance made to local housing authorities in England on or after 3 April 2018, see **16.60–16.65**.

9.6 It follows that a local housing authority should first make inquiries into whether an applicant is eligible and whether he or she is homeless or threatened with homelessness. The inquiries into whether an applicant has a priority need and whether he or she has become homeless intentionally can be carried out whilst the HA 1996, s 195[1] prevention duty or the HA 1996, s 189B[2] relief duty is being performed[3].

[1] As amended by HRA 2017, s 4(2), for applications for homelessness assistance made to local housing authorities in England on or after 3 April 2018. See **15.87–15.139**.

[2] As inserted by HRA 2017, s 5(2), for applications for homelessness assistance made to local housing authorities in England on or after 3 April 2018. See **15.138–15.195**.

[3] *Homelessness Code of Guidance for Local Authorities* (MHCLG, 2018) (the English Code), para 11.3.

9.7 Separately, a local housing authority in England has a power, but not a duty, to make inquiries into whether the applicant has a local connection with its district and, if not, whether he or she has a local connection elsewhere[1]. This is an entirely discretionary line of inquiry for the local housing authority; it can choose whether or not to make inquiries into local connection, but if it chooses not to do so, the applicant has no right to a review of that decision[2]. There are two occasions when the local housing authority might consider making inquiries into the issue of local connection:

- when making inquiries into whether the applicant is eligible for assistance and is homeless, and would therefore be owed the HA 1996, s 189B(2), relief duty[3]; and
- when making inquiries as to what duty, if any, an applicant would be owed when the HA 1996, s 189B(2) relief duty[4] has been performed and the applicant remains without accommodation, and therefore if he or she is eligible for assistance, has a priority need and has not become homeless intentionally, the HA 1996, s 193(2), main housing duty would be owed[5].

[1] HA 1996, s 184(2).

[2] *Hackney London Borough Council v Sareen* [2003] EWCA Civ 351, (2003) 35 HLR 54, CA.

[3] As inserted by HRA 2017, s 5(2), for applications for homelessness assistance made to local housing authorities in England on or after 3 April 2018. See **15.138–15.195**.

[4] As inserted by HRA 2017, s 5(2), for applications for homelessness assistance made to local housing authorities in England on or after 3 April 2018. See **15.138–15.195**.

[5] See **16.94–16.199**.

9.8 If the conditions for referral at HA 1996, s 198(2)[1], (2ZA)[2] or (4)[3] are made out, then the local housing authority may refer the applicant's case to another local housing authority for either the HA 1996, s 189B(2)[4], relief duty or the HA 1996, s 193(2), main housing duty to be performed[5].

[1] Conditions for referral as a result of local connection, see **14.43–14.122**.

2   Conditions for referral as a result of acceptance of private rented sector offer within two years prior to the date of the application for homelessness assistance, see **14.123–14.137**.

3   Conditions for referral as a result of having been placed by another local housing authority within a prescribed period, see **14.138–14.150**.

4   As inserted by HRA 2017, s 5(2), for applications for homelessness assistance made to local housing authorities in England on or after 3 April 2018. See **15.138–15.195**.

5   HA 1996, s 198(A1), as inserted by HRA 2017, s 5(8), for applications for homelessness assistance made to local housing authorities in England on or after 3 April 2018, permits a local housing authority to refer the HA 1996, s 189B(2) (as inserted by HRA 2017, s 5(2), for applications for homelessness assistance made to local housing authorities in England on or after 3 April 2018) to another local housing authority, see **15.139–15.142** and **16.15**. HA 1996, s 198(1) permits a local housing authority to refer performance of the HA 1996, s 193(2), main housing duty to another local housing authority, see **16.16**.

9.9 The trigger for the making of inquiries into the applicant's eligibility and whether any duty is owed to him or her is extremely low[1]. Any information that causes the local housing authority to have reason to believe that the applicant *may* be homeless or *may* be threatened with homelessness is sufficient. An applicant does not need to be applying explicitly for homelessness assistance.

1   See *R (Aweys) v Birmingham City Council* [2007] EWHC 52 (Admin), [2007] HLR 27, Admin Ct at [8] per Collins J; and *R (Edwards) v Birmingham City Council* [2016] EWHC 173 (Admin), [2016] HLR 11, Admin Ct per Hickinbottom J at [39]. See also **8.75–8.76** and **16.37–16.45**.

9.10 The scope of the compulsory inquiries may appear to be quite limited. For example, inquiries only need be made to determine 'whether' a duty is owed and, therefore, inquiries need not necessarily be made as to the way in which it is appropriate to perform the duty. However, the new HA 1996, s 189A[1] duties to make an assessment of the applicant's case[2] and record a personalised housing plan[3] mean that the local housing authority will be able to gather enough information to enable it to ask, and answer, the statutory questions and also determine how to perform what duty, if any, is owed to the applicant. This is reflected in the new Homelessness Code of Guidance for Local Authorities[4], (the English Code). There is very little guidance on the making of 'inquiries', whereas a chapter is devoted to how to obtain information to be contained in assessments and personalised housing plans[5].

1   As inserted by HRA 2017, s 3(1), for applications for homelessness assistance made to local housing authorities in England on or after 3 April 2018. See **15.62–15.86**.

2   HA 1996, s 189A(1), as inserted by HRA 2017, s 3(1), for applications for homelessness assistance made to local housing authorities in England on or after 3 April 2018. See **15.62–15.86**.

3   HA 1996, s 189A(4)–(7), as inserted by HRA 2017, s 3(1), for applications for homelessness assistance made to local housing authorities in England on or after 3 April 2018. See **15.72–15.80**.

4   MHCLG 2018

5   English Code, chapter 11.

9.11 The legal obligation is to inquire into the possible application of *every* relevant duty under HA 1996, Pt 7[1] regarding the applicant's circumstances. That would include, for example, whether the duty to protect the applicant's possessions had been triggered[2]. This minimum requirement should not be overlooked.

¹   As amended by HRA 2017, for applications for homelessness assistance made to local housing authorities in England on or after 3 April 2018.
²   HA 1996, s 211, as amended by HRA 2017, s 5(12), for applications for homelessness assistance made to local housing authorities in England on or after 3 April 2018. See **16.228–16.309**.

Local housing authorities in Wales

9.12 As with local housing authorities in England, once a person has applied to a local housing authority in Wales for accommodation, or for help in retaining or obtaining accommodation, and it appears to the local housing authority that he or she may be homeless¹, or threatened with homelessness², the local housing authority must assess whether or not the applicant is eligible for help³. The only circumstance in which the local housing authority can refuse to carry out an assessment of the person's case is if it is satisfied that the person's circumstances have not changed materially since that assessment was carried out, and there is no new information that materially affects that assessment⁴.

¹   As defined at Housing (Wales)Act 2014 (H(W)A 2014), ss 55–57, see Chapter 10.
²   As defined at H(W)A 2014, s 55(4), see **10.144–10.147**.
³   H(W)A 2014, s 62(1).
⁴   H(W)A 2014, s 62(2), see **8.80–8.82** and **8.85–8.91**.

9.13 While it is assessing that initial issue¹, or once it has assessed that the applicant is eligible for help, the local housing authority should also assess:

(1)   the circumstances that caused the applicant to be homeless or threatened with homelessness²;

(2)   the applicant's housing needs and those of the applicant's household³;

(3)   the support needed for the applicant and his or her household to be able to retain accommodation which is currently available, or which may become available⁴; and

(4)   whether or not the local housing authority has any duty to the applicant under H(W)A 2014, Pt 2⁵.

¹   *Code of Guidance for Local Authorities on the Allocation of Accommodation and Homelessness* (Welsh Government, March 2016), (the Welsh Code), see the CD Rom with this book. Paragraphs 10.15–10.16 make the point that 'provisions of eligibility are complex and may take some time to assess' and so the assessment of the other matters should take place whilst the local housing authority is assessing eligibility.
²   H(W)A 2014, s 62(5)(a); Welsh Code, paras 10.21–10.22.
³   H(W)A 2014, s 62(5)(b); Welsh Code, paras 10.23–10.24.
⁴   H(W)A 2014, s 62(5)(c); Welsh Code, paras 10.25–10.29.
⁵   H(W)A 2014, s 62(5)(d); Welsh Code, paras 10.30–10.31.

9.14 In order to be able to complete its assessment, the local housing authority in Wales must seek to identify the outcome that the applicant wishes to achieve. It should also assess whether exercising any of the local housing authority's functions under Housing (Wales) Act 2014, Pt 2 (H(W)A 2014) could contribute to the achievement of that outcome¹. Templates for assessment can be found at Annexes 15–17 of the Welsh Code².

1   H(W)A 2014, s 62(6); Welsh Code, paras 10.32–10.38. The Code advises; '[t]he Act is clear
     that there is no expectation that the Authority must meet the wishes of the applicant unless it
     is able to do so within the functions detailed in the chapter and within the constraints of the
     local housing market and their own resources' (para 10.36).
2   See the CD Rom with this book.

Structure of this chapter and terminology

9.15 The terminology used by HA 1996, Pt 7¹, and by H(W)A 2014, Pt 2, is
somewhat confusing. Local housing authorities in England are required to
make 'inquiries' into the various matters required at HA 1996, s 184(1). If
those inquiries result in a decision that an applicant is eligible and is either
threatened with homelessness, or homeless, then the local housing authority
has a duty at HA 1996, s 189A(1), to make 'an assessment of the applicant's case'². The 'assessment' of the applicant's case, and associated personalised housing plan, will assist the local housing authority in its decision as to
how to perform any duty owed to the applicant.

1   As amended by HRA 2017 for applications for homelessness assistance made to local housing
     authorities in England on or after 3 April 2018.
2   HA 1996, s 189A(1), as inserted by HRA 2017, s 3(1), for applications for homelessness
     assistance made to local housing authorities in England on or after 3 April 2018. See
     15.62–15.86.

9.16 However, H(W)A 2014, s 62, requires a local housing authority in Wales
to 'carry out an assessment of a person's case' in order to decide whether an
applicant is eligible for help and, if so, whether the local housing authority has
any duty to the applicant¹. H(W)A 2014, Pt 2, uses the word 'assessment' in
this context to mean the same process as making 'inquiries' under HA 1996,
s 184. If the applicant is assessed as being eligible for help, the local housing
authority must also assess:

- the circumstances that have caused the applicant to be homeless or
  threatened with homelessness;
- the housing needs of the applicant and any person with whom the
  applicant lives or might reasonably be expected to live;
- the support needed for the applicant and any person with whom the
  applicant lives or might reasonably be expected to live to retain
  accommodation which is or may become available; and
- whether or not the authority has any duty to the applicant².

1   H(W)A 2014, s 62(1), (3) and (4), see **9.12–9.14**.
2   H(W)A 2014, s 62(5), see **9.13**.

9.17 H(W)A 2014, Pt 2, uses the word 'assessment' to mean both the process
of making inquiries (into whether the applicant is eligible for help and, if so,
whether the local housing authority has a duty to the applicant) and the
process of drawing up an assessment of the applicant's case in order to assist
the local housing authority in its decision as to how to perform any duty owed
to the applicant.

9.18 Where we use the word 'assessment' in the context of applications for
homelessness assistance made under HA 1996, Pt 7¹, to local housing

authorities in England, we are referring to the assessment of the applicant's case required to be made under HA 1996, s 189A[2]. Where we use the word 'assessment' in the context of applications for homelessness assistance made under H(W)A 2014, Pt 2, to local housing authorities in Wales, we are referring either to the process of 'assessment' in the sense of either making inquiries to establish what duty, if any, is owed to the applicant or to the process of gathering information to assist the local housing authority in deciding how to perform any duty owed.

[1] As amended by HRA 2017 for applications for homelessness assistance made to local housing authorities in England on or after 3 April 2018.

[2] As inserted by HRA 2017, s 3(1), for applications for homelessness assistance made to local housing authorities in England on or after 3 April 2018. See **15.62–15.86**.

9.19 Considerable guidance as to how these inquiries or assessments should be carried out is provided in each of the Codes[1].

[1] English Code, chapter 11; Welsh Code, chapter 10.

The sequence of inquiries

9.20 The process of making inquiries may be undertaken in stages, reflecting the sequence of duties in the statutory schemes[1]. For example, the first statutory inquiry is as to whether the applicant is 'eligible'[2]. If the local housing authority decides that an applicant is not eligible for assistance, it is not required to make any further inquiries. It would be a waste of time and effort if the local housing authority had to embark on detailed inquiries into other matters, because no duty is owed to an applicant who is ineligible for assistance, beyond the duty to notify the applicant of the reasons for that decision[3]. Treating eligibility as a discrete first issue may therefore lead to a saving of time and resources. However, if the applicant may be eligible but the question of eligibility cannot be inquired into and resolved immediately, at least some preliminary further inquiries will be necessary in order for the local housing authority to determine whether the applicant may also be homeless and may have a priority need and thus be the subject of a duty to provide interim accommodation[4].

[1] Prior to the coming into force of H(W)A 2014, Pt 2, for applications for homelessness assistance made to local housing authorities in Wales on or after 27 April 2015, and prior to the amendments to HA 1996, Pt 7, inserted by HRA 2017, for applications for homelessness assistance made to local housing authorities in England on or after 3 April 2018, there was some debate about whether the statutory schemes permitted inquiries to be undertaken in stages, or whether all the various questions had to be asked and answered in one decision-making process: see *Crawley Borough Council v B* (2000) 32 HLR 636, CA and previous editions of this book (Luba, Davies and Johnston, 4th edn, 2016). However, given that both statutory schemes now provide for duties to be owed to eligible applicants who are either homeless or threatened with homelessness, irrespective of whether those applicants also have a priority need and whether they have become homeless intentionally, it must follow that local housing authorities in both England and Wales can first make inquiries into the issues of an applicant's eligibility and whether he or she is homeless or threatened with homelessness, and can postpone the other issues until the question arises of what other duty, if any, may be owed to the applicant. See CHAPTERS 15 AND 16 for the duties that may be owed by local housing authorities in England and CHAPTER 17 for the duties that may be owed by local housing authorities in Wales.

[2] HA 1996, s 184(1)(a); H(W)A 2014, s 62(4). See CHAPTER 11.

³ HA 1996, s 184(3) and English Code, para 11.3; H(W)A 2014, s 63(1); and Welsh Code, para 10.14.
⁴ HA 1996, s 188(1); H(W)A 2014, s 68(1). English Code, paras 15.4–15.6; Welsh Code, paras 10.13–10.14. See also **16.37–16.80** (England) and **17.118–17.134** (Wales).

9.21 If a local housing authority in England decides, as a result of its inquiries, that an applicant is eligible for assistance, it must then inquire into whether it owes him or her a duty under HA 1996, Pt 7¹. The immediate duties that it might owe are:

• either the HA 1996, s 195(2)², prevention duty (if the applicant is threatened with homelessness) or HA 1996, s 189B(2)³, relief duty (if the applicant is homeless); and
• the duty to make an assess of the applicant's case and record a personalised housing plan⁴.

¹ HA 1996, s 184(1)(b).
² As amended by HRA 2017, s 4(2), for applications for homelessness assistance made to local housing authorities in England on or after 3 April 2018. See **15.87–15.137**.
³ As inserted by HRA 2017, s 5(2), for applications for homelessness assistance made to local housing authorities in England on or after 3 April 2018. See **15.138–15.195**.
⁴ HA 1996, s 189A, as inserted by HRA 2017, s 3(1), for applications for homelessness assistance made to local housing authorities in England on or after 3 April 2018. See **15.62–15.86**.

9.22 So the local housing authority must inquire into and decide whether the applicant is homeless or threatened with homelessness. If the applicant is neither homeless nor threatened with homelessness, no further duty will be owed under HA 1996, Pt 7¹. No further inquiries need be made and the applicant will be notified accordingly that no duty is owed and provided with the reasons for that decision².

¹ As amended by HRA 2017, for applications for homelessness assistance made to local housing authorities in England on or after 3 April 2018..
² HA 1996, s 184(3); English Code, paras 11.3–11.6.

9.23 If a local housing authority in Wales has assessed that the applicant is eligible for help, it must then make an assessment of the applicant's circumstances, housing need, and need for support. It should seek to identify the outcome that the applicant wishes to achieve, and whether the exercise of any of the local housing authority's functions at H(W)A 2014, Pt 2, could contribute to the achievement of that outcome¹. The local housing authority must also assess whether or not it has any duty to the applicant under H(W)A 2014, Pt 2². In order to assess whether any duty is owed, the local housing authority must first decide whether the applicant is homeless or threatened with homelessness. If the applicant is not homeless or threatened with homelessness, no duty will be owed beyond that of notifying the applicant of the local housing authority's decision, with reasons for that decision³.

¹ H(W)A 2014, s 62(4) and (5); Welsh Code, paras 10.15–10.38.
² H(W)A 2014, s 62(4)(d); Welsh Code, paras 10.30–10.31.
³ H(W)A 2014, s 63(1).

9.24 If the applicant is both eligible for assistance¹ and threatened with homelessness², the local housing authority will owe the applicant a duty to take reasonable steps to help the applicant to secure that accommodation does not cease to be available for his or her occupation[3]. If the applicant is both eligible for assistance[4] and homeless[5], the local housing authority will owe the applicant a duty to take reasonable steps to help the applicant to secure that suitable accommodation becomes available for his or her occupation[6]. In both cases, Local housing authorities will also owe a duty to make an assessment of the applicant's case and, for local housing authorities in England, try to agree a personalised housing plan with the applicant[7].

[1]   See CHAPTER 11.
[2]   See **10.144–10.147.**
[3]   HA 1996, s 195(2) (as amended by HRA 2017, s 4(2), for applications for homelessness assistance made to local housing authorities in England on or after 3 April 2018), see **15.87–15.137;** H(W)A 2014, s 66(1), see **17.45–17.72.**
[4]   See CHAPTER 11.
[5]   See CHAPTER 10.
[6]   HA 1996, s 189B(2) (as inserted by HRA 2017, s 5(2), for applications for homelessness assistance made to local housing authorities in England on or after 3 April 2018), see **15.138–15.195;** H(W)A 2014, s 73(1), see **17.73–17.143.**
[7]   HA 1996, s 189A, as inserted by HRA 2017, s 3, for applications for homelessness assistance made to local housing authorities in England on or after 3 April 2018, see **15.62–15.86;** H(W)A 2014, s 62(5)(a), (b) and (c), see **9.12–9.15.**

9.25 It is only once the HA 1996, s 189B(2)[1], or H(W)A 2014, s 73(1) relief duty has come to an end, and the applicant remains homeless and eligible for assistance, that any other duty might arise. In order to decide what further duty, if any, is owed[2], local housing authorities must inquire into and determine two further issues in respect of most applicants:

(1)   whether the applicant has a priority need[3]; and
(2)   whether the applicant became homeless intentionally[4].

[1]   As inserted by HRA 2017, s 5,(2) for applications for homelessness assistance made to local housing authorities in England on or after 3 April 2018.
[2]   HA 1996, s 184(1)(b); H(W)A 2014, s 62(5)(d).
[3]   See CHAPTER 12.
[4]   See CHAPTER 13.

9.26 Where an applicant had made an application for homelessness assistance to a local housing authority in England and had accepted a private rented sector offer[1], if the applicant subsequently makes a further application for homelessness assistance to a local housing authority in England within two years of the date of acceptance of that offer, he or she need not have a priority need in order to be entitled to the HA 1996, s 193(2) main housing duty[2]. This does not apply where the HA 1996, s 193(2) main housing duty would not be owed were it not for the presence in the applicant's household of a 'restricted person'[3]. If the applicant's household contains a restricted person in those circumstances, he or she must have a priority need in order to be entitled to the HA 1996, s 193(2), main housing duty[4].

[1]   HA 1996, s 193(7AA)–(7AC). See **16.161–16.180.**
[2]   HA 1996, s 195A(1) . See **8.100–8.107** and **16.47–16.50.**
[3]   HA 1996, s 195A(5) as amended by HRA 2017, s 4(4) for applications for homelessness assistance made to local housing authorities in England on or after 3 April 2018. For more on this special provision for re-applications, see English Code, paras 18.16–18.26; and **9.94–9.100.** For 'restricted person' see HA 1996, s 184(7) at **9.54–9.56** and **11.163–11.167.**

---

[4] For 'restricted person' see **9.54–9.56** and **11.163–11.67**. For 'priority' need, see Chapter **12**.

9.27 It follows that the local housing authority need only make inquiries into whether the applicant's household contains a restricted person if it has already accepted that the HA 1996, s 193(2) main housing duty is owed to the applicant. If the duty is not owed, there is no need to make inquiries into the presence of a restricted person. It also follows that, if the HA 1996, s 193(2) main housing duty in HA 1996, s 193(2), would be owed whether or not the applicant's household included a restricted person, there is no obligation to make inquiries into the presence of the restricted person[1].

[1] For the duties owed to such 'restricted cases': see HA 1996, s 193(3B) and **16.180–16.183** (England); H(W)A 2014, s 76(5) and **17.177** (Wales).

Inquiries into local connection

9.28 If the local housing authority decides to exercise its discretionary power to inquire into whether an applicant has a local connection[1], care must be taken in deciding when to make such inquiries.

[1] HA 1996, s 184(2), see **9.28–9.30**.

9.29 Local housing authorities in England may refer performance of either of two duties if the conditions for referral are satisfied[1]. Those duties are:

- the HA 1996, s 189B(2), relief duty to take reasonable steps to help an applicant to secure that suitable accommodation becomes available for his or her occupation[2]; and
- the HA 1996, s 193(2), main housing duty to secure that accommodation is available for the applicant's occupation[3].

[1] HA 1996, s 198 as amended by HRA 2017, s 5(8), for applications for homelessness assistance made to local housing authorities in England on or after 3 April 2018. See **15.139–15.146** and **16.13–16.17**.
[2] HA 1996, s 189B(2) (as inserted by HRA 2017, s 5(2), for applications for homelessness assistance made to local housing authorities in England on or after 3 April 2018), see **15.138–15.195**. The power to refer is at HA 1996, 198(A1), as inserted by HRA 2017, s 5(8), for applications for homelessness assistance made to local housing authorities in England on or after 3 April 2018. See **15.139–15.146** and **16.13–16.15**.
[3] HA 1996, s 193(2), see **16.94–16.199**. The power to refer is at HA 1996, s 198(1), see **16.16**.

9.30 Local housing authorities in Wales may refer performance of the H(W)A 2014, s 73(1) relief duty, but only in respect of applicants who have a priority need and have not become homeless intentionally[1].

[1] H(W)A 2014, s 80(1), see **14.32**.

Burden of proof

9.31 The burden of making inquiries rests on the local housing authority. It is for the local housing authority to make the inquiries necessary to 'satisfy' itself whether the applicant is 'eligible' and then, if satisfied that she or he is eligible, to make the inquiries necessary to satisfy itself whether any duty is owed under

HA 1996, Pt 7[1], or H(W)A 2014, Pt 2[2].

[1] As amended by HRA 2017 for applications for homelessness assistance made to local housing authorities in England on or after 3 April 2018, see CHAPTERS 15 AND 16.

[2] HA 1996, s 184(1); the language used in H(W)A 2014, Pt 2, refers to the duty on the local housing authority to 'carry out an assessment of a person's case', including 'whether or not the authority has any duty to the applicant': H(W)A 2014, s 62(1) and (5)(d).

9.32 It is not for the applicant to 'prove' his or her case[1]. This point has been reiterated in decisions of the courts and in successive editions of the Codes[2]. The applicant can obviously be asked, or invited, to cooperate with the inquiries and to provide information, but an application cannot be rejected simply because the applicant has not provided some document or other material considered necessary to prove part of his or her case. It follows that the local housing authority cannot suspend inquiries or transfer its responsibilities onto the applicant by such practices as refusing to make a decision unless the applicant obtains a letter from a person with whom he or she recently resided, or a medical report, or a copy of a police or accident report[3].

[1] *R v Woodspring Borough Council ex p Walters* (1984) 16 HLR 73, QBD.

[2] Welsh Code, para 10.22. The 2018 edition of the English Code contains this advice in relation to the issue of whether or not the applicant became homeless intentionally: English Code, para 9.5.

[3] See, for example, *Complaints against Southwark London Borough Council*, 10 000 207, 10 004 245 and 11 000 195, 22 May 2012, (2012) August *Legal Action*, p 27. H(W)A 2014, s 79(5) permits the local housing authority to notify the applicant that any duty owed to him or her has come to an end because the local housing authority is satisfied that the applicant is unreasonably failing to cooperate with the authority in exercise of any of the functions under H(W)A 2014, Pt 2. Guidance in Welsh Code, at paras 15.86–15.89, refers to the test of unreasonably failing to cooperate entirely in relation to the applicant failing to cooperate with the duties to help the applicant, rather than the applicant failing to cooperate with the assessment. See **17.195–17.197**.

9.33 The correct approach was summarised in *R v Gravesham Borough Council ex p Winchester*[1]. The burden lies on local housing authorities to make appropriate inquiries in a caring and sympathetic way. Such inquiries should be pursued rigorously and fairly, but there is no duty to conduct 'CID type inquiries'. Applicants should be given an opportunity to explain matters which local housing authorities consider may weigh substantially against them[2].

[1] *R v Gravesham Borough Council ex p Winchester* (1986) 18 HLR 207, QBD.

[2] See **9.42–9.49**. For an example where a decision was quashed because the decision-maker had not obtained the applicant's full account, see *Mondeh v Southwark London Borough Council* (2010) November *Legal Action*, p 19, Lambeth County Court.

9.34 Very infrequently, an applicant will simply make an application and then refuse to cooperate in the conduct of inquiries, or refuse to provide any but the barest details of himself or herself, or of his or her circumstances. This is not a position that any applicant who was sensibly advised would take, and, if adopted, might suggest that there were issues relating to the applicant's capacity to conduct his or her affairs[1].

[1] *AB v Leicester City Council* [2009] EWCA Civ 192, CA. For a similar instance of lack of cooperation in the context of a challenge to a decision of a local authority's adult care services, see *R (WG) v Leicester City Council* [2011] EWHC 189 (Admin), [2011] EWCA Civ 483 and [2011] EWCA Civ 861, CA. For the circumstances in which local housing authorities can

notify an applicant of a decision that the duty owed has come to an end as a result of the applicant's deliberate and unreasonable refusal to co-operate, see **15.196–15.221** (England) and **17.195–17.197** (Wales).

9.35 At the end of the inquiries there is unlikely to be any remaining doubt or uncertainty as to whether an applicant is 'eligible', or over most of the decisions as to what duties, if any, are owed. The local housing authority will be able to determine whether it is satisfied that the applicant is 'eligible', 'threatened with homelessness', 'homeless', and has a 'priority need'. However, the burden of proof may be decisive where the issue is whether the applicant has become homeless intentionally. On that matter, the legal question is whether the local housing authority is *not* satisfied that the applicant became homeless, or threatened with homelessness, intentionally[1]. Accordingly, on that question, if there is doubt or uncertainty, the issue must be resolved in the applicant's favour.

[1] HA 1996, s 193(1) and English Code, para 9.5; H(W)A 2014, s 75(2)(d) and Welsh Code, para 17.12; and see **13.19–13.28**.

Scope of inquiries

9.36 The legal obligation on a local housing authority in England is to make 'such inquiries as are necessary'[1]. But who decides which inquiries are 'necessary'? The courts have repeatedly indicated that it is for the local housing authority to decide what inquiries it considers 'necessary' to undertake. A local housing authority will only err in law if it has failed to make an inquiry that no reasonable local housing authority would have regarded as unnecessary[2].

[1] HA 1996, s 184(1), as explained in *R v Kensington and Chelsea Royal London Borough Council ex p Bayani* (1990) 22 HLR 406, CA. The duty on a local housing authority in Wales is to 'carry out an assessment of a person's case': H(W)A 2014, s 62(1).
[2] See *R v Nottingham City Council ex p Costello* (1989) 21 HLR 301, QBD; *R v Kensington and Chelsea Royal London Borough Council ex p Bayani* (1990) 22 HLR 406, CA; and *Cramp v Hastings Borough Council* [2005] EWCA Civ 1005, [2005] HLR 48, CA.

9.37 The local housing authority must ensure that it has, in the course of its inquiries, taken all of the applicant's circumstances into account and come to an overall, or composite, view. Whilst inquiries into different aspects, such as medical factors, may be made by different officers of the local housing authority, the final decision should be taken by an officer who has all of the information available[1].

[1] *R v Lewisham London Borough Council ex p Dolan* (1993) 25 HLR 68, QBD.

9.38 Although it is for the local housing authority to decide what inquiries are necessary, its decision must still be lawful. A judge sitting in the Administrative Court found that it was 'highly arguable' that no lawful inquiries had been conducted, in a case where the applicant had attended council offices to make an application for homelessness assistance, supported by a report from his GP setting out his medical condition and the GP's opinion that he was vulnerable[1]. The applicant had been interviewed on the same day that he attended, and, at the end of a 'relatively short interview', the interviewing officer printed off, signed and handed him a written decision purporting to be made under HA

1996, s 184(3), notifying him that the local housing authority did not consider him to have a priority need. The judge commented that inquiries into mental health issues and issues arising from historic mistreatment of former asylum seekers would normally require consultation with the applicant's medical advisers and the relevant mental health services, would usually require a further assessment and report from a psychiatrist, and could be expected to extend to a detailed inquiry into the applicant's way of life prior to his or her homelessness. It would have been impossible for any of those inquiries to have been undertaken during the initial screening interview[2].

1   See **9.70–9.80, 12.76–12.125** (England) and **12.199–12.206** (Wales).
2   *R (IA) v Westminster City Council* [2013] EWHC 1273 (QB), (2013) July/August *Legal Action*, p 23, QBD.

9.39 Local housing authorities are required by HA 1996, s 182, and H(W)A 2014, s 98(1), to take into account the guidance contained in the Codes of Guidance[1]. For this purpose, local housing authorities need to be able to refer to the current version of the relevant Codes[2]. If the local housing authority decides to disregard the guidance in the Codes or other guidance, the onus lies on the local housing authority to justify that decision[3]. However, there is no obligation on a local housing authority to identify each paragraph of the relevant Code which bears upon the decision, provided that, reading the decision as a whole, it is plain that the decision-maker had regard to the guidance[4].

1   If the Secretary of State additionally issues any Code of Practice, a local housing authority in England must have regard to it: HA 1996, s 214A(12) (as inserted by HRA 2017, s 11, for applications for homelessness assistance made to local housing authorities in England on or after 3 April 2018).
2   See *R v Newham London Borough Council ex p Bones* (1993) 25 HLR 357, QBD, where a decision based on an out-of-date edition of the Code was quashed. In *Mondeh v Southwark London Borough Council* (2010) November *Legal Action*, p 19, Lambeth County Court, a review decision was quashed, in part because the reviewing officer had failed to address the Code of Guidance and had failed to give reasons for departing from its guidance. See also *Walsh v Haringey London Borough Council* (2014) July/August *Legal Action*, p 56, Clerkenwell and Shoreditch County Court.
3   *De Falco v Crawley Borough Council* [1980] QB 460, CA.
4   *Balog v Birmingham City Council* [2013] EWCA Civ 1582, [2014] HLR 14, CA; see also *Farah v Hillingdon London Borough Council* [2014] EWCA Civ 359, [2014] HLR 24, CA, where one of the errors of the law in the decision was that there was no reference to the Code.

9.40 In fixing the scope, form and manner of making its inquiries, a local housing authority must bear in mind its obligations under equalities legis-lation. The Equality Act 2010, s 149(1) contains the Public Sector Equality Duty (PSED) which requires local housing authorities in both England and in Wales to:

'have due regard to the need to—
(a)   eliminate discrimination, harassment, victimisation and any other conduct that is prohibited by or under this Act;
(b)   advance equality of opportunity between persons who share a relevant protected characteristic[1] and persons who do not share it;

(c)   foster good relations between persons who share a relevant protected characteristic and persons who do not share it.'

¹ The relevant protected characteristics for the purposes of Equality Act 2010, s 149(1), are: age, disability, gender re-assignment, pregnancy and/or maternity, race, religion and/or belief, sex, and sexual orientation: Equality Act 2010: s 149(7). An additional protected characteristic in the Equality Act 2010 is marriage and/or civil partnership, Equality Act 2010, s 4, but this is not a 'relevant' protected characteristic for the purposes of the public sector equality duty at Equality Act 2010, s 149(1).

9.41 The courts have held that decision-makers must take steps to take account of any disability or any other protected characteristic in the Equality Act 2010 which may be relevant to the decision being considered[1]. This is the case even if the disability or other protected characteristic is not obvious to the decision-maker. If there appears to be a protected characteristic, which has some relevance to the decisions being considered, at each stage of the decision-making the local housing authority must have the equality duty well in mind. The local housing authority should consider whether the applicant (or a member of his or her household) has a relevant protected characteristic, the extent of that protected characteristic and the likely effect of the protected characteristic, when taken together with any other functions, on the applicant or the member of his or her household[2]. The relevant principles are summarised by a Court of Appeal judge as follows:

'First, the aim of the PSED (as of other equality duties) is to bring equality issues into the main-stream, so that they become an essential element in public decision making: . . . In *Bracking* , at [59], McCombe LJ said:

"It seems to have been the intention of Parliament that these considerations of equality of opportunity (where they arise) are now to be placed at the centre of formulation of policy by all public authorities, side by side with all other pressing circumstances of whatever magnitude."

That was a case about formulation of policy, but the underlying principle applies equally to public authority decision-making of any kind.

Secondly, the duty is a matter of substance rather than of form. It requires that the decision maker be aware of the duty to have due regard to the relevant matters: see per Aikens LJ in Brown at [91]: "It involves a conscious approach and state of mind."

. . . The duty must be exercised in substance, with rigour and with an open mind. It is not a question of ticking boxes: . . . "The question in every case is whether the decision-maker has in substance had due regard to the relevant statutory needs. Just as the use of a mantra referring to the statutory provision does not of itself show that the duty as being performed, so too a failure to refer expressly to the statute does not of itself show that the duty has not been performed."

Third, the concept of due regard is to be distinguished from a requirement to give the PSED considerations specific weight. It is not a duty to achieve a particular result . . . In Hurley , Elias LJ said this at [78]:

"The concept of 'due regard' requires the court to ensure that there has been a proper and conscientious focus on the statutory criteria, but if that is done, the court cannot interfere with the decision simply because it would have given greater weight to the equality implications of the decision than did the decision maker"[3].'

¹   *Pieretti v Enfield London Borough Council* [2010] EWCA Civ 1140, [2011] HLR 3, CA considering the statutory predecessor to Equality Act 2010, s 149 which was Disability Discrimination Act 1995, s 49; *Hotak v Southwark London Borough Council, Kanu v Southwark London Borough Council, Johnson v Solihull Metropolitan Borough Council* [2015] UKSC 30, [2016] AC 811, SC; and *Hackney London Borough Council v Haque* [2017] EWCA Civ 4, [2017] HLR 14, CA.
²   *Hotak v Southwark London Borough Council, Kanu v Southwark London Borough Council, Johnson v Solihull Metropolitan Borough Council* [2015] UKSC 30, [2016] AC 811, SC per Lord Neuberger at [78].
³   *Hackney London Borough Council v Haque* [2017] EWCA Civ 4, [2017] HLR 14, CA per Briggs LJ at [20]–[23].

Interviewing the applicant

9.42   A local housing authority is obviously obliged to give the applicant the opportunity to explain his or her circumstances fully. Whether or not procedural fairness requires that an applicant be interviewed is a decision for the local housing authority. In particular, if the local housing authority accepts the applicant's facts and circumstances, but takes a different view on the questions that it has to decide, there is no obligation to put that view to the applicant for comment[1]. However, a view of certain facts that could lead to a decision against the applicant's interests should normally be put to him or her before the decision is made[2]. In *Royal Borough of Windsor and Maidenhead v Hemans*[3], Toulson LJ said: '[i]t is striking that at no time was [the applicant], either directly or through her solicitors, given the opportunity to meet the suggestion, if the review officer really had it in mind, that this account was essentially fictitious'[4]. One county court judge has decided that, where an applicant's credibility is at issue, he or she should be personally interviewed by the officer making the relevant decision, not by another officer[5]. In some circumstances, an interview would be essential, particularly where the local housing authority is considering disbelieving the applicant's account[6].

¹   *Tetteh v Kingston-upon-Thames Royal London Borough Council* [2004] EWCA Civ 1775, [2005] HLR 21, CA.
²   Welsh Code, paras 10.21–10.22. See also *R v Wyre Borough Council ex p Joyce* (1983) 11 HLR 73, QBD and *R v Dacorum Borough Council ex p Brown* (1989) 21 HLR 405, QBD.
³   [2010] EWCA Civ 374, [2011] HLR 25, CA.
⁴   Toulson LJ at [56].
⁵   *N v Allerdale Borough Council* (2008) October *Legal Action*, p 38, Carlisle County Court.
⁶   *R v Hackney London Borough Council ex p Decordova* (1994) 27 HLR 108, QBD; *Burr v Hastings Borough Council* [2008] EWCA Civ 1217, (2009) January *Legal Action*, p 27, CA; and *Royal Borough of Windsor and Maidenhead v Hemans* [2010] EWCA Civ 374, [2011] HLR 25, CA. See also Welsh Code, para 10.22.

9.43   Generally, the local housing authority will interview the applicant face to face, although there is no reason why the local housing authority should not put questions to the applicant by letter[1].

¹   English Code, paras 11.14–11.15. In *Rowley v Rugby Borough Council* [2007] EWCA Civ 483, [2007] HLR 40, CA, a local housing authority had not made an error of law when it asked the applicant to confirm what it understood to be her version of events on a tear-off slip, and then relied upon that confirmation.

9.44 A local housing authority in England was severely criticised by the Local Government Ombudsman for failing to use interpreters in all of its interviews with a particular applicant[1]. In another case, an applicant with impaired hearing was not provided with sufficient assistance during the inquiries[2].

[1] *Complaint against Waltham Forest London Borough Council*, 03/A/15819, 9 November 2005.
[2] *Complaint against Redbridge London Borough Council*, 07/A/03275, 23 March 2009 (2009) May *Legal Action*, p 26.

9.45 The local housing authority's inquiries and, in particular, any interview of the applicant, should be conducted in a 'caring and sympathetic way'[1]. It is for the local housing authority to decide how it conducts any interview, how long it lasts and what questions are asked. An error of law will only be made out if the style of questioning has the effect of inhibiting the applicant from putting forward his or her case or any facts which might assist the application[2].

[1] *R v Gravesham Borough Council ex p Winchester* (1986) 18 HLR 207, QBD. See also English Code, para 11.9 'Applicants should be encouraged to share information without fear that this will reduce their chances of receiving support, and questions should be asked in a sensitive way and with an awareness that the applicant may be reluctant to disclose personal details if they lack confidence that their circumstances will be understood and considered sympathetically'. See also specific guidance for interviewing victims of domestic violence at English Code para 21.23.
[2] *R v Tower Hamlets London Borough Council ex p Khatun (Shafia)* (1996) 27 HLR 465, CA.

9.46 The local housing authority is not required to accept what the applicant says at face value[1]. If the applicant's response raises a relevant matter of fact that the local housing authority is not prepared simply to accept, the local housing authority must investigate it[2]. If there is any doubt, and the matter cannot be resolved by further reasonable inquiries, the question should be resolved in the applicant's favour, at least where it relates to whether or not the applicant had become homeless intentionally[3].

[1] *R v Kensington and Chelsea Royal London Borough Council ex p Cunha* (1989) 21 HLR 16, QBD.
[2] See *R v Tower Hamlets London Borough Council ex p Bibi* (1991) 23 HLR 500, QBD; *R v Northampton Borough Council ex p Clarkson* (1992) 24 HLR 529, QBD; *R v Newham London Borough Council ex p Bones* (1993) 25 HLR 357, QBD; *R v Kensington and Chelsea Royal London Borough Council ex p Silchenstedt* (1996) 29 HLR 728, QBD; and *Forbes v Lambeth London Borough Council* (2000) July *Legal Action*, p 30, Lambeth County Court.
[3] *R v Gravesham Borough Council ex p Winchester* (1986) 18 HLR 207, QBD; English Code, para 9.5; Welsh Code, para 17.12. See also **9.31–9.35**.

9.47 Statements from third parties containing material contrary to the applicant's case should be put to the applicant for comment before the local housing authority decides whether or not it accepts those statements. Usually this can be achieved by simply showing the applicant the statements. Guidance on the situation which arises where it is important not to disclose the identity of the third party is given in *R v Poole Borough Council ex p Cooper*[1]. It may be that the applicant is able to provide reasons why the adverse information from the third party cannot be relied upon[2]. Adverse medical evidence, whether from the local housing authority's own medical adviser or the applicant's doctor(s), should also be put to the applicant for comment before a decision is reached[3]. If the local housing authority is relying on factual information in relation to the applicant's case which conflicts with the applicant's own account, that information should be put to the applicant for comment[4].

1   (1994) 27 HLR 605, QBD.
2   See *R v Ealing London Borough Council ex p Chanter* (1992) December *Legal Action*, p 22, QBD, where the applicant's sister had informed the local housing authority that the applicant had left accommodation voluntarily but, had the statement been put to the applicant, she would have told the local housing authority of long-standing hostility between herself and her sister.
3   *R v Newham London Borough Council ex p Lumley* (2001) 33 HLR 11, QBD, and *Begum (Amirun) v Tower Hamlets London Borough Council* [2002] EWHC 633, (2003) 35 HLR 8, QBD. A careful distinction should be drawn between adverse medical evidence and adverse medical opinion. See **9.70–9.80** for a fuller discussion on the proper conduct of medical inquiries.
4   See *Lane and Ginda v Islington London Borough Council* (2001) April *Legal Action*, p 21, Clerkenwell County Court, where the local housing authority's failure to put information as to the frequency of lift breakdown to the applicant before deciding that accommodation offered was 'suitable' resulted in the decision being quashed. See also English Code, para 18.33: 'In cases where contradictory factual accounts are put before the housing authority, and it prefers one account to another, the decisions letter should explain why a particular account was preferred.'

9.48 The local housing authority is entitled to rely upon the applicant's own statement or statements. However, if there is ambiguity or subsequent contradiction of a statement by the applicant, the local housing authority should give the applicant an opportunity to challenge its interpretation of his or her earlier statement[1]. It is not for the applicant to volunteer matters that may or may not be relevant. It is for the local housing authority, through interview and other inquiries, to identify those relevant matters and then make the necessary inquiries into them[2]. Where an interview would not yield more information than is already known to the local housing authority, an interview will not be a necessary part of the duty to make inquiries[3].

1   *Robinson v Brent London Borough Council* (1999) 31 HLR 1015, CA.
2   *R v Tower Hamlets London Borough Council ex p Ullah* (1992) 24 HLR 680, QBD; the Welsh Code advises that there may be factors that make it difficult for applicants to explain their situations fully: Welsh Code, para 10.21.
3   *Kacar v Enfield London Borough Council* (2001) 33 HLR 64, CA and *Tetteh v Kingston-upon-Thames Royal London Borough Council* [2004] EWCA Civ 1775, [2005] HLR 21, CA.

9.49 In addition, once the local housing authority is satisfied that the applicant is eligible for assistance and is either threatened with homelessness, or is homeless, the local housing authority is under a duty to make an assessment of the applicant's case and to draw up a personalised housing plan[1]. Both Codes of Guidance are predicated on the assumption that an assessment of needs will require a face-to-face interview[2].

1   HA 1996, s 189A, as inserted by HRA 2017, s 3(1), for applications for homelessness assistance made to local housing authorities in England on or after 3 April 2018, see **15.62–15.86**. For local housing authorities in Wales, the duty to assess is owed once an applicant has applied to a local housing authority for accommodation or for help in retaining or obtaining accommodation and it appears to the local housing authority that the person may be homeless or threatened with homelessness, and the local housing authority is satisfied that, if the person has been assessed on a previous occasion, the person's circumstances have not changed materially and there is no new information that materially affects the previous

assessment: H(W)A 2014, s 62(1) and (2). Once the local housing authority is satisfied that the applicant is eligible for help, it is under a duty to carry out a more detailed assessment: H(W)A 2014, s 62(5), see **9.12–9.14**.
2   English Code, para 11.14; Welsh Code, chapter 10.

Timescale

9.50 There is no time limit prescribed by HA 1996, Pt 7[1] or by H(W)A 2014, Pt 2, for the completion of inquiries. The Codes work on the premise that the obligation to inquire or to assess is triggered as soon as the applicant gives the local housing authority reason to believe that he or she may be homeless, or may be threatened with homelessness[2]. Previous editions of the English Code encouraged local housing authorities to carry out their inquiries 'as quickly as possible' notify the applicant of their decision within 33 working days, counted from the date on which the application was received[3]. There is no advice on specific timescale in the current edition of the English Code because the assessment of the applicant's case will depend on the applicant's particular circumstances[4]. The only recommendation arises in the context of the decision as to what duty, if any, might be owed when the HA 1996, s 189B(2)[5], relief duty comes to an end. In those circumstances, the English Code advises that local housing authorities should not delay completing their inquiries. It should be possible to notify the applicant on the 57th day[6]. If significant further investigations are required, the English Code advises that inquiries should be completed and a decision notified within a maximum of 15 working days after the end of the 56-day period[7].

1   As amended by HRA 2017 for applications for homelessness assistance made to local housing authorities in England on or after 3 April 2018.
2   English Code, paras 18.82–18.33; Welsh Code, paras 10.8–10.9.
3   2006 English Code, para 6.16.
4   English Code, paras 11.24–11.28.
5   As inserted by HRA 2017, s 5(2), for applications for homelessness assistance made to local housing authorities in England on or after 3 April 2018, see **15.138–15.195**.
6   The day after the 56-day period for the performance of the HA 1996, s 189B(2) (as inserted by HRA 2017, s 5(2), for application for homelessness assistance made to local housing authorities in England on or after 3 April 2018) relief duty.
7   English Code, para 14.16.

9.51 The Welsh Code advises that the duty to assess arises as soon as the conditions at H(W)A 2014, s 62(1), are satisfied[1], and that, if there is any doubt, the local housing authority should begin the assessment process[2]. The Welsh Code also recommends that each stage of the assessment should be completed, and the outcome should be notified to the applicant, within 10 working days, although the priority is that the assessment and the decision should be correct[3].

1   See **9.12–9.14**.
2   Welsh Code, paras 10.8–10.9.
3   Welsh Code, paras 10.5 and 10.53–10.54.

9.52 It is unlawful for a local housing authority to postpone the taking of a decision once it has reached the conclusion of its inquiries (or to extend the inquiry process artificially) simply in order to avoid a duty. Most commonly, this might arise where a 17-year-old makes an application for homelessness assistance shortly before his or her eighteenth birthday[1].

1   *Robinson v Hammersmith & Fulham London Borough Council* [2006] EWCA Civ 1122,
    [2007] HLR 7, CA. While 17-year-olds have a priority need by virtue of their age, that is not
    the position with 18-year-olds: Homelessness (Priority Need for Accommodation) (England)
    Order 2002, SI 2002/2051, art 3 and H(W)A 2014, s 70(1)(d) and see **12.137–12.159**
    (England) and **12.212–12.213** (Wales). In *R (Raw) v Lambeth London Borough Council*
    [2010] EWHC 507 (Admin), (2011) May *Legal Action*, p 24, Admin Ct, the judge considered
    that a practice of deferring or ceasing inquiries where an applicant for homelessness assistance
    had been referred to a rent deposit scheme would also be an illegitimate approach and an
    impermissible reason for not performing the duty to inquire. See also, in a different context,
    R (Edwards) v Birmingham City Council [2016] EWHC 173 (Admin), [2016] HLR 11, Admin
    Ct per Hickinbottom J at [44]. See also **8.15**.

9.53 If the local housing authority simply fails to progress or complete its
inquiries, or fails to notify the decision made on the conclusion of its inquiries
to the applicant, the applicant is left in a limbo situation[1]. As no decision has
been notified, the applicant does not have the right to request a review of it.
Instead, an applicant would need to bring judicial review proceedings for a
mandatory order requiring the local housing authority to complete its inquiries
and notify its decision by a specified date[2]. Alternatively, the applicant could
complain through the local housing authority's complaints procedure and
ultimately to the Local Government and Social Care Ombudsman or Public
Services Ombudsman for Wales who can recommend that inquiries be
concluded and/or that the applicant should be compensated for delays which
amount to maladministration[3].

1   If no decision is reached and notified to the applicant, then any accommodation that had been
    secured for the applicant under the duty at HA 1996, s 188(1), or H(W)A 2014, s 68(2), will
    continue to be occupied under that duty (see **16.38–16.80** (England) and **17.118–17.134**
    (Wales)). In *O'Callaghan v Southwark London Borough Council* (2010) May *Legal Action*,
    p 23, Lambeth County Court, the applicant was in that position. She subsequently lost her
    accommodation. On a further application for homelessness assistance, the local housing
    authority's decision that she had become homeless intentionally was wrong in law, as she
    could not have become homeless intentionally from accommodation secured under HA 1996,
    s 188(1). See also *Complaint against Newham London Borough Council*, 13 005 484,
    17 March 2014 (2014) June *Legal* Action, p 40, where the Ombudsman awarded £750
    compensation for, among other faults, a failure to notify acceptance of the HA 1996, s 193(2),
    main housing duty and *Complaint against Lambeth London Borough Council*, 16 005 834,
    15 August 2017, (2017) November *Legal Action*, p 41, where £3,000 compensation was
    recommended for a delay of almost a year, and for 20 months' occupation of unsuitable
    accommodation..
2   In *R v Lambeth London Borough Council ex p Weir* [2001] EWHC 121 (Admin), (2001) June
    Legal Action, p 26, Admin Ct, the local housing authority was required to notify the applicant
    within 14 days after a 20-month delay; in *R v Brent London Borough Council ex p Miyanger*
    (1996) 29 HLR 628, QBD, the local housing authority was required to make a decision within
    28 days and notify the applicant within a further three days, after the local housing authority
    had failed to comply with an agreement made three months earlier that a decision would be
    made. See **19.306–19.333** for judicial review.
3   The Local Government Ombudsman described a local housing authority's failure to reach a
    decision in one case as 'clearly unacceptable' and 'a failure to fulfil its statutory responsibili-
    ties': *Complaint against Hounslow London Borough Council*, 10 019 388, 5 October 2011,
    (2011) December *Legal Action*, p 29. See also *Complaint against Hounslow London
    Borough Council*, 11 008 191, 28 August 2012 (2012) November *Legal Action*, p 14 where
    maladministration was found for, amongst other failings, a delay of approximately three
    months in reaching a decision; *Complaint against Birmingham City Council*, 13 017 548,
    (2014) October *Legal Action*, p 50, where £400 was awarded for a delay of six months;
    Complaint against Hounslow London Borough Council, 13 008 825, (2014) December *Legal
    Action*, p 34, where £5,000 compensation was awarded for delay of over 12 months;
    Complaint against Lambeth London Borough Council, 14 014 884, 8 December 2015, (2016)

June *Legal Action*, p 42, where £150 compensation was agreed for a three month delay; and *Complaint against Lambeth London Borough Council*, 16 005 834, 15 August 2017 (2017), November, *Legal Action*, p 42, where the delay was almost a year. See **19.336–19.340**.

The special rules for restricted persons

9.54 Where the applicant's household includes a 'restricted person'[1], there may be additional inquiries to be made and additional notification duties[2].

[1] HA 1996, s 184(7); H(W)A 2014, s 63(5). See **9.54–9.56** and **11.163–11.167**.
[2] HA 1996, s 184(3A) as amended by HRA 2017, ss 4(3) and 5(3) for applications for homelessness assistance made to local housing authorities in England on or after 3 April 2018, and English Code, paras 7.25–7.28; H(W)A 2014, s 63(2), and Welsh Code, para 10.59. See **9.126–9.130**.

9.55 A 'restricted person' is defined as a person:

- who is not eligible for assistance under HA 1996, Pt 7[1] or H(W)A 2014, Pt 2[2]; and
- who is subject to immigration control within the meaning of the Asylum and Immigration Act 1996[3]; and either
- who does not have leave to enter or remain in the UK; or
- who has leave to enter or remain in the UK but is subject to a condition to maintain and accommodate himself or herself, and any dependent, without recourse to public funds[4].

[1] As amended by HRA 2017 for applications for homelessness assistance made to local housing authorities in England on or after 3 April 2018.
[2] See Chapter **11**.
[3] See **11.26–11.31** and **11.101**.
[4] HA 1996, s 184(7); H(W)A 2014, s 63(5).

9.56 It follows that British nationals, some Commonwealth nationals with the right of abode in the UK and most EEA nationals and their family members cannot be restricted persons[1].

[1] See **11.26–11.31**. The difference between those who are owed a main housing duty (HA 1996, s 193(2)) or duty to secure accommodation for an applicant in priority need (H(W)A 2014, s 75(2)) because of the presence in his or her household of a restricted person, and other applicants owed the same duty, is that the local housing authority is required to bring the duty in a restricted case to an end by making a private rented sector offer so far as reasonably practicable, whereas it may, but is not required to, make a private rented sector offer to other applicants (HA 1996, s 193(7AA)–(7AD), H(W)A 2014, s 76(5)). See **16.180–16.185** (England) and **17.177** (Wales).

Particular situations

Violence, harassment or abuse

9.57 There is a specific chapter in the English Code contains guidance on providing homelessness services to people who have experienced, or are at risk of, domestic violence or abuse[1]. The Code contains guidance that it is essential that inquiries do not provoke further violence and abuse. Local housing authorities are warned against approaching the alleged perpetrator. Information may be sought from the applicant, his or her friends or relatives, from adult care or children's services, or from the police[2].

1   English Code, chapter 21.
2   English Code, para 21.21; Welsh Code, para 10.22.

9.58 If the violence or abuse alleged is *domestic* violence or abuse, local housing authorities are reminded that the applicant 'may be in considerable distress'. Any interview should be conducted by an officer who is trained to deal with domestic violence allegations, and the applicant should have the option of requesting an officer of the same sex as him or her[1]. Local housing authorities are advised that applicants alleging domestic violence may not be able to produce independent evidence of the violence. Whilst a local housing authority may seek corroboration, it should not reject the applicant's account merely because there is no evidence of complaints to the police or other agencies[2]. Local housing authorities are reminded that the term 'violence' should not be given a restrictive meaning and that the test to be applied is not whether violence or abuse occurred in the past but whether it is probable that there will be violence, threats of violence that are likely to be carried out, or abuse, if the applicant continues to occupy his or her home[3].

1   English Code, para 21.23; Welsh Code, paras 8.21–8.26.
2   *Hawa Abdilah Ali v Newham London Borough Council* (2000) November *Legal Action*, p 23, Bow County Court; English Code, para 21.21.
3   English Code, paras 21.19–21.20; Welsh Code, paras 8.21–8.26. See also *Bond v Leicester City Council* [2001] EWCA Civ 1544, (2002) 34 HLR 6, CA. See further **10.79–10.91** (England) and **10.79–10.80, 10.79–10.98**(Wales).

9.59 A local housing authority must investigate accounts of violence, harassment or abuse given by the applicant when it is making its inquiries into whether accommodation is or was reasonable for the applicant to occupy[1]. A local housing authority cannot refuse to investigate these accounts merely because the applicant had failed to raise them at an earlier stage[2].

1   *R v Northampton Borough Council ex p Clarkson* (1992) 24 HLR 529, QBD, where the local housing authority's decision that an applicant had become homeless intentionally was quashed, as it had failed to make inquiries into her account that her brother had sexually harassed her at the accommodation.
2   *R v Hackney London Borough Council ex p Decordova* (1994) 27 HLR 108, QBD.

9.60 If the local housing authority is considering disbelieving an applicant because of contradictions or inconsistencies in his or her account, or because of information derived from other sources, those contradictions or inconsistencies should be put to the applicant for explanation[1].

1   *R v Camden London Borough Council ex p Mohammed* (1997) 30 HLR 315, QBD. See **9.42**.

Modern slavery and trafficking

9.61 The English Code contains a specific chapter giving guidance on assisting applicants who may have been subject to modern slavery, or trafficked[1]. In relation to inquiries, it advises that applicants may be in considerable distress, and local housing authority officers should have appropriate training to enable them to conduct interviews. Applicants should be given the option of being interviewed by a person of the same sex as them, if they wish[2].

1 English Code, chapter 25.
2 English Code, paras 25.15.

Financial problems

9.62 If accommodation has been lost as a result of the applicant accruing rent or mortgage arrears, the local housing authority will need to make inquiries into the applicant's financial affairs. Those same issues may also be relevant to the question of whether accommodation currently occupied by the applicant is reasonable for him or her to continue to occupy[1].

1 For local housing authorities in England, Homelessness (Suitability of Accommodation) Order 1996, SI 1996/3204 at Appendix 2; English Code, paras 6.28 and 9.18–9.19. For local housing authorities in Wales, H(W)A 2014, s 59(2); Welsh Code, paras 8.29–8.30 and 17.18–17.19. See 10.107–10.109.

9.63 The local housing authority should examine why the applicant had fallen into arrears and give him or her an opportunity to explain the cause of the arrears, their extent and any arrangements made to repay them[1]. The local housing authority should investigate whether an applicant knew about the availability of housing benefit or other relevant welfare benefits, whether housing benefit was claimed and if not, why not[2]. In a case where the applicants had not disputed the landlord's claim to possession on the grounds that they were in arrears, but had subsequently argued that the contractual rent was lower than that put forward to the court, and therefore they were not in arrears, the local housing authority was not obliged to make inquiries into the actual level of the contractual rent. The court would not have made a possession order if the contractual rent had been the amount stated by the applicants[3].

1 *R v Wyre Borough Council ex p Joyce* (1983) 11 HLR 73, QBD.
2 *R v Tower Hamlets London Borough Council ex p Saber* (1992) 24 HLR 611, QBD.
3 *Green v Croydon London Borough Council* [2007] EWCA Civ 1367, [2008] HLR 28, CA. See also *Sheppard v Richmond-upon-Thames Royal London Borough Council* [2012] EWCA Civ 302, (2012) June *Legal Action*, p 38, CA.

9.64 If an applicant gave up his or her accommodation due to financial pressures, the local housing authority must determine the extent of those pressures, eg what debts may have been owed by the applicant and what the arrangements for repayment were. If loans were taken out to support a business venture, it is relevant to inquire into what the applicant knew or ought to have known about the business's prospects[1]. The local housing authority must consider fully whether or not an applicant could have afforded to have remained in his or her accommodation, but need not engage in detailed arithmetical calculations or verification of itemised expenses[2].

1 *R v Exeter City Council ex p Tranckle* (1993) 26 HLR 244, QBD.
2 *R v Brent London Borough Council ex p Grossett* (1994) 28 HLR 9, CA; and *Bernard v Enfield London Borough Council* [2001] EWCA Civ 1831, (2002) 34 HLR 46, CA.

9.65 The Court of Appeal has said that the right question for a local housing authority to determine was whether the rent was affordable for an applicant, and therefore whether it was reasonable for her to have continued to occupy the property. The issues of whether the applicant may in fact have spent part of her benefits on other things apart from basic expenses, or have failed to pay the whole of her housing benefit to her landlord, were not strictly relevant if the accommodation was never in fact affordable on the applicant's income. The local housing authority's decision had been wrong not to give reasons for its decision that certain items of expenditure had been considered by the decision-maker to be non-essential items[1].

1   *Farah v Hillingdon London Borough Council* [2014] EWCA Civ 359, [2014] HLR 24, CA. See also *Balog v Birmingham City Council* [2013] EWCA Civ 1582, [2014] HLR 14, CA, where the issue of affordability had been lawfully assessed by the local housing authority; and *Samuels v Birmingham City Council* [2015] EWCA Civ 1051, [2015] HLR 47, CA. Permission has been granted to Ms Samuels to appeal to The Supreme Court. At the time of writing, the appeal has yet to be heard.

Loss of assured shorthold tenancy

9.66 The most frequently occurring reason in England for the loss of the last settled home, leading to an application for homelessness assistance, is where a landlord has obtained a mandatory order for possession under Housing Act 1988, s 21, against an assured shorthold tenant[1]. Where an applicant for homelessness assistance to a local housing authority in England has received a valid Housing Act 1988, s 21, notice, he or she will be threatened with homelessness[2] during the 56-day period leading up to the date of expiry of the notice, and the HA 1996, s 195(2)[3], prevention duty will be owed. The local housing authority should make inquiries to satisfy themselves that the notice is valid[4].

1   Table 774, *Statutory Homelessness Live Tables*, MHCLG. In Wales, loss of an assured shorthold tenancy was a significant cause of homelessness, but not the most frequent cause: *Table: Households accepted as homeless by main reason for loss of last settled accommodation*, Welsh Government, 2015 (the Welsh Government no longer publishes statistics on the causes of homelessness).
2   HA 1996, s 175(5), as inserted by HRA 2017, s 1(3), for applications for homelessness assistance made to local housing authorities in England on or after 3 April 2018; see **10.146**.
3   As amended by HRA 2017, s 4(2), for applications for homelessness assistance made to local housing authorities in England on or after 3 April 2018; see **15.87–15.137**.
4   The availability of defences to a claim for possession brought after expiry of the date for possession in a Housing Act 1988, s 21, notice is beyond the scope of this work. Readers are referred to *Defending Possession Proceedings* (Luba, Madge, McConnell, Gallagher, Madge-Wyld, Legal Action Group, 8th edn, 2016).

9.67 After the date for expiry of the notice, the applicant may no longer be threatened with homelessness, but instead have become homeless[1]. The Secretary of State's position, as recommended in the English Code, is that if the local housing authority is satisfied that the landlord intends to seek possession and that further efforts from the local housing authority to resolve the situation and persuade the landlord to allow the tenant to remain in the property are unlikely to be successful and there would be no defence to an application for a possession order, then it is unlikely to be reasonable for the applicant to continue to occupy beyond the expiration date in the notice, (unless the local housing authority is taking steps to persuade the landlord to allow the tenant to continue to occupy the accommodation for a reasonable period to provide an opportunity for alternative accommodation to be found)[2].

In addition, the Secretary of State's view is that it is highly unlikely to be reasonable for the applicant to continue to occupy once a court has made an order for possession and that local housing authorities should not consider it reasonable for an applicant to remain in occupation until the point when a warrant or writ is issued[3]. The local housing authority will need to make inquiries into all of these issues.

[1]   Which would mean that the HA 1996, s 195(2), as amended by HRA 2017, s 4(2), for applications for homelessness assistance made to local housing authorities in England on or after 3 April 2018), prevention duty has come to an end: HA 1996, s 195(8)(c) (as amended by HRA 2017, s 4(2), for applications for homelessness assistance made to local housing authorities in England on or after 3 April 2018) and the HA 1996, s 189B(2) (as inserted by HRA 2017, s 5(2), for applications for homelessness assistance made to local housing authorities in England on or after 3 April 2018) would apply, see **15.113–15.117**.
[2]   English Code, para 6.36.
[3]   English Code, paras 6.37–6.38.

9.68 If the local housing authority decides that the applicant is homeless[1], it is entitled to consider the reasons why the landlord wanted possession of the property and whether those reasons could be said to be as a result of the applicant's deliberate act or omission (for example, in accruing rent arrears) and whether or not the applicant has become homeless intentionally[2].

[1]   Either because the accommodation is not reasonable to continue to occupy while the landlord brings possession proceedings, see **10.110–10.116**, or because the landlord has obtained and executed a possession order.
[2]   *Bratton v Croydon London Borough Council* [2002] EWCA Civ 1492, (2002) December *Legal Action*, p 22, CA; see **13.201–13.2016**.

Acquiescence

9.69 In general, if a household has lost accommodation as a result of the deliberate act or omission of one of its members (eg by the one who was the tenant or owner accruing rent or mortgage arrears or engaging in nuisance behaviour), the local housing authority is entitled to assume that the other one acquiesced in that behaviour[1]. However, if there is any suggestion to the contrary, the local housing authority must investigate whether there was in fact such acquiescence in that particular case[2].

[1]   *R v North Devon District Council ex p Lewis* [1981] 1 WLR 328, QBD.
[2]   *R v Eastleigh Borough Council ex p Beattie (No 2)* (1984) 17 HLR 168, QBD; English Code, paras 9.9–9.11. See **13.95–13.99**.

Medical conditions

9.70 A local housing authority may need to make inquiries into an applicant's medical condition in order to decide whether he or she has a priority need[1], whether previous accommodation was reasonable for the applicant to continue to occupy[2], or whether accommodation currently occupied or offered for occupation is suitable for the applicant's needs[3].

[1]   See **12.76–12.125** (England) and **12.199–12.206** (Wales).
[2]   See **10.73–10.134** and **13.162–13.180**.
[3]   See CHAPTER **18** of this book.

9.71 Where the local housing authority has to make decisions on both medical and non-medical aspects, it cannot treat the two aspects entirely separately. It must come to an overall, or composite, assessment of the applicant's circumstances[1].

[1]   *R v Lewisham London Borough Council ex p Dolan* (1993) 25 HLR 68, QBD; and *Crossley v City of Westminster* [2006] EWCA Civ 140, [2006] HLR 26, CA.

9.72 In 2013, the Universities of York and Heriot Watt published research into medical evidence and decision-making in applications for homelessness assistance to local housing authorities in England: ' "*You can judge them on how they look . . .* ", *Homelessness Officers, Medical evidence and Decision-Making in England*'[1]. The research found that decision-makers were often influenced by their own initial impressions of applicants. Physical infirmity, such as walking with a stick, shortness of breath or amputated limbs, was seen as a strong indicator of vulnerability even before any information had been collected. Investigating officers could be suspicious of an applicant's behaviour, particularly if he or she appeared to be 'too clever' or knew 'the system' too well. It was routine to seek the views of the applicant's GP, and sometimes the views of hospital consultants, but medical professionals who were treating the applicant were perceived to be less objective than the medical advisers to the local housing authority. A significant amount of reliance was placed on the medication, and dosages, prescribed. Often decision-makers would look up the medication on the internet themselves rather than obtain expert advice. The researchers conclude that authoritative letters from an applicant's medical advisers should specify the length of time that the adviser has known the applicant, the degree of familiarity with his or her condition, the diagnosis, the medication prescribed and an explanation of any particular drug or dosage. They also suggest that the adviser should comment on the effect or likely impact of street homelessness on the diagnosed conditions, and how and why the prognosis might be worsened by street homelessness.

[1]   Bretheron, Hunter and Johnson ' "*You can judge them on how they look . . .* ", *Homelessness Officers, Medical evidence and Decision-Making in England*' (2013) *European Journal of Homelessness*, Vol 7, No 1, p 69. For a summary of the research see (2013) October *Legal Action*, p 28. See also **12.92–12.101**.

USE OF MEDICAL ADVISERS

9.73 Where a medical issue is raised by the applicant, or is apparent from the information available, the local housing authority should obtain medical evidence[1]. A local housing authority can obtain the opinion of its own medical adviser, or any medical evidence, but any decisions on the facts and the overall assessment should each be made by the local housing authority itself and not delegated to the medical adviser[2]. If the inquiries indicate that the applicant is anxious or depressed or has some other mental health condition, it may be appropriate to obtain specialist psychiatric evidence[3].

[1]   *Osmani v Camden London Borough Council* [2004] EWCA Civ 1706, [2005] HLR 22, CA.
[2]   *R v Lambeth London Borough Council ex p Walters* (1994) 26 HLR 170, QBD; *Osmani v Camden London Borough Council* [2004] EWCA Civ 1706, [2005] HLR 22, CA; *Cramp v Hastings Borough Council* [2005] EWCA Civ 1005, [2005] HLR 48, CA; and *Shala v Birmingham City Council* [2007] EWCA Civ 624, [2008] HLR 8, CA. Where an adviser had informed the local housing authority that more evidence was required, and the decision-maker

had known that a further report would be produced, it was wrong in law for the local housing authority to make its decision without waiting for that report or obtaining further evidence itself: *Woldeab v Southwark London Borough Council* (2011), November *Legal Action*, p 39, Lambeth County Court.

3   *R v Brent London Borough Council ex p McManus* (1993) 25 HLR 643, QBD. But see *Wells v Tower Hamlets London Borough Council* [2006] EWCA Civ 755, (2006) September *Legal Action*, p 14, CA, where the local housing authority was entitled to rely on the opinion of its own medical adviser, a GP, who had accepted (but provided a 'gloss' to) the opinion expressed by the applicant's treating psychiatrist. See also *R (IA) v Westminster City Council* [2013] EWHC 1273 (QB), (2013) July/August *Legal Action*, p 23, QBD. In *Oyebanji v Waltham Forest London Borough Council*, 22 August 2013, Central London County Court, (2014) February *Legal Action*, p 31, the local housing authority had been wrong in law to prefer the opinion of a psychiatrist who had not seen the applicant over the evidence of a practising psychotherapist who saw her regularly.

9.74 The medical adviser must act fairly in obtaining any relevant information from the applicant's own doctors and in coming to an opinion. Depending on the circumstances, the applicant's medical records should be considered and it may even be necessary for the medical adviser to examine the applicant personally or to discuss the case with the applicant's own doctor[1].

1   *R v Lambeth London Borough Council ex p Walters* (1994) 26 HLR 170, QBD; and *Shala v Birmingham City Council* [2007] EWCA Civ 624, [2008] HLR 8, CA. Whether or not a personal examination is required will depend on the particular facts. See *Khelassi v Brent London Borough Council* [2006] EWCA Civ 1825, (2007) February *Legal Action*, p 31, CA (where there had been a personal medical examination); *Shala v Birmingham City Council* [2007] EWCA Civ 624, [2008] HLR 8, CA (where the local housing authority was required to bear in mind that its medical adviser had not examined the applicant); *Wandsworth London Borough Council v Allison* [2008] EWCA Civ 354, (2008) June *Legal Action*, p 33, CA (where a personal examination was not necessary); and *R (Bauer-Czarnomski) v Ealing London Borough Council* [2010] EWHC 130 (Admin), (2010) March *Legal Action*, p 30, Admin Ct (a judicial review claim relating to an application for an allocation of social housing, see 4.98–4.100).

9.75 If there are differences of opinion between the local housing authority's medical advisers and the medical opinion put forward on behalf of the applicant, the local housing authority should seek an explanation for those differences[1]. The local housing authority should also take into account differences in medical expertise when trying to reconcile conflicting medical opinions[2]. An adverse medical opinion, including one from the applicant's own doctor(s), should normally be put to the applicant for comment[3]. So too should any medical advice that raises new issues or contentious points[4]. Where a local housing authority's policy was to 'encourage persons who have any knowledge of an applicant's medical or social history to attend' the decision-making panel, and the applicant's doctor had expressed a wish to attend, the local housing authority was severely criticised by the Local Government Ombudsman for failing to invite the doctor[5]. The final decision (for example, as to whether or not an applicant is vulnerable) is for the local housing authority, not for the medical adviser, but normally the medical adviser should be asked to address the relevant statutory test (such as vulnerability)[6].

1   *R v Kensington and Chelsea Royal London Borough Council ex p Assiter* (1996) September *Legal Action*, p 13, QBD.
2   *Yemlahi v Lambeth London Borough Council* (2000) August *Legal Action*, p 26, Wandsworth County Court; *Khelassi v Brent London Borough Council* [2006] EWCA Civ 1825, (2007) February *Legal Action*, p 31, CA; and *Shala v Birmingham City Council* [2007] EWCA Civ 624, [2008] HLR 8, CA.

3   *R v Newham London Borough Council ex p Lumley* (2001) 33 HLR 11, QBD; *Yemlahi v Lambeth London Borough Council* (2000) August *Legal Action*, p 26, Wandsworth County Court; and *R (Amirun Begum) v Tower Hamlets London Borough Council* [2002] EWHC 633 (Admin), (2003) 35 HLR 8, QBD. But see *Wells v Tower Hamlets London Borough Council* [2006] EWCA Civ 755, (2006) September *Legal Action*, p 14, CA, where the applicant's medical evidence had been accepted and the local housing authority's medical adviser had added 'a gloss'. In those circumstances, there was no obligation to put the medical adviser's comments to the applicant.

4   *Hall v Wandsworth London Borough Council* [2004] EWCA Civ 1740, [2005] HLR 23, CA.

5   *Complaint against Waltham Forest London Borough Council*, 03/A/15819, 9 November 2005.

6   English Code, paras 8.13–8.18; see also *Sicilia v Waltham Forest London Borough Council* (2002) December *Legal Action*, p 21, Bow County Court; *Ryde v Enfield London Borough Council* [2005] EWCA Civ 1281, (2006) January *Legal Action*, p 32, CA. See also, in the context of an application for an allocation of social housing, *R (Bauer-Czarnomski) v Ealing London Borough Council* [2010] EWHC 130 (Admin), March *Legal Action*, p 30, Admin Ct, where the medical adviser did overstep his remit, see **4.98–4.100**.

9.76 When the local housing authority is assessing whether an applicant is 'vulnerable', and care, health or other support needs are identified in the course of that assessment, the local housing authority should liaise with adult care services and health authorities, where appropriate, as part of its inquiries[1]. It may be necessary to obtain an assessment from the relevant specialist authority. Medical reports obtained as part of an assessment by the Department for Work and Pensions, of a person's entitlement for specific welfare benefits, may be taken into account, but the local housing authority must bear in mind that assessment of entitlement to benefits is a wholly different exercise from assessment of priority need[2].

1   English Code, para 8.25; Welsh Code, para 16.16.

2   *Mangion v Lewisham London Borough Council* [2008] EWCA Civ 1642, (2009) January *Legal Action*, p 26, CA; and *Simpson-Lowe v Croydon London Borough Council* [2012] EWCA Civ 131, (2012) April *Legal Action*, p 47, CA.

9.77 One judge said, in a case where the applicant was a former asylum-seeker who suffered from a number of mental health conditions[1]:

'Where mental health issues and issues arising from historic mistreatment of former asylum seeker are concerned, the housing authority should normally consult with the applicant's medical advisers, both present and past and with the relevant mental health services and will usually seek [to] obtain a further assessment and report from a psychiatrist. Where, as in this case, it appears that the applicant is depressed, alone, unable readily to cope with day-to-day living tasks, unemployed and possibly unemployable, has no settled links with England or the English way of life and has minimal support mechanisms at his disposal, the inquiries would be expected to extend to a detailed inquiry into the applicant's way of life prior to his homelessness.'

1   *R (IA) v Westminster City Council* [2013] EWHC 1273 (QB), (2013) July/August *Legal Action*, p 23 per HHJ Anthony Thornton QC, sitting as a deputy High Court judge, at [25]. The judge also said that, where the applicant is a former asylum-seeker: '[t]he decision-maker should . . . have sought details of the case presented to the UK Border Agency that led to the claimant being granted asylum, of the nature and contents of the psychiatric assessment and treatment he had previously received, of the reasons for the proposed counselling, of the reasons why the landlord had terminated the claimant's tenancy and of any independent evidence of the claimant's living difficulties' at [29].

9.78 The Court of Appeal has considered the issue of the use, by local housing authorities, of medical advisers[1]. It held:

'It is entirely right that local authority officers, themselves without any medical expertise, should not be expected to make their own critical evaluation of applicants' medical evidence and should have access to specialist advice about it. What would not be acceptable is seeking out advisers to support a refusal of priority need housing wherever possible[2].'

The Court of Appeal went on to remind local housing authorities that it is not the medical advisers but the local housing authorities that have the task of determining whether an applicant has a priority need (or any other medically related question). It is appropriate for medical advisers to be asked to address the specific issue which the local housing authority has to decide, and to furnish material within their professional competence which addresses that issue. It has also reminded local housing authorities that, unless their medical adviser has personally examined the applicant, his or her opinion cannot be considered expert evidence of the applicant's condition[3].

[1]   *Shala v Birmingham City Council* [2007] EWCA Civ 624, [2008] HLR 8, CA.
[2]   *Shala v Birmingham City Council* [2007] EWCA Civ 624, [2008] HLR 8, CA at [19] per Sedley LJ.
[3]   *Shala v Birmingham City Council* [2007] EWCA Civ 624, [2008] HLR 8, CA at [19]–[22] per Sedley LJ. An attempt to argue that the particular medical adviser's organisation was 'biased in favour of their paymasters' received short shrift from the Court of Appeal in *Harper v Oxford City Council* [2007] EWCA Civ 1169, (2008) January *Legal Action*, p 37, CA. In *Oyebanji v Waltham Forest London Borough Council*, 22 August 2013, Central London County Court, (2014) February *Legal Action*, p 31, the local housing authority had been wrong in law to prefer the opinion of a psychiatrist who had not seen the applicant over the evidence of a practising psychotherapist who saw her regularly. See also **12.92–12.101**.

9.79 In a separate case, the Court of Appeal has held that the role of a medical adviser is to comment 'on the medical evidence in order to enable the local authority to understand the medical issues and to evaluate for itself the evidence before it as to [the applicant's] medical condition'[1]. In that case, it was not appropriate for the medical adviser to have examined the applicant personally.

[1]   *Wandsworth London Borough Council v Allison* [2008] EWCA Civ 354, (2008) June *Legal Action*, p 33, CA per Wall LJ at [71].

9.80 An application to the Court of Appeal for permission to bring a second appeal[1], on the grounds that those two decisions of the Court of Appeal were inconsistent, was refused. The judge said:

'I do not see any inconsistency between the two decisions in [*Birmingham City Council v*] *Shala* and [*Wandsworth London Borough Council v*] *Allison*. In *Allison* the Court of Appeal helpfully set out the kind of assistance that a local authority's in-house medical adviser can give. In *Shala*, on the other hand, the Court of Appeal pointed out the limitations which exist if the in-house medical adviser instead of assisting the local authority to understand the medical expert seeks to offer conflicting expert opinion[2].'

[1]   For 'second appeals', see **19.293–19.300**.

2   *Simpson-Lowe v Croydon London Borough Council* [2012] EWCA Civ 131, (2012) April
    Legal Action, p 47, CA at [9] per Jackson LJ. See also *Nagi v Birmingham City Council* [2010]
    EWCA Civ 1391, (2011) January *Legal Action*, p 36, CA.

Public sector equality duty

9.81 If some feature of the evidence presented raises a possibility that the
applicant, or other relevant person, might have a 'disability', and that this
might be relevant to the issue under consideration, the decision-maker must
comply with the requirements of the Equality Act 2010 and take account of
that disability[1]. The same applies to any other protected characteristic that
might be relevant to the issue being inquired into[2].

1   Equality Act 2010, s 149. See English Code, para 8.17; and **12.91, 12.100, 13.70** and
    18.65–18.68 of this book.
2   The relevant protected characteristics are: age; disability; gender reassignment; pregnancy and
    maternity; race; religion or belief; sex; sexual orientation: Equality Act 2010, s 149(7).

9.82 A 'disability' is defined at Equality Act 2010, s 6, as 'a physical or mental
impairment' which 'has a substantial and long-term adverse effect on P's ability to carry out normal day-to-day activities'[1]. Where the issue of disability is
raised, local housing authorities should:

> 'focus very sharply on (i) whether the applicant is under a disability (or has another
> relevant protected characteristic), (ii) the extent of such disability, (iii) the likely
> effect of the disability, when taken together with any other features, on the
> applicant[2].'

1   Equality Act 2010, s 6. 'Substantial' means 'more than minor or trivial': Equality Act 2010,
    s 212. The effect of an impairment is long-term if (a) it has lasted for at least 12 months, (b)
    it is likely to last for at least 12 months, or (c) it is likely to last for the rest of the life of the
    person affected: Equality Act, Sch 1 para 1. Addiction to alcohol, nicotine or any other
    substance is to be treated as not amounting to an impairment, unless the addiction was
    originally the result of the administration of medically prescribed drugs or other medical
    treatment: Equality Act 2010 (Disability) Regulations, SI 2010/2128, reg 3. Cancer, HIV
    infection and multiple sclerosis are each deemed to be disabilities: Equality Act 2010, Sch 1,
    para 6.
2   *Hotak v Southwark London Borough Council* [2015] UKSC 30, [2016] AC 811, SC per
    Lord Neuberger [78].

9.83 The issue of whether or not an applicant, or other member of the
applicant's household is disabled, might relate to whether or not the applicant
has a priority need because he or she, or a member of his or her household is
vulnerable[1], whether the applicant has become homeless intentionally[2],
whether the applicant is occupying suitable accommodation[3] or to any other
points.

1   *Hotak v Southwark London Borough Council* [2015] UKSC 30, [2016] AC 811, SC, see
    12.91.
2   *Pieretti v Enfield London Borough Council* [2010] EWCA Civ 1104, [2011] HLR 3, CA, see
    13.70.
3   *Hackney London Borough Council v Haque* [2017] EWCA Civ 4, [2017] HLR 14, CA, see
    18.65–18.68.

RELEVANCE OF SUPPORT

9.84 Particular inquiries may be necessary in order to decide whether an applicant, who has been receiving support from a third party, is vulnerable[1]. Local housing authorities should not assume that the possibility or existence of support means that the applicant is not vulnerable. Rather, a local housing authority should inquire into whether the support will be available on a consistent and predictable basis. If so, the local housing authority should then consider whether the support will be sufficient to prevent the applicant from being vulnerable. Unless both of those questions are answered in the affirmative, then the applicant will be vulnerable[2].

[1] HA 1996, s 189(1)(c), see **12.76–12.125**; H(W)A 2014, ss 70(1)(c) and 71, see **12.199–12.206**.
[2] *Hotak v Southwark London Borough Council, Kanu v Southwark London Borough Council, Johnson v Solihull Metropolitan Borough* [2015] UKSC 30, [2016] AC 811, SC per Lord Neuberger at [65] and [70]; English Code, para 8.16. See **12.90**.

Overcrowded accommodation

9.85 If an applicant claims that his or her present or previous accommodation is or was overcrowded, and therefore not reasonable for him or her to continue to occupy, the local housing authority must make inquiries to determine whether the accommodation is or was overcrowded and, if so, to what extent[1]. Where there is a dispute as to the size, space or arrangement of the accommodation, inquiries should be made so that the local housing authority can make its own decision on the disputed issues[2].

[1] *R v Tower Hamlets London Borough Council ex p Bibi* (1991) 23 HLR 500, QBD. See **10.122–10.123**.
[2] *R v Kensington and Chelsea Royal London Borough Council ex p Silchenstedt* (1997) 29 HLR 728, QBD.

Best interests of any children

9.86 The Children Act 2004 requires all local authorities, including local housing authorities, to discharge their functions having regard to the need to safeguard and promote the welfare of children[1]. This duty is colloquially referred to as the 'best interests' duty. Whilst the duty does not arise in all of the decisions that a local housing authority has to make[2], the Supreme Court has held that it will always arise when offers of accommodation are made to applicants whose households include minor children[3]. Local housing authorities are required to consider the significance of any disruption caused by the location of the accommodation to the education of the applicant or any member of his or her household[4]. The Supreme Court has held that it is not enough for a decision-maker simply to ask whether any of the children are approaching their GCSE or other externally assessed examinations. The decision-maker should identify the principal needs of the children, both individually and collectively, and have regard to the need to safeguard and promote the children's welfare. The local housing authority should also explain, either by reference to a published policy, or in its decision letter, the choices made about the location of accommodation (or any other factors relating to suitability) that affect the welfare of the children[5].

[1]   Children Act 2004, s 11(2) for local authorities in England; s 28(2) for local authorities in Wales.
[2]   It will not affect, for example, whether or not an applicant has become homeless intentionally: *Huzrat v Hounslow London Borough Council* [2013] EWCA Civ 1865, [2014] HLR 17, CA, see **13.169**.
[3]   *Nzolameso v City of Westminster Council* [2015] UKSC 22, [2015] 2 All ER 942, [2015] HLR 22, SC.
[4]   Homelessness (Suitability of Accommodation) (England) Order 2012, SI 2012/2601, art 2(b), see **18.48–18.61**; Homelessness (Suitability of Accommodation) (Wales) Order 2015/1268, art 3(f), see **18.48** and **18.60–18.64**.
[5]   *Nzolameso v City of Westminster Council* [2015] UKSC 22, [2015] 2 All ER 942, [2015] HLR 22, SC per Baroness Hale at [22]–[30].

9.87 The Administrative Court has considered the position of school-age children who are being accommodated, by a local housing authority, outside of the local housing authority's district and may have to change schools. In those cases, the local housing authority must have contemporary records showing that it evaluated the likely impact of transfer on the educational welfare of the child, and how it conducted that evaluation. It must be able to show that it had liaised with the education department of the receiving local housing authority and that it had satisfied that adequate educational arrangements had been, or would be, put in place[1].

[1]   R *(E) v Islington London Borough Council* [2017] EWHC 1440 (Admin) per Ben Emerson QC sitting as a deputy High Court judge at [120]–[122], and discussed further at **18.57**.

Additional matters for assessment

9.88 Local housing authorities in both England and Wales are now required to consider a number of additional issues. The local housing authority must assess:

(a)   the circumstances that have caused the applicant to be homeless or threatened with homelessness;
(b)   the housing needs of the applicant and of any members of his or her household; and
(c)   the support needed for the applicant and for his or her household in order to retain accommodation which is or may become available[1].

[1]   HA 1996, s 189A(2), inserted by HRA 2017, s 3(1), for applications for homelessness assistance made to local housing authorities in England on or after 3 April 2018; see English Code, chapter 11, and see **15.67–15.69**; H(W)A 2014, s 62(5)(a), (b) and (c); Welsh Code, paras 10.21–10.29, see **9.13**.

DECISIONS ON APPLICATIONS

Overview

9.89 Once the local housing authority has completed its inquiries into an application, it is required to notify the applicant of its decision (in England) or of the outcome of its assessment (in Wales)[1]. Every application therefore results in notification of a decision. As a result of the new focus in both England and

Wales of early intervention, and the new duties so that all eligible applicants are now helped to prevent their own homelessness, or to find suitable accommodation, local housing authorities are now likely to notify an applicant of a series of decisions, rather than just one decision[2]. Those decisions will include:

- a decision that the applicant is ineligible for assistance[3];
- a decision that the applicant is eligible for assistance and is threatened with homelessness[4] or is homeless[5], so that the HA 1996, s 195(2)[6] or H(W)A 2014, s 68(1)[7] prevention or HA 1996, s 189B(2)[8] or H(W)A 2014, s 73(1)[9], relief duty is owed[10];
- a decision that the HA 1996, s 195(2)[11] or H(W)A 2014, s 68(1)[12] prevention or HA 1996, s 189B(2)[13] or H(W)A 2014, s 73(1)[14], relief duty has come to an end[15]; and
- a decision as to what duty, if any, is subsequently owed to the applicant[16].

[1] HA 1996, s 184(3) and English Code, paras 18.29–18.33; H(W)A 2014, s 63(1) and Welsh Code, paras 10.5 and 10.53–10.58. See **9.90–9.94**.
[2] See **9.97–9.107**.
[3] HA 1996, s 184(1)(a); H(W)A 2014, s 62(4). See Chapter **11** for eligible for assistance.
[4] HA 1996, s 175(4) and (5), as amended and inserted by HRA 2017, s 1(2) and (3), for applications for homelessness assistance made to local housing authorities in England on or after 3 April 2018; H(W)A 2014, s 55(4), see **10.144–10.147**.
[5] HA 1996, s 175–177; H(W)A 2014, ss 55–58, see Chapter **10**.
[6] As amended by HRA 2017, s 4(2), for applications for homelessness assistance made to local housing authorities in England on or after 3 April 2018, see **15.87–15.137**.
[7] See **17.45–17.72**.
[8] As inserted by HRA 2017, s 5(2), for applications for homelessness assistance made to local housing authorities in England on or after 3 April 2018, see **15.138–15.195**.
[9] See **17.73–17.143**.
[10] HA 1996, s 184(1)(b); H(W)A 2014, s 62(5)(d).
[11] As amended by HRA 2017, s 4(2), for applications for homelessness assistance made to local housing authorities in England on or after 3 April 2018, see **15.87–15.137**.
[12] See **17.45–17.72**.
[13] As inserted by HRA 2017, s 5(2), for applications for homelessness assistance made to local housing authorities in England on or after 3 April 2018, see **15.138–15.195**.
[14] See **17.73–17.143**.
[15] For prevention duty coming to an end: HA 1996, s 195(5)–(10), as amended by HRA 2017, s 4(2), for applications for homelessness assistance made to local housing authorities in England on or after 3 April 2018, see **15.98–15.132**; and H(W)A 2014, s 69, see **17.56–17.72**. For relief duty coming to an end: HA 1996, s 189B(5)–(9), as inserted by HRA 2017, s 5(2), for applications for homelessness assistance made to local housing authorities in England on or after 3 April 2018, see **15.151–15.189** and H(W)A 2014, s 74, see **17.84–17.119**.
[16] HA 1996, s 184(1)(b); H(W)A 2014, s 62(5)(d).

Notification of decisions

9.90 The requirements as to the content of the decision or decisions are given in HA 1996, s 184, or H(W)A 2014, s 63. For local housing authorities in England, the colloquialism 'a section 184 notice' or 'section 184 letter' is commonly used to refer to a local housing authority's notification of a decision on an application. There is no question of applicants being given the result informally in lieu of a written notification. Every applicant, even if she or he is found to be not eligible or not homeless, is entitled to a written decision. Even those successful in their application obtain a written record of that success[1]. The English Code advises that notifications 'should be clearly written in plain language'. They should include information .about any rights to request a review, and the timescale in which to do so. The notifications might also include information about independent advice services that available[2]. The English Code also notes that more than one notification might be required, and sometimes those notifications could be combined in one letter[3].

[1] The Local Government Ombudsman found maladministration when a local housing authority fails to notify the applicant of the decision on his or her application for homelessness assistance. £200 was recommended as compensation for a failure to notify a HA 1996, s 184, decision at all: *Investigation into complaint against Bristol City Council*, 12 015 826, 4 July 2013, (2013) September *Legal Action*, p 30; and £750 was recommended for a failure to notify a decision and secure suitable interim accommodation: *Investigation into complaint against London Borough of Newham*, 13 005 484, 17 March 2014, (2014) June *Legal Action*, p 40.
[2] English Code, para 18.29, see also Welsh Code, para 10.56.
[3] English Code, para 18.31. Somewhat surprisingly, this is the only reference in the English Code to the likelihood that, for applications for homelessness assistance made to local housing authorities in England on or after 3 April 2018, there are likely to be more than one notification, or s 184 decision.

9.91 The local housing authority is under an obligation, when making its decision, to consider the facts and the law in existence at the date of the decision. This means that any change of circumstances between the date of the application for homelessness assistance and the date of the decision must be taken into account. So, where an applicant for homelessness assistance had obtained a suitable assured shorthold tenancy before the HA 1996, s 184 decision had been made, the local housing authority was entitled to decide that the applicant was not homeless[1].

[1] *Hanton-Rhouila v Westminster City Council* [2010] EWCA Civ 1334, [2011] HLR 12, CA.

9.92 There is one circumstance in which it might be important to distinguish between the date on which the decision was actually made and the date when it was put in writing and 'notified' to the applicant. If either the facts or the law changes in an interval between the actual making of the decision and putting it in writing, it will be the facts and law that existed at the date of the actual making of the decision that are relevant, not those existing at the date of the written notification[1].

[1] *Robinson v Hammersmith & Fulham London Borough Council* [2006] EWCA Civ 1122, [2007] HLR 7, CA. See **12.136–12.139.**

9.93 In one case, the local housing authority concluded, on the day before an applicant's eighteenth birthday, that she did not have a priority need. The decision was actually put in writing on the following day. The Court of Appeal held that the decision was made on the day before the birthday, and therefore, applying the facts and law at that date, the local housing authority should have concluded that the applicant had a priority need by reason of her age[1].

[1] *Robinson v Hammersmith & Fulham London Borough Council* [2006] EWCA Civ 1122, [2007] HLR 7, CA. See **12.136–12.139.**

9.94 However, time limits attaching to rights to request a review (and, subsequently, to appeal) run from the date when the written decision is 'notified' to the applicant[1]. This is likely to be a date different from, and later than, either the actual date of the decision, or the date of the written decision. Notification refers to receipt of the decision by the applicant or by his or her agents, not the date on the letter[2]. If the notification is not actually received by the applicant, then it is treated as having been given to him or her if it is made available at the local housing authority's office for a reasonable period for collection by the applicant or by his or her agents[3]. In those circumstances, the date of notification would be the end of the reasonable period.

[1] HA 1996, s 202(3); H(W)A 2014, s 85(5).
[2] See **19.110**.
[3] HA 1996, s 184(6); English Code, para 18.30.

Time in which to notify decisions

9.95 There is no statutory time limit within which the decision reached on the application must be notified[1]. HA 1996, Pt 7[2] assumes that notice of the decision will be given by the local housing authorities 'on completing their inquiries', which suggests immediately[3]. That formulation also does not take account of the likelihood that the applicant may now be notified of more than one decision[4]. The present English Code reproduces the statutory formula: notification of a decision must be given 'when a housing authority has completed its inquiries'[5]. The Welsh Code recommends that local housing authorities should aim to complete each stage of the assessment and notify the applicant of the decision as soon as possible, and that in most cases this should be achieved within 10 working days. The emphasis, however, is on the correctness of the decision and the recommended timescale could be extended where the case is complex or information is difficult to clarify[6].

[1] See **9.50–9.52**.
[2] As amended by HRA 2017 for applications for homelessness assistance made to local housing authorities in England on or after 3 April 2018.
[3] HA 1996, s 184(3). H(W)A 2014, s 63(1) uses the formulation 'notify the applicant of the outcome of its assessment'.
[4] See **9.97–9.107**.
[5] English Code, para 18.32. A decision which was reached 11 months after the applicant had been interviewed, and where the applicant's circumstances had changed during those 11 months, was held to be 'manifestly' flawed, and the special procedure under the then Allocation of Housing and Homelessness (Review Procedures) Regulations 1999, SI 1999/71, reg 8(2) should have been implemented: *Lambeth London Borough Council v Johnston* [2008] EWCA Civ 690, [2009] HLR 10, CA. See **19.150–19.165**. See also *Complaint against Hounslow London Borough Council*, 10 019 388, 5 October 2011, (2011) December *Legal Action*, p 29; *Complaint against Birmingham City Council*, 13 017 548, (2014) October *Legal Action*, p 50; *Complaint against Hounslow London Borough Council*, 13 008 825, (2014) December *Legal Action*, p 34; and *Complaint against Lambeth London Borough Council*, 16 005 834, 15 August 2017 (2017) November *Legal Action*, p 41. The Commissioner for Complaints investigating the Northern Ireland Housing Executive recommended £4,000 for a delay of a year: Complaint 200700491, 6 November 2008, (2009) April *Legal Action*, p 22.
[6] Welsh Code, paras 10.5 and 10.54.

9.96 The only recommended timescale in the English Code refers to the decision as to what duty, if any, might be owed to the applicant when the HA 1996, s 189B(2)[1], relief duty comes to an end, and if the applicant remains homeless and has a priority need. In those circumstances, the English Code advises that local housing authorities should not delay completing their inquiries. It may be possible to notify the applicant the day after the 56-day period for the performance of the HA 1996, s 189B(2)[2], relief duty ie on the 57th day. If significant further investigations are required, the English Code advises that inquiries should be completed and a decision notified within a maximum of 15 working days (which would be three weeks) after the end of the 56-day period[3].

1　As inserted by HRA 2017 s 5(2), for applications for homelessness assistance made to local housing authorities in England on or after 3 April 2018, see **15.138–15.195**.
2　For the ending of the HA 1996, s 189B(2), relief duty after 56 days, see HA 1996, s 189B(7)(b) as inserted by HRA 2017 s 5(2), for applications for homelessness assistance made to local housing authorities in England on or after 3 April 2018, see **15.166–15.168**.
3　English Code, para 14.16.

Sequence of decisions

9.97 As a result of the new duties on local housing authorities in both England and Wales to help all applicants who are eligible for assistance and are either threatened with homelessness or homeless, it seems likely that local housing authorities will have to notify the applicant of a series of decisions. Those decisions include:

- a decision that the applicant is ineligible for assistance[1];
- a decision that the applicant is eligible for assistance and is threatened with homelessness[2] or is homeless[3], so that the HA 1996, s 195(2)[4] or H(W)A 2014, s 66(1)[5] prevention or HA 1996, s 189B(2)[6] or H(W)A 2014, s 73(1)[7], relief duty is owed[8];
- a decision that the HA 1996, s 195(2)[9] or H(W)A 2014, s 66(1)[10] prevention or HA 1996, s 189B(2)[11] or H(W)A 2014, s 73(1)[12], relief duty has come to an end[13]; and
- a decision as to what duty, if any, is subsequently owed to the applicant[14].

1　HA 1996, s 184(1)(a); H(W)A 2014, s 62(4). See Chapter 11 for eligible for assistance.
2　HA 1996, s 175(4) and (5), as amended and inserted by HRA 2017, s 1(2) and (3), for applications for homelessness assistance made to local housing authorities in England on or after 3 April 2018; H(W)A 2014, s 55(4), see **10.144–10.147**.
3　HA 1996, s 175–177; H(W)A 2014, ss 55–58, see Chapter 10.
4　As amended by HRA 2017, s 4(2), for applications for homelessness assistance made to local housing authorities in England on or after 3 April 2018, see **16.161–16.180**.
5　See **17.45–17.72**.
6　As inserted by HRA 2017, s 5(2), for applications for homelessness assistance made to local housing authorities in England on or after 3 April 2018, see **15.138–15.195**.
7　See **17.73–17.143**.
8　HA 1996, s 184(1)(b); H(W)A 2014, s 62(5)(d).
9　As amended by HRA 2017, s 4(2), for applications for homelessness assistance made to local housing authorities in England on or after 3 April 2018, see **16.161–16.180**.
10　See **17.45–17.72**.
11　As inserted by HRA 2017, s 5(2), for applications for homelessness assistance made to local housing authorities in England on or after 3 April 2018, see **15.138–15.195**.
12　See **17.73–17.143**.
13　HA 1996, 195(5)–(10), as amended by HRA 2017, s 4(2), for applications for homelessness assistance made to local housing authorities in England on or after 3 April 2018, see **15.98–15.132**; HA 1996, 189B(5)–(9), as inserted by HRA 2017, s 5(2), for applications for homelessness assistance made to local housing authorities in England on or after 3 April 2018, see **15.151–15.189**; H(W)A 2014, s 67, see **17.56–17.72**, and H(W)A 2014, s 74, see **17.84–17.119**.

14 HA 1996, s 184(1)(b); H(W)A 2014, s 62(5)(d).

9.98 The first decision for local housing authorities in both England and Wales will be whether the applicant is eligible for assistance[1]. If the applicant is not eligible, the decision must be notified to him or her with reasons[2]. If the local housing authority had been accommodating the applicant, under its interim accommodation duty[3], because it had reason to believe that the applicant may be eligible for assistance, may be homeless and may have a priority need, notification of this decision will bring the interim accommodation duty to an end[4].

1   HA 1996, s 184(1)(a); H(W)A 2014, s 62(4). See Chapter 10 for 'eligible for assistance'.
2   HA 1996, s 184(3) and English Code, para 18.33; H(W)A 2014, s 63(1) and Welsh Code, para 10.56.
3   HA 1996, s 188(1), see **16.37–16.80**; H(W)A 2014, s 68(1), see **17.118–17.134**.
4   HA 1996, s 188(1ZA)(a), (1ZB)(a), as inserted by HRA 2017, s 5(8), for applications for homelessness assistance made to local housing authorities in England on or after 3 April 2018, see **16.56–16.59**; H(W)A 2014, s 69(2), see **17.128–17.133**.

9.99 If the applicant is eligible, the local housing authority will then consider what duty, if any, is owed to the applicant[1]. This will require, in the first instance, consideration of whether the applicant is homeless or threatened with homelessness. If the applicant is neither homeless, nor threatened with homelessness, the decision that no duty is owed will be notified to the applicant with reasons[2]. If the local housing authority had been accommodating the applicant, under its interim accommodation duty[3], because it had reason to believe that the applicant may be eligible for assistance, may be homeless and may have a priority need, notification of this decision will bring the interim accommodation duty to an end[4].

1   HA 1996, s 184(1)(b); H(W)A 2014, s 62(5)(d).
2   HA 1996, s 184(3) and English Code, para 18.33; H(W)A 2014, s 63(1) and Welsh Code, para 10.56.
3   HA 1996, s 188(1), see **16.37–16.80**; H(W)A 2014, s 68(1), see **17.118–17.134**.
4   HA 1996, s 188(1ZA)(a), (1ZB)(a), as inserted by HRA 2017, s 5(8), for applications for homelessness assistance made to local housing authorities in England on or after 3 April 2018, see **16.56–16.59**; H(W)A 2014, s 69(2), see **17.128–17.133**.

9.100 If the applicant is either threatened with homelessness or homeless, a local housing authority in England will owe him or her two duties:

•   A duty to make an assessment of the applicant's case[1]; and
•   A duty to help the applicant prevent his or her homelessness[2], or to help the applicant secure accommodation[3].

This decision that these two duties are owed must be notified to the applicant[4]. There is no requirement to give reasons for the decision[5].

1   HA 1996, s 189A(1), as inserted by HRA 2017, s 3, for applications for homelessness assistance made to local housing authorities in England on or after 3 April 2018; see **15.62–15.86**.
2   HA 1996, s 195(2), as amended by HRA 2017, s 4(2), for applications for homelessness assistance made to local housing authorities in England on or after 3 April 2018; see **15.87–15.137**.
3   HA 1996, s 189B(2), as inserted by HRA 2017, s 5(2), for applications for homelessness assistance made to local housing authorities in England on or after 3 April 2018 see **15.138–15.195**.

⁴ HA 1996, s 184(3).
⁵ Because the statutory formulation is 'so far as any issue is decided against his interests, inform him of the reasons for their decision': HA 1996, s 184(3).

9.101 If the local housing authority in England has decided that the applicant is eligible for assistance and is homeless, and that the conditions are met for the applicant to be referred to another local housing authority for performance of the relief duty, that decision must be notified to the applicant with reasons[1].

[1] HA 1996, s 198(A1), as inserted by HRA 2017, s 5(8), for applications for homelessness assistance made to local housing authorities in England on or after 3 April 2018; see **15.139–15.146**. There is no right for the applicant to request a review of this decision to refer: HA 1996, s 202(1) (as amended by HRA 2017, s 9, for applications for homelessness assistance made to local housing authorities in England on or after 3 April 2018) does not include this decision in the list of decisions which can be subject to a request for a review.

9.102 Subsequently, local housing authorities will notify the applicant of its decision that either the HA 1996, s 195(2)[1] or H(W)A 2014, s 66(1)[2], prevention duty or the HA 1996, s 189B(2)[3] or H(W)A 2014, s 73(1)[4], relief duty has come to an end[5]. This decision must be notified with reasons[6]. The only exception is where the HA 1996, s 189B(2)[7], relief duty has come to an end after 56 days[8] and the applicant remains homeless and the local housing authority is satisfied that he or she has a priority need and is not satisfied that he or she has become homeless intentionally, so the HA 1996, s 193(2), main housing duty will be owed[9]. The decision that the HA 1996, s 189B(2)[10], relief duty has come to an end in these circumstances need not be notified[11]. However, the applicant will be notified of the subsequent decision that the HA 1996, s 193(2), main housing duty is owed to him or her[12].

[1] As amended by HRA 2017, s 4(2), for applications for homelessness assistance made to local housing authorities in England on or after 3 April 2018; see **15.87–15.137**.
[2] See **17.45–17.72**.
[3] As inserted by HRA 2017, s 5(2), for applications for homelessness assistance made to local housing authorities in England on or after 3 April 2018 see **15.138–15.195**.
[4] See **17.73–17.143**.
[5] HA 1996, 195(5)–(10), as amended by HRA 2017, s 4(2), for applications for homelessness assistance made to local housing authorities in England on or after 3 April 2018, see **15.98–15.132**; HA 1996, 189B(5)–(9), as inserted by HRA 2017, s 5(2), for applications for homelessness assistance made to local housing authorities in England on or after 3 April 2018, see **15.151–15.189**; H(W)A 2014, s 69, see **17.56–17.72**, and H(W)A 2014, s 74, see **17.84–17.119**.
[6] HA 1996, s 195(7), as amended by HRA 2017, s 4(2), for applications for homelessness assistance made to local housing authorities in England on or after 3 April 2018; English Code, paras 14.37–14.39; see **15.98–15.103** of this book; H(W)A 2014, ss 67(1) and 84(1); Welsh Code, paras 15.94–15.98; see **17.57** of this book; HA 1996, s 189B(6), as inserted by HRA 2017, s 5(2), for applications for homelessness assistance made to local housing authorities in England on or after 3 April 2018; English Code, paras 14.40–14.42; see **15.152–15.158** of this book; H(W)A 2014, ss 74(1) and 84(1); Welsh Code, paras 15.94–15.98; see **17.85** of this book.
[7] As inserted by HRA 2017, s 5(2), for applications for homelessness assistance made to local housing authorities in England on or after 3 April 2018 see **15.138–15.195**.
[8] HA 1996, s 189B(7)(b), as inserted by HRA 2017, s 5(2), for applications for homelessness assistance made to local housing authorities in England on or after 3 April 2018 see **15.166–15.168**.
[9] See **15.160–15.161**.
[10] As inserted by HRA 2017, s 5(2), for applications for homelessness assistance made to local housing authorities in England on or after 3 April 2018 see **15.138–15.195**.
[11] HA 1996, s 189B(4), as inserted by HRA 2017, s 5(2), for applications for homelessness assistance made to local housing authorities in England on or after 3 April 2018 see **15.160**.

[12] HA 1996, s 184(1)(b) and (3).

9.103 If the applicant remains, or there is the local housing authority has reason to believe that the applicant may be homeless, a local housing authority will have to notify the applicant of what duty, if any, is now owed to the applicant[1]. That might be notification of a decision that the applicant is not homeless[2].

[1] HA 1996, s 184(1)(b) and (3); H(W)A 2014, ss 62(9) and 63(1); Welsh Code paras 10.44–10.49.
[2] HA 1996, s 184(1)(b) and (3); H(W)A 2014, ss 62(9) and 63(1).

9.104 If the local housing authority is satisfied that the applicant is homeless, and that the HA 1996, s 189B(2)[1] or H(W)A 2014, s 73(1)[2], relief duty has come to an end, there will then be consideration of whether the applicant has a priority need, whether he or she has become homeless intentionally and the circumstances in which the HA 1996, s 189B(2)[3], or H(W)A 2014, s 73(1)[4] relief duty came to an end[5]. If any of those decisions are decided against the applicant's interests, the decision must be notified with reasons[6].

[1] As inserted by HRA 2017, s 5(2), for applications for homelessness assistance made to local housing authorities in England on or after 3 April 2018 see **15.138–15.195**.
[2] See **17.73–17.143**.
[3] As inserted by HRA 2017, s 5(2), for applications for homelessness assistance made to local housing authorities in England on or after 3 April 2018 see **15.138–15.195**.
[4] See **17.73–17.143**.
[5] For local housing authorities in England, the HA 1996, s 193(2), main housing duty to the applicant will not be owed if the HA 1996, s 189B(2) (as inserted by HRA 2017, s 5(2), for applications for homelessness assistance made to local housing authorities in England on or after 3 April 2018) relief duty came to an end because the applicant refused a final accommodation or final Pt 6 offer: HA 1996, s 189B(9)(a) and 193A (as inserted by HRA 2017, ss 5(2) and 7(1), for applications for homelessness assistance made to local housing authorities in England on or after 3 April 2018), see **15.181–15.188**. For local housing authorities in Wales, the H(W)A 2014, s 75(1), main housing duty will not be owed if the H(W)A 2014, s 73(1) relief duty came to an end as a result of the applicant having refused an offer of suitable accommodation: H(W)A 2014, ss 74(5) and 75(1). See **17.109–17.117** and **17.146**.
[6] HA 1996, s 184(1)(b) and (3); H(W)A 2014, s 63(1).

9.105 For local housing authorities in England, the decision might be one of the following:

- That the applicant is homeless but he or she does not have a priority need, so no further duty is owed[1];
- That the applicant is homeless and has a priority need and the HA 1996, s 189B(2)[2], relief duty came to an end because the applicant refused a final accommodation duty[3] or final Pt 6 offer[4], so the HA 1996, s 193(2), main housing duty is not owed[5];
- That the applicant is homeless and has a priority need and has become homeless intentionally, so the short-term duty to accommodate at HA 1996, s 190(2), is owed[6];
- That the applicant is homeless and has a priority need, and has not become homeless intentionally, and the local housing authority has notified him or her of a decision that he or she has deliberately and unreasonably refused to co-operate[7], so that the accommodation duty at HA 1996, s 193C[8] is owed;

- That the applicant is homeless and has a priority need and has not become homeless intentionally and that the local housing authority consider that the conditions are met for referral of the applicant's case to another local housing authority, and that it intends to notify or has notified the other local housing authority of that decision[9]; or

- That the applicant is homeless and has a priority need, and has not become homeless intentionally, so the HA 1996, s 193(2) main housing duty is owed[10].

[1] Because the duties owed after the HA 1996, s 189B(2) (as inserted by HRA 2017, s 5(2), for applications for homelessness assistance made to local housing authorities in England on or after 3 April 2018) relief duty comes to an end are only owed to applicants who have a priority need.

[2] As inserted by HRA 2017, s 5(2), for applications for homelessness assistance made to local housing authorities in England on or after 3 April 2018 see **15.138–15.195**.

[3] HA 1996, s 193A(4), as inserted by HRA 2017, s 7(1), for applications for homelessness assistance made to local housing authorities in England on or after 3 April 2018 see **15.181–15.184**.

[4] HA 1996, s 193A(5), as inserted by HRA 2017, s 7(1), for applications for homelessness assistance made to local housing authorities in England on or after 3 April 2018 see **15.185–15.187**.

[5] HA 1996, ss 189B(9)(a) and 193A(1), as inserted by HRA 2017, ss 5(2) and 7(1), for applications for homelessness assistance made to local housing authorities in England on or after 3 April 2018 see **16.95**.

[6] As amended by HRA 2017, s 5(5), for applications for homelessness assistance made to local housing authorities in England on or after 3 April 2018 see **16.81–16.93**.

[7] HA 1996, ss 189B(9)(b) and 193B, as inserted by HRA 2017, ss 5(2) and 7(1), for applications for homelessness assistance made to local housing authorities in England on or after 3 April 2018 see **15.196–15.221**.

[8] As inserted by HRA 2017, s 7(1), for applications for homelessness assistance made to local housing authorities in England on or after 3 April 2018 see **16.200–16.216**.

[9] HA 1996, ss 198(1) and 200(1), see **16.16**.

[10] See **16.94–16.199**.

9.106 The English Code advises that local housing authorities in England should not issue a decision that the HA 1996, s 193(2) main housing duty will be owed until the HA 1996, s 189B(2)[1], relief duty has come to an end[2]. The advice also states that if a duty under HA 1996, s 190(2)[3], will be owed (because the applicant has a priority need but has become homeless intentionally), that decision might be notified during the performance of the relief duty, so that the applicant is aware that the HA 1996, s 193(2) main housing duty will not be owed[4].

[1] As inserted by HRA 2017, s 5(2), for applications for homelessness assistance made to local housing authorities in England on or after 3 April 2018 see **15.138–15.195**.

[2] See **15.152–15.158**.

[3] As amended by HRA 2017, s 5(5), for applications for homelessness assistance made to local housing authorities in England on or after 3 April 2018 see **16.81–16.93**.

[4] English Code, paras 13.10–13.11.

9.107 For local housing authorities in Wales, the decision might be one of the following:

- That the applicant is homeless but he or she does not have a priority need, so no further duty is owed[1];

- That the applicant is homeless and has a priority need and the H(W)A 2014, s 73(1) relief duty came to an end because the applicant has suitable accommodation available for his or her occupation or refused an offer of suitable accommodation[2] and so the H(W)A 2014, s 75(1) main housing duty is not owed[3];

- That the applicant is homeless and has a priority need and has become homeless intentionally, so the short-term duty to accommodate is owed[4];

- That the applicant is homeless and has a priority need and has not become homeless intentionally and that the local housing authority consider that the conditions are met for referral of the applicant's case to another local housing authority, and that it intends to notify or has notified the other local housing authority of that decision[5]; or

- That the applicant is homeless and has a priority need, and has not become homeless intentionally, so the H(W)A 2014, s 75(1) main housing duty is owed[6].

[1] Because the duties owed after the H(W)A 2014, s 73(1), relief duty comes to an end are only owed to applicants who have a priority need.
[2] H(W)A 2014, s 74(4) and (5),
[3] H(W)A 2014, s 75(1) see **17.146–17.199**.
[4] H(W)A 2014, s 68(3)–(6), see **17.124–17.127**.
[5] H(W)A 2014, s 80(1), see **14.32**.
[6] See **17.146–17.199**.

Contents of decision

9.108 The decision (in England) or outcome of the assessment (in Wales) must be put in writing[1]. If any issue has been decided against the applicant's interests, the local housing authority must not only notify that decision but also inform the applicant in writing of the reasons for its decision[2]. The duty to give reasons applies to all decisions that the local housing authority is obliged to make on an application (decisions as to whether the applicant is 'eligible', whether a duty is owed, and, if so, what duty) and to any decision that it chooses to make as to whether the applicant has a local connection[3]. However, to make sense in practice, this obligation is interpreted to mean that any adverse finding on any issue decided in the course of working out what duty is owed must be explained by reasons. Therefore, it is not sufficient for a local housing authority in England simply to notify a positive decision that the duty owed is the limited duty in HA 1996, s 190(2)[4]. It must explain, with reasons, why the applicant is not owed the HA 1996, s 193(2) main housing duty[5].

[1] HA 1996, s 184(6) and English Code, para 18.29; H(W)A 2014, s 63(4)(b) and Welsh Code, para 10.53.
[2] HA 1996, s 184(3) and English Code, para 18.33; H(W)A 2014, s 63(1) and Welsh Code, para 10.56.
[3] HA 1996, s 184(4), H(W)A 2014, s 63(3). Where a local housing authority found that an applicant did not have a priority need, but failed to make any decision as to whether or not he was homeless, the Local Government Ombudsman said that the decision was defective: *Complaint against Waltham Forest London Borough Council*, 03/A/15819, 9 November 2005, Annual Digest of Cases 2005/06, LGO.
[4] As amended by HRA 2017, s 5(5), for applications for homelessness assistance made to local housing authorities in England on or after 3 April 2018, duty to accommodate owed to applicants who are homeless, eligible for assistance, have a priority need, have become homeless intentionally and in respect of whom the HA 1996, s 189B(2) (as inserted by HRA

2017, s 5(2), for applications for homelessness assistance made to local housing authorities in England on or after 3 April 2018) relief duty has come to an end: HA 1996, s 190(1).
5   As to the detail required to be given see **9.111–9.125.**

9.109 The decision is limited to whether or not the statutory criteria are met and, as a result of those findings, what duty (if any) is owed to the applicant[1]. The local housing authority cannot impose further requirements on an applicant or suggest that a duty is conditional upon the applicant doing something, such as surrendering an existing tenancy[2].

1   Although the assessment of the applicant's case will contain much broader information: HA 1996, s 189A(1)–(3) (as inserted by HRA 2017, s 3(1), for applications for homelessness assistance made to local housing authorities in England on or after 3 April 2018) for local housing authorities in England, see **15.62–15.86;** H(W)A 2014, s 62 for local housing authorities in Wales, see **9.12–9.14.**
2   *R (Hammia) v Wandsworth London Borough Council* [2005] EWHC 1127 (Admin), [2005] HLR 45, Admin Ct. However, conditions may attach to the duty to protect the applicant's possessions: see **16.288–16.309** (England) and **17.199–17.205** (Wales).

9.110 Whether the decision notified by the local housing authority is favourable or unfavourable, the notification letter must inform the applicant of his or her right to request a review and also of the 21-day period within which any request for a review must be made[1].

1   HA 1996, s 184(5) and English Code, para 18.29; H(W)A 2014 s 63(4)(a) and Welsh Code, para 10.56.

Reasons

9.111 All decisions that are required to be notified in writing must also contain reasons for any issue that was decided against an applicant's interests[1]. The Codes recommend that the reasons for the decision are explained clearly and fully and that any assistance that can be made available to the applicant is also clearly set out. If the applicant has difficulty in understanding the decision, the local housing authority should consider arranging for a member of staff to explain the decision in person[2].

1   HA 1996, ss 184(3), (4), 203(4); H(W)A 2014, ss 63(1), (3), 84(1)(b), 86(4).
2   English Code, para 18.29; Welsh Code, para 10.58.

9.112 The reasons given must be proper, intelligible and adequate and relate to the substantive issues raised by the applicant[1]. An applicant is entitled to reasons so that he or she can understand, clearly, why he or she has not succeeded and can properly assess any prospects of challenging that decision[2]. In addition, adequate reasons serve to indicate that:

' . . . the decision-maker has gone through the right process of thinking in arriving at its conclusion[3].'

1   *Re Poyser and Mills' Arbitration* [1964] 2 QB 467, QBD; *Westminster City Council v Great Portland Estates plc* [1985] AC 661, HL; and *South Bucks District Council v Porter (No 2)* [2004] UKHL 33, [2004] 1 WLR 1953, HL.
2   *R v Croydon London Borough Council ex p Graham* (1993) 26 HLR 286, CA; *R v Camden London Borough Council ex p Mohammed* (1998) 30 HLR 315, QBD; and *Shire v Birmingham City Council* (2003) March *Legal Action*, p 30, Birmingham County Court.

Reasons in the s 184 decision also permit the applicant to address them in his or her request for a review: *Connors v Birmingham City Council* (2010) May *Legal Action*, p 25, Birmingham County Court.

3   *R v Newham London Borough Council ex p Qureshi* (1998) March *Legal Action*, p 14, QBD.

9.113 It is important, when considering whether or not the reasons are proper, intelligible and adequate, to read the decision letter as a whole. The court should not take an over-technical or over-critical approach. Lord Neuberger of Abbotsbury said in *Holmes-Moorhouse v Richmond upon Thames Royal London Borough Council*[1]:

'a judge should not adopt an unfair or unrealistic approach when considering or interpreting such review decisions. Although they may often be checked by people with legal experience or qualifications before they are sent out, review decisions are prepared by housing officers, who occupy a post of considerable responsibility and who have substantial experience in the housing field, but they are not lawyers. It is not therefore appropriate to subject their decisions to the same sort of analysis as may be applied to a contract drafted by solicitors, to an Act of Parliament, or to a court's judgment[2].'

1   [2009] UKHL 7, [2009] 1 WLR 413, HL.
2   *Holmes-Moorhouse v Richmond-upon-Thames Royal London Borough Council* [2009] UKHL 7, [2009] 1 WLR 413, HL, at [47]. The point applies to all decisions, not just to review decisions.

9.114 He added[1]:

'Accordingly, a benevolent approach should be adopted to the interpretation of review decisions. The court should not take too technical a view of the language used, or search for inconsistencies, or adopt a nit-picking approach, when confronted with an appeal against a review decision. That is not to say that the court should approve incomprehensible or misguided reasoning, but it should be realistic and practical in its approach to the interpretation of review decisions.

Further . . . a decision can often survive despite the existence of an error in the reasoning advanced to support it. For example, sometimes the error is irrelevant to the outcome; sometimes it is too trivial (objectively, or in the eyes of the decision-maker) to affect the outcome; sometimes it is obvious from the rest of the reasoning, read as a whole, that the decision would have been the same notwithstanding the error; sometimes, there is more than one reason for the conclusion, and the error only undermines one of the reasons; sometimes, the decision is the only one which could rationally have been reached.'

1   *Holmes-Moorhouse v Richmond-upon-Thames Royal London Borough Council* [2009] UKHL 7, [2009] 1 WLR 413, HL, at [50]–[51]. Again, the point applies to all decisions, not just to review decisions.

9.115 The Supreme Court considered the duty to give reasons in two cases decided in 2015. In the case of *Hotak v Southwark London Borough Council, Kanu v Southwark London Borough Council, Johnson v Solihull Metropolitan Borough Council*[1] Lord Neuberger said that he strongly maintained the views he had expressed in *Holmes-Moorhouse v Richmond upon Thames Royal London Borough Council*[2], but that, in cases where the public sector equality duty is engaged[3], the decision or review decision should show that the decision-maker had sharply focused on the duty, and on any relevant protected characteristic[4].

1   [2015] UKSC 30, [2016] AC 811, SC.
2   [2009] UKHL 7, [2009] 1 WLR 413, HL.
3   Equality Act 2010, s 149, see **9.81–9.83**, **12.91**, **12.100**, **13.70** and **18.65–18.68**.
4   *Hotak v Southwark London Borough Council, Kanu v Southwark London Borough Council, Johnson v Solihull Metropolitan Borough Council* [2015] UKSC 30, [2016] AC 811, SC per Lord Neuberger at [78]–[79], see **9.81–9.83** and **13.70** for the Equality Act 2010 and protected characteristics.

9.116 In *Nzolameso v Westminster City Council*[1], Baroness Hale said[2]:

'it must be clear from the decision that proper consideration has been given to the relevant matters required by [HA 1996] and the Code. While the court should not adopt an overly technical or "nit-picking" approach to the reasons given in the decision, these do have to be adequate to fulfil their basic function. It has long been established that an obligation to give reasons for a decision is imposed so that the persons affected by the decision may know why they have won or lost and, in particular, may be able to judge whether the decision is valid and therefore unchallengeable or invalid and therefore open to challenge . . . Nor, without a proper explanation, can the court know whether the authority have properly fulfilled their statutory obligations.'

1   [2015] UKSC 22, [2015] 2 All ER 942, [2015] HLR 22, SC.
2   *Nzolameso v City of Westminster Council* [2015] UKSC 22, [2015] 2 All ER 942, [2015] HLR 22, SC per Baroness Hale at [32].

9.117 In *Poshteh v Kensington & Chelsea Royal London Borough Council*[1], Lord Carnwath JSC, giving the leading judgment, reiterated the warning in *Holmes-Moorhouse v Richmond upon Thames London Borough Council*[2]. The decision, read as a whole, must address the relevant issues, including those required under the Equality Act 2010[3], but care must be taken not to engage in 'over-zealous linguistic analysis'[4].

1   [2017] UKSC 30, [2017] 2 WLR 1417, SC.
2   [2009] UKHL 7, [2009] 2 WLR 1413, HL.
3   See **9.81–9.83**.
4   *Poshteh v Kensington & Chelsea Royal London Borough Council* [2017] UKSC 30, [2017] 2 WLR 1417, SC per Lord Carnwath JSC at [39]–[41].

9.118 Merely reciting the relevant legal formula set out in HA 1996, Pt 7[1], or H(W)A 2014, Pt 2, and stating that the applicant does not meet it, will not amount to giving adequate and sufficient reasons[2]. For example, where a local housing authority is satisfied that an applicant has become homeless intentionally, the decision letter should state:

(1)   when the local housing authority considers that the applicant became homeless;
(2)   why he or she become homeless;
(3)   whether the loss of accommodation was caused by the deliberate act (or failure to act) on the part of the applicant, including consideration of whether the applicant was ignorant of a relevant fact in good faith[3];
(4)   whether the accommodation lost was 'available' for the applicant's occupation[4];
(5)   why it would have been reasonable for the applicant to have continued to occupy the accommodation; and[5]

(6)   whether the applicant's current homelessness was caused by his or her intentional conduct or whether the causal chain has been broken by subsequent events[6].

1   As amended by HRA 2017 for applications for homelessness assistance made to local housing authorities in England on or after 3 April 2018.
2   *R v Camden London Borough Council ex p Adair* (1996) 29 HLR 236, QBD; and *R v Islington London Borough Council ex p Trail* (1993) Times, 27 May, QBD.
3   *O'Connor v Kensington & Chelsea Royal London Borough Council* [2004] EWCA Civ 394, [2004] HLR 33, CA. See **13.56–13.64**.
4   HA 1996, s 175(1); H(W)A 2014, s 55(1). See **10.17–10.32** and **13.155–13.161**.
5   *R v Gloucester City Council ex p Miles* (1985) 17 HLR 292, CA.
6   *Haile v Waltham Forest London Borough Council* [2015] UKSC 34, [2015] AC 1471, SC, see **13.100–13.131**.

9.119 The deliberate act or omission of the applicant which is said to have caused the homelessness should be identified, even though the findings can be expressed simply and briefly[1]. Where the central issue is whether it would have been reasonable for the applicant to have continued to occupy the previous accommodation, the decision letter should state what factors were considered in deciding that it would have been reasonable to continue to occupy and specifically address the reasons given by the applicant for leaving[2].

1   *R v Hillingdon London Borough Council ex p H* (1988) 20 HLR 554, QBD.
2   *R v Tower Hamlets London Borough Council ex p Monaf* (1988) 20 HLR 529, CA; and *R v Tower Hamlets London Borough Council ex p Ojo* (1991) 23 HLR 488, QBD.

9.120 Where the issue of whether the accommodation is, or was, reasonable for the applicant to continue to occupy requires consideration of whether he or she could afford to pay the rent, the decision letter should set out any amounts of the applicant's expenditure which the local housing authority considered to be excessive or unnecessary. In some cases, where the applicant has produced and relied on a justification for the expenditure, a more detailed explanation of the reasons for rejecting that material may be required[1]. Where the local housing authority had concluded that it was not probable that the applicant would be at risk of violence if she had continued to occupy the accommodation[2], its decision was deficient in that it did not explain why it had come to that conclusion given the applicant's account that she had seen her violent husband in the area of her accommodation[3].

1   *Farah v Hillingdon London Borough Council* [2014] EWCA Civ 359, [2014] HLR 24, CA.
2   HA 1996, s 177(1), see **10.79–10.91** (England); H(W)A 2014, s 57(1), see **10.79–10.80** and **10.97–10.98** (Wales).
3   *H v Southwark London Borough Council*, Central London Civil Trial Centre, 30 January 2014, (2014) March *Legal Action*, p 23.

9.121 Where there are medical issues, the decision letter should give reasons for rejecting any medical opinions[1].

1   *R v Kensington and Chelsea Royal London Borough Council ex p CAmpbell* (1995) 28 HLR 160, QBD. In *Al-Kabi v Southwark London Borough Council*, (2008) March *Legal Action*, p 21, Lambeth County Court, a decision letter was found to be defective for its failure to mention the medical evidence at all, and no reasons were given for the local housing authority's decision to reject the undisputed medical evidence.

9.122 Where a local housing authority has made a decision that its duty to the applicant has come to an end, as a result of the applicant's refusal of suitable accommodation[1], and the offer of accommodation was located outside of its district, the issue may be whether or not that accommodation was suitable for the needs of the applicant and of his or her household[2]. Any decision that the accommodation is or was suitable should set out what accommodation was available in the local housing authority's district or why no such accommodation had been offered. It should also show that the decision-maker was aware that, if it is not reasonably practicable to offer accommodation in the local housing authority's own district, the obligation is to offer accommodation as near as possible to that district. In addition, the Supreme Court has recommended that local housing authorities adopt policies for procuring sufficient units of accommodation which set out how those units will be allocated. Where there is an anticipated shortfall of accommodation in the local housing authority's district, the policy should explain the factors which will be taken into account in offering accommodation outside of the district[3]. A decision letter should also demonstrate that a local housing authority, when placing families with school-age children in another local housing authority's district, has made satisfactory arrangements to safeguard a child's educational welfare, and specifically show that the local housing authority has liaised with the education department of the receiving local authority and satisfied itself that educational arrangements are in place[4].

[1] HA 1996, ss 189B(7)(c), or (9)(a) (as inserted by HRA 2017, s 5(2), for applications for homelessness assistance made to local housing authorities in England on or after 3 April 2018), see **15.169–15.173** and **15.181–15.188**; HA 1996, ss 193(5), (7) and (7AA)–(7AC), see **16.114–16.123, 16.142–16.152** and **16.163–16.179**; HA 1996, s 195(8)(d) (as amended by HRA 2017, s 4(2), for applications for homelessness assistance made to local housing authorities in England on or after 3 April 2018), see **15.118–15.122**; HA 1996, s 193C(6) (as inserted by HRA 2017, s 7(1), for applications for homelessness assistance made to local housing authorities in England on or after 3 April 2018), see **16.205–16.216**; (H(W)A 2014, ss 67(4), 74(5) and 76(3), see **17.66–17.72, 17.109–17.117** and **17.165–17.179**.
[2] As required by HA 1996, s 206(1), see **18.48–18.61** (England); H(W)A 2014, Pt 2, see **18.48, 18.60–18.64** (Wales).
[3] *Nzolameso v City of Westminster Council* [2015] UKSC 22, [2015] 2 All ER 942, [2015] HLR 22, SC.
[4] R (E) *v Islington London Borough Council* [2017] EWHC 1440 (Admin), Admin Ct see **18.57**.

9.123 The decision letter should address any issues raised that fall within the public sector equality duty[1] and show that the decision-maker had sharply focused on the relevant protected characteristics and the issues raised relating to the characteristic[2]. However, a failure expressly to mention the public sector equality duty will not necessarily mean that the decision-maker has failed to comply with the duty if the decision, read as a whole, shows that the decision-maker had addressed the relevant questions[3].

[1] Equality Act 2010, s 149, see **9.81–9.83, 12.91, 12.100, 13.70, 18.65–18.68**.
[2] *Hotak v Southwark London Borough Council* [2015] UKSC 30, [2017] AC 811, SC per Lord Neuberger [78], see **12.91**.
[3] *Hackney London Borough Council v Haque* [2017] EWCA Civ 4, [2017] HLR 14, CA.

9.124 Where there are contradictory factual accounts put before the local housing authority, and it prefers one account to another, the decision letter should explain that that was the case, and why a particular account was preferred[1]. If a decision letter fails to refer to part of the applicant's case, the inference will be that the local housing authority has failed to have regard to that matter[2].

1   *R v Wandsworth London Borough Council ex p Dodia* (1997) 30 HLR 562, QBD; English Code, para 18.33.
2   *R (Jeylani) v Waltham Forest London Borough Council* [2002] EWHC 487 (Admin), (2002) May *Legal Action*, p 30, Admin Ct.

9.125 Notifications of decisions that the duty has come to an end must also include the reasons for the decision, and inform the applicant of his or her right to request a review of the decision and of the time within which the request must be made[1].

1   For local housing authorities in England: HA 1996, ss 189B(6), 193B(3) and 195(7) (as inserted and amended by HRA 2017 ss 4(2), 5(2) and 7(1) for applications for homelessness assistance made to local housing authorities in England on or after 3 April 2018) and English Code, paras 18.34–18.35; H(W)A 2014, s 84(1) and Welsh Code, paras 15.94–15.95.

The special rules for notifying decisions which involve restricted persons

9.126 There is an additional notification duty on local housing authorities where:

(1)   the applicant's household includes a restricted person[1]; and
(2)   the local housing authority has decided that the HA 1996, s 193(2)[2] or H(W)A 2014, s 75(1), main housing duty[3], is only owed because of the presence of the restricted person.

1   HA 1996, s 184(3A) and (7); H(W)A 2014, s 63(2) and (5). For 'restricted person', see **9.54–9.56** and **11.163–11.167**.
2   See **16.94–16.199**.
3   See **17.146–17.199**.

9.127 In those circumstances, the applicant becomes a 'restricted case'[1]. There is a requirement on local housing authorities to bring the HA 1996, s 193(2), or H(W)A 2014, s 75(1), main housing duty, or the duty to secure accommodation, to an end by making a private rented sector offer, so far as reasonably practicable[2].

1   HA 1996, s 193(3B), see **16.180–16.185**; H(W)A 2014, s 76(5), see **17.177**.
2   HA 1996, s 193(7AD); H(W)A 2014, s 76(5).

9.128 The additional notification duty only arises if:

•   the local housing authority decides that the applicant is, or would be, owed the HA 1996, s 193(2), or H(W)A 2014, s 75(1), main housing duty[1]; and
•   that duty is only owed to the applicant *because of* the presence of the restricted person in the applicant's household[2].

1   H(W)A 2014, s 75(2), see **17.146–17.199**.
2   HA 1996, s 184(3A); H(W)A 2014 s 63(2).

9.129 If those two conditions are met, the local housing authority must:

- inform the applicant that the decision that he or she is, or will be, owed the HA 1996, s 193(2) or H(W)A 2014, s 75(1), main housing duty was reached having regard to the restricted person in the applicant's household;
- include the name of the restricted person;
- explain why the person is a restricted person; and
- explain the effect of the modification to the HA 1996, s 193(2), or H(W)A 2014, s 75(1), main housing duty as a result of HA 1996, s 193(7AD), or H(W)A 2014, s 76(5)[1].

[1] HA 1996, s 184(3A); H(W)A 2014, s 63(2). For the modification to the main housing duty in England as a result of HA 1996, s 193(7AD) and s 195(4A), see **16.180–16.185**. For the modification in Wales, at H(W)A 2014, s 76(5), see **17.177**.

9.130 The additional notification duty does not apply in all cases where the applicant's household includes a restricted person. If the HA 1996, s 193(2), or H(W)A 2014, s 75(1) main housing duty to secure accommodation for applicants who have a priority need[1], is not owed, the additional notification duty does not apply. Nor does it apply if those duties would have arisen despite the presence in the applicant's household of a restricted person[2].

[1] H(W)A 2014, s 75(2), see **17.146–17.199**.
[2] See **9.126**.

The special rules for notification of a decision that the applicant has deliberately and unreasonably refused to co-operate

Local housing authorities in England

9.131 Where local housing authorities in England owe an applicant a HA 1996, s 195(2)[1] prevention or a HA 1996, s 189B(2)[2], relief duty, those duties can come to an end where a local housing authority notifies an applicant of a decision that he or she has deliberately and unreasonably refused to co-operate[3]. That notification cannot be given unless:

- the local housing authority has first given the applicant a warning that he or she has deliberately and unreasonably refused to take any steps that he or she had agreed to take under the personalised housing plan, or that had been recorded by the local housing authority in the personalised housing plan as a step that it would be reasonable to require the applicant to take[4];
- the warning states that, if the applicant deliberately and unreasonably refuses to take any of these steps after receiving the warning, the local housing authority intends to give the notice that of its decision that he or she has deliberately and unreasonably refused to co-operate;
- the warning explains the consequences of giving such notice, ie that the relevant duty will come to an end[5]; and
- a reasonable period has elapsed since the warning was given[6].

[1] As amended by HRA 2017, s 4, for applications for homelessness assistance made to local housing authorities in England on or 3 April 2018. See **15.87–15.137**.
[2] As inserted by HRA 2017, s 5(2), for applications for homelessness assistance made to local housing authorities in England on or after 3 April 2018. See **15.138–15.195**.

3   HA 1996, ss 189B(9)(b) and 195(10), as inserted and amended by HRA 2017, ss 4(2) and 5(2),
     for applications for homelessness assistance made to local housing authorities in England on
     or 3 April 2018. See English Code, paras 14.43–14.59 and **15.196–15.221** of this book.

4   HA 1996, s 193B(5), as inserted by HRA 2017, s 7(1), for applications for homelessness
     assistance made to local housing authorities in England on or 3 April 2018 and see
     15.203–15.205. See HA 1996, s 189A(4) and (6), as inserted by HRA 2017, s 3(1), for
     applications for homelessness assistance made to local housing authorities in England on or
     after 3 April 2018 for the steps that an applicant has agreed to take or is recorded as required
     by the local housing authority to take. See **15.207**.

5   HA 1996, s 193B(5)(b) and (c), as inserted by HRA 2017, s 7(1), for applications for
     homelessness assistance made to local housing authorities in England on or after 3 April 2018;
     and English Code, para 14.44. See **15.207**.

6   HA 1996, s 193B(4)(b), as inserted by HRA 2017, s 7(1), for applications for homelessness
     assistance made to local housing authorities in England on or 3 April 2018 and see **15.208**.

9.132 The local housing authority can subsequently give a notice to the applicant of its decision that the applicant has deliberately and unreasonably refused to take any step[1]. That notice must contain reasons for the local housing authority's decision, explain the effect of the decision and inform the applicant that he or she has the right to request a review of the decision[2]. The notice cannot be given to the applicant until a reasonable period has elapsed since the warning was given, so that the applicant has time to comply with the warning[3]. The English Code advises that there is no set reasonable period but local housing authorities should ensure sufficient time is given to allow the applicant to rectify the non-co-operation. The length of the reasonable period will therefore vary according to the applicant's particular needs and circumstances[4].

1   HA 1996, s 193B(2), as inserted by HRA 2017, s 7(1), for applications for homelessness
     assistance made to local housing authorities in England on or 3 April 2018; English Code
     paras 14.42 and 14.54–14.59. See **15.209**.

2   HA 1996, s 193B(3), as inserted by HRA 2017, s 7(1), for applications for homelessness
     assistance made to local housing authorities in England on or after 3 April 2018. See
     15.212–15.213.

3   HA 1996, s 193B(4), as inserted by HRA 2017, s 7(1), for applications for homelessness
     assistance made to local housing authorities in England on or after 3 April 2018. See **15.210**.

4   English Code, para 14.44.

9.133 The consequences of a local housing authority notifying the applicant of a decision that he or she has deliberately and unreasonably failed to co-operate are that the HA 1996, s 195(2)[1] prevention duty or the HA 1996, s 189B(2)[2] relief duty owed to the applicant will come to an end[3].

1   As amended by HRA 2017, s 4(2), for applications for homelessness assistance made to local
     housing authorities in England on or 3 April 2018, see **15.87–15.137**.

2   As inserted by HRA 2017, s 5(2), for applications for homelessness assistance made to local
     housing authorities in England on or 3 April 2018, see **15.138–15.195**.

3   HA 1996, s 193C(2), as inserted by HRA 2017, s 7(1), for applications for homelessness
     assistance made to local housing authorities in England on or 3 April 2018, see **15.132** and
     15.189.

9.134 The local housing authority will then to notify the applicant as to what other duty, if any, is owed to him or her[1]. If the local housing authority is satisfied that an applicant is homeless, eligible for assistance, has a priority need and are satisfied that he or she has become homeless intentionally, the HA 1996, s 190(2)(a) short-term accommodation duty will arise[2]. If the local housing authority is satisfied that an applicant is homeless, eligible for assistance, has a priority need and are not satisfied that he or she has become homeless intentionally, the HA 1996, s 193(2) main housing duty will not arise, but the local housing authority will owe the applicant a duty to secure accommodation under HA 1996, s 193C[3]. That duty can be brought to an end if the applicant accepts or refuses a final accommodation offer of suitable accommodation (a fixed-term assured shorthold tenancy of at least six months) or a final Pt 6 offer, or in certain other circumstances[4].

[1]   HA 1996, s 184(1)(b) and (3).
[2]   As amended by HRA 2017, s 5(5), for applications for homelessness assistance made to local housing authorities in England on or after 3 April 2018. See **16.81–16.93**.
[3]   As inserted by HRA 2017, s 7(1), for applications for homelessness assistance made to local housing authorities in England on or after 3 April 2018. See **16.200–16.216**.
[4]   HA 1996, s 193C(5) and (6), as inserted by HRA 2017, s 7(1), for applications for homelessness assistance made to local housing authorities in England on or 3 April 2018. See English Code, para 14.48 and **16.204–16.214** of this book.

Local housing authorities in Wales

9.135 Local housing authorities in Wales can notify an applicant of a decision that it is satisfied that he or she is unreasonably failing to co-operate with it in connection in performance of any of the functions at H(W)A 2014, Pt 2[1].

[1]   H(W)A 2014, s 79(5), see Welsh Code, paras 15.86–15.89; see **17.195–17.197**. Note that the Welsh Code stresses that every effort to obtain the co-operation of the applicant should first be made: Welsh Code, para 15.87.

9.136 That decision must be notified to the applicant with the following information:

- that the local housing authority no longer regards itself as being subject to the relevant duty;
- the reasons for that decision;
- the applicant's right to request a review of that decision; and
- the time within which the request for a review must be made[1].

[1]   H(W)A 2014, s 84(1); Welsh Code, paras 15.93–15.98, see **17.195–17.197**.

Insufficient reasons

9.137 A properly notified decision should give sufficient reasons for the applicant to understand why she or he has been unsuccessful on an issue and to enable the applicant to assess whether to make, and how best to frame, an application for review[1].

[1]   See further discussion on 'reasons' at **9.111–9.125**.

9.138 If the applicant considers that the reasoning given is insufficient to explain the decision, she or he could simply ignore the deficiency and apply for a review[1]. If the reasons given in a subsequent review decision are sufficient, the failure to comply with the requirement to give reasons in the initial decision will generally be cured by the reasons in the review decision (but not always)[2].

[1]   See **19.12–19.85**.

² *Simpson v Brent London Borough Council* (2000) November *Legal Action*, p 23, Willesden County Court; and *R (Lynch) v Lambeth London Borough Council* [2006] EWHC 2737 (Admin), [2007] HLR 15, Admin Ct.

9.139 However, where the paucity of reasons in the initial decision means that the applicant cannot make a properly informed assessment as to whether to request a review, or how best to frame a review request, there will be a real need to secure the proper reasons. In the first instance, the applicant might simply ask the local housing authority to give, or to supplement, its reasons. If the local housing authority's response does not provide adequate reasons, then the applicant may want to seek a judicial review and a declaration that the obligation to give reasons has not been complied with, in breach of the legal requirement. The courts will be slow to intervene unless it is clear that the deficiency in the reasons is such as to render any attempt to use the statutory review mechanism unfair because the applicant simply does not know what was found against him or her, and what the case is that needs to be met[1]. As a fall-back, to protect against the eventuality that the court may find the reasons adequate, the applicant may want to lodge a formal request for a review within the 21-day time limit and invite the local housing authority to defer the conclusion of the review until the outcome of the judicial review proceedings.

¹ *R v Camden London Borough Council ex p Mohammed* (1998) 30 HLR 315, QBD. See Baroness Hale in *Nzolameso v City of Westminster Council* [2015] UKSC 22, [2015] 2 All ER 942, [2015] HLR 22, SC, at [32] emphasising that the obligation to give reasons for a decision is so that the person affected may know whether he or she has won or lost, and may be able to judge whether the decision is valid, or invalid and open to challenge.

The effect of a decision

Local housing authorities in England

9.140 When a local housing authority in England has concluded its inquiries and notified the applicant of its decision as whether he or she is eligible, whether he or she is owed the HA 1996, s 195(2)[1] prevention or HA 1996, s 189B(2)[2], relief duty, then (unless the applicant requests a review of the decision) that can be the end of the immediate matters to be inquired into and notified to the applicant. Once the local housing authority has accepted a duty towards the applicant, it cannot subsequently reconsider its decision if the applicant's circumstances change (if, for example, he or she ceases to have a priority need).[3] If, for a local housing authority in England, the HA 1996, s 184 decision has been obtained by the applicant's fraud or deception, or is the result of a fundamental mistake over the facts prevailing at the date of the decision, the local housing authority may revisit and re-open its decision.[4] For local housing authorities in Wales, H(W)A 2014, s 79(3) permits a local housing authority to decide that its duty has come to an end if it is satisfied that a mistake of fact led to the applicant being notified that a duty was owed.[5]

¹ As amended by HRA 2017, s 4(2), for applications for homelessness assistance made to local housing authorities in England on or after 3 April 2018, see **15.87–15.137**.
² As inserted by HRA 2017, s 5(2), for applications for homelessness assistance made to local housing authorities in England on or after 3 April 2018, see **15.138 –15.195**.

3 *R v Brent London Borough Council ex p Sadiq* (2001) 33 HLR 47, QBD, unless the duty is that owed under HA 1996, s 193(2) and the change of circumstances is one of the events set out at HA 1996, s 193(6). See **16.124–16.141**.

4 *R v Southwark London Borough Council ex p Dagou* (1995) 28 HLR 72, QBD; *Crawley Borough Council v B* (2000) 32 HLR 636, CA; and *Porteous v West Dorset District Council* [2004] EWCA Civ 244, [2004] HLR 30, CA. For a discussion of the limited circumstances in which s 184 decisions might be withdrawn unilaterally by a local housing authority, see Ian Loveland 'Homelessness reviews: when can local authorities withdraw s 184 decisions?' (2007) March *Legal Action*, p 20.

5 H(W)A 2014, s 79(3); Welsh Code, paras 15.80–15.83; see **17.193**.

9.141 Once the notification has been given that a duty is owed, then the local housing authority has to ensure that it plays its part, by taking the reasonable steps which are recorded in the personalised housing plan[1], to help the applicant prevent his or her homelessness, or secure new accommodation. Those duties are conditional upon the applicant playing his or her part, so that if the applicant has deliberately and unreasonably refused to co-operate, the local housing authority can notify the applicant of its decision that the relevant duty had come to an end for that reason[2].

1 HA 1996, s 189A(4)–(6), as inserted by HRA 2017, s 3(1), for applications for homelessness assistance made to local housing authorities in England on or after 3 April 2018, see **15.62–15.86**.

2 HA 1996, ss 193B and 193C(2), as inserted by HRA 2017, s 7(1), for applications for homelessness assistance made to local housing authorities in England on or after 3 April 2018, see **15.196–15.221** and **16.200–16.215**.

9.142 If, once the HA 1996, s 195(2)[1] prevention or HA 1996, s 189B(2)[2], relief duties have ended, the applicant remains homeless and the local housing authority notifies him or her that it owes an accommodation duty[3], then the local housing authority must ensure that it performs that duty. Any accommodation duty owed cannot be postponed, or made conditional upon the applicant complying with certain requirements[4].

1 As amended by HRA 2017, s 4(2), for applications for homelessness assistance made to local housing authorities in England on or after 3 April 2018, see **15.87–15.137**.

2 As inserted by HRA 2017, s 5(2), for applications for homelessness assistance made to local housing authorities in England on or after 3 April 2018, see **15.138–15.195**.

3 Accommodation duties are only owed where the local housing authority is satisfied that the applicant has a priority need. The accommodation duty owed could be: (a) the duty to secure short-term accommodation where the applicant is homeless, eligible for assistance, has a priority need and has become homeless intentionally (HA 1996, s 190(2)(a), as amended by HRA 2017, s 5(5), for applications for homelessness assistance made to local housing authorities in England on or after 3 April 2018), see **16.81–16.93**; (b) the main housing duty where the applicant is homeless, eligible for assistance, has a priority need and has not become homeless intentionally (HA 1996, s 193(2)), see **16.94–16.199**; or (c) the duty to secure accommodation where the applicant is homeless, eligible for assistance, has a priority need, has not become homeless intentionally and has deliberately and unreasonably refused to co-operate (HA 1996, s 193C(4), as inserted by HRA 2017, s 7(1), for applications for homelessness assistance made to local housing authorities in England on or after 3 April 2018), see **16.200–16.216**.

4 *R (Hammia) v Wandsworth London Borough Council* [2005] EWHC 1127 (Admin), [2005] HLR 45, Admin Ct.

Local housing authorities in Wales

9.143 For local housing authorities in Wales, in general, once the outcome of the assessment has been notified, then, as with local housing authorities in England, the decision as to what duty is owed cannot be changed[1]. However, the assessment will be reviewed once the duties owed under H(W)A 2014, s 66(1) or s 73(1) have been performed[2]. In addition, H(W)A 2014, s 79, permits a local housing authority to decide that any duty owed to the applicant has come to an end if:

- the local housing authority is no longer satisfied that the applicant is eligible for help[3];
- the local housing authority is satisfied that a mistake of fact led to the applicant being notified that a duty was owed[4];
- the local housing authority is satisfied that the applicant has withdrawn his or her application[5]; or
- the local housing authority is satisfied that the applicant is unreasonably failing to cooperate with it in connection with its performance of any of the functions in H(W)A 2014, Pt 2[6].

[1] Welsh Code, paras 10.50–10.52.
[2] H(W)A 2014, s 62(9), see **17.31**.
[3] H(W)A 2014, s 79(2); Welsh Code, para 15.79; see **17.192**. For 'eligible for help', see CHAPTER **11**.
[4] H(W)A 2014, s 79(3); Welsh Code, paras 15.80–15.83; see **17.193**.
[5] H(W)A 2014, s 79(4); Welsh Code, paras 15.84–15.85; see **17.194**.
[6] H(W)A 2014, s 79(5); Welsh Code, paras 15.86–15.89; see **17.195–17.197**.

DECISIONS PENDING THE OUTCOME OF AN APPLICATION

9.144 Not every decision made by a local housing authority in the course of dealing with an application must be notified to the applicant in writing, let alone with reasons given. In the course of dealing with an application for homelessness assistance, the local housing authority may well take a number of decisions of importance to the applicant. For example:

(1) whether to accept an application for homelessness assistance[1];
(2) whether to provide interim accommodation pending a decision on the application[2];
(3) what interim accommodation to provide;
(4) for local housing authorities in England, whether to withdraw the interim accommodation, perhaps because the applicant has rejected it[3];
(5) whether to conduct an interview in the course of inquiries;
(6) which matters to inquire into;
(7) whether to explore local connection issues;
(8) and many more.

[1] In *R (May) v Birmingham City Council* [2012] EWHC 1399 (Admin), (2012) July *Legal Action*, p 41, the local housing authority initially notified the prospective applicant that she had the right to request a review of its decision not to accept a repeat application for homelessness assistance. This was clearly wrong and the prospective applicant successfully challenged the local housing authority through judicial review, rather than through an appeal to the county court. For 'repeat applications', see **8.80–8.82** and **8.85–8.91**. For 'judicial review', see **19.306–19.333**. For 'appeal to the county court', see **19.214–19.276**. Even though H(W)A 2014, s 62(2) contains a statutory test allowing local housing authority in Wales to

refuse to carry out an assessment of a person's case if the application is a repeat application, there is no duty in H(W)A 2014, Pt 2, requiring the local housing authority to notify the applicant in writing of its decision.

2 HA 1996, s 188(1); H(W)A 2014, s 68(1).

3 For local housing authorities in Wales, H(W)A 2014, s 69(1) provides that an applicant must be notified, in accordance with H(W)A 2014, s 84(1), of any decision that the interim duty to secure accommodation has come to an end. The applicant has the right to request a review of the decision: H(W)A 2014, s 85(1)(c).

9.145 None of these decisions need be put in writing by the local housing authority. None of them give rise to an opportunity for a statutory review. If a local housing authority is asked for a written notification and/or reasons for one of these decisions, it may provide them. On any challenge to the relevant decision (in proceedings brought by judicial review) it would be helpful to the local housing authority to be able to point to a contemporaneous written explanation to the applicant as to why it had reached the decision under challenge[1].

1 See *Complaint against Newham London Borough Council*, 11 000 383, 8 March 2012 (2012) May *Legal Action*, p 34, where the Local Government Ombudsman found maladministration and stated: '[i]t is good practice to record reasons for a refusal to provide interim accommodation' (para 50).

Reviews of assessments

Local housing authorities in England

9.146 Local housing authorities in England are under a duty to make an assessment of an applicant's case if the applicant is eligible for assistance and is either threatened with homelessness or is homeless[1]. The contents of that assessment will inform the local housing authority as to what steps it should take in order to perform the duty it owes to the applicant and help the applicant prevent his or her homelessness, or secure new accommodation.

1 HA 1996, s 189A(1), inserted by HRA 2017, s 3(1), for applications for homelessness assistance made to local housing authorities in England on or after 3 April 2018. See 15.62–15.86.

9.147 After the assessment has been made, the local housing authority must try to agree with the applicant the steps that he or she is required to take for the purposes of securing accommodation. Those steps must be recorded in writing and the applicant's agreement or refusal must also be recorded[1].

1 HA 1996, s 189A(4)–(6), inserted by HRA 2017, s 3(1), for applications for homelessness assistance made to local housing authorities in England on or after 3 April 2018. See 15.72–15.80.

9.148 The local housing authority is required to keep under review:

- its assessment of the applicant's case; and
- the appropriateness of the agreement and of the steps that both the applicant and the local housing authority have agreed to take; or
- where there has been no agreement, the steps which the local housing authority has recorded would be reasonable for the applicant to take, and the steps that the local housing authority are to take[1].

The English Code also advises that the local housing authority should arrange to review the assessment and the personalised housing plan[2] if it believes that the applicant is not co-operating[3].

1   HA 1996, s 189A(9), inserted by HRA 2017, s 3(1), for applications for homelessness assistance made to local housing authorities in England on or after 3 April 2018. See English Code, paras 11.29–11.36 and **15.73** of this book.
2   Which contains the record of the steps that both parties have agreed to take, or the local housing authority has recorded as reasonable to require the applicant to take: HA 1996, s 189A(4)–(6) for applications for homelessness assistance made to local housing authorities in England on or after 3 April 2018. See **15.72–15.80**.
3   English Code, para 11.33.

9.149 The duty to keep these matters under review continues until the local housing authority considers that it no longer owes the applicant any duty under HA 1996, Pt 7, as amended by HRA 2017[1]. It follows that the assessment should remain in place and under review throughout the time when the applicant is being helped and/or accommodated by the local housing authority under HA 1996, Pt 7[2], duties.

1   HA 1996, s 189A(9), inserted by HRA 2017, s 3(1), for applications for homelessness assistance made to local housing authorities in England on or after 3 April 2018. See **15.87–15.80**.
2   As amended by HRA 2017, s 4(2), for applications for homelessness assistance made to local housing authorities in England on or after 3 April 2018.

9.150 If the local housing authority's assessment of the three issues that it is required to consider changes, then it must notify the applicant in writing of how that assessment has changed[1]. If the local housing authority's assessment of other aspects of the applicant's case changes, the local housing authority must notify the applicant in writing of those changes only if it considers it appropriate to do so[2].

1   HA 1996, s 189A(10)(a)), inserted by HRA 2017, s 3(1), for applications for homelessness assistance made to local housing authorities in England on or after 3 April 2018. See English Code, para 11.34 and **15.84** of this book.
2   HA 1996, s 189A(10)(b)), inserted by HRA 2017, s 3(1), for applications for homelessness assistance made to local housing authorities in England on or after 3 April 2018. See **15.84**.

Local housing authorities in Wales

9.151 A local housing authority in Wales must keep its assessment under review throughout the period when it considers that it owes the applicant any duty under H(W)A 2014, Pt 2, or before it has decided that a duty is owed but where it considers that it may owe the applicant a duty[1]. 'Review' in this context does not mean a formal review of a decision[2], but a reconsideration. It follows that an assessment of an applicant's case by a local housing authority in Wales can be constantly changed and updated to deal with changing circumstances. However, that does not entitle a local housing authority to decide that an applicant's circumstances have changed once a duty has been accepted such that a duty is no longer owed (for example, if he or she did have a priority need and no longer has it)[3].

1   H(W)A 2014, s 62(8); Welsh Code, paras 10.44–10.49.
2   Which would fall under H(W)A 2014, s 85(1).

³   Welsh Code, paras 10.50–10.52.

9.152 A local housing authority in Wales is also required to review its assessment in two specified cases:

- Case 1: where an applicant has been notified that the duty under H(W)A 2014, s 66¹ prevention duty is owed and it appears to the local housing authority that the duty has or is likely to come to an end because the applicant is homeless; and
- Case 2: where an applicant has been notified that the duty under H(W)A 2014, s 73², relief duty is owed to him or her, and it appears to the local housing authority that the duty has or is likely to come to an end in circumstances where a duty may be owed to him or her under H(W)A 2014, s 75, main housing duty³.

¹   See **17.45–17.72**.
²   See **17.73–17.143**.
³   H(W)A 2014, s 62(9). See **17.31**.

9.153 The requirement to review the assessment arises because, when the assessment is initially undertaken, the local housing authority will have been assessing whether the applicant is eligible for help and, if so, whether he or she is homeless or threatened with homelessness. That is all the information that the local housing authority needs in order to determine whether the duties in H(WA) 2014, s 66(1) or 73(1), apply. Once those duties come to an end, the local housing authority will have to assess whether or not the applicant has a priority need and (if regard is being had to the test) whether the applicant has become homeless intentionally, so as to determine whether the duty to accommodate under H(W)A 2014, s 75(1), is owed to the applicant¹. The local housing authority is required to notify the outcome of the review of the assessment to the applicant and give reasons for any issues decided against the applicant's interests².

¹   Welsh Code, paras 10.44–10.49
²   H(W)A 2014, s 63(1).

ADDITIONAL INQUIRIES AND DECISIONS

9.154 The decision or decisions notified to the applicant are unlikely to be the only important decision that has to be made by a local housing authority, particularly where the initial decision is that the applicant *is* owed a duty under HA 1996, Pt 7¹, or under H(W)A 2014, Pt 2. Some of those decisions are required to be notified to the applicant in writing; and some are not required to be notified in writing.

¹   As amended by HRA 2017 for applications for homelessness assistance made to local housing authorities in England on or after 3 April 2018.

Additional decisions that are required to be notified in writing

Local housing authorities in England

9.155 After a local housing authority has notified an applicant of its decision:

- as to whether or not he or she is eligible for assistance[1]; and, if so
- as to whether or not a duty, if any, is owed[2]; and if so
- which duty,

various other issues which the local housing authority will have to consider, and come to decisions about, will arise. Some of those issues are subject to specific notification requirements under HA 1996, Pt 7[3].

[1] HA 1996, s 184(1)(a), see **9.20**.
[2] HA 1996, s 184(1)(b), see **9.21–9.22**.
[3] As amended by HRA 2017 for applications for homelessness assistance made to local housing authorities in England on or after 3 April 2018.

9.156 In respect of some other decisions, there is no specific notification requirements, but assistance can be drawn from other provisions of HA 1996, Pt 7[1]. It is probably safe to suggest that the proper inference to be drawn from the structure of the statutory provisions on the 'right to request a review'[2] is that, at least in respect of the decisions that are potentially subject to a right of review, the local housing authority must notify (ie put in writing) those decisions. Moreover, the structure of HA 1996, s 202[3] suggests that all reviewable decisions will have been notified in writing[4]. Although there is no express obligation to give reasons for all of the decisions which carry a right to request a review, it makes good administrative sense for reasons to be given.

[1] As amended by HRA 2017 for applications for homelessness assistance made to local housing authorities in England on or after 3 April 2018.
[2] HA 1996, s 202(1), as amended by HRA 2017, s 9, for applications for homelessness assistance made to local housing authorities in England on or after 3 April 2018. See **19.8–19.69**.
[3] As amended by HRA 2017, s 9, for applications for homelessness assistance made to local housing authorities in England on or after 3 April 2018, see **19.8–19.69**.
[4] See, in particular, HA 1996, s 202(3). See **19.86–19.89**.

9.157 The other decisions that may arise during the process of an application for homelessness assistance are:

- whether the interim accommodation duty at HA 1996, s 188(1) has come to an end;
- whether the conditions for referral are made out and, if so, whether the local housing authority will refer performance of the relevant duty;
- the suitability of accommodation secured under any accommodation duty; and
- whether the relevant duty has come to an end.

We discuss these decision in the following paragraphs[1].

[1] See **9.158–9.160** for decisions relating to the interim accommodation, **9.161–9.162** for decisions relating to the conditions for referral, **9.163–9.165** for decision relating to the suitability of accommodation and **9.166–9.167** for decisions relating to the ending of the relevant duty.

DECISIONS RELATING TO THE INTERIM ACCOMMODATION DUTY

9.158 The duty to secure interim accommodation can be brought to an end in the following circumstances[1]:

- where the local housing authority has notified the applicant of its decision that it does not owe him or her a HA 1996, s 189B(2)[2], relief duty, because he or she is either not eligible for assistance or is not homeless[3];
- where the local housing authority has notified the applicant of its decision that, upon the HA 1996, s 189B(2)[4], relief duty coming to an end, no accommodation duty under HA 1996, ss 190[5] or 193[6], will be owed, because he or she does not have a priority need[7];
- where HA 1996, s 189B(2)[8], relief duty has come to an end and the local housing authority has notified the applicant of its decision as to what duty, if any, is owed to the applicant[9]; or
- where the applicant has rejected an offer of suitable interim accommodation[10].

[1] HA 1996, s 188, as amended by HRA 2017, s 5(4), for applications for homelessness assistance made to local housing authorities in England on or after 3 April 2018, see **16.37–16.80**.
[2] As inserted by HRA 2017, s 5(2), for applications for homelessness assistance made to local housing authorities in England on or after 3 April 2018, see **15.138–15.195**.
[3] HA 1996, s 188(1ZA)(a) and (1ZB)(a), as inserted by HRA 2017, s 5(4), for applications for homelessness assistance made to local housing authorities in England on or after 3 April 2018, see **16.56–16.59**.
[4] As inserted by HRA 2017, s 5(2), for applications for homelessness assistance made to local housing authorities in England on or after 3 April 2018, see **15.138–15.139**.
[5] As amended by HRA 2017, s 5(5), for applications for homelessness assistance made to local housing authorities in England on or after 3 April 2018; the short-term accommodation duty owed to applicants who are homelessness, eligible for assistance, have a priority need and have become homeless intentionally, see **16.81–16.93**.
[6] The main housing duty owed to applicants who are homelessness, eligible for assistance, have a priority need and have not become homeless intentionally, see **16.94–16.199**.
[7] HA 1996, s 188(1ZA)(b), as inserted by HRA 2017, s 5(4), for applications for homelessness assistance made to local housing authorities in England on or after 3 April 2018, see **16.60–16.65**.
[8] As inserted by HRA 2017, s 5(2), for applications for homelessness assistance made to local housing authorities in England on or after 3 April 2018, see **15.138–15.195**.
[9] HA 1996, s 188(1ZB)(b), as inserted by HRA 2017, s 5(4), for applications for homelessness assistance made to local housing authorities in England on or after 3 April 2018, see **16.60–16.65**. The various duties that could be owed to the applicant are: (a) the short-term accommodation duty owed to applicants who are homelessness, eligible for assistance, have a priority need and have become homeless intentionally: HA 1996, s 190(2), (as amended by HRA 2017, s 5(5), for applications for homelessness assistance made to local housing authorities in England on or after 3 April 2018) see **16.81–16.93**; (b) the main housing duty at HA 1996, s 193(2), owed to applicants who are homelessness, eligible for assistance, have a priority need and have not become homeless intentionally see **16.94–16.199**; or (c) the accommodation duty owed to applicants who are homelessness, eligible for assistance, have a, priority need, have not become homeless intentionally and have deliberately and unreasonably refused to co-operate at HA 1996, s 193C(4) (as inserted by HRA 2017, s 7(1), for applications for homelessness assistance made to local housing authorities in England on or after 3 April 2018), see **16.200–16.216**. Each of these duties depend upon the local housing authority being satisfied that the applicant has a priority need. There is an exception for applicants who have made a fresh application for homelessness assistance within two years of acceptance of a private rented sector offer made in order to bring the HA 1996, s 193(2) main housing duty to an end: HA 1996, s 193(7AA). Those applicants do not need to have a priority need in order to be owed the HA 1996, s 193(2), main housing duty: HA 1996, ss 188(1A) and

195A(1) (as amended by HRA 2017, s 4(4), for applications for homelessness assistance made to local housing authorities in England on or after 3 April 2018), see **8.100–8.107**.

[10] *R (Brooks) v Islington London Borough Council* [2015] EWHC 2657 (Admin), [2016] HLR 2, Admin Ct, see **16.66–16.69**.

9.159 There is no requirement on the local housing authority specifically to notify the applicant that the interim accommodation duty has come to an end. The first, second and third circumstance each depend upon notification of the principal s 184(1) decision[1]. It would be expected that contents of the s 184(1) decision would include information about the interim accommodation duty coming to an end[2]. There is no right to request a review of any decision that the interim accommodation duty has come to an end, but the applicant does have a right to request a review of the HA 1996, s 184, decision that triggered the interim accommodation duty coming to an end[3].

[1] Whether he or she is eligible for assistance, and whether a duty, and if so, what duty is owed to the applicant.
[2] See **9.140–9.143**.
[3] HA 1996, s 202(1)(a), (b), (ba)(ii) (as inserted by HRA 2017, s 9, for applications for homelessness assistance made to local housing authorities in England on or after 3 April 2018), see **19.15–19.17**.

9.160 In relation to the fourth circumstance, there are no notification requirements specified in HA 1996, Pt 7[1]. However, it would be expected that the local housing authority would inform the applicant that his or her refusal of the interim accommodation offered means that no further interim accommodation would be secured under HA 1996, s 188(1). If the applicant wishes to dispute that decision, whether in relation to the suitability of the accommodation secured or on any other issues, his or her remedy would be a claim in judicial review, arguing that the local housing authority has made an error of law[2].

[1] As amended by HRA 2017, s 5(8), for applications for homelessness assistance made to local housing authorities in England on or after 3 April 2018.
[2] See **16.74–16.80** for disputes in relation to the HA 1996, s 188(1), interim accommodation duty and see **19.306–19.333** for judicial review.

DECISIONS RELATING TO THE CONDITIONS FOR REFERRAL

9.161 A local housing authority must notify the applicant of the following decisions[1]:

- that it considers that the conditions are met for referral of the HA 1996, s 189B(2)[2], relief duty to another local housing authority and intends to notify or has notified the other local housing authority of that opinion[3];
- that it has been decided, by agreement between the two local housing authorities or following a referee's decision[4], that the conditions for referral of the HA 1996, s 189B(2)[5], relief duty are met[6];
- that it has been decided that the conditions for referral of the HA 1996, s 189B(2)[7], relief duty are not met[8];
- that it considers that the conditions are met for referral of the HA 1996, s 193(2), main housing duty[9] to another local housing authority and intends to notify or has notified the other local housing authority of that opinion[10]; and

- that it has been decided, by agreement between the two local housing authorities or following a referee's decision[11], that the conditions for referral of the HA 1996, s 193(2), main housing duty[12] are met[13]; and
- that it has been decided that the conditions for referral of the HA 1996, s 193(2), main housing duty[14] are not met[15].

1   HA 1996, s 198 (as amended by HRA 2017, s 5(8), for applications for homelessness assistance made to local housing authorities in England on or after 3 April 2018), see **14.155–14.163**.
2   As inserted by HRA 2017, s 5(2), for applications for homelessness assistance made to local housing authorities in England on or after 3 April 2018, see **15.138–15.195**.
3   HA 1996, ss 184(4), 198(A1) and 199A(1) (as amended and inserted by HRA 2017, s 5(3), (8) and (9), for applications for homelessness assistance made to local housing authorities in England on or after 3 April 2018); a decision that must be notified with reasons (HA 1996, s 184(4), as amended and inserted by HRA 2017, s 5(3), for applications for homelessness assistance made to local housing authorities in England on or after 3 April 2018), see **14.155–14.161**.
4   HA 1996, s 198(5), see **14.176–14.190**.
5   As inserted by HRA 2017, s 5(2), for applications for homelessness assistance made to local housing authorities in England on or after 3 April 2018, see **15.138–15.195**.
6   HA 1996, s 199A(3) (as inserted by HRA 2017, s 5(9), for applications for homelessness assistance made to local housing authorities in England on or after 3 April 2018); a decision that must be notified with reasons, see **14.155–14.161** and **14.176–14.190**.
7   As inserted by HRA 2017, s 5(2), for applications for homelessness assistance made to local housing authorities in England on or after 3 April 2018, see **15.138–15.195**.
8   HA 1996, s 199A(3) (as inserted by HRA 2017, s 5(9), for applications for homelessness assistance made to local housing authorities in England on or after 3 April 2018; a decision that must be notified with reasons, see **14.155–14.161** and **14.176–14.190**.
9   See **14.26** and **14.155–14.161**.
10   HA 1996, ss 198(1) and 200(1) (as amended by HRA 2017, s 5(10), for applications for homelessness assistance made to local housing authorities in England on or after 3 April 2018): a decision that need not contain reasons, see **14.155**.
11   HA 1996, s 198(5), see **14.184–14.190**.
12   See **16.94–16.199**.
13   HA 1996, s 200(2) (as amended by HRA 2017, s 5(10), for applications for homelessness assistance made to local housing authorities in England on or after 3 April 2018): a decision that must be notified with reasons, see **14.155**.
14   See **16.94–16.199**.
15   HA 1996, s 200(2) (as amended by HRA 2017, s 5(10), for applications for homelessness assistance made to local housing authorities in England on or after 3 April 2018): a decision that must be notified with reasons, see **14.155–14.160**.

9.162 HA 1996, Pt 7[1], provides that all but the fourth of those notifications[2] must contain reasons for the local housing authority's decision. In addition, the applicant has the right to request a review of all but the first decision[3]. Notifications of the second, third, fourth, fifth and sixth decision must therefore inform the applicant of his or her right to request a review and of the time within the request must be made[4].

1   As amended by HRA 2017 for applications for homelessness assistance made to local housing authorities in England on or after 3 April 2018.
2   The decision that the local housing authority considers that the conditions are met for referral of the HA 1996, s 193(2), main housing duty to another local housing authority and intends to notify or has notified the other local housing authority of that opinion: HA 1996, s 198(1) and 200(1) (as amended by HRA 2017, s 5(10), for applications for homelessness assistance made to local housing authorities in England on or after 3 April 2018).
3   HA 1996, s 202(1)(c), (d) and (e), see **19.49–19.58**.

⁴ HA 1996, ss 184(5), 199A(3) (as inserted by HRA 2017, s 5(9), for applications for homelessness assistance made to local housing authorities in England on or after 3 April 2018), 200(2) and (3), see **19.86–19.89**.

DECISIONS AS TO THE SUITABILITY OF ACCOMMODATION

9.163 The decision as to suitability of accommodation offered under any of the duties or powers in HA 1996, Pt 7[1], is not specifically required to be notified in writing, nor is it the subject of any obligation to give reasons. Nor, indeed, is there any express obligation on the local housing authority to make inquiries into the issue of suitability (although, because it is a public authority, it must have regard to all relevant considerations and otherwise comply with the ordinary principles of administrative law). The Court of Appeal has held that there is no obligation on a local housing authority to give reasons for its decision that an offer of accommodation is suitable in the offer letter[2].

¹ As amended by HRA 2017 for applications for homelessness assistance made to local housing authorities in England on or after 3 April 2018.
² *Akhtar v Birmingham City Council* [2011] EWCA Civ 383, [2011] HLR 28, CA; and *Solihull Metropolitan Borough Council v Khan* [2014] EWCA Civ 41, [2014] HLR 33, CA.

9.164 The issue of suitability arises not only in relation to any letter offering accommodation, but also in relation to any decision by a local housing authority that its duty has come to an end, because the applicant has refused an offer of suitable accommodation. That decision should normally be notified in writing, because there is a right to request a review of that decision[1], but there is no obligation to give reasons in the decision letter for the local housing authority's decision that the accommodation offered was suitable[2].

¹ HA 1996, s 202(1)(b) as amended by HRA 2017, s 9, for applications for homelessness assistance made to local housing authorities in England on or after 3 April 2018, see **19.15–19.17**. *Warsame v Hounslow London Borough Council* (2000) 32 HLR 335, CA.
² *Solihull Metropolitan Borough Council v Khan* [2014] EWCA Civ 41, [2014] HLR 33, CA.

9.165 However, where the issue of suitability relates to anything other than HA 1996, s 188 interim accommodation, the applicant has a right to request a review of the local housing authority's assessment of suitability[1]. Any decision made on review, if decided against the interests of the applicant, must contain reasons for that decision[2].

¹ HA 1996, s 202(1)(f), (g) and (h), as amended by HRA 2017, s 9, for applications for homelessness assistance made to local housing authorities in England on or after 3 April 2018, see **19.59–19.69**.
² HA 1996, s 203(4)(a); see **19.180–19.184**.

DECISIONS NOTIFYING THAT THE DUTY HAS COME TO AN END

9.166 The local housing authority must notify the applicant, in writing, of any decision that certain duties have come to an end. The notification must also specify the circumstances that have led to the decision, the applicant's right to request a review of the decision and the time limit in which to do so[1].Those decisions are:

- any decision that the HA 1996, s 195(2)[2], prevention duty has come to an end by reason of the one of the circumstances at HA 1996, s 195(8) or (10)[3];
- any decision that the HA 1996, s 189B(2)[4], relief duty has come to an end by reason of the one of the circumstances at HA 1996, s 189B(7) or (9)[5];
- any decision that the HA 1996, s 193(2), main housing duty[6] has come to an end by reason of one of the events at HA 1996, s 193(5)–(7AA)[7]; and
- any decision that the HA 1996, s 193C(4)[8], accommodation duty has come to an end by reason of one of the events at HA 1996, s 193C(5)–(6)[9].

[1] HA 1996, ss 189B(6) and 195(7), as inserted and amended by HRA 2017, ss 4(2) and 5(2), for applications for homelessness assistance made to local housing authorities in England on or after 3 April 2018.
[2] As amended by HRA 2017, s 4(2), for applications for homelessness assistance made to local housing authorities in England on or after 3 April 2018.
[3] As amended by HRA 2017, s 4(2), for applications for homelessness assistance made to local housing authorities in England on or after 3 April 2018, see **15.87–15.137**.
[4] As inserted by HRA 2017, s 5(2), for applications for homelessness assistance made to local housing authorities in England on or after 3 April 2018.
[5] As inserted by HRA 2017, s 5(2), for applications for homelessness assistance made to local housing authorities in England on or after 3 April 2018, see **15.138–15.195**.
[6] See **16.94–16.199**.
[7] See **16.113–16.179**.
[8] As inserted by HRA 2017, s 7(1), for applications for homelessness assistance made to local housing authorities in England on or after 3 April 2018. Duty to secure accommodation for applicants who are homeless, eligible for assistance, have a priority need, have not become homeless intentionally and have deliberately and unreasonably refused to co-operate: see **16.200–16.216**.
[9] As inserted by HRA 2017, s 7(1), for applications for homelessness assistance made to local housing authorities in England on or after 3 April 2018, see **16.204–16.216**.

9.167 Several of those circumstances are as a result of the applicant having refused an offer of suitable accommodation. Most, but not all, offers must include information about the possible consequences of refusal or acceptance of the offer, and of the applicant's right to request a review of the suitability of the accommodation. Those offers are:

- a final accommodation offer[1] made in order to bring the HA 1996, s 189B(2)[2], relief duty to an end[3];
- a final Pt 6 offer[4] made in order to bring the HA 1996, s 189B(2)[5], relief duty to an end[6];
- an offer of accommodation made under the HA 1996, s 193(2) main housing duty[7];
- a final offer of Pt 6 accommodation made in order to bring the HA 1996, s 193(2) main housing duty to an end[8];
- a private rented sector offer made in order to bring the HA 1996, s 193(2) main housing duty to an end[9];
- a final accommodation offer[10] made in order to bring the HA 1996, s 193C(4)[11], accommodation duty to an end[12]; and
- a final Pt 6 offer[13] made in order to bring the HA 1996, s 193C(4)[14],

duty to an end[15].

1   Defined at HA 1996, s 193A(4), as inserted by HRA 2017, s 7(1), for applications for homelessness assistance made to local housing authorities in England on or after 3 April 2018, see **15.181–15.184**.
2   As inserted by HRA 2017, s 5(2), for applications for homelessness assistance made to local housing authorities in England on or after 3 April 2018 see **15.138–15.195**.
3   HA 1996, ss 189B(9) and 193A(1)(b), as inserted by HRA 2017, ss 5(2) and 7(1), for applications for homelessness assistance made to local housing authorities in England on or after 3 April 2018, see **15.181–15.184**.
4   Defined at HA 1996, s 193A(5), as inserted by HRA 2017, s 7(1), for applications for homelessness assistance made to local housing authorities in England on or after 3 April 2018, see **15.185–15.188**.
5   As inserted by HRA 2017, s 5(2), for applications for homelessness assistance made to local housing authorities in England on or after 3 April 2018, see **15.138–15.195**.
6   HA 1996, ss 189B(9) and 193A(1)(b), as inserted by HRA 2017, ss 5(2) and 7(1), for applications for homelessness assistance made to local housing authorities in England on or after 3 April 2018, see **15.185–15.188**.
7   HA 1996, s 193(5), see **16.114–16.124**.
8   HA 1996, s 193(7), see **16.142–16.152**.
9   HA 1996, s 193(7AA), see **16.153–16.179**.
10 Defined at HA 1996, s 193C(7), as inserted by HRA 2017, s 7(1), for applications for homelessness assistance made to local housing authorities in England on or after 3 April 2018, see **16.206**.
11 As inserted by HRA 2017, s 7(1), for applications for homelessness assistance made to local housing authorities in England on or after 3 April 2018, see **16.200–16.216**.
12 HA 1996, s 193C(6)(a), as inserted by HRA 2017, s 7(1), for applications for homelessness assistance made to local housing authorities in England on or after 3 April 2018, see **16.205–16.209**.
13 Defined at HA 1996, s 193C(8), as inserted by HRA 2017, s 7(1), for applications for homelessness assistance made to local housing authorities in England on or after 3 April 2018, see **16.211**.
14 As inserted by HRA 2017, s 7(1), for applications for homelessness assistance made to local housing authorities in England on or after 3 April 2018, see **16.200–16.216**.
15 HA 1996, s 193C(6)(b), as inserted by HRA 2017, s 7(1), for applications for homelessness assistance made to local housing authorities in England on or after 3 April 2018, see **16.210–16.215**.

Local housing authorities in Wales

9.168 H(W)A 2014, Pt 2, contains a rigorous structure for notification of decisions after the H(W)A 2014, s 62 assessment has been notified to the applicant[1]. These include:

(1)   a decision to refer an application to another local housing authority under the local connection provisions (because the local housing authority making the referral has assessed the applicant as having a priority need and as not having become homeless intentionally and believes that the conditions for referral may be met)[2];

(2)   a decision that the conditions for referral of an application to another local housing authority are actually met[3]; and

(3)   a decision that any of the local housing authority's duties to help to prevent homelessness[4], to help to secure accommodation[5], to secure accommodation for applicants who have a priority need[6], or the interim duty to secure accommodation for homeless applicants who may have a priority need[7], have come to an end[8].

All of these decisions must be notified in writing, with reasons, and inform the applicant of his or her right to request a review and of the time within which such a request must be made[9].

1   See **9.12–914** and **9.143**.
2   H(W)A 2014, s 63(3); Welsh Code, para 18.22: a decision which must be notified with reasons. See **14.162–14.163**.
3   H(W)A 2014, s 82(2); Welsh Code, para 18.24: a decision which must be notified with reasons. See **14.162–14.163**.
4   H(W)A 2014, s 66(1); see **17.45–17.72**.
5   H(W)A 2014, s 73(1); see **17.73–17.143**.
6   H(W)A 2014, s 75(1); see **17.146–17.199**.
7   H(W)A 2014, s 68(1); see **17.118–17.134**.
8   H(W)A 2014, s 84(1); Welsh Code, chapter 15.
9   H(W)A 2014, ss 63(3), 82(2), 84(1).

9.169 A decision that the local housing authority's duty to secure or help to secure accommodation has come to an end might be for one of various different reasons:

(1)   each duty contains a list of circumstances where the duty will come to an end[1]; or

(2)   as a result of any of the circumstances specified in H(W)A 2014, s 79[2].

1   The circumstances in which the duty in H(W)A 2014, s 66(1), comes to an end are set out in H(W)A 2014, s 67, see **17.56–17.72**; the circumstances in which the duty in H(W)A 2014, s 68, comes to an end are set out in H(W)A 2014, s 69, see **17.128–17.133**; the circumstances in which the duty in H(W)A 2014, s 73(1), comes to an end are set out in H(W)A 2014, s 74, see **17.84–17.117**; the circumstances in which the duty in H(W)A 2014, s 75(1), comes to an end are set out in H(W)A 2014, s 76, see **17.158–17.188**.
2   H(W)A 2014, s 79, see **17.189–17.197**.

9.170 The circumstances specified in H(W)A 2014, s 79, are where the local housing authority has notified the applicant of any of the following:

- that it is no longer satisfied that the applicant is eligible for help[1];
- that it is satisfied that a mistake of fact had led to the applicant being notified under H(W)A 2014, s 63(1), that a duty was owed to him or her[2];
- that it is satisfied that the applicant has withdrawn his or her application[3]; or
- that it is satisfied that the applicant is unreasonably failing to cooperate with the local housing authority in connection with the exercise of any of the local housing authority's functions under H(W)A 2014, Pt 2[4].

1   H(W)A 2014, s 79(2); Welsh Code, paras 15.79; see **17.192**.
2   H(W)A 2014, s 79(3); Welsh Code, paras 15.80–15.83; see **17.193**.
3   H(W)A 2014, s 79(4); Welsh Code, paras 15.84–15.85; see **17.194**.
4   H(W)A 2014, s 79(5); Welsh Code, paras 15.86–15.89; see **17.195–17.197**.

9.171 Where a local housing authority in Wales is satisfied that its duty has come to an end, it must notify the applicant in writing that it no longer regards itself as being subject to the relevant duty, of the reasons why, of the right to request a review and of the time within which the request must be made[1]. Where the decision is that the duty under H(W)A 2014, s 73(1) has come to an end at the end of the 56-day period[2], or has come to an end because the local housing authority is satisfied that reasonable steps have been taken to secure that suitable accommodation is available for occupation by the applicant[3], the notification must include notice of the steps taken by the local housing authority to help to secure that suitable accommodation would be available for occupation by the applicant[4]. The applicant has the right to request a review of any decision that the duties have ended and, if relevant, of whether or not reasonable steps were taken during the period when the H(W)A 2014, s 73(1) duty was owed[5].

[1] H(W)A 2014, s 84(1); Welsh Code, paras 15.93–15.98.
[2] H(W)A 2014, s 74(2).
[3] H(W)A 2014, s 74(3); Welsh Code, paras 15.53–15.54. The Code advises that local housing authorities should be 'cautious' when using this mechanism to bring the duty to an end.
[4] H(W)A 2014, s 84(2).
[5] H(W)A 2014, s 85(1)(c) and (2).

9.172 The decision must be notified to the applicant in writing[1]. Where a notice is not received by an applicant, he or she may be treated as having been notified if the notice was made available at the local housing authority's office for a reasonable period for collection by the applicant or by someone on his or her behalf[2].

[1] H(W)A 2014, s 84(3); Welsh Code, paras 15.93–15.98.
[2] H(W)A 2014, s 84(4).

9.173 A local housing authority in Wales may not decide that its duty has come to an end as a result of an applicant refusing an offer of accommodation unless the local housing authority is satisfied that the applicant had been notified in writing of the possible consequences of refusal or acceptance of the offer before he or she refused the offer[1].

[1] H(W)A 2014, s 67(4)(a), see **17.66–17.72**; s 69(7), see **17.129**, and **17.172**; s 74(5), see **17.109–17.119**; and s 76(3), see **17.165–17.177**.

Decisions not required to be notified in writing

9.174 This still leaves a large number of decisions which will be made by a local housing authority in England or in Wales in the course of its dealings with an applicant which are not the subject of any express requirement:

(1)   to make inquiries;
(2)   to notify the decision in writing; or
(3)   to give reasons.

9.175 Those are the decisions in relation to which there is no explicit statutory requirement under HA 1996, s 184, H(W)A 2014, Pt 2, or elsewhere[1], and no right to a statutory review[2]. Accordingly, these decisions are subject only to the normal constraints of good administration and administrative law. An applicant aggrieved by any such decision could use the complaints procedure, complain to the relevant Ombudsman and/or bring proceedings for judicial review.

[1] See **9.90–9.94**.
[2] See **19.12–19.85**.

Chapter 10

HOMELESS OR THREATENED WITH HOMELESSNESS

Contents

INTRODUCTION

10.1 The main statutory duties set out in Pt 7 of the Housing Act 1996 (HA 1996) as amended by the Homelessness Reduction Act 2017[1] (HRA 2017) and Pt 2 of the Housing (Wales) Act 2014 (H(W)A 2014) are owed only to those whom a local housing authority is satisfied are either 'homeless' or 'threatened with homelessness'. Each of those terms is very tightly defined by HA 1996, Pt 7[2] and H(W)A 2014, Pt 2, so that there is no room for alternative terminology, such as 'rooflessness', or for more colloquial approaches such as whether someone has 'a place to sleep' or 'a home of their own'. As this chapter demonstrates, the tightness of the legal definitions can produce some surprising results: even the owner of a mansion could, in certain circumstances, be 'homeless' for the purposes of HA 1996, Pt 7[3] and H(W)A 2014, Pt 2.

[1]   For applications for homelessness assistance made to local housing authorities in England on or after 3 April 2018. See the Homelessness Reduction Act 2017 (Commencement and Transitional and Savings Provisions) Regulations 2018, SI 2018/167, reg 3.

[2]   As amended by HRA 2017, for applications for homelessness assistance made to local housing authorities in England on or after 3 April 2018.

[3]   As amended by HRA 2017, for applications for homelessness assistance made to local housing authorities in England on or after 3 April 2018.

DEFINITION OF 'HOMELESS'

Overview

10.2 The legal definition of 'homeless' is contained in four inter-related sections of HA 1996, Pt 7[1] and H(W)A 2014, Pt 2[2]. Taken together, these sections provide that a person is homeless if he or she:

(1)   has no accommodation physically available for him or her to occupy in the UK or elsewhere[3]; or

(2)   has no accommodation available which he or she is legally entitled to occupy[4]; or

(3)   has accommodation which is available and which he or she is entitled to occupy, but cannot secure entry to that accommodation[5]; or

(4)   has accommodation available, which he or she is entitled to occupy, but that accommodation consists of a moveable structure and there is no place where the applicant is entitled or permitted both to place and reside in it[6]; or

(5)   has accommodation available, which he or she is entitled to occupy and entry can be secured to it, but that accommodation is not reasonable to continue to occupy[7].

[1]   As amended by HRA 2017, for applications for homelessness assistance made to local housing authorities in England on or after 3 April 2018.
[2]   Housing Act 1996, ss 175–178 as amended by HRA 2017, for applications for homelessness assistance made to local housing authorities in England on or after 3 April 2018; Housing (Wales) Act 2014, ss 55–58.
[3]   HA 1996, s 175(1); H(W)A 2014, s 55(1).
[4]   HA 1996, s 175(1)(a)–(c); H(W)A 2014, s 55(1)(a)–(c).
[5]   HA 1996, s 175(2)(a); H(W)A 2014, s 55(2)(a).
[6]   HA 1996, s 175(2)(b); H(W)A 2014, s 55(2)(b).
[7]   HA 1996, s 175(3); H(W)A 2014, s 55(3).

10.3 In practice, the easiest way to apply the statutory definition is to start from the presumption that everyone is homeless. Then to ask whether, on the facts, *all* of the following conditions are satisfied:

(1)   there is 'accommodation'[1]; and
(2)   it is 'available' for the applicant's occupation[2]; and
(3)   the applicant has some right to occupy it[3]; and
(4)   the applicant can physically enter it[4]; and
(5)   it would be reasonable for the applicant to continue to occupy it[5].

[1]   See **10.8–10.16**.
[2]   See **10.17–10.32**.
[3]   See **10.33–10.65**.
[4]   See **10.73–10.134**.
[5]   See **11.73–11.129**.

10.4 Only if *all* of those conditions are fulfilled can the applicant be said not to be 'homeless'. There is an extra condition which must be satisfied if the relevant accommodation is 'a moveable structure'[1].

[1]   Discussed at **10.68–10.72**.

10.5 The question for the local housing authority is whether the applicant is homeless at the date of the making of the decision on his or her application. If an applicant for homelessness assistance has obtained accommodation, meeting the conditions described either at HA 1996, ss 175–178[1] or (as appropriate) at H(W)A 2014, ss 55–58, after he or she has made the application, but before the making of the decision on that application, he or she will no longer be homeless[2].

[1]   As amended by HRA 2017, for applications for homelessness assistance made to local housing authorities in England on or after 3 April 2018.
[2]   *Hanton-Rhouila v Westminster City Council* [2010] EWCA Civ 1334, [2011] HLR 12, CA. Unless the accommodation is being provided by the local housing authority itself in performance of its housing duties; see **10.13**.

10.6 There is a special deeming provision for applicants who are re-applying for homelessness assistance within two years of acceptance of a private rented sector offer[1]. Applicants in those circumstances who have been served with a valid Housing Act 1988, s 21 notice are to be treated as homeless from the date on which the notice expires[2]. There is no equivalent deeming provision in H(W)A 2014, Pt 2, for applicants in Wales.

[1]   'Private rented sector offers' are defined at HA 1996 s 193(7AC). See **16.153–16.179**. See further **8.100–8.107** in relation to applications for homelessness assistance to a local housing authority in England made within two years of the date of acceptance of the private rented sector.
[2]   HA 1996, s 195A(2) as amended by HRA 2017, s 4(4), for applications for homelessness assistance made to local housing authorities in England on or after 3 April 2018. See **10.116**.

10.7 In the following paragraphs each of the conditions which form the component parts of the statutory definition of 'homeless' are examined in turn.

The meaning of 'accommodation'

10.8 The question is not 'does the applicant have an "address"[1]?' or 'does he or she have somewhere to stay?' but rather 'does the applicant have "accommodation"?'

[1]   *Tickner v Mole Valley District Council* [1980] LAG Bull 187, CA.

10.9 HA 1996, Pt 7[1] and H(W)A 2014, Pt 2 give no definition of this term. The standard dictionary definitions refer to 'lodgings' or 'living quarters'[2]. In practice, ordinary English usage tends to refer to 'accommodation' as shelter with a degree of permanence.

[1]   As amended by HRA 2017, for applications for homelessness assistance made to local housing authorities in England on or after 3 April 2018.
[2]   For example, in the *Chambers Dictionary* (revised 13th edn).

10.10 It is for the local housing authority to decide whether what it is considering constitutes 'accommodation'. Houses or flats (or parts of them) are not the only units that the local housing authority can regard as falling within the meaning of 'accommodation'. In *R v Hillingdon London Borough Council ex p Puhlhofer*[1], the courts upheld a local housing authority's decision that a modest hotel room in a bed and breakfast guest house occupied by a husband and wife and their two children (later described as a 'single cramped and squalid bedroom')[2] was 'accommodation'.

[1]   *R v Hillingdon London Borough Council ex p Puhlhofer* [1986] AC 484, HL.
[2]   *R v Brent London Borough Council ex p Awua* [1996] 1 AC 55, HL at 68B–D per Lord Hoffmann.

10.11 This does not mean that anything pressed into service for sleeping in can constitute 'accommodation'. Examples not constituting 'accommodation' canvassed in the case law include 'Diogenes' barrel'[1] and 'a potting shed'[2]. It would be hard to describe a cardboard box in a shop doorway, a factory where a homeless worker was allowed to sleep overnight, or a car used to sleep in as 'accommodation'. Even though a prison cell is physically capable of accommodating a prisoner, it cannot be treated as 'accommodation' for the purposes of the definition of 'homeless'[3].

[1]   *R v Hillingdon London Borough Council ex p Puhlhofer* [1986] AC 484, HL per Lord Brightman at 517, also referred to in *R v Newham London Borough Council ex p Ojuri (No 2)* (1999) 31 HLR 452, QBD by Collins J. In *Moran v Manchester City Council, Richards v Ipswich Borough Council* [2008] EWCA Civ 378, [2008] HLR 39, CA at [28] Wilson LJ described Lord Brightman's reference to Diogenes' barrel as a phrase 'which, with respect, was neatly apt but has since become hackneyed by repetition'.

[2]   *R v Hillingdon London Borough Council ex p Puhlhofer* [1986] AC 484, HL per Ackner LJ (giving judgment in the Court of Appeal) at 491.

[3]   *Stewart v London Borough of Lambeth* [2002] EWCA Civ 753, [2002] HLR 40, CA and *R (B) v Southwark London Borough Council* [2003] EWHC 1678 (Admin), (2004) 36 HLR 3, Admin Ct. In *Rageb v Kensington and Chelsea Royal Borough Council* [2017] EWCA Civ 360, CA, the Court of Appeal refused permission to appeal to an applicant who sought to argue that this principle should be extended to property which he was required to occupy by the terms of his licence, following his release from prison.

10.12 From 1982 until 2008, the approach of the courts was that *crisis accommodation* should not fall within the definition of 'accommodation' for these purposes. This approach was based on a 1982 decision that women's refuges did not fall within the definition[1]. The approach was reviewed, and held to be wrong, by the Court of Appeal in 2008 in *Moran v Manchester City Council, Richards v Ipswich Borough Council*[2]. The House of Lords subsequently considered an appeal in that case and decided that women's refuges were not reasonable for women to continue to occupy indefinitely. As a result, the House of Lords held that there was no need to consider, in reaching its own decision in that case, whether other refuges and hostels, or other forms of shelter such as prison cells or hospital wards, were 'accommodation' or not[3]. The question of whether other forms of crisis accommodation should fall within the definition of 'accommodation' remains open[4].

[1]   *R v Ealing London Borough Council ex p Sidhu* (1982) 2 HLR 41, QBD, applying *Williams v Cynon Valley Borough Council* [1980] LAG Bull 16.

[2]   [2008] EWCA Civ 378, [2008] HLR 39, CA. See also *NJ v Wandsworth London Borough Council* [2013] EWCA Civ 1373, [2014] HLR 6, CA, where the Court of Appeal held that accommodation at a women's refuge could constitute residence of a person's 'own choice' for the purposes of building a local connection. See **14.60**.

[3]   *Ali & others v Birmingham City Council, Moran v Manchester City Council* [2009] UKHL 36, [2009] 1 WLR 1506, HL at [52] and [56] per Baroness Hale.

[4]   In *Horwitz v Bath and North East Somerset Council* [2013] EWCA Civ 839, (2015) September *Legal Action*, p 30, CA, the Court of Appeal granted the applicant permission to bring a second appeal against a decision that accommodation provided on an emergency basis at a nursing home is 'accommodation' for the purposes of the statutory definition. It appears that the appeal never proceeded.

10.13 For policy reasons, accommodation provided by a local housing authority under the interim duty to accommodate[1], or under its powers to provide accommodation pending review[2] or pending appeal[3], is not 'accommodation' for the purposes of the statutory definition. An applicant is still homeless even if occupying such interim accommodation[4].

¹ HA 1996, s 188(1); H(W)A 2014, s 68(1). See **16.37–16.73** and **17.118–17.133**.
² HA 1996, s 188(3) as amended by HRA 2017, s 5(4), for applications for homelessness assistance made to local housing authorities in England on or after 3 April 2018; H(W)A 2014, s 69(11). See **16.233–16.257** and **17.134**.
³ HA 1996, s 204(4) as amended by HRA 2017, s 4(6), for applications for homelessness assistance made to local housing authorities in England on or after 3 April 2018; H(W)A 2014, s 88(5). See 16.258–16.277 and 17.135–17.137.
⁴ *R (Alam) v Tower Hamlets London Borough Council* [2009] EWHC 44, (2009) March *Legal Action*, p 24. In *Ali & others v Birmingham City Council, Moran v Manchester City Council* [2009] UKHL 36, [2009] 1 WLR 1506, HL, Manchester City Council accepted that an applicant remained homeless while occupying interim accommodation provided under HA 1996, s 188(1): see Baroness Hale at [55]. In *O'Callaghan v Southwark London Borough Council* (2010) May *Legal Action*, p 23, Lambeth County Court, an applicant who was occupying interim accommodation secured under the local housing authority's duty at HA 1996, s 188(1) could not have become homeless intentionally when she subsequently lost the accommodation, because she had remained 'homeless' throughout the period of occupation of the accommodation.

10.14 But some circumstances can generate real issues as to whether the subject matter is 'accommodation'. For example, is a tent or a beach hut, which a family has been forced to occupy for several weeks, 'accommodation'?

10.15 These issues on the meaning of 'accommodation' are brought into sharper focus by the globalisation of the definition of homelessness. Until 1996 the question was whether the applicant had 'accommodation' in England, Scotland or Wales. Now the question is whether the applicant has 'accommodation' in the United Kingdom (bringing Northern Ireland within scope)[1] or 'elsewhere', ie anywhere in the world[2]. As a result, the question 'Is it "accommodation"?' must now be applied to a wider range of forms of habitation.

¹ See **11.28** and Box 1.
² HA 1996, s 175(1); H(W)A 2014, s 55(1).

10.16 If the local housing authority has decided that the applicant has 'accommodation', the next inquiry is whether it is 'available for his occupation'[1].

¹ HA 1996, s 175(1); H(W)A 2014, s 55(1).

The meaning of 'available for occupation'

10.17 The local housing authority must consider first whether the accommodation is factually 'available'. If so, the second consideration is whether the accommodation is 'available for' the applicant's occupation and for the occupation of all members of the applicant's household as defined by HA 1996, s 176 and H(W)A 2014, s 56.

The factual test

10.18 The factual question is the most straightforward: is the particular accommodation 'available' to the applicant as a matter of fact? Accommodation which is hypothetically or notionally available will not suffice: the language of HA 1996, Pt 7[1] and H(W)A 2014, Pt 2, which use the present tense, 'is not apt to refer to unspecified accommodation which may in the future become available'[2]. HA 1996, Pt 7[3] and H(W)A 2014, Pt 2, specifically deal with situations where admission to the accommodation is physically barred so that the applicant cannot secure entry to it[4]. But factual 'availability' can embrace broader issues, especially given that the accommodation under consideration might be anywhere in the world. In *Begum v Tower Hamlets London Borough Council*[5], the accommodation being considered was a room in the applicant's father-in-law's house in Bangladesh. The court was satisfied that if the applicant had said to the local housing authority that she could not get to Bangladesh (eg because of her lack of means) or could not enter that country (eg because of her immigration status) the local housing authority would have had to decide whether the accommodation was in fact 'available' to her:

> 'To hold that it is available to her because it is legally and physically hers to occupy, without regard to the question of whether she has any way of getting there, is not only to take leave of reality; it is to drain the word "available" of any meaning[6].'

[1] As amended by HRA 2017, for applications for homelessness assistance made to local housing authorities in England on or after 3 April 2018.
[2] *Johnston v Westminster City Council* [2015] EWCA Civ 554, [2015] PTSR 1557, CA per Gloster LJ at [27]. In that case Westminster found that the applicant was not homeless, as he was owed the HA 1996, s 193(2) main housing duty by another local housing authority. The Court of Appeal held that this was wrong in law since no accommodation had actually been made available at the time of the decision.
[3] As amended by HRA 2017, for applications for homelessness assistance made to local housing authorities in England on or after 3 April 2018.
[4] HA 1996, s 175(2)(a); H(W)A 2014, s 55(2)(a); see **10.66–10.72**.
[5] *Begum v Tower Hamlets London Borough Council* (2000) 32 HLR 445, CA.
[6] *Begum v Tower Hamlets London Borough Council* (2000) 32 HLR 445, CA at 464 per Sedley LJ. It should be noted that the majority of the Court of Appeal in *Begum v Tower Hamlets London Borough Council* said that the issue of whether or not accommodation was reasonable for an applicant to occupy was not relevant where the applicant was not actually occupying the accommodation. That has now been held to be wrong by the Court of Appeal in *Maloba v Waltham Forest London Borough Council* [2007] EWCA Civ 1281, , [2008] 2 All ER 701, [2008] HLR 408, CA. See **10.74**.

10.19 So, if there is accommodation that the applicant has the right to occupy, but it is not in fact 'available', the applicant is homeless. Those granted refugee status in the UK because they cannot return to their countries of origin may have perfectly good homes in those countries but would be 'homeless' here because their accommodation is not 'available'. Likewise, the issue of whether accommodation is 'available' is raised where:

(1) a person leaves his or her home in search of work, travels to the other end of the country and expends all his or her resources looking for work, leaving him or her unable to return home;

(2) a person is the subject of a banning order under anti-terrorism legislation preventing him or her from returning to a country (or a part of this country) in which his or her home is situated; or

(3) a person is prohibited by a court order (such as an injunction or closure order) from entering the premises or geographic area in which his or her

home is situated[1].

[1] Some of these examples were cited in *Begum v Tower Hamlets London Borough Council* (2000) 32 HLR 445, CA at 464 per Sedley LJ.

10.20 In each of these cases, although the applicant would have accommodation which he or she is legally entitled to occupy, the accommodation would not be 'available' for his or her occupation.

The special statutory definition

10.21 If there is accommodation factually available to the applicant, the next question is whether the special statutory definition of 'available' is met[1]. Accommodation only counts as available if it is available for occupation not only by the applicant but also by those people who normally reside with the applicant as members of his or her family and also by any other person who might reasonably be expected to reside with the applicant[2].

[1] HA 1996, s 176; H(W)A 2014, s 56.
[2] HA 1996, s 176; H(W)A 2014, s 56.

10.22 In effect, this means that accommodation will only be considered available if it is available to occupy by both the applicant and all of the other members of his or her household. The purpose of the provision is clear: a person is to be considered homeless *unless* there is accommodation sufficient in its factual and legal capacity to accommodate the applicant's entire household. So the local housing authority first needs to establish the extent of the relevant household and then consider whether there is accommodation available for all those persons to occupy together[1].

[1] Where a household has to live in separate units of accommodation, the accommodation will be available for occupation by the applicant and all members of his or her household (as defined by HA 1996, s 176 and H(W)A 2014, s 56) if and only if the units are 'so located that they enable the family to live "together" in practical terms'. *Sharif v Camden London Borough Council* [2013] UKSC 10, [2013] HLR 16, SC per Lord Carnwath at [17]. In that case the family of three, who were accommodated in two separate units on the same floor of a hostel, were deemed to be accommodated 'together' for the purposes of HA 1996, s 176. See **18.10–18.11**.

Members of the applicant's household

10.23 Two different groups of people could fall within the applicant's household for these purposes:

(1) Group One – those who normally reside with the applicant as a member of the applicant's family[1].
(2) Group Two – any other persons who might reasonably be expected to reside with the applicant[2].

[1] HA 1996, s 176(a); H(W)A 2014, s 56(1)(a).
[2] HA 1996, s 176(b); H(W)A 2014, s 56(1)(b).

Group One: 'normally resides with him as a member of his family'

10.24 To fall within Group One a person must fulfil two conditions[1]:

- he or she must normally reside with the applicant; and
- must do so as a member of the applicant's family.

[1] HA 1996, s 176(a); H(W)A 2014, s 56(1)(a).

10.25 There is no additional condition that it must be 'reasonable' for that person to reside with the applicant[1]. The local housing authority may or may not think it reasonable for the applicant to be normally residing, as part of one family unit, with a host of relatives, in-laws, or even friends and others. But the local housing authority's opinion is irrelevant. The conditions raise simple factual questions for decision – who is living with the applicant and why – not issues of judgment.

[1] *Homelessness Code of Guidance for Local Authorities* (Ministry of Housing, Communities and Local Government, February 2018) (the English Code), para 6.7, at APPENDIX 2 of this book; *Code of Guidance for Local Authorities on the Allocation of Accommodation and Homelessness* (Welsh Government, March 2016) (the Welsh Code), para 8.7 on the CD Rom with this book. See further *R v Newham London Borough Council ex p Khan and Hussain* (2001) 33 HLR 269, QBD, where the local housing authority's decision that two adult sisters, who both occupied accommodation together along with their husbands and children, did not normally reside together was held to be irrational.

10.26 To fall within the first condition, it is necessary that the person concerned 'resides with' the applicant. Someone who is simply a regular visitor to the applicant's home will not fall within the definition[1]. A very short period of temporary residence with the applicant is also unlikely to suffice, because the person must 'normally' reside with the applicant. Finally, there is no requirement that the person who normally lives with the applicant is literally doing so at the time of the application for homelessness assistance. Children will still 'normally reside' with their mother even if she fled the family home in fear of domestic violence a few days earlier. An elderly person unable to return from hospital to his or her normal home will 'normally reside with' those with whom he or she was living before going into hospital.

[1] See further discussion of 'resides with' at **12.54–12.57**.

10.27 The second condition is that the person normally resides with the applicant 'as a member of his [or her] family'[1]. This term is not defined in HA 1996, Pt 7[2] or H(W)A 2014, Pt 2. Indeed, a definition of 'family' would not help, as the test is whether the person lived with the applicant 'as' a member of the applicant's family. The question is not whether the other person *is* a member of the applicant's family.

[1] HA 1996, s 176(a); H(W)A 2014, s 56(1)(a).
[2] As amended by HRA 2017, for applications for homelessness assistance made to local housing authorities in England on or after 3 April 2018.

10.28 Limited help is to be found in the Codes of Guidance, which advise that '[t]he phrase "as a member of his [or her] family" will include those with close blood or marital relationships and cohabiting partners (including same sex partners)'[1].

[1] English Code, para 6.7; Welsh Code, para 8.7.

Group Two: 'any other person who might reasonably be expected to reside with him'

10.29 The second group who may qualify for these purposes as members of the applicant's household (Group Two) contains three potential sub-groups. These comprise[1]:

(1) *any member of the applicant's family not normally residing with him or her, but who might reasonably be expected to reside with the applicant.* For example, a dependent child who has been living with his or her mother but who is, by arrangement between the separated parents, to begin living with his or her father (the applicant) will fall within this category[2]. As the Codes helpfully emphasise, the question of who the child is to reside with is nowadays more likely to be dealt with by parental agreement than by court order[3]. Another example might be a married couple, or civil partners, who have to live apart, with their respective parents, because they have nowhere they can live together[4]. It must be remembered that one purpose of HA 1996, Pt 7 and of H(W)A 2014, Pt 2 is 'bringing families together'[5].

(2) *someone already normally residing with the applicant (but not as a member of his or her family) who might reasonably be expected to continue to reside with the applicant.* This might be a lodger, nanny, carer, friend of the family or anyone else who has been living with the applicant but not 'as' a family member. Obviously the fact that the person is already actually residing with the applicant will be a powerful factor when the local housing authority decides whether it is reasonable for him or her to continue to live with the applicant.

(3) *someone who is not a member of the applicant's family and does not normally live with the applicant but who might reasonably be expected to reside with the applicant.* This sub-group will embrace those who wish to live with the applicant but do not currently do so. The classic example is the prospective carer[6] who wishes to live with and look after the applicant. But the classic example can sometimes cause a local housing authority to believe that the relevant question is whether the applicant needs a companion or carer. That is not the correct approach[7]. The question is simple: 'Is it reasonable to expect this person to reside with the applicant?'

[1] HA 1996, s 176(b); H(W)A 2014, s 56(1)(b).
[2] For further examples where the person is a dependent child, see **12.58–12.75**.
[3] English Code, para 6.9; Welsh Code, para 8.8. See *Holmes-Moorhouse v Richmond upon Thames Royal London Borough Council* [2009] UKHL 7, [2009] 1 WLR 413, HL for a discussion on 'reside with' in the context of the priority need test. See **12.54–12.57**.
[4] As was the case in *R v Westminster City Council ex p Chambers* [1982] 6 HLR 24, QBD.
[5] *Din v Wandsworth London Borough Council* [1983] 1 AC 657, HL at 663 per Lord Wilberforce.
[6] *R v Kensington and Chelsea Royal London Borough Council ex p Kassam* (1994) 26 HLR 455, QBD; and *R v Hackney London Borough Council ex p Tonnicodi* (1998) 30 HLR 916, QBD.

[7]   *R v Hackney London Borough Council ex p Tonnicodi* (1998) 30 HLR 916, QBD.

10.30 The Codes give two further examples of those who will fall within the second group of household members (Group Two):

- foster children[1]; and
- companions for elderly or disabled applicants.

The Codes advise that those people might reasonably be expected to reside with an applicant[2].

[1]   Although the correct approach in the authors' view should be that current foster children would fall within Group One, and prospective foster children within Group Two.
[2]   English Code, para 6.8; Welsh Code para 8.7.

APPLICATION OF THE SPECIAL STATUTORY DEFINITION

10.31 Once the local housing authority has identified the total number of people forming the applicant's household (ie the composite of Groups One and Two), it can return to the central task of determining whether the applicant is 'homeless'. The relevant question posed by HA 1996, Pt 7[1] and by H(W)A 2014, Pt 2 is then whether the accommodation under consideration is available not just for occupation by the applicant but also for occupation by all the members of the applicant's household[2].

[1]   As amended by HRA 2017, for applications for homelessness assistance made to local housing authorities in England on or after 3 April 2018.
[2]   HA 1996, s 176; H(W)A 2014, s 56.

10.32 This is essentially a factual issue about practical and legal availability. If the only accommodation available to a male applicant is a shared room with four other men in a men-only hostel, he will be homeless if his household now includes a female (for example, a woman he has just married or a wife with whom he has been reunited)[1] and he does not have other accommodation into which he can move. Likewise, if a husband and wife have a home together, but the husband is prevented from returning to it by some legal restriction (such as a court order obtained by a third party) the wife will be 'homeless' on her application to the local housing authority, because her home is no longer available to a member of her family with whom she normally resides.

[1]   As was the case in *R v Hillingdon London Borough Council ex p Islam* [1983] 1 AC 688, HL.

The meaning of 'entitled to occupy'

10.33 Assuming that the local housing authority is satisfied that there is accommodation[1] available to the applicant and his or her household[2], the next question is whether the applicant has some sort of right or legal entitlement to occupy the accommodation[3].

[1]   See **10.8–10.16**.
[2]   See **10.17–10.32**.
[3]   HA 1996, s 175(1); H(W)A 2014, s 55(1).

10.34 An applicant will have a relevant entitlement to occupy accommodation only if he or she has the right to occupy it by reason of one of the following:

- a legal interest in it[1]; or
- the benefit of an order of a court that he or she is entitled to occupy it[2]; or
- an express or implied licence to occupy it[3]; or
- some legal protection preventing the applicant from being evicted from it[4].

1. HA 1996, s 175(1)(a), H(W)A 2014, s 55(1)(a).
2. HA 1996, s 175(1)(a); H(W)A 2014, s 55(1)(a).
3. HA 1996, s 175(1)(b); H(W)A 2014, s 55(1)(b).
4. HA 1996, s 175(1)(c); H(W)A 2014, s 55(1)(c).

10.35 If an applicant rids himself or herself of the right to occupy his or her only available accommodation (eg by selling owned property or by assigning or ending a lease or tenancy), then he or she will be homeless but is likely to be found to have become homeless intentionally[1].

1. *R v Wandsworth London Borough Council ex p Oteng* (1994) 26 HLR 413, CA. See CHAPTER 13.

10.36 Each of the relevant forms of right to occupy requires close consideration.

' . . . an interest in it'

10.37 This first alternative is satisfied if the applicant has a legal interest in the accommodation[1]. That might be freehold or leasehold ownership or a tenancy. Unless the applicant enjoys some other right to occupy the accommodation, he or she will become homeless when the legal interest is brought to an end. For example, a joint tenant's legal interest will end on the expiry of a notice to quit given by the other joint tenant[2].

1. HA 1996, s 175(1)(a); H(W)A 2014, s 55(1)(a).
2. *Fletcher v Brent London Borough Council* [2006] EWCA Civ 960, [2007] HLR 12, CA.

10.38 However, a legal interest only counts for these purposes if, by virtue of it, the applicant is entitled to occupy the accommodation. It is not sufficient for the local housing authority to establish that the applicant owns the accommodation. He or she may have let or sub-let it to others who are, as a result, the people entitled to occupy it, whereas the applicant is not. The local housing authority could not, in those circumstances, avoid finding that the applicant is homeless by advising him or her to repossess the property let out to tenants. The applicant is 'homeless' now[1].

1. Such a scenario occurred in *R (Miah) v Tower Hamlets London Borough Council* (2013) May *Legal Action*, p 36, Clerkenwell and Shoreditch County Court, where the applicant was the owner of a house let to a tenant. On her application for homelessness assistance, the local housing authority initially decided that she was not homeless because she owned the house. An appeal to the County Court against that decision was allowed on the basis that the house was not 'available' to her.

' . . . an order of a court'

10.39 A person may be entitled to occupy accommodation under an order of a court[1], if, for example, he or she has the protection of a court order granting him or her the right to occupy in family proceedings, or (more unusually) a court has made a declaration that the person has a beneficial interest in the land carrying a right to immediate occupation[2].

[1] HA 1996, s 175(1)(a); H(W)A 2014, s 55(1)(a).
[2] Family Law Act 1996, ss 30–40; Trusts of Land and Appointment of Trustees Act 1996, ss 12 and 14.

' . . . express or implied licence to occupy'

10.40 A licence[1] is simply permission to occupy. The person giving the permission is a licensor; the person given the permission is the licensee. An express licence arises when permission to occupy is explicitly given verbally or in writing. An implied licence exists when permission to occupy has never been expressly granted but can simply be inferred or assumed (for example, very few parents expressly say to their young children 'you can live with me' – such permission is to be inferred).

[1] HA 1996, s 175(1)(b); H(W)A 2014, s 55(1)(b).

10.41 Sometimes, the permission will have been granted in return for the payment of money or provision of services. More often, the licence will be a bare licence, the simple grant of permission to occupy without any money or services paid in return. Examples of licensees given in the Codes are lodgers, employees who have service occupancies (ie accommodation that they occupy in order to do their jobs), those living with relatives and those staying in hospital[1]. Precisely because 'licence' simply means 'permission' it can be applied to accommodation anywhere in the world without the need to refer to the property laws of the relevant country.

[1] English Code, paras 6.10(b) and 6.11; Welsh Code para 8.9(ii).

10.42 The task for the local housing authority is to identify whether the applicant 'has' (present tense) an express or implied licence to occupy the relevant accommodation[1]. This means that a licence that an applicant did have in the past, or could get in the future, is quite irrelevant to the question of whether he or she is homeless now. Even if the local housing authority can identify accommodation that the applicant has recently occupied under a licence (which has ended), and where a further licence is being offered, the applicant will still be 'homeless'. So, where a former live-in housekeeper, having lost her employment and the licence to occupy accommodation, had been offered re-employment and a further licence, she was still homeless at the date of her application[2]. Likewise, an applicant who has a licence to occupy a night shelter for one night only is homeless during the day, even if he or she could secure another licence for another night in the same shelter[3].

[1] HA 1996, s 175(1)(b); H(W)A 2014 s 55(1)(b).
[2] *R v Kensington and Chelsea Royal London Borough Council ex p Minton* (1988) 20 HLR 648, QBD.

³   *R v Waveney District Council ex p Bowers* [1983] QB 238, CA. The decision that the applicant was homeless in these circumstances was made at first instance by Stephen Brown J (as he then was) and was not subject to appeal to the Court of Appeal. The first instance decision is at (1982) The Times, May 25.

10.43 If an applicant occupies accommodation under an express or an implied licence, she or he will normally be entitled to four weeks' written notice to end that licence[1]. If the statutory requirement of four weeks' notice does not apply[2], the notice period will be whatever is stated in any written licence agreement. If there is no such agreement, the licence can be ended by reasonable notice[3], which can be given verbally. In certain circumstances 'you've got 10 minutes to leave my house' could be sufficient reasonable notice to end a licence.

1   Protection from Eviction Act 1977, s 5.
2   There are a wide range of circumstances in which it will not, such as where the licensee shares accommodation with the licensor. See *R v Hammersmith & Fulham London Borough Council ex p O'Sullivan* [1991] EGCS 110, QBD and Protection from Eviction Act 1977, s 3A.
3   *Minister of Health v Bellotti* [1944] KB 298, [1944] 1 All ER 238, CA; *Gibson v Douglas* [2016] EWCA Civ 1266; [2017] HLR 11.

10.44 Once the licence has ended (ie any fixed term, or notice period, has expired), the former licensee will be a trespasser in the accommodation. Some ex-licensees will be protected by the Protection from Eviction Act 1977 from eviction without a court order and may therefore not be immediately homeless (because there is a restriction on the former licensor recovering possession)[1].

1   See **10.56–10.65** and **10.110–11.116**.

10.45 For those licensees who are *not* protected by the Protection from Eviction Act 1977[1], homelessness will arise immediately the licence ends, even if they do not actually move out. In such cases, the Codes correctly advise local housing authorities that if the licence has been determined, but the occupier remains in occupation as a trespasser, the occupier will be homeless[2]. The Codes give, as examples, the termination of licences to those who have been living with friends or relatives, in hostels or hospitals, or former employees occupying premises under a service occupancy whose contracts of employment have ended[3]. Each of those examples may fall outside the protection of the Protection from Eviction Act 1977[4].

1   Protection from Eviction Act 1977, s 3A defines licences and tenancies which are excluded from protection.
2   English Code, para 6.11; Welsh Code, paras 8.10 and 8.14. See also *R v Surrey Heath Borough Council ex p Li* (1984) 16 HLR 79, QBD, where the local housing authority's advice to a former licensee asked to leave service accommodation – that he could remain in occupation until a possession order was obtained – was held to be wrong, and a decision that the applicant was not homeless was quashed.
3   English Code, paras 6.11–6.12; Welsh Code, para 8.10.
4   Protection from Eviction Act 1977, ss 3–3A. Note, that some forms of accommodation that are not listed expressly in PEA 1977, s 3A may still fall outside of the protection of that Act, where the accommodation is not classed as a 'dwelling' within the meaning of PEA 1977, s 3. See *R (N) v Lewisham London Borough Council* [2014] UKSC 62, [2015] HLR 6, SC. Further, the position in relation to service occupiers can be complex and dependent on the terms of the contract of employment. See *Hertfordshire County Council v Davies* [2017] 1 WLR 4395, [2017] HLR 33, QBD.

10.46 The Court of Appeal has held that, where a secure tenant leaves his or her accommodation, and the landlord subsequently terminates the tenancy by service of a notice to quit, but has refrained from taking possession proceedings, the former tenant becomes a licensee during the 'period of grace' before proceedings are brought[1]. This is a difficult decision to construe. If the tenant was occupying the accommodation as his or her only or principal home at the date of expiry of the notice to quit, then the notice would not have determined the tenancy and the tenant would have continued to enjoy security of tenure[2]. If, on the other hand, the tenant had not been occupying his or her accommodation at that date[3], then he or she was not a residential occupier and was not entitled to the protection offered by the Protection from Eviction Act 1977. In effect, this former tenant was being offered a chance to return to the accommodation, even though the previous tenancy had been terminated. It is hard to see how that chance can be construed as a licence.

1   *Porteous v West Dorset District Council* [2004] EWCA Civ 244, [2004] HLR 30, CA.
2   Housing Act 1985, ss 81–82 for secure tenancies; Housing Act 1988, ss 1 and 5 for assured tenancies.
3   As was the case in *Porteous v West Dorset District Council* [2004] EWCA Civ 244, [2004] HLR 30, CA.

10.47 Various Local Government Ombudsman investigations have found maladministration where applicants who did not enjoy protection under the Protection from Eviction Act 1977 were wrongly told that they were not homeless until possession orders were obtained against them[1].

1   See for example *Complaint against Ealing London Borough Council*, 90/A/1038, where the local housing authority was invited to repay to the complainants the legal costs that they had been ordered to pay to their resident landlord by the court in the possession proceedings, having been wrongly told by the local housing authority that they should await a court order.

10.48 One of the most common causes of homelessness is the termination of a licence to occupy the home of a friend or relative with whom the applicant has been staying. Many such applicants apply to local housing authorities reporting simply that they have been 'asked to leave'. Quite properly, the Codes recommend that where someone reports being asked to leave accommodation by family or friends the local housing authority 'will need to consider carefully whether the applicant's licence to occupy has in fact been revoked' (so that the applicant is 'homeless') or whether, instead, the request to leave is merely a warning of an intention to terminate the licence at some future date (in which case the applicant may not be homeless, although he or she may be threatened with homelessness)[1].

1   English Code, para 6.12; Welsh Code, para 8.11.

10.49 Beyond that, the Codes offer a confusing mix of advice on best practice in such cases. Local housing authorities are warned that there may be genuine difficulties between the guest and host that could be resolved with help. The Codes go on to suggest that local housing authorities should consider providing support, arranging family mediation services, or assisting the applicant to find alternative accommodation. Local housing authorities are reminded that they should be sensitive to the possibility that applicants may be at risk of violence or abuse if they return home[1]. The English Code also warns that there may be collusion in order to assist the applicant to obtain housing from the local housing authority[2]. But all this guidance leaves unasked and unanswered the important central question: whether the permission to occupy (ie the licence) has been ended or not ended[3].

[1]   English Code, para 6.13; Welsh Code, para 8.12.
[2]   English Code, para 6.16.
[3]   In *Abdullah v Westminster City Council* [2011] EWCA Civ 1171, [2012] HLR 5, CA, the local housing authority was not wrong in law to find that an applicant still had an implied licence to occupy where the joint tenants of the property (her mother and her husband) had asked her to leave but not taken any steps to enforce that request, and the applicant would have had matrimonial home rights to enforce her right to occupy the property. See also *Complaint against Newham London Borough Council*, 11 000 388, 8 March 2012 (2012) May *Legal Action*, p 34. See **10.124**.

10.50 All too often the resolution of that simple question is deferred (quite improperly) by requiring the friend or relative, who has already told the applicant to leave, to confirm it in writing or by suggesting that a home visit at some later date will be necessary. As indicated above, save in those cases covered by the Protection from Eviction Act 1977, there is no need for notice terminating a licence to be given in writing[1]. If the licence has been terminated, the applicant has no home to visit. Worse still, applicants are sometimes told that the local housing authority will not even entertain applications for homelessness assistance without the applicants themselves producing a letter from their former hosts requiring them to leave. This practice is, of course, an unlawful attempt to reverse the burden imposed on the local housing authority to undertake the inquiries itself[2], and the Welsh Code specifically precludes such practices[3].

[1]   See **10.45**.
[2]   See **10.22**–**10.26**. *R v Woodspring District Council ex p Walters* (1984) 16 HLR 73, QBD is one example, albeit not concerning applicants living with friends or relatives.
[3]   Welsh Code, para 8.11.

10.51 Sadly, it is often young people asked to leave their parental home (frequently in sudden and traumatic circumstances), who find it most difficult to achieve prompt decisions as to whether they are 'homeless' because their licence has been determined. A young person who has been told by his or her parent 'Get out now and never set your foot in this house again' is plainly 'homeless'.

10.52 The English Code contains specific guidance on dealing with 16- and 17-year-olds in this situation[1]. The Secretary of State's view is that local housing authorities should cooperate with children's services, with the latter being the 'lead agency', in order to 'prevent homelessness and support young people to remain within the family network, wherever it is safe and appropriate to do so.' Family mediation, external support or the offer of assistance in securing alternative accommodation are suggested as means by which homelessness may be prevented[2]. Though, such general guidance can blur the real question: whether the licence to occupy has been ended or not. If it has, the young person is 'homeless'[3].

[1]   English Code, para 6.15.
[2]   English Code, para 6.14.

3   In which case, the guidance given in the English Code may be relevant to the steps taken by the local housing authority to help to secure that accommodation becomes available for the young person. See **15.138–15.189**.

10.53 Similar recommendations in the previous version of the statutory guidance were considered by the House of Lords in *R (M) v Hammersmith & Fulham London Borough Council*[1]. Giving the leading judgment, Baroness Hale noted the risk of collusion but added that 'any mediation or reconciliation will need careful brokering and housing authorities may wish to seek the assistance of social services in all such cases'[2].

1   [2008] UKHL 14, [2008] 1 WLR 535, HL.
2   *R (M) v Hammersmith & Fulham London Borough Council* [2008] UKHL 14, [2008] 1 WLR 535, HL at [26] and [27], quoting the previous version of the English Code, paras 12.9 and 12.11. See also *R (G) v Southwark London Borough Council* [2009] UKHL 26, [2009] 1 WLR 2399, HL. As a result of these two House of Lords' decisions, the Secretaries of State in England and the Welsh Assembly Government issued guidance to housing and children's services departments: *Provision of Accommodation for 16 and 17 year old young people who may be homeless and/or require Accommodation* (April 2010, CLG and DCSF) and *Provision of Accommodation for 16 and 17 year old young people who may be homeless* (September 2010, Welsh Assembly Government). The former guidance has since been replaced with *Prevention of homelessness and provision of accommodation for 16 and 17 year old young people who may be homeless and/or require accommodation* (April 2018, MHCLG and DfE). The guidance is on the CD Rom with this book. See also **12.133–12.159** (England) and **12.212–12.213** (Wales).

10.54 The Court of Appeal has considered the position of a 17-year-old, approaching her eighteenth birthday, who made an application for homelessness assistance having been asked to leave the family home by her mother[1]. The local housing authority delayed making its decision until the day before her eighteenth birthday and then, unlawfully, decided that she did not have a priority need[2]. The Court of Appeal acknowledged that 'an authority is entitled to have time to check the genuineness of the decision to exclude the child, and indeed the reasons given by the child for being excluded, for example where there may have been collusion'[3]. However, 'it cannot be right that an authority can persuade a family into mediation while a child is 17 and then use the time that the mediation would take to deprive the child of a right that it would have had without mediation'[4]. If the child genuinely has had his or her licence withdrawn, he or she will be homeless.

1   *Robinson v Hammersmith & Fulham London Borough Council* [2006] EWCA Civ 1122, [2007] HLR 7, CA.
2   See **12.133–12.159** (England) and **12.212–12.213** (Wales).
3   *Robinson v Hammersmith & Fulham London Borough Council* [2006] EWCA Civ 1122, [2007] HLR 7, CA at [39] per Waller LJ.
4   *Robinson v Hammersmith & Fulham London Borough Council* [2006] EWCA Civ 1122, [2007] HLR 7, CA at [41] per Waller LJ.

10.55 In such circumstances the better approach may be for the local housing authority to accept that the applicant is homeless and then perform HA 1996, s 189B(2)[1] or H(W)A 2014, s 73, relief duty to help the applicant to secure that suitable accommodation becomes available for his or her occupation, by achieving a 'reconciliation' under which the applicant can in future live either with his or her parents or with members of the wider family[2].

[1] As inserted by HRA 2017, s 5(2), for applications for homelessness assistance made to local housing authorities in England on or after 3 April 2018. See **15.138–15.189** and English Code, para 11.23.
[2] *Robinson v Hammersmith & Fulham London Borough Council* [2006] EWCA Civ 1122, [2007] HLR 7, CA per Waller LJ at [41]. See further **13.138–13.143** and English Code, para 11.23.

' . . . *enactment or rule of law*'

10.56 Even if an applicant does not have any legal interest in, or licence to occupy, his or her accommodation, she or he may nevertheless be entitled to live there under an 'enactment' or 'rule of law' permitting his or her occupation or preventing another person from obtaining possession[1]. Such occupation is treated for the purposes of HA 1996, Pt 7[2] and H(W)A 2014, Pt 2 as though it was under a right to occupy and may prevent the applicant from being homeless.

[1] HA 1996, s 175(1)(c); H(W)A 2014, s 55(1)(c).
[2] As amended by HRA 2017, for applications for homelessness assistance made to local housing authorities in England on or after 3 April 2018.

10.57 An 'enactment' in this context would normally mean an Act of Parliament. But in HA 1996, Pt 7[1] and H(W)A 2014, Pt 2 it is defined to include 'an enactment comprised in subordinate legislation (within the meaning of the Interpretation Act 1978)'[2]. This wide definition brings in orders, rules, regulations, by-laws, schemes, warrants and other instruments made under any Act of Parliament[3]. So, if any of those give a right to occupy, or inhibit someone else from recovering possession, the applicant may not be homeless.

[1] As amended by HRA 2017, for applications for homelessness assistance made to local housing authorities in England on or after 3 April 2018.
[2] HA 1996, s 230; H(W)A 2014, s 99.
[3] Interpretation Act 1978, s 21.

10.58 A 'rule of law' is not defined in HA 1996, Pt 7[1] or in H(W)A 2014, Pt 2. In contrast to 'enactment', it probably means a judge-made rule of common law, eg the rule that a licence to occupy may not normally be ended without giving reasonable notice.

[1] As amended by HRA 2017, for applications for homelessness assistance made to local housing authorities in England on or after 3 April 2018.

10.59 Some Acts of Parliament expressly provide that individuals who are otherwise without rights may remain in possession. The classic example is the Rent Act 1977. Statutory tenants, whose contractual tenancies have ended, enjoy a personal right under the Rent Act 1977 not to be evicted without a court order, and thus fall within this category[1]. The Codes specifically refer to Rent Act statutory tenants because their personal right to remain is created by statute[2]. A statutory tenant remains under the protection of the Rent Act 1977 and the Protection from Eviction Act 1977 not just until a possession order has been obtained against him or her, but until the point of actual eviction by court bailiffs[3].

1   Rent Act 1977, s 2.
2   English Code, para 6.10(c); Welsh Code, para 8.9(iii).
3   *Haniff v Robinson* [1993] QB 419, CA.

10.60 Other Acts of Parliament provide that tenancies cannot be ended without landlords obtaining possession orders. This is the case for introductory, demoted, secure and assured (including assured shorthold) tenants[1]. Even where former tenants remain in occupation as trespassers, they are not 'homeless', because a different form of enactment, the procedural rules of court, restricts them from being ousted other than by a bailiff's warrant. They do not lose the benefit of that enactment until the bailiffs actually turn them out[2].

1   Housing Act 1985, Part 4 governs secure tenants; Housing Act 1988, Part 1 governs assured tenants.
2   There are complex provisions, which are beyond the scope of this text, governing when tenancies end on or after the making of a possession order. All assured tenants remain tenants until any possession order is executed against them (*Knowsley Housing Trust v White* [2008] UKHL 70, [2009] HLR 17, HL). Since 20 May 2009, secure tenants have been in the same position (Housing Act 1985, s 82 as amended by Housing and Regeneration Act 2008, s 299 and Sch 11). There were certain 'tolerated trespassers' who had originally been secure tenants until they were subject to outright or suspended possession orders made before 20 May 2009. Most of them became holders of 'replacement tenancies' on 20 May 2009 (Housing and Regeneration Act 2008, Sch 11, Part 2).

10.61 Anyone who is occupying premises where a possession order has been obtained but has not yet been executed will remain entitled to occupy those premises under an enactment or rule of law, until actually evicted by the bailiffs[1].

1   *R (Sacupima) v Newham London Borough Council* (2001) 33 HLR 2, CA. However this does not necessarily mean that the individual is not homeless, or that the local housing authority from which he or she has sought homelessness assistance do not owe him or her a duty. If the possession order is to be executed within 56 days, the applicant will be threatened with homelessness. See **10.144–10.147**. Alternatively, the applicant might be homeless because it is not reasonable for him or her, and his or her household, to continue to occupy the accommodation until the date of the eviction, see **10.110–11.116**. On 9 December 2015 the Court of Appeal granted permission to appeal in the case of *Michalczyk v London Borough of Southwark* [2015] EWCA Civ 1501, to explore whether there was any inconsistency between the approach in *Sacupima* whereby an applicant is still deemed to have an entitlement to occupy his or her accommodation under an 'enactment or rule of law' until the possession order is executed and the approach discussed at **10.111** and **10.113** whereby a local housing authority may, nevertheless, decide that the applicant is homeless as the accommodation is not reasonable for him or her to continue to occupy. At the time of writing the appeal has not yet taken place.

10.62 It is not possible to set out in this text details of all the primary and secondary legislation giving rights to remain in occupation of accommodation or restricting the rights of others to recover possession. Spouses, civil partners[1], and cohabitants may have rights to remain in their homes under the Family Law Act 1996[2].

1   The Civil Partnership Act 2004 introduced registration of civil partnerships for same-sex couples, in force from 5 December 2005. The Marriage (Same Sex Couples) Act 2013 legalised same-sex marriage from 13 March 2014.
2   Those matrimonial home rights need not have been exercised in order to give a person a right to remain. Where a woman was asked to leave by her mother and her husband, who were the

joint tenants of the property, she was not homeless because she could bring a claim under Family Law Act 1996, s 30, to enforce her right of occupation in the property: *Abdullah v Westminster City Council* [2011] EWCA Civ 1171, [2012] HLR 5, CA. If she had obtained an order, she would be not homeless by virtue of HA 1996, s 175(2)(a), see **10.39**. See also **10.49** fn 3 for the additional factual background to *Abdullah v Westminster City Council* [2011] EWCA Civ 1171, [2012] HLR 5, CA.

10.63 It must not be assumed that all residential occupiers have the benefit of enactments or rules of law enabling them to remain in occupation or restricting others from recovering possession. True trespassers – squatters who have entered property without authority – have no such rights and are 'homeless' throughout.

10.64 Even in relation to former tenants and licensees, the Protection from Eviction Act 1977 is not comprehensive. There are very many occupiers who are excepted from its protection and will become 'homeless' as soon as their tenancies or licences end. That is precisely because there is no legal right to remain, nor any restriction on their eviction. A list of those excluded from the Protection from Eviction Act 1977 is found at s 3A of that Act[1]. It includes those living with resident landlords, occupying holiday lets or subject to licences granted not for money or money's worth[2].

[1] Note, that some forms of accommodation that are not listed expressly in PEA 1977, s 3A may still fall outside of the protection of that Act, where the accommodation is not classed as a 'dwelling' within the meaning of PEA 1977, s 3. See *R (N) v Lewisham London Borough Council* [2014] UKSC 62, [2015] HLR 6, SC.
[2] Protection from Eviction Act 1977, s 3A.

10.65 There are many people – owners, tenants, former tenants and former licensees – who have no defence to an inevitable possession order, but who do have the benefit of the protection of an enactment or rule of law preventing their eviction. They will not automatically be 'homeless' (in that they have accommodation that they are entitled to occupy)[1] unless they are re-applying for homelessness assistance to a local housing authority in England within two years of acceptance of a private rented sector offer[2] and have been served with a valid Housing Act 1988, s 21 notice[3]. However, if the mortgage lender, landlord, former landlord or former licensor is taking steps to obtain a possession order, it may not be reasonable for them to continue in occupation and they may nevertheless be 'homeless'[4].

[1] Protection from Eviction Act 1977, s 3; HA 1996, s 175(1)(c); H(W)A 2014, s 55(1)(c).
[2] A 'private rented sector offer' is defined at HA 1996, s 193(7AC). See **16.153–16.179**.
[3] In which case the applicant is deemed to be homeless from the date on which the notice expires: HA 1996, s 195A(2).
[4] English Code, paras 6.18–6.19 and 6.29–6.38; Welsh Code, paras 8.14 and 8.31. See **10.110–11.116**.

Can the applicant secure entry to the accommodation?

10.66 Even if there is 'accommodation'[1] which is 'available'[2] and which the applicant is 'entitled to occupy'[3], he or she will still be homeless if he or she is physically barred from entering the property[4]. The examples given in the Codes are where an occupier has been illegally evicted, or comes home to find his or her accommodation occupied by squatters[5]. But those examples are far from exhaustive. The property may be cut off temporarily by floodwaters or sealed behind a police barrier. An emergency may have rendered it temporarily impossible to enter the property. Whatever the cause, if the applicant physically cannot enter (and has no other accommodation meeting the legal definition) he or she is 'homeless'.

1   See **10.8–10.16**.
2   See **10.17–10.32**.
3   See **10.33–10.65**.
4   HA 1996, s 175(2)(a); H(W)A 2014, s 55(2)(a).
5   English Code, para 6.20; Welsh Code, para 8.16. See also *Nipa Begum v Tower Hamlets London Borough Council* (2000) 32 HLR 445, CA.

10.67 Even though practical or legal remedies to gain entry at some later stage will usually be available to the applicant, he or she remains homeless until entry can be secured. Local housing authorities cannot, therefore, decide that the applicant is not homeless because he or she has not yet exhausted all legal and practical remedies to secure entry (although they can, of course, give advice on the remedies available). To put it in the language of the English Code, ' . . . an authority cannot refuse to assist an applicant who is homeless and eligible for assistance under Pt 7 simply because such remedies are available'[1].

1   English Code, para 6.21. See also Welsh Code, para 8.17 which stipulates that the local housing authority 'must treat the applicant as homeless until re-entry is secured'.

The special rule for mobile homes

10.68 A local housing authority may find that an applicant has 'accommodation' in the form of a moveable structure (eg a mobile home or towing caravan), or in the form of a vehicle or vessel designed for, or adapted for, human habitation. The latter category includes not only purpose built caravanettes and houseboats but also adapted or converted buses, lorries, vans and boats.

10.69 An applicant who has a right to occupy such accommodation, which is available to him or her, will be homeless unless he or she has a place where he or she is permitted or entitled both to place it and to reside in it. Simply having a place to put or park the mobile home is not enough. The applicant must also be entitled to live in it at that location.

10.70 Typically, a mobile home occupier has a licence to station and live in his or her home on a particular plot or to tie up and live in his or her boat at a particular mooring. The Codes advise that, where an applicant has an itinerant lifestyle, the site or mooring need not be permanent in order to avoid homelessness[1]. But it is quite common for those with mobile homes to have no permission to stay anywhere. Such travellers would obviously be 'homeless', however comfortable their mobile accommodation.

1   English Code, para 6.22; Welsh Code, para 8.18.

10.71 A person who has a licence to bring his or her mobile home onto a particular piece of land to live in it has an entitlement or permission to 'place it and to reside in it' and would therefore not be homeless[1]. So, a houseboat owner with permission to use and live in the houseboat on a particular waterway is not homeless[2]. If the licence then expires, but no proceedings are brought and he or she continues to occupy the land (or water), he or she may or may not be homeless, depending upon whether it can be inferred from the landowners' inaction that the permission is continuing[3]. If an occupier is required to leave a site, but has another site to go to, he or she will not be homeless[4]. If, on the other hand, an occupier is required to leave and has no alternative provision in place, he or she will be homeless[5]. An occupier who is camping unlawfully, and never had the right or permission to occupy the land, is homeless throughout[6].

[1]   HA 1996, s 175(2)(b); H(W)A 2014, s 55(2)(b).
[2]   *R v Hillingdon London Borough Council ex p Bax* (1992) December *Legal Action*, p 21, QBD.
[3]   *R (O'Donoghue) v Brighton and Hove City Council* [2003] EWHC (Admin) 129, (2003) April *Legal Action*, p 27, Admin Ct and [2003] EWCA Civ 459, (2003) May *Legal Action*, p 35, CA.
[4]   *R v Chiltern District Council ex p Roberts* (1991) 23 HLR 387, QBD.
[5]   As would have been the case in *Jones v Canal and River Trust* [2017] EWCA Civ 135, [2017] HLR 24, CA; a possession claim where the relief sought by the Canal and River Trust would have required Mr Jones to remove his boat from the Kennet and Avon canal and refrain from using it on any of the extensive network of waterways which are controlled by the Trust.
[6]   *Higgs v Brighton and Hove City Council* [2003] EWCA Civ 895, [2004] HLR 2, CA. This was the factual situation in *R (Plant) v Somerset County Council and Taunton Deane Borough Council* [2016] EWHC 1245 (Admin), [2016] HLR 24, CA, where Mr Plant, without permission, moved his motor home and workshop on to land owned by Somerset Council. Taunton Deane Borough Council later accepted the main housing duty at HA 1996, s 193(2) toward him.

10.72 Local Government Ombudsman investigations have found maladministration where caravan-dwellers were subject to imminent eviction proceedings but the local housing authorities refused to accept them as homeless[1].

[1]   For example, *Complaint against Boston Borough Council*, 518/L/85 and *Complaint against East Lindsey District Council*, 88/B/1216.

Is the accommodation reasonable for the applicant to continue to occupy?

10.73 If the applicant has 'accommodation'[1] which is 'available'[2], which he or she is 'entitled to occupy'[3], and to which entry can be secured[4], that would, before 1986, have been sufficient to demonstrate that he or she was not homeless. But that approach could and did produce absurd results. It paid no attention to the quality, condition or appropriateness of the accommodation for the applicant and his or her family. The narrowness of the definition was amply demonstrated by the finding in the *Puhlhofer*[5] case that a family of four occupying a small squalid single room in a guest house was not homeless. As a direct response to that decision, in 1986, Parliament enlarged the definition of 'homeless' so that, as well as fulfilling all other parts of the statutory definition, the accommodation in question also has to be 'reasonable' for the applicant to continue to occupy[6].

[1]   See 10.8–10.16.
[2]   See 10.17–10.32.
[3]   See 10.33–10.65.
[4]   See 10.66–10.72.
[5]   *R v Hillingdon London Borough Council ex p Puhlhofer* [1986] AC 484, HL.

6   HA 1996, s 175(3); H(W)A 2014, s 55(3).

10.74 The words 'continue to occupy' refer to Parliament's intention to deal specifically with accommodation that an applicant already 'has', and is therefore occupying, rather than accommodation that the applicant has left[1]. The Court of Appeal has held that the words 'continue to occupy' mean that the question of reasonableness of occupation is relevant to any accommodation that is 'available' to the applicant, whether or not she or he is actually occupying it[2].

1   *R v Brent London Borough Council ex p Awua* [1996] 1 AC 55, HL at 67 per Lord Hoffmann.
2   *Waltham Forest London Borough Council v Maloba* [2007] EWCA Civ 1271, [2008] HLR 26, CA, which considered the dicta in *Begum v Tower Hamlets London Borough Council* (2000) 32 HLR 445, CA and held that *Begum* was wrongly decided on this point.

10.75 The words 'continue to occupy' look to occupation over time and suggest an element of looking to the future. This means that accommodation could be considered not to be reasonable to continue to occupy, even though the occupiers could get by in it for a little while longer[1].

1   *Ali & others v Birmingham City Council, Moran v Manchester City Council* [2009] UKHL 36, [2009] 1 WLR 1506, HL per Baroness Hale at [36]–[39].

10.76 The words ' . . . shall not be treated as having accommodation unless it is accommodation which would be reasonable for him to continue to occupy' used in HA 1996, s 175(3) and H(W)A 2014, s 55(3), might suggest that a local housing authority had to probe, with the applicant, every conceivable aspect of the existing property to establish whether or not it was reasonable to occupy. That would be unworkable. A local housing authority must always consider whether or not the accommodation is affordable for the applicant[1]. A local housing authority must also make inquiries into any other material before it that might lead it to conclude that the accommodation would not be reasonable to continue to occupy.

1   Homelessness (Suitability of Accommodation) Order 1996, SI 1996/3204; H(W)A 2014, s 57(3)(b). See **10.107–10.109** and Appendix 2 and Appendix 3 respectively.

10.77 Once a finding has been made that accommodation is not reasonable for an applicant to continue to occupy, the applicant is homeless and, providing he or she is also eligible for assistance[1], the HA 1996, s 189B(2)[2] or H(W)A 2014, s 73, relief duty will be owed[3]. The local housing authority cannot impose any additional conditions, such as requiring the applicant to terminate his or her tenancy, before performing the relevant duty[4].

1   HA 1996, s 185; H(W)A 2014, s 61. See Chapter 11.
2   As inserted by HRA 2017, s 5(2), for applications for homelessness assistance made to local housing authorities in England on or after 3 April 2018.
3   See **15.138–15.189** and **17.73–17.117**.
4   *R (Hammia) v Wandsworth London Borough Council* [2005] EWHC 1127 (Admin), [2005] HLR 45, Admin Ct. See **9.140–9.143**.

10.78 There are two distinct circumstances in which accommodation will not be reasonable for the applicant to continue to occupy:

(1)   where the circumstances are such that HA 1996, Pt 7[1] or H(W)A 2014, Pt 2 *deems* the accommodation to be unreasonable to continue to occupy[2]; or

(2)   where the circumstances are such that, *as a matter of fact*, the accommodation is not reasonable to continue to occupy[3].

[1]   As amended by HRA 2017, for applications for homelessness assistance made to local housing authorities in England on or after 3 April 2018.
[2]   See **10.79–10.98.**
[3]   See **10.99–10.133.**

Deemed unreasonableness

10.79 If it is 'probable' that continued occupation of the accommodation will lead to 'domestic violence or other violence' (for applicants in England) or 'abuse' (for applicants in Wales) against the applicant or against a member of the applicant's household[1], the accommodation is deemed not to be reasonable for the applicant to continue to occupy and the applicant is homeless[2]. The local housing authority's inquiries are simply confined to finding the facts necessary to answer the question of whether such violence or abuse is probable. Note that there are certain differences between the deeming provisions in England[3] and Wales[4].

[1]   HA 1996, s 177(1)(a) and (b); H(W)A 2014, s 57(1) and (2). For this purpose household membership is defined at H(W)A 2014, s 57(2). See **10.21–10.32.**
[2]   HA 1996, s 177(1); H(W)A 2014, s 57(1). According to St Mungo's Broadway, a charity that assists homeless persons, over half of its female clients have experienced domestic violence, *Rough Justice: uncovering social policies that create homelessness* (Commonweal housing, 2014).
[3]   See **10.81–10.91.**
[4]   See **10.92–10.98.**

10.80 Situations of violence and abuse are currently the only circumstances in which accommodation is deemed to be unreasonable to continue to occupy. There is provision within HA 1996, Pt 7[1] and in H(W)A 2014, Pt 2 for the Secretary of State and the Welsh Ministers, respectively, to specify by order other circumstances in which accommodation should be regarded, as a matter of law, as reasonable or not reasonable for the applicant to continue to occupy[2]. This power has not yet been exercised either in England or in Wales.

[1]   As amended by HRA 2017, for applications for homelessness assistance made to local housing authorities in England on or after 3 April 2018.
[2]   HA 1996, s 177(3)(a); H(W)A 2014, s 57(4).

ENGLAND

10.81 For the purposes of the deeming provision, 'violence' means 'violence from another person; or threats of violence from another person which are likely to be carried out'[1]. Although HA 1996, Pt 7[2] refers to 'threats' of violence, this can include a single threat of violence[3]. It is 'domestic violence' if the violence or threats of violence come from 'a person who is associated with the victim'[4].

[1]   HA 1996, s 177(1A).

² As amended by HRA 2017, for applications for homelessness assistance made to local housing
authorities in England on or after 3 April 2018.
³ Interpretation Act 1978, s 6(c): ' . . . unless the contrary intention appears . . . words in
the singular include the plural and words in the plural include the singular.'
⁴ HA 1996, s 177(1A).

10.82 The modern approach is to understand 'violence' as a very broad
concept. The English Code records the Secretary of State's opinion that 'the
term "violence" should not be given a restrictive meaning' and that:

> '"domestic violence" should be understood to include threatening behaviour,
> violence or abuse (psychological, physical, sexual, financial or emotional) between
> persons who are, or have been, intimate partners, family members or members of the
> same household, regardless of gender or sexuality¹.'

¹ English Code, para 21.19. See more generally English Code, para 6.24 and chapter 21. See
APPENDIX 2.

10.83 The Supreme Court has held that the term 'domestic violence' should be
interpreted in the same sense as it is used in family proceedings: '[d]omestic
violence includes physical violence, threatening or intimidating behaviour and
any other form of abuse which, directly or indirectly may give rise to the risk
of harm'¹. It follows that, where it is probable that an applicant would be
subject to abuse that may give rise to harm, but would not necessarily be
subject to physical violence, she or he will be deemed to be homeless under HA
1996, s 177(1) if that abuse comes from a person who is associated with the
victim. The Supreme Court declined to decide whether this extended definition
of violence should also apply to people who might be fleeing from violence that
was not domestic violence, as the question did not arise on the facts of that
case². The matter has since fallen for consideration by the Court of Appeal,
which determined that the extended definition of violence should also be
applied to violence that is not domestic violence³. However, conduct will not
normally be capable of being described as 'violent', as opposed to merely
anti-social, unless it is of such a nature and seriousness as to be liable to cause
psychological harm. The phrase connotes something more than transient upset
or distress⁴.

¹ *Yemshaw v Hounslow London Borough Council* [2011] UKSC 3, [2011] 1 WLR 433, [2011]
HLR 16, SC, Baroness Hale at [28] quoting the *Practice Direction (Residence and Contact
Orders: Domestic Violence) (No 2)* [2009] 1 WLR 251.
² *Yemshaw v Hounslow London Borough Council* [2011] UKSC 3, [2011] 1 WLR 433, [2011]
HLR 16, SC, Baroness Hale said: '[p]eople who are at risk of intimidating or harmful
behaviour from their near neighbours are equally worthy of protection as are those who run
the same risk from their relatives. But it may be less likely that they will suffer harm as a result
of the abusive behaviour of their neighbours than it is in the domestic context. In practice, the
threshold of seriousness may be higher' at [35]. The wording of the English Code potentially
contains the same distinction: English Code, para 21.19.
³ *Hussain v Waltham Forest London Borough Council* [2015] EWCA Civ 14, [2015] HLR
16, CA.
⁴ *Hussain v Waltham Forest London Borough Council* [2015] EWCA Civ 14, [2015] HLR
16, CA per Underhill LJ at [32].

10.84 The English Code contains a chapter dedicated to assisting local
housing authorities in England with the identification and management of
cases involving domestic violence¹. Applying the extended definition of

domestic violence advocated by the Supreme Court in *Yemshaw v Hounslow London Borough Council*[2], the English Code advises local housing authorities to be alive to (among other things) controlling and coercive behaviour, financial emotional abuse and 'so-called honour based abuse', including forced marriage and female genital mutilation[3] and reminds decision makers that 'the impacts may be different on different groups of people'[4].

[1] English Code, chapter 21 incorporating much of the material previously found in the *Supplementary guidance on domestic abuse and homelessness* (Department for Communities and Local Government, November 2014) which has now been withdrawn.
[2] [2011] UKSC 3, [2011] 1 WLR 433, [2011] HLR 16, SC.
[3] English Code, paras 21.4–21.7.
[4] English Code, para 21.9.

10.85 'A person who is associated with the victim' is exhaustively defined in HA 1996, s 178. If the relationship between the perpetrator and the victim does not fall within the statutory definition, the violence cannot be domestic violence (but will be 'other violence'). The English Code reiterates that the question of whether the violence is 'domestic' or not turns on the relationship between the perpetrator and the victim; not on where the violence took place[1]. The statutory definition of 'associated person' is very widely drawn, so as to include both existing and former spouses, civil partners, cohabitants, any person who has lived in the same household as the victim, any blood relation or relation by marriage, cohabitation or civil partnership, and any person who shares the parentage of, or parental responsibility for, a child with the victim (including adoptive parents in their relationship to natural parents)[2].

[1] English Code, paras 21.2.
[2] Civil Partnership Act 2004, s 81 and Sch 8, para 61 amended HA 1996, s 178 to include references to civil partnerships and same sex couples living together as though they were civil partners, in force from 5 December 2005. Paragraph 21.18 of the English Code contains an up-to-date list, but wrongly omits relatives of a civil partner or former civil partner (para 21.18(e)).

10.86 Before the implementation of the Homelessness Act 2002, only 'domestic' violence led to a deeming that it would not be reasonable for an applicant to continue to occupy accommodation. Since the amendment made by the Homelessness Act 2002, which inserted 'or other violence' into the deeming section, it is no longer necessary for local housing authorities to distinguish between domestic or other violence for the purposes of taking a decision on whether an applicant is homeless[1]. Where it is probable that continued occupation of the accommodation will lead to violence or threats of violence that are likely to be carried out against the applicant or a member of his or her household, that accommodation cannot be reasonable for the applicant to continue to occupy, whoever the violence (or threat of it) comes from. Following the decision of the Court of Appeal in *Hussain v Waltham Forest London Borough Council*[2], the distinction between 'domestic' violence and 'other violence' is of relatively little practical significance, save in circumstances where a local housing authority is considering a referral under the local connection provisions[3].

[1] Homelessness Act 2002, s 10. During its passage the Minister specifically referred to racial violence as falling within this provision (*Hansard*, SC, 10 July 2001, Sally Keeble MP).
[2] *Hussain v Waltham Forest London Borough Council* [2015] EWCA Civ 14, [2015] HLR 16, CA.

3   See **14.107–14.119**.

10.87 The test is not whether there has been violence in the past, or whether violence will definitely occur in the future. The question for the local housing authority is whether it is 'probable' that continued occupation of the accommodation would lead either to violence, or to threats of violence which are likely to be carried out. The Court of Appeal set aside a local housing authority's decision that an applicant was not homeless because she could have invoked legal remedies in order to prevent a recurrence of domestic violence. The local housing authority had asked itself the wrong question and had taken into account wider considerations (including whether the applicant had acted reasonably) rather than confining itself to the probability of her being subject to violence or threats of violence likely to be carried out if she remained in her accommodation[1]. 'Probable' means 'more likely than not'. 'Likely' in the context of 'threats of violence' includes 'a real or serious possibility'[2]. If, therefore, it is more likely than not that an applicant's continued occupation of his or her home will lead to violence, or to threats of violence where there is a real or serious possibility that those threats will be carried out, the applicant will be homeless.

1   *Bond v Leicester City Council* [2001] EWCA Civ 1544, [2002] HLR 6, CA.
2   *Bond v Leicester City Council* [2001] EWCA Civ 1544, [2002] HLR 6, CA per Hale LJ at [35].

10.88 Local housing authorities are entitled to advise applicants about any legal or practical remedies (obtaining injunctions, improving security, etc), but such remedies should only be pursued where the applicant wishes to do so and local housing authorities should be mindful that injunctions may not be effective in deterring some perpetrators[1]. The safety of the applicant and his or her household must be the primary consideration at all stages[2]. Local housing authorities are also advised that the fact that violence has not yet occurred does not mean that it is not likely to occur; and that (particularly in cases of domestic violence) they should not necessarily expect direct evidence of violence to be available from the applicant[3].

1   English Code, paras 21.27 and 21.29–21.30.
2   English Code, para 21.31. This need for safety will necessitate careful inquiries into the application. See Chapter **9**. In *Purewal v Ealing London Borough Council* [2013] EWCA Civ 1579, [2014] HLR 5, CA, a review decision that an applicant was not homeless, because it was not probable that she would be subject to sexual assault or rape from a neighbour if she continued to occupy her accommodation, was quashed. The local housing authority had failed to make all necessary inquiries into the issue. Specifically, it had failed to obtain a copy of key witness statement which the applicant had given to the police.
3   English Code, para 21.21. See **9.57–9.60**.

10.89 The definition of 'violence 'and 'threats of violence' as coming 'from another person' means that the risk of self-harm from continued occupation of accommodation does not put an applicant into this deemed unreasonableness category (although any risk of self-harm may be relevant to the broader test of whether the accommodation is reasonable to continue to occupy, as a matter of fact).

10.90 The local housing authority cannot take into account, when determining whether an applicant falls within this deemed unreasonableness category, general housing circumstances prevailing in its district. The local housing authority can only consider the applicant's individual circumstances and that of his or her household.

10.91 Where there is harassment falling short of actual violence or threats of violence that are likely to be carried out, the accommodation will not be deemed to be unreasonable for the applicant and members of his or her household to continue to occupy, but may be as a matter of fact unreasonable for them to continue to occupy[1].

[1]   See **10.129**.

WALES

10.92 The position for local housing authorities in Wales is very similar to that for local housing authorities in England and H(W)A 2014, ss 57–58, correspond closely with HA 1996, ss 177–178.

10.93 Under H(W)A 2014, s 57(1) it is not reasonable for a person to continue to occupy accommodation if it is 'probable that it will lead to the person, or a member of the person's household, being subjected to abuse'.

10.94 Probable, in the context of the risk of a person being subjected to abuse, means 'more likely than not'. 'Likely' in the context of 'threats of violence' includes 'a real or serious possibility'[1].

[1]   *Bond v Leicester City Council* [2002] EWCA Civ 1544, [2002] HLR 6, CA.

10.95 Abuse has been defined in H(W)A 2014, s 58 to reflect the extended definition of domestic violence given in *Yemshaw v Hounslow London Borough* Council[1]. Specifically 'abuse' means physical violence, threatening or intimidating behaviour and any other form of abuse which, directly or indirectly, may give rise to the risk of harm[2]. The Welsh Code advises that the likelihood of a threat of abuse being carried out should not be based on whether there has been actual abuse in the past[3]. In cases involving abuse, local housing authorities may wish to inform applicants of the option of seeking an injunction, but there is no obligation for the applicant then to do so[4].

[1]   [2011] UKSC 3, [2011] 1 WLR 433, [2011] HLR 16, SC. See **10.83**.
[2]   H(W)A 2014, s 58(1).
[3]   Welsh Code, para 8.23.
[4]   Welsh Code, para 8.24.

10.96 Abuse is 'domestic abuse' where the victim is 'associated with the abuser'[1]. The abuser will be associated with the victim where he or she falls within one of the relationships listed in H(W)A 2014, s 58(2). The list is exhaustive. The relationships set out in that section mirror those in HA 1996, s 178, though the wording has been modernised[2]. Surprisingly, given that domestic abuse will often occur in the context of a parent and child, the word 'child' is left undefined. However, it may be inferred from H(W)A 2014, s 96, which refers to children and persons under 18 synonymously, that, as under HA 1996, s 178, a child is a person under the age of 18.

[1]   H(W)A 2014, s 58(1).

² *Housing (Wales) Bill, Explanatory Memorandum* (Welsh Government, November 2013), p 158.

10.97 'Member of a person's household' means a person who normally resides with the applicant as member of his or her family, or any other person who might reasonably be expected to reside with the applicant¹.

¹ H(W)A 2014, s 57(2). See discussion at **10.24–10.30**.

10.98 The most obvious distinction between this particular aspect of the respective regimes under H(W)A 2014, Pt 2 and HA 1996, Pt 7¹ is that under H(W)A 2014, s 57 the terms 'violence' and 'domestic violence' as used in HA 1996, s 177 have been substituted with 'abuse' and 'domestic abuse'. The purpose of this amendment was said to be in order 'to reflect the way case law has interpreted the 1996 Act'². Actually, this amendment, which was enacted prior to the decision in *Hussain v Waltham Forest London Borough Council*³, went rather further than the existing case law which had, hitherto, refrained from applying the extended definition of violence, outside of the domestic context⁴. However, the decision of the Court of Appeal in *Hussain v Waltham Forest London Borough Council*⁵ means that this distinction is now of little, if any, practical significance and that the deemed unreasonableness provisions in both England and Wales are virtually identical.

¹ As amended by HRA 2017, for applications for homelessness assistance made to local housing authorities in England on or after 3 April 2018.
² *Housing (Wales) Bill, Explanatory Memorandum* (Welsh Government, November 2013) 158. See also Welsh Code, para 8.22.
³ [2015] EWCA Civ 14, [2015] HLR 16, CA.
⁴ See *Yemshaw v Hounslow London Borough Council* [2011] UKSC 3, [2011] 1 WLR 433, [2011] HLR 16, SC, and **10.83**.
⁵ [2015] EWCA Civ 14, [2015] HLR 16, CA. See **10.83**.

Factual unreasonableness

10.99 As a matter of fact, accommodation may not be reasonable for an applicant to continue to occupy. This is a much broader question for a local housing authority to determine than the relatively narrow deemed unreasonableness category. It is always required to consider whether or not the accommodation is 'affordable' for the applicant¹. It should also take into account any other relevant matters, including all those raised by the applicant. In making its decision as to whether or not the accommodation is reasonable for the applicant to continue to occupy, the local housing authority may, but is not obliged to, have regard to the general housing circumstances prevailing in its district².

¹ HA 1996, s 177(3)(b); Homelessness (Suitability of Accommodation) Order 1996, SI 1996/3204 at Appendix 2; H(W)A 2014, s 57(3)(b).
² HA 1996, s 177(2); H(W)A 2014, s 57(3)(a).

10.100 The phrase 'reasonable to continue to occupy' is also used as part of the definition of intentional homelessness¹. Case law and guidance relating to that part of the definition of intentional homelessness applies to the interpretation of the same phrase in relation to homelessness.

[1] HA 1996, s 191(1), discussed at **13.162–13.180**.

10.101 Both Codes contain the advice that '[t]here is no simple test of reasonableness'[1]. Each case will require an individual assessment involving consideration of the applicant's circumstances and (if the local housing authority elects to have regard to them) the general housing conditions in the district.

[1] English Code, para 6.23; Welsh Code, para 8.20.

10.102 As already noted, a local housing authority must always consider whether the applicant can afford to occupy the accommodation, and should then also consider any other relevant issues, whether raised directly by the applicant or becoming apparent during the local housing authority's inquiries. Examples of matters that might be relevant are given in the Codes, but the scope of the local housing authority's inquiries is not confined to those examples[1]. Any matter that appears to be relevant must be considered. The question of reasonableness is not limited to the characteristics of the accommodation alone; it can include other factors such as whether the applicant has access to employment or to welfare benefits in the place (or country) where the accommodation is located[2].

[1] English Code, paras 6.26–6.40; Welsh Code, paras 8.21–8.31.
[2] *R v Hammersmith and Fulham London Borough Council ex p Duro-Rama* (1983) 9 HLR 71, QBD; and *R v Gravesham Borough Council ex p Winchester* (1986) 18 HLR 207, QBD.

10.103 The Court of Appeal has set out a useful list of indicative factors that might be taken into account when considering whether any accommodation is reasonable to continue to occupy[1]. The House of Lords allowed an appeal in that case against the Court of Appeal's decision that women's refuges were accommodation that might be reasonable to continue to occupy, but did not specifically overrule the list[2]. Those factors are:

- the size, type and quality of the available accommodation, including the extent of any need to share its facilities;
- the terms of the agreement by which it is made available;
- the ability to afford it;
- the appropriateness of its location for an applicant and child (if any);
- the extent of its facilities;
- its appropriateness in the light of any particular characteristics (including as to health);
- the length of time for which the applicant has already occupied it;
- the state of physical and emotional health of the applicant while in occupation of it; and
- the length of time for which, unless accepted as homeless, they might expect to continue to occupy it[3].

[1] *Moran v Manchester City Council* [2008] EWCA Civ 378, [2008] HLR 39, CA.
[2] *Ali & others v Birmingham City Council, Moran v Manchester City Council* [2009] UKHL 36, [2009] 1 WLR 1506, HL.
[3] *Moran v Manchester City Council* [2008] EWCA Civ 378, [2008] HLR 39, CA per Wilson LJ at [49].

GENERAL CIRCUMSTANCES PREVAILING IN RELATION TO HOUSING IN THE
LOCAL HOUSING AUTHORITY'S DISTRICT

10.104 The local housing authority may, but is not obliged to, take into account 'the general circumstances prevailing in relation to housing in the district of the local housing authority to whom [the applicant] has applied'[1]. The Codes give two examples of when such a comparison might be appropriate: where the application is based on the physical condition of the property, or on overcrowding[2]. Other circumstances that local housing authorities have lawfully taken into account include the demands for housing in the local housing authority's area[3], its capacity to absorb and accommodate homeless families[4], the shortage of supply[5], and conflicts of lifestyle in multi-occupied homes[6]. A reasonably up-to-date picture of general housing conditions in a local housing authority's district will be available from the local housing authority's own local homelessness review[7]. Local housing authorities should ensure that they are taking into account 'general' housing conditions, rather than applying a narrower test. A decision that compared the applicant's degree of overcrowding only with that of others on the local housing register was overturned because those others were, by definition, in the most housing need[8].

[1] HA 1996, s 177(2); H(W)A 2014, s 57(3)(a).
[2] English Code, paras 6.26–6.27; Welsh Code, para 8.29 which adds a third: 'type of accommodation'. See **10.117–10.121** for physical conditions and **10.122–10.123** for over-crowding.
[3] *Noh v Hammersmith & Fulham London Borough Council* [2001] EWCA Civ 905, [2002] HLR 54, CA.
[4] *Noh v Hammersmith & Fulham London Borough Council* [2001] EWCA Civ 905, [2002] HLR 54, CA.
[5] *R v Kensington and Chelsea Royal London Borough Council ex p Moncada* (1997) 29 HLR 289, QBD.
[6] *R v Brent London Borough Council ex p Yusuf* (1997) 29 HLR 48, QBD; *R v Brent London Borough Council ex p Bariise* (1999) 31 HLR 50, CA.
[7] See **7.97–7.126**.
[8] *Chawa v Kensington and Chelsea Royal London Borough Council* (2012) January *Legal Action*, p 21, Central London County Court.

10.105 It is the local housing authority that is in the best position to assess the seriousness of the general conditions relating to housing in its area, and the extent to which an applicant's complaints might take his or her case out of the norm and make it unreasonable to continue in occupation[1]. It follows that applicants who apply to hard-pressed local housing authorities will find that satisfying the local housing authority that accommodation is not reasonable for them to continue to occupy is a harder task than if they had applied to local housing authorities with more accommodation available[2].

[1] *R v Brent London Borough Council ex p Bariise* (1999) 31 HLR 50, CA.
[2] See *Harouki v Kensington and Chelsea Royal London Borough Council* [2007] EWCA Civ 1000, [2008] HLR 16, CA for one such example.

10.106 The following paragraphs deal with the more common situations in which questions arise about factual reasonableness to continue to occupy.

AFFORDABILITY

10.107 Accommodation is not reasonable for an applicant to continue to occupy if the cost of paying for it would deprive the applicant of the means to provide for 'the ordinary necessities of life'[1]. What constitutes 'the ordinary necessities of life' is a question of fact and can vary according to each applicant's needs[2]. Care must be taken in evaluating these needs. A broad assertion by a local housing authority that an applicant's expenditure is exaggerated and that his or her accommodation is affordable, without any consideration of which items of expenditure could be reduced or why, will not be lawful[3]. The guidance in the Codes is also relevant. The English Code advises (in the context of assessing the suitability[4] of accommodation) that local housing authorities consider 'whether the applicant can afford the housing costs without being deprived of basic essentials such as food, clothing, heating, transport and other essentials specific to their circumstances'[5]. The Welsh Code provides that 'the Secretary of State recommends that housing authorities regard accommodation as not being affordable if the applicant would be left with a residual income which would be less than the level of income support or income-based jobseekers allowance that is applicable in respect of the applicant, or would be applicable if he or she was entitled to claim such benefit'[6]. Where an applicant is in receipt of other benefits, such as child benefit or child tax credit, there is no rule of law that such benefits are not intended to be used toward housing, or that there is no flexibility within such income for the payment of housing costs[7].

1   *R v Wandsworth London Borough Council ex p Hawthorne* [1994] 1 WLR 1442, CA; and *R v Brent London Borough Council ex p Baruwa* (1997) 29 HLR 915, CA. See English Code, para 6.29, which uses the phrase 'reasonable living expenses'.
2   *R v Hillingdon London Borough Council ex p Tinn* (1988) 20 HLR 305, QBD.
3   *Farah v Hillingdon London Borough Council* [2014] EWCA Civ 359, [2014] HLR 24, CA.
4   See CHAPTER 18.
5   English Code, para 17.45.
6   Welsh Code, para 19.28. When applying this paragraph, local housing authorities should not confine themselves to those specified benefits which only apply to adult claimants, but also consider the level of equivalent benefits paid in respect of the entire household, such as child tax credits: *Eryurekler v Hackney London Borough Council* (2010) May *Legal Action*, p 24, Clerkenwell and Shoreditch County Court. Specific reference to this particular passage of the Code may not be needed as long as the local housing authority adopts 'the kind of analysis' envisaged in the Code: *Birmingham City Council v Balog* [2013] EWCA Civ 1582, [2014] HLR 14, CA per Kitchin LJ at [50].
7   *Samuels v Birmingham City Council* [2015] EWCA Civ 1051, [2016] PTSR 558, CA. The Supreme Court has granted permission to appeal against this decision.

10.108 A local housing authority in England is specifically required by statutory instrument to consider the whole of the applicant's financial resources as against the cost of the accommodation, any child support or other payments that the applicant is required to make, and all the applicant's other reasonable living expenses[1].

1   Homelessness (Suitability of Accommodation) Order 1996, SI 1996/3204, reg 2. See APPENDIX 2.

10.109 These considerations are mirrored at H(W)A 2014, s 59(2)[1] and in the Welsh Code[2]. The Welsh Code also advises local housing authorities to be mindful of the changes in entitlement to housing benefit that have taken effect since April 2011, stipulating that 'households should not be penalised for the loss of accommodation where it was due to an unavoidable change in their welfare benefits that led to the accommodation becoming unaffordable'[3]. In practice, a similar approach has been adopted by the county court[4] in the context of HA 1996, Pt 7[5].

[1] In the context of suitability.
[2] Welsh Code, para 8.29.
[3] Welsh Code, para 8.30.
[4] In *Magoury v Brent London Borough Council* (2016) February *Legal Action*, p 46, County Court at Central London, a finding that the applicant had become homeless intentionally was quashed where there had been a failure to consider whether she would have become homeless anyway as a result of the benefit cap. Similarly, *Barker v Watford City Council* (2017) July/August *Legal Action*, p 42, County Court at Central London, involved a finding that the applicant had become homeless intentionally in circumstances where she had lost her accommodation as a result of welfare reforms which left a shortfall between her housing benefit award and her rent. The local housing authority decided that the applicant's property was affordable, and therefore reasonable to continue to occupy, as she could have applied for discretionary housing payments. The decision was quashed on appeal. The local housing authority had failed to make any inquiries to establish whether such an application would succeed or for how long any award would be made See **13.77**.
[5] As amended by HRA 2017, for applications for homelessness assistance made to local housing authorities in England on or after 3 April 2018.

IMMINENT OR ACTUAL POSSESSION PROCEEDINGS

10.110 The approach to be taken where an applicant facing imminent or actual possession proceedings seeks homelessness assistance varies slightly as between local housing authorities in England and in Wales. It is convenient to set out the position in Wales first.

Wales

10.111 In Wales, where an applicant is entitled to occupy rented accommodation, because no possession order has yet been obtained, but possession proceedings are imminent or have been started, the local housing authority should consider whether in those circumstances it is reasonable for the applicant to continue to occupy until the possession order has been obtained, and executed. Factors that the local housing authority should take into account include: the general cost to the local housing authority of accepting the applicant as 'homeless' at that stage; the position of the tenant; the position of the landlord; the likelihood that the landlord will actually proceed (or continue) with the possession claim; the burden on the courts of unnecessary proceedings where there is no defence to a claim for possession; and the general housing circumstances prevailing in the local housing authority's district[1]. The Welsh Code suggests that it is unlikely to be reasonable for an assured shorthold tenant (who has received a proper statutory notice)[2] to continue to occupy where the local housing authority is satisfied that the landlord intends to seek possession and where there would be no defence to a possession claim[3]. This guidance would also apply to other occupiers faced with imminent possession proceedings to which they have no defence and who would therefore become liable to pay the costs of those proceedings[4]. Similarly, case law has stressed that 'it is undesirable that a tenant, or an ex-tenant, in those circumstances should be required to hang on till the bitter end and require a court order'[5]. However, the decision as to the imminence of possession proceedings, and whether or not an applicant would have a defence, is a question of fact for the local housing authority[6].

1 Welsh Code, para 8.31(a).
2 Complying with Housing Act 1988, s 21.
3 Welsh Code, para 8.31(a). The Welsh Code disapplies this advice where the local housing authority is taking steps to persuade the landlord to withdraw the notice or to allow the tenant to continue to occupy the accommodation for a reasonable period.
4 Such as introductory tenants, demoted tenants, non-secure tenants, occupiers whose former tenancies were determined by notices to quit, and other former common-law tenants.
5 *R v Croydon London Borough Council ex p Jarvis* (1994) 26 HLR 194, QBD per Collins J at 205.
6 *R v Bradford Metropolitan Borough Council ex p Parveen* (1996) 28 HLR 681, QBD. See also *Goddard v Torridge District Council* (1982) January *Legal Action*, p 9; *R v Portsmouth City Council ex p Knight* (1983) 10 HLR 115, QBD; and *R v Surrey Heath Borough Council ex p Li* (1984) 16 HLR 69, QBD. In *Khadija Ali v Bristol City Council* (2007) October *Legal Action*, p 26, Bristol County Court, the review decision was defective because there was no reference to the guidance given in the Code, or any explanation of the reviewing officer's decision to depart from it.

England

10.112 From 2006 onward the English Code[1] contained similar guidance to that which is applicable in Wales[2]. But despite this clear guidance it was not unusual for local housing authorities to advise occupiers facing imminent or actual possession proceedings to remain in occupation until a court order was obtained and executed[3]. This prompted the then Minister of State for Housing and Planning, Brandon Lewis MP, to write to all local housing authorities in England in June 2016, urging them to follow the guidance set out in the English Code and to avoid 'routinely . . . advising tenants to stay until the bailiffs arrive'[4]. It was the mischief identified here which the new HA 1996, s 175(5)[5] seeks to remedy. HA 1996, s 175(5)[6] applies to applicants who have been served with a valid Housing Act 1988, s 21 notice. Such applicants are deemed to be threatened with homelessness throughout the 56-day period leading up to the expiry of the notice[7]. This means that the applicant will be owed the HA 1996, s 195(2)[8] prevention duty and that the local housing authority must take reasonable steps to help the applicant to secure that accommodation does not cease to be available for his or her occupation. Those reasonable steps might include negotiating with the landlord for a further assured shorthold tenancy. The idea behind this duty is to 'tackle the bad practice whereby some local authorities advise tenants to remain in properties until the bailiffs arrive' and to 'help to reduce evictions from privately rented accommodation and facilitate less disruptive moves to alternative housing when tenants do have to move out'[9].

1 English Code, paras 6.29–6.38.
2 *Homelessness Code of Guidance for Local Authorities* (Department for Communities and Local Government, Department for Education and Skills, Department of Health, July 2006), paras 8.30–8.32a. (See **10.111** for the guidance applicable in Wales.)
3 See for example *Complaint against Eastbourne Borough Council*, 14 016 569, 29 February 2016 (2016) September *Legal Action*, p 37.
4 Brandon Lewis MP, Minister of State for Housing and Planning, letter to Local Housing Authority CEOs, June 2016.
5 As inserted by HRA 2017, s 1(3) for applications for homelessness assistance made to local housing authorities in England on or after 3 April 2018.

[6] As inserted by HRA 2017, s 1(3) for applications for homelessness assistance made to local housing authorities in England on or after 3 April 2018.

[7] See **10.144–10.147.**

[8] As amended by HRA 2017, s 4 for applications for homelessness assistance made to local housing authorities in England on or after 3 April 2018. See **15.87–15.137.**

[9] Homelessness Reduction Bill (Seventh sitting), *Hansard*, HC Deb, Cols 158–159, 17 January 2017, Marcus Jones (Parliamentary Under-Secretary of State for Communities and Local Government).

10.113 This new deeming provision applies only to occupiers who have been served with a valid notice under HA 1988, s 21 which is due to expire with 56 days. Accordingly, when a local housing authority in England receives an application for homelessness assistance from an occupier who has been served with:

- a notice other than one under HA 1998, s 21;
- a notice under HA 1988, s 21 that is not valid;
- a notice under HA 1988, s 21 that will expire in excess of 56 days[1]; or
- a notice under HA 1988, s 21 notice that has expired[2],

it should continue to treat that application in accordance with the principles that applied prior to the coming into force of HA 1996, s 175(5)[3] and consider whether, in the circumstances, it is reasonable for the applicant to continue to occupy the accommodation[4]. If it is not reasonable for the applicant to continue to occupy the accommodation then he or she will be homeless.

[1] In this scenario, the deeming provision under HA 1996, s 175(5) as inserted by HRA 2017, s 1(3) for applications for homelessness assistance made to local housing authorities in England on or after 3 April 2018, will still apply but only once sufficient time has passed so that the notice is within 56 days of expiry.

[2] The effect of the HA 1988, s 21 duty expiring during the performance of the HA 1996, s 195(2), prevention duty is discussed at **15.111.** In outline, although the applicant will no longer fall within the scope of HA 1996, s 175(5) (as inserted by HRA 2017, s 1(3) for applications for homelessness assistance made to local housing authorities in England on or after 3 April 2018) the local housing authority must continue to take reasonable steps to help him or her to secure that accommodation does not cease to be available for his or her occupation. He or she cannot be "timed out" of the prevention duty'. See HA 1996, s 195(5)–(6) (as inserted by HRA 2017, s 4(2) for applications for homelessness assistance made to local housing authorities in England on or after 3 April 2018) and English Code, para 6.30. This allows the applicant to retain the benefit of the prevention duty *unless* the local housing authority concludes that matters have actually reached the stage where the applicant might now properly be regarded as homeless rather than threatened with homelessness. Importantly, the expiry of the HA 1988, s 21 notice does not compel a conclusion that the applicant has transitioned from being threatened with homelessness to being homeless. Whether that transition has taken place will depend on the circumstances of the case. See English Code, paras 6.31–6.32.

[3] As inserted by HRA 2017, s 1(3) for applications for homelessness assistance made to local housing authorities in England on or after 3 April 2018.

[4] See English Code, paras 6.32–6.33 for factors that may be relevant to this assessment and **10.111** on the approach in Wales, which reflects the approach in England prior to the coming into force of HA 1996, s 175(5), as inserted by HRA 2017, s 1(3) for applications for homelessness assistance made to local housing authorities in England on or after 3 April 2018.

10.114 The Secretary of State advises that where an applicant who has been served with a valid notice under HA 1988, s 21 would have no defence to possession proceedings, and where the local housing authority is satisfied that further efforts to persuade the landlord to allow the applicant to stay in the property would be unlikely to succeed, then it is unlikely to be reasonable for the applicant to continue to occupy the accommodation beyond the expiry of the notice[1]. The combined effect of HA 1996, s 175(5)[2] and the guidance given in the English Code, is that an applicant served with a valid HA 1988, s 21 notice, will be threatened with homelessness in the 56-day period leading up to the expiry of the notice and is likely to be homeless thereafter.

[1]   English Code, para 6.35.
[2]   As inserted by HRA 2017, s 1(3) for applications for homelessness assistance made to local housing authorities in England on or after 3 April 2018.

10.115 In all cases, irrespective of the legal basis of the possession proceedings (ie whether the proceedings have been brought pursuant to HA 1988, s 21 or otherwise), the practice of requiring an applicant to remain in his or her accommodation after the making of a possession order is deprecated. In particular, the English Code provides that:

- it is highly unlikely to be reasonable for the applicant to continue to occupy once a court has issued an order for possession[1];
- local housing authorities should not consider it reasonable for an applicant to remain in occupation up until the point at which a court issues a warrant or writ to enforce an order for possession[2]; and
- local housing authorities should ensure that homeless families and vulnerable individuals who are owed an accommodation duty[3] are not evicted through the enforcement of an order for possession a result of a failure by the authority to make suitable accommodation available to them[4].

[1]   English Code, para 6.36.
[2]   English Code, para 6.37.
[3]   See CHAPTER 16.
[4]   English Code, para 6.38.

10.116 A further distinction as between the law in England and in Wales is that under HA 1996, Pt 7[1] applicants to local housing authorities in England who are re-applying for homelessness assistance within two years of acceptance of a private rented sector offer[2] and who have been served with a valid HA 1988, s 21 notice will be deemed to be homeless from the date of the expiry of the notice[3].

[1]   As amended by HRA 2017, for applications for homelessness assistance made to local housing authorities in England on or after 3 April 2018.
[2]   'Private rented sector offers' are defined at HA 1996, s 193(7AC). See **16.153–16.179**.
[3]   HA 1996, s 195A(2) as amended by HRA 2017, s 4(4) for applications for homelessness assistance made to local housing authorities in England on or after 3 April 2018. See **8.100–8.107** and **10.135–10.143**.

PHYSICAL CONDITIONS

10.117 The English Code suggests that the local housing authority ask itself:

' . . . whether the condition of the property was so bad in comparison with other accommodation in the district that it would not be reasonable to expect someone to continue to live there[1].'

[1] English Code, para 6.26. Though this requirement to consider the physical condition of the property does not necessarily require a hazard assessment under the Housing Act 2004. Such an assessment may be necessary in considering whether the accommodation is suitable within the meaning of HA 1996, s 206 and s 210 and H(W)A 2014, s 59. See CHAPTER 18. But the questions of whether accommodation is 'reasonable . . . to continue to occupy' and whether it is 'suitable' are distinct, though they will often lead to the same result. See *Temur v Hackney London Borough Council* [2014] EWCA Civ 877, [2014] HLR 39, CA, dealing with both the requirement for a hazard assessment and the distinction between 'suitability' and 'reasonable to continue to occupy'.

10.118 The Welsh Code repeats that proposed test, but also refers to the question of whether the property is unsuitable for human habitation and to the Housing, Health and Safety Rating System[1]. It also draws attention to the particular needs of disabled people, and the needs of children[2].

[1] Housing Act 2004, Part 1.
[2] Welsh Code, para 8.27(i). In contrast to the position under HA 1996, Part 7 (as amended by HRA 2017 for applications for homelessness assistance made to local housing authorities in England on or after 3 April 2018) set out at **10.117** fn 1, the Welsh Code advises that consideration of the physical condition of the property will always require an inspection of the property and an assessment in accordance with the Housing, Health and Safety Rating System.

10.119 The English Code also refers to 'the physical characteristics of the accommodation' being reasonable for the particular applicant (eg a wheelchair user) to continue to occupy[1]. It is in this context that the public sector equality duty under Equality Act 2010, s 149 may become relevant. Where the applicant has a disability which is relevant to the question of whether accommodation is reasonable for his or her continued occupation, then the public sector equality duty will be engaged. In such circumstances the local housing authority will need to 'focus very sharply' on the matters relevant to the performance of this duty[2]. In practice this is likely to require a similar approach to that which is required in assessing whether or not accommodation provided to a disabled person is suitable within the meaning of HA 1996, s 206[3].

[1] English Code, para 6.39(a).
[2] See *Kanu v Southwark London Borough Council* [2015] UKSC 30, [2015] 2 WLR 1341, SC per Lord Neuberger at [78], discussed further at **12.91** and **12.100**.
[3] See *London Borough of Hackney v Haque* [2017] EWCA Civ 4, [2017] PTSR 769, CA per Briggs LJ at [43], *Chatokai v Salford City Council* (2017) July/August *Legal Action*, p 42, County Court at Manchester and **18.65–18.68**.

10.120 Whether or not a property has adequate fire prevention and escape facilities, in comparison with other properties in the local housing authority's district, is a relevant consideration[1]. A vandalised property was, on the facts of a particular case, found to be not reasonable for the applicant to continue to occupy[2]. A damp beach chalet, which a pregnant applicant had been told would be unsafe for her baby, was held not to be reasonable to continue to occupy, given the clear medical advice[3].

1 *R v Kensington and Chelsea Royal London Borough Council ex p Ben-El-Mabrouk* (1995) 27 HLR 564, CA; and *R v Haringey London Borough Council ex p Flynn* (1995), (1995) June *Legal Action*, p 21, QBD.
2 *City of Gloucester v Miles* (1985) 17 HLR 292, CA.
3 *R v Medina Borough Council ex p Dee* (1992) 24 HLR 562, QBD. See also *Bavi v Waltham Forest London Borough Council* [2009] EWCA Civ 551, (2009) August *Legal Action*, p 37, CA, where the local housing authority had properly considered all the relevant defects, including rising dampness, and found that the applicant was not homeless, and *Nagi v Birmingham City Council* [2010] EWCA Civ 1391, (2011) January *Legal Action*, p 36, CA, where a local housing authority was not wrong in law to find that accommodation which had internal stairs and was accessed by a steep slope was reasonable to continue to be occupied by a couple where the wife had epilepsy and a mobility problem.

10.121 Local housing authorities are entitled to compare the physical conditions of the applicant's accommodation with the general physical conditions of housing in their districts[1].

1 HA 1996, s 177(2); H(W)A 2014, s 57(3)(a). For examples, see *R v Brent London Borough Council ex parte Yusuf* (1997) 29 HLR 48, QBD; *R v Brent London Borough Council ex p Bariise* (1999) 31 HLR 50, CA; *R (Lynch) v Lambeth London Borough Council* [2006] EWHC 2737 (Admin), [2007] HLR 15, Admin Ct. See 10.104–10.106.

OVERCROWDING

10.122 When considering the question of overcrowding, local housing authorities should consider all the different aspects of the statutory overcrowding test at Housing Act 1985, ss 324–326[1]. They must not limit themselves to whether the property is statutorily overcrowded, although that can be a key or contributing factor to their decision on reasonableness[2]. They should also consider any overcrowding that does not amount to statutory overcrowding, any medical needs and any other matters relevant to the impact of overcrowding[3]. The extent to which the accommodation may be a 'hazard', as defined by Housing Act 2004[4], and the severity of that hazard, may also be relevant[5].

1 *Elrify v Westminster City Council* [2007] EWCA Civ 332, [2007] HLR 36, CA. In *Elmer v London Borough of Wandsworth* [2016] EWCA Civ 1278, CA, the Court of Appeal refused the appellant permission to appeal against a decision that the local housing authority were not required to measure the dimensions of the rooms in the property to evaluate whether there had been statutory overcrowding, where that issue had not been raised on review.
2 English Code, para 6.27; Welsh Code, para 8.27(ii).
3 *R v Westminster City Council ex p Alouat* (1989) 21 HLR 477, QBD.
4 Housing Act 2004, ss 1–2.
5 *Khadija Ali v Bristol City Council* (2007) October *Legal Action*, p 26, Bristol County Court; and see also *Hashi v Birmingham City Council* (2010) November *Legal Action*, p 19, Birmingham County Court, where there had been a total reliance or an over-reliance on the test of statutory overcrowding and a failure to give a rational explanation for rejecting independent advice that there was a Category 1 hazard.

10.123 Even when accommodation is statutorily overcrowded, a local housing authority may be entitled to find that it is reasonable to continue to occupy, taking into account the general housing circumstances prevailing in its district[1]. However, a decision that an overcrowded property was reasonable to continue to occupy because the overcrowding was a result of the increasing size of the applicant's family was quashed. It was a value judgment that had no place in the statutory scheme. The reason for the overcrowding is simply not relevant to whether or not the property is reasonable to continue to occupy[2]. A local housing authority is entitled to compare the degree of overcrowding with the general housing circumstances prevailing in its district, including the general degree of overcrowding in its district[3], but it should ensure that it addresses the particular degree of overcrowding experienced by the applicant. Merely asserting the general prevalence of overcrowding in the district without evidence showing the numbers of households experiencing a similar degree of overcrowding to that experienced by the applicant is not sufficient[4].

[1] *Harouki v Kensington and Chelsea Royal London Borough Council* [2007] EWCA Civ 1000, [2008] HLR 16, CA, where an applicant was statutorily overcrowded and thus committing an offence (Housing Act 1985, s 327). It should be noted that the extent to which the accommodation might constitute a 'hazard' within the meaning of the Housing Act 2004 was not considered.

[2] *R v Eastleigh Borough Council ex p Beattie (No 1)* (1983) 10 HLR 134, QBD; *R v Eastleigh Borough Council ex p Beattie (No 2)* (1985) 17 HLR 168, QBD; and *R v Tower Hamlets London Borough Council ex p Hoque* (1993) The Times, July 20, QBD.

[3] *R v Tower Hamlets London Borough Council ex p Monaf* (1988) 20 HLR 529, CA; *R v Tower Hamlets London Borough Council ex p Ojo* (1991) 23 HLR 488, QBD; *R v Tower Hamlets London Borough Council ex p Uddin* (1993) June *Legal Action*, p 15, QBD; *Osei v Southwark London Borough Council* [2007] EWCA Civ 787, [2008] HLR 15, CA; *Harouki v Kensington and Chelsea Royal London Borough Council* [2007] EWCA Civ 1000, [2008] HLR 16, CA; *Mohamoud v Greenwich London Borough Council* (2003) January *Legal Action*, p 23, Woolwich County Court; *Khadija Ali v Bristol City Council* (2007) October *Legal Action*, p 26, Bristol County Court; and *Chawa v Kensington and Chelsea Royal London Borough Council* (2012) January *Legal Action*, p 21, Central London County Court.

[4] *Mohamoud v Greenwich London Borough Council* (2003) January *Legal Action*, p 23, Woolwich County Court; and *Khadija Ali v Bristol City Council* (2007) October *Legal Action*, p 26, Bristol County Court.

RELATIONSHIP BREAKDOWN

10.124 A local housing authority's decision that it was reasonable for an ex-husband to occupy his former matrimonial home with his ex-wife and her new boyfriend, given the general housing circumstances prevailing in its district, was held not to contain errors of law. Although it was undesirable for a divorced couple to have to live together, the local housing authority was entitled to take into account the shortage of accommodation in its district[1].

[1] *R v Kensington and Chelsea Royal London Borough Council ex p Moncada* (1997) 29 HLR 289, QBD. See also *Abdullah v Westminster City Council* [2011] EWCA Civ 1171, [2012] HLR 5, CA and **10.49** fn 3.

TYPES OF ACCOMMODATION

10.125 Short-term crisis-type accommodation, such as women's refuges, direct access hostels and night shelters should not be considered accommodation that is reasonable to continue to occupy in the medium and long term (assuming that such facilities are capable of constituting 'accommodation' at all)[1].

[1] English Code, para 6.39(b); Welsh Code, paras 8.26 and 8.27(iii)–8.28. The House of Lords, when considering the special position of women's refuges in *Ali & others v Birmingham City Council, Moran v Manchester City Council* [2009] UKHL 36, [2009] 1 WLR 1506, HL, held that since refuges were not reasonable for women to continue to occupy indefinitely, they

did not need to decide whether refuges were 'accommodation' within the meaning of HA 1996, s 175. See also **10.8–10.16**.

10.126 The House of Lords has held that women's refuges, in particular, should not be considered reasonable to continue to occupy indefinitely. Baroness Hale said:

' . . . a refuge is not simply crisis intervention for a few nights. It is a safe haven in which to find peace and support. But it is not a place to live. There are rules which are necessary for the protection of residents but make it impossible to live a normal family life. It is a place to gather one's strength and one's thoughts and to decide what to do with one's life[1].'

1   *Ali & others v Birmingham City Council, Moran v Manchester City Council* [2009] UKHL 36, [2009] 1 WLR 1506, HL at [43].

TENURE

10.127 Accommodation need not be subject to any security of tenure for it to be accommodation which is reasonable for the applicant to continue to occupy. The mere fact that accommodation is temporary will not, in itself, render accommodation not reasonable to continue to occupy[1]. If accommodation is so precarious that the occupier is likely to have to leave within 56 days then the applicant will in any event be threatened with homelessness[2].

1   *R v Brent London Borough Council ex p Awua* [1996] AC 55, HL.
2   HA 1996, s 175(4) as amended by HRA 2017, s 1(2) for applications for homelessness assistance made to local housing authorities in England on or after 3 April 2018; H(W)A 2014, s 55(4); see **10.144–10.147**.

FORMER MEMBERS OF THE ARMED FORCES

10.128 Former members of the armed forces, who were provided with accommodation during their service, are likely to lose that accommodation upon discharge. The Ministry of Defence will usually issue a Certificate of Cessation of Entitlement to Occupy Service Living Accommodation, which contains a date on which entitlement to occupy service quarters will end. The Codes recommend that local housing authorities should accept the date in the Certificate as being the date upon which an applicant becomes homeless, and should not insist upon the Ministry of Defence obtaining possession orders[1]. They add that the 6-month notice period before the date of cessation in the certificate can be used to ensure that service personnel receive advice on housing options available to them. If this advice does not result in the applicant obtaining alternative accommodation by the beginning of the 56-day period leading up to the date of cessation, the applicant will be threatened with homeless and will be entitled to have his or her application for homelessness assistance determined in accordance with HA 1996, Pt 7[2] or H(W)A 2014, Pt 2.

1   English Code, para 24.8; Welsh Code, para 8.31(b).
2   As amended by HRA 2017, for applications for homelessness assistance made to local housing authorities in England on or after 3 April 2018.

HARASSMENT FALLING SHORT OF VIOLENCE

10.129 Where there is harassment falling short of actual violence[1] or threats of violence that are likely to be carried out, the English Code recommends that local housing authorities should 'consider carefully' the question of whether or not it would be reasonable for the applicant and his or her household to continue to occupy. Examples of verbal abuse, damage to property or the risk of intimidation of witnesses in criminal proceedings are given[2]. In Wales, such harassment may constitute 'abuse'[3].

[1] Applying the extended definition approved by the Court of Appeal in *Hussain v Waltham Forest London Borough Council* [2015] EWCA Civ 14, [2015] HLR 16, CA. See **10.83**.
[2] English Code, para 6.39(c).
[3] See **10.92–10.98**.

ACCOMMODATION OVERSEAS

10.130 Where the applicant has accommodation available to him or her overseas[1], the question of whether it is reasonable to occupy the accommodation requires consideration of all relevant matters, including the affordability of the accommodation, its physical condition, etc. The local housing authority should not limit itself to the issue of the accommodation's size and facilities. Any risk of violence to the applicant, the location of the accommodation, the applicant's personal circumstances, financial circumstances and employment prospects are also relevant[2]. The local housing authority will also need to consider the applicant's Art 8[3] rights, the extent to which leaving the UK would interfere with his or her private or family life and whether that impact is proportionate. If the impact of the local housing authority's decision would or might involve a child or children having to relocate to another country, the local housing authority must also consider whether relocating would be in the best interests of the child. Those best interests are to be given primacy[4].

[1] See **10.15**.
[2] *R v Hammersmith & Fulham London Borough Council ex p Duro-Rama* (1983) 9 HLR 71, QBD; *R v Camden London Borough Council ex p Aranda* (1998) 30 HLR 76, CA; *R v Kensington and Chelsea Royal London Borough Council ex p Bayani* (1990) 22 HLR 406, CA; *R v Newham London Borough Council ex p Ajayi* (1996) 28 HLR 25, QBD; *Waltham Forest London Borough Council v Maloba* [2007] EWCA Civ 1291, [2008] HLR 26, CA, where a decision that it was reasonable for a family to occupy accommodation in Uganda, when the husband had lived in the UK for 10 years and had acquired British citizenship, was held to be a decision that no reasonable local housing authority would have come to on those particular facts; and *CM v Westminster City Council* (2017) February *Legal Action*, p 50, County Court at Central London.
[3] The 'right to respect for his private and family life' at Human Rights Act 1998, Sch 1, Art 8.
[4] *Kumaning v Haringey London Borough Council* (2012) April *Legal Action*, p 47, Central London County Court. The Supreme Court held in *ZH (Tanzania) v Secretary of State for the Home Department* [2011] UKSC 4, [2011] 2 AC 166, SC, that a child's best interests must be given primacy. See *Nzolameso v Westminster City Council* [2015] UKSC 22, [2015] HLR 22, SC for the most authoritative guidance on the relevance of the best interests of the child to decision-making under HA 1996, Pt 7 and H(W)A 2014, Pt 2. See further **9.87–9.87** and **18.56–18.57**.

10.131 When considering the location, physical characteristics, etc, of the accommodation abroad, the local housing authority is entitled to take into account the general circumstances prevailing in relation to housing in its own district. The comparison is not with general housing circumstances in the area in which the accommodation is located[1].

[1] *R v Tower Hamlets London Borough Council ex p Monaf* (1988) 20 HLR 529, CA; *R v Newham London Borough Council ex p Tower Hamlets London Borough Council* [1991] 1 WLR 1032, (1991) 23 HLR 62, CA; and *Osei v Southwark London Borough Council* [2007] EWCA Civ 787, [2008] HLR 15, CA.

ACCOMMODATION OBTAINED BY DECEPTION

10.132 It will not be reasonable for an applicant to continue to occupy accommodation which has been obtained by deception. In *Chishimba v Kensington and Chelsea Royal London Borough Council*[1] the applicant, a Namibian national, had obtained accommodation under HA 1996, Pt 7 using a counterfeit passport. Her deception was later uncovered and a possession order was made against her. The local housing authority took the view that it would have been reasonable for her to continue to occupy the accommodation it had provided. This decision was upheld on review and on appeal. The Court of Appeal allowed a second appeal holding that it could not have been reasonable for her to occupy accommodation which she never had any lawful right to occupy.

[1] [2013] EWCA Civ 786, [2013] HLR 34, CA. The Court of Appeal in this case approved and applied the earlier case of *R v Exeter City Council ex p Gliddon* (1984) HLR 103, QBD, where the applicants had obtained accommodation by misleading their landlord about their income.

OTHER CIRCUMSTANCES

10.133 It is impossible to set out and examine all of the many factors that may cause accommodation to be, or to have become, unreasonable for an applicant to continue to occupy. That is precisely why the local housing authority will have to examine carefully any matter raised by the applicant. Applicants may advance highly subjective reasons for not wanting to continue in occupation of a particular property[1]. For example, a factor considered by the Court of Appeal in one case was the location of the accommodation in relation to the applicant's place of employment[2]. The question for the local housing authority is not 'Would it be reasonable for this applicant to leave this property?' but rather 'Would it be reasonable for the applicant to continue in occupation?' Even when faced with what might seem to be compelling personal objections to the applicant continuing to occupy accommodation, a local housing authority may be able to point to general housing conditions in its area to demonstrate that it would be reasonable for the applicant to stay on.

[1] In *R v Nottingham City Council ex p Costello* (1989) 21 HLR 301, QBD, the issue was whether the accommodation was troubled by poltergeists (either actually or in the applicant's belief) and therefore not reasonable to continue to occupy. In *EC v Westminster City Council* (2017) May *Legal Action*, p 43, County Court at Central London the issue (which the local housing authority had failed to properly consider) was whether the severe impact of a mother's grief after her son had been killed in a hit-and-run accident outside the family home, meant that it was not reasonable for her to continue to occupy the property.

[2] *Hemans v Royal Borough of Windsor and Maidenhead* [2011] EWCA Civ 374, [2011] HLR 25, CA.

Reasonable for whom?

10.134 When a local housing authority is considering whether accommodation is 'available' for the applicant, HA 1996, Pt 7[1] and H(W)A 2014, Pt 2 require it to consider availability for all others in the applicant's household[2]. In contrast, when considering the reasonableness of continued occupation, the focus is only on the reasonableness of *the applicant* continuing in occupation, and not on whether or not it is reasonable for his or her *household* to continue in occupation. HA 1996, Pt 7[3] and H(W)A 2014, Pt 2 expressly address the others in the household for the purposes of deemed unreasonableness (violence, threats of violence or abuse)[4], but not otherwise. However, this does not mean that, in cases not involving violence or abuse, the circumstances of the applicant's household can be ignored. An applicant may very commonly assert that the factor causing the accommodation to be no longer reasonable for his or her occupation is the medical or other situation of a different member of his or her household. The phrase 'reasonable for the person to continue to occupy'[5] is plainly broad enough to encompass such considerations. It follows that the local housing authority must make inquiries sufficient to determine whether, in view of those matters, the accommodation is not reasonable for the applicant to continue to occupy[6].

[1] As amended by HRA 2017, for applications for homelessness assistance made to local housing authorities in England on or after 3 April 2018.
[2] See **10.21–10.32**.
[3] As amended by HRA 2017, for applications for homelessness assistance made to local housing authorities in England on or after 3 April 2018.
[4] HA 1996, s 177(1); H(W)A 2014, s 57(1).
[5] HA 1996, s 175(4) as amended by HRA 2017, s 1(2), for applications for homelessness assistance made to local housing authorities in England on or after 3 April 2018; H(W)A 2014, s 55(4).
[6] See *R v Westminster City Council ex p Bishop* (1993) 25 HLR 459, CA; English Code, para 9.22 (dealing with the same issue in the context of becoming homeless intentionally).

The special position for applicants to local housing authorities in England re-applying within two years of acceptance of a private rented sector offer

10.135 As a result of the amendments to HA 1996, Pt 7, made by Localism Act 2011, ss 148–149, local housing authorities in England can make a 'private rented sector offer'[1] to an applicant whose application for homelessness assistance was made on or after 9 November 2012 and who is owed the HA 1996, s 193(2), main housing duty[2]. If the private rented sector offer is suitable for the needs of the applicant and of his or her household[3], and if the applicant has been informed in writing of the matters set out at HA 1996, s 193(7AB), the HA 1996, s 193(2) main housing duty will come to an end whether the applicant accepts or refuses the private rented sector offer[4].

[1] HA 1996, s 193(7AC). See **16.153–16.179**.
[2] For 'main housing duty', see **16.94–16.199**.
[3] HA 1996, s 193(7F), for suitability see CHAPTER 18.
[4] HA 1996, s 193(7AA). See **16.153–16.179**. It should be noted that the 'private rented sector offer' is not the only avenue by which a duty owed to an applicant for homelessness assistance to a local housing authority in England may be brought to an end by means of accommodation being secured for him or her in the private rented sector. In fact, the amendments to HA 1996, Pt 7 made by the HRA 2017 (for applications for homelessness assistance made to local housing authorities in England on or after 3 April 2018) mean that discharge into the private

rented sector is likely to become more common. But the 'private rented sector offer' is the only such avenue which places the applicant in a more advantageous position if he or she re-applies for homelessness assistance within two years of accepting such an offer. See Chapter 16 for a full discussion of the various duties that may be owed to a homeless applicant and the various ways in which they may be brought to an end.

10.136 Where an applicant has accepted a private rented sector offer[1], and subsequently makes a fresh application for homelessness assistance to a local housing authority in England within two years of the date of his or her acceptance of the offer, having been given a valid Housing Act 1988, s 21 notice, he or she will be deemed to be homeless at the date of expiry of the notice[2].

[1] HA 1996, s 193(7AA)–(7AC).
[2] HA 1996, s 195A(2). Note, that as a result of the new HA 1996, s 175(5) (inserted by HRA 2017 s 1(3) for applications for homelessness assistance made to local housing authorities in England on or after 3 April 2018) *any* applicant who has been served with a valid HA 1988, s 21 notice will be deemed to be threatened with homelessness in the 56-day period preceding the expiry of the notice. See **10.112** and **10.144–10.147**.

10.137 To obtain the benefit of this provision, the fresh application must be made within two years of the date of acceptance of the private rented sector offer, not the date when the tenancy is granted or when it actually began[1].

[1] HA 1996, s 195A(1).

10.138 Providing he or she is eligible for assistance[1], the local housing authority will owe the HA 1996, s 189B(2)[2] relief duty, and must take reasonable steps to help the applicant to secure that suitable accommodation becomes available for his or her occupation. Those reasonable steps might include negotiating with the landlord for a further assured shorthold tenancy.

[1] See Chapter 11.
[2] As inserted by HRA 2017, s 5(2) for applications for homelessness assistance made to local housing authorities in England on or after 3 April 2018. See **15.138–15.189**.

10.139 However, if the performance of the HA 1996, s 189B(2)[1] relief duty does not result in suitable accommodation becoming available for the applicant's occupation then, when the HA 1996, s 189B(2)[2] relief duty comes to an end, the local housing authority will have to secure alternative accommodation for the applicant and his or her household pursuant to the HA 1996, s 193(2) main housing duty 'regardless of whether the applicant has a priority need'[3].

[1] As inserted by HRA 2017, s 5(2) for applications for homelessness assistance made to local housing authorities in England on or after 3 April 2018. See **15.138–15.189**.
[2] As inserted by HRA 2017, s 5(2) for applications for homelessness assistance made to local housing authorities in England on or after 3 April 2018. See **15.138–15.189**.
[3] HA 1996, s 195A(1).

10.140 For that reason, it is important not to delay the making of an application. If the applicant were to wait to make his or her application until after two years from the date of his or her acceptance of the private rented sector offer had elapsed, this special deeming provision would not apply[1].

[1] The applicant will have been advised of the importance of making a further application within two years of the date of his or her acceptance of the private rented sector offer when the offer

was first made (HA 1996, s 193(7AB)(c)). This notification provision does not apply to applicants who were restricted cases (HA 1996, s 193(7AB)(c)).

10.141 This special provision does not apply to applicants to whom the main housing duty at HA 1996, s 193(2) is only owed because of the presence in his or her household of a restricted person[1]. Applicants in those circumstances would have to be homeless applying the usual rules and also have a priority need in order to be owed the HA 1996, s 193(2) main housing duty.

[1] HA 1996, s 195A(5) as amended by HRA 2017, s 4(4) for applications for homelessness assistance made to local housing authorities in England on or after 3 April 2018. For 'restricted person' see HA 1996, s 184(7) and **9.54–9.56, 9.126–9.130** and **11.163–11.164**.

10.142 This special deeming provision only applies once. If an applicant in these circumstances accepts a further private rented sector offer and that accommodation subsequently comes to an end within two years of the date of that acceptance, the usual rules governing whether or not the applicant is homeless would apply and the applicant would need to have a priority need in order to be owed the HA 1996, s 193(2) main housing duty[1].

[1] HA 1996, s 195A(6) as amended by HRA 2017, s 4(4) for applications for homelessness assistance made to local housing authorities in England on or after 3 April 2018.

10.143 In Wales the duty to secure accommodation under H(W)A 2014, s 75(1), may be brought to an end[1] by acceptance of an offer of suitable accommodation under an assured tenancy (including an assured shorthold tenancy)[2] or by rejection of a private rented sector offer[3] as defined in H(W)A 2014, s 76(4). However, there is no equivalent deeming provision under H(W)A 2014, Pt 2. Applicants in Wales who accept an offer of an assured shorthold tenancy and are subsequently given a valid Housing Act 1988, s 21 notice, must, on later re-applications, satisfy the same conditions as any other applicant who applies to a local housing authority for help in retaining or obtaining accommodation.

[1] See **17.158–17.197**.
[2] H(W)A 2014, s 76(2)(b). See **17.161–17.164**.
[3] H(W)A 2014, s 76(3)(b). See **17.165–17.178**.

THREATENED WITH HOMELESSNESS

10.144 If it is likely that an applicant will become homeless (within the extended definition explained in this Chapter) within 56 days, that person is 'threatened with homelessness'[1]. In practice, many homeless applicants are likely to be threatened with homelessness rather than being actually homeless when they first make their application to a local housing authority for accommodation or assistance in obtaining accommodation. The Codes advise that local housing authorities should not wait for homelessness to be imminent before providing assistance[2].

[1] HA 1996, s 175(4) as amended by HRA 2017, s 1(2) for applications for homelessness assistance made to local housing authorities in England on or after 3 April 2018; H(W)A 2014, s 55(4).
[2] English Code, para 11.6. Welsh Code, paras 8.4–8.5.

10.145 Where a local housing authority has reason to believe that an applicant 'may be threatened with homelessness', it is subject to the duty to accept the application and either make inquiries (where the application is made to a local housing authority in England)[1] or undertake an assessment (where the application is made to a local housing authority in Wales)[2]. If, upon concluding its inquiries or its assessment, the local housing authority decides that the applicant is eligible and threatened with homelessness then, irrespective of the personal circumstances of the applicant, a single duty arises to take reasonable steps to help to secure that accommodation does not cease to be available for the applicant's occupation[3]. Where the application is made to a local housing authority in England, a further duty will also be owed, to assess the applicant's case and prepare a personalised housing plan[4].

[1] HA 1996, s 184(1). *R v Newham London Borough Council ex p Khan & Hussain* (2001) 33 HLR 269, QBD. See also **8.69–8.74**.
[2] H(W)A 2014, s 62(1). See also **9.12–9.14**.
[3] HA 1996, s 195(2) as amended by HRA 2017, s 4(2) for applications for homelessness assistance made to local housing authorities in England on or after 3 April 2018; H(W)A 2014, ss 65–66(1). See **15.87–15.137** (England) and **17.45–17.72** (Wales).
[4] HA 1996, s 189A as inserted by HRA 2017, s 3(1) for applications for homelessness assistance made to local housing authorities in England on or after 3 April 2018. See **15.62–15.86**.

10.146 There is obviously a wide range of circumstances in which an applicant may face the prospect of homelessness within 56 days. One of the more common arises where an applicant has been served with a Housing Act 1988, s 21 notice. An applicant for homelessness assistance to a local housing authority in England who has been served with a valid Housing Act 1988, s 21 notice will be deemed to be threatened with homelessness throughout the 56-day period leading up to the expiry of the notice[1]. Another common scenario is where an applicant has been informed that a court has issued a warrant for his or her eviction and there are fewer than 56 days left before the date scheduled for execution of the warrant[2]. If an applicant in these circumstances is not already homeless, he or she will be threatened with homelessness[3].

[1] HA 1996, s 175(5), as inserted by HRA 2017, s 1(3) for applications for applications for homelessness assistance made to local housing authorities in England on or after 3 April 2018. See **10.112**.
[2] *R (Sacupima) v Newham London Borough Council* (2001) 33 HLR 2, CA.
[3] See **10.110–11.116** for further discussion of the effect of imminent or actual possession proceedings.

10.147 Prior to the coming into force of H(W)A 2014, Pt 2 and the amendments to HA 1996, Pt 7 introduced by HRA 2017[1], a person would have been regarded as being threatened with homelessness where it was likely that he or she would become homeless within 28 days[2]. The duty owed to such a person would vary according to whether he or she had a priority need[3] and whether he or she had become threatened with homeless intentionally[4]. The extension of the time period during which a person is to be regarded as threatened with homelessness and the widening of the scope of the duty owed to such applicants denote a clear policy shift in both England and Wales, placing a greater emphasis on 'prevention'[5], ie assisting applicants at an early stage[6], and increasing the help available to those who would previously have received only limited assistance, with the intention that fewer households should experience the trauma of homelessness[7].

1   For applications for homelessness assistance made to local housing authorities in England on or after 3 April 2018.
2   For a discussion of the rules applicable in Wales prior to the coming into force of H(W)A 2014, Pt 2 see the third edition of this book (Jan Luba QC and Liz Davies, 3rd edn, 2012) and for the rules applicable in England prior to the coming into force of the amendments to HA 1996, Pt 7 introduced by HRA 2017, see the fourth edition (Jan Luba QC, Liz Davies and Connor Johnston, 4th edn, 2016).
3   See CHAPTER 12.
4   See CHAPTER 13 on becoming homeless intentionally.
5   See **15.87–15.137** and **17.45–17.72** for a full discussion of the scope of the new prevention duties.
6   English Code, para 1.9; Welsh Code, para 8.4.
7   Welsh Code, p 97 and paras 12.1–12.3.

Chapter 11

ELIGIBILITY FOR ASSISTANCE

Contents

INTRODUCTION

Overview

11.1 Not everyone qualifies for help from a local housing authority under the homelessness provisions. There is an 'eligibility' test and, because of that, one of the first inquiries that a local housing authority must make of an applicant for assistance is whether he or she is eligible to obtain any help at all[1].

[1] Housing Act 1996, s 184(1)(a); Housing (Wales) Act 2014, s 62(4).

11.2 As this chapter will demonstrate, 'eligibility' normally (but not exclusively) depends on the immigration status of the person seeking assistance. For this reason, both those who advise the homeless, and the staff who receive and determine their applications, need a familiarity with the homelessness eligibility rules set out here, and also with the basic rules of UK immigration control[1]. Self-evidently, a system which discriminates between potential service-users on the basis of nationality may lay itself open to a complaint of discrimination. Not surprisingly, the impact of the anti-discrimination provisions of the Human Rights Act, Sch 1, Art 14 on the eligibility test has already been explored in the courts[2].

[1] Immigration law is beyond the scope of this book. Standard texts include MacDonald and Toal *MacDonald's Immigration Law and Practice* (9th edn, 2015).
[2] *R (Morris) v Westminster City Council* [2005] EWCA Civ 1184, [2006] HLR 8, CA; *Bah v UK* App No 56328/07 [2011] ECHR 1448, [2012] HLR 2, ECtHR. See **11.154–11.156**.

11.3 The normal rule is that anyone is able to apply for help to any local housing authority, whatever his or her connection with the district of that particular local housing authority (or even if he or she has no connection with the UK at all). When the homelessness safety net was first brought into law by the Housing (Homeless Persons) Act 1977, it contained no eligibility test at all. Anyone from anywhere could apply[1]. It was left to the courts to identify the first ineligible categories: those who had entered the country unlawfully and those who, having entered lawfully, remained unlawfully in the UK[2].

1   *R v Hillingdon London Borough Council ex p Streeting* [1980] 3 All ER 413, [1980] 1 WLR 1425, CA.
2   See *R v Hillingdon London Borough Council ex p Streeting* [1980] 3 All ER 413, [1980] 1 WLR 1425, CA per Lord Denning MR at 1434.

11.4 But nowadays the modern statutory regime contains sophisticated exclusion provisions. The general rule, that homelessness assistance is available to all, is preserved. However, the Housing Act 1996 (HA 1996), Pt 7, at ss 185 and 186, and Housing (Wales) Act 2014 (H(W)A 2014), Pt 2, at s 61 and Sch 2, provide for the exclusion of specific categories of applicants. As a result, eligibility is defined in the negative. A person is *not excluded* from homelessness assistance *unless* caught by the provisions of either HA 1996, s 185 or s 186 or H(W)A 2014, Sch 2, paras 1 and 2[1].

1   HA 1996, s 183(2); H(W)A 2014, s 99.

11.5 The largest excluded group comprises those rendered ineligible either by HA 1996, s 185, or by H(W)A 2014, Sch 2, para 1, which both contain two categories of 'persons from abroad'. They are:

(1)   'persons subject to immigration control'; and
(2)   'other persons from abroad'.

11.6 Anyone falling within the first category will be excluded from homelessness assistance, unless he or she is within one of the classes of persons prescribed as eligible by regulations[1]. Anyone falling within the second category will be excluded from homelessness assistance if he or she is not habitually resident[2], unless he or she falls within one of the groups of people prescribed as exempt from the habitual residence test[3], or falls within the two other classes of people[4] prescribed as excluded by the regulations[5].

1   HA 1996, s 185(2); H(W)A 2014, Sch 2, para 1(2). The relevant Regulations for England are the Allocation of Housing and Homelessness (Eligibility) (England) Regulations 2006, SI 2006/1294 (as amended), reg 5. The relevant regulations for Wales are the Allocation of Housing and Homelessness (Eligibility) (Wales) Regulations 2014, SI 2014/ 2603 (W 257), reg 5, which apply to the H(W)A 2014, Pt 2 by virtue of the saving provision contained in the Housing (Wales) Act 2014 (Commencement No 3 and Transitory, Transitional and Saving Provisions) Order 2015, SI 2015/1272 (W 88), art 5, both on the CD Rom with this book. See **11.101–11.121.**
2   See **11.130–11.136.**
3   See **11.137–11.40.**
4   See **11.141–11.153.**
5   HA 1996, s 185(3); SI 2006/1294, reg 6; H(W)A 2014, Sch 2, para 1(4); SI 2014/2603 (W 257), reg 6.

11.7 Though there are separate regulations governing eligibility for homelessness assistance in England and Wales respectively, the classes of eligible person contained within those regulations are identical. But this has not always been the case. In England, the current relevant regulations apply to applications for homelessness assistance made on or after 1 June 2006[1]. In Wales, the current regulations apply to applications made on or after 31 October 2014[2]. For applications to local housing authorities made *before* 1 June 2006 (England) or 31 October 2014 (Wales), the relevant regulations were considered in previous editions of this book[3].

[1]   SI 2006/1294, reg 8.
[2]   SI 2014/2603 (W 257), reg 8.
[3]   Luba & Davies (2006, 1st edn; 2010, 2nd edn; 2012, 3rd edn).

11.8 Often the most difficult question to answer in determining whether an applicant is eligible for homelessness assistance is whether he or she is subject to immigration control. This is the linchpin of eligibility, since it is necessary to answer this question in order to determine whether the applicant falls into either of the two categories of 'persons from abroad' rendered ineligible by HA 1996, s 185, or by H(W)A 2014, Sch 2, para 1, and if so which one. This difficulty can be particularly acute in instances where the applicant may have a right to reside as, or deriving from, an EEA national[1]. The law relating to the eligibility of EEA nationals is particularly complex and requires understanding not only of the Regulations made under HA 1996, s 185(2) and (3) and H(W)A 2014, Sch 2, paras 1(2) and (4), but also of the immigration status of EEA nationals and their family members. With that in mind, the remainder of this chapter is structured as follows:

- first, we will consider who is, and is not, a person subject to immigration control (including a discussion of the various EEA rights of residence)[2];
- second, we will go on to discuss the rules that must then be applied to determine whether an applicant is eligible[3];
- third, we will review the further, self-contained, sets of rules that must be applied in those cases where the applicant has an ineligible household member, or where the application for homelessness assistance is made to a local housing authority in the Isles of Scilly[4].

[1]   It is to be expected that the law relating to the rights of EEA nationals to reside in the UK and the rules governing their eligibility for homelessness assistance will change significantly following Brexit. What these changes may be and when they may come into effect are, at the time of writing, a matter of speculation. This chapter states the law currently in force.
[2]   See **11.26–11.93**.
[3]   See **11.94–11.172**.
[4]   See **11.154–11.174**.

11.9 The other provisions relating to eligibility, HA 1996, s 186 and H(W)A 2014, Sch 2, para 2, catch the ever-diminishing number of pre-April 2000 asylum seekers who are eligible for homelessness assistance. The provisions will be repealed when the last of those cases passes through the asylum system[1]. At the date of writing the fifth edition of this book, any applicant who fell within these provisions would have made his or her application for homelessness assistance over 17 years previously. This edition does not contain commentary on these provisions. Readers who might still need that commentary are referred to the first or second editions of this book[2].

[1]   Immigration and Asylum Act 1999, ss 117(5), 169(3) and Sch 16; H(W)A 2014, Sch 2, para 2(1).

² Luba & Davies (2006, 1st edn; 2010, 2nd edn).

Eligible for what?

11.10 Applicants seeking homelessness assistance from local housing authorities in England who are not eligible are excluded from almost all the forms of assistance available under HA 1996, Pt 7[1] as amended by the Homelessness Reduction Act 2017 (HRA 2017)[2]. This is because HA 1996, Pt 7 defines 'assistance' to mean:

> ' . . . the benefit of any function under the following provisions of this Part relating to accommodation or assistance in obtaining accommodation[3].'

Someone who is not eligible will not be entitled to assistance under any of the duties or powers set out from HA 1996, s 188[4] onwards.

[1]   HA 1995, s 185(1).
[2]   For applications for homelessness assistance made to local housing authorities in England on or after 3 April 2018: Homelessness Reduction Act 2017 (Commencement and Transitional and Savings Provisions) Regulations 2018, SI 2018/167, reg 3.
[3]   HA 1996, s 183(2).
[4]   As amended by HRA 2017, s 5(4), for applications for homelessness assistance made to local housing authorities in England on or after 3 April 2018.

11.11 Applicants seeking homelessness assistance from local housing authorities in Wales who are not eligible are expressly excluded from the duties at H(W)A 2014, ss 66, 68, 73 and 75[1] only[2]. Functionally, this is very similar to the position faced by applicants in England. In Wales, such applicants will be excluded from the majority of forms of assistance under H(W)A 2014, Pt 2[3].

[1]   See **17.45–17.72, 17.118–17.133, 17.73–17.117** and **17.146–17.197** for the respective duties.
[2]   H(W)A 2014, Sch 2, para 1(1).
[3]   The distinction is that these applicants are still, notionally, entitled to seek interim accommodation pending review under H(W)A 2014, s 69(11), which finds it counterpart in HA 1996, s 188(3). It seems unlikely that the distinction will have any practical impact. The power to provide accommodation pending review is discretionary and in circumstances where there is no dispute that the applicant for homelessness assistance is not eligible, it seems inconceivable that this discretion would be exercised in his or her favour.

11.12 Applicants for homelessness assistance in either England or Wales who are not eligible, will still be able to obtain advice and information about homelessness (and about the prevention of homelessness) from the local housing authority, free of charge[1].

[1]   HA 1996, ss 179(1), as amended by HRA 2017, s 2, for applications for homelessness assistance made to local housing authorities in England on or after 3 April 2018, and 183(3); H(W)A 2014, ss 60(1), 61 and Sch 2, para 1(1). See CHAPTER 8 and **8.4–8.13**. The *Homelessness Code of Guidance for Local Authorities* (Ministry of Housing, Communities and Local Government, 2018) (the English Code), para 14.32 suggests that 'where an applicant is found not to be eligible for assistance, the housing authority must provide, or secure the provision, of information and advice as set out in section 179'. See further CHAPTER 20 for other help which may be available to an ineligible applicant from his or her local authority.

11.13 This very wide definition of the exclusion from assistance under HA 1996, Pt 7[1] and H(W)A 2014, Pt 2 makes it all the more important that the provisions of HA 1996, s 185 and H(W)A 2014, Sch 2, para 1 (and the regulations made under them) are looked at very carefully to ensure that only those whom HA 1996, Pt 7[2] and H(W)A 2014, Pt 2 define as ineligible are in fact excluded.

1   As amended by HRA 2017, for applications for homelessness assistance made to local housing authorities in England on or after 3 April 2018.
2   As amended by HRA 2017, for applications for homelessness assistance made to local housing authorities in England on or after 3 April 2018.

Going in and out of eligibility

11.14 Because eligibility is linked to immigration status, which can change, it is possible for an applicant's eligibility also to change.

11.15 The *first crucial date* for determining eligibility is the date on which the local housing authority reaches its decision as to whether the applicant is 'eligible'[1]. If there is then a review of that decision, the critical date becomes the date of the review decision[2]. It would be maladministration and unlawful for a local housing authority deliberately to delay its inquiries in the hope that an applicant's eligibility might change[3], although it may be sensible in particular circumstances to delay a determination of eligibility if a decision of the immigration authorities is a matter of hours or days away. If, at the first crucial date, the applicant is 'eligible', then the appropriate service under HA 1996, Pt 7[4] or H(W)A 2014, Pt 2 must be provided.

1   Unless the applicant has applied for homelessness assistance before 1 June 2006 (local housing authorities in England) or 31 October 2014 (local housing authorities in Wales), in which case transitional provisions state that his or her eligibility will be determined by the relevant Regulations in force at the date of his or her application (Allocation of Housing and Homelessness (Eligibility) (England) Regulations 2006, SI 2006/1294, reg 8; Allocation of Housing and Homelessness (Eligibility) (Wales) Regulations 2014, SI 2014/2603 (W 257), reg 8.
2   *Ealing London Borough Council v Surdonja* [2001] QB 97, CA; and *Mohammed v Hammersmith and Fulham London Borough Council* [2001] UKHL 57, [2002] 1 AC 547, HL.
3   *Robinson v Hammersmith & Fulham London Borough Council* [2006] EWCA Civ 1122, [2007] HLR 7, CA.
4   As amended by HRA 2017, for applications for homelessness assistance made to local housing authorities in England on or after 3 April 2018.

11.16 The *second crucial date* is the date on which the applicant's immigration status changes. The consequences of a change in immigration status (which vary according to whether the application for homelessness assistance is made in England or Wales and which duty is owed at the time) are as follows:

- if the applicant is owed the HA 1996, s 195(2)[1] or H(W)A 2014, s 66[2] prevention duty then that duty will end upon the applicant being given notice that the local housing authority is satisfied that he or she is no longer eligible for assistance[3];
- if the applicant is owed the HA 1996, s 188(1)[4] or H(W)A 2014, s 68[5] interim accommodation duty then that duty will end upon the applicant being given notice that the local housing authority is satisfied that he or she is no longer eligible for assistance[6];

- if the applicant is owed the HA 1996, s 189B(2)[7] or H(W)A 2014, s 73[8] relief duty then that duty will end upon the applicant being given notice that the local housing authority is satisfied that he or she is no longer eligible for assistance[9];
- if the applicant is owed the HA 1996, s 193(2)[10] or H(W)A 2014, s 75[11] main housing duty then that duty will end upon the applicant ceasing to be eligible for assistance (England)[12] or being given notice that the local housing authority is satisfied that he or she is no longer eligible for assistance (Wales)[13];
- if the applicant is owed the HA 1996, s 190(2)[14] short-term accommodation duty then the fact that the applicant is no longer eligible for assistance will be of no effect[15];
- if the applicant is owed the HA 1996, s 193C(4) accommodation duty[16], owed to applicants who have deliberately and unreasonably refused to co-operate, then that duty will end upon the applicant ceasing to be eligible for assistance[17];
- if the homeless applicant has passed through HA 1996, Pt 7[18] or H(W)A 2014, Pt 2 into longer-term social housing allocated under HA 1996, Pt 6, or has accepted an offer of accommodation in the private sector which brought the duty owed to him or her to an end, the change in eligibility does not impact directly on his or her status as a tenant. However, the underlying change in the person's immigration status which led to the change in his or her eligibility may well have a knock on effect on his or her legal right to maintain any tenancy[19].

---

[1] As inserted by HRA 2017, s 4(2), for applications for homelessness assistance made to local housing authorities in England on or after 3 April 2018. See **15.87–15.137.**

[2] See **17.45–17.72.**

[3] HA 1996, s 195(5) and (8)(e), as amended by HRA 2017, s 4(2), for applications for homelessness assistance made to local housing authorities in England on or after 3 April 2018; H(W)A 2014, s 79(1) and (2). See **15.126–15.127** and **17.192.**

[4] As amended by HRA 2017, s 5(4), or applications for homelessness assistance made to local housing authorities in England on or after 3 April 2018. See **16.37–16.73.**

[5] See **17.118–17.133.**

[6] HA 1996, s 188(1ZA)(a) and (1ZB)(a), as inserted by HRA 2017, s 5(4), for applications for homelessness assistance made to local housing authorities in England on or after 3 April 2018; H(W)A 2014, s 79(1) and (2). See **16.56–16.65** and **17.192.**

[7] As inserted by HRA 2017, s 5(2), or applications for homelessness assistance made to local housing authorities in England on or after 3 April 2018. See **15.138–15.189.**

[8] See **17.73–7.117.**

[9] HA 1996, s 189B(5) and (7)(e), as inserted by HRA 2017, s 5(2), for applications for homelessness assistance made to local housing authorities in England on or after 3 April 2018; H(W)A 2014, s 79(1) and (2). See **15.178–15.179** and **17.192.**

[10] See **16.94–16.199.**

[11] See **17.146–17.197.**

[12] See **16.124–16.126.** On the strict wording of HA 1996, s 193(6)(a), it would appear that the duty automatically ceases. See *Faizi v Brent London Borough Council* [2015] EWHC 2449 (Admin), Admin Ct dealing with the analogous provision under HA 1996, s 193(5). However, normally a decision that the applicant is no longer eligible should be notified to the applicant in the usual way (providing reasons and notifying him or her of the right to a review). See *Tower Hamlets London Borough Council v Deugi* [2006] EWCA Civ 159, [2006] HLR 28, CA at [33], where May LJ doubted whether a loss of eligibility required a decision under HA 1996, s 193(6)(a), since the local housing authority had no discretion, but recognised that there may be a dispute over the decision that eligibility has been lost.

[13] H(W)A 2014, s 79(1) and (2). See **17.192.**

[14] As amended by HRA 2017, s 5(5), for applications for homelessness assistance made on or after 3 April 2018. See **16.81–16.93.**

15 Presumably this reflects the practical reality that this is a short-term duty which would have come to an end after a reasonable period, in any event.

16 As inserted by HRA 2017, s 7(1) for applications for homelessness assistance made on or after 3 April 2018. See **16.200–16.216.**

17 HA 1996, s 193C(5)(a) as inserted by HRA 2017, s 7(1) for applications for homelessness assistance made on or after 3 April 2018. See fn 12 and **16.204.**

18 As amended by HRA 2017, for applications for homelessness assistance made to local housing authorities in England on or after 3 April 2018.

19 The Immigration Act 2014, Pt 3 places significant restrictions on the rights of certain nationals from outside of the EEA and Switzerland to rent accommodation in the UK in the private sector. Under the Immigration Act 2014, ss 20–28 a landlord who rents premises to an individual who is disqualified as a result of his or her immigration status from occupying premises under a residential tenancy agreement may be required to pay a financial penalty. This includes the situation where a person becomes disqualified as a result of a change in his or her immigration status during the course of their tenancy: Immigration Act 2014, s 22(5).

11.17 In either England or Wales, if an applicant who is being helped or accommodated under HA 1996, Pt 7[1] or H(W)A 2014, Pt 2, becomes ineligible owing to a change in his or her immigration status, this does not mean that he or she is instantly put out onto the streets. The expectation is that public authorities will behave reasonably which (in this context) means that accommodation provision should at least be continued for such time as gives the applicant a fair chance to find somewhere else to live[2].

1 As amended by HRA 2017, for applications for homelessness assistance made to local housing authorities in England on or after 3 April 2018.

2 *R v Secretary of State for the Environment ex p Shelter and the Refugee Council* [1997] COD 49, QBD; and *R v Newham London Borough Council ex p Ojuri (No 5)* (1999) 31 HLR 631, QBD. See further **16.71–16.73.**

11.18 Where an ineligible applicant (or an applicant who becomes ineligible) has children under the age of 18 (or is himself or herself a child), the local housing authority should make arrangements to refer the applicant's case to the relevant children's services authority or department, so that they can consider the exercise of their statutory duties and powers to protect children[1].

1 HA 1996, s 213A as amended by HRA 2017, s 4(7) for applications for homelessness assistance made on or after 3 April 2018; H(W)A 2014, s 96. See also *R (Badu) v Lambeth London Borough Council* [2005] EWCA Civ 1184, [2006] HLR 8, CA, and CHAPTER 20 for the range of statutory powers and duties available to children's services authorities.

11.19 Any applicant who is found to be ineligible for homelessness assistance may re-apply for homelessness assistance if his or her circumstances change such that he or she may have become eligible again[1].

1 Local housing authorities in England must accept fresh applications where there are 'new facts' that are not merely fanciful or trivial (*Begum v Tower Hamlets London Borough Council* [2005] EWCA Civ 340, [2005] HLR 34, CA; and *R (May) v Birmingham City Council* [2012] EWHC 1399 (Admin), (2012) July Legal Action, p 41, Admin Ct). See **8.78–8.83** and English Code, paras 18.11–18.13. Local housing authorities in Wales must accept fresh applications where there has been a material change in the applicant's circumstances or where there is new information that would affect the local housing authority's previous assessment: H(W)A 2014, s 62(1) and (2). See **8.84** and *Code of Guidance for Local Authorities on the Allocation of Accommodation and Homelessness* (Welsh Government, March 2016) (the Welsh Code), paras 10.10–10.12.

Whose eligibility?

11.20 The eligibility test is primarily directed to working out whether the applicant is eligible for, or excluded from, homelessness services. If the applicant is found not to be eligible, that will (subject to any review or appeal) be an end to his or her attempt to obtain homelessness services, even if other members of his or her household are plainly eligible for such services. The proper course in that situation is for the other household member(s) to apply to the local housing authority on behalf of the household[1]. However, where the applicant is eligible but a member of his or her household is not, then the special rules on disregarding ineligible household members or the rules on restricted persons may apply[2].

1   Any accommodation duty owed to the new applicant will extend to accommodating everyone else who falls within the definition of 'household' at HA 1996, s 176 and H(W)A 2014, s 56 (see **10.21–10.32**).
2   See **11.157–11.172**.

Making inquiries into eligibility

11.21 To work out whether either of the two statutory exclusion provisions (either at HA 1996, ss 185 and 186 or H(W)A 2014, Sch 2, paras 1 and 2) apply, it is first necessary to know something of the nationality and immigration status of the applicant. Inquiries[1] need to be made sensitively and without applying any form of discriminatory approach as between different applicants[2].

1   For a general discussion on the duty to make inquiries see CHAPTER 9.
2   English Code, para 7.4; Welsh Code, para 7.3.

11.22 Detailed discussion of an applicant's immigration status is outside the scope of this book, but some guidance in this complex area is provided at CHAPTER 7 and Annex 1 of the English Code and Chapter 7 and Annexes 4–6 of the Welsh Code.

11.23 The resolution of any uncertainty about an applicant's immigration or asylum status, or about the relevant dates (eg of entry into the UK or application for asylum) may require the help of the Home Office[1]. Local housing authorities are advised to contact the Home Office if there is any uncertainty arising from an application[2]. The Welsh Code recommends that the applicant is informed that an inquiry will be made before doing so[3]. This allows the applicant an opportunity to withdraw his or her application for homelessness assistance if she or he does not want such an inquiry to be made.

1   Contact details can be found at Welsh Code, Annex 5.
2   English Code, para 7.11; Welsh Code, para 7.15.
3   Welsh Code, para 7.15.

11.24 The Home Office is required to provide local housing authorities, on request, with information about whether a person falls within any particular statutory category (eg within Immigration and Asylum Act 1999, s 115)[1] or any other information required to enable local housing authorities to determine whether applicants are eligible for assistance[2]. Most requests for information are made, and the responses to them given, by telephone. Having regard to the complexity of the subject matter and the importance of accuracy, it may be sensible for a local housing authority receiving complex information from the Home Office (particularly if it is going to be used to make or support an adverse eligibility decision) to ask that the Home Office provide the information in writing. The Home Office need not provide written confirmation unless the request itself is in writing[3]. A local housing authority is entitled to rely on the Home Office's view of an applicant's current immigration status, and need not make inquiries as to, for example, the possible outcome of a pending appeal[4]. The Home Office may advise on an applicant's immigration status, but the decision on eligibility is for the local housing authority itself.

[1] Which excludes 'persons subject to immigration control' from housing benefit and is referred to at HA 1996, s 185(2A) and H(W)A 2014, Sch 2, para 1(3).
[2] HA 1996, s 187(1) and (2); H(W)A 2014, Sch 2, paras 3(1) and (2).
[3] HA 1996, s 187(2); H(W)A 2014, Sch 2, para 3(2).
[4] *Burns v Southwark London Borough Council* [2004] EWHC 1901 (Admin), [2004] All ER (D) 328 (Jul), Admin Ct.

11.25 If the Home Office does provide information to a local housing authority, it is then under a continuing obligation to notify that local housing authority, in writing, if there are any subsequent applications, decisions or other changes of circumstance affecting the particular applicant's status[1]. This continuing obligation is obviously of crucial importance if the applicant's immigration status is under review (or awaiting an initial decision or subject to an appeal) when the local housing authority makes its first request for information.

[1] HA 1996, s 187(3); H(W)A 2014, Sch 2, para 3(3). From the wording, it appears that the Home Office is obliged to notify these changes of circumstances in writing, whether or not the information originally provided was provided in writing or verbally.

WHO IS, AND IS NOT, SUBJECT TO IMMIGRATION CONTROL?

Overview

11.26 The starting point is the special meaning of 'subject to immigration control'. It means 'a person who is subject to immigration control within the meaning of the Asylum and Immigration Act 1996'[1]. The Asylum and Immigration Act 1996 itself states:

'. . . "person subject to immigration control" means a person who under the 1971 Act requires leave to enter or remain in the United Kingdom (whether or not such leave has been given)[2].'

For these purposes, it is important to emphasise that a person (usually an EEA national or a person claiming to exercise rights derived from an EEA national) who does not require leave to enter but who does require leave to remain, is a person subject to immigration control[3]. It is only a person who requires neither leave to enter nor leave to remain who is not subject to immigration control.

[1] HA 1996, s 185(2).
[2] Asylum and Immigration Act 1996, s 13(2).
[3] *Abdi v Barnet London Borough Council, Ismail v Barnet London Borough Council* [2006] EWCA Civ 383, [2006] HLR 23, CA. *See also Ehiabor v Kensington & Chelsea Royal London*

Borough Council [2008] EWCA Civ 1074, [2008] All ER (D) 104 (May), CA, where a child born in the UK, without British Citizenship, to a Nigerian mother was found to be subject to immigration control: although he was not required to apply for leave to remain in order to stay in the country, had he left the country and sought to return he would have required leave to enter. The Court of Appeal, at [25] endorsed a concession made on the part of the Appellant that the expression 'person from abroad' refers to a person who is ineligible for assistance under HA 1996, s 185(2)-(4): 'such a person may have physically come to this country from a foreign country. However, he need not necessarily have done so.' See further *Ismail v Newham London Borough Council* [2018] EWCA Civ 665, CA: another case concerning a child born in the UK.

11.27 Tracing that route back to the Immigration Act 1971[1] reveals that:

- British citizens;
- Commonwealth citizens with the right of abode in the UK;
- European Economic Area (EEA) nationals and Swiss nationals exercising certain Treaty rights[2] (see Box 2 at **11.29**);
- people exercising rights derived from EEA or Swiss nationals exercising certain Treaty rights[3];
- certain people who are exempt from immigration control under the Immigration Acts (diplomats and their family members based in the UK, and some military personnel); and
- Irish citizens with a Common Travel Area[4] entitlement,

do *not* require leave to enter or remain in the UK and therefore cannot be 'persons subject to immigration control'[5].

[1] Immigration Act 1971, ss 1–3.

[2] Immigration Act 1988, s 7; Immigration (European Economic Area) Regulations 2016, SI 2016/1052, regs 13–15 at APPENDIX 2. From 1 June 2002, Swiss nationals have had the same rights to freedom of movement and social security within the EEA as EEA nationals and so Swiss nationals fall within the definition of EEA nationals at Immigration (European Economic Area) Regulations 2016, SI 2016/1052, reg 2. All references to 'EEA nationals' in this book include Swiss nationals.

[3] Immigration (European Economic Area) Regulations 2016, SI 2016/1052, reg 16. See **11.32–11.93**.

[4] See Box 1. In the case of *McCarthy v Brent London Borough Council* (2016) November *Legal Action*, p 41, County Court at Central London the local housing authority unsuccessfully sought to persuade the court that Irish Citizens with a Common Travel Area entitlement were subject to immigration control.

[5] Immigration Act 1971, ss 1–3; Immigration Act 1988, s 7; Immigration (European Economic Area) Regulations 2016, SI 2016/1052. See English Code, paras 7.8–7.9. It is to be expected that the law relating to the rights of EEA nationals to reside in the UK will change significantly following Brexit. What these changes may be and when they may come into effect are, at the time of writing, a matter of speculation. This chapter states the law currently in force.

11.28 The legal definition of the term 'the United Kingdom' and its related parts is given in Box 1.

Box 1

Key Geographic Terms:

England: counties established by Local Government Act 1972, s 1, Greater London area and the Isles of Scilly[1].

Great Britain: England, Wales, and Scotland[2].

United Kingdom: England, Wales, Scotland and Northern Ireland[3].

Common Travel Area (CTA): England, Wales, Scotland, Northern Ireland, Republic of Ireland, Isle of Man, and the Channel Islands[4].

---

[1] Interpretation Act 1978, s 5 and Sch 1.
[2] Union of Scotland Act 1706.
[3] Interpretation Act 1978, s 5 and Sch 1.
[4] Immigration Act 1971, s 1(3).

11.29 Box 2 shows which countries are members of the European Union (EU) and/or members of the wider European Economic Area (EEA)[1]. For these purposes, nationals of Iceland, Liechtenstein, Norway, and Switzerland have the same rights to enter or reside as nationals of most of the EU Member States[2]. Rights for nationals of Croatia[3] are slightly different from those enjoyed by nationals of other EEA states[4]. We refer throughout this chapter to nationals of EEA Member States, by which we mean all the EU Member States, plus the three additional EEA Member States and Switzerland.

Box 2

The European Union (EU):

Member States: Austria, Belgium, Bulgaria, Croatia, Cyprus, Czech Republic, Denmark, Estonia, Finland, France, Germany, Greece, Hungary, Ireland, Italy, Latvia, Lithuania, Luxembourg, Malta, Netherlands, Poland, Portugal, Romania, Slovakia, Slovenia, Spain, Sweden and the UK.

The European Economic Area (EEA):

All EU States[5] plus Iceland, Liechtenstein and Norway.

Switzerland is not part of the EEA, but its nationals are treated as EEA nationals for these purposes[6].

---

[1] Croatia acceded to the EU on 1 July 2013. Albania, Montenegro, Serbia, Turkey and the former Yugoslav Republic of Macedonia are 'candidate countries' for accession to the EU. Bosnia and Herzegovina, and Kosovo are potential 'candidate countries'. See www.europa.eu/about-eu/countries/index_en.htm for an up-to-date list. The UK is expected to leave the EU in due course.

2   Immigration (European Economic Area) Regulations 2016, SI 2016/1052. See Appendix 2 of this book.
3   See **11.88–11.92**.
4   The nationals of new member states are typically treated differently upon accession to the EU. Rights for nationals of the eight 2004 Accession States ('A8 states') were initially subject to derogation between 1 May 2004 and 30 April 2009 (Accession (Immigration and Worker Registration) Regulations 2004, SI 2004/1219). This period was subsequently extended to 30 April 2011 (Accession (Immigration and Worker Registration) (Amendment) Regulations 2009, SI 2009/892). This extension was recently held to be unlawful by the Court of Appeal in *Secretary of State for Work and Pensions v Gubeladze* [2017] EWCA Civ 1751, CA. The nature and extent of the practical ramifications of this decision remain to be seen. But, in any event, from 1 May 2011 nationals of the A8 member states have been treated in the same way as nationals of any other EEA member state, save that retained worker status is slightly different. The A8 states were the Czech Republic, Estonia, Hungary, Latvia, Lithuania, Poland, Slovakia and Slovenia. Rights for nationals of the two 2007 Accession States ('A2 states') were subject to derogation between 1 January 2007 and 31 December 2013 (Accession (Immigration and Worker Registration) Regulations 2006, SI 2006/3317). From 1 January 2014 nationals of the A2 member states have been treated in the same way as nationals of any other EEA member state, save that retained worker status is slightly different. The A2 states were Romania and Bulgaria. Rights for Croatian nationals have been subject to derogation since 1 July 2013. After 30 June 2018, Croatian nationals are to be treated in the same way as other EEA nationals. See **111.88–11.92**.
5   The Channel Islands, Isle of Man and Gibraltar are not part of the EEA but are within the EU.
6   Immigration (European Economic Area) Regulations 2016, SI 2016/1052, reg 2.

11.30 Obviously, the lists given in these boxes will fluctuate from time to time. The most up-to-date list is at Annex 4 of the Welsh Code.

11.31 In some instances it will be easy to establish whether an individual falls within the list at **11.29**. For example, it will often be fairly easy to establish whether an individual has British citizenship, from which it can then be concluded that he or she is not subject to immigration control. Difficulties tend to arise in cases involving EEA nationals. In these cases it is not sufficient to inquire whether the individual has citizenship of a country within the EEA in order to determine whether he or she is subject to immigration control. In addition to that inquiry it will be necessary to establish whether he or she is exercising EU Treaty rights, or has derived a right to reside from another person who is exercising his or her EU Treaty rights. Answering these questions is rarely straightforward. For that reason, the remainder of this part of the chapter will be given over to discussing the various rights to reside available to EEA nationals and their family members[1].

1   See **11.32–11.93**.

Rights to reside for EEA nationals and their family members

11.32 The principal rights of residence are those recognised in domestic law by the Immigration (European Economic Area) Regulations 2016, regs 13–16[1]. Those regulations are derived from the Freedom of Movement in the European Union Directive[2]. The Court of Justice of the European Union (CJEU) has held that European Union Treaties and Regulations can confer rights of residence directly, whether or not those rights are specifically found in domestic law[3]. The specific rights that the CJEU has recognised in recent years have been given effect in domestic legislation, to some extent in Immigration (European Economic Area) Regulations 2016, reg 16 which contains the concept of 'derivative rights'[4]. However, the principle remains that EU Treaties and EU Regulations can confer rights of residence directly and there may be other rights of residence which have not yet been considered by legislators or by the CJEU[5]. Nationals of EEA member states who have never exercised any right of freedom of movement under EU Treaty rights are not beneficiaries of rights of free movement under EU Directive 2004/38/EC[6].

¹ SI 2016/1052, at Appendix 2. References in Allocation of Housing and Homelessness (Eligibility) (England) Regulations 2006, SI 2006/1294 (at Appendix 2) to Immigration (European Economic Area) Regulations 2006, SI 2006/1003 should be read as referring to Immigration (European Economic Area) Regulations 2016, SI 2016/1052. See SI 2016/1052, Sch 7, para 1.
² Directive 2004/38/EC.
³ *Baumbast & R v Secretary of State for the Home Department* [2002] ECR I-7091, ECJ; *Harrow London Borough Council v Ibrahim* [2010] EUECJ 310–08, [2010] HLR 31, CJEU and *Teixeira v Lambeth London Borough Council* [2010] EUECJ 48008, [2010] HLR 32, CJEU.
⁴ SI 2016/1052, reg 16. See **11.66–11.87**.
⁵ See **11.93**.
⁶ *McCarthy v SSHD* [2011] C-434/09, [2011] All ER (EC) 729, CJEU.

11.33 The Immigration (European Economic Area) Regulations 2016 confer four rights of residence:

- an initial right of residence[1];
- an extended right of residence[2];
- a permanent right of residence;[3] and
- a derivative right of residence[4].

¹ SI 2016/1052, reg 13. See **11.35–11.36**.
² SI 2016/1052, reg 14. See **11.37–11.60**.
³ SI 2016/1052, reg 15. See **11.61–11.65**.
⁴ SI 2016/1052, reg 16. See **11.66–11.87**.

11.34 Each will be examined in turn. Rights of residence will be most readily apparent where the person has a registration certificate or residence card issued by the Secretary of State. However, the registration certificate or residence card is simply confirmation of the person's right, rather than the conferring of a right to reside. Where there is no residence certificate or residence card, local housing authorities will have to decide for themselves whether someone has a right of residence under EU law[1].

¹ *Secretary of State for Work and Pensions v Dias* [2011] C-325/09, [2011] 3 CMLR 1103, CJEU. Indeed, the registration certificate or residence card will only prove the holder's right of residence at the date of issue of the document, SI 2016/1052, regs 17(8) and 18(7).

The 'initial right of residence'

11.35 Regulation 13[1] of the Immigration (European Economic Area) Regulations 2016[2] gives all EEA nationals and their family members[3] an initial right of residence in the UK for a period not exceeding three months, upon condition that each person has a valid identity card issued by an EEA member state or a valid passport.

¹ Immigration (European Economic Area) Regulations 2016, SI 2016/1052, reg 13. The rules on eligibility for individuals with this right of residence are set out at **11.141–11.153**.
² SI 2016/1052.

3   Including 'family member who has retained the right of residence'. 'Family member' is defined
    at SI 2016/1052, reg 7 and 'family member who has retained the right of residence' at SI
    2016/1052, reg 10. See **11.54–11.60**.

11.36 There is an exception where the Secretary of State has decided that a
person's removal is justified for the purposes of public policy, public security or
public health, where the person has become an unreasonable burden on the
social assistance system of the UK or where the person has misused his or her
right to reside[1].

1   SI 2016/1052, reg 13(3) and (4).

The 'extended right of residence'

11.37 'Qualified persons' and their family members[1], including family members who have retained the right of residence[2], are entitled to an 'extended
right of residence' in the UK for so long as they remain qualified persons and/or
family members of qualified persons.[3]

1   As defined at Immigration (European Economic Area) Regulations 2016, SI 2016/1052, reg 7.
    See **11.54–11.60**.
2   As defined at SI 2016/1052, reg 10. See **11.60**.
3   SI 2016/1052, reg 14. The rules on eligibility for individuals with this right of residence are set
    out at **12.122–11.140**.

11.38 'Qualified person' is defined at reg 6 of the Immigration (European
Economic Area) Regulations 2016[1] as being a person who is an EEA national
and, in the UK, is:

- a job-seeker[2]; or
- a worker[3]; or
- a self-employed person[4]; or
- a self-sufficient person[5]; or
- a student[6].

Each of these concepts will now be explored in turn.

1   SI 2016/1052.
2   Defined at SI 2016/1052, reg 6(1). See **11.39**.
3   Defined at SI 2016/1052, regs 4(1)(a) and 6(2)–(3). See **11.40–11.46**.
4   Defined at SI 2016/1052, regs 4(1)(b) and 6(4). See **11.47–11.49**.
5   Defined at SI 2016/1052, reg 4(1)(c). See **11.50–11.52**.
6   Defined at SI 2016/1052, reg 4(1)(d). See **11.53**.

'JOB-SEEKER'

11.39 A 'job-seeker'[1] is defined as 'a person who enters the UK in order to
seek employment and can provide evidence that he is seeking employment and
has a genuine chance of being engaged'[2].

1   Defined at Immigration (European Economic Area) Regulations 2016, SI 2016/1052, reg 6(1).
2   SI 2016/1052, reg 6(1) and (5)–(7). See English Code, para 7.14(b).

'WORKER'

11.40 In order to qualify as a 'worker'[1] under this provision, the person must first be a national of an EEA Member State[2]. The term 'worker' is not defined in HA 1996, Pt 7[3] or regulations and nor is it exhaustively defined in EU legislation. The CJEU has emphasised that a narrow approach should *not* be taken:

> '[I]t is settled case law that the concept of worker has a specific Community meaning and must not be interpreted narrowly. It must be defined in accordance with objective criteria which distinguish an employment relationship by reference to the rights and duties of the person concerned. In order to be treated as a worker, a person must pursue an activity which is genuine and effective, to the exclusion of activities on such a small scale as to be regarded as purely marginal and ancillary. The essential feature of an employment relationship is that for a certain period of time a person performs services for and under the direction of another person in return for which he receives remuneration. By contrast, neither the *sui generis* nature of the employment relationship under national law, nor the level of productivity of the person concerned, the origin of the funds from which the remuneration is paid or the limited amount of the remuneration can have any consequence in regard to whether the person is a worker for the purposes of Community law . . . [4].'

[1] Defined at Immigration (European Economic Area) Regulations 2016, SI 2016/1052, regs 4(1)(a) and 6(2)–(3).
[2] See Box 2 at **11.29**.
[3] As amended by HRA 2017, for applications for homelessness assistance made to local housing authorities in England on or after 3 April 2018.
[4] *Kurz* [2002] ECR I-10691, para 32. See also *Vatsouras* [2009] ECR 1–4585.

11.41 A person will be a worker if he or she is actually working in the UK, whether full- or part-time. Any genuine and effective work should count, so long as it is not so irregular and/or so limited that it is a purely marginal and ancillary activity[1].

[1] *Levin* 53/81 [1982] ECR 1035; *Kempf* Case 139/85 [1986] ECR 1741; *Raulin* Case C-357/89 [1992] ECR 1027.

11.42 A person will retain the status of a worker for the purposes of these regulations[1] if he or she:

- has worked in the UK (at any time and even for a short period) but has become temporarily incapable of work as a result of an illness or accident[2]; or
- has worked in the UK for one year or more before becoming involuntarily unemployed, is registered as a jobseeker and either has been unemployed for no more than six months or can provide 'compelling evidence' that he or she is continuing to seek employment and has a genuine chance of being engaged[3]; or
- has worked in the UK for less than one year before becoming involuntarily unemployed and is registered as a jobseeker and has been unemployed for no more than six months[4]; or
- has worked in the UK (at any time and even for a short period), but has become involuntarily unemployed and has embarked on vocational training[5]; or

- has worked in the UK (at any time and even for a short period) and voluntarily given up work in the UK to take up vocational training related to his or her previous job[6].

1   Immigration (European Economic Area) Regulations 2016, SI 2016/1052, reg 6(2) based on *Scrivner Case 122/84* [1985] ECR 1027. Note that A8 workers requiring registration who had not completed 12 months' registered employment before 1 May 2011 do not retain worker status under this regulation on account of work done before that date. Any work which he or she does after 1 May 2011 will count for these purposes (SI 2016/1052, Sch 4, para 2). The same rule applies with the necessary changes made, to A2 nationals who had not completed 12 months' registered employment before 1 June 2014 (SI 2016/1052, Sch 4, para 2). Note also that this extended definition of 'worker' does not apply where a person is claiming a derivative right of residence, derived from his or her parent being a worker (SI 2016/1052, reg 16(7)(b) (see **11.76–11.79**)).
2   SI 2016/1052, reg 6(2)(a).
3   SI 2016/1052, reg 6(2)(b) and (7).
4   SI 2016/1052, reg 6(2)(c) and (3).
5   *Lair* Case 39/86 [1988] ECR 3161; and *Raulin* Case C-357/89 [1992] ECR 1027. SI 2016/1052, reg 6(2)(d).
6   *Raulin* Case C-357/89 [1992] ECR 1027. SI 2016/1052, reg 6(2)(e).

11.43 The Court of Appeal has held, in relation to both workers and self-employed persons[1], that if someone's illness means that he or she is unlikely to be able to work in the foreseeable future, then there are no realistic prospects of him or her being able to return to work and he or she is no longer a worker or a self-employed person[2].

1   See **11.47–11.49** for 'self-employed persons'.
2   *Konodyba v Kensington & Chelsea Royal London Borough Council* [2012] EWCA Civ 982, [2012] HLR 45 CA. See also *Samin v Westminster City Council* [2012] EWCA Civ 1468, [2013] HLR 7, CA, upheld by the Supreme Court in the conjoined appeals of *Samin v Westminster City Council, Mirga v Secretary of State for Work and Pensions* [2016] UKSC 1, [2016] 1 WLR 481, SC. The court held that the regulations denying support to former workers in these cases did not result in unlawful discrimination contrary to the Treaty on the Functioning of the EU.

11.44 Attempts to argue that people who have never worked in the UK are, nevertheless, 'workers' for the purpose of entitlement to job-seeker's allowance and Children Act assistance have failed[1]. A job-seeker who has never worked is not, therefore a 'worker'. Students and au pairs, working part-time, have been held by the Court of Appeal and the CJEU to be 'workers'[2].

1   *Collins v Secretary of State for Work and Pensions*, C-138/02 ECJ, 23 March 2004; and *Ali v SSHD* [2006] EWCA Civ 484, [2006] 3 CMLR 326, [2006] ELR 423, CA.
2   *Ozturk v Secretary of State for the Home Department* C-294/06 [2006] EWCA Civ 541, [2007] 1 WLR 508, CA, judgment 24 January 2008, ECJ.

11.45 The question as to whether an applicant is or is not a worker, is a question of fact for the local housing authority. In *R (Mohamed) v Harrow London Borough Council*[1], it was held that the local housing authority had not made any errors of law in concluding that a woman who had worked part-time for three months, finishing a year before her application for homelessness assistance, spoke little or no English, had two small children to look after and had not registered with an employment agency was not and had not retained the status of being a 'worker'. In *Barry v Southwark London Borough Council*[2], the local housing authority was wrong to decide that an applicant was not a 'worker' during a two-week period when he was employed by Group 4 Securicor for stewarding duties at the Wimbledon All England Tennis Championships. The work done was of economic value, there were PAYE deductions from his pay and the services provided by him to his employer were real and actual, and not merely marginal and ancillary[3]. In another case of a part-time worker earning a low income, the local housing authority made an error of law when it applied a test of whether the work produced enough income to cover 'reasonable living expenses'. The question of whether work is 'effective' is to be looked at from the view of the value of the work to the employer and not to the employee[4].

[1]   [2005] EWHC 3194 (Admin), [2006] HLR 18, Admin Ct.
[2]   [2008] EWCA Civ 1440, [2009] HLR 30, CA.
[3]   [2008] EWCA Civ 1440, [2009] HLR 30, CA per Arden LJ at [23].
[4]   *Amin v Brent London Borough Council* (2011) August *Legal Action*, p 41, Wandsworth County Court.

11.46 Expanding the definition of worker, the CJEU has held that a woman who gives up work because of the physical constraints of pregnancy and the aftermath of childbirth will retain her status as a 'worker', providing she is able to return to work or find another job within a reasonable period after the birth of her child[1].

[1]   *Saint Prix v Secretary of State for Work and Pensions* Case C507/12, [2014] PTSR 1448, CJEU. See *CS v Barnet London Borough Council* [2015] UKUT 0502 (AAC), UT and *Obulor v Secretary of State for the Home Department* [2015] UKUT 540 (IAC), UT for guidance on the application of these principles.

'Self-employed person'

11.47 A 'self-employed person'[1] is defined as 'a person who establishes himself in order to pursue activity as a self-employed person in accordance with Art 49 of the Treaty on the Functioning of the European Union'[2]. Article 49 refers to 'freedom of establishment', which is itself defined as 'the right to take up and pursue activities as self-employed persons and to set up and manage undertakings'. Self-employment is not confined to periods of actual work; a person remains self-employed if he or she is engaged on administrative, marketing or other tasks required to run or promote his or her business[3].

[1]   Defined at Immigration (European Economic Area) Regulations 2016, SI 2016/1052, regs 4(1)(b) and 6(4).
[2]   Immigration (European Economic Area) Regulations 2016, SI 2016/1052, reg 4(1)(b). The Treaty referred to is the Treaty of Lisbon (Official Journal C326, 26 October 2012).
[3]   *Secretary of State for Work and Pensions v JS (IS)* [2010] UKUT 240 (AAC), (2011) March *Legal Action*, p 21, UT.

11.48 In considering who is, and is not, a self-employed person the CJEU has an analagous approach to that which has been taken in respect of workers[1]:

'According to settled case law, the pursuit of an activity as an employed person or the provision of services for remuneration must be regarded as an economic activity within the meaning of Art. 2 of the EC Treaty (now, after amendment, Art. 2 EC), provided that the work performed is genuine and effective and not such as to be regarded as purely marginal and ancillary.

Since the essential characteristic of an employment relationship within the meaning of Art. 48 of the EC Treaty (now, after amendment, Art.39 EC) is the fact that for a certain period of time a person performs services for and under the direction of another person in return for which he receives remuneration, any activity which a person performs outside a relationship of subordination must be classified as an activity pursued in a self employed capacity for the purposes of Art.52 of the Treaty[2].'

[1]   See **11.40–11.46** for 'workers'.
[2]   *Jany* C-268/99, [2003] 2 CMLR 1, paras 33–34.

11.49 A person remains a self-employed person if he or she is temporarily unable to pursue his or her self-employment activity as a result of illness or accident[1]. But the Court of Appeal has held, in relation to both self-employed persons and workers, that if someone's illness means that he or she is unlikely to be able to work in the foreseeable future, then there are no realistic prospects of him or her being able to return to work and he or she is no longer a worker or a self-employed person[2]. A person will also retain his or her self-employed status where he or she has been compelled, because of an absence of work owing to circumstances beyond his or her control, to register as a jobseeker with the relevant employment office, having previously been self-employed for more than one year[3].

[1]   SI 2016/1052, reg 6(4).
[2]   *Konodyba v Kensington & Chelsea Royal London Borough Council* [2012] EWCA Civ 982, [2012] HLR 45 CA, and *Samin v Westminster City Council* [2012] EWCA Civ 1468, [2013] HLR 7, CA. The latter decision was upheld by the Supreme Court in the conjoined appeals of *Samin v Westminster City Council, Mirga v Secretary of State for Work and Pensions* [2016] UKSC 1, [2016] 1 WLR 481, SC. The court held that the regulations denying support to former workers in these cases did not result in unlawful discrimination contrary to the Treaty on the Functioning of the EU.
[3]   *Gusa v Minister for Social Protection* C-442/16, CJEU.

'SELF-SUFFICIENT PERSON'

11.50 A 'self-sufficient person'[1] is defined at Immigration (European Economic Area) Regulations 2016[2], reg 4(1)(c) as a person who has:

• sufficient resources not to become a burden on the social assistance system of the UK during his or her period of residence; and
• comprehensive sickness insurance cover in the UK.

[1]   Defined at Immigration (European Economic Area) Regulations 2016, SI 2016/1052, reg 4(1)(c).
[2]   SI 2016/1052.

11.51 The person's resources must be sufficient to ensure that his or her family members[1] also do not become a burden on the UK's social assistance system[2]. This does not mean that the person, or his or her family member, cannot have any recourse at all to the social assistance system on the UK. EU law has made it clear that the test is:

'as long as the beneficiaries of the right of residence do not become an unreasonable burden on the social assistance system of the host Member State they should not be expelled . . . The host Member State should examine whether it is a case of temporary difficulties and take into account the duration of residence, the personal circumstances and the amount of aid granted in order to consider whether the beneficiary has become an unreasonable burden on its social assistance system and to proceed to his expulsion'[3].

This means that a person, or his or her family member, who has a temporary need for homelessness assistance will not necessarily be 'an unreasonable burden' on the social assistance system of the UK, and may be able to make an application for homelessness assistance whilst still retaining his or her status as a self-sufficient person, (or as a family member of a self-sufficient person) and hence remaining a qualified person.

[1]   As defined at SI 2016/1052, reg 4(2).
[2]   SI 2016/1052, reg 4(3)(a). Resources will be regarded as sufficient in the circumstances set out in SI 2016/1052, reg 4.
[3]   Directive 2004/38/EC(16)). See also para 2.3.1 of Commission of the European Communities Communication to the European Parliament and the Council on guidance for better transposition and application of Directive 2004/38/EC on the right of citizens of the Union and their family members to move and reside freely within the territory of the Member States, COM009313 final and SI 2016/1052, reg 4(3).

11.52 The person's comprehensive sickness insurance must also cover his or her family members[1]. Comprehensive sickness insurance cover does not include the public healthcare system of the host state. That is, entitlement to free NHS treatment will not be sufficient[2].

[1]   SI 2016/1052, reg 4(3)(b).
[2]   *Ahmad v Secretary of State for the Home Department* [2014] EWCA Civ 998, [2015] 1 WLR 953, CA.

'STUDENT'

11.53 A student[1] is defined as a person who:

•   is enrolled for the principal purpose of following a course of study (which includes vocational training) at a public or private establishment which is financed from public funds or accredited by the Secretary of State;

•   has comprehensive sickness insurance cover in the United Kingdom; and

•   has assured the Secretary of State that he or she has sufficient resources not to become a burden on the UK's social assistance system[2].

The latter two requirements mirror those which are applicable to self-sufficient persons[3] meaning a person might retain his or her status as a student and a qualified person whilst also having a temporary need for homelessness assistance.

[1]   Defined at Immigration (European Economic Area) Regulations 2016, SI 2016/1052, reg 4(1)(d).
[2]   SI 2016/1052, reg 4(1)(d).
[3]   See **11.50–11.52**.

'FAMILY MEMBER'

11.54 'Family members'[1] are defined at Immigration (European Economic Area) Regulations 2016[2], reg 7 as:

- the EEA national's spouse or civil partner[3];
- any direct descendants of the EEA national, or of his or her spouse or civil partner, who are under 21, or who are dependent on the qualifying person, or his or her spouse or civil partner[4];
- any dependent direct relatives in the ascending line of the EEA national or his or her spouse or civil partner[5]; and
- any extended family member who has been issued with an EEA family permit, a registration certificate or residence card and continues to satisfy the conditions for the issue of the document[6].

[1] Defined at Immigration (European Economic Area) Regulations 2016, SI 2016/1052, reg 7.
[2] SI 2016/1052.
[3] SI 2016/1052, reg 7(1)(a). A 'spouse' means a person who is formally contracted to a legal marriage (*Netherlands v Reed 59/85* [1986] ECR 1283, ECJ; *R v Secretary of State for the Home Department ex p Monro-Lopez* [2007] Imm AR 11, QBD; and *Diatta v Land Berlin* [1986] 2 CMLR 164, ECJ). 'Civil partnership' is defined at Civil Partnership Act 2004, s 1. In both cases, the emphasis is on the legal condition, not on whether or not the parties continue to live together. A marriage or civil partnership only ends upon death, divorce, annulment, or dissolution of the civil partnership. A party to a marriage of convenience, or to a civil partnership of convenience, is excluded from the definition; SI 2016/1052, reg 2(1)).
[4] SI 2016/1052, reg 7(1)(b).
[5] SI 2016/1052, reg 7(1)(c).
[6] SI 2016/1052, reg 7(3). For 'extended family member', see **11.58–11.59**.

11.55 There are special rules for students[1].

[1] SI 2016/1052, reg 7(2).

11.56 'Family members' thus include children who are under 21, dependent children who are 21 or older, dependent parents, parents-in-law, and parents of a qualifying person's civil partner[1]. So long as children aged 21 or over are 'dependent' on the qualifying person, their ages are irrelevant. Children who are not dependent on the qualifying person, but are nevertheless under 21 (for example, an 18-year-old who is working) also fall within the definition.

[1] The inclusion of the word 'direct' in SI 2016/1052, reg 7 encompasses grandchildren (and hence grandparents) but not nephews or nieces (or, conversely, aunts or uncles): *Bigia v Entry Clearance Officer* [2009] EWCA Civ 79, CA per Maurice Kay LJ at [9].

11.57 Cohabiting partners, whether of the same sex or different sex, do *not* fall within the definition of 'spouse' or 'civil partner'. For cohabiting partners to be 'family members', they must be:

- the partner of an EEA national; and
- in a 'durable relationship' with him or her; and
- have been issued with an EEA family permit, registration certificate or residence card[1].

[1] SI 2016/1052, regs 7(3) and 8(5).

11.58 Other types of relationship could fall within the definition of 'extended family members'[1]. An 'extended family member' is one of the following:

(1)   a relative of an EEA national, or of his or her spouse or civil partner[2]:

(a) who is residing in a country other than the UK and is dependent upon the EEA national or is a member of his or her household; or

(b) who was residing in a country other than the UK and was dependent upon the EEA national or was a member of his or her household and is accompanying the EEA national to the UK or wishes to join the EEA national in the UK; or

(c) who was residing in a country other than the UK and was dependent upon the EEA national or was a member of his or her household and who has joined the EEA national in the UK and continues to be dependent upon the EEA national or to be a member of his or her household; or

(2) a relative of an EEA national or of his or her spouse or civil partner and who, on serious health grounds strictly requires the personal care of the EEA national, his or her spouse or civil partner; or

(3) a relative of an EEA national who would meet the requirements in the immigration rules (other than those relating to entry clearance) for indefinite leave to enter or remain in the UK as a dependent relative of the EEA national were the EEA national a person who is present and settled in the UK; or

(4) a partner (other than a civil partner) of an EEA national if he or she can prove that he or she is in a 'durable relationship'[3] with the EEA national[4].

[1]   SI 2016/1052, reg 8. See also *Secretary of State for the Home Department v Rahman* [2013] QB 249, [2013] 2 WLR 230, CJEU.
[2]   See SI 2016/1052, reg 2(1) for 'spouse' and for 'civil partner'. See also **11.54** fn 3.
[3]   See SI 2016/1052, reg 2(1) for 'durable partner'.
[4]   SI 2016/1052, reg 8.

11.59 If an extended family member of a qualified person or of an EEA national has been issued with an EEA family permit, a registration certificate or a residence card, he or she is to be treated as a 'family member' of a qualified person or of an EEA national for so long as he or she continues to fall within the definition of an 'extended family member' and so long as the documentation has not ceased to be valid or been revoked[1].

[1]   SI 2016/1052, reg 7(3). Note the differential treatment of EEA nationals who are students at SI 2016/1052, reg 7(2).

11.60 A person who was a family member of a qualified person, or of an EEA national with the permanent right of residence, and who had resided in the UK in accordance with the regulations for at least a year immediately before the death of the qualified person or of the EEA national with the permanent right of residence, may have 'retained the right of residence'[1] if the qualified person subsequently dies or ceases to reside in the UK. Similarly, if a person was a spouse or civil partner of a qualified person, and they have divorced or terminated the civil partnership, he or she may have 'retained the right of residence'. If that is the case, the surviving person (or former spouse or civil partner) may be entitled to the extended right of residence, even though he or she is not a qualifying person[2].

[1]   SI 2016/1052, reg 10. The provisions are complex and care should be taken to apply the exact wording of the regulations.

² SI 2016/1052, reg 14(3).

The 'permanent right of residence'

11.61 The permanent right of residence[1] is defined at Immigration (European Economic Area) Regulations 2016[2], reg 15(1)[3]. There are six categories of people who can acquire 'permanent rights of residence':

(1) an EEA national who has resided in the UK in accordance with the regulations for a continuous period of five years[4];

(2) a family member of an EEA national who is not himself or herself an EEA national but who has resided in the UK with the EEA national in accordance with the regulations for a continuous period of five years[5];

(3) a worker or self-employed person who has ceased activity[6];

(4) a family member of a worker or self-employed person who has ceased activity[7];

(5) a person who was the family member of a worker or self-employed person where:

    (a) the worker or self-employed person has died, and

    (b) the family member resided with him or her immediately before his or her death, and

    (c) the worker or self-employed person had resided continuously in the UK for at least the two years immediately before his or her death, or the death was the result of an accident at work or an occupational disease[8]; and

(6) a person who:

    (a) has resided in the UK in accordance with the regulations for a continuous period of five years, and

    (b) was, at the end of that period, a family member who has retained the right of residence[9].

For 'family member', see **11.54–11.60.**

1 Immigration (European Economic Area) Regulations 2016, SI 2016/1052, reg 15(1). The rules on eligibility for individuals with this right of residence are set out at **11.122–11.140.**
2 SI 2016/1052.
3 SI 2016/1052.
4 SI 2016/1052, reg 15(1)(a). Residence as a result of a derivative right of residence does not constitute residence for these purposes (SI 2016/1052, reg 15(2)). For 'derivative right of residence' see **11.66–11.87.**
5 SI 2016/1052, reg 15(1)(b). See **11.63–11.65** on continuity of residence.
6 SI 2016/1052, reg 15(1)(c). Note that 'worker or self-employed person who has ceased activity' is defined at SI 2016/1052, reg 5. The requirement for three years' residence which forms part of that definition (see SI 2016/1052, reg 5(2)(c)) necessitates three years' *lawful* residence. See *Secretary of State for Work and Pensions v Gubeladze* [2017] EWCA Civ 1751, CA dealing with the correct interpretation of the Freedom of Movement in the European Union Directive, Directive 2004/38/EC, Arts 16 and 17 which have been transposed into domestic legislation in SI 2016/1052, regs 15 and 5 respectively.
7 SI 2016/1052, reg 15(1)(d).
8 SI 2016/1052, reg 15(1)(e). See **11.63–11.65** on continuity of residence.
9 SI 2016/1052, reg 15(1)(f). For 'a family member who has retained the right of residence', see **11.60.** See **11.63–11.65** on continuity of residence.

11.62 The continuous period of five years' residence, which is a prerequisite of several of these categories, can be at any time, including before the Immigration (European Economic Area) Regulations 2006[1] came into force in 2006, provided that at all times during that five-year period the applicant was residing lawfully, in accordance with EU law[2].

[1]   SI 2006/1003 (which preceded SI 2016/1052).
[2]   See *SSWP v Lassal* C-162/09 [2011] 1 CMLR 972, CJEU and *SSWP v Dias* [2011] C-325/09, [2011] 3 CMLR 1103, CJEU.

11.63 Continuity of residence for these purposes is to be interpreted in accordance with SI 2016/1052, reg 3 which allows for periods of absence from the United Kingdom which do not exceed six months in total in any year, among other things, while also providing that continuity of residence shall be broken by a period of imprisonment[1].

[1]   See SI 2016/1052 reg 3(2)–(4) for the complete list of events that are deemed to break (or not break) a person's continuity of residence.

11.64 The concept of continuity of residence has also fallen for consideration by the courts in a number of cases. In *Secretary of State for the Home Department v Ojo*[1] the Court of Appeal held that a woman who had resided in the UK continuously for a period of five years, had not acquired the permanent right of residence as she had not been lawfully resident (as a family member) for the entirety of that period. Moore-Bick LJ (with whom the rest of the court agreed) observed that 'the acquisition of a permanent right of residence depends on continuous residence in a qualifying status and the Directive makes no provision for changes in status'[2]. In reaching this decision he drew a distinction between continuity of *residence* and continuity of *status*, and refused to draw an analogy with Immigration (European Economic Area) Regulations 2006[3], reg 3(2), which provides that certain breaks in a person's residence will not affect the continuity of that residence[4]. The acquisition of the permanent right of residence is based on an EU citizen's integration into a member state, and it is the continuity of *lawful* residence which satisfies the need for integration[5]. Similarly, in *Poltari v Southwark London Borough Council*[6], Jackson LJ refused permission to appeal against a decision that a homeless applicant had not acquired the permanent right to reside as she did not have comprehensive sickness insurance cover during the five-year period.

[1]   [2015] EWCA Civ 1301, CA.
[2]   [2015] EWCA Civ 1301, CA per Moore-Bick LJ at [20].
[3]   SI 2006/1006. The predecessor of SI 2016/1052, reg 3(2).
[4]   See **11.63**.
[5]   [2015] EWCA Civ 1301, CA per Moore-Bick LJ at [18].
[6]   [2015] EWCA Civ 300, CA.

11.65 In contrast, more recently, in *OB v Secretary of State for Work and Pensions (ESA)*[1] it was suggested by Judge Rowlands that:

'regulation 15 should be interpreted as requiring continuity of residence, but not necessarily continuity of residence in accordance with the Directive or as a qualified person. However, where a person's right of permanent residence under regulation 15 depends on his or her having resided in the United Kingdom as a qualified person, the aggregate of any periods of residence as a qualified person must amount to at least five years[2].'

The appellant in that case had breaks in the continuity of her residence as a qualified person as a result of periods of study where she did not have comprehensive sickness insurance cover. The judge took the view that in light of the importance of integration in this context, periods of study within a member state without a right of residence, could not have been intended to 'affect continuity in the sense of wiping out the credit gained from any previous residence of the claimant as a qualified person'[3]. *Ojo* does not appear to have been cited in *OB*, and the principles applied in the latter decision should perhaps be treated with a degree of caution, though the two cases are plainly distinguishable on the facts.

[1]   [2017] UKUT 0255 (AAC), UT.
[2]   [2017] UKUT 0255 (AAC), UT at [30].
[3]   See [2017] UKUT 0255 (AAC), UT at [27]–[30]. See further **11.53** and **11.52** on the need for comprehensive sickness insurance cover.

The 'derivative right of residence'

11.66 The derivative rights of residence[1] recognised in Immigration (European Economic Area) Regulations 2016, reg 16[2] are based on declarations by the CJEU of various EU Treaty rights. There are five different derivative rights of residence[3] which may be held by the following individuals:

- a primary carer of an EEA national child who is self-sufficient[4];
- a child in education in the UK who is a child of an EEA national[5];
- a primary carer of a child in education who is a child of an EEA national[6];
- a primary carer of a British citizen residing in the UK where the British citizen would be unable to reside in the UK or another EEA member state if the primary carer left the UK for an indefinite period[7];
- a child whose primary carer is also the primary carer of an EEA national child who is self-sufficient, of a child in education who is a child of an EEA national or of a British citizen child who would be unable to reside in the UK or another EEA member state if the primary carer left the UK for an indefinite period[8].

[1]   Defined at Immigration (European Economic Area) Regulations 2016, SI 2016/1052, reg 16. These derivative rights of residence were declared as EU Treaty rights of residence by the CJEU in various decisions and have now been incorporated into domestic regulation. The rules on eligibility for individuals with this right of residence are set out at **11.141–11.153**.
[2]   SI 2016/1052, reg 16.
[3]   SI 2016/1052, reg 16(2), (3), (4), (5) and (6).
[4]   SI 2016/1052, reg 16(2). See **11.73–11.75**.
[5]   SI 2016/1052, reg 16(3). See **11.76–11.77**.
[6]   SI 2016/1052, reg 16(4). See **11.78–11.79**.
[7]   SI 2016/1052, reg 16(5). See **11.80–11.85**.
[8]   SI 2016/1052, reg 16(6). See **11.86–11.87**.

11.67 It should be noted that these derivative rights can only be exercised in certain circumstances, such as when a child is in education or needs a primary carer. If the relevant circumstance comes to an end, and the holder of the derivative right of residence has no claim on any other right of residence under the regulations or EU law, he or she will no longer have any right to reside.

11.68 Residence in the UK as a result of the exercise of a derivative right of residence does not constitute 'residence' for the purpose of acquiring a permanent right of residence[1].

1   SI 2016/1052, reg 15(2). For permanent right of residence, see **11.61–11.65**.

11.69 None of these derivative rights require the recipient to be a national of an EEA member state. Indeed, the rights will often be exercised by people who are not nationals of the UK or of any other EEA member state[1].

1   By SI 2016/1052, reg 16(1), a derivative right can only be exercised by a person who is not an 'exempt person', as defined by reg 16(7). In broad terms this means that only those who have no other right to reside can exercise a derivative right of residence, for example, nationals of EEA member states who do not have one of the other rights of residence discussed at **11.35–11.65**. The particular derivative right of residence identified in SI 2016/1052, reg 16(5), 'the Zambrano right of residence' (see **11.80–11.85**), can only be enjoyed by a national of a non-EEA member state.

11.70 These 'derivative' rights of residence identify rights which, among other outcomes, enable former workers and other formerly qualified persons to exercise a right to reside. They provide that a child who is in education because of the exercise of his or her parent's right of residence as a worker derives a right of residence from his or her parent's right[1]. The child's right would be meaningless if his or her primary carer could not also enjoy a right of residence and so the first and third rights are derived from the exercise of the child's right[2]. A primary carer's right of residence would also be meaningless if his or her children, for whom he or she is the primary carer, did not also have a right of residence[3].

1   SI 2016/1052, reg 16(3). See **11.76–11.77**.
2   SI 2016/1052, reg 16(2) and (4). See **11.73–11.75** and **11.78–11.79**.
3   SI 2016/1052, reg 16(6). See **11.86–11.87**.

11.71 A derivative right of residence is not contingent on any declaration or grant of leave by the Secretary of State. The right will exist as long as the conditions set out in reg 16 are satisfied[1]. However, a derivative right of residence can be withdrawn or cancelled by the Secretary of State on the grounds that it is conducive to the public good to do so[2].

1   *R (Sanneh) v Secretary of State for Work and Pensions* [2015] EWCA Civ 49, [2015] HLR 27, CA. An appeal by one of the Claimants in that case (on another issue) was dismissed by the Supreme Court in *R (HC) v Secretary of State for Work and Pensions* [2017] UKSC 73, [2017] 3 WLR 1486, SC.
2   SI 2016/1052, reg 16(12).

11.72 Neither of the Codes give any substantive guidance on any of these derivative rights, or even on the cases decided by the CJEU which gave rise to the Regulation[1]. Each right will now be discussed in turn.

1   SI 2016/1052, reg 16. Although brief reference is made to *Zambrano v Office national de l'emploi* C34/09, [2012] QB 265, CJEU in the Welsh Code, para 7.11(iv).

A PRIMARY CARER OF AN EEA NATIONAL CHILD WHO IS SELF-SUFFICIENT

11.73 A person will have a derivative right to reside[1] in the UK if he or she is:

* not an exempt person[2];
* the primary carer of an EEA national; and

- the EEA national is:
  - under the age of 18;
  - is residing in the UK as a self-sufficient person[3]; and
  - would be unable to remain in the UK if the primary carer left the UK for an indefinite period[4].

[1] SI 2016/1052, reg 16(2).
[2] 'Exempt person' is defined as a person who has a right to reside in the UK as a result of any other provision of SI 2016/1052, or who has a right of abode in the UK by virtue of s 2 Immigration Act 1971 or who has indefinite leave to enter or remain in the UK or has been exempted from these provisions: SI 2016/1052, reg 16(7).
[3] For 'self-sufficient person' see SI 2016/1052, reg 4(1)(c) and **11.50–11.52**.
[4] SI 2016/1052, reg 16(2). This right was declared by the CJEU in October 2004 in *Chen v UK* (C-200/02, [2005] All ER (EC) 129, ECJ).

11.74 The primary carer need not be a national of an EEA member state but the child must be. A 'primary carer' is defined as a direct relative or legal guardian of the child and either has primary responsibility for the child's care or shares responsibility equally with another person who is not an exempt person[1]. 'Responsibility' requires more than a financial contribution towards care[2].

[1] SI 2016/1052, reg 16(8).
[2] SI 2016/1052, reg 16(11). See also the additional definitions regarding shared care at SI 2016/1052, reg 16(9) and (10).

11.75 This right will cease if:

- the person is no longer the primary carer of the child;
- the child reaches the age of 18;
- the child is no longer in the UK or is no longer self-sufficient;
- the child ceases to need a primary carer.

A CHILD IN EDUCATION IN THE UK WHO IS A CHILD OF AN EEA NATIONAL

11.76 A person will have a derivative right to reside[1] in the UK if he or she is:

- not an exempt person[2];
- any of his or her parents is an EEA national who resides or has resided in the UK;
- he or she resides, or has resided, in the UK at a time when his or her EEA national parent was residing in the UK as a worker[3]; and
- he or she is in education in the UK[4].

[1] SI 2016/1052, reg 16(3).
[2] See **11.73** fn 3.
[3] For 'worker', see SI 2016/1052, reg 4(1)(a) and **11.40–11.46**. Note that the extended definition of 'worker' at reg 6(2) does not apply to this regulation (reg 16(7)(b)).
[4] SI 2016/1052, reg 16(3).

11.77 The child need not himself or herself be a national of an EEA member state but one of his or her parents must be. Furthermore, that parent must have resided in the UK as a worker. The child must have been, at some point, in education at a time when his or her parent was in the UK. There is no requirement that the parent should still be in the UK, or should still be a worker[1]. Note that the word 'child' is used here to describe the relationship between the person enjoying the derivative right to reside and his or her EEA national parent[2], since the right arises, in part, from the existence of that relationship. But the word 'child' is not actually used in Immigration (European Economic Area) Regulations 2016, reg 16(3) and there is no suggestion in the regulation that the right ceases when the child turns 18. However, it will cease when he or she ceases to be in education, whether that occurs before or after his or her eighteenth birthday. 'Education' does not include nursery education[3].

[1]   Indeed it is likely that the parent is either no longer in the UK, or no longer has any EU rights of residence, as otherwise the child would probably be a family member and be entitled to the same right of residence as his or her parent.
[2]   As opposed to being a reference to his or her age.
[3]   SI 2016/1052, reg 16(7)(a). This right was declared by the CJEU in *R (Bidar) v Ealing London Borough Council* C209–03, [2005] QB 812, ECJ.

A PRIMARY CARER OF A CHILD IN EDUCATION WHO IS A CHILD OF AN EEA NATIONAL

11.78 The primary carer of a child who has the derivative right described at **11.76–11.77** will also have a derivative right of residence[1]. That right exists where:

•   the primary carer is not an exempt person[2];
•   the child of an EEA national parent resides, or has resided, in the UK at a time when the parent was residing here as a worker;
•   the child is in education in the UK;
•   the child has a primary carer; and
•   the child would be unable to continue to be educated in the UK if the primary carer left the UK for an indefinite period[3].

[1]   SI 2016/1052, reg 16(4).
[2]   See **11.73** fn 3.
[3]   SI 2016/1052, reg 16(4).

11.79 For 'primary carer', see **11.74**. For 'education', see **11.77**. This right ends when:

•   the person ceases to be the child's primary carer;
•   the child ceases to need a primary carer; or
•   the child ceases to be in education[1].

[1]   This right was declared by the CJEU in several cases: *Baumbast & R v SSHD* [2002] ECR 1–7091, ECJ; *Ibrahim v Harrow London Borough Council* C-310/08, [2010] HLR 31, CJEU; and *Teixeira v Lambeth London Borough Council*, C4–380/08, [2010] HLR 32, CJEU.

A PRIMARY CARER OF A BRITISH CITIZEN RESIDING IN THE UK WHERE THE BRITISH CITIZEN WOULD BE UNABLE TO RESIDE IN THE UK OR ANOTHER EEA MEMBER STATE IF THE PRIMARY CARER LEFT THE UK FOR AN INDEFINITE PERIOD

11.80 A person will have a derivative right of residence[1] in the UK if he or she is:

- not an exempt person[2];
- the primary carer of a British citizen;
- the British citizen for whom he or she cares is residing in the UK; and
- the British citizen would be unable to reside in the UK or in another EEA member state if his or her primary carer left the UK for an indefinite period[3].

[1]   SI 2016/1052, reg 16(5).
[2]   See **11.73** fn 3.
[3]   SI 2016/1052, reg 16(5).

11.81 For 'primary carer', see **11.74**. This derivative right of residence was recognised by CJEU in the case of *Zambrano v Office national de l'emploi*[1].

[1]   C34/9, [2012] QB 265, CJEU.

11.82 The circumstances in which this derivative right of residence will arise have been considered by the courts in a number of cases. In *Harrison v Secretary of State for the Home Department*[1], the Court of Appeal held that the principle in *Zambrano* did not cover anything short of the situation where an EU citizen would be forced to leave the EU. In particular, it would not arise in circumstances where an EU citizen is not forced, as a matter of substance, to follow the non-EU national out of the EU, but where his or her continuing residence in the EU is affected because, for example, his or her quality of life is diminished[2].

[1]   [2012] EWCA Civ 1736, [2013] 2 CMLR 23, CA.
[2]   *Harrison v Secretary of State for the Home Department* [2012] EWCA Civ 1736, [2013] 2 CMLR 23, CA per Elias LJ at paras 55 and 63.

11.83 In *Hines v Lambeth London Borough Council*[1] the Court of Appeal, applying the decision in *Harrison v Secretary of State for the Home Department*[2], held that a non-EU national would only be granted a derivative right to reside as the primary carer of a British citizen, if that British citizen would be effectively compelled to leave the United Kingdom if the primary carer were required to leave. Where the British citizen was a child, the welfare of that child, including any impairment of his or her quality of life, should be taken into account in considering whether he or she would be effectively compelled to leave. But his or her welfare could not be the paramount consideration because that would be flatly inconsistent with the statutory test under Immigration (European Economic Area) Regulations 2006, reg 15A(4A)[3].

[1]   [2014] EWCA Civ 660, [2014] 1 WLR 4112, CA.
[2]   [2012] EWCA Civ 1736, [2013] 2 CMLR 23, CA.
[3]   *Hines v Lambeth London Borough Council* [2014] EWCA Civ 660, [2014] HLR 32, CA per Vos LJ at paras 21–25. SI 2006/1003, reg 15A has since been replaced by SI 2016/1052, reg 16.

11.84 In *R (Sanneh) v Secretary of State for Work and Pensions*[1] the High Court held that the availability of support under the Children Act 1989, s 17[2] to a child who was a British citizen, could be taken into account in assessing whether the effect of a national measure was such that she would be forced to leave the EU, in contravention of the Zambrano right of residence. In that case the claimant was the mother of a British citizen. She sought to challenge regulations excluding her from mainstream social security benefits on the basis that without those benefits she would be compelled to leave the EU owing to a lack of means and that her daughter would be forced to leave with her. Her application for judicial review was dismissed, as 'realistically, the Claimant was not going to leave the United Kingdom in the foreseeable future, because the Council's s 17 support would inevitably ensure that neither EU law nor European human rights law would be breached'[3].

1 [2013] EWHC 793 (Admin), Admin Ct, upheld by the Court of Appeal in *R (Sanneh) v Secretary of State for Work and Pensions* [2015] EWCA Civ 49, [2015] HLR 27, CA and by the Supreme Court in *R (HC) v Secretary of State for Work and Pensions* [2017] UKSC 73, [2017] 3 WLR 1486, SC.
2 See **20.39–20.57**.
3 [2013] EWHC 793 (Admin), Admin Ct per Hickinbottom J at para 97.

11.85 The beneficiaries of this derivative right of residence will be adults who are not nationals of any EEA member state. They will be entitled to the derivative right of residence for so long as they are a primary carer of a British citizen child or adult who needs a primary carer. The right will cease if:

- the person ceases to be the primary carer of the British citizen;
- the British citizen no longer requires the primary carer; or
- either the British citizen or his or her primary carer has a right of residence in another EEA member state.

A CHILD WHOSE PRIMARY CARER IS ALSO A PRIMARY CARER OF A EEA NA-TIONAL CHILD WHO IS SELF-SUFFICIENT OR OF A CHILD IN EDUCATION WHO IS A CHILD OF AN EEA NATIONAL OR OF A BRITISH CITIZEN CHILD WHO WOULD BE UNABLE TO RESIDE IN THE UK OR ANOTHER EEA MEMBER STATE IF THE PRIMARY CARER LEFT THE UK FOR AN INDEFINITE PERIOD

11.86 The child of a person who has a derivative right to reside as a primary carer of a child who is an EEA national and is self-sufficient[1], or of a child in education who is a child of an EEA national[2], or of a British citizen child who would be unable to reside in the UK or another EEA member state if the primary carer left the UK for an indefinite period[3] will also have a derivative right of residence so long as[4]:

- the child is not an exempt person[5];
- the child entitled to this derivative right is under the age of 18;
- his or her primary carer is entitled to the derivative right to reside in the UK by virtue of either reg 16(2)[6], (4)[7] or (5)[8] of SI 2016/1052;
- the child does not have leave to enter or remain in the UK; and
- if the child left the UK for an indefinite period, his or her primary carer would be prevented from residing in the UK[9].

1 SI 2016/1052, reg 16(2). See **11.73–11.75**.
2 SI 2016/1052, reg 16(4). See **11.78–11.79**.
3 SI 2016/1052, reg 16(5). See **11.80–11.85**.
4 SI 2016/1052, reg 16(6).
5 See **11.73** fn 3.
6 A primary carer of an EEA national child who is self-sufficient: see **11.73–11.75**.
7 A primary carer of a child in education in the UK who is a child of an EEA national: see **11.78–11.79**.
8 A *Zambrano* Carer: see **11.80–11.85**.

11.86 *Eligibility for Assistance*

9   SI 2016/1052, reg 16(6).

11.87 For 'primary carer', see **11.74**. For 'self-sufficient', see **11.50–11.52**. For 'education', see **11.77**. The child entitled to the derivative right does not have to be related by blood or marriage either to his or her primary carer or to the child from whose right to reside the primary carer's right is derived. However, the primary carer must be the primary carer of both children. This right ends when:

- the child reaches the age of 18;
- the derivative right of residence of the child's primary carer comes to an end[1];
- the child acquires leave to enter or remain in the UK or an EEA right of residence; or
- the child ceases to need a primary carer.

1   See **11.75**, **11.79** and **11.85**.

The special rules for Croatian nationals

11.88 Croatia, which acceded to the EU on 1 July 2013, is the newest member of the EU. The rules[1] governing the circumstances in which a Croatian national will acquire one of the various rights of residence available to EEA nationals[2] are slightly different to those which apply to nationals of other EEA states. A Croatian national (save for certain exceptions discussed at **11.91**) will be classed as an 'Accession State national subject to worker authorisation', as defined by the Accession of Croatia (Immigration and Worker Authorisation) Regulations 2013[3] during the first 12 months of his or her employment.

1   Accession of Croatia (Immigration and Worker Authorisation) Regulations 2013, SI 2013/1460. The rules on eligibility for individuals with this right of residence are set out at **12.122–11.140**.
2   See **11.35–11.87**.
3   SI 2013/1460, reg 2(1).

11.89 An Accession State national subject to worker authorisation and authorised in accordance with the Accession Regulations 2013[1] will only be classed as a worker[2] during such time as he or she holds an Accession Worker authorisation document and is working in accordance with the conditions set out in that document[3]. The document normally issued is an EEA registration card[4]. In addition, a Croatian national who is a job-seeker[5] will not have any right of residence[6]. The combined effect of these rules is that a Croation national will *only* have a right to reside as long as he or she holds an Accession Worker authorisation document and is working in accordance with that document. Residence that does not meet these requirements will not be regarded as lawful residence for the purposes of acquiring a permanent right to reside[7] under SI 2016/1052, reg 15(1)(c)[8].

1   Accession of Croatia (Immigration and Worker Authorisation) Regulations 2013, SI 2013/1460.
2   See **11.40–11.46**.
3   SI 2013/1460, reg 5.
4   SI 2013/1460, reg 7.
5   See **11.39**.

6   SI 2013/1460, reg 5.
7   See **11.61–11.65**.
8   *Secretary of State for Work and Pensions v Gubeladze* [2017] EWCA Civ 1751, CA, dealing with the correct interpretation of the Freedom of Movement in the European Union Directive, Directive 2004/38/EC, Arts 16 and 17 which have been transposed into domestic legislation in SI 2016/1052, regs 15 and 5 respectively.

11.90 After 30 June 2018, Croatian nationals are to be treated in the same way as other EEA nationals[1].

1   SI 2013/1460, reg 1(2) and reg 5. The Secretary of State has the power to make regulations to extend this period pursuant to European Union (Croatian Accession and Irish Protocol) Act 2013, s 4. However, at the time of writing this power had not been exercised and UK Visas and Immigration had indicated that it would not be: see https://www.gov.uk/government/pub lications/guidance-for-croatian-nationals-on-getting-permission-to-work-in-the-uk (last accessed on 22 May 2018).

11.91 Not all Croatian nationals fall within the definition of 'an Accession State national subject to worker authorisation'. They should be treated in the same way as other EEA nationals if they fall into one of these categories:

- a person who, on 30 June 2013, had leave to enter or remain without any restriction on taking employment other than a condition restricting his or her employment as a doctor or dentist in training or as a sports coach[1]; or
- a person who has legally worked in the UK without interruption for a period of 12 months[2]; or
- a person who is also a national of the UK or of another EEA Member State (other than Croatia)[3]; or
- a person who is at the same time a national of Bulgaria or Romania who is subject to worker authorisation within the meaning of Accession (Immigration and Authorisation) Regulations 2006, reg 2(7)[4]; or
- a spouse, civil partner, unmarried or same-sex partner or child under 18 of a person who has leave to remain under the Immigration Act 1971 that allows him or her to live and work in the UK[5]; or
- a spouse, civil partner, unmarried or same-sex partner of a UK national or of a person settled in the UK[6]; or
- a diplomat or family member of a diplomat[7]; or
- a person who is exempt from the provisions of the Immigration Act 1971 by virtue of an order made under Immigration Act 1971, s 8(2)[8]; or
- a person who has a permanent right of residence pursuant to Immigration (European Economic Area) Regulations 2016, reg 15[9]; or
- a person who is the family member of an EEA national who has a right to reside in the United Kingdom[10]. Though where the EEA national is himself or herself subject to worker authorisation under SI 2013/1460 or is a Bulgarian or Romanian national subject to worker authorisation under Accession (Immigration and Authorisation) Regulations 2006[11], this exemption will only apply where the former is the spouse, civil partner, unmarried or same-sex partner of the latter or where the latter is a dependant under the age of 21 who is a direct descendant of the former, or of his or her spouse or civil partner; or

- a person who holds a registration certificate to the effect that he or she is a highly skilled person and has unconditional access to the labour market[12]; or
- a person who is in the UK as a student, and *either* holds a registration certificate that includes a statement that he or she is a student who may work in the UK whilst a student, and who is working not more than 20 hours a week during term time (unless following a course of vocational training)[13], *or* has leave to enter or remain under Immigration Act 1971 as a student and who is working in accordance with any conditions attached to that leave[14]; or
- a 'posted worker'[15].

1 SI 2013/1460, reg 2(2).
2 SI 2013/1460, reg 2(3), (4) and (5). This is the case whether the 12-month period ends on 30 June 2013, falls partly before and partly after 30 June 2013, or wholly after 30 June 2013.
3 SI 2013/1460, reg 2(6).
4 SI 2006/3317; SI 2013/1460, reg 2(7).
5 SI 2013/1460, reg 2(8).
6 SI 2006/3317, reg 2(9).
7 SI 2013/1460, reg 2(10).
8 SI 2013/1460, reg 2(11).
9 SI 2013/1460, reg 2(12). For 'permanent right of residence' see **11.61–11.65**.
10 SI 2013/1460, reg 2(13) and (14). For 'family member', see **11.54–11.60**. For 'right to reside', see **11.35–11.87**.
11 SI 2006/3317.
12 SI 2013/1460, reg 2(15).
13 He or she may work full-time during vacations (SI 2013/1460, reg 2(17)(b)).
14 SI 2013/1460, reg 2(16) and (17). A person falling within this class may work during the period of four months following the end of his or her course providing his or her EEA registration card was issued prior to the end of the course and includes a statement specifying that he or she may work during this period: SI 2013/460, reg 2(18).
15 SI 2013/1460, reg 2(19) and (20). A 'posted worker' is a worker who, for a limited period, is working in the territory of a different member state from that where he or she normally works (Directive 96/71/EC, Arts 1 and 3).

11.92 Any national of Croatia who falls within one of these categories will fall to be treated as any other EEA national would be[1].

1 SI 2013/1460, regs 2(1) and 5.

EU rights of residence not contained in domestic Regulations

11.93 There may be rights of residence, that are not specifically identified in the Immigration (European Economic Area) Regulations 2016[1]. Such rights may potentially arise under a variety of provisions including Arts 20, 21 and 56 of the Treaty on the Functioning of the EU[2].

1 SI 2016/1052.
2 Article 20 on the rights of nationals of EU member states to be EU citizens; Art 21 on the rights of EU citizens to move and reside as EU citizens; Art 56 on the freedom to provide and receive services. The Scottish Court of Session, in the case of *O v Aberdeen City Council* [2017] CSOH 9, 2017 SLT 181, has recently rejected an attempt to argue that a homeless EEA national applicant, who was not a qualified person but who was a victim of trafficking, had a right to reside under Art 21 of the Treaty on the Functioning of the EU. See [44]–[49].

WORKING OUT WHETHER THE APPLICANT IS ELIGIBLE

Overview

11.94 The main provisions governing eligibility and exclusion are HA 1996, s 185(1) and its counterpart, H(W)A 2014, Sch 2, para 1(1)[1]. They provide that 'a person from abroad who is ineligible for housing assistance' is not eligible for assistance from a local housing authority under the homelessness provisions in HA 1996, Pt 7[2] and H(W)A 2014, ss 66, 68, 73 or 75 respectively. Working out who is, and who is not, caught by that term is therefore crucial in deciding whether homelessness services can be provided.

[1] *R (Morris) v Westminster City Council* [2005] EWCA Civ 1184, [2006] HLR 8, CA per Sedley LJ at [13] and [14].
[2] As amended by HRA 2017, for applications for homelessness assistance made to local housing authorities in England on or after 3 April 2018.

11.95 There are two categories of 'persons from abroad' for the purposes of HA 1996, s 185 and H(W)A 2014, Sch 2, para 1.

(1) Those subject to immigration control[1]:
  - are *not eligible* for assistance;
  - *unless* they fall within a class prescribed as 'eligible' in regulations made by the Secretary of State or the Welsh Ministers[2].
(2) Those not subject to immigration control but who are nevertheless prescribed by regulations as being 'persons from abroad':
  - are *not eligible* if they are not habitually resident in the Common Travel Area *unless* they are prescribed as exempt from the habitual residence test; and
  - are *not eligible* if they are prescribed as ineligible because of their particular rights of residence under European Union law[3].

[1] See **11.26–11.93** for discussion of whether a person is, or is not, subject to immigration control.
[2] HA 1996, s 185(2); H(W)A 2014, Sch 2, para 1(2).
[3] HA 1996, s 185(3); H(W)A 2014, Sch 2, para 1(3).

11.96 As is apparent from the terms of these provisions, the general rule is that people from abroad are excluded. But the Secretary of State and the Welsh Ministers each have the power to make regulations exempting some people from abroad from that exclusory rule[1]. They each also have the power to make regulations excluding people who would otherwise be eligible. Each of these powers has been exercised in both England and Wales.

[1] They cannot designate as eligible any person who is excluded from entitlement to universal credit or housing benefit by the Immigration and Asylum Act 1999, s 115 (HA 1996, s 185(2A); H(W)A 2014, Sch 2, para 1(3)). Immigration and Asylum Act 1999, s 115 prescribes that 'a person subject to immigration control' is not eligible for universal credit or housing benefit unless he or she falls within one of the classes of people prescribed by the Secretary of State. Classes of persons subject to immigration control who are entitled to housing benefit are prescribed in the Social Security (Immigration and Asylum) Consequential Amendment Regulations 2000, SI 2000/636, reg 2 and Sch 1, Pt 1 and the Housing Benefit Regulations 2006, SI 2006/213, reg 10(3B).

11.97 For England, the Secretary of State has made the Allocation of Housing and Homelessness (Eligibility) (England) Regulations 2006[1], which apply to all applications for homelessness assistance made to local housing authorities in England made on or after 1 June 2006[2]. Those regulations have since been made amended by:

- the Allocation of Housing and Homelessness (Eligibility) (England) (Amendment) Regulations 2006[3]; and
- the Allocation of Housing and Homelessness (Eligibility) (England) (Miscellaneous Provisions) Regulations 2006[4]; and
- the Allocation of Housing and Homelessness (Eligibility) (England) (Amendment No 2) Regulations 2006[5]; and
- the Allocation of Housing and Homelessness (Eligibility) (England) (Amendment) Regulations 2009[6]; and
- the Allocation of Housing and Homelessness (Eligibility) (England) (Amendment) Regulations 2012[7]; and
- the Allocation of Housing and Homelessness (Eligibility) (England) (Amendment) Regulations 2013[8]; and
- the Allocation of Housing and Homelessness (Eligibility) (England) (Amendment) Regulations 2014[9].
- the Allocation of Housing and Homelessness (Eligibility) (England) (Amendment) Regulations 2016[10].

[1] SI 2006/1294. References in these Regulations to the Immigration (European Economic Area) Regulations 2006, SI 2006/1003 should be read as referring to the Immigration (European Economic Area) Regulations 2016, SI 2016/1052. See SI 2016/1052, Sch 7, para 1.

[2] Any applications for homelessness assistance made before 1 June 2006 to local housing authorities in England are determined according to the Homelessness (England) Regulations 2000, SI 2000/701, amended by the Allocation of Housing and Homelessness (Amendment) (England) Regulations 2004, SI 2004/1235, and further amended by the Allocation of Housing and Homelessness (Amendment) (England) Regulations 2006, SI 2006/1093. See previous editions of this book.

[3] SI 2006/2007, in force for applications made to local housing authorities in England made on or after 25 July 2006.

[4] SI 2006/2527, in force for applications made to local housing authorities in England made on or after 9 October 2006.

[5] SI 2006/3340, in force for applications made to local housing authorities in England made on or after 1 January 2007.

[6] SI 2009/358, in force for applications made to local housing authorities in England made on or after 18 March 2009.

[7] SI 2012/2588, in force for applications made to local housing authorities in England on or after 8 November 2012.

[8] SI 2013/1467, in force for applications made to local housing authorities in England on or after 1 July 2013.

[9] SI 2014/435. In force from 31 March 2014. The regulations contain no transitional provisions and presumably apply to any application outstanding at that date irrespective of when the application was made.

[10] SI 2016/965. In force from 30 October 2016. The regulations contain no transitional provisions and presumably apply to any application outstanding at that date irrespective of when the application was made.

11.98 Appendix 2 of this book contains the text of the Allocation of Housing and Homelessness (Eligibility) (England) Regulations 2006[1], as amended by all of the above regulations. Guidance is provided at Chapter 7 of the English Code.

[1] SI 2006/1294.

11.99 In Wales, the Welsh Ministers have made the Allocation of Housing and Homelessness (Eligibility) (Wales) Regulations 2014[1], which apply to all applications for homelessness assistance to local housing authorities in Wales made on or after 31 October 2014[2]. These Regulations were originally enacted under HA 1996, Pt 7 but now apply to the H(W)A 2014, Pt 2 by virtue of the saving provision contained in the Housing (Wales) Act 2014 (Commencement No 3 and Transitory, Transitional and Saving Provisions) Order 2015, art 5[3]. These have been amended by the Allocation of Housing and Homelessness (Eligibility) (Wales) (Amendment) Regulations 2017[4].

[1] SI 2014/2603 (W 257).
[2] For the relevant regulations in Wales before 31 October 2014, see previous editions of this book.
[3] SI 2015/1272 (W 88).
[4] SI 2017/698 (W 164). In force from 22 June 2017.

11.100 The regulations in both England and Wales (which are now virtually identical, although historically there were differences) set out classes of persons who are subject to immigration control but are prescribed as eligible nevertheless. They also set out classes of persons who are not subject to immigration control, but are nevertheless ineligible. Each of the two categories of persons from abroad (those subject to immigration control and those not subject to such control) needs careful examination.

Category One: those who are subject to immigration control

11.101 The starting point is that:

' . . . a person who is subject to immigration control within the meaning of the Asylum and Immigration Act 1996 is not eligible for housing assistance unless he is of a class prescribed by regulations made by the Secretary of State[1].'

[1] HA 1996, s 185(2); H(W)A 2014, Sch 1, para 1(2).

The exclusionary rule

11.102 The basic rule is that 'a person subject to immigration control'[1] is *not eligible*. The exceptions to this exclusionary rule are contained in classes set out in regulations. Allocation of Housing and Homelessness (Eligibility) (England) Regulations 2006[2], reg 5 and Allocation of Housing and Homelessness (Eligibility) (Wales) Regulations 2014[3], reg 5 prescribe that the following classes of persons from abroad are eligible even though they are subject to immigration control:

(1)   Class A[4]: a person recorded by the Secretary of State as a refugee and who has leave to enter or remain in the UK.
(2)   Class B[5]: a person who has:
        (a)   exceptional leave to enter or remain in the UK granted outside of the provisions of the Immigration Rules; and
        (b)   whose leave is not subject to conditions requiring him or her to maintain and accommodate himself or herself and any dependents without recourse to public funds.

(3)   Class C[6]: a person who:
     (a)   is habitually resident in the CTA[7]; and
     (b)   has current leave to enter or remain in the UK which is not subject to any limitation or condition; but
     (c)   is not a person who:
          (i)   has been given leave to enter or remain in the UK upon a written undertaking from a sponsor that he or she will be responsible for maintenance and accommodation; and
          (ii)   has been resident in the CTA for less than five years beginning on the date of entry or the date of the undertaking (whichever is the later date); and
          (iii) whose sponsor is still alive.

(4)   Class D[8]: a person who has humanitarian protection granted under the Immigration Rules.

(5)   Class F[9]: Afghan citizens granted leave to enter under Immigration Rules, para 276BA1[10] who are habitually resident in the CTA.

(6)   Class G[11]: A person who has limited leave to enter or remain in the United Kingdom on family or private life grounds under Art 8 of the European Convention on Human Rights, such leave granted:
     (a)   under para 276BE(1), para 276DG or Appendix FM of the Immigration Rules[12], and
     (b)   who is not subject to a condition requiring that person to maintain and accommodate himself, and any person dependent upon him, without recourse to public funds[13].

---

[1]   See **11.26–11.93** for discussion of how to determine whether a person is subject to immigration control.
[2]   SI 2006/1294.
[3]   SI 2014/2603 (W 257).
[4]   SI 2006/1294, reg 5(1)(a); SI 2014/2603 (W 257), reg 5(1)(a). See **11.106–11.108**.
[5]   SI 2006/1294, reg 5(1)(b); SI 2014/2603 (W 257), reg 5(1)(b). See **11.109–11.111**.
[6]   SI 2006/1294, reg 5(1)(c); SI 2014/2603 (W 257), reg 5(1)(c). See **1.112–11.114**.
[7]   See Box 1 at **11.28**.
[8]   SI 2006/1294, reg 5(1)(d); SI 2014/2603 (W 257), reg 5(1)(d). See **11.115**.
[9]   SI 2006/1294, reg 5(1)(f); SI 2014/2603 (W 257), reg 5(1)(f). See **12.116**. Note that Class E has been repealed, which is why the classes skip from D to F.
[10] *Immigration Rules*, HC 395, (23 May 1994 as amended.).
[11] SI 2006/1294, reg 5(1)(g); SI 2014/2603 (W 257), reg 5(1)(g). See **11.117–11.120**.
[12] Immigration Rules, HC 395, (23 May 1994 as amended.).
[13] The requirements of SI 2006/1294, reg 5(1)(g), strictly, do not make grammatical sense: a point highlighted in the Joint Committee on Statutory Instruments Thirteenth Report of Session 2016–17, 16 November 2016 at para 2.4. However, if one avoids an overly technical reading, the scope of the class is clear. This grammatical error has been avoided in SI 2014/2603 (W 257), reg 5(1)(g).

11.103 Extremely limited guidance on the scope of Classes A–G is given in the English Code at para 7.12. Slightly more in depth guidance is given in the Welsh Code at para 7.8[1]. The classes are individually considered at **11.106–11.121**.

[1]   Though the Welsh Code pre-dates the introduction of class G.

11.104 A number of the Classes contain terms that are defined by the regulations or by case law. For the meaning of:

•   'Common Travel Area (CTA)' see Box 1 at **11.28**;

- 'habitually resident' see **11.130–11.136**;
- 'UK' see Box 1 at **11.28**.

11.105 Even if an applicant is eligible under any of these six Classes, any members of his or her household who are not eligible are to be disregarded for the purposes of deciding whether the applicant is homeless and whether he or she has a priority need[1].

[1] HA 1996, s 185(4); H(W)A 2014, Sch 2, para 1(4). See **11.158–11.167**.

Exemptions from the exclusionary rule

CLASS A: REFUGEES

11.106 If a former asylum seeker has been granted refugee status by the Secretary of State, he or she will also have the 'leave to enter or remain in the UK' required for Class A purposes and will be eligible for homelessness assistance, welfare benefits, community care services and for an allocation of social housing according to the same criteria as those applicable to British citizens. Leave may be granted either for an indefinite period or limited for five years[1].

[1] Allocation of Housing and Homelessness (Eligibility) (England) Regulations 2006, SI 2006/1294, reg 5(1)(a); Allocation of Housing and Homelessness (Eligibility) (Wales) Regulations 2014, SI 2014/2603 (W 257), reg 5(1)(a).

11.107 It is not unusual for someone to be granted refugee status and then to apply for his or her family to come to the UK. The family enters the UK with the refugee acting as their sponsor[1]. A refugee is entitled to such family reunion[2], and so the usual rules regarding maintenance and accommodation (which would normally involve a condition of 'no recourse to public funds') do not apply to a refugee's family members.

[1] See *R (Jimaali) v Haringey London Borough Council* (2002) November *Legal Action*, p 24, Admin Ct for discussion of the specific meaning and effect of the word sponsor in this context.
[2] See *Immigration Rules*, HC 395 (23 May 1994 as amended), paras 352A–352F.

11.108 Once a former asylum-seeker is granted refugee status, any accommodation which was provided by the Home Office[1] under Immigration and Asylum Act 1999, Pt 6 will be withdrawn. If the asylum-seeker was occupying accommodation provided by the Home Office under Immigration and Asylum Act 1999, s 95 (the main duty to provide support to asylum-seekers), he or she will have a local connection with the local housing authority in whose district the accommodation was situated[2]. This does not preclude the former asylum-seeker from establishing a local connection, or several local connections, elsewhere, whether by residence, family associations, employment or special circumstances. He or she might then have a local connection with more than one local housing authority.

[1] Formerly the National Asylum Support Service or 'NASS'.
[2] HA 1996, s 199(6); H(W)A 2014, s 81(5). See **14.88–14.95**.

CLASS B: EXCEPTIONAL LEAVE TO ENTER OR REMAIN

11.109 'Exceptional leave to enter or remain'[1] was generally a status granted to asylum-seekers whose claim for full refugee status had not succeeded but where the Home Office recognised that there were compelling humanitarian and/or compassionate circumstances that required that the applicant should be allowed to stay in the UK. From 1 April 2003, the Home Office has called leave granted in those circumstances 'humanitarian protection' or 'discretionary leave'[2]. Viewed broadly, anyone who was granted leave to enter or remain when the Secretary of State has recognised that he or she does not fully meet the requirements of the Immigration Rules has been treated 'exceptionally' and may be said to have been granted 'exceptional leave' and the expectation of the Ministry of Housing, Communities and Local Government is that such persons should fall within Class B[3]. Leave is normally, but not always, granted for a period of 30 months.

[1]   Allocation of Housing and Homelessness (Eligibility) (England) Regulations 2006, SI 2006/1294, reg 5(1)(b); Allocation of Housing and Homelessness (Eligibility) (Wales) Regulations 2014, SI 2014/2603 (W 257), reg 5(1)(b).

[2]   Letter from the Homelessness Directorate (Office of the Deputy Prime Minister) to Chief Executives and Housing Directors of English local housing authorities, dated 25 March 2003, at APPENDIX 2.

[3]   See Letter from the Homelessness Directorate (Office of the Deputy Prime Minister) to Chief Executives and Housing Directors of English local housing authorities, dated 25 March 2003 and Letter from the Department of Communities and Local Government to Chief Executives and Chief Housing Officers of Local Authorities in England, dated 21 October 2016, at APPENDIX 2.

11.110 People with exceptional leave to enter or remain will be eligible for homelessness assistance unless that leave is subject to a condition requiring them to maintain and accommodate themselves (and their dependents) without recourse to public funds. The presence or absence of such a condition will be manifest from the document (or stamp) containing the grant of leave itself.

11.111 Unless they fall within the prohibition of 'no recourse to public funds', they will not only be entitled to homelessness assistance but also to welfare benefits and community care services, and can apply for an allocation of social housing.

CLASS C: A PERSON WITH CURRENT LEAVE TO ENTER OR REMAIN IN THE UK WITH NO CONDITION OR LIMITATION AND WHO IS HABITUALLY RESIDENT IN THE COMMON TRAVEL AREA

11.112 The type of leave contemplated by this Class is commonly referred to as 'indefinite leave to enter or remain'[1] and cannot be granted subject to conditions[2]. Anyone granted indefinite leave to enter or remain will be eligible if he or she is also habitually resident in the CTA[3].

[1]   Allocation of Housing and Homelessness (Eligibility) (England) Regulations 2006, SI 2006/1294, reg 5(1)(c); Allocation of Housing and Homelessness (Eligibility) (Wales) Regulations 2014, SI 2014/2603 (W 257), reg 5(1)(c). See also English Code, para 7.12(c) and Welsh Code, para 7.8(iii).

[2]   Immigration Act 1971, s 3(1)(b) and (c).

³ For the meaning of 'habitually resident', see **11.130–11.136**. For the 'Common Travel Area', see Box 1 at **11.28**.

11.113 If leave to enter or remain has been granted on the basis of a written undertaking that a sponsor would be responsible for the applicant's maintenance and accommodation, the applicant will *not* be eligible for homeless assistance under Class C for five years running from:

- the date of his or her arrival in the UK; or
- the date the sponsorship undertaking was given;

starting from whichever is the later event[1].

¹ SI 2006/1294, reg 5(1)(c)(ii); SI 2014/2603 (W 257), reg 5(1)(c)(ii).

11.114 After those five years, or if the sponsor (or at least one of several sponsors) dies within the five years[1], an applicant will be eligible under this class (subject to satisfying the test of habitual residence)[2].

¹ SI 2006/1294, reg 5(1)(c)(iii); SI 2014/2603 (W 257), reg 5(1)(c)(ii).
² See **11.130–11.136**.

CLASS D: A PERSON GRANTED HUMANITARIAN PROTECTION UNDER THE IMMIGRATION RULES

11.115 'Humanitarian protection'[1] is granted to those people whose claims for asylum do not succeed, but who have international protection needs (ie they face a serious risk of the death penalty, unlawful killing, torture, inhuman or degrading treatment or punishment if removed from the UK). The status must be granted pursuant to the Immigration Rules[2]. People with humanitarian protection are entitled to family reunion in the same way as refugees[3].

¹ Allocation of Housing and Homelessness (Eligibility) (England) Regulations 2006, SI 2006/1294, reg 5(1)(d); Allocation of Housing and Homelessness (Eligibility) (Wales) Regulations 2014, SI 2014/2603 (W 257), reg 5(1)(d). See also Welsh Code, para 7.8(iv).
² See *Immigration Rules*, HC 395, paras 339C–339H (23 May 1994, as amended).
³ *Immigration Rules*, HC 395, paras 352FA–352FI. See **11.107**.

CLASS F: AFGHAN CITIZENS GRANTED LEAVE TO ENTER UNDER IMMIGRATION RULES, PARA 276BA1, WHO ARE HABITUALLY RESIDENT IN THE CTA

11.116 This class[1] consists of persons habitually resident[2] in the CTA[3] who have limited leave to enter the United Kingdom as a relevant Afghan citizen under para 276BA1 of the Immigration Rules[4]. This is a niche category of leave offered to locally engaged staff in Afghanistan who worked in particularly challenging or dangerous roles in Helmand province[5].

¹ Allocation of Housing and Homelessness (Eligibility) (England) Regulations 2006, SI 2006/1294, reg 5(1)(f); Allocation of Housing and Homelessness (Eligibility) (Wales) Regulations 2014, SI 2014/2603 (W 257), reg 5(1)(f).
² See **11.130–11.136**.
³ See Box 1 at **11.28**.
⁴ *Immigration Rules*, HC 395 (23 May 1994 as amended).

CLASS G: PERSON WHO HAS LIMITED LEAVE TO ENTER OR REMAIN IN THE UK ON FAMILY OR PRIVATE LIFE GROUNDS UNDER ARTICLE 8, WHO IS NOT SUBJECT TO A NO RECOURSE TO PUBLIC FUNDS CONDITION

11.117 To fall within this class a person must[1]:

(a) have limited leave to enter or remain in the United Kingdom on family or private life grounds under Art 8 of the European Convention on Human Rights, such leave granted under paragraph 276BE(1), paragraph 276DG or Appendix FM of the Immigration Rules[2], and

(b) not be subject to a condition requiring that person to maintain and accommodate himself, and any person dependent upon him, without recourse to public funds[3].

This class was introduced in 2016 in England and 2017 in Wales[4]. The purpose of the amendment was to ensure that homeless persons who have been granted limited leave to remain under paragraph 276BE(1), paragraph 276DG or Appendix FM of the Immigration Rules to the Immigration Rules, who are not subject to a no recourse to public funds condition are able to access homelessness assistance under HA 1996, Pt 7[5] or H(W)A 2014, Pt 2.

[1] The Allocation of Housing and Homelessness (Eligibility) (England) Regulations 2006, SI 2006/1294, reg 5(1)(g); the Allocation of Housing and Homelessness (Eligibility) (Wales) Regulations 2014, SI 2014/2603 (W 257), reg 5(1)(g).
[2] Immigration Rules, HC 395 (23 May 1994, as amended).
[3] The requirements of SI 2006/1294, reg 5(1)(g), strictly, do not make grammatical sense: a point highlighted in the Joint Committee on Statutory Instruments Thirteenth Report of Session 2016–17, 16 November 2016 at para 2.4. However, if one refrains from an overly technical reading, the scope of the class is clear and the requirements have been set out here so as to avoid reproducing the error. This grammatical error has been avoided in SI 2014/2603 (W 257), reg 5(1)(g).
[4] SI 2016/1294, reg 5(1)(g) was added by the the Allocation of Housing and Homelessness (Eligibility) (England) (Amendment) Regulations 2016, FN SI 2016/965, in force from 30 October 2016. SI 2014/2603 (W 257), reg 5(1)(g) was added by the Allocation of Housing and Homelessness (Eligibility) (Wales) (Amendment) Regulations 2017, SI 2017/698 (W 164).
[5] As amended by HRA 2017, for applications for homelessness assistance made to local housing authorities in England on or after 3 April 2018.

11.118 The need for the amendments arose from the fact that until July 2012, those seeking leave to remain in the UK relying on Art 8 grounds, would typically have been granted leave outside of the Immigration Rules. As such they would have been eligible for homelessness assistance, under class B provided they were not subject to a no recourse to public funds condition[1].

[1] See Letter from the Homelessness Directorate (Office of the Deputy Prime Minister) to Chief Executives and Housing Directors of English local housing authorities, dated 25 March 2003 and Letter from the Department of Communities and Local Government to Chief Executives and Chief Housing Officers of Local Authorities in England, dated 21 October 2016.

11.119 But in July 2012, the Home Office introduced various new provisions into the Immigration Rules to deal with these cases[1]. Thereafter most Art 8 applications were dealt with within the rules, under para 276BE(1), paragraph 276DG or Appendix FM. The Home Secretary retained a discretion to grant leave outside of the rules where the requirements of the rules were not met, but the grant of leave was still necessary to avoid a breach of Art 8.

1 See *R (Nagre) v Secretary of State for the Home Department* [2013] EWHC 720 (Admin), Admin Ct per Sales J at [7]–[12] and *R (NS) v Secretary of State for the Home Department* [2014] EWHC 1971 (Admin), [2014] Imm AR 1153, Admin Ct per Kenneth Parker J at [54]–[56], for the background to the changes to the Immigration Rules.

11.120 The unintended consequence of this change to the Immigration Rules was that homeless persons granted leave to remain on Art 8 grounds outside of the rules were treated more favourably than those granted Art 8 leave within the rules. On a literal interpretation of class B the former were eligible for assistance whereas the latter were not. On the face of it there was no particular justification for this differential treatment. This led to a number of challenges[1] and, in due course, the amendment of the regulations to remove this inconsistency[2].

1 For example, *Samuels v Lewisham LBC* (2016) September *Legal Action*, pp 37–38, County Court at Central London.
2 See Letter from the Department of Communities and Local Government to Chief Executives and Chief Housing Officers of Local Authorities in England, dated 21 October 2016, at Appendix 2.

11.121 If a person who is subject to immigration control is *not* within any of the Classes A–G described above, and made his or her application for homelessness assistance on or after 1 June 2006 (to a local housing authority in England) or 31 October 2014 (to a local housing authority in Wales), he or she is *not* 'eligible' for homelessness assistance.

Category Two: other 'persons from abroad'

11.122 Ordinarily, persons not subject to immigration control[1] would be eligible for homelessness assistance. However, the Secretary of State and Welsh Ministers are permitted to make regulations treating some people who are not subject to immigration control as 'persons from abroad' and therefore ineligible for homelessness assistance. Both have exercised these powers.

1 See **11.26–11.93** for detailed discussion of how to determine who is, and is not, subject to immigration control.

11.123 In the Allocation of Housing and Homelessness (Eligibility) (England) Regulations 2006[1] and the Allocation of Housing and Homelessness (Eligibility) (Wales) Regulations 2014[2] the Secretary of State and the Welsh Ministers have exercised their powers to treat some people who are not subject to immigration control as 'persons from abroad'[3]. This means that some British citizens, nationals of EEA Member States, and others who are exempt from immigration control may nevertheless be denied homelessness assistance on the grounds that they are 'not eligible'. The primary function of these provisions is to confine homelessness assistance to the ordinary residents of the UK, ie those habitually resident here, and to EEA nationals exercising Treaty rights.

1   SI 2006/1294, as amended. In force for applications for homelessness assistance made to local housing authorities in England on or after 1 June 2006.

2   SI 2014/2603, (W 257). In force for applications for homelessness assistance made to local housing authorities in Wales on or after 31 October 2014.

3   For applications for homelessness assistance made before 1 June 2006 in England and before 31 October 2014 in Wales, see the first and third editions of this book respectively.

11.124 Allocation of Housing and Homelessness (Eligibility) (England) Regulations 2006, reg 6 and Allocation of Housing and Homelessness (Eligibility) (Wales) Regulations 2014, reg 6 establish three classes of people who are to be treated as 'persons from abroad' and therefore *ineligible* for housing assistance despite not being subject to immigration control. They are described in the English Code at para 7.13 and in the Welsh Code at paras 7.9–7.12.

11.125 The *first class*[1] comprises persons who are 'not habitually resident'[2] in the CTA[3]. But that test of habitual residence is subject to a number of exemptions[4].

1   Allocation of Housing and Homelessness (Eligibility) (England) Regulations 2006, SI 2006/1294, reg 6(1)(a); Allocation of Housing and Homelessness (Eligibility) (Wales) Regulations 2014, SI 2014/2603 (W 257), reg 6(1)(a).

2   See **11.130–11.136**.

3   See Box 1 at **11.28**.

4   See **11.137–11.140**.

11.126 The *second class* Comprises EEA nationals and their family members whose only right to reside in the UK is derived from:

- their status as job-seekers;
- their status as family members of job-seekers;
- the exercise of the initial right to reside in the UK for a period not exceeding three months;
- the exercise of a derivative right to reside in the UK as the primary carer of a British citizen; or
- the exercise of a right to reside derived from Art 20 of the Treaty on the Functioning of the EU[1].

1   SI 2006/1294, reg 6(1)(b); SI 2014/2603 (W 257), reg 6(1)(b). See **11.141–11.148**.

11.127 The *third class* Comprises EEA nationals and their family members whose only right to reside in the rest of the CTA (Channel Islands, Isle of Man or the Republic of Ireland) is derived from:

- their status as job-seekers;
- their status as family members of job-seekers;
- the exercise of the initial right to reside in the UK for a period not exceeding three months;
- the exercise of a derivative right to reside in the CTA as the primary carer of an Irish or British citizen;
- the exercise of a right to reside derived from Art 20 of the Treaty on the Functioning of the EU[1].

1   SI 2006/1294, reg 6(1)(c); SI 2014/2603 (W 257), reg 6(1)(c). See **11.149–11.153**.

11.128 Each of the three classes will be examined in turn.

11.129 Note that even if an applicant is eligible under any of these three classes, any members of his or her household who are not eligible will be classed as restricted persons, which may modify the nature of any duty owed to the applicant[1].

¹ See **11.157–11.172**.

The first class: not habitually resident

11.130 'Habitual residence'[1] does not refer to someone's immigration status. A person may be a British citizen, but if he or she is not habitually resident in the CTA[2], he or she will not be eligible[3]. Nor is the term 'habitual residence' defined in either HA 1996, Pt 7[4], H(W)A 2014, Pt 2 or in the regulations[5]. It is a question of fact for the local housing authority to decide. Happily, there is some guidance in the Codes of Guidance[6].

¹ SI 2006/1294, reg 6(1)(a); SI 2014/2603 (W 257), reg 6(1)(a).
² See Box 1 at **11.28**.
³ Unless he or she is exempt from the habitual residence test. See **11.137–11.140**.
⁴ As amended by HRA 2017, for applications for homelessness assistance made to local housing authorities in England on or after 3 April 2018.
⁵ SI 2006/1294 and SI 2014/2603 (W 257).
⁶ English Code, paras 7.14(a), 7.18–7.20 and Annex 1; Welsh Code, paras 7.13 and 2.18–2.24 and Annex 6.

11.131 A person who is not habitually resident will also not be entitled to non-contributory social security benefits. If the person is receiving one of those social security benefits, it must follow that the Department for Work and Pensions (DWP) has determined that he or she is habitually resident[1]. A determination by the DWP is not necessarily binding on a local housing authority[2] but in the interests of good administration and consistent decision making, such a determination should certainly be taken into account by the local housing authority during the decision making process[3] and reasons should be given if the local housing authority elects to depart from the determination[4].

¹ A person who has a derivative right of residence contained at SI 2016/1052, reg 16(5) (the 'Zambrano' right of residence) is treated as not habitually resident for the purposes of entitlement to income support, jobseeker's allowance, state pension credit, and housing benefit (SI 2012/ 2587, in force 8 November 2012) and for universal credit (SI 2013/376, reg 9). See **11.145** fn 3.
² In *Mangion v Lewisham London Borough Council* [2008] EWCA Civ 1642, (2009) January *Legal Action*, p 26, CA and *Simpson-Lowe v Croydon London Borough Council* [2012] EWCA Civ 131, (2012) April *Legal Action*, p 47, CA the Court of Appeal took the view that the findings of the DWP relating to eligibility for disability benefits were not binding on a local housing authority when assessing vulnerability: see **9.76**. However, that was because different legal tests applied in the different legal contexts under consideration. With habitual residence, the same test is applied by both the DWP and the local housing authority.
³ See *R (Clue) v Birmingham City Council* [2010] EWCA Civ 460, [2011] 1 WLR 99, CA on the importance of consistent decision making across government departments and local authorities.
⁴ See **9.111–9.125** on the duty to give reasons.

11.132 There are two aspects required to be present in order to constitute habitual residence:

(1)   a settled purpose of establishing residence in one of the territories of the CTA[1]; and

(2)   an appreciable period of such residence.

[1]   For 'CTA', see **11.28**, Box 1.

11.133 Whether each aspect is satisfied is a question of fact for the local housing authority to decide. The Codes advise that normally, if someone has lived in one of the territories of the CTA for two years continuously prior to his or her application for homelessness assistance, he or she should be considered to be habitually resident without further inquiry[1]. However, that should not be taken as meaning that a person cannot be habitually resident if he or she has lived in one of the territories of the CTA for less than two years. The point is simply that there is little point in a local housing authority wasting resources by making inquiries into whether or not an applicant who came to the UK more than two years ago is habitually resident. In *R (Paul-Coker) v Southwark London Borough Council*[2], a number of instances where people had been resident for periods of time that were shorter than two years, but had been sufficient to constitute 'an appreciable period', were cited to the judge. He said: '[i]t is therefore clear that what constitutes an appreciable period of time for these purposes will vary from case to case and will depend on the facts of the individual case'[3]. In that particular case the local housing authority was wrong in law to have directed itself that an applicant had to have been resident for six months before she could be considered to be habitually resident.

[1]   English Code, para 7.19 and Annex 1, para 1; Welsh Code, paras 2.22 and 7.13 and Annex 6, para 4.
[2]   [2006] EWHC 497 (Admin), [2006] HLR 32, Admin Ct.
[3]   *R (Paul-Coker) v Southwark London Borough Council* [2006] EWHC 497 (Admin), [2006] HLR 32, Admin Ct, Forbes J at [22].

11.134 Establishing a 'settled purpose' will obviously involve consideration of an applicant's subjective intentions and motivations. Someone in stable employment may be more likely to be able to establish his or her 'settled purpose' to be habitually resident than someone who is in transitory employment, or dependent on benefit. However, local housing authorities must be careful not to give too much weight to an applicant's lack of finances and not enough weight to other factors such as the applicant's nationality, ties with the UK, and future intentions[1].

[1]   *Barnet London Borough Council v Shah* [1983] 2 AC 309, HL; and *Olokunboro v Croydon London Borough Council* (2003) February *Legal Action*, p 37, Croydon County Court.

11.135 What constitutes an 'appreciable period of residence' likewise varies according to the circumstances of each individual's case. If a former British resident returns to the UK after living and working abroad, she or he may be habitually resident from the first day of his or her return[1]. When someone is coming to live in the UK for the first time, there must be an appreciable period of residence before habitual residence is obtained. To determine how long that period of residence should be in any particular case, local housing authorities should consider all the circumstances, including:

•   whether the person is seeking to bring any family members to the CTA;

- whether he or she has brought his or her personal property and possessions to the CTA;
- whether he or she has done everything necessary to establish a residence before coming;
- whether he or she has a right of abode; and
- what 'durable ties' there are with the CTA[2].

[1] *Swaddling v Adjudication Officer* [1999] All ER (EC) 217 ECJ; and see CIS/1304/1997 and CJSA/5394/1998; and English Code, para 7.20 and Annex 1, paras 7–8.
[2] *Nessa v Chief Adjudication Officer* [1999] 1 WLR 1937, HL.

11.136 In *R (Paul-Coker) v Southwark London Borough Council*[1], the local housing authority erred in failing to take into account that the applicant had, in fact, been resident for seven months, had given birth to a child who was a British national, had spent her formative years in the UK and had returned for extended holidays in the three years preceding her arrival, that she had travelled to the UK on a one-way ticket and had family and friends in the UK. All of those factors should have been considered.

[1] [2006] EWHC 497 (Admin), [2006] HLR 32, Admin Ct.

EXEMPTIONS FROM THE HABITUAL RESIDENCE TEST

11.137 The following people are eligible for assistance even if they are not habitually resident:

- an EEA national who is a worker[1]; or
- an EEA national who is self-employed[2]; or
- until 30 June 2018[3], a person who is an Accession State national subject to worker authorisation who is authorised in accordance with the Accession Regulations 2013[4](a Croatian national')[5]; or
- a family member of an EEA national who is a worker, a self-employed person, or an Accession State national subject to worker authorisation who is authorised in accordance with the Accession Regulations 2013[6]; or
- a person who has one of certain permanent rights to reside in the UK[7]; or
- a person who is in the UK as a result of having been deported, expelled or otherwise removed by compulsion of law from another country to the UK[8].

[1] Allocation of Housing and Homelessness (Eligibility) (England) Regulations 2006, SI 2006/1294, reg 6(2)(a); Allocation of Housing and Homelessness (Eligibility) (Wales) Regulations 2014, SI 2014/2603 (W 257), reg 6(2)(a). For 'worker' see **11.40–11.46**.
[2] SI 2006/1294, reg 6(2)(b); SI 2014/2603 (W 257), reg 6(2)(b). For 'self-employed' see **11.47–11.49**.
[3] The Secretary of State has the power to make regulations to extend this period pursuant to European Union (Croatian Accession and Irish Protocol) Act 2013, s 4. At the time of writing this power had not been exercised and UK Visas and Immigration have indicated that it will not be exercised in future: https://www.gov.uk/government/publications/guidance-for-croatian -nationals-on-getting-permission-to-work-in-the-uk (last accessed on 22 May 2018).
[4] Accession of Croatia (Immigration and Worker Authorisation) Regulations 2013, SI 2013/1460.
[5] SI 2006/1294, reg 6(2)(c)(ii); SI 2014/2603 (W 257), reg 6(2)(c)(ii). For 'Accession State national subject to worker authorisation' see **11.88–11.92**.

6 SI 2006/1294, reg 6(2)(d); SI 2014/2603 (W 257), reg 6(2)(d). For 'worker' see **11.40–11.46**. For 'self-employed' person see **11.47–11.49**. For 'family member' see **11.54–11.60**. For 'Accession State national subject to worker authorisation' see **11.88–11.92**.
7 SI 2006/1294, reg 6(2)(e); SI 2014/2603 (W 257), reg 6(2)(e). For 'permanent right of residence' see **11.61–11.65**.
8 SI 2006/1294, reg 6(2)(g); SI 2014/2603 (W 257), reg 6(2)(f). This group of persons, who are eligible even if not habitually resident, is probably small. The inclusion of this group brings eligibility for homelessness assistance into line with eligibility for housing benefit.

11.138 Most of these exemptions refer to those persons exercising rights of freedom of movement enjoyed under European Union law and contained in the Immigration (European Economic Area) Regulations 2016[1], which are the current regulations transposing European Union freedom of movement legislation into domestic law.

1 SI 2016/1052.

11.139 The penultimate exemption requires some elaboration. This exemption from the habitual residence test only applies to three sub-classes of persons who are entitled to a permanent right of residence[1]. Those three sub-classes are:

(1) an EEA national who was a worker or self-employed person who has ceased activity[2];
(2) the family member of such an EEA national[3]; and
(3) a person who was:
- the family member of an EEA national who was a worker or self-employed person; and
- the EEA national has died; and
- the family member had resided with the EEA national immediately before his or her death; and
- either the EEA national had resided in the UK for at least two years immediately before his or her death; or
- the death was the result of an accident at work or an occupational disease[4].

1 For 'permanent right of residence' see **11.61–11.65**.
2 Immigration (European Economic Area) Regulations 2016, SI 2016/1052, reg 15(1)(c).
3 SI 2016/1052, reg 15(1)(d).
4 SI 2016/1052, reg 15(1)(e).

11.140 'Worker or self-employed person who has ceased activity' is defined at Immigration (European Economic Area) Regulations 2016, reg 5[1]. For 'family member', see **11.54–11.60**. For 'worker', see **11.40–11.46**. For 'self-employed person' see **11.47–11.49**. A person with a permanent right of residence who does not fall within any of these sub-classes set out at **11.139** will have to satisfy the habitual residence test in order to be eligible.

1 SI 2016/1052.

The second class: EEA nationals with certain rights to reside in the UK

11.141 If an EEA national is[1]:

(a) a job-seeker[2];

(b) a family member[3] of a job-seeker;

(c) only entitled to remain in the UK by virtue of the initial right to reside for three months[4];

(d) has a derivative right to reside because he or she is the primary carer of a British citizen[5]; or

(e) has a right to reside derived from Art 20 of the Treaty on the Functioning of the EU, where the right to reside arises because a British citizen would otherwise be deprived of the genuine enjoyment of the substance of those rights as a EU citizen[6],

he or she cannot be eligible[7]. For those EEA nationals who fall within this class the habitual residence test is not relevant: anyone who falls exclusively within this class cannot be eligible for homelessness assistance irrespective of where he or she habitually resides.

[1] Allocation of Housing and Homelessness (Eligibility) (England) Regulations 2006, SI 2006/1294, reg 6(1)(b); Allocation of Housing and Homelessness (Eligibility) (Wales) Regulations 2014, SI 2014/2603 (W 257), reg 6(1)(b). See also English Code, para 7.14(b)–(e); Welsh Code, para 7.11(ii)–(iv).

[2] See **11.39**.

[3] See **11.54–11.60**.

[4] See **11.35–11.36**.

[5] SI 2016/1052, reg 16(5), see **11.80–11.85**.

[6] See **11.93**.

[7] SI 2006/1294, reg 6(1)(b); SI 2014/2603 (W 257), reg 6(1)(b). Persons falling within the fourth and fifth categories are not eligible if their applications for homelessness assistance were made to local housing authorities in England on or after 8 November 2012 (SI 2012/2588, reg 3). See letter DCLG to Chief Housing Officers of Local Authorities in England, 17 October 2012, at Appendix 2. Persons falling within these categories applying for homelessness assistance to local housing authorities in Wales will not be eligible if the application was made on or after 31 October 2014, SI 2014/2603 (W 257), reg 8. For applications pre-dating 8 November 2012 (in England) and 31 October 2014 (in Wales) see *Pryce v Southwark London Borough Council* [2012] EWCA 1572, [2013] 1 WLR 996, [2013] HLR 10, CA.

11.142 So, this second class operates to ensure that any EEA national, or family member of an EEA national, whose *only* right of residence in the UK is the initial three-month right of residence is not eligible for homelessness assistance.

11.143 It also excludes job-seekers[1] from homelessness assistance. EEA nationals who are 'job-seekers' are 'qualified persons'[2] and therefore are entitled to the extended right of residence[3]. If a job-seeker had previously been employed, he or she may still be a 'worker' in certain circumstances and is potentially eligible because of the 'worker' status[4]. However, if a person's *only* claim to the extended right of residence is because of his or her status as a 'job-seeker', or as a family member[5] of a job-seeker, he or she will not be eligible.

[1] See **11.39**.

[2] See **11.38**.

[3] See **11.37–11.60**.

[4] SI 2016/1052, reg 6(2). See **11.42–11.46**.

[5] See **11.54–11.60**.

11.144 For applications for homelessness assistance made to local housing authorities in England on or after 8 November 2012[1], or to local housing authorities in Wales on or after 31 October 2014[2], there are two additional exclusions from eligibility.

1   SI 2012/2588, reg 3.
2   SI 2014/2603 (W 257), reg 8.

11.145 First, a person who is entitled to an EU right of residence that is derived from being the primary carer of a British national is excluded[1]. He or she is also treated as not habitually resident and thus excluded from receiving non-contributory benefits[2] including housing benefit[3]. He or she is also excluded from eligibility for an allocation of social housing[4]. The 'derivative right of residence' which forms the basis of this exclusion was recognised by the CJEU in the case of *Zambrano v Office national de l'emploi*[5], and is now identified in the Immigration (European Economic Area) Regulations 2016[6], see **11.80–11.85**. People entitled to any of the four other derivative rights of residence in reg 16 of the Immigration (European Economic Area) Regulations 2016[7] do not fall within this second class of people excluded from eligibility.

1   SI 2006/1294, reg 6(1)(b)(iii); SI 2014/2603 (W 257), reg 6(1)(b)(iii). This exclusion reverses the effect of *Pryce v Southwark London Borough Council* [2012] EWCA 1572, [2013] 1 WLR 996, [2013] HLR 10, CA. See further T Vaneghan 'The Pryce of Eligibility' *Legal Action*, February 2013, pp 31–32 for commentary on the background to, and legality of, these regulations. See **11.80–11.85** for a discussion of this derivative right to reside.
2   Social Security (Habitual Residence) (Amendment) Regulations 2012, SI 2012/2587, and Universal Credit Regulations 2013, SI 2013/376, reg 9. A challenge to these regulations as discriminatory was unsuccessful in *R (Sanneh) v Secretary of State for Work and Pensions* [2015] EWCA Civ 49, [2015] HLR 27, CA. That decision was upheld by the Supreme Court in An appeal by one of the Claimants in that case (on another issue) was dismissed by the Supreme Court in *R (HC) v Secretary of State for Work and Pensions* [2017] UKSC 73, [2017] 3 WLR 1486, SC. There is no exclusion prohibiting the person who has this derivative right of residence from working. However, if the person is not in or cannot work (not least because of his or her caring responsibilities) and the household is destitute, the recourse is likely to be to adult care or children's services for financial and accommodation assistance. See CHAPTER 20.
3   Note that the transitional provisions contained in SI 2012/2588 are not matched by those in SI 2012/2587. This creates a predicament whereby applicants for homelessness assistance in England prior to 8 November 2012 relying on this derivative right of residence may be eligible for assistance under HA 1996, Pt 7 but ineligible for housing benefit. In such cases it may be appropriate for a local housing authority to consider charging a 'peppercorn' rent; *R (Yekini) v Southwark London Borough Council* [2014] EWHC 2096 (Admin), (2014) September *Legal Action*, p 50, Admin Ct. See **16.25**.
4   SI 2006/1294, reg 4(1)(b) and (c) (England); SI 2014/2603 (W 257), reg 4(1)(b)(iii) and (iv) (Wales). See **3.12–3.75**.
5   C34/09, [2012] QB 265, CJEU.
6   SI 2016/1052, reg 16(5).
7   SI 2016/1052. See **11.73–11.79** and **11.86–11.87**.

11.146 Second, a person who has a right derived from Art 20 of the Treaty on the Functioning of the EU, in a case where the right to reside arises because a British citizen would otherwise be deprived of the genuine enjoyment of the substance of his or her rights as an EU citizen, is also excluded from eligibility[1]. This new provision appears to exclude those with certain rights of residence arising from Art 20 which have not, as yet, been identified in the Immigration (European Economic Area) Regulations[2], but which are subsequently declared by the CJEU. Article 20 of the Treaty contains the right of nationals of EU member states to be citizens of the EU and to move and reside freely within the territories of the EU Member States. This provision does not exclude all the rights of EU residence that might, in the future, be recognised in CJEU case-law but simply those that are:

- derived from Art 20 of the Treaty; and
- arise because otherwise a British citizen would be deprived of the genuine enjoyment of the substance of his or her rights under EU law.

1 SI 2006/1294, reg 6(1)(b)(iv); SI 2014/2603 (W 257), reg 6(1)(b)(iv).
2 SI 2016/1052.

11.147 For rights declared by the CJEU, see **11.93**[1].

1 The DCLG has written to Chief Housing Officers of Local Authorities in England in relation to these rights, see letter dated 17 October 2012 at Appendix **2**.

11.148 If a person has more than one right of residence, such as being both a job-seeker and being the family member of a worker or self-employed person, then his or her right to reside is not 'only' derived from his or her status as a job-seeker, or from any of the other four provisions in this second class, and he or she will not fall within this second class of persons (not subject to immigration control) who are not eligible for homelessness assistance.

The third class: EEA nationals with certain rights to reside in the CTA

11.149 This third class[1] refers to an EEA nationals whose only right to reside in the rest of the Common Travel Area arises from:

(a) his or her status a job-seeker;
(b) his or her status as the family member of a job-seeker;
(c) an entitlement to remain in the UK by virtue of the initial right to reside for three months;
(d) having a derivative right to reside because he or she is the primary carer of a British or Irish citizen; or
(e) having a right to reside derived from Art 20 of the Treaty on the Functioning of the EU, where the right to reside arises because a British or Irish citizen in the Common Travel Area would otherwise be deprived of the genuine enjoyment of the substance of his or her rights as an EU citizen.

An applicant who falls within one of these categories will not be eligible for assistance[2].

1 Allocation of Housing and Homelessness (Eligibility) (England) Regulations 2006, SI 2006/1294, reg 6(1)(c); Allocation of Housing and Homelessness (Eligibility) (Wales) Regulations 2014, SI 2014/2603 (W 257), reg 6(1)(c). See also English Code, para 7.14(f); Welsh Code, para 7.11(v).
2 SI 2006/1294, reg 6(1)(c); SI 2014/2603 (W 257), reg 6(1)(c).

11.150 For 'job-seeker', see **11.39**. For 'family member', see **11.54–11.60**. For 'initial right to reside', see **11.35–11.36**. For 'Common Travel Area' see Box 1 at **11.28**. For 'persons with a right to reside derived from Art 20 of the Treaty on the Functioning of the EU', see **11.93**.

11.151 The derivative right to reside referred to in this class is not identified in the Immigration (European Economic Area) Regulations 2016[1]. It arises as a result of the CJEU's decision in *Zambrano v Office national de l'emploi*[2]. That decision recognized rights of residence which are directly effective in the remainder of the CTA: ie the Channel Islands, Isle of Man and the Republic of Ireland. A person will have this derivative right of residence if he or she is the primary carer of a British citizen residing in the Channels Islands or the Isle of Man, or of an Irish citizen residing in the Republic of Ireland, and the British or Irish citizen would have to leave those countries and would not be able to reside in any other EU member state if his or her primary carer did not have an EU right of residence.

1 SI 2016/1052.
2 C34/09, [2012] QB 265, CJEU.

11.152 The exclusion from eligibility for homelessness assistance for those people exercising the derivative right of residence or other rights of residence derived from Art 20 applies to applications for homelessness assistance made to local housing authorities in England on or after 8 November 2012[1] and to local housing authorities in Wales on or after 31 October 2014[2].

1 SI 2012/2588, reg 3.
2 SI 2014/2603 (W 257), reg 8.

11.153 As with the second class, if a person has more than one right of residence, then his or her right to reside is not 'only' derived from his or her status as a jobseeker, or from the other four provisions in this class, and he or she will not fall within this third class of persons (not subject to immigration control) who are not eligible for homelessness assistance.

FURTHER RULES ON ELIGIBILITY

Disregard of ineligible members of the household

Overview

11.154 Even if an applicant is eligible for assistance, not all of the members of his or her household will necessarily also be eligible. HA 1996, s 185(4) and H(W)A 2014, Sch 2, para 1(5) provide that, for certain applicants, any member of his or her household who is not eligible for assistance must be disregarded when the local housing authority is considering whether the applicant is homeless or threatened with homelessness, or whether the applicant has a priority need[1].

1 HA 1996, s 185(4); H(W)A 2014, Sch 2, para 1(5).

11.155 HA 1996, s 185(4) as originally enacted was declared incompatible with the Human Rights Act 1998, Sch 1, Art 14[1]. The reason was because its wording at that time provided for a difference in treatment between applicants on the grounds of national origin or on grounds of a combination of one or more of nationality, immigration control, settled residence or social welfare, and that difference in treatment could prevent the applicant and his or her child from being able to enjoy their right to respect for their home and family life (Art 8) and was therefore discriminatory (Art 14). In the context of a British citizen with a young dependent child who was subject to immigration control, the court found that the difference in treatment was not justified. However, until the government took action to remedy the incompatibility, local housing authorities were required to continue to operate HA 1996, s 185(4)[2]. The changes to the law made necessary by the judgment came into force in both England and Wales on 2 March 2009[3] and applied to applications for homelessness assistance made on or after that date[4].

[1] *R (Morris) v Westminster City Council* [2005] EWCA 1184, [2006] HLR 8, CA.
[2] Human Rights Act 1998, s 4(6)(a).
[3] The rules affecting Wales have since been reenacted in H(W)A 2014, Sch 2, para 1(5) and (6).
[4] HA 1996, s 185(4) and (5) as amended and inserted by s 314 and Sch 15 Housing and Regeneration Act 2008.

11.156 Some two and a half years after the new rules came into force, the European Court of Human Rights (ECtHR) considered the same question in the context of an applicant from Sierra Leone with indefinite leave to remain whose dependent son had been granted leave to come to the UK on the express proviso that he should have no recourse to public funds. The issue was whether the previous rules (and, by implication, the current rules)[1] violated an applicant's right to respect for his or her private and family life and home (Art 8) and was discriminatory (contrary to Art 14). The ECtHR found that there was differential treatment between applicants who rely for priority need status on people who are in the UK unlawfully or subject to a condition that they do not have recourse to public funds, and those applicants who rely for priority need on people not subject to the same immigration restriction. It found that the differential treatment was reasonably and objectively justified by the need to allocate the scarce stock of social housing available and that it could be legitimate when allocating social housing to have regard to the immigration status of those who are in need of social housing. Accordingly there was no violation of Art 14 taken in conjunction with Art 8[2].

[1] The change to the rules as a result of the decision in *R (Morris) v Westminster City Council* [2005] EWCA 1184, [2006] HLR 8, CA did not extent to applicants, such as Ms Bah, from outside of the EEA and Switzerland.
[2] *Bah v UK* App No 56328/07 [2011] ECHR 1448, [2012] HLR 2, ECtHR. The current rules were subject to a challenge by means of an application to the ECtHR in the case of *Ijaola-Jokesenumi v UK*, App no 45996/11 [2012] ECHR 652, (2012) September *Legal Action*, p 29. However, the claim was struck out following an agreed settlement between the parties and the ECtHR did not adjudicate on the merits of the case. See (2014) November *Legal Action*, p 41.

The rules on disregarding household members

11.157 The current rules came into force on 2 March 2009 and apply to applications for homelessness assistance made on or after that date to local housing authorities in England and in Wales[1]. They are found at HA 1996, s 185(4) and (5)[2] and H(W)A 2014, Sch 2, para 1(5) and (6). Neither Code of Guidance contains any guidance on the subject.

[1] Applications to local housing authorities in England after 2 March 2009 will be dealt with under HA 1996, s 185(4) and (5). Applications to local housing authorities in Wales after 2 March 2009 but before 27 April 2015 will be dealt with under HA 1996, s 185(4) and (5). Applications to local housing authorities in Wales after 31 October 2014 will be dealt with under H(W)A 2014, Sch 2, paras 1(5) and (6). This distinction is a technical one: there is no substantive difference between the provisions under HA 1996 and H(W)A 2014.

[2]   As amended by Housing and Regeneration Act 2008, s 314 and Sch 15.

THE DISREGARD WHERE THE APPLICANT IS A PERSON SUBJECT TO IMMIGRA-
TION CONTROL

11.158 For applications to local housing authorities made on or after 2 March 2009[1], this disregard of non-eligible household members *only* applies where the eligible *applicant* is:

- subject to immigration control[2];
- eligible as a result of falling within one of the classes of people prescribed as eligible by Regulation[3]; and
- not a national of an EEA state or of Switzerland[4].

[1]   The date applies to applications to local housing authorities in both England and Wales (Housing and Regeneration Act 2008, s 314 and Sch 15).
[2]   See **11.26–11.93.**
[3]   For applications to local housing authorities in England, the classes are Classes A–G at Allocation of Housing and Homelessness (Eligibility) (England) 2006, SI 2006/1294, reg 5(1). For applications to local housing authorities in Wales, the classes are Classes A–G at Allocation of Housing and Homelessness (Eligibility) (Wales) 2014, SI 2014/2603 (W 257), reg 5(1). See **11.106–11.121.**
[4]   HA 1996, s 184(5); H(W)A 2014, Sch 2, para 1(6).

11.159 If the applicant has all of those characteristics, any ineligible members of his or her household must be disregarded when the local housing authority is considering whether the applicant is homeless or threatened with homelessness, or whether the applicant has a priority need[1]. For example, when a local housing authority is considering whether overcrowded accommodation is reasonable for the applicant and his or her household to continue to occupy for the purpose of deciding whether the applicant is homeless or threatened with homelessness, ineligible members of the household cannot be considered. Even more importantly, if an applicant's children or other family members are all persons from abroad and ineligible for assistance, they cannot provide the applicant with a priority need[2].

[1]   HA 1996, s 185(4); H(W)A 2014, Sch 2, para 1(5).
[2]   *R (Morris) v Westminster City Council* [2005] EWCA 1184, [2006] HLR 8, CA. This rule was challenged by means of an application to the ECtHR in the case of *Ijaola-Jokesenumi v UK*, App no 45996/11 [2012] ECHR 652, (2012) September *Legal Action*, p 29. However, the claim was struck out following an agreed settlement between the parties and the ECtHR did not adjudicate on the merits of the case. See (2014) November *Legal Action*, p 41.

11.160 It does not follow, however, that those members of an applicant's household who are not eligible are to be disregarded for all purposes. When it comes to the discharge of the local housing authority's duty by the provision of suitable accommodation, that accommodation must be suitable for the needs of the applicant and his or her household, even if the household includes persons who are not eligible for assistance[1].

[1]   HA 1996, s 176; H(W)A 2014, s 56.

11.161 In addition, local authorities have a range of other statutory duties and powers under which they may provide accommodation, particularly where there are dependent children[1]. If a household is caught by HA 1996, s 185(4) or H(W)A 2014, Sch 2, para 1(5), and none of any dependent children or other vulnerable members are eligible and so cannot confer a priority need, local authorities may consider using those other statutory duties and powers in order to provide accommodation. But they may not do so simply with the object of circumventing the restriction in HA 1996, s 185(4) or H(W)A 2014, Sch 2, para 1(5)[2].

[1] See Chapter 20.
[2] *R (Badu) v Lambeth London Borough Council* [2005] EWCA Civ 1184, [2006] HLR 8, CA; and see Chapter 20 for the range of statutory powers and duties available to local authorities.

DISREGARD ABOLISHED WHERE THE APPLICANT IS NOT A PERSON SUBJECT TO IMMIGRATION CONTROL

11.162 The disregard of ineligible household members does not apply if the applicant is not a person subject to immigration control[1]. The applicant will be entitled to have the whole of his or her household assessed for the purposes of determining whether he or she is homeless and whether he or she has a priority need, irrespective of the immigration status of the people in his or her household.

[1] HA 1996, s 185(4) and (5); H(W)A 2014, Sch 2, paras 1(5) and (6). See **11.26–11.93**.

11.163 However, if there are ineligible members of an applicant's household in those circumstances, the ineligible members are known as 'restricted persons' and, in some circumstances, the duty owed to the applicant may be modified as a result of that person's presence in the household[1]. For applications to a local housing authority in England made on or after 9 November 2012, the modifications are less significant than prior to that date, as a result of the amendments to HA 1996, s 193 made by the Localism Act 2011, ss 148–149. These amendments did not take effect in Wales but the coming into force of H(W)A 2014, Pt 2 on 27 April 2015 has had the same effect.

[1] HA 1996, s 184(7); H(W)A 2014, s 63(5). For the duties owed to 'restricted cases' by local housing authorities, see **16.180–16.185** (England) and **17.177** (Wales). See English Code, paras 7.25–7.28 and Welsh Code, paras 15.73–15.74.

11.164 A 'restricted person' is defined as a person:

- who is not eligible for assistance under HA 1996, Pt 7[1] or H(W)A 2014, Pt 2; and
- who is subject to immigration control within the meaning of the Asylum and Immigration Act 1996[2]; and
- who either does not have leave to enter or remain in the UK; or
- whose leave to enter or remain in the UK is subject to a condition to maintain and accommodate himself or herself, and any dependents, without recourse to public funds[3].

[1] As amended by HRA 2017, for applications for homelessness assistance made to local housing authorities in England on or after 3 April 2018.
[2] See **11.26–11.93**.
[3] HA 1996, s 184(7); H(W)A 2014, s 63(5). For an example of a 'restricted case' and 'restricted person', see *Lekpo-Bozua v Hackney London Borough Council* [2010] EWCA Civ 909, [2010] HLR 46, CA.

11.165 If the applicant is owed the HA 1996, s 193(2) main housing duty[1] (in England) or the H(W)A 2014, s 75 duty[2] (in Wales) and that duty is only owed to the applicant because of the presence in his or her household of a restricted person, the local housing authority has additional notification duties[3]. It must notify the applicant that the main housing duty, or H(W)A 2014, s 75 duty, is owed on the basis of the restricted person's presence in the applicant's household, must name the restricted person, must explain why that person is a restricted person, and must explain the effects of the modifications to the relevant duty. In those circumstances, the applicant's case becomes known as 'a restricted case'[4].

1   HA 1996, s 193(2). See **16.94–16.199**.
2   H(W)A 2014, s 75. See **17.146–17.197**.
3   HA 1996, s 184(3A); H(W)A 2014, s 63(2). See **9.54–9.56**.
4   HA 1996, s 193(3B); H(W)A 2014, s 76(5). See English Code, para 7.25.

11.166 The mere presence of a restricted person in an applicant's household is not sufficient for the applicant's case to become a restricted case. The applicant's case *only* becomes a restricted case if the presence of the restricted person has either:

- caused the applicant to become homeless or threatened with homelessness[1]; or
- caused the applicant to have a priority need.

1   If, for example, the presence of the restricted person or persons has brought the level of overcrowding in the applicant's household to such an extent that it is not reasonable for the applicant to continue to occupy (HA 1996, s 175(3); H(W)A 2014, s 55(3)): see **10.122–10.123**. Or where the applicant is homeless because accommodation is not available for the occupation of the applicant together with the restricted person. (HA 1996, s 176; H(W)A 2014, s 56): see **10.17–10.32**. In practical terms it seems unlikely that the presence of a restricted person could ever cause a person to become threatened with homelessness, though the legislation does, technically, cater for this possibility.

11.167 If the applicant would have been homeless or threatened with homelessness, and/or had a priority need, whether or not he or she had the restricted person in his or her household, his or her case will not be a restricted case.

Duties owed to restricted cases

11.168 Since the amendments to HA 1996, s 193 made by Localism Act 2011, s 148, which apply to applications for homelessness assistance made to a local housing authority in England on or after 9 November 2012[1], and the coming into force of H(W)A 2014, which applies to applications for homelessness assistance made to a local housing authority in Wales on or after 27 April 2015, the distinction between restricted cases and other applicants has become less significant. This is because HA 1996, Pt 7[2] and H(W)A Pt 2 both now allow for the HA 1996, s 193(2) main housing duty (in England) and the H(W)A 2014, s 75 duty (in Wales) to be brought to an end by a private rented sector offer in any case, irrespective of the eligibility of the members of the applicant's household[3]. The increased recourse to the private rented sector which the Homelessness Reduction Act 2017[4] seeks to promote is likely to reduce the significance of the distinction between restricted cases and other applicants further[5].

[1] See previous editions of this text (Luba & Davies (1st edn, 2006; 2nd edn, 2010; 3rd edn, 2012)) for applications made prior to this date.
[2] As amended by HRA 2017, for applications for homelessness assistance made to local housing authorities in England on or after 3 April 2018.
[3] See HA 1996, s 193(7AA) (**16.153–16.179**); H(W)A 2014, s 76(3)(b) (**17.173–17.177**).
[4] The amendments made to HA 1996, Pt 7 by the HRA 2017 apply to applications for homelessness assistance made to local housing authorities in England on or after 3 April 2018.
[5] See Chapter 16 for the various ways in which the duties owed to applicants for homelessness assistance to local housing authorities in England may be brought to an end.

11.169 If an applicant is a 'restricted case'[1], the local housing authority is required to bring the HA 1996, s 193(2) main housing duty (in England) or the H(W)A 2014, s 75 duty (in Wales) to an end by making a private rented sector offer, so far as is reasonably practicable[2]. Any regulations made by the Secretary of State in respect of England[3], specifying a minimum period greater than 12 months for a private rented sector offer need not apply to restricted cases[4], so if, in a regulation in the future, a longer minimum period is specified for most applicants in England owed the main housing duty, restricted cases may still be made a private rented sector offer of a 12-month fixed-term tenancy[5].

[1] HA 1996, s 193(3B); H(W)A 2014, s 76(5). See **11.163–11.166**.
[2] HA 1996, s 193(7AD); H(W)A 2014, s 76(5). See English Code, para 7.25.
[3] The power to make such regulations in England is found in HA 1996, s 193(10). There is no equivalent power in H(W)A 2014, Pt 2.
[4] HA 1996, s 193(11)(b).
[5] At the date of writing, all applicants in England can be made a private rented sector offer for a minimum term of 12 months. See **16.153–16.179**.

11.170 A further distinction which applies only to applications made in England is that an applicant who is a restricted case need not have been informed in writing of the effect under HA 1996, s 195A[1] of a further application to a local housing authority within two years of acceptance of a private rented sector offer[2]. This is because the special provisions at HA 1996, s 195A[3], which provide for the interim accommodation duty at HA 1996, s 188 and/or the main housing duty at HA 1996, s 193 to be owed regardless of whether the applicant has a priority need[4], do not apply where the main housing duty would not apply without having regard to the presence of a restricted person in the applicant's household[5]. Under H(W)A 2014, Pt 2, there is no equivalent provision to HA 1996, s 195A[6] and so these issues do not arise in respect of applications for homelessness assistance made in Wales.

[1] As amended by HRA 2017, s 4(4) for applications for homelessness assistance made to local housing authorities in England on or after 3 April 2018. See **8.100–8.107**.
[2] HA 1996, s 193(7AB)(c). See **16.153–16.179**.
[3] As amended by HRA 2017, s 4(4) for applications for homelessness assistance made to local housing authorities in England on or after 3 April 2018. See **8.100–8.107**.
[4] HA 1996, ss 188(1A) and 195A(1).
[5] HA 1996, s 195A(5) as amended by HRA 2017, s 4(4) for applications for homelessness assistance made to local housing authorities in England on or after 3 April 2018. See **8.100–8.107**.
[6] As amended by HRA 2017, s 4(4) for applications for homelessness assistance made to local housing authorities in England on or after 3 April 2018.

11.171 The wording of HA 1996, s 195A[1] is somewhat confusing. It provides that if the local housing authority would not have been satisfied that the applicant was homeless and eligible and had not become homeless intentionally had it not had 'regard to a restricted person', then the special provisions do not apply and the applicant must also have a priority need in order to be entitled to the main housing duty. So if an applicant would have been unintentionally homeless and eligible for assistance whether or not a restricted person was in his or her household, he or she will still be entitled to the special provisions and to the main housing duty without having to show a priority need. From the wording of the subsection, it appears that it is only if the presence of the restricted person has rendered the applicant homeless[2], that the applicant would also need to have a priority need in order to be entitled to the main housing duty.

[1] As amended by HRA 2017, s 4(4) for applications for homelessness assistance made to local housing authorities in England on or after 3 April 2018.
[2] Perhaps because the arrival of the restricted person has made the accommodation overcrowded and unreasonable to occupy or because his or her presence has resulted in the landlord requiring possession.

11.172 If the applicant who makes a further application for homelessness assistance to a local housing authority in England within two years of the date of his or her acceptance of a private rented sector offer is only entitled to the main housing duty because of the presence in his or her household of a restricted person, he or she will again be regarded as a 'restricted case'[1]. The modifications to the main housing duty will apply and the local housing authority will be required, so far as is reasonably practicable, to make a private rented sector offer to the applicant[2], and will not be required to notify him or her of the special provision at HA 1996, s 195A[3].

[1] HA 1996, s 193(3B).
[2] HA 1996, s 193(7AD).
[3] HA 1996, s 193(7AB)(c).

The Isles of Scilly

11.173 The Isles of Scilly are administratively part of England[1], but special measures have been taken to protect the very limited stock of social housing on those islands. HA 1996[2] enables the Secretary of State to make an order adapting HA 1996, Pt 7[3] in its application to the Isles of Scilly and that power has been used to make special provisions governing eligibility for applicants applying for homelessness assistance there[4].

[1] Interpretation Act 1978, s 5 and Sch 1.
[2] HA 1996, s 225(1).
[3] As amended by HRA 2017, for applications for homelessness assistance made to local housing authorities in England on or after 3 April 2018.
[4] Homelessness (Isles of Scilly) Order 1997, SI 1997/797.

11.174 The order amends HA 1996, ss 183–218[1], to provide that a person is not eligible for homelessness assistance from the authorities in the Isles of Scilly unless he or she has been resident in the district of the Isles of Scilly for a total period of two years and six months during the period of three years immediately prior to the application[2]. If an applicant is eligible, by virtue of having resided in the Isles of Scilly for that period, he or she is also deemed to have a local connection with the Isles of Scilly[3].

[1] As amended by HRA 2017, for applications for homelessness assistance made to local housing authorities in England on or after 3 April 2018.
[2] SI 1997/797, reg 2(2).
[3] SI 1997/797, reg 2(3). See also **14.226–14.229**.

Chapter 12

PRIORITY NEED

Contents

INTRODUCTION

12.1 For the large part of the four decades following the enactment of the Housing (Homeless Persons) Act 1977, the question of whether or not an applicant had a priority need was of central importance to the determination of his or her homelessness application and the help which he or she would receive in consequence of this determination. The answer to that question dictated whether or not the help provided to the applicant might be restricted to the provision of advice and assistance, often limited in extent and variable in quality[1], or might extend to having accommodation secured for his or her occupation. As Crisis put it:

> The Housing (Homeless Persons) Act (1977) made local authorities responsible for the long-term rehousing of some groups of homeless people for the first time. The Act defined which groups of homeless people were considered to have a 'priority need' and therefore might be owed a statutory duty to be secured settled accommodation by local authorities. This is commonly referred to as the 'main homelessness duty'. The 1977 Act ushered in a transformative legal change for many homeless people but also created a longstanding distinction between those defined as priority need who are owed the main homelessness duty (predominantly families with dependent children) and those who are not (predominantly single people, including couples without dependent children)[2].

---

[1] See *Turned Away* (Crisis, 2014).

[2] *The homelessness legislation: an independent review of the legal duties owed to homeless people* (Crisis, 2015), p 8. This review contained the draft legislation which went on to form the basis of the Homelessness Reduction Bill, introduced to Parliament by means of a Private Member's Bill by Bob Blackman MP.

12.2 It was this 'longstanding distinction' which the Housing (Wales) Act 2014[1] (H(W)A 2014), Pt 2 and the amendments to the Housing Act 1996 (HA 1996), Pt 7 made by the Homelessness Reduction Act 2017[2] (HRA 2017) sought to address. One of the stated aims of the H(W)A 2014, Pt 2 was to 'extend the help available to people by improving services for those who are not in priority need'[3]. Likewise, the HRA 2017, the drafting of which was modelled on H(W)A 2014, Pt 2, was intended to 'create a more robust package of advice and assistance to prevent and relieve homelessness for all applicants regardless of priority need status'[4].

[1] For applications for homelessness assistance made to local housing authorities in Wales on or after 27 April 2015. See Housing (Wales) Act (Commencement No 3 and Transitory Transitional and Saving Provisions) Order 2015, SI 2015/1272 (W 88).

[2] For applications for homelessness assistance made to local housing authorities in England on or after 3 April 2018. See Homelessness Reduction Act 2017 (Commencement and Transitional and Savings Provisions) Regulations 2018, SI 2018/167, reg 3.

[3] *Housing (Wales) Bill, Explanatory Memorandum* (Welsh Government, November 2013) p 16.

[4] *The homelessness legislation: an independent review of the legal duties owed to homeless people* (Crisis, 2015), p 20. See **12.1** fn 3.

12.3 The legislation sought to achieve this by means of two separate duties owed to any applicant who is eligible for assistance and either threatened with homelessness or homeless, irrespective of whether he or she has a priority need. Respectively these are:

- the HA 1996, s 195(2) and H(W)A 2014, s 66 prevention[1] duty to take reasonable steps to help the applicant secure that suitable accommodation does not cease to be available for his or her occupation;
- the HA 1996, s 189B(2) and H(W)A 2014, s 73 relief[2] duty to take reasonable steps to help the applicant secure that suitable accommodation becomes available for his or her occupation.

[1] HA 1996, s 195(2) as amended by HRA 2017, s 4(2) for applications for homelessness assistance made to local housing authorities in England on or after 3 April 2018; H(W)A 2017, s 66(1). See **15.87–15.137** and **17.45–17.72.**

[2] HA 1996, s 189B(2) as inserted by HRA 2017, s 5(2) for applications for homelessness assistance made to local housing authorities in England on or after 3 April 2018; H(W)A 2017, s 73(1). See **15.138–15.189** and **17.73–17.117.**

12.4 As a consequence, the question of whether or not an applicant for homelessness assistance has a priority need is of less significance for applicants for homelessness assistance than it used to be. However, despite the fact that applicants who do not have a priority need should now receive rather more effective help than used to be the case, the question of whether or not the applicant has a priority need remains a significant one and will still need to be addressed in most, if not all, cases[1]. The complex body of rules which dictate whether or not an applicant has a priority need form the subject of this chapter.

[1] See **12.5–12.21.**

When and why it matters

12.5 To understand when and why the question of priority need may (or may not) be significant it helps to consider the application and decision making process in stages.

The application stage

12.6 At the outset of an application for homelessness assistance, the local housing authority must take a preliminary view about priority need. If the local housing authority has reason to believe that the applicant may have a priority need and may also be homeless and eligible, it *must* provide interim accommodation while it works out what duty under HA 1996, Pt 7 or H(W)A 2014, Pt 2 (if any) the applicant is owed[1]. The threshold for the provision of interim accommodation is very low; any 'reason to believe' that an applicant may have a priority need is sufficient. There have been findings of maladministration against local housing authorities which turned away applicants, telling them to obtain medical evidence, and, as a result, failed to discharge their duty to provide interim accommodation[2]. The burden of making inquiries rests on the local housing authority; it is not for the applicant to have to prove his or her case[3].

1 HA 1996, s 188(1)–(1ZB) as amended by HRA 2017, s 5(4)(a) for applications for homelessness assistance made to local housing authorities in England on or after 3 April 2018; H(W)A 2014, s 68(1) and (2). See also *Homelessness Code of Guidance for Local Authorities* (Ministry of Housing, Communities and Local Government, February 2018) (the English Code), paras 15.4–15.6, at Appendix 2 of this book and *Code of Guidance for Local Authorities on the Allocation of Accommodation and Homelessness* (Welsh Government, March 2016), para 11.3, on the CD Rom with this book. The interim duties are more fully discussed at **16.37–16.73** and **17.118–17.133**.

2 *Complaint against Southwark London Borough Council*, 14 002 981, 9 October 2014 (2015) April *Legal Action*, p 46; *Complaint against Haringey London Borough Council*, 13 019 000, 10 July 2014 (2015) March *Legal Action*, p 45; *Complaint against Tunbridge Wells Borough Council*, 89/A/2825; *Complaint against Ealing London Borough Council*, 90/A/2032; *Complaint against Kingston upon Hull City Council*, 90/C/2893; *Complaint against Eastleigh Borough Council*, 06/B/7896; *Complaint against Hammersmith & Fulham London Borough Council*, 09 001 262, 21 January 2010, (2010) March *Legal Action*, p 31; *Complaint against Richmond upon Thames Royal London Borough Council*, 10 009 069, 10 February 2011, (2011) April *Legal Action*, p 30; *Complaint against Hounslow London Borough Council*, 10 019 388, 5 October 2011 (2011) December *Legal Action*, p 29; and *Complaint against Hounslow London Borough Council*, 11 008 191, 28 August 2012 (2012) November *Legal Action*, p 14, *Complaint against Eastbourne Borough Council*, 14 016 059, 29 February 2016 (2016) September *Legal Action*, p 37, *Complaint against Barnet London Borough Council*, 16 002 971, 8 March 2017 (2017) May *Legal Action*, p 37.

3 See **9.31–9.35**.

The decision stage

12.7 There are various decision which a local housing authority may need to make in the course of considering a homelessness application and we will consider each of the possible decisions in the order in which they may arise. A local housing authority will not necessarily need to make all of these decisions in every case. Much will depend upon the applicant's situation at the time he or she makes his or her application for homelessness assistance and the effectiveness of the help provided by the local housing authority following his or her application. But a local housing authority will have to make at least one these decisions following the receipt of an application for homelessness assistance.

The first decision – whether or not the prevention duty is owed

12.8 The HA 1996, s 195(2) or H(W)A 2014, s 66 prevention[1] duty will be owed to any applicant who is threatened with homelessness[2] and eligible for assistance[3], irrespective of whether he or she has a priority need. In deciding whether or not this duty is owed, the local housing authority is not required to consider whether or not the applicant has a priority need. However, if the applicant is owed this duty then the local housing authority must also make an assessment of his or her case with a view to identifying what steps should be taken to help the applicant to retain his or her accommodation[4]. In practice, this assessment is likely to involve some consideration of the matters relevant to whether or not the applicant has a priority need.

[1]   HA 1996, s 195(2) as amended by HRA 2017, s 4(2) for applications for homelessness assistance made to local housing authorities in England on or after 3 April 2018; H(W)A 2017, s 66(1). See **15.87–15.137** and **17.45–17.72**.
[2]   See **10.144–10.147**.
[3]   See Chapter **11**.
[4]   HA 1996, s 189A(2) as inserted by HRA 2017, s 3(1) for applications for homelessness assistance made to local housing authorities in England on or after 3 April 2018; H(W)A 2014, s 62(1) and (5). See **15.62–15.86** and **9.13**.

The second decision – whether or not the relief duty is owed

12.9 The HA 1996, s 189B(2) or H(W)A 2014, s 73 relief[1] duty will be owed to any applicant who is homeless[2] and eligible for assistance[3], irrespective of whether he or she has a priority need. In deciding whether or not this duty is owed, the local housing authority is not required to consider whether or not the applicant has a priority need. However, if the applicant is owed this duty then the local housing authority must also make an assessment of his or her case with a view to identifying what steps should be taken to help the applicant to secure accommodation[4]. In practice, this assessment is likely to involve some consideration of the matters relevant to whether or not the applicant has a priority need.

[1]   HA 1996, s 189B(2) as inserted by HRA 2017, s 5(2) for applications for homelessness assistance made to local housing authorities in England on or after 3 April 2018; H(W)A 2017, s 73(1). See **15.138–15.189** and **17.73–17.117**.
[2]   See Chapter **10**.
[3]   See Chapter **11**.
[4]   HA 1996, s 189A(2) as inserted by HRA 2017, s 3(1) for applications for homelessness assistance made to local housing authorities in England on or after 3 April 2018; H(W)A 2014, s 62(1) and (5). See **15.62–15.86** and **9.13**.

The third decision – what duty is owed after the relief duty comes to an end

12.10 The question of whether the applicant has a priority need will assume critical importance in those cases where the applicant has been found to be homeless and eligible for assistance, but the HA 1996, s 189B(2) or H(W)A 2014, s 73 relief[1] duty has come to an end and the applicant has not yet been successful in obtaining accommodation. In these cases the question of what, if any, duty the applicant will be owed next will turn on whether he or she has a priority need.

1   HA 1996, s 189B(2) as inserted by HRA 2017, s 5(2) for applications for homelessness assistance made to local housing authorities in England on or after 3 April 2018; H(W)A 2017, s 73(1). See **15.138–15.189** and **17.73–17.117**.

12.11 If the applicant has a priority need, did not become homeless intentionally[1] and is still homeless (England) or without suitable accommodation available to him or her which is likely to remain available for at least six months (Wales), then the HA 1996, s 193(2), main housing duty or the H(W)A 2014, s 75 duty will be owed[2], providing that the relief duty did not come to an end by reason of certain specified acts or omissions on the part of the applicant[3]. This means that the local housing authority must secure that accommodation is available for the applicant's occupation. The Welsh Code describes this function as a 'safety net for those applicants deemed to be most in need'[4].

1   See Chapter 13.
2   HA 1996, s 193(2); H(W)A 2014, s 75(1). See **16.94–16.199** and **17.146–17.197**. Note that for applicants for homelessness assistance to local housing authorities in Wales, the local housing authority will only consider whether the applicant has become homeless intentionally where the decision making process set out at **13.252–13.255** has been followed. Otherwise the local housing authority will not consider this issue and the applicant will be owed the H(W)A 2014, s 75 duty irrespective of whether he or she became homeless intentionally: see H(W)A 2014, s 75(1) and (2).
3   Specifically, in relation to applications for homelessness assistance made to a local housing authority in England, the HA 1996, s 193(2) main housing duty will not apply where the HA 1996, s 189B(2) relief duty (as inserted by HRA 2017, s 5(2) for applications for homelessness assistance made to local housing authorities in England on or after 3 April 2018) has come to end by reason of the applicant refusing a 'final accommodation offer' (defined by HA 1996, s 193A(4) as inserted by HRA 2017, s 7(1) for applications for homelessness assistance made to local housing authorities in England on or after 3 April 2018) or a 'final Pt 6 offer' (defined by HA 1996, s 193A(5) as inserted by HRA 2017, s 7(1) for applications for homelessness assistance made to local housing authorities in England on or after 3 April 2018) or where notice has been given under HA 1996 s 193B(2) (as inserted by HRA 2017, s 7(1) for applications for homelessness assistance made to local housing authorities in England on or after 3 April 2018) that the applicant has deliberately and unreasonably refused to take any step recorded in his or her personal plan under HA 1996, s 189A (as inserted by HRA 2017, s 3(1) for applications for homelessness assistance made to local housing authorities in England on or after 3 April 2018). See HA 1996, s 193(1A) (as inserted by HRA 2017, s 7(2) for applications for homelessness assistance made to local housing authorities in England on or after 3 April 2018). In relation to applications for homelessness assistance made to local housing authorities in Wales, the H(W)A 2014, s 75 duty will not apply where the relief duty has come to an end by virtue of H(W)A 2014, s 74(5) as a result of the applicant refusing an offer of suitable accommodation. See H(W)A 2015, s 75(1).
4   Welsh Code, para 16.2.

12.12 For applicants to local housing authorities in England where the applicant has a priority need and did not become homeless intentionally, but the relief duty came to an end by virtue of HA 1996, s 193C(2)[1] after notice was given under HA 1996 s 193B(2)[2] that the applicant had deliberately and unreasonably refused to take any step recorded in his or her personal plan[3], the HA 1996, s 193(2) main housing duty will not apply[4]. Instead the applicant will be owed the duty at HA 1996, s 193C(4)[5]. This means that the local housing authority will be required to secure that accommodation is available for occupation by the applicant. In practice this is very similar to the HA 1996, s 193(2) main housing duty. This distinction lies in the different ways in which the two duties may be brought to an end[6].

1   As inserted by HRA 2017, s 7(1) for applications for homelessness assistance made to local
     housing authorities in England on or after 3 April 2018.
2   As inserted by HRA 2017, s 7(1) for applications for homelessness assistance made to local
     housing authorities in England on or after 3 April 2018.
3   Produced under HA 1996, s 189A as inserted by HRA 2017, s 3(1) for applications for
     homelessness assistance made to local housing authorities in England on or after 3 April 2018.
     See **15.62–15.86**.
4   HA 1996, s 193(1A) as inserted by HRA 2017, s 7(2) for applications for homelessness
     assistance made to local housing authorities in England on or after 3 April 2018.
5   As inserted by HRA 2017, s 7(1) for applications for homelessness assistance made to local
     housing authorities in England on or after 3 April 2018.
6   Contrast HA 1996, s 193C(5) and (6) (as inserted by HRA 2017, s 7(1) for applications for
     homelessness assistance made to local housing authorities in England on or after 3 April 2018)
     with HA 1996, s 193(5)–(7) and (7AA). See further **16.113–16.189** and **16.204–16.216**
     respectively.

12.13 If the applicant has a priority need but became homeless intentionally
then, if the application was made to a local housing authority in England, the
local housing authority must secure that accommodation is available for the
applicant's occupation for such period as they consider will give him or her a
reasonable opportunity of securing accommodation, and secure that he or she
is provided with advice and assistance in any attempts he or she may make to
secure that accommodation becomes available for his or her occupation[1].
Alternatively, if the application was made to a local housing authority in
Wales, the local housing authority will owe no further duty[2]. If the applicant
does not have a priority need then no further duty will be owed.

1   HA 1996, s 190(2). See **16.81–16.93**.
2   Note that H(W)A 2014, s 75(3) is not yet in force. According to the Welsh Code, para 14.8
     it is anticipated that this section will be brought into force in 2019. When this happens the
     duty to secure accommodation under H(W)A 2014, s 75(3) to those applicants who have a
     priority need who became homeless intentionally will be extended. See **17.2**.

12.14 In England, the local housing authority is *not*, at this stage, concerned
with whether the applicant had a priority need at the date of *application*, but
rather with whether she or he has a priority need at the date of the *decision* as
to what (if any) HA 1996, Pt 7[1] duty is, or will be, owed once the HA 1996,
s 189B(2) relief[2] duty comes to an end. If there has been a change of
circumstances between the making of the application and the date of the
decision, the local housing authority must take that change into account. In
one case, which reached the Court of Appeal, the applicant had had a priority
need at the date of application and for the following six days, but not at the
date of the decision[3].

1   As amended by HRA 2017, for applications for homelessness assistance made to local housing
     authorities in England on or after 3 April 2018.
2   HA 1996, s 189B(2) (as inserted by HRA 2017, s 5(2) for applications for homelessness
     assistance made to local housing authorities in England on or after 3 April 2018). See
     15.138–15.189.
3   *R v Kensington and Chelsea Royal London Borough Council ex p Amarfio* (1995) 27 HLR
     543, CA.

12.15 The question for the local housing authority is whether, at the date of
its decision (or, if a review has been requested, at the date of the review
decision) the applicant has a priority need[1]. The local housing authority must

not improperly delay making its decision (or concluding its review) in order to see whether the applicant might meanwhile lose an apparent priority need[2]. It is not at all unusual for an applicant to have one form of priority need at the date of application (eg pregnancy) and another at the date of decision or review (eg a dependent child).

[1]   *Mohammed v Hammersmith and Fulham London Borough Council* [2001] UKHL 57, [2002] 1 AC 547, HL. See English Code, para 8.4.
[2]   *Robinson v Hammersmith & Fulham London Borough Council* [2006] EWCA Civ 1122, [2007] HLR 7, CA. See English Code, para 8.4.

12.16 In contrast, the position for local housing authorities in Wales varies according to which category of priority need the applicant falls within. Where priority need status is dependent on establishing that the applicant is between 16 and 21 years old[1], then the local housing authority must rely on his or her age at the date of application[2]. Otherwise the position is the same as under HA 1996, Pt 7[3]: the applicant's status must be considered as of the time of the decision as to what duty, if any, is or, will be, owed to him or her following the performance of the relief duty[4].

[1]   H(W)A 2014, s 70(1)(f), (g) and (h). See **12.212–12.213**, **12.214–12.216** and **12.217–12.219** respectively. This avoids the situation whereby a young person loses priority need status as a result of unavoidable delay in processing his or her application.
[2]   Welsh Code, paras 16.40 and 16.46.
[3]   As amended by HRA 2017, for applications for homelessness assistance made to local housing authorities in England on or after 3 April 2018.
[4]   H(W)A 2014, s 73(1). See **17.73–17.117**.

After the decision

12.17 Once the local housing authority has reached a decision that the applicant has a priority need and has identified what duty it therefore owes to the applicant, that duty will not be displaced by any later change in the applicant's priority need (unless a review has been sought and the change takes place between the original decision and conclusion of the review[1]). The schemes of HA 1996, Pt 7 and H(W)A 2014, Pt 2 do not permit a concluded duty to be re-opened simply because priority need is later lost. Once a duty has been accepted, save for very limited exceptions[2], the duty continues until it is discharged[3].

[1]   *Temur v Hackney LBC* [2014] EWCA Civ 877, [2014] HLR 39, CA. English Code, para 8.4
[2]   Such as where fraud or deception on the part of the applicant has been discovered. See **9.143** and **16.103**.
[3]   *R v Brent London Borough Council ex p Sadiq* (2001) 33 HLR 47, QBD. English Code, para 8.4; Welsh Code, para 14.7(iii).

12.18 However, the manner in which the local housing authority's duty to the applicant is performed may be affected if priority need is lost. An obvious example would be where the applicant is provided with temporary four-bedroom accommodation because four dependent children, who are residing with him or her, confer a priority need. If those children all leave, the local housing authority will be entitled to perform its duty by providing smaller accommodation.

12.19 *Priority Need*

On a new application

12.19 If the applicant has been owed the HA 1996, s 193(2) main housing duty[1] or H(W)A 2014, s 75 duty[2] and that duty ends, the applicant may apply again[3]. It is quite irrelevant that the applicant had a priority need on his or her earlier application. What is important is whether she or he may have a priority need at the date of the new application and at the date of the decision on that new application.

[1] See **16.94–16.199**.
[2] See **17.146–17.197**.
[3] HA 1996, s 193(9). See **8.77–8.91**. There is no equivalent provision in H(W)A 2014, Pt 2, but the only limit which is placed on further applications in contained in H(W)A 2014, s 62(2).

12.20 If the applicant was not owed the HA 1996, s 193(2) main housing duty or the H(W)A 2014, s 75 duty on the initial application (because she or he had no priority need) but has now applied again, it will be critically important whether she or he has since acquired a priority need. Subsequently acquiring a priority need may constitute a change of the factual position so that the local housing authority is required to entertain and inquire into the new application[1].

[1] *R (Van der Stolk) v Camden London Borough Council* [2002] EWHC 1261 (Admin), (2002) July *Legal Action*, p 26, Admin Ct; H(W)A 2014, s 62(2).

12.21 An applicant whose earlier application for homelessness assistance was made to a local housing authority in England on or after 9 November 2012, who had accepted a private rented sector offer[1], and who subsequently makes a fresh application for homelessness assistance to a local housing authority in England within two years of the date of accepting the offer, will generally not need to have a priority need in order to be entitled to the HA 1996, s 193(2) main housing duty again. He or she will still have to be homeless, eligible for assistance, and the local housing authority not be satisfied that he or she became homeless intentionally in order to be entitled to that duty[2]. The exception is where a local housing authority in England is only satisfied that the applicant is homeless or eligible for assistance, and is not satisfied that he or she became homeless intentionally, as a result of the presence in his or her household of a 'restricted person'[3]. Where that is the case, the applicant must still have a priority need in order to be entitled to the main housing duty[4]. Generally, it will be the very presence of the restricted person in the applicant's household that will give the applicant a priority need.

[1] HA 1996, s 193(7AA)–(7AC) defines 'private rented sector offers'. See **16.153–16.179**.
[2] HA 1996, s 195A as amended by HRA 2017, s 4(4) for applications for homelessness assistance made to local housing authorities in England on or after 3 April 2018. See **8.100–8.107**.
[3] As defined at HA 1996, s 184(7). See **11.163–11.164**.
[4] HA 1996, s 195A(5) as amended by HRA 2017, s 4(4) for applications for homelessness assistance made to local housing authorities in England on or after 3 April 2018. See **8.100–8.107**.

OVERVIEW OF THE STATUTORY SCHEME

England

12.22 The concept and definition of 'priority need' was first given statutory expression in the Housing (Homeless Persons) Act 1977 and is now found in very similar (but not precisely the same) terms in HA 1996, s 189(1). HA 1996, Pt 7[1] sets out four different categories. If the applicant falls into any one of the four categories, he or she has a priority need.

[1] As amended by HRA 2017, for applications for homelessness assistance made to local housing authorities in England on or after 3 April 2018.

12.23 Those categories are:

- a pregnant woman or a person with whom she resides or might reasonably be expected to reside[1];
- a person with whom dependent children reside or might reasonably be expected to reside[2];
- a person who is vulnerable as a result of old age, mental illness or mental handicap or physical disability or other special reason, or with whom such a person resides or might reasonably be expected to reside[3]; and
- a person who is homeless or threatened with homelessness as a result of an emergency such as flood, fire or other disaster[4].

[1] HA 1996, s 189(1)(a). See **12.37–12.40**.
[2] HA 1996, s 189(1)(b). See **12.41–12.75**.
[3] HA 1996, s 189(1)(c). See **12.76–12.125**.
[4] HA 1996, s 189(1)(d). See **12.126–12.131**.

12.24 Each of these four categories is examined in more detail at **12.37–12.131**.

12.25 The Secretary of State is given powers under HA 1996, Pt 7[1], to specify further categories of priority need and to amend or repeal any part of the four statutory categories[2]. For more than 20 years, the statutory categories remained unchanged. In 2002, however, further categories were added by the Secretary of State.

[1] As amended by HRA 2017, for applications for homelessness assistance made to local housing authorities in England on or after 3 April 2018.
[2] HA 1996, s 189(2).

12.26 The Homelessness (Priority Need for Accommodation) (England) Order 2002[1], made by the Secretary of State, came into force from 31 July 2002. It adds six *additional* categories to those at HA 1996, s 189(1). In summary they cover:

(1)   a child aged 16 or 17, subject to exceptions[2];
(2)   a young person under 21, who has been looked after, accommodated or fostered, but who is not a student in full-time education[3];
(3)   a person over 21 who is vulnerable as a result of having been looked after, accommodated or fostered[4];

(4)   a person who is vulnerable as a result of having served in the armed forces[5];

(5)   a person who is vulnerable as a result of having been imprisoned[6]; and

(6)   a person who is vulnerable as a result of ceasing to occupy accommodation because of actual or threatened violence[7].

[1]   SI 2002/2051.
[2]   SI 2002/2051, art 3. Since the making of this Order, both case-law and government guidance have directed that a homeless child in these circumstances will generally be considered 'a child in need' (Children Act 1989, s 20) so a duty to secure accommodation will be owed by a children's services authority. Most importantly, the guidance emphasises that local housing authorities and children's services authorities should work together and co-operate in order to meet the accommodation and other needs of children and young people. See **12.133–12.159**.
[3]   SI 2002/2051, art 4. See **12.160–12.165**.
[4]   SI 2002/2051, art 5(1). See **12.170–12.173**.
[5]   SI 2002/2051, art 5(2). See **12.174–12.179**.
[6]   SI 2002/2051, art 5(3). See **12.189–12.186**.
[7]   SI 2002/2051, art 6. See **12.187–12.194**.

12.27 Each of these six categories is examined in more detail at **12.133–12.194**.

12.28 The English Code has a separate chapter giving guidance on the priority need categories applicable to local housing authorities in England[1].

[1]   English Code, chapter 8.

Wales

12.29 In Wales, the categories of priority need are contained wholly in H(W)A 2014, s 70. In summary, the 10 categories are:

- a pregnant woman or a person with whom she resides or might reasonably be expected to reside[1];
- a person with whom a dependent child resides or might reasonably be expected to reside[2];
- a person who is vulnerable as a result of some special reason (eg old age, physical or mental illness or physical or mental disability) or a person with whom such a person resides or might reasonably be expected to reside[3];
- a person who is homeless or threatened with homelessness as a result of an emergency such as flood, fire or other disaster or a person with whom such a person resides or might reasonably be expected to reside[4];
- a person who is homeless as a result of being subject to domestic abuse or a person with whom such a person resides or might reasonably be expected to reside[5];
- a 16- or 17-year-old (at the time of application), or a person with whom such a person resides or might reasonably be expected to reside[6];
- a young person aged 18, 19 or 20 (at the time of application), who is at particular risk of sexual or financial exploitation, or a person with whom such a person resides or might reasonably be expected to reside[7];
- a young person aged 18, 19 or 20 (at the time of application), who has been looked after, accommodated or fostered, or a person with whom such a person resides or might reasonably be expected to reside[8];

- a person who is homeless after leaving the armed forces, or a person with whom such a person resides or might reasonably be expected to reside[9]; and

- a person who is vulnerable as a result of having been imprisoned, or a person with whom such a person resides or might reasonably be expected to reside[10].

1   H(W)A 2014, s 70(1)(a). See **12.197**.
2   H(W)A 2014, s 70(1)(b). See **12.198**.
3   H(W)A 2014, s 70(1)(c). See **12.199–12.206**.
4   H(W)A 2014, s 70(1)(d). See **12.207**.
5   H(W)A 2014, s 70(1)(e). See **12.208–12.211**.
6   H(W)A 2014, s 70(1)(f). See **12.212–12.213**.
7   H(W)A 2014, s 70(1)(g). See **12.214–12.216**.
8   H(W)A 2014, s 70(1)(h). See **12.217–12.219**.
9   H(W)A 2014, s 70(1)(i). See **12.220–12.222**.
10   H(W)A 2014, s 70(1)(j). See **12.223–12.228**.

12.30 Each of these categories is examined in more detail at **12.197–12.228**. The Welsh Code has a separate chapter giving guidance on the priority need categories applicable in Wales[1].

1   Welsh Code, chapter 16.

How do the categories work?

12.31 An applicant may acquire a priority need in one of two ways: (1) by reliance on their own personal circumstances; or (2) in some cases, by reliance on the personal circumstances of others. The statutory categories make the available routes clear.

12.32 For local housing authorities in England, in some cases, the applicant will only acquire a priority need if he or she personally meets the qualifying conditions. For example, if priority need arises from homelessness caused by an emergency, it must be the applicant who has been personally rendered homeless by the emergency[1]. For those cases there is no mechanism whereby another member of the applicant's household who falls within one of those priority need categories could confer priority need upon the applicant. In that situation, the proper course is for the application to be made by any person who does fall within any of those categories. Any housing duty he or she is owed will be met by accommodation being provided to all members of his or her household (including non-priority members)[2]. For example, if a childless couple is considering making an application for homelessness assistance to a local housing authority in England, and one of the two is vulnerable as a result of having been in care, having served in the armed forces, or having been imprisoned, it is that person who should be the applicant.

1   HA 1996, s 189(1)(d). See **12.126–12.131**.
2   HA 1996, s 176; H(W)A 2014, s 56. See *R (Ogbeni) v Tower Hamlets London Borough Council* [2008] EWHC 2444 (Admin), (2008) October *Legal Action*, p 37, Admin Ct, where a 17-year-old applicant had a priority need and was entitled to the main housing duty. The local housing authority was required to secure accommodation for both him and his aunt, who had normally resided with him as a member of his family.

12.33 For other cases for local housing authorities in England, and all cases for local housing authorities in Wales, the applicant may acquire priority need as a result of another person's circumstances. For example, in both jurisdictions, when it comes to pregnancy or the statutory category of vulnerability, the applicant will be in priority need either if he or she personally is in that condition or if it applies to any person with whom the applicant resides or might reasonably be expected to reside.

12.34 If the applicant is a person subject to immigration control[1] who is eligible for assistance[2] and is not a British or EEA national, and if the applicant has (or may have) a priority need only because a person with whom he or she resides, or might reasonably be expected to reside, is pregnant, vulnerable or a dependent child, that person must be 'eligible' for assistance[3]. Otherwise the person is invisible, for the purposes of assessing priority need, to the local housing authority[4].

1   See **11.26–11.93**.
2   By virtue of falling within one of Classes A–G at reg 5 of the Allocation of Housing and Homelessness (Eligibility) (England) Regulations 2006, SI 2006/1294 or reg 5 of the Allocation of Housing and Homelessness (Eligibility) (Wales) Regulations 2014, SI 2014/2603 (W 257) (see **11.106–11.121**).
3   HA 1996, s 185(4) and (5); H(W)A 2014, Sch 2, para 1(5)–(6); *Kaya v Haringey London Borough Council* [2001] EWCA Civ 677, [2002] HLR 1, CA.
4   HA 1996, s 185(4) and (5); H(W)A 2014, Sch 2, para 1(5)–(6). See **11.157–11.172**.

12.35 If the applicant has a priority need *only* because of the presence in his or her household of a 'restricted person'[1], the applicant is known as a 'restricted case'[2]. All applicants whose applications for homelessness assistance were made on or after 9 November 2012 to a local housing authority in England, or on or after 27 April 2015 to a local housing authority in Wales, can be made private rented sector offers[3]. And the amendments made to HA 1996, Pt 7 by HRA 2017[4] increase further the scope for the duties owed to applicants for homelessness assistance to local authorities in England to be discharged by means of the applicant being helped to secure accommodation in the private sector[5]. However, HA 1996, s 193(7AD) and H(W)A 2014, s 76(5) require a local housing authority to make an applicant who is a restricted case a 'private rented sector offer' 'so far as reasonably practicable'.

1   As defined at HA 1996, s 184(7) and H(W)A 2014, s 63(5). See **11.163–11.164**.
2   HA 1996, s 193(3B); H(W)A 2014, s 76(5). See **11.165–11.166**.
3   HA 1996, s 193(7AA)–(7AC); H(W)A 2014, s 76(3)–(4). See **16.153–16.179** and **17.173–17.177**.
4   For applications for homelessness assistance made to local housing authorities in England on or after 3 April 2018.
5   See CHAPTER 15 and CHAPTER 16 on the ways in which the various duties owed to applicants for homelessness assistance to local authorities in England may be brought to an end.

ENGLAND

The statutory categories in Housing Act 1996, s 189(1)

12.36 These categories apply to applicants to local housing authorities in England.

Pregnancy

12.37 It is a question of fact whether an applicant, or someone who resides with or might reasonably be expected to reside with him or her, is pregnant[1] at the date of the local housing authority's decision[2]. The length of the pregnancy is not an issue. Nor is the age of the pregnant woman.

[1]   HA 1996, s 189(1)(a).
[2]   English Code, para 8.5.

12.38 It is for the local housing authority to undertake such sensitive inquiries as it considers necessary to satisfy itself whether a woman is pregnant. It is not for the applicant to prove pregnancy in any particular way (or at all). Obviously, as the English Code advises, the normal confirmation of pregnancy issued by a GP or midwife should be accepted as sufficient evidence of pregnancy[1].

[1]   English Code, para 8.5.

12.39 If the pregnant woman is not herself the applicant, the applicant will have a priority need if he or she resides with the pregnant woman or might reasonably be expected to reside with her. This would include the non-pregnant partner in a couple who had not previously lived together, but who now, in the light of the pregnancy, intend to do so. In those circumstances, it is for the local housing authority to determine whether such a couple might reasonably be expected to reside together, although it might be thought manifestly reasonable if the partner is the father of the expected child[1]. Self-evidently, both same sex and different sex couples can fall within this statutory definition.

[1]   A single man argued that this category discriminated against single men by giving preferential treatment to women who are pregnant. A County Court judge and subsequently a Court of Appeal judge dismissed the argument. The preferential treatment given to pregnant women is justified by their particular vulnerability while pregnant and by society's need to protect unborn children: *Thorburne v Oxford City Council* [2010] EWCA Civ 957, (2010) October *Legal Action*, p 32, CA.

12.40 If the pregnancy ends *before* the decision is made, there will be no priority need under this category, although local housing authorities are advised to consider whether the woman is vulnerable for some other special reason where there has been a miscarriage or termination[1]. Conversely, if the pregnancy ends *after* the decision has been made, the local housing authority will continue to owe its acknowledged duty towards the applicant, whether or not a child has been born. There is an obligation on the applicant to notify any relevant change of circumstance occurring during the assessment process[2].

[1]   English Code, para 8.5.
[2]   HA 1996, s 214(2).

Dependent child or children

12.41 Dependent children[1] cannot be applicants for homelessness assistance in their own right[2]. Where an application is made which involves dependent children, the question for the local housing authority is whether the applicant is someone with whom dependent children reside or with whom they might reasonably be expected to reside.

¹   HA 1996, s 189(1)(b).
²   *R v Oldham Metropolitan Borough Council ex p Garlick* [1993] AC 509, HL and *R (SD) v Oxford City Council* [2015] EWHC 1871 (Admin), (2015) October *Legal* Action, p 41, Admin Ct. See **8.40–8.46**.

12.42 That question itself breaks down into several parts:

(1)   Is there a 'child' or 'children'?
(2)   Is that child, or are those children, 'dependent'?
(3)   Does the dependent child, or do the dependent children, reside with the applicant?
(4)   If not, might that child or those children be reasonably expected to reside with the applicant?

12.43 Advice on this priority need category is set out in the English Code, paras 10.6–10.11.

12.44 It is no part of the statutory requirement that the dependent children are the applicant's children. The English Code makes this plain: 'dependent children need not necessarily be the applicant's own children'¹. The Code does suggest that there must be something in the nature of a parent/child relationship, referring to adoptive, foster or step relationships². However, nothing in HA 1996, Pt 7³, requires a relationship of this nature or any form of relationship between the applicant and the dependent child.

¹   English Code, para 8.8.
²   English Code, para 8.8.
³   As amended by HRA 2017, for applications for homelessness assistance made to local housing authorities in England on or after 3 April 2018.

'CHILDREN'

12.45 HA 1996, Pt 7¹ does not specify an age at which a child ceases to be a 'child' for the purposes of this priority need category²; so there is no statutory maximum age. The critical question is not the child's age, but the date at which the child (of whatever age) ceases to be 'dependent'³.

¹   As amended by HRA 2017, for applications for homelessness assistance made to local housing authorities in England on or after 3 April 2018.
²   Contrast with HA 1996, s 178(3). See English Code, para 8.7.
³   See **12.51–12.53**.

12.46 One judge has expressed the view that the word 'child' should be construed in a narrower rather than a broader sense. He suggested that:

' . . . "children" cannot be taken to refer to children of any age but to those who have not, or perhaps have only just, attained their majority¹.'

¹   *R v Kensington and Chelsea Royal London Borough Council ex p Amarfio* (1995) 27 HLR 543, CA per Nourse LJ at 545.

12.47 The English Code refers to the phrase 'dependent children' as embracing 'all children under 16', and also:

' . . . all children aged 16–18 who are in, or are about to begin, full-time education or training or who for other reasons are unable to support themselves and who live at home[1].'

This wording suggests that adults aged 18 can be 'children' for the purposes of HA 1996, Pt 7[2].

1   English Code, para 8.7.
2   As amended by HRA 2017, for applications for homelessness assistance made to local housing authorities in England on or after 3 April 2018.

12.48 In *Miah v Newham London Borough Council*[1], the Court of Appeal was dealing with a 'child' of 18. It refused the local housing authority permission to appeal against a decision that she was a dependent child. The court accepted that, applying the guidance in the English Code, the words could include children of any age up to the child's nineteenth birthday and would therefore include someone in his or her eighteenth year.

1   *Miah v Newham London Borough Council* [2001] EWCA Civ 487, (2001) June *Legal Action*, p 25, CA.

12.49 The fact that the English Code, which is not determinative of the meaning of HA 1996, Pt 7[1], offers no guidance concerning those who have reached their nineteenth birthday does not *necessarily* mean that a person of 19 or older could not be a dependent child. However, in *James v Waltham Forest London Borough Council*[2] a judge of the county court disagreed, taking the view that the English Code provides an exhaustive statement of those who may be regarded a dependent children, and that the applicant's 19-year-old son could not confer a priority need on her.

1   As amended by HRA 2017, for applications for homelessness assistance made to local housing authorities in England on or after 3 April 2018.
2   (2017) October *Legal Action*, p 33, CA.

12.50 In any event, it would be an extreme use of language to suggest that a person who had married could simultaneously be a 'dependent child' of his or her spouse for the purposes of this priority need provision. The Court of Appeal has decided that a 17-year-old wife was not a 'dependent child' and, as a result, her husband did not fall within this priority need category[1]. The better course, now, would be for the 16- or 17-year-old wife to be the applicant, as she would have a priority need under the Priority Need Order[2] and the husband would be accommodated with her in performance of any duty to accommodate her.

1   *Hackney London Borough Council v Ekinci* [2001] EWCA Civ 776, (2002) 34 HLR 2, CA.
2   Homelessness (Priority Need for Accommodation) (England) Order 2002, SI 2002/2051, art 3 (see **12.133–12.159**) at APPENDIX 2.

DEPENDENT

12.51 The term 'dependent' is also not defined in HA 1996, Pt 7[1]. While it obviously includes financial dependence, local housing authorities are reminded by the English Code and the case-law that children may be financially independent, but not yet mature enough to live independently from their parents. They will therefore still be 'dependent' for these purposes[2].

1   As amended by HRA 2017, for applications for homelessness assistance made to local housing authorities in England on or after 3 April 2018. Note that the phrase 'dependant of an asylum seeker' has a specific meaning set out at HA 1996, s 186(4), which is applicable to that section only. For a discussion of the meaning of 'dependent' in the planning context see [19]–[34] of *Shortt v Secretary of State for Communities and Local Government* [2014] EWHC 2480 (Admin), [2015] JPL 75, Admin Ct, where Hickinbottom J rejected a contention that the concept was limited to financial dependence.

2   English Code, para 8.7; *R v Kensington and Chelsea Royal London Borough Council ex p Amarfio* (1995) 27 HLR 543, CA.

12.52 HA 1996, Pt 7[1] does not say that the dependent child must be dependent on the applicant. On the face of it, the statutory language could be satisfied if a dependent child is living with the applicant, even if the child is wholly dependent on another. An example would be two brothers who live together, the eldest being in full-time employment, and the younger being financially supported by his parents who are abroad but send money. In such a case, the older brother would have a priority need, even though his brother was not financially dependent on him or her. The point is probably academic since, in this and any other similar examples, the younger brother would be likely to have some emotional dependence on his older brother.

1   As amended by HRA 2017, for applications for homelessness assistance made to local housing authorities in England on or after 3 April 2018.

12.53 The English Code advises that 'there must be actual dependence on the applicant' although the dependence need not be wholly or exclusively on the applicant, suggesting that a child may be dependent upon more than one person[1]. This wording, which was not in the older editions of the English Code prior to 2006, reflects the statutory language originally used in the Housing (Homeless Persons) Act 1977, when the category was defined as 'if he has dependent children who are residing with him or who might reasonably be expected to reside with him'[2]. Indeed, in 1996, a judge decided that this language did require that there be at least some dependency by the child on the applicant[3]. However, that decision does not, strictly speaking, apply to the definition in HA 1996, Pt 7[4], and there is nothing in the case law on HA 1996, Pt 7[5] to suggest that this priority need category can only be met if the child is dependent on the applicant, rather than upon someone else.

1   English Code, para 8.6.
2   Housing (Homeless Persons) Act 1977, s 2(1)(a).
3   *R v Westminster City Council ex p Bishop* (1997) 29 HLR 546, QBD at 551–4. The decision is complicated, because the language considered by the judge was not that in the Housing (Homeless Persons) Act 1977 but instead that in the Housing Act 1985, where the relevant category was said to be 'with whom dependent children reside' – removing 'he has'. However, the Housing Act 1985 was a consolidating Act and so the judge held that the language used was not intended to change the original statutory meaning. HA 1996, which reproduces the language of the Housing Act 1985 (and not the language of the Housing (Homeless Persons) Act 1977) is not a consolidating Act, but replaces the legislative scheme in the Housing Act 1985. The language of HA 1996, Pt 7 (as amended by HRA 2017, for applications for homelessness assistance made to local housing authorities in England on or after 3 April 2018) is not, therefore, subject to the same construction and can be considered afresh.
4   As amended by HRA 2017, for applications for homelessness assistance made to local housing authorities in England on or after 3 April 2018.

5   As amended by HRA 2017, for applications for homelessness assistance made to local housing
    authorities in England on or after 3 April 2018.

'RESIDES WITH' THE APPLICANT

12.54 The next question for the local housing authority is whether the dependent child actually resides with the applicant. This is a straightforward question of fact. If a child does in fact reside with the applicant, the question of whether or not the child 'might reasonably be expected' to reside with him or her does not arise[1].

1   *R v Hillingdon London Borough Council ex p Islam* [1983] 1 AC 688, HL (a decision on
    priority need at first instance and that aspect of the judgment not subject to appeal); *R v
    Lambeth London Borough Council ex p Ly* (1986) 19 HLR 51, QBD; *R v Lambeth London
    Borough Council ex p Bodunrin* (1992) 24 HLR 647, QBD; and *Oxford City Council v Bull*
    [2011] EWCA Civ 609, [2011] HLR 35, [2012] 1 WLR 203, CA.

12.55 The word 'reside' would not normally be used to describe a situation in which one person is visiting another, or even staying with them for a short time, such as for a holiday although the English Code, perhaps, goes too far in suggesting that there must be:

> ' . . . some degree of permanence or regularity, rather than a temporary arrangement whereby the children are merely staying with the applicant for a limited period[1].'

1   English Code, para 8.6. There is no case law directly on point though *R v Lewisham London
    Borough Council ex p Creppy* (1992) 24 HLR 121, CA touches on the issue obliquely.
    However, the requirement for 'permanence or regularity' stipulated in the Code corresponds
    more naturally with the phrase '*normally* resides with . . . ' (as used in HA 1996, s 176(a)
    for example) rather than 'resides with . . . '. Both formulations are contained in HA 1996,
    Pt 7 (as amended by HRA 2017, for applications for homelessness assistance made to local
    housing authorities in England on or after 3 April 2018) implying that they are distinct
    concepts. This is reinforced by the difference in wording employed in the current and previous
    editions of the English Code. The *Homelessness Code of Guidance for Local Authorities*
    (Department for Communities and Local Government, Department for Education and Skills,
    Department of Health, July 2006), at para 10.6, spoke of applicants having a priority need 'if
    they have one or more dependent children who normally live with them'. The word 'normally'
    has been omitted from para 8.6 of the 2018 edition of the English Code.

12.56 The English Code reminds local housing authorities that residence does not have to be full-time and that a child can be considered to reside with either or both parents, providing there is 'some regularity' to the arrangement[1].

1   English Code, para 8.10.

12.57 Children who are temporarily away from the applicant on holiday or for other purposes would ordinarily be said to 'reside with' the applicant during their absence, not with the person with whom they are staying[1].

1   *See R v Lewisham London Borough Council ex p Creppy* (1992) 24 HLR 121, CA and
    Halonen v Westminster City Council (1997) September *Legal Action*, p 19, Central
    London County Court.

'REASONABLY EXPECTED TO RESIDE' WITH THE APPLICANT

12.58 Even if no dependent child is actually residing with him or her, an applicant will have priority need if at least one dependent child might reasonably be expected to reside with him or her[1]. This covers the situation where the applicant and the dependent child (or children) are not currently living together but might reasonably be expected to live together in future. It will come into play where, for example, children are in the care of children's services or staying with relatives, but would return to live with their parents if the parents obtain accommodation. In assessing whether a child might reasonably be expected to reside with the applicant, the best interests of the child will be of relevance and the duty under Children Act 2004, s 11 will be engaged[2]. In this vein, the English Code advises that local housing authorities should take into account 'the specific needs of the child, including whether suitable accommodation is available to them with their other parent'[3].

1   HA 1996, s 189(1)(b).
2   See **9.86–9.87**.
3   English Code, para 8.11.

12.59 Where children are in the care of a children's services authority (whether voluntarily or under the terms of a care order) and are not currently living with the applicant, local housing authorities are advised that liaison with the children's services authority[1] is essential and that there should be joint consideration before the local housing authority reaches its decision[2].

1   Or children's services department, in the case of a unitary authority.
2   English Code, para 8.12.

12.60 The correct approach to the question of whether it is reasonable to expect a person who does not currently live with an applicant to live with him or her is more fully discussed in CHAPTER 10[1].

1   See **10.29–10.32**.

SEPARATED PARENTS AND DEPENDENT CHILDREN

12.61 Most of the difficult decisions on the 'dependent children' priority need category arise where the application is made by one of two parents who are separated. The local housing authority will have to consider three questions:

(1)   Is there a child who is dependent ('dependency')?
(2)   If so, does the child reside with the applicant ('residence')?
(3)   If not, is the child reasonably expected to reside with the applicant in the future ('future residence')[1]?

1   *R v Port Talbot Borough Council ex p McCarthy* (1990) 23 HLR 207, CA.

DEPENDENCY

12.62 As already indicated, HA 1996, Pt 7[1] itself does not require that the child be dependent on the applicant[2]. However, in cases where parents are separated, the expectation will be that the child is at least to some extent dependent on the parent who is applying to the local housing authority for homelessness assistance. Where a local housing authority found on the facts of a particular case that a child was exclusively dependent upon his mother (who received both child benefit and income support for the child) and not the father (who was the applicant), the father's challenge to that decision was dismissed[3]. However, the question for the local housing authority is not whether the child is wholly and exclusively dependent upon the applicant, or upon its other parent[4], but simply whether the child is dependent. The question of dependency has been described as 'fact-sensitive to a very large degree'[5].

[1] As amended by HRA 2017, for applications for homelessness assistance made to local housing authorities in England on or after 3 April 2018.
[2] See **12.51–12.53**.
[3] *R v Westminster City Council ex p Bishop* (1997) 29 HLR 546, QBD and see **12.53** fn 3.
[4] *R v Lambeth London Borough Council ex p Vagliviello* (1991) 22 HLR 392, CA.
[5] *McGrath v Camden London Borough Council* [2007] EWCA Civ 1269, (2008) January *Legal Action*, p 37, CA.

RESIDENCE AND CO-RESIDENCE

12.63 When considering whether a child resides with the applicant, the local housing authority should consider all the circumstances, including whether or not a court order has been made in respect of where the child should reside. An issue about where a child resides, or might reasonably be expected to reside, might arise where a child's two parents are separated, or in any other circumstance where more than one adult is involved in bringing up the child, such as different sets of foster parents, adoptive parents, grandparents or other members of the child's family.

RESIDENCE ORDERS

12.64 Where a residence order in favour of one of the parents has been made, the English Code advises that the local housing authority should normally follow the provisions of the order and treat the child as residing with the person identified in the order[1].

[1] English Code, para 8.9.

12.65 Nowadays, it is not unusual for family courts to make shared residence orders, either after a contested hearing between the parents, or by consent[1]. Shared residence orders can be made even when the child does not divide his or her time equally between the parents[2]. This is recognised in the current version of the English Code, which no longer advises that it is exceptional for a child to reside with both parents[3].

[1] Children Act 1989, s 8. As recognised by the House of Lords in *Holmes-Moorhouse v Richmond upon Thames Royal London Borough Council* [2009] UKHL 7, [2009] 1 WLR 413, HL per Lord Hoffmann at [7].
[2] See *D v D* [2000] EWCA Civ 3009, [2001] 1 FLR 495, CA.
[3] English Code, para 8.10. The 2002 English Code contained similar advice at para 8.10 (*Homelessness Code of Guidance for Local Authorities (England)* (Department of Health and Office of the Deputy Prime Minister), July 2002) but concluded 'it would only be in very exceptional cases though that a child might be considered to reside with both parents'. This last sentence was omitted from the 2006 and 2018 versions of the English Code. In *Holmes-Moorhouse v Richmond upon Thames Royal London Borough Council* [2009] UKHL 7, [2009] 1 WLR 413, HL at [11], Lord Hoffmann described the paragraph in the

2002 Code as 'muddling in its reasoning' and saying little as to what considerations the local housing authority should take into account.

INFORMAL ARRANGEMENTS

12.66 Where no court order has been obtained, the local housing authority cannot just refuse to consider the question of a child's residence until a court makes such an order[1]. The local housing authority must consider all the present circumstances of the case. It is looking to see whether the child resides with the applicant; it is not enough that the child visits the applicant. A court order or parental agreement for staying contact does not make the visiting child resident or co-resident with the applicant, because 'staying access does not equal residence'[2] and 'the staying access will not amount to residence with their father'[3].

[1] *R v Ealing London Borough Council ex p Sidhu* (1982) 2 HLR 45, QBD.
[2] *R v Port Talbot Borough Council ex p McCarthy* (1991) 23 HLR 207, CA per Butler-Sloss LJ at 210.
[3] *R v Port Talbot Borough Council ex p McCarthy* (1991) 23 HLR 207, CA per Dillon LJ at 211.

12.67 A child need not live full-time with the applicant in order to 'reside' with him or her. The child may divide his or her time between the two parents. However, there should be 'some regularity' to the arrangement[1]. The possibility that the child may be residing with both of his or her separated parents was previously described by the courts as 'unlikely to be the normal arrangement'[2], as 'a remote possibility', or 'a very rare case'[3]. However, the current edition of the English Code reflects a more modern and flexible approach: 'where parents separate, there will generally be a presumption towards shared residence though this will not always be on the basis of an equal amount of time being spent with both parents'[4].

[1] English Code, para 8.10.
[2] *R v Port Talbot Borough Council ex p McCarthy* (1991) 23 HLR 207, CA per Butler-Sloss LJ at 210.
[3] *R v Lambeth London Borough Council ex p Vaglivello* (1990) 22 HLR 392, CA per Purchas LJ at 397.
[4] English Code, para 8.10.

12.68 Local housing authorities which have considered where a child's 'main' residence is, or which parent has a 'greater' responsibility, have been held to be wrong in law[1]. But where a local housing authority applied the correct test ('Does the child reside with the applicant?'), its decision that an applicant's children did not reside with him (even though they spent three or four nights each week with him) was not wrong in law[2].

[1] *R v Kingswood Borough Council ex p Smith-Morse* [1995] 2 FLR 137, QBD, and *R v Leeds City Council ex p Collier* (1998) June *Legal Action*, p 14, QBD.
[2] *R v Oxford City Council ex p Doyle* (1998) 30 HLR 506, QBD.

12.69 In *Oxford City Council v Bull*[1], three children moved from living with their mother in adequate accommodation to live with their father in a single room. He made an application for homelessness assistance shortly afterwards. The local housing authority accommodated the father and the three children in interim accommodation[2]. It subsequently decided that the children were not residing with their father and that the arrangements in the interim accommodation should not be taken into account. The Court of Appeal held that the local housing authority's decision was wrong in law. The period in interim accommodation constituted 'residence' for the purposes of HA 1996, s 189(1)(b)[3]. Accordingly, by the date of the review decision, the children were and had been 'residing with' their father. The interim accommodation was 'where [the children] kept their clothes and possessions. It was their main home, from which they went to school. It is quite true that the children went to stay with their mother regularly, but that does not detract from the fact that they resided at their father's house'[4].

[1]   [2011] EWCA Civ 609, [2012] 1 WLR 203, CA.
[2]   HA 1996, s 188(1) as amended by HRA 2017, s 5(4) for applications for homelessness assistance made to local housing authorities in England on or after 3 April 2018. See **16.37–16.73**.
[3]   Relying on *Mohamed v Hammersmith & Fulham London Borough Council* [2011] UKHL 57, [2002]1 AC 547, HL. See **14.56–14.58**.
[4]   Jackson LJ at [39]. However, the father had become homeless intentionally because his decision to permit the children to move in with him was his own deliberate conduct which led to his being required to leave his previous accommodation. See **13.159**.

12.70 It is often very difficult to say whether a child is residing with an applicant (as distinct from visiting), and a sensitive home visit by an officer can provide the local housing authority with much useful information. But even when the facts are established, two officers of the same local housing authority (and, indeed, of different local housing authorities) can legitimately reach different conclusions. For example, in one case[1] a visiting officer found the child with the applicant at his flat and the presence of 'many personal effects, toothbrush and paste, clothing and food' belonging to the child. The visiting officer concluded that this (together with assertions by both the separated parents that the child was residing with the applicant) established that the child was therefore living with the applicant. Her recommendation was reversed by her superior, who took a different view of the facts. The case amply demonstrates why, in this context, an initial adverse decision could usefully be subject to the review procedure[2] in almost all cases. If the initial adverse decision is upheld on review, it may be sensible to apply to a different local housing authority with the prospect of receiving a more favourable decision.

[1]   *R v Westminster City Council ex p Bishop* (1997) 29 HLR 546, QBD.
[2]   Described at **19.8–19.213**.

FUTURE RESIDENCE

12.71 If the child is not currently residing with the applicant, the local housing authority should next consider whether it is reasonable to expect the child to reside with him or her in the future. This issue will often arise in the context of a child whose parents have separated, but may be relevant if the child is living with foster parents, or there are potential adoptive parents, or other members of the child's family wishes to be involved in the child's up-bringing.

12.72 It may be that there is a genuine arrangement between the separated parents that the child should reside with the applicant once the applicant has suitable accommodation. Again, this is a question of fact for the local housing authority. Its decision letter should show that it has separately considered the questions:

(1)   Is the child now residing with the applicant?

(2)   If not, is it reasonable to expect the child to reside with the applicant in the future[1]?

[1]   For an illustration of a legal challenge prompted by the failure to distinguish these two questions, see *R v Port Talbot Borough Council ex p McCarthy* (1997) 23 HLR 207, CA.

12.73 In some cases, family courts have made shared residence orders, either after a contested hearing between the parents, or by consent. What should happen when the parents have a shared residence order but one parent is homeless and has made an application for homelessness assistance to a local housing authority? His or her children do not actually reside with him or her.

12.74 This scenario was considered by the House of Lords in *Holmes-Moorhouse v Richmond upon Thames Royal London Borough Council*[1]. In that case, the Court of Appeal had held that once a family court had decided in contested proceedings that residence should be shared, and had made an order to that effect, the local housing authority could not deny that the children might reasonably be expected to live with the father (who was applying for homelessness assistance) as well as with their mother. The House of Lords overturned the Court of Appeal's decision. It held that when the local housing authority is deciding whether dependent children might reasonably be expected to reside with a homeless parent, the local housing authority is entitled to take into account the fact that housing is a scarce resource, and to have regard to the social purposes of HA 1996, Pt 7, to the claims of other homeless applicants and the scale of the local housing authority's own responsibilities. The question for the local housing authority is whether it is reasonably to be expected, in the context of a scheme for housing the homeless, that children who already have a home with one parent should also be able to reside with their other parent. The existence of a shared residence order is relevant, but not a determinative factor. It added that the paramount consideration for family courts, when deciding issues about the upbringing of a child, is the child's welfare under Children Act 1989. A local housing authority should not intervene in family proceedings to argue against a court making a shared residence order, but the family court should not make a shared residence order unless it appears reasonably likely that both parties will have accommodation in which the children can reside.

[1]   [2009] UKHL 7, [2009] 1 WLR 413, HL.

12.75 In *El Goure v Kensington & Chelsea Royal London Borough Council*[1], the Court of Appeal held that Lord Hoffmann's reference in *Holmes-Moorhouse v Richmond upon Thames Royal London Borough Council*[2] to it only being reasonable for a child to reside with both his or her separated parents 'in exceptional circumstances' was not intended to provide an additional test and the correct test was 'the statutory test of reasonable expectation of residence'[3].

[1]   [2012] EWCA Civ 670, [2012] HLR 36, CA.
[2]   [2009] UKHL 7, [2009] 1 WLR 413, HL.

3   Per Mummery LJ at [44].

Vulnerability

12.76 To meet this category of priority need the relevant person (the applicant or a person with whom the applicant resides or might reasonably be expected to reside) must[1]:

(1)   be currently 'vulnerable'; and
(2)   be vulnerable by reason of one of the prescribed statutory matters.

1   HA 1996, s 189(1)(c).

'VULNERABLE'

12.77 The term 'vulnerable' is not defined in HA 1996, Pt 7[1]. Its meaning was explained by the Court of Appeal in *R v Camden London Borough Council ex p Pereira*[2]. That definition was repeatedly followed and applied in later cases, such as *Osmani v Camden London Borough Council*[3] and was reproduced in the previous version of the English Code[4]. A person was taken to be 'vulnerable' if he or she was less able to fend for himself or herself than an ordinary homeless person and so would suffer injury or detriment in circumstances in which the ordinary homeless person would not. This gloss on the plain words of the HA 1996, s 189(1)(c) brought homelessness law to the point 'where decision-makers were saying, of people who clearly had serious mental or physical disabilities, that "you are not vulnerable, because you are no more vulnerable than the usual run of street homeless people in our locality"'[5].

1   As amended by HRA 2017, for applications for homelessness assistance made to local housing authorities in England on or after 3 April 2018.
2   *R v Camden London Borough Council ex p Pereira* (1999) 31 HLR 317, CA, reconciling the earlier and somewhat contradictory authorities of *R v Waveney District Council ex p Bowers* [1982] 3 WLR 661, CA; *R v Lambeth London Borough Council ex p Carroll* (1987) 20 HLR 142, QBD; and *R v Westminster City Council ex p Ortiz* (1993) 27 HLR 364, CA.
3   [2004] EWCA Civ 1706, [2005] HLR 22, CA per Auld LJ at [38].
4   *Homelessness Code of Guidance for Local Authorities* (Department for Communities and Local Government, Department for Education and Skills, Department of Health, July 2006), para 10.13.
5   *Hotak v Southwark London Borough Council, Kanu v Southwark London Borough Council & Johnson v Solihull Metropolitan Borough Council* [2015] UKSC 30, [2016] AC 811, SC per Baroness Hale at [91].

12.78 This was turned on its head in May 2015 following the decision of the Supreme Court in the conjoined appeals of *Hotak v Southwark London Borough Council, Kanu v Southwark London Borough Council & Johnson v Solihull Metropolitan Borough Council*[1]. Interestingly, the Supreme Court did go so far as to say that the decision in *R v Camden London Borough Council ex p Pereira*[2] was wrong. The observations on the meaning of vulnerability made in that case were, according to Lord Neuberger 'simply intended to be guidance to Camden housing authority as to how to approach Mr Pereira's application' and the real error lay in the fact that the guidance had not been 'properly understood' and had wrongly been 'treated in some decisions of courts and reviewing officers almost as a statutory definition'[3]. Nevertheless, as will be seen from the discussion that follows at **12.82–12.91**, the approach advocated by the Supreme Court differs significantly from that which had been taken in the cases following *R v Camden London Borough Council ex p Pereira*.[4] As a consequence, all of the previous case law on vulnerability needs to be read carefully in light of the changes wrought by the Supreme Court's judgment and should be applied with caution.

[1] [2015] UKSC 30, [2016] AC 811, SC. In *Hemley and Croydon London Borough Council* (unreported) 25 July 2017, CA, the Court of Appeal dismissed an appeal by the local housing authority which sought to argue that a review decision applying the *Pereira* test would have been the same even if the guidance in *Hotak v Southwark London Borough Council, Kanu v Southwark London Borough Council & Johnson v Solihull Metropolitan Borough Council* had been applied. Lewison LJ observed at [14] that 'a person may yet be vulnerable even though she can fend for herself' and that 'the review might have led to a different outcome if the correct test had been applied.'

[2] *R v Camden London Borough Council ex p Pereira* (1999) 31 HLR 317, CA.

[3] *Hotak v Southwark London Borough Council, Kanu v Southwark London Borough Council & Johnson v Solihull Metropolitan Borough Council* [2015] UKSC 30, [2016] AC 811, SC at [49] and [57]. The Court of Appeal has, subsequently, been rather less deferential to the earlier case law referring to the comparator relied on in *R v Camden London Borough Council ex p Pereira* (1999) 31 HLR 317, CA as 'wrong' (*Panayiotou v Waltham Forest London Borough Council, Smith v Haringey London Borough Council* [2017] EWCA Civ 1624, [2017] HLR 48, CA at [33]) and 'not the right test' (*Rother District Council v Freeman-Roach* [2018] EWCA Civ 368, (2018) April *Legal Action*, p 39, CA at [18].)

[4] *R v Camden London Borough Council ex p Pereira* (1999) 31 HLR 317, CA.

12.79 The First Appellant in the Supreme Court was Sifatullah Hotak: a 23-year-old Afghan refugee suffering from learning disabilities, depression and post-traumatic stress disorder. He was heavily reliant on personal support from his 24-year-old brother Ezatullah. Sifatullah made an application for homelessness assistance to Southwark London Borough Council, with Ezatullah as a member of his household. Southwark decided that Sifatullah's medical conditions were sufficiently serious for him to be vulnerable within the meaning of HA 1996, s 189(1)(c) if he were a single applicant but that as long as he was with his brother he would not be vulnerable since Ezatullah 'would not allow circumstances to arise whereby his brother is placed at risk'[1]. The decision was upheld on appeal to the County Court and to the Court of Appeal[2].

[1] *Hotak v Southwark London Borough Council* [2013] EWCA Civ 515, [2013] HLR 32, CA per Pitchford LJ at [6].

[2] *Hotak v Southwark London Borough Council* [2013] EWCA Civ 515, [2013] HLR 32, CA.

12.80 The Second Appellant, Mr Johnson, described himself as a persistent criminal offender, and a recovering heroin addict who was prescribed methadone for his addiction. His addiction underpinned his offending. He made an application for homelessness assistance to Solihull Metropolitan Borough Council but was found not to be vulnerable. This was upheld on review. The review decision noted that '[t]here is, therefore, a chance that if you were street homeless or even accommodated that you would return to using drugs. Even if you do slip back to using drugs this would not necessarily be anything unusual in relation to homeless people. For example, Homeless Link's Survey of Needs and Provision (SNAP) 2010 found that drug issues were among the issues most frequently affecting the users of homelessness services. SNAP 2010 found that 92% of homelessness services are working with people who are experiencing problems with drugs . . . Given the above I am not satisfied that your drug history makes you vulnerable'[1]. The decision was upheld on appeal to the County Court and to the Court of Appeal[2].

[1] *Johnson v Solihull Metropolitan Borough Council* [2013] EWCA Civ 752, [2013] HLR 39, CA per Arden LJ at [12].
[2] *Johnson v Solihull Metropolitan Borough Council* [2013] EWCA Civ 752, [2013] HLR 39, CA.

12.81 The Third Appellant, Mr Kanu suffered from a number of health conditions, including hepatitis B, back pain affecting his mobility, high blood pressure, haemorrhoids and a mental disorder which involved suicidal ideations. He made an application for homelessness assistance to Southwark London Borough Council having been evicted from his previous accommodation, which he had occupied with this wife and adult son, because it was required by the landlord for redevelopment. On review it was decided that although Mr Kanu might have been vulnerable as an individual applicant, the availability of support from his wife and son meant that he did not have a priority need. With regard to the public sector equality duty under Equality Act 2010, s 149[1] the decision accepted that Mr Kanu might be disabled and indicated that inquiries had been made into his medical conditions as a consequence, but that Equality Act 2010, s 149 did not override the underlying decision that he was not vulnerable. The decision was quashed on appeal to the county court. The Court of Appeal allowed Southwark's appeal against the decision of the county court[2]. In all three cases the guidance on vulnerability given by the Court of Appeal in *R v Camden London Borough Council ex p Pereira* in 1999[3] was applied.

[1] See **9.81–9.83** and **12.100**.
[2] *Kanu v Southwark London Borough Council* [2014] EWCA Civ 1085, [2014] HLR 40, CA.
[3] *R v Camden London Borough Council ex p Pereira* (1999) 31 HLR 317, CA. See **12.77**.

12.82 In the Supreme Court, three issues arose for consideration: (i) whether the test for vulnerability for the purposes of HA 1996, s 189(1)(c) involved a comparator and, if so, who that comparator should be; (ii) in assessing vulnerability, whether it was permissible to take into account the support which would be provided by a family member or member of the applicant's household; and (iii) what effect, if any, the public sector equality duty under Equality Act 2010, s 149 has on the determination of vulnerability.

12.83 On the first issue, the Supreme Court, departing from the formulation applied in *R v Camden London Borough Council ex p Pereira*[1], held that the test of vulnerability under HA 1996, s 189(1)(c) involved a comparison with an ordinary person if made homeless, as opposed to an ordinary homeless person. The comparison is with ordinary people generally, not ordinary people locally. Where an applicant is 'significantly more vulnerable' than an ordinary person if made homeless, or 'more at risk of harm without accommodation than an ordinary person would be', then he or she will be classed as vulnerable[2]. When applying the test, a local housing authority should not rely on statistics as to the characteristics of the ordinary person[3]. The resources of the local housing authority have no relevance to the assessment of vulnerability[4]. This test has now been incorporated into the English Code[5].

[1] *R v Camden London Borough Council ex p Pereira* (1999) 31 HLR 317, CA. See **12.77**.

2   *Hotak v Southwark London Borough Council, Kanu v Southwark London Borough Council
    & Johnson v Solihull Metropolitan Borough Council* [2015] UKSC 30, [2016] AC 811, SC per
    Lord Neuberger at [53] and [57]–[58] and per Baroness Hale at [93].
3   *Hotak v Southwark London Borough Council, Kanu v Southwark London Borough Council
    & Johnson v Solihull Metropolitan Borough Council* [2015] UKSC 30, [2016] AC 811, SC per
    Lord Neuberger at [43] and [84].
4   *Hotak v Southwark London Borough Council, Kanu v Southwark London Borough Council
    & Johnson v Solihull Metropolitan Borough Council* [2015] UKSC 30, [2016] AC 811, SC per
    Lord Neuberger at [39].
5   English Code, para 8.15.

12.84 The meaning of the word 'significantly'[1] in this context caused some initial difficulty following the decision in *Hotak v Southwark London Borough Council, Kanu v Southwark London Borough Council & Johnson v Solihull Metropolitan Borough Council*[2]. It is a word with several possible meanings which may vary according to the context in which it is used. Perhaps unsurprisingly a number of appeals were brought in the county court, following the Supreme Court's decision, challenging the way in which local housing authorities had evaluated the significance of a particular vulnerability or the adequacy of reasons given to explain what the word significantly was thought to mean[3]. The approach adopted by the county court in considering these appeals was not entirely consistent.

1   As used by Lord Neuberger at [53].
2   [2015] UKSC 30, [2016] AC 811, SC.
3   See for *example HB v Haringey London Borough Council* (2016) January *Legal Action*, p 46,
    the County Court at Mayors and City of London, *Mohammed v Southwark London
    Borough Council* (2016) July/August *Legal Action*, p 48, the County Court at Central
    London, *Ward v Haringey London Borough Council* (2016) September *Legal Action*, p 38,
    the County Court at Central London, *SS v Waltham Forest London Borough Council* (2016)
    November *Legal Action*, p 41, County Court at Central London, *DT v Lambeth London
    Borough Council* (2016) December/January *Legal Action*, p 41, the County Court at Central
    London.

12.85 It is to be hoped that the difficulties posed by this issue have now been resolved by the Court of Appeal in the conjoined appeals in *Panayiotou v Waltham Forest London Borough Council, Smith v Haringey London Borough Council*[1]. In that case Lewison LJ explained that the use of the word significant denoted a qualitative rather than a quantitative test:

> 'I do not, therefore consider that Lord Neuberger can have used "significantly" in such a way as to introduce for the first time a quantitative threshold, particularly in the light of his warning about glossing the statute. Rather, in my opinion, he was using the adverb in a qualitative sense. In other words, the question to be asked is whether, when compared to an ordinary person if made homeless, the applicant, in consequence of a characteristic within section 189(1)(c), would suffer or be at risk of suffering harm or detriment which the ordinary person would not suffer or be at risk of suffering such that the harm or detriment would make a noticeable difference to his ability to deal with the consequences of homelessness. To put it another way, what Lord Neuberger must have meant was that an applicant would be vulnerable if he were at risk of more harm in a significant way. Whether the test is met in relation to any given set of facts is a question of evaluative judgment for the reviewer[2].'

The danger with this kind of guidance (as the court observed)[3] is that it may simply replace 'one imprecise formulation of the test with another' posing a risk[4] of 'further semantic debate about the boundaries of meaning of the synonym'.

1 [2017] EWCA Civ 1624, [2017] HLR 48, CA.
2 *Panayiotou v Waltham Forest London Borough Council, Smith v Haringey London Borough Council* [2017] EWCA Civ 1624, [2017] HLR 48, CA at [64].
3 *Panayiotou v Waltham Forest London Borough Council, Smith v Haringey London Borough Council* [2017] EWCA Civ 1624, [2017] HLR 48, CA per Lewison LJ at [47] and [50].
4 Adopting the words of Lord Hughes at [37] of *R v Golds* [2016] UKSC 61, [2016] 1 WLR 5231, SC.

12.86 With that note of caution, the guidance would appear to suggest that the significance of an applicant's vulnerability is primarily a question of its *relevance*. Specifically, its relevance to the applicant's ability to deal with the consequences of homelessness. A vulnerability will be relevant in this context, if it manifests itself in the form of 'an impairment of a person's ability to find accommodation or, if he cannot find it, to deal with the lack of it'. The latter might take the form of 'an expectation that a person's physical or mental health would deteriorate; or it may be exposure to some external risk such as the risk of exploitation by others'[1]. The assessment of these issues involves an evaluative judgment on the part of the local housing authority[2]. To give a practical example, a fear of heights might not be regarded as 'significant' in this context. The reason being that it is unlikely to be relevant to an applicant's ability to find accommodation. Similarly, homelessness is unlikely to involve any exposure to heights. The fear of heights, however severe, has little relevance in this context[3].

1 *Panayiotou v Waltham Forest London Borough Council, Smith v Haringey London Borough Council* [2017] EWCA Civ 1624, [2017] HLR 48, CA per Lewison LJ at [44].
2 *Panayiotou v Waltham Forest London Borough Council, Smith v Haringey London Borough Council* [2017] EWCA Civ 1624, [2017] HLR 48, CA per Lewison LJ at [50] and [64].
3 In contrast, a fear of heights may well be relevant to the suitability of any accommodation secured for his or her occupation. See CHAPTER 18.

12.87 This is not to say that any *relevant* vulnerability will be sufficient to meet the statutory criteria. The harm or detriment which the applicant would suffer (or be at risk of suffering) must have a *noticeable* impact on his or her ability to deal with the consequences of homelessness and, to satisfy the comparative element of the test, must not be something which the ordinary person would experience[1].

1 *Panayiotou v Waltham Forest London Borough Council, Smith v Haringey London Borough Council* [2017] EWCA Civ 1624, [2017] HLR 48, CA at [64].

12.88 However, a proper application of the statutory test should not focus solely on the degree of magnitude of the harm that the applicant might suffer. That is, applying the test correctly is not as simple as asking whether the effect of a condition or characteristic is 'more than minor or trivial', or at the other end of the spectrum, whether it would result in 'more harm plus', since that would be a quantitative assessment of the type deprecated by the court.

12.89 Drawing these threads together it might be said that an applicant who, if without accommodation, will suffer (or be at risk of suffering) from harm that:

- will impact on his or her ability to find accommodation or deal with the lack of it;

- will be noticeable in extent; and
- would not be experienced by the ordinary person;

might properly be regarded as being at 'risk of more harm in a significant way' and therefore vulnerable. Provided that this harm (or risk of harm) is the result of one of the statutory causes[1] then he or she will have a priority need as a result of HA 1996, s 189(1)(c). A local housing authority which has properly applied this approach will not generally be faulted simply because 'it failed to define 'vulnerable' or 'significantly' or failed to list the attributes of the ordinary person if made homeless'[2].

[1] See **12.102–12.125**.
[2] *Rother District Council v Freeman-Roach* [2018] EWCA Civ 368, (2018) April *Legal Action*, p 39, CA per Rose J at [35].

12.90 On the second of the three issues addressed by the Supreme Court *in Hotak v Southwark London Borough Council, Kanu v Southwark London Borough Council & Johnson v Solihull Metropolitan Borough Council*[1], it was decided that support provided by a family or household member can be taken into account in assessing vulnerability. But the local housing authority must be satisfied that such support will be available on a consistent and predictable basis and will be sufficient to prevent the applicant from being vulnerable[2]. The answer to this question must be based on evidence not presumptions[3].

[1] [2015] UKSC 30, [2016] AC 811, SC.
[2] *Hotak v Southwark London Borough Council, Kanu v Southwark London Borough Council & Johnson v Solihull Metropolitan Borough Council* [2015] UKSC 30, [2016] AC 811, SC per Lord Neuberger at [65] and [69]. See also English Code, para 8.15.
[3] *Hotak v Southwark London Borough Council, Kanu v Southwark London Borough Council & Johnson v Solihull Metropolitan Borough Council* [2015] UKSC 30, [2016] AC 811, SC per Lord Neuberger at [70].

12.91 On the third point, it was decided that the public sector equality duty is complementary to the duty under HA 1996, s 189(1)(c). When assessing whether an applicant with an actual or possible disability is vulnerable, each stage of the decision-making process should be carried out with the duty well in mind and the duty 'must be exercised in substance, with rigour, and with an open mind'[1].

[1] *Hotak v Southwark London Borough Council, Kanu v Southwark London Borough Council & Johnson v Solihull Metropolitan Borough Council* [2015] UKSC 30, [2016] AC 811, SC per Lord Neuberger at [78]. See further See also English Code, para 8.17 and **12.100**.

MAKING INQUIRIES INTO WHETHER A PERSON IS VULNERABLE

12.92 Whether a person is 'vulnerable' is a question of fact and degree for the local housing authority to determine. It is not a question that can be delegated to a doctor, nurse, consultant or anyone else[1].

[1] *R v Lambeth London Borough Council ex p Walters* (1994) 26 HLR 170, QBD; *Osmani v Camden London Borough Council* [2004] EWCA Civ 1706, [2005] HLR 22, CA; and *Cramp v Hastings Borough Council* [2005] EWCA Civ 1005, [2005] HLR 48, CA.

12.93 A local housing authority will usually need to make inquiries[1] into the applicant's medical condition in order to determine vulnerability. The local housing authority should take account of any medical evidence it receives[2] and may seek its own medical adviser's view. Indeed,

' . . . where the applicant claims to be vulnerable for medical reasons or where on making proper inquiries it is apparent to the authorities that such is his claim, it is both proper and necessary . . . to take and consider a medical opinion, unless the applicant's condition renders him so obviously vulnerable that that is not necessary[3].'

[1] See also **9.70–9.80**.
[2] English Code, para 8.25.
[3] *R v Lambeth London Borough Council ex p Carroll* (1988) 20 HLR 142, QBD per Webster J at 150. In particular, in cases where the applicant claims to be vulnerable as a result of mental health issues, medical evidence is likely to be essential. See *R (IA) v Westminster City Council* [2013] EWHC 1273 (Admin), (2013) July *Legal Action*, p 23, Admin Ct. See further English Code, para 8.25.

12.94 Very often the medical evidence will be helpful in identifying the physical disability, mental handicap or mental illness, but less useful on whether the applicant satisfies the definition of 'vulnerable'. That is a question for a local housing authority, not a doctor. If a view is expressed by a medical expert, that view is merely one consideration which may influence the local housing authority's own conclusion, but it is certainly not bound by it[1]. Likewise, the local housing authority's own medical adviser may express a view on 'vulnerability', but the local housing authority should not merely rubber-stamp that view[2]. Where there is competing medical evidence, the evaluation of it is a matter for the local housing authority[3]. Sufficient reasons must be given where a decision is taken to depart from the medical evidence, or to prefer one piece over another[4]. A local housing authority relying on its own medical adviser is not bound to refer each and every medical document to the adviser but must do so where there is a 'demonstrable need', for example where a new report is obtained which is materially different to the documents which have already been referred to the adviser[5].

[1] *Chowdhoury v Newham London Borough Council* [2004] EWCA Civ 8, (2004) March *Legal Action*, p 25, CA; *Cramp v Hastings Borough Council* [2005] EWCA Civ 1005, [2005] HLR 48, CA; and *R (Bauer-Czarnomski) v Ealing London Borough Council* [2010] EWHC Admin 130, (2010) March *Legal Action, p 30, Admin Ct* (the latter was in respect of an application for an allocation of social housing, see **4.99**).
[2] *R v Wandsworth London Borough Council ex p Banbury* (1987) 19 HLR 76, QBD; and *R v Lambeth London Borough Council ex p Carroll* (1988) 20 HLR 142, QBD.
[3] *Mehmet v Wandsworth London Borough Council* [2004] EWCA Civ 1560, (2005) January *Legal Action*, p 28, CA.
[4] *Hall v Wandsworth London Borough Council, Carter v Wandsworth London Borough Council* [2004] EWCA Civ 1740, [2005] HLR 23, CA; *Qoraishi v Westminster City Council* (2014) June Legal Action, pp 38–39, Central London County Court.
[5] *Simms v Islington London Borough Council* [2008] EWCA Civ 1083, [2009] HLR 20, CA per Ward LJ at [31].

12.95 In keeping with the general burden that applies to the making of inquiries[1], it is for the local housing authority to make all necessary inquiries into the person's medical condition, not for the applicant to produce medical evidence. The applicant may, however, be expected to give written consent to the local housing authority's medical advisers to seek medical information or inspect medical records. The local housing authority is under a duty to act fairly in its gathering of, and use of, medical information. That includes a requirement to put adverse medical opinions to the applicant for comment before an initial decision is reached[2].

1   See **9.31–9.35**.
2   *Yemlahi v Lambeth London Borough Council* (2000) August *Legal Action*, p 26, Wandsworth County Court; *Thorne v Winchester City Council* (2000) April *Legal Action*, p 32, CA; and *R v Newham London Borough Council ex p Lumley* (2001) 33 HLR 11, QBD. There is however, no absolute requirement that the applicant should always have 'the last word' in respect of medical advice. See *Bellouti v Wandsworth London Borough Council* [2005] EWCA Civ 602, [2005] HLR 46, CA. The requirements of procedural fairness are context specific.

12.96 There has been some judicial consideration of the role of medical advisers to local housing authorities. A local housing authority is entitled to obtain its own expert opinion, but care has to be taken not to appear to be using professional medical advisers simply to provide or shore up reasons for a negative decision[1]. Where there is a conflict between medical opinions, the local housing authority must bear in mind the respective qualifications of the experts[2]. The local housing authority's medical adviser has the function of enabling the local housing authority to understand the medical issues and to evaluate for itself the expert evidence from the applicant's medical advisers. In the absence of an examination of the patient, the local housing authority's medical adviser's advice cannot itself constitute expert evidence of an applicant's condition. The local housing authority must take any absence of a personal examination of the applicant into account[3]. If a medical adviser has not personally examined the applicant, he or she could consider discussing the applicant's condition with his or her treating doctors[4].

1   *Hall v Wandsworth London Borough Council, Carter v Wandsworth London Borough Council* [2004] EWCA Civ 1740, [2005] HLR 23, CA; *Shala v Birmingham City Council* [2007] EWCA Civ 624, [2008] HLR 8, CA.
2   *R v Newham London Borough Council ex p Lumley* (2001) 33 HLR 11, QBD; *Khelassi v Brent London Borough Council* [2006] EWCA Civ 1825, CA; and *Shala v Birmingham City Council* [2007] EWCA Civ 624, [2008] HLR 8, CA. All of those cases concerned medical evidence from a psychiatrist which had been evaluated by a GP advising the local housing authority.
3   The need to accord due weight to those medical professionals who have personal experience of the applicant is important and sometimes overlooked: research has disclosed a perception among some local housing authorities that applicants' GPs were lacking in objectivity and more likely to be 'on the side of the applicant' (J Bretherton, C Hunter and S Johnsen '"You can judge them on how they look . . . " Homelessness Officers, Medical Evidence and Decision Making in England' (2013) 7 *European Journal of Homelessness* 1, 69–92 at 83). See also *Medical evidence in homelessness cases* (2013) October *Legal Action*, pp 28–30.
4   *Shala v Birmingham City Council* [2007] EWCA Civ 624, [2008] HLR 8, CA per Sedley LJ at [23]. The Court of Appeal made these comments in relation to the use of medical advisers from the organisation, Nowmedical, which is regularly used by local housing authorities. However, the Court of Appeal refused permission to bring a second appeal where the applicant was arguing that advice from Nowmedical should not be relied upon by local housing authorities in any circumstances (*Harper v Oxford City Council* [2007] EWCA Civ 1169, (2008) January *Legal Action*, p 37, CA). See *Thomas v Lambeth London Borough Council* (2017) November *Legal Action*, p 42, County Court at Central London for a case exposing the potential pitfalls in reliance on such advice.

12.97 Recent examples of cases where the content of medical advice obtained by a local housing authority has received judicial consideration include *Thomas v Lambeth London Borough Council*[1], where the judge expressed the view that 'it is unhelpful for these reports to identify problems that the appellant is not alleged to be suffering from . . . and then reach a conclusion based on the absence of those factors', and *R (J and L) v Hillingdon London Borough Council*[2], where the judge stressed the need for such advice to be confined to the medical issues in the case. That case involved a young autistic boy with challenging behaviour, who was prone to trips and falls. He lived with his mother by a busy road. A social worker had assessed him as being at risk of being run over on the road outside the house. Medical advice relied on by the local housing authority in the course of its decision making criticised the social worker for requesting rehousing on behalf of the family, suggesting this 'may pose a risk of unhelpfully raising expectations', and expressed the view that 'maintaining any child's safety on a road remains a normal parenting role' and not something that would render the property unsuitable. Nicklin J described the medical advice as 'very unimpressive' in so far as it provided 'superficial answers to issues that had no medical dimension and upon which he should not have been commenting at all[3]'.

1   (2017) November *Legal Action*, p 42, County Court at Central London.
2   [2017] EWHC 3411, Admin Ct.
3   [2017] EWHC 3411, Admin Ct at [34] and [64].

12.98 It is for the local housing authority to decide what inquiries are necessary and what weight to give to the various pieces of medical evidence[1] though, where relevant medical evidence (or an opinion expressed therein) has been rejected, reasons should be given to explain why[2]. A local housing authority's decision is only susceptible to challenge for failure to make all necessary inquiries if no reasonable local housing authority would have failed to regard certain additional inquiries as necessary[3]. Inquiries by local housing authorities in these 'medical' cases are further considered at **9.70–9.80**.

1   *Wandsworth London Borough Council v Allison* [2008] EWCA Civ 354, (2008) June *Legal Action*, p 33, CA.
2   *Carter v Wandsworth London Borough Council* [2004] EWCA Civ 1740, [2005] HLR 23, CA; *DT v Lambeth London Borough Council* (2016) December/January *Legal Action*, p 41, the County Court at Central London.
3   *Cramp v Hastings Borough Council* [2005] EWCA Civ 1005, [2005] HLR 48, CA; and see **9.36–9.41**.

12.99 Medical reports obtained as part of an assessment by the Department for Work and Pensions of a person's entitlement to specific welfare benefits may be taken into account by the local housing authority, but the local housing authority must bear in mind that assessment of eligibility for benefits is a wholly different exercise from assessment of priority need[1].

1   *Mangion v Lewisham London Borough Council* [2008] EWCA Civ 1642, (2009) January *Legal Action*, p 26, CA; and *Simpson-Lowe v Croydon London Borough Council* [2012] EWCA Civ 131, (2012) April *Legal Action*, p 47, CA. See **9.76**.

12.100 There will obviously be a close relationship between the issue of vulnerability and a possible disability that the applicant, or a member of the applicant's household, might have[1]. This relationship will require the local housing authority to be alive to the requirements of the public sector equality duty under Equality Act 2010, s 149[2]. The local housing authority must always take due steps to consider any disability (or other protected characteristic) that might be relevant[3]. The public sector equality duty is not confined to circumstances where the disability is 'obvious'. The decision-maker must make inquiries into the issue of disability if some feature of the evidence presented raises a 'real possibility' that the applicant (or a member of his or her household) might be disabled and that disability (or other protected characteristic) is relevant to the decision under consideration[4]. This is a question of fact for the local housing authority[5]. The duty must be kept in mind at every stage of the decision-making process and 'must be exercised in substance, with rigour, and with an open mind'. This will require the decision maker to 'focus very sharply' on: (i) whether the applicant is under a disability (or has another protected characteristic); (ii) the extent of such disability; (iii) the likely effect of the disability, when taken together with any other features, on the applicant when homeless; and (iv) whether the applicant is, as a result, vulnerable[6]. A court in assessing whether this duty has been complied with should not resort to 'over-zealous linguistic analysis'[7]. However, in order to properly discharge the duty sufficient reasons must be given so that on a 'stand-back' reading of the decision, it can be seen that the relevant questions have been addressed[8].

[1] For vulnerable as a result of a mental or physical impairment, see **12.106–12.115**.

[2] For an overview of the requirements of the public sector equality duty generally and in the context of HA 1996, Pt 7 (as amended by HRA 2017, for applications for homelessness assistance made to local housing authorities in England on or after 3 April 2018) see *Hackney London Borough Council v Haque* [2017] EWCA Civ 4, [2017] HLR 14, CA per Briggs LJ at [18]–[24] and [32]–[36]. See further **18.65–18.68** on the requirements of the public sector equality duty in the context of decisions on the suitability of accommodation. Examples of recent cases where the county court has found that the public sector equality duty has not been properly discharged in assessing vulnerability include *Hosseini v Westminster City Council* (2015) October *Legal Action*, p 42, County Court at Central London; *Barrett v Westminster City Council* (2016) February *Legal Action*, p 45, County Court at Central London; *SS v Waltham Forest London Borough Council* (2016) November *Legal Action*, p 41, County Court at Central London; *MQ v Southwark London Borough Council* (2016) December *Legal Action*, p 42, County Court at Central London.

[3] See Equality Act 2010, ss 5–12 and s 149. Although the case law on the public sector equality duty has, in the main, been focused on those who may be vulnerable as a result of a disability, it is important to recall that disability is not the only protected characteristic. In *SS v Waltham Forest London Borough Council* (2016) November *Legal Action*, p 41, County Court at Central London and in *MQ v Southwark London Borough Council* (2016) December *Legal Action*, p 42, County Court at Central London the court found there had been a breach of the public sector equality duty with regard to the applicant's sex.

[4] *Pieretti v Enfield London Borough Council* [2010] EWCA Civ 1104, [2011] HLR 3, CA. Lord Neuberger, at [78] of *Kanu v Southwark London Borough Council* [2015] UKSC 30, [2016] AC 811, SC, spoke of the duty being engaged in instances of 'actual or possible' disability.

[5] See *Birmingham City Council v Wilson* [2016] EWCA Civ 1137, [2017] HLR 4, CA per Sales LJ at [38]–[40].

[6] *Kanu v Southwark London Borough Council* [2015] UKSC 30, [2016] AC 811, SC per Lord Neuberger at [78].

[7] See *Poshteh v Kensington and Chelsea Royal London Borough Council* [2017] UKSC 36, [2017] AC 624, SC per Lord Carnwath at [39] following the approach advocated by the House of Lords in *Holmes-Moorhouse v Richmond upon Thames Royal London Borough Council* [2009] UKHL 7, [2009] 1 WLR 413, HL.

[8] See *Hackney London Borough Council v Haque* [2017] EWCA Civ 4, [2017] HLR 14, CA per Briggs LJ at [51] and *Kanu v Southwark London Borough Council* [2015] UKSC 30, [2016] AC 811, SC per Lord Neuberger at [78]–[79].

12.101 Once the local housing authority is satisfied that there is 'vulnerability', the next step is for it to decide on the cause[1]. For there to be priority need, the vulnerability must have arisen as a result of one of the specified statutory causes[2] or one of the additional causes set out in the Priority Need Order[3]. If the relevant person is vulnerable, but the cause of the vulnerability cannot be put into one of the specified categories, the relevant person may still be vulnerable for some 'other special reason'[4].

[1] In *Hotak v Southwark London Borough Council, Kanu v Southwark London Borough Council & Johnson v Solihull Metropolitan Borough Council* [2015] UKSC 30, [2016] AC 811, SC at [46], Lord Neuberger considered that whether or not this requires a one or two stage test to be applied will probably depend on the facts of the case in hand but that 'the one stage test will probably be more practical in most cases'.
[2] HA 1996, s 189(1)(c). See **12.102**.
[3] SI 2002/2051. See **12.102**.
[4] HA 1996, s 189(1)(c). See **12.116–12.125**.

THE STATUTORY CAUSES

12.102 A range of potential causes of vulnerability are set out in HA 1996, Pt 7[1], and in the Homelessness (Priority Need for Accommodation) (England) Order 2002[2], including 'old age', 'physical disability' and many others. But a person does not accrue priority need simply by achieving 'old age' or by reason of having a 'physical disability', etc. Neither being 100 years old nor having lost a limb (or even two) automatically qualifies a relevant person as having priority need. The specified statutory causes are relevant only in that they could give rise to a vulnerability that counts for priority need purposes. The test is not whether an applicant, or a member of his or her household, falls within the ambit of one of these causes, but whether he or she is vulnerable and, if so, whether the vulnerability is the result of one of the specified reasons (or the result of some 'other special reason'). The full list is:

(1)   old age[3];
(2)   mental illness[4];
(3)   mental handicap[5];
(4)   physical disability[6];
(5)   other special reason[7];
(6)   having been looked after, accommodated or fostered[8];
(7)   having been in the armed forces[9];
(8)   having been imprisoned[10]; or
(9)   having been driven from home by actual or threatened violence[11].

[1] As amended by HRA 2017, for applications for homelessness assistance made to local housing authorities in England on or after 3 April 2018.
[2] SI 2002/2051. See **12.133–12.194**.
[3] See **12.104–12.105**.
[4] See **12.106–12.110**.
[5] See **12.106–12.110**.
[6] See **12.111–12.115**.
[7] See **12.116–12.125**.
[8] See **12.170–12.173**.
[9] See **12.174–12.179**.
[10] See **12.189–12.186**.
[11] See **12.187–12.194**.

12.103 The vulnerability need not be *wholly* the result of one of the specified matters listed above. Many vulnerable individuals will have been rendered vulnerable by several causes or by a combination of factors. Some causal factors may be in the list, others not. The statutory test is satisfied if at least one of the listed matters contributes to the vulnerability. So, in one case[1], the court considered that a man who had been reduced to a state of vulnerability by alcoholism would not normally, by that reason alone, have qualified. But he had suffered a severe head injury a year prior to his application and the medical advice was that this had caused 'some persistent disability made worse by his drinking habits'. The court said that whether the brain injury was described as a 'mental handicap' or 'other special reason', it was 'another important factor' in the applicant's current vulnerability and made the 'whole difference' so as to bring him into the priority need category. In another case, a man who had an addiction to hard drugs, partly as a result of having spent most of his childhood in care, might be 'vulnerable' as a result of the combination of difficulties he suffered from[2].

[1]   *R v Waveney District Council ex p Bowers* [1983] QB 238, CA.
[2]   *Crossley v City of Westminster* [2006] EWCA Civ 140, [2006] HLR 26, CA. See further **12.123**.

Old age

12.104 'Old age' is not defined in HA 1996, Pt 7[1]. The English Code advises that 'it may be that as a result of old age the applicant would be significantly more vulnerable than an ordinary person would be if homeless' but that local housing authorities 'should not use a fixed age beyond which vulnerability occurs automatically (or below which it can be ruled out)' and that each case should be considered on its individual circumstances[2].' Such guidance is of little practical value and local housing authorities are left to determine for themselves whether a person can be said to be 'old' for these purposes.

[1]   As amended by HRA 2017, for applications for homelessness assistance made to local housing authorities in England on or after 3 April 2018.
[2]   English Code, para 8.24.

12.105 Earlier editions of the English Code had suggested particular ages but this only produced unhelpful rigidity. For example, an early Code suggested that men reaching 65, should be accepted. 'Taken literally this would mean that a healthy man of 64 would not be vulnerable while the same man at 65 would be'[1]. Not surprisingly, therefore, there is no specific guidance offered by the current Code, nor by any reported cases, as to what constitutes 'old age'.

[1]   *R v Waveney District Council ex p Bowers* [1983] QB 238, CA per Waller LJ at 245.

Mental illness or (mental) handicap

12.106 The statutory term 'mental illness or handicap' plainly includes a wide range of conditions[1]. Mental illness and mental handicap are, however, two very different things. The reference to 'handicap' is dated. In more modern language this could be described as 'learning disability' which is the phrase currently employed in the English Code[2]. In determining whether there is such illness or handicap contributing to current vulnerability, a local housing authority will need to have regard to any advice from medical professionals, social services or current providers of care and support[3]. Local housing authorities will need to have in place arrangements for liaising with social services and mental health services. Advice from these agencies should be sought where necessary. Consideration should also be given to joint assessments with these agencies or the use of a trained mental health practitioner as part of the assessment team[4].

[1] In considering this statutory cause of vulnerability, local authorities will need to be alive to the possibility that the public sector equality duty under Equality Act 2010, s 149 may be engaged. See **12.100**.
[2] English Code, paras 8.13(b) and 8.25–8.27.
[3] English Code, para 8.25.
[4] English Code, paras 8.25–8.27.

12.107 Those discharged from hospitals following a period of treatment for mental illness are likely to be vulnerable[1]. Although health authorities are supposed to make appropriate pre-discharge arrangements[2] and help with housing may be available from the NHS under the Care Programme Approach[3], if the applicant is actually vulnerable, the fact that such arrangements should have been (or could have been) made is irrelevant[4].

[1] English Code, paras 8.26.
[2] Mental Health Act 1983, s 117. See **20.99–20.104**.
[3] English Code, para 8.26.
[4] See **12.90** for the relevance of third-party support in assessing vulnerability.

12.108 Local housing authorities should clearly distinguish, in the decision letter dealing with this category of priority need, between any mental illness and any mental handicap[1].

[1] *R v Bath City Council ex p Sangermano* (1985) 17 HLR 94, QBD.

12.109 Where there is more than one mental condition, the local housing authority must consider the combined impact of the various conditions on the applicant, as well as any physical disability or other conditions that cumulatively might render the applicant vulnerable[1].

[1] *Crossley v Westminster City Council* [2006] EWCA Civ 140, [2006] HLR 26, CA.

12.110 A wide range of conditions have been explored in the case law as potentially or actually falling within the terms 'mental illness' and 'handicap'. These include:

(1)   accidental brain injury[1];
(2)   'subnormal' intelligence (without any psychiatric disturbance or psychiatric history)[2];
(3)   depression[3];
(4)   epilepsy[4];
(5)   persecutory delusion disorder and lack of insight[5];
(6)   severe poly-drug dependence syndrome[6]; and
(7)   post-traumatic stress disorder[7].

[1] *R v Waveney District Council ex p Bowers* [1983] QB 238, CA; and *R v Lambeth London Borough Council ex p Carroll* (1988) 20 HLR 142, QBD.
[2] *R v Bath City Council ex p Sangermano* (1985) 17 HLR 94, QBD.

[3] *Griffin v City of Westminster Council* [2004] EWCA Civ 108, [2004] HLR 32 CA;
 Chowdhoury v Newham London Borough Council [2004] EWCA Civ 08, (2004) March
 Legal Action, p 25, CA; *Hall v Wandsworth London Borough Council* [2004] EWCA Civ
 1740, [2005] HLR 23, CA; *Osmani v Camden London Borough Council* [2004] EWCA Civ
 1706, [2005] HLR 22, CA; *Shala v Birmingham City Council* [2007] EWCA Civ 624, [2008]
 HLR 8, CA; *Faulkner v Westminster City Council* (2014) June Legal Action, pp 38–39,
 Central London County Court; and *Qoraishi v Westminster City Council* (2014) July/August
 Legal Action, p 55, Central London County Court.
[4] *R v Wandsworth London Borough Council ex p Banbury* (1986) 19 HLR 76, QBD; and *R v
 Reigate and Banstead District Council ex p Di Domenico* (1988) 20 HLR 153, QBD.
[5] *R v Greenwich London Borough Council ex p Dukic* (1996) 29 HLR 87, QBD.
[6] *R v Camden London Borough Council ex p Pereira* (1999) 31 HLR 317, CA.
[7] *Shala v Birmingham City Council* [2007] EWCA Civ 624, [2008] HLR 8, CA; and *Sesay v
 Islington London Borough Council* (2009) September *Legal Action*, p 25, Clerkenwell and
 Shoreditch County Court; and *Hotak v Southwark London Borough Council*, [2015] UKSC
 30, [2016] AC 811, SC.

Physical disability

12.111 Physical disabilities[1] that have an adverse impact on an applicant's susceptibility to harm when homeless may be readily discernible, but the
English Code recommends that medical or social services advice should be
sought wherever necessary[2].

[1] In considering this statutory cause of vulnerability, local authorities will need to be alive to the
 possibility that the public sector equality duty under Equality Act 2010, s 149 may be engaged.
 See **12.100**.
[2] English Code, paras 8.25 and 8.27.

12.112 There is no requirement that any particular degree of disability is
present, nor that it is of any particular duration. The phrase 'substantial
disability' is not part of the statutory rubric[1]. The question is simply whether
the relevant person is vulnerable wholly or partly by reason of his or her
current physical disability[2].

[1] *R v Lambeth London Borough Council ex p Carroll* (1988) 20 HLR 142, QBD per Webster J
 at 145.
[2] In *Wandsworth London Borough Council v Brown* [2005] EWCA Civ 907, the Court of
 Appeal refused permission to appeal against a first-instance judge's order varying the local
 housing authority's decision from one of no priority need to a decision that the applicant had
 a priority need. The applicant suffered from 'extreme sciatica, back pain, asthma, severe
 psoriasis and dermatitis and narcolepsy' and an 'extreme combination of a variety of very
 different ailments', which made the case unusual and one in which there could be only one
 conclusion – that he was vulnerable.

12.113 A local housing authority is not bound to treat someone as vulnerable
as a result of a physical disability simply because the Department for Work and
Pensions has awarded that person a benefit such as Disability Living Allowance or Personal Independence Payments[1].

[1] *Mangion v Lewisham London Borough Council* [2008] EWCA Civ 1642, (2009) January
 Legal Action, p 26, CA; and *Simpson-Lowe v Croydon London Borough Council* [2012]
 EWCA Civ 131, (2012) April *Legal Action*, p 47, CA. See **9.76**.

12.114 Where there is more than one physical disability, the local housing
authority must consider the combined impact of the various conditions on the
applicant, as well as any other conditions, such as mental illness or handicap,

that cumulatively might render the applicant vulnerable[1].

1   *Crossley v Westminster City Council* [2006] EWCA Civ 140, [2006] HLR 26, CA.

12.115 HA 1996, Pt 7[1] does not specifically deal with vulnerability arising through physical illness. Plainly, a person suffering from, for example, influenza may be rendered 'vulnerable' in the relevant sense. But unless the local housing authority is prepared to accept the fact of physical illness as some 'other special reason'[2], vulnerability caused by it will not attract a finding of 'priority need'. On the other hand there will be circumstances in which acute long-term illness itself amounts to disability[3].

1   As amended by HRA 2017, for applications for homelessness assistance made to local housing authorities in England on or after 3 April 2018.
2   See **12.116–12.125**.
3   For example, Equality Act 2010, Sch 1, para 6 which deems cancer, HIV infection and multiple sclerosis to be disabilities for the purposes of Equality Act 2010.

Other special reason

12.116 If a person is vulnerable, but not by reason of any of the factors specified in HA 1996, Pt 7, or the English Priority Need Order[1], the question is whether he or she is vulnerable by reason of some 'other special reason' or reasons[2]. This term is not defined in HA 1996, Pt 7[3], or in the English Code. It is a free-standing category, and is not limited to physical or mental factors.

1   SI 2002/2051. See **12.132–12.194**.
2   HA 1996, s 189(1)(c).
3   As amended by HRA 2017, for applications for homelessness assistance made to local housing authorities in England on or after 3 April 2018.

12.117 In *R v Kensington and Chelsea Royal London Borough Council ex p Kihara*[1], the Court of Appeal held that 'special' means that the difficulties faced must be of an unusual degree of gravity. Asylum-seekers who were homeless, had no right to receive welfare benefits, had no income or capital, no family or friends, no opportunity to work and, in some cases, spoke no English were plainly in priority need for some 'other special reason'[2].

1   (1997) 29 HLR 147, CA.
2   Since 3 April 2000, most asylum seekers who are destitute are not eligible for homelessness assistance and receive support and accommodation from the Home Office. See **11.101–11.121**.

12.118 There are no set or pre-determined groups of people who would fall within this category. Local housing authorities should keep an open mind, and consider the whole of an applicant's circumstances[1].

1   English Code, paras 8.38–8.42.

12.119 Whilst reminding local housing authorities of the need to consider the relevant individual's circumstances, the English Code does give a number of examples of people whose circumstances might amount to their being vulnerable for an 'other special reason'. A number of cases have also come before the courts.

12.120 Young people who do not fall within any other category of priority may be vulnerable for some 'other special reason', and local housing authorities should consider the degree of support available to a young person, along with the cost and practicalities of finding and maintaining a home for the first time. Young people who were forced to leave the parental home, or who left it because of violence or sexual abuse, are particularly likely to be vulnerable[1]. In England, former care-leavers who are vulnerable as a result of having been looked after, accommodated or fostered have a priority need under the Priority Need Order[2].

1   English Code, para 8.40. See also the Scottish cases of *Kelly v Monklands District Council* 1985 SLT 165, OH; and *Wilson v Nithsdale District Council* 1992 SLT 1131, OH.
2   SI 2002/2051, art 5(1). See **12.170–12.173**.

12.121 People who flee their homes as a result of harassment that falls short of actual violence or threats of violence may be vulnerable for an 'other special reason'. Witnesses who may be at risk of intimidation could also fall within this category[1].

1   English Code, para 8.41.

12.122 The previous edition of the English Code suggested that former asylum-seekers may fall within this category if they are vulnerable[1]. Their experience of persecution in their country of origin and/or severe hardship in reaching the UK would be relevant, and local housing authorities should be sensitive to the fact that former asylum-seekers may be reluctant to discuss some of their experiences[2].

1   The Refugee Council has provided a helpful guide for those working with refugees seeking accommodation under HA 1996, Pt 7. See *Making homelessness applications for refugees in England: a guide for anyone supporting newly recognised single refugees* (Chloe Morgan and Eve Bartlett, May 2017). Vulnerability is dealt with at pp 13–15. The guide pre-dates the amendments to HA 1996, Pt 7 introduced by as amended by HRA 2017 (for applications for homelessness assistance made to local housing authorities in England on or after 3 April 2018) though much of the material remains useful for local housing authorities and practitioners working with refugees.
2   *Homelessness Code of Guidance for Local Authorities* (Department for Communities and Local Government, Department for Education and Skills, Department of Health, July 2006), para 10.35. This paragraph has not been reproduced in the 2018 version of the English Code but the underlying logic remains good and the situation of former asylum seekers is one that has been recognised by the courts. See for example *Al-Oumian v Brent London Borough Council*(1999) June *Legal Action*, p 24, Willesden County Court; *Shala v Birmingham City Council* [2007] EWCA Civ 624, [2008] HLR 8, CA; *Al-Kabi v Southwark London Borough Council* (2008) March *Legal Action*, p 21, Lambeth County Court; and *Sesay v Islington London Borough Council* (2008) September *Legal Action*, p 25, Clerkenwell and Shoreditch County Court.

12.123 Drug or alcohol addiction and the risk of relapsing could fall within this 'other special reason' category if the relevant person is vulnerable as a result of it[1]. In *R v Waveney District Council ex p Bowers*[2], the Court of Appeal held that self-induced alcoholism would not normally result in a finding of 'vulnerability'. This was described as a 'grey area' in *Crossley v City of Westminster*[3]. Giving the judgment of the court, Sedley LJ said: 'drug addiction by itself, for all its personal and social consequences, cannot amount to a special reason for vulnerability which is capable of being addressed by housing'[4]. However in *Johnson v Solihull Metropolitan Borough Council* the

Supreme Court was prepared to assume, without deciding, that actual or potential problems with drugs fall within the expression 'other special reason'[5]. The local housing authority should, in any event, consider whether there are other factors, including the possibility of harm suffered as a result of relapse into drug addiction if the applicant is on the streets, or the lack of family support available to the applicant, which would render the applicant 'vulnerable' for an 'other special reason'. In *Crossley v City of Westminster*,[6] the applicant's combination of problems – he had spent his childhood from the age of three in care, he had developed his addiction to heroin at the age of 13, he had been sleeping rough from the age of 17, with short spells in hostels and in prison, he was chronically depressed and suffered from asthma and hepatitis C – were described as 'stark facts' pointing to a decision that he was vulnerable[7].

[1]   *R v Camden London Borough Council ex p Pereira* (1999) 31 HLR 317, CA; *R v Westminster City Council ex p Ortiz* (1993) 27 HLR 364, CA; *Hoolaghan v Motherwell District Council* 1997 CLY 6114, OH; *Tetteh v Kingston Royal London Borough Council* [2004] EWCA Civ 1775, [2005] HLR 21, CA; and *Ryde v Enfield London Borough Council* [2005] EWCA Civ 1281, (2005) January *Legal Action*, p 32, CA.
[2]   [1983] QB 238, CA.
[3]   [2006] EWCA Civ 140, [2006] HLR 26, CA.
[4]   [2006] EWCA Civ 140, [2006] HLR 26, CA at [30].
[5]   *Johnson v Solihull Metropolitan Borough Council* [2015] UKSC 30, [2016] AC 811 per Lord Neuberger at [85].
[6]   [2006] EWCA Civ 140, [2006] HLR 26, CA.
[7]   Another case involving multiple problems, including drug misuse, was *Payne v Kingston upon Thames Royal London Borough Council* (2008) March *Legal Action*, p 21, Central London Civil Justice Centre, where a decision that a single woman, who had been a victim of abuse and domestic violence, and had a history of mental health problems and of drug misuse, was not vulnerable was quashed.

12.124 Victims of trafficking, within the meaning of Art 4 of the Council of Europe Convention on Action Against Trafficking in Human Beings[1], may also fall within the 'other special reason' category, where the applicant's vulnerability arises from his or her status as a trafficking victim. This potential cause of vulnerability is not one that has been considered by the courts in the context of Housing Act 1996, Pt 7[2]. However, the Supreme Court has recognised that there is an emerging and 'prominent strain of current public policy against trafficking and in favour of the protection of its victims'[3]. In addition, the European Court of Human Rights has held that Art 4 of the European Convention on Human Rights places states under a positive obligation to provide practical and effective protection against trafficking and exploitation in general and specific measures of protection[4]. Local housing authorities must act compatibly with those rights contained in the European Convention on Human Rights as are set out in the Human Rights Act 1998, Sch 1[5], and so will need to be alive to the particular vulnerabilities of trafficking victims and the risk that they may face of being re-trafficked if they are without accommodation, in order to ensure compliance with Art 4[6].

[1]   CETS No 197.
[2]   As amended by HRA 2017, for applications for homelessness assistance made to local housing authorities in England on or after 3 April 2018. The topic has received some consideration in Scotland, in the case of *O v Aberdeen City Council* [2017] CSOH 9, 2017 SLT 181, where the Court of Session rejected an attempt to argue that Art 4 of the European Convention on Human Rights gave rise to a general obligation to accommodate homeless victims of trafficking under Housing (Scotland) Act 1987, Pt 2, who would not otherwise have been

eligible for homeless assistance on the basis of their immigration status. See further *XPQ v Hammersmith and Fulham London Borough Council* [2018] EWHC 1391 (QB) which involved an (unsuccesful) claim for damages arising from an alleged failure to provide suitable accommodation. In that case, the High Court considered the interplay between HA 1996, Pt 7, the Council of Europe Convention on Action Against Trafficking in Human Beings and the EU Directive on Preventing and Combating Trafficking in Human Beings, 2011/36/EU.

3   *Hounga v Allen* [2014] UKSC 47, [2014] 1 WLR 2889 per Lord Wilson JSC at [52].
4   *Rantsev v Cyprus and Russia* (2010) 51 EHRR 1.
5   Human Rights Act 1998, s 6.
6   For an insight into some of the difficulties in accessing accommodation faced by victims of trafficking see *Life Beyond the Safe House For Survivors of Modern Slavery in London* (Human Trafficking Foundation, July 2015).

12.125 This is reflected in the English Code which stipulates that local housing authorities should ensure that staff have an awareness of 'the possibility that applicants may be victims of trafficking or of modern slavery, and are able to assess whether or not they are vulnerable as a result'[1]. Further guidance is contained in chapter 21 of the English Code which is dedicated to victims of modern slavery and trafficking. Local housing authorities are reminded that applicants who are victims of trafficking may be in considerable distress and that appropriate training would benefit those staff conducting interviews[2]. Applicants should be given the option of being interviewed by someone of the same sex[3]. And in assessing vulnerability, local housing authorities should take account of any advice from specialist agencies providing services to the applicant and be mindful that 'if a victim of modern slavery is threatened with homelessness or is homeless this significantly increases their risk to being re-trafficked or exposed to further exploitation'[4].

1   English Code, para 8.42.
2   English Code, para 25.15.
3   English Code, para 25.15.
4   English Code, para 25.17.

Homeless 'as a result of an emergency'

12.126 Any applicant (the only relevant person under this category) will have a priority need if currently homeless (or threatened with homelessness) as a 'result of an emergency such as a flood, fire or other disaster'[1]. There are therefore two questions for the local housing authority:

(1)   Is the applicant's present or threatened homelessness 'as a result of' an emergency?
(2)   If so, was the emergency one of a relevant type?

1   HA 1996, s 189(1)(d).

CAUSE AND EFFECT

12.127 The 'emergency' must cause the actual or prospective loss of accommodation and therefore the current or threatened homelessness. The category is intended to deal with sudden emergencies rather than the loss of accommodation that has been anticipated for some time[1]. If the person is already 'homeless', in the technical sense used in HA 1996, Pt 7[2], before the emergency occurs, then the homelessness did not result from the emergency. For example, in one case, a caravan-dweller suddenly lost his caravan. But the caravan had been on a site where he had not had permission to station it or occupy it. So he had been homeless when the loss of the caravan occurred. Whilst the sudden loss of his home was 'an emergency', it did not cause his homelessness[3]. In another case, a local housing authority's decision that the applicant had become homeless as a result of the withdrawal of accommodation provided to him as an asylum-seeker, rather than as a result of his losing his home in Darfur, was not wrong in law. He was not therefore homeless as a result of an emergency[4].

[1] *R v Walsall Metropolitan Borough Council ex p Price* [1996] CLY 3068, QBD; and *R v Camden London Borough Council ex p Wait* (1986) 18 HLR 434, QBD.
[2] As amended by HRA 2017, for applications for homelessness assistance made to local housing authorities in England on or after 3 April 2018. See CHAPTER **11**.
[3] *Higgs v Brighton and Hove City Council* [2003] EWCA Civ 895, [2004] HLR 2, CA.
[4] *Sadiq v Hackney London Borough Council* [2007] EWCA Civ 1507, (2008) April *Legal Action*, p 34, CA.

12.128 On the other hand, if a person loses his or her home as the result of an emergency, it is irrelevant (to the question of priority need) that he or she might have been made homeless anyway at a later date[1]. So, a person who is in no other sense in 'priority need' will be within this category if made homeless by an emergency (such as a fire) even if that occurs just before an imminent eviction from his or her accommodation for massive rent or mortgage arrears.

[1] *R v Camden London Borough Council ex p Wait* (1986) 18 HLR 434, QBD.

WHAT TYPE OF EMERGENCY?

12.129 The words used at HA 1996, s 189(1)(d) are 'emergency such as a flood, fire or other disaster'. The courts have held that this wording means that the emergency must have some physical nature, such as a flood, fire or some similar event. But the flood or fire or other disaster need not have been naturally caused. The person made homeless by flooding from a burst communal water tank is as much in priority need as the person made homeless by reason of sea or river flooding. The person made homeless by an arsonist or by a fire caused by faulty electric wiring is as much in priority need as the victim made homeless by a forest fire or lightning strike. Homelessness caused by a sudden gas leak or explosion is likewise the result of an emergency. A person whose mobile home is stolen from its lawful pitch, site or mooring is also within this provision[1].

[1] *Higgs v Brighton and Hove City Council* [2003] EWCA Civ 895, [2004] HLR 2, CA.

12.130 On the other hand, homelessness resulting from the enforcement of a demolition order is not the result of an emergency[1]. Likewise, an unlawful eviction (where the locks were changed and the applicant's belongings placed outside) did not constitute some 'other disaster' falling within the term 'emergency'[2].

[1] *Noble v South Herefordshire District Council* (1985) 17 HLR 80, CA.
[2] *R v Bristol City Council ex p Bradic* (1995) 27 HLR 584, CA.

12.131 The volcanic eruptions in Montserrat were an obvious example of an 'emergency' that fell within this subsection, and people fleeing from the eruption which caused the loss of their home were found to have a priority need[1]. The devastating fire at the Grenfell Tower in West London in June 2017, would be another. Where a person resides in any building which has been made subject to an order of the magistrates' court under the Greater London Council (General Powers) Act 1984, s 37[2] or s 38[3], he or she is deemed to have a priority need by virtue of an emergency[4].

1   *Telesford v Ealing London Borough Council* (2000) August *Legal Action*, p 26, Brentford County Court.
2   Removal of occupants of dangerous buildings in outer London.
3   Removal of occupants of buildings in vicinity of dangerous structures, etc.
4   Greater London Council (General Powers) Act 1984, s 39.

Additional categories in England: the Priority Need Order

12.132 The Homelessness (Priority Need for Accommodation) (England) Order 2002 (the Order)[1] came into force on 31 July 2002. Under the Order, there are six extra categories of people who have a priority need in addition to the four categories set out in HA 1996, Pt 7[2] itself[3]. These additional categories only operate to confer priority need on the applicant personally.

1   SI 2002/2051 at Appendix 2.
2   As amended by HRA 2017, for applications for homelessness assistance made to local housing authorities in England on or after 3 April 2018.
3   SI 2002/2051, arts 3–6.

A person aged 16 or 17

12.133 A young person, who is aged 16 or 17[1], has a priority need simply by virtue of his or her age[2]. There is no additional requirement that he or she be 'vulnerable' or fall into any of the other priority need categories of HA 1996, Pt 7[3], or the Order. There are only two exceptions specified in the Order:

(1)   'relevant' children; or
(2)   children who ought to be being accommodated by a children's services authority which owes them duties under the Children Act 1989, s 20.

1   SI 2002/2051, art 3.
2   See English Code, paras 8.19–8.23.
3   As amended by HRA 2017, for applications for homelessness assistance made to local housing authorities in England on or after 3 April 2018.

AGE

12.134 In most cases, the child's age is unlikely to be in any doubt. If there is doubt, a local housing authority will have to make its own decision on the child's age, relying on the applicant's appearance, family and educational background and any ethnic or cultural considerations[1].

1   *R (B) v Merton London Borough Council* [2003] EWHC 1689 (Admin), [2003] 4 All R 295. In the context of the provision of accommodation under Children Act 1989, s 20, the Supreme Court has held that if a child disagrees with a children's services' authori-

ty's assessment of his or her age, the child can bring judicial review proceedings and, unlike most claims in judicial review, ask the court to review the evidence available and make its own decision as to what age he or she is (*R (A) v Croydon London Borough Council, R (M) v Lambeth London Borough Council* [2009] UKSC 8, [2009] 1 WLR 2557, SC). The question of how this might fit into the review and appeal provisions of HA 1996, Pt 7, as amended by HRA 2017 for applications for homelessness assistance made to local housing authorities in England on or after 3 April 2018 (see Chapter 19) is not one that has been addressed by the courts. In practice the question may be academic as most age disputed minors tend to seek accommodation from children's services in the first instance. Where children's services have completed their own age assessment a local housing authority would be entitled to have regard to this.

12.135 The local housing authority must decide whether the child is 16 or 17 at the date of its initial decision or review decision, rather than at the date of application. The Local Government Ombudsman has found maladministration where local housing authorities have refused to help 17-year-olds who were attempting to make applications for homelessness assistance[1].

[1]　See *Complaint against South Tyneside Metropolitan Borough Council*, 04/C/18995, 12 December 2005, where £2,000 compensation was recommended after the local housing authority failed to give a 17-year-old a homeless application form to complete or provide him with any interim accommodation. He returned after two months, by which time he had turned 18 and no longer had a priority need.

12.136 What should happen when a 17-year-old, approaching his or her eighteenth birthday, makes an application for homelessness assistance? The Court of Appeal considered these circumstances in *Robinson v Hammersmith & Fulham London Borough Council*[1]. Although the guidance given in that case pre-dates the amendments to HA 1996, Pt 7 introduced by HRA 2017[2], it remains relevant for any local housing authority considering whether or not a 17-year-old applicant has a priority need and what further duty (if any) he or she will be owed when the HA 1996, s 189B(2)[3] relief duty comes an end. The guidance given by the Court of Appeal was in three parts.

[1]　[2006] EWCA Civ 1122, [2007] HLR 7, CA.
[2]　For applications for homelessness assistance made to local housing authorities in England on or after 3 April 2018.
[3]　As inserted by HRA 2017, s 5(2) for applications for homelessness assistance made to local housing authorities in England on or after 3 April 2018.

12.137 First, the making of decisions on applications for homelessness assistance should not be postponed[1]. The issue of the applicant's priority need is a very straightforward question of fact, which would not normally take much time to determine. The Court of Appeal said:

> 'in the case of a 17-year-old child, it would not . . . be lawful for a local authority to postpone the taking of a decision even for a short period on the basis that by postponing that decision the child will have reached the age of 18 before the decision is taken[2].'

[1]　English Code, para 8.4 and 14.16.
[2]　*Robinson v Hammersmith & Fulham London Borough Council* [2006] EWCA Civ 1122, [2007] HLR 7, CA per Waller LJ at [38]. See also *R (MM) v Lewisham London Borough Council* [2009] EWHC 416 (Admin), (2009) April *Legal Action*, p 23, Admin Ct, where the local housing authority simply failed to make a decision on an application from a 17-year-old for over four months. The Administrative Court judge said, 'I would urge the defendant to take action to ensure that . . . steps are taken to ensure that the imminence of

a child attaining 18 years is not taken as a basis for failing to take action and . . . there is due and proper contact between its housing authority and its social services authority'.

12.138 Second, a local housing authority cannot find that a young person approaching his or her eighteenth birthday does not have a priority need because he or she is 'so nearly 18 that the difference between 18 and 17, should be ignored'[1]. If, at the date of the decision, the young person is, as a matter of fact, 17 (even if the following day is his or her eighteenth birthday), he or she has a priority need.

[1]   *Robinson v Hammersmith & Fulham London Borough Council* [2006] EWCA Civ 1122, [2007] HLR 7, CA per Waller LJ at [29].

12.139 Third, where the young person requests a review of any negative decision, but turns 18 before the review is concluded, it is not lawful for the local housing authority simply to state that, at the date of the review decision, the young person does not have a priority need:

'if the original decision was unlawful . . . the review decision should have so held and made a decision that would have restored to the appellant the rights she would have had if the decision had been lawful[1].'

[1]   *Robinson v Hammersmith & Fulham London Borough Council* [2006] EWCA Civ 1122, [2007] HLR 7, CA per Waller LJ at [32].

THE EXCEPTIONS

12.140 Both of the exceptions to this category are designed to ensure that young people to whom children's services have owed duties in the past, or do owe a present duty to accommodate by virtue of Children Act 1989, s 20, should be the responsibility of children's services. This is because young people in those circumstances are likely to have needs over and above the simple need for a roof over their heads, and those needs are best met by children's services[1]. As Baroness Hale put it in the House of Lords:

'It is, perhaps, possible to envisage circumstances in which a 16 or 17 year old who is temporarily without accommodation is nevertheless not in need within the meaning of section 17(10): perhaps a child whose home has been temporarily damaged by fire or flood who can well afford hotel accommodation while it is repaired . . . But it cannot seriously be suggested that a child excluded from home who is "sofa surfing" in this way, more often sleeping in cars, snatching showers and washing his clothes when he can, is not in need[2].'

[1]   *R (M) v Hammersmith & Fulham London Borough Council* [2008] UKHL 14, [2008] 1 WLR 535, HL per Baroness Hale at [31]; *R (G) v Southwark London Borough Council* [2009] UKHL 26, [2009] 1 WLR 2399, HL; and *R (TG) v Lambeth London Borough Council* [2011] EWCA Civ 526, [2011] HLR 33, CA. See *Prevention of homelessness and provision of accommodation for 16 and 17 year old young people who may be homeless and/or require accommodation* (April 2018, MHCLG and DfE) on the CD Rom with this book.
[2]   *R (G) v Southwark London Borough Council* [2009] UKHL 26, [2009] 1 WLR 2399, HL per Baroness Hale at [28]. For an example of a young person who was accommodated by the local housing authority under HA 1996, s 193(2) main housing duty rather than by children's services, see *R (B) v Nottingham City Council* [2011] EWHC 2933 (Admin), (2011) December *Legal Action*, p 30, Admin Ct. The local housing authority was not wrong in law

on the facts of that particular case when it decided that a pregnant 16-year-old was not a child in need.

12.141 Following the two significant House of Lords' decisions on the housing needs of 16- and 17-year-olds[1], the UK Government issued statutory guidance in April 2010: *Provision of Accommodation for 16 and 17 year old young people who may be homeless and/or require accommodation*[2]. This was replaced in April 2018 by *Prevention of homelessness and provision of accommodation for 16 and 17 year old young people who may be homeless and/or require accommodation* (the Homeless 16/17 guidance)[3]. The guidance reinforces the decisions of the House of Lords: the duty 'under section 20 of the 1989 [Children] Act . . . takes precedence over the duties in the 1996 [Housing] Act'[4], and so primary responsibility for homeless teenagers will lie with children's services.

[1]   *R (M) v Hammersmith & Fulham London Borough Council* [2008] UKHL 14, [2008] 1 WLR 535, HL; and *R (G) v Southwark London Borough Council* [2009] UKHL 26, [2009] 1 WLR 2399, HL.
[2]   April 2010, CLG and Children, Schools and Families.
[3]   April 2018, MHCLG and DfE. HA 1996, s 182 requires that local housing authorities take the guidance into account when exercising their HA 1996 Pt 7 functions. Similarly, the Local Authority Social Services Act 1970, s 7 requires children's services' departments to take the guidance into account when exercising children's services' functions. See **12.151–12.159**.
[4]   Homeless 16/17 guidance, para 1.2.

12.142 The case law and government guidance have all emphasised joint working between local housing authorities and children's services. However, investigations by Shelter[1] and the magazine *Inside Housing*[2] have found that 'a substantial number of vulnerable children are still suffering from a failure of co-ordination between these two departments within a number of local authorities' in England[3]. The issue of joint working is explored further at **12.150–12.159**.

[1]   Referred to in *R (TG) v Lambeth London Borough Council* [2011] EWCA Civ 526, [2011] HLR 33, CA per Wilson LJ at [5].
[2]   'Who Cares?', *Inside Housing*, 7 January 2011. See also *No excuses: preventing homelessness for the next generation* (Homeless Link, 2013), 'Councils illegally housing teenagers in B&B's', BBC Newsnight, 29 August 2013, *Complaint against Kent County Council* 09/017/510, *Complaint against Dover District Council* 09/017/512, 31 July 2012 (case of a 17-year-old who spent nine months living in a tent), 'From Pillar to Post', *Inside Housing*, 21 June 2013 and 'Homeless teenagers failed by councils', *Inside Housing*, 21 June 2013. The latter investigation found that in the first seven months of 2012, 59% (3,418) of 5,789 teenagers who approached 112 councils were sent straight to housing departments rather than children's services.
[3]   *R (TG) v Lambeth London Borough Council* [2011] EWCA Civ 526, [2011] HLR 33, CA per Wilson LJ at [5].

Relevant child

12.143 A 16- or 17-year-old does not have automatic priority need if he or she is 'a relevant child', defined by the Children Act 1989, s 23A(2), as any child, aged 16 or 17, who was formerly being looked after by any local authority for a prescribed period of time while of a prescribed age, but who is no longer being looked after[1]. This exception, as described in the English Code[2], is satisfied only if:

(1)   the child is 16 or 17; and

(2)   the child was 'looked after'[3] by a children's services authority:

    (a)   for at least 13 weeks,

    (b)   after the age of 14[4]; and

(3)   has been looked after while he or she was 16 or 17; and

(4)   is no longer being looked after.

[1]   Children Act 1989, Sch 2, para 19B; Care Leavers (England) Regulations 2010, SI 2010/2571, reg 3.

[2]   English Code, para 8.21.

[3]   See **12.149**.

[4]   See Care Planning, Placement and Care Review Regulations 2010, SI 2010/959, reg 40.

12.144 As the English Code itself foreshadows[1], each of these elements is subject to close technical definition in the Children Act 1989 (as amended) and in the Care Leavers (England) Regulations 2010[2]. If the terms of the exception appear to be satisfied, the local housing authority should obviously refer to the precise wording of the Children Act 1989 and the regulations to confirm the actual position. Although the Code recommends joint working between the local housing authority and children's services[3], the decision as to whether the child meets the technical definition of 'relevant child' is for the local housing authority to make and not for children's services to decide.

[1]   English Code, para 8.21.

[2]   SI 2010/2571, reg 3.

[3]   English Code, para 8.23.

A child owed duties under the Children Act 1989, s 20

12.145 A 16- or 17-year-old does not have automatic priority need if she or he is a person to whom a children's services authority 'owe a duty to provide accommodation' under the Children Act 1989, s 20[1]. Note that the exception only applies if the duty 'is' owed (that is currently owed). That the duty was owed in the past or might be owed in the future is irrelevant, save to the extent that a child who was owed a duty under Children Act 1989, s 20 in the past may be a relevant child[2]. A children's services authority is not obliged to notify a decision that it owes a young person the duty under Children Act 1989, s 20 in writing, so there is unlikely to be a convenient short-cut for inquiries by simply requesting sight of such a document.

[1]   SI 2001/2051, art 3(2).

[2]   See **12.143–12.144**.

12.146 Children owed duties under the Children Act 1989, s 20 are those children who appear to a children's services authority to require accommodation either:

(1)   because they are 16 or over and their welfare is otherwise likely to be seriously prejudiced; or

(2)   because they have no parents or other people who are able to provide accommodation for them.

12.147 Where a child has been provided with accommodation by children's services, there may be some doubt as to whether that accommodation was provided under the duty at Children Act 1989, s 20, or the power at Children Act 1989, s 17[1]. The courts have held that where accommodation has been provided as a result of a young person falling within the test at Children Act, s 20, the local authority cannot side-step its responsibility by recording or arguing that it was in fact acting under the Children Act 1989, s 17 power or some other legislation[2]. Equally, the children's services authority cannot side-step its responsibility by telling a child aged 16 or 17 who falls within the criteria at Children Act 1989, s 20 to make an application for homelessness assistance[3].

[1] See **20.39–20.57** for Children Act 1989, s 17; and **20.58–20.64** for Children Act 1989, s 20.
[2] *Southwark London Borough Council v D* [2007] EWCA Civ 182, (2007) 10 CCLR 280, CA; *R (H) v Wandsworth London Borough Council, R (Barhanu) v Hackney London Borough Council, R (B) v Islington London Borough Council* [2007] EWHC 1082 (Admin), (2007) 10 CCLR 441, Admin Ct; *R (L) v Nottinghamshire County Council* [2007] EWHC 2364 (Admin); *R (M) v Hammersmith & Fulham LBC* [2008] UKHL 14, [2008] 1 WLR 535; *R (G) v Southwark LBC* [2009] UKHL 26; [2009] 1 WLR 1299; *R (TG) v Lambeth London Borough Council* [2011] EWCA Civ 527, [2011] 4 All R 453.
[3] *R (G) v Southwark London Borough Council* [2009] UKHL 26, [2009] 1 WLR 2399, HL; *R (MM) v Lewisham London Borough Council* [2009] EWHC 416 (Admin), (2009) April *Legal Action*, p 23, Admin Ct *and R (TG) v Lambeth London Borough Council* [2011] EWCA Civ 526, [2011] HLR 33, CA. The Local Government Ombudsman recommended that a local authority pay a teenager £7,000 for its failure to provide her with services under Children Act 1989, s 20 and for being content for her to be dealt with solely by the housing department (*Complaint against Waltham Forest London Borough Council*, 08 016 986, 21 October 2009, (2010) February *Legal Action*, p 34).

CHILDREN'S SERVICES' DUTIES TOWARDS RELEVANT CHILDREN AND 'LOOKED AFTER' CHILDREN

12.148 The thrust of the amendments made to the Children Act 1989 by the Children (Leaving Care) Act 2000 is that children's services authorities should be responsible for meeting the accommodation and other needs of young people who have been in, but are no longer in, the care system (at least until they reach 18), or who have been 'looked after' under Children Act 1989, s 20. To accord such 16- and 17-year-olds priority need would shift the responsibility for accommodating young people on to local housing authorities when children's services should be arranging accommodation[1]. This policy aim is reinforced by the Homeless 16/17 guidance.

[1] *R (G) v Southwark London Borough Council* [2009] UKHL 26, [2009] 1 WLR 2399, HL.

12.149 Where a child is in the care of a local authority, or is accommodated under the Children Act 1989, s 20 for a continuous period of more than 24 hours, he or she then becomes a 'looked after' child[1]. The children's services authority is then responsible for safeguarding and promoting the child's welfare, including his or her educational achievement[2], and for maintaining the child in other respects apart from providing accommodation[3]. In addition, if the 'looked after' 16- or 17-year-old has been looked after by the children's services authority for a total of 13 weeks or more at any time since the age of 14, he or she is entitled to services under the Children (Leaving Care) Act 2000. Those services include an assessment of the child's future needs, preparation of a detailed pathway plan for him or her, and a personal adviser[4]. The services may continue until the young person reaches the age of 25[5]. It is precisely because of these obligations of children's services towards 16- and 17-year-olds that the exceptions to this priority need category have been made.

1   Children Act 1989, s 22(1).
2   Children Act 1989, s 22(3) and (3A).
3   Children Act 1989, s 22B.
4   Children Act 1989, s 23B.
5   Children Act 1989, ss 23C(6)–(7) and 23CZB (as inserted by Children and Social Work Act 2017, s 3).

JOINT WORKING BETWEEN HOUSING AND CHILDREN'S SERVICES

12.150 The English Code recommends that local housing authorities and children's services agree written joint protocols, in respect of 16- and 17-year-olds, setting out 'clear, practical arrangements for providing services that are centered on young people and their families and prevent young people from being passed over and back between housing and children's services authorities'[1]. This reflects the House of Lords' view that, when a 16- or 17-year-old presents himself or herself to the housing department as homeless, the housing department must make a referral to the children's services department as part of its ongoing inquiries into whether or not the young person has a priority need, or is a relevant child or is owed a Children Act 1989, s 20 duty. The children's services department should then carry out its own assessment in accordance with its responsibilities under the Children Act 1989[2]. It is because 'relevant children' and children entitled to a Children Act 1989, s 20 duty have needs over and above the simple need for a roof over their heads that the Priority Need Order clearly contemplates that children's services should take the long term responsibility[3].

1   English Code, para 8.23.
2   *R (M) v Hammersmith & Fulham London Borough Council* [2008] UKHL 14, [2008] 1 WLR 535, HL per Baroness Hale at [29]. See **20.39–20.68** for children's services' responsibilities.
3   *R (M) v Hammersmith & Fulham London Borough Council* [2008] UKHL 14, [2008] 1 WLR 535, HL per Baroness Hale at [31]. See also *R (G) v Southwark London Borough Council* [2009] UKHL 26, [2009] 1 WLR 2399, HL.

12.151 The Homeless 16/17 guidance, also emphasises the need for a joint approach, underpinned by a joint protocol, to prevent 16- and 17-year-olds in crisis from being passed between housing and children's services departments unnecessarily[1]. The Guidance addresses various scenarios that housing and children's services departments may encounter when approached by a 16- or 17-year-old who may be homeless.

1   Homeless 16/17 guidance, Chapter 6.

12.152 To facilitate joint working, children's services may ask local housing authorities to 'help in the exercise of any of their functions' under Children Act 1989 and local housing authorities are required to comply with the request where possible[1]. Similarly local housing authorities can ask children's services authorities to assist them in discharging their functions under HA 1996, Pt 7[2], and children's services authorities should co-operate by rendering such assistance as is reasonable in the circumstances[3].

1   Children Act 1989, s 27. This duty to cooperate does not apply in circumstances where the local housing authority and children's services form a part of the same unitary authority. See

R (C1 and C2) v Hackney London Borough Council [2014] EWHC 3670 (Admin), Admin Ct. However, the guidance issued by the Secretary of State in *Working Together to Safeguard Children* (HM Government, March 2015), requires a similar degree of co-operation between departments in the same authority. See *R (M) v Islington London Borough Council* [2016] EWHC 332 (Admin), [2016] HLR 19, Admin Ct per Collins J at [14]–[15].
2   As amended by HRA 2017, for applications for homelessness assistance made to local housing authorities in England on or after 3 April 2018.
3   HA 1996, s 213(1)(b).

Initial approach made to the local housing authority

12.153 Where the young person first approaches the local housing authority, it has a duty to accept an application for homelessness assistance, to make inquiries into that application and to secure interim accommodation where there is reason to believe that the young person may be eligible for assistance, may be homeless and may be 16 or 17 years old[1]. The Homeless 16/17 guidance advises that bed and breakfast accommodation is unsuitable for 16- and 17-year-olds[2].

1   HA 1996, s 188(1) as amended by HRA 2017, s 5(4) for applications for homelessness assistance made to local housing authorities in England on or after 3 April 2018. See also Homeless 16/17 guidance, paras 4.1–4.2.
2   Homeless 16/17 guidance, para 5.10. See also *Complaint against Lancashire County Council*, 13 020 158, 5 August 2015, where Lancashire County Council placed a 16-year old in bed and breakfast accommodation following his release on bail, in breach of the guidance and against the recommendation of the Youth Offending Team. The Ombudsman made a finding of 'fault causing injustice'.

12.154 The local housing authority should then make a referral to children's services for an assessment[1]. The Homeless 16/17 guidance emphasises that this referral should be made in a 'timely manner'[2] and that, in those cases where the young person is not eligible for assistance or is a relevant child[3], 'immediate arrangements must be made for them to receive assistance from children's services'[4].

1   Homeless 16/17 guidance, paras 4.4–4.6, 4.13 and 4.14. Guidance on the approach to be taken in circumstances where the young person is reluctant to engage with this process is given at para 4.7. Consent for a referral in the other direction is dealt with expressly by HA 1996, s 213B as inserted by HRA 2017, s 10 for applications for homelessness assistance made to local housing authorities in England on or after 3 April 2018.
2   Homeless 16/17 guidance, para 4.4.
3   See **12.143–12.144**.
4   Homeless 16/17 guidance, para 4.5.

12.155 The duties owed by the local housing authority do not end upon the making of the referral to children's services. Having accepted an application for homelessness assistance, the local housing authority must still make inquiries into the application and notify the applicant of its decision[1]. If these inquiries lead the local housing authority to conclude that the young person is eligible for assistance and threatened with homelessness the the HA 1996, s 195(2)[2] prevention duty (to take reasonable steps to help the applicant secure that suitable accommodation does not cease to be available for his or her occupation) will be owed. Alternatively if the inquiries lead to the conclusion that the young person is eligible for assistance and homeless then the HA 1996, s 189B(2) relief[3] duty (to take reasonable steps to help the applicant secure that suitable accommodation becomes available for his or her occupation) will be owed. In either case the young person will also be entitled to an assessment of his case and a personalised housing plan under HA 1996, s 189A.[4] In broad terms, the Homeless 16/17 guidance anticipates that these various duties may be discharged by the local housing authority co-operating with children's services to ensure that suitable accommodation is provided by children's services.[5] But until that occurs the young person, if homeless, will need to be accommodated by the local housing authority[6]. Once the HA 1996 s 195(2)[7] prevention duty or s 189B(2) relief[8] duty have come to an end, the local housing authority will need to make a decision as to what, if any, duty is owed next. Where children's services, having carried out their assessment of the young person's needs, have decided that he or she is a child in need of accommodation, they have a duty under Children Act 1989, s 20 to provide accommodation[9]. Since a child who has been provided with accommodation under Children Act 1989, s 20 will no longer be homeless the local housing authority can simply notify the applicant of its decision that he or she is not homeless and that no duty is owed[10]. Alternatively, if children's services have concluded that they do not owe the young person a duty, then he or she will have a priority need[11] and 'housing services duties under Part 7 of the 1996 Act will continue'[12].

[1] HA 1996, s 184(1) and (3). See CHAPTER 9.
[2] HA 1996, s 195(2) as amended by HRA 2017, s 4(2) for applications for homelessness assistance made to local housing authorities in England on or after 3 April 2018. See **15.87–15.137**.
[3] HA 1996, s 189B(2) as inserted by HRA 2017, s 5(2) for applications for homelessness assistance made to local housing authorities in England on or after 3 April 2018. See **15.138–15.189**.
[4] HA 1996, s 189A as inserted by HRA 2017, s 3(1) for applications for homelessness assistance made to local housing authorities in England on or after 3 April 2018. See **15.62–15.86**.
[5] Homeless 16/17 guidance, paras 4.12–4.18.
[6] HA 1996, s 188 as amended by HRA 2017, s 5(4) for applications for homelessness assistance made to local housing authorities in England on or after 3 April 2018. See **16.37–16.73**.
[7] HA 1996, s 195(2) as amended by HRA 2017, s 4(2) for applications for homelessness assistance made to local housing authorities in England on or after 3 April 2018. See **15.87–15.137**.
[8] HA 1996, s 189B(2) as inserted by HRA 2017, s 5(2) for applications for homelessness assistance made to local housing authorities in England on or after 3 April 2018. See **15.138–15.189**.
[9] See **12.146**.
[10] Homeless 16/17 guidance, para 4.18(a).
[11] See **12.133**.
[12] Homeless 16/17 guidance, para 4.8. See CHAPTER 16 for the duties that may be owed.

Initial approach made to children's services

12.156 Where a 16- or 17-year-old first approaches children's services, either directly or through a referral by another agency, and he or she appears to be homeless or at risk of homelessness, children's services must assess whether the young person is a child in need and whether any duty is owed to him or her to provide accommodation under Children Act 1989[1]. If it appears that the young person has nowhere safe to stay that night, children's services must secure suitable emergency accommodation for him or her[2]. Bed and breakfast accommodation is not considered suitable accommodation, even for emergencies[3]. Children's services should also, with the young person's consent, refer his or her case to the local housing authority under HA 1996, s 213B[4]. The referral should include a summary of any initial assessment together with an indication of what assistance, if any, housing services might provide[5]. When the local housing authority receives a referral from children's services the two services should work together to ensure that the needs of the young person are met. The making of this referral 'does not diminish children's services responsibilities' rather 'it should be used to help strengthen communication between children's and housing services'[6].

[1] Homeless 16/17 guidance, para 3.1.
[2] Homeless 16/17 guidance, para 3.4
[3] See **12.153** fn 2.
[4] HA 1996, s 213B(2)–(3) as inserted by HRA 2017, s 10 for applications for homelessness assistance made to local housing authorities in England on or after 3 April 2018 and the Homelessness (Review Procedure etc.) Regulations 2018, SI 2018/223, reg 10 and Sch 1, para 10. See **15.229–15.230**. See further Homeless 16/17 guidance, paras 3.63–3.64.
[5] Homeless 16/17 guidance, para 3.64.
[6] Homeless 16/17 guidance, para 3.65.

12.157 The Homeless 16/17 guidance advises that where a young person requires accommodation as a result of one of the factors at Children Act 1989, s 20(1)(a)–(c) or (3), then that young person must be provided with accommodation by children's services[1]. This is not 'simply a matter for local policy'[2]. That young person then, after a period of 24-hours, becomes a 'looked after' child and will be entitled to all the duties owed to looked-after children[3]. The acceptance of the duty under Children Act 1989, s 20 means that the young person will not have a priority need under the Priority Need Order[4].

[1] Homeless 16/17 guidance, para 3.12.
[2] Homeless 16/17 guidance, para 3.11.
[3] Homeless 16/17 guidance, para 3.12. See **12.149**.
[4] Art 3(2), SI 2002/2051.

12.158 If the young person refuses accommodation offered under Children Act 1989, s 20, children's services must be clear that his or her decision has been reached after having been provided with 'all relevant information' and that she or he is competent to make the decision[1]. Once accommodation has been lost because the young person has refused it, and he or she does not have any other accommodation, he or she will be homeless within the definition at HA 1996, ss 175–177[2]. In these circumstances, once again, children's services would need to refer the young person's case, with his her consent, to the local housing authority under HA 1996, s 213B[3]. Upon receipt of the referral, the local housing authority should then make its inquiries and notify the young person of its decision[4]. Providing the young person is eligible for assistance then he or she will be owed the HA 1996, s 189B(2)[5] relief duty. A young person in these circumstances will also have a priority need[6] and should not be considered to have become homeless intentionally simply because of failing to take up an offer of accommodation from children's services[7]. This means that if the young person remains homeless at the time the HA 1996, s 189B(2)[8] relief duty comes to an end[9], then the local housing authority will owe him or her the HA 1996, s 193(2) main housing duty[10].

[1] Homeless 16/17 guidance, para 3.49. English Code, para 8.23.
[2] See CHAPTER 10.

3   HA 1996, s 213B(2)–(3) as inserted by HRA 2017, s 10 for applications for homelessness assistance made to local housing authorities in England on or after 3 April 2018 and the Homelessness (Review Procedure etc.) Regulations 2018, SI 2018/223, reg 10 and Sch 1, para 10. See **15.229–15.230**.

4   HA 1996, s 184(1) and (3).

5   As inserted by HRA 2017, s 5(2) for applications for homelessness assistance made to local housing authorities in England on or after 3 April 2018. See **15.138–15.189**.

6   Homelessness (Priority Need for Accommodation) (England) Order SI 2002/2051, art 3.

7   Homeless 16/17 guidance, para 4.21 and **13.114–13.117**. See also, by analogy, *Johnston v City of Westminster* [2015] EWCA Civ 554, [2015] HLR 35, CA, where the applicant was owed the main housing duty by Eastbourne Borough Council as a result of a referral made under the local connection provisions (see CHAPTER **14**) but had never been actually been offered accommodation or accommodated by Eastbourne. The Court of Appeal rejected a contention by the City of Westminster that the applicant was not homeless.

8   As inserted by HRA 2017, s 5(2) for applications for homelessness assistance made to local housing authorities in England on or after 3 April 2018. See **15.138–15.150**.

9   See **15.151–15.189**.

10 See **16.94–16.199**. See further Homeless 16/17, para 4.25.

12.159 Where accommodation is provided to the young person under one of the duties in HA 1996 Pt 7[1], that is not necessarily the end of children's services' responsibilities. They should consider whether the child is still 'a child in need' and, if so, produce a child in need plan setting out the services that will be provided in order to meet his or her needs[2].

1   As amended by HRA 2017, for applications for homelessness assistance made to local housing authorities in England on or after 3 April 2018.

2   Homeless 16/17 guidance, para 3.50.

A young person under 21

12.160 A young person who:

- is under 21; and
- was looked after, accommodated or fostered at any time between the ages of 16–18;

will have a priority need provided that he or she is not a 'relevant student'[1]. In non-technical language, the criteria are likely to be fulfilled by recent care leavers who are not yet 21. If the applicant falls within this priority need category, he or she does not also need to be 'vulnerable' or fall into any other category.

1   Homelessness (Priority Need for Accommodation) (England) Order 2002, SI 2002/2051, art 4. See English Code, para 22.21. See, generally, *On my own: the accommodation needs of young people leaving care in England* (Barnardos, 2013) for research into the particular problems faced by this group.

12.161 The term 'looked after, accommodated or fostered'[1] takes its meaning from the Children Act 1989, s 24(2)[2]. It encompasses those who have been:

- looked after by a local authority;
- accommodated by or on behalf of a voluntary organisation;
- accommodated in a private children's home;
- accommodated for a consecutive period of at least three months:
  - by a local health board, special health authority or by a local authority in the exercise of education functions; or

- in any care home or independent hospital or in any accommodation provided pursuant to arrangements made under the National Health Service Act 2006 by a National Health Service trust or an NHS foundation trust, or by a local authority in Wales in the exercise of education functions; or
- privately fostered[3].

A child will have been 'looked after' by a local authority if he or she was:

- in its care; or
- provided with accommodation by the local authority in the exercise of any of its social services functions (within the meaning the Local Authority Social Services Act 1970) apart from Children Act 1989, ss 17, 23B and 24B;

for a continuous period of more than 24 hours[4].

[1] SI 2002/2051, art 1(3).
[2] SI 2002/2051, art 1(3).
[3] Children Act 1989, s 24(2). See also English Code, para 8.28.
[4] Children Act 1989, s 22(1)–(2). See also *R (Berhe) v Hillingdon London Borough Council and Secretary of State for Education and Skills* [2003] EWHC 2075 (Admin), [2003] All ER (D) 01 Sep, Admin Ct, for an example of a dispute over whether children provided with accommodation by children's services had been 'looked after'.

12.162 As long as the applicant was 'looked after, accommodated or fostered' at some stage when he or she was 16, 17 or 18 years old, the criteria will be met. No minimum period of time during which he or she was 'looked after, accommodated or fostered' is prescribed.

12.163 Many of these former care leavers will be owed duties of support by children's services under Children Act 1989, ss 23C–24D including the duty to prepare and review a pathway plan, and to appoint a personal adviser[1]. Where a care leaver falls within this category but is not owed the HA 1996, s 193(2) main housing duty[2], for example because he or she has become homeless intentionally[3], he or she may be entitled to accommodation under Children Act 1989, s 23C(4)(c)[4].

[1] Children Act 1989, ss 23C–24D.
[2] See **16.94–16.199**.
[3] See **Chapter 13**.
[4] See generally *SO v Barking and Dagenham London Borough Council* [2010] EWCA Civ 1101, [2011] 1 WLR 1283, CA.

12.164 The exception to this category of priority need is where the applicant is a 'relevant student'[1]. That term is only met by a person:

(1) who is a care leaver;
(2) who is under 25;
(3) to whom s 24B(3) of the Children Act 1989 applies;
(4) who is in full time higher or further education; and
(5) whose term time accommodation is unavailable during vacation[2].

[1] SI 2002/2051, art 4(1).
[2] SI 2002/2051, art 1(3). See also English Code, para 8.29.

12.165 Children's services authorities continue to have duties to provide accommodation to those young people who meet these very specific conditions, and for that reason they are not accorded priority need under this provision[1]. However, an applicant for homelessness assistance to a local housing authority in England who is a 'relevant student' should not simply be turned away to the children's services authority which should be accommodating them. The appropriate course would be to accept the application, make due inquiries and refer the applicant to children's services in performance of the HA 1996, s 189B(2)[2] relief duty.

1 Children Act 1989, s 24B(5).
2 As inserted by HRA 2017, s 5(2) for applications for homelessness assistance made to local housing authorities in England on or after 3 April 2018. See **15.138–15.189**.

Vulnerability: institutional backgrounds

12.166 People applying to local housing authorities in England and who are 'vulnerable' as a result of:

- having been 'looked after, accommodated or fostered' (and who are aged 21 or over and not 'relevant students')[1]; or
- having been a member of Her Majesty's regular naval, military or air forces; or
- having served a custodial sentence, been committed for contempt of court or other kindred offences, or having been remanded in custody,

all have a priority need[2]. Each sub-category is described in more detail in the following paragraphs.

1 See **12.171**.
2 SI 2002/2051, art 5.

12.167 To qualify, the applicant must be 'vulnerable' as defined in *Hotak, Johnson and Kanu*[1]. So, simply having been in the military, in care, or in prison is not enough. The applicant must be vulnerable, and that vulnerability must be the result, in whole or in part, of having been in care, in custody or in the military.

1 *Hotak v Southwark London Borough Council, Kanu v Southwark London Borough Council & Johnson v Solihull Metropolitan Borough Council* [2015] UKSC 30, [2016] AC 811, SC, and see **12.77–12.91**.

12.168 The provisions do not require any immediate link between the end of military service, imprisonment or care and the application for homelessness assistance. They direct attention to the present vulnerability of the applicant. Although a person may be particularly vulnerable when first released, discharged, or at the point of leaving care, that may not be the only time at which he or she experiences relevant vulnerability. The provisions of the English Priority Need Order[1] will be met by any current vulnerability that is the result of the experience of a period in care, in the military or in prison, even if that period ended many months or years earlier.

1 SI 2002/2051, art 5.

12.169 Unlike the category of 'vulnerable' persons set out in HA 1996, s 189(1)(c) this category of priority need can only be satisfied if the applicant personally is vulnerable for these reasons. A member of the applicant's household who is vulnerable as a result of one of these reasons does not confer priority need on the applicant. Obviously, in those circumstances, it would make sense for the vulnerable individual to apply in his or her own right for accommodation for his or her household.

A FORMER CARE LEAVER AGED 21 OR OVER

12.170 The local housing authority must address the following questions[1]:

(1)   Is the person aged 21 or over?
(2)   Was he or she formerly looked after, accommodated or fostered?
(3)   Is he or she a relevant student?
(4)   Is he or she vulnerable?
(5)   Is that vulnerability *as a result of* having been looked after, accommodated or fostered[2]?

[1]   SI 2002/2051, art 5(1). English Code, paras 8.28–8.31 and 22.20–22.23
[2]   English Code, para 8.27.

12.171 The meanings of 'looked after, accommodated or fostered' and 'relevant student' are defined in the English Priority Need Order[1]. If the applicant is a 'relevant student' he or she cannot qualify under this category.

[1]   SI 2002/2051, art 1(3). See English Code, para 8.28.

12.172 Unlike the category of care leavers aged 18, 19 and 20[1], there is no requirement, for those aged 21 or over, that their period in care should have been at any particular age. The effects of a traumatic period in care (at any age) may only manifest themselves later in life.

[1]   See **12.160–12.165**.

12.173 The first three questions are therefore simple questions of fact for the local housing authority to determine. By contrast, determining:

(1)   whether the applicant is vulnerable; and
(2)   whether that vulnerability is *as a result of* having been 'looked after, accommodated or fostered',

require much more difficult judgments. The English Code recommends that local housing authorities consider:

(1)   the length of time that the applicant was 'looked after, accommodated or fostered';
(2)   the reasons why the applicant was 'looked after, accommodated or fostered';
(3)   the length of time since that ended;
(4)   whether the applicant has been able to obtain or maintain accommodation since then; and
(5)   whether the applicant has existing support networks, particularly family, friends or a mentor[1].

The English Code also emphasises that particular care should be taken in assessing those who may potentially fall within this class and that local housing authorities 'should take into account whether, if homeless, they would be at particular risk of exploitation, abuse or involvement in offending behaviour'[2].

¹ English Code, para 22.22.
² English Code, para 22.23.

A person who is vulnerable as a result of having been a member of the armed forces

12.174 The questions for the local housing authority are[1]:

(1)   Was the applicant a member of the armed forces?
(2)   Is he or she vulnerable?
(3)   Is that vulnerability *as a result of* having been a member of the armed forces?

¹ SI 2002/2051, art 5(2). English Code, paras 8.31–8.32 and 24.8–24.9

12.175 The first question is a very straightforward question of fact, although military service is very broadly defined. The English Priority Need Order[1] refers to membership of 'Her Majesty's regular naval, military or air forces' without linking back to the much more technical definition previously used in HA 1996, s 199(4)[2]. It is difficult to see how the words could be met by a person who has been in anything other than the British armed services.

¹ SI 2002/2051.
² Repealed by Housing and Regeneration Act 2008, ss 315((b), 321(1), Sch 16.

12.176 The next question is whether a person is 'vulnerable' as defined in *Hotak, Johnson and Kanu*[1].

¹ *Hotak v Southwark London Borough Council, Kanu v Southwark London Borough Council & Johnson v Solihull Metropolitan Borough Council* [2015] UKSC 30, [2016] AC 811, SC. See **12.77–12.91**.

12.177 The final question is whether the applicant is vulnerable *as a result of* time spent in the armed forces. Local housing authorities are advised to consider:

(1)   the length of time spent in the forces (they should not assume that vulnerability cannot occur after even a short period of service);
(2)   the type of service that the applicant was engaged in (those on active service might find it more difficult to cope with civilian life);
(3)   whether the applicant spent any time in a military hospital (possibly an indicator of a serious health problem or of post-traumatic stress);
(4)   whether the forces' medical and welfare advisers judged the individual to be particularly vulnerable and issued a Medical History Release Form;
(5)   the length of time since discharge; and
(6)   whether the applicant has any existing support networks, particularly

family or friends[1].

[1] English Code, para 24.10.

12.178 Some applicants (who have served for a long period or who have been medically discharged) ought to have been offered assistance with resettlement by the armed forces[1]. This does not mean that they are to be turned away by the local housing authority or redirected to their former unit. In any event, such assistance from the armed forces is directed to the point of discharge, not to any later need for accommodation.

[1] English Code, para 24.5.

12.179 The H(W)A 2014, s 70 does not contain the additional requirement of vulnerability[1]. Former members of the armed forces who may not be vulnerable might consider directing an application (or a further application) to a local housing authority in Wales.

[1] See **12.77–12.91**.

A former prisoner who is vulnerable

12.180 The questions for the local housing authority in dealing with an applicant who may fall within this category follow the same pattern as described for the previous two categories[1]:

(1)   Is he or she vulnerable?
(2)   If so, is the vulnerability *as a result of* having served a custodial sentence, having been committed for contempt of court (or other kindred offences), or having been remanded in custody?

[1] SI 2002/2051, art 5(3). English Code, paras 8.34–8.35 and 23.17–23.20.

12.181 The term 'custodial sentence' is defined to include:

* a sentence of imprisonment for those aged 21 or over;
* a sentence of detention for those aged under 18;
* a sentence of detention for public protection for those under 18 who commit serious offences;
* a sentence of detention for those under 18 who commit certain violent or sexual offences;
* a sentence of custody for life for persons under 21;
* a sentence of detention in a young offender institution for those aged between 18 and 21; and
* a detention and training order[1].

[1] Powers of Criminal Courts (Sentencing) Act 2000, s 76; the references to sentence of custody for life and sentences of detention in a young offender institution are due to be repealed by the Criminal Justice and Court Services Act 2000, but no date for their repeal has yet been appointed (Criminal Justice and Court Services Act 2000, s 80(1)).

12.182 Being 'committed for contempt of court' refers to punishment under the inherent jurisdiction of the court to commit, and 'other kindred offences' refers to committals under the court's statutory powers[1]. Being 'remanded in custody' refers to being remanded by an order of the court, being remanded to youth detention accommodation under the Legal Aid, Sentencing and Punishment of Offenders Act 2012, s 91(4), or being remanded, admitted or removed to hospital under the sentences available under the Mental Health Act 1983[2].

1   Such as that at County Courts Act 1984, s 118.
2   Referred to in the Order as being defined by the Powers of Criminal Courts (Sentencing) Act 2000, s 88. That section has been repealed and the definition is now found at Criminal Justice Act 2003, s 242(2). The references to the Mental Health Act 1983 are to the powers at ss 35, 36, 38 or 48, Mental Health Act 1983.

12.183 The English Code recommends that, in determining 'vulnerability', and whether it is the result of imprisonment or custody, local housing authorities should consider:

(1)   the length of time served (it should not be assumed that vulnerability could not occur as a result of a short period of imprisonment);

(2)   whether the applicant is receiving supervision from a criminal justice agency and any advice received from such an agency;

(3)   the length of time since release;

(4)   the extent to which the applicant has been able to obtain and maintain accommodation during that time; and

(5)   whether the applicant has existing support networks, particularly family or friends, and how much of a positive influence those networks are likely to be[1].

1   English Code, para 23.19.

12.184 In one county court decision, the judge found that the local housing authority had been wrong to reject the opinion of a prison officer that the applicant was institutionalised[1], and had also been wrong to find that the applicant had a history of managing to secure housing when, in fact, his only accommodation in recent years had been insecure accommodation with a friend and he had previously been recalled to prison because he had not managed to secure housing[2].

1   The English Code, para 23.20 now expressly recommends that the assessments of offender managers and the like are taken into account.
2   *Kelly v City of Westminster Council* (2008) December *Legal Action*, p 27, Central London County Court.

12.185 Former prisoners who have a priority need for this reason may still be found to have become homeless intentionally by the local housing authority if their homelessness arose as a result of their deliberate acts or omissions (which led them to prison and to lose their previous accommodation)[1].

1   *R v Hounslow London Borough Council ex p R* (1997) 29 HLR 939, QBD; and *Stewart v Lambeth London Borough Council* [2002] EWCA Civ 753, [2002] HLR 40, CA. See 13.237–13.238.

12.186 There is a considerable body of literature on some of the problems faced by ex-offenders in trying to find accommodation on their release from prison[1]. The importance of this category of priority need arises from the close link between homelessness and offending. According to a survey conducted by the Ministry of Justice, 15% of prisoners surveyed reported being homeless before custody and 60% of prisoners felt that having a place to live following release was important in stopping them reoffending in future[2].

1   For example, *Locked Out* (Citizens' Advice Bureau, March 2007); *Homelessness Prevention and meeting housing need for ex-offenders: a Guide to Good Practice* (CLG, 2009); *Accommodation, Homelessness and re-offending of prisoners, results from the surveying prisoner crime reduction survey* (Ministry of Justice, 2012); *Finding and Sustaining a Home in the Private Rented Sector – the essentials a guide for front-line staff working with homeless offenders* (Crisis, 2012); *Housing Ex-offenders* (House of Commons Library, SN/SP/2989, 16 April 2014); *Homelessness prevention for care leavers, prison leavers and survivors of domestic violence* (APPG for Ending Homelessness, July 2017).
2   *Accommodation, homelessness and reoffending of prisoners: results from the Surveying Prisoner Crime Reduction (SPCR) survey* (MOJ, 2012).

A person who is vulnerable as a result of fleeing violence or threats of violence

12.187 The questions for the local housing authority when dealing with an applicant who may fall within this category are[1]:

(1)   Did the person cease to occupy accommodation as a result of violence from another person or threats of violence from another person which were likely to be carried out?
(2)   Is the person vulnerable?
(3)   Is that vulnerability *as a result of* having ceased to occupy accommodation because of violence from another person or threats of violence from another person which were likely to be carried out?

1   SI 2002/2051, art 6. English Code, paras 8.36–8.37 and 21.32–21.34.

12.188 Although this category was intended primarily to benefit people without children who had been subject to domestic violence, its terms include people fleeing accommodation as a result of any type of violence (except self-inflicted harm). The English Code refers to all forms of violence, including racially motivated violence[1]. The Supreme Court has held that where violence is 'domestic violence'[2], the definition of violence should be interpreted in the same sense as it is used in family proceedings: '"Domestic violence" includes physical violence, threatening or intimidating behaviour and any other form of abuse which, directly or indirectly may give rise to the risk of harm[3].' This approach is reflected in the English Code[4]. The Court of Appeal has held that this extended definition of violence should also apply to people who are fleeing from violence that is not domestic violence[5].

1   English Code, para 21.31.
2   See **10.83**.
3   *Yemshaw v Hounslow London Borough Council* [2011] UKSC 3, [2011] 1 WLR 433, [2011] HLR 16, SC, Baroness Hale at [28] quoting the *Practice Direction (Residence and Contact Orders: Domestic Violence (No 2)* [2009] 1 WLR 251.
4   English Code, para 21.19.
5   *Hussain v Waltham Forest London Borough Council* [2015] EWCA Civ 14, [2015] HLR 16, CA. For further discussion of 'domestic violence' and 'violence', and the background to these decisions, see **10.81–10.91**.

12.189 The English Code recommends that:

- the safety of the applicant and ensuring his or her confidentiality are of paramount concern;
- inquiries should not be made of the perpetrator; and
- the correct approach is to consider the probability of violence, and not actions which the applicant could take (such as injunctions against the perpetrators)[1].

[1] English Code, paras 8.36, 21.21, 21.31 and 21.33.

12.190 This reflects the approach taken in relation to the question whether it would be reasonable for the applicant to continue to occupy accommodation in which violence is being experienced or threatened[1].

[1] See 10.81–10.91.

12.191 In considering whether an applicant is vulnerable for this reason, local housing authorities are advised to take into account:

(1) the nature of the violence or threats (whether a single but significant incident or a number of incidents over an extended period of time which have a cumulative effect);

(2) the impact and likely effects of the violence or threats on the applicant's physical and mental health and well-being;

(3) whether the applicant has any existing support networks, particularly by way of family or friends; and

(4) the continuing threat from the perpetrator[1].

[1] English Code, para 21.34.

12.192 Considering an applicant who claimed to have left his home because of threats of violence[1], a county court judge held that the local housing authority should consider the following:

- Did the applicant leave his or her home due to threats?
- Were those threats likely to be carried out?
- Was he or she vulnerable?

In relation to the third question, the judge held that a person who is subject to threats of violence, and who is street homeless, is less likely to be able to protect himself or herself[2].

[1] Not domestic violence.
[2] *Logan v Havering London Borough Council* (2007) May *Legal Action*, p 31, Romford County Court.

12.193 To qualify under this category, the applicant must have actually left accommodation and have left it because of the violence or threatened violence. This need not be, but is very likely to have been, the accommodation which he or she had most recently occupied.

12.194 The H(W)A 2014, s 70 does not contain the additional requirement of vulnerability[1]. A person who has been subject to domestic abuse who is not vulnerable and does not have a dependent child might consider directing an application for homelessness assistance (or a further application) to a local housing authority in Wales.

¹   H(W)A 2014, s 70(1)(e).

WALES

The statutory categories in H(W)A 2014, s 70

12.195 In *Wales*, the categories of priority need are wholly contained in H(W)A 2014, s 70. This section codifies, with some amendments, the four categories set out in HA 1996, s 189(1) and those six categories which, prior to the coming into force of H(W)A 2014, were set out in the Homeless Persons (Priority Need) (Wales) Order 2001¹. With the exception of the category relating to prisoners², the intention behind H(W)A 2014, s 70 was to consolidate the existing categories, modernising the language where appropriate, rather than to effect any substantial change to the law³.

¹   SI 2001/607 (W 30). See Luba & Davies (2012, 3rd edn).
²   See **12.223–12.228**.
³   *Housing (Wales) Bill, Explanatory Memorandum* (Welsh Government, November 2013) p 160.

12.196 In contrast to the position for applicants to local housing authorities in England, in each of the categories under H(W)A 2012, s 70 an applicant will have a priority need if either he or she, or any person with whom he or she resides or might reasonably be expected to reside¹, falls within the relevant category. The categories are set out below. There is considerable overlap with the categories under HA 1996, s 189(1) and reference back to the relevant sections is made where appropriate.

¹   See H(W)A 2014, s 56 and **10.21–10.32**.

Pregnancy

12.197 This category¹ corresponds precisely with HA 1996, s 189(1)(a)². The Welsh Code advises local housing authorities that in the event that a pregnant woman suffers a miscarriage or terminates her pregnancy during the assessment of her application, then the local housing authority should consider whether she continues to have a priority need for any other reason, for example, on the basis that she is vulnerable within the meaning of H(W)A 2014, s 70(1)(c)³.

¹   H(W)A 2014, s 70(1)(a). See also Welsh Code, para 16.3.
²   See **12.37–12.40**.
³   Welsh Code, para 16.5.

Dependent child

12.198 Aside from a minor variation[1] in the wording, this category[2] corresponds precisely with HA 1996, s 189(1)(b)[3].

[1] The singular 'child' has been used in H(W)A 2014, s 70(1)(b), rather than 'children'. The distinction is of no practical effect since words in the singular include the plural and vice versa (Interpretation Act 1978, s 6(c)).
[2] H(W)A 2014, s 70(1)(b). See also Welsh Code, paras 16.6–16.8.
[3] See **12.41–12.75**.

Vulnerable

12.199 An applicant, or a person with whom he or she resides or might reasonably be expected to reside will fall within this category if he or she is vulnerable[1] as a result of some special reason (eg old age, physical or mental illness or physical or mental disability).

[1] H(W)A 2014, s 70(1)(c). See also Welsh Code, paras 16.11–16.33 and 16.71–16.78.

THE STATUTORY CAUSES OF VULNERABILITY

12.200 Under H(W)A 2014, s 70(1)(c) the statutory causes of vulnerability are old age, physical or mental illness and physical or mental disability. This list of statutory causes is expressed to be non-exhaustive meaning that a person may be vulnerable as a result of any one of the specified statutory causes or as a result of another unspecified special reason[1]. This may be contrasted with HA 1996, s 189(1)(c), where 'special reason' is a distinct statutory cause of vulnerability[2] separate to the express statutory causes of old age, physical disability or mental illness etc. It seems unlikely that this minor change in the phraseology was intended to have any effect as the objective underpinning H(W)A 2014, s 70 was to consolidate the existing categories of priority need, modernising the language where appropriate, rather than to effect any substantial change to the law[3].

[1] See further Welsh Code, paras 16.12–16.13 and 16.18.
[2] See **12.116–13.125**.
[3] *Housing (Wales) Bill, Explanatory Memorandum* (Welsh Government, November 2013) p 160.

12.201 Guidance is given in the Welsh Code on the assessment of individuals who may be vulnerable as a result of old age[1], mental or physical illness or disability (including autistic spectrum disorder)[2], as well as those who are in receipt of psychiatric services[3], the chronically sick[4], victims of abuse[5], rough sleepers[6] and former asylum seekers[7]. In relation to old age the Welsh Code advises that 'Authorities should normally consider applicants over 60 to be vulnerable'[8]. While in relation to rough sleepers, the Welsh Code directs that 'people who are sleeping rough are likely to be vulnerable due to the health and social implications of their situation'[9].

[1] Welsh Code, para 16.20.
[2] Welsh Code, para 16.21–16.25.
[3] Welsh Code, para 16.26.
[4] Welsh Code, para 16.27.
[5] Welsh Code, para 16.28.

6   Welsh Code, para 16.29–16.30.
7   Welsh Code, para 16.31–16.33.
8   Welsh Code, para 16.20.
9   Welsh Code, para 16.29.

The meaning of 'vulnerable'

12.202 Unlike HA 1996, Pt 7[1], H(W)A 2014, Pt 2 contains a definition of vulnerable at H(W)A 2014, s 71. A person will be deemed to be vulnerable if he or she:

- would be less able to fend for himself or herself if the person were to become street homeless than would an ordinary homeless person who becomes street homeless; and
- this reduced ability is the result of some special reason (eg old age, physical or mental illness or physical or mental disability); and
- this would lead to the person suffering more harm than would be suffered by the ordinary homeless person[2].

1   As amended by HRA 2017, for applications for homelessness assistance made to local housing authorities in England on or after 3 April 2018.
2   H(W)A 2014, s 71(1).

12.203 This is the test for vulnerability under H(W)A 2014, s 71 represents the statutory codification of the *Pereira* test[1]. The comparison with the 'ordinary homeless person' under H(W)A 2014, s 71 is to be contrasted with the 'ordinary person who is homeless', which is the relevant comparator under HA 1996, s 189(1)(c) following the decision of the Supreme Court in *Hotak, Johnson and Kanu*[2]. However, the Welsh Code makes clear that while local housing authorities should use the 'ordinary homeless person' as the comparator, the 'ordinary homeless person' should not be equated with a 'chronic rough sleeper with the associated social, mental and physical health problems that they can display'[3]. From this it might be inferred that the ordinary homeless person is a person who does not suffer from these problems. Building on this, the Welsh Code advises that 'people who are sleeping rough are likely to be very vulnerable due to the health and social implications of their situation'[4].

1   *R v Camden London Borough Council ex p Pereira* (1999) 31 HLR 317, CA. See **12.77** above.
2   *Hotak v Southwark London Borough Council, Kanu v Southwark London Borough Council & Johnson v Solihull Metropolitan Borough Council* [2015] UKSC 30, [2016] AC 811, SC, and see **12.77–12.91**.
3   Welsh Code, para 16.73.
4   Welsh Code, para 16.29.

12.204 'Street homeless' in the context of H(W)A 2014, s 71, means that the person has no accommodation available for his or her occupation in the United Kingdom or elsewhere, which the person:

- is entitled to occupy by virtue of an interest in it or by virtue of an order of a court;
- has an express or implied licence to occupy; or

- occupies as a residence by virtue of any enactment or rule of law giving the person the right to remain in occupation or restricting the right of another person to recover possession[1].

The extended definition of homelessness at H(W)A 2014, ss 55–56 does not apply to the definition of 'street homeless'[2]. That is, the test for vulnerability envisions that the person in question, literally, has no accommodation available. Whether or not the person actually is, or is likely to become, street homeless has no bearing on the application of the test for vulnerability[3].

[1]   H(W)A 2014, s 71(2).
[2]   H(W)A 2014, s 71(2).
[3]   H(W)A 2014, s 71(1).

12.205 Since the test for vulnerability under H(W)A 2014, s 71 codifies the *Pereira* test[1], the correct approach to vulnerability under this section might be assumed to mirror the approach to vulnerability adopted under HA 1996, s 189(1)(c) prior to the decision of the Supreme Court in *Hotak, Johnson and Kanu*[2]. For example, in *Pereira* it was said that the material sense in which the person must be less well able to 'fend' for himself or herself is in coping with his or her actual (or threatened) homelessness[3]. Obviously, that test will be satisfied by a person whose circumstances are such that he or she is not able to obtain housing unaided and is thus unable to deal with homelessness in the ordinary way[4]. There need not be actual injury or detriment. An increase in the risk of injury or other harm is itself a 'detriment'. 'Injury or detriment' can include physical injury, a deterioration of a person's mental condition, or the risk of self-harm[5].

[1]   *R v Camden London Borough Council ex p Pereira* (1999) 31 HLR 317, CA. See **12.87**.
[2]   *Hotak v Southwark London Borough Council, Kanu v Southwark London Borough Council & Johnson v Solihull Metropolitan Borough Council* [2015] UKSC 30, [2016] AC 811, SC, and see **12.77–12.91**.
[3]   *R v Camden London Borough Council ex p Pereira* (1998) 31 HLR 317, CA per Hobhouse LJ at 330.
[4]   *R v Camden London Borough Council ex p Pereira* (1998) 31 HLR 317, CA per Hobhouse LJ at 330.
[5]   *Griffin v City of Westminster Council* [2004] EWCA Civ 108, CA, [2004] HLR 32, CA; *Gentle v Wandsworth London Borough Council* [2005] EWCA Civ 1377, (2006) January *Legal Action*, p 32, CA; and *Khelassi v Brent London Borough Council* [2006] EWCA Civ 1825, CA.

12.206 However, in some respects the guidance in the Welsh Code has sought to reflect the guidance given in *Hotak, Johnson and Kanu*[1]. For example the Welsh Code emphasises that local housing authorities should not simply 'compare the vulnerable with the vulnerable' in carrying out the comparative exercise and should only take into account third-party support where it is available on a consistent and predictable basis[2]. Giving an overview of the approach to be taken in assessing vulnerability the relevant sections of the Welsh Code conclude by advising that:

> 'In order to establish the basis of this test the Local Authority must first understand the likely harm or detriment an ordinary homeless person would face if they were to become street homeless and their ability to fend for themselves. This should be based on the ordinary person who is in need of accommodation. This would be the starting point for any comparison.

Once they have established the harm or detriment that the ordinary homeless person would experience and their ability to fend for themselves when street homeless, they will need to compare this to the applicant. If the applicant or any other person reasonably expected to reside would be less able to fend for themselves AND thus suffer more harm as result of the special reason (Mental Health, Substance misuse, etc.) then they would be considered "Vulnerable" as set out in section 70 (c) and (j)[3].'

[1] *Hotak v Southwark London Borough Council, Kanu v Southwark London Borough Council & Johnson v Solihull Metropolitan Borough Council* [2015] UKSC 30, [2016] AC 811, SC, and see **12.77–12.91**.
[2] Welsh Code, paras 16.73–16.74.
[3] Welsh Code, paras 16.77–16.78.

Homeless 'as a result of an emergency'

12.207 This category[1] corresponds precisely with HA 1996, s 189(1)(d) save that it has been extended to include those with whom the applicant resides or might reasonably be expected to reside[2].

[1] H(W)A 2014, s 70(1)(d). See also Welsh Code, para 16.34.
[2] See **12.126–12.131**.

Homeless as a result of domestic abuse

12.208 The questions for the local housing authority when dealing with an applicant, or a person with whom an applicant resides or might reasonably be expected to reside, who may fall within this category[1] are:

- is he or she homeless;
- has he or she been subjected to domestic abuse; and
- if so, is the homelessness a result of the domestic abuse?

[1] H(W)A 2014, s 70(1)(e). See also Welsh Code, para 16.35–16.39.

12.209 Unlike the equivalent category in the English Order[1], there is no need for the applicant to be vulnerable as a result of having fled accommodation in order to qualify in this category.

[1] SI 2002/2051, art 6. See **12.187–12.194**.

12.210 Unlike the equivalent category in the English Order[1], the requirement is for the person to be homeless. It is not necessary for the person to have physically ceased to occupy his or her accommodation. It will suffice that the accommodation is not reasonable for him or her to continue to occupy[2]. This enables an applicant to apply for accommodation and quickly be accepted as homeless, in priority need and unintentionally homeless, whilst still at home. He or she will therefore be able to receive the benefit of the H(W)A 2014, s 73 duty[3] and the H(W)A 2014, s 75 duty[4] thereafter, without necessarily having to be provided with interim accommodation first.

[1] SI 2002/2051, art 6. See See **12.187–12.194**.
[2] H(W)A 2014, s 55(3) and s 57. See further CHAPTER 10 for the definition of homelessness.
[3] See **17.73–17.117**.

⁴   See **17.146–17.197**.

12.211 It will be noted that in contrast to the position under the English Order, the abuse must be domestic in nature. Domestic abuse has the meaning given in H(W)A 2014, s 58¹, that is, the extended definition adopted by the Supreme Court in *Yemshaw v Hounslow London Borough Council*²: 'physical violence, threatening or intimidating behaviour and any other form of abuse which, directly or indirectly may give rise to the risk of harm'³.

¹   H(W)A 2014, s 99.
²   [2011] UKSC 3, [2011] 1 WLR 433, [2011] HLR 16, SC.
³   See **10.83**.

A person aged 16 or 17

12.212 This category embraces all 16- and 17-year-olds¹ and those with whom they reside or might reasonably be expected to reside. In contrast to the situation under the English Priority Need Order², there are no exceptions to this category³. There is certainly no requirement that the applicant be vulnerable or separated from his or her parents. It is simply being aged 16 or 17 that gives rise to the priority need. Note, in contrast to the position for those who apply to local housing authorities in England for homelessness assistance, the requirement is that the person is aged 16 or 17 at the time of application, rather than the time of the initial decision or review. This point is emphasised in the Welsh Code which states that 'it is important to note that a person who is 16 or 17 at the time they are applying to a Local Housing Authority for accommodation retains their priority need should they turn 18 at any point during the assessment'⁴. This avoids the problems discussed at **12.136–12.139**, whereby delay on the part of a local housing authority might in certain circumstances, deprive an applicant of his or her rights.

¹   SI 2001/607, art 4; H(W)A 2014, s 70(1)(f). See also Welsh Code, paras 16.40–16.44.
²   SI 2002/2051, art 3.
³   See **13.145–13.152** and Welsh Code, paras 16.40–16.44.
⁴   Welsh Code, para 16.40.

12.213 Despite the breadth of this category, the intention of the Welsh Government is that the primary responsibility for accommodating 16- and 17-year-olds, as is the case in England¹, should lie with children's services². Specifically, 16- and 17-year-olds who are without accommodation will generally be accommodated under the Social Services and Well-being (Wales) Act 2014³. Joint working between local housing authorities is encouraged in order to achieve this⁴. In instances where the young person exercises their right to refuse assistance from children's services then the local housing authority will owe him or her a duty under H(W)A 2014, ss 73 or 75⁵.

¹   See **12.133–12.159**.
²   Welsh Code, para 16.41 and Social Services and Well-being (Wales) Act 2014 Pt 6 *Code of Practice (Looked After and Accommodated Children)* (Welsh Government, 2015), para 545.
³   See **20.85–20.98**.
⁴   Welsh Code, para 16.41 and Social Services and Well-being (Wales) Act 2014 Pt 6 *Code of Practice (Looked After and Accommodated Children)* (Welsh Government, 2015), para 582.
⁵   Social Services and Well-being (Wales) Act 2014 Pt 6 *Code of Practice (Looked After and Accommodated Children)* (Welsh Government, 2015), para 585.

A person aged 18, 19 or 20 at particular risk of exploitation

12.214 If an applicant, or a person with whom he or she resides or might reasonably be expected to reside[1]:

- is aged 18 or over, but under 21; and
- is at particular risk of sexual or financial exploitation,

then he or she will have a priority need.

[1] H(W)A 2014, s 70(1)(g). See also Welsh Code, paras 16.45–16.48.

12.215 Note that the person must be at 'particular' risk for the terms of H(W)A 2014, s 70(1)(g) to be satisfied, not merely subject to the general risk of sexual or financial exploitation that any young person may face. Presumably this additional criterion will be satisfied by some personal characteristic of the person (eg drug or alcohol dependency), some special feature of his or her local area (eg prevalent street prostitution) or any aspect of his or her personal circumstances which places the applicant at a greater than normal level or risk. Although a young person need not have been exploited in the past in order to fall within this category, the Welsh Code emphasises that 'where young persons have a history of being sexually or financially exploited, they should normally be regarded as vulnerable and in priority need'[1]. However, the Code goes on to warn that 'it is not good practice for Authorities to always expect evidence of sexual or financial exploitation'[2].

[1] Welsh Code, para 16.48.
[2] Welsh Code, para 16.48.

12.216 A person who is deemed to be at risk who turns 21 during the assessment process will still fall within this category[1].

[1] Welsh Code, para 16.46.

A person aged 18, 19 or 20 who has been looked after, accommodated or fostered

12.217 If an applicant, or a person with whom he or she resides or might reasonably be expected to reside[1]:

- is aged 18 or over, but under 21; and
- was 'looked after, accommodated or fostered' at any time while under the age of 18,

then he or she will have a priority need.

[1] H(W)A 2014, s 70(1)(h). See also Welsh Code, paras 16.49–16.56.

12.218 The definition of 'looked after, accommodated or fostered' is given in H(W)A 2014, s 70(2) and is very broad. Although the shorthand commonly used for this rubric is 'care leaver', there is no requirement that the person has been in care. For example, the definition is met if the person has at some time in the past been 'privately fostered'[1].

[1] H(W)A 2014, s 70(2)(e).

12.219 There is no minimum period of time during which the person must have been looked after, accommodated or fostered in order to qualify[1]. Nor is there any specified age at which he or she must have been looked after, accommodated or fostered. Any young person (now aged 18, 19 or 20), who was 'looked after, accommodated or fostered' at any point in his or her life, for any period, will fall within this category.

[1] Welsh Code, para 16.51. To have been 'looked-after' a child must have been accommodated continuously for a period of 24 hours or more: see Children Act 1989, s 22 and Social Services and Well-being Act 2014, s 74.

A person homeless after leaving the armed forces of the Crown

12.220 This category is met by any applicant, or a person with whom an applicant resides or might reasonably be expected to reside, who is a former member of the armed forces and[1]:

(1)   is homeless; and
(2)   has been homeless since leaving the armed forces.

[1] H(W)A 2014, s 70(1)(i). See also Welsh Code, paras 16.57–16.63.

12.221 Unlike the English equivalent category[1], there is no requirement that the person be 'vulnerable', whether by reason of service in the forces or otherwise.

[1] SI 2002/2051, art 5(2). See **12.174–12.179**.

12.222 Only service in the 'regular armed forces of the Crown' satisfies the condition for this category. The definition of 'armed forces' used is set out in H(W)A 2014, s 99[1]. The length of time since discharge is not in point; the issue is whether the applicant has remained homeless since he or she was discharged. Though strictly the wording of H(W)A 2014, s 70(1)(i) requires the applicant, or the person with whom the applicant resides or might reasonably be expected to reside, to have been homeless since the point of discharge, the Welsh Code has interpreted this as a more relaxed requirement that he or she should have 'failed to secure suitable permanent accommodation' since leaving the armed forces[2]. The Welsh Code advises that local housing authorities should recognise this criterion as being satisfied where the individual has been unable to secure either an assured (including assured shorthold), introductory or secure tenancy, or permanent accommodation with family or friends[3].

[1] Which refers to the regular forces as defined by the Armed Forces Act 2006, s 374.
[2] Welsh Code, para 16.60.
[3] Welsh Code, paras 16.60–16.61.

A former prisoner who is vulnerable

12.223 The questions for the local housing authority in dealing with an applicant, or a person with whom he or she resides or might reasonably be expected to reside, who may fall within this category are[1]:

(1)   Is he or she vulnerable;

(2)   If so, is the vulnerability *as a result of* having served a custodial sentence, having been committed or remanded in custody by court order, or having been remanded to youth detention accommodation under Legal Aid, Sentencing and Punishment of Offenders Act 2012, s 91(4);

(3)   If so, does he or she have a local connection with the area of the local housing authority?

[1]   H(W)A 2014, s 70(1)(j). See also Welsh Code, paras 16.64–16.70.

12.224 The term 'custodial sentence' is defined to include:

- a sentence of imprisonment for those aged 21 or over;
- a sentence of detention for those aged under 18;
- a sentence of detention for public protection for those under 18 who commit serious offences;
- a sentence of detention for those under 18 who commit certain violent or sexual offences;
- a sentence of custody for life for persons under 21;
- a sentence of detention in a young offender institution for those aged between 18 and 21; and
- a detention and training order[1].

Being committed to custody by an order of a court refers to punishment under the inherent jurisdiction of the court to commit and 'to committals under the court's statutory powers[2].

[1]   Powers of Criminal Courts (Sentencing) Act 2000, s 76; the references to sentence of custody for life and sentences of detention in a young offender institution are due to be repealed by the Criminal Justice and Court Services Act 2000, but no date for their repeal has yet been appointed (Criminal Justice and Court Services Act 2000, s 80(1)).
[2]   Such as that at County Courts Act 1984, s 118.

12.225 Unlike the English Priority Need Order[1], the ambit of the phrase 'remanded in . . . custody' in H(W)A 2014, s 70(1)(j) is left undefined. Youth detention accommodation is defined in H(W)A 2014, s 99 and includes a secure children's home, a secure training centre and a young offender's institution.

[1]   SI 2002/2051, art 5(1)(c).

12.226 The inclusion of a 'local connection' requirement, which has been reproduced from the Homeless Persons (Priority Need) (Wales) Order 2002[1], reflects a concern expressed during the passage of the Homelessness Act 2002 through Parliament, when MPs representing constituencies containing sizeable prisons were anxious that their local housing authorities should not suddenly receive a host of applications from former prisoners. The solution in England was to restrict the extension of priority need to those former prisoners who were 'vulnerable' as a result of their imprisonment. The solution in Wales was to require that former prisoners must have a local connection with the local housing authority to which they apply in order to obtain the benefit of this priority need category[2]. As can be seen, the requirement for the person to be vulnerable, which was not a requirement under Homeless Persons (Priority Need) (Wales) Order 2002[3], has now been introduced in H(W)A 2014, s 70(1)(j). The rationale behind this amendment was to 'redress the balance of priority need status for vulnerable applicants by amending the priority need status of former prisoners'[4], thereby bringing the position in Wales closer in-line with that in England.

1   SI 2001/607, art 7(1).
2   See *Code of Guidance for Local Authorities Allocation of Accommodation and Homelessness 2012* (Welsh Government, August 2012), paras 14.58–14.60.
3   SI 2001/607, art 7(1).
4   *Housing (Wales) Bill, Explanatory Memorandum* (Welsh Government, November 2013), p 16.

12.227 Local connection to an area is defined at H(W)A 2014, s 81[1]. A person has a local connection with the area of a local housing authority in circumstances where he or she has a connection with it because the person is, or in the past was, normally resident there, because the person is employed there, because of family associations, or because of special circumstances[2]. But local connection cannot be acquired by residence as a result of detention under the authority of an enactment in that area[3]. A former prisoner would, therefore, not acquire a local connection in the area where his or her prison was situated, unless he or she had acquired a local connection with that area for a reason other than residence, eg by employment (either before or after the period of imprisonment)[4]. Recognising the problems this may cause for ex-prisoners who wish to make a fresh start in a new area post-release, or those who cannot return home owing to licence conditions, the Welsh Code recommends that local housing authorities should consider having reciprocal arrangements with another area, whereby a former prisoner could be accommodated outside of the area to which he or she has applied as homeless[5].

1   See **14.43–14.122**.
2   H(W)A 2014, s 81(2).
3   H(W)A 2014, s 81(3). See **14.62**.
4   H(W)A 2014, s 81(3). See **14.67–14.71**.
5   Welsh Code, para 16.68.

12.228 A prisoner who has no local connection with the local housing authority to which the application is made may of course still argue that he or she is vulnerable for another special reason within the meaning of H(W)A 2014, s 70(1)(c), in which case the lack of local connection will not be a bar to establishing a priority need[1].

1   Welsh Code, para 16.70.

Chapter 13

BECOMING HOMELESS INTENTIONALLY

Contents

INTRODUCTION

England

13.1 When a local housing authority in England has determined that an applicant is homeless and that she or he is eligible for assistance, the relief duty under Housing Act 1996 (HA 1996), s 189B(2)[1] is owed to the applicant meaning that the local housing authority must take reasonable steps to help the applicant secure that suitable accommodation becomes available for his or her occupation. If the applicant is still homeless at the time this duty comes to an end, whether any further duty is owed (and if so, which one) will depend on whether the applicant has a priority need[2] and whether she or he has become homeless intentionally.

1   Housing Act 1996, s 189B(2) as inserted by the Homelessness Reduction Act 2017, s 5(2) for applications for homelessness assistance made to local housing authorities in England on or after 3 April 2018. See **15.138–15.189**.
2   See CHAPTER 13.

13.2 For the first 20 years of statutory homelessness provision in the UK (1977–1997), the decision as to whether or not the homelessness of a priority need applicant had come about 'intentionally' was pivotal. Those who had not become homeless intentionally were treated as entitled to a permanent home. Those who had become homeless intentionally would merely be given temporary accommodation and then only for a very short period. Disputes about whether an applicant had become homeless 'intentionally' accordingly dominated the work of housing advisers and homelessness officers, and formed the bulk of the reported court cases on the statutory provisions. To be found to have become 'homeless intentionally' was to be given what one judge described as the 'mark of Cain'[1].

1   *Din v Wandsworth London Borough Council* (unreported) 23 June 1981, CA per Ackner LJ, quoted in *Lambert v Ealing London Borough Council* [1982] 1 WLR 550, CA per Lord Denning MR at 557.

13.3 Much has changed since the early days of homelessness law. First, a decision of the House of Lords in 1996 exploded the myth that those applicants who had become homeless unintentionally were entitled to be provided with permanent homes under the statutory homelessness provisions[1]. Second, the new statutory framework of HA 1996, Pt 7 as originally enacted made it clear that the highest duty owed to any applicant would be met by the provision of temporary accommodation only[2]. Third, changes to the arrangements for allocation of social housing (made by the Homelessness Act 2002) required local housing authorities to give a preference to all homeless people, including those who have become homeless intentionally[3]. Fourth, changes to HA 1996, Pt 7 (made by the Localism Act 2011) allowed local housing authorities to bring the main housing duty[4] to an end by making them an offer of suitable private rented accommodation[5]. So even applicants who are not found to have become homeless intentionally may have accommodation secured for them in the private rented sector. Fifth, the coming into force of the Homelessness Reduction Act 2017 (HRA 2017)[6] has broadened the scope of the duties under HA 1996, Pt 7 with the effect that the HA 1996, s 195(2)[7] prevention duty and the s 189B(2)[8] relief duty are owed to all eligible[9] applicants who are, respectively, threatened with homelessness or homeless, irrespective of whether the applicant became homeless (or threatened with homelessness) intentionally[10].

1   *R v Brent London Borough Council ex p Awua* [1996] AC 55, HL.
2   HA 1996, s 193(2). See **16.94–16.199**.
3   HA 1996, s 166A(3)(a) and (b). See **4.58–4.79**.
4   HA 1996, s 193(2), see **16.94–16.199**.
5   For 'private rented sector offers', see **16.153–16.179**.
6   For applications for homelessness assistance made to local housing authorities in England on or after 3 April 2018: Homelessness Reduction Act 2017 (Commencement and Transitional and Savings Provisions) Regulations 2018, SI 2018/167, reg 3.

[7]   As amended by HRA 2017, s 4(2) for applications for homelessness assistance made to local housing authorities in England on or after 3 April 2018. See **15.87–15.137**.

[8]   As inserted by HRA 2017, s 5(2) for applications for homelessness assistance made to local housing authorities in England on or after 3 April 2018. See **15.138–15.189**.

[9]   See CHAPTER **11**.

[10]   In fact, the concept of 'becoming threatened with homelessness intentionally' has been abolished by HRA 2017, s 4(5) entirely (for applications for homelessness assistance made to local housing authorities in England on or after 3 April 2018) which repealed HA 1996, s 196.

13.4 These factors have reduced the significance of a finding that an applicant has become homeless intentionally. However, the changes have certainly not rendered the question of 'becoming homeless intentionally' altogether academic. Statistically, the numbers affected are significant[1]. And much still turns on whether homelessness was intentional[2]. The English Code explains the policy reasoning behind the different duties owed to those applicants found to have become homeless intentionally and those found not to have become homeless intentionally:

'This reflects the general expectation that, wherever possible, people should take responsibility for their own accommodation needs and ensure that they do not behave in a way which might lead to the loss of their accommodation[3].'

[1]   *Table 770: Decisions taken by local authorities under the Housing Act 1996 on applications by eligible households* (DCLG) shows that the number of decisions where the applicant had a priority need and had become homeless intentionally had been 3% of applications for homelessness assistance each year from 1998–2002. From 2003, the proportion started rising to a high of 9% for 2016–17. This 9% comprised 9,850 households. No figures are collected for those applicants found not to have a priority need and to have become homeless intentionally.

[2]   See **13.8–13.10**.

[3]   *Homelessness Code of Guidance for Local Authorities* (Department for Communities and Local Government, 2018) (the English Code), para 9.3, at APPENDIX **2** of this book.

13.5 However, even an adverse finding that homelessness has been brought about 'intentionally' is simply the result of one local housing authority having applied a complex statutory test and its own judgment to the facts of the application. Two equally reasonable local housing authorities may quite lawfully reach different conclusions on the same statutory test and the same set of facts. This means that there are often prospects for an applicant, who has been found to have become homeless intentionally by one local housing authority, to apply to another local housing authority and find that a different conclusion will be reached[1].

[1]   See **8.55–8.63**.

13.6 Likewise, it is important to appreciate that the adverse finding is one that is applicable only so long as the period of homelessness lasts. A person who is found to have become homeless intentionally may render that finding irrelevant to any future incidence of homelessness by, for example, obtaining settled accommodation[1]. This limited life of a finding of becoming homeless intentionally means that a fresh application can always be made to a local housing authority for assistance under HA 1996, Pt 7, unless the facts are precisely the same on the new application as upon the last application[2]. Obviously, to save repeating what may have been extensive recent investigations on a previous application, the local housing authority is entitled initially to rely on its original finding that the applicant had become homeless intentionally and to confine its inquiries to whether there has been any intervening settled accommodation or other factual change since the earlier finding[3].

1   For 'settled accommodation' see **13.136–13.146**. More generally, for the ways in which an applicant becoming homeless intentionally may be rendered irrelevant by subsequent events see **13.133–13.154**.
2   *R v Harrow London Borough Council ex p Fahia* (1996) 30 HLR 1124, HL; and *Begum v Tower Hamlets London Borough Council* [2005] EWCA Civ 340, [2005] HLR 34, CA. See **8.77–9.91**.
3   See English Code, para 18.11.

13.7 There is no special provision dispensing with this question of whether an applicant has become homeless intentionally where he or she has made a fresh application for homelessness assistance to a local housing authority in England within two years of acceptance of a private rented sector offer[1]. Even though inquiry into priority need is dispensed with[2], the HA 1996, s 193(2)[3] main housing duty will only apply where the local housing authority is 'not satisfied that the applicant became homeless intentionally'. Local housing authorities will therefore be permitted to examine the reasons why the applicant has lost his or her accommodation.

1   HA 1996, s 193(7AA). See **16.153–16.179**.
2   See **8.100–8.107**.
3   See **16.94–16.199**.

13.8 An applicant who is homeless but is not found to have become homeless intentionally and who does have a priority need will, if he or she is still homeless at the time the HA 1996, s 189B(2)[1] relief duty comes to an end, generally be owed the HA 1996, s 193(2)[2] main housing duty. That duty requires the local housing authority 'to secure that accommodation is available for occupation by the applicant'[3]. There are a number of exceptions to this general rule, which are discussed at **16.95**[4]. Of particular significance is the exception at HA 1996, s 193(1A)(b)[5]. In circumstances where the HA 1996, s 189B(2)[6] relief duty came to an end as a result of the applicant being given notice of his or her deliberate and unreasonable failure to cooperate[7], he or she will be owed the HA 1996, s 193C(4)[8] accommodation duty instead.

1   As inserted by HRA 2017, s 5(2) for applications for homelessness assistance made to local housing authorities in England on or after 3 April 2018. See **15.138–15.189**.
2   See **16.94–16.199**.
3   HA 1996, s 193(2). See **16.94–16.199**.
4   In overview, the main housing duty will not be owed where the relief duty has come to an end in the circumstances set out in HA 1996, s 193(1A) as inserted by HRA 2017, s 7(2) for applications for homelessness assistance made to local housing authorities in England on or after 3 April 2018. That is, where the relief duty has come to end by reason of the applicant refusing a 'final accommodation offer' (defined by HA 1996, s 193A(4) as inserted by HRA 2017, s 7(1) for applications for homelessness assistance made to local housing authorities in England on or after 3 April 2018) or a 'final Pt 6 offer' (defined by HA 1996, s 193A(5) as inserted by HRA 2017, s 7(1) for applications for homelessness assistance made to local housing authorities in England on or after 3 April 2018) or where notice has been given under HA 1996 s 193B(2) (as inserted by HRA 2017, s 7(1) for applications for homelessness assistance made to local housing authorities in England on or after 3 April 2018) that the applicant has deliberately and unreasonably refused to take any step recorded in his or her

personal plan under HA 1996, s 189A (as inserted by HRA 2017, s 3(1) for applications for homelessness assistance made to local housing authorities in England on or after 3 April 2018).

⁵   As inserted by HRA 2017, s 7(2) for applications for homelessness assistance made to local housing authorities in England on or after 3 April 2018.

⁶   As inserted by HRA 2017, s 5(2) for applications for homelessness assistance made to local housing authorities in England on or after 3 April 2018. See **15.138–15.189**.

⁷   HA 1996, ss 193B(2) and 193C(2) as inserted by HRA 2017, s 7(1) for applications for homelessness assistance made to local housing authorities in England on or after 3 April 2018. See **15.196–15.221**.

⁸   As inserted by HRA 2017, s 7(1) for applications for homelessness assistance made to local housing authorities in England on or after 3 April 2018. See **16.200–16.216**.

13.9 In contrast, an applicant who became homeless intentionally and who has a priority need will be owed lesser duties[1]:

' . . . to secure that accommodation is available for his occupation for such period as they consider will give him a reasonable opportunity of securing accommodation[2].'

and to

' . . . provide him with (or secure that he is provided with) advice and assistance in any attempts he may make to secure that accommodation becomes available for his occupation[3].'

¹   See English Code, paras 15.13–15.15.

²   HA 1996, s 190(2)(a) as amended by HRA 2017, s 5(5) for applications for homelessness assistance made to local housing authorities in England on or after 3 April 2018. English Code, para 9.4. See **16.81–16.93**.

³   HA 1996, s 190(2)(b) as amended by HRA 2017, s 5(5) for applications for homelessness assistance made to local housing authorities in England on or after 3 April 2018. English Code, para 9.4. See **15.231**.

13.10 An applicant who does not have a priority need will be owed no further duty, irrespective of whether he or she became homeless intentionally. To mitigate the hardship caused to those falling within this class the English Code suggests that 'the authority may want to consider continuing the relief duty for longer[1].'

¹   Considerations relevant to the exercise of this discretion will include the needs of the applicant and the risk of him or her sleeping rough. English Code, para 14.19.

13.11 Further discussion as to the extent of these various duties, and the methods of performing them, is provided at CHAPTER 16.

Wales

13.12 In Wales, under the Housing (Wales) Act 2014 (H(W)A 2014), Pt 2, the consequences of a finding that an applicant has become homeless intentionally are similar. Indeed, the amendments to HA 1996, Pt 7 introduced by HRA 2017[1] were modelled on H(W)A 2014, Pt 2, the stated aim of which was to 'extend the help available' to applicants for homelessness assistance in Wales 'by improving services for those who are not in priority need and those who are found to be intentionally homeless' and to 'provide greater protection for children in households who are found to have caused their own homelessness'[2].

[1] For applications for homelessness assistance made to local housing authorities in England on or after 3 April 2018.

[2] *Housing (Wales) Bill, Explanatory Memorandum* (Welsh Government, November 2013), p 16.

13.13 As is the case in England, all eligible applicants who are threatened with homelessness will be entitled to the prevention duty, irrespective of whether they have become threatened with homelessness intentionally[1]. Likewise, all eligible homeless applicants are entitled to the relief duty irrespective of whether they became homeless intentionally[2].

[1] Housing (Wales) Act 2014, s 66(1). See **17.45–17.72**.

[2] H(W)A 2014, s 73(1). See **17.73–17.117**.

13.14 The principal distinction between HA 1996, Pt 7[1] and H(W)A 2014, Pt 2 is that a local housing authority in Wales may choose to have regard to whether particular categories of person have become homeless intentionally[2]. The idea behind this approach is to put the onus on local housing authorities to 'opt into having regard to intentionality rather than opt out' with the intention that local housing authorities 'will eventually move away from the use of intentionality'[3]. The procedure which a local housing authority must follow in order to 'opt into' having regard to whether a category of person became homeless intentionally is set out at **13.252–13.255**.

[1] As amended by HRA 2017, for applications for homelessness assistance made to local housing authorities in England on or after 3 April 2018.

[2] H(W)A 2015, s 78. See **13.252–13.255**.

[3] *Code of Guidance for Local Authorities on the Allocation of Accommodation and Homelessness* (Welsh Government, March 2016) (the Welsh Code), para 17.1. See the CD Rom with this book.

13.15 Whether or not such a decision is made is a matter of discretion for each local housing authority: a local housing authority is not obliged to make a decision to 'have regard to intentionality'[1]. Where a local housing authority has made a decision to 'opt into' having regard to whether a category of person became homeless intentionally and has given appropriate notice of that decision, the local housing authority must consider whether every applicant falling within the relevant category has become homeless intentionally[2]. They may only cease doing so if a subsequent decision is taken to stop having regard to whether or not applicants falling into the category specified in the notice have become homeless intentionally[3] and notice of that decision is then properly publicised[4]. If the local housing authority has decided to 'have regard to intentionality' in respect of a category of person to which the applicant belongs then, when the H(W)A 2014, s 73[5] relief duty comes to an end, if the applicant is homeless[6], eligible for help[7], has a priority need[8] and did not become homeless intentionally, the local housing authority must secure that suitable accommodation is available for his or her occupation[9]. Conversely, if the applicant did become homeless intentionally then the H(W)A 2015, s 75 duty will not arise, and no further duty will be owed[10].

[1] H(W)A 2014, s 78(2).

2   H(W)A 2014, s 78(4). The principle behind this provision is that all applicants must be treated alike: there is no power to make an exception and overlook whether a particular applicant has become homeless intentionally.
3   H(W)A 2014, s 78(3)(a).
4   See **13.252–13.255.**
5   See **17.73–17.117.**
6   See CHAPTER 10.
7   See CHAPTER 11.
8   See CHAPTER 12.
9   H(W)A 2014, s 75(1) and (2). See **17.146–17.197.**
10 H(W)A 2014, s 75(3) contains an exception to this rule, whereby certain categories of priority need applicant may be owed the duty under H(W)A 2014, s 75(1) even if they became homeless intentionally. However, this section is not yet in force. The Welsh Government intends to bring H(W)A 2014, s 75(3) into force in 2019; Welsh Code, para 14.10.

13.16 Where a local housing authority has not made a decision to 'opt into' having regard to whether the category of persons to which the applicant belongs became homeless intentionally, or has not given appropriate notice of that decision, then the local housing authority is not entitled to have regard to whether the applicant became homeless intentionally[1]. In this situation, when the relief duty[2] comes to an end, the local housing authority must secure that suitable accommodation is available for his or her occupation, providing that he or she is homeless, eligible for help, and has a priority need[3]. Whether the applicant became homeless intentionally is irrelevant.

1   H(W)A 2014, s 78(2). See **13.252–13.255.**
2   H(W)A 2014, s 73(1). See **17.73–17.117.**
3   H(W)A 2014, s 75(1) and (2).

The structure of this chapter

13.17 In this chapter, first, we consider the test used by local housing authorities in England and Wales to determine whether or not someone has become homeless intentionally[1], and then outline some of the common scenarios in which an applicant may or may not be found to have become homeless intentionally[2]. The test for determining whether a person has become homeless intentionally is identical under HA 1996, Pt 7[3] and H(W)A 2014, Pt 2, and so applications to local housing authorities in England and Wales will be dealt with together.

1   See **13.29–13.187.**
2   See **13.188–13.251.**
3   As amended by HRA 2017, for applications for homelessness assistance made to local housing authorities in England on or after 3 April 2018.

13.18 We then go on to consider the rules unique to H(W)A 2014, Pt 2, governing the circumstances where a local housing authority is entitled to have regard to intentionality[1].

1   See **13.252–13.255.**

MAKING INQUIRIES INTO 'BECOMING HOMELESS INTENTIONALLY'

13.19 A local housing authority must conduct such inquiries into an application as will enable it to determine what duty under HA 1996, Pt 7 or H(W)A 2014, Pt 2 (if any) is owed[1]. But this will not necessarily require a local housing authority to consider whether the applicant has become homeless intentionally in every case.

[1] HA 1996, s 184(1)(b); H(W)A 2014, s 62(5).

13.20 For applications made to local housing authorities in England, or for applications made to local housing authorities in Wales where the local housing authority has made a decision to have regard to whether an applicant has become homeless intentionally[1], whether the applicant has become homeless intentionally is not relevant in deciding whether the applicant is entitled to the prevention duty[2] or the relief duty[3]. The issue becomes relevant at the later stage where the relief duty is coming to an end and it falls to the local housing authority to determine what further duty, if any, is owed[4]. An applicant who does not have a priority need will be owed no further duty[5]. Whereas an applicant who does have a priority need will be 'owed a lesser duty if they have become homeless intentionally than would be owed to them if they were homeless unintentionally'[6].

[1] See **13.252–13.255**.
[2] HA 1996, s 195(2) as amended by HRA 2017, s 4(2) for applications for homelessness assistance made to local housing authorities in England on or after 3 April 2018; H(W)A 2014, s 66(1). See **15.87–15.137** and **17.45–17.72**.
[3] HA 1996, s 189B(2) as inserted by HRA 2017, s 5(2) for applications for homelessness assistance made to local housing authorities in England on or after 3 April 2018; H(W)A 2014, s 73(1). See **15.138–15.189** and **17.73–17.117**. Note though, that for applications for homelessness assistance made to local housing authorities in England, the assessment of the applicant's case under HA 1996, s 189A(1) (as inserted by HRA 2017, s 3(1) for applications for homelessness assistance made to local housing authorities in England on or after 3 April 2018) must include an assessment of the circumstances that caused him or her to become homeless or threatened with homelessness. See HA 1996, s 189A(2)(a). In practice this assessment is likely to overlap to some extent with the inquiries necessary to determine whether the applicant became homeless intentionally even if it does not bear on the performance of the prevention or relief duties. See English Code, para 11.8.
[4] See Welsh Code, para 17.37. See **16.81–16.216** and **17.146–17.197** for the duties that may be owed by local housing authorities in England and Wales respectively, when the relief duty comes to an end.
[5] As such, where a local housing authority has decided that an applicant does not have a priority need it need not necessarily make further inquiries to determine whether the applicant became homeless intentionally.
[6] English Code, para 9.3.

13.21 The Codes provide differing advice as to precisely when a local housing authority should carry out its inquiries to determine whether an applicant became homeless intentionally. The English Code encourages local housing authorities to conclude their inquiries into whether the applicant became homeless intentionally, while the the HA 1996, s 189B(2)[1] relief duty is being performed. The rationale appears to be that an applicant who has been forewarned of the fact that he or she has become homeless intentionally and will not be owed a long-term accommodation duty may be more diligent in his or her efforts to find accommodation:

'Housing authorities may issue a section 184 decision to the applicant, that when the relief duty ends they will owe them a duty under section 190 because they have a priority need but are intentionally homeless. Although the section 190 duty cannot commence until the relief duty has come to an end, the authority may wish to alert an applicant that the main housing duty will not be owed. It may be beneficial to review the personalised housing plan at this point to help maximise joint efforts to relieve homelessness[2].'

[1] As inserted by HRA 2017, s 5(2) for applications for homelessness assistance made to local housing authorities in England on or after 3 April 2018. See **15.138–15.189.**
[2] English Code, para 13.11.

13.22 In contrast, the Welsh Code advises that until the local housing authority is required to determine whether the applicant became homeless intentionally, it should not spend time investigating the issue 'to the detriment of focussing on problem solving through the use of reasonable steps to help the applicant to prevent homelessness or to help secure accommodation'[1]. However, the Welsh Code acknowledges that 'the Act does not say that a Local Housing Authority is not allowed to look at intentionality at any point during its assessment' and suggests that if it becomes clear at an early stage that an applicant might later be found to have become homeless intentionally, then he or she should be notified by letter that the local housing authority is minded to find him or her intentionally homeless, and given the opportunity to provide any further explanation or evidence[2]. This latter approach is closer to that which is recommended by the English Code.

[1] Welsh Code, para 17.36.
[2] Welsh Code, para 17.35.

13.23 For applications made to local housing authorities in Wales, where the local housing authority has not made a decision to have regard to whether an applicant has become homeless intentionally[1] inquiries into whether the applicant became homeless intentionally may legitimately be dispensed with since it will have no bearing on the outcome of the application[2].

[1] H(W)A 2014, s 78 and Welsh Code, paras 17.1–17.11. See **13.252–13.255.** There is no equivalent provision under HA 1996, Pt 7.
[2] Welsh Code, para 17.34.

13.24 Obviously, an individual and applicant-centred approach to the question is required in both England and Wales. Local housing authorities should not adopt general policies which seek to predetermine that particular classes of applicant (eg tenants of the local housing authority who were evicted for arrears of rent or anti-social behaviour) will or will not be found to have become homeless intentionally[1]. Local housing authorities should make all necessary inquiries about each particular application and reach a decision in the light of those inquiries. When dealing with applications for homelessness assistance from care leavers, the English Code advises that local housing authorities should make inquiries of the relevant children's services authority and obtain advice and assistance as to the young person's emotional and mental well-being, maturity and general ability to understand the impact of his or her actions[2]. If there is doubt about the matter at the conclusion of initial inquiries, then either inquiries should continue until the matter is free of doubt, or the benefit of the doubt should be given to the applicant and he or she should be found not to have become homeless intentionally[3]. Where the events which the local housing authority is inquiring into occurred some years earlier and the facts are unclear, it may not be possible for the local housing authority to satisfy itself that the applicant became homeless intentionally[4].

[1]   English Code, para 9.6; Welsh Code, para 17.12.
[2]   English Code, para 22.17.
[3]   *R v Thurrock Borough Council ex p Williams* (1981) 1 HLR 128, QBD, and see **9.35**.
[4]   English Code, para 9.6; Welsh Code, para 17.12.

13.25 Any decision that an applicant has become homeless intentionally should be accompanied by clear reasons for that finding, even though the formal decision being notified to the applicant is only the decision as to what precise HA 1996, Pt 7[1] or H(W)A 2014, Pt 2 duty the applicant is owed[2].

[1]   As amended by HRA 2017, for applications for homelessness assistance made to local housing authorities in England on or after 3 April 2018.
[2]   English Code, para 18.33; Welsh Code, para 10.56; and *Southall v West Wiltshire District Council* (2002) October *Legal Action*, p 31, Swindon County Court.

13.26 The burden of making the inquiries rests with the local housing authority. It is not for the applicant to prove his or her case, and satisfy the local housing authority that she or he did not become homeless intentionally. This was reinforced by the Court of Appeal in *O'Connor v Kensington and Chelsea Royal London Borough Council*[1], where it was held that a local housing authority, when considering the question of whether the applicant had become homeless intentionally, should consider whether the applicant had been unaware of a relevant fact in good faith, regardless of whether this latter point had been raised by the applicant. A later Court of Appeal decision refined the point, adding that the decision-maker need not consider matters that were not raised by the applicant, unless those matters were within 'the circumstances of obviousness'[2].

[1]   *O'Connor v Kensington and Chelsea Royal London Borough Council*, [2004] EWCA Civ 394, [2004] HLR 37, CA per Sedley LJ at [37] and per Waller LJ at [54].
[2]   *Aw-Aden v Birmingham City Council* [2005] EWCA Civ 1834, (2006) July *Legal Action*, p 29, CA per Maurice Kay LJ at [12]. See *Bury Metropolitan Borough Council v Gibbons* [2010] EWCA Civ 327, [2010] HLR 33, CA, where one of the reasons why the review decision was held to be unlawful was that the decision-maker had failed to consider whether, on the facts, the applicant had been, in good faith, unaware of relevant facts, namely the availability of housing benefit and his right to remain in possession until a possession order had been made.

13.27 The English Code suggests that there is one exception to the general rule about the burden of proof: if an applicant is seeking to establish that he or she did not acquiesce in the deliberate actions of another member of his her household (who has already been found, or is likely to be found, to have caused the homelessness of the household), acquiescence may be assumed in the absence of material which indicates to the contrary[1]. This reflects the approach advocated by the courts: where there is any material that indicates that the applicant may not have acquiesced, the local housing authority must make inquiries in the usual way[2]. The Welsh Code puts matters more simply, stating that the local housing authority 'must satisfy itself that the applicant acquiesced in the behaviour that led to the homelessness in order to find them intentionally homeless[3].'

1 English Code, para 9.5. This marks a departure from (or at least a clarification of) the previous edition of the English Code which had suggested, at para 11.5, that that applicant would 'need to demonstrate that he or she was not involved in the acts or omissions that led to homelessness, and did not have control over them.'
2 *R v North Devon District Council ex parte Lewis* [1981] 1 WLR 328 per Woolf J at 333; *R v West Dorset District Council ex parte Phillips* (1985) 17 HLR 336, QBD; and *N v Allerdale Borough Council* (2008) October *Legal Action*, p 38, Carlisle County Court.
3 Welsh Code, para 17.13.

13.28 If, during its inquiries, a local housing authority in England has reason to believe that an applicant whose household includes children under 18 *might* be found to have become homeless intentionally, it is under a duty to ask the applicant to give consent for his or her circumstances to be referred to the children's services authority, and then (if consent is given) to make that referral[1]. For local housing authorities in Wales, the equivalent duty arises where the household includes children under 18 and the local housing authority has reason to believe that the H(W)A 2014, s 75 duty is not likely to apply to the applicant[2]. This will enable children's services to begin planning what assistance it might provide for the household if the local housing authority's final conclusion is that the applicant did become homeless intentionally. In both England and Wales, the local housing authority is obliged to follow up the referral by advising the children's services authority of the decision that it actually reaches on the application for homelessness assistance[3].

1 HA 1996, s 213A(1)–(3) as amended by HRA 2017, s 4(7) for applications made to local housing authorities in England on or after 3 April 2018. See **15.229–15.230**.
2 H(W)A 2014, s 96(1)(b) and Welsh Code, paras 17.47–17.49. See **17.212–17.215**.
3 HA 1996, s 213A(2) and (3); H(W)A 2014, s 96(2).

THE STATUTORY MEANING

Overview

13.29 In the homelessness provisions of HA 1996, Pt 7 and H(W)A 2014, Pt 2, the word 'intentionally' is not given its ordinary or dictionary meaning. It has a very tightly prescribed statutory meaning. Most obviously this is because, in the ordinary use of language, an applicant's homelessness is very often brought about, not by an intentional act of the applicant, but rather by the intentional act of another party (such as a landlord, parent or court bailiff) who has deliberately ejected the applicant. Moreover, it is something of a contradiction to suggest that an applicant has become homeless intentionally, since the whole point of the applicant making an application for homelessness assistance is to avoid or end his or her state of homelessness.

13.30 As Lord Denning MR observed, in one of the earliest homelessness cases:

'Many people would have thought that [the applicant's] conduct, however deplorable, was not 'deliberate' in the sense required by . . . [the Act]. She did not deliberately do anything to get herself turned out[1].'

[1]   *R v Slough Borough Council ex p Ealing London Borough Council* [1981] 1 QB 801, CA at 809.

13.31 Similarly, Lord Lowry said:

'No one really becomes homeless or threatened with homelessness intentionally; the word is a convenient label to describe the result of acting or failing to act as described in [the Act][1]'

[1]   *Din v Wandsworth London Borough Council* [1983] 1 AC 657, HL at 679, referring to Housing (Homeless Persons) Act 1977, s 17, containing the same definition of 'becoming homeless intentionally' as in HA 1996, s 191(1).

13.32 The statutory definition of 'becoming homeless intentionally' under HA 1996, s 191, is that:

' . . . a person becomes homeless intentionally if he deliberately does or fails to do anything in consequence of which he ceases to occupy accommodation which is available for his occupation and which it would have been reasonable for him to continue to occupy[1].'

[1]   HA 1996, s 191(1).

13.33 Similarly, by virtue of H(W)A 2014, s 77(1) and 77(2) a person is homeless intentionally if[1]:

' . . . the person deliberately does or fails to do anything in consequence of which the person ceases to occupy accommodation which is available for the person's occupation and which it would have been reasonable for the person to continue to occupy.'

[1]   H(W)A 2014, s 77(2).

13.34 This complex composite definition has been described as part of a statutory 'semantic nightmare'[1].

[1]   *Roughead v Falkirk District Council* 1979 SCOLAG 188 per Sheriff Sinclair.

13.35 Because each and every element of the composite must be in place before a local housing authority can be satisfied that an applicant 'became homeless intentionally', initial expectations (when the phrase was first enacted) were that it would only be satisfied infrequently. The first edition of the *Code of Guidance* in 1978 indicated that the number of applicants falling foul of it was 'expected to be small'[1].

[1]   *Code of Guidance* (Department of Environment, 1978), para 2.19.

13.36 The statutory formulation is most practically approached by treating it as having six elements. To ensure that they are all in place, the local housing authority needs to address six questions in the course of its inquiries and decision-making. The necessary premise for the questions is that the applicant is currently homeless (ignoring, of course, any interim accommodation that the local housing authority may have provided):

(1)   Was there a deliberate act or omission (which does not include an act or omission in good faith by a person unaware of a material fact)[1]?

(2)   Was that a deliberate act or omission by the applicant[2]?

(3)   Was it as a consequence of that deliberate act or omission that the applicant ceased to occupy accommodation[3]?

(4)   Is the deliberate act (or omission), and the cessation of occupation it caused, an operative cause of the present homelessness[4]?

(5)   Was that accommodation available for the applicant's occupation and for occupation by members of the applicant's family who normally resided with the applicant and by persons with whom the applicant might reasonably have been expected to reside[5]?

(6)   Would it have been reasonable for the applicant to have continued to occupy the accommodation[6]?

[1]   See **13.42–13.94**.
[2]   See **13.95–13.99**.
[3]   See **13.112–13.132**.
[4]   See **13.133–13.154**.
[5]   See **13.155–13.161**.
[6]   See **13.162–13.180**.

13.37 The fourth question, strictly, is not a part of the statutory formulation contained in HA 1996, s 191(1) and H(W)A 2014, s 77(2). However, adopting the approach set down by the Supreme Court in *Haile v Waltham Forest London Borough Council*[1] it is necessary to ask this additional question to determine whether or not an applicant is owed the main housing duty under HA 1996, s 193(2)[2] or the duty to secure accommodation pursuant to H(W)A 2015, s 75(1)[3].

[1]   [2015] UKSC 34, [2015] AC 1471, SC. See **13.100–13.111**.
[2]   See **16.94–16.199**.
[3]   See **17.146–17.197**.

13.38 If the local housing authority's answer to *each* of these six questions is 'Yes', then the applicant will have 'become homeless intentionally'. If the answer to *any* of them is 'No', the applicant cannot, at the time of application or review, be regarded as having become homeless intentionally.

13.39 There is, in addition, a category of applicants who are *deemed* to have become homeless intentionally if their application is made to a local housing authority in England, and who *are* intentionally homeless if their application is to a local housing authority in Wales[1]. In these circumstances the six-question approach is not to be applied. An applicant '*is*' intentionally homeless (Wales) or is '*treated as*' becoming homeless intentionally (England) if:

(1)   he or she has (in the past) entered into an arrangement to give up accommodation;

(2)   it was accommodation which it would have been reasonable to continue to occupy;

(3)   the purpose of the arrangement was to trigger entitlement to help under HA 1996, Pt 7[2] or H(W)A 2014, Pt 2; and

(4) there is no other good reason why the applicant is homeless[3].

[1] In this instance the use of the deeming provision for applications in England is a semantic difference only.
[2] As amended by HRA 2017, for applications for homelessness assistance made to local housing authorities in England on or after 3 April 2018.
[3] HA 1996, s 191(3); H(W)A 2014, s 77(1) and (4). See also English Code, paras 9.8 and 9.28–9.29; Welsh Code, para 17.30; and **13.181–13.187**.

13.40 This provision is obviously designed to prevent collusive arrangements, but in practice is hardly ever used. Not only are the conditions tightly drawn, but they only deem (England) or define (Wales) the 'person' who 'enters into' the arrangement as having become homeless intentionally[1]. Its effect can therefore be avoided by a different member of the homeless household making the application for homelessness assistance[2].

[1] HA 1996, s 191(3)(a); H(W)A 2014, s 77(4).
[2] Discussed further at **13.95**.

13.41 The following paragraphs address, in turn, each of the six elements of the composite statutory definition of 'becoming homeless intentionally'.

Was there a deliberate act or omission?

A deliberate act or omission

13.42 The first step in the statutory definition is that the applicant 'deliberately does or fails to do anything' which results in his or her loss of accommodation[1]. There is no definition of 'deliberate act' or 'deliberate omission' in HA 1996, Pt 7[2] or H(W)A 2014, Pt 2[3]. Instead, HA 1996, Pt 7[4] and H(W)A 2014, Pt 2, stipulate that some acts or omissions are not to be treated as deliberate, by providing that:

' . . . an act or omission in good faith on the part of a person who was unaware of any relevant fact shall not be treated as deliberate[5].'

[1] HA 1996, s 191(1); H(W)A 2014, s 77(2).
[2] As amended by HRA 2017, for applications for homelessness assistance made to local housing authorities in England on or after 3 April 2018.
[3] The dictionary definition of 'deliberate' is 'intentional', which, in the context of HA 1996, s 191 and H(W)A 2014, s 77, seems to take one round in circles (*Shorter Oxford English Dictionary*, 2007).
[4] As amended by HRA 2017, for applications for homelessness assistance made to local housing authorities in England on or after 3 April 2018.
[5] HA 1996, s 191(2); H(W)A 2014, s 77(3).

13.43 So the word 'deliberate' in this setting must connote a free election to act (or fail to act) in a particular way by a person in possession of all the relevant facts. As one English judge has put it:

'I am satisfied from a consideration of the whole of the section . . . that "deliberately" is used in the ordinary sense of the word and is not to be narrowly construed. In particular the provisions of [the] subsection . . . indicate that "deliberately" means "after a consideration of all the relevant facts"[1].'

[1]   *Devenport v Salford City Council* (1983) 8 HLR 54, CA per Waller LJ.

13.44 The most obvious example of an act 'deliberately' done arises where an applicant has surrendered, or given notice on, his or her tenancy, or sold his or her house, and made no provision for future accommodation[1]. The most obvious example of a 'deliberate' omission would be failure to pay housing costs notwithstanding having the means and opportunity to pay them.

[1]   See *Dyson v Kerrier District Council* [1980] 1 WLR 1205, CA (a case in which the applicant gave up long-term accommodation for a precarious winter let); and *F v Birmingham City Council* [2006] EWC Civ 1427, [2007] HLR 18, CA, where a tenant gave up her secure tenancy for unaffordable private rented accommodation.

13.45 The English Code of Guidance introduces the notions of 'force' and 'fault':

'An act or omission should not generally be treated as deliberate, even where deliberately carried out, if it was forced upon the applicant through no fault of their own[1].'

[1]   English Code, para 9.16; there is no equivalent in the Welsh Code.

13.46 Adopting the approach in this guidance and adding a non-statutory gloss to HA 1996, Pt 7[1] itself, a non-deliberate act could therefore occur either when:

(1)   someone was forced to do something; or
(2)   someone may have chosen to act in a particular way, but did so in ignorance of all the relevant facts[2].

[1]   As amended by HRA 2017, for applications for homelessness assistance made to local housing authorities in England on or after 3 April 2018.
[2]   The important question of an applicant's mental capacity at the time of the act or omission in this context is discussed at **13.66–13.75**.

13.47 An example of the former would arise where the applicant had deliberately vacated accommodation, but did so because remaining there would lead to him or her experiencing further violence from a neighbour. Similarly, an applicant's choice to spend his or her last available money to buy food for hungry children rather than paying the rent is not, for the purposes of the legislation, 'deliberate'[1]. On the latter set of facts, a local housing authority argued:

'a person does or fails to do something "deliberately" if he makes a considered choice between two courses of action or inaction, either of which he is able to take. Thus, if he makes a considered decision to apply the only money he has in his pocket in maintaining his children instead of paying it to his landlord, he deliberately fails to pay the rent[2].'

[1]   As happened in *R v Wandsworth London Borough Council ex p Hawthorne* (1995) 27 HLR 59, CA. See also *Adekunle v Islington London Borough Council* (2009) November *Legal Action*, p 25, Mayor's and City of London County Court, where the local housing authority had decided that the applicant's choice to sell her house in the face of serious financial

difficulties was 'a conscious and deliberate decision' which fell within the definition of 'deliberate act'. The judge said that view was 'mistaken and wrong' in the circumstances where a person's conscious decision is taken 'in a situation where there is no realistic alternative'.

2   *R v Wandsworth London Borough Council ex p Hawthorne* (1995) 27 HLR 59, CA at 63.

13.48 This submission was rejected. The Court of Appeal said:

'The purpose of . . . the . . . Act is to house the homeless. Admittedly it is no part of that purpose to house those whose homelessness has been brought upon them by their own fault. But equally it is no part of it to refuse housing to those whose homelessness has been brought upon them without fault on their part, for example by disability, sickness, poverty or even a simple inability to make ends meet[1].'

1   *R v Wandsworth London Borough Council ex p Hawthorne* (1995) 27 HLR 59, CA per Nourse LJ at 63.

Unaware of a relevant fact

13.49 The proviso dealing with ignorance of material facts can be difficult to operate in practice. First, the local housing authority must identify whether the fact of which the applicant was ignorant was 'relevant'. Second, assuming that there was ignorance of a relevant fact, it must ask whether the applicant acted 'in good faith'[1].

1   HA 1996, s 191(2); H(W)A 2014, s 77(3).

13.50 As one judge has observed, the proviso is:

' . . . not without its difficulties. It is to be noted that the test is not the reasonableness of the applicant's actions, but whether they were taken in ignorance. This may seem unjust. A person who takes the trouble to find out all the relevant facts, but makes a reasonable but mistaken judgment, cannot apparently claim the benefit of the section; a person who makes no enquiries at all and therefore acts in ignorance, may be able to do so. The omission of a test of reasonableness has been criticised in the courts (see for example *R v Tower Hamlets London Borough Council ex p Rouf*)[1] but the section remains unamended[2].'

1   *R v Tower Hamlets London Borough Council ex p Rouf* (1991) 23 HLR 460, CA.
2   *R v Westminster City Council ex p Obeid* (1996) 29 HLR 389, QBD per Carnwath J at 394.

13.51 In using the words 'any relevant fact', Parliament has indicated that it intended a wide construction to be given to that phrase[1]. But 'relevant' to what? In *R v Westminster City Council ex p N-Dormadingar*[2], the court explained that a fact is relevant where, had the applicant been aware of it, he or she would have taken it into account in deciding whether to give up the accommodation. The court also observed that the fact must be sufficiently clear and definite for its existence to be objectively determined. But this may be easier said than done. A person may have deliberately given up his or her existing home in the mistaken belief that there would be accommodation (or employment capable of funding accommodation) in a place to which he or she then moved. If that person was factually wrong about the availability of other accommodation (or employment) can that render the giving up of the original home not a 'deliberate' act?

1   *R v Hammersmith and Fulham London Borough Council ex p Lusi* (1991) 23 HLR 260, QBD per Roch J at 269.
2   *R v Westminster City Council ex p N-Dormadingar* (1997) Times, 20 November, QBD.

13.52 For example, in one case, a young woman gave up her home overseas to come to the UK in the mistaken belief that her family would accommodate her here. In another, a businessman gave up his home in the UK to move abroad in the mistaken belief that he would be pursuing a sound business venture overseas capable of financing alternative accommodation there. Both were ignorant of the true facts, but were these facts 'relevant' to the giving up of their homes? In both cases, the judges decided that they were 'relevant facts' that were capable of triggering the application of the proviso to what was otherwise manifestly the deliberate giving-up of their homes[1].

1   *R v Wandsworth London Borough Council ex p Rose* (1983) 11 HLR 105, QBD, and *R v Hammersmith and Fulham London Borough Council ex p Lusi* (1991) 23 HLR 260, QBD.

13.53 Building on this, the courts have subsequently drawn a distinction between 'matters of hope' in relation to the prospects of future housing or employment, and relevant facts[1]. In the case of a scientist who gave up accommodation in Belgium to come to the UK, the Court of Appeal described his prospects of finding suitable employment as resting on 'little more than a wing and a prayer'[2]. The question of good faith simply did not arise, because the scientist's over-optimism did not constitute a relevant fact[3]. Similarly, in another case, the failure to see that withholding a small part of the rent to fund a replacement washing machine would lead to the non-renewal of the tenancy, did not amount to ignorance of a relevant fact[4]. Longmore LJ commented that HA 1996, s 191(2) was intended to deal with a 'genuine mistake or misapprehension of existing fact not with future events which may or may not occur'[5] and while a mistaken belief might suffice, 'the belief has to be a belief in an existing fact, not a misplaced belief in the likelihood of the happening or otherwise of future event'[6]. Endorsing this approach, in the case of *da Trindade v Hackney London Borough Council*[7], Sales LJ explained that:

> ' . . . an applicant who seeks to bring herself within section 191(2) where the future has not worked out as expected by her, has to show that at the time of her action or omission to act referred to in section 191(1), she had an active belief that a specific state of affairs would arise or continue in the future based on a genuine investigation about those prospects, and not on mere aspiration. Her belief about her current prospects regarding the future can then properly be regarded as belief about a current relevant fact (the apparent good prospects that the future will work out as she expects), such that if that belief can be seen to be unjustified by what a fully informed appreciation of her prospects at the time would have revealed, her mistake will qualify as unawareness of a relevant fact for the purposes of section 191(2)[8].'

1   See *R v Westminster City Council ex p Obeid* (1996) 29 HLR 389, QBD; *Aw-Aden v Birmingham City Council* [2005] EWCA Civ 1834, (2006) July *Legal Action*, p 29, CA; *F v Birmingham City Council* [2006] EWCA Civ 1427, [2007] HLR 18, CA; *Ugiagbe v Southwark London Borough Council* [2009] EWCA Civ 31, [2009] HLR 35, CA; *Enfield London Borough Council v Najim* [2015] EWCA Civ 319, [2015] HLR 19, CA; *da Trindade v Hackney London Borough Council* [2017] EWCA Civ 942, [2017] HLR 37, CA.

2   *Aw-Aden v Birmingham City Council* [2005] EWCA Civ 1834, (2006) July *Legal Action*,
     p 29, CA per Maurice Kay LJ at [11].
3   Similarly, in *F v Birmingham City Council* [2006] EWCA Civ 1427, [2007] HLR 18, CA,
     where a young woman had 'closed her eyes to the obvious', in that case that housing benefit
     would not be available for the whole of the contractual rent, there was no relevant fact and
     thus the issue of whether she had acted in good faith did not arise for consideration.
4   *Enfield London Borough Council v Najim* [2015] EWCA Civ 319, [2015] HLR 19, CA.
     Permission to appeal was refused by the Supreme Court on 27 July 2015 with the observations
     that 'the issue turned mainly on the factual evaluation made by the reviewing officer and
     the Court of Appeal was plainly right about section 191(2).'
5   *Enfield London Borough Council v Najim* [2015] EWCA Civ 319, [2015] HLR 19, CA per
     Longmore LJ at [32].
6   *Enfield London Borough Council v Najim* [2015] EWCA Civ 319, [2015] HLR 19, CA per
     Longmore LJ at [34].
7   [2017] EWCA Civ 942, [2017] HLR 37, CA.
8   *da Trindade v Hackney London Borough Council* [2017] EWCA Civ 942, [2017] HLR
     37, CA per Sales LJ at [26].

13.54 Note that what the individual has been ignorant of must have been a 'fact', and not the legal consequences of that fact. For example, an applicant who decides not to pay his or her housing costs, in the mistaken belief that this (and the consequent eviction) will not prejudice any subsequent application for homelessness assistance, has not acted in ignorance of any fact but rather in ignorance of the legal consequences of the deliberate omission to pay[1]. A secure tenant who leaves her home in fear of threats of violence cannot be said to have been unaware of the 'fact' that her security of tenure would be lost in her absence. That is not a fact but 'a legal result of the factual departure which she made'[2]. Likewise, it has been suggested that ignorance of legal rights is not ignorance of a 'fact'[3]. The Codes contain some confusing advice regarding the scenario of a former tenant who left his or her home in response to a valid notice from the landlord where the former tenant was genuinely unaware that he or she had a legal right to remain until a possession order is made (and even until execution of the subsequent warrant). This scenario is described as 'a general example of an act made in good faith' even though the tenant had 'the belief that they had no legal right to continue to occupy the accommodation', which suggests an ignorance of the legal position[4]. More obviously, if, as a matter of fact, an applicant had to do something by a particular date to retain his or her home and did not understand that there was such a deadline, the applicant's failure to act will not have been deliberate, as it was in ignorance of a relevant 'fact'[5].

1   *R v Eastleigh Borough Council ex p Beattie (No 2)* (1984) 17 HLR 168, QBD.
2   *R v Croydon London Borough Council ex p Toth* (1987) 20 HLR 576, CA per O'Connor LJ
     at 582.
3   *Brown v Hamilton District Council* 1983 SLT 397 per Lord Fraser and *R v Harrow London
     Borough Council ex p Weingold* (unreported) 24 August 1992, QBD.
4   English Code, para 9.24; Welsh Code, para 17.25. See also **13.62** for two other examples
     which appear at first sight to relate to ignorance of the law, but where the Codes advise that
     they might also be ignorance of a material fact.
5   *R v Christchurch Borough Council ex p Conway* (1987) 19 HLR 238, QBD. In *Abdullahi v
     Brent London Borough Council* [2007] EWCA Civ 885, (2007) October *Legal Action*,
     p 26, CA, a woman's ignorance of her responsibility to pay the shortfall between her
     contractual rent and housing benefit was held to be a relevant fact and the issue of whether she
     had acted in good faith should have been considered by the local housing authority.

13.55 Another scenario considered by the courts is where an applicant approaches a local housing authority for help with his or her housing situation and is either given the wrong advice, or not given any advice at all. In both *Ugiagbe v Southwark London Borough Council*[1] and *Bury Metropolitan Borough Council v Gibbons*[2], assured shorthold tenants who had been given notices requiring possession by their landlords approached their local housing authorities. Neither of them were given advice that they were entitled to remain in their properties until a possession order had been made against them. They each left their accommodation upon the expiration of the notice. On their subsequent applications for homelessness assistance, they were found to have become homeless intentionally. The Court of Appeal found in each case that the local housing authorities' failure to give the correct advice had meant that they had not been acting 'deliberately', within the meaning of the statutory provisions, when they left their tenancies.

1   [2009] EWCA Civ 31, [2009] HLR 35, CA.
2   [2010] EWCA Civ 327, [2010] HLR 33, CA.

Good faith

13.56 'Good faith' is a phrase introducing similar complexity[1]. HA 1996, Pt 7[2] and H(W)A 2014, Pt 2, couple lack of awareness and 'good faith'. The test on lack of awareness is subjective: 'was *the applicant* unaware of any relevant fact?' rather than 'would a reasonable person have been unaware of that fact[3]?' Then, if there was lack of awareness, the applicant must addition-ally have acted in 'good faith' for the act not to be considered 'deliberate' for the purposes of the definition of becoming homelessness intentionally.

1   HA 1996, s 191(2); H(W)A 2014, s 77(3).
2   As amended by HRA 2017, for applications for homelessness assistance made to local housing authorities in England on or after 3 April 2018.
3   *O'Connor v Kensington and Chelsea Royal London Borough Council* [2004] EWCA Civ 394, [2004] HLR 37, CA per Sedley LJ at [30] and [34].

13.57 A mistake of judgment may constitute an act in good faith, but not those instances based on 'wilful ignorance'[1] nor those based on 'mere aspiration'[2]. As the Court of Appeal put it in one case:

' . . . the statutory dividing line . . . comes not at the point where the applicant's ignorance of a relevant fact was due to his own unreasonable conduct, but at the point where, for example, by shutting his eyes to the obvious he can be said not to have acted in good faith[3].'

1   *O'Connor v Kensington and Chelsea Royal London Borough Council* [2004] EWCA Civ 394, [2004] HLR 37, CA per Sedley LJ at [30].
2   *R v Westminster City Council ex p Obeid* (1996) 29 HLR 389, QBD per Carnwath J at 397.
3   *O'Connor v Kensington and Chelsea Royal London Borough Council* [2004] EWCA Civ 394, [2004] HLR 37, CA per Sedley LJ at [34]. See further *da Trindade v Hackney London Borough Council* [2017] EWCA Civ 942, [2017] HLR 37, CA, at [35]–[36].

13.58 There is a degree of overlap in the circumstances in which a belief as to future prospects will constitute a 'relevant fact'[1] and those in which an applicant will be found to have acted in 'good faith'. An applicant who has carried out a genuine investigation of his or her future prospects is likely to have acted in good faith, even if the future does not turn out as planned[2].

1   See **13.49–13.55**.

2   See further *da Trindade v Hackney London Borough Council* [2017] EWCA Civ 942, [2017] HLR 37, CA per Sales LJ at [35]–[36].

13.59 If there is dishonesty, the act or omission cannot have been made in good faith[1]. Lloyd LJ has said in the Court of Appeal:

> 'the use of the phrase "good faith" carries a connotation of some kind of impropriety, or some element of misuse or abuse of the legislation. It is aimed at protecting local housing authorities from finding that they owe the full duty under Pt 7 of the 1996 Act to a person who, despite some relevant ignorance, ought to be regarded as intentionally homeless . . . Dishonesty is the most obvious kind of conduct which it would catch, and wilful blindness in the Nelsonian sense comes close to that[2].'

1   English Code, para 9.25; *R v Barnet London Borough Council ex p Rughooputh* (1993) 25 HLR 607, CA.
2   *Ugiagbe v Southwark London Borough Council* [2009] EWCA Civ 31, [2009] HLR, 35 CA per Lloyd LJ at [27].

13.60 'Foolish or imprudent' or unreasonable behaviour is not sufficient to put a person into the category of not acting in good faith[1]. Conversely, a 'laudable or understandable motive' on the part of the applicant will not be sufficient to establish that he or she acted in good faith[2].

1   *Ugiagbe v Southwark London Borough Council* [2009] EWCA Civ 31, [2009] HLR, 35 CA per Lloyd LJ at [26].
2   *da Trindade v Hackney London Borough Council* [2017] EWCA Civ 942, [2017] HLR 37, CA at [34] per Sales LJ.

13.61 Both Codes give examples of acts or omissions that could be made in good faith[1]:

(1)   a person accrues rent arrears, unaware that he or she may be entitled to housing benefit or other social security benefits;

(2)   an owner-occupier, faced with foreclosure or possession proceedings to which there is no defence, sells or surrenders the property before a possession order is obtained; and

(3)   a tenant faced with possession proceedings to which there is no defence surrenders the property to the landlord.

1   English Code, para 9.26; Welsh Code, para 17.26.

13.62 The latter two examples could be analysed as ignorance of the legal right to remain in the property. In relation to the last example, the Welsh Code advises that the ignorance might be of 'the general pressure on the authority for housing' – a matter of fact rather than law[1].

1   Welsh Code, para 17.26(iii). See further English Code, para 9.27.

13.63 Note that the adverb 'deliberately' governs only the act or omission itself, not the outcome, or consequences, of the act or omission. The question is not: 'Has the applicant deliberately become homeless?' but rather: 'Has the applicant deliberately done something, or failed to do something, as a result of which he or she is now homeless[1]?'

[1]   *Devenport v Salford City Council* (1983) 8 HLR 54, CA.

13.64 Whilst each case must be considered on its own facts, the Codes and the courts have considered a number of different scenarios that provide some useful guidance[1]. Each is examined below.

[1]   English Code, paras 9.16–9.20; Welsh Code, paras 17.15–17.26.

Acts or omissions not generally considered 'deliberate'

13.65 The Codes of Guidance suggest several circumstances in which acts or omissions of applicants 'should not' be considered to be 'deliberate'[1].

[1]   English Code, para 9.17; Welsh Code, para 17.17.

(1) Incapacity

13.66 The Codes advise that where the local housing authority has reason to believe that an applicant was incapable of managing his or her affairs, for example by reason of age, mental illness or disability, his or her act or failure to act at that time should not be considered to have been 'deliberate'[1]. The formulations in the Codes suggest that both the very old and the very young might be considered incapable as a result of their age[2]. Applying this approach, if the applicant was incapable at the date when the act or omission was committed, he or she will not have become homeless intentionally.

[1]   English Code, para 9.17(b); Welsh Code, para 17.17(ii).
[2]   Earlier editions of the Codes referred to 'old age' rather than 'age'.

13.67 This guidance in the Codes should not be taken as meaning that young people and children cannot be found to have become homeless intentionally even when their deliberate acts were committed when they were children. In *Denton v Southwark London Borough Council*[1], the Court of Appeal upheld a finding by the local housing authority that a young person had become homeless intentionally as a result of his deliberate actions when he was 21. Similarly *White v Southwark London Borough Council*[2], a Court of Appeal judge said that actions of children as young as 13 might be 'deliberate acts'[3].However, the statutory guidance *Prevention of homelessness and provision of accommodation for 16 and 17 year old young people who may be homeless and/or require accommodation*[4] emphasises that 'Housing authorities will need to be mindful that a homeless 16–17 year old might not have the ability to understand the full consequences of their actions and choices that would be expected of an adult'[5].

[1]   [2007] EWCA Civ 623, [2008] HLR 11, CA.
[2]   [2008] EWCA Civ 792, (2008) October *Legal Action*, p 37, CA.
[3]   Sir Peter Gibson, dismissing an application for permission to bring a second appeal. Note that guidance from both the UK Government (*Prevention of homelessness and provision of accommodation for 16 and 17 year old young people who may be homeless and/or require accommodation*) and the Welsh Government (*Social Services and Well-being (Wales) Act 2014 Pt 6 Code of Practice (Looked After and Accommodated Children)*), each advise that young people who have refused accommodation provided by children's services and who have lost

such accommodation as a result should not be treated as having acted deliberately (English Guidance, para 4.21; Welsh Guidance, para 587).

⁴ April 2018, MHCLG and DfE. HA 1996, s 182 requires that local housing authorities take the guidance into account when exercising their HA 1996 Pt 7 functions. Similarly, the Local Authority Social Services Act 1970, s 7 requires children's services' departments to take the guidance into account when exercising children's services' functions.

⁵ *Prevention of homelessness and provision of accommodation for 16 and 17 year old young people who may be homeless and/or require accommodation*, para 4.20.

13.68 On the other hand however, the English Code advises that 'all attempts should be made by housing authorities to avoid the impact of intentionally homeless decisions in relation to care leavers aged 18–25'[1]. To this end, local housing authorities should consult with the relevant children's services authority and obtain advice and assistance as to the young person's emotional and mental well-being, maturity and general ability to understand the impact of his or her actions[2].

¹ English Code, para 22.17.
² English Code, para 22.17.

13.69 Both the English and Welsh Codes were published many years after the principles and structured approach to determining capacity contained in the Mental Capacity Act 2005 (MCA 2005), ss 1–3 came into force. It is therefore surprising that neither Code makes any reference to the MCA 2005. The modern approach to capacity, set out in MCA 2005, ss 1–3, is that 'a person must be assumed to have capacity unless it is established that he lacks capacity'[1] When deciding whether or not a person has capacity to make a decision, the test is issue-specific. In other words the question is whether the person has or had the capacity to make that particular decision, not whether he or she can make other (simpler or more complex) decisions[2]. An impairment or disturbance in the functioning of the mind or brain, which leads to the person being incapable of making a decision, may be permanent or temporary[3]. This very structured, careful approach should be applied by a local housing authority decision-maker considering whether or not an applicant for homelessness assistance had capacity at the date of commission of his or her deliberate act (or his or her omission to act).

¹ MCA 2005, s 1(2). See further WB *(a protected party through her litigation friend the Official Solicitor) v W District Council* [2018] EWCA Civ 928, CA for a discussion of the relationship between HA 1996, Pt 7 and MCA 2005.
² MCA 2005, s 3.
³ MCA 2005, s 2.

13.70 Local housing authorities should also bear in mind their public sector equality duty in the Equality Act 2010, s 149[1]. Local housing authorities should be making inquiries into the issue of capacity if there is any feature of the evidence presented to them that raises a real possibility that the applicant was disabled where that is relevant to the issue of whether he or she acted deliberately[2].

¹ See **4.206–4.230** and **12.100**.
² *Pieretti v Enfield London Borough Council* [2010] EWCA Civ 1104, [2011] HLR 3, CA. See also *Brown v Southwark London Borough Council* (2016) February *Legal Action*, pp 45–46, County Court at Central London. In *Kanu v Southwark London Borough Council* [2015] UKSC 30, [2015] HLR 23, SC, Lord Neuberger said at [78] that the duty would be engaged in any case where there is an 'actual or possible disability'. See **12.100**. See also *The public*

sector equality duty, homelessness and the Pieretti principles (Local Government Lawyer, 16 January 2013) reporting the case of *Holmes v Leicester City Council* in the Birmingham County Court.

13.71 Even if the applicant appears (at the date of his or her application) to be capable, he or she may have been temporarily incapable at the date that he or she committed the act or at the date when he or she omitted to act.

13.72 Although the phrasing in the Codes appears to reflect part of the priority need test for 'vulnerability'[1], it does not follow, just because an applicant has been found to be vulnerable (and therefore to have a priority need) at the date of the application for homelessness assistance, that he or she was incapable at the time when the accommodation was lost[2].

[1] HA 1996, s 189(1)(c); H(W)A 2014, s 70(1)(c); see **12.76–12.125** and **12.202–12.206**.
[2] *R v Wirral Metropolitan Borough Council ex p Bell* (1995) 27 HLR 234, QBD.

(2) LIMITED CAPACITY, FRAILTY OR VULNERABILITY

13.73 Even if the applicant is generally capable of managing his or her own affairs and had a measure of capacity at the relevant time, the English Code advises local housing authorities to consider whether the particular act or omission leading to the loss of accommodation was 'the result of limited mental capacity; or a temporary aberration or aberrations caused by mental illness or frailty'[1].

[1] English Code, para 9.17(c); *Hijazi v Kensington and Chelsea Royal London Borough Council* [2003] EWCA Civ 692, [2003] HLR 72, CA.

13.74 The English Code advises that a temporary aberration or aberrations may have been caused by an assessed substance abuse problem and that, in those circumstances, an act or omission should not be considered as deliberate[1].

[1] See *Kendall v City of Westminster Council* (2009) November *Legal Action*, p 25, Central London County Court. It is not clear what the English Code means by 'assessed' and whether there has to have been some formal process of assessment.

13.75 The Welsh Code deals with these various issues under the heading of 'vulnerability'[1]. The Code perhaps goes too far in suggesting that this means vulnerability within the meaning of H(W)A 2014, s 71[2]. It advises that local housing authorities might consider what advice and support was made available to someone who could be considered to be vulnerable before he or she became homeless. If advice and support was offered, in order to prevent homelessness, but this was disregarded by the applicant, he or she might be considered to have become homeless intentionally. If the advice and support was not available to a vulnerable person, and he or she was not be able to manage his or her affairs without that advice and support, he or she could be considered not to have acted deliberately[3].

[1] Welsh Code, para 17.17(iii).
[2] Welsh Code, para 17.17(iii). There is nothing within H(W)A 2014, Pt 2 or the case law to support that particular interpretation of the word 'deliberate'.

Welsh Code, para 17.21–17.23: the advice applies where the person's acts or omissions led to the loss of accommodation which he or she was occupying, not, of course, to any failure to accept advice designed to find alternative accommodation.

(3) LACKING FORESIGHT OR PRUDENCE

13.76 The act or omission may have been imprudent or have been a result of lack of foresight. If the applicant acted in good faith, it will not generally be considered that such act or omission was deliberate[1].

[1] English Code, para 9.17(e); Welsh Code, para 17.17(iv).

(4) FINANCIAL DIFFICULTIES BEYOND THE APPLICANT'S CONTROL

13.77 The Codes give examples of a tenant not paying the rent as a result of housing benefit or universal credit delays, or financial difficulties which were beyond the applicant's control[1]. Where the applicant was genuinely unable to keep up rent (or mortgage) payments, even after claiming benefits, and there was no further financial help available, giving up possession of the home would not generally be considered deliberate[2]. However, in those circumstances, the local housing authority is entitled to consider why the arrears accrued and the applicant's ability to meet the commitment to pay housing costs at the time that it was taken on[3]. That is because the 'act' of the applicant, which may have ultimately caused his or her homelessness, could have been the taking out of an impossible rent or mortgage commitment in the first place. The Welsh Code also advises that changes to the welfare benefit system may result in increased numbers of people struggling to meet their housing costs and that applicants should not be penalised where their previously affordable accommodation became unaffordable as a result of changes in the local housing allowance or housing benefit[4]. In practice, a similar approach has been adopted by the County Court in the context of HA 1996, Pt 7[5].

[1] English Code, para 9.17(a); Welsh Code, paras 17.17(i) and 17.18. See **13.189–13.198**.
[2] English Code, para 9.18; Welsh Code, paras 17.17(i) and 17.18. For an example, see *Adekunle v Islington London Borough Council* (2009) November *Legal Action*, p 25, Mayor's and City of London County Court.
[3] English Code, para 9.19; Welsh Code, para 17.19. See *William v Wandsworth London Borough Council* [2006] EWCA Civ 535, [2006] HLR 42, CA.
[4] Welsh Code, para 8.30.
[5] In *Magoury v Brent London Borough Council* (2016) February *Legal Action*, p 46, County Court at Central London, a finding that the applicant had become homeless intentionally was quashed where there had been a failure to consider whether she would have become homeless anyway as a result of the benefit cap set under the Welfare Reform Act 2012, Pt 5. Similarly, *Barker v Watford City Council* (2017) July/August *Legal Action*, p 42, County Court at Central London, involved a finding that the applicant had become homeless intentionally in circumstances where she had lost her accommodation as a result of welfare reforms which left a shortfall between her housing benefit award and her rent. The local housing authority decided that the applicant's property was affordable, and therefore reasonable to continue to occupy, as she could have applied for discretionary housing payments. The decision was quashed on appeal. The local housing authority had failed to make any inquiries to establish whether such an application would succeed or for how long any award would be made.

(5) UNDER DURESS

13.78 The English Code advises that an act or omission made when the applicant was under duress should not generally be considered deliberate[1]. There is no further explanation. An example would presumably be someone subjected to domestic violence who is required by his or her partner to give up any legal interest in the home[2].

[1] English Code, para 9.17(d).
[2] See 14.216–14.226.

(6) SERVING A PRISON SENTENCE

13.79 The Welsh Code gives an example of a prisoner who has just served a sentence (and presumably lost his or her accommodation during the term of imprisonment) for offences which were not in themselves breaches of his or her tenancy agreement[1]. This reflects the Welsh Government's view that 'the actions that caused the person to be imprisoned . . . should not be considered as grounds for regarding him or her as intentionally homeless', unless the offence which resulted in the sentence of imprisonment was a direct breach of the prisoner's tenancy agreement and led to the landlord obtaining possession of the property[2].

[1] Welsh Code, para 17.26(ii). See **13.237–13.238**.
[2] Welsh Code, para 17.26(ii).

13.80 In England, the tendency has been to treat the criminal act as having been 'deliberate', but then to focus on whether it was causative of the homelessness[1]. The English Code does however remind local housing authorities to 'consider each case in the light of all the facts and circumstances' and to avoid a 'blanket policy which assumes that people who have lost accommodation whilst in custody will or will not be assessed as intentionally homeless[2].'

[1] English Code, para 23.21. See **13.237**.
[2] English Code, para 23.22.

Acts or omissions that may be regarded as 'deliberate'

13.81 The Codes of Guidance suggest a number of circumstances in which acts or omissions of applicants 'may be regarded as deliberate'[1].

[1] English Code, para 9.20; Welsh Code, para 17.23.

(1) VOLUNTARY SALE OR VOLUNTARY NON-PAYMENT OF HOUSING COSTS

13.82 If an applicant has chosen to sell his or her home where there was no risk of losing it, that action will generally be treated as having been 'deliberate'[1]. The question of whether any resultant homelessness was intentional will turn on other aspects of the statutory definition, eg whether it would have been reasonable to have continued in occupation of that home[2].

[1] English Code, para 9.20(a); Welsh Code, para 17.23(i).
[2] See **13.162–13.180**.

13.83 Where a home has been lost for failure to meet liabilities for housing costs and where any rent or mortgage arrears accrued as a result of a 'wilful and persistent refusal to pay', the omission to pay will generally be treated as having been 'deliberate'[1]. The Codes' emphasis on persistent and wilful default underscores the obvious point that non-payment caused by lack of funds will not be deliberate[2]. 'Wilful default' in making payment, however, is sufficient to establish a deliberate omission[3].

[1] English Code, para 9.20(b); Welsh Code, para 17.23(ii). For examples, see *William v Wandsworth London Borough Council* [2006] EWCA Civ 535, [2006] HLR 42, CA and *Watchman v Ipswich Borough Council* [2007] EWCA Civ 348, [2007] HLR 33, CA. See **13.189–13.198**.

[2] See **13.189–13.198**.

[3] *R v Wyre Borough Council ex p Joyce* (1983) 11 HLR 73, QBD, discussed at **13.197**.

(2) Neglecting affairs

13.84 An omission may be regarded as deliberate where the applicant 'could be said to have significantly neglected their affairs having disregarded sound advice from qualified people'[1]. Into the scope of this example would fall an applicant who temporarily left accommodation without making arrangements for the rent to be paid in his or her absence[2]. Similarly, in *Viackiene v Tower Hamlets London Borough Council*[3] a joint tenant who declined an offer from her landlord to assist her in replacing her impecunious co-tenant, was found to have acted deliberately when she was subsequently evicted for rent arrears.

[1] English Code, para 9.20(c); Welsh Code, para 17.23(iii).

[2] *R v Wycombe District Council ex p Mahsood* (1988) 20 HLR 683, QBD.

[3] [2013] EWCA Civ 1764, [2014] HLR 13, CA.

13.85 The courts have held that, where someone had been given inaccurate advice, or no advice at all, from a local housing authority and had therefore acted in ignorance of his or her legal rights, then the applicant's actions should not be construed as 'deliberate'[1].

[1] *Ugiagbe v Southwark London Borough Council* [2009] EWCA Civ 31, [2009] HLR 35, CA; *Bury Metropolitan Borough Council v Gibbons* [2010] EWCA Civ 327, [2010] HLR 33, CA. See **13.55**.

(3) Giving up a home

13.86 The Codes advise that voluntary surrender of adequate accommodation in this country or abroad which it would have been reasonable for the applicant to continue to occupy may be regarded as a deliberate act[1]. Again, whether the applicant is likely to be found to have become homeless intentionally will turn on other parts of the statutory definition and, in particular, on whether it would have been reasonable to have continued occupying the accommodation given up[2].

[1] English Code, para 9.20(d); Welsh Code, para 17.23(iv). See **13.234**.

[2] For an unusual example involving joint owners see *Bellamy v Hounslow London Borough Council* [2006] EWCA Civ 535, [2006] HLR 42, CA. See **13.98** and **13.176**.

13.87 Where a father had permitted his three children to move from perfectly suitable accommodation with their mother to his one room accommodation, and, as a result of the presence of the children, he was then required to leave by his landlord, his conduct had been deliberate[1].

[1]   *Oxford City Council v Bull* [2011] EWCA Civ 609, [2011] HLR 35, [2012] 1 WLR 203, CA. See **12.69**.

(4)   Eviction for anti-social behaviour

13.88 The Codes suggest that where someone is evicted because of anti-social behaviour, nuisance to neighbours or harassment, that behaviour may be treated as having been deliberate[1]. The nuisance or anti-social behaviour that brought about the eviction will often have been the deliberate 'act' of the applicant. In other cases, the applicant's deliberate 'omission' may have been his or her failure to control or remove the perpetrator of the nuisance, thus constituting his or her acquiescence in the perpetrator's nuisance behaviour[2]. In such cases, a local housing authority is entitled to consider the behaviour of the family as a whole and to come to a decision that the applicant had either acquiesced in, or failed to prevent, the nuisance behaviour which had resulted in the family's eviction[3]. A tenant subject to a possession order on the grounds of waste to the property or deterioration of the furniture may also be considered to have committed a deliberate act (damage) or omission (failure to maintain)[4].

[1]   English Code, para 9.20(e); Welsh Code, para 17.23(v). See **13.201–13.206**.
[2]   *Devenport v Salford City Council* (1983) 8 HLR 54, CA, and *R v Swansea City Council ex p John* (1982) 9 HLR 56, QBD. See **13.95–13.99**.
[3]   *R v East Hertfordshire District Council ex p Bannon* (1986) 18 HLR 515, QBD.
[4]   *R v Sevenoaks District Council ex p Reynolds* (1990) 22 HLR 250, CA.

13.89 Local housing authorities need not restrict their application of this guidance to cases where tenants enjoying security of tenure have been subject to possession orders under one or more of the 'fault' grounds for possession[1]. If a private landlord refuses to renew an assured shorthold tenancy, and subsequently obtains a possession order following service of a notice given under the Housing Act 1988, s 21, the local housing authority is entitled to consider the reason for the landlord seeking possession. If it was due to the fault of the tenant, or members of the tenant's household, the loss of accommodation may be found to have been caused by the deliberate act of, or omission by, the tenant[2].

[1]   Housing Act 1988, Sch 2, Pt 1 and Housing Act 1985, Sch 2.
[2]   *R v Rochester upon Medway City Council ex p Williams* (1994) 26 HLR 588, QBD; *R v Nottingham City Council ex p Edwards* (1999) 31 HLR 33, QBD; *Sheppard v Richmond upon Thames Royal London Borough* [2012] EWCA Civ 302, (2012) June *Legal Action*, p 36, CA; and *Enfield London Borough Council v Najim* [2015] EWCA Civ 319, [2015] HLR 19, CA.

(5)   Inflicting violence

13.90 Perpetrators of 'violence' or 'threats of violence', as defined by HA 1996, Pt 7[1], or 'abuse' as defined by H(W)A 2014, Pt 2[2], who are evicted because of their behaviour, may be considered to have committed a deliberate act[3]. Such an eviction may arise from the former landlord applying for possession on one or more of the grounds that specifically relate to nuisance, criminal convictions or domestic violence[4], or as a result of the victim of domestic violence either:

(1)   obtaining an occupation order in family court proceedings requiring the perpetrator to leave[5]; or

(2)   bringing the tenancy to an end by notice.

[1]   As amended by HRA 2017, for applications for homelessness assistance made to local housing authorities in England on or after 3 April 2018. See HA 1996, s 177(1) and (1A). See **10.81–10.91**.
[2]   H(W)A 2014, s 57(1) and 58(1). See **10.92–10.98**.
[3]   English Code, para 9.20(f); the Welsh Code, para 17.23(vi). See **13.216** and **13.221**.
[4]   Housing Act 1985, Sch 2, Grounds 2 and 2A; Housing Act 1988, Sch 2, Grounds 14 and 14A.
[5]   Family Law Act 1996, s 33.

(6)   GIVING UP TIED ACCOMMODATION

13.91 Where an applicant has been living in tied accommodation and leaves his or her job, thereby losing the accommodation, the local housing authority may well find that there has been a 'deliberate' act[1]. The Codes advise local housing authorities to consider whether it would have been reasonable for the employee to have continued in the employment and/or reasonable to have continued to occupy the accommodation. If the applicant has been dismissed, the local housing authority should make inquiries to ascertain whether the acts or omissions leading to the applicant's dismissal were the applicant's 'deliberate' acts or omissions. The English Code recommends that former members of the armed forces, who are required to vacate service quarters as a result of giving notice to leave the service, should not be considered to have become homeless intentionally[2].

[1]   English Code, para 9.20(g); Welsh Code, para 17.23(vii); and *R v Kyle and Carrick District Council ex p Speck* 1993 GWD 1566, OH.
[2]   English Code, para 24.11.

Summary of 'deliberate' act or omission

13.92 In summary, a 'deliberate' act or omission is one that:

• is freely made;
• by a person (the applicant) in possession of all the relevant facts;
• who is not forced to act (or fail to act); and
• who is not unaware of a relevant fact.

13.93 If the applicant was unaware of a relevant fact, his or her act or omission will not be considered deliberate if he or she acted in good faith, ie he or she was genuinely ignorant of that relevant fact and that ignorance was not based on an unrealistic degree of optimism, a shutting of eyes to the obvious, or on dishonesty.

13.94 Even if the local housing authority finds that this limb of the test is satisfied, it cannot find that the applicant has become homeless intentionally unless the other five limbs[1] are also made out.

[1] See **13.36**.

Was the deliberate act or omission by the applicant?

13.95 Each applicant is entitled to individual consideration of his or her application. This means that even where one member of a household has been found to have become homeless intentionally, an application from another member must still be individually considered providing that he or she has the legal capacity to make an application[1]. For this reason it is inappropriate to use the term 'intentionally homeless family'. An applicant can only be found to have become homeless intentionally if it was his or her deliberate act or omission that caused the homelessness[2]. However, where an applicant has acquiesced to the deliberate act or omission of another which led to the loss of accommodation, then the applicant's failure to prevent the other from acting or failing to act in a particular way may be characterised as a deliberate act or omission on the part of the applicant. In this way an applicant may assume responsibility for the conduct of another.

[1] See **8.42** and note the distinct rules for 16- and 17-year-olds. A child aged 16 or 17 years old who is dependents on parents who have become homeless intentionally cannot circumvent the rules on becoming homeless intentionally by making an application on behalf of the household. In such a case the local housing authority should still accept the application and determine whether or not the child is, as a matter of fact, a dependant. But where the child is found to be dependent on his or her parents, the child will not have a priority need, thereby limiting the extent of duties that will be owed to the household. See *R (SD) v Oxford City Council* [2015] EWHC 1871 (Admin), (2015) October *Legal Action*, p 41, Admin Ct.

[2] English Code, para 9.9; Welsh Code, para 17.15; *R v North Devon District Council ex p Lewis* [1981] 1 WLR 328, QBD, and *City of Gloucester v Miles* (1985) 17 HLR 292, CA.

13.96 In instances where one member of the household's conduct has been such that he or she would be regarded as having deliberately acted or failed to act in such a way as to cause the homelessness, there is an evidential presumption (or a local housing authority is entitled to make an assumption or draw an inference), in the absence of any material indicating the contrary, that the other household members were party to that conduct[1]. However, once there are positive assertions by an applicant (or some other evidence) that there was no acquiescence, such as one partner asserting that he or she had always protested at the other partner's failure to pay the rent or mortgage, that will be sufficient to rebut the presumption and the local housing authority must inquire into the issue fully[2].

[1] English Code, paras 9.5 and 9.11; Welsh Code, para 17.13. See further *R v North Devon District Council ex p Lewis* [1981] 1 WLR 328, QBD.

[2] *R v West Dorset District Council ex p Phillips* (1985) 17 HLR 336, QBD; *R v Eastleigh Borough Council ex p Beattie (No 2)* (1984) 17 HLR 168, QBD; *R v East Northamptonshire Borough Council ex p Spruce* (1988) 20 HLR 508, QBD; *R v Thanet District Council ex p Groves* (1990) 22 HLR 223, QBD; *Quinton v East Hertfordshire District Council* (2003) April *Legal Action*, p 27, Luton County Court; and *N v Allerdale Borough Council* (2008) October *Legal Action*, p 38, Carlisle County Court.

13.97 The case law is replete with examples of everyday situations in which the question has arisen as to whether the applicant acquiesced in the conduct of another household member. This includes situations in which the other household member has:

- failed to pay the rent in circumstances where both partners were involved in managing the household's finances[1];
- terminated a joint tenancy[2];
- given up his or her job (to which tied accommodation was linked)[3];
- changed jobs (from one to which future re-housing was linked to another with no promise of re-housing)[4];
- misspent the money earmarked for housing costs (whether on drink, drugs or gambling)[5];
- caused nuisance or annoyance to others[6]; or
- as head of the household, taken the family from secure to insecure accommodation[7]; or
- withheld the rent in the mistaken belief that there was an entitlement to do so on account of disrepair[8]; or
- re-mortgaged the home to such an extent that the debt became unmanageable[9].

[1] *R v Barnet London Borough Council ex p O'Connor* (1990) 22 HLR 486, QBD; and *R v Nottingham City Council ex p Caine* (1996) 28 HLR 374, CA, where, in both cases, the local housing authority was entitled to find acquiescence.

[2] *R v Penwith District Council ex p Trevena* (1984) 17 HLR 526, QBD, where a decision that the former joint tenant remaining in occupation had acquiesced was held to be one that no reasonable local housing authority would have come to.

[3] *R v North Devon DC ex p Lewis* [1981] 1 WLR 328, QBD, where it was held that, on the evidence, the local housing authority was entitled to find acquiescence.

[4] *R v Mole Valley DC ex p Burton* (1989) 20 HLR 479, QBD, where the decision that the applicant had acquiesced in that behaviour was quashed. She had known of the behaviour but had also acted in good faith in believing his assurances that they would qualify for council housing.

[5] *R v West Dorset DC ex p Phillips* (1984) 17 HLR 336, QBD, where a decision that the wife had acquiesced (when she had informed the local housing authority that she did not know about the non-payment and had always said that the husband's drinking would lead to trouble) was quashed.

[6] *Smith v Bristol City Council* [1981] LAG Bull 287, CA; *Devenport v Salford City Council* (1983) 8 HLR 54, CA, where there was acquiescence; *R v Swansea City Council ex p John* (1982) 9 HLR 56, QBD, where a finding that the wife had acquiesced by failing to remove her husband who had caused nuisance was upheld; *R v East Hertfordshire District Council ex p Bannon* (1986) 18 HLR 515, QBD, where a finding that the conduct of the whole of the family was to blame and therefore the applicant had acquiesced was upheld; and *N v Allerdale Borough Council* (2008) October *Legal Action*, p 38, Carlisle County Court, where the local housing authority's inquiries into whether a mother had acquiesced in her son's anti-social behaviour were inadequate.

[7] *R v Tower Hamlets London Borough Council ex p Khatun (Asma)* (1993) 27 HLR 344, CA, where the wife was found to have acquiesced by having been content to leave the decisions to her husband.

[8] *R v Nottingham City Council ex p Caine* (1995) 28 HLR 374, CA, where the decision that the applicant had acquiesced was upheld, as she must have known of the non-payment. See also *Enfield London Borough Council v Najim* [2015] EWCA Civ 319, [2015] HLR 19, CA.

[9] *R v Barnet London Borough Council ex p O'Connor* (1990) 22 HLR 486, QBD, where the decision that the wife had acquiesced was upheld – she had said that she left financial matters to her husband, but had signed two mortgage applications on which she had made false representations.

13.98 In summary, the deliberate act or omission must have been by the applicant. In cases where the deliberate act or omission was by another member of the applicant's household, a local housing authority is entitled to presume that the applicant acquiesced in that conduct unless there is an assertion, or evidence, that the applicant did not acquiesce. Where there is an assertion, or evidence, that the applicant did not acquiesce, the local housing authority must then make full inquiries into the issue[1].

1   In the unusual case of *Bellamy v Hounslow London Borough Council* [2006] EWCA Civ 535, [2006] HLR 42, CA, the applicant's account was that she was not aware that she, as a legal joint owner of her home with her mother, had a power to object to a sale. The local housing authority did not believe the applicant and the Court of Appeal held that the local housing authority had been entitled not to believe her.

13.99 Even if the local housing authority finds that this limb of the test is satisfied, it cannot find that the applicant has become homeless intentionally unless the other five limbs[1] are also made out.

1   See **13.36**.

Causation

13.100 Causation in the law has been described as a 'notoriously difficult'[1] subject, and this is certainly so when it comes to judging whether a person has become homeless intentionally. In this context, there are two situations in which the issue of causation arises. Firstly, in deciding whether or not the applicant ceased to occupy accommodation in consequence his or her deliberate act or omission[2]. Secondly, in deciding whether the applicant's deliberate act (or omission), and the cessation of occupation it caused, remains an operative cause of the present homelessness[3]. Before turning to these two respective topics, we begin with some general remarks regarding the Supreme Court decision in *Haile v Waltham Forest London Borough Council*[4] - which provides the most authoritative guidance on causation in the context of becoming homeless intentionally – to show the relationship between these two questions of causation and how it is that the second question, which does not obviously form part of the statutory rubric[5], arises at all.

1   *R v Hackney London Borough Council ex p Ajayi* (1997) 30 HLR 473, QBD at 479 per Dyson J, subsequently approved by the Court of Appeal in *William v Wandsworth London Borough Council* [2006] EWCA Civ 535, [2006] HLR 42, CA and in *Watchman v Ipswich Borough Council* [2007] EWCA Civ 348, [2007] HLR 33, CA.
2   See **13.112–13.132**.
3   See **13.133–13.154**.
4   [2015] UKSC 34, [2015] AC 1471, SC. See M. Hutchings '*Haile v Waltham Forest LBC* - Intentional homelessness, queue jumping and the "I would have been homeless anyway" argument' (2015) *Journal of Housing Law* 18(6), 116–118 for an interesting commentary on the case.
5   HA 1996, s 191; H(W)A 2014, s 77.

13.101 Ms Haile was an assured shorthold tenant of a room. It was a term of her tenancy that only one person could reside in the room. The tenancy also entitled her to use of the kitchen shared with other residents. She became unhappy with the accommodation, moved out and later applied to Waltham Forest London Borough Council as homeless. Ms Haile informed Waltham Forest on a number of occasions that she had moved out of the accommodation owing to unpleasant smells caused by the other residents cooking. Subsequently Ms Haile gave birth to a girl. At this juncture, if she had still be living in the room, she would have had to move out in any event since the tenancy agreement would not have permitted her to reside there with her daughter.

13.102 Several months later Waltham Forest issued a decision finding that Ms Haile had become homeless intentionally. This decision was upheld on review and on appeal to the County Court. The Court of Appeal dismissed a second appeal[1] on the basis that the decision of the House of Lords in *Din v Wandsworth London Borough Council*[2], involving the analogous provisions under the Housing (Homeless Persons) Act 1977, remained binding and was determinative of the issue. The decision as to whether an applicant has become homeless intentionally, the Court of Appeal said, was to be made based on the facts as they existed at the time the applicant left his or her accommodation. If the applicant became homeless intentionally at that point, the fact that subsequent developments would have rendered him or her homeless in any event was irrelevant.

1   [2014] EWCA Civ 792, [2014] HLR 37, CA.
2   [1983] AC 657, HL.

13.103 The Supreme Court[1] allowed Ms Haile's appeal. It held that in deciding whether a person is owed the main housing duty under HA 1996, s 193(2), or the duty to secure accommodation pursuant to H(W)A 2015, s 75(2)[2], in circumstances where a question arises as to whether the applicant has become homeless intentionally, a two-stage test should be applied in considering causation[3].

1   Lord Carnwath dissenting.
2   The case was decided under HA 1996, s 191 but the reasoning would apply with equal force to H(W)A 2014, s 77 which is drafted in similar terms.
3   [2015] UKSC 34, [2015] AC 1471, SC per Lord Reed at [25].

13.104 First, the local housing authority should consider whether the applicant became homeless intentionally within the meaning of HA 1996, s 191(1) and H(W)A 2014, s 77(2), ie whether he or she deliberately failed to do anything in consequence of which he or she ceased to occupy accommodation. This issue is dealt with at **13.112–13.132**.

13.105 Second, the local housing authority should consider for the purposes of HA 1996, s 193(1) and H(W)A 2014, s 75(2)(d), whether the applicant's *current* homelessness, has been caused by his or her intentional conduct or whether the causal chain has been broken by subsequent events. This issue is dealt with at **13.133–13.154**.

13.106 The causal chain will be broken in the following circumstances:

* where it can no longer 'reasonably be said' that 'but for' the applicant's conduct he or she would not currently be homeless; or
* where the 'proximate cause of the homelessness is an event which is unconnected to the applicant's own earlier conduct, and in the absence of which homelessness would probably not have occurred'[1].

1   *Haile v Waltham Forest London Borough Council* [2015] UKSC 34, [2015] AC 1471, SC per Lord Reed at [63].

13.107 This approach was consistent with the purpose of the legislative provisions which is to prevent applicants 'queue jumping' and obtaining accommodation by deliberately making themselves homeless[1]. In Ms Haile's case it could not be said that 'but for' her deliberate conduct in leaving the room she would not have been homeless since she would have become homeless in any event following the subsequent birth of her child[2]. *Din* was distinguished on the 'narrow ground' that there was no such later causative event in that case, 'merely a possibility that one might well have occurred'[3].

[1]   *Haile v Waltham Forest London Borough Council* [2015] UKSC 34, [2015] AC 1471, SC per Lord Reed at [22].
[2]   *Haile v Waltham Forest London Borough Council* [2015] UKSC 34, [2015] AC 1471, SC per Lord Reed at [67].
[3]   *Haile v Waltham Forest London Borough Council* [2015] UKSC 34, [2015] AC 1471, SC per Lord Neuberger at [79]–[80].

13.108 The distinction between the two stages of the test in *Haile v Waltham Forest London Borough Council*[1] is significant though certainly not straightforward. To understand the nature of the two-stage test, it may assist to consider a timeline. At the beginning of the timeline there is a deliberate act or omission by the applicant. At the centre of the timeline there is the point at which the applicant ceases to occupy his or her accommodation. The timeline ends at the date of the local housing authority's review decision.

[1]   [2015] UKSC 34, [2015] AC 1471, SC.

13.109 The first stage of the test[1] is concerned with the first half of the time-line, and involves consideration of events prior to the cessation of occupation. The local housing authority must consider whether the applicant's deliberate act was the cause of his or her ceasing to occupy the accommodation. In some cases there may be multiple factors which all contributed toward the applicant giving up his or her accommodation and the local housing authority must determine the operative cause[2]. In other cases there may be an intervening event that occurred between the deliberate act and the cessation of occupation and the local housing authority must consider whether this has broken the causal chain[3]. This part of the test reflects the orthodox approach to assessing intentional homelessness which had hitherto prevailed[4].

[1]   See **13.112–13.132**.
[2]   See **13.119–13.128**.
[3]   See **13.129–13.130**.
[4]   *Din v Wandsworth London Borough Council* [1983] AC 657, HL.

13.110 Where the operative cause of the cessation of occupation was a deliberate act or omission of the applicant it falls to the local housing authority to move on to the second stage. The second stage of the test[1] involves the second half of the time line and involves consideration of whether there has been a supervening event that has happened since the applicant ceased to occupy the accommodation meaning that his or her deliberate act can no longer reasonably be regarded as the operative cause of his current homelessness at the time of application or review[2]. This aspect of the test 'has to be understood as being implicit if absurd consequences are to be avoided'[3]. For example, an elderly man who becomes homeless when his care home was closed cannot be intended to be denied assistance under HA 1996, Pt 7 or H(W)A 2014, Pt 2 merely because, 60 years earlier, he was evicted from his student digs for holding rowdy parties[4].

1   See **13.133–13.154**.
2   *Haile v Waltham Forest London Borough Council* [2015] UKSC 34, [2015] AC 1471, SC per Lord Neuberger at [76].
3   *Haile v Waltham Forest London Borough Council* [2015] UKSC 34, [2015] AC 1471, SC per Lord Reed at [28].
4   See *Haile v Waltham Forest London Borough Council* [2015] UKSC 34, [2015] AC 1471, SC per Lord Reed at [23]. Presumably in this scenario the causal chain would have been broken by the supervening period in settled accommodation. See **13.136–13.146**.

13.111 It is this second stage of the test which is the novel aspect of the court's decision, and marks the real development in the law. Strictly, the notion that the causal chain may be broken by subsequent events is not a new one. For example, the occupation of 'settled accommodation'[1], following an earlier loss of accommodation is a well-established means by which the causal chain may be broken. But the Supreme Court in *Haile v Waltham Forest London Borough Council*[2], for the first time, has provided a clear explanation, rooted in the language of HA 1996, Pt 7[3], to explain how and why the causal chain may be broken, and in doing so has confirmed unequivocally that supervening events other than a period of time spent in settled accommodation may suffice to break the causal chain. We will now consider the two stages of the test in detail.

1   See **13.136–13.146**.
2   [2015] UKSC 34, [2015] AC 1471, SC.
3   As amended by HRA 2017, for applications for homelessness assistance made to local housing authorities in England on or after 3 April 2018.

Was it as a consequence of a deliberate act or omission that the applicant ceased to occupy accommodation?

13.112 This requires consideration of two elements:

(1)   Has there been any cessation of occupation at all?
(2)   If so, did the deliberate act or omission cause the cessation of occupation?

13.113 Only if both are answered affirmatively will this limb of the statutory definition be made out.

Has there been any cessation of occupation at all?

13.114 The deliberate act or omission must have the consequence that the applicant 'ceases to occupy' accommodation[1]. Accordingly, the applicant must have actually occupied the accommodation the loss of which was caused by his or her deliberate act or omission[2]. Failing to take up an offer of accommodation will not suffice[3]. Likewise 'the mere right to possession is not enough'[4]. However, at the other end of the spectrum, there need not have been continuous occupation at all times, but the accommodation must at least have been at the disposal of the applicant and available for his or her occupation at the time it was given up[5].

1   HA 1996, s 191(1); H(W)A 2014, s 77(2).
2   *R v Westminster City Council ex p Chambers* (1982) 6 HLR 24, QBD, and *Din v Wandsworth London Borough Council* [1983] 1 AC 657, HL.
3   English Code, para 9.12.
4   *Lee-Lawrence v Penwith District Council* [2006] EWCA Civ 1672, (2006) July *Legal Action*, p 29, CA per Arden LJ at [16].
5   See the unusual facts of *R v Westminster City Council ex p Khan* (1991) 23 HLR 230, QBD, where the applicant had not actually occupied the accommodation, but it was held to have been at her disposal and available for her occupation; and see *Lee-Lawrence v Penwith District Council* [2006] EWCA Civ 1672, (2006) July *Legal Action*, p 29, CA, where holding the keys to a house provided on a tenancy and claiming housing benefit in order to pay the rent was held to be sufficient evidence to uphold a finding of occupation for the purposes of HA 1996, s 191(1).

13.115 The accommodation the applicant has ceased to occupy may have been anywhere in the world; local housing authorities are not restricted to considering accommodation the applicant has occupied in the UK[1].

1   English Code, para 9.12.

13.116 It follows that decisions by applicants:

(1)   to rid themselves of accommodation that they have not occupied; or
(2)   not to accept accommodation offered to them to occupy,

cannot result in findings that they have become homeless intentionally. In *R v Wandsworth London Borough Council ex p Oteng*[1], the applicant left a home that she shared with her two sisters and, over two years later, she transferred her interest in the property to her mother. The local housing authority decided that she had become homeless intentionally as a result of voluntarily transferring her interest. The Court of Appeal rejected that approach. The transfer of interest had not caused the applicant to cease to occupy the accommodation – that had occurred two years earlier[2].

1   *R v Wandsworth London Borough Council ex p Oteng* (1994) 26 HLR 413, CA. See also *R v Westminster City Council ex p De Souza* (1997) 29 HLR 649, QBD.
2   In *Quaid v Westminster City Council* (2008) February *Legal Action*, p 41, Central London County Court, the applicant had committed offences while he was street homeless. He subsequently acquired a place at a Salvation Army hostel. He was convicted of those offences, sent to prison and lost the hostel place. The local housing authority found that he had become homeless intentionally as a result of the offences committed. The decision was varied to a decision that he had not become homeless intentionally. The commission of the offences had not caused the loss of the hostel place.

13.117 Applying the correct approach, homeless applicants in temporary accommodation provided under HA 1996, Pt 7[1] who refuse offers of accommodation cannot become homeless intentionally from the accommodation that they refuse, as they have never occupied it (although they may be found to have become homeless intentionally from temporary accommodation lost as a result of their refusal of other accommodation)[2]. However, in such cases, local housing authorities should consider whether it was the refusal that caused the loss of the temporary accommodation, or whether there was some other reason for its loss[3].

1   As amended by HRA 2017, for applications for homelessness assistance made to local housing authorities in England on or after 3 April 2018.

2 English Code, para 9.12. See also *R v Brent London Borough Council ex p Awua* [1996] AC 55, HL and *Johnston v Westminster City Council* [2015] EWCA Civ 554, (2015) *Legal Action*, p 54, CA (**10.18–10.20**) for another example of the issues that may arise in this type of situation. In the latter case Westminster found that the applicant was not homeless, as he was owed the main housing duty by another local housing authority. The Court of Appeal held that this was wrong in law. The fact that another local housing authority was willing to provide unspecified accommodation did not prevent the applicant from qualifying as homeless, since no such accommodation had actually been made available at the time of the decision.

3 *Sonde v Newham London Borough Council* (1999) June *Legal Action*, p 24, Bow County Court; and *R (Dragic) v Wandsworth London Borough Council* [2012] EWHC 1241 (Admin), (2012) July *Legal Action*, p 42, Admin Ct. See **13.248–13.251**.

Did the act or omission cause the cessation of occupation?

13.118 This is the first stage of the two-stage test identified by the Supreme Court in *Haile v Waltham Forest London Borough Council*[1].

1 [2015] UKSC 34, [2015] AC 1471, SC. See **13.100–13.111** for an overview of the two-stage test and a detailed explanation of the decision in *Haile v Waltham Forest London Borough Council* [2015] UKSC 34, [2015] AC 1471, SC. See **13.133–13.154** for the second stage of the two-stage test.

IDENTIFYING THE EFFECTIVE OR OPERATIVE CAUSES OF THE LOSS OF ACCOMMODATION

13.119 In most situations, there will be a number of events that, taken together, caused the applicant to cease to occupy the accommodation. Some of those events may not be the direct cause of the loss of the accommodation, but may have started off the chain of events that led to the loss of accommodation (linear causation). Sometimes there will be a number of independent contributing factors operating at the same time (parallel causation)[1].

1 See *Noel v Hillingdon London Borough Council* [2013] EWCA Civ 1602, [2014] HLR 10, CA, *Chishimba v Kensington and Chelsea Royal London Borough Council* [2013] EWCA Civ 786, [2013] HLR 34, CA and *Enfield London Borough Council v Najim* [2015] EWCA Civ 319, [2015] HLR 19, CA.

13.120 HA 1996, Pt 7[1] and H(W)A 2014, Pt 2 use the word 'anything' to refer to what has been done (or failed to be done)[2]. However, the subject of inquiry is not every act or omission in which the applicant engaged at the time she or he became homeless, or in the lead-up to that time. HA 1996, Pt 7[3] and H(W)A 2014, Pt 2 are concerned only with the doing of (or failure to do) something 'in consequence of which' the applicant ceased to occupy his or her accommodation.

1 As amended by HRA 2017, for applications for homelessness assistance made to local housing authorities in England on or after 3 April 2018.
2 HA 1996, s 191(1); H(W)A 2014, s 77(2).
3 As amended by HRA 2017, for applications for homelessness assistance made to local housing authorities in England on or after 3 April 2018.

13.121 It is necessary, therefore, to identify the operative or effective[1] cause of the loss of accommodation, and then to consider whether that was the applicant's deliberate act or omission[2]. This should be answered in a practical, common-sense way. It is more than a 'but-for' test[3]. The operative cause can be doing (or failing to do) 'anything'[4]. Where there are multiple parallel causes, if just one of the causes was the applicant's deliberate act or omission, that will be sufficient for the applicant to fall within this limb of the definition of having become homeless intentionally[5]. This is a question of fact for the local housing authority to determine[6].

1   The words 'effective' and 'operative' have been used interchangeably in the case law.
2   See **13.42–13.94**.
3   *Noel v Hillingdon London Borough Council* [2013] EWCA Civ 1602, [2014] HLR 10, CA per Lewison LJ at [9]; *Chishimba v Kensington and Chelsea Royal London Borough Council* [2013] EWCA Civ 786, [2013] HLR 34, CA per Lewison LJ at [7].
4   HA 1996, s 191(1); H(W)A 2014, s 77(2). See *Enfield London Borough Council v Najim* [2015] EWCA Civ 319, [2015] HLR 19, CA.
5   *O'Connor v Kensington and Chelsea Royal London Borough Council* [2004] EWCA Civ 394, [2004] HLR 37, CA. For example, in *Noel v Hillingdon London Borough Council* [2013] EWCA Civ 1602, [2014] HLR 10, CA, the local housing authority was entitled to find that it was a failure to apply for an increase in housing benefit that was the effective cause of the applicant's homelessness rather than the taking of an unaffordable tenancy.
6   *Noel v Hillingdon London Borough Council* [2013] EWCA Civ 1602, [2014] HLR 10, CA per Lewison LJ at [11]; *Chishimba v Royal Borough of Kensington and Chelsea* [2013] EWCA Civ 786, [2013] HLR 34, CA per Lewison LJ at [9].

13.122 Various judges have commented on the difficulties involved in establishing the cause or causes of the loss of accommodation. In *R v Hackney London Borough Council ex p Ajayi*[1], Dyson J said:

'Questions of causation are notoriously difficult and, in my judgment, the Court should be slow to intervene to strike down the decisions of administrative bodies on such questions and should do so only in clear cases. I cannot accept that the effective cause should always be regarded in these cases as the chronologically immediate or proximate cause. In some cases, the cause closest in point of time will be regarded as the effective cause . . . In others, the cause closest in time will be not so regarded[2].'

1   (1997) 30 HLR 473, QBD.
2   *R v Hackney London Borough Council ex p Ajayi* (1997) 30 HLR 473, QBD per Dyson J at 479, subsequently approved by the Court of Appeal in *William v Wandsworth London Borough Council* [2006] EWCA Civ 535, [2006] HLR 42, CA and in *Watchman v Ipswich Borough Council* [2007] EWCA Civ 348, [2007] HLR 33, CA.

13.123 In *O'Connor v Kensington and Chelsea Royal London Borough Council*[1] the applicant's father was terminally ill and the whole family travelled to Ireland to his bedside, starting off a chain of events that eventually resulted in the loss of their accommodation in London. The father's illness was not an act or omission of the applicants and, although the decision to travel to Ireland was the applicants' act:

' . . . nobody but a logician would say that it was in consequence of the family's going to Ireland to see a sick relative that they lost their accommodation[2].'

1   [2004] EWCA Civ 394, [2004] HLR 37, CA.
2   [2004] EWCA Civ 394, [2004] HLR 37, CA per Sedley LJ at [27].

The 'reasonable likelihood' test

13.124 A loss of accommodation must have occurred as a consequence of the applicant's deliberate act or omission. This does not mean that there needs to be any immediate link between the nature of the act done (or the omission) and the loss of accommodation. In *Chishimba v Kensington and Chelsea Royal London Borough Council*, in relation to instances of linear causation, Lewison LJ observed that 'if a series of dominoes falls over it does not matter that the applicant did not knock over the last domino if he set the domino effect in motion'[1]. An applicant who deliberately gambles at a casino and loses every resource he or she has, has done an act (the gambling) that is in itself entirely unrelated to the accommodation subsequently lost for failure to pay housing costs. A convicted international drug dealer who, while in prison, has his or her house confiscated and sold as a proceed of crime, has done an act (criminal drug dealing) wholly unrelated to the former home. The issue, however, is not whether the loss of the home was the intended consequence of the deliberate act or omission but whether it is *a* consequence[2].

1   [2013] EWCA Civ 786, [2013] HLR 34, CA per Lewison LJ at [9].
2   *Noel v Hillingdon London Borough Council* [2013] EWCA Civ 1602, [2014] HLR 10, CA per Lewison LJ at [7]; *Chishimba v Royal Borough of Kensington and Chelsea* [2013] EWCA Civ 786, [2013] HLR 34, CA per Lewison LJ at [7].

13.125 This is not to say that acts or omissions wholly removed from any connection at all with the eventual loss of accommodation can always be counted if they, as a matter of fact, did 'cause' that loss. Without any sensible restraint on the plain words, absurd decisions might be made, eg that a father who chastised his son too harshly for the liking of the mother (who then excluded the father from her home) had lost his accommodation in consequence of the deliberate act of chastisement[1]. In cases of linear causation, the courts have, accordingly, striven to identify a narrower basis on which the link between the act and its consequences must be made out rather than a simple test of strict causation. Through the case law a test of 'reasonable likelihood' has emerged by way of a control mechanism[2]. The question to be posed is: 'Was the loss of the accommodation the reasonably likely result of what the applicant did?' Rather more straightforwardly, one judge has suggested that the correct approach is:

- to look at what the applicant did;
- find that the ultimate result was loss of accommodation; and
- then to ask 'if the fair-minded bystander could say to himself, "He asked for it"[3].

1   *R v Westminster City Council ex p Reid* (1994) 26 HLR 690, QBD.
2   *R v Hounslow London Borough Council ex p R* (1997) 29 HLR 939, QBD.
3   *Robinson v Torbay District Council* [1982] 1 All ER 726, QBD per HHJ Goodall at 731.

13.126 This approach of 'reasonable likelihood' has been approved by the Court of Appeal[1] and subsumed into the English Code[2], and is to be preferred to a test of whether the act done was too 'remote' from the resultant loss of accommodation[3].

1   *Devenport v Salford City Council* (1983) 8 HLR 54, CA; *R v Westminster City Council ex p Reid* (1994) 26 HLR 691, CA; *Stewart v Lambeth London Borough Council* [2002]

EWCA Civ 753, [2002] HLR 40, CA; and *Watchman v Ipswich Borough Council* [2007] EWCA Civ 348, [2007] HLR 33, CA.

2 English Code, para 9.13.

3 *R v Thanet District Council ex p Reeve* (1981) 6 HLR 31, QBD.

13.127 A helpful formulation of the correct approach given by the Court of Appeal is:

'What is called for, then, in a case where there are potentially multiple causes of an applicant's homelessness, is a careful judgment on the particular facts looking to see whether homelessness is shown to have been a likely consequence of the applicant's deliberate act, bearing in mind that it is the applicant's own responsibility for his homelessness that the statute is looking for. The precise question to be asked and answered of course relates to the time when the applicant in fact became homeless: that is the result of their Lordships' decision in Din[1].'

1 *Watchman v Ipswich Borough Council* [2007] EWCA Civ 348, [2007] HLR 33, CA per Laws LJ at [22], referring to *Din v Wandsworth London Borough Council* [1983]1 AC 657, HL.

13.128 Applying this approach, former prisoners, who are homeless on their release, face being found to have become homeless intentionally if the reasonably likely result of their deliberate acts in committing criminal offences, viewed objectively, was a sentence of imprisonment resulting in the loss of their accommodation[1].

1 *R v Hounslow London Borough Council ex p R* (1997) 29 HLR 939, QBD; *Minchin v Sheffield City Council* (2000) The Times, 26 August, CA, and *Stewart v Lambeth London Borough Council* [2002] EWCA Civ 753, (2002) 34 HLR 40, CA. See further English Code, paras 23.21–23.22. The Welsh Code, however, advises local housing authorities in Wales against finding that the applicant became homeless intentionally in such circumstances, unless the acts, which led to the applicant's imprisonment, were also breaches of his or her tenancy and led to the landlord obtaining possession of the property: Welsh Code, para 17.26. See 13.237–13.238.

INTERVENING EVENTS

13.129 The causative link between the deliberate act or omission and the actual loss of accommodation must be in place throughout. An independent act or omission of a third party that actually causes the loss of accommodation will break that link. For example, an applicant may be on the brink of having his or her home repossessed for non-payment of rent or a mortgage, but if, on the eve of eviction, the house is burnt down by a third party, the homelessness cannot have been intentional, as it was not a consequence of the applicant's omission to pay[1]. In *Gloucester City Council v Miles*[2], the applicant left her home, but (because she did not give up her tenancy) she was not homeless. Finding her gone, her husband vandalised the home, rendering it uninhabitable; his act rendered her homeless. As Stephenson LJ put it:

'The relevant questions – when, how and why did she become homeless – admit of only one answer: on vandalisation of her home[3].'

1 See *Cox v Brent London Borough Council* [2015] EWCA Civ 1551, CA, however for a variation on this set of facts, where the Court of Appeal refused permission to bring a second appeal against a finding that the applicant had become homeless intentionally.

13.130 Again, loss of accommodation by prisoners can provide classic examples of the operation of these provisions. Many prisoners will find difficulty in paying rent for their homes whilst they are in custody. Rent arrears and consequent loss of the tenancy may be inevitable[1]. But if the landlord wrongfully repossesses without a court order, it will be that illegal eviction that actually causes the homelessness and the prisoner cannot have become homeless intentionally[2]. If the prisoner asks a third party to pay the rent and that third party fails to pay, that may, depending on the facts, result in a decision that the prisoner became homeless intentionally (because the prisoner has failed to make an effective arrangement)[3], or in a decision that the prisoner became homeless unintentionally (where a proper and genuine arrangement is frustrated by the third party stealing the prisoner's money rather than paying the rent).

[1] The Welsh Code, however, advises local housing authorities in Wales against finding that the applicant became homeless intentionally in such circumstances, unless the acts, which led to the applicant's imprisonment, were also breaches of his or her tenancy and led to the landlord obtaining possession of the property: Welsh Code, para 17.26(ii).

[2] *Wilkins v Barnet London Borough Council* (1998) December *Legal Action*, p 27, Watford County Court.

[3] *Stewart v Lambeth London Borough Council* [2002] EWCA Civ 753, [2002] HLR 40, CA.

Summary

13.131 In summary, the deliberate act or omission by the applicant must have *caused* him or her actually to *cease to occupy* accommodation. An applicant's decision to rid himself or herself of accommodation that he or she was not occupying, or to refuse an offer of accommodation, cannot fall within this limb of the test since there will have been no *cessation of occupation*. In deciding whether the deliberate act or omission *caused* the cessation of occupation, the following principles should be taken into account:

- the task is to identify the real or effective cause of the homelessness, which should be approached in a practical common-sense way;
- where there are a number of independent factors which separately contributed to the loss of accommodation (parallel causation) it suffices if one of them is the deliberate act or omission of the applicant. This is a question of fact for the local housing authority;
- where a sequence of connected events led to the cessation of occupation (linear causation or 'the domino effect'), the control mechanism is whether it was reasonably likely that the act or omission would result in homelessness; and
- the causal chain will be broken by an intervening independent act or omission of a third party.

13.132 Even if the local housing authority finds that this limb of the test is satisfied, it cannot find that the applicant has become homeless intentionally unless the other five limbs[1] are also made out.

1 See **13.36**.

Is the deliberate act (or omission), and the cessation of occupation it caused, an operative cause of the present homelessness?

13.133 Particularly in those cases where there has been a significant passage of time or change in circumstances between an applicant ceasing to occupy accommodation and applying as homeless, it may be necessary to consider whether his or her deliberate act (or omission), and the cessation of occupation it caused, remains an operative cause of the present homelessness[1]. This is the second stage of the two-stage test set down by the Supreme Court in *Haile v Waltham Forest London Borough Council*[2]. It requires the local housing authority to consider for the purposes of HA 1996, s 193(1) and H(W)A 2014, s 75(2)(d), whether the applicant's current homelessness, has been caused by his or her intentional conduct or whether the causal chain has been broken by subsequent events.

1 The question of causation also arises in the context of the earlier decision as to whether or not the applicant ceased to occupy accommodation in consequence his or her deliberate act or omission. See **13.112–13.132**.
2 [2015] UKSC 34, [2015] AC 1471, SC. See **13.100–13.111** for an overview of the two-stage test and a detailed explanation of the decision in *Haile v Waltham Forest London Borough Council* [2015] UKSC 34, [2015] AC 1471, SC. See **13.112–13.132** for the first stage of the two-stage test.

13.134 The causal chain will be broken in the following circumstances:

*   where it can no longer 'reasonably be said' that 'but for' the applicant's conduct he or she would not currently be homeless; or
*   where the 'proximate cause of the homelessness is an event which is unconnected to the applicant's own earlier conduct, and in the absence of which homelessness would probably not have occurred'[1].

1 *Haile v Waltham Forest London Borough Council* [2015] UKSC 34, [2015] AC 1471, SC per Lord Reed at [63].

13.135 The remainder of this section of this chapter will consider the concept of 'settled accommodation', one of the well-established means by which the causal chain may be broken, before going on to consider other events that may break the causal chain.

Supervening events - settled accommodation

13.136 The Supreme Court in *Haile v Waltham Forest London Borough Council*[1] endorsed the well-established principle, that an applicant's deliberate act (or omission), and the cessation of occupation it caused, will no longer be regarded as an operative cause of his or her present homelessness, where he or she has spent a subsequent period in 'settled accommodation'[2]. The English Code advises that local housing authorities look back only to 'the last period of settled accommodation' and examine why the applicant left that[3].

1   [2015] UKSC 34, [2015] AC 1471, SC.
2   [2015] UKSC 34, [2015] AC 1471, SC per Lord Reed at [11].
3   English Code, para 9.13. The Welsh Code contains a paucity of guidance on this issue. See Welsh Code, para 17.32.

13.137 The advice in the English Code echoes the approach taken by the courts. They have decided that past intentional homelessness can be expunged by the subsequent acquisition of 'settled' accommodation. The phrase was first coined by Ackner LJ in *Din v Wandsworth London Borough Council*[1]. He said:

'To remove his self-imposed disqualification, he must therefore have achieved what can be loosely described as "a settled residence", as opposed to what from the outset is known . . . to be only temporary accommodation. What amounts to "a settled residence" is a question of fact and degree depending upon the circumstances of each individual case.'

1   *Din v Wandsworth London Borough Council* (unreported) 23 June 1981, CA, quoted by Lord Denning MR in *Lambert v Ealing London Borough Council* [1982] 1 WLR 550, CA at 557.

13.138 Consequently, where housing was lost in circumstances meeting the statutory definition of becoming homeless intentionally, a local housing authority's inquiries can be limited to determining those circumstances and then to whether there has been any settled accommodation since that loss of accommodation. The local housing authority is entitled to ignore the acquisition and loss of temporary or insecure accommodation (even if occupation of such accommodation brought the applicant's state of homelessness to an end for a time) and may track back to the loss of the last settled accommodation. That loss, looking at the whole history, may be the real reason for the present homelessness[1].

1   In accordance with the principle that it is not for the applicant to prove his or her case (see **9.31–9.35** and **13.19–13.28**), the local housing authority must consider whether the facts as disclosed by the applicant amount to there being intervening settled accommodation, whether or not the applicant has specifically raised the point (*Black v Wandsworth London Borough Council* (2008) February *Legal Action*, p 41, Lambeth County Court).

13.139 Not surprisingly, a whole body of case law has developed as to the circumstances in which accommodation is to be treated as 'settled' for the purpose of applying this test. While the matter is one primarily for the local housing authority itself to determine on the facts of the particular application, it should take a careful and measured approach. In the words of one judge[1]:

'Given the grave difficulty of securing settled accommodation, and given too that the clear legislative objective underlying the concept of intentionality – to discourage people from needlessly leaving their accommodation and becoming homeless – is surely sufficiently achieved without too protracted a period of consequential disqualification from re-housing, it is much to be hoped that housing authorities will in general interpret benevolently the character of accommodation secured by applicants after a finding of intentionality, namely as to whether or not it is settled.'

[1] *R v Merton London Borough Council ex p Ruffle* (1988) 21 HLR 361, QBD per Simon Brown J at 366–367.

13.140 More recently the Court of Appeal has commented that[1]:

' . . . the length of the period of accommodation relied on is not conclusive as to whether it should be treated as settled in the sense described in Din and the subsequent cases in which the test has been applied. What the applicant needs to establish is a period of occupation under either a licence or a tenancy which has at its outset or during its term a real prospect of continuation for a significant or indefinite period of time so that the applicant's transition from his earlier accommodation cannot be said to have put him into a more precarious position than he previously enjoyed.'

[1] *Doka v Southwark London Borough Council* [2017] EWCA Civ 1532, [2017] HLR 47, CA per Patten LJ at [18].

13.141 The case-law has thrown up many helpful illustrations of what some local housing authorities have respectively considered unsettled and settled accommodation for these purposes.

NOT USUALLY TREATED AS 'SETTLED' ACCOMMODATION

13.142 The following have not usually been treated as settled accommodation:

- holiday lets[1];
- out of season (or winter) lettings[2];
- bed and breakfast or other short-term hostel style accommodation[3];
- tied accommodation linked to short fixed-term employment[4];
- a temporary stay with relatives[5];
- decrepit caravans[6];
- lodging in a council house[7];
- accommodation in another country in breach of immigration laws[8];
- moving in temporarily with a cohabitant[9];
- a statutorily overcrowded and unaffordable assured shorthold tenancy[10];
- precarious occupation, whether as a bare licensee or as an unlawful sub-tenant[11];
- occupation in a caravan on a site without permission[12];
- a licence originally granted pursuant to the HA 1996, s 190(2) short-term accommodation duty[13]; or
- a non-secure tenancy provided in performance of the HA 1996, s 193(2) main housing duty[14].

[1] *Lambert v Ealing London Borough Council* [1982] 1 WLR 550, CA.
[2] *Dyson v Kerrier District Council* [1980] 1 WLR 1205, CA.
[3] *R v Harrow London Borough Council ex p Holland, R v Rushcliffe District Council ex p Summerson* (1992) 25 HLR 577, QBD.
[4] *R v Dacorum District Council ex p Wright* (unreported) 16 October 1991, QBD.
[5] *De Falco v Crawley Borough Council* [1980] QB 460, CA.

[6]   *Davis v Kingston Royal London Borough Council* (1981) The Times 28 March, CA.
[7]   *R v Merton London Borough Council ex p Ruffle* (1988) 21 HLR 361, QBD, and *Mazzaccherini v Argyll and Bute District Council* (1987) SCLR 475.
[8]   *R v Croydon London Borough Council ex p Easom* (1992) 25 HLR 262, QBD.
[9]   *R v Purbeck District Council ex p Cadney* (1986) 17 HLR 534, QBD; *C v Stirling Council* [2016] CSOH 55, [2016] Hous LR 58, Outer House.
[10] *Mohamed v Westminster City Council* [2005] EWCA Civ 796, [2005] HLR 47, CA.
[11] *Gilby v Westminster City Council* [2007] EWCA Civ 604, [2008] HLR 7, CA. See also *Doka v Southwark London Borough Council* [2017] EWCA Civ 1532, [2017] HLR 47, CA.
[12] *Stewart v Kingston upon Thames RLBC* [2007] EWCA Civ 565, [2007] HLR 42, CA.
[13] *Huda v London Borough of Redbridge* [2016] EWCA Civ 709, [2016] HLR 30, CA.
[14] *Ali v Haringey London Borough Council* [2008] EWCA Civ 132, (2008) April *Legal Action*, p 34, CA. For 'main housing duty' see **16.94–16.199**.

Usually treated as settled accommodation

13.143 The following have usually been treated as settled accommodation:

- freehold or leasehold ownership;
- a tenancy enjoying security of tenure;
- an indefinite licence or permission to occupy;
- returning to long-term occupation of the parental home[1];
- indefinite stay with friends or relatives[2]; or
- tied accommodation as a long-term employee.

[1]   *Robson v Kyle and Carrick District Council* (1994) SCLR 259.
[2]   *Krishnan v Hillingdon London Borough Council* (1981) SCOLAG January 1981, p 137, and *Black v Wandsworth London Borough Council* (2008) February *Legal Action*, p 41, Lambeth County Court.

13.144 The most difficult application of the test of 'settled' accommodation arises where an applicant who became homeless intentionally has subsequently obtained a tenancy with a private sector landlord. Since February 1997, any such letting will have been on an assured shorthold tenancy (AST) involving hardly any security of tenure. The Court of Appeal has rejected the proposition that, because an AST is the normal or default tenancy in the private sector, it must always count as 'settled'[1]. The true question for the local housing authority is whether, having regard to the circumstances and terms of its creation, the AST can properly be treated as having provided 'settled' accommodation for the applicant.

[1]   *Knight v Vale Royal District Council* [2003] EWCA Civ 1258, [2004] HLR 9, CA.

13.145 The material consideration is (generally) the position at the date of commencement of the new accommodation, 'since if the causal link is broken at that point nothing that happens thereafter will mend it'[1]. Of course, the reverse is also true. An arrangement may not have been 'settled' at the outset, but may become so at a later stage (eg when an originally short-term tenancy is renewed for an extended term) and it is at that stage that the causal link from previously having become homeless intentionally may be severed.

[1]   *R v Westminster City Council ex p Obeid* (1996) 29 HLR 389, QBD per Carnwath J at 400.

13.146 Properly understood, the application of the 'settled' accommodation test is all about cause and effect. The search is for a causal link between past deliberate loss of accommodation and the present homelessness. The local housing authority is really asking itself whether the earlier intentional act is causative of the present homelessness. It will usually conclude that it is, unless there has been some intermediate 'settled' accommodation.

Other supervening events breaking the causal link

13.147 Prior to the decision of the Supreme Court in *Haile v Waltham Forest London Borough Council*[1] there was a degree of uncertainty as to whether there might potentially be other circumstances in which the causal chain between present unintentional homelessness and having become homelessness intentionally in the past could be broken. In *R v Brent London Borough Council ex p Awua*[2], Lord Hoffman reached no concluded view. He said the jurisprudence concerning 'settled' accommodation[3]:

'... is well-established (it was approved by this House in Din's case) and nothing I have said is intended to cast any doubt upon it, although I would wish to reserve the question of whether the occupation of a settled residence is the sole and exclusive method by which the causal link can be broken[4].'

[1] [2015] UKSC 34, [2015] AC 1471, SC.
[2] *R v Brent London Borough Council ex p Awua* [1996] AC 55, HL.
[3] *R v Brent London Borough Council ex p Awua* [1996] AC 55 per Lord Hoffmann referring to *Din v Wandsworth London Borough Council* [1983] 1 AC 657, HL.
[4] See further *R v Harrow London Borough Council ex p Fahia* [1998] 1 WLR 1396, HL at 1129 per Lord Browne-Wilkinson, where the House of Lords declined to express a view.

13.148 The matter has now been settled beyond doubt by the decision of the Supreme Court in *Haile v Waltham Forest London Borough Council*[1]. The causal chain may be broken by other events[2]. The following cases provide examples of other events that may be sufficient to break the causal chain.

[1] [2015] UKSC 34, [2015] AC 1471, SC.
[2] See English Code, para 9.14. The test to be applied in determining whether the causal chain has been broken is set out at **13.134**. This present section is concerned with discussing the particular instances where the courts have found the test to be satisfied and the causal chain broken.

13.149 In *R v Basingstoke and Deane District Council ex p Bassett*[1], the applicant and her husband gave up secure accommodation to go and stay with her husband's relations. The marriage then broke down, she left her in-laws' house and became homeless. She had not had any intervening settled accommodation and the local housing authority considered that she had therefore become homeless intentionally. Taylor J held that the final homelessness resulted from the breakdown of the marriage, not from the decision to give up the settled accommodation[2].

[1] (1983) 10 HLR 125, QBD. Approved by the Supreme Court in *Haile v Waltham Forest London Borough Council* [2015] UKSC 34, [2015] AC 1471, SC per Lord Reed at [47].
[2] See also *Blackstock v Birmingham City Council* (2008) March *Legal Action*, p 22, Birmingham County Court and *R v Harrow London Borough Council ex p Louis* (1997) June *Legal Action*, p 23, QBD for further examples of cases where an applicant gives up accommodation in the UK in order to emigrate and then later returns to the UK.

13.150 *R v Harrow London Borough Council ex p Fahia*[1] concerned an applicant who was found to have deliberately procured her own eviction from accommodation in Harrow of which she was the tenant. She was then provided by the authority with temporary accommodation in a guest house, where she remained for over a year. Her housing benefit was then reduced by half, on the basis that her rent was too high. The landlord then told her that she would be evicted. At first instance, Mr Roger Toulson QC, sitting as a deputy judge, held that the authority had erred in failing to consider whether the causal connection between the applicant's deliberately procuring her eviction from her accommodation in Harrow, and her homelessness on being evicted from the guest house, had been broken by the reduction in her benefit[2].

1   (1997) 29 HLR 94, QBD. Approved by the Supreme Court in *Haile v Waltham Forest London Borough Council* [2015] UKSC 34, [2015] AC 1471, SC per Lord Reed at [49]–[51].
2   A similar approach was taken in *Magoury v Brent London Borough Council* (2016) February *Legal Action*, p 46, County Court at Central London, where a finding that the applicant had become homeless intentionally was quashed where there had been a failure to consider whether she would have become homeless anyway as a result of the benefit cap set under the Welfare Reform Act, Pt 5.

13.151 In *R v Camden London Borough Council ex p Aranda*[1] the applicant and her husband surrendered their tenancy of a house in Camden and moved to Colombia, where they obtained accommodation. On arrival in Colombia, the applicant was deserted by her husband. With no prospect of employment in Colombia, and no entitlement to social security benefits, she returned to Camden and applied for housing. It was held by the Court of Appeal that the causal connection between her deliberately giving up the accommodation in Camden, and her homelessness after leaving the accommodation in Colombia, had been broken by her husband's desertion.

1   (1997) 30 HLR 76, CA. Approved by the Supreme Court in *Haile v Waltham Forest London Borough Council* [2015] UKSC 34, [2015] AC 1471, SC per Lord Reed at [52].

13.152 The case of *R v Hackney London Borough Council ex p Ajayi*[1] involved an applicant who left settled accommodation in Nigeria to come to the United Kingdom, where she lived in overcrowded short-term accommodation. She was given notice to leave after she became pregnant. She challenged the local housing authority's decision that she had become homeless intentionally as a result of having left the accommodation in Nigeria, and argued that the true cause of her homelessness was her pregnancy. On the facts of that particular case, Dyson J held that the local housing authority had been entitled to decide that the effective cause of the applicant's homelessness was her action in leaving Nigeria.

1   (1997) 30 HLR 473, QBD. Approved by the Supreme Court in *Haile v Waltham Forest London Borough Council* [2015] UKSC 34, [2015] AC 1471, SC per Lord Reed at [53].

13.153 Another example of a case where the causal chain was not broken by a supervening event was *Stewart v Lambeth London Borough Council*[1]. In that case the applicant ceased to occupy his council flat when he was convicted of a drugs offence and sentenced to imprisonment. While in prison, he was evicted from the flat for non-payment of rent. He had arranged with his sister that the rent should continue to be paid while he was in prison, but she failed to implement the arrangement. It was held that the causal chain connecting his deliberate conduct in committing the offence to his homelessness on release from prison had not been broken. It was accepted that the position might have been different if the arrangement had been implemented for a time but had then broken down.

1   [2002] EWCA Civ 753, [2002] HLR 747, CA. Approved by the Supreme Court in *Haile v Waltham Forest London Borough Council* [2015] UKSC 34, [2015] AC 1471, SC per Lord Reed at [54].

13.154 *Haile v Waltham Forest London Borough Council*[1] involved a case where an assured shorthold tenant ceased to occupy her room in a shared property, complaining of smells from the other residents' cooking. This act would have been sufficient for her to be regarded as having become homeless intentionally. However, by the time of the review decision she had given birth to a baby girl. The consequence of this was that she would no longer have been able to occupy the room in any event as her tenancy agreement would not have permitted her to reside there with her daughter. The Supreme Court accepted that her deliberate act in leaving the accommodation could no longer be regarded as the cause of her current homelessness and that the causal chain had been broken by the birth of her child[2].

1   [2015] UKSC 34, [2015] AC 1471, SC.
2   [2015] UKSC 34, [2015] AC 1471, SC per Lord Reed at [67].

Was the accommodation available for the applicant?

13.155 If the applicant deliberately did (or failed to do) something in consequence of which he or she ceased to occupy accommodation, the next question for consideration is whether the accommodation lost was accommodation that was available for his or her occupation[1].

1   See English Code, para 9.21.

13.156 In HA 1996, Pt 7[1] and H(W)A 2014, Pt 2 the phrase 'available for his occupation' has a special meaning. The statutory definition relates both to the physical availability of the accommodation and to the nature and extent of the applicant's right to occupy it[2]. The same definition is used in determining whether an applicant is 'homeless'. The detail has already been explored in CHAPTER 10. The following paragraphs contain only a brief summary.

1   As amended by HRA 2017, for applications for homelessness assistance made to local housing authorities in England on or after 3 April 2018.
2   HA 1996, s 175(1) and s 176; H(W)A 2014, ss 55(1) and 56. See also English Code, paras 6.5–6.9; Welsh Code, paras 8.6–8.8. See further 10.17–10.65.

13.157 The accommodation must have been available for occupation by the applicant and by any person who normally resided with the applicant as a member of the applicant's family, and also by any person who might reasonably have been expected to reside with the applicant at the date it was lost[1].

1   See HA 1996, s 176 and H(W)A 2014, s 56 for the definition of the applicant's household. See also *R v Wimborne Borough Council ex p Curtis* (1986) 18 HLR 79, QBD; *R v Hammersmith*

and *Fulham London Borough Council ex p O'Sullivan* [1991] EGCS 110, QBD; and *R v Peterborough City Council ex p Carr* (1990) 22 HLR 206, QBD. See also 10.29–10.32.

13.158 The function of this provision is to prevent a finding that the applicant has become homeless intentionally when what the applicant has lost was accommodation that could not actually accommodate his or her household. Frequently, it is applied to split or separated households that have no accommodation in which they can live together. For example:

- A head of household who left his or her home country and took up a hostel room for a single person in the UK will not become homeless intentionally when he or she is later asked to leave that hostel once the family arrives (because the single person's hostel was not accommodation 'available' to the family)[1].

- Two young people living in their respective parental homes may develop a relationship and have a child. If neither set of parents will accommodate their child's partner, neither of the two will become homeless intentionally when the parental home is lost (eg on ejection following a family dispute) because neither partner had accommodation 'available' to accommodate the other[2].

[1]   *R v Westminster City Council ex p Ali* (1983) 11 HLR 83, QBD.
[2]   *R v Peterborough City Council ex p Carr* (1990) 22 HLR 206, QBD.

13.159 However, a father who permitted his three children to leave perfectly satisfactory accommodation that they were occupying with their mother so as to move into his one-room accommodation with him was held to have become homeless intentionally. His deliberate conduct in letting them move in subsequently led to his landlord requiring the family to leave the one room. The distinction between this case and the first example above is that, before the children moved in to live with their father, they did not reside with him and nor was it reasonable to expect that they would do so[1].

[1]   *Oxford City Council v Bull* [2011] EWCA Civ 609, [2011] HLR 35, [2012] 1 WLR 203, CA.

13.160 In summary, the accommodation must have been actually available both for the applicant and any person who normally resided with him or her as a member of his or her family and for any person who might reasonably have been expected to reside with him or her at the date it was lost.

13.161 Even if the local housing authority finds that this limb of the test is satisfied, it cannot find that the applicant has become homeless intentionally unless the other five limbs[1] are also made out.

[1]   See **13.36**.

Would it have been reasonable for the applicant to have continued to occupy the accommodation?

13.162 To reach this stage in the application of the 'becoming homeless intentionally' test, the local housing authority must have satisfied itself that it was by his or her own deliberate act (or failure to act) that the applicant ceased to occupy available accommodation. The last issue to be settled is whether it would (at the point at which the deliberate act was done) have been reasonable for the applicant to have remained in occupation[1]. It cannot be over-emphasised that the question is not 'Was it reasonable for the applicant to leave?' but rather 'Was it reasonable for the applicant to have continued in occupation?'

[1] English Code, para 9.22.

13.163 This reasonableness aspect of the test is the parallel of the part of the definition of 'homelessness' which uses exactly the same rubric[1]. Cases decided on whether an applicant is homeless or not homeless, having regard to the reasonableness of continued occupation, are therefore equally relevant to decisions as to whether a person became homelessness intentionally.

[1] HA 1996, s 175(3); H(W)A 2014, s 55(3). See also English Code, paras 8.18–8.32; Welsh Code, paras 6.23–6.41. See further **10.73–10.124** for a more detailed discussion of this statutory requirement.

13.164 The question of whether accommodation was 'reasonable to continue to occupy' involves consideration of all the circumstances at the time of the applicant's deliberate act or omission, and is not limited to the physical quality of the accommodation that the applicant has ceased to occupy[1].

[1] *R v Broxbourne Borough Council ex p Willmoth* (1989) 22 HLR 118, CA. See *Moran v Manchester City Council, Richards v Ipswich Borough Council* [2008] EWCA Civ 378 per Wilson LJ at [49]–[50]. The case went to the House of Lords, which decided the discrete issue that women's refuges could not be accommodation that was reasonable for an applicant and her household to continue to occupy: *Ali & others v Birmingham City Council, Moran v Manchester City Council* [2009] UKHL 36, [2009] 1 WLR 1506, HL. However, their Lordships did not specifically overrule the list of general considerations set out by Wilson LJ at [49]. See **10.103**.

13.165 When considering whether accommodation was reasonable for the applicant to continue to occupy, a local housing authority is directed by HA 1996, Pt 7[1] and H(W)A 2014, Pt 2 only to the reasonableness of *the applicant* remaining in occupation. But the local housing authority must also consider whether it was reasonable for other members of the applicant's household to continue to occupy the accommodation as an element in determining whether it was reasonable for the applicant to remain in occupation[2]. If there is an issue as to whether the accommodation lost would not have been reasonable for other persons in the household to continue to occupy, the local housing authority must resolve that issue. In *R v Westminster City Council ex p Bishop*[3] the local housing authority was satisfied that it would have been reasonable for the applicant herself to have remained in occupation of the former home, but the court found that the issue of whether it would have been reasonable for her dependent daughter to have remained had not been properly considered by the local housing authority[4]. Rose LJ said:

' . . . accommodation can only be regarded as available for an applicant's occupation if both she and those members of her family who normally live with her can reasonably be expected to occupy it. Accordingly, although I accept that the question of reasonableness of continued occupation within [s 191(1)] has to be looked at in relation to the applicant herself, if, in the present case, it was reasonable for her daughter to leave, it could not, in my view, be said that it was reasonable for the applicant to have remained alone. The daughter's position was, therefore, as it seems to me, of great significance[5].'

1   As amended by HRA 2017, for applications for homelessness assistance made to local housing authorities in England on or after 3 April 2018.
2   See **10.21–10.32.**
3   (1993) 25 HLR 459, CA.
4   *R v Westminster City Council ex p Bishop* (1993) 25 HLR 459, CA. See **10.135.**
5   *R v Westminster City Council ex p Bishop* (1993) 25 HLR 459, CA at 465.

13.166 Accordingly, the English Code advises that, as part of determining whether it was reasonable to have continued to occupy, a local housing authority will find it 'necessary' to consider the circumstances of both the applicant 'and the household' in each case[1].

1   English Code, para 9.22. See also **10.22.**

13.167 There is an important distinction, prescribed by HA 1996, Pt 7[1] and H(W)A 2014, Pt 2, between the test of 'reasonable to continue to occupy' to be applied where an applicant has ceased to occupy accommodation because of *violence* (England) or *abuse* (Wales) and all other cases. Where it is probable that the applicant (or a member of his or her household) would have been subject to violence or abuse if he or she had continued to occupy accommodation, as a matter of law that accommodation cannot be regarded as having been reasonable for the him or her to continue to occupy[2].

1   As amended by HRA 2017, for applications for homelessness assistance made to local housing authorities in England on or after 3 April 2018.
2   HA 1996, s 177(1); H(W)A 2014, s 57(1). *Bond v Leicester City Council* [2001] EWCA Civ 1544, (2002) 34 HLR 6, CA. English Code, paras 21.16–21.20; Welsh Code, paras 8.21–8.26. See **10.79–10.98** and **13.207–13.216.** 'Violence' (whether domestic or otherwise) should be given a broad interpretation, including 'physical violence, threatening or intimidating behaviour and any other form of abuse which, directly or indirectly may give rise to the risk of harm'. See *Yemshaw v Hounslow London Borough Council* [2011] UKSC 3, [2011] 1 WLR 433, [2011] HLR 16, SC, Baroness Hale at [28] quoting the *Practice Direction (Residence and Contact Orders: Domestic Violence (No 2)* [2009] 1 WLR 251 and *Hussain v Waltham Forest London Borough Council* [2015] EWCA Civ 14, [2015] HLR 16, CA. The definition of abuse in H(W)A 2014, s 58(1) reflects this. See **10.83** and **10.95–10.98.**

13.168 In all other cases, including cases of harassment that falls short of violence or abuse, the local housing authority should consider all the circumstances in determining whether it would have been reasonable for the applicant to have continued in occupation. Those circumstances could include:

• the availability or otherwise of alternative remedies to tackle the problem that drove the applicant to leave;
• the possibility of it being reasonable for the applicant to have continued to occupy the accommodation for at least the period it would have taken to arrange alternative accommodation; and
• any other relevant matters.

13.169 The local housing authority is specifically required to consider whether the accommodation that the applicant has ceased to occupy was *affordable* for him or her[1]. Obviously, whether or not accommodation was 'affordable' will be a critical factor where accommodation has been lost by reason of mortgage default or rent arrears[2]. Accommodation is not reasonable for an applicant to continue to occupy if the cost of paying for it would deprive the applicant of the means to provide for 'the ordinary necessities of life'[3]. Care must be taken in determining whether accommodation is affordable. In *Farah v Hillingdon London Borough Council*[4] a finding that the applicant had become homeless intentionally was quashed where it was based on a broad assertion by the local housing authority that the applicant's expenditure was exaggerated and that her accommodation was affordable, without any explanation of which items of expenditure could be reduced or why. A local housing authority that fails to consider affordability when determining whether or not accommodation had been reasonable for the applicant to continue to occupy will find its decision quashed[5]. The application of Children Act 2004, s 11 and the 'best interests of the child' principle will generally be of limited relevance to the evaluation of affordability[6]. The income which an applicant receives from welfare benefits will be of obvious relevance in considering affordability. But where an applicant is in receipt of benefits such as child benefit or child tax credit, there is no rule of law that such benefits are not intended to be used toward housing, or that there is no flexibility within such income for the payment of housing costs[7].

[1]   Homelessness (Suitability of Accommodation) Order 1996, SI 1996/3204; H(W)A 2014, s 57(3)(b). See **10.107** and **18.44–18.46**.
[2]   For example, *Barker v Watford City Council* (2017) July/August *Legal Action*, p 42, County Court at Central London, which involved a finding that the applicant had become homeless intentionally in circumstances where she had lost her accommodation as a result of welfare reforms which left a shortfall between her housing benefit award and her rent. The local housing authority decided that the applicant's property was affordable, and therefore reasonable to continue to occupy, as she could have applied for discretionary housing payments. The decision was quashed on appeal. The local housing authority had failed to make any inquiries to establish whether such an application would succeed or for how long any award would be made.
[3]   *R v Wandsworth London Borough Council ex p Hawthorne* [1994] 1 WLR 1442, CA; and *R v Brent London Borough Council ex p Baruwa* (1997) 29 HLR 915, CA. See English Code, paras 6.28 and 17.45; Welsh Code, paras 8.31–8.32.
[4]   *Farah v Hillingdon London Borough Council* [2014] EWCA Civ 359, [2014] HLR 24, CA.
[5]   *Carthew v Exeter City Council* [2012] EWCA Civ 1913, [2013] HLR 19; *Odunsi v Brent London Borough Council* [1999] CLY 3063, Willesden County Court.
[6]   *Huzrat v Hounslow London Borough Council* [2013] EWCA Civ 1865, [2014] HLR, CA. These principles are more likely to be relevant where the local housing authority has to make an exercise of judgment or discretion as opposed to purely factual decisions. See *Nzolameso v Westminster City Council* [2015] UKSC 22, [2015] HLR 22, SC per Baroness Hale at [25], discussed at **18.52**, and *Mohamoud v Kensington and Chelsea Royal London Borough Council* [2015] EWCA Civ 780, [2015] HLR 38, CA.
[7]   *Samuels v Birmingham City Council* [2015] EWCA Civ 1051, [2016] PTSR 558, CA.

13.170 In the specific case of women's refuges, the House of Lords has held that it would not be reasonable for a woman to continue to occupy a refuge indefinitely. Even if she is asked to leave the refuge because of her own deliberate act, therefore, she should not be found to have become homeless intentionally[1].

[1]   *Ali & others v Birmingham City Council, Moran v Manchester City Council* [2009] UKHL 36, [2009] 1 WLR 1506, HL.

13.171 It will not be reasonable for an applicant to continue to occupy accommodation which has been obtained by deception. In *Chishimba v Kensington and Chelsea Royal London Borough Council*[1] the applicant, a

Namibian national, had obtained accommodation under HA 1996, Pt 7 using a counterfeit passport. Her deception was later uncovered and a possession order was made against her. On a subsequent application for homelessness assistance the local housing authority took the view that she had become homeless intentionally. This decision was upheld on review and on appeal to the county court. The Court of Appeal allowed a second appeal holding that it could not have been reasonable for her to continue to occupy accommodation, which she never had any lawful right to occupy.

1   [2013] EWCA Civ 786, [2013] HLR 34, CA. The Court of Appeal in *Chishimba* approved and applied the earlier case of *R v Exeter City Council ex p Gliddon* (1984) HLR 103, QBD, where the applicants had obtained accommodation by misleading their landlord about their income.

13.172 On the face of it, the question whether it was reasonable for a particular applicant to have continued in occupation is directed to the specific circumstances of that applicant. However, HA 1996, Pt 7[1] and H(W)A 2014, Pt 2 each allow a local housing authority to inject a comparative element by comparing the situation that faces the applicant with the *general circumstances in relation to housing* in its area. A local housing authority, when determining whether it was reasonable for the applicant to have continued in occupation, is permitted (but not required) to have regard to general housing circumstances in its area[2]. This element of comparison is also a feature of the definition of being 'homeless'[3].

1   As amended by HRA 2017, for applications for homelessness assistance made to local housing authorities in England on or after 3 April 2018.
2   HA 1996, s 177(2); H(W)A 2014, s 57(3)(a).
3   See **10.104–10.105**.

13.173 Where the accommodation that the applicant has ceased to occupy was not within the local housing authority's district, and particularly if the accommodation was outside the UK, the question for the local housing authority is not: 'Was the accommodation reasonable to continue to occupy given general housing circumstances prevailing in the area where the accommodation was situated?' Instead, the question is: 'Was the accommodation reasonable to continue to occupy given the general housing circumstances prevailing in our own area?' This necessitates a balancing exercise[1] which should include consideration of the prospects available to the applicant in the accommodation that he or she has ceased to occupy, including employment prospects, the availability of welfare benefits, the applicant's financial position, and the space and arrangement (and any overcrowding) of that accommodation[2]. Strict application of this test could mean that an applicant who ceases to occupy accommodation in an area of acute housing need would be best advised to direct an application for homelessness assistance to an area where the general circumstances in relation to housing are much better, in the hope of then being referred back to the first area once a duty to secure accommodation has been accepted[3].

1   *R v Tower Hamlets London Borough Council ex p Monaf* (1988) 20 HLR 529, CA, and *De Falco v Crawley Borough Council* [1980] QB 460, CA.
2   *R v Tower Hamlets London Borough Council ex p Ojo* (1991) 23 HLR 488, QBD, and *Osei v Southwark London Borough Council* [2007] EWCA Civ 787, [2008] HLR 15, CA.

³ However, judicially developed control measures in relation to the law on referral of applications (see **14.176–14.183**) have made it somewhat more difficult for applicants to expect referral back to the first area by this route.

13.174 Where a local housing authority has elected to take general housing circumstances prevailing in its district into account, the courts will be loath to interfere with its assessment of those circumstances. It is the local housing authority that is in the best position to judge the seriousness of any housing crisis in its district and to determine whether the applicant's particular complaints about his or her previous accommodation took him or her out of the norm of difficult housing circumstances in the district[1].

¹ *R v Brent London Borough Council ex p Bariise* (1999) 31 HLR 50, CA.

13.175 For their part, applicants must be careful not to jump the gun. The question for the local housing authority is: 'Was the accommodation reasonable for the applicant and members of his or her household to continue to occupy at the date of the applicant's deliberate act or omission?'. So an applicant who faces the prospect, perhaps in the relatively near future, that the accommodation may become unreasonable to continue to occupy, would perhaps be best advised to wait until he or she is within 56 days of that situation crystallising and then make an application on the basis that he or she has become threatened with homelessness. However, following the decision in *Haile v Waltham Forest London Borough Council*[1] an applicant who ceases to occupy accommodation which subsequent events would have rendered unreasonable for the applicant to continue to occupy, will not have become homeless intentionally[2].

¹ [2015] UKSC 34, [2015] AC 1471, SC. See **13.100–13.111**.
² In *Magoury v Brent London Borough Council* (2016) February *Legal Action*, p 46, County Court at Central London, a finding that the applicant had become homeless intentionally was quashed where there had been a failure to consider whether she would have become homeless anyway as a result of the benefit cap set under the Welfare Reform Act 2012, Pt 5 rendering the property unaffordable.

13.176 Although the statutory formula appears to suggest that the relevant date, when considering whether it was 'reasonable for him to continue to occupy', is the date when the applicant ceases to be in occupation of the accommodation, the better view is that the test should be applied as at the date of the earlier act or omission (if any) that caused the accommodation to be lost. For example, as at the date of actual eviction, the defaulting mortgage borrower may have faced such a level of repayments as to make it impossible to say that it would be reasonable to have continued in occupation[1]. Nevertheless, the applicant may have become homeless intentionally if it would have been reasonable to have continued in occupation at the date when the property was unwisely remortgaged or the borrowing was increased so that the level of instalments became unmanageable[2].

¹ See English Code, paras 6.29 and 17.45.
² In *Bellamy v Hounslow London Borough Council* [2006] EWCA Civ 535, [2006] HLR 42, CA, the Court of Appeal held that it would have been reasonable for a joint legal owner to remain in the property whilst she contested any application for sale that her co-owner might make.

13.177 The Court of Appeal has held that the question whether it would have been reasonable for the applicant to continue in occupation of particular accommodation should be considered in light of all the facts that occurred *before* the applicant's deliberate act or omission which led to the loss of the accommodation. The local housing authority must ignore later deliberate acts or omissions when deciding whether it was reasonable for the applicant to continue in occupation[1]. Though this approach may require some adjustment following the decision in *Haile v Waltham Forest London Borough Council*[2].

[1] *Denton v Southwark London Borough Council* [2007] EWCA Civ 623, [2008] HLR 11, CA.
[2] [2015] UKSC 34, [2015] AC 1471, SC. See **13.100–13.111**.

13.178 In summary, for an applicant to have become homeless intentionally, the accommodation that he or she was occupying, and lost, must have been reasonable for him or her to continue to occupy. The accommodation must also have been reasonable for anyone who normally resides with the applicant as a member of his or her family and for any other person who might reasonably have been expected to reside with the applicant to continue to occupy. Accommodation cannot have been reasonable for an applicant to continue to occupy if it was probable that continued occupation would have led to violence (England) or abuse (Wales) against the applicant or a member of his or her household. In all other cases, the local housing authority has to make a decision as to whether or not the accommodation was factually reasonable for the applicant and his or her household to continue to occupy, taking account, if it chooses, of the general housing circumstances prevailing in its area.

13.179 The relevant date, when considering whether it was reasonable for the applicant to continue to occupy accommodation, should, in the first instance, be the date of the deliberate act or omission that caused the loss of accommodation[1]. But if events following the cessation of occupation would have rendered the accommodation not reasonable to continue to occupy this may suffice to sever the causal chain[2].

[1] See **13.42–13.94**.
[2] See *Haile v Waltham Forest London Borough Council*. [2015] UKSC 34, [2015] AC 1471, SC discussed at **13.100–13.111**.

13.180 Even if the local housing authority finds that this limb of the test is satisfied, it cannot find that the applicant has become homeless intentionally unless the other five limbs[1] are also made out.

[1] See **13.36**.

ENTERING INTO AN ARRANGEMENT TO CEASE TO OCCUPY ACCOMMODATION

13.181 Until 1997, an applicant could only be considered to have become homeless intentionally by falling foul of the multi-part statutory definition considered at **13.36**. However, HA 1996, s 191(3) introduced a wholly new and separate class of intentional homelessness. If the statutory requirements of that category are met, then the applicant is deemed to have become homeless intentionally without consideration of the six-part definition. For applicants to local housing authorities in Wales this class is contained in H(W)A 2014, s 77(4).

13.182 Under these provisions, if a local housing authority decides that an applicant entered into an arrangement by which he or she was required to leave accommodation, and that the purpose of that arrangement was to enable the applicant to receive homelessness assistance, he or she will have become homeless intentionally[1].

[1]   HA 1996, s 191(3); H(W)A 2014, s 77(4).

13.183 The essential elements are that:

(1)   the applicant is homeless;
(2)   he or she had previously entered into an arrangement under which she or he would be required to leave accommodation;
(3)   the accommodation to which that arrangement applied would have been reasonable to continue to occupy;
(4)   the purpose of the arrangement was to enable the applicant to become entitled to HA 1996, Pt 7[1] or H(W)A 2014, Pt 2 assistance; and
(5)   there is no other good reason for the applicant's present homelessness[2].

[1]   As amended by HRA 2017, for applications for homelessness assistance made to local housing authorities in England on or after 3 April 2018.
[2]   HA 1996, s 191(3); H(W)A 2014, s 77(4).

13.184 The Codes refer, by way of example, to collusion 'with friends or relatives' and 'between landlords and tenants'[1].

[1]   English Code, para 9.28; Welsh Code, para 17.30.

13.185 The statutory provision is obviously directed to preventing collusion to bring about homelessness that would result in HA 1996, Pt 7[1] or H(W)A 2014, Pt 2 duties. Collusion could occur in informal arrangements, between friends or relations, or in the more formal relationship between landlord and tenant. Even if there has been collusion, the applicant will not have become homeless intentionally if the accommodation given up was not reasonable for the applicant to continue to occupy[2]. If the applicant was staying with friends or relatives, the relationship may have broken down to such an extent that the accommodation became unreasonable to continue to occupy.

[1]   As amended by HRA 2017, for applications for homelessness assistance made to local housing authorities in England on or after 3 April 2018.
[2]   See **13.162–13.180**.

13.186 The Codes advise that an 'other good reason' why an applicant may be homeless might include overcrowding, or an obvious breakdown in relations between the applicant and his or her host[1]. In those circumstances, an applicant will not be caught by this provision.

[1]   English Code, para 9.29; Welsh Code, para 17.30.

13.187 Local housing authorities must be satisfied that collusion exists and should not rely on hearsay or unfounded suspicions if they are to find that the applicant became homeless intentionally under this provision. As already noted[1], the provision is hardly ever used in practice by local housing authorities to sustain a decision that the applicant became homeless intentionally, and it can be avoided altogether by ensuring that the application for homelessness assistance is made by someone other than the person who entered into the arrangement.

[1]   See 13.39–13.40.

PARTICULAR SCENARIOS

13.188 This section of the chapter seeks to apply the above analysis of the statutory definition of 'becoming homeless intentionally' to common factual circumstances in which local housing authorities may be called upon to apply those tests. A number of the examples cited turn on the issue of whether the applicant's accommodation was reasonable for him or her to continue to occupy. Readers may find it useful to refer to the more detailed exposition of this topic in CHAPTER 10[1].

[1]   See 10.73–10.134.

Rent or mortgage arrears

13.189 The local housing authority will need to consider why it was that the applicant accrued the rent or mortgage arrears that caused the loss of accommodation. If the applicant had simply refused to pay the rent or mortgage payments and had spent the money elsewhere, that would constitute a deliberate act (spending it) or omission (to pay it towards housing costs) necessary to satisfy the first part of the definition of becoming homeless intentionally[1].

[1]   See *William v Wandsworth London Borough Council* [2006] EWCA Civ 535, [2006] HLR 42, CA; and *Bury Metropolitan Borough Council v Gibbons* [2010] EWCA Civ 327, [2010] HLR 33, CA.

13.190 But the enquiry cannot stop there, because if the accommodation was unaffordable for the applicant, in that he or she could not afford the housing costs as well as meet the ordinary necessities of life, the property would not have been reasonable for the applicant and the members of his or her household to continue to occupy[1]. A local housing authority that fails to inquire into this will have erred in law[2]. What constitute 'the ordinary necessities of life' may vary according to the individual circumstances of each applicant and is a question of fact for the local housing authority to decide. For local housing authorities in England a number of considerations relevant to this assessment are set out in a statutory order[3]. Care must be taken in performing this assessment. In *Farah v Hillingdon London Borough Council*[4] a finding that the applicant had become homeless intentionally was quashed as it was based on a broad assertion by the local housing authority that the applicant's expenditure was exaggerated and that her accommodation is affordable, without any explanation of which items of expenditure could be reduced or why. While a local housing authority must have regard to the relevant passages of the Codes dealing with affordability, explicit reference to each specific passage will not be needed as long as the local housing authority adopts 'the kind of analysis' envisaged by the Codes[5]. The application of Children Act 2004, s 11 and the 'best interests of the child' principle are unlikely to be relevant to the evaluation of affordability[6].

1   Homelessness (Suitability of Accommodation) Order, SI 1996/3204 at APPENDIX 2; H(W)A 2014, s 59(2). English Code, paras 6.28, 9.22 and 17.45; Welsh Code, paras 8.30–8.31. See also *R v Hillingdon London Borough Council ex p Tinn* (1988) 20 HLR 305, QBD; *R v Wandsworth London Borough Council ex p Hawthorne* [1994] 1 WLR 1442, CA; *R v Brent London Borough Council ex p Baruwa* (1997) 29 HLR 915, CA; *Saunders v Hammersmith and Fulham London Borough Council* [1999] CLY 3058, West London County Court; and *Bernard v Enfield London Borough Council* [2001] EWCA Civ 1831, (2002) 34 HLR 46, CA, *Birmingham City Council v Balog* [2013] EWCA Civ 1582, [2014] HLR 14, CA; and **10.102** and **10.107–10.109**. For affordability in relation to suitability, see **18.44–18.46**.
2   *Carthew v Exeter City Council* [2012] EWCA Civ 1913, [2013] HLR 19, CA. See also *Barker v Watford City Council* (2017) *Legal Action July/August*, p 42, County Court at Central London.
3   Homelessness (Suitability of Accommodation) Order, SI 1996/3204.
4   *Farah v Hillingdon London Borough Council* [2014] EWCA Civ 359, [2014] HLR 24, CA.
5   *Birmingham City Council v Balog* [2013] EWCA Civ 1582, [2014] HLR 14, CA per Kitchin LJ at [50].
6   *Huzrat v Hounslow London Borough Council* [2013] EWCA Civ 1865, [2014] HLR, CA. These principles are more likely to be relevant where the local housing authority has to make an exercise of judgment or discretion as opposed to purely factual decisions. See *Nzolameso v Westminster City Council* [2015] UKSC 22, [2015] HLR 22, SC per Baroness Hale at [25], discussed at **18.52–18.56**, and *Mohamoud v Kensington and Chelsea Royal London Borough Council* [2015] EWCA Civ 780, [2015] HLR 38, CA.

13.191 Of course, the two elements of: (i) a deliberate act; and (ii) the reasonableness of continued occupation may overlap. That is particularly likely where the deliberate act of the applicant has itself arguably rendered the accommodation unaffordable. The local housing authority is entitled to consider the applicant's financial position both when he or she first obtained the accommodation, and throughout the occupation of that property. So, for example, if the applicant had been able to afford the mortgage for the accommodation when it was first acquired, but had later taken on an additional loan that became unaffordable, that decision to extend the lending or remortgage the property could properly be described as a deliberate act which, eventually, led to the loss of accommodation[1]. Equally, if the applicant's financial difficulties occurred as a result of his or her raising a secured loan to finance an unsuccessful business venture (which led to inability to meet repayments), the local housing authority would be entitled to consider the prospects of that venture as they appeared at the time that the mortgage was taken out[2]. If the applicant genuinely believed that the business venture would be sound, he or she will have acted in good faith in taking out a mortgage to finance it. However, if that judgment involved an unrealistic degree of optimism or any dishonesty, he or she will not have acted in good faith[3]. Two Court of Appeal decisions have upheld local housing authorities' decisions that the taking out of a mortgage that was unaffordable was a deliberate act which subsequently rendered the applicants homeless and therefore they had become homeless intentionally[4].

1   *R v Barnet London Borough Council ex p Rughooputh* (1993) 25 HLR 607, CA; and *R v Wandsworth London Borough Council ex p Onwudiwe* (1993) 26 HLR 302, CA.
2   *R v Exeter City Council ex p Tranckle* (1994) 26 HLR 244, CA; and *R v Warrington Borough Council ex p Bryant* (2000) October *Legal Action*, p 24, QBD.

3 English Code, para 9.25. See also *R v Hammersmith and Fulham London Borough Council ex p Lusi* (1991) 23 HLR 260, QBD, *Enfield London Borough Council v Najim* [2015] EWCA Civ 319, [2015] HLR 19, CA and **13.56–13.64.**

4 *William v Wandsworth London Borough Council* [2006] EWCA Civ 535, [2006] HLR 42, CA; and *Watchman v Ipswich Borough Council* [2007] EWCA Civ 348, [2007] HLR 33, CA.

13.192 If an applicant was receiving welfare benefits to help with the accommodation costs, the local housing authority should not simply assume that the housing costs were therefore affordable, but should still look at all the circumstances. Even if the applicant failed to use his or her available welfare benefits to pay his or her rent or mortgage, the property might still be unaffordable in any event due to the shortfall between the benefit received and the contractual rent or mortgage payments[1].

1 *R v Shrewsbury and Atcham Borough Council ex p Griffiths* (1993) 25 HLR 613, QBD; *R v Brent London Borough Council ex p Grossett* (1996) 28 HLR 9, CA; *Ahmed v Westminster City Council* (1999) June *Legal Action*, p 24, Central London County Court; and *Odunsi v Brent London Borough Council* [1999] CLY 3063, Willesden County Court.

13.193 If the applicant failed to apply for benefit to which he or she would have been entitled, that would generally be considered to have been a deliberate omission[1]. However, if he or she was genuinely unaware of his or her entitlement to benefit, he or she may not have been guilty of deliberate omission if she or he acted in good faith[2].

1 *Noel v Hillingdon London Borough Council* [2013] EWCA Civ 1602, [2014] HLR 10, CA. However a local housing authority may need to obtain evidence to establish that an entitlement existed. See *Barker v Watford City Council* (2017) July/August *Legal Action*, p 42, Country Court at Central London.

2 *R v Tower Hamlets London Borough Council ex p Saber* (1992) 24 HLR 611, QBD; and *R v Westminster City Council ex p Moozary-Oraky* (1993) 26 HLR 213, QBD; *Bury Metropolitan Borough Council v Gibbons* [2010] EWCA Civ 327, [2010] HLR 33, CA; and *Essex v Birmingham City Council* (2012) August *Legal Action*, p 28, Birmingham County Court. Note that in *F v Birmingham City Council* [2006] EWCA Civ 1427, [2007] HLR 18, CA, a tenant had 'closed her eyes to the obvious' when she gave up a secure tenancy for a private rented tenancy in ignorance of the fact that housing benefit would not cover the whole of the contractual rent and therefore the issue of good faith did not arise. In different circumstances, in *Abdullahi v Brent London Borough Council* [2007] EWCA Civ 885, (2007) October *Legal Action*, p 26, CA, an assured tenant's ignorance of the shortfall between contractual rent and housing benefit was a relevant fact which required consideration of whether she had acted in good faith. For 'relevant fact', see **13.49–13.55.** For 'good faith', see **13.56–13.64.**

13.194 The Codes advise that non-payment of rent due to housing benefit or universal credit delays which were beyond the applicant's control should not generally be considered deliberate[1]. This guidance must refer to situations where a landlord is entitled to a mandatory order of possession, either based on rent arrears[2] or as a result of a notice requiring possession[3], and the court had no discretion to adjourn or refuse a possession order, even though the arrears might be due to be paid by a late determination of housing benefit entitlement[4]. The Welsh Code advises that 'households should not be penalised for the loss of accommodation where it was due to an unavoidable change in their welfare benefits that led to the accommodation becoming unaffordable'[5].

1 English Code, para 9.17(a); Welsh Code, para 17.17(i).
2 Housing Act 1988, Sch 2, Ground 8.
3 Housing Act 1988, s 21.

13.195 Occupiers in financial difficulties would do well to approach the local housing authority for help at an early stage. They certainly cannot assume that, if they leave the accommodation because of financial difficulties, they will not be found to have become homeless intentionally. If they have left, the local housing authority will consider whether leaving the accommodation was the only option available to them, ie whether or not it would have been reasonable to have continued in occupation at the date when they left. In *Viackiene v Tower Hamlets London Borough Council*¹ a joint tenant who turned down the option of assistance from her landlord in replacing her impecunious co-tenant, was found to have acted deliberately when she was subsequently evicted for rent arrears. If the applicant is still in the accommodation then the prevention duty may be engaged². A failure by the local housing authority to properly perform the prevention duty may mean that the applicant should not be regarded as having become homeless intentionally when he or she subsequently leaves the accommodation³. Whether or not this is the case will turn on whether or not it is the applicant's deliberate act or the local housing authority's failure to properly perform the prevention duty which is properly to be regarded as the operative cause of the applicant's cessation of occupation⁴.

¹ [2013] EWCA Civ 1764, [2014] HLR 13, CA.
² HA 1996, s 195(2) as inserted by HRA 2017, s 4(2) for applications for homelessness assistance made to local housing authorities in England on or after 3 April 2018; H(W)A 2014, s 66(1). See **15.87–15.137** and **17.45–17.72**.
³ *Bury Metropolitan Borough Council v Gibbons* [2010] EWCA Civ 327, [2010] HLR 33, CA.
⁴ See **13.119–13.130**.

13.196 The local housing authority is, accordingly, entitled to consider how desperate the applicant's financial position was and whether, for example, his or her creditors were actually threatening to recover loans or obtain possession of the accommodation or not¹. The correct approach has been crisply stated in this way:

> 'As a matter of common sense, it seems to me that it cannot be reasonable for a person to continue to occupy accommodation when they can no longer discharge their fiscal obligations in relation to that accommodation, that is to say, pay the rent and make the mortgage repayments, without so straining their resources as to deprive themselves of the ordinary necessities of life, such as food, clothing, heat, transport and so forth².'

¹ *R v Tower Hamlets London Borough Council ex p Ullah* (1992) 24 HLR 680, QBD; and *R v Westminster City Council ex p Ali* (1997) 29 HLR 580, QBD.
² *R v Hillingdon London Borough Council ex p Tinn* (1988) 20 HLR 305, QBD at 308 per Kennedy J. See, more recently, *Adekunle v Islington London Borough Council* (2009) November *Legal Action*, p 25, Mayor's and City of London County Court.

13.197 A local housing authority is entitled to presume that, where one partner in a household accrued rent or mortgage arrears, the other partner acquiesced in that behaviour[1]. If, however, the applicant asserts that he or she did not acquiesce or puts forward some relevant material, the local housing authority must make inquiries into that assertion[2]. Where the applicant has been actively involved in the family finances, the local housing authority may be entitled to find that he or she acquiesced in a decision not to pay the rent or mortgage arrears, or to over-extend the family budget[3].

1 See the discussion on acquiescence at **13.95–13.99**.
2 *R v Wyre Borough Council ex p Joyce* (1983) 11 HLR 73, QBD; *R v West Dorset District Council ex p Phillips* (1985) 17 HLR 336, QBD; *R v Eastleigh Borough Council ex p Beattie (No 2)* (1985) 17 HLR 168 QBD; *R v East Northamptonshire Borough Council* (1988) 20 HLR 508, QBD; *R v Thanet District Council ex p Groves* (1990) 22 HLR 223, QBD; and *Quinton v East Hertfordshire District Council* (2003) April *Legal Action*, p 27, Luton County Court.
3 *R v Barnet London Borough Council ex p O'Connor* (1990) 22 HLR 486, QBD; and *R v Nottingham City Council ex p Caine* (1996) 28 HLR 374, CA.

13.198 Decisions as to whether or not the applicant could have afforded to pay both the housing costs and the ordinary necessities of life apply equally to accommodation that has been lost outside the UK. If an applicant gives up accommodation overseas in order to migrate to the UK for economic reasons, the question for the local housing authority is whether or not the applicant could have afforded to pay his or her housing costs and the ordinary necessities of life in the overseas accommodation. If not, the accommodation will not have been reasonable for the applicant and members of his or her household to have continued to occupy[1].

1 *R v Islington London Borough Council ex p Bibi* (1996) 29 HLR 498, QBD.

Tenants facing possession proceedings

13.199 Most landlords cannot lawfully obtain possession of tenanted premises without obtaining an order for possession[1]. The legal proceedings may not be the tenant's fault, there may be no defence and the tenant may be anxious to leave before a court hearing, not least to avoid liability for court costs. If the tenant chooses to leave, that may be a perfectly reasonable thing to do, but there may still be a finding that he or she became homeless intentionally if it would have been reasonable to have remained in occupation[2]. The question of whether or not accommodation will be regarded as reasonable to continue to occupy in circumstances where the occupier is facing actual or imminent possession proceedings is discussed in depth at **10.110–11.116**. There are few hard and fast rules[3] but the English Code stresses that it is highly unlikely to be reasonable for an applicant to continue to occupy accommodation beyond the date given for possession in any possession order[4] and that local housing authorities should not consider it reasonable for an applicant to remain in occupation up until the point at which a court issues a warrant or writ to enforce an order for possession[5]. Similarly, accommodation occupied by an applicant facing possession proceedings to which he or she has no defence may well not be reasonable to continue to occupy[6].

1 Protection from Eviction Act 1977, ss 1–3.

2   In *Ugiagbe v Southwark London Borough Council* [2009] EWCA Civ 31, [2009] HLR
    35, CA, an assured shorthold tenant left the premises before the landlord served a Housing Act
    1988, s 21 notice or started possession proceedings. Having been told by the landlord to leave,
    she sought advice from a local housing authority advice centre which told her to go to the
    Homeless Persons Unit who would put her into temporary accommodation. The advice centre
    did not tell her that she had the right to remain in the property until the landlord obtained a
    possession order. Had she gone to the Homeless Persons Unit, she would have been advised
    accordingly. The Court of Appeal found that she was ignorant of a relevant fact (her security
    of tenure) and that her failure to obtain that advice had been in good faith. See also *Bury
    Metropolitan Borough Council v Gibbons* [2010] EWCA Civ 327, [2010] HLR 33, CA.
3   Save that an applicant who is re-applying within two years of acceptance of a private rented
    sector offer (see **16.153–16.179**) who has been served with a valid Housing Act 1988, s 21
    notice will be deemed to be homeless from the expiry of the notice: HA 1996, s 195A(2).
4   English Code, para 6.36.
5   English Code, para 6.37.
6   English Code, para 6.35; Welsh Code, para 8.31.

13.200 Of course, the local housing authority is also entitled to take into account the landlord's reasons for seeking possession[1] and this issue may be critical in determining whether an applicant in these circumstances has become homeless intentionally. If a deliberate act or ommission on the part of the applicant led the landlord to seek possession, and the accommodation was reasonable to continue to occupy at the time of that deliberate act or ommission, then the fact that the subsequent possession proceedings rendered the property unreasonable to continue to occupy will not save the applicant from a finding that he or she became homeless intentionally.

1   See **10.110–11.116** and **13.201–13.206**.

Loss of accommodation as a result of a possession order

13.201 As already referred to[1], most owner-occupiers and tenants of rented accommodation are entitled not to be evicted unless a possession order has been made against them. In one sense, occupiers who leave or are evicted from property as a result of a possession order cannot be said to have become homeless intentionally. They have been required to leave by a court, against their wishes.

1   See **10.56–10.65**.

13.202 However, applying the 'effective cause'[1] and 'reasonable likelihood'[2] tests described above, local housing authorities are entitled to consider the reasons for the bringing of possession proceedings[3]. Possession proceedings themselves fall into three categories:

* claims for possession where the reason is said to be some fault by the tenant;
* claims for possession where there is no obligation on the landlord to show fault; and
* claims for possession brought by lenders.

1   See **13.119–13.123**.
2   See **13.124–13.128**.

3   *Devenport v Salford City Council* (1988) 8 HLR 54, CA; *Bratton v Croydon London Borough Council* [2002] EWCA Civ 1494, (2002) December *Legal Action*, p 22, CA; and *Enfield London Borough Council v Najim* [2015] EWCA Civ 319, [2015] HLR 19, CA.

13.203 The Court of Appeal has declined an invitation to hold that a local housing authority is always obliged to accept what is said on the face of a possession order (such as the correct figures for the arrears)[1]. However, it would be unusual for a local housing authority to come to a different decision from the facts as determined by the judge and recorded on the face of the order. There may, however, be a number of matters that were not raised before or considered by a judge hearing the possession claim that could be relevant to the question of whether the occupier has become homeless intentionally.

1   *Green v Croydon London Borough Council* [2007] EWCA Civ 1367, (2008) *Legal Action*, p 41, CA.

13.204 Where the claim for possession is brought by a landlord who alleges fault on the part of a secure or assured tenant[1], the court hearing the claim for possession will determine whether there has been fault, so as to entitle the landlord to possession, and will normally consider whether it is reasonable to make an order for possession and whether the order should be postponed on terms[2]. A tenant evicted as a result of one of these 'fault-based' grounds for possession may well find that the local housing authority decides that he or she has become homeless intentionally for the same reason that the court decided to make a possession order[3]. Common scenarios include where the tenant has accrued rent arrears or has been found responsible for nuisance behaviour[4]. Normally, in these fault-based claims for possession, the tenant will have had the opportunity to put everything that is relevant to a decision as to whether he or she had become homeless intentionally to the judge hearing the possession claim, and so it would be unusual for there to be additional relevant facts to be put before the local housing authority.

1   Under Housing Act 1985, s 84A (as inserted by the Anti-Social Behaviour, Crime and Policing Act 2014) or Sch 2, Pt 1 (secure tenants) or Housing Act 1988, Sch 2, Grounds 8, 10, 11, 12, 13, 14, 14ZA, 14A, 15, or 17 (assured tenants).
2   The exceptions are Housing Act 1985, s 84A and Housing Act 1988, Sch 2, Ground 8, where the landlord is entitled to possession if the statutory conditions are satisfied: ie the court has no discretion.
3   An exception to this might be where a tenant was evicted for high levels of rent arrears caused by events beyond his or her control.
4   For cases concerning rent arrears, see: *R v Wandsworth London Borough Council ex p Hawthorne* [1994] 1 WLR 1442, CA; *R v Brent London Borough Council ex p Baruwa* (1997) 29 HLR 915, CA; and *R v Newham London Borough Council ex p Campbell* (1994) 26 HLR 183, QBD (where the real cause of homelessness was not the reason for the making of the possession order). For cases concerning nuisance behaviour, see: *Devenport v Salford City Council* (1983) 8 HLR 54, CA; *R v Swansea City Council ex p John* (1983) 9 HLR 56, QBD (where the tenant had acquiesced in her partner's nuisance behaviour and so had become homeless intentionally); *Griffiths v St Helens Metropolitan Borough Council* [2004] 142 Housing Aid Update, St Helens County Court, noted at Madge & Madge-Wyld *Housing Law Casebook* (LAG, 6th edn, 2015), T23.5 (where the tenant had tried to stop her children's misconduct and had not become homeless intentionally); and *Walcot v Lambeth London Borough Council* [2006] EWCA Civ 809, (2006) September *Legal Action*, p 14, CA. In *Sheppard v Richmond-upon-Thames Royal London Borough Council* [2012] EWCA Civ 302, (2012) June *Legal Action*, p 36, CA, the possession order had been made because of the tenant's breach of her tenancy agreement by refusing to allow gas safety checks.

13.205 Where the possession claim has been brought without any need for the landlord to show that the tenant is at fault, such as possession proceedings brought under Housing Act 1988, s 21 against assured shorthold tenants, or proceedings by local housing authorities against introductory, demoted or non-secure tenants, then very little information may have been put before the judge. The local housing authority is entitled to consider the reasons for the landlord's decision to bring (and continue) possession proceedings and, of course, must hear the tenant's side of the story. If those reasons are because of the fault of the tenant, he or she may have become homeless intentionally, even though the possession claim was not brought on any of the fault-based grounds[1].

[1]   *Bratton v Croydon London Borough Council* [2002] EWCA Civ 1494, (2002) December *Legal Action*, p 22, CA. See *Houghton v Sheffield City Council* [2006] EWCA Civ 1799, (2007) March *Legal Action*, p 18, where a local housing authority was wrong to find that a tenant who had reduced arrears from £1,000 to £7, but was still subject to a possession order, had become homeless intentionally.

13.206 Where the occupier is evicted as a result of mortgage foreclosure proceedings, the reason for the bringing of the proceedings will have been the occupier's accrued arrears under the mortgage, and the local housing authority will be entitled to consider the reasons for those arrears and for the decision to take out the mortgage in the first place[1].

[1]   See **13.189–13.198**.

Leaving accommodation because of violence or abuse

Violence or abuse

13.207 As a matter of law, if the local housing authority finds that it is probable that, if the applicant had continued to occupy his or her accommodation, he or she or a member of his or her household would have been subject to violence (England) or abuse (Wales), the accommodation cannot have been reasonable for the applicant and members of his or her household to continue to occupy[1]. The applicant was already 'homeless' and was therefore able to leave without a finding that he or she has become homeless intentionally.

[1]   HA 1996, s 177(1); H(W)A 2014, s 57(1). See also English Code, paras 6.24, 9.22 and 21.16–21.20; Welsh Code, paras 8.21–8.26 and 17.26(i)). *Bond v Leicester City Council* [2001] EWCA Civ 1544, (2002) 34 HLR 6, CA. See **10.79–10.98**.

13.208 For applicants to local housing authorities in England, 'violence' (which includes 'threats of violence') can include sexual or physical abuse from another member of the family[1] or any other form of actual or threatened violence. The courts have held that 'violence' (whether domestic[2] or otherwise) should be given a broad interpretation including 'physical violence, threatening or intimidating behaviour and any other form of abuse which, directly or indirectly may give rise to the risk of harm'[3]. For applicants to local housing authorities in Wales, 'abuse' under H(W)A 2014, s 57 is defined in similar terms[4].

[1]   *R v Northampton Borough Council ex p Clarkson* (1992) 24 HLR 529, QBD.

2   Defined by reference to the relationship between the perpetrator and the victim (HA 1996, s 177(1A) and s 178), see **10.85** and **10.96**.
3   *Yemshaw v Hounslow London Borough Council* [2011] UKSC 3, [2011] 1 WLR 433, [2011] HLR 16, SC, Baroness Hale at [28] quoting the *Practice Direction (Residence and Contact Orders: Domestic Violence (No 2)* [2009] 1 WLR 251 and *Hussain v Waltham Forest London Borough Council* [2015] EWCA Civ 14, [2015] HLR 16, CA. See further **10.83**.
4   H(W)A 2014, s 58(1).

13.209 A failure to pursue legal remedies against the perpetrator because of fears of reprisal, or because the applicant was unaware of the remedies available, should not generally be considered a deliberate omission if the applicant was acting in good faith[1].

1   English Code, paras 21.27 and 21.30 (reminding local housing authorities that such remedies are merely an 'option' and may not be effective); Welsh Code, para 17.26(i).

13.210 Where a woman leaves her accommodation because of domestic violence, and goes to a women's refuge, the refuge will not be reasonable to continue to occupy indefinitely[1]. Consequently, in determining whether she became homeless intentionally, the local housing authority should look back to the reasons why the woman left her accommodation, and whether it was due to violence or abuse, as defined at HA 1996, s 177(1) and H(W)A 2014, s 58(1) respectively.

1   *Ali & others v Birmingham City Council, Moran v Manchester City Council* [2009] UKHL 36, [2009] 1 WLR 1506, HL.

Harassment not amounting to violence or abuse

13.211 If the applicant says that he or she left accommodation due to harassment, on a scale that does not amount to violence or abuse, the local housing authority should determine whether, in all the circumstances, including (if it chooses) taking into account general housing conditions in its district, the accommodation was reasonable for the applicant to continue to occupy[1]. Many of the cases that considered this point were decided before the enactment of the current statutory formula, 'reasonable for him to continue to occupy' in respect of violence or abuse[2]. Those cases now only apply to a lower level of harassment: one that does not amount to violence or abuse.

1   English Code, para 6.39(c).
2   HA 1996, ss 175(3), 177(1); H(W)A 2014, s 55(3), s 57(1). See **10.79–10.98**.

13.212 When considering non-violent, and non-abusive harassment cases, local housing authorities are entitled to make inquiries into whether or not the applicant could have arranged to move away (eg by arranging a sale or through a transfer), and the extent to which it might be reasonable for the applicant to have continued to occupy the accommodation whilst that move was arranged[1]. Similarly, local housing authorities are entitled to consider whether it would have been reasonable for the applicant to have continued to occupy the accommodation with police protection rather than to have simply left[2].

1   *R v Hillingdon London Borough Council ex p H* (1988) 20 HLR 554, QBD, and *R v Newham London Borough Council ex p McIlroy* (1991) 23 HLR 570, QBD.

13.213 Once an applicant has raised the issues of violence or abuse and/or lower-level harassment, the local housing authority has a duty to make all necessary inquiries of all agencies that have been involved[1]. The English Code stresses that great care must be taken in interviewing applicants in these circumstances[2]. The burden rests on the local housing authority and not on the applicant[3]. The local housing authority must make a finding of fact as to whether or not it accepts the applicant's account of events[4]. If significant matters are to be held against the applicant, they should first be put to him or her for comment[5]. Having made that finding of fact, the local housing authority should then consider whether it was probable that continued occupation of the accommodation would have led to violence or abuse against the applicant. If it was probable, the accommodation was not reasonable to continue to occupy and the applicant cannot have become homeless intentionally. If violence or abuse were not probable, the local housing authority should consider whether, in all the circumstances, it was reasonable for the applicant to have continued to occupy the accommodation. If the applicant's account is accepted, the local housing authority should give proper, adequate and intelligible reasons if it concludes that the accommodation was, in any event, reasonable for the applicant to continue to occupy[6].

1   *Hawa Abdilah Ali v Newham London Borough Council* (2000) November *Legal Action*, p 23, Bow County Court; *Purewal v Ealing London Borough Council* [2013] EWCA Civ 1579, [2014] HLR 5.
2   English Code, para 21.23.
3   *R v Barnet London Borough Council ex p Babalola* (1995) 28 HLR 196, QBD.
4   *R v Newham London Borough Council ex p Bones* (1993) 25 HLR 357, QBD. See *Eren v Haringey London Borough Council* [2007] EWCA Civ 1796, (2007) June *Legal Action*, p 38, CA, and *Rodrigues v Barking & Dagenham London Borough Council* [2008] EWCA Civ 271, (2008) June *Legal Action*, p 33, CA, for examples of cases where the local housing authority did not believe the applicant and *H v Southwark London Borough Council* (2014) March *Legal Action*, p 23, Central London Civil Trial Centre, where it was unclear whether the local housing authority had accepted the applicant's account.
5   *R v Brent London Borough Council ex p McManus* (1995) 25 HLR 643, QBD.
6   *R v Westminster City Council ex p Ermakov* [1996] 2 All ER 302, CA.

13.214 The question for the local housing authority is whether it was reasonable for the applicant to continue to occupy the accommodation[1]. If the violence or abuse was directed against a member of the household, rather than the applicant, the accommodation will not have been reasonable for the applicant to continue to occupy[2]. Where the behaviour is harassment which does not amount to violence or abuse, and is directed against a member of the household rather than the applicant, the local housing authority must take this into account. Such accommodation will generally not be reasonable for the applicant to continue to occupy[3].

1   See **10.73–10.134**.
2   HA 1996, s 177(1), H(W)A 2014, s 57(1).
3   *R v Westminster City Council ex p Bishop* (1997) 29 HLR 546, QBD.

13.215 Where the applicant has actually been responsible for violence, abuse, harassment or nuisance behaviour and has lost his or her home as a result, he or she will generally be considered to have committed a deliberate act leading to the loss of accommodation[1]. An applicant who has not directly participated in nuisance behaviour carried out by another household member may have acquiesced if he or she failed to take any steps to prevent the behaviour[2].

1   English Code, para 9.20(f); Welsh Code, para 17.23(vi). See also *Devenport v Salford City Council* (1983) 8 HLR 54, CA, and *R v Swansea City Council ex p John* (1983) 9 HLR 56, QBD.
2   See **13.95–13.99**.

13.216 However, if the accommodation has been lost for any other reason, not related to the applicant's deliberate act, even though the applicant has also been guilty of violent behaviour, he or she will not have become homeless intentionally[1]. If the applicant's own behaviour has led to the harassment, that behaviour can constitute a deliberate act, and he or she could be found to have become homeless intentionally[2].

1   *R v Westminster City Council ex p Reid* (1994) 26 HLR 690, QBD; *R v Leeds City Council ex p Collier* (1998) June *Legal Action*, p 14, QBD; and *Demirtas v Islington London Borough Council* (2003) April *Legal Action*, p 27, Mayor's and City of London County Court.
2   *R v Hammersmith and Fulham London Borough Council ex p P* (1990) 22 HLR 21, QBD.

Exclusion by friends or relatives

13.217 Where people are living with friends or relatives, but are not themselves the tenant or owner of the accommodation, they are usually bare licensees or tenants with no statutory protection[1]. Their host will be entitled to require them to leave, provided that the licence or tenancy is terminated upon reasonable notice, which might be 24 hours or even less.

1   Such as the protection normally provided by the Protection from Eviction Act 1977, s 3.

13.218 The local housing authority is entitled in these cases to consider the reasons for the host's decision to exclude. It is not unusual for guests in these circumstances to have been staying with their hosts in overcrowded accommodation and for the accommodation therefore not to have been reasonable for the guests to continue to occupy[1].

1   See **13.162–13.180** for 'reasonable to continue to occupy' and **13.222–13.227** for unsatisfactory accommodation.

13.219 It might, however, have been the applicant's own conduct that led to the decision to exclude him or her from accommodation that would otherwise have been reasonable for him or her to continue to occupy. In *Denton v Southwark London Borough Council*[1], the Court of Appeal held that a 21-year-old had become homeless intentionally after his mother had excluded him because of his unreasonable conduct. Arden LJ said:

'it is essential when people live together, that they show appropriate respect for each other's needs and follow any requests that one reasonably makes to the other. This is not a case where the mother was laying down inappropriate rules[2].'

The situation would be different if the mother's rules had been unreasonable[3].

1   [2007] EWCA Civ 623, [2008] HLR 11, CA.

2   *Denton v Southwark London Borough Council* [2007] EWCA Civ 623, [2008] HLR 11, CA per Arden LJ at [21].
3   In *White v Southwark London Borough Council* [2008] EWCA Civ 792, (2008) October *Legal Action*, p 37, CA, the Court of Appeal said that actions of children as young as 13 might be 'deliberate acts' and could be considered, even if the applicant was currently an independent young person. See also *Hassan v Brent London Borough Council* [2008] EWCA Civ 1385, (2009) February *Legal Action*, p 32, CA.

13.220 The fact that accommodation was unreasonable to continue to occupy when the applicant left, will not save him or her from a finding that he or she became homeless intentionally if the accommodation had become unreasonable to continue to occupy as a result of his or her behaviour[1].

1   *Denton v Southwark London Borough Council* [2007] EWCA Civ 623, [2008] HLR 11, CA.

13.221 Perpetrators of domestic violence or abuse who are excluded from, or lose, their family home as a result of such violence or abuse could be found to have become homeless intentionally[1].

1   English Code, para 9.20(f); Welsh Code, para 17.23(vi).

Unsatisfactory accommodation

13.222 When considering the accommodation from which the applicant became (or is about to become) homeless, a local housing authority should consider the property's physical conditions and any overcrowding when deciding whether the accommodation was reasonable for the applicant (and members of his or her household) to have continued to occupy[1].

1   English Code, paras 6.26–6.27 and 6.39(a); Welsh Code, para 8.27. See further 10.117–10.123.

13.223 Local housing authorities are entitled to have regard to the conditions prevailing in their district when considering the question of reasonableness of continued occupation[1]. This is the case whether the relevant accommodation is in the local housing authority's own district, elsewhere in the UK, or outside the UK[2]. The local housing authority should not rely on assertions as to the general level of overcrowding or unfitness in its district, but should address itself to the particular degree of overcrowding or unfitness experienced by the applicant[3].

1   HA 1996, s 177(2); H(W)A 2014, s 57(3)(b); *R v Brent London Borough Council ex p Bariise* (1999) 31 HLR 50, CA.
2   *R v Tower Hamlets London Borough Council ex p Monaf* (1988) 20 HLR 529, CA; *R v Tower Hamlets London Borough Council ex p Ojo* (1991) 23 HLR 488, QBD; *R v Tower Hamlets London Borough Council ex p Bibi* (1991) 23 HLR 500, QBD; and *Osei v Southwark London Borough Council* [2007] EWCA Civ 787, [2008] HLR 15, CA.
3   *Mohamoud v Greenwich London Borough Council* (2003) January *Legal Action*, p 23, Woolwich County Court.

13.224 Overcrowding which may render accommodation unreasonable for continued occupation is not restricted to statutory overcrowding[1]. If there are any medical needs arising as a result of the overcrowding or the physical condition of the property, they are relevant to the question of whether it would have been reasonable to continue to occupy.

1   *R v Westminster City Council ex p Alouat* (1989) 21 HLR 477, QBD.

13.225 Even when taking into account general housing conditions in its district, a local housing authority would normally be wrong to conclude that it would have been reasonable for a husband, wife and four children to have continued to occupy one room[1]. However, a local housing authority's decision that it would be reasonable, taking into account the shortage of accommodation in its district, for a separated husband to continue to occupy the same accommodation as his wife and her new boyfriend was not wrong in law[2]. In addition, where three children had satisfactory accommodation with their mother, and their father permitted them to leave that accommodation and live with him in his one-room accommodation (so that his landlord required them to leave), the father's actions in permitting his children to leave satisfactory accommodation so as to reside with him were held to be deliberate and he had become homeless intentionally[3].

1   *R v Hillingdon London Borough Council ex p Islam* [1983] 1 AC 688, HL, although the opposite conclusion was held not to be wrong in law in *R v Tower Hamlets London Borough Council ex p Uddin* (1993) June *Legal Action*, p 15, QBD. See also *R v Harrow London Borough Council ex p Louis* (1997) June *Legal Action*, p 23, QBD; and *R v Kensington and Chelsea Royal London Borough Council ex p Silchenstedt* (1997) 29 HLR 728, QBD.
2   *R v Kensington and Chelsea Royal London Borough Council ex p Moncada* (1996) 29 HLR 289, QBD.
3   *Oxford City Council v Bull* [2011] EWCA Civ 609, [2011] HLR 35, [2012] 1 WLR 203, CA.

13.226 It is not appropriate for a local housing authority to conclude that the applicant has become homeless intentionally where the accommodation had become overcrowded (and is no longer reasonable to continue to occupy) as a result of the applicant's deliberate acts in having more children, or otherwise expanding his or her family[1].

1   *R v Eastleigh Borough Council ex p Beattie (No 1)* (1984) 10 HLR 134, QBD; and *R v Tower Hamlets London Borough Council ex p Hoque* (1993) Times 20 July, QBD.

13.227 Other issues arising on the question of whether accommodation might not have been reasonable to have continued to occupy include the adequacy of fire prevention and escape facilities at the property and/or whether the accommodation was fit for human habitation[1].

1   *R v Kensington and Chelsea Royal London Borough Council ex p Ben-El-Mabrouk* (1995) 27 HLR 564, CA; and *R v Haringey London Borough Council ex p Flynn* (1995) June *Legal Action*, p 21, QBD.

Medical needs

13.228 An applicant's medical needs can render the accommodation that the applicant has ceased to occupy unreasonable to have continued to occupy[1].

1   See further 10.119.

13.229 Where medical issues are raised in relation to whether or not accommodation was reasonable to continue to occupy, the local housing authority is under a duty to inquire into them[1]. The local housing authority must consider the medical needs of the applicant and of all members of his or her household, together with any other factors which may, cumulatively, have resulted in the accommodation having been unreasonable to continue to occupy[2].

1   *R v Wycombe District Council ex p Homes* (1990) 22 HLR 150, QBD. The Welsh Code advises that local housing authorities should also consider a person's vulnerability: paras 17.17(iii).
2   *R v Westminster City Council ex p Bishop* (1993) 25 HLR 459, CA.

13.230 It has been held that where an applicant leaves accommodation that he or she anticipates will in the future become unreasonable to continue to occupy (such as where a pregnant applicant has been told that the property will not be suitable for her baby), he or she may still have become homeless intentionally if, at the particular time when the applicant left, the property was then reasonable to continue to occupy at least for some further period[1]. It is likely that such cases will be decided differently following the decision of the Supreme Court in *Haile v Waltham Forest London Borough Council*[2]. A supervening event, following the loss of accommodation, which would have rendered the accommodation unreasonable to continue to occupy will be sufficient to break the causal chain between the applicant's deliberate act and his or her current homelessness[3].

1   *R v Brent London Borough Council ex p Yusuf* (1997) 29 HLR 48, QBD; but see also *R v Medina District Council ex p Dee* (1992) 24 HLR 562, QBD.
2   [2015] UKSC 34, [2015] AC 1471, SC.
3   See **13.133–13.154**.

13.231 The location of the accommodation and its effect on the applicant's state of health, or the health of members of his or her household, can be relevant and can render accommodation not reasonable for continued occupation, although in making its assessment the local housing authority would be entitled to take into account general housing conditions in its own area[1].

1   *R v Waltham Forest London Borough Council ex p Green* (1997) December *Legal Action*, p 15, QBD.

13.232 The question for the local housing authority is not whether an applicant's medical needs, or those of his or her family members, would be better served elsewhere, but whether their medical needs rendered the accommodation unreasonable to continue to occupy at the date when the applicant left it[1].

1   *R v Wandsworth London Borough Council ex p Nimako-Boateng* (1984) 11 HLR 95, QBD.

Employment and other social or economic prospects

13.233 The opportunities for employment (and any other financial prospects) that were available to the applicant at the accommodation may need to be taken into account in determining whether it would have been reasonable for him or her to have continued to occupy it[1]. Relevant matters may include employment prospects, any available capital or savings, debts, the availability of social security benefits and any other means of support, as well as the extent to which the applicant was socially isolated and any effect on his or her health as a result[2].

¹ *R v Kensington and Chelsea Royal London Borough Council ex p Bayani* (1990) 22 HLR 406, CA.

² *R v Hammersmith and Fulham London Borough Council ex p Duro-Rama* (1983) 9 HLR 71, QBD; *R v Kensington and Chelsea Royal London Borough Council ex p Cunha* (1989) 21 HLR 16, QBD; *R v Camden London Borough Council ex p Aranda* (1997) 30 HLR 76, CA; *R v Camden London Borough Council ex p Cosmo* (1997) 30 HLR 817, QBD; *R v Wandsworth London Borough Council ex p Dodia* (1998) 30 HLR 562, QBD; *Kacar v Enfield London Borough Council* (2001) 33 HLR 5, CA; *Mohammed v Waltham Forest London Borough Council* (2002) October *Legal Action*, p 30, Bow County Court (permission to appeal refused by CA at [2002] EWCA Civ 1241, (2002) December *Legal Action*, p 22); and *Aw-Aden v Birmingham City Council* [2005] EWCA 1834, (2006) July *Legal Action*, p 29, CA.

13.234 Frequently, cases on this point will relate either to applicants migrating to the UK from elsewhere in the world for economic reasons, or to UK residents deciding to emigrate and then returning to the UK, again for economic reasons. The question for the local housing authority is not whether it was reasonable for the applicant to seek to live in (or return to) the UK, but rather whether it would have been reasonable to have continued to occupy the accommodation overseas. Local housing authorities should avoid decisions containing such phrases as 'you brought your family to the UK without making reasonable provision for their accommodation', as they suggest that the wrong issue is being addressed. The true focus of inquiry is whether it would have been reasonable for the applicant and his or her household to have remained in their accommodation overseas. The issue for the local housing authority is not why the applicant has left a particular country to come to the UK, but why he or she has left the particular accommodation in that country[1].

¹ *R v Westminster City Council ex p Guilarte* (1994) June *Legal Action*, p 13, QBD.

13.235 Where the applicant raises the issue of the lack of employment prospects if he or she had continued to occupy his or her previous accommodation, the local housing authority is bound to make inquiries into that issue to see whether it would in fact have been reasonable for the applicant to have remained in occupation[1].

¹ *Bowen v Lambeth London Borough Council* (1999) December *Legal Action*, p 22, Lambeth County Court; and *R v Westminster City Council ex p Augustin* (1993) 25 HLR 281, CA.

13.236 If the applicant has lost tied accommodation as a result of his or her employment having come to an end, the local housing authority is entitled to consider whether his or her deliberate act or omission (in resigning or on being dismissed for misconduct) led to the loss of employment and hence the loss of accommodation[1]. Even if it finds such a deliberate act or omission, it must of course go on to consider whether the accommodation was available to the applicant and reasonable for him or her to have continued to occupy.

¹ English Code, para 9.20(g); Welsh Code, para 17.23(vii). See also *R v Kyle and Carrick District Council ex p Speck* 1993 GWD 1566, OH.

Ex-prisoners

13.237 The courts have held that the commission of a criminal offence, where the reasonably likely result is that the applicant will be sent to prison, can constitute a deliberate act as a consequence of which the applicant's accommodation may have been lost. As a result, local housing authorities are entitled to find that a prisoner who loses his or her accommodation during the period of imprisonment because of inability to keep up payments for an unoccupied home has become homeless intentionally[1]. This conclusion was held not be wrong in law even in the case of a prisoner who made arrangements with his sister that she would pay the rent and a contribution to the arrears (required under a suspended possession order) during his sentence, when she then failed to honour the agreement[2].

1   *R v Hounslow London Borough Council ex p R* (1997) 29 HLR 939, QBD; and *Minchin v Sheffield City Council* (2000) Times, 26 April, CA. In *Minchin v Sheffield City Council*, the fact that the applicant had moved house after the commission of offences was irrelevant to her subsequently being found to have become homeless intentionally. In *Quaid v Westminster City Council* (2008) February *Legal Action*, p 41, Central London County Court, the applicant had not become homeless intentionally because he had committed offences when street homeless. It was not reasonably likely at the time that he had committed the offences that he would lose accommodation acquired after the offences had been committed. See also English Code, paras 23.21–23.22.
2   *Stewart v Lambeth London Borough Council* [2002] EWCA Civ 753, [2002] 34 HLR 40, CA.

13.238 The Welsh Code advises that applicants who have just served a prison sentence and who find themselves homeless on release should not be considered to have become homeless intentionally unless the offences were themselves breaches of their previous tenancy agreement and led to the loss of their accommodation[1].

1   Welsh Code, para 17.26(ii).

Becoming homeless intentionally from accommodation provided under the prevention or relief duties

13.239 The amendments to HA 1996, Pt 7 introduced by the HRA 2017[1] include two important new duties:

- the HA 1996, s 195(2)[2] prevention duty, to take reasonable steps to help the applicant secure that suitable accommodation does not cease to be available for his or her occupation; and
- the HA 1996, s 189B(2)[3] relief duty, to take reasonable steps to help the applicant secure that suitable accommodation becomes available for his or her occupation for at least six months.

Neither of these duties requires a local housing authority to accommodate an applicant. However, a local housing authority has a *power* to provide accommodation under either of these duties[4].

1   For applications for homelessness assistance made to local housing authorities in England on or after 3 April 2018.
2   As amended by HRA 2017, s 4(2) for applications for homelessness assistance made to local housing authorities in England on or after 3 April 2018. See **15.87–15.137**.

³ As inserted by HRA 2017, s 5(2), for applications for homelessness assistance made to local housing authorities in England on or after 3 April 2018. See **15.138–15.189**.

⁴ See HA 1996, s 205(3) as inserted by HRA 2017, s 6 for applications for homelessness assistance made to local housing authorities in England on or after 3 April 2018.

13.240 Where accommodation *is* provided, HA 1996, Pt 7¹ provides that the duty in question shall come to an end where the applicant becomes homeless intentionally from that accommodation².

¹ As amended by HRA 2017, for applications for homelessness assistance made to local housing authorities in England on or after 3 April 2018.

² HA 1996, s 195(8)(e) (as amended by HRA 2017, s 4(2) for applications for homelessness assistance made to local housing authorities in England on or after 3 April 2018), see **15.123–15.125**; HA 1996, s 189B(7)(d) (as inserted by HRA 2017, s 5(2) for applications for homelessness assistance made to local housing authorities in England on or after 3 April 2018), see **15.174–15.177**.

13.241 It remains to be seen how frequently, if at all, applicants will be found to have become homeless intentionally from such accommodation. There are a number of reasons why such findings may be rare. This is acknowledged in the English Code, para 14.30 of which suggests that 'there will be very limited circumstances in which the duty is brought to an end' in this manner.

13.242 First, the financial pressures on local housing authorities may mean that discretionary accommodation is provided under these provisions relatively rarely. It is to be remembered that an applicant who is owed the HA 1996, s 195(2)¹ prevention duty has not yet become homeless and that an applicant who is owed the HA 1996, s 189B(2)² relief duty and appears to have a priority need will already have been provided with interim accommodation under HA 1996, s 188(1)³. These two cohorts will not, therefore, have an immediate need for accommodation. In view of this, the number of applicants who are owed the HA 1996, s 195(2)⁴, or HA 1996, s 189B (2)⁵, relief duty, and whom the local housing authority consider it appropriate or necessary to accommodate, is likely to be small.

¹ As amended by HRA 2017, s 4(2) for applications for homelessness assistance made to local housing authorities in England on or after 3 April 2018. See **15.87–15.137**.

² As inserted by HRA 2017, s 5(2), for applications for homelessness assistance made to local housing authorities in England on or after 3 April 2018. See **15.138–15.189**.

³ As amended by HRA 2017, s 5(4) for applications for homelessness assistance made to local housing authorities in England on or after 3 April 2018. It is well-established that an applicant who is occupying interim accommodation under HA 1996, s 188(1) is still homeless: See **10.13**.

⁴ As amended by HRA 2017, s 4(2) for applications for homelessness assistance made to local housing authorities in England on or after 3 April 2018. See **15.87–15.137**.

⁵ As inserted by HRA 2017, s 5(2), for applications for homelessness assistance made to local housing authorities in England on or after 3 April 2018. See **15.138–15.189**.

13.243 Second, accommodation provided under the HA 1996, s 195(2)¹ prevention duty or HA 1996, s 189B(2)² relief duty is likely to be short term in nature, and therefore probably precarious in tenure. This is evident from the fact that these duties are typically expected to come to an end after 56 days³ and so accommodation provided in performance of the duty would not be expected to last longer than this. Accommodation of this nature is relatively unlikely to be considered be reasonable to continue to occupy[4].

1 As amended by HRA 2017, s 4(2) for applications for homelessness assistance made to local housing authorities in England on or after 3 April 2018. See **15.87–15.137**.
2 As inserted by HRA 2017, s 5(2), for applications for homelessness assistance made to local housing authorities in England on or after 3 April 2018. See **15.138–15.189**.
3 HA 1996, s 195(8)(b) (as amended by HRA 2017, s 4(2) for applications for homelessness assistance made to local housing authorities in England on or after 3 April 2018), see **15.110–15.112**. HA 1996, s 189B(4) and (7)(b) (as inserted by HRA 2017, s 5(2) for applications for homelessness assistance made to local housing authorities in England on or after 3 April 2018), see **15.166–15.168**.
4 See **13.162–13.180**. Pursuant to HA 1996, s 191, a person can only become homeless intentionally from accommodation which is available for his occupation and which it would have been reasonable for him to continue to occupy.

13.244 Third, and by the same token, if by any chance accommodation *were* to be provided pursuant to either of these duties for a longer period, and that accommodation was both suitable and likely to be available for six months or more, then that by itself would have been sufficient to bring the duty in question to an end[1]. This precludes the possibility of the duty subsequently being brought to an end by the applicant becoming homeless intentionally.

1 HA 1996, s 195(8)(a) (as amended by HRA 2017, s 4(2) for applications for homelessness assistance made to local housing authorities in England on or after 3 April 2018), see **15.105–15.109**; HA 1996, s 189B(7)(a) (as inserted by HRA 2017, s 5(2) for applications for homelessness assistance made to local housing authorities in England on or after 3 April 2018), see **15.162–15.165**. See English Code, para 14.30: 'In most cases where such accommodation has been secured the housing authority will already have notified the applicant that the prevention or relief duty has come to an end'. The Code goes on to suggest that the applicant might become homeless intentionally in these circumstances if he or she surrendered or was excluded from the accommodation prior to being notified that the provision of accommodation had brought the duty to an end.

13.245 Fourth, and finally, in connection with the HA 1996, s 189B(2)[1] relief duty there is a policy consideration which might make it necessary to interpret the legislation is such a way as to make it *impossible* for an applicant to become homeless intentionally from accommodation provided under this duty. It is well-established that an applicant who is occupying interim accommodation under HA 1996, s 188(1)[2] is still to be regarded as homeless[3]. One of the reasons why the legislation is interpreted in this way is to avoid absurdity. If an applicant were not to be considered homeless then he or she would 'lose the protection of Pt 7'[4] since the interim accommodation duty is a temporary expedient to accommodate applicants who appear to be homeless and eligible and have a priority need, while the local housing authority makes the inquiries necessary to determine whether a longer-term accommodation duty is owed. All of this would become redundant were the applicant to lose his or her status as homeless once placed in interim accommodation. The same points might be made in respect of the HA 1996, s 189B(2)[5] relief duty. If the accommodation offered is suitable and reasonably likely to be available for at least six months, the HA 1996, s 189B(2)[6] relief duty can be brought to an end under HA 1996, s 189B(7)(a)[7]. If it is not, then the applicant remains entitled to the benefit of the HA 1996, s 189B(2)[8] relief duty. How, though, can a local housing authority meaningfully be expected to take reasonable steps to relieve the homelessness of someone who is no longer regarded as homeless? And how could any further duty be owed upon the relief duty coming to an end?

1 As inserted by HRA 2017, s 5(2), for applications for homelessness assistance made to local housing authorities in England on or after 3 April 2018. See **15.138–15.189**.

2 As amended by HRA 2017, s 5(4) for applications for homelessness assistance made to local housing authorities in England on or after 3 April 2018.

3 See **10.13**.

4 *R (Alam) v Tower Hamlets London Borough Council* [2009] EWHC 44, (2009) March *Legal Action*, p 24 at [15].

5 As inserted by HRA 2017, s 5(2), for applications for homelessness assistance made to local housing authorities in England on or after 3 April 2018. See **15.138–15.189**.

6 As inserted by HRA 2017, s 5(2), for applications for homelessness assistance made to local housing authorities in England on or after 3 April 2018. See **15.138–15.189**.

7 As amended by HRA 2017, s 4(2) for applications for homelessness assistance made to local housing authorities in England on or after 3 April 2018.

8 As inserted by HRA 2017, s 5(2), for applications for homelessness assistance made to local housing authorities in England on or after 3 April 2018. See **15.138–15.189**.

13.246 Given this, in order to avoid absurdity[1] it might be necessary to adopt an interpretation of the HA 1996, s 189B(2)[2] relief duty which has the result that an applicant is still to be regarded as homeless whilst in interim accommodation provided under the HA 1996, s 189B(2)[3] relief duty. The consequence of this would be that an applicant can *never* become homeless intentionally from such accommodation[4].

1 Legislation should generally be construed so as to avoid absurdity. See *Bennion on Statutory Interpretation* (Lexis Nexis, 6th edn 2013), at para 312.

2 As inserted by HRA 2017, s 5(2), for applications for homelessness assistance made to local housing authorities in England on or after 3 April 2018. See **15.138–15.189**.

3 As inserted by HRA 2017, s 5(2), for applications for homelessness assistance made to local housing authorities in England on or after 3 April 2018. See **15.138–15.189**.

4 A court might be reluctant to adopt such an interpretation lightly as that would mean that HA 1996, s 189B(7)(d) is redundant. This would run counter to the well-established principle of 'effective interpretation' which stipulates that legislation must be construed so that its provisions are given force and effect rather than being rendered nugatory: *Bennion on Statutory Interpretation* (Lexis Nexis, 6th edn 2013), at para 198.

13.247 The answer to this conundrum is by no means obvious. But, in view of the practical reality that accommodation is likely to be provided under the HA 1996, s 195(2)[1] prevention duty or HA 1996, s 189B(2)[2] relief duty only rarely, it may be that this issue is of no more than academic interest.

1 As amended by HRA 2017, s 4(2) for applications for homelessness assistance made to local housing authorities in England on or after 3 April 2018. See **15.87–15.137**.

2 As inserted by HRA 2017, s 5(2), for applications for homelessness assistance made to local housing authorities in England on or after 3 April 2018. See **15.138–15.189**.

Accommodation withdrawn by a local housing authority on completion of its homeless duty

13.248 An applicant is still homeless while occupying interim accommodation[1] under HA 1996, s 188(1)[2] or H(W)A 2014, s 68(1)[3]. As such he or she cannot be regarded as having become homeless intentionally from any such accommodation. Similarly accommodation provided by the local housing authority under the various short-term accommodation duties[4] or powers[5], may well be of such limited duration and precarious tenure that it is cannot properly be regarded as reasonable for the applicant to continue to occupy[6].

1. See **10.13**.
2. As amended by HRA 2017, s 5(4) for applications for homelessness assistance made on or after 3 April 2017.
3. *R (Alam) v Tower Hamlets London Borough Council* [2009] EWHC 44, (2009) March *Legal Action*, p 24. In *Ali & others v Birmingham City Council, Moran v Manchester City Council* [2009] UKHL 36, [2009] 1 WLR 1506, HL, Manchester City Council accepted that an applicant remained homeless while occupying interim accommodation provided under HA 1996, s 188(1): see Baroness Hale at [55]. In *O'Callaghan v Southwark London Borough Council* (2010) May *Legal Action*, p 23, Lambeth County Court, an applicant who was occupying interim accommodation secured under the local housing authority's duty at HA 1996, s 188(1) could not have become homeless intentionally when she subsequently lost the accommodation, because she had remained 'homeless' throughout the period of occupation of the accommodation.
4. HA 1996, s 190(2)(a) as amended by HRA 2017, s 5(5) for applications for homelessness assistance made on or after 3 April 2017 (see **16.81–16.93**); HA 1996, s 199A(2) as inserted by HRA 2017, s 5(9) for applications for homelessness assistance made on or after 3 April 2017 (see **16.217–16.224**); HA 1996, s 200(1) as amended by HRA 2017, s 5(10) for applications for homelessness assistance made on or after 3 April 2017 (see **16.225–16.232**); and H(W)A 2014, s 82(1) (see **17.138–17.145**).
5. HA 1996, s 188(3) (see **16.233–16.257**), s 199A(6) as inserted by HRA 2017, s 5(9) for applications for homelessness assistance made on or after 3 April 2017 (see **16.223–16.224**), s 200(5) (see **16.231–16.231**), and s 204(4) (see **16.258–16.277**); H(W)A 2014, s 69(11) (see **17.134**), s 73 (see **17.79**), s 82(6) (see **17.138–17.145**) and s 88(5) (see **17.135–17.137**).
6. See **13.162–13.180**.

13.249 However, where an applicant loses accommodation provided under the HA 1996, s 193(2)[1] or H(W)A 2014, s 75[2] main housing duty or the HA 1996, s 193C(4)[3] accommodation duty owed to those who have deliberately and unreasonably refused to cooperate, the question may subsequently arise of whether that accommodation was lost as a result of the deliberate act or omission of the applicant[4].

1. See **16.94–16.199**.
2. See **17.146–17.197**.
3. As inserted by HRA 2017, s 7(1) for applications for homelessness assistance made to local housing authorities in England on or after 3 April 2018. See **16.200–16.216**.
4. For repeat applications see **9.77–9.91**. Acceptance of the application, however, does not prevent a local housing authority from determining that the applicant has become homeless intentionally. For such a scenario, see *R (Dragic) v Wandsworth London Borough Council* [2012] EWHC 1241 (Admin), (2012) July *Legal Action*, p 42, Admin Ct.

13.250 That was the situation in the landmark case of *R v Brent London Borough Council ex p Awua*[1]. The House of Lords held that there was no requirement that the accommodation lost by a person who had become homeless intentionally should have been settled accommodation. As a result, Ms Awua had become homeless intentionally because she had lost the accommodation temporarily provided to her under the main housing duty as a result of her having refused an offer of other accommodation[2].

1. [1996] AC 55, (1995) 27 HLR 453, HL.
2. See *Amanuel v Southwark London Borough Council* [2007] EWCA Civ 854, (2007) September *Legal Action*, p 18, CA; and *Ali v Haringey London Borough Council* [2008] EWCA Civ 132, (2008) April *Legal Action*, p 34, CA. Care must be taken to identify the reason for the loss of the accommodation: see *Bolah v Croydon London Borough Council* (2008) February *Legal Action*, p 40, Lambeth County Court. In *Keita v Southwark London Borough Council* [2008] EWCA Civ 963, (2008) October *Legal Action*, p 38, CA, the accommodation lost had not been provided under homelessness duties, but was terminated by the landlord charity after the applicant had refused an offer of accommodation. Where young

people aged 16 or 17 years old refuse offers of accommodation provided under Children Act 1989, s 20 duties, statutory guidance advises that they should not be considered to have become homeless intentionally when accommodation is subsequently withdrawn as a result of that refusal: *Prevention of homelessness and provision of accommodation for 16 and 17 year old young people who may be homeless and/or require accommodation* (MHCLG and DofE, April 2018), para 4.21; *Social Services and Well-being (Wales) Act 2014 Pt 6 Code of Practice (Looked After and Accommodated Children)* (Welsh Government, 2015), para 587.

13.251 This type of situation can easily arise as the HA 1996, s 193(2)[1] and H(W)A 2014, s 75[2] main housing duty and the HA 1996, s 193C(4)[3] accommodation duty owed to those who have deliberately and unreasonably refused to cooperate, can all be brought to an end as a result of an applicant's refusal to accept certain types of offer of suitable accommodation[4]. An applicant faced with such an offer but concerned about the suitability of the accommodation would be well-advised to accept the offer accommodation and then request a review[5] of its suitability, lest he or she find that the duty owed to him or her has come to an end and that any subsequent application for homelessness assistance results in a finding that he or she became homeless intentionally. However, in that scenario, the local housing authority could not simply infer from the refusal that the applicant had become homeless intentionally. It would still need to satisfy itself that the six elements of the statutory test were satisfied[6].

[1] See **16.94–16.199**.
[2] See **17.146–17.197**.
[3] As inserted by HRA 2017, s 7(1) for applications for homelessness assistance made to local housing authorities in England on or after 3 April 2018. See **16.200–16.216**.
[4] See **16.94–16.199, 17.146–17.197** and **16.200–16.216**.
[5] See **Chapter 19**.
[6] See **13.36**.

WALES: DECIDING TO 'HAVE REGARD TO INTENTIONALITY'

13.252 For applicants to local housing authorities in Wales, the foregoing sections of this chapter will *only* be of relevance if a decision has been made by the local housing authority to whom the application is made, to 'have regard to intentionality'[1]. If no such decision has been made, the question of whether an applicant has become homeless intentionally will not arise for consideration[2]. This is one of the key innovations of H(W)A 2014, Pt 2. The explanatory notes to H(W)A 2014 state that:

'It is intended that local authorities will be allowed to apply the intentionality test for all applicants, or none, or for certain priority need categories. This will allow for a gradual reduction in the application of intentionality to vulnerable groups[3].'

[1] H(W)A 2014, s 78. Brought into force on 1 July 2015 by Housing (Wales) Act 2014 (Commencement No 3 and Transitory, Transitional and Saving Provisions) Order 2015, SI 2015/1272 (W 88), art 3 but subject to para 29 of the Schedule to SI 2015/1272.
[2] This feature of H(W)A 2014, Pt 2 might conceivably provide a motivation for applicants to direct their applications to local housing authorities in Wales rather than England. However, at the time of writing it is understood that most local housing authorities in Wales have signalled their intention to 'have regard to intentionality' to some extent.
[3] *Housing (Wales) Bill, Explanatory Memorandum* (Welsh Government, November 2013) p 162. See also Welsh Code, para 17.1.

13.253 In order to have regard to whether an applicant has become homeless intentionally for the purposes of H(W)A 2014, ss 68 and 75, first, the Welsh Ministers must, by regulations, specify a category or categories of applicant for that purpose[1]. The relevant regulations are the Homelessness (Intentionality) (Specified Categories) (Wales) Regulations 2015[2] which came into force on 27 April 2015[3]. The categories mirror precisely the categories of persons who may have a priority need under H(W)A 2014, s 70[4].

[1]   H(W)A 2014, s 78(1).
[2]   SI 2015/1265 (W 85).
[3]   Homelessness (Intentionality) (Specified Categories) (Wales) Regulations 2015, SI 2015/1265 (W 85), reg 1(2).
[4]   SI 2015/1265 (W 85), reg 2; Welsh Code, para 17.6. See **12.195–12.228** for the priority need categories. The reason that the categories correspond is that the issue of intentionality can only be relevant to those who have a priority need, by virtue of H(W)A 2014, s 75(2) and (3). See **17.146–17.197**.

13.254 A local housing authority is then entitled to have regard to whether an applicant has become homeless intentionally if and only if three conditions are satisfied:

(1)   the applicant falls within a category specified in the regulations[1];
(2)   the local housing authority has decided to have regard to whether or not applicants in that category[2] have become homeless intentionally[3]; and
(3)   the authority has published a notice of that decision which specifies the category[4]. The written notice must specify the list of specified categories of applicants and the reasons for having regard to those categories and be provided to the Welsh Ministers no less than 14 days prior to the implementation of the decision[5]. The notice must also be published on the authority's website (if it has one), and at the offices where homelessness applications are received, no less than 14 days prior to the implementation of the decision[6]. A local housing authority must also take reasonable steps to notify its decision to applicants and their advisers, and to such public or local authorities, voluntary organisations or other persons as it considers appropriate, and must make a copy of the notice of its decision available, without charge, to applicants who will be affected by the decision[7].

[1]   H(W)A 2014, s 78(2)(a).
[2]   The local housing authority is free to be selective in choosing which of the categories it wishes to have regard to. It is not a question of 'all or nothing'. See H(W)A 2014, s 78(2)(a).
[3]   H(W)A 2014, s 78(2)(a).
[4]   H(W)A 2014, s 78(2)(b).
[5]   SI 2015/1265 (W 85), reg 3; Welsh Code, para 17.8.
[6]   SI 2015/1265 (W 85), reg 4; Welsh Code, para 17.9.
[7]   SI 2015/1265 (W 85), reg 4.

13.255 Whether or not such a decision is made is a matter of discretion for each local housing authority: a local housing authority is not obliged to make a decision to 'have regard to intentionality'[1]. But where such a decision has been made, and where a local housing authority has published a notice under H(W)A 2014, s 78(3), the local housing authority must consider whether the applicant has become homeless intentionally in every case[2] unless and until a decision is taken to stop having regard to whether or not applicants falling into the category specified in the notice have become homeless intentionally[3] and a notice of the decision specifying the category has been published[4]. Where a local housing authority has not made such a decision, or has not published a notice of that decision in accordance with H(W)A 2014, s 78(2)(b) and Homelessness (Intentionality) (Specified Categories) (Wales) Regulations 2015, regs 3 and 4, then the local housing authority is not entitled to have regard to whether the applicant became homeless intentionally[5].

1   H(W)A 2014, s 78(2).
2   H(W)A 2014, s 78(4). The principle behind this provision is that all applicants must be treated alike: there is no power to make an exception and overlook whether a particular applicant has become homeless intentionally.
3   H(W)A 2014, s 78(3)(a).
4   H(W)A 2014, s 78(3)(b).
5   H(W)A 2014, s 78(2).

Chapter 14

REFERRAL BETWEEN LOCAL HOUSING AUTHORITIES

Contents

INTRODUCTION

14.1 The referral provisions in the Housing Act 1996 (HA 1996), Pt 7 as amended by the Homelessness Reduction Act 2017 (HRA 2017)[1] and the Housing Wales Act 2014 (H(W)A 2014), Pt 2 ensure that responsibility for accommodating those who are homeless is spread fairly between local housing authorities. Without a coherent set of rules governing which local housing

675

authority owes a housing duty, homeless applicants would end up in the same position as their predecessors under the Poor Laws, when:

> ' . . . each parish was responsible for the relief of those who were poor and unable to work. When a poor man moved from one parish to another, the question arose: which parish was responsible? The disputes, Blackstone tells us, "created an infinity of expensive lawsuits between contending neighbourhoods, concerning those settlements and removals"[2].'

[1] For applications for homelessness assistance made to local housing authorities in England on or after 3 April 2018: Homelessness Reduction Act 2017 (Commencement and Transitional and Savings Provisions) Regulations 2018, SI 2018/167, reg 3.

[2] *R v Slough Borough Council ex p Ealing London Borough Council* [1981] QB 801, CA at 808 per Lord Denning, cited in *R (J) v Worcestershire County Council* [2013] EWHC 3845 (Admin), [2014] PTSR 537, Admin Ct at [27] per Holman J.

14.2 In order to avoid intractable disputes (including 'expensive lawsuits'), HA 1996, Pt 7[1] and H(W)A 2014, Pt 2 lay out the conditions under which local housing authorities can transfer responsibility for applicants by referring them to other local housing authorities.

[1] As amended by HRA 2017, for applications for homelessness assistance made to local housing authorities in England on or after 3 April 2018.

14.3 For applications for homelessness assistance made to local housing authorities in England on or after 3 April 2018, there are two stages during the application process at which the conditions may be satisfied and a homeless applicant may be referred to another local housing authority. The first is at the point where it has been established that the applicant is homeless[1] and eligible for assistance[2] and that, unless his or her case is referred, he or she would be owed the HA 1996, s 189B(2)[3] relief duty to take reasonable steps to help the applicant secure that suitable accommodation becomes available for his or her occupation[4]. The second is at the point where the relief duty has come to an end and it has also been established that the applicant has a priority need[5], did not become homeless intentionally[6] and, unless his or her case is referred, would be owed the HA 1996, s 193(2)[7] main housing duty[8].

[1] See CHAPTER 10.

[2] See CHAPTER 11.

[3] As inserted by HRA 2017, s 5(2) for applications for homelessness assistance made to local housing authorities in England on or after 3 April 2018. See **15.138–15.189**.

[4] HA 1996, s 198(A1) as inserted by HA 1996, s 5(8) for applications for homelessness assistance made to local housing authorities in England on or after 3 April 2018. A referral at this stage can only be made to another local housing authority in England. See **14.155–14.161** and **14.166–14.171**.

[5] See CHAPTER 12.

[6] See CHAPTER 13.

[7] See **16.94–16.199**. An applicant who is homeless, eligible for assistance, has a priority need and did not become homeless intentionally will be owed the main housing duty unless the relief duty came to end by virtue of the applicant having refused a 'final accommodation offer' (see **15.181–15.184**) or a 'final Pt 6 offer' (see **15.185–15.188**), or having been given notice that he or she has deliberately and unreasonably refused to cooperate (see **15.196–15.221**): HA 1996, s 193(1A) as inserted by HRA 2017, s 7(2) for applications for homelessness assistance made to local housing authorities in England on or after 3 April 2018.

[8] HA 1996, s 198(1). A referral at this stage can be made to another local housing authority in England or to a local housing authority in Wales. See **14.155–14.163** and **14.166–14.175**.

14.4 For applications for homelessness assistance made to local housing authorities in Wales, there is only one stage during the application process at which the conditions may be satisfied and a homeless applicant may be referred to another local housing authority. That is at the point where it has been established that the applicant is homeless and eligible for assistance and that, unless his or her case is referred, he or she would be owed the H(W)A 2014, s 73[1] relief duty to take reasonable steps to help the applicant secure that suitable accommodation becomes available for his or her occupation[2]. *But,* in contrast to applications for homelessness assistance made to local housing authorities in England, the application may only be referred at this stage where the local housing authority has *also* decided that the applicant has a priority need and did not become homeless intentionally[3].

[1] See **17.73–17.117**.
[2] H(W)A 2014, s 80(1)–(2). See **14.162–14.163** and **14.172–14.175**.
[3] H(W)A 2014, s 80(1)(b).

14.5 In very broad terms, there are three sets of circumstances in which a local housing authority in England can refer an applicant for homelessness assistance to another local housing authority[1]. These are:

(1)   where the applicant and his or her household have no connection with the area to which the application for homelessness assistance has been made but do have a connection with another area to which they can safely be returned[2];

(2)   where an applicant had accepted a private rented sector offer[3] from one local housing authority of accommodation located in the district of another local housing authority, and the applicant has made another application for homelessness assistance to the other local housing authority in England within two years of the date of acceptance[4]; or

(3)   where the applicant has been recently placed in the local housing authority's area by another local housing authority in England or Wales acting under its homelessness functions, but has become homeless again[5].

[1] There are special additional rules permitting local housing authorities to refer certain asylum-seekers to another local housing authority that has agreed to accept the referral. These rules only apply to applicants whose applications for homelessness assistance were made on or before 3 April 2000. For a discussion of those rules see the first or second editions of this book (Jan Luba QC and Liz Davies, 1st edn, 2006; 2nd edn, 2010).
[2] HA 1996, s 198(2) and (2A). See **14.43–14.122**.
[3] HA 1996, s 193(7AA)–(7AC). See **16.153–16.179**.
[4] HA 1996, s 198(2ZA) and (2A). See **14.123–14.137**.
[5] HA 1996, s 198(4) and (4A). See **14.138–14.150**.

14.6 Local housing authorities in Wales may only refer a homeless applicant to another local housing authority, in either England or Wales, where the first set of conditions for referral are met[1].

[1] H(W)A 2014, s 80(1) and (3). See **14.43–14.122**.

14.7 If the statutory conditions are satisfied, responsibility for a homeless applicant can be transferred from one local housing authority to another.

14.8 Several judges have remarked on the parallels with the Poor Laws:

' . . . it is all very reminiscent of the operation of the Poor Law of the nineteenth century and before, all dressed up in modern language[1].'

'Given the pressures on many housing authorities, the natural tendency would be to try to export the homeless whenever possible. Moving the needy beyond the parish boundary has a long history[2].'

' . . . there are echoes of the old Poor Laws, under which parishes contended that paupers were settled in a parish other than their own: see Holdsworth, A History of English Law, vol X, p 257 et passim[3].'

[1] *R v Hammersmith and Fulham London Borough Council ex p O'Brien* (1985) 17 HLR 471, QBD at 474 per Glidewell J.
[2] *R v Slough Borough Council ex p Khan* (1995) 27 HLR 492, QBD at 496 per Mr Roger Toulson QC.
[3] *Al-Ameri v Kensington and Chelsea Royal London Borough Council* [2004] UKHL 4, [2004] 2 AC 159, HL per Lord Bingham at [3].

14.9 Local housing authorities are not required to use these provisions. They are free to accept all those who apply to them. So, although they have power to make inquiries into an applicant's connection with another district if they wish, there is no obligation upon them to do so[1].

[1] HA 1996, s 184(2). *Homelessness Code of Guidance for Local Authorities* (Department for Communities and Local Government, 2018) (the English Code), paras 10.15 and 10.32. For local housing authorities in Wales there is no equivalent provision under H(W)A 2014, Pt 2 governing the making of inquiries into the applicant's connection with another area. However, the power to make such inquiries must be implicit in H(W)A 2014, s 80 since the referral mechanism contained in H(W)A 2014, ss 80–83 would be inoperable without it. And since there is no express duty to make these inquiries in H(W)A 2014, Pt 2 it must be the case that these inquiries are discretionary. See also *Code of Guidance for Local Authorities on the Allocation of Accommodation and Homelessness* (Welsh Government, March 2016) (the Welsh Code) on the CD Rom with this book, paras 18.1 and 18.6.

14.10 However, if local housing authorities do choose to make those inquiries, the tests that they must apply to determine whether a referral can be made are strictly defined at HA 1996, s 198(2), (2ZA), (2A), and (4) and at H(W)A 2014, s 80(3) and (4). If the conditions are not met, no referral to another local housing authority can be made and the first-approached local housing authority must perform either the relief duty[1] (England and Wales) or the main housing duty[2] (England) (depending on the stage the application has reached). If the local housing authority decides that the conditions are met, it retains a discretion, even at that stage, as to whether or not to make a referral. There is no obligation to do so.

[1] HA 1996, s 189B(2) as inserted by the HRA 2017, s 5(2) for applications for homelessness assistance made to local housing authorities in England on or after 3 April 2018; H(W)A 2014, s 73(1). See **15.138–15.189** and **17.73–17.117**.
[2] HA 1996, s 193(2). See **16.94–16.199**.

14.11 Accordingly, there are potentially three decisions for a local housing authority to make in relation to each applicant:

(1) whether or not to make inquiries into the question of any local connection at all; if so,

(2)   whether the conditions for referral as defined at either HA 1996, s 198(2), (2ZA), (2A), and (4) or at H(W)A 2014, s 80(3) and (4) are met; and, if so,

(3)   whether or not to notify another local housing authority of its opinion that the conditions are met.

As explained at **14.3–14.4**, for applications made to local housing authorities in England there are two stages at which a referral can potentially be made and where a local housing authority may be called upon to consider these three questions. For applications made to local housing authorities in Wales there is only one stage at which a referral can potentially be made, at which point these questions may be considered.

14.12 For applications made to local housing authorities in England, if the referral is made at the first stage, where the relief duty[1] would otherwise be owed, the applicant has a right to be accommodated throughout the decision making process only where there is reason to believe that he or she may have a priority need[2]. Otherwise there is no duty to accommodate the applicant. The duty to accommodate falls initially on the first-approached local housing authority and then on the local housing authority to which the referral is made[3].

[1]   HA 1996, s 189B(2) as inserted by HRA 2017, s 5(2) for applications for homelessness assistance made to local housing authorities in England on or after 3 April 2018. See **15.138–15.189**.
[2]   HA 1996, s 199A as inserted by HRA 2017, s 5(9) for applications for homelessness assistance made to local housing authorities in England on or after 3 April 2018.
[3]   HA 1996, ss 199A(2) and (5) (as inserted by HRA 2017, s 5(9) for applications for homelessness assistance made to local housing authorities in England on or after 3 April 2018) and 188(1) (as amended by HRA 2017, s 5(4) for applications for homelessness assistance made to local housing authorities in England on or after 3 April 2018). See **14.166–14.171**.

14.13 If the referral is made at the second stage, where the main housing duty[1] would otherwise be owed, the applicant has a right to be accommodated throughout the decision making process. Again, the duty to accommodate falls initially on the first-approached local housing authority, and then on the local housing authority to which the referral is made[2].

[1]   HA 1996, s 193(2). See **16.94–16.199**.
[2]   HA 1996, ss 200(1) (as amended by HRA 2017, s 5(10) for applications for homelessness assistance made to local housing authorities in England on or after 3 April 2018) and (4) and H(W)A 2014, s 83(2). See **14.166–14.171**.

14.14 For applications made to local housing authorities in Wales at the stage where the relief duty[1] would otherwise be owed, the applicant affected has a right to be accommodated throughout the decision-making process, initially by the first-approached local housing authority and subsequently by the local housing authority to which the referral is made[2].

[1]   H(W)A 2014, s 73(1). See **17.73–17.117**.
[2]   H(W)A 2014, ss 82(4) and 68(3); HA 1996, s 201A(2). See **14.172–14.175**.

14.15 Applicants are most likely to seek assistance from the local housing authority for the district in which they want to live and so would be expected to dispute a decision to refer them to another local housing authority. It is therefore no surprise that applicants are entitled to request reviews of several of the decisions involved in the referral process.

14.16 For applications for homelessness assistance to local housing authorities in England, where the referral is made at the first stage, where the relief duty[1] would otherwise be owed, the applicant has only limited review rights, restricted to the issue of whether the conditions are met for the referral of his or her case[2]. If the decision on review contains an error of law then the applicant may appeal to the county court[3].

[1]   HA 1996, s 189B(2) as inserted by HRA 2017, s 5(2) for applications for homelessness assistance made to local housing authorities in England on or after 3 April 2018. See **15.138–15.189**.
[2]   HA 1996, s 202(1)(d). See **19.55–19.57**.
[3]   HA 1996, s 204(1). See **19.214–19.276**.

14.17 In contrast, if the referral is made at the second stage, where the main housing duty[1] would otherwise be owed, the applicant may request reviews of any decision that he or she should be referred to another local housing authority, any decision that the conditions for referral are made out, and any decision as to the duties owed to him or her as a result[2]. Again, if any of those review decisions contain an error of law, the applicant may appeal to the county court[3]. Applicants for homelessness assistance to local housing authorities in Wales have a similar range of review and appeal rights[4].

[1]   HA 1996, s 193(2). See **16.94–16.199**.
[2]   HA 1996, s 202(1)(c), (d) and (e). See **19.49–19.58**.
[3]   HA 1996, s 204(1). See **19.214–19.276**.
[4]   H(W)A 2014, s 85(1)(c); H(W)A 2014, s 88(1). See **19.77–19.80** and **19.214–19.276**.

14.18 It will be seen from this that, for applications made to local housing authorities in England, there is a lack of parity in the review rights available as between referrals made at the first and second stage. The reason for this lack of parity is not clear. Presumably, an applicant who is dissatisfied with any decision that he or she should be referred to another local housing authority, or any decision as to the duties owed to him or her as a result of the conditions for referral being satisfied, would be entitled to seek judicial review[1]. However, in practice it seems likely that the majority of disputes in this context will fall within the ambit of HA 1996, s 202(1)(d), which provides a right to review of any decision under HA 1996, s 198(5) as to whether the conditions are met for the referral of the applicant's case[2].

[1]   See **19.306–19.327**.
[2]   See **19.55–19.57**.

14.19 In order to avoid applicants being caught in 'a game of battledore and shuttlecock – with the homeless the shuttlecock and the housing authorities wielding the battledore'[1], local housing authorities are obliged to accept a referral if the conditions for referral are met. If the local housing authority, which has been asked to accept a referral, disputes whether the conditions are met, a referee can be appointed[2]. Those arrangements are described in detail in *Procedures for referrals of homeless applicants to another local authority* (the Local Authorities Agreement)[3]. The local housing authorities involved are then bound by the referee's decision. However, the applicant still has the right to request a review of this decision (and subsequently to appeal to the county court on a point of law)[4].

1   *R v Slough Borough Council ex p Ealing London Borough Council* [1981] QB 801, CA at 808 per Lord Denning.
2   This process does not allow the local housing authority which has been asked to accept the referral to challenge the referring local housing authority's assessment of the underlying issues such as whether the applicant is homeless or eligible for assistance. Any such challenge would need to be brought by way of judicial review. See **14.180–14.182**.
3   Guidelines agreed by the Local Government Association, Convention of Scottish Local Authorities, and Welsh Local Government Association. The guidelines are referred to in the English Code, para 10.2 and in the Welsh Code, para 18.27–18.30 and can be found at **Appendix 2**.
4   HA 1996, s 202(1)(d); H(W)A 2014, s 85(1)(c). See **14.197–14.204, 19.55–19.57, 19.77–19.80** and **19.214–19.276**.

14.20 There are special additional rules concerning former asylum-seekers who occupied accommodation provided by the Home Office in Scotland and subsequently made applications for homelessness assistance to local housing authorities in England. In those cases, local housing authorities in England will not be subject to the main housing duty[1] when the relief duty[2] comes to an end, but instead may provide accommodation for a limited period and provide advice and assistance to help the applicant apply to a local authority in Scotland, or make other arrangements for accommodation[3]. These rules are discussed towards the end of this chapter[4].

1   HA 1996, s 193(2). See **16.94–16.199**.
2   HA 1996, s 189B(2) as inserted by H(W)A 2014, s 5(2) for applications for homelessness assistance made or after 3 April 2018. See **15.138–15.189**.
3   Asylum and Immigration (Treatment of Claimants etc) Act 2004, s 11(2) and (3). See **14.212–14.220**.
4   See **14.212–14.220**.

14.21 Throughout this chapter, we use the statutory terms of 'notifying local housing authority' and 'notified local housing authority' to indicate respectively the local housing authority first receiving the application for homelessness assistance and subsequently making the referral (the 'notifying local housing authority'), and the local housing authority receiving the referral (the 'notified local housing authority').

14.22 The chapter concludes with a review of cross-border referrals and the circumstances in which applicants may be accommodated outside the district in which they sought to be accommodated but without the local housing authority invoking the statutory referral procedure.

THE RIGHT TO MAKE AN APPLICATION FOR HOMELESSNESS ASSISTANCE TO ANY LOCAL HOUSING AUTHORITY

14.23 A homeless person is free to apply to any local housing authority in England, Wales or Scotland (or to the Housing Executive in Northern Ireland) for assistance with accommodation. There is no prior condition that the applicant must apply to the local housing authority for any particular district. There is no filter that prevents an applicant who has no connection with a particular local housing authority from applying to that local housing authority. Once the application for homelessness assistance has been made, and there is reason to believe that the applicant may be homeless or threatened with homelessness, the local housing authority must conduct inquiries and make its decision as to whether or not the applicant is eligible and, if so, whether a duty and (if so) what duty, is owed to the applicant under HA 1996, Pt 7[1] or H(W)A 2014, Pt 2[2]. Any local housing authority that tells an applicant that he or she has applied to the wrong local housing authority, that he or she cannot apply to that particular local housing authority, or that no inquiries will be made because he or she does not appear to have a connection with its district, is acting unlawfully[3].

[1]   As amended by HRA 2017, for applications for homelessness assistance made to local housing authorities in England on or after 3 April 2018.
[2]   HA 1996, s 184(1); H(W)A 2014, s 63(1), (4) and (5).
[3]   *R v Slough Borough Council ex p Ealing London Borough Council* [1981] QB 801, CA; and *R v Tower Hamlets London Borough Council ex p Camden London Borough Council* (1988) 21 HLR 197, QBD.

POWER OF A LOCAL HOUSING AUTHORITY TO MAKE INQUIRIES INTO THE CONDITIONS FOR REFERRAL

Introduction

14.24 As soon as a local housing authority has 'reason to believe' that an applicant for assistance under HA 1996, Pt 7 or H(W)A 2014, Pt 2 may be homeless or threatened with homelessness, it must make inquiries (England) or commence an assessment (Wales) to satisfy itself whether the applicant is eligible and whether any duty, and if so what duty, is owed to the applicant[1]. It *may* also make inquiries into whether the applicant has a 'local connection' with the district of any other local housing authority in England, Wales or (for applicants to local housing authorities in England) Scotland[2]. However, there is no obligation to make those latter inquiries. Even if the applicant self-evidently has no connection with the local housing authority to which he or she has applied, and has an obvious connection with another local housing authority, the first local housing authority can choose not to make inquiries into that connection.

[1]   HA 1996, s 184(1); H(W)A 2014, s 63(1), (4) and (5). See **9.1–9.14**.
[2]   HA 1996, s 184(2). See **9.28–9.30**. For local housing authorities in Wales there is no equivalent provision under H(W)A 2014, Pt 2 governing the making of inquiries into the applicant's connection with another area. However, the power to make such inquiries must be implicit in H(W)A 2014, s 80 since the referral mechanism contained in H(W)A 2014, ss 80–83 would be inoperable without it. And since there is no express duty to make these inquiries in H(W)A 2014, Pt 2 it must be the case that these inquiries are discretionary. See Welsh Code, paras 18.1 and 18.6.

14.25 Applicants cannot insist that the local housing authority to which they apply makes inquiries into their local connection. If the local housing authority decides not to make those inquiries, the applicant has no right to request a review of that decision, as it is not a decision that falls within one of the categories of decisions capable of review[1]. Any legal challenge could only be brought by judicial review[2]. Although many local housing authorities, anxious to reduce pressure on their resources, will want to consider the possibility of referring an applicant to another local housing authority, local housing authorities are also entitled to assume that an applicant has applied to the local housing authority in whose district he or she would want to be housed[3].

1 HA 1996, s 202(1) as amended by HRA 2017, s 9(2) for applications for homelessness assistance made to local housing authorities in England on or after 3 April 2018; H(W)A 2014, s 85(1)(c). See *Hackney London Borough Council v Sareen* [2003] EWCA Civ 351, [2003] HLR 54, CA.
2 See **19.306–19.327**.
3 *Hackney London Borough Council v Sareen* [2003] EWCA Civ 351, [2003] HLR 54, CA at [42] per Auld LJ.

What inquiries can the local housing authority make?

14.26 If the local housing authority does choose to make inquiries into the applicant's local connection, the results of those inquiries will only become relevant once the local housing authority has concluded that it would otherwise owe the relief duty[1] or the main housing duty[2] under HA 1996, Pt 7[3] or the relief duty under H(W)A 2014, Pt 2[4].

1 HA 1996, s 189B(2) as inserted by HRA 2017, s 5(2) for applications made to local housing authorities in England on or after 3 April 2018. See **15.138–15.189**.
2 HA 1996, s 193(2). See **16.94–16.199**.
3 As amended by HRA 2017, for applications for homelessness assistance made to local housing authorities in England on or after 3 April 2018.
4 H(W)A 2014, s 73(1). See **17.73–17.117**.

14.27 For applications for homelessness assistance made to local housing authorities in Wales, the conditions for referral only apply to those applicants who are homeless, eligible, have a priority need and did not become homeless intentionally. As such it may make practical sense for a local housing authority in Wales not to make inquiries into any local connection until it has completed the remainder of its inquiries and made decisions upon them. If an applicant appears to have become homeless intentionally or not to have a priority need, there is no point devoting additional resources to making wasteful inquiries into the question of local connection. In contrast, for applications for homelessness assistance made to local housing authorities in England, the conditions for referral can apply to any applicant who is homeless and eligible, to whom the relief duty would otherwise be owed[1]. Local housing authorities in England might therefore properly inquire into an applicant's local connection at an earlier stage then would be the case if the application had been made to a local housing authority in Wales.

1 HA 1996, s 198(A1) as inserted by HRA 2017, s 5(8) for applications made to local housing authorities in England on or after 3 April 2018.

England

14.28 A local housing authority in England may only make inquiries into whether the applicant has a local connection with the district of any other local housing authority in England, Wales or Scotland[1]. A local connection with a local housing authority elsewhere is not relevant[2]. In particular, a connection with other parts of the UK (eg Northern Ireland)[3] would not trigger the referral provisions in HA 1996, s 198[4].

1 HA 1996, s 184(2).
2 *R v Westminster City Council ex p Esmail* (1989) June *Legal Action*, p 25, QBD.
3 See Box 1 at **11.28**. See also **14.239**.
4 As amended by HRA 2017, s 5(8) for applications made to local housing authorities in England on or after 3 April 2018.

14.29 Curiously, HA 1996, Pt 7[1] limits the subject matter of the discretionary inquiries to whether the applicant himself or herself has a connection elsewhere[2]. A local housing authority which confined its inquiries only to that question would find it impossible to determine whether the conditions for referral to another local housing authority were in fact satisfied or not. As the remainder of this chapter indicates, the referral conditions are detailed and complex and go well beyond the question of whether the applicant personally has a local connection with the district of another local housing authority. The local housing authority which receives an application for homelessness assistance, and wishes to pursue the possibility of referring the applicant's case, will need to know whether:

(1) the applicant or any member of his or her household has a local connection with its own area[3];

(2) the applicant or any member of his or her household has a local connection with another local housing authority's area[4];

(3) the applicant had been placed in its area as a result of having accepted a private rented sector offer[5] from another local housing authority and subsequently made his or her application for homelessness assistance within two years of the date of acceptance[6];

(4) the applicant (or any member of his or her household) would be at risk of actual or threatened violence if returned to another area[7]; and

(5) the applicant had been placed in its area by another local housing authority acting under the homelessness provisions of HA 1996, Pt 7[8] or H(W)A 2014, Pt 2[9].

1 As amended by HRA 2017 for applications made to local housing authorities in England on or after 3 April 2018.
2 HA 1996, s 184(2).
3 HA 1996, s 198(2)(a). See **14.43–14.106**.
4 HA 1996, s 198(2)(b). See **14.43–14.106**.
5 HA 1996, s 193(7AA). See **16.153–16.179**.
6 HA 1996, s 198(2ZA). See **14.123–14.137**.
7 HA 1996, s 198(2)(c). See **14.107–14.119**.
8 As amended by HRA 2017, for applications for homelessness assistance made to local housing authorities in England on or after 3 April 2018. HA 1996, s 198(4).
9 HA 1996, s 198(4A). See **15.131–15.144**.

14.30 Self-evidently, inquiries into those matters would go well beyond the scope of those expressly mentioned in HA 1996, s 184(2), and so the power to make these inquiries must therefore be implicit in the scheme of HA 1996, Pt 7 since the referral mechanisms would be inoperable otherwise.

14.31 Accordingly, where the local housing authority has received an application for homelessness assistance, has opted to make inquiries into the matter and has discovered that the applicant has a local connection elsewhere, it cannot simply assume that all the other ingredients of the conditions for a referral are made out. It must go on to explore whether the other conditions for referral are satisfied[1].

[1] *R v Slough Borough Council ex p Khan* (1995) 27 HLR 492, QBD; and *R v Greenwich London Borough Council ex p Patterson* (1994) 26 HLR 159, CA.

Wales

14.32 In contrast to local housing authorities in England[1], a local housing authority in Wales has no express power to make inquiries into any element of the conditions for referral. However, the power to make inquiries into whether the conditions for referral are met must be implicit in H(W)A 2014, Pt 2, since the referral mechanism contained in H(W)A 2014, ss 80–83 would be inoperable without it. Since there is no express duty to make these inquiries in H(W)A 2014, Pt 2 it must be the case that these inquiries are discretionary. In line with the principle that any discretion conferred by statute must be exercised to promote the policy and object of that statute[2] the scope of these inquiries must therefore be limited to England and Wales since there is no mechanism under H(W)A 2014, Pt 2 to make a referral elsewhere[3]. It follows that a local housing authority in Wales which receives an application for homelessness assistance, and wishes to pursue the possibility of referring the applicant's case, has the power (and will need) to inquire into whether:

(1) the applicant or any member of his or her household has a local connection with its own area[4];

(2) the applicant or any member of his or her household has a local connection with another local housing authority's area[5];

(3) the applicant or any member of his or her household would be at risk of actual or threatened violence if returned to another area[6].

[1] See **14.29–14.31**.
[2] *Padfield v Minister of Agriculture, Fisheries and Food* [1968] AC 997, [1968] 2 WLR 924, HL.
[3] H(W)A 2014, s 80(1)(a).
[4] H(W)A 2014, s 80(3)(a). See **14.43–14.106**.
[5] H(W)A 2014, s 80(3)(b). See **14.43–14.106**.
[6] H(W)A 2014, s 80(3)(c). See **14.107–14.119**.

THE CONDITIONS FOR REFERRAL

Introduction

14.33 For applications made to local housing authorities in England, the preliminary condition for any referral is that the local housing authority in receipt of the application for homelessness assistance is satisfied that it would itself owe the applicant either the HA 1996, s 189B(2)[1] relief duty or the HA 1996, s 193(2) main housing duty[2]. For applications made to local housing authorities in Wales, the preliminary condition for any referral is that the local housing authority in receipt of the application is satisfied that it would itself owe the applicant the H(W)A 2014, s 73[3] relief duty and the applicant has a priority need and did not become homeless intentionally[4].

[1] As inserted by HRA 2017, s 5(2) for applications made to local housing authorities in England on or after 3 April 2018. See **15.138–15.189**.
[2] HA 1996, 198(1).
[3] See **17.73–17.117**.

⁴   H(W)A 2014, ss 73 and 80(1). Note, the explicit requirement that an applicant to a local housing authority in Wales should have a priority need and should not have become homeless intentionally was originally intended, prior to the enactment of HRA 2017, to ensure parity across the referral mechanisms between England and Wales, since these requirements are essential to the existence of the main housing duty under HA 1996, s 193(2). Following the amendments to HA 1996, Pt 7 made by HRA 2017 there is no longer complete parity across the referral mechanisms. In particular, the case of an applicant who is owed the relief duty contained in HA 1996, s 189B(2) (as inserted by HRA 2017, s 5(2) for applications for homelessness assistance made to local housing authorities in England on or after 3 April 2018) by a local housing authority in England can only be referred to another local housing authority in England. See HA 1996, s 198(A1) as inserted by HRA 2017, s 5(8) for applications for homelessness assistance made to local housing authorities in England on or after 3 April 2018.

14.34 Beyond that, the detailed conditions for referral are set out in HA 1996, s 198[1] (as amended by HRA 2017, s 5) and H(W)A 2014, s 80. There are three separate and alternative sets of conditions for referral. The first set of conditions applies to referrals throughout England and Wales. The second set of conditions applies only to referrals between local housing authorities in England. The third set of conditions applies to referrals by local housing authorities in England to local housing authorities in England and Wales.

¹   As amended by HRA 2017, s 5(8) for applications for homelessness assistance made to local housing authorities in England on or after 3 April 2018.

14.35 The *first* set of 'conditions for referral' are found in HA 1996, s 198(2) and (2A) and in H(W)A 2014, s 80(3) and (4). It applies to referrals throughout England and Wales. The conditions are that:

(1)   neither the applicant nor any person who might reasonably be expected to reside with the applicant has a local connection with the district[1] of the local housing authority to which the application for homelessness assistance was made; and

(2)   either the applicant or a person who might reasonably be expected to reside with the applicant has a local connection with the district of another local housing authority in England, Wales or (for applications to local housing authorities in England) Scotland; and

(3)   neither the applicant nor any person who might reasonably be expected to reside with the applicant will run the risk of domestic violence (England) or domestic abuse (Wales) in that other district; and

(4)   neither the applicant nor any person who might reasonably be expected to reside with the applicant has suffered violence (England) or abuse (Wales) in the district of that other local housing authority; or,

(5)   if violence (England) or abuse (Wales) has been suffered, it is not probable that a return to that district will lead to further violence or abuse of a similar kind against that person.

¹   HA 1996, Pt 7 uses the phrase 'district of a local housing authority'. This has the meaning given in Housing Act 1985 (HA 1996, ss 217 and 218). H(W)A 2014, Pt 2 uses the phrase 'area of a local housing authority'. The phrase is undefined. It must be the case that the two phrases are intended to have an identical meaning: consistency is needed for the cross-border referral mechanisms to work harmoniously. The word 'district' will be used throughout this chapter for the sake of simplicity.

14.36 This set of conditions requires additional consideration of the concepts of 'local connection'[1], and 'violence' or 'abuse' (domestic or otherwise)[2].

[1]   See **14.43–14.106**.
[2]   HA 1996, s 198(3); H(W)A 2014, s 58(1) and s 99. See **14.107–14.119**. There must also be
      a determination by the local housing authority as to those persons with whom the applicant
      'might reasonably be expected to reside' – a phrase that is not confined to those with whom
      the applicant is, or has been, living immediately prior to the application for homelessness
      assistance. See **10.29–10.30**.

14.37 The *second* set of 'conditions for referral' is to be found in HA 1996,
s 198(2ZA) and (2A). It applies only to referrals within England. The
conditions are that:

(1)   the applicant accepted a private rented sector offer made by one local
      housing authority (authority A); and
(2)   within two years of the date of acceptance, the applicant makes an
      application for homelessness assistance to authority B; and
(3)   neither the applicant nor any person who might reasonably be expected
      to reside with the applicant will run the risk of domestic violence in the
      district of authority A; and
(4)   neither the applicant nor any person who might reasonably be expected
      to reside with him or her has suffered violence in the district of
      authority A; or
(5)   if violence has been suffered, it is not probable that a return to the
      district of authority A will lead to further violence of a similar kind
      against that person[1].

[1]   HA 1996, s 198(2ZA) and (2A). See **14.123–14.137**.

14.38 The *third* set of 'conditions for referral' is to be found in HA 1996,
s 198(4) and (4A). It applies only to referrals made by local housing authorities
in England to local housing authorities in England or Wales.

14.39 The conditions are that:

(1)   the applicant was placed in accommodation in the district of the local
      housing authority to which he or she has now applied (authority A) by
      another local housing authority (authority B); and
(2)   that placement was made in pursuance of authority B's functions under
      HA 1996, Pt 7 or H(W)A 2014, Pt 2; and
(3)   the application for homelessness assistance to authority A is made
      within a prescribed period.

14.40 The prescribed period is the total of five years plus the period between
the date of the applicant's application for homelessness assistance to authority B and the date when the applicant was placed in authority A[1].

[1]   Allocation of Housing and Homelessness (Miscellaneous Provisions) (England) Regula-
      tions 2006, SI 2006/2527, reg 3, for applications to local housing authorities made on or after
      9 October 2006. See Appendix 2.

14.41 If this third set of conditions is met, the applicant can be referred by
authority A to authority B. There is no additional requirement on authority A
to consider whether the applicant ever had a local connection with authority B
or has, more recently, acquired a local connection with its district. Nor is there

any requirement to consider whether the applicant or any member of his or her household would be subject to domestic or other violence in the district of authority B.

14.42 Each set of conditions for referral is now separately considered.

The first set of conditions for referral – 'local connection'

Overview

14.43 The lynchpin of the first set of referral conditions is the concept of 'local connection'[1] with the district of a local housing authority. That phrase is not itself defined by HA 1996, Pt 7[2] or H(W)A 2014, Pt 2. The legislation simply limits the relevant methods by which a local connection can be acquired to one or more of the circumstances specified in HA 1996, s 199 or H(W)A 2014, s 81. As a result of amendments to HA 1996, Pt 7 made by HRA 2017[3] the circumstances in which a person may acquire a local connection to a local housing authority in England are no longer identical to the circumstances in which a person may acquire a local connection to a local housing authority in Wales. There are now two additional situations in which an applicant for homelessness assistance under HA 1996, Pt 7[4] may have a local connection to a local housing authority in England.

[1]   HA 1996, s 198(2) and (2A); H(W)A 2014, s 80(3) and (4).
[2]   As amended by HRA 2017, for applications for homelessness assistance made to local housing authorities in England on or after 3 April 2018.
[3]   For applications for homelessness assistance made to local housing authorities in England on or after 3 April 2018.
[4]   As amended by HRA 2017, for applications for homelessness assistance made to local housing authorities in England on or after 3 April 2018.

14.44 The circumstances in which a homeless applicant may have a local connection with the district of a local housing authority in England or Wales are that:

(1)   the person is, or was in the past, normally resident in a district and his or her residence there is, or was, of his or her own choice[1];
(2)   the person is employed in the district[2];
(3)   the person has a connection with the district through family associations[3];
(4)   the person has a connection with the district through special circumstances[4];
(5)   the person was provided with accommodation in the district (in England or Wales) under s 95 of the Immigration and Asylum Act 1999 (dispersal of asylum-seekers)[5].

The additional circumstances in which an applicant for homelessness assistance under HA 1996, Pt 7[6] may have a local connection with the district of a local housing authority in England only are that:

(6)   the person is owed a duty under Children Act 1989, s 23C[7] by a local authority in England[8] and either that local authority is also the local housing authority for the district or, alternatively, the district of the local housing authority falls within the area of the local authority[9]; or

(7)   the person is under 21 and was normally resident in the district of a local housing authority in England for a continuous period of at least two years, some or all of which fell before the person attained the age of 16, as a result of being accommodated under Children Act 1989, s 22A[10].

1   HA 1996, s 199(1)(a); H(W)A 2014, s 81(2)(a). See **14.56–14.66.**
2   HA 1996, s 199(1)(b); H(W)A 2014, s 81(2)(b). See **14.67–14.71.**
3   HA 1996, s 199(1)(c); H(W)A 2014, s 81(2)(c). See **14.72–14.81.**
4   HA 1996, s 199(1)(d); H(W)A 2014, s 81(2)(d). See **14.82–14.87.**
5   HA 1996, s 199(6); H(W)A 2014, s 81(5). See **14.88–14.94.**
6   As amended by HRA 2017, for applications for homelessness assistance made to local housing authorities in England on or after 3 April 2018.
7   See **20.65.**
8   As defined in Children Act 1989, s 105. See HA 1996, s 199(9) as inserted by HRA 2017, s 8 for applications for homelessness assistance made to local housing authorities in England on or after 3 April 2018.
9   HA 1996, s 199(8) as inserted by HRA 2017, s 8 for applications for homelessness assistance made to local housing authorities in England on or after 3 April 2018. See **14.95–14.99.**
10   HA 1996, ss 199(10)–(11) as inserted by HRA 2017, s 8 for applications for homelessness assistance made to local housing authorities in England on or after 3 April 2018. See **14.100–14.103.** Children Act 1989, s 22A provides for accommodation for children in care.

14.45 Each of the above circumstances will be examined in turn in this chapter.

14.46 When considering whether the circumstances sufficient to establish a 'local connection' are made out, a local housing authority must have regard to HA 1996, Pt 7[1], H(W)A 2014, Pt 2 and the relevant Code of Guidance. In addition, local housing authorities have also agreed and adopted additional guidance as to the interpretation of some of these statutory provisions[2]. The House of Lords has confirmed that local housing authorities are entitled to consider that additional guidance when making their decisions[3]. As Chadwick LJ put it in a later case:

> 'It is desirable that the notified authority – who is being asked to assume the burden of providing accommodation for the applicant in the place of the notifying authority – should be able to accept the view of the notifying authority both that the applicant has no local connection with the district of the notifying authority and that the applicant does have a local connection with their own district. Ready agreement is unlikely to be achieved on those two points unless both the notifying authority and the notified authority are able to approach the question from a common basis. It is the need for that common basis which, as it seems to me, provides the imperative for all authorities to apply the guidelines "generally to all applications which come before them"[4].'

1   As amended by HRA 2017, for applications for homelessness assistance made to local housing authorities in England on or after 3 April 2018.
2   The Local Authorities Agreement. See **14.19** fn 3.
3   *R v Eastleigh Borough Council ex p Betts* [1983] 2 AC 613, HL at 627 per Lord Brightman. Referring to an earlier version of the guidance.
4   *Ozbek v Ipswich Borough Council* [2006] EWCA Civ 534, [2006] HLR 41, CA at [39] per Chadwick LJ.

14.47 If they do take the guidance into account, local housing authorities must still ensure that they consider the applicant's individual circumstances, particularly any exceptional circumstances, before reaching a decision[1].

¹ *R v Harrow London Borough Council ex p Carter* (1992) 26 HLR 32, QBD.

14.48 If they embark on inquiries into local connection at all, local housing authorities should consider each of the five (Wales) or seven (England) circumstances in which an applicant, or a member of his or her household, may acquire a local connection[1]. It is not sufficient merely to establish that a local connection has been acquired by *the applicant* with the district of another local housing authority through one of the specified categories. The local housing authority must go on to consider what other local connections the applicant or his or her household members may have. Consideration of all the categories might reveal that the applicant, or a member of his or her household, has a local connection with the very local housing authority to which he or she applied. If that is the case, the conditions for referral will not be met. Alternatively, it might be the case that the applicant or a member of his or her household has a local connection with more than one local housing authority (other than that to which he or she applied), in which case the conditions for referral are met, but the applicant's preference[2] is relevant when deciding which local housing authority should be notified by the local housing authority to whom the applicant has applied[3].

¹ *R v Slough Borough Council ex p Khan* (1995) 27 HLR 492, QBD.
² English Code, para 10.34; Welsh Code, para 18.10.
³ Local Authorities Agreement, para 4.11.

14.49 The House of Lords held in *Mohammed v Hammersmith and Fulham London Borough Council*[1] that the relevant date for determining whether an applicant has a local connection, and with which local housing authority, is the date of the decision that the local housing authority (or local housing authorities jointly, or a referee) makes on the question or (if a review is requested) the date of the review decision. Although in that case, the House of Lords was concerned with the definition of 'normally resident', the principle must apply to any of the other statutory circumstances that fall to be considered. So, if an applicant acquires a family association or becomes employed in a local housing authority's district after his or her application for homelessness assistance but before the date of decision, or even the review decision, the question of local connection must be considered on the facts at that later date, not as at the date of application. More commonly, of course, the applicant might have been 'resident' in the local housing authority's district for long enough since applying to have established a local connection[2] by the time of the initial decision or review decision, even though the period of residence in the district prior to the application for homelessness assistance had not been long enough to establish such a local connection[3].

¹ [2001] UKHL 57, [2002] 1 AC 547, HL.
² Under HA 1996, s 199(1)(a) or H(W)A 2014, s 81(2)(a).
³ See, for example, *Fetaj v Lambeth London Borough Council* (2002) September *Legal Action*, p 31, Lambeth County Court.

14.50 It is possible for a person not to have a local connection with any local housing authority in England, Wales or Scotland. The example given in the Welsh Code is where a person has 'had an unsettled way of life for many years"[1]. Former prisoners, former long-term hospital residents, former service-men or servicewomen, etc, may likewise not have a local connection with any district at all. Neither would someone newly arrived in the UK, with no prior period of residence in England, Wales or Scotland, who was not employed and who had no family associations here. If there is no local connection anywhere, the conditions for referral are not met and the applicant remains the responsibility of the local housing authority to which he or she applied[2].

[1] Welsh Code, para 18.19.
[2] English Code, para 10.35; Welsh Code, para 18.19.

14.51 Four additional points about local connection must be made before the individual ingredients are considered further.

14.52 First, HA 1996, Pt 7[1] and H(W)A 2014, Pt 2 do not exhaustively define 'local connection'. Most obviously, a person may have a local connection with an area but it may arise from circumstances falling outside the prescribed list of circumstances. If that is the case, that connection would not fall within the definition of 'local connection' for the purposes of HA 1996, Pt 7[2] or H(W)A 2014, Pt 2. For example, the connection a person has with an area because it was the place of his or her birth would be immaterial: 'A local connection not founded upon any of the four stated factors is irrelevant'[3].

[1] As amended by HRA 2017, for applications for homelessness assistance made to local housing authorities in England on or after 3 April 2018.
[2] As amended by HRA 2017, for applications for homelessness assistance made to local housing authorities in England on or after 3 April 2018.
[3] *R v Eastleigh Borough Council ex p Betts* [1983] 2 AC 613, HL per Lord Brightman. There are now seven stated factors in England and five in Wales, see **14.4**.

14.53 Second, a 'local connection' with a district is something more than simply *a* connection by residence, employment, etc. While one of the seven (England) or five (Wales) prescribed circumstances is a necessary pre-condition for a local connection, it is not sufficient alone to establish a local connection. For example, a person may have employment in an area, but it may be of only a transient or very part-time nature. A person may have 'family associations' with an area because his or her parents live there, but might be estranged from their parents and not have seen or spoken to them for years. What is required is that the connection of a person (eg by having been 'normally resident', 'employed', or having 'family associations' in an area) is of sufficient quality to amount to a present 'local connection'. As the House of Lords has put it, a local connection is a connection which has been built up or established so as to have become 'a connection in real terms'[1].

[1] *R v Eastleigh Borough Council ex p Betts* [1983] 2 AC 613, HL per Lord Brightman. See *X v Ealing London Borough Council* (2010) November *Legal Action*, p 19, Brent-ford County Court, for an example of a connection based on special circumstances amounting to a connection in real terms, see **14.85**.

14.54 Third, different local connections may be of different comparative strengths. For example, a person might be said to have a stronger local connection with the place in which she or he lives than with the place where she or he works. If the applicant (or anyone who might reasonably be expected to live with him or her) has *any* local connection (based on one or more of the statutory circumstances) with the local housing authority to which an application for homelessness assistance has been made, the strength of that local connection is irrelevant. The conditions for referral will not be made out and the referral provisions cannot be used, even if the applicant has a much stronger local connection with another local housing authority[1]. But where there is no local connection with the district of the local housing authority applied to, but local connections with two or more other districts, the applicant's preference, will be a factor for the first local housing authority in determining to which other local housing authority it should direct the referral[2].

[1] English Code, para 10.33; Welsh Code, para 18.10.
[2] English Code, para 10.34; Welsh Code, para 18.10.

14.55 Fourth, the relevant local connection is with the 'district'[1] of a local housing authority. That must mean with any part of the geographical area of that authority. So, a person who lives (and has always lived) just inside the boundaries of Borough A will have a local connection with that borough even if, in practice, most of his or her time is spent in neighbouring Borough B (for shopping, education, recreation or leisure purposes). None of the interesting questions which might arise in relation to local connection when district boundaries are moved (eg by implementation of recommendations of the Boundary Commission) have yet been considered by the courts.

[1] See **14.35** fn 1.

The relevant statutory circumstances

(1) Normal residence of his or her own choice

14.56 A person must have been 'normally resident'[1] in a district in order to acquire a local connection with that district by having lived there. 'Normal residence' is to be understood as meaning 'the place where at the relevant time the person in fact resides'[2]. There is no need for the place to be a permanent home, or even to be the place where a person most wants to be living.

> 'So long as that place where he eats and sleeps is voluntarily accepted by him, the reason why he is there rather than somewhere else does not prevent that place from being his normal residence. He may not like it, he may prefer some other place, but that place is for the relevant time the place where he normally resides. If a person, having no other accommodation, takes his few belongings and moves into a barn for a period to work on a farm that is where during that period he is normally resident, however much he might prefer some more permanent or better accommodation. In a sense it is "shelter" but it is also where he resides[3].'

[1] HA 1996, s 199(1)(a); H(W)A 2014, s 81(2)(a).
[2] *Mohamed v Hammersmith and Fulham London Borough Council* [2001] UKHL 57, [2002] 1 AC 547, HL at [17] per Lord Slynn.
[3] *Mohamed v Hammersmith and Fulham London Borough Council* [2001] UKHL 57, [2002] 1 AC 547, HL at [17] per Lord Slynn.

14.57 Applying this approach, even occupation of interim accommodation, provided under a local housing authority's homelessness duties, constitutes 'normal residence'[1]. Likewise, occupation of accommodation provided under community care or other duties will be accommodation in which the applicant normally resides. At a county court level it has been held that normal residence does not necessarily equate to lawful residence. A victim of trafficking who had lived for several years in an area without any leave to remain in the UK, before applying for asylum and obtaining refugee status, could be classed as normally resident during that time[2].

1   Applying this same approach, a person occupying interim accommodation provided by local housing authority A in the area of local housing authority B, would not be considered to be normally resident in the district of local housing authority A. In *Adam v Waltham Forest London Borough Council* [2016] EWCA Civ 248, CA, the Court of Appeal refused permission to bring a second appeal in which the applicant sought to argue otherwise. An applicant accommodated in such circumstances might nevertheless have a local connection with local housing authority A on the basis of special circumstances. See **14.82–14.87**.
2   *Nakiyingi v Lambeth London Borough Council* (2014) March *Legal Action*, p 24, Central London County Court.

14.58 The assessment that has to be made in a 'residence' case:

' . . . is not whether the homeless person is now or was in the past normally resident in the area of the notifying authority, but whether the applicant has now a local connection with either area based upon the fact that he is now or was in the past normally resident in that area[1].'

1   *R v Eastleigh Borough Council ex p Betts* [1983] 2 AC 613, HL per Lord Brightman.

14.59 The Local Authorities' Agreement[1] suggests that a working definition of normal residence sufficient to establish a 'local connection' should be residence for at least six months in an area during the previous 12 months, or for not less than three years during the previous five-year period[2]. Local housing authorities may apply that working definition, although each case must be considered on its own particular facts[3].

1   See **14.19** fn 3.
2   Local Authorities Agreement, para 4.3(i).
3   *R v Eastleigh Borough Council ex p Betts* [1983] 2 AC 613, HL.

14.60 The concept of normal residence being 'of his own choice' was considered by the House of Lords in *Al-Ameri v Kensington and Chelsea Royal London Borough Council*[1]. It decided that 'choice' in this context refers to a person's choice to go and live in a particular district. The district must have been selected by the individual, rather than by some other person (for example, by an official or a Secretary of State)[2]. The particular situation in *Al-Ameri* (asylum-seekers occupying accommodation provided under the then National Asylum Support Service (NASS) scheme) has since been specifically addressed by legislation[3]. However, the general definition of 'his own choice' remains. The reasoning of the House of Lords suggests, for example, that children moved from one district to another by their parents or by social services would not have been resident in the new district 'of their own choice'[4]. This latter scenario has now been partially addressed by the amendments made to HA 1996, Pt 7 by HRA 2017[5]. The Court of Appeal has held that residence in a women's refuge is capable of being residence of a person's own choice[6].

1   *Al-Ameri v Kensington and Chelsea Royal London Borough Council* [2004] UKHL 4, [2004] 2 AC 159, HLR.

2   See *Al-Ameri v Kensington and Chelsea Royal London Borough Council* [2004] UKHL 4,
     [2004] 2 AC 159, HLR at [57] per Lord Scott.
3   HA 1996, s 199(6) and (7) as amended. See **15.86–15.92**.
4   See also Local Authorities Agreement, para 4.3(iii).
5   By HA 1996, ss 199(10)–(11) as inserted by HA 1996, s 8 for applications for homelessness
     assistance made to local housing authorities in England on or after 3 April 2018. See
     14.95–14.103.
6   *Wandsworth London Borough Council v NJ* [2013] EWCA Civ 1373, [2014] HLR 6, CA.

14.61 This freedom of choice aspect cannot be extrapolated too far. A person
who moves from one area to another as a consequence of his or her employer
relocating might be said to be simply falling in line with a choice made by
another, and the point could be made with even more force about the
employee's partner. However, in reality, the employee has chosen to move
rather than to resign and the employee's partner has chosen to follow. Their
residence is, accordingly, of their 'own choice'. Much more acute difficulties
arise with the 'own choice' concept when an applicant to the local housing
authority for District A has become resident in District A as a result of having
been placed there by District B in pursuance of its statutory duties to
accommodate the applicant. Those statutory obligations might include the
making of a private rented sector offer to the applicant[1]. In one sense this was
not residence of the applicant's 'own choice'. On the other hand, the applicant
was not obliged to accept the accommodation in District A as offered by
District B[2].

1   HA 1996, s 193(7AA)–(7AC); H(W)A 2014, s 76(3)–(4). See **16.153–16.179** (England) and
     17.173–17.177 (Wales).
2   This problem is side-stepped for local housing authorities in England by the second and third
     set of referral conditions available to District A when this scenario arises (HA 1996,
     s 198(2ZA), (4) and (4A)). See **14.123–14.137** and **14.138–14.150**.

Exceptions to normal residence of his or her own choice

Detention

14.62 Residence in a district is not 'of his own choice' if it occurs because a
person is detained under the authority of an Act of Parliament (England) or an
enactment (Wales)[1]. This refers to any form of detention authorised by statute
and therefore embraces detention, for example, as a result of having been
remanded in custody[2], having been given a custodial sentence[3], or having been
detained under the Mental Health Act 1983[4]. Periods of residence in a district
prior to detention are not excluded and can count towards normal residence
for the purposes of HA 1996, Pt 7[5] and H(W)A 2014, Pt 2[6]. This exception
encompasses spouses or other family members of detainees, who come to
reside in the district in order to be close to their detained relative. Therefore,
the person who moves from District A to District B to be near her partner, who
is detained in District B, cannot acquire a local connection with District B
unless either:

(1)   a connection other than through normal residence is available (eg she
       becomes employed in District B); or
(2)   there is a period of fresh residence (eg if she remained in District B after
       her partner was released, or after she had ended the relationship but

chose to remain in the district).

1 HA 1996, s 199(3)(b); H(W)A 2014, s 81(3). See H(W)A 2014, s 99 for the definition of 'an enactment'.
2 Criminal Justice Act 2003, s 242(2).
3 Powers of Criminal Courts (Sentencing) Act 2000, s 76. See English Code, paras 10.40 and 23.22–23.24 for more general guidance on local connection referrals for those with an offending history.
4 Mental Health Act 1983, ss 2–3.
5 As amended by HRA 2017, for applications for homelessness assistance made to local housing authorities in England on or after 3 April 2018.
6 Welsh Code, para 18.14.

Other exceptions

14.63 The Secretary of State and the Welsh Ministers have the power to specify circumstances in which residence in a district is not to be treated as being of a person's own choice[1]. To date, neither the Secretary of State nor the Welsh Ministers have exercised that power.

1 HA 1996, s 199(5)(b); H(W)A 2014, s 81(4)(b).

14.64 Previous editions of the Local Authorities' Agreement recommended that local housing authorities also treat time spent in hospital or time spent in an institution in which households are accepted only for a limited period (eg mother and baby homes, refuges, rehabilitation centres) as exceptions for the purposes of determining local connection. These examples, not repeated in the current edition, illustrate the point that having normal residence of one's own choice in an area is not sufficient. Such residence must have the character, additionally, of establishing a 'local connection' with a local housing authority's district. The examples given were of normal residence of choice which *may* be thought, as a general rule, not to be of sufficient character to establish a local connection.

Former asylum-seekers

14.65 Former asylum-seekers who previously lived in accommodation provided by the Home Office under s 95 of the Immigration and Asylum Act 1999 (formerly known as 'NASS accommodation') do not reside in that district of their own choice[1]. However, asylum-seekers who occupied accommodation provided under IAA 1999, s 95 (the main duty to provide accommodation and support) are deemed to have a local connection with the local housing authority in whose district that accommodation is situated[2]. This deeming provision does not apply to asylum-seekers who only occupied accommodation provided under IAA 1999, s 98 (temporary support) or s 4 (hard cases support), nor to asylum-seekers who were provided with accommodation by local authorities under the Asylum Seekers (Interim Provisions) Regulations 1999[3].

1 *Al-Ameri v Kensington and Chelsea Royal London Borough Council* [2004] UKHL 4, [2004] 2 AC 159, HLR.
2 By HA 1996, s 199(6); H(W)A 2014, s 81(5). English Code, paras 10.23–10.25; Welsh Code, paras 18.16–18.18. See **14.88–14.94**.

³ SI 1999/3056. See further *Ciftci v Haringey London Borough Council* (2004) January *Legal Action*, p 32, Central London County Court.

14.66 Scottish law provides that residence in accommodation provided under IAA 1999, s 95 cannot constitute residence 'of his own choice', and so asylum seekers dispersed to Scotland by the Home Office do not, as a matter of law, acquire a local connection with a local authority in Scotland under this provision[1].

¹ Housing (Scotland) Act 1987, s 27 as amended by Homelessness etc (Scotland) Act 2003, s 7. As a result, there are lesser duties imposed on local housing authorities in England who receive applications for homelessness assistance from asylum seekers previously dispersed to Scotland (see **14.212–14.220**). The Scottish Ministers have the power to suspend Housing (Scotland) Act 1987, s 27, so as to end referral between local housing authorities (Homelessness etc (Scotland) Act 2003, s 8). They have not as yet exercised this power, see **15.238**. English Code, paras 10.26–10.29.

(2) EMPLOYMENT

14.67 An applicant, or a member of his or her household, who is employed in a district may acquire a local connection with that district by virtue of that employment[1]. The English Code suggests that the person must actually work in the district, in the sense of being physically present, for the employment to establish a local connection, and so it would not be sufficient, as in the case of a peripatetic employee, for the employer's head office to be located there[2].

¹ HA 1996, s 199(1)(b); H(W)A 2014, s 81(2)(b).
² English Code, para 10.8, although this is a difficult approach to apply to employment that is mobile, such as taxi-drivers or Deliveroo riders.

14.68 HA 1996, Pt 7[1], H(W)A 2014, Pt 2 and the English Code all use the present tense ('is employed')[2]. The question is therefore whether the applicant, or a member of his or her household, is employed in the relevant district at the date of the initial decision or review decision[3]. However, the simple fact of such current employment will not necessarily establish a local connection in itself. To build up and establish a local connection there will usually need to have been 'a period of employment'[4], although HA 1996, Pt 7[5] and H(W)A 2014, Pt 2 and the English Code do not suggest any particular period of employment. If the person's connection with an area is through past employment that will count, if at all, only if it amounts to 'special circumstances'[6].

¹ As amended by HRA 2017, for applications for homelessness assistance made to local housing authorities in England on or after 3 April 2018.
² HA 1996, s 199(1)(b); H(W)A 2014, s 81(2)(b).
³ *R v Ealing London Borough Council ex p Fox* (1998) The Times, 9 March, QBD.
⁴ *Betts v Eastleigh Borough Council* [1983] 2 AC 613, HL at 627 per Lord Brightman.
⁵ As amended by HRA 2017, for applications for homelessness assistance made to local housing authorities in England on or after 3 April 2018.
⁶ HA 1996, s 199(1)(d); H(W)A 2014, s 81(2)(d). See also **14.82–14.87**.

14.69 Further, the Local Authorities' Agreement suggests that, if it is to found a local connection, employment should not be of a casual nature. It then suggests that employers be asked for confirmation of both the fact of employment and its non-casual nature[1]. This inquiry is obviously unnecessary if the applicant can produce a written statement of the terms and conditions of employment or a fixed-term contract.

¹   Local Authorities Agreement, para 4.3(ii).

14.70 Employment can be full-time or part-time and include both paid and unpaid employment[1]. For example, an unpaid pastor in a church has been held to have a local connection with a district by virtue of that employment[2].

¹   *R v Ealing London Borough Council ex p Fox* (1998) The Times, 9 March, QBD.
²   *Sarac v Camden London Borough Council* (2002) June *Legal Action*, p 28, Central London County Court.

14.71 There is provision for the Secretary of State or the Welsh Ministers to specify other circumstances in which a person is not to be treated as employed in a district, but this power has not been exercised in either jurisdiction[1].

¹   HA 1996, s 199(5)(a); H(W)A 2014, s 81(4)(a).

(3)   FAMILY ASSOCIATIONS

14.72 An applicant, or a member of his or her household, may have a local connection with a district if he or she has family associations with that district[1]. 'Family associations' are not defined in HA 1996, Pt 7[2] or H(W)A 2014, Pt 2. The Local Authorities' Agreement suggests that the phrase should 'normally' be understood to refer to 'parents, adult children or brothers and sisters' and that only in 'exceptional circumstances' should the place of residence of other relatives be taken into account[3]. In the past, this approach (which was also contained in earlier versions of the Local Authorities Agreement) received a measure of judicial support:

> 'In my opinion family associations do not extend beyond parents, adult children or brothers and sisters. First cousins once removed (or cousins of any description) cannot provide the necessary connection[4].'

¹   HA 1996, s 199(1)(c); H(W)A 2014, s 81(2)(c).
²   As amended by HRA 2017, for applications for homelessness assistance made to local housing authorities in England on or after 3 April 2018.
³   Local Authorities Agreement, para 4.3(iii).
⁴   *R v Hammersmith and Fulham London Borough Council ex p Avdic* (1996) 28 HLR 897, QBD at 899 per Tucker J, confirmed on appeal at (1998) 30 HLR 1, CA.

14.73 In *R v Hammersmith and Fulham London Borough Council ex p Avdic*, it had been conceded that a first cousin once removed did not amount to a 'family association'. In a later case, *R v Ealing London Borough Council ex p Fox*, that expression of judicial opinion was directly followed and a local housing authority's decision that an uncle did not constitute a sufficiently close relative to establish a 'family association' was held not to be wrong in law[1].

¹   (1998) The Times, 9 March, QBD.

14.74 However, the better and more recent view, which has also received some support from the Court of Appeal, is that the question falls to be decided having regard to the fact-specific characteristics of the individual case:

697

' . . . the starting point is the position of the applicant and his household and, in having regard to both "family association" and "special circumstances", while we do not discourage general rules such as are to be found in the Local Authority Agreement, we note that Parliament left those broad phrases undefined and to be judged as a matter of fact and degree in every case. For instance, the actual closeness of the family association may count for more than the precise degree of consanguinity[1].'

[1] *Surdonja v Ealing London Borough Council* (2000) 32 HLR 481, CA at 489 per Henry LJ. Other cases have stressed the importance of the local housing authority's role in fact-finding, see, for example, *Bellis v Woking Borough Council* [2005] EWCA Civ 1671, (2006) February *Legal Action*, p 31, CA, where there was no error of law in the local housing authority's rejection of contact with a separated father as 'family association'.

14.75 In *Ozbek v Ipswich Borough Council*[1], the Court of Appeal specifically rejected a submission that only near relatives could found the basis for a local connection because of 'family associations'. Considering the judicial observations in *R v Hammersmith & Fulham London Borough Council ex p Avdic*[2], Chadwick LJ said that those observations were not authority for the proposition that only near relatives (parents, siblings, children) could provide a 'family association' and said that the relevant question is:

'whether, in the particular circumstances of the individual case, the bond between the applicant and one or more members of the extended family was of such a nature that it would be appropriate to regard those members of the extended family as "near relatives" in the sense in which that concept is recognised in the Referral Guidelines[3].'

[1] [2006] EWCA Civ 534, [2006] HLR 41, CA.
[2] (1996) 28 HLR 897, QBD; see **14.72–14.73**.
[3] *Ozbek v Ipswich Borough Council* [2006] EWCA Civ 534, [2006] HLR 41, CA at [43]–[44] and [49] per Chadwick LJ. By 'Referral Guidelines' the court was referring to the Local Authorities Agreement.

14.76 Sedley LJ said that, if the judge in *Avdic* had meant to confine 'family association' to near relatives, he was wrong and his judgment should not be followed in that regard. He gave examples of relatives whose presence might found a 'family association' as 'grandparents or uncles and aunts by whom the applicant had been brought up' and emphasised that 'the character of the family association must be at least as relevant – probably more relevant – than the degree of consanguinity'[1].

[1] *Ozbek v Ipswich Borough Council* [2006] EWCA Civ 534, [2006] HLR 41, CA at [64] per Sedley LJ.

14.77 Accordingly, the family relationship does not have to be one of blood or marriage. For example, an unmarried step-parent has been held to be a sufficiently close relative to provide a family association[1].

[1] *Munting v Hammersmith and Fulham London Borough Council* (1998) March *Legal Action*, p 15, West London County Court.

14.78 The current edition of the English Code shows that the Secretary of State takes a similar view:

' . . . where the applicant raises family associations, this may extend beyond partners, parents, adult children or siblings. They may include associations with other family members such as step-parents, grandparents, grandchildren, aunts or uncles provided there are sufficiently close links in the form of frequent contact, commitment or dependency. Family associations should be determined with regard to the fact-specific circumstances of the individual case. For example, the actual closeness of the family association may count for more than the degree of blood relation[1].'

[1] English Code, para 10.9. There is no specific guidance in the Welsh Code.

14.79 Local housing authorities, certainly in England, are therefore advised against applying the guidelines in the Local Authorities' Agreement rigidly and should follow the guidance in the English Code[1].

[1] Local housing authorities in Wales, even though not subject to the same guidance, should certainly ensure that they apply the Court of Appeal's approach in *Ozbek v Ipswich Borough Council* [2006] EWCA Civ 534, [2006] HLR 41, CA.

14.80 The Local Authorities' Agreement recommends that, in order to give rise to a local connection, the family members relied upon as 'family associations' should have been resident in the district for a period of at least five years at the date of application for homelessness assistance[1]. But no rule to this effect is contained in HA 1996 Pt 7[2] or H(W)A 2014, Pt 2, and the individual circumstances of a particular case might indicate that a shorter period of residence by a relation is sufficient. Local housing authorities need to guard against the temptation simply to apply the five-year yardstick to every case[3]. This is particularly so in the cases of refugees or other recent arrivals to the UK, where local housing authorities should bear in mind that the relatives may not have had five years in which to build up a residence period in any district in the UK[4].

[1] Local Authorities Agreement, para 4.3(iii).
[2] As amended by HRA 2017, for applications for homelessness assistance made to local housing authorities in England on or after 3 April 2018.
[3] See *R v Harrow London Borough Council ex p Carter* (1992) 26 HLR 32, QBD at 37, where the applicant's sister had lived in the Harrow area for only four years. Roger Henderson QC, sitting as a deputy High Court judge, said: 'It will be seen that that clause of the agreement, if applied rigidly, would mean that a family association would not normally arise if a homeless person's sister had been resident in Harrow for less than five years, but the agreement would not preclude this abnormally. Thus, to say without more ado that Mrs Carter had no local connection with Harrow because her sister had lived in Harrow for between four and five years would have been erroneous (a) because the agreement is no more than a guideline, (b) because the agreement did not so provide and (c) because, in Mrs Carter's predicament with four small children, any form of sisterly support might well make a significant difference in coping with her parental responsibilities'.
[4] *Ozbek v Ipswich Borough Council* [2006] EWCA Civ 534 [2006] HLR 41, (2006) June *Legal Action*, p 36, CA, at [46] per Chadwick LJ and at [65], per Sedley LJ.

14.81 The 'family associations' variant of local connection is an acknowledgment of 'the continuity of support that family associations can give'[1]. Accordingly, a local housing authority should not be relying on it in order to identify a connection with an area other than one where the applicant positively wants to live[2]. The applicant would generally need to indicate a wish to be near those members of his or her family for a local connection to be acquired through 'family associations'. As the Local Authorities' Agreement sensibly acknowledges, a referral should not be made under 'family associations' if the applicant objects to being referred to a district in which other members of his or her family live[3].

1   *Surdonja v Ealing London Borough Council* (2000) 32 HLR 481, CA at 485 per Henry LJ.
2   English Code, para 10.9.
3   Local Authorities Agreement, para 4.3(iii).

(4)   Special circumstances

14.82 A person may have a local connection with a particular district if his or her connection with it arises because of 'special circumstances'[1]. Unsurprisingly, these are not defined in HA 1996, Pt 7[2] or H(W)A 2014, Pt 2. The deliberately wide term embraces 'all special circumstances which can contribute to such a socially beneficial "local connection"' with an area[3].

1   HA 1996, s 199(1)(d); H(W)A 2014, s 81(2)(d).
2   As amended by HRA 2017, for applications for homelessness assistance made to local housing authorities in England on or after 3 April 2018.
3   *Surdonja v Ealing London Borough Council* (2000) 32 HLR 481, CA at 485 per Henry LJ.

14.83 The English Code gives as an example 'the need to be near special medical or support services which are available only in a particular district'[1].

1   English Code, para 10.11.

14.84 The Local Authorities' Agreement suggests that this category 'may be particularly relevant in dealing with people who have been in prison or in hospital' and gives an example of a person seeking to return to an area where he or she was brought up or lived for a considerable length of time[1].

1   Local Authorities Agreement, para 4.3(iv).

14.85 Absent a statutory definition, and with only limited guidance given by the Codes and the Local Authorities' Agreement, it is no surprise to find that a wide range of circumstances have been advanced (often unsuccessfully) as being sufficiently 'special' for these purposes. These include:

- the need to visit a particular mosque and attend a particular school[1];
- medical advice that an applicant needed to live in a warmer area[2];
- residence (not for a sufficient period to constitute normal residence under HA 1996, s 199(1)(a) or H(W)A 2014, s 81(2)(a)), first with the man with whom the applicant believed that she was going to live permanently and, secondly, in a woman's refuge[3];
- the need to remain in the London area to receive medical treatment (the local housing authority was entitled to take the view that the medical treatment required was also available in the notified local housing authority's district)[4];
- the applicant's need for care and assistance would not be met in the notified local housing authority's district[5];
- the applicant's traumatic experiences before fleeing as a refugee, the existence of an ethnic minority community of same-language speakers in the local housing authority's district, and enrolment at a local college[6];

- the fact that the applicant's children had special educational needs and were making rapid progress at a particular local school[7];
- a fear of leaving the area by reason of the risk of violence that might be experienced elsewhere[8];
- membership of a church community around which the applicant's social life revolved[9];
- 14 years' previous residence in the area in which the applicants' children had attended school and in which the family still had friends[10]; and
- a former asylum-seeker's decision to seek accommodation in an area because her daughter had secured a bursary to study at a private school in that area, and where the daughter had been in that school for three months[11].

[1] *R v Westminster City Council ex p Benniche* (1996) 29 HLR 230, CA, where the local housing authority's decision of 'no special circumstances' on the facts was not wrong in law.

[2] *R v East Devon District Council ex p Robb* (1997) 30 HLR 922, QBD, where the local housing authority was wrong in law not to have considered this as a potentially special circumstance.

[3] *R v Southwark London Borough Council ex p Hughes* (1998) 30 HLR 1082, QBD, where the local housing authority was wrong in law not to have considered this as a potentially special circumstance.

[4] *R v Hammersmith and Fulham London Borough Council ex p Avdic* (1998) 30 HLR 1, CA, where the local housing authority's decision of no special circumstances on the facts was not wrong in law.

[5] *Connor v Brighton and Hove Council* [1998] EWCA Civ 1396, (1999) August *Legal Action*, p 29, CA, where the local housing authority's decision of no special circumstances on the facts was not wrong in law.

[6] *R v Kensington and Chelsea Royal London Borough Council ex p Bishop* (unreported) 11 February 1983, QBD.

[7] *R v Harrow London Borough Council ex p Carter* (1992) 26 HLR 32, QBD, where the local housing authority should have considered those circumstances.

[8] *R v Islington London Borough Council ex p Adigun* (1986) 20 HLR 600, QBD, where the local housing authority's decision of no special circumstances on the facts was not wrong in law.

[9] *R v White Horse District Council ex p Smith and Hay* (1984) 17 HLR 160, QBD, where the local housing authority's decision of no special circumstances on the facts was not wrong in law. See also *R (Gebremarium) v Westminster City Council* [2009] EWHC 2254 (Admin), (2009) November *Legal Action*, p 26, Admin Ct.

[10] *R v Waltham Forest London Borough Council ex p Koutsoudis* (unreported) 1 September 1986, QBD.

[11] *X v Ealing London Borough Council* (2010) November *Legal Action*, p 19, Brentford County Court where the local housing authority's decision that there were no special circumstances was wrong in law, and no reasonable local housing authority could have decided other than that the applicant had a local connection.

14.86 The generally strict line taken by the courts (rejecting most of the above challenges to decisions of local housing authorities) reflects the fact that Parliament has left it to local housing authorities to determine whether there are sufficiently 'special' circumstances to amount to a local connection. However, a local housing authority must not gloss the statutory language by seeking some extra-special or particularly pressing 'special circumstances'. For example, a local housing authority considering an application based on a 'special circumstances' connection was held to have misdirected itself by looking for 'an essential compassionate, social or support need' to be in a particular area[1]. Policy considerations that might be relevant to the decision whether to exercise the discretion to make a referral, will not be relevant to a decision as to whether an applicant has a local connection as the result of special circumstances[2].

1 *Surdonja v Ealing London Borough Council* (2000) 32 HLR 481, CA at 494 per Henry LJ.
2 *Salmani v Southwark London Borough Council* (2013) July/August *Legal Action*, p 23, Lambeth County Court.

14.87 Local housing authorities are advised in the Local Authorities' Agreement that, if they are referring on the basis that an applicant has no local connection with their area, but does have a local connection with another area under this category, they should only do so with the prior consent of the notified local housing authority[1].

1 Local Authorities Agreement, para 4.4.

(5)   DEEMED 'LOCAL CONNECTION' FOR SOME FORMER ASYLUM-SEEKERS

14.88 By virtue of amendments made to HA 1996, Pt 7 in 2005 (and subsequently enacted in H(W)A 2014, Pt 2), a 'local connection' is deemed to have been acquired by a person with the district of any local housing authority in England or Wales in which he or she, while an asylum-seeker, was provided with accommodation under s 95 of the Immigration and Asylum Act 1999[1]. The accommodation could have been provided 'at any time', ie before or after this provision for deemed local connection was enacted[2].

1 HA 1996, s 199(6); (H(W)A 2014, s 81(5). See English Code, paras 10.23–10.25.
2 HA 1996, s 199(6); H(W)A 2014, s 81(5).

14.89 The effect of this deeming provision is that former asylum-seekers, who previously occupied accommodation provided by the Home Office, will acquire a local connection with the local housing authority in whose district the Home Office accommodation was situated[1].

1 As was the case in *Ozbek v Ipswich Borough Council* [2006] EWCA Civ 534, [2006] HLR 41, CA, where the applicant had a local connection with Portsmouth, having lived in NASS accommodation there for just under three months. In *Danesh v Kensington & Chelsea Royal London Borough Council* [2006] EWCA Civ 1404, [2007] HLR 17, CA, the applicant had spent 14 months in Home Office accommodation. See also *R (Gebremarium) v Westminster City Council* [2009] EWHC 2254 (Admin), (2009) November *Legal Action*, p 26, Admin Ct.

14.90 Since HA 1996, s 199(6) and H(W)A 2014, s 81(5) both specify 'at any time', a former asylum-seeker will retain a local connection with that district forever. Even if the Home Office accommodation came to an end some considerable time before the applicant's subsequent application for homelessness assistance, and even if the applicant had since then moved around the country and acquired a local connection with other local housing authorities, he or she will retain a local connection with that original district. It appears that the local connection cannot be lost, although it becomes of less importance if the former asylum-seeker is able to establish a local connection with another local housing authority (for example, by employment) and makes the application for homelessness assistance there[1].

1 English Code, para 10.25. For an example of a former asylum-seeker who had both a local connection because of special circumstances with the district of the local housing authority to

which she had applied, and a deemed local connection with another local housing authority because of occupying accommodation there which had been provided under Immigration and Asylum Act 1999, s 95, see *X v Ealing London Borough Council* (2010) November *Legal Action*, p 19, Brentford County Court.

14.91 The lifetime acquisition of deemed local connection applies not just to the asylum-seeker, but also, it would seem, to every member of his or her household who had been 'provided with' Home Office accommodation in that area. Applying that deemed local connection to a homeless applicant's household means that any member of the applicant's household who had, in the past, been provided with Home Office accommodation, whether in his or her own right or as part of the household of an asylum-seeker, therefore acquires a local connection. Nor does there appear to be any minimum period during which the asylum-seeker must occupy the Home Office accommodation for it to trigger a deemed local connection[1].

1   So, if a person moves into Home Office accommodation in District A on a Monday (having lived in District B for the previous nine months), is accorded refugee status on the Tuesday, and that accommodation burns down on the Wednesday, he or she will have a local connection with District A, and his or her application for homelessness assistance made on Thursday to District A could not be referred to District B or anywhere else.

14.92 There are two statutory qualifications to the deemed local connection triggered by occupation of Home Office accommodation. First, the deemed local connection is only acquired with the district in which the *last* accommodation provided by the Home Office was situated. If the asylum-seeker was moved around by the Home Office, it is only the last accommodation that can be considered as giving rise to the deemed local connection[1]. Second, accommodation provided by the Home Office in an accommodation centre[2] cannot constitute accommodation by which an applicant acquires a deemed local connection[3].

1   HA 1996, s 199(7)(a); H(W)A 2014, s 81(6)(a). See English Code, para 10.24(a).
2   Nationality, Immigration and Asylum Act 2002, s 22; English Code, para 10.24(b). Plans to build accommodation centres were abandoned by the then Labour government and s 22 has never been brought into force.
3   HA 1996, s 199(7)(b); H(W)A 2014, s 81(6)(b).

14.93 The deemed local connection category specifically refers to accommodation which was provided under s 95 of the Immigration and Asylum Act 1999 (IAA 1999). That is the main statutory power available to the Secretary of State to provide accommodation to asylum-seekers. It does not refer to other temporary accommodation, including accommodation provided under IAA 1999, s 98[1], or to hard cases support[2], or to accommodation provided by local authorities[3]. Former asylum-seekers who were accommodated only under one of these latter provisions, therefore, will not have acquired a deemed local connection.

1   Immigration and Asylum Act 1999, s 98. See *Berhane v Lambeth London Borough Council* [2007] EWHC 2702 (QB), (2008) March *Legal Action*, p 21, QBD.
2   Immigration and Asylum Act 1999, s 4.
3   SI 1999/3056.

14.94 The deemed local connection provisions are only part of homelessness legislation for *England* and *Wales* – there is no such deeming provision in

Scotland. Instead, Home Office accommodation provided under IAA 1999, s 95 in Scotland is specifically not capable of giving rise to a local connection by virtue of normal residence because it is not 'residence of his own choice'[1]. Asylum-seekers who occupied Home Office accommodation in Scotland do not, therefore, acquire a local connection with the local authority in Scotland for the area in which that accommodation is situated, by virtue of such residence alone. Instead, for a local housing authority in England considering an application from a former asylum seeker who had been provided with accommodation under IAA 1999, s 95, the main housing duty under HA 1996, s 193(2) to provide accommodation (if owed by a local housing authority in England to a former resident of Home Office accommodation in Scotland) is modified by s 11(2) and (3) of the Asylum and Immigration (Treatment of Claimants etc) Act 2004, so that a former asylum-seeker is provided with accommodation for a period, giving him or her a reasonable opportunity of securing accommodation, and is given advice and assistance either to apply to a local authority in Scotland as homeless or to find his or her own accommodation[2]. These rules are discussed later in this chapter[3].

[1] Housing (Scotland) Act 1987, s 27, as amended.
[2] Asylum and Immigration (Treatment of Claimants etc) Act 2004, s 11(2) and (3); English Code, paras 10.26–10.29.
[3] See **14.212–14.220**. Note there is no modification to the HA 1996, s 189B(2) relief duty, as inserted by HRA 2017, s 5(2) for applications for homelessness assistance made to local housing authorities in England on or after 3 April 2018.

Deemed 'local connection' for certain care leavers owed a duty under Children Act 1989, s 23C

14.95 By virtue of amendments made to HA 1996, Pt 7 by HRA 2017, a local connection is deemed to have been acquired by a young person to whom a duty is owed under Children Act 1989, s 23C by a local authority[1]. That duty is owed to any young person between the ages of 18 and 21[2] or 25[3] who was looked after[4] by the local authority for a period of 13 weeks or more, beginning after his or her 14th birthday and ending after his or her 16th birthday[5]. A young person who is owed the duty under Children Act 1989, s 23C is known as a 'former relevant child'[6]. He or she will be entitled to a personal advisor, a pathway plan and various other forms of assistance[7].

[1] HA 1996, ss 199(8)–(9) as inserted by HRA 2017, s 8 for applications for homelessness assistance made to local housing authorities in England on or after 3 April 2018. See English Code, paras 10.17–10.18.
[2] See Children Act 1989 ss 23C(1) and (6).
[3] The duty may continue after the young person has reached the age of 21 if he or she is pursuing a programme of education which is set out in his or her pathway plan. See Children Act 1989 s 23C(7).
[4] As defined by Children Act 1989, s 22.
[5] See Children Act 1989, s 23C(1); Children Act 1989, Sch 2, para 19B; Children Act 1989 s 23A; and Care Planning, Placement and Care Review Regulations 2010, SI 2010/959, reg 40.
[6] Children Act 1989, s 23C(1).
[7] Children Act 1989, s 23C(2)–(5). See further **20.65**.

14.96 While a local authority in England have a duty towards a young person under Children Act 1989, s 23C, if the local authority is a local housing authority, the young person is deemed to have a local connection with that district[1]. If the local authority is not a local housing authority then the young person is deemed to have a local connection with every district of a local housing authority that falls within the area of the local authority[2].

[1] HA 1996, s 199(8)(a) as inserted by HRA 2017, s 8 for applications for homelessness assistance made to local housing authorities in England on or after 3 April 2018. 'Local authority' in this context has the same meaning as in Children Act 1989, s 105. See HA 1996, s 199(9) as inserted by HRA 2017, s 8 for applications for homelessness assistance made to local housing authorities in England on or after 3 April 2018.

[2] HA 1996, s 199(8)(b) as inserted by HRA 2017, s 8 for applications for homelessness assistance made to local housing authorities in England on or after 3 April 2018.

14.97 HA 1996, s 199(8) is a deeming provision. That is, a person who satisfies the requirements of HA 1996, s 199(8) is deemed to have a local connection with a district irrespective of the actual strength of his or her connection with the area.

14.98 The local connection is deemed to exist only while the duty under Children Act 1989, s 23C is owed. Typically the duty will end when the young person reaches the age of 21 or when his or her programme of education finishes[1]. When the duty comes to an end the young person will no longer be deemed to have a local connection with the district. Though he or she may still have a local connection acquired in one or more of the other circumstances specified in HA 1996, s 199[2].

[1] See **14.95** fn 3.
[2] See **14.44**.

14.99 This deemed local connection provision is only part of the homelessness legislation for England under HA 1996, Pt 7[1] and applies solely to referrals between local housing authorities in England[2]. There is no such deeming provision in Wales under H(W)A 2014, Pt 2.

[1] As amended by HRA 2017, for applications for homelessness assistance made to local housing authorities in England on or after 3 April 2018.
[2] HA 1996, s 199(8) as inserted by HRA 2017, s 8 for applications for homelessness assistance made to local housing authorities in England on or after 3 April 2018.

DEEMED 'LOCAL CONNECTION' FOR CERTAIN CARE LEAVERS WHO HAVE BEEN ACCOMMODATED UNDER CHILDREN ACT 1989, S 22A

14.100 By virtue of amendments made to HA 1996, Pt 7 by HRA 2017[1], a young person under the age of 21 who, by virtue of being accommodated under Children Act 1989, s 22A[2], was normally resident in the district of a local housing authority in England for a continuous period of at least two years, some or all of which fell before the person attained the age of 16, is deemed to have a local connection with that district[3].

[1] For applications for homelessness assistance made to local housing authorities in England on or after 3 April 2018.
[2] HA 1996, ss 199(10)–(11) as inserted by HRA 2017, s 8 for applications for homelessness assistance made to local housing authorities in England on or after 3 April 2018. See English Code, paras 10.17–10.18.
[3] HA 1996, s 199(10) as inserted by HRA 2017, s 8 for applications for homelessness assistance made to local housing authorities in England on or after 3 April 2018.

14.101 There is no requirement that the young person should have been normally resident in the district by his or her own choice[1]. Indeed, in many cases the residence will not have been of his or her choosing[2].

1 Contrast HA 1996, s 199(10) with s 199(1)(a).
2 See **14.60**.

14.102 HA 1996, s 199(10)[1] is a deeming provision. That is, a person who satisfies the requirements of HA 1996, s 199(10)[2] is deemed to have a local connection with a district irrespective of the actual strength of his or her connection with the area. This deemed local connection will cease upon the young person reaching the age of 21[3], though he or she may still have a local connection acquired in one or more of the other circumstances specified in HA 1996, s 199[4].

1 As inserted by HRA 2017, s 8 for applications for homelessness assistance made to local housing authorities in England on or after 3 April 2018.
2 As inserted by HRA 2017, s 8 for applications for homelessness assistance made to local housing authorities in England on or after 3 April 2018.
3 HA 1996, s 199(11) as inserted by HRA 2017, s 8 for applications for homelessness assistance made to local housing authorities in England on or after 3 April 2018.
4 See **14.44**.

14.103 This deemed local connection provision is only part of the homelessness legislation for England under HA 1996, Pt 7[1] and applies solely to referrals between local housing authorities in England[2]. There is no such deeming provision in Wales under H(W)A 2014, Pt 2.

1 As amended by HRA 2017, for applications for homelessness assistance made to local housing authorities in England on or after 3 April 2018.
2 HA 1996, s 199(10) as inserted by HRA 2017, s 8 for applications for homelessness assistance made to local housing authorities in England on or after 3 April 2018.

Who acquires a local connection?

14.104 A relevant local connection may have been acquired (or deemed to have been acquired) by the applicant or by any person who might reasonably be expected to reside with the applicant[1].

1 HA 1996, s 198(2); H(W)A 2014, s 80(3). See also English Code, para 10.35; Local Authorities Agreement, para 4.3; Welsh Code, paras 18.5 and 18.9. The question of whether it is reasonable to expect a person to reside with the applicant arises both in relation to homelessness and priority need and is discussed at **10.29–10.30, 12.58–12.75**.

14.105 Any local housing authority choosing to investigate the question of local connection must obviously, therefore, make inquiries into any potential local connection that any of the people who might reasonably be expected to reside with the applicant might have, either with its own district or any other district in England, Wales or (for applications to local housing authorities in England) Scotland.

14.106 The extent of any local connection enjoyed by any other member of the household (if that local connection is different from any enjoyed by the applicant) could be relevant in various scenarios. For example:

(1) The applicant has no local connection with the local housing authority to which she or he has applied and does have a local connection with another local housing authority, but a member of his or her household has a local connection with the local housing authority to which the application has been made: the conditions for referral are not met and the applicant cannot be referred.

(2) Neither the applicant nor any member of his or her household has a local connection with the local housing authority to which he or she has applied, the applicant has a local connection with another local housing authority and a member of the applicant's household has a local connection with a different local housing authority: the conditions for referral are met, but the local housing authority dealing with the application has a discretion as to which local housing authority it will refer the applicant to (if it decides to make any referral)[1].

(3) The applicant has a connection with the local housing authority applied to, but a member of the household has a stronger connection with the district of another local housing authority. There can be no referral – the connection of the other household member(s) is irrelevant.

[1] See **15.151–15.154**.

Risk of violence or abuse (domestic or otherwise)

14.107 If the applicant is owed the HA 1996, s 189B(2) relief duty[1] or the HA 1996, s 193(2)[2] main housing duty (England) or is owed the H(W)A 2014, s 73 duty[3], has a priority need and did not become homeless intentionally, (Wales) and he or she, or a member of his or her household:

(1) does not have a local connection with the district of the local housing authority to which the application is made; and

(2) does have a local connection with the district of another local housing authority in England, Wales or (for applications to local housing authorities in England) Scotland,

the local housing authority in receipt of the application, and which has opted to consider local connection questions, must then inquire into whether or not:

(1) the applicant, or any member of his or her household, would run the risk of domestic violence (England) or domestic abuse (Wales) in that other local housing authority's district; and

(2) the applicant, or any member of his or her household, had suffered violence or abuse in the district of that other local housing authority and it is probable that there would be further violence or abuse of a similar kind if he or she returned to that district.[4]

[1] As inserted by the HRA 2017, s 5(2) for applications for homelessness assistance made to local housing authorities in England on or after 3 April 2018. See **15.138–15.189**.
[2] See **16.94–16.199**.
[3] See **17.73–17.117**.
[4] HA 1996, s 198(2)(c), (2A) and (3); H(W)A 2014, s 198(3)(c) and (4).

14.108 The local housing authority is obliged to make inquiries itself into the risk of violence or abuse (domestic or otherwise); it is not sufficient for it to wait for the applicant to volunteer any relevant information[1].

[1]   *R v Greenwich London Borough Council ex p Patterson* (1994) 26 HLR 159, CA.

14.109 The wording of the statutory provisions puts victims of domestic violence or domestic abuse in a slightly different position from victims of other violence or abuse.

14.110 Under HA 1996, Pt 7[1], 'violence' means 'violence from another person or threats of violence from another person which are likely to be carried out'[2]. The courts have decided that violence (whether domestic or otherwise) should be given a broad definition, encompassing not just physical violence but also 'threatening or intimidating behaviour and any other form of abuse which, directly or indirectly may give rise to the risk of harm'[3]. The broad definition has been adopted in the English Code[4].

[1]   As amended by HRA 2017, for applications for homelessness assistance made to local housing authorities in England on or after 3 April 2018.
[2]   HA 1996, s 198(3). The definition is the same as that applying to the definition of homelessness at HA 1996, s 177(1). See **10.79–10.91**.
[3]   *Yemshaw v Hounslow London Borough Council* [2011] UKSC 3, [2011] 1 WLR 433, [2011] HLR 16, SC, Baroness Hale at [28] (quoting the *Practice Direction (Residence and Contact Orders: Domestic Violence (No 2)* [2009] 1 WLR 251) and *Hussain v Waltham Forest London Borough Council* [2015] EWCA Civ 14, [2015] HLR 16, CA.
[4]   English Code, paras 21.2–21.7 and 21.19. See **10.83**.

14.111 For local housing authorities in Wales, the word 'abuse' has been used in place of the word 'violence'. 'Abuse' has been defined in H(W)A 2014, s 58(1)[1] as 'physical violence, threatening or intimidating behaviour and any other form of abuse which, directly or indirectly, may give rise to the risk of harm'[2], reflecting the approach under HA 1996, Pt 7[3].

[1]   H(W)A 2014, s 99.
[2]   See further Welsh Code, paras 3.114 and 18.20–18.21.
[3]   As amended by HRA 2017, for applications for homelessness assistance made to local housing authorities in England on or after 3 April 2018. See further **10.91–10.98**.

DOMESTIC VIOLENCE OR ABUSE

14.112 Violence or abuse is 'domestic' in nature if it is from a person who is associated with the victim[1]. The phrase 'a person who is associated with the victim' is defined at HA 1996, s 178 and H(W)A 2014, s 58(2) and includes:

- spouses and former spouses;
- civil partners and former civil partners;
- cohabitants and former cohabitants (heterosexual or same-sex);
- people who live or used to live in the same household;
- relatives;
- people who have agreed to marry each other or to enter into a civil partnership; and
- people who share the parentage of, or parental responsibility for, a child (including the relationship between natural and adoptive parents)[2].

[1]   HA 1996, s 198(3); H(W)A 2014, s 58(1).

2 Civil Partnership Act 2004, s 81 and Sch 8, para 61 amended HA 1996, s 178 to include references to civil partnerships and same-sex couples living together as though they were civil partners, in force from 5 December 2005.

14.113 The definition also includes adoptive and natural parents of a child, step-relatives, grandparents and grandchildren, siblings, uncles, aunts, nieces and nephews, and in-laws or former in-laws (including relatives of a civil partner or former civil partner)[1]. Under H(W)A 2014, Pt 2 the definition also includes people who have had an intimate personal relationship with each other of significant duration[2].

1 HA 1996, s 178(1), (2), (3); H(W)A 2014, s 58(2), (3) and (5). See also **10.85** and **10.96**.
2 H(W)A 2014, s 58(2).

14.114 If the issue of domestic violence or abuse is the subject of inquiries, the question is whether the applicant, or a member of the applicant's household, will run the risk of domestic violence or abuse in the district of the local housing authority intended to be notified[1]. It follows, therefore, that that person need not actually have been subject in the past to actual or threatened domestic violence or abuse there. Obviously, if there has been domestic violence or abuse, the relevant question to ask is whether it will recur. However, even where there has been no domestic violence or abuse in the past, if there is information that leads to the conclusion that the person would be at risk of violence or abuse from an associated person, the conditions for referral are not made out.

1 HA 1996, s 198(2)(c); H(W)A 2014, s 80(3)(c).

OTHER VIOLENCE OR ABUSE

14.115 If there is no *domestic* violence or abuse, the test is slightly different (although the Codes of Guidance do not draw attention to, or give guidance upon, the difference.)[1] There must have been violence, as defined by HA 1996[2], or abuse, as defined by H(W)A 2014[3], suffered in the district of the local housing authority likely to be notified, and it must be probable that the return to that district will lead to further violence or abuse of a similar kind[4]. The past violence or abuse may have been carried out by any person, not being a person 'associated' with the victim.

1 English Code, paras 10.52–10.54; Welsh Code, paras 18.20–18.21.
2 HA 1996, s 198(3). See **14.110**.
3 H(W)A 2014, s 58(1). See **14.111**.
4 HA 1996, s 198(2A); H(W)A 2014, s 80(4).

14.116 It follows that there are two questions for the local housing authority:

(1)   Has there been violence or abuse?
(2)   Is it 'probable'[1] that the victim's return to the notified local housing authority's district will lead to further violence or abuse of a similar kind against the same victim?

1 'Probable' means 'more likely than not' (*Bond v Leicester City Council* [2001] EWCA Civ 1544, [2002] HLR 6, CA).

14.117 The local housing authority is entitled to take the applicant's perceptions, fears or concerns into account, but it is for the local housing authority to decide the facts, in order to answer these two questions objectively[1].

[1]   *Danesh v Kensington & Chelsea Royal London Borough Council* [2006] EWCA Civ 1404, [2007] HLR 17, CA at [26] per Neuberger LJ.

14.118 Where there is a probability of violence or abuse, other than domestic violence or abuse, which is of a different kind to that previously experienced, the test will not be made out. Similarly, if any violence or abuse in the future were to be directed against another member of the household, the test will not be made out. Although there would be no statutory bar on a local housing authority referring a victim back to an area in which a different kind of non-domestic violence or abuse was likely to be suffered by another member of the household, it might be expected that a local housing authority would exercise its discretion *not* to refer in those circumstances.

14.119 The factual decisions as to:

(1)   whether there is a risk of domestic violence or domestic abuse; or
(2)   whether other violence or abuse occurred in the past; and
(3)   whether it is probable that there will be further violence or abuse of a similar kind in future,

are for the local housing authority to make, and its decisions will be upheld by the courts, provided that it lawfully applies the correct statutory tests[1].

[1]   *R v Islington London Borough Council ex p Adigun* (1988) 20 HLR 600, QBD; *Danesh v Kensington & Chelsea Royal London Borough Council* [2006] EWCA Civ 1404, [2007] HLR 17, CA.

Conditions for referral by reason of local connection – a summary

14.120 Only if:

* the applicant is owed the HA 1996, s 189B(2)[1] relief duty or the HA 1996, s 193(2) main housing duty[2], (England) or is owed the H(W)A 2014, s 73 duty[3] relief duty, has a priority need and did not become homeless intentionally, (Wales); and
* neither the applicant, nor any member of his or her household, has a local connection with the district of the local housing authority to which he or she has applied; and
* either the applicant, or a member of his or her household, has a local connection with the district of another local housing authority in England, Wales or (for applications to local housing authorities in England) Scotland; and
* there is no risk of domestic violence or domestic abuse to the applicant or any member of his or her household in the district of the other local housing authority; and
* neither the applicant, nor any member of his or her household, had suffered violence or abuse the other local housing authority's district; and

• if either the applicant, or a member of his or her household, had suffered violence or abuse in the other local housing authority's district, it is not probable that there will be further violence or abuse of a similar kind against that person,

are the conditions for referral under the local connection route made out.

[1] As inserted by the HRA 2017, s 5(2) for applications for homelessness assistance made to local housing authorities in England on or after 3 April 2018. See **15.138–15.189**. Note, the case of an applicant who is owed the relief duty by a local housing authority in England can only be referred to another local housing authority in England. See HA 1996, s 198(A1) as inserted by HRA 2017, s 5(8) for applications for homelessness assistance made to local housing authorities in England on or after 3 April 2018.

[2] See **16.94–16.199**.

[3] See **17.73–17.117**.

14.121 Where the conditions for referral are met, and there is a local connection with *two or more* different local housing authorities (not including the local housing authority which received the application), the original local housing authority has a discretion as to which of the other local housing authorities it should refer the applicant to (if any). When considering that discretion, it should take into account the applicant's own preference[1].

[1] English Code, para 10.34; Welsh Code, para 18.10.

14.122 Even if all the conditions for a referral are made out, the local housing authority is under no obligation to refer and has an unqualified discretion as to whether or not to refer[1].

[1] See **14.151–14.154**.

The second set of conditions for referral – private rented sector offers

Introduction

14.123 The second set of circumstances[1] in which the conditions for referral are met is much more self-contained and has nothing to do with the statutory definition of 'local connection'[2]. It arises where:

(1) an applicant had made an application for homelessness assistance on or after 9 November 2012 to a local housing authority in England; and

(2) the applicant accepted a private rented sector offer[3] from that local housing authority of accommodation located in the district of another local housing authority in England; and

(3) the applicant subsequently made an application for homelessness assistance to the second local housing authority in England within two years of the date of acceptance of that offer[4].

[1] HA 1996, s 198(2ZA) and (2A).

[2] See **14.43–14.122**.

[3] HA 1996, s 193(7AA)–(7AC). See **16.153–16.179**.

[4] HA 1996 198(2ZA) and (2A).

14.124 Its purpose is to ensure that applicants in those circumstances – who benefit from special provisions whereby the main housing duty will be owed to most applicants whether or not they have a priority need[1] – remain the responsibility of the local housing authority which made the private rented sector offer. In particular, the availability of private rented sector offers and the restrictions on housing benefit make it likely that local housing authorities operating in areas of high private sector rents will make private rented sector offers in districts where rents are less expensive. If the assured shorthold tenancies secured under these arrangements end within two years of the date of acceptance, it is the local housing authority which made the private rented sector offer which will subsequently owe a main housing duty to the applicant[2].

1   HA 1996, s 195A(1). See **8.100–8.107**. There is no equivalent provision in H(W)A 2014.
2   HA 1996, s 195A as amended by HRA 2017, s 4(4) for applications for homelessness assistance made to local housing authorities in England on or after 3 April 2018. See **8.100–8.107**.

14.125 This set of conditions applies where both the first application and the subsequent application for homelessness assistance were made to local housing authorities in England. The first application for homelessness assistance must have been made on or after 9 November 2012[1].

1   Localism Act 2011 (Commencement No 2 and Transitional Provisions) (England) Order 2012, SI 2012/2599.

14.126 This second set of conditions for referral does not apply in Scotland or Wales and cannot be used by a local housing authority in England to refer an applicant to a local authority in Scotland or Wales[1].

1   Because HA 1996, s 198(2ZA) only applies to local housing authorities in England. Housing (Scotland) Act 1987, s 33 (the Scottish equivalent to HA 1996, s 198) and H(W)A 2014, Pt 2 do not contain an equivalent provision to HA 1996, s 198(2ZA).

14.127 The provisions of the Local Authorities' Agreement will apply, where relevant, to any disputes between local housing authorities as to whether or not this set of conditions for referral is met[1].

1   Local Authorities Agreement, para 10.1.

The second set of conditions

14.128 The second set of conditions[1] for a referral will be met where[2]:

(1)   the applicant had previously applied to a local housing authority in England (authority A) on or after 9 November 2012[3];
(2)   authority A had made the applicant a private rented sector offer[4] in order to bring the main housing duty to an end[5];
(3)   the applicant accepted the private rented sector offer[6];
(4)   the applicant makes an application for homelessness assistance to authority B within two years of the date of his or her acceptance of the offer[7];
(5)   neither the applicant nor any member of the applicant's household will run the risk of domestic violence in the district of authority A[8];

(6)　　neither the applicant, nor any member of his or her household, had suffered violence or threats of violence that were likely to be carried out in the district of authority A[9]; and

(7)　　if either the applicant, or a member of his or her household, had suffered violence in the district, of authority A, it is not probable that there will be further violence of a similar kind against that person[10].

1　English Code, para 10.54.
2　HA 1996, s 198(2ZA).
3　The date when the amendments to HA 1996 made by LA 2011, ss 148–149 came into force (see Localism Act 2011 (Commencement No 2 and Transitional Provisions) (England) Order 2012, SI 2012/2599).
4　HA 1996, s 193(7AA).
5　HA 1996, ss 193(7AA)–(7AC). See **16.153–16.179**.
6　HA 1996, s 193(7AA)(a).
7　See **8.100–8.107**.
8　See **14.107–14.119**.
9　See **14.107–14.119**.
10　See **14.107–14.119**.

14.129 It should be noted that the relevant two-year period is that between the date of the applicant's acceptance of the private rented sector offer from authority A and the date of his or her application for homelessness assistance to authority B. It is not from the date of the commencement of the tenancy.

14.130 The applicant will also be entitled to the benefit of the special provisions in HA 1996, s 195A[1]. For most applicants, they will not need to have a priority need in order to be entitled to the main housing duty[2]. If they are given a valid HA 1988, s 21 notice, they will also be deemed to be homelessness on the date on which the notice expires[3]. These special provisions only apply on the first occasion when an applicant makes an application within two years of acceptance of a private rented sector offer[4]. If the applicant subsequently accepts a second private rented sector offer, there are no special provisions if the applicant later makes a fresh application for homelessness assistance.

1　See **8.100–8.107**.
2　HA 1996, s 195A(1). See **8.100–8.107**. The exception is where the applicant is only owed the main housing duty because of the presence in his or her household of a 'restricted person' (defined at HA 1996, s 184(7), see **11.163–11.164**). If that is the case, the applicant must still have a priority need in order to be entitled to the main housing duty (HA 1996 s 195A(5)). See **16.180–16.185**.
3　HA 1996, s 195A(2). See **8.100–8.107**. For priority need, see Chapter **12**.
4　HA 1996, s 195A(6) as amended by HRA 2017, for applications for homelessness assistance made to local housing authorities in England on or after 3 April 2018. See **8.100–8.107** and **10.135–10.143**.

14.131 Unlike the special provisions in HA 1996, s 195A[1], this set of conditions for referral applies to all applicants who have accepted a private rented sector offer from one local housing authority and then make an application for homelessness assistance to another local housing authority within two years of acceptance. It does not matter whether the application being considered follows a first acceptance of a private rented sector offer, or a second, third or fourth acceptance. If the application for homelessness assistance is made within two years of any acceptance of a private rented sector offer, this set of conditions for referral will apply.

¹ See **8.100–8.107**.

14.132 This set of conditions does not require the applicant to be currently living in the private rented sector accommodation, which he or she had accepted. It may be that the tenancy has ended and the applicant has managed to find his or her own accommodation, whether another assured shorthold tenancy or some much more insecure arrangement. If the application for homelessness assistance is made within two years of the date of acceptance of the private rented sector offer, this set of conditions for referral will apply.

14.133 The second set of conditions for referral is not satisfied if the application for homelessness assistance is made to authority B more than two years after the date of acceptance of the private rented sector offer. If the application is made on the two-year anniversary itself, or any time after that, this set of conditions for referral will not apply and the only relevant set of conditions would be those relating to 'local connection'¹.

¹ HA 1996, s 198(2) and (2A), see **14.43–14.122**.

14.134 The second set of conditions is also not satisfied if the applicant is someone other than the person who accepted the private rented sector offer¹. The special provisions at HA 1996, s 195A² only apply to re-applications made by the same person who had accepted the private rented sector offer³. So if the household would need to take advantage of those special provisions (perhaps because there is no longer any member of a household who has a priority need)⁴, the application should be made by the person who had accepted the private rented sector offer. On the other hand, if there is no benefit to the household in the special provisions at HA 1996, s 195A⁵ (because any member of the household would have a priority need⁶), and the household would wish to avoid a referral back to authority A, the applicant could be a different member of the household from the one who had accepted the private rented sector offer.

¹ HA 1996, s 198(2ZA).
² As amended by HRA 2017, s 4(4) for applications for homelessness assistance made to local housing authorities in England on or after 3 April 2018. See **8.100–8.107**.
³ HA 1996 s 195A as amended by HRA 2017, s 4(4) for applications for homelessness assistance made to local housing authorities in England on or after 3 April 2018. See **8.100–8.107**.
⁴ See Chapter **12**.
⁵ As amended by HRA 2017, s 4(4) for applications for homelessness assistance made to local housing authorities in England on or after 3 April 2018.
⁶ See Chapter **12** for 'priority need' and see **16.191–16.199** for the duties owed under HA 1996 s 195A.

14.135 It must be emphasised that the conditions stipulated are conditions for formal referral. Authority B cannot merely turn the applicant away to apply for himself or herself at authority A. The referral can only be made after authority B has satisfied itself, on completion of inquiries, that it would otherwise owe the applicant the HA 1996, s 189B(2)¹ relief duty or the HA 1996, s 193(2)² main housing duty. The duty which may arise to provide interim accommodation pending the outcome of those inquiries³, remains on authority B.

1   As inserted by the HRA 2017, s 5(2) for applications for homelessness assistance made to local housing authorities in England on or after 3 April 2018. See **15.138–15.189**.
2   HA 1996, s 193(2). See **16.94–16.199**.
3   HA 1996, s 188(1). See **16.37–16.73**.

14.136 Authority B must make inquiries into all the limbs of the test in HA 1996, s 198(2ZA) and (2A)[1]. The conditions for referral will not be satisfied merely by authority B establishing that the applicant had accepted a private rented sector offer from authority A and that the application for homelessness assistance was made within two years of the date of the acceptance. Authority B must also inquire into whether the applicant or any member of his or her household will run the risk of domestic violence in the district of authority A, whether the applicant, or any member of his or her household, had suffered violence in the district of authority A; and (if either the applicant, or a member of his or her household, had suffered violence in the district of authority A) whether is probable that there will be further violence of a similar kind against that person[2].

1   See **14.128**.
2   HA 1996, ss 198(2ZA)(b) and (2A). See **14.107–14.119**.

14.137 It should also be remembered that authority B retains a discretion whether or not to refer the applicant to authority A[1]. It may be that, even if this set of conditions for referral are made out, if the applicant also has a local connection with authority B, it would be reasonable on the facts of a particular case for authority B to decide not to refer him or her to authority A.

1   HA 1998, s 198(1). See **14.151–14.154**.

The third set of conditions for referral – out of district placements

Introduction

14.138 The third set of conditions[1] for referral arises where an applicant has previously been placed by another local housing authority in England or Wales in the district of a local housing authority in England, to which a new application for homelessness assistance is being made. It is different from the second set of conditions for referral in that it applies where an applicant was occupying accommodation secured in performance of HA 1996, Pt 7[2] or H(W)A 2014, Pt 2 duties rather than having accepted a private rented sector offer which brought those duties to an end[3].

1   HA 1996, s 198(4) and (4A).
2   As amended by HRA 2017, for applications for homelessness assistance made to local housing authorities in England on or after 3 April 2018.
3   HA 1996 ss 193(7AA)–(7AC). See **16.153–16.179** for the provisions by which acceptance of a private rented sector offer in England brings the main housing duty to an end. See **14.123–14.137** for the second set of conditions for referral.

14.139 Its purpose is to underscore the statutory presumption that homeless households should be accommodated in the district to which they first apply by ensuring that a local housing authority cannot relieve itself of some future responsibility by placing the applicant outside its own district[1]. It was enacted in HA 1996, Pt 7 to meet the phenomenon of increasing numbers of local housing authorities placing their homeless households in other local housing authorities' districts. These conditions for referral no longer apply to applications made to local housing authorities in Wales. H(W)A 2014, Pt 2 contains no equivalent provision to HA 1996, s 198(4).

[1] HA 1996, s 208(1); H(W)A 2014, s 91(1). See **15.244–15.251** and **18.47–18.63.**

14.140 The Codes and the Local Authorities Agreement are silent on what should happen if a local housing authority in England wishes to refer under these conditions to a local housing authority in Wales[1].

[1] See **15.222–15.225.**

14.141 This third set of conditions for referral does not apply in Scotland and cannot be used by a local housing authority in England to refer an applicant to a local authority in Scotland[1].

[1] Because HA 1996, s 198(4) and (4A) only apply to applicants accommodated by local housing authorities in England and Wales under HA 1996, Pt 7 (as amended by HRA 2017, for applications for homelessness assistance made to local housing authorities in England on or after 3 April 2018) or H(W)A 2014, Pt 2, and Housing (Scotland) Act 1987, s 33 (the Scottish equivalent to HA 1996, s 198) does not contain an equivalent provision to HA 1996, s 198(4). See **15.230–15.233.**

The third set of conditions

14.142 The conditions for a referral will be met where:

(1)   the applicant applies to local housing authority B for homelessness assistance;

(2)   the applicant had previously been placed in the district of local housing authority B by local housing authority A in performance of any of authority A's homelessness functions under HA 1996, Pt 7 or H(W)A 2014, Pt 2; and

(3)   the current application is made within a prescribed period running from the date of the application for homelessness assistance to authority A; and

(4)   the HA 1996, s 189B(2)[1] relief duty or the HA 1996, s 193(2)[2] main housing duty would be owed to the applicant by authority B[3].

[1] As inserted by the HRA 2017, s 5(2) for applications for homelessness assistance made to local housing authorities in England on or after 3 April 2018. See **15.138–15.189.**
[2] See **16.94–16.199.**
[3] HA 1996, s 198(4) and (4A).

14.143 The currently prescribed period is five years *plus* any period between the date of the applicant's original application to authority A and the date of being placed in the accommodation in authority B's district[1]. This aggregate period is then applied running backwards from the date of the application to authority B (not from the date of authority B's decision on that application)[2].

[1] Allocation of Housing and Homelessness (Miscellaneous Provisions) Regulations 2006, SI 2006/2527, reg 3. Local Authorities Agreement, para 3.6.

So, if the applicant applied to local housing authority A on 3 June 2009 and was placed in the district of local housing authority B on 3 January 2010 (six months later) the prescribed period would not have expired until 3 January 2015 (five years and six months in all). If he or she applied to authority B on 30 August 2014, the conditions for referral to authority A will be met, even if authority B's decision is taken several weeks or months later. If he or she applied to authority B on 1 September 2015, the conditions for referral will not be met.

14.144 This set of conditions for referral applies regardless of which of authority A's statutory homelessness functions it was carrying out when it provided the accommodation. Throughout the whole of the prescribed period, authority A retains responsibility for that applicant. A local housing authority which moves a homeless household over a series of districts (eg interim accommodation in District B, followed by short-term temporary accommodation in District C, and then longer term temporary accommodation in District D) will find that it is triggering a new prescribed period of responsibility on each move.

14.145 This third set of conditions for referral may be satisfied whether the applicant has become homeless from the accommodation actually provided by authority A or from some other accommodation in authority B's district. An applicant provided with accommodation in authority B's district by authority A may have found his or her own accommodation in authority B's district. Or he or she may have found accommodation elsewhere. However, if he or she becomes homeless again and applies to authority B within the prescribed period, the conditions for referral will be met and authority B may refer his or her application back to authority A.

14.146 It has already been noted that the statutory scope of initial inquiries that a local housing authority undertakes on an application for homelessness assistance has not been expressly expanded to include the information required to make out this third set of conditions for referral[1]. Certainly there is no obligation on an applicant to volunteer (without being asked) the fact that he or she came into the local housing authority's district on placement by another local housing authority.

[1] See **14.29**.

14.147 As with the second set of conditions for referral[1], it must be emphasised that these are conditions for formal referral. Authority B cannot merely turn the applicant away to apply for himself or herself at authority A. The referral can only be made after authority B has satisfied itself, on completion of inquiries, that it would otherwise owe the applicant the HA 1996, s 189B(2)[2] relief duty or the HA 1996, s 193(2)[3] main housing duty. The duty which may arise to provide interim accommodation pending the outcome of those inquiries[4], remains on authority B.

[1] HA 1996, s 198(2ZA) and (2A). See **14.123–14.137**.
[2] As inserted by the HRA 2017, s 5(2) for applications for homelessness assistance made to local housing authorities in England on or after 3 April 2018. See **15.138–15.189**.
[3] See **16.94–16.199**.
[4] HA 1996, s 188(1). See **16.37–16.73**.

14.148 Since this third set of conditions for referral is separate from the conditions governing a local connection referral under the first set of conditions, it must follow that there is no strict need for authority B to consider whether the applicant might be at risk of domestic or other violence if he or she is referred back to authority A. However, authority B retains a discretion whether or not to refer[1], once it has decided that the conditions are met, and any risk of violence would be relevant to the exercise of that discretion.

[1]   See **14.151–14.154**.

14.149 It must also follow that, even if the applicant has acquired a local connection with the district of authority B, by residence, employment, family association or special circumstances, the third set of conditions for referral is still met. Although, if the applicant has a local connection with authority B, particularly if he or she is employed in that district or has family associations, this should be a relevant consideration when authority B is deciding whether or not to exercise its discretion to refer.

14.150 The third set of conditions for referral is only met if the applicant to authority B was also the applicant to authority A. They do not apply to people with whom the applicant resides or might reasonably be expected to reside. This suggests that, if the placement in the district of authority B was as a result of authority A's duty owed to one member of the household, another member of the household could apply to authority B and the third set of conditions for referral would not be made out.

THE DECISION WHETHER OR NOT TO REFER

14.151 Once a local housing authority has decided that one of the three sets of conditions for referral is met, it must then decide whether or not to notify the other local housing authority of its opinion[1]. A local housing authority that failed properly to consider its discretion whether to refer, having determined that the conditions for referral were met, would have erred in law[2]. However, given the shortfall between housing supply and demand in many areas, there is nothing to prevent a local housing authority from adopting a general policy that it will normally refer an applicant in respect of whom the conditions are fulfilled, provided that it ensures that it considers any particular circumstances of an individual case that would suggest that a departure from the general policy should be made[3].

[1]   HA 1996, s 198(1); H(W)A 2014, s 80(1)–(2).
[2]   *R v East Devon District Council ex p Robb* (1997) 30 HLR 922, QBD.
[3]   English Code, para 10.32.

14.152 Obviously, the applicant's personal circumstances (including any risk of violence that does not fall within any of the statutory criteria prohibiting referral) are relevant to the local housing authority's decision whether or not to notify[1]. There will be other cases in which the conditions for a referral are only tenuously met and where, for that reason and perhaps others, it would not be right to use the power to refer. In those and other cases, the local housing authority will want to consider 'whether it is in the public interest' to accept the relevant duty or to make a referral, taking into account the public expenditure involved and whether a referral involves disruption to an applicant's employment or education, etc[2]. In a case involving former asylum-seekers, who had a local connection by reason of having occupied accommodation provided by the Home Office, the notifying local housing authority was entitled to take into account the burden on its own resources and the importance of giving effect to Parliament's intention in respect of the dispersal of asylum-seekers. Absence of family or friends in the district of the notified local housing authority was not a sufficient reason for the notifying local housing authority to decide against making a referral[3].

1   *R v Harrow London Borough Council ex p Carter* (1994) 26 HLR 32, QBD.
2   Local Authorities' Agreement, para 3.7.
3   *Ozbek v Ipswich Borough Council* [2006] EWCA Civ 534, [2006] HLR 41, CA at [61] per Chadwick LJ; see **14.75–14.77**.

14.153 In addition, when considering a referral, local housing authorities may take into account, where it is relevant, the general housing circumstances prevailing in the district of the local housing authority potentially to be notified[1]. Where the applicant or a member of his or her household has a local connection with more than one local housing authority (other than the local housing authority to which the application has been made), the notifying local housing authority should weigh up all relevant factors which will include the applicant's own preference[2].

1   Local Authorities' Agreement, para 3.7. See *R v Newham London Borough Council ex p Tower Hamlets London Borough Council* [1991] 1 WLR 1032, CA.
2   English Code, para 10.34; Welsh Code, para 18.10.

14.154 There is no requirement on any local housing authority to notify another local housing authority of an application for homelessness assistance, even where it has decided that the conditions for referral are met. Local housing authorities are free to accept all those to whom they owe the relief duty[1] or the main housing duty[2] (England) or the H(W)A 2014, s 73 duty[3], (Wales) regardless of whether any set of the conditions for referral is met[4].

1   HA 1996, s 189B(2) as inserted by the HRA 2017, s 5(2) for applications for homelessness assistance made to local housing authorities in England on or after 3 April 2018. See **15.138–15.189**.
2   HA 1996, s 193(2). See **16.94–16.199**.
3   See **17.73–17.117**.
4   English Code, para 10.32; Welsh Code, para 18.1.

NOTIFICATION DUTIES

Notification to the applicant

England

14.155 Where referral to another local housing authority is being pursued by a local housing authority in England, there are two occasions on which the local housing authority which received the application may need to notify the applicant of its decision[1]:

(1)   'the first notification': when it has decided that the conditions for referral are met, and that it intends to notify, or has notified, another local housing authority of that opinion[2]; and

(2)   'the second notification': when it has later been decided (by the two local housing authorities agreeing, or by a referee) that the conditions

for referral are or are not met[3].

1   See also **9.90–9.139**.
2   HA 1996, s 184(4) (as amended by HRA 2017, s 5(3) for applications for homelessness assistance made to local housing authorities in England on or after 3 April 2018) and s 200(1) and (1A) (as amended by HRA 2017, s 5(10) for applications for homelessness assistance made to local housing authorities in England on or after 3 April 2018).
3   HA 1996, s 199A(3) (as inserted by HRA 2017, s 5(9) for applications for homelessness assistance made to local housing authorities in England on or after 3 April 2018) and s 200(2); H(W)A 2014, s 82(2).

14.156 Where the referral is made at the stage where the HA 1996, s 189B(2)[1] relief duty would be owed, the first notification is mandatory[2]. However, if the referral is made at the stage where the HA 1996, s 193(2)[3] main housing duty would be owed, the first notification is discretionary[4]. The second notification is mandatory, irrespective of whether the referral has been made at the stage where the relief duty or the main housing duty would be owed[5].

1   As inserted by HRA 2017, s 5(2) for applications for homelessness assistance made to local housing authorities in England on or after 3 April 2018. See **15.138–15.189**.
2   HA 1996, s 184(4) as amended by HRA 2017, s 5(3) for applications for homelessness assistance made to local housing authorities in England on or after 3 April 2018.
3   See **17.146–17.197**.
4   HA 1996, ss 200(1) and (1A) as amended by HRA 2017, s 5(10) for applications for homelessness assistance made to local housing authorities in England on or after 3 April 2018. Note that this notification cannot be issued until the relief duty has come to an end.
5   HA 1996, s 199A(3) (as inserted by HRA 2017, s 5(9) for applications for homelessness assistance made to local housing authorities in England on or after 3 April 2018) and s 200(2).

14.157 There is no obvious reason for the lack of parity in notification requirements as between the two stages. The English Code, rather that drawing attention to the lack of parity, seems to proceed on the assumption that applicants will notified at every opportunity[1]. As has been shown, the position is a little more complex than this. But while not strictly accurate, the advice in the English Code might be understood as an example of best practice.

1   English Code, paras 10.39 and 10.47–10.48.

14.158 The first notification duty enables a local housing authority, in effect, to give the applicant a 'minded to refer' notification so that all the issues can be explored with the applicant before another local housing authority is troubled with what might transpire to be an inappropriate or impermissible referral[1]. Alternatively, if the question of referral appears straightforward, it permits one local housing authority to give notice of referral to another straight away, whilst simultaneously also notifying the applicant that this has been done.

1   When the purpose of the first notification is viewed in this way it might be thought that a local housing authority would be well-advised to issue the first notification in all cases prior to contacting the other local housing authority, irrespective of whether it is under a duty to do so, in order to ensure that it has before it all of the material which is relevant to the decision to refer, prior to making the decision.

14.159 If the referral is made at the stage when the HA 1996, s 189B(2)[1] relief duty would be owed, the local housing authority, in issuing the applicant with the first notification, is required to inform the applicant of his or her right to request a review of that decision[2]. But there is in fact no such right of review[3] and any challenge would need to be brought by way of judicial review[4].

1   As inserted by HRA 2017, s 5(2) for applications for homelessness assistance made to local housing authorities in England on or after 3 April 2018. See **15.138–15.189**.
2   HA 1996, s 184(5).
3   Note the limits of HA 1996, s 202(1)(c). See further English Code, para 10.56.
4   See **19.306–19.327**.

14.160 In contrast, there is a right to request a review of any decision to notify a local housing authority that the conditions for referral are satisfied at the stage where the HA 1996,s 193(2)[1] main housing duty would be owed[2]. But, as discussed at **14.156**, a local housing authority is not required to issue the applicant with the first notification in these circumstances, and even if it chooses to do so it is not required to inform him or her of the right to request a review[3].

1   HA 1996, s 193(2). See **16.94–16.199**.
2   HA 1996, s 202(1)(c). English Code, para 10.56.
3   HA 1996, ss 200(1) and (1A) as amended by HRA 2017, s 5(10) for applications for homelessness assistance made to local housing authorities in England on or after 3 April 2018.

14.161 This mismatch in the notification duties and review rights can only sensibly be attributed to a drafting error in the legislation. The potential for hardship caused by this mismatch may be mitigated to some extent by the fact that an applicant has the right to request a review of any decision as to whether the conditions for referral are, or are not, met (at whatever stage the referral is made)[1] and the second notification must inform the applicant of this right and of the 21-day period in which the review must be requested[2].

1   HA 1996, s 200(1)(e). English Code, para 10.56.
2   HA 1996, s 199A(3) (as inserted by HRA 2017, s 5(9) for applications for homelessness assistance made to local housing authorities in England on or after 3 April 2018) and s 200(2).

Wales

14.162 Where referral to another local housing authority is being pursued by a local housing authority in Wales, there are (as is the case in England) two occasions on which the local housing authority which received the application may need to notify the applicant of its decision[1]:

(1)   'the first notification': when it has decided that the conditions for referral are met, and that it intends to notify, or has notified, another local housing authority of that opinion[2]; and

(2)   'the second notification': when it has later been decided (by the two local housing authorities agreeing, or by a referee) that the conditions for referral are or are not met[3].

1   See Welsh Code, paras 18.22–18.26.
2   H(W)A 2014, s 63(3).
3   H(W)A 2014, s 82(2).

14.163 Both notifications are mandatory. The local housing authority 'must' notify the applicant of both of these decisions[1]. Each notification must inform the applicant that he or she has a right to request a review of the decision and of the 21-day period in which a review must be requested[2].

1   H(W)A 2014, ss 63(3) and 82(2).
2   H(W)A 2014, ss 63(4), 82(2) and 84.

Notification procedures between local housing authorities

14.164 Once the notifying local housing authority has formed the opinion that the conditions for referral are met and decided that a referral should be made, it is advised first to contact the local housing authority which it intends to notify by telephone and then confirm the notification in writing[1]. A pro-forma written notification is provided in the Local Authorities' Agreement. Each local housing authority is expected to have a nominated officer to deal with such notifications as are received[2]. Unless there is likely to be a dispute between the local housing authorities, the notified local housing authority should immediately start to make appropriate arrangements to provide accommodation and not wait for the written confirmation to arrive[3]. If it does accept responsibility (or is found by a referee to be responsible), the notified local housing authority should reimburse the notifying local housing authority for the cost of the accommodation it has provided to the applicant, unless there has been undue delay in making the referral[4].

1   Local Authorities' Agreement, para 6.1.
2   Local Authorities' Agreement, para 6.2.
3   Local Authorities' Agreement, para 6.1.
4   Local Authorities' Agreement, para 7.4.

14.165 The notified local housing authority should reply to the notifying local housing authority (confirming whether or not it accepts responsibility) within ten days of receiving the written confirmation of notification[1].

1   Local Authorities' Agreement, para 6.5.

DUTIES OWED TO AN APPLICANT WHOSE CASE IS REFERRED

England

14.166 For applications made to local housing authorities in England, once the first notification[1] has been given to the applicant, any duty which the notifying local housing authority may have under HA 1996, s 188(1)[2] to provide interim accommodation for the applicant comes to an end and the notifying local housing authority is not subject to either the HA 1996, s 189B(2)[3] relief duty or the HA 1996, s 193(2)[4] main housing duty (as the case may be) from that point on[5]. This does not mean that the applicant is left without accommodation. Where the first notification has been given at the stage where the HA 1996, s 189B(2)[6] relief duty would be owed, the notifying local housing authority must continue to secure that accommodation is available for the applicant's occupation under HA 1996, s 199A(2)[7] until the second notification has been given, provided that it has reason to believe that the applicant may have a priority need[8]. Similarly, where the first notification has been given at the stage where the HA 1996, s 193(2)[9] main housing duty would be owed, the notifying local housing authority must continue to secure that accommodation is available for the applicant's occupation under HA 1996, s 200(1) until the second notification has been given[10].

1   See **14.155**.
2   As amended by HRA 2017, s 5(4) for applications for homelessness assistance made to local housing authorities in England on or after 3 April 2018. See **16.37–16.73**.
3   As inserted by HRA 2017, s 5(2) for applications for homelessness assistance made to local housing authorities in England on or after 3 April 2018. See **15.138–15.189**.
4   See **16.94–16.199**.
5   HA 1996, s 199A(1) (as inserted by HRA 2017, s 5(9) for applications for homelessness assistance made to local housing authorities in England on or after 3 April 2018) and s 200(1).
6   As inserted by HRA 2017, s 5(2) for applications for homelessness assistance made to local housing authorities in England on or after 3 April 2018. See **15.138–15.189**.
7   As inserted by HRA 2017, s 5(9) for applications for homelessness assistance made to local housing authorities in England on or after 3 April 2018.
8   See **16.217–16.224** and English Code, para 10.40
9   See **16.94–16.199**.
10 See **16.225–16.232**.

14.167 If, after the first notification, it is decided that the conditions for referral are *not* met, the notifying local housing authority will, upon the second notification[1] being given, be required to pick up where it left off and perform either the HA 1996, s 189B(2)[2] relief duty or the HA 1996, s 193(2)[3] main housing duty (as the case may be)[4]. In respect of the HA 1996, s 189B(2)[5] relief duty, the notifying local housing authority will, if it has reason to believe that the applicant has a priority need, be required to secure accommodation for his or her occupation while the duty is performed[6]. The 56-day period for the performance of the HA 1996, s 189B(2)[7] relief duty will run from the date of the second notification[8].

1   See **14.155**.
2   As inserted by HRA 2017, s 5(2) for applications for homelessness assistance made to local housing authorities in England on or after 3 April 2018. See **15.138–15.189**.
3   See **16.94–16.199**.
4   HA 1996, s 199A(4)(a) (as inserted by HRA 2017, s 5(9) for applications for homelessness assistance made to local housing authorities in England on or after 3 April 2018) and s 200(3). See English Code, paras 10.44 and 10.49.
5   As inserted by HRA 2017, s 5(2) for applications for homelessness assistance made to local housing authorities in England on or after 3 April 2018. See **15.138–15.189**.
6   HA 1996, s 199A(4)(c) as inserted by HRA 2017, s 5(9) for applications for homelessness assistance made to local housing authorities in England on or after 3 April 2018.
7   As inserted by HRA 2017, s 5(2) for applications for homelessness assistance made to local housing authorities in England on or after 3 April 2018. See **15.138–15.189**.
8   HA 1996, s 199A(4)(b) as inserted by HRA 2017, s 5(9) for applications for homelessness assistance made to local housing authorities in England on or after 3 April 2018. See further **15.160–15.161** and **15.166–15.168**.

14.168 Alternatively, if, after the first notification, it is decided that the conditions for referral *are* met, the duties that would otherwise be applicable had the case not been referred, pass to the notified local housing authority[1].

1   See English Code, paras 10.40–10.41 and 10.48.

14.169 Specifically, where the referral has been made at the stage where the HA 1996, s 189B(2)[1] relief duty would be owed by the notifying local housing authority, upon the second notification being given the duties owed by the notifying local housing authority come to an end and the applicant will be treated as having made his or her homeless application to the notified authority on that date[2]. Since the notifying local housing authority will already have decided that the applicant is homeless and eligible for assistance, and the notified local housing authority will only be permitted to revisit these findings in very limited circumstances[3], this has the legal consequence that the notified local housing authority will owe the applicant the HA 1996, s 189B(2)[4] relief duty from that point on[5]. To facilitate the performance of this duty the notifying local housing authority is required to provide the notified local housing authority with copies of any assessment of the applicant's case which it may have carried out pursuant to HA 1996, s 189A[6], together with any revisions to that assessment[7]. Further, where it appears to the notified local housing authority that the applicant has a priority need, it must secure that accommodation is available for his or her occupation[8].

1   As inserted by HRA 2017, s 5(2) for applications for homelessness assistance made to local housing authorities in England on or after 3 April 2018. See **15.138–15.189**.
2   HA 1996, ss 199A(5)(a) and (b) as inserted by HRA 2017, s 5(9) for applications for homelessness assistance made to local housing authorities in England on or after 3 April 2018.
3   Set out in HA 1996, s 199A(5)(c) as inserted by HRA 2017, s 5(9) for applications for homelessness assistance made to local housing authorities in England on or after 3 April 2018. See **14.179**.
4   As inserted by HRA 2017, s 5(2) for applications for homelessness assistance made to local housing authorities in England on or after 3 April 2018. See **15.138–15.189**.
5   HA 1996, s 189B(2) as inserted by HRA 2017, s 5(2) for applications for homelessness assistance made to local housing authorities in England on or after 3 April 2018. See **15.138–15.189**.
6   As inserted by HRA 2017, s 3(1) for applications for homelessness assistance made to local housing authorities in England on or after 3 April 2018. See **15.62–15.86**.
7   HA 1996, s 199A(5)(d) as inserted by HRA 2017, s 5(9) for applications for homelessness assistance made to local housing authorities in England on or after 3 April 2018. See English Code, para 10.43.
8   HA 1996, s 188(1) as amended by HRA 2017, s 5(4) for applications for homelessness assistance made to local housing authorities in England on or after 3 April 2018. See **16.37–16.73**.

14.170 Where the referral has been made at the stage where the HA 1996, s 193(2)[1] main housing duty would be owed, the notified local housing authority will, upon the second notification being given, be subject to the HA 1996, s 193(2)[2] main housing duty (England) or the H(W)A 2014, s 73 duty (Wales)[3].

1   See **16.94–16.199**.
2   See **16.94–16.199**.
3   HA 1996, s 200(4); H(W)A 2014, s 83(2). See English Code, para 10.48. In Wales, the notified authority will at this juncture become subject to the duty to accommodate under H(W)A 2014, s 68(1) and (3).

14.171 If the applicant requests a review following notification[1], the notifying local housing authority has a power, but not a duty, to provide accommodation pending the determination of the review (and a similar power to provide accommodation pending the determination of any appeal against that review decision)[2].

1   See English Code, para 10.56 and also **19.55–19.57**.
2   HA 1996, ss 199A(6) (as inserted by HRA 2017, s 5(9) for applications for homelessness assistance made to local housing authorities in England on or after 3 April 2018) 200(5) and 204(4) (as amended by HRA 2017, s 5(11) for applications for homelessness assistance made to local housing authorities in England on or after 3 April 2018). See English Code, para 10.57

and *R (Gebremarium) v Westminster City Council* [2009] EWHC 2254 (Admin), (2009) November *Legal Action*, p 26, Admin Ct, where the Administrative Court refused permission to seek a judicial review against Westminster's decision not to provide accommodation under HA 1996, s 200(5) pending a s 202 review of its decision to refer the claimant to Cardiff. See also **16.233–16.277**.

Wales

14.172 Once the first notification[1] has been given to the applicant, the notifying local housing authority's duty to provide interim accommodation for the applicant comes to an end[2]. In its place, a duty to provide accommodation under H(W)A 2014, s 82(1) arises on the notifying local housing authority[3].

[1] See **14.162**.
[2] H(W)A 2014, ss 69(2) or (3) and 73(2).
[3] See **17.138–17.145**.

14.173 If, after the first notification, it is decided that the conditions for referral are *not* met, the notifying local housing authority will, upon the second notification[1] being given, be required to pick up where it left off and perform the H(W)A 2014, s 73 duty[2].

[1] See **14.162**.
[2] H(W)A 2014, s 82(3). The duty to provide interim accommodation under H(W)A 2014, s 68(1) will also apply.

14.174 Alternatively, if, after the first notification, it is decided that the conditions for referral *are* met, the duties that would otherwise be applicable had the case not been referred, pass to the notified local housing authority. Specifically, once the second notification has been given to the applicant, the notifying local housing authority is no longer under a duty to provide accommodation for the applicant[1] and the duty to provide accommodation passes to the notified local housing authority[2].

[1] H(W)A 2014, s 82(1) and (5). Welsh Code, para 18.22.
[2] H(W)A 2014, ss 68(1), (3) and 82(4) (for referrals within Wales); HA 1996, s 201A(2) (for referrals from Wales to England).

14.175 If the applicant requests a review following notification[1], the notifying local housing authority has a power, but not a duty, to provide accommodation pending the determination of the review (and a similar power to provide accommodation pending the determination of any appeal against that review decision)[2]. The Welsh Code recommends that applicants who have a priority need (which would include any applicant whose case is being referred) should be accommodated during the review process[3].

[1] See also **19.55–19.57**.
[2] H(W)A 2014, ss 82(6) and 88(5). See Welsh Code, para 18.24–18.25. See also **17.134–17.137**.
[3] Welsh Code, para 18.25.

DISPUTES BETWEEN LOCAL HOUSING AUTHORITIES

14.176 Where the notified local housing authority disagrees with the opinion of the notifying local housing authority, as to whether the conditions for a referral are made out, there is a special procedure for resolution of the dispute[1].

[1]   See **14.184–14.190**.

14.177 However, the notified local housing authority may have a more fundamental disagreement with the referral. It may disagree with one or more of the notifying local housing authority's earlier decisions: that the applicant is homeless and eligible for assistance, or that the applicant has a priority need and did not become homeless intentionally. In other words, it may dispute the proposition that the applicant is owed the HA 1996, s 189B(2)[1] relief duty or the HA 1996, s 193(2)[2] main housing duty (England) or the H(W)A 2014, s 73 duty[3] (Wales). The sense of grievance may be particularly strong when the notified local housing authority had previously accepted an application by the very same applicant, but had decided a duty was not owed (perhaps because the notified local housing authority had decided that the applicant had become homeless intentionally). The prospect of the applicant then applying to a different local housing authority, with which he or she has no local connection, and that local housing authority inquiring into the same facts, but coming to a different conclusion and then referring the performance of the duty back to the original local housing authority is not one that the original local housing authority would find attractive. Although this may seem harsh to the notified local housing authority, an essential premise is that the notifying local housing authority has investigated all the circumstances 'with the same degree of care and thoroughness . . . as it would for any other case'[4].

[1]   As inserted by HRA 2017, s 5(2) for applications for homelessness assistance made to local housing authorities in England on or after 3 April 2018. See **15.138–15.189**.
[2]   See **16.94–16.199**.
[3]   See **17.73–17.117**.
[4]   Local Authorities' Agreement, para 6.3.

14.178 The courts have traditionally made it very clear that, once a local housing authority has determined that a duty is owed, and has notified another local housing authority that the conditions for referral are met, the notified local housing authority cannot re-open or go behind the inquiries and decisions made by the notifying authority as to the existence of that duty[1].

[1]   *R v Slough Borough Council ex p Ealing London Borough Council* [1981] QB 801, CA.

14.179 As a result of amendments made to the HA 1996, Pt 7 by HRA 2017[1], a limited exception to this principle arises in circumstances where an applicant's case has been referred at the stage where the HA 1996, s 189B(2)[2] relief duty would have been owed. In these circumstances the notified local housing authority will be entitled to revisit the notifying local housing authority's conclusions that the applicant is either homeless, eligible for assistance or did not become homeless intentionally if (and only if):

- the applicant's circumstances have changed, or new information has come to light, since the notifying local housing authority's decision; and

• the change in circumstances or new information justifies the notified local housing authority in reaching a different decision[3].

In these circumstances, the notified local housing authority is not entitled to refuse to accept the referral[4]. Rather, the duty which it owes as a result of the acceptance of the referral will be modified according to the outcome of any new decision.

---

1 For applications for homelessness assistance made to local housing authorities in England on or after 3 April 2018.
2 As inserted by HRA 2017, s 5(2) for applications for homelessness assistance made to local housing authorities in England on or after 3 April 2018. See **15.138–15.189**.
3 HA 1996, s 199A(5)(c) as inserted by HRA 2017, s 5(9) for applications for homelessness assistance made to local housing authorities in England on or after 3 April 2018; English Code, para 10.42.
4 HA 1996, s 199A(5)(a) as inserted by HRA 2017, s 5(9) for applications for homelessness assistance made to local housing authorities in England on or after 3 April 2018.

14.180 In other circumstances, where this exception does not apply[1], if the notified local housing authority remains dissatisfied with the notifying local housing authority's decision making, the notified local housing authority can challenge, through judicial review, the lawfulness of the inquiries made by the notifying local housing authority before it came to its decision that a duty was owed, or the legality of the decision itself. In *R v Tower Hamlets London Borough Council ex p Camden London Borough Council*[2], the notifying local housing authority (Camden) should have made inquiries of the notified local housing authority (Tower Hamlets) and considered Tower Hamlets' reasons for finding that the applicant had become homeless intentionally, before making its own decision that a main housing duty was owed. In *R v Newham London Borough Council ex p Tower Hamlets London Borough Council*[3], Newham notified Tower Hamlets of its intention to refer an applicant whom Tower Hamlets had previously found to have become homeless intentionally. Tower Hamlets successfully challenged the lawfulness of Newham's inquiries into the question of whether the applicant had become homeless intentionally.

---

1 For example, where the referral has been made at the stage where the HA 1996, s 193(2) main housing duty would be owed. See English Code, para 10.50.
2 (1989) 21 HLR 197, QBD.
3 [1991] 1 WLR 1032, CA.

14.181 Where an applicant applies to the notifying local housing authority after refusing an offer of accommodation from the notified local housing authority (and the notified local housing authority had decided that its duty to the applicant had come to an end), the notifying local housing authority must accept the new application save where it is based on exactly the same facts as the first application[1]. Once the application has been accepted the local housing authority must make inquiries to determine what duty if any is owed to the applicant. If it is decided that a duty is owed then the notifying local housing authority may seek to refer the applicant's case, once again. If the notified local housing authority disputes, but does not challenge in the courts, the lawfulness of the notifying local housing authority's decision that a duty would be owed, it cannot simply refuse to accept the referral[2]. Nor can it seek to raise the matter as part of the procedures for resolving disputes over whether the conditions for referral are satisfied. It is bound by the notifying local housing authority's decision unless that decision is withdrawn or is successfully challenged, and quashed, in judicial review proceedings[3]. An applicant should never be required to bring his or her own legal proceedings to compel a local housing authority to act on a referral.

1   *R (Royal Borough of Kensington and Chelsea) v London Borough of Ealing and Ms Hacene-Blidi (Interested Party)* [2017] EWHC 24 (Admin), [2017] PTSR 1029, Admin Ct following the approach in *Rikha Begum v LB of Tower Hamlets* [2005] EWCA Civ 340, [2005] HLR 34, CA (see **8.77–8.91**) and holding that the approach in *R v Hammersmith and Fulham London Borough Council ex p O'Brien* (1985) 17 HLR 471, QBD (which required a 'new incidence of homelessness' was no longer good law.

2   *R (Royal Borough of Kensington and Chelsea) v London Borough of Ealing and Ms Hacene-Blidi (Interested Party)* [2017] EWHC 24 (Admin), [2017] PTSR 1029, Admin Ct. In that case the High Court quashed Ealing's refusal to accept a referral, in circumstances where no challenge had been brought to the rationality of Kensington and Chelsea's decision that the applicant was owed the main housing duty under HA 1996, s 193(2) 1996.

3   *R (Bantamagbari) v Westminster City Council* [2003] EWHC 1350 (Admin), (2003) July *Legal Action*, p 27, Admin Ct; and *R (Enfield London Borough Council) v Broxbourne Borough Council* [2004] EWHC 1053 (Admin), (2004) May *Legal Action*, p 26, Admin Ct. Alternatively, if the exception at HA 1996, s 199A(5)(c) (as inserted by HRA 2017, s 5(9) for applications for homelessness assistance made to local housing authorities in England on or after 3 April 2018) applies, then it may be entitled to revisit the decision as to what duty is owed to the applicant, following the acceptance of the referral.

14.182 In circumstances where the notified local housing authority is successful in persuading the notifying local housing authority to withdraw a referral on the basis that its underlying decision making as to the duty owed to an applicant is flawed, this does not entitle the notifying local housing authority to revisit its decision. This situation arose in *R (Sambotin) v Brent London Borough Council*[1]. Mr Sambotin applied as homeless to Brent London Borough Council, who accepted the HA 1996, s 193(2)[2] main housing duty but referred his case to Waltham Forest London Borough Council. Waltham Forest refused to accept the referral on the basis that it did not accept that the applicant was eligible[3] for homelessness assistance. Brent then withdrew the referral and proceeded to revisit its earlier decision, substituting it for finding that that the applicant was not eligible. On Mr Sambotin's application for judicial review, the High Court quashed Brent's decision. Absent fraud or deception on the part of the applicant or a fundamental mistake of fact, there was no power to revisit a decision once made[4].

1   *R (Sambotin) v Brent London Borough Council* [2017] EWHC 1190 (Admin), [2017] PTSR 1154, Admin Ct.
2   See **16.94–16.199**.
3   See CHAPTER **11**.
4   Applying the approach in *Porteous v West Dorset District Council* [2004] EWCA Civ 244, [2004] HLR 30, CA. See **9.140**.

14.183 The notified local housing authority can, however, perfectly properly dispute the notifying local housing authority's opinion that the conditions for referral are met. The following paragraphs explain the procedure involved.

Determining disputes about whether the conditions for referral are met

14.184 The arrangements for resolving disputes between local housing authorities as to whether any of the three sets of conditions for referral are met have been negotiated and agreed between the organisations representing local authorities in England, Wales and Scotland and have been approved by the Secretary of State in the Homelessness (Decisions on Referrals) Order 1998[1].

[1] SI 1998/1578, made under the Secretary of State's powers at HA 1996, s 198(5) and approving the *Guidelines for Local Authorities and Referees Agreement*. By virtue of the Homelessness (Review Procedure) (Wales) Regulations 2015 SI 2015/1266 (W 86), reg 7 (see the CD Rom with this book), the Homelessness (Decisions on Referrals) Order 1998, SI 1998/1578 is to be treated as if it had been made under H(W)A 2014, s 80(5)(b) and (6)(b), thereby transposing the arrangements for resolving disputes they contain into Welsh law. See further Welsh Code, paras 18.27–18.30.

14.185 If the notified local housing authority wishes to challenge the referral, in the sense of contending that the conditions for referral are not made out, it must state its written reasons in full within ten days of receiving the referral notification[1]. On receipt of that response, the notifying local housing authority may accept the notified local housing authority's position and withdraw the referral.

[1] Local Authorities Agreement, para 10.1.

14.186 However, if there is no agreement between the two local housing authorities, the question of whether the conditions for referral are met should be decided by a referee. The referee should be appointed within 21 days of notification to the notified local housing authority of the referral[1]. The local housing authorities agree to be bound by the referee's decision. The two local housing authorities may themselves find and appoint an agreed referee, but if they cannot agree on the identity of the referee, one will be appointed by the chairperson of their appropriate local government organisation[2]. The request for a referee to be appointed should be jointly made, or can be made by the notifying local housing authority alone if the notified local housing authority has failed to agree to accept the referral within six weeks of the referral having been made[3].

[1] Local Authorities Agreement, para 10.3.
[2] There is a small panel of referees established by the local authority organisations to perform this function. The list of panel members is maintained by the Local Government Association.
[3] Local Authorities Agreement, paras 10.5–10.6.

14.187 The referee, once appointed, invites both local housing authorities to submit representations within 14 working days. Each local housing authority will have the opportunity to consider the other's representations, and to comment in writing on those representations within a further 10 working days. If the representations are insufficient, the referee can invite further representations on any issue that he or she considers necessary. Although the applicant is not a party to this particular aspect of the dispute, he or she should be sent the local housing authorities' representations. It is up to the referee whether the applicant should be invited to comment, or to make written representations. The referee may choose to hold an oral hearing and the Local Authorities' Agreement advises that an oral hearing might be necessary or more convenient where the applicant is illiterate, where English is not his or her first language, or where further information is necessary for the issues to be resolved[1].

[1] Local Authorities Agreement, paras 15.1–15.4.

14.188 The referee's decision must be given in writing. The Local Authorities' Agreement recommends that the decision should be reached 'as quickly as possible' and normally within one month from receipt of both the local housing authorities' written representations[1]. The decision should record the issues, the referee's findings of fact, the decision and the reasons for the decision. Copies should be sent to both local housing authorities and the appropriate local government organisation. The notifying local housing authority should inform the applicant of the decision[2]. One judge described the aims of the procedure in this way:

> 'the legislature intended that these matters should be disposed of within a particular specified time frame and "as quickly as possible" and "promptly". It is also obvious from the terms of that guidance that it is, as one would expect, contemplated by the legislature that the relevant applicant should be kept informed of what is going on, to a reasonable extent[3].'

1   Local Authorities Agreement, para 14.5.
2   Local Authorities Agreement, paras 18.2.
3   *Berhane v Lambeth London Borough Council* [2007] EWHC 2702 (QB), (2008) March *Legal Action*, p 21, QBD, at [36] per Eady J.

14.189 The applicant may then request a review of the referee's decision, in which case a reviewer will have to be appointed by agreement between the two local housing authorities; this would commonly be another referee from the panel maintained by the local authority associations[1].

1   Allocation of Housing and Homelessness (Review Procedures) Regulations 1999, SI 1999/71, reg 7, see APPENDIX 2; Homelessness (Review Procedure) (Wales) Regulations 2015, SI 2015/1266 (W 86), reg 4, on the CD Rom with this book. See also **19.131–19.137**.

14.190 The written decisions of the referees are collected by the local government associations and distributed among other members of the panel of referees (no doubt to encourage consistency of decision-making). They are not officially published. By the end of 2004 only some 120 decisions had been made by referees since the inception of the scheme in 1977. The great bulk had been made in the early years and over the past decade no more than a handful of disputes has been resolved by referees each year[1].

1   In November 1980 the then London Boroughs Association produced an indexed Digest covering decisions 1–25. A supplement in May 1982 added decisions 26–43. A second update in December 1986 added and indexed decisions up to No 60. However, production of the Digest ceased with the issue of a final supplement in 1993 (which added decisions up to and including No 89 to the text). For an analysis of the operation of the local connection referrals during these years see R Thornton 'Who Houses? Homelessness, Local Connection and Inter-Authority Referrals Under HA 1985, s 67' [1994] 16 Journal of Social Welfare and Family Law 19.

CHALLENGES BY THE APPLICANT

Right to request a review

14.191 The applicant has the right to request the review of a number of the decisions that a local housing authority may make in connection with referral procedures, including:

(1) a decision made by the local housing authority to which the applicant applied, at the point where the HA 1996, s 193(2)[1] main housing duty (England) or H(W)A 2014, s 73[2] relief duty (Wales) would be owed, to notify another local housing authority[3];

(2) any decision reached, by agreement between the two local housing authorities or by a referee's decision, that the conditions for referral are met[4]; and

(3) any decision[5] by either of the two local housing authorities as to which of them is subject to the HA 1996, s 193(2)[6] main housing duty (England) or the H(W)A 2014, s 73[7] relief duty(Wales)[8].

1 See **16.94–16.199**.
2 See **17.73–17.117**.
3 HA 1996, s 202(1)(c); H(W)A 2014, s 85(1)(c). See **19.49–19.54**. For applications made to local housing authorities in England there is no right to review of a decision to refer an applicant at the point where the relief duty under HA 1996, s 189B(2) (as inserted by HRA 2017, s 5(2) for applications for homelessness assistance made to local housing authorities in England on or after 3 April 2018) would be owed. See English Code, para 10.56.
4 HA 1996, s 202(1)(d); H(W)A 2014, s 85(1)(c). See **19.55–19.57**.
5 Under HA 1996, s 200(3) or (4) or under H(W)A 2014, s 80(3) or (4).
6 See **17.146–17.197**.
7 See **17.73–17.117**.
8 HA 1996, s 202(1)(e); H(W)A 2014, s 85(1)(c). Now redundant: see **19.58**.

14.192 Those rights, read together with the requirements of notification to the applicant[1], have the effect that, during the referral process, the applicant could substantively challenge decisions to make a referral on two occasions and on a number of issues. It will be recalled that the applicant may receive up to two decisions:

(1) a decision made by the local housing authority to which he or she applied to notify another local housing authority[2]; and then

(2) a decision reached by agreement between the two local housing authorities or by a referee that the conditions for referral are met[3].

1 See **14.155–14.163**.
2 HA 1996, s 184(4) (as amended by HRA 2017, s 5(3) for applications for homelessness assistance made to local housing authorities in England on or after 3 April 2018) and ss 200(1) and (1A) (as amended by HRA 2017, s 5(10) for applications for homelessness assistance made to local housing authorities in England on or after 3 April 2018); H(W)A 2014, s 63(3).
3 HA 1996, s 199A(3) (as inserted by HRA 2017, s 5(9) for applications for homelessness assistance made to local housing authorities in England on or after 3 April 2018) and s 200(2); H(W)A 2014, s 82(2).

14.193 For applications for homelessness assistance made to local housing authorities in Wales, the local housing authority is required to notify the applicant of both of these decisions[1] and both decisions can be challenged by the applicant making a request for a review should he or she wish to do so.

1 See **14.163**.

14.194 For applications for homelessness assistance made to local housing authorities in England the position is more complicated and varies according to the point at which the applicant's case is referred.

14.195 Where the referral is made at the stage where the HA 1996, s 189B(2)[1] relief duty would be owed, the local housing authority is required to notify the applicant of the first decision[2]. However, if the referral is made at the stage where the HA 1996, s 193(2)[3] main housing duty would be owed, the local housing authority has a discretion as to whether to notify the applicant of the first decision[4]. Incongruously, there is a right to a review of the first decision only where the referral is made at the stage where the HA 1996, s 193(2)[5] main housing duty would be owed, and not where the referral is made at the stage where the HA 1996, s 189B(2)[6] relief duty would be owed[7].

[1]   As inserted by HRA 2017, s 5(2) for applications for homelessness assistance made to local housing authorities in England on or after 3 April 2018. See **15.138–15.189**.
[2]   HA 1996, s 184(4) as amended by HRA 2017, s 5(3) for applications for homelessness assistance made to local housing authorities in England on or after 3 April 2018.
[3]   See **16.94–16.199**.
[4]   HA 1996, ss 200(1) and (1A) as amended by HRA 2017, s 5(10) for applications for homelessness assistance made to local housing authorities in England on or after 3 April 2018. Note that this notification cannot be issued until the relief duty has come to an end.
[5]   See **16.94–16.199**.
[6]   As inserted by HRA 2017, s 5(2) for applications for homelessness assistance made to local housing authorities in England on or after 3 April 2018. See **15.138–15.189**.
[7]   HA 1996, s 202(1)(c). See English Code, para 10.56.

14.196 In contrast, the second decision must be notified to the applicant, irrespective of whether the referral has been made at the stage where the HA 1996, s 189B(2)[1] relief duty or the HA 1996, s 193(2)[2] main housing duty would be owed[3]. There is a right to a review of the second decision in all cases[4].

[1]   As inserted by HRA 2017, s 5(2) for applications for homelessness assistance made to local housing authorities in England on or after 3 April 2018. See **15.138–15.189**.
[2]   See **16.94–16.199**.
[3]   HA 1996, s 199A(3) (as inserted by HRA 2017, s 5(9) for applications for homelessness assistance made to local housing authorities in England on or after 3 April 2018) and s 200(2).
[4]   HA 1996, ss 202(1)(d). The mismatch between the notification duties and corresponding review rights is discussed in more detail at **14.155–14.161**.

Right to a review of whether the first set of conditions for referral are satisfied

14.197 The applicant has, in effect, the right to request a review in relation to a local connection referral made at the stage where the HA 1996, s 193(2)[1] main housing duty (England) or the H(W)A 2014, s 73[2] relief duty (Wales) would be owed, *of the notifying local housing authority's decision* that:

(1)   the applicant, or a member of his or her household, has no local connection with it[3]; or

(2)   the applicant, or a member of his or her household, has a local connection with the district of another local housing authority[4]; or

(3)   the applicant, or a member of his or her household, will not run the risk of domestic violence in the district of the other local housing authority[5]; or

(4)   the applicant, or a member of his or her household, has not suffered violence in the district of the other local housing authority[6]; or

(5)   the applicant, or a member of his or her household, has suffered violence, but it is not probable that any return to the other local housing authority's district will lead to further violence of a similar kind against the victim[7]; or

(6)   the other local housing authority should be notified of the local housing authority's decision that the conditions for referral are met[8].

1   See **16.94–16.199**.
2   See **17.73–17.117**.
3   HA 1996, s 198(2)(a). See **14.43–14.122**.
4   HA 1996, s 198(2)(b). See **14.43–14.122**.
5   HA 1996, s 198(2)(c). See **14.107–14.119**.
6   HA 1996, s 198(2A). See **14.107–14.119**.
7   HA 1996, s 198(2A). See **14.107–14.119**.
8   HA 1996, s 198(1). See **14.151–14.154**.

14.198 In addition, the applicant has the right to request a review in all cases, following a referral, *of the local housing authorities' agreement*, or *of a referee's decision*, that:

(1)   the applicant, or a member of his or her household, has no local connection with the local housing authority to which he or she applied[1]; or

(2)   the applicant, or a member of his or her household, has a local connection with the district of another local housing authority[2]; or

(3)   the applicant, or a member of his or her household, will not run the risk of domestic violence in the district of the other local housing authority[3]; or

(4)   the applicant or a member of his or her household, has not suffered violence in the other local housing authority's district[4]; or

(5)   the applicant, or a member of his or her household, has suffered violence, but it is not probable that any return to the other local housing authority's district will lead to further violence of a similar kind against the victim[5].

1   HA 1996, s 198(2)(a). See **14.43–14.122**.
2   HA 1996, s 198(2)(b). See **14.43–14.122**.
3   HA 1996, s 198(2)(c). See **14.107–14.119**.
4   HA 1996, s 198(2A). See **14.107–14.119**.
5   HA 1996, s 198(2A). See **14.107–14.119**.

Right to a review of whether the second set of conditions for referral are satisfied

14.199 In relation to the second set of conditions for referral between local housing authorities in England[1], the applicant, where the referral has been made at the stage where the HA 1996, s 193(2)[2] main housing duty would be owed, has the right to request a review *of the notifying local housing authority's decision* that:

(1)   he or she accepted a private rented sector offer[3] from another local housing authority and has made his or her application for homelessness assistance within two years of the date of acceptance[4]; or

(2)   he or she, or a member of his or her household, will not run the risk of domestic violence in the district of the other local housing authority[5]; or

(3)   he or she, or a member of his or her household, has not suffered violence in the district of the other local housing authority[6]; or

(4)   he or she, or a member of his or her household, has suffered violence, but it is not probable that any return to the other local housing authority's district will lead to further violence of a similar kind against the victim[7]; or

(5)   the other local housing authority should be notified of the local housing authority's decision that the conditions for referral are met[8].

[1]   HA 1996 s 198(2ZA) and (2A). See **14.123–14.137.**
[2]   See **16.94–16.199.**
[3]   HA 1996, s 193(7AA). See **16.153–16.179.**
[4]   HA 1996, s 198(2ZA)(a). See **8.100–8.107** and **14.123–14.137.**
[5]   HA 1996, s 198(2ZA)(b). See **14.107–14.119** and **14.128–14.137.**
[6]   HA 1996, s 198(2A). See **14.107–14.119** and **14.128–14.137.**
[7]   HA 1996, s 198(2A). See **14.107–14.119** and **14.128–14.137.**
[8]   HA 1996, s 198(1). See **14.151–14.154.**

14.200 In addition, the applicant has the right to request a review in all cases, following a referral, *of the local housing authorities' agreement*, or *of a referee's decision*, that:

(1)   he or she accepted a private rented sector offer[1] from another local housing authority and has made his or her application for homelessness assistance within two years of the date of acceptance[2]; or

(2)   he or she, or a member of his or her household, will not run the risk of domestic violence in the district of the other local housing authority[3]; or

(3)   he or she, or a member of his or her household, has not suffered violence in the district of the other local housing authority[4]; or

(4)   he or she, or a member of his or her household, has suffered violence, but it is not probable that any return to the other local housing authority's district will lead to further violence of a similar kind against the victim[5].

[1]   HA 1996, s 193(7AA). See **16.153–16.179.**
[2]   HA 1996, s 198(2ZA)(a). See **8.100–8.107** and **14.123–14.137.**
[3]   HA 1996 s 198(2ZA)(b). See **14.107–14.119** and **14.128–14.137.**
[4]   HA 1996 s 198(2A). See **14.107–14.119** and **14.128–14.137.**
[5]   HA 1996, s 198(2A). See **14.107–14.119** and **14.128–14.137.**

Right to a review of whether the third set of conditions for referral are satisfied

14.201 For applicants to local housing authorities in England, in relation to the third set of conditions for referral[1], the applicant, where the referral has been made at the stage where the HA 1996, s 193(2)[2] main housing duty would be owed, has the right to request a review of any decision *by the notifying local housing authority* (authority B) that:

(1)   the applicant was, on a previous application to authority A, placed in the district of authority B in performance of authority A's homelessness functions; or

(2)   the previous application to authority A was made within the prescribed period of the application to authority B; or

(3)   authority B should notify authority A of its decision that these

conditions for referral are met.

¹   HA 1996, s 198(4). See **14.138–14.150**.
²   See **16.94–16.199**.

14.202 In addition, the applicant has the right to request a review in all cases, following a referral, of *the local housing authorities' agreement*, or *of a referee's decision*, that:

(1)   the applicant was on a previous application to authority A placed in the district of authority B in performance of authority A's homelessness functions; or

(2)   the previous application was within the prescribed period.

Circumstances where there is no right to a review

14.203 However, there is *no* statutory right to request a review of any of the other decisions involved in the process, including:

(1)   a decision, by the local housing authority to which he or she has applied, to make or not to make inquiries into local connection or the other conditions of referral¹;

(2)   a decision by the local housing authority that the conditions of referral are met, but that another local housing authority should not be notified of the application²;

(3)   a decision by a local housing authority in England to refer the applicant's case at the stage where the HA 1996, s 189B(2)³ relief duty would be owed⁴; and

(4)   a decision by the notifying local housing authority not to exercise its power to provide accommodation pending determination of a request for a review of the decision made by the two local housing authorities jointly or by the referee⁵.

¹   HA 1996, s 184(2) (England); *Hackney London Borough Council v Sareen* [2003] EWCA Civ 351, [2003] HLR 54, CA. For local housing authorities in Wales there is no equivalent provision under H(W)A 2014, Pt 2 governing the making of inquiries into the applicant's connection with another area. However, the power to make such inquiries must be implicit in the scheme of H(W)A 2014, Pt 2 since the referral mechanism contained in H(W)A 2014, ss 80–83 would be inoperable without it. And since there is no express duty to make these inquiries in H(W)A 2014, Pt 2 it must be the case that these inquiries are discretionary. See Welsh Code, paras 18.1 and 18.6. See **14.24–14.25**.
²   HA 1996, s 198(1); H(W)A 2014, s 80(2). See **14.151–14.154**.
³   As inserted by HRA 2017, s 5(2) for applications for homelessness assistance made to local housing authorities in England on or after 3 April 2018. See **15.138–15.189**.
⁴   HA 1996, s 198(A1) as inserted by HRA 2017, s 5(8) for applications for homelessness assistance made to local housing authorities in England on or after 3 April 2018. See English Code, para 10.56.
⁵   HA 1996, s 200(5); H(W)A 2014, s 82(6). See *R (Gebremarium) v Westminster City Council* [2009] EWHC 2254 (Admin), (2009) November *Legal Action*, p 26, Admin Ct for an example of an unsuccessful challenge in judicial review to Westminster's decision not to exercise its HA 1996, s 200(5) power pending a review of its decision to refer her to Cardiff. See also **14.171** and **14.175**.

14.204 Challenges to those four types of decision can only be brought by way of a judicial review[1].

¹   See **19.306–19.327**.

Review procedure

14.205 The procedure for requesting a review of any decision by the notifying local housing authority is the same as for any other request for a review, and the reviewer will be appointed by the notifying local housing authority in the usual way[1]. The right to request a review arises upon notification to the applicant of a reviewable decision[2].

¹   See **19.104–19.108** and **19.131–19.137**.
²   *Berhane v Lambeth London Borough Council* [2007] EWHC 2702 (QB), (2008) March *Legal Action*, p 21, QBD.

14.206 If the request is to review a decision made as to whether the conditions for referral are met, the decision will have been made either by agreement between the notifying and notified local housing authorities, or by a referee. In either case, the request should be made to the notifying local housing authority[1].

¹   Allocation of Housing and Homelessness (Review Procedures) Regulations 1999, SI 1999/71, reg 6(1)(b); Homelessness (Review Procedure) (Wales) Regulations 2015, SI 2015/1266 (W 86), regs 2(1) and 1(3)(b).

14.207 If the decision was one made by agreement between the two local housing authorities, then the review must be undertaken by them jointly[1]. Presumably this will mean an arrangement for a joint committee or a joint panel of officers, or contracting out to a reviewer independent of both.

¹   SI 1999/71, reg 1(2)(b)(i).

14.208 If a referee made the decision, then the reviewer should be a person jointly appointed by the local housing authorities within 5 working days from the day on which the review request was received by the notifying local housing authority[1]. This appointee could be anyone to whom both local housing authorities are prepared to entrust the review process who has no personal interest in the dispute, no connection to the applicant and is not employed by either authority or a council tax payer in either area[2]. If an appointment is not agreed within that time frame, the notifying local housing authority (which has received the review request) has a further 5 working days to ask the chair of the Local Government Association (LGA)[3] to appoint another referee[4]. The chair of the LGA must then appoint a referee within a further seven days from among the membership of a panel appointed by the LGA[5]. That person then undertakes the review. Although this may appear to be a very tight time frame[6], the membership of the panel comprises only a handful of referees, one of whom is already eliminated because he or she took the decision[7]. Whether appointed by the local housing authorities or by the LGA, the reviewer will in this chapter be referred to as to the 'appointed' reviewer[8].

¹   SI 1999/71, reg 7(1); SI 2015/1266 (W 86), reg 4(2).
²   Local Authorities Agreement, paras 13.1–13.3.

3   Or Convention of Scottish Local Authorities, if the notified authority is in Scotland.
4   SI 1999/71, reg 7(2); SI 2015/1266 (W 86), reg 4(2); Local Authorities Agreement, para 13.1.
5   SI 1999/71, reg 7(2)(b) and (3); SI 2015/1266 (W 86), reg 4(2)(b) and (3).
6   SI 1999/71, reg 7(7) and SI 2015/1266 (W 86), reg 1(3) define 'working day'.
7   SI 1999/71, reg 7(6); SI 2015/1266 (W 86), reg 4(6).
8   SI 1999/71, reg 7 and SI 2015/1266 (W 86), reg 4 refer to the reviewer appointed in these
     circumstances as 'the appointed person'.

14.209 Once the appointed reviewer has been appointed, the local housing authorities should supply the reasons for the decision under review, together with information and evidence in support. The appointed reviewer will inform the applicant of the procedure to be followed during the review process and that he or she may make written representations. The request for a review and representations made by the applicant should be sent to the local housing authorities and they should be invited to respond. If there is thought to be a deficiency or irregularity in the original decision, further written or oral representations should be invited[1].

1   SI 1999/71, reg 8; SI 2015/1266 (W 86), reg 5; and see **19.150–19.165**.

14.210 If the appointed reviewer is a person appointed by agreement between the two local housing authorities, the review decision must be notified to the applicant within ten weeks from the date of the request for the review[1]. If the appointed reviewer was appointed from a panel, the period is 12 weeks for notification to the applicant, and the review decision will be notified to the local housing authorities one week prior to notification to the applicant, in order to give the local housing authorities concerned time to notify a review decision within the 12-week period[2].

1   SI 1999/71, reg 9(1)(b); SI 2015/1266 (W 86), reg 6(1)(b).
2   SI 1999/71, reg 9(1)(c) and (3); SI 2015/1266 (W 86), reg 6(1)(b) and (c).

14.211 Once the review has been determined, and the decision on review notified to the applicant, the applicant may appeal to the county court against the review decision. The exercise of this right is entirely separate from any dispute that may be going on between the two local housing authorities. In one case, the county court judge's decision to adjourn the appeal whilst the notifying and notified local housing authorities sought to resolve their dispute was criticised by an appeal judge because it 'denies the appellant effective access to the court, where there is, or is likely to be, undue delay on the part of the relevant respondent'[1].

1   *Berhane v Lambeth London Borough Council* [2007] EWHC 2702 (QBD), (2008) March
     Legal Action, p 21, QBD, at [43] per Eady J.

The power to assist former asylum-seekers who occupied Home Office accommodation in Scotland

14.212 Former asylum-seekers who leave accommodation in Scotland provided by the Home Office under the Immigration and Asylum Act 1999, s 95 and then apply as homeless to local housing authorities in England will not normally have a local connection with the district of the local authority in

Scotland (unless by reason of employment, family associations, or some other special circumstance).

14.213 Providing the applicant is homeless[1] and eligible for assistance[2], he or she will be owed the HA 1996, s 189B(2)[3] relief duty by the local housing authority in England to which he or she has applied. Normally, when the HA 1996, s 189B(2)[4] relief duty comes to an end, an applicant who remains homeless and has a priority need[5] would be owed the HA 1996, s 193(2)[6] main housing duty. However, legislation passed in 2004 provides that where local housing authorities in England would otherwise owe the HA 1996, s 193(2)[7] main housing duty towards these former asylum-seekers, the duty does not apply[8]. There is no equivalent provision under H(W)A 2014, Pt 2.

[1]   See CHAPTER 10.
[2]   See CHAPTER 11.
[3]   As inserted by HRA 2017, s 5(2) for applications for homelessness assistance made to local housing authorities in England on or after 3 April 2018. See **15.138–15.189**.
[4]   As inserted by HRA 2017, s 5(2) for applications for homelessness assistance made to local housing authorities in England on or after 3 April 2018. See **15.138–15.189**.
[5]   See CHAPTER 12.
[6]   See **16.94–16.199**.
[7]   See **16.94–16.199**.
[8]   Asylum and Immigration (Treatment of Claimants etc) Act 2004, s 11(2) and (3).

14.214 Instead, the local housing authority in England has a power (but no duty):

- to provide accommodation for the former asylum-seeker for a period that would give him or her a reasonable opportunity of obtaining accommodation; and
- to provide advice and assistance with any attempts he or she may make to obtain his or her own accommodation[1].

[1]   Asylum and Immigration (Treatment of Claimants etc) Act 2004, s 11(3)(b).

14.215 The idea is that the former asylum-seeker will either obtain his or her own accommodation in England, with assistance from the local housing authority (if the local housing authority chooses to provide it), or will return to Scotland and make an application for homelessness assistance to a local authority in Scotland[1]. Indeed, the English Code specifically suggests that the local housing authority consider:

> 'providing such advice and assistance as would enable the applicant to make an application for housing to the Scottish authority in the district where the section 95 accommodation was last provided, or to another Scottish authority of the applicant's choice[2].'

[1]   Since an application for homelessness assistance can be made in any manner and should not require completion of the local housing authority's standard form, the former asylum-seeker could be assisted to make an application to any local authority in Scotland by writing, by fax, or even by email. There should be no need to leave any accommodation provided by the local housing authority in England or in Wales until the local authority in Scotland has notified the applicant that the application for homelessness assistance has been received and that suitable accommodation will be provided.
[2]   English Code, para 10.29.

14.216 Since, under Scottish law, the former asylum-seeker will most likely have no local connection with any local housing authority in England, Wales or Scotland, a local authority in Scotland will be subject to the main housing duty. There is no need for the former asylum-seeker to apply to the Scottish local authority in Scotland in whose district he or she had been accommodated by the Home Office[1]. He or she could apply to any Scottish local authority.

1   English Code, para 10.29.

14.217 The surprising effect of this provision is to put a former asylum-seeker who was dispersed to Scotland by the Home Office but has become homeless unintentionally from Home Office accommodation and wishes to apply for accommodation to a local housing authority in England in a worse position than a person who has become homeless intentionally. At least an applicant who has become homeless intentionally would (if he or she had a priority need) be owed the HA 1996, s 190(2) short term accommodation duty[1] when the HA 1996, s 189B(2)[2] relief duty came to an end.

1   See **16.81–16.93**.
2   As inserted by HRA 2017, s 5(2) for applications for homelessness assistance made to local housing authorities in England on or after 3 April 2018. See **15.138–15.189**.

14.218 Any decision by the local housing authority that such an applicant is caught by these provisions and not owed the HA 1996, s 193(2)[1] main housing dutywould be a decision as to 'what duty (if any) is owed'. The applicant would have a right to request a review of that decision under HA 1996, s 202(1)(b).

1   See **16.94–16.199**.

14.219 The powers given to local housing authorities in England under the Asylum and Immigration (Treatment of Claimants etc) Act 2004 (whether or not to provide accommodation and/or whether or not to provide advice and assistance) are discretionary powers and carry no statutory right to request a review. If a local housing authority decided not to exercise these powers, any challenge could only be brought on a point of law in judicial review proceedings[1].

1   See **19.306–19.327** for judicial review.

14.220 An applicant who had been provided with accommodation under the interim duty owed by the local housing authority in England would be entitled to reasonable notice of the termination of that accommodation[1].

1   HA 1996, s 188(1); *R v Newham London Borough Council ex p Ojuri (No 5)* (1999) 31 HLR 631, QBD applying *R v Secretary of State for the Environment ex p Shelter* [1997] COD 49, QB.

CROSS-BORDER REFERRALS

14.221 All the countries of the UK[1] operate statutory homelessness schemes. This book is concerned only with the detailed schemes for England and Wales found in HA 1996, Pt 7[2] and H(W)A 2014, Pt 2, respectively. But cross-border referrals may arise between local housing authorities in England or in Wales and when local housing authorities in England or in Wales make referrals to, or are asked to receive referrals from, other countries in the UK.

[1]   England, Wales, Scotland and Northern Ireland. See Interpretation Act 1978, s 5 and Sch 1; and see Box 1 at **11.28**.
[2]   As amended by HRA 2017, for applications for homelessness assistance made to local housing authorities in England on or after 3 April 2018.

Referrals within England and Wales

14.222 The referral arrangements in HA 1996, Pt 7[1] and H(W)A 2014, Pt 2 govern all referrals between local housing authorities in England or Wales. They apply to referrals between:

- a local housing authority in Wales and one or more other local housing authorities in Wales;
- a local housing authority in England and one or more other local housing authorities in England;
- a local housing authority in England and one or more local housing authorities in Wales; and
- a local housing authority in Wales and one or more local housing authorities in England.

[1]   As amended by HRA 2017, for applications for homelessness assistance made to local housing authorities in England on or after 3 April 2018.

14.223 However, the schemes under HA 1996, Pt 7[1] and H(W)A 2014, Pt 2 are not identical. For example the case of an applicant who is owed the HA 1996, s 189B(2)[2] relief duty by a local housing authority in England can only be referred to another local housing authority in England[3]. The net result is a potential for disparity between the treatment of an application for homelessness assistance by a local housing authority in Wales as compared to that by a local housing authority in England. An applicant to a local housing authority in Wales might well be accepted as having priority need in circumstances in which no priority need would be found by a local housing authority in England (because of the differences between the priority need classes)[4]. The result may be that the conditions of referral from Wales to England are made out where the conditions for referral of the same application from England to Wales would not be, since the main housing duty under HA 1996, s 193(2) would not be owed.

[1]   As amended by HRA 2017, for applications for homelessness assistance made to local housing authorities in England on or after 3 April 2018.
[2]   As inserted by HRA 2017, s 5(2) for applications for homelessness assistance made to local housing authorities in England on or after 3 April 2018. See **15.138–15.189**.
[3]   HA 1996, s 198(A1) as inserted by HRA 2017, s 5(8) for applications for homelessness assistance made to local housing authorities in England on or after 3 April 2018.
[4]   See **12.132–12.194** (English Priority Need Order), and contrast **12.195–12.2228** (H(W)A 2014, s 70).

14.224 These nuances cannot, however, make any difference to the application of the first set of referral conditions discussed in this chapter[1]. For example, if a local housing authority in Wales finds that it owes the H(W)A

2014, s 73 duty to an applicant who has a priority need, who has not become homeless intentionally, who has no local connection with its district but who does have a local connection with a local housing authority in England (and would run no risk of violence by returning there), it may make a referral. No doubt, in considering the exercise of its discretion whether to refer[2], it might wish to take into account that, on the same facts, the notified local housing authority might not have owed the main housing duty at all.

[1] See **14.43–14.122**.
[2] See **14.151–14.154**.

14.225 However, as this chapter has described, an applicant to a local housing authority in England who had previously accepted a private rented sector offer[1] from a local housing authority could be referred back to that local housing authority under the secondset of conditions for referral[2]. Likewise, an applicant to a local housing authority in England who was placed in the local housing authority's district by another local housing authority in England or Wales pursuant to its functions under HA 1996, Pt 7[3] or H(W)A 2014, Pt 2 could be referred back to the first local housing authority under the third set of conditions for referral[4]. This is not the case for applications made to local housing authorities in Wales. A local housing authority in Wales would have no power to refer the applicant's case back to another local housing authority in Wales or to a local housing authority in England in these circumstances.

[1] HA 1996, s 193(7AA). See **16.153–16.179**.
[2] HA 1996, s 198(2ZA) and (2A). See **14.123–14.137**.
[3] As amended by HRA 2017, for applications for homelessness assistance made to local housing authorities in England on or after 3 April 2018.
[4] HA 1996, s 198(4) and (4A). See **14.138–14.150**.

Referrals to the Isles of Scilly

14.226 The Isles of Scilly are administratively part of England[1], but special measures have been taken to protect the very limited stock of social housing on those islands. HA 1996[2] enables the Secretary of State to make an order adapting HA 1996, Pt 7[3] in its application to the Isles of Scilly, and that power has been used[4]. So, for example, there are special provisions governing eligibility for applicants applying there[5].

[1] Interpretation Act 1978, s 5 and Sch 1.
[2] HA 1996, s 225(1).
[3] As amended by HRA 2017, for applications for homelessness assistance made to local housing authorities in England on or after 3 April 2018.
[4] Homelessness (Isles of Scilly) Order 1997, SI 1997/797.
[5] Discussed at **11.173–11.174**.

14.227 To prevent these eligibility rules being circumvented by an application directed initially to a local housing authority elsewhere, modifications have been made by Order to arrangements for referral by other local housing authorities to the Isles of Scilly Council.

14.228 If a homeless applicant applies to a local housing authority elsewhere in England or in Wales and the conditions for a local connection referral to the Council of the Isles of Scilly would otherwise be met, they are displaced by special rules. The intended effect of the Order[1] is that the applicant will only have a local connection with the Isles of Scilly if she or he has resided in the district of the Isles of Scilly Council for two years and six months during the three years prior to the date that the latest application for homelessness assistance is made. If that period of residence is established, there is a deemed local connection in place of the normal local connection provisions[2].

[1]   Which is not well drafted.
[2]   HA 1996, s 199(1).

14.229 It is recognised that the Isles of Scilly may need to accommodate some of its homeless applicants on the mainland. As a result, local housing authorities in England can refer back to the islands if the second or third set of conditions for a referral is made out[1]. This is because the HA 1996, s 225(2) power to modify HA 1996, Pt 7[2] has not been used in relation to this set of conditions.

[1]   See **14.123–14.150**. However, for either of the second or third conditions for referral to apply, the Isles of Scilly would have had to have made private rented sector offers of accommodation or to have secured accommodation for an applicant in the district of a local housing authority in England, which seems unlikely.
[2]   As amended by HRA 2017, for applications for homelessness assistance made to local housing authorities in England on or after 3 April 2018.

Referrals to Scotland

14.230 The provisions of HA 1996, Pt 7 enable local housing authorities in England to make referrals to local authorities in Scotland in a similar way as they might make a referral to another local housing authority in Wales. There is no equivalent provision under H(W)A 2014, Pt 2. The Local Authorities' Agreement[1] was drawn up with the co-operation of the Confederation of Scottish Local Authorities (CoSLA) and applies in the same way to referrals to local authorities in Scotland as it would to any other referral.

[1]   See **14.19** fn 3.

14.231 The Local Authorities' Agreement provides that, where there is a cross-border dispute, the relevant law to be applied is that relevant to the location of the notified local housing authority[1]. This only applies to the issue of whether or not the conditions for referral are or are not made out, and not to any other disagreements that the notified local housing authority may have with the decision of the notifying local housing authority[2].

[1]   Local Authorities Agreement, para 11.2.
[2]   See **14.176–14.183**.

14.232 The only procedural difference is that if the notified local authority (in Scotland) does not accept that the conditions for referral are made out and is unable to agree with the notifying local housing authority (in England or in Wales) on the identity of a referee to resolve the dispute, then it is CoSLA which appoints a referee in default of such agreement[1]. The adjudication will then be governed by the procedural rules in the Homelessness (Decisions on

Referrals) (Scotland) Order 1998[2].

1 Local Authorities Agreement, para 11.4.
2 Homelessness (Decisions on Referrals) (Scotland) Order 1998, SI 1998/1603.

14.233 If the conditions for a referral are not made out, a local housing authority in England may nevertheless invite a local authority in Scotland to assist in the discharge of HA 1996, Pt 7[1] functions. The local authority in Scotland would be bound to co-operate with that request to such extent as was reasonable in the particular circumstances[2]. A local housing authority in Wales would also be entitled to make such a request but there would be no statutory obligation on the local housing authority in Scotland to cooperate[3].

1 As amended by HRA 2017, for applications for homelessness assistance made to local housing authorities in England on or after 3 April 2018.
2 HA 1996, s 213(1).
3 H(W)A 2014, s 95.

Referrals from Scotland to England

14.234 The capacity of a local authority in Scotland to refer an application for homelessness assistance to a local housing authority in England will primarily be regulated by the law of Scotland (which is beyond the scope of this book). Note that under Housing (Scotland) Act 1987, s 33(1) a local housing authority in Scotland may refer a case to England *or* Wales. However, under H(W)A 2014, Pt 2 there is no corresponding provision to receive such a referral. Contrast this with HA 1996, ss 201 and 201A (for local housing authorities in England to receive referrals from Scotland and Wales) and H(W)A 2014, s 83 (for local housing authorities in Wales to receive referrals from England). As such it is very difficult to see how the referral mechanism from Scotland to Wales can possibly operate.

14.235 It should be noted that there are several differences in the operation of homelessness provisions, including those relating to referrals, as between Scotland and England. For example:

- the priority need test has been abolished in Scotland[1];
- applicants in Scotland have no statutory right to seek a review of a decision to refer them to a local housing authority in England or Wales;
- the second and third sets of conditions for a statutory referral (reference back to a local housing authority which made a private rented sector offer or placed the applicant in the present local housing authority's area)[2] do not extend to Scotland[3]; and
- the deemed local connection for residents of Home Office accommodation[4] is not part of the law of Scotland.

1 Homelessness (Abolition of Priority Need Test) (Scotland) Order 2012, SI 2012/330.
2 Second set of conditions at HA 1996, s 198(2ZA) and (2A). See **14.123–14.137**. Third set of conditions at HA 1996, s 198(4). See paras **14.138–14.150**.
3 Because HA 1996, Pt 7, as amended by HRA 2017, for applications for homelessness assistance made to local housing authorities in England on or after 3 April 2018, (and in particular HA 1996, s 193(7AA)) does not apply to Scotland.
4 HA 1996, s 199(6) and (7), added by Asylum and Immigration (Treatment of Claimants etc) Act 2004, s 11(1).

14.236 However, if a local authority in Scotland (applying the law of Scotland) forms the opinion that the conditions for a referral to a local housing authority in England are met, it may notify the local housing authority in England to that effect. If the notified local housing authority accepts that the conditions for a referral are satisfied, then the application is referred in the normal way. If the local housing authority in England does not accept that the necessary conditions are satisfied, a referee will be appointed by agreement or in default by the Local Government Association[1]. The adjudication will then be governed by the procedural rules in the Homelessness (Decisions on Referrals) Order[2].

[1]   Local Authorities Agreement, para 10.3.
[2]   SI 1998/1603. See Local Authorities Agreement, para 11.4.

14.237 If the conditions for a referral are not made out, a local authority in Scotland may nevertheless invite a local housing authority in England or Wales to assist in the discharge of its homelessness duties. The local housing authority in England or in Wales would be bound to co-operate with that request to such extent as was reasonable in the particular circumstances[1].

[1]   HA 1996, s 213.

14.238 The Homelessness etc (Scotland) Act 2003 contains powers under which ministers of the Scottish Executive may effectively abolish the referral powers of local authorities in Scotland so that responsibility for a homeless person in Scotland will remain with the local authority to which an applicant first applies[1]. The powers have yet to be used.

[1]   Homelessness (Scotland) Act 2003, s 8.

Northern Ireland

14.239 Northern Ireland has its own self-contained legislative scheme for homelessness[1]. No doubt because there is a single authority dealing with applications for homelessness assistance in Northern Ireland (the Housing Executive), there are no 'local connection' or other referral provisions in the scheme. There is no power for the Executive to refer an application to a local housing authority in England, Scotland or Wales. Likewise, there is no power to make a referral in the other direction. Any referral could therefore only be through informal, co-operative arrangements[2].

[1]   Housing (Northern Ireland) Order 1988, SI 1988/1990, as amended.
[2]   See **14.241–14.257**.

The Isle of Man

14.240 The Isle of Man has its own separate jurisdiction and, indeed, a self-contained legislative scheme defining the right of residence[1]. There are no legislative powers permitting referrals from the Isle of Man to local housing authorities in England or in Wales, or vice versa. Any referral could only, therefore, be informal through co-operative mechanisms, and the Isle of Man would be unlikely to co-operate unless the applicant had the right to reside under its statutes.

[1]   Residence Act 2001, s 9 (not yet brought into effect).

INFORMAL REFERRALS

14.241 This chapter has been primarily concerned with the formal mechanisms by which a local housing authority can refer a homelessness applicant to another local housing authority to be accommodated in another local housing authority's district. Where those provisions do not apply, the normal rule is that the local housing authority that has accepted the application must accommodate the applicant in its own district[1].

[1]   HA 1996, s 208(1); H(W)A 2014, s 91(1).

14.242 But there is a wide range of circumstances beyond those covered by the formal referral arrangements when the provision of accommodation in the area of another local housing authority may be appropriate. For example:

- the applicant may not be safe (in that there is a risk of domestic or other violence) in the district of the local housing authority which has accepted his or her application and with which she or he may enjoy a local connection[1]; or
- the applicant may have other compelling reasons (eg relating to health or education or the need to be near a carer) for asking that local housing authority to provide accommodation in another local housing authority's district; or
- the local housing authority may simply be unable to provide any accommodation which is suitable for the applicant in its own district; or
- the local housing authority may have sought to make a referral under the formal provisions, and then been satisfied by the notified local housing authority's response that the conditions for referral were not made out, yet the applicant may still wish to be accommodated in the other local housing authority's area.

[1]   English Code, para 17.54.

14.243 The following paragraphs explore the extent to which there is scope under HA 1996, Pt 7[1] and H(W)A 2014, Pt 2 for a local housing authority to provide accommodation in another local housing authority's district outside the tailor-made referral provisions.

[1]   As amended by HRA 2017, for applications for homelessness assistance made to local housing authorities in England on or after 3 April 2018.

Unilateral placements in another district

14.244 Strictly, a local housing authority which has accepted a responsibility to accommodate an applicant, but finds that it is not 'reasonably practicable' to accommodate that applicant in its own district, can provide accommodation in the district of another local housing authority (provided that it is suitable), and may do so without any prior reference to that other local housing authority at all[1]. A local housing authority might be tempted to do precisely that when it comes to its most needy and vulnerable applicants, so that the burden of meeting their special needs (for example, in relation to education or adult care or children's services) falls on another district[2].

1   HA 1996, s 208(1); H(W)A 2014, s 91(1).
2   See the comments of Latham LJ in *R v Newham London Borough Council ex p Sacupima* (2001) 33 HLR 2, CA at [31]. And see *R (AM) v Havering London Borough Council and Tower Hamlets London Borough Council* [2015] EWHC 1004 (Admin), (2015) May *Legal Action*, p 46, Admin Ct for an example of a dispute between two unitary authorities in this type of situation.

14.245 The legality of such placements fell for consideration by the Supreme Court in *Nzolameso v City of Westminster Council*[1]. The judgment reaffirms the significance of the requirement on local housing authorities to place applicants within their own district so far as is reasonably practicable. 'Reasonably practicable' is a stronger duty than an obligation simply to act reasonably. If it is not reasonably practicable to secure accommodation within the local housing authority's own district, it should try to place the household as close as possible to where it was previously living[2]. Ideally, each local housing authority should maintain and publish a policy of procuring units of accommodation within its own district and a separate policy on how those units of accommodation would be allocated[3].

1   [2015] UKSC 22, [2015] HLR 22, SC. See **18.53–18.57**.
2   *Nzolameso v City of Westminster Council*, [2015] UKSC 22, [2015] HLR 22, SC per Baroness Hale at [10].
3   *Nzolameso v City of Westminster Council*, [2015] UKSC 22, [2015] HLR 22, SC per Baroness Hale at [36]–[40].

14.246 Where an 'out of district'[1] placement is made, HA 1996, Pt 7[2] and H(W)A 2014, Pt 2 require the placing local housing authority to give notice of any such placement to the other local housing authority[3]. Notice is not required in advance but must be given within 14 days of the provision of accommodation in the notified local housing authority's district[4].

1   English Code, paras 17.46–17.61.There is no comparable guidance in the Welsh Code addressing specifically the operation of H(W)A 2014, s 91, though the location of accommodation more generally is dealt with at paras 19.13–19.24.
2   As amended by HRA 2017, for applications for homelessness assistance made to local housing authorities in England on or after 3 April 2018.
3   HA 1996, s 208(2); H(W)A 2014, s 91(2).
4   HA 1996, s 208(4); H(W)A 2014, s 91(4).

14.247 HA 1996, Pt 7[1] and H(W)A 2014, Pt 2, set out the formal requirements of the notice (name of applicant, address of the accommodation, etc) including the provision of the date on which accommodation was provided to the applicant[2].

1   As amended by HRA 2017, for applications for homelessness assistance made to local housing authorities in England on or after 3 April 2018.
2   HA 1996, s 208(3); H(W)A 2014, s 91(3).

14.248 The duty to notify an 'out of district' placement applies whenever a local housing authority is discharging any accommodation duty owed under HA 1996, Pt 7[1] or H(W)A 2014, Pt 2 by securing accommodation in another district, whether the accommodation being provided is provided by a social or private sector landlord or anyone else. Thus, it is not confined to placement of those owed the main housing duty under HA 1996, s 193(2) or the H(W)A 2014, s 73 duty. For example, it applies whenever accommodation is being provided on an interim basis pending a decision on an application[2]. Experience suggests that, particularly in relation to interim accommodation where there can be a reasonably rapid turnover of households, the notification duty is honoured in the breach[3].

[1] As amended by HRA 2017, for applications for homelessness assistance made to local housing authorities in England on or after 3 April 2018.
[2] HA 1996, s 188(1); H(W)A 2014, s 68(1). See **16.37–16.73**.
[3] See *R (AM) v Havering London Borough Council and Tower Hamlets London Borough Council* [2015] EWHC 1004 (Admin) (2015) May *Legal Action*, p 46, Admin Ct at [3] per Cobb J for an instance of a failure to comply with this duty.

14.249 The duty to notify does not apply where a local housing authority in England owes the main housing duty to an applicant and makes him or her a private rented sector offer in the district of another local housing authority[1]. This is surprising as the second local housing authority will become responsible for education, adult care or children's services and any other needs that the applicant and his or her household has. In addition, in England, if the applicant makes a further application for homelessness assistance to the second local housing authority more than two years after he or she had accepted the private rented sector offer, any duty to accommodate under HA 1996, Pt 7 will fall on the second local housing authority[2].

[1] HA 1996, s 193(7AA)–(7AC). See **16.153–16.179**.
[2] Because the second set of conditions for referral at HA 1996 s 198(2ZA) and (2) will not be met. See **14.123–14.137**.

14.250 The simple dispatch of a notice is not sufficient to relieve the placing local housing authority of any responsibility for the homeless household[1]. The English Code reminds placing local housing authorities to consider the particular needs of a household being accommodated out of the area and advises that households who need adult care or children's services support or need to maintain links with specialist medical services, special schools or other essential services within the authority's district should be given priority for accommodation within that district[2].

[1] See *R (E) v Islington London Borough Council* [2017] EWHC 1440 (Admin), (2017) 20 CCLR 148, Admin Ct for the procedural requirements in instances where there are children in the household.
[2] English Code, para 17.56.

14.251 Where a household is placed in a different district from the district of the local housing authority to which it applied, it might be prudent for that household to apply for long-term social housing under *both* local housing authorities' allocation schemes.

Placements by co-operation between local housing authorities

14.252 HA 1996, Pt 7[1], H(W)A 2014, Pt 2, the Codes and the Local Authorities' Agreement are all replete with references to the need for local housing authorities to co-operate with one another in their dealings with homeless applicants. Obviously, it is particularly important for local housing authorities to co-operate where a homeless household is being re-located from the district of the local housing authority to which it applied to another local housing authority's district.

1   As amended by HRA 2017, for applications for homelessness assistance made to local housing authorities in England on or after 3 April 2018.

14.253 The legislation facilitates that necessary co-operation in two ways. First, HA 1996, Pt 7[1] requires any local housing authority receiving a request for assistance in discharging HA 1996, Pt 7[2] functions from another local housing authority, to give such assistance as is reasonable in the circumstances[3]. The corresponding provision under H(W)A 2014, Pt 2 requires a local housing authority receiving a request to cooperate save to the extent that such cooperation would be incompatible with that local housing authority's own duties or otherwise have an adverse effect on the exercise of its functions: a stronger duty[4]. Secondly, HA 1996, Pt 7[5] and H(W)A 2014, Pt 2 enable a local housing authority to perform its housing functions by securing accommodation for the applicant from some other person than the local housing authority itself[6]. That other person might be a different local housing authority.

1   As amended by HRA 2017, for applications for homelessness assistance made to local housing authorities in England on or after 3 April 2018.
2   As amended by HRA 2017, for applications for homelessness assistance made to local housing authorities in England on or after 3 April 2018.
3   HA 1996, s 213(1). See also English Code, para 16.13–16.14.
4   H(W)A 2014, s 95(2) or (3).
5   As amended by HRA 2017, for applications for homelessness assistance made to local housing authorities in England on or after 3 April 2018.
6   HA 1996, s 206(1)(b); H(W)A 2014, s 64(1).

14.254 The most frequent instance of local housing authorities co-operating occurs when local housing authorities with surplus accommodation make that stock available to other local housing authorities. These arrangements are particularly encouraged by the Codes[1]. Increasingly sophisticated schemes have been developed to match homeless applicants who apply to high demand areas with accommodation in lower demand areas (even though they may have previously had no connection with those areas). Most of those schemes work on the premise that the applicant is willing to take up the opportunity of a home elsewhere.

1   English Code, Chapter 2 and para 16.15 generally on the importance of joint working; Welsh Code, paras 6.1–6.12

14.255 The power given to local housing authorities to make private rented sector offers[1], coupled with the restrictions on the levels of housing benefit paid to claimants, make it more likely that local housing authorities in districts where private rents are high will make private rented sector offers in districts where the rents are comparatively cheaper. The effects of such placements have yet to be fully researched.

1   HA 1996, s 193(7AA); H(W)A 2014, s 76(3). See **16.153–16.179** and **17.173–17.177**.

14.256 It is not permissible for the local housing authority (to which an applicant has applied) to use the mere existence or activation of these co-operative arrangements as a purported performance of its own duties[1]. However, where a local housing authority has satisfied itself that another local housing authority is prepared to accommodate the applicant and that the accommodation to be provided for the applicant will be suitable, the main housing duty owed to an applicant can be performed upon the other local housing authority accepting that it would accommodate him or her[2].

[1] See *R v Bromley London Borough Council ex p Cafun* (2001) January *Legal Action*, p 27, Admin Ct, where Bromley had told the applicant that Greenwich, its neighbouring borough, would accommodate her. The court held that simple activation of the co-operative arrangements between the two boroughs was not enough. Bromley had to ensure that accommodation suitable for that particular applicant was actually going to be provided by Greenwich before its duty could be said to have been performed. Had *Bromley* satisfied itself that was the case, placing her in Greenwich would potentially have been lawful and its duty would have been discharged.

[2] *R v Bristol City Council ex p Browne* [1979] 1 WLR 1437, QBD. Though note that a specific unit of accommodation would need to have been made available. The hypothetical existence of a unit of accommodation based on the fact that the other local housing authority had accepted a duty would not suffice. See *Johnston v Westminster City Council* [2015] EWCA Civ 554, (2015) *Legal Action*, p 54, CA.

14.257 The second common form of co-operative out-of-district placements is a reciprocal arrangement, whereby one local housing authority agrees to accommodate an applicant who has applied as homeless elsewhere, and, in response, can place one of its homeless applicants in the transferring local housing authority's district. The Codes advise local housing authorities that this form of co-operation is particularly appropriate where an applicant has 'special housing needs' which can better be met in one area than another, or where the applicant needs be placed elsewhere to avoid the risk of violence in the area of the local housing authority to which he or she applied[1]. The Local Authorities' Agreement also promotes such reciprocal arrangements where, for one reason or another, a strict application of the formal referral rules would not result in a successful referral[2].

[1] English Code, para 16.15. Welsh Code, para 19.32 advises that a reason to place out of area might include where the applicant or a member of his or her household has been at risk of abuse, or where ex-offenders or drug/alcohol users would benefit from being accommodated outside the district to help break links with previous contacts who could exert a negative influence.

[2] For example, where the only ground for a local connection with the notified local housing authority would be 'special circumstances' or where a local connection is made out with the notifying local housing authority but the applicant does not wish to live in that local housing authority's area: Local Authorities Agreement, paras 4.4 and 6.4.

Chapter 15

DUTIES ON LOCAL HOUSING AUTHORITIES IN ENGLAND TO HELP APPLICANTS PREVENT OR RELIEVE HOMELESSNESS AND OTHER NON-ACCOMMODATION DUTIES

Contents

INTRODUCTION

15.1 The Homelessness Reduction Act 2017 (HRA 2017) broadens the range of duties owed by local housing authorities in England under the Housing Act 1996, Pt 7 (HA 1996) in very significant ways. Local housing authorities in England now owe duties to help and support eligible applicants who are homeless, or threatened with homelessness, regardless of whether those applicants also have a priority need or became homeless intentionally[1]. These duties are intended to provide much more assistance to applicants who are trying to retain their accommodation, or are looking for new accommodation, than the previous duties of 'advice and assistance' provided in practice[2]. These new duties do not require a local housing authority to secure accommodation for the applicant, although interim accommodation must be secured while the duties are being performed if the local housing authority has reason to believe that the applicant may be homeless, may be eligible for assistance and may have a priority need[3].

[1] For 'eligible for assistance', see Chapter 11; for 'homeless', see Housing Act 1996 (HA 1996), s 175–177 and Chapter 10; for 'threatened with homelessness', see HA 1996, s 175(4) and (5), as amended and inserted by Homelessness Reduction Act 2017 (HRA 2017), s 1(2) and (3), for applications for homelessness assistance on or after 3 April 2018, see **10.144–10.147**.

[2] HA 1996, ss 190(2)(b) and (3), 192(2), and 195(5), prior to amendment by HRA 2017, see previous editions of *Housing Allocation and Homelessness: Law and Practice* (Luba, Davies and Johnston, Jordan Publishing, 4th edn, 2016).

[3] HA 1996, s 188, as amended by HRA 2017, s 5(4), for applications for homelessness assistance on or after 3 April 2018, see **16.37–16.80**. For accommodation duties, see Chapter 16.

15.2 HRA 2017 operates by substantially amending HA 1996, Pt 7[1]. The changes came into force on 3 April 2018[2] and apply to all applications for homelessness assistance, made on or after that date[3]. A new *Homelessness Code of Guidance for Local Authorities* (the English Code) was published on 22 February 2018 and amended in June 2018[4]. Chapters 11–14 of the English Code provide guidance on the contents of this chapter[5]. We begin this chapter by providing an overview of the duties that fall short of the immediate provision of accommodation[6], before considering the background to HRA 2017 that led to the expansion of these duties and some of the key concepts underpinning it[7]. We will then go on to consider the duties in detail[8].

[1] See Appendix 2 of this book for HA 1996, Pt 7, as amended by HRA 2017, for applications for homelessness assistance made on or after 3 April 2018

[2] Homelessness Reduction Act (Commencement and Transitional and Savings Provisions) Regulations 2018, SI 2018/167, reg 3, at Appendix 2 of this book.

³ Homelessness Reduction Act (Commencement and Transitional and Savings Provisions) Regulations 2018, SI 2018/167, reg 4.
⁴ *Homelessness Code of Guidance for Local Authorities* (MHCLG, February 2018) (the English Code).
⁵ Chapter 11 of the English Code: Assessments and personalised plans, see **15.62–15.86**; Chapter 12 of the English Code: Duty in cases of threatened homelessness (the prevention duty), see **15.87–15.137**; Chapter 13 of the English Code: Relief Duty, see **15.138–15.195**; and Chapter 14 of the English Code: Ending the prevention and relief duties, see **15.98–15.133** and **15.151–15.190**.
⁶ See **15.3–15.12**.
⁷ See **15.13–15.61**.
⁸ See **15.62–15.232**.

OVERVIEW

15.3 HRA 2017 amends HA 1996, Pt 7[1], with the effect that local housing authorities owe duties to *all* eligible applicants as long as they are either threatened with homelessness or homeless. In accordance with Parliament's intention to encourage early intervention, the definition of 'threatened with homelessness' has been expanded by amendments to HA 1996, s 175 made by HRA 2017[2]. Each eligible applicant who is either homeless or threatened with homelessness is owed a duty under which the local housing authority must assess his or her case and formulate a personalised housing plan[3].

¹ For applications for homelessness assistance made on or after 3 April 2018.
² HA 1996, s 175(4) and (5) as amended and inserted by HRA 2017, s 1(2) and (3), for applications for homelessness assistance made on or after 3 April 2018, see **10.144–10.147**.
³ HA 1996, s 189A, inserted by HRA 2017, s 3, for applications for homelessness assistance made on or after 3 April 2018, see **15.62–15.86**. For 'eligible for assistance', see CHAPTER 11; for 'homeless', see HA 1996, s 175–177 and CHAPTER 10; for 'threatened with homelessness', see HA 1996, s 175(4) and (5), as amended and inserted by HRA 2017, s 1(2) and (3), for applications for homelessness assistance made on or after 3 April 2018, see **10.144–10.147**.

15.4 Eligible applicants who are threatened with homelessness will be owed the HA 1996, s 195(2)[1], prevention duty which requires local housing authorities to take reasonable steps to help them secure that their accommodation does not cease to be available for their occupation[2]. This is not entirely new. A duty to take reasonable steps to secure that accommodation did not cease to be available existed previously[3], but the group to whom the duty is owed has been enlarged, and HA 1996, Pt 7[4], now requires the local housing authority to take reasonable steps to *help* to secure that accommodation does not cease to be available[5].

¹ As amended by HRA 2017, s 4(2) for applications for homelessness assistance made on or after 3 April 2018, see **15.87–15.137**.
² HA 1996, s 195(2), amended by HRA 2017, s 4(2), for applications for homelessness assistance made on or after 3 April 2018, see English Code, chapter 12 and **15.87–15.97**.
³ HA 1996, s 195(2), prior to amendment by HRA 2017, required a local housing authority to take reasonable steps to secure that accommodation did not cease to be available for an applicant's occupation if the local housing authority was satisfied that an applicant was threatened with homelessness, eligible for assistance, had a priority need and was not satisfied that he or she had become homeless intentionally.
⁴ As amended by HRA 2017 for applications for homelessness assistance made on or after 3 April 2018.
⁵ HA 1996, s 195(2), as amended by HRA 2017, s 4(2), for applications for homelessness assistance made on or after 3 April 2018, see English Code, chapter 12, and **15.87–15.97**.

15.5 Eligible applicants who are homeless will be owed the HA 1996, s 189B(2)[1], relief duty which requires local authorities to take reasonable steps to help them secure that suitable accommodation becomes available for their occupation[2]. This is an entirely new duty. Where the local housing authority has reason to believe that an applicant to whom the HA 1996, s 189B(2), relief duty is owed may have a priority need, it is under a duty to secure interim accommodation for the applicant and all members of his or her household during the performance of that duty[3].

[1] As inserted by HRA 2017, s 5(2), for applications for homelessness assistance made on or after 3 April 2018, see **15.138–15.195**.
[2] HA 1996, s 189B(2), inserted by HRA 2017, s 5(2), for applications for homelessness assistance made on or after 3 April 2018, see English Code, chapter 13 and **15.138–15.195**.
[3] HA 1996, s 188, as amended by HRA 2017, s 5(4), for applications for homelessness assistance made on or after 3 April 2018, see **16.37–16.80**.

15.6 The HA 1996, s 195(2)[1] prevention and HA 1996, s 189B(2)[2] relief duties can each be brought to an end in a number of ways, which we discuss in detail later on in the chapter[3].

[1] As amended by HRA 2017, s 4(2) for applications for homelessness assistance made on or after 3 April 2018.
[2] As inserted by HRA 2017, s 5(2) for applications for homelessness assistance made on or after 3 April 2018.
[3] See **15.98–15.133** for the events that bring the HA 1996, s 195(2) (as amended by HRA 2017, s 4(2), for applications for homelessness assistance made on or after 3 April 2018) prevention duty to an end; see **15.151–15.189** for the events that bring the HA 1996, s 189B(2) (as inserted by HRA 2017, s 5(2), for applications for homelessness assistance made on or after 3 April 2018) relief duty to an end.

15.7 HRA 2017, s 7(1)[1] also inserts provisions into HA 1996, Pt 7, permitting a local housing authority to notify the applicant of a decision that he or she has deliberately and unreasonably refused to co-operate[2]. Notification of a decision to this effect will bring the HA 1996, s 195(2)[3], prevention duty or the HA 1996, s 189B(2)[4], relief duty to an end[5]. If the applicant is threatened with homelessness, no further duty will be owed. If the applicant is homeless, but does not have a priority need, no further duty will be owed.

[1] In force for applications for homelessness assistance made on or after 3 April 2018.
[2] HA 1996, s 193B, inserted by HRA 2017, s 7(1), for applications for homelessness assistance made on or after 3 April 2018, see **15.196–15.221**.
[3] As amended by HRA 2017, s 4(2), for applications for homelessness assistance made on or after 3 April 2018, see **15.87–15.137**.
[4] As inserted by HRA 2017, s 5(2), for applications for homelessness assistance made on or after 3 April 2018, see **15.138–15.195**.
[5] HA 1996, s 193A(2), as inserted by HRA 2017, s 7(1), for applications for homelessness assistance made on or after 3 April 2018. See **15.132** and **15.189**.

15.8 If the applicant is homeless and has a priority need, one of two duties will be owed:

- where the local housing authority is satisfied that the applicant has become homeless intentionally, a duty to secure accommodation for such period as the local housing authority considers will give him or her a reasonable opportunity of securing his or her own accommodation and a duty to provide advice and assistance in any attempts the applicant may make in securing accommodation[1]; or

- where the local housing authority is not satisfied that the applicant has become homeless intentionally, a duty to secure accommodation which can be brought to an end on the occurrence of various events, including if the applicant accepts or refuses[2] a suitable final accommodation offer[3] or final Pt 6[4] offer.

[1] HA 1996, s 190(2), as amended by HRA 2017, s 5(5), for applications for homelessness assistance made on or after 3 April 2018 see **16.81–16.93**.

[2] HA 1996, s 193C(4), inserted by HRA 2017, s 7(1), for applications for homelessness assistance made on or after 3 April 2018, see **16.200–16.216**.

[3] Defined at HA 1996, s 193C(7), as inserted by HRA 2017, s 7(1), for applications for homelessness assistance made on or after 3 April 2018, see **16.206**.

[4] Defined at HA 1996, s 193C(8), as inserted by HRA 2017, s 7(1), for applications for homelessness assistance made on or after 3 April 2018, see **16.211**.

15.9 A new HA 1996, s 213B[1], imposes a duty on specified public authorities to notify local housing authorities in England of people who are or may be homeless or threatened with homelessness. The relevant public authorities are specified in reg 10 of and the Schedule to the Homelessness (Review Procedure etc) Regulations 2018[2]. Whilst the HA 1996, s 213B[3], duty comes into force on 3 April 2018, the list of specified public authorities does not come into force until 1 October 2018[4]. This duty is discussed at **15.222–15.228**.

[1] As inserted by HRA 2017, s 10, from 12 February 2018 (but only to enable the exercise of the power under HA 1996, s 213B(4) to make regulations) and otherwise from 3 April 2018.

[2] SI 2018/223, see APPENDIX 2 and **15.222–15.228**.

[3] As inserted by HRA 2017, s 10, from 12 February 2018 (but only to enable the exercise of the power under HA 1996, s 213B(4) to make regulations) and otherwise from 3 April 2018.

[4] SI 2018/223, regs 1(3) and 10.

15.10 There is also a duty at HA 1996, s 213A[1], on a local housing authority to refer an applicant to children's services if his or her household includes a child and the local housing authority has reason to believe that he or she may not be eligible for assistance or that he or she has become homeless intentionally. This duty is discussed at **15.229** and **16.280–16.288**.

[1] As amended by HRA 2017, s 4(7), for applications for homelessness assistance made on or after 3 April 2018.

15.11 Under HA 1996, Pt 7[1], there is a duty to provide advice and assistance to the applicant. This is separate to the new, and more substantive, duties to take reasonable steps to help the applicant retain or secure accommodation[2]. The duty to provide advice and assistance is owed to an applicant who is homeless, eligible for assistance, has a priority need, has become homeless intentionally and in respect of whom the local housing authority's HA 1996, s 189B(2), relief duty has come to an end[3]. As well as being obliged to secure accommodation for the applicant for such period as the local housing authority considers will give him or her a reasonable opportunity of securing his or her own accommodation[4], the local housing authority must provide the applicant, or secure that he or she is provided with, advice and assistance in any attempts she or he may make to secure accommodation[5]. We discuss this duty at **15.231**.

[1] As amended by HRA 2017, for applications for homelessness assistance made on or after 3 April 2018.

² HA 1996, ss 189B(2) relief duty and 195(2) prevention duty, as inserted and amended by HRA 2017, ss 5(2) and 4(2), for applications for homelessness assistance made on or after 3 April 2018. See **15.87–15.137** for prevention duty and **15.138–15.195** for relief duty.

³ HA 1996, s 190(1), as amended by HRA 2017, s 5(5), for applications for homelessness assistance made on or after 3 April 2018. See **16.81–16.93**.

⁴ HA 1996, s 190(2)(a), as amended by HRA 2017, s 5(5), for applications for homelessness assistance made on or after 3 April 2018. See **16.81–16.93**.

⁵ HA 1996, s 190(2)(a), (4) and (5), as amended by HRA 2017, s 5(5), for applications for homelessness assistance made on or after 3 April 2018. See **15.231**.

15.12 Finally, there is also a duty on the local housing authority to protect an applicant's property where the local housing authority is subject to a duty to the applicant under HA 1996, Pt 7[1], and has reason to believe that there is a danger of loss of, or damage to, his or her personal property[2]. This duty is discussed at **16.288–16.309**.

¹ As amended by HRA 2017, for applications for homelessness assistance made on or after 3 April 2018.

² HA 1996, ss 211–212, as amended by HRA 2017, s 5(12), for applications for homelessness assistance made on or after 3 April 2018. See **16.288–16.309**.

THE NEW LANDSCAPE: THE HOMELESSNESS REDUCTION ACT 2017

Law and practice before the Homelessness Reduction Act 2017

15.13 For many years, there had been criticism of HA 1996, Pt 7, and of its statutory predecessors for providing little help to applicants who did not have a priority need[1]. Whilst there had always been a duty to provide advice and assistance to those applicants[2], this duty tended to be neglected by local housing authorities. As long ago as 2002, the government had acknowledged that it should 'consider the varying standards of homelessness advice services in order to promote good practice across all local authorities'[3].

¹ For 'priority need', see CHAPTER 12.

² HA 1996, s 190(3), repealed by HRA 2017, s 5(5)(c) and HA 1996, s 192(2), repealed by HRA 2017, s 5(6), for applications for homelessness assistance made on or after 3 April 2018.

³ *More than a Roof: A report into Tackling Homelessness* (Department for Transport, Local Government and the Regions, March 2002).

15.14 That acknowledgement led in 2003 to amendments to HA 1996, Pt 7, inserted by the Homelessness Act 2002[1]. As a result of those amendments, where a local housing authority owed an applicant a duty to provide him or her with advice and assistance in any attempts he or she might make to secure accommodation, it was required first to make an assessment of the applicant's housing needs[2]. The advice and assistance subsequently provided had to include information about the likely availability in the local housing authority's district of types of accommodation appropriate to the applicant's housing needs, including the location and sources of such types of accommodation[3].

¹ The Explanatory Notes to the Homelessness Act 2002 stated at [55]: 'There are amendments to sections 190, 192 and 195 which place stronger duties on authorities to provide advice and assistance to applicants who are homeless or threatened with homelessness, but who either do not have priority need or have become homeless or threatened with homelessness intention-

ally. The amendments set out specific requirements for an assessment of the applicant's housing needs and the provision of information about the likely availability of appropriate accommodation'.

[2]   HA 1996, s 190(4) and (5), inserted by Homelessness Act 2002, s 18(1), Sch 1, and amended by HRA 2017, ss 3(2) and 5(5), for applications for homelessness assistance made on or after 3 April 2018; HA 1996, s 192(4) and (5), inserted by Homelessness Act 2002, s 18(1), Sch 1, and repealed by HRA 2017, s 5(6), for applications for homelessness assistance made on or after 3 April 2018.

[3]   HA 1996, ss 190(5) and 192(5), prior to amendment and repeal by HRA 2017, s 5(5) and (6), for applications for homelessness assistance made on or after 3 April 2018.

15.15 However, there were concerns that assessments were not being undertaken adequately or at all. Research conducted in 2009 by Crisis, the national charity for homeless people, found that only very superficial assessments were taking place[1]. A mystery shopper exercise undertaken by Crisis in 2014 found that, in over a third of visits to local housing authorities by single homeless people seeking assistance, no assessments were carried out. Even where assessments were carried out, the assistance provided was minimal[2]. In one case[3], a High Court judge found that the local housing authority's purported assessment was either non-existent or patently inadequate. The local housing authority had found that the applicant did not have a priority need. Towards the end of its HA 1996, s 184, decision letter[4], it had advised the applicant to refer to information that had been previously given to her, and had given her a telephone number to apply to be registered on a scheme for long-term places in hostels. The judge found that the local housing authority could not demonstrate that the HA 1996, s 184, decision letter constituted an assessment of the 'nuts and bolts' of the applicant's housing needs.

[1]   *No one's priority: the treatment of single homeless people by local authority homelessness services* (Crisis, 2009).
[2]   *Turned away: The treatment of single homeless people by local authority homelessness services in England* (Dobie, Sanders & Teixeira, Crisis, 2014).
[3]   *R (S (Albania)) v Waltham Forest London Borough Council* [2016] EWHC 1240 (Admin), [2016] HLR 41, Admin Ct.
[4]   See **9.89–9.110**.

15.16 In addition, there was concern that advice intended to prevent homelessness was instead operating so as to prevent applicants from making applications for homelessness assistance. It was common for applicants who did not appear to have a priority need simply to be given written information, or even turned away without help or the opportunity to speak to a housing adviser. From 2014, Crisis began to lobby for a change in the English law, arguing for early intervention to be put on a statutory footing and for local housing authorities to be required to take action to relieve homelessness experienced by anyone in their district[1].

[1]   *No one turned away: changing the law to prevent and tackle homelessness* (Gousey, Crisis, 2016).

Origins of the Homelessness Reduction Act 2017

15.17 On 27 April 2015, the Housing (Wales) Act 2014, Pt 2, (H(W)A 2014) came into force for local housing authorities in Wales[1]. H(W)A 2014, Pt 2, introduced statutory duties requiring local housing authorities in Wales to help an eligible applicant who is threatened with homelessness avoid becoming homeless[2] and to help an eligible homeless applicant to secure his or her own accommodation[3]. These duties apply whether or not an applicant has a priority need, or has become homeless intentionally[4].

[1]   See CHAPTER 17 of this book.
[2]   H(W)A 2014, s 66(1), see **17.45–17.72**.
[3]   H(W)A 2014, s 73(1), see **17.73–17.143**.
[4]   See CHAPTER 12 for priority need and CHAPTER 13 for 'becoming homeless intentionally'.

15.18 In 2016, Crisis prepared a draft Homelessness Reduction Bill, based on the concepts in H(W)A 2014, Pt 2. Bob Blackman MP introduced the Bill as a Private Members' Bill in 2016, and it gained cross-party support, receiving Royal Assent on 27 April 2017. Its substantive provisions were brought into force for applications for homelessness assistance made to local housing authorities on or after 3 April 2018[1]. The then DCLG[2] consulted on a draft Homelessness Code of Guidance for local authorities between October and December 2017 and the MHCLG published the final version on 22 February 2018[3].

[1]   Homelessness Reduction Act (Commencement and Transitional and Savings Provisions) Regulations 2018, SI 2018/167, reg 3.
[2]   Subsequently the MHCLG.
[3]   See APPENDIX 2.

15.19 A new HA 1996, s 214A[1] allows the Secretary of State to issue one or more Codes of Practice, in addition to the Code of Guidance. A draft of any Code of Practice must first be laid before Parliament, and can be issued by the Secretary of State if no negative resolution is made by Parliament within 40 days[2]. Local housing authorities must have regard to those Codes of Practice when exercising functions under HA 1996, Pt 7[3]. It is understood that the MHCLG's intention is to use this facility to complement the English Code, and provide examples of good practice[4].

[1]   As inserted by HRA 2017, s 10, and in force from 12 February 2018 for the purpose of making Regulations, and from 3 April 2018.
[2]   HA 1996, s 214A(5), as inserted by HRA 2017, s 10, and in force from 3 April 2018.
[3]   HA 1996, s 214A(12), as inserted by HRA 2017, s 10, and in force from 3 April 2018.
[4]   Policy fact-sheet Codes of Practice (DCLG November 2017).

The new approach to dealing with homelessness

Early intervention

15.20 The aim, as characterised by Crisis, of the amendments made by HRA 2017 to HA 1996, Pt 7, is to 'ensure that more robust prevention work . . . is provided at a much earlier point, irrespective of priority need status'[1]. Local housing authorities must now assist applicants for homelessness assistance well before they become homeless, by complying with the HA 1996, s 195(2)[2], prevention duty, owed to all applicants who are eligible for assistance and are threatened with homelessness[3]. If that assistance is successful, then the applicant will never have to face actual homelessness. He or she would be assisted either to retain his or her current accommodation, or to secure new accommodation and so move straight from one to the other. If the applicant does become homeless - or was homeless when he or she first approached the local housing authority - the local housing authority must then take reasonable steps to help him or her secure accommodation: this is the HA 1996, s 189B(2)[4], relief duty, owed to all applicants who are eligible for assistance and are homeless[5].

1   *No one turned away: changing the law to prevent and tackle homelessness* (Gousey, Crisis, 2016).
2   As amended by HRA 2017, s 4(2), for applications for homelessness assistance made to local housing authorities in England on or after 3 April 2018.
3   See **15.87–15.37**.
4   As inserted by HRA 2017, s 5(2) for applications for homelessness assistance made on or after 3 April 2018.
5   See **15.138–15.195**.

15.21 It is only if the HA 1996, s 189B(2)[1], relief duty fails to achieve the applicant obtaining suitable accommodation that the distinction between applicants with priority need and those without will become crucial[2]. At that stage the local housing authority will be obliged to secure that accommodation is available for the former (albeit for a limited period if the local housing authority is satisfied that they have also become homeless intentionally)[3], but will not be obliged to do so for the latter.

1   As inserted by HRA 2017, s 5(2) for applications for homelessness assistance made on or after 3 April 2018.
2   Although it is not without relevance earlier in the process, as the duty to secure interim accommodation only arises if the local housing authority has reason to believe that the applicant may have a priority need: HA 1996, s 188(1), as amended by HRA 2017, s 5(4), for applications for homelessness assistance made on or after 3 April 2018. See **16.37–16.80**
3   HA 1996, s 190(2)(a), as amended by HRA 2017, s 5(5), for applications for homelessness assistance made to local housing authorities on or after 3 April 2018: duty to secure accommodation for such period as the local housing authority consider will give the applicant a reasonable opportunity of securing his or her own accommodation, owed to applicants who have a priority need and who have become homeless intentionally, see **16.81–16.93**; HA 1996, s 193(2): the main housing duty to secure accommodation owed to applicants who have a priority need and who have not become homeless intentionally, see **16.94–16.199**; HA 1996, s 193C(4), as inserted by HRA 2017, s 7(1), for applications for homelessness assistance made to local housing authorities on or after 3 April 2018: duty to secure accommodation owed to applicants who have a priority need and who have not become homeless intentionally, and who have deliberately and unreasonably refused to co-operate, see **16.200–16.216**.

How does a local housing authority 'help' an applicant?

15.22 Both the HA 1996, s 195(2)[1], prevention duty and the HA 1996, s 189B(2)[2], relief duty require the local housing authority to 'take reasonable steps to help the applicant to secure' that accommodation either does not cease to be available, or becomes available, for his or her occupation. What does this phrase mean?

1   Amended by HRA 2017, s 4(2), for applications for homelessness assistance made on or after 3 April 2018, see **15.87–15.137**.
2   Inserted by HRA 2017, s 5(2), for applications for homelessness assistance made on or after 3 April 2018, see **15.138–15.195**.

15.23 It does not mean that the local housing authority must actually provide accommodation, either directly from its own stock or by making arrangements with a private landlord. The duties merely require a local housing authority to 'help the applicant to secure', not to 'secure'.

15.24 Equally it does not preclude the local housing authority from providing accommodation. The local housing authority may, for example, accommodate the applicant itself, in temporary accommodation or through its allocation scheme[1].

[1] The applicant will have a reasonable preference, by virtue of being a person who is owed a duty under HA 1996, s 195(2), as amended by HRA 2017, s 4(2), for applications for homelessness assistance made on or after 3 April 2018: HA 1996, s 166A(3)(b); or by virtue of being a person who is homeless: HA 1996, s 166(3)(a) and (b), see **4.58–4.79**.

15.25 In contrast to H(W)A 2014, Pt 2, there is no definition of the phrase 'help to secure'[1], in HA 1996, Pt 7, as amended by HRA 2017[2]. Assistance must therefore be found in the English Code, which contains the following general suggestions:

- attempting mediation or conciliation where an applicant is threatened with parental or family exclusion;
- assessing whether applicants with rent arrears might be entitled to Discretionary Housing Payments;
- providing support to applicants, whether financial or otherwise, to access private rented accommodation;
- assisting people at risk of violence and abuse wishing to stay safely in their home through provision of 'sanctuary' or other measures; or
- helping to secure or securing an immediate safe place to stay for people who are sleeping rough or at high risk of sleeping rough[3].

[1] In contrast, see H(W)A 2014, s 65, see **17.36–17.40**.
[2] For applications for homelessness assistance made on or after 3 April 2018.
[3] All at para 11.23 English Code.

15.26 The local housing authority may provide these services itself, or it may arrange for the applicant to receive these services from another organisation or individual, such as housing advice agencies, private registered providers of social housing, voluntary sector organisations, or private landlords[1]. However, the local housing authority must ensure that the applicant is actually provided with these services, and that they are tailored so as to assist him or her either to retain his or her own home, or to find another home. Provision of generic information should not be acceptable[2].

[1] HA 1996, s 179(1) as amended by HRA 2017, s 2, in force from 3 April 2018, see **8.4–8.13**.
[2] See English Code, chapter 11 and in particular para 11.18: 'these steps should be tailored to the household'.

Use of the private rented sector

15.27 Since November 2012, local housing authorities have been able to bring the HA 1996, s 193(2), main housing duty[1] to an end by making the applicant a private rented sector offer[2]. The amendments to HA 1996, Pt 7, made by HRA 2017[3] allow local housing authorities to make much greater use of the private rented sector.

[1] See **16.94–16.199**.

2   HA 1996, s 193(7AA)–(7AC), see **16.161–16.180**.
3   For applications for homelessness assistance made on or after 3 April 2018.

15.28 Local housing authorities can use private rented accommodation for three different functions:

- where they are helping an applicant to secure his or her own accommodation[1], such accommodation is likely to be accommodation in the private rented sector;
- where they are under a duty to secure accommodation for the applicant[2], that accommodation might also be in the private rented sector; and
- where they are making certain offers of suitable accommodation to applicants with a view to bringing the relevant duty owed to an end, namely:
  - a final accommodation offer[3], which is defined as an offer of an assured shorthold tenancy for a minimum period of six months made by a private landlord, will bring the HA 1996, s 189B(2)[4], relief duty or HA 1996, s 193C(4)[5] duty to an end[6]; or
  - a private rented sector offer[7], which is defined as an offer of an assured shorthold tenancy for a minimum period of 12 months made by a private landlord will bring the HA 1996, s 193(2), main housing duty to an end[8].

1   HA 1996, s 189B(2), as inserted by HRA 2017, s 5(2), see **15.138–15.195**; and HA 1996, s 195(2), as amended by HRA 2017, s 4(2), for applications for homelessness assistance made on or after 3 April 2018, see **15.87–15.137**.
2   The various accommodation duties are: the interim accommodation duties at HA 1996, ss 188(1), 199A(2) and 200(1), as amended and inserted by HRA 2017, ss 5(4), (9) and (10), for applications for homelessness assistance made on or after 3 April 2018, see **16.37–16.80** and **16.217–16.222**; the short-term accommodation duty owed to applicants who are homeless, eligible for assistance, have a priority need and have become homeless intentionally at HA 1996, s 190(2)(a), as amended by HRA 2017, s 5(5), for applications for homelessness assistance made on or after 3 April 2018, see **16.81–16.93**; the main housing duty owed to applicants who are homeless, eligible for assistance, have a priority need and have not become homeless intentionally at HA 1996, s 193(2), see **16.94–16.199**; and the accommodation duty owed to applicants who are homeless, eligible for assistance, have a priority need and have not become homeless intentionally and who have deliberately and unreasonably refused to co-operate at HA 1996, s 193C(4), as inserted by HRA 2017, s 7(1), for applications for homelessness assistance made on or after 3 April 2018, see **16.200–16.216**.
3   As defined at HA 1996, ss 193A(4), and 193C(7), inserted by HRA 2017, s 7(1), for applications for homelessness assistance made on or after 3 April 2018, see **15.181** and **16.206**.
4   As inserted by HRA 2017, s 5(2), for applications for homelessness assistance made on or after 3 April 2018.
5   As inserted by HRA 2017, s 7(1), for applications for homelessness assistance made on or after 3 April 2018. Duty owed to applicants who are homeless, eligible for assistance, have a priority need and have not become homeless intentionally and who have deliberately and unreasonably refused to co-operate: HA 1996, ss 193B and 193C, inserted by HRA 2017, s 7(1), for applications for homelessness assistance made on or after 3 April 2018, see **16.200–16.216**.
6   HA 1996, ss 189B(9)(a), and 193A(1)–(3), as inserted by HRA 2017, ss 5(2) and 7(1), for applications for homelessness assistance made on or after 3 April 2018, see **16.205–16.219**.
7   As defined at HA 1996, s 193(7AC), see **16.154**.
8   Duty owed to applicants who are homeless, eligible for assistance, have a priority need and have not become homeless intentionally and where the HA 1996, s 189B(2), relief duty

(inserted by HRA 2017, s 5(2), for applications for homelessness assistance made on or after 3 April 2018) has come to an end: HA 1996, s 193(7AA)–(7AC), see **16.153–16.180**.

15.29 The English Code reminds local housing authorities that enabling applicants to 'exercise some choice over the accommodation offered' is likely to increase acceptances and secure the co-operation of both applicants and landlords[1]. It encourages local housing authorities to 'develop a private rented sector access scheme which provides opportunities for all applicants, including those who do not have a priority need, to access private rented accommodation'. Support provided by the local housing authority through such a scheme could include offers of guarantees and paying deposits[2]. The English Code also reminds local housing authorities of the need to identify shared housing options for younger people[3].

1   English Code, para 16.18.
2   English Code, para 16.19.
3   English Code, para 16.19. With some exceptions, single people under the age of 35 who are renting privately are only entitled to the Local Housing Allowance rate for housing benefit for a single room in a shared house.

15.30 Special rules apply where private rented sector accommodation is being made available:

- under HA 1996, s 193(7F) to end the HA 1996, s 193(2) main housing duty[1];
- as a 'final accommodation offer' under HA 1996, s 193A(4) or HA 1996, s 193C(6)(a)[2] to end the HA 1996, s 189B(2)[3] relief duty or the HA 1996, s 193C(4)[4] accommodation duty; or
- for an applicant with a priority need where that accommodation has been secured by the local housing authority in performance of the HA 1996, s 195(2)[5] prevention duty or HA 1996, s 189B(2)[6] relief duty.

1   See **16.153–16.180**.
2   As inserted by HRA 2017, s 7(1), for applications for homelessness assistance made on or after 3 April 2018 date, see **15.181–15.184** and **16.205–16.209**.
3   Inserted by HRA 2017, s 5(2), for applications for homelessness assistance made on or after 3 April 2018, see **15.138–15.195**.
4   As inserted by HRA 2017, s 7(1), for applications for homelessness assistance made on or after 3 April 2018.
5   As amended by HRA 2017, s 4(2) for applications for homelessness assistance made on or after 3 April 2018, see **15.87–15.137**
6   As inserted by HRA 2017, s 5(2) for applications for homelessness assistance made on or after 3 April 2018.

15.31 In those situations, the local housing authority must be satisfied that the requirements specified at art 3 of the Homelessness (Suitability of Accommodation) (England) Order 2012 are met[1]. These relate to the physical condition of the accommodation and to the landlord's fitness to let the accommodation.

1   Homelessness (Suitability of Accommodation) (England) Order 2012, SI 2012/2601, art 3, as amended by HRA 2017, s 12(4), for applications for homelessness assistance made on or after 3 April 2018, see APPENDIX 2 and **18.70–18.79**.

Availability and suitability of accommodation

15.32 The HA 1996, s 189B(2)[1], relief duty specifically requires the local housing authority to take reasonable steps to help the applicant to secure that 'suitable' accommodation becomes 'available' for his or her occupation for at least six months[2]. In addition, both the HA 1996, s 189B(2)[3], relief duty, and the HA 1996, s 195(2)[4], prevention duty will come to an end if the local housing authority is satisfied that the applicant has 'suitable' accommodation which there are reasonable prospects to believe will be 'available' for occupation for at least six months[5], or has refused an offer of such accommodation[6].

[1] As inserted by HRA 2017, s 5(2), for applications for homelessness assistance made on or after 3 April 2018, see **15.138–15.195.**
[2] Or such longer period, not exceeding 12 months, as may be prescribed by the Secretary of State, see **15.105** and **15.169.**
[3] As inserted by HRA 2017, s 5(2), for applications for homelessness assistance made on or after 3 April 2018, see **15.138–15.195.**
[4] HA 1996, s 195(2), as amended by HRA s 4(2), for applications for homelessness assistance made on or after 3 April 2018, see **15.87–15.137.**
[5] Or such longer period, not exceeding 12 months, as may be prescribed by the Secretary of State, see **15.105** and **15.118.**
[6] HRA 1996, ss 189B(7)(a) and (c), inserted by HRA 2017, s 5(2), and 195(8)(a) and (d), inserted by HRA 2017, s 4(2), for applications for homelessness assistance made on or after 3 April 2018. See English Code, paras 14.5–14.12 and 14.23–14.28 and **15.169–15.173** and **15.118–15.122**

15.33 The requirement that accommodation should be 'available' for the applicant's occupation' mirrors the test which is applied to determine whether an applicant is homeless at HA 1996, ss 175–176[1]. An applicant is homeless if he or she does not have accommodation which is both factually and legally 'available' for his or her occupation[2]. Accommodation must be available for occupation not only by the applicant but also by all members of his or her household[3]. In this context, household means any other person who normally resides with the applicant as a member of his or her family and any other person who might reasonably be expected to reside with the applicant[4].

[1] See **10.17–10.30.**
[2] HA 1996, s 175(1)–(2), see **10.17–10.72.**
[3] By s 206(1) Housing Act 1996, a local housing authority must discharge its functions by (among other things) securing that suitable accommodation is 'available'. This refers to HA 1996, s 176: 'accommodation shall be regarded as available only if it is available for occupation by [the applicant] together with any other person who normally resides with him as a member of his family, or any other person who might reasonably be expected to reside with him'. The combined effect of these two provisions is that suitable accommodation must be available for the applicant and his household, which carries with it the implication that the accommodation must be suitable for all such persons, and not solely the applicant. See English Code, paras 16.3 and 17.2 and *R v Newham London Borough Council ex parte Sacupima* [2001] 1 WLR 563, CA, at [28]–[32].
[4] HA 1996, s 176, see **10.23–10.30.**

15.34 The accommodation must actually be available for the applicant to occupy. A promise or offer of accommodation, to be made available in the future, will not be sufficient for the local housing authority to be 'satisfied' that the applicant currently has 'suitable accommodation available for occupation'[1]. Similarly, assisting the applicant simply to join the local housing authority's allocation scheme without actually securing accommodation would not bring the duty to an end.

¹ HA 1996, ss 195(8)(a)(i) and 189B(7)(a)(i), as amended and inserted by HRA 2017, ss 4(2) and 5(2), for applications for homelessness assistance made on or after 3 April 2018.

15.35 Although accommodation must be suitable¹ and there must be a 'reasonable prospect' of it being 'available for occupation for at least six months'², HA 1996, s 189B(2)³, does not specify accommodation of any particular type or tenure⁴. It could, for example, be accommodation provided under the local housing authority's allocation scheme, (provided by either the local housing authority or a private registered provider of social housing). More frequently, it will be an assured shorthold tenancy in the private rented sector, or even a licence granted by family or friends to occupy accommodation⁵.

¹ See CHAPTER 18
² Or such longer period, not exceeding 12 months as may be prescribed by the Secretary of State.
³ As inserted by HRA 2017, s 5(2), for applications for homelessness assistance made on or after 3 April 2018, see **15.138–15.195**.
⁴ HA 1996, s 189B(7)(a) and c), as inserted by HRA 2017, s 5(2), and HA 1996, s 195(8)(a) and (d) as amended by HRA 2017, s 4(2), for applications for homelessness assistance made on or after 3 April 2018.
⁵ English Code paras 14.8–14.10.

15.36 The English Code contains advice that applicants should be given a reasonable period in which to consider offers of accommodation. There is no set reasonable period: the length will depend on each applicant's circumstances. It also contains advice that applicants should be given the opportunity to view the accommodation or (if it is not practical to travel) that sufficient information about the property and the locality should be made available¹. In addition, the opportunity to consider more than one property could play an important part in the process of exploring what options are realistically available and what compromises an applicant may want to make².

¹ English Code, paras 14.5–14.6.
² English Code, para 14.28.

15.37 The period of 'six months'¹ is the minimum period for which the accommodation must be available. It could, obviously, be available for a longer period. The six-month period starts from different points depending on whether the applicant is in possession of, or has refused, the accommodation:

- if the applicant currently has suitable accommodation available, then there must be a reasonable prospect that there will be suitable accommodation available for at least six months² from the date the local housing authority gives notice to the applicant bringing the duty to an end³; or
- if the applicant refused an offer of suitable accommodation, then there must have been a reasonable prospect that suitable accommodation would have been available for at least six months⁴ from the date of the refusal⁵.

¹ Or such longer period, not exceeding 12 months, as may be prescribed by the Secretary of State.
² Or such longer period, not exceeding 12 months as may be prescribed by the Secretary of State.

³ HA 1996, s 189B(7)(a), as inserted by HRA 2017, s 4(2) and HA 1996, s 195(8)(a), as amended by HRA 2017, s 5(2) for applications for homelessness assistance made on or after 3 April 2018.
⁴ Or such longer period, not exceeding 12 months as may be prescribed by the Secretary of State.
⁵ HA 1996, s 189B(7)(c), as inserted by HRA 2017, s 4(2) and HA 1996, s 195(8)(d), as amended by HRA 2017, s 5(2) for applications for homelessness assistance made on or after 3 April 2018.

15.38 The English Code encourages local housing authorities to adopt policies favouring longer tenancies than the legal minimum where market conditions in their area allow, and advises that minimum tenancy lengths should be 12 months so as to provide more stability, particularly but not exclusively for families who have children¹.

¹ English Code, para 14.7.

15.39 If the accommodation is situated outside the local housing authority's district, the local housing authority must take into account the distance of the accommodation from its district. Whether the accommodation is situated inside or outside the local housing authority's district, it should also take into account the significance of any disruption which would be caused by the location of the accommodation to the employment, caring responsibilities or education of the applicant and members of his or her household, the proximity and accessibility of the accommodation to medical facilities and other support which are currently used or provided to the applicant or members of his or her household and which are essentially to the well-being of that person, and the proximity and accessibility of the accommodation to local services, amenities and transport¹.

¹ Homelessness (Suitability of Accommodation) (England) Order 2012, SI 2012/2601, art 2; see Appendix 2 and **18.48–18.61**.

TO WHOM ARE THE DUTIES OWED?

15.40 Every applicant is owed at least one duty: the duty that the local housing authority must notify a decision on his or her application¹.

¹ HA 1996, s 184(1) and (3), see English Code, paras 11.3 and **18.32–18.33** and **9.89**.

Applicants who are not eligible for assistance

15.41 Beyond that initial notification, if an applicant is not eligible for assistance¹, no further duty is owed to him or her, although he or she may receive advice from the local housing authority's homelessness service². If the local housing authority had been providing interim accommodation for the applicant³, the interim accommodation duty will come to an end upon notification from the local housing authority⁴.

¹ HA 1996, s 185, see Chapter **11**.
² HA 1996, s 179, as amended by HRA 2017, s 2, in force from 3 April 2018; see English Code, chapter 3 and para 14.32 and **8.4–8.14**.
³ HA 1996, s 188(1), as amended by HRA 2017, s 5(4) for applications for homelessness assistance made on or after 3 April 2018, see **16.37–16.50**.

Applicants who are eligible for assistance

15.42 Any duties owed to eligible applicants will depend on whether they are threatened with homelessness, or homeless. If an applicant is neither threatened with homelessness, nor homeless, no duty is owed.

15.43 For ease of reference, the main duties and powers listed below have been divided up by reference to those key findings:

- Local housing authorities owe the following duties to all *eligible applicants who are threatened with homelessness*:
  — the duty to make an assessment of the applicant's case[1];
  — the duty to formulate a personalised housing plan[2]; and
  — the duty to take reasonable steps to help the applicant secure that accommodation does not cease to be available (the HA 1996, s 195(2) prevention duty)[3].
- Local housing authorities owe the following duties to all *eligible applicants who are homeless*:
  — the duty to make an assessment of the applicant's case[4];
  — the duty to formulate a personalised housing plan[5];
  — the duty to take reasonable steps to help the applicant secure that suitable accommodation becomes available for his or her occupation (the HA 1996, s 189B(2) relief duty) *unless* the local housing authority refers the applicant to another local housing authority[6]; and
  — if there is reason to believe that the applicant may have a priority need, the duty to secure interim accommodation[7].

[1] HA 1996, s 189A(1), as inserted by HRA 2017, s 3(1), for applications for homelessness assistance made on or after 3 April 2018, see English Code, chapter 11 and **15.62–15.69**.
[2] HA 1996, s 189A(4)–(6), as inserted by HRA 2017, s 3(1), for applications for homelessness assistance made on or after 3 April 2018, see English Code, chapter 11 and **15.70–15.80**.
[3] HA 1996, s 195(2), as amended by HRA 2017, s 4(2), for applications for homelessness assistance made on or after 3 April 2018, see English Code, chapter 12 and **15.87–15.137**.
[4] HA 1996, s 189A(1), as inserted by HRA 2017, s 3(1), for applications for homelessness assistance made on or after 3 April 2018, see English Code, chapter 11 and **15.62–15.69**.
[5] HA 1996, s 189A(4)–(6), as inserted by HRA 2017, s 3(1), for applications for homelessness assistance made on or after 3 April 2018, see English Code, chapter 11 and **15.70–15.80**.
[6] HA 1996, s 189B(2), as inserted by HRA 2017, s 5(2), for applications for homelessness assistance made on or after 3 April 2018, see English Code, chapter 13 and **15.138–15.195**.
[7] HA 1996, s 188(1), as amended by HRA 217, s 5(4) for applications for homelessness assistance made on or after 3 April 2018. See **16.37–16.50**.

15.44 The HA 1996, s 189B(2) relief duty will not be owed if the local housing authority refers[1] the applicant's case to another local housing authority in England[2]. In that case, however, two further duties arise:

- a duty to notify the applicant that the local housing authority have referred or intend to refer him or her and to inform the applicant of the reasons[3]; and

• if there is reason to believe that the applicant may have a priority need, a duty to secure interim accommodation until the applicant is notified of the decision as to whether or not the conditions for referral are met[4].

The duty to carry out an assessment of the applicant's case and to agree a personalised housing plan remain on the first local housing authority and cannot be referred. If the applicant's case is to be referred to another local housing authority, the notifying local housing authority should send a copy of the assessment and the personalised housing plan, if completed, to the notified local housing authority[5].

[1] HA 1996, s 198(A1), as inserted by HRA 2017, s 5(8), for applications for homelessness assistance made on or after 3 April 2018, see English Code, para 13.4 and **16.15**.

[2] HA 1996, s 189B(2), as inserted by HRA 2017, s 5(2), for applications for homelessness assistance made on or after 3 April 2018, see English Code, chapter 13 and **16.15**. Unlike the ability to refer performance of the HA 1996, s 193(2), main housing duty, performance of the HA 1996, s 189B(2), (as inserted by HRA 2017, s 5(2) for applications for homelessness assistance made on or after 3 April 2018) relief duty cannot be referred to local housing authorities in Wales or Scotland: HA 1996, s 198(A1) (inserted by HRA 2017, s 5(8), for applications for homelessness assistance made on or after 3 April 2018), see English Code, paras 10.36–10.44 and 13.4, and see **16.15**.

[3] HA 1996, s 184(4), as amended by HRA 2017, s 5(3), for applications for homelessness assistance made on or after 3 April 2018, see **14.28–14.31**.

[4] HA 1996, s 199A(2), as inserted by HRA 2017, s 5(9), for applications for homelessness assistance made on or after 3 April 2018, see English Code, paras 15.16 and 15.59–15.61.

[5] English Code, para 10.43.

HOW DO THE DUTIES FIT TOGETHER?

15.45 Under HA 1996, Pt 7, prior to its amendment by HRA 2017, an applicant would apply as homeless to the local housing authority and in due course be issued with a decision under HA 1996, s 184(3), notifying him or her what duty, if any, the local housing authority considered that it owed. The position has now changed.

15.46 An applicant may move through several duties. Moreover, the applicant is likely to receive a number of different decisions under HA 1996, s 184(3), before the application process is concluded. The English Code recognises that more than one notification may be required in any given case[1].

[1] English Code, paras 18. 29–18.31.

15.47 The first decision the local housing authority will be required to make is whether there is reason to believe the applicant may be homeless, eligible, and have a priority need. If so, a duty arises to secure interim accommodation[1]. This does not require a HA 1996, s 184(3) decision.

[1] HA 1996, s 188(1), as amended by HRA 2017, s 5(4), for homelessness assistance made on or after 3 April 2018. See **16.37–16.50**.

15.48 The local housing authority will then need to decide whether the applicant is eligible and whether he or she is homeless or threatened with homelessness. If both these criteria are met, the local housing will owe the applicant two duties and must notify the applicant in accordance with HA 1996, s 184(3):

- the HA 1996, s 189A(1)[1] duty to assess his or her case and formulate a personalised housing plan; and
- either:
  - the HA 1996, s 195(2)[2] prevention duty; or
  - the HA 1996, s 189B(2)[3] relief duty.

[1] As inserted by HRA 2017, s 3(1), for applications for homelessness assistance made on or after 3 April 2018.
[2] As amended by HRA 2017, s 4(2), for applications for homelessness assistance made on or after 3 April 2018.
[3] As inserted by HRA 2017, s 5(2), for applications for homelessness assistance made on or after 3 April 2018.

15.49 If the applicant is threatened with homelessness then, whilst the HA 1996, s 195(2)[1] prevention duty is being performed, the local housing authority will need to decide what duty might be owed when the HA 1996, s 195(2) prevention duty has come to an end. The various scenarios would be as follows:

- where homelessness has been prevented, or the applicant has become ineligible, no further duty will be owed;
- where the applicant remains threatened with homelessness at the end of the HA 1996, s 195(2)[2] prevention duty, but has not become homeless, then no further duty will be owed[3];
- If the applicant has become homeless by the end of the HA 1996, s 195(2)[4] prevention duty then the HA 1996, s 189B(2)[5], relief duty will arise[6].

[1] As amended by HRA 2017, s 4(2), for applications for homelessness assistance made on or after 3 April 2018.
[2] As amended by HRA 2017, s 4(2), for applications for homelessness assistance made on or after 3 April 2018.
[3] Unless the applicant has been served with a valid Housing Act 1988 s 21 notice that either will expire within 56 days, or has expired, and is in respect of the only accommodation that is available for his or her occupation: HA 1996, s 195(6), as amended by HRA 2017, s 4(2), for applications for homelessness assistance made on or after 3 April 2018. If that is the case, the HA 1996, s 195(2) prevention duty continues to be owed. See **15.111**.
[4] As amended by HRA 2017, s 4(2), for applications for homelessness assistance made on or after 3 April 2018.
[5] As inserted by HRA 2017, s 5(2), for applications for homelessness assistance made on or after 3 April 2018. English Code, para 14.20 advises that the local housing authority will 'want to provide a seamless transition between the prevention and relief duties'.
[6] HA 1996, s 189B(1), as inserted by HRA 2017, s 5(2), for applications for homelessness assistance made on or after 3 April 2018.

15.50 If the applicant is homeless[1], then the HA 1996, s 189B(2)[2] relief duty arises[3]. If the action taken pursuant to the HA 1996, s 189B(2)[4] relief duty successfully relieves the applicant's homelessness, then no further duty will be owed.

[1] Either because he or she was homeless at the date of the application for homelessness assistance, or because he or she was formerly threatened with homelessness and has since become homeless.
[2] As inserted by HRA 2017, s 5(2), for applications for homelessness assistance made on or after 3 April 2018.
[3] The applicant will have received a notification under HA 1996, s 184(3), that the HA 1996, s 189B(2), relief duty is owed.

15.51 If, however, the applicant remains homeless at the point when the HA
1996, s 189B(2)[1], relief duty ends, then the local housing authority will have
to decide what final duty is applicable:

- where the applicant has become ineligible, no duty arises;
- where the applicant does not have a priority need, no duty arises,
  - unless the applicant has made a fresh application for homeless-
    ness assistance within two years of accepting a private rented
    sector offer[2], and the local housing authority is also satisfied that
    the applicant has not become homeless intentionally, in which
    case the HA 1996, s 193(2), main housing duty will be owed[3];
- if the applicant has a priority need but became homeless intentionally,
  the local housing authority must secure that accommodation is available for a reasonable period and also provide advice and assistance[4];
- if the applicant has a priority need and did not become homeless
  intentionally, then the HA 1996, s 193(2) main housing duty will be
  owed unless:
  - during the course of the HA 1996, s 189B(2)[5] relief duty, the
    applicant refused a final accommodation offer[6] or a final Pt 6
    offer[7]. In this situation, the main housing duty does not apply
    and no further duty will be owed[8]; or
  - during the course of the HA 1996, s 189B(2)[9] relief duty, the
    local housing authority gave notice to the applicant stating that
    it considered he or she had deliberately and unreasonably failed
    to take a step under his or her personalised housing plan[10]. In
    this situation, the HA 1996, s 193(2), main housing duty does
    not apply but the local housing authority must secure that
    accommodation is available under HA 1996, s 193C(4)[11].

Whenever the local housing authority has to decide what further duty, if any,
is owed, it must notify the applicant of its decision under HA 1996, s 184(3).

1 As inserted by HRA 2017, s 5(2), for applications for homelessness assistance made on or after
   3 April 2018.
2 As defined at HA 1996, s 193(7AC), see **16.154**.
3 HA 1996, s 195A(1), see **8.100–8.107**. This special provision does not apply where the local
   housing authority would not be satisfied that the HA 1996, s 193(2), main housing duty
   applies without having regard to a restricted person: HA 1996, s 195A(5), as amended by
   HRA 2017, s 4(4), for applications for homelessness assistance made on or after 3 April 2018.
   See **16.47–16.50**.
4 Under HA 1996, s 190(2), as amended by HRA 2017, s 5(5) for applications for homelessness
   assistance made on or after 3 April 2018.
5 As inserted by HRA 2017, s 5(2), for applications for homelessness assistance made on or after
   3 April 2018.
6 As defined at HA 1996, s 193A(4), as inserted by HRA 2017, s 7(1), for applications for
   homelessness assistance made on or after 3 April 2018.
7 As defined at HA 1996, s 193A(5), as inserted by HRA 2017, s 7(1) for applications for
   homelessness assistance made on or after 3 April 2018.
8 HA 1996, s 193A(3), as inserted by HRA 2017, s 7(1) for applications for homelessness
   assistance made on or after 3 April 2018.
9 As inserted by HRA 2017, s 5(2), for applications for homelessness assistance made on or after
   3 April 2018.
10 HA 1996, s 193B, as inserted by HRA 2017, s 7(1), for applications for homelessness
   assistance made on or after 3 April 2018.

[11] As inserted by HRA 2017, s 7(1), for applications for homelessness assistance made on or after 3 April 2018.

15.52 If no further duty is owed to the applicant, and the applicant remains homeless, he or she could make a fresh application for homelessness assistance[1]. Unless the factual circumstances are the same as those when the first application for homelessness assistance was disposed of[2], then the local housing authority must accept the application, make inquiries into what duty might be owed, and (if there is reason to believe that the applicant may be eligible for assistance, may be homeless and may have a priority need), secure interim accommodation[3]. The English Code contains advice that in the majority of re-application cases where the applicant has previously refused an offer of suitable accommodation, the local housing authority will be entitled to rely on the ending of its duties following the refusal of accommodation. It is only if the applicant's factual circumstances have changed that the local housing authority must accept a fresh application[4].

[1] HA 1996, s 183(1), see **8.80–8.82** and **8.85–8.91**.
[2] See **8.80–8.82** and **8.85** and **8.91**.
[3] HA 1996, s 188(1), see **16.37–16.50**.
[4] English Code, para 18.12.

Interim accommodation

15.53 Where the local housing authority has reason to believe that an applicant may be homeless, may be eligible for assistance and may have a priority need[1], it has a duty to secure interim accommodation[2] for the applicant and his or her household whilst it carries out its inquiries and then during the performance of the HA 1996, s 189B(2)[3], relief duty[4]. The words 'reason to believe' and 'may' mean that the threshold is very low[5].

[1] Unless the applicant has made a fresh application for homelessness assistance within two years of having accepted a private rented sector offer (HA 1996, s 193(7AA)–(7AC), see **16.154**), in which case the applicant will not normally need a possible priority need in order to be entitled to the interim accommodation duty: HA 1996, ss 188(1A) and 195A(1), as amended by HRA 2017, s 5(4) and 4(4), for applications for homelessness assistance made on or after 3 April 2018, see **8.100–8.107** and **16.47–16.50**.
[2] HA 1996, s 188(1), as amended by HRA 2017, s 5(4), for applications for homelessness assistance made on or after 3 April 2018. See English Code, paras 15.4–15.12, and see **16.37–16.80**.
[3] As inserted by HRA 2017, s 5(2), for applications for homelessness assistance made on or after 3 April 2018.
[4] HA 1996, s 188(1), see **16.37–16.50**.
[5] See *R (Aweys) v Birmingham City Council* [2007] EWHC 52 (Admin), [2007] HLR 27, Admin Ct; and *R (Kelly & Mehari) v Birmingham City Council* [2009] EWHC 3240 (Admin), (2010) January *Legal Action*, p 35, Admin Ct; and **16.37**.

15.54 Where a local housing authority decides that an applicant does *not* have a priority need:

- the interim accommodation duty will come to an end when the applicant is notified of a decision that the HA 1996, s 189B(2)[1], relief duty is not owed, because the applicant is either not homeless or is not eligible for assistance[2]; or

- the interim accommodation duty will come to an end during the performance of the HA 1996, s 189B(2)[3], relief duty upon notification to the applicant that no duty will be owed to him or her under HA 1996, ss 190(2)[4] or 193(2)[5] because he or she does not have a priority need[6].

[1] As inserted by HRA 2017, s 5(2), for applications for homelessness assistance made on or after 3 April 2018.

[2] HA 1996, s 188(1ZA)(a), as inserted by HRA 2017, s 5(4), for applications for homelessness assistance made on or after 3 April 2018.

[3] As inserted by HRA 2017, s 5(2), for applications for homelessness assistance made on or after 3 April 2018.

[4] As amended by HRA 2017, s 5(5), for applications for homelessness assistance made on or after 3 April 2018. Duty to secure accommodation for such period as the local housing authority considers will give the applicant a reasonable opportunity of securing his or her own accommodation, owed to applicants who have a priority need and who have become homeless intentionally, see **16.81–16.93**.

[5] Main housing duty, owed to applicants who have a priority need and who have not become homeless intentionally, see **16.94–16.199**.

[6] HA 1996, s 188(1ZA)(b), as inserted by HRA 2017, s 5(4), for applications for homelessness assistance made on or after 3 April 2018, see **16.56–16.59**.

15.55 In any other case, the interim accommodation duty will come to an end upon any of the following events occurring:

- the applicant is notified of a decision that the HA 1996, s 189B(2)[1], relief duty is not owed, because the applicant is either not homeless or is not eligible for assistance[2];
- the ending of the HA 1996, s 189B(2)[3], relief duty[4]; or
- the applicant has been notified of the local housing authority's decision as to what duty, if any, will be owed to him or her upon the ending of the HA 1996, s 189B(2)[5], relief duty[6].

Where the applicant was owed the HA 1996, s 189B(2)[7], relief duty and it has come to an end because the applicant has accepted or refused[8] a final accommodation offer[9] or a final Pt 6 offer[10], and the applicant has requested a review of the suitability of that offer[11], the interim accommodation duty continues until the review decision has been notified to the applicant[12].

[1] As inserted by HRA 2017, s 5(2), for applications for homelessness assistance made on or after 3 April 2018, see **15.138–15.195**.

[2] HA 1996, s 188(1ZB)(a), as inserted by HRA 2017, s 5(4), for applications for homelessness assistance made on or after 3 April 2018.

[3] As inserted by HRA 2017, s 5(2), for applications for homelessness assistance made on or after 3 April 2018, see **15.138–15.195**.

[4] HA 1996, s 188(1ZB)(a), as inserted by HRA 2017, s 5(4), for applications for homelessness assistance made to local housing authorities in England on or after 3 April 2018, see **16.61**.

[5] As inserted by HRA 2017, s 5(2), for applications for homelessness assistance made on or after 3 April 2018, see **15.138–15.195**.

[6] HA 1996, s 188(1ZB)(a) and (b), as inserted by HRA 2017, s 5(4), for applications for homelessness assistance made on or after 3 April 2018, see **16.62–16.65**.

[7] As inserted by HRA 2017, s 5(2), for applications for homelessness assistance made on or after 3 April 2018, see **15.138–15.195**.

[8] HA 1996, s 189B(9)(a), as inserted by HRA 2017, s 5(2), for applications for homelessness assistance made on or after 3 April 2018, see **15.162–15.165** and **15.181–15.184**.

[9] As defined at HA 1996, s 193A(4), as inserted by HRA 2017, s 7(1), for applications for homelessness assistance made on or after 3 April 2018, see **15.181**.

[10] As defined at HA 1996, s 193A(5), as inserted by HRA 2017, s 7(1), for applications for homelessness assistance made on or after 3 April 2018, see **15.185**.

¹¹ HA 1996, s 202(1)(h), as inserted by HRA 2017, s 9, for applications for homelessness assistance made on or after 3 April 2018, see **19.65–19.69**.
¹² HA 1996, s 188(2A), as inserted by HRA 2017, s 5(4), for applications for homelessness assistance made on or after 3 April 2018 see **15.184** and **15.188**.

Applicants who have re-applied for homelessness assistance within two years of acceptance of a private rented sector offer

15.56 Special provisions apply where an applicant, having accepted a private rented sector offer[1] made by a local housing authority in response to an earlier application for homelessness assistance, makes a fresh application for homelessness assistance within two years of the date of his or her acceptance of the offer[2]. Most applicants in these circumstances will be entitled to the HA 1996, s 193(2), main housing duty whether or not they have a priority need provided that the local housing authority is satisfied that they are homeless, eligible, and did not become homeless intentionally[3].

¹ As defined at HA 1996, s 193(7AC), see **16.154**.
² HA 1996, s 195A, as amended by HRA 2017, s 4(4), for applications for homelessness assistance made on or after 3 April 2018, see **8.100–8.107** and **16.47–16.50**.
³ HA 1996, s 195A(1). The exception is where the local housing authority would not be satisfied that the HA 1996, s 193(2), main housing duty is owed without having regard to a restricted person: HA 1996, s 195A(5), as amended by HRA 2017, s 4(4), for applications for homelessness assistance made on or after 3 April 2018, see **8.102**.

15.57 If, therefore, before a final decision has been made, the local housing authority has reason to believe that the HA 1996, s 193(2), main housing duty will apply[1], it is under a duty to secure interim accommodation for the applicant and his or her household[2]. This duty applies whether or not there is any reason to believe that the applicant has a priority need[3].

¹ HA 1996, s 195A(1), as amended by HRA 2017, s 4(4), for applications for homelessness assistance made on or after 3 April 2018, see **8.100–8.107**.
² HA 1996, s 188(1A), as amended by HRA 2017, s 5(4), for applications for homelessness assistance made on or after 3 April 2018, see **16.47–16.50**.
³ HA 1996, s 195A(1), see **8.100–8.107**.

15.58 Applicants in these circumstances must be provided with interim accommodation. That duty comes to an end upon any of the following events occurring:

- the applicant is notified of a decision that the HA 1996, s 189B(2)[1], relief duty is not owed, because the applicant is either not homeless or is not eligible for assistance[2];
- the ending of the HA 1996, s 189B(2)[3], relief duty[4]; or
- the applicant is notified of the local housing authority's decision as to what duty, if any, will be owed to him or her upon the ending of the HA 1996, s 189B(2)[5], relief duty[6].

¹ As inserted by HRA 2017, s 5(2), for applications for homelessness assistance made on or after 3 April 2018. See **15.138–15.195**.
² HA 1996, s 188(1ZB)(a), as inserted by HRA 2017, s 5(4), for applications for homelessness assistance made on or after 3 April 2018.
³ As inserted by HRA 2017, s 5(2), for applications for homelessness assistance made on or after 3 April 2018, see **15.138–15.195**.

⁴ HA 1996, s 188(1ZB)(a), as inserted by HRA 2017, s 5(4), for applications for homelessness assistance made to local housing authorities in England on or after 3 April 2018, see **16.60–16.61.**

⁵ As inserted by HRA 2017, s 5(2), for applications for homelessness assistance made on or after 3 April 2018, see **15.138–15.195.**

⁶ HA 1996, s 188(1ZB)(a) and (b), as inserted by HRA 2017, s 5(4), for applications for homelessness assistance made on or after 3 April 2018, see **16.51–16.65.**

Applicants referred to another local housing authority

15.59 Where a local housing authority decides to notify an applicant that the conditions for referral¹ are met, usually by reason of his or her local connection with the district and the local housing authority², so that the HA 1996, s 189B(2)³, relief duty will be performed by another local housing authority, the first local housing authority's duty to secure interim accommodation under HA 1996, s 188⁴ will come to an end⁵. However, if the first local housing authority has reason to believe that the applicant may have a priority need then it will continue to be under a duty to secure accommodation for the applicant and his or her household⁶. That duty continues until the applicant is notified of the decision as to whether or not the conditions for referral of his or her case are met⁷.

¹ At HA 1996, s 198(A1) or (1), as amended by HRA 2017, s 5(8), for applications for homelessness assistance made on or after 3 April 2018, see **15.139–15.146.**

² HA 1996, s 198(2) and 199 (as amended by HRA 2017, s 8, for application for homelessness assistance made on or after 3 April 2018), see Chapter 14.

³ As inserted by HRA 2017, s 5(2), for applications for homelessness assistance made on or after 3 April 2018, see **14.43–14.122.**

⁴ As amended by HRA 2017, s 5(4), for applications for homelessness assistance made on or after 3 April 2018.

⁵ HA 1996, s 199A(1) as inserted by HRA s 5(9), for applications for homelessness assistance made on or after 3 April 2018, and HA 1996, s 200(1), see **14.33–14.42.**

⁶ HA 1996, s 199A(2), as inserted by HRA 2017, s 5(9), for applications for homelessness assistance made on or after 3 April 2018, see **16.15.**

⁷ HA 1996, s 199A(2), as inserted by HRA 2017, s 5(9), for applications for homelessness assistance made on or after 3 April 2018, see **16.15.** If the applicant was already accommodated by the first local housing authority under the HA 1996, s 188(1) interim accommodation duty, then the first local housing authority had already decided that it had reason to believe that the applicant may have a priority need.

15.60 If it is decided that the conditions for referral are met, and if the notified local housing authority has reason to believe that the applicant may have a priority need, it becomes subject to an interim accommodation duty to accommodate the applicant¹.

¹ HA 1996, ss 188 and 199A(5), as amended and inserted by HRA 2017, s 5 (4) and (9), for applications for homelessness assistance made on or after 3 April 2018, see **16.15.**

15.61 If it is decided that the conditions for referral are not met, the first local housing authority becomes subject to the HA 1996, s 189B(2)¹, relief duty and, if there is reason to believe that the applicant may have a priority need, to the the interim accommodation duty². This ends upon the later of:

- the HA 1996, s 189B(2)³ relief duty coming to an end; or
- the local housing authority deciding what further duty, if any, it owes

after the HA 1996, s 189B(2)[4] duty ends[5].

1   As inserted by HRA 2017, s 5(2), for applications for homelessness assistance made on or after
     3 April 2018, see **15.138–15.195**.
2   HA 1996, s 199A(4)(c), as inserted by HRA 2017, s 5(8) for applications for homelessness
     assistance made on or after 3 April 2018.
3   As inserted by HRA 2017, s 5(2), for applications for homelessness assistance made on or after
     3 April 2018, see **15.138–15.195**.
4   As inserted by HRA 2017, s 5(2), for applications for homelessness assistance made on or after
     3 April 2018, see **15.138–15.195**.
5   HA 1996, s 199A(4), as inserted by HRA 2017, s 5(9), for applications for homelessness
     assistance made on or after 3 April 2018, see **16.51**.

ASSESSMENTS AND PERSONALISED PLANS

Duty to make an assessment of the applicant's case

15.62 The duty to make an assessment of an applicant's case[1] is owed to applicants whom the local housing authority is satisfied are[2]:

- eligible for assistance[3]; and
- threatened with homelessness[4]; or
- homeless[5].

1   HA 1996, s 189A(1), as inserted by HRA 2017, s 3(1), for applications for homelessness
     assistance made on or after 3 April 2018, see English Code, chapter 11.
2   HA 1996, s 189A(1), as inserted by HRA 2017, s 3(1), for applications for homelessness
     assistance made on or after 3 April 2018.
3   HA 1996, s 185, see CHAPTER 11.
4   HA 1996, s 175(4) and (5) as amended and inserted by HRA 2017, s 1(2) and (3), for
     applications for homelessness assistance made on or after 3 April 2018, see **10.144–10.147**.
5   HA 1996, ss 175–177, see CHAPTER 10.

When does the duty arise?

15.63 The duty to assess arises as soon as the local housing authority is satisfied of these matters[1]. Concurrently, once the local housing authority is satisfied that these conditions are met, it will also owe a duty either to help the applicant prevent his or her homelessness[2] or to help the applicant secure suitable accommodation for his or her occupation[3]. The local housing authority must notify the applicant in writing of the decision that one of these two duties, as well as the duty to assess his or her case, is owed to him or her[4].

1   HA 1996, s 189A(1), as inserted by HRA 2017, s 3(1), for applications for homelessness
     assistance made on or after 3 April 2018, see English Code, paras 11.3–11.4.
2   HA 1996, s 195(2), as amended by HRA 2017, s 4(2), for applications for homelessness
     assistance made on or after 3 April 2018, see **15.87–15.137**.
3   HA 1996, s 189B(2), as inserted by HRA 2017, s 5(2), for applications for homelessness
     assistance made on or after 3 April 2018, see **15.138–153195**.
4   HA 1996, s 184(1) and (3), see English Code, paras 18.32–18.33 and **9.90–9.94**.

15.64 If the local housing authority has 'reason to believe' that an applicant 'may' be homeless, 'may' be eligible for assistance and 'may' have a priority need, it is also under a duty to secure interim accommodation for the applicant and his or her household[1]. The local housing authority must provide this accommodation whilst it complies with HA 1996, s 189A[2] duty, unless, during the performance of that duty, it notifies the applicant that it is satisfied that he or she does not have a priority need[3].

1   HA 1996, s 188(1), see English Code, para 13.3 and **16.37–16.50**.
2   As inserted by HRA 2017, s 3(1), for applications for homelessness assistance made on or after 3 April 2018.
3   See **16.51–16.80** for the ways in which the HA 1996, s 188(1) interim accommodation duty can come to an end.

Duty towards applicants who are referred under the conditions for referral

15.65 If the local housing authority would be subject to the HA 1996, s 189B(2)[1], relief duty but considers that the conditions for referral of the applicant's case for performance of HA 1996, s 189B(2), relief duty might be met[2], it remains under a duty to carry out an assessment of the applicant's case and, potentially, to proceed to produce a personalised housing plan with the applicant[3]. It is only once it has been determined, by agreement or by a referee's decision, that the conditions for referral are met that the notifying local housing authority ceases to be under a duty under HA 1996, s 189A[4]. Once that decision has been made, and the applicant has been notified of that decision, the notified local housing authority becomes subject to the HA 1996, s 189A duty and any other duties under HA 1996, Pt 7, and the notifying local housing authority owes no further duties[5].

1   As inserted by HRA 2017, s 5(2), for applications for homelessness assistance made on or after 3 April 2018, see **15.138–15.195**.
2   HA 1996, s 198, see Chapter **14**.
3   HA 1996, s 199A(1) (as inserted by HRA 2017, s 5(9) for applications for homelessness assistance made on or after 3 April 2018) states that where the local housing authority notify an applicant that they have notified or intend to notify another local housing authority under HA 1996, s 198(A1) (as inserted by HRA 2017, s 5(8) for applications for homelessness assistance made on or after 3 April 2018) the notifying local housing authority will not be subject to the HA 1996, s 188(1) interim accommodation duty or the HA 1996, s 189B(2) (as inserted by HRA 2017, s 5(2), for applications for homelessness assistance made on or after 3 April 2018) relief duty. The ommision HA 1996, s 189A (as inserted by HRA 2017, s 3(1), for applications for homelessness assistance made on or after 3 April 2018) means that the duties imposed by this section continue.
4   As inserted by HRA 2017, s 3(1), for applications for homelessness assistance made on or after 3 April 2018.
5   HA 1996, s 199A(5)(a) and (b), as inserted by HRA 2017, s 5(9), for applications for homelessness assistance made on or after 3 April 2018, see **15.139–15.146**.

15.66 The English Code advises that the notifying local housing authority should give to the notified local housing authority a copy of the applicant's assessment of his or her case and, if the applicant consents, a copy of the personalised housing plan in so far as that remains relevant[1].

1   English Code, paras 10.36–10.44, particularly para 10.43.

Contents of the assessment

15.67 HA 1996, s 189A(2)[1], requires the local housing authority to assess:

- the circumstances that caused the applicant to become homeless[2] or threatened with homelessness[3];

- the housing needs of the applicant including, in particular, what accommodation would be suitable[4] for the applicant and any persons with whom the applicant resides or might reasonably be expected to reside ('other relevant persons'); and
- what support would be necessary for the applicant and any other relevant persons to be able to have and retain suitable accommodation.

[1]   As inserted by HRA 2017, s 3(1), for applications for homelessness assistance made on or after 3 April 2018, see English Code, paras 11.7–11.12.
[2]   HA 1996, ss 175–177, see CHAPTER 10.
[3]   HA 1996, s 175(4)–(5), as amended and inserted by HRA 2017, s 1(2) and (3), for applications for homelessness assistance made on or after 3 April 2018, see **10.144–10.147**.
[4]   For 'suitable accommodation' see CHAPTER 18.

15.68 The English Code advises that when considering the circumstances leading to a threat of homelessness, local housing authorities will need to make inquiries into an applicant's accommodation history, at least as far as back as his or her last settled address and the events that led to him or her being threatened with or becoming homeless[1]. When assessing the applicant's housing needs, local housing authorities will need to consider all the members of the applicant's household and their needs. That should include an assessment of the size and type of accommodation required, any requirements necessary to meet the needs of any disabled people, any specific medical needs, and also the location. The applicant's wishes and preferences should be considered and recorded, whether or not there is a reasonable prospect of accommodation being available that would meet them[2]. The assessment of support needs should be holistic and comprehensive, not limited to those needs which are most apparent or which have already been notified to the local housing authority by a referral agency. Applicants should be sensitively encouraged to discuss their needs and local housing authorities should be aware of the support that can be provided by health or social care services[3]. The English Code also contains guidance on the arrangements for carrying out assessments and recommends at least one face to face interview[4].

[1]   English Code, paras 11.8–11.9.
[2]   English Code, para 11.10.
[3]   English Code, paras 11.11–11.12. For young people aged 16 or 17, there is specific guidance as to the contents of assessment, see *Prevention of Homelessness and Provision of Accommodation for 16 and 17 year old young people who may be homeless and/or require accommodation* (MHCLG and Department for Education, April 2018), chapter 4.
[4]   English Code, paras 11.13–11.16.

15.69 The contents of the assessment will assist the local housing authority in deciding what steps to take to help the applicant to prevent his or her homelessness[1], or to secure that accommodation becomes available for his or her occupation, together with the members of his or her household[2].

[1]   HA 1996, s 195(3), as amended by HRA 2017, s 4(2), for applications for homelessness assistance made on or after 3 April 2018, see **15.91–15.96**.
[2]   HA 1996, s 189B(3), as inserted by HRA 2017, s 5(2), for applications for homelessness assistance made on or after 3 April 2018, see **15.144–15.149**.

15.70 Once the assessment has been drawn up it must be notified, in writing, to the applicant[1]. If the notification is not received by the applicant, then it is treated as having been given to him or her if it is made available at the local housing authority's office for a reasonable period for collection by or on behalf of the applicant[2].

[1]   HA 1996, s 189A(3), as inserted by HRA 2017, s 3(1), for applications for homelessness assistance made on or after 3 April 2018, see English Code, para 11.24.
[2]   HA 1996, s 189A(12), as amended by HRA 2017, s 3(1), for applications for homelessness assistance made on or after 3 April 2018.

15.71 There is no right to request a review of the contents of the assessment. However, the applicant does have the right to request a review of the local housing authority's decision as to what steps it will take, either to help the applicant prevent his or her homelessness[1], or to help the applicant secure his or her own accommodation[2]. Those steps will be set out in the personalised housing plan drawn up following the assessment[3].

[1]   HA 1996, s 195(2), as amended by HRA 2017, s 4(2), for applications for homelessness assistance made on or after 3 April 2018, see **15.87–15.137**. The right to request a review is at HA 1996, s 202(1)(bc)(i), as inserted by HRA 2017, s 9, for applications for homelessness assistance made on or after 3 April 2018, see English Code, para 11.36 and **19.36–19.41**.
[2]   HA 1996, s 189B(2), as inserted by HRA 2017, s 5(2), for applications for homelessness assistance made on or after 3 April 2018, see **15.138–15.195**. The right to request a review is at HA 1996, s 202(1)(ba)(i), as inserted by HRA 2017, s 9, for applications for homelessness assistance made on or after 3 April 2018, see English Code, para 11.36 and **19.18 –19.23**.
[3]   HA 1996, s 189A(4) - (6), as inserted by HRA 2017, s 3(1), for applications for homelessness assistance made on or after 3 April 2018, see English Code, paras 11.18–11.23 and **15.72–15.80**.

Personalised housing plans

15.72 After the assessment has been completed, the local housing authority and the applicant should try to agree what steps each of them will take in order to secure that the applicant and members of his or her household 'have and are able to retain' suitable accommodation[1]. If the local housing authority and the applicant agree on the steps each of them should take, that agreement should be recorded in writing[2].

[1]   HA 1996, s 189A(4), as inserted by HRA 2017, s 3(1), for applications for homelessness assistance made on or after 3 April 2018.
[2]   HA 1996, s 189A(5), as inserted by HRA 2017, s 3(1), for applications for homelessness assistance made on or after 3 April 2018.

15.73 If they do not agree, then the local housing authority must record in writing:

•   the reasons why they could not agree;
•   what steps the local housing authority considers it would be reasonable to require the applicant to take; and
•   what steps the local housing authority is to take[1].

[1]   HA 1996, s 189A(6) as inserted by HRA 2017, s 3(1), for applications for homelessness assistance made on or after 3 April 2018.

15.74 Whether or not the steps are agreed, the local housing authority can also include in the written record any advice for the applicant that it considers appropriate. That advice can include any steps that the local housing authority considers it would be a good idea for the applicant to take, but which he or she is not required to take[1].

> [1] HA 1996, s 189A(7), as inserted by HRA 2017, s 3(1), for applications for homelessness assistance made on or after 3 April 2018.

15.75 The local housing authority must give the applicant a copy of the written record[1]. This written record is the applicant's 'personalised plan', also known as the 'personalised housing plan'[2].

> [1] HA 1996, s 189A(8), as inserted by HRA 2017, s 3(1), for applications for homelessness assistance made on or after 3 April 2018.
> [2] HA 1996, s 189A (as inserted by HRA 2017, s 3(1), for applications for homelessness assistance made on or after 3 April 2018) is headed 'personalised plan' while the English Code uses the phrase 'personalised housing plan', para 11.20. The two terms refer to the same document.

15.76 The English Code advises that the personalised housing plans should be realistic and that local housing authorities should provide sufficient information and advice for applicants to make informed and realistic choices. Applicants should be encouraged to extend the areas in which they are searching for accommodation and to consider different types of properties[1]. The type of reasonable steps that a local housing authority might consider taking are discussed at **15.22–15.26**, **15.91–15.96** and **15.144–15.149** of this book.[2]

> [1] English Code, para 11.20.
> [2] There is specific guidance as to contents of personal housing plans for young people aged 16 or 17 in *Prevention of Homelessness and Provision of Accommodation for 16 and 17 year old young people who may be homeless and/or require accommodation* (MHCLG and Department for Education, April 2018), chapter 4.

15.77 This record of what steps the applicant is to take, whether agreed or otherwise, is important. If the applicant subsequently fails to take any of those steps, he or she could be notified by the local housing authority of a decision that he or she has deliberately and unreasonably refused to co-operate[1]. The consequence of such a decision is that any HA 1996, s 195(2)[2], prevention duty, or any HA 1996, s 189B(2)[3], relief duty owed will come to an end[4] and the HA 1996, s 193(2), main housing duty, if it would otherwise have been owed, will not apply[5]. Instead, for applicants who have a priority need and who have not become homeless intentionally, a duty to secure accommodation will arise under HA 1996, s 193C(4)[6], which can be ended by (among other circumstances) the making of a final accommodation offer[7].

> [1] HA 1996, s 193B(2), as inserted by HRA 2017, s 7(1), for applications for homelessness assistance made on or after 3 April 2018, see **15.196–15.221**. The decision must be preceded by a relevant warning giving the applicant a reasonable period in which to comply: HA 1996, s 193B(4) and (5), as inserted by HRA 2017, s 7(1), for applications for homelessness assistance made on or after 3 April 2018, see **15.196–15.221**.
> [2] As amended by HRA 2017, s 4(2), for applications for homelessness assistance made on or after 3 April 2018, see **15.87–15.137**.
> [3] As inserted by HRA 2017, s 5(2), for applications for homelessness assistance made on or after 3 April 2018, see **15.138–15.195**.
> [4] For the HA 1996, s 195(2), prevention duty coming to an end, see HA 1996, ss 195(10), and 193C(2) as amended and inserted by HRA 2017, ss 4(2) and 7(1), for applications for homelessness assistance made on or after 3 April 2018, see **15.98–15.132**. For the HA 1996,

s 189B(2), relief duty coming to an end, see HA 1996, s 189B(9)(b) and 193C(2), as inserted by HRA 2017, s 5(2) and 7(1), for applications for homelessness assistance made on or after 3 April 2018, see **15.151–15.189**.

5   HA 1996, s 193C(4), as inserted by HRA 2017, s 7(1), for applications for homelessness assistance made on or after 3 April 2018, see **16.200–16.216**.

6   As inserted by HRA 2017, s 7(1), for applications for homelessness assistance made on or after 3 April 2018, see **16.200–16.216**.

7   HA 1996, s 193C(4) and (6), as inserted by HRA 2017, s 7(1), for applications for homelessness assistance made on or after 3 April 2018, see **16.204–16.209**.

15.78 The applicant has a right to request a review of any of the steps that the local housing authority has recorded that it will take in order to help him or her secure and retain accommodation[1].

[1]   HA 1996, s 202(1)(ba)(i) and (bc)(i) as inserted by HRA 2017, s 9, for applications for homelessness assistance made on or after 3 April 2018, see English Code, para 11.36 and **19.18–19.23** and **19.36–19.41**.

15.79 The position in respect of the steps that the *applicant* is to take to secure and retain accommodation is less clear. The right to request a review at HA 1996, s 202(1)(ba)(i) and (bc)(i)[1] refers to any decision of a local housing authority as to the steps 'they' are to take. 'They' appears to refer back to 'the local housing authority' only and therefore there seems to be no right to request a review of the steps the applicant is to take. This is surprising given the significant implications if the applicant is subsequently found to have deliberately and unreasonably refused to co-operate as a result of his or her failure to take any of those steps, but the authors' view is that this is the natural meaning of the provision. However, it is noted that the English Code is more ambiguous and refers to a right to request a review of the reasonable steps, in general, rather than those specified to be taken by the local housing authority[2].

[1]   As inserted by HRA 2017, s 9, for applications for homelessness assistance made on or after 3 April 2018, see **19.18–19.23** and **19.36–19.41**.

[2]   English Code, para 11.36. The authors' view is that the plain wording of HA 1996, s 202(1)(ba)(i) and (bc)(i) (as inserted by HRA 2017, s 9, for applications for homelessness assistance made on or after 3 April 2018) should prevail.

15.80 The applicant does, however, have a right to request a review of any decision of a local housing authority to give notice that he or she has deliberately and unreasonably refused to take a required step under the personalised housing plan[1]. This provides an avenue, albeit at a later stage, for an applicant to challenge the steps which he or she has been required to take.

[1]   HA 1996, s 202(1)(bb) as inserted by HRA 2017, s 9, for applications for homelessness assistance made on or after 3 April 2018, see **19.30–19.35**.

Continuing review of assessment and personalised housing plan

15.81 The local housing authority must keep the contents of both the assessment and the personalised housing plan under review at all times whilst the local housing authority continues to owe any duty towards the applicant[1]. In this context, 'review' means a continuing re-assessment of the contents, rather than the 'review' requested against an adverse decision[2].

1   HA 1996, s 189A(9) as inserted by HRA 2017, s 3(1), for applications for homelessness assistance made on or after 3 April 2018, see English Code, paras 11.32–11.35. It should be noted that the English Code advises that local housing authorities should keep the assessment and personalised housing plan under review throughout the prevention and relief stages, implying that there is no need to review them if the applicant is subsequently accommodated under other duties.
2   HA 1996, s 202(1), as amended by HRA 2017, s 9, for applications for homelessness assistance made on or after 3 April 2018, see **19.8–19.69**.

15.82 The duty to keep the assessment and personalised housing plan under review continues even where the local housing authority intends to refer the applicant to another local housing authority for performance of the HA 1996, s 189B(2)[1], relief duty or performance of the HA 1996, s 193(2) main housing duty[2]. It only ends in those circumstances once it has been decided that the conditions for referral are made out[3]. The assessment and personalised housing plan will have been sent to the notified local housing authority and the duty to keep those documents under review will be owed by the notified local housing authority[4].

1   As inserted by HRA 2017, s 5(2), for applications for homelessness assistance made to local housing authorities in England on or after 3 April 2018, see **15.138–15.195**.
2   HA 1996, s 198(A1) and (1) as inserted and amended by HRA 2017, s 5(8), for applications for homelessness assistance made to local housing authorities in England on or after 3 April 2018, see CHAPTER **14**. The duties to accommodate in these circumstances are at HA 1996, s 199A(2), as amended by HRA 2017, s 5(9), for applications for homelessness assistance made to local housing authorities in England on or after 3 April 2018, and HA 1996, s 200(1), see **15.139–15.146**.
3   HA 1996, s 199A(5)(b), as inserted by HRA 2017, s 5(9) for applications for homelessness assistance made to local housing authorities in England on or after 3 April 2018.
4   HA 1996, 199A(5)(a) and (b). The English Code suggests that the applicant's consent will be needed for a copy of his or her personalised plan to be sent to the notified local housing authority: English Code, para 10.43.

15.83 The English Code contains advice that local housing authorities should establish timescales for reviewing plans and those timescales are likely to vary according to each applicant's individual needs and circumstances. In addition, if a personalised housing plan is agreed when the applicant is threatened with homelessness, it must be reviewed if the applicant subsequently becomes homeless[1]. A local housing authority should also initiate a review if it becomes aware that any information provided was inaccurate, or if there is new information or a relevant change in the applicant's circumstances or if it believes that the applicant is not co-operating with the personalised housing plan[2].

1   English Code, para 11.32.
2   English Code, para 11.33.

15.84 If the local housing authority's assessment of the applicant's case changes, the local housing authority may be under a duty to notify the applicant of that change in writing. If the change is to the assessment of any of the three matters that it was required to assess by HA 1996, s 189A(2)[1], then the applicant must be notified in writing of the change[2]. Otherwise, the local housing authority is required to notify the applicant in writing of any other changes to the assessment of his or her case that it considers it appropriate[3]. The notification of the changes might take the form of a revised written assessment, or, more simply, a letter setting out the changes.

[1]   The three statutory matters are: the circumstances that caused the applicant to become homeless or threatened with homelessness; the housing needs of the applicant including in particular what accommodation would be suitable for the applicant and for other relevant persons; and what support would be necessary for the applicant and any other relevant persons to be able to have and retain suitable accommodation: HA 1996, s 189A(2) as inserted by HRA 2017, s 3(1), for applications for homelessness assistance made on or after 3 April 2018, see 15.67.
[2]   HA 1996, s 189A(10)(a) as inserted by HRA 2017, s 3(1), for applications for homelessness assistance made on or after 3 April 2018, see English Code, para 11.34.
[3]   HA 1996, s 189A(10)(b) as inserted by HRA 2017, s 3(1), for applications for homelessness assistance made on or after 3 April 2018.

15.85 If the local housing authority decides that any of the steps that were recorded as required of the applicant, whether by agreement or otherwise, or any steps to be taken by the local housing authority, are no longer appropriate, it must notify the applicant of that decision in writing[1]. The effect of that notification is that any subsequent failure by the applicant to take those steps should be disregarded and so should not be the basis of any decision that he or she has deliberately and unreasonably refused to co-operate[2]. The applicant should still be taking any steps remaining in the personalised housing plan which have not been notified to him or her as no longer appropriate[3].

[1]   HA 1996, s 189A(11)(a) as inserted by HRA 2017, s 3(1), for applications for homelessness assistance made on or after 3 April 2018, see English Code, para 11.34.
[2]   HA 1996, ss 189A(11)(b) and 193B(2) as inserted by HRA 2017, ss 3(1) and 7(1), for applications for homelessness assistance made on or after 3 April 2018, see 15.196–15.221.
[3]   HA 1996, s 189A(11)(c) as inserted by HRA 2017, s 3(1), for applications for homelessness assistance made on or after 3 April 2018.

15.86 As already noted[1], the applicant does not, in the authors' view, have a right to request a review of the local housing authority's decision as to what steps he or she is required to take. It follows that there is no right to request a review of any decision that any of those steps are no longer appropriate. Nor is there any right to request a review of a decision that the local housing authority no longer has to keep the assessment or personalised housing plan under review. However, he or she would be able to request a review of a decision that the steps that were to be taken by the local housing authority were not reasonable steps[2].

[1]   See 15.71 and 15.79.
[2]   HA 1996, s 202(1)(ba)(i) and (bc)(i), as inserted by HRA 2017, s 99(2), for applications for homelessness assistance made on or after 3 April 2018, see 19.18–19.23 and 19.36–19.40.

DUTY TO TAKE REASONABLE STEPS TO HELP THE APPLICANT SECURE THAT ACCOMMODATION DOES NOT CEASE TO BE AVAILABLE: 'THE PREVENTION DUTY'

Applicants entitled to the duty

15.87 The HA 1996, s 195(2)[1], prevention duty is owed to all applicants whom the local housing authority is satisfied are:

- eligible for assistance[2]; and
- threatened with homelessness[3].

[1] As amended by HRA 2017, s 4(2), for applications for homelessness assistance made on or after 3 April 2018; see English Code, chapter 12.
[2] HA 1996, s 185, see Chapter 11.
[3] HA 1996, s 175(4) and (5) as amended and inserted by HRA 2017, s 1(2) and (3), for applications for homelessness assistance made on or after 3 April 2018. See **10.144–10.147**.

15.88 All applicants who are eligible, and who are likely to become homeless within 56 days[1], or who have received a valid Housing Act 1988, s 21, notice which expires within 56 days[2], are entitled to this duty. There is no additional test of whether an applicant has a priority need, or whether or not he or she has become threatened with homelessness intentionally.

[1] HA 1996, s 175(4), as amended by HRA 2017, s 1(2), for applications for homelessness assistance made on or after 3 April 2018. See **10.144–10.145**.
[2] HA 1996, s 175(5), as inserted by HRA 2017, s 1(3), for applications for homelessness assistance made on or after 3 April 2018. See **10.145–10.147**.

15.89 The duty arises as soon as the local housing authority is satisfied that an applicant is threatened with homelessness and is eligible for assistance[1].

[1] HA 1996, s 195(1), as amended by HRA 2017, s 4(2), for applications for homelessness assistance made on or after 3 April 2018; English Code, para 12.2.

15.90 The local housing authority must notify the applicant in writing of its decision that the HA 1996, s 195(2)[1], prevention duty is owed to him or her[2]. If the written decision is notified later than the date on which the local housing authority actually came to that decision, that is not a reason for the local housing authority to delay performing its duty.

[1] As amended by HRA 2017, s 4(2), for applications for homelessness assistance made on or after 3 April 2018.
[2] HA 1996, s 184(1) and (3), see **9.90–9.94**.

Performing the duty

15.91 The duty requires the local housing authority to 'take reasonable steps to help the applicant to secure that accommodation does not cease to be available for the applicant's occupation'[1]. The meaning of 'take reasonable steps to help the applicant to secure' and 'available for occupation' is discussed at **15.22–15.40**.

[1] HA 1996, s 195(2), as amended by HRA 2017, s 4(2), for applications for homelessness assistance made on or after 3 April 2018.

15.92 When the local housing authority is deciding what steps it will take, it must have regard to its assessment of the applicant's case under HA 1996, s 189A[1]. In the course of the assessment (which may be ongoing), the local housing authority will have considered the circumstances that caused the applicant to become threatened with homelessness, his or her housing needs together with those of his her household, and what support would be necessary for the applicant and his household to have or retain suitable accommodation[2]. This should therefore ensure that the local housing authority is aware of the information necessary to determine what steps might reasonably be taken to help the applicant secure that accommodation does not cease to be available. Those reasonable steps will then have been set out in the personalised housing plan, drawn up following the assessment[3].

1   HA 1996, s 195(3), as amended by HRA 2017, s 4(2), for applications for homelessness assistance made on or after 3 April 2018. See HA 1996, s 189A, as inserted by HRA, s 3(1), for applications for homelessness assistance made on or after 3 April 2018, and **15.62–15.86**.
2   HA 1996, s 189A(2), as inserted by HRA 2017, s 3(1), for applications for homelessness assistance made on or after 3 April 2018. See **15.62 –15.71**.
3   HA 1996, s 189A(4)(b) and (6)(b), as inserted by HRA 2017, s 3(1), for applications for homelessness assistance made on or after 3 April 2018. See English Code, paras 11.18–11.23 and **15.71–15.86**. There is specific guidance as to how to perform the prevention duty when dealing with young people aged 16 or 17 in *Prevention of Homelessness and Provision of Accommodation for 16 and 17 year old young people who may be homeless and/or require accommodation* (MHCLG and Department for Education, April 2018), chapter 4.

15.93   The applicant has the right to request a review of the steps that the local housing authority has decided that it is to take under this duty[1]. This is the opportunity for the applicant to challenge the local housing authority if he or she believes that it is not taking sufficient or appropriate steps to help him or her find or retain accommodation.

1   HA 1996, s 202(1)(bc)(i), as amended by HRA 2017, s 9, for applications for homelessness assistance made on or after 3 April 2018. See **19.36–19.41**.

15.94   The English Code advises that the first option to be explored should be enabling the applicant to remain in his or her current home where suitable. It gives examples of when interim accommodation can be provided whilst action is taken to enable an applicant to remain in his or her home, for example if sanctuary measures are to be installed or emergency repairs carried out, or whilst action is taken to reinstate a tenant who has been illegally evicted. If this is not possible, the focus should be on helping to secure alternative accommodation that he or she can move into in a planned way, which may require taking steps to extend the stay in the current accommodation until he or she can move[1]. There is specific guidance in the English Code as to how to perform the HA 1996, s 195(2)[2], prevention duty when dealing with applicants who have been subject to domestic abuse[3] and when dealing with applicants who have an offending history[4].

1   English Code, paras 12.3–12.4.
2   As amended by HRA 2017, s 4(2), for applications for homelessness assistance made on or after 3 April 2018.
3   English Code, paras 21.10–21.15.
4   English Code, paras 23.11–23.13.

15.95   Provided that the applicant is able to move directly from his or her existing accommodation into new, suitable accommodation, then the local housing authority will have performed its duty to the applicant. Of course, if there is an intervening period when the applicant has no accommodation, the applicant will no longer be threatened with homelessness and the local housing authority may give notice bringing the HA 1996, s 195(2)[1], prevention duty to an end[2]. The applicant will be homeless and the HA 1996, s 189B(2)[3], relief duty will apply.

[1]   As amended by HRA 2017, s 4(2), for applications for homelessness assistance made on or
      after 3 April 2018.
[2]   HA 1996, s 195(8)(c), as amended by HRA 2017, s 4(2), for applications for homelessness
      assistance made on or after 3 April 2018, see **15.113–15.117.**
[3]   As inserted by HRA 2017, s 5(2), for applications for homelessness assistance made on or after
      3 April 2018. See **15.183–15.195.**

15.96 HA 1996, s 195(4)[1], specifically provides that this duty to help the
applicant secure that accommodation does not cease to be available does not
affect any right of the local housing authority to secure vacant possession of
any accommodation. In other words, if a council tenant is due to be evicted
from his or her council home within 56 days and is eligible for assistance, the
duty arises to help the tenant to secure that the accommodation does not cease
to be available. But that duty does not prevent the local housing authority from
continuing to exercise its functions as landlord, and so proceeding with an
eviction. However, since the duty will be owed, efficient allocation of resources
might involve the local housing authority, when seeking to exercise its
homelessness functions, liaising with its housing department with a view to
preventing the eviction if possible by, for example, assisting to resolve housing
benefit problems, providing debt and budgeting advice, helping to pay the
tenant's rent arrears or providing any other service that might enable the
tenant to remain in his or her home.

[1]   As amended by HRA 2017, s 4(2), for applications for homelessness assistance made on or
      after 3 April 2018.

Interim accommodation

15.97 Since the applicant is threatened with homelessness, but not actually
homeless, there is no duty to secure interim accommodation[1].

[1]   See **16.37–16.50.**

How does the duty to prevent homelessness come to an end?

15.98 The local housing authority can bring the HA 1996, s 195(2)[1],
prevention duty to an end in the following eight circumstances[2]:

(1)   it is satisfied that the applicant has suitable accommodation available
      for his or her occupation and a reasonable prospect of having suitable
      accommodation available for occupation for at least six months[3];
(2)   it has complied with the HA 1996, s 195(2)[4], prevention duty for a
      period of 56 days beginning with the day on which the local housing
      authority is first satisfied that the duty is owed *unless* the applicant has
      been served with a valid Housing Act 1988, s 21, notice which will
      either expire within 56 days or has already expired[5];
(3)   it is satisfied that the applicant has become homeless[6];

(4)   it is satisfied that the applicant has refused an offer of suitable accommodation and, on the date of the refusal, there was a reasonable prospect that suitable accommodation would be available for occupation by the applicant for at least six months[7];

(5)   it is satisfied that the applicant has become homeless intentionally from any accommodation that had been made available to the applicant as a result of the local housing authority's exercise of its functions under the HA 1996, 195(2)[8], prevention duty[9];

(6)   it is satisfied that the applicant is no longer eligible for assistance[10];

(7)   it is satisfied that the applicant has withdrawn his or her application for homelessness assistance[11]; or

(8)   it considers that he or she has deliberately and unreasonably refused to co-operate following a warning[12].

[1]   As amended by HRA 2017, s 4(2), for applications for homelessness assistance made on or after 3 April 2018.

[2]   English Code, chapter 14.

[3]   HA 1996, s 195(8)(a), as amended by HRA 2017, s 4(2), for applications for homelessness assistance made on or after 3 April 2018. See English Code, paras 14.5–14.12 and **15.105–15.109**. The period of six months could be extended to a longer period of no more than 12 months if the Secretary of State so prescribes: HA 1996, s 195(8)(a), as amended by HRA 2017, s 4(2), for applications for homelessness assistance made on or after 3 April 2018.

[4]   As amended by HRA 2017, s 4(2), for applications for homelessness assistance made on or after 3 April 2018.

[5]   HA 1996, s 195(6) and (8)(b), as amended by HRA 2017, s 4(2), for applications for homelessness assistance on or after 3 April 2018; see English Code, paras 14.13–14.19 and **15.110–15.112**.

[6]   HA 1996, s 195(8)(c), as amended by HRA 2017, s 4(2), for applications for homelessness assistance made on or after 3 April 2018. See English Code, paras 14.20–14.22 and **15.113–15.117**.

[7]   HA 1996, s 195(8)(d), as amended by HRA 2017, s 4(2), for applications for homelessness assistance made on or after 3 April 2018. See English Code, paras 14.23–14.28 and **15.118–15.125**. The period of six months could be extended to a longer period of no more than 12 months if the Secretary of State so prescribes: HA 1996, s 195(8)(d), as amended by HRA 2017, s 4(2), for applications for homelessness assistance made on or after 3 April 2018.

[8]   As amended by HRA 2017, s 4(2), for applications for homelessness assistance made on or after 3 April 2018.

[9]   HA 1996, s 195(8)(e), as amended by HRA 2017, s 4(2), for applications for homelessness assistance made on or after 3 April 2018. See English Code, paras 14.29–14.31 and **15.126**.

[10]   HA 1996, s 195(8)(f), as amended by HRA 2017, s 4(2), for applications for homelessness assistance made on or after 3 April 2018. See English Code, para 14.32 and **12.127–15.127**.

[11]   HA 1996, s 195(8)(g) as inserted and amended by HRA 2017, s 4(2), for applications for homelessness assistance made to local housing authorities in England on or after 3 April 2018. See English Code, paras 14.33–14.34 and **15.128–15.131**.

[12]   HA 1996, s 193B(2) and 195(10), as inserted and amended by HRA 2017, s 7(1) and 4(2), for applications for homelessness assistance made on or after 3 April 2018. See English Code, paras 14.35–14.36 and 14.43–14.59 and **15.132** and **15.196–15.218**.

15.99 All of these circumstances require some form of notice to be given to the applicant before the duty can be ended.

15.100 In the eighth circumstance[1], the applicant must be given a written notice setting out the reasons for the notice, the effect of the notice, his or her right to request a review and the period of 21 days in which to request the review[2]. The giving of the notice, which is discretionary[3], automatically brings the duty to an end[4].

[1]   Where the local housing authority considers that the applicant has deliberately and unreasonably refused to co-operate.

[2]   HA 1996, s 193B(3), as inserted by HRA 2017, s 7(1), for applications for homelessness assistance made on or after 3 April 2018. See **15.207–15.212**.
[3]   HA 1996, s 193B(2), as inserted by HRA 2017, s 7(1), for applications for homelessness assistance made on or after 3 April 2018.
[4]   HA 1996, s 193C(2), as inserted by HRA 2017, s 7(1), for applications for homelessness assistance made on or after 3 April 2018, see English Code, paras 14.35–14.36 and see **15.216–15.218**.

15.101 In all other cases, the duty does not come to an end until the applicant is given notice in writing of the decision bringing the duty to an end[1]. That notification must:

- specify which of the circumstances, set out at **15.98**, has occurred;
- inform the applicant that he or she has the right to request a review of the decision to bring the duty to an end[2]; and
- inform the applicant of the 21-day period within which the request must be made[3].

If no notification is given[4], or if the notification does not contain all of that information, the duty continues[5]. Whilst there is no statutory requirement that reasons be given for the decision, procedural fairness is likely to require that the local housing authority explain why they consider the circumstance in question applies[6].

[1]   HA 1996, s 195(5) and (7), as amended by HRA 2017, s 4(2), for applications for homelessness assistance made on or after 3 April 2018. See English Code, paras 14.37–14.39 and **15.209–15.211**.
[2]   HA 1996, s 201(1)(bc), as amended by HRA 2017, s 9, for applications for homelessness assistance made on or after 3 April 2018. See **19.30–19.35**.
[3]   HA 1996, s 195(5) and (7), as amended by HRA 2017, s 4(2), for applications for homelessness assistance made on or after 3 April 2018. See **15.214–15.215**.
[4]   Because the decision is not put in writing, or is not received by the applicant, or is not made available at the local housing authority's office for a reasonable period for collection, see **15.211**.
[5]   HA 1996, s 195(5) and (7), as amended by HRA 2017, s 4(2), for applications for homelessness assistance made on or after 3 April 2018. See **15.211**.
[6]   See **9.111–9.125** and **9.137–9.140**.

15.102 The decision must be notified in writing to the applicant[1]. If the notification is not received by the applicant, then it is treated as having been given to the applicant if it is made available at the local housing authority's office for a reasonable period for collection by or on behalf of the applicant[2].

[1]   HA 1996, s 195(9), as amended by HRA 2017, s 4(2), for applications for homelessness assistance made on or after 3 April 2018, see **15.99–15.102**.
[2]   HA 1996, s 195(9), as amended by HRA 2017, s 4(2), for applications for homelessness assistance made on or after 3 April 2018, see **15.211**.

15.103 The decision to serve a notice ending the duty[1] is a discretionary one. Even if the statutory criteria are met, the local housing authority may decide not to end the duty[2].

[1]   Whether under HA 1996, s 195(5) or s 193B(2), as amended by HRA 2017, s 4(2) and inserted by HRA 2017, s 7(1), for applications for homelessness assistance made on or after 3 April 2018.

15.104 Each of these events will now be considered in more detail.

Suitable accommodation is available for occupation by the applicant and there is a reasonable prospect that accommodation will be available for at least six months

15.105 The HA 1996, s 195(2)[1], prevention duty can be brought to an end if the local housing authority is satisfied that *all* of the following conditions are met:

- the applicant has suitable accommodation[2];
- the accommodation is available for occupation[3] by the applicant, and by all the members of his or her household[4]; and
- there is a reasonable prospect that suitable accommodation will be available for the applicant's occupation for at least six months[5].

The local housing authority must be 'satisfied' of all these different requirements[6]. This requires something more on the local housing authority's part than simply an assumption.

1   As amended by HRA 2017, s 4(2), for applications for homelessness assistance made on or after 3 April 2018.
2   For 'suitable' accommodation, see CHAPTER **18**.
3   As defined at HA 1996, ss 175–177, see CHAPTER **10**.
4   As defined at HA 1996, s 176, see **10.21–10.33**.
5   HA 1996, s 195(8)(a), as amended by HRA 2017, s 4(2), for applications for homelessness assistance made on or after 3 April 2018. The period of six months could be extended to a longer period of no more than 12 months if the Secretary of State so prescribes: HA 1996, s 195(8)(a), as amended by HRA 2017, s 4(2), for applications for homelessness assistance made on or after 3 April 2018.
6   HA 1996, s 195(8), as amended by HRA 2017, s 4(2), for applications for homelessness assistance made on or after 3 April 2018.

15.106 The accommodation that has become available might be the applicant's existing home, from which the applicant had originally been threatened with homelessness[1]. For example, the local housing authority might have helped the applicant to negotiate a new tenancy with his or her landlord. Alternatively, the applicant might have been helped to secure new accommodation.

1   HA 1996, s 175(4) and (5), as amended by HRA 2017, s 4(2), for applications for homelessness assistance made on or after 3 April 2018. See **10.144–10.147**.

15.107 HA 1996, s 195(8)(a)[1] does not stipulate that it should be the same unit of accommodation which must be available for six months, as long as some suitable accommodation is available. Potentially then, the requirement might be met by means of two or more units of accommodation available one after the other for an aggregate period of six months or more. However, where a local housing authority is considering accommodation which is not yet available, it will need a sufficient basis to be 'satisfied' that there is a 'reasonable prospect' it will be available. The English Code advises that where

787

an applicant with support needs is placed in short term accommodation, as part of a planned accommodation and support pathway, there should be a clear, documented expectation that he or she will be supported to make a planned move directly to more supported accommodation or independent accommodation[2].

1   As amended by HRA 2017, s 4(2), for applications for homelessness assistance made on or after 3 April 2018.
2   English Code, paras 14.11.

15.108 As already observed, there must be 'a reasonable prospect' that the accommodation will continue to be available for at least six months[1]. What is 'a reasonable prospect? Obviously if the applicant is granted a fixed-term tenancy, for a term of six months or more, the local housing authority could be satisfied that there is a reasonable prospect that the accommodation will continue to be available for that period. In the case of more informal arrangements, such as accommodation provided by family or friends, the local housing authority would want something more than a mere assurance that it might be available for that period. The English Code contains advice to deal with two specific circumstances:

- where the applicant is permitted to remain in his or her existing accommodation by the landlord, but a Housing Act 1988, s 21 notice was previously issued, the landlord should be asked to issue a new tenancy. If he or she refuses, the local housing authority could secure written confirmation that the applicant can remain on condition that he or she complies with documented conditions. Provided that the local housing authority has a reasonable expectation that the applicant can comply, the guidance in the English Code is that there is likely to be a reasonable prospect of availability[2];
- where the applicant is staying with friends or family, the local housing authority must satisfy itself that the accommodation will be available for at least six months, either with an open-ended agreement (perhaps with reasonable conditions) or an agreement that the applicant can stay until he or she has secured alternative accommodation[3].

1   HA 1996, s 195(8)(a)(ii), as amended by HRA 2017, s 4(2), for applications for homelessness assistance made on or after 3 April 2018. The period of six months could be extended to a longer period of no more than 12 months if the Secretary of State so prescribes: HA 1996, s 195(8)(a), as amended by HRA 2017, s 4(2), for applications for homelessness assistance made on or after 3 April 2018.
2   English Code, paras 14.8–14.9.
3   English Code, para 14.10.

15.109 The period of six months begins on the day when the local housing authority notifies the applicant of its decision that the duty has come to an end (or has made the notification available for collection at its office)[1].

1   HA 1996, s 195(5), (8)(a)(i)(ii) and (9), as amended by HRA 2017, s 4(2), for applications for homelessness assistance made on or after 3 April 2018. See **15.37–15.38**.

The local housing authority has complied with its HA 1996, s 195(2) prevention duty for a period of 56 days

15.110 The HA 1996, s 195(2)[1], prevention duty can be brought to an end where the local housing authority is satisfied that:

- it has complied with the duty to take 'reasonable steps' for a period of 56 days[2];
- that period began on the day on which the local housing authority was first satisfied that the duty was owed[3]; and
- the applicant has not been served with a valid Housing Act 1988, s 21, notice which is due to expire within 56 days, or has expired[4].

The local housing authority must be 'satisfied' of all these different requirements[5].

[1]   As amended by HRA 2017, s 4(2), for applications for homelessness assistance made on or after 3 April 2018.
[2]   HA 1996, s 195(8)(b), as amended by HRA 2017, s 4(2), for applications for homelessness assistance made on or after 3 April 2018; English Code, paras 14.13–14.19.
[3]   HA 1996, ss 195(1) and (8)(b), as amended by HRA 2017, s 4(2), for applications for homelessness assistance made on or after 3 April 2018. For the possible distinction between the local housing authority being satisfied that the duty was owed, and the notification of that decision to the applicant, see **15.137**.
[4]   HA 1996, s 195(6), as amended by HRA 2017, s 4(2), for applications for homelessness assistance made on or after 3 April 2018. The HA 1988, s 21 notice in this context must relate to the only accommodation that is available for the applicant's occupation.
[5]   HA 1996, s 195(8), as amended by HRA 2017, s 4(2), for applications for homelessness assistance made on or after 3 April 2018.

15.111 If, at the end of the 56-day period in which the local housing authority was performing its HA 1996, s 195(2)[1], prevention duty, the applicant is still threatened with homelessness, there is generally no longer any duty on the local housing authority to continue to help the applicant. However, if the applicant was served with a valid Housing Act 1988, s 21, notice in respect of the only accommodation which is available for his or her occupation, and that notice either has expired, or is due to expire within 56 days, the local housing authority cannot bring its duty to an end on this ground[2]. It must continue to take reasonable steps to help the applicant secure that accommodation does not cease to be available. The Housing Act 1988, s 21, notice might have been served on the applicant on or before the applicant made his or her application for homelessness assistance, and might be the reason why the local housing authority was satisfied that the applicant was threatened with homelessness[3]. Alternatively, the applicant might have made his or her application for homelessness assistance and have been found to have been threatened with homelessness for some other reason, but later received a valid Housing Act 1988, s 21, notice.

[1]   As amended by HRA 2017, s 4(2), for applications for homelessness assistance made on or after 3 April 2018.
[2]   HA 1996, s 195(6), as amended by HRA 2017, s 4(2), for applications for homelessness assistance made on or after 3 April 2018; English Code, paras 14.13.
[3]   HA 1996, s 175(5), as inserted by HRA 2017, s 1(3), for applications for homelessness assistance made on or after 3 April 2018. See **10.147**.

15.112 If the applicant remains threatened with homelessness for some reason other than having been served with a valid Housing Act 1988, s 21, notice[1], and the local housing authority has not been able to help the applicant resolve the situation within 56 days, the local housing authority is no longer under a duty to continue to help the applicant. However, the English Code makes it clear that a local housing authority may choose to continue the duty for a longer period, and that local housing authorities should not have blanket policies of ending the duty after 56 days. In each case, the applicant's circumstances should be taken into account. It is in both the applicant's and the local housing authority's interests to continue the HA 1996, s 195(2)[2] prevention duty, in order to work to help the applicant avoid homelessness, since if the applicant becomes homeless a HA 1996, s 189B(2)[3], relief duty will arise[4].

[1] Such as having been told to leave by a licensor, or being subject to a possession order which has not yet been enforced. See **10.144–10.146.**
[2] As amended by HRA 2017, s 4(2), for applications for homelessness assistance made on or after 3 April 2018.
[3] As inserted by HRA 2017, s 5(2), for applications for homelessness assistance made on or after 3 April 2018; see **15.138–15.195.**
[4] English Code, paras 14.15–14.18.

The applicant has become homeless

15.113 If, despite the steps taken by both the applicant and the local housing authority, the applicant becomes homeless, the HA 1996, s 195(2)[1], prevention duty can be brought to an end. The local housing authority must be 'satisfied' that the applicant has become homeless[2].

[1] As amended by HRA 2017, s 4(2), for applications for homelessness assistance made on or after 3 April 2018.
[2] HA 1996, s 195(8)(c), as amended by HRA 2017, s 4(2), for applications for homelessness assistance made on or after 3 April 2018; English Code, paras 14.20–14.22.

15.114 The definition of 'homeless' is at HA 1996, ss 175–177[1]. The applicant might have become homeless because he or she has left the accommodation, whether voluntarily or not. Alternatively the accommodation might have become unreasonable for the applicant and his or her household to continue to occupy[2].

[1] See CHAPTER 10.
[2] HA 1996, s 175(3), see **10.73–10.134.**

15.115 Although the HA 1996, s 195(2)[1], prevention duty will have ended, this does not mean that the applicant can be abandoned by the local housing authority. The change in circumstances from the applicant having been threatened with homelessness to becoming homeless will mean that the local housing authority must review its assessment of the applicant's case and notify the applicant in writing accordingly[2].

[1] As amended by HRA 2017, s 4(2), for applications for homelessness assistance made on or after 3 April 2018.
[2] HA 1996, s 189A(2)(a) and (10)(a), as inserted by HRA 2017, s 3(1), for applications for homelessness assistance made on or after 3 April 2018. See English Code, para 14.22 and **15.81–15.86.**

15.116 Provided that the applicant remains eligible for assistance[1], the local housing authority will now owe the applicant the HA 1996, s 189B(2)[2], relief duty to take reasonable steps to secure that suitable accommodation becomes available for the applicant's occupation, and for the members of his or her household. The English Code advises that the local housing authority will want to provide a 'seamless transition' between the two duties[3].

1   HA 1996, s 185, see CHAPTER 10.
2   As inserted by HRA 2017, s 5(2), for applications for homelessness assistance made on or after 3 April 2018. See **15.138–15.195**.
3   English Code, para 14.20.

15.117 In addition, if the local housing authority has reason to believe that the applicant may have a priority need, the local housing authority will have a duty to secure interim accommodation for the applicant and the members of his or her household[1]. The English Code advises that this should be arranged as a priority[2].

1   HA 1996, s 188(1), (1ZA) and (1ZB), as inserted by HRA 2017, s 5(4), for applications for homelessness assistance made on or after 3 April 2018. See **16.37–16.50**.
2   English Code, para 14.21.

The applicant has refused an offer of suitable accommodation where there was a reasonable prospect that it would be available for occupation for at least six months

15.118 The HA 1996, s 195(2)[1], prevention duty can be brought to an end if the local housing authority is satisfied that:

- the applicant was made an offer of accommodation;
- the accommodation was suitable for the needs of the applicant and members of his or her household[2];
- the applicant refused the offer; and
- on the date of refusal, there was a reasonable prospect that suitable accommodation would be available for occupation[3] by the applicant and all the members of his or her household[4] for at least six months[5].

The local housing authority must be 'satisfied' of all these different requirements[6]. This requires something more on the local housing authority's part than simply an assumption.

1   As amended by HRA 2017, s 4(2), for applications for homelessness assistance made on or after 3 April 2018.
2   For 'suitable' accommodation, see CHAPTER 18. By s 206(1) Housing Act 1996, a local housing authority must discharge its functions by (among other things) securing that suitable accommodation is 'available'. This refers to HA 1996, s 176: 'accommodation shall be regarded as available only if it is available for occupation by [the applicant] together with any other person who normally resides with him as a member of his family, or any other person who might reasonably be expected to reside with him'. The combined effect of these two provisions is that suitable accommodation must be available for the applicant and his household, which carries with it the implication that the accommodation must be suitable for all such persons, and not solely the applicant. See English Code, paras 16.3 and 17.2 and *R v Newham London Borough Council ex parte Sacupima* [2001] 1 WLR 563, CA, at [28]–[32].
3   As defined at HA 1996, s 175–177, see CHAPTER 10.
4   As defined at HA 1996, s 176, see **10.21–10.32**.
5   HA 1996, s 195(8)(d), as amended by HRA 2017, s 4(2), for applications for homelessness assistance made on or after 3 April 2018. The period of six months could be extended to a longer period of no more than 12 months if the Secretary of State so prescribes: HA 1996,

s 195(8)(d), as amended by HRA 2017, s 4(2), for applications for homelessness assistance made on or after 3 April 2018. See **15.37–15.38**.
[6] HA 1996, s 195(8), as amended by HRA 2017, s 4(2), for applications for homelessness assistance made on or after 3 April 2018.

15.119 The meanings of 'suitable' and 'available' accommodation are discussed at **15.32–15.35**. Readers are also referred to the discussion of HA 1996, s 195(8)(a)[1], which allows the local housing authority to bring the HA 1996, s 195(2)[2] prevention duty to an end when the equivalent offer is accepted[3].

[1] As amended by HRA 2017, s 4(2), for applications for homelessness assistance made on or after 3 April 2018.
[2] As amended by HRA 2017, s 4(2), for applications for homelessness assistance made on or after 3 April 2018.
[3] See **15.105–15.109**.

15.120 Normally this offer of alternative accommodation will have been as a result of the local housing authority's help given to the applicant to prevent his or her homelessness. It might be that the local housing authority had been able to persuade the applicant's existing landlord to make the applicant an offer of a new tenancy of the current home. It might have been that the offer came from the local housing authority, under its allocation scheme, or from a private registered provider[1]. Or the offer might have come from family or friends making suitable accommodation available on an informal basis[2].

[1] The applicant will have been entitled to a reasonable preference under the local housing authority's allocation scheme because the HA 1996, s 195(2), as amended by HRA 2017, s 4(2), for applications for homelessness assistance made on or after 3 April 2018, prevention duty was owed to him or her: HA 1996, s 166A(3)(b), see **4.67–4.79**.
[2] See **15.35**.

15.121 There is nothing in HA 1996, s 195[1], setting out any form in which the offer must have been made. There is no requirement that the offer was made in writing, or that it was accompanied with an explanation of the consequences of refusal.

[1] As amended by HRA 2017, s 4(2), for applications for homelessness assistance made on or after 3 April 2018.

15.122 Given that the local housing authority must be 'satisfied' that all of these conditions are met, this requires a local housing authority to consider carefully any reasons that are put forward by the applicant, or are otherwise apparent to the local housing authority, as to why the accommodation offered might not have been suitable. The local housing authority will also need a sufficient basis to be 'satisfied' that there was a reasonable prospect that the accommodation would have been available for occupation for at least six months[1]. The period of six months begins from the date when the applicant refused the offer of accommodation.

[1] The period of six months could be extended to a longer period of no more than 12 months if the Secretary of State so prescribes: HA 1996, s 195(8)(d), as amended by HRA 2017, s 4(2), for applications for homelessness assistance made on or after 3 April 2018, see **15.37–15.38**.

The applicant has become homeless intentionally from any accommodation made available to him or her as a result of the local housing authority's exercise of its functions under the HA 1996, s 195(2), prevention duty

15.123 The HA 1996, s 195(2)[1], prevention duty can be brought to an end when the local housing authority is satisfied that:

- the applicant occupied accommodation made available to him or her pursuant to the local housing authority's functions under the HA 1996, s 195(2)[2], prevention duty[3];
- the applicant has ceased to occupy that accommodation;
- the cessation of occupation was due to a deliberate act or omission (which does not include an act or omission in good faith by a person unaware of a material fact);
- that deliberate act, or omission, was by the applicant;
- that deliberate act or omission was an operative cause of the applicant's homelessness;
- the accommodation was available for the applicant's occupation, and for the members of his or her household; and
- the accommodation was reasonable for the applicant and his or her household to continue to occupy[4].

[1] As amended by HRA 2017, s 4(2) for applications for homelessness assistance made on or after 3 April 2018.
[2] As amended by HRA 2017, s 4(2) for applications for homelessness assistance made on or after 3 April 2018.
[3] HA 1996, s 195(8)(e), as amended by HRA 2017, s 4(2), for applications for homelessness assistance made on or after 3 April 2018; English Code, paras 14.29–14.31.
[4] These last six conditions are the elements of the 'becoming homeless intentionally' test at HA 1996, s 191, see Chapter **13**.

15.124 The local housing authority must be 'satisfied' that all these conditions are made out[1]. If there is any doubt, the duty will not have ended.

[1] HA 1996, s 195(8), as amended by HRA 2017, s 4(2), for applications for homelessness assistance made on or after 3 April 2018.

15.125 The first condition makes it clear that the accommodation that the applicant has ceased to occupy must have been made available to the applicant pursuant to the HA 1996, s 195(2)[1], prevention duty. It would be unusual for the local housing authority to have secured accommodation for the applicant under this duty, first, because the applicant is threatened with homelessness, and not actually homeless, and secondly because the duty is only to take reasonable steps to help the applicant prevent his or her homelessness[2]. The cases in which a local housing authority regards it as 'reasonable' to secure accommodation for an applicant who is not yet homeless will probably be rare. This means that instances where an applicant has become homeless intentionally from any such accommodation are likely to be rarer still.

[1] As amended by HRA 2017, s 4(2), for applications for homelessness assistance made to local housing authorities on or after 3 April 2018, see **15.87–15.137**.
[2] There is a power to secure accommodation at HA 1996, s 205(3), as inserted by HRA 2017, s 5(12), for applications for homelessness assistance made to local housing authorities on or after 3 April 2018 and English Code, para 14.30, envisages the possibility, see **13.239–13.247** and **16.278–16.279**.

The applicant is no longer eligible for assistance

15.126 The local housing authority must be 'satisfied' that the applicant is no longer eligible for assistance[1]. 'Eligible for assistance' is defined at HA 1996, s 185, and discussed at Chapter 11. The HA 1996, s 193(2) main housing duty can come to an end for this reason[2] and readers are referred to the discussion at Chapter 16[3].

[1] HA 1996, s 195(8)(f), as amended by HRA 2017, s 4(2), for applications for homelessness assistance made on or after 3 April 2018; English Code, para 14.33.
[2] HA 1996, s 193(6)(a).
[3] See **16.124–16.127**. For an example of the HA 1996, s 193(2), main housing duty coming to an end for this reason, see *Tower Hamlets London Borough Council v Deugi* [2006] EWCA Civ 159, [2006] HLR 28, CA.

15.127 If the applicant's household includes a child aged under 18, the applicant will be asked to consent to a referral of the essential facts of his or her case to children's services. The English Code contains advice that when interim accommodation is brought to an end, the period of notice should take account of the applicant's needs and of the time required for him or her to access assistance, and that the local housing authority should consider having arrangements in place to manage a transition in responsibility from housing to adult or children's services, so that there is no break in the provision of accommodation[1].

[1] English Code, para 14.32.

The applicant has withdrawn his or her application

15.128 The local housing authority must be 'satisfied' that the applicant has withdrawn his or her application[1]. It cannot rely on ambiguity. An unequivocal written warning would be sufficient for the local housing authority to be satisfied. But what if the wording is ambiguous? What if the applicant simply falls silent and fails to respond to communications from the local housing authority? Or if he or she verbally informs the local housing adviser that he or she has withdrawn, or intends to withdraw, the application? Can those circumstances be interpreted as the applicant withdrawing his or her application?

[1] HA 1996, s 195(8)(g), as amended by HRA 2017, s 4(2), for applications for homelessness assistance made to local housing authorities in England on or after 3 April 2018; English Code, paras 14.33–14.34.

15.129 The only guidance in the English Code is in relation to the situation where the applicant fails to keep in contact with the local housing authority. In those circumstances, it recommends that local housing authorities should have procedures in place to attempt to maintain or regain contact with applicants, and should use a variety of communication channels[1].

[1] English Code, para 14.31.

15.130 The local housing authority's decision that the duty has come to an end for this reason must be notified to the applicant in writing[1]. If the applicant were to respond to this notification, and dispute the decision, that would probably be sufficient for the local housing authority to find that the applicant has not withdrawn his or her application.

1   HA 1996, s 195(5) and (7), as amended by HRA 2017, s 4(2), for applications for homelessness assistance made on or after 3 April 2018.

15.131 In addition, the applicant has the right to request a review of this decision that the duty has come to an end[1]. If the applicant requests a review disputing the decision, that very action may suggest that the application has not in fact been withdrawn.

1   HA 1996, s 202(1)(bc)(ii), as amended by HRA 2017, s 9, for applications for homelessness assistance made on or after 3 April 2018. See **19.42–19.48**.

Decision that an applicant has deliberately and unreasonably refused to co-operate

15.132 A new provision at HA 1996, s 193B[1], permits a local housing authority to decide that an applicant has deliberately and unreasonably refused to co-operate[2]. The consequences of this decision are that the HA 1996, s 195(2)[3], prevention duty will come to an end[4]. This provision is further discussed at **15.196–15.221**.

1   As inserted by HRA 2017, s 7(1), for applications for homelessness assistance made on or after 3 April 2018.
2   HA 1996, s 193B(2), as inserted by HRA 2017, s 7(1), for applications for homelessness assistance made on or after 3 April 2018; English Code, paras 14.35–14.36 and 14.43–14.59.
3   As amended by HRA 2017, s 4(2), for applications for homelessness assistance made on or after 3 April 2018.
4   HA 1996, s 193C(2) as inserted by HRA 2017, s 7(1), for applications for homelessness assistance made on or after 3 April 2018. See **15.216–15.218**.

The right to request a review

15.133 The applicant has the right to request a review[1] of the following decisions made by the local housing authority that might be relevant to the HA 1996, s 195(2)[2], prevention duty:

* whether or not he or she is eligible for assistance[3];
* whether or not the HA 1996, s 195(2)[4], prevention duty is owed[5];
* what steps the local housing authority is to take in order to perform its HA 1996, s 195(2)[6] prevention duty[7];
* whether or not any accommodation offered in discharge of the HA 1996, s 195(2)[8], prevention duty is suitable[9];
* to give notice to the applicant that the HA 1996, s 195(2)[10], prevention duty has come to an end because the local housing authority is satisfied that one of the circumstances set out in HA 1996, s 195(8) has occurred[11]; and
* to give notice to the applicant of a decision under HA 1996, s 193B(2)[12], that he or she has deliberately and unreasonably refused to

co-operate[13].

1   HA 1996, s 202(1), as amended by HRA 2017, s 9, for applications for homelessness assistance made on or after 3 April 2018. See **19.8–19.69** for a discussion of the right to review and procedure.
2   As inserted by HRA 2017, s 4(2), for applications for homelessness assistance made on or after 3 April 2018.
3   HA 1996, s 202(1)(a), as amended by HRA 2017, s 9, for applications for homelessness assistance made on or after 3 April 2018. For 'eligible for assistance' see HA 1996, s 185, and CHAPTER **11**. See **19.14**.
4   As amended by HRA 2017, s 4(2), for applications for homelessness assistance made on or after 3 April 2018. See **15.87–15.137**.
5   HA 1996, s 202(1)(b), as amended by HRA 2017, s 9, for applications for homelessness assistance made on or after 3 April 2018. See **19.15–19.17**.
6   As amended by HRA 2017, s 4(2), for applications for homelessness assistance made on or after 3 April 2018. See **15.87–15.137**.
7   HA 1996, s 202(1)(bc)(i), as inserted by HRA 2017, s 9, for applications for homelessness assistance made on or after 3 April 2018. See **19.36–19.41**. For the steps to be taken by the local housing authority, see HA 1996, s 189A(4)(b) and (6)(c), as inserted by HRA 2017, s 3(1), for applications for homelessness assistance made on or after 3 April 2018. See **15.91–15.96**.
8   As amended by HRA 2017, s 4(2), for applications for homelessness assistance made on or after 3 April 2018. See **15.87–15.137**.
9   HA 1996, s 202(1)(f), see **19.59–19.62**.
10   As amended by HRA 2017, s 4(2), for applications for homelessness assistance made on or after 3 April 2018. See **15.87–15.137**.
11   As amended by HRA 2017, s 4(2), for applications for homelessness assistance made on or after 3 April 2018. See **15.92–15.132**. HA 1996, s 202(1)(bc)(ii), as inserted by HRA 2017, s 9, for applications for homelessness assistance made on or after 3 April 2018. See **19.42–19.48**. For the circumstances that bring the HA 1996, s 195(2), prevention duty to an end, see HA 1996, s 195(8) and (10), as amended by HRA 2017, s 4(2), for applications for homelessness assistance made on or after 3 April 2018. See **19.42–19.48**.
12   As inserted by HRA 2017, s 7(1), for applications for homelessness assistance made on or after 3 April 2018. See **15.196–15.221**.
13   HA 1996, s 202(1)(bb), as inserted by HRA 2017, s 9, for applications for homelessness assistance made on or after 3 April 2018. See **19.30–19.35**.

15.134 If the applicant wishes to request a review of the suitability of accommodation offered, then caution would suggest that the applicant should accept the offer of accommodation[1]. If the review is unsuccessful, the applicant will at least have some accommodation. If the applicant refuses the accommodation and the review is unsuccessful, he or she may be without any accommodation at all[2].

1   The right to accept whilst also requesting a review is at HA 1996, s 202(1)(g) and (h), as inserted by HRA 2017, s 9, for applications for homelessness assistance made on or after 3 April 2018, see **19.90–19.99**.
2   There is nothing at HA 1996, s 202(1) (as amended by HRA 2017, s 9 for applications for homelessness assistance made on or after 3 April 2018) which specifically provides for an applicant who is made an offer of accommodation under the HA 1996, s 195(2) (as amended by HRA 2017, s 4(2), for applications for homelessness assistance made on or after 3 April 2018) prevention duty both to accept the accommodation offered and to request a review of its suitability. However, if the applicant is contemplating refusing an offer of accommodation, he or she would be advised to accept the offer instead and then, when notified of the local housing authority's decision that the HA 1996, s 195(2) (as amended by HRA 2017, s 4(2), for applications for homelessness assistance made on or after 3 April 2018) prevention duty has come to an end because the applicant has accepted an offer of suitable accommodation, which is available for occupation for at least six months (under HA 1996, s 195(8)(a), as amended by HRA 2017, s 4(2), for applications for homelessness assistance made on or after 3 April 2018), the applicant would have a right to request a review of that decision and to make representations as to why the accommodation was not suitable: HA 1996, s 202(1(b) (as

amended by HRA 2017, s 9, for applications for homelessness assistance made on or after 3 April 2018).

15.135 A review must be requested within 21 days of the applicant being notified of the relevant decision, which is the date when the applicant received the decision. If the applicant did not receive the notice, and the local housing authority made the notice available at its office for a reasonable period for collection by or on behalf of the applicant, the date of notification will be the end of that period[1].

[1] HA 1996, s 195(9), as amended by HRA 2017, s 4(2) and s 193B(8), as inserted by HRA 2017, s 7(1), for applications for homelessness assistance made on or after 3 April 2018.

What happens after the HA 1996, s 195(2) prevention duty has ended?

15.136 The fact that the HA 1996, s 195(2) prevention duty has come to an end does not necessarily mean that no further duty will be owed to the applicant. What happens next for the applicant depends on what his or her circumstances are:

- If the applicant has become ineligible for assistance, then no further duty will be owed.
- If the applicant has secured accommodation, then he or she will not be homeless or threatened with homelessness, and no further duty will be owed.
- If the applicant remains threatened with homelessness, then he or she will be owed no further duty[1].
- If the applicant has become homeless, then the HA 1996, s 189B(2)[2] relief duty arises. This applies even if, for example, the applicant refused an offer of suitable accommodation[3]. There is no need for the applicant to make a fresh application for homelessness assistance because the local housing authority will have notified the applicant that the HA 1996, s 195(2)[4], prevention duty has come to an end because the applicant has become homeless[5]. The local housing authority will also have notified the applicant that its assessment of his or her case has changed, because he or she was previously threatened with homelessness, and is now homeless[6].

[1] Unless the applicant has been served with a valid Housing Act 1988, s 21, notice that either will expire within 56 days or has expired, and is in respect of the only accommodation that is available for his or her occupation. In those circumstances, the HA 1996, s 195(2), prevention duty continues: HA 1996, s 195(6), as amended by HRA 2017, s 4(2), for applications for homelessness assistance made on or after 3 April 2018. See **15.111**.
[2] As inserted by HRA 2017, s 5(2), for applications for homelessness assistance made on or after 3 April 2018.
[3] See **15.118–15.122**.
[4] As amended by HRA 2017, s 4(2), for applications for homelessness assistance made on or after 3 April 2018.
[5] HA 1996, s 195(8)(c), as amended by HRA 2017, s 4(2), for applications for homelessness assistance made on or after 3 April 2018, see **15.123–15.125**.
[6] HA 1996, s 189A(10), as inserted by HRA 2017, s 3(1), for applications for homelessness assistance made on or after 3 April 2018. English Code, paras 11.32–11.35 and 14.20–14.22, see **8.80–8.82** and **8.85–8.91**.

15.137 Even if no further duty is owed, the applicant may make a further application for homelessness assistance. If the factual circumstances are not the same as they were at the time when the earlier application for homelessness assistance was disposed of (namely the circumstances at the time the HA 1996, s 195(2)[1], prevention duty came to an end), the local housing authority must accept the application and make inquiries into what duty, if any, is owed to the applicant[2].

[1]   As amended by HRA 2017, s 4(2), for applications for homelessness assistance made on or after 3 April 2018.
[2]   The English Code contains advice that in the majority of re-application cases where the applicant has previously refused an offer of suitable accommodation, the local housing authority will be entitled to rely on the ending of its duty. However, if the applicant's factual circumstances have changed, the local housing authority must accept the fresh application: English Code, paras 18.11–13.13 and particularly para 18.12. See **8.80–8.82** and **8.85–8.91** for discussion of further applications.

DUTY TO TAKE REASONABLE STEPS TO HELP THE APPLICANT TO SECURE THAT SUITABLE ACCOMMODATION BECOMES AVAILABLE FOR HIS OR HER OCCUPATION: 'THE RELIEF DUTY'

Applicants entitled to the duty

15.138 The HA 1996, s 189B(2)[1], relief duty is owed to applicants whom the local housing authority is satisfied are[2]:

- eligible for assistance[3]; and
- homeless[4].

However, where a local housing authority has notified the applicant that it intends to notify, or has notified, another local housing authority of its opinion that the conditions are met for the referral of the applicant's case to that other local housing authority, the HA 1996, s 189B(2)[5], relief duty will not be owed to the applicant[6].

[1]   As inserted by HRA 2017, s 5(2), for applications for homelessness assistance made on or after 3 April 2018; English Code, chapter 13.
[2]   HA 1996, s 189B(1) and (2), as inserted by HRA 2017, s 5(2), for applications for homelessness assistance made on or after 3 April 2018.
[3]   HA 1996, s 185, see Chapter **11**.
[4]   HA 1996, ss 175–177, see Chapter **10**.
[5]   As inserted by HRA 2017, s 5(2), for applications for homelessness assistance made on or after 3 April 2018.
[6]   HA 1996, ss 189B(2) and 199A(1), as inserted by HRA 2017, s 5(2) and (9), for applications for homelessness assistance made on or after 3 April 2018, see **15.139–15.146**.

Referral of HA 1996, s 189B(2), relief duty to another local housing authority

15.139 If the local housing authority decides that the conditions for referral to another local housing authority are met, it may choose to refer the applicant's case to another local housing authority for that local housing authority to perform the HA 1996, s 189B(2)[1], relief duty.[2] Once it has notified the applicant that it has notified, or intends to notify, another local housing authority of its opinion that the conditions for referral are met, it is not subject to the HA 1996, s 189B(2)[3] relief duty[4]. The applicant does not have the right to request a review of that decision[5].

[1]   As inserted by HRA 2017, s 5(2), for applications for homelessness assistance made on or after 3 April 2018, see **15.138–15.195**.
[2]   HA 1996, s 198(A1) as inserted by HRA 2017, s 5(2), for applications for homelessness assistance made on or after 3 April 2018, and HA 1996, s 198(2)–(4).
[3]   As inserted by HRA 2017, s 5(2), for applications for homelessness assistance made on or after 3 April 2018.
[4]   HA 1996, s 199A(1)(b), as inserted by HRA 2017, s 5(9), for applications for homelessness assistance made on or after 3 April 2018; English Code, para 13.4.
[5]   Because the only right to request a review of a decision to notify another local housing authority applies to decisions made under HA 1996, s 198(1), which permits a local housing authority to refer performance of the HA 1996, s 193(2) main housing duty: HA 202(1)(c), see **19.49–19.54**.

15.140 The conditions for referral are discussed at CHAPTER 14. Even if the local housing authority is satisfied that the conditions for referral are met, it retains a discretion whether or not to refer the performance of the HA 1996, s 189B(2)[1], relief duty to the other local housing authority[2].

[1]   As inserted by HRA 2017, s 5(2), for applications for homelessness assistance made on or after 3 April 2018.
[2]   HA 1996, s 198(A1), as inserted by HRA 2017, s 5(8), for applications for homelessness assistance made on or after 3 April 2018, see English Code, para 10.30 and 13.4.

15.141 If it is decided that the conditions for referral are met[1], the applicant will be notified by the notifying local housing authority of that decision and the reasons for it[2]. The applicant will have the right to request a review of that decision[3]. Performance of the HA 1996, s 189B(2)[4], relief duty will become the responsibility of the notified local housing authority[5]. The notifying local housing authority should send to the notified local housing authority its assessment of the applicant's case and the personalised housing plan, if completed[6].

[1]   By agreement between the two local housing authorities, or by a referee's decision, see HA 1996, s 198(5) and **14.176–14.190**.
[2]   HA 1996, s 199A(3), as inserted by HRA 2017, s 5(9), for applications for homelessness assistance made on or after 3 April 2018.
[3]   HA 1996, s 202(1)(d), see **19.55–19.57**.
[4]   As inserted by HRA 2017, s 5(2), for applications for homelessness assistance made on or after 3 April 2018.
[5]   HA 1996, s 199A(5), as inserted by HRA 2017, s 5(9), for applications for homelessness assistance made on or after 3 April 2018.
[6]   English Code, para 10.43. The English Code suggests that the applicant's consent will be needed for a copy of his or her personalised plan to be sent to the notified local housing authority.

15.142 If it is decided that the conditions for referral are not met, the applicant will be notified of that decision and the notifying local housing authority becomes subject to the HA 1996, s 189B(2)[1], relief duty[2]. The 56-day period during which the local housing authority should perform the HA 1996, s 189B(2)[3], relief duty will commence from the day when the applicant is notified of the decision that the conditions for referral are not met[4].

[1]   As inserted by HRA 2017, s 5(2), for applications for homelessness assistance made on or after 3 April 2018.

² HA 1996, s 199A(4)(a), as inserted by HRA 2017, s 5(9), for applications for homelessness assistance made on or after 3 April 2018.
³ As inserted by HRA 2017, s 5(2), for applications for homelessness assistance made on or after 3 April 2018.
⁴ HA 1996, s 189B(4) and (7)(b), as inserted by HRA 2017, s 5(2), for applications for homelessness assistance made on or after 3 April 2018, see **15.160–15.161** and **15.166–15.168**. HA 1996, s 199A(4)(b), as inserted by HRA 2017, s 5(9), for applications for homelessness assistance made on or after 3 April 2018.

When does the duty arise?

15.143 The duty arises as soon as the local housing authority is satisfied that an applicant is homeless and is eligible for assistance[1]. The local housing authority must notify the applicant in writing of its decision that the HA 1996, s 189B(2)[2], relief duty is owed to him or her[3]. However, the duty arises as soon as the local housing authority is 'satisfied' that these conditions are met, rather than on the date of notification[4]. If the written decision is notified later than the date on which the local housing authority has concluded that it is 'satisfied' that the applicant is eligible for assistance and is homeless, that is not a reason for the local housing authority to delay in performing its duty[5].

¹ HA 1996, s 189B(1), as inserted by HRA 2017, s 5(2), for applications for homelessness assistance made on or after 3 April 2018; English Code, para 13.2.
² As inserted by HRA 2017, s 5(2), for applications for homelessness assistance made on or after 3 April 2018.
³ HA 1996, s 184(1) and (3), see **9.89–9.126**.
⁴ HA 1996, s 189B(1), as inserted by HRA 2017, s 5(2), for applications for homelessness assistance made on or after 3 April 2018.
⁵ See *Robinson v Hammersmith & Fulham London Borough Council* [2006] EWCA Civ 1122, [2006] 1 WLR 3295, [2007] HLR 7, CA, for an example of a decision being taken on one day, and notification on another day, and see **9.93** and **12.136–12.139**.

Performing the duty

15.144 The duty on the local housing authority is to 'take reasonable steps to help the applicant to secure that suitable accommodation becomes available for the applicant's occupation' for at least six months[1]. The meaning of 'take reasonable steps to help the applicant to secure' is discussed at **15.22–15.26** and the meaning of 'available for occupation' is discussed at **15.32–15.39**.

¹ HA 1996, s 189B(2), as inserted by HRA 2017, s 5(2), for applications for homelessness assistance made on or after 3 April 2018. The period may be extended by the Secretary of State to up to twelve months: HA 1996, s 189B(2), as inserted by HRA 2017, s 5(2), for applications for homelessness assistance made on or after 3 April 2018.

15.145 When the local housing authority is deciding what steps it will take, it must have regard to the assessment of the applicant's case that it will have already undertaken[1]. In the course of the assessment (which may be ongoing), the local housing authority will have considered the circumstances that caused the applicant to become homeless, his or her housing needs, together with those of his or her household, and what support would be necessary for the applicant to find suitable accommodation. The information in the assessment should ensure that the local housing authority is aware of all the information necessary to determine what steps might reasonably be taken to help the applicant secure accommodation. Those 'reasonable steps' will then have been set out in the personalised housing plan, drawn up following the assessment[2].

1   HA 1996, s 189B(3), as inserted by HRA 2017, s 5(2), for applications for homelessness assistance made on or after 3 April 2018. See HA 1996, s 189A, as inserted by HRA, s 3(1), for applications for homelessness assistance made on or after 3 April 2018, and see **15.62–15.71**.
2   HA 1996, s 189A(4)(b) and (6)(b), as inserted by HRA 2017, s 3(1), for applications for homelessness assistance made on or after 3 April 2018. See English Code, paras 11.18–11.23 and para 13.7, and **15.72–15.80**. There is specific guidance as to how to perform the relief duty when dealing with young people aged 16 or 17 in *Prevention of Homelessness and Provision of Accommodation for 16 and 17 year old young people who may be homeless and/or require accommodation* (MHCLG and Department for Education, April 2018), chapter 4.

15.146 The applicant has the right to request a review of the steps that the local housing authority has decided that it is to take under this duty[1]. This is the opportunity for the applicant to challenge the local housing authority if he or she believes that it is not taking sufficient or appropriate steps to help him or her secure accommodation.

1   HA 1996, s 202(1)(ba)(i), as amended by HRA 2017, s 9, for applications for homelessness assistance made on or after 3 April 2018. See **19.18–19.23**.

15.147 The aim is to help the applicant find his or her own accommodation, whether that is social housing, accommodation in the private rented sector or accommodation through some other route such as an informal arrangement from family or friends[1].

1   The applicant will be entitled to reasonable preference within the local housing allocation scheme, because he or she is homeless: HA 1996, s 166A(3)(a), see **4.58–4.66**.

15.148 The English Code contains specific advice on supporting people who are sleeping rough[1]. It also advises that where homelessness is relieved, but the applicant's needs put him or her at risk of a further threat of homelessness, the local housing authority should work with other support services to help the applicant[2].

1   English Code, para 13.7.
2   English Code, para 13.8.

15.149 Any accommodation which is secured must be:

- suitable for the needs of the applicant and the members of his or her household[1];
- available for occupation by the applicant and the members of his or her household[2]; and
- available for occupation for at least six months[3].

The meanings of 'suitable accommodation' and 'available for occupation' are discussed at **15.32–15.39** and Chapter **18**.

1   HA 1996, s 189B(2), as inserted by HRA 2017, s 5(2), for applications for homelessness assistance made on or after 3 April 2018, and HA 1996, s 206(1), see Chapter **18**. By s 206(1) Housing Act 1996, a local housing authority must discharge its functions by (among other things) securing that suitable accommodation is 'available'. This refers to HA 1996, s 176: 'accommodation shall be regarded as available only if it is available for occupation by [the applicant] together with any other person who normally resides with him as a member of his

family, or any other person who might reasonably be expected to reside with him'. The combined effect of these two provisions is that suitable accommodation must be available for the applicant and his household, which carries with it the implication that the accommodation must be suitable for all such persons, and not solely the applicant. See English Code, paras 16.3 and 17.2 and *R v Newham London Borough Council ex parte Sacupima* [2001] 1 WLR 563, CA, at [28]–[32].

2   'Available' is defined at HA 1996, s 175(1) as meaning some legal entitlement to occupy, see **10.17–10.32**.

3   HA 1996, s 189B(2), as inserted by HRA 2017, s 5(2), for applications for homelessness assistance made on or after 3 April 2018. See **8.100–8.107**, **15.56–15.58** and **16.47–16.50** for the special provisions which apply where an applicant is re-applying within two years of acceptance of a private rented sector offer.

Interim accommodation

15.150 If the local housing authority has 'reason to believe' that an applicant 'may' be homeless, 'may' be eligible for assistance and 'may' have a priority need, it is under a duty to secure interim accommodation for the applicant and his or her household[1]. The local housing authority must provide this accommodation whilst it complies with the HA 1996, s 189B(2)[2], relief duty, unless, whilst it is complying, it concludes that the applicant does not have a priority need and notifies the applicant of its decision that, once the HA 1996, s 189B(2)[3], relief duty has come to an end, no further duty will therefore be owed[4].

1   HA 1996, s 188(1), see English Code, para 13.3 and **16.37–16.50**.
2   As inserted by HRA 2017, s 5(2), for applications for homelessness assistance made on or after 3 April 2018.
3   As inserted by HRA 2017, s 5(2), for applications for homelessness assistance made on or after 3 April 2018.
4   HA 1996, s 188(1ZA)(b), as inserted by HRA 2017, s 5(4), for applications for homelessness assistance made on or after 3 April 2018.

How does the HA 1996, s 189B(2), relief duty come to an end

15.151 There are ten circumstances in which the HA 1996, s 189B[1] relief duty can come to an end[2]. They are:

(1)   the local housing authority is satisfied that the applicant has a priority need and has not become homeless intentionally, and 56 days have passed since the day on which the local housing authority was first satisfied that the duty was owed. In this case, the duty will end automatically when the 56 day period has ended[3];

(2)   the local housing authority is satisfied that the applicant has suitable accommodation available for occupation and that there is a reasonable prospect of suitable accommodation being available for occupation for at least six months[4];

(3)   the local housing authority has complied with the relief duty at HA 1996, s 189B(2)[5], for a period of 56 days beginning with the day on which the local housing authority was first satisfied that the duty is owed[6];

(4) the local housing authority is satisfied that the applicant has refused an offer of suitable accommodation and, on the date of the refusal, there was a reasonable prospect that suitable accommodation would be available for occupation by the applicant for at least six months[7];

(5) the local housing authority is satisfied that the applicant has become homeless intentionally from any accommodation that had been made available to the applicant as a result of the local housing authority's exercise of its functions under the HA 1996, s 189B(2)[8], relief duty[9];

(6) the local housing authority is satisfied that the applicant is no longer eligible for assistance[10];

(7) the local housing authority is satisfied that the applicant has withdrawn his or her application for homelessness assistance[11];

(8) the applicant has refused a final accommodation offer, having been informed of the consequences of refusal and of his or her right to request a review of the suitability of the accommodation[12];

(9) the applicant has refused a final Pt 6 offer, having been informed of the consequences of refusal and of his or her right to request a review of the suitability of the accommodation[13]; or

(10) the local housing authority considers that the applicant has deliberately and unreasonably refused to co-operate following a warning[14].

[1] As inserted by HRA 2017, s 5(2), for applications for homelessness assistance made on or after 3 April 2018. See **15.138–15.195**.

[2] HA 1996, s 189B(4)–(9), as inserted by HRA 2017, s 5(2), for applications for homelessness assistance made on or after 3 April 2018 and see English Code, chapter 14.

[3] HA 1996, s 189B(4), as inserted by HRA 2017, s 5(2), for applications for homelessness assistance made on or after 3 April 2018; English Code, paras 14.2–14.3. There is no requirement that the local housing authority notifies the applicant of this circumstance. See **15.160–15.161**.

[4] HA 1996, s 189B(7)(a), as inserted by HRA 2017, s 5(2), for applications for homelessness assistance made on or after 3 April 2018; English Code, paras 14.5–14.12. See **15.162–15.165**. The period of six months could be extended to a longer period of no more than 12 months if the Secretary of State so prescribes: HA 1996, s 189B(7)(a), as amended by HRA 2017, s 5(2), for applications for homelessness assistance made on or after 3 April 2018, see **15.37–15.38**.

[5] As inserted by HRA 2017, s 5(2), for applications for homelessness assistance made on or after 3 April 2018. See **15.138–15.195**.

[6] HA 1996, s 189B(7)(b), as inserted by HRA 2017, s 5(2), for applications for homelessness assistance made on or after 3 April 2018.See English Code, paras 14.13–14.19 and 15.166–15.168. The local housing authority can choose to continue to deliver the HA 1996, s 189B(2), relief duty for longer than 56 days, except where the applicant has a priority need and has not become homeless intentionally: HA 1996, s 189B(4) (as inserted by HRA 2017, s 5(2), for applications for homelessness assistance made on or after 3 April 2018), see English Code, para 14.15.

[7] HA 1996, s 189B(7)(c), as inserted by HRA 2017, s 5(2), for applications for homelessness assistance made on or after 3 April 2018; English Code, paras 14.23–14.28. See **15.169–15.173**. The period of six months could be extended to a longer period of no more than 12 months if the Secretary of State so prescribes: HA 1996, s 189B(7)(c), as inserted by HRA 2017, s 5(2), for applications for homelessness assistance made on or after 3 April 2018, see **15.37–15.38**.

[8] As inserted by HRA 2017, s 5(2), for applications for homelessness assistance made on or after 3 April 2018.

[9] HA 1996, s 189B(7)(d), as inserted by HRA 2017, s 5(2), for applications for homelessness assistance made on or after 3 April 2018; English Code, paras 14.29–14.31. See **15.174–15.177**.

[10] HA 1996, s 189B(7)(e), as inserted by HRA 2017, s 5(2), for applications for homelessness assistance made on or after 3 April 2018; English Code, para 14.32. See **15.178–15.179**.

11 HA 1996, s s 189B(7)(f) as inserted by HRA 2017, s 5(2), for applications for homelessness assistance made on or after 3 April 2018; English Code, paras 14.33–14.34. See **15.180**.

12 HA 1996, ss 189B(9)(a) and 193A(2) as inserted by HRA 2017, s 5(2) and 7(1), for applications for homelessness assistance made on or after 3 April 2018; English Code, para 14.26 and CHAPTER 15. See **15.181–15.184**.

13 HA 1996, ss 189B(9)(a) and 193A(2) as inserted by HRA 2017, s 5(2) and 7(1), for applications for homelessness assistance made on or after 3 April 2018; English Code, para 14.26. See **15.185–15.188**.

14 HA 1996, ss 189B(9)(b) and 193C(2), as inserted by HRA 2017, s s 5(2) and 7(1), for applications for homelessness assistance made on or after 3 April 2018; English Code, paras 14.35–14.36 and 14.43–14.5. See **15.189** and **15.196–15.221**.

When the applicant must be notified in writing

15.152 There is no obligation to notify the applicant of the first circumstance[1]. It is an automatic consequence at the end of the 56 day period that the HA 1996, s 189B(2), relief duty ends where an applicant has a priority need and has not become homeless intentionally. The HA 1996, s 193(2), main housing duty will arise[2].

1 HA 1996, s 189B(4), as inserted by HRA 2017, s 5(2), for applications for homelessness assistance made on or after 3 April 2018, see English Code, para 14.3 and see **15.160–15.161**.
2 See **16.94–16.199**.

15.153 For the second to seventh circumstances inclusive, the applicant must be notified in writing of the local housing authority's decision that the relevant circumstances have been met[1]. The duty does not come to an end until that notification has been given.

1 HA 1996, s 189B(5)–(8), as inserted by HRA 2017, s 5(2), for applications for homelessness assistance made on or after 3 April 2018. See English Code, paras 14.40–14.41; and see **15.162–15.189**.

15.154 That notification must:

• specify which of the circumstances apply that have brought the duty to an end[1];
• inform the applicant that he or she has the right to request a review of the decision[2]; and
• inform the applicant of the 21-day period within which the request must be made[3].

1 HA 1996, s 189B(6)(a), as inserted by HRA 2017, s 5(2), for applications for homelessness assistance made on or after 3 April 2018. See **15.151**.
2 HA 1996, s 189B(6)(b), as inserted by HRA 2017, s 5(2), for applications for homelessness assistance made on or after 3 April 2018.HA 1996, s 202(1)(ba)(ii), as amended by HRA 2017, s 9, for applications for homelessness assistance made on or after 3 April 2018. See **19.24–19.29**.
3 HA 1996, s 189B(6)(b), as inserted by HRA 2017, s 5(2), for applications for homelessness assistance made on or after 3 April 2018. See **15.190–15.192**.

15.155 If no notification is made[1], or if the notification does not contain all of that information, the duty continues[2].

1 Because the decision is not put in writing, or is not received by the applicant, or is not made available at the applicant's office for a reasonable period for collection, see **15.152–15.159**.

2   HA 1996, s 189B(5) and (6), as inserted by HRA 2017, s 5(2), for applications for
     homelessness assistance made on or after 3 April 2018. See **15.152–15.159**.

15.156 Whilst there is no statutory requirement that reasons be given for the
decision, procedural fairness is likely to require that the local housing
authority explain why they consider the circumstance in question applies[1]. If
the notification is not received by the applicant, then it is treated as having
been given to the applicant if it is made available at the applicant's office for
a reasonable period for collection by or on behalf of the applicant[2]. The
decision to serve a notice is discretionary. Even if the statutory criteria are met,
the local housing authority may decide not to end the duty[3].

1   See **9.111–9.125** and **9.137–9.140**.
2   HA 1996, s 189B(8), as inserted by HRA 2017, s 5(2), for applications for homelessness
     assistance made on or after 3 April 2018, see **15.152–15.159**.
3   Because HA 1996, s 189B(5) (as inserted by HRA 2017, s 5(2), for applications for
     homelessness assistance made on or after 3 April 2018) contains the word 'may'.

15.157 In respect of the eighth and ninth circumstances[1], there is no need for
notification to be given under HA 1996, s 189B(5)–(7)[2]. However, the
applicant will have been informed of the consequences of refusal and of his or
her right to request a review[3]. A final Pt 6 offer must be made in writing[4] and
it would be expected that a final accommodation offer would also be made in
writing. The duty ends when the offer is refused[5].

1   Both at HA 1996, s 189B(9)(a), as inserted by HRA 2017, s 5(2), for applications for
     homelessness assistance made on or after 3 April 2018, see **15.181–15.184** for the eighth
     circumstance and **15.185–15.188** for the ninth circumstance.
2   As inserted by HRA 2017, s 5(2), for applications for homelessness assistance made on or after
     3 April 2018.
3   HA 1996, s 193A(1), (4)–(5), as inserted by HRA 2017, s 7(1), for applications for
     homelessness assistance made on or after 3 April 2018 and English Code, para 14.26. See
     15.152–15.159.
4   HA 1996, s 193A(5), as inserted by HRA 2017, s 7(1), for applications for homelessness
     assistance made on or after 3 April 2018, see **15.185**.
5   HA 1996, s 193A(2), as inserted by HRA 2017, s 7(1), for applications for homelessness
     assistance made on or after 3 April 2018.

15.158 In the tenth circumstance[1], the applicant will have been given a written
notice setting out the reasons for the notice, the effect of the notice, his or her
right to request a review and the period of 21 days in which to request the
review[2]. The giving of the notice, which is discretionary[3], brings the duty to an
end[4].

1   HA 1996, ss 189B(9)(b), and 193C(2), as inserted by HRA 2017, ss 5(2) and 7(1), for
     applications for homelessness assistance made on or after 3 April 2018, see **15.189** and
     15.196–15.221.
2   HA 1996, s 193B(3), as inserted by HRA 2017, s 7(1), for applications for homelessness
     assistance made on or after 3 April 2018. See **15.152–15.195**.
3   HA 1996, s 193B(2), as inserted by HRA 2017, s 7(1), for applications for homelessness
     assistance made on or after 3 April 2018.
4   HA 1996, s 193C(2), as inserted by HRA 2017, s 7(1), for applications for homelessness
     assistance made on or after 3 April 2018, see English Code, paras 14.35–14.36 and see **15.189**
     and **15.219–15.221**.

15.159 Each of these circumstances will now be considered in more detail.

Applicant has a priority need and did not become homeless intentionally and 56 days have passed

15.160 The HA 1996, s 189B(2)[1], relief duty will come to an end if[2]:

- the local housing authority is satisfied that the applicant has a priority need[3];
- the local housing authority is not satisfied that the applicant became homeless intentionally[4]; and
- 56 days have passed since the HA 1996, s 189B(2)[5], relief duty arose.

The duty ends automatically when these criteria are met and no written notification is needed, although the local housing authority must inform the applicant in writing of its decision that he or she has a priority need and did not become homeless intentionally[6]. It would also have notified the applicant in writing that its assessment of the applicant's case has changed[7].

[1] As inserted by HRA 2017, s 5(2), for applications for homelessness assistance made on or after 3 April 2018.
[2] HA 1996, s 189B(4), as inserted by HRA 2017, s 5(2), for applications for homelessness assistance made on or after 3 April 2018; English Code, paras 14.2–14.3.
[3] See CHAPTER 12.
[4] See CHAPTER 13.
[5] As inserted by HRA 2017, s 5(2), for applications for homelessness assistance made on or after 3 April 2018.
[6] HA 1996, s 184(1) and (3), and see 9.89–9.125.
[7] HA 1996, s 189A(10), as inserted by HRA 2017, s 3(1), for applications for homelessness assistance made on or after 3 April 2018, see English Code, paras 11.32–11.34 and 15.81–15.86.

15.161 This provision brings the HA 1996, s 189B(2)[1], relief duty automatically to an end even if the local housing authority has not taken any reasonable steps to help the applicant. It only applies to applicants who would be owed the HA 1996, s 193(2) main housing duty. There is no discretion available to the local housing authority to extend the period for compliance with the HA 1996, s 189B(2)[2], relief duty and thus postpone the HA 1996, s 193(2), main housing duty[3].

[1] As inserted by HRA 2017, s 5(2), for applications for homelessness assistance made on or after 3 April 2018.
[2] As inserted by HRA 2017, s 5(2), for applications for homelessness assistance made on or after 3 April 2018.
[3] See 16.94–16.199.

Suitable accommodation is available for occupation by the applicant and there is a reasonable prospect that the accommodation will be available for at least six months

15.162 The HA 1996, s 189B(2)[1], relief duty will come to an end if the local housing authority is satisfied that *all* of the following conditions are met:

- that the applicant has accommodation that is suitable for his or her needs and those of the members of his or her household[2];
- that the accommodation is available for occupation[3] by the applicant, and by all the members of his or her household[4]; and
- that there is a reasonable prospect that suitable accommodation will be

available for the applicant's occupation for at least six months[5].

[1]   As inserted by HRA 2017, s 5(2), for applications for homelessness assistance made on or after 3 April 2018.

[2]   For 'suitable' accommodation, see CHAPTER 18. By s 206(1) Housing Act 1996, a local housing authority must discharge its functions by (among other things) securing that suitable accommodation is 'available'. This refers to HA 1996, s 176: 'accommodation shall be regarded as available only if it is available for occupation by [the applicant] together with any other person who normally resides with him as a member of his family, or any other person who might reasonably be expected to reside with him'. The combined effect of these two provisions is that suitable accommodation must be available for the applicant and his household, which carries with it the implication that the accommodation must be suitable for all such persons, and not solely the applicant. See English Code, paras 16.3 and 17.2 and *R v Newham London Borough Council ex parte Sacupima* [2001] 1 WLR 563, CA, at [28]–[32].

[3]   As defined at HA 1996, ss 175–177, see CHAPTER 10.

[4]   As defined at HA 1996, s 176, see **10.21–10.32**.

[5]   HA 1996, s 189B(7)(a), as inserted by HRA 2017, s 5(2), for applications for homelessness assistance made on or after 3 April 2018. The period of six months could be extended to a longer period of no more than 12 months if the Secretary of State so prescribes: HA 1996, s 189B(7)(a), as inserted by HRA 2017, s 5(2), for applications for homelessness assistance made on or after 3 April 2018.

15.163 The local housing authority must be 'satisfied' of all these different requirements[1]. This requires something more on the local housing authority's part than simply an assumption. If there is any doubt, the duty will not have come to an end.

[1]   HA 1996, s 189B(7), as inserted by HRA 2017, s 5(2), for applications for homelessness assistance made on or after 3 April 2018.

15.164 The meanings of 'suitable' and 'available' accommodation are is discussed at **15.32–15.39**. As already observed, there must be 'a reasonable prospect' that the accommodation will continue to be available for at least six months[1]. What is 'a reasonable prospect? Obviously if the applicant is granted a fixed-term tenancy, for a term of six months or more, the local housing authority could be satisfied that there is a reasonable prospect that the accommodation will continue to be available for that period. In the case of more informal arrangements, such as accommodation provided by family or friends, the local housing authority would want something more than a mere assurance that it might be available for that period. The English Code contains advice to deal with two specific circumstances:

- where the applicant is permitted to remain in his or her existing accommodation by the landlord, but a Housing Act 1988, s 21 notice was previously issued, in those circumstances the landlord should be asked to issue a new tenancy. If he or she refuses, the local housing authority could secure written confirmation that the applicant can remain on condition that he or she complies with documented conditions. Provided that the local housing authority has a reasonable expectation that the applicant can comply, the guidance in the English Code is that there is likely to be a reasonable prospect of availability[2];

- where the applicant is staying with friends or family, the local housing authority must satisfy itself that the accommodation will be available for at least six months, either with an open-ended agreement (perhaps with reasonable conditions) or an agreement that the applicant can stay until he or she has secured alternative accommodation[3].

1   HA 1996, s 189B(7)(a)(ii), as inserted by HRA 2017, s 5(2), for applications for homelessness assistance made on or after 3 April 2018. The period of six months could be extended to a longer period of no more than 12 months if the Secretary of State so prescribes: HA 1996, s 189B(7)(a), as inserted by HRA 2017, s 5(2), for applications for homelessness assistance made on or after 3 April 2018.
2   English Code, paras 14.8–14.9.
3   English Code, para 14.10.

15.165   The period of six months begins on the date of the notice bringing the duty to an end[1].

1   HA 1996, s 189B(5), (7)(a)(ii) and (8), as inserted by HRA 2017, s 5(2), for applications for homelessness assistance made on or after 3 April 2018. See **15.153**.

The local housing authority has complied with its HA 1996, s 189B(2) relief duty for a period of 56 days

15.166   The HA 1996, s 189B(2)[1], relief duty will come to an end where the local housing authority is satisfied that *all* of the following conditions are met[2]:

- it has complied with the duty;
- a period of 56 days has ended; and
- the 56 day period began on the day on which the local housing authority was first satisfied that the duty was owed[3].

1   As inserted by HRA 2017, s 5(2), for applications for homelessness assistance made on or after 3 April 2018.
2   HA 1996, s 189B(7)(b), as inserted by HRA 2017, s 5(2), for applications for homelessness assistance made on or after 3 April 2018; English Code, paras 14.14–14.19.
3   HA 1996, s 189B(1), as inserted by HRA 2017, s 5(2), for applications for homelessness assistance made on or after 3 April 2018. For the potential distinction between the date when the local housing authority was satisfied that the duty was owed, and the notification of that decision to the applicant, see **9.93**.

15.167   The local housing authority must be 'satisfied' of all of these conditions[1]. It does not matter whether the outcome of the local housing authority's compliance has been that the applicant has actually secured accommodation or not[2]. However, the local housing authority must be 'satisfied' that it has actually complied, ie that it has taken reasonable steps to help the applicant. If the local housing authority has done nothing during the 56 days, it has not complied with the HA 1996, s 189B(2)[3], relief duty and so the duty will not end at the close of the 56 day period.

1   HA 1996, s 189B(7), as inserted by HRA 2017, s 5(2), for applications for homelessness assistance made on or after 3 April 2018.
2   HA 1996, s 189B(7)(b), as inserted by HRA 2017, s 5(2), for applications for homelessness assistance made on or after 3 April 2018.
3   As inserted by HRA 2017, s 5(2), for applications for homelessness assistance made on or after 3 April 2018.

15.168   The English Code makes it clear that a local housing authority may choose to continue to provide help to the applicant for a longer period, and that local housing authorities should not have blanket policies of ending the duty after 56 days[1]. In each case, the applicant's circumstances should be taken into account, including his or her needs, the risk of him or her sleeping rough, the prospects of him or her securing accommodation, along with the local housing authority's resources and any wider implications of bringing the duty to an end, such as an applicant with children being referred to children's services[2].

1   Except where the applicant has a priority need and has not become homeless intentionally, in which case the duty will automatically end after 56 days: HA 1996, s 189B(4), as inserted by HRA 2017, s 5(2), for applications for homelessness assistance made on or after 3 April 2018, see **15.160–15.161**.
2   English Code, paras 14.15–14.19.

The applicant has refused an offer of suitable accommodation where there was a reasonable prospect that it would be available for occupation for at least six months

15.169 The HA 1996, s 189B(2)[1], relief duty will come to an end if the local housing authority is satisfied that:

• the applicant was made an offer of accommodation;
• the accommodation was suitable for the needs of the applicant and members of his or her household[2];
• the applicant refused the offer;
• on the date of refusal, there was a reasonable prospect that suitable accommodation would be available for occupation[3] by the applicant and all the members of his or her household[4] for at least six months[5].

1   As inserted by HRA 2017, s 5(2), for applications for homelessness assistance made on or after 3 April 2018.
2   For 'suitable' accommodation, see CHAPTER 18. By s 206(1) Housing Act 1996, a local housing authority must discharge its functions by (among other things) securing that suitable accommodation is 'available'. This refers to HA 1996, s 176: 'accommodation shall be regarded as available only if it is available for occupation by [the applicant] together with any other person who normally resides with him as a member of his family, or any other person who might reasonably be expected to reside with him'. The combined effect of these two provisions is that suitable accommodation must be available for the applicant and his household, which carries with it the implication that the accommodation must be suitable for all such persons, and not solely the applicant. See English Code, paras 16.3 and 17.2 and *R v Newham London Borough Council ex parte Sacupima* [2001] 1 WLR 563, CA, at [28]–[32].
3   As defined at HA 1996, ss 175–177, see CHAPTER 10.
4   As defined at HA 1996, s 176, see **10.21–10.32**.
5   HA 1996, s 189B(7)(c), as inserted by HRA 2017, s 5(2), for applications for homelessness assistance made on or after 3 April 2018. The period of six months could be extended to a longer period of no more than 12 months if the Secretary of State so prescribes: HA 1996, s 189B(7)(c), as inserted by HRA 2017, s 5(2), for applications for homelessness assistance made on or after 3 April 2018.

15.170 The local housing authority must be 'satisfied' of all these different requirements[1]. This requires something more on the local housing authority's part than simply an assumption. If there is any doubt, the duty will not have come to an end.

1   HA 1996, s 189B(7), as inserted by HRA 2017, s 5(2), for applications for homelessness assistance made on or after 3 April 2018.

15.171 The meanings of 'suitable' and 'available' accommodation are discussed at **15.32–15.39**. The issue of how the local housing authority can be satisfied that there was a reasonable prospect that the accommodation would be available for at least six months is discussed at **15.37**.

15.172 There is no requirement that the offer should have come from the local housing authority itself. It might have come from a private landlord, from family or friends making suitable accommodation available on an informal basis. Equally, the offer might have come from the local housing authority, through it's allocation scheme.

15.173 Given that the local housing authority must be 'satisfied' that all of these conditions are met, this requires a local housing authority to consider carefully any reasons that are put forward by the applicant, or that are otherwise apparent to the local housing authority, as to why the accommodation offered might not have been suitable. The local housing authority will also need a sufficient basis to be 'satisfied' that there was a reasonable prospect that the accommodation would have been available for occupation for at least six months[1]. The period of six months begins from the date when the applicant refused the offer of accommodation[2]. Finally, it would also have to be 'satisfied' that the applicant had actually refused the offer of accommodation[3].

[1]   The period of six months could be extended to a longer period of no more than 12 months if the Secretary of State so prescribes: HA 1996, s 189B(7)(c), as inserted by HRA 2017, s 5(2), for applications for homelessness assistance made on or after 3 April 2018.

[2]   HA 1996, s 189B(7)(c), as inserted by HRA 2017, s 5(2), for applications for homelessness assistance made on or after 3 April 2018.

[3]   For an example where the local housing authority was wrong in law to characterise the applicant's response as a refusal, see *Ciercierska v Brent London Borough Council* (2016) *Legal Action*, October, p 41, County Court at Central London.

The applicant has become homeless intentionally from any accommodation made available to him or her as a result of the local housing authority's exercise of its functions under the HA 1996, s 189B(2) relief duty

15.174 The HA 1996, s 189B(2)[1], relief duty will come to an end when the local housing authority is satisfied that *all* of the following apply[2]:

- the applicant occupied accommodation made available to him or her pursuant to the local housing authority's functions under the HA 1996, s 189B(2)[3], relief duty;
- the applicant has ceased to occupy that accommodation;
- the cessation of occupation was due to a deliberate act or omission (which does not include an act or omission in good faith by a person unaware of a material fact);
- that deliberate act, or omission, was by the applicant;
- that deliberate act or omission was an operative cause of the applicant's homelessness;
- the accommodation was available for the applicant's occupation, and for the members of his or her household; and
- the accommodation was reasonable for the applicant and his or her household to continue to occupy.

The local housing authority must be 'satisfied' that all these conditions are made out[4]. If there is any doubt, the duty will not have ended.

¹ As inserted by HRA 2017, s 5(2) for applications for homelessness assistance made on or after 3 April 2018.
² HA 1996, s 189B(7)(d), as inserted by HRA 2017, s 5(2), for applications for homelessness assistance made on or after 3 April 2018; English Code, paras 14.23–14.23.
³ As inserted by HRA 2017, s 5(2), for applications for homelessness assistance made on or after 3 April 2018.
⁴ HA 1996, s 189B(7), as inserted by HRA 2017, s 5(2), for applications for homelessness assistance made on or after 3 April 2018.

15.175 The first condition makes it clear that the accommodation that the applicant has ceased to occupy must have been provided to the applicant pursuant to the HA 1996, s 189B(2)[1], relief duty.

¹ As inserted by HRA 2017, s 5(2), for applications for homelessness assistance made on or after 3 April 2018.see **15.138–15.195**.

15.176 The six latter conditions comprise the definition of 'becoming homeless intentionally' at HA 1996, s 191[1]. The HA 1996, s 193(2) main housing duty can come to an end for the same reason[2] and readers are referred to the discussion at CHAPTER 16[3].

¹ See CHAPTER 13.
² HA 1996, s 193(6)(b)
³ See **16.124–16.126**. See also the ending of the HA 1996, s 195(2), (as amended by HRA 2017, s 4(2), for applications for homelessness assistance made on or after 3 April 2018) prevention duty for this reason: **15.126–15.127**.

15.177 It remains to be seen how much practical relevance this provision will be. The local housing authority is not obliged to provide accommodation under the HA 1996, s 189B(2)[1] relief duty, although there is a power to do so at HA 1996, s 205(3)[2]. So the number of applicants likely to be accommodated under this duty may not be large. Moreover, it is well-established that an applicant in interim accommodation remains homeless and therefore cannot become homeless intentionally from it[3]. It would appear likely that in order for the accommodation provided under the HA 1996, s 189B(2)[4] relief duty to be accommodation from which it is possible to become homeless intentionally, it would have to have some degree of permanence, in which case the HA 1996, s 189B(2)[5] relief duty is likely to have been brought to an end under one of the other provisions long before the applicant becomes homeless intentionally from it.

¹ As inserted by HRA 2017, s 5(2), for applications for homelessness assistance made on or after 3 April 2018.
² As inserted by HRA 2017, s 6, for applications for homelessness assistance made on or after 3 April 2018.
³ *R (Alam) v Tower Hamlets London Borough Council* [2009] EWHC 44, (2009) March *Legal Action*, p 24 and *O'Callaghan v Southwark London Borough Council* (2010) May *Legal Action*, p 23.
⁴ As inserted by HRA 2017, s 5(2), for applications for homelessness assistance made to local authorities on or after 3 April 2018, see **15.138–15.195**.
⁵ As inserted by HRA 2017, s 5(2), for applications for homelessness assistance made to local authorities on or after 3 April 2018, see **15.138–15.195**.

The applicant is no longer eligible for assistance

15.178 The local housing authority must be 'satisfied' that the applicant is no longer eligible for assistance[1]. 'Eligible for assistance' is defined at HA 1996, s 185, and discussed at Chapter 11. The HA 1996 s 193(2), main housing duty can come to an end for this reason[2] and readers are referred to the discussion at Chapter 16[3].

---

[1]   HA 1996, s 189B(7)(e), as inserted by HRA 2017, s 5(2), for applications for homelessness assistance made to local housing authorities in England on or after 3 April 2018; English Code, para 14.32.
[2]   HA 1996, s 193(6)(a).
[3]   See **16.124–16.125**. For an example of the HA 1996, s 193(2), main housing duty coming to an end for this reason, see *Tower Hamlets London Borough Council v Deugi* [2006] EWCA Civ 159, [2006] HLR 28, CA. See also the ending of the HA 1996, s 195(2), (as amended by HRA 2017, s 4(2), for applications for homelessness assistance made on or after 3 April 2018), prevention duty for this reason: **15.126–15.127**.

15.179 Where the applicant's household includes a child aged under 18, and the local housing authority has reason to believe that the applicant may not be eligible for assistance[1], the applicant will be asked to consent to a referral of the essential facts of his or her case to children's services[2] The English Code contains advice that when interim accommodation is brought to an end, the period of notice should take account of the applicant's needs and of the time required for him or her to access assistance, and that the local housing authority should consider having arrangements in place to manage a transition in responsibility from housing to adult or children's services, so that there is no break in the provision of accommodation[3].

---

[1]   HA 1996, s 213A(1)(a), see **15.229–15.230** and **16.280–16.287**.
[2]   HA 1996, s 213A(2), see **16.281–16.283**.
[3]   English Code, para 14.32.

The applicant has withdrawn his or her application

15.180 The equivalent provision which brings to an end the HA 196, s 195(2)[1] prevention duty is discussed at **15.128–15.131**. The local housing authority's decision that the duty has come to an end for this reason must be notified to the applicant in writing[2]. If the applicant were to respond to this notification, that would be an indication in itself that he or she has not withdrawn his or her application. Similarly, the applicant has the right to request a review of this decision that the duty has come to an end[3], and any such request might suggest that the application has not in fact been withdrawn.[4]

---

[1]   As amended by HRA 2017, s 4(2) for applications for homelessness assistance made on or after 3 April 2018.
[2]   HA 1996, s 189B(5), (6) and (8), as inserted by HRA 2017, s 5(2), for applications for homelessness assistance made on or after 3 April 2018. See **15.155**.
[3]   HA 1996, s 202(1)(ba)(ii), as amended by HRA 2017, s 9, for applications for homelessness assistance made on or after 3 April 2018. See **19.24–19.29**.
[4]   HA 1996, s 189B(7)(f), as inserted by HRA 2017, s 5(2), for applications for homelessness assistance made on or after 3 April 2018; English Code, paras 14.33–14.34.

The applicant has refused a final accommodation offer

15.181 The HA 1996, s 189B(2)[1], relief duty will come to an end where[2]:

- the applicant has received an offer of accommodation;
- the applicant had been informed of the consequences of refusal and of his or her right to request a review of the suitability of accommodation[3];
- that offer was of an assured shorthold tenancy made by a private landlord to the applicant in relation to any accommodation which is, or may become, available for the applicant's occupation[4];
- the offer was made, with the approval of the local housing authority, in pursuance of arrangements made by it in discharge of its HA 1996, s 189B(2)[5], relief duty[6];
- the tenancy was for a fixed-term of at least six months[7];
- the applicant has refused the offer[8];
- the local housing authority is satisfied that the accommodation was suitable for the needs of the applicant and of his or her household[9]; and
- the local housing authority is satisfied that the applicant was not under contractual or other obligations in respect of his or her existing accommodation which he or she could not bring to an end before being required to take up the offer[10].

[1]   As inserted by HRA 2017, s 5(2), for applications for homelessness assistance made on or after 3 April 2018.
[2]   HA 1996, ss 189B(9)(a) and 193A(2), as inserted by HRA 2017, ss 5(2) and 7(1), for applications for homelessness assistance made on or after 3 April 2018.
[3]   HA 1996, s 193A(1)(b), as inserted by HRA 2017, s 7(1), for applications for homelessness assistance made on or after 3 April 2018.
[4]   HA 1996, s 193A(4)(a), as inserted by HRA 2017, s 7(1), for applications for homelessness assistance made on or after 3 April 2018.
[5]   As inserted by HRA 2017, s 5(2), for applications for homelessness assistance made on or after 3 April 2018.
[6]   HA 1996, s 193A(4)(b), as inserted by HRA 2017, s 7(1),), for applications for homelessness assistance made on or after 3 April 2018.
[7]   HA 1996, s 193A(4)(c), as inserted by HRA 2017, s 7(1), for applications for homelessness assistance made on or after 3 April 2018.
[8]   HA 1996, s 193A(1)(b)(i), as inserted by HRA 2017, s 7(1), for applications for homelessness assistance made on or after 3 April 2018
[9]   HA 1996, s 193A(6), as inserted by HRA 2017, s 7(1), for applications for homelessness assistance made on or after 3 April 2018, and s 206. For suitability, see Chapter **18**.
[10]   HA 1996, s 193A(7), as inserted by HRA 2017, s 7(1), for applications for homelessness assistance made on or after 3 April 2018.

15.182 In order to approve the making of a final accommodation offer, the local housing authority must be 'satisfied' that the accommodation is suitable for the applicant and that he or she is not under contractual or other obligations preventing him or her from taking up the accommodation[1]. Whilst there is no specific requirement in HA 1996, Pt 7[2], that the local housing authority must be 'satisfied' about the other conditions, that does not mean that the local housing authority could operate simply on an assumption. For the duty to come to an end for this reason, the local housing authority must come to a decision that all the conditions are met which means, in effect, that it must be satisfied that each one is met.

[1]   HA 1996, s 193A(6), inserted by HRA 2017, s 7(1), for applications for homelessness assistance made on or after 3 April 2018.

[2]   As amended by HRA 2017 for applications for homelessness assistance made on or after 3 April 2018.

15.183 There is nothing in HA 1996, s 193A[1], setting out any form in which the offer must be made. However, it would be expected that the offer will be made in writing. Similarly, there is nothing that requires that the information given to the applicant (of the consequences of refusal and of his or her right to request a review of the suitability) is given in writing, but again it should be expected as good administrative practice. The meanings of 'suitable accommodation' and 'available for occupation' are discussed at **15.32–15.39** and CHAPTER **18**.

[1]   As inserted by HRA 2017, s 7(1), for applications for homelessness assistance made on or after 3 April 2018.

15.184 A special provision applies in relation to applicants who have been occupying interim accommodation and who have refused a final accommodation offer in these circumstances. If the applicant requests a review of the suitability of the final accommodation offer, and the local housing authority either has reason to believe that the applicant has a priority need, or is satisfied that he or she does have a priority need, the local housing authority will continue to be under a duty to secure interim accommodation until the review decision has been notified to the applicant[1]. Unlike the usual position where an applicant who has interim accommodation requests a review, this is not a discretionary power exercised by the local housing authority but a duty to continue to secure interim accommodation[2].

[1]   HA 1996, s 188(2A), as inserted by HRA 2017, s 5(4) for applications for homelessness assistance made on or after 3 April 2018. See **16.51**.
[2]   HA 1996, s 188(2A) as inserted by HRA 2017, s 5(4), for applications for homelessness assistance made on or after 3 April 2018, see **16.51**.

The applicant has refused a final Pt 6 offer

15.185 The HA 1996, s 189B(2)[1], relief duty will come to an end where[2]:

- the applicant has received an offer of accommodation;
- the applicant had been informed of the consequences of refusal and of his or her right to request a review of the suitability of accommodation[3];
- that offer was an offer of accommodation under HA 1996, Pt 6 ('allocation of housing accommodation')[4];
- the offer was made in writing by the local housing authority in discharge of its HA 1996, s 189B(2)[5], relief duty[6];
- the offer stated that it was a final offer for the purposes of HA 1996, s 193A[7];
- the applicant has refused the offer of accommodation[8];
- the local housing authority is satisfied that the accommodation was suitable for the needs of the applicant and of his or her household[9]; and
- the local housing authority is satisfied that the applicant was not under contractual or other obligations in respect of his or her existing accommodation which he or she could not bring to an end before being

required to take up the offer[10].

1   As inserted by HRA 2017, s 5(2), for applications for homelessness assistance made on or after 3 April 2018.
2   HA 1996, ss 189B(9)(a),and 193A(2), as inserted by HRA 2017, ss 5(2) and 7(1), for applications for homelessness assistance made on or after 3 April 2018; there is limited guidance in the English Code, see paras 14.25, and 15.46–15.48.
3   HA 1996, s 193A(1)(b), as inserted by HRA 2017, s 7(1), for applications for homelessness assistance made on or after 3 April 2018.
4   HA 1996, s 193A(5), as inserted by HRA 2017, s 7(1), for applications for homelessness assistance made on or after 3 April 2018. See CHAPTERS 1–6 for HA 1996, Pt 6, allocation of social housing.
5   As inserted by HRA 2017, s 5(2), for applications for homelessness assistance made on or after 3 April 2018.
6   HA 1996, s 193A(5)(a), as inserted by HRA 2017, s 7(1), for applications for homelessness assistance made on or after 3 April 2018.
7   HA 1996, s 193A(5)(b), as inserted by HRA 2017, s 7(1), for applications for homelessness assistance made on or after 3 April 2018.
8   HA 1996, s 193A(1)(b)(ii), as inserted by HRA 2017, s 7(1), for applications for homelessness assistance made on or 3 April 2018
9   HA 1996, s 193A(6), as inserted by HRA 2017, s 7(1), for applications for homelessness assistance made on or after 3 April 2018, and s 206. For suitability, see CHAPTER 18 and 15.32–15.39.
10   HA 1996, s 193A(7), as inserted by HRA 2017, s 7(1), for applications for homelessness assistance made on or after 3 April 2018.

15.186 In order to make a final HA 1996, Pt 6 offer, the local housing authority must be 'satisfied' that the accommodation is suitable for the applicant and that he or she is not under contractual or other obligations preventing him or her from taking up the accommodation[1]. The meanings of 'suitable accommodation' and 'available for occupation' are discussed at **15.32–15.39** and CHAPTER 18.

1   HA 1996, s 193A(6), inserted by HRA 2017, s 7(1), for applications for homelessness assistance made on or after 3 April 2018.

15.187 The offer must be made in writing and state that it is a final offer for these purposes[1]. Although there is nothing in HA 1996, Pt 7[2], requiring that the information given to the applicant (of the consequences of refusal and of his or her right to request a review of the suitability) should be in writing, this would be expected as good administrative practice.

1   HA 1996, s 193A(5)(a)–(b), as inserted by HRA 2017, s 7(1), for applications for homelessness assistance made on or after 3 April 2018.
2   As amended by HRA 2017 for applications for homelessness assistance made on or after 3 April 2018.

15.188 A special provision applies in relation to applicants who have been occupying interim accommodation. If the applicant requests a review of the suitability of the final Pt 6 offer, and the local housing authority either has reason to believe that the applicant has a priority need, or is satisfied that he or she does have a priority need, the local housing authority will continue to be under a duty to secure interim accommodation until the review decision has been notified to the applicant[1]. Unlike the usual position where an applicant who has interim accommodation requests a review, this is not a discretionary decision exercised by the local housing authority but a duty to continue to secure interim accommodation[2].

1   HA 1996, s 188(2A), as inserted by HRA 2017, s 5(4) for applications for homelessness assistance made on or after 3 April 2018.See **16.51**.
2   HA 1996, s 188(2A), as inserted by HRA 2017, s 5(4) for applications for homelessness assistance made on or after 3 April 2018.See **16.51**.

Decision that an applicant has deliberately and unreasonably refused to co-operate

15.189 If the local housing authority has notified an applicant under HA 1996, s 193B(2)[1], that it considers that he or she has deliberately and unreasonably failed to co-operate[2], then the HA 1996, s 189B(2)[3], relief duty will come to an end for this reason. This notification is discussed at **15.196–15.221**.

1   As inserted by HRA 2017, s 7(1), for applications for homelessness assistance made on or after 3 April 2018.
2   HA 1996, ss 189B(9)(b) and 193C(2), as inserted by HRA 2017, ss 5(2), and 7(1), for applications for homelessness assistance made on or after 3 April 2018; English Code, paras 14.35–14.36 and 14.43–14.59. See **15.196–15.221**.
3   As inserted by HRA 2017, s 5(2), for applications for homelessness assistance made on or after 3 April 2018.

The right to request a review

15.190 The applicant has the right to request a review[1] of the following decisions made by the local housing authority that might be relevant to this duty:

- whether or not he or she is eligible for assistance[2];
- whether or not the HA 1996, s 189B(2)[3], relief duty is owed[4];
- what steps the local housing authority is to take in order to perform its HA 1996, s 189B(2)[5] relief duty[6];
- any decision, by agreement between local housing authorities or following a referee's decision, under HA 1996, s 198(5)[7], that the conditions for referral[8] are met and that the performance of the HA 1996, s 189B(2)[9], relief duty will be referred to another local housing authority[10];
- any decision as to the suitability of any accommodation offered to the applicant in order to bring the HA 1996, s 189B(2)[11], relief duty to an end[12];
- any decision as to the suitability of accommodation offered by a way of a final accommodation offer[13];
- any decision as to the suitability of accommodation offered by a way of a final Pt 6 offer[14];
- any decision that the HA 1996, s 189B(2)[15], relief duty has come to an end under HA 1996, s 189B(4)[16] because the applicant has a priority need, did not become homeless intentionally, and 56 days have passed[17];
- any decision to give notice to the applicant that the HA 1996, s 189B(2)[18], relief duty has come to an end because the local housing authority is satisfied that one of the circumstances at HA 1996, s 189B(7)[19] applies[20]; and

- any decision to give notice to the applicant of a decision under HA 1996, s 193B(2)[21], that he or she has deliberately and unreasonably refused to co-operate[22].

[1] HA 1996, s 202(1), as amended by HRA 2017, s 9, for applications for homelessness assistance made on or after 3 April 2018. See **19.12–19.69** for a discussion of the right to review and procedure.

[2] HA 1996, s 202(1)(a), as amended by HRA 2017, s 9, for applications for homelessness assistance made on or after 3 April 2018. See 19.14. For 'eligible for assistance' see CHAPTER **11**.

[3] As inserted by HRA 2017, s 5(2), for applications for homelessness assistance made on or after 3 April 2018. See **15.138–15.195**.

[4] HA 1996, s 202(1)(b), as amended by HRA 2017, s 9, for applications for homelessness assistance made on or after 3 April 2018. See **19.15–19.17**.

[5] As inserted by HRA 2017, s 5(2), for applications for homelessness assistance made on or after 3 April 2018. See **15.138–15.195**.

[6] HA 1996, s 202(1)(ba)(i), as inserted by HRA 2017, s 9, for applications for homelessness assistance made on or after 3 April 2018. See **19.18–19.23**. For the steps to be taken by the local housing authority, see HA 1996, s 189A(4)(b) and (6)(c), as inserted by HRA 2017, s 3(1), for applications for homelessness assistance made on or after 3 April 2018. See **15.72–15.80**.

[7] See **14.176–14.190**.

[8] HA 1996, s 198(2), (2ZA) or (4), see **14.43–14.122**.

[9] As inserted by HRA 2017, s 5(2), for applications for homelessness assistance made on or after 3 April 2018. See **15.138–15.195**.

[10] HA 1996, s 202(1)(d), as amended by HRA 2017, s 9, for applications for homelessness assistance made on or after 3 April 2018. See **19.55–19.57**.

[11] As inserted by HRA 2017, s 5(2), for applications for homelessness assistance made on or after 3 April 2018. See **15.162–15.165** and **15.169–15.173**.

[12] HA 1996, s 202(1)(f), as amended by HRA 2017, s 9, for applications for homelessness assistance made on or after 3 April 2018. See **19.59–19.62**. For the circumstances when the local housing authority might offer suitable accommodation to the applicant, see HA 1996, s 189B(7)(a) and (c), as inserted by HRA 2017, s 5(2), for applications for homelessness assistance made on or after 3 April 2018. See **15.162–15.165** and **15.169–15.173**.

[13] HA 1996, s 202(1)(h), as amended by HRA 2017, s 9, for applications for homelessness assistance made on or after 3 April 2018. See **19.65–19.69**. For final accommodation offer, see HA 1996, s 193A(4), as inserted by HRA 2017, s 7(1), for applications for homelessness assistance made on or after 3 April 2018. See **15.181–15.184**.

[14] HA 1996, s 202(1)(h), as amended by HRA 2017, s 9, for applications for homelessness assistance made on or after 3 April 2018. See **19.65–19.69**. For final Pt 6 offer, see HA 1996, s 193A(5), as inserted by HRA 2017, s 7(1), for applications for homelessness assistance made on or after 3 April 2018. See **15.185–15.188**.

[15] As inserted by HRA 2017, s 5(2), for applications for homelessness assistance made on or after 3 April 2018. See **15.138–15.195**.

[16] As inserted by HRA 2017, s 5(2), for applications for homelessness assistance made on or after 3 April 2018.

[17] HA 1996, s 202(1)(b), as amended by HRA 2017, s 9(2) for applications for homelessness assistance made on or after 3 April 2018.

[18] As inserted by HRA 2017, s 5(2), for applications for homelessness assistance made on or after 3 April 2018. See **15.138–15.195**.

[19] As inserted by HRA 2017, s 5(2), for applications for homelessness assistance made on or after 3 April 2018. See **15.138–15.195**.

[20] HA 1996, s 202(1)(ba)(ii), as inserted by HRA 2017, s 9, for applications for homelessness assistance made on or after 3 April 2018. See **19.24–19.30**. For the circumstances that bring the HA 1996, s 189B(2), relief duty to an end, see HA 1996, s 189B(7), as inserted by HRA 2017, s 5(2), for applications for homelessness assistance made on or after 3 April 2018. See **15.151–15.195**.

[21] As inserted by HRA 2017, s 7(1), for applications for homelessness assistance made on or after 3 April 2018. See **15.196–15.221**.

[22] HA 1996, s 202(1)(bb), as inserted by HRA 2017, s 9, for applications for homelessness assistance made on or after 3 April 2018. See **19.30–19.35**.

15.191 If the applicant wishes to request a review of the suitability of accommodation offered, then caution would suggest that the applicant should accept the accommodation. The right to request a review of any decision as to the suitability of either a final accommodation offer[1] or final Pt 6 offer[2] applies whether the applicant has accepted or refused the offer[3]. However, those are not the only offers of accommodation which can bring the HA 1996, s 189B(2)[4], relief duty to an end. The duty can also end where the local housing authority is satisfied that the applicant has refused an offer of suitable accommodation and there was a reasonable prospect that suitable accommodation would be available for his or her occupation for a period of at least six months[5]. If the applicant is contemplating refusing an offer in these circumstances, the safer course would be to accept the accommodation and then, when notified of the local housing authority's decision that the HA 1996, s 189B(2), relief duty has come to an end because of his or her acceptance[6], request a review of the suitability of the accommodation[7]. If the review is unsuccessful, the applicant will at least have some accommodation. If the applicant refuses the accommodation and the review is unsuccessful, he or she may be without any accommodation at all. The cautious approach would therefore always be to accept the offer and request a review of the suitability of accommodation offered.

[1] HA 1996, s 193A(4), as inserted by HRA 2017, s 7(1), for applications for homelessness assistance made on or after 3 April 2018. See **15.181–15.184**.
[2] HA 1996, s 193A(5), as inserted by HRA 2017, s 7(1), for applications for homelessness assistance made on or after 3 April 2018. See **15.185–15.188**.
[3] HA 1996, s 202(1B), as inserted by HRA 2017, s 9, for applications for homelessness assistance made on or after 3 April 2018. See **19.90–19.99**.
[4] As inserted by HRA 2017, s 5(2), for applications for homelessness assistance made on or after 3 April 2018.
[5] HA 1996, s 189B(7)(c), as amended by HRA 2017, s 5(2), for applications for homelessness assistance made on or after 3 April 2018, see **15.169–15.174**.
[6] HA 1996, s 189B(7)(a), as amended by HRA 2017, s 5(2), for applications for homelessness assistance made on or after 3 April 2018, see **15.162–15.166**.
[7] HA 1996, s 202(1)(b), , as amended by HRA 2017, s 9, for applications for homelessness assistance made on or after 3 April 2018, see **19.15–19.17**.

15.192 A review must be requested within 21 days of the applicant being notified of the relevant decision, which is the date when the applicant received the decision[1]. If the applicant did not receive the notice, and the local housing authority made the notice available at its office for a reasonable period for collection by or on behalf of the applicant, the date of notification will be the end of that period[2].

[1] HA 1996, s 202(3), see **19.109–19.115**.
[2] HA 1996, s 189B(8), as inserted by HRA 2017, s 5(2), and s 193B(8), as inserted by HRA 2017, s 7(1), for applications for homelessness assistance made on or after 3 April 2018. The exact wording is 'treated as having been given to the applicant if it is made available at the authority's office for a reasonable period for collection'. This suggests that the date when it is to be treated as having been given, ie notified, is the end of the reasonable period, rather than the date when the notice was first left.

What happens after the HA 1996, s 189B(2) relief duty has ended?

15.193 The applicant's position when the HA 1996, s 189B(2)[1] relief duty ends depends on his or her circumstances.

¹ As inserted by HRA 2017, s 5(2), for applications for homelessness assistance made on or after 3 April 2018. See **15.138–15.195**.

15.194 If the applicant is no longer eligible or homeless, no further duty will be owed. If the applicant is eligible and homeless but does not have a priority end, no further duty will be owed. If the applicant is eligible, homeless, and has a priority need, but became homeless intentionally, the local housing authority must secure accommodation for the applicant for such period as it considers will give him or her a reasonable opportunity of securing his or her own accommodation, and must provide advice and assistance[1].

¹ HA 1996, s 190(2)(a) and (b), as amended by HRA 2017, s 5(5), for applications for homelessness assistance made on or after 3 April 2018, see **15.231** and **16.81–16.93**. Paragraph 14.30 of the English Code advises that applicants for whom the HA 1996, s 189B(2) relief duty was ended because they became homeless intentionally from accommodation made available under that duty will be found to have become homeless intentionally for the purposes of HA 1996, s 190(2). However, this is open to question, see **13.239–13.247**.

15.195 If the applicant is eligible, homeless, and has a priority need, and did not become homeless intentionally, then he or she will be owed the HA 1996, s 193(2) main housing duty[1] unless one of the following applies:

- the HA 1996, s 189B(2)[2] relief duty came to an end under HA 1996, s 193A(2)[3] following the refusal of a final accommodation offer or a final Pt 6 offer. In this case, the HA 1996, s 193 main housing duty will not apply. No further duty will be owed[4].
- the HA 1996, s 189B(2)[5] relief duty came to an end under HA 1996, s 193C(2)[6] following the applicant's deliberate and unreasonable refusal to co-operate. In this case, the main housing duty does not apply but the local housing authority must secure that accommodation is available under the duty at HA 1996, s 193C(4)[7].

Even if no further duty is owed, the applicant may make a further application for homelessness assistance. If the factual circumstances are not the same as they were at the time when the earlier application for homelessness assistance was disposed of (i.e. when the HA 1996, s 189B(2)[8], relief duty came to an end), the local housing authority must accept the application and make inquiries into what duty, if any, is owed to the applicant[9].

¹ See **16.94–16.199**.
² As inserted by HRA 2017, s 5(2), for applications for homelessness assistance made on or after 3 April 2018. See **15.138–15.195**.
³ As inserted by HRA 2017, s 7(1), for applications for homelessness assistance made on or after 3 April 2018.
⁴ If the applicant had been occupying interim accommodation, and requests a review of the suitability of the final accommodation offer or final Pt 6 offer, the interim accommodation will continue until the applicant has been notified of the decision on review: HA 1996, s 188(2A), for applications for homelessness assistance made on or after 3 April 2018. See **16.51**.
⁵ As inserted by HRA 2017, s 5(2), for applications for homelessness assistance made on or after 3 April 2018. See **15.138–15.195**.
⁶ As inserted by HRA 2017, s 7(1), for applications for homelessness assistance made on or after 3 April 2018. See **15.189** and **15.196–15.221**.

7   As inserted by HRA 2017, s 7(1), for applications for homelessness assistance made on or after 3 April 2018. The ways in which that duty will come to an end are discussed at **16.204–16.216**.

8   As inserted by HRA 2017, s 5(2), for applications for homelessness assistance made on or after 3 April 2018.

9   See **8.80–8.82** and **8.85–8.91**. The English Code contains advice that in the majority of re-application cases where the applicant has previously refused an offer of suitable accommodation, the local housing authority will be entitled to rely on the ending of its duty. However, if the applicant's factual circumstances have changed, the local housing authority must accept the fresh application: English Code, paras 18.11–18.13 and particularly para 18.12.

DECISION THAT AN APPLICANT HAS DELIBERATELY AND UNREASONABLY REFUSED TO CO-OPERATE

Overview

15.196 A new provision at HA 1996, s 193B[1] permits a local housing authority to decide that an applicant has deliberately and unreasonably refused to co-operate[2]. The applicant must first have been warned that the local housing authority considers that he or she has deliberately and unreasonably refused to take an appropriate step. The applicant must also have been warned as to the consequences of such a decision, and have been given a reasonable period in which to take the step[3]. The step, or steps, referred to are those that the applicant either agreed to take when he or she and the local housing authority agreed his or her personalised housing plan[4], or, if there was no agreement, the steps recorded by the local housing authority in the personalised housing plan as being reasonable to require the applicant to take[5].

1   As inserted by HRA 2017, s 7(1), for applications for homelessness assistance made on or after 3 April 2018.

2   HA 1996, s 193B(2), as inserted by HRA 2017, s 7(1), for applications for homelessness assistance made on or after 3 April 2018. See **15.196–15.221**.

3   HA 1996, s 193B(4) and (5) as inserted by HRA 2017, s 7(1), for applications for homelessness assistance made on or after 3 April 2018. See **15.203–15.210**.

4   HA 1996, s 189A(4)(a), as inserted by HRA 2017, s 3(1), for applications for homelessness assistance made on or after 3 April 2018. See **15.72–15.80** and **15.203–15.206**.

5   HA 1996, s 189A(6)(b), as inserted by HRA 2017, s 3(1), for applications for homelessness assistance made on or after 3 April 2018. See **15.73**. HA 1996, s 193B((2) and (5)(a), as inserted by HRA 2017, s 7(1), for applications for homelessness assistance made on or after 3 April 2018. See **15.203–15.206**.

15.197 The consequences of this decision are that the HA 1996, s 195(2)[1], prevention or HA 1996, s 189B(2)[2], relief duties will come to an end[3]. A decision that the applicant has deliberately and unreasonably refused to co-operate cannot bring any other duties, such as the HA 1996, s 193(2), main housing duty, to an end.

1   As amended by HRA 2017, s 4(2), for applications for homelessness assistance made on or after 3 April 2018.

2   As inserted by HRA 2017, s 5(2), for applications for homelessness assistance made on or after 3 April 2018, see **15.138–15.195**.

3   HA 1996, s 189B(9)(b) as inserted by HRA 2017, s 5(2) and HA 1996, s 195(10), as amended by HRA 2017, s 4(2), for applications for homelessness assistance made on or after 3 April 2018. See **15.132**, **15.189** and **15.216**.

15.198 Where the HA 1996, s 195(2)[1], prevention or HA 1996, s 189B(2)[2], relief duties come to an end for this reason, no further duty will be owed unless the local housing authority is satisfied that the applicant remains eligible for assistance[3], is homeless[4], and has a priority need[5]. If any of those conditions are not met, then no further duty is owed to the applicant. If all of those conditions are met, the local housing authority will owe the applicant a duty to secure accommodation for him or her. Which accommodation duty will be owed will depend on whether or not the local housing authority is satisfied that the applicant has become homeless intentionally[6].

1   As amended by HRA 2017, s 4(2), for applications for homelessness assistance made on or after 3 April 2018.
2   As inserted by HRA 2017, s 5(2), for applications for homelessness assistance made on or after 3 April 2018.
3   HA 1996, s 185, see CHAPTER 11.
4   HA 1996, ss 175–177, see CHAPTER 10.
5   HA 1996, s 189(1) and Homelessness (Priority Need for Accommodation) (England) Order 2002, SI 2002/2051, see CHAPTER 12.
6   HA 1996, s 191, see CHAPTER 13.

15.199 If the local housing authority is satisfied that the applicant is eligible for assistance, is homeless, has a priority need and has become homeless intentionally, then the duty at HA 1996, s 190(2)[1], to secure accommodation for such period as the local housing authority considers will give the applicant a reasonable opportunity of securing his or her own accommodation, and to provide advice and assistance will be owed[2].

1   As amended by HRA 2017, s 5(5), for applications for homelessness assistance made on or after 3 April 2018.
2   HA 1996, s 190(2), as amended by HRA 2017, s 5(5), for applications for homelessness assistance made on or after 3 April 2018. See **16.81–16.93**.

15.200 If the local housing authority is satisfied that the applicant is eligible for assistance, is homeless, has a priority need and is not satisfied that the applicant has become homeless intentionally, then the HA 1996, s 193(2), main housing duty will not apply because of the decision that the applicant has deliberately and unreasonably refused to co-operate[1]. Instead, the local housing authority has a different duty, at HA 1996, s 193C(4)[2], to secure that accommodation is available for occupation by the applicant and the members of his or her household[3]. That duty will come to an end if the applicant is offered, and accepts or refuses, a final accommodation offer[4] or a final Pt 6 offer[5], having been informed of the consequences of refusal or acceptance and of his or her right to request a review of the suitability of the offer[6]. The duty will also come to an end if the local housing authority is satisfied that the applicant is no longer eligible for assistance[7], or has become homeless intentionally from accommodation made available[8], or has accepted an offer of an assured tenancy from a private landlord[9], or has voluntarily ceased to occupy as his or her only or principal home the accommodation made available for his or her occupation[10].

1   HA 1996, s 193C(4), as inserted by HRA 2017, s 7(1), for applications for homelessness assistance made on or after 3 April 2018, see **16.200–16.216**.
2   As inserted by HRA 2017, s 7(1), for applications for homelessness assistance made on or after 3 April 2018.
3   HA 1996, s 193C(4), as inserted by HRA 2017, s 7(1), for applications for homelessness assistance made on or after 3 April 2018. See **16.200–16.216**.

4   Defined at HA 1996, s 193C(7), as inserted by HRA 2017, s 7(1), for applications for
     homelessness assistance made on or after 3 April 2018. See **16.205–16.209.**
5   Defined at HA 1996, s 193C(8), as inserted by HRA 2017, s 7(1), for applications for
     homelessness assistance made on or after 3 April 2018. See **16.210–16.214.**
6   HA 1996, s 193C(6), as inserted by HRA 2017, s 7(1), for applications for homelessness
     assistance made on or after 3 April 2018. See **16.204–16.216.**
7   HA 1996, s 193C(5)(a), as inserted by HRA 2017, s 7(1), for applications for homelessness
     assistance made on or after 3 April 2018. See **16.204.** For 'eligible for assistance', see HA
     1996, s 185, and Chapter 11.
8   HA 1996, s 193C(5)(b), as inserted by HRA 2017, s 7(1), for applications for homelessness
     assistance made on or after 3 April 2018. See **16.204.** For 'becoming homeless intentionally',
     see HA 1996, s 191, and Chapter 13.
9   HA 1996, s 193C(5)(c), as inserted by HRA 2017, s 7(1), for applications for homelessness
     assistance made on or after 3April 2018. See **16.204.**
10   HA 1996, s 193C(5)(d), as inserted by HRA 2017, s 7(1), for applications for homelessness
     assistance made on or after 3 April 2018. See **16.204.**

15.201 The applicant has the right to request a review of any decision that he
or she has deliberately and unreasonably refused to co-operate[1].

1   HA 1996, s 202(1)(bb), as inserted by HRA 2017, s 9(2), for applications for homelessness
     assistance made on or after 3 April 2018. See **19.30–19.35.**

15.202 Each local housing authority must develop a procedure to be followed
when issuing the relevant warning, or the final decision, or both, under HA
1996, s 193B[1]. That procedure must be in writing, and must be kept under
review[2]. The final notice of a decision that an applicant has deliberately and
unreasonably refused to co-operate, given under HA 1996, s 193B(2)[3], will
involve two people. One officer decides to issue the decision and then another
officer, known as the 'appropriate person', who is of at least equivalent
seniority to the first officer, must authorise it. The appropriate person must
work for the local housing authority (or in another department in the local
authority), or work under a contract for the local housing authority, and must
not previously have been involved in the decision to give the notice[4].

1   As inserted by HRA 2017, s 7(1), for applications for homelessness assistance made on or after
     3 April 2018.
2   Homelessness (Review Procedure etc) Regulations 2018, SI 2018/223, reg 2; English Code,
     para 14.56.
3   As inserted by HRA 2017, s 7(1), for applications for homelessness assistance made on or after
     3 April 2018.
4   Homelessness (Review Procedure etc) Regulations 2018, SI 2018/223, reg 3; English Code,
     paras 14.57–14.59.

The steps which the applicant has agreed, or was required, to take

15.203 After the local housing authority had notified the applicant of its
assessment of his or her case under HA 1996, s 189A(3)[1], it will then try to
agree with the applicant the steps that he or she is required to take in order to
retain or secure suitable accommodation. It will also record the steps that it has
argued to take for the same purpose[2]. This record is known as the personalised
housing plan[3].

1   As inserted by HRA 2017, s 3(1), for applications for homelessness assistance made on or after
     3 April 2018 See **15.62–15.86.**

² HA 1996, s 189A(4), as inserted by HRA 2017, s 3(1), for applications for homelessness assistance made on or after 3 April 2018. See **15.72–15.80**.

³ HA 1996, s 189A, as inserted by HRA 2017, s 3(1), for applications for homelessness assistance made on or after 3 April 2018; English Code, chapter 11. See **15.72–15.80**.

15.204 It is only if the applicant has refused to take any of the steps recorded as either agreed, or as required by the local housing authority, in the personalised housing plan that the local housing authority can decide that he or she has deliberately and unreasonably refused to co-operate[1]. The local housing authority cannot come to this decision in respect of any steps which it may have advised the applicant to take, but are not recorded as either agreed or required from the applicant.

¹ See **15.72–15.80**.

15.205 The local housing authority can only activate this procedure if it considers that the applicant has refused to take the specified step, and that refusal was deliberate and unreasonable. If the applicant was, for example, unaware of the requirement to take the step, then his or her failure to do so would not be a refusal, nor would it be deliberate, or unreasonable.

15.206 The English Code reminds local housing authorities that they must have regard to the particular circumstances and needs of the applicant in deciding whether refusal by the applicant is unreasonable. It also advises that, both before the procedure is invoked, and during its use, local housing authorities should make reasonable efforts to obtain the applicant's co-operation, including seeking to understand the reasons for any lack of co-operation. Local housing authorities should review their assessment of the applicant's case and the appropriateness of the steps in the personalised housing plans. They should also explain to the applicant the consequences of not co-operating before they take the formal stage of serving him or her with a relevant warning. They should also seek to involve any other support services. If the applicant is street homeless or is insecurely housed, then particular difficulties in managing communications should be taken into account[1].

¹ English Code, paras 14.51–14.53.

The two-stage process

The relevant warning

15.207 The first stage is that the local housing authority must serve the applicant with a 'relevant warning'[1]. This is defined as a notice which:

- is given by the local housing authority to the applicant;
- is given after the applicant has deliberately and unreasonably refused to take any step that he or she had agreed to take or that was recorded by the local housing authority as reasonable to require him or her to take;
- warns the applicant that, if he or she deliberately and unreasonably refuses to take any such step after receiving the notice, the local housing authority intends to give notice that he or she has deliberately and unreasonably refused to co-operate; and

- explains the consequence of a notice that he or she has deliberately and unreasonably refused to co-operate.

The warning notice must be in writing. If the notice is not received by the applicant, it is treated as having been given to him or her if it was made available at the local housing authority's office for a reasonable period for collection by or on behalf of the applicant[2].

[1] HA 1996, s 193B(5), as inserted by HRA 2017, s 7(1), for applications for homelessness assistance made on or after 3 April 2018. English Code, para 14.55.
[2] HA 1996, s 193B(8), as inserted by HRA 2017, s 7(1), for applications for homelessness assistance made on or after 3 April 2018.

The reasonable period

15.208 The applicant must then have a 'reasonable period' within which to comply ie to take the step required of him or her[1]. The English Code advises that there is no set reasonable period but that local housing authorities should ensure that the applicant has sufficient time to rectify his or her non-co-operation. The length of that sufficient time will vary according to the applicant's particular needs and circumstances[2].

[1] HA 1996, s 193B(4)(b), as inserted by HRA 2017, s 7(1), for applications for homelessness assistance made on or after 3 April 2018.
[2] English Code, para 14.44.

The notice that an applicant has deliberately and unreasonably refused to co-operate

15.209 If the applicant has not taken the step required by the end of the reasonable period, the local housing authority can then give him or her notice of its decision that he or she has deliberately and unreasonably refused to take the step and thus has deliberately and unreasonably refused to co-operate[1].

[1] HA 1996, s 193B(2), as inserted by HRA 2017, s 7(1), for applications for homelessness assistance made on or after 3 April 2018.

Procedure for authorising the notice

15.210 The decision to give the notice must be made by two separate people working for, or on behalf of, the local housing authority. One officer will make the decision to give the notice. This could be the same officer as made the decision to give the applicant a warning. A second officer, known as the 'authorised person', must then authorise the decision to give the notice. That 'authorised person' must be of at least equivalent seniority to the first officer and must not have been involved in the officer's decision to give notice[1]. He or she should either be employed by the local housing authority, work under a contract with the local housing authority, be supplied as an agency worker or be seconded to work for the local housing authority[2]. There is no requirement that the authorised person be employed in the housing department of the local housing authority[3].

[1] There is no provision prohibiting the authorised person from having been involved in the decision to give the applicant a warning.

²   Homelessness (Review Procedure etc) Regulations 2018, SI 2018/223, reg 3.
³   English Code, paras 14.56–14.59. Para 14.58 advises that it may be appropriate for an officer within children's services to be the authorised person in the case of a care-leaver.

15.211 The notice must be in writing. If the notice is not received by the applicant, it is treated as having been given to him or her if it was made available at the local housing authority's office for a reasonable period for collection by or on behalf of the applicant[1]. The period of 21 days within which the applicant must request a review runs from the date of notification, which means the date when the notice was actually received[2]. If the notice was not received at all, then the date of notification (and therefore the beginning of the 21 day period) should be the end of the reasonable period during which the notice was made available for collection at the local housing authority's office rather than the date of the notice or when it was first made available[3].

¹   HA 1996, s 193B(8), as inserted by HRA 2017, s 7(1), for applications for homelessness assistance made on or after 3 April 2018.
²   HA 1996, s 202(3), see **19.109–19.115**.
³   HA 1996, s 193B(8), as inserted by HRA 2017, s 7(1), for applications for homelessness assistance made on or after 3 April 2018.The exact wording is 'treated as having been given to the applicant if it is made available at the authority's office for a reasonable period for collection'. This suggests that the date when it is to be treated as having been given, ie notified, is the end of the reasonable period, rather than the date when the notice was first left.

What does 'deliberately and unreasonably' mean?

15.212 HA 1996, s 193B[1], provides that the local housing authority must be satisfied that the applicant's failure to take the required step is more than a mere omission. The local housing authority must consider the applicant's personal circumstances and his or her needs[2]. It should not confine itself to those circumstances and needs identified in the HA 1996, s 189A[3], assessment of the applicant's case.

¹   As inserted by HRA 2017, s 7(1), for applications for homelessness assistance made on or after 3 April 2018.
²   HA 1996, s 193B(6), as inserted by HRA 2017, s 7(1), for applications for homelessness assistance made on or after 3 April 2018.
³   As inserted by HRA 2017, s 3(1), for applications for homelessness assistance made on or after 3 April 2018.

15.213 The English Code contains detailed advice at paras 14.49–14.53, including advice that the local housing authority must be satisfied of the following matters:

- that the steps recorded in the personalised housing plans were reasonable in the context of the applicant's particular circumstances and needs;
- that the applicant understood what was required of him or her in order to fulfil those reasonable steps and is therefore in a position to make a deliberate refusal;
- that the applicant is not refusing to co-operate as a result of a mental illness or other health need, for which he or she is not being provided with support, or as a result of a difficulty in communicating; and

- the applicant's refusal to co-operate with any steps was unreasonable in the context of his or her particular circumstances and needs (examples are given about failing to attend appointments or view properties)[1].

It also contains advice on applicants who might have particular needs, and particular reasons why their actions should not be regarded as deliberate and unreasonable refusals to co-operate[2].

1   English Code, para 14.53.
2   English Code, chapter 21 for people who have experienced domestic abuse; chapter 22 for care-leavers; chapter 23 for people with an offending history; chapter 24 for former members of the armed forces; and chapter 25 for people who have experienced modern slavery or have been trafficked.

The right to request a review

15.214 The applicant has the right to request a review of the local housing authority's decision that he or she has deliberately and unreasonably refused to co-operate[1].

1   HA 1996, s 202(1)(bb), as inserted by HRA 2017, s 9, for applications for homelessness assistance made on or after 3 April 2018, see **19.30–19.35**.

15.215 The review must be requested within 21 days of notification, which is the date when the applicant received the notice[1]. If the applicant did not receive the notice, and the local housing authority made the notice available at its office for a reasonable period for collection by or on behalf of the applicant, the date of notification will be the end of that period[2].

1   HA 1996, s 202(3), see **19.109–19.115**.
2   HA 1996, s 193B(8), as inserted by HRA 2017, s 7(1), for applications for homelessness assistance made on or after 3 April 2018. The exact wording is 'treated as having been given to the applicant if it is made available at the authority's office for a reasonable period for collection'. This suggests that the date when it is to be treated as having been given, ie notified, is the end of the reasonable period, rather than the date when the notice was first left.

Consequences of a decision that the applicant has deliberately and unreasonably refused to co-operate

15.216 A notice of a decision that the applicant has deliberately and unreasonably refused to co-operate can only be served on an applicant who is owed either the HA 1996, s 195(2)[1], prevention duty or the HA 1996, s 189B(2)[2], relief duty. In each case, the relevant duty will come to an end[3]. What happens next to the applicant depends on which duty he or she was owed and, if he or she was owed the HA 1996, s 189B(2)[4], relief duty, whether or not he or she has a priority need and whether he or she became homeless intentionally.

1   As amended by HRA 2017, s 4(2), for applications for homelessness assistance made on or after 3 April 2018. See **15.87–15.137**.
2   As inserted by HRA 2017, s 5(2), for applications for homelessness assistance made on or after 3 April 2018. See **15.138–15.195**.
3   HA 1996, s 193C(2), as inserted by HRA 2017, s 7(1), for applications for homelessness assistance made on or after 3 April 2018.

4   As inserted by HRA 2017, s 5(2), for applications for homelessness assistance made on or after
     3 April 2018. See **15.138–15.195**.

The end of the HA 1996, s 195(2), prevention duty

15.217 If the applicant was owed the HA 1996, s 195(2)[1], prevention duty,
then he or she was threatened with homelessness. No further duty will arise
under HA 1996, Pt 7[2]. If he or she remains threatened with homelessness, he
or she could make a fresh application for assistance. The local housing
authority must accept a fresh application if the factual circumstances are not
the same as those on the disposal of his or her first application[3].

1   As amended by HRA 2017, s 4(2), for applications for homelessness assistance made on or
     after 3 April 2018. See **15.87–15.137**.
2   As amended by HRA 2017 for applications for homelessness assistance made on or after
     3 April 2018.
3   HA 1996, s 183(1), see English Code, para 18.12 and **8.80–8.82** and **8.85–8.91**.

15.218 If the applicant subsequently becomes homeless, the factual circumstances will not be the same as on his or her first application and so he or she
could make a fresh application for homelessness assistance. If he or she is
homeless and eligible for assistance, the local housing authority will owe the
applicant the HA 1996, s 189B(2)[1], relief duty. If the local housing authority
has reason to believe that the applicant may be homeless, may be eligible for
assistance and may have a priority need, it will owe a duty to secure interim
accommodation[2].

1   As inserted by HRA 2017, s 5(2), for applications for homelessness assistance made on or after
     3 April 2018. See **15.138–15.195**.
2   HA 1996, s 188(1), (1ZA) and (1ZB), as inserted by HRA 2017, s 5(4), for applications for
     homelessness assistance made on or after 3 April 2018. See **16.37–16.50**.

The ending of the HA 1996, s 189B(2), relief duty

15.219 If the applicant was owed the HA 1996, s 189B(2)[1], relief duty, then
he or she is homeless. If the local housing authority is satisfied that the
applicant does not have a priority need, then no further duty is owed. The
applicant could make a fresh application for assistance. The local housing
authority must accept a fresh application if the factual circumstances are not
the same as those on disposal of his or her first application[2].

1   As inserted by HRA 2017, s 5(2), for applications for homelessness assistance made on or after
     3 April 2018. See English Code, para 18.12 and **15.137–15.195**.
2   HA 1996, s 183(1), see **8.80–8.82** and **8.85–8.91**.

15.220 If the local housing authority is satisfied that the applicant has a
priority need, then it must also consider whether or not the applicant became
homeless intentionally. Where the applicant is homeless, eligible for assistance,
has a priority need, and has become homeless intentionally, the local housing
authority will owe the applicant:

- a duty to secure that accommodation is available for his or her occupation for such period as it considers will give him or her a reasonable opportunity of securing accommodation for his or her occupation[1]; and
- a duty to provide the applicant, or secure that he or she is provided with, advice and assistance in any attempt he or she may make to secure that accommodation becomes available for his or her occupation[2].

[1]   HA 1996, s 190(2)(a), as amended by HRA 2017, s 5(5), for applications for homelessness assistance made on or after 3 April 2018. See **16.81–16.93**.
[2]   HA 1996, s 190(2)(b), as amended by HRA 2017, s 5(5), for applications for homelessness assistance made on or after 3 April 2018. See **15.231**.

15.221 Where the local housing authority is satisfied that the applicant is homeless, eligible for assistance and has a priority need and is not satisfied that the applicant became homeless intentionally, and the local housing authority is also satisfied that the relevant duty came to an end because the applicant had deliberately and unreasonably refused to co-operate[1], then the main housing duty at HA 1996, s 193(2)[2], will not be owed[3]. Instead, the local housing authority will owe the applicant a different duty, under HA 1996, s 193C(4)[4], to secure accommodation for the applicant's occupation. This accommodation duty is discussed at **16.200–16.216**.

[1]   See **15.196–15.221**.
[2]   See **15.196–15.221**.
[3]   HA 1996, s 193C(3) and (4), as inserted by HRA 2017, s 7(1), for applications for homelessness assistance made on or after 3 April 2018.
[4]   As inserted by HRA 2017, s 7(1), for applications for homelessness assistance made on or after 3 April 2018.

REFERRAL DUTIES

Duty on public authority to notify a local housing authority

15.222 A new HA 1996, s 213B[1], creates a duty on other public authorities to take steps to refer a person who is or may be homeless or threatened with homelessness to a local housing authority for the purposes of allowing him or her to make an application for homelessness assistance. Public authorities are defined as 'a person (other than a local housing authority) who has functions of a public nature'[2]. The public authorities specified as subject to this duty are set out at Homelessness (Review Procedure etc) Regulations 2018, reg 10 and Sch 1[3]. They are:

- a governor of a prison within the meaning of Prison Act 1952, s 53(1);
- a director of a contracted out prison within the meaning of Criminal Justice Act 1991, s 84(4);
- a governor of a young offender institution provided under Prison Act 1952 s 43(1)(a);
- a governor of a secure training centre provided under Prison Act 1952, s 43(1)(b);
- a director of a contracted out secure training centre within the meaning of Criminal Justice and Public Order Act 1994, s 15;

- a principal of a secure college provided under of Prison Act 1952, s 43(1)(c);
- a youth offending team established under Crime and Disorder Act 1998, s 39(1);
- a provider of probation services;
- an officer designated for these purposes by the Secretary of State for Work and Pensions employed at a Jobcentre Plus office; a social services authority;
- a person who performs a function of a local authority pursuant to a direction under Education Act 1996, s 497A(4) or (4A) applying to social services functions relating to children under Children Act 2004, s 50, and relating to childcare by Childcare Act 2006, s 15;[4]
- a NHS Trust and an NHS Foundation Trust in relation to emergency departments, urgent treatment centres and in-patient treatment; and
- the Secretary of State for Defence in relation to members of the regular armed forces.

Although the referral duty came into force on 3 April 2018, the list of specified public authorities does not come into force until 1 October 2018[5]. This is presumably to allow the specified public authorities a period in which to prepare for the referral duty.

[1]   Inserted by HRA, s 10, from 3 April 2018; English Code, chapter 4.
[2]   HA 1996, s 213B(5), as inserted by HRA, s 10, from 3 April 2018.
[3]   SI 2018/223, at Appendix 2.
[4]   There is specific guidance as to the duty to refer when dealing with young people aged 16 or 17 in *Prevention of Homelessness and Provision of Accommodation for 16 and 17 year old young people who may be homeless and/or require accommodation* (MHCLG and Department for Education, April 2018), paras 3.62–3.63.
[5]   SI 2018/223, regs 1(3) and 10.

15.223 The duty applies when one of those bodies is exercising functions in respect of a person, and also considers that person is or may be homeless or threatened with homelessness. Those functions could be the provision of criminal justice, health care, social care, or education.

15.224 The threshold is met when the public authority considers that a person is or may be homeless or threatened with homelessness[1]. That requires a public authority to be aware that homelessness does not mean just that a person might lack a roof over his or her head. It also applies where accommodation might not be reasonable to continue to occupy[2], or might not be available for the occupation of members of the person's family, or by people with whom he or she might reasonably be expected to reside[3]. The public authority should also be aware of the two definitions of 'threatened with homelessness': that a person is likely to become homeless within 56 days or that a person has been served with a valid Housing Act 1988, s 21, notice which expires within 56 days[4]. The test is that a person 'is or may be' homeless, so if in doubt, it should be assumed that a person is homeless.

[1]   HA 1996, s 213B(1), as inserted by HRA 2017, s 10, from 3 April 2018.
[2]   HA 1996, s 175(3), see **10.73–10.134**.
[3]   HA 1996, s 176, see **10.21–10.32**.
[4]   HA 1996, s 175(4) and (5), as inserted by HRA 2017, s 1(2) and (3), for applications for homelessness assistance made on or after 3 April 2018. See **10.144–10.147**.

15.225 If the relevant public authority does come to that conclusion, it must ask the person to agree that it should notify a local housing authority in England of its opinion (that the person is or may be homeless or threatened with homelessness). It should also ask the person how he or she may be contacted by the local housing authority, and ask him or her to identify which local housing authority should be notified[1]. The public authority cannot make the referral unless the person consents and identifies which local housing authority in England should be notified[2]. The English Code contains a procedure for referrals, to be set up by the local housing authority and agreed with local service partners[3].

[1]   HA 1996, s 213B(2), as inserted by HRA 2017, s 10, from 3 April 2018.
[2]   HA 1996, s 213B(3), as inserted by HRA 2017, s 10, from 3 April 2018; English Code, para 4.1.
[3]   English Code, paras 4.5–4.12

15.226 Once the notification has been sent, the onus will be on the local housing authority then to make contact with the person, and to invite him or her to make an application for homelessness assistance[1]. This is the reason for including the person's contact details in the notification.

[1]   HA 1996, s 183(1), see **8.14–8.110**.

15.227 Receipt of the notification, containing information that the person is or may be homeless or threatened with homelessness, might constitute an application for homelessness assistance under HA 1996, s 183(1) meaning that the local housing authority's obligations under HA 1996, Pt 7[1], would apply. The immediate obligations would be for the local housing authority to make inquiries into whether the person is eligible for assistance and if so, what duty, if any is owed[2], and to secure interim accommodation if it has reason to believe that the person may be eligible for assistance, may be homeless and may have a priority need[3].

[1]   As amended by HRA 2017, for applications for homelessness assistance made on or after 3 April 2018.
[2]   HA 1996, s 184(1), see **9.89–9.143**.
[3]   HA 1996, s 188(1), as amended by HRA 2017, s 5(4), for applications for homelessness assistance made on or after 3 April 2018, see **16.20–16.50**.

15.228 The English Code, however, does not advise that the receipt of a referral constitutes an application for homelessness assistance. Instead, it advises that the local housing authority should try to make contact with the person and that an application for homelessness assistance is only triggered once contact has been achieved, and details are received that give the local housing authority reason to believe that the person may be homeless or threatened with homelessness[1]. The authors of this book consider that this advice fails to recognise that the referral itself can give the local housing authority reason to believe that the person may be homeless or threatened with homelessness, and thus that the referral itself constitutes an application for the purposes of HA 1996, s 183(1). In those circumstances, the duty at HA 1996, s 183(1), to start to make inquiries and to consider whether interim accommodation should be secured applies once the local housing authority has received the referral[2].

1 English Code, paras 4.19–4.20
2 See **16.20–16.50**.

Duty on local housing authority to refer in cases involving children

15.229 Where a local housing authority has reason to believe that an applicant with whom a child normally resides or might reasonably be expected to reside may be ineligible or may have become intentionally homeless[1], the local housing authority must invite the applicant to consent to the referral of the essential facts of his or her case to children's services[2]. If consent is given, the referral must be made[3]. The local housing authority must provide children's services with the essential facts of the applicant's case and the subsequent decision that is made on his or her homelessness application[4]. This duty is discussed in more detail at **16.280–16.287**.

1 HA 1996, s 213A(1), as amended by HRA 2017, s 44, for applications for homelessness assistance made on or after 3 April 2018.
2 HA 1996, s 213A(2)(a) and 3(b), as amended by HRA 2017, s 4(7), for applications for homelessness assistance on or after 3 April 2018.
3 HA 1996, s 213A(2)(b) and 3(b), as amended by HRA 2017, s 4(7), for applications for homelessness assistance made on or after 3 April 2018.
4 HA 1996, s 213A(2)(b) and (3)(b), as amended by HRA 2017, s 4(7), for applications for homelessness assistance made on or after 3 April 2018.

15.230 In addition to this referral duty, local housing authorities are obliged to co-operate with social services. Where social services are aware of a decision by a local housing authority that the applicant is ineligible for assistance or became homeless intentionally, they may request the local housing authority provide them with advice and assistance. The local housing authority must provide such advice and assistance as is reasonable[1].

1 HA 1996, s 213A(5) and (6), as amended by HRA 2017, s 4(7), for applications for homelessness assistance made on or after 3 April 2018.

ADVICE AND ASSISTANCE DUTY OWED TO APPLICANTS WHO HAVE A PRIORITY NEED AND HAVE BECOME HOMELESS INTENTIONALLY

15.231 The duty to provide advice and assistance remains in HA 1996, Pt 7, as amended by HRA 2017[1], for one group of applicants only: those in respect of whom a local housing authority is satisfied that they are homeless, eligible for assistance, have a priority need and have become homeless intentionally. The duty to secure advice and assistance applies when the local housing authority's HA 1996, s 189B(2)[2], relief duty has come to an end[3]. At that point, the local housing authority must provide the applicant with advice and assistance in any attempt he or she may make to secure that accommodation becomes available for his or her occupation[4]. The local housing authority is also under a duty to secure that accommodation is available for the applicant and for his or her household for such period as it considers will give him a reasonable opportunity of securing his or her own accommodation[5]. In deciding what advice and assistance is to be provided under this duty, the local housing authority must have regard to its assessment of the applicant's case under HA 1996, s 189A[6]. The advice and assistance must include information about the likely availability in the local housing authority's district of types of accommodation appropriate to the applicant's housing needs, including the location and sources of such types of accommodation[7].

[1]   For applications for homelessness assistance made on or after 3 April 2018.
[2]   As inserted by HRA 2017, s 5(2), for applications for homelessness assistance made on or after 3 April 2018, see **15.138–15.195**.
[3]   For the events which bring the HA 1996, s 189B(2), relief duty to an end, see HA 1996, s 189B(4), (7) and (9), as inserted by HRA 2017, s 5(2), for applications for homelessness assistance made on or after 3 April 2018, see **15.151–15.189**. Strangely, there is no guidance as to this remaining advice and assistance duty in the English Code.
[4]   HA 1996, s 190(2)(b) as amended by HRA 2017, s 5(5), for applications for homelessness assistance made on or after 3 April 2018.
[5]   HA 1996, s 190(2)(a), as amended by HRA 2017, s 5(5), for applications for homelessness assistance made on or after 3 April 2018, see **16.81–16.93**.
[6]   As inserted by HRA 2017, s 3(1), for applications for homelessness assistance made on or after 3 April 2018, see **15.62–15.86**. HA 1996, s 190(4), as amended by HRA 2017, s 5(5), for applications for homelessness assistance made on or after 3 April 2018.
[7]   HA 1996, s 190(5), as amended by HRA 2017, s 5(5), for applications for homelessness assistance made on or after 3 April 2018.

DUTY TO PROTECT APPLICANT'S PROPERTY

15.232 The local housing authority must take reasonable steps to prevent the loss of or damage to an applicant's personal property where[1]:

- the local housing authority have reason to believe there is a danger of loss of, or damage to, the property;
- that danger arises from the applicant's inability to protect or deal with his or her property;
- no other suitable arrangements are in place; and
- the local housing authority are or were subject to a duty to accommodate the applicant under HA 1996, ss 188[2] (interim accommodation duty), 189B[3] (relief duty), 190[4] (duty to persons found to be homeless intentionally), 193[5] (main housing duty), 195[6] (duty to persons threatened with homelessness prevention duty), or 200[7] (duties to applicants whose case is considered for referral to another local housing authority)[8].

This duty is discussed in more detail at **16.288–16.309**.

[1]   HA 1996, ss 211–212, as amended by HRA 2017, s 5(12), for applications for homelessness assistance made on or after 3 April 2018.
[2]   As amended by HRA 2017, s 5, for applications for homelessness assistance made on or after 3 April 2018.
[3]   As inserted by HRA 2017, s 5(2) for applications for homelessness assistance made on or after 3 April 2018.
[4]   As amended by HRA 2017, ss 3 and 5, for applications for homelessness assistance made on or after 3 April 2018.
[5]   As amended by HRA 2017, ss 5 and 7, for applications for homelessness assistance made on or after 3 April 2018.
[6]   As amended by HRA 2017, s 4, for applications for homelessness assistance made on or after 3 April 2018.

7   As amended by HRA 2017, s 5, for applications for homelessness assistance made on or after 3 April 2018.
8   HA 1996, s 211(1)–(2) as amended by HRA 2017, s 5(2) for applications for homelessness assistance made on or after 3 April 2018.

Chapter 16

ACCOMMODATION – DUTIES AND POWERS ON LOCAL HOUSING AUTHORITIES IN ENGLAND

Contents

INTRODUCTION

16.1 In this chapter, we consider the powers and duties, in the Housing Act 1996 (HA 1996), Pt 7, as amended by the Homelessness Reduction Act 2017 (HRA 2017), on local housing authorities in England[1] to secure accommodation for homeless applicants. The amendments to HA 1996, Pt 7, inserted by HRA 2017[2], require a change in approach by both local housing authorities and advisers. In particular, the HA 1996, s 195(2)[3] prevention duty and the s 189B(2)[4] relief duty, discussed in detail in CHAPTER 15, mark a shift in policy away from local housing authorities securing accommodation for eligible, homeless applicants in favour of helping those applicants retain or secure accommodation for themselves. The shift is a significant one: from 1977, when the Housing (Homeless Persons) Act 1977 was enacted, until 2018 when the HRA 2017 came into force, whether or not a local housing authority would be required to secure accommodation for a homeless applicant could properly be described as the ultimate question underpinning each successive statutory homelessness scheme[5]. The policy behind the HRA 2017 is that of early intervention, so that applicants can be assisted either to keep their existing accommodation or to find alternative accommodation without having to experience 'the stress and experience of a homelessness crisis'[6]. The second policy aim is to help all applicants, regardless of whether they have a priority need or have become homelessness intentionally[7]. However, that 'help' does not extend to a duty to accommodate all those applicants.

---

[1] See CHAPTER 17 for the duties on local housing authorities in Wales to secure accommodation for the applicant under Housing (Wales) Act 2014, Pt 2.

[2] In force from 3 April 2018: Homelessness Reduction Act 2017 (Commencement and Transitional and Savings Provisions) Regulations 2018, SI 2018/167, reg 3; see APPENDIX 2.

[3] As amended by Homelessness Reduction Act 2017 (HRA 2017), s 4(2) for applications for homelessness assistance made on or after 3 April 2018.

[4] As inserted by HRA 2017, s 5(2) for applications for homelessness assistance made on or after 3 April 2018.

[5] Housing (Homeless Persons) Act 1977; Housing Act 1985, Pt 3; Housing Act 1996, Pt 7 (HA 1996), (prior to the amendments introduced by HRA 2017, for applications for homelessness assistance made on or after 3 April 2018).

[6] Policy fact sheet: homelessness prevention duty (DCLG, 2017).

[7] The HA 1996, s 195(2) (as amended by HRA 2017, s 4(2) for applications for homelessness assistance made on or after 3 April 2018) prevention duty is owed to all applicants who are threatened with homelessness and are eligible for assistance, see **15.87–15.137**; the HA 1996, s 189B(2) (as inserted by HRA 2017, s 5(2) for applications for homelessness assistance made

on or after 3 April 2018) prevention duty is owed to all applicants who are threatened with homelessness and are eligible for assistance, see **15.138–15.195**.

16.2 Accommodation will only now be secured by the local housing authority in those cases where the performance of the HA 1996, s 195(2)[1] prevention duty or the s 189B(2)[2] relief duty has not been effective in helping the applicant to retain or secure accommodation for him or herself. That is, if the performance of the HA 1996, s 195(2)[3] prevention duty or the s 189B(2)[4] relief duty is successful and the applicant retains or secures accommodation, the issue of accommodation being provided by the local housing authority will no longer arise.

[1] As amended by HRA 2017, s 4(2) for applications for homelessness assistance made on or after 3 April 2018.
[2] As inserted by HRA 2017, s 5(2) for applications for homelessness assistance made on or after 3 April 2018.
[3] As amended by HRA 2017, s 4(2) for applications for homelessness assistance made on or after 3 April 2018.
[4] As inserted by HRA 2017, s 5(2) for applications for homelessness assistance made on or after 3 April 2018.

16.3 This shift in policy goes hand in hand with another longer-term trend: the increased use of the private rented sector as a means of tackling statutory homelessness as an alternative to the allocation of social housing or the provision of any other form of permanent or indefinite accommodation[1]. Putting it another way, an application for homelessness assistance can no longer be seen as an automatic gateway to 'council housing', as it is colloquially known.

[1] Pursuant to HA 1996, Part 6. For the allocation of social housing prior to April 1997 see **1.14–1.15**.

The shift away from provision of accommodation to helping an applicant secure accommodation

16.4 In 1981, when the House of Lords handed down its landmark decision on the circumstances in which a person is to be regarded as having become homeless intentionally[1] in the case of *Din v Wandsworth London Borough Council*[2], there was (or at least there was seen to be) a clear link between applications for homelessness assistance and the allocation of social housing. In the words of Lord Bridge:

'A homeless person who has a priority need can look to the relevant housing authority to secure that accommodation becomes available for his occupation. This throws a heavy burden on already hard-pressed housing authorities in areas, of which Wandsworth is undoubtedly one, where there is a desperate shortage of housing accommodation and a long housing waiting list. It may also no doubt engender a sense of grievance among those on that list who either have no priority need or cannot claim to be homeless, although their existing accommodation is far from satisfactory, to see others going to the head of the queue[3].'

[1] See Chapter 13 on becoming homeless intentionally.
[2] [1983] 1 AC 657, AC. The case turned on the construction of Housing (Homeless Persons) Act 1977, s 17.

3   *Din v Wandsworth London Borough Council* [1983] 1 AC 657, 680, AC.

16.5 But in 1996, the House of Lords, when they were next called upon to consider the circumstances in which a person is to be regarded as having become homeless intentionally[1], exploded the idea that those applicants who had not become homeless intentionally were entitled to be provided with permanent homes under the statutory homelessness provisions contained in Housing Act 1985, Pt 3:

> '[T]he duty of the local housing authority to an unintentionally homeless person in priority need under section 65(2) is simply to secure that accommodation becomes available for his occupation. Under the substituted section 69(1), the accommodation must be 'suitable,' but this does not import any requirement of permanence . . . there is no reason why temporary accommodation should ipso facto be unsuitable. If the tenure is so precarious that the person is likely to have to leave within 28 days without any alternative accommodation being available, then he remains threatened with homelessness and the council has not discharged its duty. Otherwise it seems to me that the term for which the accommodation is provided is a matter for the council to decide. In some cases, such as a person in priority need because he is old, mentally ill or handicapped (section 59(1)(c)), the council may decide to provide permanent accommodation as soon as reasonably possible. In other cases, such as the pregnant woman in my earlier example, it may prefer to use temporary accommodation and wait and see. But provided that the decision is not *Wednesbury* unreasonable (*Associated Provincial Picture Houses Ltd. v. Wednesday Corporation* [1948] 1 K.B. 233), I do not think that the courts should lay down requirements as to security of tenure[2].'

[1]   This time, under the provisions of Housing Act 1985, Pt 3.
[2]   *R v Brent London Borough Council ex p Awua* [1996] AC 55, AC at 72 per Lord Hoffmann.

16.6 Subsequently, the statutory framework in HA 1996, Pt 7 made it clear that the highest duty owed to any applicant would be met by the provision of temporary accommodation only[1]. The Homelessness Act 2002 then introduced a new mechanism by which this duty might be brought to an end: the acceptance of an offer of an assured non-shorthold tenancy from a private landlord[2]. For 'restricted cases' only[3], further amendments to HA 1996, Pt 7 introduced by the Housing and Regeneration Act 2008[4] provided that this duty could be brought to an end by means of a 'private accommodation offer' of an assured shorthold tenancy[5]. Further changes to HA 1996, Pt 7 made by the Localism Act 2011[6] then allowed local housing authorities to bring the HA 1996, s 193(2), main housing duty[7] to an end in *any* case by means of a 'private rented sector offer' of an assured shorthold tenancy[8]. Then finally, the changes to the HA 1996, Pt 7 introduced by HRA 2017[9] encourage the use of the private rented sector still further as a means of bringing the HA 1996, s 195(2)[10] prevention duty, the s 189B(2)[11] relief duty or the s 193C(4)(c)[12] accommodation duty to an end[13].

[1]   HA 1996, s 193(2). See **16.94–16.199**.
[2]   HA 1996, s 193(6)(cc), as inserted by Homelessness Act 2002, s 7(2).
[3]   A niche status defined by reference to the immigration status of certain members of the applicant's household. See **16.180–16.183**.
[4]   Housing and Regeneration Act 2008, Sch 15, Pt 1, para 5.
[5]   As defined by HA 1996, s 193(7AA) in force between 2 March 2009 and 8 November 2012.
[6]   Localism Act 2011, s 148. In force from 9 November 2012.
[7]   HA 1996, s 193(2), see **16.94–16.199**.

8   As defined by HA 1996, s 193(7AC). See **16.153–16.180**. Though this marked a significant change, its practical effect should not be overstated: only around 1% of applicants owed the HA 1996, s 193(2), main housing duty are made private rented sector offers. See Table 777, *Immediate outcome of decision by local authority to accept household as unintentionally homeless, eligible and in priority need* (DCLG, September 2017).

9   For applications for homelessness assistance made on or after 3 April 2018.

10 As amended by HRA 2017, s 4(2) for applications for homelessness assistance made on or after 3 April 2018.

11 As inserted by HRA 2017, s 5(2) for applications for homelessness assistance made on or after 3 April 2018.

12 Duty owed to applicants who have a priority need and have not become homeless intentionally, but who have deliberately and unreasonably refused to co-operate. As inserted by HRA 2017, s 7(1) for applications for homelessness assistance made on or after 3 April 2018. See **16.200–16.216**.

13 The various ways in which these duties may be brought to an end by means of the acceptance or refusal of suitable accommodation in the private sector are discussed in detail at **15.98–15.132** (for the prevention duty), **15.151–15.190** (for the relief duty), and **16.204–16.215** (for the accommodation duty): HA 1996, ss 189B(2), 193C(4) and 195(2), as inserted and amended by HRA 2017, ss 4(2), 5(2) and 7(1), for applications for homelessness assistance made on or after 3 April 2018.

16.7 The effect of the new provisions introduced by HRA 2017[1], if they operate effectively, is that a homeless applicant is likely to be helped to secure (or retain) suitable accommodation in the private sector, rather than being made an offer of permanent social housing. This is not to say that the link between the duties owed to homeless applicants under HA 1997, Pt 7[2] and the allocation of social housing under HA 1996, Pt 6[3] has been severed entirely. Local housing authority allocation schemes must still give 'reasonable preference' to those who are homeless under HA 1996, Pt 7[4] and to those who are owed certain specific duties under HA 1996, Pt 7[5], when it comes to allocating social housing[6]. And the allocation of social housing under HA 1996, Pt 6 to a homeless applicant remains one of the ways in which the HA 1996, s 193(2)[7] main housing duty may be brought to an end[8]. But if not severed, the link has certainly become frayed. This might be seen as part of a wider policy shift away from the provision of accommodation by local housing authorities as a long-term solution by which to meet housing need, and instead implementation of a shorter term solution to cope with emergencies and facilitate access to the private rented sector[9].

1   For applications for homelessness assistance made on or after 3 April 2018.

2   As amended by HRA 2017, for applications for homelessness assistance made on or after 3 April 2018.

3   See **Part 1** of this book.

4   As amended by HRA 2017, for applications for homelessness assistance made on or after 3 April 2018.

5   As amended by HRA 2017, for applications for homelessness assistance made on or after 3 April 2018.

6   Applicants who are 'homeless' will be entitled to a reasonable preference under HA 1996, s 166A(3)(a) as will applicants who are owed any of the duties at HA 1996, ss 190(2), 193(2), or 195(2) (as amended by HRA 2017, s 4(2), for applications for homelessness assistance made on or after 3 April 2018). See **4.58–4.79**.

7   See **16.94–16.199**.

8   HA 1996, s 193(6)(c) and (7). See **16.130–16.135** and **16.142–16.152**.

9   Evidence for this wider policy shift can be found in Housing and Planning Act 2016, s 118 and Sch 7 ('Secure tenancies etc: phasing out of tenancies for life'), and s 119 and Sch 8, which restrict succession rights to secure, introductory and demoted tenancies. At the date of writing, these provisions have not been brought into force and there seem to be no immediate plans to do so.

16.8 Clearly, then, the nature of the accommodation which a homeless applicant may expect to obtain under HA 1997, Pt 7[1], and the circumstances in which a local housing authority will be under a duty to secure that accommodation, as opposed to helping the applicant to secure it, have changed significantly in the years since 1977. The duties to help a homeless applicant retain or secure accommodation form the subject of CHAPTER 15. The duties (and powers) on local housing authorities to secure accommodation form the subject of this chapter.

[1] As amended by HRA 2017, for applications for homelessness assistance made on or after 3 April 2018.

THE DUTIES AND POWERS IN OUTLINE

The interim accommodation duty

16.9 The first accommodation duty which may arise upon an application for homelessness assistance having been made is the interim duty to secure accommodation for applicants whom the local housing authority have reason to believe may be homeless, eligible for assistance and have a priority need[1]. Before the amendments to HA 1996, Pt 7 made by HRA 2017 came into force[2], the operation of this duty was a relatively simple matter. The duty would be owed as soon as the local housing authority had reason to believe that the applicant satisfied the relevant criteria, and it would end upon the local housing authority concluding its inquiries and deciding what further duty, if any, the applicant was owed. Now the operation of the duty is considerably more complex. The complexity arises from the operation of the HA 1996, s 189B(2)[3], relief duty to help the applicant secure accommodation for him or herself, which may be owed at the same time as the interim accommodation duty under HA 1996, s 188(1)[4]. The new duties have increased the number of decisions which a local housing authority is required to make in the course of considering an application for homelessness assistance[5]. As a result there is a greater variety of events which may cause the interim accommodation duty to come to an end.

[1] HA 1996, s 188(1), as amended by HRA 2017, s 5(4), for applications for homelessness assistance made on or after 3 April 2018.
[2] On 3 April 2018: Homelessness Reduction Act 2017 (Commencement and Transitional and Savings Provisions) Regulations 2018, SI 2018/167, reg 3.
[3] As inserted by HRA 2017, s 5(2), for applications for homelessness assistance made on or after 3 April 2018.
[4] As amended by HRA 2017, s 5(4) for applications for homelessness assistance made on or after 3 April 2018.
[5] See CHAPTER 9 of this book.

16.10 The precise circumstances in which the interim accommodation duty will be owed and the ways in which it may come to an end are analysed in detail at **16.51–16.80**. In overview, the duty operates as follows:

- Where the applicant has made an application for homelessness assistance, and the local housing authority has reason to believe that he or she may be homeless, may be eligible for assistance and may have a priority need, the interim accommodation duty is owed[1].

- Where the local housing authority, having made inquiries, satisfies itself that an applicant does not have a priority need, the interim accommodation duty continues until either:
  - the applicant is notified of the local housing authority's decision that the HA 1996, s 189B(2)[2], relief duty is not owed (because the applicant is either not eligible for assistance or is not homeless)[3]; or
  - the applicant is notified of the local housing authority's decision that, when the HA 1996, s 189B(2)[4], relief duty comes to an end, no further accommodation duty will be owed under the HA 1996, s 190(2)[5], short-term duty, or the HA 1996, s 193(2)[6], main housing duty[7].
- Where the local housing authority is satisfied that an applicant does have a priority need, or continues to have reason to believe that he or she may have a priority need, the interim accommodation duty continues until the later of:
  - the HA 1996, s 189B(2)[8], relief duty coming to an end[9];
  - the applicant being notified of the local housing authority's decision that the HA 1996, s 189B(2)[10], relief duty is not owed (because the applicant is either not eligible for assistance or is not homeless)[11]; or
  - the applicant being notified of the local housing authority's decision as to what further duty (if any) will be owed to him or her when the HA 1996, s 189B(2)[12], relief duty comes to an end[13].
- Where the applicant requests a review under HA 1996, s 202(1)(h)[14] of the suitability of accommodation offered to him or her by way of a final accommodation offer[15] or final Pt 6 offer[16], having accepted or refused the offer, the interim accommodation duty will continue until the decision on review has been notified to the applicant[17].
- Where the applicant has made an application for homelessness assistance within two years of acceptance of a private rented sector offer[18], and the local housing authority has reason to believe that he or she may be homeless and may be eligible for assistance, the interim accommodation duty will arise irrespective of whether the applicant has a priority need and will continue until the later of[19]:
  - the HA 1996 s 189B(2)[20], relief duty coming to an end[21];
  - the applicant being notified of the local housing authority's decision that the HA 1996, s 189B(2)[22], relief duty is not owed, because the applicant is either not eligible for assistance or is not homeless[23]; or
  - the applicant being notified of the local housing authority's decision as to what further duty (if any) will be owed to him or her when the HA 1996, s 189B(2)[24], relief duty comes to an end[25].

Where the applicant's case is referred to another local housing authority under HA 1996, s 198[26] different rules apply. An outline of the rules is at **16.15–16.16**. The rules are analysed in detail at **16.217–16.232**.

---

[1]   HA 1996, s 188(1). See **16.37–16.50**.
[2]   As inserted by HRA 2017, s 5(2), for applications for homelessness assistance made on or after 3 April 2018.
[3]   HA 1996, s 188(1ZA)(a), as inserted by HRA 2017, s 5(4), for applications for homelessness assistance made on or after 3 April 2018. See **16.57** and **16.61**.

[4] As inserted by HRA 2017, s 5(2), for applications for homelessness assistance made on or after 3 April 2018.

[5] As amended by HRA 2017, s 5(5), for applications for homelessness assistance made on or after 3 April 2018. See **16.81–16.93**.

[6] See **16.94–16.199**.

[7] HA 1996, s 188(1ZA)(b), as inserted by HRA 2017, s 5(4), for applications for homelessness assistance made on or after 3 April 2018, see **16.58**.

[8] As inserted by HRA 2017, s 5(2), for applications for homelessness assistance made on or after 3 April 2018.

[9] HA 1996, s 188(1ZB)(a), as inserted by HRA 2017, s 5(4), for applications for homelessness assistance made on or after 3 April 2018. See **16.61**.

[10] As inserted by HRA 2017, s 5(2), for applications for homelessness assistance made on or after 3 April 2018.

[11] HA 1996, s 188(1ZB)(a), as inserted by HRA 2017, s 5(4), for applications for homelessness assistance made on or after 3 April 2018. See **16.61**.

[12] As inserted by HRA 2017, s 5(2), for applications for homelessness assistance made on or after 3 April 2018.

[13] HA 1996, s 188(1ZB)(b), as inserted by HRA 2017, s 5(4), for applications for homelessness assistance made on or after 3 April 2018, see **16.62**.

[14] As inserted by HRA 2017, s 9(2) for applications for homelessness assistance made on or after 3 April 2018. See **19.65–19.69**.

[15] As defined at HA 1996, s 193A(4), as inserted by HRA 2017, s 7(1), for applications for homelessness assistance made on or after 3 April 2018. See **15.181–15.184**.

[16] As defined at HA 1996, s 193A(5), as inserted by HRA 2017, s 7(1), for applications for homelessness assistance made on or after 3 April 2018. See **15.185–15.188**.

[17] HA 1996, s 188(1ZB) and (2A), as inserted by HRA 2017, s 5(4) for applications for homelessness assistance made on or after 3 April 2018. The local housing authority must continue either to have reason to believe that the applicant may have a priority need, or be satisfied that the applicant has a priority need.

[18] For private rented sector offer, see HA 1996, s 193(7AA)–(7AC), and **16.153–16.180**.

[19] HA 1996, s 188(1A), as amended by HRA 2017, s 5(4), for applications for homelessness assistance made on or after 3 April 2018.

[20] As inserted by HRA 2017, s 5(2), for applications for homelessness assistance made on or after 3 April 2018.

[21] HA 1996, s 188(1ZB)(a), as amended by HRA 2017, s 5(4), for applications for homelessness assistance made on or after 3 April 2018. See **16.61**.

[22] As inserted by HRA 2017, s 5(2), for applications for homelessness assistance made on or after 3 April 2018.

[23] HA 1996, s 188(1ZB)(a), as amended by HRA 2017, s 5(4), for applications for homelessness assistance made on or after 3 April 2018. See **16.61**.

[24] As inserted by HRA 2017, s 5(2), for applications for homelessness assistance made on or after 3 April 2018.

[25] HA 1996, s 188(1ZB)(b), as amended by HRA 2017, s 5(4), for applications for homelessness assistance made on or after 3 April 2018. See **16.62**.

[26] As amended by HRA 2017, s 5(8) for applications for homelessness assistance made on or after 3 April 2018.

The HA 1996, s 190(2), short-term accommodation duty

16.11 Once the HA 1996, s 189B(2)[1], relief duty has come to an end, if the local housing authority is satisfied that the applicant is homeless, eligible for assistance, has a priority need, and has become homeless intentionally it will owe the applicant a duty to:

- secure accommodation for such period as it considers will give him or her a reasonable opportunity of securing accommodation for his or her occupation; and
- provide, or secure the provision of, advice and assistance in any attempts he or she may make to secure accommodation[2].

These duties are discussed in detail at **15.23** and **16.81–16.93**.

¹   As inserted by HRA 2017, s 5(2), for applications for homelessness assistance made on or after
3 April 2018.
²   HA 1996, s 190(2), as amended by HRA 2017, s 5(5), for applications for homelessness
assistance made on or after 3 April 2018. See **16.81–16.93**.

The HA 1996, s 193(2), main housing duty

16.12 Once the HA 1996, s 189B(2)¹, relief duty has come to an end, if the
local housing authority is satisfied that the applicant is homeless, eligible for
assistance, has a priority need, and is not satisfied that the applicant has
become homeless intentionally, then it will normally owe him or her the HA
1996, s 193(2) main housing duty to secure accommodation for his or her
occupation². This duty will continue until one of the events at HA 1996,
s 193(5)–(7AA), occurs.

¹   As inserted by HRA 2017, s 5(2), for applications for homelessness assistance made on or after
3 April 2018.
²   See **16.94–16.199**.

16.13 The HA 1996, s 193(2), duty is not, however, owed to the following
applicants, even though they are homeless, eligible for assistance, have a
priority need and have not become homeless intentionally:

- applicants who are to be referred to another local housing authority
  under the conditions for referral: a duty to accommodate under HA
  1996, s 200(1) arises¹;
- applicants who have refused a final accommodation offer² or final Pt 6
  offer³ made to them during the performance of the HA 1996,
  s 189B(2)⁴, relief duty: no accommodation duty arises⁵; and
- applicants who have been notified of the local housing authority's decision that they have deliberately and unreasonably refused to
  co-operate⁶: a duty to accommodate under HA 1996, s 193C(4)⁷ arises.

The s 193(2) main housing duty is discussed in detail at **16.94–16.199**.

¹   HA 1996, ss 193(2) and 200(1), see **16.225–16.232**.
²   As defined at HA 1996, s 193A(4), as inserted by HRA 2017, s 7(1) for applications for
homelessness assistance made on or after 3 April 2018. See **15.181**.
³   As defined at HA 1996, s 193A(5), as inserted by HRA 2017, s 7(1) for applications for
homelessness assistance made on or after 3 April 2018. See **15.185**.
⁴   As inserted by HRA 2017, s 5(2), for applications for homelessness assistance made on or after
3 April 2018.
⁵   HA 1996, s 193A(3), as inserted by HRA 2017, s 7(1) for applications for homelessness
assistance made on or after 3 April 2018. See **15.181–15.188**.
⁶   HA 1996, s 193B, as inserted by HRA 2017, s 7(1) for applications for homelessness assistance
made on or after 3 April 2018. See **15.196–15.221**.
⁷   As inserted by HRA 2017, s 7(1) for applications for homelessness assistance made on or after
3 April 2018. See **16.200–16.216**.

The HA 1996, s 193C(4) duty to accommodate applicants who have deliberately and unreasonably refused to cooperate

16.14 If the HA 1996, s 189B(2)[1], relief duty has come to an end because the local housing authority has given notice, in accordance with HA 1996, s 193B[2], that the applicant has deliberately and unreasonably refused to cooperate[3], then whether any further duty is owed to the applicant will depend on his or her personal circumstances. If the applicant has a priority need and has not become homeless intentionally, then the local housing authority will be required to accommodate him or her under HA 1996, s 193C(4)[4]. That duty will continue until one of the events at HA 1996, s 193C(5)–(6)[5] occurs: typically the acceptance or refusal by the applicant of a final accommodation offer[6]. If the applicant has a priority need but has become homeless intentionally, then he or she will be owed the HA 1996, s 190(2)[7] short-term accommodation duty. This duty is discussed in detail at **16.200–16.216**.

[1] As inserted by HRA 2017, s 5(2), for applications for homelessness assistance made on or after 3 April 2018.
[2] As inserted by HRA 2017, s 7(1), for applications for homelessness assistance made on or after 3 April 2018.
[3] HA 1996, s 193C(2) as inserted by HRA 2017, s 7(1), for applications for homelessness assistance made on or after 3 April 2018. See **16.200–16.216**.
[4] As inserted by HRA 2017, s 7(1) for applications for homelessness assistance made on or after 3 April 2018. See **16.200–16.216**.
[5] As inserted by HRA 2017, s 7(1), for applications for homelessness assistance made on or after 3 April 2018. See **16.204–16.215**.
[6] HA 1996, s 193C(4), as inserted by HRA 2017, s 7(1), for applications for homelessness assistance made on or after 3 April 2018. See **16.205–16.209**.
[7] As amended by HRA 2017, s 5(5) for applications for homelessness assistance made on or after 3 April 2018.

Accommodation duties owed where the applicant's case is referred to another local housing authority

Referral of the HA 1996, s 189B(2), relief duty

16.15 Where the local housing authority would be subject to the HA 1996, s 189B(2)[1], relief duty but have notified the applicant that they intend to notify, or have notified, another local housing authority that the conditions for the referral of his or her case[2] are met, and have reason to believe that the applicant has a priority need:

- the interim accommodation duty comes to an end[3];
- there is a duty on the notifying local housing authority to accommodate the applicant until it has been decided whether the conditions for referral are met[4];
- if it is decided that the conditions for referral are met[5], the notified local housing authority becomes subject to the HA 1996, s 189B(2)[6], relief duty and also to the duty to secure interim accommodation, if there is reason to believe that the applicant may have a priority need[7]; and
- if it is decided that the conditions for referral are not met, then the performance of the HA 1996, s 189B(2)[8], relief duty will revert to the notifying local housing authority, along with a further duty to secure

interim accommodation[9].

¹ As inserted by HRA 2017, s 5(2), for applications for homelessness assistance made on or after 3 April 2018.
² HA 1996, s 198(A1), as inserted by HRA 2017, s 5(8), for applications for homelessness assistance made on or after 3 April 2018. See **16.217–16.224**.
³ HA 1996, s 199A(1), as inserted by HRA 2017, s 5(9), for applications for homelessness assistance made on or after 3 April 2018. See **16.217–16.224**.
⁴ HA 1996, s 199A(2), as inserted by HRA 2017, s 5(9), for applications for homelessness assistance made on or after 3 April 2018. See **16.217–16.224**.
⁵ HA 1996, s 198(5). See **14.176–14.190**.
⁶ As inserted by HRA 2017, s 5(2), for applications for homelessness assistance made on or after 3 April 2018.
⁷ HA 1996, s 199A(5), as inserted by HRA 2017, s 5(9), for applications for homelessness assistance made on or after 3 April 2018. See **16.217–16.224**.
⁸ As inserted by HRA 2017, s 5(2), for applications for homelessness assistance made on or after 3 April 2018.
⁹ HA 1996, s 199A(4), as inserted by HRA 2017, s 5(9), for applications for homelessness assistance made on or after 3 April 2018. See **16.217–16.224**.

Referral of HA 1996, s 193(2), main housing duty

16.16 Where the local housing authority would be subject to the HA 1996, s 193(2), main housing duty[1] but have notified the applicant that they intend to notify, or have notified, another local housing authority that the conditions for the referral of his or her case[2] are met:

- the interim accommodation duty comes to an end[3];
- there is a duty on the notifying local housing authority to accommodate the applicant until it has been decided whether the conditions for referral are met[4];
- if it is decided that the conditions for referral are met[5], the notified local housing authority becomes subject to the HA 1996, s 193(2), main housing duty[6]; and
- if it is decided that the conditions for referral are not met, then the performance of the HA 1996, s 193(2), main housing duty will revert to the notifying local housing authority[7].

¹ See **16.94–16.199**.
² HA 1996, s 198(1). See **14.43–14.122**.
³ HA 1996, s 200(1). See **16.225–16.232**.
⁴ HA 1996, s 200(1). See **16.225–16.232**.
⁵ HA 1996, s 198(5). See **14.176–14.190**.
⁶ HA 1996, s 200(4). See **16.225–16.232**.
⁷ HA 1996, s 200(3). See **16.225–16.232**.

Powers to accommodate

16.17 A local housing authority also has three different powers to secure accommodation for a homeless applicant:

- a power to accommodate pending a decision on review[1];
- a power to accommodate pending the determination of an appeal[2]; and
- a power to secure accommodation in performance of the HA 1996, s 195(2)[3], prevention duty or the s 189B(2)[4], relief duty[5].

These powers are discussed in detail at **16.233–16.279**.

[1] HA 1996, s 188(3), as amended by HRA 2017, s 5(4), for applications for homelessness assistance made on or after 3 April 2018, see **16.233–16.257**.

[2] HA 1996, s 204(4), as amended by HRA 2017, ss 4(6) and 5(11), for applications for homelessness assistance made on or after 3 April 2018, see **16.258–16.277**.

[3] As amended by HRA 2017, s 4(2), for applications for homelessness assistance made on or after 3 April 2018. See **15.87–15.137**.

[4] As inserted by HRA 2017, s 5(2), for applications for homelessness assistance made on or after 3 April 2018. See **15.138–15.195**.

[5] HA 1996, s 205(3), as inserted by HRA 2017, s 6, for applications for homelessness assistance made on or after 3 April 2018, see **16.278–16.279**.

GENERAL ISSUES ABOUT ACCOMMODATION

16.18 Before we discuss the accommodation duties in detail, we consider some general points that apply to accommodation secured under any of the duties or powers referred to at **16.9–16.17**.

Accommodation for whom?

16.19 All of the duties to secure accommodation are owed to the applicant. However, the accommodation secured must be *'available'* for the applicant's occupation. This means 'available' as defined in HA 1996, s 176. That is, the accommodation must be available for the occupation of both the applicant and of those who normally reside with the applicant as a member of his or her family, or anyone who might be reasonably be expected to reside with the applicant[1]. The accommodation must also be *'suitable'* for the applicant and his or her household[2]. Usually, this will require the local housing authority to secure one unit of accommodation, which all the members of the household can occupy together. In some circumstances, more than one unit of accommodation might properly be secured, providing that such an arrangement allows the applicant and his or her household to 'live together'[3].

[1] HA 1996, s 176; *Homelessness Code of Guidance for Local Authorities* (Ministry of Housing, Communities & Local Government, 2018) (the English Code), para 16.6. See **10.21–10.32**.

[2] See **16.20** and CHAPTER **18**.

[3] *Sharif v Camden London Borough Council* [2013] UKSC 10, [2013] HLR 16 per Lord Carnwath at [17], discussed at **18.11**.

Suitability

16.20 A local housing authority which is subject to a duty to secure accommodation (or is using its powers to secure such accommodation) is not obliged to provide the applicant with local housing authority housing. It may secure accommodation in any of the following three ways:

(1) by providing suitable accommodation itself;
(2) by arranging for someone else to secure suitable accommodation; or
(3) by giving the applicant such advice and assistance as secures that suitable accommodation is made available by someone else[1].

[1] HA 1996, s 206(1).

16.21 In all cases, any accommodation secured under HA 1996, Pt 7[1] must be suitable for the applicant, and for the members of the applicant's household[2]. Whether or not the accommodation is 'suitable' is primarily a matter for the local housing authority, but consideration of suitability must focus on whether the accommodation is suitable for the particular applicant. The issue of whether accommodation is 'suitable', including issues such as terms, tenure, location and duration of occupation are discussed in detail in CHAPTER 18.

[1]   As amended by HRA 2017, for applications for homelessness assistance made on or after 3 April 2018
[2]   See English Code, para 17.2.

Charging for accommodation

16.22 The local housing authority can secure accommodation for applicants free of charge. More usually it will require the applicant to pay whatever amount the local housing authority considers he or she can reasonably afford. The local housing authority has power to require the applicant to pay 'such reasonable charges as they may determine' in respect of the accommodation secured, by itself or by another person[1]. Where the local housing authority is itself paying for the accommodation[2], it can require the applicant to pay 'such reasonable amount' towards the cost as it may determine[3].

[1]   HA 1996, s 206(2)(a) and (b).
[2]   For example, where it is paying rent for accommodation that it is leasing from a private owner.
[3]   HA 1996, s 206(2)(b).

16.23 The local housing authority's performance of its duty to secure accommodation is not contingent upon the applicant paying any charges imposed[1]. Obviously, if an unpaid charge leads to loss of the accommodation, this may give rise to a further incidence of homelessness.

[1]   *R v Tower Hamlets London Borough Council ex p Khalique* (1994) 26 ACR 517, QBD at 523.

16.24 What is a 'reasonable' charge or amount will vary according to the type, nature and extent of the accommodation and the personal circumstances of the applicant[1]. Indeed, local housing authorities are required to consider 'affordability' as a function of 'suitability' whenever they secure accommodation[2]. Plainly, it would not be reasonable to impose a level of charges that pushed the applicant below subsistence levels of income and the English Code advises that in determining suitability, local housing authorities will need to 'consider whether the applicant can afford the housing costs without being deprived of basic essentials'[3].

[1]   *R (Best) v Oxford City Council* [2009] EWHC 608 (Admin), (2009) May *Legal Action*, p 27, Admin Ct, where, on the facts, the local housing authority was entitled to find that the applicant did have the resources to pay charges.
[2]   Homelessness (Suitability of Accommodation) Order 1996, SI 1996/3204. See **18.44–18.47** and APPENDIX 2.
[3]   English Code, para 17.45. See *Samuels v Birmingham City Council* [2015] EWCA Civ 1051, [2015] HLR 41, CA, which considered the wording of the guidance in the previous edition of the Code (Homelessness Code of Guidance for Local Authorities 2006) in relation to the test

of 'becoming homeless intentionally'. At the date of writing, Ms Samuels has been granted permission to appeal to the Supreme Court.

16.25 What if an applicant has no income, or very limited income, from which to pay housing costs? In a case where the applicant was not eligible for housing benefit[1], the local housing authority considered that its HA 1996, s 193(2), main housing duty[2] had come to an end. She and her children had been evicted from her temporary accommodation because she could not afford to pay the charges on her accommodation. On her claim in judicial review, the judge held that the HA 1996, s 193(2) main housing duty had not ended. He said that, in the circumstances where an applicant is owed the main housing duty but is unable to pay reasonable charges, the local housing authority had three options:

'The first option is the discretion which I have described, as to a nil or nominal rent or charge for the purposes of [HA 1996] section 206(2). The second is that the housing assistance secured for the purposes of the 1996 Act could continue to be housing provided by the local housing authority, but with the relevant rental met by assistance in cash made available by social services in the context of a 1989 [Children] Act section 17 assessment. In those circumstances, were that the approach taken, the rent would continue to be charged, the means would be made available for the protection of the children, and the local authority would in that sense be able to balance its books. That could have clear implications for questions as to eviction. The third option is that the 1989 [Children] Act duty, being a duty not to house but to secure that accommodation is available, could be discharged through securing and being satisfied that provision is being made available through accommodation under section 17(6) of the 1989 Act[3].'

It follows that, if an applicant cannot afford to pay any charges, the local housing authority must perform its duty, and secure accommodation, in any event, and either charge a nil or nominal rent, or arrange for other sources of funding, which might include contributions from children's services, to pay for its charges. This point is likely to become increasingly important as changes to welfare benefits, especially the benefit cap[4], leave individuals with insufficient resources to pay otherwise reasonable housing costs.

[1] Because of her status as a '*Zambrano* carer', see **11.80–11.85**. Applicants who have that status have not been eligible for assistance since 12 November 2012, see **11.144–11.145**.
[2] See **16.94–16.199**.
[3] *R (Yekini) v Southwark London Borough Council* [2014] EWHC 2096 (Admin), (2014) September *Legal Action*, p 50, Admin Ct per Michael Fordham QC, sitting as a deputy High Court judge, at [69].
[4] Welfare Reform Act 2012, s 96.

16.26 There is no right to a statutory review of the amount charged by the local housing authority unless:

(1)   it could be said that the level of charging rendered the accommodation 'unsuitable'; and
(2)   the accommodation is being secured under one of the duties which carry a right to a review of its suitability[1].

[1] HA 1996, s 202(1)(f) (as amended by HRA 2017, s 9, for applications for homelessness assistance made on or after 3 April 2018) gives a right to request a review of the suitability of accommodation secured under HA 1996, ss 190(2) (as amended by HRA 2017, s 5(5), for applications for homelessness assistance made on or after 3 April 2018), 193(2) and 195 (as amended by HRA 2017, s 4(2), for applications for homelessness assistance made on or after

3 April 2018), or any offer of HA 1996, Pt 6 accommodation (see **19.59–19.62**). The right to request a review of the suitability of private rented sector offers is at HA 1996, s 202(1)(g) (as amended by HRA 2017, s 9, for applications for homelessness assistance made on or after 3 April 2018), see **19.63–19.64**. The right to request a review of the suitability of accommodation offered as a final accommodation offer or a final Part 6 offer is at HA 1996, s 202(1)(h) (as inserted by HRA 2017, s 9, for applications for homelessness assistance made on or after 3 April 2018), see **19.65–19.69**.

16.27 Otherwise, the amount of the charge can be disputed through the local housing authority's complaints procedure, and thereafter with a complaint to the Local Government and Social Care Ombudsman, or (where an error of law is alleged) by a challenge by way of judicial review[1].

1   For complaints see **19.333–19.339** and for judicial review, see **19.306–19.332**.

Viewing accommodation

16.28 The English Code contains a recommendation from the Secretary of State that applicants should be:

'given the chance to view accommodation that is offered on anything other than an interim basis, before being required to decide whether they accept or refuse an offer, and before being required to sign any written agreement relating to the accommodation[1].'

This suggests that local housing authorities should normally give the applicant an opportunity to view accommodation, even though they are not strictly required to under HA 1996, Pt 7[2]. The English Code also recommends that, where offers of accommodation are made outside of the local housing authority's district, particular care should be taken to ensure that applicants have sufficient information about the location of the accommodation and the services that would be available to them there[3]. Applicants should also be given a reasonable period to consider any offer made before a reaching a decision. The appropriate length of time depends on the applicant's circumstances. Local housing authorities should take into account that:

- applicants may wish to seek advice; and
- applicants may not be familiar with the property offered[4].

If the applicant is in hospital or temporarily absent, the local housing authority should take that into account[5].

1   English Code, para 15.46.
2   As amended by HRA 2017 for applications for homelessness assistance made on or after 3 April 2018.
3   English Code, para 15.46.
4   English Code, para, 15.48.
5   English Code, para 15.48.

Termination of accommodation

16.29 Once any duty to secure accommodation has ended, or a local housing authority decides that it will no longer exercise a power to secure interim accommodation, the applicant's legal right to occupation of the accommodation may need to be brought to an end.

16.30 The length of any notice period that the applicant is entitled to be given if he or she is required to leave the accommodation depends first on the terms of the licence or tenancy under which she or he has been occupying it. She or he cannot be excluded on shorter notice than is provided for in that tenancy or licence agreement. What further protection (if any) that the applicant is entitled to is likely to vary according to the duty or power under which he or she is accommodated, the type of accommodation in question, and the nature of his or her occupation agreement. We discuss the different obligations governing termination of accommodation under the relevant duty[1].

[1] For termination of interim accommodation, see **16.51–16.74**; for termination of accommodation secured under the HA 1996, s 190(2), short-term accommodation duty, see **16.90–16.93**; for termination of accommodation secured under the HA 1996, s 193(2), main housing duty, see **16.102–16.190**; for termination of accommodation secured under the HA 1996, s 193C(4), duty to accommodate those who have deliberately and unreasonably failed to co-operate, see **16.204–16.216**.

Compensation claims

16.31 Challenges to decisions as to whether an accommodation duty is owed to an applicant[1], to refusals to exercise any powers to secure accommodation[2], and to decisions to bring any duties to an end[3] are dealt with elsewhere in this chapter. Challenges to the suitability of accommodation offered are considered in CHAPTER 18[4].

[1] For challenges to refusals to secure interim accommodation under HA 1996, s 188(1), see **16.74–16.80**; for challenges to decisions concerning accommodation secured pending referral of the HA 1996, s 189B(2), relief duty to another local housing authority under HA 1996, s 199A (as inserted by HRA 2017, s 5(9), for applications for homelessness assistance made on or after 3 April 2018), see **16.223**; for challenges to decisions concerning accommodation secured pending referral of the HA 1996, s 193(2), main housing duty to another local housing authority under HA 1996, s 200 (as amended by HRA 2017, s 5(10), for applications for homelessness assistance made on or after 3 April 2018), see **16.231**; for challenges to decisions as to whether the short-term duty at HA 1996, s 190(2)(a) (as amended by HRA 2017, s 5(5), for applications for homelessness assistance made on or after 3 April 2018) is owed, see **19.15–19.17**; for challenges to decisions as to whether the HA 1996, s 193(2) main housing duty is owed, see **19.15–19.17**; for challenges to decisions as to whether the HA 1996, s 193C(4) (as inserted by HRA 2017, s 7(1), for applications for homelessness assistance made on or after 3 April 2018) duty is owed towards applicants who have deliberately and unreasonably refused to co-operate, see **19.30–19.35**.

[2] For challenges to refusals to secure accommodation pending review under HA 1996, s 188(3) (as amended by HRA 2017, s 5(4), for applications for homelessness assistance made on or after 3 April 2018), see **16.248–16.257**; for challenges to refusals to secure accommodation pending appeal under HA 1996, s 204(4) (as amended by HRA 2017, ss 4(6) and 5(11), for applications for homelessness assistance made on or after 3 April 2018), see **16.266–16.277**.

[3] For challenges to decisions to bring interim accommodation to an end under HA 1996, s 188(1ZA) or (1ZB) (as inserted by HRA 2017, s 5(4), for applications for homelessness assistance made on or after 3 April 2018), see **16.74–16.80**; for challenges to decisions to bring the HA 1996, s 193(2) main housing duty to an end, see **19.15–19.17**; for challenges to decisions to bring the HA 1996, s 193C(4) (as inserted by HRA 2017, s 7(1), for applications for homelessness assistance made on or after 3 April 2018) duty towards applicants who have deliberately and unreasonably refused to co-operate to an end, see **19.15–19.17**.

[4] For challenges to the suitability of interim accommodation, see **16.17**; for challenges to the suitability of accommodation secured under HA 1996, s 193(2), main housing duty see **19.59–19.62**.

16.32 Whilst those remedies are available to an applicant, so that the local housing authority's decisions can be scrutinised, and it can be required to remedy any unlawfulness, an applicant may feel that having to experience a local housing authority's unlawful conduct requires some recompense. Where a local housing authority wrongly fails to secure interim accommodation, in breach of its statutory duty so to do, the applicant cannot sue for compensation for loss in respect of that breach of statutory duty[1] nor can he or she recover damages for that breach as an ancillary remedy in a claim by way of judicial review[2]. Nor can the applicant recover damages for any breach of the right to respect for his or her home[3] because, by definition, she or he has, at this point, no home to 'respect'. The right to 'respect for his home' does not encompass a right to a home[4]. There may be a legal right to compensation[5] if the breach of duty reduces the applicant to circumstances amounting to inhuman or degrading treatment[6], or infringes his or her right to respect for private or family life[7].

[1] *O'Rourke v Camden London Borough Council* [1998] AC 188, AC.
[2] *R v Ealing London Borough Council ex p Parkinson* (1997) 29 HLR 179, QBD per Laws J. In some circumstances, it might be possible to claim damages for the tort of misfeasance in public office. In the only attempt known to the authors of a claim for damages for this tort being brought in connection with homelessness duties, the judge said: '[w]hilst . . . I would be reluctant to conclude that a claim for misfeasance in a public office could *never* be brought in a situation that reflects a breach of Part 7, the circumstances in which such a claim could successfully be brought would . . . be extremely limited' (*R (Kharzai & others) v Birmingham City Council* [2010] EWHC 2576 (Admin), (2010) December *Legal Action*, p 37, Admin Ct per Foskett J at [44]).
[3] Protected by European Convention on Human Rights: Human Rights Act 1998, Sch 1, Art 8.
[4] *O'Rourke v UK (Application 39022/97)* (unreported) 26 June 2001, ECtHR.
[5] Human Rights Act 1998, s 8(2).
[6] Human Rights Act 1998, Sch 1, Art 3; see **19.328–19.333** and **20.110–20.123**; *O'Rourke v UK (Application 39022/97)* (unreported) 26 June 2001, ECtHR.
[7] Human Rights Act 1998, Sch 1, Art 8. See *R (B) v Southwark London Borough Council (No 2)* (2004) January *Legal Action*, p 32, in which the local housing authority settled a claim for compensation for £3,000 where the failure to secure interim accommodation caused the applicant to stay in prison unnecessarily for an additional weekend.

16.33 The absence of a general right to compensation in these circumstances makes it even more important that the applicant promptly obtains a mandatory order in judicial review proceedings requiring the local housing authority to perform its duty. Normally, any financial or other loss caused in the period before an order is obtained could only be recovered through a complaint under the local housing authority's own complaints procedure (or thereafter by further complaint to the Local Government and Social Care Ombudsman)[1].

[1] See **19.333–19.339**.

16.34 Even where an applicant has been provided with interim accommodation, the local housing authority will be in breach of its statutory duties if the accommodation is not 'suitable'[1]. Again, the normal rule is that the applicant cannot sue for recompense[2]. However, where the standard of accommodation is so unsuitable that it infringes an applicant's right to respect for his or her home, family or private life, damages could be awarded for breach of the Human Rights Act 1998, Sch 1, Art 8(1)[3]. Where the evidence shows that the conditions of the accommodation do infringe an applicant's rights under Art

8(1), the burden rests on the local housing authority to show that the interference with those rights was justified and proportionate under Art 8(2)[4].

1   HA 1996, s 206(1). See CHAPTER 18.
2   *R v Ealing London Borough Council ex p Parkinson* (1997) 29 ACR 179, QBD.
3   Human Rights Act 1998, s 8, Sch 1; *R (Bernard) v Enfield London Borough Council* [2002] EWHC 2282 (Admin), (2003) 35 ACR 27, Admin Ct, see **19.328–19.332**.
4   *R (Yumsak) v Enfield London Borough Council* [2002] EWHC 280 (Admin), [2003] HLR 1, Admin Ct.

16.35 Precisely because Art 8(1) does not provide a right to a home[1], merely the right to respect for the applicant's existing home, any claims brought under it are likely to relate to the interference, as a result of the condition of the accommodation, with the applicant's right to respect for his or her family or private life[2]. For example, placing a London family in interim accommodation in Birmingham, when the child needed to retain contact with her father in London, was found to be contrary to the family's right to respect for their family life[3]. On the other hand, a claim for damages for 29 weeks spent in grossly overcrowded and unsuitable accommodation did not succeed as the applicant was not deprived of her home, she was not separated from her children and the health problems caused by the unsuitable accommodation were not so grave as to constitute an interference with her private life[4]. Damages were awarded for breach of the applicant's right to respect for her family and private life where a wheelchair-bound woman was restricted to a single room in unsuitable temporary accommodation for over two years[5]. However, where an elderly woman had been effectively confined to her bedroom as a result of the steepness of the stairs in the family's temporary accommodation, and had missed the family interaction that took place principally in the kitchen, the local housing authority was held not to have interfered with her right to respect for her family life. It had secured accommodation, made offers of alternative accommodation that had been rejected, and had provided practical help. The obligations under Human Rights Act 1998, Sch 1, imposed on the local housing authority did not extend to creating a set of circumstances in which all major impediments to the full enjoyment of family life were removed[6].

1   See **19.331** and **20.119–20.123**.
2   *R (Morris) v Newham London Borough Council* [2002] EWHC 1262 (Admin), (2002) July *Legal Action*, p 27, Admin Ct.
3   *R (Yumsak) v Enfield London Borough Council* [2002] EWHC 280 (Admin), [2003] HLR 1, Admin Ct.
4   *R (Morris) v Newham London Borough Council* [2002] EWHC 1262 (Admin), (2002) July *Legal Action*, p 27, Admin Ct.
5   *R (Bernard) v Enfield London Borough Council* [2002] EWHC 2282 (Admin), (2003) 35 ACR 27, Admin Ct.
6   *Anufrijeva v Southwark London Borough Council* [2003] EWCA Civ 1406, CA, [2004] 1 All ER 833, CA. See also *R (McDonagh) v Enfield London Borough Council* [2018] EWHC 1287 (Admin), Admin Ct.

16.36 Alternatively, complaint could be made to the Local Government and Social Care Ombudsman that the local housing authority has been guilty of maladministration. Indeed, any awards of compensation for interference with an applicant's rights under Art 8(1) of the Human Rights Act 1998, Sch 1, are likely to be assessed by reference to the sums recommended as compensation for maladministration by the Local Government and Social Care Ombudsman in other cases[1].

1   *R (Bernard) v Enfield London Borough Council* [2002] EWHC 2282 (Admin), (2003) 35 ACR 27, Admin Ct. For an example of compensation recommended by the Local Government Ombudsman for unsuitable interim accommodation, see *Complaint against Brent London Borough* Council 13 008 940 (2014) October *Legal* Action, p 50. See **19.336–19.340**.

THE INITIAL DUTY TO SECURE INTERIM ACCOMMODATION

To whom is the duty owed?

16.37 The initial duty to secure interim accommodation[1] is triggered when the local housing authority has 'reason to believe' that an applicant may be 'homeless'[2], may be 'eligible for assistance'[3], and may have a 'priority need'[4]. This is a very low threshold[5]. The governing word is 'may', which must be understood to apply to all the elements of the statutory formula. So the threshold is met when a local housing authority has reason to believe that an applicant:

- 'may' be homeless; and also
- 'may' be eligible; and also
- 'may' have a priority need.

1   HA 1996, s 188(1); Code, paras 15.11–15.12, and 15.19–15.22.
2   See Chapter 10.
3   See Chapter 11.
4   See Chapter 12.
5   See *R (Kelly & Mehari) v Birmingham City Council* [2009] EWHC 3240 (Admin), (2010) January *Legal Action*, p 35, Admin Ct; English Code, para 15.5; See **8.75–8.76**. See also decisions by the then Local Government Ombudsman where local housing authorities were guilty of maladministration for failing to secure interim accommodation: *Complaints against Kent County Council and Dover District Council*, 09 017 510 and 09 017 512, 31 July 2012, (2012) October *Legal Action*, p 38; *Complaint against Newham London Borough Council* 11 022 307, 27 November 2012 (2013) January *Legal Action*, p 41; *Complaint against Newham London Borough Council*, 13 005 484, 17 March 2014, (2014) June *Legal Action*, p 40; *Complaint against Eastbourne Borough Council* 14 016 569, 29 February 2016, (2016) September *Legal Action*, p 37 and *Complaint against Barnet London Borough Council* 16 002 971, 8 March 2017 (2017) May *Legal Action*, p 42 . See also *Serious Case Review in respect of 'Robert'*, North Yorkshire Safeguarding Adults Board, November 2013, (2013) March *Legal Action*, p 21 and the judicial review claim in respect of Southwark's London Borough Council's 'unfair policies and practices': *R (XX) v Southwark London Borough Council* (2015) May *Legal Action*, p 45. See **16.74–16.80**.

16.38 These are some of the issues that the local housing authority will be making inquiries into, in due course, in order to determine what duty (if any) is ultimately owed to the applicant under HA 1996, Pt 7[1].

1   As amended by HRA 2017.

16.39 Four additional points should be noted. First, no interim accommodation duty is owed to an applicant who may be simply 'threatened with' homelessness[1]. An applicant who is eligible for assistance and is threatened with homelessness will be owed the HA 1996, s 195(2)[2], prevention duty requiring the local housing authority to take reasonable steps to help him or her secure that accommodation does not cease to be available for his or her occupation, but will not normally need interim accommodation because he or she is not yet homeless[3].

1   As defined in HA 1996, s 175(4), see **10.144–10.147**.
2   As amended by HRA 2017, s 4(2), for applications for homelessness assistance made on or after 3 April 2018, see **15.87–15.137**.
3   There is, however, a power to secure that accommodation is available in discharge of the HA 1996, s 195(2), prevention duty (as amended by HRA 2017, s 4(2) for applications for homelessness assistance made on or after 3 April 2018). See HA 1996, s 205(3) (as inserted by HRA 2017, s 6, for applications for homelessness assistance made on or after 3 April 2018) and English Code, paras 15.33–15.35. See further **15.184–15.188** and **16.278–16.279**.

16.40 Second, the question whether the initial duty is owed may arise not only when the initial application is made but also at any stage before the local housing authority's final decision on the application has been notified to the applicant. For example, where a local housing authority is making its inquiries into an application made by an applicant who appears to be threatened with homelessness, it is not under a duty to secure interim accommodation[1]. However, if, before the local housing authority has concluded its inquiries and notified the applicant of its decision, the situation changes and the local housing authority has reason to believe that the applicant may actually be homeless (and there is also reason to believe that the applicant may be eligible and may have a priority need), the duty to secure interim accommodation is immediately triggered.

1   HA 1996, ss 184(1) and 188(1).

16.41 Third, the initial duty arises irrespective of any local connection the applicant may have with any other local housing authority[1].

1   HA 1996, s 188(2); English Code, para 15.6.

16.42 Fourth, the initial duty to secure interim accommodation is not a duty capable of being referred to another local housing authority under the conditions for referral described in CHAPTER 14[1].

1   Where the local housing authority is satisfied that the applicant is homeless and is eligible for assistance, and also considers that the conditions for referral of the performance of the HA 1996, s 189B(2) (as inserted by HRA 2017, s 5(2), for applications for homelessness assistance made on or after 3 April 2018), relief duty are met, and that it intends to notify another local housing authority of its opinion (HA 1996, s 198(A1), as inserted by HRA 2017, s 5(8), for applications for homelessness assistance made on or after 3 April 2018), then the local housing authority is no longer subject to a duty to secure interim accommodation at HA 1996, s 188(1): HA 1996, s 199A(1)(a) (as inserted by HRA 2017, s 5(9), for applications for homelessness assistance made on or after 3 April 2018). Instead, if it continues to have reason to believe that the applicant may have a priority need, the notifying local housing authority must secure accommodation for the applicant until he or she has been notified of the decision as to whether the conditions for referral of his or her case are met: HA 1996, s 199A(2), as inserted by HRA 2017, s 5(9), for applications for homelessness assistance made on or after 3 April 2018. See **16.217–16.224**.

16.43 If the local housing authority does have reason to believe that the applicant may be homeless, may be eligible and may have a priority need, the duty to secure initial interim accommodation is an absolute one. The local housing authority must secure that accommodation is available; it cannot postpone that duty, which is triggered as soon as the requisite 'reason to believe' is present. One local housing authority's application form contained the following instruction to its officers: 'unless the applicant and family are at risk of harm, they should be advised to return to the homeless address whereby a visiting officer will attend the property'. As a result of that instruction, the local housing authority failed to engage with the criteria at HA 1996, s 188(1) and failed to provide accommodation to applicants for homelessness assistance whom it had reason to believe may be homeless, may be eligible and may have a priority need. A judge said:

'The approach of the Council to their obligations under Section 188 at the very least lacks legal coherence and a proper consideration of the relevant Section 188 criteria. So far as the Council are concerned that failure had and, insofar as that practice continues, continues to have, the effect of avoiding their obligations under Section 188[1].'

[1] *R (Kelly & Mehari) v Birmingham City Council* [2009] EWHC 3240 (Admin), (2010) January *Legal Action*, p 35, Admin Ct at [40] per Hickinbottom J.

16.44 The same local housing authority was later alleged to be operating a variety of systems in order to avoid the duty to secure interim accommodation. In a subsequent case, it agreed that apparent instructions that 'all single homeless . . . must be referred to the appropriate funded support service. We should not be completing a homeless application' were unlawful[1].

[1] *R (Khazai) v Birmingham City Council* [2010] EWHC 2576 (Admin), (2010) December *Legal Action*, p 37, Admin Ct.

16.45 There was also a suggestion that the same local housing authority was encouraging its officers to make a decision on an application for homelessness assistance on the same day as the application was received, so that the duty to secure interim accommodation at HA 1996, s 188(1) would not arise. The judge said:

'[t]here is no doubt that a blanket 'same day' policy, which requires a decision on the homeless application and, in consequence, the interim accommodation all in one day would be unlawful . . . it would only be "in the most straightforward of cases that a decision can be reached on the same day as the application itself"[1].'

[1] *R (Khazai) v Birmingham City Council* [2010] EWHC 2576 (Admin), (2010) December *Legal Action*, p 37, Admin Ct per Foskett J at [47] quoting from the instruction to local housing authority staff that was under scrutiny. See also *R (IA) v Westminster City Council* [2013] EWHC 1273(Admin), (2013) July/August *Legal Action*, p 23, Admin Ct, where the decision that the applicant did not have a priority need had been notified to him on the same day as his application for homelessness assistance. The judge found that the claimant had a 'highly arguable' case that no lawful inquiry under HA 1996, s 184(1) had been conducted. He went on to say that 'it follows that the claimant has good prospects of showing that the defendant is in breach of its [HA 1996] section 188(1) duty in not providing the claimant with interim accommodation pending the provision of a lawful [HA 1996] section 184 decision' per Judge Anthony Thornton QC, sitting as a deputy judge of the High Court, at [27] and [31]. See also *R (XX) v Southwark London Borough Council* (2015) May *Legal Action*, p 45; and see decisions by the Ombudsmen finding maladministration discussed at **8.75–8.76**. In 2016, Hickinbottom J found that Birmingham City Council's up to date policies did not show that there was a systematic failure to comply with duties under Part 7, HA 1996: *R (Edwards) v Birmingham City Council* [2016] EWHC 173 (Admin), [2016] HLR 11, Admin Ct.

16.46 If the local housing authority refuses to secure initial interim accommodation when the statutory conditions are fulfilled or, before the duty ends, withdraws any accommodation secured and accepted by the applicant, it is in breach of its statutory duty. The applicant is entitled to bring judicial review proceedings for a mandatory order that accommodation be secured immediately[1].

1 See **16.74–16.80**. See also *R (Brooks) v Islington London Borough Council* [2015] EWHC 2657 (Admin) per Lewis J at [30].

The duty to secure interim accommodation where there is a re-application for homelessness assistance within two years of acceptance of a private rented sector offer

16.47 Special provisions apply where an applicant, having accepted a private rented sector offer[1] made by a local housing authority in response to an earlier application for homelessness assistance[2], makes a fresh application for homelessness assistance to a local housing authority within two years of the date of his or her acceptance of the offer.

1 HA 1996, s 193(7AA)–(7AC), See **16.153–16.162**.
2 HA 1996, s 188(1A) as amended by HRA 2017, s 5(4), for applications for homelessness assistance made on or after 3 April 2018; English Code, paras 18.16–18.20; see Appendix 2.

16.48 If the local housing authority has reason to believe that the HA 1996, s 193(2), main housing duty[1] may apply in these circumstances, it is under a duty to secure interim accommodation for the applicant and his or her household[2]. This duty applies whether or not there is any reason to believe that the applicant has a priority need. This is because most applicants in these circumstances will be entitled to the HA 1996, s 193(2), main housing duty whether or not they have a priority need[3].

1 See **16.94–16.199**.
2 HA 1996, s 188(1A), as amended by HRA 2017, s 5(4), for applications for homelessness assistance made on or after 3 April 2018; see English Code, para 15.10.
3 HA 1996, s 195A(1). See **8.100–8.107** and **15.56–15.58**. The exception is where the local housing authority would not be satisfied that the HA 1996, s 193(2), main housing duty is owed without having regard to a restricted person (HA 1996, s 195A(5)). In those cases, there would have to be reason to believe that the applicant might have a priority need. See **8.102**.

16.49 In order for the HA 1996, s 193(2), main housing duty to apply, the local housing authority will only have to be satisfied that the applicant:

- is homeless;
- is eligible for assistance; and
- did not become homeless intentionally[1].

Obviously for the duty to secure *interim* accommodation to apply in these circumstances, the local housing authority need not be satisfied of any of these tests. It just has to have 'reason to believe' that the applicant may pass each of those conditions. The threshold is a low one[2].

1 HA 1996, s 195A(1). See **8.100–8.107** and **15.56–15.58**.
2 See **8.75–8.76** and **16.37**.

16.50 An applicant to whom these special provisions apply is threatened with homelessness throughout the 56-day period leading up to the expiry of a valid

Housing Act 1988, s 21 notice[1], and is deemed to be homeless upon the expiry of the notice[2]. Accordingly, such applicants may make fresh applications for homelessness assistance while they are still occupying their private rented accommodation. The interim accommodation duty will apply once the date stipulated in the notice for giving up possession has been reached[3]. In those circumstances, it may be possible for the local housing authority to perform that duty by arranging with the landlord for the applicant and his or her household to remain in the private rented accommodation. However, if the applicant is required to leave that accommodation, the local housing authority will have to secure interim accommodation for him or her.

[1]   HA 1996, s 175(5), as inserted by HRA 2017, s 1(3), for applications for homelessness assistance made on or after 3 April 2018. See **10.145–10.147**.
[2]   HA 1996, s 195A(2).
[3]   HA 1996, s 195A(2).

Ending the duty to secure interim accommodation

Overview

16.51 The duty to secure interim accommodation will come to an end in the circumstances set out below.

- Where the local housing authority, having made inquiries, satisfies itself that an applicant does not have a priority need, the interim accommodation duty continues until either:
    - the applicant is notified of the local housing authority's decision that the HA 1996, s 189B(2)[1], relief duty is not owed (because the applicant is either not eligible for assistance or is not homeless)[2]; or
    - the applicant is notified of the local housing authority's decision that, when the HA 1996, s 189B(2)[3], relief duty comes to an end, no further accommodation duty will be owed under the HA 1996, s 190(2)[4], short-term duty, or the HA 1996, s 193(2)[5], main housing duty[6].
- Where the local housing authority is satisfied that an applicant does have a priority need, or continues to have reason to believe that he or she may have a priority need, the interim accommodation duty continues until the later of:
    - the HA 1996, s 189B(2)[7], relief duty coming to an end[8];
    - the applicant being notified of the local housing authority's decision that the HA 1996, s 189B(2)[9], relief duty is not owed (because the applicant is either not eligible for assistance or is not homeless)[10]; or
    - the applicant being notified of the local housing authority's decision as to what further duty (if any) will be owed to him or her when the HA 1996, s 189B(2)[11], relief duty comes to an end[12].
- Where the applicant requests a review under HA 1996, s 202(1)(h)[13] of the suitability of accommodation offered to him or her by way of a final accommodation offer[14] or final Pt 6 offer[15]:
    - the interim accommodation duty will continue until the decision on review has been notified to the applicant[16].

- Where the applicant has made an application for homelessness assistance within two years of acceptance of a private rented sector offer[17], and the local housing authority has reason to believe that he or she may be homeless and may be eligible for assistance, the interim accommodation duty will arise irrespective of whether the applicant has a priority need and will continue until the later of[18]:
  - the HA 1996 s 189B(2)[19], relief duty coming to an end[20];
  - the applicant being notified of the local housing authority's decision that the HA 1996, s 189B(2)[21], relief duty is not owed (because the applicant is either not eligible for assistance or is not homeless)[22]; or
  - the applicant being notified of the local housing authority's decision as to what further duty (if any) will be owed to him or her when the HA 1996, s 189B(2)[23], relief duty comes to an end[24].

[1] As inserted by HRA 2017, s 5(2), for applications for homelessness assistance made on or after 3 April 2018.

[2] HA 1996, s 188(1ZA)(a), as inserted by HRA 2017, s 5(4), for applications for homelessness assistance made on or after 3 April 2018. See **16.57**.

[3] As inserted by HRA 2017, s 5(2), for applications for homelessness assistance made on or after 3 April 2018.

[4] As amended by HRA 2017, s 5(5), for applications for homelessness assistance made on or after 3 April 2018. See **16.81–16.93**.

[5] See **16.94–16.199**.

[6] HA 1996, s 188(1ZA)(b), as inserted by HRA 2017, s 5(4), for applications for homelessness assistance made on or after 3 April 2018, see **16.58**.

[7] As inserted by HRA 2017, s 5(2), for applications for homelessness assistance made on or after 3 April 2018.

[8] HA 1996, s 188(1ZB)(a), as inserted by HRA 2017, s 5(4), for applications for homelessness assistance made on or after 3 April 2018. See **16.61**.

[9] As inserted by HRA 2017, s 5(2), for applications for homelessness assistance made on or after 3 April 2018.

[10] HA 1996, s 188(1ZB)(a), as inserted by HRA 2017, s 5(4), for applications for homelessness assistance made on or after 3 April 2018. See **16.61**.

[11] As inserted by HRA 2017, s 5(2), for applications for homelessness assistance made on or after 3 April 2018.

[12] HA 1996, s 188(1ZB)(b), as inserted by HRA 2017, s 5(4), for applications for homelessness assistance made on or after 3 April 2018, See **16.62**.

[13] As inserted by HRA 2017, s 9(2) for applications for homelessness assistance made on or after 3 April 2018. See **19.65–19.69**.

[14] As defined at HA 1996, s 193A(4), as inserted by HRA 2017, s 7(1), for applications for homelessness assistance made on or after 3 April 2018. See **15.181**.

[15] As defined at HA 1996, s 193A(5), as inserted by HRA 2017, s 7(1), for applications for homelessness assistance made on or after 3 April 2018. See **15.185**.

[16] HA 1996, s 188(1ZB) and (2A), as inserted by HRA 2017, s 5(4) for applications for homelessness assistance made on or after 3 April 2018. See **15.184–15.188**.

[17] For private rented sector offer, see HA 1996, s 193(7AA)–(7AC), and **16.153–16.180**.

[18] HA 1996, s 188(1A), as amended by HRA 2017, s 5(4), for applications for homelessness assistance made on or after 3 April 2018. See **8.100–8.107** and **15.56–15.58**.

[19] As inserted by HRA 2017, s 5(2), for applications for homelessness assistance made on or after 3 April 2018.

[20] HA 1996, s 188(1ZB)(1), as amended by HRA 2017, s 5(4), for applications for homelessness assistance made on or after 3 April 2018. See **16.62**.

[21] As inserted by HRA 2017, s 5(2), for applications for homelessness assistance made on or after 3 April 2018.

[22] HA 1996, s 188(1ZB)(a), as amended by HRA 2017, s 5(4), for applications for homelessness assistance made on or after 3 April 2018. See **16.61**.

[23] As inserted by HRA 2017, s 5(2), for applications for homelessness assistance made on or after 3 April 2018.

24 HA 1996, s 188(1ZB)(b), as amended by HRA 2017, s 5(4), for applications for homelessness assistance made on or after 3 April 2018. See **16.62**.

16.52 These circumstances are all set out expressly in HA 1996, Pt 7[1]. A further situation, not expressly contemplated within HA 1996, Pt 7[2], but which has been considered by the High Court and by the English Code, is where the applicant refuses interim accommodation[3]. Each of these circumstances will be considered in turn. But first we will discuss the duties owed by a local housing authority to notify the applicant that the duty has ended.

1 As amended by HRA 2017 for applications for homelessness assistance made on or after 3 April 2018.
2 As amended by HRA 2017 for applications for homelessness assistance made on or after 3 April 2018.
3 *R (Brooks) v Islington London Borough Council* [2015] EWHC 2657 (Admin), [2016] HLR 2, Admin Ct; English Code, para 15.22. See **16.66–16.69**.

Notification duties

16.53 There is no specific provision in HA 1996, Pt 7[1], requiring the local housing authority to notify the applicant of any decision that the interim accommodation duty has come to an end. However, in most circumstances the applicant will know that the interim accommodation is due to end because he or she will have received a notification informing him or her of one or more of the following:

- that the HA 1996, s 189B(2)[2], relief duty is not owed[3];
- that the HA 1996, s 189B(2)[4], relief duty has come to an end[5]; and/or
- of what further duty, if any, will be owed when the HA 1996, s 189B(2)[6], relief duty comes to an end[7].

Each of those decisions contains a right to request a review if the decision is adverse[8]. Normally, requesting a review will not prevent the interim accommodation duty from coming to an end[9]. The local housing authority has a power to continue to secure accommodation if the applicant requests a review of either of those decisions[10].

1 As amended by HRA 2017 for applications for homelessness assistance made on or after 3 April 2018.
2 As inserted by HRA 2017, s 5(2), for applications for homelessness assistance made on or after 3 April 2018.
3 HA 1996, s 184(3) and ss 188(1ZA)(a) and (1ZB)(a), as amended by HRA 2017, s 5(4) for applications for homelessness assistance made on or after 3 April 2018.
4 As inserted by HRA 2017, s 5(2), for applications for homelessness assistance made on or after 3 April 2018.
5 HA 1996, s 184(3) and s 188(1ZB)(a), as amended by HRA 2017, s 5(4) for applications for homelessness assistance made on or after 3 April 2018.
6 As inserted by HRA 2017, s 5(2), for applications for homelessness assistance made on or after 3 April 2018.
7 HA 1996, s 184(3) and ss 188(1ZA)(b) and (1ZB)(b), as amended by HRA 2017, s 5(4) for applications for homelessness assistance made on or after 3 April 2018.
8 HA 1996, s 202(1)(a) or (b) as amended by HRA 2017, s 9(2) for applications for homelessness assistance made on or after 3 April 2018. See **19.14–19.17**.
9 HA 1996, s 188(3), as amended by HRA 2017, s 5(4), for applications for homelessness assistance made on or after 3 April 2018.

¹⁰ HA 1996, s 188(3), as amended by HRA 2017, s 5(4), for applications for homelessness assistance made on or after 3 April 2018, see **16.233–16.257**.

16.54 There is an exception to this rule at HA 1996, s 188(2A)¹. Where the HA 1996, s 189B(2)², relief duty has come to an end because the applicant has refused a final accommodation offer³ or a final Pt 6 offer⁴, but has requested a review of the suitability of the accommodation offered, the HA 1996, s 189B(2)⁵, relief duty does not come to an end until the applicant is notified of the decision on review⁶. Consequently, unless the local housing authority is satisfied that the applicant does *not* have a priority need, and have notified him or her of that, the interim accommodation duty will continue until the review has concluded⁷.

¹   As inserted by HRA 2017, s 5(4) for applications for homelessness assistance on or after 3 April 2018.
²   As inserted by HRA 2107 s 5(2), for applications for homelessness assistance made on or before 3 April 2018, see **15.138–15.195**.
³   Defined at HA 1996, s 193A(4), as inserted by HRA 2017, s 7(1), for applications for homelessness assistance made on or after 3 April 2018. See **15.181**.
⁴   Defined at HA 1996, s 193A(5), as inserted by HRA 2017, s 7(1), for applications for homelessness assistance made on or after 3 April 2018. See **15.185**.
⁵   As inserted by HRA 2017, s 5(2), for applications for homelessness assistance made on or after 3 April 2018.
⁶   HA 1996, s 188(2A), as inserted by HRA 2017, s 5(4), for applications for homelessness assistance made on or after 3 April 2018.
⁷   HA 1996, ss 188(1ZA) and (1ZB), as inserted by HRA 2017, s 5(4) for applications for homelessness assistance made on or after 3 April 2018.

16.55 The fact that the initial interim accommodation duty is brought to an end by notification of the decision on the application for homelessness assistance does not mean that the accommodation that has been secured will be instantly withdrawn. At the very least, 'reasonable' notice will be required¹. Alternatively, the local housing authority may have to continue to secure accommodation for the applicant in performance of one of its other duties² or may choose to continue to secure accommodation in the exercise of a power³.

¹   See **16.29–16.30**.
²   See **16.11–16.16**.
³   See **15.184–15.188**.

Applicants with no priority need

16.56 Where the local housing authority, having made inquiries, satisfies itself that an applicant does not have a priority need¹, the interim accommodation duty will end upon:

•   the applicant being notified of the local housing authority's decision that the HA 1996, s 189B(2)², relief duty is not owed (because the applicant is either not eligible for assistance or is not homeless)³; or
•   the applicant being notified of the local housing authority's decision that, when the HA 1996, s 189B(2)⁴, relief duty comes to an end, no further accommodation duty will be owed under the HA 1996, s 190(2)⁵, short-term duty, or the HA 1996, s 193(2)⁶, main housing duty⁷.

¹   See English Code paras 15.8–15.9.

²   As inserted by HRA 2017, s 5(2), for applications for homelessness assistance made on or after 3 April 2018.
³   HA 1996, s 188(1ZA)(a), as inserted by HRA 2017, s 5(4), for applications for homelessness assistance made on or after 3 April 2018. See **16.57**.
⁴   As inserted by HRA 2017, s 5(2), for applications for homelessness assistance made on or after 3 April 2018.
⁵   As amended by HRA 2017, s 5(5), for applications for homelessness assistance made on or after 3 April 2018. See **16.81–16.93**.
⁶   See **16.94–16.199**.
⁷   HA 1996, s 188(1ZA)(b), as inserted by HRA 2017, s 5(4), for applications for homelessness assistance made on or after 3 April 2018, see **16.58**.

16.57 An applicant who does not have a priority need will continue to be owed the HA 1996, s 189B(2)[1], relief duty if he or she is homeless and eligible for assistance, but no further duty thereafter. An applicant who has no priority need and is either not homeless or is ineligible for assistance will be owed no duty at all. In either scenario, the applicant will need to be notified of the local housing authority's decision and upon that notification the interim accommodation duty will come to an end[2].

¹   As inserted by HRA 2017, s 5(2), for applications for homelessness assistance made on or after 3 April 2018.
²   HA 1996, s 188(1ZA), as inserted by HRA 2017, s 5(4), for applications for homelessness assistance made on or after 3 April 2018.

16.58 So, in instances where the applicant is found not to have a priority need, the HA 1996, s 189B(2)[1], relief duty and the interim accommodation duty are not coterminous. The local housing authority does continue to help the applicant must secure accommodation, but does not have to accommodate him or her while doing so. The English Code suggests that:

'. . . an applicant who the housing authority has found to be not in priority need within the 56 day 'relief stage' will no longer be owed a section 188(1) interim duty to accommodate, but will continue to be owed a section 189B(2) relief duty until that duty ends *or is found not to be owed*[2].' [Emphasis added]

The italicized parts of this sentence are apt to mislead. In those cases where the HA 1996, s 189B(2)[3], relief duty is found not to be owed, the '56 day 'relief stage" will never have begun. So it is wrong to suggest that the interim accommodation duty could end during the 56-day period in those cases. But, those cases aside, the underlying point that, in non-priority need cases, the interim accommodation duty may end, while the HA 1996, s 189B(2)[4], relief duty continues, is correct.

¹   As inserted by HRA 2017, s 5(2), for applications for homelessness assistance made on or after 3 April 2018.
²   English Code, para 15.9.
³   As inserted by HRA 2017, s 5(2), for applications for homelessness assistance made on or after 3 April 2018.
⁴   As inserted by HRA 2017, s 5(2), for applications for homelessness assistance made on or after 3 April 2018.

16.59 An applicant has the right to request a review of a decision:

- that he or she is not eligible for assistance;
- that he or she is not owed (or is no longer owed) the HA 1996, s 189B(2)[1], relief duty; and

- that he or she is not owed the HA 1996, s 190(2)[2], short-term duty, or the HA 1996, s 193(2)[3], main housing duty[4].

The local housing authority is not required to accommodate the applicant pending the notification of the review decision but has a power to do so[5].

[1] As inserted by HRA 2017, s 5(2), for applications for homelessness assistance made on or after 3 April 2018.
[2] As amended by HRA 2017, s 5(5), for applications for homelessness assistance made on or after 3 April 2018. See **16.81–16.93**.
[3] See **16.94–16.199**.
[4] HA 1996, s 202(1)(a) and (b) as amended by HRA 2017, s 9(2) for applications for homelessness assistance on or after 3 April 2018.
[5] HA 1996, s 188(3) as amended by HRA 2017, s 5(4) for applications for homelessness assistance on or after 3 April 2018, see **16.233–16.257**.

Applicants who have, or whom the local housing authority has reason to believe may have, a priority need

16.60 For all other applicants, where there is either reason to believe that they may have a priority need, or where the local housing authority is satisfied that they do have a priority need, the interim accommodation duty will end upon the later of:

- the HA 1996, s 189B(2)[1], relief duty coming to an end[2];
- the applicant being notified of the local housing authority's decision that the HA 1996, s 189B(2)[3], relief duty is not owed (because the applicant is either not eligible for assistance or is not homeless)[4]; or
- the applicant being notified of the local housing authority's decision as to what further duty (if any) will be owed to him or her when the HA 1996, s 189B(2)[5], relief duty comes to an end[6].

[1] As inserted by HRA 2017, s 5(2), for applications for homelessness assistance made on or after 3 April 2018.
[2] HA 1996, s 188(1ZB)(a), as inserted by HRA 2017, s 5(4), for applications for homelessness assistance made on or after 3 April 2018. See **16.61**.
[3] As inserted by HRA 2017, s 5(2), for applications for homelessness assistance made on or after 3 April 2018.
[4] HA 1996, s 188(1ZB)(a), as inserted by HRA 2017, s 5(4), for applications for homelessness assistance made on or after 3 April 2018. See **16.61**.
[5] As inserted by HRA 2017, s 5(2), for applications for homelessness assistance made on or after 3 April 2018.
[6] HA 1996, s 188(1ZB)(b), as inserted by HRA 2017, s 5(4), for applications for homelessness assistance made on or after 3 April 2018, see English Code, paras 15.10–15.11 and see **16.62**.

16.61 As to the first of these events, the circumstances in which the HA 1996, s 189B(2)[1], relief duty will come to an end are set out at HA 1996, s 189B(4)–(9)[2] and discussed at **15.151–15.189**. In relation to the second of these events, no HA 1996, s 189B(2)[3], relief duty will be owed in circumstances where the applicant is either found not to be eligible for assistance or not to be homeless.

[1] As inserted by HRA 2017, s 5(2), for applications for homelessness assistance made on or after 3 April 2018.
[2] As inserted by HRA 2017, s 5(2), for applications for homelessness assistance made on or after 3 April 2018.

[3]   As inserted by HRA 2017, s 5(2), for applications for homelessness assistance made on or after 3 April 2018.

16.62 Turning to the third of these events, if any duty is owed to an applicant once the HA 1996, s 189B(2)[1], relief duty has come to an end, it would be one of:

- the HA 1996, s 190(2)[2], short-term accommodation duty: owed to applicants who have a priority need but have become homeless intentionally[3];
- the HA 1996, s 193(2), main housing duty: owed to applicants who have a priority need who have not become homeless intentionally[4]; or
- the HA 1996, s 193C(4)[5], duty to accommodate: owed to applicants who have a priority need, who have not become homeless intentionally but who have deliberately and unreasonably refused to co-operate with the local housing authority[6].

[1]   As inserted by HRA 2017, s 5(2), for applications for homelessness assistance made on or after 3 April 2018.
[2]   As amended by HRA 2017, s 5(5), for applications for homelessness assistance made on or after 3 April 2018. See **16.81–16.93**.
[3]   See **16.81–16.93**.
[4]   See **16.94–16.199**.
[5]   As inserted by HRA 2017, s 7(1), for applications for homelessness assistance made on or after 3 April 2018.
[6]   See **16.200–16.216**.

16.63 The interim accommodation duty will come to an end 'upon the later of' one of the three events at **16.60** occurring. Each of these events must be notified to the applicant in writing[1]. Until the relevant notification has been given, the duty will continue[2]. The English Code advises that an applicant should simply receive one notification if possible, combining notification of the HA 1996, s 189B(2), relief duty coming to an end with notification of what additional duty is owed to the applicant:

> 'Housing authorities are advised against issuing a section 184 notification accepting the section 193 (main housing duty) during the relief stage. The section 193 duty cannot commence until the relief duty has come to an end and issuing notification during the relief stage might detract from activities to relieve their homelessness[3].'

[1]   See HA 1996, s 188(1ZB), as inserted by HRA 2017, s 5(4) for applications for homelessness assistance made on or after 3 April 2018.
[2]   This might be taken to suggest that an applicant could receive three separate notifications and that the interim accommodation duty will end upon receipt of the third notification. But this is not the case. The second event is mutually exclusive to the first and third events: in cases where the applicant is notified that the HA 1996, s 189B(2), (as inserted by HRA 2017, s 5(2) for applications for homelessness assistance made on or after 3 April 2018) relief duty is not owed, there will be no question of subsequently notifying him or her that the HA 1996, s 189B(2), (as inserted by HRA 2017, s 5(2) for applications for homelessness assistance made on or after 3 April 2018) relief duty has come to an end, or what, if any, duty will be owed after the HA 1996, s 189B(2), (as inserted by HRA 2017, s 5(2) for applications for homelessness assistance made on or after 3 April 2018) relief duty has ended. Further, in practice, it is likely that notification of the first and third events will be combined. That is, the local housing authority will choose to combine the notification that the HA 1996, s 189B(2), (as inserted by HRA 2017, s 5(2) for applications for homelessness assistance made on or after 3 April 2018) relief duty has come to an end with notification of what, if any, duty will be owed next.

3   English Code, para 13.10. The implication is that an applicant who is informed that he or she will be owed the HA 1996, s 193(2), main housing duty might lose the motivation to take steps to secure accommodation for himself or herself.

16.64 An applicant has the right to request a review of a decision that he or she is not eligible for assistance, that he or she is not owed (or no longer owed) the HA 1996, s 189B(2)[1], relief duty and that he or she is not owed the HA 1996, s 190(2)[2], short-term duty, or the HA 1996, s 193(2)[3], main housing duty[4]. The local housing authority is not required to accommodate the applicant pending the notification of the review decision but has a power to do so[5].

If the HA 1996, s 189B(2) relief duty,[6] has come to an end because the applicant has referred a final accommodation offer[7] or a final Pt 6 offer[8], and the applicant has requested a review of the decision that the duty has ended, the HA 1996, s 189B(2)[9] relief duty is deemed not to end until the review decision has been notified to the applicant and so the interim accommodation duty continues[10].

1   As inserted by HRA 2017, s 5(2), for applications for homelessness assistance made on or after 3 April 2018.
2   As amended by HRA 2017, s 5(5), for applications for homelessness assistance made on or after 3 April 2018. See **16.81–16.93**.
3   See **16.94–16.199**.
4   HA 1996, s 202(1)(a) and (b) as amended by HRA 2017, s 9(2) for applications for homelessness assistance nade on or after 3 April 2018.
5   HA 1996, s 188(3) as amended by HRA 2017, s 5(4) for applications for homelessness assistance made on or after 3 April 2018.
6   As inserted by HRA, s 5(2) for applications for homelessness assistance made on or after 3 April 2018. See **15.137–15.145**.
7   HA 1996, ss 189B(4)(u) and 193A(z) as inserted by HRA 2017, ss 5(2) and 7(1), for applications for homelessness assistance made on or after 3 April 2018. See **15.181–15.184**.
8   HA 1996, ss 189 (B)(9)(b) and 193A(2), as inserted by HRA 2017, ss 5(2) and 7(1), for applications for homelessness assistnace made on or after 3 April 2018,. See **15.185–15.188**.
9   As inserted by HRA, s 5(2) for applications for homelessness assistance made on or after 3 April 2018. See **15.137–15.145**.
10   HA 1996, s 188(2A) as inserted by HRA 2017, s 5(4), for applications for homelessness assistance made on or after 3 April 2108.

16.65 In effect, therefore, in most priority need (or apparent priority need) cases, the interim accommodation duty will end either when the local housing authority notifies the applicant that the HA 1996, s 189B(2)[1], relief duty is not owed, or when the HA 1996, s 189B(2)[2], relief duty comes to an end. So the HA 1996, s 189B(2)[3], relief duty and the HA 1996, s 188, interim accommodation duty are likely to be coterminous in most priority need (or apparent priority need) cases[4].

1   As inserted by HRA 2017, s 5(2), for applications for homelessness assistance made on or after 3 April 2018.
2   As inserted by HRA 2017, s 5(2), for applications for homelessness assistance made on or after 3 April 2018.
3   As inserted by HRA 2017, s 5(2), for applications for homelessness assistance made on or after 3 April 2018.
4   The only situation in which this would not be the case is if the local housing authority chose to give the applicant notice under HA 1996, s 189B(5) (as inserted by HRA 2017, s 5(2) for applications for homelessness assistance made on or after 3 April 2018) bringing the HA 1996, s 189B(2), relief duty (as inserted by HRA 2017, s 5(2) for applications for homelessness assistance made on or after 3 April 2018) to an end, but chose to notify the applicant what

duty (if any) is owed to him or her next, at some later stage. As discussed at **16.63**, it seems likely that most local housing authorities will choose to combine these notifications.

The applicant refuses interim accommodation

16.66 Circumstances, set out *expressly* in HA 1996, Pt 7[1], in which the interim accommodation duty comes to an end, are dealt with at **16.51–16.65**. A further situation, not expressly contemplated within HA 1996, Pt 7[2] was considered by the High Court prior to the amendment of HA 1996, Pt 7 by HRA 2017[3]. The circumstance was that the applicant had refused[4] interim accommodation[5]. In this situation, the High Court held that:

> 'The authority will have performed the duty owed under section 188 of the Act if the authority offers suitable accommodation, or secures the offer of suitable accommodation by another person, which is intended to be available to the applicant until the authority have completed their inquiries and notified the applicant of their decision as to whether a duty is owed. If the applicant does not take up the offer of accommodation, then he cannot require the authority to take different and further steps to perform the duty again[6].'

The exception to this principle is where the applicant rejects accommodation but a subsequent change in circumstances renders the accommodation unsuitable. In that case, the local housing authority will be required to secure alternative accommodation[7].

[1] As amended by HRA 2017 for applications for homelessness assistance made on or after 3 April 2018.
[2] As amended by HRA 2017 for applications for homelessness assistance made on or after 3 April 2018.
[3] For applications for homelessness assistance more on or after or after 3 April 2018.
[4] English Code, para 15.22.
[5] *R (Brooks) v Islington London Borough Council* [2015] EWHC 2657 (Admin), [2016] HLR 2, Admin Ct.
[6] *R (Brooks) v Islington London Borough Council* [2015] EWHC 2657 (Admin), [2016] HLR 2, Admin Ct at [31] per Lewis J.
[7] *R (Brooks) v Islington London Borough Council* [2015] EWHC 2657 (Admin), [2016] HLR 2, Admin Ct at [32] per Lewis J.

16.67 An attempt to codify these principles is contained in the English Code which provides that:

> 'Where an applicant rejects an offer of interim accommodation (or accepts and moves into the interim accommodation and then later rejects it), this will bring the housing authority's interim accommodation duty to an end – unless it is reactivated by any change of circumstances[1].'

[1] English Code, para 15.22.

16.68 Whether these principles still hold good following the amendment of HA 1996, Pt 7 by HRA 2017[1] may be open to question. The reasoning of Lewis J in *R (Brooks) v Islington London Borough Council*[2] was based, in part, on the earlier decision of in *R v Westminster City Council ex p Chambers*[3]. In *R (Royal London Borough of Kensington and Chelsea) v London Borough of Ealing and Ms Hacene-Blidi*[4], HHJ Karen Walden-Smith, sitting as a deputy High Court judge, held that *R v Westminster City Council ex p Chambers* was no longer good law on this issue and the reasoning in that decision could not be applied to the HA 1996, s 193(2), main housing duty[5]. Now that HA 1996, s 188 has been amended by HRA 2017, s 5(4) to insert a series of express statutory provisions as to cessation of duty[6], if *Chambers* is no longer good law, then the reasoning of Lewis J in *Brooks* may be undermined[7].

1   For applications for homelessness assistance on or after 3 April 2018.
2   [2015] EWHC 2657 (Admin), [2016] HLR 2, Admin Ct.
3   (1982) 6 HLR 24, QBD. That case, which 'created the concept of discharge of duty', involved an applicant who refused an offer of accommodation under Housing (Homeless Persons) Act 1977, s 4(5) duty owed to applicants who had a priority need and who had not become homeless intentionally. McCullough J held that, although there was no express statutory provision as to the cessation of duty contained in the Housing (Homeless Persons) Act 1977, the local housing authority were not obliged to secure alternative accommodation. They had performed the duty by 'making available to him accommodation' and were required to do no more.
4   [2017] EWHC 24 (Admin), [2017] PTSR 1029, Admin Ct.
5   This was because, among other things, HA 1996, s 193 differed from Housing (Homeless Persons) Act 1977, s 4 in that the former does contain express statutory provision as to the cessation of duty. As such, HA 1996, Pt 7 could be regarded as a complete statutory scheme 'in which there is no place for any judicial overlay'.
6   HA 1996, s 188(1ZA)–(1ZB), as inserted by HRA 2017, s 5(4) for applications for homelessness assistance made on or after 3 April 2018.
7   The answer to this question may lie in the distinction drawn by Lewis J in *R (Brooks) v Islington London Borough Council* between the *existence* of the HA 1996, s 188(1) duty and the *performance* of the duty. The duty will *exist* until one of the events specified in HA 1996, s 188(1ZA)–(1ZB) occurs. However, the duty can be *performed* by securing a single offer of suitable accommodation. That interpretation might be taken to reflect 'the realities . . . of the competing claims for the provision of accommodation, which is often a scare resource' [43]. But the answer is not clear cut and it may be that the courts are required to consider this question before long.

16.69 In the meantime, (and irrespective of the answer to this question) applicants would be well-advised to be cautious before refusing an offer of interim accommodation. Conversely, local housing authorities will certainly be required to ensure that the applicant has actually rejected the accommodation before deciding that their initial interim accommodation duty has come to an end. One local housing authority was subject to judicial review proceedings when it refused to secure further interim accommodation, insisting that the applicant had rejected the accommodation, after the applicant had arrived at the accommodation a day late[1]. Likewise, where it is said that the applicant's conduct has manifested an implied rejection of the accommodation[2], the local housing authority should normally give the applicant a warning and an opportunity to provide an explanation for his or her conduct[3]. Particular sensitivity will be needed when the applicant is in poor mental health (a phenomenon that is not infrequent, given the stressful nature of homelessness). In those circumstances, where an applicant might have behaved in a way that led him or her to be excluded from interim accommodation, whether the accommodation provided was suitable for the applicant's needs will be relevant to whether the duty owed to him or her has been properly performed[4].

1   *R (Carstens) v Basildon District Council* (2006) CO/923/2006, (2007) September *Legal Action*, p 18, Admin Ct.
2   For example, if the applicant flouts the terms on which the accommodation is available or, in extreme cases, damages or destroys the accommodation.
3   *R v Kensington and Chelsea Royal London Borough Council ex p Kujtim* [1999] 4 All ER 161, (2000) 32 HLR 579, CA.

4   See *R (Lindsay) v Watford Borough Council*, unreported, 17 October 2017, Admin Ct, where the applicant, who suffered from depression and severe epilepsy, was required to leave hotel accommodation having allegedly assaulted a member of staff. The Administrative Court judge held that there was a serious issue to be tried as to whether the accommodation provided had been suitable and whether, therefore, the local housing authority had discharged its duty under HA 1996, s 188(1).

Consequences of decision that the duty to secure interim accommodation has come to an end

16.70 The duty to secure interim accommodation is separate from the other duties that a local housing authority is likely to owe to an applicant who is homeless at an early stage in the progress of the application for homelessness assistance. Those duties are:

- to make inquiries into the application and to notify the applicant of a decision as to whether he or she is eligible for assistance and, if so, whether any duty is owed to him or her[1];
- if the applicant is eligible for assistance,to make an assessment of his or her case and draw up a personalised housing plan;[2] and
- if the applicant is eligible for assistance, to take reasonable steps to help him or her to secure that accommodation becomes available for his or her occupation[3].

Those duties continue even if there is no further duty to secure interim accommodation.

1   HA 1996, s 184(1) and (3). See **9.89–9.142**.
2   HA 1996, s 189A, as inserted by HRA 2017, s 3(1), for applications for homelessness assistance made on or after 3 April 2018. See **15.62–15.71**.
3   HA 1996, s 189B(2), as inserted by HRA 2017, s 5(2), for applications for homelessness assistance made on or after 3 April 2018. See **15.138–15.195**.

Termination of interim accommodation

16.71 Almost by definition, any agreement for occupation of 'interim' accommodation will provide for quite short notice. Ordinarily, whatever the agreement itself says, those tenancies and licences that fall within the scope of the Protection from Eviction Act 1977 can only be terminated by the landlord on at least four weeks' written notice and the landlord will require a possession order from the court before he or she is entitled to obtain possession. But much of the accommodation secured as interim accommodation is provided under licences excluded from that protection[1]. In particular, a licence to occupy a local authority hostel is excluded from protection[2], and so all that the local housing authority or the hostel manager need do is give the applicant reasonable notice to leave[3].

1   Protection from Eviction Act 1977, s 3A lists the exclusions.
2   Protection from Eviction Act 1977, s 3A(8).
3   *Minister of Health v Bellotti* [1944] 1 KB 298, CA. See further *Gibson v Douglas* [2016] EWCA Civ 1266, CA at [20]–[21] per Sir James Munby for an *obiter* discussion on the length of notice that may be required to terminate a licence.

16.72 Even in respect of the types of accommodation which might otherwise ordinarily fall within the scope of the Protection from Eviction Act 1977 (such as self-contained accommodation), the courts have not been inclined to apply the provisions of the Protection from Eviction Act 1977 to interim accommodation which is occupied under a licence. The approach taken has been that it is incompatible with a scheme for interim accommodation that the occupier should be entitled to four weeks' notice and then to the benefit of the further inevitable delay while possession is obtained through the courts[1].

[1]   *Mohammed v Manek and Kensington and Chelsea Royal London Borough Council* (1995) 27 HLR 439, CA; *Gibson v Paddington Churches Housing Association* (2003) November *Legal Action*, p 16, Central London County Court; *Desnousse v Newham London Borough Council* [2006] EWCA Civ 547, [2006] HLR 38, CA; and *R (CN) v Lewisham London Borough Council, R (ZN) v Newham London Borough Council* [2014] UKSC 62, [2015] AC 1259, SC. See English Code, paras 15.19–15.21.

16.73 Even if there is no minimum notice required and no need to obtain a possession order, this does not mean that the local housing authority can simply eject applicants accommodated on an interim basis. Local housing authorities must act reasonably, as any public authority would. The obligation to behave reasonably requires that the applicant be given at least some opportunity to find some other accommodation before the interim accommodation is withdrawn[1]. Reasonable notice in those circumstances should obviously be more than 24 hours[2] and periods of six or seven days have also been held to be too short to constitute reasonable notice[3]. In one case, a judge suggested that the reasonable notice ought to be at least the period the local housing authority would have given to applicants who have a priority need and have become homeless intentionally occupying accommodation secured under HA 1996, s 190(2)(a)[4].

[1]   English Code, paras 15.19–15.21; and *R v Secretary of State for the Environment ex p Shelter* [1997] COD 49, QBD, applied in *R v Newham London Borough Council ex p Ojuri (No 5)* (1999) 31 ACR 631, QBD and in *R (AM) v Tower Hamlets London Borough Council and Havering London Borough Council* [2015] EWHC 1004 Admin Ct, (2015) May *Legal Action*, p 46, Admin Ct per Cobb J at [35].
[2]   *R v Newham London Borough Council ex p Ojuri (No 5)* (1999) 31 ACR 631, QBD.
[3]   *R v Newham London Borough Council ex p Pembele* (1999) January *Legal Action*, p 27, QBD; *R v Westminster City Council ex p Abdulkadir* (1999) August *Legal Action*, p 29, QBD, although in *R v Newham London Borough Council ex p Lumley* (2001) 33 ACR 11, QBD, it was said *obiter* that 6 clear days' notice would not be unreasonable for a young single man.
[4]   *R v Secretary of State for the Environment ex parte Shelter* [1997] COD 49, QB. See **16.81–16.93** for the duty at HA 1996, s 190(2)(a) (as now amended by HRA 2017, s 5(5), for applications for homelessness assistance made on or after 3 April 2018).

Challenges to decisions concerning interim accommodation

16.74 None of the decisions that a local housing authority might make in relation to its duty to secure 'interim' accommodation are subject to the statutory review procedure at HA 1996, s 202(1)[1]. None of the following decisions about the provision of interim accommodation, which may be among the most critical to be made concerning an applicant, are covered by the statutory review procedure:

(1)   a decision that no duty to secure interim accommodation is owed;
(2)   a decision as to how a duty to secure interim accommodation will be performed;

(3)   a decision as to which members of the applicant's household will be accommodated under the duty;

(4)   a decision as to whether the interim accommodation is suitable; or

(5)   a decision that the interim accommodation duty is no longer owed.

[1]   As amended by HRA 2017, s 9, for applications for homelessness assistance made on or after 3 April 2018, see **19.12–19.69**.

16.75 There is no statutory obligation to notify the applicant of these decisions (in writing or otherwise), nor is there a statutory obligation to give reasons for those decisions[1].

[1]   It is obviously good administrative practice for decisions to be recorded in writing and, where appropriate, to be explained by written reasons.

16.76 Although these decisions, if disputed, could be the subject of a formal complaint to the local housing authority under its complaints procedure and (ultimately) to the Local Government and Social Care Ombudsman, the applicant will usually need the urgent provision of suitable interim accommodation, and this can only be obtained (if at all) by a legal challenge to the relevant decision.

16.77 Any challenge to the local housing authority's decision that it does not have 'reason to believe' that an applicant 'may' be homeless, 'may' be eligible for assistance and 'may' have a priority need, can only be brought by judicial review[1].

[1]   See **19.306–19.333**.

16.78 Any challenge to the suitability of accommodation secured under the duty to secure interim accommodation (or any of the other decisions listed) can only be brought by judicial review[1]. There is no right to request a statutory review of the suitability of interim accommodation and no appeal to the county court on such an issue.

[1]   See **19.306–19.333**.

16.79 When the local housing authority agrees that it has reason to believe that the applicant may be homeless, may be eligible for assistance and may have a priority need, but is nevertheless failing to comply with its acknowledged statutory duty, the appropriate procedure is to bring a claim for judicial review[1], including an application for both an interim and final mandatory order requiring the local housing authority to comply with its statutory duty.

[1]   See **19.306–19.333**.

16.80 There is no right to request a review of any decision that the interim accommodation duty is not owed, or has come to an end. However, there are rights to request reviews of the decisions that may have led the local housing authority to notify the applicant that it no longer owes him or her the interim accommodation duties[1]. The local housing authority is not required to accommodate the applicant pending the notification of the review decision but has a power to do so[2].

1   HA 1996, s 202(1)(a) and s 202(1)(b) as amended by HRA 2017, s 9(2), for applications for homelessness assistance made on or after 3 April 2018. See **19.14–19.17**.

2   HA 1996, s 188(3) as amended by HRA 2017, s 5(4) for applications for homelessness assistance on or after 3 April 2018. See **16.233–16.257**. Unless the reason for the HA 1996, s 189B(2), (as inserted by HRA 2017, s 5(2), for applications for homelessness assistance made on or after 3 April 2018) relief duty coming to an end is because the applicant refused a final accommodation offer or final Part 6 offer: HA 1996, ss 189B(2)(a) and 193A(2) (as inserted by HRA 2017, ss 5(2) and 7(1), for applications for homelessness assistance made on or after 3 April 2018). If that is the case, then the HA 1996, s 189B(2) (as inserted by HRA 2017, s 5(2), for applications for homelessness assistance made on or after 3 April 2018) relief duty continues while the applicant requests a review of the decision that the duty has ended, and, if the local housing authority still has reason to believe that the applicant may have a priority need, the interim accommodation duty continues: HA 1996, s 188(2A), as inserted by HRA 2017, s 5(4), for applications for homelessness assistance made on or after 3 April 2018, see **15.184–15.188** and **16.64**.

THE HA 1996, S 190(2), SHORT-TERM ACCOMMODATION DUTY

16.81 This duty[1], which arises once the HA 1996, s 189B(2)[2], relief duty has come to an end, is owed to an applicant in respect of whom the local housing authority is satisfied that he or she[3]:

- is eligible for assistance[4];
- is homeless[5];
- has become homeless intentionally[6]; and
- has a priority need[7].

1   HA 1996, s190(2), as amended by HRA 2017, s 5(5) for applications for homelessness assistance made on or after 3 April 2018.

2   As inserted by HRA 2017, s 5(2), for applications for homelessness assistance made on or after 3 April 2018.

3   HA 1996, s 190(1), as amended by HRA 2017, s 5(5), for applications for homelessness assistance made on or after 3 April 2018.

4   HA 1996, s 185, see Chapter **11**.

5   HA 1996, ss 175–177, see Chapter **10**.

6   HA 1996, s 191, see Chapter **13**.

7   HA 1996, s 189(1) and Homelessness (Priority Need for Accommodation) (England) Order 2002, SI 2002/2051, see Chapter **12** and Appendix **2**.

16.82 The duty is triggered as soon as those conditions are fulfilled, although the local housing authority will provide written notification to the applicant indicating that this is the duty that it owes to him or her[1]. The duty owed by the local housing authority is to secure accommodation 'for such period as they consider will give him a reasonable opportunity of securing accommodation for his occupation'[2]. The accommodation secured for this period must meet all the usual requirements[3].

1   HA 1996, s 184(3). See **9.90–9.94**. Where a local housing authority had rejected the contention that it owed this duty to accommodate an applicant whom it had found to have become homeless intentionally, it was ordered to pay the costs of the applicant's judicial review claim. The prospect of the local housing authority losing the judicial review was 'towards the obvious end of the spectrum': per Walker J in *R (Dumbaya) v Lewisham London Borough Council* [2008] EWHC 1852 (Admin), (2008) September *Legal Action*, p 25, Admin Ct.

2   HA 1996, s 190(2)(a), as amended by HRA 2017, s 5(5), for applications for homelessness assistance made on or after 3 April 2018.

16.83 Concurrently, the local housing authority also has a duty to provide, or secure that the applicant is provided with, advice and assistance in any attempt he or she may make to secure that accommodation is available for his or her occupation¹. This advice and assistance is to be provided in addition to the help that the local housing authority will already have provided during the performance of the HA 1996, s 189B(2)², relief duty³. In deciding what advice and assistance to provide, HA 1996, s 190(4)⁴, provides that the local housing authority must have regard to its assessment of the applicant's case under HA 1996, 189A⁵. The advice and assistance must include information about the likely availability in the local housing authority's district of types of accommodation appropriate to the applicant's housing needs, including in particular the location and sources of such types of accommodation⁶. This advice and assistance duty is discussed further at **15.231**.

¹   HA 1996, s 190(2)(b), as amended by HRA 2017, s 5(5), for applications for homelessness assistance made on or after 3 April 2018. See **15.231**.
²   As inserted by HRA 2017, s 5(2), for applications for homelessness assistance made on or after 3 April 2018. See **15.138–15.195**.
³   This is evident from the fact that the duty to provide this advice and assistance only arises after the HA 189B(2), relief duty (as inserted by HRA 2017, s 5(2) for applications for homelessness assistance made on or after 3 April 2018) has come to an end.
⁴   As inserted by HRA 2017, s 5(5), for applications for homelessness assistance made on or after 3 April 2018. See **15.231–15.232**.
⁵   As inserted by HRA 2017, s 3(1), for applications for homelessness assistance made on or after 3 April 2018. See **15.62–15.71**.
⁶   HA 1996, s 190(5), as amended by HRA 2017, s 5(5), for applications for homelessness assistance made on or after 3 April 2018.

16.84 The applicant owed these duties is likely to have been provided with interim accommodation pending the decision on his or her application and the subsequent performance of the HA 1996, s 189B(2)¹, relief duty². In that situation, the usual course will be for the local housing authority to continue the provision of that same accommodation for whatever further period it has decided will satisfy its duty. If it has not previously secured accommodation, it must do so for that same period.

¹   As inserted by HRA 2017, s 5(2), for applications for homelessness assistance made on or after 3 April 2018.
²   HA 1996, s 188(1) and (1B), as inserted by HRA 2017, s 5(4), for applications for homelessness assistance made on or after 3 April 2018, see **16.37–16.50**.

16.85 Local housing authorities, having strategic responsibility for housing in their districts, are uniquely well placed to determine what sort of period an applicant will require in order to have a 'reasonable opportunity' of finding housing locally. The duty is not to secure accommodation for as long as it actually takes the applicant to find his or her own housing. It is instead to secure accommodation for the period that the local housing authority considers will give the applicant a 'reasonable opportunity' to find and secure accommodation for himself or herself.

16.86 The English Code advises that local housing authorities, when determining the length of the period, should take into account:

- the particular needs and circumstances of the applicant and any resources available to him or her to secure accommodation, which might include any health or support needs that make it more difficult for the applicant to find and secure accommodation and any support available from the applicant's family or social network;
- the housing circumstances in the local area and the length of time it might reasonably take to secure accommodation, including the efforts previously made by both the local housing authority and the applicant to relieve his or her homelessness and why those efforts have not proved successful; and
- any arrangements that have already been made by the applicant to secure accommodation which are likely to be successful within a reasonable timescale, and whether it would be appropriate to accommodate the applicant in the meantime[1].

1 English Code, para 15.15.

16.87 Some of these issues will have already been addressed within the HA 1996, s 189A(1)[1], assessment of the applicant's needs and from the personalised housing plan agreed with the applicant, or recorded by the local housing authority[2]. This personalised approach should end the practice, to the extent it still exists, of providing a standardised period of accommodation without any proper assessment of the applicant's needs and resources.

1 As inserted by HRA 2017, s 3(1), for applications for homelessness assistance made on or after 3 April 2018. See **15.62–15.71**.
2 HA 1996, s 189A(4) and (6), as inserted by HRA 2017, s 3(1), for applications for homelessness assistance made on or after 3 April 2018. See **15.72–15.80**.

16.88 Plainly the period required will be longer in areas of housing shortage. Some examples considered by the courts are:

- a period of four days for an applicant with a family was considered to be unlawfully short and a period of months might be expected[1];
- an initial decision to give a single parent of three children six or seven days' accommodation could not be considered reasonable, but there was no error of law in the local housing authority's subsequent decision not to extend the period beyond 28 days[2];
- where a judge decided that accommodation secured[3] the duty would only have been for a maximum period of three months, so that the judicial review claim was academic[4];
- where a judge decided that he should grant an interim injunction requiring the local housing authority to continue to secure accommodation for the applicant, where the evidence was that within a week the claimant would be able to clear previous arrears, secure housing benefit and with the help of a bond scheme, secure a private sector tenancy[5]; and
- where a judge held that it was not wrong in law for a local housing authority to decide that a 28-day period was a 'reasonable period' for a single mother with a 4-year-old son[6] to secure accommodation for their occupation.

1 *De Falco v Crawley Borough Council* [1980] QB 460, AC.

2   R *(Nipyo) v Croydon London Borough Council* [2008] EWHC 847 (Admin), [2008] HLR 37, Admin Ct.

3   Prior to amendment by HRA 2017.

4   *Newman v Croydon London Borough Council* [2008] EWCA Civ 1176, (2009) April *Legal Action*, p 22, CA.

5   R *(Anwar) v Manchester City Council* [2009] EWHC 2876 (Admin), (2010) January *Legal Action*, p 36, Admin Ct.

6   R *(Savage) v Hillingdon London Borough Council* [2010] EWHC 88 (Admin), March *Legal Action*, p 31, Admin Ct.

16.89 The Court of Appeal has held that, when considering what period would give the applicant a 'reasonable opportunity' for securing accommodation for his or her occupation, the local housing authority should consider what is reasonable from an applicant's standpoint, having regard to his or her circumstances and in the context of accommodation potentially available. Considerations peculiar to the local housing authority, such as the extent of its resources and the other demands on its resources, are not to be taken into account when determining the length of the period[1].

1   R *(Conville) v Richmond upon Thames London Borough Council* [2006] EWCA Civ 718, [2006] HLR 45, CA.

Termination of accommodation secured under the HA 1996, s 190(2), short-term accommodation duty

16.90 The duty at HA 1996, s 190(2)[1], owed to applicants who are homeless, eligible for assistance, have a priority need and have become homeless intentionally is to secure accommodation for the applicant's occupation for such period as the local housing authority considers will give him or her a reasonable opportunity of securing accommodation for his or her own occupation. The duty arises after the HA 1996, s 189B(2)[2], relief duty has come to an end[3].

1   As amended by HRA 2017, s 5(5), for applications for homelessness assistance made on or after 3 April 2018.

2   As inserted by HRA 2017, s 5(2), for applications for homelessness assistance made on or after 3 April 2018. See **15.138–15.195**.

3   HA 1996, s 190(1), as amended by HRA 2017, s 5(5), for applications for homelessness assistance made on or after 3 April 2018.

16.91 Accommodation secured under this duty is usually provided under a licence and for a short period of time[1]. In *R (CN) v Lewisham London Borough Council*[2], the Supreme Court held that the Protection from Eviction Act 1977 would not generally apply to such accommodation. The licence to occupy the accommodation can therefore be terminated on reasonable notice, but with no obligation on the licensor to obtain a possession order[3].

1   See **16.29–16.30**.

2   [2014] UKSC 62, [2015] AC 1259, SC

3   Protection from Eviction Act 1977, s 3; *R (CN) v Lewisham London Borough Council, R (ZN) v Newham London Borough Council* [2014] UKSC 62, [2015] AC 1259, SC; Code paras 15.19–15.21; see **16.29–16.30**.

16.92 Where the applicant's household includes a person under 18, the applicant should be invited to consent to a referral to children's services for assistance under Children Act 1989[1].

[1] HA 1996, s 213A(1), as amended by HRA 2017, s 4(7), for applications for homelessness assistance made on or after 3 April 2018, Code, para 15.21, see **16.280–16.287**.

16.93 If the applicant wants to challenge the local housing authority's decision as to the length of the period that it considers will give him or her 'a reasonable opportunity' of securing his or her own accommodation, he or she must bring a claim for judicial review. This is because it is a dispute over the way in which the local housing authority is performing its duty, not over what duty, if any, is owed to the applicant, and so the statutory right to request a review is not available[1].

[1] *R (Conville) v Richmond upon Thames London Borough Council* [2006] EWCA Civ 718, [2006] HLR 45, CA. For judicial review, see **19.306–19.333**.

THE HA 1996, S 193(2) MAIN HOUSING DUTY

16.94 The highest duty to secure accommodation that can be owed under HA 1996, s 193(2)[1] is often colloquially called the 'full housing duty', but HA 1996, Pt 7[2] refers to it as the 'main housing duty'[3]. We use the statutory language to refer to the duty throughout this chapter and this book.

[1] HA 1996, s 193, as amended by HRA 2017, ss 5(7) and 7(2), for applications for homelessness assistance made on or after 3 April 2018; English Code, paras 15.39–15.43.
[2] As amended by HRA 2017, for applications for homelessness assistance made on or after 3 April 2018.
[3] For example in HA 1996, s 200(3).

To whom is the duty owed?

16.95 The HA 1996, s 193(2) 'main housing duty' is owed to applicants whom the local housing authority is satisfied[1]:

- are homeless[2];
- are eligible for assistance[3];
- have not become homeless intentionally[4]; and
- have a priority need[5].

The duty will only arise once the HA 1996, s 189B(2)[6], relief duty has come to an end[7]. But it will not be owed in circumstances where:

- the HA 1996, s 189B(2)[8], relief duty came to an end because the applicant refused a final accommodation offer[9] or a final Pt 6[10] offer[11];
- the HA 1996, s 189B(2)[12], relief duty came to an end because of the applicant's deliberate and unreasonable refusal to co-operate[13]; or
- the local housing authority has notified the applicant that they have notified, or intend to notify, another local housing authority that the conditions for referral[14] of his or her case are met[15].

[1] HA 1996, s 193(1) and (1A), as amended by HRA 2017, s 5(7), for applications for homelessness assistance made on or after 3 April 2018; English Code, para 15.39.
[2] HA 1996, s 185, see CHAPTER **11**.
[3] HA 1996, ss 175–177, see CHAPTER **10**.
[4] HA 1996, s 191, see CHAPTER **13**.

⁵ HA 1996, s 189(1) and Homelessness (Priority Need for Accommodation) (England) Order 2002, SI 2002/2051, see Chapter **12** and Appendix **2**. There is an exception from the requirement that an applicant must have a priority need in order to be owed the HA 1996, s 193(2), main housing duty where the applicant is making a fresh application for homelessness assistance within two years of the date of acceptance by the applicant of a private rented sector offer (HA 1996, s 195A, as amended by HRA 2017, s 4(4), for applications for homelessness assistance made on or after 3 April 2018), see **8.100–8.107**, **15.56–15.58** and **16.47–16.50**. It should be noted that where the HA 1996, s 193(2), main housing duty would only be owed to the applicant because of the presence of a restricted person, the applicant must still have a priority need in order to be owed the main housing duty (HA 1996, s 195A(5) as amended by HRA 2017, s 4(4), for applications for homelessness assistance made on or after 3 April 2018), see **8.102**.

⁶ As inserted by HRA 2017, s 5(2), for applications for homelessness assistance made on or after 3 April 2018.

⁷ See **15.151–15.195**.

⁸ As inserted by HRA 2017, s 5(2), for applications for homelessness assistance made on or after 3 April 2018.

⁹ As defined at HA 1996, s 193A(4), as inserted by HRA 2017, s 7(1), for applications for homelessness assistance made on or after 3 April 2018. See **15.181**.

¹⁰ As defined at HA 1996, s 193A(5), as inserted by HRA 2017, s 7(1), for applications for homelessness assistance made on or after 3 April 2018. See **15.185**.

¹¹ HA 1996, s 193A(3), as inserted by HRA 2017, s 7(1), for applications for homelessness assistance made on or after 3 April 2018, see **15.181–15.89**.

¹² As inserted by HRA 2017, s 5(2), for applications for homelessness assistance made on or after 3 April 2018.

¹³ HA 1996, s 193C(4), as inserted by HRA 2017, s 7(1), for applications for homelessness assistance made on or after 3 April 2018. See **16.200–16.216** for the duty that will be owed instead in these circumstances.

¹⁴ See Chapter **14**.

¹⁵ HA 1996, s 200(1). See **16.225–16.232** for the duty that will be owed instead in these circumstances.

16.96 The duty is 'to secure that accommodation is available for occupation by the applicant' and by his or her household (ie by all other persons who normally reside with the applicant as a member of his or her family, or who might reasonably be expected to reside with the applicant)[1].

¹ HA 1996, s 176; English Code, para 15.40. This extension of the duty to the other household members is considered at **10.21–10.32**. See *R (Ogbeni) v Tower Hamlets London Borough Council* [2008] EWHC 2444 (Admin), (2008) October *Legal Action*, p 37, Admin Ct, where the local housing authority was wrong to refuse to secure accommodation for a 17-year-old applicant and his aunt, who normally resided with him as a member of his family.

16.97 The duty is not limited to any particular minimum or maximum period. Nor is it a duty to provide a lasting home. HA 1996, Pt 7[1] is a safety net statutory scheme designed to resolve or prevent homelessness. The HA 1996, s 193(2), 'main housing duty' is the highest form of that safety net. Under that duty, accommodation is secured until the applicant is able, with any appropriate assistance, to resolve his or her longer-term housing needs[2]. That longer-term need might be met by the provision of a tenancy of social housing[3], in which case the applicant will need the assistance of HA 1996, Pt 6 (Allocation of Housing Accommodation) described in Chapters **1–6**, or accommodation in the private rented sector[4].

¹ As amended by HRA 2017, for applications for homelessness assistance made on or after 3 April 2018.

² Or other events, specified at HA 1996, s 193(5) and (6), occur. See **16.114–16.141**.

³ HA 1996, s 193(6)(c) or (7). See **16.131–16.135** and **16.142–16.152**.

4   HA 1996, s 193(7AA)–(7AC). See **16.153–16.180**.

When does the duty start?

16.98 The HA 1996, s 193(2), main housing duty is triggered as soon as the local housing authority is satisfied that the HA 1996, s 189B(2)[1], relief duty has come to an end[2], and all the other components required to activate the duty are in place.

1   As inserted by HRA 2017, s 5(2), for applications for homelessness assistance made on or after 3 April 2018. See **15.138–15.195**.
2   HA 1996, s 193(1)(c), as amended by HRA 2017, s 5(7), for applications for homelessness assistance made on or after 3 April 2018.

16.99 Whilst the commencement of the duty is not dependent on notification being given to the applicant, because it is owed as soon as the local housing authority is 'satisfied' that the components are in place[1], the applicant will have been notified of the local housing authority's decision that the HA 1996, s 189B(2)[2], relief duty has come to an end[3].

1   HA 1996, s 193(1), as amended by HRA 2017, s 5(7), for applications for homelessness assistance made on or after 3 April 2018.
2   As inserted by HRA 2017, s 5(2), for applications for homelessness assistance made on or after 3 April 2018.
3   HA 1996, s 189B(5) and (6), as inserted by HRA 2017, s 5(2), for applications for homelessness assistance made on or after 3 April 2018. See **15.151–15.159**.

16.100 The duty is an unqualified one and, once the components are in place, its performance cannot be deferred. A local housing authority must secure accommodation, and it must be suitable, from the date the duty is first owed. The local housing authority cannot avoid the immediate performance of the duty by reference to the other demands on its housing services or its available stock[1]. The whole point of the safety net duty is that it kicks in immediately once its components are met.

1   *Codona v Mid-Bedfordshire District Council* [2004] EWCA Civ 925, [2005] HLR 1, CA at [36] per Auld LJ.

16.101 If the local housing authority fails to secure suitable accommodation, the applicant can apply for a mandatory order in judicial review proceedings requiring the local housing authority to comply with its duty[1]. If the breach of duty is technical or minor, and the local housing authority can demonstrate it has done its best to comply with the duty, permission to bring a judicial review claim may be refused[2].

1   See **19.312**.
2   *R v Newham London Borough Council ex p Sacupima* (2000) 33 ACR 2, CA, at [17].

How can the duty end?

16.102 When the local housing authority owes the HA 1996, s 193(2), main housing duty to secure accommodation for the applicant, that duty can only end if one of the events set out in HA 1996, s 193(5)–(7AA) occurs[1]. The list of those events is exhaustive. If there is a change of circumstances not featuring among the events specified, the duty is not brought to an end[2]. For example, where an applicant who had a priority need and was entitled to the HA 1996, s 193(2), main housing duty had a change of circumstances such that he no longer had a priority need, the local housing authority still had a duty towards him, because such a change is not among the listed events[3]. Similarly, where an applicant is owed the HA 1996, s 193(2), main housing duty but is unable to afford the charges levied on the accommodation, the HA 1996, s 193(2), main housing duty does not come to an end (because an inability to afford the charges is not among the listed events)[4].

[1]   HA 1996, s 193(5)–(7AA); English Code paras 15.41–15.42. See **16.104** and **16.113–16.183**.
[2]   *R v Hackney London Borough Council ex p K* (1997) 30 HLR 760, CA.
[3]   *R v Brent London Borough Council ex p Sadiq* (2001) 33 HLR 525, QBD.
[4]   *R (Yekini) v Southwark London Borough Council* [2014] EWHC 2096 (Admin), (2014) September *Legal Action*, p 50, Admin Ct. See **16.25**.

16.103 Of course, if the local housing authority discovers that its decision that the HA 1996, s 193(2), main housing duty is owed was obtained as a result of fraud, or made under a fundamental mistake of fact, it may re-open that decision and, on further inquiries, may decide that it does not owe the HA 1996, s 193(2), main housing duty after all[1].

[1]   *Porteous v West Dorset District Council* [2004] EWCA Civ 244, [2004] HLR 30, CA. See **9.140**.

16.104 The events that can cause the duty to end are:

(1)   the refusal by an applicant of suitable accommodation secured in performance of the HA 1996, s 193(2), main housing duty[1];
(2)   the applicant ceasing to be eligible for assistance[2];
(3)   the applicant becoming homeless intentionally from his or her HA 1996, s 193(2), main housing duty accommodation[3];
(4)   the applicant accepting an offer of a tenancy made under HA 1996, Pt 6[4];
(5)   the applicant accepting an offer of an assured, but not an assured shorthold, tenancy from a private landlord, including a private registered provider[5];
(6)   the applicant voluntarily ceasing to occupy his or her HA 1996, s 193(2), main housing duty accommodation as his or her only or principal home[6];
(7)   the applicant refusing a final offer of suitable accommodation made under HA 1996, Pt 6[7];
(8)   the applicant accepting a private rented sector offer[8]; or
(9)   the applicant refusing a private rented sector offer[9].

[1]   HA 1996, s 193(5). See **16.114–16.123**.
[2]   HA 1996, s 193(6)(a). See **16.124–16.126**.
[3]   HA 1996, s 193(6)(b). See **16.127–16.129**.
[4]   HA 1996, s 193(6)(c). See **16.130–16.135**.
[5]   HA 1996, s 193(6)(cc). See **16.136–16.139**.
[6]   HA 1996, s 193(6)(d). See **16.140–16.141**.
[7]   HA 1996, s 193(7)–(7A). See **16.142–16.152**.
[8]   HA 1996, s 193(7AA)(a). See **16.153–16.162**.
[9]   HA 1996, s 193(7AA)(b)–(7AC). See **16.163–16.185**.

16.105 From this list it is clear that the duty may end when the applicant *refuses* three types of offer of suitable accommodation:

- an offer of accommodation made in performance of the HA 1996, s 193(2), main housing duty itself[1];
- a final offer made under HA 1996, Pt 6[2]; or
- a private rented sector offer[3].

[1]   HA 1996, s 193(5). See **16.114–16.123.**
[2]   HA 1996, s 193(7) and (7A). See **16.142–16.152.**
[3]   HA 1996, s 193(7AA)–(7AC), see **16.163–16.185.**

16.106 If, unusually, an offer of accommodation is made outside of these provisions, an applicant would be free to refuse it without fear that the HA 1996, s 193(2), main housing duty would end. Because the consequence of refusal of any of these offers can be to bring the HA 1996, s 193(2), main housing duty to an end, applicants contemplating refusing an offer, and their advisers, should first ensure that they are very clear whether the offer is being made under any of these three provisions or not.

Decisions and challenges about ending the main housing duty

16.107 There is a common misconception that it is for the local housing authority to decide whether or not the HA 1996, s 193(2), main housing duty has ended. In fact, HA 1996, Pt 7[1], simply prescribes that, on the happening of one of the events listed above, the local housing authority 'shall cease to be subject to the duty'[2]. In other words, the HA 1996, s 193(2), main housing duty ends automatically and without any need for a freestanding decision to that effect by the local housing authority. In consequence, there is no obligation on a local housing authority to 'notify' any such decision to the applicant[3].

[1]   As amended by HRA 2017, for applications for homelessness assistance made on or after 3 April 2018..
[2]   HA 1996, s 193(5), (6), (7) and (7AA).
[3]   There is one exception: if the duty ends for the reason given at HA 1996, s 193(5), (refusal of an offer of accommodation made in performance of the HA 1996, s 193(2), main housing duty), the local housing authority is required to notify the applicant that it regards itself as ceasing to be subject to the HA 1996, s 193(2), main housing duty.

16.108 However, many of the events which terminate the HA 1996, s 193(2), main housing duty are dependent upon the local housing authority being 'satisfied' that a particular situation has come about (eg that accommodation refused by the applicant was suitable)[1]. Most local housing authorities will notify the applicant of their conclusions and indicate that, as a result, they consider that the HA 1996, s 193(2), main housing duty has ended. These are colloquially called 'discharge of duty' letters.

[1]   HA 1996, s 193(5) and (7).

16.109 A decision made by a local housing authority that events have occurred that bring to an end the HA 1996, s 193(2), main housing duty owed to the applicant has been held to constitute a decision as to 'what duty (if any) is owed to him'. The applicant therefore has a right to request a review of the decision to treat the HA 1996, s 193(2), main housing duty as at an end[1].

1   HA 1996, s 202(1)(b), as amended by HRA 2017, s 9(2), for applications for homelessness assistance made on or after 3 April 2018. *Warsame v Hounslow London Borough Council* (2000) 32 HLR 335, CA.

16.110 Quite apart from this general right to a statutory review of any decision that events have occurred which bring the HA 1996, s 193(2), main housing duty to an end, the applicant also has a separate freestanding right to request a review of any decision that accommodation offered in performance of the HA 1996, s 193(2), main housing duty, as a final offer under HA 1996, Pt 6, or as a private rented offer[1] is suitable[2]. If an applicant receives an offer of accommodation under any of the three provisions, and he or she believes that the accommodation is not suitable, there is the right both to request a review of the decision that the property is suitable, and to accept the property in any event[3]. This must usually be the sensible course of action for an applicant to take. Otherwise, she or he may lose the suitability review and find that the offer has meanwhile been withdrawn[4].

1   HA 1996, s 193(7AA)–(7AC). See **16.153–16.185**.
2   HA 1996, s 202(1)(f) and (g), as amended by HRA 2017, s 9(2), for applications for homelessness assistance made on or after 3 April 2018. See **19.59–19.62**.
3   HA 1996, s 202(1A).
4   The Court of Appeal has made it clear that, once an offer of accommodation has been refused and the local housing authority has decided that its duty has come to an end, there is no obligation on the local housing authority to keep the accommodation available for the applicant while a review is being carried out (*Osseily v Westminster City Council* [2007] EWCA Civ 1108, [2008] HLR 18, CA).

16.111 Where the local housing authority has decided to end its duty because the applicant has refused an offer of suitable accommodation[1], and the applicant then requests a review of that decision (as he or she is entitled to do), the scope of the review will be different from the scope of reviews of other decisions. The normal rule for reviews is that the reviewing officer should consider all the facts, law and circumstances as at the date of the review decision[2]. The Court of Appeal has considered whether the normal rule should apply to cases involving refusals of offers. In *Osseily v Westminster City Council*[3], it held that there was no obligation on the local housing authority to keep open the offer of accommodation until the review had been determined. In *Omar v Westminster City Council*[4], the Court of Appeal considered the position where, at the date of refusal, the accommodation was unsuitable, but subsequent events had rendered it suitable by the date of the review decision. The Court of Appeal held that:

> 'the correct question for the reviewer is whether the council were right, as at the date of that original decision; and for that purpose what they should be examining is the facts that existed as of that date, albeit they may discover what facts existed as at that date, between the date of that original decision and the date of review[5].'

1   For a refusal of HA 1996, s 193(2), main housing duty accommodation (HA 1996, s 193(5)), see **16.114–16.123**. For a refusal of a final offer of Part 6 accommodation (HA 1996, s 193(7) and (7A)), see **16.142–16.152**. For a refusal of private rented sector offered accommodation (HA 1996, s 193(7AA)–(7AC)), see **16.163–16.185**.
2   *Mohammed v Hammersmith & Fulham London Borough Council* [2001] UKHL 57, [2002] 1 AC 547, AC; and *Crawley Borough Council v B* (2000) 32 HLR 636, CA. See

19.166–19.174 for scope of review in general and **19.174** for scope of review where the applicant has refused an offer of accommodation.

3   [2007] EWCA Civ 1108, [2008] HLR 18, CA.
4   [2008] EWCA Civ 421, [2008] HLR 36, CA.
5   *Omar v Westminster City Council* [2008] EWCA Civ 421, [2008] HLR 36, CA at [32] per Waller LJ, see **19.174**.

16.112 A third decision of the Court of Appeal concerned accommodation which, at the date when the applicant was required to accept it, was not suitable but there were works proposed that would render it suitable. In *Boreh v Ealing London Borough Council*[1], the Court of Appeal held that there would only be an offer of suitable accommodation in those circumstances if the offer was accompanied with certain, binding and enforceable assurances about what work would be carried out after acceptance and before occupation[2]. A reviewing officer should not take into account the works subsequently carried out if they had not been contained in such assurances.

1   [2008] EWCA Civ 1176, [2009] HLR 22, CA.
2   The Court of Appeal in *Boreh v Ealing London Borough Council* [2008] EWCA Civ 1176, [2009] HLR 22, CA, did not specify that the assurances must be to the effect that the works would be carried out before the accommodation is to be occupied. However, it follows that if the accommodation before works were carried out was not suitable for occupation by the applicant, then the works should be carried out before occupation commences. See also *Norris v Milton Keynes Council* [2010] EWCA Civ 77, (2010) April *Legal Action*, p 26, CA.

The events that may cause the HA 1996, s 193(2), main housing duty to end

16.113 HA 1996, s 193(5)–(7AA) contains a list of nine events which may cause the main housing duty to come to an end.

(1)   Refusal of HA 1996, s 193(2), main housing duty accommodation

16.114 For the HA 1996, s 193(2), main housing duty to end for this reason, HA 1996, s 193(5) prescribes a number of fairly strict conditions which must all be fulfilled. These conditions are that[1]:

(1)   the accommodation has been offered in performance of the HA 1996, s 193(2), main housing duty[2];
(2)   the local housing authority is satisfied that it is 'suitable' accommodation;
(3)   the applicant has been informed of the consequences of refusal or acceptance of the offer;
(4)   the applicant has been informed of the right to seek a review of the suitability of the offered accommodation;
(5)   the applicant refuses the offer; and
(6)   the local housing authority notifies the applicant that it regards the HA 1996, s 193(2), main housing duty as having ended as a result of the refusal[3].

1   HA 1996, s 193(5); English Code, para 15.41(e).
2   The exact text is 'not an offer of accommodation under Part 6 or a private rented sector offer' (HA 1996, s 193(5)).

³ HA 1996, s 193(5). See English Code, para 15.41(e).

16.115 Where a fixed-term assured shorthold tenancy is offered in performance of the HA 1996, s 193(2), main housing duty, the Court of Appeal has held that the local housing authority should explain in the offer letter that:

> 'the authority acknowledges the accommodation would be temporary if the private landlord lawfully exercises his right to recover possession after the end of the fixed term and that, if that happens and assuming that the applicant's circumstances have not materially changed, the authority accepts that it would again become obliged to perform its duty under the section to secure that accommodation is available for occupation by the applicant¹.'

¹ *Griffiths v St Helens Council* [2006] EWCA Civ 160, [2006] HLR 29, CA at [42] per May LJ. The offer letter should make it clear that the assured shorthold tenancy is not a private rented sector offer, but an offer made under the HA 1996, s 193(2), main housing duty.

16.116 The conditions refer to two sets of rights to request a review:

(a)   a review of the decision as to suitability¹; and
(b)   a review of the decision that the duty is regarded as ended².

¹ HA 1996, s 202(1)(f), as amended by HRA 2017, s 9(2) for applications for homelessness assistance made on or after 3 April 2018. See **19.59–19.62**.
² HA 1996, s 202(1)(b), as amended by HRA 2017, s 9(2) for applications for homelessness assistance made on or after 3 April 2018. See **19.15–19.17**. For the specific considerations where an offer has been refused, see **19.174**.

16.117 This reflects the fact that the applicant will have received two letters. The first letter will have offered the accommodation on the basis that it was suitable, outlined the right to seek a review of suitability, and warned of the consequences of refusal. The second, following a refusal, will have notified the applicant of the fact that the local housing authority considered that the main housing duty had ended. Because an applicant can request a review whilst simultaneously accepting the accommodation (and thus preserve his or her position), it should become less common for the second letter to be sent¹. In *Ali v Birmingham City Council*², the Court of Appeal held that '"inform" in [HA 1996, Pt 7] is . . . to be construed as requiring information to be conveyed in understandable English' and that 'notify' requires the giving of a notice which imports a degree of formality³. The Local Government Ombudsman⁴ found maladministration following a complaint where the offer letter containing notification of the consequences of refusal was sent on the day that the applicant verbally refused an offer of a tenancy made under HA 1996, Pt 6, and was not received by her until three days after the refusal⁵.

¹ HA 1996, s 202(1A).
² [2009] EWCA Civ 1279, [2011] HLR 17, CA.
³ *Ali v Birmingham City Council* [2009] EWCA Civ 1279, [2011] HLR 17, CA at [39] per Sir Anthony May.
⁴ Now the Local Government and Social Care Ombudsman.
⁵ *Complaint against Forest Heath District Council*, 13 019 785, (2014/15) December/January *Legal Action*, p 35. See also *Complaint against Bournemouth Borough Council*, 14 020 077, 16 December 2015, (2016) June, *Legal Action*, p 42, where the local housing authority had failed to inform the applicant in writing of the consequences of accepting or refusing the offer, it had not formally responded to his reasons for refusing the offer and failed to explain why it was satisfied that the accommodation was suitable, the discharge of duty letter did not correctly state his review rights, an officer had wrongly told the applicant that he could only

request a review if he accepted the offer and moved into the property, and the local housing authority did not notify him in writing of its decision to end the HA 1996, s 211, duty to protect his possessions and did not give reasons for that decision.

16.118 There is no obligation for the information to be given to the applicant in the same letter as the offer. It may have been provided in an earlier communication. The Court of Appeal has held that it is 'essentially a matter of fact and degree' whether or not any period between the notification and the offer itself means that the applicant has or has not been informed of his or her statutory rights. In the case considered by the Court of Appeal[1], there had been a month between the information being conveyed to the applicant and the offer being made, with no other relevant events occurring during that month. If there was a longer period between the information being conveyed and the offer being made, and especially if there had been other correspondence during that period between the local housing authority and the applicant, it might be the length of that period meant that the applicant had been not been informed of the consequences before refusing the offer of accommodation[2].

1   *Vilvarasa v Harrow London Borough Council* [2010] EWCA Civ 1278, [2011] HLR 12, CA.
2   *Vilvarasa v Harrow London Borough Council* [2010] EWCA Civ 1278, [2011] HLR 12, CA per Munby LJ at [23]. In relation to offers of HA 1996, Pt 6 accommodation, the Court of Appeal has held that there is no obligation on the local housing authority to explain, in the offer letter, its reasons for concluding that the accommodation offered is suitable: *Solihull Metropolitan Borough Council v Khan* [2014] EWCA Civ 41, [2014] HLR 33, CA.

16.119 A decision by the local housing authority that its HA 1996, s 193(2), main housing duty has come to an end as a result of this provision could arise at any time during the performance of the HA 1996, s 193(2) main housing duty. So, where an applicant is offered a move from his or her current accommodation secured under the HA 1996, s 193(2), main housing duty to other suitable accommodation and refuses to move, he or she may find that the HA 1996, s 193(2), main housing duty has come to an end[1]. If the applicant is notified that the HA 1996, s 193(2), main housing duty has come to an end as a result of his or her refusal of HA 1996, s 193(2), main housing duty accommodation, local housing authorities should be alert to the possibility that an applicant's request for a review might either be made in respect solely of the suitability of the offer[2] or have been made in respect of an actual or anticipated decision that the duty has come to an end. So the applicant might request a review because he or she believes that he or she did not refuse the offer, or had not been informed of the consequences of refusal or acceptance of the offer[3]. The local housing authority must ensure that it deals with all the issues that arise on a HA 1996, s 193(5) decision that the duty has ended and not confine the review only to the issue of suitability of the accommodation[4].

1   *Muse v Brent London Borough Council* [2008] EWCA Civ 1447, (2009) February *Legal Action*, p 32, CA; *Vilvarasa v Harrow London Borough Council* [2010] EWCA Civ 1278, [2011] HLR 12, CA; and *Nzamy v Brent London Borough Council* [2011] EWCA Civ 283, [2011] HLR 20, CA.
2   Under HA 1996, s 202(1)(f), as amended by HRA 2017, s 9(2), for applications for homelessness assistance made on or after 3 April 2018. See **19.59–19.62**.
3   For an example where the local housing authority was wrong in law to characterise the applicant's response to a private rented sector offer as a refusal (HA 1996, s 193(7AA)–(7AC), see **16.163–16.185**), see *Ciercierska v Brent London Borough Council* (2016), *Legal Action*, October, p 41, County Court at Central London.

4   *Nzamy v Brent London Borough Council* [2011] EWCA Civ 283, [2011] HLR 20, CA.

16.120 The key issue for the applicant is likely to be the suitability or otherwise of the accommodation offered[1]. It may be that accommodation offered was not suitable at the date when it fell to be accepted, eg if it was not wheelchair-accessible. If accompanied by certain, binding and enforceable assurances about the work to be carried out after acceptance but before occupation, the accommodation may be suitable and a refusal of the offer may result in the ending of the HA 1996, s 193(2), main housing duty under this provision[2]. However, where no such assurance had been given by the date for acceptance, it will not have been an offer of suitable accommodation[3].

1   See Chapter 18.
2   *Boreh v Ealing London Borough Council* [2008] EWCA Civ 1176, [2009] HLR 22, CA; and *Norris v Milton Keynes Council* [2010] EWCA Civ 77, (2010) April *Legal Action*, p 26, CA.
3   In one case, the applicant refused an offer of HA 1996, s 193(2), main housing duty accommodation, arguing that she had a legitimate expectation that any offer of alternative accommodation made to her would be an offer of suitable Part 6 accommodation. The local housing authority had previously made her three offers of HA 1996, Part 6 accommodation, all of which were acknowledged not to be suitable for her. The Court of Appeal held that the fact that the local housing authority had made her a number of offers of permanent accommodation did not prevent it from making an offer of temporary accommodation and the applicant did not have a legitimate expectation that she would only be offered permanent accommodation: *Obiorah v Lewisham London Borough Council* [2013] EWCA Civ 325, [2013] HLR 35, CA.

16.121 The location of the accommodation offered is relevant to whether or not the accommodation is suitable[1]. Accommodation should be offered in the local housing authority's district so far as is reasonably practicable[2]. If that is not practicable, the local housing authority should try to secure accommodation as close as possible to its own district, and to where the applicant was previously living[3]. Article 2 of the Homelessness (Suitability of Accommodation) (England) Order 2012[4] contains a checklist of factors which the local housing authority must consider before it can treat the offer of accommodation as suitable[5].

1   Homelessness (Suitability of Accommodation) (England) Order 2012, SI 2012/2601 art 2 and English Code, paras 17.46–17.61. See Appendix 2 and Chapter 18 of this book.
2   HA 1996, s 208(1), see **18.48–18.61**.
3   English Code, para 17.47.
4   SI 2012/2601. See Appendix 2.
5   *Nzolameso v City of Westminster Council* [2015] UKSC 22, [2015] 2 All ER 942, [2015] HLR 22, SC. For a detailed discussion of these provisions, see **9.86–9.87** and **18.48–18.61**.

16.122 The expectation is that, following receipt of the offer of HA 1996, s 193(2), main housing duty accommodation, the applicant should have a reasonable opportunity to consider the offer and inspect the accommodation. This reflects best practice as set out in the English Code[1]. However, circumstances might compel the local housing authority to require an immediate acceptance or rejection of the offer, even if the applicant has not had the opportunity to see it or consider it. The safeguards, if the local housing authority insists on an immediate acceptance or rejection, are that:

(1)   the local housing authority must have satisfied itself that the accommodation is suitable[2];

(2)   it must have notified the applicant of the right to a review[3]; and

(3)   the applicant can both accept and seek a review[4].

The Court of Appeal has held (in a decision that pre-dates guidance given in the current and previous editions of the English Code) that these safeguards are sufficiently compliant with the statutory scheme, and that there is no separate right for applicants to view, and comment on, the accommodation before being required to accept or reject it[5].

1   English Code, para 15.46.
2   HA 1996, s 193(5)(a).
3   HA 1996, s 193(5)(a).
4   HA 1996, s 202(1)(f), as amended by HRA 2017, s 9, for applications for homelessness
      assistance made on or after 3 April 2018, and (1A). See **19.59–19.62** and **19.90–19.99**.
5   *R (Khatun) v Newham London Borough Council* [2004] EWCA 55, [2004] HLR 29, CA. In
      Abed v Westminster City Council [2011] EWCA Civ 1406, (2012) January *Legal Action*, p 21,
      CA, the Court of Appeal held that any deficiency leading up to the offer of accommodation to
      the applicant, such as a failure to assess the suitability of accommodation, could be made good
      by the review process.

16.123 The key ingredient to the ending of the HA 1996, s 193(2), main housing duty under this first route is that the applicant has *refused* the accommodation offered. The statutory wording is that the applicant 'refuses' an offer – not simply fails to accept it. This must mean something more than that the applicant has not replied to the making of an offer. The local housing authority must be able to identify something that amounts to unequivocal rejection following receipt of the offer[1].

1   *R v Haringey London Borough Council ex p Muslu* (2001) February *Legal Action*, p 29, QBD.
      See also *R (Faizi) v Brent London Borough Council* [2015] EWHC 2449 (Admin), (2015)
      September *Legal Action*, p 54, Admin Ct, where Haddon-Cave J said '[t]he subsection
      provides in terms that, as from the moment of refusal, the duty of the authority "ceases"'
      at [17]. For an example where the local housing authority was wrong in law to characterise the
      applicant's response to a private rented sector offer as a refusal (HA 1996, s 193(7AA)–(7AC),
      see **16.163–16.85**), see *Ciercierska v Brent London Borough Council* (2016) October, *Legal
      Action*, p 41, County Court at Central London.

(2)   Because the applicant ceases to be eligible

16.124 When an applicant ceases to be eligible[1] for homelessness assistance, the HA 1996, s 193(2), main housing duty ends. Eligibility is primarily determined by immigration status[2], so the trigger to the ending of the HA 1996, s 193(2), main housing duty in these circumstances will normally be a change in that status[3].

1   HA 1996, s 193(6)(a). English Code, para 15.42(a).
2   See CHAPTER 11.
3   As happened in *Tower Hamlets London Borough Council v Deugi* [2006] EWCA Civ 159,
      [2006] HLR 28, CA, where the applicant had originally been eligible as a result of being the
      primary carer of a dependent child who was in full-time education. See **11.78–11.79**. She
      ceased to be eligible when the child left full-time education.

16.125 HA 1996, s 193(6)(a) makes it clear that the issue is whether *the applicant* has ceased to be eligible. The HA 1996, s 193(2), main housing duty does not end if it is some other member of the applicant's household who ceases to be eligible for assistance, even if it is the very household member whose presence conferred priority need on the applicant in the first place. In those circumstances, the HA 1996, s 193(2), main housing duty will continue.

16.126 There is some debate as to whether or not a local housing authority needs to make a decision that the HA 1996, s 193(2), main housing duty has ended because the applicant is no longer eligible, since the issue is not a matter of discretion[1]. It is recognised, however, that the question of whether the applicant has ceased to be eligible may be disputed, and in those circumstances it would seem right for there to be a decision by the local housing authority, which can then be the subject of a request for a statutory review[2].

[1] See the comments by May LJ in *Tower Hamlets London Borough Council v Deugi* [2006] EWCA Civ 159, [2006] HLR 28, CA, at [33].
[2] HA 1996, s 202(1)(a) and (b), as amended by HRA 2017, s 9(2), for applications for homelessness assistance made on or after 3 April 2018. See **19.14–19.17**.

(3) Because the applicant becomes homeless intentionally from the main housing duty accommodation

16.127 When the local housing authority is deciding whether the HA 1996, s 193(2) main housing duty has ended for this reason, it should apply the definition of intentional homelessness[1] contained in HA 1996, s 191[2]. In *Orejudos v Kensington and Chelsea Royal London Borough Council*[3] the applicant was absent, despite warnings, on ten different occasions (over a period of more than a year) from hostel accommodation provided in performance of the main housing duty. In breach of the conditions of his occupancy, he had failed to give reasons for his absences in advance. The local housing authority terminated his booking, decided that he had become homeless intentionally and concluded that its duty toward him had ended. That decision was upheld on review, on appeal to the county court and on a further appeal to the Court of Appeal[4]. Similarly, where an applicant lost her HA 1996, s 193(2), main housing duty accommodation because she did not pay the rent, and the local housing authority rejected her argument that she did not have the resources to pay for the accommodation, she had become homeless intentionally from the main housing duty accommodation[5]. It is, of course, a necessary pre-requisite that the applicant has actually been rendered homeless by termination of any rights to occupy the HA 1996, s 193(2), main housing duty accommodation. The duty does not end simply because the applicant has become threatened with homelessness intentionally. Nor will it end in circumstances where the applicant has never taken up occupation of the accommodation[6]. The local housing authority must also be satisfied that the HA 1996, s 193(2), main housing duty accommodation provided was suitable for the applicant[7]. If it was not suitable, then the local housing authority will not have been properly performing the HA 1996, s 193(2) main housing duty in the first place[8].

[1] HA 1996, s 193(6)(b); English Code, para 15.42(b)..
[2] See **Chapter 13**.
[3] [2003] EWCA Civ 1967, [2004] HLR 23, CA.
[4] *Orejudos v Kensington and Chelsea Royal London Borough Council* [2003] EWCA Civ 1967, [2004] HLR 23, CA.
[5] *R (Best) v Oxford City Council* [2009] EWHC 608 (Admin), (2009) May *Legal Action*, p 27, Admin Ct.
[6] *R v Westminster City Council ex p Chambers* (1982) 6 ACR 24, QBD.

[7] See HA 1996, s 206, **16.20–16.21** and Chapter **18**.

[8] See, in the context of accommodation secured under the HA 1996, s 188(1) interim accommodation duty, *R (Lindsay) v Watford Borough Council*, unreported, 17 October 2017, Admin Ct, where the applicant, who suffered from depression and severe epilepsy, was required to leave hotel accommodation having allegedly assaulted a member of staff. The Administrative Court judge held that there was a serious issue to be tried as to whether the accommodation provided had been suitable, whether it was therefore sufficient for HA 1996, s 188(1), accommodation and, accordingly, whether the local housing authority had properly discharged its duty under HA 1996, s 188(1).

16.128 The applicant has a right to request that the local housing authority reviews its decision that the HA 1996, s 193(2), main housing duty has ended for this reason[1].

[1] HA 1996, s 202(1)(b), as amended by HRA 2017, s 9(2), for applications for homelessness assistance made on or after 3 April 2018. See **19.15–19.17**.

16.129 In one case, an applicant argued that, once his HA 1996, s 193(2), main housing duty accommodation had ended under this provision, the local housing authority should provide him with accommodation for such period as would give him a reasonable opportunity to secure his own accommodation[1]. By the time the appeal was heard, the applicant had been accommodated by friends and relatives for six months and the appeal was dismissed by the county court judge on the basis that it had become academic and futile. The Court of Appeal refused permission to appeal on the grounds that the decision had been justified on the facts, but reserved for another occasion whether a different result might be required in 'a starker case[2]'.

[1] HA 1996, s 190(2)(a), now amended by HRA 2017, s 5(5) for applications for homelessness assistance made on or after 3 April 2018. See **16.81–16.93**.

[2] *Newman v Croydon London Borough Council* [2008] EWCA Civ 1591, (2009) *Legal Action*, p 22, CA. See *also R (Dragic) v Wandsworth London Borough Council* [2012] EWHC 1241 (Admin), (2012) July *Legal Action*, p 42, Admin Ct, where the applicants took the route of re-applying after the HR 1996, s 193(2) main housing duty had come to an end, the local housing authority accepted that they were entitled to make fresh applications for homelessness assistance and notified them of its decision that they had become homeless intentionally.

(4)   Acceptance of a HA 1996, Pt 6 offer

16.130 An applicant owed the HA 1996, s 193(2) main housing duty will normally have applied to the same local housing authority for an allocation of a social housing tenancy under the provisions of HA 1996, Pt 6 ('Allocation of housing accommodation')[1].

[1] HA 1996, s 193(6)(c). See English Code, para 15.41(a). See Chapters **1–6**.

16.131 Because all homeless persons (including those owed the HA 1996, s 193(2), main housing duty) are entitled to a reasonable preference in an allocation scheme[1], an offer under HA 1996, Pt 6 could be made quite quickly. In some circumstances, a HA 1996, Pt 6 offer could be made immediately upon the HA 1996, s 193(2), main housing duty being triggered, not least because the applicant might have been using the period of the HA 1996, s 189B(2)[2], relief duty[3] to place bids under a choice-based lettings scheme. If that offer is accepted, then it may not be necessary to secure any accommodation under the HA 1996, s 193(2), main housing duty at all.

¹ See **4.58–4.79**.
² As inserted by HRA 2017, s 5(2), for applications for homelessness assistance made on or after 3 April 2018
³ See **15.138–15.150**.

16.132 Where the applicant has been provided with accommodation from a local housing authority or from a private registered provider under the HA 1996, s 193(2), main housing duty, the subsequent offer under HA 1996, Pt 6 might be of a tenancy of the very same property. If that offer is accepted, the local housing authority, or private registered provider will notify the applicant of his or her new tenancy status.

16.133 Since the introduction of choice-based lettings in some allocation schemes¹, the expectation has been that an applicant is free to bid for properties without any penalties or risks to his or her temporary accommodation. Precisely for this reason, there is no requirement in HA 1996, Pt 7², that *all* the HA 1996, Pt 6 offers made to an applicant should be of 'suitable' accommodation or that any reasons are required to be given by the applicant for refusal of those offers. There is no right to a statutory review of the suitability of offers that are *not* expressed to be 'final' offers.

¹ See **5.6–5.47**.
² As amended by HRA 2017 for applications for homelessness assistance made on or after 3 April 2018.

16.134 An applicant who accepts an offer made under HA 1996, Pt 6, only to find subsequently that it is unsuitable, will simply apply for a transfer to alternative accommodation in the ordinary way¹. When a 'final' offer is made under HA 1996, Pt 6, the applicant will need to be cautious. If a local housing authority's policy is to make one offer, then the only offer made to someone owed the HA 1996, s 193(2), main housing duty will be 'a final offer', and there may be consequences if the applicant refuses it².

¹ See **2.55–2.65** and **5.77–5.82**.
² HA 1996, s 193(7) and (7A). See **16.142–16.152**.

16.135 The applicant has a right to request that the local housing authority reviews its decision that the duty has ended for this reason¹. However, since the HA 1996, s 193(2), main housing duty only ends as a result of the voluntary acceptance by the applicant of accommodation, it would seem unlikely that the applicant would want to challenge such a decision.

¹ HA 1996, s 202(1)(b). See **19.15–19.17**.

(5)   Acceptance of an offer of an assured tenancy

16.136 The HA 1996, s 193(2), main housing duty will end if the applicant accepts an assured tenancy¹ offered by a private landlord (including by a private registered provider). In this context, assured tenancy does not include an assured shorthold tenancy². It follows that it would also not be a private rented sector offer³.

¹ HA 1996, s 193(6)(cc). See English Code, para 15.41(b).

²   HA 1996, s 193(6)(cc).
³   Because a 'private rented sector offer' can only be an offer of an assured shorthold tenancy:
    HA 1996, s 193(7AA)–(7AC). See **16.154**.

16.137 The offer will have been made other than as a result of a nomination under the local housing authority's allocation scheme (HA 1996, Pt 6)¹. Such an offer may have been elicited from a private sector landlord by a local housing authority seeking homes for its homeless households. Or it may have come from a private registered provider to which the applicant had applied directly for a tenancy².

¹   Because the acceptance of HA 1996, Part 6 offers is dealt with separately in HA 1996,
    s 193(6)(c), see **16.130–16.135**.
²   See CHAPTER 6.

16.138 An offer of an assured tenancy, made separately from the HA 1996, Pt 6 process, may be refused by the applicant with no adverse consequences upon the HA 1996, s 193(2), main housing duty, unless the accommodation is subsequently re-offered to him or her as a final HA 1996, Pt 6 offer¹. The local housing authority cannot make a 'final' offer of HA 1996, Pt 6 accommodation without first being satisfied that the accommodation is suitable for the applicant and his or her household².

¹   See **16.142–16.152**.
²   HA 1996, s 193(7F). See **16.147–16.149**.

16.139 The applicant has a right to request that the local housing authority reviews its decision that the duty has ended for this reason¹. However, since the HA 1996, s 193(2) main housing duty only ends as a result of the voluntary acceptance by the applicant of accommodation, it would seem unlikely that the applicant would want to challenge such a decision.

¹   HA 1996, s 202(1)(b), as amended by HRA 2017, s 9(2) for applications for homelessness
    assistance made on or after 3 April 2018. See **19.15–19.17**.

(6)   Because the applicant voluntarily ceases to occupy the HA 1996, s 193(2), main housing duty accommodation

16.140 The HA 1996, s 193(2), main housing duty will come to an end where the applicant voluntarily ceases to occupy¹, as his or her only or principal home, the accommodation made available under the HA 1996, s 193(2), main housing duty. The test to be applied in relation to the cessation of occupation is the same test as that used for determining whether a tenant of social housing has lost security of tenure because he or she no longer occupies accommodation as his or her only or principal home². The test is not met, and the HA 1996, s 193(2), main housing duty will not have ended, merely because the applicant has been staying somewhere else temporarily³. Additionally, if the applicant has ceased to occupy, he or she must have done so 'voluntarily'. This requirement is especially important where the applicant has been accommodated because she or he is vulnerable as a result of mental illness⁴. Its presence corresponds to the requirement in the definition of 'becoming homeless intentionally' that the applicant's actions must have been 'deliberate'⁵.

¹   HA 1996, s 193(6)(d). See English Code, para 15.42(c).

² Housing Act 1985, s 81 (secure tenants) and Housing Act 1988, s 1 (assured tenants). See *Islington London Borough Council v Boyle* [2011] EWCA Civ 1450, [2012] HLR 18, CA.
³ *Crawley Borough Council v Sawyer* (1987) 20 HLR 98, CA.
⁴ As was the case in *R v Kensington and Chelsea Royal London Borough Council ex p Kujtim* (1999) 32 HLR 579, CA. See also *R (Lindsay) v Watford Borough Council*, unreported, 17 October 2017, Admin Ct.
⁵ HA 1996, s 191(1). See **13.42–13.94**.

16.141 The applicant has a right to request that the local housing authority reviews its decision that the main housing duty has ended for this reason[1].

¹ HA 1996, s 202(1)(b), as amended by HRA 2017, s 9(2) for applications for homelessness assistance made on or after 3 April 2018. See **19.15–19.17**.

(7)   Refusal of a final offer made under HA 1996, Pt 6

16.142 Where the applicant refuses an offer of accommodation[1] made under HA 1996, Pt 6, the HA 1996, 193(2), main housing duty will end if the following requirements are all fulfilled:

(1)   the applicant was offered accommodation under HA 1996, Pt 6[2];
(2)   the offer was made in writing[3];
(3)   the offer stated that it was a 'final offer for the purposes of section 193(7)'[4];
(4)   the local housing authority had satisfied itself that the accommodation was 'suitable' for the applicant[5];
(5)   the applicant is not under contractual or other obligations in respect of his or her existing accommodation which he or she cannot bring to an end before being required to take up the offer[6];
(6)   the applicant had been informed of the possible consequences of refusal or acceptance of the offer[7];
(7)   the applicant had been told of the right to request a review of the suitability of the accommodation[8]; and
(8)   the offer was refused[9].

¹ HA 1996, s 193(7) and (7A). See English Code, para 15.41(d).
² HA 1996, s 193(7).
³ HA 1996, s 193(7A).
⁴ HA 1996, s 193(7A).
⁵ HA 1996, s 193(7F)(a).
⁶ HA 1996, s 193(7F) and (8). HA 1996, s 193(7F) as originally enacted contained a requirement that the local housing authority must also be satisfied that it would have been reasonable for the applicant to have accepted the accommodation.
⁷ HA 1996, s 193(7).
⁸ HA 1996, s 193(7).
⁹ HA 1996, s 193(7).

16.143 This possible avenue to the ending of the HA 1996, s 193(2), main housing duty only applies to a 'final offer' of HA 1996, Pt 6 Accommodation.

NOTIFICATION OF THE FINAL OFFER

16.144 The applicant will know whether or not the offer is a 'final offer' because the written notification must not only state that it is, but must also state that it is being treated as such for the purposes of the specific subsection in HA 1996, Pt 7[1]. Meeting all of these different requirements, which enables the local housing authority to bring the HA 1996, s 193(2), main housing duty to an end under this route, requires careful organisation by the allocation staff and the homelessness staff[2].

[1]   The letter need not contain the exact words in HA 1996, s 193(7), provided that it conveys every matter of substance required by s 193(7): *Omar v Birmingham City Council* [2007] EWCA Civ 610, [2007] HLR 43, CA.

[2]   Particularly so where these functions are separately managed within the particular local housing authority. See *Complaint against Forest Heath District Council*, 13 019 785, 17 July 2014, (2014/15) December/January *Legal Action*, p 35, where the Local Government Ombudsman found maladministration when an applicant had been verbally offered accommodation under HA 1996, Part 6 which she had refused. The letter setting out that it was a final offer, and the consequences of refusal, was dated the same day as her refusal and received by her three days later.

16.145 The formula for the ending of the HA 1996, s 193(2), main housing duty by refusal of a final offer of accommodation offered under HA 1996, Pt 6 potentially triggers two sets of rights to request a review:

(1)   a right to request a review of the decision as to suitability[1]; and
(2)   a right to request a review of the decision that the duty is regarded as ended[2].

[1]   HA 1996, s 202(1)(f), as amended by HRA 2017, s 9(2) for applications for homelessness assistance made on or after 3 April 2018. See **19.59–19.62**.

[2]   HA 1996, s 202(1)(b), as amended by HRA 2017, s 9(2) for applications for homelessness assistance made on or after 3 April 2018. See **19.15–19.17**. For the specific considerations where an offer has been refused, see **19.174**.

16.146 This reflects the fact that the applicant will have received two letters. The first will have offered the accommodation on the basis that it was a final offer, outlined the right to seek a review of suitability, and warned of the consequences of refusal[1]. The second, following a refusal, will have notified the applicant that the local housing authority considers the HR 1996, s 193(2), main housing duty to have come to an end. The Court of Appeal has held that it is desirable for all the issues arising on refusal to be reviewed at the same time. It should be made clear to the applicant that he or she has a right to a review of the suitability of the accommodation alone and/or of all the other elements of HA 1996, s 193(7) and (7A)[2]. Because an applicant can both request a review and also simultaneously accept the accommodation (and thus preserve his or her position), it should be less common for the stage to be reached at which the second letter comes to be sent[3].

[1]   This letter need not contain the reasons for the local housing authority's decision that the offer of accommodation is suitable: *Solihull Metropolitan Borough Council v Khan* [2014] EWCA Civ 41, [2014] HLR 33, CA.

[2]   *Ravichandran v Lewisham London Borough Council* [2010] EWCA Civ 755, [2010] HLR 42, CA. While the specific point that the Court of Appeal was considering (whether it had been reasonable for the applicants to accept the offer) no longer arises following the amendments to HA 1996, s 193(7F) by Localism Act 2011, s 148(9), the general point that applicants should not be deprived of a review decision that considers all the separate elements of a HA 1996, s 193(7) decision still applies.

[3]   HA 1996, s 202(1A). See **19.90–19.99**. Where this occurs, the duty will have come to an end because the applicant has accepted an offer made under HA 1996, Part 6, see **16.130–16.135**.

SUITABLE ACCOMMODATION

16.147 The local housing authority cannot make a 'final' offer of HA 1996, Pt 6 accommodation without first being satisfied that the accommodation is suitable for the applicant and his or her household[1]. There is no obligation on the local housing authority to give reasons for its decision that the offer is suitable at this stage[2]. The applicant will have been notified that if he or she refuses the final offer, the HA 1996, s 193(2), main housing duty may come to an end. He or she will also know that the safest course is to accept the offer, even if he or she considers it to be unsuitable, and to request a review of the suitability[3]. It follows that it is good practice for an applicant to be informed of his or her right to accept the offer whilst requesting a review of its suitability. Indeed, the Local Government Ombudsman[4] has found maladministration in one case where the local housing authority failed to inform the applicant in writing of his right to request a review of the suitability of the accommodation offered[5].

[1] HA 1996, s 193(7F). See English Code, paras 14.21–14.22 and **16.20–16.21**.
[2] *Solihull Metropolitan Borough Council v Khan* [2014] EWCA Civ 41, [2014] HLR 33, CA.
[3] HA 1996, ss 202(1)(f) (as amended by HRA 2017, s 9(2) for applications for homelessness assistance made on or after 3 April 2018) and (1A). See **19.15–19.17** and **19.166–19.174**.
[4] Now the Local Government and Social Care Ombudsman.
[5] *Complaint against Isle of Wight Council*, 12 001 189, 14 January 2014, (2014) March *Legal Action*, p 24.

16.148 The question of suitability of accommodation is considered in CHAPTER **18**. The location of the accommodation offered is relevant to whether or not the accommodation is suitable[1]. Accommodation should be offered in the local housing authority's district so far as is reasonably practicable[2]. If that is not practicable, the local housing authority should try to secure accommodation as close as possible to its own district, and to where the applicant was previously living[3]. Article 2 of the Homelessness (Suitability of Accommodation) (England) Order 2012[4] contains a checklist of factors which the local housing authority must consider before it can show that the offer of accommodation was suitable[5].

[1] Homelessness (Suitability of Accommodation) (England) Order 2012, SI 2012/2601, art 2. See APPENDIX **2** and **18.48–18.61**.
[2] HA 1996, s 208(1), see **18.48–18.61**.
[3] English Code, paras 17.46–17.61.
[4] SI 2012/2601. See **18.50** and APPENDIX **2**.
[5] See also *Nzolameso v City of Westminster Council* [2015] UKSC 22, [2015] 2 All ER 942, [2015] HLR 22, SC. For a detailed discussion of these provisions, see **18.48–18.61**.

VIEWING THE PROPERTY

16.149 Although the Court of Appeal has held that there is no obligation on a local housing authority to allow the applicant to view the property before accepting an offer of accommodation made to bring the HA 1996, s 193(2), main housing duty to an end[1], the English Code contains advice that applicants should be given the chance to view accommodation before required to decide on whether they accept or refuse the accommodation and before being required to sign any written agreement. It also contains advice that applicants should be given a reasonable period in which to consider offers of accommodation. The length of the reasonable period would depend on the applicant's particular circumstances[2].

---

[1] *R (Khatun) v Newham London Borough Council* [2004] EWCA Civ 55, [2005] QB 37, CA.
[2] English Code, paras 15.46–15.48.

CONTRACTUAL OR OTHER OBLIGATIONS

16.150 Since the coming into force of the amendments to HA 1996, s 193(7F), by Localism Act 2011, s 148(9)[1], the elements of HA 1996, s 193(7) will not be made out where the applicant is:

- under contractual or other obligations in respect of his or her existing accommodation; and
- not able to bring those obligations to an end before being required to take up the offer[2].

---

[1] Applicable to applications for homelessness assistance made on or after 9 November 2012: Localism Act 2011 (Commencement No 2 and Transitional Provisions) (England) Order 2012, SI 2012/2599. Prior to those amendments, the local housing authority was also obliged to consider whether it would be reasonable for the applicant to accept the offer of accommodation.
[2] HA 1996, s 193(7F) and (8). See English Code, para 15.47.

16.151 This means that if an applicant cannot end the term of his or her tenancy or licence in order to take up the offer of HA 1996, Pt 6 accommodation, even though that accommodation is suitable and all the other elements of HA 1996, s 193(7) are made out, the local housing authority cannot decide that its HA 1996, s 193(2), main housing duty has come to an end as a result of the applicant's refusal of the offer. In practice, this is likely to apply to applicants who are occupying HA 1996, s 193(2), main housing duty accommodation on a fixed-term tenancy, with no break clause.

REFUSAL OF OFFER

16.152 The key ingredient for ending the duty in these circumstances is that the applicant has *refused* the HA 1996, Pt 6 accommodation offered. The wording in HA 1996, s 193(7) is that the applicant 'refuses' a final offer. It is not sufficient that there has been a simple failure to accept it. This must mean something more than that the applicant has failed to respond to an offer made to him or her. The local housing authority must be able to identify something that amounts to unequivocal rejection following receipt of the offer[1].

---

[1] *R v Haringey London Borough Council ex p Muslu* (2001) February *Legal Action*, p 29, QBD. For an example where the local housing authority was wrong in law to characterise the applicant's response to a private rented sector offer as a refusal, see *Ciercierska v Brent London Borough Council* (2016), *Legal Action*, October, p 41, County Court at Central London.

(8)   Acceptance of a private rented sector offer

16.153 Since November 2012, local housing authorities have been able to make private rented sector offers[1] to those applicants owed the HA 1996, s 193(2), main housing duty[2]. Advice from the Secretary of State about private rented sector offers is contained at paras 17.11–17.29 of the English Code.

1   HA 1996, s 193(7AA)–(7AC); English Code, para 15.41(c).
2   Applicants whose applications for homelessness assistance were made on or after 9 November 2012: Localism Act 2011 (Commencement No 2 and Transitional Provisions) (England) Order 2012, SI 2012/2599. Applicants whose applications were made before 9 November 2012 can be made a qualifying offer of an assured shorthold tenancy, but there are no consequences if they refuse those offers: HA 1996, s 193(7B) and (7C) prior to repeal by Localism Act 2011, s 148 and Sch 25.

16.154 A 'private rented sector offer' is defined at HA 1996, s 193(7AC) as being:

(a)   an offer of an assured shorthold tenancy made by a private landlord to the applicant in relation to any accommodation which is, or may become, available for the applicant's occupation;

(b)   made, with the approval of the local housing authority, in pursuance of arrangements made by the authority with the landlord with a view to bringing the local housing authority's main housing duty to an end; and

(c)   the tenancy being offered is a fixed-term tenancy (within the meaning of Housing Act 1988 Pt 1) for a period of at least 12 months.

16.155 Power is given to the Secretary of State to provide by regulations that the minimum term may be increased from 12 months[1]. That power has not been exercised. However, local housing authorities can choose to make private rented sector offers of tenancies with terms longer than the minimum of 12 months.

1   HA 1996, s 193(10)–(12).

16.156 Local housing authorities may choose to make private rented sector offers to applicants who are owed the HA 1996, s 193(2), main housing duty. However, where the applicant is a restricted case[1], HA 1996, s 193(7AD) requires local housing authorities to bring the HA 1996, s 193(2), main housing duty to an end by making a private rented sector offer 'so far as reasonably practicable'[2].

1   HA 1996, s 193(3B), see **9.56–9.56, 11.163–11.167** and **16.180–16.183**.
2   See English Code, para 15.43.

16.157 The accommodation offered by way of a private rented sector offer must be suitable for the needs of the applicant and the members of his or her household[1]. In addition to all the general considerations provided by HA 1996, Pt 7[2], and by case law, the Secretary of State has made the Homelessness (Suitability of Accommodation) (England) Order 2012[3] which contains specific prescriptions regarding the physical characteristics and the management of a property offered by way of a private rented sector offer[4].

1   HA 1996, s 193(7F). See Chapter 18 for general considerations regarding suitability.
2   As amended by HRA 2017, for applications for homelessness assistance made on or after 3 April 2018.

³   SI 2012/2601, art 3, as amended by HRA 2017, s 12, for applications for homelessness assistance made on or after 3 April 2018.
⁴   See Chapter **18** for general considerations on suitability and **18.69–18.79** for the specific requirements in relation to a private rented sector offer. See English Code, paras 17.11–17.29.

16.158 The applicant will know that this is an offer designed to bring the HA 1996, s 193(2), main housing duty to an end, rather than an offer of HA 1996, s 193(2), main housing duty accommodation, because of the special notification requirements.

16.159 Before or, at the latest, at the same time as the private rented sector offer is made, the local housing authority must:

(1)   inform the applicant in writing[1] of the possible consequences of refusal or acceptance of the offer[2];

(2)   inform the applicant in writing of his or her right to request a review of the suitability of the private rented sector offer[3];

(3)   unless the applicant is a 'restricted case'[4], inform him or her in writing of the effect of the special provisions in HA 1996, s 195A[5] on a further application for homelessness assistance to a local housing authority in England within two years of the date of acceptance of the offer[6];

(4)   be satisfied that the offer is 'suitable' for the applicant and his or her household[7]; and

(5)   be satisfied that the applicant is not under contractual or other obligations in respect of his or her existing accommodation, or, if he or she is, that he or she is able to bring those obligations to an end before being required to take up the offer[8].

¹   The letter need not contain the exact words in HA 1996, s 193(7AB), provided that it conveys every matter of substance required by s 193(7A) and (7B) (*Omar v Birmingham City Council* [2007] EWCA Civ 610, [2007] HLR 43, CA). It also need not contain any reasons for the local housing authority's decision that the accommodation offered is suitable for the applicant: *Solihull Metropolitan Borough Council v Khan* [2014] EWCA Civ 41, [2014] HLR 33 CA.
²   HA 1996, s 193(7AA)–(7AB).
³   HA 1996, s 193(7AA)–(7AB).
⁴   HA 1996, s 193(3B). See **9.54–9.56, 11.163–11.167** and **16.180–16.183**.
⁵   As amended by HRA 2017, s 4(2) for applications for homelessness assistance made on or after 3 April 2018.
⁶   HA 1996, s 193(7AA)–(7AB); for the special provisions governing a re-application for homelessness assistance within two years of acceptance of a private rented sector offer, see HA 1996, s 195A, as amended by HRA 2017, s ,4(2) for applications for homelessness assistance made on or after 3 April 2018. See **8.100–8.107, 15.56–15.58** and **16.47–16.50**.
⁷   HA 1996, s 193(7F). For 'suitability' in general, see Chapter **18**. For the specific requirements governing the suitability of a private rented sector offer, see **18.69–18.79**.
⁸   HA 1996, s 193(7F) and (8), see **16.150–16.151**.

16.160 If the applicant accepts the offer, all that the local housing authority has to do is to notify the applicant that the HA 1996, s 193(2), main housing duty has come to an end as a result of his or her acceptance[1].

¹   HA 1996, s 193(7AA).

VIEWING THE PROPERTY

16.161 Although the Court of Appeal has held that there is no obligation on a local housing authority to allow the applicant to view the property before accepting an offer of accommodation made to bring the HA 1996, s 193(2), main housing duty to an end[1], the English Code contains advice that applicants should be given the chance to view accommodation before required to decide on whether they accept or refuse the accommodation and before being required to sign any written agreement. It also contains advice that applicants should be given a reasonable period in which to consider offers of accommodation. The length of the reasonable period would depend on the applicant's particular circumstances[2].

1 *R (Khatun) v Newham London Borough Council* [2004] EWCA Civ 55, [2005] QB 37, CA.
2 English Code, paras 15.46–15.48.

16.162 The applicant might wish to request a review of the suitability of the accommodation offered[1]. As with other offers which bring the HA 1996, s 193(2), main housing duty to an end, he or she should usually be advised both to accept the offer and to request a review simultaneously[2]. The question arises as to what happens if the applicant, having accepted the fixed-term tenancy, is then informed by the local housing authority that his or her request for a review has been successful and the local housing authority agrees that the accommodation was not suitable? The applicant at that point may wish to terminate the tenancy but will not be able to do so unless the terms of the tenancy contain a break clause. Alternatively, it may be that the accommodation is not suitable for a private rented sector offer, but might be considered suitable accommodation for accommodation made available under the HR 1996, s 193(2), main housing duty[3]. A third possibility might be that the local housing authority intervenes and pays the landlord any rent for the remaining period of the term of the tenancy, so that the applicant can move out of the accommodation without incurring debt.

1 HA 1996, s 202(1)(g), as amended by HRA 2017, s 9(2), for applications for homelessness assistance made on or after 3 April 2018. See **19.63–19.64**.
2 HA 1996, s 202(1A), see **19.166–19.174**.
3 On the basis that expected duration of occupation is relevant to whether or not accommodation is suitable (*Ali v Birmingham City Council, Moran v Manchester City Council* [2009] UKHL 36, [2009] 1 WLR 1506, [2009] HLR 41, AC) and so accommodation that was not suitable for the term of the private rented sector offer could be suitable as performance of the main housing duty in HA 1996, s 193(2). See **18.62–18.88**.

(9) Refusal of a private rented sector offer

16.163 Since November 2012, local housing authorities have been able to make private rented sector offers[1] to those applicants owed the HA 1996, s 193(2), main housing duty[2]. Advice from the Secretary of State about private rented sector offers is contained at paras 17.11–17.29 of the English Code.

1 HA 1996, s 193(7AA)–(7AC), English Code, paras 15.41(c) and **17.11–17.29**.
2 Applicants whose applications for homelessness assistance were made on or after 9 November 2012: Localism Act 2011 (Commencement No 2 and Transitional Provisions) (England) Order 2012, SI 2012/2599. Applicants whose applications were made before 9 November 2012 can be made a qualifying offer of an assured shorthold tenancy, but there are no consequences if they refuse those offers: HA 1996, s 193(7B) and (7C) prior to repeal by Localism Act 2011, s 148 and Sch 25.

16.164 A 'private rented sector offer' is defined at HA 1996, s 193(7AC) as being:

(a)   an offer of an assured shorthold tenancy made by a private landlord to the applicant in relation to any accommodation which is, or may become, available for the applicant's occupation;

(b)   made, with the approval of the local housing authority, in pursuance of arrangements made by the authority with the landlord with a view to bringing the local housing authority's main housing duty to an end; and

(c)   the tenancy being offered is a fixed-term tenancy (within the meaning of Housing Act 1988, Pt 1) for a period of at least 12 months.

16.165 Power is given to the Secretary of State to provide by regulations that the minimum term may be increased from 12 months[1]. That power has not been exercised. However, local housing authorities can choose to make private rented sector offers of tenancies with terms longer than the minimum of 12 months.

1   HA 1996, s 193(10)–(12).

16.166 Local housing authorities may choose to make private rented sector offers to applicants who are owed the HA 1996, s 193(2), main housing duty. However, where the applicant is a restricted case[1], HA 1996, s 193(7AD) requires local housing authorities to bring the HA 1996, s 193(2), main housing duty to an end by making a private rented sector offer 'so far as reasonably practicable'[2].

1   HA 1996, s 193(3B), see **9.54–9.56, 11.163–11.167** and **16.180–16.183**.
2   See English Code, para 15.43.

16.167 The accommodation offered by way of a private rented sector offer must be suitable for the needs of the applicant and the members of his or her household[1]. In addition to all the general considerations provided by HA 1996, Pt 7[2], and by case law[3], the Secretary of State has made the Homelessness (Suitability of Accommodation) (England) Order 2012[4] which contains specific prescriptions regarding the physical characteristics and the management of a property offered by way of a private rented sector offer[5].

1   HA 1996, s 193(7F). See Chapter **18** for general considerations regarding suitability.
2   As amended by HRA 2017.
3   See Chapter **18** for case law on suitability.
4   SI 2012/2601, Art 3, as amended by HRA 2017, s 12, for applications for homelessness assistance made on or after 3 April 2018.
5   See Chapter **18** for general considerations on suitability and **18.69–18.79** for the specific requirements in relation to a private rented sector offer. See English Code, paras 17.11–17.29.

First notification to the applicant

16.168 The applicant will know that this is an offer designed to bring the HA 1996, s 193(2), main housing duty to an end, rather than an offer of HA 1996, s 193(2), main housing duty accommodation, because of the special notification requirements. The special notification requirements are designed to ensure that the applicant is fully informed of the consequences if he or she decides to refuse the offer.

16.169 The first notification to the applicant will have been on, or before, the private rented sector offer was made to the applicant. By the time of the offer, the local housing authority must have:

(1)   informed the applicant in writing[1] of the possible consequences of refusal or acceptance of the offer[2];

(2)   informed the applicant in writing of his or her right to request a review of the suitability of the private rented sector offer[3];

(3)   unless the applicant is a 'restricted case'[4], informed him or her in writing of the effect of the special provisions in HA 1996, s 195A[5] on a further application for homelessness assistance to a local housing authority in England within two years of the date of acceptance of the offer[6];

(4)   been satisfied that the offer is 'suitable' for the applicant and his or her household[7]; and

(5)   been satisfied that the applicant is not under contractual or other obligations in respect of his or her existing accommodation, or, if he or she is, that he or she is able to bring those obligations to an end before being required to take up the offer[8].

---

[1]   The letter need not contain the exact words in HA 1996, s 193(7AB), provided that it conveys every matter of substance required by s 193(7A) and (7B) (*Omar v Birmingham City Council* [2007] EWCA Civ 610, [2007] HLR 43, CA). It also need not contain any reasons for the local housing authority's decision that the accommodation offered is suitable for the applicant: *Solihull Metropolitan Borough Council v Khan* [2014] EWCA Civ 41, [2014] HLR 33 CA.

[2]   HA 1996, s 193(7AA)–(7AB).

[3]   HA 1996, s 193(7AA)–(7AB).

[4]   HA 1996, s 193(3B). See **9.54–9.56, 11.163–11.167** and **16.180–16.183**.

[5]   As amended by HRA 2017, s 4(4), for applications for homelessness assistance made on or after 3 April 2018.

[6]   HA 1996, s 193(7AA)–(7AB); for the special provisions governing a re-application for homelessness assistance within two years of acceptance of a private rented sector offer, see HA 1996, s 195A, as amended by HRA 2017, s ,4(2) for applications for homelessness assistance made on or after 3 April 2018. See **8.100–8.107, 15.56–15.58** and **16.47–16.50**.

[7]   HA 1996, s 193(7F). For 'suitability' in general, see Chapter **18**. For the specific requirements governing the suitability of a private rented sector offer, see **18.69–18.79**.

[8]   HA 1996, s 193(7F) and (8), see **16.150–16.151**.

16.170 If an applicant, having received the required information, refuses the private rented sector offer, and the local housing authority is not willing to make him or her another offer, or to continue to secure accommodation under the HA 1996, s 193(2), main housing duty, it will notify him or her accordingly. That second notification will contain the local housing authority's decision that the HA 1996, s 193(2), main housing duty has ended as a result of the applicant's refusal and its reasons for that decision. The issues to be addressed by the local housing authority are:

(1)   whether the applicant was informed in writing of the possible consequences of refusal or acceptance of the private rented sector offer, of his or her right to request a review of the suitability of the accommodation and (in most cases) of the effect under HA 1996, s 195A[1] of a further application to a local housing within two years of acceptance of the offer[2];

(2)   whether the accommodation offered qualified as a private rented sector offer[3];

(3)   whether the applicant refused the offer[4];

(4)   whether the offer was suitable for the needs of the applicant and of his or her household[5];

(5)   whether the applicant was under contractual or other obligations in relation to his or her existing accommodation[6]; and

(6)   if the applicant was under such contractual or other obligations, whether he or she was able to bring those obligations to an end before being required to take up the tenancy[7].

[1]   As amended by HRA 2017, s 4(2), for applications for homelessness assistance made on or after 3 April 2018. See **8.100–8.107**, **15.56–15.58** and **16.47–16.50**.
[2]   HA 1996, s 193(7AB).
[3]   HA 1996, s 193(7AC). See **16.154**.
[4]   HA 1996, s 193(7AA)(b).
[5]   HA 1996, s 193(7F). For 'suitability', see Chapter **18**. For the specific issues relating to suitability of private rented sector offers, see **18.69–18.79**.
[6]   HA 1996, s 193(7F) and (8). See **16.150–16.151**.
[7]   HA 1996, s 193(8).

16.171   The local housing authority will also inform the applicant of his or her right to request a review of the decision that the HA 1996, s 193(2), main housing duty has come to an end[1] and of the time within which the request for the review should be made.

[1]   HA 1996, s 202(1)(b), as amended by HRA 2017, s 9(2), for applications for homelessness assistance made on or after 3 April 2018. See **19.15–19.17**.

16.172   The applicant might wish to request a review of the suitability of the accommodation offered[1]. As with other offers which bring the HA 1996, s 193(2), main housing duty to an end, he or she should usually be advised both to accept the offer and to request a review simultaneously[2].

[1]   HA 1996, s 202(1)(g), as amended by HRA 2017, s 9(2), for applications for homelessness assistance made on or after 3 April 2018. See **19.63–19.64**.
[2]   HA 1996, s 202(1A), see **19.90–19.99**.

16.173   A significant issue for most applicants who refuse private rented sector offers is likely to have been the suitability of that offer, but it may be that the applicant is challenging another part of the local housing authority's decision, for example disputing whether the accommodation offered was a private rented sector offer, or whether he or she could have brought his or her contractual obligations to an end. The key ingredient for ending the duty in these circumstances is that the applicant has *refused* the private rented sector offer. The wording in HA 1996, s 193(7AA)(b) is that the applicant 'refuses' a private rented sector offer. It is not sufficient that there has been a simple failure to accept it. This must mean something more than that the applicant has failed to respond to an offer made to him or her. The local housing authority must be able to identify something that amounts to unequivocal rejection following receipt of the offer[1].

[1]   *R v Haringey London Borough Council ex p Muslu* (2001) February *Legal Action*, p 29, QBD; for an example where the local housing authority was wrong in law to characterise the applicant's response to a private rented sector offer as a refusal, see *Ciercierska v Brent London Borough Council* (2016), *Legal Action*, October, p 41, County Court at Central London.

VIEWING THE PROPERTY

16.174 Although the Court of Appeal has held that there is no obligation on a local housing authority to allow the applicant to view the property before accepting an offer of accommodation made to bring the HA 1996, s 193(2), main housing duty to an end[1], the English Code contains advice that applicants should be given the chance to view accommodation before being required to decide on whether they accept or refuse the accommodation and before being required to sign any written agreement. It also contains advice that applicants should be given a reasonable period in which to consider offers of accommodation. The length of the reasonable period would depend on the applicant's particular circumstances[2].

[1]   *R (Khatun) v Newham London Borough Council* [2004] EWCA Civ 55, [2005] QB 37, CA.
[2]   English Code, paras 15.46–15.48.

SUITABILITY OF PRIVATE RENTED SECTOR OFFERS

16.175 During the passage through Parliament of the Localism Act 2011, concern was raised about the possible cost, quality and location of accommodation offered by way of private rented sector offers. The Homelessness (Suitability of Accommodation) (England) Order 2012[1] contains a list of ten factors relating to the physical condition of the property and the character of the landlord. Each of those factors must be complied with before a local housing authority can be satisfied that the accommodation offered is suitable[2].

[1]   SI 2012/2601.
[2]   See **18.70–18.76**. See also English Code, paras 17.13–17.14.

16.176 The location of the accommodation offered is relevant to whether or not the accommodation is suitable[1]. Accommodation should be offered in the local housing authority's district so far as is reasonably practicable[2]. If that is not practicable, the local housing authority should try to secure accommodation as close as possible to its own district, and to where the applicant was previously living[3].

[1]   Homelessness (Suitability of Accommodation) (England) Order 2012, SI 2012/2601, art 2, as amended by HRA 2017, s 12, for applications for homelessness assistance made on or after 3 April 2018, and English Code, paras 17.46–17.59. See **18.48–18.61**.
[2]   HA 1996, s 208(1). See **18.52**.
[3]   English Code, paras 17.46–17.59.

16.177 The English Code contains guidance on both the ten-point checklist for private rented sector offers[1] and on the location of the accommodation[2]. In addition, local housing authorities are directed by specific statutory instrument[3] to consider the applicant's financial resources (including any welfare benefits) and the total costs of the accommodation. If the accommodation is not affordable, it will not be suitable[4]. The English Code also contains guidance on the cost of accommodation[5].

[1]   English Code, paras 17.11–17.22. See **18.72–18.79** and APPENDIX **2**.
[2]   English Code, paras 17.46–17.59. See **18.48–18.61** and APPENDIX **2**.
[3]   Homelessness (Suitability of Accommodation) Order 1996, SI 1996/3204, at APPENDIX **2**.
[4]   SI 1996/3204, art 2.

⁵   English Code, paras 17.44–17.45. For more on 'affordability', see **18.45–18.47**.

16.178 In 2014, Shelter and Crisis published a joint report: *A Roof over My Head, the final report of the Sustain project*[1]. The report contained research into the experiences and well-being of people who had been rehoused into the private rented sector following a period of homelessness. The report found that two-thirds of people were unhappy with their private rented tenancies. Key issues were the condition of the property and having to deal with problem landlords. Some people were moved into very cramped, unsuitable accommodation. People on low incomes felt vulnerable because they were less likely to be able to afford alternative accommodation when they needed to move. People with vulnerabilities found it particularly hard to cope with private rented sector accommodation. In response, the then Under-Secretary of State, Kris Hopkins MP, wrote to the leaders of local housing authorities in East and South East London, Greater Manchester and East Sussex on 28 February 2014[2]. He reiterated the provisions of art 3 of the Homelessness (Suitability of Accommodation) (England) Order 2012[3], the effect of which should mean that only 'good-quality private rented sector accommodation' would be used to bring the main housing duty to an end. He also drew attention to local housing authorities' powers in relation to enforcement of housing standards in the private rented sector.

[1]   *A Roof Over My Head: the final report of the Sustain project* (Crisis & Shelter, 2014).
[2]   The regions where the research had been carried out.
[3]   See **18.72–18.79**.

16.179 An applicant may raise on review any other issue, relating to the accommodation offered and/or to his or her personal circumstances or those of any member of his or her household, as a reason why the accommodation offered is not suitable for him or her and his or her household[1].

[1]   English Code, chapter 17 contains guidance on suitability. See Chapter 18.

The special rules for 'restricted cases'

The definition of a 'restricted case'

16.180 The HA 1996, s 193(2), main housing duty applies differently to applicants who are 'restricted cases'. An applicant is a 'restricted case'[1] where:

- the applicant is eligible[2];
- the applicant's household contains a 'restricted person'[3]; and
- it is the presence in the household of the restricted person that has led to the main housing duty having been accepted[4].

[1]   HA 1996, s 193(3B).
[2]   See Chapter 11.
[3]   HA 1996, s 184(7), see **9.54–9.56** and **11.163–11.167**.
[4]   HA 1996, s 193(3B).

16.181 A 'restricted person'[1] is defined as a person:

- who is not eligible for assistance under HA 1996, Pt 7[2];

- who is subject to immigration control within the meaning of the Asylum and Immigration Act 1996[3]; and
- who either does not have leave to enter or remain in the UK[4]; or
- whose leave to enter or remain in the UK is subject to a condition to maintain and accommodate himself, and any dependents, without recourse to public funds[5].

[1] HA 1996, s 184(7).
[2] See Chapter 11.
[3] See **11.101** and **11.26–11.31**.
[4] HR 1996, s 184(7)(c)(i).
[5] HR 1996, s 184(7)(c)(ii).

16.182 Importantly, a restricted case only arises where the applicant's entitlement to the HA 1996, s 193(2), main housing duty is *solely* because of the presence in the applicant's household of a restricted person. For example, if it was only the presence of the restricted person that resulted in the applicant becoming homeless, or having a priority need, the applicant's case would be a restricted case. However, if the applicant would be entitled to the HA 1996, s 193(2), main housing duty regardless of the presence of the restricted person (if, for example, the applicant himself or herself had a priority need, or there were other members of the applicant's household whose presence entitled the applicant to a priority need), the applicant's case would not be a restricted case.

16.183 The applicant will know whether his or her case is a 'restricted case', because the local housing authority is required to notify him or her that the HA 1996, s 193(2), main housing duty is owed because of the presence in his or her household of a restricted person[1]. The applicant will have the right to request a review of any decision that he or she is a 'restricted case'[2].

[1] HA 1996, s 184(3A), as amended by HRA 2017, s 4(3), for applications for homelessness assistance made on or after 3 April 2018. See **9.54–9.56**.
[2] Such a decision would be a decision as to 'what duty (if any)' is owed to the applicant and therefore carries a right to request a review at HA 1996, s 202(1)(b), as amended by HRA 2017, s 9(2), for applications for homelessness assistance made on or after 3 April 2018. See **19.15–19.17**.

Modifications to the HA 1996, s 193(2), main housing duty

16.184 For restricted cases, the HA 1996, s 193(2), main housing duty is modified in two ways:

(1) the local housing authority is required, so far as reasonably practicable, to bring its HR 1996, s 193(2) main housing duty to an end by making the applicant a private rented sector offer[1]; and

(2) where an applicant is made a private rented sector offer, he or she need not be informed in writing of the effect under HA 1996, s 195A[2] of a further application to a local housing authority within two years of acceptance of the offer[3].

[1] HA 1996, s 193(7AD); English Code, para 15.43. See **16.152**.
[2] As amended by HRA 2017, s 4(4), for applications for homelessness assistance made on or after 3 April 2018.
[3] HA 1996, s 193(7AB)(c).

16.185 The reason for this second modification is because part of the special provisions in HA 1996, s 195A[1] do not apply to an applicant to whom the HA 1996, s 193(2), main housing duty is only owed because of the presence in his or her household of a restricted person[2].

1   As amended by HRA 2017, s 4(4), for applications for homelessness assistance made on or after 3 April 2018. See **8.100–8.107**, **15.56–15.58** and **16.47–16.50**.
2   HA 1996, s 195A(5), as amended by HRA 2017, s 4(4), for applications for homelessness assistance made on or after 3 April 2018. See **8.100–8.107**, **15.56–15.58** and **16.47–16.50**.

Termination of accommodation secured under the HA 1996, s 193(2), main housing duty

16.186 Accommodation secured under the HA 1996, s 193(2), main housing duty[1] is usually provided for a longer period than accommodation provided under the other more short-term duties under HA 1996, Pt 7[2]. A variety of types of accommodation might be used in order to perform the duty. For example: hostel accommodation provided either under a tenancy or a licence; accommodation let to the applicant by the local housing authority under a non-secure tenancy (either the local housing authority's own stock or accommodation leased by the local housing authority from a private landlord); accommodation provided directly by a private landlord under an assured shorthold tenancy agreement; or accommodation provided by a private registered provider[3].

1   See **16.94–16.199**.
2   As amended by HRA 2017 for application for homelessness assistance made on or before 3 April 2018.
3   See **18.155–18.162**.

16.187 If the accommodation has been provided under an assured shorthold tenancy agreement, then the procedure for recovering possession set out in Housing Act 1988, Pt 1 would need to be followed by the landlord. That is, service of the relevant notice, followed by an application to the Court for a possession order. If the accommodation is provided by the local housing authority under a non-secure tenancy agreement, it is generally accepted that the accommodation will have been a 'dwelling' and so the tenancy must be terminated by notice to quit, in accordance with Protection from Eviction Act 1977, s 5, and an application for a possession order must be made[1].

1   Protection from Eviction Act 1977, ss 3 and 5.

16.188 What if the accommodation is provided under a licence? If the accommodation provider wants possession, the licence must be terminated in accordance with its own terms. Whether or not there must be a four-week notice to quit[1], followed by an application to court for a possession order[2], will depend on whether or not the applicant is occupying the accommodation as a 'dwelling'. If the accommodation is occupied as a dwelling, the Protection from Eviction Act 1977 will apply[3].

1   Protection from Eviction Act 1977, s 5.
2   Protection from Eviction Act 1977, s 3.
3   Protection from Eviction Act 1977, s 3.

16.189 In *Bucknall v Dacorum Borough Council*[1] the High Court considered the position of an applicant who occupied accommodation under a licence. The accommodation had been secured for her initially under the HA 1996, s 188(1), interim accommodation duty[2]. She then continued to occupy the same accommodation once the HA 1996, s 193(2), main housing duty[3] had been accepted. Six weeks after the notification that the HA 1996, s 193(2), main housing duty was owed, the local housing authority made Ms Bucknall an offer of alternative accommodation, which she refused, and so the HA 1996, s 193(2), main housing duty came to an end[4]. Four months later, the local housing authority served a notice to quit purporting to terminate the licence[5]. The High Court judge held that whether or not accommodation occupied in these circumstances was a 'dwelling' was a question of fact, depending on the particular circumstances. In this case, the original purpose of the arrangement had been overtaken by the subsequent acceptance of the HA 1996, s 193(2), main housing duty, Ms Bucknall had expected to occupy the accommodation for an indefinite period until she was made an offer of private accommodation and she could reasonably have regarded it as her home. In those circumstances, the accommodation was a 'dwelling' and the Protection from Eviction Act 1977 applied[6].

[1]   [2017] EWHC 2094 (QB), [2017] HLR 40, QBD.
[2]   See **16.37–16.50**.
[3]   See **16.49–16.199**.
[4]   HA 1996, s 193(5). See **16.114–16.123**.
[5]   The notice was defective and did not comply with all the requirements of Protection from Eviction Act 1977, s 5.
[6]   There may be other circumstances when accommodation occupied under the HA 1996, s 193(2), main housing duty might not be a 'dwelling', for example if the notification to the applicant that the HA 1996, s 193(2), main housing duty was owed included a notification that an offer of alternative accommodation would be made within seven days. Each case will, however, be fact specific.

Re-applying after the HA 1996, s 193(2), main housing duty ends

16.190 An applicant in respect of whom the HA 1996, s 193(2), main housing duty has ended is free to make a new application for homelessness assistance to the same local housing authority, or any local housing other authority, at any time[1].

[1]   HA 1996, s 193(9). See **8.50–8.82** and **8.85–8.91**.

The special rules for applicants re-applying within two years of acceptance of a private rented sector offer

16.191 The introduction of the facility for local housing authorities to end the HA 1996, s 193(2) main housing duty[1] by making private rented sector offers[2], of tenancies of only 12 months duration[3], raised the spectre of applicants for homelessness assistance constantly re-applying for homelessness assistance. As each private let came to an end, an applicant would once again apply for homelessness assistance and would need to pass, once again, through the obstacle course of HA 1996, Pt 7[4] before being owed another HA 1996, s 193(2), main housing duty and made just another short-term private rented sector offer[5].

1   HA 1996, s 193(2), see **16.94–16.199**.
2   HA 1996, s 193(7AA)–(7AC). See **16.153–16.185**.
3   HA 1996, s 193(7AC)(c). See **16.154**.
4   As amended by HRA 2017 for applications for homelessness assistance made on or after 3 April 2018.
5   HA 1996, s 195A (as amended by HRA 2017, s 4(4), for applications for homelessness assistance made on or after 3 April 2018); English Code, paras 18.16–18.20. See **8.100–8.107** and **15.56–15.58**.

16.192 To meet this possibility, at least in part, the Localism Act 2011 amended HA 1996, Pt 7, by inserting HA 1996, 195A[1]. In short, it provides that the HA 1996, s 193(2), main housing duty remains with the placing local authority for a 2-year period'.[2] This is achieved by arranging that if an applicant becomes homeless within two years of the acceptance of a suitable private rented sector offer, and applies again for homelessness assistance, he or she will be fast-tracked through HA 1996, Pt 7[3] to the HA 1996, s 193(2), main housing duty again with the benefit of special provisions and, most particularly:

(1)   irrespective of whether he or she still has a priority need for accommodation; and

(2)   without needing to face possession proceedings brought by the private sector landlord.

1   Subsequently amended by HRA 2017, s 4(4), for applications for homelessness assistance made on or after 3 April 2018. See **8.100–8.107**, **15.56–15.58** and **16.47–16.50**.
2   Parliamentary Under-Secretary of State for Communities and Local Government (Andrew Stunell MP), *Hansard*, Public Bill Committee on the Localism Bill, 3 March 2011, col 787.
3   As amended by HRA 2017 for applications for homelessness assistance made on or after 3 April 2018.

16.193 The first special provision is that he or she will not normally require a priority need in order to be owed the HA 1996, s 193(2), main housing duty[1]. The exception to this special provision is where the applicant would only be owed the HA 1996, s 193(2), main housing duty because of the presence in his or her household of a restricted person[2]. Even if this is the case, the presence of the restricted person might give the applicant a priority need and so he or she would be then owed the HA 1996, s 193(2), main housing duty.

1   HA 1996, s 195A(1) (as amended by HRA 2017, s 4(4), for applications for homelessness assistance made on or after 3 April 2018); English Code, para 18.16. See **8.101**.
2   HA 1996, s 195A(5) (as amended by HRA 2017, s 4(4), for applications for homelessness assistance made on or after 3 April 2018); English Code, para 18.26. See **8.102**. For 'restricted person', see **9.54–9.56** and **11.163–11.167**.

16.194 The second special provision is that applicants are deemed to be homeless on the day on which any Housing Act 1988, s 21, notice which has been served on them expires[1].

1   HA 1996, s 195A(2), as amended by HRA 2017, s 4(4), for applications for homelessness assistance made on or after 3 April 2018. See **10.145–10.147** for the effect of service of a Housing Act 1988, s 21 notice in other cases.

16.195 An applicant should therefore make his or her application for homelessness assistance as soon as he or she is given a valid Housing Act 1988, s 21 notice by the private sector landlord. If the notice is valid, the local housing authority must accept that he or she is threatened with homelessness[1]. There may be some further inquiries to be carried out, for example as to whether the applicant remains eligible for assistance[2]. However, if the local housing authority is able to carry out any necessary further inquiries and make its decision on the application before the Housing Act 1988, s 21 notice expires – or in other words, whilst the applicant remains threatened with homelessness, as opposed to being actually homeless – it will be subject to the HA 1996, s 195(2)[3], prevention duty.

[1]   HA 1996, s 175(5), as inserted by HRA 2017, s 1(3), for applications for homelessness assistance made on or after 3 April 2018. See **10.145–10.147**.
[2]   HA 1996, s 185. See Chapter **11**.
[3]   As amended by HRA 2017, s 4(2), for applications for homelessness assistance made on or after 3 April 2018. See **15.87–15.137**.

16.196 If the decision on the application for homelessness assistance is taken on or after the date on which the notice expires, the applicant will be deemed to be homeless[1]. The HA 1996, s 195(2) prevention duty[77] will come to an end[55]. If there is reason to believe that he or she remains eligible for assistance, the HA 1996, s 188(1), interim accommodation duty will apply without any consideration of whether there is reason to believe that the applicant may have a priority need[2]. Subsequently, if the local housing authority satisfies itself that the applicant remains eligible for assistance, the HA 1996, s 189B(2)[3], relief duty will be owed and the interim accommodation duty will continue until the HA 1996, s 189B(2)[4], relief duty comes to an end or the applicant is notified what duty, if any, will be owed once the HA 1996, s 189B(2)[5], relief duty has ended (whichever is the later event)[6]. Following this, if the applicant remains homeless, and did not become homeless intentionally, he or she will then be owed the HA 1996, s 193(2), main housing duty[7].

[1]   HA 1996, s 195A(2), as amended by HRA 2017, s 4(4), for applications for homelessness assistance made on or after 3 April 2018. See **8.105–8.106**.
[77] As amended by HRA 2017, s 9(2), for applications for homelessness assistance made on or after 3 April 2018. See **15.87–15.137**.
[55] HA 1996, s 195(8)(c), as amended by HRA 2017, s 4(2), for applications foe homelessness assistance made on or after 3 April 2018. See **15.113–15.117**.
[2]   HA 1996, s 188(1A) (as amended by HRA 2017, s 5(4), for applications for homelessness assistance made on or after 3 April 2018); English Code paras 15.10 and 18.27–18.28. See **8.106** and **16.47–16.50**.
[3]   As inserted by HRA 2017, s 5(2), for applications for homelessness assistance made on or after 3 April 2018. See **15.138–15.195**.
[4]   As inserted by HRA 2017, s 5(2), for applications for homelessness assistance made on or after 3 April 2018.
[5]   As inserted by HRA 2017, s 5(2), for applications for homelessness assistance made on or after 3 April 2018.
[6]   HA 1996, s 188(1A), as amended by HRA 2017, s 5(4), for applications for homelessness assistance made on or after 3 April 2018. See **8.106** and **16.47–16.50**.
[7]   HA 1996, s 195A(1) (as amended by HRA 2017, s 4(4), for applications for homelessness assistance made on or after 3 April 2018); English Code, para 18.16. See **8.101**.

16.197 If the accommodation secured by the private rented sector offer was in the district of authority A, but had been offered to the applicant by authority B, and the applicant makes his or her further application for homelessness assistance to authority A, authority A can refer the performance of either the HA 1996, s 189B(2)[1], relief duty or the HA 1996, s 193(2), main housing duty back to authority B provided that neither the applicant nor any member of his or her household will run the risk of domestic or other violence in the district of authority B[2].

[1] As inserted by HRA 2017, s 5(2), for applications for homelessness assistance made on or after 3 April 2018.
[2] HA 1996, s 198(A1) (as inserted by HRA 2017, s 5(8), for applications for homelessness assistance made on or after 3 April 2018), (1), (2ZA) and (2A); English Code, paras 18.21–18.25. See **14.123–14.127**.

16.198 As already noted, the special rules do not exclude consideration of whether the applicant is eligible for assistance, and of whether he or she became homeless intentionally. If the applicant is not eligible for assistance, then no duty will be owed[1]. If the applicant is found to have become homeless intentionally from the private rented accommodation, eg because it was his or her actions that led the landlord to serve a Housing Act 1988, s 21 notice, then the applicant will be entitled to the HA 1996, s 189B(2)[2], relief duty and, when that comes to an end, if the applicant also has a priority need, to short-term accommodation under HA 1996, s 190(2)(a)[3]. It may be that the local housing authority can arrange with the private landlord that the accommodation previously occupied as a result of the private rented sector offer can now be offered to the applicant again, perhaps if the local housing authority's assistance were to include help with rent in advance or a rent guarantee.

[1] HA 1996, s 183(2).
[2] As inserted by HRA 2017, s 5(2), for applications for homelessness assistance made on or after 3 April 2018. See **15.138–15.195**.
[3] See **16.81–16.93**. The special provision at HA 1996, s 195A(1) only excludes priority need from consideration if the applicant is entitled to the HA 1996, s 193(2), main housing duty. It does not apply where the local housing authority is satisfied that the applicant has become homeless intentionally and so the issue of priority need will be relevant to whether or not the local housing authority owes a short-term duty to accommodate under HA 1996, s 190(2)(a), as amended by HRA 2017, s 5(5), for applications for homelessness assistance made on or after 3 April 2018. See English Code, para 18.20.

16.199 These special provisions only apply once[1]. If, on a re-application within two years of acceptance of a private rented sector offer, the applicant accepts another private rented sector offer (which might be of the same or different accommodation), and that subsequently comes to an end, he or she will have to apply in the usual way and will need to have a priority need in order to be owed any of the accommodation duties.

[1] HA 1996, s 195A(6) (as amended by HRA 2017, s 4(4), for applications for homelessness assistance made on or after 3 April 2018); English Code para 18.26.

THE HA 1996, S 193C(4) ACCOMMODATION DUTY OWED TO APPLICANTS WHO HAVE DELIBERATELY AND UNREASONABLY REFUSED TO CO-OPERATE

16.200 Where the local housing authority has notified an applicant of its decision that he or she has deliberately and unreasonably refused to co-operate[1], any HA 1996, s 195(2)[2], prevention duty or HA 1996, s 189B(2)[3], relief duty owed to the applicant will come to an end[4]. For many applicants this will mark the end of the road: no further duty will be owed[5]. But a proportion of applicants may, notwithstanding their conduct, be owed the HA 1996, s 193C(4)[6] accommodation duty.

[1]   HA 1996, s 193B(2), as inserted by HRA 2017, s 7(1), for applications for homelessness assistance made on or after 3 April 2018. See **15.196–15.216**.

[2]   As amended by HRA 2017, s 4(2), for applications for homelessness assistance made on or after 3 April 2018. See **15.87–15.137**.

[3]   As inserted by HRA 2017, s 5(2), for applications for homelessness assistance made on or after 3 April 2018. See **15.138–15.195**.

[4]   HA 1996, s 193C(2), as inserted by HRA 2017, s 7(1), for applications for homelessness assistance made on or after 3 April 2018. See **15.216–15.221**.

[5]   Though the applicant may be entitled to make a fresh homelessness application. See **15.218–15.219**.

[6]   As inserted by HRA 2017, s 7(1), for applications for homelessness assistance made on or after 3 April 2018; English Code, paras 15.36–15.38.

To whom is the duty owed?

16.201 The HA 1996, s 193C(4)[1] accommodation duty can only arise where the local housing authority[2]:

- owed the applicant the HA 1996, s 195(2)[3], prevention duty or the HA 1996, s 189B(2)[4], relief duty; and
- has given the applicant a notice in accordance with HA 1996, s 193B(2)–(6)[5].

That notice will have informed the applicant of the local housing authority's opinion that he or she had deliberately and unreasonably refused to take any step set out in his or her personalised housing plan[6]. The giving of this notice has the effect of bringing the HA 1996, s 195(2)[7], prevention duty or the HA 1996, s 189B(2)[8], relief duty to an end[9].

[1]   As inserted by HRA 2017, s 7(1), for applications for homelessness assistance made on or after 3 April 2018.

[2]   HA 1996, s 193B(1), as inserted by HRA 2017, s 7(1), for applications for homelessness assistance made on or after 3 April 2018.

[3]   As amended by HRA 2017, s 4(2), for applications for homelessness assistance made on or after 3 April 2018. See **15.87–15.137**.

[4]   As inserted by HRA 2017, s 5(2), for applications for homelessness assistance made on or after 3 April 2018. See **15.138–15.195**.

[5]   As inserted by HRA 2017, s 7(1), for applications for homelessness assistance made on or after 3 April 2018. See **15.207–15.211**.

[6]   HA 1996, s 193B(2)–(3), as inserted by HRA 2017, s 7(1), for applications for homelessness assistance made on or after 3 April 2018; see **15.203–15.206**. For personalised housing plan see **15.72–15.80**.

[7]   As amended by HRA 2017, s 4(2), for applications for homelessness assistance made on or after 3 April 2018. See **15.87–15.137**.

[8]   As inserted by HRA 2017, s 5(2), for applications for homelessness assistance made on or after 3 April 2018. See **15.138–15.195**.

[9]   HA 1996, s 193C(1)–(2), as inserted by HRA 2017, s 7(1), for applications for homelessness assistance made on or after 3 April 2018. See **15.216–15.221**.

16.202 In these circumstances, the local housing authority will be required to secure that accommodation is available for the applicant, if:

- the local housing authority is satisfied that he or she is homeless;

- the local housing authority is satisfied that he or she is eligible for assistance;
- the local housing authority is satisfied that he or she has a priority need; and
- the local housing authority is not satisfied that he or she became homeless intentionally[1].

It will be noted that this is the counterpart to the HA 1996, s 193(2) main housing duty[2]. But for the applicant's unreasonable conduct, that duty would have been owed instead[3]. The distinction between the two duties lies in the manner in which they may be brought to an end[4].

[1]   HA 1996, s 193C(4) (as inserted by HRA 2017, s 7(1), for applications for homelessness assistance made on or after 3 April 2018); English Code, paras 15.36–15.38.
[2]   See **16.114–16.118** for the ways in which the HA 1996, s 193(2) main housing duty can be brought to an end; and see **16.204–16.218** for the ways in which the duty at HA 1996, s 193C(4) can be brought to an end.
[3]   HA 1996, s 193C(4), as inserted by HRA 2017, s 7(1), for applications for homelessness assistance made on or after 3 April 2018.
[4]   See **15.196–15.221**.

When does the duty start?

16.203 The duty to accommodate commences as soon as the notice that a local housing authority considers that an applicant has deliberately and unreasonably refused to co-operate has been given to him or her[1]. For a notice to be 'given', it must be in writing[2]. If it is not actually received by the applicant, having been physically handed over to him or her, or sent by post, or by email, then it is treated as having been given to him or her if it is made available at the local housing authority's office for a reasonable period for collection by the applicant, or on his or her behalf[3].

[1]   HA 1996, ss 193B(1) and 193C(1), (2) and (4), as inserted by HRA 2017, s 7(1), for applications for homelessness assistance made on or after 3 April 2018.
[2]   HA 1996, s 193B(8), as inserted by HRA 2017, s 7(1), for applications for homelessness assistance made on or after 3 April 2018.
[3]   HA 1996, s 193B(8), as inserted by HRA 2017, s 7(1), for applications for homelessness assistance made on or after 3 April 2018.

How can the duty end?

16.204 The HA 1996, s 193C(4)[1] duty to accommodate will come to an end when any of the following events occurs:

- the applicant ceases to be eligible for assistance[2];
- the applicant becomes homeless intentionally from accommodation made available for his or her occupation[3];
- the applicant accepts an offer of an assured tenancy from a private landlord[4];
- the applicant otherwise voluntarily ceases to occupy, as his or her only or principal home, the accommodation made available for his or her occupation[5];

- the applicant, having been informed of the possible consequences of refusal or acceptance, and of his or her right to request a review of the suitability of accommodation, refuses a final accommodation offer[6];

- the applicant, having been informed of the possible consequences of refusal or acceptance, and of his or her right to request a review of the suitability of accommodation, accepts a final accommodation offer[7];

- the applicant, having been informed of the possible consequences of refusal or acceptance, and of his or her right to request a review of the suitability of accommodation, refuses a final Pt 6 offer[8]; or

- the applicant, having been informed of the possible consequences of refusal or acceptance, and of his or her right to request a review of the suitability of accommodation, accepts a final Pt 6 offer[9].

The first four events are also events that would cause the HA 1996, s 193(2), main housing duty to come to an end and are discussed in the sections of this chapter dealing with that duty[10].

[1]   As inserted by HRA 2017, s 7(1), for applications for homelessness assistance made on or after 3 April 2018.
[2]   HA 1996, s 193C(5)(a), as inserted by HRA 2017, s 7(1), for applications for homelessness assistance made on or after 3 April 2018; English Code para 15.38(a). See **16.124–16.126**.
[3]   HA 1996, s 193C(5)(b), as inserted by HRA 2017, s 7(1), for applications for homelessness assistance made on or after 3 April 2018; English Code para 15.38(b). See **16.127–16.130**.
[4]   HA 1996, s 193C(5)(c), as inserted by HRA 2017, s 7(1), for applications for homelessness assistance made on or after 3 April 2018; English Code para 15.38(c). See **16.136–16.139**.
[5]   HA 1996, s 193C(5)(d), as inserted by HRA 2017, s 7(1), for applications for homelessness assistance made on or after 3 April 2018; English Code para 15.38(d). See **16.140–16.141**.
[6]   HA 1996, s 193C(6)(a), as inserted by HRA 2017, s 7(1), for applications for homelessness assistance made on or after 3 April 2018; English Code para 15.37. See **16.205–16.209** and **16.214–16.215**.
[7]   HA 1996, s 193C(6)(a), as inserted by HRA 2017, s 7(1), for applications for homelessness assistance made on or after 3 April 2018; English Code para 15.37. See **16.205–16.209** and **16.214–16.215**.
[8]   HA 1996, s 193C(6)(b), as inserted by HRA 2017, s 7(1), for applications for homelessness assistance made on or after 3 April 2018; English Code para 15.37. See **16.210–16.215**.
[9]   HA 1996, s 193C(6)(b), as inserted by HRA 2017, s 7(1), for applications for homelessness assistance made on or after 3 April 2018; English Code para 15.37. See **16.210–16.215**.
[10] HA 1996, s 193(6). For the applicant ceasing to be eligible for assistance, see **16.124–16.126**. For the applicant becoming homeless intentionally from accommodation made available for his or her occupation see **16.127–16.130**. For the applicant accepting an offer of an assured tenancy from a private landlord, see **16.136–16.139**. For the applicant otherwise voluntarily ceasing to occupy, as his or her only or principal home, the accommodation made available for his or her occupation, see **16.140–16.141**.

A final accommodation offer

16.205 The HA 1996, s 193C(4)[1], accommodation duty will come to an end where the applicant refuses or accepts a final accommodation offer[2]. Since the applicant has the right to request a review of the suitability of the accommodation offered, whilst also accepting the offer, acceptance must always be the safest course of action[3].

[1]   As inserted by HRA 2017, s 7(1), for applications for homelessness assistance made on or after 3 April 2018.
[2]   HA 1996, s 193C(6)(a), as inserted by HRA 2017, s 7(1), for applications for homelessness assistance made on or after 3 April 2018; English Code, para 15.37.

3   HA 1996, s 202(1)(h) and (1B), as inserted by HRA 2017, s 9, for applications for homelessness assistance made on or after 3 April 2018. See **19.65–19.69** and **19.90–19.99**.

16.206 An offer will be a 'final accommodation offer' if:

- it is an offer of an assured shorthold tenancy made by a private landlord to the applicant in relation to any accommodation which is, or may become, available for the applicant's occupation;
- it is made with the approval of the local housing authority in pursuance of arrangements made by the local housing authority with a view to bringing the HA 1996, s 193C(4)[1], accommodation duty to an end; and
- the tenancy offered is a fixed term tenancy, (within the meaning of Pt 1, Housing Act 1988), for a period of at least six months[2].

1   As inserted by HRA 2017, s 7(1), for applications for homelessness assistance made on or after 3 April 2018.
2   HA 1996, s 193C(7), as inserted by HRA 2017, s 7(1), for applications for homelessness assistance made on or after 3 April 2018.

16.207 Local housing authorities can choose to make final accommodation offers of tenancies with terms longer than the minimum of six months. The accommodation offered must be suitable for the needs of the applicant[1]. In addition to the general requirements of suitability[2], the Homelessness (Suitability of Accommodation) (England) Order 2012[3] applies to final accommodation offers. Art 3 contains specific requirements relating to the physical characteristics and management of the accommodation[4].

1   HA 1996, s 193C(9), as inserted by HRA 2017, s 7(1), for applications for homelessness assistance made on or after 3 April 2018.
2   See CHAPTER 18.
3   SI 2012/2601, as amended by HRA 2017, s 12, for applications for homelessness assistance made on or after 3 April 2018
4   See **18.70–1.79** for these requirements and see further English Code, paras 17.11–17.22.

16.208 A local housing authority may not approve a final accommodation offer unless it is satisfied that the applicant is not under any contractual or other obligations in respect of his or her existing accommodation, or, that if he or she is, he or she is able to bring those obligations to an end before being required to take up the offer[1].

1   HA 1996, s 193C(9) and (10), as inserted by HRA 2017, s 7(1), for applications for homelessness assistance made on or after 3 April 2018; English Code, para 15.37; see **16.205–16.215**.

16.209 The applicant will know that this is an offer designed to bring the HA 1996, s 193C(4), duty to an end, rather than an offer of HA 1996, s 193C(4), accommodation, because of the special notification requirements. In particular, the offer (or a document preceding or accompanying the offer) must:

- inform the applicant of the possible consequences of refusal or acceptance of the offer[1]; and
- inform the applicant in writing of his or her right to request a review of the suitability of the accommodation[2].

1   HA 1996, s 193C(6), as inserted by HRA 2017, s 7(1), for applications for homelessness assistance made on or after 3 April 2018. The letter need not contain the exact words in HA

1996, s 193C(6), provided that it conveys the substance of the requirements. See *Omar v Birmingham City Council* [2007] EWCA Civ 610, [2007] HLR 43, CA.

2   HA 1996, s 193C(6), as inserted by HRA 2017, s 7(1), for applications for homelessness assistance made on or after 3 April 2018. The letter need not, however, contain the local housing authority's reasons for being satisfied that the accommodation offered is suitable for the applicant: *Solihull Metropolitan Borough Council v Khan* [2014] EWCA Civ 41, [2014] HLR 33 CA.

A final Pt 6 offer

16.210 The HA 1996, s 193C(4)[1], duty will come to an end where the applicant refuses or accepts a final Pt 6 offer[2]. Since the applicant has the right to request a review of the suitability of the accommodation offered, whilst also accepting the offer, acceptance must always be the safest course of action[3].

1   As inserted by HRA 2017, s 7(1), for applications for homelessness assistance made on or after 3 April 2018.
2   HA 1996, s 193C(6)(b), as inserted by HRA 2017, s 7(1), for applications for homelessness assistance made on or after 3 April 2018; English Code, para 15.37.
3   HA 1996, s 202(1)(h) and (1B), as inserted by HRA 2017, s 9, for applications for homelessness assistance made on or after 3 April 2018. See **19.69–19.69** and **19.90–19.99**.

16.211 A final Pt 6 offer is defined as:

*   an offer of accommodation under HA 1996, Pt 6 (allocation of social housing);
*   that is made in writing; and
*   that states that it is a final offer for the purposes of HA 1996, s 193C[1].

1   HA 1996, s 193C(8), as inserted by HRA 2017, s 7(1), for applications for homelessness assistance made on or after 3 April 2018.

16.212 In addition, the offer (or a document preceding or accompanying the offer) must:

*   inform the applicant of the possible consequences of refusal or acceptance of the offer[1]; and
*   inform the applicant in writing of his or her right to request a review of the suitability of the accommodation[2].

1   HA 1996, s 193C(6), as inserted by HRA 2017, s 7(1), for applications for homelessness assistance made on or after 3 April 2018. The letter need not contain the exact words in HA 1996, s 193C(6), provided that it conveys the substance of the requirements. See *Omar v Birmingham City Council* [2007] EWCA Civ 610, [2007] HLR 43, CA.
2   HA 1996, s 193C(6), as inserted by HRA 2017, s 7(1), for applications for homelessness assistance made on or after 3 April 2018. The letter need not, however, contain the local housing authority's reasons for being satisfied that the accommodation offered is suitable for the applicant: *Solihull Metropolitan Borough Council v Khan* [2014] EWCA Civ 41, [2014] HLR 33 CA.

16.213 The accommodation offered must be suitable for the needs of the applicant[1]. In addition, a local housing authority may not make a final Pt 6 offer unless it is satisfied that the applicant is not under any contractual or other obligations in respect of his or her existing accommodation, or, that if he or she is, he or she is able to bring those obligations to an end before being required to take up the offer[2].

1   HA 1996, s 193C(9), as inserted by HRA 2017, s 7(1), for applications for homelessness assistance made on or after 3 April 2018. See CHAPTER 18 for the general requirements of suitability.

2   HA 1996, s 193C(9) and (10), as inserted by HRA 2017, s 7(1), for applications for homelessness assistance made on or after 3 April 2018; English Code, para 15.37; see **16.205–16.215**.

Acceptance or refusal of the offer

16.214 If the applicant accepts or refuses a final accommodation offer or a final Pt 6 offer, the HA 1996, s 193C(4)[1], duty will come to an end automatically, without any further notification being required[2]. The deliberate use of the word 'refuse' in this context connotes something more than a simple failure to accept or respond to an offer. The local housing authority must be able to identify something that amounts to unequivocal rejection following receipt of the offer[3].

1   As inserted by HRA 2017, s 7(1), for applications for homelessness assistance made on or after 3 April 2018.

2   HA 1996, s 193C(6), as inserted by HRA 2017, s 7(1), for applications for homelessness assistance made on or after 3 April 2018.

3   *R v Haringey London Borough Council ex p Muslu* (2001) February *Legal Action*, p 29, QBD; for an example where the local housing authority was wrong in law to characterise the applicant's response to a private rented sector offer as a refusal, see *Ciercierska v Brent London Borough Council* (2016), *Legal Action*, October, p 41, County Court at Central London.

16.215 The applicant might wish to request a review of the suitability of the accommodation offered[1]. As with other offers, he or she should usually be advised both to accept the offer and to request a review simultaneously[2]. The question arises as to what happens if the applicant, having accepted a fixed-term tenancy, is then informed by the local housing authority that his or her request for a review has been successful and the local housing authority agrees that the accommodation was not suitable? The applicant at that point may wish to terminate the tenancy but will not be able to do so unless the terms of the tenancy contain a break clause[3].

1   HA 1996, s 202(1)(h), as inserted by HRA 2017, s 9(2), for applications for homelessness assistance made on or after 3 April 2018. See **19.65–19.69**.

2   HA 1996, s 202(1B), as inserted by HRA 2017, s 9(2), for applications for homelessness assistance made on or after 3 April 2018. See **19.90–19.99**.

3   See further discussion in relation to private rented sector offers at **18.175**.

Termination of accommodation secured under the HA 1996, s 193C(4), duty to accommodate those who have deliberately and unreasonably failed to co-operate

16.216 Unlike accommodation secured under the HA 1996, s 188(1), interim accommodation duty[1], or the HA 1996, s 190(2), duty[2], this duty is not inevitably short-term. The accommodation might be occupied for an indefinite period. Whether the accommodation is occupied as a 'dwelling', thereby attracting the protection of the Protection from Eviction Act 1977, is likely to be a question of fact, which will require consideration of all of the circumstances[3]. If the Protection from Eviction Act 1977 does not apply, the accommodation provider will have to terminate the licence under which the accommodation is occupied in accordance with its terms and upon reasonable notice[4].

1   See **16.37–16.50**.
2   See **16.81–16.89**.
3   See **16.29–16.30**.
4   See **16.30**.

ACCOMMODATION DUTIES OWED WHERE THE APPLICANT'S CASE IS REFERRED TO ANOTHER LOCAL HOUSING AUTHORITY

Referral of the applicant's case at the stage when the HA 1996, s 189B(2) relief duty would be owed

16.217 Whichever local housing authority an applicant applies to, if that local housing authority has reason to believe that the applicant may be homeless, eligible for assistance, and have a priority need, the duty to secure initial interim accommodation is triggered[1]. Interim accommodation must be secured, irrespective of whether or not the applicant appears to have a local connection with the local housing authority[2]. That duty continues while it carries out its inquiries.

1   See **16.37–16.50**. In the case of an application for homelessness assistance made within two years of acceptance of a private rented sector offer, the duty to secure interim accommodation applies whether or not there is reason to believe that the applicant may have a priority need (HA 1996, s 188(1A), as amended by HRA 2017, ss 5(4), for applications for homelessness assistance made on or after 3 April 2018). See **16.47–16.50**.
2   HA 1996, s 188(2).

16.218 If the local housing authority's conclusion upon those inquiries is that the applicant:

(1)   is homeless; and
(2)   is eligible for assistance;

it would normally be subject to the HA 1996, s 189B(2)[1], relief duty[2]. But if it considers that the conditions for referral of the applicant's case to another local housing authority in England[3] are made out, it may notify the other local housing authority that it holds that opinion[4]. The notifying local housing authority ('the first local housing authority') must notify the applicant that it has notified, or intends to notify, another local housing authority ('the second local housing authority') of its opinion[5].

1   As inserted by HRA 2017, s 5(2), for applications for homelessness assistance made on or after 3 April 2018.
2   See **15.138-15.195**.
3   The HA 1996, s 189(B)(2) (as inserted by HRA 2017, s 5(2), for applications for homelessness assistance made on or after 3 April 2018) relief duty cannot be referred to a local housing authority in Wales or to a local authority in Scotland: HA 1996, s 198(A1) (as inserted by HRA 2017, s 5(8), for applications for homelessness assistance made on or after 3 April 2018).
4   HA 1996, s 198(A1), as inserted by HRA 2017, s 5(8), for applications for homelessness assistance made on or after 3 April 2018. See **15.139–15.142**.

⁵ HA 1996, s 184(4), as amended by HRA 2017, s 5(3), for applications for homelessness assistance made on or after 3 April 2018. See **15.139**.

16.219 The effect of these two notices is:

(a) to bring to an end the initial interim duty to accommodate; and

(b) to defer the performance of the HA 1996, s 189B(2)¹, relief duty until the applicant has been notified whether or not the conditions for referral are met².

¹ As inserted by HRA 2017, s 5(2), for applications for homelessness assistance made on or after 3 April 2018. See **15.138–15.195**.

² HA 1996, s 199A(1) as inserted by HRA 2017, s 5(9), for applications for homelessness assistance made on or after 3 April 2018.

16.220 HA 1996, Pt 7¹, creates a further interim duty on the first local housing authority so that it is required to continue to accommodate the applicant if it has reason to believe that he or she may have a priority need². That further interim duty ends only when the applicant receives a further notice from the first local housing authority. That further notice will contain the final decision that the conditions of referral are, or are not, met³. That decision will have been reached either by agreement between the two local housing authorities or, if there is a dispute between them, by a referee⁴. Whilst any dispute between the two local housing authorities remains, the first local housing authority remains under the duty to secure interim accommodation until the dispute is resolved⁵.

¹ As amended by HRA 2017 for applications for homelessness assistance made on or after 3 April 2018.

² HA 1996, s 199A(2), as inserted by HRA 2017, s 5(9), for applications for homelessness assistance made on or after 3 April 2018. See English Code, paras 18.21–18.25.

³ HA 1996, s 199A(3) as inserted by HRA 2017, s 5(9), for applications for homelessness assistance made on or after 3 April 2018.

⁴ HA 1996, s 198(5).

⁵ HA 1996, s 199A(2), as inserted by HRA 2017, s 5(9), for applications for homelessness assistance made on or after 3 April 2018.

16.221 If the applicant is notified of a decision that the conditions for referral are *not* met, then the first local housing authority continues to owe an interim duty to accommodate until either the HA 1996, s 189B(2), relief duty has come to an end or the applicant has been notified as to what other duty he or she might be owed¹.

¹ Whichever is the later event: HA 1996, s 199A(4)(c), as inserted by HRA 2017, s 5(9), for applications for homelessness assistance made on or after 3 April 2018.

16.222 If, however, the applicant is notified that both local housing authorities agree (or it has been determined by arbitration) that the conditions for referral *are* met, then the interim duty to accommodate on the first local housing authority comes to an end. The second local housing authority is then subject to the HA 1996, s 189B(2), relief duty and also, provided that the second local housing authority also has reason to believe that the applicant may have a priority need, to secure interim accommodation for the applicant[1].

[1]   HA 1996, s 199A(5) and (6), as inserted by HRA 2017, s 5(9), for applications for homelessness assistance made on or after 3 April 2018.

16.223 If the applicant requests a review of the decision to refer, and asks to remain in accommodation secured by the first local housing authority while the review is considered, the first local housing authority has no further duty but does have a power to continue to secure interim accommodation pending review and, later, pending any appeal to the county court[1]. The refusal to exercise that power cannot be subject to a statutory review or an appeal to the courts. Any challenge would have to be by way of judicial review.

[1]   HA 1996, ss 199A(6) and 204(4), as inserted and amended by HRA 2017, ss 5(9) and (11), and 4(6), for applications for homelessness assistance made on or after 3 April 2018.

16.224 Obviously, when the first local housing authority considers whether or not to exercise its discretion to secure interim accommodation in these circumstances, one of the factors that it will take into account is the fact that there is an existing duty on the second local housing authority to perform the HA 1996, s 189B(2), relief duty and (provided that the second local housing authority has reason to believe that the applicant may have a priority need) to secure interim accommodation, meaning that the applicant has accommodation available for his or her occupation.

Referral of the applicant's case at the stage when the HA 1996, s 193(2) main housing duty would be owed

16.225 Whichever local housing authority an applicant applies to, if that local housing authority has reason to believe that the applicant may be homeless, eligible for assistance, and have a priority need, the duty to secure initial interim accommodation is triggered[1]. Interim accommodation must be secured, irrespective of whether or not the applicant appears to have a local connection with the local housing authority[2]. That duty continues while it carries out its inquiries.

[1]   See **16.37–16.50**. In the case of an application for homelessness assistance made within two years of acceptance of a private rented sector offer, the duty to secure interim accommodation applies whether or not there is reason to believe that the applicant may have a priority need (HA 1996, s 188(1A), as amended by HRA 2017, s 5(4), for applications for homelessness assistance made on or after 3 April 2018). See **16.47–16.50**.
[2]   HA 1996, s 188(2).

16.226 Once the HA 1996, s 189B(2)[1], relief duty has come to an end, if the local housing authority is satisfied that the applicant:

(1)   is homeless;
(2)   is eligible;
(3)   has a priority need; and
(4)   did not become homeless intentionally,

it would normally be subject to the HA 1996, s 193(2) main housing duty[2]. But if it considers that the conditions for referral of the applicant's case to another local housing authority (in England, Wales or Scotland) are made out, it may notify the other local housing authority that it holds that opinion[3]. The notifying local housing authority ('the first local housing authority') may, in such a case, notify the applicant that it has notified, or intends to notify, another local housing authority ('the second local housing authority') of its opinion[4]. The notification cannot be given to the applicant until the HA 1996, s 189B(2)[5], relief duty has come to an end[6].

[1]   As inserted by HRA 2017, s 5(2), for applications for homelessness assistance made on or after 3 April 2018. See **15.138–15.195**.
[2]   HA 1996, s 193(2). Where the applicant is making an application for homelessness assistance within two years of the acceptance by him or her of a private rented sector offer, the main housing duty will apply whether or not the applicant has a priority need (HA 1996, s 195A(1)). See **16.94–16.112** for the HA 1996, s 193(2) main housing duty and **16.191–16.199** for the special rules for applicants re-applying within two years of acceptance of a private rented sector offer.
[3]   HA 1996, s 198(1). See **14.164–14.165**.
[4]   HA 1996, s 200(1). See **14.155–14.162**.
[5]   As inserted by HRA 2017, s 5(2), for applications for homelessness assistance made on or after 3 April 2018.
[6]   HA 1996, s 200(1A), as inserted by HRA 2017, s 5(10), for applications for homelessness assistance made on or after 3 April 2018.

16.227 The effect of these two notices is:

(a)   to bring to an end the initial interim duty to accommodate[1]; and

(b)   to defer the performance of the HA 1996, s 193(2), main housing duty[2] until the applicant has been notified whether or not the conditions for referral are met[3].

[1]   By the notification to the applicant under HA 1996, ss 184(4) (as amended by HRA 2017, s 5(3), for applications for homelessness assistance made on or after 3 April 2018) and 200(1).
[2]   See **16.94–16.101**.
[3]   HA 1996, s 200(1).

16.228 HA 1996, Pt 7[1], therefore, creates a further interim duty on the first local housing authority so that it is required to continue to accommodate the applicant[2]. That further interim duty, which has been triggered by a notice given to the applicant by the first local housing authority, ends only when the applicant receives a further notice from the first local housing authority. That further notice will contain the final decision that the conditions of referral are, or are not, met[3]. That decision will have been reached either by agreement between the two local housing authorities or, if there is a dispute between them, by a referee[4]. Whilst any dispute between the two local housing authorities remains, the first local housing authority remains under the duty to secure interim accommodation until the dispute is resolved[5].

[1]   As amended by HRA 2017, for applications for homelessness assistance made on or after 3 April 2018.
[2]   HA 1996, s 200(1). See English Code, paras 10.30 and 15.16.
[3]   HA 1996, s 200(1).
[4]   HA 1996, s 198(5).
[5]   HA 1996, s 200(1).

16.229 If the applicant is notified of a decision that the conditions for referral are *not* met, then the interim duty falls away and is replaced by the main housing duty[1] owed by the first local housing authority[2].

1   HA 1996, s 193(2), see **16.94–16.101**.
2   HA 1996, s 200(3).

16.230 If, however, the applicant is notified that both local housing authorities agree (or it has been determined by arbitration) that the conditions for referral *are* met, then the interim duty to accommodate on the first local housing authority comes to an end. The second local housing authority is then subject to a duty to secure accommodation for the applicant under the HR 1996, s 193(2) main housing duty[1].

1   HA 1996, s 200(4) where the second local housing authority is a local housing authority in England. See also *Johnston v City of Westminster Council* [2015] EWCA Civ 554, [2015] HLR 35, CA. If the second local housing authority is a local housing authority in Wales, the second local housing authority will be under a duty to secure interim accommodation and to help the applicant to secure his or her own accommodation: Housing (Wales) Act 2014, ss 68, 73 and 83(2), see **14.172–14.175**.

16.231 If the applicant requests a review of the decision to refer, and asks to remain in accommodation secured by the first local housing authority while the review is considered, the first local housing authority has no further duty but does have a power to continue to secure interim accommodation pending review and, later, pending any appeal to the county court[1]. The refusal to exercise that power cannot be subject to a statutory review or an appeal to the courts. Any challenge would have to be by way of judicial review[2].

1   HA 1996, ss 200(5) and 204(4), as amended by HRA 2017, ss 4(6) and 5(11), for applications for homelessness assistance made on or after 3 April 2018.
2   Examples of unsuccessful applications for permission to bring judicial review proceedings to challenge a local housing authority's decision not to secure accommodation pending review of a decision that the applicant should be referred to another local housing authority can be found at *R (Gebremarium) v Westminster City Council* [2009] EWHC 2254 (Admin), (2009) November *Legal Action*, p 26, Admin Ct and *R (Fadol) v Westminster City Council* [2012] EWHC 1399 (Admin), (2012) July *Legal Action*, p 42, Admin Ct.

16.232 Obviously, when the first local housing authority considers whether or not to exercise its discretion to secure interim accommodation in these circumstances, one of the factors that it will take into account is the fact that there is an existing duty on the second local housing authority to secure accommodation and that therefore, if the applicant is willing to take it up, he or she will no longer be homeless[1].

1   See *Johnston v City of Westminster Council* [2015] EWCA Civ 554, [2015] HLR 35, CA.

POWERS TO SECURE ACCOMMODATION

Accommodation pending review

16.233 Some of the decisions made by a local housing authority on an application for homelessness assistance under HA 1996 Pt 7[1], carry a right to a statutory review[2]. In most cases, if the applicant requests a review of such a decision, the local housing authority has a power, but not a duty, to secure accommodation until the review has been concluded[3].

1   As amended by HRA 2017 for applications for homelessness assistance made on or after 3 April 2018.

2   HA 1996, ss 202(1), as amended by HRA 2017, s 9(2), for applications for homelessness assistance made on or after 3 April 2018. See also **19.12–19.69**.

3   HA 1996, s 188(3) as amended by HRA 2017, s 5(4), for applications for homelessness assistance made on or after 3 April 2018; English Code, paras 15.25–15.27. The exception is where the applicant was accommodated during the performance of the HA 1996, s 189B(2) (as inserted by HRA 2017, s 5(2), for applications for homelessness assistance made on or after 3 April 2018) relief duty, has refused a final accommodation offer or final Part 6 offer and has requested a review of the suitability of the offer. In those circumstances the HA 1996, s 189B(2) (as inserted by HRA 2017, s 5(2), for applications for homelessness assistance made on or after 3 April 2018) relief duty is deemed not to come to an end, and provided the local housing authority continues to have reason to believe that the applicant may have a priority need, the interim accommodation duty continues until notification of the review: HA 1996, s 188(2A) (as inserted by HRA 2017, s 5(4), for applications for homelessness assistance made on or after 3 April 2018), see **16.64–16.239**.

16.234 That power can be exercised irrespective of the nature of the decision which is being reviewed (provided it is a decision which may be subject to statutory review) and regardless of whether the applicant has previously had any accommodation (interim or otherwise) secured for him or her by the local housing authority.

16.235 The local housing authority is not required automatically to consider the exercise of the power every time it receives a request for review. An applicant who wants interim accommodation, pending a decision on the review, should ask for it. There is no need for the request to be made in writing or on any particular form.

16.236 Once a request has been made, a local housing authority that refuses even to consider, or simply fails to consider, the exercise of its power would be acting unlawfully and may be vulnerable to a judicial review challenge[1]. Likewise, a local housing authority which decided *never* to exercise the discretionary power to accommodate pending review would be unlawfully fettering that discretion.

1   For challenges to a refusal to exercise the power, see **16.248–16.257**.

16.237 Busy local housing authorities, receiving large numbers of requests for reviews, may receive almost as many requests for accommodation pending decisions on those reviews. Although each such application must be given individual consideration, local housing authorities may draw up and apply policies governing the circumstances when they will exercise their powers to secure such accommodation. Local housing authorities that adopt policies restricting the provision of discretionary interim accommodation pending review to 'exceptional circumstances' are not necessarily acting unlawfully. But any such policy must be flexible enough to ensure that individual consideration is given to the circumstances of each applicant requesting interim accommodation pending review[1].

1   English Code, paras 15.25–15.27.

16.238 Whether or not it might represent best practice, it is not unlawful for the decision-maker who made the original decision that is the subject of the review also to make the decision as to whether or not accommodation will be secured pending a statutory review[1].

1   *R (Abdi) v Lambeth London Borough Council* [2007] EWHC 1681 (Admin), [2008] HLR 5, Admin Ct.

The exception

16.239 The exception to the principle that accommodation pending review is discretionary is where the applicant requests a review under HA 1996, s 202(1)(h)[1] of the suitability of accommodation offered to him by way of a final accommodation offer[2] or final Pt 6 offer[3]. This is one of the ways in which the HA 1996, s 189B(2)[4], relief duty may come to an end[5]. In this scenario, the HA 1996, s 189B(2)[6], relief duty will continue until the decision on review has been notified to the applicant[7]. In such cases, where the applicant has a priority need or the local housing authority has reason to believe he may have a priority need, the local housing authority will be required to continue to accommodate the applicant until he or she has been notified of that decision[8].

1   As inserted by HRA 2017, s 9(2) for applications for homelessness assistance made on or after 3 April 2018. See **16.248–16.257**.
2   As defined at HA 1996, s 193A(4), as inserted by HRA 2017, s 7(1), for applications for homelessness assistance made on or after 3 April 2018. See **15.181–15.184**.
3   As defined at HA 1996, s 193A(5), as inserted by HRA 2017, s 7(1), for applications for homelessness assistance made on or after 3 April 2018. See **15.185–15.188**.
4   As inserted by HRA 2017, s 5(2), for applications for homelessness assistance made on or after 3 April 2018.
5   See **15.181–15.188**.
6   As inserted by HRA 2017, s 5(2), for applications for homelessness assistance made on or after 3 April 2018.
7   HA 1996, s 188(2A), as inserted by HRA 2017, s 5(4) for applications for homelessness assistance made on or after 3 April 2018.
8   HA 1996, s 188(1ZB), as inserted by HRA 2017, s 5(4) for applications for homelessness assistance made on or after 3 April 2018.

The factors to be considered for the exercise of the power

16.240 When a local housing authority considers the individual circumstances of each applicant, it must always take into account:

- the strength of the applicant's case on review;
- whether any new material, information or argument has become known to the local housing authority since the decision which is the subject of the review was made;
- the personal circumstances of the applicant and the consequences for him or her if accommodation is not secured; and
- any other relevant considerations[1].

1   *R v Camden London Borough Council ex p Mohammed* (1998) 30 ACR 315, QBD; and *R v Newham London Borough Council ex p Lumley* (2001) 33 ACR 11, QBD; English Code, para 15.26.

16.241 The task of taking into account these various factors is often referred to as the '*Mohammed* balancing exercise' (after the name of the case in which the factors were set out)[1].

[1]   *R v Camden London Borough Council ex p Mohammed* (1998) 30 ACR 315, QBD.

16.242 Additional considerations arise if the applicant's household includes children. In such cases, the duty on local authorities, including local housing authorities, to safeguard and promote the welfare of any children found at Children Act 2004, s 11(2) will be engaged. The Supreme Court, in *Nzolameso v City of Westminster City Council*[1], held that, when a local housing authority is making a decision which involves an exercise of discretion, or an evaluation, the duty to promote and safeguard the children's welfare, colloquially referred to as 'the best interests duty', should always be considered. The duty is *a* primary but not the only consideration. The decision-maker should identify the principal needs of the children, both individually and collectively, and have regard to the need to safeguard and promote their welfare when making any decision[2]. A local housing authority should be able to evidence the discharge of this duty by reference to contemporaneous records[3] and explain any choices that it makes that affect the welfare of children in the household, preferably by reference to published policies setting out how it makes such decisions[4]. Where the local housing authority has decided not to secure accommodation pending review for an applicant whose household includes dependent children, or for an applicant who is aged 16 or 17, this will usually be in the context of the local housing authority having decided that the applicant is not eligible for assistance, or has become homeless intentionally. In those circumstances, the local housing authority should ask the applicant for consent to notify the children's services department or authority[5].

[1]   [2015] UKSC 22, [2015] 2 All ER 942, [2015] HLR 22, SC per Baroness Hale at [22]–[30].
[2]   *Nzolameso v City of Westminster Council* [2015] UKSC 22, [2015] 2 All ER 942, [2015] HLR 22, SC, per Baroness Hale at [22]–[30].
[3]   *R (E) v Islington London Borough Council* [2017] EWHC 1440 (Admin), Admin Ct.
[4]   *Nzolameso v City of Westminster Council* [2015] UKSC 22, [2015] 2 All ER 942, [2015] HLR 22, SC, per Baroness Hale at [30].
[5]   HA 1996, s 213A as amended by HRA 2017, s 4(7), for applications for homelessness assistance made on or after 3 April 2018, see **16.280–16.288**. See also *Mohamoud v Kensington & Chelsea Royal London Borough Council, Saleem v Wandsworth London Borough Council* [2015] EWCA Civ 780, [2016] PTSR 289, CA. Children's services have a general duty, under Children Act 1989, s 17, to safeguard and promote the welfare of children within their area who are in need. It is well-established that if a child is in need of accommodation, children's services could provide services to meet that need, including arranging for the child to be accommodated along with his or her parents. 16- and 17-year-olds who are homeless are likely to be considered 'children in need' who appear to require accommodation and accommodation should be provided for them by children's services under the Children Act 1989, s 20. Children's services' powers and duties are discussed further at CHAPTER 20.

16.243 Additional considerations will also apply in cases where there is a 'real possibility' that the applicant, or a member of his household, has a disability within the meaning of Equality Act 2010, s 6. In such cases the public sector equality duty under Equality Act 2010, s 149 will be engaged[1]. In one case, a local housing authority's refusal to secure accommodation pending review was held to be unlawful, in part, because the decision appeared 'to be the work of someone who is not carrying out the conscientious requirements under the public sector equality duty referred to by Lord Neuberger in the *Hotak* decision and it can properly be read as simply paying lip service to the points put'[2]. The public sector equality duty can also be engaged on other grounds, as well as disability, such as age, race, or sex[3].

1   *Hotak v Southwark London Borough Council, Kanu v Southwark London Borough Council, Johnson v Solihull Metropolitan Borough Council* [2015] UKSC 30, [2016] AC 811, SC.

2   *R (Barrett) v Westminster City Council* [2015] EWHC 2515 (Admin), (2015) October *Legal Action*, p 42 at [34] per John Bowers QC, sitting as a deputy High Court judge.

3   Equality Act 2010, s 149(7). See **9.81–9.83**.

16.244 Where a local housing authority has been provided with new information (in the sense that it was not available when the decision which is the subject of the review was made), the officer deciding on the request for interim accommodation pending review should consider the extent to which that material affects the strength of the applicant's case on review[1]. In deciding whether to exercise its power to secure interim accommodation pending review, a local housing authority is also entitled to take into account the demands on its resources involved in securing interim accommodation, the scarcity of accommodation and the demand for accommodation from other homeless applicants (provided that it does also consider the applicant's individual circumstances)[2].

1   *R v Newham London Borough Council ex p Lumley* (2001) 33 ACR 11, QBD.

2   *R (Cole) v Enfield London Borough Council* [2003] EWHC 1454 (Admin), (2003) August *Legal Action*, p 32, Admin Ct. For examples of local housing authorities correctly applying the 'Mohammed factors', see *R (Lusamba) v Islington London Borough Council* [2008] EWHC 1149 (Admin), (2008) July *Legal Action*, p 22, Admin Ct; *R (Sadek) v Westminster City Council* [2012] EWCA Civ 803, (2012) August *Legal Action*, p 28, Admin Ct and *R(TJ) v Birmingham City Council* [2012] EWHC 2731 (Admin), (2012) December *Legal Action*, p 30.

16.245 In *R (Paul-Coker) v Southwark London Borough Council*[1], the local housing authority had decided that the applicant was not eligible because she was not habitually resident in the UK[2]. She requested interim accommodation pending a review and her solicitors made a number of representations, both in relation to her personal circumstances and by providing new information that could have an effect on the review decision. The Administrative Court held that 'there was a complete absence of any explanation or reasoning in the decision letter dealing with these various important aspects of the case' and that the local housing authority, whilst referring to the *Mohammed* balancing exercise, had actually only paid 'lip-service' to it[3]. This decision reminds local housing authorities that 'lip-service' is not good enough. They must actually consider the representations made in support of the request for interim accommodation pending review and consider them in relation to the *Mohammed* factors, and any other factors that may arise for consideration.

1   [2006] EWHC 497 (Admin), [2006] HLR 32, Admin Ct.

2   See **11.130–11.136**.

3   *R (Paul-Coker) v Southwark London Borough Council* [2006] EWHC 497 (Admin), [2006] HLR 32, Admin Ct at [49] per Forbes J and see *R (Barrett) v Westminster City Council* [2015] EWHC 2515 (Admin), (2015) October *Legal Action*, p 42, Admin Ct.

16.246 In another case, the local housing authority's decision not to secure accommodation pending review had relied on documentation that had not been mentioned in the HA 1996, s 184, decision letter. The judge decided that there was an arguable case that relying on new information, and not giving the applicant an opportunity to comment on it, was an error of law[1].

[1]   *R (Miah) v Westminster City Council* [2012] EWHC 3563 (Admin), (2013) February *Legal Action*, p 36, Admin Ct.

Circumstances when power to secure accommodation pending review is restricted

16.247 The benefit of the power to secure interim accommodation pending a statutory review, and pending an appeal to the county court[1], is not available to[2]:

- nationals of other European Economic Area (EEA) states;
- refugees given refugee status by other states (including EEA states);
- former asylum-seekers who have failed to co-operate with removal directions;
- people who are unlawfully present in the UK; and
- failed asylum-seekers with dependent children,

unless the local housing authority decides that securing accommodation is necessary in order to prevent a breach of the applicant's rights under the European Convention on Human Rights or under European Union law[3]. If interim accommodation is requested for former asylum-seekers who have failed to co-operate with removal directions, those who are unlawfully present in the UK, or for certain failed asylum-seekers with dependent children, local housing authorities are required to inform the Home Office[4].

[1]   HA s 204(4). See **16.258–16.278**.
[2]   English Code, para 15.24.
[3]   Nationality Immigration and Asylum Act 2002, s 54, Sch 3, paras 1 and 3; see English Code, para 15.24 and see also **16.56, 20.35–20.38** and **20.50–20.57**. See also *R (Mohammed) v Harrow London Borough Council* [2005] EWHC 3194 (Admin), [2006] HLR 18, Admin Ct, where the local housing authority's decision that accommodation was not 'necessary' to avoid a breach of European Union rights, as the claimant was not a worker or work-seeker and therefore not exercising those rights, contained no error of law. Note that these categories are due to be amended by Immigration Act 2016, Sch 12, para 9. At the time of writing it is not known when these amendments will come into force.
[4]   Nationality Immigration and Asylum Act 2002, Sch 3, para 14; English Code, para 15.24. It is unlikely that any of those classes of people would be eligible for assistance. See Chapter 11.

Challenges to refusal to exercise power to secure interim accommodation pending review

16.248 Where a local housing authority has:

- failed to consider a request for interim accommodation pending review;
- refused to secure interim accommodation pending a review;
- decided to secure interim accommodation for a limited period only; or
- decided to withdraw interim accommodation that had been secured pending the review, before the notification of the review decision,

the appropriate avenue for the applicant to challenge any of these decisions is to bring a judicial review claim. In order to succeed, the applicant must show that the local housing authority's decision (or failure to make one) was wrong in law.

16.249 Challenges to local housing authorities' decisions not to exercise a discretionary power are generally much more difficult for the applicant than bringing a claim for breach of statutory duty. The courts can be particularly reluctant to intervene where Parliament has left local housing authorities free of duties and enjoying a discretion to exercise (or not exercise) powers[1].

1   See *R (Tesfay) v Birmingham City Council* [2013] EWCA Civ 1509, (2014) February *Legal Action*, p 31, CA.

16.250 The principles that a local housing authority must consider when deciding whether or not to secure interim accommodation pending review are set out at **16.240–16.246**.

16.251 On applying for permission to bring a claim by way of judicial review, the applicant can also apply for an interim injunction requiring the local housing authority to secure accommodation pending the determination of the judicial review proceedings. The test that the Administrative Court will apply in considering whether or not to make an interim injunction is two-fold:

(1)   whether the applicant has a strong prima facie case[1]; and
(2)   the likely consequences to each party of the granting or withholding of interim relief and the wider public interest[2].

The onus is on the applicant to demonstrate that he or she has a strong prima facie case, where he or she is applying for an interim injunction[3].

1   *De Falco v Crawley Borough Council* [1980] QB 460, CA; *R v Kensington and Chelsea Royal London Borough Council ex parte Hammell* [1989] 1 QB 518, CA; *Francis v Kensington and Chelsea Royal London Borough Council* [2003] EWCA Civ 443, [2003] HLR 50; and *Putans v Tower Hamlets London Borough Council* [2006] EWHC 1634 (Ch), [2007] HLR 10, ChD at [52] per Michael Briggs QC.
2   *R v Kensington and Chelsea Royal London Borough Council ex parte Hammell* [1989] 1 QB 518, CA. And see further *R (Medical Justice) v Secretary of State for the Home Department* [2010] EWHC 1425 (Admin), [2010] ACD 70, Admin Ct per Cranston J at [12]–[16] for a discussion of the 'wider public interest' in public law claims. See also **19.315–19.320**.
3   *R (Omatoyo) v City of Westminster Council* [2006] EWHC 2572 (Admin), (2006) December *Legal Action*, p 21, Admin Ct.

16.252 In cases of emergency, where the applicant is or is about to be street homeless, an application for an interim injunction can be made out of hours and over the telephone to a duty Administrative Court judge. In *R (Lawer) v Restormel Borough Council*[1], the applicant's legal representatives were re-minded that applications in these circumstances are exceptional and of the importance of their duties:

•   to make full and frank disclosure of all the relevant documents to the judge; and
•   to ensure that there has been compliance with the pre-action protocol in judicial review claims and service on the local housing authori-ty's legal department[2].

1   [2007] EWHC 2299 (Admin), [2008] HLR 20, Admin Ct.
2   See **20.262** and **19.319**. And see also *R (Sadek) v Westminster City Council* [2012] EWCA Civ 803, (2012) August *Legal Action*, p 28, Admin Ct.

16.253 Legal representatives should ensure that the Administrative Court has been provided with all the information required, as set out in the prescribed forms. In particular, reasons for any urgency must be explained, along with the time when the need for urgent consideration was first appreciated and the efforts made to notify the defendant. The consequences for legal representatives of failing to comply with those obligations can be severe[1].

[1] *R (Hamid) v Secretary of State for the Home Department* [2012] EWHC 3070 (Admin), Admin Ct.

16.254 In practice, if the Administrative Court judge considers that the claim for judicial review is a strong prima facie case, the judge is also likely to make an interim injunction, since otherwise the applicant would be homeless. However, the consequences of making the interim order against the local housing authority, and its effect on other applicants should also be considered[1].

[1] *De Falco v Crawley Borough Council* [1980] QB 460, CA per Lord Bridge at 481.

16.255 Many judicial review claims against refusals to secure interim accommodation are disposed of at the time of, or shortly after, consideration of whether or not permission should be granted to bring the claim. If permission is refused, unless there is to be an appeal, that is the end of the matter for the applicant. If permission is granted, and an interim injunction made requiring the local housing authority to accommodate the applicant until the judicial review claim has been determined[1], many local housing authorities will then agree to accommodate pending review. Even if there is no agreement, it is not unusual for the review decision to be notified to the applicant before the judicial review claim has been finally heard, and so the claim for judicial review becomes academic.

[1] Permission is granted where there is a reasonably arguable case. An interim mandatory injunction requires the claimant to show that he or she has a strong prima facie case. The fact that permission has been granted, whilst not determinative, is certainly a relevant factor when the court considers whether an interim injunction should continue (*R (Omatoyo) v City of Westminster Council* [2006] EWHC 2572 (Admin), (2006) December *Legal Action*, p 21, Admin Ct).

16.256 If the judicial review claim does proceed to a full hearing, the claim might be dismissed (if there is no error of law). If the claim succeeds, and the Administrative Court decides that the local housing authority did make an error of law in one or more of its decisions, it can set the decision aside (a 'quashing order'). The local housing authority will either have to reconsider its decision or the Administrative Court may make a mandatory order requiring the local housing authority to secure accommodation until the review decision has been notified to the applicant.

16.257 The case of *R (Paul-Coker) v Southwark London Borough Council*[1] is an example of the Administrative Court deciding that a local housing authority, when it referred to the criteria involved in the *Mohammed* balancing-exercise, was in fact paying 'lip-service' to them. The refusal to exercise the power to secure accommodation in that case was unlawful[2].

[1] *R (Paul-Coker) v Southwark London Borough Council* [2006] EWHC 497 (Admin), [2006] HLR 32, Admin Ct; and see **16.245**.

² See also *R (Miah) v Westminster City Council* [2012] EWHC 3563 (Admin), (2013) February *Legal Action*, p 36, Admin Ct; *R (S) v Brent London Borough* Council [2014] EWHC 3742, (2015) March *Legal Action*, p 45, Admin Ct; *R (Hatami) v Southwark London Borough Council* [2015] EWHC 899 (Admin); and *R (Barrett) v Westminster City Council* [2015] EWHC 2515 (Admin), (2015) October *Legal Action* p 42, Admin Ct.

Accommodation pending appeal

Appeals to the county court

16.258 Review decisions (and original decisions which can be subject to a statutory review) can be appealed to the county court[1]. The fact that an applicant might lodge or has lodged an appeal does not impose a duty on the local housing authority to accommodate the applicant pending the hearing of that appeal. Sadly, in many areas, appeals cannot be heard for some weeks or months after they are lodged[2].

¹ HA 1996, s 204(1). See **19.214–19.276**.
² HA 1996, s 204(4) as amended by HRA 2017, ss 4(6) and 5(11), for applications for homelessness assistance made on or after 3 April 2018; English Code, paras 15.28–15.32.

16.259 However, there is a discretionary power available for the local housing authority to secure interim accommodation at two stages:

(1)   during the 21-day period between notification of the review decision and the normal deadline for issue of a county court appeal[1]; and/or

(2)   pending the determination of the appeal itself, once made[2].

¹ HA 1996, s 204(4)(a).
² HA 1996, s 204(4)(b).

16.260 The power can only be used where the local housing authority has already[1] owed one of the following duties to the applicant:

•   the duty to secure interim accommodation[2];
•   the HA 1996, s 190(2), short-term accommodation duty owed to an applicant who has a priority need but has been found to have become homeless intentionally[3];
•   the duty to secure accommodation pending referral of the HA 1996, s 189B(2)[4], relief duty, under the 'conditions for referral' provisions[5]; or
•   the duty to secure accommodation pending referral of the HA 1996, s 193(2)[6], main housing duty, under the 'conditions for referral' provisions[7].

¹ HA 1996, s 204(4).
² HA 1996, s 188(1) and (1A) as amended by HRA 2017, s 5(4) for applications for homelessness assistance made on or after 3 April 2018. See **16.37–16.50**.
³ HA 1996, s 190(2), as amended by HRA 2017, s 5(5), for applications for homelessness assistance made on or after 3 April 2018 . See **16.81–16.93**.
⁴ As inserted by HRA 2017, s 5(2), for applications for homelessness assistance made on or after 3 April 2018. See **15.138–15.195**.
⁵ HA 1996, s 199A, as amended by HRA 2017, s 5(9), for applications for homelessness assistance made on or after 3 April 2018. See **16.217–16.224**.
⁶ See **16.94**.

7   HA 1996, s 200, as amended by HRA 2017, s 5(10), for applications for homelessness assistance made on or after 3 April 2018. See **16.225-16.232.**

16.261 The common thread running through the list is that the applicant either has, or the local housing authority initially had reason to believe that he or she might have, a priority need. Where the local housing authority has not been subject to any of those duties, there is no power under HA 1996, Pt 7[1], for a local housing authority to secure interim accommodation pending appeal. Where the power is available, an applicant may invite the local housing authority to exercise it while an appeal is being considered, prepared, or later, once the appeal has been lodged.

1   As amended by HRA 2017 for applications for homelessness assistance made on or after 3 April 2018.

16.262 When considering whether or not to exercise a power to accommodate pending appeal to the county court, a local housing authority should carry out the same balancing exercise as it is required to undertake when considering a request for interim accommodation pending review. This is discussed in detail at **16.242–16.246.** In overview, it should consider all the relevant circumstances, and any new information, material or argument. It is required to consider the applicant's grounds of appeal, as part of its consideration of the merits of the case, but would not normally be expected to refer to any of the grounds of appeal in its decision letter, unless there is some important and striking ground which requires specific comment[1]. In addition, it will need to consider the applicant's personal and household circumstances, the need to safeguard and promote the welfare of any children involved, the public sector equality duty under Equality Act 2010, s 149 (if applicable) along with the terms of any general policy it has adopted governing its discretion (if any), and the resources available[2].

1   *Lewis v Havering London Borough Council* [2006] EWCA Civ 1793, [2007] HLR 20, CA.
2   English Code, paras 15.28–15.32. For the possibility of challenging a refusal to accommodate pending appeal, see **16.266–16.277** and **19.280–19.292.**

Onward appeals

16.263 The power in HA 1996, s 204(4), can also be exercised by the local housing authority to continue to secure accommodation in the event of an appeal from the decision of a county court judge to the Court of Appeal, or further, to the Supreme Court. When the local housing authority is deciding whether to exercise its power to secure accommodation pending determination of an appeal to the Court of Appeal, it must again direct itself in accordance with the same principles discussed at **16.242–16.246.** When considering whether or not to secure interim accommodation, the local housing authority is entitled to take into account the prospects of the Court of Appeal granting permission to bring a second appeal[1], and, if permission was granted, the applicant's prospects of success on appeal[2].

1   See **19.293–19.298.**
2   *R(Nzolameso) v City of Westminster Council* [2014] EWHC 409 (Admin), (2014) April *Legal Action*, p 27, Admin Ct.

16.264 If the local housing authority refuses to secure interim accommodation, and the HA 1996, s 204(1) appeal has been finally determined, at least in the county court, then the right to appeal against the refusal to secure interim accommodation in HA 1996, s 204A(1) is not available[1]. The Court of Appeal does not have any inherent power to order that the local housing authority secure accommodation pending the determination of the appeal to the Court of Appeal (or the Supreme Court). Accordingly, any challenge to the local housing authority's refusal to secure interim accommodation pending determination of an appeal to the Court of Appeal, or subsequently to the Supreme Court, must be brought by judicial review[2].

[1]   Nor is it available where the HA 1996, s 204 appeal is against an original decision (HA 1996, s 204(1)(b)). In those circumstances, a dis-satisfied applicant should challenge any refusal to secure accommodation by way of judicial review: *Davis v Watford Borough Council* [2018] EWCA Civ 529, CA, see **19.281**.

[2]   *Johnson v City of Westminster Council* [2013] EWCA Civ 773, [2013] HLR 45, CA.

Circumstances when power to secure accommodation pending appeal is restricted

16.265 This power to secure interim accommodation pending appeal to the county court is not available to:

- nationals of other EEA states;
- refugees given refugee status by other EEA states;
- former asylum-seekers who have failed to co-operate with removal directions;
- people who are unlawfully present in the UK; and
- failed asylum-seekers with dependent children,

unless the local housing authority considers it necessary in order to prevent a breach of rights under the European Convention on Human Rights or European Union law[1].

[1]   Nationality Immigration and Asylum Act 2002, s 54 and Sch 3, paras 1 and 3; see **16.47–16.48, 20.35–20.38** and **20.50–20.57**, and English Code, para 15.24. Note that these categories are due to be amended by Immigration Act 2016, Sch 12, para 9. At the time of writing it is not known when these amendments will come into force. If accommodation is requested by a former asylum-seeker who has failed to co-operate with removal directions, anyone unlawfully present in the UK or a failed asylum-seeker with dependent children, the local housing authority is under an obligation to inform the Home Office (Nationality, Immigration and Asylum Act 2002, Sch 3, para 14; English Code, para 15.24). In practice, there are very few people who might be eligible who would also fall within one of those three categories (see Chapter 11).

Challenges to refusal to exercise a power to secure interim accommodation pending appeal

16.266 If the local housing authority refuses to secure interim accommodation pending appeal (or if it decides to secure interim accommodation for a limited period only), there is no right to a statutory review of that decision. Instead, the applicant has the right to appeal against that refusal. The appeal lies to the county court on a point of law[1]. To distinguish this appeal from the main or substantive appeal (usually brought against the review decision of the local housing authority) it is described in the paragraphs that follow as the 'accommodation appeal'. However, where the HA 1996, s 204 appeal is against an original decision under HA 1996, s 204(1)(b), the HA 1996, s 204A appeal route is not available. In those circumstances, a dis-satisfied applicant should challenge any refusal to secure accommodation by way of judicial review[2].

[1] HA 1996, s 204A(2). See **19.280–19.292.**
[2] *Davis v Watford Borough Council* [2018] EWCA Civ 529, CA, see **19.281.**

16.267 The principles that a local housing authority must consider when deciding whether or not to secure interim accommodation pending appeal are set out at **16.242–16.246.**

16.268 The accommodation appeal may be against:

(1)   the refusal to accommodate at all pending appeal;
(2)   a decision to exercise the power to accommodate only for a limited period; or
(3)   a decision to withdraw interim accommodation that had been secured pending appeal[1].

[1]   HA 1996, s 204A(2).

16.269 There is no appeal on the facts. The applicant must show that the local housing authority's refusal, decision, or withdrawal was wrong in law. The court will adopt the principles applied generally in judicial review claims when it considers the lawfulness of the local housing authority's decision-making[1].

[1]   HA 1996, s 204A(4)(b). See **19.281.**

16.270 Prior to 30 September 2002, challenges to refusals to secure accommodation pending appeal were brought by way of judicial review[1]. The Court of Appeal had held that if the guidance given in *R v Camden London Borough Council ex p Mohammed*[2] had been followed by a local housing authority, when considering whether or not to secure interim accommodation pending appeal, challenges to the exercise of that discretion were likely to be futile, and applications for judicial review should only be brought in exceptional cases. The appropriate step for an applicant without accommodation was to seek to expedite the hearing of his or her substantive appeal, rather than challenge the refusal to accommodate pending appeal[3].

[1]   *Ali v Westminster City Council* [1999] 1 WLR 384, (1999) 31 ACR 349, CA.
[2]   *R v Camden London Borough Council ex p Mohammed* (1998) 30 ACR 315, QBD. See also **16.240–16.247.**
[3]   *R v Brighton and Hove Borough Council ex p Nacion* (1999) 31 ACR 1095, CA.

16.271 The Court of Appeal has taken the same approach now that challenges to refusals are brought by way of a county court appeal rather than by way of judicial review[1]. If the local housing authority has properly directed itself in accordance with the *Mohammed* principles[2], the court will not intervene. The county court hearing an accommodation appeal should not embark on a consideration of the merits of the main or substantive appeal[3].

[1]   *Francis v Kensington and Chelsea Royal London Borough Council* [2003] EWCA Civ 443, [2003] 35 ACR 50, CA; *Brookes v Croydon London Borough Council* [2004] EWCA Civ 439, (2004) June *Legal Action*, p 31, CA. However, in the scenario where an applicant has issued

an appeal in the County Court under HA 1996, s 204(1)(b), having requested a review but not been notified of the decision on review (see **16.240–16.247**), and has sought and been refused interim accommodation pending the determination of that appeal (HA 1996, s 204(4), as amended by HRA 2017, ss 4(6) and 5(11) for applications for homelessness assistance made on or after 3 April 2018), the appropriate course of action is for the applicant to challenge the refusal of interim accommodation by way of judicial review: *Davis v Watford Borough Council* [2018] EWCA Civ 529, CA.

2   *R v Camden London Borough Council ex p Mohammed* (1998) 30 ACR 315, QBD. See also **16.240–16.246**.

3   For a recent example, see *Rother District Council v Freeman-Roach* [2018] EWCA Civ 368, CA per Rose J at [41]–[44].

16.272 The decision in *Francis v Kensington and Chelsea Royal London Borough Council*[1], begs the question as to what 'properly directed itself' means. Certainly, where a local housing authority fails to consider, at all, a request for accommodation pending appeal, it cannot be said to have properly considered the right factors, and must therefore have erred in law. Conversely, where a local housing authority has set out the *Mohammed* factors and carefully considered each of those, along with any other relevant factors and points raised by the applicant, then the decision is unlikely to be wrong in law. In practice, the decision in *Francis* means that accommodation appeals may now be rarely brought, but in the rare cases in which they may justifiably be brought they may well succeed[2].

1   [2003] EWCA Civ 443, [2003] 35 ACR 50, CA.

2   As did the applicants in *Onyaebor v Newham London Borough Council* (2004) May *Legal Action*, p 27, Bow County Court; and *Quadir v Tower Hamlets London Borough Council* (2011), (2012) April *Legal Action*, p 47, Central London Civil Justice Centre. For an example of an appeal which did not succeed, see *Hafiz & Haque v Westminster City Council* [2012] EWHC 1392 (QB), (2012) July *Legal Action*, p 42, QBD.

16.273 If the accommodation appeal succeeds, the court may quash the decision appealed against. At that point, the court may either refer the matter back to the local housing authority for re-consideration of the request for accommodation pending appeal, or it may make an order requiring the local housing authority to secure interim accommodation. It can only make the latter order if it is satisfied that:

' . . . failure to exercise the section 204(4) power in accordance with the order would substantially prejudice the applicant's ability to pursue the main appeal[1].'

1   HA 1996, s 204A(6).

16.274 This is a strikingly different test from that governing the local housing authority's own exercise of discretion. The determinative factor for the court can only be the ability of the applicant to pursue his or her main or substantive appeal with or without the provision of accommodation. While an applicant's other personal circumstances may be relevant, they cannot be determinative[1].

1   For example, in *Quadir v Tower Hamlets London Borough Council* (2011), (2012) April *Legal Action*, p 47, Central London Civil Justice Centre, the appeal against the refusal to secure accommodation pending appeal was successful, and the local housing authority's refusal was quashed by the judge. However, the judge did not consider that the strict test

in HA 1996, s 204A(6) was satisfied and did not make an order requiring the local housing authority to secure interim accommodation.

16.275 An order to accommodate made by the court cannot extend beyond the conclusion of the main appeal. In other words, the county court has no jurisdiction to order the provision of accommodation pending any further appeal beyond the county court[1].

[1] HA 1996, s 204A(6)(b). As a result, any challenge to a decision by a local housing authority not to secure accommodation pending determination of an appeal to the Court of Appeal, or subsequently to the Supreme Court, must be brought by way of judicial review: *Johnson v Westminster City Council* [2013] EWCA Civ 773, [2013] HLR 45, CA.

16.276 Accommodation appeals, like main or substantive appeals, can only be heard by a circuit judge or recorder, not by a district judge[1]. Applications for interim orders, requiring the provision of accommodation pending determination of the accommodation appeal, can be made before the full accommodation appeal is heard. A judge hearing an interlocutory application will have to decide:

(1) whether there is an arguable error of law in the decision being appealed against; and, if so,

(2) whether, arguably, the ability of the applicant to pursue his or her main appeal would be substantially prejudiced if accommodation were not secured.

[1] CPR Pt 2, PD2B, para 9.

16.277 An interim order can only be made if the judge takes the view that the applicant has a strong prima facie case in respect of quashing the refusal to accommodate and in obtaining an order requiring the local housing authority to secure accommodation pending the determination of the HA 1996, s 204 appeal[1].

[1] HA 1996, s 204A(4)(a); and see *Hafiz & Haque v Westminster City Council* [2012] EWHC 1392 (QB), (2012) July *Legal Action*, p 42, QBD.

Power to secure accommodation under the HA 1996, s 195(2), prevention or HA 1996, s 189B(2), relief duties

16.278 The HA 1996, s 195(2)[1], prevention duty and the HA 1996, s 189B(2)[2], relief duty will be owed to applicants who are eligible for assistance and who are, respectively, either threatened with homelessness or are homeless. As already discussed[3], these duties do not require the local housing authority to secure accommodation for the applicant; the duty in each case is to help the applicant secure his or her accommodation. However, HA 1996, 205(3)[4], makes it clear that the local housing authority has the power to secure that accommodation is available in the performance of these functions if it takes the view that this is an appropriate course.

[1] As amended by HRA 2017, s 4(2), for applications for homelessness assistance made on or after 3 April 2018. See **15.84–15.137**.

[2] As inserted by HRA 2017, s 5(2), for applications for homelessness assistance made on or after 3 April 2018. See **15.138–15.195**.

³ See **15.22–15.27**.
⁴ As inserted by HRA 2017, s 6, for applications for homelessness assistance made on or after 3 April 2018. See English Code, paras 15.33–15.35.

16.279 The Code advises that this power provides more flexibility for local housing authorities to pursue appropriate housing options for those who are owed either of these duties. It suggests that local housing authorities might use the power to deliver accommodation services for groups that are at higher risk of homelessness, for example young people with low incomes. The power might also be used to provide additional help to those least able to secure accommodation directly from a private landlord, such as people with an offending history or with a mental health problem[1].

There is no right to request a review of any decision not to exercise this power in the applicant's favour. Consequently, any challenge would have to be by judicial review[2], or by internal complaint and subsequently to the Local Government and Social Care Ombudsman[3].

¹ English Code, paras 15.34–15.35.
² See **19.306–19.332**.
³ See **19.333–19.340**.

ADDITIONAL DUTIES AND POWERS

Duties to applicants whose household includes a person under 18

16.280 Special provision is made in HA 1996, Pt 7[1] for situations in which it appears to a local housing authority that it will be unlikely to owe a duty to a family with dependent children. The objective is to ensure that in those cases, where HA 1996, Pt 7[2], will not provide the necessary safety net, the alternative safety net of provision of accommodation for children (under the Children Act 1989) is ready to be used by the time the family is facing imminent homelessness.

¹ As amended by HRA 2017 for applications for homelessness assistance made on or after 3 April 2018.
² As amended by HRA 2017 for applications for homelessness assistance made on or after 3 April 2018.

16.281 Where the applicant's household[1] includes a person under the age of 18, and the local housing authority has reason to believe that the applicant:

(1) may not be eligible for assistance; or

(2) may have become homeless intentionally[2],

the local housing authority must ask the applicant to consent to the referral of the essential facts of his or her case to the local children's services department or authority[3]. The local housing authority should not wait until its actual decision is made on the application under HA 1996, Pt 7[4], but must obtain consent when it simply has reason to believe that it may not be able to help the applicant, which will usually be almost immediately after the application for homelessness assistance has been made.

¹ In this context, the word 'household' is used to mean those persons who normally reside with the applicant as a member of his or her family, and any other persons who might reasonably be expected to reside with the applicant; see HA 1996, s 176 and **10.21–10.32**.

² HA 1996, s 213A(1), as amended by HRA 2017, s 4(7), for applications for homelessness assistance made on or after 3 April 2018; English Code, para 15.12.

³ HA 1996, s 213A(2).

⁴ As amended by HRA 2017 for applications for homelessness assistance made on or after 3 April 2018.

16.282 This obligation is not triggered where the application is received from a lone applicant who is under 18, because such cases are covered by different liaison arrangements[1].

¹ See **12.133–12.159**. See also *R (M) v Hammersmith & Fulham London Borough Council* [2008] UKHL 14, [2008] 1 WLR 535, SC; *R (G) v Southwark London Borough Council* [2009] UKHL 26, [2009] 1 WLR, 2399, SC and *Prevention of homelessness and provision of accommodation for 16 and 17-year-old young people who may be homeless and/or require Accommodation*, (April 2018, MHCLG and Department for Education), on the CD Rom with this book.

16.283 Once the consent has been given, the essential facts and details of the application and of the subsequent HA 1996, Pt 7[1] decision must be communicated to the children's services authority[2]. This early notification obligation applies to unitary authorities (thus requiring notification between departments) as well as to separate local housing authorities and children's services authorities[3]. Children's services should be alerted as quickly as possible, so as to have an opportunity to consider the case and plan their response well before the local housing authority has concluded its inquiries and reached any negative HA 1996, Pt 7[4] decision. The English Code advises that local housing authorities should consider having arrangements in place to manage the transition in responsibilities, so that there is no break in provision of accommodation[5].

¹ As amended by HRA 2017 for applications for homelessness assistance made on or after 3 April 2018.

² HA 1996, s 213A(1) and (2), as amended by HRA 2017, s 4(7), for applications for homelessness assistance made on or after 3 April 2018 . See also English Code, chapter 13 for guidance.

³ HA 1996, s 213A(3).

⁴ As amended by HRA 2017 for applications for homelessness assistance made on or after 3 April 2018.

⁵ English Code, para 15.12.

16.284 If the applicant does not give his or her consent, the local housing authority may still disclose information about an application to the children's services department if it has reason to believe that a child is, or may be, at risk of significant harm[1].

¹ HA 1996, s 213A(4). See also English Code, para 13.7.

16.285 HA 1996, Pt 7[1], contains a provision designed to ensure that the local housing authority cannot simply wash its hands of the applicant and pass responsibility to children's services. In the case of an applicant whose household includes a person under 18 and whom the local housing authority has decided:

- is ineligible for assistance; or
- has become homeless intentionally;

the children's services authority can call upon the local housing authority to provide such advice and assistance as is reasonable in the circumstances to help with the exercise of any children's services functions under Pt 3 of the Children Act 1989[2]. In this way it is intended that there should be a seamless scheme of social welfare provision for the most vulnerable families. In a Parliamentary debate initiated by a former housing minister, the then government spelt out its understanding that the scheme should work in this way[3].

[1] As amended by HRA 2017 for applications for homelessness assistance made on or after 3 April 2018.
[2] HA 1996, s 213A(5) and (6), as amended by HRA 2017, s 4(7), for applications for homelessness assistance made on or after 3 April 2018. See also Children Act 1989, s 27, where a local authority can request the help of a local housing authority in the exercise of their functions. In *R (M) v Islington London Borough Council* [2016] EWCA Civ 1028, [2016] HLR 19, Admin Ct, the Administrative Court held that this provision did not apply directly between departments in a unitary authority, although it was reasonable to assume that departments within a unitary authority were expected to co-operate.
[3] *Hansard*, HC Deb, vol 417, cols 1092–1098 (6 February 2004).

16.286 Any disagreement between the local housing authority and the children's services authority should be resolved by discussion and negotiation and not by litigation[1]. Where a local housing authority had placed an applicant and his household in a different district, and the accommodation was due to come to an end as a result of the local housing authority being satisfied that the applicant had become homeless intentionally, the Administrative Court found that there was a duty on both local authorities to assess the children's needs. The duty lay on the first local authority's children's services department because, following a notification under HA 1996, s 213A, it had commenced, but not completed, an assessment of needs under Children Act 1989, s 17. The duty also lay on the second local housing authority's children's services' department because it had been wrong to conclude that the children, who were facing eviction from the temporary accommodation, were not in need[2].

[1] *R v Northavon District Council ex p Smith* [1994] 2 AC 402, AC at 410 per Lord Templeman.
[2] *R (AM) v Havering London Borough Council and Tower Hamlets London Borough Council* [2015] EWHC 1004 (Admin) (2015) May *Legal Action*, p 46, Admin Ct.

16.287 The assistance that the applicant, or, more particularly, the applicant's children, can expect to receive from children's services under the Children Act 1989 is outlined in CHAPTER 20[1].

[1] See 20.39–20.71.

Duties and powers to protect the applicant's property

Introduction

16.288 The provisions of HA 1996, Pt 7[1], recognise that a safety net scheme of assistance for the homeless will not be comprehensive if all it achieves is shelter for the people involved. Most applicants who are actually homeless or threatened with homelessness will also have at least a few personal possessions that need safeguarding, ranging from a single bag containing a change of clothes at one extreme to a full house of furniture, personal possessions and pets at the other. HA 1996, Pt 7[2], imposes duties, and provides powers, for the safeguarding of these possessions[3].

[1] As amended by HRA 2017 for applications for homelessness assistance made on or after 3 April 2018.
[2] As amended by HRA 2017 for applications for homelessness assistance made on or after 3 April 2018.
[3] HA 1996, ss 211, (as amended by HRA 2017, s 5(12), for applications for homelessness assistance made on or after 3 April 2018) and 212; English Code, chapter 20.

When duties are owed

16.289 A duty is owed to certain applicants[1] where the local housing authority has reason to believe that:

(1) there is a danger of loss of, or damage to, any of the applicant's personal property;
(2) the danger arises because the applicant is unable to protect or deal with that property; and
(3) no other suitable arrangements have been or are being made[2].

[1] Identified at HA 1996, s 211(2), as amended by HRA 2017, s 5(12), for applications for homelessness assistance made on or after 3 April 2018. See **16.291**.
[2] HA 1996, s 211(1). See English Code, para 20.2.

16.290 'Danger' in this context means a genuine or real danger. That is, something more than a possible danger, a slight risk or remote possibility of injury. It denotes a 'likelihood of harm'[1]. The duty will not therefore be triggered simply because property was left behind in a secure locked flat which was regularly visited by the applicant or by others on his or her behalf, giving rise to no greater risk of burglary than that experienced by a householder who is temporarily away from home[2]. Of course, the situation would be entirely different if the flat were insecure with 'a front door opened and banging in the wind', or the property was 'left in the gutter' after an eviction[3].

[1] *Deadman v Southwark London Borough Council* (2001) 33 HLR 75, CA at [20] per Ward LJ. See English Code, para 20.6.
[2] *Deadman v Southwark London Borough Council* (2001) 33 HLR 75, CA at [21] per Ward LJ.
[3] *Deadman v Southwark London Borough Council* (2001) 33 HLR 75, CA at [25] per Ward LJ.

16.291 If the local housing authority is or has been subject to:

(1) the HA 1996, s 188[1] interim duty to accommodate;
(2) the HA 1996, s 189B(2)[2], relief duty;
(3) the HA 1996, s 195(2)[3], prevention duty;
(4) the HA 1996, s 190(2) short-term accommodation duty[4];
(5) the HA 1996, s 193(2), main housing duty[5]; or
(6) any of the accommodation duties owed towards applicants where the HA 1996, s 193(2) main housing duty is being considered for referral[6],

it owes an applicant the duty to take reasonable steps to prevent the loss of property or prevent or mitigate any damage to it[7].

[1] As amended by HRA 2017, s 5(4), for applications for homelessness assistance made on or after 3 April 2018. See **16.37–16.50**.

2   As inserted by HRA 2017, s 5(2), for applications for homelessness assistance made on or after 3 April 2018. See **15.138–15.195**.

3   As amended by HRA 2017, s 4(2), for applications for homelessness assistance made on or after 3 April 2018. See **15.84–15.137**.

4   As amended by HRA 2017, s 5(5), for applications for homelessness assistance made on or after 3 April 2018. See **16.81–16.93**.

5   See **16.94–16.101**.

6   HA 1996, s 200, as amended by HRA 2017, s 5(10), for applications for homelessness assistance made on or after 3 April 2018. See **16.225–16.232**.

7   HA 1996, s 211(2), as amended by HRA 2017, s 5(12), for applications for homelessness assistance made on or after 3 April 2018.

16.292 This list contains some surprising omissions. It does not include the HA 1996, s 193C(4)[1], duty to accommodate applicants who have deliberately and unreasonably refused to co-operate. Nor does it include the duty to accommodate an applicant where the local housing authority is considering the referral of the HA 1996, s 189B(2)[2], relief duty[3]. However, in each of those cases, the local housing authority is likely to have owed the HA 1996, s 188(1), interim accommodation duty. Even if no prescribed duty is or was owed to an applicant[4], the local housing authority has a power to take any steps it considers reasonable in order to protect personal property[5].

1   As inserted by HRA 2017, s 7(1), for applications for homelessness assistance made on or after 3 April 2018. See **16.200–16.218**.

2   As inserted by HRA 2017, s 5(2), for applications for homelessness assistance made on or after 3 April 2018. See **15.138–15.195**.

3   HA 1996, s 199A, as inserted by HRA 2017, s 5(9), for applications for homelessness assistance made on or after 3 April 2018. See **16.217–16.224**.

4   Because he or she has been found not to be homeless or threatened with homelessness, or not to be eligible for assistance, and was never provided with interim accommodation.

5   HA 1996, s 211(3); English Code, para 20.4

16.293 The local housing authority should therefore start by asking and answering the following questions:

(1)   Is there a danger of loss or damage?

(2)   Is that because the applicant is unable to protect or deal with his or her possessions?

(3)   Is that because no other suitable arrangements have been made or are being made?

16.294 The local housing authority is only under the duty imposed by HA 1996, Pt 7[1], if all of the questions are answered positively.

1   As amended by HRA 2017 for applications for homelessness assistance made on or after 3 April 2018.

16.295 If the applicant seeks to challenge a local housing authority's decision that all or any of the questions are to be answered 'NO', the only challenge would lie in a claim by judicial review on the basis that the local housing authority's decision was wrong in law[1].

1   *Deadman v Southwark London Borough Council* (2001) 33 HLR 75, CA. There is no right to request a statutory review in respect of any of the functions of the local housing authority that relate to the protection of possessions.

16.296 If the answer to all three questions is 'Yes', then the next question for the local housing authority is whether it owes or has owed the applicant any of the duties identified at **16.291**. If it has done, even if that duty has since ended, it remains under a duty to take reasonable steps to prevent any loss of, or damage to, the property. If the local housing authority never owed the applicant any of those duties, it may still choose to take reasonable steps to prevent loss or damage.

The extent of the duties to prevent loss or damage

16.297 The local housing authority can deal with the personal property in any way that is reasonably necessary in order to prevent or mitigate loss or damage to it. This includes storing the property itself, or arranging for it to be stored by some other person[1]. If the applicant's previous home is still available, the local housing authority may be able to arrange for the personal property to remain there if it can be adequately protected[2].

[1] HA 1996, s 212(1).
[2] English Code, para 20.9.

16.298 The local housing authority has the right to impose conditions before it will take any steps to deal with personal property. These conditions can include levying reasonable charges[1] and specifying in what circumstances the local housing authority may dispose of the property (usually upon reasonable notice to the applicant or if the applicant loses touch with the local housing authority and cannot be traced)[2].

[1] HA 1996, s 211(4)(a) and English Code, para 20.10. See **16.22–16.27** for a discussion of reasonable charges for accommodation.
[2] HA 1996, s 211(4). English Code, para 20.10.

16.299 In order to perform the duty and protect the property, the local housing authority is entitled to enter the applicant's usual or last place of residence at all reasonable times[1].

[1] HA 1996, s 212(1)(a).

Which possessions must be protected?

16.300 The powers and duties are concerned with the 'personal property' of the applicant. This is enlarged by HA 1996, Pt 7[1] to embrace the 'personal property of any person who might reasonably be expected to reside with him'[2]. That terminology echoes wording used elsewhere in HA 1996, Pt 7[3]. It is wide enough to include those with whom an applicant resides and others with whom an applicant proposes to reside.

[1] As amended by HRA 2017 for applications for homelessness assistance made on or after 3 April 2018.
[2] HA 1996, s 211(5).
[3] As amended by HRA 2017 for applications for homelessness assistance made on or after 3 April 2018. See **10.21–10.32**.

16.301 The term 'personal property' is not defined in HA 1996, Pt 7[1]. Given the wide variety of ways in which individuals accumulate possessions, the range will be enormous. In *R v Chiltern District Council ex p Roberts*[2], the applicants were travelling showmen and the question arose as to whether their fairground equipment constituted their 'personal property'. Although, in the event, the case did not turn on the point, the judge said of 'personal property':

> 'I am inclined to the view that it would not extend to equipment used by an applicant in his business, at any rate where the business is conducted other than at the relevant accommodation . . . The adjective "personal" is used to distinguish not only from real property, but from property used for commercial purposes, particularly if used elsewhere[3].'

[1] As amended by HRA 2017 for applications for homelessness assistance made on or after 3 April 2018.
[2] (1990) 23 HLR 387, QBD.
[3] *R v Chiltern District Council ex p Roberts* (1990) 23 HLR 387, QBD, at 396, per Pill J.

16.302 Nowadays, local housing authorities will want to avoid too restrictive a definition of personal property. Otherwise, they may run the risk of breaching the obligation on public authorities to take positive measures to prevent individuals losing their possessions contrary to the Human Rights Act, Sch 1, Art 1, First Protocol[1].

[1] Human Rights Act 1998, Sch 1.

16.303 The most controversial issues in day-to-day practice arise where the personal possessions include pets. No local housing authority would deny that a goldfish bowl was 'personal property' – so, no less, the goldfish inside it. The safeguard for a local housing authority faced with a menagerie of cats, dogs and other pets is the power to impose, in advance, a condition that the applicant pays a reasonable charge for the action it takes[1]. Obviously, for applicants on a low income, the amount that is 'a reasonable charge' for them to pay may not meet the full cost to the local housing authority. But even the poorest applicant will have been paying something to feed the pets and so could be expected to pay a weekly charge equivalent to that amount so as to contribute to kennelling or other fees. Local housing authorities troubled by the need to arrange kennelling for a few dogs should sympathise with Harlow District Council, which faced the prospect of dealing with a homeless applicant with 56 cats[2].

[1] HA 1996, s 211(4)(a).
[2] *Harlow District Council v Sewell* [2000] EHLR 122.

The ending of the duties

16.304 In most cases, the duty to protect possessions will end at the same time as the most common form of the termination of several of the duties, ie with the applicant's move to a longer-term home[1]. There will usually be a notification that a duty has come to an end. But this is not necessarily so. In one case, the main housing duty ended by the applicant becoming homeless intentionally from his accommodation secured under HA 1996, Pt 7. The duty to protect his possessions did not cease, and the local housing authority which had wrongly disposed of his personal possessions later agreed to pay £6,000 compensation and waive its storage charges[2].

1 HA 1996, s 212(3)–(5); English Code paras 20.11–20.12.
2 *Complaint against Sutton London Borough Council*, 03/B/6452, 9 December 2004, (2005) April *Legal Action*, p 30; see also *Complaint against Bournemouth Borough Council*, 14 20 077, 16 December 2015 (2016) June *Legal Action*, p 42, where the decision that the HA 1996, s 193(2), main housing duty had come to an end because of the applicant's refusal of accommodation was defective and the local housing authority had been wrong to withdraw storage arrangements.

16.305 If the applicant requests that his or her property is moved to a particular address (whether it is the applicant's new long-term home or anywhere else), and the local housing authority agrees, the duty will have ended once the property has been moved. The authority must inform the applicant that this will be the case before it agrees to move the property[1].

1 HA 1996, s 212(2); English Code, para 20.11.

16.306 Otherwise, the duty ceases if the local housing authority no longer has reason to believe that there is a threat of loss of, or damage to, the applicant's property. For example, there may have been a change of circumstances in that the applicant has found accommodation or has become able to afford to pay private storage charges.

16.307 Once the duty has ended, the local housing authority retains a power to continue to store any property previously in storage, upon the same or modified conditions[1].

1 HA 1996, s 212(3); English Code, para 20.11.

16.308 If the local housing authority is no longer under the duty, and/or no longer intends to exercise the power, to store the property, it must notify the applicant of that fact. The notification must include the reasons for the decision that the duty no longer applies[1].

1 HA 1996, s 212(4); English Code, para 20.12.

16.309 Once the local housing authority has accepted a duty, then it is under a private law obligation to the applicant as bailee of his or her goods until the obligation is discharged and the goods are collected[1]. If property is damaged or destroyed, the applicant would be entitled to bring a private law action for damages for breach of that duty, conversion and/or trespass to goods. The local housing authority may have a defence available if it can show that it took all reasonable steps to prevent the loss or damage, or if the loss or damage was not reasonably foreseeable.

1 *Mitchell v Ealing London Borough Council* [1979] QB 1, QBD.

Chapter 17

DUTIES TO ASSIST THE HOMELESS ON LOCAL HOUSING AUTHORITIES IN WALES

Contents

HOUSING (WALES) ACT 2014, PT 2

17.1 The Housing (Wales) Act 2014 (H(W)A 2014), Pt 2, came into force on 27 April 2015, with the exception of H(W)A 2014, ss 75(3) and 78[1]. Anyone who applied to a local housing authority in Wales for accommodation or for help in retaining or obtaining accommodation on or after 27 April 2015 is assessed under H(W)A 2014, Pt 2. Applicants whose applications for homelessness assistance were made to a local housing authority in Wales before 27 April 2015 continue to be dealt with under Housing Act 1996, Pt 7 (HA 1996, Pt 7)[2].

[1] Housing (Wales) Act (Commencement No 3 and Transitory Transitional and Saving Provisions) Order 2015, SI 2015/1272 (W 88), see the CD Rom with this book.
[2] Housing (Wales) Act (Commencement No 3 and Transitory Transitional and Saving Provisions) Order 2015, SI 2015/1272 (W 88), art 7.

17.2 H(W)A 2014, s 75(3), which requires local housing authorities to secure accommodation for some applicants who have a priority need, whether or not they have become homeless intentionally, will not be brought into force until 2019[1]. H(W)A 2014, s 78, which requires a local housing authority to make a decision as to whether or not it will have regard to the 'becoming homeless intentionally' test came into force on 1 July 2015[2].

[1] *Code of Guidance for Local Authorities on the Allocation of Accommodation and Homelessness* (Welsh Government, March 2016) (the Welsh Code), para 14.10. See **17.24–17.26**.
[2] Housing (Wales) Act (Commencement No 3 and Transitory Transitional and Saving Provisions) Order 2015, SI 2015/1272 (W 88), arts 3 and 6; see **17.17–17.23**. From implementation in April 2015, five local housing authorities elected to disregard the 'becoming homeless intentionally' test in relation to specified groups of people: four in relation to 16- and 17-year-olds, and to care leavers, and one in respect of people who had experienced domestic abuse: *Post Implementation Evaluation of the homelessness legislation (Pt 2 of the Housing (Wales) Act 2014, Interim Report* (Welsh Government, August 2017).

OVERVIEW

Structure of H(W)A 2014, Pt 2

17.3 H(W)A 2014, Pt 2, is clearly structured and written in plain language. Each section that sets out a duty is followed by a section containing the circumstances in which that duty can come to an end. The duties are as follows:

- general duty to provide information, advice and assistance in accessing help: H(W)A 2014, s 60[1];
- duty to carry out an assessment of a person's case: H(W)A 2014, s 62(1)[2];
- prevention duty to help to prevent an applicant from becoming homeless: H(W)A 2014, s 66(1)[3];
- interim duty to secure accommodation for homeless applicants in priority need: H(W)A 2014, s 68(1)[4];
- relief duty to help to secure accommodation for homeless applicants: H(W)A 2014, s 73(1)[5];

- main housing duty to secure accommodation for applicants in priority need when the H(W)A 2014, s 73(1), relief duty ends: H(W)A 2014, s 75(1)[6];
- duties to an applicant whose case is considered for referral or referred to another local housing authority: H(W)A 2014, s 82[7]; and
- duties regarding protection of property: H(W)A 2014, ss 93–94[8].

[1] See **8.9–8.14**.
[2] See **9.12–9.14** and **9.88**.
[3] See **17.45–17.72**.
[4] See **17.118–17.134**.
[5] See **17.73–17.117**.
[6] See **17.146–17.199**.
[7] See **14.172–14.175**.
[8] See **17.199–17.205**.

17.4 After giving an initial overview of the approach to homelessness contained in H(W)A 2014, Pt 2, this chapter deals first with the H(W)A 2014, s 66(1), prevention duty owed to applications who are threatened with homelessness, and the H(W)A 2014, s 73(1), relief duty owed to applicants who are homeless. It then deals with the H(W)A 2014, s 68(1), interim accommodation duty. We then consider the H(W)A 2014, s 75(1), main housing duty for applicants who have a priority need and (if appropriate) have not become homeless intentionally and the H(W)A 2014, s 82, duties towards applicants who are referred to other local housing authorities. We then review the other circumstances that can cause any of the duties to come to an end at H(W)A 2014, s 95, finally we consider the H(W)A 2014, ss 93–94, duties to protect property, the H(W)A 2014, s 95, duty on different authorities and departments to co-operate, and the H(W)A 2014, s 96, duty to co-operate in certain cases involving children. Finally, the chapter reviews the other circumstances that can cause any of the duties to come to an end at H(W)A 2014, s 79.

17.5 Given that none of the duties described in this chapter can be owed to applicants in respect of whom the local housing authority is satisfied are not eligible for help[1], reference in this chapter to 'applicants' means applicants who are eligible.

[1] For 'eligible for help' see H(W)A 2014, s 61 and Sch 2, and see Chapter **11**.

The Welsh approach to dealing with homelessness

17.6 When it came into force on 27 April 2015, H(W)A 2014, Pt 2, contained a new approach towards homelessness duties. The thinking derived from two policy initiatives in the area of homelessness adopted by successive UK governments since 2002: early assistance to prevent homelessness and use of the private rented sector. The focus shifted away from the concept that local housing authorities should provide accommodation themselves, to the view that local housing authorities should assist people in finding and keeping their own accommodation, in the public or private rented sectors. The local housing authority became more of an enabler helping homeless people, than a provider of housing. Much of the thinking behind H(W)A 2014, Pt 2, has now been implemented for local housing authorities in England in the amendments to

HA 1996, Pt 7, inserted by the Homelessness Reduction Act 2017[1].

[1] For applications for homelessness assistance made to local housing authorities in England on
     or after 3 April 2018.

17.7 The Welsh Government published statistics for 1 April 2016 to
31 March 2017[1]. During that year, 62% of applicants who were owed the
H(W)A 2014, s 66(1), prevention duty[2] had been helped to retain accommodation, or find alternative accommodation available for at least six months.
Prevention had not helped 18% of applicants owed the duty and they had
become homeless. The remaining applicants owed the H(W)A 2014, s 66(1),
prevention duty had either withdrawn their applications (11%), been found
not to have co-operated (5%)[3] or had refused offers (3%)[4]. Of the applicants
owed the H(W)A 2014, s 73(1), relief duty[5], 41% had been helped to find
accommodation that was likely to last for six months, 37% remained homeless
at the end of the H(W)A 2014, s 73(1), relief duty and just over half of those
cases were then accommodated under the H(W)A 2014, s 75(1), main housing
duty[6]. The remaining applicants owed the H(W)A 2014, s 73(1), relief duty
had either withdrawn their applications (13%), been found not to have
co-operated (6%)[7] or had refused offers (2%)[8].

[1] Homelessness in Wales, 2016–17, Statistical First Release, 27 July 2017, Welsh Government.
[2] See **17.45–17.72**.
[3] See **17.195–17.197**.
[4] See **17.66–17.72**.
[5] See **17.73–17.143**.
[6] See **17.146–17.199**.
[7] See **17.195–17.197**.
[8] See **17.108–17.117**.

17.8 The implementation of H(W)A 2014, Pt 2, has been evaluated by both
the Welsh Government[1] and by Crisis[2]. Both reports have been broadly
positive. Local housing authorities and most service users felt that applicants
could be assisted to find alternative accommodation by use of the H(W)A
2014, s 66(1), prevention[3] and H(W)A 2014, s 73(1), relief duties[4]. Crisis
commented that the new approach has had an array of positive impacts,
including re-orientating the culture of local housing authorities towards a
more preventative, person-centred and outcome-focussed approach and providing a much better service to single homeless people in particular. It
expressed concern about the cases which fall out of the system, and particularly about those applicants who were found not to have co-operated.

[1] *Post Implementation Evaluation of the homelessness legislation (Pt 2 of the Housing (Wales)
     Act 2014), Interim Report* (Welsh Government, August 2017).
[2] *The Homelessness Monitor: Wales 2017* (Fitzpatrick, Pawson, Bramley, Wilcox, Watts and
     Wood, Crisis, September 2017).
[3] See **17.45–17.72**.
[4] See **17.73–17.117**.

Prevention and helping the applicant

17.9 In the past, in both England and Wales, duties to provide advice and
assistance were often neglected. The provisions of H(W)A 2014, Pt 2, mean
that local housing authorities in Wales will allocate resources towards early

help, advice and information, so that an applicant can be more effectively helped to find or maintain his or her own accommodation. The *Code of Guidance for Local Authorities on the Allocation of Accommodation and Homelessness*[1] (the Welsh Code') puts it in the following terms:

'The purpose of the legislation is to achieve:
- fewer households experiencing the trauma of homelessness,
- better, more targeted, prevention work,
- increased help, advice and information for households who receive limited assistance under the current legislation,
- more focus on the service user, helping them to address the causes of homelessness and make informed decisions on finding solutions to their housing problem,
- more effective use of the private rented sector as a solution to homelessness,
- a stronger emphasis on co-operation and multi-agency working, and
- greater protection provided for children in households who are homeless or threatened with homelessness as well as additional help for children leaving care[2].'

---

[1] Welsh Government, March 2016, see the CD Rom with this book.
[2] Welsh Code, Introduction to Pt 2 'homelessness'.

17.10 H(W)A 2014, Pt 2, has sought to achieve this by:

- extending the definition of 'threatened with homelessness' to someone who is likely to become homeless within 56 days, rather than the previous period of 28 days, so that there is a longer period for the local housing authority to help to prevent the applicant from becoming homeless[1];
- requiring local housing authorities to provide resources to help the applicant secure his or her own accommodation[2];
- creating duties owed to all applicants who are eligible and either threatened with homelessness or homeless, to help them secure accommodation[3];
- permitting a local housing authority to end any of the duties owed to help applicants if the applicant has either obtained or refused accommodation, including accommodation in the private rented sector provided that it is suitable and is likely to be available for a period of at least six months[4];
- requiring that interim accommodation is secured for an applicant throughout the performance of the H(W)A 2014, s 73(1), relief duty if there is reason to believe that the applicant may be homeless, eligible for help and have a priority need[5]; and
- permitting a local housing authority to bring the H(W)A 2014, s 75(1), main housing duty[6] to an end by making an offer of suitable private rented sector accommodation[7].

---

[1] H(W)A 2014, s 55(4), see **10.144–10.147**.
[2] See **17.36–17.40**.
[3] H(W)A 2014, ss 66(1) and 73(1); see **17.45–17.72** and **17.73–17.143**.
[4] H(W)A 2014, s 67(3) and (4), see **17.62–17.72**; H(W)A 2014, s 74(4) and (5), see **17.104–17.117**.
[5] H(W)A 2014, s 68(1), see **17.118–17.134**.
[6] See **17.146–17.199**.

7   H(W)A 2014, s 76(3)(b) and (4), see **17.173–17.177**.

17.11 The duties to help applicants secure accommodation are owed to nearly all applicants. The only applicants who will not be owed any duty at all are:

- those assessed by the local housing authority as neither homeless nor threatened with homelessness[1]; or
- those assessed as not being eligible for help, whether they are homeless (or threatened with homelessness) or not[2].

1   Defined in H(W)A 2014, ss 55–58 and see Chapter 10.
2   Defined in H(W)A 2014, s 61 and Sch 2 and see Chapter 11.

Accommodation duties

17.12 The duties to help an applicant to secure his or her own accommodation are augmented by duties to accommodate an applicant if he or she has, or if the local housing authority has reason to believe that he or she may have, a priority need. Those duties arise on three occasions.

Immediate duty to secure interim accommodation

17.13 When the applicant makes an application for homelessness assistance, there is a duty to secure interim accommodation for the applicant and all members of his or her household if the local housing authority has reason to believe that the applicant may be homeless, may be eligible for help and may have a priority need. That duty continues until the applicant is notified of the local housing authority's assessment of the applicant's case[1].

1   H(W)A 2014, s 68(1)–(2); Welsh Code, chapter 11. This interim duty is discussed further at **17.118–17.134**.

Continuing duty to secure interim accommodation

17.14 If the applicant is homeless, eligible for help and the local housing authority is satisfied that he or she has a priority need, or has reason to believe that he or she may have a priority need, and the applicant is being helped to secure his or her own accommodation under the H(W)A 2014, s 73(1), relief duty[1], there is a duty to continue to secure interim accommodation that duty is being performed. The interim accommodation duty will generally end either when the local housing authority notifies the applicant of a decision that the H(W)A 2014, s 73(1), relief duty is not owed to him or her[2], or when the applicant has been notified that the H(W)A 2014, s 73(1), relief duty has come to an end[3].

1   See **17.73–17.117**.
2   H(W)A 2014, s 68(2), see **17.128–17.133**.
3   H(W)A 2014, ss 68(3) and 69(3)–(5), see **17.128–17.133**. Note that if the applicant is not to be accommodated under the duty in H(W)A 2014, s 75(1), he or she must be given accommodation for a sufficient period, from the date of notification, to allow him or her a reasonable opportunity of securing his or her own accommodation: H(W)A 2014, s 69(5), see **17.124–17.127**. There are also other circumstances by which the local housing authority can

bring the interim accommodation duty to an end at H(W)A 2014, s 68(7)–(9), discussed at **17.128–17.133**.

Duty to secure accommodation for applicants in priority need

17.15 If the applicant is homeless, eligible for help, has a priority need and the H(W)A 2014, s 73(1) relief duty[1] has come to an end in certain circumstances, then the H(W)A 2014, s 75(1) main housing duty will arise[2].

1   See **17.84–17.102**.
2   See **17.146–17.199**.

17.16 The H(W)A 2014, s 75(1), main housing duty to secure accommodation for applicants who have a priority need, can currently be restricted to applicants who have not been found to have become homeless intentionally[1]. However, H(W)A 2014, Pt 2, permits local housing authorities to decide not to apply the 'becoming homeless intentionally' test[2] and the Welsh Government's intention is that it should be gradually phased out[3].

1   H(W)A 2014, s 75(2)(d), see **17.148**.
2   H(W)A 2014, s 78, see Chapter **13** for the 'becoming homeless intentionally' test.
3   Welsh Code, paras 14.10 and 17.1.

The relevance of the 'becoming homeless intentionally' test?

17.17 H(W)A 2014, Pt 2, seeks to achieve the Welsh Government's aim of gradually abolishing the 'becoming homeless intentionally' test in two ways.

Taking a decision to opt in

17.18 The starting-point is that the 'becoming homeless intentionally' test should not necessarily be applied by local housing authorities From 1 July 2015, local housing authorities have been required to take a positive decision to choose whether they will apply the test. If they do not take a positive decision to do so, then they cannot apply the test[1].

1   H(W)A 2014, s 78.

17.19 The mechanism by which local housing authorities can choose to apply the test is in H(W)A 2014, s 78, and the Homelessness (Intentionality) (Specified Categories) (Wales) Regulations 2015[1]. Guidance is given in chapter 17 of the Welsh Code. Local housing authorities may only apply the test if:

- they have taken, published and notified to the Welsh Government a decision that they will have regard to the 'becoming homeless intentionally' test in relation to applicants who fall within certain specified categories[2]; and
- the Welsh Ministers have specified those categories of person as being categories of applicants to whom the test could be applied in the Homelessness (Intentionality) (Specified Categories) (Wales) Regulations 2015[3].

1   SI 2015/1265 (W 85), see the CD Rom with this book.

[2] The decision must be notified to the Welsh Housing Minister (who will publish it) and published on the local housing authority's own website at least 14 days before the policy is to be implemented: H(W)A 2014, s 78(3) and Homelessness (Intentionality) (Specified Categories) (Wales) Regulations 2015, SI 2015/1265 (W 85), regs 3–4.

[3] H(W)A 2014, s 78(1) and (2) and Homelessness (Intentionality) (Specified Categories) (Wales) Regulations 2015.

17.20 Currently, the categories of person specified in the Homelessness (Intentionality) (Specified Categories) (Wales) Regulations 2015 as those to whom the 'becoming homeless intentionally' test can be applied are all those categories of people who have a priority need[1]. In other words, a local housing authority is free to decide that it will apply the 'becoming homeless intentionally' test to everyone who has a priority need and who it would otherwise have to accommodate under the H(W)A 2014, s 75(1) main housing duty.

[1] Homelessness (Intentionality) (Specified Categories) (Wales) Regulations 2015, reg 2; H(W)A 2014, s 70, see **12.29–12.30**.

17.21 However, a local housing authority could also choose only to apply the test to some of the specified categories of people, but not to all of the categories. The published decision must specify which categories of people the test will be applied to. The Welsh Code advises 'it may be that a Local Authority would want to gradually phase out considering intentionality and would choose to begin with certain groups such as young people, pregnant women and/or families'[1]. It may also be that, in the future, the Welsh Ministers remove some of the current categories from the list of specified categories.

[1] Welsh Code, para 17.7.

17.22 A local housing authority could, of course, decide not to apply the 'becoming homeless intentionally' test at all. Indeed, if, on or after 1 July 2015, a local housing authority has failed to make, notify and publish a decision that it will apply the test, and to which categories of people, then it cannot apply the test[1].

[1] H(W)A 2014, s 78(2); Welsh Code, paras 17.7–17.11.

17.23 Once a local housing authority has published a notice that it will have regard to the 'becoming homeless intentionally' test in respect of any or all of the categories of applicants specified in the Homelessness (Intentionality) (Specified Categories) (Wales) Regulations[1], then it must apply that test to all applicants falling within the specified category or categories[2].

[1] SI 2015/1265 (W 85).

[2] H(W)A 2014, s 78(4). From implementation in April 2015, five local housing authorities elected to disregard the 'becoming homeless intentionally' test in relation to specified groups of people: four in relation to 16- and 17-year-olds, and to care leavers, and one in respect of people who had experienced domestic abuse: *Post Implementation Evaluation of the homelessness legislation (Pt 2 of the Housing (Wales) Act 2014, Interim Report* (Welsh Government, August 2017).

The future of the 'becoming homeless intentionally' test

17.24 The second mechanism by which the Welsh Government aims to abolish the 'becoming homeless intentionally' test is contained in H(W)A 2014, s 75(3). That section has not yet been brought into force and the Welsh Government states that it does not intend to bring it into force until 2019[1].

[1] Welsh Code, para 14.10

17.25 H(W)A 2014, 75(3) provides that the H(W)A 2014, s 75(1), main housing duty[1] will apply to certain categories of applicants, even though the local housing authority might have decided that they have become homeless intentionally[2]. When it does come into force, then the H(W)A 2014, s 75(1) main housing duty, will apply to an applicant if he or she:

- has been found to have become homeless intentionally; and
- does not have suitable accommodation available for his or her occupation or, if there is accommodation, it is not likely that it will be available for occupation for a period of at least six months from notification of the end of the H(W)A 2014, s 73(1) relief duty; and
- is eligible for help; and
- has a priority need; and
- is one of:
  - a pregnant woman or a person with whom the pregnant woman resides or might reasonably be expected to reside; or
  - a person with whom dependent children reside or might reasonably be expected to reside; or
  - a person who was under 21 when his or her application for help was made, or a person with whom such a person resides or might reasonably be expected to reside; or
  - a person who was aged between 21 and 25 when his or her application for help was made, and who was looked after, accommodated or fostered while under the age of 18, or a person with whom such a person resides or might reasonably be expected to reside; and
- was not previously given an offer of accommodation by that local housing authority, as a result of a previous application for help, where the offer was made within five years of the date when the current application for help was made[3].

[1] See **17.146–17.199**.
[2] Which presumes that some local housing authorities will still be publishing their decisions to have regard to the 'becoming homeless intentionally' test in 2019.
[3] H(W)A 2014, s 75(3). Note that the last condition – an offer of accommodation made under a previous application for help – refers to offers being made specifically under H(W)A 2014, s 75, rather than to offers made under any of the duties in H(W)A 2014, Pt 2.

17.26 It will be seen that the intention is that households containing anyone aged under 21, or with former care-leavers aged under 25, should be accommodated under this duty, even though the applicant may have been found to have become homeless intentionally.

Use of the private rented sector

17.27 Until the commencement of H(W)A 2014, Pt 2, local housing authorities in Wales only had a limited ability to use private rented accommodation. H(W)A 2014, Pt 2, permits local housing authorities in Wales to make much greater use of the private rented sector. The Welsh Code states '[f]or many, the private sector will offer the only realistic opportunity of finding the type of property they need in their preferred location and local authorities should ensure that they fully engage with landlords in order to exploit this significant source of housing'[1].

---
[1]   Welsh Code, para 12.31.

17.28 The use of the private rented sector can occur in three different ways:

- if the applicant is helped to secure his or her own accommodation, that is likely to be accommodation in the private rented sector[1];
- the accommodation secured for the applicant under any of the accommodation duties in the H(W)A 2014, Pt 2, could be in the private rented sector[2]; or
- a private rented sector offer can be made to an applicant who is owed the H(W)A 2014, s 75(1), main housing duty with the consequence that the duty can come to an end if the applicant accepts or refuses it[3].

The use of private rented sector accommodation is discussed in more detail under the relevant duties[4].

---
[1]   H(W)A 2014, s 66(1), see **17.118–17.114**; H(W)A 2014, s 73(1), see **17.73–17.117**.
[2]   H(W)A 2014, s 92.
[3]   H(W)A 2014, s 76(3)(b) and (4), see **17.173–17.175**.
[4]   H(W)A 2014, s 66(1), see **17.66–17.72**; H(W)A 2014, s 73(1), see **17.104–17.117**. H(W)A 2014, s 76(3)(b), see **17.173–17.177**.

Duties to assist applicants

17.29 A list of the duties owed to applicants under H(W)A 2014, Pt 2, is set out for ease of reference:

Applicants who are eligible for assistance and threatened with homelessness:

- a duty to help to prevent the applicant from becoming homeless[1];

Applicants who are homeless:

- a duty to help to secure that suitable accommodation is available for his or her occupation[2];

Applicants who are homeless and have a priority need, or the local housing authority has reason to believe that he or she may have a priority need:

- an interim duty to secure accommodation, where reason to believe applicant may have priority need[3]; and

- a duty to help to secure accommodation coupled with the interim accommodation duty where reason to believe the applicant may have priority need[4]; or
- if the applicant has a priority need and has not become homeless intentionally, and is referred to another local housing authority[5]:
  - – a duty to notify the applicant that the local housing authority intends to refer him or her and to inform the applicant of her of the reasons for it[6]; and
  - – an interim duty to secure accommodation until the applicant is notified that the conditions for referral have been met[7]; and
  - – a duty to help to secure accommodation if the conditions for referral are not met[8]; or
  - – a power to secure accommodation if the conditions for referral are met and the applicant requests a review[9];
- an additional duty to secure accommodation when the duty to help to secure accommodation ends in certain circumstances if the applicant has a priority need and has *not* become homeless intentionally or if the local housing authority has decided not to have regard to whether an applicant has become homeless intentionally[10].

Applicants who are homeless and have a priority need, or there is reason to believe they may have a priority need, and who have become homeless intentionally:

- an interim duty to secure accommodation, where reason to believe applicant may have priority need[11]; and
- a duty to help to secure accommodation coupled with the interim accommodation duty where reason to believe that the applicant may have priority need[12]; and
- a duty to secure accommodation for a sufficient period from the date of notification that the H(W)A 2014, s 75(1), main housing duty does not apply[13] to allow the applicant a reasonable opportunity of securing accommodation for his or her occupation[14];
- an additional duty to secure accommodation when the H(W)A 2014, s 73(1), relief duty ends in certain circumstances, if the local housing authority has decided not to have regard to whether an applicant in that category has become homeless intentionally and the applicant has a priority need[15]; and
- on a date to be appointed[16], if the applicant has a priority need relating to pregnancy, dependent children, being under 21 at the date of the application or aged under 25 and had been looked after, accommodated or fostered, a H(W)A 2014, s 75(3) main housing duty when the H(W)A 2014, s 73(1), relief duty ends in certain circumstances[17].

[1]   H(W)A 2014, s 66(1); Welsh Code, chapter 12, see **17.45–17.72**.
[2]   H(W)A 2014, s 73(1); Welsh Code, chapter 13, see **17.73–17.117**.
[3]   H(W)A 2014, s 68(1); Welsh Code, chapter 11, see **17.118–17.134**.
[4]   H(W)A 2014, ss 68(3) and 73(1); Welsh Code, chapter 13, see **17.120–17.123**.
[5]   H(W)A 2014, s 80, see **17.120–17.123**.
[6]   H(W)A 2014, s 63(3) and (4), see **14.162–14.163**.
[7]   H(W)A 2014, s 82(1), see **14.172–14.175** and **17.138–17.145**.
[8]   H(W)A 2014, s 73(1) and s 82(3), see **17.138–17.145**.
[9]   H(W)A 2014, s 82(6), see **17.145**.
[10] H(W)A 2014, s 75(1) and (2), see **17.146–17.199**.

11 H(W)A 2014, s 68(1); Welsh Code, chapter 11, see **17.118–17.134.**
12 H(W)A 2014, s 73(1); Welsh Code, chapter 13, see **17.73–17.117** and **17.120–17.123.**
13 See **17.148.**
14 H(W)A 2014, s 69(3)–(6), see **17.124–17.127.**
15 H(W)A 2014, s 75(1) and (2), see **17.148.**
16 Intended to be in or around 2019: Welsh Code, para 14.10.
17 H(W)A 2014, s 75(3), see **17.24–17.26.**

NOTIFICATION DUTY

17.30 The applicant will know which, if any, of the duties in H(W)A 2014, Pt 2, will be performed by the local housing authority because he or she will have received a notice of the outcome of the local housing authority's assessment of his or her case[1]. That notice will inform the applicant whether the local housing authority will perform any of the duties in H(W)A 2014, Pt 2. The details to be contained in the notice of the outcome of assessment are discussed at CHAPTER 9.

1 H(W)A 2014, s 63(1), see **9.90–9.110.**

17.31 The local housing authority must review its assessment in two cases[1]:

- Case 1: where the local housing authority has concluded that the applicant is threatened with homelessness and that the H(W)A 2014, s 66(1), prevention duty applies[2], and it subsequently appears to the local housing authority that the duty has come or is likely to come to an end because the applicant is homeless[3]; and
- Case 2: where the local housing authority has concluded that an applicant is homeless and that the H(W)A 2014, s 73(1), relief duty applies[4], and it subsequently appears to the local housing authority that the duty has come or is likely to come to an end in circumstances where the H(W)A 2014, s 75(1), main housing duty may be owed[5].

The applicant will be notified of the outcome of the review of the assessment of his or her case.

1 H(W)A 2014, s 62(9); Welsh Code, paras 10.44–10.49 and see **9.151–9.153.**
2 H(W)A 2014, s 66(1), see **17.45–17.72.**
3 H(W)A 2014, s 67(2), see **17.55–17.61.**
4 H(W)A 2014, s 73(1), see **17.73–17.117.**
5 H(W)A 2014, s 74(2), see **17.87–17.96**; H(W)A 2014, s 74(3), see **17.96–17.103**; H(W)A 2014, s 75(1), see **17.146–17.199.**

17.32 In addition, the local housing authority must keep its assessment under review throughout the whole of the period when any of the duties in H(W)A 2014, Pt 2, apply, in case the applicant's circumstances change[1]. If the assessment is reviewed, then any change in the assessment or in the local housing authority's conclusions must be notified to the applicant[2].

1 H(W)A 2014, s 62(8); Welsh Code, para 10.44
2 H(W)A 2014, s 63(1).

17.33 The applicant will also be notified if the local housing authority concludes that any of its duties have come to an end. A duty owed to the applicant will not come to an end until the applicant has been notified of that decision[1]. The notification must comply with H(W)A 2014, s 84[2], which requires:

- that the notification is in writing[3]; and
- that the local housing authority no longer regards itself as subject to the relevant duty, the reasons why it considers that the duty has come to an end, the applicant's right to request a review and the time within which the request must be made[4]; and
- that the details of the steps taken by the local housing authority to help the applicant secure his or her accommodation are set out, where the decision is that the H(W)A 2014, s 73(1), relief duty[5] has come to an end because 56 days have expired, or because the local housing authority is satisfied that reasonable steps have been taken within a shorter period[6].

[1]   H(W)A 2014, ss 67(1), 74(1), 76(1) and 79(1) all explicitly provide that the duty comes an end 'if the applicant has been notified in accordance with' H(W)A 2014, s 84.
[2]   See Welsh Code, paras 15.94–15.98.
[3]   H(W)A 2014, s 84(3).
[4]   H(W)A 2014, s 84(1).
[5]   See **17.73–17.117**.
[6]   H(W)A 2014, s 84(2).

17.34 The notification should be received by the applicant and is only effective on receipt. If the applicant has not received the notification, he or she is treated as having been notified if the notice was made available at the local housing authority's office for a reasonable time for collection by the applicant or by someone on his or her behalf[1].

[1]   H(W)A 2014, s 84(4); Welsh Code, para 15.96.

17.35 The applicant has the right to request a review of any decision that a duty has come to an end[1]. The request for a review must be made before the end of 21 days, beginning from the day on which the applicant is notified of the decision, or such longer period as the local housing authority may agree in writing[2].

[1]   H(W)A 2014, s 85(1)(c), see **19.77–19.80**.
[2]   H(W)A 2014, s 85(5).

THE PREVENTION AND RELIEF DUTIES

Common characteristic

How to 'help to secure' accommodation

17.36 Both duties in H(W)A 2014, ss 66 and 73, contain the words 'help to secure'[1]. This phrase relates both to the H(W)A 2014, s 66(1), prevention duty[2], and to the H(W)A 2014, s 73(1), relief duty[3]. 'Help to secure' does not mean that accommodation must actually be provided, either directly by the local housing authority or through the private rented sector. It quite simply means 'help' so that the applicant can keep or find his or her accommodation. The definition of 'help to secure' in H(W)A 2014, s 65 is that:

'the authority—

(a) is required to take reasonable steps to help, having regard (among other things) to the need to make the best use of the authority's resources;

(b) is not required to secure an offer of accommodation under Pt 6 of the Housing Act 1996 (allocation of housing);

(c) is not required to otherwise provide accommodation[4].'

---

1 H(W)A 2014, s 66(1), see **17.45–17.72**; H(W)A 2014, s 73(1), see **17.73–17.117**.
2 H(W)A 2014, s 66(1), see **17.45–17.72**.
3 In H(W)A 2014, s 73(1), see **17.73–17.117**.
4 H(W)A 2014, s 65.

17.37 Guidance is given in paras 12.7–12.11 of the Welsh Code. The guidance emphasises the limitations of the duty: '[t]his does not mean that the local authority has a duty to secure accommodation and it is vital that the applicant co-operates fully in developing and undertaking a housing solution'[1].

---

1 Welsh Code, para 12.7.

17.38 H(W)A 2014, s 64 contains a non-exhaustive list of examples of the ways in which accommodation might be secured, or an applicant might be helped to secure, accommodation. Guidance is given in paras 12.12–12.55 of the Welsh Code[1].

---

1 A long list of the type of help that could be provided is given in para 12.13 of the Welsh Code, described as 'a minimum set of available interventions'.

17.39 Essentially, H(W)A 2014, s 64, permits the local housing authority:

- to provide the applicant with information and advice, including financial advice, so that he or she can find and keep his or her own accommodation[1];
- to provide the applicant with specific services, such as mediation, grant or loan payments, security measures, or advocacy, to help the applicant find or keep his or her own accommodation[2]; and/or
- to provide the applicant with accommodation, either directly or by arranging for an offer of accommodation from a registered social landlord or private landlord, or even from family or friends[3].

---

1 H(W)A 2014, s 64(2)(h).
2 H(W)A 2014, s 64(2)(a), (b), (c), (e), (f), (i).
3 H(W)A 2014, s 64(2)(g).

17.40 The local housing authority may provide these services itself, or it may arrange for the applicant to receive these services from another organisation or individual, such as debt advice agencies, or mediation providers[1]. However, the local housing authority must ensure that the applicant is provided with these services, and that they are tailored in order to assist the applicant either to retain his or her own home or to find another home. Provision of generic information should not be acceptable.

---

1 H(W)A 2014, s 64(1).

Availability and suitability of accommodation

17.41 Each of the two duties to help the applicant to keep or to secure his or her own accommodation[1] will come to an end if the local housing authority is satisfied that the applicant has suitable accommodation, which is likely to be available for his or her occupation for a period of at least six months, or has refused an offer of such accommodation[2]. There is discussion of the requirement that accommodation must be 'suitable' at CHAPTER 18[3].

1   H(W)A 2014, s 66(1), see **17.45–17.72**; and H(W)A 2014, s 73(1), see **17.73–17.117**.
2   H(W)A 2014, s 67(3) and (4), see **17.62–17.72**; H(W)A 2014, s 74(4) and (5), see **17.104–17.117**.
3   See **18.28–18.31**.

17.42 When H(W)A 2014, Pt 2, specifies that accommodation must be 'available for occupation by the applicant'[1], that means that the accommodation must be both factually and legally 'available' for occupation[2]. Accommodation must be available for occupation not only by the applicant but also by all members of his or her household. In this context, household means any person who normally resides with the applicant as a member of his or her family and any other person who might reasonably be expected to reside with the applicant[3].

1   H(W)A 2014, s 67(3) and (4), see **17.62–17.72**; H(W)A 2014, s 74(4) and (5), see **17.104–17.117**.
2   As defined in H(W)A 2014, ss 55–56, see **10.17–10.65**.
3   H(W)A 2014, s 56(1) and (2), see **10.21–10.32**.

17.43 The phrase 'accommodation is likely to be available for occupation by the applicant'[1] does not specify accommodation of any particular type or tenure. It could be accommodation provided under the local housing authority's allocation scheme, by the local housing authority or a registered social landlord. More frequently, it will be an assured shorthold tenancy in the private rented sector, or even a licence granted by family or friends to occupy accommodation[2].

1   H(W)A 2014, s 67(3) and (4), see **17.62–17.72**; H(W)A 2014, s 74(4) and (5), see **17.104–17.117**.
2   Welsh Code, paras 12.20–12.37.

17.44 The period of 'six months' is the minimum period for which the accommodation must be available. It could, obviously, be available for a longer period. The period starts from the day when the notification of the local housing authority's decision that the duty has come to an end, made under H(W)A 2014, s 84(1), is sent to the applicant or first made available for collection in the local housing authority's office[1]. The Welsh Code advises that, in the case of assured, secure or assured shorthold tenancies, the local housing authority can expect the accommodation to be available for the minimum six-month period[2]. In the case of more informal arrangements, such as accommodation provided by family or friends, or where the applicant has 'returned home', the local housing authority should satisfy itself that there is a realistic expectation that the accommodation will be available for the minimum six-month period[3].

1   H(W)A 2014, s 67(5); H(W)A 2014, s 74(7).

2   Welsh Code, para 15.11.
3   Welsh Code, para 15.10.

Duty to help to prevent homelessness

Applicants entitled to the duty

17.45 This duty is owed to an applicant whom the local housing authority is satisfied is[1]:

- threatened with homelessness[2]; and
- eligible for help[3].

1   H(W)A 2014, s 66(1); Welsh Code, chapter 12.
2   H(W)A 2014, s 55(4), see **10.144–10.147**.
3   H(W)A 2014, s 61 and Sch 2, see CHAPTER 11.

17.46 All applicants who are eligible, and who are likely to become homeless within 56 days, are entitled to this duty. The duty is not restricted to those applicants who have a priority need or who have not become homeless intentionally.

Performing the duty

17.47 The duty is to 'help to secure' that suitable accommodation does not cease to be available for the applicant's occupation[1]. The applicant is to be helped to remain in his or her existing home, if possible. If this is not possible, the applicant should be helped to find another home which he or she can move into without any intervening period of homelessness[2]. It is implicit in the wording of H(W)A 2014, s 66(1), that the existing accommodation is suitable for the needs of the applicant and of his or her household. This is because an applicant who is occupying unsuitable accommodation will normally be homeless, as the accommodation would not be reasonable for him or her to continue to occupy[3].

1   H(W)A 2014, s 66(1).
2   Welsh Code, para 12.4.
3   H(W)A 2014, s 55(3) see **10.73–10.134**.

17.48 As already noted[1], the phrase 'help to secure' is defined in H(W)A 2014, s 65, and further explained in H(W)A 2014, s 64 and Welsh Code, chapter 12. The H(W)A 2014, s 66(1), prevention duty to 'help to secure' does not require the local housing authority to provide accommodation itself, although equally it does not preclude the local housing authority from providing accommodation. More usually, the local housing authority will use some of the services set out as examples in H(W)A 2014, s 64(2), and para 12.13 of the Welsh Code, to help the applicant stay in his or her existing accommodation[2].

1   See **17.36–17.40**.
2   See **17.36–17.40**.

17.49 These services can be provided directly by the local housing authority, or by any other person such as a registered social landlord, voluntary sector organisation or private landlord[1]. The local housing authority's duty is to ensure that the applicant receives those services, from whoever provides them, and that those services are sufficient to help him or her secure that suitable accommodation does not cease to be available.

[1]   H(W)A 2014, s 64(1).

17.50 The Welsh Code advises that 'the first option to be considered should be for the client to remain at the current accommodation where suitable'[1]. This can be achieved by helping with financial options[2], consulting with a landlord to explore the possibility of a tenancy continuing or at least of the tenant remaining for a reasonable period whilst alternative accommodation can be found[3], and/or working with the local housing authority's housing benefit departmetn to prevent delays in responding to claims or to make a Discretionary Housing Payment[4]. The Welsh Code also advises that a homelessness prevention fund is a cost-effective option: '[t]his source of funding can be vital in preventing homelessness or even delaying it in order to allow a household to remain in their home until a settled housing option becomes available'[5].

[1]   Welsh Code, para 12.20.
[2]   Welsh Code, paras 12.20–12.23.
[3]   Welsh Code, para 12.38.
[4]   Welsh Code, paras 12.39–12.55.
[5]   Welsh Code, paras 12.56–12.57.

17.51 If the applicant cannot be assisted to remain in his or her existing home, then consideration should be given to finding alternative accommodation, so that the applicant can move directly, without having to undergo an intervening period of homelessness. The local housing authority is not precluded from accommodating the applicant itself, through its allocation scheme, but the Welsh Code advises that local housing authorities' allocation practices 'should not encourage the view that people have to apply as homeless to the Local Authority in order to obtain a social tenancy'[1]. The local housing authority may assist the applicant to find private rented accommodation, or obtain accommodation from a registered social landlord. Applicants should be assisted to apply to registered social landlords, to consider low cost home ownership schemes and to access the private rented sector[2]. The Welsh Code advises: '[f]or many, the private sector will offer the only realistic opportunity of finding the type of property they need in their preferred location'[3].

[1]   Welsh Code, para 12.20.
[2]   Welsh Code, paras 12.24–12.37.
[3]   Welsh Code, para 12.31.

17.52 Provided the applicant is able to move directly from his or her existing accommodation into new, suitable accommodation, then the local housing authority will have performed its duty to the applicant. Of course, if there is an intervening period when the applicant has no accommodation, the applicant will no longer be threatened with homelessness but will be homeless and the H(W)A 2014, s 66(1), prevention duty will no longer apply[1].

[1]   The duty in H(W)A 2014, s 73(1) to help to secure accommodation will apply, see **17.73–17.117**. There will be a duty to secure interim accommodation if the local housing

authority has reason to believe that the applicant may have a priority need: H(W)A 2014, s 68, see **17.120–17.124**.

17.53 The Welsh Code recognises that certain groups of people are at most risk of homelessness and require special targeted help[1]. In the case of young people who are homeless, there should be joint working with children's services[2]. Specific guidance is provided in respect of people from minority ethnic backgrounds[3], armed forces personnel and veterans[4], hospital patients[5], former prisoners[6], former asylum seekers[7], people with mental impairment or learning disabilities[8], people with mental health needs[9], people with Autistic Spectrum Disorder[10], people with a substance misuse problem[11], and people experiencing domestic disputes, abuse, violence or harassment[12]. The Welsh Code also emphasises that preventing homelessness from recurring is an important aim, and that underlying problems which led to the prospect of homelessness should be addressed in order to provide long-term solutions, and to avoid repeated episodes of homelessness[13].

1   Welsh Code, paras 12.58–12.172.
2   Welsh Code, paras 12.61–12.64, see also *Provision of accommodation for 16- and 17-year-old people who may be homeless* (Welsh Assembly Government, September 2010) on the CD Rom with this book and **12.212–12.214**.
3   Welsh Code, paras 12.65–12.70.
4   Welsh Code, paras 12.71–12.79.
5   Welsh Code, paras 12.80–12.82.
6   Welsh Code, paras 12.83–12.139, with specific guidance on resettlement of women prisoners in paras 12.124–12.130.
7   Welsh Code, paras 12.143–12.145.
8   Welsh Code, para 12.149.
9   Welsh Code, paras 12.150–12.152.
10   Welsh Code, paras 12.153–12.159
11   Welsh Code, para 12.169.
12   Welsh Code, paras 12.161–12.167.
13   Welsh Code, paras 12.168–12.170.

17.54 Obviously, the help provided will cost the local housing authority time and resources. The Welsh Code advises that 'a Local Authority may have regard to making best use of the Authority's resources', and that 'Local Authorities must ensure that resources are allocated effectively and efficiently'[1]. It also advises that resources spent on homelessness prevention could provide 'potential cost savings at a corporate level'[2]. Local housing authorities should not be so conscious of resources that they prioritise applicants who have, or might have, a priority need in order to try to avoid the costs involved in subsequently having to accommodate those applicants under H(W)A 2014, s 75(1)[3]. All applicants should be treated in the same way. However, the Welsh Code notes that applicants who have, or might have, a priority need may be people who are likely to require additional support and resources[4].

1   Welsh Code, paras 12.11, 15.19–15.29.
2   Welsh Code, para 15.20.
3   See **17.146–17.199**.
4   Welsh Code, para 15.25.

17.55 H(W)A 2014, s 66(2), specifically provides that the H(W)A 2104, s 66(1), prevention duty does not affect any right of the local housing authority to secure vacant possession of any accommodation. In other words, if a tenant is due to be evicted from his or her home rented from the local housing authority within 56 days and is eligible for help, the H(W)A 2014, s 66(1), prevention duty will be owed. But that does not prevent the local housing authority from continuing to exercise its functions as landlord and proceeding with an eviction. However, since the duty will be owed, efficient allocation of resources might involve the local housing authority, when exercising its homelessness functions, liaising with its housing department and seeking to prevent the eviction if possible, for example, by assisting to resolve housing benefit problems, by providing debt and budgeting advice, by helping to pay the tenant's rent arrears or by providing any other service that would enable the tenant to remain in his or her home.

How does the H(W)A 2014, s 66(1), prevention duty come to an end?

17.56 H(W)A 2014, s 67 specifies three separate events upon which the H(W)A 2014, s 66(1), prevention duty can come to an end. Those three events are:

- where the local housing authority is satisfied that the applicant has become homeless[1];
- where the local housing authority is satisfied that the applicant is no longer threatened with homelessness and suitable accommodation is likely to be available for occupation by the applicant for a period of at least six months[2]; or
- where the local housing authority is satisfied that the applicant has refused an offer of suitable accommodation[3].

In addition, the duty will come to an end if any of the events specified in H(W)A 2014, s 79(2)–(5) occur[4].

[1] H(W)A 2014, s 67(2), see **17.59–17.61**.
[2] H(W)A 2014, s 67(3), see **17.62–17.65**.
[3] H(W)A 2014, s 67(4), see **17.66–17.72**.
[4] See **17.189–17.197**.

17.57 The H(W)A 2014, s 66(1), prevention duty does not come to an end until the applicant is notified in writing of the local housing authority's decision that it has come to an end. That notification must:

- contain the reasons for the decision;
- inform the applicant that he or she has a right to request a review of that decision; and
- inform the applicant of the 21-day period within which the review request must be made[1].

If no notification is received, or if the notification does not contain all of that information, the H(W)A 2014, s 66(1), prevention duty has not ended[2].

[1] H(W)A 2014, s 84, see **17.33–17.35**.
[2] H(W)A 2014, s 67(1).

17.58 The applicant has the right to request a review of any decision that the H(W)A 2014, s 66(1), prevention duty has come to an end[1]. If the applicant is offered suitable accommodation which is intended to end the duty, the duty will come to an end if he or she accepts it or refuses it, provided that the accommodation is likely to be available for occupation by the applicant for at least six months[2]. In those circumstances, the cautious approach must always be to accept the accommodation and request a review of whether or not it was suitable[3].

1 H(W)A 2014, s 85(1)(c), see **19.77–19.80.**
2 As a result of H(W)A 2014, s 67(3) or (4). See **17.62–17.72.**
3 H(W)A 2014, s 85(3), see **19.100–19.101.**

THE APPLICANT HAS BECOME HOMELESS

17.59 The H(W)A 2014, s 66(1) prevention duty will come to an end if the local housing authority notifies the applicant that it is satisfied that she or he has become homeless[1]. The definition of 'homeless' is in H(W)A 2014, s 55[2]. The accommodation occupied by the applicant during the performance of the H(W)A 2014, s 66(1), prevention duty might have ceased to be available for the applicant, or it might be that the accommodation is no longer reasonable for the applicant and his or her household to continue to occupy.

1 H(W)A 2014, ss 67(1) and (2).
2 See CHAPTER 10.

17.60 Although the H(W)A 2014, s 66(1), prevention duty ends when the local housing authority is satisfied that the applicant has become homeless, this does not mean that the applicant will be abandoned by the local housing authority. The local housing authority must first review its assessment of the applicant's case[1]. Provided that the applicant is still eligible for help[2], he or she will then be owed the H(W)A 2014, s 73(1) relief duty, by which the local housing authority must help to secure that suitable accommodation is available for the applicant. So a duty to help the applicant, by providing the services suggested in H(W)A 2014, s 64(2), and chapter 13 of the Welsh Code, remains[3].

1 H(W)A 2014, s 62(9), Case 1; Welsh Code, para 15.31, see **9.151–9.153** and **17.31.**
2 See CHAPTER 11.
3 See **17.36–17.41.**

17.61 In addition, if the local housing authority is satisfied that the applicant has a priority need, or even if the local housing authority simply has 'reason to believe' that the applicant 'may' have a priority need, the H(W)A 2014, s 73(1), relief duty is augmented by the H(W)A 2014, s 68(3) interim accommodation duty[1]. So the applicant and his or her household must be provided with accommodation whilst they are being helped to secure alternative accommodation. The tests of 'reason to believe' and 'may' each have a low threshold[2]. It is only applicants in respect of whom there is no reason to believe that they may have a priority need who will not be accommodated.

1 See **17.120–17.123.**
2 See **17.118.**

THE APPLICANT IS NO LONGER THREATENED WITH HOMELESSNESS AND SUIT-
ABLE ACCOMMODATION IS LIKELY TO BE AVAILABLE FOR OCCUPATION BY
THE APPLICANT FOR A PERIOD OF AT LEAST SIX MONTHS

17.62 The H(W)A 2014, s 66(1), prevention duty will come to an end if the local housing authority is satisfied that the applicant can remain in his or her existing home and that he or she will be able to stay there for at least six months[1]. Alternatively, the applicant might have been helped to secure new accommodation which is available for at least six months. The accommodation must be suitable for the needs of the applicant and of his or her household[2]. The local housing authority must be 'satisfied' of both limbs:

- that the applicant is no longer threatened with homelessness, in other words that it is not likely that he or she will become homeless within 56 days; and
- that suitable accommodation is likely to be available for occupation by the applicant for at least six months.

[1] H(W)A 2014, s 67(3); Welsh Code, paras 15.33–15.34.
[2] H(W)A 2014, s 67(3), see Welsh Code, chapter 19 and CHAPTER 18.

17.63 This requires something more on the local housing authority's part than simply an assumption. If the applicant has been assisted to remain in his or her existing home, or has gone to stay with friends or family, the Welsh Code advises that the local housing authority should 'satisfy itself that there is a realistic expectation that this solution will last for six months and that it is not intended by the family, friends, extended family or the applicant to be a temporary arrangement'[1]. Where accommodation has been secured on a more formal basis, for example where the applicant has accepted an assured shorthold, secure or assured tenancy, the local housing authority is entitled to expect the accommodation for be available for the minimum period of six months[2].

[1] Welsh Code, para 15.10.
[2] Welsh Code, para 15.11.

17.64 The accommodation must actually be available for the applicant to move into. A promise from a private landlord of the offer of a future tenancy will not be sufficient for the local housing authority to be 'satisfied' that suitable accommodation is likely to be available. Similarly, assisting the applicant to join the local housing authority's waiting list without actually securing accommodation would not bring the duty to an end[1].

[1] Welsh Code, para 15.13.

17.65 The fact that both limbs must be satisfied gives the applicant a minimum of six months' security. The period of six months begins on the day when the local housing authority sends notification of its decision that the duty has come to an end (or first makes the notification available for collection at its office)[1].

[1] H(W)A 2014, s 67(5) and s 84; Welsh Code, para 15.13; see **17.57**.

17.66 The H(W)A 2014, s 66(1),prevention duty can only come to an end where an applicant refuses an offer of accommodation[1] if *all* of the following conditions are met:

- the applicant had been notified in writing of the possible consequences of refusal or acceptance of the offer;
- the applicant has refused an offer of accommodation;
- the local housing authority is satisfied that the offer of accommodation was suitable for the applicant and for his or her household; and
- the local housing authority is satisfied that the accommodation offered was likely to have been available for occupation by the applicant and the members of his or her household for a period of at least six months[2].

[1] H(W)A 2014, s 67(4); Welsh Code, paras 15.35–15.36.
[2] H(W)A 2014, s 67(4).

17.67 The applicant will have received at least two letters containing notifications. The applicant must first be notified of the possible consequences of refusal or acceptance of the offer. The possible consequence of refusal is that the H(W)A 2014, s 66(1), prevention duty will come to an end and that the local housing authority will not necessarily be subject to any duty to accommodate the applicant[1]. The possible consequence of acceptance is that the H(W)A 2014, s 66(1), prevention duty will come to an end. In either case, the applicant will still have the right to request a review of the suitability of the accommodation offered, even though he or she has also accepted it[2].

[1] Welsh Code, para 15.16.
[2] H(W)A 2014, s 85(3); see **19.100–19.101**. The question arises as to what the position is if the reviewing officer agrees with the applicant that the accommodation was not suitable. It must be assumed that the duty in H(W)A 2014, s 66(1) would not have come to an end and would still be owed to the applicant, because a crucial element of the event which brings the H(W)A 2014, s 66(1), prevention duty, that of 'suitable' accommodation would not have been satisfied: H(W)A 2014, s 67(4).

17.68 The first notification is likely to be contained in a letter making the offer of accommodation. The Welsh Code advises that local housing authorities must allow applicants a reasonable period for considering offers of accommodation that will bring H(W)A 2014, Pt 2, duties to an end. It also advises that there is no set reasonable period, and what is a reasonable period will depend upon an applicant's circumstances[1]. Applicants should be given an opportunity to view the accommodation before making any decision or signing any written agreement[2].

[1] Welsh Code, para 15.14.
[2] Welsh Code, para 15.15.

17.69 The second notification received by the applicant will have been the notification of the local housing authority's decision that the H(W)A 2014, s 66(1), prevention duty has come to an end because the applicant refused the offer of accommodation and that all of the circumstances in H(W)A 2014, s 67(4) apply[1]. The applicant has the right to request a review of that decision[2].

[1] H(W)A 2014, s 84(1); Welsh Code, para 15.16, see **17.57**.

² H(W)A 2014, s 85(1)(c), see **19.77–19.81**.

17.70 The offer of accommodation may have come from 'any person'¹, so it may have been an offer of an allocation of a secure, assured or introductory tenancy made by the local housing authority under HA 1996, Pt 6, or an offer of accommodation made by any other landlord (registered social landlord or private landlord) or indeed an offer of accommodation made more informally by a friend or family member². The offer may not have been arranged by the local housing authority. However, the local housing authority will have had some involvement in or knowledge of the offer, because it will have notified the applicant of the consequences of acceptance or refusal.

¹ H(W)A 2014, s 67(4)(a).
² The accommodation would have to be offered on terms that gave the applicant a right to occupy it, as defined in H(W)A 2014, s 55(1), see **10.33–10.65**.

17.71 As with the circumstances for the ending of the H(W)A 2014, s 66(1), prevention duty under H(W)A 2014, s 67(3)¹, the local housing authority must be satisfied that the accommodation would have been suitable for the applicant² and that it would have been available for occupation for a period of at least six months, beginning from the day on which the notification that the local housing authority had decided that the duty had come to an end was sent³.

¹ See **17.56–17.72**.
² See Chapter **18**.
³ H(W)A 2014, s 67(5); Welsh Code, para 15.13.

17.72 If the H(W)A 2014, s 66(1), prevention duty comes to an end for this reason, and the applicant remains threatened with homelessness, then no other duty will be owed to him or her. If he or she later becomes homeless, he or she can make a new application for homelessness assistance.

Duty to help to secure accommodation for homeless applicants

Applicants entitled to the duty

17.73 This H(W)A 2014, s 73(1), relief duty is owed to an applicant whom the local housing authority is satisfied is¹:

•   homeless²; and
•   eligible for help³.

In addition, the local housing authority must not have decided to refer the applicant to another local housing authority⁴.

¹ H(W)A 2014, s 73(1); Welsh Code, chapter 13.
² As defined in H(W)A 2014, ss 55–58, see Chapter **10**.
³ H(W)A 2014, s 61 and Sch 2, see Chapter **11**.
⁴ H(W)A 2014, s 73(1). 'Referral of case to another local housing authority' is in H(W)A 2014, s 80, and discussed at Chapter **14**.

17.74 An applicant need not be literally without a roof over his or her head for the H(W)A 2014, s 73(1), relief duty to be owed. 'Homeless' is defined in

H(W)A 2014, ss 55–58 and includes the possibility that an applicant has accommodation available for his or her occupation, but that the accommodation is not reasonable for him or her to continue to occupy[1], or that an applicant has accommodation, but it is not available for the occupation of all the members of his or her household[2].

[1]   H(W)A 2014, s 55(3), see **10.73–10.134.**
[2]   H(W)A 2014, s 56, see **10.21–10.32.**

17.75 The Welsh Code advises that the H(W)A 2014, s 73(1), relief duty is intended to help people where the H(W)A 2014, s 66(1), prevention duty[1] has not been effective, or where the applicant was already homeless when he or she approached the local housing authority[2]. In the former case, the local housing authority should review its earlier assessment of the applicant's case, on the basis that the applicant is now homeless[3].

[1]   H(W)A 2014, s 66(1), see **17.45–17.72.**
[2]   Welsh Code, para 13.1.
[3]   H(W)A 2014, s 62(9), Case 1; see **9.151–9.153** and **17.31.**

Performing the H(W)A 2014, s 73(1), relief duty

17.76 The H(W)A 2014, s 73(1), relief duty is to 'help to secure that suitable accommodation is available for occupation by an applicant'[1]. '[H]elp to secure that suitable accommodation is available' does not mean that the local housing authority must actually provide accommodation itself, or at all. The local housing authority simply has to 'help' the applicant find suitable accommodation. '[H]elp to secure' is defined in H(W)A 2014, s 65 and examples of how the local housing authority can 'help to secure' accommodation are given in H(W)A 2014, s 64 and in chapter 12 and paras 13.12–13.24 of the Welsh Code[2]. Any accommodation that is found must be available for occupation by the applicant and all members of his or her household[3]. It must also be suitable for the needs of the applicant[4].

[1]   H(W)A 2014, s 73(1).
[2]   See **17.36–17.40** for a detailed discussion.
[3]   H(W)A 2014, s 56, see **10.21–10.32.**
[4]   See CHAPTER **18.**

17.77 The H(W)A 2014, s 73(1), relief duty lasts for up to 56 days, or for a shorter period if one of the events specified in H(W)A 2014, s 74(3)–(5) occurs during the 56-day period[1].

[1]   H(W)A 2014, s 74(2).

17.78 During the 56-day period[1], the local housing authority is expected to take 'reasonable steps' to help the applicant to secure accommodation[2]. Those 'reasonable steps' might be helping to secure an offer of suitable accommodation, from the local housing authority's own stock, or from that of a registered social landlord (and so offered under HA 1996, Pt 6) or a private rented sector offer from a private landlord. Alternatively, the applicant might simply be helped by being given information, advice, loans or small grants to find his or her own accommodation[3]. The Welsh Code advises that a local housing authority that could not show that it had used the 56-day period to take reasonable steps were taken could be subject to a challenge by the applicant (by a request for a review and a subsequent appeal to the county court)[4].

1   See **17.87–17.96**.
2   H(W)A 2014, ss 65 and 73(1); Welsh Code, paras 13.8–13.10.
3   Welsh Code, paras 12.12–12.55 and 13.12–13.21. There is particular guidance for help appropriate to rough sleepers in Welsh Code, paras 13.16–13.21.
4   Welsh Code, para 15.52. There is, in addition, a freestanding right to request a review of whether or not reasonable steps were taken: H(W)A 2014, s 85(2), see **19.81–19.82**.

ACCOMMODATING THE APPLICANT

17.79 The H(W)A 2014, s 73(1), relief duty does not include a duty to accommodate all applicants whilst the is being performed[1].

1   Although, H(W)A 2014, ss 64(1) and 65, read in conjunction with each other, arguably give a local housing authority a *power* to secure accommodation during the performance of the H(W)A 2014, s 73(1), duty.

17.80 If the applicant who is owed the H(W)A 2014, s 73(1), relief duty also has a priority need, or if the local housing authority has reason to believe that he or she may have a priority need, the H(W)A 2014, s 68(1), interim accommodation duty applies during the performance of the H(W)A 2014, s 73(1), relief duty[1]. Only those applicants in respect of whom there is no reason to believe that they may have a priority need will not be accommodated under the H(W)A 2014, s 68, interim accommodation duty.

1   H(W)A 2014, s 68(3), see **17.120–17.123**.

17.81 When the H(W)A 2014, s 73(1) relief duty comes to an end, an applicant who has a priority need and still does not have suitable accommodation available, will generally be accommodated under the H(W)A 2014, s 75(1), main housing duty to secure accommodation for applicants who have a priority need[1]. The local housing authority is obliged to review its assessment of the applicant's case at the point when it appears to the local housing authority that the H(W)A 2014, s 73(1), relief duty has or is likely to come to an end and that the H(W)A 2014, s 75(1), main housing duty might be owed. It is also required to notify the applicant of the outcome of this revised assessment[2].

1   See **17.146–17.199**.
2   H(W)A 2014, s 62(9) Case 2, see **9.151–9.153** and **17.31**.

17.82 If the applicant is not entitled to the H(W)A 2014, s 75(1), main housing duty when the H(W)A 2014, s 73(1), relief duty comes to an end[1], the H(W)A 2014, s 68, interim accommodation duty will come to an end[2]. However, the interim accommodation should not be withdrawn immediately. The accommodation can only be withdrawn upon notice[3].

1   This might be for various reasons: the local housing authority might have satisfied itself that the applicant does not have a priority need; or the applicant might have suitable accommodation available for occupation for a period of six months (H(W)A 2014, s 74(4), see **17.104–17.108**) or the applicant might have refused an offer of suitable accommodation

(H(W)A 2014, s 74(5), see **17.109–17.117**) or the local housing authority might have been satisfied that the applicant had become homeless intentionally (H(W)A 2014, s 75(2)).

2   H(W)A 2014, s 69(3), see **17.128–17.134**.
3   The length of the notice should be provided for in the tenancy or licence agreement; if there is no express provision, then reasonable notice should be given: *Minister of Health v Bellotti* [1944] 1 KB 298, CA. For a recent discussion of the requirements to give notice, see *R (N) v Lewisham London Borough Council* [2014] UKSC 62, [2014] 3 WLR 1548, SC; and *Gibson v Douglas* [2016] EWC Civ 1266, [2017] HLR 11, CA.

17.83 In addition, where an applicant has a priority need, but the local housing authority is satisfied that he or she has become homeless intentionally[1], so the H(W)A 2014, s 75(1), main housing duty will not apply[2], then the accommodation should continue to be secured until the local housing authority is satisfied that it has been available to the applicant for a sufficient period to allow the applicant a reasonable opportunity of securing his or her own accommodation[3]. This provision is modelled on HA 1996, s 190(2)(a), where applicants who have a priority need but who have become homeless intentionally are entitled to interim accommodation for such period as the local housing authority considers will give him or her a reasonable opportunity of securing accommodation[4]. What constitutes a 'sufficient period' is not spelled out, either in H(W)A 2014, Pt 2, or in the Welsh Code.

1   In the circumstance where the local housing authority is having regard to the 'becoming homeless intentionally' test, see H(W)A 2014, s 78, and **13.252–13.255** and **17.18–17.23**.
2   H(W)A 2014, s 75(2)(d), see **17.148**.
3   H(W)A 2014, s 69(4) and (5); Welsh Code, paras 15.42–15.44, see **17.123–17.127**.
4   See **16.81–16.93**.

How does the H(W)A 2014, s 73(1), relief duty come to an end?

17.84 H(W)A 2014, s 74, contains a list of four circumstances in which the H(W)A 2014, s 73(1), relief duty can come to an end[1]. Those circumstances are:

- that a period of 56 days has expired[2];
- that the local housing authority is satisfied that, before the end of the 56-day period, reasonable steps have been taken to help to secure that suitable accommodation is available for the applicant[3];
- that the local housing authority is satisfied that suitable accommodation is available for occupation by the applicant for a period of at least six months[4]; or
- that the local housing authority is satisfied that the applicant has refused an offer of suitable accommodation[5].

In addition, the H(W)A 2014, s 73(1), relief duty will come to an end if any of the events in H(W)A 2014, s 79(2)–(5) occur[6].

1   Welsh Code, paras 15.1–15.29 and 15.47–15.59.
2   H(W)A 2014, s 74(2), see **17.87–17.96**.
3   H(W)A 2014, s 74(3), see **17.97–17.103**.
4   H(W)A 2014, s 74(4), see **17.104–17.108**.
5   H(W)A 2014, s 74(5), see **17.109–17.117**.
6   See **17.189–17.197**.

17.85 The H(W)A 2014, s 73(1), relief duty does not come to an end until the applicant is notified in writing:

- of the local housing authority's decision that the duty has come to an end;
- of the reasons for the decision;
- of the applicant's right to request a review of that decision; and
- of the 21-day period in which to request a review[1].

If no notification is received containing that information, the H(W)A 2014, s 73(1), relief duty continues[2].

1   H(W)A 2014, s 84, see **17.33**.
2   H(W)A 2014, s 74(1).

17.86 The applicant has the right to request a review of any decision that the H(W)A 2014, s 73(1), relief duty has come to an end[1]. If the applicant is offered suitable accommodation which is likely to be available for his or her occupation for a period of at least six months, the duty will come to an end if he or she accepts it[2] or refuses it[3]. In those circumstances, the cautious approach must normally be to accept the accommodation and request a review of whether or not it was suitable[4].

1   H(W)A 2014, s 85(1)(c), see **19.77–19.80**.
2   H(W)A 2014, s 74(4), see **17.104–17.108**.
3   H(W)A 2014, s 74(5), see **17.109–17.117**.
4   H(W)A 2014, s 85(3), see **19.83–19.85** and **19.100–19.101**.

AFTER 56 DAYS

17.87 The H(W)A 2014, s 73(1), relief duty lasts for a maximum period of 56 days[1]. It may come to an end sooner if any of the circumstances in H(W)A 2014, s 74(3)–(5) occur[2].

1   H(W)A 2014, s 74(2); Welsh Code, paras 15.48–15.52.
2   For H(W)A 2014, s 74(3), see **17.97–17.103**. For H(W)A 2014, s 74(4), see **17.104–17.108**. For H(W)A 2014, s 74(5), see **17.109–17.117**.

17.88 However, this does not entitle the local housing authority simply to wait for the end of the 56-day period. It is required actively to help the applicant to secure suitable accommodation during that period[1]. The Welsh Code advises that the local housing authority should identify the reasonable steps to be taken during that period, in partnership with the applicant, to try to secure accommodation[2]. It also advises that, if reasonable steps are not taken, and the duty subsequently comes to an end, the local housing authority could be subject to a challenge[3].

1   H(W)A 2014, ss 65(a) and 73(1).
2   Welsh Code, para 15.50.
3   Welsh Code, para 15.52. Challenges would be brought by the applicant requesting a review of whether or not reasonable steps were taken (H(W)A 2014, s 85(2)) and possibly by a subsequent appeal to the county court: H(W)A 2014, s 88(1), see **19.81–19.82**.

17.89 The 56-day period begins on the day that the applicant is sent the assessment of his or her case carried out by the local housing authority under H(W)A 2014, s 63(1), or on the day when the assessment is made available for the applicant's collection at the local housing authority's office[1].

[1] H(W)A 2014, s 74(6).

17.90 If, at the end of the 56-day period, the applicant remains homeless, or has accommodation available but it is not likely that the accommodation will be available for occupation for at least six months, the applicant will be owed a H(W)A 2014, s 75(1), main housing duty to accommodate him or her if:

- the applicant remains eligible for help;
- the applicant has a priority need; and
- either:
    - the local housing authority has not decided to have regard to the 'becoming homeless intentionally' test; or
    - if the local housing authority has had regard to the 'becoming homeless intentionally' test, it is satisfied that the applicant has not become homeless intentionally[1].

[1] H(W)A 2014, s 75(1) and (2), see **13.252–13.255** and **17.18–17.23**. From 2019, certain groups of applicants who have a priority need will be entitled to the duty to accommodate whether or not they have become homeless intentionally: H(W)A 2014, s 75(3), see **17.24–17.27**.

17.91 The applicant will know if there is a duty to accommodate him or her, because the local housing authority will have reviewed its assessment of the applicant's case and notified him or her of the outcome of that reviewed assessment[1].

[1] H(W)A 2014, s 62(9), Case 2; see **9.151–9.153** and **17.31**.

17.92 An applicant who is not entitled to the H(W)A 2014, s 75(1), main housing duty, usually because he or she does not have a priority need or, where relevant, has been found to have become homeless intentionally[1], will have to find his or her own accommodation. He or she will not be able to make a fresh application for homelessness assistance, unless his or her circumstances have changed materially since the previous assessment was made, or there is new information that materially affects the previous assessment[2].

[1] Or because he or she has accepted or refused suitable accommodation: H(W)A 2014, s 74(4) and (5), see **17.97–17.107**.
[2] H(W)A 2014, s 62(2), see **8.80–8.82** and **8.85–8.91**.

17.93 It may be that the applicant has been accommodated under the H(W)A 2014, s 68(3), interim accommodation duty and the local housing authority is satisfied that he or she has a priority need, but the H(W)A 2014, s 75(1), main housing duty does not apply, because the local housing authority has decided to have regard to the 'becoming homeless intentionally' test and is satisfied that the applicant has become homeless intentionally. At that point, the H(W)A 2014, s 68(3), interim accommodation duty will come to an end[1]. However, the interim accommodation should not be withdrawn immediately. The accommodation can only be withdrawn upon notice[2]. If the local housing authority is satisfied that the applicant has become homeless intentionally, the interim accommodation should continue for a sufficient period to allow him or her a reasonable opportunity of securing his or her own accommodation[3].

1 H(W)A 2014, s 69(3).
2 The length of the notice should be provided for in the tenancy or licence agreement; if there is no express provision, then reasonable notice should be given: *Minister of Health v Bellotti* [1944] 1 KB 298, CA. See *R (N) v Lewisham London Borough Council* [2014] UKSC 62, [2015] AC 1259, SC and *Gibson v Douglas* [2016] EWCA Civ 1266, [2017] HLR 11, CA. For a more detailed discussion, see **16.29–16.30**.
3 H(W)A 2014, s 69(4) and (5); Welsh Code, paras 15.42–15.44, see **17.124–17.128**.

17.94 The notification to the applicant of the decision that the H(W)A 2014, s 73(1), relief duty has come to an end must inform him or her that the local housing authority no longer regards itself as subject to the duty, contain the reasons why it considers that the duty has come to an end, and inform him or her of the right to request a review of that decision and the time in which the request for the review must be made[1]. The notification must also contain details of the steps taken by the local housing authority to help to secure suitable accommodation[2].

1 H(W)A 2014, s 84(1), see **17.33**.
2 H(W)A 2014, s 84(2), see **17.33**.

17.95 The applicant has the right to request a review of the decision that the duty has come to an end for this reason[1]. If the local housing authority had reason to believe that the applicant might have had a priority need, and so had been accommodating him or her during the 56-day period, it has a power to continue to accommodate pending notification of the review decision[2].

1 H(W)A 2014, s 85(1)(c), see **19.77–19.80**.
2 H(W)A 2014, s 69(11), see **17.134**.

17.96 The applicant has a separate right to request a review of whether or not reasonable steps were taken during the 56-day period to help to secure that suitable accommodation would be available for his or her occupation[1]. If the review, or subsequent appeal to the county court, results in a decision that reasonable steps were not taken, then the H(W)A 2014, s 73(1), relief duty will continue to be owed[2]. The new 56-day period will run from the day on which the review decision is notified to the applicant, or from whatever date a county court might order[3].

1 H(W)A 2014, s 85(2), see **19.81–19.82**.
2 H(W)A 2014, s 87; Welsh Code, para 20.33.
3 H(W)A 2014, s 87(2); Welsh Code, para 20.33.

REASONABLE STEPS HAVE BEEN TAKEN TO HELP TO SECURE THAT SUITABLE ACCOMMODATION IS AVAILABLE FOR OCCUPATION BY THE APPLICANT

17.97 If, during the 56-day period, the local housing authority is satisfied that reasonable steps have been taken to help to secure that suitable accommodation is available for occupation by the applicant[1], it can notify the applicant of its decision that the H(W)A 2014, s 73(1) relief duty has come to an end[2].

1 H(W)A 2014, s 74(3); Welsh Code, paras 15.53–15.56.

²   H(W)A 2014, s 74(3).

17.98 Local housing authorities should be cautious about ending the duty for this reason, rather than simply waiting until the 56-day period has come to an end. A local housing authority would have to be able to show that it had 'exhausted all reasonable steps' and should be 'able to evidence that there is no further action that can be taken to help to secure accommodation' for whatever period remains of the 56 days[1]. The Welsh Code advises that these circumstances might arise where the local housing authority had already pursued a number of reasonable steps with the applicant under the H(W)A 2014, s 66(1) prevention duty[2].

[1]   Welsh Code, para 15.53.
[2]   Welsh Code, para 15.53, see **17.45–17.72**.

17.99 If, on notification of the decision that the duty has come to an end for this reason, the applicant remains homeless or has accommodation available but it is not likely that the accommodation will be available for occupation for at least six months, the applicant will be owed a H(W)A 2014, s 75(1), main housing duty if:

- the applicant remains eligible for help;
- the applicant has a priority need; and
- either:
    - the local housing authority has not decided to have regard to the 'becoming homeless intentionally' test[1]; or
    - if the local housing authority has had regard to the 'becoming homeless 'intentionally' test, it is satisfied that the applicant has not become homeless intentionally[2].

[1]   H(W)A 2014, s 78, see **13.252–13.255** and **17.18–17.23**.
[2]   H(W)A 2014, s 75(1) and (2), see **17.148**.

17.100 The applicant will know if there is a H(W)A 2014, s 75(1), main housing duty to accommodate him or her, because the local housing authority will have reviewed its assessment of the applicant's case and notified him or her of the outcome of that review[1].

[1]   H(W)A 2014, s 62(9) Case 2, see **19.151–19.153** and **17.31**.

17.101 It may be that the applicant has been accommodated under the H(W)A 2014, s 68(3), interim accommodation duty and the local housing authority is satisfied that he or she has a priority need, but the H(W)A 2014, s 75(1), main housing duty does not apply, because the local housing authority has decided to have regard to the 'becoming homeless intentionally' test and is satisfied that the applicant has become homeless intentionally. At that point, the H(W)A 2014, s 68(3), interim accommodation duty will come to an end[1]. However, the interim accommodation should not be withdrawn immediately. The accommodation can only be withdrawn upon notice[2]. If the local housing authority is satisfied that the applicant has become homeless intentionally, the interim accommodation should continue for a sufficient period to allow him or her a reasonable opportunity of securing his or her own accommodation[3].

[1]   H(W)A 2014, s 69(3).

2   The length of the notice should be provided for in the tenancy or licence agreement; if there is no express provision, then reasonable notice should be given: *Minister of Health v Bellotti* [1944] 1 KB 298, CA. See *R (N) v Lewisham London Borough Council* [2014] UKSC 62, [2015] AC 1259, SC and *Gibson v Douglas* [2016] EWC Civ 1266, [2017] HLR 11, CA. For a more detailed discussion, see **16.29–16.30**.
3   H(W)A 2014, s 69(4) and (5); Welsh Code, paras 15.42–15.44, see **17.124–17.127**.

17.102 The notification to the applicant of the decision that the duty has come to an end must inform him or her that the local housing authority no longer regards itself as subject to the duty, contain the reasons why it considers that the duty has come to an end, and inform him or her of the right to request a review of that decision and the time in which the request for the review must be made[1]. The notification must also contain details of the steps taken by the local housing authority to help to secure suitable accommodation[2].

1   H(W)A 2014, s 84(1), see **17.33**.
2   H(W)A 2014, s 84(2), see **17.33**.

17.103 The applicant has the right to request a review of the decision that the duty has come to an end for this reason[1]. If he or she has been assessed as having a priority need, and so had been accommodated during the 56-day period, the local housing authority has a power to continue to accommodate pending notification of the review decision[2]. If the review, or subsequent appeal to the county court, contains a decision that reasonable steps were not taken, then the H(W)A 2014, s 73(1), relief duty will continue to be owed[3]. The new 56-day period will run from the day on which the review decision is notified to the applicant, or from whatever date a county court might order[4].

1   H(W)A 2014, s 85(1)(c), see **19.77–19.80**.
2   H(W)A 2014, s 69(11), see **17.134**.
3   H(W)A 2014, s 87; Welsh Code, para 20.33.
4   H(W)A 2014, 87(2).

SUITABLE ACCOMMODATION IS AVAILABLE FOR OCCUPATION BY THE APPLI-
CANT FOR A PERIOD OF AT LEAST SIX MONTHS

17.104 The H(W)A 2014, s 73(1), relief duty will come to an end where the local housing authority is satisfied that[1]:

- the applicant has accommodation available for his or her occupation (and for his or her household);
- the accommodation is suitable for the needs of the applicant and of his or her household[2]; and
- the accommodation is likely to be available for occupation by the applicant for a period of at least six months.

The Welsh Code contains advice on 'suitable accommodation'[3] and on 'likely to last for a period of six months'[4].

1   H(W)A 2014, s 74(4); Welsh Code, para 15.56.
2   See CHAPTER 18.
3   Welsh Code, paras 15.6–15.8 and chapter 19, see also CHAPTER 18.
4   Welsh Code, paras 15.9–15.13. See **17.41–17.44**.

17.105 There is no requirement that the accommodation was found as a result of any steps taken by the local housing authority[1]. No particular types or tenure of accommodation are specified. So long as the accommodation is 'accommodation available for the person's occupation'[2], any type of accommodation may be sufficient, ranging from relatively informal arrangements with family or friends, to private rented sector tenancies, to hostels and more long-term accommodation offered by way of a secure or assured tenancy[3]. However, in the case of more informal arrangements, the local housing authority should be satisfied that the accommodation will genuinely be available for a period of six months[4]. A promise of accommodation is not sufficient[5].

1 H(W)A 2014, s 74(4).
2 H(W)A 2014, s 55(1), see 10.17–10.65.
3 Welsh Code, paras 12.12–12.55 and 13.12–13.15.
4 Welsh Code, para 15.10, see 17.44.
5 Welsh Code, para 15.13.

17.106 The period of six months begins on the day on which the notification of the local housing authority's decision that the duty has come to an end for this reason is sent to the applicant, or is first made available for collection by the applicant at the local housing authority's office[1].

1 H(W)A 2014, s 74(7).

17.107 The notification to the applicant of the decision that the duty has come to an end must inform him or her that the local housing authority no longer regards itself as subject to the duty, contain the reasons why it considers that the duty has come to an end, and inform him or her of the right to request a review of that decision and the time in which the request for the review must be made[1].

1 H(W)A 2014, s 84(1), see 17.33.

17.108 The applicant has the right to request a review of the decision that the duty has come to an end for this reason[1].

1 H(W)A 2014, s 85(1)(c), see 19.77–19.80.

THE APPLICANT REFUSES AN OFFER OF SUITABLE ACCOMMODATION

17.109 The H(W)A 2014, s 73(1), relief duty will come to an end where[1]:

• the applicant had been notified of the consequences of refusal or acceptance of an offer of accommodation;
• he or she refuses an offer of accommodation from any person;
• the local housing authority is satisfied that the accommodation is suitable for the applicant and for his or her household; and
• the local housing authority is satisfied that the accommodation offered is likely to be available for occupation by the applicant and his or her household for a period of at least six months[2].

1 H(W)A 2014, s 74(5); Welsh Code, paras 15.57–15.58.
2 H(W)A 2014, s 74(5).

17.110 The applicant will have received at least two letters containing notifications. The applicant must first be notified of the possible consequences of refusal or acceptance of the offer. The possible consequence of refusal is that the H(W)A 2014, s 73(1), relief duty will come to an end and that the local housing authority will not necessarily be subject to any duty to accommodate the applicant[1]. The possible consequence of acceptance is that the H(W)A 2014, s 73(1), relief duty will come to an end.

[1] Welsh Code, para 15.16.

17.111 The first notification is likely to be contained in a letter making the offer of accommodation. The Welsh Code advises that local housing authorities must allow applicants a reasonable period for considering offers of accommodation that will bring H(W)A 2014, Pt 2, duties to an end. It also advises that there is no set reasonable period, and what is a reasonable period will depend upon an applicant's circumstances[1]. Applicants should be given an opportunity to view the accommodation before making any decision or signing any written agreement[2].

[1] Welsh Code, para 15.14.
[2] Welsh Code, para 15.15.

17.112 The second notification received by the applicant will have been the notification of the local housing authority's decision that the duty has come to an end because the applicant refused the offer of accommodation and that all of the circumstances in H(W)A 2014, s 74(5) apply[1]. The applicant has the right to request a review of that decision[2].

[1] H(W)A 2014, s 84(1); Welsh Code, para 15.16, see **17.33**.
[2] H(W)A 2014, s 85(1)(c), see **19.77–19.80**.

17.113 The applicant must have actually refused the offer. The accommodation offered must also have been suitable for the needs of the applicant and his or her household[1]. The offer of accommodation could have been made by the local housing authority itself, by a registered social landlord, by a private landlord or any other body (for example, a voluntary sector agency operating a hostel). It must have been available for occupation by the applicant for a minimum period of six months[2].

[1] See Welsh Code, chapter 19 and CHAPTER 18.
[2] See Welsh Code, paras 15.9–15.13 for accommodation available for a period of at least six months and see **17.41–17.45**.

17.114 The period of six months begins on the day on which the notification of the local housing authority's decision that the duty has come to an end for this reason is sent to the applicant, or is first made available for collection by the applicant at the local housing authority's office[1].

[1] H(W)A 2014, s 74(7).

17.115 The notification to the applicant of the decision that the duty has come to an end must inform the applicant that the local housing authority no longer regards itself as subject to the duty, contain the reasons why it considers that the duty has come to an end, inform him or her of the right to request a review of that decision and the time in which the request for the review must be made[1].

[1]   H(W)A 2014, s 84(1), see **17.33**.

17.116 Once the duty has come to an end for this reason, the applicant will not be entitled to the H(W)A 2014, s 75(1), main housing duty[1]. If the applicant has been accommodated under H(W)A 2014, s 68(3), interim accommodation duty because he or she had, or the local housing authority had reason to believe that he or she might have had, a priority need, the H(W)A 2014, s 68(3), interim accommodation duty will also come to an end[2].

[1]   H(W)A 2014, s 75(1), see **17.146–17.199**.
[2]   H(W)A 2014, s 69(3), see **17.128–17.133**.

17.117 The applicant has the right to request a review of the decision that the duty has come to an end for this reason[1]. If he or she has been assessed as having a priority need, and so had been accommodated during the performance of the H(W)A 2014, s 73(1) relief duty, the local housing authority has a power to continue to accommodate pending notification of the review decision[2].

[1]   H(W)A 2014, s 85(1)(c), see **19.77–19.80**.
[2]   H(W)A 2014, s 69(11), see **17.134**.

INTERIM ACCOMMODATION DUTIES AND POWERS

The initial duty to secure interim accommodation

17.118 Local housing authorities in Wales are under a duty to secure interim accommodation[1] if they have reason to believe that an applicant *may*:

- be homeless[2];
- be eligible for help under H(W)A 2014, Pt 2[3]; and
- have a priority need[4] for accommodation[5].

The threshold for 'reason to believe' and 'may' is a low one. If there is any doubt, then interim accommodation should be secured[6].

[1]   H(W)A 2014, ss 68(1) and (2); Welsh Code, paras 11.3–11.9.
[2]   H(W)A 2014, ss 55–58, see Chapter 10.
[3]   H(W)A 2014, s 61 and Sch 2, see Chapter 11.
[4]   H(W)A 2014, s 70, see **12.29** and **12.195–12.228**.
[5]   H(W)A 2014, s 68(2).
[6]   Welsh Code, para 11.4. See **8.75–8.76**.

17.119 The H(W)A 2014, s 68(1), interim accommodation duty only comes to an end if one of the events specified at H(W)A 2014, s 69, occurs[1]. Where a local housing authority decides that the H(W)A 2014, s 68(1) interim accommodation duty is not owed to the applicant, it must notify the applicant of that decision in writing[2]. The notification should contain the local housing authority's reasons for coming to that decision, and inform the applicant of his or her right to request a review of the decision and of the time within which such a request must be made[3]. The applicant has a right to request a review of that decision and, subsequently, to appeal to the county court on a point of law[4].

¹ See **17.128–17.33**.
² H(W)A 2014, s 69(1).
³ H(W)A 2014, s 84(1).
⁴ H(W)A 2014, s 85(1)(c) and s 88(1), see **19.77–19.80**.

The additional interim duty to secure accommodation for homeless applicants in priority need

17.120 The H(W)A 2014, s 68(1) interim accommodation duty also applies to an applicant:

- to whom the H(W)A 2014, s 73(1) relief duty[1] applies;
- where the local housing authority has reason to believe that the applicant has a priority need;
- where the local housing authority is satisfied that the applicant has a priority need; or
- where the applicant has been referred from a local housing authority in England under HA 1996, s 198(1) 'conditions for referral'[2].

¹ See **17.73–17.117**.
² H(W)A 2014, s 68(3); Welsh Code para 11.7.

17.121 This requires a local housing authority to accommodate an applicant in short-term accommodation[1]. Simultaneously, the local housing authority is helping the applicant to secure longer-term accommodation[2].

¹ H(W)A 2014, s 74(2); Welsh Code, paras 15.48–15.52.
² The longer-term accommodation should be available for occupation by the applicant for at least six months: H(W)A 2014, s 74(4) and (5); Welsh Code para 15.56, see **17.73–17.117**.

17.122 This duty will come to an end when the local housing authority notifies the applicant that the H(W)A 2014, s 73(1), relief duty comes to an end[1].

¹ H(W)A 2014, s 69(3); Welsh Code, paras 15.42–15.45. This does not exclude the local housing authority deciding that the duty has come to an end as a result of any of the other nine circumstances in H(W)A 2014, ss 69 and 79 occurring, see **17.128–17.133** and **17.189–17.197**.

17.123 If, on notification of the decision that the H(W)A 2014, s 68(1), interim accommodation duty has come to an end, the applicant remains homeless, the applicant will be owed a H(W)A 2014, s 75(1), main housing duty if:

- the applicant remains eligible for help;
- the applicant has a priority need; and
- either:
  - the local housing authority has not decided to have regard to the 'becoming homeless intentionally' test[1]; or

- if the local housing authority has had regard to the 'becoming homeless 'intentionally' test, it is satisfied that the applicant has not become homeless intentionally[2].

[1] H(W)A 2014, s 78, see **13.252–13.255** and **17.18–17.23**.
[2] H(W)A 2014, s 75(1) and (2), see **17.148**.

Interim accommodation for applicants who have a priority need and who have become homeless intentionally

17.124 If the applicant has a priority need[1], but the local housing authority is satisfied that he or she became homeless intentionally, then the H(W)A 2014, s 68(1), interim accommodation duty will not come to an end until the local housing authority is satisfied that interim accommodation has been secured for the applicant for a sufficient period to allow him or her a reasonable opportunity of securing accommodation for his or her own occupation[2]. The effect is that the local housing authority should continue to secure short-term accommodation for an applicant who has a priority need but became homeless intentionally, while the applicant makes efforts to secure his or her own accommodation.

[1] H(W)A 2014, s 69(3)–(6); Welsh Code, paras 15.42–15.45.
[2] H(W)A 2014, s 69(4) and (5). See discussion in relation to local housing authorities in England at **16.81–16.93**.

17.125 The period of further accommodation starts from the date of notification to the applicant that the H(W)A 2014, s 75(1), main housing duty was not owed to him or her[1]. The length of the period cannot be less than the 56-day period during which the local housing authority was subject to the H(W)A 2014, s 73(1), relief duty[2]. It could be a longer period, because the local housing authority must be satisfied that the accommodation had been available for a 'sufficient' period to allow the applicant a reasonable opportunity of securing accommodation for his or her occupation. The Welsh Code advises that the period for which the accommodation is available after the ending of the H(W)A 2014, s 73(1), relief duty must be 'of a reasonable time frame'[3]. While the language at H(W)A 2014, s 69(3)–(6), is slightly different to that in HA 1996, s 190(2)(a), useful reference can be made to the case-law decided in respect of that latter duty[4].

[1] H(W)A 2014, s 69(5).
[2] H(W)A 2014, 69(5) and (6). For two useful examples, see Welsh Code, paras 15.43–15.44.
[3] Welsh Code, para 15.42.
[4] See **16.81–16.93**.

17.126 When the provisions of H(W)A 2014, s 75(3), are brought into force[1], the 'becoming homeless intentionally' test will be abolished for applicants who have a priority need related to children or young people in the household[2]. At that point, an additional set of applicants will fall within this duty to secure accommodation for a sufficient period. The duty will apply where the local housing authority is satisfied that no H(W)A 2014, s 75(1), main housing duty because the local housing authority had previously secured an offer of accommodation for the applicant within the preceding five years[3].

[1] Intended by the Welsh Ministers to be in 2019, see **17.24–17.26**.
[2] Once in force, H(W)A 2014, s 75(1) and (3) will confer a duty to accommodate applicants who became homeless intentionally, who do not have suitable accommodation available for their occupation (or any such accommodation is not available for a period of six months), who are eligible for help and who have a priority need and because they are either a pregnant woman or a person with whom she resides or might reasonably be expected to reside, or a person with whom a dependent child resides or might reasonably be expected to reside, or a person who was under the age of 21 when the application for help was made or a person with whom such a person resides or might reasonably be expected to reside, or a person aged between 21 and 25 years when the application was made who was previously looked after, accommodated or fostered or a person with whom such a person resides or might reasonably be expected reside. See **17.24–17.26**.
[3] H(W)A 2014, s 69(4)(b), s 75(3)(f).

17.127 Where a local housing authority in Wales decides that the H(W)A 2014, s 68(1), interim accommodation duty has ended or is not owed to the applicant, it must notify the applicant in writing of its decision, the reasons for that decision, of the applicant's right to request a review of that decision and of the time within such a request must be made[1]. The applicant has a right to request a review of that decision and subsequently to appeal to the county court on a point of law[2].

[1] H(W)A 2014, s 69(1), s 84(1), see **17.130–17.135**.
[2] H(W)A 2014, ss 85(1)(b) and (c) and 88(1), see **19.74–19.80**.

Ending the duty to secure interim accommodation

17.128 H(W)A 2014, ss 69 and 79, contain the only circumstances in which the H(W)A 2014, s 68, interim accommodation duty comes to an end[1]. A local housing authority cannot decide that the duty has come to an end for any reason that is not provided for in those sections.

[1] H(W)A 2014, s 69; Welsh Code, paras 15.38–15.46.

17.129 The circumstances in which the H(W)A 2014, s 68, interim accommodation duty can come to an end are:

(1) the local housing authority has decided that no H(W)A 2014, s 73(1, relief duty is owed to the applicant[1];
(2) the H(W)A 2014, s 73(1) relief duty has come to an end[2];
(3) the applicant refuses an offer of accommodation secured under H(W)A 2014, s 68, which the local housing authority is satisfied is suitable for the applicant, and the applicant had been notified of the possible consequence of refusal[3];
(4) the local housing authority is satisfied that the applicant has become homeless intentionally from suitable interim accommodation made available for his or her occupation under H(W)A 2014, s 68[4];
(5) the local housing authority is satisfied that the applicant voluntarily ceased to occupy, as his or her only or principal home, suitable interim accommodation made available for his or her occupation under H(W)A 2014, s 68[5];

(6)   the local housing authority is no longer satisfied that the applicant is eligible for help[6];

(7)   the local housing authority is satisfied that a mistake of fact led to the applicant being notified that a duty was owed to him or her[7];

(8)   the local housing authority is satisfied that the applicant has withdrawn his or her application[8];

(9)   the local housing authority is satisfied that the applicant is unreasonably failing to co-operate with it in connection with the exercise of its functions under H(W)A 2014, Pt 2[9]; or

(10) the local housing authority has notified the applicant that it intends to notify, or has notified, another local housing authority in Wales or England of its opinion that the conditions are met for the referral of the applicant's case to that other authority[10].

[1]   H(W)A 2014, s 69(2). For the H(W)A 2014, s 73 duty, see **17.73–17.117**.

[2]   H(W)A 2014, s 69(3); Welsh Code, paras 15.41–15.44. It may be that the applicant is then accommodated under the duty in H(W)A 2014, s 75(1), see **17.146–17.199**. If the applicant has a priority need but the local housing authority is satisfied that he or she has become homeless intentionally, the duty to accommodate in H(W)A 2014, s 75(1) will not apply, but the local housing authority must continue to secure accommodation for a sufficient period to allow the applicant a reasonable opportunity of securing his or her accommodation: H(W)A 2014, s 69(3)–(6). See **17.124–17.127** for further discussion.

[3]   H(W)A 2014, s 69(7). For the equivalent power for local housing authorities in England, see *R (Brooks) v Islington London Borough Council* [2015] EWHC 2657 (Admin), [2016] HLR 2, Admin Ct; and **16.66–16.69**

[4]   H(W)A 2014, s 69(8). For 'becoming homeless intentionally', see Chapter 13.

[5]   H(W)A 201, s 69(9).

[6]   H(W)A 2014, ss 69(12) and 79(2) and see **17.192**. For 'eligible for help', see Chapter 11.

[7]   H(W)A 2014 ss 69(12) and 79(3) and see **17.193**.

[8]   H(W)A 2014, ss 69(12) and 79(4) and see **17.194**.

[9]   H(W)A 2014 ss 69(12) and 79(5) and see **17.195–17.197**.

[10] H(W)A 2014, s 82(1). In this case, a duty to accommodate the applicant until notification of any decision whether the conditions for referral are met arises: H(W)A 2014, s 82(1) and Welsh Code paras 18.22–18.26. See **17.120–17.123**.

17.130 If the local housing authority has decided that the H(W)A 2014, s 68(1), interim accommodation duty has come to an end because of one of those circumstances, it must notify the applicant in accordance with H(W)A 2014, s 84[1].The H(W)A 2014, s 68(1), interim accommodation duty does not end until the applicant has received that notification[2].

[1]   H(W)A 2014, s 69(1); Welsh Code, paras 15.93–15.98.

[2]   H(W)A 2014, s 69(1).

17.131 The notification must be in writing and must inform the applicant:

(1)   that the local housing authority no longer regards itself as being subject to the duty;

(2)   of the reasons why it considers that the duty has come to an end;

(3)   of the applicant's right to request a review of that decision; and

(4)   of the time within which such a request must be made[1].

[1]   H(W)A 2014, s 84(1) and (3).

17.132 If the written notice is not received by an applicant, he or she may be treated as having been notified if the notice is made available at the local housing authority's office for a reasonable period for collection by the applicant or on the applicant's behalf[1].

[1] H(W)A 2014. s 84(4); Welsh Code, para 15.96.

17.133 The applicant has the right to request a review of a decision that the H(W)A 2104, s 68(1), interim accommodation duty has come to an end[1]. If the review confirms the original decision, the applicant has the right to appeal to the county court on a point of law[2].

[1] H(W)A 2014, s 85(1)(c).
[2] H(W)A 2014, s 88(1).

Power to secure interim accommodation pending a statutory review

17.134 Local housing authorities in Wales have a power to secure, or to continue to secure, that suitable accommodation is available for an applicant's occupation pending a decision on a review[1]. When deciding whether or not to exercise that power, a local housing authority should consider:

- the merits of the applicant's case on review, and the extent to which it could be said that the decision was either one that appears to be contrary to the merits of the case, or one that required a very fine balance of judgment that could have gone either way;
- whether any new material, information or argument has been put to the local housing authority, which could have a real effect on the decision under review;
- the personal circumstances of the applicant;
- the consequences to the applicant of a decision not to exercise the discretion to accommodate;
- the public sector equality duty[2];
- the local housing authority's duty to safeguard and promote the welfare of any children; and[3]
- any other relevant considerations.

These factors are colloquially known as 'the *Mohammed* factors'[4] and are discussed further at **16.240–16.246**.

[1] H(W)A 2014, s 69(11); Welsh Code, paras 20.29–20.32. The power in H(W)A 2014, s 69(1)), is in identical terms to the power in HA 1996, s 188(3), see **16.240–16.246**.
[2] Equality Act 2010, s 149. See **9.81–9.83, 12.91, 12.100, 13.70** and **18.65–18.68**.
[3] Welsh Code, para 20.30; Children Act 2004, s 28(2); *Nzolameso v Westminster City Council* [2015] UKSC 22, [2015] 2 All ER 942, [2015] HLR 22, SC.
[4] *R v Camden London Borough Council ex parte Mohammed* (1998) 30 HLR 315, QBD.

Power to secure interim accommodation pending an appeal to the county court

17.135 Local housing authorities in Wales have a power to secure, or continue to secure, that suitable accommodation is available for an applicant's occupation pending any appeal to the county court[1]. The power is only available where the local housing authority has previously owed one of the following duties to the applicant:

(1) the H(W)A 2014, s 68(1) interim accommodation duty[2];

(2) the H(W)A 2014, s 75(1), main housing duty[3]; or

(3) the duty to secure accommodation pending referral under the 'conditions for referral' provisions[4].

[1] H(W)A 2014, s 88(5) ; Welsh Code, paras 20.42–20.45. The power in H(W)A 2014, s 88(5)), is in almost identical terms to the power in HA 1996, s 204(4) for local housing authorities in England discussed further at **16.258–16.277**.
[2] H(W)A 2014, s 68(1), see **17.118–17.119**.
[3] H(W)A 2014, s 75(1), see **17.146–17.199**.
[4] H(W)A 2014, s 82, see **17.120–17.123** and **17.138–17.145**.

17.136 The common thread running through this list is that the applicant either has, or the local housing authority initially had reason to believe that he or she might have, a priority need. If the local housing authority had not been subject to any of those duties, there is no power in H(W)A 2014, Pt 2, for a local housing authority to secure interim accommodation pending appeal.

17.137 Any challenge to a local housing authority's refusal to secure accommodation pending the determination of a county court appeal must be brought by a separate appeal, also on a point of law, to the county court under H(W)A 2014, s 89[1].

[1] See **19.280–19.292**.

Powers and duties to secure interim accommodation for applicants referred under the conditions for referral provisions

17.138 Where a local housing authority in Wales concludes that the conditions for referral[1] to another local housing authority are met[2], it must notify the applicant of that decision[3]. The notification must be in writing and contain the reasons for the local housing authority's decision, as well as informing the applicant of his or her right to request a review of the decision and of the time within the request for a review must be made[4]. The local housing authority will also notify the other local housing authority of its opinion that the conditions for referral have been met[5].

[1] H(W)A 2014, ss 82–83; Welsh Code, paras 18.22–18.26.
[2] H(W)A 2014, s 80, see CHAPTER **14**.
[3] H(W)A 2014, ss 82(2) and 84(1), see **14.162–14.163**.
[4] H(W)A 2014, s 84(1).
[5] H(W)A 2014, s 80(1) and (2).

17.139 Once that notification to the applicant has been received, the H(W)A 2014, s 68(1), interim accommodation duty will come to an end. In these cases, the H(W)A 2014, s 73(1) relief duty will not arise[1]. Instead, the local housing authority will be under a duty to continue to secure that suitable accommodation is available for occupation by the applicant until the applicant is notified of the subsequent decision – either by agreement between the two local housing authorities or after resolution of the dispute under the procedure in the Homelessness (Decisions on Referrals) Order 1998[2] – determining whether the conditions for referral are met, or not[3].

[1] H(W)A 2014, s 82(1).
[2] SI 1998/1578, see **14.176–14.190**.

³   H(W)A 2014, s 82(1).

17.140 The applicant will then receive a second notification. That notification must be given by the first local housing authority[1]. It must contain reasons for the decision that the conditions for referral are met, or are not met, and inform the applicant of his or her right to request a review and of the time within which to make the request[2].

¹   H(W)A 2014, s 82(2).
²   H(W)A 2014, s 84(1).

17.141 If the second notification informs the applicant that it has been decided that the conditions for referral are not met, then the interim accommodation duty falls away and is replaced by the H(W)A 2014, s 73(1) relief duty[1] and the H(W)A 2014, s 68(1), interim accommodation duty for applicants who have, or in respect of whom the local housing authority has reason to believe may have, a priority need under H(W)A 2014, s 68(3)[2].

¹   See **17.73–17.117**.
²   H(W)A 2014, ss 68(3) and 82(3), see **17.120–17.123**.

17.142 However, if the applicant is notified that both local housing authorities agree (or it has been determined by arbitration) that the conditions for referral are met, then the duty to accommodate on the first local housing authority comes to an end[1].

¹   H(W)A 2014, s 82(5).

17.143 If the applicant has been referred to another local housing authority in Wales, that second local housing authority will be under the H(W)A 2014, s 73(1) relief duty[1] and any H(W)A 2014, s 68(1), interim accommodation duty[2].

¹   See **17.73–17.117**.
²   H(W)A 2014, s 82(4). The H(W)A 2014, s 68(1), interim accommodation duty will be owed
    if the second local housing authority has reason to believe that the applicant may have a
    priority need.

17.144 If the applicant has been referred to a local housing authority in England, that local housing authority will be under the main housing duty in HA 1996, s 193(2)[1].

¹   HA 1996, s 201A(2). For HA 1996, s 193(2), main housing duty on local housing authorities
    in England, see **16.94–16.199**.

17.145 If the applicant requests a review of the decision to refer, and asks to remain in accommodation secured by the first local housing authority while the review is considered, the first local housing authority has no further duty to accommodate. However, it does have a power to continue to secure interim accommodation pending review and, later, pending any appeal to the county court[1]. The refusal to exercise that power cannot be subject of a statutory review or a subsequent appeal to the county court. Any challenge would have to be by way of judicial review.

[1]   H(W)A 2014, ss 82(6) and 88(5). The Welsh Code recommends that applicants who may have a priority need are accommodated whilst their request for a review is being considered: para 18.25.

DUTY TO SECURE ACCOMMODATION FOR APPLICANTS IN PRIORITY NEED

Overview of the duty

17.146 This duty replaces the previous 'main housing duty' in HA 1996, s 193(2)[1]. It is intended to provide a safety-net for applicants who are homeless, eligible for help and have a priority need[2]. However, the duty is not owed to certain applicants, even though they fulfil those conditions. Those applicants who are not owed the H(W)A 2014, s 75(1) duty are:

*   those who have been successfully helped to secure their own accommodation as a result of the H(W)A 2014, s 66(1) prevention duty[3]. and/or H(W)A 2014, s 73(1) relief duty[4];
*   those who have refused offers of suitable accommodation made under the H(W)A 2014, s 73(1) relief duty[5]; or
*   if the local housing authority is having regard to the 'becoming homeless intentionally' test, and is satisfied that the applicant has become homeless intentionally[6].

[1]   See **16.94–16.199**.
[2]   H(W)A 2014, s 75(1); Welsh Code, chapter 14.
[3]   See **17.62–17.65**.
[4]   See **17.104–17.108**.
[5]   H(W)A 2014, ss 74(5) and 75(1), see **17.109–17.117**.
[6]   H(W)A 2014, s 75(2)(d), see **13.252–13.255** and **17.19–17.23**.

17.147 Provision of accommodation under this duty will not be for the long-term. It is expected that the applicant will either find his or her own accommodation or, more frequently, will be made a private rented sector offer or an offer of a secure or an assured tenancy. Provided that any of those offers is of suitable accommodation[1], the H(W)A 2014, s 75(1), main housing duty will come to an end if the applicant accepts or refuses such an offer[2].

[1]   H(W)A 2014, s 76(2) and (3) and chapter 19 of the Welsh Code; see CHAPTER 18.
[2]   H(W)A 2014, s 76(2) for acceptance, see 17.161–17.164. H(W)A 2014, s 76(3) for refusal, see 17.165–17.179.

Applicants entitled to the duty

17.148 The H(W)A 2014, s 75(1), main housing duty is owed to applicants:

*   who were previously owed the H(W)A 2014, s 73(1) relief duty[1];
*   that duty came to an end as a result of either:
    –   the ending of the 56-day period[2];

- the local housing authority being satisfied, before the end of the 56-day period, that reasonable steps had been taken to help to secure that suitable accommodation was available for the occupation by the applicant[3];

- the local housing authority is satisfied that the applicant either:
  - does not have suitable accommodation available for occupation;
  - has suitable accommodation but it is not likely that the accommodation will be available for his or her occupation for a period of at least six months from the date of notification that the duty in H(W)A 2014, s 73 does not apply;

- the local housing authority is satisfied that the applicant is eligible for help[4];

- the local housing authority is satisfied that the applicant has a priority need[5]; and

- if the local housing authority is having regard to the 'becoming homeless intentionally' test[6], it is not satisfied that the applicant became homeless intentionally[7].

1 See **17.73–17.117**.
2 H(W)A 2014, s 74(2), see **17.87–17.96**.
3 H(W)A 2014 s 74(3), see **17.97–17.103**.
4 H(W)A 2014, s 61 and Sch 2. See CHAPTER 11.
5 H(W)A 2014, s 70; see **12.29** and **12.195–12.228**.
6 H(W)A 2014, s 78; see **13.252–13.255** and **17.18–17.23**.
7 H(W)A 2014, s 75(2).

17.149 It can be expected that anyone entitled to accommodation under H(W)A 2014, s 75(1), would already have been accommodated under the interim duty in H(W)A 2014, s 68(3)[1]. That interim accommodation duty will come to an end when the duty in H(W)A 2014, s 73(1), comes to an end[2].

1 Because the interim accommodation duty is owed to applicants whom the local housing authority is either satisfied have a priority need or where the local housing authority has reason to believe that they have a priority need: H(W)A 2014, s 68(3), see **17.120–17.123**.
2 H(W)A 2014, s 69(3), see **17.128–17.133**. Welsh Code, para 15.41, advises that the same accommodation can be used for performance of both the interim accommodation duty in H(W)A 2014, s 68(1), and performance of the subsequent H(W)A 2014, s 75(1), duty, provided that the accommodation remains suitable for the applicant and for the members of his or her household.

17.150 H(W)A 2014, s 75(3) is not due to come into force until 2019[1]. Once it does come into force, the duty to accommodate in H(W)A 2014, s 75(1), will be owed to certain categories of people who have a priority need, generally because they have dependent children, or are pregnant or young people, whether or not they have become homeless intentionally[2].

1 Welsh Code, para 14.10.
2 H(W)A 2014, s 75(3), see **17.24–17.26**.

Performing the duty

17.151 The accommodation secured under the H(W)A 2014, s 75(1), main housing duty will not be long-term accommodation, in the form of a secure or assured tenancy. It might be an assured shorthold tenancy. Accommodation secured under this duty must always be suitable for the needs of the applicant and of his or her household[1].

1   H(W)A 2014, s 64(1); see Welsh Code, chapter 19; and Chapter **18**.

Charging for accommodation

17.152 The local housing authority can secure accommodation for applicants free of charge. More usually, it will require an applicant to pay whatever amount the local housing authority considers he or she can reasonably afford. The provisions permitting a local housing authority to require an applicant to pay charges are in H(W)A 2014, s 90 and are identical[1] to the equivalent provision in HA 1996, s 205(2)[2].

1   Save that the wording is in plainer English.
2   See **16.22–16.27** for discussion.

17.153 Accommodation secured under this duty must be affordable for the applicant. If it is not affordable, it will not be suitable[1]. Guidance on charges and on affordability is given in paras 11.12–11.14 and 19.26–19.29 of the Welsh Code.

1   H(W)A 2014, s 59(2), see **18.45–18.47**.

Out of area placements

17.154 There is a presumption that the local housing authority will secure, or help to secure, accommodation for the applicant in its own district[1]. If it does not, it is under an obligation to notify the local housing authority in which the accommodated is situated[2]. These provisions are identical to those in HA 1996, s 208[3]. The Welsh Code contains advice on location in paras 19.13–19.25.

1   H(W)A 2014, s 91(1).
2   H(W)A 2014, s 91(2).
3   See **18.48**.

Terms and tenure

17.155 If accommodation is provided directly by the local housing authority, it will not be under a secure tenancy or contract[1].

1   Housing Act 1985, Sch 1, para 4 and (when in force), Renting Homes (Wales) Act 2016, Sch 2, Pt 4.

17.156 Where accommodation is provided by a private landlord, it will normally be on the terms of an assured shorthold tenancy. When the Renting Homes (Wales) Act 2016 is brought into force, Sch 2, Pt 4, will provide that accommodation provided by a private landlord under any of the accommodation duties in H(W)A 2014, Pt 2, including the H(W)A 2014, s 75(1) duty, will not normally be an occupation contract(and so have the rights provided for in the Renting Homes (Wales) Act 2016) for the first 12 months of the contract, unless the landlord gives earlier notice to the tenant that it is to be an occupation contract.

17.157 The terms of any tenancy are a matter of negotiation between the prospective tenant and landlord. If the landlord offers standard terms and conditions, the provisions of Pt 2 of the Consumer Rights Act 2015 are likely to apply[1].

1   Part 2, Consumer Rights Act 2015. See **18.99–18.107**.

How does the duty come to an end?

17.158 H(W)A 2014, s 76 specifies four separate circumstances by which the duty in H(W)A 2014, s 75(1), can come to an end[1]. Those circumstances are:

- that the applicant accepts an offer of suitable accommodation[2];
- that the applicant refuses an offer of suitable accommodation[3];
- that the local housing authority is satisfied that the applicant has become homeless intentionally from suitable interim accommodation made available for the applicant's occupation[4]; or
- that the local housing authority is satisfied that the applicant has voluntarily ceased to occupy as his or her only or principal home, suitable interim accommodation made available for the applicant's occupation[5].

1   H(W)A 2014, s 76; Welsh Code, paras 15.61–15.78.
2   H(W)A 2014, s 76(2), see **17.161–17.164**.
3   H(W)A 2014, s 76(3), see **17.165–17.179**.
4   H(W)A 2014, s 76(6), see **17.180–17.184**.
5   H(W)A 2014, s 76(7), see **17.185–17.188**.

17.159 In addition, the duty will come to an end if any of the events in H(W)A 2014, s 79(2)–(5) occur[1].

1   See **17.189–17.197**.

17.160 The duty does not come to an end until the applicant is notified in writing:

- of the local housing authority's decision that the duty has come to an end;
- of the reasons for the decision;
- of the applicant's right to request a review of that decision; and
- of the 21-day period in which to request a review[1].

If no notification is received containing that information, the duty continues[2]. The applicant has the right to request a review of the local housing authority's decision[3].

1   H(W)A 2014, s 84, see **17.33**.
2   H(W)A 2014, s 73(1).
3   H(W)A 2014, s 85(1)(c), see **19.77–19.80**.

Applicant accepts an offer of suitable accommodation

17.161 The first circumstance is where the applicant has accepted an offer of suitable accommodation[1]. The offer could be made under the provisions of HA 1996, Pt 6 ('allocation of accommodation'), in which case it would be an offer of a secure, introductory or assured tenancy granted by a local housing authority or registered social landlord[2]. Or it could be an offer made outside of HA 1996, Pt 6, of an assured tenancy (including an assured shorthold tenancy)[3]. This latter provision could apply to one of two scenarios:

- an offer of an assured tenancy made by a registered social landlord directly to the applicant, not through HA 1996, Pt 6[4]; or
- an offer of an assured shorthold tenancy, made either by a registered social landlord or by a private landlord.

[1] H(W)A 2014, s 76(2); Welsh Code, paras 15.61–15.62. See also CHAPTER 18.
[2] H(W)A 2014, s 76(2)(a).
[3] H(W)A 2014, s 76(2)(b).
[4] Technically a private landlord could offer an assured, rather than an assured shorthold tenancy, but this would be unlikely.

17.162 There are no specific notification duties or other requirements that must be complied with before the duty can come to an end[1]. The key is 'acceptance' of one of these types of tenancy. However, if the offer is made under HA 1996, Pt 6, or falls within the definition of 'private rented sector offer'[2], if the applicant refuses the offer, the local housing authority is likely to decide that the duty has come to an end because of the refusal[3]. A 'private rented sector offer' must be of a fixed-term tenancy for a minimum period of at least six months[4]. If the assured shorthold tenancy being offered is for a fixed term of less than six months or is a periodic tenancy, then the applicant may accept the offer but would be free to refuse it without any consequences.

[1] Although there are notification requirements if the local housing authority wishes to bring the duty to an end because the applicant has refused an offer: H(W)A 2014, s 76(3), see **17.169**.
[2] H(W)A 2014, s 76(4), see **17.173–17.179**.
[3] H(W)A 2014, s 76(3)(b), see **17.165–17.179**.
[4] H(W)A 2014, s 76(4)(c), see **17.173–17.177**.

17.163 The applicant has the right to accept the offer whilst also requesting a review of whether or not the accommodation offered is suitable for his or her needs[1]. Given that the consequences if the applicant refuses an offer of accommodation are that the local housing authority need no longer accommodate the applicant and his or her household, this must normally be the safest course of action.

[1] H(W)A 2014, s 85(3), see **19.77–19.80** and **19.100–19.101**.

17.164 The applicant has the right to request a review of this decision that the duty has come to an end[1]. The local housing authority has a power to secure accommodation pending the outcome of the review[2].

[1] H(W)A 2014 s 85(1)(c), see **19.77–19.80**.
[2] H(W)A 2014, s 69(11), see **17.134**. The local housing authority is unlikely to exercise that power if it is satisfied that the applicant has accepted suitable accommodation.

Applicant refuses an offer of suitable accommodation

17.165 The local housing authority can decide that the H(W)A 2014, s 75(1) main housing duty has come to an end because the applicant has refused an offer of suitable accommodation[1]. Only three specific offers of accommodation have this effect. If a different offer of accommodation is made to the applicant, the applicant is free to refuse it without consequences.

[1] H(W)A 2014, s 76(3); Welsh Code, paras 15.63–15.66. See also CHAPTER 18.

17.166 The three types of offers of accommodation are:

- an offer of suitable interim accommodation under H(W)A 2014, s 75[1];
- a private rented sector offer[2]; or
- an offer of accommodation made under HA 1996, Pt 6[3].

All accommodation offered must be 'suitable' for the needs of the applicant and the members of his or her household[4].

[1] H(W)A 2014, s 76(3)(a), see **17.172**.
[2] H(W)A 2014, s 76(3)(b), see **17.173–17.177**.
[3] H(W)A 2014, s 76(3)(c), see **17.178–17.179**.
[4] See Welsh Code, chapter 19; and CHAPTER 18.

17.167 The Welsh Code advises that, in the case of private rented offers and offers made under HA 1996, Pt 6, an applicant should receive a written offer, which states that:

- it is a final offer; and
- the local housing authority is satisfied that:
  - the accommodation is suitable;
  - the accommodation will be available for a minimum of six months; and
  - it would be reasonable for the applicant to accept the offer[1].

[1] Welsh Code, paras 15.67–15.72.

17.168 The Welsh Code also advises that applicants should be given the chance to view accommodation before being required to decide whether they will accept or refuse it, and before being required to sign any tenancy agreement[1].

[1] Welsh Code, paras 15.14–15.15.

17.169 Finally, the applicant must have been given notice in writing of the possible consequence of refusal or acceptance of the offer, and of the right to request a review of the suitability of the accommodation whilst also accepting the offer[1]. The duty cannot come to an end unless this notification has been given.

[1] H(W)A 2014, s 76(3) and 84(1). Welsh Code, paras 15.63–15.66.

17.170 The applicant has the right to accept the offer whilst also requesting a review of whether or not the accommodation offered is suitable for his or her needs[1]. Given that the consequences if the applicant refuses an offer of accommodation are that the local housing authority need no longer accommodate the applicant and his or her household, this must normally be the safest course of action.

¹ H(W)A 2014, s 85(3), see **19.77–19.80** and **19.100–19.101**.

17.171 If the applicant refuses the offer, he or she has the right to request a review of the local housing authority's decision that the duty has come to an end[1]. The local housing authority will no longer be under a duty to accommodate the applicant and his or her household but has a power to secure interim accommodation pending the outcome of the review[2].

¹ H(W)A 2014, s 85(1)(c) see **19.77–19.80**.
² H(W)A 2014, s 69(11), see **17.134**.

AN OFFER OF SUITABLE INTERIM ACCOMMODATION

17.172 The duty in H(W)A 2014, s 75(1), comes to an end if the applicant refuses suitable accommodation[1] offered by the local housing authority under that duty. This provision is similar to that in HA 1996, s 193(5), for local housing authorities in England[2]. The applicant must have been notified in writing of the possible consequences of refusal or acceptance.

¹ H(W)A 2014, s 76(3)(a); Welsh Code, para 15.63.
² See **16.114–16.123**.

A PRIVATE RENTED SECTOR OFFER

17.173 A private rented sector offer[1] is defined in H(W)A 2014, s 76(4) as:

- an offer of an assured shorthold tenancy made by a private landlord to the applicant in relation to any accommodation which is available for the applicant's occupation; and
- the offer is made with the approval of the local housing authority in pursuance of arrangements made by the local housing authority with the landlord with a view to bringing the local housing authority's duty under H(W)A 2014, s 75(1), to an end; and
- the tenancy being offered is a fixed-term tenancy for a period of at least six months[2].

¹ H(W)A 2014, s 76(3)(b); Welsh Code, paras 15.64 and 15.67–15.72.
² Welsh Code, paras 15.67–15.72.

17.174 Any offer of an assured shorthold tenancy that does not fall within this definition, most obviously a fixed term tenancy for a shorter period of six months or a periodic tenancy, will not be a private rented sector offer. The applicant can accept such an offer if he or she wishes to[1], but there will no consequences if he or she refuses the offer. A 'fixed term tenancy' is defined as 'any tenancy other than a periodic tenancy'[2].

¹ H(W)A 2014, s 76(2)(b), see **17.161–17.164**.
² H(W)A 2014, s 76(9); Housing Act 1988, s 45(1).

17.175 A private rented sector offer will not be considered suitable if one or more of the following apply:

- the local housing authority is of the view that the accommodation is not in a reasonable physical condition;
- the local housing authority is of the view that the accommodation does not comply with all statutory requirements, such as requirements relating to fire, gas, electricity, carbon monoxide or other safety, planning, and licences for houses in multiple occupation; or
- the local housing authority is of the view that the landlord is not a fit and person within the meaning of H(W)A 2014, s 20[1], to act in the capacity of landlord[2].

---

[1]   H(W)A 2014, s 20, requires a local housing authority to have regard to all matters which it considers appropriate, when deciding whether a person is a fit and proper person to be licensed to carry out lettings and/or property management activities.

[2]   Homelessness (Suitability of Accommodation) (Wales) Order 2015, SI 2015/1268, art 8; see the CD Rom with this book. See **18.173**.

17.176 The applicant will know that this is a 'private rented sector offer', designed to bring the H(W)A 2014, s 75(1) main housing duty to an end, because the written offer should state that it is a final offer, and that the local housing authority is satisfied that the accommodation is suitable, would be available for a minimum of six months and that it would be reasonable for the applicant to accept it[1]. The written notification of the consequences of refusal or acceptance could be contained in the offer, or in a separate notification.

---

[1]   Welsh Code, para 15.65.

17.177 If the applicant is a 'restricted case'[1], then the local housing authority should seek to bring the H(W)A 2014, s 75(1), main housing duty to an end by making a private rented sector offer, rather than by making an offer under HA 1996, Pt 6, 'so far as reasonably practicable'[2]. The applicant will know that he or she is regarded as a restricted case because the notice of the outcome of the local housing authority's assessment will have informed the applicant that the duty under H(W)A 2014, s 75(1), will only be owed to him or her because of the presence of the restricted person. The notice will also have explained that the presumption is that the local housing authority will make the applicant a private rented sector offer[3].

---

[1]   Defined as a case where the local housing authority would not be satisfied that it owed the H(W)A 2014, s 75(1), main housing duty without having regard to a restricted person: H(W)A 2014, s 76(5). For 'restricted person', see H(W)A 2014, s 63(5) and **9.54–9.56** and **11.163–11.167**.

[2]   H(W)A 2014, s 76(5); Welsh Code, paras 15.73–15.74.

[3]   H(W)A 2014, s 63(2), see **9.54–9.56**. If the applicant would have had a priority need in any event, without the presence of a restricted person, he or she will not be a restricted case.

AN OFFER OF ACCOMMODATION UNDER HA 1996, PT 6

17.178 An offer of accommodation made under HA 1996, Pt 6[1], will be an offer of a secure, introductory or assured tenancy. The offer might be made by the local housing authority which owes the duty in H(W)A 2014, s 75(1), or it might be made by another local housing authority. The tenancy offered might be a tenancy of the local housing authority's own stock (offered as an introductory or secure tenancy) or of an assured tenancy from a registered social landlord[2].

[1]   H(W)A 2014, s 76(3)(c); Welsh Code, paras 15.65–15.66.
[2]   See **1.23**.

17.179 The applicant will know that this is an offer of accommodation under HA 1996, Pt 6, designed to bring the H(W)A 2014, s 75(1) main housing duty to an end, because the written offer should state that it is a final offer, that the local housing authority is satisfied that the accommodation is suitable, and that it would be reasonable for the applicant to accept it. The written notification of the consequences of refusal or acceptance could be contained in the offer letter, or in a separate notification[1].

[1]   Welsh Code, para 15.65.

The applicant has become homeless intentionally from suitable interim accommodation

17.180 The H(W)A 2014, s 75(1), main housing duty will come to an end where the local housing authority notifies the applicant that it is satisfied that he or she has become homeless intentionally from suitable interim accommodation[1]. Interim accommodation is defined in H(W)A 2014, s 76(6) as either:

- accommodation that was initially made available to the applicant under the interim accommodation duty in H(W)A 2014, s 68(1), and the local housing authority then continued make it available under the H(W)A 2014, s 75(1), main housing duty; or
- accommodation that was made available to the applicant under the H(W)A 2014, s 75(1) main housing duty[2].

[1]   H(W)A 2014, s 76(6); Welsh Code, para 15.75.
[2]   H(W)A 2014, s 76(6); for accommodation secured under the interim accommodation duty in H(W)A s 68(3), see **17.118–17.127**.

17.181 H(W)A 2014, s 76(6) contains the same wording previously used in HA 1996, s 193(6)(b)[1] and requires the familiar test of 'becoming homeless intentionally' to be applied by the local housing authority[2]. It also requires the local housing authority to be 'satisfied' that the applicant became homeless intentionally. It follows that if there is doubt about the issue, that doubt must be decided in the applicant's favour[3].

[1]   See **16.127–16.129**.
[2]   H(W)A 2014, s 77; see Welsh Code, chapter 17; and see CHAPTER **13**.
[3]   See discussion concerning the equivalent provision in HA 1996, s 193(6)(b), at **16.127–16.129**.

17.182 This set of circumstances which can end the H(W)A 2014, s 75(1), main housing duty envisages a much broader range of scenarios than the applicant merely walking away from accommodation. The definition of 'becoming homeless intentionally' is wide enough to include numerous events where the accommodation ceased to be available for the applicant's occupation because of the applicant's deliberate actions or omissions, such as a failure to pay the rent, or any other fault of the applicant which led to the landlord obtaining possession of the property[1].

1   H(W)A 2014, s 77; Welsh Code, chapter 17; and see CHAPTER 13.

17.183 The interim accommodation lost must have been suitable for the needs of the applicant and of his or her household[1]. In addition, it must be the applicant's own actions or omissions which led to the loss of the accommodation, rather than the acts or omissions of a member of the applicant's household[2].

1   See CHAPTER 18.
2   Although an applicant can be found to have become homeless intentionally where he or she acquiesced in, or failed to control, deliberate actions or omissions by other members of his or her household. See **13.95–13.99**.

17.184 The applicant has the right to request a review of any decision that the H(W)A 2014, s 75(1), main housing duty has come to an end for this reason[1]. Once the decision has been notified to the applicant, the H(W)A 2014, s 75(1), main housing duty will no longer be owed but the local housing authority has a power to secure accommodation for the applicant pending the outcome of the review[2].

1   H(W)A 2014, s 85(1)(c), see **19.77–19.80**.
2   H(W)A 2014, s 69(11), see **17.134**.

Applicant has voluntarily ceased to occupy suitable interim accommodation

17.185 The H(W)A 2014, s 75(1), main housing duty will come to an end where the local housing authority is satisfied that the applicant has voluntarily ceased to occupy, as his or her only or principal home, suitable interim accommodation made available for his or her occupation[1]. Interim accommodation is defined in H(W)A 2014, s 76(7) as either:

- accommodation that was initially made available to the applicant under H(W)A 2014, s 68(1), interim accommodation duty, and the local housing authority then continued to make it available under the H(W)A 2014, s 75(1), main housing duty arose; or
- accommodation that was made available to the applicant under the H(W)A 2014, s 75(1), main housing duty[2].

1   H(W)A 2014, s 76(7); Welsh Code, para 15.76.
2   H(W)A 2014, s 76(7); for accommodation secured under the interim accommodation duty in H(W)A s 68(3), see **17.118–17.127**.

17.186 H(W)A 2014, s 76(7) is framed in the same terms as the test previously in HA 1996, s 193(6)(d)[1] and requires the local housing authority to be 'satisfied' that the applicant has voluntarily ceased to occupy the accommodation as his or her only or principal home. It follows that if there is doubt about the issue, that doubt must be decided in the applicant's favour. Occupation as his or her 'only or principal home' is the statutory test by which a tenant has security of tenure under Housing Act 1985 (secure tenancies) or

Housing Act 1988 (assured tenancies)[2].

1   See **16.140–16.141**.
2   Housing Act 1985, s 81 for secure tenancies; Housing Act 1988, s 1, for assured tenancies. Reference should be made to the case law decided under these sections. See *Crawley Borough Council v Sawyer* (1988) 20 HLR 98, CA; and *Islington London Borough Council v Boyle* [2011] EWCA Civ 1450, [2012] HLR 18, CA. See **16.140–16.141** for discussion of the same test in HA 1996, s 193(6)(d) for local housing authorities in England.

17.187 For this set of circumstances to apply, the accommodation must have been suitable for the needs of the applicant and of his or her household[1]. In addition, it must be the applicant who has voluntarily ceased to occupy the accommodation, not a member of the applicant's household.

1   See Chapter **18**.

17.188 The applicant has the right to request a review of any decision that the H(W)A 2014, s 75(1), main housing duty has come to an end for this reason[1]. Once the decision has been notified to the applicant, the H(W)A 2014, s 75(1), main housing duty will no longer be owed but the local housing authority has a power to secure accommodation for the applicant pending the outcome of the review[2].

1   H(W)A 2014, s 85(1)(c), see **19.77–19.80**.
2   H(W)A 2014, s 69(11), see **17.134**.

ADDITIONAL CIRCUMSTANCES IN WHICH THE DUTIES CAN END

17.189 The circumstances in which each of the different duties to secure accommodation, or to help to secure accommodation, can come to an end are discussed by reference to the respective duties. In addition, there are four specific circumstances that can lead to a local housing authority notifying the applicant that any of the duties under H(W)A 2014, ss 66, 68, 73 or 75 have come to an end[1].

1   H(W)A 2014, s 79; Welsh Code, paras 15.79–15.89.

17.190 Those circumstances are:

(a)   that the local housing authority is no longer satisfied that the applicant is eligible for help[1];
(b)   that the local housing authority is satisfied that a mistake of fact led to the applicant being notified under H(W)A 2014, s 63, that a duty was owed to him or her[2];
(c)   that the local housing authority is satisfied that the applicant has withdrawn his or her application[3]; or
(d)   that the local housing authority is satisfied that the applicant is unreasonably failing to co-operate with it in connection with the exercise of any of its functions under H(W)A 2014, Pt 2, as those functions apply to the applicant[4].

1   H(W)A 2014, s 79(2), see **17.192**. For 'eligible for help', see Chapter **11**.
2   H(W)A 2014, s 79(3), see **17.193**.
3   H(W)A 2014, s 79(4), see **17.194**.

⁴   H(W)A 2014, s 79(5), see **17.195–17.197.**

17.191 The decision that a duty has come to an end for any of these reasons is not effective until it is notified to the applicant in accordance with H(W)A 2014, s 84[1]. That written notification must include the reason why the local housing authority has decided that it is no longer subject to the duty and must inform the applicant of his or her right to request a review and of the 21-day time limit for requesting a review[2]. The applicant has the right to request a review of a decision that the relevant duty has come to an end for any of the above reasons[3]. If he or she had been accommodated under the H(W)A 2014, s 68(1), interim accommodation duty, the local housing authority has a power to secure accommodation pending the outcome of the review[4]. In each case, the local housing authority has to be 'satisfied' of the relevant reason for the duty coming to an end. If there is any doubt, it should be applied in the applicant's favour.

¹   H(W)A 2014, s 79(1); Welsh Code, paras 15.93–15.98. See **17.33.**
²   H(W)A 2014, s 84(1).
³   H(W)A 2014, s 85(1)(c), see **19.77–19.80.**
⁴   H(W)A 2014, s 69(11); see **17.134.**

Applicant is no longer eligible for help

17.192 An applicant must remain eligible for help at all times in order to continue to be entitled to any of the duties in H(W)A 2014, Pt 2[1]. If, at any point, an applicant who was being helped to secure accommodation, or was being accommodated under any of the duties in H(W)A 2014, finds that his or her immigration status has changed, and he or she is no longer eligible, the duty will come to an end.

¹   H(W)A 2014, s 79(2); Welsh Code, para 15.79; see Chapter 11 for 'eligible for help'.

Mistake of fact

17.193 If a local housing authority in Wales discovers that its assessment of the applicant's case was based on a mistake of fact[1], which led to the applicant having been notified that a duty was owed to him or her under H(W)A 2014, Pt 2, then any duty to help the applicant or to accommodate the applicant can come to an end. The mistake of fact may have come about as a result of a simple mistake or misunderstanding by the applicant or by anyone else. However, anyone who knowingly or recklessly makes a statement which is false in a material point, or knowingly withholds information requested by the local housing authority, and did so intending to induce the local housing authority to believe that a person is entitled to accommodation or assistance under H(W)A 2014, Pt 2, will have committed a criminal offence[2].

¹   H(W)A 2014, s 79(3); Welsh Code, paras 15.80–15.8.
²   H(W)A 2014, s 97(1); Welsh Code, paras 15.81–15.83.

Applicant has withdrawn his or her application

17.194 If the applicant expressly withdraws his or her application, putting that withdrawal in writing[1], the local housing authority can notify him or her of its decision that the duty has come to an end because of the withdrawal. What if the applicant simply falls silent, and fails to respond to communications from the local housing authority? And what if the applicant verbally advises the local housing authority that he or she has withdrawn his or her application? Can either of those circumstances be interpreted as the applicant withdrawing his or her application? The Welsh Code advises that it would be good practice for applications to be considered 'for closure' (or withdrawn) if there has been no contact with the applicant for six weeks and that if the applicant then resumes contact, that should be considered as a fresh application[2]. However, local housing authorities should be cautious about rigidly applying such a rule. The better course of action might be that if the applicant responds to notification of the local housing authority's decision that the duty has come to an end, because he or she has withdrawn his or her application by failing to maintain contact, and requests a review or otherwise contests the decision, that very response will suggest that the application has not in fact been withdrawn[3].

[1] H(W)A 2014, s 79(4); Welsh Code, paras 15.84–15.85.
[2] Welsh Code, para 15.84.
[3] *The Homelessness Statistics in Wales 2016–2017* (Welsh Government, July 2017) show that 11% of applicants owed the H(W)A 2014, s 66(1), prevention duty and 13% of applicants owed the H(W)A 2014, s 73(1), relief duty had withdrawn their application, and roughly half of each of those groups were assessed as their applications having been withdrawn due to loss of contact, rather than expressly withdrawn. A smaller percentage of applicants owed the H(W)A 2014, s 75(1), accommodation duty withdrew their applications: 3%.

Applicant is unreasonably failing to co-operate

17.195 A local housing authority should be cautious about ending the relevant duty on this basis[1]. The local housing authority must be satisfied that the applicant is 'unreasonably' failing to co-operate, rather than simply making a mistake or there being a misunderstanding. The Welsh Code notes that the local housing authority must be satisfied that any failure of co-operate is not because the applicant is vulnerable, or because he or she has a support need which is not being met[2].

[1] H(W)A 2014, s 79(5); Welsh Code, paras 15.86–15.89.
[2] Welsh Code, para 15.86.

17.196 The Welsh Code gives examples of circumstances in which an applicant might be considered unreasonably to have failed to cooperate:

- where the applicant has agreed to take certain reasonable steps but then fails to take them, without any good reason, such as agreeing to mediation and then failing to engage with it;
- where, despite every effort by the local housing authority, the applicant has failed to provide necessary information; or
- where the applicant has unreasonably failed to agree to the steps identified by the local housing authority when it is helping the applicant

to prevent his or her homelessness or secure accommodation[1].

¹ Welsh Code, para 15.86.

17.197 The Welsh Code also advises that local housing authorities should make every effort to obtain the applicant's cooperation and should explain the consequences of not cooperating. If it is considering whether or not to make a decision that the duty has come to an end for this reason, it should first explain its reasons to the applicant and give the applicant a reasonable opportunity to co-operate[1]. The Welsh Code also states that, even if the local housing authority decides that its duty has come to an end for this reason, it would be good practice for limited assistance to be offered to the applicant in order to avoid the need for the applicant to make a fresh application[2].

¹ Welsh Code, paras 15.87–15.88.
² Welsh Code, para 15.89. *The Homelessness Statistics in Wales 2016–2017* (Welsh Government, July 2017) show that 5% of applicants owed the H(W)A 2014, s 66(1), prevention duty and 8% of applicants owed the H(W)A 2014, s 73(1), relief duty had been notified that the relevant duty had come to an end due to non-co-operation. 3% of applicants owed the H(W)A 2014, s 75(1), main housing duty had been notified that the relevant duty had come to an end due to non-co-operation.

ADDITIONAL DUTIES

17.198 There are three duties in H(W)A 2014, Pt 2, that are very closely modelled on the equivalent duties on local housing authorities in England set out in HA 1996, Pt 7[1]. Those duties are discussed in detail in CHAPTER **17**. We highlight any differences between H(W)A 2014, Pt 2 and HA 1996, Pt 7[2], in relation to each duty.

¹ As amended by HRA 2017.
² As amended by HRA 2017.

Duty to protect property

17.199 This duty is equivalent to the duty in HA 1996, ss 211–212[1]. The duty applies where[2]:

- the local housing authority has reason to believe that there is a danger of loss of, or damage to, the applicant's property by reason of his or her inability to protect it or deal with it; and
- the applicant is, or has been, the beneficiary of one of the following duties:
  - the H(W)A 2014, s 66(1), prevention duty in the case of an applicant in priority need: H(W)A 2014, s 66[3];
  - the H(W)A 2014, s 68 interim accommodation duty, but only for applicants in actual or apparent priority need: H(W)A 2014, s 68[4];
  - the H(W)A 2014, s 75(1) main housing duty[5]; or
  - the duties at H(WA) 214, s 82, owed to an applicant whose case is considered for referral or is referred[6], in the case of an applicant

in priority need[7].

1.   As amended by HRA 2017, s 5(12).
2.   H(W)A 2014, s 93–94; Welsh Code, paras 11.15–11.25.
3.   See **16.288–16.309**.
4.   See **17.118–17.134**.
5.   See **17.146–17.199**.
6.   See **17.120–17.123**.
7.   H(W)A 2014, s 93(2).

17.200 The common thread between this list of duties is that the applicant either has a priority need, or at some point the local housing authority had reason to believe that he or she had a priority need[1].

1.   For priority need, see H(W)A 2014, s 70; Welsh Code, chapter 16 and **12.29** and **12.195–12.228**.

17.201 Once the local housing authority becomes subject to this duty to protect an applicant's property, the duty continues even though the duty under which the applicant has been helped, or accommodated, might itself have come to an end[1].

1.   H(W)A 2014, s 93(3).

17.202 The local housing authority also has a power, but not a duty, to protect the personal property of any applicant who is eligible for help by taking 'any steps it considers reasonable'[1]. The power arises in the same circumstances as the duty applies, that is where the local housing authority has reason to believe that there is a danger of loss of, or damage to, the applicant's personal property by reason of his or her inability to protect it or deal with it and no other suitable arrangements have been or are being made. The local housing authority could use the power to assist applicants who do not have a priority need, but whose possessions might be at risk of loss or damage.

1.   H(W)A 2014, s 93(5).

17.203 The duty under H(W)A 2014, s 93(1) is to 'take reasonable steps to prevent the loss of the personal property of the applicant or prevent or mitigate damage to it'[1]. In order to perform this duty, local housing authorities have the power to enter, at all reasonable times, the applicant's usual, or last usual, place of residence in order to deal with the applicant's personal property[2]. If a local housing authority in Wales is proposing to exercise this power, its officer must produce the valid documentation setting out his or her authority to enter the premises, if requested to do so[3]. It is a criminal offence to obstruct officers of the local housing authority who are exercising this power unless the person has a reasonable excuse for the obstruction[4]. The local housing authority is entitled to impose conditions when it performs the duty, including conditions about reasonable charges and disposal of property[5].

1.   H(W)A 2014, s 93(1); Welsh Code, paras 11.15–11.19.
2.   H(W)A 2014, s 94(1).
3.   H(W)A 2014, s 94(2). This is not a requirement for local housing authorities in England.
4.   H(W)A 2014, s 94(3).
5.   H(W)A 2014, s 93(4); Welsh Code, para 11.19; see **16.298**.

17.204 The duty comes to an end when:

- the local housing authority moves the applicant's property to a particular location, at the applicant's request and the applicant has been informed by the local housing authority that the duty has come to an end[1]; or
- the local housing authority no longer has any reason to believe that there is a danger of loss of or damage to the applicant's property by virtue of his or her inability to protect it or deal with it[2].

1 H(W)A 2014, s 94(4); Welsh Code, para 11.18.
2 H(W)A 2014, s 94(6); Welsh Code, para 11.20.

17.205 The applicant must be notified of the local housing authority's decision that it is no longer subject to the duty, or no longer willing to exercise the power, to protect possessions[1]. The applicant does not have a right to request a review of that decision, and so should initially ask the local housing authority to reconsider its decision. If that route is unsuccessful, the only avenue for challenge would be to bring a judicial review claim, challenging the lawfulness of the decision[2].

1 H(W)A 2014, s 94(8) and (9); Welsh Code, para 11.21.
2 See **19.306–19.333** for 'judicial review'.

Duties to co-operate and to provide information

17.206 There are two mechanisms by which a local housing authority can seek help with performing its functions under H(W)A 2014, Pt 2[1].

1 H(W)A 2014, s 95; Welsh Code, chapter 6.

General arrangements to promote co-operation between social services and housing departments or authorities

17.207 County councils and county borough councils in Wales are required, by H(W)A 2014, s 95(1), to make arrangements to promote general co-operation between their officers exercising social services functions and their officers exercising functions as the local housing authority. They must co-operate in order to achieve the following objectives in the local area:

(a)   the prevention of homelessness;
(b)   that suitable accommodation is or will be available for people who are or may be homeless;
(c)   that satisfactory support is available for people who are or may become homeless; and
(d)   the effective discharge of the council's functions under H(W)A 2014, Pt 2[1].

1 H(W)A 2014, s 95(1).

Specific requests for co-operation

17.208 The local housing authority may request a number of different bodies to co-operate with it in the exercise of its functions[1] under H(W)A 2014, Pt 2, ie helping the local housing authority to perform any of its duties or powers[2]. Those bodies might be located in Wales or in England. They are:

(a)   another local housing authority;
(b)   a social services authority;
(c)   a registered social landlord;
(d)   a new town corporation;
(e)   a private registered provider of social housing; or
(f)   a housing action trust[3].

The list of specified bodies is the same as appears in HA 1996, s 213, which contains the list of bodies required to co-operate with a request for assistance from a local housing authority in England[4].

[1]   H(W)A 2014, s 95(2)–(5); Welsh Code, paras 6.3–6.4.
[2]   H(W)A 2014, s 95(2).
[3]   H(W)A 2014, s 95(5).
[4]   See **15.222–15.228**. Note that H(W)A 2014, s 95, does not contain provision for a local housing authority in Wales to request a local authority in Scotland to co-operate.

17.209 This list of bodies can be amended by order of the Welsh Ministers[1]. There is detailed guidance in chapter 6 of the Welsh Code. In addition to the list of bodies specified in H(W)A 2014, s 95(5), the Welsh Code advises that local health boards are also under a duty to co-operate and that the Welsh Ministers intend to issue joint guidance on the duties of co-operation expected between local health boards and local housing authorities with regard to homeless persons[2]. The Welsh Code also advises that domestic abuse coordinators, registered social landlords, housing advice services, private rented sector representatives, Supporting People Teams, criminal justice agencies, community safety partnerships, the National Offender Management Service, Community Rehabilitation Companies, and Youth Offending Teams should be co-operating with local housing authorities in respect of tackling homelessness[3].

[1]   H(W)A 2014, s 95(6). Note that the Welsh Ministers may not add a Minister of the Crown to the list: H(W)A 2014, s 95(7).
[2]   National Health Service Act 2006, s 82 and National Health Service (Wales) Act 2006, s 12(3); Welsh Code, paras 6.21–6.22. As at 2018, no such guidance appears to have been issued.
[3]   Welsh Code, paras 6.17–6.20 and 6.23–6.35.

17.210 Once one of these bodies has received a request for co-operation , it 'must comply' with the request[1]. It can only refuse if it considers that complying would either be incompatible with its own duties or otherwise have an adverse effect on the exercise of its own functions, and it must put those reasons in writing[2]. The Welsh Code advises: '[t]he presumption is now placed clearly on the other service to co-operate unless it can demonstrate that the proposed action would be incompatible with its duties. Their reasons would have to be given in writing and it would not be sufficient to say that there were other priorities that had to take precedence'[3].

[1]   H(W)A 2014, s 95(2).

² H(W)A 2014, s 95(2) and (4). The test under HA 1996, s 213, is that a body receiving a request shall co-operate so far 'as is reasonable in the circumstances'.
³ Welsh Code, paras 6.3–6.4.

17.211 In addition, a local housing authority can request that any of the specified bodies provide it with information that it requires in order to exercise any of its functions under H(W)A 2014, Pt 2[1]. Again, the body receiving the request must comply, and provide the information. It can only refuse to do so for the same reasons as apply to refusing to co-operate, and, again, must put in writing any reasons for refusal[2].

¹ H(W)A 2014, s 95(3).
² H(W)A 2014, s 95(3) and (4).

Duty to co-operate in certain cases involving children

17.212 Where a local housing authority has reason to believe that an applicant with whom a person under the age of 18 resides, or might reasonably be expected to reside, may be ineligible for help under H(W)A 2014, Pt 2[1], or may not be owed any duty under H(W)A 2014, ss 66[2], 68[3], 73[4] or 75[5], then it must make arrangements for ensuring that the applicant is invited to consent to a referral to a social services department of the essential facts of the case[6] and, if consent is given, that the social services department is made aware of those facts and of the local housing authority's subsequent decision under H(W)A 2014, Pt 2[7]. This duty is equivalent to the duty on local housing authorities in England under HA 1996, s 213A[8].

¹ H(W)A 2014, s 61 and Sch 2; see CHAPTER 11.
² See **17.45–17.72**.
³ See **17.118–17.134**.
⁴ See **17.73–17.117**.
⁵ See **17.146–17.199**.
⁶ H(W)A 2014, s 96; Welsh Code, paras 17.47–17.49.
⁷ H(W)A 2014, s 96(1) and (2).
⁸ As amended by Homelessness Reduction Act 2017, s 4(7). See **16.280–16.287**.

17.213 This duty applies where the local housing authority has reason to believe that an applicant *may*:

- be ineligible for help[1]; or
- be homeless but no duty to secure or help to secure accommodation under H(W)A 2014, ss 68, 73 or 75 is likely to apply; or
- be threatened with homelessness but no duty under H(W)A 2014, s 66, is likely to apply[2].

¹ See CHAPTER 11.
² H(W)A 2014, s 96(1).

17.214 The list is a little odd. The Welsh Code advises that applicants who may fall under this section will be those who are homeless or threatened with homelessness, but who will not be offered assistance because they are ineligible or have become homeless intentionally[1]. Applicants who may be ineligible for help will not be entitled to any of those duties. All eligible applicants are entitled to the H(W)A 2014, s 66(1) prevention duty[2] or to the H(W)A 2014, s 73(1), relief duty[3] so this duty would apply if any of those duties come to an end[4]. Currently, the H(W)A 2014, s 75(1), main housing duty is only owed to applicants who have not become homeless intentionally and so this duty would apply to an applicant who has a priority need but has also become homeless intentionally[5]. It would also apply if the H(W)A 2014, s 75(1), main housing duty came to an end in circumstances where the applicant remained homeless or threatened with homelessness[6].

1   Welsh Code, para 17.47.
2   For the H(W)A 2014, s 66(1), prevention duty, see **17.45–17.72**.
3   Relief duty to help to secure accommodation for homeless applicants, see **17.73–17.117**.
4   H(W)A 2014, s 66(1), prevention duty ends on the occurrence of one of the events in H(W)A 2014, ss 67 and 79, see **17.59–17.72**. The H(W)A 2014, s 73(1), relief duty ends on the occurrence of one of the events in H(W)A 2014, ss 74 and 79, see **17.84–17.117**.
5   H(W)A 2014, s 75(2)(d), see **17.146**. Provided of course that the local housing authority has chosen to have regard to the 'becoming homeless intentionally' test, see **13.252–13.255** and **17.18–17.23**.
6   H(W)A 2014, s 75(1), main housing duty comes to an end on the occurrence of one of the events in H(W)A 2014, ss 76 and 79, see **17.161–17.188**.

17.215 Normally, an applicant will be asked to consent to the referral to social services[1]. However, a referral can be made without that consent if the local housing authority has concerns about a child's welfare[2].

1   H(W)A 2014, s 96(2).
2   H(W)A 2014, s 96(3); Welsh Code, para 17.48.

Chapter 18

SUITABILITY OF ACCOMMODATION

Contents

INTRODUCTION

18.1 Any accommodation offered to an applicant either in performance of any of the duties at Housing Act 1996 (HA 1996), Pt 7[1], or the Housing (Wales) Act 2014 (H(W)A 2014), Pt 2, or in order to bring any of those duties to an end, must be suitable for the needs of the applicant and of his or her household[2]. Guidance as to 'suitability' is given in the Codes of Guidance[3].

[1] As amended by Homelessness Reduction Act 2017 (HRA 2017) for applications for homelessness assistance made to local housing authorities in England on or after 3 April 2018.
[2] Housing Act 1996, s 206 (HA 1996); Housing (Wales) Act 2014, s 64 (H(W)A 2014).
[3] See *Homelessness Code of Guidance for Local Authorities* (Ministry for Housing, Communities and Local Government, 2018) (the English Code), chapters 16–17 at Appendix 2 and *Code of Guidance for Local Authorities on the Allocation of Accommodation and Homelessness* (Welsh Government, March 2016) (the Welsh Code), Chapter 19, on the CD Rom with this book.

18.2 The amendments made to HA 1996, Pt 7, by the Homelessness Reduction Act 2017 (HRA 2017)[1] mean that there are now a greater variety of circumstances in which local housing authorities may be required to secure, to may help to secure, accommodation for an applicant. The common thread running through all these situations is that any such accommodation must be suitable, even where it has been made available on a relatively informal basis, for example, where a family member of an applicant has agreed to allow the applicant to live with him or her. Any duty owed to the applicant under HA 1996, Pt 7[2], or H(W)A 2014, Pt 2, will not end if the applicant accepts or refuses accommodation that is not suitable.

[1] For applications for homelessness assistance made to local housing authorities in England on or after 3 April 2018.
[2] As amended by HRA 2017 for applications for homelessness assistance made to local housing authorities in England on or after 3 April 2018.

18.3 As later parts of this chapter demonstrate, 'suitability' is a flexible concept – what may be suitable for a few nights may not be suitable for a longer period[1]. But there is always an irreducible minimum standard below which accommodation must not fall:

> 'Although financial constraints and limited housing stock are matters that can be taken into account in determining suitability, there is a minimum and one must look at the needs and circumstances of the particular family and decide what is suitable for them, and there will be a line to be drawn below which the standard of accommodation cannot fall. If the accommodation falls below that line, and is accommodation which no reasonable local authority could consider to be suitable to the needs of the applicant, then the decision will be struck down, and an appeal to the resources argument will be of no avail[2].'

[1] English Code, para 17.9 and *Ali v Birmingham City Council* [2009] UKHL 36, [2009] 1 WLR 1506, HL per Baroness Hale at [47].
[2] *R v Newham London Borough Council ex p Sacupima* (2001) 33 HLR 2, CA, approving the first-instance decision of Dyson J, who had quoted Collins J in *R v Newham London Borough Council ex p Ojuri (No 3)* (1998) 31 HLR 452, QBD.

18.4 The courts recognise that, from time to time, local housing authorities may find it simply impossible to secure 'suitable' accommodation. Strictly, the local housing authority concerned will be immediately in breach of an acknowledged statutory duty. On any legal challenge it will need compelling evidence in order to avoid the making of a mandatory order[1]. After all, if there is no accommodation reasonable for the applicant to occupy, he or she will still be 'homeless'[2].

1 See *R v Lambeth London Borough Council ex p Touhey* (2000) 32 HLR 707, QBD and *Ali v Birmingham City Council* [2009] UKHL 36, [2009] 1 WLR 1506, HL per Lord Hope at [4].
2 HA 1996, s 175(3); H(W)A 2014, s 55(3).

18.5 In *Codona v Mid-Bedfordshire District Council*[1],Auld LJ, giving the leading judgment, surveyed the case law and held that there are three aspects to the issue of whether or not accommodation is 'suitable':

'(1) suitability to a *Wednesbury* minimum level of suitability in the nature, location and standard of condition of the accommodation having regard to the circumstances of the applicant and his or her resident family, including the duration of their likely occupation of it;

(2) the absolute nature of the duty which, though coupled with an elastic concept of suitability taking account of financial constraints and limited availability of accommodation, is not so elastic as to permit an offer below the *Wednesbury* minimum standard (or . . . outside the margin of appreciation); and

(3) special consideration, in the regulatory provision for and in decision-making in individual cases, for the housing needs of particularly vulnerable applicants such as traditional gypsies with a view, so far as practicable and when considered with all the other circumstances, to facilitating their traditional way of life[2].'

1 [2004] EWCA Civ 925, [2005] HLR 1, CA.
2 At [46].

18.6 Where the applicant for homelessness assistance is applying on the basis that, although he or she has accommodation that is available for him or her, the accommodation is not reasonable to continue to occupy[1], the accommodation might still be 'suitable' for the applicant to occupy[2]. This is because the local housing authority will have to ask, and answer, two separate questions:

(1) Is the accommodation reasonable for the applicant to continue to occupy for as long as he or she would have to do unless the local housing authority takes action? If the answer is 'No', the applicant will be homeless.

(2) If the applicant is entitled to an accommodation duty under HA 1996, Pt 7[3], or H(W)A 2014, Pt 2[4], is the accommodation suitable for him or her to occupy for the period during which the applicant can expect to live there until he or she receives an offer of alternative accommodation[5]?

If the accommodation is not reasonable for the applicant to continue to occupy for one more night, then it will also not be suitable accommodation[6].

1 HA 1996, ss 175 and 176; H(W)A 2014, ss 55(3) and 56. See **10.17–10.32** for available accommodation and **10.73–10.134** for reasonable to continue to occupy.
2 *Ali & others v Birmingham City Council, Moran v Manchester City Council* [2009] UKHL 36, [2009] 1 WLR 1506, HL.

3   As amended by HRA 2017 for applications for homelessness assistance made to local housing authorities in England on or after 3 April 2018. See CHAPTER **16** for accommodation duties owed to applicants for homelessness assistance by local housing authorities in England.

4   See CHAPTER **17** for accommodation duties owed to applicants for homelessness assistance by local housing authorities in Wales.

5   *Ali & others v Birmingham City Council, Moran v Manchester City Council* [2009] UKHL 36, [2009] 1 WLR 1506, HL at [46]–[48] per Baroness Hale. See English Code, para 17.7.

6   *Ali & others v Birmingham City Council, Moran v Manchester City Council* [2009] UKHL 36, [2009] 1 WLR 1506, HL at [47] per Baroness Hale.

'Suitable' accommodation for whom?

18.7 Any accommodation secured by a local housing authority in performance of its duties, or the exercise of its powers, under HA 1996, Pt 7[1], or H(W)A 2014, Pt 2, or offered with a view to achieving a release from its duties, must be 'suitable'. But suitable for whom?

1   As amended by HRA 2017 for applications for homelessness assistance made to local housing authorities in England on or after 3 April 2018.

18.8 The focus throughout HA 1996, Pt 7[1], and H(W)A 2014, Pt 2, is on the 'applicant'[2]. Accommodation secured for the applicant must be 'available' for him or her. 'Available' is given a special meaning, ensuring that accommodation is 'available' not only for the applicant, but also for all those people who might be included in his or her household[3]. There is no precise mirroring of this expanded approach, beyond the needs of the individual applicant, in the treatment of 'suitability'.

1   As amended by HRA 2017 for applications for homelessness assistance made to local housing authorities in England on or after 3 April 2018.

2   See HA 1996, s 193(2) or H(W)A 2014, s 75(1) for examples.

3   As defined in HA 1996, s 176 or H(W)A 2014, s 56. See **10.21–10.32**. See *R (Ogbeni) v Tower Hamlets London Borough Council* [2008] EWHC 2444 (Admin), (2008) October *Legal Action*, p 37, Admin Ct.

18.9 However, when dealing with 'suitability', HA 1996, Pt 7[1] refers to suitability for 'a person' rather than for 'the applicant'[2]. It follows that the determination of suitability requires regard not only for the individual needs of the applicant, but also for the needs of all those other persons who are members of the applicant's family who normally reside with him or her or who might reasonably be expected to reside with him or her[3]. This is certainly the approach taken in the Codes of Guidance, which, when dealing with suitability, specifically direct attention not only to the applicant but also to others in his or her family or household[4].

1   As amended by HRA 2017 for applications for homelessness assistance made to local housing authorities in England on or after 3 April 2018.

2   HA 1996, s 210(1). The equivalent provision in H(W)A 2014, s 64(1), retains the language of 'applicant'.

3   HA 1996, ss 176, 206 and 210; H(W)A 2014, ss 56, 59 and 64(1) and (2). Although H(W)A 2014 uses different language, the same point applies.

4   English Code, para 16.6; Welsh Code, paras 19.4 and 19.11 (referring to 'household'). In *R (McCammon-Mckenzie) v Southwark London Borough Council* [2004] EWHC 612 (Admin), [2004] All ER (D) 174 (Mar), Admin Ct, accommodation was not suitable for the

applicant because her 16-year-old son could not occupy it with her (and had been taken into care as a result).

18.10 In 2001, the Court of Appeal proceeded on the uncontested assumption that the accommodation:

' . . . has to be suitable for the particular homeless person *and his or her family*. There is no doubt that the question of whether or not the accommodation is suitable requires an assessment of all the qualities of the accommodation in the light of the needs and requirements of the homeless person *and his or her family*[1].'

'Family' was there used by the court in the sense of the household for whom accommodation must be made available[2].

[1] *R v Newham London Borough Council ex p Sacupima* (2001) 33 HLR 2, CA at [28] per Latham LJ (emphasis added). The Court of Appeal has also referred to 'suitability' as 'having regard to the circumstances of the occupant and his or her resident family' (*Codona v Mid-Bedfordshire District Council* [2004] EWCA Civ 925, [2005] HLR 1, CA at [46] per Auld LJ). The House of Lords in *Ali & others v Birmingham City Council, Moran v Manchester City Council* [2009] UKHL 36, [2009] 1 WLR 1506, HL also referred to 'homeless families' rather than to 'applicants'.
[2] *R v Newham London Borough Council ex p Sacupima* (2001) 33 HLR 2, CA at [32].

18.11 In 2013, the Supreme Court confirmed this approach in *Sharif v Camden London Borough Council*[1]: '[i]t is still a fundamental objective of the Act to ensure that families can "live together" in the true sense'[2].

[1] [2013] UKSC 10, [2013] HLR 16, SC.
[2] Lord Carnwath at [23]. See also *Nzolameso v City of Westminster Council* [2015] UKSC 22, [2015] 2 All ER 942, [2015] HLR 22 per Baroness Hale at [13].

'Suitable' accommodation from whom?

18.12 When performing a duty (or exercising a power) to secure accommodation, a local housing authority need not provide the particular accommodation itself. Both HA 1996, Pt 7[1] and H(W)A 2014, Pt 2, enable the securing of accommodation to be achieved in any one of three ways. These are[2]:

(1)   By the local housing authority itself providing the accommodation[3]. This might be, for example, by providing council-owned housing, a place in a council-run hostel or supported housing scheme, or accommodation that the local housing authority has itself rented from a private owner[4].

(2)   By obtaining accommodation for the applicant from some other person[5]. The other person may be a private landlord, a private registered provider in England or registered social landlord in Wales, another local housing authority, an adult care and children's services authority, a voluntary organisation or anyone else[6].

(3)   By giving the applicant such advice and assistance that she or he is able to obtain accommodation from another person[7]. This would include helping an applicant to purchase accommodation from another person using her or his own funds, or giving advice and assistance so that an owner can obtain possession of his or her property from tenants[8].

[1] As amended by HRA 2017 for applications for homelessness assistance made to local housing authorities in England on or after 3 April 2018.

2   HA 1996, s 206(1); H(W)A 2014, s 64(1).
3   HA 1996, s 206(1)(a); H(W)A 2014, s 64(1)(b).
4   English Code, paras 16.10–16.11; Welsh Code, para 13.14.
5   HA 1996, s 206(1)(b); H(W)A 2014, s 64(1)(a).
6   English Code, paras 16.12–16.28; Welsh Code, para 13.14.
7   HA 1996, s 206(1)(c); H(W)A 2014, s 64(1)(c) and (2)(h).
8   English Code, para 16.9; *R (Miah) v Tower Hamlets London Borough Council* [2014] EWCA Civ 1029, (2014) September *Legal Action*, p 50, CA.

18.13 It is the local housing authority, and not the applicant, that chooses which of the three options will be used. For some local housing authorities (those which have transferred all their housing stock and other accommodation to new owners), only the latter two options will be available.

18.14 Where the local housing authority is relying on an offer of 'suitable' accommodation to release it from the duties owed under HA 1996, Pt 7[1], or H(W)A 2014, Pt 2, that offer may be of local housing authority accommodation (its own or obtained from another local housing authority) or of private registered provider or registered social landlord property, or of a tenancy made available by a private landlord.

1   As amended by HRA 2017 for applications for homelessness assistance made to local housing authorities in England on or after 3 April 2018.

Suitability in general

18.15 In determining whether accommodation is 'suitable', local housing authorities must consider the applicant and his or her household's particular individual needs. A general assessment of what accommodation may be suitable could be made in advance (for example, that a unit of accommodation of a particular size or type is likely to be required). However, the question posed by both HA 1996, Pt 7[1] and H(W)A 2014, Pt 2, is whether the specific property secured for, or offered to, the applicant is 'suitable'[2]. Accordingly, local housing authorities cannot adopt blanket policies prescribing that certain types of accommodation will be suitable in certain circumstances[3]. If the applicant raises a reason why the accommodation that has been secured or offered is not suitable, the local housing authority must consider that particular reason. It cannot restrict itself to general considerations of whether the accommodation would be suitable for the average or ordinary applicant[4].

1   As amended by HRA 2017 for applications for homelessness assistance made to local housing authorities in England on or after 3 April 2018.
2   *R v Lambeth London Borough Council ex p Touhey* (1999) 32 HLR 707, QBD, at 716, 723 and 727 per Richards J.
3   English Code, para 17.9; Welsh Code, para 19.11.
4   *R v Brent London Borough Council ex p Omar* (1991) 23 HLR 446, QBD.

18.16 The duty to secure suitable accommodation is a continuing one. If an applicant's circumstances change, so that the accommodation secured in performance of a power or duty ceases to be suitable, the local housing authority has a duty to secure other, suitable accommodation[1].

1   *R (Zaher) v Westminster City Council* [2003] EWHC 101 Admin, [2003] All ER (D) 253 (Jan), Admin Ct; *R v Newham London Borough Council ex p Mashuda Begum* (1999) 32 HLR 808, QBD; and English Code, para 17.8. An applicant in this situation, faced with a

move from unsuitable accommodation to accommodation that the local housing authority has secured for him or her and has decided is suitable, will be at risk of the local housing authority deciding that its main housing duty has come to an end under HA 1996, s 193(5) or H(W)A 2014, s 76(3)(a) if he or she refuses the offer of suitable accommodation (*Muse v Brent London Borough Council* [2008] EWCA Civ 1447, (2009) February *Legal Action*, p 32, CA; *Vilvarasa v Harrow London Borough Council* [2010] EWCA Civ 1278, [2011] HLR 12, CA; *Nzamy v Brent London Borough Council* [2011] EWCA Civ 283, [2011] HLR 20, CA and *Sharif v Camden London Borough Council* [2013] UKSC 10, [2013] HLR 16, SC). For the ending of the HA 1996, s 193(2) main housing duty under HA 1996, s 193(5) see **16.114–16.124** (England) and for the ending of the H(W)A 2014, s 75(1), main housing duty under H(W)A 2014, s 76(3)(a), see **17.165–17.173**.

Disputes over 'suitability'

Avenues for challenge

RIGHTS TO REQUEST A REVIEW

18.17 Although all accommodation secured or arranged under the duties to help to secure under HA 1996, Pt 7[1] or under H(W)A 2014, Pt 2, must be 'suitable', not every decision about suitability is amenable to the statutory review procedure[2].

[1]   As amended by HRA 2017 for applications for homelessness assistance made to local housing authorities in England on or after 3 April 2018.
[2]   HA 1996, s 202(1), as amended by HRA 2017, s 9, for applications for homelessness assistance to a local housing authority in England on or after 3 April 2018; H(W)A 2014, s 85(1). See **19.12–19.69** for a full description of that procedure.

18.18 In both England and in Wales, the applicant has the right to request a review of a decision by the local housing authority that accommodation offered to him or her is suitable in the following scenarios:

(1)   accommodation secured in the 'discharge'[1] of the HA 1996, s 189B(2)[2], relief duty, the HA 1996, s 190(2)[3] short-term accommodation duty, the HA 1996, s 193(2) main housing duty[4], the HA 1996, s 193C(4)[5], accommodation duty, or the HA 1996, s 195(2)[6], prevention duty; or under the H(W)A 2014, s 66(1) prevention duty[7], the H(W)A 2014, s 68(1) interim accommodation duty[8], the H(W)A 2014, s 73(1) relief duty[9], or the H(W)A 2014, s 75(1) main housing duty[10]; or

(2)   if he or she has accepted or refused accommodation secured in the 'discharge' of any of those duties and the local housing authority has notified him or her that the duty has come to an end[11].

(3)   a final offer of HA 1996, Pt 6 accommodation[12] made in order to bring the HA 1996, s 193(2) or H(W)A 2014, s 75(1) main housing duties to an end[13]; or

(4)   a private rented sector offer[14] made in order to bring the HA 1996, s 193(2) or H(W)A 2014, s 75(1) main housing duties to an end[15].

[1]   In this context, 'discharge' means 'performance' of the duty.
[2]   As inserted by HRA 2017, s 5(2), for applications for homelessness assistance to a local housing authority in England on or after 3 April 2018. It would be unusual for accommodation to have been secured under this duty. See **15.138–15.195**.
[3]   As amended by HRA 2017, s 5(5), for applications for homelessness assistance to a local housing authority in England on or after 3 April 2018. See **16.81–16.93**.

4 See **16.94–16.199**.
5 As inserted by HRA 2017, s 7(1), for applications for homelessness assistance to a local
   housing authority in England on or after 3 April 2018. See **16.200–16.216**.
6 As amended by HRA 2017, s 4(2), for applications for homelessness assistance to a local
   housing authority in England on or after 3 April 2018. It would be unusual for accommodation to have been secured under this duty, see **15.87–15.137**.
7 See **17.45–17.72**.
8 See **17.118–17.134**.
9 See **17.73–17.117**.
10 HA 1996, s 202(1)(f), as amended by HRA 2017, s 9, for applications for homelessness
   assistance to a local housing authority in England on or after 3 April 2018, and (1A); H(W)A
   2014, s 85(3), see **19.59–19.62**.
11 HA 1996, s 202(1)(b), as amended by HRA 2017, s 9, for applications for homelessness
   assistance to a local housing authority in England on or after 3 April 2018; H(W)A 2014,
   s 85(2)(c).
12 HA 1996, s 193(7), see **16.142–16.152**. H(W)A 2014, s 76(2), see **17.178–17.179**.
13 HA 1996, s 202(1)(f), as amended by HRA 2017, s 9, for applications for homelessness
   assistance to a local housing authority in England on or after 3 April 2018, and (1A); H(W)A
   2014, s 85(3), see **19.59–19.62**.
14 HA 1996, s 193(7AA)–(7AC), see **16.153–16.180**. H(W)A 2014, s 76(3)(b), see
   17.173–17.175.
15 HA 1996, s 202(1)(g), as amended by HRA 2017, s 9, for applications for homelessness
   assistance to a local housing authority in England on or after 3 April 2018; H(W)A 2014,
   s 85(1)(c), see **19.63–19.64**.

18.19 There are additional rights to request a review in respect of certain offers of accommodation made by local housing authorities in England:

- where the applicant is made a final accommodation offer[1] made in order to bring the HA 1996, s 189B(2)[2], relief duty to an end[3], he or she could accept or refuse the offer and request a review[4];
- where the applicant is made a final Pt 6 offer[5] made in order to bring the HA 1996, s 189B(2)[6], relief duty to an end[7], he or she could accept or refuse the offer and request a review[8];
- where the applicant is made a final accommodation offer[9] made in order to bring the HA 1996, s 193C(4)[10] accommodation duty to an end[11], he or she could accept or refuse the offer and request a review[12]; or
- where the applicant is made a final Pt 6 offer[13] made in order to bring the HA 1996, s 193C(4)[14] accommodation duty to an end[15], he or she could accept or refuse the offer and request a review[16].

1 As defined at HA 1996, s 193A(4), as inserted by HRA 2017, s 7(1), for applications for
   homelessness assistance to a local housing authority in England on or after 3 April 2018, see
   15.181–15.184.
2 As inserted by HRA 2017, s 5(2), for applications for homelessness assistance to a local
   housing authority in England on or after 3 April 2018.
3 HA 1996, ss 189B(9)(a) and 193A(2), as inserted by HRA 2017, ss 5(2) and 7(1), for
   applications for homelessness assistance to a local housing authority in England on or after
   3 April 2018, see **15.181–15.184**.
4 HA 1996, s 202(1)(h) and (1B), as inserted by HRA 2017, s 9, for applications for
   homelessness assistance to a local housing authority in England on or after 3 April 2018.
5 As defined at HA 1996, s 193A(5) as inserted by HRA 2017, s 7(1), for applications for
   homelessness assistance to a local housing authority in England on or after 3 April 2018, see
   15.185–15.188.
6 As inserted by HRA 2017, s 5(2), for applications for homelessness assistance to a local
   housing authority in England on or after 3 April 2018.

⁷ HA 1996, s 189B(9)(a) and 193A(2), as inserted by HRA 2017, ss 5(2) and 7(1), for applications for homelessness assistance to a local housing authority in England on or after 3 April 2018, see **15.185–15.188.**

⁸ HA 1996, s 202(1)(h) and (1B), as inserted by HRA 2017, s 9, for applications for homelessness assistance to a local housing authority in England on or after 3 April 2018.

⁹ As defined at HA 1996, s 193C(7), as inserted by HRA 2017, s 7(1), for applications for homelessness assistance to a local housing authority in England on or after 3 April 2018, see **16.205–16.209.**

¹⁰ As inserted by HRA 2017, s 7(1), for applications for homelessness assistance to a local housing authority in England on or after 3 April 2018.

¹¹ HA 1996, s 193C(6), as inserted by HRA 2017, s 7(1), for applications for homelessness assistance to a local housing authority in England on or after 3 April 2018, see **16.205–16.209.**

¹² HA 1996, s 202(1)(h) and (1B), as inserted by HRA 2017, s 9, for applications for homelessness assistance to a local housing authority in England on or after 3 April 2018.

¹³ As defined at HA 1996, s 193C(8), as inserted by HRA 2017, s 7(1), for applications for homelessness assistance to a local housing authority in England on or after 3 April 2018, see **16.210–16.213.**

¹⁴ As inserted by HRA 2017, s 7(1), for applications for homelessness assistance to a local housing authority in England on or after 3 April 2018.

¹⁵ HA 1996, s 193C(6), as inserted by HRA 2017, s 7(1), for applications for homelessness assistance to a local housing authority in England on or after 3 April 2018, see **16.210–16.213.**

¹⁶ HA 1996, s 202(1)(h) and (1B), as inserted by HRA 2017, s 9, for applications for homelessness assistance to a local housing authority in England on or after 3 April 2018.

18.20 It is plain, therefore, that there is no right to a statutory review of the suitability of accommodation offered in the exercise of a power[1]. Equally, there is no right to a review of the suitability of interim accommodation secured by a local housing authority in England under the duty in HA 1996, s 188(1)[2].

[1] Any challenge would have to be brought by way of judicial review.
[2] See **16.37–16.50.** There is a right to request a review of the suitability of interim accommodation secured under H(W)A 2014, s 68(1) at H(W)A 2014, s 85(3).

18.21 If a review on suitability is available and has been requested by the applicant, but is either unsuccessful or has not been determined by the local housing authority, the applicant can appeal to the county court on a point of law[1].

[1] HA 1996, s 204(1); H(W)A 2014, s 88(1). See **19.214–19.276.**

18.22 'Suitability' decisions that do not fall within the scope of the statutory review scheme will need to be challenged by way of judicial review proceedings or under the local housing authority's complaints procedure[1].

[1] See **19.306–19.340.**

18.23 If the local housing authority and the applicant are agreed that accommodation which has been offered or secured is *not* suitable, the appropriate procedure in order to obtain suitable accommodation is for the applicant to bring judicial review proceedings for a mandatory order requiring the local housing authority to secure such suitable accommodation. That remedy is discretionary. The Administrative Court could refuse permission to seek judicial review if the breach of statutory duty was not particularly significant and of short duration[1], or could refuse to make a mandatory order if the local housing authority demonstrated that it was doing all that it could to secure suitable accommodation[2]. But if there is plain and continuing failure and no clear evidence that everything possible is being done, the

Administrative Court should grant a mandatory order[3].

[1] *R v Newham London Borough Council ex p Sacupima* (2001) 33 HLR 2, CA at [17].
[2] *R v Lambeth London Borough Council ex p Touhey* (2000) 32 HLR 707, QBD; and *Ali v Birmingham City Council* [2009] UKHL 36, [2009] 1 WLR 1506, HL per Lord Hope at [4].
[3] *R v Newham London Borough Council ex p Mashuda Begum* (2000) 32 HLR 808, QBD; and *R (McCammon-Mckenzie) v Southwark London Borough Council* [2004] EWHC 612 (Admin), [2004] All ER (D) 174 (Mar), Admin Ct.

Grounds for challenge

18.24 The question of whether or not accommodation is 'suitable' is a factual one for the local housing authority to ask and answer. It is not for the applicant, the applicant's adviser, or for a judge to determine. Any applicant wishing to challenge the decision in the courts, and to argue that no reasonable local housing authority would have found that the accommodation was suitable for his or her needs, has a high hurdle to overcome[1]. A challenge may have a better prospect of success if it attacks the local housing authority's procedure in reaching its decision, or alleges a failure to consider a specific point raised, or a failure to have regard to a matter which ought to have been taken into account.

[1] *R v Haringey London Borough Council ex p Karaman* (1996) 29 HLR 366, QBD. See also *Watson v Wandsworth London Borough Council* [2010] EWCA Civ 1558, [2011] HLR 9, CA, where a first-instance judge's decision that a review decision that accommodation was suitable had been perverse was overturned by the Court of Appeal.

FACTORS THAT THE LOCAL HOUSING AUTHORITY MUST TAKE INTO ACCOUNT

Local housing authorities in England

18.25 As a matter of law, when determining whether particular accommodation is 'suitable', local housing authorities in England are required to consider seven matters:

(1) the provisions of the Housing Act 1985 relating to slum clearance and overcrowding[1];
(2) the provisions of Pts 1–4 of the Housing Act 2004 relating to housing conditions, houses in multiple occupation and licensing of accommodation[2];
(3) the affordability of the accommodation[3];
(4) the location of the accommodation[4]; a
(5) the public sector equality duty in Equality Act 2010, s 149[5];
(6) if the applicant is a child, or there are children in the applicant's household, the duty to safeguard and promote the welfare of children in Children Act 2004, s 11[6];
(7) in respect of school-age children, the duty in the Human Rights Act 1998 that no person shall be denied the right to education[7];
(8) the guidance given in the Code of Guidance[8]; and
(9) the relevant content (if any) of their own homelessness strategies[9].

[1] HA 1996, s 210(1); Housing Act 1985, Pts 9 and 10; also now referred to as 'demolition' or 'closing' and 'overcrowding' See **18.35–18.37**.

2   HA 1985, s 210(1); Housing Act 2004 Pts 1–4. See **18.38–18.44**.
3   HA 1996, s 210(2) and Homelessness (Suitability of Accommodation) Order 1996, SI 1996/3204. See **18.45–18.47** and Appendix 2.
4   Homelessness (Suitability of Accommodation) (England) Order 2012, SI 2012/2601, art 2, see Appendix 2, and see **18.48–18.64**.
5   *Pieretti v Enfield London Borough Council* [2010] EWCA Civ 1104, [2011] HLR 3, CA; *Hotak v Southwark London Borough Council* [2015] UKSC 30, SC per Lord Neuberger at[72]–[80]; *Wilson v Birmingham City Council,* [2016] EWCA Civ 1137, [2017] HLR 4, CA; *Hackney London Borough Council v Haque* [2017] EWCA Civ 4, [2017] HLR 14, CA; and *Poshteh v Kensington & Chelsea Royal London Borough Council* [2017] UKSC 36, [2017] AC 624, and see **18.65–18.68**.
6   *Nzolameso v City of Westminster Council* [2015] UKSC 22, [2015] 2 All ER 952, [2015] HLR 22, SC
7   Human Rights Act 1998, Sch 1, Pt 2, Art 2; and *R (E) v Islington London Borough Council* [2017] EWHC 1440 (Admin)
8   HA 1996, s 182(2). Guidance on suitability is at English Code, chapter 17.
9   Homelessness Act 2002, s 1(5)). See **7.89–7.90**.

18.26 Local housing authorities in England should also be aware that bed and breakfast accommodation made available under their duties to secure accommodation is deemed not to be suitable for applicants with family commitments, unless no other accommodation is available (and even then for at most only a six-week period)[1].

1   Homelessness (Suitability of Accommodation) (England) Order 2003, SI 2003/3326. See **18.131–18.146** and Appendix 2.

18.27 Local housing authorities in England making any of the following offers must also take into account 10 factors relating to physical condition and management of the property[1]:

- A private rented sector offer made under HA 1996, s 193(7AA)[2];
- A final accommodation made under HA 1996, s 193A(1)(b)(i)[3];
- A final accommodation offer made under HA 1996, s 193C(6)(a)[4]; or
- Any accommodation secured in discharge of the HA 1996, s 195(2)[5], prevention or HA 1996, s 189B(2)[6], relief duties, where the accommodation is made available under a tenancy with a private landlord, to an applicant who has a priority need.

1   Homelessness (Suitability of Accommodation) (England) Order 2012, SI 2012/2601, art 3, as amended by HRA 2017, s 12, for applications for homelessness assistance made to a local housing authority in England on or after 3 April 2018; see **18.70–18.79**. See Appendix 2.
2   See **16.153–16.180**.
3   As inserted by HRA 2017, s 7(1), for applications for homelessness assistance made to a local housing authority in England on or after 3 April 2018; see **15.181–15.184**.
4   As inserted by HRA 2017, s 7(1), for applications for homelessness assistance made to a local housing authority in England on or after 3 April 2018; see **16.205–16.209**.
5   As amended by HRA 2017, s 4(2), for applications for homelessness assistance made to a local housing authority in England on or after 3 April 2018; see **15.87–15.137**.
6   As inserted by HRA 2017, s 5(2), for applications for homelessness assistance made to a local housing authority in England on or after 3 April 2018; see **15.138–15.195**.

Local housing authorities in Wales

18.28 Local housing authorities in Wales are required to take the following into account when considering whether or not accommodation is suitable:

(1)   the provisions of the Housing Act 1985 relating to slum clearance and overcrowding[1];

(2)   the provisions of Pts 1–4 of the Housing Act 2004 relating to housing conditions, houses in multiple occupation and licensing of accommodation[2];

(3)   the provisions of H(W)A 2014, Pt 1, which relate to the regulation of private rented housing and require private landlords to be registered[3];

(4)   the affordability of the accommodation is affordable[4];

(5)   the location of the accommodation[5];

(6)   the public sector equality duty in Equality Act 2010, s 149[6]; and

(7)   if the applicant is a child, or there are children in the applicant's household, the duty to safeguard and promote the welfare of children in Children Act 2004, s 28[7];

(8)   the guidance given in the Code of Guidance[8]; and

(9)   the relevant content (if any) of their own homelessness strategies[9].

[1]   H(W)A 2014, s 59(1)(a) and (b), see **18.35–18.37**. 'Slum clearance' is also now referred to as 'demolition' or 'closing'.

[2]   H(W)A 2014, s 59(1)(c), (d), (e) and (f), see **18.38–18.44**.

[3]   H(W)A 2014, s 59(1)(g), see **18.81**.

[4]   H(W)A 2014, s 59(2), see **18.45–18.47**.

[5]   Homelessness (Suitability of Accommodation) (Wales) Order 2015/1268 (W 87), art 3, see **18.62–18.64**. See the CD Rom with this book.

[6]   *Pieretti v Enfield London Borough Council* [2010] EWCA Civ 1104, [2011] HLR 3, CA; and see **18.65–18.68**.

[7]   Note also the obligation in the Human Rights Act 1998 that no person shall be denied the right to education: Sch 1, Pt 2, Art 2.

[8]   H(W)A 2014 s 98(1); Welsh Code, chapter 19.

[9]   H(W)A 2014, s 50(4). See **7.89–7.90**.

18.29 When considering whether accommodation is suitable for any applicant who has, or may have, a priority need, a local housing authority in Wales must also consider:

(1)   the specific health needs of the applicant or of any members of his or her household;

(2)   the proximity and accessibility of family support;

(3)   any disability of the applicant or of any members of his or her household;

(4)   the proximity and accessibility of medical facilities and other support services which are currently used by or provided to the applicant or a member of his or her household and are essential to that person's well-being; and

(5)   the proximity of alleged perpetrators and victims of domestic abuse[1].

[1]   SI 2015/1268, art 3, see **18.63–18.64** and the CD Rom with this book.

18.30 Local housing authorities in Wales considering the making of a private rented sector offer[1] must also take into account three additional factors relating to physical condition, safety requirements and the fitness of the landlord[2].

[1]   H(W)A 2014, s 76(4), see **17.173–17.175**.

[2]   SI 2015/1268, art 8, see **18.80** and the CD Rom with this book.

18.31 Local housing authorities in Wales are prohibited from using bed and breakfast accommodation and other shared accommodation for any applicant who has, or may have, a priority need, except for very tightly defined periods of no more than two or six weeks (depending on the standard of the accommodation)[1].

[1] SI 2015/1268, arts 4–7, see **18.147–18.154** and the CD Rom with this book.

General points

18.32 The local housing authority's file notes, if not the terms of any letter written to the applicant, should demonstrate that these mandatory factors have been considered in respect of each unit of accommodation offered or secured. The presence of these factors in the statutory scheme ensures that a local housing authority cannot rely on accommodation offered unless it has informed itself, at least, of the physical attributes of the specific accommodation, its cost and, if situated outside of the district, specific considerations relating to its location[1].

[1] English Code, para 17.58; See *Nzolameso v City of Westminster Council* [2015] UKSC 22, [2015] 2 All ER 952, [2015] HLR 22, SC, where the local housing authority's letters, including the review decision, did not contain sufficient information to show that consideration had been given to the relevant statutory factors per Baroness Hale at [36]–[37]; and see also *R (E) v Islington London Borough Council* [2017] EWHC 1440 (Admin), Admin Ct where the file notes were deficient.

18.33 Beyond the mandatory matters, however, numerous judicial decisions – reviewed and applied by the Court of Appeal in *Codona v Mid-Bedfordshire District Council*[1] – have confirmed that 'suitability' has 'a broad meaning'.

'It must, as a matter of common-sense encompass considerations of the range, nature and location of accommodation as well as of its standard of condition and the likely duration of the applicant's occupancy of it. Standards of the condition of property are clearly important[2].'

[1] [2004] EWCA Civ 925, [2005] HLR 1, CA.
[2] Auld LJ at [34].

18.34 In the rest of this chapter, we consider first the mandatory matters set out at **18.35–18.61** and **18.65–18.79** (England) and **18.35–18.48**, **18.62–18.70** and **18.80–18.81**(Wales); second, the suitability of private rented sector offers in both England[1] and Wales[2], and the suitability of final accommodation offers and other offers of accommodation made by private landlords to applicants who have a priority need in England[3]; third, the additional statutory factors for local housing authorities in Wales[4]; and fourth the broader range of matters relevant to 'suitability'[5]. The specific statutory factors governing the use of bed and breakfast accommodation[6] and of shared accommodation[7] are discussed at **18.131–18.146** (England) and **18.131–18.135** and **18.147–18.154** (Wales).

[1] See **18.69–18.79**.
[2] See **18.80–18.81**.
[3] See **18.108–18.110–18.111**.
[4] H(W)A 2014, s 59(1)(g). See **18.80–18.81** and **18.112**.

⁵   See **18.82–18.122.**
⁶   Homelessness (Suitability of Accommodation) (England) Order 2003/3326 for local housing authorities in England see **18.136–18.146;** SI 2015/1268, arts 4 and 6–7 for local housing authorities in Wales, see **18.147–18.151** and the CD Rom with this book.
⁷   SI 2015/1268, arts 5–7 for local housing authorities in Wales, see **18.152–18.154** and the CD Rom with this book.

Mandatory matters for local housing authorities in England and Wales

Demolition, clearance or overcrowding

18.35 The provisions of the Housing Act 1985 direct local housing authorities to take action where dwelling houses in their districts are in such condition as to require demolition or clearance or where they are statutorily overcrowded[1].

¹   Housing Act 1985, Pts 9 and 10. See English Code, paras 17.25–17.26.

18.36 These strategic responsibilities would be wholly undermined if homeless households were to be placed in such poor or overcrowded premises at the initiative of the very same local housing authority. For that reason, the local housing authority is required by HA 1996, Pt 7[1] or H(W)A 2014, Pt 2, to 'have regard to' those statutory provisions addressing such housing conditions when considering what would be 'suitable' accommodation[2].

¹   As amended by HRA 2017 for applications for homelessness assistance made to local housing authorities in England on or after 3 April 2018.
²   HA 1996, s 210(1); H(W)A 2014, s 59(1)(a) and (b).

18.37 Neither HA 1996, Pt 7[1], nor H(W)A 2014, Pt 2, expressly states that accommodation which fails to meet statutory minimum standards or would be statutorily overcrowded is unsuitable. It follows, therefore, that a local housing authority could determine that the state of the accommodation contravenes the statutory standards, but that it is still suitable, although it would seem that the local housing authority would need some compelling reasons for such a determination.

¹   As amended by HRA 2017 for applications for homelessness assistance made to local housing authorities in England on or after 3 April 2018.

Housing conditions, houses in multiple occupation and licensing of accommodation

18.38 The Housing Act 2004 amended the statutory rubric regarding the mandatory considerations on the question of 'suitability' with effect from 6 April 2006 in England (16 June 2006 in Wales). From those dates, local housing authorities should have regard to 'slum clearance and overcrowding and Pts 1 to 4 of the Housing Act'[1]. The following paragraphs provide only a summary outline of the scope of Pts 1–4 of the Housing Act 2004 to which attention is drawn[2].

¹   HA 1996, s 210(1); H(W)A 2014, s 59(1)(c), (d), (e) and (f).
²   Useful summaries are given in paras 19.6–19.10 and 19.35–19.38 of the Welsh Code; the English Code contains briefer references at paras 17.23–17.24.

18.39 Part 1 of the Housing Act 2004[1] contains duties and powers enabling local housing authorities to inspect the condition of residential premises in their areas and to assess them for hazards. A 'hazard' is a risk of harm to the health of an actual or potential occupier deriving from a deficiency in the dwelling or neighbouring land. Where there are hazards identified as 'Category One' hazards, the local housing authority will be under a duty to take enforcement action. Where there are 'Category Two' hazards, the local housing authority has a power, not a duty, to require remedial action. The hazards relate to physiological requirements (damp and mould growth, excess cold or heat, pollutants), psychological requirements (relating to space, security, light and noise), protection against infection and protection against accident. The assessment of hazards is a complex process, including an assessment of the likelihood of an occurrence, the risk to health and safety of an actual or potential occupant, and the spread of possible harms[2].

[1] Housing Act 2004, ss 1–54.
[2] English Code, para 17.23; Welsh Code, para 19.7.

18.40 Neither the Housing Act 2004, HA 1996, s 210, nor H(W)A 2014, Pt 2, provide that accommodation will be, as a matter of law, unsuitable if it constitutes a Category One or Category Two hazard. However, the Codes contain recommendations that, as a minimum, local housing authorities should ensure that accommodation secured under HA 1996, Pt 7[1] or H(W)A 2014, Pt 2, duties is free of Category One hazards[2]. This should not be read as guidance that 'suitable accommodation' can contain Category Two hazards. The local housing authority should still normally consider the condition of the building and the risk to health and safety when deciding whether it is suitable[3]. However, it is for the local housing authority to decide whether an inspection and formal hazard assessment would provide it with any more information than it already had available, when making a decision on whether or not accommodation is suitable[4].

[1] As amended by HRA 2017 for applications for homelessness assistance made to local housing authorities in England on or after 3 April 2018.
[2] English Code, para 17.24; Welsh Code, para 19.37.
[3] In *Firoozmand v Lambeth London Borough Council* [2015] EWCA Civ 952, [2015] HLR 45, CA, the Court of Appeal considered the local housing authority's obligation to 'have regard' to Pts 1–4 of the Housing Act 2004. It held that where, following the making of a complaint, the local housing authority had come to the conclusion that an inspection of the premises would be appropriate, or had come under a duty to carry out an inspection following an official complaint, then the local housing authority must take those circumstances into account when deciding whether the accommodation would be suitable. However, the local housing authority was not required *always* to carry out a full hazard inspection and assessment. It is a matter for the local housing authority whether the potential scale of the problem makes it inappropriate to offer accommodation to the applicant before a full hazard assessment had been undertaken, bearing in mind the possible delay involved in undertaking a full assessment, measured against the apparent seriousness of the problem.
[4] *Firoozmand v Lambeth London Borough Council* [2015] EWCA Civ 952, [2015] HLR 45, CA.

18.41 Part 2[1] of the Housing Act 2004 requires that some houses in multiple occupation (HMOs), which include privately owned bed and breakfast and hostel accommodation, should be licensed by local housing authorities. For a licence to be granted, the local housing authority must be satisfied that the house is reasonably suitable for occupation by a specified number of persons or households, that the proposed licence holder and manager are both fit and proper persons and that the proposed management arrangements are satisfactory[2].

1   Housing Act 2004, ss 55–78.
2   English Code, paras 17.27–17.29; Welsh Code, paras 19.9, 19.46–19.49 and 19.55. There are different regulations governing standards of management in England and in Wales.

18.42 Local housing authorities also have a discretionary power, in Pt 3[1] of the Housing Act 2004, to designate areas in their districts as areas where there will be a requirement for the licensing of all privately rented housing.

1   Housing Act 2004, ss 79–100.

18.43 Where a local housing authority decides that there is no reasonable prospect of being able to grant a licence for a property under Pts 2 or 3 of the Housing Act 2004, Pt 4[1] of Housing Act 2004 obliges the local housing authority to make a management order, taking over the management of the property. The local housing authority may also make management orders in respect of HMOs which do not fall within Pts 2 or 3 of the Housing Act 2004 and so do not require licences. Management orders may also be made where the local housing authority believes that they are necessary for the health and safety of the occupiers of the property, or of others in the vicinity. Local housing authorities can make interim management orders (for a maximum period of 12 months) and final management orders (maximum period five years).

1   Housing Act 2004, ss 101–147.

18.44 There is nothing in the statutory schemes (HA 1996, Pt 7[1], H(W)A 2014, Pt 2, and Housing Act 2004, Pts 2–4) explicitly providing that a house in multiple occupation which does not comply with these provisions is not 'suitable' accommodation. It would be difficult to describe a dwelling for which the owner does not have the requisite licence, or where he or she is in breach of the licence conditions, as 'suitable'[2]. Although where the accommodation is being offered by a local housing authority in England as a private rented sector offer[3], a private accommodation offer[4], or under either the HA 1996, s 189B(2)[5] relief duty or HA 1996, s 195(2) prevention duty[6] to an applicant who has a priority need, a house in multiple occupation which is subject to licensing and is not licensed will be not be suitable[7]. The Welsh Code does contain advice that accommodation in a house of multiple occupation that is subject to the licensing scheme, and is not licensed, is not suitable[8].

1   As amended by HRA 2017 for applications for homelessness assistance made to local housing authorities in England on or after 3 April 2018.
2   English Code, paras 17.27–17.29; see **18.155–18.156**.
3   HA 1996, s 193(7AC), see **16.153–16.180**.
4   HA 1996, ss 193A(4) or 193C(6), as inserted by HRA 2017, s 7(1), for applications for homelessness assistance made to local housing authorities in England on or after 3 April 2018, see **15.181–15.184** and **16.205–16.209**.
5   As inserted by HRA 2017, s 5(2), for applications for homelessness assistance made to local housing authorities in England on or after 3 April 2018.
6   As amended by HRA 2017, s 4(2), for applications for homelessness assistance made to local housing authorities in England on or after 3 April 2018.

7 Art 3(1)(f) of SI 2012/2601 (as amended by HRA 2017, s 12, for applications for homelessness
   assistance made to local housing authorities in England on or after 3 April 2018).
8 Welsh Code, para 19.55.

Affordability

18.45 Local housing authorities in England and in Wales must take into
account whether or not the accommodation is affordable for a person[1]. If the
accommodation is not affordable, it will not be suitable[2]. Local housing
authorities in England are directed, by specific statutory order, to consider an
applicant's financial resources (including any available social security benefits),
and the total costs of the accommodation, in determining whether particular
accommodation would be 'suitable'[3]. Local housing authorities in Wales are
directed towards the same calculation by H(W)A 2014, s 59(2) supplemented
by advice in the Welsh Code[4].

1 Homelessness (Suitability of Accommodation) Order 1996, SI 1996/3204 for local housing
   authorities in England, see APPENDIX 2; H(W)A 2014, s 59(2) for local housing authorities in
   Wales.
2 *R (Yekini) v Southwark London Borough Council* [2014] EWHC 2096 (Admin), (2014)
   September *Legal Action*, p 50, Admin Ct.
3 Homelessness (Suitability of Accommodation) Order 1996, SI 1996/3204, see APPENDIX 2.
4 Welsh Code, paras 19.26–19.29.

18.46 The English Code simply advises that local housing authorities in
England will need to consider whether the applicant can afford the housing
cost without being deprived of basic essentials[1]. The Welsh Code is more
robust and contains advice that not only will accommodation be unsuitable if
the applicant would be unable to afford basic essentials, but also that it will
not be suitable if his or her net income, after payment of housing costs, would
be significantly less than income support or jobseekers allowance levels[2]. If
there is likely to be a substantial shortfall between housing benefit and the
contractual rent, which the applicant would have to find from his or her own
resources, the local housing authority will have to consider whether that
shortfall is affordable, taking into account all forms of income and all
reasonable expenses[3].

1 English Code, paras 17.44–17.45.
2 Welsh Code, para 19.28.
3 See *Eryurekler v Hackney London Borough Council* (2010) May *Legal Action*, p 24,
   Clerkenwell & Shoreditch County Court. See also *Balog v Birmingham City Council* [2013]
   EWCA Civ 1582, [2014] HLR 14, CA, and *Farah v Hillingdon London Borough Council*
   [2014] EWCA Civ 359, [2014] HLR 24, CA. See also *Samuels v Birmingham City Council*
   [2015] EWCA Civ 1051, [2015] HLR 47, CA, where the applicant has been granted
   permission to appeal to the Supreme Court.

18.47 There are some applicants who might not be able to afford anything
more than a nominal payment towards their housing costs[1]. The fact that an
applicant cannot pay for his or her housing costs does not allow the local
housing authority to bring any duty to accommodate the applicant to an end.
Local housing authorities should consider finding accommodation elsewhere,
at a cheaper rent, or charging a nil or nominal amount in rent if the
accommodation is secured from their own stock, or assisting the applicant to
obtain other funding (such as from children's services under Children Act

1989, s 17)[2] to pay the rent or indeed pay the rent themselves[3].

[1]   Examples might be applicants who are subject to the benefit cap.
[2]   See **20.39–20.68** or under the Social Services and Well-Being Act 2014 (Wales), see **20.85–20.98**.
[3]   *R (Yekini) v Southwark London Borough Council* [2014] EWHC 2096 (Admin), (2014) September *Legal Action*, p 50, Admin Ct per Michael Fordham QC sitting as a deputy High Court judge at [69].

Location of accommodation

18.48 Local housing authorities in England and in Wales are all required to secure accommodation for the applicant, and for his or her household, within their own districts so far as is reasonably practicable[1]. In both cases, if accommodation is to be secured outside of their own districts, they must give notice to the local housing authority in whose district the accommodation is situated[2]. This is because the local housing authority in whose district the accommodation is situated will become responsible for any social services', or education, responsibilities[3].

[1]   HA 1996, s 208(1); H(W)A 2014, s 91(1), see also **14.244–14.251**.
[2]   HA 1996, s 208(2); H(W)A 2014, s 91(2).
[3]   *R (AM) v Havering London Borough Council and Tower Hamlets London Borough Council* [2015] EWHC 1004 (Admin) (2015) May *Legal Action*, p 46, Admin Ct; *R (E) v Islington London Borough Council* [2017] EWHC 1440 (Admin) (2017) September, *Legal Action*, p 35. See **20.42**.

LOCAL HOUSING AUTHORITIES IN ENGLAND

18.49 Local housing authorities in England are directed by Art 2 of the Homelessness (Suitability of Accommodation) (England) Order 2012[1], (the Order) to take into account the location of the accommodation secured. Guidance is given in the English Code, paras 17.46–17.61[2].

[1]   SI 2012/2601, see APPENDIX 2.
[2]   See APPENDIX 2.

18.50 The Order[1] contains a non-exhaustive list of factors relating to the location of any accommodation. The local housing authority must take into account:

- where the accommodation is situated outside of its district, the distance of the accommodation from its district;
- the significance of any disruption which would be caused by the location of the accommodation to the employment, caring responsibilities or education of the applicant or of members of the applicant's household;
- the proximity and accessibility of the accommodation to medical facilities and other support which are currently used by or provided to the applicant, or used by or provided to members of the applicant's household, and which are essential to the applicant's well-being or to the well-being of members of the applicant's household; and
- the proximity and accessibility of the accommodation to local services,

amenities and transport[2].

[1]   SI 2012/2601.
[2]   SI 2012/2601, art 2.

18.51 These four factors must be considered by the local housing authority. The local housing authority must also, of course, consider any other factors regarding the location of the accommodation that might be relevant to its suitability, whether those other factors are already known to the local housing authority or are raised by the applicant.

18.52 Local housing authorities are reminded, in the Code that the starting point is that they should, so far as is reasonably practicable, secure accommodation within their own district[1]. If that is not possible, local housing authorities must take into account the distance of the accommodation to be secured from their own district. If accommodation which is otherwise suitable and affordable is available nearer to the local housing authority's district than the accommodation which has been secured, that accommodation is unlikely to be suitable unless the local housing authority has a justifiable reason for securing that accommodation, or the applicant has specified a preference[2]. When local housing authorities are assessing whether or not suitable accommodation might be available in their own districts, they should consider not only the current availability but also look to the future and consider whether suitable accommodation closer to the home borough might become available and, if so, within what period[3].

[1]   HA 1996, s 208(1), English Code, para 17.46.
[2]   English Code, para 17.47.
[3]   *Barakte v Brent London Borough Council* (2016) (2017) April *Legal Action*, p 42, County Court at Central London.

18.53 The Supreme Court considered art 2 of the Order in *Nzolameso v City of Westminster Council*[1]. The judgment reaffirms the significance of the obligation on local housing authorities to place applicants within their own district so far as is reasonably practicable. 'Reasonably practicable' is a stronger duty than an obligation simply to act reasonably. If it is not reasonably practicable to secure accommodation within the local housing authority's own district, it should try to place the applicant as close as possible to where he or she was previously living[2]. Ideally, each local housing authority should maintain and publish a policy of procuring units of accommodation within its own district and a separate policy on the allocation of those units. The factors that the local housing authority will rely on in deciding which applicants will be offered accommodation within its own district should be set out in the published policy. When local housing authorities are making offers of accommodation, the offer letter should show that the local housing authority has considered the four factors at art 2 of the Order, and has assessed how practicable it would be for the applicant to move out of the area, whether there were any inquiries made to ascertain whether school places would be available, and whether any medical conditions had been considered. The offer letter should also indicate that the local housing authority had recognised that, if accommodation could not be secured within its own district, there was an obligation to offer accommodation as close to the district as possible[3].

[1]   [2015] UKSC 22, [2015] 2 All ER 942, [2015] HLR 22, SC.

2   *Nzolameso v City of Westminster Council* [2015] UKSC 22, [2015] 2 All ER 942, [2015] HLR
    22, SC per Baroness Hale at [10].
3   *Nzolameso v City of Westminster Council* [2015] UKSC 22, [2015] 2 All ER 942, [2015] HLR
    22, SC per Baroness Hale at [36]–[40].

18.54 There is substantial guidance on location in the English Code[1]. Generally, local housing authorities should try to secure accommodation that is as close as possible to where an applicant was previously living. Where possible, they should try to ensure that the applicant can retain established links with schools, doctors, social workers and other key services and support[2]. The Secretary of State advises that applicants whose household has a need for social services support, or a need to maintain links with other essential services within the borough, such as families whose children are subject to safeguarding arrangements, should be given particular attention to try and ensure that their accommodation is located in or close to the local housing authority's own district. Similarly, careful consideration should be given to applicants with a mental illness or learning disability who may have a particular need to remain in a specific area, such as a need to maintain links with health services professionals or existing informal support networks or community links[3]. Letters containing offers of accommodation should clearly set out why a local housing authority has considered a particular property to be suitable, taking into account the applicant's needs and those of his or her household. Any offer letter should state how any medical needs will be met in a new district, how the impact on education on any school-age children has been assessed and what arrangements have been made for their education in the new district[4].

1   English Code, paras 17.46–17.61.
2   English Code, para 17.48.
3   English Code, para 17.56.
4   English Code para 17.58.

18.55 When considering the significance of disruption to employment, caring responsibilities and education, local housing authorities should take account of a person's need to reach his or her normal workplace from the accommodation secured (rather than expect the person to change employment), and should take account of the type and importance of the care that household members provide and the likely impact that withdrawal of that care would cause (including any cost implications)[1].

1   English Code, para 17.49

18.56 When considering the significance of disruption to education, local housing authorities have a number of additional obligations. Article 2, Protocol 1 of the European Convention on Human Rights[1] states 'no person shall be denied the right to education.' This means that public authorities, including local housing authorities, should not deny effective access to the general educational facilities available[2]. In addition, the duty at Children Act 2004, s 11(2) requires public authorities, including local housing authorities, to ensure that '(a) their functions are discharged having regard to the need to safeguard and promote the welfare of children; and (b) any services provided by another person pursuant to arrangements made by the person or body in discharge of their functions are provided having regard to that need'[3].

1   Human Rights Act 1998, Sch 1.

² *R (E) v Islington London Borough Council* [2017] EWHC 1440 (Admin) (2017) September, *Legal Action*, p 35, Admin Ct per Deputy High Court Judge Ben Emmerson QC at [25], citing *A v Headteacher and Governors of Lord Grey School* [2006] UKHL 14, [2006] AC 363, HL.
³ Children Act 2004, s 11(2). See Baroness Hale in *R (HC) v Secretary of State for Work and Pensions* [2017] UKSC 73, [2017] 3 WLR 1486, SC, where she emphasised the need both to safeguard and to promote the welfare of children at [46].

18.57 As interpreted by the Supreme Court in *Nzolameso v City of Westminster Council*[1], the Children Act 2004, s 11, duty, together with the requirements of art 2 of the Order, mean that local housing authorities need to address their minds to the educational consequences which follow any relocation and keep records of the factors they have taken into account and the process which by which the decision was reached. In *R (E) v Islington London Borough Council*[2], a deputy High Court judge held that those legal obligations mean that the local housing authority has a continuing duty to satisfy itself, throughout the period of any temporary placement outside of its district, that the receiving authority has taken (and will continue to take) the necessary steps to safeguard the child's educational welfare, that it must show that it has liaised with the education department of the receiving authority and satisfied itself that suitable arrangements were or will be in place, and that it has records demonstrating that it had taken those steps[3].

¹ [2015] UKSC 22, [2015] HLR 22, SC.
² [2017] EWHC 1440 (Admin), (2017) 20 CCL Rep 148, Admin Ct.
³ *R (E) v Islington London Borough Council*, [2017] EWHC 1440 (Admin), (2017) 20 CCL Rep 148, Admin Ct per Deputy High Court Judge Ben Emmerson QC at [116]–[120].

18.58 The English Code advises that local housing authorities should take into account the need to minimise disruption to the education of young people, particularly at critical points such as leading up to taking GCSE or equivalent examinations. They should also liaise with the receiving authority and make every reasonable effort to ensure arrangements are or will be put in place to meet a child's educational needs[1]. However, this should not be read as suggesting that disruption will not be caused if the child is not at GCSE or similar examination level[2].

¹ English Code, paras 17.50–17.51.
² See *Begum v Tower Hamlets London Borough Council* (2015) (2016) September *Legal Action*, p 38, County Court at Central London, where the local housing authority had failed to consider the needs and well-being of the children, who were undertaking a daily commute of five hours to school and back and had failed to consider the disruption that would be caused to their education by being forced to change school; and *Forsythe-Young v Redbridge London Borough Council* (2015), (2016) February *Legal Action*, p 46, County Court at Central London, where there had been non consideration of the distances necessary to travel in order for the child to continue at her current school and no consideration of alternative schools that would be available or of which school would be best for her.

18.59 When taking account of the proximity and accessibility of medical facilities and other support provided to the applicant and to his or her household, local housing authorities should consider the potential impact on the health and well-being of the person receiving those facilities or support if they were no longer accessible. They should consider whether similar facilities are accessible and available near the accommodation being offered, and whether there would be any specific difficulties in the person using those essential facilities[1].

[1] English Code, para 17.52

18.60 Local housing authorities should avoid placing applicants in isolated accommodation away from public transport, shops and other facilities, where possible[1].

[1] English Code, para 17.53.

18.61 The English Code advises that, in some cases, there might be clear benefits for an applicant to be accommodated outside of the local housing authority's district, for example where he or she (or a member of his or her household) would be at risk of violence in that district, where ex-offenders or substance abusers would benefit from being able to break links with previous contacts, or where an applicant might be able to find employment outside of the current district[1].

[1] English Code, paras 17.54–17.55.

LOCAL HOUSING AUTHORITIES IN WALES

18.62 As with local housing authorities in England, the starting point for local housing authorities in Wales is that accommodation should be secured within the local housing authority's own area, so far as is reasonably practicable[1]. Since the wording of the prohibition on placing outside a local housing authority's own district in H(W)A 2014, Pt 2, is identical to the wording in HA 1996, Pt 7, which was considered by the Supreme Court in *Nzolameso v City of Westminster Council*[2],.the Supreme Court's decision that 'reasonably practicable' is a stronger obligation than simply being reasonable applies equally to local housing authorities in Wales[3].

[1] H(W)A 2014, s 91(1). See discussion at **18.48**.
[2] [2015] UKSC 22, [2015] 2 All ER 942, [2015] HLR 22, SC.
[3] *Nzolameso v City of Westminster Council* [2015] UKSC 22, [2015] 2 All ER 942, [2015] HLR 22, SC per Baroness Hale at [19].

18.63 Local housing authorities in Wales are required to take into account, when considering whether accommodation is suitable for any applicant who has, or may have, a priority need:

(a) the specific health needs of an applicant and of the members of his or her household;
(b) the proximity and accessibility of family support;
(c) any disability of the applicant or of any member of his or her household;
(d) the proximity and accessibility of medical facilities and other support services which are currently used by or provided to the applicant or to a member of his or her household and which are essential to that person's well-being;
(e) where the accommodation is situated outside the area of the local housing authority, the distance of the accommodation from the local housing authority's area;

(f)   the significance of any disruption which would be caused by the location of the accommodation to the employment, caring responsibilities or education of the applicant or any member of his or her household; and

(g)   the proximity of alleged perpetrators and victims of domestic abuse[1].

---

[1]   Homelessness (Suitability of Accommodation) (Wales) Order 2015, SI 2015/1268 (W 87), art 3, see the CD Rom with this book.

18.64 However, the Welsh Code does not confine itself to guidance on those specific points. It advises that the suitability of the location for all members of the household must be considered by the local housing authority[1]. Where accommodation is located outside of the local housing authority's district, the requirement to take into account the distance means that accommodation will not be suitable if there is accommodation which is closer, and is also suitable and affordable[2]. The Code provides advice on assessing the significance of disruption to employment, caring responsibilities and education and on the proximity of a perpetrator of alleged domestic or other abuse[3].

---

[1]   Guidance on location is given in Welsh Code, paras 19.13–19.25.
[2]   Accommodation located further away could be suitable if the applicant had specified a preference for it: Welsh Code, para 19.14.
[3]   Welsh Code, paras 19.15–19.25. For considerations in relation to education, see *R (E) v Islington London Borough Council* (2107) EWHC 1440 (Admin), (2017) 20 CCL Rep 148, Admin Ct and the discussion at **18.57–18.58**.

Public sector equality duty

18.65 The Equality Act 2010, s 149 requires all public authorities, including local housing authorities, to have:

'due regard to the need to—
(a)   eliminate discrimination, harassment, victimisation and any other conduct that is prohibited by or under this Act;
(b)   advance equality of opportunity between persons who share a relevant protected characteristic and persons who do not share it;
(c)   foster good relations between persons who share a relevant protected characteristic and persons who do not share it'[1].

---

[1]   Equality Act 2010, s 149(1). The 'relevant protected characteristics' for the purposes of Equality Act 2010, s 149(1) are: age; disability; gender reassignment; pregnancy and maternity; race; religion or belief; sex; sexual orientation (Equality Act 2010, s 149(7)).

18.66 They must have such 'due regard' when exercising any of their functions under HA 1996, Pt 7[1] or H(W)A 2014, Pt 2[2]. So the duty to have 'due regard' to these equality issues applies not only when a local housing authority is deciding policy questions but also when any decisions are taken in respect of individual applications[3]. In *Hotak v Southwark London Borough Council*[4], the Supreme Court held that a local housing authority decision-maker should 'focus very sharply' on whether an applicant has a protected characteristic under Equality Act 2010, and the extent of the protected characteristic[5].

---

[1]   As amended by HRA 2017 for applications for homelessness assistance made to local housing authorities in England on or after 3 April 2018.

2   *Hotak v Southwark London Borough Council* [2015] UKSC 30, [2016] AC 811, SC per Lord Neuberger at [76].

3   *Pieretti v Enfield London Borough Council* [2010] EWCA Civ 1104, [2011] HLR 3, CA; *Hotak v Southwark London Borough Council* [2015] UKSC 30, [2016] AC 811, SC per Lord Neuberger [72]–[80]; *Hackney London Borough Council v Haque* [2017] EWCA Civ 4, [2017] HLR 14, CA; and *Poshteh v Kensington & Chelsea Royal London Borough Council* [2017] UKSC 36, [2017] AC 624, SC.

4   [2015] UKSC 30, [2016] AC 811, SC.

5   *Hotak v Southwark London Borough Council* [2015] UKSC 30, [2016] AC 811, SC per Lord Neuberger at [78].

18.67 The Court of Appeal considered what the public sector equality duty requires, in the context of local housing authorities assessing the suitability of accommodation, in *Hackney London Borough Council v Haque*[1]. It held that the duty required the decision-maker:

(i)   to recognise that the applicant had a disability or other relevant protected characteristic;

(ii)   to focus on specific aspects of his or her impairment or characteristics to the extent that they were relevant to the suitability of the accommodation;

(iii)   to focus on the disadvantages he or she might suffer when compared to a person without those impairments or characteristics;

(iv)   to focus on his or her accommodation needs arising from those impairments and the extent to which the accommodation met those needs;

(v)   to recognise that the applicant's particular needs might require him to be treated more favourably than a person without a disability or without that protected characteristic; and

(vi)   to review the suitability of the accommodation, paying due regard to those matters[2].

1   [2017] EWCA Civ 4, [2017] HLR 14, CA.

2   *Hackney London Borough Council v Haque* [2017] EWCA Civ 4, [2017] HLR 14, CA per Briggs LJ at [42]–[47]. The guidance was subsequently applied in *Chatokai v Salford City Council* (2017) July/August *Legal Action*, p 42, County Court at Manchester, where the reviewing officer had failed to consider whether it was reasonable for the applicant to continue to occupy his accommodation, and thus whether he was homeless as a result of HA 1996, s 175(3) 'through the prism of his subjectively experienced dysfunction'.

18.68 The local housing authority will need to inquire in any case where some feature of the evidence presents a real possibility that the applicant or a member of his or her household has protected characteristic which is relevant to the matter in issue[1]. Whether the evidence presents this real possibility is a question of fact for the local housing authority[2].

1   *Pieretti v Enfield London Borough Council* [2010] EWCA Civ 1104, [2011] HLR 3, CA, at [35].

2   *Wilson v Birmingham City Council* [2016] EWCA Civ 1137, [2017] HLR 4, CA, at [33].

Offers of accommodation in the private rented sector

18.69 Local housing authorities in both England and in Wales can bring their HA 1996, s 193(2) or H(W)A 2014, s 75(1), main housing duties to an end by making the applicant a private rented sector offer of suitable accommodation[1].

In both countries, there are factors specified by statutory instrument that a local housing authority must be satisfied about before such accommodation could be suitable. For local housing authorities in England, those specified factors also apply to final accommodation offers[2] and to other offers of accommodation in the private rented sector made to applicants who have a priority need[3].

[1] HA 1996, s 193(7AA), see **16.153–16.180**; H(W)A 2014, s 76(3)(b), see **17.173–17.177**.
[2] Defined at HA 1996, ss 193A(4) and 193C(7), as inserted by HRA 2017, s 7(1), for applications for homelessness assistance made to a local housing authority in England on or after 3 April 2018.
[3] Homelessness (Suitability of Accommodation) Order 2012, SI 2012/2601, art 3, as amended by HRA 2017, s 12, for applications for homelessness assistance made to a local housing authority in England on or after 3 April 2018, see **18.108**.

Local housing authorities in England

THE STANDARDS REQUIRED BY ART 3

18.70 Article 3 of the Homelessness (Suitability of Accommodation) (England) Order 2012[1] provides that most offers of accommodation in the private rented sector made to an applicant who has a priority need will only be suitable if the local housing authority is satisfied of all of the following:

(a) that the accommodation is in a reasonable physical condition;
(b) that the electrical equipment supplied with the accommodation meets the requirements of regs 5 and 7 of the Electrical Equipment (Safety) Regulations 1994[2];
(c) that the landlord has taken reasonable fire safety precautions with the accommodation and any furnishings supplied with it;
(d) that the landlord has taken reasonable precautions to prevent the possibility of carbon monoxide poisoning in the accommodation;
(e) that the landlord is a fit and proper person to act in the capacity of landlord, following consideration of whether he or she has:
    (i) committed any offence involving fraud or other dishonesty, or violence or drugs, or any offence listed in Sch 3 to the Sexual Offences Act 2003[3];
    (ii) practised unlawful discrimination (on grounds of sex, race, age, disability, marriage or civil partnership, pregnancy or maternity, religion or belief, sexual orientation, gender identity or gender reassignment) in, or in connection with, the carrying out of any business;
    (iii) contravened any provision of the law relating to housing or of landlord or tenant law; and
    (iv) acted otherwise than in accordance with any applicable code of practice for the management of a house in multiple occupation, approved under Housing Act 2004, s 233;
(f) that where it is a house in multiple occupation subject to licensing under Housing Act 2004, s 55, it is licensed;
(g) that where it is a house in multiple occupation subject to additional licensing under Housing Act 2004, s 54, it has that additional licence;
(h) that the property has a valid Energy Performance Certificate;

(i)   that the property has a current gas safety record in accordance with Gas Safety (Installation and Use) Regulations 1998[4]; and

(j)   that the landlord has provided a written tenancy agreement which he or she proposes to use for the purposes of a private rented sector offer and the local housing authority considers the agreement to be adequate[5].

[1]   SI 2012/2601, as amended by HRA 2017, s 12, for applications for homelessness assistance made to a local housing authority in England on or after 3 April 2018. See APPENDIX 2.

[2]   SI 1994/3260. The Regulations require electrical equipment to be safe and in conformity either with EU harmonised standards or UK domestic standards.

[3]   The Schedule as amended specifies 175 offences which are to be notified as sexual offences under Sexual Offences Act 2003, Pt 2.

[4]   SI 1998/2451.

[5]   SI 2012/2601, art 3(1), as amended by HRA 2017, s 12, for applications for homelessness assistance made to a local housing authority in England on or after 3 April 2018. See APPENDIX 2.

18.71 Guidance is given in the English Code at paras 17.11–17.22[1]. Local housing authorities are advised to ensure that the property has been visited either by one of their officers or someone acting on their behalf. In determining whether the accommodation is in 'reasonable physical condition'[2], the English Code advises that attention should be paid to signs of damp, mould, indications that the property would be cold and any other physical signs that would indicate that it is not in reasonable physical condition[3].

[1]   See APPENDIX 2.

[2]   SI 2012/2601, art 3(1)(a), as amended by HRA 2017, s 12, for applications for homelessness assistance made to a local housing authority in England on or after 3 April 2018.

[3]   English Code, para 17.16.

18.72 A visual inspection of the electrical equipment, checking for obvious signs of loose wiring, cracked or broken sockets, or lights switches that do not work, is said to be indicative that the relevant regulations have been applied[1]. Landlords, owners or agents are required to carry out a fire risk assessment of the common parts and implement and maintain appropriate and adequate fire safety measures[2]. They should put in place appropriate management and maintenance systems to ensure that any fire safety equipment, or equipment which may represent a fire hazard, is maintained in good working order and in accordance with the manufacturer's instructions. Furniture and furnishings supplied must comply with the Furniture and Furnishings (Fire) (Safety) Regulations 1988[3]. Landlords are required to have at least one smoke alarm installed on every storey of their properties and a carbon monoxide alarm in any room containing a solid fuel burning appliance, and must make sure that the alarms are in working order at the start of each new tenancy[4]. The accommodation must also have a valid energy performance certificate and a current gas safety record[5]. Local housing authorities should satisfy themselves that the relevant regulations have been adhered to[6].

[1]   SI 2012/2601, art 3(1)(b), as amended by HRA 2017, s 12, for applications for homelessness assistance made to a local housing authority in England on or after 3 April 2018.

[2]   SI 2012/2601, art 3(1)(c), as amended by HRA 2017, s 12, for applications for homelessness assistance made to a local housing authority in England on or after 3 April 2018.

[3]   SI 1998/1324, as amended.

[4]   SI 2012/2601, art 3(1)(d), as amended by HRA 2017, s 12, for applications for homelessness assistance made to a local housing authority in England on or after 3 April 2018.

⁵ SI 2012/2601, art 3(1)(h) and (i), as amended by HRA 2017, s 12, for applications for homelessness assistance made to a local housing authority in England on or after 3 April 2018; English Code, para 17.14.
⁶ English Code paras 17.17–17.19.

18.73 Local housing authorities must satisfy themselves that landlords are fit and proper people to act in that capacity[1]. This includes considering whether the landlord has committed any relevant criminal offence, practised unlawful discrimination in or in connection with the carrying on of any business, contravened any provision of housing law or acted contrary to any applicable code of practice for the management of a House in Multiple Occupation (HMO). Where the accommodation is outside of the local housing authority's district, there should be liaison with the relevant district[2].

1 SI 2012/2601, art 3(1)(e), as amended by HRA 2017, s 12, for applications for homelessness assistance made to a local housing authority in England on or after 3 April 2018.
2 English Code, paras 17.20–17.21.

18.74 Any HMO that is required to be licensed will not be suitable accommodation unless it is licensed[1]. Local housing authorities should be satisfied that a HMO is suitable for the number of households or occupants it is licensed for and that it meets statutory standards relating to shared amenities and facilities[2].

1 SI 2012/2601, art 3(1)(f) and (g), as amended by HRA 2017, s 12, for applications for homelessness assistance made to a local housing authority in England on or after 3 April 2018.
2 English Code, paras 17.27–17.29; the standards are at Housing Act 2004, ss 254–275 and Licensing and Management of Houses in Multiple Occupation and Other Houses (Miscellaneous Provisions) (England) Regulations 2006, SI 206/373.

18.75 Local housing authorities should ensure that the landlord has provided to them, in advance, the written tenancy agreement to be used for the purposes of a private rented sector offer[1].

1 SI 2012/2601, art 3(1)(j), as amended by HRA 2017, s 12, for applications for homelessness assistance made to a local housing authority in England on or after 3 April 2018; English Code, para 17.14(e).

18.76 In addition, the English Code recommends that local housing authorities remind prospective landlords, and tenants, that landlords are required to place any deposit in a tenancy deposit scheme[1].

1 English Code, para 17.22. This is not part of the 10-point checklist in SI 2012/2601, Art 3.

OFFERS OF ACCOMMODATION TO WHICH ART 3 STANDARDS APPLY

18.77 These standards apply to[1]:

- private rented sector offers made under HA 1996, s 193(7AA)[2], in order to bring the HA 1996, s 193(2), main housing duty[3] to an end[4];
- final accommodation offers as defined at HA 1996, s 193A(4)[5], made under HA 1996, s 193A(1)(b)[6], in order to bring the HA 1996, s 189B(2)[7], relief duty to an end[8];

- final accommodation offers as defined at HA 1996, s 193C(7)[9], made under HA 1996, s 193C(6)[10], in order to bring the HA 1996, s 193C(4)[11], accommodation duty owed to applicants who have deliberately and unreasonably refused to co-operate to an end[12]; and
- any accommodation which is made available for occupation under a tenancy with a private landlord and is secured for a person who has a priority need under the HA 1996, s 195(2)[13], prevention or HA 1996, s 189B(2)[14], relief duties[15].

[1] SI 2012/2601, art 3(2), as amended by HRA 2017, s 12, for applications for homelessness assistance made to a local housing authority in England on or after 3 April 2018.
[2] See **16.153–16.180.**
[3] See **16.94–16.199.**
[4] SI 2012/2601, art 3(2)(a), as inserted by HRA 2017, s 12(4), for applications for homelessness assistance made to a local housing authority in England on or after 3 April 2018, see **16.153–16.180.**
[5] As inserted by HRA 2017, s 7(1), for applications for homelessness assistance made to a local housing authority in England on or after 3 April 2018, see **15.181–15.184.**
[6] As inserted by HRA 2017, s 7(1), for applications for homelessness assistance made to a local housing authority in England on or after 3 April 2018, see **15.181–15.184.**
[7] As inserted by HRA 2017, s 4(2), for applications for homelessness assistance made to a local housing authority in England on or after 3 April 2018, see **15.138–15.195.**
[8] SI 2012/2601, Art 3(2)(b), as inserted by HRA 2017, s 12(4), for applications for homelessness assistance made to a local housing authority in England on or after 3 April 2018, see **15.181–15.184.**
[9] As inserted by HRA 2017, s 7(1), for applications for homelessness assistance made to a local housing authority in England on or after 3 April 2018, see **16.205–16.209.**
[10] As inserted by HRA 2017, s 7(1), for applications for homelessness assistance made to a local housing authority in England on or after 3 April 2018, see **16.205–16.209.**
[11] As inserted by HRA 2017, s 7(1), for applications for homelessness assistance made to a local housing authority in England on or after 3 April 2018, see **16.200–16.216.**
[12] SI 2012/2601, Art 3(2)(b), as inserted by HRA 2017, s 12(4), for applications for homelessness assistance made to a local housing authority in England on or after 3 April 2018, see **16.200–16.216.**
[13] As amended by HRA 2017, s 5(2), for applications for homelessness assistance made to a local housing authority in England on or after 3 April 2018, see **15.87–15.137.**
[14] As inserted by HRA 2017, s 4(2), for applications for homelessness assistance made to a local housing authority in England on or after 3 April 2018, see **15.138–15.195.**
[15] SI 2012/2601, Art 3(2)(c), as inserted by HRA 2017, s 12(4), for applications for homelessness assistance made to a local housing authority in England on or after 3 April 2018, see **16.278–16.279.**

18.78 This last category would include any accommodation made available by a private landlord which the local housing authority is satisfied is, or would have been, available for the applicant's occupation for at least six months. The common thread between these four groups is that the applicant will have a priority need. In general, the standards do not apply to applicants who do not have a priority need[1].

[1] It is possible that an applicant could be made a final accommodation offer designed to bring the HA 1996, s 189B(2) (as inserted by HRA 2017, s 5(2), for applications for homelessness assistance made to local housing authorities in England on or after 3 April 2018) relief duty to an end, even if he or she does not have a priority need: HA 1996, ss 189B(9)(a) and 193A(1)(b) as inserted by HRA 2017, ss 5(2) and 7(1), for applications for homelessness assistance made to local housing authorities in England on or after 3 April 2018). See **15.181–15.184.**

18.79 Even if the standards do not apply, because the applicant has found the accommodation or because he or she does not have a priority need, the

Secretary of State expects local housing authorities to make reasonable efforts to ensure private rented accommodation is safe and in reasonable condition[1].

[1]   English Code, para 17.15.

Local housing authorities in Wales

18.80 A private rented sector offer made by a local housing authority in Wales[1] and intended to bring the H(W)A 2014, s 75(1) main housing duty to an end[2] will not be of 'suitable' accommodation if any one or more of the following apply:

(1)   the local housing authority is of the view that the accommodation is not in reasonable physical condition;

(2)   the local housing authority is of the view that the accommodation does not comply with all statutory requirements, such as, where applicable, requirements relating to fire, gas, electrical, carbon monoxide and other safety; planning; and licences for houses in multiple occupation; or

(3)   the local housing authority is of the view that the landlord is not a fit and proper person within the meaning of H(W)A 2014, s 20, to act in the capacity of landlord[3].

Guidance is given in paras 19.35–19.55 of the Welsh Code. The standards do not apply to other offers of accommodation.

[1]   H(W)A 2014, s 76(4), see **17.173–17.177**.
[2]   H(W)A 2014, s 76(3)(b), see **17.165–17.171**.
[3]   Homelessness (Suitability of Accommodation) (Wales) Order 2015, SI 2015/1268 (W 87), art 8, see the CD Rom with this book.

Additional statutory factors for local housing authorities in Wales

18.81 Local housing authorities in Wales are additionally directed to consider the provisions of H(W)A 2014, Pt 1[1] when assessing the suitability of accommodation. This requires all landlords letting 'domestic tenancies'[2] to be registered for each dwelling that is let, or marketed to be let, and licensed to let premises and to carry out property management activities. The requirements to be registered and licensed do not apply to local housing authorities[3] or to registered social landlords or housing associations[4]. In order to obtain a licence, the landlord must be a 'fit and proper person'[5].

[1]   H(W)A 2014, s 59(1)(g); Welsh Code, paras 19.6–19.10 and 19.35–19.55.
[2]   Defined in H(W)A 2014, s 2(1).
[3]   Because the definition of 'domestic tenancy' refers to assured, including assured shorthold, tenancies and to regulated tenancies: H(W)A 2014, s 2(1).
[4]   H(W)A 2014, ss 4 and 8.
[5]   H(W)A 2014, ss 19–20.

PARTICULAR ASPECTS OF 'SUITABILITY'

Expected duration of occupation

18.82 The length of time that an applicant and his or her household is expected to occupy any accommodation secured under HA 1996, Pt 7[1], or H(W)A 2014, Pt 2, duties or powers, is relevant to the standard of the accommodation and its location:

> 'What is suitable for occupation in the short term may not be suitable for occupation in the medium term, and what is suitable for occupation in the medium term may not be suitable for occupation in the longer term[2].'

---

[1] As amended by HRA 2017 for applications for homelessness assistance made to a local housing authority in England on or after 3 April 2018.

[2] *Ali & others v Birmingham City Council, Moran v Manchester City Council* [2009] UKHL 36, [2009] 1 WLR 1506, HL, at [47] per Baroness Hale. See also English Code, para 17.7.

18.83 If the accommodation offered is a final offer of accommodation made under HA 1996, Pt 6[1] or H(W)A 2014, Pt 2[2], it would not necessarily be unreasonable for the local housing authority, when considering 'suitability', to expect the applicant to change schools, doctors, etc, although each case has to be considered on its individual facts[3]. However, it could be far more disruptive for an applicant offered accommodation under HA 1996, Pt 7[4], or H(W)A 2014, Pt 2, to have to make those changes, as he or she would only be occupying the accommodation until the duties under HA 1996, Pt 7[5] or H(W)A 2014, Pt 2, ended. It might also be disruptive for an applicant made a private rented sector offer[6], a final accommodation offer[7] or other accommodation in the private sector to have to make those changes, since the applicant may not have any legal right to occupy the accommodation offered for more than six or 12 months. Similarly, it may be appropriate for an applicant to tolerate certain conditions for the short-term which would not be appropriate, and would render the accommodation unsuitable, if those conditions were to be experienced in the long-term[8].

---

[1] Relied upon to release the local housing authority from the HA 1996, s 189B(2), relief duty: HA 1996, ss 189B(9)(a) and 193A(1)(b) (as inserted by HRA 2017, ss 5(2) and 7(1), for applications for homelessness assistance made to a local housing authority in England on or after 3 April 2018) see **15.185–15.188**. Or from the HA 1996 s 193(2) main housing duty: HA 1996, s 193(6)(c) or (7), see **16.130–16.135** and **16.142–16.152**. Or from the HA 1996, s 193C(4) accommodation duty to applicants who have unreasonably and deliberately refused to co-operate: HA 1996, s 193C(6)(b) (as inserted by HRA 2017, s 7(1), for applications for homelessness assistance made to a local housing authority in England on or after 3 April 2018, see **16.210–16.213**.

[2] Relied upon to release the local housing authority from the H(W)A 2014 s 75(1) main housing duty: H(W)A 2014, s 76(2)(a) and (3)(c), see **17.178–17.179**.

[3] *R v South Holland District Council ex p Baxter* (1998) 30 HLR 1069, QBD; and *Williams v Birmingham City Council* [2007] EWCA Civ 691, [2008] HLR 4, CA.

[4] As amended by HRA 2017 for applications for homelessness assistance made to a local housing authority in England on or after 3 April 2018.

[5] As amended by HRA 2017 for applications for homelessness assistance made to a local housing authority in England on or after 3 April 2018.

[6] HA 1996, s 193(7AC), see **16.153–16.180**; H(W)A 2014, s 76(4), see **17.173–17.177**.

[7] HA 1996, ss 193A(4) and 193C(6), as inserted by HRA 2017, s 7(1), for applications for homelessness assistance made to a local housing authority in England on or after 3 April 2018, see **15.181–15.184** and **16.205–16.209**.

[8] English Code, para 17.7.

18.84 It is for those reasons that local housing authorities in both England and in Wales are required to consider the significance of any disruption. For local housing authorities in England, the Homelessness (Suitability of Accommodation) (England) Order 2012[1] specifically requires them to consider the issue of the significance of any disruption to employment, caring responsibilities or education for the applicant and any member of his or her household[2]. There is guidance at paras 17.46–17.61 of the English Code[3].

[1]   SI 2012/2601, as amended by HRA 2017, s 12, for applications for homelessness assistance made to a local housing authority in England on or after 3 April 2018, see APPENDIX 2.
[2]   SI 2012/2601, art 2.
[3]   See APPENDIX 2.

18.85 For local housing authorities in Wales, the Homelessness (Suitability of Accommodation) (Wales) Order 2015, art 3(f), similarly requires them to take into account the significance of any disruption which would be caused by the location of the accommodation to the employment, caring responsibilities or education of the applicant or of any member of his or her household[1].

[1]   SI 2015/12668, art 3(f), on the CD Rom with this book; Welsh Code, paras 19.13–19.25.

Space and arrangement

18.86 The English Code provides that space and arrangement of the accommodation are 'key factors' in determining its suitability[1]. But that, like the judicial pronouncement from which it is drawn[2], is not intended to suggest to the local housing authority that it must do anything other than consider *all* relevant matters.

[1]   English Code, para 17.4; not in Welsh Code.
[2]   *R v Brent London Borough Council ex p Awua* [1996] AC 55, HL at 72 per Lord Hoffmann.

18.87 Particular issues in relation to space and arrangement of accommodation can arise where there are children in the household, or elderly or disabled persons[1]. Accommodation which is not suitable and requires adaptations could be suitable accommodation if the offer is accompanied with certain, binding and enforceable assurances as to the adaptations to be carried out before the accommodation is to be occupied in order to render it suitable[2].

[1]   English Code, para 17.5.
[2]   *Boreh v Ealing London Borough Council* [2008] EWCA Civ 1176, [2009] HLR 22, CA.

18.88 Where there are children, issues such as insecure door and window locks, access to a dangerous balcony, and inoperative fire doors will be relevant. They could produce a genuine risk to the health or safety of a child, and the local housing authority would be under a duty to consider those matters[1]. Where the applicant, or any member of his or her household, is disabled, then the accessibility of the accommodation itself is relevant, as is the internal layout in terms of the provision of accessible bathroom and toilet facilities[2].

[1]   *R v Newham London Borough Council ex p Gentle* (1993) 26 HLR 466, QBD.
[2]   *R (Amirun Begum) v Tower Hamlets London Borough Council* [2002] EWHC 633 (Admin), (2003) 35 HLR 8, Admin Ct; and *Boreh v Ealing London Borough Council* [2008] EWCA Civ

1176, [2009] HLR 22, CA. See also the somewhat surprising decision in *McDermott v Croydon London Borough Council* [2011] EWCA Civ 1696 (2012) April *Legal Action*, p 47, CA, that there was no error of law where a local housing authority had decided that accommodation was suitable even where a disabled man could not access the kitchen, since his disability prevented him from using the kitchen facilities even if he could get access. In another case, the Local Government Ombudsman found that there was maladministration where an applicant occupied a second floor flat without lift access. During the course of his occupation there, he had become paralysed and had to use a wheelchair. The local housing authority acknowledged that the accommodation had become unsuitable but had only identified one alternative property in a six-month period and thus deprived him of suitable temporary accommodation for over six months: *Complaint against Newham London Borough Council*, 13 017 531, 3 June 2014 (2014) October *Legal Action*, p 51.

18.89 In one case, a local housing authority offered a five-bedroom house with one combined bathroom and toilet to an applicant to occupy with her husband, her ten children and two other family members. The applicant said that this accommodation could not be suitable as it would involve 14 people sharing one toilet. Rejecting that claim, the judge said that, when determining what is suitable accommodation, the local housing authority is entitled to take account of any general shortage of accommodation available to it in its district and the nature of the accommodation actually available to it[1].

[1]   *R v Camden London Borough Council ex p Jibril* (1997) 29 HLR 785, QBD.

18.90 The Supreme Court has considered whether the obligation to secure suitable accommodation for an applicant and all the members of his or her household[1] requires a local housing authority always to secure one unit of accommodation, for occupation by all the household members. In *Sharif v Camden London Borough Council*[2], the Supreme Court held that the test was whether or not the household could 'live together'. That test would be satisfied by a single unit of accommodation in which the 'family' could live together. But, depending on the individual circumstances, it could also be satisfied by two units of accommodation if they are located so that they enable the family to live 'together' in practical terms. That is a factual test, to be decided by the local housing authority. The issue, where there is more than one unit of accommodation, is whether they are close enough together to enable the household to 'eat and share time together as a family'. However, if accommodation did not permit the family to 'live together' in that sense, then it would not be suitable[3].

[1]   As defined at HA 1996, s 176 or H(W)A 2014, s 56, see 10.21–10.32.
[2]   [2013] UKSC 10, [2013] HLR 16, SC.
[3]   *Sharif v Camden London Borough Council* [2013] UKSC 10, [2013] HLR 16, SC per Lord Carnwath at [17] and [23] and Baroness Hale at [30].

18.91 A parent who has staying contact with his or her children, rather than the children actually residing with him or her, will not normally be entitled to expect a bedroom for the children[1]. Where a local housing authority's allocation scheme provided for an additional bedroom if the applicant needed overnight care, which was not given by a member of the applicant's household, the local housing authority should apply its scheme and consider *any* evidence supporting a need for an additional bedroom[2].

[1] *Holmes-Moorhouse v Richmond-upon-Thames Royal London Borough Council* [2009] UKHL 7, [2009] 1 WLR 413, HL; *Dixon v Haringey London Borough Council* [2013] EWCA Civ 1050, (2013) October *Legal Action*, p 35, CA.
[2] *Walsh v Haringey London Borough Council* (2014) July/August, *Legal Action*, p 56, Clerkenwell & Shoreditch County Court.

Standard of accommodation

18.92 Although the courts have recognised a minimum standard of suitability below which accommodation must not fall[1], once that threshold is met it is for the local housing authority to determine the standard of the accommodation offered or secured. It must be remembered that even the 'main housing duty' under HA 1996, s 193(2), or under H(W)A 2014, s 75(1), is only the safety net provision of temporary accommodation until the applicant's longer term housing needs are resolved. It would be wrong to raise expectations that this short-term accommodation will be of a high standard.

[1] See **18.3–18.6**.

18.93 A local housing authority is entitled to have regard to the 'realities' in terms of the accommodation it can offer in areas of high demand where, therefore, 'a high standard of suitability cannot be obtained'[1]. The statutory references to 'slum clearance' and 'overcrowding' as mandatory consider-ations[2] indicate 'a relatively modest minimum standard that is relevant to the determination of suitability'[3].

[1] *R v Brent London Borough Council ex p Omar* (1991) 23 HLR 446, QBD, at 459 per Henry J.
[2] See **18.35–18.37**. The Local Government Ombudsman found maladministration when an applicant was told to accept accommodation that was 'filthy' and in such a state as to be 'stomach turning'. The local housing authority paid the applicant £2,450 on the Ombuds-man's recommendation in recognition of the distress caused (*Complaint against Nottingham City Council*, 05/C/02965, 19 April 2007).
[3] *R v Camden London Borough Council ex p Jibril* (1997) 29 HLR 785, QBD, at 792 per Stephen Richards sitting as a deputy High Court judge.

18.94 Obviously, once the applicant has taken up occupation of the accom-modation, he or she can rely on the express or implied provisions of the tenancy agreement to secure any necessary repairs. Disrepair, and any other problems with the standard of the property (eg lack of soundproofing), can also be addressed by inviting the local Environmental Health Officer to inspect the accommodation.

18.95 Where the accommodation is offered under the allocation arrange-ments in HA 1996, Pt 6 (normally of long-term housing accommodation), a higher standard might be expected before the accommodation was to be considered 'suitable'.

Medical needs

18.96 The medical needs of the applicant and his or her household are clearly relevant to the question of suitability. When considering the suitability of accommodation offered to an applicant who has raised both medical and non-medical reasons as to why it might not be suitable, the local housing authority must take an overall or composite view of the applicant's needs[1].

[1]   *R v Lewisham London Borough Council ex p Dolan* (1993) 25 HLR 68, QBD.

18.97 Some examples of court decisions where the issue was whether the accommodation was suitable given the applicant's medical circumstances are:

- where an applicant suffering from post-traumatic stress disorder rejected an offer of accommodation situated on the twenty-seventh floor, the local housing authority was under a duty to consider the medical evidence properly[1];
- where an applicant with vertigo had a panic attack and collapsed in the lift after viewing a flat on the 16th floor of a tower block, the local housing authority acted irrationally in deciding the property was suitable[2];
- where no medical evidence had been provided in support of an assertion that the applicant's child had a fear of heights, and there was nothing forthcoming in response to specific inquiries and a minded-to letter, the local housing authority was not wrong in law to conclude that any problems that the child might not have were not such that the applicant thought she should obtain a medical diagnosis[3];
- where an applicant produced evidence that she had suffered a violent sexual assault on a housing estate, the local housing authority was under a duty to consider that evidence when deciding whether the offer of accommodation on an estate was suitable[4];
- where a local housing authority had decided that a property on the third or fourth floor, with no access by lift, was suitable for a single parent who suffered from back problems and who had two young children, that decision was quashed because it had failed to have proper or adequate regard to the medical evidence[5];
- a local housing authority made no error of law in offering a maisonette with 13 internal steps to an applicant who suffered chronic back pain, even though there was medical evidence that climbing stairs would aggravate her back pain[6];
- a local housing authority was wrong in law not to have obtained any information as to the risk to an applicant who suffered from epilepsy of occupying a small studio-bedsit property, where she said that she was at greater risk of injury during a fit than she would have been had she had larger accommodation[7];
- where the applicant suffered from severe post-traumatic disorder and her treating psychotherapist had advised that the accommodation offered could do serious damage to her, and set back her psychological progress, the local housing authority was wrong in law to prefer the opinion of a psychiatrist, who had not met or examined the applicant, over that of the treating psychotherapist[8]; and
- where the reviewing officer had considered the medical evidence but had concluded that it was based on assertions, made by the applicant to her medical advisers about the layout of the property, which did not match the facts, the local housing authority was not wrong in law to

conclude that the accommodation was suitable[9].

1   *R v Kensington and Chelsea Royal London Borough Council ex p Campbell* (1996) 28 HLR 160, QBD.
2   *El Dinnaoui v Westminster City Council* [2013] EWCA Civ 231, [2013] HLR 23, CA, where the medical evidence made it clear that the applicant's wife had a fear of heights.
3   *Wilson v Birmingham City Council* [2016] EWCA Civ 1137, [2017] HLR 4, CA.
4   *R v Islington London Borough Council ex p Thomas* (1997) 30 HLR 111, QBD, although, once the local housing authority had considered the medical evidence and decided that the offer was suitable, its decision was upheld.
5   *R v Haringey London Borough Council ex p Sampaio* (1999) 31 HLR 1, QBD.
6   *Abdi v Wandsworth London Borough Council* [2006] EWCA Civ 1099, (2006) October *Legal Action*, p 26, CA.
7   *Nazokkar v Barnet London Borough Council* (2011), February *Legal Action*, p 45, Central London Civil Trial Centre.
8   *Oyebanji v Waltham Forest London Borough Council* (2013) Central London County Court, (2014) February *Legal Action*, p 31.
9   *Poshteh v Kensington & Chelsea Royal London Borough Council* [2017] UKSC 36, [2017] AC 64, SC.

18.98 Local housing authorities in Wales are directed to consider:

- the specific health needs of the applicant, and those of the members of his or her household;
- the proximity and accessibility of family support;
- any disability of the applicant, and those of the members of his or her household; and
- the proximity and accessibility of medical facilities and other support services, which are currently used by a person or by a member of his or her household and which are essential to that person's well-being[1].

1   Homelessness (Suitability of Accommodation) (Wales) Order 2015, SI 2015/1268 (W 87), art 3; Welsh Code, paras 19.15–19.19, see **18.63** and the CD Rom with this book.

Terms and tenure

Contractual terms

18.99 When accommodation is being secured in performance of any of the accommodation duties or power at HA 1996, Pt 7[1], of H(W)A 2014, Pt 2, there are no requirements for accommodation to be secured or offered on any particular terms, or with any security of tenure, in order for it to be 'suitable'[2]. However, if the accommodation is being offered on 'standard terms' set by the accommodation provider, those terms must be 'fair'[3]. There are minimum requirements for accommodation secured from a private landlords, and offered in certain circumstances[4].

1   As amended by HRA 2017 for applications for homelessness assistance made to local housing authorities in England on or after 3 April 2018.
2   Save that it must be affordable; see **18.45–18.47**.
3   In that they must not contravene the Consumer Rights Act 2015: *R (Khatun) v Newham London Borough Council* [2004] EWCA Civ 55, [2004] HLR 29, CA.
4   See **18.69–18.80**.

Tenure

18.100 If the accommodation is self-contained premises, occupation is likely to be under a tenancy rather than on a licence. But even then the fairly minimal protection of the Protection from Eviction Act 1977 may not be available in respect of accommodation secured under HA 1996, Pt 7, or H(W)A 2014, Pt 2[1].

[1]   As amended by HRA 2017 for applications for homelessness assistance made to local housing authorities in England on or after 3 April 2018. See *R (N) v Lewisham London Borough Council* [2014] UKSC 62, [2015] AC 1259, SC, and the discussion at **16.29–16.30**.

18.101 Although local housing authority accommodation can be secured under HA 1996, Pt 7[1], or under H(W)A 2014, Pt 2, it cannot be made available on a secure or introductory tenancy[2]. Likewise, accommodation rented by the local housing authority from a private owner and sub-let to the occupier will not be offered under a secure or introductory tenancy[3]. The occupier will simply be a bare contractual tenant.

[1]   As amended by HRA 2017 for applications for homelessness assistance made to local housing authorities in England on or after 3 April 2018.
[2]   Housing Act 1985, Sch 1, para 4. English Code, paras 16.10–16.11. See *Westminster City Council v Boraliu* [2007] EWCA Civ 1339, [2008] HLR 42, CA.
[3]   Housing Act 1985, Sch 1, para 6. English Code, paras 16.25–16.28.

18.102 Accommodation obtained from a private landlord or a private registered provider or registered social landlord will not be offered on a full assured tenancy. So applicants will normally occupy their accommodation under, at best, assured shorthold tenancies[1]. An assured shorthold tenancy offered in performance of the HA 1996, s 193(2), main housing duty was held by the Court of Appeal, in principle, to constitute an offer of suitable accommodation[2].

[1]   HA 1996, s 209; H(W)A 2014, s 92(2). English Code, paras 16.23–16.24.
[2]   *Griffiths v St Helens Council* [2006] EWCA Civ 160, [2006] HLR 29, CA, see **16.115**.

18.103 The absence of any particular requirement for a minimum term, or for any security or stability, might enable a local housing authority to perform its duties under HA 1996, Pt 7[1], or H(W)A 2014, Pt 2, by moving an applicant through a succession of very short-term placements. However, each unit of accommodation must itself be suitable. Furthermore, the very fact that the accommodation offered is yet another short-term placement, with minimum stability for the applicant, could, depending on the particular circumstances, render the accommodation 'not suitable'.

[1]   As amended by HRA 2017 for applications for homelessness assistance made to local housing authorities in England on or after 3 April 2018.

18.104 In a landmark case decided under the homelessness provisions of Pt 3 of the Housing Act 1985[1], the House of Lords held that a local housing authority was not required to provide permanent accommodation in performing its duty to applicants for homelessness assistance. Lord Hoffmann said:

'[T]here is no reason why temporary accommodation should ipso facto be unsuitable. If the tenure is so precarious that the person is likely to have to leave within 28 days without any alternative accommodation being available, then he remains

threatened with homelessness and the council has not discharged its duty. Otherwise, it seems to me that the term for which the accommodation is provided is a
matter for the council to decide. Provided that the decision is not *Wednesbury*
unreasonable . . . I do not think that the courts should lay down requirements as
to security of tenure[2].'

[1]   *R v Brent London Borough Council ex p Awua* [1996] AC 55, HL. Prior to this decision, it
had been widely assumed that the duty in s 65(2) of the Housing Act 1985 to secure suitable
accommodation for applicants required local housing authorities to grant secure tenancies
from their own stock.
[2]   *R v Brent London Borough Council ex p Awua* [1996] AC 55, HL at 72 per Lord Hoffmann.

18.105 Following on from that decision, the Court of Appeal held that a local
housing authority could perform its duty to secure 'suitable' accommodation
by arranging assured shorthold tenancies for applicants[1]. Evans LJ considered
that the tenure of the accommodation secured could be relevant to the local
housing authority's decision as to whether or not the accommodation was
'suitable' and held:

'[T]he House of Lords' ruling that there is no requirement of permanence does not
lead to the conclusion that there is no temporal requirement whatever. In my
judgment the question of tenure is not left to the unfettered discretion of the [local
housing] authority: its decision must be proportionate to the relevant circumstances
of the particular case. These include, in my judgment, both the needs of the applicant
and the situation in the local housing market[2].'

[1]   *R v Wandsworth London Borough Council ex p Mansoor & Wingrove* (1996) 29 HLR
801, CA. All of these cases were considering the duty to secure suitable accommodation under
s 65(2) of the Housing Act 1985 which was the statutory predecessor to HA 1996, s 193(2).
[2]   *R v Wandsworth London Borough Council ex p Mansoor & Wingrove* (1996) 29 HLR
801, CA, at 811 per Evans LJ, followed and quoted with approval by Laws J when considering
the duty under Housing Act 1985, s 65(2) in *R v Lambeth London Borough Council
ex p Ekpo-Wedderman* (1998) 31 HLR 498, QBD; and by Richards J in *R v Lambeth London
Borough Council ex p Touhey* (1999) 32 HLR 707, QBD.

18.106 Between 1997 and 2012 in England (1997 and 2015 in Wales),
accommodation offered with a view to releasing the local housing authority
from the HA 1996, s 193(2), main housing duty was usually offered as an
assured, introductory or secure tenancy, made under the local housing
authority's housing allocation scheme adopted pursuant to HA 1996, Pt 6[1].
From 9 November 2012, local housing authorities in England have been
released from the HA 1996, s 193(2), main housing duty by the making of a
private rented sector offer as well as by making final offers under HA 1996,
Pt 6, if they choose to do so[2]. Local housing authorities in Wales have been able
to make private rented sector offers in order to release themselves from the
main housing duty to applicants who have applied for help for accommodation on or after 27 April 2015[3].

[1]   HA 1996, s 193(7); H(W)A 2014, s 76(2) and (3)(c), see **16.142–16.152**.
[2]   HA 1996, s 193(7AA)–(7AC), see **16.153–16.180**.
[3]   H(W)A 2014, s 76(3)(c) and (4), see **17.173–17.177**.

18.107 Now, in both England and Wales, private rented accommodation
could be offered at various stages in the process of an application for
homelessness assistance made under HA 1996, Pt 7, or H(W)A, Pt 2.

Use of private rented accommodation

Local housing authorities in England

18.108 For local housing authorities in England, offers of private rented accommodation can be made at any of these stages:

- in order to bring the HA 1996, s 195(2)[1], prevention duty to an end[2];
- under the interim accommodation duty at HA 1996, s 188(1)[3];
- in order to bring the HA 1996, s 189B(2)[4], relief duty to an end[5];
- bringing the HA 1996, s 189B(2)[6], relief duty to an end by making a final accommodation offer[7];
- performing any of the accommodation duties at HA 1996, ss 190(2)(a)[8], 193(2)[9], or 193C(4)[10];
- bringing the HA 1996, s 193(2), main housing duty to an end by making a private rented sector offer[11] or an offer of an assured tenancy from a private landlord[12]; or
- bringing the HA 1996, s 193C(4)[13], duty to an end by making a final accommodation offer[14].

[1] As amended by HRA 2017, s 4(2), for applications for homelessness assistance made to local housing authorities in England on or after 3 April 2018, see **15.87–15.137**.
[2] HA 1996, s 195(8)(a) and (d), as amended by HRA 2017, s 4(2), for applications for homelessness assistance made to local housing authorities in England on or after 3 April 2018, see **15.105–15.109** and **15.118–15.122**.
[3] See **16.37–16.50**.
[4] As inserted by HRA 2017, s 5(2), for applications for homelessness assistance made to local housing authorities in England on or after 3 April 2018, see **15.138–15.195**.
[5] HA 1996, s 189B(5) and (7)(a) and (c), as inserted by HRA 2017, s 5(2), for applications for homelessness assistance made to local housing authorities in England on or after 3 April 2018, see **15.162–15.165** and **15.169–15.174**.
[6] As inserted by HRA 2017, s 5(2), for applications for homelessness assistance made to local housing authorities in England on or before 3 April 2018, see **15.138–15.195**.
[7] HA 1996, s 193A(1)(b) and (4), as inserted by HRA 2017, s 7(1), for applications for homelessness assistance made to local housing authorities in England on or after 3 April 2018, see **15.181–15.184**.
[8] As amended by HRA 2017, s 5(5), for applications for homelessness assistance made to local housing authorities in England on or after 3 April 2018: duty to secure accommodation for applicants who are homeless, eligible for assistance, have a priority need and have become homeless intentionally, see **16.81–16.93**.
[9] Main housing duty to secure accommodation for applicants who are homeless, eligible for assistance, have a priority need and have not become homeless intentionally, see **16.94–16.199**.
[10] As inserted by HRA 2017, s 7(1), for applications for homelessness assistance made to local housing authorities in England on or after 3 April 2018: duty to secure accommodation for applicants who are homeless, eligible for assistance, have a priority need and have not become homeless intentionally and have deliberately and unreasonably refused to co-operate; see **16.200–16.216**.
[11] HA 1996, s 193(7AA)–(7AC), see **16.153–16.180**.
[12] HA 1996, s 193(6)(cc), see **16.136–16.139**.
[13] As inserted by HRA 2017, s 7(1), for applications for homelessness assistance made to local housing authorities in England on or after 3 April 2018, duty to secure accommodation for applicants who are homeless, eligible for assistance, have a priority need and have not become homeless intentionally and have deliberately and unreasonably refused to co-operate; see **16.200–16.216**.
[14] HA 1996, s 193C(6)(a) and (7), as inserted by HRA 2017, s 7(1), for applications for homelessness assistance made to local housing authorities in England on or after 3 April 2018, see **16.205–16.209**.

Local housing authorities in Wales

18.109 Local housing authorities in Wales can make the following offers of private accommodation:

- offers of, or arrangements for, accommodation made available by a private landlord which is suitable and likely to be available for the applicant's occupation for at least six months, offered in order to bring the H(W)A 2014, s 66(1), prevention duty[1] to an end[2];
- offers of interim accommodation under H(W)A 2014, s 68(1)[3];
- offers of, or arrangements for, accommodation made available by a private landlord which is suitable and likely to be available for the applicant's occupation for at least six months, offered in order to bring the H(W)A 2014, s 73(1), relief duty[4] to an end[5];
- offers of accommodation secured under the H(W)A 2014, s 75(1), main housing duty[6]; or
- private rented sector offers[7] offered in order to bring the H(W)A 2014, s 75(1), main housing duty to an end[8].

[1] See **17.45–17.72**.
[2] H(W)A 2014, s 67(3) and (4) , see **17.62–17.72**.
[3] See **17.118–17.134**.
[4] See **17.73–17.117**.
[5] H(W)A 2014, s 74(4) and (5) , see **17.104–17.117**.
[6] See **17.146–17.199**.
[7] H(W)A 2014, s 76(4), see **17.173–17.177**.
[8] H(W)A 2014, s 76(3)(b), see **17.161–17.171**.

MINIMUM TERMS OF PRIVATE RENTED TENANCIES

18.110 Both HA 1996, Pt 7[1], and H(W)A 2014, Pt 2, do contain some minimum requirements in relation to term and tenure[2].

[1] As inserted by HRA 2017, s 5(2), for applications for homelessness assistance made on or after 3 April 2018.
[2] Rather than a tenancy with no security of tenure, as defined at Housing Act 1988, Sch 1.

Local housing authorities in England

18.111 For local housing authorities in England:

- a 'private rented sector offer' must be of an assured shorthold tenancy and have a minimum fixed term of at least 12 months[1];
- a 'final accommodation offer' must be of an assured shorthold tenancy and have a minimum fixed term of at least six months[2]; and
- other accommodation provided in order to bring the HA 1996, s 195(2)[3], prevention duty or the HA 1996, s 189B(2)[4], relief duty to an end need not be of any particular tenure but there must be a reasonable prospect that it, or other suitable accommodation, will be available for the applicant for at least six months[5].

[1] HA 1996, s 193(7AC), see **17.109**. See also **18.70–18.79** for the specific factors relating to suitability of private rented sector offers.
[2] HA 1996, ss 193A(4) and 193C(7) as inserted by HRA 2017, s 7(1), for applications for homelessness assistance made on or after 3 April 2018, see **15.181–15.184** and **16.205–16.209**.

3   As amended by HRA 2017, s 4(2), for applications for homelessness assistance made on or
    after 3 April 2018, see **15.87–15.137**.
4   As inserted by HRA 2017, s 5(2), for applications for homelessness assistance made on or after
    3 April 2018, see **15.138–15.195**.
5   HA 1996, ss 189B(7)(a) and (c) and 195(8)(a) and (d),as inserted and amended by HRA 2017,
    ss 5(2) and 4(2), for applications for homelessness assistance made on or after 3 April 2018,
    see **15.105–15.109**, **15.117–15.122**, and **15.162–15.173**.

Local housing authorities in Wales

18.112 A private rented sector offer made with the approval of a local housing
authority in Wales in order to bring the H(W)A 2014, s 75(1) main housing
duty to an end must be of an assured shorthold tenancy for a minimum period
of six months[1].

1   H(W)A 2014, s 76(4)(c), see **17.173–17.177** (Wales).

INFORMATION ON PRIVATE TENANCIES REQUIRED TO BE GIVEN TO THE APPLICANT

18.113 In 2006, the Court of Appeal considered the distinction between local
housing authorities offering assured shorthold tenancies under what were then
known as 'qualifying offers'[1] (so bringing the main housing duty to an end if
accepted by the applicant)[2] and offering them in performance of the main
housing duty in HA 1996, s 193(2)[3]. Considering 'qualifying offers'[4], May LJ
said:

> 'The elaborate provisions for a qualifying offer of an assured shorthold tenancy
> from a private landlord in sub-section (7B) are there to recognise that, on the one
> hand, assured shorthold tenancies from private landlords have their disadvantages
> – the rent is not controlled and the tenure is technically insecure – but, on the other
> hand, some homeless applicants may reasonably prefer to accept the offer of such a
> tenancy rather than remain in temporary accommodation for a long time until they
> may be offered secure accommodation under Pt 6. Some homeless applicants may
> therefore be prepared to accept an offer of an assured shorthold tenancy from a
> private landlord as the permanent accommodation which in practice it is often
> capable of being. But they must only do so with their eyes fully open, and the local
> housing authority must be satisfied that it is reasonable for the applicant to accept
> the offer. Applicants are entitled to reject the offer. But if they do accept it, the local
> housing authority's duty ceases[5].'

1   HA 1996, s 193(7B), prior to amendment by Localism Act 2011, s 148. See previous editions
    of this book.
2   HA 1996, s 193(7B)–(7D) for applicants whose applications for homelessness assistance were
    made before 9 November 2012 to local housing authorities in England or before 27 April 2015
    to local housing authorities in Wales.
3   *Griffiths v St Helens Council* [2006] EWCA Civ 160, [2006] HLR 29, CA.
4   HA 1996, s 193(7B), prior to amendment by Localism Act 2011, s 148.
5   *Griffiths v St Helens Council* [2006] EWCA Civ 160, [2006] HLR 29, CA at [36].

18.114 When an assured shorthold tenancy is offered in performance of the
HA 1996, s 193(2) main housing duty[1], it:

> 'may be technically insecure, but may in practice extend for a number of years. If the
> applicant accepts the offer and the accommodation subsequently ceases to be

available, the authority's duty will have to be performed again, assuming that the applicant's circumstances have not otherwise relevantly changed[2].'

[1]   Or the H(W)A 2014, s 75(1) main housing duty.
[2]   *Griffiths v St Helens Council* [2006] EWCA Civ 160, [2006] HLR 29, CA at [38].

18.115 Local housing authorities should be careful to inform applicants whether an assured shorthold tenancy is being offered to them as a performance of the main housing duty[1] or in order to bring that duty to an end in the circumstances described at **16.153–16.180** (England) or **17.173–17.177** (Wales). A number of these offers require specific information to be contained in the offer[2].

[1]   HA 1996, s 193(2) and (5); H(W)A 2014, ss 75(1) and 76 (3)(a). See **16.114–16.123** (England) and **17.172** (Wales).
[2]   The relevant notification requirements are discussed under the paragraphs dealing with the various different types of offers.

Offers of secure tenancies

18.116 Where an applicant has been given an assurance that she or he would be offered a secure tenancy[1], that assurance might constitute a legitimate expectation[2]. The local housing authority is then under a duty, when considering what accommodation is suitable for the needs of the applicant and his or her household, to take into account the applicant's legitimate expectation to be offered a secure tenancy. That does not amount to a duty to give the applicant automatic priority above other applicants on the local housing authority's allocation scheme, but it does require the local housing authority to adopt some method, such as the provision of additional points, to reflect that legitimate expectation[3].

[1]   Or a secure contract, when Renting Homes (Wales) Act 2016 comes into force.
[2]   Where such assurances have been given, they were usually given to applicants under Housing Act 1985, Pt III: the previous homelessness provisions.
[3]   *R (Bibi and Al-Nashed) v Newham London Borough Council* [2001] EWCA Civ 607, (2001) 33 HLR 955, CA; *R (Ibrahim) v Redbridge London Borough Council* [2002] EWHC 2756 (Admin), (2003) February *Legal Action*, p 35, Admin Ct; and *R (Bibi) v Newham London Borough Council* [2003] EWHC 1860 (Admin), (2003) September *Legal Action*, p 28, Admin Ct. See also *R (Alansi) v Newham London Borough Council*, [2013] EWHC 3722 (Admin), [2014] HLR 25, Admin Ct, where there was no legitimate expectation. See **4.50–4.53.**

The applicant's views

18.117 The decision on suitability is for the local housing authority to make. Neither HA 1996, Pt 7[1], nor H(W)A 2014, Pt 2, prescribes any specific inquiries to be undertaken before a local housing authority can determine whether particular accommodation will be suitable for a particular applicant. It need only ensure that it has had regard to the prescribed matters it is required to consider in every case[2], and to any other matters relevant to the circumstances of a particular case. Indeed, a local housing authority may decide that the applicant's views as to suitability can be sufficiently aired at the review stage[3].

1 As amended by HRA 2017 for applications for homelessness assistance made to a local
   housing authority in England on or after 3 April 2018.
2 See **18.25–18.31**.
3 *R (Khatun) v Newham London Borough Council* [2004] EWCA Civ 55, [2005] HLR 29, CA.
   See also *Abed v Westminster City Council* [2011] EWCA Civ 1406, (2012) January *Legal
   Action*, p 21, CA.

18.118 A local housing authority may, if it wishes, invite the applicant's views
on any general issues affecting the suitability of accommodation for him or her,
or on a specific proposed offer or provision of accommodation. Indeed, both
the Codes contain advice that applicants should be given a chance to view the
accommodation before being required to accept or refuse it[1]. An applicant
should be given a reasonable period when deciding whether or not to accept it,
particularly when refusal or acceptance of the offer would have the effect of
bringing a duty to an end. There is no set reasonable period; the length will
depend on the applicant's circumstances[2].

1 English Code, paras 14.6 and 15.46–15.49; Welsh Code, para 15.15.
2 English Code, para 15.48; Welsh Code, para 15.14.

Other considerations

18.119 The factors relevant to the question of whether or not accommodation
offered to the applicant is suitable could encompass any issue raised by the
applicant. A local housing authority cannot confine itself to consideration of
the factors prescribed by HA 1996, Pt 7[1], or H(W)A 2014, Pt 2, or the
Regulations made under those provisions. Where a basement property on a
large housing estate reminded the applicant, who was a refugee, of the prison
in which she had been confined and tortured, the court quashed the local
housing authority's decision that the accommodation was suitable, holding
that this was an exceptional case[2].

1 As amended by HRA 2017 for applications for homelessness assistance made to local housing
   authorities in England on or after 3 April 2018.
2 *R v Brent London Borough Council ex p Omar* (1991) 23 HLR 446, QBD. But see *Poshteh
   v Kensington & Chelsea Royal London Borough Council* [2017] UKSC 36, [2017] AC 624,
   SC, where, on the particular facts, the review decision did not contain an error of law in its
   finding that the layout of the accommodation was not such that it recreated the conditions in
   which the applicant had been detained, and was not likely to have a significant impact on her
   mental health.

18.120 Where accommodation that was suitable when offered was then
occupied by squatters before the applicant had been able to move in, it was
held to be no longer suitable[1]. A local housing authority's decision, however,
that squatted accommodation would be suitable once it had been repossessed
and refurbished was held not to contain errors of law[2].

1 *R v Lambeth London Borough Council ex p Campbell* (1994) 26 HLR 618, QBD.
2 *R v Ealing London Borough Council ex p Denny* (1995) 27 HLR 424, QBD.

18.121 Where an applicant had a cultural aversion to conventional bricks and
mortar accommodation (having lived a nomadic lifestyle all her life), an offer
of conventional housing was held to be unsuitable for her needs. The local

housing authority had failed to accord sufficient respect to her rights under the Human Rights Act 1998, Sch 1, Art 8(1)[1]. However, if no sites or pitches are available, the local housing authority is not in breach of its statutory duty, nor of the applicant's rights under the Human Rights Act 1998 by making an offer of conventional accommodation unless that accommodation falls below the *Wednesbury* minimum standards of suitability[2].

1   *R (Price) v Carmarthenshire County Council* [2003] EWHC 42 (Admin), (2003) March *Legal Action*, p 30, Admin Ct.
2   *Codona v Mid-Bedfordshire District Council* [2004] EWCA Civ 925, [2005] HLR 1, CA. See also English Code, paras 16.43–16.45; Welsh Code, para 19.11; *Thompson v Mendip District Council* (2010) April 2011 *Legal Action*, p 31, Taunton County Court; *Sheridan v Basildon Borough Council* [2012] EWCA Civ 335, [2012] HLR 19, CA; and *Slattery v Basildon Borough Council* [2014] EWCA Civ 30, [2014] HLR 16, CA. See **18.184–18.191**.

18.122 The Codes recommend that local housing authorities should be 'sensitive' to the importance of pets to some applicants, particularly elderly people and/or rough sleepers, when considering the suitability of accommodation offered[1]. If pets cannot be accommodated with the applicant, separate provision to kennel or otherwise look after them would fall under a local housing authority's duty to protect the applicant's property[2].

1   English Code, para 17.62; Welsh Code, paras 11.22–11.25.
2   HA 1996, ss 211–212; see **16.288–16.309**; H(W)A 2014, ss 93–94, see **17.199–17.205**.

TYPES OF ACCOMMODATION THAT MAY BE 'SUITABLE'

18.123 The English Code offers considerable guidance as to the types of accommodation that might be used by a local housing authority seeking to perform duties owed under HA 1996, Pt 7[1] to secure 'suitable' accommodation[2].

1   As amended by HRA 2017 for applications for homelessness assistance made to a local housing authority in England on or after 3 April 2018.
2   English Code, chapters 16 and 17. See Appendix 2. The Welsh Code contains a list of types of accommodation that could be obtained through the duty to help the applicant secure accommodation: Welsh Code, para 13.14.

18.124 The following review deals first with the forms of accommodation least likely to be suitable and progresses to accommodation more likely to be suitable.

Homeless at home

18.125 Many applications under HA 1996, Pt 7[1], or H(W)A 2014, Pt 2 are made by individuals who have been asked to leave the homes of friends or relatives with whom they have been staying. An applicant who indicates that he or she has been asked to leave such accommodation plainly gives a local housing authority 'reason to believe' that he or she 'may' be homeless. If there is reason to believe that he or she may also be eligible and may have a priority need, then the duty to secure interim accommodation is triggered[2].

1   As amended by HRA 2017 2017 for applications for homelessness assistance made to a local housing authority in England on or after 3 April 2018.

²   HA 1996, s 188(1); H(W)A 2014, s 68(1). See also **16.37–16.80** and **17.118–17.134**.

18.126 In that situation the local housing authority may consider performing its interim duty by arranging[1] for the friend or relative to provide further accommodation, at least until it concludes its inquiries and notifies its decision to the applicant. Often friends or relatives are prepared to do this, on the assumption (which is not always correct) that this will only be for a matter of days. From the applicant's perspective, remaining where he or she is may be more attractive than other forms of interim accommodation that the local housing authority might provide. For obvious reasons, this common form of performance of the interim accommodation duty is called 'homeless at home'[2].

¹   Under HA 1996, s 206(1)(b) or (c); or under H(W)A 2014, ss 64(1)(a) or (c) and 66. See **18.12–18.14**.
²   The HA 1996, s 195(2) (as amended by HRA 2017, s 4(2), for applications for homelessness assistance to local housing authorities in England made on or after 3 April 2018), and the H(W)A 2014, s 66(1) prevention duties specifically envisage helping an applicant to stay in his or her accommodation. See **15.91–15.96**.

18.127 The arrangement is not altogether easy to square with the scheme of HA 1996, Pt 7[1], or H(W)A 2014, Pt 2, not least because the readiness of the friend or relative to accommodate may suggest that there was no homelessness or threat of homelessness in the first place (or that the original request to leave was part of an arrangement to take advantage of HA 1996, Pt 7[2] or H(W)A 2014, Pt 2)[3].

¹   As amended by HRA 2017 for applications for homelessness assistance made to a local housing authority in England on or after 3 April 2018.
²   As amended by HRA 2017 for applications for homelessness assistance made to a local housing authority in England on or after 3 April 2018.
³   See **10.2–10.7** and **13.181–13.187**.

18.128 However, in practice these issues are overlooked. 'Homeless at home' has been a feature of the provision of interim accommodation for homeless applicants for over 40 years. Furthermore, even though local housing authorities make substantial financial savings by performing their duty in this way, rather than by paying for alternative forms of accommodation, it is very rare for a local housing authority to offer or pay anything to friends or relatives for providing this service. Many friends and relatives fail to make such payment a term for their co-operation.

18.129 It is important that the 'homeless at home' arrangement is made in the correct way. The accommodation must be 'secured' by the local housing authority[1]. It is not sufficient for an applicant to be told 'go back and see if they will let you stay until we make our decision'. It is for the local housing authority to ensure that accommodation is available, not for the applicant to take a chance that it might be. Plainly, the local housing authority must also make sufficient investigations to satisfy itself that the 'homeless at home' arrangement can secure 'suitable' accommodation for the applicant.

¹   HA 1996, ss 188(1) and 206(1); H(W)A 2014, ss 64(1)(b) and 68.

18.130 Where an applicant has made his or her application for homelessness assistance on the basis that he or she has accommodation available, but that accommodation is not reasonable for him or her to continue to occupy[1], it may still be suitable for the purposes of interim accommodation or even whilst the HA 1996, s 193(2)[2], or H(W)A 2014, s 75(1)[3], main housing duties are being performed. That is because the local housing authority is required to consider whether the accommodation is reasonable to occupy in the long term, even if the applicant could remain there in the short term[4]. However, if the accommodation is not reasonable for the applicant to continue to occupy for one more night, then it will not be suitable accommodation and the local housing authority should secure an alternative form of accommodation in performance of its interim duty[5].

[1] HA 1996, ss 175 and 176; H(W)A 2014, ss 55(3) and 56, see **10.73–10.134**.
[2] See **16.94–16.199**.
[3] See **17.146–17.199**.
[4] *Ali & others v Birmingham City Council, Moran v Manchester City Council* [2009] UKHL 36, [2009] 1 WLR 1506, HL.
[5] See English Code, para 17.7; see *R (Edwards) v Birmingham City Council* [2016] EWHC 173 (Admin), [2016] HLR 11, Admin Ct.

Bed and breakfast accommodation

Generally

18.131 In general, bed and breakfast accommodation should only be regarded as suitable accommodation for an applicant when emergency accommodation is required at very short notice, and there is simply no better accommodation available. It should only be used as a last resort and for the shortest period possible[1].

[1] English Code, paras 16.29; 17.30–17.43; Welsh Code, para 19.57.

18.132 Bed and breakfast accommodation allocated to a family with six children, in a hostel where the other residents were single men with histories of drug abuse, psychiatric illness and violent behaviour, was held not to be suitable for the family's needs[1]. In a case where the applicant had occupied bed and breakfast accommodation for over 18 months, in circumstances where her 16-year-old son could not live there and had been taken into care, the Administrative Court held that 'the time has now come when the claimant cannot expect to return to hostel accommodation'[2].

[1] *Driver v Purbeck District Council* (1999) 10 CLD 407, Bournemouth County Court.
[2] *R (McCammon-Mckenzie) v Southwark London Borough Council* [2004] EWHC 612 (Admin), [2004] All ER (D) 174 (Mar), Admin Ct, at [15] per Keith J.

18.133 Relevant considerations as to whether bed and breakfast accommodation may be suitable include:

(1) the length of time that the applicant and his or her household are expected to occupy it;

(2) the efforts made by the local housing authority to find other suitable accommodation;

(3) the degree of likelihood of suitable accommodation becoming available in the near future; and

(4) any other factors affecting the individual applicant.

However, lack of resources available to the local housing authority is not a relevant consideration[1].

[1]   *R (Khan) v Newham London Borough Council* [2001] EWHC (Admin) 589, (2001) October *Legal Action*, p 16, Admin Ct.

18.134 Where bed and breakfast accommodation has been secured, local housing authorities should ensure that the accommodation is of a good standard. Bed and breakfast accommodation will normally be provided in a building which falls within the definition of a house in multiple occupation[1]. Minimum standards are set out in the Codes of Guidance[2].

[1]   Housing Act 2004, s 254.
[2]   English Code, paras 17.27–17.29 and 17.42–17.43; Welsh Code, paras 19.56–19.62. See **18.38–18.44**.

18.135 If bed and breakfast accommodation has been secured under the local housing authority's duty to secure suitable interim accommodation[1], and the local housing authority subsequently accepts a main housing duty[2], it must consider anew whether or not the bed and breakfast accommodation is suitable for the needs of the applicant and his or her household with reference to that new duty[3].

[1]   HA 1996, s 188(1), see **16.37–16.50**; H(W)A 2014, ss 68(1) and (3), see **17.118–17.134**.
[2]   HA 1996, s 193(2); H(W)A 2014, s 75(1). See **16.94–16.101** (England) and **17.146–17.157** (Wales).
[3]   *R (Chowdhury) v Newham London Borough Council* (2002) November *Legal Action*, p 24, Admin Ct (permission hearing); and *R (Cano) v Kensington and Chelsea Royal London Borough Council* [2002] EWHC 436 (Admin), (2002) December *Legal Action*, p 22, Admin Ct.

The special rules in England

18.136 For local housing authorities in England, bed and breakfast accommodation is deemed to be unsuitable for applicants with family commitments[1]. It can only be used at all where 'no accommodation other than bed and breakfast is available'[2] and even then for no longer than a total period of six weeks[3]. Where an applicant has been referred from one local housing authority to another under the conditions of referral[4], any period spent in accommodation secured by the notifying local housing authority will be disregarded when calculating the total period of occupation.

[1]   Homelessness (Suitability of Accommodation) (England) Order 2003, SI 2003/3326. See Appendix 2.
[2]   SI 2003/3326, art 4(1)(a). English Code, paras 17.31–17.40.
[3]   SI 2003/3326, art 4(1)(b).
[4]   See Chapter 14.

18.137 It follows that a local housing authority is required to satisfy itself that no other accommodation is available before it can use bed and breakfast accommodation for an applicant with family commitments. The English Code is unclear how a local housing authority in England can demonstrate that 'no other accommodation' can be secured for the applicant in order to be able to justify its use of bed and breakfast. It simply advises that, in making the determination that no other accommodation can be secured, local housing authorities should take account of the cost to the local housing authority in securing accommodation, its affordability and location. A local housing authority is not under an obligation to include accommodation which is to be allocated under its allocation scheme when considering whether there is any alternative accommodation[1]. This suggests that a local housing authority could decide to secure bed and breakfast accommodation even though an empty council home or a stay at a five-star hotel might be technically 'available'. The authors suggest that, for a local housing authority to demonstrate that no other accommodation was available, it must show that it has done more than merely check with its usual providers of short-term accommodation. It should have considered all possible means of providing accommodation other than bed and breakfast, including considering whether it has any empty properties that could be made available, and making inquiries of all potential providers, both in its own district and any other districts where it would be suitable for the applicant and his or her household to be located for the expected duration[2].

[1] English Code, para 17.36.
[2] A useful analogy might be made with the obligation on a local housing authority to secure accommodation within its own district, so far as reasonably practicable: HA 1996, s 208(1); H(W)A 2014, s 91(1), see **18.48**. In *Nzolameso v City of Westminster Council* [2015] UKSC 22, [2015] 2 All ER 942, [2015] HLR 22, SC, the Supreme Court held that the local housing authority could not show, from its decisions on the suitability of the accommodation offered, that it had complied with the relevant obligations concerning location of accommodation, see **18.53**. Baroness Hale said that ideally each local housing authority should have, and keep up to date, a policy on procuring sufficient units of temporary accommodation and setting out how those units would be allocated. Arguably, a local housing authority would need to do the same thing in order to be able to demonstrate that no other suitable accommodation was available before securing bed and breakfast accommodation.

18.138 It should also be noted that the obligation is a continuing one throughout the six-week period. It may be that no accommodation other than bed and breakfast is available for the first night after the local housing authority has come under a duty to secure accommodation, and so bed and breakfast accommodation will not be deemed to be unsuitable. That does not mean, however, that the local housing authority is then relieved of its obligation to consider whether any other accommodation is available after the first night. It cannot simply leave the applicant and his or her household in the bed and breakfast accommodation for a total period of six weeks[1].

[1] The six-week period 'does not allow the temporarily accommodating council to sit back – it must make all efforts to find suitable accommodation' said Collins J in *R (Nagaye) v Bristol City Council* (2005) CO/3477/2005, (2005) August *Legal Action*, p 19, Admin Ct (consideration of permission).

18.139 'Applicants with family commitments' are defined as applicants who are pregnant, or with whom a pregnant woman resides or might reasonably be expected to reside, or applicants with whom dependent children reside or might reasonably be expected to reside[1].

[1] SI 2003/3326, art 2. English Code, para 17.32.

18.140 'Bed and breakfast accommodation' is defined as accommodation which is not separate, self-contained premises and where any one of a toilet, personal washing facilities or cooking facilities are shared between more than one household[1]. It does not include accommodation owned or managed by a local housing authority, a private registered provider or a voluntary organisation, and so use of bed and breakfast establishments owned by any of those organisations is not, as a matter of law, deemed unsuitable (although it may still be unsuitable for the particular needs of a specific applicant)[2].

[1]   SI 2003/3326, art 2. English Code, para 17.33.
[2]   SI 2003/3326, art 2.

18.141 This prohibition on the use of bed and breakfast by local housing authorities in England does not apply where accommodation is being secured in the exercise of a power, eg the power to accommodate pending a review or appeal[1].

[1]   SI 2003/3326, art 1(2).

18.142 Since 2013, DCLG and now MHCLG has published quarterly statistics on families in bed and breakfast accommodation for more than six weeks[1]. These statistics show a significant increase in the use of bed and breakfast accommodation, and in the numbers of families with children occupying such accommodation for more than six weeks, from 2010[2].

[1]   Table 793, DCLG. The figures date from 2007, but figures for the years 2007–2012 were only published in June 2013, following a Freedom of Information Act request.
[2]   As of June 2017, there were 6,660 households in bed and breakfast accommodation. Those included households urgently displaced from 14 June 2017 as a result of the Grenfell Tower fire. Excluding the Grenfell households, 2,710 households had dependent children and 1,200 of those had been living there for more than six weeks: Statutory Homelessness Statistics, April – June 2017 (DCLG, September 2017).

18.143 The Local Government and Social Care Ombudsman found several local housing authorities, principally London Borough Councils, to be guilty of maladministration for securing bed and breakfast accommodation for applicants with family commitments for periods substantially exceeding six weeks[1]. By October 2013, the then Ombudsman had become so concerned that she published a focus report: *No Place like home: Councils' use of unsuitable bed and breakfast accommodation for homeless families and young people*[2]. She said that over the previous two years, the Ombudsman service had seen a 14% increase in the number of complaints about local housing authority homelessness services, and amongst those, an increasing number of cases where bed and breakfast accommodation had been inappropriately used as a stop-gap to house people. She noted the effect of poor accommodation on children's lives[3]. She also gave a number of examples where local housing authorities:

- had failed to consider alternatives to bed and breakfast accommodation;
- had failed to plan to secure enough emergency and temporary accommodation to meet demand in the future;
- had accommodated significant numbers of families for more than six weeks;
- had no flexible approach to moving families out of bed and breakfast; or
- had not engaged in a joined-up approach (with children's services) to

secure suitable accommodation to young people.

¹   See *Complaint against Croydon London Borough Council*, 11 05 774, 12 December 2012
(2013) February *Legal Action*, p 35; *Complaint against Croydon London Borough Council*,
11 010 420, 1 February 2013 (2013) April *Legal Action*, p 45; *Complaint against Birmingham
City Council*, 12 001 546, 28 May 2013 (2013) July/August, *Legal Action*, p 23; *Complaints
against Westminster City Council*, 12 009 140 and 12 013 552, 13 September 2013, (2013)
November, *Legal Action*, p 33; *Complaints against Ealing London Borough Council*, 12 004
331 and 12 011 635, 22 November 2013 (2014) February, *Legal Action*, p 30; *Complaints
against Croydon London Borough Council*, 13 008 594, 17 March 2014 and 13 006 148,
9 April 2014 (2014) October *Legal Action*, p 51; *Complaint against Lambeth London
Borough Council*, 16 005 834, 15 August 2017 .
²   Local Government Ombudsman, October 2013.
³   From a report by Shelter: *Chance of a Lifetime: the impact of bad housing on children's lives*
(2006, Shelter).

18.144 The Ombudsman advised that local housing authorities should use a
range of targeted and coordinated measures to prevent homelessness arising,
should discuss with the applicant at the outset any alternatives to bed and
breakfast accommodation, and should have arrangements in place for cooperation between homelessness services and children's services in all cases
involving families and young people. Where use of bed and breakfast
accommodation was unavoidable, she advised that applicants should be
notified that the law says that it is unsuitable and that the local housing
authority must secure alternative accommodation within six weeks. She also
recommended that local housing authorities should have systems to prioritise
sourcing alternative suitable accommodation for families in bed and breakfast
within the six weeks, and should keep clear records in each case of what has
been done to find alternative suitable accommodation. Where families are in
bed and breakfast accommodation for more than six weeks, local housing
authorities should have a strategy in place so as to tackle the problem within
a reasonable timescale. Councillors should be regularly informed of the local
housing authority's performance regarding placement of families and young
people in bed and breakfast accommodation. Despite this focus report, the
Ombudsman has continued to find instances of local housing authorities using
bed and breakfast accommodation in circumstances that can amount to
maladministration[1]. The Ombudsman was so concerned about the continued
placement of applicants with family commitments in bed and breakfast
accommodation that he published *Still No Place like Home* in December
2017[2]. In the foreword, the Ombudsman said: 'our cases show some people are
still spending far, far too long in unsuitable accommodation – two and a half
years in one case. We are also routinely seeing people housed in poorly
maintained accommodation with significant damp or infestations'.

¹   See *Complaint against Lancashire County Council*, 13 020 158, 5 August 2015 (2015)
October *Legal Action*, p 42.
²   *Still No Place like Home*, Local Government and Social Care Ombudsman, December 2017.

18.145 In 2013, Shelter published *Nowhere to go, the scandal of homeless
children in B&Bs*[1]. It quoted the DCLG statistics for children living in bed and
breakfast accommodation, and the numbers of families who had been living
there for more than six weeks. It also interviewed 25 families who were, or
recently had been, living in bed and breakfast accommodation. It found that
living in bed and breakfast accommodation can result in children feeling
unsafe or witnessing traumatic events, that the lack of amenities for normal

family life can damage children's physical or mental health, that children's education can be affected, that living in bed and breakfast accommodation can be expensive, and make it harder for family members to find work, and that the lack of space and privacy can mean that children struggle to enjoy day-to-day aspects of family life. It recommended that the Government urgently consider exempting homeless households in temporary accommodation from the household benefit cap, so as to make it easier for local housing authorities to secure local self-contained accommodation, and the rates paid for leased temporary accommodation, the local housing allowance level and universal credit should all be reviewed. Shelter also recommended that, in the long-term, both central and local government should take a more strategic approach to preventing homelessness by ensuring that there is an adequate supply of genuinely affordable homes for families who cannot afford to buy or pay private sector rents and ensuring there is adequate funding for high quality advice and advocacy to prevent families from losing their homes.

[1]   Shelter, October 2013.

18.146 The Secretary of State has advised, in statutory guidance, that bed and breakfast accommodation is not considered to be suitable accommodation in any circumstances for the needs of homeless 16- and 17-year-olds[1]. Despite that guidance, children's services authorities have been found guilty of maladministration for using bed and breakfast accommodation for 'looked-after' children[2].

[1]   *Prevention of Homelessness and Provision of accommodation for 16 and 17 year old young people who may be homeless and/or require Accommodation*, (April 2018, MHCLG and Department for Education), see the CD Rom with this book. See also English Code, para 17.39; and **12.133–12.159**.
[2]   See *Complaint against Lancashire County Council*, 13 020 158, 5 August 2015 (2015) October *Legal Action*, p 42. See **12.143–12.147** for 'looked-after' children.

The special rules in Wales

18.147 When H(W)A 2014, Pt 2, came into force on 27 April 2015, the Welsh Government issued the Homelessness (Suitability of Accommodation) (Wales) Order 2015[1]. This new statutory instrument also came into effect on 27 April 2015. It contains limits on the use of bed and breakfast accommodation and, separately, other 'shared accommodation'.

[1]   SI 2015/1268 (W 87), see the CD Rom with this book.

18.148 'Bed and breakfast accommodation' has the same statutory definition in Wales as it does in England[1]. The Welsh Order requires that 'bed and breakfast accommodation' must meet one of two standards – the 'basic' or the 'higher' standard – in order to be 'suitable'[2].

[1]   SI 2015/1268, art 2, see the CD Rom with this book; Welsh Code, para 19.75; and see **18.131–18.135**.
[2]   Detailed guidance is given in Welsh Code, paras 19.73–19.107.

18.149 'Basic standard' is defined as accommodation that meets all the prescribed statutory requirements and has a manager who has been deemed by the local housing authority to be a fit and proper person with the ability to manage bed and breakfast accommodation[1]. 'Higher standard' is basic standard accommodation which also complies with various additional standards relating to minimum amounts of space, adequate heating, facilities for storing and cooking food, exclusive washing and toilet facilities, lockable entrance doors, a common room and appropriate standards of management[2].

[1] SI 2015/1268, art 2; Welsh Code, para 19.82.
[2] SI 2015/1268, art 2 and Schedule; Welsh Code, para 19.82.

18.150 There is also an additional category of 'small Bed and Breakfast accommodation', defined as bed and breakfast accommodation where the manager resides on the premises and there are fewer than seven bedrooms available for letting[1].

[1] SI 2015/1268, art 2; Welsh Code, para 19.77.

18.151 Since 7 April 2008, bed and breakfast accommodation has not been regarded as suitable for any applicant who has a priority need unless it is occupied for no more than two weeks (basic standard) or six weeks (higher standard)[1]. If an offer of suitable alternative accommodation has been made during those periods and the person has chosen to remain in his or her bed and breakfast accommodation, higher standard small bed and breakfast accommodation can be considered suitable for an indefinite period[2]. In the case of basic standard small bed and breakfast accommodation, two offers of suitable alternative accommodation must be made and refused for it to be considered suitable indefinitely[3].

[1] SI 2015/1268, arts 4 and 7(1); Welsh Code, paras 19.78–19.81.
[2] SI 2015/1268, arts 4 and 7(1); Welsh Code, para 19.79.
[3] SI 2015/1268, arts 4 and 7(1); Welsh Code, para 19.79.

18.152 The Welsh Order also effectively outlaws use of 'shared accommodation', which it defines as accommodation which is not separate and self-contained premises, and where at least one of a toilet, personal washing facilities or cooking facilities are shared between more than one household, provided that it is not an institution registered under the Care Standards Act 2000[1]. Unlike 'bed and breakfast accommodation', 'shared accommodation' can be owned or managed by local housing authorities, registered social landlords or voluntary organisations[2].

[1] SI 2015/1268, arts 2 and 5; Welsh Code, para 19.31.
[2] SI 2015/1268 (W 87), art 2; Welsh Code, para 19.81.

18.153 'Shared accommodation' is not regarded as suitable for an applicant who has a priority need unless it meets the higher standard[1]. Basic standard shared accommodation may be regarded as suitable for a period of no more than two weeks, or for a six-week period if during the initial two-week period an offer of suitable alternative accommodation has been made but the person has chosen to remain in the basic standard shared accommodation[2].

[1] SI 2015/1268, art 5, Welsh Code, para 19.81.
[2] SI 2015/1268, arts 5 and 7(2); Welsh Code, para 19.81; in the case of an applicant who is occupying temporary accommodation which is used wholly or mainly to provide temporary accommodation to people who have left their homes as a result of a domestic abuse, and which is not managed by a local housing authority or a profit-making organisation, the offer of

suitable alternative accommodation (rejected by the applicant) could be made at any time during the six-week period.

18.154 Although the Explanatory Notes to the Homelessness (Suitability of Accommodation) (Wales) Order 2015[1] and the Welsh Code[2] both state that the prohibition applies only to accommodation secured under H(W)A 2014, Pt 2, *duties* (and therefore not to accommodation secured under any powers), there is nothing in the Order that contains such a restriction. The plain wording of the Order appears to apply the prohibition to accommodation secured either under H(W)A 2014, Pt 2, *duties* to secure accommodation or under H(W)A 2014, Pt 2, *powers* to secure accommodation. The prohibitions do not apply where the applicant has, or may have, a priority need as a result of an emergency[3]. They also do not apply if the local housing authority has offered suitable accommodation to the applicant but the applicant has decided to accept other accommodation[4]. If an applicant is referred from one local housing authority to another under the conditions of referral[5], the period spent in accommodation secured by the notifying local housing authority will be disregarded when calculating the total period of occupation[6].

[1]   SI 2015/1268.
[2]   Welsh Code, para 19.80.
[3]   SI 2015/1268, art 6.
[4]   SI 2015/1268, art 6.
[5]   See CHAPTER 14.
[6]   Homelessness (Suitability of Accommodation) (Wales) Order 2015, SI 2015/1268, art 7(5).

Hostels

18.155 The English Code recommends that providing accommodation in a hostel may be a means of securing suitable accommodation for applicants in order to meet specific accommodation and support needs, particularly young people or adults who need a period of stability and individual support to help them to prepare to live independently[1]. The Welsh Code does not specifically refer to hostels but contains detailed guidance on the standards to be met in shared housing and/or in houses of multiple occupation before the accommodation can be considered to be suitable[2]. The hostels referred to are not the night shelter variety that simply secure accommodation overnight, leaving the applicant homeless again the next day[3]. Some hostels, if privately run, will fall within the English or Welsh definition of 'bed and breakfast' accommodation[4]. Since 7 April 2008, privately run hostels in Wales have been likely to fall within the definition of 'shared accommodation'[5]. Hostels are also likely to fall within the definition of houses in multiple occupation[6] and be subject to Pts 1–4 of the Housing Act 2004[7].

[1]   English Code, paras 16.33–16.39.
[2]   Welsh Code, paras 19.35–19.38.
[3]   *R v Waveney District Council ex p Bowers* [1983] QB 238, CA.
[4]   For bed and breakfast accommodation generally, see **18.131–18.135**. For the English rules, see **18.136–18.146**. For the Welsh rules, see **18.147–18.154**.
[5]   See **18.152–18.153**.
[6]   Housing Act 2004, s 254.
[7]   See **18.38–18.44**.

Lodgings

18.156 Some young applicants, particularly those who are vulnerable, may benefit from lodgings rather than hostel or self-contained accommodation. Generally, such lodgings would be offered by landlords who provide a service for young people with support needs[1].

1   English Code, para 16.32; Welsh Code, para 19.65.

Women's refuges

18.157 Women's refuges should generally be considered as emergency accommodation only and not be used to perform accommodation duties under HA 1996, Pt 7[1] or H(W)A 2014, Pt 2[2]. Whether or not a particular refuge is suitable for a particular woman and her household will depend on the characteristics of the refuge and the applicant. The English Code advises local housing authorities that placements in a refuge should generally be for the short term, except where a longer period of support is required to enable applicants to prepare to manage independently. The English Code contains a chapter on providing homelessness services to people who have experienced domestic violence or abuse or are at risk of domestic violence or abuse, including advice on securing suitable accommodation[3].

1   As amended by HRA 2017 for applications for homelessness assistance made to local housing authorities in England on or after 3 April 2018.
2   See **10.12** and **10.126**. See also Baroness Hale in *Ali & others v Birmingham City Council, Moran v Manchester City Council* [2009] UKHL 36, [2009] 1 WLR 1506, HL, when she said, referring to submissions made by the Women's Aid Federation of England and Wales: 'They point out that a refuge is not simply crisis intervention for a few nights. It is a safe haven in which to find peace and support. But it is not a place to live. There are rules which are necessary for the protection of residents but make it impossible to live a normal family life. It is a place to gather one's strength and one's thoughts and to decide what to do with one's life.' at [43].
3   English Code, paras 16.40–16.41 and Chapter 21, paras 21.34–21.36. See **18.192–18.193**.

Mobile homes

18.158 Mobile homes are unlikely to be suitable for families with children, for the elderly, or for disabled applicants. Generally, if used at all, they should be used for emergency accommodation, when the local housing authority has not had an opportunity to arrange anything else. Holiday caravans should not be regarded as suitable at all[1].

1   English Code, paras 16.43–16.45; Welsh Code, para 19.65.

18.159 If the applicant normally occupies moveable accommodation and is homeless because she or he has no place at which to place the moveable home and reside in it[1], the local housing authority is not required to provide a site or berth itself, but should consider whether sites, berths or pitches are reasonably available[2]. These may be its own sites, sites provided by other local housing authorities (in which case provision can be made by arrangement with the appropriate local housing authority), or private sites on which the local housing authority has been able to persuade the owner to receive the applicant and his or her home[3].

1   HA 1996, s 175(2)(b); H(W)A 2014, s 55(2)(b). See **10.68–10.72**.
2   English Code, para 16.44.
3   HA 1996, s 206(1)(a)–(c); H(W)A 2014, s 64(1)(a)–(c).

18.160 Where an applicant has a strong cultural aversion to living in bricks and mortar accommodation, the only accommodation that would be suitable for his or her needs would be the provision of mobile or caravan accommodation, or a site on which to put the caravan or other mobile accommodation[1]. However, if no sites or pitches are available, the local housing authority is not in breach of its statutory duty, nor of the applicant's rights under the Human Rights Act 1998 by making an offer of conventional accommodation unless that accommodation falls below the *Wednesbury* minimum standards of suitability[2].

1   *R (Price) v Carmarthenshire County Council* [2003] EWHC 42 (Admin), (2003) March *Legal Action*, p 31, Admin Ct; *Codona v Mid-Bedfordshire District Council* [2004] EWCA Civ 925, [2005] HLR 1, CA; *Thompson v Mendip District Council* (2010) April 2011 *Legal Action*, p 31, Taunton County Court; *Sheridan v Basildon Borough Council* [2012] EWCA Civ 335, [2012] HLR 19, CA; *Slattery v Basildon Borough Council* [2014] EWCA Civ 30, [2014] HLR 16, CA. However, note that 'if there is no prospect of a suitable site for the time being, there may be no alternative solution' (English Code, para 16.44; Welsh Code, paras 19.11–19.12).
2   *Codona v Mid-Bedfordshire District Council* [2004] EWCA Civ 925, [2005] HLR 1, CA. See also English Code, paras 16.43–16.45; Welsh Code, para 19.11; *Thompson v Mendip District Council* (2010) April 2011 *Legal Action*, p 31, Taunton County Court; *Sheridan v Basildon Borough Council* [2012] EWCA Civ 335, [2012] HLR 19, CA; and *Slattery v Basildon Borough Council* [2014] EWCA Civ 30, [2014] HLR 16, CA. See **18.02–18.06**.

Accommodation leased from a private landlord

18.161 Local housing authorities are able to lease accommodation from private owners, and then let it themselves to applicants who are owed a housing duty. This option is known as 'private sector leasing'[1]. Although the applicant becomes a tenant of the local housing authority, the tenancy is not an introductory or secure tenancy[2].

1   English Code, paras 16.25–16.28.
2   Housing Act 1985, Sch 1, para 6. *Westminster City Council v Boraliu* [2007] EWCA Civ 1339, [2008] HLR 42, CA. See **18.101–18.107**.

18.162 The English Code encourages local housing authorities to test approaches that would enable such accommodation let as temporary accommodation to become settled accommodation[1]. That eventual offer could be a private sector rented offer[2] designed to bring the HA 1996, s 193(2) main housing duty[3] to an end or a final accommodation offer[4] designed to bring the HA 1996, s 189B(2)[5], relief duty or the HA 1996, s 193C(4)[6], accommodation duty to an end. The Welsh Code encourages greater use of the private rented sector generally, particularly by use of private rented sector offers[7].

1   English Code, paras 16.25–16.28. The implication is that, once the lease of the private rented accommodation let to the local housing authority expires, the local housing authority could negotiate with the private landlord to see if he or she would be willing to make an offer of a tenancy of that same accommodation.
2   HA 1996, s 193(7AC), see **16.153**; H(W)A 2014, s 76(4), see **17.172**.
3   HA 1996, s 193(7AA)–(7AC), see **16.153–16.180**.

⁴ As defined at HA 1996, ss 193A(4) and 193C(7), as inserted by HRA 2017, s 7(1) for applications for homelessness assistance made to local housing authorities' in England on or after 3 April 2018, see **15.181** and **16.206**.

⁵ As inserted by HRA 2017, s 5(2) for applications for homelessness assistance made to local housing authorities in England on or after 3 April 2018, see **15.138–15.195**.

⁶ As inserted by HRA 2017, s 7(1) for applications for homelessness assistance made to local housing authorities in England on or after 3 April 2018; duty owed to applicants who are homeless, eligible for assistance, have a priority need, have not become homeless intentionally and who have deliberately and unreasonably refused to co-operate, see **16.200–16.216**.

⁷ Welsh Code, paras 12.20–12.33.

Local housing authority properties

18.163 Local housing authorities can use their own stock (if they have any) to secure accommodation in order to perform their duties under HA 1996, Pt 7¹ or H(W)A 2014, Pt 2². Tenancies granted by local housing authorities in performance of their own homelessness duties will not be secure or introductory tenancies³.

¹ As amended by HRA 2017 for applications for homelessness assistance made to a local housing authority in England on or after 3 April 2018.

² HA 1996, s 206(1)(a); H(W)A 2014, s 64(1)(b). See also English Code, paras 16.10–16.11.

³ Housing Act 1985, Sch 1, para 4. See English Code, para 16.11. See also *Wandsworth London Borough Council v Tompkins* [2015] EWCA Civ 846, CA.

Accommodation provided by other local housing authorities or social landlords

18.164 Local housing authorities may request other local housing authorities, other social landlords and/or social services authorities to assist them in the performance of their duties by providing accommodation for applicants who are owed housing duties. If requested by a local housing authority in England, those bodies must co-operate and render assistance so far as is reasonable in the circumstances¹. Where requests for co-operation are made by a local housing authority in Wales, the recipient must comply unless it considers that doing so would be incompatible with its own duties or have an adverse effect on its functions. If it refuses to comply for one of those reasons it must put the refusal in writing, with reasons². Other local housing authorities and social landlords could therefore assist either by providing temporary accommodation to meet a duty owed under HA 1996, Pt 7³, or under H(W)A 2014, Pt 2, or by agreeing to accept a nomination made under the local housing authority's allocation scheme, thus enabling the local housing authority which owes the duty under HA 1996, Pt 7⁴ or under H(W)A 2014, Pt 2, to make the applicant an offer of HA 1996, Pt 6 accommodation, so as to release it from its HA 1996, Pt 7⁵ or H(W)A 2014, Pt 2, duties.

¹ HA 1996, s 213; English Code, para 16.12.

² H(W)A 2014, s 95(2) and (3); Welsh Code, chapter 6. See **17.208–17.211**.

³ As amended by HRA 2017 for applications for homelessness assistance made to a local housing authority in England on or after 3 April 2018.

⁴ As amended by HRA 2017 for applications for homelessness assistance made to a local housing authority in England on or after 3 April 2018.

⁵ As amended by HRA 2017 for applications for homelessness assistance made to a local housing authority in England on or after 3 April 2018. The offer would be made as a final Pt 6

offer defined at HA 1996, ss 193(7A), 193A(5) or 193C(8) in order to bring the HA 1996, s 189B(2) relief duty, the HA 1996, s 193(2) main housing duty or the HA 1996, s 193C(4) duty to an end, as inserted by HRA 2017, ss 5(2) and 7(1) for applications for homelessness assistance made to a local housing authority in England on or after 3 April 2018, see **16.142–16.152, 15.185–15.188** and **16.210–16.213**.

18.165 A local housing authority cannot normally discharge its responsibility to secure 'suitable' accommodation by leaving the identification of the actual unit of accommodation to another local housing authority or social housing landlord. The decision about 'suitability' remains with the local housing authority which owes the duty under HA 1996, Pt 7[1] or under H(W)A 2014, Pt 2, so it must be able to assess the suitability of a specific property[2].

[1]   As amended by HRA 2017 for applications for homelessness assistance made to a local housing authority in England on or after 3 April 2018.

[2]   *R (Cafun) v Bromley London Borough Council* [2000] All ER (D) 1425, Admin Ct.

18.166 If temporary accommodation is obtained from another local housing authority, the housing duty owed towards the applicant remains with the first local housing authority to which the applicant applied.

18.167 These voluntary arrangements are different from the arrangements for the referral of an applicant under the conditions for referral[1]. The Codes advise that accommodation secured under such voluntary, and often reciprocal, arrangements is particularly appropriate for the needs of applicants who might be at risk of violence or serious harassment in the area of the local housing authority to which they applied[2].

[1]   See Chapter 14.

[2]   English Code, para 16.15; Welsh Code, para 19.23.

Accommodation provided by private registered providers or by registered social landlords

18.168 As already noted[1], local housing authorities can discharge their duty to secure accommodation by ensuring that suitable accommodation is obtained from another person[2]. That might be a private landlord or a private registered provider or registered social landlord.

[1]   See **18.12–18.14**.

[2]   HA 1996, s 206(1)(b); H(W)A 2014, s 64(1)(a).

18.169 Private registered providers and registered social landlords are required by HA 1996, s 213(1)(a) and by H(W)A 2014, s 95, and by regulatory guidance to provide assistance to local housing authorities in the carrying out of those local housing authorities' homelessness duties[1].

[1]   HA 1996, s 213; H(W)A 2014, ss 95(2)–(5). See also English Code, paras 16.13–16.15; Welsh Code, chapter 6. *Neighbourhood and Community Standard* (Homes and Communities Agency, 2012) published by Homes England as part of the regulated standards for private registered providers of social housing in England. There is not the same emphasis in the *Regulatory Framework for Housing Associations Registered in Wales* (Welsh Government 2017).

18.170 Where nomination arrangements have been set up, an offer of an assured, or an assured shorthold, tenancy from a private registered provider or registered social landlord could be made under the local housing authority's allocation scheme. Those offers would therefore be capable of amounting to a final offer of accommodation made under HA 1996, Pt 6, or under H(W)A 2014, Pt 2, sufficient to release the local housing authority from the main housing duty or (for local housing authorities in England) as a final Pt 6 offer[1] offer[2] to bring the HA 1996, s 189B(2)[3], relief duty or the HA 1996, s 193C(4)[4] accommodation duty to an end[5].

1   HA 1996, ss 193A(5) and 193C(8), as inserted by HRA 2017, s 7(1) for applications for homelessness assistance made to a local housing authority in England on or after 3 April 2018, see **15.185–15.188** and **16.210–16.213**.
2   HA 1996, ss 193A(4) and 193C(7), as inserted by HRA 2017, s 7(1) for applications for homelessness assistance made to a local housing authority in England on or after 3 April 2018, see **15.181–15.184** and **16.205–16.209**.
3   As inserted by HRA 2017, s 5(2) for applications for homelessness assistance made to a local housing authority in England on or after 3 April 2018, see **15.138–15.195**.
4   As inserted by HRA 2017, s 7(1) for applications for homelessness assistance made to a local housing authority in England on or after 3 April 2018, see **16.200–16.216**.
5   HA 1996, ss 189B(9)(a), 193(6)(c), (cc) and (7)–(7A), 193A(2) and 193C(6), (as inserted by HRA 2017, ss 5(2) and 7(1) for applications for homelessness assistance made to a local housing authority in England on or after 3 April 2018,) see **15.185–15.188, 16.130–16.140, 16.142–16.152** and **16.210–16.213**; H(W)A 2014, ss 76(2)(a) and (3)(c), see **17.161–17.164** and **17.177–17.179**.

Accommodation provided by private landlords

18.171 Private landlords can also make accommodation available to help the local housing authority meet duties owed under HA 1996, Pt 7[1] or under H(W)A 2014, Pt 2. The Court of Appeal has held that assured shorthold tenancies can be secured under the local housing authority's main housing duty[2], provided that, if the accommodation subsequently ceases to be available and the applicant's circumstances have not changed, the local housing authority acknowledges that its main housing duty will have to be performed again[3]. For a fuller discussion of the circumstances in which private rented accommodation can be secured under HA 1996, Pt 7[4], or H(W)A 2014, Pt 2, see **18.69–18.81** and **18.108–18.115**.

1   As amended by HRA 2017 for applications for homelessness assistance made to a local housing authority in England on or after 3 April 2018.
2   HA 1996, s 193(2), see **16.94–16.123**; H(W)A 2014, s 75(1), see **17.51**.
3   *Griffiths v St Helens Council* [2006] EWCA Civ 160, [2006] HLR 29, CA.
4   As amended by HRA 2017 for applications for homelessness assistance made to a local housing authority in England on or after 3 April 2018.

18.172 It is not unusual for there to be confusion as to the identity of the landlord in these circumstances. Accommodation is often secured under tripartite arrangements between a property owner, a local housing authority and an applicant[1]. That accommodation could either have been leased by the local housing authority from the private landlord[2], or the local housing authority may have arranged for the applicant to be granted a tenancy by the property owner. The identity of the landlord is therefore a question of fact[3].

1   *Apczynski v Hounslow London Borough Council* [2006] EWCA Civ 1833, (2007) April *Legal Action*, p 21, CA, at [6] per Neuberger LJ. In that case, the applicant occupied a room in a hotel owned by a private company, having been booked into the hotel by the local housing authority in performance of its housing duty owed to the applicant. He brought a claim against the local housing authority for damages for disrepair to the room. His claim was dismissed because the local housing authority was not his landlord.
2   See **18.161–18.162**.
3   *Apczynski v Hounslow London Borough Council* [2006] EWCA Civ 1833, (2007) April *Legal Action*, p 21, CA.

18.173 In both England and Wales, there are specific factors to be considered regarding the suitability of private rented accommodation. In England, the Secretary of State has made the Homelessness (Suitability of Accommodation) (England) Order 2012[1] containing a non-exhaustive list of four factors to be considered regarding the location of the accommodation and ten specific tests on the physical condition of the property and the standard of management of it before private rented accommodation can be considered to be suitable[2]. The ten specific tests apply to private rented sector offers[3], final accommodation offers[4] or any other accommodation made available by a private landlord to an applicant who has a priority need in order to perform or to bring the HA 1996, s 195(2)[5], prevention or HA 1996, s 189B(2)[6], relief duties to an end[7]. The Welsh Government has made the Homelessness (Suitability of Accommodation) (Wales) Order 2015[8] which contains a non-exhaustive list of seven factors to be considered principally in relation to location of the accommodation and three tests to be made before a private rented sector offer can be considered to be suitable[9].

1   SI 2012/2601, As amended by HRA 2017, s 12, for applications for homelessness assistance made to a local housing authority in England on or after 3 April 2018: English Code, paras 17.11–17.21. See Appendix 2.
2   See **18.70–18.80**.
3   HA 1996, s 193(7AA), see **16.153**.
4   HA 1996, ss 193A(4) and 193C(7), as inserted by HRA 2017, s 7(1) for applications for homelessness assistance made to a local housing authority in England on or after 3 April 2018, see **15.181–15.184** and **16.205–16.209**.
5   As amended by HRA 2017, s 4(2) for applications for homelessness assistance made to a local housing authority in England on or after 3 April 2018, see **15.87–15.137**.
6   As inserted by HRA 2017, s 5(2) for applications for homelessness assistance made to a local housing authority in England on or after 3 April 2018, see **15.138–15.195**.
7   HA 1996, ss 189B(9)(a),193(6)(cc) and (7AA)–(7AC), 193A(1)(b) and 193C(6), as inserted by HRA 2017, ss 5(2) and 7(1) for applications for homelessness assistance made to a local housing authority in England on or after 3 April 2018, see **15.181–15.184, 16.136–16.139, 16.153–16.180** and **16.205–16.209**.
8   SI 2015/1268 (W 87), see the CD Rom with this book.
9   See **18.80**.

18.174 An applicant will know whether an assured shorthold tenancy is being offered to him or her in performance of the main housing duty, or other accommodation duties[1] or as a private rented sector offer or final accommodation offer because there are specific notification requirements, see **15.181, 16.114, 16.169** and **16.209** for notification requirements by local housing authorities in England and **17.167–17.169** for notification requirements by local housing authorities in Wales

¹   HA 1996, ss 193(2) and (5), 193C(4), as inserted by HRA 2017, s 7(1) for applications for homelessness assistance made to a local housing authority in England on or after 3 April 2018. See **16.94–16.13** and **16.200–16.216**.

18.175 Where the applicant has the right to request a review of the suitability of accommodation¹, any fixed-term tenancy should contain a break clause in order to be suitable. Otherwise what happens if the applicant accepts the offer and requests a review of the suitability of accommodation and the review is successful? Without a break clause, the applicant remains contractually committed to pay rent for the remainder of the term.

¹   HA 1996, s 202(1)(f) and (1A); see **19.59–19.62** and **19.190–19.199**; H(W)A 2014, s 85(3), see **19.83–19.85** and **19.100–19.101**.

PARTICULAR APPLICANTS AND THEIR NEEDS

18.176 Precisely because the question of 'suitability' requires a person-centred approach, considerable statutory guidance is offered for those cases in which the provision of accommodation will need to be handled with particular sensitivity.

18.177 The Codes identify that some applicants may need support from adult care or children's services to assist them to maintain the accommodation which is to be secured. The applicant's needs and the support that the local housing authority and any other agencies might provide to help the applicant find and keep accommodation will be recorded in the personal housing plan or assessment¹.

¹   HA 1996, s 189A, as as inserted by HRA 2017, s 37(1) for applications for homelessness assistance made to a local housing authority in England on or after 3 April 2018 and English Code, chapter 11, see **15.62–15.86**; H(W)A 2014, s 62(5) and (6) and Welsh Code, paras 12.61–12.64, see **17.30–17.35**. The Local Government Ombudsman found maladministration where a vulnerable applicant who was being moved from one unit of temporary accommodation to another ended up with overlapping liabilities to pay rent. The Ombudsman said '[a]lthough the council says it offered and provided a degree of support, there apparently is not evidence to support substantial support and other advice' (*Complaint against Birmingham City Council*, 10 000 145, 20 December 2010, (2011) March *Legal Action*, p 28).

Young people

18.178 Providing 'suitable' accommodation for young people can superficially seem difficult because of the rule that minors (persons aged under 18) cannot be the legal owners of an interest in land, which includes a tenancy. But they can be beneficial owners under a trust, and a tenancy granted to a young person takes effect as the grant of that tenancy on trust for the young person. The English Code states that there needs to be sufficient support in place and a licence agreement may be more appropriate¹. This was also the view of the Court of Appeal which discussed the difficulties of granting a tenancy on trust to a minor, and suggested that licences to occupy accommodation where the minor does not have exclusive possession of that accommodation should normally be granted[2]. Alternatively, the authors suggest, a tenancy could contain a declaration of trust appointing another person as the legal owner and trustee of the land.

[1] English Code, para 16.46. See also *Complaint against Dover District Council*, 09 017 510, 31 July 2012 (2012) October *Legal Action*, p 36.
[2] *Alexander-David v Hammersmith & Fulham London Borough Council* [2009] EWCA Civ 259, [2009] HLR 39, CA.

18.179 Some homeless young people may need help with managing tenancies or with household budgeting. Close liaison with the children's services team is recommended as essential. Other young people may benefit from supported accommodation before they are sufficiently independent to manage a tenancy, although local housing authorities are reminded that they must consider each applicant's individual circumstances and not just assume that supported accommodation will be suitable for all young people. Generally, if the minor is also a parent, semi-independent accommodation with support is recommended. If the young parent is aged less than 16, she or he should always be referred to children's services for an assessment of his or her care needs[1].

[1] English Code, paras 8.19–8.23; Welsh Code, paras 12.61–12.64.

18.180 In *R (M) v Hammersmith & Fulham London Borough Council*[1], the House of Lords held that local housing authorities should always refer children, aged less than 18 years, for an assessment by children's services. The expectation is that, unless the child's need for accommodation is relatively short-term, the responsibility for providing accommodation should be met by children's services under Children Act 1989, s 20, and so the child will receive not just accommodation but also additional assistance to help and support him or her in the transition to independent adult living. The House of Lords stressed joint working between local housing authorities and children's services.

[1] [2008] UKHL 17, [2008] 1 WLR 535, HL, see 8.45–8.46 and 12.150–12.159.

18.181 The referral to children's services does not avoid the local housing authority's duty to secure accommodation for the child while children's services carry out an assessment and consider whether he or she is a child in need pursuant to Children Act 1989, s 20 (or under the Social Services and Well-Being (Wales) Act 2014)[1]. This emphasis on joint working between local housing authorities and children's services' authorities was reiterated by the House of Lords in *R (G) v Southwark London Borough Council*[2], where the children's services' department was criticised for referring a homeless 17-year-old to the housing department, to make an application for homelessness assistance, rather than assessing the child's needs under the Children Act 1989. Both the UK Government and the Welsh Government subsequently published statutory guidance to local housing authorities and children's services. Each set of guidance emphasises that homeless children are likely to be children 'in need' and services should primarily be provided under Children Act 1989[3]. If the child is being accommodated under HA 1996, Pt 7[4] or H(W)A 2014, Pt 2, duties, each set of guidance advises that bed and breakfast accommodation would not be suitable.

¹ See **12.145–12.159** (England) and **12.212–12.213** (Wales) and **20.58–20.64** (England) and **20.85–20.98** (Wales).

² [2009] UKHL 26, [2008] 1 WLR 1299, HL.

³ *Prevention of Homelessness and Provision of Accommodation for 16 and 17 year old young people who may be homeless and/or require accommodation*, (April 2018, MHCLG and Department for Education) and *Provision of Accommodation for 16 and 17 year old young people who may be homeless* (Welsh Assembly Government, September 2010) both on the CD Rom with this book. See also **12.145–12.159** (England) and **12.212–12.213** (Wales).

⁴ As amended by HRA 2017 for applications for homelessness assistance made to a local housing authority in England on or after 3 April 2018.

Care leavers

18.182 The English Code contains a specific chapter on duties towards care-leaves and guidance is given on the suitability of accommodation for this group¹. Local housing authorities should work with children's services. When considering suitability, they should bear in mind that care leavers who are homeless may lack skills in managing their affairs and may require help with managing their own accommodation and operating a household budget. There should be no blanket presumption that a young person aged 18 who has left care will be ready for his or her own tenancy. Bed and breakfast accommodation, including hotels and nightly let accommodation with shared facilities, is not considered suitable and should only be used in exceptional circumstances. Supported lodgings, supported accommodation or independent accommodation with visiting support could be suitable, depending on the particular applicant's needs. When considering the location of accommodation, local housing authorities should take into account that a care leaver may want to live as near as possible to a significant adult such as a friend or ex-foster carer, or may need to avoid certain locations due to childhood experiences or associations².

¹ English Code, chapter 22, advice on suitable accommodation is at paras 22.24–22.29.

² English Code, paras 22.24–22.29. See **12.160–12.173** (England) and **12.217–12.219** (Wales) for the priority need awarded to care leavers and see **14.195–14.103** for the local connection referrals in England specifically relating to care leavers.

Families with children

18.183 When offering or securing accommodation for families with children, local housing authorities in England are advised to ensure that families with children who are subject to safeguarding arrangements should be given particular attention to try to ensure that accommodation is located in or close to the local housing authority's own district¹. Where there are school age children, and the local housing authority is considering placing the applicant outside of its district, it should liaise with the receiving authority and make every reasonable effort to ensure that arrangements are or will be put in place to meet the child's educational needs. The local housing authority should keep records of how it has assessed the impact on the child's education and what arrangements have been made for the child's education².

¹ English Code para 17.56.

2   English Code, paras 17.51 and 17.58; *R (E) v Islington London Borough Council* [2017] EWHC 1440 (Admin), (2017) 20 CCL Rep 148, see **18.56–18.58**.

Gypsies and travellers

18.184 Local housing authorities are advised to consider the needs and lifestyles of applicants who are gypsies or travellers when considering how to secure suitable accommodation. Where an applicant has a 'cultural aversion to the prospect of "bricks and mortar" accommodation', local housing authorities are advised that sites, or pitches, should be provided[1]. It is for the local housing authority to determine whether a particular applicant has 'a cultural aversion'.

1   *R (Price) v Carmarthenshire County Council* [2003] EWHC 42 (Admin), (2003) March *Legal Action*, p 31, Admin Ct, and see *Codona v Mid-Bedfordshire District Council* [2004] EWCA Civ 925, [2005] HLR 1, CA. English Code, paras 16.43–16.45; Welsh Code, para 19.11. See **18.158–18.160**.

18.185 In determining whether there is a 'cultural aversion', local housing authorities should:

'carefully . . . examine a gypsy's claim for such special consideration and, if satisfied that it is genuine, whether in all the circumstances of the case, it should attempt to meet it, and, if so, how. Those circumstances should, of course, include the likely duration of occupation in respect of which an offer is to be made[1].'

1   *Codona v Mid-Bedfordshire District Council* [2004] EWCA Civ 925, [2005] HLR 1, CA at [49] per Auld LJ.

18.186 In particular, a local housing authority should consider:

(1)   whether the applicant and his or her family lived in a caravan;
(2)   whether they subscribe to a gypsy culture;
(3)   whether they are itinerant or nomadic for a substantial part of the year;
(4)   whether itinerancy is linked to their livelihood; and
(5)   whether they subscribe to the relevant features of the gypsy life[1].

1   *Codona v Mid-Bedfordshire District Council* [2004] EWCA Civ 925, [2005] HLR 1, CA, at [49]–[51] per Auld LJ. In that case, it was not wrong in law for the local housing authority to conclude on the facts that 'bricks and mortar' accommodation could be secured for a short time. See also *Slattery v Basildon Borough Council* [2014] EWCA Civ 30, [2014] HLR 16, CA, where the Court of Appeal upheld the local housing authority's finding that the applicant's depression was related to the circumstances of her eviction, rather than to the possibility of being accommodated in 'bricks and mortar' accommodation.

18.187 The English Code adds, drawing on decisions of the European Court of Human Rights[1], that local housing authorities must give consideration to their obligations to act consistently with the Human Rights Act 1998, and in particular the applicant's right to respect for his or her private and family life, and his or her home[2].

1   For example, *Chapman v United Kingdom* (2001) 33 EHRR 18, ECtHR.
2   English Code, para 16.44, referring to Art 8 of the European Convention on Human Rights and the Human Rights Act 1998, Sch 1.

18.188 Local housing authorities will have to address whether or not sites are available on four different occasions:

(1) in determining whether or not they have 'reason to believe' that an applicant may be homeless, in that there is no place where the applicant is entitled or permitted to place and live in his or her mobile home or caravan – if so, and if they also have 'reason to believe' that an applicant may be eligible and may have a priority need, they have a duty to secure suitable interim accommodation pending notification of their decision[1];

(2) in determining whether or not the applicant is actually homeless or threatened with homelessness according to the statutory test[2];

(3) in carrying out their assessment of the applicant's case and drawing up his or her personalised housing plan[3];

(4) in determining, what suitable accommodation could be offered to the applicant in performance of any accommodation duty[4]; and

(5) in determining whether any duty has come to an end[5].

[1] HA 1996, s 188(1), see **16.37–16.50**; H(W)A 2014, s 68(1), see **17.118–17.134**.
[2] HA 1996, s 175(2)(b); H(W)A 2014, s 55(2)(b). See Chapter 10 in general and in particular **10.68–10.72**.
[3] HA 1996, s 189A, as inserted by HRA 2017, s 3(1), for applications for homelessness assistance made to local housing authorities in England on or after 3 April 2018.
[4] HA 1996, ss 188(1), 190(2)(a) 193(2), or 193C(4), as inserted by HRA 2017, s 7(1), for applications for homelessness assistance made to local housing authorities in England on or after 3 April 2018; H(W)A 2014, s 75(1).
[5] HA 1996, ss 189B(5), (7)(a) and (c), (9)(a), 193(5)–(7F), 193A(1), 193C(6), as inserted by HRA 2017, ss 5(2) and 7(1), for applications for homelessness assistance made to local housing authorities in England on or after 3 April 2018 see **15.162–15.165**, **15.169–15.173**, **15.181–15.184**, **16.113–16.185**, **16.240**, **16.215**; H(W)A 2014, ss 76(2) and (3), see **17.158–17.179**.

18.189 If, during any part of this process, a place on an acceptable permanent site becomes available, is suitable for the applicant's needs, and has been secured for him or her to occupy, the applicant will no longer be 'homeless', as there will be somewhere where he or she is entitled or permitted to park his or her mobile home or caravan and to live in it. If this arrangement comprises suitable accommodation for the applicant, and there is a reasonable prospect that the arrangement will be available for at least six months, the prevention or relief duties will come to an end[1].

[1] HA 1996, ss 195(8)(a) and (d),189B(7)(a) and (c), as amended and inserted by HRA 2017, ss 4(2) and 5(2), for applications for homelessness assistance made to local housing authorities in England on or after 3 April 2018, see **15.105–15.109**, **15.118–15.122**, **15.162–15.165** and **15.169–15.173**.

18.190 If no permanent site is available, the local housing authority's duty is to secure 'suitable' accommodation. The starting point is that, if the applicant is accepted as having a cultural aversion to bricks and mortar, a temporary site should be found, so that, at least, 'suitable' accommodation has been secured[1].

[1] *Thompson v Mendip District Council* (2010) April 2011 *Legal Action*, p 31, Taunton County Court.

18.191 But, given the shortage of permanent and temporary sites for travellers, what if no site is available? The Court of Appeal has held that:

'where land is not available, or cannot readily be made available, on which a gypsy applicant can station his or her caravan, it is open to a local authority to provide other accommodation of the conventional bricks and mortar kind, providing that it satisfies the *Wednesbury* minimum line of suitability[1].'

The Codes contain the same advice[2].

[1]   *Codona v Mid-Bedfordshire District Council* [2004] EWCA Civ 925, [2005] HLR 1, CA, at [47] per Auld LJ. Followed and applied in *Lee v Rhondda Cynon Taf CBC* [2008] EWCA Civ 1013, (2008) November *Legal Action*, p 20, CA and in *Sheridan v Basildon Borough Council* [2012] EWCA Civ 335, [2012] HLR 19, CA.

[2]   English Code, para 16.44; Welsh Code, para 19.12.

People who have experienced or at risk of domestic violence or abuse

18.192 HA 1996, Pt 7[1] and H(W)A 2014, Pt 2, contain provisions to recognise the specific circumstances in which people who have experienced or are at risk of domestic violence or abuse are homeless[2], may have a priority need[3] and may not be referred under the conditions for referral[4]. But, incongruously, neither HA 1996, Pt 7[5], nor H(W)A 2014, Pt 2, contain any specific requirements as to what accommodation might be suitable for people who have experienced or are at risk of domestic abuse.

[1]   As amended by HRA 2017 for applications for homelessness assistance made to a local housing authority in England on or after 3 April 2018.

[2]   HA 1996, s 177(1); H(W)A 2014, s 57(1), see **10.79–10.98**.

[3]   Homelessness (Priority Need for Accommodation) (England) Order 2002, SI 2002/2015, art 6 and H(W)A 2014, s 70(1)(e), see **12.187–12.194** (England) and **12.208–12.211** (Wales)

[4]   HA 1996, s 198(2), (2ZA) and (2A); H(W)A 2014, s 80(3) and (4), see **14.107–14.114**.

[5]   As amended by HRA 2017 for applications for homelessness assistance made to a local housing authority in England on or after 3 April 2018.

18.193 The English Code contains a chapter advising local housing authorities in England on specific issues relating to such people[1]. Within that it advises that consideration should be given to safe temporary accommodation, planning for victims to remain in or return to their homes, or finding accommodation that cannot be found by the perpetrator and which has security measures and appropriately staff to protect the occupants[2]. Refuges may be the most appropriate choice for people at risk from highly dangerous perpetrators but refuges should not be seen simply as a substitute for other forms of temporary accommodation[3].

[1]   English Code, chapter 21.

[2]   The English Code advises 'in all cases involving violence the safety of the applicant and their household should be the primary consideration at all stages of decision making as to whether or not the applicant remains in their own home' para 21.31 [bold in original].

[3]   English Code, paras 21.35–21.37.

People with an offending history

18.194 The English Code[1] contains a chapter advising local housing authorities in England on specific issues relating to people with an offending history[2]. It advises a multi-agency approach for securing accommodation, so that local housing authorities take the advice of the probation service or the Multi Agency Public Protection Agency. There may be particular issues concerning the location of accommodation and also support needs[3].

1 English Code, chapter 23.
2 Homelessness (Priority Need for Accommodation) (England) Order 2002, SI 2002/2015, art 5(3) and H(W)A 2014, s 70(1)(j), see **12.180–12.186** (England) and **12.223–12.226** (Wales).
3 English Code, paras 22.26–23.28.

People who have experienced or at risk of modern slavery or trafficking

18.195 These are no specific provisions in either HA 1996, Pt 7[1] or H(W)A 2014, Pt 2, contain provisions to recognise the specific circumstances in which people who have experienced or are at risk of modern slavery or trafficking might have a priority need[2]. However, the English Code contains a chapter advising local housing authorities in England on specific issues relating to people who are in this position[3]. It advises that local housing authorities should consider what accommodation options would be the most appropriate for each person on a case by case basis. If there is no option but emergency hostel or bed and breakfast accommodation, the accommodation should be gender-specific and have appropriate security measures. Risks of violence or racial harassment should be borne in mind, along with the risk of possible re-trafficking. There could be benefits in accommodation being secured outside the local housing authority's own district[4].

1 As amended by HRA 2017 for applications for homelessness assistance made to a local housing authority in England on or after 3 April 2018.
2 The issue would be whether they were vulnerable, see HA 1996, s 189(1)(c) and H(W)A 2014, ss 70(1)(c) and 71, see **12.76–12.125** (England) and **12.199–12.206** (Wales).
3 English Code, chapter 25.
4 English Code, paras 25.20–25.22.

ADVICE AND ASSISTANCE WHICH SECURES SUITABLE ACCOMMODATION

18.196 As already noted[1], as an alternative to providing accommodation (or arranging for someone else to secure accommodation), a local housing authority may discharge its duty to secure that suitable accommodation is available for the applicant and his or her household by:

'. . . giving him such advice and assistance as will secure that suitable accommodation is available from some other person[2].'

1 See **18.12**.
2 HA 1996, s 206(1)(c); H(W)A 2014, s 64(1)(b) and (2)(h).

18.197 This is different from the distinct duty under HA 1996, Pt 7[1] on local housing authorities in England to provide advice and assistance to applicants who have a priority need and have become homeless intentionally[2]. It is also different from the HA 1996, s 195(2)[3] or H(W)A 2014, s 66(1)[4], prevention and HA 1996 s 189B(2)[5] or H(W)A 2014, s 73(1)[6] relief duties.

[1] As amended by HRA 2017 for applications for homelessness assistance made to a local housing authority in England on or after 3 April 2018.
[2] HA 1996, ss 190(2)(b) as amended by HRA 2017, s 5(5), for applications for homelessness assistance made to local housing authorities in England on or after 3 April 2018. See **15.231**.
[3] As amended by HRA 2017, s 4(2) for applications for homelessness assistance made to local housing authorities in England on or after 3 April 2018, see **15.87–15.137**.
[4] See **17.45–17.72**.
[5] As inserted by HRA 2017, s 5(2) for applications for homelessness assistance made to local housing authorities in England on or after 3 April 2018, see **15.138–15.195**.
[6] See **17.73–17.117**.

18.198 If the advice and assistance provided under HA 1996, s 206(1)(c) or help provided under H(W)A 2014, s 64(2)(h) enables the applicant to succeed in obtaining suitable accommodation that is likely to be available for his or her occupation normally for at least six months, the local housing authority's duty to him or her under HA 1996, Pt 7[1], or under H(W)A 2014, Pt 2, will have been performed. Both Codes of Guidance contain chapters on the help that can be given to the applicant under the duties to help the applicant to secure accommodation[2].

[1] As amended by HRA 2017 for applications for homelessness assistance made to a local housing authority in England on or after 3 April 2018.
[2] English Code, chapters 12–14; Welsh Code, chapters 12 and 13.

SUITABILITY: DECISIONS AND CHALLENGES

Decisions

18.199 Save in the exceptional cases mentioned at **16.114**, there is no strict requirement for a local housing authority to notify its decision that it considers particular accommodation secured in performance of a duty owed under HA 1996, Pt 7[1] or H(W)A 2014, Pt 2 (or under a power) to be 'suitable' for the applicant. Nor is there any duty to provide reasons for such a decision[2].

[1] As amended by HRA 2017 for applications for homelessness assistance made to a local housing authority in England on or after 3 April 2018.
[2] See *Solihull Metropolitan Borough Council v Khan* [2014] EWCA Civ 41, [2014] HLR 33, CA.

18.200 Usually, however, such a decision will be notified in writing if:

(1)   an applicant is being told that accommodation initially secured under an interim duty is subsequently being treated as suitable accommodation secured in performance of a different accommodation duty (if an applicant remains in the same accommodation during different stages of the local housing authority's handling of his or her application under HA 1996, Pt 7[1] or H(W)A 2014, Pt 2), since the local housing authority is under a duty at each stage to consider whether the accommodation is suitable for an applicant's needs[2];

(2)   for local housing authorities in England, the accommodation is being offered as a final accommodation offer[3];

(3)   for local housing authorities in England, the accommodation is being offered as a final Pt 6 offer[4];

(4)   the accommodation is being offered in performance of the HA 1996, s 193(2), or H(W)A 2014, s 75(1), main housing duty[5];

(5)   the accommodation is a private rented sector offer[6]; or

(6)   the accommodation is a Pt 6 offer[7];

(7)   the applicant has raised a concern or complaint about the accommodation secured or offered; or

(8)   there is some other reason why it would be good administrative practice to give such a notice.

[1]   As amended by HRA 2017, for applications for homelessness assistance made to a local housing authority in England on or after 3 April 2018.

[2]   *R v Lambeth London Borough Council ex p Touhey* (2000) 32 HLR 707, QBD.

[3]   HA 1996, ss 193A(4), or 193C(7), as inserted by HRA 2017, s 7(1), for applications for homelessness assistance made to a local housing authority in England on or after 3 April 2018; see **15.181–15.184** and **16.205–16.209.**

[4]   HA 1996, ss 193A(5), or 193C(8), as inserted by HRA 2017, s 7(1), for applications for homelessness assistance made to a local housing authority in England on or after 3 April 2018; see **15.185–15.189** and **16.210–16.213.**

[5]   HA 1996, s 193(2) and (5), see **16.94–16.123**; H(W)A 2014, s 76(3)(a), see **17.165–17.172.**

[6]   HA 1996, s 193(7AA), see **16.153**; H(W)A 2014, s 76(3)(b), see **17.173.**

[7]   HA 1996, s 193(7), see **16.142–16.152**; H(W)A 2014, s 76(3)(c), see **17.178–17.179.**

18.201 For local housing authorities in England making offers of HA 1996, s 193(2) main housing duty accommodation, private rented sector offers, final accommodation offers, or final Pt 6 offers, the applicant must be advised of any right to review the local housing authority's decision that the accommodation offered was 'suitable'[1]. It would be good practice to inform applicants in other circumstances of the right to request a review. It would also be good practice to inform applicants of the time within which the right to request a review should be exercised, in order to ensure that the right is effective.

[1]   HA 1996, ss 193(7AB), 193A(1)(b) and 193C(6), as inserted by HRA 2017, s 7(1), for applications for homelessness assistance made to a local housing authority in England on or after 3 April 2018; see **16.114–16.123, 16.153–16.180, 15.181–15.184, 16.205–16.209 15.185–15.188** and **16.210–16.213.**

18.202 There is no obligation on local housing authorities in Wales to inform applicants of their right to request a review of the suitability of any offers made, at the time of making the offer, but again it would be considered to be good practice to do so.

Statutory reviews

Statutory reviews in England

18.203 As already noted[1], an applicant to a local housing authority in England has the right to request a statutory review of any the local housing authority's decisions that accommodation offered to him or her under HA 1996, ss 189B[2], 190(2)[3], 193[4], or 193C[5] is suitable[6]. He or she also has the right to request a review of any decision that any duty has come to an end, including where the duty has come to an end as a result of the applicant's acceptance or refusal of accommodation[7]. Additionally, the applicant may seek a review of the 'suitability' of:

*   a final accommodation offer[8];

- a final Pt 6 offer[9];
- a final offer of accommodation made under HA 1996, Pt 6 where that is being relied upon to bring a main housing duty to an end; or[10]
- a private rented sector offer[11].

Where an applicant has requested a review of the suitability of a final accommodation offer[12] or a final Pt offer[13], offered in order to bring the HA 1996, s 189B(2)[14], relief duty to an end[15], and the applicant had been occupying interim accommodation, the HA 1996, s 189B(2)[16], relief duty does not end until the decision on review has been notified to the applicant[17]. The duty to secure interim accommodation will not come to an end until the decision on review has been notified to the applicant[18].

[1] See **16.114**.
[2] As inserted by HRA 2017, s 5(2), for applications for homelessness assistance made to a local housing authority in England on or after 3 April 2018, see **15.138–15.195**.
[3] As amended by HRA 2017, s 5(5), for applications for homelessness assistance made to a local housing authority in England on or after 3 April 2018, see **16.81–16.93**.
[4] HA 1996, s 193(2), main housing duty, see **16.94–16.199**.
[5] As inserted by HRA 2017, s 7(1), for applications for homelessness assistance made to a local housing authority in England on or after 3 April 2018, see **16.200–16.216**.
[6] HA 1996, s 202(1)(f) and (1A), as amended by HRA 2017, s 9, for applications for homelessness assistance made to a local housing authority in England on or after 3 April 2018. See **19.59–19.62** and **19.190–19.199**.
[7] HA 1996, s 202(1)(b), as amended by HRA 2017, s 9, for applications for homelessness assistance made to a local housing authority in England on or after 3 April 2018. See **19.15–19.17**.
[8] HA 1996, ss 193A(4), or 193C(7), and s 202(1)(h) and (1B) as inserted by HRA 2017, ss 7(1) and (9), for applications for homelessness assistance made to a local housing authority in England on or after 3 April 2018; see **15.181–15.184, 16.205–16.209, 19.65–19.69** and **19.90–19.99**.
[9] HA 1996, ss 193A(5), or 193C(8), and s 202(1)(h) and (1B) as inserted by HRA 2017, ss 7(1) and (9), for applications for homelessness assistance made to a local housing authority in England on or after 3 April 2018; see **15.185–15.189, 16.210–16.213, 19.65–19.69** and **19.90–19.99**.
[10] HA 1996, s 202(1)(f), as amended by HRA 2017, s 9, for applications for homelessness assistance made to a local housing authority in England on or after 3 April 2018. See **19.59–19.62**.
[11] HA 1996, s 202(1)(g), as amended by HRA 2017, s 9, for applications for homelessness assistance made to a local housing authority in England on or after 3 April 2018.
[12] HA 1996, s 193A(4), and s 202(1)(h) and (1B) as inserted by HRA 2017, ss 7(1) and (9), for applications for homelessness assistance made to a local housing authority in England on or after 3 April 2018; see **15.181–15.184, 19.65–19.69** and **19.90–19.99**.
[13] HA 1996, s 193A(5), and s 202(1)(h) and (1B) as inserted by HRA 2017, ss 7(1) and (9), for applications for homelessness assistance made to a local housing authority in England on or after 3 April 2018; see **15.185–15.189, 19.65–19.69** and **19.90–19.99**.
[14] As inserted by HRA 2017, s 5(2), for applications for homelessness assistance made to a local housing authority in England on or after 3 April 2018; see **15.138–15.195**.
[15] HA 1996, ss 189B(9)(a) and 193A(2), as inserted by HRA 2017, ss 5(2) and 7(1), for applications for homelessness assistance made to a local housing authority in England on or after 3 April 2018; see **15.181–15.189**.
[16] As inserted by HRA 2017, s 5(2), for applications for homelessness assistance made to a local housing authority in England on or after 3 April 2018; see **15.138–15.195**.
[17] HA 1996, s 188(2A), as inserted by HRA 2017, s 5(4), for applications for homelessness assistance made to a local housing authority in England on or after 3 April 2018; see **15.184–15.188**.
[18] HA 1996, s 188(2A), as inserted by HRA 2017, s 5(4), for applications for homelessness assistance made to a local housing authority in England on or after 3 April 2018; see **15.184–15.188**. Unless the applicant were to be notified of the local housing authority's decision that it was satisfied that he or she does not have a priority need: HA 1996,

s 188(1ZA)(b), as inserted by HRA 2017, s 5(4), for applications for homelessness assistance made to a local housing authority in England on or after 3 April 2018; see **16.56–16.59**.

18.204 An applicant can, at any time, request that the local housing authority reconsider its decision that the accommodation secured under HA 1996, Pt 7[1] or under H(W)A 2014, Pt 2, is suitable. An applicant might need to take that step if accommodation that was originally suitable for the applicant when first occupied has become unsuitable as a result of a change in the applicant's circumstances[2].

1   As amended by HRA 2017, for applications for homelessness assistance made to a local housing authority in England on or after 3 April 2018.
2   *R v Southwark London Borough Council ex p Campisi* (1999) 31 HLR 560, CA; and *R v Newham London Borough Council ex p Mashuda Begum* (1999) 32 HLR 808, QBD. In *Muse v Brent London Borough Council* [2008] EWCA Civ 1447, (2009) February *Legal Action*, p 32, CA, the applicant refused to move from main housing duty accommodation which had become unsuitable to new accommodation offered to her which the local housing authority had decided was suitable for her and her household. As a result, the local housing authority's main housing duty to her came to an end under HA 1996, s 193(5) (see **16.114–16.123**).

Statutory reviews in Wales

18.205 Applicants to local housing authorities in Wales can request a statutory review of the decision that accommodation offered under any of the duties in H(W)A 2014, Pt 2 is suitable[1]. Unlike applicants to local housing authorities in England, they can request a review of the suitability of accommodation secured under the H(W)A 2014, s 68(1) interim accommodation duty[2]. They can also request a review of any decision that accommodation offered to them in order to end any of those duties is suitable[3]. They have the right to accept the accommodation offered under any of the duties in H(W)A 2014, Pt 2, while also requesting a review[4].

1   H(W)A 2014, s 85(3), see **19.100–19.101**.
2   H(W)A 2014, s 85(3).
3   H(W)A 2014, s 85(1)(a), see **19.83–19.85**.
4   H(W)A 2014, s 85(3), see **19.100–19.101**.

Offers which end duties

Local housing authorities in England

18.206 Seven types of offer of 'suitable' accommodation raise special issues. If these offers are refused by an applicant, the making of the offer can bring to an end the relevant duty owed under HA 1996, Pt 7[1]. They are:

(1)   a final accommodation offer[2] made in order to bring the HA 1996, s 189B(2)[3], relief duty to an end[4];
(2)   a final Pt 6 offer[5] made in order to bring the HA 1996, s 189B(2)[6], relief duty to an end[7];
(3)   a final accommodation offer[8] made in order to bring the HA 1996, s 193C(4)[9], duty to an end[10];
(4)   a final Pt 6 offer[11] made in order to bring the HA 1996, s 193C(4)[12], duty to an end[13];

(5)   an offer of suitable accommodation in performance of the HA 1996, s 193(2), main housing duty[14];

(6)   a final offer of suitable accommodation made through the allocation arrangements in HA 1996, Pt 6[15]; and

(7)   a private rented sector offer[16].

[1]   As amended by HRA 2017, for applications for homelessness assistance made to a local housing authority in England on or after 3 April 2018.

[2]   HA 1996, s 193A(4), as inserted by HRA 2017, ss 7(1), for applications for homelessness assistance made to a local housing authority in England on or after 3 April 2018; see **15.181–15.184**.

[3]   As inserted by HRA 2017, s 5(2), for applications for homelessness assistance made to a local housing authority in England on or after 3 April 2018; see **15.138–15.195**.

[4]   HA 1996, ss 189B(9)(a) and 193A(2), as inserted by HRA 2017, ss 5(2) and 7(1), for applications for homelessness assistance made to a local housing authority in England on or after 3 April 2018; see **15.181–15.184**.

[5]   HA 1996, s 193A(5), as inserted by HRA 2017, s 7(1), for applications for homelessness assistance made to a local housing authority in England on or after 3 April 2018; see **15.185–15.189**.

[6]   As inserted by HRA 2017, s 5(2), for applications for homelessness assistance made to a local housing authority in England on or after 3 April 2018; see **15.135–15.195**.

[7]   HA 1996, ss 189B(9)(a) and 193A(2), as inserted by HRA 2017, ss 5(2) and 7(1), for applications for homelessness assistance made to a local housing authority in England on or after 3 April 2018; see **15.185–15.189**.

[8]   HA 1996, s 193C(7), as inserted by HRA 2017, s 7(1), for applications for homelessness assistance made to a local housing authority in England on or after 3 April 2018; see **16.205–16.209**.

[9]   As inserted by HRA 2017, s 7(1), for applications for homelessness assistance made to a local housing authority in England on or after 3 April 2018: duty to secure accommodation to applicants who are homeless, eligible for assistance, have a priority need, have not become homeless intentionally and have deliberately and unreasonably refused to co-operate, see **16.200–16.216**.

[10]   HA 1996, s 193C(6), as inserted by HRA 2017, s 7(1), for applications for homelessness assistance made to a local housing authority in England on or after 3 April 2018; see **16.205–16.209**.

[11]   HA 1996, s 193C(8), as inserted by HRA 2017, s 7(1), for applications for homelessness assistance made to a local housing authority in England on or after 3 April 2018; see **16.210–16.213**.

[12]   As inserted by HRA 2017, s 7(1), for applications for homelessness assistance made to a local housing authority in England on or after 3 April 2018: duty to secure accommodation to applicants who are homeless, eligible for assistance, have a priority need, have not become homeless intentionally and have deliberately and unreasonably refused to co-operate, see **16.200–16.216**.

[13]   HA 1996, s 193C(6), as inserted by HRA 2017, s 7(1), for applications for homelessness assistance made to a local housing authority in England on or after 3 April 2018; see **16.210–16.213**.

[14]   HA 1996, s 193(5), see **16.114–16.123**.

[15]   HA 1996, s 193(7) see **16.142–16.152**.

[16]   HA 1996, s 193(7AC), see **16.153–16.180**.

18.207 Because these offers are of crucial importance, they are subject to special preconditions before they operate to bring relevant duties to an end[1].

[1]   See **16.114, 16.117–16.119, 16.144–16.146, 16.168–16.173**.

18.208 They also, exceptionally, confer on the applicant the right to request a review of the suitability of the accommodation whilst simultaneously accepting it[1]. Given the serious consequences which may follow if an offer is refused but is later upheld as 'suitable', accepting the offer while also requesting a review of the decision that the accommodation offered was suitable must normally be the advisable course of action.

1   HA 1996, ss 202(1A) and (1B), as inserted by HRA 2017, s 9, for applications for homelessness assistance made to a local housing authority in England on or after 3 April 2018, see **19.90–19.99**.

18.209 Even if the applicant has not requested a review of a decision that accommodation offered in one of these ways is suitable, he or she is still entitled to a review of any later decision (if one is made) that the duty on the local housing authority has ended by reason of the refusal of that accommodation[1]. If the applicant's reasons for refusing the offer are that the accommodation is not suitable, the local housing authority must consider his or her representations to that effect on review.

1   HA 1996, s 202(1)(b), as amended by HRA 2017, s 9, for applications for homelessness assistance made to a local housing authority in England on or after 3 April 2018, see **19.15–19.17** and see *Warsame v Hounslow London Borough Council* (2000) 32 HLR 335, CA.

18.210 The general rules governing what facts, law and other circumstances the reviewing officer should consider are modified in relation to reviews of decisions to end a duty as a result of the applicant having refused an offer of accommodation that the local housing authority has considered to be suitable for the applicant and his or her household. The reviewing officer is required to look at the facts that existed at the date of the applicant's refusal of the offer, albeit that some of those facts might only come to the local housing authority's attention after the refusal[1].

1   *Osseily v Westminster City Council* [2007] EWCA Civ 1108, [2008] HLR 18, CA; and *Omar v Westminster City Council* [2008] EWCA Civ 421, [2008] HLR 36, CA. See **20.136**.

18.211 In *Nzolameso v City of Westminster Council*[1], the Supreme Court held that the local housing authority's letter containing its decision that the HA 1996, s 193(2), main housing duty had come to an end because the applicant had refused an offer of suitable accommodation[2] could not demonstrate that it had considered the location of the accommodation, the applicant's needs and all of the issues in art 2 of the Homelessness (Suitability of Accommodation) (England) Order 2012[3]. There was no indication that the reviewing officer recognised, in particular, the obligation to offer accommodation as close to the local housing authority's district as possible (if it was not reasonably practicable to offer accommodation within its district)[4].

1   [2015] UKSC 22, [2015] 2 All ER 942, [2015] HLR 22, SC.
2   HA 1996, s 193(5), see **16.114–16.123**.
3   SI 2012/2601, see **18.48–18.61**.
4   *Nzolameso v City of Westminster Council* [2015] UKSC 22, [2015] 2 All ER 942, [2015] HLR 22 per Baroness Hale at [35]–[37].

Local housing authorities in Wales

18.212 Six types of offer of accommodation raise special issues. If these offers are refused by an applicant, the making of the offer can bring to an end the relevant duty owed under H(W)A 2014, Pt 2. They are:

- an offer of accommodation made in order to bring the H(W)A 2014, s 66(1), prevention duty to an end[1];
- an offer of accommodation made in order to bring the H(W)A 2014, s 73(1), relief duty to an end[2];
- an offer of accommodation made in performance of the H(W)A 2014, s 68(1), interim accommodation duty[3];
- an offer of suitable accommodation made in performance of the H(W)A 2014, s 75(1), main housing duty[4];
- a final offer of suitable accommodation made through the allocation arrangements in HA 1996, Pt 6[5]; and
- a private rented sector offer[6].

As for applicants to local housing authorities in England, the applicant has the right to accept the offer whilst simultaneously requesting a review of the suitability[7]. Given the serious consequences which may follow if an offer is refused, but is later upheld as suitable, accepting the offer whilst also requesting a review of the decision that the accommodation offered was suitable must normally be the advisable course of action[8].

[1]   H(W)A 2014, s 67(4), see **17.66–17.72**.
[2]   H(W)A 2014, s 74(5), see **17.109–17.118**.
[3]   H(W)A 2014, s 69(7), see **17.129**.
[4]   H(W)A 2014, s 76(3)(a), see **17.165–17.171**.
[5]   H(W)A 2014, s 76(3)(c), see **17.178–17.179**.
[6]   H(W)A 2014, s 76(3)(b), see **17.172–17.177**.
[7]   H(W)A 2014, s 85(3), see **19.100–19.101**.
[8]   For further discussion, see **17.165–17.171**.

Legal challenges

18.213 There is no explicit duty to assess the suitability of the accommodation in relation to the applicant's needs before making the offer of accommodation. Nor is there any duty on the local housing authority to give the reasons, in its letter offering the accommodation, why it considers that the accommodation is suitable[1].

[1]   *Solihull Metropolitan Borough Council v Khan* [2014] EWCA Civ 41, [2014] HLR 33, CA.

Disputes over suitability

18.214 It is expected that, if the accommodation appears to the applicant to be unsuitable, the applicant will have the opportunity to raise reasons why the accommodation is or was not suitable during the review process[1]. However, it makes good administrative sense for a local housing authority to satisfy itself as to the suitability of accommodation to be offered, *before* making the offer, not least in order to minimise dissatisfaction and the prospect of a review.

[1]   *Abed v Westminster City Council* [2011] EWCA Civ 1406, (2012) January *Legal Action*, p 21, CA; and *Nzolameso v City of Westminster Council* [2015] UKSC 22, [2015] 2 All ER 942, [2015] HLR 22 per Baroness Hale at [35]–[37].

18.215 Where the local housing authority decides on review that the accommodation was suitable for the applicant, it has a duty to give reasons for that decision. Those reasons must be adequate and intelligible to the applicant and must address the issues relating to suitability raised by the applicant and by the legislation[1]. Where a review decision is in the applicant's favour, the review officer is not required to give reasons for the decision that the accommodation was not suitable[2].

[1]   HA 1996, s 203(4); H(W)A 2014, s 86(4). See **19.181**.
[2]   *Akhtar v Birmingham City Council* [2011] EWCA Civ 383, [2011] HLR 28, CA.

18.216 If the review decision confirms that the accommodation offered was suitable, the applicant may appeal to the county court on a point of law[1]. An applicant can only seek to challenge a particular decision that the accommodation was suitable for his or her needs. The courts will not entertain a challenge to the local housing authority's policy on certain types of offers in the abstract[2].

[1]   HA 1996, s 204(1); H(W)A 2014, s 88(1). See **19.214–19.276**.
[2]   *R v Westminster City Council ex p Tansey* (1988) 21 HLR 57, CA.

Failure to secure suitable accommodation

18.217 If the local housing authority agrees that the accommodation is not suitable for the needs of the applicant and members of his or her household but does not secure any alternative accommodation, the applicant's remedy is to bring a claim in judicial review for a mandatory order requiring the local housing authority to secure suitable accommodation[1].

[1]   *R v Newham London Borough Council ex p Mashuda Begum* (1999) 32 HLR 808, QBD. See also **18.23** and **19.306–19.333**.

18.218 If the dispute between the applicant and the local housing authority as to the suitability of accommodation does not attract a right to request a review[1], the applicant's remedy is to bring a claim by way of judicial review proceedings arguing that the local housing authority's decision is wrong in law, or to invoke the local housing authority's complaints procedure[2].

[1]   See **18.20**.
[2]   See **19.306–19.333** for judicial review, and **19.333–19.340** for complaints.

Handling 'suitability' disputes

18.219 The general conduct of reviews, appeals and court challenges is dealt with in CHAPTER 19, but several specific points can be made about the conduct of cases which concern 'suitability' issues.

18.220 Where an applicant pursuing a review raises new information as part of his or her argument that the accommodation is unsuitable, the reviewing officer must take that information into account. If the fact that the information was not previously raised causes the reviewing officer to disbelieve the applicant, the reviewing officer must put those concerns to the applicant and give him or her an opportunity to deal with them[1]. If the reviewing officer is relying on inconsistencies in the applicant's account, those too should be put to the applicant for explanation[2]. If a reviewing officer, in the course of deliberations into whether or not accommodation offered was suitable, obtains information from a third party causing him or her to believe that the accommodation was suitable, the information should be put to the applicant for comment[3].

[1] *R v Hackney London Borough Council ex p Decordova* (1995) 27 HLR 108, QBD.
[2] *R v Camden London Borough Council ex p Mohammed* (1998) 30 HLR 315, QBD.
[3] *R v Southwark London Borough Council ex p Ryder* (1995) September *Legal Action*, p 15, CA (refusal of permission to appeal).

18.221 Where both medical and non-medical considerations are raised as reasons for the refusal of an offer, the local housing authority must take an overall or composite view of those reasons as affecting the suitability of the accommodation for the individual applicant[1]. If there is conflicting medical evidence or opinion, the local housing authority is under a duty to act fairly and not merely to rely on the view of its medical adviser without explaining why it had rejected the contrary views of other medical practitioners[2]. It should also put to the applicant for comment any adverse medical views on which it is proposing to rely[3]. Where a consultant's report was rejected after referral to the local housing authority's medical adviser, the subsequent decision of the local housing authority was quashed because it had failed to give reasons for rejecting the report[4]. Where the local housing authority does not make its own investigations into the applicant's medical condition or obtain its own medical advice, it is bound by the medical evidence on suitability submitted by the applicant[5].

[1] *R v Lewisham London Borough Council ex p Dolan* (1993) 25 HLR 68, QBD.
[2] *R v Kensington and Chelsea Royal London Borough Council ex p Assister* (1996) September *Legal Action*, p 13, QBD.
[3] *R v Newham London Borough Council ex p Lumley* (2001) 33 HLR 124, QBD; and *R (Amirun Begum) v Tower Hamlets London Borough Council* [2002] EWHC 633 (Admin), (2003) 33 HLR 8, Admin Ct.
[4] *R v Kensington and Chelsea Royal London Borough Council ex p Campbell* (1996) 28 HLR 160, QBD.
[5] *R v Haringey London Borough Council ex p Karaman* (1997) 29 HLR 366, QBD.

18.222 The letter containing the decision or review decision should be able to demonstrate that the local housing authority had not only considered all the issues on suitability raised by the applicant, but had also considered the relevant law, before deciding that its duty had come to an end. In the case of accommodation located outside of the local housing authority's district, the letter should show the local housing authority's assessment of how practicable it would be for the applicant and his or her household to move out of the area, what inquiries had been made to ascertain whether school places would be available (if relevant)[1] and what the applicant's particular medical conditions required. It should also indicate what accommodation was available in the local housing district, why that had not been offered to the applicant and should make it clear that the local housing authority had understood that there is an obligation to offer accommodation as close to its district as possible[2].

[1] *R (E) v Islington London Borough Council* [2017] EWHC 1440, (2017) 20 CCL Rep 148, Admin Ct.
[2] *Nzolameso v City of Westminster Council* [2015] UKSC 22, [2015] 2 All ER 942, [2015] HLR 22, SC per Baroness Hale at [35]–[37], considering the statutory test in art 2 of the

Homelessness (Suitability of Accommodation) (England) Order 2012, SI 2012/2601, see **18.57**.

18.223 Where an applicant has accepted the accommodation and simultaneously sought a review of the suitability, the reviewing officer should consider all the circumstances at the date of the review[1]. It follows that, if there have been any developments between the date of the request for a review and the reviewing officer's decision, and those developments might render the accommodation unsuitable, they should be considered[2].

[1] *Mohamed v Hammersmith & Fulham London Borough Council* [2001] UKHL 57, [2002] 1 AC 547, HL. See *Omar v Westminster City Council* [2008] EWCA Civ 421, [2008] HLR 36, CA, and **18.210** and **19.174** for the relevant considerations when an applicant has refused an offer of accommodation.
[2] *Omar v Westminster City Council* [2008] EWCA Civ 421, [2008] HLR 36, CA, at [25] per Waller LJ.

18.224 If a review is determined in the applicant's favour, and the reviewing officer decides that the accommodation offered to the applicant, and accepted by him or her, is not suitable, then the local housing authority must take steps to secure that suitable accommodation is available. The Ombudsman has found maladministration, and recommended compensation of £1,400, where there had been a delay in dealing with a review and a subsequent delay in identifying a suitable alternative property when the review succeeded[1].

[1] *Complaint against Haringey London Borough Council* 14 03 002, 14 March 2015, (2015) September *Legal Action*, p 54.

Chapter 19

REVIEWING AND APPEALING HOMELESSNESS DECISIONS

Contents

INTRODUCTION

19.1 Inevitably, some applicants are disappointed with the decisions made by local housing authorities on their applications for assistance under the Housing Act 1996, Pt 7[1] (HA 1996) ('Homelessness') or under the Housing (Wales) Act 2014, Pt 2 (H(W)A 2014) ('Homelessness'). Others may be concerned at the way in which they have been treated by a local housing authority or the way in which it has performed its obligations.

[1] As amended by Homelessness Reduction Act 2017 (HRA 2017) for applications for homelessness assistance made to local housing authorities in England on or after 3 April 2018.

19.2 Disputes about the content of decisions were not addressed at all in the earliest versions of the statutory homelessness provisions. From 1977 onwards, those who were disappointed sought recourse to the courts, initially by ordinary civil claims in the county courts and in the Chancery and Queen's Bench Divisions of the High Court. But from the early 1980s, challenges to decisions could only be made by bringing judicial review proceedings in the Crown Office List of the High Court, now the Administrative Court. As a result, challenges were confined to claims alleging breach by the local housing authority of administrative law principles.

19.3 Only a modest number of judicial review applications were brought, but, partly at least to reduce the numbers of those challenges, later versions of the Codes of Guidance encouraged local housing authorities to establish and operate their own in-house mechanisms to review disputed decisions. Applicants who expressed concern about decisions on their applications could then request an extra-statutory, internal review of those decisions by the relevant local housing authority. The approach was widely adopted by local housing authorities, but in practice did little to diminish the numbers of judicial review applications to the courts.

19.4 The current regime in HA 1996, Pt 7[1] and, for local housing authorities in Wales, in H(W)A 2014, Pt 2, built on both approaches (in-house reviews and access to the courts to challenge the contents of unlawful decisions). First, HA 1996, Pt 7[2] and H(W)A 2014, Pt 2, each contain a statutory scheme for internal review by a local housing authority of some of its own decisions. Second, most legal challenges are diverted away from the High Court to the county court, where there is a limited right of appeal against those decisions capable of being subject to statutory review. Third, judicial review remains available for a residual category of disputes under HA 1996, Pt 7 or H(W)A 2014, Pt 2, in particular those relating to non-reviewable decisions. Concerns that this three-pronged arrangement for challenging decisions might not comply with the 'fair hearing' requirements of the European Convention on Human Rights were quickly put to rest by the House of Lords[3]. Since then, in 2010 and again in 2017, the Supreme Court has held that decision-making on an application for homelessness assistance did not involve a determination of the applicant's 'civil rights' and therefore that Art 6(1) of the European Convention on Human Rights did not apply[4].

[1]   As amended by HRA 2017, for applications for homelessness assistance made to local housing authorities in England on or after 3 April 2018.

[2]   As amended by HRA 2017, for applications for homelessness assistance made to local housing authorities in England on or after 3 April 2018.

[3]   European Convention on Human Rights, Art 6; Human Rights Act 1998, Sch 1, Art 6. *Runa Begum v Tower Hamlets London Borough Council* [2003] UKHL 5, [2003] 2 AC 430, HL.

[4]   *Ali v Birmingham City Council* [2010] UKSC 8, [2010] 2 AC 39, SC and *Poshteh v Kensington & Chelsea Royal London Borough Council* [2017] UKSC 36, [2017] 624, SC; see also *Fazia Ali v UK* (App No 40378, 20 October 2015) where the European Court of Human Rights took a different view.

19.5 Where the applicant's concern is over the way in which his or her application has been handled, or the way in which the duties owed have been performed, HA 1996, Pt 7[1] and H(W)A 2014, Pt 2, provide no means of redress. For that, the applicant must look first to the local housing authority's own complaints procedure. That procedure is underscored by:

(1)   a right of further complaint to the Local Commissioner for Administration[2] or to the Public Services Ombudsman for Wales;

(2)   the local housing authority's own monitoring officer, who deals with alleged maladministration or unlawful conduct[3]; and

(3)   an enhanced statutory power permitting local authorities to give

compensation to complainants[4].

1   As amended by HRA 2017, for applications for homelessness assistance made to local housing authorities in England on or after 3 April 2018.
2   Known as 'the Local Government and Social Care Ombudsman'.
3   Local Government and Housing Act 1989, ss 5 and 5A, which are each slightly modified for the two different jurisdictions in England and in Wales.
4   Local Government Act 2000, s 92.

19.6 Of course, in the process of performing its functions under HA 1996, Pt 7[1], or H(W)A 2014, Pt 2, the local housing authority may also infringe the applicant's rights under the European Convention on Human Rights (giving rise to a possible claim under the Human Rights Act 1998)[2] or be guilty of discrimination on the grounds of one or more of the eight protected characteristics set out in the Equality Act 2010[3]. A full consideration of such specialist claims is beyond the scope of this book. In addition, if the local housing authority is not performing its acknowledged duty under HA 1996, Pt 7[4], or H(W)A 2014, Pt 2, or is failing to consider exercising an available power, the Administrative Court can grant a mandatory order in judicial review proceedings, requiring it to perform its statutory obligations[5].

1   As amended by HRA 2017, for applications for homelessness assistance made to local housing authorities in England on or after 3 April 2018.
2   See **20.110–20.123**.
3   Equality Act 2010, ss 5–12.
4   As amended by HRA 2017, for applications for homelessness assistance made to local housing authorities in England on or after 3 April 2018.
5   See **19.312**.

19.7 Any particular application for homelessness assistance may trigger more than one of the different possibilities for redress. This chapter considers each potential remedy in turn. The reader will need to consider the portfolio as a whole before deciding which remedy, or which selection of remedies, to pursue.

REVIEWS

Statutory reviews

An overview

19.8 Where an applicant is disappointed with a decision made by the local housing authority on his or her application for homelessness assistance, the statutory review processes provided by HA 1996, Pt 7[1] and H(W)A 2014, Pt 2, may give that applicant an opportunity to have all the relevant facts and the law reconsidered by the local housing authority[2]. In most cases, the reviewing officer must look at all the circumstances afresh, and as they exist at the date of the review decision. The process is not confined to considering matters as they stood when the applicant first applied or as at the date of the initial decision[3]. The statutory review is, therefore, the opportunity for the applicant to have his or her case completely re-examined by the local housing authority itself[4].

1   As amended by HRA 2017, for applications for homelessness assistance made to local housing authorities in England on or after 3 April 2018.

2   HA 1996, ss 202–203, as amended by HRA 2017, s 9, for applications for homelessness assistance made to local housing authorities in England on or after 3 April 2018; H(W)A 2014 ss 85–87.

3   *Mohammed v Hammersmith and Fulham London Borough Council* [2001] UKHL 57, [2002] 1 AC 547, HL.

4   Case law has developed two exceptions to the general rule that a reviewing officer considers all the circumstances at the date of the review decision. The first exception is where the decision made under HA 1996, s 184 or the assessment under H(W)A 2014, s 63(1) was unlawful, and had deprived the applicant of rights that he or she would have had if there had been a lawful decision, so that the reviewing officer should restore those rights (*Robinson v Hammersmith & Fulham London Borough Council* [2006] EWCA Civ 1122, [2007] HLR 7, CA). See **9.93–9.94** and **12.136–12.139**. The second exception is where the review relates to a decision that the local housing authority's duty to the applicant has come to an end, because the applicant has refused an offer of suitable accommodation, see **15.118–15.123, 15.169–15.173, 15.181–15.188, 16.114–16.123, 16.142–16.152, 16.163–16.179** and **16.205–16.216** (England) and **17.66–17.72, 17.109–17.117, 17.129, 17.165–17.179** (Wales)). In those circumstances, the reviewing officer should consider the facts and circumstances as at the date of the refusal (*Omar v Westminster City Council* [2008] EWCA Civ 421, [2008] HLR 36, CA). See **16.111**.

19.9 There is no free-standing right to a review of *every* adverse decision made by a local housing authority under HA 1996, Pt 7[1] or H(W)A 2014, Pt 2. The statutory review schemes apply only to a specific band of decisions[2]. However, nothing in either HA 1996, Pt 7[3] or H(W)A 2014, Pt 2, prevents a local housing authority from adopting its own informal arrangements enabling it to look again at any other decisions about which applicants express concern. Such informal reviews are no part of the statutory scheme, but can nevertheless help to reduce the number of formal complaints or claims for judicial review[4]. HA 1996, Pt 7[5], and H(W)A 2014, Pt 2, only permit one statutory review of any particular decision. A review decision cannot itself be the subject of a statutory review[6].

1   As amended by HRA 2017, for applications for homelessness assistance made to local housing authorities in England on or after 3 April 2018.

2   See **19.12–19.70** (England) and **19.71–19.86** (Wales).

3   As amended by HRA 2017, for applications for homelessness assistance made to local housing authorities in England on or after 3 April 2018.

4   See **19.306–19.340**.

5   As amended by HRA 2017, for applications for homelessness assistance made to local housing authorities in England on or after 3 April 2018.

6   HA 1996, s 202(2); H(W)A 2014, s 85(4). See also **19.202–19.209**.

19.10 When the scheme of statutory reviews was first introduced by HA 1996, Pt 7[1], it was hoped that this new regime would be monitored so as to establish its success or failure. Regrettably, there has been very little feedback on whether or not the scheme of statutory reviews has been a success.

1   At the date of commencement (20 January 1997), HA 1996, Pt 7, applied to local housing authorities in both England and in Wales. From 27 April 2015, applications for help for accommodation or for finding or retaining accommodation made to a local housing authority in Wales fall under H(W)A 2014, Pt 2.

19.11 The first government-commissioned research targeted a geographic area in which there had been relatively little review activity[1]. The little empirical information that is available has come mainly through independent academic research[2]. In 2011, the magazine *Inside Housing* published the result of its own investigations, showing that, on average, 42% of initial decisions that reached the review stage were overturned by the reviewing officer[3].

1   Atkinson et al *A Regional Study of Local Authority and Court Processes in Homelessness Cases* (Faculty of Law, University of Leicester, Department of Constitutional Affairs, 1999).
2   Cowan, Halliday and Hunter 'Homelessness reviews – findings published' (2002) July *Legal Action*, p 6; and 'Homeless applicants and internal reviews' (2003) March *Legal Action*, p 8; Cowan, Dymond, Halliday, and Hunter 'Reconsidering mandatory reconsideration' *Public Law*, April 2017, 215–234 confirm a substantial attrition rate between initial applications, internal reviews and subsequent appeals. They also found evidence that, the higher the internal review caseload of local housing authorities, the more likely those local housing authorities were to consider that internal review improved the quality of their ongoing initial decision-making.
3   Inside Housing, 23 September 2011.

Which decisions by a local housing authority in England can be reviewed?

19.12 An applicant who is dissatisfied with a local housing authority's decision in his or her case can only request a review if the decision falls into one of the categories specified at HA 1996, s 202(1)[1]. Between them, these categories encompass many of the most important decisions that a local housing authority is likely to make on an application. We consider each of the categories in turn.

1   As amended by HRA 2017, s 9, for applications for homelessness assistance made to local housing authorities in England on or after 3 April 2018.

19.13 If a local housing authority's decision does not fall into one of the specified categories, there is no right to request a statutory review, and any legal challenge to the decision itself can only be by way of judicial review[1]. The procedure to be followed on review is set out at Homelessness (Review Procedure etc.) Regulations 2018[2] and Chapter 19 of the English Code.

1   See **19.306–19.332**.
2   SI 2018/223, see Appendix 2. These Regulations apply to requests for review made on or after 3 April 2018: reg 11(2) SI 2018/223. Requests for review made before 3 April 2018 are governed by the Allocation of Housing and Homelessness (Review Procedures) Regulations 1999, SI 1999/71.

(1)   Any decision as to the applicant's 'eligibility' for assistance

19.14 'Eligibility' is primarily a matter of immigration status and is fully discussed in Chapter 11. The decision capable of statutory review is the decision of the local housing authority, not any decision of the immigration or benefits authorities on essentially the same subject matter[1].

1   HA 1996, s 202(1)(a), English Code, para 19.3(a).

(2)   Any decision as to what duty (if any) is owed to the applicant

19.15 The right to a review is only available in respect of decisions as to whether a duty is owed[1] under the following sections of HA 1996, Pt 7[2]:

- the HA 1996, s 189B(2)[3], relief duty to take reasonable steps to help the applicant to secure that suitable accommodation becomes available for his or her occupation[4];

- the HA 1996, s 190(2)(a), duty to accommodate applicants who are homeless, eligible for assistance, have a priority need, have become homeless intentionally and in respect of whom the HA 1996, s 189B(2), relief duty[5] has come to an end[6];
- the HA 1996, s 193(2), main housing duty[7];
- the HA 1996, s 193C(4)[8], duty to accommodate applicants who are homeless, eligible for assistance, have a priority need, have not become homeless intentionally and who have deliberately and unreasonably refused to co-operate[9]; and
- the HA 1996, s 195(2)[10], prevention duty to take reasonable steps to help the applicant secure that accommodation does not cease to be available for his or her occupation[11].

[1] HA 1996, s 202(1)(b), as amended by HRA 2017, s 9, for applications for homelessness assistance made to local housing authorities in England on or after 3 April 2018, English Code, para 19.3(b).

[2] As amended by HRA 2017, for applications for homelessness assistance made to local housing authorities in England on or after 3 April 2018.

[3] As inserted by HRA 2017, s 5(2), for applications for homelessness assistance made to local housing authorities in England on or after 3 April 2018.

[4] HA 1996, s 189B(2), as inserted by HRA 2017, s 5(2), for applications for homelessness assistance made to local housing authorities in England on or after 3 April 2018, see **15.138–15.195**.

[5] As inserted by HRA 2017, s 5(2), for applications for homelessness assistance made to local housing authorities in England on or after 3 April 2018.

[6] HA 1996, s 190(2), as amended by HRA 2017, s 5(5), for applications for homelessness assistance made to local housing authorities in England on or after 3 April 2018: see **16.81–16.93**.

[7] HA 1996s, 193(2), duty to accommodate applicants who are homeless, eligible for assistance, have a priority need, have not become homeless intentionally and in respect of whom the HA 1996, s 189B(2), relief duty has come to an end, see **16.94–16.199**.

[8] As inserted by HRA 2017, s 7(1), for applications for homelessness assistance to local housing authorities in England on or after 3 April 2018.

[9] HA 1996, s 193C(4), as inserted by HRA 2017, s 7(1), for applications for homelessness assistance made to local housing authorities in England on or after 3 April 2018, see **16.200–16.216**.

[10] As amended by HRA 2017, s 4(2), for applications for homelessness assistance to local housing authorities in England on or after 3 April 2018.

[11] HA 1996, s 195(2), as amended by HRA 2017, s 4(2), for applications for homelessness assistance made to local housing authorities in England on or after 3 April 2018, see **15.87–15.137**.

19.16 The applicant will know whether or not the decision falls within one of the categories which entitle him or her to request a review, as he or she will receive a written notification, informing him or her of the right to request a review and of the time within which the request must be made[1].

[1] See **9.90**.

19.17 This category is also broad enough to include a right to a review of any decision that a duty once owed (under one of the specified sections) is no longer owed[1]. Some decisions by which a duty can come to an end contain separate rights to request a review and so do not need to be reviewed under this category[2]. Accordingly, this category includes:

- any decision of a local housing authority that the HA 1996, s 193(2), main housing duty[3] has come to an end by reason of one of the events at HA 1996, s 193(5)–(7AA)[4] inclusive[5]; and
- any decision of a local housing authority that the HA 1996, s 193C(4)[6], accommodation duty[7] has come to an end by reason of one of the events at HA 1996[8], s 193C(5)–(6)[9] inclusive[10].

[1] *Warsame v Hounslow London Borough Council* (2000) 32 HLR 335, CA. Note the special rules regarding the scope of the review where the decision is that an accommodation duty has come to an end as a result of the applicant having refused an offer of accommodation. See **16.111**.

[2] Any decision that the HA 1996, s 189B(2),(as inserted by HRA 2017, s 5(2), for applications for homelessness assistance made to local housing authorities in England on or after 3 April 2018) relief duty has come to an end has a right to request a review at HA 1996, s 202(1)(ba)(ii) (as inserted by HRA 2017, s 9, for applications for homelessness assistance made to local housing authorities in England on or after 3 April 2018), see **19.24–19.29**. Any decision that the HA 1996, s 195(2),(as amended by HRA 2017, s 4(2), for applications for homelessness assistance made to local housing authorities in England on or after 3 April 2018) prevention duty has come to an end has a right to request a review at HA 1996, s 202(1)(bc)(ii) (as inserted by HRA 2017, s 9, for applications for homelessness assistance made to local housing authorities in England on or after 3 April 2018), see **19.42–19.48**.

[3] See **16.94–16.199**.

[4] See **16.113–16.199**.

[5] See **16.200–16.216**.

[6] As inserted by HRA 2017, s 7(1), for applications for homelessness assistance made to local housing authorities in England on or after 3 April 2018.

[7] Duty to accommodate applicants who are homeless, eligible for assistance, have a priority need have not become homeless intentionally and who have deliberately and unreasonably refused to co-operate, see **16.200–16.216**.

[8] As inserted by HRA 2017, s 7(1), for applications for homelessness assistance made to local housing authorities in England on or after 3 April 2018.

[9] As inserted by HRA 2017, s 7(1), for applications for homelessness assistance made to local housing authorities in England on or after 3 April 2018; see **16.204–16.215**.

[10] See **19.15–19.17**.

(3) Any decision of the local housing authority as to the steps it is to take under HA 1996, s 189B(2), relief duty

19.18 Once the local housing authority is satisfied that an applicant is eligible for assistance and is homeless, so that the HA 1996, s 189B(2)[1], relief duty is owed, the local housing authority is under a separate duty[2] to make an assessment of the applicant's case and to notify the applicant in writing of the assessment[3]. It is also under a duty to try to agree a personalised housing plan with the applicant[4]. That personalised housing plan will include the steps that the local housing authority is to take in order to help the applicant to secure that suitable accommodation becomes available for his or her occupation[5], and the steps that either the applicant agrees to take for the same purpose[6], or the local housing authority considers that it would be reasonable to require him or her to take[7]. The plan must be recorded in writing and given to the applicant[8].

[1] As inserted by HRA 2017, s 5(2), for applications for homelessness assistance made to local housing authorities in England on or after 3 April 2018, see **15.138–15.195**.

[2] HA 1996, s 202(1)(ba)(i), as inserted by HRA 2017, s 9, for applications for homelessness assistance made to local housing authorities in England on or after 3 April 2018, English Code, para 19.3(e).

[3] HA 1996, s 189A(1) and (3), as inserted by HRA 2017, s 3(1), for applications for homelessness assistance made to local housing authorities in England on or after 3 April 2018, see **15.62–15.71**.

4   HA 1996, s 189A(4)–(6) inclusive, as inserted by HRA 2017, s 3(1), for applications for homelessness assistance made to local housing authorities in England on or after 3 April 2018, see **15.72–15.86**.
5   HA 1996, s 189A(4)(b), (5) and (6)(c), as inserted by HRA 2017, s 3(1), for applications for homelessness assistance made to local housing authorities in England on or after 3 April 2018, see **15.72–15.86**.
6   HA 1996, s 189A(4)(a) and (5), as inserted by HRA 2017, s 3(1), for applications for homelessness assistance made to local housing authorities in England on or after 3 April 2018, see **15.72**.
7   HA 1996, s 189A(6)(b), as inserted by HRA 2017, s 3(1), for applications for homelessness assistance made to local housing authorities in England on or after 3 April 2018, see **15.73**.
8   HA 1996, s 189A(5), (6) and (8), as inserted by HRA 2017, s 3(1), for applications for homelessness assistance made to local housing authorities in England on or after 3 April 2018, see **15.75**.

19.19 This right to request a review allows an applicant to ask for a reconsideration of the steps that the local housing authority has decided that it should take. It does not permit the applicant to ask for a reconsideration of the steps that he has agreed, or more relevantly, is recorded as required to take[1]. This is an opportunity for the applicant to make representations as to what would actually help him or her to find and keep his or her own accommodation.

1   A challenge to the steps that an applicant has agreed, or is required, to take can only be brought after the event, ie if notice of a decision that the applicant has deliberately and unreasonably refused to co-operate is served on him or her under HA 1996, s 193B(1), as inserted by HRA 2017, s 7(1), for applications for homelessness assistance made to local housing authorities in England on or after 3 April 2018, see **15.196–15.221**. The right to request a review of that decision is at HA 1996, s 202(1)(bb), as inserted by HRA 2017, s 9, for applications for homelessness assistance made to local housing authorities in England on or after 3 April 2018, see **19.30–19.35**.

19.20 The steps that the local housing authority have decided, or agreed, to take will dictate to how it performs the HA 1996, s 189B(2)[1], relief duty. Indeed, these steps, together with those agreed by the applicant or required to be taken by him or her, will comprise the personalised plan setting out how the local housing authority will help the applicant to secure his or her own accommodation. If the applicant is dis-satisfied with the steps to be taken by the local housing authority in the personalised housing plan, he or she should therefore exercise his or her right to request a review.

1   As inserted by HRA 2017, s 5(2), for applications for homelessness assistance made to local housing authorities in England on or after 3 April 2018, see **15.138–15.195**.

19.21 The 21-day period within which to request a review will begin on the day when the written record of the personal housing plan is given to the applicant or the end of the period when it is made available for collection at the local housing authority's office[1].

1   HA 1996, ss 189A(8) and (12), as inserted by HRA 2017, s 3(1), for applications for homelessness assistance made to local housing authorities in England on or after 3 April 2018, and 202(3) see **15.70** and **15.75**.

19.22 There is a short period prescribed for the completion of the review. The applicant will have two weeks from the date he or she requested the review in which to provide representations. That period could be extended by written agreement between the applicant and the reviewer[1]. The review decision itself must be notified to the applicant three weeks from the date when the review request was made (not received) or, if a minded-to letter[2] had been sent, three weeks from the applicant's response to the minded-to letter[3]. The applicant and the reviewer could agree in writing that there will be a longer period for notification of the review decision[4].

1   SI 2018/223, reg 5(3)(b)(i); English Code, para 19.15. See **19.188–19.189**.
2   Under SI 2018/223, reg 7(2), see **19.150–19.165**.
3   SI 2018/223, reg 9(1)(a)(i); English Code, para 19.23.
4   SI 2018/223, reg 9(1).

19.23 The reviewing officer will consider the facts and circumstances as they exist at the date of the review, so any new developments, or any information that was not previously known to the local housing authority, can be taken into account[1]. This is an opportunity for the applicant to ask for additional, or different, steps to be taken by the local housing authority, and, essentially, to ask for the personalised housing plan to be reconsidered.

1   See **19.166–19.174**.

(4)   ANY DECISION OF THE LOCAL HOUSING AUTHORITY TO GIVE NOTICE TO THE APPLICANT UNDER HA 1996, s 189B(5), THAT THE HA 1996, s 189B(2) RELIEF DUTY HAS COME TO AN END

19.24 The local housing authority can give notice to the applicant of a decision that the HA 1996, s 189B(2)[1], relief duty has come to an end if it is satisfied of any of the following[2]:

- that the applicant has suitable accommodation available for occupation and there is a reasonable prospect of having suitable accommodation available for occupation for at least six months[3];
- that the local housing authority has complied with the HA 1996, s 189B(2)[4], relief duty for a period of 56 days beginning with the day that the local housing authority was first satisfied that the duty was owed, and the 56 day period has ended[5];
- that the applicant has refused an offer of suitable accommodation and, on the date of refusal, there was a reasonable prospect that suitable accommodation would be available for occupation for at least six months[6];
- that the applicant has become homeless intentionally from any accommodation that was made available to him or her as a result of the exercise of the local housing authority's HA 1996, s 189B(2)[7], relief functions[8];
- that the applicant is no longer eligible for assistance[9]; or
- that the applicant has withdrawn his or her application for homelessness assistance[10].

1   As inserted by HRA 2017, s 5(2), for applications for homelessness assistance made to local housing authorities in England on or after 3 April 2018, see **15.138–15.195**.
2   HA 1996, s 202(1)(ba)(ii), as inserted by HRA 2017, s 9, for applications for homelessness assistance made to local housing authorities in England on or after 3 April 2018, English Code, para 19.3(f).
3   HA 1996, s 189B(7)(a), as inserted by HRA 2017, s 5(2), for applications for homelessness assistance made to local housing authorities in England on or after 3 April 2018, see

15.162–15.165. There is provision by which the Secretary of State can prescribe a longer period, not exceeding 12 months. This power has not been exercised.

⁴ As inserted by HRA 2017, s 5(2), for applications for homelessness assistance made to local housing authorities in England on or after 3 April 2018, see **15.138–15.195**.

⁵ HA 1996, s 189B(7)(b), as inserted by HRA 2017, s 5(2), for applications for homelessness assistance made to local housing authorities in England on or after 3 April 2018, see **15.166–15.168**.

⁶ HA 1996, s 189B(7)(c), as inserted by HRA 2017, s 5(2), for applications for homelessness assistance made to local housing authorities in England on or after 3 April 2018, see **15.169–15.173**. There is provision by which the Secretary of State can prescribe a longer period, not exceeding 12 months. This power has not been exercised.

⁷ As inserted by HRA 2017, s 5(2), for applications for homelessness assistance made to local housing authorities in England on or after 3 April 2018, see **15.138–15.195**.

⁸ HA 1996, s 189B(7)(d), as inserted by HRA 2017, s 5(2), for applications for homelessness assistance made to local housing authorities in England on or after 3 April 2018, see **15.174–15.177**.

⁹ HA 1996, s 189B(7)(e), as inserted by HRA 2017, s 5(2), for applications for homelessness assistance made to local housing authorities in England on or after 3 April 2018, see **15.178–15.179**.

¹⁰ HA 1996, s 189B(7)(f), as inserted by HRA 2017, s 5(2), for applications for homelessness assistance made to local housing authorities in England on or after 3 April 2018, see **15.180**.

19.25 The applicant will have been notified in writing of any such decision[1]. That notification must specify which of the circumstances applies, and inform the applicant of his or her right to request a review and of the 21 day period within which the request must be made[2]. The 21 day period will run from the date of notification, ie the date when the applicant actually receives the notification[3] or, if the notification is not received by the applicant, after a reasonable period from it having been made available at the local housing authority's for collection[4].

¹ HA 1996, s 189B(5), (6) and (8), as inserted by HRA 2017, s 5(2), for applications for homelessness assistance made to local housing authorities in England on or after 3 April 2018, see **15.152–15.159**.

² HA 1996, s 189B(6), as inserted by HRA 2017, s 5(2), for applications for homelessness assistance made to local housing authorities in England on or after 3 April 2018, see **15.153**.

³ HA 1996, s 202(3), see **19.109–19.115**.

⁴ HA 1996, s 189B(8), as inserted by HRA 2017, s 5(2), for applications for homelessness assistance made to local housing authorities in England on or after 3 April 2018, see **15.154**.

19.26 Two of the circumstances refer to the applicant either having suitable accommodation[1], or having refused an offer of suitable accommodation[2]. HA 1996, s 202(1)(f)[3], permits an applicant to request a review of the suitability of that accommodation. However, there is no express stipulation that an applicant requesting a review under HA 1996, s 202(1)(ba)(ii)[4], is permitted both to accept the accommodation and to request a review[5].

¹ HA 1996, s 189B(7)(a), as inserted by HRA 2017, s 5(2), for applications for homelessness assistance made to local housing authorities in England on or after 3 April 2018, see **15.162–15.165**.

² HA 1996, s 189B(7)(c), as inserted by HRA 2017, s 5(2), for applications for homelessness assistance made to local housing authorities in England on or after 3 April 2018, see **15.169–15.174**.

³ As amended by HRA 2017, s 9, for applications for homelessness assistance made to local housing authorities in England on or after 3 April 2018, see **19.59–19.62** and **19.90–19.99**.

⁴ As amended by HRA 2017, s 9, for applications for homelessness assistance made to local housing authorities in England on or after 3 April 2018.

⁵ HA 1996, s 202(1A) and (1B) (as amended by HRA 2017, s 9, for applications for homelessness assistance made to local housing authorities in England on or after 3 April 2018)

refer to the applicant being able to accept offers and to request a review of their suitability where those offers are made under HA 1996, s 193(5), (7), (7AA) or final accommodation offers or final PArt 6 offers made under HA 1996, ss 193A or 193C (as inserted by HRA 2017, s 7(1), for applications for homelessness assistance made to local housing authorities in England on or after 3 April 2018).

19.27 An applicant who has been offered accommodation, and considers the accommodation to be unsuitable should accept the offer. If he or she refuses the offer, and a subsequent review upholds the original decision and concludes that the accommodation was suitable, the applicant will no longer be owed the HA 1996, s 189B(2)[1], relief duty and may face the prospect of being homeless.

[1] As inserted by HRA 2017, s 5(2), for applications for homelessness assistance made to local housing authorities in England on or after 3 April 2018, see **15.138–15.195.**

19.28 Having accepted the offer, he or she will then receive notification of a decision that the HA 1996, s 189B(2)[1], relief duty has come to an end as a result of his or her acceptance of the offer under HA 1996, s 189B(7)(a)[2]. That notification would entitle the applicant then to request a review and to make representations to the effect that the duty has not come to an end because the accommodation offered, and accepted, is not suitable. Or to make any other representations the applicant felt to be relevant. If the reviewing officer agrees that the accommodation is not suitable, the HA 1996, s 189B(2)[3], relief duty will not have ended. If the reviewing officer decides that the accommodation is suitable, and upholds the original decision, the applicant will at least not be homeless.

[1] As inserted by HRA 2017, s 5(2), for applications for homelessness assistance made to local housing authorities in England on or after 3 April 2018.
[2] As inserted by HRA 2017, s 5(2), for applications for homelessness assistance made to local housing authorities in England on or after 3 April 2018, see **15.162–15.165.**
[3] As inserted by HRA 2017, s 5(2), for applications for homelessness assistance made to local housing authorities in England on or after 3 April 2018.

19.29 It should be noted that the HA 1996, s 189B(2)[1], relief duty can also come to an end in four other circumstances:

- where the local housing authority is satisfied that the applicant has a priority need and is not satisfied that the applicant has become homeless intentionally and the HA 1996, s 189B(2)[2], relief duty has come to an end at the end of 56 days from the date when the local housing authority was first satisfied that the HA 1996, s 189B(2)[3], relief duty was owed[4];
- where the applicant has refused a final accommodation offer[5] made under HA 1996, s 193A(1)[6]; or
- where the applicant has refused a final Pt 6 offer[7] made under HA 1996, s 193A(1)[8]; or
- where an applicant has been given a notice of the local housing authority's decision that he or she has deliberately and unreasonably refused to co-operate[9].

These mechanisms for the ending of the HA 1996, s 189B(2)[10], relief duty do not fall within the scope of this right to request a review, but there are separate rights to request reviews of those decisions at HA 1996, s 202(1)(b), (bb), and (h)[11].

[1] As inserted by HRA 2017, s 5(2), for applications for homelessness assistance made to local housing authorities in England on or after 3 April 2018.

[2] As inserted by HRA 2017, s 5(2), for applications for homelessness assistance made to local housing authorities in England on or after 3 April 2018.

[3] As inserted by HRA 2017, s 5(2), for applications for homelessness assistance made to local housing authorities in England on or after 3 April 2018.

[4] HA 1996, s 189B(4) (as inserted by HRA 2017, s 5(2), for applications for homelessness assistance made to local housing authorities in England on or after 3 April 2018). In these circumstances the HA 1996, s 193(2), main housing duty will be owed to the applicant. If the applicant wished to dispute the decision that the HA 1996, s 189B(2) relief duty had come to an end and that the HA 1996, s 193(2), main housing duty was owed, the right to request a review is under HA 1996, s 202(1)(b) (as amended by HRA 2017, s 9, for applications for homelessness assistance made to local housing authorities in England on or after 3 April 2018), see **15.160–15.161**.

[5] As defined at HA 1996, s 193A(4), as inserted by HRA 2017, s 7(1), for applications for homelessness assistance made to local housing authorities in England on or after 3 April 2018, see **15.181–15.184**.

[6] HA 1996, s 189B(9)(a), as inserted by HRA 2017, s 5(2), for applications for homelessness assistance made to local housing authorities in England on or after 3 April 2018, see **15.181–15.184**.

[7] As defined at HA 1996, s 193A(5), as inserted by HRA 2017, s 7(1), for applications for homelessness assistance made to local housing authorities in England on or after 3 April 2018, see **15.185–15.189**.

[8] HA 1996, s 189B(9)(a), as inserted by HRA 2017, s 5(2), for applications for homelessness assistance made to local housing authorities in England on or after 3 April 2018, see **15.185–15.189**.

[9] HA 1996, s 189B(9)(b), as inserted by HRA 2017, s 5(2), for applications for homelessness assistance made to local housing authorities in England on or after 3 April 2018, see **15.189** and **15.196–15.221**.

[10] As inserted by HRA 2017, s 5(2), for applications for homelessness assistance made to local housing authorities in England on or after 3 April 2018.

[11] As amended by HRA 2017, s 9, for applications for homelessness assistance made to local housing authorities in England on or after 3 April 2018), see **19.15–19.17, 19.30–19.35** and **19.65–19.69**.

(5) Any decision of the local housing authority to give notice to the applicant under HA 1996, s 193B(2), that the applicant has deliberately and unreasonably refused to co-operate

19.30 Section 193B(2)[1] permits a local housing authority to give notice to an applicant of its decision that he or she has deliberately and unreasonably refused to co-operate[2]. The only basis on which the local housing authority can reach that decision is if it considers that the applicant has deliberately and unreasonably refused to take any step, either that he or she had agreed to in the personalised housing plan[3], or that the local housing authority had recorded that it was reasonable to require him or her to take[4]. Guidance as to what might constitute a deliberate and unreasonable refusal is given in the English Code[5].

[1] As inserted by HRA 2017, s 7(1), for applications for homelessness assistance made to local housing authorities in England on or after 3 April 2018, see **15.196–15.221**.

[2] HA 1996, s 202(1)(bb), as inserted by HRA 2017, s 9, for applications for homelessness assistance made to local housing authorities in England on or after 3 April 2018, English Code, para 19.3(g).

[3] HA 1996, s 189A(4)(a), as inserted by HRA 2017, s 3(1), for applications for homelessness assistance made to local housing authorities in England on or after 3 April 2018, see **15.72**.

⁴ HA 1996, s 189A(6)(b), as inserted by HRA 2017, s 3(1), for applications for homelessness assistance made to local housing authorities in England on or after 3 April 2018, see **15.73**.
⁵ English Code, paras 14.43–14.59.

19.31 The request for a review must be made within 21 days of notification of the decision that the applicant has deliberately and unreasonably refused to co-operate¹. That period runs either from the date on which the applicant has received the notice or, if the notice is not received by the applicant, after it has been made available at the local housing authority's office for a reasonable period for collection².

¹ HA 1996, s 202(3), see **19.109–19.115**.
² HA 1996, s 193B(8), as inserted by HRA 2017, s 7(1), for applications for homelessness assistance made to local housing authorities in England on or after 3 April 2018, see **15.211**.

19.32 There is no right to request a review of the warning notice given before the decision was notified¹. The applicant does not have any opportunity, at this stage or even earlier, when the personalised housing plan is being drawn up², to challenge the steps which he or she has either agreed to, or, more likely, is required to take under the personalised housing plan³. The applicant could consider a claim in judicial review in order to challenge the decisions as to those steps, or the decision to send a warning notice⁴.

¹ HA 1996, s 193B(5) (as inserted by HRA 2017, s 7(1), for applications for homelessness assistance made to local housing authorities in England on or after 3 April 2018), see **15.207**.
² See **15.72–15.80**.
³ HA 1996, s 189A(4) (a) and (6)(b), as inserted by HRA 2017, s 3(1), for applications for homelessness assistance made to local housing authorities in England on or after 3 April 2018, see **15.72–15.73**.
⁴ See **19.306–19.332**.

19.33 It follows that the *only* statutory opportunity that the applicant has to challenge the steps that he or she is required to take under the personalised housing plan is after a notice that he or she has deliberately and unreasonably refused to co-operate has been served on him or her. Of course, he or she may have raised issues about those steps at an earlier stage, when the personal housing plan was being drawn up¹. However, there is no opportunity for the applicant formally to require another housing officer, or a senior officer of the local housing authority, to review what steps he or she is required to take. Those steps will only be reconsidered after the applicant is said to have deliberately and unreasonably refused to take them, a notice to that effect has been served, and the applicant requests a review.

¹ HA 1996, s 189A(4)–(6) inclusive, as inserted by HRA 2017, s 3(1), for applications for homelessness assistance made to local housing authorities in England on or after 3 April 2018, see **15.72–15.80**.

19.34 There is a short period prescribed for the completion of the review. The applicant will have two weeks from the date he or she requested the review in which to provide representations. That period could be extended by written agreement between the applicant and the reviewer¹. The review decision itself must be notified to the applicant three weeks from the date when the review request was made (not received) or, if a minded-to letter² had been sent, three weeks from the applicant's response to the minded-to letter³. The applicant and the reviewer could agree in writing that there will be a longer period for notification of the review decision[4].

1   SI 2018/223, reg 5(3)(b)(i); English Code, para 19.15. See **19.188–19.189**.
2   Under SI 2018/223, reg 7(2), see **19.150–19.165**.
3   SI 2018/223, reg 9(1)(a)(i); English Code, para 19.23.
4   SI 2018/223, reg 9(1).

19.35 The reviewing officer will consider the facts and circumstances as they exist at the date of the review, so any new developments, or any information that was not previously known to the local housing authority, can be taken into account[1]. This is an opportunity for the applicant to make the case that the steps that he or she either agreed to take, or, more likely, was required to take were not reasonable or not realistic, and, essentially, to ask for the personalised housing plan to be reconsidered.

1   See **19.166–19.174**.

(6)   ANY DECISION OF THE LOCAL HOUSING AUTHORITY AS TO THE STEPS IT IS TO TAKE UNDER HA 1996, S 195(2), PREVENTION DUTY

19.36 Once the local housing authority is satisfied that an applicant is eligible for assistance and is threatened with homelessness, so that the HA 1996, s 195(2)[1], prevention duty is owed, the local housing authority is under a separate duty[2] to make an assessment of the applicant's case and to notify that assessment in writing[3]. It is also under a duty to try to agree a personalised housing plan with the applicant[4]. That personalised housing plan will include the steps that the local housing authority is to take in order to help the applicant to secure that suitable accommodation does not cease to become available for his or her occupation[5], and the steps that either the applicant agrees to take for the same purpose[6], or the local housing authority considers would be reasonable for him or her to take[7]. The plan must be recorded in writing and given to the applicant[8].

1   As amended by HRA 2017, s 4(2), for applications for homelessness assistance made to local housing authorities in England on or after 3 April 2018, see **15.87–15.137**.
2   HA 1996, s 202(1)(bc)(i), as inserted by HRA 2017, s 9, for applications for homelessness assistance made to local housing authorities in England on or after 3 April 2018; English Code, para 19.3(c).
3   HA 1996, s 189A(1) and (3), as inserted by HRA 2017, s 3(1), for applications for homelessness assistance made to local housing authorities in England on or after 3 April 2018, see **15.62–15.71**.
4   HA 1996, s 189A(4)–(6) inclusive, as inserted by HRA 2017, s 3(1), for applications for homelessness assistance made to local housing authorities in England on or after 3 April 2018, see **15.72–15.86**.
5   HA 1996, s 189A(4)(b) and (6)(c), as inserted by HRA 2017, s 3(1), for applications for homelessness assistance made to local housing authorities in England on or after 3 April 2018, see **15.72–15.74**.
6   HA 1996, s 189A(4)(a), as inserted by HRA 2017, s 3(1), for applications for homelessness assistance made to local housing authorities in England on or after 3 April 2018, see **15.72**.
7   HA 1996, s 189A(6)(b), as inserted by HRA 2017, s 3(1), for applications for homelessness assistance made to local housing authorities in England on or after 3 April 2018, see **15.73**.
8   HA 1996, s 189A(5), (6) and (8), as inserted by HRA 2017, s 3(1), for applications for homelessness assistance made to local housing authorities in England on or after 3 April 2018, see **15.74–15.75**.

19.37 This right to request a review allows an applicant to ask for a reconsideration of the steps that the local housing authority has decided that it should take. It does not permit the applicant to ask for a reconsideration of the steps that he or she has agreed, or more relevantly, is recorded as being required to take[1].

1   A challenge to the steps that an applicant has agreed, or is required, to take can only be brought after the event, ie if notice of a decision that the applicant has deliberately and unreasonably refused to co-operate is served on him or her under HA 1996, s 193B(1), as inserted by HRA 2017, s 7(1), for applications for homelessness assistance made to local housing authorities in England on or after 3 April 2018, see **15.196–15.221**.The right to request a review of that decision is at HA 1996, s 202(1)(bb), as inserted by HRA 2017, s 9, for applications for homelessness assistance made to local housing authorities in England on or after 3 April 2018, see **19.30–19.35**.

19.38 The steps that the local housing authority have decided, or agreed, to take will dictate how it performs the HA 1996, s 195(2)[1], prevention duty. Indeed, these steps, together with those agreed by the applicant or required to be taken by him or her, will comprise the personalised housing plan, setting out how the local housing authority and the applicant will work together either to secure his or her existing accommodation or to find alternative accommodation[2]. If the applicant is dis-satisfied with the steps to be taken by the local housing authority in the personalised housing plan, he or she should therefore exercise his or her right to request a review.

1   As amended by HRA 2017, s 4(2), for applications for homelessness assistance made to local housing authorities in England on or after 3 April 2018, see **15.87–15.135**.
2   HA 1996, s 189A(5), (6) and (8), as inserted by HRA 2017, s 3(1), for applications for homelessness assistance made to local housing authorities in England on or after 3 April 2018, see **15.72–15.80**.

19.39 The 21-day period within which to request a review will begin on the day when the written record of the personalised housing plan is given to the applicant, or at the end of the period when the record is left for collection at the local housing authority's office[1].

1   HA 1996, ss 189A(8) and (12), as inserted by HRA 2017, s 3(1), for applications for homelessness assistance made to local housing authorities in England on or after 3 April 2018, and 202(3) see 15.75 and **19.109–19.115**.

19.40 There is a short period prescribed for the completion of the review. The applicant will have two weeks from the date he or she requested the review in which to provide representations. That period could be extended by written agreement between the applicant and the reviewer[1]. The review decision itself must be notified to the applicant three weeks from the date when the review request was made (not received) or, if a minded-to letter[2] had been sent, three weeks from the applicant's response to the minded-to letter[3]. The applicant and the reviewer could agree in writing that there will be a longer period for notification of the review decision[4].

1   SI 2018/223, reg 5(3)(b)(i); English Code, para 19.15. See **19.188–19.189**.
2   Under SI 2018/223, reg 7(2), see **19.150–19.165**.
3   SI 2018/223, reg 9(1)(a)(i); English Code, para 19.23.
4   SI 2018/223, reg 9(1).

19.41 The reviewing officer will consider the whole of the facts and circumstances available at the date of the review, so any new developments, or any information that was not previously known to the local housing authority, can be taken into account[1]. This is an opportunity for the applicant to ask for additional, or different, steps to be taken and, essentially, to ask for the plan to be reconsidered.

[1]   See **19.166–19.174**.

---

(7)   ANY DECISION OF THE LOCAL HOUSING AUTHORITY TO GIVE NOTICE
TO THE APPLICANT UNDER HA 1996, s 195(5), THAT THE HA 1996,
s 195(2) PREVENTION DUTY HAS COME TO AN END

19.42 The local housing authority can give notice to the applicant of a decision that the HA 1996, s 195(2)[1], prevention duty has come to an end if it is satisfied of any of the following[2]:

- that the applicant has suitable accommodation available for occupation and there is a reasonable prospect of having suitable accommodation available for occupation for at least six months[3];
- that the local housing authority has complied with the HA 1996, s 195(2)[4], prevention duty for a period of 56 days beginning with the day that the local housing authority was first satisfied that the duty was owed, and the 56 day period has ended, unless the applicant has been served with a valid Housing Act 1998 s 21 notice[5];
- that the applicant has become homeless[6];
- that the applicant has refused an offer of suitable accommodation and, on the date of refusal, there was a reasonable prospect that suitable accommodation would be available for occupation for at least six months[7];
- that the applicant has become homeless intentionally from any accommodation that was made available to him or her as a result of the exercise of the local housing authority's HA 1996, s 195(2)[8], prevention functions[9];
- that the applicant is no longer eligible for assistance[10]; or
- that the applicant has withdrawn his or her application for homelessness assistance[11].

[1]   As amended by HRA 2017, s 4(2), for applications for homelessness assistance made to local housing authorities in England on or after 3 April 2018, see **15.87–15.135**.

[2]   HA 1996, s 202(1)(bc)(ii), as inserted by HRA 2017, s 9, for applications for homelessness assistance made to local housing authorities in England on or after 3 April 2018, English Code, para **19.3(d)**.

[3]   HA 1996, s 195(8)(a), as amended by HRA 2017, s 4(2), for applications for homelessness assistance made to local housing authorities in England on or after 3 April 2018, see **15.105–15.109**. There is provision by which the Secretary of State can prescribe a longer period, not exceeding 12 months. This power has not been exercised.

[4]   As amended by HRA 2017, s 4(2), for applications for homelessness assistance made to local housing authorities in England on or after 3 April 2018, see **15.87–15.135**.

[5]   HA 1996, s 195(6) and (8)(b), as inserted by HRA 2017, s 5(2), for applications for homelessness assistance made to local housing authorities in England on or after 3 April 2018, see **15.110–15.112**.

[6]   HA 1996, s 195(8)(c), as amended by HRA 2017, s 4(2), for applications for homelessness assistance made to local housing authorities in England on or after 3 April 2018, see **15.113–15.117**.

7   HA 1996, s 195(8)(d), as amended by HRA 2017, s 4(2), for applications for homelessness assistance made to local housing authorities in England on or after 3 April 2018, see **15.118–15.122**. There is provision by which the Secretary of State can prescribe a longer period, not exceeding 12 months. This power has not been exercised.

8   As amended by HRA 2017, s 4(2), for applications for homelessness assistance made to local housing authorities in England on or after 3 April 2018, see **15.87–15.135**.

9   HA 1996, s 195(8)(e), as amended by HRA 2017, s 4(2), for applications for homelessness assistance made to local housing authorities in England on or after 3 April 2018, see **15.123–15.125**.

10 HA 1996, s 195(8)(f), as amended by HRA 2017, s 4(2), for applications for homelessness assistance made to local housing authorities in England on or after 3 April 2018, see **15.126–15.127**.

11 HA 1996, s 195(8)(g), as inserted by HRA 2017, s 4(2), for applications for homelessness assistance made to local housing authorities in England on or after 3 April 2018, see **15.128–15.131**.

19.43 The applicant will have been notified in writing of the decision[1]. That notification must specify which of the circumstances apply, and inform the applicant of his or her right to request a review and of the 21-day period within which the request must be made[2]. The 21-day period will run from the date of notification, ie the date when the applicant actually receives the notification[3] or, if the notification is not received by the applicant, after a reasonable period from it having been made available at the local housing authorities for collection[4].

1   HA 1996, s 195(5) and (7)(a), as amended by HRA 2017, s 4(2), for applications for homelessness assistance made to local housing authorities in England on or after 3 April 2018, see **15.100–15.103**.

2   HA 1996, s 195(7), as amended by HRA 2017, s 4(2), for applications for homelessness assistance made to local housing authorities in England on or after 3 April 2018, see **15.101**.

3   HA 1996, s 202(3), see **19.109–19.115**.

4   HA 1996, s 195(9), as amended by HRA 2017, s 4(2), for applications for homelessness assistance made to local housing authorities in England on or after 3 April 2018, see **15.102**.

19.44 Two of the circumstances refer to the applicant either having suitable accommodation[1], or having refused an offer of suitable accommodation[2]. HA 1996, s 202(1)(f)[3], permits an applicant to request a review of the suitability of that accommodation. However, there is no express stipulation that an applicant requesting a review under HA 1996, s 202(1)(bc)(ii)[4], is permitted both to accept the accommodation and to request a review[5].

1   HA 1996, s 195(8)(a), as amended by HRA 2017, s 4(2), for applications for homelessness assistance made to local housing authorities in England on or after 3 April 2018, see **15.105–15.109**.

2   HA 1996, s 195(8)(d), as amended by HRA 2017, s 4(2), for applications for homelessness assistance made to local housing authorities in England on or after 3 April 2018, see **15.118–15.122**.

3   As amended by HRA 2017, s 9, for applications for homelessness assistance made to local housing authorities in England on or after 3 April 2018, see **19.59–19.62**.

4   As amended by HRA 2017, s 9, for applications for homelessness assistance made to local housing authorities in England on or after 3 April 2018.

5   HA 1996, s 202(1A) and (1B) (as amended by HRA 2017, s 9, for applications for homelessness assistance made to local housing authorities in England on or after 3 April 2018) refer to the applicant being able to accept offers and to request a review of their suitability where those offers are made under HA 1996, s 193(5), (7), (7AA) or final accommodation offers or final Part 6 offers made under HA 1996, ss 193A or 193C (as inserted by HRA 2017, s 7(1), for applications for homelessness assistance made to local housing authorities in England on or after 3 April 2018).

19.45 An applicant who has been offered accommodation, and considers the accommodation to be unsuitable should accept the offer. If he or she refuses the offer, and a subsequent review upholds the original decision and concludes that the accommodation was suitable, the applicant will no longer be owed the HA 1996, s 195(2)[1], prevention duty.

[1]   As amended by HRA 2017, s 4(2), for applications for homelessness assistance made to local housing authorities in England on or after 3 April 2018, see **15.87–15.135**.

19.46 Having accepted the offer, he or she will then receive notification of a decision that the HA 1996, s 195(2)[1], prevention duty has come to an end as a result of his or her acceptance of the offer under HA 1996, s 195(8)(a)[2]. That notification would entitle the applicant then to request a review and to make representations to the effect that the duty has not come to an end because the accommodation offered, and accepted, is not suitable. Or to make any other representations the applicant felt to be relevant. If the reviewing officer agrees that the accommodation is not suitable, the HA 1996, s 195(2)[3], prevention duty will not have ended. If the reviewing officer decides that the accommodation is suitable, and upholds the original decision, the applicant will at least not be facing the prospect of imminent homelessness.

[1]   As amended by HRA 2017, s 4(2), for applications for homelessness assistance made to local housing authorities in England on or after 3 April 2018.
[2]   As amended by HRA 2017, s 4(2), for applications for homelessness assistance made to local housing authorities in England on or after 3 April 2018, see **15.101**.
[3]   As amended by HRA 2017, s 4(2), for applications for homelessness assistance made to local housing authorities in England on or after 3 April 2018.

19.47 There is a short period prescribed for the completion of the review. The applicant will have two weeks from the date he or she requested the review in which to provide representations. That period could be extended by written agreement between the applicant and the reviewer[1]. The review decision itself must be notified to the applicant three weeks from the date when the review request was made (not received) or, if a minded-to letter[2] had been sent, three weeks from the applicant's response to the minded-to letter[3]. The applicant and the reviewer could agree in writing that there will be a longer period for notification of the review decision[4].

[1]   SI 2018/223, reg 5(3)(b)(i); English Code, para 19.15.
[2]   Under SI 2018/223, reg 7(2), see **19.150–19.156**.
[3]   SI 2018/223, reg 9(1)(a)(i); English Code, para 19.23.
[4]   SI 2018/223, reg 9(1).

19.48 It should be noted that the HA 1996, s 195(2)[1], prevention duty can also come to an end where an applicant has been given a notice that he or she has deliberately and unreasonably refused to co-operate[2]. This mechanism for the ending of the duty does not fall within the scope of this right to request a review, but there is a separate right to request a review at HA 1996, s 202(1)(bb)[3].

[1]   As amended by HRA 2017, s 4(2), for applications for homelessness assistance made to local housing authorities in England on or after 3 April 2018.
[2]   HA 1996, s 195(10), as amended by HRA 2017, s 4(2), for applications for homelessness assistance made to local housing authorities in England on or after 3 April 2018.

³   As amended by HRA 2017, s 9, for applications for homelessness assistance made to local
    housing authorities in England on or after 3 April 2018, see **19.30–19.35**.

(8)   ANY DECISION TO NOTIFY ANOTHER LOCAL HOUSING AUTHORITY UN-
DER HA 1996, S 198(1)

19.49 Under HA 1996, s 198(1)¹ ('conditions for referral')², a local housing
authority can initiate the procedure for the referral of the performance of the
HA 1996, s 193(2), main housing duty³ to another local housing authority⁴.
The procedure starts when the local housing authority that has received the
application notifies the other local housing authority that it believes that one
of the three conditions for a referral is made out.

¹   HA 1996, s 202(1)(c), English Code, para 19.3(h).
²   See CHAPTER **14**.
³   See **16.94–16.199**.
⁴   HA 1996, s 198(2)–(4), see **14.151–14.154**.

19.50 As a result of amendments to HA 1996, Pt 7¹, made by HRA 2017,
there is no obligation on the notifying local housing authority to give to the
applicant that such a notification is going to be made or has been made². It
follows that the applicant will also not be informed the right to seek a review
of the decision to notify. However, there is provision to notify the applicant
that the local housing authority intends to notify another local housing author
or has already done so³.

¹   For applications for homelessness assistance made to local housing authorities in England on
    or after 2018.
²   HA 1996, s 184(5), as amended by HRA 2017, s 5(10), for applications for homelessness
    assistance made to local housing authorities in England on or after 3 April 2018.
³   HA 1996, s 200(1), see **14.155–14.161**.

19.51 The applicant has the right to request a review once the notifying local
housing authority has made two decisions on his or her application. The
applicant will have been notified of that decision by the notifying local housing
authority and notified of his or her right to request a review.¹ The decisions are:

(1)   that it considers that the conditions for referral are met; and
(2)   that it is going to exercise its discretion to notify the other local housing
        authority on that basis².

The applicant's request for a review can cause either or both of those decisions
to be reconsidered.

¹   HA 1996, s 184(4) and (5), see **14.155–14.156**.
²   HA 1996, s 198(1), see **14.151–14.154**.

19.52 It follows that the review request can be made before the notification is
actually sent from the first to the second local housing authority. In those
circumstances, it may be sensible for the first local housing authority to
conduct and determine the review before it notifies the second local housing
authority, as, if the review is successful and the decision set aside, there may be
no need to notify. This is particularly true if the applicant is challenging a
decision as to which (of several) local housing authorities he or she should be

referred[1].

[1]   In *Berhane v Lambeth London Borough Council* [2007] EWHC 2702 (QBD), (2008) March *Legal Action*, p 28, QBD, the High Court criticised a county court judge's decision to adjourn the applicant's appeal against a decision to notify another local housing authority until the two local housing authorities had resolved their dispute as to whether or not the conditions for referral were made out. Where there had been undue delay on the part of the notifying local housing authority, it was wrong, and deprived the applicant of effective access to the courts, to wait for the referee's decision. This decision emphasises that the applicant's right to challenge a decision to refer him or her to another local housing authority is entirely separate from the procedure used by two local housing authorities to resolve disputes between themselves. See **14.176–14.190** for disputes between two local housing authorities; and see **14.191–14.211** for challenges by the applicant.

19.53 Where the second local housing authority is notified before a review is requested, or concluded, any response it makes does not affect the applicant's right to a review or the conclusions of that review.

19.54 There is no right available, either under this category or any other, to review a decision *not* to notify another local housing authority under the referral provisions[1]. Nor is there is any right to request a review of a decision to notify another local housing authority to refer the performance of the HA 1996, s 189B(2)[2], relief duty under HA 1996, s 198(A1)[3]. If the applicant is notified[4] of a decision to refer the HA 1996, s 189B(2)[5], relief duty and wishes to challenge that decision, he or she would have to wait for the decision to be made between the two local housing authorities as to whether the conditions for referral are met[6].

[1]   *Sareen v Hackney London Borough Council* [2003] EWCA Civ 351, [2003] HLR 54, CA.
[2]   As inserted by HRA 2017, s 5(2), for applications for homelessness assistance made to local housing authorities in England on or after 3 April 2018, see **15.138–15.195**.
[3]   As inserted by HRA 2017, s 5(8), for applications for homelessness assistance made to local housing authorities in England on or after 3 April 2018, see **15.139–15.142** and **16.217–16.224**.
[4]   Under HA 1996, s 184(4), as amended by HRA 2017, s 5(3), for applications for homelessness assistance made to local housing authorities in England on or after 3 April 2018.
[5]   As inserted by HRA 2017, s 5(2), for applications for homelessness assistance made to local housing authorities in England on or after 3 April 2018, see **15.138–15.195**.
[6]   HA 1996, s 198(5), see **14.176–14.190**. The right to request a review is at HA 1996, s 202(1)(d), see **19.55–19.57**.

(9)   Any decision under HA 1996, s 198(5) as to whether the conditions for referral are met

19.55 The right to request a review of the decision set out in the preceding category enables an applicant to challenge the opinion of the notifying local housing authority that the conditions for referral are made out[1]. This additional category confers a right to a review of the *final decision* as to whether the referral conditions are actually made out. The applicant therefore has a right to request a review of either one of two decisions:

- a decision that the conditions are met, or are not met, for the referral of the HA 1996, s 189B(2)[2], relief duty to another local housing authority[3]; or
- a decision that the conditions are met, or are not met, for the referral of the HA 1996, s 193(2), main housing duty[4] to another local housing

authority[5].

1   HA 1996, s 202(1)(d), English Code, para 19.3(i).
2   As inserted by HRA 2017, s 5(2), for applications for homelessness assistance made to local housing authorities in England on or after 3 April 2018, see **15.138–15.195**.
3   HA 1996, s 198(A1), as inserted by HRA 2017, s 5(8), for applications for homelessness assistance made to local housing authorities in England on or after 3 April 2018, and 198(5), see **15.139–15.142**.
4   See CHAPTER 14 and **16.225–16.232**.
5   HA 1996, s 198(1) and (5), see **14.176–14.19**.

19.56 The final decision arises *after* the first local housing authority has notified the second local housing authority. They may either agree between them that the conditions are made out (or that they are not), or, if they cannot agree, they may invite a referee to decide the matter under the disputes procedure.

19.57 There are special modifications made to the ordinary review procedures where the request for a review is in respect of either a joint decision or a referee's decision[1].

1   HA 1996, s 202(4); SI 2018/223, regs 5(2) and (4), (6) and 9(2), see APPENDIX 2. English Code, para 19.6; and see **14.206–14.211** and **19.192–19.193**.

(10)   ANY DECISION UNDER HA 1996, S 200(3) OR (4)

19.58 In the light of amendments made to HA 1996, s 200(3) and (4)[1] by the Homelessness Act 2002, this category is arguably redundant. The only decision to which these two subsections now refer is the final decision that the conditions for referral are or are not met and those can be raised under the previous category. However, for clarity, this provides a right to request a review of any decision that:

- the conditions for referral of the main housing duty to another local housing authority are not met and so the notifying local housing authority is subject to the main housing duty[2]; or
- the conditions for referral of the main housing duty are met and a notified local housing authority in either England or Wales is subject to the main housing duty[3].

1   HA 1996, s 202(1)(e), English Code, para 19.3(j), which describes this category as relating to decisions that the conditions for referral of the main housing duty are not met, or that the conditions for referral of the main housing duty to a local housing authority in Wales are met.
2   HA 1996, s 200(3), see **14.167**.
3   HA 1996, s 200(4), see **14.168**.

(11)   ANY DECISION AS TO THE SUITABILITY OF ACCOMMODATION

19.59 This category concerns decisions as to the suitability of accommodation[1] offered to the applicant in performance of the following duties owed under HA 1996, Pt 7[2]:

- the HA 1996, s 189B(2)[3], relief duty to take reasonable steps to help the applicant to secure that suitable accommodation becomes available for his or her occupation[4];

- the HA 1996, s 1930(2)(a), duty to accommodate applicants who are homeless, eligible for assistance, have a priority need, have become homeless intentionally and in respect of whom the HA 1996, s 189B(2), relief duty[5] has come to an end[6];
- the HA 1996, s 193(2), main housing duty[7];
- the HA 1996, s 193C(4)[8], duty to accommodate applicants who are homeless, eligible for assistance, have a priority need, have not become homeless intentionally and who have deliberately and unreasonably refused to co-operate[9];
- the HA 1996, s 195(2)[10], prevention duty to take reasonable steps to help the applicant secure that accommodation does not cease to be available for his or her occupation[11];
- the HA 1996, s 193(2), main housing duty owed to an applicant where it has been decided that the conditions for referral of his or her case are not met[12]; and
- the HA 1996, s 193(2), main housing duty owed to an applicant by the notified local housing authority where it has been decided that the conditions for referral of his or her case are met[13].

[1] HA 1996, s 202(1)(f), as amended by HRA 2017, s 9, for applications for homelessness assistance made to local housing authorities in England on or after 3 April 2018, English Code, para 19.3(k).

[2] As amended by HRA 2017, for applications for homelessness assistance made to local housing authorities in England on or after 3 April 2018.

[3] As inserted by HRA 2017, s 5(2), for applications for homelessness assistance made to local housing authorities in England on or after 3 April 2018.

[4] HA 1996, s 189B(2), as inserted by HRA 2017, s 5(2), for applications for homelessness assistance made to local housing authorities in England on or after 3 April 2018. It would be unusual for accommodation to be secured to the applicant under this duty, see **16.278–16.279**.

[5] As inserted by HRA 2017, s 5(2), for applications for homelessness assistance made to local housing authorities in England on or after 3 April 2018.

[6] HA 1996, s 190(2), as amended by HRA 2017, s 5(5), for applications for homelessness assistance made to local housing authorities in England on or after 3 April 2018, see **16.81–16.93**.

[7] HA 1996s, 193(2), duty to accommodate applicants who are homeless, eligible for assistance, have a priority need, have not become homeless intentionally and in respect of whom the HA 1996, s 189B(2), relief duty has come to an end, see **16.94–16.199**.

[8] As inserted by HRA 2017, s 7(1), for applications for homelessness assistance made to local housing authorities in England on or after 3 April 2018.

[9] HA 1996, s 193C(4), as inserted by HRA 2017, s 7(1), for applications for homelessness assistance made to local housing authorities in England on or after 3 April 2018, see **16.200–16.216**.

[10] As amended by HRA 2017, s 4(2), for applications for homelessness assistance made to local housing authorities in England on or after 3 April 2018.

[11] HA 1996s, 195(2), as amended by HRA 2017, s 4(2), for applications for homelessness assistance made to local housing authorities in England on or after 3 April 2018, see **15.87–15.137**.

[12] HA 1996, s 200(3), see **14.167**.

[13] HA 1996, s 200(4), see **14.168**.

19.60 The meaning of 'suitability' in respect of the accommodation offered under the statutory provisions referred to in this category is considered in Chapter 18.

19.61 In addition, those provisions of HA 1996, Pt 7[1] obliging the local housing authority to provide some form of *interim* accommodation, or giving the local housing authority *powers* to provide accommodation, are omitted from this category. As a result, there is no right to a review of a decision as to the suitability of accommodation provided:

(1)   under the duty to secure pre-decision accommodation[2];
(2)   under the duty to secure interim accommodation during the perfor-
        mance of the HA 1996, s 189B(2)[3], relief duty[4];
(3)   under the duty to secure accommodation pending the outcome of a
        local connection referral for referral of the HA 1996, s 189B(2)[5], relief
        duty[6];
(4)   under the duty to secure accommodation pending the outcome of a
        local connection referral for referral of the HA 1996, s 193(2), main
        housing duty[7]; or
(5)   under the power to accommodate pending review[8];
(6)   under the power to accommodate pending a review of the referral of the
        HA 1996, s 189B(2)[9], relief duty[10];
(7)   under the power to accommodate pending a review of the referral of the
        HA 1996, s 193(2), main housing duty[11]; or
(8)   under the power to accommodate pending appeal[12].

[1]   As amended by HRA 2017, for applications for homelessness assistance made to local housing authorities in England on or after 3 April 2018.
[2]   HA 1996, s 188(1) and 188(1A), as amended by HRA 2017, s 5(4), for applications for homelessness assistance made to local housing authorities in England on or after 3 April 2018. See **16.37–16.50**.
[3]   As inserted by HRA 2017, s 5(2), for applications for homelessness assistance made to local housing authorities in England on or after 3 April 2018.
[4]   HA 1996, s 188(1), (1ZA), (1ZB), and (1A), as amended by HRA 2017, s 5(4), for applications for homelessness assistance made to local housing authorities in England on or after 3 April 2018; see **16.37–16.80**.
[5]   As inserted by HRA 2017, s 5(2), for applications for homelessness assistance made to local housing authorities in England on or after 3 April 2018.
[6]   HA 1996, s 199A(2), as inserted by HRA 2017, s 5(9), for applications for homelessness assistance made to local housing authorities in England on or after 3 April 2018. See **15.139–15.146** and **16.217–16.224**.
[7]   HA 1996, s 200(1). See **16.225–16.232**.
[8]   HA 1996, s 188(3), as amended by HRA 2017, s 5(4), for applications for homelessness assistance made to local housing authorities in England on or after 3 April 2018. See **16.33–16.257**.
[9]   As inserted by HRA 2017, s 5(2), for applications for homelessness assistance made to local housing authorities in England on or after 3 April 2018.
[10] HA 1996, s 199A(6), as inserted by HRA 2017, s 5(9), for applications for homelessness assistance made to local housing authorities in England on or after 3 April 2018. See **16.223**.
[11] HA 1996, s 200(5). See **16.231**.
[12] HA 1996, s 204(4), as amended by HRA 2017, ss 4(6) and 5(11), for applications for homelessness assistance made to local housing authorities in England on or after 3 April 2018. See **16.257–16.279**.

19.62 Finally, this review category does not give everyone made an offer of accommodation under HA 1996, Pt 6 a right to a review of its suitability. The only HA 1996, Pt 6 offer addressed here is a final offer made to an applicant owed the HA 1996, s 193(2) main housing duty, where the refusal of that offer may bring that duty to an end[1]. If other offers, not expressed as 'final offers' of Pt 6 accommodation, and therefore not bringing the s 193(2) main housing duty to an end, have been made, there is no right to request a review of the suitability of the accommodation offered. The suitability of final Pt 6 offers[2], made in order to bring the HA 1996, s 189B(2)[3], relief duty or the HA 1996, s 193C(4)[4], accommodation duty to an end[5], can be raised in a request for a review brought under HA 1996, s 202(1)(h)[6].

1   HA 1996, s 193(7), see **16.142–16.152**. For rights to accept the offer of PArt 6 accommodation and simultaneously request a review, see **19.90–19.99**.
2   As defined at HA 1996, ss 193A(5) or 193C(8), as inserted by HRA 2017, s 7(1), for applications for homelessness assistance made to local housing authorities in England on or after 3 April 2018. See **15.185–15.189** and **16.210–16.213**.
3   As inserted by HRA 2017, s 5(2), for applications for homelessness assistance made to local housing authorities in England on or after 3 April 2018.
4   As inserted by HRA 2017, s 7(1), for applications for homelessness assistance made to local housing authorities in England on or after 3 April 2018.See **16.200–16.216**.
5   HA 1996, ss 189B(9)(a) and 193C(6)(b), as inserted by HRA 2017, ss 5(2) and 7(1), for applications for homelessness assistance made to local housing authorities in England on or after 3 April 2018.
6   As inserted by HRA 2017, s 9, for applications for homelessness assistance made to local housing authorities in England on or after 3 April 2018, see **19.65–19.69**.

(12)   ANY DECISION AS TO THE SUITABILITY OF ACCOMMODATION CONTAINED IN A PRIVATE RENTED SECTOR OFFER

19.63 This provision[1] applies to applicants who have been made a private rented sector offer[2] in order to bring the HA 1996, s 193(2), main housing duty to an end[3]. For 'private rented sector offer', see **16.153–16.180**. For 'suitability', see CHAPTER **18**.

1   HA 1996, s 202(1)(g) as amended by HRA 2017, s 9, for applications for homelessness assistance made to a local housing authority in England on or after 3 April 2018, English Code, para 19.3(l).
2   HA 1996, s 193(7AC).
3   Private rented sector offers can only be made to applicants whose applications for homelessness assistance were made on or after 9 November 2012: Localism Act 2011 (Commencement No 2 and Transitional Provisions) (England) Order 2012, SI 2012/2599.

19.64 As with other disputes over the suitability of an offer of accommodation, the applicant has the right both to accept the offer and to request a review of its suitability[1]. This must normally be the sensible course of action[2]. Here, the applicant is being required to enter into a fixed-term assured shorthold tenancy[3]. He or she will need a break clause to be contained in the tenancy, so as to permit the applicant to terminate the tenancy before the end of the fixed term upon notice to the landlord, if the outcome of the review (or any subsequent appeal) is a decision that the private rented sector offer was unsuitable.

1   HA 1996, s 202(1A).
2   See **19.90–19.99**.
3   HA 1996, s 193(7AC).

(13)   ANY DECISION AS TO THE SUITABILITY OF ACCOMMODATION CONTAINED IN A FINAL ACCOMMODATION OFFER OR A FINAL PT 6 OFFER

19.65 Final accommodation offers[1] and final Pt 6 offers[2] can be made in two circumstances[3]:

- in order to bring the HA 1996, s 189B(2)[4], relief duty to an end[5]; and
- in order to bring the HA 1996, s 193C(4),[6] accommodation duty to an

end[7].

1   Defined at HA 1996, ss 193A(4) and 193C(7) (as inserted by HRA 2017, s 7(1), for applications for homelessness assistance made to a local housing authority in England on or after 3 April 2018), see **15.181–15.184** and **16.205–16.209**.
2   Defined at HA 1996, ss 193A(5) and 193C(8) (as inserted by HRA 2017, s 7(1), for applications for homelessness assistance made to a local housing authority in England on or after 3 April 2018), see **15.185–15.189** and **16.210–16.213**. These categories of final Pt 6 offers are different from final Pt 6 offers intended to bring the HA 1996, s 193(2), main housing duty to an end under HA 1996, s 193(7), see **16.142–16.152**.
3   HA 1996, s 202(1)(h) as inserted by HRA 2017, s 9, for applications for homelessness assistance made to a local housing authority in England on or after 3 April 2018, English Code, para 19.3(m).
4   As inserted by HRA 2017, s 5(2), for applications for homelessness assistance made to a local housing authority in England on or after 3 April 2018, see **15.138–15.195**.
5   HA 1996, ss 189B(9)(a) and 193A(1) and (2), as inserted by HRA 2017, ss 5(2) and 7(1), for applications for homelessness assistance made to a local housing authority in England on or after 3 April 2018, see **15.181–15.189**.
6   As inserted by HRA 2017, s 7(1), for applications for homelessness assistance made to a local housing authority in England on or after 3 April 2018. Duty owed to applicants who are homeless, eligible for assistance, have a priority need, have not become homeless intentionally and who have deliberately and unreasonably refused to co-operate, see **16.200–16.216**.
7   HA 1996, s 193C(6), as inserted by HRA 2017, ss 5(2) and 7(1), for applications for homelessness assistance made to a local housing authority in England on or after 3 April 2018, see **16.204–16.215**.

19.66 Final accommodation offers are defined, in similar terms, in both HA 1996, ss 193A and 193C[1], as being:

•   an offer of an assured shorthold tenancy made by a private landlord to the applicant in relation to any accommodation which is, or may become, available for the applicant's occupation;
•   made, with the approval of the local housing authority, in pursuance of arrangements made by the local housing authority in discharge of its HA 1996, s 189B(2)[2], relief duty or with a view to bringing its HA 1996, s 193C(4)[3] accommodation duty to an end; and
•   the tenancy offer is a fixed term tenancy within the meaning of Housing Act 1988, Pt 1, for a period of at least six months[4].

1   As inserted by HRA 2017, s 7(1), for applications for homelessness assistance made to a local housing authority in England on or after 3 April 2018.
2   As inserted by HRA 2017, s 5(2), for applications for homelessness assistance made to a local housing authority in England on or after 3 April 2018, see **15.138–15.195**.
3   As inserted by HRA 2017, s 7(1), for applications for homelessness assistance made to a local housing authority in England on or after 3 April 2018, see **16.200–16.216**.
4   HA 1996, ss 193A(4) and 193C(7), as inserted by HRA 2017, s 7(1), for applications for homelessness assistance made to a local housing authority in England on or after 3 April 2018, see **15.181–15.184** and **16.205–16.209**.

19.67 The local housing authority must be satisfied that the final accommodation offer is suitable for the needs of the applicant and his or her household and that the applicant is not under contractual or other obligations in respect of his or her existing accommodation which he or she is not able to bring to an end before being required to take up the offer[1]. In addition to all of the other considerations relating to suitability[2], a final accommodation offer must comply with all the criteria at Homelessness (Suitability of Accommodation) (England) Order 2012, art 3[3] in order to be suitable. It should be noted that the applicant is being required to enter into a fixed-term assured shorthold tenancy[4]. He or she will need a break clause to be contained in the tenancy, so as to permit the applicant to terminate the tenancy before the end of the fixed term upon notice to the landlord, if the outcome of the review (or any subsequent appeal) is a decision that the private rented sector offer was unsuitable.

[1] HA 1996, ss 193A(6) and (7) and 193C(9) and (10), as inserted by HRA 2017, s 7(1), for applications for homelessness assistance made to a local housing authority in England on or after 3 April 2018, see **16**.
[2] See **15.182** and **16.208**.
[3] SI 2012/2601, as amended by HRA 2017, s 12, for applications for homelessness assistance made to a local housing authority in England on or after 3 April 2018, see **18.70–18.79**.
[4] HA 1996, ss 193A(4)(c) and 193C (7)(c), as inserted by HRA 2017, s 7(1), for applications for homelessness assistance made to a local housing authority in England on or after 3 April 2018,

19.68 Final Pt 6 offers are also defined in similar in both HA 1996, ss 193A and 193C[1], as being:

- an offer of accommodation under HA 1996, Pt 6 (allocation of housing);
- made in writing in discharge of the local housing authority's HA 1996, s 189B(2)[2], relief duty or with a view to bringing its HA 1996, s 193C(4)[3] accommodation duty to an end; and
- stating that it is a final offer for those purposes[4].

The local housing authority must be satisfied that the final PArt 6 offer is suitable for the needs of the applicant and his or her household and that the applicant is not under contractual or other obligations in respect of his or her existing accommodation which he or she is not able to bring to an end before being required to take up the offer[5].

[1] As inserted by HRA 2017, s 7(1), for applications for homelessness assistance made to a local housing authority in England on or after 3 April 2018.
[2] As inserted by HRA 2017, s 5(2), for applications for homelessness assistance made to a local housing authority in England on or after 3 April 2018, see **15.138–15.195**.
[3] As inserted by HRA 2017, s 7(1), for applications for homelessness assistance made to a local housing authority in England on or after 3 April 2018, see **16.200–16.216**.
[4] HA 1996, ss 193A(5) and 193C(8), as inserted by HRA 2017, s 7(1), for applications for homelessness assistance made to a local housing authority in England on or after 3 April 2018., see **15.185–15.189** and **16.210–16.213**.
[5] HA 1996, ss 193A(6) and (7) and 193C(9) and (10), as inserted by HRA 2017, s 7(1), for applications for homelessness assistance made to a local housing authority in England on or after 3 April 2018, see **19.90–19.99**.

19.69 As with other disputes over the suitability of an offer of accommodation, the applicant has the right both to accept the offer and to request a review of its suitability[1]. This must normally be the sensible course of action[2].

[1] HA 1996, s 202(1B) as inserted by HRA 2017, s 9, for applications for homelessness assistance made to a local housing authority in England on or after 3 April 2018.
[2] See **19.90–19.99**.

Which decisions by a local housing authority in Wales can be reviewed?

19.70 The right to request a review, where an applicant is dissatisfied with a local housing authority's decision, applies where the decision falls within one of five specified categories[1]. We consider each of the categories in turn.

[1] H(W)A 2014, s 85(1) and (2). *Code of Guidance for Local Authorities on the Allocation of Accommodation and Homelessness* (Welsh Government, March 2016) (the Welsh Code), para 20.3 on the CD Rom with this book.

19.71 If a local housing authority's decision does not fall into one of the specified categories, there is no right to request a statutory review, and any legal challenge to the decision itself can only be by way of judicial review[1].

[1] See **19.306–19.332.**

19.72 The applicant will know whether or not the decision falls within one of the categories which entitle him or her to request a review, because the notice of the outcome of the local housing authority's assessment will inform the applicant of his or her right to request a review and of the time within which the request must be made[1].

[1] H(W)A 2014, s 63(4)(a). See **10.139–10.145.**

(1) ANY DECISION AS TO THE APPLICANT'S 'ELIGIBILITY' FOR HELP

19.73 'Eligibility' for help[1] is primarily a matter of immigration status and is fully discussed in CHAPTER 11. The decision capable of statutory review is the decision of the local housing authority, not any decision of the immigration or benefits authorities on essentially the same subject matter[2].

[1] H(W)A 2014, s 61 and Sch 2.
[2] H(W)A 2014, s 85(1)(a); Welsh Code, para 20.3(a).

(2) ANY DECISION THAT A DUTY IS NOT OWED TO THE APPLICANT

19.74 The right to a review is available in respect of a decision that any of the following duties under H(W)A 2014, Pt 2, is not owed to the applicant[1]:

- the H(W)A 2014, s 66(1), prevention duty[2];
- the H(W)A 2014, s 68(1), interim accommodation duty for homeless applicants who may be homeless, may be eligible for help, and may have a priority need[3];
- the H(W)A 2014, s 73(1), relief duty[4]; or
- the H(W)A 2014, s 75(1), main housing duty for applicants in priority need when the duty in H(W)A 2014, s 73 ends: (H(W)A 2014, s 75(1))[5].

[1] H(W)A 2014, s 85(1)(b); Welsh Code, para 20.3(b).
[2] See **17.45–17.72.**
[3] See **17.118–17.134.**
[4] See **17.73–17.117.**
[5] See **17.146–17.199.**

19.75 It follows that the applicant will have the right to request a review if the local housing authority has notified him or her of its assessment[1] that he or she is not homeless or threatened with homelessness, or does not have a priority need, or (in the case of the duty in H(W)A 2014, s 75(2)) is satisfied that the applicant has become homeless intentionally.

¹   H(W)A 2014, s 63(1), see **19.12–19.14**.

19.76 Unlike the law governing local housing authorities in England, the list of duties includes the H(W)A 2014, s 68(1), interim duty to secure accommodation for the applicant¹. For that duty not to apply, the local housing authority would have to have no reason to believe that the applicant might be homeless, might be eligible for help or might have a priority need. If there is any doubt as to any of those matters, interim accommodation should have been secured².

¹   The duty at H(W)A 2014, s 68(1).
²   H(W)A 2014, s 68(2), see **16.66–16.67**.

(3)   ANY DECISION OF THE LOCAL HOUSING AUTHORITY THAT A DUTY OWED TO THE APPLICANT HAS COME TO AN END

19.77 This category applies where the applicant has been notified of a local housing authority's decision that a duty owed to him or her has come to an end¹. The specified duties are:

- the H(W)A 2014, s 66(1), prevention duty²;
- the H(W)A 2014, s 68(1), interim accommodation³;
- the H(W)A 2014, s 73(1), relief duty⁴; or
- the H(W)A 2014, s 75(1) main housing duty⁵.

¹   H(W)A 2014, s 85(1)(c); Welsh Code, para 20.3(c).
²   The events which bring the H(W)A 2014, s 66(1), prevention duty to an end are at H(W)A 2014, s 67, and see **17.56–17.72**.
³   The events which bring the H(W)A 2014, s 68(1), interim accommodation duty to an end are at H(W)A 2014, s 69, and see **17.128–17.133**.
⁴   The events which bring the H(W)A 2014, s 73(1), relief duty to an end are at H(W)A 2014, s 74, and see **17.84–17.117**.
⁵   The events which bring the H(W)A 2014, s 75(1), main housing duty to an end are at H(W)A 2014, s 76, and see **17.158–17.188**.

19.78 The wording of the subsection states that the right to request a review also applies:

- to any decision to refer the applicant's case to another local housing authority; and
- to any decision that the conditions for referral are met¹.

¹   H(W)A 2014, s 85(1)(c); see CHAPTER **14** for conditions for referral.

19.79 Any of the specified duties could also come to an end if one of the circumstances in H(W)A 2014, s 79, occurs. Those circumstances are:

- where the local housing authority is no longer satisfied that the applicant is eligible for help¹;
- where the local housing authority is satisfied that a mistake of fact led to the applicant being notified under H(W)A 2014, s 63, that a duty was owed to him or her²;
- where the local housing authority is satisfied that the applicant has withdrawn his or her application³; or

- where the local housing authority is satisfied that the applicant is unreasonably failing to cooperate with it in connection with the exercise of its functions under H(W)A 2014, Pt 2, as they apply to the applicant[4].

1   H(W)A 2014, s 79(2); for 'eligible for help', see CHAPTER **11**; for the duty coming to an end for this reason, see **17.192**.
2   H(W)A 2014, s 79(3); see **17.193**.
3   H(W)A 2014, s 79(4); see **17.194**.
4   H(W)A 2014, s 79(5); see **17.195–17.197**.

19.80 In all cases, the relevant duty only comes to an end once the applicant has been notified in writing of the local housing authority's decision to that effect[1]. That notification must contain:

- the local housing authority's decision that it no longer regards itself as subject to the relevant duty;
- the reasons why it considers that the duty has come to an end;
- the applicant's right to request a review; and
- the time within which the request for a review must be made[2].

1   H(W)A 2014, s 67(1), s 69(1), s 74(1), s 76(1) and s 79(1).
2   H(W)A 2014, s 84(1).

(4)   WHETHER OR NOT REASONABLE STEPS WERE TAKEN

19.81 If the local housing authority has decided that the duty under H(W)A 2014, s 73(1) has come to an end because the 56-day period has ended[1] or because the local housing authority is satisfied that reasonable steps have been taken[2] to help to secure that suitable accommodation is available for occupation by the applicant[3], the written notification that the duty has come to an end[4] must include notice of those steps taken by the local housing authority[5]. The applicant has a right to request a review of whether or not reasonable steps were taken during the 56-day period. This is a separate right from the right to request a review of the decision that the duty has come to an end[6].

1   H(W)A 2014, s 74(2), see **17.87–17.96**.
2   H(W)A 2014, s 85(2); Welsh Code, para 20.3(d).
3   H(W)A 2014, s 74(3), see **17.97–17.103**.
4   H(W)A 2014, s 84(1) and (3).
5   H(W)A 2014, s 84(2), see **17.102**.
6   H(W)A 2014, s 85(1)(c); Welsh Code, paras 20.17–20.22.

19.82 H(W)A 2014, s 87, provides that if the review decision, or subsequent appeal to the county court, concludes that reasonable steps were not taken, and so the duty under H(W)A 2014, s 73(1)[1] continues to apply, a new 56-day period for the performance of the duty will arise, starting on the day when the review decision is notified to the applicant, or on a date that the county court orders[2].

1   See **17.73–17.117**.
2   H(W)A 2014, s 87; Welsh Code, para 20.33.

(5) Suitability of accommodation offered

19.83 An applicant has the right to request a review of the suitability of any accommodation offered[1] under any of the duties in H(W)A 2014, Pt 2[2].

1   H(W)A 2014, s 85(3); Welsh Code, para 20.3(h).
2   H(W)A 2014, s 66(1): duty to help to prevent an applicant from becoming homeless, see **17.45–17.72.** H(W)A 2014, s 68: interim duty to secure accommodation for homeless applicants in priority need, see **17.118–17.134.** H(W)A 2014, s 73(1): duty to help to secure accommodation for homeless applicants, see **17.73–17.117.** H(W)A 2014, s 75(1): duty to secure accommodation for applicants in priority need when the H(W)A 2014, s 73 duty ends, see **17.146–17.199.** H(W)A 2014, s 82(1): duty to secure suitable accommodation until the applicant is notified of the decision whether the conditions for referral are met, see **17.120–17.123.**

19.84 This category refers to accommodation offered either in order to perform any of the duties, or offered in order to bring any of the duties to an end, whether the applicant has refused or accepted the offer of accommodation[1]. The applicant has the right both to accept the offer and to request a review of its suitability[2]. This must normally be the sensible course of action for the applicant[3]. Unlike applicants to local housing authorities in England, an applicant may request a review of the suitability of any interim accommodation offered under the H(W)A 2014, s 68(1) duty[4].

1   H(W)A 2014, s 67(4) refusal of offer of accommodation by an applicant who is threatened with homelessness, see **17.66–17.72.** H(W)A 2014, s 69(7) refusal of suitable interim accommodation, see **17.129.** H(W)A 2014, s 74(5) refusal of an offer of suitable accommodation, see **17.109–17.117.** H(W)A 2014, s 76(2): applicant accepts an offer of suitable accommodation under HA 1996, Pt 6 or an offer of suitable accommodation under an assured tenancy, including an assured shorthold tenancy, see **17.161–17.164.** H(W)A 2014, s 76(3): refusal of suitable interim accommodation under H(W)A 2014, s 75(1) or of a private rented sector offer or of an offer of accommodation under HA 1996, Pt 6, see **17.172–17.179.**
2   H(W)A 2014, s 85(3).
3   See **19.100–19.101.**
4   See **19.83–19.85.**

19.85 This category does not give the applicant a right to request a review of the suitability of accommodation offered under a *power* to secure accommodation[1].

1   H(W)A 2014, s 85(3) refers only to 'accommodation in, or in connection with, the discharge of any duty under this chapter'.

Notifying rights to request a review

19.86 It might be expected that, whenever a local housing authority takes *any* decision that carries a statutory right to a review, it should be required to notify the applicant not only of the decision, but also of the applicant's right to request a review and the time limit within which he or she should make the request. However, this is not always the case.

19.87 For local housing authorities in England, the following notifications must inform the applicant of his or her right to request a review and of the time limit within which to make the request:

•   decisions as to whether an applicant is eligible for assistance[1];

- decisions as to whether any duty, and if so what duty, is owed to the applicant[2];
- decisions that the HA 1996, s 195(2)[3], prevention duty has come to an end as a result of one of the circumstances specified at HA 1996, s 195(7)(a)–(g)[4] inclusive[5];
- decisions that the HA 1996, s 189B(2)[6], relief duty has come to an end as a result of one of the circumstances specified at HA 1996, s 189B(8)(a)–(f)[7] inclusive[8];
- notification of the consequences of refusal of a a final accommodation offer[9] or a final PArt 6 offer[10] made in order to bring the HA 1996, s 189B(2)[11], relief duty to an end[12];
- notification of an offer of accommodation made under the HA 1996, s 193(2), main housing duty and of the consequences of refusal or acceptance[13];
- notification of a final offer of PArt 6 accommodation made under HA 1996, s 193(7), and of the consequences of refusal or acceptance[14];
- notification of a private rented sector offer under HA 1996, s 193(7AA), and of the consequences of refusal or acceptance[15];
- a notice of the local housing authority's decision that the applicant has deliberately and unreasonably refused to co-operate[16]; and
- decisions that the HA 1996, s 193C(4)[17], accommodation duty has come to an end as a result of the applicant having refused a final accommodation offer[18] or a final Pt 6 offer[19].

[1] HA 1996, s 184(1)(a) and (5), see **9.108–9.110**.
[2] HA 1996, s 184(1)(b) and (5), see **9.108–9.110**.
[3] As amended by HRA 2017, s 4(2), for applications to local housing authorities in England made on or after 3 April 2018, see **15.87–15.137**.
[4] As amended by HRA 2017, s 4(2), for applications to local housing authorities in England made on or after 3 April 2018.
[5] HA 1996, s 195(7)(b), as amended by HRA 2017, s 4(2), for applications to local housing authorities in England made on or after 3 April 2018, see **15.98–15.131**.
[6] As inserted by HRA 2017, s 5(2), for applications to local housing authorities in England made on or after 3 April 2018, see **15.138–15.195**.
[7] As inserted by HRA 2017, s 5(2), for applications to local housing authorities in England made on or after 3 April 2018, see **15.151–15.180**.
[8] HA 1996, s 189B(6)(b), as inserted by HRA 2017, s 5(2), for applications to local housing authorities in England made on or after 3 April 2018, see **15.151–15.180**.
[9] Defined at HA 1996, s 193A(4), as inserted by HRA 2017, s 7(1), for applications to local housing authorities in England made on or after 3 April 2018, see **15.181–15.184**.
[10] Defined at HA 1996, s 193A(5), as inserted by HRA 2017, s 7(1), for applications to local housing authorities in England made on or after 3 April 2018, see **15.185–15.189**; HA 1996, s 193A(1)(b), as inserted by HRA 2017, s 7(1), for applications to local housing authorities in England made on or after 3 April 2018, see **15.181–15.189**.
[11] As inserted by HRA 2017, s 5(2), for applications to local housing authorities in England made on or after 3 April 2018, see **15.138–15.195**.
[12] HA 1996, s 193A(1)(b), as inserted by HRA 2017, s 7(1), for applications to local housing authorities in England made on or after 3 April 2018, see **15.181–15.189**.
[13] HA 1996, s 193(5)(a), see **16.114–16.123**.
[14] HA 1996, s 193(7), see **16.142–16.152**.
[15] HA 1996, s 193(7AA) and (7AB), see **16.153–16.180**.
[16] HA 1996, s 193B(3)(b), as inserted by HRA 2017, s 7(1), for applications to local housing authorities in England made on or after 3 April 2018, see **15.196–15.221**.
[17] As inserted by HRA 2017, s 7(1), for applications to local housing authorities in England made on or after 3 April 2018, see **16.200–16.216**.
[18] Defined at HA 1996, s 193C(7), as inserted by HRA 2017, s 7(1), for applications to local housing authorities in England made on or after 3 April 2018, see **16.205–16.209**.

¹⁹ Defined at HA 1996, s 193C(8), as inserted by HRA 2017, s 7(1), for applications to local housing authorities in England made on or after 3 April 2018, see **16.210–16.213**; HA 1996, s 193C(6), as inserted by HRA 2017, s 7(1), for applications to local housing authorities in England made on or after 3 April 2018, see **16.205–16.215**.

19.88 Even in those cases, there is no requirement that the applicant should also be informed of any advice or other help available to assist him or her in pursuing a review. There is no obligation to inform the applicant about the procedure at this stage[1]. Nor is there any obligation to provide a pro-forma on which the applicant can request a review. Notification can be given either directly to the applicant or, where the applicant has signed a form of authority appointing solicitors or other advisers as his or her agents, to those agents[2].

1   Only when a review has been requested is the local housing authority obliged to notify the applicant of the procedure: SI 2018/ 223, reg 5(3)(c), at Appendix **2**.
2   *Dharmaraj v Hounslow London Borough Council* [2011] EWCA Civ 312, [2011] HLR 18, CA.

19.89 Local housing authorities in Wales are required to notify the applicant of their assessment of his or her case[1] and also of any decision that any of the duties have come to an end[2]. Both of those notifications must be in writing, contain the reasons for the decision, inform the applicant of his or her right to request a review of the decision and of the time within which to request the review[3].

1   H(W)A 2014, s 63(1), see **9.108–9.110**.
2   H(W)A 2014, s 84(1), see **9.169**.
3   H(W)A 2014, s 63(4), see **9.100**; H(W)A 2014, s 84(1), see **9.169**.

Seeking a review and also accepting Accommodation

England

19.90 Where an applicant to a local housing authority in England requests[1]:

- a review of the suitability of accommodation provided for him or her under the HA 1996, s 193(2), main housing duty[2];
- a review of the suitability of a final offer of accommodation made under HA 1996, Pt 6[3];
- a review of the suitability of a private rented sector offer[4];
- a review of the suitability of a final accommodation offer[5]; or
- a review of the suitability of a final Pt 6 offer[6],

he or she has the right to accept the offer while also requesting the review[7].

1   HA 1996, s 202(1)(f), (g) and (h), as amended and inserted by HRA 2017, s 9, for applications to local housing authorities in England made on or after 3 April 2018, see **19.59–19.69**.
2   HA 1996, s 193(2) and (5), see **16.114–16.123**.
3   HA 1996, s 193(7), see **16.142–16.152**.
4   HA 1996, s 193(7AC), see **16.153–16.180**.
5   Defined at HA 1996, ss 193A(4) and 193C(7), as inserted by HRA 2017, s 7(1), for applications to local housing authorities in England made on or after 3 April 2018, see **15.181–15.184** and **16.205–16.209**.
6   Defined at HA 1996, ss 193A(5) and 193C(8), as inserted by HRA 2017, s 7(1), for applications to local housing authorities in England made on or after 3 April 2018, see **15.185–15.189** and **16.209–16.213**.

⁷   HA 1996, s 202(1A) and (1B), as inserted by HRA 2017, s 9, for applications to local housing
    authorities in England made on or after 3 April 2018.

19.91 The way in which the applicant's options might be put in the notification has been neatly summarised as follows:

'[T]he choice which has to be presented to a person to whom an offer is made has to be in substance to this effect: you may accept or refuse a house. In either event you are entitled to seek a review of the decision to make this offer to you. If, though, you refuse to accept this accommodation you will not be able to retract your refusal, so that if the review goes against you, we shall be discharged of any duty towards you. On the other hand, if the review goes in your favour, we shall, in the light of the review decision, have to make you a different offer or reconsider our position.¹'

¹   *R v Tower Hamlets London Borough Council ex p Mbidi* (2000) April *Legal Action*, p 32,
    QBD per Jowitt J.

19.92 If the local housing authority fails to provide this information, it risks a subsequent complaint that the whole procedure has been unfair¹.

¹   See *Akhtar & Naseem v Manchester City Council* (2003) April *Legal Action*, p 28,
    Manchester County Court, but also *Ali-Ahmed v Islington London Borough Council* [2004]
    EWCA Civ 128, (2004) April *Legal Action*, p 35, CA, where the process was not unfair,
    although the offer letter did not contain this information.

19.93 Since the consequences of refusing an offer of suitable accommodation in any of these cases will be that the relevant duty owed by the local housing authority's under HA 1996, Pt 7¹, will end, and the applicant will face the possibility that he or she will be homeless and left without any help or accommodation, acceptance of the accommodation whilst simultaneously requesting a review of its suitability must normally be the prudent approach. For private rented sector offers², or final accommodation offers³, where the applicant is being required to enter into a fixed term assured shorthold tenancy⁴, the terms of the tenancy should contain a break clause, so as to permit the applicant to terminate the tenancy before the end of the fixed term upon notice to the landlord, if the outcome of the review (or any subsequent appeal) is a decision that that the accommodation was unsuitable.

¹   As amended by HRA 2017, for applications for homelessness assistance made to local housing
    authorities in England on or after 3 April 2018.
²   HA 1996, s 193(7AC), see **16.153–16.180**.
³   Defined at HA 1996, ss 193A(4) and 193C(7), as inserted by HRA 2017, s 7(1), for
    applications to local housing authorities in England made on or after 3 April 2018, see
    15.181–15.184 and **16.205–16.209**.
⁴   HA 1996, s 193(7AC)(c), see **16.164**.

19.94 However, it is only in the case of these specific offers of accommodation¹ that the right to request a review whilst also accepting the offer is available². Applicants who are contemplating refusing accommodation arranged by a local housing authority with a view to bringing either a HA 1996, s 189B(2)³, relief duty or a HA 1996, s 195(2)⁴, prevention duty to an end have the opportunity to accept the accommodation and also request a review of its suitability⁵.

¹   HA 1996, ss 193(5), (7) and (7AA)–(7AC), 193A(1) and 193C(5) (as inserted by HRA 2017,
    s 7(1), for applications to local housing authorities in England made on or after 3 April 2018).

2   HA 1996, s 202(1A) and (1B), as inserted by HRA 2017, s 9, for applications to local housing authorities in England made on or after 3 April 2018.
3   As inserted by HRA 2017, s 5(2), for applications to local housing authorities in England made on or after 3 April 2018, see **15.138–15.195**.
4   As amended by HRA 2017, s 4(2), for applications to local housing authorities in England made on or after 3 April 2018, see **15**.
5   At HA 1996, ss 189B(7)(a) and 195(8)(a) (as inserted and amended by HRA 2017, ss 5(2) and 4(2), for applications to local housing authorities in England made on or after 3 April 2018) see **15.105–15.09** and **15.162–15.165**.

19.95 Where an applicant has rejected accommodation offered in performance of the HA 1996, s 193(2) main housing duty[1], as a final offer under HA 1996, Pt 6[2], as a private rented sector offer[3], as a final accommodation offer[4], or as a final PArt 6 offer[5] and has requested a review of its suitability and then subsequently sought to accept the offer, the decision whether to re-offer the accommodation or not is one for the local housing authority. There is no requirement on the local housing authority to keep the accommodation available for the applicant during the review process[6].

1   HA 1996, s 193(2) and (5), see **16.114–16.123**.
2   HA 1996, s 193(7) and (7A), see **16.142–16.152**.
3   HA 1996, s 193(7AA)–(7AC), see **16.153–16.180**.
4   Defined at HA 1996, ss 193A(4) and 193C(7), as inserted by HRA 2017, s 7(1), for applications to local housing authorities in England made on or after 3 April 2018, see **15.181–15.184** and **16.205–16.209**.
5   Defined at HA 1996, ss 193A(5) and 193C(8), as inserted by HRA 2017, s 7(1), for applications to local housing authorities in England made on or after 3 April 2018, see **15.185–15.189** and **16.210–16.213**.
6   *Osseily v Westminster City Council* [2007] EWCA Civ 1108, [2008] HLR 18, CA.

19.96 Where an applicant is occupying interim accommodation, secured under HA 1996, s 188(1)[1], while the local housing authority is performing its HA 1996, s 189B(2)[2], relief duty, and the applicant requests a review of a final accommodation offer[3] or a final Pt 6 offer[4], the HA 1996, s 189B(2)[5] relief duty is deemed not to come to an end until the review decision has been notified to the applicant[6]. So, unless the local housing authority were to notify the applicant during the review process that he or she does not have a priority need[7], interim accommodation must continue[8].

1   See **16.37–16.50**.
2   As inserted by HRA 2017, s 5(2), for applications to local housing authorities in England made on or after 3 April 2018, see **15.138–15.195**.
3   Defined at HA 1996, ss 193A(4), as inserted by HRA 2017, s 7(1), for applications to local housing authorities in England made on or after 3 April 2018, see **15.181–15.184**.
4   Defined at HA 1996, ss 193A(5), as inserted by HRA 2017, s 7(1), for applications to local housing authorities in England made on or after 3 April 2018, see **15.185–15.189**.
5   As inserted by HRA 2017, s 5(2), for applications to local housing authorities in England made on or after 3 April 2018, see **15.135–15.195**.
6   HA 1996, s 188(2A), as inserted by HRA 2017, s 5(4), for applications to local housing authorities in England made on or after 3 April 2018, see **15.184–15.188** and **16.239**.
7   HA 1996, s 188(1ZA)(b), as inserted by HRA 2017, s 5(4), for applications to local housing authorities in England made on or after 3 April 2018, see **16.56–16.59**.
8   HA 1996, s 188(1AB) and (2A), as inserted by HRA 2017, s 5(4), for applications to local housing authorities in England made on or after 3 April 2018, see **15.185–15.188**, **16.60–16.66** and **16.239**.

19.97 What happens if an applicant accepts accommodation offered as a final offer[1] without requesting any review, and then subsequently decides to request a review of its suitability? The present tense used in s 202(1A) and (1B)[2] suggests that the express statutory right to request a review, whilst also accepting the accommodation, remains open for the period of the statutory time limit in which to request a review[3]. Where the applicant has accepted the offer of accommodation and also requested a review of its suitability, the reviewing officer should consider all the facts and circumstances as at the date of the review decision[4].

[1] A final offer of Pt 6 accommodation or a private rented sector made in order to bring the HA 1996, s 193(2), main housing duty to an end: HA 1996, s 193(7) and (7AA). Or a final accommodation offer or final Part offer made in order to bring the HA 1996, s 189B(2), relief or HA 1996, s 193C(4), accommodation duties to an end: HA 1996, ss 193A(1) and 193C(5) (as inserted by HRA 2017, ss 5(2) and 7(1), for applications to local housing authorities in England made on or after 3 April 2018).

[2] HA 1996, s 202(1A) and (1B), as inserted by HRA 2017, s 9, for applications to local housing authorities in England made on or after 3 April 2018, see **19.90–19.99**.

[3] 21 days beginning with the date on which the applicant is notified of the local housing authority's decision: HA 1996, s 202(3); and see **19.109–19.115**.

[4] *Omar v Westminster City Council* [2008] EWCA Civ 421, [2008] HLR 36, CA at [25] per Waller LJ, see **16.111**.

19.98 If the review (or any subsequent appeal) against the decision that accommodation offered, and accepted, was suitable is successful, so that the accommodation is considered to be unsuitable, then the relevant duty under HA 1996, Pt 7[1], will not have come to an end. The accommodation might be considered to be suitable for the applicant to continue to occupy in the short-term or medium-term, since expected duration of occupation is relevant to the issue of suitability[2]. Or it might be so unsuitable that it should not be occupied by the applicant even in the short-term in which case the local housing authority will have to secure alternative accommodation which is suitable.

[1] As amended by HRA 2017, for applications to local housing authorities in England made on or after 3 April 2018.

[2] *Birmingham City Council v Ali* [2009] UKHL 36, [2009] 1 WLR 1506, HL at [47] per Baroness Hale; see **18.82–18.85**.

19.99 In contrast, the right to request a review of the suitability of accommodation being occupied by an applicant under the HA 1996, s 193(2), main housing duty remains available to the applicant throughout the period when he or she is occupying the accommodation[1].

[1] *R (Zaher) v City of Westminster Council* [2003] EWHC 101 (Admin), [2003] All ER (D) 253 (Jan), Admin Ct.

Wales

19.100 Applicants to local housing authorities in Wales have the right to accept an offer while also requesting a review of the suitability of accommodation offered either in performance of any of the duties under H(W)A 2014, Pt 2, or in order to bring any of those duties to an end[1].

[1] H(W)A 2014, s 85(3).

19.101 Applicants will have been notified of their right to request a review, and of the time within which to request it, in any decision that the duty has come to an end[1]. If the duty has come to an end because the applicant has refused:

- an offer of suitable accommodation made under H(W)A 2014, s 66(1)[2];
- an offer of suitable interim accommodation made under H(W)A 2014, s 68(1)[3];
- an offer of suitable accommodation made under H(W)A 2014, s 73(1)[4]; or
- an offer of suitable accommodation made under H(W)A 2014, s 75(1)[5];

the applicant will have been notified of the possible consequences of refusal or acceptance of the offer, before he or she receives notification of the decision that the duty has been discharged[6]. It will normally be the safest course of action to accept the offer while simultaneously requesting a review of the suitability of the accommodation offered[7].

1   H(W)A 2014, s 84(1)(c) and (d), see **17.33**.
2   H(W)A 2014, s 67(4), see **17.66–17.72**.
3   H(W)A 2014, s 69(7), see **17.129**.
4   H(W)A 2014, s 74(5), see **17.109–17.117**.
5   H(W)A 2014, s 76(3), see **17.165–17.169**.
6   H(W)A 2014, s 67(4); H(W)A 2014, s 69(7) (which only requires notification of the possible consequences of refusal); H(W)A 2014, s 74(5); and H(W)A 2014, s 76(3).
7   See **19.100–19.101**.

Who may seek a review?

19.102 The statutory review rights are only available to 'an applicant'[1]. No member of the applicant's household has that statutory right. Nor can the review process be activated by others who may have an interest in challenging the local housing authority's decision, eg a different local housing authority, a private registered provider of social housing in England or a registered social landlord in Wales, or another homeless person.

1   HA 1996, s 202(1), as amended by HRA 2017, s 9 for applications for homelessness assistance to local housing authorities in England made on or after 3 April 2018; H(W)A 2014, s 85(1).

19.103 An applicant's request for review does not need to be made personally. It may be made by someone else as the applicant's formal or informal agent (by a solicitor or anyone else asked to act on the applicant's behalf)[1].

1   As happened in *R (Sederati) v Enfield London Borough Council* [2002] EWHC 2423 (Admin), (2003) January *Legal Action*, p 23, Admin Ct, where the manager of the applicant's temporary accommodation made the request on his behalf. If the person making the request is authorised by the applicant to act as his or her agent (usually by signing a form of authority to that effect), notification of the review decision can be given to that agent (*Dharmaraj v Hounslow London Borough Council* [2011] EWCA Civ 312, [2011] HLR 18, CA). See Welsh Code, para 20.4.

How to seek a review

19.104 The obligation on a local housing authority to carry out a review is triggered 'on a request being duly made to them'[1].

[1]   HA 1996, s 202(4); H(W)A 2014, s 85(6).

19.105 Beyond those words, neither HA 1996, Pt 7[1], nor H(W)A 2014, Pt 2, say anything about the form or content of the request. In particular:

- the request need not be in writing;
- there is no prescribed form;
- the applicant need not use a form provided by the local housing authority (even if a form is available)[2];
- no grounds or reasons for requesting the review need be given[3]; and
- no particular office or officer is the specified recipient of the request.

[1]   As amended by HRA 2017 for applications for homelessness assistance to local housing authorities in England made on or after 3 April 2018.
[2]   See *Complaint against Brighton and Hove City Council*, 13 015 710, (2014) November *Legal Action*, p 41.
[3]   English Code, para 19.13.

19.106 However, it must be tolerably clear that the applicant is asking for a review of the decision made and not, for example, requesting a disciplinary investigation into the conduct of the officer(s) who took the decision[1].

[1]   See for example: *R (Taylor) v Commissioner for Local Administration* [2003] EWCA Civ 1088, (2003) September *Legal Action*, p 28, CA. In *Nzamy v Brent London Borough Council*, [2011] EWCA Civ 283, [2011] HLR 20, CA, a letter from an unrepresented applicant which set out reasons why an offer of main housing duty accommodation was unsuitable and concluded 'I ask you please to offer us a permanent accommodation for us, but until that time we can wait in our current flat', was a request that the reviewing officer should look both at the issue of whether the accommodation offered was suitable and also at the question of whether the local housing authority had validly discharged its duty: see Black LJ at [19].

19.107 The use of the words 'made to them'[1] suggests that the request must not only have been made to, but also received by, the local housing authority[2]. Simply posting a letter containing a written request for a review will probably not suffice (although a local housing authority might agree to extend the time limit for requesting a review if it was satisfied that the request had been posted in good time but was not subsequently received in time or at all)[3].

[1]   HA 1996, s 202(4); H(W)A 2014, s 85(6).
[2]   See *R (Lester) v London Rent Assessment Committee* [2003] EWCA Civ 319, [2003] 33 HLR 53, [2003] 1 WLR 1449, CA – a rent is not 'referred' to the RAC until a notice of referral is received by it.
[3]   HA 1996, s 202(3); H(W)A 2014, s 85(5). See **19.109–19.115**.

19.108 The local housing authority to which the request is to be made is normally the local housing authority that made the decision sought to be reviewed[1]. Where review is sought of a decision that the conditions for referral to another local housing authority are met[2], the request is to be made to the 'notifying local housing authority' which made the referral[3].

[1]   SI 2018/223, reg 5(1) at Appendix 2; Homelessness (Review Procedure) (Wales) Regulations 2015, SI 2015/1266 (W 86), reg 2(1)(a) at the CD Rom with this book.

² HA 1996, s 202(1)(d), see **19.55–19.57** or H(W)A 2014, ss 80(5) and 85(1)(c); see **19.77–19.80**.
³ SI 2018/223, reg 5(2); SI 2015/1266, regs 1(3)(b) and 2(1).

Time in which to request a review

19.109 The applicant has 21 days, 'beginning with the day on which he [or she] is notified of the authority's decision', in which to make the request to the local housing authority for a review¹. Because it is relatively short, the time limit needs careful consideration.

¹ HA 1996, s 202(3) and (4); H(W)A 2014, s 85(5) and (6).

19.110 The time limit begins with the day on which the original decision is 'notified'¹. So, for example, if the local housing authority's decision is received by the applicant or his or her agents on 2 April, the review request must be made to the local housing authority by midnight on 22 April². Provided that it is physically delivered to the local housing authority's offices before midnight, it will be in time, even if 22 April is not a working day, or if the office has already closed³.

¹ Which may be different from the day on which the decision was actually taken, and the day on which it was put in writing. See *Robinson v Hammersmith & Fulham London Borough Council* [2006] EWCA Civ 1122, [2007] HLR 7, CA, and **8.69** and **9.93–9.94**.
² The phrase 'beginning with' includes the day of notification as the first day of the period: *Trow v Ind Coope (West Midlands) Ltd* [1967] 2 QB 899, CA, and *Zoan v Rouamba* [2000] 1 WLR 1509, CA. See also *RJB Mining (UK) Ltd v National Union of Mineworkers (1995)* [1995] IRLR 556, CA, where the Court of Appeal held time limits couched in terms of days expire at midnight, not part of the way through a day. However, the 21-day time limit for the issue of an appeal under HA 1996, s 204 or H(W)A 2014, s 89, commences on the day after notification, see **19.244–19.245**.
³ *Van Aken v Camden London Borough Council* [2002] EWCA Civ 1724, (2003) 35 HLR 33, CA.

19.111 The local housing authority may decide that a particular request for review was not made in time and that it therefore has no duty to conduct a review. If it will not agree to extend the time, the applicant can apply for judicial review of the refusal to carry out the review. The issue of whether a request was made and, if so, whether it was made in time, will have to be resolved by the Administrative Court as a matter of fact¹.

¹ *R (Sederati) v Enfield London Borough Council* [2002] EWHC 2423 (Admin), (2003) January *Legal Action*, p 23, Admin Ct; and *R (Casey) v Restormel Borough Council* [2007] EWHC 2554 (Admin), (2008) January *Legal Action*, p 38, Admin Ct.

19.112 The local housing authority has a discretion to agree a longer period in which an applicant can request a review¹. When a local housing authority receives a request for a review made out of time, it should consider the explanation offered for the applicant's delay in making the request and the prospects of success on the review. The precise weight to be given to the balance between these two factors, and all other relevant considerations, is a matter for the local housing authority². Nothing in HA 1996, Pt 7³, in H(W)A 2014, Pt 2, or in the regulations made under them, requires the decision on extending time to be taken by the person who would be conducting the review. As a matter of fairness and good practice, however, it probably should *not* be taken by the original decision-maker[4].

¹ HA 1996, s 202(3) and English Code, para 19.4; H(W)A 2014, s 85(5); Welsh Code, para 20.7.
² *R (C) v Lewisham London Borough Council* [2003] EWCA Civ 927, [2004] HLR 4, CA; and *R (Slaiman) v Richmond upon Thames London Borough Council* [2006] EWHC 329 (Admin), [2006] HLR 20, Admin Ct.
³ As amended by HRA 2017 for applications for homelessness assistance to local housing authorities in England made on or after 3 April 2018.
⁴ It should be noted, however, that the Administrative Court, in *R (Abdi) v Lambeth London Borough Council* [2007] EWHC 1565 (Admin), [2008] HLR 5, Admin Ct, held that there was nothing in HA 1996, Pt 7, the relevant regulations, or the general law on issues of bias, that prevented an original decision-maker from deciding a request for accommodation pending review.

19.113 Most (and for applicants to local housing authorities in Wales, all) notifications of decisions carrying rights of review, will spell out the time limit[1]. A failure on the part of the local housing authority to comply with the obligation to notify the time limit would be a powerful factor in support of a request to extend time. The exact wording of HA 1996, s 184(5) (or of H(W)A 2014, s 63(2) and 84(1)) need not be duplicated but the notification must contain the substance of the information required to be notified by HA 1996, Pt 7[2] or H(W)A 2014, Pt 2[3]. If the time limit was notified and emphasised in the notification letter, any request to extend time will be more difficult to sustain.

¹ HA 1996, ss 184(5), 189B(6)(b) (as inserted by HRA 2017, s 5(2) for applications for homelessness assistance to local housing authorities in England made on or after 3 April 2018), 193B(3)(b) (as inserted by HRA 2017, s 7(1) for applications for homelessness assistance to local housing authorities in England made on or after 3 April 2018), 195(7)(b) (as amended by HRA 2017, s 4(2) for applications for homelessness assistance to local housing authorities in England made on or after 3 April 2018), 199A(3) (as inserted by HRA 2017, s 5(9) for applications for homelessness assistance to local housing authorities in England made on or after 3 April 2018), and 200(2); H(W)A 2014, ss 63(4)(a) and 84(1)(d).
² As amended by HRA 2017 for applications for homelessness assistance to local housing authorities in England made on or after 3 April 2018.
³ *Dharmaraj v Hounslow London Borough Council* [2011] EWCA Civ 312, [2011] HLR 18, CA.

19.114 If the local housing authority accedes to the request to extend time, it must notify the applicant in writing accordingly[1]. This curious provision (not mirrored by any obligation to give written notice of a refusal to extend time) is presumably intended to avoid applicants suggesting that they were verbally given an indication that a late request would be allowed.

¹ HA 1996, s 202(3); H(W)A 2014, s 85(5).

19.115 If the local housing authority refuses to extend the time limit for a review, where the request has been made late, the only challenge to that decision would be by way of judicial review[1]. A refusal to extend time is not itself a decision that can be subject to statutory review. If the decision to refuse to extend time was irrational, or for some other reason unlawful, it will be quashed and the local housing authority will be required to take the decision again on whether to extend time. In an exceptional case, the Administrative Court may even grant a mandatory order requiring the local housing authority to extend the time limit[2].

[1] As happened in *R (Casey) v Restormel Borough Council* [2007] EWHC 2554 (Admin), (2008) January *Legal Action*, p 38, Admin Ct. See also *R (Dragic) v Wandsworth London Borough Council* [2012] EWHC 1241 (Admin), (2012) July *Legal Action*, p 42, Admin Ct, where the request for a review was two weeks' late and the judge held that 'two weeks in other contexts may not be regarded as very long, but in the context of a tight time limit of three weeks, two weeks has a different complexion'. She refused the claimant permission to apply for judicial review.

[2] *R v Newham London Borough Council ex p P* (2001) January *Legal Action*, p 28, QBD, reported as *R (Patrick) v Newham London Borough Council* (2001) 4 CCLR 48, QBD.

Procedure on receipt of a request for a review

PROCEDURE LOCALLY

19.116 Only the barest outline of the procedure to be followed on review is set out in HA 1996, Pt 7[1] or in H(W)A 2014, Pt 2[2]. Little more detail is given in the current versions of the review procedure regulations for local housing authorities in England[3] and for local housing authorities in Wales[4]. Accordingly, the day-to-day procedural operation of the review process is largely left to each local housing authority to determine with the benefit of the guidance given in HA 1996, Pt 7[5], or H(W)A 2014, Pt 2, the relevant set of regulations and in the respective Codes[6].

[1] As amended by HRA 2017 for applications for homelessness assistance to local housing authorities in England made on or after 3 April 2018.

[2] HA 1996, ss 202–203 (as amended by HRA 2017, s 9 for applications for homelessness assistance to local housing authorities in England made on or after 3 April 2018); H(W)A 2014, ss 85–86.

[3] Homelessness (Review Procedure etc) Regulations 2018, SI 1999/71, see Appendix 2.

[4] Homelessness (Review Procedure) (Wales) Regulations 2015, SI 2015/1266 (W 86), see the CD Rom with this book.

[5] As amended by HRA 2017 for applications for homelessness assistance to local housing authorities in England made on or after 3 April 2018.

[6] English Code, paras 19.8–19.28; Welsh Code, paras 20.8–20.28.

19.117 The expectation is that each local housing authority will formulate and apply a written statement of its own procedure. On receipt of the review request the local housing authority must, if it has not earlier done so, notify the applicant of the 'procedure to be followed in connection with the review'[1]. Failure to comply with that obligation might undermine the fairness of the whole review process.

[1] SI 2018/223, reg 5(3); SI 2015/1268 (W 86), reg 2(2)(b). See also English Code, para 19.18; Welsh Code, para 20.12.

19.118 The Court of Appeal has considered the failure of two local housing authorities to comply with the requirement to notify the review procedure[1]. In both cases, the original decision letter had correctly notified the applicants that they had the right to request a review and had also notified them of their right to make representations and to provide new information, and that someone else could help them put their cases. It was also relevant that, in both cases, the applicants had solicitors representing them throughout the review process and that the solicitors were aware of their right to make representations on the review. Accordingly, the underlying purpose of the regulations had been achieved in that the applicants knew about their right to make representations. The judge giving the leading judgment in one of those cases said:

> 'the self-evident purpose of imposing the duty to notify is not to inform an applicant who already had professional legal advisers about the right to make representations, but to protect those who did not have professional advisers, so that they can make representations themselves, or get someone else to do it for them'[2].

As a result, the local housing authorities had not made any errors of law in their conduct of the review procedures.

1 *Maswaku v Westminster City Council* [2012] EWCA Civ 669, [2012] HLR 37, CA; and *El Goure v Kensington & Chelsea Royal London Borough Council* [2012] EWCA Civ 670, [2012] HLR 36, CA.
2 *El Goure v Kensington & Chelsea Royal London Borough Council* [2012] EWCA Civ 670, [2012] HLR 36, CA per Mummery LJ at [38].

19.119 If the review is being sought of a referee's decision[1], the person appointed to conduct the review must notify the applicant of the procedure that he or she is going to follow[2].

1 HA 1996, s 202(1)(d); H(W)A 2014, ss 80(5)(b) and 85(1)(c). See **19.55–19.57** (England) and **19.77–19.80** (Wales).
2 SI 2018/223, reg 5(4)(b); English Code, para 19.19; SI 2015/1266 (W 86), reg 2(3)(b); Welsh Code, para 20.12(ii).

Notification of time limits for certain review requests

19.120 For most review requests, there is no time limit specified for the receipt of representations. The English Code advises that representations should be made within a reasonable period to allow sufficient time for the local housing authority to complete the review within the prescribed time-frame[1].

1 English Code, para 19.17. For the prescribed time-frame, see **19.188–19.195**.

19.121 However, for local housing authorities in England, some review requests have to be completed within a short prescribed time-frame of three weeks or such longer period as may be agreed in writing[1]. As a result, the Regulations provide that the applicant must be notified that any written representations made in respect of these review requests must be made within two weeks beginning with the date on which the applicant requested the review, or such longer period as the applicant and the reviewer might agree in writing[2].

1 SI 2018/223, reg 9(1)(a), see **19.188–19.189**.
2 SI 2018/223, reg 5(3)(b), English Code, para 19.15.

19.122 The review requests that must be completed within three weeks (or longer period as agreed in writing) are:

- a review of a decision as to the steps that the local housing authority is to take under the HA 1996, s 189B(2)[1], relief duty[2];
- a review of a decision to give notice to the applicant that he or she has deliberately and unreasonably refused to co-operate[3];

- a review of a decision as to the steps that the local housing authority is to take under the HA 1996, s 195(2)[4], prevention duty[5]; and

- a review of a decision to give notice to the applicant that the HA 1996, s 195(2)[6], prevention duty has come to an end by reason of one of the events specified at HA 1996, s 195(8)[7].

[1] As inserted by HRA 2017, s 5(2), for applications for homelessness assistance to local housing authorities in England made on or after 3 April 2018.

[2] HA 1996, s 202(1)(ba)(i), as inserted by HRA 2017, s 9, for applications for homelessness assistance to local housing authorities in England made on or after 3 April 2018, **19.18–19.23.**

[3] HA 1996, s 202(1)(bb), as inserted by HRA 2017, s 9, for applications for homelessness assistance to local housing authorities in England made on or after 3 April 2018, see **19.30–19.35.**

[4] As amended by HRA 2017, s 4(2), for applications for homelessness assistance to local housing authorities in England made on or after 3 April 2018.

[5] HA 1996, s 202(1)(bc)(i), as inserted by HRA 2017, s 9, for applications for homelessness assistance to local housing authorities in England made on or after 3 April 2018, see **19.36–19.41.**

[6] As amended by HRA 2017, s 5(2), for applications for homelessness assistance to local housing authorities in England made on or after 3 April 2018.

[7] HA 1996, s 202(1)(bc)(ii), as inserted by HRA 2017, s 9, for applications for homelessness assistance to local housing authorities in England made on or after 3 April 2018, see **19.42–19.48.**

INVITING WRITTEN REPRESENTATIONS

19.123 As already noted[1], there is no requirement that the applicant should set out any grounds or reasons in the request for review. Accordingly, not least so that any particular issues can be drawn out, the regulations require that once the request for a review has been received, the local housing authority which received it must notify the applicant that he or she, or a representative, may make written representations to the local housing authority in connection with the review[2]. If the applicant has already been notified of the right to make representations, and particularly if he or she is represented by solicitors, there will be no error of law if the requirement is not strictly complied with after the request for the review has been received[3].

[1] See **19.105.**

[2] SI 2018/223, reg 5(3)(a)5(4)(a); SI 2015/1266 (W 86), regs 2(2)(a) and 2(3)(a). A notification which read 'you will be given an opportunity to make oral and/or written representations to the Panel' was described as wording which the local housing authority would be 'well advised' to reconsider, but was sufficient for the applicant to know that a review was under way and of his right to make representations (*Jama v Islington London Borough Council* [2006] EWCA Civ 45, (2006) June *Legal Action*, p 36, CA).

[3] *Maswaku v Westminster City Council* [2012] EWCA Civ 669, [2012] HLR 37, CA; and *El Goure v Kensington & Chelsea Royal London Borough Council* [2012] EWCA Civ 670, [2012] HLR 36, CA. See **19.118.**

19.124 For applicants to local housing authorities in England, there is no right in HA 1996, Pt 7[1], or in the Regulations[2] to make oral representations, except in the special circumstances where there is a deficiency or irregularity[3]. Local housing authorities in Wales must notify the applicant that he or she has the right to make representations orally, or in writing, or both orally and in writing[4].

[1] As amended by HRA 2017 for applications for homelessness assistance made to local housing authorities in England on or after 3 April 2018.

²   SI 2018/223.
³   SI 2018/223, regs 5(3)(a) and 7(2), see **19.150–19.165**.
⁴   Homelessness (Review Procedure) (Wales) Regulations 2015, SI 2015/1266 (W 86), regs 2(2)(a) and 2(3)(a); Welsh Code, paras 20.11–20.12.

19.125 The invitation to submit representations must be issued in every case, either in the original decision or after the applicant has requested a review. The invitation must be sent either to the applicant personally or to agents nominated by the applicant¹.

¹   SI 2018/223, reg 5(3)(a), English Code, para 19.14; Homelessness (Review Procedure) (Wales) Regulations 2015, SI 2015/1266 (W 86), reg 2(2)(a).

19.126 If the review is being sought of a referee's decision¹, the person appointed to conduct the review will notify the applicant of the right to make written representations direct to him or her and not to the local housing authority².

¹   HA 1996, s 202(1)(d); H(W)A 2014, ss 80(5)(b) and 85(1)(c). See **19.55–19.57** (England) and **19.77–19.80** (Wales).
²   SI 2018/223, reg 6(5); SI 2015/1266 (W 86), reg 2(3)(a).

19.127 There is no obligation on the applicant to respond to the invitation to make representations. The review will take place whether or not a response is received. For most review requests, there is no deadline prescribed for the receipt of representations, and therefore they can be submitted at any stage before the decision on review is actually made¹. For local housing authorities in England, dealing with requests for review decisions falling under HA 1996, s 202(1)(ba)(i)², (bb)³, (bc)(i)⁴, or (bc)(ii)⁵, the representations must be made within two weeks beginning with the day on which the applicant requested the review, or such longer period as the applicant and the reviewer may agree in writing⁶.

¹   See English Code, para 19.17 and Welsh Code, para 20.16.
²   Request for review of decision as to what steps the local housing authority is to take under the HA 1996, s 189B(2) (as inserted by HRA 2017, s 5(2), for applications for homelessness assistance to local housing authorities in England made on or after 3 April 2018) relief duty, see **19.18–19.23**.
³   Request for review of decision of to give notice that an applicant has deliberately and unreasonably refused to co-operate under HA 1996, s 193B(2) (as inserted by HRA 2017, s 7(1), for applications for homelessness assistance to local housing authorities in England made on or after 3 April 2018), see **19.24–19.29**.
⁴   Request for review of decision as to what steps the local housing authority is to take under the HA 1996, s 195(2) (as amended by HRA 2017, s 4(2), for applications for homelessness assistance to local housing authorities in England made on or after 3 April 2018) prevention duty, see **19.36–19.41**.
⁵   Request for review of decision that the HA 1996, s 195(2) (as amended by HRA 2017, s 4(2), for applications for homelessness assistance to local housing authorities in England made on or after 3 April 2018) prevention duty has come to an end, see **19.42–19.48**.
⁶   SI 2018/223, reg 5(3)(b) and English Code, para 19.15.

19.128 Self-evidently, if the applicant has specific criticisms of the original decision, those criticisms should be set out at the earliest possible stage so as to ensure that they are properly considered. The review process is the applicant's last opportunity to have the facts relevant to his or her application re-considered. The applicant, or his or her advisers, should therefore ensure that any fact that he or she believes might be relevant, and ought to be considered by the reviewing officer, is specifically brought to the reviewing officer's attention. It can often be helpful for the applicant, or his or her adviser, to ensure that the whole of the applicant's circumstances and representations are put together in one, full, letter, even if some or all of those representations have previously been put to the local housing authority in a more piecemeal fashion.

19.129 However, this does not mean that the reviewing officer is excused from considering points the applicant has not made. For example, even if the review request is primarily disputing whether an applicant did or did not personally do something that caused him or her to become homeless intentionally, and the reviewing officer is satisfied that the applicant did do the act in question, he or she must then go on, whether or not this point has been raised, to look at whether or not that act was 'deliberate'. That is true even if the applicant is professionally represented by experienced solicitors and has made detailed written representations which do not raise that point[1].

[1] *O'Connor v Kensington and Chelsea Royal London Borough Council* [2004] EWCA Civ 394, [2004] HLR 37, CA. A later Court of Appeal decision held that it was only those issues that fell within 'the circumstances of obviousness' that should be considered by the reviewing officer if they had not been raised by the applicant or his or her representatives (*Aw-Aden v Birmingham City Council* [2005] EWCA Civ 1834, (2005) July *Legal Action*, p 29, CA, at [12b] per Kay LJ). For another example, see *Black v Wandsworth London Borough Council* (2008) February *Legal Action*, p 41, Lambeth County Court, where the reviewing officer was obliged to consider the questions of causation and intervening settled accommodation, even though the applicant had not raised the issues, because those issues arose from the established facts before the reviewing officer.

19.130 A failure to inform the applicant of the right to make representations, either in the original decision or subsequently, would make the review process unfair, particularly if the applicant would have responded with representations[1]. The resultant review decision would be likely to be quashed on an appeal to the county court.

[1] But see *Maswaku v Westminster City Council* [2012] EWCA Civ 669, [2012] HLR 37, CA; and *El Goure v Kensington & Chelsea Royal London Borough Council* [2012] EWCA Civ 670, [2012] HLR 36, CA where the applicants had been notified of their right to make representations in the original decision and were represented by solicitors during the review process, even though they had not been notified of the procedure to be followed in connection with the review. See **19.118**.

The identity of the reviewing officer

19.131 The review decision must be made by the local housing authority which made the original decision or, in the case of a review of a joint decision that the conditions for referral to another local housing authority are met[1], by the two or more local housing authorities which made that decision[2].

[1] HA 1996, s 202(1)(d), see **19.55–19.57**; H(W)A 2014, ss 80(5)(b) and 85(1)(c); see **19.77–19.80**.
[2] HA 1996, s 202(4); H(W)A 2014, 85(6).

19.132 Neither HA 1996, Pt 7[1], H(W)A 2014, Pt 2, nor the relevant regulations, prescribe that a particular officer or committee of the local housing authority (or authorities) should undertake the review. It is therefore for the local housing authority (or authorities) to decide whether:

- to delegate the task to an officer; or
- to devolve it to a committee or subcommittee of the council[2]; or
- to contract the function out[3].

[1] As amended by HRA 2017 for applications for homelessness assistance to local housing authorities in England made on or after 3 April 2018.
[2] But not to an individual councillor.
[3] *De-Winter Heald v Brent London Borough Council* [2009] EWCA Civ 930, [2010] HLR 8, CA. See **21.35–21.38**.

19.133 For local housing authorities in England, if the original decision (which is the subject of the request for a review) was made by an officer of the local housing authority, and the local housing authority has decided that the review will also be carried out by an officer, then the local housing authority is required to ensure that the person conducting the review was not involved in the original decision and is senior to the original decision-maker[1]. Reviews of decisions made by local housing authorities in Wales can be made by an officer of the same local housing authority provided that he or she was not involved in the original decision. There is no requirement under H(W)A 2014, Pt 2, that the reviewing officer should be senior to the original decision-maker[2].

[1] HA 1996, s 203(2)(a); SI 2018/223, reg 8(2); and English Code, para 19.9. See *Butt v Hounslow London Borough Council* [2011] EWCA Civ 1327, (2012) January *Legal Action*, p 22, CA, where the judge heard oral evidence as to which officer had taken the review decision.
[2] Homelessness (Review Procedure) (Wales) Regulations 2015, SI 2015/1266 (W 86), reg 3; Welsh Code, para 20.9.

19.134 The original decision-maker is not excluded from assisting the reviewing officer or reviewing committee by, for example, writing and receiving letters, making further inquiries, or even attending a further interview or review hearing, but the review decision must be made by the reviewing officer or committee[1].

[1] *Butler v Fareham Borough Council* (2001) May *Legal Action*, p 24, CA.

19.135 In some local housing authorities, all reviews are conducted by a single senior officer. This can cause difficulties. For example, where an earlier review decision has been quashed on appeal, the same officer would be taking the new review decision. Likewise, the review might be a second one in the history of a single application where the first review decision was withdrawn. An applicant may be aggrieved if the reviewing officer on the second review is the same officer who considered his or her case at an earlier stage and reached an adverse decision on a different issue. The courts have considered how fairness might be achieved in such circumstances. In *Feld v Barnet London Borough Council*[1] and *Poor v Westminster City Council*[2] it was decided that neither the regulations nor the need to avoid bias required that any second review be conducted by a different reviewing officer. Applying the test of a 'fair-minded and intelligent observer', such an observer would conclude that reviewing officers were competent, conscientious, able to engage with issues on a reasonable and intelligent basis, and able to change their position on particular issues[3].

1   *Feld v Barnet London Borough Council* [2004] EWCA Civ 1307, [2005] HLR 9, CA.
2   *Poor v Westminster City Council* [2004] EWCA 1307, [2005] HLR 9, CA.
3   *Feld v Barnet London Borough Council, Poor v Westminster City Council* [2004] EWC Civ 1307, [2005] HLR 9, CA at [44]–[46] per Ward LJ. The test of a 'fair-minded and intelligent observer' is derived from *Porter v Magill* [2001] UKHL 67, [2002] 2 AC 257, [2002] HLR 16, HL.

19.136 If the decision subject to review was that the conditions were met for the applicant's case to be referred to another local housing authority[1], that decision will have been made either by agreement between two local housing authorities or by a referee[2]. If the decision was one made by agreement between two local housing authorities, then the review must be made by them jointly[3]. Presumably this will mean an arrangement for a joint committee or a joint panel of officers.

1   HA 1996, s 202(1)(d); H(W)A 2014, ss 80(5) and 85(1)(c).
2   English Code, para 19.11; Welsh Code, para 20.10.
3   SI 2018/223, reg 4(a); SI 2015/1266, reg 4(1).

19.137 If a referee made the original decision[1], then the reviewing officer should be a person jointly appointed by the local housing authorities within 5 working days from the day on which the review request was received by the notifying local housing authority[2]. This appointee could be anyone to whom both local housing authorities are prepared to entrust the review process[3]. If an appointment is not agreed within that time frame, the notifying local housing authority (which has received the review request) has a further 5 working days to ask the chair of the Local Government Association (LGA) or Welsh Local Government Association (WLGA) to appoint another referee[4]. The chair must then appoint a referee within a further 5 working days for local housing authorities in England, or 7 working days for local housing authorities in Wales from among the membership of a panel appointed by the LGA or WLGA[5]. That person then undertakes the review. Although this may appear to be a very tight time frame[6], the membership of the panel comprises only a handful of referees, one of whom is already eliminated because he or she took the original decision[7]. Whether the reviewing officer is appointed by the local housing authorities or by the LGA or WLGA chairs, in this chapter we will refer to that person as the 'appointed' reviewing officer[8].

1   See also **14.186–14.190** and **19.55–19.57** (England) and **19.77–19.80** (Wales).
2   SI 2018/223, reg 6(1); SI 2015/1266, reg 4(1) and (2).
3   English Code, paras 19.12 and 19.19; Welsh Code, paras 18.27–18.30.
4   SI 2018/223, reg 6(3); SI 2015/1266, reg 4(3).
5   SI 2018/223, reg 6(4); SI 2015/1266 (W 86), reg 4(2) and (3).
6   The regulations even define 'working day': SI 2018/223, reg 6(7); SI 2015/1266, reg 1(3).
7   SI 2018/223, reg 6(6); SI 2015/1266, reg 4(6).
8   SI 2018/223, reg 6(4) and SI 2015/1266, reg 4(4), each refer to the reviewing officer appointed in these circumstances as 'the appointed person'.

Conduct of the review

THE PAPER REVIEW

19.138 The reviewing officer's first task will be to gather together the relevant documents. These will consist of:

(1)   the original decision;
(2)   the request for review (if in writing);
(3)   the local housing authority's file relating to the application;
(4)   any written representations the applicant or his or her representative has made;
(5)   the relevant Code of Guidance; and
(6)   the local homelessness strategy.

19.139 An 'appointed' reviewing officer[1] will, within five working days of his or her appointment, receive files from each of the local housing authorities involved containing the original decision and the 'information and evidence on which that decision was based'[2]. Presumably, if the 'appointed' reviewing officer is reviewing a referee's decision, she or he will ask for the documents that the referee had.

[1]   See **19.131–19.138**.
[2]   2018/223, reg 6(4); Homelessness (Review Procedure) (Wales) Regulations 2015, SI 2015/1266 (W 86), reg 4(4).

19.140 The reviewing officer is required by HA 1996, Pt 7[1] or H(W)A 2014[5], Pt 2, and by the relevant regulations to consider in every case:

(a)   any representations made[2];
(b)   the relevant Code of Guidance[3]; and
(c)   the local homelessness strategy[4].

[1]   As amended by HRA 2017 for applications for homelessness assistance to local housing authorities in England made on or after 3 April 2018.
[2]   SI 2018/223, reg 7(1); SI 2015/1266, reg 5(1).
[3]   HA 1996, s 182(1); H(W)A 2014, s 98(1).
[4]   Homelessness Act 2002, s 1(5); H(W)A 2014, s 50(4), see **7.89–7.90**.

19.141 Additionally, an 'appointed' reviewing officer must distribute any representations received from the applicant to the two or more local housing authorities involved[1], and must then consider any representations they make[2].

[1]   SI 2018/223, reg 6(5); SI 2015/1266 (W 86), reg 4(5).
[2]   SI 2018/223, reg 7(1)(a); SI 2015/1266, reg 5(1)(a).

ORAL HEARING

19.142 The reviewing officer must obviously adopt and apply a fair procedure at the review stage. For local housing authorities in England, there is no general right for the applicant to have an oral hearing, or even to have a meeting or interview with the reviewing officer. It will normally be for the reviewing officer to determine whether the facts or circumstances of the particular case warrant an oral hearing[1]. Local housing authorities in Wales must offer the applicant the opportunity to make oral representations instead of, or in addition to, written representations if he or she so wishes[2].

1   SI 2018/223, reg 7(1)(a).
2   Homelessness (Review Procedure) (Wales) Regulations 2015, SI 2015/1266 (W 86), regs 2(2)(a) and (3)(a); Welsh Code, paras 20.11–20.12.

19.143 There is one circumstance in which 'an oral hearing'[1] must be convened. That occurs when:

(1)   the reviewing officer has issued a 'minded-to' letter[2]; and
(2)   the applicant responds indicating that she or he wishes to make representations orally (either personally or through a representative)[3].

1   HA 1996, s 203(2)(b); H(W)A 2014, s 86(2)(b).
2   See **19.150–19.165**.
3   SI 2018/223, reg 7(2)(b) SI 2015/1266 (W 86), reg 5(2); *Makisi v Birmingham City Council* [2011] EWCA Civ 355, [2011] HLR 27, CA, see **19.150–19.165**.

19.144 Neither HA 1996, Pt 7[1], H(W)A 2014, Pt 2, the relevant regulations, nor the Codes of Guidance, specify how an oral hearing is to be conducted. The Court of Appeal considered this in *Makisi v Birmingham City Council*[2]. It held that, where an applicant requests the right to make oral representations, he or she must be given the option of a face to face meeting with the reviewing officer. However, the applicant does not have any right to insist that any witnesses are called, or that he or she may cross-examine them. The hearing should be 'a simple and relatively brief opportunity for the applicant to make oral representations to the review officer'[3].

1   As amended by HRA 2017 for applications for homelessness assistance to local housing authorities in England made on or after 3 April 2018
2   [2011] EWCA Civ 355, [2011] HLR 27, CA.
3   Etherton LJ at [70].

FAIRNESS

19.145 The reviewing officer will consider not only the material originally before the decision-maker but also any further relevant material received. If a reviewing officer is minded to draw an adverse inference, or to call into question the applicant's credibility, or hold matters against the applicant, those should be put to the applicant for comment, especially if he or she has not already had an opportunity to comment prior to the original decision[1]. Both Codes of Guidance advise that a reviewing officer should be flexible about allowing further exchanges[2]. The reviewing officer should also consider whether there was a deficiency or irregularity in the original decision or in the manner in which it was made. If so, the special procedure should be activated[3].

1   For general principles of fairness, see *Doody v Secretary of State for the Home Department* [1994] 1 AC 531, HL per Lord Mustill at 560. These principles have been applied in the context of homelessness law in *Feld v Barnet London Borough Council, Pour v Westminster City Council* [2004] EWCA Civ 1307, [2005] HLR 9, CA, and in *Akhtar v Birmingham City Council* [2011] EWCA Civ 383, [2011] HLR 28, CA.
2   English Code, paras 19.17 and 19.24; Welsh Code, para 20.16.
3   SI 2018/223, reg 7(2); Homelessness (Review Procedure) (Wales) Regulations 2015, SI 2015/1266 (W 86), reg 5(2); see **19.150–19.165**.

19.146 Neither HA 1996, Pt 7[1], H(W)A 2014, Pt 2, nor the relevant regulations specifically require or encourage the reviewing officer to make further inquiries at his or her own initiative. The reviewing officer should, however, be prepared to make further inquiries, if necessary, and to consider asking the applicant to agree to extend the time for a review to be completed if further inquiries need to be made, or an oral hearing needs to be arranged[2]. It is a decision for the reviewing officer as to what inquiries, if any, are necessary before the reviewing officer can take and notify the decision on the review[3].

[1] As amended by HRA 2017 for applications for homelessness assistance to local housing authorities in England made on or after 3 April 2018.
[2] English Code, para 19.24; Welsh Code, para 20.16.
[3] *Cramp v Hastings Borough Council, Phillips v Camden London Borough Council* [2005] EWCA Civ 1005, [2005] HLR 48, CA. See Chapter 9.

INDEPENDENCE IN THE CONDUCT OF THE REVIEW

19.147 Review decisions are ultimately made by the very local housing authorities which made the original decisions and are usually made by staff of the local housing authorities concerned. Only where the review is conducted by an 'appointed' reviewing officer[1] will there be anything resembling independence in the review process[2].

[1] See **19.131–19.137**.
[2] In *Runa Begum v Tower Hamlets London Borough Council* [2003] UKHL 5, [2003] 2 AC 430, HL, the House of Lords held that reviewing officers employed by local housing authorities were not independent of the local housing authority. In *De-Winter Heald v Brent London Borough Council* [2009] EWCA Civ 930, [2010] HLR 8, CA, the Court of Appeal held that a reviewing officer contracted by the local housing authority to carry out the review (instead of being employed by the local housing authority) was not necessarily any more or less independent of the local housing authority than its employees were (per Stanley Burnton LJ at [52]–[54]).

19.148 The review procedure itself is therefore not compliant with the requirements of Art 6 of the European Convention on Human Rights, which provides that:

' . . . everyone is entitled to a fair and public hearing within a reasonable time by an independent and impartial tribunal established by law.'

19.149 However, the opportunity of an appeal to the county court on a point of law against the eventual review decision (and the judicial control exercisable within the appeal) safeguards the fairness of the proceedings and renders the overall process compliant with Art 6(1) of the Convention[1]. Indeed, the Supreme Court has held that decision-making on an application for homelessness assistance did not involve a determination of an applicant's 'civil rights' at all and so Art 6(1) did not apply[2].

[1] *Runa Begum v Tower Hamlets London Borough Council* [2003] UKHL 5, [2003] 2 AC 430, HL.
[2] *Ali v Birmingham City Council* [2010] UKSC 8, [2010] 2 AC 39, SC. The applicant complained to the European Court of Human Rights (ECtHR) that her right of access to a fair trial by an impartial and independent tribunal had been infringed. On, the applicant's petition to the ECtHR, a Chamber of the ECtHR held that an application for homelessness did involve a determination of the applicant's civil rights but that the availability of an appeal to the county court on a point of law rendered the process compatible with Art 6: *Ali v UK*

(2016) 63 EHRR 20. However, the Supreme Court has declined to follow the case of *Ali v UK* (2016) 63 EHRR 20, and confirmed its earlier decision that an applicant's civil rights are not determined in these circumstances: *Poshteh v Kensington & Chelsea Royal London Borough Council* [2017] UKSC 36, [2017] AC 624, SC at [37].

The special procedure where there is a deficiency or irregularity

19.150 A reviewing officer must consider, on review of the material initially collected[1], whether there was a deficiency or irregularity in the original decision or in the manner in which it was made[2]. If the reviewing officer decides that there was a deficiency or irregularity, special provisions apply[3].

[1] See **19.138**.
[2] *Lambeth London Borough Council v Johnston* [2008] EWCA Civ 690, [2009] HLR 10, CA.
[3] See Cowan 'The Judicialisation of Homelessness Law: a Study of Regulation 8(2) Allocation of Housing and Homelessness (Review Procedures) Regulations 1999' [2016] *Public Law*, April, for an interesting academic discussion of the procedure.

19.151 If the reviewing officer is satisfied that there was a deficiency or irregularity in the original decision, but is minded to make a decision in favour of the applicant, the reviewing officer may immediately proceed to make that review decision.

19.152 If, however, the reviewing officer is satisfied that there was a deficiency or irregularity in the original decision or in the manner in which it was made, but is still minded to make a decision that is against the interests of the applicant, the reviewing officer must notify the applicant:

(1)   of his or her intention; and
(2)   of the reasons why he or she is so minded.

19.153 The reviewing officer must also give the applicant an opportunity to make representations, either orally or in writing, or both[1].

[1] HA 1996, s 203(2)(b); SI 2018/223, reg 7(2) and English Code, paras 19.20–19.22; H(W)A 2014, s 86(2)(b); Homelessness (Review Procedure) (Wales) Regulations 2015, SI 2015/1266 (W 86), reg 5(2); Welsh Code, para 20.13.

19.154 This preliminary notification ('minded-to') letter gives the applicant an opportunity to persuade the reviewing officer away from an expressed intention to reach a substituted, but nevertheless unfavourable, decision[1]. When the applicant receives this notification, he or she could respond by requesting an oral hearing, or could choose simply to make further representations in writing, or could choose to do both.

[1] In one case, the reviewing officer had given the applicant a deadline for the submission of written representations of a week from the date of the letter inviting representations. That was held to be an 'unreasonably short' period by the judge, particularly since the letter took five days to arrive, so the two days' actual notice was 'manifestly too short': *Harman v Greenwich London Borough Council* (2010) January *Legal Action*, p 36, Lambeth County Court. In another case, seven days' notice was again held to be too short: *Connors v Birmingham City Council* (2010) May *Legal Action*, p 25, Birmingham County Court.

19.155 Sending the minded-to letter is a mandatory obligation on the reviewing officer. There is no room for the reviewing officer to decide, if he or she has concluded that there was a deficiency or irregularity, not to send a 'minded-to' letter because there is no apparent benefit to the applicant. The wording of the regulations makes it clear that the duty must be complied with[1]. One Court of Appeal judge has said:

> 'The minded-to notice gives an opportunity to the applicant to try to persuade the review officer that his reasoning for his provisional conclusion is mistaken and is, at the very least, potentially of great benefit to an applicant, and to be deprived of that right is or may be seriously prejudicial.[2]'

---

1   *Lambeth London Borough Council v Johnston* [2008] EWCA Civ 690, [2009] HLR 10, CA at [51] per Rimer LJ.
2   *Banks v Royal Borough of Kingston-upon-Thames* [2008] EWCA Civ 1443, [2009] HLR 29, CA per Lawrence Collins LJ at [67], following *Lambeth London Borough Council v Johnston* [2008] EWCA Civ 690, [2009] HLR 10, CA.

19.156 The Codes provide some guidance as to the types of deficiencies or irregularities that a reviewing officer might consider render the original decision flawed. Examples given are:

(1)   failure to take into account relevant considerations;
(2)   taking into account irrelevant considerations;
(3)   failure to base the decision on the facts;
(4)   bad faith or dishonesty;
(5)   a mistake of law;
(6)   decisions that run contrary to the policy of HA 1996, Pt 7[1] (or, for local housing authorities in Wales, H(W)A 2014, Pt 2);
(7)   irrationality or unreasonableness; or
(8)   procedural unfairness, eg where an applicant has not been given a chance to comment on relevant matters[2].

---

1   As amended by HRA 2017 for applications for homelessness assistance to local housing authorities in England made on or after 3 April 2018.
2   English Code, para 19.21; Welsh Code, para 20.13.

19.157 In *Hall v Wandsworth London Borough Council*[1], the Court of Appeal considered what was meant by 'deficiency'. It held that it meant 'something lacking'. It was not limited to failings which would provide grounds for legal challenge, although it must be something sufficiently important to the fairness of the process to justify the operation of these special provisions and the 'minded-to' notification. In the two linked cases considered by the Court of Appeal, there was a deficiency in one (in that it was unclear whether the original decision-maker had applied the correct test for vulnerability). The reviewing officer should have treated that failing as a 'deficiency' and should have applied the special provisions.

---

1   [2004] EWCA Civ 1740, [2005] HLR 23, CA per Carnwath LJ at [29].

19.158 An 'irregularity' means something lacking in the manner in which the original decision was made, that is a procedural flaw or error[1].

---

1   *Hall v Wandsworth London Borough Council* [2004] EWCA Civ 1740, [2005] HLR 23, CA per Carnwath LJ at [27].

19.159 How significant should this flaw be? In *Hall v Wandsworth London Borough Council*[1], the Court of Appeal had held that the 'something lacking' must be of sufficient importance to the fairness of the procedure to justify the extra procedural safeguard involved by application of reg 8(2)[2]. In *Banks v Kingston upon Thames Royal London Borough Council*[3], the Court of Appeal said that the test of 'sufficient importance' should be understood 'in the sense that further representations made in response could have made a difference to the decision that the reviewing officer had to make'[4]. A third Court of Appeal decision, *Bury Metropolitan Borough Council v Gibbons*[5], applied the decision of *Hall v Wandsworth London Borough Council*, and the judge said: '[w]here the reviewer rejects the factual basis of the original decision and proposes to substitute a different factual basis leading to the same conclusion, it seems to me that the review has identified as "deficiency" within the meaning of regulation 8(2)'[6].

[1]   [2004] EWCA Civ 1740, [2005] HLR 23, CA.
[2]   Carnwath LJ at [29].
[3]   [2008] EWCA Civ 1443, [2009] HLR 29, CA.
[4]   Lawrence Collins LJ at [72].
[5]   [2010] EWCA Civ 327, [2010] HLR 33, CA.
[6]   Per Jackson LJ at [45].

19.160 In *Mitu v Camden London Borough Council*[1], the local housing authority argued that a flaw in the original decision would only amount to a 'deficiency' if it was a flaw in the reasoning on an issue which the reviewing officer was minded to find against the applicant and if it was sufficiently serious. The Court of Appeal, by a majority, rejected that argument as entailing writing words into the regulation which are not there. The judge giving the leading judgment said:

> '[l]ooking at the matter broadly and untechnically, it seems to me that if the reviewing officer considers that the original decision maker was wrong on an important aspect of the case, then he has identified a deficiency in the original decision . . . To hold otherwise means that the reviewing officer has the power to decide, in effect, that nothing the applicant can say will cause him to change his mind on the issue on which he has found against the applicant.'[2]

[1]   [2011] EWCA Civ 1249, [2012] HLR 10, CA.
[2]   Per Lewison LJ at [28].

19.161 There may also be a 'deficiency' that requires the activation of the special procedure[1], even where the original decision did not contain any errors in its conclusion on the facts as they stood at the time of the original decision. In *Banks v Kingston-upon-Thames Royal London Borough Council*,[2] the original decision had been that the applicant was not homeless. The applicant requested a review. Before the reviewing officer had completed the review, the applicant had been served with a notice to quit. The reviewing officer decided that the applicant was homeless but that he did not have a priority need. The Court of Appeal held that, once it was decided that the applicant was homeless, the original decision had become deficient because it had not addressed his priority need. As a result, where the reviewing officer is minded to decide the review against the interests of the applicant, reg 8(2) should operate so as to ensure that the applicant be given the opportunity to make representations[3].

1   SI 2018/223, reg 7(2) or SI 2015/1266, reg 5(2).
2   [2008] EWCA Civ 1443, [2009] HLR 29, CA.
3   See also *NJ v Wandsworth London Borough Council* [2013] EWCA Civ 1373, [2014] HLR 6, CA; and *Mohamoud v Birmingham City Council* [2014] EWCA Civ 227, [2014] HLR 22, CA.

19.162 The Codes, accordingly, advise that the reviewing officer must consider whether there is 'something lacking' in the decision under review. They suggest that significant issues which were not addressed, or addressed inadequately, which could have to led to unfairness, constitute 'something lacking'[1].

1   English Code, para 19.22; Welsh Code, para 20.13.

19.163 The Court of Appeal has considered whether or not the special procedure in reg 7(2)[1] should apply where there was 'a plainly deficient homelessness decision when the deficiency has had no adverse consequences for the applicant'[2]. The deficiency in that case was that the local housing authority's original decision had concluded that the applicant, who had a priority need, had become homeless intentionally. The decision had, erroneously, informed her that the local housing authority's duty towards her was limited to providing her with advice and assistance[3]. The decision did not notify her that the local housing authority had a duty to secure accommodation for such period as it considered would give her a reasonable opportunity of securing accommodation for herself[4]. The applicant did not suffer any detriment because the local housing authority agreed to secure accommodation pending the review, and then pending her appeal to the county court and subsequently to the Court of Appeal.

1   SI 2018/223 (England); SI 2015/1266, reg 5(2) (Wales).
2   *Ibrahim v Wandsworth London Borough* Council [2013] EWCA Civ 20, [2015] HLR 15, CA at [1].
3   HA 1996, s 190(2)(b), prior to amendment by HRA 2017, s 5(5), for applications for homelessness assistance to local housing authorities in England made on or after 3 April 2018, see **15.231**.
4   HA 1996, s 190(2)(a), prior to amendment by HRA 2017, s 5(5), for applications for homelessness assistance to local housing authorities in England made on or after 3 April 2018, see **16.81–16.93**.

19.164 The reviewing officer did not identify that there was a deficiency or irregularity in the original decision and did not apply the special procedure, although the reviewing officer did notify the applicant of the duty under HA 1996, s 190(2)(a) in the review decision. The Court of Appeal decided that, although the original decision was wrong, it did not contain a 'deficiency' for the purposes of reg 8(2) and that the reviewing officer was correct not to activate the special procedure[1].

1   *Ibrahim v Wandsworth London Borough* Council [2013] EWCA Civ 20, [2015] HLR 15, CA: the judgment contains different reasoning by the different Lord Justices. Sir Stephen Sedley, giving the leading judgment, regarded the error as a 'deficiency', but held that the county court judge was right to exercise her discretion to confirm he review decision because the deficiency was not of sufficient importance to justify engaging the special procedure. Etherton LJ held that the error was not a 'deficiency' for the purposes of the then reg 8(2) procedure because the applicant had not made any complaint about it in her representations on review and the

reviewing officer had not made the same error but had stated the HA 1996, s 190(2)(a) duty correctly. The third judge, Mummery LJ, agreed with Etherton LJ.

19.165 Examples from case-law as to when there may have been 'something lacking' include:

- where it is unclear, from the wording of the original decision, whether or not the decision-maker had applied the correct legal test[1];
- where the original decision-maker had failed to make adequate inquiries of the applicant's medical advisers and had failed to give a reasoned explanation for preferring the in-house medical advice against that of the applicant's advisers[2];
- where the original decision had not mentioned the medical evidence that had been submitted by the applicant[3];
- where the original decision had been made 11 months after the applicant had been interviewed, and by a different officer from the one who had interviewed the applicant[4];
- on a 'broad reading' of the regulations, where the original decision had become 'deficient' simply because it did not deal with a matter raised by a changed factual situation since the original decision was made[5];
- where no reasons had been given in the original decision as to why offered accommodation had been suitable[6];
- where both the applicant and the original decision maker had only viewed the accommodation, the suitability of which was subject to the request for a review, after the original decision had been made[7];
- where the reviewing officer had rejected the factual basis of the original decision;[8]
- where the original decision had simply set out the statutory elements necessary for the ending of the main housing duty under HA 1996, s 193(5)[9], and had not given any reasons for the decision[10];
- where the original decision had concluded that the applicant had become homeless intentionally without giving reasons or explaining what that meant[11];
- where the decision as to whether or not the applicant had become homeless intentionally had been overturned by the reviewing officer even though the duty owed to the applicant had not changed[12];
- where the applicant had raised new information in her representations on review which the reviewing officer had been inclined not to accept[13]; and
- where the applicant had raised new information in her representations on review, to the effect that she had been confused about the number of offers she would receive[14]; and
- where the applicant had raised new information in response to a minded to letter which had not been considered in the original decision, a further minded to letter should have been sent[15].

[1]   *Hall v Wandsworth London Borough Council* [2004] EWCA Civ 1740, [2005] HLR 23, CA.
[2]   *Benson v Lewisham London Borough Council* (2007) October *Legal Action*, p 26, Central London County Court; and see *Lloyd v Birmingham City Council* [2016] EWCA Civ 1348, (2017) *Legal Action* February, p 50, CA, where a Recorder and the CA dismissed submissions that receipt of medical evidence undermining the applicant's claim to have suffered a heart attack required a minded to letter.
[3]   *Al-Kabi v Southwark London Borough Council* (2008) March *Legal Action*, p 21, Lambeth County Court.

4   *Lambeth London Borough Council v Johnston* [2008] EWCA Civ 690, [2009] HLR 10, CA.
5   *Banks v Kingston upon Thames Royal London Borough Council* [2008] EWCA Civ 1443, [2009] HLR 29, CA.
6   *Connors v Birmingham City Council* (2010) *Legal Action* May, p 25, Birmingham County Court.
7   *Norris v Milton Keynes City Council* [2010] EWCA Civ 77, April *Legal Action*, p 26, CA.
8   *Bury Metropolitan Borough Council v Gibbons* [2010] EWCA Civ 327, [2010] HLR 33, CA.
9   See **16.113–16.179**.
10 *Makisi v Birmingham City Council* [2011] EWCA Civ 355, [2011] HLR 27, CA.
11 *Yosief v Birmingham City Council* [2011] EWCA Civ 355, [2011] HLR 27, CA, heard and reported at the same time as *Makisi v Birmingham City Council*. Note that in the third of these cases considered together by the Court of Appeal (*Nagi v Birmingham City Council*), the Court of Appeal found that there had not been a deficiency in the original decision even though the letter was 'poorly worded'. Despite that, the decision had addressed all the important aspects and could not have left a reasonable reader with any real doubt as to the basis of the decision (Etherton LJ at [77]).
12 *Mitu v Camden London Borough Council* [2011] EWCA Civ 1249, [2012] HLR 10, CA.
13 *NJ v Wandsworth London Borough Council* [2013] EWCA Civ 1373, [2014] HLR 6, CA.
14 *Mohamoud v Birmingham City Council* [2014] EWCA Civ 227, [2014] HLR 22, CA.
15 *Begum v Birmingham City Council* [2017] EW Misc 10(CC), *Legal Action*, September, p 34, County Court at Birmingham.

Scope of the review

19.166 It is not possible for an applicant to restrict the scope of the review only to a specific part of the decision that she or he has asked to be reviewed. This is particularly important where the original decision falls under the second category of reviewable decisions, ie a decision as to 'what duty, if any' is owed to the applicant[1]. The general rule is that the reviewing officer is charged with the task of considering the whole matter (of whether any duty is owed) afresh on the latest material available[2]. There are two potential scenarios in which this can create difficulties for applicants.

1   HA 1996, s 202(1)(b), as amended by HRA 2017, s 9, for applications for homelessness assistance to local housing authorities in England made on or after 3 April 2018; see **19.15–19.17**. Or, for applications to local housing authorities in Wales, where the decision is that 'a duty is not owed to the applicant': H(W)A 2014, s 85(1)(b), see **19.74–19.76**.
2   *Temur v Hackney London Borough Council* [2014] EWCA Civ 877, [2014] HLR 39, CA.

19.167 First, an applicant owed the benefit of a duty as a result of the original decision may find that the reviewing officer concludes (on consideration of the same material) that he or she is owed not a higher but a lesser duty. For example, the original decision may have been that the applicant was eligible, homeless, and in priority need, but had become homeless intentionally. The reviewing officer, on reconsideration, may conclude that the applicant did not become homeless intentionally but has never had a priority need, and that therefore there is no accommodation duty at all. The 'minded-to' procedure ought to ensure that the applicant is not taken by surprise by such a decision[1].

1   See **19.150–19.165**.

19.168 Second, the applicant may find that new information, or a change of circumstances between the original decision and the conclusion of the review, undermines the benefits of the original decision. For example, the original decision may have been that the applicant was eligible, homeless, and had a priority need but had become homeless intentionally. The reviewing officer may be satisfied (by either new information or a change of circumstances) that the applicant is not eligible or no longer has a priority need. Even if the original decision was correct on the facts available at the time, the new information or change of circumstances renders the original decision subject to a 'deficiency'. The reviewing officer should send a 'minded-to' letter inviting the applicant to make representations if the reviewing officer is minded to decide the review against the interests of the applicant[1].

1 SI 2018/223, reg 7(2); SI 2015/1266, reg 5(2); and *Banks v Kingston-upon-Thames Royal London Borough Council* [2008] EWCA Civ 1443, [2009] HLR 29, CA. In *Temur v Hackney London Borough Council* [2014] EWCA Civ 877, [2014] HLR 39, CA, the original decision had found that the applicant was homeless and eligible for assistance but did not have a priority need. By the time of the review decision, the applicant had obtained an assured shorthold tenancy of a bed-sitting room and her daughter had come to live with her. The reviewing officer, having used the special procedure in reg 8(2), decided that the applicant was not homeless. See **19.150–19.165**.

19.169 A difficult situation arises where the applicant is not provided with accommodation pending review[1] and then has obtained his or her own accommodation before the conclusion of the review. If the applicant has managed to obtain something better than emergency accommodation, the reviewing officer will be entitled – indeed required – to conclude that the applicant is not homeless as at the date of the decision on review[2].

1 See **16.233–16.257** (England) and **17.134** (Wales).
2 See CHAPTER 10. This is exactly what happened in *Temur v Hackney London Borough Council* [2014] EWCA Civ 877, [2014] HLR 39, CA.

19.170 Another difficult situation is where the applicant has accepted a private rented sector offer[1] or a final accommodation offer[2] and simultaneously requested a review of its suitability[3]. The applicant will have entered into a fixed-term assured shorthold tenancy and so he or she will be liable to the landlord for the rent for the whole of the term. What happens if the reviewing officer agrees with the applicant that the accommodation is not suitable for the applicant? Arguably, in order to provide for this situation, all private rented sector offers should contain break clauses, exercisable by the applicant. Otherwise, the applicant would either have to pay large sums of money to the landlord to be released from the agreement, or would have to remain living in accommodation which is agreed not to be suitable[4].

1 HA 1996, s 193(7AA)–(7AC), see **16.153–16.180**; H(W)A s 76(3)(b) and (4), see **17.173–17.177**.
2 As defined at HA 1996, ss 193A(4) and 193C(7), as inserted by HRA 2017, s 7(1), for applications for homelessness assistance to local housing authorities in England made on or after 3 April 2018, and made in order to bring the HA 1996, s 189B(2), relief duty or HA 1996, s 193C(4) accommodation duty to an end: HA 1996, ss 193A(1) and 193C(6)(a), as inserted by HRA 2017, s 7(1), for applications for homelessness assistance to local housing authorities in England made on or after 3 April 2018, see **15.181–15.184** and **16.205–16.209**.
3 HA 1996, ss 202(1)(g) and (h), as amended and inserted by HRA 2017, s 9, for applications for homelessness assistance to local housing authorities in England made on or after 3 April 2018, see **19.63–19.64**; H(W)A 2014, s 85(3), see **19.83–19.85**.
4 This scenario is not addressed at all in either Code of Guidance.

19.171 Obviously, any new information or change of circumstances could equally well work in an applicant's favour. Between the request for, and conclusion of, the review, he or she may have acquired priority need status, established a new local connection or had any other change of circumstance which could produce a more favourable review decision[1]. Provided that this material comes to the attention of the reviewing officer, it must be taken into account[2].

1   *Mohammed v Hammersmith and Fulham London Borough Council* [2001] UKHL 57, [2002] 1 AC 547, HL.
2   *Temur v Hackney London Borough Council* [2014] EWCA Civ 877, [2014] HLR 39, CA per Jackson LJ at [35]. If that is the case, the review decision will be favourable for the applicant and the special procedure need not be activated.

19.172 There are two exceptions to the general rule that the reviewing officer must consider the whole matter on the latest material available.

19.173 First, the Court of Appeal has held that, where the original decision was unlawful and had deprived the applicant of a benefit to which he or she would have been entitled had the original decision been lawfully taken, the reviewing officer should take a different approach from the normal course of considering all the facts and law at the date of the review decision. In those circumstances, the reviewing officer should restore to the applicant the rights he or she would have had if the decision had been lawful, even if the applicant's circumstances have changed such that he or she would normally not be entitled to that benefit[1]. The obvious example, and that considered by the Court of Appeal, is where a 17-year-old is notified that he or she does not have a priority need, requests a review and the review is decided after his or her eighteenth birthday[2]. These unusual circumstances apply where the original decision was unlawful, in this case because the 17-year-old could not have been anything other than in priority need at the date of the original decision. The position if, for example, the original decision had been that the 17-year-old had a priority need but had become homeless intentionally, and a reviewing officer is considering the position after the applicant's eighteenth birthday, is much more difficult. The original decision was not unlawful, certainly as far as the priority need part of the decision is concerned. Should the reviewing officer confine himself or herself to considering the part of the decision that did not relate to priority need? The Court of Appeal's approach in *Crawley Borough Council v B*[3] suggests not and that all of the circumstances that go towards a decision as to what duty, if any, is owed to the applicant should be considered by the reviewing officer as at the date of the review[4]. In those circumstances, reg 7(2)[5] requires the reviewing officer to send the applicant a 'minded-to' letter if he or she is minded to decide the review against the interests of the applicant[6].

1   *Robinson v Hammersmith & Fulham London Borough Council* [2006] EWCA Civ 1122, [2007] HLR 7, CA at [32] per Waller LJ, drawing on dicta in *Crawley Borough Council v B* [2000] 32 HLR 636, CA at 651, per Chadwick LJ.
2   See **12.133–12.159** (England) and **12.212–12.213** (Wales).
3   (2000) 32 HLR 636, CA.
4   See also *Temur v Hackney London Borough Council* [2014] EWCA Civ 877, [2014] HLR 39, CA.
5   SI 2018/223; SI 2015/1266, reg 5(2) for local housing authorities in Wales, see **19.150–19.165**.
6   *Banks v Kingston-upon-Thames Royal London Borough Council* [2008] EWCA Civ 1443, [2009] HLR 29, CA.

19.174 Second, where the reviewing officer is considering the applicant's reasons for refusing an offer of accommodation, the reviewing officer should consider the facts and circumstances that existed at the date of the refusal, not at the date of the review. Some of those facts may only come to the attention of the local housing authority after the date of the refusal, but the correct question for the reviewing officer is what facts existed at the date of the refusal[1].

1 *Osseily v Westminster City Council* [2007] EWCA Civ 1108, [2008] HLR 18, CA; *Omar v Westminster City Council* [2008] EWCA Civ 421, [2008] HLR 36, CA. See **16.111.**

Effect of a review against a decision as to steps to be taken to help the applicant

Local housing authorities in England

19.175 As previously noted[1], an applicant to a local housing authority in England can request a review of what steps the local housing authority has decided are reasonable for it to take either under the HA 1996, s 195(2)[2], prevention duty or under the HA 1996, s 189B(2)[3] relief duty. A short time-frame is prescribed for completion of these review decisions: representations must be made within two weeks from the date when the review is requested, and the decision on review must be notified within three weeks from receipt of the representations or, if no representations are made, from the date when the review was requested[4]. Each time limit can be extended by written agreement between the applicant and the reviewer[5].

1 See **19.18–19.23** and **19.36–19.41.**
2 As amended by HRA 2017, s 4(2), for applications for homelessness assistance to local housing authorities in England made on or after 3 April 2018, see **15.87–15.137.** The right to request a review is at HA 1996, s 202(1)(bc)(i), as inserted by HRA 2017, s 9, for applications for homelessness assistance to local housing authorities in England made on or after 3 April 2018, see **19.36–19.41.**
3 As inserted by HRA 2017, s 5(2), for applications for homelessness assistance to local housing authorities in England made on or after 3 April 2018, see **15.138–15.195.** The right to request a review is at HA 1996, s 202(1)(ba)(i), as inserted by HRA 2017, s 9, for applications for homelessness assistance to local housing authorities in England made on or after 3 April 2018, see **19.18–19.23.**
4 SI 2018/223, regs 5(3)(b) and 9(1)(a).
5 SI 2018/223, regs 5(3)(b) and 9(1)(a)

19.176 The Code of Guidance advises local housing authorities to encourage applicants to raise any concerns they have about the steps, which will be contained in the personalised housing plan[1], more informally so that they can resolve disagreements. However, this does not, of course, restrict an applicant's right to request a review of the steps set out in the personalised hosing plan[2].

1 HA 1996, s 189A(4)(b) and (6)(c), as inserted by HRA 2017, s 3(1), for applications for homelessness assistance to local housing authorities in England made on or after 3 April 2018, see **15.72–15.80.**
2 English Code, para 11.36.

19.177 The question arises as to what happens if the review decision is to the effect that the steps proposed, and being undertaken by the local housing authority, are not reasonable. Arguably, that would mean that the 56 day period should commence from the date of the review decision, or even from a later date if the reviewer does not decide what steps would be reasonable but simply requires the original decision-maker to reconsider the steps in the personalized housing plan.[1]The English Code is much more ambiguous than that. It advises that 'review officers are recommended to use their discretion to assess the impact of the failure across the whole period of the relevant duty and make recommendations which seek to remedy this'[2].

[1]   This is the effect of a review decision for local housing authorities in Wales, see **19.81–19.82**.
[2]   English Code, paras 19.34–19.35.

Local housing authorities in Wales

19.178 As previously noted[1], an applicant to a local housing authority in Wales can request a review of whether reasonable steps were taken by the local housing authority in performance of its H(W)A 2014, s 73(1), duty to help the applicant to secure accommodation[2]. This right to request a review arises if the local housing authority has decided that the duty has come to an end, either because the 56-day period has expired or earlier than 56 days if the local housing authority is satisfied that reasonable steps have been taken to secure that suitable accommodation is available for occupation by the applicant[3]. Detailed guidance on the procedure when a review is sought of a local housing authority's decision that reasonable steps were taken is in the Welsh Code[4].

[1]   See **19.81–19.82**.
[2]   H(W)A 2014, s 73(1), see **17.76–17.78**.
[3]   H(W)A 2014, ss 74 (2) and (3) and 85(2).
[4]   Welsh Code, paras 20.17–20.22

19.179 If the review decision confirms that reasonable steps had not been taken, then the duty in H(W)A 2014, s 73(1), has not come to an end, and a new 56-day period should commence from the date when the review decision is notified to the applicant[1].

[1]   H(W)A 2014, s 87; Welsh Code, para 20.33.

Notification of the review decision

19.180 Every review decision must be notified to the applicant or to his or her authorised agent by the local housing authority or authorities concerned, even if the review has been conducted by an 'appointed' reviewing officer[1]. That notice must be given in writing[2]. If the local housing authority is for some reason unable to give the applicant the written notice, it may make the review decision available for collection at its office for a reasonable period, and that can constitute notification[3]. It is important to establish the exact date of notification, because the very tight 21-day time-limit for the filing of an appeal to the county court runs from the date of notification. If there is any doubt as to the exact date of notification, the county court judge will have to determine the date. In those circumstances, if there might be any doubt as to the correct deadline, an applicant should be advised to apply for an extension of time when he or she issues his or her Appellant's Notice, in case the judge finds that the appeal has been issued out of time[4].

1   HA 1996, s 203(3); English Code, paras 19.29–19.31; H(W)A 2014, s 86(3); Welsh Code, paras 20.25–20.28.
2   HA 1996, s 203(8); H(W)A 2014, s 86(7).
3   HA 1996, s 203(8); H(W)A 2014, s 86(7).
4   HA 1996, s 204(2A); H(W)A 2014, s 88(3). See **19.251–19.255**.

19.181 The local housing authority must notify the applicant of the reasons for the review decision[1] if the review decision:

- confirms the original decision against the interests of the applicant on any issue;
- confirms the original decision to give a notice of referral under the conditions for referral[2];
- confirms the original decision that the conditions are met for referral of the applicant's case[3];
- (for local housing authorities in England) confirms that reasonable steps are being taken under the HA 1996, ss 189B(2)[4], relief or 195(2)[5], prevention duties[6]; or
- (for local housing authorities in Wales) confirms that reasonable steps were taken to help to secure that suitable accommodation would be available for the applicant under the H(W)A 2014, s 73(1) duty[7].

In any other case, where applicants would be expected to be pleased with the review decision, reasons are not required to be given[8]. It might, however, be expected that an 'appointed' reviewing officer[9] would have given written reasons to the local housing authorities involved and that they would be passed on to the applicant.

1   HA 1996, s 203(4); H(W)A s 86(4). For 'reasons' see **9.111–9.139**.
2   See **19.49–19.54** and **19.77–19.80**.
3   See **19.55–19.57** (England) and **19.77–19.80** (Wales).
4   As inserted by HRA 2017, s 5(2), for applications for homelessness assistance to local housing authorities in England made on or after 3 April 2018.
5   As amended by HRA 2017, s 4(2), for applications for homelessness assistance to local housing authorities in England made on or after 3 April 2018.
6   HA 1996, s 202(1)(ba)(i) and (bc)(i), as inserted by HRA 2017, s 9, for applications for homelessness assistance to local housing authorities in England made on or after 3 April 2018, see **19.18–19.23** and **19.36–19.41**.
7   H(W)A 2014, s 85(2), see **19.81–19.82**.
8   *Akhtar v Birmingham City Council* [2011] EWCA Civ 383, [2011] HLR 28, CA.
9   See **19.131–19.137**.

19.182 Whatever the outcome of the review, the same notice of the review decision must also inform the applicant of the right to appeal to the county court on a point of law and of the 21-day period in which the appeal must be made[1].

1   HA 1996, s 203(5); H(W)A 2014, s 86(5). The exact wording of this sub-section need not be set out so long as the substance is conveyed: *Dharmaraj v Hounslow London Borough Council* [2011] EWCA Civ 312, [2011] HLR 18, CA. It may seem surprising that this information has to be notified even in a review decision which decides all the issues in the applicant's favour but the wording in both HA 1996, 203(5) and H(W)A 2014, s 86(5) is '[i]n any case . . . '.

19.183 A review decision notification that fails to provide either the reasons for the decision or the information about rights to appeal (where those are required) will not be effective as a review decision.[1] This will mean that the review has not been concluded.

[1] HA 1996, s 203(6); H(W)A 2014, s 85(6).

19.184 The applicant's remedy in that case might be to appeal on a point of law against the original decision (because there is no review decision)[1]. However, the better course might be to invite the reviewing officer to conclude the review properly by giving the required notice, seizing the opportunity to put forward any additional material before that notice is given[2].

[1] HA 1996, s 204(1)(b); H(W)A s 88(1)(b). See **19.222–19.223**.
[2] See **19.224**. The Local Government Ombudsman found maladministration where a local housing authority failed to notify the applicant of her right of appeal: *Complaint against Croydon London Borough Council* 13 002 818, 6 November 2013 (2014) February *Legal Action*, p 32; and *Complaint against Kingston upon Hull City Council*, 13 002 073, 23 January 2014 (2014) March *Legal Action*, p 24 where the review decision additionally failed to give reasons for deciding the issue against the applicant's interests.

Time scale for completion of the review

LOCAL HOUSING AUTHORITIES IN ENGLAND

19.185 For local housing authorities in England, the Regulations prescribe different time limits, depending on the different decisions which are subject to the request for a review. The different time limits are separately discussed below.

19.186 In most of the cases below[1], the period runs from day on which the applicant made his or her request for a review, not the date on which the request was received[2]. The period for notification of the review decision can be extended by written agreement between the applicant and the reviewer[3]. This allows for flexibility and also the certainty provided by a written record of the agreement which contains the period of the extension. The wording of reg 9(1) was considered to be 'defective drafting' by the House of Lords and House of Commons Joint Committee on Statutory Instruments[4].

[1] The three week period for notification runs from either the date on which the request for the review was made, or the date on which representations were received, see **19.189**.
[2] SI 2018/223, reg 9(1).
[3] SI 2018/223, reg 9(1).
[4] House of Lords and House of Commons Joint Committee on Statutory Instruments (Eighteenth Report of Session 2017–19, 28 March 2018). The Joint Committee stated that the wording was not grammatical and did not achieve the purpose of HA 1996, s 203(7), which allows regulations make provision as to the period in which the review must be carried out and notice given of the decision. The Joint Committee noted the MHCLG's explanation that reg 9(1) has the effect of making provision for the period in which the review must be carried out, but it did not agree. The Joint Committee said: 'Regulation 9(1) could have stated expressly that notice is to be given within the period specified; or it could simply have stated that the period for the purpose of section 203 is a specified number of weeks; but it does neither one nor the other. Stating that notice must be given "a period of X weeks" is not the same as stating that it must be given within that period.'

19.187 The time limit of 21 days for bringing an appeal to the county court against a review decision[1] runs from the date of written notification of the review decision to the applicant or to his or her agent[2]. That must mean the date on which the review decision is received if it is sent by post, and not the date of posting or the date on the letter itself[3].

[1] See **19.244–19.245.**
[2] HA 1996, s 204(2); H(W)A 2014, s 88(2). For review decisions notified to agents, see *Dharmaraj v Hounslow London Borough Council* [2011] EWCA Civ 312, [2011] HLR 18, CA.
[3] *Demetri v Westminster City Council* (1999) 32 HLR 470, CA, at 471, in which the review decision was posted on 7 December but not received until 17 December. See *Lambeth London Borough Council v Namegembe* [2006] EWHC 3608 (Ch), (2007) February *Legal Action*, p 31, ChD, and *Dawkins v Central Bedfordshire Council* [2013] EWHC 4757 (QB), (2013) September *Legal Action*, p 31, QBD, for examples of a judge having to determine conflicts of fact between the parties as to when a review decision had been received by the applicant.

Review decisions which must be notified within three weeks

19.188 The three-week time limit applies to the following requests for a review:

- in respect of a decision as to steps that the local housing authority is to take under the HA 1996, s 189B(2)[1], relief duty[2];
- in respect of a decision to give notice to the applicant that he or she has deliberately and unreasonably refused to co-operate, where the effect of the decision is to bring the HA 1996, s 195(2)[3] prevention duty to an end[4];
- in respect of a decision as to the steps that the local housing authority is to take under the HA 1996, s 195(2)[5], prevention duty[6]; or
- in respect of a decision to give notice to the applicant that the HA 1996, s 195(2)[7], prevention duty has come to an end[8].

[1] As inserted by HRA 2017, s 5(2), for applications for homelessness assistance to local housing authorities in England made on or after 3 April 2018.
[2] HA 1996, s 202(1)(ba)(i), as inserted by HRA 2017, s 9, for applications for homelessness assistance to local housing authorities in England made on or after 3 April 2018, see **19.18–19.23.**
[3] As amended by HRA 2017, s 4(2), for applications for homelessness assistance to local housing authorities in England made on or after 3 April 2018.
[4] HA 1996, s 202(1)(bb), as inserted by HRA 2017, s 9, for applications for homelessness assistance to local housing authorities in England made on or after 3 April 2018, see **19.30–19.35.**
[5] As amended by HRA 2017, s 4(2), for applications for homelessness assistance to local housing authorities in England made on or after 3 April 2018.
[6] HA 1996, s 202(1)(bc)(i), as inserted by HRA 2017, s 9, for applications for homelessness assistance to local housing authorities in England made on or after 3 April 2018, see **19.36–19.41.**
[7] As amended by HRA 2017, s 4(2), for applications for homelessness assistance to local housing authorities in England made on or after 3 April 2018.
[8] HA 1996, s 202(1)(bc)(ii), as inserted by HRA 2017, s 9, for applications for homelessness assistance to local housing authorities in England made on or after 3 April 2018, see **19.42–19.48.**

19.189 The review decision must be notified to the applicant within three weeks of one of the following dates:

- the date on which the applicant requested the review if the applicant made no further representations; or
- the date on which the applicant made representations in response to the reviewer's notification that he or she could make representations[1].

[1]   SI 2018/223, reg 9(1)(a) and English Code, para 19.23.

Review decisions which must be notified within eight weeks

19.190 The eight-week time limit applies to the following requests for a review:

- in respect of a decision as to the applicant's eligibility for assistance[1];
- in respect of a decision as what duty (if any) is owed to the applicant[2];
- in respect of a decision to give notice to the applicant that the HA 1996, s 189B(2)[3], relief duty has come to an end[4];
- in respect of a decision to give notice to the applicant that he or she has deliberately and unreasonably refused to co-operate, where the effect of the decision is to bring the HA 1996, s 189B(2)[5] relief duty to an end[6];
- in respect of a decision to notify another local housing authority for referral of the HA 1996, s 193(2), main housing duty[7];
- in respect of a decision that the conditions for referral of the applicant's case are or are not met[8];
- in respect of a decision that the conditions for referral of the HA 1996, s 193(2), main housing duty are, or are not, met[9];
- in respect of a decision as to the suitability of accommodation offered in discharge of the duties at HA 1996, ss 189B(2)[10], 190(2)[11], 193(2), 193C(4)[12], 195(2)[13], 200(3) or (4), or a final PArt 6 offer made under HA 1996, s 193(7)[14];
- in respect of a decision as to the suitability of a private rented sector offer made under HA 1996, s 193(7AA)[15]; or
- in respect of a decision as to the suitability of a final accommodation offer[16] or a final PArt 6 offer[17] made under HA 1996, ss 193A(1) or 193C(6)[18].

The review decision must be notified to the applicant within eight weeks of the date on which the applicant requested the review[19].

[1]   HA 1996, s 202(1)(a), see **19.14**.
[2]   HA 1996, s 202(1)(b), as amended by HRA 2017, s 9, for applications for homelessness assistance to local housing authorities in England made on or after 3 April 2018, see **19.15–19.17**.
[3]   As inserted by HRA 2017, s 5(2), for applications for homelessness assistance to local housing authorities in England made on or after 3 April 2018.
[4]   HA 1996, s 202(1)(ba)(ii), as inserted by HRA 2017, s 9, for applications for homelessness assistance to local housing authorities in England made on or after 3 April 2018, see **19.24–19.29**.
[5]   As inserted by HRA 2017, s 5(2), for applications for homelessness assistance to local housing authorities in England made on or after 3 April 2018.
[6]   HA 1996, s 202(1)(bb), as inserted by HRA 2017, s 9, for applications for homelessness assistance to local housing authorities in England made on or after 3 April 2018, see **19.30–19.35**.
[7]   HA 1996, s 202(1)(c), see **19.49–19.54**.
[8]   HA 1996, s 202(1)(d), see **19.55–19.57**.
[9]   HA 1996, s 202(1)(e), see **19.58**.

[10] As inserted by HRA 2017, s 5(2), for applications for homelessness assistance to local housing authorities in England made on or after 3 April 2018.

[11] As amended by HRA 2017, s 5(5), for applications for homelessness assistance to local housing authorities in England made on or after 3 April 2018.

[12] As inserted by HRA 2017, s 7(1), for applications for homelessness assistance to local housing authorities in England made on or after 3 April 2018.

[13] As amended by HRA 2017, s 4(2), for applications for homelessness assistance to local housing authorities in England made on or after 3 April 2018.

[14] HA 1996, s 202(1)(f), see **19.59–19.62**.

[15] HA 1996, s 202(1)(g), see **19.63–19.64**.

[16] As defined at HA 1996, ss 193A(4) or 193C(7), as inserted by HRA 2017, s 7(1), for applications for homelessness assistance to local housing authorities in England made on or after 3 April 2018, see **15.181–15.184** and **16.205–16.209**.

[17] As defined at HA 1996, ss 193A(5) or 193C(8), as inserted by HRA 2017, s 7(1), for applications for homelessness assistance to local housing authorities in England made on or after 3 April 2018, see **15.184–15.189** and **16.210–16.218**.

[18] As inserted by HRA 2017, s 7(1), for applications for homelessness assistance to local housing authorities in England made on or after 3 April 2018, see **15.181–15.189** and **16.200–16.216**. HA 1996, s 202(h), as inserted by HRA 2017, s 9, for applications for homelessness assistance to local housing authorities in England made on or after 3 April 2018, see **19.65–19.69**.

[19] SI 2018/223, reg 9(1)(b) and English Code, para 19.23.

Review decisions which must be notified within ten weeks

19.191 A ten-week time limit applies to the request for a review of a decision that the conditions for referral of the applicant's case are met[1], and the review has been carried out by the notifying local housing authority and the notified local housing authority[2]. The review decision must be notified to the applicant within ten weeks of the date on which the applicant requested the review.

[1] HA 1996, s 202(1)(d), see **19.55–19.57**.
[2] SI 2018/223, reg 9(1)(c) and English Code, para 19.23.

Review decisions which must be notified within twelve weeks

19.192 A 12-week time limit applies to the request for a review of a decision that the conditions for referral of the applicant's case are met when the original decision had been made by a referee[1], and the review has been carried out by a person appointed by the notifying local housing authority and the notified local housing authority or appointed by the Local Government Association[2]. The review decision must be notified to the applicant within 12 weeks of the date on which the applicant requested the review.

[1] HA 1996, s 202(1)(d), see **19.55–19.57**.
[2] SI 2018/223, regs 6 and 9(1)(d) and English Code, para 19.23.

19.193 Since responsibility for notifying the applicant of the review decision is on the two local housing authorities concerned, not the appointed person, the appointed person must send the review to the local housing authorities one week either eleven-weeks after the review was requested, or, if a longer period had been agreed, no later than one week before the expiry of that period[1]. This gives the local housing authorities sufficient time to notify the applicant within the 12-week period[2].

[1] SI 2018/223, reg 9(2).

²   SI 2015/1266, reg 6(1)(a).

LOCAL HOUSING AUTHORITIES IN WALES

19.194 In most cases, the time limit is that the review decision must be notified to the applicant within eight weeks from the receipt of the request for a review. Different time limits apply if the review has been sought of a decision that the conditions for a referral to another local housing authority are met[1]. If the review is of a decision made by the two local housing authorities involved, the review period is ten weeks[2]. If the review is of a decision made by a referee, the period is 12 weeks[3]. In the latter case, in order to give the local housing authorities concerned time to notify a review decision within the 12-week period, the 'appointed' reviewing officer must notify them of his or her decision within 11 weeks[4].

¹   H(W)A 2014, ss 80(5) and 85(1)(c); and see **19.77–19.80**.
²   SI 2015/1266 (W 86), reg 6(1)(b).
³   SI 2015/1266, reg 6(1)(c).
⁴   SI 2015/1266, reg 6(3).

19.195 The period for completion of a review can be longer than these prescribed periods if both the applicant and local housing authority agree in writing that the period should be extended[1]. The time limit of 21 days for bringing an appeal to the county court against a review decision[2] runs from the date of written notification of the review decision to the applicant or to his or her agent[3].

¹   SI 2015/1266, reg 6(2).
²   See **19.244–19.245**.
³   H(W)A 2014, s 88(2). For review decisions notified to agents, see *Dharmaraj v Hounslow London Borough Council* [2011] EWCA Civ 312, [2011] HLR 18, CA.

Remedies for failure to complete the review in time

19.196 If no review decision has been notified by the end of the prescribed (or any agreed extended) period, the applicant has 21 days from the end of that period in which to bring an appeal against the original decision on a point of law[1].

¹   HA 1996, s 204(1)(b) and (2); H(W)A 2014, s 88(1)(b) and (2).

19.197 However, it may be that pursuing an appeal on a point of law against the original decision is not the most appropriate option available to the applicant. The original decision may have been one that the local housing authority was lawfully entitled to take. But the applicant may disagree with the factual conclusions or may have submitted new information in the course of the review process which might alter the local housing authority's approach. In these cases, what the applicant requires is a reconsideration of the facts relevant to his or her application, not an appeal on a point of law. The local housing authority's failure to complete the review will have prevented the applicant from having his or her case reconsidered on its facts.

19.198 The appropriate procedure in these circumstances would be for the applicant to apply by way of judicial review proceedings for a mandatory order requiring the local housing authority to complete the review and to notify the applicant of its decision on review[1].

1   *R (Aguiar) v Newham London Borough Council* [2002] EWHC 1325 (Admin), (2002) September *Legal Action*, p 31, Admin Ct.

19.199 It may be sensible for the applicant to lodge an appellant's notice against the original decision in any event[1], and then request that the appeal is stayed until the judicial review application (seeking a review decision) has been determined[2]. If the applicant does not succeed in obtaining a review decision through the judicial review process, his or her appeal against the original decision will still have been issued within the time limit.

1   HA 1996, s 204(1)(b) H(W)A 2014, s 88(1)(b).
2   See **19.306–19.332.**

Extra-statutory reviews

Preliminary reviews

19.200 As already noted[1], prior to the introduction of HA 1996, Pt 7[2], many local housing authorities had adopted informal local review procedures where decisions were disputed.

1   See **19.1–19.7.**
2   HA 1996, Pt 7, applied to local housing authorities in England and in Wales from its commencement on 20 January 1997. For applications for homelessness assistance to local housing authorities in Wales, H(W)A 2014, Pt 2, came into force on 27 April 2015.

19.201 Since 1997, as the statutory review process has become more familiar, the use of these informal preliminary reviews and of multi-layered reviewing has declined and, to the best of the authors' knowledge, no local housing authority in England or Wales operates a multi-staged scheme. Of course, local housing authorities may still offer informal extra-statutory reviews of those decisions which carry no right to a statutory review[1].

1   See **19.12–19.70** for decisions by local housing authorities in England that carry a right to request a review; see **9.71–19.86** for decisions by local housing authorities in Wales that carry a right to request a review.

Second reviews

19.202 There is no statutory provision for any further review of a review decision, and there is no right to request a statutory review of a review decision[1].

1   HA 1996, s 202(2); H(W)A 2014, s 85(4).

19.203 A local housing authority is not precluded from reconsidering its decision on review, if the applicant consents, just as it is not precluded from reconsidering any other decision[1]. But if the review is reconsidered, the exercise is simply an extra-statutory reconsideration. It is not a statutory review, and is not, and cannot be, a second statutory review.

[1]   *R v Westminster City Council ex p Ellioua* (1998) 31 HLR 440, CA.

19.204 The local housing authority may be prepared voluntarily to carry out an additional, extra-statutory reconsideration if, for example:

(1)   new relevant information has come to light since the review decision; or

(2)   an appeal against the review decision is likely to be mounted so that an early reconsideration would be a sensible opportunity to ensure the review decision is likely to survive judicial scrutiny; or

(3)   there is some other good reason to justify looking at the matter again.

19.205 If the applicant is requesting that the local housing authority look again at the review decision, he or she should seek to dissuade the local housing authority from conducting only an informal or extra-statutory reconsideration. Instead, the applicant should ask the local housing authority to agree to treat the first review decision as withdrawn and the statutory review process as re-opened. The applicant should ask that the local housing authority confirms in writing that it is proceeding on this basis. That confirmation should also contain written agreement to any necessary extension of the time limit for completion of that review (if the original time limit has expired or is about to expire).

19.206 The applicant will need to take this course because only a true review decision, and not an extra-statutory reconsideration, can be subject to an appeal to the county court[1].

[1]   *Demetri v Westminster City Council* (2000) 32 HLR 470, CA.

19.207 If the local housing authority only agrees to an informal reconsideration, the applicant who wishes to preserve his or her position should bring an appeal against the statutory review decision. That appeal must be lodged within the normal 21-day period, even if the local housing authority has agreed to carry out an informal reconsideration of the review decision.

19.208 Theoretically, the decisions not to withdraw a review decision and/or not to undertake an extra-statutory reconsideration are amenable to judicial review. However, save in the most exceptional case, any such challenge is highly unlikely to be successful[1]. The better course would be to bring an appeal against the review decision or, if necessary, apply for an extension of time within which to bring that appeal[2].

[1]   Exceptionally, a claim for judicial review succeeded in quashing the local housing authority's informal reconsideration in *R (Van Der Stolk) v Camden London Borough Council* [2002] EWHC 1261 (Admin), (2002) July *Legal Action*, p 26, Admin Ct. In *R v Westminster City Council ex p Ellioua* (1999) 31 HLR 440, CA, the applicant's claim for judicial review of a refusal to reconsider did not succeed; the county court was the correct forum for an appeal against the statutory review decision. In *R (C) v Lewisham London Borough Council* [2003] EWCA Civ 927, (2004) 36 HLR 4, CA, the Court of Appeal held that the local housing authority's exercise of its extra-statutory discretion in considering an extension of time in which to request a review, a further reconsideration of a review decision or a further extension of time is close to being an absolute discretion and unlikely to be amenable to challenge by judicial review; and see *R (Slaiman) v Richmond upon Thames London Borough Council* [2006] EWHC 329 (Admin), [2006] HLR 20, Admin Ct, where a similar challenge failed.

[2]   See **19.244–19.245** and **19.306–19.332**.

19.209 Of course, a review decision only affects the position between the applicant and the particular reviewing local housing authority. An applicant unable or unwilling to challenge an adverse review decision of a local housing authority in the county court is always free to apply to a different local housing authority[1].

---

[1] The local housing authority receiving the second application for homelessness assistance can take into account any decisions or review decisions made by previous local housing authorities but must reach its own conclusions. See **9.50–9.56**.

Accommodation pending the outcome of the review

19.210 The local housing authority has a discretion, but not a duty, to provide accommodation for the applicant and the members of his or her household during the review process[1]. The discretion is available whether or not the applicant has been accommodated prior to the original decision.

---

[1] HA 1996, ss 188(3), 199A(6), as amended and inserted by HRA 2017, s 5(4) and (9), for applications for homelessness assistance to local housing authorities in England made on or after 3 April 2018, and 200(5); H(W)A 2014, ss 69(11) and 88(5). See also English Code, paras 15.25–15.27; Welsh Code, paras 20.29–20.32. See **16.233–16.257** (England) and **17.134** (Wales).

19.211 The local housing authority is under no obligation to consider, in every case, whether it should exercise the power. An applicant who wants accommodation pending the review should ask for it[1].

---

[1] *R (Ahmed) v Waltham Forest London Borough Council* [2001] EWHC 540 (Admin), (2001) October *Legal Action*, p 17, Admin Ct.

19.212 If the local housing authority declines to exercise this power, a court will only intervene if the local housing authority has made an error of law in considering the exercise of its discretion (or has failed to consider the request for accommodation at all). Any challenge to the local housing authority's exercise or non-exercise of discretion can only be made by way of judicial review proceedings[1].

---

[1] See **19.306–19.332**.

19.213 Full descriptions of the powers to accommodate pending review, its various features and the scope for challenges to decisions are given in CHAPTER 16 (England) and CHAPTER 17 (Wales).[1]

---

[1] See **16.233–16.257** (England) and **17.134** (Wales).

APPEALS

Right to appeal

19.214 As already noted[1], prior to HA 1996, Pt 7[2] all legal challenges to local housing authority decisions made under the statutory homelessness provisions were brought by way of judicial review. Since 20 January 1997, challenges to most decisions are pursued instead by way of an appeal on a point of law to the county court[3].

1   See **19.1–19.7**.
2   HA 1996, Pt 7, applied to local housing authorities in England and in Wales from its
     commencement on 20 January 1997. H(W)A 2014, Pt 2, applies for applications for
     homelessness assistance made to local housing authorities in Wales on or after 27 April 2015.
3   HA 1996, s 204(1); H(W)A 2014, s 88(1). See also English Code, paras 19.37–19.40
     Welsh Code, paras 20.35–20.41.

19.215 However, there is no free-standing or general right of appeal to the
county court against every decision made under HA 1996, Pt 7[1] or H(W)A
2014, Pt 2. The prerequisites (examined in more detail below) for a county
court appeal against a substantive HA 1996, Pt 7[2] or H(W)A 2014, Pt 2,
decision are that:

(1)   the initial decision must have been a reviewable decision[3];
(2)   the applicant must have made a request for a review[4];
(3)   the review decision must have been properly notified[5];
(4)   the time limit for proper notification of a review decision must have
       expired[6];
(5)   the appeal must be on a point of law[7]; and
(6)   the appeal must be brought within the prescribed time limit (or such
       extension of it as the court may allow)[8].

1   As amended by HRA 2017, for applications for homelessness assistance to local housing
     authorities in England made on or after 3 April 2018.
2   As amended by HRA 2017, for applications for homelessness assistance to local housing
     authorities in England made on or after 3 April 2018.
3   See **19.12–19.70** for decisions made by local housing authorities in England that carry the
     right to request a review; see **19.71–19.86** for decisions made by local housing authorities in
     Wales that carry the right to request a review, and see **19.217–19.218**.
4   See **19.102–19.103**.
5   See **19.180–19.184**.
6   See **19.185–19.195**.
7   See **19.225–19.231**.
8   See **19.244–19.256**.

19.216 There is no need for the applicant to first obtain permission to appeal
from the court (or from anyone else)[1].

1   See *Buxton v Charnwood District Council* [2004] EWCA Civ 612, (2004) July *Legal Action*,
     p 19, CA, where the Court of Appeal made clear its disapproval of a local county
     court's practice of holding a preliminary consideration of the merits of HA 1996, s 204
     appeals.

Was the initial decision a reviewable decision?

19.217 An appeal can only be brought against one of the decisions set out in
the categories of decision conferring the right to request a review which are
listed at HA 1996, s 202(1)[1] or H(W)A 2014, s 85(1)–(3)[2].

1   As amended by HRA 2017, s 9, for applications for homelessness assistance to local housing
     authorities in England made on or after 3 April 2018.
2   *Hackney London Borough Council v Sareen* [2003] EWCA Civ 351, (2003) 35 HLR 54, CA.
     See **19.12–19.70** for decisions made by local housing authorities in England that carry the
     right to request a review; see **19.71–19.86** for decisions made by local housing authorities in
     Wales that carry the right to request a review.

19.218 If the decision does not fall into one of the categories specified, the applicant had no right to request a statutory review and has no right to bring a county court appeal. The appropriate challenge to any such decision is made by a claim for judicial review[1].

1   See **19.306–19.332.**

Did the applicant make the request for a review?

19.219 The statutory appeal rights are only available to 'an applicant'[1]. No member of the applicant's household, however closely related, has that statutory right. In *Lewis v Brent London Borough Council*[2], one of two joint applicants appealed to the county court, relying on the strength of the other joint applicant's case (her husband). The appeal was dismissed and the Court of Appeal refused permission to appeal, holding that the husband was not a party to the proceedings and the wife could not rely, in her own case, on any error in the decision relating to her husband. Nor can the appeal process be activated by others who may have an interest in challenging the local housing authority's original or review decision, eg a different local housing authority, a private registered provider or registered social landlord, or another homeless person.

1   HA 1996, s 204(1); H(W)A 2014, s 88(1).
2   [2005] EWCA Civ 605, (2005) July *Legal Action*, p 29, CA.

19.220 In addition, the applicant must actually have requested a statutory review in order to be able to bring an appeal[1]. If the applicant did not request a review of a reviewable decision, no appeal is available. The applicant in that situation could only reinstate his or her appeal rights by first asking the local housing authority to review its original decision. If the time limit for making a review request has expired, the local housing authority will also have to agree to extend the time limit for the making of the review request[2].

1   HA 1996, s 204(1); H(W)A 2014, s 88(1).
2   See **19.109–19.115.**

Was the review decision properly notified?

19.221 Because the right of appeal is only available to an applicant who has sought a review, the appeal will normally be brought against the review decision[1].

1   HA 1996, s 204(1)(a); H(W)A 2014, s 88(1)(a).

Has the time limit for proper notification of a review decision expired?

19.222 However, if the local housing authority has failed to notify the applicant of its review decision within the prescribed time limit (or any agreed extension of that time limit), the applicant can bring an appeal against the original decision, which was the subject of the request for the review[1]. This important provision prevents the applicant from being denied access to the courts by the local housing authority unduly prolonging the review procedure.

[1]   HA 1996, s 204(1)(b); H(W)A 2014, s 88(1)(b).

19.223 Even if the local housing authority has attempted to notify a review decision in time, a negative review decision is of no effect unless it has been communicated by written notice:

•   containing reasons for the review decision;
•   informing the applicant of the right to appeal; and
•   setting out the time limit for an appeal[1].

[1]   See **19.181**.

19.224 Faced with a review decision which is invalid by reason of non-compliance with one or more of these provisions, the applicant can appeal against the original decision (although adding an appeal against the defective review decision in the alternative in the Appellant's Notice might be a sensible precaution)[1]. Alternatively, if the applicant requires consideration of the facts relevant to his or her application, rather than an appeal on a point of law, he or she could apply by way of judicial review proceedings for a mandatory order requiring the local housing authority to complete the review and notify the applicant of its decision on review[2].

[1]   In *Bellamy v Hounslow London Borough Council* (reported under the name of *William v Wandsworth London Borough Council, Bellamy v Hounslow London Borough Council* [2006] EWCA Civ 535, [2006] HLR 42, CA), no review decision had been notified within the statutory time limits and the applicant appealed against the original decision. Before the appeal was heard in the county court, the local housing authority notified the applicant of its review decision. The appeal was then brought against both the original and the review decision. The Court of Appeal, considering an appeal against the decision of the county court judge, doubted whether HA 1996, s 204 conferred a right of appeal against the original decision once the review decision had been notified (albeit late), and approved the first-instance judge's decision to treat the appeal as being against the review decision. See **19.214–19.216**.

[2]   See **19.312**.

What is a 'point of law'?

19.225 Appeals can only be brought on a point of law 'arising from the decision' appealed against[1].

[1]   HA 1996, s 204(1); H(W)A 2014, s 88(1).

19.226 Points of law include any of the grounds of challenge that would normally be available in judicial review proceedings. Traditionally those grounds for judicial review have been classified as 'illegality', 'irrationality' and 'procedural impropriety'[1].

[1]   *Council of Civil Service Unions v Minister for the Civil Service* [1985] AC 374, HL.

19.227 A point of law can be properly said to arise from any decision that:

•   is based on a misconstruction of HA 1996, Pt 7[1] or H(W)A 2014, Pt 2, or of the relevant regulations;

- is *ultra vires*, ie beyond or in excess of the local housing authority's powers;
- is irrational;
- is taken in breach of natural justice;
- is the result of bias or bad faith;
- is reached without all necessary inquiries having been undertaken;
- is reached where there is no evidence to support factual findings made;
- is reached without regard to relevant factors;
- has failed to have regard to relevant factors; or
- gives inadequate reasons[2].

[1] As amended by HRA 2017, for applications for homelessness assistance to local housing authorities in England made on or after 3 April 2018.

[2] *Nipa Begum v Tower Hamlets London Borough Council*, (2000) 32 HLR 445, CA; see also *Runa Begum v Tower Hamlets* [2003] UKHL 5, [2006] AC 430, HL at 439 per Lord Bingham and at 426 per Lord Millett.

19.228 Questions of fact, as distinct from questions of law, are for the local housing authority to decide[1], unless the local housing authority's decision cannot be supported (in which case it will have made an error of law). Lord Millett in *Runa Begum v Tower Hamlets London Borough Council*[2] summarised the distinction between disputes of law and disputes of fact:

'A decision may be quashed if it is based on a finding of fact or inference from the facts which is perverse or irrational; or there was no evidence to support it; or it was made by reference to irrelevant factors or without regard to relevant factors. It is not necessary to identify a specific error of law; if the decision cannot be supported the court will infer that the decision-making authority misunderstood or overlooked relevant evidence or misdirected itself in law. The court cannot substitute its own findings of fact for those of the decision-making authority if there was evidence to support them; and the questions as to the weight to be given to a particular piece of evidence and the credibility of witnesses are for the decision-making authority and not the court.'

[1] *Puhlhofer v Hillingdon London Borough Council* [1986] AC 484, HL.

[2] [2003] UKHL 5, [2006] 2 AC 430, HL at 462 per Lord Millett. See also Wall LJ in *Wandsworth London Borough Council v Allison* [2008] EWCA Civ 354, (2008) June *Legal Action*, p 33, CA at [65].

19.229 Procedural errors in the making of inquiries, or in the making of the decision or review decision, are errors of law and can render the relevant decision unlawful. However, procedural unfairness in the appeal process, such as a failure to provide a copy of the applicant's housing file until six days before the county court hearing, does not necessarily render the decision under appeal wrong in law[1].

[1] *Goodger v Ealing London Borough Council* [2002] EWCA Civ 751, (2003) 35 HLR 6, CA.

19.230 What happens when the appellant is arguing that the review decision was based on a mistake of fact? In administrative law, there are two competing lines of authority. One argues that the issue of a mistaken fact should be absorbed into a traditional error of law approach, in that the decision-maker must have taken account of an irrelevant consideration, or failed to provide adequate or intelligible reasons, or failed to base the decision upon any evidence[1]. The other, more modern, approach holds that a mistake of fact giving rise to unfairness to the applicant can be a separate head of challenge in an appeal on a point of law. This latter view has prevailed in the context of asylum appeals[2]. The High Court has held that decisions about housing assistance fall within the scope of this principle[3]. There would ordinarily be four requirements that must be met before a mistake of fact could render a local housing authority's decision unfair and therefore unlawful:

- there must have been a mistake as to an existing fact, including a mistake as to the availability of evidence on a particular matter;
- the fact or evidence must have been 'established' in the sense that it was uncontentious and objectively verifiable;
- the applicant (or his or her advisers) must not have been responsible for the mistake; and
- the mistake must have played a material, but not necessarily decisive, part in the reasoning for the decision[4].

[1] *Wandsworth London Borough Council v A* [2000] 1 WLR 1246, CA at 1255 per Buxton LJ; and *R v London Residuary Body ex p Inner London Education Authority* (1987) *The Times*, July 24, CA per Watkins LJ.

[2] *E v Home Office* [2004] EWCA Civ 49, [2004] QB 1044, CA.

[3] *Richmond-upon-Thames Royal London Borough Council v Kubicek* [2012] EWHC 3292 (QB), (2013) January *Legal Action*, p 42 per Leggatt J at [26].

[4] *E v Secretary of State for the Home Department* [2004] EWCA Civ 49, [2004] QB 1044, CA at [66] per Carnwath LJ; and see also the analysis by Leggatt J in *Richmond-upon-Thames Royal London Borough Council v Kubicek* [2012] EWHC 3292 (QB) (2013) January *Legal Action*, p 42 at [22]–[30].

19.231 Chadwick LJ put it succinctly in *Williams v Wandsworth London Borough Council*[1]:

'where what is alleged is a misconstruction of ascertained facts, "obvious perversity" is required before the court can properly interfere with the authority's findings of fact.'

[1] [2006] EWCA Civ 535, [2006] HLR 42, CA at [20] per Chadwick LJ.

Disputed facts

19.232 Should the court hear evidence as to factual issues that are contested between the parties? It is well-established that discretionary decisions, such as whether accommodation is suitable for the needs of the applicant and of his or her household, involve evaluative judgments and should be left to the local housing authority and its officers to determine (subject to the court ensuring that no errors of law were made)[1]. However what about factual decisions that do not involve those evaluative judgments but instead require the local housing authority's officer to make a determination of hard fact, such as the age of a person, or whether or not the applicant had been 'notified' as required by HA 1996, Pt 7[2] or H(W)A 2014, Pt 2? The Supreme Court and the Court of Appeal have held that there is no scope for a court which is hearing an appeal on a point of law, brought under HA 1996, s 204, to determine factual disagreements for itself. The judge should only decide whether or not the conclusion of a reviewing officer is wrong in law, and is not entitled to consider the factual issues[3].

1 *Ali v Birmingham City Council* [2010] UKSC 8, [2010] 2 AC 39, SC. The applicant complained to the European Court of Human Rights (ECtHR) that her right of access to a fair trial by an impartial and independent tribunal had been infringed. On, the applicant's petition to the ECtHR, a Chamber of the ECtHR held that an application for homelessness did involve a determination of the applicant's civil rights but that the availability of an appeal to the county court on a point of law rendered the process compatible with Art 6: *Ali v UK* (2016) 63 EHRR 20. However, the Supreme Court has declined to follow the case of *Ali v UK* (2016) 63 EHRR 20, and confirmed its earlier decision that an applicant's civil rights are not determined in these circumstances: *Poshteh v Kensington & Chelsea Royal London Borough Council* [2017] UKSC 36, [2017] AC 624, SC at [37].
2 As amended by HRA 2017, for applications for homelessness assistance to local housing authorities in England made on or after 3 April 2018.
3 *Ali v Birmingham City Council* [2010] UKSC 8, [2010] 2 AC 39, SC; *Bubb v Wandsworth London Borough Council* [2011] EWCA Civ, 1285, [2012] HLR 13, CA and *Richmond-upon-Thames Royal London Borough Council v Kubicek* [2012] EWHC 3292 (QB) (2013) January *Legal Action*, p 42, QBD. A judge retains jurisdiction to consider whether, as a matter of fact, the applicant has complied with the procedural requirements for bringing an appeal under HA 1996, s 204, for example whether the appeal has been issued within the 21-day time limit, or the disputed identity of the reviewing officer, see *Butt v Hounslow London Borough Council* [2011] EWCA Civ 1327, (2012) January *Legal Action*, p 22, CA. In *R (Edwards) v Birmingham City Council* [2016] EWHC 173 (Admin), [2016] HLR 11, Admin Ct, the Administrative Court judge rejected a submission that the test at HA 1996, ss 183(1) and 188(1) of whether the local housing authorities has 'reason to believe' that an applicant may be homeless was a question of hard-edged fact, to be determined by a Court, and instead found that it was a value judgment to be determined by the local housing authority, at [69]–[71].

19.233 A recent review of the earlier case-law by the High Court concluded that there are two purposes for which factual evidence may be relevant on an appeal:

- to show how the review decision was reached, including what material was before the reviewing officer and what procedure was followed, this may be relevant where the allegation is that there was a failure to comply with the requirements of natural justice[1]; or
- to demonstrate that the decision subject to appeal was based on a material error of fact giving rise to unfairness[2].

1 *Richmond-upon-Thames Royal London Borough Council v Kubicek* [2012] EWHC 3292 (QB) (2013) January *Legal Action*, p 42, QBD per Leggatt J at [18]–[19] relying on *Butt v Hounslow London Borough Council* [2011] EWCA Civ 1327, (2012) January *Legal Action*, p 22, CA.
2 *Richmond-upon-Thames Royal London Borough Council v Kubicek* [2012] EWHC 3292 (QB) (2013) January *Legal Action*, p 42, QBD per Leggatt J at [21]–[29].

Fresh evidence

19.234 The starting-point is that a county court will not generally admit fresh evidence on an appeal at all. However, if an applicant is seeking to argue that the local housing authority made a mistake of fact, such as to amount to an error of law[1], or that it failed to carry out all necessary inquiries, or there has been some procedural impropriety, he or she may have to present new information to the court in order to show that one of the local housing authority's factual conclusions was based on a mistake of fact, or a failure to carry out necessary inquiries[2]. The authorities on the presentation of new information have been described as 'unusually fact-sensitive' rather than laying down general propositions of law. Even if the evidence put forward passes the relevance test[3], the party seeking to rely on that evidence also has to address the traditional test for the submission of new information on an appeal which can be found in *Ladd v Marshall*[4]. That case decided that the court will only permit new evidence to be produced at an appeal stage if:

(1)   it is evidence that could not have been obtained without reasonable diligence for use at trial (or, in a homelessness context, at the review or original decision stage);

(2)   the evidence would probably have an important (although it need not be decisive) influence on the outcome; and

(3)   the evidence is such as is apparently credible[5].

1   See **19.225–19.231**.
2   In *Cramp v Hastings Borough Council* [2005] EWCA Civ 1005, [2005] HLR 48, CA, the Court of Appeal overturned county court decisions that inadequate inquiries had been made, and noted that the inquiries said by the appellants' solicitors to be necessary in the grounds of appeal had not been suggested by those same solicitors during the review process.
3   See **19.233**.
4   [1954] 1 WLR 1489, CA.
5   See *Richmond-upon-Thames Royal London Borough Council v Kubicek* [2012] EWHC 3292 (QB) (2013) January *Legal Action*, p 42, QBD, for an application of the *Ladd v Marshall* test on admitting fresh evidence.

19.235 In *Cramp v Hastings Borough Council*,[1] the Court of Appeal warned that:

'judges in the county court need to be astute to ensure that evidential material over and above the contents of the housing file and the reviewing officer's decision is limited to that which is necessary to illuminate the points of law that are to be relied on in the appeal, or the issue of what, if any, relief ought to be granted. An undisciplined approach to the admission of new evidence may lead to the danger that the reviewing officer is found guilty of an error of law for not taking into account evidence that was never before her, notwithstanding the applicant's opportunity to make representations about the original decision.[2]'

1   [2005] EWCA Civ 1005, [2005] HLR 48, CA.
2   At [71] per Brooke LJ.

19.236 If fresh evidence is admitted, it will generally be in the form of witness statements and not oral evidence, so there will be no cross-examination[1].

1   *Bubb v Wandsworth London Borough Council* [2011] EWCA Civ, 1285, [2012] HLR 13, CA per Lord Neuberger MR at [24]–[26].

Paying for an appeal

19.237 Taking cases to court is not cheap, and an appeal in the county court is no exception. The court fee for issuing the appeal is £140[1], and the normal rule is that the unsuccessful party will pay the other party's legal costs, so there is a considerable financial risk. Usually, appeals take a day, or half a day, of court time and require considerable preparation.

1   At the time of writing, although it may increase. This can be waived where a litigant in person can satisfy a disposable capital and monthly income test: Civil Proceedings Fees Order 2008,

SI 2008/1053, art 5 and Sch 2, as amended. The up-to-date figures are at www.justice.gov.uk/courts/fees/.

19.238 Some applicants will qualify for free preliminary advice from a lawyer or legal adviser under the Legal Help scheme. If an appeal is thought to have merit, application can be made for full legal aid (certificate for legal representation) to fund the appeal[1]. Specialist housing solicitors and agencies with Legal Aid Agency (LAA) housing contracts will be able to grant emergency legal aid so that work on an appeal can start quickly. The criteria under which the LAA will grant public funding for homelessness appeals are set out in regs 53–56 of the Civil Legal Aid (Merits Criteria) Regulations[2]. As already noted, the normal rule is that the unsuccessful party will pay the other party's legal costs[3].

[1] Legal Aid Sentencing and Punishment of Offenders Act 2012, s 9 and Sch 1, para 34.
[2] SI 2013/104.
[3] See *Waltham Forest London Borough Council v Maloba* [2007] EWCA Civ 1281, [2008] HLR 26, CA, where the local housing authority argued unsuccessfully that there should be a general practice on HA 1996, s 204 appeals that any order for costs made against a local housing authority should be subject to a stay until after the re-determination of the decision under appeal and any subsequent appeal from that re-determination. If the losing party is in receipt of legal aid, the court will postpone determination of the amount which he or she should pay: Legal Aid Sentencing and Punishment of Offenders Act 2012, s 26.

19.239 It is not unusual for appeals brought either under HA 1996, s 204[1], or under H(W)A 2014, s 88, to be settled after the appeal has been issued, but before the hearing of the appeal. Usually the local housing authority will agree that the review decision should be quashed and therefore that a new review decision should be made. What should be the normal order as to costs in such circumstances? The principles can be found in *R (M) v Croydon London Borough Council*[2]. The general rule is that a successful party who obtains all the relief he or she sought, whether by consent or after a contested hearing, is entitled to have his or her costs paid by the unsuccessful party. This general rule applies in judicial review claims and appeals brought under HA 1996, s 204[3], or H(W)A 2014, s 88[4] as it does in other areas of civil litigation. Each case turns on its own facts. A case might have an unusual feature which could justify departing from the usual costs order. The Court of Appeal has identified four types of case:

- Case (i): where the claimant has been wholly successful either following a contested hearing or pursuant to a settlement: the claimant should, as the successful party, recover his or her costs unless there are special circumstances;
- Case (ii): the claimant has only succeeded in part, whether following a contested hearing, or pursuant to a settlement: when deciding how to allocate liability for costs, the court will normally consider how reasonable the claimant was in pursuing the unsuccessful part of the claim, how important that part of the claim was compared to the successful part of the claim, and how much the costs were increased as a result of the claimant pursuing the unsuccessful part of the claim; where there has been a trial, the court will be in a reasonably good position to make those findings; where there has been a settlement, the

court may be able to form a view as to the appropriate costs orders but 'there is often much to be said for concluding that there is no order for costs'[5];

- Case (iii): where there has been some compromise which does not actually reflect the claimant's claims: the court is often unable to gauge whether there is a successful party and there may be an even more powerful argument that the position should be no order for costs; but it may also be sensible to look at the underlying claims and inquire whether it was tolerably clear who would have won, if the matter had not settled; if it is tolerably clear who would have won, that may strongly support a contention that that party did better out of the settlement, and therefore did win and should be awarded his or her costs[6]; and
- Case (iv): where the appeal has become academic as a result of new evidence produced after the review decision, either the local housing authority should recover its costs, or there should be no order for costs, depending on an assessment on whether the local housing authority would have succeeded or not[7].

[1] As amended by HRA 2017, s 4(6), for applications for homelessness assistance made to local housing authorities in England on or after 3 April 2018.
[2] [2012] EWCA Civ 595, [2012] 1 WLR 2607, CA.
[3] As amended by HRA 2017, s 4(6), for applications for homelessness assistance made to local housing authorities in England on or after 3 April 2018.
[4] *Unichi v Southwark London Borough Council* [2013] EWHC 3681 (QB), (2013) December *Legal Action*, p 34, QBD.
[5] *R (M) v Croydon London Borough Council* [2012] EWCA Civ 595, [2012] 1 WLR 2607, CA per Lord Neuberger at [61]–[62].
[6] *R (M) v Croydon London Borough Council* [2012] EWCA Civ 595, [2012] 1 WLR 2607, CA per Lord Neuberger at [61]–[63].
[7] *Lopes v Croydon London Borough Council* [2016] EWCA Civ 465, CA, reported as *Handley & Evans v Lake Jackson Solicitors (A Firm)*, [2016] EWCA Civ 465, [2016] 1 WLR 3138, CA per Christopher Clarke LJ at [70], followed by *Croydon London Borough Council v Lopes* [2017] EWHC 33 (QB), [2017] HLR 15, QBD.

19.240 The Court of Appeal has also observed that parties should be willing to try to agree not only the substantive issues in the case, but also the position on costs. Where a judge cannot fairly and sensibly make a decision on the liability for costs without spending disproportionate time, the default position should be an order that there be no order for costs[1].

[1] Which has the effect that each party pays his or her own costs or, if a party is receiving legal aid, the LAA will pay that party's costs: CPR PD44, para 4.2. For one example of a decision that the costs order should be no order for costs, see *Ersus v Redbridge London Borough Council* [2016] EWHC 1025 (QB).

19.241 These principles were applied to appeals brought under HA 1996, s 204[1], or under H(W)A 2014, s 88, in *Unichi v Southwark London Borough Council*[2].

[1] As amended by HRA 2017, s 4(6), for applications for homelessness assistance made to local housing authorities in England on or after 3 April 2018.
[2] [2013] EWHC 3681 (QB) (2013) December *Legal Action*, p 34, QBD. See also *Harripaul v Lewisham London Borough Council* [2012] EWCA Civ 266, [2012] HLR 24, CA, decided before the Court of Appeal delivered judgment in *R (M) v Croydon London Borough Council* [2012] EWCA Civ 595, [2012] 1 WLR 2607, CA.

19.242 Part of the Court of Appeal's reasoning in *R (M) v Croydon London Borough Council*[1] relied on the fact that, in judicial review claims, the claimant will have sent a letter before claim in accordance with the Pre-Action Protocol for Judicial Review. There is no equivalent pre-action protocol for appeals brought under HA 1996, s 204[2] or H(W)A 2014, s 88. However, advisers could consider sending any draft grounds of appeal to the local housing authority before the appeal has to be issued, so as to give the local housing authority an opportunity to consider the merits of the appeal. Or, if the appeal has to be issued urgently in order to comply with the 21-day deadline, advisers could consider issuing the appeal and asking for a stay so as to provide the local housing authority with an opportunity to consider the grounds of appeal, and the merits of the appeal.

[1] [2012] EWCA Civ 595, [2012] 1 WLR 2607, CA.
[2] As amended by HRA 2017, s 4(6), for applications for homelessness assistance made to local housing authorities in England on or after 3 April 2018.

19.243 Since December 2013, the Administrative Court has published guidance which applies where parties have settled a judicial review claim, but have been unable to agree the issue of costs[1]. The Guidance provides for a judge to decide liability for costs on the basis of written submissions from the parties. The Guidance does not directly apply to appeals brought under HA 1996, s 204[2] or H(W)A 2014, s 88. However, it can be taken to represent best practice in order to avoid accruing legal costs. The Guidance provides that if the parties are able to agree settlement of all issues in the case except for those of costs, they could jointly apply to the court for an order permitting them to file written submissions on the issue of costs and for those submissions to be considered by a judge without holding an oral hearing[3].

[1] *Guidance as to how the parties should assist the court when applications for costs are made following settlement of claims for judicial review* (Administrative Court office, December 2013). See also *The Administrative Court Judicial Review Guide 2017*, Judiciary for England and Wales, July 2017, chapter 23.
[2] As amended by HRA 2017, s 4(6), for applications for homelessness assistance made to local housing authorities in England on or after 3 April 2018.
[3] The practice in the County Court sitting in Central London is for costs to be determined in a short hearing, rather than on the basis of written submissions.

How an appeal is brought

Time limit

19.244 If the appeal is being made against a decision reached on review, the appeal must be brought within 21 days of the appellant being 'notified' of the review decision[1]. The time limit therefore begins to run on the day after the notice of review decision is actually received by the appellant or by his or her agent rather than the date on the review decision letter or the date it was sent[2]. The last day of the 21-day period is the twenty-first day from the date of receipt, so that if a review decision is received on 4 July, the last day for bringing the appeal is 25 July[3].

[1] HA 1996, s 204(2); H(W)A 2014, s 88(2).
[2] *Aadan v Brent London Borough Council* (2000) 32 HLR 848, CA at 851 per Chadwick LJ. This is a different calculation to the time limit for receipt of requests for review, where HA

1996, s 202(3) and H(W)A 2014, s 85(5) specifically state that the 21-day period begins from the date of receipt of the original decision: 'beginning with the day' see **19.109–19.115**.
3   *Aadan v Brent London Borough Council* (1999) 32 HLR 848, CA.

19.245 If the appeal is brought in respect of an original decision made under HA 1996, s 184(3) or notice of assessment made under H(W)A 2014, s 63(1)[1], the appeal must be brought within 21 days of the date on which the review of that decision should have been notified. This time limit will therefore be calculated from the last day of the time limit for the conclusion of the review[2]. As already noted[3], that will usually be a date eight weeks after the date on which the request for a review was made, meaning that an appeal against an original decision should be brought within 21 days from the end of the eight-week period[4].

1   See **19.215**.
2   HA 1996, s 204(2); H(W)A 2014, s 88(2).
3   See **19.185–19.195**.
4   Note the different time limits for notification of the review decision for different types of review decisions made by local housing authorities in England, see **19.188–19.193**.

Bringing the appeal

19.246 The procedure for the appeal brought under HA 1996, s 204[1], or under H(W)A 2014, s 88, is governed primarily by CPR Pt 52 and PD52A, PD52B and PD52D, para 28.

1   As amended by HRA 2017, s 4(6) and 5(11), for applications for homelessness assistance made to local housing authorities in England on or after 3 April 2018.

19.247 An appeal is brought when an Appellant's Notice (court form N161) is filed at the county court[1]. 'Filing' means 'delivering it, by post or otherwise, to the court office'[2]. The form can be sent by fax or, in certain specified courts, by email or by online form[3]. Although criticised by the Court of Appeal[4], Practice Directions 5A and 5B specify that, where a fax or email is received after 4pm on a working day, the document sent should not be recorded as 'filed' until the next working day[5]. However, documents physically posted through a court's letterbox after close of business on a working day, but before midnight, are 'filed' on that day, and not on the following working day[6]. Where the final day falls on a non-working day, the period in which the form must be filed ends on the next day on which the court office is open[7].

1   PD52A, para 4.2.
2   CPR 2.3(1) and 5.5 and PD5B.
3   CPR, PD5B.
4   *Van Aken v Camden London Borough Council* [2002] EWCA Civ 1724, (2003) 35 HLR 33, CA per Ward LJ at [60].
5   PD5A, para 5.3(6); PD5B, para 4.2.
6   *Van Aken v Camden London Borough Council* [2002] EWCA Civ 1724, (2003) 35 HLR 33, CA.
7   CPR 2.8(5); *Aadan v Brent London Borough Council* (2000) 32 HLR 848, CA.

19.248 If there is any dispute over the date on which the appellant was notified of the review decision (or as to the date on which the time limit for review expired), the court itself will have to decide the question of the correct date, and go on to decide whether or not the appeal was filed within the 21-day time limit[1].

[1] See *Bakare v Waltham Forest London Borough Council* (1998) December *Legal Action*, p 27, Bow County Court, where the local housing authority put in evidence as to the method and likely date of delivery and the appellant had no contrary evidence. The court held that he had been notified more than 21 days before the appeal had been filed; *Lambeth London Borough Council v Namegembe* [2006] EWHC 3608 (Ch), (2007) February *Legal Action*, p 31, ChD; and the unusual case of *Dawkins v Central Bedfordshire Council* [2013] EWHC 4757 (QB) (2013) September *Legal Action*, p 31, QBD. These decisions are made under the county court's own jurisdiction to apply the Civil Procedure Rules and are different from the prohibition on courts making factual decisions in areas that were the province of the local housing authority's decision-maker, see **19.232–19.233**.

19.249 As already noted[1], notification is treated as having occurred if the decision has been made available at the local housing authority's office for a reasonable period for collection[2]. However, this deeming provision only applies where the review decision has *not* been sent to the appellant.

[1] See **19.180**.
[2] HA 1996, s 203(8); H(W)A 2014, s 86(7).

Extending the time limit

19.250 The county court may give permission for an appeal to be brought after the end of the 21-day period if it is satisfied that there was a good reason[1]:

- for the failure to bring the appeal in time; and
- (where permission is sought after the expiry of the deadline for issue) for any delay in applying for permission to extend time[2].

Permission may be applied for either during the 21-day period, or after it has ended[3].

[1] HA 1996, s 204(2A); H(W)A 2014, s 88(3).
[2] HA 1996, s 204(2A); H(W)A 2014, s 88(3).
[3] HA 1996, s 204(2A); H(W)A 2014, s 88(3).

19.251 If the appellant is seeking permission to extend time that application should be made in the Appellant's Notice and should be supported by a witness statement explaining the good reason for the failure to bring the appeal in time and for any delay since the time limit expired[1].

[1] CPR 52 and PD52B, paras 3.1–3.3.

19.252 The court may give permission to extend time before the expiry of the 21-day period.[1] This provision might be thought helpful where it is appreciated that the time limit is about to expire but an Appellant's Notice cannot be prepared in time. But if the applicant can manage to lodge an application to extend the time limit, it is difficult to envisage a case in which the applicant (or his or her advisers) could not have filed even a very basic Appellant's Notice. Indeed, a professional adviser may be in difficulties if no such Appellant's Notice is filed in time, because it is always possible that a time extension, for which an application is made instead, will be refused.

[1] HA 1996, s 204(2A)(a); H(W)A 2014, s 88(3)(a).

19.253 If the concern is that it is getting late on a working day, and that day is the last day of the 21-day time limit, some comfort can be taken from the Court of Appeal's decision in *Van Aken v Camden London Borough Council*[1]. The appellant's advisers, confronted with the imminent expiry of the 21-day period, should aim to file the notice of appeal by posting it through the letterbox of the court (if one exists) at any time until midnight of that twenty-first day, rather than apply for permission to extend time.

[1]   *Van Aken v Camden London Borough Council* [2002] EWCA Civ 1724, [2003] 35 HLR 33, CA. See also **19.244–19.245**.

19.254 In *Short v Birmingham City Council*[1], the High Court upheld the county court judge's approach to whether or not to grant permission to appeal out of time. The court should first consider the reasons for delay and only consider the merits of the appeal, and the hardship to the applicant, if there were good reasons for that delay. In *Barrett v Southwark London Borough Council*[2], the judge said 'good reason is a phrase in common parlance, which . . . does not need elaboration[3]' and that all the circumstances were relevant[4]. Once it had been decided that there was 'good reason', permission should be given, unless the appeal is 'hopeless'[5]. In *Peake v Hackney London Borough Council*[6], the High Court upheld a decision of a county court judge to refuse permission. It held that it was not helpful to talk of an objective or subjective test; the court must be satisfied whether there is good reason. Whether a reason or combination of reasons amounts to a good reason is a question of fact, involving a value judgment. The circumstances of the individual applicant may be relevant if there is a link between those characteristics and the failure to bring the appeal in time. The judge should first identify the reasons for the failure to bring the appeal in time and for any delay in applying for permission, and then determine whether or not those reasons are good reasons in the particular case[7].

[1]   [2004] EWHC 2112 (QB), [2005] HLR 6, QBD.
[2]   [2008] EWHC 1568 (Comm), QBD.
[3]   *Barrett v Southwark London Borough Council* [2008] EWHC 1568 (Comm), (2008) September *Legal Action*, p 26, QBD at [24] per Sir Thomas Morrison.
[4]   In *Barrett v Southwark London Borough Council* [2008] EWHC 1568 (Comm), (2008) September *Legal Action*, p 26, QBD, permission was given to bring an appeal four weeks late, where a profoundly deaf applicant had made diligent attempts to obtain legal advice and had continued to try to find legal representation, even though she had received unfavourable advice.
[5]   *Barrett v Southwark London Borough Council* [2008] EWHC 1568 (Comm), (2008) September *Legal Action*, p 26, QBD at [28] per Sir Thomas Morrison.
[6]   [2013] EWHC 2528 (QB).
[7]   *Peake v Hackney London Borough Council* [2013] EWHC 2528 (QB), (2013) September *Legal Action*, p 31, QBD per Lewis J at [16]–[19]. See *Ali & Grover v Ealing London Borough Council* (2013) November *Legal Action*, p 33, Brentford County Court, for an example of a county court judge finding that there was a good reason both for the one day's delay in filing the notice of appeal and for the delay in making the application to extend time; and see also *Ranza v Northern Ireland Housing Executive* [2015] NIQB 13, where there was good reason for a delay of three days.

19.255 The Court must consider both limbs of the test before granting permission. In *Poorsalehy v Wandsworth London Borough Council*[1], the court found that there was a good reason for the delay of one working day in filing the appeal, but that there was no evidence of any reasons for the delay in applying for permission. It followed that the applicant had failed to discharge the burden of explaining to the court the delay in applying for permission[2].

1   [2013] EWHC 3687 (QB), (2013) December *Legal Action*, p 34, QBD,
2   In that case, the applicant argued that the irresistible inference, given the facts of the case, was that it was his legal representatives who were responsible for the delay in making the application and not him. The High Court was not prepared to draw that inference without evidence. He also found that there was no rule of law that delay by legal representatives would exculpate the applicant and, by inference, always amount to 'good reason'. Each case must depend on the evidence available on the particular facts. See also *Lounis v Newham London Borough Council* [2016] EWHC 1857 (QB) where the judge was not wrong in law to refuse to draw an inference, without there being any evidence, that because the applicant had handed the review decision to apparently competent solicitors within the time-limit, incompetence by the solicitors should be inferred.

Procedure

19.256 The Civil Procedure Rules (CPR) and Practice Directions (PD) (particularly CPR 52 and PDs 52A, 52B and 52D) govern the procedure for the county court appeal[1]. The appellant should file and serve the following documents:

- the Appellant's Notice on form N161 plus two additional copies for the court and a copy for the respondent;
- grounds of appeal attached to the N161;
- a copy of the decision subject to the appeal; and
- proposed case management directions[2].

1   General procedure is at PD52A. Procedure for county court appeals is at PD52B. Specific requirements for HA 1996, s 204 (as amended by HRA 2017, s 4(6), for applications for homelessness assistance made to local housing authorities in England on or after 3 April 2018), or H(W)A 2014, s 88, appeals are at para 28 of PD52D.
2   PD52B, para 4.2) and PD52D, para 28.1

19.257 If the appellant has not received the whole of the homelessness file from the local housing authority, then an application should be made in the Appellant's Notice for a direction requiring the local housing authority (which in the appeal will be described as 'the respondent') to disclose it. The application can be made in the proposed case management directions which are filed when the Appellant's Notice is issued[1]. The case management directions will normally propose that respondent disclose the whole of the homelessness file within a specified time (usually 14 days), that the appellant may amend his or her grounds of appeal, if required, within 14 days of receipt of the disclosure and should file and serve a skeleton argument and any witness statements within the same period, and that the respondent file and serve its skeleton argument and any witness statements 14 days from receipt of the appellant's skeleton argument[2].

1   PD52D, para 28.1 and **19.256**.
2   See **19.232–19.236** for the limited circumstances when witness statements might be admitted.

19.258 The respondent should consider the proposed case management directions and either agree them or file and serve its own proposed directions within 14 days of having been served with the Appellant's Notice. It should also disclose any documents relevant to the appeal which had not previously been disclosed within the same 14-day period[1].

1   PD52D, para 28.1(5).

19.259 As soon as practicable, and in any event within 35 days of the filing of the Appellant's Notice, the appellant should file an appeal bundle which contains:

- a copy of the Appellant's Notice;
- a copy of the appellant's skeleton argument and any skeleton argument filed at that stage by the respondent;
- a copy of the decision subject to the appeal;
- any witness statements; and
- any other relevant documents such as extracts from the homelessness file, if received from the local housing authority, and any relevant correspondence[1].

1   PD52B, para 6.4. In *Cramp v Hastings Borough Council* [2005] EWCA Civ 1005, [2005] HLR 48, CA, the Court of Appeal stated that it was 'thoroughly bad practice to state the barest possible grounds in the original notice of appeal . . . and then to delay formulating and serving very substantial amended grounds of appeal for five months so that they surfaced for the first time less than a week before the appeal hearing' (Brooke LJ at [72]). It also said that the appeal bundle should be limited to the grounds of appeal, the decision being appealed and only those documents which the appellant reasonably considers necessary to enable the appeal court to reach its decision on the hearing. Documents extraneous to the issues to be considered on appeal must be excluded, and it was quite wrong to photocopy the entire contents of a bulky housing file regardless of whether it was necessary to do so.

19.260 The usual practice is that witness statements need not be filed by either party. If the points of law raised can be determined solely on the contents of the review decision and the relevant parts of the homelessness file, there will be no need for any witness statement by the applicant. If, on the other hand, one of the points of law is that the local housing authority has failed to make all necessary inquiries, it can be helpful for the applicant to make a witness statement in which he or she sets out what inquiries should have been made and, if possible, what the results of those inquiries would have been. If the local housing authority is satisfied that its review decision is correct, there will normally be no need for a witness statement from the reviewing officer or any other officer. Sometimes local housing authorities will want to put in witness statements, usually by the decision-maker, to explain or elucidate the reasons contained in the written decision. The purpose and admissibility of those witness statements (formerly affidavits) was considered in detail by the Court of Appeal in *R v Westminster City Council ex p Ermakov*[1]. Where the contents of the witness statement serve to elucidate the reasons contained in the decision letter, they will be admissible. Examples of circumstances in which evidence might elucidate, rather than alter, the original decision were said to include where: 'an error has been made in transcription or expression, or a word or words inadvertently omitted, or where the language used may be in some way lacking in clarity.[2]' Where, however, the contents fundamentally alter the reasons in the decision letter, they should not be admitted.

1   *R v Westminster City Council ex p Ermakov* (1996) 28 HLR 819, [1996] 2 All ER 302, CA.

2   *R v Westminster City Council ex p Ermakov* (1996) 28 HLR 819, [1996] 2 All ER 302, CA at 315H per Hutchison LJ; and see also *R v Westminster City Council ex p Khanam* (unreported) 9 May 1997, QBD, and *Hijazi v Kensington and Chelsea Royal London Borough Council* [2003] EWCA Civ 692, [2003] HLR 72, CA. In *Swords v Secretary of State for Communities and Local Government* [2007] EWCA Civ 795, [2008] HLR 17, CA, the Court of Appeal approved five reasons for admitting a witness statement into evidence, including '[i] it must, as a matter of common sense, be easier for a decision-maker to secure permission to make a belated assertion that she took into account a factor to which she had not previously referred but gave it no weight than that she gave weight to a factor to which she had not previously referred; for in the former case the lack of previous reference would be inherently less significant': Wilson LJ at [47].

19.261 In *Bellamy v Hounslow London Borough Council*[1], the Court of Appeal made some cautionary remarks about the use of witness statements in second appeals[2], which also hold true for first-instance appeals to the county court:

> 'Witness statements are a proper vehicle for relevant and admissible evidence going to the issue before the court, and for nothing else. Argument is for advocates. Innuendo has no place at all.[3]'

1   Reported under the name of *William v Wandsworth London Borough Council, Bellamy v Hounslow London Borough Council* [2006] EWCA Civ 535, [2006] HLR 42, CA.
2   See **19.293–19.303**.
3   *Bellamy v Hounslow London Borough Council* [2006] EWCA Civ 535, [2006] HLR 42, CA at [80] per Sedley LJ.

19.262 Once the homelessness file has been disclosed, any witness statements and skeleton arguments have been filed, and a bundle of documents has been prepared[1], the appeal will generally be ready for hearing. The hearing itself will consist of oral argument, based on the skeleton arguments. Since the appeal is on a point of law, there is not generally any need for live evidence to be given[2].

1   See **19.259**. Advocates preparing a bundle of statutes and authorities should bear in mind the comments of Lord CArnwath, JSC, in *Poshteh v Kensington & Chelsea Royal London Borough Council* [2017] UKSC 36, [2017] AC 624, SC [44]–[47] warning against a proliferation of authorities.
2   See **19.232–19.236**.

19.263 Homelessness appeals may only be heard by a circuit judge, not a district judge[1].

1   CPR Pt 2 and PD2B, para 9.

Powers of the county court on an appeal

19.264 If the court concludes that there has been an error of law, it may confirm, quash or vary the decision which is the subject of the appeal[1]. If there is no error of law, it will dismiss the appeal.

1   HA 1996, s 204(3); H(W)A 2014, s 88(4).

Confirming the decision

19.265 The court is only entitled to confirm a decision that contains an error of law in one of two circumstances:

(1)   if it is satisfied that a properly directed local housing authority, which did not make the same error of law, would inevitably have reached the same decision[1]; or

(2)   if it is satisfied that the bringing of the appeal was an abuse of process in the sense that bringing the appeal was for practical purposes 'pointless', even though there was some irregularity in the decision appealed against[2].

[1]   The test is one of inevitability. If there is any real possibility of a different conclusion being reached, it is wrong for the court to confirm the decision: *Ali and Nessa v Newham London Borough Council* [2001] EWCA Civ 73, [2002] HLR 20, CA.

[2]   *O'Connor v Kensington and Chelsea Royal London Borough Council* [2004] EWCA Civ 394, [2004] HLR 37, CA at [42]–[43] per Waller LJ and Carnwath LJ, giving majority judgments on this point (Sedley LJ dissenting). In *Ugiagbe v Southwark London Borough Council* [2009] EWCA Civ 31, [2009] HLR 35, CA, by the time the appeal reached the Court of Appeal, the applicant had found herself accommodation. The Court of Appeal rejected the local housing authority's submission that the appeal was academic. Because there was a risk that the applicant might again become homeless, it quashed the review decision, see Lloyd LJ at [30]–[32].

Quashing the decision

19.266 Normally, where there is an error of law, the court will simply quash the decision that has been the subject of the appeal. If a review decision is quashed on appeal, then the review process will not have been concluded because no legally correct review decision has been reached. The reviewing officer will need to re-open the review and the applicant and the local housing authority will need to agree in writing a new deadline for the completion of the review (as the original prescribed time limit will inevitably have expired by this stage)[1].

[1]   See **19.185–19.195**. If, however, the local housing authority has applied for permission to bring a second appeal, the Court of Appeal has suggested that both parties should agree that the new review decision should not be notified until the appeal process has been concluded: *William v Wandsworth London Borough Council* [2006] EWCA Civ 535, [2006] HLR 42, CA at [42] per Chadwick LJ.

19.267 If the decision quashed on appeal is the original decision, then the local housing authority will have to take a fresh decision, having carried out such further inquiries as it considers necessary. It is by no means inevitable that, following a successful appeal, the new decision reached will be different in effect from the one quashed. In either case, the reviewing officer or the local housing authority must make the fresh decision on the basis of the facts and information as they stand at the date of that new decision, which may be very different from how they stood at the date of the quashed decision or even at the date of the quashing.

Varying the decision

19.268 It is unusual for the court to exercise its power to *vary* the decision appealed against. It may do so where it is satisfied, on the evidence, that there was only one lawful conclusion for the local housing authority to have reached, or, as Sedley LJ has put it: 'where the decision was erroneous in law and only a contrary decision was lawfully possible'[1]. In *Purewal v Ealing London Borough Council*[2], Sullivan LJ said: '[t]he normal consequence of a decision being flawed because of a failure to take into consideration relevant factors is that the decision is quashed and the matter is remitted to the decision taker to reconsider the matter, taking into account the factors which were omitted from the previous, unlawful decision. [Counsel for the local authority] accepts that there may be cases in which the material that the decision taker has not considered is so compelling that it could rationally lead to only one conclusion, and that in such a case the court may vary the decision to give effect to that sole, permissible conclusion'[3].

[1]   *Ozbek v Ipswich Borough Council* [2006] EWCA Civ 534, [2006] HLR 41 CA at [63] per Sedley LJ; see also *Deugi v Tower Hamlets London Borough Council* [2006] EWCA Civ 159, [2006] HLR 28, CA per May LJ at [36].

[2]   [2013] EWCA Civ 1579, [2014] HLR 5, CA

[3]   *Purewal v Ealing London Borough Council* [2013] EWCA Civ 1579, [2014] HLR 5, CA per Sullivan LJ at [16]. See also *Johnston v City of Westminster Council* [2015] EWCA Civ 554, [2015] HLR 35, CA, where the Court of Appeal directed itself that a county court was not limited to allowing or dismissing the appeal but may make such order varying the decision as it thought fit per Gloster LJ at [39]. In that case, part of the review decision was varied and the remainder of the decision confirmed.

19.269 In *Bond v Leicester City Council*[1], the Court of Appeal held that, had the local housing authority asked itself the right question, it was 'more likely than not' that it would have found that the applicant was homeless and the court varied the decision accordingly. In *Ekwuru v Westminster City Council*[2], the Court of Appeal held that, where the local housing authority had conceded that three successive statutory review decisions had been wrong in law, and there was no material which would entitle it to reach a conclusion other than that the applicant had not become homeless intentionally, it would exceptionally vary the latest decision rather than quash it[3].

[1]   [2001] EWCA Civ 1544, [2002] HLR 6, CA.

[2]   *Ekwuru v Westminster City Council* [2003] EWCA Civ 1293, [2004] HLR 13, CA.

[3]   See also the following cases in which the power to vary was used: *Woodrow v Lewisham London Borough Council* (2000) November *Legal Action*, p 23, Woolwich County Court; *Mohammed v Waltham Forest London Borough Council* (2002) October *Legal Action*, p 30, Bow County Court; *Yousif v Newham London Borough Council* (2002) December *Legal Action*, p 22, Bow County Court; *Bond v Leicester City Council* [2001] EWCA Civ 1544, [2002] HLR 6, CA; *Lane and Ginda v Islington London Borough Council* (2001) April *Legal Action*, p 21, Clerkenwell County Court; *Fetaj v Lambeth London Borough Council* (2002) September *Legal Action*, p 31, Lambeth County Court; *Houghton v Sheffield City Council* [2006] EWCA Civ 1799, (2007) March *Legal Action*, p 18, CA; *Benson v Lewisham London Borough Council* (2007) October *Legal Action*, p 26, Central London County Court; *Bolah v Croydon London Borough Council* (2008) February *Legal Action*, p 40, Central London County Court; *Quaid v Westminster City Council* (2008) February *Legal Action*, p 41, Central London County Court; *Adekunle v Islington London Borough Council* (2009) November *Legal Action*, p 25, Mayor's and City of London County Court; *Villiers v Lewisham London Borough Council* (2009) November *Legal Action*, p 26, Central London County Court; *O'Callaghan v Southwark London Borough Council* (2010) May *Legal Action*, p 23, Lambeth County Court; *Abdi v Waltham Forest London Borough Council*

(2012), (2013) January *Legal Action*, p 42, Bow County Court; and *Johnston v City of Westminster Council* [2015] EWCA Civ 554, [2015] HLR 35, CA.

19.270 In *Tower Hamlets London Borough Council v Deugi*[1], the local housing authority had conceded that its decision that the applicant was not eligible was wrong, and the Court of Appeal held that varying the decision would provide some enduring benefit to the applicant, and so the county court judge was correct to vary it. In *Slater v Lewisham London Borough Council*[2], the Court of Appeal agreed with the county court judge that there was no real prospect that the local housing authority, acting rationally and with the benefit of any further inquiries it might make, could conclude that it was reasonable for an offer of accommodation to be accepted, and it upheld the county court judge's decision to vary a review decision to a finding that the duty to provide accommodation had not been discharged.

[1]   [2006] EWCA Civ 159, [2006] HLR 28, CA.
[2]   [2006] EWCA Civ 394, [2006] HLR 37, CA.

19.271 The House of Lords varied a review decision in *Moran v Manchester City Council*[1], having found that the applicant could not have become homeless intentionally from a women's refuge, because, as a matter of law, the refuge in that case had not been reasonable for the applicant to continue to occupy[2].

[1]   *Ali & others v Birmingham City Council, Moran v Manchester City Council* [2009] UKHL 36, [2009] 1 WLR 1506, HL at [65]–[66] per Baroness Hale.
[2]   See **10.126**.

19.272 It may also be appropriate to use this power where the behaviour of the local housing authority has been open to criticism, eg where it has repeatedly made and then withdrawn defective decisions[1].

[1]   *Mohamud v Lambeth London Borough Council* (2002) May *Legal Action*, p 30, Wandsworth County Court. In *Wandsworth London Borough Council v Brown* [2005] EWCA Civ 907, (2005) *Legal Action*, p 16, CA, the county court judge varied a decision that the appellant was not 'vulnerable', which he held to be perverse, to a decision that he was 'vulnerable'. The local housing authority was refused permission to bring a second appeal, as no important point of principle was raised; see **19.293**.

19.273 The county court does not have any power to make a mandatory order to require that certain steps are taken or procedures are followed, in contrast to the power available to the Administrative Court on judicial review[1]. So, where a county court judge had allowed an appeal and ordered that a further review be conducted by a different reviewing officer, he had exceeded his powers[2]. In any event, there should be no need for any additional order or direction. The statutory scheme makes it tolerably clear what should occur after a decision is confirmed, varied or quashed.

[1]   Except where the court is considering an appeal brought under H(W)A 2014, s 88, against a review decision by a local housing authority in Wales that reasonable steps had been taken to help to secure that suitable alternative accommodation would be available for the applicant's occupation, see **19.275–19.276**.
[2]   *Adan v Newham London Borough Council* [2001] EWCA Civ 1916, (2002) 34 HLR 28, CA.

Powers on appeals against review decisions that reasonable steps had been taken to help to secure that suitable alternative accommodation would be available for the applicant's occupation

LOCAL HOUSING AUTHORITIES IN ENGLAND

19.274 As previously noted, an applicant has the right to request a review of a local housing authority's decision as to what steps it is to take under the HA 1996, s 189B(2)[1], relief or HA 1996, s 195(2)[2], prevention duties[3]. It follows that an applicant has the right to appeal on a point of law against any review decision that he or she is dis-satisfied with[4]. The question arises as to what order the court can make if the appeal is successful. There are no additional powers provided under these amendments to HA 1996, Pt 7, made by HRA 2017[5]. The judge has the usual powers available to him or her, to confirm, quash or vary the review decision[6]. Essentially if the court considered that reasonable steps had not been, or were not being, taken, he or she could quash the review decision (so that a new review decision would have to be notified) or vary the review decision and set out what reasonable steps should be taken. Unlike the position of appeals brought against review decisions by local housing authorities in Wales[7], there is no specific provision providing that the 56–day period should start again.

[1] As inserted by HRA 2017, s 5(2), for applications for homelessness assistance made to local housing authorities in England on or after 3 April 2018.
[2] As amended by HRA 2017, s 4(2), for applications for homelessness assistance made to local housing authorities in England on or after 3 April 2018.
[3] HA 1996, s 202(1)(ba)(i) and (bc)(i), as inserted by HRA 2017, s 9, for applications for homelessness assistance made to local housing authorities in England on or after 3 April 2018, see **19.18–19.23** and **19.36–19.41**.
[4] HA 1996, s 204(1).
[5] For applications for homelessness assistance made to local housing authorities in England on or after 3 April 2018.
[6] HA 1996, s 204(3).
[7] See **19.275–19.276**.

LOCAL HOUSING AUTHORITIES IN WALES

19.275 As already noted[1], an applicant to a local housing authority in Wales can request a review[2] of whether reasonable steps were taken by the local housing authority in performance of its duty to help the applicant to secure accommodation[3] if the local housing authority has decided that the duty has come to an end, either because the 56-day period has expired[4] or earlier than 56 days if the local housing authority is satisfied that reasonable steps have been taken to secure that suitable accommodation is available for occupation by the applicant[5].

[1] See **19.81–19.82**.
[2] H(W)A 2014, s 85(2), see **19.81–19.82**.
[3] H(W)A 2014, s 73(1), see **17.73–17.117**.
[4] H(W)A 2014, s 74(2), see **17.87–17.96**.
[5] H(W)A 2014, ss 74(3), see **17.97–17.103** and s 85(2).

19.276 If the applicant subsequently appeals against a review decision which decides that reasonable steps had been taken, and the court allows the appeal and decides that reasonable steps had not been taken, the duty in H(W)A 2014, s 73(1), has not come to an end, and a new 56-day period will commence. The court has the power to decide what date that period should start from[1].

[1] H(W)A 2014, s 87(2).

Accommodation pending appeal

19.277 The local housing authority has a power, but not a duty, to provide accommodation pending the making or determination of a county court appeal. The scope and exercise of the power is detailed in CHAPTER 16 and CHAPTER 17[1].

[1] See **16.258–16.277** (England) and **17.135–17.137** (Wales).

19.278 The power is triggered as soon as the period for an appeal starts to run, so the applicant need not actually have lodged an appeal before inviting the local housing authority to provide accommodation (or to continue accommodation). The local housing authority can only exercise its discretion to provide accommodation[1], if it previously owed the appellant one of the following duties to provide accommodation:

- the interim accommodation duty at HA 1996, s 188[2], or H(W)A 2014, s 68;
- the short-term accommodation duty at HA 1996, s 190[3], or H(W)A 2014, ss 68(1) and 69(8);
- (for local housing authorities in England), the interim accommodation duty at HA 1996, s 199A[4];
- the interim accommodation duty at HA 1996, s 200[5], or H(W)A 2014, s 82; or
- (for local housing authorities in Wales), H(W)A 2014, s 75 main housing duty[6].

[1] HA 1996, s 204(4); H(W)A 2014, s 88(5).
[2] As amended by HRA 2017, s 5(4), for applications for homelessness assistance to local housing authorities in England made on or after 3 April 2018; see **16.37–16.50**.
[3] As amended by HRA 2017, s 5(5), for applications for homelessness assistance to local housing authorities in England made on or after 3 April 2018; accommodation for those who have a priority need and have become homeless intentionally. See **16.81–16.93**.
[4] As inserted by HRA 2017, s 5(9), for applications for homelessness assistance to local housing authorities in England made on or after 3 April 2018; duty to accommodate applicant pending referral of HA 1996, s 189B(2) relief duty (as inserted by HRA 2017, s 5(2), for applications for homelessness assistance to local housing authorities in England made on or after 3 April 2018), see **16.217–16.224**.
[5] As amended by HRA 2017, s 5(10), for applications for homelessness assistance to local housing authorities in England made on or after 3 April 2018; duty to accommodate applicant pending referral of HA 1996, s 193(2), main housing duty. See **16.225–16.232**.
[6] Duty to secure accommodation for applicants in priority need, see **17.146–17.199**.

19.279 When considering whether or not to exercise its discretion to provide accommodation pending an appeal, the local housing authority should take into account the factors set out in *R v Camden London Borough Council ex p Mohammed*[1], ie the prospects of success on appeal[2], the appellant's personal circumstances, any new information, the consequences for the applicant if accommodation is not secured, the duty to safeguard and promote the welfare of children, the public sector equality duty and any other relevant considerations[3].

1 *R v Camden London Borough Council ex p Mohammed* (1998) 30 HLR 315, QBD.
2 *R v Newham London Borough Council ex p Lumley* (2001) 33 HLR 124, QBD.
3 See **16.240–16.246**. This power to provide accommodation pending appeal to the county court is not available for local housing authorities in England for use in respect of certain applicants from other EEA states, persons with refugee status from other EEA states, failed asylum-seekers, or people unlawfully present in the UK, unless the local housing authority considers it necessary in order to prevent a breach of rights under the European Convention on Human Rights or European Community law: Nationality, Immigration and Asylum Act 2002, s 54 and Sch 3, para 1, in force from 8 January 2003. For an example of an unsuccessful attempt to challenge a refusal to secure accommodation pending appeal for such a person (with complicated procedural points involved) see *R (Kondoyba) v Kensington & Chelsea Royal London Borough Council* [2011] EWHC 2653 (Admin), (2011) December *Legal Action*, p 30, Admin Ct.

Appeals against refusal to provide accommodation

19.280 If the local housing authority refuses to provide accommodation pending the determination of the appeal, or decides to provide accommodation only for a limited period, the appellant may appeal to the county court against that decision on a point of law[1]. This is a separate appeal from the main homelessness appeal and, for ease of reference, is referred to by the section number which contains the right to appeal: 'section 204A' (or, for local housing authorities in Wales, H(W)A 2014, s 89 appeals).

1 HA 1996, s 204A; H(W)A 2014, s 89.

19.281 The principles to be applied in a HA 1996, s 204A[1] appeal are the same as those applied in HA 1996, s 204[2] appeals[3] and in judicial review[4]. The HA 1996, s 204A appeal procedure does not apply where the applicant's HA 1996, s 204 appeal is brought against an original decision under HA 1996, s 204(1)(b) rather than against a review decision[5].

1 Or H(W)A 2014, s 89.
2 As amended by HRA 2017, ss 4(6) and 5(11), for applications for homelessness assistance to local housing authorities in England made on or after 3 April 2018.
3 H(W)A 2014, s 88.
4 HA 1996 s 204A(4); H(W)A 2014, s 89(5).
5 See *Davis v Watford Borough Council* [2018] EWCA Civ 529 and **19.291–19.292**. The case was decided under HA 1996, s 204A, as it applies to local housing authorities in England. It would be a matter for the courts whether the same principles apply to H(W)A 2014, 2014, s 89 appeals, for local housing authorities in Wales.

19.282 Prior to 30 September 2002, any challenge to a refusal to provide accommodation pending appeal could only be brought by judicial review and the case law from that period is still instructive[1]. The Court of Appeal in *R v Brighton & Hove Council ex p Nacion*[2] held that where the local housing authority had followed the guidance in *Mohammed*[3], any challenges arguing that the refusal to provide accommodation was wrong in law were likely to be futile, and applications should be strongly discouraged. The appropriate remedy for an appellant would normally be to apply to expedite the county court homelessness appeal, rather than bring judicial review proceedings.

1   *Ali v Westminster City Council* (1999) 31 HLR 349, CA.
2   (1999) 31 HLR 1095, CA.
3   *R v Camden London Borough Council ex p Mohammed* (1998) 30 HLR 315, QBD.

19.283 After the HA 1996, s 204A appeal procedure was introduced[1], the Court of Appeal considered the scope of those appeals in *Francis v Kensington and Chelsea Royal London Borough Council*[2]. In that case, the Court of Appeal applied its previous decision in *Nacion*[3] to appeals against the refusal of accommodation pending a homelessness appeal. It held that, unless the court considers that the local housing authority has failed to direct itself in accordance with *Mohammed*[4], it should not intervene. Where the local housing authority has not properly directed itself, the decision should be quashed and the court should consider whether to exercise its power to order the local housing authority to provide accommodation pending the determination of the appeal[5]. The court should not embark on a review of the merits of the main appeal. The local housing authority is required to consider the applicant's grounds of appeal, as part of its consideration of the merits of the case, but would not normally be expected to refer to any of the grounds of appeal in its decision letter unless there is some important and striking ground which requires specific comment[6].

1   By Homelessness Act 2002, s 11, with effect from 30 September 2002. For applications for homelessness assistance made to local housing authorities in Wales on or after 27 April 2015, the procedure is at H(W)A 2014, s 89.
2   [2003] EWCA Civ 443, (2003) 35 HLR 50, CA.
3   *R v Brighton & Hove Council ex p Nacion* (1999) 31 HLR 1095, CA.
4   *R v Camden London Borough Council ex p Mohammed* (1998) 30 HLR 315, QBD. See **16.240–16.246**.
5   Confirmed again by the Court of Appeal in *Brookes v Croydon London Borough Council* [2004] EWCA Civ 439, (2004) June *Legal Action*, p 31, CA and reviewed in *R (Kondoyba) v Kensington & Chelsea Royal London Borough Council* [2011] EWHC 2653 (Admin), (2011) December *Legal Action*, p 30, Admin Ct per HHJ Robinson at [44]–[45].
6   *Lewis v Havering London Borough Council* [2006] EWCA Civ 1793, [2007] HLR 20, CA.

19.284 In the light of the pronouncements made in these judicial review and Court of Appeal cases, if the local housing authority has considered the *relevant* factors and applied them to the appellant's circumstances, an appeal against the refusal to accommodate pending appeal is unlikely to be successful. That is not to suggest that on a HA 1996, s 204A, or H(W)A 2014, s 89, appeal in an appropriate case a court would not quash a decision to refuse to accommodate[1]. There must be proper consideration of the *Mohammed*[2] factors and, if appropriate, of the local housing authority's duty to safeguard and promote the welfare of any children[3]. Simply referring to them was described in one case as paying only 'lip-service', and a refusal to accommodate pending review was quashed[4].

1   See *Onyaebor v Newham London Borough Council* (2004) May *Legal Action*, p 27, Bow County Court, and *Quadir v Tower Hamlets London Borough Council* (2011), (2012) April *Legal Action*, p 42, Central London Civil Justice Centre for examples of successful HA 1996, s 204A appeals.
2   *R v Camden London Borough Council ex p Mohammed* (1998) 30 HLR 315, QBD.
3   Children Act 2004, ss 11(2) (England) and 28(2) (Wales); *Nzolameso v City of Westminster Council* [2015] UKSC 22, [2015] 2 All ER 942, [2015] HLR 22, SC.

4   *R (Paul-Coker) v Lewisham London Borough Council* [2006] EWHC 497 (Admin), [2006] HLR 32. See **16.240–16.246** for detailed discussion of the relevant factors when a local housing authority is considering whether or not to exercise its power to secure accommodation pending determination of any review decision and pending determination of any appeal.

19.285 The HA 1996, s 204A or H(W)A 2014, s 89, appeal is only available in respect of a 'decision' not to accommodate pending an appeal. Where a local housing authority has failed altogether to make a decision on a request for accommodation pending appeal, the appropriate procedure is to seek a judicial review of the failure to make a decision. This has been described as a 'serious weakness' in the drafting of the section[1].

1   Robert Duddridge 'House of Bricks or House of Sticks: Some thoughts on the new s 204A of the Housing Act 1996' [2003] JHL 11.

Procedure

19.286 There is no time limit prescribed in HA 1996, Pt 7[1], or H(W)A 2014, Pt 2, for the filing of an Appellant's Notice in a HA 1996, s 204A or H(W)A 2014, s 89, appeal against a refusal to accommodate pending appeal. The limit is therefore the 21-day period generally applied by the procedure rules to appeals[2]. If possible, the appellant should file one Appellant's Notice (form N161) containing both the main homelessness appeal and the HA 1996 s 204A or H(W)A 2014, s 89, appeal[3]. Otherwise, the HA 1996 s 204A or H(W)A 2014, s 89, appeal can be brought on a separate form N161[4]. The appellant should comply with CPR Pt 52 and PDs 52A, 52B and 52D. See **19.256–19.263** for the documents required to be filed and served.

1   As amended by HRA 2017 for applications for homelessness assistance made to local housing authorities in England on or after 3 April 2018.
2   CPR 52.12(2)(b).
3   PD52D, para 28.1(1).
4   PD52D, para 28.2.

19.287 If a HA 1996, s 204A or H(W)A 2014, s 89, appeal is brought, the need for a speedy judicial decision is obvious. The whole point is to provide accommodation urgently. An application can therefore be made for an interim injunction requiring that the local housing authority provide accommodation until the HA 1996, s 204A, or H(W)A 2014, s 89, appeal is determined. The matters to be considered on the application for an interim injunction would include:

(1)   the merits of the HA 1996, s 204A or H(W)A 2014, s 89, appeal itself and whether the applicant has a strong prima facie case[1];

(2)   whether or not the appellant's ability to pursue the main homelessness appeal would be substantially prejudiced if no interim order was made[2]; and

(3)   consideration of the likely consequences to each party of the granting or withholding of interim relief[3].

1   *Putans v Tower Hamlets London Borough Council* [2006] EWHC 1634 (Ch), [2007] HLR 10, ChD at [52] per Michael Briggs QC, applying the principles in *American Cyanamid Co v Ethicon Ltd* [1975] AC 396, HL to HA 1996, s 204A.
2   HA 1996, s 204A(6)(a); H(W)A 2014, s 89(7)(a).

3   *De Falco v Crawley Borough Council* [1980] QB 460, CA; and *R v Kensington and Chelsea Royal London Borough Council ex parte Hammell* [1989] 1 QB 518, CA.

19.288 An application can be made in the Appellant's Notice for an urgent injunction requiring the local housing authority to secure that accommodation is available for the applicant's occupation. If, exceptionally, the court were to make an order to that effect without giving the parties notice of any hearing, the appellant must serve his or her Appellant's Notice and a copy of the order on the respondent. The court would normally fix a hearing date when it will reconsider whether the order should continue[1].

1   PD52D, paras 28.3 and 28.4.

19.289 Appeals under HA 1996, s 204A or H(W)A 2014, s 89, can only be heard by a circuit judge[1]. The appeal may not be brought after the determination of the main homelessness appeal[2].

1   CPR Pt 2 and PD2B, para 9.
2   HA 1996, s 204A(3); H(W)A 2014, s 89(3).

19.290 At the final hearing of the HA 1996, s 204A or H(W)A 2014, s 89, appeal, the court may either confirm or quash the decision made by the local housing authority (refusing accommodation pending the main appeal)[1]. Variation is not a possibility. If the court quashes the decision, it may order that the local housing authority provides that accommodation is available for the appellant until the main appeal has been determined, or any earlier specified time. It can only order the local housing authority to provide accommodation if it is satisfied that the appellant's ability to pursue the main appeal would otherwise be substantially prejudiced[2].

1   HA 1996, s 204A(4)(b); H(W)A 2014, s 89(4)(b).
2   HA 1996, s 204A(5) and (6); H(W)A 2014, s 89(6) and (7). For an example where the court quashed the decision under appeal, but declined to make an injunction requiring the local housing authority to provide accommodation, see *Quadir v Tower Hamlets London Borough Council* (2011), (2012) April *Legal Action*, p 42, Central London Civil Justice Centre. For a recent decision where the Court of Appeal held that the judge had been wrong to uphold a HA 1996, s 204A, appeal, see *Rother District Council v Freeman-Roach* [2018] EWCA Civ 368, CA.

Refusal of interim accommodation where no review decision

19.291 As previously noted, an appeal on a point of law can be brought under HA 1996, 204(1)(b), or H(W)A 2014, s 88(1)(b), where the applicant has requested a review and the review decision has not been notified to him or her. In these cases, the appeal is against the original decision[1]. In these circumstances, the applicant may require, and request, interim accommodation pending the review decision[2]. If interim accommodation is refused, the applicant may want to challenge that decision.

1   See **19.222–19.224**.
2   HA 1996, s 204(4), (as amended by HRA 2017, s 4(6) and 5(11), for applications to local housing authorities in England made on or after 3 April 2018; H(W)A 2014, s 89(5), see **19.210–19.213**.

19.292 The Court of Appeal has held that the interim accommodation appeal process under HA 1996, s 204A or H(W)A 2014, s 89, is not available in these circumstances[1]. Accordingly, any challenge must be brought by judicial review[2].

1 *Davis v Watford Borough Council* [2018] EWCA Civ 529, CA.
2 See **19.306–19.332** for judicial review.

Appeal to the Court of Appeal

The test for bringing a second appeal

19.293 Any appeals against orders of the county court determining a main homelessness appeal or a HA 1996, s 204A or H(W)A 2014, s 89, appeal are *second* appeals and can only be made to the Court of Appeal[1]. Such appeals require permission to appeal. Permission can be given only by the Court of Appeal itself and will only be given if the appeal raises 'an important point of principle or practice', or there is 'some other compelling reason' for the Court of Appeal to hear it[2]. In *Uphill v BRB (Residuary) Ltd*[3], the Court of Appeal considered the general principles to be applied when deciding whether to give permission to bring a second appeal.

1 *Azimi v Newham London Borough Council* (2001) 33 HLR 51, CA. See **19.303–19.305** for the circumstances where an appeal against an order made in HA 1996, s 204 appeal proceedings is to be made to the High Court.
2 CPR 52.7(2).
3 [2005] EWCA Civ 60, [2005] 1 WLR 2070, CA.

19.294 It held that permission should only be granted in exceptional cases. When permission was sought under the first limb ('an important point of principle or practice'), it could be granted where such an important point had not yet been determined by a higher court, but would not be granted where the contention was merely that an established point of principle or practice had not been correctly applied[1]. As far as the second limb was concerned ('some other compelling reason'), the starting point was that the prospects of success had to be very high. Even if they were very high, the decision against which the appellant sought permission to appeal had to be inconsistent with the authority of a higher court or tainted with some procedural irregularity leading to unfairness before permission would be given[2].

1 For an example where permission was refused as there was no important point of principle or practice arising on the appeal, see *Selvarajah v Croydon London Borough Council* [2014] EWCA Civ 498, (2014) June *Legal Action*, p 38, CA.
2 Another instance of the Court of Appeal considering whether or not to grant permission to bring a second appeal, outside of the homelessness context, is *Esure Insurance Ltd v Direct Line Insurance Ltd plc* [2008] EWCA Civ 842, [2009] Bus LR 438, CA, where the complexity of the case and the real prospect of showing that the first-instance judge had incorrectly exercised his appellate function were held to constitute 'compelling reasons' for permitting a second appeal. The fact that an applicant is facing the prospect of street homeless is not an 'other compelling reason' justifying the grant of permission: *Selvarajah v Croydon London Borough Council* [2014] EWCA Civ 498, (2014) June *Legal Action*, p 38, CA.

19.295 The Court of Appeal considered the second limb of the test ('some other compelling reason') in *Cramp v Hastings Borough Council*[1]. It held that there was a good prospect of success on a second appeal because the first-instance judge had appeared to substitute his own view for that of the local housing authority. There was evidence before the Court of Appeal that the extent of inquiries needed to be undertaken by the local housing authority was a matter of great concern to it and had implications for its resources. Those two points together were 'compelling reasons' sufficient to justify a second appeal[2].

1   The permission hearing is at [2005] EWCA Civ 439, CA.
2   Carnwath LJ quoted by Brooke LJ in the full appeal: *Cramp v Hastings Borough Council* [2005] EWCA Civ 1005, [2005] HLR 48, CA, at [34].

19.296 In *Camden London Borough Council v Phillips*[1], the Court of Appeal granted the local housing authority permission to appeal (having heard the full appeal in *Cramp v Hastings Borough Council*, which had been listed for hearing on the same day). It noted that the guidance in *Uphill v BRB Residuary Board Ltd*[2] was not exhaustive and should not require the Court of Appeal to feel that there is a:

'fetter on its power to put things right if it has occasion to believe that things are going wrong in an important way in the practical operation of the statutory scheme in Pt 7 of the 1996 Act.[3]'

1   Heard with the full appeal of *Cramp v Hastings Borough Council* [2005] EWCA Civ 1005, [2005] HLR 48, CA.
2   [2005] EWCA Civ 60, [2005] 1 WLR 2070, CA.
3   Brooke LJ at [66].

19.297 The issues in both *Camden London Borough Council v Phillips* and *Cramp v Hastings Borough Council* raised an important point of practice. The Court of Appeal noted:

'a worrying tendency in judges at that level to overlook the fact that it will never be easy for a judge to say that an experienced senior housing officer on a homelessness review, who has considered all the reports readily available, and all the representations made by the applicant's solicitors, has made an error of law when she considered that it was unnecessary to put in train further detailed inquiries, not suggested by the applicant's solicitors, before she could properly make a decision on the review. The need to correct that tendency raises an important point of practice.[1]'

1   Brooke LJ at [68].

19.298 In *William v Wandsworth London Borough Council*[1], the Court of Appeal was concerned with a second appeal which had been brought by the local housing authority. Noting that the local housing authority had made a new review decision between the date of the county court appeal and the date on which permission to bring a second appeal was given, the Court of Appeal criticised the local housing authority's failure to inform the court that it had carried out a further review as 'verging on abuse' and doubted that permission would have been given, had the Court of Appeal been informed that a new review decision had been made. The new review decision had been made because both the applicant's lawyers and the local housing authority's lawyers believed that HA 1996, s 202(4) and the regulations required it to be made, once the previous review decision had been quashed by the county court judge. Chadwick LJ described this as an unsatisfactory position and said that:

'the parties should . . . take the sensible and obvious course of agreeing that performance of the duty imposed on the authority by section 202(4) of the Act should await the outcome of the application [for permission], or the appeal (as the case may be).[2]'

1   [2006] EWCA Civ 535, [2006] HLR 42, CA.
2   *William v Wandsworth London Borough Council* [2006] EWCA Civ 535, [2006] HLR 42, CA at [42]–[43] per Chadwick LJ.

Procedure on a second appeal

19.299 An application for permission to bring a second appeal should be made within the Appellant's Notice, and must be filed at the Court of Appeal within 21 days of the judgment or order appealed from[1]. The county court does not have the power to grant or refuse permission to appeal, but does have the power to order that the time within which an Appellant's Notice is to be filed is extended[2]. Applications for permission do not need to be supported by witness statements, but if a witness statement is filed in support of the application for permission, or any other application, 'fairness requires it to be sent to the intended respondent' and, if it is the local housing authority which is seeking permission to appeal, it should bear in mind that the other party is likely to be without legal representation at the time and so those preparing a witness statement have a particular responsibility 'to ensure that it is relevant to the specific question whether permission to appeal should be granted, and that it is not argumentative and so far as practicable not contentious'[3]. The respondent is permitted, and indeed encouraged, to file and serve a brief statement of any reasons why permission should be refused. That statement should be filed and served within 14 days of service on the respondent of the appellant's notice or skeleton argument, whichever is the later document[4].

1   CPR 52.4. PD52C, paras 14–20 contain the procedure for a second appeal to the Court of Appeal.
2   CPR 52.12(2)(a).
3   *William v Wandsworth London Borough Council* [2006] EWCA Civ 535, [2006] HLR 42, CA at [80]–[81] per Sedley LJ; see **19.232–19.236** on contents of witness statements in general.
4   PD52C, para 19(1).

19.300 Once permission has been granted, the focus for the Court of Appeal on hearing the appeal will be on errors of law in the local housing authority's decision that was the original subject of the appeal, rather than confining itself to considering possible errors of law made by the county court judge on hearing the appeal[1].

1   *Danesh v Kensington & Chelsea Royal London Borough Council* [2006] EWCA Civ 1404, [2006] 1 WLR 69, CA per Neuberger LJ at [30]; *Bubb v Wandsworth London Borough Council* [2011] EWCA Civ 1285, [2012] HLR 13, CA per Neuberger MR at [31]; and *Mohamoud v Birmingham City Council* [2014] EWCA Civ 227, [2014] HLR 22, CA per Proudman J at [24].

Accommodation pending appeal to the Court of Appeal

19.301 The Court of Appeal has no power to order that the local housing authority secure, or continue to secure, accommodation for the applicant pending determination of any appeal to the Court of Appeal[1].

[1]   *Johnson v City of Westminster Council* [2013] EWCA Civ 773, [2013] HLR 45, CA

19.302 The local housing authority's power to provide accommodation for the appellant continues until any second appeal is finally determined, and so it may agree to provide accommodation until the determination of an appeal to the Court of Appeal[1]. When making its decision, it should again take into account the factors in *R v Camden London Borough Council ex parte Mohammed*[2]. If the local housing authority refuses to provide accommodation pending an appeal to the Court of Appeal, there is no power under HA 1996, s 204A or H(W)A 2014, s 89, for the county court to entertain an appeal against that refusal. In the absence of such a power, the more straightforward course is for the applicant to challenge by way of judicial review the decision not to provide accommodation pending the second appeal to the Court of Appeal[3]. If the Court of Appeal (or Supreme Court in the case of an appeal to the Supreme Court) has granted permission, that will be an additional relevant factor for the local housing authority to consider in deciding whether to exercise its discretion to accommodate pending appeal[4].

[1]   HA 1996, s 204(4)(b); H(W)A 2014, s 88(5)(b).
[2]   (1998) 30 HLR 315, QBD. See **16.240–16.246**.
[3]   For an (unsuccessful) example see *R (Nzolameso) v Westminster City Council* [2014] EWHC 409 (Admin) (2014) April *Legal Action*, p 27; despite the local housing authority's view on the prospects of the appeal, the applicant succeeded in the Supreme Court on the substantive issue on appeal: *R (Nzolameso) v Westminster City Council* [2015] UKSC 22, [2015] 2 All ER 942, [2015] HLR 22, SC, see **19.306–19.332**.
[4]   *R (Nzolameso) v City of Westminster Council* [2015] EWHC 799 (Admin), Admin Ct.

Appeals from the county court to the High Court

19.303 A decision made on appeal by the county court is a second appeal and appeal will lie to the Court of Appeal[1]. However, during the course of a HA 1996, s 204[2] or H(W)A 2014, s 89, appeal, the judge might make decisions which are not, themselves, decisions on appeal. Any appeal against any of those decisions would not be a second appeal and appeal lies to the High Court, not to the Court of Appeal[3].

[1]   Access to Justice Act 1999 (Destination of Appeals) Order 2016, SI 2016/917, art 6, see **19.293–19.298**.
[2]   As amended by HRA 2017, s 4(6), for applications for homelessness assistance made to local housing authority in England on or after 3 April 2018.
[3]   Access to Justice Act 1999 (Destination of Appeals) Order 2016, SI 2016/917, art 5, see **19.293–19.298**.

19.304 The procedure for the bringing of an appeal to the High Court is at CPR 52 and PDs 52A – 52B. An appellant's notice must be filed at the High Court within 21 days of the decision being appealed against, or such longer time as the County Court may have ordered[1]. The County Court must normally have been asked for permission to appeal. If the County Court refuses permission, then application can be made to the High Court for permission[2]. Permission for appeal may be given only where the Court considers that the appeal would have a real prospect of success or there is some other compelling reason for the appeal to be heard[3]. Once permission has been given, the procedural requirements set out at PD 52B apply.

1   CPR 52.12(2).
2   CPR 52.3(a).
3   CPR 52.6(1).

19.305 Decisions made during the course of a HA 1996, s 204[1], or H(W)A 2014, s 89 appeal which are not themselves decisions made on appeal would include:

- a decision made on an application to extend the time for filing the appeal under HA 1996, s 204(2A), or H(W)A 2014, s 88(3)[2]; and
- a decision as to the costs of the appeal, whether made without a hearing and on the judge, having received written submissions, or at the end of a hearing[3].

Any appeal against any of these decisions must be made to the High Court.

1   As amended by HRA 2017, ss 4(6) and 5(11), for applications for homelessness assistance made to local housing authority in England on or after 3 April 2018.
2   *Short v Birmingham City Council* [2004] EWHC 2112 (QB), [2005] HLR 6, QBD, see **19.250–19.255**.
3   *Unichi v Southwark London Borough Council* [2013] EWHC 3681 (QB); and *Lopes v Croydon London Borough Council* [2016] EWCA Civ 465, reported as *Handley & Evans v Lake Jackson Solicitors (A Firm)*, [2016] EWCA Civ 465, [2016] 1 WLR 3138, CA.

JUDICIAL REVIEW

Introduction

19.306 Local housing authority decisions made under HA 1996, Pt 7[1] or under H(W)A 2014, Pt 2, that do not carry with them a right to request a review can only be challenged (in the courts) in judicial review proceedings.

1   As amended by HRA 2017 for applications for homelessness assistance made to local housing authorities in England on or after 3 April 2018.

19.307 Complaints that the applicant has been treated unsatisfactorily, but where no error of law in the actual decision reached is alleged, should be raised within the local housing authority's internal complaints procedure[1]. If the treatment amounts to maladministration, the Local Government and Social Care Ombudsman or Public Services Ombudsman for Wales can investigate, once the internal complaints procedure has been exhausted[2].

1   See **19.333–19.335**.
2   See **19.336–19.340**.

Procedure

19.308 The procedure for judicial review is set out in the Civil Procedure Rules at CPR 54 and PDs 54A and 54D. Only a short summary of that procedure can be given here. Before the procedure is adopted, it will be expected that any applicant has complied with the Pre-Action Protocol for

Judicial Review[1].

[1]   See **19.319**.

19.309 In order to bring a claim by way of judicial review, the applicant must obtain permission from the Administrative Court[1]. The application for permission[2] is first considered on the papers. The local housing authority has an opportunity to put its brief case to the judge on paper in an Acknowledgment of Service[3]. If permission is refused on the papers, the applicant has the right to renew his or her application for permission at an oral hearing, unless the application has been marked as 'totally without merit'[4].

[1]   CPR 54.4.
[2]   Made on claim form N461.
[3]   Form N462.
[4]   CPR 54.12(3) and (7).

19.310 Claims should be brought promptly, and in any event within three months of the decision being challenged (although the court does have the discretion to extend time where there is a good reason for the delay)[1]. Delay can be a reason in itself for refusing permission. Judicial review is not available, and permission will be refused, if there is an alternative avenue for redress available to the applicant.

[1]   CPR 54.5(1) and CPR 3.1(2)(a). The parties themselves cannot extend time by agreement: CPR 54.5(2).

19.311 If permission is granted, the local housing authority has the opportunity to put in its own evidence and submissions, and a full hearing will take place.

19.312 If the court finds that the decision was made in breach of the usual administrative law principles, it can:

(1)   quash the decision and remit the matter back to the local housing authority for reconsideration;
(2)   make a mandatory order requiring the local housing authority to act in a certain way;
(3)   make a prohibitory order setting out how the local housing authority may not act; or
(4)   make an injunction[1].

[1]   CPR r 54.2.

19.313 Judicial review is a discretionary remedy and, even if the court finds that an error of law was made, it may still decide, in all the circumstances, not to make any order. Situations where the court might decide not to make any order could include:

•   where there had been undue delay;
•   where it would be pointless to quash a decision because the decision had been completely overtaken by events; or
•   where granting a remedy would cause substantial hardship to any person or would be detrimental to good administration[1].

In addition, the court must refuse to grant relief if it appears to the court to be highly likely that the outcome for the applicant would not have been substantially different if the conduct complained of had not occurred[2].

1 Senior Courts Act 1981, s 31(6); and *R (Edwards) v Environmental Agency* [2008] UKHL 22, SC.
2 Senior Courts Act 1981, s 31(2)A; see *R (Logan) v Havering London Borough Council* [2015] EWHC 3193 (Admin).

19.314 Since 2 October 2000, when the Human Rights Act 1998 came into force, it has also been possible to claim damages for breach of human rights within judicial review proceedings[1]. Judicial review proceedings cannot, however, be brought solely to claim damages[2].

1 See **19.328–19.333**.
2 CPR 54.3(2).

Obtaining interim remedies

19.315 In many judicial review claims relating to a local housing authority's decisions under HA 1996, Pt 7[1], or under H(W)A 2014, Pt 2, the applicant will have an immediate need for accommodation. The judicial review claim is likely to wait months before a full hearing. Even the application for permission to bring the claim may not be considered for several weeks.

1 As amended by HRA 2017 for applications for homelessness assistance made to local housing authorities in England on or after 3 April 2018.

19.316 At all times during the progress of the judicial review claim, the Administrative Court has a discretion to grant an interim injunction requiring the local housing authority whose decision is under challenge to accommodate the applicant, and his or her household, until the judicial review claim has been heard or determined[1]. Indeed, in cases of extreme urgency, it is possible to obtain an interim injunction out-of-hours from the duty judge, upon the applicant and his or her legal advisers undertaking to issue the judicial review claim within a specified period (usually less than 24 hours).

1 The power to make an injunction is in CPR 54.2. The Administrative Court's interim powers are in CPR 25.1(1) and include the power to make an interim injunction (CPR 25.1(1)(a)).

19.317 The test that the Administrative Court will apply in considering whether or not to make an interim injunction is three-fold:

(1) whether the applicant has a strong prima facie case[1];
(2) the likely consequences to each party of the granting or withholding of interim relief; and
(3) the wider public interest[2].

1 *De Falco v Crawley Borough Council* [1980] QB 460, CA; *R v Kensington and Chelsea Royal London Borough Council ex parte Hammell* [1989] 1 QB 518, CA; *Francis v Kensington and Chelsea Royal London Borough Council* [2003] EWCA Civ 443, [2003] HLR 50; and *Putans v Tower Hamlets London Borough Council* [2006] EWHC 1634 (Ch), [2007] HLR 10, ChD at [52] per Michael Briggs QC.
2 *R v Kensington and Chelsea Royal London Borough Council ex parte Hammell* [1989] 1 QB 518, CA. And see further *R (Medical Justice) v Secretary of State for the Home Department*

[2010] EWHC 1425 (Admin), [2010] ACD 70, Admin Ct per Cranston J at [12]–[16] for a discussion of the 'wider public interest' in public law claims.

19.318 Where the application for an interim injunction is made in an emergency, and without notice to the local housing authority, the following principles should be borne in mind:

(1)   that the granting of an injunction without notice is 'an exceptional remedy'[1], and normally appropriate only if the case is genuinely one of emergency or other great urgency;

(2)   even then, it should normally be possible to give some informal notice to the other party;

(3)   the claimant applying for an injunction, and his or her legal representatives, are under a heavy duty to make full and frank disclosure of all matters relevant to the claim, whether matters of fact or of law;

(4)   the duty to make full and frank disclosure includes a duty to make proper inquiries before making the application, so that the claimant, and his or her legal representatives, disclose all the material facts; and

(5)   proper disclosure means identifying all relevant documents for the judge, taking the judge to the particular passages in those documents, and taking appropriate steps to ensure that the judge appreciates the significance of what he or she is being asked to read, or is being told[2].

¹   *R (Lawer) v Restormel Borough Council* [2007] EWHC 2299 (Admin), [2008] HLR 20, Admin Ct at [62] per Munby J, quoting *Moat Housing Group South Ltd v Harris* [2005] EWCA Civ 287, [2005] HLR 33, CA.

²   *R (Lawer) v Restormel Borough Council* [2007] EWHC 2299 (Admin), [2008] HLR 20, Admin Ct at [62]–[69] per Munby J. For another example where the claimant had failed to comply with the duty to make full and frank disclosure, see *R (Kondyba) v Kensington & Chelsea Royal London Borough Council* [2011] EWHC 2653 (Admin), (2011) December *Legal Action*, p 30, Admin Ct.

19.319 Legal representatives are also reminded of the importance of complying with the Pre-Action Protocol for Judicial Review, which requires that the claimant's representatives give notice of the intention to bring judicial review proceedings to the local housing authority's legal department. Even if the matter is too urgent to comply with the time limits required in the protocol, some warning to the legal department should be given[1]. Legal advisers should also be aware of the guidance given in the immigration case of *R (Hamid) v SSHD*[2], stressing the exceptional nature of applications for injunctions made without notice to the other side, and the need for strict compliance with the rules requiring completion of Court forms.

¹   *R (Lawer) v Restormel Borough Council* [2007] EWHC 2299 (Admin), [2008] HLR 20, Admin Ct at [81]–[82] per Munby J.

²   [2012] EWHC 3070 (Admin), [2013] ACD 27, Admin Ct.

19.320 An interim injunction obtained without notice to the local housing authority will usually contain a provision permitting the local housing authority to apply to vary or discharge the injunction upon a short period of notice to the claimant or his or her legal representatives. Such applications should be considered relatively urgently by the Administrative Court[1].

[1]   *R (Casey) v Restormel Borough Council* [2007] EWHC 2554 (Admin), (2008) January *Legal Action*, p 38, Admin Ct. The urgency application must be made on form N463.

Judicial review as a substitute for a county court appeal

19.321 Where an appeal to the county court is available, it is only in really exceptional circumstances that the Administrative Court will give permission for a judicial review claim to be brought[1]. Missing the 21-day deadline for the county court appeal[2] is not generally an exceptional circumstance[3], and particularly so now that the county court has power to extend that deadline[4].

[1]   *R v Brent London Borough Council ex p O'Connor* (1998) 31 HLR 923, QBD.
[2]   See **19.244–19.245**.
[3]   *R v Brent London Borough Council ex p O'Connor* (1999) 31 HLR 923, QBD; *R v Waltham Forest London Borough Council ex p Abdullahi* (1999) May *Legal Action*, p 29, QBD; and *R v Hillingdon London Borough Council ex p Rahim* (2000), (2000) May *Legal Action*, p 30, QBD.
[4]   See **19.250–19.255**.

19.322 In one case, permission to bring a claim in judicial review was given where there was an arguable error of law and the applicant had unsuccessfully tried to issue a notice of appeal in the county court (but had wrongly made an application within possession proceedings instead)[1]. In another case, permission was given, and the judicial review claim succeeded, where the local housing authority had refused to consider fresh information, produced after the review decision, concerning the applicant's mental health, which was relevant to the decision that he had become homeless intentionally[2].

[1]   *R v Lambeth London Borough Council ex p Alleyne* (1999), (1999) June *Legal Action*, p 24, CA.
[2]   *R (Van der Stolk) v Camden London Borough Council* [2002] EWHC 1261 (Admin), (2002) July *Legal Action*, p 26, Admin Ct.

19.323 However, permission was refused to an applicant who had been found to have become homeless intentionally, had then withdrawn his request for a review, made a fresh application and then claimed that the local housing authority had failed to provide him with interim accommodation in accordance with the interim pre-decision duty[1]. Likewise, permission will be refused in cases where the applicant seeks to dispute the suitability of accommodation and where a right to a review of suitability is available under the review category at HA 1996, s 202(1)(f), (g), or (h)[2] or H(W)A 2014, s 85(3)[3]. An applicant also failed in a judicial review claim where she sought to challenge an original decision which contained inadequate reasons. The Administrative Court held that the proper route to challenge such deficiencies was by requesting a review and subsequently appealing to the county court[4].

[1]   *R (Campbell) v Enfield London Borough Council* [2001] EWHC 357 (Admin), Admin Ct.
[2]   As amended and inserted by HRA 2017, s 9, for applications for homelessness assistance made to local housing authorities in England on or after 3 April 2018, see **19.59–19.69**.
[3]   *R (Cano) v Kensington and Chelsea Royal London Borough Council* [2002] EWHC 1922 (Admin), (2002) December *Legal Action*, p 22, Admin Ct. See also **19.59–19.69** (England) and **19.100–19.101** (Wales).

[4]   *R (Lynch) v Lambeth London Borough Council* [2006] EWHC 2737 (Admin), [2007] HLR 15, Admin Ct. Unusually, the claimant had also issued a HA 1996, s 204 appeal to the county court, which was transferred to the High Court and heard with the judicial review claim.

Judicial review where there can be no county court appeal

19.324 There may be several reasons why a county court appeal is not available and the applicant may need to bring a claim for judicial review. They include:

(1)   where he or she wishes to challenge a decision which does not carry the right to request a statutory review;

(2)   if the local housing authority fails to comply with its acknowledged statutory duty, a judicial review claim can be brought for a mandatory order requiring the local housing authority to comply; or

(3)   if the local housing authority simply fails to take a decision on a request or application made to it, a judicial review claim can be brought for a mandatory order requiring the local housing authority to make the decision.

19.325 Subjects for judicial review can therefore include:

(1)   a local housing authority refusing to accept an application under HA 1996, Pt 7[1] or H(W)A 2014, Pt 2[2];

(2)   a local housing authority's failure to make the necessary inquiries or to notify the applicant of the decision on those inquiries[3];

(3)   a local housing authority's refusal to secure interim accommodation pending an initial decision[4];

(4)   a local housing authority's decision not to secure accommodation pending a decision on review[5];

(5)   a local housing authority's decision not to secure interim accommodation[6] pending an appeal under HA 1996, 204(1)(b) or H(W)A 2014, s 89(1)b)[7];

(6)   for applicants to local housing authorities in England, any dispute as to whether or not accommodation provided under an interim duty is suitable[8];

(7)   any failure to provide suitable accommodation in discharge of any of its statutory duties (where the local housing authority either fails to provide accommodation at all or provides accommodation that it is agreed is unsuitable for the needs of the applicant and his or her household)[9];

(8)   any dispute as to the length of the period that would provide an applicant who has a priority need and who had become homeless intentionally with 'a reasonable opportunity of securing accommodation'[10];

(9)   for applicants to local housing authorities in England, any challenge to the contents of the assessment of the applicant's case[11];

(10)   for applicants to local housing authorities in England, any challenge to the steps recorded in the personal housing plan as required to be taken by the applicant[12];

(11) for applicants to local housing authorities in England, any decision to warn the applicant of its opinion that he or she has deliberately and unreasonably refused to take any step required or agreed[13];

(12) any refusal to consider whether or not the conditions are met for the referral of the applicant's case to another local housing authority[14];

(13) any decision not to allow the applicant to request a review outside the 21-day period[15]; and

(14) any failure to complete a statutory review or to notify the applicant of the decision on review[16].

---

[1] As amended by HRA 2017 for applications for homelessness assistance made to local housing authorities in England on or after 3 April 2018.

[2] HA 1996, s 183(1); H(W)A 2014, s 62(1); for examples see *R (Hoyte) v Southwark London Borough Council* [2016] EWHC 1665 (Admin), [2016] HLR 35, Admin Ct; and *R (Abdulrahman) v Hillingdon London Borough Council* [2016] EWHC 2647 (Admin), [2017] HLR 1, Admin Ct.

[3] HA 1996, s 184, as amended by HRA 2017, ss 4(3) and 5(3), for applications for homelessness assistance made to local housing authorities in England on or after 3 April 2018, see **9.1–9.11**; H(W)A 2014 ss 62 and 63; see **9.12–9.14**.

[4] HA 1996, s 188(1) or s 188(1A), as amended by HRA 2017, s 5(4), for applications for homelessness assistance made to local housing authorities in England on or after 3 April 2018, see **16.37–16.50**; H(W)A 2014, s 68(1), see **17.118–17.137**.

[5] HA 1996, s 188(3), as amended by HRA 2017, s 5(4), for applications for homelessness assistance made to local housing authorities in England on or after 3 April 2018, see **16.233–16.257**; H(W)A 2014, s 69(11), see **17.134**. See also *R v Camden London Borough Council ex p Mohammed* (1998) 30 HLR 315, QBD; and *R (IA) v City of Westminster Council* [2013] EWHC 1273 (Admin) (2013) July/August *Legal Action*, p 23, Admin Ct.

[6] Under its power at HA 1996, s 204(4) (as amended by HRA 2017, ss 4(6) and 5(11), for applications for homelessness assistance made to local housing authorities in England on or after 3 April 2018) or H(W)A 2014, s 89(5), see **16.258–16.277** (England), **17.135–17.137** (Wales).

[7] Appeals against original decisions where a review has been requested but has not been notified, see **19.215**.

[8] *R (Sacupima) v Newham London Borough Council* (2001) 33 HLR 2, CA. See **16.74–16.80**. H(W)A 2014, s 85(3), permits an applicant to a local housing authority in Wales to request a review of a decision that accommodation secured under the interim accommodation duty in H(W)A 2014, s 68(1), is suitable, see **19.83–19.85**.

[9] *R v Newham London Borough Council ex p Begum (Mashuda)* (2000) 32 HLR 808, QBD. See also *R (Dumbaya) v Lewisham London Borough Council* [2008] EWHC 1852 (Admin), (2008) September *Legal Action*, p 25, Admin Ct, where the local housing authority had failed to provide short-term accommodation under HA 1996, s 190(2)(a) to the claimant, whom it had found to have a priority need and to have become homeless intentionally. The local housing authority was ordered to pay the claimant's costs of bringing the judicial review. See **19.217–19.218**.

[10] HA 1996, s 190(2)(a) and H(W)A 2014, s 69(5). See *R (Conville) v Richmond upon Thames London Borough Council* [2006] EWCA Civ 718, [2006] HLR 45, CA, a decision of the Court of Appeal, containing, in the authors' opinion, the correct approach on forum; and *R (Nipyo) v Croydon London Borough Council* [2008] EWHC 847, [2008] HLR 37, Admin Ct. See **16.81–16.93**.

[11] HA 1996, s 189A(1), as inserted by HRA 2017, s 3(1), for applications for homelessness assistance made to local housing authorities in England on or after 3 April 2018, see **15.62–15.72**.

[12] HA 1996, s 189A(4) and (6)(b), as inserted by HRA 2017, s 7(1), for applications for homelessness assistance made to local housing authorities in England on or after 3 April 2018, see **15.72–15.86**.

[13] HA 1996, 193B(4)(a) and (5), as inserted by HRA 2017, s 3(1), for applications for homelessness assistance made to local housing authorities in England on or after 3 April 2018, see **15.72–15.86**.

[14] *Hackney London Borough Council v Sareen* [2003] EWCA Civ 351, [2003] HLR 54, CA. See **14.25**.

[15] *R (C) v Lewisham London Borough Council* [2003] EWCA Civ 927, [2004] HLR 4, CA; *R (Slaiman) v Richmond upon Thames London Borough Council* [2006] EWHC 329 (Admin), [2006] HLR 20, Admin Ct; *R (Casey) v Restormel Borough Council* [2007] EWHC 2554 (Admin), (2008) January *Legal Action*, p 38, Admin Ct; and *R (Dragic) v Wandsworth London Borough Council* [2012] EWHC 1241(Admin) (2012) July *Legal Action*, p 42, Admin Ct. See **19.109–19.115**.

[16] HA 1996, ss 202(4) and 203; H(W)A 2014, ss 85(6) and 86, see **19.196–19.199**.

19.326 The last of these provides a good example of the usefulness of judicial review in the operation of HA 1996, Pt 7[1] and of H(W)A 2014, Pt 2. Where an applicant has requested a review, but the local housing authority has failed to complete the review or to notify him or her of the review decision, the applicant can appeal to the county court if there was an error of law in the original decision[2]. However, if there is no error of law in the original decision, but the applicant wants his or her case reconsidered, or has provided new information, then an appeal to the county court will not be the appropriate course. The applicant's remedy in those circumstances is to apply for a mandatory order in judicial review proceedings requiring the local housing authority to complete the review and notify him or her of the review decision.

[1] As amended by HRA 2017 for applications for homelessness assistance made to local housing authorities in England on or after 3 April 2018.

[2] HA 1996, s 204(1)(b); H(W)A 2014, s 88(1)(b), see **19.196–19.197**.

19.327 Judicial review may also be available where the applicant is challenging the local housing authority's policy on some aspect of HA 1996, Pt 7[1] or H(W)A 2014, Pt 2[2]. Although the court retains a discretion to consider disputes on policy matters that have become academic for the individual applicant (because matters have moved on, or the local housing authority has conceded the applicant's claim), it should only do so if that would be in the public interest and the appropriate procedural steps have been taken[3].

[1] As amended by HRA 2017 for applications for homelessness assistance made to local housing authorities in England on or after 3 April 2018.

[2] For example, *R (Khatun) v Newham London Borough Council* [2004] EWCA Civ 55, [2004] HLR 29, CA, where the applicants challenged the local housing authority's policy that offers of accommodation made under HA 1996, s 193 had to be accepted or rejected before they were viewed; *R (Calgin) v Enfield London Borough Council* [2005] EWHC 1716 (Admin), [2006] HLR 4, Admin Ct, where the challenge was to the local housing authority's policy of securing accommodation outside its district; and *Ali & others v Birmingham City Council* [2009] UKHL 36, [2009] 1 WLR 1506, HL, where the challenge was to the local housing authority's policy on securing accommodation for the applicants under the HA 1996, s 193(2), main housing duty in accommodation which was not reasonable to continue to occupy.

[3] *R (Tshikangu) v Newham London Borough Council* (2001) The Times, April 27, QBD. See *R (Morris) v Westminster City Council* [2004] EWHC 1199 (Admin) for an example of permission to continue a claim for judicial review which had become academic. The substantive point was subsequently decided by the Court of Appeal in *R (Morris) v Westminster City Council* [2005] EWCA Civ 1184, [2006] HLR 8, CA.

Claims for damages

19.328 If an applicant for accommodation under HA 1996, Pt 7[1] or H(W)A 2014, Pt 2, is not dealt with properly by a local housing authority, he or she may suffer considerable personal loss and hardship. Ordinarily, the law would provide a right to recompense through an award of financial compensation or damages at the suit of the individual who had suffered loss. That is *not* the case for applicants seeking assistance under HA 1996, Pt 7[2] or under H(W)A 2014, Pt 2.

1   As amended by HRA 2017 for applications for homelessness assistance made to local housing authorities in England on or after 3 April 2018.
2   As amended by HRA 2017 for applications for homelessness assistance made to local housing authorities in England on or after 3 April 2018.

19.329 The House of Lords decision in *O'Rourke v Camden London Borough Council*[1] established that damages were not available at common law for a local housing authority's breach of its statutory duty owed to a homeless person. The local housing authority, when dealing with an application for homelessness assistance, is implementing a scheme of social welfare that is intended to confer benefits at public expense on the grounds of public policy. To implement the scheme involves the local housing authority making discretionary decisions as to whether to provide accommodation and the type of accommodation to be provided. The House of Lords decided that it was unlikely that Parliament had intended that any errors of judgment made by the local housing authority in those circumstances would give rise to an obligation to make financial reparation.

1   *O'Rourke v Camden London Borough Council* [1998] AC 188, HL.

19.330 Since 2 October 2000, it has been possible for damages to be claimed for breach of an applicant's human rights where the court is satisfied that the award is necessary to afford 'just satisfaction' to the applicant[1]. This has been used to explore possible compensation claims in recent years. A failure to provide suitable accommodation does not breach the applicant's right to respect for his or her home[2]. It might, in particular circumstances, breach the applicant's right to respect for his or her family or private life under Art 8 of the European Convention on Human Rights[3]. Damages should be assessed on the basis that they should not be a lesser amount than damages that would be awarded for a claim in tort, and using the amount of compensation awarded by the Local Government Ombudsmen as a reference point[4].

1   Human Rights Act 1998, s 8(1) and (2). See J Compton 'Claiming Damages: a public law perspective' (2006) March *Legal Action*, p 23.
2   *R (Morris) v Newham London Borough Council* [2002] EWHC 1262 (Admin); and *Chapman v UK* (2001) 33 EHRR 18, ECtHR.
3   Human Rights Act 1998, Sch 1, Art 8. See *R (Bernard) v Enfield London Borough Council* [2002] EWHC 2282 (Admin), (2003) 35 HLR 2, Admin Ct.
4   *Anufrijeva v Southwark London Borough Council* [2003] EWCA Civ 1406, [2004] HLR 22, CA.

19.331 The Court of Appeal in *Anufrijeva v Southwark London Borough Council*[1] considered the circumstances in which damages should be awarded for breach of an applicant's rights under Art 8. In considering the extent to which Art 8(1) imposed a positive obligation on states to provide public assistance, it concluded that generally a failure to provide welfare support was unlikely to infringe a single applicant's rights under Art 8 if it did not also infringe his or her rights under Art 3 (not to be subjected to inhuman or degrading treatment). However, where families were involved, the applicant's right to respect for his or her family life might be more easily infringed.

Before a local housing authority could be held to have failed to respect an applicant's private or family life, there had to be an element of culpability, involving at the very least knowledge by the local housing authority that the applicant's private or family life was at risk. For maladministration to infringe an applicant's Art 8 rights, the consequences (that the maladministration would lead to lack of respect for the applicant's private or family life) must be serious and foreseeable.[2] Damages would be awarded, taking into account Judicial Studies Board Guidelines, Criminal Injuries Compensation awards, and awards by the Parliamentary and Local Government Ombudsmen for maladministration.

[1] *Anufrijeva v Southwark London Borough Council* [2003] EWCA Civ 1406, [2004] HLR 22, CA.

[2] See also *R (McDonagh) v Enfield London Borough Council* [2018] EWHC 1287 (Admin), where an Administrative Court judge decided that Art 8 had not been infringed when a mother and her disabled child were living in a property where the child could not access the bathroom or toilet.

19.332 In a case relating to prisoners' rights, the House of Lords considered generally the principles under which damages for breach of Convention rights should be awarded. It held that in many cases, the finding that there had been a violation should be 'just satisfaction' for the applicant. Where the finding in itself was not sufficient for there to be 'just satisfaction', damages should be assessed in accordance with the amounts awarded by the European Court of Human Rights[1].

[1] *R (Greenfield) v Secretary of State for the Home Department* [2005] UKHL 14, [2005] 1 WLR 673, HL; and *Van Colle v Chief Constable of Hertfordshire Police* [2007] EWCA Civ 325, [2007] 1 WLR 1821, CA.

COMPLAINTS

Local complaints procedures

19.333 Every local housing authority will have a procedure for entertaining complaints made by those using its services, including the homeless. A procedure leaflet and complaint form should be readily available on request. This process will enable the HA 1996, Pt 7[1] or H(W)A 2014, Pt 2, applicant to log concerns which do not attack the merits of local housing authority decisions, but rather raise matters such as staff (mis)conduct, unfair treatment, delay, incompetence and the like.

[1] As amended by HRA 2017 for applications for homelessness assistance made to local housing authorities in England on or after 3 April 2018.

19.334 Every local housing authority will have designated one of its most senior officials as the statutory monitoring officer[1]. That person is responsible for ensuring that the local housing authority's services are administered lawfully and without maladministration. Advisers assisting those who have been poorly dealt with under HA 1996, Pt 7[2], or H(W)A 2014, Part 2, should direct their complaints to the monitoring officer. For example, in one case a local housing authority reached an incorrect decision and resisted an appeal which had overwhelming merit. On receipt of a complaint from the trial judge, the local monitoring officer engaged an independent firm of solicitors to scrutinise what had gone wrong. As a result of their report, procedures were changed and the complainant received compensation[3].

¹   Local Government and Housing Act 1989, ss 5 and 5A.
²   As amended by HRA 2017 for applications for homelessness assistance made to local housing authorities in England on or after 3 April 2018.
³   *Mohamud v Lambeth London Borough Council* (2003) March *Legal Action*, p 31.

19.335 Every local housing authority has a specific power to pay compensation, or provide some other suitable remedy, to any complainant who has been adversely affected by council action or inaction which may amount to maladministration[1].

¹   Local Government Act 2000, s 92.

Complaints to the Ombudsmen

19.336 Complaints can be made to the Local Government and Social Care Ombudsman (or Public Services Ombudsman for Wales) where it is alleged that the applicant has been subject to maladministration[1]. The complaint can be made informally, but the Local Government and Social Care Ombudsman's website publishes useful information as to how to complain.

¹   See English Code, paras 19.30–19.32; Welsh Code, paras 20.46–20.48.

19.337 A complaint to the Local Government and Social Care Ombudsman must be made within 12 months of the maladministration complained of, and the applicant should first complain through the local housing authority's internal complaints procedure[1]. If the applicant has not made an internal complaint before complaining to the Local Government and Social Care Ombudsman, the Ombudsman will refer the complaint to the local housing authority's internal complaints procedure before investigating it.

¹   See **19.333–19.336**.

19.338 The Local Government and Social Care Ombudsman has the power to make recommendations, if he or she concludes that maladministration has occurred, and can recommend that the local housing authority compensate the applicant. The current rate for the 'distress' element alone in homelessness cases is in the general range of £500–£2000[1].

¹   Recent awards have included: £300 *Complaint against Newham London Borough*, 11 000 383, 16 March 2012 (2012) May *Legal Action*, p 34; £5,050 *Complaint against Dover District Council*, 09 017 510, 31 July 2012 (2012) October *Legal Action*, p 38; £1,000 to each complainant in *Complaint against Westminster City Council*, 12 009 140, 13 September 2013 (2013) November *Legal Action*, p 33 (use of bed and breakfast accommodation for period in excess of six weeks; £1,750 and £2,000 *Complaints against Ealing London Borough Council* 12 004 331 and 12 011 635, 22 November 2013 (2014) February *Legal Action*, p 30 (bed and breakfast for more than six weeks); £200–£250 per month Complaints *against Croydon London Borough Council*, 13 08 594 and 13 006 148, 17 March 2014 (bed and breakfast for more than six weeks); £750 *Complaint against Newham London Borough Council*, 13 005 484, 17 March 2014 (2014) June *Legal Action*, p 40 (offer of accommodation in Birmingham); £2,100 *Complaint against Newham London Borough Council*, 13 017 531, 3 June 2014 (2014) October *Legal Action*, p 51 (leaving the complainant in unsuitable accommodation); £500 for a failure to notify a written decision on an application for

homelessness assistance and £200 to the applicant's father to reflect his time and trouble in complaining on behalf of his daughter *Complaint against Barnet London Borough Council* 16 002 971, 8 March 2017 (2017), *Legal Action*, May, p 42; and £500 for a failure to notify a decision on a suitability review *Complaint against Kettering Borough Council*, 16 012 028, 3 August 2017 (2017) November *Legal Action*, p 42.

19.339 Reports of individual investigations by the Ombudsmen can be found at the Local Government and Social Care Ombudsman's website and many are noted in the monthly article Recent Developments in Housing Law in *Legal Action*. Since April 2013, the Ombudsmen have published on their website the text of all complaints made to them in homelessness cases.

19.340 For complaints involving local housing authorities in Wales, applicants should, having exhausted the local housing authority's internal complaints procedure, seek an investigation by the Public Services Ombudsman for Wales. In 2006, the Public Services Ombudsman for Wales produced a comprehensive report on the practices of local housing authorities in Wales relating to homelessness[1] and the Ombudsman has since published many investigation reports on homelessness complaints.

[1] *Housing Allocations and Homelessness, a special report by the Local Government Ombudsman for Wales* (Public Services Ombudsman for Wales, 2006). See **7.26**.

Chapter 20

OTHER HELP WITH ACCOMMODATION FROM LOCAL AUTHORITIES

Contents

INTRODUCTION

20.1 The *homelessness* provisions in Housing Act 1996 (HA 1996), Pt 7[1] and Housing (Wales) Act 2014, (H(W)A 2014), are intended to ensure that local housing authorities provide short-term accommodation for those in the most urgent housing need. The *allocation* provisions in HA 1996, Pt 6 are intended to facilitate the sensible distribution of longer-term homes in social housing by local housing authorities. Taken together, the objective of HA 1996, Pts 6 and 7[2], and H(W)A 2014, Pt 2, is to ensure that local housing authorities can help most people in housing need by providing them with temporary accommodation and/or by helping them find alternative homes.

[1] As amended by HRA 2017, for applications for homelessness assistance made to local housing authorities in England on or after 3 April 2018.
[2] As amended by HRA 2017, for applications for homelessness assistance made to local housing authorities in England on or after 3 April 2018.

20.2 Although HA 1996, Pts 6 and 7[1], and H(W)A 2014, Pt 2, are the primary statutory means by which local authorities meet housing need, they are not the only statutory provisions that allow local authorities to help with accommodation.

[1] As amended by HRA 2017, for applications for homelessness assistance made to local housing authorities in England on or after 3 April 2018.

20.3 This chapter focuses on help that local authorities (both local housing authorities and other authorities) can, and in some cases must, give to those needing accommodation, either by the local authorities providing accommodation themselves, or by helping applicants to find it. Initially, the chapter outlines the general power to help (available in almost all cases) before turning separately to consider the special powers and duties that apply, in turn, to adults, young people and children, first in England and then in Wales. These powers and duties have been subject to considerable change in recent years. In England, the relevant provisions of the National Assistance Act 1948 have been replaced by the Care Act 2014 which came into force on 1 April 2015[1]. While in Wales, the relevant provisions of both the National Assistance Act 1948 and the Children Act 1989 have been replaced by the Social Services and Well-being (Wales) Act 2014 which came into force on 6 April 2016[2]. Consequently, this chapter will consider in turn the law in England and then in Wales, under these statutes. The chapter concludes with a brief review of the duties to provide accommodation (in both England and Wales) under the Mental Health Act 1983 and the duties to accommodate those displaced from their homes in emergencies, in other circumstances of involuntary displacement, and under the Human Rights Act 1998.

[1] Care Act 2014 (Commencement No 4) Order 2015, SI 2015/993, art 2, subject to the transitional and saving provisions contained in Care Act 2014 (Transitional Provision) Order 2015, SI 2015/995, art 2.
[2] Social Services and Well-being (Wales) Act 2014 (Commencement No 3, Savings and Transitional Provisions) Order 2016, SI 2016/412 (W 130), art 2, subject to the transitional and saving provisions contained in art 3 and art 4.

20.4 This chapter cannot, however, cover all the help available to meet housing need. Apart from the powers and duties reviewed here, both central and local government departments have developed other arrangements to assist people in housing need. Central government's housing policy in England is the responsibility of the Ministry of Housing, Communities and Local Government (MHCLG). In Wales, the Welsh Government has responsibility for housing policy. Those in need of accommodation can also apply directly to other social sector providers such as private registered providers in England or registered social landlords in Wales, charitable trusts and co-operatives, and to private landlords[1]. For those on low incomes wishing to become tenants, housing benefit or, latterly, universal credit is available to help with the cost of renting[2]. On a more limited basis, the cost of mortgage interest can be claimed through the income support scheme, so that the poorest owner-occupiers can remain in their homes, and there are several schemes to assist those on low incomes with house purchase. There is also a wholly separate statutory scheme that provides accommodation for individuals seeking asylum in the UK[3]. It is not possible to set out here the details of all these different arrangements. Rather, this chapter concentrates on the powers and duties of local authorities to provide accommodation directly, or secure the provision of accommodation by others.

[1]   See *Code of Guidance for Local Authorities on the Allocation of Accommodation and Homelessness* (Welsh Government, March 2016) (the Welsh Code) at the CD Rom with this book, Annex 12 on the duties on private registered providers and registered social landlords to co-operate with local housing authorities and see Chapter 6.

[2]   There have been considerable changes to the availability and amount of housing benefit in recent years and prospective tenants should always obtain a pre-tenancy determination which will inform them how much housing benefit they will be entitled to.

[3]   Immigration and Asylum Act 1999, Pt 6, which set up the scheme formerly known as the National Asylum Support Service (NASS), now operated by the Home Office. The extent of that scheme is outside the scope of this book, except in so far as there is an interplay with statutory powers and duties exercised by local housing authorities. A detailed guide can be found in Walker, Lawrence and Gellner's *Benefits for Migrants Handbook* (CPAG, 9th edn, 2017). Note that there are outstanding amendments to this scheme contained in the Immigration Act 2016. It is not clear if or when the Home Office intends to bring these amendments into force.

GENERAL POWER FOR LOCAL AUTHORITIES TO HELP WITH ACCOMMODATION

20.5 Because they are statutory bodies, local authorities can only undertake functions conferred on them by legislation. The legislative provision concerned with accommodation has developed incrementally for over a century. This has produced a veritable hotchpotch of powers and duties enabling local authorities to give help with housing and other social needs, including the provisions of what are now HA 1996, Pts 6 and 7[1] and H(W)A 2014, Pt 2. However, for cases falling outside the major provisions of those Parts, a local authority would have to scrabble about to identify some other discrete source of statutory power before it could know whether, when and how it could help to provide accommodation.

[1]   As amended by HRA 2017, for applications for homelessness assistance made to local housing authorities in England on or after 3 April 2018.

20.6 Parliament adopted a wholly new approach when it enacted the Local Government Act 2000 (LGA 2000). This gave local authorities in both England and Wales wide-ranging statutory powers to meet local social needs, expressed as a power to promote economic, social and environmental 'well-being'[1]. The UK government's guidance suggested that this general power in LGA 2000, s 2, should be seen as a 'power of first resort' which could be 'wide ranging' and would lead to the abandonment of the 'traditionally cautious approach'[2].

[1]   Local Government Act 2000, s 2.

[2]   *Power to promote or improve economic, social or environmental well-being* (ODPM Guidance, 2000), Chapter 1, paras 6–7 and 10.

20.7 Since 4 April 2012, as a result of amendment by the Localism Act 2011, this power has only been available to local authorities in Wales[1]. In England, it has been replaced by the more limited (though still general) power under the Localism Act 2011, s 1, which endows local authorities in England with the power to do anything which individuals generally may do[2].

[1]   Localism Act 2011, s 1 and Sch 1.

2   Localism Act 2011, s 1(1).

Wales

20.8 An individual who needs accommodation (or aid with obtaining accommodation), and is unable or unwilling to obtain help through HA 1996, Pt 7[1] or H(W)A 2014, Pt 2, can ask any local authority in Wales (including a local housing authority) to provide assistance under the general power in LGA 2000, s 2. There is no prescribed application process governing the request for help (no statutory form and not even a requirement that an application be made in writing). However, it makes good sense for any request for help to include a reference to the statutory provision.

1   As amended by HRA 2017, for applications for homelessness assistance made to local housing authorities in England on or after 3 April 2018.

20.9 Under LGA 2000, s 2, local authorities in Wales have the power to do 'anything' that they consider is likely to achieve the improvement or promotion of the 'social well-being' of their area[1]. That includes 'anything' for the benefit of, or in relation to, any person resident in, or simply present in, the local authority's area[2].

1   LGA 2000, s 2(1)(b).
2   LGA 2000, s 2(2)(b).

20.10 To put the scope for assistance with housing beyond doubt, LGA 2000, specifically provides that the power includes a power to give 'financial assistance to any person'[1] (so as to enable that person to find his or her own accommodation) and a power to provide 'accommodation to any person'[2].

1   LGA 2000, s 2(4)(b).
2   LGA 2000, s 2(4)(f).

20.11 Local authorities in Wales can therefore be asked to exercise this power in order to provide accommodation either directly or indirectly, or to assist with financial help in obtaining accommodation, eg with the costs of rental deposits or rent-in-advance, etc. In *R (J) v Enfield London Borough Council*[1], the court found that the power under LGA 2000, s 2 permitted the local authority to help with payments so that a family could obtain accommodation. The power has also been used to offer financial assistance for travel arrangements to an applicant who could not afford to fund those travel arrangements[2]. The power is by no means restricted to local housing authorities – others (eg county councils and local councils) have equal access to the power[3].

1   *R (J) v Enfield London Borough Council* [2002] EWHC 432 (Admin), (2002) 34 HLR 38, Admin Ct.
2   *R (Grant) v Lambeth LBC* [2004] EWCA Civ 1171, [2005] HLR 27, CA.
3   LGA 2000, s 1, as amended by Local Government and Public Involvement in Health Act 2002, s 77, defines 'local authority'.

20.12 It must be emphasised that LGA 2000, s 2 contains only a power and not a duty. A local authority in Wales cannot be compelled to provide help under this section, save where the exercise of the power is necessary in order to avoid a breach of a person's human rights contrary to Human Rights Act 1998 (HRA 1998), s 6[1]. The LGA 2000 contains no mechanism for statutory review or appeal against decisions about whether to exercise the power or how to exercise it. Nor does it provide any quality criteria, such as a requirement that any accommodation provided must be reasonable or suitable.

[1]   See **20.110–20.123**.

20.13 Anyone disappointed by the refusal to exercise the power, or a decision to exercise it in a particular way, can invoke the local authority's own complaints procedure and, if still dissatisfied, complain to the Public Services Ombudsman for Wales[1]. Alternatively, if the local authority is behaving irrationally, or in some other way unlawfully, a challenge could be brought in judicial review proceedings[2].

[1]   See **19.333–19.340**.
[2]   See *R (Theophilus) v Lewisham London Borough Council* [2002] EWHC 1371, [2002] 3 All ER 851, QBD as an example of a successful challenge to the refusal of an application for LGA 2000, s 2 assistance. And see **19.306–19.327** for judicial review.

20.14 However, there is an important qualification. Local authorities cannot use LGA 2000, s 2 to do anything that they are prevented from doing by a prohibition, restriction or limitation contained in some other enactment[1]. So, for example, a local housing authority in Wales cannot use the power to allocate an individual a secure tenancy if such an allocation would be outside the terms of the local housing authority's own allocation scheme, because to do so would breach a statutory prohibition[2]. Likewise, the power cannot be used by a local authority in Wales to assist with housing (or with the costs of housing) for an adult or child who is barred from help with accommodation under the Social Services and Well-being (Wales) Act 2014[3].

[1]   LGA 2000, s 3(1).
[2]   The prohibition in HA 1996, s 167(8).
[3]   See **20.69–20.98**. See *R (Khan) v Oxfordshire County Council* [2004] EWCA 309, [2004] HLR 41, CA, *R(MK) v Barking and Dagenham London Borough Council* [2013] EWHC 3486 (Admin), Admin Ct, and *R (GS) v Camden London Borough Council* [2016] EWHC 1762 (Admin), [2016] HLR 43, Admin Ct for a discussion of the way in which this statutory qualification operates. Note though, the latter two cases were decided under the analogous provisions of the Care Act 2014. See **20.19–20.38**.

England

20.15 On 4 April 2012, the power under LGA 2000, s 2 was replaced in England by the more limited (though still general) power under the Localism Act 2011, s 1, which endows local authorities in England with the power to do anything which individuals generally may do[1]. Building on the approach in LGA 2000, s 2, local authorities cannot use Localism Act 2011, s 1 to do anything:

- which the local authority is unable to do by virtue of a prohibition, restriction or other limitation contained in an enactment pre-dating the Localism Act 2011;

• which the local authority is unable to do by virtue of a prohibition, restriction or other limitation contained in an enactment post-dating the Localism Act 2011 which excludes the use of the general power, excludes the use of all of the local authority's powers, or excludes the use of all of the local authority's powers with named exceptions that do not include the general power[2].

¹ Localism Act 2011, s 1(1).
² Localism Act 2011, s 2(2).

20.16 By way of illustration, the High Court held in *R(MK) v Barking and Dagenham London Borough Council*[1], that a local authority had no power under Localism Act 2011, s 1, to accommodate a young adult, who had overstayed in the UK illegally, with her aunt and cousins. Accommodation could not have been provided to the entire extended family under the Asylum Act 1999 or the Children Act 1989. So to have provided her with accommodation with her family in these circumstances would have been to circumvent those statutory schemes.

¹ [2013] EWHC 3486 (Admin), Admin Ct. See also *R (AM) v Havering London Borough Council and Tower Hamlets London Borough Council* [2015] EWHC 1004 (Admin), [2015] PTSR 1242.

20.17 In contrast, in *R (GS) v Camden London Borough Council*[1], the High Court held that the provision of accommodation was necessary under the Localism Act, s 1 in order to avoid a breach of European Convention on Human Rights, Art 3[2] in respect of a homeless Swiss national who suffered from physical and mental health problems (and was unable to work as a result) who was ineligible for support under the Care Act 2014[3].

¹ [2016] EWHC 1762 (Admin), [2016] HLR 43, Admin Ct.
² See **20.113–20.118**.
³ See **20.19–20.38**.

20.18 The different outcome in these two cases turned on the differing application of the the limitation contained in Localism Act 2011, s 2(2) to the Children Act 1989 and the Care Act 2014 respectively[1]. In broad terms where an enactment pre-dating the Localism Act 2011 does not allow a local authority to act in a certain way, then the general power may not be used to circumvent that restriction. But, for enactments that post-date the Localism Act, unless the enactment specifically rules out the use of the general power, then it remains available.

¹ See *R (GS) v Camden London Borough Council* [2016] EWHC 1762 (Admin), [2016] HLR 43, Admin Ct at [51]–[62] per Mr Peter Marquand sitting as a deputy High Court judge.

SPECIFIC POWERS FOR LOCAL AUTHORITIES TO HELP WITH ACCOMMODATION: ENGLAND

Adults

Powers and duties under the Care Act 2014

20.19 Implementing the recommendations of the Law Commission report on Adult Social Care[1], the powers and duties to provide accommodation under the National Assistance Act 1948, s 21 (together with a host of other statutory provisions governing adult social care) have been consolidated and modernised to produce the Care Act 2014 (CA 2014)[2]. The CA 2014 came into force on 1 April 2015[3]. The CA 2014 is a comprehensive and detailed piece of legislation enacting wide-ranging reforms across the field of adult social care. What follows is no more than a basic overview of those functions within the CA 2014 under which vulnerable adults can access accommodation, and how they can go about doing so[4]. The statutory provisions referred to below should be read in conjunction with the relevant passages of the Care and Support Statutory Guidance (the Guidance)[5].

[1] Law Com 326, HC 941, May 2011.
[2] The CA 2014 applies to adults only. The responsibility for arranging accommodation for children in England falls principally under the Children Act 1989. See **20.39–20.68**.
[3] Care Act 2014 (Commencement No 4) Order 2015, SI 2015/993, art 2, subject to the transitional and saving provisions contained in Care Act 2014 (Transitional Provision) Order 2015, SI 2015/995, art 2.
[4] For further reading see T Spencer-Lane *Care Act Manual* (1st edn, Sweet and Maxwell 2014).
[5] *Care and Support Statutory Guidance* (Department of Health, June 2014). Statutory Guidance issued under Care Act 2014, s 78.

THE POWER/DUTY TO PROVIDE ACCOMMODATION

20.20 The duty to provide accommodation, along with a range of other services, is contained in CA 2014, s 18. Under CA 2014, s 18(1) and (5) a local authority is required to provide 'care and support' to an adult, which may include accommodation[1], if:

- he or she is ordinarily resident in the local authority's area, or is present in its area but of no settled residence; and
- he or she has a need for care and support which meets the eligibility criteria; and
- he or she meets the detailed financial criteria set out in CA 2014, Pt 1[2].

[1] CA 2014, s 8.
[2] CA 2014, s 18.

Ordinary residence

20.21 Whether a person is ordinarily resident in the local authority's area is to be determined in accordance with CA 2014, s 39. This section does not seek to define the term 'ordinary residence' but provides that a person will be deemed to be ordinarily resident in certain circumstances, such as where he or she is provided with accommodation under the Mental Health Act 1983, s 117[1]. The prior case law on ordinary residence under National Assistance Act 1948, Pt 3 will remain applicable outside of the particular scenarios dealt with in CA 2014, s 39[2].

[1] See 20.99–20.104.
[2] See *R (Cornwall Council) v Secretary of State for Health* [2015] UKSC 46, [2016] AC 137, SC on how to determine ordinary residence. Although that was a case concerning ordinary residence under NAA 1948, Lord Carnwath at [38] indicated that the same approach would apply under the Care Act 2014.

A need for care and support

20.22 Whether a person has a need for care and support which meets the eligibility criteria is to be determined in accordance with CA 2014, s 13. Needs are deemed to meet the eligibility criteria if they are of a description specified in regulations made under CA 2014, s 13(7) and (8), or form part of a combination of needs described in the regulations[1]. The relevant regulations are the Care and Support (Eligibility Criteria) Regulations 2015[2]. The regulations provide that an adult's needs will meet the eligibility criteria if:

- the adult's needs arise from or are related to a physical or mental impairment or illness; and
- as a result of the adult's needs the adult is unable to achieve two or more specified outcomes; and
- as a consequence there is, or is likely to be, a significant impact on the adult's well-being[3].

As to the meaning of 'need', Morris J, in the case of *R (Luke Davey) v Oxfordshire County Council*[4] explained that the term:

' . . . denotes something more than merely "want" but falls far short of "cannot survive without". The words "are in need of", refers to present needs and not the future. The duty should not be extended to a person who does not currently satisfy a requirement simply because he will or may do so in the future.[5]'

[1] CA 2014, 13(7).
[2] Care and Support (Eligibility Criteria) Regulations 2015, SI 2015/315.
[3] SI 2015/315, reg 2(1).
[4] [2017] EWHC 354 (Admin), [2017] PTSR 904. Upheld by the Court of Appeal in *R (Luke Davey) v Oxfordshire County Council* [2017] EWCA 1308, (2017) 20 CCLR 303, CA
[5] *R (Luke Davey) v Oxfordshire County Council* [2017] EWHC 354 (Admin), [2017] PTSR 904 at [57] per Morris J.

20.23 The specified outcomes are:

- managing and maintaining nutrition;
- maintaining personal hygiene;
- managing toilet needs;
- being appropriately clothed;
- being able to make use of the adult's home safely;
- maintaining a habitable home environment;
- developing and maintaining family or other personal relationships;
- accessing and engaging in work, training, education or volunteering;
- making use of necessary facilities or services in the local community including public transport, and recreational facilities or services; and

- carrying out any caring responsibilities the adult has for a child[1].

[1] SI 2015/315, reg 2(2).

20.24 In this context an adult is to be regarded as being 'unable to achieve an outcome' if he or she:

- is unable to achieve it without assistance;
- is able to achieve it without assistance but doing so causes the adult significant pain, distress or anxiety;
- is able to achieve it without assistance but doing so endangers or is likely to endanger the health or safety of the adult, or of others; or
- is able to achieve it without assistance but takes significantly longer to do so than would normally be expected[1].

As to the meaning of the word 'significant', the Guidance explains that:

> The term 'significant' is not defined by the regulations, and must therefore be understood to have its everyday meaning. Local authorities will have to consider whether the adult's needs and their consequent inability to achieve the relevant outcomes will have an important, consequential effect on their daily lives, their independence and their wellbeing[2].

[1] SI 2015/315, reg 2(3).
[2] Guidance, para 6.109.

Financial eligibility

20.25 Whether a person meets the financial criteria for care and support under either CA 2014, s 18(1) or (5) is calculated in accordance with CA 2014, ss 14–18 and the Care and Support (Charging and Assessment of Resources) Regulations 2014[1]. The detail of the financial eligibility criteria is beyond the scope of this book.

[1] Care and Support (Charging and Assessment of Resources) Regulations 2014, SI 2014/2672.

The duty to meet eligible needs

20.26 Where a person who is ordinarily resident has a need for care and support for which he or she is financially eligible, a local authority will be required to meet those of his or her needs for care and support which satisfy the eligibility criteria[1]. But the question of how to meet those needs is a matter for the local authority[2]. It follows that if a person requires accommodation in order to meet a need for care and support which satisfies the eligibility criteria, the local authority must secure accommodation for him or her, either by providing accommodation itself, by arranging for another to provide it or by making direct payments to the person in order for him or her to pay for it[3]. In *R (SG) v Haringey London Borough Council*[4] (the first case relying on the accommodation provisions under CA 2014), the judge took the view that a local authority would be compelled to provide accommodation, where the care and support needed were of a type normally provided in the home, and would be 'effectively useless' without the provision of accommodation[5]. On the other hand, if a person has a need for care and support which does not meet the eligibility criteria, or if the local authority can meet his or her needs otherwise than by the provision of accommodation, the local authority will not be required to secure accommodation. In *R (GS) v Camden LBC*[6], Peter Marquand QC, sitting as a deputy High Court judge, held that a need for accommodation by itself does not constitute a need for care and support.

[1]   CA 2014, s 18(1) or (5).
[2]   CA 2014, s 8.
[3]   CA 2014, s 8(2).
[4]   [2015] EWHC Civ 2579 (Admin), 18 CCLR 444, Admin Ct. Upheld on appeal in *R (SG) v Haringey London Borough Council* [2017] EWCA Civ 322, CA.
[5]   Following the approach taken in respect of National Assistance Act 1948, s 21, by the Supreme Court in *R (SL) v Westminster City Council* [2013] UKSC 27, [2013] 1 WLR 1445, SC.
[6]   [2016] EWHC 1762 (Admin), [2016] HLR 43.

20.27 Where the person has a need for care and support which the local authority is not required to meet under CA 2014, s 18, the local authority retains a power to meet that need, so long as the person in question is ordinarily resident in the local authority's area, or is present in its area but of no settled residence[1]. A vulnerable[2] homeless person without accommodation who does not meet the CA 2014 eligibility criteria might consider requesting that the local authority exercise its discretion to accommodate him or her in any event.

[1]   CA 2014, s 19(1).
[2]   Used here in the non-technical sense, in contrast to CHAPTER **12**.

20.28 The powers and duties under CA 2014, ss 18–19 are residual. That is, a local authority is not permitted to do anything under these sections which it is required to do under the Housing Act 1996 or the National Health Service Act 2006 save, in the latter case, where the provision of care and support under CA 2014, ss 18–19 is merely incidental to the provision of health services by the NHS[1].

[1]   CA 2014, ss 22 and 23.

ASSESSMENT AND CARE PLANNING

20.29 The duty to assess a person's needs for care and support under CA 2014, Pt 1 is contained in CA 2014, s 9. The duty will arise where 'it appears' to the local authority that the person 'may have needs for care and support'[1]. That is a low threshold. In urgent cases, the local authority has a discretion to provide services while the assessment is being carried out, irrespective of whether the person is ordinarily resident in its area[2].

[1]   CA 2014, s 9(1). See Guidance, para 6.13.
[2]   CA 2014, s 19(3).

20.30 The assessment should be carried out in accordance with the requirements set out in CA 2014, s 9 and regulations made by the Secretary of State under CA 2014, s 12. The relevant regulations are the Care and Support (Assessment) Regulations 2014[1]. The assessment of children who are likely to have a need for care and support after becoming 18 is governed by CA 2014, ss 58–59[2]. There is no fixed time period in which the assessment must be completed. Rather it should be undertaken over a reasonable and appropriate timescale[3].

[1] Care and Support (Assessment) Regulations 2014, SI 2014/2827.
[2] See further **20.39–20.68** for the duties owed to children and young persons under Children Act 1989.
[3] Guidance, para 6.29.

20.31 There are certain general requirements set out in the Care and Support (Assessment) Regulations 2014[1] with which a lawful assessment must comply[2]. For example, an assessment must be carried out in a way that is 'appropriate and proportionate to the needs and circumstances of the person to whom it relates' and in carrying out the assessment, a local authority must have regard to the wishes and preferences of that person[3]. A lawful assessment should also expressly address the well-being principle[4]. A failure to carry out an assessment, if the threshold is made out, is a breach of the local authority's statutory duty. It can be enforced by bringing a claim by way of judicial review seeking a mandatory order requiring the local authority to carry out an assessment[5].

[1] Care and Support (Assessment) Regulations 2014, SI 2014/2827.
[2] Care and Support (Assessment) Regulations 2014, SI 2014/2827, reg 3. See further Guidance, para 6.3.
[3] Care and Support (Assessment) Regulations 2014, SI 2014/2827, reg 3(1) and (2).
[4] *R (JF) v the London Borough of Merton* [2017] EWHC 1519 (Admin), (2017) 20 CCLR 241, Admin Ct and *R (Luke Davey) v Oxfordshire County Council* [2017] EWHC 354 (Admin), [2017] PTSR 904, Admin Ct at [20]–[22] upheld by the Court of Appeal in *R (Luke Davey) v Oxfordshire County Council* [2017] EWCA 1308, (2017) 20 CCLR 303, CA. See **20.34** for the well-being principle.
[5] See **19.306–19.327** on practice and procedure for judicial review claims.

20.32 The duty to assess is not confined to the local authority in whose area the person is ordinarily resident. Whenever a person presents to a local authority and it appears that the person may have a need for care and support, the duty to assess will arise[1]. However, since the duty to provide care and support under CA 2014, s 18 will only be owed by the local authority in whose area the person is ordinarily resident[2] he or she would be well advised to direct his or her application to that local authority. Any dispute as to which local authority owes the duty to assess should be decided by the Secretary of State for Health[3].

[1] CA 2014, s 9(1).
[2] Save in those cases where the person has no settled residence (CA 2014, s 18(1)).
[3] CA 2014, s 40.

20.33 Upon completion of the assessment, if the local authority concludes that it is required to provide care and support pursuant to CA 2014, s 18, it must prepare a care and support plan[1]. The plan must meet the requirements set out in CA 2014, s 25. It should be completed within a reasonable period[2] and kept under review[3].

[1] CA 2014, s 24.
[2] Guidance, para 10.84 and *R (D) v Brent LBC* [2015] EWHC 3224 (Admin), Admit Ct at [27].
[3] CA 2014, s 27(4).

THE WELL-BEING PRINCIPLE

20.34 The powers and duties outlined at **20.19–20.33** are all subject to the general duty under CA 2014, s 1 to promote the person's well-being. 'Well-being' is defined in CA 2014, s 1(2) and includes such matters as 'well-being so far as relating to . . . the suitability of living accommodation.'[1] The well-being principle has been described as 'the most important section of the Act'[2] and the Guidance makes clear that 'housing has a vital role to play' in securing a person's well-being[3].

[1] See further Guidance, para 4.91.
[2] *R (Luke Davey) v Oxfordshire County Council* [2017] EWCA 1308, (2017) 20 CCLR 303, CA at [48] per Bean LJ.
[3] Guidance, para 15.58.

PERSONS FROM ABROAD

20.35 A person subject to immigration control who is excluded from benefits[1], and whose need for care and support has arisen solely because of destitution or because of the physical effects or the anticipated physical effects of destitution cannot be provided with care and support under CA 2014, Pt 1[2]. Accommodation for those who are seeking asylum is the responsibility of the Home Office.

[1] By Immigration and Asylum Act 1999, s 115.
[2] CA 2014, s 21(1).

20.36 There is an additional prohibition on providing support (including accommodation) under CA 2014, Pt 1 to persons who fall within one of the following five classes of persons from abroad[1]:

- refugees granted refugee status by another state of the European Economic Area (EEA)[2];
- nationals of another state of the EEA;
- asylum-seekers whose claims for asylum have failed and who have failed to cooperate with removal directions;
- persons who are not asylum-seekers and are unlawfully present in the UK; and
- failed asylum-seekers with dependent children, where those families have been certified by the Secretary of State as not having taken reasonable steps to leave the UK[3].

[1] Nationality, Immigration and Asylum Act 2002, s 54 and Sch 3 as amended by the Care Act 2014 and Children and Families Act 2014 (Consequential Amendments) Order 2015, SI 2015/914.
[2] For a list of EEA states, see **11.29**, Box 2.
[3] Nationality, Immigration and Asylum Act 2002, s 54 and Sch 3; Withholding and Withdrawal of Support (Travel Assistance and Temporary Accommodation) Regulations 2002, SI 2002/3078.

20.37 There are two exceptions to that general prohibition:

(1) where the support is necessary to prevent an interference with a person's human rights under the European Convention[1]; or

(2)   for the first two classes of people, provision of support can be made in the form of assistance with travel arrangements to their home countries[2]. Adults with dependent children may receive limited temporary accommodation while they await implementation of the travel arrangements[3].

[1]   Nationality, Immigration and Asylum Act 2002, Sch 3, para 3. See *R (Limbuela) v Secretary of State for the Home Department* [2005] UKHL 66, [2006] 1 AC 396, HL, as to the operation of this threshold. For cases raising issues as to breach of Art 8 rights (which generally involve adults with dependent children), see **20.55–20.56**. The Court of Appeal held in *R (Clue) v Birmingham City Council* [2010] EWCA Civ 460, [2011] 1 WLR 99, CA, that where an applicant had made an application for leave to remain in the UK, that claim was not hopeless or abusive and that claim would be forfeited if he or she had to leave the UK before it was decided, it would be a breach of human rights to refuse support.

[2]   SI 2002/3078, reg 3; there is no obligation to provide assistance with travel arrangements to the third and fourth classes, who are expected to comply with removal directions.

[3]   See **20.51–20.54**.

20.38 If a request is made for support by anyone falling within one of the third, fourth or fifth classes, the local authority is obliged to inform the Home Office[1].

[1]   Nationality, Immigration and Asylum Act 2002, Sch 3, para 14.

Children and young people

Powers and duties under the Children Act 1989

20.39 Local children's services authorities have a duty, under the Children Act 1989 (CA 1989),[1] s 17(1) to safeguard and promote the welfare of children[2] within their area who are in need[3]. So far as is consistent with that duty, they must promote the upbringing of such children by their families by providing a range and level of services appropriate to those children's needs. This duty is a target duty, meaning that it is owed generally to children within the children's services authority's area. The children's services authority has a substantial discretion as to how it performs that duty.

[1]   At the time of writing, there are significant outstanding amendments to the Children Act 1989, Pt 3, contained in the Immigration Act 2016, which will change and curtail the support available to certain young migrants and their families. See C Johnston '*Housing difficulties for destitute migrant families unresolved*' (2016) November *Legal Action*. The Home Office has not given any indication of when (if at all) these amendments will come into force. For a fuller treatment of the powers and duties under the Children Act 1989, Pt 3 see Wise et al *Children in need: local authority support for children and families* (LAG, 2nd edn, 2013).

[2]   Children Act 1989, s 105 defines a child as 'a person under the age of 18'.

[3]   In discharging this duty a children's services authority is not bound by the provisions of the *Homelessness Code of Guidance for Local Authorities* (Ministry of Housing, Communities and Local Government, February 2018) found at APPENDIX 2. See *R (C, T, M, U) v Southwark London Borough Council* [2014] EWHC 3983 (Admin), Admin Ct.

ASSESSMENT

20.40 Children's services authorities must first assess whether or not a child is 'in need'. The children's services authority is under a duty to take reasonable steps to assess the needs of any child within its area who appears to be in need.

If it fails to do so, a mandatory order can be sought in judicial review compelling it to do so[1]. Where there is a material change in the circumstances upon which the conclusions of the assessment are based, then the local authority may need to carry out a reassessment[2].

[1] *R (AB and SB) v Nottinghamshire County Council* (2001) 4 CCLR 295, QBD. See also *R (G) v Barnet London Borough Council* [2003] UKHL 57, [2004] 2 AC 208, HL per Lord Nicholls at [32].
[2] *R(ES) v Barking and Dagenham LBC* [2013] EWHC 691 (Admin), Admin Ct and *R (CO) v Lewisham LBC* [2017] EWHC 1676 (Admin), Admin Ct.

20.41 The concept of being 'in need' is defined at CA 1989, s 17(10). A child is in need if he or she is disabled or if, without the provision of local authority services, the child is unlikely to achieve or maintain a reasonable standard of health or development, or his or her health or development is likely to be significantly impaired. Guidance to children's services' authorities in England is provided in *Working together to safeguard children*[1]. It is well established that a child without accommodation is 'child in need' and that the provision of accommodation can be a service to meet that need[2].

[1] *Working together to safeguard children* (HM Government, March 2015).
[2] CA 1989, s 17(6) and (10). See for example *R v Northavon District Council ex p Smith* [1994] 2 AC 402, HL; *R (G) v Barnet London Borough Council, R (W) v Lambeth London Borough Council, R (A) v Lambeth London Borough Council* [2003] UKHL 57, [2004] 2 AC 208, [2003] 3 WLR 1194, HL; and *R (AM) v Havering London Borough Council and Tower Hamlets London Borough Council* [2015] EWHC 1004 (Admin), [2015] PTSR 1242, Admin Ct.

20.42 The duty imposed on a children's services authority by CA 1989, s 17(1) is to provide services appropriate to the needs of children within its area. 'Within their area' means that the child must be actually physically present. So the duty will be owed by the children's services authority for the area where the child lives or where he or she attends school[1] though the services provided pursuant to the assessment may be provided outside of the area of the local authority responsible for providing those services[2].

[1] *R (Stewart) v Wandsworth London Borough Council, Hammersmith & Fulham London Borough Council and Lambeth London Borough Council* [2001] EWHC 709 (Admin), (2001) 4 CCLR 446, Admin Ct. See also *R (M) v Barking & Dagenham London Borough Council* [2002] EWHC 2663 (Admin), (2003) 6 CCLR 87, Admin Ct.
[2] *R (J) v Worcestershire CC* [2014] EWCA Civ 1518, [2015] PTSR 127, CA, and *R (AM) v Havering London Borough Council and Tower Hamlets London Borough Council* [2015] EWHC 1004 (Admin), [2015] PTSR 1242, Admin Ct.

20.43 Where a homeless family with children is found not to be eligible for assistance under HA 1996, Pt 7[1], or the adults are found to have become homeless intentionally so that there is no main housing duty on the local housing authority to provide accommodation, the local housing authority must ask the applicant to consent to the family being referred to the local children's services authority or department[2]. Even if the applicant refuses, the local housing authority must still make the referral if it considers that the child is, or may be, at risk of significant harm[3]. When a referral is received, the children's services authority is entitled to request advice and assistance from the local housing authority[4]. A local housing authority that has placed a homeless family outside its own district should refer the family (if it is found to be ineligible or the adult members are found to have become homeless intentionally) to its own children's services department or authority[5]. It may, of course, also seek the assistance of the children's services authority for the district in which the family has been placed, under the general provisions for co-operation in HA 1996, s 213[6].

[1] As amended by Homelessness Reduction Act 2017 (HRA 2017), for applications for homelessness assistance made to local housing authorities in England on or after 3 April 2018.
[2] HA 1996, s 213A as amended by HRA 2017, s 4(7) for applications for homelessness assistance made to local housing authorities in England on or after 3 April 2018. See **15.229–15.230**.
[3] HA 1996, s 213A(4). See also English Code, Chapter 13.
[4] HA 1996, s 213A(5) as amended by HRA 2017, s 4(7) for applications for homelessness assistance made to local housing authorities in England on or after 3 April 2018.
[5] *R (Ambrose) v Westminster City Council* (2011) July *Legal Action*, p 21, Admin Ct.
[6] See **15.230**.

20.44 Once the children's services department is aware that the child may be in need, the child's needs *must* be assessed. If the child appears to be 'in need', there is a duty to assess, which should not be deferred[1]. The content of a lawful assessment has been considered in a number of cases including *R (AB and SB) v Nottingham City Council*[2].

[1] *R (J) v Newham London Borough Council* [2001] EWHC 992 (Admin), (2002) 5 CCLR 303.
[2] [2001] EWHC Admin 235, (2001) 4 CCLR 295, Admin Ct. See *R (U (Children)) v Milton Keynes Council* [2017] EWHC 3050 (Admin), Admin Ct and *R (Stewart) v Birmingham City Council* [2018] EWHC 61 (Admin), Admin Ct for the relevance of the restrictions on the right to rent contained in Immigration Act 2014, s 21, to the assessment of the needs of those seeking accommodation under CA 1989, s 17.

20.45 Findings of fact within the assessment are for the local authority to make. Further, a local authority may be entitled to draw adverse inferences where a parent has failed to provide information during the assessment process, providing that he or she has been given a fair opportunity to respond to any concerns[1].

[1] See for example *R (O) v Lewisham London Borough Council* [2017] EWHC 2015 (Admin), Admin Ct and *R (AC) v Lambeth London Borough Council* [2017] EWHC 1796 (Admin), Admin Ct (where there was no impropriety in the assessment process) and *R (S and J) v Haringey London Borough Council* [2016] EWHC 2692 (Admin), Admin Ct, *R (OK) v Barking and Dagenham London Borough Council* [2017] EWHC 2092 (Admin), Admin Ct and *R (CO) v Lewisham London Borough Council* [2017] EWHC 1676 (Admin), Admin Ct (where a lack of procedural fairness led to the quashing of the decisions).

Services

20.46 After the assessment has been carried out, services to meet the child's identified needs may be provided. Services for the child's family or any member of his or her family may also be provided, with a view to safeguarding or promoting the child's welfare[1]. Those services can include drawing up and implementing plans to remedy inadequate accommodation[2], or the provision of a roof over the child's head if he or she is facing literal homelessness[3]. Cash can, in exceptional circumstances, be provided[4]. Therefore, in practice, a child's need for accommodation with his or her family could result in the children's services authority assisting the family financially with a deposit or rent guarantee so that they can find accommodation in the private sector[5].

Other forms of assistance could include moving a child and his or her family from inadequate to adequate accommodation[6]. It is sometimes (although not often) the case that children's services' authorities will offer accommodation to the child, or children, alone under CA 1989, s 20[7] rather than offering assistance to the whole of the family. This practice was first considered by the House of Lords in *R (A) v Lambeth London Borough Council, R (W) v Lambeth London Borough Council and R (G) v Barnet London Borough Council*[8] and found, in principle, to be lawful.

[1]   CA 1989, s 17(3).
[2]   *R v Ealing London Borough Council ex p C (A Minor)* (2000) 3 CCLR 132, CA.
[3]   Where accommodation is provided under CA 1989, s 17, there is no express requirement that such accommodation should be suitable. However local authorities, as public bodies, should only exercise their powers to promote the purpose of the statute and must act reasonably in doing so 'which may to a large extent come to, in effect, a requirement of suitability.' See *R (Yekini) v Southwark London Borough Council* [2014] EWHC 2096 (Admin) at [47] per Michael Fordham QC sitting as a deputy High Court judge.
[4]   CA 1989, s 17(6). There are a number of cases where the courts have been called upon to adjudicate on the adequacy of support provided under CA 1989, s 17(6). See for example *R (PO) v Newham LBC* [2014] EWHC 2561 (Admin), (2014) 17 CCLR 325, Admin Ct and *R (C, T, M, U) v Southwark LBC* [2016] EWCA Civ 707, [2016] HLR 36, CA. The thrust of the case law is that the setting of levels of support with reference to benefits provided under other statutory regimes without any individualized assessment of need is likely to be unlawful.
[5]   *R v Barking and Dagenham London Borough Council ex p Ebuki* (2001) March *Legal Action*, p 30, Admin Ct. For an example where a children's services authority should have considered its powers to assist with rent in the private rented sector more carefully, see *R (S) v Plymouth City Council* [2009] EWHC 1499 (Admin) October *Legal Action*, p 26, Admin Ct and [2010] EWCA Civ 1490, (2010) March *Legal Action*, p 31, CA, (refusal of permission to appeal).
[6]   *R v Tower Hamlets London Borough Council ex p Bradford* (1997) 1 CCLR 294, CA. See also *R (Mooney) v Southwark London Borough Council* [2006] EWHC 1912 (Admin), (2006) September *Legal Action*, p 14, Admin Ct.
[7]   See 20.58–20.64.
[8]   *R (G) v Barnet London Borough Council, R (W) v Lambeth London Borough Council, R (A) v Lambeth London Borough Council* [2003] UKHL 57, [2004] 2 AC 208, HL.

20.47 The three cases considered by the House of Lords in *R (A) v Lambeth London Borough Council, R (W) v Lambeth London Borough Council and R (G) v Barnet London Borough Council*[1] illustrate the types of assistance with housing need that can be sought under CA 1989, s 17. In *A*, two severely disabled children, whose mother was a secure tenant, needed to move to larger and safer accommodation. In *W*, the child's mother had been found to have become homeless intentionally. She argued that her child was in need of emergency accommodation (and that it was in the child's best interests for the two of them to be accommodated together). In *G*, the child's mother was homeless and not eligible for homelessness assistance, as she was not habitually resident in the UK. The assessment of the child's needs had resulted in the local authority offering to pay for travel to the family's home country, which the mother had refused. The children in *W* and *G*, therefore, both had immediate needs for accommodation with (it was argued) their parents, and the children in *A* had a need for suitable long-term accommodation. In both *W* and *G*, the local authorities were offering accommodation to the children alone, without their mothers, pursuant to their duty under CA 1989, s 20.

[1]   *R (G) v Barnet London Borough Council, R (W) v Lambeth London Borough Council, R (A) v Lambeth London Borough Council* [2003] UKHL 57, [2004] 2 AC 208, HL.

20.48 The House of Lords confirmed that accommodation could be provided under CA 1989, s 17 powers, a position also legislated for by Parliament, which had amended s 17(6) to include specific reference to 'accommodation'[1]. It held, however, that the duty under CA 1989, s 17 was a 'target duty' and therefore there was no means by which an individual child could require that the local authority provide him or her with particular services under that section. In A's case, there was no power for the court to order that the local authority obtain suitable accommodation for the children. The House of Lords also emphasised that the decisions, as to whether a child was in need and what services should be provided to meet those needs, were decisions for the local authority. In particular, local authorities are entitled to operate certain policies such as (in the case of G) offering to return the family to their home country and providing accommodation only for the child if the offer is refused. In W, the local authority had not been acting unreasonably when it decided that the child was not in need of accommodation (as her mother had relatives with whom they could stay) and that, if the mother failed to make her own arrangements for accommodation, it would provide accommodation for the child but not the family.

[1]   Adoption and Children Act 2002, s 116(1), in force from 7 November 2002 and enacted after the Court of Appeal decision in *R (A) v Lambeth London Borough Council* [2002] EWCA Civ 540, (2002) 34 HLR 13, CA, which had held that there was no such power and was subsequently overturned by the House of Lords.

20.49 However, this is not to say that a decision to accommodate a homeless child separately from his or her parents under CA 1989, s 20, rather than accommodating the family together under CA 1989, s 17(6) will be lawful in every case. Indeed, in many cases it will not be. Local authorities remain under an obligation to consider the individual needs of each child, and an assessment of those needs should form the basis of the local authority's decision making. Any refusal to provide services to meet those needs identified in the assessment will be subject to review on conventional grounds of reasonableness and proportionality[1] and will be subject to 'strict and, it may be, sceptical scrutiny'[2]. This level of scrutiny may be characterised as a consequence of the enactment of Children Act 2004, s 11, which requires local authorities to put in place arrangements to safeguard and promote the welfare of children, reflecting the requirement under Art 3 of the UN Convention on the Rights of the Child that the best interests of the child shall be a primary consideration[3]. Children Act 2004, s 11, requires decision makers, in addition, to demonstrate how the local authority has had regard to the need to safeguard *and* promote the welfare of children both individually and collectively, and that any adverse impact on their welfare is proportionate[4]. In *R (HC) v Secretary of State for Work and Pensions*[5], Baroness Hale observed that 'Safeguarding is not enough: their welfare has to be actively promoted'.

[1]   *R (G) v Barnet London Borough Council, R (W) v Lambeth London Borough Council, R (A) v Lambeth London Borough Council* [2003] UKHL 57, [2004] 2 AC 208, [2003] 3 WLR 1194, [2004] HLR 10, HL per Lord Scott at [135].
[2]   *R (VC) v Newcastle City Council* [2011] EWHC 2673 (Admin), [2012] PTSR 546 per Munby LJ at [26]. See also *R (AM) v Havering London Borough Council and Tower Hamlets London Borough Council* [2015] EWHC 1004 (Admin), [2015] PTSR 1242.
[3]   *ZH (Tanzania) v Home Secretary* [2011] UKSC 4, [2011] 2 AC 166, SC per Baroness Hale at [23]. See further *Nzolameso v City of Westminster Council* [2015] UKSC 22, [2015] HLR 22, SC discussed at **18.53–18.57**.

4   See *R (C, T, M, U) v Southwark LBC* [2016] EWCA Civ 707, [2016] HLR 36, CA at [15].
5   [2017] UKSC 73, [2017] 3 WLR 1486, SC.

CHILDREN OF PERSONS FROM ABROAD

20.50 There used to be no general prohibition on providing services under CA 1989, s 17 to children who were persons from abroad, or whose parents were persons from abroad. Prior to 6 December 1999, asylum-seekers whose families included dependent children were provided with accommodation and services by local authorities under CA 1989, s 17. As from 6 December 1999, the statutory basis for providing accommodation and services fell under the Asylum Support (Interim Provisions) Regulations 1999[1] and, from 3 April 2000, local authorities have been prevented from providing CA 1989, s 17 assistance to the children of asylum-seekers[2]. Even if the children have needs that would normally bring them within the scope of CA 1989, s 17(1) (eg disability), the provision of adequate accommodation and support for the family remains the responsibility of the Home Office[3]. The situation is different in cases involving the children of failed asylum seekers. In those cases, the family may be entitled to support from the Home Office under the Immigration and Asylum Act 1999, s 4, but this does not exonerate the children's services authority from performing its powers and duties under CA 1989, s 17[4].

1   Asylum Support (Interim Provisions) Regulations 1999, SI 1999/3056.
2   Immigration and Asylum Act 1999, s 122(5), to be substituted by s 122(3), but not yet in force (Nationality, Immigration and Asylum Act 2002, s 47).
3   *R (A) v NASS and Waltham Forest London Borough Council* [2003] EWCA Civ 1473, [2004] HLR 24, CA.
4   *R (VC) v Newcastle City Council & SSHD* [2011] EWHC 2673 (Admin), [2012] PTSR 546. Note however, a member of this cohort is likely to be affected by the restrictions set out at 20.51–20.53.

20.51 On 8 January 2003, s 54 and Sch 3 of the Nationality, Immigration and Asylum Act 2002 came into force, along with the Withholding and Withdrawal of Support (Travel Assistance and Temporary Accommodation) Regulations 2002[1]. These provisions apply to five classes of people:

(1)   refugees given refugee status by another state of the EEA;
(2)   nationals of another state of the EEA;
(3)   asylum-seekers whose claims for asylum have failed and who have failed to co-operate with removal directions;
(4)   persons who are not asylum-seekers and are unlawfully present in the UK; and
(5)   failed asylum-seekers with dependent children where those families have been certified by the Secretary of State as not having taken reasonable steps to leave the UK[2].

1   SI 2002/3078.
2   Nationality Immigration and Asylum Act 2002, s 54 and Sch 3; and SI 2002/3078. For a list of EEA states, see **11.29**, Box 2.

20.52 People in the first, second and fourth categories who have dependent children are entitled to limited support under CA 1989, s 17[1]. Children's services authorities can provide assistance with travel arrangements for families in the first two categories to return to their home countries and can provide support and accommodation until they travel[2]. They may also provide support and accommodation for families in the fourth category until those people make their own arrangements to travel. If the families do not leave the UK, accommodation and support will cease. The children will be entitled to accommodation and support under CA 1989, s 20, but their parents will not be entitled to any services. If a request is made for support by anyone falling within one of the third, fourth or fifth classes, the local children's services authority is obliged to inform the Home Office[3].

[1]   SI 2002/3078, reg 3(2) and (3). See *Practice Guidance for Local Authorities assessing and supporting children and families and former looked-after children who have No Recourse to Public Funds for Support from Local Authorities under Children Act 1989* (No Recourse to Public Funds Network, December 2011).
[2]   SI 2002/3078, reg 3(1).
[3]   Nationality Immigration and Asylum Act 2002, Sch 3, para 14.

20.53 When these restrictions were first enacted, guidance issued by the Secretary of State (to which children's services authorities must have regard)[1] stated that it was preferable that accommodation was only provided for a limited period, with maximum periods suggested of five days for families falling within the first two categories and ten days for families falling into the fourth category from the date when they first presented to the children's services authority for support. In the case of *R (M) v Islington London Borough Council*[2], the majority of the Court of Appeal held that the periods 5 and ten days suggested in the Secretary of State's guidance did not preclude a local authority from providing accommodation for a longer period.

[1]   SI 2002/3078, reg 4(4).
[2]   [2004] EWCA Civ 235, [2004] 4 All ER 709, CA.

20.54 Children's services authorities are not prevented from providing accommodation and support to anyone falling within one of these five categories if it is necessary to do so in order to prevent a breach of that individual's European Convention rights or European Union Treaty rights[1]. They should also take into account Home Office policy where the claimant might potentially be entitled to remain in the UK.

[1]   Nationality, Immigration and Asylum Act 2002, Sch 3, para 3.

20.55 The possibility of a breach of an individual's European Convention rights usually relates to his or her rights under Art 6 (right to a fair trial) and/or Art 8 (right to respect for private and family life). In *R (Clue) v Birmingham City Council*[1], the Court of Appeal held that children's services authorities should adopt the following approach:

• the first enquiry is to ascertain the applicant's immigration status;
• if the applicant is a person in the UK in breach of immigration laws and is not an asylum-seeker, the next question is to decide whether the family is destitute; if so
• the next consideration is whether there is any impediment to the family returning to its country of origin (and if the only impediment is financial, the children's services authority can assist with funds);

- if it is said that there would be a breach of European Convention rights if the family were to return, and if the applicant has not applied to the Home Office for leave to remain in the UK, the children's services authority must consider whether the applicant enjoys a private or family life in the UK within the meaning of Art 8(1) and, if so, whether a return to the country of origin would constitute an interference with that right. Relevant to that question is the length of time the family has spent in the UK and the degree to which the children may have spent their formative years in the UK;
- where a person has made an application for leave to remain in the UK, children's services authorities should not undertake their own assessment of how the Secretary of State will determine the application for leave, unless the application is hopeless or abusive; and
- it follows that where a return to the country of origin would involve having to abandon the application for leave to remain, there is a legal impediment preventing the applicant from returning.

[1] [2010] EWCA Civ 460, [2011] 1 WLR 99, CA. See also *KA (Nigeria) v Essex County Council* [2013] EWHC 43 (Admin), [2013] 1 WLR 1163 (Admin Ct).

20.56 Earlier cases considered the potential for a breach of the right to respect for family life. In *R (M) v Islington London Borough Council*[1], the children's services authority's decision to provide support by returning the mother and child to the mother's home country of Guyana was held to be wrong in law because the children's services authority had failed to consider the child's right to respect for her family life, in that she might lose contact with her father, who was to remain in the UK and thus it might be necessary to provide support in order to prevent a breach of the child's European Convention rights[2].

[1] *R (M) v Islington London Borough Council* [2004] EWCA Civ 235, [2004] 4 All ER 709, CA.
[2] In *R (K) v Lambeth London Borough Council* [2003] EWCA Civ 1150, [2004] HLR 15, CA, the Court of Appeal held that neither Art 3 nor Art 8 of the European Convention on Human Rights imposed a duty on the UK to provide support to foreign nationals who are permitted to enter the country but are in a position freely to return home. See also *R (Blackburn-Smith) v Lambeth London Borough Council* [2007] EWHC 767 (Admin), (2007) October *Legal Action*, p 27, Admin Ct.

20.57 In *R (Conde) v Lambeth London Borough Council*[1], the court considered the position of an EEA national who was seeking work, and held that children's services authorities considering applications from EEA nationals should always ensure that those applicants are not exercising any rights under European Union Treaties, although it was unlikely that work-seekers applying for housing or Children Act accommodation would be exercising European Union Treaty rights.

[1] [2005] EWHC 62 (Admin), [2005] HLR 29, Admin Ct. See also **11.32–11.93** for EEA rights of residence.

INDIVIDUAL CHILDREN

20.58 By CA 1989, s 20(1), children's services authorities are required to provide accommodation for any children in need within their area who appear to them to require accommodation as a result of:

(1)   there being no one who has parental responsibility for them; or

(2)   their having been lost or abandoned; or

(3)   the person who had been caring for them being prevented from providing suitable accommodation or care[1].

---

[1]   This is the most commonly used and cited accommodation duty under CA 1989, s 20. However, CA 1989, s 20(3) also requires a local authority to accommodate any child in need within its area who has reached the age of 16 and whose welfare is likely to be 'seriously prejudiced' if the local authority do not provide him or her with accommodation.

20.59 In *R (M) v Gateshead Metropolitan Borough Council*[1], Dyson LJ described the duty as:

> 'an absolute duty to provide accommodation for any child in need where one of the specified circumstances exists. It is a precise and specific duty. There is no scope of discretion as to whether or not to provide accommodation at all. Thus where it appears to the local authority that there is a child in need, for example, as a result of there being no person who has parental responsibility, the local authority has an absolute obligation to provide some accommodation for that child. Section 20, says nothing about the type of accommodation that must be provided: that is left to the discretion of the local authority[2].'

---

[1]   [2006] EWCA Civ 221, [2006] QB 650, CA.

[2]   *R (M) v Gateshead Metropolitan Borough Council* [2006] EWCA Civ 221, [2006] 1 QB 650, CA at [33] per Dyson LJ.

20.60 CA 1989, s 20 poses a series of questions for the children's services authority to ask and answer:

(1)   Is the applicant a child?

(2)   If so, is the applicant a child in need, which might mean that he or she lacks accommodation?

(3)   If so, is the child within the children's services authority's area[1]?

(4)   If so, does he or she appear to the children's services authority to require accommodation?

(5)   If so, is that because of one of the three statutory reasons (which can include the circumstance where a child is excluded from the parental home by his or her parent)?

(6)   If so, what are the child's wishes and feelings regarding the provision of accommodation for him or her? and

(7)   What consideration should be given to the child's wishes and feelings[2]?

---

[1]   See *R (Liverpool City Council) v Hillingdon London Borough Council and AK* [2008] EWCA Civ 43, [2009] LGR 289, CA; and *R (A) v Leicester City Council and Hillingdon London Borough Council* [2009] EWHC 2351 (Admin), (2009) November *Legal Action*, p 26, Admin Ct, for examples of disputes between local authorities about the area a child is in.

[2]   *R (G) v Southwark London Borough Council* [2009] UKHL 26, [2009] 1 WLR 2399, HL at [28] per Baroness Hale.

20.61 If the answers to those questions indicate that the child falls within CA 1989, s 20(1), accommodation must be provided by the children's services authority. The children's services authority should not be 'side-stepping' its responsibilities, for example by simply advising a child to make an application for homelessness assistance to a local housing authority[1].

1   A homeless child who has a priority need (see Chapter 12) will almost certainly be a 'child in need' for the purposes of CA 1989 and local housing authorities should refer children who approach them for assistance with homelessness to children's services as well as complying with their duties under HA 1996, Pt 7 (as amended by HRA 2017, for applications for homelessness assistance made to local housing authorities in England on or after 3 April 2018) but the primary responsibility is likely to fall on children's services authorities. See *R (M) v Hammersmith & Fulham London Borough Council* [2008] UKHL 14, 1 WLR 535, HL; *R (G) v Southwark London Borough Council* [2009] UKHL 26, [2009] 1 WLR 2399, HL; and *R(TG) v Lambeth London Borough Council* [2010] EWHC 907 (Admin), [2011] HLR 33, Admin Ct. See **12.150–12.159** for a fuller commentary on joint working between housing and children's services.

20.62 The duty is owed to the individual child, and for these purposes a child is defined as a person who is not yet 18 years old[1]. The children's services authority will initially assess whether or not a person claiming to be a child without parental support is in fact aged less than 18. Useful guidance on the assessment of the child's age is provided by *R (B) v Merton London Borough Council*[2]. However, if the child disagrees with the children's services authority's assessment of his or her age, he or she can bring judicial review proceedings and, unlike most claims in judicial review, ask the court to review the evidence available and make its own decision as to what age he or she is[3].

1   CA 1989, s 105.
2   *R (B) v Merton London Borough Council* [2003] EWHC 1689 (Admin), [2003] 4 All ER 280, Admin Ct.
3   *R (A) v Croydon London Borough Council, R (M) v Lambeth London Borough Council* [2009] UKSC 8, [2009] 1 WLR 2557, SC. Since this important decision of the Supreme Court, there are various decisions of the Court of Appeal, Administrative Court and Upper Tribunal containing the court's own assessment of a claimant's age and guidance on how the courts should be carrying out that assessment. A detailed survey of those cases is beyond the scope of this book.

20.63 There are no restrictions on the grounds of immigration status to providing CA 1989, s 20 accommodation to children. Asylum-seeking children who are unaccompanied are entitled to the same care and after-care duties as any other children[1].

1   *R (Berhe) v Hillingdon London Borough Council* [2003] EWHC 2075 (Admin), [2004] 1 FLR 439, Admin Ct; and *R (SO) v Barking & Dagenham London Borough Council* [2010] EWCA Civ 1101, [2011] HLR 4, CA.

20.64 Children who are provided with accommodation under CA 1989, s 20 are entitled to certain assistance beyond their eighteenth birthday[1]. This is not the case for children provided with help with accommodation under CA 1989, s 17. In *R (H) v Wandsworth London Borough Council*[2], the court held that where a local authority actually provided accommodation to a child whom it had identified as a 'child in need', that accommodation was provided under CA 1989, s 20 and it was not for the children's services authority, or even the child, to characterise that accommodation as provided under CA 1989, s 17[3]. A child may have been provided with accommodation under CA 1989, s 20, even when he or she is assisted to live with relatives[4], placed in respite care or in a residential specialist placement.

1   See **12.148–12.149, 12.160–12.165** and **20.65–20.66**.

2   [2007] EWHC 1082 (Admin), [2007] 2 FCR 378, Admin Ct. See also *R (S) v Sutton London Borough Council* [2007] EWCA Civ 790, (2007) September *Legal Action*, p 19, CA.

3   See further *R (M) v Hammersmith & Fulham LBC* [2008] UKHL 14, [2008] 1 WLR 535, HL per Baroness Hale at [42]; *R (G) v Southwark LBC* [2009] UKHL 26, 1 WLR 1299, HL per Baroness Hale at [9]; *R (LW) v North Lincolnshire Council* [2008] EWHC 2299 (Admin), [2008] 2 FLR 2150; *R (FL) v Lambeth London Borough Council* [2010] EWHC 49, (2010) March *Legal Action*, p 31, Admin Ct; *R (TG) v Lambeth London Borough Council* [2010] EWHC 907 (Admin), [2011] HLR 33, Admin Ct; and *Prevention of homelessness and provision of accommodation for 16 and 17 year old young people who may be homeless and/or require accommodation* (MHCLG and DfE, April 2018). See further **12.147** and also *R (GE) (Eritrea) v Secretary of State for the Home Department and Bedford Borough Council* [2014] EWCA Civ 1490, [2015] PTSR 854, CA, *R (A) v Enfield London Borough Council* [2016] EWHC 567 (Admin), [2016] HLR 3, Admin Ct and *R (BM) v Hackney London Borough Council* [2016] EWHC 3338 (Admin), Admin Ct for remedies that may be available retrospectively where a local authority has acted unlawfully in failing to accommodate a child under CA 1989, s 20.

4   See *R (Cunningham) v Hertfordshire City Council* [2016] EWCA Civ 1108, [2017] 1 WLR 2153, CA for the most recent guidance on this type of case.

YOUNG PEOPLE

20.65 Children owed CA 1989, s 20 duties are entitled to accommodation until the age of 18 and thereafter (subject to certain conditions) to the benefits of the amendments to CA 1989 made by the Children (Leaving Care) Act 2000, the Children and Social Work Act 2017 and the regulations and guidance made under CA 1989. The children's services authority must prepare a pathway plan assessing the child's need for advice, assistance and support both before and after the authority ceases to look after the child[1]. That pathway plan should include consideration of the young person's needs for accommodation and how accommodation is to be provided[2]. The children's services authority will itself need to secure accommodation for the young person where his or her welfare requires it, or arrange for accommodation to be provided[3]. The children's services authority must also provide a personal adviser and pay for certain education-related expenses[4]. These obligations continue to be owed until young person reaches the age of 21 and certain of the obligations may continue until the young person reaches the age of 25[5].

1   CA 1989, s 23E.
2   See *R (J) v Caerphilly County Borough Council* [2005] EWHC 586, [2005] 2 FCR 157, Admin Ct.
3   CA 1989, s 23C(4)(c) and *R (SO) v Barking & Dagenham London Borough Council* [2010] EWCA Civ 1101, [2011] HLR 4, CA.
4   CA 1989, ss 23C–23D.
5   Children Act 1989, ss 23C(6)–(7) and 23CZB (as inserted by Children and Social Work Act 2017, s 3).

20.66 There are no restrictions on the grounds of immigration status to these services provided to young people[1].

1   *R (Binomughisa) v Southwark London Borough Council* [2006] EWHC 2254 (Admin), [2007] 1 FLR 916.

PERFORMING OBLIGATIONS UNDER THE CHILDREN ACT 1989

20.67 Once a children's services authority has identified a child's need for accommodation and has either acknowledged a duty to provide it (under CA 1989, s 20) or decided to exercise a power to provide it (under CA 1989, s 17) the crucial next step is to find that accommodation. The children's services authority is most unlikely to have units of residential accommodation simply standing ready to meet demand.

20.68 Where what is needed is ordinary housing, the children's services authority (or department) needs to be able to call upon others. Co-operation can be expected from the local housing authority (or department) as a result of the statutory requirement upon local housing authorities to assist, on request[1]. Similar expectations as to co-operation are imposed on local private registered providers or registered social landlords, not least by the requirements of their regulatory bodies. Beyond assistance from local housing authorities and private registered providers or registered social landlords, a children's services authority will either need to pay for housing itself (by purchasing or renting from the private sector) or help to finance the acquisition by the child, or his or her family, of suitable accommodation, usually by assisting with a deposit and rent guarantee[2].

[1] CA 1989, s 27. Note that this statutory duty to co-operate does not apply when the local housing authority and the children's services authority fall under the auspices of the same unitary authority, *R (C1 and C2) v Hackney London Borough Council* [2014] EWHC 3670 (Admin), Admin Ct. However, the guidance issued by the Secretary of State in *Working Together to Safeguard Children* (HM Government, March 2015), requires a similar degree of co-operation between departments in the same authority. See *R (M) v Islington London Borough Council* [2016] EWHC 332 (Admin), [2016] HLR 19, Admin Ct at [14]–[15] per Collins J.
[2] See *R (S) v Plymouth City Council* [2009] EWHC 1499 (Admin), (2009) October *Legal Action*, p 26, Admin Ct and [2010] EWCA Civ 1490, (2010) March *Legal Action*, p 31, CA (refusal of permission to appeal).

SPECIFIC POWERS FOR LOCAL AUTHORITIES TO HELP WITH ACCOMMODATION: WALES

20.69 On 6 April 2016 the Social Services and Well-being (Wales) Act 2014 (SSWBA 2014) came into force replacing CA 1989 and the National Assistance Act 1948, Pt 3 as the single principal piece of legislation governing support for children and young people, and adult social care, in Wales[1]. In this section, adults and then children will be dealt with in turn.

[1] Social Services and Well-being (Wales) Act 2014 (Commencement No 3, Savings and Transitional Provisions) Order 2016, SI 2016/412 (W 130), art 2, subject to the transitional and saving provisions contained in art 3 and art 4.

20.70 SSWBA 2014 is a comprehensive and detailed piece of legislation and what follows is no more than a basic overview of those functions within it by which people might access accommodation, and how they can go about doing so. SSWBA 2014 should be read together with the various codes of practice and statutory guidance issued under SSWBA 2014, s 145 which are available on the Welsh Government website.

20.71 One of the more innovative features of SSWBA 2014 is the inclusion of a number of 'overarching duties' to which officials exercising functions under SSWBA 2014 will be subject. These include (but are not limited to):

- the need to promote the well-being of people who need care and support[1];
- the need to have regard to the importance of promoting and respecting the dignity of a person who needs care and support[2];
- the need to have regard, in an appropriate case, to the United Nations Convention on the Rights of the Child[3].

A local authority exercising any the functions under the SSWBA 2014 set out at **20.72–20.98** will be subject to these duties.

[1] SSWBA 2014, s 5(1).
[2] SSWBA 2014, s 6(1) and (2).
[3] SSWBA 2014, s 7(2).

Adults

Powers and duties to provide accommodation

20.72 By SSWBA 2014, s 3(2) an adult is defined as a person who is aged 18 or over. The duty to provide accommodation to certain adults, along with a range of other services, is contained in SSWBA 2014, s 35. A local authority is required to provide 'care and support' to an adult under SSWBA 2014, s 35(1), which may include accommodation[1], if:

- he or she is ordinarily resident in the local authority's area, or is within its area but of no settled residence;
- he or she has a need for care and support which meets the eligibility criteria *or* the local authority considers it necessary to meet his or her needs in order to protect him or her from abuse or neglect, or a risk of abuse or neglect; and
- he or she meets the financial eligibility criteria[2].

[1] SSWBA 2014, s 34(2).
[2] SSWBA 2014, s 35.

20.73 Whether a person is ordinarily resident in the local authority's area is to be determined in accordance with SSWBA 2014, s 194. This section does not seek to define the term 'ordinary residence' but provides that a person will be deemed to be ordinarily resident in certain circumstances, such as where he or she is provided with accommodation under Mental Health Act 1983, s 117[1]. The prior case law on ordinary residence under NAA 1948, Pt 3 will presumably remain applicable outside of the particular scenarios dealt with in SSWBA 2014, s 194[2].

[1] See 20.99–20.104.
[2] See 20.21.

20.74 Whether a person has a need for care and support which meets the eligibility criteria is to be determined in accordance with SSWBA 2014, s 32. Needs are deemed to meet the eligibility criteria if they are of a description specified in regulations made under SSWBA 2014, s 32(3), or form part of a combination of needs described in the regulations[1]. In cases where a person has a need for care and support which does not meet the eligibility criteria, the local authority is required to go on to determine whether the provision of care and support is necessary in any event in order to protect the person from abuse or neglect or a risk of abuse or neglect[2].

[1] SSWBA 2014, s 32(4). The relevant regulations are the Care and Support (Eligibility) (Wales) Regulations 2015, SI 2015/1578 (W 187).
[2] SSWBA 2014, s 32(1)(b).

20.75 Whether a person is financially eligible for care and support is to be calculated in accordance with SSWBA 2014, s 35(4) and Pt 5 and the Care and Support (Financial Assessment) (Wales) Regulations 2015[1].

[1] SI 2015/1844 (W 272).

20.76 Where a person satisfies these three conditions then a local authority will be required to meet those of his or her needs for care and support which satisfy the eligibility criteria or which need to be met in order to protect the person from abuse or neglect or a risk of abuse or neglect[1]. But the question of how to meet those needs is a matter for the local authority[2].

[1] SSWBA 2014, s 35(1) and (3).
[2] SSWBA 2014, s 34.

20.77 It follows that where a person requires accommodation in order to meet his or her eligible needs, or to protect him or her from abuse or neglect, or a risk of abuse or neglect, then the local authority must secure accommodation for him or her, either by providing accommodation itself or by arranging for another to provide it[1]. On the other hand if a person has a need for care and support which does not meet the eligibility criteria, if there is no risk of abuse or neglect, or if the local authority can meet his or her needs otherwise than by the provision of accommodation, the local authority will not be required to secure accommodation.

[1] SSWBA 2014, s 34(1).

20.78 Where the person has a need for care and support which the local authority is not required to meet under SSWBA 2014, s 35, the local authority retains a discretion whether to meet that need, so long as the person in question is ordinarily resident in the local authority's area, or is present in its area but of no settled residence[1]. Hence, a vulnerable[2] homeless person without accommodation who does not meet the eligibility criteria in SSWBA 2014 and who is not at risk of abuse or neglect might consider asking the local authority to exercise its discretion to accommodate him or her in any event.

[1] SSWBA 2014, s 36(1).
[2] Used here in the non-technical sense, in contrast to Chapter **12**.

20.79 A person subject to immigration control who is excluded from benefits[1], whose need for care and support has arisen solely because of destitution or because of the physical effects or the anticipated physical effects of destitution, cannot be provided with care and support under SSWBA 2014, ss 35 or 36[2].

Accommodation for those who are seeking asylum is the responsibility of the Home Office. As with the CA 1989, s 17, and CA 2014, Pt 1 there is an additional prohibition on providing residential accommodation to persons who fall within one of five specified classes of persons from abroad[3].

[1] By Immigration and Asylum Act 1999, s 115.
[2] SSWBA 2014, s 46.
[3] Nationality, Immigration and Asylum Act 2002, s 54 and Sch 3, para 1(o). See **20.35–20.38** and **20.50–20.57** for a discussion of the classes of person affected by this prohibition, and the exceptions to it.

20.80 The powers and duties under SSWBA 2014, ss 35–36 are residual. That is, a local authority is not permitted to do anything under these sections which it is required to do under H(W)A 2014, under any enactment specified in regulations or under a health enactment, save, in the case of a health enactment, where the provision is merely incidental to care and support provided under SSWBA 2014, ss 35–36[1].

[1] SSWBA 2014, ss 47–48. 'Health enactment' is defined in SSWBA 2014, s 47(10).

THE DUTY TO ASSESS

20.81 The duty to assess a person's needs for care and support under SSWBA 2014, s 35 and 36 is contained in SSWBA 2014, s 19. The duty will arise where 'it appears' to the local authority that the person 'may have needs for care and support'[1]: a low threshold. The local authority has a discretion to provide services while the assessment is being carried out providing that the person is *either* within the area *or* is outside of the area but ordinarily resides in the area[2]. This discretion is not confined to urgent cases.

[1] SSWBA 2014, s 19(1).
[2] SSWBA 2014, s 36(1) and (3).

20.82 The assessment should be carried out in accordance with the requirements set out in SSWBA 2014, s 19 and the Care and Support (Assessment) (Wales) Regulations 2015[1].

[1] SI 2015/1305 (W 111). See SSWBA 2014, s 30.

20.83 A failure to carry out an assessment, if the threshold is satisfied, is a breach of the local authority's statutory duty. It can be enforced by bringing a claim by way of judicial review seeking a mandatory order requiring the local authority to carry out an assessment[1].

[1] See **19.306–19.327** on practice and procedure for judicial review claims.

20.84 The duty to assess is not confined to the local authority in whose area the person is ordinarily resident[1]. However, since the duty to provide care and support under SSWBA 2014, s 35 will only be owed by the local authority in whose area the person is ordinarily resident[2] he or she would be well advised to direct his or her application to that local authority. Any dispute as to which local authority owes the duty to assess should be decided by the Welsh Ministers[3].

[1] SSWBA 2014, s 19(2).

²   Save in those cases where the person has no settled residence (SSWBA 2014, s 35(1)).
³   SSWBA 2014, s 195.

Children and young people

The duties to provide accommodation

20.85 By SSWBA 2014, s 3(3) a child is defined as a person who is aged under-18. There are two principal provisions within SSWBA 2014 under which a child may be accommodated. The first is SSWBA 2014, s 76(1) which requires a local authority to provide accommodation for any child within its area who appears to require accommodation as a result of:

- there being no person who has parental responsibility for the child;
- the child being lost or having been abandoned; or
- the person who has been caring for the child being prevented (whether or not permanently, and for whatever reason) from providing the child with suitable accommodation or care.

20.86 This is supplemented by SSWBA 2014, s 76(3) which requires a local authority to provide accommodation for any child within its area who has reached the age of 16 and whose well-being the authority considers is likely to be seriously prejudiced if it does not provide the child with accommodation.

20.87 The duties under SSWBA 2014, s 76 mirror the duties under CA 1989, s 20 and it may be assumed that the same approach to decision making under that section should be applied[1]. A child who is looked-after[2] under SSWBA 2014, s 76 will be owed additional duties under SSWBA 2014, ss 78–86 and may be owed further duties as a care-leaver following his or her 18th birthday[3].

¹   See **20.58–20.64** and Welsh Code, para 16.41.
²   Within the meaning of SSWBA 2014, s 74.
³   See **20.98**.

20.88 There are no restrictions on the grounds of immigration status to providing SSWBA 2014, s 76 accommodation to children.

20.89 The second of the principal duties owed to children is in SSWBA 2014, s 37. This is a duty to provide 'care and support' to a child, which may include accommodation[1], if:

- he or she is within the local authority's area; and
- he or she has a need for care and support which meets the eligibility criteria; or
- the local authority considers it necessary to meet his or her needs in order to protect him or her from abuse or neglect or any other harm, or a risk of abuse, neglect or other harm[2].

¹   SSWBA 2014, s 34(2).
²   SSWBA 2014, s 37.

20.90 This duty is secondary to the duty under SSWBA 2014, s 76. By virtue of SSWBA 2014, s 37(6), the duty does not apply to a child who is looked-after by a local authority. This is an indicator that where the conditions in SSWBA

2014, s 76 are met in respect of an individual child, the local authority should accommodate that child under SSWBA 2014, s 76 and not under SSWBA 2014, s 37(6). In view of the additional services which must be provided to a looked-after child under SSWBA 2014, ss 78–86, which effectively place the local authority in the shoes of the absent parent, it seems likely that SSWBA 2014, s 76 was intended to take precedence over SSWBA 2014, s 37 in those cases where an individual child seeks accommodation.[1]

[1]   See, by analogy, 20.60–20.64 in respect of the position under CA 1989, Pt 3.

20.91 The wording of SSWBA 2014, s 37, which obliges a local authority to provide such care and support as is necessary to 'meet a child's needs' is wide enough to permit a local authority to accommodate a child with his or her family under this provision, where that is necessary to meet the child's needs. In contrast with CA 1989, s 17[1], the duty under SSWBA 2014, s 37 is a specific duty rather than a target duty. If the child is assessed as having eligible needs for care and support or as requiring care and support to protect him or her from abuse, neglect or any other harm, or a risk of abuse, neglect or other harm, then the duty *will* be owed.

[1]   See 20.39–20.57.

20.92 In view of the position adopted by the House of Lords and Supreme Court to the effect that a child without accommodation is a 'child in need' for the purposes of CA 1989, s 17[1], it seems reasonable to assume that a child without accommodation may be taken to be at risk of 'harm' for the purposes of SSWBA 2014, s 37(3)[2].

[1]   *R v Northavon District Council ex p Smith* [1994] 2 AC 402, HL; and *R (G) v Barnet London Borough Council, R (W) v Lambeth London Borough Council, R (A) v Lambeth London Borough Council* [2003] UKHL 57, [2004] 2 AC 208, HL.
[2]   By CA 1989, s 17(10) a child shall be taken to be in need if 'his health or development is likely to be significantly impaired, or further impaired, without the provision for him of . . . services'. This might be equated with the concept of 'harm' in SSWBA 2014, s 37(3).

20.93 The duty to provide care and support under SSWBA 2014, s 37 is subject to the five exclusions set out in Nationality, Asylum and Immigration Act 2002, Sch 3, affecting the ability of certain persons from abroad to access certain community care services[1].

[1]   Nationality, Asylum and Immigration Act 2002, s 54 and Sch 3, para 1(o).

20.94 Where a local housing authority has reason to believe that a family with children are homeless or threatened with homelessness but are ineligible for help under H(W)A 2014, Pt 2 or, for any other reason, are not likely to be owed a duty under H(W)A 2014, ss 66, 68, 73 or 75[1], then local housing authority must ask the applicant to consent to the family being referred to the local children's services department[2], who may then consider whether an accommodation duty under SSWBA 2014 has arisen. Even if the applicant refuses, the local housing authority must still make the referral if it considers that the child is, or may be, at risk of significant harm[3]. When a referral is received, the children's services authority is entitled to request advice and assistance from the local housing authority[4]. A local housing authority that has placed a homeless family outside its own district should refer the family (if it is found to be ineligible or the adult members are found to have become homeless intentionally) to its own children's services department or authority[5]. It may, of course, also seek the assistance of the children's services authority for the district in which the family has been placed, under the general provisions for co-operation in H(W)A 2014, s 95[6].

[1] See CHAPTER 17.
[2] H(W)A 2014, s 96.
[3] H(W)A 2014, s 96(4).
[4] H(W)A 2014, s 96(4).
[5] *R (Ambrose) v Westminster City Council* (2011) July *Legal Action*, p 21, Admin Ct.
[6] See **17.208–17.211**.

THE DUTY TO ASSESS

20.95 The duty to assess a child's needs for care and support is contained in SSWBA 2014, s 21. The duty will arise where 'it appears' to the local authority that the person 'may need care and support in addition to, or instead of, the care and support provided by the child's family'[1]. This is a low threshold. The local authority has a discretion to provide services while the assessment is being carried out providing that the child is *either* within the area *or* is outside of the area but ordinarily resides in the area[2]. This discretion is not confined to urgent cases.

[1] SSWBA 2014, s 21(1).
[2] SSWBA 2014, s 38(1) and (3).

20.96 The assessment should be carried out in accordance with the requirements set out in SSWBA 2014, s 21 and the Care and Support (Assessment) (Wales) Regulations 2015[1].

[1] SI 2015/1305 (W 111). See SSWBA, s 30.

20.97 A failure to carry out an assessment, if the threshold is made out, is a breach of the local authority's statutory duty. It can be enforced by bringing a claim by way of judicial review seeking a mandatory order requiring the local authority to carry out an assessment[1].

[1] See **19.306–19.327** on practice and procedure for judicial review claims.

YOUNG PEOPLE

20.98 Various categories of young person up to the age of 21[1], who have previously been looked after by a local authority, are set out in SSWBA 2014, s 104. The responsible local authority[2] will owe a range of additional duties to young people falling within these categories. These duties are set out in SSWBA 2014, ss 105–115, and include the provision of a personal adviser, a pathway plan, and, where required, accommodation or a contribution toward the cost of accommodation.

[1] Or 25 if the young person in question has informed the responsible local authority that he or she is or intends to pursue a course of education or training.
[2] Defined in accordance with SSWBA 2014, 104(5).

POWERS AND DUTIES UNDER THE MENTAL HEALTH ACT 1983

20.99 Special statutory provision is made to meet the accommodation needs of adults in England and Wales who are, or who have recently been, mentally ill. The Mental Health Act 1983, s 117 (MHA 1983[1]) imposes a duty on local authorities in England and in Wales to provide after-care services for any person who has left hospital, having been detained, or who has been subject to certain hospital orders made in criminal proceedings[2]. This duty rests jointly on the relevant clinical commissioning group or local health board and on the local authority, and they are expected to co-operate in ensuring that services are provided. The local authority which owes the duty is the local authority for the area, in England or Wales, in which the person concerned was ordinarily resident prior to his or her detention[3]. Where a person was ordinarily resident somewhere other than England or Wales prior to his or her detention, or where he or she had no place of ordinary residence, then the duty will be owed by the local authority for the area in which the person concerned is resident or to which he or she is sent on discharge from the hospital in which he or she was detained[4]. The term 'resident' is used in contradistinction to the term 'ordinarily resident' and the two terms do not, therefore, have the same meaning. A patient is not 'resident' for these purposes in the hospital or other facility in which he or she was compulsorily detained[5]. Where a person has been made subject to a hospital order with restrictions, conditionally discharged, recalled to a hospital, and then conditionally discharged for a second time, for the purposes of MHA 1983, s 117(3)(c) he or she should be treated as 'resident in the area' of the local authority in which he or she lived before the original hospital order was made[6].

[1] As amended by Health and Social Care Act 2012, s 40.
[2] A description of the much broader provision in the Mental Health Act 1983, as amended by the Mental Capacity Act 2005 and Mental Health Act 2007, consolidating the health services to which mentally ill patients are entitled, is beyond the scope of this book.
[3] MHA 1983, s 117(3)(a) and (b). See *R (Cornwall Council) v Secretary of State for Health* [2015] UKSC 46, [2016] AC 137, SC for the most authoritative guidance on how to determine ordinary residence. Local authorities in England will also need to have regard to CA 2014, s 39, while local authorities in Wales will need to consider SSWBA 2014, s 194.
[4] MHA 1983, s 117(3)(c).
[5] *R (Hertfordshire County Council) v Hammersmith & Fulham London Borough Council & JM* [2011] EWCA Civ 77, (2011) 14 CCLR 224, CA. See also *R (Sunderland City Council) v South Tyneside County Council* [2012] EWCA Civ 1232.
[6] *R (Wiltshire County Council) v Hertfordshire County Council* [2014] EWCA Civ 712, (2014) 17 CCLR 258, CA.

20.100 Guidance on this duty for local authorities in England is provided in *After-Care Under the Mental Health Act 1983: section 117 after-care services*[1].

[1] LAC (2000) 3, Department of Health and Chapter 33 of the *Code of Practice: Mental Health Act 1983* (Department of Heath, 2015). There is also LAC(96)8 *Guidance on supervised discharge (after-care under supervision) and related provisions* (Department of Heath 1996). In Wales, guidance is given in Chapter 33 of the *Mental Health Act 1983: Code of Practice for Wales* (Welsh Government, 2016).

20.101 It is unlawful for a clinical commissioning group, health authority or local authority to fail to take steps to prepare a package of after-care services so as to enable discharge to take place from residential accommodation provided under the MHA 1983[1]. However, the duty at MHA 1983, s 117 is not absolute; all that local authorities are required to do is to use their best endeavours to provide after-care services. In those circumstances, if no package is set up despite the local authority using its best endeavours, and the consequence is that the patient remains detained rather than being released into the community, there is no illegality or breach of the patient's human rights[2]. Similarly, where there is a genuine inability to provide accommodation, because of the particular needs of the applicant and the absence of suitable accommodation, no unlawfulness or illegal detention will arise[3].

1   *R v Ealing London Borough Council ex p Fox* [1993] 3 All ER 170, QBD.
2   *R (K) v Camden and Islington Health Authority* [2001] EWCA Civ 240, (2001) 4 CCLR 170, CA.
3   *R (W) v Doncaster Metropolitan Borough Council* [2004] EWCA Civ 378, CA.

20.102 The duty to provide after-care services is a duty to provide services that are necessary to meet any needs arising from the person's mental disorder[1]. Those services can include the provision of ordinary accommodation if accommodation is necessary to meet the person's needs[2]. Importantly, local authorities are not permitted to charge for after-care services provided under MHA 1983, s 117 and are not permitted to refuse to provide accommodation on the grounds of lack of resources[3]. A corollary of this is that where a person has been awarded tortious damages toward his or her future care needs, a local authority is not entitled to insist that he or she should exhaust those sums before after-care services are funded under MHA 1983, s 117[4].

1   *R (Mwanza) v Greenwich London Borough Council & Bromley London Borough Council* [2010] EWHC 1462 (Admin), (2010) 13 CCLR 454, Admin Ct.
2   *Clunis v Camden and Islington Health Authority* [1998] QB 978, (1998) 1 CCLR 215, CA.
3   *R v Richmond London Borough Council ex p Watson, R v Manchester City Council ex p Stennett* [2002] UKHL 34, [2002] 2 AC 1127, HL.
4   *R (Tinsley) v Manchester City Council* [2017] EWCA Civ 1704, (2017) 20 CCLR 455, CA.

20.103 If the person has left hospital subject to supervised community treatment, the duty continues for the whole of the supervision period[1]. If he or she is not subject to supervision, the duty continues until the local authority is satisfied that he or she is no longer in need of MHA 1983, s 117, services[2].

1   See Mental Health Act 1983, ss 17A–17G for provisions about supervised community treatment.
2   *R (Mwanza) v Greenwich London Borough Council & Bromley London Borough Council* [2010] EWHC 1462 (Admin), (2010) 13 CCLR 454, Admin Ct.

20.104 Voluntary patients and those patients detained for assessment under MHA 1983, s 2 are not entitled to the benefit of the MHA 1983, s 117 duty. If, on leaving hospital, they are in need of community care services and accommodation, they can require that the local authority assesses their needs under SSWBA 2014 (Wales)[1] or CA 2014 (England)[2] and that the local authority then provides community care services to meet those needs, which may include assistance with finding accommodation[3].

1   See **20.81–20.84**.
2   See **20.29–20.33**.
3   *R (B) v Camden London Borough Council and Camden & Islington Mental Health and Social Care Trust* [2005] EWHC 1366 (Admin), [2005] MHLR 258, Admin Ct. See **20.26–20.27** and **20.72–20.84**.

POWERS AND DUTIES UNDER THE HOUSING ACT 1985 AND THE LAND COMPENSATION ACT 1973

Displaced occupiers

20.105 Quite apart from the requirements of HA 1996, Pts 6 and 7[1] and H(W)A 2014, Pt 2, local housing authorities can be required, in certain circumstances, to provide accommodation to existing tenants, or owner-occupiers who are faced with loss of their homes.

[1] As amended by HRA 2017, for applications for homelessness assistance made to local housing authorities in England on or after 3 April 2018.

20.106 If the local housing authority is the landlord of a secure tenant, and is bringing possession proceedings against that tenant under statutory grounds 9–16 inclusive[1], it must make suitable alternative accommodation available for the tenant and his or her family in order to obtain an order for possession from the court. The accommodation need not be provided by that, or any, local housing authority landlord; it may be provided by a private registered provider or registered social landlord or even by a private landlord on an assured tenancy. What is 'suitable' accommodation for these purposes is determined by Sch 2, Pt 4 of the Housing Act 1985. If no suitable accommodation is available from another provider, the local housing authority itself will have to provide the accommodation if it wishes to obtain possession.

[1] Housing Act 1985, Sch 2.

20.107 More generally, where any person is 'displaced from residential accommodation' as a result of a local housing authority compulsorily purchasing land, making a housing order or making improvements to or redeveloping land, the local housing authority will be under a duty to provide suitable alternative residential accommodation on reasonable terms, if no such accommodation is otherwise available to the person displaced[1]. That duty does not require the local housing authority to put the displaced person to the top of its allocation scheme, thereby achieving priority over those who may have been waiting some considerable time. The provision of temporary accommodation until more permanent housing becomes available is sufficient to comply with the duty[2]. In order to give local housing authorities maximum flexibility, the provision of suitable alternative accommodation under this duty does not constitute an 'allocation' for the purposes of HA 1996, Pt 6, and the local housing authority does not have to comply with the requirements of HA 1996, Pt 6 or its own allocation scheme before making it available[3].

[1] Land Compensation Act 1973, s 39(1).
[2] *R v Bristol Corporation ex p Hendy* [1974] 1 All ER 1047, CA; *R v East Hertfordshire District Council ex p Smith* (1990) 23 HLR 26, CA.
[3] Allocation of Housing (England) Regulations 2002, SI 2002/3264, reg 3(2); and Allocation of Housing (Wales) Regulations 2003, SI 2003/239 (W 36), reg 3(a), both made under HA 1996, s 160(4). See also **1.27**.

DEFECTIVE DWELLING-HOUSES

20.108 Special statutory provision is made for the re-housing of those who currently occupy, but need to leave, defective homes which were purchased from local housing authorities under right-to-buy arrangements. Local housing authorities have to take responsibility for those defective dwelling-houses in their areas[1], including the re-purchase of a defective dwelling-house where an individual is entitled to that assistance[2]. Where such a property is occupied, the local housing authority will then become subject to housing obligations towards that occupier. If the property is occupied by its owner or by a statutory Rent Act 1977 tenant, the local housing authority is required to grant the occupier a secure tenancy of that property or, if the dwelling-house is not safe for occupation or the local housing authority intends to demolish or reconstruct it within a reasonable time, a different property[3]. If the property is occupied by a contractual tenant, who is either protected under the Rent Act 1977 or an assured tenant protected by the Housing Act 1988, the local housing authority acquires the landlord's interest under the tenancy and the status of the tenancy changes to that of a secure tenancy[4]. Again, if there is to be reconstruction or the house is unsafe, the tenant must be re-housed.

1   Housing Act 1985, Pt XVI, 'Assistance for Owners of Defective Housing'.
2   Housing Act 1985, ss 547–553 and Sch 20.
3   These provisions only apply if the occupier makes a written request for the grant of a tenancy: Housing Act 1985, ss 554–557.
4   Housing Act 1985, s 553.

20.109 The grant of a secure tenancy to a former owner-occupier or statutory tenant in these circumstances does not constitute an 'allocation' for the purposes of HA 1996, Pt 6, and so the local housing authority does not have to comply with the normal requirements of HA 1996, Pt 6 or its allocation scheme, before granting such a tenancy[1].

1   SI 2003/3264, reg 3(3); SI 2003/239, reg 3(b), both made under HA 1996, s 160(4).

POWERS AND DUTIES UNDER THE HUMAN RIGHTS ACT 1998

20.110 Since 2 October 2000, all local housing authorities, along with all other public authorities, have had to refrain from acting in a way which is incompatible with the main provisions of the European Convention on Human Rights[1]. Private registered providers and registered social landlords may constitute public authorities for the purposes of allocating and terminating tenancies of social housing[2].

1   Human Rights Act 1998, s 6.
2   *R (Weaver) v London & Quadrant Housing Trust* [2009] EWCA Civ 587, [2009] HLR 40, CA.

20.111 Two Articles of the European Convention are particularly relevant to the subject of this book: an individual's absolute right not to be subjected to inhuman or degrading treatment (Art 3) and the qualified right to respect for his or her home, family life, private life and correspondence (Art 8)[1].

1   Human Rights Act 1998, s 6 and Sch 1. See further *XPQ v Hammersmith and Fulham London Borough Council* [2018] EWHC 1391 (QB), for an example of how Art 4 may be relevant.

That case involved an (unsuccessful) claim for damages arising from an alleged failure to provide suitable accommodation to a victim of human trafficking.

20.112 Each of these Articles may give an individual the right to insist on a local housing authority or other public authority providing adequate accommodation where he or she has none. In practice this accommodation is likely to be provided pursuant to the Local Government Act 2000 (Wales) or the Localism Act 2011 (England)[1], because if the individual were entitled to accommodation under another statute then it is unlikely that he or she would be in such dire circumstances as to require accommodation in order to avoid a breach of his or her human rights. Human rights considerations may however still arise in other statutory contexts, for example when a local authority is considering whether to exercise a power under CA 1989, CA 2014 (England) or SSWBA 2014 (Wales)[2].

[1] See **20.5–20.18**.
[2] See **20.39–20.68**, **20.19–20.38** and **20.69–20.98** respectively.

Article 3

20.113 For a breach of the Human Rights Act 1998 (HRA 1998), Sch 1, Art 3 to be made out, there must be either:

' . . . ill-treatment that attains a minimum level of severity and involves actual bodily injury or intense physical or mental suffering',

or treatment that:

' . . . humiliates or debases an individual showing lack of respect for, or diminishing, his or her human dignity or arouses feelings of fear, anguish or inferiority capable of breaking an individual's moral and physical resistance.[1]'

[1] *Pretty v UK* (2002) 35 EHRR 1, ECtHR.

20.114 If the failure to provide accommodation would reduce an individual to this condition, then public authorities may have to take measures to avoid that situation arising[1].

[1] But see **20.118**.

20.115 Prior to the implementation of the HRA 1998, the European Court of Human Rights considered the application of Art 3 in the case of a homeless person who was entitled to work and to claim benefits. He had been evicted from a night shelter due to his behaviour and had thereafter spent 14 months on the streets (essentially by his own choice). It was held that he had not demonstrated a minimum level of suffering sufficient to breach Art 3[1].

[1] *O'Rourke v UK (Application No 39022/97)* (2001), ECtHR.

20.116 An attempt, in *R (Bernard) v Enfield London Borough Council*[1], to establish that the provision of grossly unsuitable temporary accommodation, which failed to meet the assessed needs of a disabled woman, was in breach of

Art 3 was not successful.

¹ R *(Bernard) v Enfield London Borough Council* [2002] EWHC 2282 (Admin), (2003) 35 HLR 27, Admin Ct.

20.117 The courts in England and Wales have considered the extent to which the failure of public authorities to provide shelter and subsistence can infringe Art 3¹. It is not enough for there to be a risk, or even a real risk, of Art 3, suffering occurring; it must actually be occurring or be about to occur². Physical ill health or psychological disturbance arising from a lack of a roof over the individual's head can constitute a condition that amounts to inhuman or degrading treatment³. The courts will seek to establish whether the entire package of deprivation is so severe that it can properly be described as inhuman or degrading treatment. The threshold of severity would, in the ordinary way, be crossed where a person deprived of subsistence and restricted from work is obliged to sleep in the street, or is seriously hungry, or is unable to sustain the most basic level of hygiene⁴. A recent example of a case where this threshold was found to be met is *R (GS) v Camden London Borough Council*⁵. In that case the High Court held that the provision of accommodation was necessary under the Localism Act 2011, s 1 in order to avoid a breach of Art 3 in respect of a homeless Swiss national who suffered from physical and mental health problems (and was unable to work as a result) who was ineligible for support CA 2014⁶.

¹ R *(Limbuela) v Secretary of State for the Home Department* [2005] UKHL 66, [2006] 1 AC 396, HL (in the context of destitute asylum seekers) and *R (de Almeida) v Kensington and Chelsea Royal London Borough Council* [2012] EWHC 1082 (Admin), (2012) 15 CCLR 318, Admin Ct (in the context of a terminally ill EEA national seeking accommodation under NAA 1948, s 21(1)).
² R *(Q) v Secretary of State for the Home Department* [2003] EWCA Civ 364, [2004] QB 36, CA.
³ R *(T) v Secretary of State for the Home Department* [2003] EWCA Civ 1285, (2003) 7 CCLR 53, CA at [17] per Kennedy LJ, referring to the condition of S, an applicant in the first instance decision.
⁴ R *(Limbuela) v Secretary of State for the Home Department* [2005] UKHL 66, [2006] 1 AC 396, HL.
⁵ [2016] EWHC 1762 (Admin), [2016] HLR 43, Admin Ct.
⁶ See **20.26**.

20.118 Since local authorities, as public authorities, are subject to the obligation not to submit an individual to inhuman or degrading treatment, arguably they have a responsibility to provide accommodation to anyone in their area whose suffering is verging on being inhuman or degrading treatment¹. It is important to note, however, that the threshold is a strict one. A person must have no access to any form of support (including welfare benefits) and not be able to work, whether through physical or legal incapacity. The human rights obligation to support destitute asylum-seekers is undertaken by the Secretary of State; a local authority's obligation, therefore, would only extend to a destitute person in its area who was not entitled to asylum support or any other statutory scheme providing support, was prohibited from claiming welfare benefits, who had no access to employment, and was without any form of shelter or private means of subsistence².

¹ In *R (Limbuela) v Secretary of State for the Home Department* [2005] UKHL 66, [2006] 1 AC 396, HL, the Secretary of State was held to be under a statutory duty to provide support to an

asylum-seeker in order to avoid a breach of his or her European Convention rights. See also *R (EW) v Secretary of State for the Home Department* [2009] EWHC 2957, (2010) January *Legal Action*, p 35, Admin Ct.

2 It would be surprising if this level of destitution were to be experienced by a British national, or a person with leave to remain in the UK and whose leave permitted him or her to claim welfare benefits. The scenario might be more likely to arise in the case of a person who does not have leave to remain in the UK, or whose leave is dependent upon him or her having no recourse to public funds. In those circumstances, local authorities might in any event have statutory duties to assist an adult applicant and certainly have powers and duties to assist and accommodate children (Children Act 1989, ss 17 and 20). See **20.19–20.38** and **20.72–20.84** for adult care and **20.39–20.68** and **20.85–20.98** for children's services. If an adult applicant is seeking help from a local authority in order to avoid destitution, it is a matter for the local authority how it provides that help. In the case of a person without leave to remain in the UK, that help might consist of assisting him or her to return to his or her country of origin or making those arrangements with the Home Office.

Article 8

20.119 Claims centering on a public authority's obligation not to interfere with an individual's right to respect for his or her home, family, private life and correspondence under HRA 1998, Sch 1, Art 8 have had rather more success since the introduction of the HRA 1998. Article 8:

' . . . concerns rights of central importance to the individual's identity, self-determination, physical and moral integrity, maintenance of relationships with others and a settled and secure place in the community.[1]'

1 *Connors v UK* [2004] HLR 52, ECHR, at 82.

20.120 It is well established in European human rights law that Art 8 does not contain a positive *general* obligation on central or local government to provide every individual with a home[1] though there will be exceptional cases where accommodation will need to be provided to avoid a breach of Art 8. *R (de Almeida) v Kensington and Chelsea Royal London Borough Council*[2] was one such case. In that case, the High Court found that a local authority's refusal to provide accommodation under NAA 1948, s 21(1) to a terminally ill Portuguese national with advanced and untreatable HIV/AIDS, combined with hepatitis C and cancer, was incompatible with his rights under both Arts 3 and 8.

1 See, among others, *Marzari v Italy* [1999] 28 EHRR CD 175, ECHR; *O'Rourke v UK (Application No 00039022/97)*, ECtHR.
2 [2012] EWHC 1082 (Admin), (2012) 15 CCLR 318, Admin Ct.

20.121 Where accommodation is provided by public authorities it must not be of such standard or condition as to amount to a lack of respect within Art 8. Nor must it be allowed to fall to such a standard once occupied[1]. Furthermore, if an individual is left without any accommodation, with the result that his or her family is fractured or private life is adversely affected, Art 8 may be engaged. This possibility has already been explored by the European Court of Human Rights in relation to a severely disabled individual[2].

1 *Lee v Leeds City Council* [2002] 1 WLR 1488, [2002] HLR 17, CA.
2 *Marzari v Italy* [1999] 28 EHRR CD 175, ECtHR.

20.122 The conditions of the accommodation provided by the local authority in *R (Bernard) v Enfield London Borough Council*[1] were sufficiently demeaning to breach the applicant's right to respect for her private and family life under Art 8. However, in *R (Anufrijeva) v Southwark London Borough Council*[2], a local authority was found not to have interfered with an elderly woman's right to respect for her home, her family life or her private life, by virtue of the nature of temporary accommodation it had provided[3]. The court held that before a public authority could be held to have failed to respect an applicant's private or family life, there had to be an element of culpability, involving (at the very least) knowledge by the public authority that the applicant's private or family life was at risk.

[1] *R (Bernard) v Enfield London Borough Council* [2002] EWHC 2282 (Admin), (2003) 35 HLR 27, Admin Ct.

[2] *R (Anufrijeva) v Southwark London Borough Council* [2003] EWCA Civ 1406, [2004] 2 WLR 603, CA.

[3] See further *R (McDonagh) v Enfield London Borough Council* [2018] EWHC 1287 (Admin), Admin Ct where a failure to provide suitable accommodation for a family with a severely disabled young child, in breach of HA 1996, s 188(1), for a period in excess of two years, was found not to have resulted in a breach of Art 8.

20.123 The right to respect for an applicant's home, protected by Art 8(1), can be relevant in a separate context. Where an occupier faces possession proceedings in respect of his or her home, the court has a duty to consider whether the making of a possession order is proportionate if that point is taken by the occupier[1].

[1] *Manchester City Council v Pinnock* [2010] UKSC 45, [2011] 2 AC 104, SC. See Luba, Madge, McConnell, Gallagher and Madge-Wyld *Defending Possession Proceedings* (8th edn, LAG 2016).

Chapter 21

CONTRACTING OUT OF HOMELESSNESS AND ALLOCATION FUNCTIONS

Contents

INTRODUCTION

21.1 The major duties and powers discussed in this book are those which are the responsibility of local housing authorities under the provisions of the Housing Act 1996 (HA 1996), Parts 6 ('Allocation of Housing Accommodation') and 7[1] ('Homelessness') in England. For local housing authorities in Wales, the relevant provisions are HA 1996, Part 6 and Housing (Wales) Act 2014 (HWA 2014), Part 2, ('Homelessness'). Those local housing authorities must ensure that:

(1)   they comply with the law;
(2)   they perform the duties required by HA 1996[2] or H(W)A 2014, Part 2; and
(3)   they lawfully exercise the powers given to them by HA 1996[3] or H(W)A 2014, Part 2.

---

[1]   As amended by Homelessness Reduction Act 2017 (HRA 2017) for applications for homelessness assistance made to local housing authorities in England on or after 3 April 2018.
[2]   As amended by HRA 2017 for applications for homelessness assistance made to local housing authorities in England on or after 3 April 2018.
[3]   As amended by HRA 2017 for applications for homelessness assistance made to local housing authorities in England on or after 3 April 2018.

21.2 If the performance of a duty or exercise of a power has been contracted out, it will be the local housing authority itself that is answerable to the courts or the Ombudsmen[1]. The local housing authority cannot escape that responsibility by reference to, or reliance upon, some other body.

1   In England, the Local Government and Social Care Ombudsman. In Wales, the Public Services
     Ombudsman for Wales.

THE MOVE TOWARDS CONTRACTING OUT

21.3 A local housing authority is free to decide for itself how it wishes to organise the performance of its duties and the exercise of its powers. Traditionally, staff directly employed by the local housing authority would carry out those functions on behalf of the local housing authority.

21.4 In recent years, however, more and more local housing authorities have chosen to employ private contractors, frequently local private registered providers in England or registered social landlords in Wales, to carry out those functions for them. Even when they engage contractors, local housing authorities remain responsible for those contractors' actions and also remain responsible to applicants for homelessness assistance, and to applicants for social housing, for any lapses made either by their own staff or by the contractors' staff. Therefore, in order to protect their position, local housing authorities are sensibly advised to build into the contracts between themselves and the private contractors robust penalty and escape clauses, in case of poor performance by the contractors[1]. So assured, more and more local housing authorities have been contracting out their homelessness and allocation functions.

1   *Homelessness Code of Guidance for Local Authorities* (MHCLG, 2018) (the English Code),
     chapter 5; *Code of Guidance for Local Authorities on the Allocation of Accommodation and
     Homelessness 2012* (Welsh Government, March 2016) (the Welsh Code), Annex 9, on
     CD-Rom.

THE RELEVANCE OF STOCK TRANSFER

21.5 Over 150 local housing authorities chose (with the consent of their tenants and the approval of the Secretary of State) to transfer all of their own housing stock to private registered providers or registered social landlords[1]. The law and guidance governing stock transfer itself is complex and outside the scope of this book. However, three particular points arise concerning homelessness and allocation of social housing following such a stock transfer.

1   H Pawson et al *The impacts of housing stock transfers in urban Britain* (Joseph Rowntree
     Press, 2009). The frequency of large-scale voluntary transfer has declined since 2009 and there
     have been none at all in England since July 2012.

21.6 First, even though a local housing authority no longer has any housing stock, and therefore cannot grant secure or introductory tenancies, it is still responsible for receiving and determining applications for homelessness assistance and for deciding (in response to an application for an allocation) who is to be nominated to private registered providers or registered social landlords for the grant of any assured tenancies (including nominations to any landlords who have acquired the local housing authority's own stock). It must, therefore, still have an allocation scheme and make those nominations in accordance with that scheme.

21.7 Second, some local housing authorities, having transferred the whole of their housing stock, have also contracted out their homelessness and/or allocation functions, usually to the transferee private registered provider or registered social landlord. Applicants may find that, for all intents and purposes, they appear to be dealing exclusively with staff working for a private registered provider or registered social landlord, from the moment that they apply (for homelessness assistance or under the local housing authority's allocation scheme), up to receiving an offer of accommodation from that same private registered provider or registered social landlord. Despite that appearance, decisions that are made under one of the local housing authority's statutory functions remain the responsibility of the local housing authority.

21.8 Third, the statutory obligations on a private registered provider or registered social landlord to co-operate with a local housing authority from which it has acquired housing stock[1] do not mean that the purchasing private registered provider or registered social landlord is itself obliged to operate an allocation scheme in the same terms as that which would have been operated by the local housing authority. A private registered provider or registered social landlord will normally be required by the terms of the stock transfer contract to ensure that a certain proportion of its housing stock is available for the local housing authority to nominate applicants to. However, the private registered provider or registered social landlord may also operate its own policies governing which applicants it will accept in relation to the rest of its stock.

[1] For example, HA 1996, s 213, see **14.252–14.257**; H(W)A 2014, s 95, see **17.208–17.211**.

21.9 Homes England, which regulates private registered providers in England, previously expected private registered providers to 'co-operate with local authorities' strategic housing functions, and their duties to meet identified local housing needs. This includes assistance with local authorities' homelessness duties, and meeting obligations in nominations agreements[1]. The extent of co-operation now required by Homes England is that 'registered providers shall co-operate with relevant partners to help promote social, environmental and economic wellbeing in the areas where they own properties' and that they should 'co-operate with local partnership arrangements and strategic housing functions of local authorities where they are able to assist them in achieving their objectives'[2].

[1] *Tenancy Standard*, Homes and Communities Agency, April 2012, para 2.1.1, no longer published.
[2] *Neighbourhood and Community Standard*, Homes and Communities Agency, April 2012, paras 1.2 and 2.2(b).

21.10 Where a local housing authority requests a private registered provider or registered social landlord to co-operate in offering accommodation to people with priority under the local housing authority's allocation scheme, then the provider or landlord should co-operate to such extent as is reasonable[1]. Similarly, if there is a request from a local housing authority in England to a private registered provider to co-operate in performing their homelessness functions, the provider or landlord should co-operate by rendering such assistance as is reasonable in the circumstances[2].

[1] HA 1996, s 170.

²   HA 1996, s 213.

21.11 In Wales, there is an assumption that registered social landlords will co-operate with any request for assistance or request for information from a local housing authority in performing its homelessness functions. The registered social landlord must comply with the request, unless it considers that cooperating would be incompatible with its own duties or have an adverse effect on its own functions[1]. If that is the case, it must reply in writing, giving reasons for the refusal[2].

¹   H(W)A 2014, s 95(2) and (3). *The Regulatory Framework for Housing Associations Registered in Wales* (Welsh Government, December 2011) stated that registered social landlords should 'work with other organisations to prevent and alleviate homelessness' (Part B). There is no equivalent requirement governing co-operation in the current *The Regulatory Framework for Housing Associations Registered in Wales* (Welsh Government, May 2017).
²   H(W)A 2014, s 95(4) and (5), see **17.208–17.211**. The Welsh Code advises that 'it is important that the Local Authority has comprehensive agreements in place with each of its housing association partners covering the range of its expectations', para 6.9.

THE DIFFERENT LEGAL STRUCTURES GOVERNING CONTRACTING OUT

21.12 When local housing authorities deliver their own homelessness and allocation services, they do so under HA 1996, Parts 6 and 7[1], or under H(W)A 2014, Part 2, and the Codes of Guidance issued by the Secretary of State and the Welsh Government pursuant to those statutory provisions. The legal basis for contracting out to any contractor is explained below under sub-headings that deal separately with allocation and homelessness functions. In practice, most of the contractors engaged by local housing authorities (for either or both of the functions) are private registered providers or registered social landlords.

¹   As amended by HRA 2017 for applications for homelessness assistance made to local housing authorities in England on or after 3 April 2018.

21.13 Private registered providers and registered social landlords do not have the same statutory powers and duties as local housing authorities. They are simply required by HA 1996 to 'co-operate' in the delivery of the local housing authority's homelessness and allocation functions 'to such extent as is reasonable in the circumstances', if requested to do so by the local housing authority[1].

¹   HA 1996, ss 170 (applicable to private registered providers and registered social landlords dealing with allocations by local housing authorities in both England and Wales) and 213(1) (applicable to private registered providers dealing with applications for homelessness assistance made to local housing authorities in England). H(W)A 2014, s 95, creates an obligation on registered social landlords to co-operate over applications for homelessness assistance made to local housing authorities in Wales, see **17.208–17.211**.

21.14 Whether or not the local housing authority has disposed of its stock, if it has contracted out the HA 1996, Part 6 and/or the HA 1996, Part 7[1] or H(W)A 2014, Part 2, functions, the instrument regulating each private registered provider's or registered social landlord's (or other contractor's) relationship with the local housing authority is the contract by which the private registered provider, registered social landlord or other contractor agrees to deliver the local housing authority's homelessness or allocation service (or both) at a price. Again, guidance is provided by government on the contents of that contract, particularly where it forms part of an overall arrangement for stock transfer[2]. Clearly, the terms of the contract will govern the standard of the service to be provided and, in cases of stock transfer, the extent to which the private registered provider or registered social landlord must make its vacancies available for nomination by the local housing authority.

[1] As amended by HRA 2017 for applications for homelessness assistance made to local housing authorities in England on or after 3 April 2018.
[2] *Housing Transfer Manual*: period to 31 March 2016 (DCLG, Homes and Communities Agency, Mayor of London, 2014); *Housing Transfer Guidelines* (Welsh Assembly Government, 2009).

21.15 Where, exceptionally, the local housing authority contracts out its HA 1996, Part 6 or Part 7[1] functions or H(W)A 2014, Part 2, functions to another local authority, the legal basis for that process is given by the Local Government Act 1972, s 101 and the exact scope of the functions contracted out will be shown in the contract itself.

[1] As amended by HRA 2017 for applications for homelessness assistance made to local housing authorities in England on or after 2018.

21.16 Any complaints by members of the public about the services provided by contractors acting on behalf of local housing authorities in respect of HA 1996[1] or H(W)A 2014, Part 2, functions are made against the local housing authorities themselves, not the contractors. Accordingly, any member of the public wishing to complain should use first the local housing authority's complaints procedure[2] and then complain to the Ombudsmen[3].

[1] As amended by HRA 2017 for applications for homelessness assistance made to local housing authorities in England on or after 3 April 2018.
[2] See **19.333–19.336**.
[3] See **19.337–19.340**. Note that a local housing authority was found guilty of serious maladministration by the Ombudsman when a housing association to which it had contracted out some of its homelessness responsibilities advised an applicant that complaints should be made to the Independent Housing Ombudsman and not to the Local Government Ombudsman (*Complaint against East Dorset District Council*, 05/B/08409, 22 June 2006).

HOMELESSNESS

The statutory basis governing contracting out of homelessness functions

Background to the present arrangements

21.17 As a matter of strict law, a local housing authority consists only of its elected councillors. In practice, no local housing authority, whatever its size, expects the majority of its functions (except general policy-making) to be carried out by its elected councillors. The Local Government Act 1972 permits the elected councillors to delegate the performance of the local housing authority's functions to its own officers (staff employed directly by the local housing authority) and to other local authorities[1].

1 Local Government Act 1972, s 101.

21.18 In the homelessness context, between 1985 and 1996, the statutory regime recognised a form of quasi-delegation[1]. The legislation provided that where a local housing authority requested a registered housing association to assist it with the discharge of its homelessness functions, the association should co-operate in rendering such assistance as was reasonable in the circumstances.

1 Housing Act 1985, s 72, repealed by HA 1996, s 227, Sch 19 (with effect from 20 January 1997).

21.19 However, in recent years, many local housing authorities have actually employed private registered providers, registered social landlords or other private contractors to assist with the performance of their duties (and some have gone so far as to transfer the whole or part of their housing stock to the same or different contractors)[1].

1 Governed by separate statutory powers: see **21.50–21.53**.

21.20 In 1994 and 1995, the High Court considered the extent to which a local housing authority could contract out its homelessness functions. In *R v West Dorset District Council and West Dorset Housing Association ex p Gerrard*[1], the local housing authority had transferred all its stock to the housing association with which it also contracted for the provision of a homelessness advice and investigation service. On receipt of a summary report from the association, a local housing authority officer decided that the applicant in that case was not homeless. A deputy High Court judge held that the local housing authority remained responsible for taking 'an active and dominant part in the investigative process' even after contracting out. Since the local housing authority had not itself carried out any part of the inquiries into the applicant's application for homelessness assistance (and, in addition, relevant representations made by the applicant's solicitor had not been brought to the officer's attention), the decision was quashed. Indeed, the whole administration of the local housing authority's homelessness duties was held to be unlawful. A subsequent appeal against that judgment was dismissed by consent in the Court of Appeal.

1 (1995) 27 HLR 150, QBD.

21.21 Some 10 months later, another deputy High Court judge considered the same issue in *R v Hertsmere Borough Council ex p Woolgar*[1]. That local housing authority had transferred its stock to two housing associations. A different decision (the suitability of accommodation offered) was under scrutiny, but the judge held that the same statutory framework applied. He went on to consider Housing Act 1985, s 72[2], the guidance offered in the Code[3], and government guidelines on transfer of housing stock[4], all of which clearly envisaged that:

- both the homelessness functions and a local housing authority's housing stock could be transferred;
- that the local housing authority should retain responsibility for decisions made under its homelessness duties; and

- that the local housing authority should retain at least some nomination rights to its former housing.

¹ (1995) 27 HLR 703, QBD.
² See **21.18**.
³ At that time Department of Environment's *Code of Guidance*, para 11.7.
⁴ *Large Scale Voluntary Transfers Guidelines* (Department of the Environment, December 1993).

21.22 Having considered those materials, he held that the decision in *Gerrard* had been made without any scrutiny of the government's guidelines and was therefore made *per incuriam*¹. As a result, Hertsmere Borough Council's scheme for delivering its homelessness duties, which amounted to its homelessness functions being carried out by a registered social landlord (now a private registered provider) and the accommodation offered being provided by that same landlord, was held to be lawful.

¹ Without awareness of authority that might have made a difference to the court's decision.

The modern framework

HA 1996, Pt 7

21.23 The judicial uncertainty created by these two conflicting decisions was soon resolved by Parliament¹. The modern legislative framework permitting a local housing authority to contract out its homelessness functions is found in the Deregulation and Contracting Out Act 1994, s 70. Under that Act, the Secretary of State has made the Local Authorities (Contracting Out of Allocation of Housing and Homelessness Functions) Order 1996². Local housing authorities are now permitted to contract out the bulk of their homelessness functions³.

¹ HA 1996, Pt 7, was the statutory framework for applications for homelessness assistance made to local housing authorities in both England and Wales until 27 April 2015, when H(W)A 2014, Pt 2 (homelessness) came into effect for applications for homelessness assistance made to local housing authorities in Wales.
² SI 1996/3205, as amended by the Housing (Wales) Act 2014 (Consequential Amendments) Regulations 2015, SI 2015/752 (W 59) reproduced at Appendix 2. See also English Code, chapter 21; Welsh Code, Annex 9, for guidance.
³ Except those listed at **21.26**.

21.24 Particular conditions related to the carrying out of those functions can be (and should be) included in the contract itself, so that standards of performance are prescribed. The Deregulation and Contracting Out Act 1994 provides that the contract cannot be for a period of more than 10 years, and may be for any shorter period¹. The contract must also provide that it can be revoked at any time by the Minister or by the local housing authority². The local housing authority remains responsible for any acts or omissions made by the contractor in the performance of the local housing authority's homelessness functions, unless the contractor is in breach of the conditions specified in the contract or the contractor has committed a criminal offence.

¹ Deregulation and Contracting Out Act 1994, s 69(5)(a).
² Deregulation and Contracting Out Act 1994, s 69(5)(b).

21.25 In *Runa Begum v Tower Hamlets London Borough Council*[1], the House of Lords considered whether such a contractor could be considered 'independent' of the local housing authority for the purposes of the European Convention on Human Rights, Art 6(1)[2]. If contractors were held to be 'independent' for those purposes, review decisions that were being taken by officers employed by the local housing authority (who were obviously not independent) could, instead, be taken by contracted individuals or organisations in order to obtain the necessary measure of independence. The House of Lords held that a contractor, whose services could be dispensed with, was probably no more independent than an officer employed directly by the local housing authority. However, Lord Bingham, in an *obiter* paragraph, added that he had very considerable doubt whether the resolution of applications for review fell within a local housing authority's relevant functions and therefore could be contracted out at all[3]. Since then, the Court of Appeal has held that the making of review decisions *is* a function that can be contracted by a local housing authority: *De-Winter Heald v Brent London Borough Council*[4]. More recently the Court of Appeal held that the public sector equality duty on local housing authorities at Equality Act 2010, s 149[5], was not a function that could be contracted out, but that the application of the public sector equality duty within the local housing authority's homelessness functions did not amount to a delegation of the duty[6].

[1] *Runa Begum v Tower Hamlets London Borough Council* [2003] UKHL 5, [2003] 2 AC 430, HL.
[2] Which provides that civil rights are to be determined by a body independent of the parties. The Supreme Court has held that decision-making on applications for homelessness assistance does not involve a determination of an applicant's 'civil rights' and so Art 6(1) does not apply: *Ali v Birmingham City Council* [2010] UKSC 8, [2010] 2 AC 39, SC; and *Poshteh v Kensington & Chelsea Royal London Borough Council* [2017] UKSC 36, [2017] 624, SC; see also *Fazia Ali v UK* (App No 40378, 20 October 2015) ECtHR, where the European Court of Human Rights took a different view.
[3] [2003] UKHL 5, [2003] 2 AC 430, HL at [10] per Lord Bingham.
[4] [2009] EWCA Civ 930, [2010] HLR 8, CA. See **21.35–21.36.**
[5] See **9.81–9.83, 12.91, 12.100, 13.70** and **18.65–18.68.**
[6] *Smith v Haringey London Borough Council*, reported with *Panayiotou v Waltham Forest London Borough Council* [2017] EWCA Civ 1624, [2017] HLR 48, CA per Lewison LJ at [72]–[80].

21.26 The local housing authority may *not* contract out four specified functions:

(1)   for local housing authorities in England, their power to provide finance to a person or organisation so that housing advice and information is provided on the local housing authority's behalf[1];

(2)   for local housing authorities in England, their power to assist such a person or organisation by providing premises, furniture, or its own housing staff[2];

(3)   for local housing authorities in England, their power to finance, or provide premises, furniture or the services of its staff, to a voluntary organisation concerned with homelessness or matters relating to homelessness[3]; and

(4)   for local housing authorities in both England and Wales, their obligation to render assistance if asked by another local housing authority to assist it in the discharge of that local housing authority's HA 1996, Pt 7[4]

or H(W)A 2014, Pt 2, functions[5].

1   HA 1996, s 179(3), as inserted by HRA 2017, s 2, for applications for homelessness assistance
    made to local housing authorities in England on or after 3 April 2018; Local Authorities
    (Contracting Out of Allocation of Housing and Homelessness Functions) Order 1996,
    SI 1996/3205, art 3 and Sch 2.
2   HA 1996, s 179(4), as inserted by HRA 2017, s 2, for applications for homelessness assistance
    made to local housing authorities in England on or after 3 April 2018; SI 1996/3205, art 3 and
    Sch 2.
3   HA 1996, s 180; SI 1996/3205, art 3 and Sch 2.
4   As amended by HRA 2017 for applications for homelessness assistance made to local housing
    authorities in England on or after 3 April 2018.
5   HA 1996, s 213; H(W)A 2014, s 95; SI 1996/3205, art 3 and Sch 2.

21.27 In addition, local housing authorities in England cannot contract out
their obligations under Homelessness Act 2002, ss 1–4 to carry out homelessness reviews and strategies[1].

1   See **7.180–7.182** and English Code, para 5.7. It seems from the wording of the Local
    Authorities (Contracting Out of Allocation of Housing and Homelessness Functions) Order
    1996, SI 1996/3205 as amended by the Housing (Wales) Act 2014 (Consequential
    Amendments) Regulations 2015, SI 2015/752 (W 59) that local housing authorities in Wales
    can contract out these functions.

21.28 Where a local housing authority has contracted out its function of
making review decisions, the review decision is only lawful if the process of
contracting out complied with the statutory obligations. In *Shacklady v
Flintshire County Council*[1], the local housing authority could not produce any
written authorisation in respect of the contract. The judge found that the
absence of any written record containing a period of appointment was a
serious departure from the statutory requirements and could not be waived.
The authorisation to the contractor was therefore invalid and the review
decision was a nullity. In *England v Westminster City Council*[2], the courts
found that the review decision had not been actually contracted out. The
private registered provider involved had provided information to the reviewing
officer but had not made the decision[3].

1   (2010) November *Legal Action*, p 26, Mold County Court.
2   [2010] EWCA Civ 106, (2010) April *Legal Action*, p 26, CA.
3   See also *Hussain v Waltham Forest London Borough Council* [2015] EWCA Civ 14, [2015]
    1 WLR 2912, [2015] HLR 16, CA, for a recent example of a review decision being taken by
    an agency contracted to manage the local housing authority's functions under HA 1996, Pt 7.

21.29 As already noted[1], the obligation on private registered providers, social
services' authorities, or other local housing authorities which receive requests
for assistance from a local housing authority in England is to 'co-operate in
rendering such assistance in the discharge of the functions to which the request
relates as is reasonable in the circumstances'[2].

1   See **21.8–21.11**.
2   HA 1996, s 213(1) and (2).

H(W)A 2014, Pt 2

21.30 There are fewer restrictions limiting which functions in H(W)A 2014,
Pt 2, can be contracted out by a local housing authority in Wales. Indeed, the

only function that cannot be contracted out is the obligation on a local housing authority to co-operate when it has received a request for co-operation, or for information, from a local housing authority in Wales[1].

[1]   Local Authorities (Contracting Out of Allocation of Housing and Homelessness Functions) Order 1996, SI 1996/3205, art 3 and Sch 2 as amended by the Housing (Wales) Act (Consequential Amendments) Regulations 2015, SI 2015/752 (W 59). The request would be made under H(W)A 2014, s 95, see **22.11**.

21.31 A local housing authority in Wales may make a request for co-operation so that it can receive help in order to achieve any or all of the following objectives:

- the prevention of homelessness;
- that suitable accommodation is or will be available for people who are or may become homeless;
- that satisfactory support is available for people who are or may become homeless; or
- effective performance of any function under H(W)A 2014, Pt 2[1].

[1]   H(W)A 2014, s 95(1).

21.32 The request can be made to any other local housing authority, to a social services authority, to a registered social landlord, a new town corporation, a private registered provider of social housing or a housing action trust. The request can be directed to any of those bodies, whether in Wales or in England[1]. A local housing authority in Wales can also request that any of those bodies provide it with information required for the exercise of its functions under H(W)A 2014, Pt 2[2].

[1]   H(W)A 2014, s 95(5).
[2]   H(W)A 2014, s 95(3).

21.33 When the request for assistance or for information is received, the recipient must comply unless it considers that doing so would either be incompatible with the recipient's own duties or would otherwise have an adverse effect on the exercise of the recipient's functions[1]. If that is the case, the recipient must put in writing to the local housing authority the reasons for its decision[2]. Guidance is given in chapter 6 of the Welsh Code and the point is succinctly expressed: 'the default position will be that the partner organisation will co-operate to meet a request for assistance'[3].

[1]   H(W)A 2014, s 95(2) and (3).
[2]   H(W)A 2014, s 95(4).
[3]   Welsh Code, para 6.4.

21.34 Unlike local housing authorities in England[1], there is no prohibition on a local housing authority contracting out its duties to carry out a homelessness review and formulate a homelessness strategy[2].

[1]   See **21.27**.
[2]   H(W)A 2014, ss 50–52, see **21.30**.

Case law on contracting out of a review decision

21.35 As already noted[1], at least one senior judge in 2003 thought that the decision-making involved in the review process might not be something that could be contracted out[2]. However, three different cases decided by the Court of Appeal and High Court have confirmed that there is nothing unlawful in a review decision being taken by an individual who was not employed by the local housing authority.

1   See **21.25**.
2   *Runa Begum v Tower Hamlets London Borough Council* [2003] UKHL 5, [2003] 2 AC 430, HL per Lord Bingham at [10].

21.36 In *De-Winter Heald v Brent London Borough Council*[1], the local housing authority had delegated the decision-making on a request for a review to an external 'reviews manager' and his company. The Court of Appeal considered the Local Authorities (Contracting Out of Allocation of Housing and Homelessness Functions) Order 1996[2]. It noted the functions in art 3 and Sch 2 that could not be contracted out by a local housing authority. The decision-making required once a request for a review had been received was not amongst those functions excluded from being contracted out. It followed that the decision-making and notification of a decision made on review could be lawfully contracted out by a local housing authority. The local housing authority, of course, remains responsible for the consequences of that review decision.

1   [2009] EWCA Civ 930, [2010] HLR 8, CA.
2   SI 1996/3205.

21.37 In *Tachie v Welwyn Hatfield Borough Council*[1], the local housing authority had contracted out all of its homelessness functions under HA 1996, Part 7, to an arms-length management organisation. The judge noted that the Deregulation and Contracting Out Act 1994, s 70, is 'wide enough to cover the entirety of the . . . homelessness functions, whether or not the latter comprise "discretionary decision-making"'[2]. He then considered the Local Authorities (Contracting Out of Allocation of Housing and Homelessness Functions) Order 1996[3] and noted that the specified homelessness functions that could not be contracted out did not include the making of review decisions and so there was no general prohibition on that function being contracted out. He noted that para **21.2** of the English Code suggested that 'making strategic decisions' should not be contracted out. He concluded that decisions made on review were 'evaluative judgments which entail an assessment and interpretation of the available material, and the drawing of inferential conclusions from the facts'. They were evaluative, but not policy or strategic decision-making[4]. It followed that there was no prohibition on contracting out the function of decision-making on review.

1   [2013] EWHC 3972 (QB), [2014] PTSR 662, QBD.
2   *Tachie v Welwyn Hatfield Borough Council* [2013] EWHC 3972 (QB), [2014] PTSR 662, QBD per Jay J at [23].
3   SI 1996/3205.
4   *Tachie v Welwyn Hatfield Borough Council* [2013] EWHC 3972 (QB), [2014] PTSR 662, QBD per Jay J at [26]–[27].

21.38 In *Smith v Haringey London Borough Council*,[1] the appellant argued that Equality Act 2010, s 149, did not permit a local housing authority to contract out decisions in which the public sector equality duty was engaged, because that duty was not delegable[2]. The Court of Appeal accepted that the duty was not delegable, but held that the effect of contracting out is that the function in question shall be treated as having been exercised by the local housing authority. So the principle that the public sector equality duty could not be delegated had not been breached[3]. The Court also heard, and dismissed arguments that the local housing authority had failed to adopt the correct method of contracting out decisions, in breach of its own constitutional requirements, and that in deciding to contract the homelessness decision-making functions, the local housing authority had not considered the public sector equality duty[4].

[1] Reported *with Panayiotou v Waltham Forest London Borough Council* [2017] EWCA Civ 1624, [2017] HLR 48, CA.
[2] Equality Act 2010, s 149, see **9.81–9.83, 12.91, 12.100, 13.70** and **18.65–18.68**.
[3] Lewison LJ at [72]–[80].
[4] Lewison LJ at [81]–[88]. The court also suggested that such issues should not be raised in HA 1996, s 204 appeals [90]. See also *Servis v Newham London Borough Council* [2018] EWHC 1547 (QB), where the High Court upheld a refusal to order specific disclosure of documents relating to the contracting out process which had been sought in order to sustain a similar challenge. The documents sought were not relevant to any of the applications existing grounds of appeal and the circuit judge had not erred in refusing to order disclosure.

Using a contractor's accommodation for the homeless

21.39 Different statutory provisions govern a local housing authority's ability to use accommodation from other providers in order to perform its HA 1996, Part 7[1] or H(W)A 2014, Part 2, duties to applicants for homelessness assistance. As an alternative to providing the applicant with its own accommodation, HA 1996, s 206, and H(W)A 2014, s 68, permit a local housing authority to perform its duty to provide accommodation for an applicant and members of his or her household, by securing that the applicant obtains suitable accommodation 'from some other person' or, even, merely by 'giving him such advice and assistance as will secure that suitable accommodation is available from some other person'[2]. If the latter course is taken, then the local housing authority must ensure that the advice and assistance does actually secure that suitable accommodation is obtained. If not, the local housing authority's duty to secure accommodation from its own stock or from some other person remains[3]. These provisions have given local housing authorities considerable flexibility to arrange for accommodation for the homeless to be supplied, under contract, by private registered providers, registered social landlords and other private contractors.

[1] As amended by HRA 2017 for applications for homelessness assistance made to local housing authorities in England on or after 3 April 2018.
[2] HA 1996, s 206(1)(b) and (c); H(W)A 2014, s 64(1)(a) and (c).
[3] See **19.8–19.10**.

21.40 The ability to secure accommodation 'from some other person' allows a local housing authority to arrange for a private landlord, a private registered provider or registered social landlord to grant a tenancy directly to an applicant in performance of any duty to accommodate the applicant[1]. HA 1996, s 193 and H(W)A 2014, s 76 also allow the local housing authority to bring the main housing duty to an end when an applicant accepts an offer of an assured tenancy from a private registered provider or registered social landlord[2]. Local housing authorities in England can also bring their duties to an end when:

- they are satisfied that the applicant has suitable accommodation available for his or her occupation and there is a reasonable prospect that suitable accommodation will be available for at least six months[3];
- they are satisfied that the applicant has refused an offer suitable accommodation which was available for his or her occupation and there was a reasonable prospect that suitable accommodation will be available for at least six months[4];
- the applicant has refused a final accommodation offer[5] made in order to bring the HA 1996, s189B(2),[6] relief duty or the HA 1996, s 193C(4),[7] accommodation duty to an end[8]; or
- the applicant has accepted or refused a private rented sector offer[9] made in order to bring the HA 1996, s 193(2), main housing duty[10] to an end[11].

[1] HA 1996, s 206(1)(b); H(W)A 2014, s 64(a) and (c) and see *R (on the application of Khatun) v Newham London Borough Council* [2004] EWCA Civ 55, [2004] HLR 29, CA at [91] per Laws LJ.
[2] HA 1996, s 193(6)(cc), see **16.136–16.139**; H(W)A 2014, s 76(2)(b), see **17.161–17.164**.
[3] HA 1996, ss 189B(5) and (7)(a) and 195(5) and (8)(a), as inserted and amended by HRA 2017, ss 4(2) and 5(2), for applications for homelessness assistance made to local housing authorities in England on or after 3 April 2018, see **15.162–15.165** and **15.105–15.109**.
[4] HA 1996, ss 189B(7)(c) and 195(8)(d), as inserted and amended by HRA 2017, ss 4(2) and 5(2), for applications for homelessness assistance made to local housing authorities in England on or after 3 April 2018, see **15.169–15.173** and **15.118–15.122**.
[5] As defined at HA 1996, ss 193A(4) or 193C(7), inserted by HRA 2017, s 7(1), for applications for homelessness assistance made to local housing authorities in England on or after 3 April 2018, see **15.181–15.184** and **16.205–16.209**.
[6] As inserted by HRA 2017, s 5(2), for applications for homelessness assistance made to local housing authorities in England on or after 3 April 2018, see **15.138–15.195**.
[7] As inserted by HRA 2017, s 7(1), for applications for homelessness assistance made to local housing authorities in England on or after 3 April 2018; duty to accommodate applicants who are homeless, eligible for assistance, have a priority need, have not become homeless intentionally and who have deliberately and unreasonably refused to co-operate, see **16.200–16.216**.
[8] HA 1996, ss 189B(9)(a), 193A(1), and 193C(6)(a), as inserted by HRA 2017, ss 5(2) and 7(1), for applications for homelessness assistance made to local housing authorities in England on or after 3 April 2018, see **15.181–15.184** and **16.205–16.209**.
[9] As defined at HA 1996, s 193(7AC), see **16.153–16.180**.
[10] See **16.94–16.199**.
[11] HA 1996, s 193(7AA), see **16.153–16.180**.

Ensuring that the private contractor maintains the appropriate level of service

21.41 Given that the local housing authority remains responsible for the calibre and correctness of its homelessness decisions, even when the inquiries and recommendations leading to those decisions have been made by a private contractor, it is vital for a local housing authority to be able to rely upon the quality of the service provided by the contractor. That safeguard should be contained in the contract between the local housing authority and the contractor. The Audit Commission noted (in the context of stock transfer):

> ' . . . few [authorities] have experience of contracting out these services, and there is rarely time during the hectic [stock] transfer process to review them, decide their best location and draw up a good contract. As a result, some contracts are poorly written or difficult to monitor. Attention can focus on "maintaining" minimum service rather than improvement[1].'

[1]   *Housing after Transfer, the Local Authority Role* (The Audit Commission, 2002), Chapter 3, para 64.

21.42 The *Housing Transfer Manual: period to 31 March 2016*[1] contains some guidance on drawing up the contract in para 6.11. There should be a plain English summary of its contents. Where either party is to provide services to the other, the terms should be set out in service level agreements.

[1]   DCLG, Homes & Communities Agency and Mayor of London, 2014.

ALLOCATION OF ACCOMMODATION

21.43 The same statutory framework applies to the contracting out of the functions involved in the allocation of social housing. The Local Authorities (Contracting Out of Allocation of Housing and Homelessness Functions) Order 1996,[1] made by the Secretary of State under the Deregulation and Contracting Out Act 1994, s 70, permits local housing authorities to contract out the bulk of their functions involved in the allocation of social housing under HA 1996, Part 6. Many local housing authorities have disposed of the whole of their housing stock to local private registered providers or registered social landlords, so that the local housing authority's allocations are made by nomination to private registered providers or registered social landlords for assured tenancies, or to other local housing authorities.

[1]   SI 1996/3205, reproduced in Appendix 1.

21.44 The overall policy of the allocation scheme is for the local housing authority to determine, subject to complying with HA 1996, Part 6, the regulations and the Codes. The House of Lords has noted that '[h]ousing allocation policy is a difficult exercise which requires not only social and political sensitivity and judgment, but also local expertise and knowledge'[1]. Policy decisions on the allocation scheme are political decisions.

[1]   *Ahmad v Newham London Borough Council* [2009] UKHL 14, [2009] HLR 41, HL at [47] per Lord Neuberger.

21.45 It follows that the local housing authority is responsible for general policy decisions on:

(1)   whether or not it will offer 'choice' in its allocation scheme, or provide applicants with the opportunity to express preferences[1];

(2)   whether it will frame the scheme so as to give additional preferences within the reasonable preference categories and, if so, based on what criteria[2];

(3)   on what principles it will prioritise different applicants within the reasonable preference categories;[3] and

(4)   whether it will provide for the allocation of accommodation to persons of a particular description and, if so, what accommodation, and to whom[4].

[1]   HA 1996, s 166A(2) for local housing authorities in England; HA 1996, s 167(1A) for local housing authorities in Wales. See **5.6–5.47**.

[2]   HA 1996, s 166A(3) for local housing authorities in England; HA 1996, s 167(2) for local housing authorities in Wales. See **4.29–4112**.

[3]   HA 1996, s 166A(3) for local housing authorities in England; HA 1996, s 167(2) for local housing authorities in Wales. See **4.113–4.147**.

[4]   HA 1996, s 166A(6)(b) for local housing authorities in England; HA 1996, s 167(2E)(b) for local housing authorities in Wales. See **4.165–4.192**.

Functions

21.46 Having drawn up its allocation scheme, the local housing authority may contract out nearly all of its *functions* under HA 1996, Part 6 to a contractor. The contractor's staff, therefore, could receive an application, ensure that the applicant is given the information to which he or she is entitled, provide advice and assistance with the making of an application, process the application, make any decisions required to be made in respect of the application and, in accordance with the policy, arrange for the selection of a secure or introductory tenant, or nominate the applicant to a private registered provider or registered social landlord for an assured tenancy. At each stage the contractor will be taking the practical steps, but the local housing authority remains liable for the decisions.

21.47 The local housing authority cannot contract out the duties:

(1)   to determine the terms of its allocation scheme;

(2)   to allocate in accordance with that scheme; and

(3)   to make the scheme available for inspection[1].

[1]   HA 1996, s 166A(13) for local housing authorities in England; HA 1996, s 167(7) for local housing authorities in Wales. See **1.23–1.51**. These sections refer to adopting or altering an allocation scheme and to consulting private registered providers and registered social landlords. See also HA 1996, s 168(2); SI 1996/3205, art 2 and Sch 1.

21.48 If the contractor's staff fail to treat an applicant in accordance with the local housing authority's scheme, it is the local housing authority that will be answerable for that failure.

21.49 In the unreported case of *R (Uddin) v Tower Hamlets London Borough Council*[1], Mr Uddin was a tenant of a private registered provider who needed a transfer to larger accommodation. The local housing authority and private registered provider operated a common housing register and it was the private registered provider which made the decisions on his application for a transfer. The applicant argued that the private registered provider was not authorised by the local housing authority to make the decision. It appears that the local housing authority did not have any contemporaneous documents authorising the private registered provider to make the decision. It sought to ratify previous decisions retrospectively and made a resolution authorising future contracting out of decision-making under its allocation scheme. The case was subsequently settled[2].

¹   CO/8098/2008.
²   See '*Contracting out Decision-making: Unanswered Questions*', David Cowan [2010] 13 JHL 24.

Stock transfers and nominations to private registered providers or registered social landlords

21.50 Where a local housing authority is proposing a large scale voluntary transfer of its own stock, so that there will no longer be any council-owned accommodation in its district, any future allocation made under its allocation scheme will be by way of a nomination to a private registered provider or registered social landlord for an assured tenancy. In order to ensure that it can continue to comply with its statutory duty to maintain an allocation scheme, and to allocate accommodation, the local housing authority must ensure that the purchasing private registered provider(s) or registered social landlord(s) will accept its nominations[1].

¹   See CHAPTER 6.

21.51 There are statutory duties and contractual obligations requiring that private registered providers and registered social landlords co-operate with local housing authorities to ensure that a certain amount of their available accommodation is provided to people nominated by local housing authorities. If a local housing authority requests that a private registered provider or registered social landlord co-operates with it by offering accommodation to people on the local housing authority's allocation scheme, the private registered provider or registered social landlord is under a statutory duty to co-operate 'to such extent as is reasonable in the circumstances'[1]. In addition, when the local housing authority has transferred its own stock to the private registered provider or registered social landlord, after the process of government approval, consultation and balloting, it will have done so in a contract. The local housing authority should ensure that the terms of the contract provide that the private registered provider or registered social landlord will make a certain proportion of its empty properties available for people nominated by the local housing authority under its allocation scheme[2]. Any proposed transfer that does not include a contractual obligation on the private registered provider or registered social landlord to make a specified proportion of empty accommodation available for allocation is unlikely to receive government approval.

¹   HA 1996, s 170.
²   *Housing Transfer Manual: period to 31 March 2016* (DCLG, Homes and Communities Agency, Mayor of London, 2014), para 6.11.

21.52 Private registered providers and registered social landlords, including stock transfer associations, can therefore operate quotas under which a proportion (which can be up to 100%) of their vacancies will be allocated on the basis of the local housing authority's nominations. The remaining part of their vacancies will be allocated by the private registered provider or registered social landlord itself, either to its own tenants seeking transfers or to people who have applied directly to the private registered provider or registered social landlord for accommodation.

21.53 Generally, if a private registered provider or registered social landlord supplies a proportion of its empty stock for local housing authority nominations, it should not impose its own conditions on the type of applicant nominated, and should be contractually obliged to accept anyone whom the local housing authority nominates. However, when it comes to the remainder of the vacancies, private registered providers and registered social landlords will make their own decisions as to who is to be offered each vacancy. Each private registered provider and registered social landlord, therefore, must have its own policy governing transfer applications (from its own tenants) and any applications made to it directly rather than through the local housing authority.

Appendix 1

ENGLAND: ALLOCATION

Contents

Statutes

HOUSING ACT 1996

PART VI
ALLOCATION OF HOUSING ACCOMMODATION

Introductory

A1.1

159 Allocation of housing accommodation

(1) A local housing authority shall comply with the provisions of this Part in allocating housing accommodation.

(2) For the purposes of this Part a local housing authority allocate housing accommodation when they—

(a) select a person to be a secure or introductory tenant of housing accommodation held by them,

(b) nominate a person to be a secure or introductory tenant of housing accommodation held by another person, or

(c) nominate a person to be an assured tenant of housing accommodation held by [a private registered provider of social housing or] a registered social landlord.

(3) The reference in subsection (2)(a) to selecting a person to be a secure tenant includes deciding to exercise any power to notify an existing tenant or licensee that his tenancy or licence is to be a secure tenancy.

(4) The references in subsection (2)(b) and (c) to nominating a person include nominating a person in pursuance of any arrangements (whether legally enforceable or not) to require that housing accommodation, or a specified amount of housing accommodation, is made available to a person or one of a number of persons nominated by the authority.

[(4A) Subject to subsection (4B), the provisions of this Part do not apply to an allocation of housing accommodation by a local housing authority in England to a person who is already—

(a) a secure or introductory tenant, or

(b) an assured tenant of housing accommodation held by a private registered provider of social housing or a registered social landlord.

(4B) The provisions of this Part apply to an allocation of housing accommodation by a local housing authority in England to a person who falls within subsection (4A)(a) or (b) if—

(a) the allocation involves a transfer of housing accommodation for that person,

(b) the application for the transfer is made by that person, and

(c) the authority is satisfied that the person is to be given reasonable preference under section 166A(3).]

[(5) The provisions of this Part do not apply to an allocation of housing accommodation [by a local housing authority in Wales] to a person who is already a secure or introductory tenant unless the allocation involves a transfer of housing accommodation for that person and is made on his application.]

(7) Subject to the provisions of this Part, a local housing authority may allocate housing accommodation in such manner as they consider appropriate.

NOTES

Amendment

Sub-s (2): in para (c) words "a private registered provider of social housing or" in square brackets inserted by SI 2010/866, art 5, Sch 2, paras 81, 100.

Date in force: 1 April 2010: see SI 2010/866, art 1(2); for transitional provisions and savings see art 6, Sch 3, paras 1, 3, 4 thereto.

Sub-ss (4A), (4B): inserted by the Localism Act 2011, s 145(1), (2).

Date in force (for certain purposes): 15 January 2012: see SI 2012/57, art 4(1)(j).

Date in force (for remaining purposes): 18 June 2012: see SI 2012/1463, art 3.

Sub-s (5): substituted, for sub-ss (5), (6) as originally enacted, by the Homelessness Act 2002, s 13.

Date in force (in relation to Wales): 27 January 2003: see SI 2002/1736, art 2(2), Schedule, Pt 2.

Date in force (in relation to England): 31 January 2003: see SI 2002/3114, art 3.

Sub-s (5): words "by a local housing authority in Wales" in square brackets inserted by the Localism Act 2011, s 145(1), (3).

Date in force (for certain purposes): 15 January 2012: see SI 2012/57, art 4(1)(j).

Date in force (for remaining purposes): 18 June 2012: see SI 2012/1463, art 3.

160 Cases where provisions about allocation do not apply

(1)   The provisions of this Part about the allocation of housing accommodation do not apply in the following cases.

(2)   They do not apply where a secure tenancy—

    (a)   vests under section 89 of the Housing Act 1985 (succession to periodic secure tenancy on death of tenant),

    (b)   remains a secure tenancy by virtue of section 90 of that Act (devolution of term certain of secure tenancy on death of tenant),

    (c)   is assigned under section 92 of that Act (assignment of secure tenancy by way of exchange),

    (d)   is assigned to a person who would be qualified to succeed the secure tenant if the secure tenant died immediately before the assignment,

    [(da)   is granted in response to a request under section 158 of the Localism Act 2011 (transfer of tenancy), or]

    (e)   vests or is otherwise disposed of in pursuance of an order made under—

        (i)   section 24 of the Matrimonial Causes Act 1973 (property adjustment orders in connection with matrimonial proceedings),

        (ii)   section 17(1) of the Matrimonial and Family Proceedings Act 1984 (property adjustment orders after overseas divorce, &c), . . .

        (iii)   paragraph 1 of Schedule 1 to the Children Act 1989 (orders for financial relief against parents)[, or

        (iv)   Part 2 of Schedule 5, or paragraph 9(2) or (3) of Schedule 7, to the Civil Partnership Act 2004 (property adjustment orders in connection with civil partnership proceedings or after overseas dissolution of civil partnership, etc)].

(3)   They do not apply where an introductory tenancy—

    (a)   becomes a secure tenancy on ceasing to be an introductory tenancy,

    (b)   vests under section 133(2) (succession to introductory tenancy on death of tenant),

    (c)   is assigned to a person who would be qualified to succeed the introductory tenant if the introductory tenant died immediately before the assignment, or

    (d)   vests or is otherwise disposed of in pursuance of an order made under—

        (i)   section 24 of the Matrimonial Causes Act 1973 (property adjustment orders in connection with matrimonial proceedings),

        (ii)   section 17(1) of the Matrimonial and Family Proceedings Act 1984 (property adjustment orders after overseas divorce, &c), . . .

        (iii)   paragraph 1 of Schedule 1 to the Children Act 1989 (orders for financial relief against parents)[, or

        (iv)   Part 2 of Schedule 5, or paragraph 9(2) or (3) of Schedule 7, to the Civil Partnership Act 2004 (property adjustment orders in connection with civil partnership proceedings or after overseas dissolution of civil partnership, etc)].

(4)   They do not apply in such other cases as the Secretary of State may prescribe by regulations.

(5)   The regulations may be framed so as to make the exclusion of the provisions of this Part about the allocation of housing accommodation subject to such restrictions or conditions as may be specified.

In particular, those provisions may be excluded—

      (a)   in relation to specified descriptions of persons, or

      (b)   in relation to housing accommodation of a specified description or a specified proportion of housing accommodation of any specified description.

NOTES

Amendment

Sub-s (2): para (da) inserted by virtue of the Localism Act 2011, s 159(7).
    Date in force: 1 April 2012: see SI 2012/628, art 6(a).
Sub-s (2): in para (e)(ii) word omitted repealed by the Civil Partnership Act 2004, s 261(4), Sch 30.
    Date in force: 5 December 2005: see SI 2005/3175, art 2(6).
Sub-s (2): para (e)(iv) and word ", or" immediately preceding it inserted by the Civil Partnership Act 2004, s 81, Sch 8, para 60.
    Date in force: 5 December 2005: see SI 2005/3175, art 2(1), Sch 1.
Sub-s (3): in para (d)(ii) word omitted repealed by the Civil Partnership Act 2004, s 261(4), Sch 30.
    Date in force: 5 December 2005: see SI 2005/3175, art 2(6).
Sub-s (3): para (d)(iv) and word ", or" immediately preceding it inserted by the Civil Partnership Act 2004, s 81, Sch 8, para 60.
    Date in force: 5 December 2005: see SI 2005/3175, art 2(1), Sch 1.

[Eligibility for allocation of housing accommodation]

[160ZA Allocation only to eligible and qualifying persons: England]

[(1)   A local housing authority in England shall not allocate housing accommodation—

      (a)   to a person from abroad who is ineligible for an allocation of housing accommodation by virtue of subsection (2) or (4), or

      (b)   to two or more persons jointly if any of them is a person mentioned in paragraph (a).

(2)   A person subject to immigration control within the meaning of the Asylum and Immigration Act 1996 is ineligible for an allocation of housing accommodation by a local housing authority in England unless he is of a class prescribed by regulations made by the Secretary of State.

(3)   No person who is excluded from entitlement to [universal credit or] housing benefit by section 115 of the Immigration and Asylum Act 1999 (exclusion from benefits) shall be included in any class prescribed under subsection (2).

(4)   The Secretary of State may by regulations prescribe other classes of persons from abroad who are ineligible to be allocated housing accommodation by local housing authorities in England.

(5)   Nothing in subsection (2) or (4) affects the eligibility of a person who falls within section 159(4B).

(6) Except as provided by subsection (1), a person may be allocated housing accommodation by a local housing authority in England (whether on his application or otherwise) if that person—

    (a)   is a qualifying person within the meaning of subsection (7), or

    (b)   is one of two or more persons who apply for accommodation jointly, and one or more of the other persons is a qualifying person within the meaning of subsection (7).

(7) Subject to subsections (2) and (4) and any regulations under subsection (8), a local housing authority may decide what classes of persons are, or are not, qualifying persons.

(8) The Secretary of State may by regulations—

    (a)   prescribe classes of persons who are, or are not, to be treated as qualifying persons by local housing authorities in England, and

    (b)   prescribe criteria that may not be used by local housing authorities in England in deciding what classes of persons are not qualifying persons.

(9) If a local housing authority in England decide that an applicant for housing accommodation—

    (a)   is ineligible for an allocation by them by virtue of subsection (2) or (4), or

    (b)   is not a qualifying person,

they shall notify the applicant of their decision and the grounds for it.

(10) That notice shall be given in writing and, if not received by the applicant, shall be treated as having been given if it is made available at the authority's office for a reasonable period for collection by him or on his behalf.

(11) A person who is not being treated as a qualifying person may (if he considers that he should be treated as a qualifying person) make a fresh application to the authority for an allocation of housing accommodation by them.]

NOTES

Amendment

    Cross-heading: inserted by the Homelessness Act 2002, s 14(2); for effect see s 14(3), (4) thereof.

        Date in force (in relation to England in so far as it confers powers to make regulations): 5 December 2002: see SI 2002/3114, art 2.

        Date in force (in relation to Wales): 27 January 2003: see SI 2002/1736, art 2(2), Schedule, Pt 2.

        Date in force (in relation to England for remaining purposes): 31 January 2003: see SI 2002/3114, art 3.

    Inserted by the Localism Act 2011, s 146(1).

        Date in force (for certain purposes): 15 January 2012: see SI 2012/57, art 4(1)(k).

        Date in force (for remaining purposes): 18 June 2012: see SI 2012/1463, art 3.

    Sub-s (3): words "universal credit or" in square brackets inserted by SI 2013/630, reg 12(1), (3).

        Date in force: 29 April 2013: see SI 2013/630, reg 1(2).

[160A Allocation only to eligible persons[: Wales]]

[(1) A local housing authority [in Wales] shall not allocate housing accommodation—

    (a)   to a person from abroad who is ineligible for an allocation of housing accommodation by virtue of subsection (3) or (5);

    (b)   to a person who the authority have decided is to be treated as ineligible for such an allocation by virtue of subsection (7); or

    (c)   to two or more persons jointly if any of them is a person mentioned in paragraph (a) or (b).

(2) Except as provided by subsection (1), any person may be allocated housing accommodation by a local housing authority [in Wales] (whether on his application or otherwise).

(3)   A person subject to immigration control within the meaning of the Asylum and Immigration Act 1996 (c 49) is (subject to subsection (6)) ineligible for an allocation of housing accommodation by a local housing authority [in Wales] unless he is of a class prescribed by regulations made by the Secretary of State.

(4)   No person who is excluded from entitlement to [universal credit or] housing benefit by section 115 of the Immigration and Asylum Act 1999 (c 33) (exclusion from benefits) shall be included in any class prescribed under subsection (3).

(5)   The Secretary of State may by regulations prescribe other classes of persons from abroad who are (subject to subsection (6)) ineligible for an allocation of housing accommodation, either in relation to local housing authorities [in Wales] generally or any particular local housing authority [in Wales].

(6)   Nothing in subsection (3) or (5) affects the eligibility of a person who is already—

    (a)   a secure or introductory tenant;

    (b)   an assured tenant of housing accommodation allocated to him by a local housing authority [in Wales].

(7)   A local housing authority [in Wales] may decide that an applicant is to be treated as ineligible for an allocation of housing accommodation by them if they are satisfied that—

    (a)   he, or a member of his household, has been guilty of unacceptable behaviour serious enough to make him unsuitable to be a tenant of the authority; and

    (b)   in the circumstances at the time his application is considered, he is unsuitable to be a tenant of the authority by reason of that behaviour.

(8)   The only behaviour which may be regarded by the authority as unacceptable for the purposes of subsection (7)(a) is—

    (a)   behaviour of the person concerned which would (if he were a secure tenant of the authority) entitle the authority to a possession order under section 84 of the Housing Act 1985 (c 68) on any ground mentioned in Part 1 of Schedule 2 to that Act (other than ground 8); or

    [(aa)   behaviour of the person concerned which would (if he were a secure tenant of the authority) entitle the authority to a possession order under section 84A of the Housing Act 1985; or]

    (b)   behaviour of a member of his household which would (if he were a person residing with a secure tenant of the authority) entitle the authority to [a possession order of the type referred to in paragraph (a) or (aa)].

(9)   If a local housing authority [in Wales] decide that an applicant for housing accommodation—

    (a)   is ineligible for an allocation by them by virtue of subsection (3) or (5); or

    (b)   is to be treated as ineligible for such an allocation by virtue of subsection (7),

they shall notify the applicant of their decision and the grounds for it.

(10)   That notice shall be given in writing and, if not received by the applicant, shall be treated as having been given if it is made available at the authority's office for a reasonable period for collection by him or on his behalf.

(11)   A person who is being treated by a local housing authority [in Wales] as ineligible by virtue of subsection (7) may (if he considers that he should no longer be treated as ineligible by the authority) make a fresh application to the authority for an allocation of housing accommodation by them.]

NOTES

Amendment

Inserted by the Homelessness Act 2002, s 14(2); for effect see s 14(3), (4) thereof.
Date in force (in relation to England in so far as it confers powers to make regulations): 5 December 2002: see SI 2002/3114, art 2.

Date in force (in relation to Wales): 27 January 2003: see SI 2002/1736, art 2(2), Schedule, Pt 2.
Date in force (in relation to England for remaining purposes): 31 January 2003: see SI 2002/3114, art 3.
Section heading: word ": Wales" in square brackets inserted by the Localism Act 2011, s 146(2)(a).
Date in force (for certain purposes): 15 January 2012: see SI 2012/57, art 4(1)(k).
Date in force (for remaining purposes): 18 June 2012: see SI 2012/1463, art 3.
Sub-ss (1)–(3): words "in Wales" in square brackets inserted by the Localism Act 2011, s 146(2)(b)–(d).
Date in force (for certain purposes): 15 January 2012: see SI 2012/57, art 4(1)(k).
Date in force (for remaining purposes): 18 June 2012: see SI 2012/1463, art 3.
Sub-s (4): words "universal credit or" in square brackets inserted by SI 2013/630, reg 12(1), (4).
Date in force: 29 April 2013: see SI 2013/630, reg 1(2).
Sub-ss (5)–(7): words "in Wales" in square brackets in both places they occur inserted by the Localism Act 2011, s 146(2)(e)–(g).
Date in force (for certain purposes): 15 January 2012: see SI 2012/57, art 4(1)(k).
Date in force (for remaining purposes): 18 June 2012: see SI 2012/1463, art 3.
Sub-s (8): para (aa) inserted by SI 2015/1321, art 2(1), (2)(a).
Date in force: 19 May 2015: see SI 2015/1321, art 1.
Sub-s (8): in para (b) words "a possession order of the type referred to in paragraph (a) or (aa)" in square brackets substituted by SI 2015/1321, art 2(1), (2)(b).
Date in force: 19 May 2015: see SI 2015/1321, art 1.
Sub-ss (9), (11): words "in Wales" in square brackets inserted by the Localism Act 2011, s 146(2)(h), (i).
Date in force (for certain purposes): 15 January 2012: see SI 2012/57, art 4(1)(k).
Date in force (for remaining purposes): 18 June 2012: see SI 2012/1463, art 3.

. . .

161–165

. . .

NOTES

Amendment

Repealed by the Homelessness Act 2002, ss 14(1), 18(2), Sch 2; for effect see s 14(3), (4) thereof.
Date in force (in relation to Wales): 27 January 2003: see SI 2002/1736, art 2(2), Schedule, Pt 2.
Date in force (in relation to England): 31 January 2003: see SI 2002/3114, art 3.

[Applications for housing accommodation]

[166 Applications for housing accommodation]

[(1) A local housing authority shall secure that—

    (a)   advice and information is available free of charge to persons in their district about the right to make an application for an allocation of housing accommodation; and

    (b)   any necessary assistance in making such an application is available free of charge to persons in their district who are likely to have difficulty in doing so without assistance.

[(1A) A local housing authority in England shall secure that an applicant for an allocation of housing accommodation is informed that he has the rights mentioned in section 166A(9).]

(2) A local housing authority [in Wales] shall secure that an applicant for an allocation of housing accommodation is informed that he has the rights mentioned in section 167(4A).

(3) Every application made to a local housing authority for an allocation of housing accommodation shall (if made in accordance with the procedural requirements of the authority's allocation scheme) be considered by the authority.

(4) The fact that a person is an applicant for an allocation of housing accommodation shall not be divulged (without his consent) to any other member of the public.

(5) In this Part "district" in relation to a local housing authority has the same meaning as in the Housing Act 1985 (c 68).]

NOTES

Amendment

Substituted by the Homelessness Act 2002, s 15.
> Date in force (in relation to Wales): 27 January 2003: see SI 2002/1736, art 2(2), Schedule, Pt 2.
> Date in force (in relation to England): 31 January 2003: see SI 2002/3114, art 3.
Sub-s (1A): inserted by the Localism Act 2011, s 147(1), (2)(a).
> Date in force (for certain purposes): 15 January 2012: see SI 2012/57, art 4(1)(k); for transitional provisions see arts 6, 11 thereof.
> Date in force (for remaining purposes): 18 June 2012: see SI 2012/1463, art 3.
Sub-s (2): words "in Wales" in square brackets inserted by the Localism Act 2011, s 147(1), (2)(b).
> Date in force (for certain purposes): 15 January 2012: see SI 2012/57, art 4(1)(k); for transitional provisions see arts 6, 11 thereof.
> Date in force (for remaining purposes): 18 June 2012: see SI 2012/1463, art 3.

[Allocation schemes]

[166A Allocation in accordance with allocation scheme: England]

[(1) Every local housing authority in England must have a scheme (their "allocation scheme") for determining priorities, and as to the procedure to be followed, in allocating housing accommodation.

For this purpose "procedure" includes all aspects of the allocation process, including the persons or descriptions of persons by whom decisions are taken.

(2) The scheme must include a statement of the authority's policy on offering people who are to be allocated housing accommodation—

> (a)   a choice of housing accommodation; or
> (b)   the opportunity to express preferences about the housing accommodation to be allocated to them.

(3) As regards priorities, the scheme shall, subject to subsection (4), be framed so as to secure that reasonable preference is given to—

> (a)   people who are homeless (within the meaning of Part 7);
> (b)   people who are owed a duty by any local housing authority under section 190(2), 193(2) or 195(2) (or under section 65(2) or 68(2) of the Housing Act 1985) or who are occupying accommodation secured by any such authority under section 192(3);
> (c)   people occupying insanitary or overcrowded housing or otherwise living in unsatisfactory housing conditions;
> (d)   people who need to move on medical or welfare grounds (including any grounds relating to a disability); and
> (e)   people who need to move to a particular locality in the district of the authority, where failure to meet that need would cause hardship (to themselves or to others).

The scheme may also be framed so as to give additional preference to particular descriptions of [people within one or more of paragraphs (a) to (e)] (being descriptions of people with urgent housing needs).

[The scheme must be framed so as to give additional preference to a person with urgent housing needs who falls within one or more of paragraphs (a) to (e) and who—

> (i)   is serving in the regular forces and is suffering from a serious injury, illness or disability which is attributable (wholly or partly) to the person's service,

(ii)   formerly served in the regular forces,

(iii)   has recently ceased, or will cease to be entitled, to reside in accommodation provided by the Ministry of Defence following the death of that person's spouse or civil partner who has served in the regular forces and whose death was attributable (wholly or partly) to that service, or

(iv)   is serving or has served in the reserve forces and is suffering from a serious injury, illness or disability which is attributable (wholly or partly) to the person's service.

For this purpose "the regular forces" and "the reserve forces" have the meanings given by section 374 of the Armed Forces Act 2006.]

(4)   People are to be disregarded for the purposes of subsection (3) if they would not have fallen within paragraph (a) or (b) of that subsection without the local housing authority having had regard to a restricted person (within the meaning of Part 7).

(5)   The scheme may contain provision for determining priorities in allocating housing accommodation to people within subsection (3); and the factors which the scheme may allow to be taken into account include—

(a)   the financial resources available to a person to meet his housing costs;

(b)   any behaviour of a person (or of a member of his household) which affects his suitability to be a tenant;

(c)   any local connection (within the meaning of section 199) which exists between a person and the authority's district.

(6)   Subject to subsection (3), the scheme may contain provision about the allocation of particular housing accommodation—

(a)   to a person who makes a specific application for that accommodation;

(b)   to persons of a particular description (whether or not they are within subsection (3)).

(7)   The Secretary of State may by regulations—

(a)   specify further descriptions of people to whom preference is to be given as mentioned in subsection (3), or

(b)   amend or repeal any part of subsection (3).

(8)   The Secretary of State may by regulations specify factors which a local housing authority in England must not take into account in allocating housing accommodation.

(9)   The scheme must be framed so as to secure that an applicant for an allocation of housing accommodation—

(a)   has the right to request such general information as will enable him to assess—

(i)   how his application is likely to be treated under the scheme (including in particular whether he is likely to be regarded as a member of a group of people who are to be given preference by virtue of subsection (3)); and

(ii)   whether housing accommodation appropriate to his needs is likely to be made available to him and, if so, how long it is likely to be before such accommodation becomes available for allocation to him;

(b)   has the right to request the authority to inform him of any decision about the facts of his case which is likely to be, or has been, taken into account in considering whether to allocate housing accommodation to him; and

(c)   has the right to request a review of a decision mentioned in paragraph (b), or in section 160ZA(9), and to be informed of the decision on the review and the grounds for it.

(10)   As regards the procedure to be followed, the scheme must be framed in accordance with such principles as the Secretary of State may prescribe by regulations.

(11)   Subject to the above provisions, and to any regulations made under them, the authority may decide on what principles the scheme is to be framed.

(12)   A local housing authority in England must, in preparing or modifying their allocation scheme, have regard to—

- (a)   their current homelessness strategy under section 1 of the Homelessness Act 2002,
- (b)   their current tenancy strategy under section 150 of the Localism Act 2011, and
- (c)   in the case of an authority that is a London borough council, the London housing strategy.

(13)   Before adopting an allocation scheme, or making an alteration to their scheme reflecting a major change of policy, a local housing authority in England must—

- (a)   send a copy of the draft scheme, or proposed alteration, to every private registered provider of social housing and registered social landlord with which they have nomination arrangements (see section 159(4)), and
- (b)   afford those persons a reasonable opportunity to comment on the proposals.

(14)   A local housing authority in England shall not allocate housing accommodation except in accordance with their allocation scheme.]

NOTES

Amendment

Cross-heading: substituted by the Localism Act 2011, s 147(1), (3).
   Date in force (for certain purposes): 15 January 2012: see SI 2012/57, art 4(1)(k); for transitional provisions see arts 6, 11 thereof.
   Date in force (for remaining purposes): 18 June 2012: see SI 2012/1463, art 3.
Inserted by the Localism Act 2011, s 147(1), (4).
   Date in force (for certain purposes): 15 January 2012: see SI 2012/57, art 4(1)(k); for transitional provisions see arts 6, 11 thereof.
   Date in force (for remaining purposes): 18 June 2012: see SI 2012/1463, art 3.
Sub-s (3): words "people within one or more of paragraphs (a) to (e)" in square brackets substituted by SI 2012/2989, reg 2(a).
   Date in force: 30 November 2012: see SI 2012/2989, reg 1.
Sub-s (3): words from "The scheme must" to "Armed Forces Act 2006." in square brackets inserted by SI 2012/2989, reg 2(b).
   Date in force: 30 November 2012: see SI 2012/2989, reg 1.

167 Allocation in accordance with allocation scheme[: Wales]

(1)   Every local housing authority [in Wales] shall have a scheme (their "allocation scheme") for determining priorities, and as to the procedure to be followed, in allocating housing accommodation.

   For this purpose "procedure" includes all aspects of the allocation process, including the persons or descriptions of persons by whom decisions are to be taken.

[(1A)   The scheme shall include a statement of the authority's policy on offering people who are to be allocated housing accommodation—

- (a)   a choice of housing accommodation; or
- (b)   the opportunity to express preferences about the housing accommodation to be allocated to them.]

[(2)   As regards priorities, the scheme shall[, subject to subsection (2ZA),] be framed so as to secure that reasonable preference is given to—

- (a)   people who are homeless [(within the meaning of Part 2 of the Housing (Wales) Act 2014)];
- [(b)   people who are owed any duty by a local housing authority under section 66, 73 or 75 of the Housing (Wales) Act 2014;]
- (c)   people occupying insanitary or overcrowded housing or otherwise living in unsatisfactory housing conditions;

(d)   people who need to move on medical or welfare grounds [(including grounds relating to a disability)]; and

(e)   people who need to move to a particular locality in the district of the authority, where failure to meet that need would cause hardship (to themselves or to others).

The scheme may also be framed so as to give additional preference to particular descriptions of people within this subsection (being descriptions of people with urgent housing needs).

[(2ZA) People are to be disregarded for the purposes of subsection (2) if they would not have fallen within paragraph (a) or (b) of that subsection without the local housing authority having had regard to a restricted person (within the meaning of [Part 2 of the Housing (Wales) Act 2014]).]

(2A) The scheme may contain provision for determining priorities in allocating housing accommodation to people within subsection (2); and the factors which the scheme may allow to be taken into account include—

(a)   the financial resources available to a person to meet his housing costs;

(b)   any behaviour of a person (or of a member of his household) which affects his suitability to be a tenant;

(c)   any local connection (within the meaning of [section 81 of the Housing (Wales) Act 2014]) which exists between a person and the authority's district.

(2B) Nothing in subsection (2) requires the scheme to provide for any preference to be given to people the authority have decided are people to whom subsection (2C) applies.

(2C) This subsection applies to a person if the authority are satisfied that—

(a)   he, or a member of his household, has been guilty of unacceptable behaviour serious enough to make him unsuitable to be a tenant of the authority; and

(b)   in the circumstances at the time his case is considered, he deserves by reason of that behaviour not to be treated as a member of a group of people who are to be given preference by virtue of subsection (2).

(2D) Subsection (8) of section 160A applies for the purposes of subsection (2C)(a) above as it applies for the purposes of subsection (7)(a) of that section.

(2E) Subject to subsection (2), the scheme may contain provision about the allocation of particular housing accommodation—

(a)   to a person who makes a specific application for that accommodation;

(b)   to persons of a particular description (whether or not they are within subsection (2)).]

(3) The Secretary of State may by regulations—

(a)   specify further descriptions of people to whom preference is to be given as mentioned in subsection (2), or

(b)   amend or repeal any part of subsection (2).

(4) The Secretary of State may by regulations specify factors which a local housing authority [in Wales] shall not take into account in allocating housing accommodation.

[(4A) The scheme shall be framed so as to secure that an applicant for an allocation of housing accommodation—

(a)   has the right to request such general information as will enable him to assess—

(i)   how his application is likely to be treated under the scheme (including in particular whether he is likely to be regarded as a member of a group of people who are to be given preference by virtue of subsection (2)); and

(ii)   whether housing accommodation appropriate to his needs is likely to be made available to him and, if so, how long it is likely to be before such accommodation becomes available for allocation to him;

(b)   is notified in writing of any decision that he is a person to whom subsection (2C) applies and the grounds for it;

(c)   has the right to request the authority to inform him of any decision about the facts of his case which is likely to be, or has been, taken into account in considering whether to allocate housing accommodation to him; and

(d)   has the right to request a review of a decision mentioned in paragraph (b) or (c), or in section 160A(9), and to be informed of the decision on the review and the grounds for it.]

(5)   As regards the procedure to be followed, the scheme shall be framed in accordance with such principles as the Secretary of State may prescribe by regulations.

(6)   Subject to the above provisions, and to any regulations made under them, the authority may decide on what principles the scheme is to be framed.

(7)   Before adopting an allocation scheme, or making an alteration to their scheme reflecting a major change of policy, a local housing authority [in Wales] shall—

(a)   send a copy of the draft scheme, or proposed alteration, to every [private registered provider of social housing and] registered social landlord with which they have nomination arrangements (see section 159(4)), and

(b)   afford those persons a reasonable opportunity to comment on the proposals.

(8)   A local housing authority [in Wales] shall not allocate housing accommodation except in accordance with their allocation scheme.

NOTES

Amendment

Section heading: word ": Wales" in square brackets inserted by the Localism Act 2011, s 147(1), (5)(a).
    Date in force (for certain purposes): 15 January 2012: see SI 2012/57, art 4(1)(k); for transitional provisions see arts 6, 11 thereof.
    Date in force (for remaining purposes): 18 June 2012: see SI 2012/1463, art 3.
Sub-s (1): words "in Wales" in square brackets inserted by the Localism Act 2011, s 147(1), (5)(b).
    Date in force (for certain purposes): 15 January 2012: see SI 2012/57, art 4(1)(k); for transitional provisions see arts 6, 11 thereof.
    Date in force (for remaining purposes): 18 June 2012: see SI 2012/1463, art 3.
Sub-s (1A): inserted by the Homelessness Act 2002, s 16(1), (2).
    Date in force (in relation to Wales): 27 January 2003: see SI 2002/1736, art 2(2), Schedule, Pt 2.
    Date in force (in relation to England): 31 January 2003: see SI 2002/3114, art 3.
Sub-ss (2), (2A)–(2E): substituted, for sub-s (2) as originally enacted, by the Homelessness Act 2002, s 16(1), (3).
    Date in force (in relation to Wales): 27 January 2003: see SI 2002/1736, art 2(2), Schedule, Pt 2.
    Date in force (in relation to England): 31 January 2003: see SI 2002/3114, art 3.
Sub-s (2): words ", subject to subsection (2ZA)," in square brackets inserted by the Housing and Regeneration Act 2008, s 314, Sch 15, Pt 1, paras 1, 2(1), (2).
    Date in force: 2 March 2009 (except in relation to applications for an allocation of social housing or housing assistance (homelessness) or for accommodation made before that date): see SI 2009/415, art 2.
Sub-s (2): in para (a) words "(within the meaning of Part 2 of the Housing (Wales) Act 2014)" in square brackets substituted, in relation to Wales, by the Housing (Wales) Act 2014, s 100, Sch 3, Pt 1, paras 2, 3(a)(i).
    Date in force: 27 April 2015: see SI 2015/1272, art 2, Schedule, paras 51, 53.
Sub-s (2): para (b) substituted, in relation to Wales, by the Housing (Wales) Act 2014, s 100, Sch 3, Pt 1, paras 2, 3(a)(ii).
    Date in force: 27 April 2015: see SI 2015/1272, art 2, Schedule, paras 51, 53.
Sub-s (2): in para (d) words "(including grounds relating to a disability)" in square brackets inserted by the Housing Act 2004, s 223.
    Date in force (in relation to England): 27 April 2005: see SI 2005/1120, art 2.

Date in force (in relation to Wales): to be appointed: see the Housing Act 2004, s 270(4), (5)(c).

Sub-s (2ZA): inserted by the Housing and Regeneration Act 2008, s 314, Sch 15, Pt 1, paras 1, 2(1), (3).

Date in force: 2 March 2009 (except in relation to applications for an allocation of social housing or housing assistance (homelessness) or for accommodation made before that date): see SI 2009/415, art 2.

Sub-s (2ZA): words "Part 2 of the Housing (Wales) Act 2014" in square brackets substituted, in relation to Wales, by the Housing (Wales) Act 2014, s 100, Sch 3, Pt 1, paras 2, 3(b).

Date in force: 27 April 2015: see SI 2015/1272, art 2, Schedule, paras 51, 53.

Sub-s (2A): in para (c) words "section 81 of the Housing (Wales) Act 2014" in square brackets substituted, in relation to Wales, by the Housing (Wales) Act 2014, s 100, Sch 3, Pt 1, paras 2, 3(c).

Date in force: 27 April 2015: see SI 2015/1272, art 2, Schedule, paras 51, 53.

Sub-s (4): words "in Wales" in square brackets inserted by the Localism Act 2011, s 147(1), (5)(c).

Date in force (for certain purposes): 15 January 2012: see SI 2012/57, art 4(1)(k); for transitional provisions see arts 6, 11 thereof.

Date in force (for remaining purposes): 18 June 2012: see SI 2012/1463, art 3.

Sub-s (4A): inserted by the Homelessness Act 2002, s 16(1), (4).

Date in force (in relation to Wales): 27 January 2003: see SI 2002/1736, art 2(2), Schedule, Pt 2.

Date in force (in relation to England): 31 January 2003: see SI 2002/3114, art 3.

Sub-s (7): words "in Wales" in square brackets inserted by the Localism Act 2011, s 147(1), (5)(d).

Date in force (for certain purposes): 15 January 2012: see SI 2012/57, art 4(1)(k); for transitional provisions see arts 6, 11 thereof.

Date in force (for remaining purposes): 18 June 2012: see SI 2012/1463, art 3.

Sub-s (7): in para (a) words "private registered provider of social housing and" in square brackets inserted by SI 2010/866, art 5, Sch 2, paras 81, 101.

Date in force: 1 April 2010: see SI 2010/866, art 1(2); for transitional provisions and savings see art 6, Sch 3, paras 1, 3, 4 thereto.

Sub-s (8): words "in Wales" in square brackets inserted by the Localism Act 2011, s 147(1), (5)(e).

Date in force (for certain purposes): 15 January 2012: see SI 2012/57, art 4(1)(k); for transitional provisions see arts 6, 11 thereof.

Date in force (for remaining purposes): 18 June 2012: see SI 2012/1463, art 3.

168 Information about allocation scheme

(1) A local housing authority shall publish a summary of their allocation scheme and provide a copy of the summary free of charge to any member of the public who asks for one.

(2) The authority shall make the scheme available for inspection at their principal office and shall provide a copy of the scheme, on payment of a reasonable fee, to any member of the public who asks for one.

(3) When the authority make an alteration to their scheme reflecting a major change of policy, they shall within a reasonable period of time [take such steps as they consider reasonable to bring the effect of the alteration to the attention of those likely to be affected by it].

NOTES

Amendment

Sub-s (3): words from "take such steps" to "affected by it" in square brackets substituted by the Homelessness Act 2002, s 18(1), Sch 1, paras 2, 4.

Date in force (in relation to Wales): 27 January 2003: see SI 2002/1736, art 2(2), Schedule, Pt 2.

Date in force (in relation to England): 31 January 2003: by virtue of SI 2002/3114, art 3.

Supplementary

169 Guidance to authorities by the Secretary of State

(1)   In the exercise of their functions under this Part, local housing authorities shall have regard to such guidance as may from time to time be given by the Secretary of State.

(2)   The Secretary of State may give guidance generally or to specified descriptions of authorities.

170 Co-operation between [certain] social landlords and local housing authorities

Where a local housing authority so request, a [private registered provider of social housing or] registered social landlord shall co-operate to such extent as is reasonable in the circumstances in offering accommodation to [people with priority under the authority's allocation scheme].

NOTES

Amendment

> Section heading: word "certain" in square brackets substituted by SI 2010/866, art 5, Sch 2, paras 81, 102(b).
>> Date in force: 1 April 2010: see SI 2010/866, art 1(2); for transitional provisions and savings see art 6, Sch 3, paras 1, 3, 4 thereto.
> Words "private registered provider of social housing or" in square brackets inserted by SI 2010/866, art 5, Sch 2, paras 81, 102(a).
>> Date in force: 1 April 2010: see SI 2010/866, art 1(2); for transitional provisions and savings see art 6, Sch 3, paras 1, 3, 4 thereto.
> Words "people with priority under the authority's allocation scheme" in square brackets substituted by the Homelessness Act 2002, s 18(1), Sch 1, paras 2, 5.
>> Date in force (in relation to Wales): 27 January 2003: see SI 2002/1736, art 2(2), Schedule, Pt 2.
>> Date in force (in relation to England): 31 January 2003: by virtue of SI 2002/3114, art 3.

171 False statements and withholding information

(1)   A person commits an offence if, in connection with the exercise by a local housing authority of their functions under this Part—

    (a)   he knowingly or recklessly makes a statement which is false in a material particular, or

    (b)   he knowingly withholds information which the authority have reasonably required him to give in connection with the exercise of those functions.

(2)   A person guilty of an offence under this section is liable on summary conviction to a fine not exceeding level 5 on the standard scale.

172 Regulations

(1)   Regulations under this Part shall be made by statutory instrument.

(2)   No regulations shall be made under section [166A(7) or] 167(3) (regulations amending provisions about priorities in allocating housing accommodation) unless a draft of the regulations has been laid before and approved by a resolution of each House of Parliament.

(3)   Any other regulations under this Part shall be subject to annulment in pursuance of a resolution of either House of Parliament.

(4)   Regulations under this Part may contain such incidental, supplementary and transitional provisions as appear to the Secretary of State appropriate, and may make different provision for different cases including different provision for different areas.

NOTES

Amendment

> Sub-s (2): words "166A(7) or" in square brackets inserted by the Localism Act 2011, s 147(1), (6).

Date in force: 15 January 2012: see SI 2012/57, art 4(1)(l).

173 Consequential amendments: Part VI

The enactments mentioned in Schedule 16 have effect with the amendments specified there which are consequential on the provisions of this Part.

174 Index of defined expressions: Part VI

The following Table shows provisions defining or otherwise explaining expressions used in this Part (other than provisions defining or explaining an expression used in the same section)—

allocation (of housing)	section 159(2)
allocation scheme	Section [166A and] 167
assured tenancy	section 230
[district (of local housing authority)	section 166(5)]
. . .	< . . . >
introductory tenancy and introductory tenant	section 230 and 124
local housing authority	section 230
. . .	< . . . >
registered social landlord	section 230 and 2
secure tenancy and secure tenant	section 230

NOTES

Amendment

In entry relating to "allocation scheme" in column 2 words "166A and" in square brackets Inserted by the Localism Act 2011, s 147(1), (7).
Date in force: 18 June 2012: see SI 2012/1463, art 3.
Entry relating to "district (of local housing authority)" inserted by the Homelessness Act 2002, s 18(1), Sch 1, paras 2, 6.
Date in force (in relation to Wales): 27 January 2003: see SI 2002/1736, art 2(2), Schedule, Pt 2.
Date in force (in relation to England): 31 January 2003: by virtue of SI 2002/3114, art 3.
Entries relating to "housing register" and "qualifying person" (omitted) repealed by the Homelessness Act 2002, s 18(2), Sch 2.
Date in force (in relation to Wales): 27 January 2003: see SI 2002/1736, art 2(2), Schedule, Pt 2.
Date in force (in relation to England): 31 January 2003: by virtue of SI 2002/3114, art 3.

ALLOCATION OF ACCOMMODATION: GUIDANCE FOR LOCAL HOUSING AUTHORITIES IN ENGLAND (2012)

Contents

Ministerial Foreword

MINISTERIAL FOREWORD

A1.2

Social housing is of enormous importance - for the millions who live in it now, and the many more who look to it to provide the support they need in future – and the way it is allocated is key to creating communities where people choose to live and are able to prosper.

Under the previous Government housing waiting lists almost doubled, with many people left languishing on waiting lists for years. That is why we have taken decisive steps to tackle this problem, including an affordable homes programme set to exceed expectations and deliver up to 170,000 new homes and lever in £19.5 billion of new investment – in stark contrast to the net reduction of 421,000 affordable homes for rent from 1997 to 2010. Through the Localism Act 2011 we have introduced the most radical reform to social housing for a generation.

The new freedoms in the Localism Act which allow councils to better manage their waiting lists and promote mobility for existing social tenants came into force on 18 June. This guidance will assist councils to make full use of these new freedoms - and the existing flexibilities within the allocation legislation - to encourage work and mobility, and to tailor their allocation priorities to meet local needs and local circumstances.

The guidance makes clear that we expect social homes to go to people who genuinely need them, such as hard working families and those who are looking to adopt or foster a child in need of a stable family; and not to those who do not, such as people who already own a home that is suitable for them to use.

Through the Military Covenant, the Government has made clear its responsibility to support our Armed Forces in return for the important contribution they make to the country. This guidance will assist councils to ensure that Service families get the priority for social housing they deserve.

The guidance encourages councils to adopt a modern measure of overcrowding and encourages them to give appropriate priority to tenants who want to downsize, helping them move to smaller, more manageable properties and freeing up precious social housing for crowded families.

I know that an increasing number of councils are already starting to think creatively about how social housing can change people's lives. This guidance will help others follow suit.

It is half the size of the previous guidance it replaces and is evidence of the Government's commitment to 'cutting red tape'. It is also an important part of the

Government's commitment to make the social housing system more flexible and responsive, to get the best out of our four million social homes, and to make the system fairer for all.

Rt Hon Grant Shapps, MP

CHAPTER 1

Scope of guidance and definition of an allocation

1.1 This guidance is issued to local housing authorities ('housing authorities') in England under s 169 of the Housing Act 1996 ('the 1996 Act'). Housing authorities are required to have regard to it in exercising their functions under Part 6 of the 1996 Act ('Part 6'). In so far as this guidance comments on the law, it can only reflect the Department's understanding at the time of issue.

1.2 This guidance replaces all previous guidance on social housing allocations.

Definition of an 'allocation'

1.3 For the purposes of Part 6, a housing authority allocates accommodation when it:

- selects a person to be a secure or introductory tenant of accommodation held by that authority
- nominates a person to be a secure or introductory tenant of accommodation held by another housing authority
- nominates a person to be an assured tenant of accommodation held by a Private Registered Provider (or Registered Social Landlord in Wales) (s 159(2))

1.4 The term 'assured tenant' includes a person with an assured shorthold tenancy, including of an Affordable Rent property.[1] 'Secure tenant' includes a person with a flexible tenancy granted under s 107A of the Housing Act 1985.[2]

Allocations to existing tenants

1.5 Provisions in relation to existing tenants are contained in s 159(4A) and (4B). These provide that Part 6 does not apply to an allocation of accommodation by a housing authority to a tenant of a local authority or Private Registered Provider unless:

- the allocation involves a transfer made at the tenant's request, and
- the authority is satisfied that the tenant has reasonable preference.

Accordingly, social tenants applying to the housing authority for a transfer who are considered to have reasonable preference for an allocation must be treated on the same basis as new applicants in accordance with the requirements of s 166A(3).

1.6 Transfers at the tenant's request, where the authority is satisfied the tenant does not have reasonable preference, do not fall within Part 6 and housing authorities may set their own transfer policies in relation to these tenants. Authorities should consider how to make the best use of this flexibility. Providing tenants with greater opportunities to move within the social sector can help promote social and economic mobility and make the best use of social housing stock.

1.7 Authorities should consider the importance of giving social tenants who under-occupy their accommodation appropriate priority for a transfer. This will be important in light of the measure in the Welfare Reform Act 2012 which will reduce Housing Benefit entitlement for working age social sector tenants who under-occupy their property (measured in accordance with the Local Housing Allowance size criteria) from April 2013.[3] Authorities should also consider whether there are other provisions that might make it more difficult for under-occupiers to move, such as a prohibition against tenants with minor rent arrears transferring, and the scope for removing or revising these in relation to under-occupiers.

1.8 Housing authorities may decide to operate a separate allocation system for transferring tenants who are not in the reasonable preference categories (with a separate waiting list and lettings policy) or to continue with a single allocation system which covers all applicants but which, for example, rewards transferring tenants with a good tenancy record, or gives a degree of priority to those who want to move for work.

1.9 Transfers that the housing authority initiates for management purposes do not fall within Part 6. These would include a temporary decant to allow repairs to a property to be carried out. The renewal of a flexible tenancy in the same property also does not fall within Part 6; neither do mutual exchanges between existing tenants, including exchanges between secure and assured tenants and those with flexible tenancies (under s 107A of the Housing Act 1985). Other specific exemptions from the provisions of Part 6 are set out in s 160 of the 1996 Act and the Allocation of Housing (England) Regulations 2002 (SI 2002/3264).

---

[1]   Affordable Rent is not subject to the national rent regime but is subject to other rent controls that require a rent (including service charges, where applicable) of no more than 80% of the local market rent.

[2]   Inserted by s 154 of the Localism Act 2011.

[3]   The LHA size criteria allow one bedroom for each: adult couple; any other adult (aged 16 or over); two children of the same sex aged 10 or over; two children under 10 regardless of sex; any other child.

CHAPTER 2

Overview of the amendments to Part 6 made by the Localism Act 2011

2.1 The Localism Act 2011 introduces significant amendments to Part 6. The main policy objectives behind these amendments are to:

- enable housing authorities to better manage their housing waiting list by giving them the power to determine which applicants do or do not qualify for an allocation of social housing. Authorities will be able to operate a more focused list which better reflects local circumstances and can be understood more readily by local people. It will also be easier for authorities to manage unrealistic expectations by excluding people who have little or no prospect of being allocated accommodation;
- make it easier for existing social tenants to move by removing the constraints of Part 6 from those social tenants who apply to the housing authority for a transfer, unless they have reasonable preference. Housing authorities will be able to strike a balance between meeting the needs of existing tenants and new applicants for social housing, while making best use of their stock. Part 6 continues to apply to transferring tenants with reasonable preference, ensuring they continue to receive priority under the authority's allocation scheme;
- maintain the protection provided by the statutory reasonable preference criteria – ensuring that priority for social housing goes to those in the greatest need.

2.2 The detailed changes to Part 6 contained in the Localism Act 2011 are set out in the following paragraphs.

2.3 By virtue of new s 159(4B) the term 'allocation' continues to apply to a transfer at the request of an existing secure, introductory or assured tenant where the authority is satisfied that he or she has 'reasonable preference' for an allocation. Existing secure, introductory and assured tenants seeking a transfer who are not considered to have reasonable preference are now outside the scope of Part 6 (s 159(4A)).

2.4 New s 160ZA replaces s 160A in relation to allocations by housing authorities in England. Social housing may only be allocated to 'qualifying persons' and housing authorities are given the power to determine what classes of persons are or are not qualified to be allocated housing (s 160ZA(6) and (7)). These requirements are in addition to the provisions on eligibility in respect of persons from abroad (s 160ZA(2) and (4)) which continue to be set centrally. The power for a housing authority to decide that an applicant is to be treated as ineligible by reason of unacceptable behaviour serious enough to make him unsuitable to be a tenant is redundant and has therefore been repealed.

2.5 New s 166A requires housing authorities in England to allocate accommodation in accordance with a scheme which must be framed to ensure that certain categories of applicants are given reasonable preference. With certain exceptions, s 166A replicates the provisions in s 167 which continues to apply to allocations by housing authorities in Wales. Section 166A(9) includes a new requirement for an allocation scheme to give a right to review a decision on qualification in s 160AZ(9), and to be informed of the decision on the review and the grounds for it. This is in addition to the existing right to review a decision on eligibility. Section 166A(12) is new and provides that authorities must have regard to their homelessness and tenancy strategies when framing their allocation scheme.

2.6 The provisions in s 167 which allow for no preference to be given to a person guilty of serious unacceptable behaviour (s 167(2B) – (2D)) are not reproduced in s 166A. However, the power to take behaviour – whether good or poor - into account in determining priorities between people in the reasonable preference categories remains (new s 166A(5)(b)).

2.7 The requirement for an allocation scheme to contain a statement of the authority's policy on offering a choice of accommodation or the opportunity to express preferences about their accommodation is retained (s 166A(2)). However, the requirement to provide a copy of this statement to people to whom they owe a homelessness duty (under s 193(3A) or s 195(3A) of the 1996 Act) is repealed.[1]

---

[1]   Section 148(2) and s 149(3) of the Localism Act 2011.

CHAPTER 3

Eligibility and qualification

3.1 Housing authorities must consider all applications made in accordance with the procedural requirements of the authority's allocation scheme (s 166(3)). In considering applications, authorities must ascertain:

- if an applicant is eligible for an allocation of accommodation, and
- if he or she qualifies for an allocation of accommodation.

Eligibility

3.2 An applicant may be ineligible for an allocation of accommodation under s 160ZA(2) or (4). Authorities are advised to consider applicants' eligibility at the time of the initial application and again when considering making an allocation to them, particularly where a substantial amount of time has elapsed since the original application.

Joint Tenancies

3.3   Under s 160ZA(1)(b), a housing authority must not grant a joint tenancy to two or more people if any one of them is a person from abroad who is ineligible. However, where two or more people apply and one of them is eligible, the authority may grant a tenancy to the person who is eligible. In addition, while ineligible family members must not be granted a tenancy, they may be taken into account in determining the size of accommodation which is to be allocated.

Existing Tenants

3.4   The eligibility provisions do not apply to applicants who are already secure or introductory tenants or assured tenants of a Private Registered Provider. Most transferring tenants fall outside the scope of the allocation legislation (s 159(4A)); while those who are considered to have reasonable preference for an allocation are specifically exempted from the eligibility provisions by virtue of s 160ZA(5).

Persons from abroad

3.5   A person may not be allocated accommodation under Part 6 if he or she is a person from abroad who is ineligible for an allocation under s 160ZA of the 1996 Act. There are two categories for the purposes of s 160ZA:

(i)   *a person subject to immigration control* - such a person is not eligible for an allocation of accommodation unless he or she comes within a class prescribed in regulations made by the Secretary of State (s 160ZA(2)), and

(ii)   *a person from abroad other than a person subject to immigration control* – regulations may provide for other descriptions of persons from abroad who, although not subject to immigration control, are to be treated as ineligible for an allocation of accommodation (s 160ZA(4)).

3.6   The regulations setting out which classes of persons from abroad are eligible or ineligible for an allocation are the Allocation of Housing and Homelessness (Eligibility) (England) Regulations 2006 (SI 2006 No.1294) ('the Eligibility Regulations').

Persons subject to immigration control

3.7   The term 'person subject to immigration control' is defined in s 13(2) of the Asylum and Immigration Act 1996 as a person who under the Immigration Act 1971 requires leave to enter or remain in the United Kingdom (whether or not such leave has been given).

3.8   The following categories of persons do not require leave to enter or remain in the UK:

(i)   British citizens
(ii)   certain Commonwealth citizens with a right of abode in the UK
(iii)   Irish citizens, who are not subject to immigration control in the UK because the Republic of Ireland forms part of the Common Travel Area (see paragraph 3.11 (iii) below) with the UK which allows free movement
(iv)   EEA nationals,[1] and their family members, who have a right to reside in the UK that derives from EU law. Whether an EEA national (or family member) has a particular right to reside in the UK (or another Member State) will depend on the circumstances, particularly their economic status (e.g. whether he or she is a worker, self-employed, a student, or economically inactive)
(v)   persons who are exempt from immigration control under the Immigration Acts, including diplomats and their family members based in the UK, and some military personnel.

3.9   Any person who does not fall within one of the four categories in paragraph 3.11 will be a person subject to immigration control and will be ineligible for an allocation of accommodation unless they fall within a class of persons prescribed by regulation 3 of the Eligibility Regulations (see further below).

3.10 If there is any uncertainty about an applicant's immigration status, housing authorities are recommended to contact the UK Border Agency (UKBA). UKBA provides a service to housing authorities to confirm the immigration status of an applicant from abroad (non asylum seekers) by email at LA@UKBA.gsi.gov.uk. Where UKBA indicates the applicant may be an asylum seeker, enquiries of their status can be made to the Immigration Enquiry Bureau helpline on 0870 606 7766.

3.11 Regulation 3 of the Eligibility Regulations provides that the following classes of persons subject to immigration control are eligible for an allocation of accommodation:

(i)   *a person granted refugee status*: granted 5 years' limited leave to remain in the UK

(ii)   *a person granted exceptional leave to enter or remain in the UK without condition that they and any dependants should make no recourse to public funds*: granted for a limited period where there are compelling humanitarian or compassionate circumstances for allowing them to stay. However, if leave is granted on condition that the applicant and any dependants are not a charge on public funds, the applicant will not be eligible for an allocation of accommodation. Exceptional leave to remain (granted at the Secretary of State's discretion outside the Immigration Rules) now takes the form of 'discretionary leave'.

(iii)   *a person with current leave to enter or remain in the UK with no condition or limitation, and who is habitually resident in the UK, the Channel Islands, the Isle of Man or the Republic of Ireland* (the Common Travel Area): such a person will have indefinite leave to enter (ILE) or remain (ILR) and is regarded as having settled status. However, where ILE or ILR status is granted as a result of an undertaking that a sponsor will be responsible for the applicant's maintenance and accommodation, the person must have been resident in the Common Travel Area for five years since the date of entry - or the date of the sponsorship undertaking, whichever is later - to be eligible. Where all sponsors have died within the first five years, the applicant will be eligible for an allocation of accommodation.

(iv)   *a person who has humanitarian protection granted under the Immigration Rules:*[2] a form of leave granted to persons who do not qualify for refugee status but would face a real risk of suffering serious harm if returned to their state of origin (see paragraphs 339C–344C of the Immigration Rules (HC 395)).

Other persons from abroad who may be ineligible for an allocation

3.12 By virtue of regulation 4 of the Eligibility Regulations, a person who is not subject to immigration control and who falls within one of the following descriptions is to be treated as a person from abroad who is ineligible for an allocation of accommodation:

(i)   a person who is not habitually resident in the Common Travel Area (subject to certain exceptions - see paragraph 3.14 below)

(ii)   a person whose only right to reside in the UK is derived from his status as a jobseeker (or his status as the family member of a jobseeker). 'Jobseeker' has the same meaning as in regulation 6(1) of the Immigration (European Economic Area) Regulations 2006 (SI 2006/1003) ('the EEA Regulations')

(iii)   a person whose only right to reside in the UK is an initial right to reside for a period not exceeding three months under regulation 13 of the EEA Regulations

(iv)   a person whose only right to reside in the Common Travel Area is a right equivalent to one of the rights mentioned in (ii) or (iii) above and which is derived from EU Treaty rights.

3.13 See annex 2 for guidance on rights to reside in the UK derived from EU law.

3.14 The following persons from abroad are eligible for an allocation of accommodation even if they are not habitually resident in the Common Travel Area:

(a)   an EEA national who is in the UK as a worker (which has the same meaning as in regulation 6(1) of the EEA Regulations)

(b)   an EEA national who is in the UK as a self-employed person (which has the same meaning as in regulation 6(1) of the EEA Regulations)

(c)   a person who is treated as a worker for the purposes of regulation 6(1) of the EEA Regulations, pursuant to the Accession (Immigration and Worker Authorisation) Regulations 2006 (ie nationals of Bulgaria and Romania required to be authorised by the Home Office to work until they have accrued 12 months uninterrupted authorised work)[3]

(d)   a person who is a family member of a person referred to in (a) to (c) above

(e)   a person with a right to reside permanently in the UK by virtue of regulation 15(c), (d) or (e) of the EEA Regulations

(f)   a person who left Montserrat after 1 November 1995 because of the effect of volcanic activity there

(g)   a person who is in the UK as a result of his deportation, expulsion or other removal by compulsion of law from another country to the UK. This could include EEA nationals, if the person was settled in the UK and exercising EU Treaty rights prior to deportation from the third country. Where deportation occurs, most countries will signal this in the person's passport.

3.15   A person who is no longer working or no longer in self-employment will retain his or her status as a worker or self-employed person in certain circumstances. However, accession state workers requiring authorisation will generally only be treated as a worker when they are actually working as authorised and will not retain 'worker' status between jobs until they have accrued 12 months continuous authorised employment. 'Family member' does not include a person who is an extended family member who is treated as a family member by virtue of regulation 7(3) of the EEA Regulations (see annexes 2 and 3 for further guidance).

3.16   The term 'habitual residence' is intended to convey a degree of permanence in the person's residence in the Common Travel Area; it implies an association between the individual and the place of residence and relies substantially on fact.

3.17   Applicants who have been resident in the Common Travel Area continuously during the two year period prior to their housing application are likely to be habitually resident (periods of temporary absence, e.g. visits abroad for holidays or to visit relatives may be disregarded). Where two years' continuous residency has not been established, housing authorities will need to conduct further enquiries to determine whether the applicant is habitually resident (see annex 4 for further guidance).

Qualification

3. 18   Housing authorities may only allocate accommodation to people who are defined as 'qualifying persons' (s 160ZA(6)(a)). Subject to the requirement not to allocate to persons from abroad who are ineligible and the exception for members of the Armed and Reserve Forces in paragraph 3.27 below, a housing authority may decide the classes of people who are, or are not, qualifying persons.

3.19   Housing authorities are encouraged to adopt a housing options approach as part of a move to a managed waiting list. A strong and pro-active housing options approach brings several benefits: people are offered support to access the housing solution which best meets their needs (which might be private rented housing, low cost home ownership or help to stay put); expectations about accessing social housing are properly managed; and social housing is focused on those who need it most. A lower waiting list can also be a by-product.

3.20   In framing their qualification criteria, authorities will need to have regard to their duties under the equalities legislation, as well as the requirement in s 166A(3) to give overall priority for an allocation to people in the reasonable preference categories.

3.21   Housing authorities should avoid setting criteria which disqualify groups of people whose members are likely to be accorded reasonable preference for social housing, for example on medical or welfare grounds. However, authorities may wish to adopt criteria which would disqualify individuals who satisfy the reasonable preference requirements. This could be the case, for example, if applicants are disqualified on a ground of anti-social behaviour.

3.22   When deciding what classes of people do not qualify for an allocation, authorities should consider the implications of excluding all members of such groups. For instance, when framing residency criteria, authorities may wish to consider the position of people who are moving into the district to take up work or to escape violence, or homeless applicants or children in care who are placed out of borough.

3.23 The Government believes that authorities should avoid allocating social housing to people who already own their own homes. Where they do so, this should only be in exceptional circumstances; for example, for elderly owner occupiers who cannot stay in their own home and need to move into sheltered accommodation.

3.24 There may be sound policy reasons for applying different qualification criteria in relation to existing tenants from those which apply to new applicants. For example, where residency requirements are imposed, authorities may wish to ensure they do not restrict the ability of existing social tenants to move to take up work or to downsize to a smaller home. Authorities may decide to apply different qualification criteria in relation to particular types of stock, for example properties which might otherwise be hard to let.

3.25 Whatever general criteria housing authorities use to define the classes of persons who do not qualify for social housing, there may be exceptional circumstances where it is necessary to disapply these criteria in the case of individual applicants. An example might be an intimidated witness[4] who needs to move quickly to another local authority district. Authorities are encouraged to make explicit provision for dealing with exceptional cases within their qualification rules.

3.26 As with eligibility, authorities are advised to consider whether an applicant qualifies for an allocation at the time of the initial application and when considering making an allocation, particularly where a long time has elapsed since the original application.

Members of the Armed Forces and the Reserve Forces

3.27 Subject to Parliamentary scrutiny, we will regulate to provide that authorities must not disqualify the following applicants on the grounds that they do not have a local connection[5] with the authority's district:

(a) members of the Armed Forces and former Service personnel, where the application is made within five[6] years of discharge

(b) bereaved spouses and civil partners of members of the Armed Forces leaving Services Family Accommodation following the death of their spouse or partner

(c) serving or former members of the Reserve Forces who need to move because of a serious injury, medical condition or disability sustained as a result of their service.

3.28 These provisions recognise the special position of members of the Armed Forces (and their families) whose employment requires them to be mobile and who are likely therefore to be particularly disadvantaged by local connection requirements; as well as those injured reservists who may need to move to another local authority district to access treatment, care or support.

Joint tenants

3.29 In the case of an allocation to two or more persons jointly, at least one of the persons must be a qualifying person (s 160ZA(6)(b)) and all of them must be eligible.

Fresh applications

3.30 Applicants who have previously been deemed not to qualify may make a fresh application if they consider they should now be treated as qualifying, but it will be for the applicant to show that his or her circumstances have changed (s 160ZA(11)).

Reviews of decisions on eligibility and qualification

3.31 For guidance on decisions and reviews see Chapter 5.

¹ European Economic Area nationals are nationals of any EU member state (except the UK), and nationals of Iceland, Norway, Liechtenstein and Switzerland.

² Inserted by the Allocation of Housing and Homelessness (Miscellaneous Provisions) (England) Regulations 2006.

³ As of 1 May 2011, nationals of the 8 Eastern European countries (A8 nationals) which acceded to the EU in 2004 are no longer required to register with the Workers Registration Scheme in order to work in the UK. Regulation 4(2)(c) of the Eligibility Regulations no longer applies to applications from A8 workers as of that date. Rather applications from A8 workers should be considered on the same basis as those from other EU workers under regulation 4(2)(a).

⁴ 'Intimidated witnesses include Protected Persons as specified in Section 82 and schedule 5 of the Serious Organised Crime and Police Act 2005'.

⁵ As defined by s.199 of the 1996 Act.

⁶ 5 years reflects guidelines issued by the local authorities associations which propose a working definition of normal residence for the purposes of establishing a local connection (see paragraph 4.1(i) to Annex 18 of the Homelessness Code of Guidance 2006).

CHAPTER 4

Framing an allocation scheme

4.1 Housing authorities are required by s 166A(1) to have an allocation scheme for determining priorities, and for defining the procedures to be followed in allocating housing accommodation; and they must allocate in accordance with that scheme (s 166A(14)). All aspects of the allocation process must be covered in the scheme, including the people by whom decisions are taken. In the Secretary of State's view, qualification criteria form part of an allocation scheme.

4.2 All housing authorities must have an allocation scheme, regardless of whether they own housing stock and whether they contract out the delivery of any of their allocation functions (see further Chapter 6). When framing or modifying their scheme, authorities must have regard to their current tenancy and homelessness strategies (s 166A(12)).

Choice and preference options

4.3 An allocation scheme must include a statement as to the housing authority's policy on offering people a choice of accommodation or the opportunity to express preferences about the accommodation to be allocated to them (s 166A). It is for housing authorities to determine their policy on providing choice or the ability to express preferences.

Reasonable preference

4.4 In framing their allocation scheme to determine allocation priorities, housing authorities must ensure that reasonable preference is given to the following categories of people (s 166A(3):

(a) people who are homeless within the meaning of Part 7 of the 1996 Act (including those who are intentionally homeless and those not in priority need)

(b) people who are owed a duty by any housing authority under section 190(2), 193(2) or 195(2) of the 1996 Act (or under section 65(2) or 68(2) of the Housing Act 1985) or who are occupying accommodation secured by any housing authority under s 192(3)

(c) people occupying insanitary or overcrowded housing or otherwise living in unsatisfactory housing conditions

(d) people who need to move on medical or welfare grounds, including grounds relating to a disability,¹ and

(e)   people who need to move to a particular locality in the district of the housing authority, where failure to meet that need would cause hardship (to themselves or others).

4.5   In framing their allocation scheme to give effect to s 166A(3), housing authorities should have regard to the following considerations:

• the scheme must be framed so as to give reasonable preference to applicants who fall within the categories set out in s 166A(3), over those who do not

• although there is no requirement to give equal weight to each of the reasonable preference categories, authorities will need to demonstrate that, overall, reasonable preference has been given to all of them

• there is no requirement for housing authorities to frame their scheme to afford greater priority to applicants who fall within more than one reasonable preference category (cumulative preference) over those who have reasonable preference on a single, non-urgent basis.[2]

Otherwise, it is for housing authorities to decide how to give effect to the provisions of s 166A(3) in their allocation scheme.

Restricted persons

4.6   Applicants should not be given reasonable preference under paragraph (a) or (b) of s 166A(3) if they would only qualify for reasonable preference by taking into account a 'restricted person' within the meaning of Part 7 (s 166A(4)). A restricted person is a person subject to immigration control who is not eligible for homelessness assistance because he or she does not have leave to enter or remain in the UK or has leave which is subject to a 'no recourse to public funds' condition (s 184(7) of the 1996 Act).

Homeless or owed a homelessness duty

4.7   The requirement for housing authorities to frame their allocation scheme to give reasonable preference to people who are owed certain homeless duties remains the case, notwithstanding the amendments to Part 7 made by the Localism Act which give authorities the power to end the main homelessness duty with an offer of private rented accommodation, without requiring the applicant's consent.

Overcrowding

4.8   The Secretary of State takes the view that the bedroom standard is an appropriate measure of overcrowding for allocation purposes, and recommends that all housing authorities should adopt this as a minimum. The bedroom standard allocates a separate bedroom to each:

• married or cohabiting couple
• adult aged 21 years or more
• pair of adolescents aged 10–20 years of the same sex
• pair of children aged under 10 years regardless of sex.

Medical and welfare grounds

4.9   The medical and welfare reasonable preference category includes people who need to move because of their disability or access needs, and this includes people with a learning disability as well as those with a physical disability.

4.10   'Welfare grounds' would encompass a wide range of needs, including, but not limited to, the need to:

• provide a secure base from which a care leaver, or a person who is moving on from a drug or alcohol recovery programme, can build a stable life

• provide accommodation, with appropriate care and support, for those who could not be expected to find their own accommodation, such as young adults with learning disabilities who wish to live independently in the community

- provide or receive care or support. This would include foster carers, those approved to adopt, or those being assessed for approval to foster or adopt, who need to move to a larger home in order to accommodate a looked after child or a child who was previously looked after by a local authority. It would also include special guardians, holders of a residence order and family and friends carers who are not foster carers but who have taken on the care of a child because the parents are unable to provide care.

Hardship grounds

4.11 This would include, for example, a person who needs to move to a different locality in order to give or receive care, to access specialised medical treatment, or to take up a particular employment, education or training opportunity.

4.12 Possible indicators of the criteria which apply to reasonable preference categories (c) and (d) are given in annex 1.

Additional preference

4.13 Section 166A(3) gives housing authorities the power to frame their allocation scheme to give additional preference to particular descriptions of people who fall within the statutory reasonable preference categories and have urgent housing needs. All housing authorities must consider, in the light of local circumstances, the need to give effect to this provision. Examples of people with urgent housing needs to whom housing authorities should consider giving additional preference within their allocation scheme include:

- those who need to move urgently because of a life threatening illness or sudden disability
- families in severe overcrowding which poses a serious health hazard
- those who are homeless and require urgent re-housing as a result of violence or threats of violence, including intimidated witnesses, and those escaping serious anti-social behaviour or domestic violence.

Members of the Armed and Reserve Forces

4.14 Subject to parliamentary approval, we will regulate to require authorities to frame their allocation scheme to give additional preference to the following categories of people who fall within one or more of the reasonable preference categories and who have urgent housing needs:

(a) former members of the Armed Forces
(b) serving members of the Armed Forces who need to move because of a serious injury, medical condition or disability sustained as a result of their service
(c) bereaved spouses and civil partners of members of the Armed Forces leaving Services Family Accommodation following the death of their spouse or partner
(d) serving or former members of the Reserve Forces who need to move because of a serious injury, medical condition or disability sustained as a result of their service.

Determining priorities between households with a similar level of need

4.15 Authorities may frame their allocation scheme to take into account factors in determining relative priorities between applicants in the reasonable (or additional) preference categories (s 166A(5)). Examples of such factors are given in the legislation: financial resources, behaviour and local connection. However, these examples are not exclusive and authorities may take into account other factors instead or as well as these.

Financial resources available to a person to meet his housing costs

4.16 This would enable a housing authority, for example, to give less priority to owner occupiers (wherever the property is situated).

Behaviour

4.17 This would allow for greater priority to be given to applicants who have been model tenants or have benefited the community, for example.

Local connection

4.18 Local connection is defined by s 199 of the 1996 Act. A person has a local connection because of normal residence (current or previous) of their own choice, employment, family associations, or special circumstances. Residence is not of a person's choice if it is the consequence of being detained in prison or in hospital under the Mental Health Act. As a result of changes to s 199 introduced in 2008[3] a person serving in the Armed Forces can establish a local connection with a local authority district through residence or employment there, in the same way as a civilian.

Including local priorities alongside the statutory reasonable preference categories

4.19 As the House of Lords made clear in the case of *R (on application of Ahmad) v Newham LBC*,[4] s 166A(3)[5] only requires that the people encompassed within that section are given 'reasonable preference'. It 'does not require that they should be given absolute priority over everyone else'.[6] This means that an allocation scheme may provide for other factors than those set out in s 166A(3) to be taken into account in determining which applicants are to be given preference under a scheme, provided that:

- they do not dominate the scheme, and
- overall, the scheme operates to give reasonable preference to those in the statutory reasonable preference categories over those who are not.

The Secretary of State would encourage authorities to consider the scope to take advantage of this flexibility to meet local needs and local priorities.

4.20 The House of Lords also made clear that, where an allocation scheme complies with the reasonable preference requirements and any other statutory requirements, the courts should be very slow to interfere on the ground of alleged irrationality.[7]

Local lettings policies

4.21 Section 166A(6)(b) of the 1996 Act enables housing authorities to allocate particular accommodation to people of a particular description, whether or not they fall within the reasonable preference categories, provided that overall the authority is able to demonstrate compliance with the requirements of s 166A(3). This is the statutory basis for so-called 'local lettings policies' which may be used to achieve a wide variety of housing management and policy objectives.

Households affected by the under-occupation measure

4.22 When framing the rules which determine the size of property to allocate to different households and in different circumstances, housing authorities are free to set their own criteria, provided they do not result in a household being statutorily overcrowded. However, in setting these criteria, authorities will want to take account of the provision in the Welfare Reform Act 2012 which will reduce Housing Benefit to under-occupiers.

4.23 Social tenants affected by the under-occupation measure may choose to move to more suitably sized accommodation in the private rented sector. One way to encourage tenants to consider this option might be to ensure they are given some degree of preference for an allocation if they apply for a new social tenancy at a later date.

Members of the Armed Forces

4.24 Authorities are also strongly encouraged to take into account the needs of all serving or former Service personnel when framing their allocation schemes, and to give sympathetic consideration to the housing needs of family members of serving or former Service personnel who may themselves have been disadvantaged by the requirements of military service and, in particular, the need to move from base to base. This would be in line with terms of the Government's Armed Forces Covenant published in May 2011.

4.25 Examples of ways in which authorities can ensure that Service personnel and their families are given appropriate priority, include:

- using the flexibility within the allocation legislation to set local priorities alongside the statutory reasonable preference categories so as to give preference, for example, to those who have recently left, or are close to leaving, the Armed Forces[8] (see paragraph 4.19 above)
- using the power to determine priorities between applicants in the reasonable preference categories, so that applicants in housing need who have served in the Armed Forces are given greater priority for social housing over those who have not (see paragraph 4.15 above)
- if taking into account an applicant's financial resources in determining priorities between households with a similar level of need (see paragraph 4.16 above), disregarding any lump sum received by a member of the Armed Forces as compensation for an injury or disability sustained on active service
- setting aside a proportion of properties for former members of the Armed Forces under a local lettings policy (see paragraph 4.21 above).

4.26 A number of organisations provide specialist housing and support for veterans, such as the Royal British Legion, Stoll, Haig Homes, Alabare and Norcare, and housing authorities are encouraged to liaise with them to ensure that former Service personnel are able to access the housing option which best suits their needs.

Households in work or seeking work

4.27 Local authorities are urged to consider how they can use their allocation policies to support those households who want to work, as well as those who – while unable to engage in paid employment - are contributing to their community in other ways, for example, through voluntary work. The flexibilities which authorities are encouraged to make use of to meet the needs of Service personnel would apply equally here. This might involve, for example, framing an allocation scheme to give some preference to households who are in low paid work or employment-related training, even where they are not in the reasonable preference categories; or to give greater priority to those households in the reasonable preference categories who are also in work or who can demonstrate that they are actively seeking work. Alternatively, it might involve using local lettings policies to ensure that specific properties, or a specified proportion of properties, are allocated to households in particular types of employment where, for example, skills are in short supply.

4.28 Authorities should also consider how best they can make use of the new power to offer flexible tenancies to support households who are in low paid work, and incentivise others to take up employment opportunities.

Carers

4.29 In making accommodation offers to applicants who receive support from carers who do not reside with them but may need to stay overnight, housing authorities should, wherever possible, take account of the applicant's need for a spare bedroom.

Prospective adopters and foster carers

4.30 When considering housing applications from prospective foster carers or adopters who would require an extra bedroom to accommodate a foster or adoptive child, authorities will wish to weigh up the risk that the application to foster or adopt may be unsuccessful (leading to the property being under-occupied), against the wider benefits which would be realised if the placement was successful.

4.31 Children's services have a duty under s.22G of the Children Act 1989 to ensure sufficient accommodation to meet the needs of the looked after children in their area. Authorities should work together with children's services to best meet the needs of prospective and approved foster carers and adopters, so that children's services can meet their s.22G duty. One way to strike an appropriate balance would be to set aside a quota of properties each year for people who need to move to larger accommodation in order to foster or adopt a child on the recommendation of children's services.

4.32 The advice in paragraph 4.22 is particularly relevant in relation to prospective foster carers, as foster children are not taken into account in determining the household size for the purposes of the under-occupation measure in the Welfare Reform Act. However, current and prospective foster carers affected by the measure may be eligible to apply for a Discretionary Housing Payment.

General information about particular applications

4.33 Under s166A(9), allocation schemes must be framed so as to give applicants the right to request from housing authorities general information that will enable them to assess:

(a) how their application is likely to be treated under the scheme and, in particular, whether they are likely to have reasonable preference
(b) whether accommodation appropriate to their needs is likely to be made available and, if so, how long it is likely to be before such accommodation becomes available.

Notification about decisions and the right to a review of a decision

4.34 An allocation scheme must be framed so as to give applicants the right to be informed of certain decisions and the right to review certain decisions (s 166A(9)). For further advice on decisions and reviews, see Chapter 5.

---

1   The words 'including grounds relating to a disability' were added by the Housing Act 2004.
2   *R (on application of Ahmad) v London Borough of Newham* [2009] UKHL 14, [2009] HLR 31.
3   Amendment to s.199 of the 1996 Act made by s 315 of the Housing and Regeneration Act 2008.
4   [2009] UKHL 14.
5   Previously s 167(2), which continues to apply to allocations by housing authorities in Wales.
6   Baroness Hale at para [18].
7   Lord Neuberger at para [55].
8   MoD issues a Certificate of Cessation of Entitlement to Occupy Service Living Accommodation 6 months before discharge.

CHAPTER 5

Allocation scheme management

Publishing and consulting on allocation schemes

5.1 Housing authorities must publish a summary of their allocation scheme and, if requested, provide a free copy of it (s 168(1)). They must also make the full scheme available for inspection at their principal office and, if requested, provide a copy of it on payment of a reasonable fee (s 168(2)).

5.2 When an alteration is made to a scheme reflecting a major change of policy, an authority must ensure within a reasonable time that those likely to be affected by the change have the effect brought to their attention, taking such steps as the housing authority considers reasonable (s 168(3)). A major policy change would include, for example, any amendment affecting the relative priority of a large number of applicants or a significant alteration to procedures. Housing authorities should be aware that they still have certain duties under s 106 of the Housing Act 1985.

5.3 Section 166A(13) requires authorities, before adopting an allocation scheme, or altering a scheme to reflect a major change of policy, to:

- send a copy of the draft scheme, or proposed alteration, to every Private Registered Provider[1] with which they have nomination arrangements, and
- ensure they have a reasonable opportunity to comment on the proposals.

Advice and information

5.4 Housing authorities must ensure that advice and information is available free of charge to everyone in their district about the right to apply for an allocation of accommodation (s 166(1)(a)). This would include general information about application procedures; as well as information about qualification and prioritisation criteria.

5.5 If a person is likely to have difficulty making an application without assistance, the authority must secure that any necessary assistance is available free of charge (s 166(1)(b)).

5.6 Housing authorities must inform applicants that they have the right to the following general information (s 166(1A)):

- information that will enable them to assess how their application is likely to be treated under the authority's allocation scheme, and, in particular, whether they are likely to fall within the reasonable preference categories, and
- information about whether accommodation appropriate to their needs is likely to be made available to them and, if so, how long it is likely to be before such accommodation becomes available. Maintaining a database of housing suitable for applicants with access needs would assist with this.

5.7 Section 166(4) prohibits housing authorities from divulging to other members of the public that a person is an applicant for social housing, unless they have the applicant's consent. Furthermore, authorities should process any personal data they hold about applicants consistently with the Data Protection Act 1998. If authorities are unclear about their obligations and responsibilities under the Data Protection Act they should contact the Information Commissioner.

Elected Members' Involvement in Allocation Decisions

5.8 The Allocation of Housing (Procedure) Regulations 1997 (SI 1997/483) prevent an elected Member from being part of a decision-making body at the time an allocation decision is made, when either:

- the accommodation concerned is situated in their division or electoral ward, or
- the person subject to the decision has their sole or main residence there

5.9 The regulations do not prevent an elected Member from representing their constituents in front of the decision making body, or from participating in the decision making body's deliberations prior to its decision. The regulations also do not prevent elected Members' involvement in policy decisions that affect the generality of housing accommodation in their division or electoral ward rather than individual allocations; for example, a decision that certain types of property should be prioritised for older people.

Offences related to information given or withheld by applicants

5.10 Section 171 makes it an offence for anyone, in connection with the exercise by a housing authority of its functions under Part 6, to:

- knowingly or recklessly give false information
- knowingly withhold information which the housing authority has reasonably required the applicant to give in connection with the exercise of those functions.

5.11 The circumstances in which an offence is committed could include providing false information:

- on an application form for social housing
- in response to a request for further information in support of the application
- during review proceedings.

5.12 Ground 5 in Schedule 2 to the Housing Act 1985 (as amended by s 146 of the 1996 Act) enables a housing authority to seek possession of a tenancy granted as a result of a false statement by the tenant or a person acting at the tenant's instigation.

Fraudulent or incorrect allocations

5.13 Authorities may also wish to take action to minimise the risk of staff allocating incorrectly or even fraudulently, for example to applicants who do not have sufficient priority under the allocation scheme or do not meet the authority's qualification criteria. Appropriate steps might include vetting staff who take allocation decisions or providing for decisions to be validated by employing senior staff to undertake random checks.

Decisions and reviews

Information about decisions and reviews

5.14 Housing authorities must inform applicants that they have the right to information about certain decisions which are taken in respect of their application and the right to review those decisions (s 166(1A)).

5.15 By virtue of s 160ZA (9) and (10) housing authorities must notify an applicant in writing of any decision that he or she:

- is ineligible for an allocation of accommodation under s 160ZA(2) or (4), or
- is not a qualifying person under s 160ZA(7).

5.16 The notification must give clear grounds for the decision based on the relevant facts of the case. Section 160ZA(10) provides that, where a notification is not received by an applicant, it can be treated as having been given to him or her, if it is made available at the housing authority's office for a reasonable period. Where an authority considers that an applicant may have difficulty in understanding the implications of a decision on ineligibility or disqualification, it would be good practice to make arrangements for the information to be explained verbally in addition to providing a written notice.

5.17 Applicants also have the right, on request, to be informed of any decision about the facts of their case which has been, or is likely to be, taken into account in considering whether to make an allocation to them (s 166A(9)(b)).

5.18 Under s 166A(9)(c) applicants have the right to request a review of any of the decisions mentioned in paragraphs 5.15 and 5.17 above and to be informed of the decision on the review and the grounds for it.

Procedures on review

5.19 Review procedures should be clearly set out, including timescales for each stage of the process, and must accord with the principles of transparency and fairness. Failure to put in place a fair procedure for reviews, which allows for all relevant factors to be considered, could result in a judicial review of any decision reached. The following are general principles of good administrative practice:

(i) Applicants should be notified of the timescale within which they must request a review. 21 days from the date the applicant is notified of the decision is well-established as a reasonable timescale. A housing authority should retain the discretion to extend this time limit in exceptional circumstances.

(ii)   Applicants should be notified that the request for review should be made in writing, and that it would also be acceptable for the request to be submitted by a representative on their behalf. Applicants should also be advised of the information which should accompany the request.

(iii)   Authorities should consider whether to advise that provision can be made for verbal representations, as well as written submissions, to be made.

(iv)   The review should be carried out by an officer who is senior to the person who made the original decision. Alternatively, authorities may wish to appoint a panel to consider the review. If so, it should not include any person involved in the original decision.

(v)   The review should be considered on the basis of the authority's allocation scheme, any legal requirements and all relevant information. This should include information provided by the applicant on any relevant developments since the original decision was made – for instance, the settlement of arrears or establishment of a repayment plan, or departure of a member of the household responsible for anti-social behavior.

(vi)   Reviews should be completed wherever practicable within a set deadline. Eight weeks is suggested as a reasonable timescale. The applicant should be notified of any extension to this deadline and the reasons for this.

(vii)   Applicants must be notified in writing of the outcome of the review. The notification must set out the reasons for the decision. This will assist the applicant and the authority if, for example, the applicant is not satisfied with the outcome and decides to seek a judicial review or to take their case to the Local Government Ombudsman.

---

[1]   And, where relevant, every Registered Social Landlord in Wales with which they have nomination arrangements.

CHAPTER 6

Private Registered Providers and contracting out

Working with Private Registered Providers

6.1   Private Registered Providers have a duty under s 170 to cooperate with housing authorities – where the authority requests it - to such extent as is reasonable in the circumstances in offering accommodation to people with priority under the authority's allocation scheme. Similarly, s.213 provides that, where a Private Registered Provider has been requested by a housing authority to assist them in the discharge of their homelessness functions under Part 7, it must cooperate to the same extent.

6.2   Housing authorities must comply with the requirements of Part 6 when they nominate an applicant to be the tenant of a Private Registered Provider. A housing authority nominates for these purposes when it does so 'in pursuance of any arrangements (whether legally enforceable or not) to require that housing accommodation, or a specified amount of housing accommodation, is made available to a person or one of a number of persons nominated by the authority' (s 159(4)).

6.3   Nomination agreements should set out the proportion of lettings that will be made available; any criteria which the Private Registered Provider has adopted for accepting or rejecting nominees; and how any disputes will be resolved. Housing authorities will want to put in place arrangements to monitor effective delivery of the nomination agreement so they can demonstrate they are meeting their obligations under Part 6.

6.4   The Secretary of State expects that Affordable Rent homes will be allocated in the same way as social rent properties and that existing lettings arrangements operated by housing authorities and Private Registered Providers will continue to apply. The statutory and regulatory framework for allocations provides scope for local flexibility, and authorities and Private Registered Providers may wish to exercise this discretion in relation to Affordable Rent in order to meet local needs and priorities effectively.

Contracting Out

6.5 The *Local Authorities (Contracting Out of Allocation of Housing and Homelessness Functions) Order 1996* (SI 1996/3205) – made under s.70 of the Deregulation and Contracting Out Act 1994 ('the 1994 Act') – enables housing authorities to contract out certain functions under Part 6. In essence, it allows the contracting out of administrative functions, leaving the responsibility for strategic decisions with the housing authority.

6.6 Schedule 1 to the Order lists allocation functions which may not be contracted out:

- adopting or altering the allocation scheme, including the principles on which the scheme is framed, and consulting Private Registered Providers,
- making the allocation scheme available at the authority's principal office.

6.7 The Order therefore provides that the majority of functions under Part 6 may be contracted out. These include:

(i)   making enquiries about and deciding a person's eligibility for an allocation
(ii)   carrying out reviews of decisions
(iii) securing that advice and information is available free of charge on how to apply for housing
(iv)   securing that assistance is available free of charge to people likely to have difficulty in making a housing application without such assistance, and
(v)   making individual allocations in accordance with the allocation scheme.

6.8 The 1994 Act provides that a contract:

(i)   may authorise a contractor to carry out only part of the function concerned
(ii)   may specify that the contractor is authorised to carry out functions only in certain cases or areas specified in the contract
(iii) may include conditions relating to the carrying out of the functions, for example prescribing standards of performance
(iv)   shall be for a period not exceeding 10 years and may be revoked at any time by the Minister or the housing authority. Any subsisting contract is to be treated as having been repudiated in these circumstances
(v)   shall not prevent the authority from exercising the functions to which the contract relates.

6.9 The 1994 Act also provides that the authority is responsible for any act or omission of the contractor in exercising functions under the contract, except where:

- the contractor fails to fulfil conditions specified in the contract relating to the exercise of the function
- criminal proceedings are brought in respect of the contractor's act or omission.

6.10 Where a housing authority has delegated or contracted out the operation of its allocation functions to an external contractor, the contractor must be made aware of the provisions of Part 6 and advised how the legislation and this guidance apply to them.

6.11 Where there is an arrangement in force under s 101 of the Local Government Act 1972 by virtue of which one authority exercises the functions of another, the 1994 Act provides that the authority exercising the function is not allowed to contract it out without the principal authority's consent.

ANNEX 1

Indicators of criteria in reasonable preference categories (c) & (d)

Housing authorities may devise their own indicators of the criteria in the reasonable preference categories. The following list is included for illustrative purposes and to assist housing authorities in this task. It is by no means comprehensive or exhaustive, and housing authorities may have other, local factors to consider and include as indicators of the categories.

Insanitary, overcrowded and unsatisfactory housing conditions

Lacking bathroom or kitchen

Lacking inside WC

Lacking cold or hot water supplies, electricity, gas, or adequate heating

Lack of access to a garden for young children

Sharing living room, kitchen, bathroom/WC

Property in disrepair Poor internal or external arrangements

Young children in flats above ground floor

People who need to move on medical or welfare grounds (criteria may apply to any member of the household)

A mental illness or disorder

A physical or learning disability

Chronic or progressive medical conditions (e.g. MS, HIV/AIDS)

Infirmity due to old age

The need to give or receive care

The need to recover from the effects of violence or threats of violence, or physical, emotional or sexual abuse

Ability to fend for self restricted for other reasons

Young people at risk

People with behavioural difficulties

Need for adapted housing and/or extra facilities, bedroom or bathroom

Need for improved heating (on medical grounds)

Need for sheltered housing (on medical grounds)

Need for ground floor accommodation (on medical grounds)

Need to be near friends/relatives or medical facility on medical grounds

Need to move following hospitalisation or long term care

ANNEX 2

Rights to reside in the UK derived from EU Law

1. EEA nationals and their family members who have a right to reside in the UK that derives from EU law are not persons subject to immigration control. This means that they will be eligible for an allocation of accommodation under Part 6 unless they fall within one of the categories of persons to be treated as a person from abroad who is ineligible for an allocation of accommodation by virtue of regulation 4 of the Eligibility Regulations.

General

Nationals of EU countries

2. Nationals of EU countries enjoy a number of different rights to reside in other Member States, including the UK. These rights derive from the EU Treaties, EU

secondary legislation (in particular *Directive 2004/38*), and the case law of the European Court of Justice.

3. Whether an individual EU national has a right to reside in the UK will depend on his or her circumstances, particularly his or her economic status (e.g. whether employed, self-employed, seeking work, a student, or economically inactive etc).

NATIONALS OF BULGARIA AND ROMANIA - THE A2 ACCESSION STATES

4. A slightly different regime applies to EU nationals who are nationals of Bulgaria and Romania which acceded to the EU on 1 January 2007. Bulgaria and Romania are referred to in this guidance as the A2 accession states.

THE IMMIGRATION (EUROPEAN ECONOMIC AREA) REGULATIONS 2006

5. The *Immigration (European Economic Area) Regulations 2006* ('the EEA Regulations' – SI 2006/1003) implement into UK domestic law *Directive 2004/38*. Broadly, the EEA Regulations provide that EU nationals have the right to reside in the UK without the requirement for leave to remain under the Immigration Act 1971 for the first 3 months of their residence, and for longer, if they are a 'qualified person' or they have acquired a permanent right of residence.

NATIONALS OF ICELAND, LIECHTENSTEIN AND NORWAY, AND SWITZERLAND

6. The EEA Regulations extend the same rights to reside in the UK to nationals of Iceland, Liechtenstein and Norway as those afforded to EU nationals. (The EU countries plus Iceland, Liechtenstein and Norway together comprise the EEA.) The EEA Regulations also extend the same rights to reside in the UK to nationals of Switzerland. For the purposes of this guidance, 'EEA nationals' means nationals of any of the EU member states (excluding the UK), and nationals of Iceland, Norway, Liechtenstein and Switzerland.

Initial 3 months residence

7. Regulation 13 of the EEA Regulations provides that EEA nationals have the right to reside in the UK for a period of up to 3 months without any conditions or formalities other than holding a valid identity card or passport. Therefore, during their first 3 months of residence in the UK, EEA nationals will not be subject to immigration control (unless the right to reside is lost following a decision by an immigration officer in accordance with regulation 13(3) of the EEA Regulations).

8. However, regulations 4(1)(b)(ii) and (c) of the Eligibility Regulations provide that a person who is not subject to immigration control is not eligible for an allocation of accommodation if:

(i)   his or her **only** right to reside in the UK is an initial right to reside for a period not exceeding 3 months under regulation 13 of the EEA Regulations, or

(ii)   his or her **only** right to reside in the Channel Islands, the Isle of Man or the Republic of Ireland (the Common Travel Area) is a right equivalent to the right mentioned in (i) above which is derived from the EU Treaty

Rights of residence for 'qualified persons'

9. Regulation 14 of the EEA Regulations provides that 'qualified persons' have the right to reside in the UK so long as they remain a qualified person. Under regulation 6 of the EEA Regulations, 'qualified person' means:

(a)   a jobseeker

(b)   a worker
(c)   a self-employed person
(d)   a self-sufficient person
(e)   a student

Jobseekers

10. For the purposes of regulation 6(1)(a) of the EEA Regulations, 'jobseeker' means a person who enters the UK in order to seek employment and can provide evidence that he or she is seeking employment and has a genuine chance of being employed.

11. Nationals of Bulgaria and Romania who need to be authorised to work do not have a right to reside in the UK as a jobseeker.[1] However, they may have a right to reside by virtue of another status, e.g. as a self-sufficient person.

12. Although a person who is a jobseeker is not subject to immigration control, regulation 4 of the Eligibility Regulations provides that a person is not eligible for an allocation of accommodation if:

(i)   his or her **only** right to reside in the UK is derived from his or her status as a jobseeker or the family member of a jobseeker, or
(ii)   his or her **only** right to reside in the Channel Islands, the Common Travel Area is a right equivalent to the right mentioned in (i) above which is derived from the Treaty establishing the European Community.

Workers

13. In order to be a worker for the purposes of the EEA Regulations, a person must be employed. That is to say, he or she is obliged to provide services for another person in return for monetary reward and is subject to the control of that other person as regards the way in which the work is to be done.

14. Activity as an employed person may include part time work, seasonal work and cross-border work (ie. where a worker is established in another Member State and travels to work in the UK). However, case-law provides that the employment must be effective and genuine economic activity, and not on such a small scale as to be regarded as purely marginal and ancillary.

15. Provided the employment is effective and genuine economic activity, the fact that a person's level of remuneration may be below the level of subsistence or below the national minimum wage, or the fact that a person may be receiving financial assistance from public benefits, would not exclude that person from being a 'worker'.

16. A person who is a worker is not subject to immigration control, and is eligible for an allocation of accommodation whether or not he or she is habitually resident in the Common Travel Area.

RETENTION OF WORKER STATUS

17. A person who is no longer working does not cease to be treated as a 'worker' for the purpose of regulation 6(1)(b) of the EEA Regulations, if he or she:

(a)   is temporarily unable to work as the result of an illness or accident; or
(b)   is recorded as involuntarily unemployed after having being employed in the UK, provided that he or she has registered as a jobseeker with the relevant employment office, and:
    (i)   was employed for one year or more before becoming unemployed, or
    (ii)   has been unemployed for no more than 6 months, or
    (iii)   can provide evidence that he or she is seeking employment in the UK and has a genuine chance of being engaged; or

(c)   is involuntarily unemployed and has embarked on vocational training; or

(d)   has voluntarily ceased working and embarked on vocational training that is related to his or her previous employment.

A2 STATE WORKERS REQUIRING AUTHORISATION WHO ARE TREATED AS WORKERS

18. By virtue of the *Accession (Immigration and Worker Authorisation) Regulations 2006* ('the Accession Regulations'), nationals of the A2 states (with certain exceptions) must obtain authorisation to work in the UK until they have accrued a period of 12 months continuous employment.

19. An A2 national requiring authorisation is only treated as a worker if he or she is actually working and:

(i)   holds an accession worker authorisation document, and

(ii)   is working in accordance with the conditions set out in that document (regulation 9(1) of the Accession Regulations).

20. Authorities may need to contact the employer named in the authorisation document, to confirm that the applicant continues to be employed.

Self-employed persons

21. 'Self-employed person' means a person who establishes himself in the UK in order to pursue activity as a self-employed person in accordance with Article 49 of the Treaty on the Functioning of the European Union.

22. A self-employed person should be able to confirm that he or she is pursuing activity as a self-employed person by providing documents relating to their business. A person who is no longer in self-employment does not cease to be treated as a self-employed person for the purposes of regulation 6(1)(c) of the EEA regulations, if he or she is temporarily unable to pursue his or her activity as a self-employed person as the result of an illness or accident.

23. A2 nationals are not required to be authorised in order to establish themselves in the UK as a self-employed person.

24. A person who is a self-employed is not subject to immigration control and is eligible for an allocation of accommodation whether or not he or she is habitually resident in the Common Travel Area.

Self-sufficient persons

25. Regulation 4(1)(c) of the EEA regulations defines 'self-sufficient person' as a person who has:

(i)   sufficient resources not to become a burden on the social assistance system of the UK during his or her period of residence, and

(ii)   comprehensive sickness insurance cover in the UK.

26. By regulation 4(4) of the EEA Regulations, the resources of a person who is a self-sufficient person (or a student – see below) and, where applicable, any family members, are to be regarded as sufficient if (a) they exceed the maximum level of resources which a UK national and his or her family members may possess if he or she is to become eligible for social assistance under the UK benefit system or, if (a) does not apply, (b) taking into account the personal situation of the person concerned and, where applicable, any family members, it appears to the decision maker that the resources of the person or persons concerned should be regarded as sufficient.

27. Where an EEA national applies for an allocation of accommodation as a

self-sufficient person and does not appear to meet the conditions of regulation 4(1)(c) of the EEA regulations, the housing authority will need to consider whether he or she may have some other right to reside in the UK.

28. Where the applicant does not meet the conditions of regulation 4(1)(c) but has previously done so during his or her residence in the UK, the case should be referred to the Home Office for clarification of their status.

29. A person who is a self-sufficient person is not subject to immigration control, but must be habitually resident in the Common Travel Area to be eligible for an allocation of accommodation.

Students

30. Regulation 4(1)(d) of the EEA regulations defines 'student' as a person who:

(a)   is enrolled at a private or public establishment included on the Register of Education and Training Providers,[2] or is financed from public funds, for the principal purpose of following a course of study, including vocational training, and
(b)   has comprehensive sickness insurance cover in the UK, and
(c)   assures the Secretary of State, by means of a declaration or such equivalent means as the person may choose, that he or she (and if applicable his or her family members) has sufficient resources not to become a burden on the social assistance system of the UK during his or her period of residence.

31. A person who is a student is not subject to immigration control but must be habitually resident in the Common Travel Area to be eligible for an allocation of accommodation.

Permanent right of residence

32. Regulation 15 of the EEA Regulations provides that the following persons shall acquire the right to reside in the UK permanently:

(a)   an EEA national who has resided in the UK in accordance with the EEA regulations for a continuous period of 5 years
(b)   a non-EEA national who is a family member of an EEA national and who has resided in the UK with the EEA national in accordance with the EEA regulations for a continuous period of 5 years
(c)   a worker or self-employed person who has ceased activity (see regulation 5 of the EEA Regulations for the definition of worker or self-employed person who has ceased activity)
(d)   the family member of a worker or self-employed person who has ceased activity
(e)   a person who was the family member of a worker or self-employed person who has died, where the family member resided with the worker or self-employed person immediately before the death and the worker or self-employed person had resided continuously in the UK for at least 2 years before the death (or the death was the result of an accident at work or an occupational disease)
(f)   a person who has resided in the UK in accordance with the EEA regulations for a continuous period of 5 years, and at the end of that period was a family member who has retained the right of residence (see regulation 10 of the EEA Regulations for the definition of a family member who has retained the right of residence).

Once acquired, the right of permanent residence can be lost through absence from the UK for a period exceeding two consecutive years.

33. A person with a right to reside permanently in the UK arising from (c), (d) or (e) above is eligible for an allocation of accommodation whether or not he or she is

habitually resident in the Common Travel Area. Persons with a permanent right to reside by virtue of (a), (b), or (f) must be habitually resident to be eligible.

Rights of residence for certain family members

The right to reside

34. Regulation 14 of the EEA Regulations provides that the following family members are entitled to reside in the UK:

(i)   a family member of a qualified person residing in the UK
(ii)   a family member of an EEA national with a permanent right of residence under regulation 15
(iii)   a family member who has retained the right of residence (see regulation 10 of the EEA Regulations for the definition).

35. A person who has a right to reside in the UK as the family member of an EEA national under the EEA Regulations will not be subject to immigration control. The eligibility of such a person for an allocation of accommodation should therefore be considered in accordance with regulation 4 of the Eligibility Regulations.

36. When considering the eligibility of a family member, housing authorities should consider whether the person has acquired a right to reside in their own right, for example a permanent right to reside under regulation 15 of the EEA Regulations.

Who is a 'family member'?

37. Regulation 7 of the EEA regulations provides that the following persons are treated as the family members of another person (with certain exceptions for students – see below):

(a)   the spouse of the person
(b)   the civil partner of the person
(c)   a direct descendant of the person, or of the person's spouse or civil partner, who is under the age of 21
(d)   a direct descendant of the person, or of the person's spouse or civil partner, who is over 21 and dependent on the person, or the spouse or civil partner
(e)   an ascendant relative of the person, or of the person's spouse or civil partner, who is dependent on the person or the spouse or civil partner
(f)   a person who is an extended family member and is treated as a family member by virtue of regulation 7(3) of the EEA regulations (see below).

FAMILY MEMBERS OF STUDENTS

38. Regulation 7(2) of the EEA regulations provides that a person who falls within (c), (d) or (e) above shall not be treated as a family member of a student residing in the UK after the period of 3 months beginning on the date the student is admitted to the UK unless:

(i)   in the case of paragraph 37(c) and (d) above, the person is the dependant child of the student, or of the spouse or civil partner, or
(ii)   the student is also a qualified person (for the purposes of regulation 6(1) of the EEA regulations) other than as a student.

EXTENDED FAMILY MEMBERS

39. Broadly, extended family members will be persons who:

(a)   do not fall within any of the categories (a) to (e) in paragraph 37 above, and

(b) are either a relative of an EEA national (or of the EEA national's spouse or civil partner) or the partner of an EEA national, and

(c) have been issued with an EEA family permit, a registration certificate or a residence card which is valid and has not been revoked.

Family members' eligibility for an allocation of accommodation

RELATIONSHIP WITH OTHER RIGHTS TO RESIDE

40. This section concerns the eligibility of an applicant for an allocation of accommodation whose right to reside is derived from his or her status as the family member of an EEA national with a right to reside. In some cases, a family member will have acquired a right to reside in his or her own right. In particular, a person who arrived in the UK as the family member of an EEA national may have subsequently acquired a permanent right of residence under regulation 15 of the EEA Regulations, as outlined in paragraph 32 (a) – (f) above. The eligibility for an allocation of accommodation of those with a permanent right of residence is discussed at paragraphs 32 and 33.

FAMILY MEMBERS WHO MUST BE HABITUALLY RESIDENT

41. For family members with a right to reside under regulation 14 of the EEA Regulations, the following categories of persons must be habitually resident in the UK, the Channel Islands, the Isle of Man or the Republic of Ireland in order to be eligible for an allocation of accommodation:

(a) a person whose right to reside derives from their status as a family member of an EEA national who is a self-sufficient person for the purposes of regulation 6(1)(d) of the EEA regulations

(b) a person whose right to reside derives from their status as a family member of an EEA national who is a student for the purposes of regulation 6(1)(e) of the EEA regulations

(c) a person whose right to reside is dependent on their status as a family member of an EEA national with a permanent right to reside

(d) a person whose right to reside is dependent on their status as a family member who has retained the right of residence.

FAMILY MEMBERS WHO ARE EXEMPT FROM THE HABITUAL RESIDENCE REQUIREMENT

42. A person with a right to reside under regulation 14 as a family member of an EEA national who is a worker or a self-employed person for the purposes of regulation 6(1) of the EEA regulations is exempted from the requirement to be habitually resident by regulation 4(2)(d) of the Eligibility Regulations. However, authorities should note that an extended family member (see above) is not counted as a family member for the purposes of regulation 4(2)(d) of the Eligibility Regulations (see regulation 2(3) of the Eligibility Regulations).

Family members of UK nationals exercising rights under the EU Treaty

43. There are some limited cases in which the non-EEA family member of a UK national may have a right to reside under EU law. Under regulation 9 of the EEA Regulations, the family member of a UK national should be treated as an EEA family member where the following conditions are met:

(i) the UK national is residing in an EEA State as a worker or self-employed person, or was so residing before returning to the UK, and

(ii)   if the family member of the UK national is his spouse or civil partner, the parties are living together in the EEA State, or had entered into a marriage or civil partnership and were living together in that State before the UK national returned to the UK.

44. Where the family member of a UK national is to be treated as an EEA family member by virtue of regulation 9 of the EEA Regulations, that person is not subject to immigration control, and his or her eligibility for an allocation of accommodation should therefore be determined in accordance with regulation 4 of the Eligibility Regulations.

¹   Regulation 6(2) of the *Accession (Immigration and Worker Authorisation) Regulations 2006* (SI 2006/3317).

²   Now known as the Register of Sponsors and held by UKBA.

ANNEX 3

Worker authorisation scheme

1. Bulgaria and Romania ('the A2') acceded to the European Union on 1 January 2007. A2 nationals have the right to move freely among all EU Member States. However, under the EU Accession Treaty for Bulgaria and Romania existing Member States can impose limitations on the rights of A2 nationals to access their labour markets (and the associated rights of residence) for a transitional period.

The Accession (Immigration and Worker Authorisation) Regulations 2006

2. Under the *Accession (Immigration and Worker Authorisation) Regulations 2006* (SI 2006/3317) ('the Accession Regulations'), nationals of the A2 States (with certain exceptions set out in paragraph 9 below) are required to be authorised to work by the Home Office if they work in the UK during the transitional period. While looking for work (or between jobs) their right to reside will be conditional on them being self-sufficient and not imposing an unreasonable burden on the UK social assistance system. These conditions cease to apply once they have worked in the UK continuously and legally for 12 months.

3. The Accession Regulations also give workers from the A2 states the right to reside in the UK. This means that workers from the A2 states have the same right to equal treatment as other EEA workers while they are working in accordance with work authorisation requirements or are exempt from those requirements.

The worker authorisation scheme

4. Nationals of A2 states who wish to work in the UK (except those who are exempt from the requirement) must have an accession worker authorisation document and must be working in accordance with the conditions set out in that document.

5. Nationals of the A2 states who are self-employed are not required to be authorised if they are working that capacity.

6. The following constitute worker authorisation documents:

(i)   a passport or other travel document endorsed to show that the person was given leave to enter or remain in the UK before 1 January 2007, subject to a condition restricting his or her employment in the UK to a particular employer or category of employment

(ii)   If the leave to enter or remain expires before the person qualifies to be exempt from the work authorisation requirements, or they wish to engage in employment other than the job for which the leave was granted, they will need to obtain an accession worker card

(iii)   a seasonal agricultural work card issued by the Home Office under the Seasonal Agricultural Workers Scheme. The card is valid for 6 months from the date the person starts work for the agricultural employer specified in the card

(iv)   an accession worker card issued by the Home Office.

7. The accession worker card is valid for as long as the person continues to work for the employer specified in the card. If the person changes employer, he or she must apply for a new accession worker card.

8. The worker authorisation scheme is a transitional measure. The Accession Regulations provide for the scheme to operate for up to five years from 1 January 2007 (i.e. until 31 December 2011). However, there is provision for the scheme to be extended for a further two years in the event of a serious disturbance to the labour market. The decision was taken on 23 November 2011 to maintain transitional controls on Romanian and Bulgarian workers until the end of 2013.

A2 nationals exempt from worker authorisation

9. The following are the categories of A2 nationals who are <u>not</u> required to obtain authorisation to work:

- those who are classified as highly skilled persons and hold a registration certificate allowing them unconditional access to the UK labour market
- those working legally, and without interruption, in the UK for a period of 12 months or more ending on 31 December 2006 (for example, they may have been already present in the UK as a work permit holder before accession)
- those who had leave to enter the UK under the Immigration Act 1971 on 31 December 2006 and that leave does not place any restrictions on taking employment in the United Kingdom (for example, a person may have been given leave to remain as the spouse of a British citizen or as the dependant of a work permit holder)
- those who are providing services in the UK on behalf of an employer established elsewhere in the EEA
- those who are also a national of the UK or another EEA state (other than an A2 state)
- those who are a spouse or civil partner of a national of the UK or a person settled in the UK
- those who are the spouse, civil partner or child under 18 of a person who has limited leave to enter or remain in the UK and that leave allows that person to work in the UK
- those who are a family member (spouse, civil partner or dependant child) of an EEA national who has a right to reside in the UK under the EEA Regulations, including those who are the family member (spouse, civil partner or descendant (under 21 or dependant)) of an A2 national who is working in accordance with worker authorisation requirements
- those who have a permanent right to reside in the UK under regulation 15 of the EEA Regulations
- those who are in the UK as a student and are permitted to work for 20 hours a week, provided they are in possession of a registration certificate confirming that they are exercising a Treaty right as a student.

10. In addition, where a person has worked legally in the UK without interruption for a 12 month period falling wholly or partly after 31 December 2006, they will be free from the requirement to seek authorisation. At that stage, they will be able to apply to the Home Office for an EEA residence permit to confirm their right to equal treatment on the same basis as other EEA nationals.

12 months' uninterrupted work

11. In order to establish '12 months' uninterrupted work' an A2 worker must have been working legally in the UK at the beginning and end of the 12 month period. The 12 month period does not have to run continuously. However, any intervening period in which an A2 national is not legally working must not exceed 30 days in total. If more than 30 days between periods of employment occur before a 12-month period of uninterrupted employment is established, a fresh period of 12 months' uninterrupted employment would need to commence from that point.

12. There is no restriction on the number of different authorised jobs (or employers) that a worker can have during a 12-month period of continuous employment.

Highly skilled workers

13. A national of an A2 state is not required to be authorised under the worker authorisation scheme, if he is a highly skilled worker who has been given a registration certificate by the Home Office which includes a statement that he or she has unconditional access to the UK labour market.

ANNEX 4

Habitual residence

1. In practice, when considering housing applications from persons subject to the habitual residence test, it is only necessary to investigate habitual residence if the applicant has arrived or returned to live in the UK during the two year period prior to making the application.

Definition of habitual residence

2. The term 'habitual residence' is not defined in legislation. Housing authorities should always consider the overall circumstances of a case to determine whether someone is habitually resident in the Common Travel Area.

General principles

3. When deciding whether a person is habitually resident, consideration must be given to all the facts of each case in a common sense way. It should be remembered that:

- the test focuses on the fact and nature of residence
- a person who is not resident somewhere cannot be habitually resident there
- residence is a more settled state than mere physical presence in a country. To be resident a person must be seen to be making a home. It need not be the only home or a permanent home but it must be a genuine home for the time being. For example, a short stay visitor or person receiving short term medical treatment is not resident
- the most important factors for habitual residence are length, continuity and general nature of actual residence rather than intention
- the practicality of a person's arrangements for residence is a necessary part of determining whether it can be described as settled and habitual
- established habitual residents who have periods of temporary or occasional absence of long or short duration may still be habitually resident during such absences.

Action on receipt of an application

Applicant came to live in the UK during the previous two years

4. If it appears that the applicant came to live in the UK during the previous two years, authorities should make further enquiries to decide if the applicant is habitually resident, or can be treated as such.

Factors to consider

5. The applicant's stated reasons and intentions for coming to the UK will be relevant to the question of whether he or she is habitually resident. If the applicant's stated intention is to live in the UK, and not return to the country from which they came, that intention must be consistent with their actions.

6. To decide whether an applicant is habitually resident in the UK, authorities should consider the factors set out below. However, these do not provide an exhaustive check list of the questions or factors that need to be considered. Further enquiries may be needed. The circumstances of each case will dictate what information is needed, and all relevant factors should be taken into account.

Why has the applicant come to the UK?

7. If the applicant is returning to the UK after a period spent abroad, and it can be established that the applicant was previously habitually resident in the UK and is returning to resume his or her former period of habitual residence, he or she will be immediately habitually resident.

8. In determining whether an applicant is returning to resume a former period of habitual residence authorities should consider:

- when the applicant left the UK
- how long the applicant lived in the UK before leaving
- why the applicant left the UK
- how long the applicant intended to remain abroad
- why the applicant returned
- whether the applicant's partner and children, if any, also left the UK
- whether the applicant kept accommodation in the UK
- if the applicant owned property, whether it was let, and whether the lease was timed to coincide with the applicant's return to the UK
- what links the applicant kept with the UK
- whether there have been other brief absences
- why the applicant has come back to the UK.

9. If the applicant has arrived in the UK within the previous two years and is not resuming a period of habitual residence, consideration should be given to his or her reasons for coming to the UK, and in particular to the factors set out below.

Applicant is joining family or friends

10. If the applicant has come to the UK to join or rejoin family or friends, authorities should consider:

- whether the applicant has sold or given up any property abroad
- whether the applicant has bought or rented accommodation or is staying with friends
- whether the move to the UK is intended to be permanent.

Applicant's plans

11. Authorities should consider the applicant's plans, e.g:

- if the applicant plans to remain in the UK, whether their stated plan is consistent with their actions
- whether any arrangements were made for employment and accommodation (even if unsuccessful) before the applicant arrived in the UK
- whether the applicant bought a one-way ticket
- whether the applicant brought all their belongings
- whether there is evidence of links with the UK, e.g. membership of clubs.

12. The fact that a person may intend to live in the UK for the foreseeable future does not, of itself, mean that habitual residence has been established. However, the applicant's intentions along with other factors, for example the disposal of property abroad, may indicate that the applicant is habitually resident in the UK.

13. An applicant who intends to reside in the UK for only a short period, for example for a holiday or to visit friends is unlikely to be habitually resident in the UK.

Length of residence in another country

14. Authorities should consider the length and continuity of an applicant's residence in another country:

- whether the applicant has any remaining ties with his or her former country of residence
- whether the applicant stayed in different countries outside the UK.

15. It is possible that a person may own a property abroad but still be habitually resident in the UK. A person who has a home or close family in another country would normally retain habitual residence in that country. A person who has previously lived in several different countries but has now moved permanently to the UK may be habitually resident here.

Centre of interest

16. An applicant is likely to be habitually resident in the Common Travel Area despite spending time abroad, if his or her centre of interest is located in one of these places.

17. People who maintain their centre of interest in the Common Travel Area for example a home, a job, friends, membership of clubs, are likely to be habitually resident there. People who have retained their centre of interest in another country and have no particular ties with the Common Travel Area are unlikely to be habitually resident.

18. Authorities should take the following into account when deciding the centre of interest:

- home
- family ties
- club memberships
- finance accounts

19. If the centre of interest appears to be in the Common Travel Area but the applicant has a home somewhere else, authorities should consider the applicant's intentions regarding the property.

20. It is not uncommon for a person to live in one country but have property abroad that they do not intend to sell. Where such a person has lived in the Common Travel Area for many years, the fact that they have property elsewhere does not necessarily mean that they intend to leave, or that the applicant's centre of interest is elsewhere.

PROVIDING SOCIAL HOUSING FOR LOCAL PEOPLE: STATUTORY GUIDANCE ON SOCIAL HOUSING ALLOCATIONS FOR LOCAL AUTHORITIES IN ENGLAND (2013)

A1.3

December 2013 Department for Communities and Local Government

INTRODUCTION

(1) This is guidance by the Secretary of State for Communities and Local Government under section 169 of the Housing Act 1996 (the 1996 Act). Local housing authorities (housing authorities) are required to have regard to it in exercising their functions under Part 6 of the 1996 Act.

(2) It is in addition to the Guidance for Local Housing Authorities in England on the Allocation of Accommodation issued in June 2012 (the 2012 guidance).

(3) References to sections in this guidance are references to sections in the 1996 Act.

(4) Housing authorities are encouraged to review their existing allocation policies and revise them, where appropriate, in the light of this guidance as soon as possible.

PURPOSE OF THE GUIDANCE

(5) Social housing – stable and affordable – is of enormous importance for the millions who live in it now and for those who look to it to provide the support they need in future. The way it is allocated is key to creating communities where people choose to live and are able to prosper.

(6) The Government has made clear that we expect social homes to go to people who genuinely need and deserve them. That is why the Localism Act has maintained the protection provided by the statutory reasonable preference criteria which ensure that priority for social housing continues to be given to those in the greatest housing need.

(7) The Localism Act has also given back to local authorities the freedom to better manage their social housing waiting list, as well as providing authorities with greater flexibility to enable them to tackle homelessness by providing homeless households with suitable private sector accommodation. Local authorities can now decide who qualifies for social housing in their area, and can develop solutions which make best use of the social housing stock. This guidance is intended to assist housing authorities to make full use of the flexibilities within the allocation legislation to better meet the needs of their local residents and their local communities.

(8) The Government has also taken decisive steps to increase the supply of affordable housing, with £19.5 billion of public and private investment in the current Spending Review, and up to £23.3 billion more money invested from 2015 to 2018 alongside receipts from Right to Buy sales.

(9) This investment in new affordable housing will help to meet housing need. We now want to see local authorities take an approach to social housing allocations which gives greater priority to those in need who have invested in and demonstrated a commitment to their local community.

(10) The Prime Minister has made clear the Government's determination to tackle the widespread perception that the way social housing is allocated is unfair, and to address concerns that the system favours households who have little connection to the local area over local people and members of the Armed

Forces. Another important aim of this guidance, therefore, is to encourage authorities to be open and transparent about who is applying for and being allocated social housing in their area.

QUALIFICATION FOR SOCIAL HOUSING

(11) Section 160ZA(6) provides that housing authorities may only allocate accommodation to people who are defined as 'qualifying persons' and section 160ZA(7) gives them the power to decide the classes of people who are, or are not, qualifying persons.

(12) The Government is of the view that, in deciding who qualifies or does not qualify for social housing, local authorities should ensure that they prioritise applicants who can demonstrate a close association with their local area. Social housing is a scarce resource, and the Government believes that it is appropriate, proportionate and in the public interest to restrict access in this way, to ensure that, as far as possible, sufficient affordable housing is available for those amongst the local population who are on low incomes or otherwise disadvantaged and who would find it particularly difficult to find a home on the open market.

(13) Some housing authorities have decided to include a residency requirement as part of their qualification criteria, requiring the applicant (or member of the applicant's household) to have lived within the authority's district for a specified period of time in order to qualify for an allocation of social housing. The Secretary of State believes that including a residency requirement is appropriate and strongly encourages all housing authorities to adopt such an approach. The Secretary of State believes that a reasonable period of residency would be at least two years.

(14) We are aware that in some parts of the country, housing authorities share a common allocation policy with their neighbours and may wish to adopt a broader residency test which would be met if an applicant lives in any of the partners' districts. Such an approach might be particularly appropriate where an established housing market area spans a number of local authority districts, and could help promote labour mobility within a wider geographical area.

(15) Housing authorities may wish to consider whether there is a need to adopt other qualification criteria alongside a residency requirement to enable and ensure that applicants who are not currently resident in the district who can still demonstrate a strong association to the local area are able to qualify. Examples of such criteria might include:

family association – for example, where the applicant has close family who live in the district and who have done so for a minimum period of time employment in the district – for example, where the applicant or member of their household is currently employed in the district and has worked there for a certain number of years

(16) Whatever qualification criteria for social housing authorities adopt, they will need to have regard to their duties under the Equality Act 2010, as well as their duties under other relevant legislation such as s.225 of the Housing Act 2004.

(17) Housing authorities are reminded of the desirability of operating a housing options approach (see paragraph 3.19 of the 2012 guidance) as part of a move to a managed waiting list. In this way, people who have not lived in the area long enough to qualify for social housing can be provided with advice and any necessary support to help them find appropriate alternative solutions.

PROVIDING FOR EXCEPTIONS

(18) Housing authorities should consider the need to provide for exceptions from their residency requirement; and must make an exception for certain members of the regular and reserve Armed Forces – see further at paragraph 23 below.

Providing for appropriate exceptions when framing residency requirements would be in line with paragraphs 3.22 and 3.24 of the 2012 guidance.

(19)   It is important that housing authorities retain the flexibility to take proper account of special circumstances. This can include providing protection to people who need to move away from another area, to escape violence or harm; as well as enabling those who need to return, such as homeless families and care leavers whom the authority have housed outside their district, and those who need support to rehabilitate and integrate back into the community.

(20)   There may also be sound policy reasons not to apply a residency test to existing social tenants seeking to move between local authorities. Housing authorities should assist in tackling under-occupation, for example allowing tenants to move if they wish to downsize to a smaller social home. There may also be sound housing management reasons to disapply a residency test for hard to let stock.

(21)   These examples are not intended to be exhaustive and housing authorities may wish to consider providing for other appropriate exceptions in the light of local circumstances. In addition, authorities retain a discretion to deal with individual cases where there are exceptional circumstances.

(22)   The Government wants to increase opportunities for hardworking households. That is why we have announced an intention to introduce a Right to Move for social tenants seeking to move to take up a job or be closer to their work, whether within the local authority district or across local authority boundaries. We will consult on options for implementing this policy in Spring 2014. In the meantime, we expect housing authorities to make appropriate exceptions to their residency test for social tenants so as not to impede labour market mobility.

MEMBERS OF THE ARMED FORCES

(23)   The Government is committed to ensuring that Service personnel and their families have access to appropriate accommodation when they leave the Armed Forces. The Allocation of Housing (Qualification Criteria for Armed Forces) (England) Regulations 2012 SI 2012/1869) ensure that, where housing authorities decide to use a local connection[1] requirement as a qualification criterion, they must not apply that criterion to the following persons so as to disqualify them from an allocation of social housing:
   (a)   those who are currently serving in the regular forces or who were serving in the regular forces at any time in the five years preceding their application for an allocation of social housing
   (b)   bereaved spouses or civil partners of those serving in the regular forces where (i) the bereaved spouse or civil partner has recently ceased, or will cease to be entitled, to reside in Ministry of Defence accommodation following the death of their service spouse or civil partner, and (ii) the death was wholly or partly attributable to their service
   (c)   existing or former members of the reserve forces who are suffering from a serious injury, illness, or disability which is wholly or partly attributable to their service

(24)   The Regulations give effect to the Government's commitment that those who serve in the regular and reserve Armed Forces are not disadvantaged in their access to social housing by the requirements of their service.

(25)   When adopting a residency test, we expect housing authorities to also consider the wider needs of the Armed Forces community, and to be sympathetic to changing family circumstances, recognising, for example, that the spouses and partners of Service personnel can also be disadvantaged by the need to move from base to base.

---

[1]   As defined by s.199 of the 1996 Act. A person has a local connection with the district of a housing authority if he has a connection because of normal residence there (either current or

previous) of his own choice, employment there, family connections or special circumstances.

PRIORITISING LOCAL CONNECTION

(26) Housing authorities have the ability to take account of any local connection between the applicant and their district when determining relative priorities between households who are on the waiting list (s 166A(5)). For these purposes, local connection is defined by reference to s 199 of the 1996 Act.

(27) Housing authorities should consider whether, in the light of local circumstances, there is a need to take advantage of this flexibility, in addition to applying a residency requirement as part of their qualification criteria. Examples of circumstances in which the power might be useful would include:

- dealing sensitively with lettings in rural villages by giving priority to those with a local connection to the parish, as part of a local lettings policy (section 166A(6)(b) – see paragraph 4.21 of the 2012 guidance)
- where a group of housing authorities apply a wider residency qualification test, to give greater priority to people who live or work (or have close family) in any of the partner authorities' own district

INFORMATION ABOUT ALLOCATIONS

(28) It is important that applicants and the wider community understand how social housing is allocated in their area, and that they know who is getting that social housing, so that they can see that the allocation system is fair and the authority is complying with its allocation scheme. We would encourage housing authorities to consider how accurate and anonymised information on waiting list applicants and lettings outcomes could be routinely published, to strengthen public confidence in the fairness of their allocation scheme.

RIGHT TO MOVE: STATUTORY GUIDANCE ON SOCIAL HOUSING ALLOCATIONS FOR LOCAL HOUSING AUTHORITIES IN ENGLAND (2015)

A1.4

March 2015 Department for Communities and Local Government

INTRODUCTION

(1) This is guidance by the Secretary of State for Communities and Local Government under section 169 of the Housing Act 1996 ('the 1996 Act'). Local housing authorities (housing authorities) are required to have regard to it in exercising their functions under Part 6 of the 1996 Act.

(2) It is in addition to the Guidance for Local Housing Authorities in England on the Allocation of Accommodation issued in June 2012 ('the 2012 guidance').

(3) References to sections in this guidance are references to sections in the 1996 Act.

(4) Housing authorities are encouraged to review their existing allocation policies and revise them, where appropriate, in the light of this guidance as soon as possible.

PURPOSE OF THE GUIDANCE

(5) The Government is committed to increasing mobility for social tenants to enable tenants to meet their aspirations, and to support them into work. We want to ensure that tenants are not prevented from taking up an employment opportunity because they cannot find a suitable place to live, recognising that long term unemployment is damaging for individuals and communities. That is why in the Autumn Statement 2013 we set out our intention to introduce a Right to Move for social tenants who need to move to take up a job or live closer to employment or training.

(6) We've already taken some important steps in the right direction. *HomeSwap Direct* is helping social tenants search for a new home across the country. Through the Localism Act, we have given local authorities the freedom to make better use of the social housing stock by taking transferring tenants who are not in housing need out of the allocation legislation, allowing authorities to develop appropriate policies for transferring tenants, without the risk of challenge from those in greater need on the waiting list.

(7) The Government has also taken decisive steps to increase the supply of affordable housing. The current Affordable Homes Programme is on track to deliver 170,000 homes between 2011 and 2015 with £19.5 billion of public and private investment. A further £38 billion of public and private investment will help deliver another 275,000 new affordable homes between 2015 and 2020.

(8) To give effect to the Right to Move we have introduced regulations to prevent local authorities applying a local connection test that could disadvantage tenants who need to move across local authority boundaries for work related reasons. This guidance is intended to assist local authorities to implement these regulations.

(9) The Government has made clear that we expect social homes to go to people who genuinely need and deserve them. That is why the Localism Act has

maintained the protection provided by the statutory reasonable preference criteria which ensure that priority for social housing continues to be given to those in the greatest housing need.

(10) Another important aim of this guidance, therefore, is to assist local authorities to apply the allocation legislation to ensure that tenants who need to move within or across local authority boundaries are given appropriate priority under local authorities' allocation schemes.

QUALIFICATION

(11) Section 160ZA(7) provides that local authorities may decide who does or does not qualify for an allocation of social housing, subject to any regulations made under subsection 8 which provides that the Secretary of State may prescribe that certain classes of persons are or are not qualifying persons, or that certain criteria cannot be taken into account in deciding who qualifies.

(12) Subject to parliamentary scrutiny, the Allocation of Housing (Qualification Criteria for Right to Move) (England) Regulations 2015 (SI 2015/967) ('the qualification regulations 2015') will come into force on 20 April. These provide that local authorities must not disqualify certain persons on the grounds that they do not have a local connection with the authority's district. Specifically, a local connection may not be applied to existing social tenants seeking to transfer from another local authority district in England who:

- have reasonable preference under s 166(3)(e) because of a need to move to the local authority's district to avoid hardship, and
- need to move because the tenant works in the district, or
- need to move to take up an offer of work

(13) This will ensure that existing tenants who are seeking to move between local authority areas in England in order to be closer to their work, or to take up an offer of work (hereafter referred to together as 'work related reasons'), will not be disadvantaged.

(14) We have made a similar provision for certain members of the Armed Forces community, by regulating to prevent local authorities from applying a local connection requirement to disqualify them,[1] in order to give effect to the Government's commitment that those who serve in the Armed Forces are not disadvantaged in their access to social housing by the need to move from base to base. Aside from members of the Armed Forces and transferring tenants who will benefit from the Right to Move, the Government has made clear that we expect local authorities to ensure that only long standing local residents, or those with a well established local association should qualify for social housing, and has issued statutory guidance to ensure that local authorities apply a residency test to social housing of at least two years.[2]

---

[1] The Allocation of Housing (Qualification Criteria for Armed Forces) (England) Regulations 2012 (SI 2012/1869).

[2] Providing Social Housing for Local People: Statutory guidance on social housing allocations for local authorities in England.

Local connection

(15) Local connection is defined by s 199. A person has a local connection because of normal residence (current or previous) of their own choice, employment, family associations, or special circumstances.

Need to move

(16) The qualification regulations 2015 apply to transferring tenants who have reasonable preference under s 166A(3)(e), that is to say the local authority is

satisfied that they need to move to a particular locality in the district of the housing authority, where failure to meet that need would cause hardship (to themselves or others).

(17) The local authority must ensure, therefore, not simply that the tenant needs to move for work, but that, if they were unable to do so, it would cause them hardship.

(18) Local authorities must be satisfied that the tenant needs, rather than wishes, to move for work related reasons. In the Secretary of State's view the factors that local authorities should take into account in determining whether a tenant needs to move to be closer to work or to take up a job offer include:

- the distance and/or time taken to travel between work and home
- the availability and affordability of transport, taking into account level of earnings
- the nature of the work and whether similar opportunities are available closer to home
- other personal factors, such as medical conditions and child care, which would be affected if the tenant could not move
- the length of the work contract
- whether failure to move would result in the loss of an opportunity to improve their employment circumstances or prospects, for example, by taking up a better job, a promotion, or an apprenticeship

(19) This is not an exhaustive list and local authorities may wish to consider providing for other appropriate factors to take into account in the light of local circumstances.

Work

(20) The qualification regulations 2015 only apply if work is not short-term or marginal in nature, nor ancillary to work in another district. Voluntary work is also excluded.

Short-term

(21) In determining whether work is short-term, the Secretary of State considers that the following are relevant considerations:
- *whether work is regular or intermittent*
This is likely to be particularly relevant in the case of the self-employed.
- *the period of employment and whether or not work was intended to be short-term or long-term at the outset*
In the Secretary of State's view a contract of employment that was intended to last for less than 12 months could be considered to be short-term.

Marginal

(22) The following considerations would be relevant in determining whether work is marginal:
- *the number of hours worked*
In the Secretary of State's view employment of less than 16 hours a week could be considered to be marginal in nature. This is the threshold below which a person may be able to claim Income Support and the threshold for a single person's entitlement to Working Tax Credit.
- *the level of earnings*

(23) Local authorities should take into account all the relevant factors when reaching a decision. The fact that a tenant only works 15 hours a week, for example, may not be determinative if they are able to demonstrate that the work is regular and the remuneration is substantial.

Ancillary

(24) Work must not be ancillary to work in another local authority's district. This means that, if the person works occasionally in the local authority's district, even if the pattern of work is regular, but their main place of work is in a different local authority's district, the work is excluded from the ambit of these regulations.

(25) A further relevant consideration would be whether the tenant is expected eventually to return to work in the original local authority district. If a local authority has reason to believe this is the case, they should seek verification from the tenant's employer.

(26) A person who seeks to move into a local authority to be closer to work in a neighbouring authority – for example, where the transport links are better in the first local authority's area – is also excluded from these regulations. However, there is nothing to prevent local authorities looking sympathetically on tenants seeking to move into their authority's district for this reason, if they choose to do so.

Voluntary work

(27) The regulations exclude voluntary work. Voluntary work means work where no payment is received or the only payment is in respect of any expenses reasonably incurred.

Apprenticeship

(28) The term 'work' includes an apprenticeship. This is because an apprenticeship normally takes place under an apprenticeship agreement which is an employment contract (specifically a contract of service).

Genuine intention to take up an offer of work

(29) Where the tenant has been offered a job and needs to move to take it up, they must be able to demonstrate to the local authority's satisfaction that they have a genuine intention to take up the offer.

(30) Local authorities may wish to ask to see a letter of acceptance and may wish to contact the employer to verify the position. Authorities may also wish to seek clarification from the tenant by interviewing them over the telephone or in person.

Verification and evidence

(31) Local authorities will want to satisfy themselves that the work or job-offer is genuine and should seek appropriate documentary evidence.

(32) Appropriate evidence could include:
- a contract of employment
- wage/salary slips covering a certain period of time, or bank statements (this is likely to be particularly relevant in the case of zero-hours contracts)
- tax and benefits information – eg proof that the applicant is in receipt of working tax credit (if eligible)
- a formal offer letter

(33) Additionally, local authorities may wish to contact the employer to verify the position.

(34)   Authorities are strongly advised to consider whether an applicant qualifies for an allocation under the qualification regulations 2015 both at the time of the initial application and when considering making an allocation.

PRIORITISATION

(35)   The qualification regulations will ensure that tenants who need to move between local authority districts for work related reasons are not disadvantaged by a local connection test. However, to deliver the Right to Move, it is also important that tenants who need to move for work, within or across local authority boundaries, are given appropriate priority under local authorities' allocation schemes.

Hardship reasonable preference

(36)   Section 166A(3) provides that housing authorities must frame their allocation scheme to ensure that reasonable preference is given to people who need to move to a particular locality in the authority's district, where failure to meet that need would cause hardship (to themselves or others).

(37)   Paragraph 4.11 of the 2012 guidance sets out the Secretary of State's view that 'hardship' would include, for example, a person who needs to move to a different locality to take up a particular employment, education or training opportunity.

(38)   This guidance goes further and strongly encourages all local authorities to apply the hardship reasonable preference category to tenants who are seeking to transfer and who need to move within the local authority district or from another local authority district to be closer to work, or to take up an offer of work.

(39)   In considering whether a transferring tenant needs to move for work related reasons to avoid hardship to themselves (or others), they may wish to take account of the guidance set out in paragraphs 16 to 34 above.

(40)   Where a tenant is seeking to move within the same local authority district, local authorities are encouraged to take a more flexible approach. This is because the tenant is already accommodated in the district and any move to another social home will therefore be broadly stock neutral (that is to say the transfer creates another void which can be used to meet other housing needs). In particular, local authorities should consider whether or not the issue of whether work is short-term, marginal, ancillary or voluntary carries the same weight in relation to a within district move.

Setting aside a proportion of lets for cross-boundary moves

(41)   In framing their allocation scheme to determine their allocation priorities, local authorities will wish to strike a balance between the interests of transferring tenants who need to move into their district for work related reasons and the demand from other applicants in identified housing need.

(42)   The Secretary of State considers that an appropriate way to do so would be for a local authority to set a quota for the proportion of properties that it expects to allocate each year to transferring tenants who need to move into their district for work related reasons ('the Right to Move quota'). The Secretary of State strongly encourages all local authorities to adopt such an approach and considers that an appropriate quota would be at least 1%.

(43)   Local authorities should publish the quota as part of their allocation scheme, together with their rationale for adopting the specific percentage. They should review and revise the proportion as appropriate, in the light of changing circumstances.

(44)   Local authorities may wish to set aside a higher proportion than 1%. Authorities that decide to set a quota that is lower than 1%, should be ready to explain publicly why they have chosen to do so.

(45)   It is important that local authorities are open and accountable, to their own tenants and the wider community as well as to tenants seeking to move into the area for work related reasons. Accordingly, local authorities are encouraged to report locally on demand for and lettings outcomes in relation to the Right to Move quota.

Area based choice based lettings schemes

We are aware that in some parts of the country, local authorities participate in area-based choice based lettings schemes that bring together a number of authorities and Private Registered Providers of social housing, often with a common allocation policy that applies to all the partner local authorities.

We consider that such schemes provide an excellent basis for cross-boundary mobility, particularly as housing and employment markets are likely to be similar across the partner authorities. Accordingly, we strongly encourage all local authorities that participate in area-based choice based lettings schemes to consider how they can provide for tenants to move between partner authorities for work related reasons, for example, by providing for a quota of lettings to be made available for this group.

LOCAL AUTHORITIES (CONTRACTING OUT OF ALLOCATION OF HOUSING AND HOMELESS-NESS FUNCTIONS) ORDER 1996

SI 1996/3205

A1.5

1 Citation, commencement and interpretation

(1)   This Order may be cited as the Local Authorities (Contracting Out of Allocation of Housing and Homelessness Functions) Order 1996.

(2)   This article and article 3 of this Order shall come into force on 20th January 1997 and article 2 of this Order shall come into force on 1st April 1997.

(3)   In this Order—

"the Act" means the Housing Act 1996;

"an authority" means a local housing authority as defined in the Housing Act 1985.

(4)   Any expressions used in this Order which are also used in the Act have the same meaning as they have in the Act.

2 Contracting out of allocation of housing functions

Any function of an authority which is conferred by or under Part VI of the Act (allocation of housing accommodation), except one which is listed in Schedule 1 to this Order, may be exercised by, or by employees of, such person (if any) as may be authorised in that behalf by the authority whose function it is.

3 Contracting out of homelessness functions

Any function of an authority which is conferred by or under Part VII of the Act (homelessness) [or Chapter 2 of Part 2 of the Housing (Wales) Act 2014 (help for people who are homeless or threatened with homelessness)], except one which is listed in Schedule 2 to this Order, may be exercised by, or by employees of, such person (if any) as may be authorised in that behalf by the authority whose function it is.

NOTES

Amendment

Words from "or Chapter 2" to "threatened with homelessness)" in square brackets inserted, in relation to Wales, by SI 2015/752, reg 2(1), (2).

Date in force: 27 April 2015: see SI 2015/752, reg 1.

SCHEDULE 1

ALLOCATION OF HOUSING FUNCTIONS OF A LOCAL HOUSING AUTHORITY EXCLUDED FROM CONTRACTING OUT

Article 2

Functions conferred by or under any of the following provisions of the Act:

(a)   section 161(4) (classes of persons qualifying for allocations);

(b)   section 162 (the housing register) so far as they relate to any decision about the form of the register;

(c)   section 167 (allocation in accordance with allocation scheme) so far as they relate to adopting or altering an allocation scheme (including decisions on what principles the scheme is to be framed) and to the functions in subsection (7) of that section;

(d) section 168(2) (information about allocation scheme) so far as they relate to making the allocation scheme available for inspection at the authority's principal office.

SCHEDULE 2

HOMELESSNESS FUNCTIONS OF A LOCAL HOUSING AUTHORITY
EXCLUDED FROM CONTRACTING OUT

Article 3

Functions conferred by or under any of the following provisions of the Act:

(a) section 179(2) and (3) (duty of local housing authority to provide advisory services);
(b) section 180 (assistance for voluntary organisations);
(c) section 213 (co-operation between relevant housing authorities and bodies).

[Functions conferred by or under section 95 of the Housing (Wales) Act 2014.]

NOTES

Amendment

Words from "Functions conferred by" to "Housing (Wales) Act 2014." in square brackets inserted, in relation to Wales, by SI 2015/752, reg 2(1), (3).
Date in force: 27 April 2015: see SI 2015/752, reg 1.

ALLOCATION OF HOUSING (PROCEDURE) REGULATIONS 1997

SI 1997/483

A1.6

1 Citation and commencement

These Regulations may be cited as the Allocation of Housing (Procedure) Regulations 1997 and shall come into force on 1st April 1997.

2 Interpretation

In these Regulations—

"allocation decision" means a decision to allocate housing accommodation;

"authority" means a local housing authority in England;

"decision-making body" means an authority or a committee or sub-committee of an authority.

3 Allocation scheme procedure

(1) As regards the procedure to be followed, an authority's allocation scheme shall be framed in accordance with the principle prescribed in this regulation.

(2) A member of an authority who has been elected for the electoral division or ward in which—

(a) the housing accommodation in relation to which an allocation decision falls to be made is situated, or

(b) the person in relation to whom that decision falls to be made has his sole or main residence,

shall not, at the time the allocation decision is made, be included in the persons constituting the decision-making body.

ALLOCATION OF HOUSING (ENGLAND) REGULATIONS 2002

SI 2002/3264

A1.7

1 Citation, commencement and application
(1) These Regulations may be cited as the Allocation of Housing (England) Regulations 2002 and shall come into force on 31st January 2003.
(2) These Regulations apply in England only.

2 Interpretation
In these Regulations—
  "the Act" means the Housing Act 1996;
  "the Common Travel Area" means the United Kingdom, the Channel Islands, the Isle of Man and the Republic of Ireland collectively; and
  ["family intervention tenancy"—

  (a)   in relation to a tenancy granted by a local housing authority, has the meaning given by paragraph 4ZA(3) of Schedule 1 to the Housing Act 1985;

  (b)   in relation to a tenancy granted by a registered social landlord [or a private registered provider of social housing], has the meaning given by paragraph 12ZA(3) of Part 1 of Schedule 1 to the Housing Act 1988;]

  "the immigration rules" means the rules laid down as mentioned in section 3(2) of the Immigration Act 1971 (general provisions for regulation and control).

NOTES

Amendment

Definition "family intervention tenancy" inserted by SI 2008/3015, reg 2(1), (2).
  Date in force: 1 January 2009: see SI 2008/3015, reg 1(1).
In definition "family intervention tenancy" in para (b) words "or a private registered provider of social housing" in square brackets inserted by SI 2010/671, art 4, Sch 1, para 29.
  Date in force: 1 April 2010 (being the date on which the Housing and Regeneration Act 2008, s 111 came into force): see SI 2010/671, art 1(2), and SI 2010/862, art 2; for transitional provisions and savings see SI 2010/671, art 5, Sch 2, paras 1, 2, 5, 6 and SI 2010/862, arts 2, 3, Schedule, paras 1–5.

3 Cases where the provisions of Part 6 of the Act do not apply
(1) The provisions of Part 6 of the Act about the allocation of housing accommodation do not apply in the following cases.
(2) They do not apply where a local housing authority secures the provision of suitable alternative accommodation under section 39 of the Land Compensation Act 1973 (duty to rehouse residential occupiers).
(3) They do not apply in relation to the grant of a secure tenancy under sections 554 and 555 of the Housing Act 1985 (grant of tenancy to former owner-occupier or statutory tenant of defective dwelling-house).
[(4) They do not apply in relation to the allocation of housing accommodation by a local housing authority to a person who lawfully occupies accommodation let on a family intervention tenancy.]

NOTES

Amendment

Para (4): inserted by SI 2008/3015, reg 2(1), (3).

Date in force: 1 January 2009: see SI 2008/3015, reg 1(1).

4, 5 . . .

. . .

NOTES

Amendment

Revoked by SI 2006/1294, reg 7, Schedule.
Date in force: 1 June 2006: see SI 2006/1294, reg 1(1); for transitional provisions see reg 8 thereof.

6 Revocation

The Allocation of Housing (England) Regulations 2000 are revoked.

ALLOCATION OF HOUSING (QUALIFICATION CRITERIA FOR ARMED FORCES) (ENGLAND) REGULATIONS 2012

SI 2012/1869

A1.8

1 Citation and commencement
(1) These Regulations may be cited as the Allocation of Housing (Qualification Criteria for Armed Forces) (England) Regulations 2012.
(2) These Regulations come into force on 24th August 2012.

2 Interpretation
In these Regulations—
"the 1996 Act" means the Housing Act 1996;
"local connection" has the meaning given by section 199 of the 1996 Act; and
"regular forces" and "reserve forces" have the meanings given by section 374 of the Armed Forces Act 2006.

3 Criterion that may not be used in deciding what classes of persons are not qualifying persons
(1) In deciding what classes of persons are not qualifying persons under section 160ZA(7) of the 1996 Act, a local housing authority in England may not use the criterion set out in paragraph (2).
(2) The criterion is that a relevant person must have a local connection to the district of a local housing authority.
(3) A relevant person is a person who—
    (a)   is serving in the regular forces or who has served in the regular forces within five years of the date of their application for an allocation of housing under Part 6 of the 1996 Act;
    (b)   has recently ceased, or will cease to be entitled, to reside in accommodation provided by the Ministry of Defence following the death of that person's spouse or civil partner where—
        (i)   the spouse or civil partner has served in the regular forces; and
        (ii)   their death was attributable (wholly or partly) to that service; or
    (c)   is serving or has served in the reserve forces and who is suffering from a serious injury, illness or disability which is attributable (wholly or partly) to that service.

HOUSING ACT 1996 (ADDITIONAL PREFERENCE FOR ARMED FORCES) (ENGLAND) REGULATIONS 2012

SI 2012/2989

A1.9

1 Citation and commencement

These Regulations may be cited as the Housing Act 1996 (Additional Preference for Armed Forces) (England) Regulations 2012 and come into force on the day after the day on which they are made.

2 Amendment of section 166A(3) of the Housing Act 1996

Section 166A(3) of the Housing Act 1996 (Allocation in accordance with allocation scheme: England) is amended as follows—

(a) in the sentence following the end of paragraph (e) (beginning with "The scheme may also be framed") for "people within this subsection" substitute "people within one or more of paragraphs (a) to (e)";

(b) at the end of that sentence, insert—

"The scheme must be framed so as to give additional preference to a person with urgent housing needs who falls within one or more of paragraphs (a) to (e) and who—

(i) is serving in the regular forces and is suffering from a serious injury, illness or disability which is attributable (wholly or partly) to the person's service,

(ii) formerly served in the regular forces,

(iii) has recently ceased, or will cease to be entitled, to reside in accommodation provided by the Ministry of Defence following the death of that person's spouse or civil partner who has served in the regular forces and whose death was attributable (wholly or partly) to that service, or

(iv) is serving or has served in the reserve forces and is suffering from a serious injury, illness or disability which is attributable (wholly or partly) to the person's service.

For this purpose "the regular forces" and "the reserve forces" have the meanings given by section 374 of the Armed Forces Act 2006.".

ALLOCATION OF HOUSING (QUALIFICATION CRITERIA FOR RIGHT TO MOVE) (ENGLAND) REGULATIONS 2015

SI 2015/967

A1.10

1 Citation, commencement and application

(1) These Regulations may be cited as the Allocation of Housing (Qualification Criteria for Right to Move) (England) Regulations 2015.

(2) These Regulations come into force on 20th April 2015.

(3) These Regulations apply in relation to England only.

2 Interpretation

Any reference in these Regulations to a section is a reference to a section of the Housing Act 1996.

3 Criterion that may not be used in deciding what classes of persons are not qualifying persons

(1) In deciding whether a person is a qualifying person under section 160ZA(7), a local housing authority may not use the criterion set out in paragraph (2) if the allocation involves a transfer of housing accommodation for that person from the district of another local housing authority in England.

(2) The criterion is that a relevant person must have a local connection with the district of the local housing authority.

(3) In this regulation "local connection" has the meaning given by section 199.

4 Relevant person

For the purposes of regulation 3, a relevant person is a person who—

    (a)   falls within section 159(4A)(a) or (b),

    (b)   is to be given reasonable preference under section 166A(3)(e), and

    (c)   has a need to move falling within regulation 5(1).

5 Need to move

(1) Subject to paragraph (2), for the purposes of regulation 4, a relevant person has a need to move because the relevant person—

    (a)   works in the district of the local housing authority, or

    (b)

        (i)   has been offered work in the district of the local housing authority, and

        (ii)   the authority is satisfied that the relevant person has a genuine intention of taking up the offer of work.

(2) This regulation does not apply if the need to move is associated with work or the offer of work which is—

    (a)   short-term or marginal in nature,

    (b)   ancillary to work in another district, or

    (c)   voluntary work.

(3) In this regulation "voluntary work" means work where no payment is received by the relevant person or the only payment due to be made to the relevant person by virtue of being so engaged is a payment in respect of any expenses reasonably incurred by the relevant person in the course of being so engaged.

Appendix 2

ENGLAND: HOMELESSNESS

Contents

Statutes

Statutory Guidance

Regulations and Orders

England: Homelessness

HOUSING ACT 1996

PART VII
HOMELESSNESS[: ENGLAND]

Homelessness and threatened homelessness

A2.1

175 Homelessness and threatened homelessness

(1)   A person is homeless if he has no accommodation available for his occupation, in the United Kingdom or elsewhere, which he—

(a)   is entitled to occupy by virtue of an interest in it or by virtue of an order of a court,

(b)   has an express or implied licence to occupy, or

(c)   occupies as a residence by virtue of any enactment or rule of law giving him the right to remain in occupation or restricting the right of another person to recover possession.

(2)   A person is also homeless if he has accommodation but—

(a)   he cannot secure entry to it, or

(b)   it consists of a moveable structure, vehicle or vessel designed or adapted for human habitation and there is no place where he is entitled or permitted both to place it and to reside in it.

(3)   A person shall not be treated as having accommodation unless it is accommodation which it would be reasonable for him to continue to occupy.

(4)   A person is threatened with homelessness if it is likely that he will become homeless within [56] days.

[(5)   A person is also threatened with homelessness if—

(a)   a valid notice has been given to the person under section 21 of the Housing Act 1988 (orders for possession on expiry or termination of assured shorthold tenancy) in respect of the only accommodation the person has that is available for the person's occupation, and

(b)   that notice will expire within 56 days.]

NOTES

Amendment

Part heading: word ": England" in square brackets inserted, in relation to Wales, by the Housing (Wales) Act 2014, s 100, Sch 3, Pt 1, paras 2, 4.

Date in force: 27 April 2015: see SI 2015/1272, art 2, Schedule, paras 51, 53; for a transitional provision, see art 7.

Sub-s (4): reference to "56" in square brackets substituted by the Homelessness Reduction Act 2017, s 1(1), (2).

Date in force: 3 April 2018: see SI 2018/167, reg 3(a); for transitional and savings provisions see reg 4(1).

Sub-s (5): inserted by the Homelessness Reduction Act 2017, s 1(1), (3).

Date in force: 3 April 2018: see SI 2018/167, reg 3(a); for transitional and savings provisions see reg 4(1).

176 Meaning of accommodation available for occupation

Accommodation shall be regarded as available for a person's occupation only if it is available for occupation by him together with—

(a)   any other person who normally resides with him as a member of his family, or

(b)   any other person who might reasonably be expected to reside with him.

References in this Part to securing that accommodation is available for a person's occupation shall be construed accordingly.

177 Whether it is reasonable to continue to occupy accommodation

(1) It is not reasonable for a person to continue to occupy accommodation if it is probable that this will lead to domestic violence [or other violence] against him, or against—

(a) a person who normally resides with him as a member of his family, or

(b) any other person who might reasonably be expected to reside with him.

[(1A) For this purpose "violence" means—

(a) violence from another person; or

(b) threats of violence from another person which are likely to be carried out;

and violence is "domestic violence" if it is from a person who is associated with the victim.]

(2) In determining whether it would be, or would have been, reasonable for a person to continue to occupy accommodation, regard may be had to the general circumstances prevailing in relation to housing in the district of the local housing authority to whom he has applied for accommodation or for assistance in obtaining accommodation.

(3) The Secretary of State may by order specify—

(a) other circumstances in which it is to be regarded as reasonable or not reasonable for a person to continue to occupy accommodation, and

(b) other matters to be taken into account or disregarded in determining whether it would be, or would have been, reasonable for a person to continue to occupy accommodation.

NOTES

Amendment

Sub-s (1): words "or other violence" in square brackets inserted by the Homelessness Act 2002, s 10(1)(a).
Date in force (in relation to England): 31 July 2002: see SI 2002/1799, art 2.
Date in force (in relation to Wales): 30 September 2002: see SI 2002/1736, art 2(1), Schedule, Pt 1.
Sub-s (1A) substituted, for sub-s (1) proviso as originally enacted, by the Homelessness Act 2002, s 10(1)(b).
Date in force (in relation to England): 31 July 2002: see SI 2002/1799, art 2.
Date in force (in relation to Wales): 30 September 2002: see SI 2002/1736, art 2(1), Schedule, Pt 1.

178 Meaning of associated person

(1) For the purposes of this Part, a person is associated with another person if—

(a) they are or have been married to each other;

[(aa) they are or have been civil partners of each other;]

(b) they are cohabitants or former cohabitants;

(c) they live or have lived in the same household;

(d) they are relatives;

(e) they have agreed to marry one another (whether or not that agreement has been terminated);

[(ea) they have entered into a civil partnership agreement between them (whether or not that agreement has been terminated);]

(f) in relation to a child, each of them is a parent of the child or has, or has had, parental responsibility for the child.

(2) If a child has been adopted or [falls within subsection (2A)], two persons are also associated with each other for the purposes of this Part if—

(a) one is a natural parent of the child or a parent of such a natural parent, and

(b)   the other is the child or a person—

    (i)   who has become a parent of the child by virtue of an adoption order or who has applied for an adoption order, or

    (ii)   with whom the child has at any time been placed for adoption.

[(2A)   A child falls within this subsection if—

(a)   an adoption agency, within the meaning of section 2 of the Adoption and Children Act 2002, is authorised to place him for adoption under section 19 of that Act (placing children with parental consent) or he has become the subject of an order under section 21 of that Act (placement orders), or

(b)   he is freed for adoption by virtue of an order made—

    (i)   in England and Wales, under section 18 of the Adoption Act 1976,

    (ii)   in Scotland, under section 18 of the Adoption (Scotland) Act 1978, or

    (iii)   in Northern Ireland, under Article 17(1) or 18(1) of the Adoption (Northern Ireland) Order 1987.]

(3)   In this section—

["adoption order" means an adoption order within the meaning of section 72(1) of the Adoption Act 1976 or section 46(1) of the Adoption and Children Act 2002;]

"child" means a person under the age of 18 years;

["civil partnership agreement" has the meaning given by section 73 of the Civil Partnership Act 2004;]

["cohabitants" means—

(a)   a man and a woman who, although not married to each other, are living together as husband and wife, or

(b)   two people of the same sex who, although not civil partners of each other, are living together as if they were civil partners;

and "former cohabitants" shall be construed accordingly;]

"parental responsibility" has the same meaning as in the Children Act 1989; and

"relative", in relation to a person, means—

(a)   the father, mother, stepfather, stepmother, son, daughter, stepson, stepdaughter, grandmother, grandfather, grandson or granddaughter of that person or of that person's [spouse, civil partner, former spouse or former civil partner], or

(b)   the brother, sister, uncle, aunt, niece or nephew (whether of the full blood or of the half blood or by [marriage or civil partnership]) of that person or of that person's [spouse, civil partner, former spouse or former civil partner],

and includes, in relation to a person who is living or has lived with another person as husband and wife, a person who would fall within paragraph (a) or (b) if the parties were married to each other.

NOTES

Amendment

Sub-s (1): para (aa) inserted by the Civil Partnership Act 2004, s 81, Sch 8, para 61(1), (2).
Date in force: 5 December 2005: see SI 2005/3175, art 2(1), Sch 1.
Sub-s (1): para (ea) inserted by the Civil Partnership Act 2004, s 81, Sch 8, para 61(1), (3).
Date in force: 5 December 2005: see SI 2005/3175, art 2(1), Sch 1.
Sub-s (2): words "falls within subsection (2A)" in square brackets substituted by the Adoption and Children Act 2002, s 139(1), Sch 3, paras 89, 90.
Date in force: 30 December 2005: see SI 2005/2213, art 2(o).
Sub-s (2A): inserted by the Adoption and Children Act 2002, s 139(1), Sch 3, paras 89, 91.
Date in force: 30 December 2005: see SI 2005/2213, art 2(o).

Sub-s (3): definition "adoption order" substituted by the Adoption and Children Act 2002,
s 139(1), Sch 3, paras 89, 92.
　　　　Date in force: 30 December 2005: see SI 2005/2213, art 2(o).
Sub-s (3): definition "civil partnership agreement" inserted by the Civil Partnership Act 2004,
s 81, Sch 8, para 61(1), (4).
　　　　Date in force: 5 December 2005: see SI 2005/3175, art 2(1), Sch 1.
Sub-s (3): definition "cohabitants" substituted by the Civil Partnership Act 2004, s 81, Sch
8, para 61(1), (5).
　　　　Date in force: 5 December 2005: see SI 2005/3175, art 2(1), Sch 1.
Sub-s (3): in definition "relative" in paras (a), (b) words "spouse, civil partner, former spouse
or former civil partner" in square brackets substituted by the Civil Partnership Act 2004,
s 81, Sch 8, para 61(1), (6).
　　　　Date in force: 5 December 2005: see SI 2005/3175, art 2(1), Sch 1.
Sub-s (3): in definition "relative" in para (b) words "marriage or civil partnership" in square
brackets substituted by the Civil Partnership Act 2004, s 81, Sch 8, para 61(1), (7).
　　　　Date in force: 5 December 2005: see SI 2005/3175, art 2(1), Sch 1.

General functions in relation to homelessness or threatened homelessness

[179 Duty of local housing authority in England to provide advisory services]

[(1)　Each local housing authority in England must provide or secure the provision of
a service, available free of charge to any person in the authority's district, providing
information and advice on—

(a)　preventing homelessness,

(b)　securing accommodation when homeless,

(c)　the rights of persons who are homeless or threatened with homelessness,
and the duties of the authority, under this Part,

(d)　any help that is available from the authority or anyone else, whether
under this Part or otherwise, for persons in the authority's district who
are homeless or may become homeless (whether or not they are
threatened with homelessness), and

(e)　how to access that help.

(2)　The service must be designed to meet the needs of persons in the
authority's district including, in particular, the needs of—

(a)　persons released from prison or youth detention accommodation,

(b)　care leavers,

(c)　former members of the regular armed forces,

(d)　victims of domestic abuse,

(e)　persons leaving hospital,

(f)　persons suffering from a mental illness or impairment, and

(g)　any other group that the authority identify as being at particular risk of
homelessness in the authority's district.

(3)　The authority may give to any person by whom the service is provided on behalf
of the authority assistance by way of grant or loan.

(4)　The authority may also assist any such person—

(a)　by permitting the person to use premises belonging to the authority,

(b)　by making available furniture or other goods, whether by way of gift,
loan or otherwise, and

(c)　by making available the services of staff employed by the authority.

(5)　In this section—

"care leavers" means persons who are former relevant children (within the
meaning given by section 23C(1) of the Children Act 1989);

"domestic abuse" means—

(a)　physical violence,

(b)　threatening, intimidating, coercive or controlling behaviour, or

(c)　emotional, financial, sexual or any other form of abuse,
　　　where the victim is associated with the abuser;

"financial abuse" includes—

(a)   having money or other property stolen,

(b)   being defrauded,

(c)   being put under pressure in relation to money or other property, and

(d)   having money or other property misused;

"hospital" has the same meaning as in the National Health Service Act 2006 (see section 275(1) of that Act);

"regular armed forces" means the regular forces as defined by section 374 of the Armed Forces Act 2006;

"youth detention accommodation" means—

(a)   a secure children's home,

(b)   a secure training centre,

(c)   a secure college,

(d)   a young offender institution,

(e)   accommodation provided by or on behalf of a local authority for the purpose of restricting the liberty of children;

(f)   accommodation provided for that purpose under section 82(5) of the Children Act 1989, or

(g)   accommodation, or accommodation of a description, for the time being specified by order under section 107(1)(e) of the Powers of Criminal Courts (Sentencing) Act 2000 (youth detention accommodation for the purposes of detention and training orders).]

NOTES

Amendment

Substituted by the Homelessness Reduction Act 2017, s 2.
     Date in force: 3 April 2018: see SI 2018/167, reg 3(b).

180 Assistance for voluntary organisations

(1)   The Secretary of State or a local housing authority [in England] may give assistance by way of grant or loan to voluntary organisations concerned with homelessness or matters relating to homelessness.

(2)   A local housing authority may also assist any such organisation—

(a)   by permitting them to use premises belonging to the authority,

(b)   by making available furniture or other goods, whether by way of gift, loan or otherwise, and

(c)   by making available the services of staff employed by the authority.

(3)   A "voluntary organisation" means a body (other than a public or local authority) whose activities are not carried on for profit.

NOTES

Amendment

Sub-s (1): words "in England" in square brackets inserted, in relation to Wales, by the Housing (Wales) Act 2014, s 100, Sch 3, Pt 1, paras 2, 6.
     Date in force: 27 April 2015: see SI 2015/1272, art 2, Schedule, paras 51, 53; for a transitional provision, see art 7.

181 Terms and conditions of assistance

(1)   This section has effect as to the terms and conditions on which assistance is given under section 179 or 180.

(2)   Assistance shall be on such terms, and subject to such conditions, as the person giving the assistance may determine.

(3)   No assistance shall be given unless the person to whom it is given undertakes—

(a)   to use the money, furniture or other goods or premises for a specified purpose, and

(b)   to provide such information as may reasonably be required as to the manner in which the assistance is being used.

The person giving the assistance may require such information by notice in writing, which shall be complied with within 21 days beginning with the date on which the notice is served.

(4)   The conditions subject to which assistance is given shall in all cases include conditions requiring the person to whom the assistance is given—

(a)   to keep proper books of account and have them audited in such manner as may be specified,

(b)   to keep records indicating how he has used the money, furniture or other goods or premises, and

(c)   to submit the books of account and records for inspection by the person giving the assistance.

(5)   If it appears to the person giving the assistance that the person to whom it was given has failed to carry out his undertaking as to the purpose for which the assistance was to be used, he shall take all reasonable steps to recover from that person an amount equal to the amount of the assistance.

(6)   He must first serve on the person to whom the assistance was given a notice specifying the amount which in his opinion is recoverable and the basis on which that amount has been calculated.

182 Guidance by the Secretary of State

(1)   In the exercise of their functions relating to homelessness and the prevention of homelessness, a local housing authority or social services authority [in England] shall have regard to such guidance as may from time to time be given by the Secretary of State.

(2)   The Secretary of State may give guidance either generally or to specified descriptions of authorities.

NOTES

Amendment

Sub-s (1): words "in England" in square brackets inserted, in relation to Wales, by the Housing (Wales) Act 2014, s 100, Sch 3, Pt 1, paras 2, 7.
        Date in force: 27 April 2015: see SI 2015/1272, art 2, Schedule, paras 51, 53; for a transitional provision, see art 7.

Application for assistance in case of homelessness or threatened homelessness

183 Application for assistance

(1)   The following provisions of this Part apply where a person applies to a local housing authority [in England] for accommodation, or for assistance in obtaining accommodation, and the authority have reason to believe that he is or may be homeless or threatened with homelessness.

(2)   In this Part—

"applicant" means a person making such an application,

"assistance under this Part" means the benefit of any function under the following provisions of this Part relating to accommodation or assistance in obtaining accommodation, and

"eligible for assistance" means not excluded from such assistance by section 185 (persons from abroad not eligible for housing assistance) *or section 186 (asylum seekers and their dependants).*

(3) Nothing in this section or the following provisions of this Part affects a person's entitlement to advice and information under section 179 (duty to provide advisory services).

NOTES

Amendment

> Sub-s (1): words "in England" in square brackets inserted, in relation to Wales, by the Housing (Wales) Act 2014, s 100, Sch 3, Pt 1, paras 2, 8.
> Date in force: 27 April 2015: see SI 2015/1272, art 2, Schedule, paras 51, 53; for a transitional provision, see art 7.
> Sub-s (2): in definition "eligible for assistance" words "or section 186 (asylum seekers and their dependants)" in italics repealed by the Immigration and Asylum Act 1999, s 169(1), (3), Sch 14, para 116, Sch 16.
> Date in force: to be appointed: see the Immigration and Asylum Act 1999, s 170(4).

184 Inquiry into cases of homelessness or threatened homelessness

(1) If the local housing authority have reason to believe that an applicant may be homeless or threatened with homelessness, they shall make such inquiries as are necessary to satisfy themselves—

(a) whether he is eligible for assistance, and

(b) if so, whether any duty, and if so what duty, is owed to him under the following provisions of this Part.

(2) They may also make inquiries whether he has a local connection with the district of another local housing authority in England, Wales or Scotland.

(3) On completing their inquiries the authority shall notify the applicant of their decision and, so far as any issue is decided against his interests, inform him of the reasons for their decision.

[(3A) If the authority decide that a duty is[, or after the authority's duty to the applicant under section 189B(2) comes to an end would be,] owed to the applicant under section 193(2) . . . but would not have done so without having had regard to a restricted person, the notice under subsection (3) must also—

(a) inform the applicant that their decision was reached on that basis,

(b) include the name of the restricted person,

(c) explain why the person is a restricted person, and

(d) explain the effect of section 193(7AD) . . ..]

(4) If the authority have notified or intend to notify another local housing authority [in England under section 198(A1) (referral of cases where section 189B applies)], they shall at the same time notify the applicant of that decision and inform him of the reasons for it.

(5) A notice under subsection (3) or (4) shall also inform the applicant of his right to request a review of the decision and of the time within which such a request must be made (see section 202).

(6) Notice required to be given to a person under this section shall be given in writing and, if not received by him, shall be treated as having been given to him if it is made available at the authority's office for a reasonable period for collection by him or on his behalf.

[(7) In this Part "a restricted person" means a person—

(a) who is not eligible for assistance under this Part,

(b) who is subject to immigration control within the meaning of the Asylum and Immigration Act 1996, and

(c) either—

(i) who does not have leave to enter or remain in the United Kingdom, or

(ii) whose leave to enter or remain in the United Kingdom is subject to a condition to maintain and accommodate himself, and any dependants, without recourse to public funds.]

NOTES

Amendment

> Sub-s (3A): inserted by the Housing and Regeneration Act 2008, s 314, Sch 15, Pt 1, paras 1, 3(1), (2).
>> Date in force: 2 March 2009 (except in relation to applications for an allocation of social housing or housing assistance (homelessness) or for accommodation made before that date): see SI 2009/415, art 2.
> Sub-s (3A): words from ", or after the" to "end would be," in square brackets inserted by the Homelessness Reduction Act 2017, s 5(1), (3)(a).
>> Date in force: 3 April 2018: see SI 2018/167, reg 3(e); for transitional and savings provisions see reg 4(1).
> Sub-s (3A): words omitted repealed by the Homelessness Reduction Act 2017, s 4(1), (3)(a).
>> Date in force: 3 April 2018: see SI 2018/167, reg 3(d); for transitional and savings provisions see reg 4(1).
> Sub-s (3A): in para (d) words omitted repealed by the Homelessness Reduction Act 2017, s 4(1), (3)(b).
>> Date in force: 3 April 2018: see SI 2018/167, reg 3(d); for transitional and savings provisions see reg 4(1).
> Sub-s (4): words "in England under section 198(A1) (referral of cases where section 189B applies)" in square brackets substituted by the Homelessness Reduction Act 2017, s 5(1), (3)(b).
>> Date in force: 3 April 2018: see SI 2018/167, reg 3(e); for transitional and savings provisions see reg 4(1).
> Sub-s (7): inserted by the Housing and Regeneration Act 2008, s 314, Sch 15, Pt 1, paras 1, 3(1), (3).
>> Date in force: 2 March 2009 (except in relation to applications for an allocation of social housing or housing assistance (homelessness) or for accommodation made before that date): see SI 2009/415, art 2.

Eligibility for assistance

185 Persons from abroad not eligible for housing assistance

(1) A person is not eligible for assistance under this Part if he is a person from abroad who is ineligible for housing assistance.

(2) A person who is subject to immigration control within the meaning of the Asylum and Immigration Act 1996 is not eligible for housing assistance unless he is of a class prescribed by regulations made by the Secretary of State.

[(2A) No person who is excluded from entitlement to [universal credit or] housing benefit by section 115 of the Immigration and Asylum Act 1999 (exclusion from benefits) shall be included in any class prescribed under subsection (2).]

(3) The Secretary of State may make provision by regulations as to other descriptions of persons who are to be treated for the purposes of this Part as persons from abroad who are ineligible for housing assistance.

(4) A person from abroad who is not eligible for housing assistance shall be disregarded in determining for the purposes of this Part whether [a person falling within subsection (5)]—

> (a) is homeless or threatened with homelessness, or
> (b) has a priority need for accommodation.

[(5) A person falls within this subsection if the person—

> (a) falls within a class prescribed by regulations made under subsection (2); but
> (b) is not a national of an EEA State or Switzerland.]

NOTES

Amendment

> Sub-s (2A) (inserted by the Immigration and Asylum Act 1999, s 117(4)): substituted by the Homelessness Act 2002, s 18(1), Sch 1, paras 2, 7(1).
>> Date in force: 26 February 2002: see the Homelessness Act 2002, s 18(1), Sch 1, para 7(2).

Sub-s (2A): words "universal credit or" in square brackets inserted by SI 2013/630, reg 12(1), (5).

Date in force: 29 April 2013: see SI 2013/630, reg 1(2).

Sub-s (4): words "a person falling within subsection (5)" in square brackets substituted by the Housing and Regeneration Act 2008, s 314, Sch 15, Pt 1, paras 1, 4(1), (2).

Date in force: 2 March 2009 (except in relation to applications for an allocation of social housing or housing assistance (homelessness) or for accommodation made before that date): see SI 2009/415, art 2.

Sub-s (5): inserted by the Housing and Regeneration Act 2008, s 314, Sch 15, Pt 1, paras 1, 4(1), (3).

Date in force: 2 March 2009 (except in relation to applications for an allocation of social housing or housing assistance (homelessness) or for accommodation made before that date): see SI 2009/415, art 2.

186 *Asylum-seekers and their dependants*

(1)   An asylum-seeker, or a dependant of an asylum-seeker who is not by virtue of section 185 a person from abroad who is ineligible for housing assistance, is not eligible for assistance under this Part if he has any accommodation in the United Kingdom, however temporary, available for his occupation.

(2)   For the purposes of this section a person who makes a claim for asylum—

 (a)   becomes an asylum-seeker at the time when his claim is recorded by the Secretary of State as having been made, and

 (b)   ceases to be an asylum-seeker at the time when his claim is recorded by the Secretary of State as having been finally determined or abandoned.

(3)   For the purposes of this section a person—

 (a)   becomes a dependant of an asylum-seeker at the time when he is recorded by the Secretary of State as being a dependant of the asylum-seeker, and

 (b)   ceases to be a dependant of an asylum-seeker at the time when the person whose dependant he is ceases to be an asylum-seeker or, if it is earlier, at the time when he is recorded by the Secretary of State as ceasing to be a dependant of the asylum-seeker.

(4)   In relation to an asylum-seeker, "dependant" means a person—

 (a)   who is his spouse or a child of his under the age of eighteen, and

 (b)   who has neither a right of abode in the United Kingdom nor indefinite leave under the Immigration Act 1971 to enter or remain in the United Kingdom.

(5)   In this section a "claim for asylum" means a claim made by a person that it would be contrary to the United Kingdom's obligations under the Convention relating to the Status of Refugees done at Geneva on 28th July 1951 and the Protocol to that Convention for him to be removed from, or required to leave, the United Kingdom.

NOTES

Amendment

Repealed by the Immigration and Asylum Act 1999, ss 117(5), 169(3), Sch 16.

Date in force: to be appointed: see the Immigration and Asylum Act 1999, s 170(4).

187 Provision of information by Secretary of State

(1)   The Secretary of State shall, at the request of a local housing authority [in England], provide the authority with such information as they may require—

 (a)   as to whether a person is [a person to whom section 115 of the Immigration and Asylum Act 1999 (exclusion from benefits) applies], and

 (b)   to enable them to determine whether such a person is eligible for assistance under this Part under section 185 (persons from abroad not eligible for housing assistance).

(2)   Where that information is given otherwise than in writing, the Secretary of State shall confirm it in writing if a written request is made to him by the authority.

(3) If it appears to the Secretary of State that any application, decision or other change of circumstances has affected the status of a person about whom information was previously provided by him to a local housing authority under this section, he shall inform the authority in writing of that fact, the reason for it and the date on which the previous information became inaccurate.

NOTES

Amendment

> Sub-s (1): words "in England" in square brackets inserted, in relation to Wales, by the Housing (Wales) Act 2014, s 100, Sch 3, Pt 1, paras 2, 9.
> Date in force: 27 April 2015: see SI 2015/1272, art 2, Schedule, paras 51, 53; for a transitional provision, see art 7.
> Sub-s (1): in para (a) words from "a person to" to "from benefits) applies" in square brackets substituted by the Immigration and Asylum Act 1999, s 117(6).
> Date in force: 3 April 2000: see SI 2000/464, art 2, Schedule.

Interim duty to accommodate

188 Interim duty to accommodate in case of apparent priority need

[(1) If the local housing authority have reason to believe that an applicant may be homeless, eligible for assistance and have a priority need, they must secure that accommodation is available for the applicant's occupation.

(1ZA) In a case in which the local housing authority conclude their inquiries under section 184 and decide that the applicant does not have a priority need—

    (a)   where the authority decide that they do not owe the applicant a duty under section 189B(2), the duty under subsection (1) comes to an end when the authority notify the applicant of that decision, or

    (b)   otherwise, the duty under subsection (1) comes to an end upon the authority notifying the applicant of their decision that, upon the duty under section 189B(2) coming to an end, they do not owe the applicant any duty under section 190 or 193.

(1ZB) In any other case, the duty under subsection (1) comes to an end upon the later of—

    (a)   the duty owed to the applicant under section 189B(2) coming to an end or the authority notifying the applicant that they have decided that they do not owe the applicant a duty under that section, and

    (b)   the authority notifying the applicant of their decision as to what other duty (if any) they owe to the applicant under the following provisions of this Part upon the duty under section 189B(2) coming to an end.]

[(1A) But if the local housing authority have reason to believe that the duty under section 193(2) may apply in relation to an applicant in the circumstances referred to in section 195A(1), they shall secure that accommodation is available for the applicant's occupation [until the later of paragraph (a) or (b) of subsection (1ZB)] regardless of whether the applicant has a priority need.]

(2) The duty under this section arises irrespective of any possibility of the referral of the applicant's case to another local housing authority (see sections 198 to 200).

[(2A) For the purposes of this section, where the applicant requests a review under section 202(1)(h) of the authority's decision as to the suitability of accommodation offered to the applicant by way of a final accommodation offer or a final Part 6 offer (within the meaning of section 193A), the authority's duty to the applicant under section 189B(2) is not to be taken to have come to an end under section 193A(2) until the decision on the review has been notified to the applicant.]

(3) Otherwise, the duty under this section comes to an end in accordance with subsections (1ZA) to (1A), regardless of any review requested by the applicant under section 202.

But the authority may secure that accommodation is available for the applicant's occupation pending a decision on review.]

NOTES

Amendment

> Sub-ss (1), (1ZA), (1ZB): substituted, for sub-s (1) as originally enacted, by the Homelessness Reduction Act 2017, s 5(1), (4)(a).
>> Date in force: 3 April 2018: see SI 2018/167, reg 3(e); for transitional and savings provisions see reg 4(1).
> Sub-s (1A): inserted by the Localism Act 2011, s 149(1), (2).
>> Date in force (in relation to England): 9 November 2012: see SI 2012/2599, art 2; for transitional provisions see art 3 thereof.
> Sub-s (1A): words "until the later of paragraph (a) or (b) of subsection (1ZB)" in square brackets substituted by the Homelessness Reduction Act 2017, s 5(1), (4)(b).
>> Date in force: 3 April 2018: see SI 2018/167, reg 3(e); for transitional and savings provisions see reg 4(1).
> Sub-ss (2A), (3): substituted, for sub-s (3) as originally enacted, by the Homelessness Reduction Act 2017, s 5(1), (4)(c).
>> Date in force: 3 April 2018: see SI 2018/167, reg 3(e); for transitional and savings provisions see reg 4(1).

189 Priority need for accommodation

(1) The following have a priority need for accommodation—

    (a)   a pregnant woman or a person with whom she resides or might reasonably be expected to reside;

    (b)   a person with whom dependent children reside or might reasonably be expected to reside;

    (c)   a person who is vulnerable as a result of old age, mental illness or handicap or physical disability or other special reason, or with whom such a person resides or might reasonably be expected to reside;

    (d)   a person who is homeless or threatened with homelessness as a result of an emergency such as flood, fire or other disaster.

(2) The Secretary of State may by order—

    (a)   specify further descriptions of persons as having a priority need for accommodation, and

    (b)   amend or repeal any part of subsection (1).

(3) Before making such an order the Secretary of State shall consult such associations representing relevant authorities, and such other persons, as he considers appropriate.

(4) No such order shall be made unless a draft of it has been approved by resolution of each House of Parliament.

[Duty to assess every eligible applicant's case and agree a plan]

[189A Assessments and personalised plan]

[(1) If the local housing authority are satisfied that an applicant is—

    (a)   homeless or threatened with homelessness, and

    (b)   eligible for assistance,

the authority must make an assessment of the applicant's case.

(2) The authority's assessment of the applicant's case must include an assessment of—

    (a)   the circumstances that caused the applicant to become homeless or threatened with homelessness,

    (b)   the housing needs of the applicant including, in particular, what accommodation would be suitable for the applicant and any persons with whom the applicant resides or might reasonably be expected to reside ("other relevant persons"), and

(c)   what support would be necessary for the applicant and any other relevant persons to be able to have and retain suitable accommodation.

(3)   The authority must notify the applicant, in writing, of the assessment that the authority make.

(4)   After the assessment has been made, the authority must try to agree with the applicant—

(a)   any steps the applicant is to be required to take for the purposes of securing that the applicant and any other relevant persons have and are able to retain suitable accommodation, and

(b)   the steps the authority are to take under this Part for those purposes.

(5)   If the authority and the applicant reach an agreement, the authority must record it in writing.

(6)   If the authority and the applicant cannot reach an agreement, the authority must record in writing—

(a)   why they could not agree,

(b)   any steps the authority consider it would be reasonable to require the applicant to take for the purposes mentioned in subsection (4)(a), and

(c)   the steps the authority are to take under this Part for those purposes.

(7)   The authority may include in a written record produced under subsection (5) or (6) any advice for the applicant that the authority consider appropriate (including any steps the authority consider it would be a good idea for the applicant to take but which the applicant should not be required to take).

(8)   The authority must give to the applicant a copy of any written record produced under subsection (5) or (6).

(9)   Until such time as the authority consider that they owe the applicant no duty under any of the following sections of this Part, the authority must keep under review—

(a)   their assessment of the applicant's case, and

(b)   the appropriateness of any agreement reached under subsection (4) or steps recorded under subsection (6)(b) or (c).

(10)   If—

(a)   the authority's assessment of any of the matters mentioned in subsection (2) changes, or

(b)   the authority's assessment of the applicant's case otherwise changes such that the authority consider it appropriate to do so,

the authority must notify the applicant, in writing, of how their assessment of the applicant's case has changed (whether by providing the applicant with a revised written assessment or otherwise).

(11)   If the authority consider that any agreement reached under subsection (4) or any step recorded under subsection (6)(b) or (c) is no longer appropriate—

(a)   the authority must notify the applicant, in writing, that they consider the agreement or step is no longer appropriate,

(b)   any failure, after the notification is given, to take a step that was agreed to in the agreement or recorded under subsection (6)(b) or (c) is to be disregarded for the purposes of this Part, and

(c)   subsections (4) to (8) apply as they applied after the assessment was made.

(12)   A notification under this section or a copy of any written record produced under subsection (5) or (6), if not received by the applicant, is to be treated as having been given to the applicant if it is made available at the authority's office for a reasonable period for collection by or on behalf of the applicant.]

NOTES

Amendment

> Inserted by the Homelessness Reduction Act 2017, s 3(1).
> Date in force: 3 April 2018: see SI 2018/167, reg 3(c).

Duties to persons found to be homeless or threatened with homelessness

[189B Initial duty owed to all eligible persons who are homeless]

[(1)   This section applies where the local housing authority are satisfied that an applicant is—

(a)   homeless, and

(b)   eligible for assistance.

(2)   Unless the authority refer the application to another local housing authority in England (see section 198(A1)), the authority must take reasonable steps to help the applicant to secure that suitable accommodation becomes available for the applicant's occupation for at least—

(a)   6 months, or

(b)   such longer period not exceeding 12 months as may be prescribed.

(3)   In deciding what steps they are to take, the authority must have regard to their assessment of the applicant's case under section 189A.

(4)   Where the authority—

(a)   are satisfied that the applicant has a priority need, and

(b)   are not satisfied that the applicant became homeless intentionally,

the duty under subsection (2) comes to an end at the end of the period of 56 days beginning with the day the authority are first satisfied as mentioned in subsection (1).

(5)   If any of the circumstances mentioned in subsection (7) apply, the authority may give notice to the applicant bringing the duty under subsection (2) to an end.

(6)   The notice must—

(a)   specify which of the circumstances apply, and

(b)   inform the applicant that the applicant has a right to request a review of the authority's decision to bring the duty under subsection (2) to an end and of the time within which such a request must be made.

(7)   The circumstances are that the authority are satisfied that—

(a)   the applicant has—

  (i)   suitable accommodation available for occupation, and

  (ii)   a reasonable prospect of having suitable accommodation available for occupation for at least 6 months, or such longer period not exceeding 12 months as may be prescribed, from the date of the notice,

(b)   the authority have complied with the duty under subsection (2) and the period of 56 days beginning with the day that the authority are first satisfied as mentioned in subsection (1) has ended (whether or not the applicant has secured accommodation),

(c)   the applicant has refused an offer of suitable accommodation and, on the date of refusal, there was a reasonable prospect that suitable accommodation would be available for occupation by the applicant for at least 6 months or such longer period not exceeding 12 months as may be prescribed,

(d)   the applicant has become homeless intentionally from any accommodation that has been made available to the applicant as a result of the authority's exercise of their functions under subsection (2),

(e)   the applicant is no longer eligible for assistance, or

(f)   the applicant has withdrawn the application mentioned in section 183(1).

(8)   A notice under this section must be given in writing and, if not received by the applicant, is to be treated as having been given to the applicant if it is made available at the authority's office for a reasonable period for collection by or on behalf of the applicant.

(9)   The duty under subsection (2) can also be brought to an end under—

    (a)   section 193A (consequences of refusal of final accommodation offer or final Part 6 offer at the initial relief stage), or

    (b)   sections 193B and 193C (notices in cases of applicant's deliberate and unreasonable refusal to co-operate).]

NOTES

Amendment

> Inserted by the Homelessness Reduction Act 2017, s 5(1), (2).
> Date in force: 3 April 2018: see SI 2018/167, reg 3(e); for transitional and savings provisions see reg 4(1).

190 Duties to persons becoming homeless intentionally

[(1)   This section applies where—

    (a)   the local housing authority are satisfied that an applicant—

        (i)   is homeless and eligible for assistance, but

        (ii)   became homeless intentionally,

    (b)   the authority are also satisfied that the applicant has a priority need, and

    (c)   the authority's duty to the applicant under section 189B(2) has come to an end.]

(2)   [The authority must—]

    (a)   secure that accommodation is available for his occupation for such period as they consider will give him a reasonable opportunity of securing accommodation for his occupation, and

    (b)   provide him with [(or secure that he is provided with) advice and assistance] in any attempts he may make to secure that accommodation becomes available for his occupation.

(3)   . . .

[[(4)   In deciding what advice and assistance is to be provided under this section, the authority must have regard to their assessment of the applicant's case under section 189A.]

(5)   The advice and assistance provided under subsection (2)(b) . . . must include information about the likely availability in the authority's district of types of accommodation appropriate to the applicant's housing needs (including, in particular, the location and sources of such types of accommodation).]

NOTES

Amendment

> Sub-s (1): substituted by the Homelessness Reduction Act 2017, s 5(1), (5)(a).
> Date in force: 3 April 2018: see SI 2018/167, reg 3(e); for transitional and savings provisions see reg 4(1).
> Sub-s (2): words from "The authority must—" in square brackets substituted by the Homelessness Reduction Act 2017, s 5(1), (5)(b).
> Date in force: 3 April 2018: see SI 2018/167, reg 3(e); for transitional and savings provisions see reg 4(1).
> Sub-s (2): in para (b) words "(or secure that he is provided with) advice and assistance" in square brackets substituted by the Homelessness Act 2002, s 18(1), Sch 1, paras 2, 9.
> Date in force (in relation to England): 31 July 2002: see SI 2002/1799, art 2.
> Date in force (in relation to Wales): 30 September 2002: see SI 2002/1736, art 2(1), Schedule, Pt 1.
> Sub-s (3): repealed by the Homelessness Reduction Act 2017, s 5(1), (5)(c).
> Date in force: 3 April 2018: see SI 2018/167, reg 3(e); for transitional and savings provisions see reg 4(1).
> Sub-ss (4), (5): inserted by the Homelessness Act 2002, s 18(1), Sch 1, paras 2, 10.

Date in force (in relation to England): 31 July 2002: see SI 2002/1799, art 2.
Date in force (in relation to Wales): 30 September 2002: see SI 2002/1736, art 2(1),
Schedule, Pt 1.
Sub-s (4): substituted by the Homelessness Reduction Act 2017, s 3(2).
Date in force: 3 April 2018: see SI 2018/167, reg 3(c).
Sub-s (5): words omitted repealed by the Homelessness Reduction Act 2017, s 5(1), (5)(d).
Date in force: 3 April 2018: see SI 2018/167, reg 3(e); for transitional and savings
provisions see reg 4(1).

191 Becoming homeless intentionally

(1)   A person becomes homeless intentionally if he deliberately does or fails to do anything in consequence of which he ceases to occupy accommodation which is available for his occupation and which it would have been reasonable for him to continue to occupy.

(2)   For the purposes of subsection (1) an act or omission in good faith on the part of a person who was unaware of any relevant fact shall not be treated as deliberate.

(3)   A person shall be treated as becoming homeless intentionally if—

    (a)   he enters into an arrangement under which he is required to cease to occupy accommodation which it would have been reasonable for him to continue to occupy, and

    (b)   the purpose of the arrangement is to enable him to become entitled to assistance under this Part,

and there is no other good reason why he is homeless.

(4)   . . .

NOTES

Amendment

Sub-s (4): repealed by the Homelessness Act 2002, s 18(2), Sch 2.
Date in force (in relation to England): 31 July 2002: see SI 2002/1799, art 2.
Date in force (in relation to Wales): 30 September 2002: see SI 2002/1736, art 2(1),
Schedule, Pt 1.

192 . . .

. . .

NOTES

Amendment

Repealed by the Homelessness Reduction Act 2017, s 5(1), (6).
Date in force: 3 April 2018: see SI 2018/167, reg 3(e); for transitional and savings
provisions see reg 4(1).

193 Duty to persons with priority need who are not homeless intentionally

[(1)   This section applies where—

    (a)   the local housing authority—

        (i)   are satisfied that an applicant is homeless and eligible for assistance, and

        (ii)   are not satisfied that the applicant became homeless intentionally,

    (b)   the authority are also satisfied that the applicant has a priority need, and

    (c)   the authority's duty to the applicant under section 189B(2) has come to an end.]

[(1A)   But this section does not apply if—

    (a)   section 193A(3) disapplies this section, or

    (b)   the authority have given notice to the applicant under section 193B(2).]

(2)   Unless the authority refer the application to another local housing authority (see section 198), they shall secure that accommodation is available for occupation by the applicant.

[(3)   The authority are subject to the duty under this section until it ceases by virtue of any of the following provisions of this section.]

[(3A) . . .]

[(3B) In this section "a restricted case" means a case where the local housing authority would not be satisfied as mentioned in subsection (1) without having had regard to a restricted person.]

[(5) The local housing authority shall cease to be subject to the duty under this section if—

    (a)   the applicant, having been informed by the authority of the possible consequence of refusal or acceptance and of the right to request a review of the suitability of the accommodation, refuses an offer of accommodation which the authority are satisfied is suitable for the applicant,

    (b)   that offer of accommodation is not an offer of accommodation under Part 6 or a private rented sector offer, and

    (c)   the authority notify the applicant that they regard themselves as ceasing to be subject to the duty under this section.]

(6) The local housing authority shall cease to be subject to the duty under this section if the applicant—

    (a)   ceases to be eligible for assistance,

    (b)   becomes homeless intentionally from the accommodation made available for his occupation,

    (c)   accepts an offer of accommodation under Part VI (allocation of housing), or

    [(cc)   accepts an offer of an assured tenancy (other than an assured shorthold tenancy) from a private landlord,]

    (d)   otherwise voluntarily ceases to occupy as his only or principal home the accommodation made available for his occupation.

[(7) The local housing authority shall also cease to be subject to the duty under this section if the applicant, having been informed of the possible consequence of refusal [or acceptance] and of his right to request a review of the suitability of the accommodation, refuses a final offer of accommodation under Part 6.

(7A) An offer of accommodation under Part 6 is a final offer for the purposes of subsection (7) if it is made in writing and states that it is a final offer for the purposes of subsection (7).]

[(7AA) . . . The authority shall also cease to be subject to the duty under this section if the applicant, having been informed [in writing] of the matters mentioned in subsection (7AB)—

    (a)   accepts a [private rented sector offer], or

    (b)   refuses such an offer.

(7AB) The matters are—

    (a)   the possible consequence of refusal [or acceptance] of the offer, and

    (b)   that the applicant has the right to request a review of the suitability of the accommodation[, and

    (c)   in a case which is not a restricted case, the effect under section 195A of a further application to a local housing authority within two years of acceptance of the offer].

(7AC) For the purposes of this section an offer is a [private rented sector offer] if—

    (a)   it is an offer of an assured shorthold tenancy made by a private landlord to the applicant in relation to any accommodation which is, or may become, available for the applicant's occupation,

    (b)   it is made, with the approval of the authority, in pursuance of arrangements made by the authority with the landlord with a view to bringing the authority's duty under this section to an end, and

    (c)   the tenancy being offered is a fixed term tenancy (within the meaning of Part 1 of the Housing Act 1988) for a period of at least 12 months.

(7AD)   In a restricted case the authority shall, so far as reasonably practicable, bring their duty under this section to an end as mentioned in subsection (7AA).]

[(7B)–(7E)   . . .]

(7F)   The local housing authority shall not—

   (a)   make a final offer of accommodation under Part 6 for the purposes of subsection (7); [or]

   [(ab)   approve a [private rented sector offer];] or

   (b)   . . .,

unless they are satisfied that the accommodation is suitable for the applicant and that [subsection (8) does not apply to the applicant].]

[(8)   This subsection applies to an applicant if—

   (a)   the applicant is under contractual or other obligations in respect of the applicant's existing accommodation, and

   (b)   the applicant is not able to bring those obligations to an end before being required to take up the offer.]

(9)   A person who ceases to be owed the duty under this section may make a fresh application to the authority for accommodation or assistance in obtaining accommodation.

[(10)   The [Secretary of State] may provide by regulations that subsection (7AC)(c) is to have effect as if it referred to a period of the length specified in the regulations.

(11)   Regulations under subsection (10)—

   (a)   may not specify a period of less than 12 months, and

   (b)   may not apply to restricted cases.

(12)   . . .]

NOTES

Amendment

   Sub-s (1): substituted by the Homelessness Reduction Act 2017, s 5(1), (7).
      Date in force: 3 April 2018: see SI 2018/167, reg 3(e); for transitional and savings provisions see reg 4(1).
   Sub-s (1A): inserted by the Homelessness Reduction Act 2017, s 7(2).
      Date in force: 3 April 2018: see SI 2018/167, reg 3(g).
   Sub-s (3): substituted, for sub-ss (3), (4) as originally enacted, by the Homelessness Act 2002, s 6(1); for effect see s 6(2) thereof.
      Date in force (in relation to England): 31 July 2002: see SI 2002/1799, art 2.
      Date in force (in relation to Wales): 30 September 2002: see SI 2002/1736, art 2(1), Schedule, Pt 1.
   Sub-s (3A): inserted by the Homelessness Act 2002, s 18(1), Sch 1, paras 2, 13.
      Date in force (in relation to Wales): 30 September 2002: see SI 2002/1736, art 2(1), Schedule, Pt 1.
      Date in force (in relation to England): 31 January 2003: by virtue of SI 2002/3114, art 3.
   Sub-s (3A): repealed by the Localism Act 2011, ss 148(1), (2), 237, Sch 25, Pt 22.
      Date in force (in relation to England): 9 November 2012: see SI 2012/2599, art 2; for transitional provisions see art 3 thereof.
   Sub-s (3B): inserted by the Housing and Regeneration Act 2008, s 314, Sch 15, Pt 1, paras 1, 5(1), (3).
      Date in force: 2 March 2009 (except in relation to applications for an allocation of social housing or housing assistance (homelessness) or for accommodation made before that date): see SI 2009/415, art 2.
   Sub-s (5): substituted by the Localism Act 2011, s 148(1), (3).
      Date in force (in relation to England): 9 November 2012: see SI 2012/2599, art 2; for transitional provisions see art 3 thereof.
   Sub-s (6): para (cc) inserted by the Homelessness Act 2002, s 7(1), (2); for effect see s 7(6) thereof.
      Date in force (in relation to England): 31 July 2002: see SI 2002/1799, art 2.
      Date in force (in relation to Wales): 30 September 2002: see SI 2002/1736, art 2(1), Schedule, Pt 1.
   Sub-ss (7), (7A): substituted, for sub-s (7) as originally enacted, by the Homelessness Act 2002, s 7(1), (3); for effect see s 7(6) thereof.
      Date in force (in relation to England): 31 July 2002: see SI 2002/1799, art 2.

Date in force (in relation to Wales): 30 September 2002: see SI 2002/1736, art 2(1), Schedule, Pt 1.

Sub-s (7): words "or acceptance" in square brackets inserted by the Localism Act 2011, s 148(1), (4).

Date in force (in relation to England): 9 November 2012: see SI 2012/2599, art 2; for transitional provisions see art 3 thereof.

Sub-ss (7AA)–(7AD): inserted by the Housing and Regeneration Act 2008, s 314, Sch 15, Pt 1, paras 1, 5(1), (4).

Date in force: 2 March 2009 (except in relation to applications for an allocation of social housing or housing assistance (homelessness) or for accommodation made before that date): see SI 2009/415, art 2.

Sub-s (7AA): words "In a restricted case" in italics repealed by the Localism Act 2011, ss 148(1), (5)(a), 237, Sch 25, Pt 22.

Date in force (in relation to England): 9 November 2012: see SI 2012/2599, art 2; for transitional provisions see art 3 thereof.

Sub-s (7AA): words "in writing" in square brackets inserted by the Localism Act 2011, s 148(1), (5)(b).

Date in force (in relation to England): 9 November 2012: see SI 2012/2599, art 2; for transitional provisions see art 3 thereof.

Sub-s (7AA): in para (a) words "private rented sector offer" in square brackets substituted by the Localism Act 2011, s 148(1), (5)(c).

Date in force (in relation to England): 9 November 2012: see SI 2012/2599, art 2; for transitional provisions see art 3 thereof.

Sub-s (7AB): in para (a) words "or acceptance" in square brackets inserted by the Localism Act 2011, s 148(1), (6)(a).

Date in force (in relation to England): 9 November 2012: see SI 2012/2599, art 2; for transitional provisions see art 3 thereof.

Sub-s (7AB): para (c) and word ", and" immediately preceding it inserted by the Localism Act 2011, s 148(1), (6)(b).

Date in force (in relation to England): 9 November 2012: see SI 2012/2599, art 2; for transitional provisions see art 3 thereof.

Sub-s (7AC): words "private rented sector offer" in square brackets substituted by the Localism Act 2011, s 148(1), (7).

Date in force (in relation to England): 9 November 2012: see SI 2012/2599, art 2; for transitional provisions see art 3 thereof.

Sub-ss (7B)–(7F): inserted by the Homelessness Act 2002, s 7(1), (4); for effect see s 7(6) thereof.

Date in force (in relation to England): 31 July 2002: see SI 2002/1799, art 2.
Date in force (in relation to Wales): 30 September 2002: see SI 2002/1736, art 2(1), Schedule, Pt 1.

Sub-ss (7B)–(7E): repealed by the Localism Act 2011, ss 148(1), (8), 237, Sch 25, Pt 22.

Date in force (in relation to England): 9 November 2012: see SI 2012/2599, art 2; for transitional provisions see art 3 thereof.

Sub-s (7F): in para (a) word "or" in square brackets inserted by the Localism Act 2011, s 148(1), (9)(a).

Date in force (in relation to England): 9 November 2012: see SI 2012/2599, art 2; for transitional provisions see art 3 thereof.

Sub-s (7F): para (ab) inserted by the Housing and Regeneration Act 2008, s 314, Sch 15, Pt 1, paras 1, 5(1), (6).

Date in force: 2 March 2009 (except in relation to applications for an allocation of social housing or housing assistance (homelessness) or for accommodation made before that date): see SI 2009/415, art 2.

Sub-s (7F): in para (ab) words "private rented sector offer" in square brackets substituted by the Localism Act 2011, s 148(1), (9)(b).

Date in force (in relation to England): 9 November 2012: see SI 2012/2599, art 2; for transitional provisions see art 3 thereof.

Sub-s (7F): para (b) repealed by the Localism Act 2011, ss 148(1), (9)(c), 237, Sch 25, Pt 22.

Date in force (in relation to England): 9 November 2012: see SI 2012/2599, art 2; for transitional provisions see art 3 thereof.

Sub-s (7F): words "subsection (8) does not apply to the applicant" in square brackets substituted by the Localism Act 2011, s 148(1), (9)(d).

Date in force (in relation to England): 9 November 2012: see SI 2012/2599, art 2; for transitional provisions see art 3 thereof.

Sub-s (8): substituted by the Localism Act 2011, s 148(1), (10).

Date in force (in relation to England): 9 November 2012: see SI 2012/2599, art 2; for transitional provisions see art 3 thereof.

Sub-ss (10)–(12): inserted by the Localism Act 2011, s 148(1), (11).

Date in force (in relation to England): 9 November 2012: see SI 2012/2599, art 2; for transitional provisions see art 3 thereof.

Sub-s (10): words "Secretary of State" in square brackets substituted, in relation to Wales, by the Housing (Wales) Act 2014, s 100, Sch 3, Pt 1, paras 2, 10(a).
> Date in force: 27 April 2015: see SI 2015/1272, art 2, Schedule, paras 51, 53; for a transitional provision, see art 7.

Sub-s (12): repealed, in relation to Wales, by the Housing (Wales) Act 2014, s 100, Sch 3, Pt 1, paras 2, 10(b).
> Date in force: 27 April 2015: see SI 2015/1272, art 2, Schedule, paras 51, 53; for a transitional provision see art 7.

[193A Consequences of refusal of final accommodation offer or final Part 6 offer at the initial relief stage]

[(1) Subsections (2) and (3) apply where—

    (a)   a local housing authority owe a duty to an applicant under section 189B(2), and

    (b)   the applicant, having been informed of the consequences of refusal and of the applicant's right to request a review of the suitability of the accommodation, refuses—

        (i)   a final accommodation offer, or

        (ii)   a final Part 6 offer.

(2) The authority's duty to the applicant under section 189B(2) comes to an end.

(3) Section 193 (the main housing duty) does not apply.

(4) An offer is a "final accommodation offer" if—

    (a)   it is an offer of an assured shorthold tenancy made by a private landlord to the applicant in relation to any accommodation which is, or may become, available for the applicant's occupation,

    (b)   it is made, with the approval of the authority, in pursuance of arrangements made by the authority in the discharge of their duty under section 189B(2), and

    (c)   the tenancy being offered is a fixed term tenancy (within the meaning of Part 1 of the Housing Act 1988) for a period of at least 6 months.

(5) A "final Part 6 offer" is an offer of accommodation under Part 6 (allocation of housing) that—

    (a)   is made in writing by the authority in the discharge of their duty under section 189B(2), and

    (b)   states that it is a final offer for the purposes of this section.

(6) The authority may not approve a final accommodation offer, or make a final Part 6 offer, unless they are satisfied that the accommodation is suitable for the applicant and that subsection (7) does not apply.

(7) This subsection applies to an applicant if—

    (a)   the applicant is under contractual or other obligations in respect of the applicant's existing accommodation, and

    (b)   the applicant is not able to bring those obligations to an end before being required to take up the offer.]

NOTES

Amendment

> Inserted by the Homelessness Reduction Act 2017, s 7(1).
> > Date in force: 3 April 2018: see SI 2018/167, reg 3(g).

[193B Notices in cases of an applicant's deliberate and unreasonable refusal to co-operate]

[(1) Section 193C applies where—

    (a)   a local housing authority owe a duty to an applicant under section 189B(2) or 195(2), and

    (b)   the authority give notice to the applicant under subsection (2).

(2) A local housing authority may give a notice to an applicant under this subsection if the authority consider that the applicant has deliberately and unreasonably refused to take any step—

(a)   that the applicant agreed to take under subsection (4) of section 189A, or

(b)   that was recorded by the authority under subsection (6)(b) of that section.

(3)   A notice under subsection (2) must—

(a)   explain why the authority are giving the notice and its effect, and

(b)   inform the applicant that the applicant has a right to request a review of the authority's decision to give the notice and of the time within which such a request must be made.

(4)   The authority may not give notice to the applicant under subsection (2) unless—

(a)   the authority have given a relevant warning to the applicant, and

(b)   a reasonable period has elapsed since the warning was given.

(5)   A "relevant warning" means a notice—

(a)   given by the authority to the applicant after the applicant has deliberately and unreasonably refused to take any step—

(i)   that the applicant agreed to take under subsection (4) of section 189A, or

(ii)   that was recorded by the authority under subsection (6)(b) of that section,

(b)   that warns the applicant that, if the applicant should deliberately and unreasonably refuse to take any such step after receiving the notice, the authority intend to give notice to the applicant under subsection (2), and

(c)   that explains the consequences of such a notice being given to the applicant.

(6)   For the purposes of subsections (2) and (5), in deciding whether a refusal by the applicant is unreasonable, the authority must have regard to the particular circumstances and needs of the applicant (whether identified in the authority's assessment of the applicant's case under section 189A or not).

(7)   The Secretary of State may make provision by regulations as to the procedure to be followed by a local housing authority in connection with notices under this section.

(8)   A notice under this section must be given in writing and, if not received by the applicant, is to be treated as having been given to the applicant if it is made available at the authority's office for a reasonable period for collection by or on behalf of the applicant.]

NOTES

Amendment

> Inserted by the Homelessness Reduction Act 2017, s 7(1).
>> Date in force (for certain purposes): 12 February 2018: see SI 2018/167, reg 2(a).
>> Date in force (for remaining purposes): 3 April 2018: see SI 2018/167, reg 3(g).

[193C Notice under section 193B: consequences]

[(1)   In the circumstances mentioned in section 193B(1), this section applies in relation to a local housing authority and an applicant.

(2)   The authority's duty to the applicant under section 189B(2) or 195(2) comes to an end.

(3)   Subsection (4) applies if the authority—

(a)   are satisfied that the applicant is homeless, eligible for assistance and has a priority need, and

(b)   are not satisfied that the applicant became homeless intentionally.

(4)   Section 193 (the main housing duty) does not apply, but the authority must secure that accommodation is available for occupation by the applicant.

(5) The authority cease to be subject to the duty under subsection (4) if the applicant—

    (a)   ceases to be eligible for assistance,

    (b)   becomes homeless intentionally from accommodation made available for the applicant's occupation,

    (c)   accepts an offer of an assured tenancy from a private landlord, or

    (d)   otherwise voluntarily ceases to occupy, as the applicant's only or principal home, the accommodation made available for the applicant's occupation.

(6) The authority also cease to be subject to the duty under subsection (4) if the applicant, having been informed of the possible consequences of refusal or acceptance and of the applicant's right to request a review of the suitability of the accommodation, refuses or accepts—

    (a)   a final accommodation offer, or

    (b)   a final Part 6 offer.

(7) An offer is "a final accommodation offer" if—

    (a)   it is an offer of an assured shorthold tenancy made by a private landlord to the applicant in relation to any accommodation which is, or may become, available for the applicant's occupation,

    (b)   it is made, with the approval of the authority, in pursuance of arrangements made by the authority with a view to bringing the authority's duty under subsection (4) to an end, and

    (c)   the tenancy being offered is a fixed term tenancy (within the meaning of Part 1 of the Housing Act 1988) for a period of at least 6 months.

(8) A "final Part 6 offer" is an offer of accommodation under Part 6 (allocation of housing) that is made in writing and states that it is a final offer for the purposes of this section.

(9) The authority may not approve a final accommodation offer, or make a final Part 6 offer, unless they are satisfied that the accommodation is suitable for the applicant and that subsection (10) does not apply.

(10) This subsection applies to an applicant if—

    (a)   the applicant is under contractual or other obligations in respect of the applicant's existing accommodation, and

    (b)   the applicant is not able to bring those obligations to an end before being required to take up the offer.]

NOTES

Amendment

> Inserted by the Homelessness Reduction Act 2017, s 7(1).
>   Date in force: 3 April 2018: see SI 2018/167, reg 3(g).

194 . . .

. . .

NOTES

Amendment

> Repealed by the Homelessness Act 2002, ss 6(3), 18(2), Sch 2; for effect see s 6(4) thereof.
>   Date in force (in relation to England): 31 July 2002: see SI 2002/1799, art 2.
>   Date in force (in relation to Wales): 30 September 2002: see SI 2002/1736, art 2(1), Schedule, Pt 1.

[195 Duties in cases of threatened homelessness]

[(1) This section applies where the local housing authority are satisfied that an applicant is—

    (a)   threatened with homelessness, and

    (b)   eligible for assistance.

(2)   The authority must take reasonable steps to help the applicant to secure that accommodation does not cease to be available for the applicant's occupation.

(3)   In deciding what steps they are to take, the authority must have regard to their assessment of the applicant's case under section 189A.

(4)   Subsection (2) does not affect any right of the authority, whether by virtue of contract, enactment or rule of law, to secure vacant possession of any accommodation.

(5)   If any of the circumstances mentioned in subsection (8) apply, the authority may give notice to the applicant bringing the duty under subsection (2) to an end.

(6)   But the authority may not give notice to the applicant under subsection (5) on the basis that the circumstances in subsection (8)(b) apply if a valid notice has been given to the applicant under section 21 of the Housing Act 1988 (orders for possession on expiry or termination of assured shorthold tenancy) that—

    (a)   will expire within 56 days or has expired, and

    (b)   is in respect of the only accommodation that is available for the applicant's occupation.

(7)   The notice must—

    (a)   specify which of the circumstances apply, and

    (b)   inform the applicant that the applicant has a right to request a review of the authority's decision to bring the duty under subsection (2) to an end and of the time within which such a request must be made.

(8)   The circumstances are that the authority are satisfied that—

    (a)   the applicant has—

        (i)   suitable accommodation available for occupation, and

        (ii)   a reasonable prospect of having suitable accommodation available for occupation for at least 6 months, or such longer period not exceeding 12 months as may be prescribed, from the date of the notice,

    (b)   the authority have complied with the duty under subsection (2) and the period of 56 days beginning with the day that the authority are first satisfied as mentioned in subsection (1) has ended (whether or not the applicant is still threatened with homelessness),

    (c)   the applicant has become homeless,

    (d)   the applicant has refused an offer of suitable accommodation and, on the date of refusal, there was a reasonable prospect that suitable accommodation would be available for occupation by the applicant for at least 6 months or such longer period not exceeding 12 months as may be prescribed,

    (e)   the applicant has become homeless intentionally from any accommodation that has been made available to the applicant as a result of the authority's exercise of their functions under subsection (2),

    (f)   the applicant is no longer eligible for assistance, or

    (g)   the applicant has withdrawn the application mentioned in section 183(1).

(9)   A notice under this section must be given in writing and, if not received by the applicant, is to be treated as having been given to the applicant if it is made available at the authority's office for a reasonable period for collection by or on behalf of the applicant.

(10)   The duty under subsection (2) can also be brought to an end under sections 193B and 193C (notices in cases of applicant's deliberate and unreasonable refusal to co-operate).]

NOTES

Amendment

    Substituted by the Homelessness Reduction Act 2017, s 4(1), (2).

Date in force: 3 April 2018: see SI 2018/167, reg 3(d); for transitional and savings provisions see reg 4(1).

[195A Re-application after private rented sector offer]

[(1)   If within two years beginning with the date on which an applicant accepts an offer under section 193(7AA) (private rented sector offer), the applicant re-applies for accommodation, or for assistance in obtaining accommodation, and the local housing authority—

(a)   is satisfied that the applicant is homeless and eligible for assistance, and

(b)   is not satisfied that the applicant became homeless intentionally,

the duty under section 193(2) applies regardless of whether the applicant has a priority need.

(2)   For the purpose of subsection (1), an applicant in respect of whom a valid notice under section 21 of the Housing Act 1988 (orders for possession on expiry or termination of assured shorthold tenancy) has been given is to be treated as homeless from the date on which that notice expires.

(3)   . . .

(4)   . . .

(5)   Subsection (1) . . . does not apply to a case where the local housing authority would not be satisfied as mentioned in that subsection without having regard to a restricted person.

(6)   Subsection (1) . . . does not apply to a re-application by an applicant for accommodation, or for assistance in obtaining accommodation, if the immediately preceding application made by that applicant was one to which subsection (1) . . . applied.]

NOTES

Amendment

Inserted by the Localism Act 2011, s 149(1), (4).
    Date in force (in relation to England): 9 November 2012: see SI 2012/2599, art 2; for transitional provisions see art 3 thereof.
Sub-ss (3), (4): repealed by the Homelessness Reduction Act 2017, s 4(1), (4)(a).
    Date in force: 3 April 2018: see SI 2018/167, reg 3(d); for transitional and savings provisions see reg 4(1).
Sub-s (5): words omitted repealed by the Homelessness Reduction Act 2017, s 4(1), (4)(b).
    Date in force: 3 April 2018: see SI 2018/167, reg 3(d); for transitional and savings provisions see reg 4(1).
Sub-s (6): words omitted repealed by the Homelessness Reduction Act 2017, s 4(1), (4)(c).
    Date in force: 3 April 2018: see SI 2018/167, reg 3(d); for transitional and savings provisions see reg 4(1).

196 . . .

. . .

NOTES

Amendment

Repealed by the Homelessness Reduction Act 2017, s 4(1), (5).
    Date in force: 3 April 2018: see SI 2018/167, reg 3(d); for transitional and savings provisions see reg 4(1).

. . .

197 . . .

. . .

NOTES

Amendment

> Repealed by the Homelessness Act 2002, ss 9(1), 18(2), Sch 2; for effect see s 9(2), (3) thereof.
>> Date in force (in relation to England): 31 July 2002: see SI 2002/1799, art 2.
>> Date in force (in relation to Wales): 30 September 2002: see SI 2002/1736, art 2(1), Schedule, Pt 1.

Referral to another local housing authority

198 Referral of case to another local housing authority

[(A1) If the local housing authority would be subject to the duty under section 189B (initial duty owed to all eligible persons who are homeless) but consider that the conditions are met for referral of the case to another local housing authority in England, they may notify that other authority of their opinion.]

(1) If the local housing authority would be subject to the duty under section 193 (accommodation for those with priority need who are not homeless intentionally) but consider that the conditions are met for referral of the case to another local housing authority, they may notify that other authority of their opinion.

. . .

(2) The conditions for referral of the case to another authority are met if—

(a) neither the applicant nor any person who might reasonably be expected to reside with him has a local connection with the district of the authority to whom his application was made,

(b) the applicant or a person who might reasonably be expected to reside with him has a local connection with the district of that other authority, and

(c) neither the applicant nor any person who might reasonably be expected to reside with him will run the risk of domestic violence in that other district.

[(2ZA) The conditions for referral of the case to another authority are also met if—

(a) the application is made within the period of two years beginning with the date on which the applicant accepted an offer from the other authority under section 193(7AA) (private rented sector offer), and

(b) neither the applicant nor any person who might reasonably be expected to reside with the applicant will run the risk of domestic violence in the district of the other authority.]

[(2A) But the conditions for referral mentioned in subsection (2) [or (2ZA)] are not met if—

(a) the applicant or any person who might reasonably be expected to reside with him has suffered violence (other than domestic violence) in the district of the other authority; and

(b) it is probable that the return to that district of the victim will lead to further violence of a similar kind against him.

(3) For the purposes of subsections (2)[, (2ZA)] and (2A) "violence" means—

(a) violence from another person; or

(b) threats of violence from another person which are likely to be carried out; and violence is "domestic violence" if it is from a person who is associated with the victim.]

(4) The conditions for referral of the case to another authority are also met if—

(a) the applicant was on a previous application made to that other authority placed (in pursuance of their functions under this Part) in accommodation in the district of the authority to whom his application is now made, and

(b)   the previous application was within such period as may be prescribed of the present application.

[(4A)   Subsection (4) is to be construed, in a case where the other authority is an authority in Wales, as if the reference to "this Part" were a reference to Part 2 of the Housing (Wales) Act 2014.]

(5)   The question whether the conditions for referral of a case [which does not involve a referral to a local housing authority in Wales] are satisfied shall be decided by agreement between the notifying authority and the notified authority or, in default of agreement, in accordance with such arrangements as the Secretary of State may direct by order.

[(5A)   The question whether the conditions for referral of a case involving a referral to a local housing authority in Wales shall be decided by agreement between the notifying authority and the notified authority or, in default of agreement, in accordance with such arrangements as the Secretary of State and the Welsh Ministers may jointly direct by order.]

(6)   An order may direct that the arrangements shall be—

(a)   those agreed by any relevant authorities or associations of relevant authorities, or

(b)   in default of such agreement, such arrangements as appear to the Secretary of State [or, in the case of an order under subsection (5A), to the Secretary of State and the Welsh Ministers] to be suitable, after consultation with such associations representing relevant authorities, and such other persons, as he thinks appropriate.

(7)   [An order under this section shall not] be made unless a draft of the order has been approved by a resolution of each House of Parliament [and, in the case of a joint order, a resolution of the National Assembly for Wales].

NOTES

Amendment

Sub-s (A1): inserted by the Homelessness Reduction Act 2017, s 5(1), (8).
    Date in force: 3 April 2018: see SI 2018/167, reg 3(e); for transitional and savings provisions see reg 4(1).
Sub-s (1): words omitted repealed by the Homelessness Act 2002, s 18(2), Sch 2.
    Date in force (in relation to England): 31 July 2002: see SI 2002/1799, art 2.
    Date in force (in relation to Wales): 30 September 2002: see SI 2002/1736, art 2(1), Schedule, Pt 1.
Sub-s (2ZA): inserted by the Localism Act 2011, s 149(1), (5), (6).
    Date in force (in relation to England): 9 November 2012: see SI 2012/2599, art 2; for transitional provisions see art 3 thereof.
Sub-ss (2A), (3): substituted, for sub-s (3) as originally enacted, by the Homelessness Act 2002, s 10(2).
    Date in force (in relation to England): 31 July 2002: see SI 2002/1799, art 2.
    Date in force (in relation to Wales): 30 September 2002: see SI 2002/1736, art 2(1), Schedule, Pt 1.
Sub-s (2A): words "or (2ZA)" in square brackets inserted by the Localism Act 2011, s 149(1), (5), (7).
    Date in force (in relation to England): 9 November 2012: see SI 2012/2599, art 2; for transitional provisions see art 3 thereof.
Sub-s (3): reference to ", (2ZA)" in square brackets inserted by the Localism Act 2011, s 149(1), (5), (8).
    Date in force (in relation to England): 9 November 2012: see SI 2012/2599, art 2; for transitional provisions see art 3 thereof.
Sub-s (4A): inserted, in relation to Wales, by the Housing (Wales) Act 2014, s 100, Sch 3, Pt 1, paras 2, 11(a).
    Date in force: 27 April 2015: see SI 2015/1272, art 2, Schedule, paras 51, 53; for a transitional provision see art 7.
Sub-s (5): words from "which does not" to "authority in Wales" in square brackets inserted, in relation to Wales, by the Housing (Wales) Act 2014, s 100, Sch 3, Pt 1, paras 2, 11(b).
    Date in force: 27 April 2015: see SI 2015/1272, art 2, Schedule, paras 51, 53; for a transitional provision see art 7.
Sub-s (5A): inserted, in relation to Wales, by the Housing (Wales) Act 2014, s 100, Sch 3, Pt 1, paras 2, 11(c).

Date in force: 27 April 2015: see SI 2015/1272, art 2, Schedule, paras 51, 53; for a transitional provision see art 7.

Sub-s (6): words from "or, in the" to "the Welsh Ministers" in square brackets inserted, in relation to Wales, by the Housing (Wales) Act 2014, s 100, Sch 3, Pt 1, paras 2, 11(d).

Date in force: 27 April 2015: see SI 2015/1272, art 2, Schedule, paras 51, 53; for a transitional provision see art 7.

Sub-s (7): words "An order under this section shall not" in square brackets substituted, in relation to Wales, by the Housing (Wales) Act 2014, s 100, Sch 3, Pt 1, paras 2, 11(e)(i).

Date in force: 27 April 2015: see SI 2015/1272, art 2, Schedule, paras 51, 53; for a transitional provision see art 7.

Sub-s (7): words from "and, in the" to "Assembly for Wales" in square brackets inserted, in relation to Wales, by the Housing (Wales) Act 2014, s 100, Sch 3, Pt 1, paras 2, 11(e)(ii).

Date in force: 27 April 2015: see SI 2015/1272, art 2, Schedule, paras 51, 53; for a transitional provision see art 7.

199 Local connection

(1)   A person has a local connection with the district of a local housing authority if he has a connection with it—

    (a)   because he is, or in the past was, normally resident there, and that residence is or was of his own choice,

    (b)   because he is employed there,

    (c)   because of family associations, or

    (d)   because of special circumstances.

(2)   A person is not employed in a district if he is serving in the regular armed forces of the Crown.

(3)   Residence in a district is not of a person's own choice if—

    (a)   he becomes resident there because he, or a person who might reasonably be expected to reside with him, is serving in the regular armed forces of the Crown, or

    (b)   he, or a person who might reasonably be expected to reside with him, becomes resident there because he is detained under the authority of an Act of Parliament.

(4)   In subsections (2) and (3) "regular armed forces of the Crown" means the Royal Navy, the regular forces as defined by section 225 of the Army Act 1955 [or the regular air force as defined by section 223 of the Air Force Act 1955].

(5)   The Secretary of State may by order specify other circumstances in which—

    (a)   a person is not to be treated as employed in a district, or

    (b)   residence in a district is not to be treated as of a person's own choice.

[(6)   A person has a local connection with the district of a local housing authority if he was (at any time) provided with accommodation in that district under section 95 of the Immigration and Asylum Act 1999 (support for asylum seekers).

(7)   But subsection (6) does not apply—

    (a)   to the provision of accommodation for a person in a district of a local housing authority if he was subsequently provided with accommodation in the district of another local housing authority under section 95 of that Act, or

    (b)   to the provision of accommodation in an accommodation centre by virtue of section 22 of the Nationality, Immigration and Asylum Act 2002 (c 41) (use of accommodation centres for section 95 support).]

[(8)   While a local authority in England have a duty towards a person under section 23C of the Children Act 1989 (continuing functions in respect of former relevant children)—

    (a)   if the local authority is a local housing authority, the person has a local connection with their district, and

    (b)   otherwise, the person has a local connection with every district of a local housing authority that falls within the area of the local authority.

(9)   In subsection (8), "local authority" has the same meaning as in the Children Act 1989 (see section 105 of that Act).

(10)   Where, by virtue of being provided with accommodation under section 22A of the Children Act 1989 (provision of accommodation for children in care), a person is normally resident in the district of a local housing authority in England for a continuous period of at least two years, some or all of which falls before the person attains the age of 16, the person has a local connection with that district.

(11)   A person ceases to have a local connection with a district under subsection (10) upon attaining the age of 21 (but this does not affect whether the person has a local connection with that district under any other provision of this section).]

NOTES

Amendment

Sub-s (2): repealed by the Housing and Regeneration Act 2008, ss 315(a), 321(1), Sch 16.
   Date in force (in relation to England for certain purposes): 1 December 2008: see SI 2008/3068, arts 1(2), 4(2), (10), 5, Schedule; for transitional provisions and savings see arts 6, 9, 10 thereof.
   Date in force (in relation to Wales for certain purposes): 30 March 2009: see SI 2009/773, art 2.
   Date in force (for remaining purposes): to be appointed: see the Housing and Regeneration Act 2008, s 325(3)(b), (4).
Sub-s (3): para (a) repealed by the Housing and Regeneration Act 2008, ss 315(b), 321(1), Sch 16.
   Date in force (in relation to England for certain purposes): 1 December 2008: see SI 2008/3068, arts 1(2), 4(2), (10), 5, Schedule; for transitional provisions and savings see arts 6, 9, 10 thereof.
   Date in force (in relation to Wales for certain purposes): 30 March 2009: see SI 2009/773, art 2.
   Date in force (for remaining purposes): to be appointed: see the Housing and Regeneration Act 2008, s 325(3)(b), (4).
Sub-s (4): repealed by the Housing and Regeneration Act 2008, ss 315(c), 321(1), Sch 16.
   Date in force (in relation to England for certain purposes): 1 December 2008: see SI 2008/3068, arts 1(2), 4(2), (10), 5, Schedule; for transitional provisions and savings see arts 6, 9, 10 thereof.
   Date in force (in relation to Wales for certain purposes): 30 March 2009: see SI 2009/773, art 2.
   Date in force (for remaining purposes): to be appointed: see the Housing and Regeneration Act 2008, s 325(3)(b), (4).
Sub-s (4): words from "or the regular" to "the Air Force Act 1955" in square brackets substituted by the Armed Forces Act 2001, s 34, Sch 6, Pt 5, para 30.
   Date in force: 11 May 2001: see the Armed Forces Act 2001, s 39(3)(f).
Sub-s (5): word "other" in italics repealed by the Housing and Regeneration Act 2008, ss 315(d), 321(1), Sch 16.
   Date in force (in relation to England for certain purposes): 1 December 2008: see SI 2008/3068, arts 1(2), 4(2), (10), 5, Schedule; for transitional provisions and savings see arts 6, 9, 10 thereof.
   Date in force (in relation to Wales for certain purposes): 30 March 2009: see SI 2009/773, art 2.
   Date in force (for remaining purposes): to be appointed: see the Housing and Regeneration Act 2008, s 325(3)(b), (4).
Sub-ss (6), (7): inserted by the Asylum and Immigration (Treatment of Claimants, etc) Act 2004, s 11(1).
   Date in force: 4 January 2005: see SI 2004/2999, art 2, Schedule.
Sub-ss (8)–(11): inserted by the Homelessness Reduction Act 2017, s 8.
   Date in force: 3 April 2018: see SI 2018/167, reg 3(h).

[199A Duties to the applicant whose case is considered for referral or referred under section 198(A1)]

[(1)   Where a local housing authority ("the notifying authority") notify an applicant that they intend to notify or have notified another local housing authority in England ("the notified authority") under section 198(A1) of their opinion that the conditions are met for referral of the applicant's case to the notified authority, the notifying authority—

(a)   cease to be subject to any duty under section 188 (interim duty to accommodate in case of apparent priority need), and

(b)   are not subject to the duty under section 189B (initial duty owed to all eligible persons who are homeless).

(2)   But, if the notifying authority have reason to believe that the applicant may have a priority need, they must secure that accommodation is available for occupation by the applicant until the applicant is notified of the decision as to whether the conditions for referral of the applicant's case are met.

(3)   When it has been decided whether the conditions for referral are met, the notifying authority must give notice of the decision and the reasons for it to the applicant.

The notice must also inform the applicant of the applicant's right to request a review of the decision and of the time within which such a request must be made.

(4)   If it is decided that the conditions for referral are not met—

(a)   the notifying authority are subject to the duty under section 189B,

(b)   the references in subsections (4) and (7)(b) of that section to the day that the notifying authority are first satisfied as mentioned in subsection (1) of that section are to be read as references to the day on which notice is given under subsection (3) of this section, and

(c)   if the notifying authority have reason to believe that the applicant may have a priority need, they must secure that accommodation is available for occupation by the applicant until the later of—

(i)   the duty owed to the applicant under section 189B coming to an end, and

(ii)   the authority deciding what other duty (if any) they owe to the applicant under this Part after the duty under section 189B comes to an end.

(5)   If it is decided that the conditions for referral are met—

(a)   for the purposes of this Part, the applicant is to be treated as having made an application of the kind mentioned in section 183(1) to the notified authority on the date on which notice is given under subsection (3),

(b)   from that date, the notifying authority owes no duties to the applicant under this Part,

(c)   where the notifying authority have made a decision as to whether the applicant is eligible for assistance, is homeless or became homeless intentionally, the notified authority may only come to a different decision if they are satisfied that—

(i)   the applicant's circumstances have changed, or further information has come to light, since the notifying authority made their decision, and

(ii)   that change in circumstances, or further information, justifies the notified authority coming to a different decision to the notifying authority, and

(d)   the notifying authority must give to the notified authority copies of any notifications that the notifying authority have given to the applicant under section 189A(3) or (10) (notifications of the notifying authority's assessments of the applicant's case).

(6)   A duty under subsection (2) or paragraph (c) of subsection (4) ceases as provided in the subsection or paragraph concerned even if the applicant requests a review of the authority's decision upon which the duty ceases.

The authority may secure that accommodation is available for the applicant's occupation pending the decision on review.

(7)   A notice under this section must be given in writing and, if not received by the applicant, is to be treated as having been given to the applicant if it is made available

at the authority's office for a reasonable period for collection by or on behalf of the applicant.]

200 Duties to the applicant whose case is considered for referral or referred [under section 198(1)]

(1)   Where a local housing authority notify an applicant that they intend to notify or have notified another local housing authority [under section 198(1)] of their opinion that the conditions are met for the referral of his case to that other authority—

(a)   they cease to be subject to any duty under section 188 (interim duty to accommodate in case of apparent priority need), and

(b)   they are not subject to any duty under section 193 (the main housing duty),

but they shall secure that accommodation is available for occupation by the applicant until he is notified of the decision whether the conditions for referral of his case are met.

[(1A)   A local housing authority in England may not notify an applicant as mentioned in subsection (1) until the authority's duty to the applicant under section 189B(2) (initial duty owed to all eligible persons who are homeless) has come to an end.]

(2)   When it has been decided whether the conditions for referral are met, the notifying authority shall notify the applicant of the decision and inform him of the reasons for it.

The notice shall also inform the applicant of his right to request a review of the decision and of the time within which such a request must be made.

[(3)   If it is decided that the conditions for referral are not met, the notifying authority are subject to the duty under section 193 (the main housing duty).

(4)   If it is decided that those conditions are met [and the notified authority is not an authority in Wales], the notified authority are subject to the duty under section 193 (the main housing duty)[; for provision about cases where it is decided that those conditions are met and the notified authority is an authority in Wales, see section 83 of the Housing (Wales) Act 2014 (cases referred from a local housing authority in England)].]

(5)   The duty under subsection (1), . . . ceases as provided in that subsection even if the applicant requests a review of the authority's decision (see section 202).

The authority may [secure] that accommodation is available for the applicant's occupation pending the decision on a review.

(6)   Notice . . . given to an applicant under this section shall be given in writing and, if not received by him, shall be treated as having been given to him if it is made available at the authority's office for a reasonable period for collection by him or on his behalf.

NOTES

Amendment

Section heading: words "under section 198(1)" in square brackets inserted by the Homelessness Reduction Act 2017, s 5(1), (10)(a).
Date in force: 3 April 2018: see SI 2018/167, reg 3(e); for transitional and savings provisions see reg 4(1).
Sub-s (1): words "under section 198(1)" in square brackets inserted by the Homelessness Reduction Act 2017, s 5(1), (10)(b).
Date in force: 3 April 2018: see SI 2018/167, reg 3(e); for transitional and savings provisions see reg 4(1).
Sub-s (1A): inserted by the Homelessness Reduction Act 2017, s 5(1), (10)(c).
Date in force: 3 April 2018: see SI 2018/167, reg 3(e); for transitional and savings provisions see reg 4(1).
Sub-ss (3), (4): substituted by the Homelessness Act 2002, s 18(1), Sch 1, paras 2, 15(a).
Date in force (in relation to England): 31 July 2002: see SI 2002/1799, art 2.
Date in force (in relation to Wales): 30 September 2002: see SI 2002/1736, art 2(1), Schedule, Pt 1.

Sub-s (4): words "and the notified authority is not an authority in Wales" in square brackets inserted, in relation to Wales, by the Housing (Wales) Act 2014, s 100, Sch 3, Pt 1, paras 2, 12(a).

> Date in force: 27 April 2015: see SI 2015/1272, art 2, Schedule, paras 51, 53; for a transitional provision see art 7.

Sub-s (4): words from "; for provision about" to "authority in England)" in square brackets inserted, in relation to Wales, by the Housing (Wales) Act 2014, s 100, Sch 3, Pt 1, paras 2, 12(b).

> Date in force: 27 April 2015: see SI 2015/1272, art 2, Schedule, paras 51, 53; for a transitional provision see art 7.

Sub-s (5): words omitted repealed by the Homelessness Act 2002, s 18(2), Sch 2.

> Date in force (in relation to England): 31 July 2002: see SI 2002/1799, art 2.
> Date in force (in relation to Wales): 30 September 2002: see SI 2002/1736, art 2(1), Schedule, Pt 1.

Sub-s (5): word "secure" in square brackets substituted by the Homelessness Act 2002, s 18(1), Sch 1, paras 2, 15(b).

> Date in force (in relation to England): 31 July 2002: see SI 2002/1799, art 2.
> Date in force (in relation to Wales): 30 September 2002: see SI 2002/1736, art 2(1), Schedule, Pt 1.

Sub-s (6): words omitted repealed by the Homelessness Reduction Act 2017, s 5(1), (10)(d).

> Date in force: 3 April 2018: see SI 2018/167, reg 3(e); for transitional and savings provisions see reg 4(1).

201 Application of referral provisions to cases arising in Scotland

Sections 198 and 200 (referral of application to another local housing authority and duties to applicant whose case is considered for referral or referred) apply—

(a)   to applications referred by a local authority in Scotland in pursuance of sections 33 and 34 of the Housing (Scotland) Act 1987, and

(b)   to persons whose applications are so transferred,

as they apply to cases arising under this Part (the reference in section 198 to this Part being construed as a reference to Part II of that Act).

[201A Cases referred from a local housing authority in Wales]

[(1)   This section applies where an application has been referred by a local housing authority in Wales to a local housing authority in England under section 80 of the Housing (Wales) Act 2014 (referral of case to another local housing authority).

(2)   If it is decided that the conditions in that section for referral of the case are met, the notified authority are subject to the duty under section 193 of this Act in respect of the person whose case is referred (the main housing duty); for provision about cases where it is decided that the conditions for referral are not met, see section 82 of the Housing (Wales) Act 2014 (duties to applicant whose case is considered for referral or referred).

(3)   References in this Part to an applicant include a reference to a person to whom a duty is owed by virtue of subsection (2).]

NOTES

Amendment

> Inserted, in relation to Wales, by the Housing (Wales) Act 2014, s 100, Sch 3, Pt 1, paras 2, 13.
> > Date in force: 27 April 2015: see SI 2015/1272, art 2, Schedule, paras 51, 53; for a transitional provision see art 7.

Right to request review of decision

202 Right to request review of decision

(1)   An applicant has the right to request a review of—

(a)   any decision of a local housing authority as to his eligibility for assistance,

(b)   any decision of a local housing authority as to what duty (if any) is owed to him under sections [189B to 193C] and 195 . . . (duties to persons found to be homeless or threatened with homelessness),

[(ba)   any decision of a local housing authority—

    (i)   as to the steps they are to take under subsection (2) of section 189B, or

    (ii)   to give notice under subsection (5) of that section bringing to an end their duty to the applicant under subsection (2) of that section,

(bb)   any decision of a local housing authority to give notice to the applicant under section 193B(2) (notice given to those who deliberately and unreasonably refuse to co-operate),

(bc)   any decision of a local housing authority—

    (i)   as to the steps they are to take under subsection (2) of section 195, or

    (ii)   to give notice under subsection (5) of that section bringing to an end their duty to the applicant under subsection (2) of that section,]

(c)   any decision of a local housing authority to notify another authority under section 198(1) (referral of cases),

(d)   any decision under section 198(5) whether the conditions are met for the referral of his case,

(e)   any decision under section 200(3) or (4) (decision as to duty owed to applicant whose case is considered for referral or referred), . . .

(f)   any decision of a local housing authority as to the suitability of accommodation offered to him in discharge of their duty under any of the provisions mentioned in paragraph (b) or (e) [or as to the suitability of accommodation offered to him as mentioned in section 193(7)][, . . .

(g)   any decision of a local housing authority as to the suitability of accommodation offered to him by way of a [private rented sector offer] (within the meaning of section 193)][, or

(h)   any decision of a local housing authority as to the suitability of accommodation offered to the applicant by way of a final accommodation offer or a final Part 6 offer (within the meaning of section 193A or 193C)].

[(1A)   An applicant who is offered accommodation as mentioned in section 193(5)[, (7) or (7AA)] may under subsection (1)(f) [or (as the case may be) (g)] request a review of the suitability of the accommodation offered to him whether or not he has accepted the offer.]

[(1B)   An applicant may, under subsection (1)(h), request a review of the suitability of the accommodation offered whether or not the applicant has accepted the offer.]

(2)   There is no right to request a review of the decision reached on an earlier review.

(3)   A request for review must be made before the end of the period of 21 days beginning with the day on which he is notified of the authority's decision or such longer period as the authority may in writing allow.

(4)   On a request being duly made to them, the authority or authorities concerned shall review their decision.

NOTES

Amendment

Sub-s (1): in para (b) words "189B to 193C" in square brackets substituted by the Homelessness Reduction Act 2017, s 9(1), (2)(a)(i).

Date in force (for certain purposes): 12 February 2018: see SI 2018/167, reg 2(b).
Date in force (for remaining purposes): 3 April 2018: see SI 2018/167, reg 3(i); for transitional and savings provisions see reg 4(2).

Sub-s (1): in para (b) words omitted repealed by the Homelessness Reduction Act 2017, s 9(1), (2)(a)(ii).

Date in force (for certain purposes): 12 February 2018: see SI 2018/167, reg 2(b).
Date in force (for remaining purposes): 3 April 2018: see SI 2018/167, reg 3(i); for transitional and savings provisions see reg 4(2).

Sub-s (1): paras (ba)–(bc) inserted by the Homelessness Reduction Act 2017, s 9(1), (2)(b).

Date in force (for certain purposes): 12 February 2018: see SI 2018/167, reg 2(b).
Date in force (for remaining purposes): 3 April 2018: see SI 2018/167, reg 3(i); for transitional and savings provisions see reg 4(2).

Sub-s (1): in para (e) word omitted repealed by the Housing and Regeneration Act 2008, s 321(1), Sch 16.

Date in force: 1 December 2008: see SI 2008/3068, arts 1(2), 5, Schedule; for transitional provisions and savings see arts 6–13 thereof.

Sub-s (1): in para (f) words "or as to the suitability of accommodation offered to him as mentioned in section 193(7)" in square brackets inserted by the Homelessness Act 2002, s 8(2)(a).

Date in force: 26 February 2002: see the Homelessness Act 2002, s 8(3).

Sub-s (1): para (g) and word ", or" immediately preceding it inserted by the Housing and Regeneration Act 2008, s 314, Sch 15, Pt 1, paras 1, 7(1), (2).

Date in force: 2 March 2009 (except in relation to applications for an allocation of social housing or housing assistance (homelessness) or for accommodation made before that date): see SI 2009/415, art 2.

Sub-s (1): in para (f) word omitted repealed by the Homelessness Reduction Act 2017, s 9(1), (2)(c).

Date in force (for certain purposes): 12 February 2018: see SI 2018/167, reg 2(b).
Date in force (for remaining purposes): 3 April 2018: see SI 2018/167, reg 3(i); for transitional and savings provisions see reg 4(2).

Sub-s (1): in para (g) words "private rented sector offer" in square brackets substituted by the Localism Act 2011, s 149(1), (9).

Date in force (in relation to England): 9 November 2012: see SI 2012/2599, art 2; for transitional provisions see art 3 thereof.

Sub-s (1): para (h) and word ", or" immediately preceding it inserted by the Homelessness Reduction Act 2017, s 9(1), (2)(d).

Date in force (for certain purposes): 12 February 2018: see SI 2018/167, reg 2(b).
Date in force (for remaining purposes): 3 April 2018: see SI 2018/167, reg 3(i); for transitional and savings provisions see reg 4(2).

Sub-s (1A): inserted by the Homelessness Act 2002, s 8(2)(b).

Date in force: 26 February 2002: see the Homelessness Act 2002, s 8(3).

Sub-s (1A): words ", (7) or (7AA)" in square brackets substituted by the Housing and Regeneration Act 2008, s 314, Sch 15, Pt 1, paras 1, 7(1), (3)(a).

Date in force: 2 March 2009 (except in relation to applications for an allocation of social housing or housing assistance (homelessness) or for accommodation made before that date): see SI 2009/415, art 2.

Sub-s (1A): words "or (as the case may be) (g)" in square brackets inserted by the Housing and Regeneration Act 2008, s 314, Sch 15, Pt 1, paras 1, 7(1), (3)(b).

Date in force: 2 March 2009 (except in relation to applications for an allocation of social housing or housing assistance (homelessness) or for accommodation made before that date): see SI 2009/415, art 2.

Sub-s (1B): inserted by the Homelessness Reduction Act 2017, s 9(1), (3).

Date in force: 3 April 2018: see SI 2018/167, reg 3(i); for transitional and savings provisions see reg 4(2).

203 Procedure on a review

(1) The Secretary of State may make provision by regulations as to the procedure to be followed in connection with a review under section 202.

Nothing in the following provisions affects the generality of this power.

(2) Provision may be made by regulations—

    (a) requiring the decision on review to be made by a person of appropriate seniority who was not involved in the original decision, and

    (b) as to the circumstances in which the applicant is entitled to an oral hearing, and whether and by whom he may be represented at such a hearing.

(3) The authority, or as the case may be either of the authorities, concerned shall notify the applicant of the decision on the review.

(4) If the decision is—

(a) to confirm the original decision on any issue against the interests of the applicant, or

(b) to confirm a previous decision—

  (i) to notify another authority under section 198 (referral of cases), or

  (ii) that the conditions are met for the referral of his case,

they shall also notify him of the reasons for the decision.

(5) In any case they shall inform the applicant of his right to appeal to [the county court] on a point of law, and of the period within which such an appeal must be made (see section 204).

(6) Notice of the decision shall not be treated as given unless and until subsection (5), and where applicable subsection (4), is complied with.

(7) Provision may be made by regulations as to the period within which the review must be carried out and notice given of the decision.

(8) Notice required to be given to a person under this section shall be given in writing and, if not received by him, shall be treated as having been given if it is made available at the authority's office for a reasonable period for collection by him or on his behalf.

NOTES

Amendment

Sub-s (5): words "the county court" in square brackets substituted by the Crime and Courts Act 2013, s 17(5), Sch 9, Pt 3, para 52(1)(b), (2).
  Date in force: 22 April 2014: see SI 2014/954, art 2(a), (c); for transitional provision see art 3.

204 Right of appeal to county court on point of law

(1) If an applicant who has requested a review under section 202—

(a) is dissatisfied with the decision on the review, or

(b) is not notified of the decision on the review within the time prescribed under section 203,

he may appeal to the county court on any point of law arising from the decision or, as the case may be, the original decision.

(2) An appeal must be brought within 21 days of his being notified of the decision or, as the case may be, of the date on which he should have been notified of a decision on review.

[(2A) The court may give permission for an appeal to be brought after the end of the period allowed by subsection (2), but only if it is satisfied—

(a) where permission is sought before the end of that period, that there is a good reason for the applicant to be unable to bring the appeal in time; or

(b) where permission is sought after that time, that there was a good reason for the applicant's failure to bring the appeal in time and for any delay in applying for permission.]

(3) On appeal the court may make such order confirming, quashing or varying the decision as it thinks fit.

(4) Where the authority were under a duty under section 188, 190[, 199A] or 200 to secure that accommodation is available for the applicant's occupation[, . . . they may] secure that accommodation is so available—

(a) during the period for appealing under this section against the authority's decision, and

(b) if an appeal is brought, until the appeal (and any further appeal) is finally determined.

NOTES

Amendment

Sub-s (2A): inserted by the Homelessness Act 2002, s 18(1), Sch 1, paras 2, 17(a).

Date in force (in relation to Wales): 30 September 2002: see SI 2002/1736, art 2(1), Schedule, Pt 1.

Date in force (in relation to England): 30 September 2002 (except in relation to any case where an appeal is brought under sub-s (1) above before that date): see SI 2002/2324, arts 3, 4.

Sub-s (4): reference to ", 199A" in square brackets inserted by the Homelessness Reduction Act 2017, s 5(1), (11).

Date in force: 3 April 2018: see SI 2018/167, reg 3(e); for transitional and savings provisions see reg 4(1).

Sub-s (4): words in square brackets ending with the words "they may" in square brackets substituted by the Homelessness Act 2002, s 18(1), Sch 1, paras 2, 17(b).

Date in force (in relation to England): 31 July 2002: see SI 2002/1799, art 2.

Date in force (in relation to Wales): 30 September 2002: see SI 2002/1736, art 2(1), Schedule, Pt 1.

Sub-s (4): words omitted repealed by the Homelessness Reduction Act 2017, s 4(1), (6).

Date in force: 3 April 2018: see SI 2018/167, reg 3(d); for transitional and savings provisions see reg 4(1).

[204A Section 204(4): appeals]

[(1)   This section applies where an applicant has the right to appeal to the county court against a local housing authority's decision on a review.

(2)   If the applicant is dissatisfied with a decision by the authority—

(a)   not to exercise their power under section 204(4) ("the section 204(4) power") in his case;

(b)   to exercise that power for a limited period ending before the final determination by the county court of his appeal under section 204(1) ("the main appeal"); or

(c)   to cease exercising that power before that time,

he may appeal to the county court against the decision.

(3)   An appeal under this section may not be brought after the final determination by the county court of the main appeal.

(4)   On an appeal under this section the court—

(a)   may order the authority to secure that accommodation is available for the applicant's occupation until the determination of the appeal (or such earlier time as the court may specify); and

(b)   shall confirm or quash the decision appealed against,

and in considering whether to confirm or quash the decision the court shall apply the principles applied by the High Court on an application for judicial review.

(5)   If the court quashes the decision it may order the authority to exercise the section 204(4) power in the applicant's case for such period as may be specified in the order.

(6)   An order under subsection (5)—

(a)   may only be made if the court is satisfied that failure to exercise the section 204(4) power in accordance with the order would substantially prejudice the applicant's ability to pursue the main appeal;

(b)   may not specify any period ending after the final determination by the county court of the main appeal.]

NOTES

Amendment

Inserted by the Homelessness Act 2002, s 11.

Date in force (in relation to Wales): 30 September 2002: see SI 2002/1736, art 2(1), Schedule, Pt 1.

Date in force (in relation to England): 30 September 2002 (except in relation to any case where an appeal is brought under s 204(1) hereof before that date): see SI 2002/2324, arts 3, 4.

Supplementary provisions

205 Discharge of functions: introductory

(1) The following sections have effect in relation to the discharge by a local housing authority of their functions under this Part to secure that accommodation is available for the occupation of a person—

section 206 (general provisions),

. . .

section 208 (out-of-area placements),

section 209 (arrangements with private landlord).

(2) In [sections 206 and 208] those functions are referred to as the authority's "housing functions under this Part".

[(3) For the purposes of this section, a local housing authority's duty under section 189B(2) or 195(2) is a function of the authority to secure that accommodation is available for the occupation of a person only if the authority decide to discharge the duty by securing that accommodation is so available.]

NOTES

Amendment

Sub-s (1): words omitted repealed by the Homelessness Act 2002, s 18(2), Sch 2.
  Date in force (in relation to England): 31 July 2002: see SI 2002/1799, art 2.
  Date in force (in relation to Wales): 30 September 2002: see SI 2002/1736, art 2(1), Schedule, Pt 1.
Sub-s (2): words "sections 206 and 208" in square brackets substituted by the Homelessness Act 2002, s 18(1), Sch 1, paras 2, 18.
  Date in force (in relation to England): 31 July 2002: see SI 2002/1799, art 2.
  Date in force (in relation to Wales): 30 September 2002: see SI 2002/1736, art 2(1), Schedule, Pt 1.
Sub-s (3): inserted by the Homelessness Reduction Act 2017, s 6.
  Date in force: 3 April 2018: see SI 2018/167, reg 3(f).

206 Discharge of functions by local housing authorities

(1) A local housing authority may discharge their housing functions under this Part only in the following ways—

   (a)   by securing that suitable accommodation provided by them is available,

   (b)   by securing that he obtains suitable accommodation from some other person, or

   (c)   by giving him such advice and assistance as will secure that suitable accommodation is available from some other person.

(2) A local housing authority may require a person in relation to whom they are discharging such functions—

   (a)   to pay such reasonable charges as they may determine in respect of accommodation which they secure for his occupation (either by making it available themselves or otherwise), or

   (b)   to pay such reasonable amount as they may determine in respect of sums payable by them for accommodation made available by another person.

207 . . .

. . .

NOTES

Amendment

Repealed by the Homelessness Act 2002, s 18(2), Sch 2.
  Date in force (in relation to England): 31 July 2002: see SI 2002/1799, art 2.
  Date in force (in relation to Wales): 30 September 2002: see SI 2002/1736, art 2(1), Schedule, Pt 1.

208 Discharge of functions: out-of-area placements

(1) So far as reasonably practicable a local housing authority shall in discharging their housing functions under this Part secure that accommodation is available for the occupation of the applicant in their district.

(2) If they secure that accommodation is available for the occupation of the applicant outside their district, they shall give notice to the local housing authority in whose district the accommodation is situated.

(3) The notice shall state—

    (a)   the name of the applicant,

    (b)   the number and description of other persons who normally reside with him as a member of his family or might reasonably be expected to reside with him,

    (c)   the address of the accommodation,

    (d)   the date on which the accommodation was made available to him, and

    (e)   which function under this Part the authority was discharging in securing that the accommodation is available for his occupation.

(4) The notice must be in writing, and must be given before the end of the period of 14 days beginning with the day on which the accommodation was made available to the applicant.

[209 Discharge of interim duties: arrangements with private landlord]

[(1) This section applies where in pursuance of any of their housing functions under section 188, 190, 200 or 204(4) (interim duties) a local housing authority make arrangements with a private landlord to provide accommodation.

(2) A tenancy granted to the applicant in pursuance of the arrangements cannot be an assured tenancy before the end of the period of twelve months beginning with—

    (a)   the date on which the applicant was notified of the authority's decision under section 184(3) or 198(5); or

    (b)   if there is a review of that decision under section 202 or an appeal to the court under section 204, the date on which he is notified of the decision on review or the appeal is finally determined,

unless, before or during that period, the tenant is notified by the landlord (or in the case of joint landlords, at least one of them) that the tenancy is to be regarded as an assured shorthold tenancy or an assured tenancy other than an assured shorthold tenancy.]

NOTES

Amendment

> Substituted by the Homelessness Act 2002, s 18(1), Sch 1, paras 2, 19.
>> Date in force (in relation to England): 31 July 2002: see SI 2002/1799, art 2.
>> Date in force (in relation to Wales): 30 September 2002: see SI 2002/1736, art 2(1), Schedule, Pt 1.

210 Suitability of accommodation

(1) In determining for the purposes of this Part whether accommodation is suitable for a person, the local housing authority shall have regard to [Parts 9 and 10] of the Housing Act 1985 (slum clearance [and overcrowding) and Parts 1 to 4 of the Housing Act 2004]).

(2) The Secretary of State may by order specify—

    (a)   circumstances in which accommodation is or is not to be regarded as suitable for a person, and

    (b)   matters to be taken into account or disregarded in determining whether accommodation is suitable for a person.

NOTES

Amendment

> Sub-s (1): words "Parts 9 and 10" in square brackets substituted by the Housing Act 2004, s 265(1), Sch 15, paras 40, 43(a).
>> Date in force (in relation to England): 6 April 2006: see SI 2006/1060, arts 1(3)(c), 2(1)(d).
>> Date in force (in relation to Wales): 16 June 2006: see SI 2006/1535, arts 1(2)(c), 2(b).
> Sub-s (1): words "and overcrowding) and Parts 1 to 4 of the Housing Act 2004" in square brackets substituted by the Housing Act 2004, s 265(1), Sch 15, paras 40, 43(b).
>> Date in force (in relation to England): 6 April 2006: see SI 2006/1060, arts 1(3)(c), 2(1)(d).
>> Date in force (in relation to Wales): 16 June 2006: see SI 2006/1535, arts 1(2)(c), 2(b).

211 Protection of property of homeless persons and persons threatened with homelessness

(1) This section applies where a local housing authority have reason to believe that—

    (a)   there is danger of loss of, or damage to, any personal property of an applicant by reason of his inability to protect it or deal with it, and

    (b)   no other suitable arrangements have been or are being made.

(2) If the authority have become subject to a duty towards the applicant under—

section 188 (interim duty to accommodate),

[section 189B (initial duty owed to all eligible persons who are homeless),]

section 190, 193 or 195 (duties to persons found to be homeless or threatened with homelessness), or

section 200 (duties to applicant whose case is considered for referral or referred),

then, whether or not they are still subject to such a duty, they shall take reasonable steps to prevent the loss of the property or prevent or mitigate damage to it.

(3) If they have not become subject to such a duty, they may take any steps they consider reasonable for that purpose.

(4) The authority may decline to take action under this section except upon such conditions as they consider appropriate in the particular case, which may include conditions as to—

    (a)   the making and recovery by the authority of reasonable charges for the action taken, or

    (b)   the disposal by the authority, in such circumstances as may be specified, of property in relation to which they have taken action.

(5) References in this section to personal property of the applicant include personal property of any person who might reasonably be expected to reside with him.

(6) Section 212 contains provisions supplementing this section.

NOTES

Amendment

> Sub-s (2): words "section 189B (initial duty owed to all eligible persons who are homeless)," in square brackets inserted by the Homelessness Reduction Act 2017, s 5(1), (12).
>> Date in force: 3 April 2018: see SI 2018/167, reg 3(e); for transitional and savings provisions see reg 4(1).

212 Protection of property: supplementary provisions

(1) The authority may for the purposes of section 211 (protection of property of homeless persons or persons threatened with homelessness)—

    (a)   enter, at all reasonable times, any premises which are the usual place of residence of the applicant or which were his last usual place of residence, and

    (b)   deal with any personal property of his in any way which is reasonably necessary, in particular by storing it or arranging for its storage.

(2) Where the applicant asks the authority to move his property to a particular location nominated by him, the authority—

(a) may, if it appears to them that his request is reasonable, discharge their responsibilities under section 211 by doing as he asks, and

(b) having done so, have no further duty or power to take action under that section in relation to that property.

If such a request is made, the authority shall before complying with it inform the applicant of the consequence of their doing so.

(3) If no such request is made (or, if made, is not acted upon) the authority cease to have any duty or power to take action under section 211 when, in their opinion, there is no longer any reason to believe that there is a danger of loss of or damage to a person's personal property by reason of his inability to protect it or deal with it.

But property stored by virtue of their having taken such action may be kept in store and any conditions upon which it was taken into store continue to have effect, with any necessary modifications.

(4) Where the authority—

(a) cease to be subject to a duty to take action under section 211 in respect of an applicant's property, or

(b) cease to have power to take such action, having previously taken such action,

they shall notify the applicant of that fact and of the reason for it.

(5) The notification shall be given to the applicant—

(a) by delivering it to him, or

(b) by leaving it, or sending it to him, at his last known address.

(6) References in this section to personal property of the applicant include personal property of any person who might reasonably be expected to reside with him.

213 Co-operation between relevant housing authorities and bodies

(1) Where a local housing authority [in England]—

(a) request another relevant housing authority or body, in England, Wales or Scotland, to assist them in the discharge of their functions under this Part, or

(b) request a social services authority, in England, Wales or Scotland, to exercise any of their functions in relation to a case which the local housing authority are dealing with under this Part,

the authority or body to whom the request is made shall co-operate in rendering such assistance in the discharge of the functions to which the request relates as is reasonable in the circumstances.

(2) In subsection (1)(a) "relevant housing authority or body" means—

(a) in relation to England and Wales, a local housing authority, a new town corporation, [a private registered provider of social housing] a registered social landlord or a housing action trust;

(b) in relation to Scotland, a local authority, a development corporation, a registered housing association or Scottish Homes.

Expressions used in paragraph (a) have the same meaning as in the Housing Act 1985; and expressions used in paragraph (b) have the same meaning as in the Housing (Scotland) Act 1987.

(3) Subsection (1) above applies to a request by a local authority in Scotland under section 38 of the Housing (Scotland) Act 1987 as it applies to a request by a local housing authority in England and Wales (the references to this Part being construed, in relation to such a request, as references to Part II of that Act).

NOTES

Amendment

Sub-s (1): words "in England" in square brackets inserted, in relation to Wales, by the Housing (Wales) Act 2014, s 100, Sch 3, Pt 1, paras 2, 14.

Date in force: 27 April 2015: see SI 2015/1272, art 2, Schedule, paras 51, 53; for a transitional provision see art 7.

Sub-s (2): in para (a) words "a private registered provider of social housing" in square brackets inserted by SI 2010/866, art 5, Sch 2, paras 81, 103.

Date in force: 1 April 2010: see SI 2010/866, art 1(2); for transitional provisions and savings see art 6, Sch 3, paras 1, 3, 4 thereto.

[213A Co-operation in certain cases involving children]

[(1)   This section applies where a local housing authority have reason to believe that an applicant with whom a person under the age of 18 normally resides, or might reasonably be expected to reside—

(a)   may be ineligible for assistance; [or]

(b)   may be homeless and may have become so intentionally. . . . . .

(c)   . . ..

(2)   A local housing authority shall make arrangements for ensuring that, where this section applies—

(a)   the applicant is invited to consent to the referral of the essential facts of his case to the social services authority for the district of the housing authority (where that is a different authority); and

(b)   if the applicant has given that consent, the social services authority are made aware of those facts and of the subsequent decision of the housing authority in respect of his case.

(3)   Where the local housing authority and the social services authority for a district are the same authority (a "unitary authority"), that authority shall make arrangements for ensuring that, where this section applies—

(a)   the applicant is invited to consent to the referral to the social services department of the essential facts of his case; and

(b)   if the applicant has given that consent, the social services department is made aware of those facts and of the subsequent decision of the authority in respect of his case.

(4)   Nothing in subsection (2) or (3) affects any power apart from this section to disclose information relating to the applicant's case to the social services authority or to the social services department (as the case may be) without the consent of the applicant.

(5)   Where a social services authority—

(a)   are aware of a decision of a local housing authority that the applicant is ineligible for [assistance or became homeless intentionally], and

(b)   request the local housing authority to provide them with advice and assistance in the exercise of their social services functions under Part 3 of the Children Act 1989 [or Part 6 of the Social Services and Well-being (Wales) Act 2014],

the local housing authority shall provide them with such advice and assistance as is reasonable in the circumstances.

(6)   A unitary authority shall make arrangements for ensuring that, where they make a decision of a kind mentioned in subsection (5)(a), the housing department provide the social services department with such advice and assistance as the social services department may reasonably request.

(7)   In this section, in relation to a unitary authority—

"the housing department" means those persons responsible for the exercise of their housing functions; and

"the social services department" means those persons responsible for the exercise of their social services functions under Part 3 of the Children Act 1989 [or Part 6 of the Social Services and Well-being (Wales) Act 2014].]

NOTES

Amendment

Inserted by the Homelessness Act 2002, s 12.
Date in force (in relation to Wales): 30 September 2002: see SI 2002/1736, art 2(1), Schedule, Pt 1.
Date in force (in relation to England): 1 October 2002: see SI 2002/1799, art 3.
Sub-s (1): in para (a) word "or" in square brackets inserted by the Homelessness Reduction Act 2017, s 4(1), (7)(a)(i).
Date in force: 3 April 2018: see SI 2018/167, reg 3(d); for transitional and savings provisions see reg 4(1).
Sub-s (1): para (c) and word omitted immediately preceding it repealed by the Homelessness Reduction Act 2017, s 4(1), (7)(a)(ii).
Date in force: 3 April 2018: see SI 2018/167, reg 3(d); for transitional and savings provisions see reg 4(1).
Sub-s (5): in para (a) words "assistance or became homeless intentionally" in square brackets substituted by the Homelessness Reduction Act 2017, s 4(1), (7)(b).
Date in force: 3 April 2018: see SI 2018/167, reg 3(d); for transitional and savings provisions see reg 4(1).
Sub-s (5): in para (b) words "or Part 6 of the Social Services and Well-being (Wales) Act 2014" in square brackets inserted by SI 2016/413, regs 149, 150(a).
Date in force: 6 April 2016: see SI 2016/413, reg 2(1); for transitional provisions and savings see reg 325, Schedule.
Sub-s (7): in definition "the social services department" words "or Part 6 of the Social Services and Well-being (Wales) Act 2014" in square brackets inserted by SI 2016/413, regs 149, 150(b).
Date in force: 6 April 2016: see SI 2016/413, reg 2(1); for transitional provisions and savings see reg 325, Schedule.

[213B Duty of public authority to refer cases in England to local housing authority]

[(1)   This section applies if a specified public authority considers that a person in England in relation to whom the authority exercises functions is or may be homeless or threatened with homelessness.

(2)   The specified public authority must ask the person to agree to the authority notifying a local housing authority in England of—

(a)   the opinion mentioned in subsection (1), and

(b)   how the person may be contacted by the local housing authority.

(3)   If the person—

(a)   agrees to the specified public authority making the notification, and

(b)   identifies a local housing authority in England to which the person would like the notification to be made,

the specified public authority must notify that local housing authority of the matters mentioned in subsection (2)(a) and (b).

(4)   In this section "specified public authority" means a public authority specified, or of a description specified, in regulations made by the Secretary of State.

(5)   In subsection (4) "public authority" means a person (other than a local housing authority) who has functions of a public nature.]

NOTES

Amendment

Inserted by the Homelessness Reduction Act 2017, s 10.
Date in force (for certain purposes): 12 February 2018: see SI 2018/167, reg 2(c).
Date in force (for remaining purposes): 3 April 2018: see SI 2018/167, reg 3(j).

General provisions

214 False statements, withholding information and failure to disclose change of circumstances

(1)   It is an offence for a person, with intent to induce a local housing authority to believe in connection with the exercise of their functions under this Part that he or

another person is entitled to accommodation or assistance in accordance with the provisions of this Part, or is entitled to accommodation or assistance of a particular description—

(a)   knowingly or recklessly to make a statement which is false in a material particular, or

(b)   knowingly to withhold information which the authority have reasonably required him to give in connection with the exercise of those functions.

(2) If before an applicant receives notification of the local housing authority's decision on his application there is any change of facts material to his case, he shall notify the authority as soon as possible.

The authority shall explain to every applicant, in ordinary language, the duty imposed on him by this subsection and the effect of subsection (3).

(3)   A person who fails to comply with subsection (2) commits an offence unless he shows that he was not given the explanation required by that subsection or that he had some other reasonable excuse for non-compliance.

(4)   A person guilty of an offence under this section is liable on summary conviction to a fine not exceeding level 5 on the standard scale.

[214A Codes of practice]

[(1)   The Secretary of State may from time to time issue one or more codes of practice dealing with the functions of a local housing authority in England relating to homelessness or the prevention of homelessness.

(2)   The provision that may be made by a code of practice under this section includes, in particular, provision about—

(a)   the exercise by a local housing authority of functions under this Part;

(b)   the training of an authority's staff in relation to the exercise of those functions;

(c)   the monitoring by an authority of the exercise of those functions.

(3)   A code of practice may—

(a)   apply to all local housing authorities or to the local housing authorities specified or described in the code;

(b)   contain different provision for different kinds of local housing authority.

(4)   The Secretary of State may issue a code of practice under this section only in accordance with subsections (5) and (6).

(5)   Before issuing the code of practice, the Secretary of State must lay a draft of the code before Parliament.

(6)   If—

(a)   the Secretary of State lays a draft of the code before Parliament, and

(b)   no negative resolution is made within the 40-day period,

the Secretary of State may issue the code in the form of the draft.

(7)   For the purposes of subsection (6)—

(a)   a "negative resolution" means a resolution of either House of Parliament not to approve the draft of the code, and

(b)   "the 40-day period" means the period of 40 days beginning with the day on which the draft of the code is laid before Parliament (or, if it is not laid before each House of Parliament on the same day, the later of the two days on which it is laid).

(8)   In calculating the 40-day period, no account is to be taken of any period during which—

(a)   Parliament is dissolved or prorogued, or

(b)   both Houses are adjourned for more than four days.

(9)   The Secretary of State may—

(a)   from time to time revise and reissue a code of practice under this section;

(b)   revoke a code of practice under this section.

(10)   Subsections (4) to (6) do not apply to the reissue of a code of practice under this section.

(11)   The Secretary of State must publish the current version of each code of practice under this section in whatever manner the Secretary of State thinks fit.

(12)   A local housing authority must have regard to a code of practice under this section in exercising their functions.]

NOTES

Amendment

> Inserted by the Homelessness Reduction Act 2017, s 11.
>> Date in force: 3 April 2018: see SI 2018/167, reg 3(k).

215   Regulations and orders

(1)   In this Part "prescribed" means prescribed by regulations of the Secretary of State.

(2)   Regulations or an order under this Part may make different provision for different purposes, including different provision for different areas.

(3)   Regulations or an order under this Part shall be made by statutory instrument.

(4)   Unless required to be approved in draft, regulations or an order under this Part shall be subject to annulment in pursuance of a resolution of either House of Parliament.

216   Transitional and consequential matters

(1)   The provisions of this Part have effect in place of the provisions of Part III of the Housing Act 1985 (housing the homeless) and shall be construed as one with that Act.

(2)   Subject to any transitional provision contained in an order under section 232(4) (power to include transitional provision in commencement order), the provisions of this Part do not apply in relation to an applicant whose application for accommodation or assistance in obtaining accommodation was made before the commencement of this Part.

(3)   The enactments mentioned in Schedule 17 have effect with the amendments specified there which are consequential on the provisions of this Part.

217   Minor definitions: Part VII

(1)   In this Part, subject to subsection (2)—

> ["private landlord" means a landlord who is not within section 80(1) of the Housing Act 1985 (c 68) (the landlord condition for secure tenancies);]
>> "relevant authority" means a local housing authority or a social services authority; and
>> "social services authority" means[—
>>> (a)   in relation to England,] a local authority for the purposes of the Local Authority Social Services Act 1970, as defined in section 1 of that Act;
>>> [(b)   in relation to Wales, a local authority exercising social services functions for the purposes of the Social Services and Well-being (Wales) Act 2014].

(2)   In this Part, in relation to Scotland—

> (a)   "local housing authority" means a local authority within the meaning of the Housing (Scotland) Act 1988, and
> (b)   "social services authority" means a local authority for the purposes of the Social Work (Scotland) Act 1968.

(3)   References in this Part to the district of a local housing authority—

> (a)   have the same meaning in relation to an authority in England or Wales as in the Housing Act 1985, and

(b)   in relation to an authority in Scotland, mean the area of the local authority concerned.

NOTES

Amendment

Sub-s (1): definition "private landlord" inserted by the Homelessness Act 2002, s 18(1), Sch 1, paras 2, 20.
> Date in force (in relation to England): 31 July 2002: see SI 2002/1799, art 2.
> Date in force (in relation to Wales): 30 September 2002: see SI 2002/1736, art 2(1), Schedule, Pt 1.

Sub-s (1): in definition "social services authority" words "— (a) in relation to England," in square brackets inserted by SI 2016/413, regs 149, 151(a).
> Date in force: 6 April 2016: see SI 2016/413, reg 2(1); for transitional provisions and savings see reg 325, Schedule.

Sub-s (1): in definition "social services authority" para (b) inserted by SI 2016/413, regs 149, 151(b).
> Date in force: 6 April 2016: see SI 2016/413, reg 2(1); for transitional provisions and savings see reg 325, Schedule.

218   Index of defined expressions: Part VII

The following Table shows provisions defining or otherwise explaining expressions used in this Part (other than provisions defining or explaining an expression used in the same section)—

accommodation available for occupation	section 176
applicant	section 183(2)
assistance under this Part	section 183(2)
associated (in relation to a person)	section 178
assured tenancy and assured shorthold tenancy	section 230
district (of local housing authority)	section 217(3)
eligible for assistance	section 183(2)
homeless	section 175(1)
housing functions under this Part (in sections [206 and 208])	section 205(2)
intentionally homeless	section 191
. . .	< . . . >
local connection	section 199
local housing authority–	
-in England and Wales	section 230
-in Scotland	section 217(2)(a)
< . . . >	< . . . >
Prescribed	section 215(1)
priority need	section 189
[private landlord	section 217(1)]
Reasonable to continue to occupy accommodation	section 177
registered social landlord	section 230
relevant authority	section 217(1)
[restricted person	section 184(7)]
social services authority	section 217(1) and (2)(b)
threatened with homelessness	section 175(4)

NOTES

Amendment

In entry relating to "housing functions under this Part" words "206 and 208" in square brackets substituted by the Homelessness Act 2002, s 18(1), Sch 1, paras 2, 21(a).

Date in force (in relation to England): 31 July 2002: see SI 2002/1799, art 2.

Date in force (in relation to Wales): 30 September 2002: see SI 2002/1736, art 2(1), Schedule, Pt 1.

Entry relating to "intentionally threatened with homelessness" (omitted) repealed by the Homelessness Reduction Act 2017, s 4(1), (8).

Date in force: 3 April 2018: see SI 2018/167, reg 3(d); for transitional and savings provisions see reg 4(1).

Entry relating to "minimum period" (omitted) repealed by the Homelessness Act 2002, s 18(2), Sch 2.

Date in force (in relation to England): 31 July 2002: see SI 2002/1799, art 2.

Date in force (in relation to Wales): 30 September 2002: see SI 2002/1736, art 2(1), Schedule, Pt 1.

Entry relating to "private landlord" inserted by the Homelessness Act 2002, s 18(1), Sch 1, paras 2, 21(b).

Date in force (in relation to England): 31 July 2002: see SI 2002/1799, art 2.

Date in force (in relation to Wales): 30 September 2002: see SI 2002/1736, art 2(1), Schedule, Pt 1.

Entry relating to "restricted person" inserted by the Housing and Regeneration Act 2008, s 314, Sch 15, Pt 1, paras 1, 8.

Date in force: 2 March 2009 (except in relation to applications for an allocation of social housing or housing assistance (homelessness) or for accommodation made before that date): see SI 2009/415, art 2.

HOMELESSNESS ACT 2002

Homelessness reviews and strategies[: England]

A2.2

1 Duty of local housing authority [in England] to formulate a homelessness strategy

(1) A local housing authority [in England] ("the authority") may from time to time—

    (a)   carry out a homelessness review for their district; and

    (b)   formulate and publish a homelessness strategy based on the results of that review.

(2) The social services authority for the district of the authority (where that is a different local authority) shall give such assistance in connection with the exercise of the power under subsection (1) as the authority may reasonably require.

(3) The authority shall exercise that power so as to ensure that the first homelessness strategy for their district is published within the period of twelve months beginning with the day on which this section comes into force.

(4) The authority shall exercise that power so as to ensure that a new homelessness strategy for their district is published within the period of five years beginning with the day on which their last homelessness strategy was published.

(5) A local housing authority [in England] shall take their homelessness strategy into account in the exercise of their functions.

(6) A social services authority shall take the homelessness strategy for the district of a local housing authority into account in the exercise of their functions in relation to that district.

(7) Nothing in subsection (5) or (6) affects any duty or requirement arising apart from this section.

NOTES

Amendment

    Cross-heading: word ": England" in square brackets inserted, in relation to Wales, by the Housing (Wales) Act 2014, s 100, Sch 3, Pt 1, paras 15, 16.

        Date in force: 27 April 2015: see SI 2015/1272, art 2, Schedule, paras 51, 53.

    Section heading: words "in England" in square brackets inserted, in relation to Wales, by the Housing (Wales) Act 2014, s 100, Sch 3, Pt 1, paras 15, 17(b).

        Date in force: 27 April 2015: see SI 2015/1272, art 2, Schedule, paras 51, 53.

    Sub-s (1): words "in England" in square brackets inserted, in relation to Wales, by the Housing (Wales) Act 2014, s 100, Sch 3, Pt 1, paras 15, 17(a).

        Date in force: 27 April 2015: see SI 2015/1272, art 2, Schedule, paras 51, 53.

    Sub-s (5): words "in England" in square brackets inserted, in relation to Wales, by the Housing (Wales) Act 2014, s 100, Sch 3, Pt 1, paras 15, 17(a).

        Date in force: 27 April 2015: see SI 2015/1272, art 2, Schedule, paras 51, 53.

2 Homelessness reviews

(1) For the purposes of this Act "homelessness review" means a review by a local housing authority of—

    (a)   the levels, and likely future levels, of homelessness in their district;

    (b)   the activities which are carried out for any purpose mentioned in subsection (2) (or which contribute to their achievement); and

    (c)   the resources available to the authority, the social services authority for their district, other public authorities, voluntary organisations and other persons for such activities.

(2) Those purposes are—

    (a)   preventing homelessness in the district of the authority;

(b)   securing that accommodation is or will be available for people in the district who are or may become homeless;

(c)   providing support for people in the district—

(i)   who are or may become homeless; or

(ii)   who have been homeless and need support to prevent them becoming homeless again.

(3)   A local housing authority shall, after completing a homelessness review—

(a)   arrange for the results of the review to be available at its principal office for inspection at all reasonable hours, without charge, by members of the public; and

(b)   provide (on payment if required by the authority of a reasonable charge) a copy of those results to any member of the public who asks for one.

3   Homelessness strategies

(1)   For the purposes of this Act "homelessness strategy" means a strategy formulated by a local housing authority for—

(a)   preventing homelessness in their district;

(b)   securing that sufficient accommodation is and will be available for people in their district who are or may become homeless;

(c)   securing the satisfactory provision of support for people in their district—

(i)   who are or may become homeless; or

(ii)   who have been homeless and need support to prevent them becoming homeless again.

(2)   A homelessness strategy may include specific objectives to be pursued, and specific action planned to be taken, in the course of the exercise of—

(a)   the functions of the authority as a local housing authority; or

(b)   the functions of the social services authority for the district.

(3)   A homelessness strategy may also include provision relating to specific action which the authority expects to be taken—

(a)   by any public authority with functions (not being functions mentioned in subsection (2)) which are capable of contributing to the achievement of any of the objectives mentioned in subsection (1); or

(b)   by any voluntary organisation or other person whose activities are capable of contributing to the achievement of any of those objectives.

(4)   The inclusion in a homelessness strategy of any provision relating to action mentioned in subsection (3) requires the approval of the body or person concerned.

(5)   In formulating a homelessness strategy the authority shall consider (among other things) the extent to which any of the objectives mentioned in subsection (1) can be achieved through action involving two or more of the bodies or other persons mentioned in subsections (2) and (3).

(6)   The authority shall keep their homelessness strategy under review and may modify it from time to time.

(7)   If the authority modify their homelessness strategy, they shall publish the modifications or the strategy as modified (as they consider most appropriate).

[(7A)   In formulating or modifying a homelessness strategy, a local housing authority *in England* shall have regard to—

(a)   its current allocation scheme under section 166A of the Housing Act 1996,

(b)   its current tenancy strategy under section 150 of the Localism Act 2011, and

(c)   in the case of an authority that is a London borough council, the current London housing strategy.]

(8)   Before adopting or modifying a homelessness strategy the authority shall consult such public or local authorities, voluntary organisations or other persons as they consider appropriate.

(9)   The authority shall—

(a)   make a copy of [everything published under section 1 or] this section available at its principal office for inspection at all reasonable hours, without charge, by members of the public; and

(b)   provide (on payment if required by the authority of a reasonable charge) a copy of [anything] so published to any member of the public who asks for one.

NOTES

Amendment

Sub-s (7A): inserted by the Localism Act 2011, s 153.
    Date in force (for certain purposes): 15 January 2012: see SI 2012/57, art 4(1)(o).
    Date in force (for remaining purposes): 7 June 2012: see SI 2012/1463, art 2(g).
Sub-s (7A): words "in England" in italics repealed, in relation to Wales, by the Housing (Wales) Act 2014, s 100, Sch 3, Pt 1, paras 15, 18.
    Date in force: 27 April 2015: see SI 2015/1272, art 2, Schedule, paras 51, 53.
Sub-s (9): in para (a) words "everything published under section 1 or" in square brackets substituted by the Local Government Act 2003, s 127(1), Sch 7, para 81(a).
    Date in force: 18 November 2003: see the Local Government Act 2003, s 128(2)(e).
Sub-s (9): in para (b) word "anything" in square brackets substituted by the Local Government Act 2003, s 127(1), Sch 7, para 81(b).
    Date in force: 18 November 2003: see the Local Government Act 2003, s 128(2)(e).

4 Sections 1 to 3: interpretation

In sections 1 to 3—

"homeless" and "homelessness" have the same meaning as in Part 7 of the Housing Act 1996 (c 52) (in this Act referred to as "the 1996 Act");

"local housing authority" and "district" have the same meaning as in the Housing Act 1985 (c 68);

"social services authority" means a local authority for the purposes of the Local Authority Social Services Act 1970 (c 42) [or Part 8 of the Social Services and Well-being (Wales) Act 2014];

"support" means advice, information or assistance; and

"voluntary organisation" has the same meaning as in section 180(3) of the 1996 Act.

NOTES

Amendment

In definition "social services authority" words "or Part 8 of the Social Services and Well-being (Wales) Act 2014" in square brackets inserted by SI 2016/413, reg 187.
    Date in force: 6 April 2016: see SI 2016/413, reg 2(1); for transitional provisions and savings see reg 325, Schedule.

. . .

Supplementary

17   Wales

(1)   The reference to the 1996 Act in Schedule 1 to the National Assembly for Wales (Transfer of Functions) Order 1999 (SI 1999/672) is to be treated as referring to that Act as amended by this Act.

(2)   Subsection (1) does not affect the power to make further Orders varying or omitting that reference.

18 Minor and consequential amendments and repeals

(1)   Schedule 1 (which contains minor and consequential amendments) has effect.

(2)   Schedule 2 (which contains repeals) has effect.

19 Financial provision

There shall be paid out of money provided by Parliament any increase attributable to this Act in the sums payable out of money so provided under any other Act.

20 Commencement, transitional provision and general saving

(1)   The preceding provisions of this Act (and the Schedules), other than section 8 and paragraphs 3 and 7 of Schedule 1, come into force on such day as the Secretary of State may by order made by statutory instrument appoint; and different days may be appointed for different purposes.

(2)   The Secretary of State may by order made by statutory instrument make such transitional provisions and savings as he considers appropriate in connection with the coming into force of any provision of this Act.

(3)   The powers conferred by subsection (1) and (2) are exercisable as respects Wales by the National Assembly for Wales (and not the Secretary of State).

(4)   Nothing in this Act affects the operation of section 216(2) of the 1996 Act in relation to persons who applied for accommodation or assistance in obtaining accommodation before the commencement of Part 7 of that Act.

21 Short title, extent and application to Isles of Scilly

(1)   This Act may be cited as the Homelessness Act 2002.

(2)   This Act extends to England and Wales only.

(3)   This Act applies to the Isles of Scilly subject to such exceptions, adaptations and modifications as the Secretary of State may by order direct.

(4)   The power to make such an order is exercisable by statutory instrument subject to annulment in pursuance of a resolution of either House of Parliament.

HOMELESSNESS CODE OF GUIDANCE FOR LOCAL AUTHORITIES
(FEBRUARY 2018)

Contents

Definitions

Overview of the homelessness legislation

DEFINITIONS

A2.3

Throughout the code:

"the 1996 Act" means the Housing Act 1996;

"the 2002 Act" means the Homelessness Act 2002;

"the 2017 Act" means the Homelessness Reduction Act 2017;

"the housing authority" means the local housing authority;

"the code" means the Homelessness Code of Guidance for Local Authorities (2018);

"the Convention" means the European Convention on Human Rights;

"the Eligibility Regulations" means the Allocation of Housing and Homelessness (Eligibility) (England) Regulations 2006;

"personalised housing plans" means personalised plans;

"the 2002 Order" means the Homelessness (Priority Need for Accommodation) (England) Order 2002;

"the 2003 Order" means the Homelessness (Suitability of Accommodation) (England) Order 2003.

OVERVIEW OF THE HOMELESSNESS LEGISLATION

1   This overview provides a summary of the homelessness legislation and the duties, powers and obligations on housing authorities and others towards people who are homeless or at risk of homelessness. **It does not form part of the statutory code of guidance.**

Homelessness legislation

2   The primary homelessness legislation – that is, Part 7 of the Housing Act 1996 – provides the statutory under-pinning for action to prevent homelessness and provide assistance to people threatened with or actually homeless.

3   In 2002, the Government amended the homelessness legislation through the Homelessness Act 2002 and the *Homelessness (Priority Need for Accommodation) (England) Order 2002* to:

(a)   ensure a more strategic approach to tackling and preventing homelessness, in particular by requiring a homelessness strategy for every housing authority district; and,

(b)   strengthen the assistance available to people who are homeless or threatened with homelessness by extending the priority need categories to homeless 16 and 17 year olds; care leavers aged 18, 19 and 20; people who are vulnerable as a result of time spent in care, the armed forces, prison or custody, and people who are vulnerable because they have fled their home because of violence.

4   The Homelessness Reduction Act 2017 significantly reformed England's homelessness legislation by placing duties on local authorities to intervene at earlier stages to prevent homelessness in their areas. It also requires housing authorities to provide homelessness services to all those affected, not just those who have 'priority need.' These include:

(a)   an enhanced prevention duty extending the period a household is threatened with homelessness from 28 days to 56 days, meaning that housing authorities are required to work with people to prevent homelessness at an earlier stage; and,

1356

(b)   a new duty for those who are already homeless so that housing authorities will support households for 56 days to relieve their homelessness by helping them to secure accommodation.

Homelessness review and strategy

5   Under the Homelessness Act 2002, all housing authorities must have in place a homelessness strategy based on a review of all forms of homelessness in their district. The strategy must be renewed at least every 5 years. The social services authority must provide reasonable assistance.

6   The strategy must set out the authority's plans for the prevention of homelessness and for securing that sufficient accommodation and support are or will be available for people who become homeless or who are at risk of becoming so.

Duty to refer

7   The Homelessness Reduction Act 2017 introduced a duty on certain public authorities to refer service users who they think may be homeless or threatened with homelessness to a housing authority. The service user must give consent, and can choose which authority to be referred to. The housing authority should incorporate the duty to refer into their homelessness strategy and establish effective partnerships and working arrangements with agencies to facilitate appropriate referrals.

Duty to provide advisory services

8   The housing authority has a duty to provide advice and information about homelessness and the prevention of homelessness and the rights of homeless people or those at risk of homelessness, as well as the help that is available from the housing authority or others and how to access that help. The service should be designed with certain listed vulnerable groups in mind and authorities can provide it themselves or arrange for other agencies to do it on their behalf.

Applications and inquiries

9   Housing authorities must give proper consideration to all applications for housing assistance, and if they have reason to believe that an applicant may be homeless or threatened with homelessness, they must make inquiries to see whether they owe them any duty under Part 7 of the 1996 Act. This assessment process is important in enabling housing authorities to identify the assistance which an applicant may need, either to prevent them from becoming homeless, or to help them to find another home. In each case, the authority will need to first decide whether the applicant is eligible for assistance and threatened with or actually homeless. Certain applicants who are 'persons from abroad' are not eligible for any assistance under Part 7 except free advice and information about homelessness and the prevention of homelessness.

10   Broadly speaking, a person is *threatened with homelessness* if they are likely to become homeless within 56 days. An applicant who has been served with valid notice under section 21 of the Housing Act 1988 to end their assured shorthold tenancy is also threatened with homelessness, if the notice has expired or will expire within 56 days and is served in respect of the only accommodation that is available for them to occupy.

11   An applicant is to be considered *homeless* if they do not have accommodation that they have a legal right to occupy, which is accessible and physically available to them (and their household) and which it would be reasonable for them to continue to live in.

Assessments and personalised housing plans

12   Housing authorities have a duty to carry out an assessment in all cases where an eligible applicant is homeless or threatened with homelessness. This will identify what has caused the homelessness or threat of homelessness, the housing needs of the applicant and any support they need in order to be able to secure and retain

accommodation. Following this assessment, the housing authority must work with the person to develop a personalised housing plan which will include actions (or 'reasonable steps') to be taken by the authority and the applicant to try and prevent or relieve homelessness.

Prevention duty

13 Housing authorities have a duty to take reasonable steps to help prevent any eligible person (regardless of priority need status, intentionality and whether they have a local connection) who is threatened with homelessness from becoming homeless. This means either helping them to stay in their current accommodation or helping them to find a new place to live before they become actually homeless. The prevention duty continues for 56 days unless it is brought to an end by an event such as accommodation being secured for the person, or by their becoming homeless.

Relief duty

14 If the applicant is already homeless, or becomes homeless despite activity during the prevention stage, the reasonable steps will be focused on helping the applicant to secure accommodation. This relief duty lasts for 56 days unless ended in another way. If the housing authority has reason to believe a homeless applicant may be eligible for assistance and have a priority need they must be provided with interim accommodation.

Main housing duty

15 If homelessness is not successfully prevented or relieved, a housing authority will owe the main housing duty to applicants who are eligible, have a priority need for accommodation and are not homeless intentionally. Certain categories of household, such as pregnant women, families with children, and households that are homeless due to an emergency such as a fire or flood, have priority need if homeless. Other groups may be assessed as having priority need because they are vulnerable as a result of old age, mental ill health, physical disability, having been in prison or care or as a result of becoming homeless due to domestic abuse.

16 Under the main housing duty, housing authorities must ensure that suitable accommodation is available for the applicant and their household until the duty is brought to an end, usually through the offer of a settled home. The duty can also be brought to an end for other reasons, such as the applicant turning down a suitable offer of temporary accommodation or because they are no longer eligible for assistance. A suitable offer of a settled home (whether accepted or refused by the applicant) which would bring the main housing duty to an end includes an offer of a suitable secure or introductory tenancy with a local authority, an offer of accommodation through a private registered provider (also known as a housing association) or the offer of a suitable tenancy for at least 12 months from a private landlord made by arrangement with the local authority.

Suitable accommodation

17 Housing authorities have various powers and duties to secure accommodation for homeless applicants, either on an interim basis, to prevent or relieve homelessness, to meet the main housing duty or as a settled home. Accommodation must always be 'suitable' and there are particular standards set when private rented accommodation is secured for households which have priority need.

18 Under the *Homelessness (Suitability of Accommodation) (England) Order 2003*, Bed & Breakfast accommodation is not considered suitable for families with children and households that include a pregnant woman, except where there is no other accommodation available, and then only for a maximum of six weeks. The Secretary of State considers that Bed & Breakfast accommodation is unsuitable for 16 and 17 year olds.

Intentional homelessness

19 A person would be homeless intentionally where homelessness was the consequence of a deliberate action or omission by that person. A deliberate act might be a decision to leave the previous accommodation even though it would have been reasonable for the person (and everyone in the person's household) to continue to live there. A deliberate omission might be non-payment of rent that led to rent arrears and eviction despite the rent being affordable.

20 Where people have a priority need but are intentionally homeless the housing authority must provide advice and assistance to help them find accommodation for themselves and secure suitable accommodation for them for a period that will give them a reasonable chance of doing so.

21 If, despite this assistance, homelessness persists, any children in the household could be in need under the Children Act 1989, and the family should be referred (with consent) to the children's social services authority.

Local connection and referrals to another authority

22 Broadly speaking, for the purpose of the homelessness legislation, people may have a local connection with a district because of residence, employment or family associations in the district, or because of special circumstances. (There are exceptions, for example, residence in a district while serving a prison sentence there does not establish a local connection.) Where applicants meet the criteria for the relief duty or for the main housing duty, and the authority considers that the applicant does not have a local connection with the district but does have one somewhere else, the housing authority dealing with the application can ask the housing authority in that other district to take responsibility for the case. However, applicants cannot be referred to another housing authority if they, or any member of their household, would be at risk of violence in the district of the other authority.

23 The definition of a 'local connection' for young people leaving care was amended by the Homelessness Reduction Act 2017 so that a young homeless care leaver has a local connection to the area of the local authority that looked after them. Additional provision is made for care leavers who have been placed in accommodation, under section 22A of the Children Act 1989, in a different district to that of the children's services authority that owes them leaving care duties. If they have lived in the other district for at least 2 years, including some time before they turned 16, they will also have a local connection with that district until they are 21.

Reviews and appeals

24 Housing authorities must provide written notifications to applicants when they reach certain decisions about their case, and the reasons behind any decisions that are against the applicant's interests. Applicants can ask the housing authority to review most aspects of their decisions, and, if still dissatisfied, can appeal to the county court on a point of law.

25 Housing authorities have the power to accommodate applicants pending a review or appeal to the county court. When an applicant who is being provided with interim accommodation requests a review of the suitability of accommodation offered to end the relief duty, the authority has a duty to continue to accommodate them pending a review.

CHAPTER 1: INTRODUCTION

Purpose of the code

1.1 The Secretary of State for Ministry of Housing, Communities and Local Government is issuing this code of guidance to local housing authorities (referred to as housing authorities) in England under section 182 of the Housing Act 1996 ('the 1996 Act'). In accordance with section 182(1) of the 1996 Act, housing authorities are required to have due regard to this statutory guidance in exercising their functions relating to homelessness and prevention of homelessness, including their functions under Part 7 of the 1996 Act (as amended) and under the Homelessness Act 2002 ('the 2002 Act'). This code replaces and consolidates the previous version published in 2006 and the supplementary guidance issued in August 2009, November 2012 and November 2014.

1.2 Under section 182(1), social services authorities in England are also required to have regard to guidance given by the Secretary of State (such as this code) when exercising their functions relating to homelessness and the prevention of homelessness. Further guidance applicable to social services authorities is also issued jointly with the Secretary of State for Health and Social Care and the Secretary of State for Education.

1.3 The code provides guidance on how housing authorities should exercise their functions relating to homelessness and threatened homelessness and apply the statutory duties in practice. This is not a substitute for legislation and therefore any policy context on the law documented in the code should be considered only as the Department's understanding at the time of issue. While it is intended that the code will be updated periodically, housing authorities are expected to keep up to date with developments in legislation and case law.

1.4 The Secretary of State has the power to issue statutory codes of practice, providing further guidance on how housing authorities should deliver and monitor their homelessness and homelessness prevention functions. Any codes of practice will focus on specific functions of housing authorities in order to drive up standards.

Who is the code for?

1.5 The code is issued specifically for local authority members and staff. It is also of direct relevance to private registered providers of social housing. Private registered providers have a duty under the 1996 Act to co-operate with housing authorities in exercising their homelessness functions. Private registered providers are subject to the Regulator of Social Housing's[1] Regulatory Standards, in particular the expectation that they will co-operate with local authority strategic housing functions, as set out in the Tenancy and Home and Community Standards.

1.6 Many of the activities discussed in the code require joint planning and operational co-operation between housing authorities and social services authorities, health authorities, criminal justice agencies, voluntary sector organisations and the diverse range of bodies working in the private rented sectors – so the code is also relevant to these agencies.

---

[1] The regulation of social housing is the responsibility of the Regulation Committee, a statutory committee of the Homes and Communities Agency (HCA). The organisation refers to itself as the Regulator of Social Housing in undertaking the functions of the Regulation Committee. References in any enactment or instrument to the Regulator of Social Housing are references to the HCA acting through the Regulation Committee. Homes England is the trading name of the HCA's non-regulation functions.

Homelessness legislation

1.7 Part 7 of the 1996 Act sets out the powers and duties of housing authorities where people apply to them for accommodation or assistance in obtaining accommodation in cases of homelessness or threatened homelessness.

1.8 The Homelessness Act 2002 ('the 2002 Act') places a requirement on housing authorities in England to formulate and publish a homelessness strategy based on the results of a review of homelessness in their district. The 2002 Act also amended a number of provisions in Part 7 of the 1996 Act to strengthen the safety net for vulnerable people.

1.9 The Homelessness Reduction Act 2017 ('the 2017 Act') places a set of duties on housing authorities to intervene at earlier stages to prevent homelessness in their areas and to take reasonable steps to prevent and relieve homelessness for all eligible applicants, not just those that have priority need under the Act.

Equality

1.10 Housing authorities need to ensure that policies and decisions relating to homelessness and threatened homelessness do not amount to unlawful conduct under the Equality Act 2010 and also comply with the public sector equality duty.

1.11 The Equality Act 2010 provides protection from unlawful discrimination in the provision of goods, services and public functions, housing, transport and education in relation to the protected characteristics set out in the legislation, which are:

(a) age;
(b) disability;
(c) gender reassignment;
(d) pregnancy and maternity (which includes breastfeeding);
(e) marriage and civil partnership;
(f) race;
(g) religion or belief;
(h) sex; and,
(i) sexual orientation.

1.12 The public sector equality duty in section 149(1) of the Equality Act 2010 requires public authorities, including housing authorities, to integrate equality considerations into the decision-making process from the outset, including in the development, implementation and review of their policies and services. This includes policies and services relating to homelessness and threatened homelessness. Other agencies and bodies who carry out public functions on behalf of local authorities also have a duty to comply with the public sector equality duty in the delivery of those public functions.

1.13 Specifically, under section 149(1) Equality Act 2010, public authorities in exercising their functions (or a person exercising public functions that is not a public authority (section 149(2)) must have due regard to the need to:

(a) eliminate discrimination, harassment, victimisation and any other conduct that is prohibited by or under the Equality Act 2010;
(b) advance equality of opportunity between persons who share a relevant protected characteristic and persons who do not share it; and,
(c) foster good relations between persons who share a relevant protected characteristic and persons who do not share it.

1.14 The three limbs of the duty, listed above, apply to all protected characteristics apart from marriage and civil partnership, which is only relevant to the first limb (eliminating discrimination and so on).

1.15 In order to comply with the public sector equality duty housing authorities need to do the following:

(a) plan how to factor in equality considerations;
(b) collect sufficient information to develop a reasonable understanding of what the equality impacts might be;
(c) identify any equality impact the policy or service might have;
(d) justify any decision that it takes;
(e) re-evaluation to consider whether any alternative approaches might be possible;
(f) record how many equality impacts are taken;
(g) inform decision-makers; and,
(h) continue to review equality impacts as the policy or service is implemented or developed.

1.16 The duty to have due regard to these equality issues will also apply when decisions are taken in respect of individual applications for homelessness assistance. Applicants should receive fully considered decisions which, in accordance with the public sector equality duty, show due regard to any equality impacts of the decision.

1.17 Housing authorities are also subject to *The Equality Act 2010 (Specific Duties* *and Public Authorities) Regulations 2017* (SI 2017/353) if they are covered under Schedule 2 to those regulations, which would include most housing authorities. These regulations require public authorities to publish information to demonstrate their compliance with the public sector equality duty and set and publish equality objectives.

1.18 Further information about the Equality Act 2010 and the public sector equality duty is available from the Equality and Human Rights Commission website and the Government Equalities Office on gov.uk.

Human Rights Act 1998

1.19 In addition, when someone is receiving services from (or is on the receiving end of public functions carried out by) a public sector organisation or others who deliver services or carry out public functions on their behalf, they will also have rights under the Human Rights Act 1998.

1.20 Section 3 of the Human Rights Act 1998 specifies that when interpreting the law, so far as it is possible to do so, primary and secondary legislation must be read and given effect in a way which is compatible with the European Convention on Human Rights ('the Convention'). Section 6 of the Human Rights Act 1998 provides that it is unlawful for a public authority to act in a way which is incompatible with a Convention right. Therefore, housing authorities and other agencies that carry out public functions on behalf of housing authorities must do so in a way that is compatible with Convention rights.

1.21 Housing authorities should pay particular attention to the promotion and protection of rights of vulnerable and disadvantaged groups such as people with disabilities, ethnic minorities, victims of sexual discrimination, children and elderly people.

1.22 Schedule 1 to the Human Rights Act 1998 gives further effect to a number of Convention rights and freedoms in domestic UK law. There are three Articles which are particularly important for the purposes of this code, as follows:

(a)   Article 3 - is the prohibition of torture whereby every person has the absolute right not to be tortured or subjected to treatment or punishment that is inhuman or degrading;

(b)   Article 4 - is the prohibition of slavery and forced labour whereby every person has the right not to be held in slavery or required to perform forced labour; and,

(c)   Article 8 - is the right to respect for private and family life whereby every person has the right to respect for their private and family life, their home and their correspondence. This right can be interfered with only in specified circumstances: where it is necessary in the interests of national security, public safety or the economic well-being of the country, for the prevention of disorder or crime, for the protection of health or morals, or for the protection of the rights and freedoms of others.

1.23 Under Article 3, housing authorities have an obligation to prevent a person being subjected to treatment or punishment that is inhuman or degrading, to investigate any allegations of such treatment, and to protect vulnerable individuals who they know or should know are at risk of such treatment.

1.24 Under Article 4, housing authorities should try to ensure that their policies or decisions take measures to protect victims of modern slavery or trafficking and to protect individuals who they are aware are at risk of such treatment.

1.25 Under Article 8, housing authorities should try to ensure that their policies or decisions do not interfere with a person's right to respect for private and family life, their home and their correspondence.

1.26 If a housing authority does decide that it will be difficult to avoid interfering with someone's Article 8 rights, it will need to make sure that the policy or action is necessary, pursues one of the recognised legitimate aims and is proportionate to that aim. A housing authority may be asked to produce reasons for its decisions.

1.27 Housing authorities may also need to consider whether there are situations putting them under obligation to take active steps to promote and protect individuals' Article 8 rights from systematic interference by third parties, for example, private businesses.

1.28 Housing authorities are expected to consider the human rights implications of their actions in the exercise of their powers, or risk having their decisions overturned as a result and the planning and delivery of their services affected.

1.29 Further information about the Human Rights Act 1998 is available from the Equality and Human Rights Commission.

Safeguarding

1.30 Housing authorities have a duty to safeguard and promote the welfare of children and to co-operate to promote the well-being of all children, including 16-17 year olds, in the area as set out in the Children Act 2004.

1.31 Housing authorities also have a duty to co-operate with children's services in relation to children in need when requested to do so, as long as this is compatible with their own statutory or other duties and obligations and does not unduly prejudice the discharge of any of their functions.

1.32 Children's needs are paramount, and the welfare, needs and wishes of each child should be put first, so that every child receives the support they need.

1.33 All professionals who come into contact with children and their families must be alert to their needs and any risks of harm that individual abusers or potential abusers may pose, and respond proactively to them when dealing with their housing situation.

1.34 All professionals must share appropriate information in a timely way and can discuss any concerns about an individual child with colleagues, and with children's services. This will include identifying where current or changing housing arrangements might affect risk to children.

1.35 All professionals contribute to whatever actions are needed to safeguard and promote a child's welfare and take part in regularly reviewing the outcomes for the child against specific plans and outcomes.

1.36 The duties placed on housing authorities are set out in the Government's inter-agency statutory guidance: 'Working together to safeguard children: A guide to inter-agency working to safeguard and promote the welfare of children.' The specific duties towards 16 and 17 year olds who are at risk of homelessness or who are homeless, and the legal duties children's services authorities and housing authorities have towards them are set out in the Government's statutory guidance: 'Provision of accommodation for 16 and 17 year old young people who may be homeless and/or require accommodation.'

CHAPTER 2: HOMELESSNESS STRATEGIES AND REVIEWS

2.1 This chapter provides guidance on housing authorities' duties to carry out a homelessness review and to formulate and publish a strategy based on the results of that review.

Duty to formulate a homelessness strategy

2.2 Section 1(1) of the 2002 Act gives housing authorities the power to carry out a homelessness review for their district and formulate and publish a homelessness strategy based on the results of the review. Section 1(4) requires housing authorities to publish a new homelessness strategy, based on the results of a further homelessness review, within the period of five years beginning with the day on which their last homelessness strategy was published. However, housing authorities can conduct homelessness reviews and publish homelessness strategies more frequently if circumstances in the district change.

2.3 There was an exemption from this requirement for 'excellent authorities' as classified by the Secretary of State by virtue of the Local Authorities' Plans and Strategies (Disapplication) (England) Order 2005. This regulation was revoked by the Local Audit and Accountability Act 2014 and all housing authorities are required to publish homelessness strategies as of 01 April 2017.

2.4 In conducting a review of homelessness and to formulate a new strategy, housing authorities will need to take into account the additional duties introduced through the 2017 Act. Authorities are encouraged to take the opportunity to involve all relevant partners in developing a strategy that involves them in earlier identification and intervention to prevent homelessness.

2.5 For a homelessness strategy to be effective, housing authorities should ensure that it is consistent with other local plans and is developed with, and has the support of, all relevant local authority departments and partners. Corporate and partnership involvement in identifying strategic objectives will help to ensure all relevant departments and agencies are committed to supporting their delivery.

2.6 The homelessness strategy should link with other strategies and programmes that aim to address the wide range of factors that could contribute to homelessness in the local area. It will be important to consider how these strategies and programmes, which could encompass aspects of local health, justice or economic policy for example, can help achieve the objectives of the homelessness strategy and vice-versa.

2.7 Housing authorities should consider the benefits of cross-boundary co-operation. A county-wide approach will be particularly important in non-unitary authorities, where housing and homelessness services are provided by the district authority whilst other key services, such as social services, are delivered at the county level. Housing authorities should ensure that the homelessness strategy for their district forms part of a coherent approach to tackling homelessness with neighbouring authorities. Housing authorities may wish to collaborate to produce a joint homelessness strategy covering a sub-regional area. London boroughs should have regard to the London Housing Strategy when formulating their homelessness strategies.

2.8 Each local authority has a legal duty under the Health & Social Care Act 2012 to take such steps as it considers appropriate for improving the health of the people in its area. This includes people experiencing homelessness or at risk of homelessness. Housing authorities should ensure that their homelessness strategy is co-ordinated with the Health and Wellbeing Strategy, and that their review of homelessness informs and is informed by the Joint Strategic Needs Assessment.

2.9 To be effective the homelessness strategy will need to be based on realistic assumptions and be developed and owned jointly with partners who will be responsible for its delivery. Sections 1(5) and (6) of the 2002 Act require housing and social services authorities to take the homelessness strategy into account when exercising their functions. Authorities can combine housing and homelessness strategies in a single document where it is coherent to do so.

2.10 Housing authorities must consult public or local authorities, voluntary organisations or other persons as they consider appropriate before adopting or modifying a homelessness strategy. Housing authorities will also wish to consult with service users and specialist agencies that provide support to homeless people in the district. Section 3(4) provides that a housing authority cannot include in a homelessness strategy any specific action expected to be taken by another body or organisation without their approval.

2.11 As part of the homelessness strategy housing authorities should develop effective action plans, to help ensure that the objectives set out in the homelessness strategy are achieved. Action plans could include, for example, targets, milestones and arrangements for monitoring and evaluation.

2.12 Housing authorities must make copies of their homelessness review and the homelessness strategy available for inspection at their principal office at all reasonable hours and without charge, and the strategy must be available to any member of the public, on request (for which a reasonable charge can be made). Housing authorities are advised to publish the strategy and review documents on their website.

2.13 Housing authorities must keep their homelessness strategy under review and may modify it accordingly. Before modifying the strategy, they must consult on the same basis as required before adopting a strategy. Circumstances that might prompt modification of a homelessness strategy include but not be limited to: anything that may affect the composition of homelessness and/or the risk of homelessness in the district; anything that may change the delivery of the strategy; changes to the relationships between the partners involved in the strategy; or changes to the organisational structure of the housing authority.

Reviewing homelessness and formulating a strategy

2.14 Under section 2(1) of the 2002 Act, a homelessness review means a review by a housing authority of:

(a) the levels, and likely future levels, of homelessness in their district;
(b) the activities which are carried out for any the following purposes (or which contribute to achieving any of them):
    (i) preventing homelessness in the housing authority's district;
    (ii) securing that accommodation is or will be available for people in the district who are or may become homeless; and
    (iii) providing support for people in the district who are homeless or who may become at risk of homelessness; or who have been homeless and need support to prevent them becoming homeless again; and,
(c) the resources available to the housing authority, the social services authority for the district, other public authorities, voluntary organisations and other persons for the activities outlined in (b) above.

2.15 The purpose of the review is to determine the extent to which the population in the district is homeless or at risk of becoming homeless, assess the likely extent in the future, identify what is currently being done and by whom, and identify what resources are available, to prevent and tackle homelessness.

2.16 Housing authorities are reminded that when drawing up their homelessness strategies for preventing and reducing homelessness, they must consider the needs of all groups of people in their district who are homeless or likely to become homeless, including Gypsies and Travellers. The periodical review of housing needs under section 8 of the Housing Act 1985 is a statutory requirement on housing authorities. This requires housing authorities to assess and understand the accommodation needs of people residing or resorting to their district. Under section 124 of the Housing and Planning Act 2016, which amends section 8 of the Housing Act 1985, housing authorities have a statutory duty to consider the needs of people residing in or resorting to their district with respect to sites for caravans and the mooring of houseboats.

Identifying current and future levels of homelessness

2.17 Homelessness is defined by sections 175 to 178 of the 1996 Act. For further guidance on homelessness and threatened with homelessness see Chapter 6. The review must take account of all forms of homelessness within the meaning of the 1996 Act and should therefore consider a wide population of households who are homeless or at risk of becoming homeless. This will include people sleeping rough, and those whose accommodation and circumstances make them more likely than others to become homeless including sleeping rough.

2.18 When carrying out the review housing authorities should consider including the following as a basis for assessing current and future levels of homelessness in their district:

(a) homelessness casework records and other local sources of data;
(b) trends in homelessness approaches and in underlying causes;
(c) which cohorts may be more likely to become homeless or be threatened with homelessness;
(d) the profile of households who have experienced homelessness in their district;
(e) equality monitoring data, including that relating to homelessness applications and outcomes;

(f)   the range of factors that may affect future levels of homelessness;

(g)   the personal and structural factors that may contribute to people becoming homeless; and,

(h)   any planned legislation or local policy changes that are likely to impact on levels of homelessness for particular groups in the district.

Reviewing activities carried out and resources required

2.19   The public, private and voluntary sectors can all contribute, directly or indirectly, to the prevention of homelessness and the provision of accommodation and support for homeless people. The housing authority should therefore consider the activities of all relevant agencies and organisations, as well as the resources available to them, which may contribute to the delivery of services.

2.20   Having mapped all the current activities, the housing authority should consider whether these are appropriate and adequate to meet the aims of the strategy, and whether any realignment of resources or additional provision is needed.

Assistance from social services

2.21   In non-unitary districts, where the social services authority and the housing authority are different authorities, section 1(2) of the 2002 Act requires the social services authority to give the housing authority such assistance as may be reasonably required in carrying out a homelessness review and formulating and publishing a homelessness strategy. **Since a large proportion of people who are homeless or at risk of homelessness will be vulnerable adults or have children in their care, it will always be necessary to seek assistance from the social services authority to formulate an effective homelessness strategy.** In unitary authorities, the authority must ensure that the social services department assists the housing department in carrying out a homelessness review and formulating and publishing a homelessness strategy.

2.22   The social services authority must comply with all reasonable requests for assistance from housing authorities within their district. For the purposes of formulating a strategy, this might include providing information about the current and projected numbers of vulnerable adults within the district that might be at higher risk of homelessness, and the care, support and accommodation available to them. Children's social care services could provide, for example, future projections of young people leaving care who are likely to require accommodation and support, families provided with accommodation who are ineligible for assistance (some of which might become eligible), and the numbers of safeguarding alerts involving domestic abuse, poor housing conditions or other factors that might indicate a need for homelessness assistance.

Formulating the strategy

2.23   Having carried out a homelessness review the housing authority will be in a position to formulate its homelessness strategy based on the results of that review as required by section 1(1)(b) of the 2002 Act. In formulating its strategy, a housing authority will need to consider the necessary levels of activity required to achieve the aims set out in the paragraph below and the sufficiency of the resources available to them as revealed by the review.

2.24   Under section 3(1) of the 2002 Act a homelessness strategy means a strategy for:

(a)   preventing homelessness in the district (see paragraphs 2.25-2.29 below);

(b)   securing that sufficient accommodation is and will be available for people in the district who are or may become homeless (see paragraphs 2.30-2.56 below); and,

(c)   securing the satisfactory provision of support for people in the district who are or may become homeless or who have been homeless and need support to prevent them becoming homeless again (see paragraphs 2.57-2.75 below).

Preventing homelessness

2.25 Under section 3(1)(a) of the 2002 Act, a homelessness strategy must include a strategy for **preventing** homelessness in the district. Furthermore, the 2017 Act strengthens statutory duties to prevent homelessness for all eligible applicants, including those who do not have priority need or may be considered intentionally homelessness and regardless of local connection. The 2017 Act also creates a new duty on certain public authorities to refer users of their services who are threatened with homelessness to a housing authority of their choice, which enables earlier identification of people at risk of becoming homeless through their interactions with other services.

2.26 When developing their homelessness strategy, local authorities will wish to look beyond the statutory requirements to consider the economic and social reasons for investing in activities that prevent homelessness, and may wish to learn from other local authorities and service providers who have adopted a more preventative approach.

Reviewing homelessness prevention activities and resources

2.27 Housing authorities will need to gain a good understanding of the causes of homelessness in their district, both to inform the development of successful interventions, and to assist in securing the commitment of stakeholders who can contribute toward preventing homelessness.

2.28 Housing authorities should establish good links with service providers who have early contact with people who are at risk of becoming homeless, review and learn from their activities and consider how they might be improved. Housing authorities should also consider how they might identify and interact with those households that are not receiving services, in order to prevent homelessness.

2.29 As part of their homelessness review, housing authorities should identify resources that are allocated to activities that prevent homelessness as well as those that respond to households becoming homeless, and consider how these might be realigned. This will be particularly important for delivering the duties contained in the 2017 Act. Upstream prevention activities are likely to produce direct savings in temporary accommodation and other costs for the authority, and will also help to reduce pressures on wider services, such as health, housing and employment, in the longer term.

Formulating a strategy to prevent homelessness

2.30 Elements of a prevention strategy should include:

(a) **advice and information:** available to residents in the district, or who may return to the district, which assists them in having appropriate information or access to services that will help to prevent them becoming homeless. Maintaining a high level of awareness about housing options and homelessness amongst partner agencies will also contribute to preventing homelessness. For further guidance on advice and information on homelessness and threatened with homelessness see Chapter 3;

(b) **advice and information:** early identification: authorities should consider how they might identify people at risk of homelessness at an earlier stage, and the interventions that could be put in place to prevent them from being threatened with or becoming homeless. The 'duty to refer' (section 213B of the 1996 Act) should engage public bodies to assist with earlier identification, and housing authorities should develop local protocols or referral arrangements with appropriate agencies, whether or not they are included within that duty. For further advice on duty to refer see Chapter 4;

(c) **pre-crisis intervention:** authorities should consider whether sufficient activity is in place to intervene proactively where a household may be at risk of homelessness in the future. This might include, for example, having joint working arrangements with environmental health services to ensure tenants are not displaced through enforcement action other than in a planned way, involving children's early help services to support families at risk of losing their social housing tenancy, or funding a court duty advice service that identifies households at risk of mortgage repossession or loss of private rented accommodation;

(d) **preventing recurring homelessness:** an analysis of local data should identify applicants most at risk of repeat homelessness which will inform decisions about allocation of resources, particularly for housing related support to help sustain settled accommodation; and,

(e) **partnership arrangements:** the homelessness strategy should set out how partners will be involved in all of the above activities, and what practical arrangements are needed (for example, joint protocols and procedures) to ensure the continued commitment to joint working to prevent homelessness and improve outcomes.

Ensuring a sufficient supply of accommodation

2.31 Section 3(1)(b) of the 2002 Act provides that one of the purposes of the homelessness strategy is to secure that sufficient accommodation is and will be available for people who are or may become homeless.

2.32 A shortage of affordable housing can lead to increasing numbers of people being accommodated in temporary accommodation whilst waiting for settled housing to bring the main homelessness duty to an end. 'Settled housing' in this context will primarily be social housing and good quality private sector accommodation. For further guidance on securing accommodation see Chapter 16.

2.33 Through the homelessness review, housing authorities should estimate the likely demand for assistance to prevent or relieve homelessness, and to meet the needs of those who are owed the main housing duty. They should include within the strategy what actions are required to ensure sufficient supply of accommodation to meet the estimated need.

Reviewing accommodation needs and resources

2.34 Housing authorities need to consider the range of accommodation that is available and is likely to be required for people who are, or may become, homeless. Landlords, accommodation providers and housing developers across all sectors may contribute to the review, and to the development of a strategy for provision of accommodation in the district.

2.35 Housing authorities should review the existing supply of accommodation available to people who are homeless or at risk of homelessness and identify where there are gaps, or where existing resources do not match the most pressing needs.

2.36 This might include reviewing supply and demand for:

(a) social and affordable housing held by the housing authority and private registered providers;

(b) temporary accommodation provided on an interim basis, or under the section 193(2) main housing duty;

(c) private rented accommodation, including shared housing options for young single people;

(d) supported accommodation available for particular cohorts of people in need of accommodation with support; and,

(e) low cost home ownership schemes.

Increasing the supply of new housing

2.37 National guidance on planning and affordable housing is contained in the National Planning Policy Framework and supporting planning guidance. The Framework acts as guidance for local planning authorities both in drawing up Local Plans and making decisions about planning applications.

2.38 The Framework sets out that local planning authorities should have a clear understanding of housing needs in their area. They should prepare a Strategic Housing Market Assessment to assess their full housing needs, working with neighbouring authorities where housing market areas cross administrative boundaries.

2.39 The Framework asks local authorities to use their evidence base to ensure that their Local Plan meets the full, objectively assessed needs for market and affordable housing in the housing market area, as far as is consistent with the policies set out in the Framework.

2.40 To deliver a wide choice of high quality homes, widen opportunities for home ownership and create sustainable, inclusive and mixed communities, the Framework asks local planning authorities to:

(a) plan for a mix of housing based on current and future demographic trends, market trends and the needs of different groups in the community (such as, but not limited to, families with children, young single people, older people, people with disabilities, service families and people wishing to build their own homes);

(b) identify the size, type, tenure and range of housing that is required in particular locations, reflecting local demand;

(c) where they have identified that affordable housing is needed, set policies that meet this need within development sites, unless off-site provision or a financial contribution of broadly equivalent value can be robustly justified and the agreed approach contributes to the objective of creating mixed and balanced communities. Such policies should be sufficiently flexible to take account of changing market conditions over time.

2.41 Local planning authorities are expected to review their Plans regularly and ensure that they are kept up-to-date.

2.42 Another important means of providing affordable housing is through planning obligations, which might be sought in the context of granting planning permission for new housing development. Section 106 of the Town and Country Planning Act 1990 enables a local planning authority to seek agreement from developers to enter into planning obligations to mitigate the impact of otherwise unacceptable development. More detailed guidance on the use of planning obligations is contained within Planning Practice Guidance.

Accessing the private rented sector

2.43 Housing authorities are encouraged to work in close partnership with local landlords and to develop opportunities to expand the provision of private rented accommodation that is available to people threatened with or actually homeless. Housing authorities should engage private landlords in developing the homelessness strategy, and in identifying how they might support its delivery. There may be opportunities to provide grant funding to landlords to improve poor quality accommodation or to bring empty properties back in to use for homeless households. Housing authorities should also review their private rented access schemes to ensure they meet a broad range of needs, including for single people at risk of homelessness.

Access to social housing

2.44 In developing their homelessness strategy, housing authorities should review how allocation arrangements for their own stock, and nominations, to private registered providers contribute to preventing or relieving homelessness.

2.45 Allocations schemes will be designed to reflect local priorities and needs, but must also provide reasonable preference to people who are homeless or are owed specific homelessness duties as set out in section 166A(3) of the 1996 Act. This will include providing reasonable preference to people who are owed the prevention (section 195(2)) or relief (section 189B) duty. Housing authorities may need to review their allocations schemes in response to the 2017 Act, to ensure that they deliver the requirements of the legislation and are sufficiently geared towards preventing homelessness.

2.46 Housing authorities are encouraged to develop an annual lettings plan to match anticipated supply against applicant demand, taking into account the need to prevent homelessness and to provide settled accommodation to people owed the main housing duty. As well as considering the proportion of lettings that should be made available to applicants who are owed the main housing duty (section 193(2)), housing authorities will want to consider whether the lettings plan facilitates or reduces access to housing for groups they know to be at risk of becoming homeless in their area. Housing authorities may also wish to review what part social housing allocations should play in facilitating move-on from any supported accommodation that forms part of the authority's wider homelessness response.

2.47 The Localism Act 2011 amended Part 6 of the 1996 Act to enable housing authorities to set their own qualification criteria for applicants wishing to join their housing register, to address local priorities and needs. Authorities can also provide reduced preference to applicants because of their previous conduct, which might include anti-social behaviour or rent arrears. However, housing authorities should not apply qualification criteria which would exclude from their allocation schemes homeless households who would be entitled to reasonable preference in the allocation of housing.

2.48 Housing authorities are encouraged to keep under review the impact of their allocations policies upon people at risk of homelessness, including single people who may be less able to establish their residency or may have a history of offending or other behaviour that impacts on their ability to access social housing. It is for the authority to decide its allocation scheme based on local priorities, but in doing so it should be aware of and take into consideration the impact of policies and procedures (which may be unintentional and/or indirect) on applicants who may be at risk of homelessness in the district.

2.49 It is important that housing authorities work effectively with private registered providers to help them prevent and tackle homelessness in the district. Private registered providers have a key role to play in sustaining tenancies, reducing evictions and abandonment, and preventing homelessness through their housing management functions. All parties will wish to ensure that there are effective procedures to identify early those tenants at risk of becoming homeless and that referral processes are in place.

2.50 The Secretary of State considers that, where local authority or private registered providers stock is provided as temporary accommodation (under section 193(2)); the housing authority should give consideration to the scope for allocating the accommodation as a secure or assured tenancy, as appropriate. This is especially the case where a household has been living in a particular property for anything other than a short-term emergency stay.

Temporary accommodation

2.51 Housing authorities should review their need for and use of temporary accommodation and, where necessary, identify what improvements will be made to procurement plans within their homelessness strategy. The aim will be to maximise the supply of good quality accommodation to meet the needs of homeless households, and reduce the financial burden of temporary accommodation on the applicant, authority and public purse. Housing authorities who use bed and breakfast to accommodate families in emergencies should consider including a plan to reduce or eliminate its use. For further guidance on securing accommodation see Chapter 16.

Supported housing and refuges

2.52 Housing authorities will need to work with partners to assess the need, and plan strategically, for supported housing provision to help prevent and resolve homelessness for people with support needs, and to consider whether existing local needs are met or to commission provision (either new units or additional support) to address these needs. Supported housing should be of good quality and suitable for the needs of the client group it is intended for. For example, supported accommodation with shared facilities will not normally be suitable for longer-term placements for families with pregnant women and/or children.

2.53 Refuge provision is very important for victims of domestic abuse at high risk who need to flee from highly dangerous perpetrators, and victims will very often need to be placed in a refuge in another area in order to be safe from the perpetrator.

Housing authorities will need to work together to assess and meet the need for refuge provision across local authority boundaries, for example, across a region or sub-region, to help ensure provision for people fleeing both from and to individual housing authority areas.

Empty homes

2.54 Local authorities are encouraged to make use of their powers and the incentives available to tackle empty homes. Through the new homes bonus, local authorities can earn the same financial reward for bringing an empty home back into use as building a new one. They can also charge up to 150% council tax for a home left empty for over two years. Housing authorities may wish to consider introducing local schemes that incentivise landlords to bring empty properties back into use, for example by providing grant funding subject to the refurbished accommodation being made available for homeless households.

Disabled facilities grant

2.55 Uptake of the disabled facilities grant – a mandatory entitlement administered by housing authorities for eligible disabled people in all housing tenures – can enable homeowners to remain living an independent life at home. Authorities are required to give a decision within six months of receiving an application. The grant is subject to a maximum limit and is means tested to ensure that funding goes to those most in need.

2.56 For guidance on securing accommodation for homeless applicants see Chapter 16.

Securing the provision of support

2.57 Section 3(1)(c) of the 2002 Act provides that the homelessness strategy should secure the satisfactory provision of support for people in the district who are or may be homeless, or who have been homeless and need support to prevent them becoming homeless again.

Reviewing resources and activities to provide support

2.58 Housing authorities should consider all the current activities which contribute to the provision of support for people who are, or may be at risk of becoming, homeless and those who have been homeless and need support to prevent them becoming homeless again. The range of providers whose activities will be making a contribution to this area are likely to embrace the public, private, voluntary and charitable sectors.

2.59 The 2017 Act introduced duties for housing authorities to assess the support needs of all applicants who are homeless or threatened with homelessness, and agree a personalised housing plan which should include reasonable steps required to meet any support needs identified. This more systematic assessment arrangement for all applicants will enable the generation of much improved data on the support needs of homeless people, which can be used as part of the homelessness review and to inform the homelessness strategy as well as commissioning plans. For further guidance on assessments and personalised housing plans see Chapter 11.

2.60 Housing authorities should consider mapping support services and activities in the district to assist in developing the homelessness strategy and to identify areas, both geographic and thematic, in which services are duplicated and/or where gaps in service provision can be identified.

2.61 Housing authorities should explore how budgets and resources from a wide range of sources can be used to provide support for people in their district. Due to the cross-cutting nature of homelessness there will be opportunities, for example, for the housing authority to work with organisations specialising in primary care, substance dependency, mental health or employment and training.

2.62 In two-tier authority areas it will be necessary to engage the upper tier authority, which holds responsibility for commissioning housing related support, in identifying resources available to meet support needs across all cohorts that are at high risk of homelessness.

Formulating a strategy to provide support

2.63 In formulating their homelessness strategies, housing authorities need to recognise that for some households homelessness cannot be tackled, or prevented, solely through the provision of accommodation. Some households will require a range of support services, which may include housing related support to help them sustain their accommodation, as well as personal support relating to factors such as relationship breakdown, domestic abuse, mental health problems, drug and alcohol addiction, poverty, debt and unemployment.

2.64 Housing-related support services have a key role in preventing homelessness occurring or recurring. The types of housing-related support that households who have experienced homelessness may need include:

(a)   support in establishing a suitable home – help, advice and support in finding and maintaining suitable accommodation for independent living in the community;
(b)   support with daily living skills – help, advice and training in the day-to-day skills needed for living independently, such as budgeting and cooking;
(c)   support in accessing benefits, health and community care services – information, advice and help in claiming benefits or accessing community care or health services;
(d)   help in establishing and maintaining social support – help in rebuilding or establishing social networks that can help counter isolation and help support independent living.

Support for single people

2.65 Housing authorities will be aware that some individuals may be at particular risk of homelessness, for example young people leaving care, ex-offenders, veterans, people with mental health problems or individuals leaving hospital, and may require a broader package of resettlement support. When developing their homelessness strategies, housing authorities should consider carefully how to work effectively to prevent homelessness amongst these groups and ensure that appropriate support is available.

2.66 Housing authorities should work with key partners to assess and meet the support needs of people at risk of homelessness. Where appropriate, accommodation and support services might be jointly commissioned, with children's social care, health, criminal justice agencies and other partners, in order to share and maximise resources and ensure a more holistic service response.

2.67 Many young people who have experienced homelessness will be in particular need of support to develop skills to manage their affairs and prepare to take on and sustain a tenancy and operate a household budget. Those estranged from their family, particularly care leavers, may lack the advice and support normally available to young people.

Support for rough sleepers

2.68 In districts where there is evidence that people are sleeping rough, the homelessness strategy should include objectives to work toward eliminating rough sleeping. This would include reviewing existing support arrangements, identifying which do or do not work, and where appropriate looking for alternative ways to provide accommodation and support that might improve outcomes for people who have slept rough. Accommodation and support solutions will vary according to the profile and particular needs of rough sleepers in the district, but authorities will wish to consider whether existing arrangements are working, or whether 'Housing First' or other service models might be more effective.

2.69 Housing authorities should consider what actions will assist in preventing rough sleeping, particularly for those groups that are over represented amongst those identified as sleeping rough, which includes people who have been in care or in prison, people who have mental health problems and those with a history of drug or alcohol misuse. Housing authorities cannot tackle rough sleeping alone and should involve partners in health, social care and criminal justice, as well as third sector and charitable service providers to develop and deliver the strategy.

2.70 Housing authorities should also consider joint working with agencies to tackle issues such as street drinking, begging, drug misuse and anti-social behaviour. Such collaborative working can help reduce the numbers of people sleeping rough and provide effective services targeted at those who are homeless or at risk of becoming homeless.

Support for families

2.71 Housing authorities should consider what support is available, or could be made available to support families who are at risk of homelessness, including preventing them from becoming homeless. Early Help services commissioned or delivered by children's social care authorities can contribute to the identification of families that are struggling to maintain accommodation, and require help and support before problems escalate and they are placed at imminent risk of homelessness. Involving providers of services to children and families in developing the strategy will contribute to improving early intervention, as well as drawing in resources available to support families who become homeless or require support to access and sustain settled accommodation.

2.72 Housing authorities will also wish to involve teams responsible for delivering the 'troubled families' programme in developing and delivering a strategy that helps to prevent the most vulnerable families from becoming homeless.

Support for victims of domestic abuse

2.73 In formulating their homelessness strategies, housing authorities should consider the particular needs that victims of domestic abuse have for safe accommodation, which will include having accommodation placements available outside the district. Housing authorities should also work cooperatively with other local authorities and commissioners to provide services to tackle domestic abuse; and should involve any local Violence Against Women and Girls Forum and service provider(s) in developing the homelessness strategy.

2.74 Housing authorities should also work closely with local refuge providers to develop fair and efficient move on arrangements, and should be mindful that policies and practices do not disadvantage people who have lost settled accommodation because of domestic abuse.

Households in temporary accommodation

2.75 The provision of support to households placed in temporary accommodation is essential to ensure that they are able to continue to enjoy a reasonable quality of life and access the range of services they need. In formulating their homelessness strategies, housing authorities should consider what arrangements need to be in place to ensure that households placed in temporary accommodation, within their district or outside, are able to access relevant support services. In particular households will need to be able to access:

(a)   primary care services such as health visitors and GPs;
(b)   appropriate education services;
(c)   relevant social services; and,
(d)   employment and training services.

CHAPTER 3: ADVICE AND INFORMATION ABOUT HOMELESSNESS AND THE PREVENTION OF HOMELESSNESS

3.1 Housing authorities have a duty to provide or secure the provision of advice and information about homelessness and the prevention of homelessness, free of charge.

These services will form part of the offer to applicants who are also owed other duties under Part 7, for example the prevention and relief duties. **They must also be available to any other person in their district,** including people who are not eligible for further homelessness services as a result of their immigration status. The provision of up to date, comprehensive, tailored advice and information will play an important part in delivering the housing authority's strategy for preventing homelessness.

3.2   Housing authorities may wish to consider providing information for those who are ineligible for further homelessness services on how to access any other assistance available in the area, for example through charitable or faith groups.

3.3   Under section 179(1) of the 1996 Act, authorities must provide information and advice on:

(a)   preventing homelessness;
(b)   securing accommodation when homeless;
(c)   the rights of people who are homeless or threatened with homelessness, and the duties of the authority;
(d)   any help that is available from the authority or anyone else for people in the authority's district who are homeless or may become homeless (whether or not they are threatened with homelessness); and,
(e)   how to access that help.

3.4   Early applications for homelessness assistance maximise the time and opportunities available to prevent homelessness. Information provided through authorities' websites and other channels should therefore:

(a)   help enable people to take action themselves where possible; and,
(b)   actively encourage them to seek assistance from the authority in good time if they need it.

3.5   Section 179(2) states that housing authorities must design advice and information services to meet the needs of people within their district including, in particular, the needs of the following groups:

(a)   people released from prison or youth detention accommodation;
(b)   care leavers;
(c)   former members of the regular armed forces;
(d)   victims of domestic abuse;
(e)   people leaving hospital;
(f)   people suffering from a mental illness or impairment; and,
(g)   any other group that the authority identify as being at particular risk of homelessness in their district.

3.6   Housing authorities will need to work with other relevant statutory and non-statutory service providers to identify groups who are at particular risk and to develop appropriate provision that is accessible to those who are likely to need it. In some circumstances tailored advice and information will be best delivered in a targeted and planned way when it is most likely to be needed – for example, in preparation for leaving care, being discharged from hospital or being released from custody, but it should also be widely accessible as a universal service. Appropriate provision will need to be made to ensure accessibility for people with particular needs, including those with mobility difficulties, sight or hearing loss and learning difficulties, as well as those for whom English is not their first language.

3.7   Many people concerned about a risk of homelessness will be seeking practical advice and assistance to help them remain in their accommodation or secure alternative accommodation. Advice on the following issues may help to prevent people from becoming threatened with homelessness:

(a)   tenants' rights and rights of occupation;
(b)   what to do about harassment and threats of illegal eviction;
(c)   rights to benefits including assistance with making claims as required;
(d)   how to protect and retrieve rent deposits;
(e)   rent and mortgage arrears;
(f)   how to manage debt;

(g)   help available to people at risk of violence and abuse;
(h)   grants available for housing repair and/or adaptation;
(i)   how to obtain accommodation in the private rented sector – e.g. details of landlords and letting agents within the district, any accreditation schemes, and information on rent guarantee and deposit schemes;
(j)   how to apply for social housing; and,
(k)   how to access shared-ownership or other low cost home ownership schemes.

3.8   The legislation does not specify how housing authorities should ensure that advice and information on homelessness and the prevention of homelessness are made available. They could do this in a number of ways, for example:

(a)   provide the service themselves;
(b)   ensure that it is provided by another organisation; or,
(c)   ensure that it is provided in partnership with another organisation.
    For further guidance on contracting out homelessness functions see Chapter 5.

3.9   Under section 179(3), housing authorities may give grants or loans to other persons who are providing advice and information about homelessness and the prevention of homelessness on behalf of the housing authority. Under section 179(4), housing authorities may also assist such persons (e.g. voluntary organisations) by:

(a)   allowing them to use premises belonging to the housing authority;
(b)   making available furniture or other goods, by way of gift, loan or some other arrangement; and,
(c)   making available the services of staff employed by the housing authority.

3.10   Housing authorities should monitor the provision of advisory services to ensure they continue to meet the needs of all sections of the community and help deliver the aims of their homelessness strategy.

CHAPTER 4: THE DUTY TO REFER CASES IN ENGLAND TO HOUSING AUTHORITIES

4.1   Under section 213B the public authorities specified in regulations are required to notify a housing authority of service users they consider may be homeless or threatened with homelessness (i.e. it is likely they will become homeless within 56 days). Before making a referral a public authority must:

(a)   have consent to the referral from the individual;
(b)   allow the individual to identify the housing authority in England which they would like the notification to be made to; and,
(c)   have consent from the individual that their contact details can be supplied so the housing authority can contact them regarding the referral.

4.2   The duty to refer only applies to public authorities in England and individuals can only be referred to housing authorities in England.

4.3   The public authorities which are subject to the duty to refer are specified in *The Homelessness (Review Procedure etc.) Regulations 2018*. The public services included in the duty are as follows:

(a)   prisons;
(b)   youth offender institutions;
(c)   secure training centres;
(d)   secure colleges;
(e)   youth offending teams;
(f)   probation services (including community rehabilitation companies);
(g)   Jobcentre Plus;
(h)   social service authorities;
(i)   emergency departments;
(j)   urgent treatment centres; and,
(k)   hospitals in their function of providing inpatient care.

The Secretary of State for Defence is also subject to the duty to refer in relation to members of the regular forces. The regular forces are the Royal Navy, the Royal

Marines, the regular army and the Royal Air Force.

4.4 The most appropriate approach to discharging the duty will vary between public authorities and it is their responsibility to decide how to do so. The expected response following a disclosure from a service user that they are homeless or at risk of homelessness is for the public authority to refer the case (with consent) to a housing authority identified by the service user. Public authorities are not expected to conduct housing needs assessments as part of the section 213B duty to refer.

The procedure for referrals

4.5 The procedure for referrals should be decided by service partners in each local area. The housing authority should incorporate the duty to refer into their wider homelessness strategy and joint working arrangements and establish local arrangements with agencies in regard to referrals. These arrangements should focus on identifying people at risk of homelessness as early as possible to maximise the opportunities to prevent homelessness.

4.6 Housing authorities are responsible for setting up local procedures for managing referrals, and should ensure that all referral information is stored securely so that it can be linked to case files for use in data returns and be included in an applicant's assessment and/or personalised housing plan as appropriate.

4.7 It is recommended that housing authorities set up a single point of contact which public authorities can use for submitting referrals. This should be shared with all relevant local agencies and be clearly accessible on the housing authority website for referrals made by public authorities in different districts.

4.8 Local procedures should be tailored to each public authority. For example, arrangements with prisons should ensure that the referral is made well in advance of the release date and that, with the individual's consent, appropriate information is supplied with the referral. When designing procedures, it may be helpful to include consideration of information to be given to people being referred to help inform their decision on which housing authority they wish to be referred to. This might include information on how local connection arrangements might affect a person who is homeless and wishes to be referred to a district where they have no local connection.

4.9 Housing authorities should include information about how they will respond where the referral indicates that an individual is at risk of sleeping rough, or is already sleeping rough in their procedures for responding to referrals.

4.10 Some public authorities that are subject to the duty to refer will be required to provide accommodation for certain individuals as part of their own legal duties, for example as an element of care or supervision. Examples include social services authorities with a duty to accommodate a lone 16 or 17 year old under the Children Act 1989 or a vulnerable adult under the Care Act 2014. Housing authorities will wish to agree arrangements with relevant authorities to ensure that when they receive referrals from these authorities appropriate alternative joint working approaches are in place and the primary responsibility to provide accommodation which would prevent or address homelessness lies with the other service.

4.11 Authorities are encouraged to establish arrangements with partners that go beyond referral procedures, aiming to maximize the impact of shared efforts on positive outcomes for service users who may have multiple needs. Such arrangements can advance the objectives of partner agencies and deliver efficiencies for the public purse.

4.12 Referring authorities should be mindful that for certain individuals, rather than making a referral, it may be more appropriate to assist them to approach a housing authority directly for assistance. This might apply, for example for clients with particular support needs.

What constitutes a referral

4.13 Under section 213B the referral to a housing authority must include the individual's name and contact details and the agreed reason for referral (e.g. that the individual is homeless or at risk of homelessness).

4.14 Housing authorities may want to develop standard referral mechanisms or forms. For example, it may be helpful for public authorities to expand on the minimum legal requirement in section 213B(3) for information to be captured in a referral (that is, of the public authority's opinion that the service user is or may be homeless or threatened with homelessness and their contact details), although housing authorities should be mindful of the service context of each referring agency when considering this.

4.15 Further referral information may include:

(a)   whether an individual is already homeless, and if not when they are likely to become homeless;

(b)   whether the individual is at risk of rough sleeping on the date the referral is made and if so whether this is imminent;

(c)   risk assessment information, considering risks to the individual and to others; and,

(d)   key medical information where relevant.

Consent

4.16 Housing authorities are advised to request that referring agencies confirm that the referee has given their consent to the referral as part of referral procedures.

Multiple / repeat referrals

4.17 When establishing local arrangements, housing authorities should consider the issues of multiple and repeat referrals and agree protocols with service partners to mitigate these.

4.18 There may be circumstances in which an individual's application has been closed by the housing authority and a new referral is received shortly after. The housing authority should respond to the referral and make contact with the individual to evaluate if there has been any change in relevant facts since the last application, which would warrant inquiries being made into any new application for assistance under Part 7.

Action upon the receipt of a referral

4.19 A referral made by a public authority to the housing authority under section 213B will not in itself constitute an application for assistance under Part 7, but housing authorities should always respond to any referral received. The housing authority may wish to contact the individual via a phone-call, email or letter using the contact details provided in the referral. If a response is not received from the direct contact with the individual, the authority should provide information on accessing advice and assistance including the housing authority's website, opening hours, address and 24-hour contact details via a phone-call, email or letter.

4.20 If the housing authority's subsequent contact with the individual following receipt of the referral reveals details that provide the housing authority with reason to believe that they might be homeless or threatened with homelessness and the individual indicates they would like assistance it will trigger an application for assistance under Part 7.

CHAPTER 5: CONTRACTING OUT HOMELESSNESS FUNCTIONS

5.1 This chapter provides guidance on contracting out homelessness functions and housing authorities' statutory obligations with regard to the discharge of those functions.

5.2 The *Local Authorities (Contracting Out of Allocation of Housing and Homelessness Functions) Order 1996* (SI 1996 No. 3205) ('1996 Order') enables housing authorities to contract out certain functions under Parts 6 and 7 of the 1996 Act. The

1996 Order is made under section 70 of the Deregulation and Contracting Out Act 1994 ('1994 Act'). In essence, the 1996 Order allows the contracting out of executive functions while leaving the responsibility for making strategic decisions with the housing authority.

5.3 The 1996 Order provides that the majority of functions under Part 7 of the 1996 Act can be contracted out. These include:

(a)   making arrangements to secure that advice and information about homelessness, and the prevention of homelessness, is available free of charge within the housing authority's district;

(b)   making inquiries about and deciding a person's eligibility for assistance;

(c)   making inquiries about and deciding whether any duty and, if so, what duty is owed to a person under Part 7;

(d)   assessing eligible applicants' cases and agreeing a personalised housing plan;

(e)   undertaking prevention and relief duties owed to an applicant;

(f)   making referrals to another housing authority;

(g)   carrying out reviews of decisions; and,

(h)   securing and helping to secure accommodation to discharge homelessness duties.

5.4   Where decision-making in homelessness cases is contracted out, housing authorities may wish to consider retaining the review function under section 202 of the 1996 Act. This may provide an additional degree of independence between the initial decision and the decision on review.

5.5   The 1994 Act provides that a contract made:

(a)   may authorise a contractor to carry out only part of the function concerned;

(b)   may specify that the contractor is authorised to carry out functions only in certain cases or areas specified in the contract;

(c)   may include conditions relating to the carrying out of the functions, e.g. prescribing standards of performance;

(d)   shall be for a period not exceeding 10 years and may be revoked at any time by the Minister or the housing authority. Any subsisting contract is to be treated as having been repudiated in these circumstances; and,

(e)   shall not prevent the housing authority from exercising themselves the functions to which the contract relates.

5.6   Schedule 2 to the 1996 Order lists the homelessness functions in Part 7 of the 1996 Act that may not be contracted out, for example the provision of assistance by way of grant or loan to voluntary organisations concerned with homelessness or related matters under section 180 of the 1996 Act.

5.7   Housing authorities also cannot contract out their functions under the Homelessness Act 2002 which relate to homelessness reviews and strategies. These include:

(a)   section 1(1): carry out a homelessness review for the district, and formulate and publish a homelessness strategy based on the results of that review;

(b)   section 1(4): publish a new homelessness strategy within 5 years from the day on which their last homelessness strategy was published; and,

(c)   section 3(6): keep their homelessness strategy under review and modify it from time to time.

For further advice on homelessness reviews and strategies see Chapter 2.

5.8   Homelessness reviews and the formulation of strategies can, however, be informed by research commissioned from external organisations.

5.9   The 1994 Act also provides that the housing authority is responsible for any act or omission of the contractor in exercising functions under the contract, except:

(a)   where the contractor fails to fulfil conditions specified in the contract relating to the exercise of the function; or,

(b)   where criminal proceedings are brought in respect of the contractor's act or omission.

5.10   Where there is an arrangement in force under section 101 of the Local

Government Act 1972 whereby one housing authority exercises the functions of another, the 1994 Act provides that the authority exercising the function is not allowed to contract it out without the principal authority's consent.

5.11 Where a housing authority has contracted out the operation of any homelessness functions, the housing authority remains statutorily responsible and accountable for the discharge of those functions. This includes any public sector equality duty obligations under section 149 of the Equality Act 2010. The housing authority will therefore need to ensure that the contract provides for delivery of the homelessness functions in accordance with both the statutory obligations and the authority's own policies on tackling and preventing homelessness.

5.12 Housing authorities should ensure they have adequate contractual, monitoring and quality assurance mechanisms in place to ensure their statutory duties are being fully discharged.

CHAPTER 6: HOMELESS OR THREATENED WITH HOMELESSNESS

6.1 This chapter provides guidance on how to determine whether a person is 'homeless' or 'threatened with homelessness' for the purposes of the 1996 Act.

6.2 Under section 184, if a housing authority has reason to believe that a person applying to the housing authority for accommodation, or assistance in obtaining accommodation, may be homeless or threatened with homelessness, it must make inquiries to satisfy itself whether the applicant is eligible for assistance and if so, what duties – if any – are owed to that person. For further guidance on applications for assistance see Chapter 18.

Threatened with homelessness

6.3 Under section 175(4), a person is 'threatened with homelessness' if they are likely to become homeless within 56 days. Under section 175(5), a person is also threatened with homelessness if a valid notice under section 21 of the Housing Act 1988 has been issued in respect of the only accommodation available for their occupation, and the notice will expire within 56 days. Section 195 provides that where applicants are threatened with homelessness and eligible for assistance, housing authorities must take reasonable steps to help prevent their homelessness. For further guidance on the duty to help prevent homelessness see Chapter 12.

Homeless

6.4 There are a number of different factors that determine whether a person is homeless. Under section 175, a person is homeless if they have no accommodation in the UK or elsewhere which is available for their occupation and which that person has a legal right to occupy. A person is also homeless if they have accommodation but cannot secure entry to it, or the accommodation is a moveable structure, vehicle or vessel designed or adapted for human habitation and there is nowhere it can lawfully be placed in order to provide accommodation. A person who has accommodation is to be treated as homeless where it would not be reasonable for them to continue to occupy that accommodation. Housing authorities should ask themselves whether the person is homeless at the date of making the decision on their application.

Available for occupation

6.5 Section 176 provides that accommodation shall be treated as available for a person's occupation only if it is available for occupation by them together with:

(a)   any other person who normally resides with them as a member of the family; or,
(b)   any other person who might reasonably be expected to reside with them.

6.6 Both of these groups of people constitute members of the applicant's household, and accommodation will only be considered to be available if it is available for occupation by both the applicant and all members of their household.

6.7 The first group covers those members of the family who normally reside with the applicant. It is a question of fact as to who is living with the applicant, and housing authorities are not required to satisfy themselves that it is reasonable for this member of the family to normally reside with them. The phrase 'as a member of the family', although not defined for these purposes in legislation, will include those with close blood or marital relationships and cohabiting partners, and, where such a person is an established member of the household, the accommodation must provide for them as well.

6.8 The second group relates to any other person, and includes those who may not have been living as part of the household at the time of the application but whom it would be reasonable to expect to live with the applicant as part of their household. People in this group might include a companion for an elderly or disabled person, or children who are being fostered by the applicant or a member of their family. This group will also include those members of the family who were not living as part of the household at the time of the application but who nonetheless might reasonably be expected to form part of it.

6.9 In relation to the second group, it is for the housing authority to assess whether any other person might reasonably be expected to live with the applicant and there will be a range of situations that the authority will need to consider. Persons who would normally live with the applicant but who are unable to do so because there is no accommodation in which they can all live together should be included in the assessment. When dealing with a family which has split up, housing authorities will need to take a decision as to which members of the family normally reside, or might be expected to reside, with the applicant. A court may have made a residence order indicating with whom the children are to live, but in many cases it will be a matter of agreement between the parents and a court will not have been involved.

Legal right to occupy accommodation

6.10 Under section 175(1), a person is homeless if they have no accommodation available for occupation in the UK or somewhere else which they have a legal right to occupy by virtue of:

(a) an interest in it (e.g. as an owner, lessee or tenant) or by virtue of a court order;
(b) an express or implied licence to occupy it (e.g. as a lodger, as an employee with a service occupancy, or when living with a relative); or,
(c) any enactment or rule of law giving them the right to remain in occupation or restricting the right of another person to recover possession (e.g. a person with a right to retain occupation as a statutory tenant under the Rent Act 1977 where that person's contractual rights to occupy have expired or been terminated).

6.11 A person who has been occupying accommodation as a licensee whose licence has been terminated (and who does not have any other accommodation available for their occupation) is homeless because they no longer have a legal right to continue to occupy, despite the fact that the person may continue to occupy but as an unauthorised occupier. This may include, for example:

(a) those required to leave hostels or hospitals; or,
(b) former employees occupying premises under a service occupancy which is dependent upon contracts of employment which have ended.

People asked to leave accommodation by family or friends

6.12 Some applicants may have been asked to leave their current accommodation by family or friends with whom they have been living. In such cases, the housing authority will need to consider carefully whether the applicant's licence to occupy the accommodation has in fact been revoked, rendering the applicant homeless. Authorities are encouraged to be sensitive to situations where parents or carers have been providing a home for a family member with care or support needs (for example, a person with learning difficulties) for a number of years and who are genuinely finding it difficult to continue with that arrangement, but are reluctant to revoke their licence to occupy formally until alternative accommodation can be secured.

6.13 In some cases the applicant may be unable to stay in their accommodation and in others there may be scope for preventing or postponing homelessness, and providing them with an opportunity to plan their future accommodation with assistance from the housing authority. However, housing authorities will need to be sensitive to the possibility that for some applicants it may not be safe for them to remain in, or return to, their home because of a risk of violence or abuse.

6.14 People living with family and friends may have genuine difficulties in finding alternative accommodation that can lead to friction and disputes within their current home, culminating in a threat of homelessness. In some cases external support, or the offer of assistance with securing alternative housing, may help to reduce tension and prevent homelessness. The use of mediation services may assist here.

6.15 In cases involving 16 and 17 year olds threatened with exclusion from the family home children's services authorities will be the lead agency, but should work closely with housing authorities to prevent homelessness and support young people to remain within the family network, wherever it is safe and appropriate for them to do so.

6.16 Housing authorities will also need to be alert to the possibility of collusion where family or friends agree to revoke a licence to occupy accommodation that would have been reasonable for the person to continue to occupy, as part of an arrangement whose purpose is to enable the applicant to be entitled to assistance under Part 7. For further guidance on intentional homelessness see Chapter 9.

Tenant given notice

6.17 With certain exceptions, a person who has been occupying accommodation as a tenant and who has received a valid notice to quit, or notice that the landlord requires possession of the accommodation, would have the right to remain in occupation until a warrant for possession was executed (following the granting of an order for possession by the court). The exceptions are tenants with resident landlords and certain other tenants who do not benefit from the Protection from Eviction Act 1977.

6.18 Housing authorities should note that the fact that a tenant has a right to remain in occupation does not necessarily mean that they are not homeless. In assessing whether an applicant is homeless in cases where they are a tenant who has a right to remain in occupation pending execution of a warrant for possession, the housing authority will also need to consider whether it would be reasonable for them to continue to occupy the accommodation in the circumstances (section 175(3), 1996 Act). For guidance on cases involving service of a section 21 notice see paragraph 6.35-6.38.

6.19 Some tenants may face having to leave their accommodation because their landlord has defaulted on the mortgage of the property they rent. Where a mortgage lender starts possession proceedings, the lender is obliged to give written notice of the proceedings to the occupiers of the property before an order for possession is granted. The notice must be given after issue of the possession summons and at least 14 days before the court hearing. Housing authorities will need to consider whether it would be reasonable for an applicant to continue to occupy the accommodation after receiving notice of possession proceedings from the lender. Housing authorities should not consider it reasonable for an applicant to remain in occupation until eviction by a bailiff.

Inability to secure entry to accommodation

6.20 Under section 175(2)(a), a person is also homeless if they have a legal entitlement to accommodation, but is unable to secure entry to it, for example:

(a)   those who have been evicted illegally; or,
(b)   those whose accommodation is being occupied illegally by squatters.

6.21 Housing authorities will want to support applicants to pursue the legal remedies available to them to regain possession of their accommodation. However, an authority cannot refuse to assist an applicant who is homeless and eligible for assistance under

Part 7 simply because such remedies are available.

Accommodation consisting of a moveable structure

6.22 Section 175(2)(b) provides that a person is homeless if they have accommodation available for their occupation which is a moveable structure, vehicle or vessel designed or adapted for human habitation (e.g. a caravan or houseboat), and there is nowhere that they are entitled or permitted to place it and reside in it. The site or mooring for the moveable structure need not be permanent in order to avoid homelessness.

Reasonable to continue to occupy

6.23 Section 175(3) provides that a person shall not be treated as having accommodation unless it is accommodation which it would be reasonable for them to continue to occupy. There are a number of provisions relating to whether or not it is reasonable for someone to continue to occupy accommodation and these are discussed below. There is no simple test of reasonableness. It is for the housing authority to make a judgement on the facts of each case, taking into account the circumstances of the applicant.

Domestic abuse or other violence

6.24 Section 177(1) provides that it is not reasonable for a person to continue to occupy accommodation if it is probable that this will lead to domestic abuse or other violence against:

(a)   the applicant;
(b)   a person who normally resides with the applicant as a member of the applicant's family; or,
(c)   any other person who might reasonably be expected to reside with the applicant.

For further guidance on domestic abuse or other violence in determining whether a person is homeless see Chapter 21.

General housing circumstances in the district

6.25 Section 177(2) provides that, in determining whether it is reasonable for a person to continue to occupy accommodation, housing authorities may have regard to the general housing circumstances prevailing in the housing authority's district.

6.26 This comparison might be appropriate, for example, where it was suggested that an applicant was homeless because of poor physical conditions in their current home. In such cases it would be open to the authority to consider whether the condition of the property was so bad in comparison with other accommodation in the district that it would not be reasonable to expect someone to continue to live there.

6.27 Consideration of the general circumstances prevailing in the housing authority's district might also be appropriate in cases of homelessness due to overcrowding.

Affordability

6.28 Affordability must be considered in all cases. The *Homelessness (Suitability of Accommodation) Order 1996* (SI 1996 No.3204) requires the housing authority to consider the affordability of the accommodation for the applicant. The Order specifies, among other things, that in determining both whether it would be (or would have been) reasonable for a person to continue to occupy accommodation and whether the accommodation is suitable, a housing authority must take into account whether the accommodation is affordable for them and must, in particular, take account of:

(a)   the financial resources available to them;
(b)   the costs of the accommodation;

(c)   maintenance payments (to a spouse, former spouse or in respect of a child); and,

(d)   their reasonable living expenses

For further guidance on affordability and suitability of accommodation see Chapter 17.

Tenant given notice of intention to recover possession

6.29   In cases where the applicant has been occupying accommodation as a tenant and has received a valid notice to quit, or a notice that the landlord intends to recover possession, housing authorities should make contact with the landlord at an early stage. This will be necessary both to understand the circumstances in which the applicant has become threatened with homelessness, and to establish what reasonable steps may be taken by the housing authority and by the applicant to prevent their homelessness.

6.30   A housing authority can give notice to end the section 195(2) prevention duty where 56 days has passed since the prevention duty was accepted, whether or not the applicant is still threatened with homelessness (section 195(8)(b)). However, section 195(6) of the 1996 Act prevents an authority from doing this if the applicant has been given a valid section 21 notice which will expire within 56 days, or has already expired, in respect of the only accommodation available for the applicant's occupation. This means an applicant in these circumstances cannot be 'timed out' of the prevention duty if they remain threatened with homelessness, and the authority must continue to help the applicant to retain or secure accommodation until the prevention duty ends in another way.

6.31   However, an authority should give notice to end the section 195 prevention duty when an applicant has become homeless, triggering a section 189B relief duty. It follows that housing authorities will be required to assess at what point a tenant who has been served a valid section 21 becomes homeless and is owed a relief duty; and that expiry of a valid section 21 notice does not automatically render the person homeless for the purposes of the 1996 Act. Under section 175 of the 1996 Act, an applicant must be considered homeless if they have no accommodation to which they have a legal right to occupy that is available to them and reasonable for them to continue to occupy.

6.32   In determining whether it would be reasonable for an applicant to continue to occupy accommodation following expiry of a valid section 21 notice the authority will need to consider all the factors relevant to the case and decide the weight that each should attract. If the landlord confirms a willingness to consider delaying or halting action to recover possession if certain steps are taken, it will usually be reasonable for the tenant to remain in occupation to allow time for action to be taken which may prevent homelessness. This might include, for example, resolving problems with a benefit claim or establishing a manageable repayment schedule for rent arrears.

6.33   Authorities should not adopt a blanket policy or practice on the point at which it will no longer be reasonable for an applicant to occupy following the expiry of a section 21 notice. As well as the factors set out elsewhere in this chapter, factors which may be relevant include the preference of the applicant (who may, for example, want to remain in the property until they can move into alternative settled accommodation if there is the prospect of a timely move, or alternatively to leave the property to avoid incurring court costs); the position of the landlord; the financial impact of court action and any build up of rent arrears on both landlord and tenant; the burden on the courts of unnecessary proceedings where there is no defence to a possession claim; and the general cost to the housing authority. Housing authorities will be mindful of the need to maintain good relations with landlords providing accommodation in the district.

6.34   Throughout any period that an applicant remains in occupation whilst the landlord pursues possession action, the housing authority should keep the reasonable steps in the applicant's personalised housing plan under regular review, and maintain contact with the tenant and landlord to ascertain if there is any change in circumstances which affects whether or not it continues to be reasonable for the applicant to occupy.

6.35   The Secretary of State considers that where an applicant is:

(a)   an assured shorthold tenant who has received a valid notice in accordance with section 21 of the Housing Act 1988;

(b)   the housing authority is satisfied that the landlord intends to seek possession and further efforts from the housing authority to resolve the situation and persuade the landlord to allow the tenant to remain in the property are unlikely to be successful; and,

(c)   there would be no defence to an application for a possession order;

then it is unlikely to be reasonable for the applicant to continue to occupy beyond the expiry of a valid section 21 notice, unless the housing authority is taking steps to persuade the landlord to allow the tenant to continue to occupy the accommodation for a reasonable period to provide an opportunity for alternative accommodation to be found.

6.36   The Secretary of State considers that it is highly unlikely to be reasonable for the applicant to continue to occupy beyond the date on which the court has ordered them to leave the property and give possession to the landlord.

6.37   Housing authorities should not consider it reasonable for an applicant to remain in occupation up until the point at which a court issues a warrant or writ to enforce an order for possession.

6.38   Housing authorities should ensure that homeless families and vulnerable individuals who are owed a section 188 interim accommodation duty or section 193(2) main housing duty are not evicted through the enforcement of an order for possession as a result of a failure by the authority to make suitable accommodation available to them.

Other relevant factors

6.39   Other factors which may be relevant in determining whether it would be reasonable for an applicant to continue to occupy accommodation include:

(a)   **physical characteristics:** it would not be reasonable for an applicant to continue to occupy accommodation if the physical characteristics of the accommodation were unsuitable for the applicant because, for example, they are a wheelchair user and access was limited;

(b)   **type of accommodation:** some types of accommodation, for example women's refuges, direct access hostels and night shelters are intended to provide very short-term, temporary accommodation in a crisis and should not be regarded as being reasonable to continue to occupy in the medium and longer-term;

(c)   **people fleeing harassment:** in some cases severe harassment may fall short of actual violence or threats of violence likely to be carried out. Housing authorities should consider carefully whether it would be, or would have been, reasonable for an applicant to continue to occupy accommodation in circumstances where they have fled, or are seeking to leave, their home because of non-violent forms of harassment, for example verbal abuse or damage to property. Careful consideration should be given to applicants who may be at risk of witness intimidation. In some criminal cases the police may provide alternative accommodation for witnesses, but usually this will apply for the duration of the trial only. Witnesses may have had to give up their home or may feel unable to return to it when the trial has finished.

6.40   This is not an exhaustive list and authorities will need to take account of all relevant factors when considering whether it is reasonable for an applicant to continue to occupy accommodation.

CHAPTER 7: ELIGIBILITY FOR ASSISTANCE

7.1   This chapter provides guidance on the provisions relating to an applicant's eligibility for homelessness services.

7.2   Housing authorities have a duty to provide or secure the provision of advice and information about homelessness and the prevention of homelessness, free of charge which must be available to any person in their district. All applicants, including those who are ineligible as a result of their immigration status, will be able to access this form of assistance from the housing authority. Housing authorities should refer applicants to appropriate support which they may be entitled to where relevant. For further guidance on the provision of advice and information on homelessness and the prevention of homelessness see Chapter 3.

7.3   Part 7 of the 1996 Act includes provisions that make certain people from abroad ineligible for housing assistance. Housing authorities will therefore need to satisfy themselves that applicants are eligible before providing housing assistance. The provisions on eligibility are complex and housing authorities will need to ensure that they have procedures in place to carry out appropriate checks on housing applicants.

7.4   Housing authorities should ensure that staff who are required to screen applicants about eligibility for assistance are given training in the complexities of the housing provisions, the housing authority's duties and responsibilities under the Equality Act 2010 and are able to deal with applicants in a sensitive manner.

7.5   Local authorities are reminded that Schedule 3 to the Nationality, Immigration and Asylum Act 2002 provides that certain persons shall not be eligible for support or assistance provided through the exercise of housing authorities' powers to secure accommodation pending a review (section 188(3)) or pending an appeal to the county court (section 204(4)). For further guidance see 7.21-7.22.

Persons from abroad

7.6   A person will not be eligible for assistance under Part 7 if they are a person from abroad who is ineligible for housing assistance under section 185 of the 1996 Act. In particular:

(a)   a 'person subject to immigration control' is not eligible for housing assistance unless they come within a class prescribed in regulations made by the Secretary of State; and,

(b)   the Secretary of State can make regulations to provide for other descriptions of person from abroad who, although they are not subject to immigration control, are to be treated as ineligible for housing assistance.

7.7   The regulations that set out which classes of persons from abroad are eligible or ineligible for housing assistance are *the Allocation of Housing and Homelessness (Eligibility) (England) Regulations 2006* (SI 2006/1294) ('the Eligibility Regulations'). Persons subject to immigration control are not eligible for housing assistance unless they fall within a class of persons prescribed in regulation 5 of the Eligibility Regulations. Persons who are not subject to immigration control will be eligible for housing assistance unless they fall within a description of persons who are to be treated as persons from abroad who are ineligible for assistance by virtue of regulation 6 of the Eligibility Regulations.

Persons subject to immigration control

7.8   The term 'person subject to immigration control' is defined in section 13(2) of the Asylum and Immigration Act 1996 as a person who requires leave to enter or remain in the United Kingdom (whether or not such leave has been given).

7.9   Only the following categories of person do not require leave to enter or remain in the UK:

(a)   British citizens;
(b)   certain Commonwealth citizens with a right of abode in the UK;
(c)   citizens of an EEA country ('EEA nationals') and their family members, who have a right to reside in the UK that is derived from European Union law or any provision made under section 2(2) of the European Communities Act 1972. The question of whether an EEA national (or family member) has a right to reside in the UK (or in another Member State e.g. the Republic of Ireland) will depend on their circumstances at that particular time, e.g. whether the EEA national is, for the purposes of the Immigration (European Economic Area) Regulations 2016, a jobseeker, a worker, a self-employed person, and so on;

(d)   persons who are exempt from immigration control under the Immigration Acts, including diplomats and their family members based in the United Kingdom, and some military personnel.

For the purposes of this guidance, 'EEA nationals' means nationals of any of the EU member states (excluding the UK), and nationals of Iceland, Norway, Liechtenstein and Switzerland.

7.10   Any person who does not fall within one of the 4 categories in paragraph 7.9 above will be a person subject to immigration control and will be ineligible for housing assistance unless they fall within a class of persons prescribed by regulation 5 of the Eligibility Regulations (see paragraph 7.12 below).

7.11   If there is any uncertainty about an applicant's immigration status, it is recommended that authorities contact the Home Office. In some circumstances, local authorities may be under a duty to contact the Home Office (see paragraph 7.23).

Persons subject to immigration control who are eligible for housing assistance

7.12   Generally, persons subject to immigration control are not eligible for housing assistance. However, by virtue of regulation 5 of the Eligibility Regulations, the following classes of person subject to immigration control are eligible for housing assistance:

(a)   a person whose refugee status has been recognised by the Secretary of State and who has leave to enter and remain in the UK. Persons granted refugee status are usually granted 5 years' limited leave to remain in the UK. (Prior to 30 August 2005, it was the policy to provide immediate settlement (indefinite leave to remain) for persons granted refugee status);

(b)   a person who has discretionary leave to enter or remain in the United Kingdom granted outside the provisions of the Immigration Rules; and whose leave to enter or remain is not subject to a condition requiring them to maintain and accommodate themselves, and any person who is dependent on them, without recourse to public funds;

(c)   a person with current leave to enter or remain in the UK with no condition or limitation, and who is habitually resident in the UK, the Channel Islands, the Isle of Man or the Republic of Ireland: such a person will have indefinite leave to enter or indefinite leave to remain and will be regarded as having settled status. However, where indefinite leave to enter or indefinite leave to remain status was granted as a result of an undertaking that a sponsor would be responsible for the applicant's maintenance and accommodation, the person must have been resident in the UK, the Channel Islands, the Isle of Man or the Republic of Ireland for five years since the date of entry – or the date of the sponsorship undertaking, whichever is later – for the applicant to be eligible. Where a sponsor has (or, if there was more than one sponsor, all of the sponsors have) died within the first five years, the applicant will be eligible for housing assistance;

(d)   a person who has humanitarian protection granted under the Immigration Rules;

(e)   a person who is habitually resident in the United Kingdom, the Channel Islands, the Isle of Man or the Republic of Ireland and who has limited leave to enter the United Kingdom as a relevant Afghan citizen under paragraph 276BA1 of the Immigration Rules;

(f)   a person who has limited leave to enter or remain in the United Kingdom on family or private life grounds under Article 8 of the Human Rights Act, such leave granted under paragraph 276BE (1), paragraph 276DG or Appendix FM of the Immigration Rules, and who is not subject to a condition requiring that person to maintain and accommodate themselves, and any person dependent upon them, without recourse to public funds.

(g)   a person who is habitually resident in the United Kingdom, the Channel Islands, the Isle of Man or the Republic of Ireland and who has been transferred to the United Kingdom under section 67 of the Immigration Act 2016 and has limited leave to remain under paragraph 352ZH of the Immigration Rules. (Effective from 9th July 2018).

Asylum seekers

7.13 Under section 186 of the 1996 Act, an asylum seeker who would otherwise be eligible for housing assistance will be ineligible if they have any accommodation available in the UK for their occupation, however temporary. This exclusion is only relevant to pre-April 2000 asylum seekers who are eligible for homelessness assistance.

Other persons from abroad who are ineligible for assistance

7.14 By virtue of regulation 6 of the Eligibility Regulations, a person who is not subject to immigration control and who falls within one of the following descriptions of persons is to be treated as a person from abroad who is ineligible for housing assistance:

(a) a person who is not habitually resident in the UK, the Channel Islands, the Isle of Man or the Republic of Ireland (subject to certain exceptions – see paragraph 7.15 below);

(b) a person whose only right to reside in the UK is derived from their status as a jobseeker (or their status as the family member of a jobseeker). For this purpose, 'jobseeker' has the same meaning as for the purpose of regulation 6(1)(a) of the *Immigration (European Economic Area) Regulations 2016* (SI 2016 No. 1052) ('the EEA Regulations');

(c) a person whose only right to reside in the UK is an initial right to reside for a period not exceeding three months under regulation 13 of the EEA Regulations;

(d) a person whose only right to reside in the UK is a derivative right to reside to which they are entitled under regulation 16(1) of the EEA Regulations, but only in a case where the right exists under that regulation because the applicant satisfies the criteria in regulation 16(5) of those Regulations;

(e) a person whose only right to reside in the UK is derived from Article 20 of the Treaty on the Functioning of the European Union in a case where the right to reside arises because a British citizen would otherwise be deprived of the genuine enjoyment of the substance of the rights attaching to the status of European Union citizen (also know as 'Zambrano carers');

(f) a person whose only right to reside in the Channel Islands, the Isle of Man or the Republic of Ireland--
  (i)   is a right equivalent to one of those mentioned in sub-paragraph (b-d) above which is derived from the Treaty on the Functioning of the European Union; or
  (ii) is derived from Article 20 of the Treaty on the Functioning of the European Union, in a case where the right to reside in the Republic of Ireland arises because an Irish citizen, or in the Channel Islands or the Isle of Man arises because a British citizen also entitled to reside there and would otherwise be deprived of the genuine enjoyment of the substance of their rights as a European Union citizen.

Persons exempted from the requirement to be habitually resident

7.15 Certain persons from abroad are not subject to the requirement to be habitually resident in the UK, the Channel Islands, the Isle of Man or the Republic of Ireland. Such a person will be eligible for assistance even if not habitually resident, if they are:

(a) an EEA national who is in the UK as a worker (which has the same meaning as it does for the purposes of regulation 6(1) of the EEA Regulations);

(b) an EEA national who is in the UK as a self-employed person (which has the same meaning as it does for the purposes of regulation 6(1) of the EEA Regulations);

(c) a person who is treated as a worker for the purpose of the definition of 'qualified person' in regulation 6(1) of the EEA Regulations pursuant to regulation 5 of the *Accession of Croatia (Immigration and Worker Authorisation) Regulations 2013 (as amended)*, SI 2013/1460 (right of residence of an accession State national subject to worker authorisation);

(d) a person who is a family member of a person referred to in (a) to (c) above;

(e) a person with a right to reside permanently in the UK by virtue of regulation 15(c), (d) or (e) of the EEA Regulations;

(f)   a person who is in the UK as a result of their deportation, expulsion or other removal by compulsion of law from another country to the UK.

7.16   On (a) and (b), authorities should note that a person who is not currently working or self-employed will retain their status as a worker or self-employed person in certain circumstances. On (c), authorities should note that an accession state worker will generally only be treated as a worker if they hold an accession worker authorisation document and are working in accordance with the conditions set out in that document. On (d), authorities should note that 'family member' does not include a person who is an extended family member who is treated as a family member by virtue of regulation 7(3) of the EEA Regulations.

7.17   For further guidance on EEA right to reside see pages 6-8 of Home Office guidance on administrative removal of EEA nationals.

The habitual residence test

7.18   The term 'habitual residence' is intended to convey a degree of permanence in the person's residence in the UK, the Channel Islands, the Isle of Man or the Republic of Ireland; it implies an association between the individual and the place of residence and relies substantially on fact.

7.19   The Secretary of State considers that it is likely that applicants who have been resident in the UK, Channel Islands, the Isle of Man or the Republic of Ireland continuously during the 2-year period prior to their housing application will be habitually resident. In such cases, therefore, housing authorities may consider it unnecessary to make further enquiries to determine whether the person is habitually resident, unless there are other circumstances that need to be taken into account. A period of continuous residence in the UK, Channel Islands, the Isle of Man or the Republic of Ireland might include periods of temporary absence. Where two years' continuous residency has not been established, housing authorities will need to conduct further enquiries to determine whether the applicant is habitually resident.

7.20   A person will not generally be habitually resident anywhere unless they have taken up residence and lived there for a period. There will be cases where the person concerned is not coming to the UK for the first time, and is resuming a previous period of habitual residence. For further guidance on habitual residence see Annex 1.

Persons ineligible under certain provisions by virtue of Schedule 3 to the Nationality, Immigration and Asylum Act 2002

7.21   Section 54 of, and Schedule 3 to, the Nationality, Immigration and Asylum Act 2002 have the effect of making certain applicants for housing assistance ineligible for accommodation under section 188(3) (power to accommodate pending a review) or section 204(4) (power to accommodate pending an appeal to the county court) of the 1996 Act. The following classes of person will be ineligible for assistance under those powers:

(a)   a person who has refugee status abroad, i.e. a person:
   (i)   who does not have the nationality of an EEA State, and
   (ii)   who the government of an EEA State other than the UK has determined is entitled to protection as a refugee under the Refugee Convention;
(b)   a person who has the nationality of an EEA State other than the UK (but see paragraph 7.22 below);
(c)   a person who was (but is no longer) an asylum seeker and who fails to co-operate with removal directions issued in respect of them;
(d)   a person who is in the UK in breach of the immigration laws (within the meaning of section 50A of the British Nationality Act 1981) and is not an asylum seeker;
(e)   certain persons who are failed asylum seekers with dependent children, where the Secretary of State has certified that, in their opinion, such a person has failed without reasonable excuse to take reasonable steps to leave the UK voluntarily or place themselves in a position where they are able to leave the UK voluntarily, and that person has received the Secretary of State's certificate more than 14 days previously;

(f)   a person who is the dependant of a person who falls within class (a), (b) or (c) above.

7.22   However, section 54 and Schedule 3 do not prevent the exercise of an authority's powers under section 188(3) and section 204(4) of the 1996 Act to the extent that such exercise is necessary for the purpose of avoiding a breach of a person's rights under the European Convention of Human Rights or rights under EU Treaties. Among other things, this means that a local authority can exercise these powers to accommodate an EEA national who has a right to reside in the UK under EU law.

7.23   Paragraph 14 of Schedule 3 provides, among other things, that authorities must inform the Secretary of State where the powers under section 188(3) or section 204(4) apply, or may apply, to a person who is, or may come, within classes (c) or (d) in paragraph 7.21 by contacting the Home Office.

7.24   For further guidance, local authorities should refer to Guidance to Local Authorities and Housing Authorities about the Nationality, Immigration and Asylum Act, Section 54 and Schedule 3, and the Withholding and Withdrawal of Support (Travel Assistance and Temporary Accommodation) Regulations 2002, issued by the Home Office.

Restricted cases

7.25   A restricted case is a case where the housing authority would not be satisfied that the applicant had a priority need for accommodation without having had regard to a 'restricted person' within the household. This would be the case, for example, where an applicant who is an eligible British citizen who would not have priority need if they applied alone, does have priority need because of their dependent children who are 'restricted persons'.

7.26   A restricted person means a person who is not eligible for assistance under Part 7 of the 1996 Act and is subject to immigration control and either:

(a)   does not have leave to enter or remain in the UK; or,
(b)   does have leave but it is subject to a condition of no recourse to public funds.

7.27   In a restricted case, the housing authority must, so far as reasonably practical, bring the section 193(2) duty to an end by arranging for an offer of an assured shorthold tenancy to be made to the applicant by a private landlord (a private rented sector offer of at least 12 months in length).

7.28   Where a housing authority considers a household member of an applicant may be a restricted person who does not have leave to enter or remain in the UK, or if there is uncertainty about the immigration status of any household member, it is recommended that the authority contact the Home Office.

CHAPTER 8: PRIORITY NEED

8.1   This chapter provides guidance on the categories of applicant who have a priority need for accommodation under the homelessness legislation.

8.2   Housing authorities have duties to try and prevent or relieve homelessness for all applicants who are eligible for assistance and are homeless or threatened with homelessness, irrespective of whether or not they may have a priority need for accommodation. If a housing authority is unable to prevent an applicant from becoming homeless, or to help them to secure accommodation within the 'relief' stage, they are required to reach a decision as to whether the applicant has a priority need for accommodation.

8.3   Section 188(1) of the 1996 Act requires housing authorities to secure that accommodation is available for an applicant if they have reason to believe that the applicant **may** be homeless, eligible for assistance and have a priority need. The housing authority may bring this 'interim' accommodation duty to an end during the relief stage if they subsequently find that the applicant does not have priority need (or are not eligible or not homeless) and issues a decision that the applicant will not be owed further duties at the end of the relief duty. For further guidance on accommodation duties see chapter 15. Section 193(2) of the 1996 Act requires housing authorities to secure accommodation for applicants who have a priority need for accommodation section 189(1) and the *Homelessness (Priority Need for Accommodation) (England) Order 2002* (the '2002 Order') provide that the following categories of applicant have a priority need for accommodation:

(a) a pregnant woman or a person with whom she resides or might reasonably be expected to reside (see paragraph 8.5);

(b) a person with whom dependent children reside or might reasonably be expected to reside (see paragraphs 8.6-8.12);

(c) a person who is vulnerable as a result of old age, mental illness, learning disability or physical disability or other special reason, or with whom such a person resides or might reasonably be expected to reside (see paragraphs 8.13-8.18);

(d) a person aged 16 or 17 who is not a 'relevant child' or a child in need to whom a local authority owes a duty under section 20 of the Children Act 1989 (see paragraphs 8.19-8.23);

(e) a person under 21 who was (but is no longer) looked after, accommodated or fostered between the ages of 16 and 18 (except a person who is a 'relevant student');

(f) a person aged 21 or more who is vulnerable as a result of having been looked after, accommodated or fostered (except a person who is a 'relevant student') (see paragraphs 8.28-8.31);

(g) a person who is vulnerable as a result of having been a member of Her Majesty's regular naval, military or air forces (see paragraphs 8.32-8.33);

(h) a person who is vulnerable as a result of:
  (i) having served a custodial sentence;
  (ii) having been committed for contempt of court or any other kindred offence; or,
  (iii) having been remanded in custody;(see paragraphs 8.34-8.35);

(i) a person who is vulnerable as a result of ceasing to occupy accommodation because of violence from another person or threats of violence from another person which are likely to be carried out (see paragraphs 8.36-8.37);

(j) a person who is homeless, or threatened with homelessness, as a result of an emergency such as flood, fire or other disaster.

8.4 Once a housing authority has notified an applicant that they have a priority need and have been accepted as owed the section 193(2) duty it cannot subsequently change that decision if the applicant subsequently ceases to have a priority need (e.g. because a dependent child leaves home), except where a review has been requested and the change takes place before the review decision. Any change of circumstance prior to the decision on the homelessness application should be taken into account. However, once all the relevant inquiries are completed, the housing authority should not defer their decision on the case in anticipation of a possible change of circumstance.

Pregnant women

8.5 A pregnant woman, and anyone with whom she lives or might reasonably be expected to live, has a priority need for accommodation. This is regardless of the length of time that the woman has been pregnant. Normal confirmation of pregnancy, e.g. a letter from a medical professional, such as a midwife, should be adequate evidence of pregnancy. If a pregnant woman suffers a miscarriage or terminates her pregnancy before a decision is reached as to whether she is owed section 193(2) main housing duty the housing authority should consider whether she continues to have a priority need as a result of some other factor (e.g. she may be vulnerable as a result of another special reason – see paragraph 8.38).

Dependent children

8.6 Applicants have a priority need if one or more dependent children is living with them or might reasonably be expected to live with them. There must be actual dependence on the applicant, although the child need not be wholly and exclusively dependent on them. There must also be actual residence (or a reasonable expectation of residence) with some degree of permanence or regularity, rather than a temporary arrangement whereby the children are merely staying with the applicant for a limited period (see paragraphs 8.10 and 8.11). Similarly, the child need not be wholly and exclusively resident (or expected to reside wholly and exclusively) with the applicant.

8.7 The 1996 Act does not define dependent children, but housing authorities may wish to treat as dependent all children under 16, and all children aged 16-18 who are in, or are about to begin, full-time education or training or who for other reasons are unable to support themselves and who live at home. The meaning of dependency is not however, limited to financial dependency. Thus, while children aged 16 and over who are in full-time employment and are financially independent of their parents would not normally be considered to be dependents, housing authorities should remember that such children may not be sufficiently mature to live independently of their parents, and there may be sound reasons for considering them to be dependent. The Secretary of State considers that it will be very rare that a 16 or 17 year old child who is living at home will not be considered to be dependent.

8.8 Dependent children need not necessarily be the applicant's own children, but could, for example, be related to the applicant or their partner, or be adopted or fostered by the applicant. There must, however, be some form of parent/child relationship.

8.9 Housing authorities may receive applications from a parent who is separated from their former spouse or partner. In some cases where parents separate, the court may make a residence order indicating with which parent the child normally resides. In such cases the child may be considered to reside with the parent named in the order, and would not normally be expected to reside with the other parent. However, in many cases the parents come to an agreement themselves as to how the child is cared for, and a court order will not be required.

8.10 Residence does not have to be full-time and a child can be considered to reside with either parent or with both parents. However, there must be some regularity to the arrangement for it to establish residence. Housing authorities should be mindful that where parents separate, there will generally be a presumption towards shared residence though this will not always be on the basis of an equal amount of time being spent living with both parents.

8.11 If the child is not currently residing with the applicant, the housing authority will need to decide whether, in the circumstances in which the applicant is homeless it would be reasonable for the child to do so. An agreement for joint residency between a child's parents, or a joint residence order by a court, will not automatically lead to a conclusion that it would be reasonable for the child to reside with the parent making the application, and housing authorities will need to consider each case individually. In doing so, housing authorities should take into account the specific needs and circumstances of the child, including whether suitable accommodation is available to them with their other parent.

8.12 Where the applicant's children are being looked after by a children's social services authority, whether subject to a care order or being accommodated under a voluntary agreement, and they are not currently living with the applicant, liaison with the social services authority will be essential. Joint consideration with social services will ensure that the best interests of the applicant and the children are served. This may, for example, enable a family to be reunited subject to suitable accommodation being available.

Vulnerability

8.13 A person has a priority need for accommodation if they are vulnerable as a result of:

(a) old age;
(b) mental illness or learning disability or physical disability;
(c) having been looked after, accommodated or fostered and is aged 21 or more;

(d)   having been a member of Her Majesty's regular naval, military or air forces;
(e)   having been in custody;
(f)   ceasing to occupy accommodation because of violence from another person or threats of violence from another person which are likely to be carried out; or,
(g)   any other special reason.

8.14   In the case of (a), (b) and (g) only, a person with whom a vulnerable person lives or might reasonably be expected to live also has a priority need for accommodation and can therefore make an application on behalf of themselves and that vulnerable person.

8.15   It is a matter of evaluative judgement whether the applicant's circumstances make them vulnerable. When determining whether an applicant in any of the categories set out in paragraph 8.13 is vulnerable, the housing authority should determine whether, if homeless, the applicant would be significantly more vulnerable than an ordinary person would be if they became homeless. The assessment must be a qualitative composite one taking into account all of the relevant facts and circum-stances, and involves a consideration of the impact of homelessness on the applicant when compared to an ordinary person if made homeless. The housing authority should consider whether the applicant would suffer or be at risk of suffering harm or detriment which the ordinary person would not suffer or be at risk of suffering, such that the harm or detriment would make a noticeable difference to their ability to deal with the consequences of homelessness.

8.16   When assessing an applicant's vulnerability, a housing authority may take into account the services and support available to them from a third party, including their family. This would involve considering the needs of the applicant, the level of support being provided to them, and whether with such support they would or would not be significantly more vulnerable than an ordinary person if made homeless. In order to reach a decision that a person is not vulnerable because of the support they receive the housing authority must be satisfied that the third party will provide the support on a consistent and predictable basis. In each case a housing authority should consider whether the applicant, even with support, would be vulnerable.

8.17   Housing authorities must be mindful of the Equality Act 2010 and their public sector equality duties towards people who have a protected characteristic. For further guidance on the Equality Act 2010 see Chapter 1. If the applicant has a disability (or another relevant protected characteristic) the authority should assess the extent of such disability and the likely effect of the disability, when taken together with any other features, on the applicant if and when homeless. They will then need to decide whether the impact of this makes the applicant significantly more vulnerable as a result.

8.18   Some of the factors which may be relevant to determining whether an applicant is vulnerable are set out below.

16

and 17 year olds

8.19   The specific duties towards 16 and 17 year olds who are at risk of homelessness or who are homeless, and the legal duties children's services authorities and housing authorities have towards them are set out in the Government's statutory guidance: 'Provision of accommodation for 16 and 17 year old young people who may be homeless and/or require accommodation.'

8.20   16 and 17 year old homeless applicants have a priority need for accommodation except those who are:

(a)   a relevant child; or,
(b)   a child in need who is owed a duty under section 20 of the Children Act 1989.

8.21   A relevant child is a child aged 16 or 17 who has been looked after by a local authority for at least 13 weeks since the age of 14 and has been looked after at some time while 16 or 17 and who is not currently being looked after (i.e. an 'eligible child' for the purposes of paragraph 19B of Schedule 2 to the Children Act 1989). In addition, a child is also a relevant child if they would have been looked after by the local authority as an eligible child but for the fact that on their 16th birthday they were detained through the criminal justice system, or in hospital, or if they returned home on family placement and that has broken down (see section 23A of the Children Act 1989, section 23A and regulation 3 of the Care Leavers (England) Regulations 2010).

8.22 The primary responsibility for a child in need who requires accommodation, including a 16 and 17 year old who is homeless lies with the relevant children's services authority. The Children Act 1989 (section 20) places a duty on children's services authorities to accommodate a child in need, and in almost all circumstances a homeless 16-17 year old would be a child in need.

8.23 However, there remain circumstances when the housing authority will have duties towards a homeless 16 and 17 year olds, including when the young person, having been fully informed of the implications, and being judged to have capacity to make that decision, declines to become looked after under the Children Act and instead applies for assistance under homelessness legislation. By definition these young people are nearing adulthood where a smooth and supported transition will be necessary to protect against the risk of homelessness re-occurring. As both children's services and housing authorities have duties towards this group it is essential that services are underpinned by written joint protocols which set out clear, practical arrangements for providing services that are centered on young people and their families and prevent young people from being passed over and back between housing and children's services authorities.

Old age

8.24 Old age alone is not sufficient for the applicant to be considered vulnerable. However, it may be that as a result of old age the applicant would be significantly more vulnerable than an ordinary person would be if homeless. Housing authorities should not use a fixed age beyond which vulnerability occurs automatically (or below which it can be ruled out); each case will need to be considered in the light of the individual circumstances.

Mental illness or learning disability or physical disability

8.25 Housing authorities should have regard to any advice from medical professionals, social services or current providers of care and support. In cases where there is doubt as to the extent of any vulnerability authorities may also consider seeking a clinical opinion. However, the final decision on the question of vulnerability will rest with the housing authority. In considering whether such applicants are vulnerable, authorities will need to take account of all relevant factors including:

(a)　the nature and extent of the illness and/or disability;

(b)　the relationship between the illness and/or disability and the individual's housing difficulties; and,

(c)　the relationship between the illness and/or disability and other factors such as drug/alcohol misuse, offending behaviour, challenging behaviour, age and personality disorder.

8.26 Assessment of vulnerability due to mental health problems will require co-operation between housing authorities, social services authorities and mental health agencies. Housing authorities should consider carrying out joint assessments or using a trained mental health practitioner as part of an assessment team. NHS mental health services provide help under the Care Programme Approach (CPA) for eligible patients, including people with severe mental illness (including personality disorder), who also have problems with housing. People who are homeless on discharge from hospital following a period of treatment for mental illness are likely to be vulnerable. Effective arrangements for liaison between housing, social services and mental health services will be essential in such cases but authorities will also need to be sensitive to direct approaches from former patients who have been discharged and may be homeless.

8.27 Learning or physical disabilities or long-term or acute illnesses which give rise to vulnerability may be readily discernible, but advice from health or social services should be sought wherever necessary.

Having been looked after, accommodated or fostered and aged 21 or over

8.28 A person aged 21 or over who is vulnerable as a result of having been looked after, accommodated or fostered has a priority need (other than a person who is a 'relevant student'). The terms 'looked after, accommodated or fostered' are set out in Section 24(2) of the Children Act 1989 and this includes any person who has been:

(a) looked after by a local authority (i.e. has been subject to a care order or accommodated under a voluntary agreement);
(b) accommodated by or on behalf of a voluntary organisation;
(c) accommodated in a private children's home;
(d) accommodated for a consecutive period of at least three months:
    (i) by any Local Health Board, Special Health Authority or by a local authority in the exercise of education functions; or,
    (ii) in any care home or independent hospital or in any accommodation provided pursuant to arrangements made by the Secretary of State, the National Health Service Commissioning Board or a clinical commissioning group under the National Health Service Act 2006 or by a National Health Service trust or an NHS foundation trust, or by a local authority in Wales in the exercise of education functions; or,
(e) privately fostered.

8.29 A 'relevant student' means a care leaver under 25 to whom section 24B (3) of the Children Act 1989 applies, and who is in full-time further or higher education and whose term-time accommodation is not available during a vacation. Under section 24B(5), where a social services authority is satisfied that a person is someone to whom section 24B(3) applies and needs accommodation during a vacation they must provide accommodation or the means to enable it to be secured.

8.30 Housing authorities will need to make inquiries into an applicant's childhood history to establish whether they have been looked after, accommodated or fostered in any of these ways. If so, they will need to consider whether they are vulnerable as a result.

8.31 For further guidance on assessing vulnerability, and on providing assistance to applicants who are care leavers see Chapter 22.

Having been a member of the armed forces

8.32 A person who is vulnerable as a result of having been a member of Her Majesty's regular armed forces has a priority need for accommodation. Former members of the armed forces will include a person who was previously a member of the regular naval, military or air forces.

8.33 For further guidance on assessing vulnerability, and on providing assistance to applicants who are veterans see Chapter 24.

Having been in custody

8.34 A person who is vulnerable as a result of having served a custodial sentence, been committed for contempt of court or remanded in custody has a priority need for accommodation.

8.35 For further guidance on assessing vulnerability, and on providing assistance to applicants who have been in custody or detention see Chapter 23.

Having left accommodation because of violence

8.36 A person has a priority need if they are vulnerable as a result of having to leave accommodation because of violence from another person, or threats of violence from another person that are likely to be carried out. It will usually be apparent from the assessment of the reason for homelessness whether the applicant has had to leave accommodation because of violence or threats of violence. In cases involving violence, the safety of the applicant and ensuring confidentiality must be of paramount concern.

8.37 For further guidance on dealing with cases involving domestic violence see Chapter 21.

Other special reason

8.38 Section 189(1)(c) provides that a person has a priority need for accommodation if they are vulnerable for any 'other special reason.' The legislation envisages that vulnerability can arise because of factors that are not expressly provided for in statute. Each application must be considered in the light of the facts and circumstances of the case. Moreover, other special reasons giving rise to vulnerability are not restricted to the physical or mental characteristics of a person. Where applicants have a need for support but have no family or friends on whom they can depend they may be vulnerable as a result of another special reason.

8.39 Housing authorities must keep an open mind and should avoid blanket policies that assume that particular groups of applicants will, or will not, be vulnerable for any other special reason. Where a housing authority considers that an applicant may be vulnerable, it will be important to make an in-depth assessment of the circumstances of the case. Guidance on certain categories of applicants who may be vulnerable as a result of any other special reason is given below. The list below is not exhaustive and housing authorities must ensure that they give proper consideration to every application on the basis of the individual circumstances. In addition, housing authorities will need to be aware that an applicant may be considered vulnerable for any other special reason because of a combination of factors which taken alone may not necessarily lead to a decision that they are vulnerable (e.g. drug and alcohol problems, common mental health problems, a history of sleeping rough, no previous experience of managing a tenancy).

8.40 **Young people:** the 2002 Order makes specific provision for certain categories of young homeless people. However, there are many other young people who could be vulnerable if homeless. Most young people can expect a degree of support from families, friends or an institution (e.g. a college or university) with the practicalities and costs of finding, establishing, and managing a home for the first time. But some young people, particularly those who are forced to leave the parental home or who cannot remain there because they are being subjected to violence or sexual abuse, may lack this back-up network and be less able than others to establish and maintain a home for themselves. Moreover, a young person who is homeless without adequate financial resources to live independently may be at risk of abuse or exploitation.

8.41 **People fleeing harassment:** housing authorities should consider whether harassment falls under the general definition of domestic abuse. For further guidance see Chapter 21 and paragraphs 8.36-8.37 above. In some cases, however, severe harassment may fall short of actual violence or threats of violence likely to be carried out. Housing authorities should consider carefully whether applicants who have fled their home because of non-violent forms of harassment, for example, psychological or emotional or damage to property, are vulnerable as a result.

8.42 **Victims of trafficking and of modern slavery:** housing authorities should ensure that staff have an awareness of the possibility that applicants may be victims of trafficking or of modern slavery, and are able to assess whether or not they are vulnerable as a result. For guidance on assessing vulnerability, and on providing assistance to applicants who are victims of trafficking or modern slavery see Chapter 25.

CHAPTER 9: INTENTIONAL HOMELESSNESS

9.1 This chapter provides guidance on determining whether an applicant became homeless intentionally under section 191 of the 1996 Act.

9.2 The prevention and relief duties owed to applicants who are eligible for assistance and homeless, or threatened with homelessness, apply irrespective of whether or not they may be considered to be homeless intentionally.

9.3 Applicants who have a priority need, and whose homelessness has not been successfully relieved, are owed a lesser duty if they have become homeless intentionally than would be owed to them if they were homeless unintentionally. This reflects the general expectation that, wherever possible, people should take responsibility for their own accommodation needs and not behave in a way which might lead to the loss of their accommodation.

9.4 Where a housing authority finds an eligible applicant has a priority need but is homeless intentionally and the relief duty has come to an end, they have a duty to secure accommodation which is available to the applicant to provide reasonable opportunity for them to find their own accommodation. The authority must also provide advice and assistance in any attempts the applicant might make to secure accommodation. For further guidance on the accommodation duty owed to intentionally homeless applicants see Chapter 15.

9.5 It is for housing authorities to satisfy themselves in each individual case whether an applicant is homeless intentionally. Generally, it is not for applicants to 'prove their case.' The exception is where an applicant seeks to establish that, as a member of a household where another member has been found or is likely to be found to have caused intentional homelessness of the household, they did not acquiesce in the behaviour that led to homelessness. In such cases, acquiescence may be assumed by the housing authority in the absence of material which indicates to the contrary.

9.6 Housing authorities must not adopt general policies which seek to pre-define circumstances that do or do not amount to intentional homelessness. In each case, housing authorities must form a view in the light of all their inquiries about that particular case. Where the original loss of settled accommodation occurred some years earlier and the facts are unclear, it may not be possible for the housing authority to satisfy themselves that the applicant became homeless intentionally.

Definition of intentional homelessness

9.7 Section 191(1) provides that a person becomes homeless intentionally if ALL of the following apply:

(a) they deliberately do or fail to do anything in consequence of which they cease to occupy accommodation; and,
(b) the accommodation is available for their occupation; and,
(c) it would have been reasonable for them to continue to occupy the accommodation.

However, for this purpose, an act or omission made in good faith by someone who was unaware of any relevant fact must not be treated as deliberate (see paragraph 9.23).

9.8 Section 191(3) provides that a person must be treated as homeless intentionally if:

(a) the person enters into an arrangement under which they are required to cease to occupy accommodation which it would have been reasonable for the person to continue to occupy; and,
(b) the purpose of the arrangement is to enable the person to become entitled to assistance under Part 7; and,
(c) there is no other good reason why the person is homeless.

Whose conduct results in intentional homelessness?

9.9 Every applicant is entitled to individual consideration of their application. This includes applicants where another member of their family or household has made, or is making, a separate application. It is the applicant who must deliberately have done or failed to do something which resulted in homelessness.

9.10 Where a housing authority has found an applicant to be homeless intentionally, nothing in the 1996 Act prevents another member of their household from making a separate application. Situations may arise where one or more members of a household found to be intentionally homeless were not responsible for the actions or omissions that led to the homelessness. For example, a person may have deliberately failed to pay the rent or defaulted on the mortgage payments, which resulted in homelessness against the wishes or without the knowledge of their partner.

9.11 However, where applicants were not directly responsible for the act or omission which led to their family or household becoming homeless, but they acquiesced in that behaviour, then they may be treated as having become homeless intentionally themselves. In considering whether an applicant has acquiesced in certain behaviour, the housing authority should take into account whether the applicant could reasonably be expected to have taken that position through a fear of actual or probable violence.

Cessation of occupation

9.12 For intentional homelessness to be established there must have been actual occupation of accommodation which has ceased. However, occupation need not necessarily involve continuous occupation at all times, provided the accommodation was at the disposal of the applicant and available for their occupation. The accommodation which has been lost can be outside the UK. Housing authorities are reminded that applicants cannot be considered to have become homeless intentionally because of failing to take up an offer of accommodation. However, an applicant whose refusal of a suitable offer of accommodation brought to an end the section 193(2) duty under which they were at the time accommodated, resulting in the loss of that accommodation, may be considered to be intentionally homeless.

Consequence of a deliberate act or omission

9.13 For homelessness to be intentional, the ending of occupation of the accommodation must be a consequence of a deliberate act or omission by the applicant. Having established that there was a deliberate act or omission, the housing authority will need to decide whether the loss of the applicant's home is the reasonably likely result of that act or omission. This is a matter of cause and effect. An example would be where a person voluntarily gave up settled accommodation that it would have been reasonable for them to continue to occupy, moved into alternative accommodation of a temporary or unsettled nature and subsequently became homeless when required to leave the alternative accommodation. Housing authorities will, therefore, need to look back to the last period of settled accommodation and the reasons why the applicant left that accommodation, to determine whether the current incidence of homelessness is the reasonably likely result of a deliberate act or omission.

Ceasing to be intentionally homeless

9.14 Where a person becomes homeless intentionally, that condition may continue until the link between the causal act or omission and the intentional homelessness has been broken. It could be broken by an intervening event which, irrespective of any act or omission on the part of the applicant, would have itself led to their being homeless at the point at which the housing authority was carrying out inquiries into their application for assistance. This might be the case where, for example, an applicant gave up accommodation without sufficient good reason but at the later point at which they applied for assistance due to homelessness this accommodation would no longer have been available to them, or reasonable for them to occupy.

9.15 The causal link between a deliberate act or omission and intentional homelessness is more typically broken by a period in settled accommodation which follows the intentional homelessness. Whether accommodation is settled will depend on the circumstances of the case, with factors such as security of tenure and length of residence being relevant. Occupation of accommodation that was merely temporary rather than settled, for example, staying with friends on an insecure basis, may not be sufficient to break the link with the earlier intentional homelessness. However, a period in settled accommodation is not the only way in which a link with the earlier intentional homelessness may be broken: some other event, such as the break-up of a marriage resulting in homelessness, may be sufficient.

Deliberate act or omission

9.16   For homelessness to be intentional, the act or omission that led to the loss of accommodation must have been deliberate, and applicants must always be given the opportunity to explain such behaviour. An act or omission should not generally be treated as deliberate, even where deliberately carried out, if it is forced upon the applicant through no fault of their own. Moreover, an act or omission made in good faith where someone is genuinely ignorant of a relevant fact must not be treated as deliberate (see paragraph 9.23).

9.17   Generally, an act or omission should not be considered deliberate where, for example:

(a)   the act or omission was non-payment of rent or mortgage costs which arose from financial difficulties which were beyond the applicant's control, or were the result of Housing Benefit or Universal Credit delays;

(b)   the housing authority has reason to believe the applicant is incapable of managing their affairs, for example, by reason of age, mental illness or disability;

(c)   the act or omission was the result of limited mental capacity; or a temporary aberration or aberrations caused by mental illness, frailty, or an assessed substance misuse problem;

(d)   the act or omission was made when the applicant was under duress;

(e)   imprudence or lack of foresight on the part of an applicant led to homelessness but the act or omission was in good faith.

9.18   An applicant's actions would not amount to intentional homelessness where they have lost their home, or were obliged to sell it, because of rent or mortgage arrears resulting from significant financial difficulties, and the applicant was genuinely unable to keep up the rent or mortgage payments even after claiming benefits, and no further financial help was available.

9.19   Where an applicant has lost a former home due to rent arrears, the reasons why the arrears accrued should be fully explored, including examining the applicant's ability to pay the housing costs at the time the commitment was taken on. Similarly, in cases which involve mortgagors, housing authorities will need to look at the reasons for mortgage arrears together with the applicant's ability to pay the mortgage commitment when it was taken on, given the applicant's financial circumstances at the time.

9.20   Examples of acts or omissions which may be regarded as deliberate (unless any of the circumstances set out in paragraph 9.17 apply) include the following, where someone:

(a)   chooses to sell their home in circumstances where they are under no risk of losing it;

(b)   has lost their home because of willful and persistent refusal to pay rent or mortgage payments;

(c)   could be said to have significantly neglected their affairs having disregarded sound advice from qualified people;

(d)   voluntarily surrenders adequate accommodation in this country or abroad which it would have been reasonable for them to continue to occupy;

(e)   is evicted because of their anti-social behaviour, nuisance to neighbours or harassment;

(f)   is evicted because of violence or threats of violence or abuse by them towards another person;

(g)   leaves a job with tied accommodation and the circumstances indicate that it would have been reasonable for them to continue in the employment and reasonable to continue to occupy the accommodation.

Available for occupation

9.21   For homelessness to be intentional the accommodation must have been available for the applicant, their household and any other person reasonably expected to live with them. For further guidance on availability for occupation see Chapter 6.

Reasonable to continue to occupy the accommodation

9.22　An applicant cannot be treated as intentionally homeless unless it would have been reasonable for them to have continued to occupy the accommodation. For further guidance on reasonable to continue to occupy see Chapter 6. It will be necessary for the housing authority to give careful consideration to the circumstances of the applicant and the household, in each case, and with particular care in cases where violence and abuse has been alleged. For further guidance on domestic violence and abuse see Chapter 21.

Act or omissions in good faith

9.23　Acts or omissions made by the applicant in good faith where they were genuinely unaware of a relevant fact must not be regarded as deliberate. Provided that the applicant has acted in good faith, there is no requirement that ignorance of the relevant fact be reasonable.

9.24　A general example of an act made in good faith would be a situation where someone gave up possession of accommodation in the belief that they had no legal right to continue to occupy the accommodation and, therefore, it would not be reasonable for them to continue to occupy it. This could apply where someone leaves rented accommodation in the private sector having received a valid notice to quit or notice that the assured shorthold tenancy has come to an end and the landlord requires possession of the property, and the former tenant was genuinely unaware that they had a right to remain until the court granted an order for possession and a warrant or writ for possession to enforce it.

9.25　Where there was dishonesty there could be no question of an act or omission having been made in good faith.

9.26　Other examples of acts or omissions that could be made in good faith might include situations where:

(a)　a person gets into rent arrears, being unaware that they may be entitled to Housing Benefit, Universal Credit or other social security benefits;

(b)　an owner-occupier faced with foreclosure or possession proceedings to which there is no defence, sells before the mortgagee recovers possession through the courts or surrenders the property to the lender; or,

(c)　a tenant, faced with possession proceedings to which there would be no defence, and where the granting of a possession order would be mandatory, surrenders the property to the landlord.

9.27　In (c) although the housing authority may consider that it would have been reasonable for the tenant to continue to occupy the accommodation, the act should not be regarded as deliberate if the tenant made the decision to leave the accommodation in ignorance of relevant facts.

Applicant enters into an arrangement

9.28　Housing authorities will need to be alert to the possibility of collusion by which a person may claim that they are obliged to leave available accommodation that would have been reasonable for them to continue to occupy in order to take advantage of the homelessness legislation. Collusion is not confined to arrangements with friends or relatives but can also occur between landlords and tenants. Housing authorities, while relying on experience, nonetheless need to be satisfied that collusion exists, and must not rely on hearsay or unfounded suspicions in finding that an applicant became intentionally homeless under section 191(3).

9.29　For collusion to amount to intentional homelessness, section 191(3) specifies that there should be no other good reason for the applicant's homelessness. Examples of other good reasons include overcrowding or an obvious breakdown in relations between the applicant and their host or landlord. In some cases involving collusion the applicant may not actually be homeless, if there is no genuine need for the applicant to leave the accommodation. For further guidance on applicants asked to leave by family or friends see Chapter 6.

9.30 Specific guidance relating to intentional homelessness can also be found in the following chapters:

Chapter 21: domestic abuse;

Chapter 22: care leavers;

Chapter 23: people with an offending history;

Chapter 24: former members of the armed forces.

CHAPTER 10: LOCAL CONNECTION AND REFERRALS TO ANOTHER HOUSING AUTHORITY

10.1 This chapter provides guidance on the provisions relating to an applicant's 'local connection' with an area and explains the conditions and procedures for referring an applicant to another housing authority. The chapter includes how local connection is assessed, particular arrangements that apply for certain groups such as care leavers and former asylum seekers, the process and conditions for referrals between authorities, cross-border referrals and dealing with disputes.

Local Authorities Agreement

10.2 Local authority bodies have together agreed guidelines for local authorities on procedures for referral between them, and for resolving disputes that arise when housing authorities are unable to agree whether conditions for a referral from one authority to another are met. Although these procedures have been adopted by local authority organisations in England, Scotland and Wales, and are now widely used, housing authorities are reminded that they should consider each case individually on its own particular facts.

Assessing local connection

10.3 When a housing authority makes inquiries to determine whether an applicant is eligible for assistance and owed a duty under Part 7, it may also make inquiries under section 184(2) to establish an applicant's local connection.

10.4 Section 199(1) provides that a person has a local connection with the district of a housing authority if they have a connection with it because:

(a) they are, or were in the past, normally resident there, and that residence was of their own choice; or,
(b) they are employed there; or,
(c) they have family associations living there; or,
(d) of any special circumstances.

10.5 For the purposes of (a), above, 'normal residence' is to be understood as meaning 'the place where at the relevant time the person in fact resides.' Residence in temporary accommodation provided by a housing authority can constitute normal residence of choice and can contribute towards a local connection.

10.6 In the case of a person who is street homeless or insecurely accommodated ('sofa surfing') the housing authority will need to carry out a different type of inquiry to be satisfied as to their 'normal residence' than would be required for an applicant who has become homeless from more settled accommodation. If an applicant has no settled accommodation elsewhere, and from inquiries the authority is satisfied that they do in fact reside in the district, then there will be normal residence for the purposes of the 1996 Act.

10.7 The Local Authorities Agreement suggests that a working definition of normal residence sufficient to establish a local connection should be residence for at least 6 months in an area during the previous 12 months, or for three years during the previous five year period.

10.8 With regard to (b) the applicant should actually work in the district: it would not be sufficient that their employers' head office was located there.

10.9 For the purposes of (c), where the applicant raises family associations, this may extend beyond partners, parents, adult children or siblings. They may include associations with other family members such as step-parents, grandparents, grandchildren, aunts or uncles provided there are sufficiently close links in the form of frequent contact, commitment or dependency. Family associations should be determined with regard to the fact-specific circumstances of the individual case. For example, the actual closeness of the family association may count for more than the degree of blood relation. A housing authority should not identify a local connection through family associations with an area other than the one where the applicant positively wants to live.

10.10 The Local Authorities Agreement recommends that in order to give rise to a local connection, the family members relied upon as family associations should have been resident in the district for a period of at least five years at the date of application from homelessness assistance. Housing authorities should remain cautious in applying this guideline to every case. For example, in cases of refugees or other recent arrivals to the UK, a housing authority should bear in mind that the relatives may not have had five years in which to build up a residence period in any district in the UK.

10.11 With regard to (d), special circumstances might include the need to be near special medical or support services which are available only in a particular district.

10.12 Decisions about the application of (a) to (d) must be based on the facts at the date of the decision (or review of the decision), not the date of the application.

10.13 The test regarding local connection, as set out in section 199(1) should be applied, and the additional provisions for care leavers (see paragraph 10.17) and asylum seekers (see paragraph 10.23) where relevant, in order to establish whether the applicant has the required local connection. The fact that an applicant may satisfy one of these grounds will not necessarily mean that they have been able to establish a local connection.

10.14 The overriding consideration should always be whether the applicant has a connection 'in real terms' with an area and the housing authority must consider the applicant's individual circumstances, particularly any exceptional circumstances, before reaching a decision.

10.15 Housing authorities are not generally required to make any inquiries as to whether an applicant has a local connection with an area. However, by virtue of section 11 of the Asylum and Immigration (Treatment of Claimants, etc.) Act 2004, housing authorities will need to consider local connection in cases where the applicant is a former asylum seeker:

(a)   who was provided with accommodation in Scotland under section 95 of the Immigration and Asylum Act 1999; and,

(b)   whose accommodation was not provided in an accommodation centre by virtue of section 22 of the Nationality, Immigration and Asylum Act 2002.

10.16 In such cases, by virtue of section 11(2)(d) and (3) of the Asylum and Immigration (Treatment of Claimants, etc.) Act 2004, local connection to a district in England, Wales or Scotland will be relevant to what duty is owed under section 193. (See paragraphs 10.23 – 10.29 below).

Care leavers

10.17 Section 199(8) to (11) makes specific provisions relating to local connection for care leavers.

10.18 A young person owed leaving care duties under section 23C of the Children Act 1989 will have a local connection to the area of the children services authority that owes them the duties. If the children services authority is a county council and not a housing authority, the young person will have a local connection with every housing authority district falling within the area of the children services authority.

10.19 Where a care leaver is aged under 21 and normally lives in a different area to that of a local authority that owes them leaving care duties, and has done for at least 2 years including some time before they turned 16, the young person will also have a local connection in that area.

10.20 For further guidance on assessments and provision of services for Care Leavers see Chapter 22.

Ex-service personnel

10.21 Section 315 of the Housing and Regeneration Act 2008 amended the local connection test to enable armed forces personnel to establish a local connection in an area through residing there by choice, or being employed there, in the same way as a civilian. For further guidance on former members of the armed forces see Chapter 24.

Ex-prisoners and detainees under the Mental Health Act 1983

10.22 Detention in prison (whether convicted or not) does not establish residency of choice in the district the prison is in, and so will not create a local connection with that district. The same is true of those detained under the *Mental Health Act 1983*. For further guidance on people with an offending history see Chapter 23.

Former asylum seekers

10.23 Sections 199(6) provides that a person has a local connection with the district of a housing authority if they were (at any time) provided with accommodation there under section 95 of the *Immigration and Asylum Act 1999* (section 95 accommodation).

10.24 Under section 199(7), however, a person does not have a local connection by virtue of section 199(6):

(a)   if they have been subsequently provided with section 95 accommodation in a different area. Where a former asylum seeker has been provided with section 95 accommodation in more than one area, the local connection is with the area where accommodation was last provided; or,

(b)   if they have been provided with section 95 accommodation in an accommodation centre in the district by virtue of section 22 of the *Nationality, Immigration and Asylum Act 2002*.

10.25 A local connection with a district by virtue of section 199(6) does not override a local connection by virtue of section 199(1). Thus, a former asylum seeker who has a local connection with a district because they were provided with accommodation there under section 95 may also have a local connection elsewhere for some other reason, for example, because of employment or family associations.

Former asylum seekers provided with section 95 accommodation in Scotland

10.26 Under Scottish legislation, a person does not establish a local connection with a district in Scotland if they are resident there in section 95 accommodation. Consequently, if such a person made a homelessness application to a housing authority in England, and did not have a local connection with the district of that authority, the fact that they had been provided with section 95 accommodation in Scotland would not establish conditions for referral to the relevant local authority in Scotland.

10.27 Sections 11(2) and (3) of the Asylum and Immigration (Treatment of Claimants, etc.) Act 2004 provides that where a housing authority in England or Wales is satisfied that an applicant is eligible for assistance, unintentionally homeless and in priority need and:

(a)   the applicant has been provided with section 95 accommodation in Scotland at any time;

(b)   the section 95 accommodation was not provided in an accommodation centre by virtue of section 22 of the *Nationality, Immigration and Asylum Act 2002*;

(c)   the applicant does not have a local connection anywhere in England and Wales (within the meaning of section 199 of the 1996 Act); and,

(d)   the applicant does not have a local connection anywhere in Scotland (within the meaning of section 27 of the *Housing (Scotland) Act 1987*); then the duty to the applicant under section 193 (the main housing duty) shall not apply.

10.28   However, the authority:

(a)   may secure that accommodation is available for occupation by the applicant for a period giving them a reasonable opportunity of securing accommodation for their occupation; and,

(b)   may provide the applicant (or secure that they are provided with) advice and assistance in any attempts they may make to secure accommodation for their occupation.

10.29   When dealing with an applicant in these circumstances, housing authorities will need to take into account the wishes of the applicant but should consider providing such advice and assistance as would enable the applicant to make an application for housing to the Scottish authority in the district where the section 95 accommodation was last provided, or to another Scottish authority of the applicant's choice. If they were unintentionally homeless and in priority need, it would be open to them to apply to any Scottish housing authority and they would be owed a main housing duty.

Referrals to another housing authority

10.30   If a housing authority's inquires under section 184(2) determine that an applicant has a local connection with the district of another housing authority in England, Wales or Scotland, section 198 allows a housing authority ('the notifying authority') to refer a case to another housing authority ('the notified authority') at the point of the relief duty or main housing duty. Before making a referral the notifying authority must decide if the conditions for referral are met (see 10.32). Referrals cannot be made to Welsh or Scottish authorities where the section 189B relief duty is owed.

10.31   The Secretary of State recommends that the notified authority should respond to a referral within 10 working days.

10.32   **Referrals are discretionary only: housing authorities are not required to refer applicants to other authorities.** Housing authorities may have a policy about how they exercise their discretion to refer a case. This must not, however, extend to deciding in advance that in all cases where there is a local connection to another district the case should be referred.

10.33   There may be instances where an applicant has a local connection to the district where they applied but the housing authority considers that there is a stronger local connection elsewhere. In such cases, a housing authority can not decide to transfer responsibility to another housing authority; however, they will still be able to seek assistance from the other housing authority in securing accommodation, under section 213. For further guidance on securing accommodation see Chapter 16.

10.34   Where a person has a local connection with the districts of more than one other housing authority, the notifying housing authority should take account of the applicant's preference in deciding which housing authority to notify.

10.35   If neither an applicant, nor any person who might reasonably be expected to live with them, has a local connection with any district in Great Britain, the duty to secure accommodation or help to secure accommodation will rest with the housing authority that has received the application.

Referrals to another housing authority in England at the relief stage

10.36   Referrals cannot be made to Welsh or Scottish authorities at the relief stage - the English authority the applicant has applied to will be subject to the relief duty, if one is owed.

10.37 Section 198(A1) enables a housing authority to refer applicants who do not have a local connection to their district to another housing authority in England where they do have such a connection. Before making a referral, the notifying authority must be satisfied that the applicant is homeless and eligible for assistance and therefore owed the (section 189B) relief duty and that the conditions for referral are met (see paragraph 10.51).

10.38 Section 189B sets out the initial duties owed to all eligible people who are homeless, that is the relief duty, **unless** the authority refers the application to another housing authority. Section 199A(b) states that the housing authority is not subject to the relief duty at the point that they have notified the applicant that they intend to refer or have referred their case to another housing authority. It follows that a housing authority will owe the relief duty until such time as the applicant has been issued with this notification. If the authority believes that the applicant has no local connection and **may** have a connection elsewhere, they should take reasonable steps to try and relieve the applicant's homelessness until they issue the first notification as outlined in 10.39 below.

10.39 When the notifying authority intends to refer or have referred a case to another housing authority, there are two points at which applicants must be notified:

(a) when the notifying authority has decided that the conditions for referral are met and intend to notify, or have notified, another local authority of that opinion;

(b) when, following referral, it has been decided that the conditions for referral are or are not met. The notification must provide notice of the decision and the reasons for it.

10.40 From the date that the first notice is issued the authority will not be subject to the relief duty and will cease to be subject to the section 188 (interim accommodation) duty. However if they have reason to believe the applicant may be in priority need they will have a section 199A (2) duty to provide interim accommodation to the applicant whilst a decision is made on whether the conditions for referral are met.

10.41 From the date the second notice (b) is issued to the applicant, if it is decided that the conditions for referral are met, the applicant is to be treated as having made an application to the notified authority. At this point, the notifying authority's duties under Part 7 of the 1996 Act come to an end.

10.42 If the notifying authority has made a decision as to whether the applicant is eligible for assistance, is homeless or became homeless intentionally, the notified authority may only come to a different decision if they are satisfied that the applicants circumstances have changed; or further information has come to light since the notifying authority made their decision, and that the changes or information warrant a different decision.

10.43 The notifying authority must give the notified authority a copy of the applicant's section 189A(3) assessment and any revisions made to it, and should also (with the applicant's consent) provide any personalised housing plan that has been agreed with the applicant which remains relevant. The notifying authority should provide this documentation as quickly as possible.

10.44 If it is decided that the conditions for referral are not met the applicant's case will remain with the notifying authority and they will be subject to the relief duty under section 189(B)(2). The 56 day period of the relief duty will start from the date of the second notification.

Referrals to another housing authority in England, Wales or Scotland at the end of the relief duty

10.45 Section 198(1) enables a housing authority to refer an applicant who is owed the main housing duty but does not have a local connection to their district, to another housing authority in England, Wales or Scotland if it considers that the conditions for referral are met. Before making a referral, it is the responsibility of the notifying authority to determine that the applicant is unintentionally homeless, eligible for assistance and has a priority need; and is owed the main housing duty.

10.46 The notifying authority cannot issue a notice of referral under section 198(1) until their duties to the applicant under section 189B(2), the relief duty, have come to an end.

10.47 As set out in paragraph 10.38 above when the notifying authority intends to refer a case to another housing authority, there are two notification points. At the point that the housing authority issues the first notice which notifies the applicant that they have or will be referring their case to another housing authority the notifying authority will cease to be subject the section 188 duty to provide interim accommodation from the date of the notice and will not be subject to any duty under section 193. However, they will be subject to a section 200(1) duty to provide interim accommodation until a decision is reached on whether the conditions for referral are met.

10.48 From the date the second notice (b) is issued to the applicant, (which sets out the decision on whether the conditions for referral have been met), if it is decided that the conditions for referral are met, the notifying authority's duty to provide accommodation under section 200(1) comes to an end and the notified authority will be subject to the main housing duty.

10.49 If it is decided that the conditions for referral are not met the applicant's case will remain with the notifying authority and they will be subject to the main housing duty under section 193.

10.50 A notified authority which disagrees on a finding as to the application of the main housing duty (section 193) to the applicant must challenge the notifying authority's finding (for example as to intentionality) by way of judicial review.

Conditions for referral

10.51 Sections 198(2)(2ZA) and (4) describe the conditions which must be satisfied before a referral may be made. A notifying authority may only refer an applicant to whom the relief duty or main housing duty applies to another housing authority if all of the following are met:

(a) neither the applicant nor any person who might reasonably be expected to live with them has a local connection with its district; and,

(b) the applicant or a person who might reasonably be expected to live with them has a local connection with the district of the authority to be notified; and,

(c) none of them will be at risk of domestic or other violence, or threat of domestic or other violence which is likely to be carried out, in the district of the authority to be notified.

Or:

(a) the application is made within two years of the applicants acceptance of a private rented sector offer from the other authority under section 193(7AA); and,

(b) neither the applicant or any person who might reasonably be expected to live with them will be at risk of domestic or other violence, or threat of domestic or other violence which is likely to be carried out, in the district of the authority to be notified.

For further guidance on referrals to another housing authority in this circumstance see Chapter 18 on re-applications.

Or:

(a) the applicant was placed in the authority's district by another authority as a result of a previous homelessness application to the other authority; and,

(b) the fresh application for assistance has been made within a prescribed period of the first application.

The *Allocation of Housing and Homelessness (Miscellaneous Provisions) (England) Regulations 2006* (SI 2006 No. 2527) set out that the 'prescribed period' is the total of five years plus the period between the date of the previous application and the date the applicant was first placed in accommodation in the district of the authority to whom the application is now made.

Risk of violence

10.52 A housing authority cannot refer an applicant to another housing authority if they or anyone who might reasonably be expected to reside with them would be at risk of violence. The housing authority is under a positive duty to enquire whether the applicant would be at such a risk and, if they would, should not assume that the applicant will take steps to deal with the threat.

10.53 Section 198(3) defines violence as violence from another person or threats of violence from another person which are likely to be carried out. This is the same definition as appears in section 177 in relation to whether it is reasonable to continue to occupy accommodation and the circumstances to be considered as to whether a person runs a risk of violence are the same.

10.54 Housing authorities should be alert to the deliberate distinction which is made in section 198(3) between actual violence and threatened violence. A high standard of proof of actual violence in the past should not be imposed. The threshold is that there must be:

(a) no risk of domestic violence (actual or threatened) in the other district; and,
(b) no risk of other violence (actual or threatened) in the other district.

For further guidance on cases involving domestic abuse see Chapter 21.

Cross-border referrals

10.55 Paragraph 10.30 above sets out the circumstances under which a local housing authority can refer a case to another housing authority in Wales or Scotland, and the conditions for referral apply to all referrals. Following a referral, the Local Authorities Agreement sets out that the legislation relevant to the location of the notified authority should be applied when reaching an agreement on whether the conditions for referral are met. There are no arrangements in place to enable referrals to be made between England and Northern Ireland or the Republic of Ireland.

Applicants' rights to request a review

10.56 Applicants have the right to request a review of various decisions relating to local connection and referrals. Under section 202(1)(c), an applicant is able to request a review of a housing authority's decision to notify another housing authority that the conditions for referral are met where the main housing duty is owed (notice a – see 10.39). Applicants cannot request a review of the equivalent section 198(A1) decision at the relief stage. Applicants have a right to request a review of the decision on whether the conditions for referral are met at both the stage of the relief duty or main housing duty under section 202(1)(e) (notice b – see 10.39). For further guidance on reviews see Chapter 19.

10.57 The notifying authority's interim duty to accommodate under section 188, 199A(2) or 200(1) ends regardless of whether the applicant requests a review of a decision that the conditions for referral are met. However, where the applicant does request a review the notifying authority has powers under section 199A (6) and section 200(5) to secure that accommodation is available pending the review decision. For further guidance on powers to secure accommodation see Chapter 15.

10.58 There is no right to request a review of a decision *not* to refer a case, although a failure by a housing authority to consider whether it has the discretion to refer an applicant may be amenable to challenge though judicial review. The same is true of an unreasonable use of the discretion. For further guidance on reviews see Chapter 19.

Disputes

10.59 The question of whether the conditions for referral are met in a particular case at the point of the relief duty or the main housing duty should be decided by agreement between the housing authorities concerned (section 198(5)).

10.60 If they cannot agree, the decision should be made in accordance with such arrangements as may be directed by order of the Secretary of State (section 198(5)). The *Homelessness (Decisions on Referrals) Order 1998* (SI 1998 No. 1578) sets out that where a decision cannot be reached by agreement between the notifying authority and the notified authority, the question shall be decided by a person appointed by those authorities.

10.61 The Order directs that the arrangements to be followed in such a dispute are the arrangements agreed between the local authority associations (i.e. the Local Government Association (LGA), the Convention of Scottish Local Authorities, the Welsh Local Government Association and London Councils). The LGA has issued guidelines for housing authorities on invoking the disputes procedure.

10.62 If the authorities are unable to appoint a person to make this decision within 21 days from the date on which the notified authorities receives a notification, sections (2) to (4) of the Schedule to the Order set out the arrangements for appointing a person. These **only apply** where a housing authority in England, Wales or Scotland seek to refer a homelessness case under section 198(1) to another housing authority in England or Wales, at the point of the main housing duty and they are unable to agree to appoint a person to decide whether the conditions for referral are met. They **do not apply** where a housing authority in England seek to refer a homelessness case to another authority in England under section 198(A1) at the point of the relief duty.

10.63 The Secretary of State has issued the below guidance to set out the arrangements housing authorities should take in the event of them being unable to agree on a person to be appointed to make the decision on whether the conditions for referral of a case are met under section 198(A1) at the point of the relief duty. Housing authorities are strongly recommended to follow this guidance:

(a) if the notified and notifying authority are unable to appoint a person to make a decision on their behalf on the referral of a case within 21 days from the day on which the notified authority received a notification under section 198(A1), They should jointly request the Chair of the LGA or their nominee ('the proper officer') to appoint a person to make this decision;

(b) the Secretary of State recommends that the authorities request that the LGA appoint a person from the panel of persons they have established to decide the question of whether the conditions for a referral of a case are satisfied. The LGA are required to establish this panel under the *Homelessness (Decisions on Referrals) Order 1998* (SI 1998 No. 1578) to appoint persons to make decisions on referrals of cases under section 198(1). Housing authorities are recommended to utilise this existing procedure;

(c) if within a period of six weeks from the day on which the notified authority received a notification under section 198(A1), a person still has not been appointed, the notifying authority is recommended to request the proper officer to appoint a person from the panel specified above.

10.64 Broadly speaking, both section (2) to (4) of the Schedule to the order and the guidance above provide that in the event of two housing authorities being unable to agree on a person to be appointed to make the decision for them they should agree to make a joint request to the LGA to appoint someone. If unable to agree on that the notifying housing authority must make such a request of the LGA. In all cases relating to notifications under section 198(1) the appointed person must be drawn from a panel established by the LGA for this purpose. It is recommended that for cases relating to notification under section 198(A1) the housing authorities request that the appointed person is drawn from this panel.

10.65 Section 5, 6 and 7 of the Homelessness (Decisions on Referrals) Order 1998 sets out the procedure to be followed by the appointed person when making their decision and the arrangements for meeting associated costs. These provisions apply regardless of the means by which a person has been appointed. The appointed person must invite written representations from the notifying and notified authority and shall notify their decision and their reasons for it, in writing to the notifying authority and the notified authority. The notifying and notified authority must pay their own costs incurred in connection with these arrangements.

10.66 The *Homelessness (Decisions on Referrals) (Scotland) Order 1998*, (SI 1998 No.1603) applies under the Scottish homelessness legislation. The arrangements in the latter apply in cases where a housing authority in England, Wales or Scotland refers a homelessness case to a housing authority in Scotland, and they are unable to agree whether the conditions for referral are met.

10.67 Where an English or Welsh housing authority seek to refer a case to a Scottish housing authority, a request to the local authority association to appoint an arbitrator should be made to the Convention of Scottish Local Authorities.

CHAPTER 11: ASSESSMENTS AND PERSONALISED PLANS

11.1 This chapter provides guidance on the (section 189A of the 1996 Act) assessments that housing authorities must carry out to determine the duties owed to a person applying for assistance, and the needs and circumstances of those applicants who are eligible for assistance and homeless or threatened with homelessness. It includes guidance on personalised plans and the reasonable steps applicants and housing authorities may take to prevent or relieve homelessness.

Overview: assessments and personalised plans

11.2 The section 189A duties to assess an applicant's case and develop a personalised plan provide a framework for housing authorities and applicants to work together to identify appropriate actions to prevent or relieve the applicant's homelessness. In performing these duties, the Secretary of State considers that housing authorities should adopt a positive and collaborative approach toward applicants, taking account of their particular needs and making all reasonable efforts to engage their cooperation. Personalised plans are more frequently referred to as 'personalised housing plans', and so this term is adopted throughout this guidance.

Initial assessments

11.3 Every person applying for assistance from a housing authority stating that they are or are going to be homeless will require an initial interview. If there is reason to believe that they may be homeless or threatened with homelessness within 56 days the housing authority must carry out an assessment to determine if this is the case, and whether they are eligible for assistance. If the applicant is not eligible for assistance or if the authority is satisfied that they are not homeless or threatened with homelessness within 56 days, they must be given a written section 184 notification of the decision reached. For further guidance on eligibility see Chapter 7 and for further guidance on notifications see Chapter 18.

11.4 In some circumstances it will be possible to determine that an applicant is not threatened with homelessness at first approach, but in most cases further enquires will need to be carried out to find out more about their housing circumstances before being satisfied that they are not threatened with homelessness within 56 days. If the applicant believes they are threatened with homelessness and there is reason to believe that this is the case then further investigations will be required.

11.5 Guidance on whether a person is homeless or threatened with homelessness is provided in Chapter 6. It should be noted that applicants who have been served a valid section 21 notice to end an assured shorthold tenancy of their only available home, which expires within 56 days, are threatened with homelessness.

11.6 Housing authorities are encouraged to take a flexible approach toward applications for assistance where there is an evidenced risk of homelessness, which might not necessarily result in homelessness within 56 days. Rather than advise the applicant to return when homelessness is more imminent, the housing authority may wish to accept a prevention duty and begin to take reasonable steps to prevent homelessness. However, where there is no risk of homelessness in the foreseeable future the housing authority should offer advice and assistance to the applicant as appropriate.

Assessment of circumstances and needs (section 189A (2))

11.7 Applicants who are eligible and homeless or threatened with homelessness must have an assessment of their case, which includes assessing:

(a)   the circumstances that have caused them to be homeless or threatened with homelessness;

(b)   their housing needs, and what accommodation would be suitable for them, their household and anybody who might reasonably be expected to live with them; and,

(c)   the support that would be necessary for them, and anybody who will be living with them, to have and sustain suitable accommodation.

11.8 When assessing the **circumstances** leading to a threat of homelessness housing authorities will need applicants to provide all relevant information to inform their assessment. This will usually include enquiring into their accommodation history at least as far back as their last settled address, and the events that led to them being threatened with or becoming homeless.

11.9 Applicants should be encouraged to share information without fear that this will reduce their chances of receiving support, and questions should be asked in a sensitive way and with an awareness that the applicant may be reluctant to disclose personal details if they lack confidence that their circumstances will be understood and considered sympathetically. Housing authorities should ensure staff have sufficient skills and training to conduct assessments of applicants who may find it difficult to disclose their circumstances, including people at risk of domestic abuse, violence or hate crime.

11.10 When assessing the **housing needs** of an applicant housing authorities will need to consider the individual members of the household, and all relevant needs. This should include an assessment of the size and type of accommodation required, any requirements to meet the needs of a person who is disabled or has specific medical needs, and the location of housing that is required. The applicant's wishes and preferences should also be considered and recorded within the assessment; whether or not the housing authority believes there is a reasonable prospect of accommodation being available that will meet those wishes and preferences.

11.11 An assessment of the applicant's and household member's **support needs** should be holistic and comprehensive, and not limited to those needs which are most apparent or have been notified to the housing authority by a referral agency. Housing authorities will wish to adopt assessment tools that enable staff to tease out particular aspects of need, without appearing to take a 'checklist' approach using a list of possible needs. Some applicants may be reluctant to disclose their needs and will need sensitive encouragement to do so, with an assurance that the purpose of the assessment is to identify how the housing authority can best assist them to prevent or relieve homelessness.

11.12 Some applicants will identify care and support needs that cannot be met by the housing authority; or which require health or social care services to be provided alongside help to secure accommodation. Housing authorities should be mindful of duties under the Care Act 2014 including those relating to assessment and adult safeguarding; and the use of Care Act powers to meet urgent care and support needs where an assessment has not been completed.

Arrangements for carrying out assessments

11.13 Housing authorities should provide assessment services that are flexible to the needs of applicants. The Secretary of State considers an individual and interactive process will be required to fully and effectively assess circumstances and needs. Whilst advice and information services could be provided via an online process, housing authorities could not rely solely on such means to complete assessments into individual circumstances and needs for people who are homeless or threatened with homelessness within 56 days.

11.14   In most circumstances assessments will require at least one face to face interview. However, where that is not possible or does not meet the applicant's needs, assessments could be completed on the telephone or internet or with the assistance of a partner agency. For example, an applicant who is in prison, hospital or in other circumstances where they cannot attend an interview, could have an assessment completed through a video link or with the help of a partner agency able to complete an assessment form, provide information and assist with communication where needed.

11.15   Some applicants may find it more convenient to complete an assessment through telephone or internet interviews, but there should be an opportunity for the assessment to be completed through a face to face meeting where the applicant's needs indicate this is necessary, or if the applicant requests it.

11.16   Assessments should be specific to the applicant and the results of the assessment must be notified in writing to them.

Responding to referrals for assistance

11.17   Housing authorities will receive referrals of customers from other service providers, both statutory and non-statutory, including public authorities with a statutory duty to refer people who are homeless or threatened with homelessness. Some referring agencies will be better equipped than others to establish the threat of homelessness, or to conduct assessments of needs, and housing authorities will need to supplement the information provided within a referral with their own assessment and enquiries. For further guidance on duty to refer see Chapter 4.

Reasonable steps

11.18   Housing authorities should work alongside applicants to identify practical and reasonable steps for the housing authority and the applicant to take to help the applicant retain or secure suitable accommodation. These steps should be tailored to the household, and follow from the findings of the assessment, and must be provided to the applicant in writing as their personalised housing plan.

11.19   Housing authorities will wish to develop resources and tools that can be used regularly to address common issues, whilst also ensuring genuine personalisation in response to the wide range of circumstances and needs experienced by applicants. The Secretary of State expects this to result in significant variation in the staff time and other resources invested with each applicant in accordance with the nature and complexity of the issues they face.

11.20   Personalised housing plans should be realistic, taking account of local housing markets and the availability of relevant support services, as well as the applicant's individual needs and wishes. For example, a plan which limited the search for accommodation to a small geographic area where the applicant would like to live would be unlikely to be reasonable if there was little prospect of finding housing there that they could afford. The plan might instead enable the applicant to review accommodation prices in their preferred areas as well as extending their home search to more affordable areas and property types. In their interactions with applicants, housing authorities are encouraged to provide sufficient information and advice to encourage informed and realistic choices to be identified and agreed for inclusion in the plan.

11.21   Through their assessments, housing authorities might identify support needs that cannot be easily met from existing service provision. Improvements in assessments and data capture will enable authorities to build up better information to assess needs and inform commissioning arrangements for the future. The Secretary of State recognises that 'reasonable steps' will vary between housing authority areas, and will be affected by housing markets and availability of services to support vulnerable people. However, every authority should engage in efforts to identify and measure needs and prioritise funding for the provision of services, as well as the development of partnerships, appropriately.

11.22 It would not be reasonable to agree steps for an applicant that were reliant on them engaging with a service provision that is not currently available in the district or which is unlikely to be offered to them. If the applicant is already receiving services from an agency that might contribute to preventing or relieving homelessness, the housing authority may wish to seek the applicant's consent to involving them in developing and agreeing reasonable steps, and in delivering the personalised housing plan.

11.23 The Secretary of State expects the type of reasonable steps a housing authority might take to prevent or relieve homeless to include but not be limited to the following, irrespective of whether the applicant may have a priority need or be homeless intentionally:

(a)   attempting mediation/conciliation where an applicant is threatened with parent/family exclusion;
(b)   assessing whether applicants with rent arrears might be entitled to Discretionary Housing Payment;
(c)   providing support to applicants, whether financial or otherwise, to access private rented accommodation;
(d)   assisting people at risk of violence and abuse wishing to stay safely in their home through provision of 'sanctuary' or other measures;
(e)   helping to secure or securing an immediate safe place to stay for people who are sleeping rough or at high risk of sleeping rough.

Process and timing

11.24 Housing authorities are required to notify applicants of the assessments they have made, and also provide written personalised housing plans. In practice, these two notifications might be combined to provide a clearer response to applicants.

11.25 The duty to issue written notifications should not prevent a housing authority from taking immediate action to assist an applicant where necessary. An officer may, for example, contact a young applicant's parents or carers, perhaps through a same day home visit, if they have been asked to leave, or make immediate contact with a landlord where there is an imminent threat of eviction. In these cases prevention work would begin in parallel with the assessment and planning process, having regard to initial assessment findings and with the agreement of the applicant.

11.26 Where initial prevention or relief work is undertaken in parallel with the assessment and planning process it follows that in some cases successful prevention or relief will have been largely achieved before the assessment and personalised housing plan have been completed and the applicant has been informed in writing. Where this is the case, the record of actions taken might be included in the section 189A assessment, whilst any further steps needed to sustain the accommodation arrangements are included in the personalised housing plan.

11.27 Wherever possible and appropriate, housing authorities should prioritise efforts to prevent homelessness so that households can remain in their accommodation or, helped to secure a new home rather than becoming homeless. This might include, for example, achieving agreement for a young family to remain in the parental home pending an offer of Part 6 accommodation; or agreeing steps through which the housing authority and applicant might resolve outstanding benefit difficulties to clear or reduce rent arrears.

11.28 Housing authorities must take reasonable steps to prevent homelessness whether or not the applicant has a local connection with their area. If the applicant is actually homeless the authority may refer them to another authority where they have a local connection, and must provide copies of the assessment, and any revisions to it that have been notified to the applicant, as part of the referral arrangement. If the housing authority has agreed a personalised housing plan with the applicant they should also forward the plan to the notified authority if it has relevance, and with the applicant's consent. For further guidance on local connection see Chapter 10.

Reaching agreement and reviewing the plan (section 189A(4) to (11))

11.29 Housing authorities should make every effort to secure the agreement of applicants to their personalised housing plans. Identifying and attempting to address personal wishes and preferences will help achieve that agreement, and improve the likelihood that the plan will be successful in preventing or relieving homelessness.

11.30 If the housing authority is unable to reach an agreement with the applicant about the reasonable steps to be included in their personalised housing plan, they must record why they could not agree; and provide the written plan to the applicant indicating what steps they consider it reasonable for the applicant and the housing authority to take.

11.31 The personalised housing plan may include steps that the housing authority considers advisable for the applicant to take ('recommended steps'), but which the applicant is not required to take if they choose not to do so (section 189A(7)), as well as steps which they are required to take ('mandatory steps'). The relevant duty (prevention or relief) cannot be ended for failure to co-operate with recommended steps. The use of recommended steps might enable the authority to provide or refer the applicant to a broader range of advice and support, for example to address wider needs or to help increase their housing options in the future through employment support. Mandatory steps should be limited to those which the housing authority considers are required in order to prevent or relieve homelessness. The plan must set out clearly which steps are mandatory and which are recommended.

11.32 Assessments and personalised housing plans must be kept under review throughout the prevention and relief stages, and any amendments notified to the applicant. Housing authorities will wish to establish timescales for reviewing plans, and these are likely to vary according to individual needs and circumstances. Some applicants will need more intensive housing authority involvement to achieve a successful outcome than others, and the timescales for regular contact and reviews should reflect this. Personalised housing plans agreed during the prevention stage will need to be reviewed if an applicant subsequently becomes homelessness, enabling housing authorities and applicants to focus on steps required to help secure accommodation.

11.33 If the housing authority become aware that the information the applicant has provided for their assessment is inaccurate or if there is new information or a relevant change in the applicant's circumstances and needs there will be a need to initiate a review of the assessment and plan. The housing authority should also arrange a review if they believe the applicant is not cooperating with the personalised housing plan for whatever reason.

11.34 If the housing authority considers that their assessment of the applicant's circumstances and needs have changed, or that the agreement reached as to reasonable steps is no longer appropriate they must notify the applicant in writing. The housing authority must notify the applicant if it considers any of the agreed steps are no longer appropriate, and there will be no consequence of failure to take any of the 'removed' steps after written notification is given.

11.35 For practical purposes a review of the plan might be conducted by telephone, email or video-link, especially if the applicant is unable to or declining to attend office based appointments.

11.36 Applicants have a right under section 202 to request a review of the steps the housing authority is to take under sections 189B(2) and 195(2) which includes having regard to their personalised housing plan within the prevention and relief stages. Housing authorities should encourage applicants to raise any concerns they have about their plan and work to resolve disagreements to minimise the occasions on which the applicant will feel the need to request a review.

CHAPTER 12: DUTY IN CASES OF THREATENED HOMELESSNESS (THE PREVENTION DUTY)

12.1   Section 195 of the 1996 Act – the 'prevention duty' - places a duty on housing authorities to work with people who are threatened with homelessness within 56 days to help prevent them from becoming homelessness. This chapter provides guidance on how to fulfil the prevention duty and the ways in which it can be ended.

12.2   Housing authorities may become aware of residents who are threatened with becoming homeless but not within 56 days, and possibly not within any specified time period; and are encouraged to offer assistance where possible rather than delay providing support which may be effective in preventing homelessness.

12.3   The section 195 duty applies when the housing authority is satisfied that the applicant is both threatened with homelessness and eligible for assistance. For further guidance on eligibility see Chapter 7 and for further guidance on threatened with homelessness see Chapter 6. The housing authority is obliged to take reasonable steps to help the applicant either remains in their existing accommodation or secure alternative accommodation. For further guidance on reasonable steps see Chapter 11.

12.4   The first option to be explored with the applicant should be enabling them to remain in their current home, where suitable. Where this is not possible, the focus should be on helping to secure alternative accommodation that the applicant can move into in a planned way. This will often involve taking steps to extend an applicant's stay in their existing accommodation until they can move.

12.5   The housing authority cannot refer an applicant to another district during the prevention duty, even if the conditions for referral that would apply during the relief and main housing duties are met. For further guidance on local connection see Chapter 10. This means the housing authority is obliged to take reasonable steps to help the applicant retain their existing accommodation or secure alternative accommodation wherever that may be. If the applicant is living at distance from the housing authority to which they have applied, one reasonable step to be agreed with the applicant might be for the receiving authority to make contact with the housing authority where the applicant is living to request their assistance in efforts to prevent homelessness.

12.6   Housing authorities may find it helpful to establish protocols for collaboration with relevant neighbouring authorities to improve outcomes and efficiency in localities where applicants frequently seek help in a different district to the one where they live.

12.7   The reasonable steps taken by both the authority and the applicant to help prevent homelessness should be those set out in the personalised housing plan drawn up and reviewed as set out in section 189A of the 1996 Act. For further guidance on personalised housing plans see Chapter 11. The housing authority will need to have arrangements in place for accessible and timely communication with applicants to maximise the effectiveness of their joint efforts to prevent homelessness.

12.8   Housing authorities must take into account the needs and circumstances of the applicant as they work to fulfil the prevention duty, recognising that there are a range of factors that will affect an applicants' ability to take action to help prevent their homelessness. For some more vulnerable applicants, the factors that have contributed to their being threatened with homelessness may also affect their ability to work with the housing authority to resolve that threat. The housing authority will want to seek to understand these factors and tailor the support it provides, both directly and through engaging relevant specialist services, accordingly.

12.9   Where homelessness is prevented, but an applicant's needs may put them at risk of a further threat of homelessness, the housing authority will want to work with relevant support and specialist services to help promote sustainability.

12.10   Where an applicant has to leave their accommodation without any reasonable prospect of an imminent return, or if it otherwise ceases to be reasonable for them to occupy before a suitable alternative is available, further duties should be considered under section 189B (the relief duty).

CHAPTER 13: RELIEF DUTY

13.1   Section 189B of the 1996 Act – the 'relief duty' - requires housing authorities to help people who are homeless to secure accommodation. This chapter of the code provides guidance on how to fulfil the relief duty.

13.2 The duty applies when the housing authority is satisfied that the applicant is both homeless and eligible for assistance. The housing authority is obliged to take reasonable steps to help the applicant secure suitable accommodation with a reasonable prospect that it will be available for their occupation for at least 6 months.

13.3 Where the housing authority have reason to believe that an applicant may be homeless, eligible and have a priority need they must provide interim accommodation under section 188(1) whilst fulfilling the relief duty. For further guidance on interim duties to accommodate see Chapter 15.

13.4 If the housing authority would be subject to the relief duty but consider that the conditions are met for referral to another housing authority in England (not Scotland or Wales) they have the discretion to notify that housing authority of their opinion (section198(A1)). For further guidance on local connection see Chapter 10.

13.5 The reasonable steps to be taken by both the housing authority and the applicant to help secure accommodation must include those set out in the personalised housing plan drawn up and reviewed as set out in section 189A. For further guidance on assessments and personalised housing plans see Chapter 11. The housing authority will need to have arrangements in place for accessible and timely communication with applicants to maximise the effectiveness of their joint efforts.

13.6 Housing authorities must take into account their assessment of the applicant's case under section 189A (which includes consideration of an applicant's housing needs, circumstances leading to homelessness, and support required) as they work to fulfil the relief duty, recognising that there are a range of factors that will affect an applicant's ability to take action to secure accommodation. For some applicants, the circumstances, needs or issues that have contributed to their being homeless may also affect their ability to work with the housing authority. The housing authority's duty to have regard to the applicant's section 189A assessment will assist the authority with understanding the applicant's particular situation and tailoring the support it provides under the relief duty, both directly and through engaging relevant specialist services, accordingly.

13.7 Housing authorities will want to ensure that people who are sleeping rough and eligible for assistance are supported to apply to them for housing assistance, and should seek to prevent applicants from starting to sleep rough during the course of the relief duty. For further guidance on joint working to address rough sleeping see the homelessness strategy see Chapter 2 and for further guidance on personalised plans see Chapter 11. Specific considerations in relation to applicants who are (or are at imminent risk of) sleeping rough and are or may be owed the relief duty include:

(a) working with other agencies and/or commissioned services to ensure rough sleepers are aware of, and have support to seek, housing assistance from the authority and in the provision of appropriate accommodation and/or support;

(b) if the authority does not have reason to believe that the applicant may have a priority need and has not therefore provided interim accommodation under section 188(1), the use of discretionary powers to secure emergency accommodation to prevent nights on the streets, taking into account the risk of harm applicants may face. For further guidance on discretionary powers to secure emergency accommodation see Chapter 15;

(c) if using discretion to enquire into whether an applicant has a local connection, remembering that normal residence does not require a settled address and may include periods sleeping rough. For further guidance on local connection see Chapter 10.

13.8 Where homelessness is relieved, but an applicant's needs, as set out in the personalised housing plan, may put them at risk of a further threat of homelessness, the housing authority should work with relevant support and specialist services to help promote sustainability.

13.9 Housing authorities may conduct and complete their inquiries into the duties that will be owed to an applicant under section 193(2), the main housing duty during the period in which they are attempting to relieve homelessness under the section 189B duty. However, this activity must not detract from the housing authority's work to relieve the applicant's homelessness. **Where the housing authority considers an applicant is unlikely to be owed a section 193(2) main housing duty they must not limit or reduce the assistance they provide during the relief duty for this reason.**

13.10 Housing authorities are advised against issuing a section 184 notification accepting the section 193 (main housing duty) during the relief stage. The section 193 duty cannot commence until the relief duty has come to an end and issuing notification during the relief stage might detract from activities to relieve their homelessness.

13.11 Housing authorities may issue a section 184 decision to the applicant, that when the relief duty ends they will owe them a duty under section 190 because they have a priority need but are intentionally homeless. Although the section 190 duty cannot commence until the relief duty has come to an end, the authority may wish to alert an applicant that the main housing duty will not be owed. It may be beneficial to review the personalised housing plan at this point to help maximise joint efforts to relieve homelessness.

13.12 If the authority has provided interim accommodation under section 188 and subsequently finds that the applicant does not have a priority need during the relief duty stage, a section 184 notification that neither the main housing duty nor the section 190 duty will be owed once the relief duty ends will bring the section 188 duty to an end (section 188(1ZA)(b)). The relief duty will continue to be owed until it ends in one of the circumstances in subsections (7) or (9) of section 189B. For further guidance on interim duties to accommodate see Chapter 15, and for guidance on ending the prevention and relief duty see Chapter 14.

CHAPTER 14: ENDING THE PREVENTION AND RELIEF DUTIES

14.1 This chapter provides guidance on how the (section 195) prevention and (section 189B) relief duties come to an end.

14.2 There are seven circumstances under which both the prevention and relief duties can be brought to an end. In addition to these common circumstances the prevention duty will end where the applicant has become homeless, and the relief duty will end when 56 days has passed and the housing authority is satisfied that the applicant has a priority need and is homeless unintentionally, or on refusal of a final accommodation offer or Part 6 offer.

14.3 The housing authority must give the applicant notice in order to end the duties except under section 189B (4) where 56 days have passed since the start of the relief duty and the housing authority is satisfied the applicant has a priority need and is homeless unintentionally. For further guidance on notifications see Chapter 18 and for further guidance on reviews see Chapter 19. Guidance on bringing the duties to an end under each circumstance is set out below.

14.4 Chapter 15 provides guidance on the ending of interim accommodation duties following the end of relief duties.

Circumstances in which both prevention and relief duties may end

A - the housing authority is satisfied that the applicant has suitable accommodation available for occupation and a reasonable prospect of suitable accommodation being available for at least six months from the date of the notice. Note that the Secretary of State has a power to increase this minimum period up to a maximum of 12 months (sections 195 (8) (a) and 189B (7) (a)).

14.5 Housing authorities must allow applicants a reasonable period for considering offers of accommodation that will bring the prevention and relief duties to an end. There is no set reasonable period – housing authorities must take into account the applicant's circumstances in each case.

14.6 Applicants should be given the opportunity to view accommodation before being required to decide whether to accept or refuse an offer, and before being required to sign any written agreement relating to the accommodation (for example, a tenancy agreement). If the accommodation is in another area and it is not practical to travel to view, sufficient information about the property and the locality should be made available to them. This may, for example, include photographs and the opportunity to ask questions of the landlord or agent.

14.7 Where new tenancies are secured housing authorities are encouraged to adopt policies favouring longer tenancies than the legal minimum where market conditions in their area allow. It is recommended that, wherever possible, minimum tenancy lengths of 12 months are secured to provide more stability to individuals and particularly to families with children.

14.8 In some circumstances, determining reasonable prospect will be less clear cut. For example, a landlord may agree to allow the applicant to stay in their accommodation having previously issued a section 21 notice. Ideally in this case they would issue a new tenancy, but they may instead choose to leave the existing tenancy running, with the section 21 notice in place until it expires.

14.9 Where this is the case it is the responsibility of the housing authority to satisfy itself that there is a reasonable prospect of the accommodation being available for at least six months. This may, for example, involve securing written confirmation from the landlord that the applicant can remain in the accommodation on condition that they comply with documented conditions, and the housing authority having a reasonable expectation that the applicant is in a position to comply.

14.10 Where an applicant has remained at or returned home or gone to stay with friends or extended family, for example, through the use of mediation or negotiation, it is the responsibility of the housing authority to satisfy itself that accommodation will be available for at least six months. There may, for example, be an open ended agreement (perhaps with reasonable conditions), or an agreement that the applicant can stay until they have secured alternative accommodation (whether that happens before or after six months).

14.11 There may be other circumstances where there is a reasonable prospect of suitable accommodation being available for at least six months, but this not necessarily being the same accommodation throughout. For example, an applicant with support needs may be placed in short term supported accommodation which forms part of a planned accommodation and support pathway overseen by the housing authority. This may meet the conditions for ending the duty under this subsection if there is a clear, documented expectation that the applicant will be supported to make a planned move directly to more settled supported or independent accommodation through the pathway service.

14.12 The housing authority should take into account the support needs and vulnerabilities of an applicant, which will have been identified during assessment, in determining whether they can reasonably expect the applicant to sustain the accommodation for at least 6 months.

B - the housing authority has complied with the prevention or relief duty and 56 days have passed (regardless of whether the applicant is still threatened with homelessness in the case of the prevention duty or whether they have secured accommodation in the case of the relief duty) (sections 195 (8)(b) and 189B (7)(b)).

14.13 Under the **prevention duty** (section 195(6)), the 56 day period does not apply where the applicant has been given a valid section 21 notice that will expire within 56 days or has expired and is in respect of the only accommodation that is available for the applicant's accommodation. This is to ensure continuity of prevention services where an applicant remains in the property after the expiry of their section 21 notice or longer than 56 days from the duty starting and also remains threatened with homelessness.

14.14 Where a housing authority is satisfied that, despite the section 21 notice, the landlord has agreed not to pursue possession and there is a reasonable prospect of the accommodation being available for at least 6 months the prevention duty may be ended (section 195(8)(a)) (see paragraphs 14.7 and 14.8 above).

14.15 The housing authority can continue to deliver the **prevention or relief duty** with any applicant for longer than 56 days and issue a notice to end it under this subsection at any point after this date; as long as no other duties take precedence (for example, the relief duty takes precedence where an applicant previously owed the prevention duty becomes homeless).

14.16 Where the housing authority is satisfied that the applicant has a priority need and has become homeless unintentionally, the **relief duty** comes to an end after 56 days (section 189B (4)). Housing authorities should not delay completing their inquiries as to what further duties will be owed after the relief duty. Where the housing authority has the information it requires to make a decision as to whether the applicant is in priority need and became homeless unintentionally, it should be possible to notify the applicant on or around day 57. In cases where significant further investigations are required it is recommended that housing authorities aim to complete their inquiries and notify the applicant of their decision within a maximum of 15 working days after 56 days have passed.

14.17 Housing authorities should not have a blanket policy of ending the prevention and relief duties after 56 days where they have the discretion to continue it; instead they should in each case take the applicant's circumstances into account.

14.18 Where the applicant remains at risk of homelessness and the housing authority considers there is still the chance that homelessness can be prevented, it will be in the interests of both the applicant and the housing authority for work to continue to help the applicant avoid homelessness, whereupon they may make a new application to the housing authority for help under the relief duty.

14.19 During the relief stage, where an applicant does not have a priority need or they have a priority need and have become homeless intentionally, the authority may want to consider continuing the relief duty for longer. Considerations may include the needs of the applicant; the risk of the applicant sleeping rough; the prospects of securing accommodation within a reasonable period; the resources available to the housing authority, and any wider implications of bringing the duty to an end (for example, in the case of an applicant who has dependent children and who became homeless intentionally where Children Act duties may apply if accommodation could not be secured).

C - an applicant who was owed the prevention duty has become homeless (section 195(8)(c)).

14.20 Where an applicant in these circumstances is owed the relief duty the housing authority will want to provide a seamless transition between the prevention and relief duties, including notifying the applicant of any further duties owed to them at the same time as issuing the notice advising that the prevention duty has ended. These notifications may be combined.

14.21 Where interim accommodation is to be provided, this should be arranged as a priority. Authorities should take the opportunity to plan interim accommodation in advance whenever it is possible to do so, in order to minimise distress and disruption for the applicant and provide maximum opportunity for planning for, for example, children's journeys to school.

14.22 The housing authority and the applicant will then need to review the assessment and personalised plan undertaken under section 189A, devising new reasonable steps to help secure that accommodation becomes available for the applicant under the relief duty. For further guidance on assessments and personalised housing plans see Chapter 11.

D - the applicant has refused an offer of suitable accommodation and, on the date of refusal, there was a reasonable prospect that suitable accommodation would be available for the minimum prescribed period (sections 195(8)(d) and 189B(7)(c)).

14.23   There is an important distinction between the consequences of refusal of an offer of suitable accommodation at the prevention and relief stages.

14.24   During the **prevention stage** the housing authority can bring the prevention duty to an end but refusal does not affect any further duties that may be owed to the applicant if they become homeless.

14.25   During the **relief stage** the housing authority can bring the relief duty to an end through a suitable offer of accommodation (section 189B (7)(c)) and there will be no consequences affecting any main housing duty owed to the applicant if they refuse it.

14.26   However, the housing authority can also bring the relief duty to an end through a final **accommodation offer (section 189B (9) (a))** or a final **Part 6 offer**. Refusal of either of these two types of offer will preclude the applicant from subsequently being owed the main housing duty (section 193A (3)). A final accommodation offer must be of an assured shorthold tenancy of at least six months duration, and the applicant must have been informed of the consequences of refusal as well as the right to request a review of the suitability of the offer. For guidance on the suitability of offers see Chapter 17.

14.27   It will be up to the housing authority to decide whether or not to end the prevention or relief duty when a suitable offer, other than a final offer or Part 6 offer, is refused. In reaching their decision a housing authority should consider the applicant's circumstances, the reason for their refusal, the reasonable steps they are taking to secure accommodation that better suits their needs and preferences and, in the case of the prevention duty, the likelihood of the applicant subsequently becoming homeless and applying for help under the relief duty.

14.28   For many applicants, working with the housing authority to prevent or relieve their homelessness will provide an opportunity to explore what realistic options are available to them and consider what compromises they may wish to make in order to achieve the best option for them. The opportunity to consider more than one property can play an important part in this process.

E - the applicant has become homeless intentionally from any accommodation that has been made available to them as a result of reasonable steps taken by the housing authority during the prevention or relief duty, whichever is relevant (sections 195(8)(e) and 189B(7)(d)).

14.29   Where the prevention duty ends under this circumstance, the applicant's entitlement to the relief duty will not be affected as the relief duty applies irrespective of whether or not an applicant is considered to be intentionally homeless.

14.30   Where the applicant has a priority need and the relief duty has ended under this circumstance, the main housing duty will not apply. An applicant should only be considered intentionally homeless under this provision if they have ceased to occupy accommodation which it would have been reasonable for them to continue to occupy, and which has been provided to them within the 'reasonable steps' provisions of the Act (sections 195(2) and 189B(2)). In most cases where such accommodation has been secured the housing authority will already have notified the applicant that the prevention or relief duty has come to an end, and so there will be very limited circumstances in which the duty is brought to an end through the provision of section 195(8)(e) and 189B(7)(d). However, the provisions could apply for example, if an applicant had suitable accommodation secured as part of the housing authorities reasonable steps, and had surrendered without good reason or been excluded from that accommodation due to their actions, before the housing authority had served notice that the duty had been brought to an end under Section 195 8a or Section 189B a (suitable accommodation has been secured).

14.31   Under section 190, duties to persons becoming homeless intentionally, the housing authority will need to secure that accommodation is available for the applicant's occupation for long enough to give them a reasonable opportunity of securing accommodation and provide advice and assistance in any attempts the applicant makes to secure accommodation. This advice must have regard to the assessment the housing authority made under section 189A, assessment and personalised plans. For further guidance on intentional homelessness see Chapter 9.

F - the applicant is no longer eligible for assistance (sections 195(8)(f) and 189B(7)(e)).

14.32 In circumstances where an applicant is found not to be eligible for assistance, the housing authority must provide, or secure the provision, of information and advice as set out in section 179. For further guidance on eligibility see Chapter 7. If (section 188) interim accommodation has been provided, notice periods should take account of the needs of the applicant and the time required for them to access assistance. For households including children or particularly vulnerable adults who are owed duties under the Children Act 1989 or Care Act 2014, local authorities should consider having arrangements in place to manage a transition in responsibilities, so that there is no break in the provision of accommodation for applicants who cease to be eligible for 1996 Act support.

G - the applicant has withdrawn their application for homelessness assistance (sections 195(8)(g) and 189B(7)(f)).

14.33 Some applicants will cease contact with the authority rather than explicitly withdraw their application. It is recommended that local authorities have procedures in place to attempt to maintain or regain contact with applicants who have ceased contact prior to deciding to end the prevention or relief duty under this subsection. These efforts should take into account the circumstances and needs of the applicant, and use varied communication channels to help prevent, for example, losing contact with someone because they have lost their mobile phone. For further guidance on losing contact with applicants see Chapter 18.

14.34 It is recommended that where the housing authority considers that the applicant has withdrawn their application because they have failed to maintain contact, the duty is ended under this subsection rather than because 56 days has passed. This will help to ensure accurate data relating to the reasons why duties end.

H - deliberate and unreasonable refusal to co-operate (sections 195(10) and 189B(9)(b)).

14.35 The prevention and relief duties can also be brought to and end as a result of the applicant's deliberate and unreasonable refusal to co-operate. For further guidance on non-cooperation see Chapter 14. Where the **prevention duty** is brought to an end due to deliberate and unreasonable refusal to co-operate, the applicant's entitlements under any other section of Part 7, including the relief and main housing duties, are not affected.

14.36 Where the **relief duty** is brought to an end as a result of the applicant's deliberate and unreasonable refusal to co-operate **the main housing duty will not apply.** However, under section 193C(4) the housing authority will, be required to secure that accommodation is available for an applicant who has priority need and is unintentionally homeless, until such time as they make a final accommodation offer or a final Part 6 offer of suitable accommodation, or the duty comes to an end for another of the reasons set out in section 193C(5).

Notification to end the prevention duty

14.37 Section 195(8) provides the circumstances in which the housing authority can give notice under section 195(5) to the applicant to bring the prevention duty to an end. For further guidance on the prevention duty see Chapter 12.

14.38 The notice must specify which of the circumstances in section 195(8) apply and inform the applicant that they have a right to request a review of the housing authority's decision to bring the duty to an end, and of the time frame within which such a request must be made.

14.39 Section 195(6) prevents a housing authority from bringing the prevention duty to an end after 56 days if the applicant has been given a valid section 21 notice which will expire in 56 days or has expired, and is in respect of their only available accommodation. This means that the housing authority will continue to owe a prevention duty beyond the initial 56 days, until the applicant is served with a section 195(5) notice on the basis that another of the circumstance set out in section 195(8) applies.

Notification to end the relief duty (section 189B(7))

14.40 Section 189B(7) provides the circumstances in which the housing authority can give notice under section 189B (5) to the applicant bringing the relief duty under section 189B(2) to an end. For further guidance on the relief duty see Chapter 13.

14.41 The notice must specify which of the circumstances in section 189B(7) apply and inform the applicant that they have right to request a review of the authority's decision to bring the relief duty under section 189B(2) to an end, and of the time frame within which such a request must be made.

14.42 Housing authorities may refer an applicant's case to another housing authority in England during the relief duty if the applicant does not have a local connection with the authority to which they have applied, and does have a local connection to another district where they would not be at risk of violence. For guidance on local connection referrals see Chapter 10.

Deliberate and unreasonable refusal to co-operate (sections 193B and 193C)

14.43 Both the prevention and relief duties can be brought to an end under section 193B and section 193C if an applicant deliberately and unreasonably refuses to take any of the steps that they agreed to take, or the housing authority set out for them to take where agreement could not be reached, in their personalised housing plan (subsections (4) and (6)(b) of section 189A).

14.44 Before bringing either duty to an end by issuing a section 193B(2) notice, the housing authority must first issue a warning letting the applicant know that if they deliberately and unreasonably refuse to take any of the steps in their personalised housing plan after receiving the warning the authority intends to issue a notice bringing the prevention or relief duty, whichever is relevant, to an end. The warning must explain the consequences of a notice being given and the housing authority must allow a reasonable period after the warning is given before issuing a notice (section 193B(4) and (5)). There is no set reasonable period, but housing authorities should ensure sufficient time is given to allow the applicant to rectify the non-co-operation and prevent a notice being issued to end the prevention or relief duty. This will vary according to the particular needs and circumstances of the applicant.

14.45 Notices issued under section 193B(2) must explain why the housing authority are giving notice and its effect, and inform the applicant of their right to request a review of the decision to issue the notice (section 202(1)) and that a request for a review must be made within 21 days of being notified of that decision, or such longer period as the housing authority may allow in writing (section 202(3)).

14.46 Regulations relating to the procedure to be followed by housing authorities in connection with notices under section 193B (section 193B(7)) are set out in *The Homelessness (Review Procedure etc.) Regulations 2018* – these relate to decisions to issue a notice.

14.47 The ending of the **prevention duty** under sections 193B and 193C will not affect the housing authority's assessment of what duties are owed if the applicant subsequently seeks help having become homeless.

14.48 For applicants who are eligible for assistance, unintentionally homeless and have a priority need, the ending of the relief duty under sections 193B and 193C will mean that section 193 (the main housing duty) will not apply. However, the housing authority must secure that accommodation is available for occupation by the applicant by making a final accommodation offer or final Part 6 offer (sections 193C(4) to (10). For further guidance on accommodation duties and powers see Chapter 15.

Meaning of deliberate and unreasonable refusal

14.49 Section 193B(6) provides that the housing authority must have regard to the particular circumstances and needs of the applicant, whether or not identified in the assessment under section 189A, in deciding whether refusal by the applicant is unreasonable.

14.50 Housing authorities should make reasonable efforts to obtain the co-operation of the applicant, including seeking to understand the reasons for their lack of co-operation, before invoking and during the use of section 193B. Where an applicant appears not to be co-operating the housing authority should review their assessment of the applicant's case and the appropriateness of the steps in the personalised housing plan (section 189A(9)) and explain the consequences of not co-operating before issuing a warning under section 193B(4). For further guidance on personalised housing plans see Chapter 11.

14.51 Where the applicant is receiving support from other services, for example the leaving care team, an offender management service, or a family support service, the housing authority should alert relevant service(s) to the problem as soon as possible and seek to involve them in supporting the applicant to resolve the situation. Having local information sharing arrangements in place will facilitate this.

14.52 The housing authority should take into account any particular difficulties that the applicant may have in managing communications when considering if failure to cooperate is deliberate and unreasonable, particularly if they are street homeless or moving between temporary places to stay such as the homes of different family and friends.

14.53 The housing authority should be satisfied of the following before ending the prevention or relief duty under sections 193B and 193C:

(a)   the steps recorded in the applicant's personalised housing plan are reasonable in the context of the applicant's particular circumstances and needs;

(b)   the applicant understands what is required of them in order to fulfil the reasonable steps, and is therefore in a position to make a deliberate refusal;

(c)   the applicant is not refusing to co-operate as a result of a mental illness or other health need, for which they are not being provided with support, or because of a difficulty in communicating;

(d)   the applicant's refusal to co-operate with any step was deliberate and unreasonable in the context of their particular circumstances and needs. For example, if they prioritised attending a Jobcentre or medical appointment, or fulfilling a caring responsibility, above viewing a property, this is unlikely to constitute a deliberate and unreasonable refusal to cooperate. However, if the applicant persistently failed to attend property viewings or appointments without good reason; or they actively refused to engage with activity required to help them secure accommodation, then this might be considered deliberate and unreasonable refusal to cooperate.

Please see chapters 21–24 for client group specific considerations sections.

Notices in cases of an applicant's deliberate and unreasonable refusal to co-operate (section 193B(2))

14.54 Under section 193B(2), the housing authority may give a notice to an applicant if they consider that the applicant has deliberately and unreasonably refused to take one or more of the steps in their personalised housing plan.

14.55 Before serving this notice, the housing authority must have given a relevant warning to the applicant and a reasonable period of time has elapsed since the warning. The relevant warning must be a written notice to warn the applicant that if they deliberately and unreasonably refuse to take any step in their personalised housing plan the housing authority will issue a notice under section 193B(2), and explain the consequences of a section 193B(2) notice being served.

14.56 A housing authority must develop a procedure to be followed when issuing notices bringing their prevention or relief duties to an end under section 193B(2)). The procedure must:

(a)   be in writing;
(b)   be kept under review; and,
(c)   make provision for the decision to give a notice under section 193B(2) to be made by an officer of that housing authority and authorised by an appropriate person.

14.57 The original decision to issue the notice must be made by an officer of the housing authority and then receive authorisation by an appropriate person. An 'appropriate person' is someone of at least an equivalent seniority to the officer who made the original decision to issue a notice, and they must:

(a)   work for the housing authority or local authority; and,
(b)   not have been involved in the original decision to issue the notice.

14.58 The housing authority's procedures may provide that second sign off of the decision to issue a notice can be given by an appropriate person from another service within the local authority (or upper tier local authority). For example, in the case of a care leaver, second sign off by an officer of at least an equivalent seniority within Children's Services may be appropriate.

14.59 The appropriate person conducting the second sign off should give particular consideration as to whether the original decision to issue the notice had due regard to the circumstances and needs of the applicant, whether or not these were properly identified in the authority's assessment of the applicant's case under section 189A.

CHAPTER 15: ACCOMMODATION DUTIES AND POWERS

15.1 This chapter provides guidance on the housing authority's duties to secure accommodation for applicants, how they arise and are brought to an end; and the powers within the 1996 Act to secure accommodation for homeless households.

15.2 The chapter includes:

(a)   duties to provide interim accommodation;
(b)   powers to provide accommodation pending review or appeal;
(c)   duties to prevent and relieve homelessness, including a power to provide accommodation;
(d)   the section 193C(4) duty to secure accommodation for applicants who are homeless, eligible for assistance, have priority need and are not intentionally homeless but have deliberately and unreasonably refused to cooperate;
(e)   the section 193(2) duty to secure accommodation for applicants who are homeless, eligible for assistance, have priority need and are not intentionally homeless (the main housing duty).

Duties to provide interim accommodation

15.3 The 1996 Act provides four circumstances in which a housing authority must secure accommodation on an interim basis until a decision or other event occurs. These are set out below.

Section 188 interim duty to accommodate

15.4 Section 188(1) requires housing authorities to secure that accommodation is available for an applicant (and their household) if they have reason to believe that the applicant may:

(a)   be homeless;
(b)   be eligible for assistance; and,
(c)   have a priority need.

15.5   The threshold for triggering the section 188(1) duty is low as the housing authority only has to have a **reason to believe** (rather than being satisfied) that the applicant **may** be homeless, eligible for assistance and have a priority need.

15.6   The section 188(1) interim accommodation duty applies even where the housing authority considers the applicant may not have a local connection with their district and may have one with the district of another housing authority giving rise to the possibility of referral (section188(2)). For further guidance on local connection see Chapter 10.

Ending the section 188 interim duty

15.7   The section 188(1) interim duty comes to an end when applicants are notified of certain decisions in relation to their application.

15.8   Following inquiries, where the housing authority concludes that **an applicant does not have a priority need**, the section 188(1) duty ends when **either:**

(a)   the housing authority notifies the applicant of the decision that they do not owe a section 189B(2) relief duty; **or,**
(b)   the housing authority notifies them of a decision that, once the section 189B(2) relief duty comes to an end, they do not owe a duty under section 190 (duties to persons becoming homeless intentionally) or section 193(2) (the main housing duty owed to applicants with priority need who are not homeless intentionally).

15.9   So, an applicant who the housing authority has found to be not in priority need within the 56 day 'relief stage' will no longer be owed a section 188(1) interim duty to accommodate, but will continue to be owed a section 189B(2) relief duty until that duty ends or is found not to be owed.

15.10   For any other case (including for **applicants who have a priority need**, and for applicants who the housing authority have reason to believe will be owed a duty because they have **reapplied within two years of accepting a private rented sector offer** (for further guidance on reapplication after a private rented sector offer see Chapter 18), the section 188(1) interim duty will end at **whichever is the later of:**

(a)   the housing authority notifies them of what duty (if any) they are owed under Part 7 of the 1996 Act once the section 189B(2) relief duty comes to an end;
(b)   the housing authority notifies them that they are not owed the section 189B(2) relief duty, or that this duty has come to an end;
(c)   the housing authority notifies them of a decision following their request for a review as to the suitability of a final accommodation offer or Part 6 offer made within the section 189B relief stage.

15.11   In summary, a housing authority may bring the section 188(1) interim accommodation duty to an end within the 56 day period (the relief stage) by issuing a section 184 decision that the applicant does not have priority need; or by issuing a notification that the relief duty is not owed or has been brought to an end. If neither of these notifications is issued within the 56 day period, the section 188(1) interim accommodation duty will be brought to an end by notification of what further duties are owed, if any, under section 193 or section 190. However, in the event that the relief duty is brought to an end following refusal of a final accommodation or Part 6 offer, and the applicant requests a review as to the suitability of the accommodation offered, the section 188(1) duty will continue until a decision on the review has been notified to the applicant.

15.12   In circumstances where an applicant is found not to be eligible for assistance, the housing authority must provide, or secure the provision of, information and advice as set out in section 179. If (section 188) interim accommodation has been provided, notice periods should take account of the needs of the applicant and the time required for them to access assistance. For households including children or particularly vulnerable adults who are owed duties under the Children Act 1989 or Care Act 2014, local authorities should consider having arrangements in place to manage a transition in responsibilities, so that there is no break in the provision of accommodation for applicants who cease to be eligible for support under the1996 Act.

Section 190(2): duty to provide accommodation to applicants who are intentionally homeless

15.13   On reaching a decision that an applicant has priority need and is intentionally homeless, the housing authority must secure accommodation for a period of time that will provide a reasonable opportunity for them to find their own accommodation.

15.14   In determining the period of time for which accommodation will be secured under section 190(2) housing authorities must consider each case on its merits. A few weeks may provide the applicant with a reasonable opportunity to secure accommodation for themselves. However, some applicants might require longer and others, particularly where the housing authority provides pro-active and effective assistance, might require less time.

15.15   Housing authorities will need to take into account:

(a)   the particular needs and circumstances of the applicant and the resources available to them to secure accommodation. This might include any health or support needs that make it more difficult for the applicant to find and secure accommodation, as well as the support available from their family or social network;

(b)   the housing circumstances in the local area, and the length of time it might reasonably take to secure accommodation. In assessing this the housing authority might reflect on the efforts previously made by both the housing authority and the applicant to relieve their homelessness, and why these had not proved successful;

(c)   arrangements that have already been made by the applicant which are likely to be successful within a reasonable timescale. For example, if the applicant has secured accommodation that is not yet available to occupy or can demonstrate that accommodation will be so secured, the housing authority should consider providing section 190(2) accommodation until the applicant is able to take up the accommodation.

Section 199A(2) and section 200(1): duties to accommodate applicants with no local connection pending outcome of referral

15.16   If the housing authority has notified an applicant that it proposes to refer the case to another housing authority, the notifying authority has a duty under section 199A(2) (if referral is in the relief stage of an applicant who the authority has reason to believe may have a priority need) or section 200(1) (if referral is in the section 193 main housing duty stage of an applicant who has a priority need and is unintentionally homeless) to secure that accommodation is available for the applicant until they are notified of the decision whether the conditions for referral are met. At this point the duty under section 199A(2) or 200(1) will come to an end and a duty under section 189B or section 193(2) will be owed by either the notified housing authority or the notifying housing authority. For further guidance on referrals to another housing authority see Chapter 10.

Suitability of accommodation

15.17   Section 206(1) provides that all accommodation provided under Part 7 of the 1996 Act must be suitable for the applicant and their household, and the suitability requirements under section 210 apply. For further guidance on the suitability of accommodation see Chapter 17. Housing authorities may take into account the interim nature of a placement when assessing whether or not it is suitable; as accommodation may be suitable for a few days or weeks that would not be suitable for a longer term placement.

15.18   The applicant does not have the right to ask for a statutory review under section 202 of the housing authority's decision as to the suitability of interim accommodation, but housing authorities are reminded that such decisions could be subject to judicial review.

Ending interim accommodation arrangements

15.19 When a housing authority is satisfied that they are under no further duty to secure interim accommodation or where this duty has ended, the housing authority will need to terminate the applicant's right of occupation. In the first instance, a housing authority should look to the terms of the licence or tenancy under which interim accommodation has been provided to establish the length of the notice period required.

15.20 Interim accommodation is usually provided under licences excluded from the requirement to issue 4 weeks written notice provided by the Protection from Eviction Act 1977. The courts have applied this principle in cases where the accommodation provided was B&B accommodation in a hotel, and where it was a self-contained flat. Consequently, housing authorities are required only to provide an applicant with reasonable notice to vacate the accommodation, and do not need to apply for a possession order from the court. However, housing authorities are public bodies and so must act reasonably by giving the applicant at least some opportunity to find alternative accommodation before the interim accommodation is terminated. What is considered 'reasonable notice' would depend on the facts of the case, taking into account the circumstances of the applicant and allowing time for them to consider whether to request a review of the decision.

15.21 In cases involving applicants who have children under 18 where the housing authority have reason to believe that the applicant may be ineligible for assistance or may be homeless intentionally, the housing authority must, subject to the applicant's consent, alert the children's services authority to the case. A referral to the children's services authority may also be made without the applicant's consent where there are safeguarding concerns, in accordance with local procedures.

Refusal or loss of interim accommodation

15.22 Where an applicant rejects an offer of interim accommodation (or accepts and moves into the interim accommodation and then later rejects it), this will bring the housing authority's interim accommodation duty to an end – unless it is reactivated by any change of circumstances. Note, however, that an applicant's rejection of interim accommodation does not end other duties that the housing authority may owe under Part 7.

Discretionary powers to secure accommodation

15.23 Housing authorities have powers to secure accommodation for certain applicants who request a review of certain decisions on their case, and to certain applicants requesting accommodation pending determination of a county court appeal.

15.24 The fact that a housing authority has decided that an applicant is **not eligible** for housing assistance under Part 7 does not preclude it from exercising its powers to secure accommodation pending a review or appeal. However, housing authorities should note that section 54 of, and schedule 3 to, the Nationality, Immigration and Asylum Act 2002 prevent them from exercising their powers to accommodate an applicant pending a review or appeal to the county court, where the applicant is a person who falls within one of a number of classes of person specified in schedule 3 unless there would otherwise be a breach of the person's rights under the European Court of Human Rights or rights under EU Treaties (see paragraph 7.22). For further guidance on eligibility see Chapter 7.

Powers to accommodate pending a review

15.25 Under section 202, applicants have the right to ask for a review of a housing authority's decision on a number of issues relating to their case, and may also request that accommodation is secured for them pending a decision on the review. For further guidance on reviews see Chapter 19. Housing authorities have powers to accommodate applicants pending a decision on reviews under section 188(3), section 199A(6) and section 200(5) of the 1996 Act.

15.26 In considering whether to secure accommodation pending review housing authorities will need to balance the objective of maintaining fairness between homeless persons in circumstances where they have decided that no duty is owed to them, against proper consideration of the possibility that the applicant might be right. Housing authorities should consider the following, along with any other relevant factors:

(a)   the merits of the applicant's case that the original decision was flawed and the extent to which it can properly be said that the decision was one which was either contrary to the apparent merits or was one which involved a very fine balance of judgment;

(b)   whether any new material, information or argument has been put to them which could alter the original decision; and,

(c)   the personal circumstances of the applicant and the consequences to them of a decision not to exercise the discretion to accommodate.

15.27 Where an applicant is refused accommodation pending a review, they may seek to challenge the decision through judicial review.

Power to accommodate pending an appeal to the county court

15.28 Where an applicant is dissatisfied with a housing authority's section 202 review decision or are not notified of the review decision within the proper time limits, an applicant has the right to appeal to the county court on a point of law arising from the review decision or original homelessness decision. For further guidance on reviews see Chapter 19. Under section 204(4), housing authorities have the power to accommodate certain applicants:

(a)   during the period for making an appeal against their decision; and,

(b)   if an appeal is brought, until it and any subsequent appeals are finally determined.

15.29 This power may be exercised where the housing authority was previously under a duty to secure accommodation for the applicant's occupation under section 188, section 190, section 199A or section 200; and may be exercised whether or not the housing authority has exercised its powers to accommodate the applicant pending review.

15.30 In deciding whether to exercise this power, housing authorities will need to adopt the same approach, and consider the same factors, as for a decision whether to exercise their power to accommodate pending a review (see paragraph 15.26).

15.31 Under section 204A, applicants have a right to appeal to the county court against decisions on the use of the section 204(4) power to accommodate. This enables an appeal against decisions not to secure accommodation for them pending their main appeal, or to stop securing accommodation, or to secure accommodation for only a limited period before final determination of the main appeal by the county court).

15.32 In deciding a section 204A appeal, if the court quashes the decision of the housing authority, it may order the authority to accommodate the applicant, but only where it is satisfied that failure to do so would substantially prejudice the applicant's ability to pursue the main appeal on the homelessness decision. For further guidance on reviews see Chapter 19.

Powers to secure accommodation to prevent or relieve homelessness

15.33 Housing authorities have duties to help prevent and relieve homelessness for eligible applicants who are threatened with becoming homelessness within 56 days, or are homeless. The section 195(2) prevention duty requires authorities to take reasonable steps to help the applicant to secure that accommodation does not cease to be available to them, and the relief duty requires housing authorities to take reasonable steps to help the applicant to secure that suitable accommodation becomes available to them for at least 6 months. For further guidance on the prevention duty see Chapter 12 and for further guidance on the relief duty see Chapter 13.

15.34 Section 205(3) of the 1996 Act enables housing authorities to discharge the section 189B (2) relief and/or section 195(2) prevention duties by securing accommodation for an applicant, where it decides to do so. The power to secure accommodation to applicants to prevent or relieve homelessness, regardless of priority need status, provides more flexibility to pursue appropriate housing options for applicants.

15.35 Housing authorities might use the section 205(3) power to deliver accommodation services for groups that are at higher risk of homelessness, for example young people with low incomes. The power might also be used to provide additional help to those least able to secure accommodation directly from a private landlord, such as people with an offending history or people with a mental health problem. Housing authorities will wish to consider local priorities, needs and resources when considering how the power might best be utilised in their district.

Section 193C(4): duty to accommodate applicants who have deliberately and unreasonably refused to co-operate pending final offer

15.36 Applicants who have priority need but are no longer owed a section 189B relief duty following service of a section 193B notice due to their deliberate and unreasonable refusal to co-operate will not be owed the section 193 main housing duty but will be owed an accommodation duty under section 193C(4).

15.37 This section 193C(4) duty ends if the applicant accepts or refuses a final accommodation offer or a final Part 6 offer. A 'final accommodation offer' is an offer of an assured shorthold tenancy made by a private landlord with the approval of the housing authority, with a view to bringing the section 193C(4) duty to an end. The offer must be of a fixed term tenancy (within the meaning of Part 1 of the Housing Act 1988) of at least 6 months duration, and the accommodation must be suitable for the applicant. A 'final Part 6 offer' is a suitable housing allocation (under Part 6 of the 1996 Act) made in writing, and which states that it is a final offer for the purposes of this section. A housing authority must not approve a final accommodation offer or make a final Part 6 offer if the applicant has a contractual obligation in respect of their existing accommodation which they are unable to bring to an end before being required to take up the offer. For further guidance on suitability see Chapter 17.

15.38 The section 193C(4) duty will also end if the applicant:

(a) ceases to be eligible for assistance;
(b) becomes homeless intentionally from the accommodation provided under section 193C(4);
(c) accepts an offer of an assured tenancy from a private landlord; or,
(d) voluntarily ceases to occupy as their only or principal home, the accommodation provided.

Duty to secure accommodation under the section 193(2) 'main housing duty'

15.39 Where an applicant is unintentionally homeless, eligible for assistance and has a priority need for accommodation, the housing authority has a duty under section 193(2) to secure that accommodation is available for their occupation (unless it refers the application to another housing authority under section 198). This is commonly known as 'the main housing duty'. However, the main housing duty will not be owed to an applicant who has turned down a suitable final accommodation offer or Part 6 offer made during the section 189B(2) relief stage, or has been given notice under section 193B(2) due to their deliberate and unreasonable refusal to co-operate. For further guidance on deliberate and unreasonable refusal to co-operate see Chapter 14.

15.40 The accommodation secured must be available for occupation by the applicant together with any other person who normally resides with them as a member of their family, or any other person who might reasonably be expected to reside with them. It must be suitable for their occupation. For further guidance on suitability see Chapter 17.

15.41 The housing authority will cease to be subject to the duty under section 193(2) (the main housing duty) in the following circumstances:

(a) the applicant **accepts a suitable offer of accommodation under Part 6** (an allocation of social housing) (section 193(6) (c)). This would include an offer of an assured tenancy of a private registered provider property via the housing authority's allocation scheme;

(b) the applicant **accepts an offer of an assured tenancy** (other than an assured shorthold tenancy) from a private landlord (section 193(6) (cc)). This could include an offer of an assured tenancy made by a private registered provider;

(c) the applicant accepts or refuses a private rented sector offer - an offer of an assured shorthold tenancy of at least 12 months made by a private landlord (section 193(7AA)). For this to be the case the applicant must have been informed in writing of the possible consequences of refusing or accepting the offer, their right to request a review of the suitability of the accommodation, and the duties that would be owed to them on re-application if they became unintentionally homeless from the accommodation within two years of accepting the offer;

(d) the applicant **refuses a final offer of accommodation under Part 6** (an allocation of social housing). The main housing duty does not end unless the applicant is informed of the possible consequences of refusal and of their right to ask for a review of the suitability of the accommodation (section 193(7)), the offer is made in writing and states that it is a final offer (section 193(7A)), and the housing authority is satisfied that the accommodation is suitable and that it would be reasonable for the applicant to accept it (section 193(7F));

(e) the applicant **refuses an offer of temporary accommodation** which the housing authority is satisfied is suitable for the applicant (section 193(5)). For this to be the case the applicant must have been informed of the possible consequences of refusal and of their right to ask for a review of the suitability of the accommodation, and have been notified by the housing authority that it regards itself as having discharged its duty.

15.42 The main housing duty will also end if the applicant:

(a) **ceases to be eligible** for assistance as defined in section 185 of the 1996 Act;

(b) **becomes homeless intentionally** from accommodation made available to them under section 193. For further guidance on intentional homelessness see Chapter 9;

(c) voluntarily **ceases to occupy** as their principal home the accommodation made available under section 193.

15.43 In **restricted cases** housing authorities should, as far as is reasonably practicable, bring the section 193(2) duty to an end through the offer of a Assured Shorthold Tenancy of at least 12 months duration with a private landlord (section 193(7AD)). The applicant will not be owed a section 195A duty if they re-apply as unintentionally homeless within two years of accepting the offer. For further guidance on restricted cases see Chapter 7.

Pre-Localism Act 2011 cases

15.44 In circumstances where the housing authority accepted a section 193(2) duty on an application made before 9 November 2012, that duty cannot be brought to an end through an offer of private rented accommodation unless that offer meets the requirements of 'a qualifying offer'.

15.45 A qualifying offer must be of a fixed-term tenancy of at least 12 months duration and be accompanied by a written statement that states the term of the tenancy being offered and explains in ordinary language that there is no obligation on the applicant to accept the offer, but if the offer is accepted the housing authority will cease to be subject to the section 193 duty. The applicant must have signed a statement acknowledging that he or she has understood the written statement accompanying the offer.

Making suitable offers

15.46 The Secretary of State recommends that applicants are given the chance to view accommodation that is offered on anything other than an interim basis, before being required to decide whether they accept or refuse an offer, and before being required to sign any written agreement relating to the accommodation (e.g. a tenancy agreement). Where housing authorities are making offers of accommodation outside their district they should take particular care to ensure that applicants have sufficient information about the location of the accommodation and the services that would be available to them there and that applicants are given a reasonable amount of time to consider the offer made before reaching a decision. Under section 202(1A), an applicant who is offered accommodation can request a review of its suitability whether or not they have accepted the offer. For further guidance on suitability see Chapter 17 and for further guidance on reviews see Chapter 19.

15.47 Where an applicant has contractual or other obligations in respect of their existing accommodation (e.g. a tenancy agreement or lease), the housing authority can only reasonably expect an offer to be taken up if the applicant is able to bring those obligations to an end before being required to take up the offer (section 193(8)).

15.48 Housing authorities should allow applicants a reasonable period for considering offers of accommodation that will bring the main housing duty to an end whether accepted or refused. There is no set reasonable period; some applicants may require longer than others depending on their circumstances, whether they wish to seek advice in making their decision and whether they are already familiar with the property or locality in question. Longer periods may be required where the applicant is in hospital or temporarily absent from the district. In deciding what a reasonable period is, housing authorities must take into account the applicant's circumstances.

15.49 For further guidance on accommodation arrangements see:

(a) Chapter 16: Securing accommodation;
(b) Chapter 17: Suitability of accommodation.

CHAPTER 16: SECURING ACCOMMODATION

16.1 This chapter provides guidance on the ways in which housing authorities can ensure that suitable accommodation is available for applicants.

Securing and helping to secure accommodation

16.2 Housing authorities have various duties and powers to secure accommodation for an applicant, which require them to directly let or ensure a property owned by another landlord is made available to the applicant. The Homelessness Reduction Act 2017 introduced the duty to 'help to secure' accommodation for all applicants who are eligible for assistance and threatened with homelessness or homeless.

16.3 'Helping to secure' does not mean that the housing authority has a duty to directly find and secure the accommodation, but involves them working with applicants to agree (where possible) reasonable steps that the applicant and the housing authority can take to identify and secure suitable accommodation.

16.4 In providing 'help to secure', the housing authority is able to provide support and advice to households who are taking some responsibility for securing their own accommodation. This approach is intended to increase choice and control for applicants and allow the housing authority to help to resolve particular problems rather than direct resources at securing accommodation for households regardless of what assistance they need. It remains open to the housing authority to secure accommodation for eligible applicants where appropriate.

General considerations

16.5 Section 206(1) provides that a housing authority may discharge its housing functions under Part 7 in the following ways:

(a)   by securing that suitable accommodation provided by them is available for the applicant;
(b)   by securing that the applicant obtains suitable accommodation from some other person; or,
(c)   by giving the applicant such advice and assistance as will secure that suitable accommodation is available from some other person.

16.6   Accommodation secured must be available and suitable for occupation by the applicant and any other person who normally resides with them as a member of their family, or any other person who might reasonably be expected to reside with them. Section 208(1) requires housing authorities to secure accommodation within their district, in so far as is reasonably practicable. For further guidance on suitability of accommodation see Chapter 17.

16.7   In deciding what accommodation is to be secured, housing authorities will need to consider whether the applicant has any support needs, as identified in their (section 189A) personalised housing plan, and taking in to account any additional information available from health or social care services, or from other agencies providing services to them.

16.8   Where a housing authority has a duty under section 193(2) to secure accommodation for an applicant it should consider, where availability of suitable housing allows, securing settled (rather than temporary) accommodation that will bring the duty to an end in the immediate or short term.

16.9   Housing authorities may secure accommodation by giving advice and assistance to an applicant that will secure that accommodation becomes available for them from another person (section 206(1)(c)). However, where an authority has a duty to secure accommodation, they will need to ensure that the advice and assistance provided results in suitable accommodation actually being secured. Merely assisting the applicant in any efforts that they might make to find accommodation would not be sufficient if suitable accommodation did not actually become available.

Local authority owned accommodation

16.10   Housing authorities may secure temporary accommodation through its own stock (i.e. held under Part 2 of the Housing Act 1985). In considering whether to do so authorities will need to balance the requirements of applicants owed a duty under Part 7 against the need to provide accommodation for others who have reasonable preference for an allocation under Part 6 of the 1996 Act.

16.11   Paragraph 4 of Schedule 1 to the Housing Act 1985 provides that a tenancy granted by a housing authority in pursuance of any function under Part 7 is not a secure tenancy unless the housing authority notifies the tenant that it is such. Housing authorities are reminded that the allocation of secure and introductory tenancies must be made in accordance with their allocation scheme framed under the provisions of Part 6.

Private registered provider owned accommodation

16.12   Under section 213 of the 1996 Act, where requested by a housing authority, a private registered provider must assist the housing authority in carrying out their duties under the homelessness legislation by co-operating with them as far as is reasonable in the circumstances. Private registered providers have a duty under the 1996 Act to co-operate with housing authorities in exercising their homelessness functions. Private registered providers are subject to the Regulator of Social Housing's[1] Regulatory Standards, in particular the expectation that they will co-operate with local authorities' strategic housing function, set out in the Tenancy and Home and Community Standards.

---

[1]   The regulation of social housing is the responsibility of the Regulation Committee, a statutory committee of the Homes and Communities Agency (HCA). The organisation refers to itself as the Regulator of Social Housing in undertaking the functions of the Regulation Committee.

References in any enactment or instrument to the Regulator of Social Housing are references to the HCA acting through the Regulation Committee. Homes England is the trading name of the HCA's non-regulation functions.

Co-operation between social housing providers

16.13   Under section 213 other social landlords have a duty to co-operate, as far as is reasonable in the circumstances, with a housing authority in carrying out their housing functions under Part 7 of the 1996 Act, if asked to do so.

16.14   Housing authorities may be able to assist one another by providing temporary or settled accommodation for homeless applicants. Under section 213(1), where one housing authority requests another to help them discharge a function under Part 7, the other housing authority must co-operate in providing such assistance as far as is reasonable in the circumstances.

16.15   This could be particularly appropriate in the case of applicants who would be at risk of violence or serious harassment in the district of the housing authority to whom they have applied for assistance. Other housing authorities may also be able to provide accommodation in cases where the applicant has special housing needs and the other housing authority has accommodation available which is appropriate to those needs. Housing authorities are encouraged to consider entering into reciprocal and co-operative arrangements where these might prove beneficial to authorities and to applicants.

Privately owned accommodation

16.16   Housing authorities may seek the assistance of private landlords in providing suitable accommodation direct to applicants, as well as engaging them in schemes that enable applicants to find their own private rented accommodation.

16.17   A general consent under section 25 of the Local Government Act 1988 (The General Consent under Section 25 of the Local Government Act 1988 for Financial Assistance to any person 2010) allows housing authorities to provide financial assistance to private landlords in order to secure accommodation for people who are homeless or at risk of homelessness. This could involve, for example, making small one-off grants ('finders' fees') to landlords to encourage them to let dwellings to households owed a homelessness duty; paying rent deposits or indemnities to ensure accommodation is secured for such households; and making one-off grant payments which would prevent an eviction. There is no limit set on the amount of financial assistance that can be provided, however housing authorities are obliged to act reasonably and in accordance with their fiduciary duty to local tax and rent payers.

Private rented sector offers

16.18   Private rented accommodation can be used to prevent or relieve homelessness, or to bring the main housing duty (section 193) to an end, but in all cases enabling the applicant to exercise some choice over the accommodation offered to them is likely to increase the acceptance rate, and engage the cooperation of both applicants and landlords.

16.19   Housing authorities are encouraged to develop a private rented sector access scheme which provides opportunities for all applicants, including those who do not have a priority need, to access private rented accommodation. The level of help and support the authority is able to provide through such a scheme will vary to reflect local housing markets and available resources, but might include offers of bonds and guarantees, as well as payments towards deposits and incentives. Housing authorities will need to be mindful of the need to identify shared housing options for younger people, and will wish to work with landlords willing to provide suitable Houses in Multiple Occupation (HMOs).

16.20   Whilst housing authorities must ensure any accommodation offered to homeless applicants is suitable, there are additional suitability requirements that apply to private rented accommodation offered under section 193(7)(F) to end the main housing duty, or secured for applicants in priority need to prevent or relieve their homelessness. Private rented sector accommodation must meet the requirements of Article 3 if it is to be considered suitable when offered:

(a)   to bring to an end the section 193(2) main housing duty (section 193(7F));

(b)   as a final accommodation offer made in the 189B relief stage (sections 193A(6) and 193C(9)); or,

(c)   to an applicant who has priority need, in order to prevent or relieve their homelessness.

For further guidance on the suitability of private rented sector offers see Chapter 17.

16.21   Housing authorities may make Discretionary Housing Payments (DHP) to help an applicant secure accommodation and to meet a shortfall between the rent and the amount of Housing Benefit or Universal Credit payable to them. However, where they do this housing authorities should take into account how sustainable any arrangement will be in the longer term when considering suitability of accommodation. Payments of DHP are governed by the Discretionary Financial Assistance Regulations 2001.

16.22   Housing authorities are encouraged to secure assured shorthold tenancies of at least 12 months wherever possible, and if a private rented sector offer is being made to end the section 193 duty it must always be for a tenancy of at least 12 months and comply with other requirements of section 193(7AA).

Temporary accommodation provided by a private landlord

16.23   Section 209 governs security of tenure where a private landlord provides accommodation to assist a housing authority to discharge an interim duty. Any such accommodation is exempt from statutory security of tenure until 12 months from the date on which the applicant is notified of the authority's decision under section 184(3) or section 198(5) or from the date on which the applicant is notified of the decision on any review under section 202 or an appeal under section 204, unless the landlord notifies the applicant that the tenancy is an assured or assured shorthold tenancy.

16.24   Where a private landlord or private registered provider lets accommodation directly to an applicant to assist a housing authority to discharge any other homelessness duty, the tenancy granted will be an assured shorthold tenancy unless the tenant is notified that it is to be regarded as an assured tenancy.

Accommodation leased from a private landlord

16.25   Accommodation leased from a private landlord can provide housing authorities with a source of good quality, self-contained accommodation which can be let to applicants. When entering into leases, as when borrowing, local authority capital finance rules require authorities to be satisfied that the associated liabilities are affordable.

16.26   Housing authorities may wish to consider contracting with private registered providers for assistance in discharging their housing functions under arrangements whereby the private registered provider leases and/or manages accommodation owned by private landlords, which can be let to households to prevent or relieve homelessness or as temporary accommodation. A general consent under section 25 of the Local Government Act 1988 (The General Consent under section 25 of the Local Government Act 1988 for Financial Assistance to Registered Social Landlords or to Private Landlords to Relieve or Prevent Homelessness 2010) allows housing authorities to provide private registered providers with financial assistance in connection with such arrangements. Housing authorities must reserve the right to terminate such agreements, without penalty, after 3 years.

16.27   Housing authorities are encouraged to test approaches that would enable temporary accommodation to become settled accommodation and so reduce the uncertainty and lack of security that households in temporary accommodation can face. This could include converting private sector leased accommodation used as temporary accommodation into settled housing when the lease comes to an end. If the accommodation is suitable for the households needs, and the landlord would be prepared to let directly to them, the housing authority may wish to arrange for a section 193(7AA) private rented sector offer to end the section 193(2) duty. For further guidance on accommodation duties see Chapter 15. Similarly, where a private registered provider holds the lease of accommodation owned by a private sector landlord, the accommodation might also be offered to the applicant (if suitable) as a section 193(7AA) offer to end the main housing duty (section 193(2)).

16.28 When considering conversion of temporary into settled accommodation, the interests and needs of the household, and the affordability of the new letting arrangement for the applicant, should be taken into account before any offer is made.

Bed and breakfast accommodation

16.29 Bed and breakfast (B&B) is defined in the Homelessness Suitability Order 2003 as a form of privately owned accommodation in which residents share facilities such as kitchens, bathrooms and/or toilets, and is usually paid for on a nightly basis.

16.30 Housing authorities must not use B&B to accommodate families with children or pregnant women except where there is no alternative available, and then for a maximum period not exceeding 6 weeks. MHCLG and DfE guidance states that B&B type accommodation is never suitable for 16-17 year olds.

Privately owned 'annexe' accommodation

16.31 Some housing authorities access the private market to secure self-contained accommodation (sometimes referred to as 'annexe' accommodation) for households, which is typically paid for on a nightly basis and typically involves family members sharing a large room with one another. This type of accommodation is unlikely to be suitable for families on anything but a short-term basis.

Lodgings

16.32 Lodgings provided by householders may be suitable for some applicants. Housing authorities may wish to establish a network of such landlords in their district, and might consider operating supported lodgings schemes for people with support needs, for example young people needing to gain skills for living independently.

Hostels and supported housing

16.33 Hostels and supported housing schemes may be owned and managed by local authorities, private registered providers, charities or private landlords and may be available through direct access, local referral arrangements or as direct temporary accommodation placements. The quality of accommodation provided within hostels varies considerably, and authorities should be particularly careful when securing or helping to secure accommodation with non-commissioned providers of hostel places that are not monitored or quality assessed.

16.34 Hostel accommodation typically involves some sharing of facilities, and in some hostels this includes sharing bedrooms as well as kitchens and bathing facilities.

16.35 Where hostel accommodation is used to accommodate vulnerable young people or families with children, the Secretary of State considers that it would be inappropriate to accommodate these groups alongside vulnerable adults. Housing authorities should be alert to the risks that may be associated with placing families with children, and young people, in mixed hostel settings, and should avoid doing so in circumstances where the housing authority does not have control over all of the placements.

16.36 Hostels can offer short-term accommodation to people who are experiencing homelessness, and housing authorities will wish to ensure they make the most effective use of services available, and that accommodation is suitable for the applicants placed there. Hostel accommodation that involves families or pregnant women sharing facilities with other households will not be suitable for longer-term placements.

16.37   Supported housing is usually, although not exclusively, commissioned by a local authority or other public body in order to meet the accommodation and support needs of particular groups who require such assistance. It can provide a highly valuable source of accommodation particularly for young people and for adults who need a period of stability and individual support to help them to prepare to live independently.

16.38   Housing authorities that have commissioned supported housing services will wish to keep the uptake, utilisation and move-on arrangements for these services under regular review to ensure that they meet local needs and that resources are maximised. In two-tier local authority areas, housing authorities should ensure that evidence of homelessness and support needs is available and informs commissioning priorities at upper tier level, and that there is collaboration across the districts to ensure efficient referral and move on from supported housing services. For further guidance on homelessness strategies and reviews see Chapter 2.

16.39   A placement in a short-stay hostel or supported housing scheme will be only be sufficient to meet a housing authority's duties to prevent or relieve homelessness where there is a planned pathway to ensure that accommodation will continue to be available to them for at least 6 months.

Refuges for victims of domestic abuse

16.40   Housing authorities should develop close links with refuges within their district, and neighbouring districts, to ensure they have access to emergency accommodation for applicants who are fleeing domestic or other violence or who are at risk of such violence. Refuge placements will usually require the applicant to speak directly to the service provider, and to indicate that they want and need refuge accommodation.

16.41   Housing authorities should recognise that placing an applicant in a refuge will generally be on a short-term basis, except where a longer period of support is required to enable applicants to prepare to manage independently. Housing authorities should work together with refuge providers to ensure efficient and planned move on from refuge provision, to maximise the use of refuge spaces. For further guidance on domestic abuse see Chapter 21.

Housing First accommodation

16.42   Housing First is an approach to ending long term homelessness for people with complex needs. It has been developed specifically to meet the needs of the most challenging client groups who have previously been unable to sustain housing. Although there are some variations in approach between different providers of Housing First, the central principles include providing a home without any requirement to engage with services, flexible support available for as long as needed, enabling individuals to have choice and control, and to reduce harm.

Caravans, houseboats and other moveable accommodation

16.43   Under section 175(2) applicants are homeless if the accommodation available for their occupation is a caravan, houseboat, or other movable structure and they do not have a place where they are entitled, or permitted, to put it and live in it. If a duty to secure accommodation arises in such cases, the housing authority is not required to make equivalent accommodation available (or provide a site or berth for the applicant's own accommodation). However, the housing authority must consider whether such options are reasonably available, particularly where this would provide the most suitable solution to the applicant's accommodation needs.

16.44   The circumstances described in paragraph 16.43 will be particularly relevant in the case of Gypsies and Travellers. Where a duty to secure accommodation arises but an appropriate site is not immediately available, the housing authority may need to provide an alternative temporary solution until a suitable site, or some other suitable option, becomes available. Some Gypsies and Travellers may have a cultural aversion to the prospect of 'bricks and mortar' accommodation. In such cases, the housing authority should seek to provide an alternative solution. However, where the housing authority is satisfied that there is no prospect of a suitable site for the time being, there may be no alternative solution. Housing authorities must give consideration to the needs and lifestyle of applicants who are Gypsies and Travellers when considering their application and how best to discharge a duty to secure suitable accommodation, in line with their obligations to act consistently with the Human Rights Act 1998, and in particular the right to respect for private life, family and the home; as well as their duties under section 149 of the Equality Act 2010.

16.45 Although mobile homes may sometimes provide emergency or short-term accommodation for applicants who do not usually occupy movable accommodation, housing authorities will need to be satisfied that the accommodation is suitable for the applicant and their household, paying particular regard to their needs, requirements and circumstances and the conditions and facilities on the site. Caravans designed primarily for short-term holiday use should not be regarded as suitable as temporary accommodation for applicants.

Tenancies for minors

16.46 There are legal complications associated with the grant of a tenancy to a minor because a minor cannot hold a legal estate in land. In most cases a 16-17 year old who has become homeless will be accommodated under section 20 of the Children Act section 1989 and/or through provision of supported housing or supported lodgings, and will not be ready to manage their own tenancy until they reach adulthood. If housing authorities are securing accommodation for 16-17 year olds within social housing or private rented stock there will need to be sufficient support in place, and a license agreement may be more appropriate depending on the arrangements in place. Where a minor is considered able to manage a tenancy independently this could be granted to a minor and held on trust. Authorities will need to take into account how the terms of any tenancy will be enforced in the event that there is a breach in tenancy conditions.

CHAPTER 17: SUITABILITY OF ACCOMMODATION

17.1 This chapter provides guidance on the factors to be taken into account when determining the suitability of accommodation secured and helped to secure under the 1996 Act. This includes (temporary) accommodation secured under interim accommodation duties or the main housing duty as well as settled accommodation which would bring the prevention, relief or main housing duty to an end.

17.2 Section 206 provides that where a housing authority discharges its functions to secure that accommodation is available for an applicant the accommodation must be suitable. This applies in respect of all powers and duties to secure accommodation under Part 7, including interim duties. The accommodation must be suitable in relation to the applicant and to all members of their household who normally reside with them, or who might reasonably be expected to reside with them.

17.3 Section 210 of the 1996 Act sets out matters a housing authority must have regard to when determining suitability. Section 210(2) provides for the Secretary of State to specify by order the circumstances in which accommodation is or is not to be regarded as suitable for someone, and matters to be taken into account or disregarded in determining whether accommodation is suitable.

17.4 Space and arrangement will be key factors in determining the suitability of accommodation. However, consideration of whether accommodation is suitable will require an assessment of all aspects of the accommodation in the light of the relevant needs, requirements and circumstances of the homeless person and their household. The location of the accommodation will always be a relevant factor.

17.5 Housing authorities will need to consider carefully the suitability of accommodation for households with particular medical and/or physical needs. Physical access to and around the home, space, bathroom and kitchen facilities, access to a garden and modifications to assist people with sensory loss as well as mobility needs are all factors which might need to be taken into account.

17.6 Account will need to be taken of any social considerations relating to the applicant and their household that might affect the suitability of accommodation, including any risk of violence, racial or other harassment in a particular locality. Where domestic violence or abuse is involved and the applicant is not able to stay in the current home, housing authorities may need to consider the need for alternative accommodation whose location can be kept a secret and which has security measures and staffing to protect the occupants.

17.7 Accommodation that is suitable for a short period, for example accommodation used to discharge an interim duty pending inquiries under section 188, may not necessarily be suitable for a longer period, for example to discharge a duty under section 193(2).

17.8 Housing authorities have a continuing obligation to keep the suitability of accommodation under review, and to respond to any relevant change in circumstances which may affect suitability, until such time as the accommodation duty is brought to an end.

17.9 Housing authorities are required to assess whether accommodation is suitable for each household individually, and case records should demonstrate that they have taken the statutory requirements into account in securing the accommodation.

Standards of accommodation

17.10 Section 210(1) requires a housing authority to have regard to the following provisions when assessing the suitability of accommodation for an applicant:

(a) Parts 9 and 10 of the Housing Act 1985 (the '1985 Act') (slum clearance and overcrowding); and,

(b) Parts 1 to 4 of the Housing Act 2004 (the '2004 Act') (housing conditions, licensing of houses in multiple occupation, selective licensing of other residential accommodation, additional control provisions in relation to residential accommodation).

Suitability of private rented accommodation

17.11 Article 3 of the Homelessness (Suitability of Accommodation) (England) Order 2012 concerns the suitability of privately rented accommodation offered to certain applicants who are homeless or threatened with homelessness.

17.12 Private rented sector accommodation must meet the requirements of Article 3 if it is to be considered suitable when offered:

(a) to bring to an end the section 193(2) main housing duty (section 193(7F));

(b) as a final accommodation offer made in the 189B relief stage (sections 193A(6) and 193C(9)); or,

(c) to an applicant who has priority need, in order to prevent or relieve their homelessness.

17.13 A private rented property must not be regarded as suitable if the housing authority are of the view any of the following apply:

(a) it is not in a reasonable physical condition;

(b) electrical equipment supplied with the accommodation does not meet the requirements of Schedule 1 to the Electrical Equipment (Safety) Regulations 2016;

(c) the landlord has not taken reasonable fire safety precautions with the accommodation and any furnishings supplied with it;

(d) the landlord has not taken reasonable precautions to prevent the possibility of carbon monoxide poisoning in the accommodation (see 17.20 below);

(e) the landlord is not a fit and proper person to act in the capacity of landlord (see 17.21 below).

17.14 A private rented property must not be regarded as suitable if any of the following apply:

(a)   it is a house in multiple occupation subject to licensing under section 55 of the Housing Act 2004 and is not licensed;

(b)   it is subject to additional licensing under section 56 of the Housing Act 2004 and is not licensed;

(c)   it forms part of residential property which does not have a valid Energy Performance Certificate as required by the Energy Performance of Buildings (England and Wales) Regulations 2012;

(d)   it is or forms part of relevant premises which do not have a current gas safety record in accordance with regulation 36 of the Gas Safety (Installation and Use) Regulations 1998(e);

(e)   the landlord has not provided a written tenancy agreement to the housing authority which the landlord proposes to use for the purposes of a private rented sector offer, and which the housing authority considers to be adequate. It is expected that the housing authority should review the tenancy agreement to ensure that it sets out, ideally in a clear and comprehensible way, the tenant's obligations, for example a clear statement of the rent and other charges, and the responsibilities of the landlord, but does not contain unfair or unreasonable terms, such as call-out charges for repairs or professional cleaning at the end of the tenancy.

17.15 The particular requirements of Article 3 do not apply to accommodation secured for households that do not have priority need, or to accommodation that the authority helped the applicant to secure (for example through a bond guarantee or financial assistance) but which the applicant identified themselves. However, the Secretary of State expects housing authorities to make reasonable efforts to ensure private rented accommodation secured for applicants who do not have priority need is safe, and in reasonable condition; and that all applicants looking for their own accommodation have sufficient guidance to enable them to consider standards.

17.16 To determine whether or not accommodation meets the requirements set out in Article 3 housing authorities are advised to ensure it is visited by a local authority officer or someone acting on their behalf able to carry out an inspection. Attention should be paid to signs of damp or mould and indications that the property would be cold as well as to a visual check made of electrical installations and equipment (for example; looking for loose wiring, cracked or broken electrical sockets, light switches that do not work and appliances which do not appear to have been safety tested).

Additional health and safety requirements

17.17 The Regulatory Reform (Fire Safety) Order 2005 applies to the common or shared parts of multi occupied residential buildings. It places a duty on landlords, owners or managing agents to carry out a fire risk assessment of the common parts and implement and maintain appropriate and adequate fire safety measures to manage the risk that lives could be lost in a fire. As part of their responsibilities, landlords should put in place appropriate management and maintenance systems to ensure any fire safety equipment or equipment which may represent a fire hazard, is maintained in good working order, and in accordance with the manufacturers instructions. Landlords are also required to ensure that furniture and furnishings supplied must comply with the Furniture and Furnishings (Fire) (Safety) Regulations 1988 (as amended).

17.18 Housing authorities and fire and rescue authorities should work together to ensure the safety of domestic premises including the provision of fire safety advice to households. Housing authorities will need to satisfy themselves that these regulations have been adhered to.

17.19 Housing authorities are asked to satisfy themselves that there are reasonable precautions to prevent the possibility of carbon monoxide poisoning in the accommodation, where such a risk exists. Since 2015, private sector landlords have been required to have at least one smoke alarm installed on every storey of their properties and a carbon monoxide alarm in any room containing a solid fuel burning appliance (for example a coal fire or wood burning stove). After that, the landlord must make sure the alarms are in working order at the start of each new tenancy.

Fit and proper landlords

17.20 Housing authorities must satisfy themselves that landlords are fit and proper people to act in the capacity of a landlord. This assessment involves consideration if the landlord has:

(a) committed any offences involving fraud or other dishonesty, violence or illegal drugs, or that are listed in Schedule 3 to the Sexual Offences Act 2003(b) (offences attracting notification requirements);

(b) practised unlawful discrimination on grounds of sex, race, age, disability, marriage or civil partnership, pregnancy or maternity, religion or belief, sexual orientation, gender identity or gender reassignment in, or in connection with, the carrying on of any business;

(c) contravened any provision of the law relating to housing (including landlord or tenant law); or,

(d) acted otherwise than in accordance with any applicable code of practice for the management of a house in multiple occupation, approved under section 233 of the Housing Act 2004(c).

17.21 The Secretary of State recommends that when placing households outside of their district that the authority liaise with the receiving district to check whether that authority has taken any enforcement activity against the landlord. The Housing and Planning Act 2016 introduced a range of measures to tackle rogue landlords including a database of rogue landlords or letting agents who have been banned; convicted of certain offences; or received multiple civil penalties for housing offences. Housing authorities could check this database as part of their inquiries.

Tenancy deposit scheme

17.22 Whilst a local authority will not be able to check that a tenant's deposit has been placed in a tenancy deposit protection scheme prior to them taking the tenancy housing authorities should remind prospective landlords and tenants of their responsibilities in this area.

Housing Health and Safety Rating System (HHSRS)

17.23 Housing authorities are obliged under section 3 of the Housing Act 2004 to keep the housing conditions in their area under review with a view to identifying any action that may need to be taken by them under the Household Health and Safety Ratings System legislation (HHSRS).

17.24 When determining the suitability of accommodation secured under the homelessness legislation, housing authorities should, as a minimum, ensure that all accommodation is free of Category 1 hazards. In the case of an out of district placement it is the responsibility of the placing authority to ensure that accommodation is free of Category 1 hazards.

Overcrowding

17.25 Part 10 of the 1985 Act is intended to tackle the problems of overcrowding in dwellings. Section 324 provides a definition of overcrowding which in turn relies on the room standard specified in section 325 and the space standard in section 326. Housing authorities must be mindful of these provisions when securing or helping to secure accommodation for homeless applicants.

17.26 A room provided within an HMO may be defined as a 'dwelling' under Part 10 of the 1985 Act and the room and space standards will therefore apply. Housing authorities should also note that 'crowding and space' is one of the hazards assessed by the HHSRS. Any breach of the room and space standards under Part 10 is likely to constitute a Category 1 hazard.

Houses in Multiple Occupation (HMOs)

17.27 Housing authorities must have regard to regulations governing the required standards for any Houses in Multiple Occupation (HMO) that may be secured or helped to secure for an applicant.

17.28 A property is an HMO if it satisfies the conditions set out in sections 254(2) to (4), has been declared an HMO under section 255 or is a converted block of flats to which section 257 applies. Privately owned bed and breakfast or hostel accommodation that is used to accommodate a household pursuant to a homelessness function, and which is the household's main residence, will fall within this definition of an HMO.

17.29 A housing authority will have to be satisfied that an HMO is suitable for the number of households or occupants it is licensed for and meets statutory standards relating to shared amenities and facilities. These standards are set out in Schedule 3 to the *Licensing and Management of Houses in Multiple Occupation and Other Houses (Miscellaneous Provisions) (England) Regulations 2006* (SI No 2006/373). These 'amenity standards' will run alongside the consideration of health and safety issues under HHSRS.

Bed and breakfast accommodation

17.30 Bed and breakfast (B&B) accommodation caters for very short-term stays only and affords residents only limited privacy, and may lack or require sharing of important amenities, such as cooking and laundry facilities. Wherever possible, housing authorities should avoid using B&B accommodation as accommodation for homeless applicants, unless, in the very limited circumstances where it is likely to be the case, it is the most appropriate option for the applicant.

17.31 Living in B&B accommodation can be particularly detrimental to the health and development of children. Under section 210(2), the Secretary of State has made the *Homelessness (Suitability of Accommodation) (England) Order 2003* (SI 2003 No. 3326) ('the 2003 Order'). The 2003 Order specifies that B&B accommodation is not to be regarded as suitable for applicants with family commitments provided with accommodation under Part 7.

17.32 Housing authorities should, therefore, use B&B accommodation to discharge a duty to secure accommodation for applicants with family commitments only as a last resort and then only for a maximum of six weeks. Applicants with family commitments means an applicant:

(a) who is pregnant;
(b) with whom a pregnant woman resides or might reasonably be expected to reside; or,
(c) with whom dependent children reside or might reasonably be expected to reside.

17.33 For the purpose of the 2003 Order, B&B accommodation means accommodation (whether or not breakfast is included):

(a) which is not separate and self-contained premises; and,
(b) in which any of the following amenities is shared by more than one household:
    (i) a toilet;
    (ii) personal washing facilities; or,
    (iii) cooking facilities.

17.34 B&B accommodation does not include accommodation which is owned or managed by a housing authority, a private registered provider or a voluntary organisation as defined in section 180(3) of the 1996 Act.

17.35 The 2003 Order provides that if no alternative accommodation is available for the applicant the housing authority may accommodate the family in B&B for a period, or periods, not exceeding six weeks in result of a single homelessness application. Where B&B accommodation is secured for an applicant with family commitments, the Secretary of State considers that the authority should notify the applicant of the effect of the 2003 Order, and, in particular, that the authority will be unable to continue to secure B&B accommodation for such applicants any longer than 6 weeks, after which the authority must secure alternative, suitable accommodation.

17.36 When determining whether accommodation other than B&B accommodation is available for use, housing authorities will need to take into account, among other things, the cost to the authority of securing the accommodation, the affordability of the accommodation for the applicant and the location of the accommodation. A housing authority is under no obligation to include in its considerations accommodation which is to be allocated in accordance with its allocation scheme, published under section 167 of the 1996 Act.

17.37 If there is a significant change in an applicant's circumstances that would bring the applicant within the scope of the 2003 Order, the six week period should start from the date the authority was informed of the change of circumstances not the date the applicant was originally placed in B&B accommodation.

17.38 If the conditions for referring a case are met and another housing authority accepts responsibility for an applicant under section 200(4), any time spent in B&B accommodation before this acceptance should be disregarded in calculating the six week period.

17.39 B&B accommodation is not suitable for 16 and 17 year old applicants even on an emergency basis.

17.40 The Secretary of State considers that the limited circumstances in which B&B accommodation may provide suitable accommodation could include those where:

(a)   emergency accommodation is required at very short notice (for example to discharge an interim duty to accommodate); or,

(b)   there is simply no better alternative accommodation available and the use of B&B accommodation is necessary as a last resort.

17.41 The Secretary of State considers that where housing authorities are unable to avoid using B&B accommodation to accommodate applicants, they should ensure that such accommodation is of a good standard and is used for the shortest period possible.

Standards of B&B accommodation

17.42 Where B&B accommodation is used to accommodate an applicant and is their main residence, it falls within the definition of an HMO. Local authorities have a power under the 2004 Act to issue an HMO Declaration confirming HMO status where there is uncertainty about the status of a property.

17.43 The Government recognises that living conditions in HMOs should not only be healthy and safe but should also provide acceptable, decent standards for people who may be unrelated to each other and who are sharing basic facilities. The Government has set out in regulation the minimum 'amenity standards' required for a property to be granted an HMO licence. These standards will only apply to HMOs covered by mandatory licensing or those HMOs that will be subject to additional licensing, and will not apply to the majority of HMOs. However, housing authorities (or groups of authorities) can adopt their own local classification, amenity specification or minimum standards for B&B and other shared accommodation provided as temporary accommodation under Part 7.

Affordability

17.44 Under section 210(2), the Secretary of State has made the *Homelessness (Suitability of Accommodation) Order 1996* (SI 1996 No. 3204). The 1996 Order specifies that in determining whether it would be, or would have been, reasonable for a person to occupy accommodation and in determining whether accommodation is suitable a housing authority must take into account whether the accommodation is affordable by them, and in particular must take account of:

(a)   the financial resources available to them (i.e. all forms of income), including, but not limited to:

(i)   salary, fees and other remuneration (from such sources as investments, grants, pensions, tax credits etc.);

(ii)   social security benefits

(iii)   payments due under a court order for the making of periodical payments to a spouse or a former spouse, or to, or for the benefit of, a child;

(iv)   payments of child support maintenance due under the Child Support Act 1991;

(v)   pensions;

(vi)   contributions to the costs in respect of the accommodation which are or were made or which might reasonably be expected to be, or have been, made by other members of their household (most members can be assumed to contribute, but the amount depends on various factors including their age and income);

(vii)   financial assistance towards the costs in respect of the accommodation, including loans, provided by a local authority, voluntary organisation or other body;

(viii)   benefits derived from a policy of insurance (such as cover against unemployment or sickness);

(b)   savings and other capital sums which may be a source of income or might be available to meet accommodation expenses;

(c)   the costs in respect of the accommodation, including, but not limited to:

(i)   payments of, or by way of, rent (including rent default/property damage deposits);

(ii)   payments in respect of a licence or permission to occupy the accommodation;

(iii)   mortgage costs (including an assessment of entitlement to support for mortgage interest (SMI) in income support/income-based jobseeker's allowance/income-related employment and support allowance/universal credit);

(iv)   payments of, or by way of, service charges (e.g. maintenance or other costs required as a condition of occupation of the accommodation);

(v)   mooring charges payable for a houseboat;

(vi)   where the accommodation is a caravan or a mobile home, payments in respect of the site on which it stands;

(vii)   the amount of council tax payable in respect of the accommodation;

(viii)   payments by way of deposit or security in respect of the accommodation;

(ix)   payments required by an accommodation agency;

(d)   payments which that person is required to make under a court order for the making of periodical payments to a spouse or former spouse, or to, or for the benefit of, a child and payments of child support maintenance required to be made under the Child Support Act 1991; and,

(e)   other reasonable living expenses

17.45   Housing authorities will need to consider whether the applicant can afford the housing costs without being deprived of basic essentials such as food, clothing, heating, transport and other essentials specific to their circumstances. Housing costs should not be regarded as affordable if the applicant would be left with a residual income that is insufficient to meet these essential needs. Housing authorities may be guided by Universal Credit standard allowances when assessing the income that an applicant will require to meet essential needs aside from housing costs, but should ensure that the wishes, needs and circumstances of the applicant and their household are taken into account. The wider context of the applicant's particular circumstances should be considered when considering their household expenditure especially when these are higher than might be expected. For example, an applicant with a disabled child may have higher travel costs to ensure that the child is able to access additional support or education that they require and so this should be taken into account when assessing their essential needs, and the income that they have available for accommodation costs.

Location of accommodation

17.46   The suitability of the location for all the members of the household must be considered by the authority. Section 208(1) of the 1996 Act requires that authorities shall, in discharging their housing functions under Part 7 of the 1996 Act, in so far as is reasonably practicable, secure accommodation within the authority's own district.

17.47 Where it is not reasonably practicable to secure accommodation within district and an authority has secured accommodation outside their district, the housing authority is required to take into account the distance of that accommodation from the district of the authority. Where accommodation which is otherwise suitable and affordable is available nearer to the authority's district than the accommodation which it has secured, the accommodation which it has secured is not likely to be suitable unless the applicant has specified a preference.

17.48 Generally, where possible, housing authorities should try to secure accommodation that is as close as possible to where an applicant was previously living. Securing accommodation for an applicant in a different location can cause difficulties for some applicants. Where possible the authority should seek to retain established links with schools, doctors, social workers and other key services and support.

17.49 In assessing the significance of disruption to employment, account will need to be taken of their need to reach their normal workplace from the accommodation secured. In assessing the significance of disruption to caring responsibilities, account should be taken of the type and importance of the care household members provide and the likely impact the withdrawal would cause.

17.50 When securing accommodation for families with children housing authorities should be mindful of their duties under section 11 of the Children Act 2004 to discharge their functions with regard to the need to safeguard and promote the welfare of children. This would include minimising the disruption to the education of children and young people, particularly (but not solely) at critical points in time such as leading up to taking GCSE (or their equivalent) examinations.

17.51 Before a family that includes a school age child is placed out of district, the housing authority should liaise with the receiving authority and make every reasonable effort to ensure arrangements are or will be put in place to meet the child's educational needs. Local authorities have a duty to ensure that school places are available for children who have moved in to their area, but particular care should be taken by housing authorities when placing families that may require more support to access school places, to ensure educational needs will be met.

17.52 Account should also be taken of medical facilities and other support currently provided for the applicant and their household. Housing authorities should consider the potential impact on the health and wellbeing of an applicant or any person reasonably expected to reside with them, were such support to be removed or medical facilities were no longer accessible. They should also consider whether similar facilities are accessible and available near the accommodation being offered and whether there would be any specific difficulties in the applicant or person residing with them using those essential facilities, compared to the support they are currently receiving.

17.53 Housing authorities should avoid placing applicants in isolated accommodation away from public transport, shops and other facilities, where possible.

17.54 In some circumstances there will be clear benefits for the applicant of being accommodated outside of the district. This could occur, for example, where the applicant, and/or a member of their household, would be at risk of domestic abuse or other violence in the district and need to be accommodated elsewhere to reduce the risk of further contact with the perpetrator(s). Another example might be where, upon the advice of the relevant provider of offender management services (Probation Service, Community Rehabilitation Company or Youth Offending Team), ex-offenders or drug/alcohol users would benefit from being accommodated outside the district to help break links with previous contacts which could exert a negative influence.

17.55 There may also be advantages in enabling some applicants to access employment opportunities outside of their current district. The availability, or otherwise, of employment opportunities in the new area may help to determine if that area is suitable for the applicant.

17.56 The Secretary of State considers that applicants whose household has a need for social services support or a need to maintain links with other essential services within the borough, for example families with children who are subject to safeguarding arrangements, should be given particular attention when temporary accommodation is allocated, to try and ensure it is located in or close to the housing authorities own district. Careful consideration should be given to applicants with a mental illness or learning disability who may have a particular need to remain in a specific area, for example to maintain links with health service professionals and/or a reliance on existing informal support networks and community links. Such applicants may be less able than others to adapt to any disruption caused by being placed in accommodation in another district.

17.57 Housing authorities, particularly those that find it necessary to make out of district placements, are advised to develop policies for the procurement and allocation of temporary accommodation which will help to ensure suitability requirements are met. This would provide helpful guidance for staff responsible for identifying and making offers of accommodation, and would make local arrangements, and the challenges involved with sourcing accommodation, clearer to applicants.

17.58 When making offers of accommodation to an applicant a housing authority should make clear in the offer letter why they consider the property to be suitable, taking into account the needs of the applicant and their household. If any members of the household have health problems the authority should state how their medical needs may be met in the district where the accommodation is located. For families with school age children, the authority should set out how the impact on their education has been assessed and what arrangements have been made for their education in the area of placement.

17.59 Where a housing authority places an applicant in accommodation outside the district under any part of the Act, section 208(2) requires them to notify the authority in whose district the accommodation is situated of the placement. The notification requirement applies to all out of district placements and not just those arranged under interim accommodation duties or the section 193(2) main housing duty. The notification must include:

(a)   the name of the applicant;
(b)   the number and description of other persons who normally reside with the applicant as a member of his or her family or might reasonably be expected to do so;
(c)   the address of the accommodation;
(d)   the date on which the accommodation was made available;
(e)   which function the housing authority is discharging in securing the accommodation; and,
(f)   the notice must be given in writing within 14 days of the accommodation being made available to the applicant.

17.60 Applicants should be given a reasonable amount of time to consider offers of accommodation outside their district (for further guidance see 15.46). In considering what amount of time is to be considered reasonable, housing authorities should take into account how familiar the applicant might be with the district offered, and the length of time that the household are likely to be living there.

17.61 Housing authorities should record how decisions to place an applicant out of district have been reached, taking into account the household's collective and individual needs.

Households with pets

17.62 Housing authorities will need to be sensitive to the importance of pets to some applicants, particularly elderly people and rough sleepers who may rely on pets for companionship. Although it will not always be possible to make provision for pets, the Secretary of State recommends that housing authorities give careful consideration to this aspect when making provision for applicants who wish to retain their pet.

Right to request a review of suitability

17.63 Applicants may ask for a review on request of the housing authority's decision that the accommodation offered to them is suitable under section 202(1)(f), although this right does not apply in the case of interim accommodation secured under sections 188, 190, 200(1), 204(4). For further guidance on accommodation duties see Chapter 15. Under section 202(1A) an applicant may request a review as to suitability regardless of whether or not they accept the accommodation. This applies equally to offers of accommodation made under section 193(5) to discharge the section 193(2) main housing duty and to offers of an allocation of accommodation made under section 193(7) that would bring that duty to an end. This means that the applicant is able to ask for a review of suitability without inadvertently bringing the main housing duty to an end. Housing authorities should note that although there is no right of review of a decision on the suitability of accommodation secured under interim accommodation duties such decisions could nevertheless be subject to judicial review in the High Court. For further guidance see Chapter 19.

CHAPTER 18: APPLICATIONS, DECISIONS AND NOTIFICATIONS

18.1 This chapter provides guidance on dealing with applications for accommodation or assistance in obtaining accommodation, reapplications to a housing authority within two years of acceptance of a private rented sector offer and the circumstances in which an authority has a duty to notify an applicant of its decision.

Service provision

18.2 A need for accommodation, or assistance in obtaining accommodation, can arise at anytime. Housing authorities will therefore need to provide access to advice and assistance at all times during normal office hours, and have arrangements in place for 24 hour emergency cover, e.g. by enabling telephone access to an appropriate duty officer. The police and other relevant services should be provided with details of how to access the service outside normal office hours.

18.3 It is recommended that housing authorities should give proper consideration to the location of, and accessibility to, advice and information about homelessness and the prevention of homelessness, including the need to ensure privacy during interviews.

18.4 Housing authorities should publicise their opening hours, address, and the 24 hour contact details. For example, this information could be accessible on the housing authority's website. Translated information and interpreting services should be made available to applicants for who English is not a first language, and the availability of these services publicised to residents and community organisations. For more guidance on arrangements for carrying out assessments see 11.13 to 11.16.

Form of an application

18.5 Applications can be made to any department of the local authority and expressed in any particular form; they need not be expressed as explicitly seeking assistance under Part 7. As long as the communication seeks accommodation or assistance in obtaining accommodation and includes details that give the housing authority reason to believe that they might be homeless or threatened with homelessness, this will constitute an application.

18.6 Housing authorities should take particular attention to identify instances where information on an inquiry about a social housing allocation scheme, or an application for an allocation of housing under Part 6, provides reason to believe that the applicant might be homeless or threatened with homelessness. This should be regarded as an application for homelessness assistance.

18.7 A referral of a case made by a public authority to the housing authority under section 213B of the 1996 Act, the duty to refer, will not in itself constitute an application. However, housing authorities should make contact with the person referred and determine whether they have reason to believe that the applicant may be homeless or threatened with homelessness. For further guidance on the duty to refer see Chapter 4.

Persons making an application

18.8 An application can be made by any individual who has the mental capacity to do so. There is no statutory minimum age, but applications from dependent children should not be considered. A child aged 16-17 may make an application in their own right, and will require a Children Act 1989 assessment to be completed if they are homeless.

Applications to more than one housing authority

18.9 In some cases applicants may apply to more than one housing authority simultaneously and housing authorities should be alert to cases where an applicant is doing this. In such cases, where a housing authority has reason to believe that the applicant may be homeless or threatened with homelessness, it may wish to contact the other housing authorities involved, to agree which housing authority will take responsibility for conducting inquiries. Where another housing authority has previously made decisions about an applicant's circumstances, a housing authority considering a fresh application may wish to have regard to those decisions. However, housing authorities should not rely solely on decisions made by another housing authority and will need to make their own inquiries in order to reach an independent decision on whether any duty, and if so which duty, is owed under Part 7. Any arrangements for the discharge of any of their functions by another housing authority must comply with section 101 of the Local Government Act 1972.

Withholding or falsifying information

18.10 Under section 214, it is an offence for a person, knowingly or recklessly to make a false statement, or knowingly to withhold information, with intent to induce the housing authority to believe that they, or another person, are entitled to accommodation or assistance under Part 7. If, before the applicant receives notification of a decision, there is any change of facts material to their case, they must inform the housing authority of this as soon as possible. Housing authorities must ensure that all applicants are made aware of these obligations and that they are explained in ordinary language. Housing authorities are advised to ensure that the obligations are conveyed sensitively to avoid intimidating applicants.

Further applications

18.11 There is no period of disqualification if someone wants to make a fresh application. Where a person whose application has been previously considered and determined under Part 7 makes a fresh application, the housing authority will need to decide whether there are any new facts which render it different from the earlier application. If no new facts are revealed, or any new facts are of a trivial nature, the housing authority would not be required to consider the new application and can instead rely on its previous decision. However, where the fresh application does reveal a change in relevant facts, the housing authority must treat the fresh application in the same way as it would any other application for accommodation or assistance in obtaining accommodation under Part 7.

18.12 In the majority of re-application cases where the applicant has previously refused an offer of suitable accommodation, the housing authority will be entitled to rely on the ending of its duties following the refusal of accommodation. However, if, after the refusal of accommodation, the applicant's factual circumstances change, the housing authority can no longer rely on the completion of the earlier duty and must consider the fresh application.

18.13 For example, if an applicant makes a further application following a relationship breakdown which has changed the membership of the household, this should be treated as a new application following a factual change of circumstances.

Withdrawn applications

18.14 It is recommended that housing authorities have procedures in place for dealing with applications that are withdrawn or where someone fails to maintain contact with the housing authority after making an application. The Secretary of State considers that it would be reasonable to consider an application closed where the applicant has not responded to any form of contact for 56 days or longer. Any further approach from the applicant after this time may need to be considered as a fresh application. Where an applicant renews contact within 56 days the housing authority will need to consider any change of circumstances that may affect the application.

18.15 If an applicant dies before a decision is reached on their application, the housing authority can substitute another member of the late applicant's household as applicant upon the consent of that household member.

Reapplication to a housing authority within two years of acceptance of a private rented sector offer

18.16 Under section 195A(1) (re-application after private rented sector offer), the section 193(2) duty will apply regardless of whether the applicant has a priority need where:

(a) a person makes a re-application for assistance within two years of accepting a private rented sector offer under section 193(7AA); and,
(b) the applicant is eligible for assistance and has become homeless unintentionally.

18.17 The date from which the two years begins is the date of acceptance of the private rented sector offer, not the date when the tenancy was granted or when the applicant moved in.

18.18 Housing authorities should be aware that if, following the expiry of the initial 12 month assured shorthold tenancy, an applicant secures their own accommodation and then subsequently becomes homeless within two years of the original private rented sector offer then the re-application duty will still apply.

18.19 Given the two year re-application duty, housing authorities are advised to keep the household circumstances under review as they approach the expiry of the 12 month tenancy so they can help actively prevent homelessness wherever possible.

18.20 If the applicant is found to have become homeless intentionally but does have a priority need, the housing authority must secure short-term accommodation for the applicant under section 190(2)(a) for such period as they consider will give them a reasonable opportunity of securing accommodation.

Referrals to another housing authority

18.21 Housing authorities should note that the section 193(2) duty on re-application will apply regardless of whether or not the housing authority receiving the re-application is the same housing authority that arranged the private rented sector offer. This means that the housing authority receiving the re-application cannot simply refer the applicant to the housing authority which made the private rented sector offer but must first carry out investigations to determine whether the applicant is eligible and homeless through no fault of their own, under section 195A. It is for the receiving housing authority to establish whether the applicant has become homeless unintentionally. Once established, this matter cannot be reopened.

18.22 Once the receiving housing authority has established that the applicant is unintentionally homeless and eligible for assistance, they may refer the applicant to the housing authority that made the private rented sector offer. The conditions for referral of the case to the other housing authority are met once it has been established that the re-application has been made within two years and neither the applicant nor any person who might reasonably be expected to reside with the applicant will be at risk of violence, in the district of the other housing authority. The term 'violence' should not be given a restrictive meaning, and 'domestic violence' should be understood to include physical violence, threatening or intimidating behaviour, and any other form of abuse which directly or indirectly may give rise to harm; between persons who are, or have been, intimate partners, family members or members of the same household, regardless of gender identity or sexual orientation.

18.23 The housing authority which made the private rented sector offer will owe the reapplication duty and it will be their responsibility to secure accommodation is available for occupation by the applicant. Housing authorities are expected to respond quickly to referrals and requests for information.

18.24 Housing authorities are reminded to consider the conditions for referral of a case to another housing authority as set out under section 198(2ZA). For further guidance on referrals to another housing authority see Chapter 10 and risk of domestic abuse see Chapter 21.

18.25 Referrals regarding re-applications are not subject to any consideration of local connection.

When re-application does not apply

18.26 The provisions under section 195A do not apply in a restricted case. Additionally, these provisions do not apply in a case where the applicant has previously made a re-application which resulted in their being owed the duty under section 193(2) by virtue of section 195A(1) This effectively means that an applicant can only be owed the re-application duty once following each private rented sector offer. For further guidance on restricted cases see Chapter 7.

Interim duty to accommodate

18.27 Under section 188(1A), if the housing authority have reason to believe that the re-application duty may apply, they must secure interim accommodation for the applicant regardless of whether or not they have a priority need.

18.28 Housing authorities should note that the duty under section 188(1A) will apply regardless of whether the housing authority receiving the re-application is the same authority that arranged the private rented sector offer.

Notifications to applicants

18.29 Housing authorities are required to provide written notifications to applicants of certain decisions reached in relation to their applications under Part 7. In all cases notifications should be clearly written in plain language, and include information about the right to request a review and the timescales that apply. Housing authorities might also include information about independent advice services available to the applicant. In cases where the applicant may have difficulty understanding the implications of the decision, it is recommended that housing authorities consider arranging for a member of staff to provide and explain the notification in person.

18.30 Written notification not received by the applicant can be treated as having been given to them, if it is made available at the housing authority's office for a reasonable period that would allow it to be collected by the applicant or by someone acting on their behalf.

Combining notifications

18.31 There will be circumstances in which more than one notification will be required at the same time and it will be more practicable to combine the necessary information within one notification letter. Housing authorities will need to take particular care to ensure the information provided to the applicant is clear and comprehensive, and that they are made aware of review rights in respect of each of the decisions about which they are being notified.

Notification on decisions about duties owed section 184(3)

18.32 If a housing authority has reason to believe that a person applying for assistance may be homeless or threatened with homelessness, the housing authority must make such inquiries as are necessary to satisfy itself whether the applicant is eligible for assistance and if so, whether any duty, and if so what duty, is owed to that person under Part 7 of the 1996 Act. When a housing authority has completed its inquiries it must notify the applicant in writing of its decisions.

18.33 Where a decision is against the applicant's interests the notification must explain clearly and fully the reasons for the decision. In cases where contradictory factual accounts are put before the housing authority, and it prefers one account to another, the decisions letter should explain why a particular account was preferred.

Notification bringing duties to an end

18.34 Housing authorities can give notice to the applicant bringing their duties to an end at each stage. The conditions and requirements for these notifications are set out separately under each provision.

18.35 A notice bringing duties to an end must explain why the housing authority are giving the notice and its effect, and inform the applicant that they have a right to request a review of the authority's decision to give the notice and of the time within which such a request must be made. For further guidance on how and when the prevention and relief duties can be ended and on issuing notices in cases of an applicant's deliberate and unreasonable refusal to co-operate see Chapter 14.

CHAPTER 19: REVIEW OF DECISIONS AND APPEALS TO THE COUNTY COURT

19.1 This chapter provides guidance on the procedures to be followed when an applicant requests the housing authority to review any decision on their case.

Right to request a review

19.2 Applicants have the right to request the housing authority review their decisions on homelessness cases in some circumstances. If the request is made in accordance with section 202 the housing authority, or housing authorities, concerned must review the relevant decision.

19.3 Under section 202(1) an applicant has the right to request a review of a housing authority's decision:

(a)   of their eligibility for assistance (section 202(1)(a));
(b)   what duty (if any) is owed to them in relation to the duties owed to persons found to be homeless or threatened with homelessness (section 202(1)(b));
(c)   of the steps the housing authority are to take under section 195(2) which includes having regard to their assessment of the applicants case in the r personalised housing plan at the prevention duty (section 202(1)(bc)(i));
(d)   to give notice to bring the prevention duty to an end (section 202(1)(bc)(ii));
(e)   of the steps the housing authority are to take under section 189B(2) which includes having regard to their assessment of the applicant's case in the personalised housing plan at the relief duty (section 202(1)(ba)(i));
(f)   to give notice to bring the relief duty to an end (section 202(1)(ba)(ii));
(g)   to give notice under section 193B(2) in cases of deliberate and unreasonable refusal to co-operate (section 202(1)(bb));
(h)   to notify their case to another authority under section 198(1) (i.e. a decision to refer the applicant at the main housing duty, to another housing authority because they consider that the conditions for referral are met) (section 202(1)(c));
(i)   under section 198(5) as to whether the conditions are met for the referral of their case to another housing authority at the relief duty or main housing duty (including a decision reached either by agreement between the notifying and notified authority, or taken by a person appointed under the *Homelessness (Decisions on Referrals) Order 1998* (SI 1998 No.1578) where agreement cannot be reached) (section 202(1)(d));
(j)   under section 200(3) (i.e. where a decision is made that the conditions for referral are not met and so the notifying housing authority owe the sec-

tion 193 main housing duty) or a decision under section 200(4) (i.e. a decision that the conditions for referral to a notified authority in Wales are met and the notified authority owe the section 193 main housing duty) (section 202(1)(e));

(k)   as to the suitability of accommodation offered to the applicant under any of the provisions in paragraph (b) or (j) above or the suitability of accommodation offered under section 193(7) in relation to allocations under Part 6 [section 202(1)(f)]. Applicants can request a review of the suitability of accommodation whether or not they have accepted the offer (section 202(1B));

(l)   as to the suitability of accommodation offered to the applicant by way of a private rented sector offer under section 193 (section 202(1)(g)); or,

(m)   as to the suitability of accommodation offered to the applicant by way of a final accommodation offer or a final Part 6 offer under section 193A or 193C (section 202(1)(h)). Applicants can request a review of the suitability of accommodation whether or not they have accepted the offer.

19.4   An applicant must request a review before the end of the period of 21 days beginning with the day on which they are notified of the housing authority's decision. The housing authority may specify, in writing, a longer period during which a review may be requested.

19.5   In reviewing a decision, housing authorities will need to have regard to any information relevant to the period before the decision was made (even if only obtained afterwards) as well as any new relevant information obtained since the decision.

19.6   In the case of (i) above (a decision on whether the conditions are met for the referral of the applicant's case to another housing authority) the request for a review must be made to the notifying authority.

19.7   There is no right to request a review of a decision reached on an earlier review.

The Review Procedures Regulations

19.8   **The Allocation of Housing and Homelessness (Review Procedures) Regulations 1999 (SI 1999 No.71) have been revoked and replaced by The Homelessness (Review Procedure etc.) Regulations 2018.** These regulations set out the procedures to be followed by housing authorities in carrying out reviews under Part 7.

Who may carry out the review

19.9   A review may be carried out by the housing authority itself which made the original decision or by someone acting as an agent of the housing authority. For further guidance on contracting out homelessness functions see Chapter 5.

Where the review is to be carried out by an officer of the housing authority, the officer must not have been involved in the original decision, and they must be senior to the officer (or officers) who took that decision. Seniority for these purposes means seniority in rank or grade within the housing authority's organisational structure. The seniority provision does not apply where a committee or sub-committee of elected members took the original decision.

19.10   The same officer is able to carry out multiple reviews relating to a single case as long as they were not involved in the original decisions.

19.11   Where the decision under review is a joint decision by a notifying housing authority and the notified housing authority as to whether the conditions of referral of a case are satisfied, section 202(4) requires that the review should be carried out jointly by the two housing authorities.

19.12   Where the decision under review was taken by a person appointed by the notifying and notified authority, the review of that decision must also be carried out by a person appointed by the two authorities (see paragraph 19.25).

Written representations

19.13   An applicant is not required to provide grounds or reasons for challenging the housing authority's decision in their request for review, but should be invited to do so.

The purpose of this is to invite the applicant to state their grounds for requesting a review (if they have not already done so) and to elicit any new information and particular issues that the applicant may have in relation to their request for a review.

19.14 Regulation 5 requires the housing authority to notify the applicant that they, or someone acting on their behalf, may make written representations in connection with the request for a review.

19.15 Regulation 5 also provides that the housing authority must notify the applicant that if they chose to make written representations where the request for review relates to:

(a) the steps the housing authority is to take under sections 195(2) and 189B(2) which includes having regard to their assessment of the applicants' case in the personalised housing plan (during the prevention or relief duty) (section 202(1)(ba)(i) or (bc)(i)); or,

(b) a notice bringing the prevention duty to an end (including where the reason for this is deliberate and unreasonable refusal to co-operate) (section 202(1)(bc)(ii) and (bb));

The representations must be made to the housing authority within two weeks from the day on which the applicant requested the review. The regulations provide that this two week period is open to be extended to a longer period if the applicant and reviewing authority agree in writing.

19.16 Applicants should already have been provided with copies of their assessments and personalised housing plan which they will be able to share with any legal representatives. Housing authorities should provide further copies or any further information requested as quickly as possible to minimise delays.

19.17 Where the request for a review falls outside of the decisions listed under 19.15, written representations should be made within a reasonable period to allow sufficient time for the housing authority to respond to the review within the prescribed timeframe (see paragraph 19.23).

19.18 The housing authority must also notify the applicant of the procedure to be followed in connection with the review (if this information has not been provided earlier).

19.19 Regulation 5 also provides that:

(a) where the original decision was made jointly by the notifying and notified housing authorities under section 198(5), the notification should be made by the notifying housing authority; and,

(b) where the original decision was made by a person appointed in accordance to the *Homelessness (Decisions on Referrals) Order 1998* (SI 1998 No.1578), the notification should be made by the person appointed to carry out the review.

Oral hearings

19.20 Regulation 7 provides that in cases where a review has been requested, if the housing authority, authorities or person carrying out the review consider that there is a deficiency or irregularity in the original decision, or in the manner in which it was made, but they are minded nonetheless to make a decision that is against the applicant's interests on one or more issues, they should notify the applicant:

(a) that they are so minded and the reasons why; and,

(b) that the applicant, or someone acting on their behalf, may, within a reasonable period, make oral representations, further written representations, or both oral and written representations.

19.21 Such deficiencies or irregularities would include:

(a) failure to take into account relevant considerations and to ignore irrelevant ones;

(b) failure to base the decision on the facts;

(c) bad faith or dishonesty;

(d)   mistake of law;
(e)   decisions that run contrary to the policy of Part 7 of the 1996 Act;
(f)   irrationality or unreasonableness; or,
(g)   procedural unfairness, e.g. where an applicant has not been given a chance to comment on matters relevant to a decision.

19.22   The reviewer must consider whether there is 'something lacking' in the decision, i.e. were any significant issues not addressed or addressed inadequately, which could have led to unfairness. An original decision could subsequently be rendered deficient because of intervening events which occurred between the date of the original decision and the review decision.

Period during which review must be completed

19.23   Regulation 9 provides that the period within which the applicant (or the applicant's authorised agent) must be notified of the decision on a review is:

(a)   three weeks from the day of the request for a review, or three weeks from the day on which representations are received, where the original decision falls within section 202(1)(ba)(i), (bc), or section 202(1) (bb) and the effect of the notice is to bring the prevention duty to an end;
(b)   eight weeks from the day of the request for a review, where the original decision falls within section 202(1)(a), (b), (ba)(ii), (c), (d), (e), (f), (g), or section 202(1)(bb) and the effect of the notice is to bring the relief duty to an end;
(c)   ten weeks, where the original decision falls within section 202(1)(d) and was made jointly by two housing authorities under section 198(5) (a decision on whether the conditions for referral are met);
(d)   twelve weeks, where the original decision falls within section 202(1)(d) and it was taken by a person appointed by the notifying authority and the notified authority in accordance with the Schedule to the *Homelessness (Decisions on Referrals) Order* (SI 1998 No.1578).

The regulations provide that in all of these cases it is open to the reviewing authority to seek the applicant's agreement to an extension of the prescribed period. Any such agreement must be given in writing.

Late representations

19.24   The regulations require the reviewer(s) to consider any written representations received subject to compliance with the requirement to notify the applicant of the decision on review within the period of the review, i.e. the period prescribed in the regulations or any extended period agreed in writing between the applicant and housing authority. It may in some circumstances be necessary to make further enquiries of the applicant about information they have provided. The reviewer(s) should be flexible about allowing such further exchanges, having regard to the time limits for reviews prescribed in the regulations. If this leads to significant delays, the applicant may be approached to agree an extension in the period for the review. Similarly, if an applicant has been invited to make oral representations and this requires additional time to arrange, the applicant should be asked to agree an appropriate extension.

Procedures for reviews of section 198(5) decisions made by an appointed person

19.25   Where the original decision under section 198(5) was made by a person appointed in accordance with the Schedule to the *Homelessness (Decisions on Referrals) Order 1998* (SI 1998 No.1578), regulation 6 requires that a review must be carried out by a person appointed by the notifying authority and the notified authority. If the authorities are unable to reach agreement on an appointed person, and where the review is of the original decision on whether the conditions for referral of a case under section 198(1) are met, the review must be carried out by a person appointed from the panel by the chair of the Local Government Association (LGA), or their nominee.

19.26   The appointed person must not be the same person as the person who made the original decision and they must comply with the relevant procedures set out in the regulations. Specifically, they must invite written representations from the applicant and send copies of these to the two housing authorities, inviting them to respond. The reviewer is also required to notify in writing the two housing authorities of their decision on review and the reasons for it at least a week before the end of the prescribed period of twelve weeks (or of any extended period agreed with the applicant). This allows the housing authorities adequate time to notify the applicant of the decision before expiry of the period.

19.27 Paragraphs (2) – (4) of regulation 6 set out the procedure to be followed when the notifying and notified authority are unable to appoint a person to carry out a review by agreement. These provisions currently apply to decisions on notifications under section 198(1) at the point of the main housing duty. However local authorities are encouraged to also follow these arrangements in relation to the review of decisions on notifications under section 198(A1).

19.28 Paragraphs (2) – (4) of regulation 6 set out that if the two housing authorities fail to appoint a person to carry out the review within five working days of the date of the request for a review, the notifying housing authority must request the chair of the LGA or their nominee to appoint a person from the panel. The chair, in turn, must within seven days of that request appoint a person from the panel to undertake the review. The housing authorities are required to provide the reviewer with the reasons for the original decision, and the information on which that decision is based, within five working days of their appointment.

Notification of decision on review

19.29 Section 203 requires a housing authority to notify the applicant in writing of their decision on the review. The authority must also notify the applicant of the reasons for their decision where it:

(a) confirms the original decision on any issue against the interests of the applicant;
(b) confirms a previous decision to notify another housing authority under section 198(1) (referral of case under the main housing duty); or,
(c) confirms a previous decision that the conditions for referral in section 198 (referral of case under the relief duty or main housing duty) are met in the applicant's case.

19.30 Where the review is carried out jointly by two housing authorities under section 198(5), or by a person appointed in accordance to the *Homelessness (Decisions on Referrals) Order 1998* (SI 1998 No.1578), the notification may be made by either of the two housing authorities concerned.

19.31 At this stage, the housing authority making the notification must advise the applicant of their right to appeal to the County Court under section 204 against a review decision on a point of law, and of the period in which to appeal.

Powers to accommodate pending a review

19.32 Under section 188(2A), where an applicant refuses a final accommodation offer or a final Part 6 offer in the relief stage and requests a review under section 202(1)(h) of the housing authority's decision as to the suitability of the accommodation offered, the relief duty to the applicant continues to apply despite section 193A(2), and the housing authority must continue to provide interim accommodation for applicants in priority need until the decision on the review has been notified to the applicant.

19.33 Sections 188(3), 199A (6) and 200(5) give housing authorities powers to secure accommodation for certain applicants pending the decision on a review. For further guidance on powers to secure accommodation see Chapter 15.

Prevention and relief activity following a review decision

19.34 In circumstances where the outcome of one of the following decisions are in the applicants favour, review officers are recommended to use their discretion to assess the impact of the failure across the whole period of the relevant duty and make recommendations which seek to remedy this:

(a)   the decision on reasonable steps in the personalised housing plan; or,
(b)   the decision to issue a notice bringing the prevention or relief duties to an end.

19.35   For example, if an applicant's personalised housing plan was completed 3 days after the start of the prevention or relief duty and a review found that steps were unreasonable, the review officer may recommend that the authority work with the applicant to agree new steps and resume prevention or relief activity for a further 53 days.

19.36   Where an applicant requests a review of the authority's decision as to whether the conditions are met for the referral of their case to another housing authority at the relief stage the relief duty will rest with the notified authority whilst the review is conducted. If the review officer decides that the conditions for referral were not met and that the applicant should not have been referred to another housing authority, they are encouraged to make recommendations based on the following considerations:

(a)   the reasonable wishes of the applicant;
(b)   the relief activity that has taken place to date by both or either authorities;
(c)   how relevant this activity is in the geographical context of the notifying authority given the successful review decision; and,
(d)   whether the applicant is in priority need and therefore if they should directly proceed to the main duty after the 56 day period.

Appeals to the County Court

19.37   Section 204 provides an applicant who has requested a section 202 review with the right of appeal on a point of law to the County Court if:

(a)   they are dissatisfied with the decision on a review; or,
(b)   they are not notified of the decision on the review within the time prescribed in regulations made under section 203.

19.38   An appeal must be brought by an applicant within 21 days of:

(a)   the date on which they are notified of the decision on review; or,
(b)   the date on which they should have been notified (i.e. the date marking the end of the period for the review prescribed in the regulations, or any extended period agreed in writing by the applicant).

19.39   The court may give permission for an appeal to be brought after 21 days, but only where it is satisfied that:

(a)   (where permission is sought within the 21 day period), there is good reason for the applicant to be unable to bring the appeal in time; or,
(b)   (where permission is sought after the 21 day period has expired), there was a good reason for the applicant's failure to bring the appeal in time and for any delay in applying for permission.

19.40   On an appeal, the County Court is empowered to make an order confirming, quashing or varying the housing authority's decision as it thinks fit. It is important, therefore, that housing authorities have in place review procedures that are robust, fair, and transparent.

Power to accommodate pending an appeal to the County Court

19.41   Section 204(4) gives housing authorities the power to accommodate certain applicants during the period for making an appeal, and pending determination of the appeal and any subsequent appeal. For further guidance on powers to secure accommodation see Chapter 15.

Local Government and Social Care Ombudsman

19.42   Applicants may complain to the Local Government and Social Care Ombudsman if they consider that they have been caused injustice as a result of maladministration in relation to their application for assistance under Part 7 by a housing authority. The Ombudsman may investigate the way a decision has been made, but may not question the merits of a decision properly reached. For example, maladministration would occur where a housing authority:

(a)   took too long to do something;
(b)   did not follow their own rules or the law;
(c)   broke their promises;
(d)   treated the applicant unfairly; or,
(e)   gave the applicant the wrong information.

19.43   There are some matters an Ombudsman cannot investigate. These include:

(a)   matters the applicant knew about more than twelve months before they wrote to the Ombudsman or to a councillor, unless the Ombudsman considers it reasonable to investigate despite the delay;
(b)   matters about which the applicant has already taken court action against the housing authority, for example, an appeal to the County Court under section 204; and,
(c)   matters about which the applicant could go to court, unless the Ombudsman considers there are good reasons why the applicant could not reasonably be expected to do so.

19.44   Where there is a right of review, and/or a complaints procedure within the housing authority, the Ombudsman would expect an applicant to pursue their rights through these arrangements before making a complaint. If there is any doubt about whether the Ombudsman can look into a complaint, the applicant should seek advice from the Ombudsman's office.

CHAPTER 20: PROTECTION OF PERSONAL PROPERTY

20.1   This chapter provides guidance on the duty and powers housing authorities have to protect the personal property of an applicant.

20.2   Under section 211(1) and (2), where a housing authority has become subject to a duty to an applicant under specified provisions of Part 7 and it has reason to believe that:

(a)   there is a danger of loss of, or damage to, the applicant's personal property;
(b)   because the applicant is unable to protect it or deal with it; and,
(c)   no other suitable arrangements have been, or are being, made,

then, whether or not the housing authority is still subject to such a duty, it must take reasonable steps to prevent the loss of, or to prevent or mitigate damage to, any personal property of the applicant.

20.3   The specified provisions are:

(a)   section 188 (interim duty to accommodate);
(b)   section 189B (initial duty owed to all eligible persons who are homeless); and,
(c)   section 190, section 193 or section 195 (duties to persons found to be homeless or threatened with homelessness); or section 200 (duties to an applicant whose case is considered for referral or is referred).

20.4   In all other circumstances, housing authorities have a power to take any steps they consider reasonable to protect in the same way, an applicant's personal property (section 211(3)).

20.5   Section 212 makes provisions supplementing section 211. For the purposes of both section 211 and section 212, the personal property of an applicant includes the personal property of any person who might reasonably be expected to reside with them (section 211(5)) and section 212(6)).

20.6   A danger of loss or damage to personal property means that there is a likelihood of harm, not just that harm is a possibility. Applicants may be unable to protect their property if, for example, they are ill or are unable to afford to have it stored themselves.

20.7   Under section 212(1), in order to protect an applicant's personal property, a housing authority can enter, at all reasonable times, the applicant's current or former home, and deal with the property in any way which seems reasonably necessary.

20.8   Where a housing authority does take steps to protect personal property it must take reasonable care of it and deliver it to the owner when reasonably requested to do so. Housing authorities may find it helpful to take a log of the applicant's personal property as part of this process.

20.9   The applicant can request the housing authority to move their property to a particular location. If the housing authority considers that the request is reasonable, they may discharge their responsibilities under section 211 by doing as the applicant asks. Where such a request is met, the housing authority will have no further duty or power to protect the applicant's property, and it must inform the applicant of this consequence before complying with the request (section 212(2)).

20.10   Housing authorities may impose conditions on the assistance they provide (section 211(4)). Conditions may include making a reasonable charge for storage of property and reserving the right to dispose of property in certain circumstances specified by the housing authority – e.g. if the applicant loses touch with them and cannot be traced after a certain period (section 211(4)).

20.11   Where a request to move personal property to another location is either not made or not carried out, the duty or power to take any action under section 211 ends when the housing authority believes there is no longer any danger of loss or damage to the property because of the applicant's inability to deal with or protect it (section 212(3)). This may be the case, for example, where an applicant recovers from illness or finds accommodation where they are able to place their possessions, or becomes able to afford the storage costs themselves. However, where the housing authority has discharged the duty under section 211 by placing property in storage, it has a discretionary power to continue to keep the property in storage. Where it does so, any conditions imposed by the housing authority continue to apply and may be modified as necessary.

20.12   Where the housing authority ceases to be under a duty, or ceases to have a power, to protect an applicant's personal property under section 211, it must notify the applicant of this and give the reasons for it. The notification must be delivered to the applicant or sent to the applicant's last known address (section 212(5)). For further guidance on notifications see Chapter 18.

CHAPTER 21: DOMESTIC ABUSE

21.1   This chapter provides guidance on providing homelessness services to people who have experienced domestic violence or abuse, or are at risk of domestic violence or abuse.

Understanding domestic violence and abuse

21.2   Domestic violence or abuse is 'domestic' in nature if the perpetrator is a person who is associated with the victim. It is not limited to physical violence or confined to instances within the home.

21.3   Housing authorities must take account of the cross-government definition of domestic violence and abuse when designing and delivering services. This defines domestic violence and abuse as:

21.4   Any incident or pattern of incidents of controlling, coercive, threatening behaviour, violence or abuse between those aged 16 or over who are, or have been, intimate partners or family members regardless of gender. The abuse can encompass, but is not limited to:

(a)   **psychological** - including: intimidation, insults, isolating the person from friends and family, criticising, denying the abuse, treating the person as inferior, threatening to harm children or take them away, forced marriage;

(b)   physical - this can include: shaking, smacking, punching, kicking, presence of finger or bite marks, bruising, starving, tying up, stabbing, suffocation, throwing things, using objects as weapons, female genital mutilation. Physical effects are often in areas of the body that are covered and hidden (i.e. breasts, legs and stomach);

(c)   sexual – including rape (including the threat of rape), sexual assault, forced prostitution, ignoring religious prohibitions about sex, refusal to practise safe sex, sexual insults, passing on sexually transmitted diseases, preventing breast-feeding;

(d)   financial - not letting the person work, undermining efforts to find work or study, refusing to give money, asking for an explanation of how every penny is spent, making the person beg for money, gambling, not paying bills, building up debt in the other person's name;

(e)   emotional -- including: swearing, undermining confidence, making racist, sexist or other derogatory remarks, making the person feel unattractive, calling the person stupid or useless, eroding the person's independence, keeping them isolated from family or friends.

21.5   Controlling behaviour is a range of acts designed to make a person subordinate and/or dependent by isolating them from sources of support, exploiting their resources and capacities for personal gain, depriving them of the means needed for independence, resistance and escape and regulating their everyday behaviour.

21.6   Coercive behaviour is an act or a pattern of acts of assault, threats, humiliation and intimidation or other abuse that is used to harm, punish, or frighten their victim.

21.7   So-called honour-based abuse is also a form of domestic abuse, explained by the perpetrator of the abuse on the grounds that it was committed as a consequence of the need to protect or defend the honour of the family; it can include all the types of abuse listed above and specific crimes such as forced marriage and female genital mutilation.

21.8   Domestic violence and abuse can affect anyone regardless of their age, gender identity or reassignment, race, religion, class, sexual orientation and marital status. Housing authorities should bear in mind that the provisions of the Equality Act 2010 for public authorities apply to policies, practice and procedures relating to homelessness and domestic violence and abuse.

21.9   An important factor in ensuring that an authority develops a strong and appropriate response to domestic abuse is understanding what domestic abuse is, the context in which it takes place in and the impacts are on victims; as well as how the impacts may be different on different groups of people. Specialist training for staff and managers will help them to provide a more sensitive response and to identify, with applicants, housing options which are safe and appropriate to their needs.

Identifying abuse and preventing homelessness

21.10   Housing authorities should have policies in place to identify and respond to domestic abuse. Alongside their role in tackling homelessness authorities should take an active role in identifying victims and referring them for help and support. They are key partners in local domestic violence partnerships and should be represented at their local multi-agency risk assessment conference (MARAC).

21.11   The MARAC leads multi-agency safety planning for high-risk victims of domestic abuse. It brings together the police, independent domestic violence advisers, children's social services, health, social landlords and other relevant agencies. They share information and write a safety plan for each victim and family, which may include actions by any agency present. The housing authority should be consistently represented at the MARAC and encourage relevant social landlords to also be represented.

21.12   Victims can experience many incidents of abuse before calling the police or reporting it to another agency. Housing providers may be able to identify abuse at earlier stages and should consider how they can best provide support to their residents. By understanding the indicators of domestic abuse through training and professional development, housing officers can increase their confidence to speak to people experiencing abuse, risk assess and safety plan alongside them.

21.13   Housing authorities should also be alert to the wider role they play in ensuring victim safety. Procedures should be in place to keep all information on victims safe and secure. In many cases, particularly where extended family members or multiple perpetrators may be involved, for example in female genital mutilation, forced marriage and so called honour based violence cases, perpetrators go to great lengths to seek information on victims.

21.14 The housing authority must be alert to the possibility of employees being, or having links to, perpetrators. Housing authorities should not disclose information about an applicant to anybody outside the organisation without consent, and should be particularly alert to the need to maintain confidentiality wherever domestic abuse is involved. In some circumstances, it may be necessary to restrict access to cases where abuse is disclosed to only named members of staff. Housing authorities should also consider how they flag case files so they can identify those victims who have been referred to the MARAC and may present as homeless.

21.15 Households at risk of domestic abuse often have to leave their homes and the area where they have lived. There is a clear need for victims of abuse and their children to be able to travel to different areas in order for them to be safe from the perpetrator, and housing authorities should extend the same level of support to those from other areas as they do to their own residents.

Duties to those homeless or threatened with homelessness

21.16 Section 177(1) of the 1996 Act provides that it is not reasonable for a person to continue to occupy accommodation if it is probable that this will lead to domestic violence or other violence against:

(a)   the applicant;
(b)   a person who normally resides as a member of the applicant's family; or,
(c)   any other person who might reasonably be expected to reside with the applicant.

21.17 Section 177(1A) provides that 'violence' means violence from another person or threats of violence from another person which are likely to be carried out. 'Domestic violence' is violence or threats of violence which are likely to be carried out by a person who is associated with the victim. Domestic violence is not confined to instances within the home.

21.18 In the context of defining domestic violence, section 178 provides that, for the purposes of Part 7 of the 1996 Act, a person is associated with another if:

(a)   they are, or have been, married to each other;
(b)   they are or have been civil partners of each other;
(c)   they are, or have been, cohabitants;
(d)   they live, or have lived, in the same household;
(e)   they are relatives, i.e. father, mother, stepfather, stepmother, son, daughter, stepson, stepdaughter, grandmother, grandfather, grandson, granddaughter, brother, sister, uncle, aunt, niece or nephew (whether of full blood, or of half blood or by marriage or civil partnership) of that person or of that person's spouse or former spouse. A person is also included if they would fall into any of these categories in relation to cohabitees or former cohabitees if they were married to each other;
(f)   they have agreed to marry each other, whether or not that agreement has been terminated;
(g)   they have entered into a civil partnership agreement between them, whether or not that agreement has been terminated;
(h)   in relation to a child, each of them is a parent of the child or has, or has had, parental responsibility for the child (within the meaning of the Children Act 1989). A child is a person under 18 years of age;
(i)   if a child has been adopted or 'freed for adoption' (section 18 of the Adoption Act 1976), two persons are also associated if one is the natural parent or grandparent of the child and the other is the child or a person who has become the parent by virtue of an 'adoption order' (section 72(1), Adoption Act 1976) or has applied for an adoption order or someone with whom the child has at any time been placed for adoption.

21.19 The term 'violence' should not be given a restrictive meaning, and 'domestic violence' should be understood to include physical violence, threatening or intimidating behaviour, and any other form of abuse which directly or indirectly may give rise to harm; between persons who are, or have been, intimate partners, family members or members of the same household, regardless of gender identity or sexual orientation.

21.20 An assessment of the likelihood of a threat of violence or abuse being carried out should not be based on whether there has been actual violence or abuse in the past. Assessments must be based on the facts of the case and should be devoid of any value judgements about what an applicant should or should not do, or should or should not have done, to mitigate the risk of any violence and abuse.

21.21 It is essential that inquiries do not provoke further violence and abuse. Housing authorities **should not approach the alleged perpetrator**, since this could generate further violence and abuse. Housing authorities may, however, wish to seek information from friends and relatives of the applicant, social services, health professionals, MARACs, a domestic abuse support service or the police, as appropriate. This is not an exhaustive list and there may be other sources of evidence that would be appropriate. In some cases, corroborative evidence of actual or threatened violence may not be available, for example, because there were no adult witnesses and/or the applicant was too frightened or ashamed to report incidents to family, friend or the police. Housing authorities should not have a blanket approach toward domestic abuse which requires corroborative or police evidence to be provided.

21.22 There may be occasions where victims of abuse seek emergency assistance having left behind ID and other documentation that may be required to support their application. Housing authorities should work with police; domestic abuse agencies (as appropriate) and the applicant to ensure that essential documentation can be recovered or replaced without putting the applicant at further risk of abuse.

21.23 In many cases involving violence and abuse, the applicant may be in considerable distress and an officer trained in dealing with the particular circumstances should conduct the interview. Applicants should be given the option of being interviewed by an officer of the same sex if they so wish. Housing authorities should be aware that this may be the first time a victim has disclosed their abuse and that the period during which a victim is planning or making their exit, is often the **most dangerous time** for them and any children they have.

21.24 The following services are among those subject to the duty to refer, meaning they are required to refer service users in England they consider may be homeless or threatened with homelessness within 56 days to a housing authority, with the service user's consent:

(a)   emergency departments;
(b)   urgent treatment centres;
(c)   hospitals in their function of providing in patient care; and,
(d)   adults and children's social care services.

For further guidance on the duty to refer see Chapter 4.

Prevention and relief duties

21.25 Following an application for assistance under Part 7 of the 1996 Act, whether an applicant is threatened with homelessness or is actually homeless will be a matter for the housing authority to assess taking into account all of the relevant circumstances. For example, a person at risk of domestic violence or abuse may be threatened with homelessness because a perpetrator is soon to be released from custody (and so the person is likely to become homeless within 56 days); but would be actually homeless if the perpetrator was in the community and presented a risk to them at their home (and so it is not reasonable for the person to continue to occupy the accommodation).

21.26 When developing a personalised housing plan the housing authority should be particularly sensitive to an applicant's wishes and respectful of their judgement about the risk of abuse, unless there is evidence to the contrary. For further guidance on assessments and personalised housing plans see Chapter 11. Victims should be allowed sufficient time and space to absorb and understand the options available to them.

21.27 The reasonable steps that a housing authority might take to help an applicant to retain or secure safe accommodation might include provision of sanctuary scheme or other security measures, assistance to find alternative accommodation, or help to access legal remedies such as injunctions where these might be effective. Single people might also be assisted to access supported housing, or helped to gain more support from family and friends through the intervention of the housing authority.

21.28 Sanctuary schemes can prevent homelessness by enabling victims to remain safely in their home where it is their choice, and it is safe to do so. A sanctuary comprises enhanced security measures in the home which delay or prevent a perpetrator from gaining entry into and within a property, and allow time for the police to arrive. Use of sanctuary is not appropriate if the perpetrator lives at, or retains a legal right to enter the home, or if the victim continues to be at risk in the vicinity around the home.

21.29 Housing authorities may wish to inform applicants of the option of seeking an injunction against the perpetrator. Where applicants wish to pursue this option, authorities should inform them that they should seek legal advice and that they may be eligible for legal aid.

21.30 Housing authorities should recognise that injunctions ordering a person not to molest (non-molestation orders), or not to live in the home or enter the surrounding area (occupation orders) may not be effective in deterring some perpetrators from carrying out further violence, abuse or incursions, and applicants may not have confidence in their effectiveness. Consequently, applicants should not be expected to return home on the strength of an injunction. To ensure applicants who have experienced actual or threatened violence get the support they need, authorities should inform them of appropriate specialist organisations in the area as well as agencies offering counselling and support.

21.31 When dealing with domestic violence and abuse within the home, where the authority is the landlord, housing authorities should consider the scope for evicting the perpetrator and allowing the victim to remain in their home. However, where there would be a probability of violence if the applicant continued to occupy their present accommodation, the housing authority must treat the applicant as homeless and should not expect them to remain in, or return to, the accommodation. **In all cases involving violence the safety of the applicant and their household should be the primary consideration at all stages of decision making as to whether or not the applicant remains in their own home.**

Assessing priority need

21.32 A person has a priority need if they are vulnerable as a result of having to leave accommodation because of violence from another person, or threats of violence from another person that are likely to be carried out. (Article 6, *Homelessness (Priority Need for Accommodation) (England) Order 2002*).

21.33 It is not only domestic violence and abuse that is relevant, but all forms of violence, including racially motivated violence or threats of violence likely to be carried out. In assessing whether it is likely that threats of violence are likely to be carried out, a housing authority should only take into account the probability of violence, and not actions which the applicant could take (such as injunctions against the perpetrators).

21.34 In considering whether applicants are vulnerable as a result of leaving accommodation because of violence or threats of violence likely to be carried out, a housing authority may wish to take into account the following factors:

(a)   the nature of the violence or threats of violence (there may have been a single but significant incident or a number of incidents over an extended period of time which have had a cumulative effect);

(b)   the impact and likely effects of the violence or threats of violence on the applicant's current and future wellbeing;

    (i)   whether the applicant has any existing support networks, particularly by way of family or friends; and,

(ii)   the continuing threat from the perpetrator.

For further guidance on priority need see Chapter 8.

Providing suitable accommodation

21.35   There are a number of accommodation options for victims of domestic abuse, and housing authorities will need to consider which are most appropriate for each person on a case by case basis taking into account their circumstances and needs. This may include safe temporary accommodation and/or a managed transfer. Housing authorities may, for example, provide temporary accommodation whilst action is taken to exclude or to arrest and detain a perpetrator. Opportunities to plan for victims to remain or return to their homes are much improved by housing authorities working with partners in the MARAC o reduce risk.

21.36   For victims at risk from highly dangerous perpetrators, refuges will usually be the most appropriate choice. Refuges provide key short term, intensive support for those who flee from abuse. Given the intensity of the support and the vulnerability of the victims, attention should be paid to the length of time they spend in a refuge. Refuges are not simply a substitute for other forms of temporary accommodation. The housing authority should work with the refuge provider to consider how long a person needs to stay before the provision of other accommodation (which may be temporary in the absence of settled accommodation) may be more appropriate, potentially with floating support if needed.

21.37   Account will need to be taken of any social considerations relating to the applicant and their household that might affect the suitability of accommodation offered to them to prevent or relieve homelessness, or under the main housing duty. Any risk of violence or racial harassment in a particular locality should be taken into account. Where domestic violence is involved and the applicant is not able to stay in the current home, housing authorities may need to consider the need for accommodation that would not be found by the perpetrator (which may involve an out of district placement) and which has security measures and appropriately trained staff to protect the occupants. Housing authorities may consider implementing a reciprocal agreement with other housing authorities and providers to facilitate out of area moves for victims of domestic violence and abuse.

Local connection referrals

21.38   A housing authority cannot refer an applicant to another housing authority where they have a local connection if that person or any person who might reasonably be expected to reside with them would be at risk of violence and abuse in that other district. The housing authority is under a positive duty to enquire whether the applicant would be at such a risk and, if they would, it should not be assumed that the applicant will take steps to deal with the threat. For further guidance on local connection see Chapter 10.

21.39   Section 198(3) defines violence as violence from another person or threats of violence from another person which are likely to be carried out. Housing authorities should be alert to the deliberate distinction which is made in section 198(3) between actual violence and threatened violence. A high standard of proof of actual violence in the past should not be imposed. The threshold is that there must be:

(a)   no risk of domestic violence (actual or threatened) in the other district; and,
(b)   no risk of non-domestic violence (actual or threatened) in the other district. Nor should 'domestic violence' be interpreted restrictively.

Eligibility

21.40   People who have no recourse to public funds are not generally eligible for homelessness assistance. However, the Destitute Domestic Violence Concession supports those who have entered or stayed in the UK as a spouse, unmarried partner, same-sex or civil partner of a British Citizen, or settled citizen and this relationship has permanently broken down due to domestic violence and abuse. A victim may be eligible if:

(a)   they came to the UK or were granted leave to stay in the UK as the spouse or partner of a British Citizen or someone settled in the UK;

(b)   their relationship has permanently broken down due to domestic violence and abuse.

21.41   They can then apply to the Home Office for limited leave to remain (three months) under the Destitute Domestic Violence Concession to enable them to access public funds and advice, whilst they prepare and submit an application for indefinite leave to remain (or to make alternative arrangements).

CHAPTER 22: CARE LEAVERS

22.1   This chapter provides guidance on specific duties towards care leavers who are homeless or threatened with homelessness. It covers:

(a)   corporate parenting duties placed on housing authorities;

(b)   joint working arrangements between housing authorities and children's services authorities;

(c)   prevention and relief of homelessness;

(d)   assessing whether or not a care leaver has a priority need for accommodation; and,

(e)   the provision of suitable accommodation.

Corporate parenting duties

22.2   Local authorities have duties and powers to assist young people who are leaving and have left local authority care. As a corporate parent to all children in care and care leavers all parts of a local authority, including a housing authority, must have regard to the need:

(a)   to act in the best interests, and promote the physical and mental health and well-being, of those children and young people;

(b)   to encourage those children and young people to express their views, wishes and feelings;

(c)   to take into account the views, wishes and feelings of those children and young people;

(d)   to help those children and young people gain access to, and make the best use of, services provided by the local authority and its relevant partners;

(e)   to promote high aspirations, and seek to secure the best outcomes, for those children and young people;

(f)   for those children and young people to be safe, and for stability in their home lives, relationships and education or work; and,

(g)   to prepare those children and young people for adulthood and independent living.

Children and Social Work Act 2017 (Part 1, (1(a-g))

22.3   There is a duty on children's services authorities to appoint a Personal Adviser to provide support to care leavers until they reach their 25th birthday (except where the young person no longer wants a Personal Adviser) (Part 1(3), Children and Social Work Act 2017). The support provided by Personal Advisers should be based on the needs of the young person as set out in their statutory Pathway Plan. This may include support from a housing authority.

22.4   Any joint working arrangements between a children's services authority and a housing authority for care leavers' transition to independent living should include ensuring the delivery of effective preparation for independence with planned, sustainable moves into supported or independent accommodation. Local processes and/or practices should not involve care leavers routinely being treated as homeless when care placements come to an end in order to place the housing authority under an obligation to secure accommodation under Part 7 of the 1996 Act.

Joint working arrangements

22.5 The Secretary of State for Ministry of Housing, Communities and Local Government and the Secretary of State for Education consider that all young people leaving care should have safe and appropriate accommodation to meet their needs. By working together, housing authorities and children's services authorities can better ensure that as a corporate parent, the appropriate accommodation and support is available to care leavers.

22.6 Housing authorities, children's services authorities and other relevant departments within local authorities, are advised to develop joint protocols or procedures to ensure that each department plays a full role in providing corporate parenting support to young people leaving care. In two tier areas all housing authorities in the county should be party to these arrangements.

22.7 A joint protocol should cover arrangements for achieving planned, supportive transitions to independent living; identifying homelessness risk early and acting to prevent it, and providing a quick, safe, joined up response for care leavers who do become homeless.

Advice and information

22.8 Advisory services provided by housing authorities' under section 179 must be designed to meet the needs of care leavers in their district (section 179(2)(b)). For further guidance on the provision of advice and information on homelessness see Chapter 3. Housing authorities should work with children's services authorities and consult with care leavers themselves to ensure the advice and information is:

(a)   designed and delivered in an appropriate format for the age of the client group;
(b)   available through communication channels which care leavers are most likely to access;
(c)   understood by children's services authority staff.

22.9 It is recommended that housing options advice be made available to young people preparing to leave care to help them to make informed choices and avoid becoming homeless. Housing authorities may wish to provide training and information to social workers, Personal Advisers and others who have responsibility to support looked after young people, to ensure that the most up to date and accurate information on housing options is available to them.

Prevention and relief of homelessness

22.10 There is a duty on specified public bodies to refer to a housing authority (with consent) any household which is threatened with homelessness or is homeless within 56 days to a housing authority with the service user's consent (section 213B). The following services are among those subject to the duty to refer:

(a)   social service authorities; and,
(b)   custodial institutions, youth offending teams and probation services.

22.11 For further guidance on duty to refer see Chapter 4. Specific referral arrangements should be made for care leavers and set out in the joint protocol or procedures.

22.12 When a young person aged between 18 and 24 approaches directly or is referred to a housing authority, if it is known that they are a care leaver or the young person says they are a care leaver, then the children's services authority which has responsibility for them should be informed as soon as possible, with consent from the young person.

22.13 Where there is a duty to assess a care leaver's housing and other support needs and develop a personalised housing plan, arrangements should be in place to enable the Personal Adviser to be involved in the assessment process with the young person's consent. For further guidance on assessments and personalised housing plans see Chapter 11. Where there is no agreed local working arrangement, or where the young person has been looked after by a children's services authority which is not part of local joint protocol arrangements, the housing authority must continue without delay with the duties owed to the young person under Part 7 of the 1996 Act.

22.14 Where a care leaver has a personalised housing plan this should be informed, by their Pathway Plan (section 23C(3)(b), Children Act 1989). The Secretary of State for Ministry of Housing, Communities and Local Government considers it appropriate for housing authorities to involve a young person's Personal Adviser in assessing their needs and circumstances and developing a personalised housing plan that is appropriate to them. The young person's consent must be obtained, and it would be advisable to seek their consent for the Personal Adviser to continue to be informed and involved in efforts to prevent or relieve homelessness. The Personal Adviser may also be requested to take actions to deliver the personalised housing plan.

22.15 There are specific legal requirements in relation to local connection for care leavers (section 199(8) to (11). For further guidance on local connection see Chapter 10.

22.16 Subject to arrangements for consent, where a housing authority is concerned that a care leaver may not be co-operating with the required steps set out in the personalised housing plan this should be shared as soon as possible with the Personal Adviser to enable joint early action to remind the young person of the actions to be taken and the consequences of not doing so. For further guidance on deliberate and unreasonable refusal to co-operate see Chapter 14. Joint working to understand mitigating factors and resolve issues should continue throughout any action related to deliberate and unreasonable refusal to co-operate.

22.17 The Secretary of State for Ministry of Housing, Communities and Local Government considers that all attempts should be made by housing authorities to avoid the impact of intentionally homeless decisions in relation to care leavers aged 18 – 25. For further guidance on intentional homelessness see Chapter 9. It will be a matter for the housing authority to determine whether or not a care leaver has become homeless intentionally, taking into account all relevant facts. To inform this assessment, housing authorities should consult with the relevant children's services authority and obtain advice and information as to the young person's emotional and mental well-being, maturity and general ability to understand the impact of their actions.

22.18 The personalised housing plan should be reviewed and, the housing authority and Personal Adviser or other officer should work together with the young person to try and resolve the issues.

22.19 Children's services authorities have a duty to 'former relevant' care leavers in terms of accommodation if there are no other options available and the welfare of the care leaver requires it (section 23C (4c) Children Act 1989).

Assessing priority need

22.20 Section 193 of the 1996 Act requires housing authorities to secure accommodation for applicants who have a priority need, and whose homelessness has not been prevented or relieved.

22.21 Categories and definitions of people who have priority need are set out in Chapter 8, and include young people under 21 who were looked after between the ages of 16 and 18; and people aged 21 or more who are vulnerable as a result of having been looked after, accommodated or fostered. Both of these categories exclude 'relevant students', who are owed particular accommodation and support duties under the Children (Leaving Care) Act. It should be noted that a young person who was looked after when aged 16 or 17 will be in priority need when they are 18, 19 or 20 years old, whether or not they qualify for care leaving services from a children's services authority.

22.22 Guidance on priority need and vulnerability is contained in Chapter 8, and should be taken into account when assessing whether a person aged 21 or over is vulnerable as a result of having been looked after, accommodated or fostered. Factors that a housing authority may wish to consider include:

(a)   the length of time that the applicant was looked after, accommodated or fostered;

(b)   the reasons why they were looked after, accommodated or fostered;
(c)   the length of time since the applicant left care, and whether they have been able to obtain and maintain accommodation during any of that period;
(d)   whether the applicant has any existing support networks, particularly including family, friends or a mentor.

22.23 Housing authorities should take particular care in assessing whether a care leaver aged 21 or over is vulnerable, and should take into account whether, if homeless, they would be at particular risk of exploitation, abuse or involvement in offending behaviour as a result of having been looked after, accommodated or fostered.

Suitable accommodation for care leavers

22.24 Housing authorities and children's services authorities should adopt a shared strategic approach to the provision of suitable accommodation for care leavers.

22.25 In considering suitability, all authorities should bear in mind that care leavers who are homeless will be particularly vulnerable and in need of support. They may lack skills in managing their affairs and require help with managing their own accommodation and operating a household budget. Many care leavers are likely to lack the advice and support normally available to other young people from family, friends and a mentor.

22.26 There should be no blanket presumption that at 18 a young person who has left care will be ready for their own tenancy; this should be a matter of individual assessment. Options will be based on their individual preferences, needs, circumstances and the local provision available and might include, for example, supported lodgings, supported accommodation or independent accommodation with visiting support.

22.27 Bed and breakfast accommodation, including hotels and nightly let accommodation with shared facilities, is not considered suitable for care leavers aged under 25 and should only be used in exceptional circumstances and for short periods.

22.28 The specific needs and circumstances of care leavers should be taken into account in determining suitability of accommodation in relation to its location. For example, in the absence of strong family support networks they may wish to live as near as possible to another significant adult such as a friend or ex-foster carer; or need to avoid certain locations due to childhood experiences or associations.

22.29 Housing authorities may want to involve Personal Advisers in decisions about the suitability of accommodation and inform them prior to making an offer of accommodation, with the young person's consent. For further guidance on suitability of accommodation see Chapter 17.

CHAPTER 23: PEOPLE WITH AN OFFENDING HISTORY

23.1 This chapter provides guidance on providing homelessness services to people with an offending history.

23.2 People with an offending history are over represented amongst single people who are homeless and sleep rough, and a lack of accommodation is likely to have a negative impact on prospects for successful resettlement and rehabilitation. Female offenders often have complex needs which affect their access to suitable and sustainable accommodation on release from custody.

23.3 Housing authorities will need to work in collaboration with HM Prisons providers of probation services (National Probation Service (NPS) and Community Rehabilitation Companies (CRCs)), Youth Offending Services, as well as other relevant partners to prevent people leaving custody, or living in the community, from becoming homeless. The duty to refer introduced through the 2017 Act provides an impetus to develop effective referral arrangements and accommodation pathways that involve all relevant agencies to provide appropriate jointly planned help and support to prevent homelessness.

23.4 Housing authorities should work closely with Youth Offending Services and children's social care services to ensure joint and advanced planning around the needs of young people leaving custody. Particular care should be taken to ensure that young people aged 16-17 and care leavers aged 18-24 do not leave custody without an accommodation plan in place. This will also require cooperation between housing authorities and children's social care services in advance of release.

23.5 Housing authorities and offender management services (i.e. prisons, youth offending services and probation providers) should work together to ensure the accommodation needs of people leaving custody and those serving their sentence in the community are met. Probation providers have a responsibility to support people under their supervision to reduce reoffending. CRCs and the NPS must provide direct support to help people find accommodation. Housing authorities should continue to work with these agencies, as well as prisons and voluntary sector organisations, to ensure their clients access suitable accommodation

23.6 The following criminal justice services are subject to the duty to refer, meaning they are required to refer service users in England they consider may be homeless or threatened with homelessness within 56 days to a local housing authority, with the service user's consent:

(a) prisons (public and private);
(b) young offender institutions;
(c) secure training centres;
(d) secure colleges;
(e) youth offending teams; and,
(f) probation providers (CRCs and NPS).

For further guidance on duty to refer see Chapter 4.

Advice and information

23.7 People with an offending history generally face additional barriers in accessing housing, and therefore will need targeted advice and information to help them to secure accommodation.

23.8 Section 179(2)(a) of the 1996 Act requires authorities to provide information and advice which is designed to meet the needs of people released from prison or youth detention. Advice and information to people with an offending history may be delivered via the housing authority's website, social media, through leaflets or through dedicated advice services, and will be most effective if developed in consultation or jointly with offender management services in the district (i.e. prisons, youth offending services and probation providers). Housing authorities may also wish to consult with prisoners or people with an offending history before developing resources tailored to their particular needs.

23.9 Advice and information should reflect local circumstances and arrangements but might include:

(a) the support available to people going in to custody which will enable them to retain a tenancy or license, or to surrender it so that rent arrears do not accrue;
(b) housing benefit or universal credit entitlement for people in custody;
(c) tenancy rights and how to protect a tenancy where it is appropriate to do so;
(d) housing options for people leaving custody, including access to the social housing register, supported housing and help available to secure private rented accommodation; and,
(e) support services for people with an offending history that might help them to secure and/or to sustain accommodation on release.

23.10 It is recommended that housing advice be made available to people whilst in custody, and that housing authorities collaborate with prisons from which offenders are released to their districts, together with probation providers, to provide accessible advice on housing options available to them. For further guidance on providing advice and information see Chapter 3.

Prevention

23.11 Housing authorities should put in place arrangements that will help to prevent people with an offending history from becoming homeless. Policies and partnerships designed to reduce homelessness might include, but not be limited to, the areas set out in 23.12 to 23.15 below.

Preventing loss of accommodation due to offending behaviour:

23.12 Tenants may be at risk of becoming homeless because of their own or others' anti-social or offending behaviour. Housing authorities should ensure that their housing management procedures include early contact with a tenant who they believe may be responsible for behaviour that could result in their becoming homeless, and that private landlords and private registered providers are encouraged to alert them where tenants are threatened with eviction. Where offender management services continue to be involved with the person they should be alerted of any risk of homelessness, so that joint plans may be put in place to try and prevent homelessness and provide additional support where appropriate.

23.13 Sometimes people with an offending history, and their families, become homeless because it is no longer safe for them to remain in their tenancy. Young people, who become involved in gang related activity, whether as victims or perpetrators, sometimes face particular risks. Housing authorities should work with police, offender managers and specialist services to coordinate activity to minimise risk and prevent homelessness. This will also help reduce re-offending and promote community safety.

Preventing loss of accommodation whilst a person is in custody:

23.14 Prison services and probation providers carry out assessments to identify resettlement needs, including the need for accommodation, at the start of a prisoner's period in custody. Sentence planning arrangements require plans for resettlement to be reviewed throughout the sentence and appropriate support arranged to meet a person's needs on leaving custody.

23.15 Assessing an offender's housing needs at the start of a period in custody will help to identify if assistance is required to end, sustain or transfer an existing tenancy, access welfare support to meet rent costs while in prison, or close down an existing tenancy appropriately. Housing authorities are advised to assist the Prison service and probation providers in providing advice to prisoners and taking action to ensure they can sustain or surrender their accommodation while in custody.

Preventing homelessness on leaving custody:

23.16 If a prisoner is assessed as requiring assistance with accommodation on release, there will usually be sufficient time to consider their options and take action to try and prevent their homelessness. In most cases, but particularly with young people, contact should be made with family to try and support a return home (where safe to do so) if only on a temporary basis. Where a person preparing to leave custody cannot return to family or another safe address, housing authorities should work with the applicant and liaise with offender manager and support services to agree and to deliver reasonable steps to prevent them from becoming homeless on release.

Assessing priority need

23.17 Housing authorities have a duty to help secure accommodation for any applicant threatened with homelessness on leaving custody, irrespective of priority need. For further guidance on prevention duty see Chapter 12, for further guidance on the relief duty see Chapter 13 and for further guidance on assessments and plans see Chapter 11.

23.18 Where activity to prevent or relieve homelessness is unsuccessful the authority will need to assess whether the person has a priority need for accommodation and is owed the main housing duty. For further guidance on priority need see Chapter 8 and for further guidance on accommodation duties see Chapter 15. **A person who is vulnerable as a result of having served a custodial sentence, been committed for**

contempt of court or remanded in custody has a priority need for accommodation.

23.19   Assessments of vulnerability should be composite, taking into account all relevant factors that might contribute to a person being significantly more vulnerable if homeless than an ordinary person would be if homeless. In determining whether applicants who fall within this category are vulnerable as a result of their period in custody a housing authority will need to take into account all of the relevant factors including:

(a)   the length of time the applicant served in custody or detention (although authorities should not assume that vulnerability could not occur as a result of a short period in custody or detention);

(b)   whether the applicant is receiving supervision from a criminal justice agency e.g. the providers of probation services (NPS and CRCs) or youth offending team. Housing authorities should have regard to any advice from criminal justice agency staff regarding their view of the applicant's general vulnerability, but the final decision on the question of vulnerability for the purposes of the homelessness legislation will rest with the housing authority;

(c)   the length of time since the applicant was released from custody or detention, and the extent to which the applicant has been able to obtain and/or maintain accommodation during that time;

(d)   whether the applicant has any existing support networks and how much of a positive influence these networks are likely to be in the applicant's life.

23.20   Housing authorities should take into account the assessments of housing and support needs completed by offender management services, or voluntary organisations acting on behalf of these agencies.

Intentional homelessness

23.21   People with an offending history may apply for homelessness assistance after losing their accommodation due to a period in custody. In considering whether such an applicant is homeless intentionally the housing authority will have to decide whether:

(a)   there was a likelihood that ceasing to occupy the accommodation could reasonably have been regarded at the time as a likely consequence of committing the offence; and,

(b)   the accommodation would have otherwise continued to be available to the person at the point in time when they applied for homelessness assistance.

23.22   Housing authorities must consider each application on a case by case basis, in the light of all the facts and circumstances, including the age and maturity of the applicant, and should discuss the matter with the relevant provider of probation services. Authorities should not adopt a blanket policy which assumes that people who have lost accommodation whilst in custody will or will not be assessed as intentionally homeless.

Local connection

23.23   Housing authorities may receive applications from people leaving custody who do not have a local connection to their district but do have a connection to another local authority area. For further guidance on local connection see Chapter 10. If the applicant is eligible for assistance and threatened with homelessness the housing authority taking the application will have a section 195 prevention duty, whether or not the applicant has a local connection. Detention in prison (whether convicted or not) does not establish residency of choice in the district the prison is in, and so will not create a local connection with that district.

23.24   However, if the applicant is homeless the receiving authority may, if it is satisfied that the conditions are met, make a referral to another district where the applicant has a local connection. If the notified authority accepts that the conditions for referral are met they will take on the section 189B relief duty, as well as a duty to provide accommodation if there is reason to believe the applicant may be in priority need.

23.25 In considering whether or not a referral should be made, the authority that has taken the application should consider the particular circumstances of the applicant, and any risks involved in referring them to another local authority area. An applicant cannot be referred to another area where they would be at risk of violence. The authority will also want to take into account the considerations identified in paragraphs 23.26 and 23.27 below where relevant, before making a final decision.

Suitability of accommodation

23.26 Section 208(1) requires housing authorities to secure accommodation within their district, in so far as is reasonably practicable. There may be circumstances in which there are clear benefits for the applicant of being accommodated outside of the district. This could occur where upon the advice of the relevant provider of probation service (NPS or CRC) or through Multi Agency Public Protection Arrangements (MAPPA) it is decided that a person with an offending history should be placed outside the district to reduce risk of reoffending, or to help break links with previous contacts who could exert a negative influence.

23.27 There may also be instances where a criminal justice agency or MAPPA advise that in order to ensure appropriate distance between the applicant and their victims, the applicant should reside in a particular area, where they do not have a local connection.

23.28 When assessing the accommodation needs of a person with an offending history an authority will need to take into account their support needs, which in some cases might be complex. Young people leaving custody are likely to require accommodation with some level of support if they are to maintain their tenancy or license and avoid reoffending.

Accessing accommodation

23.29 People with an offending history face barriers to accessing accommodation across tenures. Housing authorities providing help to secure or securing accommodation should be aware of the provisions of the Rehabilitation of Offenders Act 1974 (as amended by the Legal Aid Sentencing and Punishing Offenders Act 2012). The Rehabilitation of Offenders Act 1974 sets out timescales for when convictions become spent, after which it is unlawful for social and private landlords to take spent convictions into account when determining whether the person is suitable for housing.

CHAPTER 24: FORMER MEMBERS OF THE ARMED FORCES

24.1 This chapter provides guidance on providing homelessness services to former members of the armed forces, who are referred to throughout as veterans.

24.2 Members of Her Majesty's regular naval, military and air forces are generally provided with accommodation by the Ministry of Defence (MOD), but are required to leave this when they are discharged from the service.

24.3 Housing authorities that have a significant number of service personnel stationed in their area will need to work closely with relevant partners, such as the Joint Service Housing Advice Office and MOD's resettlement services, to ascertain likely levels of need for housing assistance amongst people leaving the forces and plan their services accordingly.

24.4 The Secretary of State for Defence is subject to the duty to refer in relation to the members of the regular forces. He is required to refer members of the regular forces in England he considers may be homeless or threatened with homelessness within 56 days to a local housing authority, with the individual's consent. For further guidance on the duty to refer see Chapter 4. The regular forces are the Royal Navy, the Royal Marines, the regular army and the Royal Air Force.

Advice and information

24.5 The principal responsibility for providing housing information and advice to Service personnel lies with the armed forces up to the point of discharge and these services are delivered through the Joint Service Housing Advice Office and through the Veterans UK Online. Some people, who have served in the armed forces for a long period, and those who are medically discharged, may be offered assistance with resettlement by the MOD's resettlement staff.

24.6 Housing authorities have a duty (section 179) to provide advisory services free of charge to people in their district. The service must be designed to meet the needs of certain groups, which include former members of the regular armed forces. This duty will be particularly relevant for housing authorities who have armed forces stationed within their districts, and in these circumstances authorities are encouraged to consult with the services concerned about how best to deliver local housing advice to prevent veterans from becoming homeless. For further guidance on providing advice and information on homelessness and threatened with homelessness see Chapter 3.

Veterans required to leave service accommodation

24.7 The MOD recognises that housing authorities will need to be satisfied that entitlement to occupy service accommodation will end on a certain date in order to determine whether applicants who are service personnel and approaching their date of discharge may be homeless or threatened with homelessness.

24.8 For this purpose, the MOD issues a Certificate of Cessation of Entitlement to Occupy Service Accommodation six months before discharge. These certificates indicate the date on which entitlement to occupy service accommodation ends, and the Secretary of State considers that housing authorities should not insist upon a court order for possession to establish that entitlement to occupy has ended.

Priority need

24.9 A person who is vulnerable as a result of having been a member of Her Majesty's regular armed forces (a veteran) has a priority need for accommodation. Veterans will include a person who was previously a member of the regular naval, military or air forces.

24.10 In considering whether veterans are vulnerable (as set out in paragraph 6.9 above) as a result of their time spent in the forces, a housing authority may wish to take into account the following factors:

(a) the length of time the applicant spent in the armed forces (although authorities should not assume that vulnerability could not occur as a result of a short period of service);

(b) the type of service the applicant was engaged in (those on active service may find it more difficult to cope with civilian life);

(c) whether the applicant spent any time in a military hospital (this could be an indicator of a serious health problem or of post-traumatic stress);

(d) whether HM Forces' medical and welfare advisers have judged an individual to be particularly vulnerable in their view and have issued a Medical History Release Form giving a summary of the circumstances causing that vulnerability;

(e) the length of time since the applicant left the armed forces, and whether they have been able to obtain and/or maintain accommodation during that time; and,

(f) whether the applicant has any existing support networks, particularly by way of family or friends.

Intentional homelessness

24.11 Where service personnel are required to vacate service quarters as a result of taking up an option to give notice to leave the service, and in so doing are acting in compliance with their contractual engagement, they should not be considered to have become homeless intentionally. For further guidance on intentional homelessness see Chapter 9.

Local connection

24.12 Section 315 of the Housing and Regeneration Act 2008 amended section 199 of the 1996 Act to enable members of the armed forces to establish a local connection through residence or employment in the same way as a civilian. For further guidance on local connection see Chapter 10.

CHAPTER 25: MODERN SLAVERY

25.1 This chapter provides guidance on modern slavery in relation to applicants who are threatened with homelessness or homeless.

What is modern slavery and trafficking

25.2 Modern slavery is a serious and often hidden crime in which people are exploited for criminal gain. The impact can be devastating for victims. Modern slavery comprises slavery, servitude, and forced or compulsory labour and human trafficking. The common factors are that a victim is, or is intended to be, used or exploited for someone else's (usually financial) gain, without respect for their human rights.

25.3 Modern slavery can take many different forms. The following are types of exploitation which commonly occur in the UK and individuals may experience more than one form of abuse:

(a) **sexual exploitation**: victims are coerced into sex work or sexually abusive situations. This includes child sexual exploitation. Victims may be brought to the UK on the promise of legitimate employment, or moved around the UK to be sexually exploited. In some cases they may know they will be involved in sex work, but are forced into a type or frequency they did not agree to. Victims are more commonly female but can also be male;

(b) **domestic servitude**: domestic servitude typically involves victims working in a private family home where they are ill treated, humiliated, subjected to unbearable conditions or working hours or made to work for little or no pay. The victim could be used in this way by their own family members or partner. Again, it is very difficult for them to leave, for example because of threats, the perpetrator holding their passport, or using a position of power over the victim;

(c) **labour exploitation**: labour exploitation usually involves unacceptably low pay, poor working conditions or excessive wage deductions, but is not solely about this. In order to constitute modern slavery there will also be some form of coercion meaning that victims cannot freely leave for other employment or exercise choice over their own situation. Where the perpetrator is taking advantage of a child or vulnerable person, an offence can be committed without the element of coercion;

(d) **criminal exploitation**: criminal exploitation is the exploitation of a person to commit a crime for someone else's gain. For example victims could be coerced into shoplifting, pick-pocketing, entering into a sham marriage, benefit fraud, begging or drug cultivation such as cannabis farming;

(e) other forms of exploitation include organ or tissue removal; forced begging and illegal adoption. For further information, see Modern Slavery Awareness & Victim Identification Guidance.

Identification

25.4 Modern slavery is a highly complex crime. There is no typical victim of slavery – victims can be men, women and children of all ages, ethnicities and nationalities (including British) and cut across the population. But it is normally more prevalent amongst the most vulnerable groups, and within minority or socially excluded groups. Child victims are victims of child abuse and should therefore be treated as such using existing child protection procedures and statutory protocols.

25.5 Victims of modern slavery can be found anywhere. There are certain industries where they are currently more prevalent, such as nail bars, car washes, agriculture and fishing, building sites and the sex industry. Other high risk situations include when there is a need for a sudden injection of workers into the work force, such as seasonal staff or construction for a major event. However victims may also pass through transport hubs, health services and other public places or be found in private homes.

25.6 In all cases decision makers should be alive to the possibility that applicants for assistance under Part 7 are victims of modern slavery, or are otherwise vulnerable. Particular care should be paid to children, especially where there are doubts about the relationship with any purported guardian. **Children's social services should be alerted to any safeguarding concerns immediately.**

The National Referral Mechanism

25.7 The National Referral Mechanism (NRM) is the process by which people who may be victims of modern slavery are identified and supported by the UK Government.

25.8 Local authorities, as designated first responder organisations, should refer any individual they suspect to be a victim of modern slavery to the National Referral Mechanism (NRM). Adults have to provide informed consent to be referred to the NRM, but children do not need to consent and must be referred to the NRM if there are suspicions that the child has been a victim of modern slavery.

25.9 Following the referral of an adult or child into the NRM, an initial 'reasonable grounds' decision will be made within 5 days. If this decision is positive, the individual will be entitled to access safe accommodation provided through a central-government funded Victim Care Contract. If the person would otherwise be destitute during that 5 day period they can access emergency accommodation by contacting the Salvation Army. However, the person may be referred to the housing authority to provide accommodation if the individual is a British citizen who is homeless, eligible and has or may have a priority need.

25.10 In some instances, the adult involved may not give consent to a referral to the NRM. In this case, instead of referring the case, the local authority has a duty to notify the Home Office under section 52 of the Modern Slavery Act 2015. For further information, see Guidance for Public Authorities on Duty to Notify.

What support is provided by the National Referral Mechanism

25.11 The provision of support through the NRM is a devolved matter in the United Kingdom and differs depending on whether the victim is an adult or child. The below information covers the support offer to adult and child victims in England and Wales.

Adult support and assistance

25.12 If an adult receives a positive 'reasonable grounds' decision through the NRM, they are entitled to support for a minimum period of 45 days. This is provided through a central-government funded Victim Care Contract and includes accommodation, subsistence, counselling, access to mental, physical and dental health services, and signposting to legal services.

25.13 Whilst in support, a 'conclusive grounds' decision will be made on their case through the NRM and they will be provided with a letter setting out whether there was enough evidence to conclude that they are indeed a victim of modern slavery. The individual will then receive a short period of move-on support focused on their transition out of central government-funded support, which may include liaising with housing authorities or local homelessness services.

Children support and assistance

25.14 Children are supported locally and are not provided with support and assistance through Victim Care Contract, unless with a parent who is a potential victim. Housing authorities should refer unaccompanied children to children's services in line with local safeguarding procedures.

Applications and inquiries under Part 7

25.15 In many cases involving modern slavery or trafficking, the applicant may be in considerable distress and officers would benefit from appropriate training to enable them to conduct such interviews. Applicants should be given the option of being interviewed by an officer of the same sex if they wish.

25.16 Housing authorities should refer any individual they suspect to be a victim of modern slavery to the NRM (see paragraphs 25.7 to 25.10).

25.17 A person who has been a victim of trafficking or modern slavery may have a priority need for accommodation if they are assessed as being vulnerable according to section 189(1)(c) of the 1996 Act. In assessing whether they are vulnerable a housing authority should take into account advice from specialist agencies providing services to the applicant, such as their assigned support provider under the NRM. Many victims of modern slavery suffer from poor mental health and often lack support structures in the area they are residing. If a victim of modern slavery is threatened with homelessness or is homeless this significantly increases their risk to being re-trafficked or exposed to further exploitation. For further guidance on priority need see Chapter 8.

25.18 Section 188(1) of the 1996 Act requires housing authorities to secure that accommodation is available for an applicant if they have reason to believe that the applicant may be homeless, eligible for assistance and have a priority need. If housing authorities believe an individual may be vulnerable as a result of being a victim of modern slavery following a referral to the NRM housing authorities should ensure that accommodation is available while they are waiting for an initial 'reasonable grounds' decision.

25.19 Housing authorities may find it helpful to establish local, joint working arrangements with NRM support providers where appropriate to help identify people at risk of homelessness as early as possible and maximise the opportunities to prevent homelessness.

Suitability of accommodation

25.20 There will be a number of accommodation options for victims of modern slavery. Housing authorities should consider which are most appropriate for each person on a case by case basis taking into account their specific circumstances and needs.

25.21 Account will need to be taken of any special considerations relating to the applicant and their household or their experiences that might affect the suitability of accommodation. Where there is no other option for applicants who have suffered modern slavery but to be accommodated in an emergency hostel or bed and breakfast accommodation, the accommodation may need to be gender-specific as well as have appropriate security measures depending on their needs and circumstances. Any risk of violence or racial harassment in a particular locality should also be taken into account, and housing authorities should be mindful that individuals who have left their traffickers remain at risk of being re-trafficked.

25.22 Whilst authorities should, as far as is practicable, aim to secure accommodation within their own district, they should also recognise that there can be benefits for some applicants to be accommodated outside of the district. This could occur in cases of modern slavery or trafficking where the applicant, and/or a member of their household, would be vulnerable to further exploitation and needs to be accommodated outside the district to reduce the risk of further contact with the perpetrator(s) and to help break links which could exert a negative influence.

ANNEX 1: THE HABITUAL RESIDENCE TEST

1 In practice, when considering housing applications from persons who are subject to the habitual residence test, it is only necessary to investigate habitual residence if the applicant has arrived or returned to live in the UK during the two year period prior to making the application.

Definition of habitually resident

2 The term 'habitually resident' is not defined in legislation. Local authorities should always consider the overall circumstances of a case to determine whether someone is

habitually resident in the UK, the Channel Islands, the Isle of Man or the Republic of Ireland.

General principles

3   When deciding whether a person is habitually resident in a place, consideration must be given to all the facts of each case in a common sense way. It should be remembered that:

(a)   the test focuses on the fact and nature of residence;
(b)   a person who is not resident somewhere cannot be habitually resident there. Residence is a more settled state than mere physical presence in a country. To be resident a person must be seen to be making a home. It need not be the only home or a permanent home but it must be a genuine home for the time being. For example, a short stay visitor or a person receiving short term medical treatment is not resident;
(c)   the most important factors for habitual residence are the length, continuity and general nature of actual residence rather than intention;
(d)   the practicality of a person's arrangements for residence is a necessary part of determining whether it can be described as settled and habitual;
(e)   established habitual residents who have periods of temporary or occasional absence of long or short duration may still be habitually resident during such absences.

Action on receipt of an application

Applicant came to live in the UK during the previous two years

4   If it appears that the applicant came to live in the UK during the previous two years, authorities should make further enquiries to decide if the applicant is habitually resident, or can be treated as such.

Factors to consider

5   The applicant's stated reasons and intentions for coming to the UK will be relevant to the question of whether they are habitually resident. If the applicant's stated intention is to live in the UK, and not return to the country from which they came, that intention must be consistent with their actions.

6   To decide whether an applicant is habitually resident in the UK, authorities should consider the factors set out below. However, these do not provide an exhaustive check list of the questions or factors that need to be considered. Further enquiries may be needed. The circumstances of each case will dictate what information is needed, and all relevant factors should be taken into account.

Why has the applicant come to the UK?

7   If the applicant is returning to the UK after a period spent abroad, and it can be established that the applicant was previously habitually resident in the UK and is returning to resume their former period of habitual residence, they will be immediately habitually resident.

8   In determining whether an applicant is returning to resume a former period of habitual residence authorities should consider:

(a)   when did the applicant leave the UK?
(b)   how long did the applicant live in the UK before leaving?
(c)   why did the applicant leave the UK?
(d)   how long did the applicant intend to remain abroad?
(e)   why did the applicant return?
(f)   did the applicant's partner and children, if any, also leave the UK?
(g)   did the applicant keep accommodation in the UK?

(h)   if the applicant owned property, was it let, and was the lease timed to coincide with the applicant's return to the UK?

(i)   what links did the applicant keep with the UK?

(j)   have there been other brief absences? If yes, obtain details

(k)   why has the applicant come to the UK?

9   If the applicant has arrived in the UK within the previous two years and is not resuming a period of habitual residence, consideration should be given to their reasons for coming to the UK, and in particular to the factors set out below.

Applicant is joining family or friends

10   If the applicant has come to the UK to join or rejoin family or friends, authorities should consider:

(a)   has the applicant sold or given up any property abroad?

(b)   has the applicant bought or rented accommodation or are they staying with friends?

(c)   is the move to the UK intended to be permanent?

Applicant's plans

11   Authorities should consider the applicant's plans, e.g.:

(a)   if the applicant plans to remain in the UK, is the applicant's stated plan consistent with their actions?

(b)   were any arrangements made for employment and accommodation (even if unsuccessful) before the applicant arrived in the UK?

(c)   did the applicant buy a one-way ticket?

(d)   did the applicant bring all their belongings?

(e)   is there any evidence of links with the UK, e.g. membership of clubs?

12   The fact that a person may intend to live in the UK for the foreseeable future does not, of itself, mean that habitual residence has been established. However, the applicant's intentions along with other factors, for example the disposal of property abroad, may indicate that the applicant is habitually resident in the UK.

13   An applicant who intends to reside in the UK for only a short period, for example for a holiday or to visit friends is unlikely to be habitually resident in the UK.

Length of residence in the UK

14   To be habitually resident in a country an applicant must have actually taken up residence and lived there for a period. It is not sufficient that the applicant came to the UK voluntarily and for settled purposes. They must be resident in fact for an appropriate period of time which demonstrates that their residence has become, and is likely to remain, habitual in nature. The appropriate period of time need not be lengthy if the facts indicate that a person's residence has become habitual in nature at an early stage. In some circumstances the period can be as little as a month, but it must be a period which is more than momentary in a claimant's life history. A period of between one and three months is likely to be appropriate to demonstrate that a person's residence is habitual in nature.

Length of residence in another country

15   Authorities should consider the length and continuity of an applicant's residence in another country:

(a)   how long did the applicant live in the previous country?

(b)   does the applicant have any remaining ties with their former country of residence?

(c)   has the applicant stayed in different countries outside the UK?

16   It is possible that a person may own a property abroad but still be habitually

resident in the UK. A person who has a home or close family in another country would normally retain habitual residence in that country. A person who has previously lived in several different countries but has now moved permanently to the UK may be habitually resident here.

Centre of interest

17 An applicant is likely to be habitually resident in the UK, the Channel Islands, the Isle of Man or the Republic of Ireland, despite spending time abroad, if their centre of interest is located in one of these places.

18 People who maintain their centre of interest in the UK, the Channel Islands, the Isle of Man or the Republic of Ireland, for example a home, a job, friends, membership of clubs, are likely to be habitually resident there. People who have retained their centre of interest in another country and have no particular ties with the UK, the Channel Islands, the Isle of Man or the Republic of Ireland, are unlikely to be habitually resident in the UK, the Channel Islands, the Isle of Man or the Republic of Ireland.

19 Authorities should take the following into account when deciding the centre of interest:

(a)   home;
(b)   family ties;
(c)   club memberships;
(d)   finance accounts.

20 If the centre of interest appears to be in the UK, the Channel Islands, the Isle of Man or the Republic of Ireland but the applicant has a home somewhere else, authorities should consider the applicant's intentions regarding the property.

21 In certain cultures, e.g. the Asian culture, it is quite common for a person to live in one country but have property abroad that they do not intend to sell. Where such a person has lived in the UK, the Channel Islands, the Isle of Man or the Republic of Ireland for many years, the fact that they have property elsewhere does not necessarily mean that they intend to leave, or that the applicant's centre of interest is elsewhere.

PROCEDURES FOR REFERRALS OF HOMELESS APPLICANTS TO ANOTHER LOCAL AUTHORITY

GUIDELINES FOR LOCAL AUTHORITIES ON PROCEDURES FOR REFERRAL

A2.4

AGREED BY

LOCAL GOVERNMENT ASSOCIATION (LGA)

CONVENTION OF SCOTTISH LOCAL AUTHORITIES (COSLA)

WELSH LOCAL GOVERNMENT ASSOCIATION (WLGA)

(*"the local authority associations"*)

These procedures and guidelines concern the situation where, under Part 7 of the *Housing Act 1996*, a local housing authority consider that the conditions for referral of the case to another local housing authority are met and notifies the other authority of its opinion. Referrals are discretionary only. Housing authorities are not required to make inquiries as to whether, for example, an applicant has a local connection with another district and, where they decide to do so, there is no requirement to refer applicants to another authority if the conditions for referral are met. Authorities may have a policy about how they may exercise their discretion. However, they cannot decide in advance that a referral will be made in all cases where an applicant may, for example, have a local connection with another district.

1

Scope and purpose

1.1 These procedures and guidelines mainly concern local housing authorities in England and the legal framework which applies to them, but they also cover cross-border issues in relation to Scotland and Wales. They apply following the changes made to Part 7 of the *Housing Act 1996* by the *Homelessness Reduction Act 2017*. Authorities in England may notify another authority of their opinion that the conditions for referral are met if the notifying authority would be subject to a duty under either s 189B (the "initial" or "relief" duty) or s 193 (the "main" housing duty) of the *Housing Act 1996*; but referrals cannot be made to Scottish or Welsh authorities at the relief stage. Authorities should follow the relevant statutory provisions and have regard to governmental guidance when considering referrals; the information given below in relation to those provisions and guidance is by way of an overview only.

1.2 Section 198 of the *Housing Act 1996* provides that:

"(5) The question whether the conditions for referral of a case which does not involve a referral to a local housing authority in Wales are satisfied shall be determined by agreement between the notifying authority and the notified authority or, in default of agreement, in accordance with such arrangements as the Secretary of State may direct by order.

(5A) The question whether the conditions for referral of a case involving a referral to a local housing authority in Wales shall be decided by agreement between the notifying authority and the notified authority or, in default of agreement, in accordance with such arrangements as the Secretary of State and the Welsh Ministers may jointly direct by order.

(6) An order may direct that the arrangements shall be:

(a)   those agreed by any relevant authorities or associations of relevant authorities, or

(b)   in default of such agreement, such arrangements as appear to the Secretary of State or, in the case of an order under subsection (5A), to the Secretary of State and the Welsh Ministers to be suitable, after consultation with such associations representing relevant authorities, and such other persons, as he thinks appropriate."

1.3   Similar provision is made in s 80(5) and (6) of the *Housing (Wales) Act 2014* in relation to Wales and in s 33(4) and (5) of the *Housing (Scotland) Act 1987* in relation to Scotland. However, s 8 of the *Homelessness (Scotland) Act 2003* (not yet in force) gives Scottish ministers the power to suspend or vary the circumstances under which a homeless applicant may be referred by a Scottish local authority to another authority in Scotland. Please note any future orders made will need to be taken into account.

1.4   The LGA, CoSLA and the WLGA, the local authority associations in England, Scotland and Wales, have agreed guidelines for referrals which they recommend to local housing authorities. The relevant statutory framework contains detailed provisions in relation to referrals, including where it appears that the applicant does not have a local connection with the area of the authority receiving the housing application but does have one with another area in England, Scotland or Wales. There are, however, considerable areas of possible disagreement and dispute in determining whether the conditions of referral are met in any particular case. Although, in the last resort, disagreements can only be resolved by the courts, the associations are anxious to avoid, as far as possible, legal disputes between local authorities. The associations therefore issue these agreed guidelines on the procedures and criteria to be followed, and recommend them for general adoption by all their members. **These Guidelines are without prejudice to the duty of local authorities to treat each case on its merits and to take into account existing and future case law.** Furthermore, these Guidelines only apply to the issues of local connection and whether the conditions for referral are met.

1.5   In *R v Eastleigh BC ex p Betts* [1983] 2 AC 613, the House of Lords considered the application of the referral arrangements agreed between the local authority associations. Their Lordships decided that a rigid application of the arrangements would constitute a fetter on an authority's discretion. **The agreement could be taken into account, and applied as a guideline, provided its application to each case is given individual consideration.**

1.6   A previous version of this agreement was considered by the Court of Appeal in *Ozbek v Ipswich BC* [2006] EWCA Civ 534; [2006] HLR 41, the following being said at [37]-[38]:

"one purpose – indeed, perhaps, the principal purpose – of the Referral Guidelines and their predecessor, the Agreement on Procedures, is to facilitate agreement between authorities on the question whether the conditions for referral are met; or to provide a basis for speedy and inexpensive resolution of disputes between authorities on that question. ... [T]hat purpose is unlikely to be achieved unless authorities do follow the guidance which those guidelines provide by applying that guidance 'generally to all applications which come before them'. ... [A]n authority is not to be criticised for following that guidance in the individual case, provided that they have not closed their mind to the possibility that the particular facts of that case may require a departure from the guidance which they would apply more generally.

"... The conditions for referral – set out in s 198(2) of the 1996 Act – include (a) that the applicant does not have a local connection with the notifying authority and (b) that the applicant does have a local connection with the notified authority. It is desirable (if the statutory scheme is to work smoothly) that both notifying authority and notified authority should be able to agree on both conditions. Or, to put the point another way, it is desirable that the notified authority – who is being asked to assume the burden of providing accommodation for the applicant in the place of the notifying authority – should be able to accept the view of the notifying authority both that the applicant has no local connection with the district of the notifying authority and that the applicant does have a local connection with their own district. Ready agreement is unlikely to be achieved on those two points unless both the notifying authority and the notified authority are able to approach the question from a common basis. It is the need for that common basis which, as it seems to me, provides the imperative for all authorities to apply the guidelines 'generally to all applications which come before them'."

2

Definitions

2.1 For the purposes of this agreement, the relevant statutory definitions apply. All references in this agreement to an *"applicant"* are to be taken as references to a housing applicant to whom the relevant duty would be owed but for the decision to refer the case to another authority.

2.2 The authority to whom the applicant applies for accommodation or assistance and which decides to refer the case to another authority is the *"notifying authority"*.

2.3 Where the notifying authority consider that the conditions for referral are met, including where neither the applicant nor any person who might reasonably reside with the applicant has a local connection with its district but does have one with another local authority district and notifies the other local authority of its opinion, the authority which they notify is known as the *"notified authority"*.

2.4 The principal context in which the question of referral may arise concerns *"local connection"*, defined as explained below, but the conditions for referral may also be met in certain other cases. These guidelines provide a framework within which the referral procedures may be applied.

3

Criteria for notification

3.1 The criteria for notification are set out in the statutory framework and are addressed in governmental guidance. The following is designed to provide merely an overview.

3.2 Before a local authority can consider referring an applicant to another local authority under s 198(A1) it must first be satisfied that the applicant is

(i)   eligible for assistance and
(ii)   homeless.

3.3 Before a local authority can consider referring an applicant to another local authority under s 198(1) it must be satisfied that, in addition to meeting the two criteria noted above, the applicant also:

(i)   is in priority need and
(ii)   did not become homeless intentionally.

3.4 Before making a referral the notifying authority must be satisfied that the conditions of referral are met. Broadly, the conditions for referral will be met if:

(a)   neither the applicant nor any person who might reasonably be expected to reside with the applicant has a local connection with the district of the authority to which the application was originally made,
(b)   either the applicant or any person who might reasonably be expected to reside with the applicant has a local connection with the district of the other authority,
(c)   neither the applicant nor any person who might reasonably be expected to reside with the applicant would run the risk of domestic violence in that other district and

(d)   neither the applicant nor any person who might reasonably be expected to reside with the applicant has suffered any other violence in that other district and it is not probable that returning to that district would lead to further violence of a similar kind.

3.5   The conditions for referral will also be met if the application is made within a period of two years beginning with the date on which the applicant accepted a "private rented sector" offer from the other authority under s 193(7AA), provided that (c) and (d), above, are met.

3.6   The conditions for referral will also be met if the applicant was placed in the authority's district by another authority as a result of a previous application to that authority and the second application is made within the prescribed period (5 years) of the first.

3.7   In deciding whether or not to make a referral, authorities should also consider the Court of Appeal decision in the case of *R v Newham LBC ex p Tower Hamlets LBC* [1991] 1 WLR 1032. The notifying authority should have regard to any decisions made by the notified authority that may have a bearing on the case in question (e.g. a previous decision that the applicant was intentionally homeless) as well as any other material considerations, which should include the general housing circumstances prevailing in the district of the notifying authority and in the district of the notified authority. The notifying authority should also consider whether it is in the public interest to accept a duty to secure accommodation.

3.8   Should a local authority wish to accept a duty to secure accommodation for an applicant who does not have a local connection with its district, nothing in this agreement shall prevent the authority from providing such assistance. The decision to make a referral is discretionary and could be challenged if the discretion was considered to have been exercised unreasonably.

3.9   Under s 202 of the *Housing Act 1996*, applicants have the right to request a review of certain decisions made by the local authority about their application, including a decision to notify another authority under s 198(1) and a decision that the conditions are met for referral of the case to another authority.

4

Local connection

4.1   The test for establishing a local connection is set out in s 199 of the *Housing Act 1996* and addressed in detail in governmental guidance. The following is designed to provide merely an overview.

4.2   The relevant date for deciding whether or not a local connection has been established is not the date when the application for housing assistance was made but the date of the decision or, if there is a review, the date of the review decision (see the House of Lords' judgment in *Mohamed v Hammersmith and Fulham LBC* [2001] 1 AC 547). Moreover, if inquiries prior to a decision have been prolonged, the notifying authority should also consider whether there may have been any material change in circumstances that might affect the question of whether a local connection has been established.

4.3   A local connection may be established where the following grounds apply, subject to the exceptions below:

(i)   the applicant or a person who might reasonably be expected to reside with the applicant is, or in the past was, normally resident in the district. It is suggested that a working definition of "normal residence" should be residence for at least 6 months in the area during the previous 12 months, or for not less than 3 years during the previous 5-year period. The period taken into account should be up to the date of the authority's decision. This should include any periods living in temporary accommodation secured by the authority under s 188 (interim duty pending inquiries);

(ii)   the applicant or a person who might reasonably be expected to reside with the applicant is at present employed in the district. The local authority should obtain confirmation from the employer that the person is in employment and that the employment is not of a casual nature;

(iii)   the applicant or a person who might reasonably be expected to reside with the applicant has family associations in the district. Family associations normally arise where an applicant or a person who might reasonably be expected to reside with the applicant has parents, adult children or brothers or sisters who have been resident in the district for a period of at least 5 years at the date of the decision, and the applicant indicates a wish to be near them. Only in exceptional circumstances would the residence of relatives other than those listed above be taken to establish a local connection, but the circumstances may be sufficient and all cases will be fact-specific. The residence of dependent children in a different district from their parents would not be residence of their own choice and therefore would not establish a local connection with that district. However, a referral should not be made to another local authority on the grounds of a local connection because of family associations if the applicant objects to those grounds;

(iv)   there are special circumstances which the authority considers establish a local connection with the district. This may be particularly relevant where the applicant has been in prison or hospital and his or her circumstances do not conform to the criteria in (i) – (iii) above. Where, for example, an applicant seeks to return to a district where he or she was brought up or lived for a considerable length of time in the past, there may be grounds for considering that the applicant has a local connection with that district because of special circumstances. An authority must exercise its discretion when considering whether special circumstances apply.

4.4   A notifying authority should not refer an applicant to another authority on grounds of a local connection because of special circumstances without the prior consent of the notified authority. Alternatively, authorities may come to an informal arrangement in such cases on a reciprocal basis, subject to the agreement of the applicants.

4.5   There are certain circumstances where the local connection provisions set out above may be modified. More detail is contained in governmental guidance. See:

(i)   care leavers;
(ii)   ex-service personnel;
(iii)   ex-prisoners and detainees under the *Mental Health Act 1983*;
(iv)   former asylum seekers.

5

Procedures in making a referral

5.1   If an authority considers that the conditions for referral in s 198 *Housing Act 1996* are likely to be met in a particular case it should make any necessary enquiries in the area/s where there may be a local connection. These should be undertaken as soon as possible. An authority that is considering making a referral must investigate all the circumstances of the case with the same thoroughness as if it were not considering a referral.

5.2   Under s 184(4) *Housing Act 1996*, if a housing authority notifies or intends to notify another authority in England under s 198(A1) (*i.e.* at the relief duty stage) that it considers that the conditions for referral of a case are met, the authority must at the same time notify the applicant of this decision and the reasons for it. Under s 184(5) of the 1996 Act, the notice must also inform the applicant of his right, under s 202, to request a review of the decision and that any request must be made within 21 days, or such longer period as the authority allows in writing.

5.3   See further below as to the duty to ensure that suitable accommodation is available for occupation by the applicant, where an authority notifies an applicant, either as above under s 198(A1) or for the purposes of s 200(1) (*i.e.* at the s 193 main duty stage).

5.4 In general, the notified authority is bound by any decision made by the notifying authority as to whether the applicant is eligible, homeless, unintentionally homeless, and in priority need; there is no provision for the notified authority to challenge the decision other than by judicial review in the High Court. For notifications made under s 198(A1), however, where the notifying authority has made a decision as to whether the applicant is eligible, homeless or became homeless intentionally, the notified authority may come to a different decision but only if it is satisfied the applicant's circumstances have changed or further information has come to light since the notifying authority made its decision, and that the change in circumstances or further information justifies coming to a different decision (s 199A(5)(c)).

5.5 When it has been decided whether the conditions for referral are met, the notifying authority must notify the applicant of the decision and the reason for it (s 199A(3) and s 200(2)). The applicant must also be informed of his right to ask for a review of the decision and that any request must be made within 21 days or such longer period as the authority may allow in writing.

5.6 The local authority associations' disputes procedure should be used only where there is a disagreement over the question of whether the conditions for referral are met and not for resolving disagreement on any other matter.

6

Making the notification to the other authority

6.1 All notifications and arrangements concerning an applicant should be made by telephone and then confirmed in writing. A specimen standard notification form is attached, which authorities are advised to use. If telephone contact cannot be made, an email or fax should be sent. Where the notified authority accepts that the conditions for referral are met, it should not wait for the receipt of written confirmation of notification before making appropriate arrangements to secure accommodation for the applicant and his or her household.

6.2 Each authority should nominate an officer responsible for making decisions about applications notified by another authority. Appropriate arrangements should also be put in place to ensure cover during any absences of the designated officer.

6.3 The notified authority should normally accept the facts of the case relating to residence, employment, family associations etc., as stated by the notifying authority, unless they have clear evidence to the contrary. It is the notifying authority's duty to make inquiries into the circumstances of homelessness with the same degree of care and thoroughness before referring a case to another authority as it would for any other case.

6.4 Local authorities should try to avoid causing undue disruption to the applicant which could arise from the operation of the criteria and procedures set out above. For instance, where it is agreed that the conditions for referral are met, the two authorities involved could agree, subject to the applicants' consent, to enter into a reciprocal arrangement so as to avoid having to move a household which may already have made arrangements within the notifying authority's area for schooling, medical treatment etc. Such arrangements could involve provision via nominations to other social housing providers such as registered social landlords. Authorities are reminded that there is no requirement to refer applicants to another authority even where it is agreed that the conditions for referral are met.

6.5 Once written confirmation of notification has been received the notified authority should, within 10 days, reply to the notifying authority. If, despite reminders, there is an unreasonable delay by the notified authority in formally responding to the notification, the notifying authority may ask its local authority association to intercede on its behalf.

7

Arrangements for securing accommodation

7.1 Where an authority notifies an applicant that it intends to notify or has notified another authority of their opinion that the conditions for referral are met at the s 193 main duty stage, it has a duty under s 200(1) to ensure that suitable accommodation is available for occupation by the applicant until s/he is notified of the decision whether the conditions for referral are met. A similar duty arises under s 199A(2) where the notifying authority similarly notifies an applicant in relation to a s 198(A1) referral at the s 189B relief duty stage, but only if it has reason to believe that the applicant may have a priority need. The notifying authority may also have a duty (under s 211) to take reasonable steps for the protection of property belonging to the applicant or anyone who might reasonably be expected to reside with the applicant.

7.2 If it is decided that the conditions for referral are not met, the notifying authority will be subject to either the s 189B relief duty (see s199A(4)(a)) or the s 193 main duty (see s 200(3)), depending on whether the referral arose under s 198(A1) or s 198(1).

7.3 If it is decided that the conditions for referral are met, then either

(i)   under s 199A(5)(a), the applicant is treated as having made an application to the notified authority on the date on which the applicant is given notice that the referral conditions are met, or

(ii)   under s 200(4), the notified authority will be subject to the s 193 main duty and must ensure that suitable accommodation is available for the applicant,

as the case may be.

7.4 The local authority associations recommend that once a notified authority has accepted that the conditions of referral are met it shall reimburse the notifying authority for any expenses which may reasonably have been incurred in providing temporary accommodation, including protection of property. If the notifying authority delays unduly before advising an authority of its intention to refer an applicant then the notified authority shall only be responsible for expenses incurred after the receipt of notification. In normal circumstances a period of more than 30 working days, commencing from the date when the notifying authority had reason to believe that the applicant may be homeless or threatened with homelessness and commenced inquiries under s 184, should be considered as constituting undue delay.

8

Right of review of referral decisions

8.1 Under s 202(1)(c) *Housing Act 1996*, applicants have the right to request a review of a decision by the authority under s 198(1) to notify another authority of its opinion that the conditions for referral are met.

8.2 Further, under s 202(1)(d), applicants have the right to request a review of any decision whether the conditions for referral are met (whether the notification was made under s 198(A1) or s 198(1)).

9

Statutory procedure on review

9.1 The procedural requirements for a review are set out in the *Homelessness (Review Procedure etc) Regulations 2018 (SI 2018 No.223)*. There is some overlap between the requirements for reviews in general, considered here so far as they are relevant to referrals, and the requirements for reviews of a referee's decision under the Disputes Procedure, considered below.

9.2 The notifying authority must notify the applicant:

(i)   that the applicant, or someone acting on the applicant's behalf, may make written representations; and

(ii)   of the review procedures.

9.3   If the reviewer acting for the notifying authority considers that there is an irregularity in the original decision, or in the manner in which it was made, but is minded nonetheless to make a decision which is against the interests of the applicant, the reviewer must notify the applicant:

(i)   that the reviewer is so minded, and the reasons why; and

(ii)   that the applicant, or someone acting on the applicant's behalf, may make further written and/or oral representations.

9.4   In carrying out a review the reviewer must:

(i)   consider any representations made by, or on behalf of, the applicant;

(ii)   consider any further written and/or oral representations made by, or on behalf of, the applicant in response to a notification referred to in paragraph 9.3(ii) above; and

(iii) make a decision on the basis of the facts known at the date of the review.

9.5   In general, the applicant must be notified of the decision on a review within:

(i)   eight weeks from the date on which a request for review was made, or

(ii)   such longer period as the applicant may agree in writing.

9.6   Where the decision under review is a joint decision by the notifying housing authority and the notified housing authority, s 202(4) requires that the review be carried out jointly by the two housing authorities. In that situation, the applicant must be notified of the decision on a review within:

(i)   ten weeks from the date on which a request for review was made, or

(ii)   such longer period as the applicant may agree in writing.

9.7   Where the decision under s 198(5) was taken by a referee, the procedure is described in the *Guidelines for Invoking the Disputes Procedure*, below.

9.8   Section 204 gives applicants the right to appeal to the county court on a point of law if dissatisfied with the decision on the review (or the initial decision, if a review decision is not made within the relevant prescribed time limit).

10

Disputes between authorities

10.1   Where a notified authority considers the conditions for referral are not met it should write to the notifying authority giving its reasons in full, within 10 days. The letter should contain all the reasons for its opinion, to avoid delay and minimise any inconvenience for the applicant.

10.2   The *Homelessness (Decisions on Referrals) Order 1998* (SI 1998 No.1578) sets out the arrangements for determining whether the conditions for referral are met, should the notifying and the notified authority fail to agree.

10.3   Where two authorities cannot reach agreement on whether the conditions for referral are met they must seek to agree on a referee who will make the decision. The LGA has established an independent panel of referees for this purpose. A referee should be appointed within 21 days of the notified authority receiving the notification.

10.4   Authorities invoking the disputes procedure should, having first agreed on the proposed referee, establish that he or she is available and willing to accept the case. Each authority is then responsible for providing the referee with such information as he or she requires to reach a decision, making copies of the submission available to the applicant and ensuring prompt payment of fees and expenses. The *Guidelines for Invoking the Disputes Procedure* set out in greater detail the requirements and timescale for the disputes procedure.

10.5 If the authorities are unable to agree on the choice of a referee, they must jointly request that the LGA appoint a referee on their behalf from the independent panel.

10.6 If a referee has still not been appointed within six weeks of the notified authority receiving the referral, the notifying authority must request the LGA to appoint a referee.

10.7 The local authority associations should only be involved in the direct appointment of referees as a last resort. Under normal circumstances authorities should jointly agree the arrangements between themselves in accordance with the *Guidelines for Invoking the Disputes Procedure.*

10.8 Authorities invoking the disputes procedure should be bound by the decision of the referee, including the apportionment of fees and expenses, subject to a further decision by a referee where the applicant asks for a review of the initial decision.

11

Cross-border disputes

11.1 In Scotland, the main homelessness law is the *Housing (Scotland) Act 1987*, while in Wales it is the *Housing (Wales) Act 2014*. Both make similar provision to s 198 of the *Housing Act 1996*: s 33 of the *Housing (Scotland) Act 1987* and s 80 of the *Housing (Wales) Act 2014*. Where relevant, regard should be had to the appropriate national governmental guidance. Note that the position of former asylum seekers with regard to local connection may be quite different in Scotland from England and Wales.

11.2 Where there is a cross-border dispute, it is the legislation relevant to the location of the *notified* authority which should be applied in determining whether the conditions for referral are met.

11.3 The review procedure in Scotland and Wales respectively is governed by ss 35A and 35B of the *Housing (Scotland) Act 1987* and the *Homelessness (Review Procedure) (Wales) Regulations 2015* (SI 2015 No. 1266).

11.4 The *Homelessness (Decisions on Referrals (Scotland) Order 1998* (SI 1998 No. 1603) sets out the arrangements for determining whether the conditions for referral are met, should the notifying and the notified authority fail to agree, where the notifying authority is in Scotland. These are in the same terms as for England, but the referee is appointed through CoSLA.

GUIDELINES FOR INVOKING THE DISPUTES PROCEDURE

AGREED BY

LOCAL GOVERNMENT ASSOCIATION (LGA)

CONVENTION OF SCOTTISH LOCAL AUTHORITIES (COSLA)

WELSH LOCAL GOVERNMENT ASSOCIATION (WLGA)

"the local authority associations")

12

Determining disputes

12.1 The local authority associations have been concerned to establish an inexpensive, simple, speedy, fair and consistent way of resolving disputes between authorities arising from the referral of homeless applicants.

12.2 For the purpose of this Disputes Procedure, arbitrators are referred to as "referees". Referees will not normally be entitled to apply the criteria set out in this agreed procedure without the consent of the local authorities involved in the dispute.

Where the issues in the case are evenly balanced, referees may have regard to the wishes of the applicant.

12.3 In determining disputes referees will need to apply the relevant statutory framework and have regard to the appropriate national governmental guidance.

13

Arrangements for appointing referees

13.1 Referees will be approached by the authorities in dispute, both of which must agree that the referee should be invited to accept the appointment, to establish whether they are willing and able to act in a particular dispute. The referee should be appointed within 21 days of the notified authority receiving the referral. If the local authorities are unable to agree on the choice of referee they should contact the LGA in accordance with section 10 of the *Guidelines for Local Authorities on Procedures for Referral.*

13.2 A referee will be given an initial indication of the reason for the dispute by the relevant authorities or the local authority association. The referee's jurisdiction is limited to the issue of whether the conditions for referral are met.

13.3 A referee must not have any personal interest in the outcome of the dispute and should not accept the appointment if he or she is, or was, employed by, or is a council tax payer in, one of the disputing local authorities, or if he or she has any connection with the applicant.

14

Procedures for determining the dispute

14.1 The general procedures to be followed by a referee in determining a dispute are outlined in the Schedule to the *Homelessness (Decisions on Referrals) Order 1998* (SI 1998 No. 1578). It is recommended that the following, more detailed, procedures are applied to *all* cases.

14.2 Following appointment, the referee shall invite the notifying and notified authorities to submit written representations within a period of *fourteen* working days, specifying the closing date, and requiring them to send copies of their submission to the applicant and to the other authority involved in the dispute. Authorities must have the opportunity to see each other's written statements, and should be allowed a further period of *ten* working days to comment thereon before the referee proceeds to determine the issue. The referee may also invite further written representations from the authorities, if considered necessary.

14.3 The homeless applicant to whom the dispute relates is not a direct party to the dispute but the referee may invite written or oral representations from the applicant, or any other person, which is proper and relevant to the issue. Where the referee invites representations from a person they may be made by another person acting on the person's behalf, whether or not the other person is legally qualified.

14.4 The disputing authorities should make copies of their submissions available to the applicant. The authorities should have the opportunity to comment on any information from the applicant (or any other source) upon which the referee intends to rely in reaching his/her decision.

14.5 Since the applicant's place of abode is in question, and temporary accommodation and property storage charges may be involved, it is important that a decision should be reached as quickly as possible – normally within *a month* of the receipt of the written representations and comments from the notifying and notified authority. This period will commence at the end of the process described in paragraph 14.2. In the last resort, a referee may determine a dispute on the facts before him/her if one authority has, after reminders, failed to present its case without reasonable cause.

15

Oral hearings

15.1 Where an oral hearing is necessary or more convenient (e.g. where the applicant is illiterate, English is not his/her first language or further information is necessary to resolve issues in dispute), it is suggested that the notifying authority should be invited to present its case first, followed by the notified authority and any other persons whom the referee wishes to hear. The applicant may be invited to provide information on relevant matters. The authorities should then be given a right to reply to earlier submissions.

15.2 The referee will have to arrange the venue for the hearing and it is suggested that the offices of the notifying authority would often be the most convenient location.

15.3 Where a person has made oral representations the referee may direct either or both authorities to pay reasonable travelling expenses. The notifying and notified authorities will pay their own costs.

15.4 The referee's determination must be in writing even when there is an oral hearing.

16

Notification of determination

16.1 The written decision of the referee should set out:

(a) the issue(s) which s/he has been asked to determine
(b) the findings of fact which are relevant to the question(s) in issue
(c) the decision
(d) the reasons for the decision.

The referee's determination is binding upon the participating local authorities, subject to the applicant's right to ask for a review of the decision under s 202 of the *Housing Act 1996* (and possible right of appeal to the county court on a point of law under s 204).

17

Costs of determination

17.1 Referees will be expected to provide their own secretarial services and to obtain their own advice on points of law. The cost of so doing, however, will be costs of the determination and recoverable as such.

18

Circulation of determination

18.1 Referees should send copies of the determination to both disputing authorities and to the LGA. The LGA will circulate copies to other members of the Panel of Referees as an aid to settling future disputes and promoting consistency in decisions.

18.2 The notifying authority should inform the applicant of the outcome promptly.

19

Payment of fees and costs

19.1 The local authority associations recommend a flat rate fee of £500 per determination (including determinations made on a review) which should be paid in full and as speedily as possible after the determination has been received. However, in exceptional cases where a dispute takes a disproportionate time to resolve, a referee may negotiate a higher fee. In addition, the referee may claim the actual cost of any travelling, secretarial or other incidental expenses which s/he has incurred, including any additional costs arising from the right of review or the right of appeal to a county court on a point of law.

19.2 The LGA will determine such additional fees as may be appropriate for any additional work which may subsequently arise should there be a further dispute or appeal after the initial determination has been made or should a referee be party to an appeal, under s 204 *Housing Act 1996*, to the county court on a point of law.

19.3 The referee's fees and expenses, and any third party costs, would normally be recovered from the unsuccessful party to the dispute, although a referee may choose to apportion expenses between the disputing authorities if s/he considers it warranted. Referees are advised, when issuing invoices to local authorities, to stipulate that payment must be made within **28 days**.

20

Reopening a dispute

20.1 Once a determination on a dispute is made, a referee is not permitted to reopen the case, even though new facts may be presented to him or her, unless a fresh determination is required to rectify an error arising from a mistake or omission.

21

Review of referee's decision

21.1 Section 202(1)(d) *Housing Act 1996* gives an applicant the right to request a review of any decision made under this Dispute Procedure. The procedural requirements for a review are set out in the *Homelessness (Review Procedure etc) Regulations 2018 (SI 2018 No.223)*. There is some overlap between the requirements for reviews of a referee's decision under the Disputes Procedure, considered here, and the requirements for reviews in general, considered above so far as they are relevant to referrals.

21.2 If an applicant asks for a review of a referee's decision the notifying and notified authority must, within five working days, appoint another referee ("the reviewer") from the panel. This applies even if the original referee was appointed by the LGA. The reviewer must be a different referee from the referee who made the initial decision. If the two authorities fail to appoint a reviewer within this period then the notifying authority must, within five working days, request the LGA to appoint a reviewer and the LGA must do so within seven days of the request.

21.3 The authorities are required to provide the reviewer with the reasons for the initial decision, and the information on which the decision is based, within five working days of his or her appointment. The two authorities should decide between them who will be responsible for notifying the applicant of the reviewer's decision, once received.

21.4 The reviewer is required to:

(i)   notify the applicant that he or she, or someone acting on his or her behalf, may make written representations,
(ii)   notify the applicant of the review procedures, and
(iii)   send copies of the applicant's representations to the two authorities and invite them to respond.

21.5 If the reviewer considers that there is an irregularity in the original decision, or in the manner in which it was made, but is minded nonetheless to make a decision which is against the interests of the applicant on one or more issues, the reviewer must notify the applicant:

(a)   that the reviewer is so minded and the reasons why, and

1487

(b)   that the applicant, or someone acting on his behalf, may make further written and/or oral representations.

21.6   In carrying out a review, the reviewer is required to:

(i)   consider any representations made by, or on behalf of, the applicant,

(ii)   consider any responses to (i) above,

(iii)   consider any further written and/or oral representations made by, or on behalf of, the applicant in response to a notification referred to in paragraph 21.5(b), and

(iv)   make a decision on the basis of the facts known at the date of the review.

21.7   The applicant must be notified of the decision on a review within twelve weeks from the date on which the request for the review was made, or such longer period as the applicant may agree in writing. The two authorities must be advised in writing of the decision on the review, and the reasons for it, **at least a week before the end of the period** in order to allow them adequate time to notify the applicant. Copies of the decision should also be sent to the LGA.

22

Cross-border disputes

22.1   For cross-border cases, see Section 11 of the Guidelines, above.

PROCEDURES FOR REFERRALS OF HOMELESS APPLICANTS ON THE GROUNDS OF LOCAL CONNECTION WITH ANOTHER LOCAL AUTHORITY

Standard Notification Form

A – NOTIFYING AUTHORITY DETAILS

Contact Name

Authority

Telephone Number

Fax Number

E-mail

Address for Correspondence

B – APPLICANT DETAILS

Name of Main Applicant

Date of Birth

Current Address

C – FAMILY MEMBERS

Name	Relationship	Date of Birth

D – ADDRESSES IN LAST 5 YEARS (include dates and types of tenure)

E – PRESENT/PREVIOUS EMPLOYMENT DETAILS

Employer

Telephone No

Address

Contact Name and Job Title

Previous Employer

Date from

Date to

Address

F – REASONS FOR HOMELESSNESS

G – PRIORITY NEED CATEGORY

H – LOCAL CONNECTION DETAILS

I – WISHES OF THE APPLICANT(S) (in the context of the referral)

J – THE NOTIFYING AUTHORITY CONSIDER THE CONDITIONS FOR RE-FERRAL ARE MET BECAUSE:

K – ANY SUPPLEMENTARY INFORMATION (attach supporting documentation if relevant)

I confirm that, in accordance with the s198 Housing Act 1996, this authority considers that neither the applicant nor any person who might reasonably be expected to reside with the applicant would run the risk of domestic violence or face a probability of other violence in the district of your authority, if this referral is made.

Signed

Date

HOMELESSNESS (SUITABILITY OF ACCOMMODATION) ORDER 1996

SI 1996/3204

A2.5

1 Citation and commencement

This Order may be cited as the Homelessness (Suitability of Accommodation) Order 1996 and shall come into force on 20th January 1997.

2 Matters to be taken into account

In determining whether it would be, or would have been, reasonable for a person to continue to occupy accommodation and in determining whether accommodation is suitable for a person there shall be taken into account whether or not the accommodation is affordable for that person and, in particular, the following matters—

    (a)   the financial resources available to that person, including, but not limited to,—

        (i)   salary, fees and other remuneration;

        (ii)   social security benefits;

        (iii)   payments due under a court order for the making of periodical payments to a spouse or a former spouse, or to, or for the benefit of, a child;

        (iv)   payments of child support maintenance due under the Child Support Act 1991;

        (v)   pensions;

        (vi)   contributions to the costs in respect of the accommodation which are or were made or which might reasonably be expected to be, or have been, made by other members of his household;

        (vii)   financial assistance towards the costs in respect of the accommodation, including loans, provided by a local authority, voluntary organisation or other body;

        (viii)   benefits derived from a policy of insurance;

        (ix)   savings and other capital sums;

    (b)   the costs in respect of the accommodation, including, but not limited to,—

        (i)   payments of, or by way of, rent;

        (ii)   payments in respect of a licence or permission to occupy the accommodation;

        (iii)   mortgage costs;

        (iv)   payments of, or by way of, service charges;

        (v)   mooring charges payable for a houseboat;

        (vi)   where the accommodation is a caravan or a mobile home, payments in respect of the site on which it stands;

        (vii)   the amount of council tax payable in respect of the accommodation;

        (viii)   payments by way of deposit or security in respect of the accommodation;

        (ix)   payments required by an accommodation agency;

    (c)   payments which that person is required to make under a court order for the making of periodical payments to a spouse or a former spouse, or to, or for the benefit of, a child and payments of child support maintenance required to be made under the Child Support Act 1991;

(d)   that person's other reasonable living expenses.

[3   Circumstances in which accommodation is not to be regarded as suitable]
[For the purposes of section 197(1) of the Housing Act 1996 (duty where other suitable accommodation available), accommodation shall not be regarded as suitable unless the local housing authority are satisfied that it will be available for occupation by the applicant for at least two years beginning with the date on which he secures it.]

NOTES

Amendment

Inserted by SI 1997/1741, art 2.
     Date in force: 1 September 1997: see SI 1997/1741, art 1.

LOCAL AUTHORITIES (CONTRACTING OUT OF ALLOCATION OF HOUSING AND HOMELESS-NESS FUNCTIONS) ORDER 1996

SI 1996/3205

A2.6

1 Citation, commencement and interpretation
(1)   This Order may be cited as the Local Authorities (Contracting Out of Allocation of Housing and Homelessness Functions) Order 1996.
(2)   This article and article 3 of this Order shall come into force on 20th January 1997 and article 2 of this Order shall come into force on 1st April 1997.
(3)   In this Order—
　　　"the Act" means the Housing Act 1996;
　　　"an authority" means a local housing authority as defined in the Housing Act 1985.
(4)   Any expressions used in this Order which are also used in the Act have the same meaning as they have in the Act.

2 Contracting out of allocation of housing functions
Any function of an authority which is conferred by or under Part VI of the Act (allocation of housing accommodation), except one which is listed in Schedule 1 to this Order, may be exercised by, or by employees of, such person (if any) as may be authorised in that behalf by the authority whose function it is.

3 Contracting out of homelessness functions
Any function of an authority which is conferred by or under Part VII of the Act (homelessness) [or Chapter 2 of Part 2 of the Housing (Wales) Act 2014 (help for people who are homeless or threatened with homelessness)], except one which is listed in Schedule 2 to this Order, may be exercised by, or by employees of, such person (if any) as may be authorised in that behalf by the authority whose function it is.

NOTES

Amendment
　　Words from "or Chapter 2" to "threatened with homelessness)" in square brackets inserted, in relation to Wales, by SI 2015/752, reg 2(1), (2).
　　Date in force: 27 April 2015: see SI 2015/752, reg 1.

SCHEDULE 1

ALLOCATION OF HOUSING FUNCTIONS OF A LOCAL HOUSING AUTHORITY EXCLUDED FROM CONTRACTING OUT

Article 2
Functions conferred by or under any of the following provisions of the Act:
　　(a)　　section 161(4) (classes of persons qualifying for allocations);
　　(b)　　section 162 (the housing register) so far as they relate to any decision about the form of the register;
　　(c)　　section 167 (allocation in accordance with allocation scheme) so far as they relate to adopting or altering an allocation scheme (including decisions on what principles the scheme is to be framed) and to the functions in subsection (7) of that section;

(d)   section 168(2) (information about allocation scheme) so far as they relate to making the allocation scheme available for inspection at the authority's principal office.

SCHEDULE 2

HOMELESSNESS FUNCTIONS OF A LOCAL HOUSING AUTHORITY EXCLUDED FROM CONTRACTING OUT

Article 3

Functions conferred by or under any of the following provisions of the Act:

(a)   section 179(2) and (3) (duty of local housing authority to provide advisory services);

(b)   section 180 (assistance for voluntary organisations);

(c)   section 213 (co-operation between relevant housing authorities and bodies).

[Functions conferred by or under section 95 of the Housing (Wales) Act 2014.]

NOTES

Amendment

Words from "Functions conferred by" to "Housing (Wales) Act 2014." in square brackets inserted, in relation to Wales, by SI 2015/752, reg 2(1), (3).
Date in force: 27 April 2015: see SI 2015/752, reg 1.

HOMELESSNESS (ISLES OF SCILLY) ORDER 1997

SI 1997/797

A2.7

1 Citation, commencement and interpretation

(1) This Order may be cited as the Homelessness (Isles of Scilly) Order 1997 and shall come into force on 3rd April 1997.

(2) In this Order—

"the Act" means the Housing Act 1996;

"the Council" means the Council of the Isles of Scilly.

2 Eligibility for assistance by the Council and local connection with the district of the Council

(1) Where—

    (a) a person applies to the Council for assistance under Part VII of the Act (homelessness); or

    (b) a person applies to a local housing authority other than the Council for such assistance and, but for the provisions of paragraphs (2) and (3), the conditions specified in section 198(2) of the Act (referral of case to another authority) for referral of the case to the Council are satisfied,

sections 183 to 218 of the Act shall be subject to the following provisions of this article.

(2) A person is not eligible for assistance by the Council if he has not been resident in the district of the Council for a period of two years and six months during the period of three years immediately prior to his application.

(3) Where a person is not excluded from assistance by the Council by paragraph (2)—

    (a) he has a local connection with the district of the Council; and

    (b) section 199 of the Act (local connection) shall not apply for the purpose of determining whether he has a local connection with the district of the Council.

HOMELESSNESS (DECISIONS ON REFERRALS) ORDER 1998

SI 1998/1578

A2.8

1 Citation and commencement
This Order may be cited as the Homelessness (Decisions on Referrals) Order 1998 and shall come into force on the twenty eighth day after the day on which it is approved by resolution of each House of Parliament.

2 Arrangements for deciding whether conditions for referral are satisfied
The arrangements set out in the Schedule to this Order are those agreed by the Local Government Association, the Welsh Local Government Association, the Association of London Government and the Convention of Scottish Local Authorities, and shall be the arrangements for the purposes of section 198(5) and (6)(a) of the Housing Act 1996.

3 Revocation of order
(1) Subject to paragraph (2), the Housing (Homeless Persons) (Appropriate Arrangements) Order 1978 ("the 1978 Order") is hereby revoked.

(2) The 1978 Order shall remain in force for any case where a notified authority has received a notification under section 67(1) of the Housing Act 1985 or section 198(1) of the Housing Act 1996 (referral to another local housing authority) prior to the date on which this Order comes into force.

SCHEDULE

THE ARRANGEMENTS

Article 2

Appointment of person by agreement between notifying authority and notified authority

1

Where the question whether the conditions for referral of a case are satisfied has not been decided by agreement between the notifying authority and the notified authority, the question shall be decided by a person appointed by those authorities.

Appointment of person other than by agreement between notifying authority and notified authority

2

If within a period of 21 days commencing on the day on which the notified authority receives a notification under section 198(1) of the Housing Act 1996 a person has not been appointed in accordance with paragraph 1, the question shall be decided by a person—

    (a)   from the panel constituted in accordance with paragraph 3, and

    (b)   appointed in accordance with paragraph 4.

3

(1)   Subject to sub-paragraph (2), the Local Government Association shall establish and maintain a panel of persons from which a person may be appointed to decide the question whether the conditions for referral of a case are satisfied.

(2)   The Local Government Association shall consult such other associations of relevant authorities as they think appropriate before—

    (a)   establishing the panel,

    (b)   inviting a person to join the panel after it has been established, and

    (c)   removing a person from the panel.

4

(1)   The notifying authority and the notified authority shall jointly request the Chairman of the Local Government Association or his nominee ("the proper officer") to appoint a person from the panel.

(2)   If within a period of six weeks commencing on the day on which the notified authority receives a notification under section 198(1) of the Housing Act 1996 a person has not been appointed, the notifying authority shall request the proper officer to appoint a person from the panel.

Procedural requirements

5

(1)   Subject to the following provisions of this paragraph, the procedure for deciding whether the conditions for referral of a case are satisfied shall be determined by the appointed person.

(2)   The appointed person shall invite written representations from the notifying authority and the notified authority.

(3)   The appointed person may also invite—

    (a)   further written representations from the notifying authority and the notified authority,

    (b)   written representations from any other person, and

    (c)   oral representations from any person.

(4)   If the appointed person invites representations from any person, those representations may be made by a person acting on his behalf, whether or not legally qualified.

Notification of decision

6

The appointed person shall notify his decision, and his reasons for it, in writing to the notifying authority and the notified authority.

Costs

7

(1)   The notifying authority and the notified authority shall pay their own costs incurred in connection with the arrangements set out in this Schedule.

(2)   Where a person has made oral representations, the appointed person may give directions as to the payment by the notifying authority or the notified authority or both authorities of any travelling expenses reasonably incurred by that person.

Meaning of "appointed person"

8

In this Schedule "appointed person" means a person appointed in accordance with paragraph 1 or 4.

HOMELESSNESS (PRIORITY NEED FOR ACCOMMODATION) (ENGLAND) ORDER 2002

SI 2002/2051

A2.9

1 Citation, commencement and interpretation

(1) This Order may be cited as the Homelessness (Priority Need for Accommodation) (England) Order 2002 and shall come into force on the day after the day on which it is made.

(2) This Order extends to England only.

(3) In this Order—

"looked after, accommodated or fostered" has the meaning given by section 24(2) of the Children Act 1989 [or, as the case may be, section 104(3) of the Social Services and Well-being (Wales) Act 2014];

"relevant student" means a person to whom section 24B(3) of [the Children Act 1989 or, as the case may be, section 114(5) or 115(6) of the Social Services and Well-being (Wales) Act 2014] applies—

    (a)   who is in full-time further or higher education; and

    (b)   whose term-time accommodation is not available to him during a vacation.

NOTES

Amendment

Para (3): in definition "looked after, accommodated or fostered" words from "or, as the" to "Social Services and Well-being (Wales) Act 2014" in square brackets inserted by SI 2016/211, reg 3, Sch 3, Pt 1, paras 48, 49(a).
    Date in force: 6 April 2016: see SI 2016/211, reg 1(2).
Para (3): in definition "relevant student" words from "the Children Act 1989" to "Social Services and Well-being (Wales) Act 2014" in square brackets substituted by SI 2016/211, reg 3, Sch 3, Pt 1, paras 48, 49(b).
    Date in force: 6 April 2016: see SI 2016/211, reg 1(2).

2 Priority need for accommodation

The descriptions of person specified in the following articles have a priority need for accommodation for the purposes of Part 7 of the Housing Act 1996.

3 Children aged 16 or 17

(1) A person (other than a person to whom paragraph (2) below applies) aged sixteen or seventeen who is not a relevant child for the purposes of section 23A of the Children Act 1989 [or, as the case may be, is not a category 2 young person within the meaning of section 104(2) of the Social Services and Well-being (Wales) Act 2014].

(2) This paragraph applies to a person to whom a local authority owe a duty to provide accommodation under section 20 of that Act (provision of accommodation for children in need) [or, as the case may be, section 76 of the Social Services and Well-being (Wales) Act 2014 (accommodation for children without parents or who are lost or abandoned etc)].

NOTES

Amendment

Para (1): words from "or, as the" to "Social Services and Well-being (Wales) Act 2014" in square brackets inserted by SI 2016/211, reg 3, Sch 3, Pt 1, paras 48, 50(1), (2).
    Date in force: 6 April 2016: see SI 2016/211, reg 1(2).
Para (2): words from "or, as the" to "or abandoned etc)" in square brackets inserted by SI 2016/211, reg 3, Sch 3, Pt 1, paras 48, 50(1), (3).

Date in force: 6 April 2016: see SI 2016/211, reg 1(2).

4 Young people under 21

(1)   A person (other than a relevant student) who—

(a)   is under twenty-one; and

(b)   at any time after reaching the age of sixteen, but while still under eighteen, was, but is no longer, looked after, accommodated or fostered.

5 Vulnerability: institutional backgrounds

(1)   A person (other than a relevant student) who has reached the age of twenty-one and who is vulnerable as a result of having been looked after, accommodated or fostered.

(2)   A person who is vulnerable as a result of having been a member of Her Majesty's regular naval, military or air forces.

(3)   A person who is vulnerable as a result of—

(a)   having served a custodial sentence (within the meaning of section 76 of the Powers of Criminal Courts (Sentencing) Act 2000);

(b)   having been committed for contempt of court or any other kindred offence;

(c)   having been remanded in custody (within the meaning of paragraph (b), (c) or (d) of section 88(1) of that Act).

6 Vulnerability: fleeing violence or threats of violence

A person who is vulnerable as a result of ceasing to occupy accommodation by reason of violence from another person or threats of violence from another person which are likely to be carried out.

HOMELESSNESS (SUITABILITY OF ACCOMMODATION) (ENGLAND) ORDER 2003

SI 2003/3326

A2.10

1 Citation, commencement and application

(1)   This Order may be cited as the Homelessness (Suitability of Accommodation) (England) Order 2003 and shall come into force on 1st April 2004.

(2)   This Order applies in relation to the duties of local housing authorities in England to make accommodation available for occupation by applicants under Part 7 of the Housing Act 1996.

2 Interpretation

In this Order—

"applicant with family commitments" means an applicant—

    (a)   who is pregnant;

    (b)   with whom a pregnant woman resides or might reasonably be expected to reside; or

    (c)   with whom dependent children reside or might reasonably be expected to reside;

"B&B accommodation" means accommodation (whether or not breakfast is included)—

    (a)   which is not separate and self-contained premises; and

    (b)   in which any one of the following amenities is shared by more than one household—

        (i)   a toilet;

        (ii)   personal washing facilities;

        (iii) cooking facilities,

but does not include accommodation which is owned or managed by a local housing authority, [a non-profit registered provider of social housing] or a voluntary organisation as defined in section 180(3) of the Housing Act 1996; and

any reference to a numbered section is a reference to a section of the Housing Act 1996.

NOTES

Amendment

In definition "B&B accommodation" words "a non-profit registered provider of social housing" in square brackets substituted by SI 2010/671, art 4, Sch 1, para 36.

Date in force: 1 April 2010 (being the date on which the Housing and Regeneration Act 2008, s 111 came into force): see SI 2010/671, art 1(2), and SI 2010/862, art 2; for transitional provisions and savings see SI 2010/671, art 5, Sch 2, paras 1, 2, 5, 6 and SI 2010/862, arts 2, 3, Schedule, paras 1–5.

3 Accommodation unsuitable where there is a family commitment

Subject to the exceptions contained in article 4, B&B accommodation is not to be regarded as suitable for an applicant with family commitments where accommodation is made available for occupation—

    (a)   under section 188(1), 190(2), 193(2) or 200(1); or

    (b)   under section 195(2), where the accommodation is other than that occupied by the applicant at the time of making his application.

4 Exceptions

(1)   Article 3 does not apply—

    (a)   where no accommodation other than B&B accommodation is available for occupation by an applicant with family commitments; and

    (b)   the applicant occupies B&B accommodation for a period, or a total of periods, which does not exceed 6 weeks.

(2)   In calculating the period, or total period, of an applicant's occupation of B&B accommodation for the purposes of paragraph (1)(b), there shall be disregarded—

    (a)   any period before 1st April 2004; and

    (b)   where a local housing authority is subject to the duty under section 193 by virtue of section 200(4), any period before that authority became subject to that duty.

ALLOCATION OF HOUSING AND HOMELESS-NESS (ELIGIBILITY) (ENGLAND) REGULATIONS 2006

SI 2006/1294

A2.11

1 Citation, commencement and application
(1)   These Regulations may be cited as the Allocation of Housing and Homelessness (Eligibility) (England) Regulations 2006 and shall come into force on 1st June 2006.
(2)   These Regulations apply to England only.

2 Interpretation
(1)   In these Regulations—
   "the 1996 Act" means the Housing Act 1996;
   [. . .
   . . .]
       ["the Accession Regulations 2013" means the Accession of Croatia (Immigration and Worker Authorisation) Regulations 2013;]
       "the EEA Regulations" means the Immigration (European Economic Area) Regulations 2006;
   ["the Human Rights Convention" means the Convention for the Protection of Human Rights and Fundamental Freedoms, agreed by the Council of Europe at Rome on 4thNovember 1950 as it has effect for the time being in relation to the United Kingdom;]
       "the Immigration Rules" means the rules laid down as mentioned in section 3(2) of the Immigration Act 1971 (general provisions for regulation and control);
       "the Refugee Convention" means the Convention relating to the Status of Refugees done at Geneva on 28th July 1951, as extended by Article 1(2) of the Protocol relating to the Status of Refugees done at New York on 31st January 1967; and
       "sponsor" means a person who has given an undertaking in writing for the purposes of the Immigration Rules to be responsible for the maintenance and accommodation of another person.
(2)   For the purposes of these Regulations—
   (a)   "jobseeker", "self-employed person", and "worker" have the same meaning as for the purposes of the definition of a "qualified person" in regulation 6(1) of the EEA Regulations; and
   (b)   subject to paragraph (3), references to the family member of a jobseeker, self-employed person or worker shall be construed in accordance with regulation 7 of those Regulations.
(3)   For the purposes of regulations 4(2)(d) and 6(2)(d) "family member" does not include a person who is treated as a family member by virtue of regulation 7(3) of the EEA Regulations.
[(4)   . . .]

NOTES

Amendment

Para (1): definitions "the Accession Regulations 2004" (omitted) and "the Accession Regulations 2006" (omitted) substituted, for definition "the Accession Regulations" as originally enacted, by SI 2006/3340, reg 2(1), (2).
    Date in force: 1 January 2007: see SI 2006/3340, reg 1(1); for transitional provisions see reg 3 thereof.
Para (1): definition "the Accession Regulations 2004" (omitted) revoked by SI 2013/1467, reg 2(1), (2)(a).
    Date in force: 1 July 2013: see SI 2013/1467, reg 1(1); for transitional provisions see reg 3 thereof.
Para (1): definition "the Accession Regulations 2006" (omitted) revoked by SI 2014/435, reg 2(1), (2)(a).
    Date in force: 31 March 2014: see SI 2014/435, reg 1(1).
Para (1): definition "the Accession Regulations 2013" inserted by SI 2013/1467, reg 2(1), (2)(b).
    Date in force: 1 July 2013: see SI 2013/1467, reg 1(1); for transitional provisions see reg 3 thereof.
Para (1): definition "the Human Rights Convention" inserted by SI 2016/965, reg 2(1), (2).
    Date in force: 30 October 2016: see SI 2016/965, reg 1(1).
Para (4): inserted by SI 2006/2007, reg 2(1), (2).
    Date in force: 25 July 2006 at 1600 hours: see SI 2006/2007, reg 1(1).
Para (4): revoked by SI 2014/435, reg 2(1), (2)(b).
    Date in force: 31 March 2014: see SI 2014/435, reg 1(1).

3 Persons subject to immigration control who are eligible for an allocation of housing accommodation

The following classes of persons subject to immigration control are persons who are eligible for an allocation of housing accommodation under Part 6 of the 1996 Act—

(a)   Class A—a person who is recorded by the Secretary of State as a refugee within the definition in Article 1 of the Refugee Convention and who has leave to enter or remain in the United Kingdom;

(b)   Class B—a person—

    (i)   who has exceptional leave to enter or remain in the United Kingdom granted outside the provisions of the Immigration Rules; and

    (ii)   who is not subject to a condition requiring him to maintain and accommodate himself, and any person who is dependent on him, without recourse to public funds;

(c)   Class C—a person who is habitually resident in the United Kingdom, the Channel Islands, the Isle of Man or the Republic of Ireland and whose leave to enter or remain in the United Kingdom is not subject to any limitation or condition, other than a person—

    (i)   who has been given leave to enter or remain in the United Kingdom upon an undertaking given by his sponsor;

    (ii)   who has been resident in the United Kingdom, the Channel Islands, the Isle of Man or the Republic of Ireland for less than five years beginning on the date of entry or the date on which his sponsor gave the undertaking in respect of him, whichever date is the later; and

    (iii)   whose sponsor or, where there is more than one sponsor, at least one of whose sponsors, is still alive; . . .

[(d)   Class D—a person who has humanitarian protection granted under the Immigration Rules][; . . .

(e)   [Class E—]a person who is habitually resident in the United Kingdom, the Channel Islands, the Isle of Man or the Republic of Ireland and who has limited leave to enter the United Kingdom as a relevant Afghan citizen under paragraph 276BA1 of the Immigration Rules][; . . .

(f) Class F—a person who has limited leave to enter or remain in the United Kingdom on family or private life grounds under Article 8 of the Human Rights Convention, such leave granted—

    (i) under paragraph 276BE(1), paragraph 276DG or Appendix FM of the Immigration Rules, and

    (ii) who is not subject to a condition requiring that person to maintain and accommodate himself, and any person dependent upon him, without recourse to public funds][; and

(g) Class G—a person who is habitually resident in the United Kingdom, the Channel Islands, the Isle of Man or the Republic of Ireland and who has been transferred to the United Kingdom under section 67 of the Immigration Act 2016 and has limited leave to remain under paragraph 352ZH of the Immigration Rules.]

NOTES

Amendment

In para (c)(iii) word omitted revoked by SI 2014/435, reg 2(1), (3)(a).
    Date in force: 31 March 2014: see SI 2014/435, reg 1(1).
Para (d) substituted by SI 2006/2527, reg 2(1), (2).
    Date in force: 9 October 2006: see SI 2006/2527, reg 1(1); for transitional provisions see reg 4 thereof.
Para (e) and word omitted immediately preceding it inserted by SI 2014/435, reg 2(1), (3)(b), (c).
    Date in force: 31 March 2014: see SI 2014/435, reg 1(1).
In para (d) word omitted revoked by SI 2016/965, reg 2(1), (3)(a).
    Date in force: 30 October 2016: see SI 2016/965, reg 1(1).
In para (e) words "Class E—" in square brackets inserted by SI 2016/965, reg 2(1), (3)(b)(i).
    Date in force: 30 October 2016: see SI 2016/965, reg 1(1).
Para (f) and word "; and" immediately preceding it inserted by SI 2016/965, reg 2(1), (3)(b)(ii), (c).
    Date in force: 30 October 2016: see SI 2016/965, reg 1(1).
In para (f) word "and" omitted revoked by SI 2018/730, reg 2(1), (2)(a).
    Date in force: 9 July 2018: see SI 2018/730, reg 1.
Para (g) and word "; and" immediately preceding it inserted by SI 2018/730, reg 2(1), (2)(b), (c).
    Date in force: 9 July 2018: see SI 2018/730, reg 1.

4 Other persons from abroad who are ineligible for an allocation of housing accommodation

(1) A person who is not subject to immigration control is to be treated as a person from abroad who is ineligible for an allocation of housing accommodation under Part 6 of the 1996 Act if—

(a) subject to paragraph (2), he is not habitually resident in the United Kingdom, the Channel Islands, the Isle of Man, or the Republic of Ireland;

(b) his only right to reside in the United Kingdom—

    (i) is derived from his status as a jobseeker or the family member of a jobseeker; or

    (ii) is an initial right to reside for a period not exceeding three months under regulation 13 of the EEA Regulations; or

    [(iii) is a derivative right to reside to which he is entitled under regulation 15A(1) of the EEA Regulations, but only in a case where the right exists under that regulation because the applicant satisfies the criteria in regulation 15A(4A) of those Regulations; or

    (iv) is derived from Article 20 of the Treaty on the Functioning of the European Union, in a case where the right to reside arises because a British citizen would otherwise be deprived of the genuine enjoyment of the substance of their rights as a European Union citizen; or] [(c)　his only right to reside in the Channel Islands, the Isle of Man or the Republic of Ireland—

　　(i)　is a right equivalent to one of those mentioned in sub-paragraphs (b)(i),(ii) or (iii) which is derived from the Treaty on the Functioning of the European Union; or

　　(ii)　is derived from Article 20 of the Treaty on the Functioning of the European Union, in a case where the right to reside—

　　　　(a)　in the Republic of Ireland arises because an Irish citizen, or

　　　　(b)　in the Channel Islands or the Isle of Man arises because a British citizen also entitled to reside there

　　would otherwise be deprived of the genuine enjoyment of the substance of their rights as a European Union citizen].

(2)　The following are not to be treated as persons from abroad who are ineligible for an allocation of housing accommodation pursuant to paragraph (1)(a)—

　(a)　a worker;

　(b)　a self-employed person;

　[(c)　a person who is treated as a worker for the purpose of the definition of "qualified person" in regulation 6(1) of the EEA Regulations pursuant to
. . .—

　　(i)　. . .

　　(ii)　regulation 5 of the Accession Regulations 2013 (right of residence of an accession State national subject to worker authorisation);]

　(d)　a person who is the family member of a person specified in sub-paragraphs (a)–(c);

　(e)　a person with a right to reside permanently in the United Kingdom by virtue of regulation 15(c), (d) or (e) of the EEA Regulations; [and]

　(f)　. . .

　(g)　a person who is in the United Kingdom as a result of his deportation, expulsion or other removal by compulsion of law from another country to the United Kingdom[; . . .]

　[(h)　. . .]

　[(i)　. . .].

NOTES

Amendment

　Para (1): sub-para (b)(iii), (iv) inserted by SI 2012/2588, reg 2(1), (2).
　　Date in force: 8 November 2012: see SI 2012/2588, reg 1(1); for transitional provision see reg 3 thereof.
　Para (1): sub-para (c) substituted by SI 2012/2588, reg 2(1), (3).
　　Date in force: 8 November 2012: see SI 2012/2588, reg 1(1); for transitional provision see reg 3 thereof.
　Para (2): sub-para (c) substituted by SI 2013/1467, reg 2(1), (3).
　　Date in force: 1 July 2013: see SI 2013/1467, reg 1(1); for transitional provisions see reg 3 thereof.
　Para (2): in sub-para (c) first word omitted revoked by SI 2014/435, reg 2(1), (4)(a)(i).
　　Date in force: 31 March 2014: see SI 2014/435, reg 1(1).
　Para (2): sub-para (c)(i) revoked by SI 2014/435, reg 2(1), (4)(a)(ii).
　　Date in force: 31 March 2014: see SI 2014/435, reg 1(1).
　Para (2): in sub-para (e) word "and" in square brackets inserted by SI 2014/435, reg 2(1), (4)(b).
　　Date in force: 31 March 2014: see SI 2014/435, reg 1(1).
　Para (2): sub-para (f) revoked by SI 2014/435, reg 2(1), (4)(c).
　　Date in force: 31 March 2014: see SI 2014/435, reg 1(1).
　Para (2): in sub-para (g) semi-colon and word omitted in square brackets inserted by SI 2006/2007, reg 2(1), (4).
　　Date in force: 25 July 2006 at 1600 hours: see SI 2006/2007, reg 1(1).
　Para (2): in sub-para (g) word omitted revoked by SI 2009/358, reg 2(1), (2).
　　Date in force: 18 March 2009: see SI 2009/358, reg 1(1).
　Para (2): sub-para (h) inserted by SI 2006/2007, reg 2(1), (5).

Date in force: 25 July 2006 at 1600 hours: see SI 2006/2007, reg 1(1).
Para (2): sub-para (h) revoked by SI 2014/435, reg 2(1), (4)(c).
Date in force: 31 March 2014: see SI 2014/435, reg 1(1).
Para (2): sub-para (i) inserted by SI 2009/358, reg 2(1), (3).
Date in force: 18 March 2009: see SI 2009/358, reg 1(1).
Para (2): sub-para (i) revoked by SI 2014/435, reg 2(1), (4)(c).
Date in force: 31 March 2014: see SI 2014/435, reg 1(1).

5 Persons subject to immigration control who are eligible for housing assistance

(1)   The following classes of persons subject to immigration control are persons who are eligible for housing assistance under Part 7 of the 1996 Act—

    (a)   Class A—a person who is recorded by the Secretary of State as a refugee within the definition in Article 1 of the Refugee Convention and who has leave to enter or remain in the United Kingdom;

    (b)   Class B—a person—

        (i)   who has exceptional leave to enter or remain in the United Kingdom granted outside the provisions of the Immigration Rules; and

        (ii)   whose leave to enter or remain is not subject to a condition requiring him to maintain and accommodate himself, and any person who is dependent on him, without recourse to public funds;

    (c)   Class C—a person who is habitually resident in the United Kingdom, the Channel Islands, the Isle of Man or the Republic of Ireland and whose leave to enter or remain in the United Kingdom is not subject to any limitation or condition, other than a person—

        (i)   who has been given leave to enter or remain in the United Kingdom upon an undertaking given by his sponsor;

        (ii)   who has been resident in the United Kingdom, the Channel Islands, the Isle of Man or the Republic of Ireland for less than five years beginning on the date of entry or the date on which his sponsor gave the undertaking in respect of him, whichever date is the later; and

        (iii)   whose sponsor or, where there is more than one sponsor, at least one of whose sponsors, is still alive;

    [(d)   Class D—a person who has humanitarian protection granted under the Immigration Rules; . . .]

    (e)   . . .

    [(f)   Class F—a person who is habitually resident in the United Kingdom, the Channel Islands, the Isle of Man or the Republic of Ireland and who has limited leave to enter the United Kingdom as a relevant Afghan citizen under paragraph 276BA1 of the Immigration Rules][; . . .

    (g)   Class G—a person who has limited leave to enter or remain in the United Kingdom on family or private life grounds under Article 8 of the Human Rights Convention, such leave granted—

        (i)   under paragraph 276BE(1), paragraph 276DG or Appendix FM of the Immigration Rules, and

        (ii)   who is not subject to a condition requiring that person to maintain and accommodate himself, and any person dependent upon him, without recourse to public funds][; and.

    (h)   Class H—a person who is habitually resident in the United Kingdom, the Channel Islands, the Isle of Man or the Republic of Ireland and who has been transferred to the United Kingdom under section 67 of the Immigration Act 2016 and has limited leave to remain under paragraph 352ZH of the Immigration Rules.]

(2)   . . .

(3) . . .

NOTES

Amendment

Para (1): sub-para (d) substituted by SI 2006/2527, reg 2(1), (3).
Date in force: 9 October 2006: see SI 2006/2527, reg 1(1); for transitional provisions see reg 4 thereof.
Para (1): in sub-para (d) word omitted revoked by SI 2014/435, reg 2(1), (5)(a).
Date in force: 31 March 2014: see SI 2014/435, reg 1(1).
Para (1): sub-para (e) revoked by SI 2016/965, reg 2(1), (4)(a).
Date in force: 30 October 2016: see SI 2016/965, reg 1(1).
Para (1): sub-para (f) and word omitted immediately preceding it inserted by SI 2014/435, reg 2(1), (5)(b), (c).
Date in force: 31 March 2014: see SI 2014/435, reg 1(1).
Para (1): in sub-para (f) word "and" omitted revoked by SI 2018/730, reg 2(1), (3)(a).
Date in force: 9 July 2018: see SI 2018/730, reg 1.
Para (1): sub-para (g) and word "; and" immediately preceding it inserted by SI 2016/965, reg 2(1), (4)(b), (c).
Date in force: 30 October 2016: see SI 2016/965, reg 1(1).
Para (1): sub-para (h) and word "; and" immediately preceding it inserted by SI 2018/730, reg 2(1), (3)(b), (c).
Date in force: 9 July 2018: see SI 2018/730, reg 1.
Paras (2), (3): revoked by SI 2016/965, reg 2(1), (4)(d).
Date in force: 30 October 2016: see SI 2016/965, reg 1(1).

6 Other persons from abroad who are ineligible for housing assistance

(1)   A person who is not subject to immigration control is to be treated as a person from abroad who is ineligible for housing assistance under Part 7 of the 1996 Act if—

    (a)   subject to paragraph (2), he is not habitually resident in the United Kingdom, the Channel Islands, the Isle of Man, or the Republic of Ireland;

    (b)   his only right to reside in the United Kingdom—

        (i)   is derived from his status as a jobseeker or the family member of a jobseeker; or

        (ii)   is an initial right to reside for a period not exceeding three months under regulation 13 of the EEA Regulations; or

      [(iii)   is a derivative right to reside to which he is entitled under regulation 15A(1) of the EEA Regulations, but only in a case where the right exists under that regulation because the applicant satisfies the criteria in regulation 15A(4A) of those Regulations; or

        (iv)   is derived from Article 20 of the Treaty on the Functioning of the European Union in a case where the right to reside arises because a British citizen would otherwise be deprived of the genuine enjoyment of the substance of the rights attaching to the status of European Union citizen; or]

    [(c)   his only right to reside in the Channel Islands, the Isle of Man or the Republic of Ireland—

        (i)   is a right equivalent to one of those mentioned in sub-paragraph (b)(i),(ii) or (iii) which is derived from the Treaty on the Functioning of the European Union; or

        (ii)   is derived from Article 20 of the Treaty on the Functioning of the European Union, in a case where the right to reside—

            (a)   in the Republic of Ireland arises because an Irish citizen, or

            (b)   in the Channel Islands or the Isle of Man arises because a British citizen also entitled to reside there

        would otherwise be deprived of the genuine enjoyment of the substance of their rights as a European Union citizen].

(2)   The following are not to be treated as persons from abroad who are ineligible for housing assistance pursuant to paragraph (1)(a)—

(a)   a worker;

(b)   a self-employed person;

[(c)   a person who is treated as a worker for the purpose of the definition of "qualified person" in regulation 6(1) of the EEA Regulations pursuant to . . .—

     (i)   . . .

     (ii)   regulation 5 of the Accession Regulations 2013 (right of residence of an accession State national subject to worker authorisation);]

(d)   a person who is the family member of a person specified in sub-paragraphs (a)–(c);

(e)   a person with a right to reside permanently in the United Kingdom by virtue of regulation 15(c), (d) or (e) of the EEA Regulations; [and]

(f)   . . .

(g)   a person who is in the United Kingdom as a result of his deportation, expulsion or other removal by compulsion of law from another country to the United Kingdom[; . . .]

[(h)   . . .]

[(i)   . . .].

NOTES

Amendment

Para (1): sub-para (b)(iii), (iv) inserted by SI 2012/2588, reg 2(1), (4).
    Date in force: 8 November 2012: see SI 2012/2588, reg 1(1); for transitional provision see reg 3 thereof.
Para (1): sub-para (c) substituted by SI 2012/2588, reg 2(1), (5).
    Date in force: 8 November 2012: see SI 2012/2588, reg 1(1); for transitional provision see reg 3 thereof.
Para (2): sub-para (c) substituted by SI 2013/1467, reg 2(1), (4).
    Date in force: 1 July 2013: see SI 2013/1467, reg 1(1); for transitional provisions see reg 3 thereof.
Para (2): in sub-para (c) first word omitted revoked by SI 2014/435, reg 2(1), (6)(a)(i).
    Date in force: 31 March 2014: see SI 2014/435, reg 1(1).
Para (2): sub-para (c)(i) revoked by SI 2014/435, reg 2(1), (6)(a)(ii).
    Date in force: 31 March 2014: see SI 2014/435, reg 1(1).
Para (2): in sub-para (e) word "and" in square brackets inserted by SI 2014/435, reg 2(1), (6)(b).
    Date in force: 31 March 2014: see SI 2014/435, reg 1(1).
Para (2): sub-para (f) revoked by SI 2014/435, reg 2(1), (6)(c).
    Date in force: 31 March 2014: see SI 2014/435, reg 1(1).
Para (2): in sub-para (g) semi-colon and word omitted in square brackets inserted by SI 2006/2007, reg 2(1), (7).
    Date in force: 25 July 2006 at 1600 hours: see SI 2006/2007, reg 1(1).
Para (2): in sub-para (g) word omitted revoked by SI 2009/358, reg 2(1), (4).
    Date in force: 18 March 2009: see SI 2009/358, reg 1(1).
Para (2): sub-para (h) inserted by SI 2006/2007, reg 2(1), (8).
    Date in force: 25 July 2006 at 1600 hours: see SI 2006/2007, reg 1(1).
Para (2): sub-para (h) revoked by SI 2014/435, reg 2(1), (6)(c).
    Date in force: 31 March 2014: see SI 2014/435, reg 1(1).
Para (2): sub-para (i) inserted by SI 2009/358, reg 2(1), (5).
    Date in force: 18 March 2009: see SI 2009/358, reg 1(1).
Para (2): sub-para (i) revoked by SI 2014/435, reg 2(1), (6)(c).
    Date in force: 31 March 2014: see SI 2014/435, reg 1(1).

7 Revocation

Subject to regulation 8, the Regulations specified in column (1) of the Schedule are revoked to the extent mentioned in column (3) of the Schedule.

8 Transitional provisions

The revocations made by these Regulations shall not have effect in relation to an applicant whose application for—

(a)   an allocation of housing accommodation under Part 6 of the 1996 Act; or

(b)   housing assistance under Part 7 of the 1996 Act,

was made before 1st June 2006.

SCHEDULE

Regulation 7

Revocation schedule

(1)	(2)	(3)
Regulations Revoked	*References*	*Extent of revocation*
The Homelessness (England) Regulations 2000	SI 2000/701	The whole Regulations
The Allocation of Housing (England) Regulations 2002	SI 2002/3264	Regulations 4 and 5
The Allocation of Housing and Homelessness (Amendment) (England) Regulations 2004	SI 2004/1235	The whole Regulations
The Allocation of Housing and Homelessness (Amendment) (England) Regulations 2006	SI 2006/1093	The whole Regulations

ALLOCATION OF HOUSING AND HOMELESS-NESS (MISCELLANEOUS PROVISIONS) (ENGLAND) REGULATIONS 2006

SI 2006/2527

A2.12

1 Citation, commencement, interpretation and application

(1)   These Regulations may be cited as the Allocation of Housing and Homelessness (Miscellaneous Provisions) (England) Regulations 2006 and shall come into force on 9th October 2006.

(2)   In these Regulations, "the 1996 Act" means the Housing Act 1996.

(3)   These Regulations apply to England only.

2 Amendment of the classes of person from abroad who are eligible for an allocation of accommodation and for housing assistance

(1)   The Allocation of Housing and Homelessness (Eligibility) (England) Regulations 2006 are amended as follows.

(2)   For regulation 3(d), substitute—

> "(d)   Class D—a person who has humanitarian protection granted under the Immigration Rules.".

(3)   For regulation 5(1)(d), substitute—

> "(d)   Class D—a person who has humanitarian protection granted under the Immigration Rules; and".

3 Prescribed period for referral of case to another local housing authority

For the purposes of section 198(4)(b) of the 1996 Act (referral of case to another local housing authority), the prescribed period is the aggregate of—

> (a)   five years; and
>
> (b)   the period beginning on the date of the previous application and ending on the date on which the applicant was first placed in pursuance of that application in accommodation in the district of the authority to whom the application is now made.

4 Transitional provisions

The amendments made by these Regulations shall not have effect in relation to an applicant whose application for—

> (a)   an allocation of housing accommodation under Part 6 of the 1996 Act; or
>
> (b)   housing assistance under Part 7 of the 1996 Act,

was made before 9th October 2006.

HOMELESSNESS (SUITABILITY OF ACCOMMODATION) (ENGLAND) ORDER 2012

SI 2012/2601

A2.13

1 Citation, commencement and application

(1) This Order may be cited as the Homelessness (Suitability of Accommodation) (England) Order 2012 and comes into force on 9th November 2012.

(2) This Order applies in relation to England only.

2 Matters to be taken into account in determining whether accommodation is suitable for a person

In determining whether accommodation is suitable for a person, the local housing authority must take into account the location of the accommodation, including—

   (a)   where the accommodation is situated outside the district of the local housing authority, the distance of the accommodation from the district of the authority;

   (b)   the significance of any disruption which would be caused by the location of the accommodation to the employment, caring responsibilities or education of the person or members of the person's household;

   (c)   the proximity and accessibility of the accommodation to medical facilities and other support which—

      (i)   are currently used by or provided to the person or members of the person's household; and

      (ii)   are essential to the well-being of the person or members of the person's household; and

   (d)   the proximity and accessibility of the accommodation to local services, amenities and transport.

3 Circumstances in which accommodation is not to be regarded as suitable for a person

[(1)] For the purposes [mentioned in paragraph (2)], accommodation shall not be regarded as suitable where one or more of the following apply—

   (a)   the local housing authority are of the view that the accommodation is not in a reasonable physical condition;

   (b)   the local housing authority are of the view that any electrical equipment supplied with the accommodation does not meet the requirements of [Schedule 1 to the Electrical Equipment (Safety) Regulations 2016];

   (c)   the local housing authority are of the view that the landlord has not taken reasonable fire safety precautions with the accommodation and any furnishings supplied with it;

   (d)   the local housing authority are of the view that the landlord has not taken reasonable precautions to prevent the possibility of carbon monoxide poisoning in the accommodation;

   (e)   the local housing authority are of the view that the landlord is not a fit and proper person to act in the capacity of landlord, having considered if the person has:

      (i)   committed any offence involving fraud or other dishonesty, or violence or illegal drugs, or any offence listed in Schedule 3 to the Sexual Offences Act 2003 (offences attracting notification requirements);

     (ii)   practised unlawful discrimination on grounds of sex, race, age, disability, marriage or civil partnership, pregnancy or maternity, religion or belief, sexual orientation, gender identity or gender reassignment in, or in connection with, the carrying on of any business;

     (iii)   contravened any provision of the law relating to housing (including landlord or tenant law); or

     (iv)   acted otherwise than in accordance with any applicable code of practice for the management of a house in multiple occupation, approved under section 233 of the Housing Act 2004;

(f)   the accommodation is a house in multiple occupation subject to licensing under section 55 of the Housing Act 2004 and is not licensed;

(g)   the accommodation is a house in multiple occupation subject to additional licensing under section 56 of the Housing Act 2004 and is not licensed;

(h)   the accommodation is or forms part of residential property which does not have a valid energy performance certificate as required by the Energy Performance of Buildings (Certificates and Inspections) (England and Wales) Regulations 2007;

(i)   the accommodation is or forms part of relevant premises which do not have a current gas safety record in accordance with regulation 36 of the Gas Safety (Installation and Use) Regulations 1998; or

(j)   the landlord has not provided to the local housing authority a written tenancy agreement, which the landlord proposes to use for the purposes of a private rented sector offer, and which the local housing authority considers to be adequate.

[(2)   The purposes are—

(a)   determining, in accordance with section 193(7F) of the Housing Act 1996, whether a local housing authority may approve a private rented sector offer;

(b)   determining, in accordance with section 193A(6) or 193C(9) of that Act, whether a local housing authority may approve a final accommodation offer made by a private landlord;

(c)   determining whether any accommodation—

     (i)   secured for a person who has a priority need by a local housing authority in discharge of their functions under section 189B(2) or 195(2) of that Act, and

     (ii)   made available for occupation under a tenancy with a private landlord,

is suitable for the purposes of the section concerned.]

NOTES

Amendment

Para (1): numbered as such by the Homelessness Reduction Act 2017, s 12(1), (2).
    Date in force: 3 April 2018: see SI 2018/167, reg 3(l).
Para (1): words "mentioned in paragraph (2)" in square brackets substituted by the Homelessness Reduction Act 2017, s 12(1), (3).
    Date in force: 3 April 2018: see SI 2018/167, reg 3(l).
Para (1): in sub-para (b) words "Schedule 1 to the Electrical Equipment (Safety) Regulations 2016" in square brackets substituted by SI 2016/1101, reg 64, Sch 7, para 9.
    Date in force: 8 December 2016: see SI 2016/1101, reg 1.
Para (2): inserted by the Homelessness Reduction Act 2017, s 12(1), (4).
    Date in force: 3 April 2018: see SI 2018/167, reg 3(l).

IMMIGRATION (EUROPEAN ECONOMIC AREA) REGULATIONS 2016

SI 2016/1052

PART 1
PRELIMINARY

A2.14

1 Citation and commencement

(1) These Regulations may be cited as the Immigration (European Economic Area) Regulations 2016.

(2) These Regulations come into force—

    (a)   for the purposes of this regulation, regulation 44 and Schedule 5 (transitory provisions), on 25th November 2016;

    (b)   for all other purposes, on 1st February 2017.

2 General interpretation

(1) In these Regulations—

"the 1971 Act" means the Immigration Act 1971;

"the 1999 Act" means the Immigration and Asylum Act 1999;

"the 2002 Act" means the Nationality, Immigration and Asylum Act 2002;

"the 2006 Regulations" means the Immigration (European Economic Area) Regulations 2006;

["the 2016 Act" means the Immigration Act 2016;]

"civil partner" does not include—

    (a)   a party to a civil partnership of convenience; or

    (b)   the civil partner ("C") of a person ("P") where a spouse, civil partner or durable partner of C or P is already present in the United Kingdom;

"civil partnership of convenience" includes a civil partnership entered into for the purpose of using these Regulations, or any other right conferred by the EU Treaties, as a means to circumvent—

    (a)   immigration rules applying to non-EEA nationals (such as any applicable requirement under the 1971 Act to have leave to enter or remain in the United Kingdom); or

    (b)   any other criteria that the party to the civil partnership of convenience would otherwise have to meet in order to enjoy a right to reside under these Regulations or the EU Treaties;

"Common Travel Area" has the meaning given in section 1(3) of the 1971 Act;

"decision maker" means the Secretary of State, an immigration officer or an entry clearance officer (as the case may be);

"deportation order" means an order made under regulation 32(3);

"derivative residence card" means a card issued to a person under regulation 20;

"derivative right to reside" means a right to reside under regulation 16;

"document certifying permanent residence" means a document issued under regulation 19(1);

"durable partner" does not include—

    (a)   a party to a durable partnership of convenience; or

    (b)   the durable partner ("D") of a person ("P") where a spouse, civil partner or durable partner of D or P is already present in the

United Kingdom and where that marriage, civil partnership or durable partnership is subsisting;

"durable partnership of convenience" includes a durable partnership entered into for the purpose of using these Regulations, or any other right conferred by the EU Treaties, as a means to circumvent—

    (a)   immigration rules applying to non-EEA nationals (such as any applicable requirement under the 1971 Act to have leave to enter or remain in the United Kingdom); or

    (b)   any other criteria that the party to the durable partnership of convenience would otherwise have to meet in order to enjoy a right to reside under these Regulations or the EU Treaties;

"EEA decision" means a decision under these Regulations that concerns—

    (a)   a person's entitlement to be admitted to the United Kingdom;

    (b)   a person's entitlement to be issued with or have renewed, or not to have revoked, a registration certificate, residence card, derivative residence card, document certifying permanent residence or permanent residence card (but does not include a decision that an application for the above documentation is invalid);

    (c)   a person's removal from the United Kingdom; or

    (d)   the cancellation, under regulation 25, of a person's right to reside in the United Kingdom,

        but does not include a decision to refuse to issue a document under regulation 12(4) (issue of an EEA family permit to an extended family member), 17(5) (issue of a registration certificate to an extended family member) or 18(4) (issue of a residence card to an extended family member), a decision to reject an application under regulation 26(4) (misuse of a right to reside: material change of circumstances), or any decisions under regulation 33 (human rights considerations and interim orders to suspend removal) or 41 (temporary admission to submit case in person);

"EEA family permit" means a document issued under regulation 12;

"EEA national" means a national of an EEA State who is not also a British citizen;

"EEA State" means—

    (a)   a member State, other than the United Kingdom; or

    (b)   Liechtenstein, Iceland, Norway or Switzerland;

"entry clearance" has the meaning given in section 33(1) of the 1971 Act;

"entry clearance officer" means a person responsible for the grant or refusal of entry clearance;

"exclusion order" means an order made under regulation 23(5);

"indefinite leave", "immigration laws" and "immigration rules" have the meanings given in section 33(1) of the 1971 Act;

"marriage of convenience" includes a marriage entered into for the purpose of using these Regulations, or any other right conferred by the EU Treaties, as a means to circumvent—

    (a)   immigration rules applying to non-EEA nationals (such as any applicable requirement under the 1971 Act to have leave to enter or remain in the United Kingdom); or

    (b)   any other criteria that the party to the marriage of convenience would otherwise have to meet in order to enjoy a right to reside under these Regulations or the EU Treaties;

"military service" means service in the armed forces of an EEA State;

"permanent residence card" means a document issued under regulation 19(2);

"qualifying EEA State residence card" means a valid document called a "Residence card of a family member of a Union Citizen" issued under Article 10 of Council Directive 2004/38/EC (as applied, where relevant, by the EEA agreement) by any EEA State (except Switzerland) to a non-EEA family member of an EEA national as proof of the holder's right of residence in that State;

"registration certificate" means a certificate issued under regulation 17;

"relevant EEA national" in relation to an extended family member has the meaning given in regulation 8(6);

"residence card" means a card issued under regulation 18;

"right to reside" means a right to reside in the United Kingdom under these Regulations (or where so specified, a right to reside under a particular regulation);

"spouse" does not include—

    (a)   a party to a marriage of convenience; or

    (b)   the spouse ("S") of a person ("P") where a spouse, civil partner or durable partner of S or P is already present in the United Kingdom.

(2)   Section 11 of the 1971 Act (construction of references to entry) applies for the purpose of determining whether a person has entered the United Kingdom for the purpose of these Regulations as it applies for the purpose of determining whether a person has entered the United Kingdom for the purpose of that Act.

NOTES

Amendment

Para (1): definition "the 2016 Act" inserted by SI 2017/1242, reg 2, Schedule, para 8(1), (2). Date in force: 15 January 2018: see SI 2017/1242, reg 1.

3   Continuity of residence

(1)   This regulation applies for the purpose of calculating periods of continuous residence in the United Kingdom under these Regulations.

(2)   Continuity of residence is not affected by—

    (a)   periods of absence from the United Kingdom which do not exceed six months in total in any year;

    (b)   periods of absence from the United Kingdom on compulsory military service; or

    (c)   one absence from the United Kingdom not exceeding twelve months for an important reason such as pregnancy and childbirth, serious illness, study or vocational training or an overseas posting.

(3)   Continuity of residence is broken when—

    (a)   a person serves a sentence of imprisonment;

    (b)   a deportation or exclusion order is made in relation to a person; or

    (c)   a person is removed from the United Kingdom under these Regulations.

(4)   Paragraph (3)(a) applies, in principle, to an EEA national who has resided in the United Kingdom for at least ten years, but it does not apply where the Secretary of State considers that—

    (a)   prior to serving a sentence of imprisonment, the EEA national had forged integrating links with the United Kingdom;

    (b)   the effect of the sentence of imprisonment was not such as to break those integrating links; and

    (c)   taking into account an overall assessment of the EEA national's situation, it would not be appropriate to apply paragraph (3)(a) to the assessment of that EEA national's continuity of residence.

4   "Worker", "self-employed person", "self-sufficient person" and "student"

(1)   In these Regulations—

(a)   "worker" means a worker within the meaning of Article 45 of the Treaty on the Functioning of the European Union;

(b)   "self-employed person" means a person who is established in the United Kingdom in order to pursue activity as a self-employed person in accordance with Article 49 of the Treaty on the Functioning of the European Union;

(c)   "self-sufficient person" means a person who has—

    (i)   sufficient resources not to become a burden on the social assistance system of the United Kingdom during the person's period of residence; and

    (ii)   comprehensive sickness insurance cover in the United Kingdom;

(d)   "student" means a person who—

    (i)   is enrolled, for the principal purpose of following a course of study (including vocational training), at a public or private establishment which is—

        (aa)   financed from public funds; or

        (bb)   otherwise recognised by the Secretary of State as an establishment which has been accredited for the purpose of providing such courses or training within the law or administrative practice of the part of the United Kingdom in which the establishment is located;

    (ii)   has comprehensive sickness insurance cover in the United Kingdom; and

    (iii)   has assured the Secretary of State, by means of a declaration, or by such equivalent means as the person may choose, that the person has sufficient resources not to become a burden on the social assistance system of the United Kingdom during the person's intended period of residence.

(2)   For the purposes of paragraphs (3) and (4) below, "relevant family member" means a family member of a self-sufficient person or student who is residing in the United Kingdom and whose right to reside is dependent upon being the family member of that student or self-sufficient person.

(3)   In sub-paragraphs (1)(c) and (d)—

(a)   the requirement for the self-sufficient person or student to have sufficient resources not to become a burden on the social assistance system of the United Kingdom during the intended period of residence is only satisfied if the resources available to the student or self-sufficient person and any of their relevant family members are sufficient to avoid the self-sufficient person or student and all their relevant family members from becoming such a burden; and

(b)   the requirement for the student or self-sufficient person to have comprehensive sickness insurance cover in the United Kingdom is only satisfied if such cover extends to cover both the student or self-sufficient person and all their relevant family members.

(4)   In paragraph (1)(c) and (d) and paragraph (3), the resources of the student or self-sufficient person and, where applicable, any of their relevant family members, are to be regarded as sufficient if—

(a)   they exceed the maximum level of resources which a British citizen (including the resources of the British citizen's family members) may possess if the British citizen is to become eligible for social assistance under the United Kingdom benefit system; or

(b)   paragraph (a) does not apply but, taking into account the personal circumstances of the person concerned and, where applicable, all their relevant family members, it appears to the decision maker that the resources of the person or persons concerned should be regarded as sufficient.

(5)   For the purposes of regulation 16(2) (criteria for having a derivative right to reside), references in this regulation to "family members" includes a "primary carer" as defined in regulation 16(8).

5   "Worker or self-employed person who has ceased activity"

(1)   In these Regulations, "worker or self-employed person who has ceased activity" means an EEA national who satisfies a condition in paragraph (2), (3), (4) or (5).

(2)   The condition in this paragraph is that the person—

    (a)   terminates activity as a worker or self-employed person and—

        (i)   had reached the age of entitlement to a state pension on terminating that activity; or

        (ii)   in the case of a worker, ceases working to take early retirement;

    (b)   pursued activity as a worker or self-employed person in the United Kingdom for at least 12 months prior to the termination; and

    (c)   resided in the United Kingdom continuously for more than three years prior to the termination.

(3)   The condition in this paragraph is that the person terminates activity in the United Kingdom as a worker or self-employed person as a result of permanent incapacity to work; and—

    (a)   had resided in the United Kingdom continuously for more than two years prior to the termination; or

    (b)   the incapacity is the result of an accident at work or an occupational disease that entitles the person to a pension payable in full or in part by an institution in the United Kingdom.

(4)   The condition in this paragraph is that the person—

    (a)   is active as a worker or self-employed person in an EEA State but retains a place of residence in the United Kingdom and returns, as a rule, to that place at least once a week; and

    (b)   prior to becoming so active in the EEA State, had been continuously resident and continuously active as a worker or self-employed person in the United Kingdom for at least three years.

(5)   A person who satisfied the condition in paragraph (4)(a) but not the condition in paragraph (4)(b) must, for the purposes of paragraphs (2) and (3), be treated as being active and resident in the United Kingdom during any period during which that person is working or self-employed in the EEA State.

(6)   The conditions in paragraphs (2) and (3) as to length of residence and activity as a worker or self-employed person do not apply in relation to a person whose spouse or civil partner is a British citizen.

(7)   Subject to regulation 6(2), periods of—

    (a)   inactivity for reasons not of the person's own making;

    (b)   inactivity due to illness or accident; and

    (c)   in the case of a worker, involuntary unemployment duly recorded by the relevant employment office,

must be treated as periods of activity as a worker or self-employed person, as the case may be.

6   "Qualified person"

(1)   In these Regulations—

"jobseeker" means an EEA national who satisfies conditions A, B and, where relevant, C;

"qualified person" means a person who is an EEA national and in the United Kingdom as—

    (a)   a jobseeker;

    (b)   a worker;

    (c)   a self-employed person;

    (d)   a self-sufficient person; or

    (e)   a student;

"relevant period" means—

    (a)   in the case of a person retaining worker status under paragraph (2)(b), a continuous period of six months;

    (b)   in the case of a jobseeker, 91 days, minus the cumulative total of any days during which the person concerned previously enjoyed a right to reside as a jobseeker, not including any days prior to a continuous absence from the United Kingdom of at least 12 months.

(2)   A person who is no longer working must continue to be treated as a worker provided that the person—

    (a)   is temporarily unable to work as the result of an illness or accident;

    (b)   is in duly recorded involuntary unemployment after having been employed in the United Kingdom for at least one year, provided the person—

        (i)   has registered as a jobseeker with the relevant employment office; and

        (ii)   satisfies conditions A and B;

    (c)   is in duly recorded involuntary unemployment after having been employed in the United Kingdom for less than one year, provided the person—

        (i)   has registered as a jobseeker with the relevant employment office; and

        (ii)   satisfies conditions A and B;

    (d)   is involuntarily unemployed and has embarked on vocational training; or

    (e)   has voluntarily ceased working and has embarked on vocational training that is related to the person's previous employment.

(3)   A person to whom paragraph (2)(c) applies may only retain worker status for a maximum of six months.

(4)   A person who is no longer in self-employment continues to be treated as a self-employed person if that person is temporarily unable to engage in activities as a self-employed person as the result of an illness or accident.

(5)   Condition A is that the person—

    (a)   entered the United Kingdom in order to seek employment; or

    (b)   is present in the United Kingdom seeking employment, immediately after enjoying a right to reside under sub-paragraphs (b) to (e) of the definition of qualified person in paragraph (1) (disregarding any period during which worker status was retained pursuant to paragraph (2)(b) or (c)).

(6)   Condition B is that the person provides evidence of seeking employment and having a genuine chance of being engaged.

(7)   A person may not retain the status of—

    (a)   a worker under paragraph (2)(b); or

    (b)   a jobseeker;

for longer than the relevant period without providing compelling evidence of continuing to seek employment and having a genuine chance of being engaged.

(8)   Condition C applies where the person concerned has, previously, enjoyed a right to reside under this regulation as a result of satisfying conditions A and B—

(a)   in the case of a person to whom paragraph (2)(b) or (c) applied, for at least six months; or

(b)   in the case of a jobseeker, for at least 91 days in total,

unless the person concerned has, since enjoying the above right to reside, been continuously absent from the United Kingdom for at least 12 months.

(9)   Condition C is that the person has had a period of absence from the United Kingdom.

(10)   Where condition C applies—

(a)   paragraph (7) does not apply; and

(b)   condition B has effect as if "compelling" were inserted before "evidence".

7   "Family member"

(1)   In these Regulations, "family member" means, in relation to a person ("A")—

(a)   A's spouse or civil partner;

(b)   A's direct descendants, or the direct descendants of A's spouse or civil partner who are either—

(i)   aged under 21; or

(ii)   dependants of A, or of A's spouse or civil partner;

(c)   dependent direct relatives in A's ascending line, or in that of A's spouse or civil partner.

(2)   Where A is a student residing in the United Kingdom otherwise than under regulation 13 (initial right of residence), a person is not a family member of A under paragraph (1)(b) or (c) unless—

(a)   in the case of paragraph (1)(b), the person is the dependent child of A or of A's spouse or civil partner; or

(b)   A also falls within one of the other categories of qualified person mentioned in regulation 6(1).

(3)   A person ("B") who is an extended family member and has been issued with an EEA family permit, a registration certificate or a residence card must be treated as a family member of A, provided—

(a)   B continues to satisfy the conditions in regulation 8(2), (3), (4) or (5); and

(b)   the EEA family permit, registration certificate or residence card remains in force.

(4)   A must be an EEA national unless regulation 9 applies (family members of British citizens).

8   "Extended family member"

(1)   In these Regulations "extended family member" means a person who is not a family member of an EEA national under regulation 7(1)(a), (b) or (c) and who satisfies a condition in paragraph (2), (3), (4) or (5).

(2)   The condition in this paragraph is that the person is—

(a)   a relative of an EEA national; and

(b)   residing in a country other than the United Kingdom and is dependent upon the EEA national or is a member of the EEA national's household; and either—

(i)   is accompanying the EEA national to the United Kingdom or wants to join the EEA national in the United Kingdom; or

(ii)   has joined the EEA national in the United Kingdom and continues to be dependent upon the EEA national, or to be a member of the EEA national's household.

(3)   The condition in this paragraph is that the person is a relative of an EEA national and on serious health grounds, strictly requires the personal care of the EEA national.

(4)   The condition in this paragraph is that the person is a relative of an EEA national and would meet the requirements in the immigration rules (other than those relating to

entry clearance) for indefinite leave to enter or remain in the United Kingdom as a dependent relative of the EEA national.

(5)   The condition in this paragraph is that the person is the partner (other than a civil partner) of, and in a durable relationship with, an EEA national, and is able to prove this to the decision maker.

(6)   In these Regulations, "relevant EEA national" means, in relation to an extended family member—

    (a)   referred to in paragraph (2), (3) or (4), the EEA national to whom the extended family member is related;

    (b)   referred to in paragraph (5), the EEA national who is the durable partner of the extended family member.

(7)   In paragraphs (2) and (3), "relative of an EEA national" includes a relative of the spouse or civil partner of an EEA national where on the basis of being an extended family member a person—

    (a)   has prior to the 1st February 2017 been issued with—

        (i)   an EEA family permit;

        (ii)   a registration certificate; or

        (iii)   a residence card; and

    (b)   has since the most recent issue of a document satisfying sub-paragraph (a) been continuously resident in the United Kingdom.

9   Family members of British citizens

(1)   If the conditions in paragraph (2) are satisfied, these Regulations apply to a person who is the family member ("F") of a British citizen ("BC") as though the BC were an EEA national.

(2)   The conditions are that—

    (a)   BC—

        (i)   is residing in an EEA State as a worker, self-employed person, self-sufficient person or a student, or so resided immediately before returning to the United Kingdom; or

        (ii)   has acquired the right of permanent residence in an EEA State;

    (b)   F and BC resided together in the EEA State; and

    (c)   F and BC's residence in the EEA State was genuine.

(3)   Factors relevant to whether residence in the EEA State is or was genuine include—

    (a)   whether the centre of BC's life transferred to the EEA State;

    (b)   the length of F and BC's joint residence in the EEA State;

    (c)   the nature and quality of the F and BC's accommodation in the EEA State, and whether it is or was BC's principal residence;

    (d)   the degree of F and BC's integration in the EEA State;

    (e)   whether F's first lawful residence in the EU with BC was in the EEA State.

(4)   This regulation does not apply—

    (a)   where the purpose of the residence in the EEA State was as a means for circumventing any immigration laws applying to non-EEA nationals to which F would otherwise be subject (such as any applicable requirement under the 1971 Act to have leave to enter or remain in the United Kingdom); or

    (b)   to a person who is only eligible to be treated as a family member as a result of regulation 7(3) (extended family members treated as family members).

(5)   Where these Regulations apply to F, BC is to be treated as holding a valid passport issued by an EEA State for the purposes of the application of these Regulations to F.

(6)   In paragraph (2)(a)(ii), BC is only to be treated as having acquired the right of permanent residence in the EEA State if such residence would have led to the acquisition of that right under regulation 15, had it taken place in the United Kingdom.

(7)   For the purposes of determining whether, when treating the BC as an EEA national under these Regulations in accordance with paragraph (1), BC would be a qualified person—

- (a)   any requirement to have comprehensive sickness insurance cover in the United Kingdom still applies, save that it does not require the cover to extend to BC;
- (b)   in assessing whether BC can continue to be treated as a worker under regulation 6(2)(b) or (c), BC is not required to satisfy condition A;
- (c)   in assessing whether BC can be treated as a jobseeker as defined in regulation 6(1), BC is not required to satisfy conditions A and, where it would otherwise be relevant, condition C.

10   "Family member who has retained the right of residence"

(1)   In these Regulations, "family member who has retained the right of residence" means, subject to paragraphs (8) and (9), a person who satisfies a condition in paragraph (2), (3), (4) or (5).

(2)   The condition in this paragraph is that the person—

- (a)   was a family member of a qualified person or of an EEA national with a right of permanent residence when the qualified person or the EEA national with the right of permanent residence died;
- (b)   resided in the United Kingdom in accordance with these Regulations for at least the year immediately before the death of the qualified person or the EEA national with a right of permanent residence; and
- (c)   satisfies the condition in paragraph (6).

(3)   The condition in this paragraph is that the person—

- (a)   is the direct descendant of—
  - (i)   a qualified person or an EEA national with a right of permanent residence who has died;
  - (ii)   a person who ceased to be a qualified person on ceasing to reside in the United Kingdom;
  - (iii)   the spouse or civil partner of the qualified person or EEA national described in sub-paragraph (i) immediately preceding that qualified person or EEA national's death; or
  - (iv)   the spouse or civil partner of the person described in sub-paragraph (ii); and
- (b)   was attending an educational course in the United Kingdom immediately before the qualified person or the EEA national with a right of permanent residence died, or ceased to be a qualified person, and continues to attend such a course.

(4)   The condition in this paragraph is that the person is the parent with actual custody of a child who satisfies the condition in paragraph (3).

(5)   The condition in this paragraph is that the person ("A")—

- (a)   ceased to be a family member of a qualified person or an EEA national with a right of permanent residence on the termination of the marriage or civil partnership of A;
- (b)   was residing in the United Kingdom in accordance with these Regulations at the date of the termination;
- (c)   satisfies the condition in paragraph (6); and
- (d)   either—

      (i)   prior to the initiation of the proceedings for the termination of the marriage or the civil partnership, the marriage or civil partnership had lasted for at least three years and the parties to the marriage or civil partnership had resided in the United Kingdom for at least one year during its duration;

      (ii)   the former spouse or civil partner of the qualified person or the EEA national with a right of permanent residence has custody of a child of that qualified person or EEA national;

      (iii)   the former spouse or civil partner of the qualified person or the EEA national with a right of permanent residence has the right of access to a child of that qualified person or EEA national, where the child is under the age of 18 and where a court has ordered that such access must take place in the United Kingdom; or

      (iv)   the continued right of residence in the United Kingdom of A is warranted by particularly difficult circumstances, such as where A or another family member has been a victim of domestic violence whilst the marriage or civil partnership was subsisting.

(6)   The condition in this paragraph is that the person—

    (a)   is not an EEA national but would, if the person were an EEA national, be a worker, a self-employed person or a self-sufficient person under regulation 6; or

    (b)   is the family member of a person who falls within paragraph (a).

(7)   In this regulation, "educational course" means a course within the scope of Article 10 of Council Regulation (EU) No 492/2011.

(8)   A person ("P") does not satisfy a condition in paragraph (2), (3), (4) or (5) if, at the first time P would otherwise have satisfied the relevant condition, P had a right of permanent residence under regulation 15.

(9)   A family member who has retained the right of residence ceases to enjoy that status on acquiring a right of permanent residence under regulation 15.

PART 2
EEA RIGHTS

11 Right of admission to the United Kingdom

(1)   An EEA national must be admitted to the United Kingdom on arrival if the EEA national produces a valid national identity card or passport issued by an EEA State.

(2)   A person who is not an EEA national must be admitted to the United Kingdom if that person is—

    (a)   a family member of an EEA national and produces on arrival a valid passport and qualifying EEA State residence card, provided the conditions in regulation 23(4) (family member of EEA national must accompany or join EEA national with right to reside) are met; or

    (b)   a family member of an EEA national, a family member who has retained the right of residence, a person who meets the criteria in paragraph (5) or a person with a right of permanent residence under regulation 15 and produces on arrival—

      (i)   a valid passport; and

      (ii)   a valid EEA family permit, residence card, derivative residence card or permanent residence card.

(3)   An immigration officer must not place a stamp in the passport of a person admitted to the United Kingdom under this regulation who is not an EEA national if the person produces a residence card, a derivative residence card, a permanent residence card or a qualifying EEA State residence card.

(4)   Before an immigration officer refuses admission to the United Kingdom to a person under this regulation because the person does not produce on arrival a

document mentioned in paragraph (1) or (2), the immigration officer must provide every reasonable opportunity for the document to be obtained by, or brought to, the person or allow the person to prove by other means that the person is—

    (a)   an EEA national;

    (b)   a family member of an EEA national with a right to accompany that EEA national or join that EEA national in the United Kingdom;

    (c)   a person who meets the criteria in paragraph (5); or

    (d)   a family member who has retained the right of residence or a person with a right of permanent residence under regulation 15.

(5)   The criteria in this paragraph are that a person ("P")—

    (a)   previously resided in the United Kingdom under regulation 16(3) and would be entitled to reside in the United Kingdom under that regulation were P in the country;

    (b)   is accompanying an EEA national to, or joining an EEA national in, the United Kingdom and P would be entitled to reside in the United Kingdom under regulation 16(2) were P and the EEA national both in the United Kingdom;

    (c)   is accompanying a person ("the relevant person") to, or joining the relevant person in, the United Kingdom and—

        (i)   the relevant person is residing, or has resided, in the United Kingdom under regulation 16(3); and

        (ii)   P would be entitled to reside in the United Kingdom under regulation 16(4) were P and the relevant person both in the United Kingdom;

    (d)   is accompanying a person who meets the criteria in sub-paragraph (b) or (c) ("the relevant person") to the United Kingdom and—

        (i)   P and the relevant person are both—

            (aa)   seeking admission to the United Kingdom in reliance on this paragraph for the first time; or

            (bb)   returning to the United Kingdom having previously resided there pursuant to the same provisions of regulation 16 in reliance on which they now base their claim to admission; and

        (ii)   P would be entitled to reside in the United Kingdom under regulation 16(6) were P and the relevant person there; or

    (e)   is accompanying a British citizen to, or joining a British citizen in, the United Kingdom and P would be entitled to reside in the United Kingdom under regulation 16(5) were P and the British citizen both in the United Kingdom.

(6)   Paragraph (7) applies where—

    (a)   a person ("P") seeks admission to the United Kingdom in reliance on paragraph (5)(b), (c) or (e); and

    (b)   if P were in the United Kingdom, P would have a derived right to reside under regulation 16(8)(b)(ii).

(7)   Where this paragraph applies a person ("P") must only be regarded as meeting the criteria in paragraph (5)(b), (c) or (e) where P—

    (a)   is accompanying the person with whom P would on admission to the United Kingdom jointly share care responsibility for the purpose of regulation 16(8)(b)(ii); or

    (b)   has previously resided in the United Kingdom pursuant to regulation 16(2), (4) or (5) as a joint primary carer and seeks admission to the United Kingdom in order to reside there again on the same basis.

(8)   But this regulation is subject to regulations 23(1), (2), (3) and (4) and 31.

12 Issue of EEA family permit

(1) An entry clearance officer must issue an EEA family permit to a person who applies for one if the person is a family member of an EEA national and—

    (a)   the EEA national—

        (i)   is residing in the United Kingdom in accordance with these Regulations; or

        (ii)   will be travelling to the United Kingdom within six months of the date of the application and will be an EEA national residing in the United Kingdom in accordance with these Regulations on arrival in the United Kingdom; and

    (b)   the family member will be accompanying the EEA national to the United Kingdom or joining the EEA national there.

(2) An entry clearance officer must issue an EEA family permit to a person who applies and provides evidence demonstrating that, at the time at which the person first intends to use the EEA family permit, the person—

    (a)   would be entitled to be admitted to the United Kingdom because that person would meet the criteria in regulation 11(5); and

    (b)   will (save in the case of a person who would be entitled to be admitted to the United Kingdom because that person would meet the criteria for admission in regulation 11(5)(a)) be accompanying to, or joining in, the United Kingdom any person from whom the right to be admitted to the United Kingdom under the criteria in regulation 11(5) is derived.

(3) An entry clearance officer must issue an EEA family permit to—

    (a)   a family member who has retained the right of residence; or

    (b)   a person who is not an EEA national but who has acquired the right of permanent residence under regulation 15.

(4) An entry clearance officer may issue an EEA family permit to an extended family member of an EEA national (the relevant EEA national) who applies for one if—

    (a)   the relevant EEA national satisfies the condition in paragraph (1)(a);

    (b)   the extended family member wants to accompany the relevant EEA national to the United Kingdom or to join that EEA national there; and

    (c)   in all the circumstances, it appears to the entry clearance officer appropriate to issue the EEA family permit.

(5) Where an entry clearance officer receives an application under paragraph (4) an extensive examination of the personal circumstances of the applicant must be undertaken by the Secretary of State and if the application is refused, the entry clearance officer must give reasons justifying the refusal unless this is contrary to the interests of national security.

(6) An EEA family permit issued under this regulation must be issued free of charge and as soon as possible.

(7) But an EEA family permit must not be issued under this regulation if the applicant or the EEA national concerned is not entitled to be admitted to the United Kingdom as a result of regulation 23(1), (2) or (3) or falls to be excluded in accordance with regulation 23(5).

(8) An EEA family permit must not be issued under this regulation to a person ("A") who is the spouse, civil partner or durable partner of a person ("B") where a spouse, civil partner or durable partner of A or B holds a valid EEA family permit.

13 Initial right of residence

(1) An EEA national is entitled to reside in the United Kingdom for a period not exceeding three months beginning on the date of admission to the United Kingdom provided the EEA national holds a valid national identity card or passport issued by an EEA State.

(2) A person who is not an EEA national but is a family member who has retained the right of residence or the family member of an EEA national residing in the United Kingdom under paragraph (1) is entitled to reside in the United Kingdom provided that person holds a valid passport.

(3) An EEA national or the family member of an EEA national who is an unreasonable burden on the social assistance system of the United Kingdom does not have a right to reside under this regulation.

(4) A person who otherwise satisfies the criteria in this regulation is not entitled to a right to reside under this regulation where the Secretary of State or an immigration officer has made a decision under regulation 23(6)(b) (decision to remove on grounds of public policy, public security or public health), 24(1) (refusal to issue residence documentation etc), 25(1) (cancellation of a right of residence), 26(3) (misuse of right to reside) or 31(1) (revocation of admission), unless that decision is set aside or otherwise no longer has effect.

14 Extended right of residence

(1) A qualified person is entitled to reside in the United Kingdom for as long as that person remains a qualified person.

(2) A person ("P") who is a family member of a qualified person residing in the United Kingdom under paragraph (1) or of an EEA national with a right of permanent residence under regulation 15 is entitled to remain in the United Kingdom for so long as P remains the family member of that person or EEA national.

(3) A family member who has retained the right of residence is entitled to reside in the United Kingdom for so long as that person remains a family member who has retained the right of residence.

(4) A person who otherwise satisfies the criteria in this regulation is not entitled to a right to reside in the United Kingdom under this regulation where the Secretary of State or an immigration officer has made a decision under regulation 23(6)(b), 24(1), 25(1), 26(3) or 31(1), unless that decision is set aside or otherwise no longer has effect.

15 Right of permanent residence

(1) The following persons acquire the right to reside in the United Kingdom permanently—

    (a)   an EEA national who has resided in the United Kingdom in accordance with these Regulations for a continuous period of five years;

    (b)   a family member of an EEA national who is not an EEA national but who has resided in the United Kingdom with the EEA national in accordance with these Regulations for a continuous period of five years;

    (c)   a worker or self-employed person who has ceased activity;

    (d)   the family member of a worker or self-employed person who has ceased activity, provided—

        (i)   the person was the family member of the worker or self-employed person at the point the worker or self-employed person ceased activity; and

        (ii)   at that point, the family member enjoyed a right to reside on the basis of being the family member of that worker or self-employed person;

    (e)   a person who was the family member of a worker or self-employed person where—

        (i)   the worker or self-employed person has died;

        (ii)   the family member resided with the worker or self-employed person immediately before the death; and

        (iii)   the worker or self-employed person had resided continuously in the United Kingdom for at least two years immediately before dying or the death was the result of an accident at work or an occupational disease;

(f)   a person who—

    (i)   has resided in the United Kingdom in accordance with these Regulations for a continuous period of five years; and

    (ii)   was, at the end of the period, a family member who has retained the right of residence.

(2)   Residence in the United Kingdom as a result of a derivative right to reside does not constitute residence for the purpose of this regulation.

(3)   The right of permanent residence under this regulation is lost through absence from the United Kingdom for a period exceeding two years.

(4)   A person who satisfies the criteria in this regulation is not entitled to a right to permanent residence in the United Kingdom where the Secretary of State or an immigration officer has made a decision under regulation 23(6)(b), 24(1), 25(1), 26(3) or 31(1), unless that decision is set aside or otherwise no longer has effect.

16 Derivative right to reside

(1)   A person has a derivative right to reside during any period in which the person—

(a)   is not an exempt person; and

(b)   satisfies each of the criteria in one or more of paragraphs (2) to (6).

(2)   The criteria in this paragraph are that—

(a)   the person is the primary carer of an EEA national; and

(b)   the EEA national—

    (i)   is under the age of 18;

    (ii)   resides in the United Kingdom as a self-sufficient person; and

    (iii)   would be unable to remain in the United Kingdom if the person left the United Kingdom for an indefinite period.

(3)   The criteria in this paragraph are that—

(a)   any of the person's parents ("PP") is an EEA national who resides or has resided in the United Kingdom;

(b)   both the person and PP reside or have resided in the United Kingdom at the same time, and during such a period of residence, PP has been a worker in the United Kingdom; and

(c)   the person is in education in the United Kingdom.

(4)   The criteria in this paragraph are that—

(a)   the person is the primary carer of a person satisfying the criteria in paragraph (3) ("PPP"); and

(b)   PPP would be unable to continue to be educated in the United Kingdom if the person left the United Kingdom for an indefinite period.

(5)   The criteria in this paragraph are that—

(a)   the person is the primary carer of a British citizen ("BC");

(b)   BC is residing in the United Kingdom; and

(c)   BC would be unable to reside in the United Kingdom or in another EEA State if the person left the United Kingdom for an indefinite period.

(6)   The criteria in this paragraph are that—

(a)   the person is under the age of 18;

(b)   the person does not have leave to enter, or remain in, the United Kingdom under the 1971 Act;

(c)   the person's primary carer is entitled to a derivative right to reside in the United Kingdom under paragraph (2), (4) or (5); and

(d)   the primary carer would be prevented from residing in the United Kingdom if the person left the United Kingdom for an indefinite period.

(7)   In this regulation—

(a)   "education" excludes nursery education but does not exclude education received before the compulsory school age where that education is equivalent to the education received at or after the compulsory school age;

(b)   "worker" does not include a jobseeker or a person treated as a worker under regulation 6(2);

(c)   an "exempt person" is a person—

    (i)   who has a right to reside under another provision of these Regulations;

    (ii)   who has the right of abode under section 2 of the 1971 Act;

    (iii)   to whom section 8 of the 1971 Act, or an order made under subsection (2) of that section, applies; or

    (iv)   who has indefinite leave to enter or remain in the United Kingdom.

(8)   A person is the "primary carer" of another person ("AP") if—

    (a)   the person is a direct relative or a legal guardian of AP; and

    (b)   either—

        (i)   the person has primary responsibility for AP's care; or

        (ii)   shares equally the responsibility for AP's care with one other person who is not an exempt person.

(9)   In paragraph (2)(b)(iii), (4)(b) or (5)(c), if the role of primary carer is shared with another person in accordance with paragraph (8)(b)(ii), the words "the person" are to be read as "both primary carers".

(10)   Paragraph (9) does not apply if the person with whom care responsibility is shared acquired a derivative right to reside in the United Kingdom as a result of this regulation prior to the other person's assumption of equal care responsibility.

(11)   A person is not be regarded as having responsibility for another person's care for the purpose of paragraph (8) on the sole basis of a financial contribution towards that person's care.

(12)   A person does not have a derivative right to reside where the Secretary of State or an immigration officer has made a decision under regulation 23(6)(b), 24(1), 25(1), 26(3) or 31(1), unless that decision is set aside or otherwise no longer has effect.

HOMELESSNESS REDUCTION ACT 2017 (COMMENCEMENT AND TRANSITIONAL AND SAVINGS PROVISIONS) REGULATIONS 2018

SI 2018/167

A2.15

1 Citation and interpretation

(1) These Regulations may be cited as the Homelessness Reduction Act 2017 (Commencement and Transitional and Savings Provisions) Regulations 2018.

(2) In these Regulations "the Act" means the Homelessness Reduction Act 2017.

2 Provisions coming into force on 12th February 2018

The day appointed for the coming into force of the following provisions of the Act is 12th February 2018—

    (a)   section 7(1) (deliberate and unreasonable refusal to co-operate: duty upon giving of notice), only in so far as is necessary for enabling the exercise of the power to make regulations conferred by section 193B(7) of the Housing Act 1996;

    (b)   section 9(1) and (2) (reviews), only in so far as is necessary for enabling the exercise of the power to make regulations under section 203(1) of the Housing Act 1996 as to the procedure to be followed in relation to reviews under section 202(1)(ba) to (bc) and (h) of the Housing Act 1996;

    (c)   section 10 (duty of public authority to refer cases to local housing authority), only in so far as is necessary for enabling the exercise of the power to make regulations conferred by section 213B(4) of the Housing Act 1996.

3 Provisions coming into force on 3rd April 2018

The day appointed for the coming into force of the following provisions of the Act is 3rd April 2018—

    (a)   section 1 (meaning of "threatened with homelessness");

    (b)   section 2 (duty to provide advisory services);

    (c)   section 3 (duty to assess all eligible applicants' cases and agree a plan);

    (d)   section 4 (duty in cases of threatened homelessness);

    (e)   section 5 (duties owed to those who are homeless);

    (f)   section 6 (duties to help to secure accommodation);

    (g)   section 7 (deliberate and unreasonable refusal to co-operate: duty upon giving of notice), in so far as not already in force;

    (h)   section 8 (local connection of a care leaver);

    (i)   section 9 (reviews), in so far as not already in force;

    (j)   section 10 (duty of public authority to refer cases to local housing authority), in so far as not already in force;

    (k)   section 11 (codes of practice);

    (l)   section 12 (suitability of private rented sector accommodation).

4 Transitional and savings provisions

(1) Despite the coming into force of sections 1, 4 and 5 of the Act in accordance with regulation 3, the amendments made by those sections do not apply in relation to an

application for assistance made under section 183 of the Housing Act 1996 before 3rd April 2018.

(2)   Despite the coming into force of section 9 of the Act in accordance with regulation 3, the amendments made by that section do not apply in relation to a review requested under section 202(1) of the Housing Act 1996 before 3rd April 2018.

HOMELESSNESS (REVIEW PROCEDURE ETC) REGULATIONS 2018

SI 2018/223

PART 1
GENERAL

A2.16

1 Citation, commencement and interpretation

(1)   These Regulations may be cited as the Homelessness (Review Procedure etc) Regulations 2018.

(2)   This Part, and Parts 2, 3 and 5, come into force on 3rd April 2018.

(3)   Part 4 comes into force on 1st October 2018.

(4)   In these Regulations any reference to a section, save where the context otherwise appears, is to that section in the Housing Act 1996.

PART 2
NOTICES IN CASES OF APPLICANT'S DELIBERATE AND UNREASONABLE REFUSAL TO CO-OPERATE

2 Notice procedure

A local housing authority must ensure that its procedure in connection with notices under section 193B(2) (Notices in cases of applicant's deliberate and unreasonable refusal to co-operate)—

  (a)   is in writing,

  (b)   is kept under review, and

  (c)   makes provision which complies with regulation 3.

3 Decision to give notice

(1)   A local housing authority may not give a notice under section 193B(2) unless the decision to give the notice—

  (a)   is made by an officer of that local housing authority, and

  (b)   is authorised by an appropriate person.

(2)   For the purposes of paragraph (1)(b)—

  (a)   "appropriate person" means a person who—

    (i)   is at least as senior as the person mentioned in paragraph (1)(a),

    (ii)   works for that local housing authority or the local authority, and

    (iii)   was not involved in the decision to give the notice, and

  (b)   a person works for a local housing authority or a local authority if the person—

    (i)   works under a contract of employment with that authority,

    (ii)   works under any other contract with that authority,

    (iii)   is supplied to that authority as an agency worker (within the meaning of regulation 3 of the Agency Workers Regulations 2010), or

    (iv)   is seconded to work for that authority.

PART 3
REVIEW OF LOCAL HOUSING AUTHORITY DECISIONS UNDER SECTION 202

4 Interpretation of this Part

In this Part—

"A" means the applicant;

"the authority" means the local housing authority who made the original decision;

"notified authority" means a local housing authority who receive a notification under section 198(A1) or (1);

"notifying authority" means a local housing authority who give a notification under section 198(A1) or (1);

"original decision" means a decision of a local housing authority in relation to which a request for a review has been made;

"request for a review" means a request for a review made under section 202;

"the reviewer" means—

    (a)   where the original decision falls within section 202(1)(d)—

        (i)   the notifying authority and the notified authority, where the review is carried out by those authorities,

        (ii)   the person appointed to carry out the review in accordance with regulation 6, where the case falls within that regulation,

    (b)   where the original decision falls within any other sub-paragraph of section 202(1), the authority.

5 Request for a review and notification of review procedure

(1) A request for a review must be made to the authority where the original decision falls within—

    (a)   section 202(1)(a) (decision as to A's eligibility for assistance),

    (b)   section 202(1)(b) (decision as to what duty, if any, is owed to A under sections 189B to 193C and 195: duties to persons found to be homeless or threatened with homelessness),

    (c)   section 202(1)(ba) (decision as to the steps they are to take under section 189B(2) or to give notice under section 189B(5) to bring to an end their duty to A under section 189B(2)),

    (d)   section 202(1)(bb) (decision to give notice to A under section 193B(2): notice given to those who deliberately and unreasonably refuse to cooperate),

    (e)   section 202(1)(bc) (decision as to the steps they are to take under section 195(2) or to give notice under section 195(5) bringing to an end their duty to A under section 195(2)),

    (f)   section 202(1)(c) (decision to notify another authority under section 198(1): referral of cases),

    (g)   section 202(1)(e) (decision under section 200(3) or (4): decision as to the duty owed to A whose case is considered for referral or referred),

    (h)   section 202(1)(f) (decision as to the suitability of accommodation offered to A in discharge of their duty under any of the provisions mentioned in section 202(1)(b) or (e) or as to the suitability of accommodation offered to A as mentioned in section 193(7)),

    (i)   section 202(1)(g) (decision as to the suitability of accommodation offered to A by way of a private rented sector offer within the meaning of section 193), or

(j)   section 202(1)(h) (decision as to the suitability of accommodation offered to A by way of a final accommodation offer or a final Part 6 offer within the meaning of section 193A or 193C).

(2)   A request for a review must be made to the notifying authority where the original decision falls within section 202(1)(d) (decision under section 198(5) whether conditions are met for the referral of A's case).

(3)   Except in the case of a request for a review falling within regulation 6, the authority must—

(a)   notify A that A, or someone acting on A's behalf, may make representations in writing to the authority in connection with the review,

(b)   in the case of a request for a review falling—

(i)   within section 202(1)(ba)(i) or (bc), or

(ii)   within section 202(1)(bb) where the effect of the notice given under section 193B(2) is to bring the authority's duty to A under section 195(2) to an end,

notify A that any such representations must be made within two weeks beginning with the day on which A requested the review, or such longer period as A and the reviewer may agree in writing,

(c)   if they have not already done so, notify A of the procedure to be followed in connection with the review.

(4)   In the case of a request for a review falling within regulation 6, the person appointed in accordance with that regulation must—

(a)   notify A that A, or someone acting on A's behalf, may make representations in writing to that person in connection with the review, and

(b)   notify A of the procedure to be followed in connection with the review.

6   Initial procedure where the original decision was made under the Decisions on Referrals Order

(1)   Where the original decision under section 198(5) (whether the conditions are met for the referral of the case) was made under the Homelessness (Decisions on Referrals) Order 1998 ("the Decisions on Referrals Order"), a review of that decision must, subject to paragraph (2), be carried out by a person appointed by the notifying authority and the notified authority.

(2)   If a person is not appointed in accordance with paragraph (1) within five working days beginning with the day on which the request for a review is made, the review must be carried out by a person—

(a)   from the panel constituted in accordance with paragraph 3 of the Schedule to the Decisions on Referrals Order ("the panel"), and

(b)   appointed in accordance with paragraph (3) below.

(3)   The notifying authority must within five working days beginning with the end of the period specified in paragraph (2) request the chairman of the Local Government Association or their nominee ("the proper officer") to appoint a person from the panel and the proper officer must do so within seven days of the request.

(4)   The notifying authority and the notified authority must within five working days of the appointment of the person from the panel ("the appointed person") provide the appointed person with the reasons for the original decision and the information and evidence on which that decision was based.

(5)   The appointed person must—

(a)   send to the notifying authority and the notified authority any representations made under regulation 5, and

(b)   invite those authorities to respond to those representations.

(6)   The appointed person must not be the same person as the person who made the original decision.

(7) For the purposes of this regulation "working day" means any day other than a Saturday, a Sunday, Christmas Day, Good Friday, or a day which is a bank holiday under the Banking and Financial Dealings Act 1971 in England and Wales.

7 Procedure on a review

(1) The reviewer must, subject to compliance with the provisions of regulation 9, consider—

    (a)   any representations made under regulation 5 and, in a case falling within regulation 6, any responses to them, and

    (b)   any representations made under paragraph (2).

(2) If the reviewer considers that there is a deficiency or irregularity in the original decision, or in the manner in which it was made, but is minded nonetheless to make a decision which is against the interests of A on one or more issues, the reviewer must notify A—

    (a)   that the reviewer is so minded and the reasons why, and

    (b)   that A, or someone acting on A's behalf, may make representations to the reviewer orally or in writing, or both orally and in writing.

8 Decision on the review

(1) Paragraph (2) applies where—

    (a)   the reviewer is, or includes, the authority,

    (b)   the original decision was made by an officer of the authority, and

    (c)   the decision on the review is to be made by an officer of the authority.

(2) Where this paragraph applies, the officer making the decision on the review must be someone who—

    (a)   was not involved in the original decision, and

    (b)   is more senior than the officer who made the original decision.

9 Notification of the decision on a review

(1) Notice of the decision on a review under section 203(3) must be given to A—

    (a)   where the original decision falls within—

        (i)   section 202(1)(ba)(i) or (bc), or

        (ii)   section 202(1)(bb) and the effect of the notice given under section 193B(2) is to bring the authority's duty to A under section 195(2) to an end,

three weeks beginning with the day on which the request for the review is made or, where A makes representations under regulation 7, beginning with the day on which those representations are received,

    (b)   where the original decision falls within—

        (i)   section 202(1)(a), (b), (ba)(ii), (c), (d), (e), (f), (g), or (h), or

        (ii)   section 202(1)(bb) and the effect of the notice given under section 193B(2) is to bring the authority's duty to A under section 189B(2) to an end,

eight weeks beginning with the day on which the request for the review is made,

    (c)   where the original decision falls within section 202(1)(d) and the review is carried out by the notifying authority and the notified authority, ten weeks beginning with the day on which the request for the review is made,

    (d)   in a case falling within regulation 6, twelve weeks beginning with the day on which the request for the review is made,

or within such longer period as A and the reviewer may agree in writing.

(2) In a case falling within regulation 6, the appointed person must notify their decision on the review and the reasons for it, in writing, to the notifying authority and the notified authority—

(a)   within a period of eleven weeks beginning with the day on which the request for the review is made, or

(b)   where a longer period has been agreed in accordance with paragraph (1), by no later than one week before the expiry of that longer period.

PART 4
DUTY TO REFER

10 Specified public authorities

The public authorities set out in the Schedule are specified for the purposes of section 213B (Duty of public authority to refer cases in England to local housing authority).

PART 5
REVOCATION

11 Revocation and transitional provision

(1)   Subject to paragraph (2), the Allocation of Housing and Homelessness (Review Procedures) Regulations 1999 are revoked.

(2)   The Allocation of Housing and Homelessness (Review Procedures) Regulations 1999 continue in force in relation to any request for a review under section 202 made prior to the coming into force of this Part.

SCHEDULE
SPECIFIED PUBLIC AUTHORITIES

Regulation 10

1

The governor of a prison within the meaning given in section 53(1) of the Prison Act 1952.

2

The director of a contracted out prison within the meaning given in section 84(4) of the Criminal Justice Act 1991.

3

The governor of a young offender institution provided under section 43(1)(a) of the Prison Act 1952.

4

The governor of a secure training centre provided under section 43(1)(b) of the Prison Act 1952.

5

The director of a contracted out secure training centre within the meaning given in section 15 of the Criminal Justice and Public Order Act 1994.

6

The principal of a secure college provided under section 43(1)(c) of the Prison Act 1952.

7

A youth offending team established under section 39(1) of the Crime and Disorder Act 1998.

8

A provider of probation services.

9

An officer, designated by the Secretary of State for Work and Pensions for the purposes of section 213B, employed by the Secretary of State at an office known as a Jobcentre Plus office.

10

A social services authority.

11

A person who performs a function of a local authority pursuant to a direction under section 497A(4) or (4A) of the Education Act 1996 (which confers power on the Secretary of State to secure the proper performance of local authority education functions, and is applied to social services functions relating to children by section 50 of the Children Act 2004 and to functions relating to childcare by section 15 of the Childcare Act 2006).

12

(1) An NHS trust and an NHS foundation trust, but only in connection with the provision of the following NHS health services—

    (a)   emergency department and urgent treatment centres,

    (b)   in-patient treatment.

(2) For the purposes of paragraph (1)—

"emergency department and urgent treatment centres" includes—

    (a)   accident and emergency services provided in a hospital,

    (b)   services known as urgent treatment centres,

    (c)   any other providers of community and primary urgent care services,

"NHS foundation trust" has the meaning given in section 30 of the National Health Service Act 2006,

"NHS health services" means any kind of health services provided as part of the health service continued under, and for the purposes of, section 1(1) of the National Health Service Act 2006, and

"NHS trust" means an NHS trust established under section 25 of the National Health Service Act 2006.

13

The Secretary of State for Defence, but only in relation to members of the regular armed forces.

LETTER FROM THE HOMELESSNESS DIRECTORATE (OFFICE OF THE DEPUTY PRIME MINISTER) TO CHIEF EXECUTIVES AND HOUSING DIRECTORS OF ENGLISH LOCAL HOUSING AUTHORITIES (MARCH 2003)

A2.17

Alan Edwards
Homelessness Directorate
Zone 1/A2 Ashdown House
123 Victoria Street
London SW1E 6DE
DIRECT LINE: 020 7944 3665 alan.edwards@odpm.gsi.gov.uk

Frances Walker
Housing Management Division 1
Zone 1/H4 Eland House
Bressenden Place
London SW1E 5DU
DIRECT LINE: 020 7944 3666 frances.walker@odpm.gsi.gov.uk

Web site: www.odpm.gov.uk

25 March 2003

Dear Colleague,

ELIGIBLITY FOR HOUSING ALLOCATION AND HOMELESSNESS ASSISTANCE: NEW CATEGORIES OF LEAVE FOR PERSONS SUBJECT TO IMMIGRATION CONTROL

Please ensure that this letter is drawn to the attention of all staff dealing with applications for housing allocation and applications for homelessness assistance as soon as possible.

This letter notifies of a change to the categories of person subject to immigration control who are eligible for local authority housing with effect from 1 April 2003.

Home Office Minister Beverley Hughes announced on Friday 29 November that the policy of granting **exceptional leave** to enter or remain in the UK policy was to be abolished. It will be replaced by a new policy under which a new category of leave known as **humanitarian protection** will be granted to people who have international protection needs. Home Office Ministers will also retain a discretion to grant **discretionary leave** on an exceptional basis to people who do not have international protection needs but where there are other reasons for allowing them to stay in the UK, for example, strong compassionate grounds.

The policy change will take effect from Tuesday 1 April 2003.

Local housing authorities should note:

a) that people with **exceptional leave** to enter or remain in the UK granted prior to 1 April 2003 (and whose leave is not subject to a condition requiring them to maintain and accommodate themselves without recourse to public funds) continue to be eligible for an allocation of housing under Part 6 of the Housing Act 1996 (the 1996 Act) and eligible for homelessness assistance under Part 7 of the 1996 Act; and

b) that people granted **humanitarian protection** or **discretionary leave** (and whose leave is not subject to a condition requiring them to maintain and accommodate themselves without recourse to public funds) will be eligible for an allocation of housing under Part 6 of the Housing Act 1996 (the 1996 Act) and eligible for homelessness assistance under Part 7 of the 1996 Act.

People who fall in category (a), above, are eligible for an allocation of housing by virtue of Class B of Regulation 4 of the *Allocation of Housing (England) Regulations 2002* (SI 2002 No. 3264), and are eligible for homelessness assistance by virtue of Class B of Regulation 3 of the *Homelessness (England) Regulations 2000* (SI. 2000 No. 701).

People who fall in category (b), above, also come within the scope of Class B of Regulation 4 of the *Allocation of Housing (England) Regulations 2002* and Class B of Regulation 3 of the *Homelessness (England) Regulations 2000*. This is because **exceptional leave, humanitarian protection** and **discretionary leave** are all forms of limited leave to enter or remain in the UK granted exceptionally outside the provisions of the Immigration Rules to a person who does not qualify for leave under the Immigration Rules.

People with **exceptional leave, humanitarian protection** or **discretionary leave** (and whose leave is not subject to a condition requiring them to maintain and accommodate themselves without recourse to public funds) will also be eligible for housing benefit.

People granted humanitarian protection or discretionary leave will be issued a standard format letter by the Immigration, and Nationality Directorate (IND) at the Home Office that makes clear that they have been granted leave under one of other of these policies. The letter will be similar in format to the standard letter previously issued to people granted exceptional leave, and it will show the date on which leave to enter or remain will expire.

Authorities should note that humanitarian protection and discretionary leave will be granted for a period of up to 3 years. Towards the end of this period, leave holders will have the opportunity to apply for further leave, although there will be no presumption that such applications will be successful. If their application for an extension is made within the relevant time limits the conditions of their former leave will continue to apply until a decision is made on their application. Where authorities have allocated a secure tenancy to, or are providing temporary accommodation for, a person with humanitarian protection or discretionary leave they will need to monitor the outcome of any application to extend the period of leave. If the application is refused, and the person is not removed from the country by IND, it is possible that the person could remain in the UK unlawfully. A duty to secure accommodation under section 193 of the homelessness legislation would come to an end if the applicant ceased to be eligible for assistance. Eligibility for housing benefit would also end if their application for further leave was refused.

Authorities are urged to ensure that their partner RSLs are made aware of these changes.

Where information is required from IND, authorities should follow the arrangements at **Annex A** (also set out in Annex 10 of the Code of Guidance on the Allocation of Accommodation and Annex 21 of the Homelessness Code of Guidance for Local Authorities).

Detailed information about the new Home Office policies of Humanitarian Protection and Discretionary Leave are attached at **Annex B**.

We regret that we have been unable to provide more notice of the effect of this policy change. This is because it has only recently become clear that the new categories of leave (HP and DL) will fall within the existing provisions that relate to ELR.

Yours faithfully,

ANNEX A

How to contact the Home Office's Immigration and Nationality Directorate.

1. The Home Office's Immigration and Nationality Directorate (IND) will exchange information with Local Housing Authorities subject to relevant data protection and disclosure policy requirements being met and properly managed, provided that the information is required to assist with the carrying out of statutory functions or prevention and detection of fraud.

2. The Evidence and Enquiries Unit (EEU) will provide a service to local housing authorities to confirm the immigration status of an applicant from abroad (non-asylum seekers). In order to take advantage of the service, local housing authorities first need to register with the Evidence and Enquiries Unit, Immigration and Nationality Directorate, C Block 3rd Floor, Whitgift Centre, Wellesley Road, Croydon, CR9 2AT either by letter or **Fax: 020 8604 5783.**

3. Registration details requires by the EEU's Local Authorities' Team are;

(a)   name of enquiring local housing authority on headed paper,
(b)   job title/status of officer registering on behalf of the local housing authority,
(c)   names of local housing authority staff and their respective job titles/status who will be making enquiries on behalf of the local housing authority.

4. Once the local housing authority is registered with the EEU, then the authorised personnel can make individual enquiries by letter or fax, but replies will be returned by post.

ANNEX B

HUMANITARIAN PROTECTION

Definition

Humanitarian Protection will be granted to anyone who would, if removed, face in the country of return a serious risk to life or person arising from:

- The death penalty
- Unlawful killing; or
- Torture or inhuman or degrading treatment or punishment.

Not all Article 3 ECHR cases will fall to be granted Humanitarian Protection: for example a person with a serious medical condition whose removal could amount to a breach of Article 3 because of that condition is not in need of international protection and so would not qualify for Humanitarian Protection. Individuals who cannot be removed for this reason may qualify for Discretionary Leave. Also 'excluded persons' would not get Humanitarian Protection (see below)

Terms and Conditions of leave

A person who qualifies for Humanitarian Protection would normally be granted leave for 3 years. However, the possibility is left open for grants of leave for shorter periods, in defined category of cases where such instructions have been issued. For example where the situation in a country is fluid. It will also be possible for instructions to be issued which provide that decisions in a defined category of cases are to be suspended for a period of time.

Anyone granted Humanitarian Protection will have full access to mainstream benefits and employment. As with the current exceptional leave system, they will not have a right to automatic family reunion.

Review

There will be an avenue to apply for settlement (ILR) after 3 years if the reasons which give rise to the need for protection continue to exist.

There will be an active review at the 3 year stage. Extensions or ILR will not be granted automatically but only where the circumstances continue to justify such extensions or ILR.

Exclusions

Exclusion criteria will be applied to the Humanitarian Protection procedures, which will include, but go wider than those that apply in the 1951 Refugee Convention.

Under these exclusion criteria, we will exclude from the Humanitarian Protection procedures anyone:

- Who has committed a crime against peace, a war crime, or a crime against humanity
- Who has committed a serious crime in the UK or overseas
- Who has been guilty of acts contrary to the purposes and principles of the United Nations
- Who is a danger to national security
- Where exclusion is considered appropriate in light of their character, conduct or associations

Revocation of leave

A grant of leave would be reviewed as a result of an individual's own actions, for example where a crime has been committed, or evidence of deception comes to light or where they have demonstrated that they are no longer in need of protection.

The grant of leave would not normally be reviewed during its currency if country conditions change unless there was a separate instruction.

DISCRETIONARY LEAVE

The Home Secretary will retain the ability to allow some of those who fall outside the Humanitarian Protection Policy to stay on a discretionary basis.

This category of leave will be termed 'Discretionary Leave'. In asylum casework, Discretionary Leave will only be considered by caseworkers once a decision has been made on whether the applicant qualifies for asylum or Humanitarian Protection.

Discretionary Leave will only be granted in a number of limited circumstances:

- Cases where removal would breach Article 8 of the ECHR in the UK
- Article 3 cases where Humanitarian Protection is not granted (medical cases and certain other severe humanitarian cases)
- Unaccompanied asylum seeking children for whom no adequate reception arrangements are in place
- Other cases - where the individual circumstances are so compelling that this it is considered appropriate to grant some form of leave
- People who are excluded from being granted Humanitarian Protection but where removal is not possible, usually because of Article 3 ECHR reasons.

Anyone who does not qualify under these criteria will not be granted Discretionary Leave.

The period of leave granted will vary depending on the basis on which Discretionary Leave is granted. An initial grant of leave will be no longer than 3 years, and may sometimes be less for example unaccompanied asylum seeking children will be granted leave for three years or until their 18th birthday.

Where an extension of leave is sought after a period of Discretionary Leave the request will be subject to an active review. A person will not become eligible for settlement until they have completed 6 years on Discretionary Leave. A person who comes within the exclusion criteria would not be considered for ILR until they have spent 10 years on Discretionary Leave.

Anyone who has been refused asylum and Humanitarian Protection but granted Discretionary Leave will have full access to mainstream benefits and employment. There will be no automatic right to family reunion.

LETTER FROM THE DEPARTMENT OF COMMUNITIES AND LOCAL GOVERNMENT TO CHIEF HOUSING OFFICERS OF LOCAL AUTHORITIES IN ENGLAND (OCTOBER 2012)

A2.18

To: Chief Housing Officers of
Local Authorities in England

Dear Chief Housing Officer

This letter notifies local housing authorities that The Allocation of Housing and Homelessness (Eligibility) (England) (Amendment) Regulations 2012 (SI 2012/2588) will come into force on 8 November 2012.

These regulations (the Eligibility Amendment Regulations) are made by the Secretary of State under sections 160ZA(4), 172(4), 185(3) and 215(2) of the Housing Act 1996 (the 1996 Act) and were laid in Parliament today.

They amend regulations 4 and 6 of *The Allocation of Housing and Homelessness (Eligibility) (England) Regulations 2006* (SI 2006 No. 1294) (the Eligibility Regulations). Regulations 4 and 6 prescribe the classes of persons who are not subject to immigration control but who are to be treated as persons from abroad who are ineligible for an allocation of housing accommodation or for homelessness assistance under Parts 6 and 7 of the 1996 Act respectively.

Specifically, the Eligibility Amendment Regulations amend regulations 4 and 6 of the Eligibility Regulations to provide that the following persons are ineligible for an allocation of housing accommodation or homelessness assistance:

- Persons who have rights of residence in the UK as a result of regulation 15A(1) and (4A) of the Immigration (European Economic Area) (Amendment) (No 2) Regulations 2012 (the EEA Amendment Regulations)
- Persons who have a right derived from Article 20 of the Treaty on the Functioning of the European Union, in a case where rights of residence arise because a British citizen would otherwise be deprived of the genuine enjoyment of the substance of their rights as a European Union citizen

The Eligibility Amendment Regulations also make provision for persons who have equivalent rights of residence in the Channel Islands, the Isle of Man or the Republic of Ireland (the Common Travel Area).

The Government is making these amendments to the Eligibility Regulations following the ruling of the Court of Justice of the European Union in the case known as *Zambrano* (C-34/09 *Gerardo Ruiz Zambrano v Office national de l'emploi (ONEm)*). In that case, the Court ruled that a third country national (Mr Zambrano), who had been living and working in Belgium without a work permit, had a right of residence and right to work so that his Belgian national children were not forced to leave the EU and thereby prevented from exercising their rights as EU citizens.

Regulation 15A(1) and (4A) of the EEA Amending Regulations give effect to the *Zambrano* right by providing for a national from a non EEA country, who is resident in the UK and is the primary carer of a British citizen, to be granted a right of residence in the UK where not doing so would mean that the British citizen would have to leave the European Union.

The effect of the Eligibility Amendment Regulations is to maintain the Government's policy that non EEA nationals who are normally subject to immigration control should only have access to social housing or homelessness assistance if it accords with the Government's immigration and asylum policy, which broadly means only if they have been granted leave to enter or remain in the UK and this leave is not conditional on the person having no recourse to public funds.

The Department for Work and Pensions and HM Revenue and Customs are making similar amendments to regulations governing income-related benefits and tax credits which also come into force on 8 November.

The Eligibility Amendment Regulations are published by the Stationery Office and are available on the OPSI website at: http://www.legislation.gov.uk/2012/2588

Inquiries about the Eligibility Amendment Regulations should be addressed to Frances Walker, by telephone on 0303 444 3655 or by e-mail to: frances.walker@communities. gsi.gov.uk

A copy of this letter and the draft regulations is also being sent, by e-mail, to the homelessness strategy contact in each authority.

Yours sincerely,

LETTER FROM THE DEPARTMENT OF COMMUNITIES AND LOCAL GOVERNMENT TO CHIEF HOUSING OFFICERS OF LOCAL AUTHORITIES IN ENGLAND (MARCH 2014)

A2.19

Dear Chief Housing Officer

This letter notifies local housing authorities that The Allocation of Housing and Homelessness (Eligibility) (England) (Amendment) Regulations 2014 (SI 2014/435) will come into force on 31 March 2014.

These regulations (the Eligibility Amendment Regulations) are made by the Secretary of State under sections 160ZA (2) and (4), 172(4), 185 (2) and (3) and 215(2) of the Housing Act 1996 (the 1996 Act) and were laid before Parliament today.

They amend regulations 2, 3, 4, 5 and 6 of *The Allocation of Housing and Homelessness (Eligibility) (England) Regulations 2006* (SI 2006 No. 1294) (the Eligibility Regulations).

Regulations 3 and 5 of the Eligibility Regulations prescribe the classes of persons subject to immigration control who are to be treated as persons from abroad who are eligible for an allocation of housing accommodation or for homelessness assistance respectively.

The Eligibility Amendment Regulations amend regulations 3 and 5 to provide that the following persons are eligible for an allocation of housing accommodation or homelessness assistance: namely, certain Afghan nationals granted leave to enter or remain in the United Kingdom under paragraph 276BA1 of the Immigration Rules, provided they are habitually resident in the United Kingdom, the Channel Islands, the Isle of Man or the Republic of Ireland (the Common Travel Area).

The Government has decided to offer the opportunity to resettle in the United Kingdom to those locally engaged staff in Afghanistan who have worked in particularly dangerous and challenging roles in Helmand.

It is estimated that about 600 Afghan nationals will be eligible for resettlement under the scheme (together with their spouse or partner and dependent children, where relevant). Arrivals to the United Kingdom will be phased throughout 2014 and 2015. In order to assist those relocating to adjust to life in the United Kingdom, the Government is liaising with local authorities to provide them with accommodation and support for the first three months, funded by central Government.

The Home Office has made changes to the Immigration Rules to provide for eligible applicants to be granted five years limited leave with recourse to public funds. The effect of the Eligibility Amendment Regulations is to ensure that those Afghan citizens who have the relevant form of leave are also eligible for social housing and homelessness assistance once they are considered to be habitually resident, which is generally after three months. This is in line with existing rules for Housing Benefit.

Regulations 4 and 6 of the Eligibility Regulations prescribe the classes of persons who are not subject to immigration control but who are to be treated as persons from abroad who are ineligible for an allocation of housing accommodation or for homelessness assistance under Parts 6 and 7 of the 1996 Act respectively.

They provide that such persons should only be eligible for an allocation of housing accommodation or homelessness assistance if they are habitually resident in the Common Travel Area. However, certain categories of person are exempted from this requirement set out at regulations 4(2) and 6(2).

The Eligibility Amendment Regulations make minor changes to regulations 4 and 6 in order to remove a number of redundant and outdated provisions which dis-apply the habitual residence test in certain specific cases.

The first change relates to nationals of Bulgaria and Romania required to be authorised to work by the Home Office under the Accession (Immigration and Worker Authorisation) Regulations 2006. The worker authorisation requirements ceased to apply from 1 January 2014 when the transitional controls regulating access to the UK labour market by nationals of Bulgaria and Romania came to an end.

The second relates to persons who left Montserrat after 1st November 1995 because of the volcanic eruption there. Given the length of time that has elapsed since the volcanic eruption, it is considered that this exemption from the habitual residence test is no longer necessary to deliver the Government's policy.

The third relates to people who left the Lebanon on or after 25 July 2006 to escape the armed conflict there. This exemption was time limited and came to an end in January 2007.

The last relates to people who left Zimbabwe and arrived in Great Britain between February 2009 and March 2011 under a Government scheme open to those over 70 years of age or with health or social care needs. This provision is now redundant.

The Eligibility Amendment Regulations are published by the Stationery Office and available on the OPSI website at: http://www.legislation.gov.uk/2014/435

Enquiries about the Eligibility Amendment Regulations should be addressed to:

Frances Walker, in relation to allocations, by telephone on 0303 444 3655 or by e-mail to: frances.walker@communities.gsi.gov.uk

John Bentham, in relation to homelessness, by telephone on 0303 444 3752 or by email to: john.bentham@communities.gsi.go.uk

A copy of this letter and the regulations is also being sent, by e-mail, to the homelessness strategy contact in each authority.

Yours sincerely,

LETTER FROM THE DEPARTMENT OF COMMUNITIES AND LOCAL GOVERNMENT TO CHIEF EXECUTIVES AND CHIEF HOUSING OFFICERS OF LOCAL AUTHORITIES IN ENGLAND (OCTOBER 2016)

A2.20

Dear Chief Executive and Chief Housing Officer

This letter notifies local housing authorities that The Allocation of Housing and Homelessness (Eligibility) (England) (Amendment) Regulations 2016 (SI 2016/965) will come into force on 30 October 2016.

These regulations (the Amendment Regulations) are made by the Secretary of State under sections 160ZA(2), 172(4), 185(2) and 215(2) of the Housing Act 1996 (the 1996 Act) and were laid before Parliament on 3 October.

They amend regulations 2, 3 and 5 of *The Allocation of Housing and Homelessness (Eligibility) (England) Regulations 2006 (SI 2006 No. 1294) (the Eligibility Regulations).*

Regulations 3 and 5 of the Eligibility Regulations prescribe the classes of persons subject to immigration control who are to be treated as persons from abroad who are eligible for an allocation of housing accommodation or for homelessness assistance respectively.

The Amendment Regulations amend regulations 3 and 5 to provide that the following persons are eligible for an allocation of housing accommodation or homelessness assistance: namely, persons who have leave to enter or remain in the UK on family or private life grounds under Article 8 of the European Convention on Human Rights, granted under paragraph 276 BE(1) or 276DG of, or under Appendix FM to, the Immigration Rules, where this leave is not subject to a condition of 'no recourse to public funds'.

Before 9 July 2012 leave on family or private life grounds was one of the forms of Discretionary Leave granted outside the provisions of the Immigration Rules. Persons with this form of leave were eligible for an allocation of housing accommodation and for homelessness assistance by virtue of regulations 3(b) and 5(1)(b) of the Eligibility Regulations respectively. However, under changes made to the Immigration Rules from 9 July 2012, leave on family or private life grounds has largely been granted under the Immigration Rules. These Regulations amend the Eligibility Regulations to restore the previous position, and ensure that persons granted leave under the Immigration Rules on the grounds of family or private life are eligible for social housing and homelessness assistance, provided their leave is granted with recourse to public funds.

The Amendment Regulations also amend regulation 5 to remove redundant provisions relating to certain categories of asylum seekers whose claim for asylum was made before 3 April 2000.

Generally speaking asylum seekers are not eligible for social housing or homelessness assistance in line with the Government's wider immigration policy. Instead they are accommodated by the Home Office under the arrangements provided for in Part 6 of the Immigration and Asylum Act 1999. For a period after Part 6 of the 1999 Act came into force, transitional provisions allowed for certain categories of asylum seekers already accommodated by local authorities to continue to be supported by their local authority. These transitional provisions ceased to apply from April 2006 and, as a result, the provisions in regulation 5 are no longer required.

The Eligibility Amendment Regulations are published by the Stationery Office and are available at: http://www.legislation.gov.uk/id/uksi/2016/965

Enquiries about the Amendment Regulations should be addressed to:

Frances Walker, in relation to allocations, by telephone on 0303 444 3655 or by e-mail to: frances.walker@communities.gsi.gov.uk

John Bentham, in relation to homelessness, by telephone on 0303 444 3752 or by email to: john.bentham@communities.gsi.go.uk

Yours sincerely,

Index